SCRABBLE®

BRAND Crossword Game

WORDS

HarperCollins Publishers
Westerhill Road
Bishopbriggs
Glasgow
G64 2QT

Second Edition 2006

© HarperCollins Publishers 2006

ISBN-13 978-0-00-723315-1
ISBN-10 0-00-723315-9

Collins® is a registered trademark of
HarperCollins Publishers Limited

SCRABBLE® is a registered trademark of
J.W. Spear and Sons Ltd., a subsidiary of
Mattel, Inc., © 2006 Mattel, Inc. All rights
reserved.

www.collins.co.uk

A catalogue record for this book is
available from the British Library

About the type.
This book is set in Collins Fedra, a
typeface specially created for Collins
dictionaries by Peter Bil´ak, the type
designer.

Computing Support
Thomas Callan

Collins Corpus Programmer
Nigel Rochford

Typesetting
Wordcraft

Printed in Germany by Bercker

Acknowledgements
We would like to thank those authors and
publishers who kindly gave permission
for copyright material to be used in the
Collins Word Web. We would also like to
thank Times Newspapers Ltd for
providing valuable data.

Editorial Staff

Morven Dooner
Elaine Higgleton
Elspeth Summers

Introduction

Collins **SCRABBLE® Words** is the most complete **SCRABBLE®** wordlist
in existence. As such, it is an invaluable tool for any competitive or club
player, as well as the ultimate authority for settling disputes between
those who play with their friends and family.

More than a staggering 267,000 words are listed in Collins
SCRABBLE® Words – representing an exhaustive list of every valid
play in **SCRABBLE®**. The book is divided into two sections: Section
One contains every word of between two and nine letters, while
Section Two contains words of ten to fifteen letters. In any
SCRABBLE® game, most words will be between two and nine letters,
with longer words being formed only very rarely.

Words not listed include those spelt with an initial capital letter,
abbreviations, prefixes and suffixes, and words requiring apostrophes
and hyphens, none of which are allowed in Scrabble.

You can find definitions for all the words of between two and nine
letters in length in Collins Official **SCRABBLE®** Dictionary.

Accents
As English-language Scrabble tiles are not accented, no accents are
shown in *Collins Scrabble Words*.

Word Order
Collins Scrabble Words is an alphabetical word list, therefore any
inflected forms of a base word are given in alphabetical order, and
not after the base form, as in many dictionaries.

Offensive Terms
There may be words in *Collins Scrabble Words* that most or some players
might consider taboo or offensive. We strongly recommend that
players check meanings and suitability for general use in *Collins
English Dictionary.*

Collins would like to give warm thanks to Darryl Francis and Allan
Simmons for their enormous contribution to this wordlist. They
worked tirelessly with the editorial team to get this right. Any errors
are the responsibility of the publisher.

COLLINS SCRABBLE WORDS

2-9 LETTER WORDS

A

AA
AAH
AAHED
AAHING
AAHS
AAL
AALII
AALIIS
AALS
AARDVARK
AARDVARKS
AARDWOLF
AARGH
AARRGH
AARRGHH
AARTI
AARTIS
AAS
AASVOGEL
AASVOGELS
AB
ABA
ABAC
ABACA
ABACAS
ABACI
ABACK
ABACS
ABACTINAL
ABACTOR
ABACTORS
ABACUS
ABACUSES
ABAFT
ABAKA
ABAKAS
ABALONE
ABALONES
ABAMP
ABAMPERE
ABAMPERES
ABAMPS
ABAND
ABANDED
ABANDING
ABANDON
ABANDONED
ABANDONEE
ABANDONER
ABANDONS
ABANDS
ABAPICAL
ABAS

ABASE
ABASED
ABASEDLY
ABASEMENT
ABASER
ABASERS
ABASES
ABASH
ABASHED
ABASHEDLY
ABASHES
ABASHING
ABASHLESS
ABASHMENT
ABASIA
ABASIAS
ABASING
ABASK
ABATABLE
ABATE
ABATED
ABATEMENT
ABATER
ABATERS
ABATES
ABATING
ABATIS
ABATISES
ABATOR
ABATORS
ABATTIS
ABATTISES
ABATTOIR
ABATTOIRS
ABATTU
ABATURE
ABATURES
ABAXIAL
ABAXILE
ABAYA
ABAYAS
ABB
ABBA
ABBACIES
ABBACY
ABBAS
ABBATIAL
ABBE
ABBED
ABBES
ABBESS
ABBESSES
ABBEY

ABBEYS
ABBOT
ABBOTCIES
ABBOTCY
ABBOTS
ABBOTSHIP
ABBS
ABCEE
ABCEES
ABCOULOMB
ABDABS
ABDICABLE
ABDICANT
ABDICATE
ABDICATED
ABDICATES
ABDICATOR
ABDOMEN
ABDOMENS
ABDOMINA
ABDOMINAL
ABDUCE
ABDUCED
ABDUCENS
ABDUCENT
ABDUCES
ABDUCING
ABDUCT
ABDUCTED
ABDUCTEE
ABDUCTEES
ABDUCTING
ABDUCTION
ABDUCTOR
ABDUCTORS
ABDUCTS
ABEAM
ABEAR
ABEARING
ABEARS
ABED
ABEGGING
ABEIGH
ABELE
ABELES
ABELIA
ABELIAN
ABELIAS
ABELMOSK
ABELMOSKS
ABERNETHY
ABERRANCE
ABERRANCY

ABERRANT
ABERRANTS
ABERRATE
ABERRATED
ABERRATES
ABESSIVE
ABESSIVES
ABET
ABETMENT
ABETMENTS
ABETS
ABETTAL
ABETTALS
ABETTED
ABETTER
ABETTERS
ABETTING
ABETTOR
ABETTORS
ABEYANCE
ABEYANCES
ABEYANCY
ABEYANT
ABFARAD
ABFARADS
ABHENRIES
ABHENRY
ABHENRYS
ABHOR
ABHORRED
ABHORRENT
ABHORRER
ABHORRERS
ABHORRING
ABHORS
ABID
ABIDANCE
ABIDANCES
ABIDDEN
ABIDE
ABIDED
ABIDER
ABIDERS
ABIDES
ABIDING
ABIDINGLY
ABIDINGS
ABIES
ABIETIC
ABIGAIL
ABIGAILS
ABILITTES
ABILITY

1

ABIOGENIC	ABMHO	ABORT	ABREACTED
ABIOSES	ABMHOS	ABORTED	ABREACTS
ABIOSIS	ABNEGATE	ABORTEE	ABREAST
ABIOTIC	ABNEGATED	ABORTEES	ABREGE
ABJECT	ABNEGATES	ABORTER	ABREGES
ABJECTED	ABNEGATOR	ABORTERS	ABRI
ABJECTING	ABNORMAL	ABORTING	ABRICOCK
ABJECTION	ABNORMALS	ABORTION	ABRICOCKS
ABJECTLY	ABNORMITY	ABORTIONS	ABRIDGE
ABJECTS	ABNORMOUS	ABORTIVE	ABRIDGED
ABJOINT	ABO	ABORTS	ABRIDGER
ABJOINTED	ABOARD	ABORTUARY	ABRIDGERS
ABJOINTS	ABODE	ABORTUS	ABRIDGES
ABJURE	ABODED	ABORTUSES	ABRIDGING
ABJURED	ABODEMENT	ABOS	ABRIM
ABJURER	ABODES	ABOUGHT	ABRIN
ABJURERS	ABODING	ABOULIA	ABRINS
ABJURES	ABOHM	ABOULIAS	ABRIS
ABJURING	ABOHMS	ABOULIC	ABROACH
ABLATE	ABOIDEAU	ABOUND	ABROAD
ABLATED	ABOIDEAUS	ABOUNDED	ABROADS
ABLATES	ABOIDEAUX	ABOUNDING	ABROGABLE
ABLATING	ABOIL	ABOUNDS	ABROGATE
ABLATION	ABOITEAU	ABOUT	ABROGATED
ABLATIONS	ABOITEAUS	ABOUTS	ABROGATES
ABLATIVAL	ABOITEAUX	ABOVE	ABROGATOR
ABLATIVE	ABOLISH	ABOVES	ABROOKE
ABLATIVES	ABOLISHED	ABRACHIA	ABROOKED
ABLATOR	ABOLISHER	ABRACHIAS	ABROOKES
ABLATORS	ABOLISHES	ABRADABLE	ABROOKING
ABLAUT	ABOLITION	ABRADANT	ABROSIA
ABLAUTS	ABOLLA	ABRADANTS	ABROSIAS
ABLAZE	ABOLLAE	ABRADE	ABRUPT
ABLE	ABOLLAS	ABRADED	ABRUPTER
ABLED	ABOMA	ABRADER	ABRUPTEST
ABLEGATE	ABOMAS	ABRADERS	ABRUPTION
ABLEGATES	ABOMASA	ABRADES	ABRUPTLY
ABLEISM	ABOMASAL	ABRADING	ABRUPTS
ABLEISMS	ABOMASI	ABRAID	ABS
ABLEIST	ABOMASUM	ABRAIDED	ABSCESS
ABLEISTS	ABOMASUS	ABRAIDING	ABSCESSED
ABLER	ABOMINATE	ABRAIDS	ABSCESSES
ABLES	ABONDANCE	ABRAM	ABSCIND
ABLEST	ABOON	ABRASAX	ABSCINDED
ABLET	ABORAL	ABRASAXES	ABSCINDS
ABLETS	ABORALLY	ABRASION	ABSCISE
ABLING	ABORD	ABRASIONS	ABSCISED
ABLINGS	ABORDED	ABRASIVE	ABSCISES
ABLINS	ABORDING	ABRASIVES	ABSCISIN
ABLOOM	ABORDS	ABRAXAS	ABSCISING
ABLOW	ABORE	ABRAXASES	ABSCISINS
ABLUENT	ABORIGEN	ABRAY	ABSCISS
ABLUENTS	ABORIGENS	ABRAYED	ABSCISSA
ABLUSH	ABORIGIN	ABRAYING	ABSCISSAE
ABLUTED	ABORIGINE	ABRAYS	ABSCISSAS
ABLUTION	ABORIGINS	ABRAZO	ABSCISSE
ABLUTIONS	ABORNE	ABRAZOS	ABSCISSES
ABLY	ABORNING	ABREACT	ABSCISSIN

ABSCOND	ABSTRICTS	ABYES	ACARIDIAN
ABSCONDED	ABSTRUSE	ABYING	ACARIDS
ABSCONDER	ABSTRUSER	ABYS	ACARINE
ABSCONDS	ABSURD	ABYSM	ACARINES
ABSEIL	ABSURDER	ABYSMAL	ACAROID
ABSEILED	ABSURDEST	ABYSMALLY	ACAROLOGY
ABSEILING	ABSURDISM	ABYSMS	ACARPOUS
ABSEILS	ABSURDIST	ABYSS	ACARUS
ABSENCE	ABSURDITY	ABYSSAL	ACATER
ABSENCES	ABSURDLY	ABYSSES	ACATERS
ABSENT	ABSURDS	ACACIA	ACATES
ABSENTED	ABTHANE	ACACIAS	ACATOUR
ABSENTEE	ABTHANES	ACADEME	ACATOURS
ABSENTEES	ABUBBLE	ACADEMES	ACAUDAL
ABSENTER	ABUILDING	ACADEMIA	ACAUDATE
ABSENTERS	ABULIA	ACADEMIAS	ACAULINE
ABSENTING	ABULIAS	ACADEMIC	ACAULOSE
ABSENTLY	ABULIC	ACADEMICS	ACAULOUS
ABSENTS	ABUNA	ACADEMIES	ACCA
ABSEY	ABUNAS	ACADEMISM	ACCABLE
ABSEYS	ABUNDANCE	ACADEMIST	ACCAS
ABSINTH	ABUNDANCY	ACADEMY	ACCEDE
ABSINTHE	ABUNDANT	ACAI	ACCEDED
ABSINTHES	ABUNE	ACAIS	ACCEDENCE
ABSINTHS	ABURST	ACAJOU	ACCEDER
ABSIT	ABUSABLE	ACAJOUS	ACCEDERS
ABSITS	ABUSAGE	ACALCULIA	ACCEDES
ABSOLUTE	ABUSAGES	ACALEPH	ACCEDING
ABSOLUTER	ABUSE	ACALEPHAE	ACCEND
ABSOLUTES	ABUSED	ACALEPHAN	ACCENDED
ABSOLVE	ABUSER	ACALEPHE	ACCENDING
ABSOLVED	ABUSERS	ACALEPHES	ACCENDS
ABSOLVENT	ABUSES	ACALEPHS	ACCENSION
ABSOLVER	ABUSING	ACANTH	ACCENT
ABSOLVERS	ABUSION	ACANTHA	ACCENTED
ABSOLVES	ABUSIONS	ACANTHAE	ACCENTING
ABSOLVING	ABUSIVE	ACANTHAS	ACCENTOR
ABSONANT	ABUSIVELY	ACANTHI	ACCENTORS
ABSORB	ABUT	ACANTHIN	ACCENTS
ABSORBANT	ABUTILON	ACANTHINE	ACCENTUAL
ABSORBATE	ABUTILONS	ACANTHINS	ACCEPT
ABSORBED	ABUTMENT	ACANTHOID	ACCEPTANT
ABSORBENT	ABUTMENTS	ACANTHOUS	ACCEPTED
ABSORBER	ABUTS	ACANTHS	ACCEPTEE
ABSORBERS	ABUTTAL	ACANTHUS	ACCEPTEES
ABSORBING	ABUTTALS	ACAPNIA	ACCEPTER
ABSORBS	ABUTTED	ACAPNIAS	ACCEPTERS
ABSTAIN	ABUTTER	ACARBOSE	ACCEPTING
ABSTAINED	ABUTTERS	ACARBOSES	ACCEPTIVE
ABSTAINER	ABUTTING	ACARI	ACCEPTOR
ABSTAINS	ABUZZ	ACARIAN	ACCEPTORS
ABSTERGE	ABVOLT	ACARIASES	ACCEPTS
ABSTERGED	ABVOLTS	ACARIASIS	ACCESS
ABSTERGES	ABWATT	ACARICIDE	ACCESSARY
ABSTINENT	ABWATTS	ACARID	ACCESSED
ABSTRACT	ABY	ACARIDAN	ACCESSES
ABSTRACTS	ABYE	ACARIDANS	ACCESSING
ABSTRICT	ABYEING	ACARIDEAN	ACCESSION

3

ACCESSORY	ACCOUNTS	ACED	ACETUM
ACCIDENCE	ACCOURAGE	ACEDIA	ACETYL
ACCIDENT	ACCOURT	ACEDIAS	ACETYLATE
ACCIDENTS	ACCOURTED	ACELDAMA	ACETYLENE
ACCIDIA	ACCOURTS	ACELDAMAS	ACETYLIC
ACCIDIAS	ACCOUTER	ACELLULAR	ACETYLIDE
ACCIDIE	ACCOUTERS	ACENTRIC	ACETYLS
ACCIDIES	ACCOUTRE	ACEPHALIC	ACH
ACCINGE	ACCOUTRED	ACEQUIA	ACHAENIA
ACCINGED	ACCOUTRES	ACEQUIAS	ACHAENIUM
ACCINGES	ACCOY	ACER	ACHAGE
ACCINGING	ACCOYED	ACERATE	ACHAGES
ACCIPITER	ACCOYING	ACERATED	ACHALASIA
ACCITE	ACCOYLD	ACERB	ACHARNE
ACCITED	ACCOYS	ACERBATE	ACHARYA
ACCITES	ACCREDIT	ACERBATED	ACHARYAS
ACCITING	ACCREDITS	ACERBATES	ACHATES
ACCLAIM	ACCRETE	ACERBER	ACHE
ACCLAIMED	ACCRETED	ACERBEST	ACHED
ACCLAIMER	ACCRETES	ACERBIC	ACHENE
ACCLAIMS	ACCRETING	ACERBITY	ACHENES
ACCLIMATE	ACCRETION	ACEROLA	ACHENIA
ACCLIVITY	ACCRETIVE	ACEROLAS	ACHENIAL
ACCLIVOUS	ACCREW	ACEROSE	ACHENIUM
ACCLOY	ACCREWED	ACEROUS	ACHENIUMS
ACCLOYED	ACCREWING	ACERS	ACHES
ACCLOYING	ACCREWS	ACERVATE	ACHIER
ACCLOYS	ACCROIDES	ACERVULI	ACHIEST
ACCOAST	ACCRUABLE	ACERVULUS	ACHIEVE
ACCOASTED	ACCRUAL	ACES	ACHIEVED
ACCOASTS	ACCRUALS	ACESCENCE	ACHIEVER
ACCOIED	ACCRUE	ACESCENCY	ACHIEVERS
ACCOIL	ACCRUED	ACESCENT	ACHIEVES
ACCOILS	ACCRUES	ACESCENTS	ACHIEVING
ACCOLADE	ACCRUING	ACETA	ACHILLEA
ACCOLADED	ACCUMBENT	ACETABULA	ACHILLEAS
ACCOLADES	ACCURACY	ACETAL	ACHIMENES
ACCOMPANY	ACCURATE	ACETALS	ACHINESS
ACCOMPT	ACCURSE	ACETAMID	ACHING
ACCOMPTED	ACCURSED	ACETAMIDE	ACHINGLY
ACCOMPTS	ACCURSES	ACETAMIDS	ACHINGS
ACCORAGE	ACCURSING	ACETATE	ACHIOTE
ACCORAGED	ACCURST	ACETATED	ACHIOTES
ACCORAGES	ACCUSABLE	ACETATES	ACHIRAL
ACCORD	ACCUSABLY	ACETIC	ACHKAN
ACCORDANT	ACCUSAL	ACETIFIED	ACHKANS
ACCORDED	ACCUSALS	ACETIFIER	ACHOLIA
ACCORDER	ACCUSANT	ACETIFIES	ACHOLIAS
ACCORDERS	ACCUSANTS	ACETIFY	ACHOO
ACCORDING	ACCUSE	ACETIN	ACHROMAT
ACCORDION	ACCUSED	ACETINS	ACHROMATS
ACCORDS	ACCUSER	ACETONE	ACHROMIC
ACCOST	ACCUSERS	ACETONES	ACHROMOUS
ACCOSTED	ACCUSES	ACETONIC	ACHY
ACCOSTING	ACCUSING	ACETOSE	ACICULA
ACCOSTS	ACCUSTOM	ACETOUS	ACICULAE
ACCOUNT	ACCUSTOMS	ACETOXYL	ACICULAR
ACCOUNTED	ACE	ACETOXYLS	ACICULAS

4

ACICULATE	ACMATIC	ACQUISTS	ACROPHOBE
ACICULUM	ACME	ACQUIT	ACROPHONY
ACICULUMS	ACMES	ACQUITE	ACROPOLIS
ACID	ACMIC	ACQUITES	ACROSOMAL
ACIDEMIA	ACMITE	ACQUITING	ACROSOME
ACIDEMIAS	ACMITES	ACQUITS	ACROSOMES
ACIDER	ACNE	ACQUITTAL	ACROSPIRE
ACIDEST	ACNED	ACQUITTED	ACROSS
ACIDFREAK	ACNES	ACQUITTER	ACROSTIC
ACIDHEAD	ACNODAL	ACRASIA	ACROSTICS
ACIDHEADS	ACNODE	ACRASIAS	ACROTER
ACIDIC	ACNODES	ACRASIN	ACROTERIA
ACIDIER	ACOCK	ACRASINS	ACROTERS
ACIDIEST	ACOELOUS	ACRATIC	ACROTIC
ACIDIFIED	ACOEMETI	ACRAWL	ACROTISM
ACIDIFIER	ACOLD	ACRE	ACROTISMS
ACIDIFIES	ACOLUTHIC	ACREAGE	ACRYLATE
ACIDIFY	ACOLYTE	ACREAGES	ACRYLATES
ACIDITIES	ACOLYTES	ACRED	ACRYLIC
ACIDITY	ACOLYTH	ACRES	ACRYLICS
ACIDLY	ACOLYTHS	ACRID	ACRYLYL
ACIDNESS	ACONITE	ACRIDER	ACRYLYLS
ACIDOPHIL	ACONITES	ACRIDEST	ACT
ACIDOSES	ACONITIC	ACRIDIN	ACTA
ACIDOSIS	ACONITINE	ACRIDINE	ACTABLE
ACIDOTIC	ACONITUM	ACRIDINES	ACTANT
ACIDS	ACONITUMS	ACRIDINS	ACTANTS
ACIDULATE	ACORN	ACRIDITY	ACTED
ACIDULENT	ACORNED	ACRIDLY	ACTIN
ACIDULOUS	ACORNS	ACRIDNESS	ACTINAL
ACIDURIA	ACOSMISM	ACRIMONY	ACTINALLY
ACIDURIAS	ACOSMISMS	ACRITARCH	ACTING
ACIDY	ACOSMIST	ACRITICAL	ACTINGS
ACIERAGE	ACOSMISTS	ACROBAT	ACTINIA
ACIERAGES	ACOUCHI	ACROBATIC	ACTINIAE
ACIERATE	ACOUCHIES	ACROBATS	ACTINIAN
ACIERATED	ACOUCHIS	ACRODONT	ACTINIANS
ACIERATES	ACOUCHY	ACRODONTS	ACTINIAS
ACIFORM	ACOUSTIC	ACRODROME	ACTINIC
ACINAR	ACOUSTICS	ACROGEN	ACTINIDE
ACING	ACQUAINT	ACROGENIC	ACTINIDES
ACINI	ACQUAINTS	ACROGENS	ACTINISM
ACINIC	ACQUEST	ACROLECT	ACTINISMS
ACINIFORM	ACQUESTS	ACROLECTS	ACTINIUM
ACINOSE	ACQUIESCE	ACROLEIN	ACTINIUMS
ACINOUS	ACQUIGHT	ACROLEINS	ACTINOID
ACINUS	ACQUIGHTS	ACROLITH	ACTINOIDS
ACKEE	ACQUIRAL	ACROLITHS	ACTINON
ACKEES	ACQUIRALS	ACROMIA	ACTINONS
ACKER	ACQUIRE	ACROMIAL	ACTINOPOD
ACKERS	ACQUIRED	ACROMION	ACTINS
ACKNEW	ACQUIREE	ACRONIC	ACTION
ACKNOW	ACQUIREES	ACRONICAL	ACTIONED
ACKNOWING	ACQUIRER	ACRONYCAL	ACTIONER
ACKNOWN	ACQUIRERS	ACRONYM	ACTIONERS
ACKNOWNE	ACQUIRES	ACRONYMIC	ACTIONING
ACKNOWS	ACQUIRING	ACRONYMS	ACTIONIST
ACLINIC	ACQUIST	ACROPETAL	ACTIONS

ACTIVATE	ACUMINOUS	ADDABLE	ADDUCIBLE
ACTIVATED	ACUPOINT	ADDAX	ADDUCING
ACTIVATES	ACUPOINTS	ADDAXES	ADDUCT
ACTIVATOR	ACUSHLA	ADDEBTED	ADDUCTED
ACTIVE	ACUSHLAS	ADDED	ADDUCTING
ACTIVELY	ACUTANCE	ADDEDLY	ADDUCTION
ACTIVES	ACUTANCES	ADDEEM	ADDUCTIVE
ACTIVISE	ACUTE	ADDEEMED	ADDUCTOR
ACTIVISED	ACUTELY	ADDEEMING	ADDUCTORS
ACTIVISES	ACUTENESS	ADDEEMS	ADDUCTS
ACTIVISM	ACUTER	ADDEND	ADDY
ACTIVISMS	ACUTES	ADDENDA	ADEEM
ACTIVIST	ACUTEST	ADDENDS	ADEEMED
ACTIVISTS	ACYCLIC	ADDENDUM	ADEEMING
ACTIVITY	ACYCLOVIR	ADDENDUMS	ADEEMS
ACTIVIZE	ACYL	ADDER	ADEMPTION
ACTIVIZED	ACYLATE	ADDERS	ADENINE
ACTIVIZES	ACYLATED	ADDERWORT	ADENINES
ACTON	ACYLATES	ADDIBLE	ADENITIS
ACTONS	ACYLATING	ADDICT	ADENOID
ACTOR	ACYLATION	ADDICTED	ADENOIDAL
ACTORISH	ACYLOIN	ADDICTING	ADENOIDS
ACTORLY	ACYLOINS	ADDICTION	ADENOMA
ACTORS	ACYLS	ADDICTIVE	ADENOMAS
ACTRESS	AD	ADDICTS	ADENOMATA
ACTRESSES	ADAGE	ADDIES	ADENOSES
ACTRESSY	ADAGES	ADDING	ADENOSINE
ACTS	ADAGIAL	ADDIO	ADENOSIS
ACTUAL	ADAGIO	ADDIOS	ADENYL
ACTUALISE	ADAGIOS	ADDITION	ADENYLIC
ACTUALIST	ADAMANCE	ADDITIONS	ADENYLS
ACTUALITE	ADAMANCES	ADDITIVE	ADEPT
ACTUALITY	ADAMANCY	ADDITIVES	ADEPTER
ACTUALIZE	ADAMANT	ADDITORY	ADEPTEST
ACTUALLY	ADAMANTLY	ADDLE	ADEPTLY
ACTUALS	ADAMANTS	ADDLED	ADEPTNESS
ACTUARIAL	ADAMSITE	ADDLEMENT	ADEPTS
ACTUARIES	ADAMSITES	ADDLES	ADEQUACY
ACTUARY	ADAPT	ADDLING	ADEQUATE
ACTUATE	ADAPTABLE	ADDOOM	ADERMIN
ACTUATED	ADAPTED	ADDOOMED	ADERMINS
ACTUATES	ADAPTER	ADDOOMING	ADESPOTA
ACTUATING	ADAPTERS	ADDOOMS	ADESSIVE
ACTUATION	ADAPTING	ADDORSED	ADESSIVES
ACTUATOR	ADAPTION	ADDRESS	ADHAN
ACTUATORS	ADAPTIONS	ADDRESSED	ADHANS
ACTURE	ADAPTIVE	ADDRESSEE	ADHARMA
ACTURES	ADAPTOGEN	ADDRESSER	ADHARMAS
ACUATE	ADAPTOR	ADDRESSES	ADHERABLE
ACUITIES	ADAPTORS	ADDRESSOR	ADHERE
ACUITY	ADAPTS	ADDREST	ADHERED
ACULEATE	ADAW	ADDS	ADHERENCE
ACULEATED	ADAWED	ADDUCE	ADHEREND
ACULEI	ADAWING	ADDUCED	ADHERENDS
ACULEUS	ADAWS	ADDUCENT	ADHERENT
ACUMEN	ADAXIAL	ADDUCER	ADHERENTS
ACUMENS	ADAYS	ADDUCERS	ADHERER
ACUMINATE	ADD	ADDUCES	ADHERERS

ADHERES	ADJURORS	ADNASCENT	ADPRESS
ADHERING	ADJUST	ADNATE	ADPRESSED
ADHESION	ADJUSTED	ADNATION	ADPRESSES
ADHESIONS	ADJUSTER	ADNATIONS	ADRAD
ADHESIVE	ADJUSTERS	ADNEXA	ADREAD
ADHESIVES	ADJUSTING	ADNEXAL	ADREADED
ADHIBIT	ADJUSTIVE	ADNOMINAL	ADREADING
ADHIBITED	ADJUSTOR	ADNOUN	ADREADS
ADHIBITS	ADJUSTORS	ADNOUNS	ADRED
ADHOCRACY	ADJUSTS	ADO	ADRENAL
ADIABATIC	ADJUTAGE	ADOBE	ADRENALIN
ADIAPHORA	ADJUTAGES	ADOBELIKE	ADRENALLY
ADIEU	ADJUTANCY	ADOBES	ADRENALS
ADIEUS	ADJUTANT	ADOBO	ADRIFT
ADIEUX	ADJUTANTS	ADOBOS	ADROIT
ADIOS	ADJUVANCY	ADONIS	ADROITER
ADIPIC	ADJUVANT	ADONISE	ADROITEST
ADIPOCERE	ADJUVANTS	ADONISED	ADROITLY
ADIPOCYTE	ADLAND	ADONISES	ADRY
ADIPOSE	ADLANDS	ADONISING	ADS
ADIPOSES	ADMAN	ADONIZE	ADSCRIPT
ADIPOSIS	ADMASS	ADONIZED	ADSCRIPTS
ADIPOSITY	ADMASSES	ADONIZES	ADSORB
ADIPOUS	ADMEASURE	ADONIZING	ADSORBATE
ADIPSIA	ADMEN	ADOORS	ADSORBED
ADIPSIAS	ADMIN	ADOPT	ADSORBENT
ADIT	ADMINICLE	ADOPTABLE	ADSORBER
ADITS	ADMINS	ADOPTED	ADSORBERS
ADJACENCE	ADMIRABLE	ADOPTEE	ADSORBING
ADJACENCY	ADMIRABLY	ADOPTEES	ADSORBS
ADJACENT	ADMIRAL	ADOPTER	ADSUKI
ADJACENTS	ADMIRALS	ADOPTERS	ADSUKIS
ADJECTIVE	ADMIRALTY	ADOPTING	ADSUM
ADJIGO	ADMIRANCE	ADOPTION	ADUKI
ADJIGOS	ADMIRE	ADOPTIONS	ADUKIS
ADJOIN	ADMIRED	ADOPTIOUS	ADULARIA
ADJOINED	ADMIRER	ADOPTIVE	ADULARIAS
ADJOINING	ADMIRERS	ADOPTS	ADULATE
ADJOINS	ADMIRES	ADORABLE	ADULATED
ADJOINT	ADMIRING	ADORABLY	ADULATES
ADJOINTS	ADMISSION	ADORATION	ADULATING
ADJOURN	ADMISSIVE	ADORE	ADULATION
ADJOURNED	ADMIT	ADORED	ADULATOR
ADJOURNS	ADMITS	ADORER	ADULATORS
ADJUDGE	ADMITTED	ADORERS	ADULATORY
ADJUDGED	ADMITTEE	ADORES	ADULT
ADJUDGES	ADMITTEES	ADORING	ADULTERER
ADJUDGING	ADMITTER	ADORINGLY	ADULTERY
ADJUNCT	ADMITTERS	ADORN	ADULTESE
ADJUNCTLY	ADMITTING	ADORNED	ADULTESES
ADJUNCTS	ADMIX	ADORNER	ADULTHOOD
ADJURE	ADMIXED	ADORNERS	ADULTLIKE
ADJURED	ADMIXES	ADORNING	ADULTLY
ADJURER	ADMIXING	ADORNMENT	ADULTNESS
ADJURERS	ADMIXT	ADORNS	ADULTRESS
ADJURES	ADMIXTURE	ADOS	ADULTS
ADJURING	ADMONISH	ADOWN	ADUMBRAL
ADJUROR	ADMONITOR	ADOZE	ADUMBRATE

ADUNC	ADVISEE	AEGIRITE	AEROBIUM
ADUNCATE	ADVISEES	AEGIRITES	AEROBOMB
ADUNCATED	ADVISER	AEGIS	AEROBOMBS
ADUNCITY	ADVISERS	AEGISES	AEROBRAKE
ADUNCOUS	ADVISES	AEGLOGUE	AEROBUS
ADUST	ADVISING	AEGLOGUES	AEROBUSES
ADUSTED	ADVISINGS	AEGROTAT	AERODART
ADUSTING	ADVISOR	AEGROTATS	AERODARTS
ADUSTS	ADVISORS	AEMULE	AERODROME
ADVANCE	ADVISORY	AEMULED	AERODUCT
ADVANCED	ADVOCAAT	AEMULES	AERODUCTS
ADVANCER	ADVOCAATS	AEMULING	AERODYNE
ADVANCERS	ADVOCACY	AENEOUS	AERODYNES
ADVANCES	ADVOCATE	AENEUS	AEROFOIL
ADVANCING	ADVOCATED	AEOLIAN	AEROFOILS
ADVANTAGE	ADVOCATES	AEOLIPILE	AEROGEL
ADVECT	ADVOCATOR	AEOLIPYLE	AEROGELS
ADVECTED	ADVOUTRER	AEON	AEROGRAM
ADVECTING	ADVOUTRY	AEONIAN	AEROGRAMS
ADVECTION	ADVOWSON	AEONIC	AEROGRAPH
ADVECTIVE	ADVOWSONS	AEONS	AEROLITE
ADVECTS	ADWARD	AEPYORNIS	AEROLITES
ADVENE	ADWARDED	AEQUORIN	AEROLITH
ADVENED	ADWARDING	AEQUORINS	AEROLITHS
ADVENES	ADWARDS	AERATE	AEROLITIC
ADVENING	ADWARE	AERATED	AEROLOGIC
ADVENT	ADWARES	AERATES	AEROLOGY
ADVENTIVE	ADWOMAN	AERATING	AEROMANCY
ADVENTS	ADWOMEN	AERATION	AEROMETER
ADVENTURE	ADYNAMIA	AERATIONS	AEROMETRY
ADVERB	ADYNAMIAS	AERATOR	AEROMOTOR
ADVERBIAL	ADYNAMIC	AERATORS	AERONAUT
ADVERBS	ADYTA	AERIAL	AERONAUTS
ADVERSARY	ADYTUM	AERIALIST	AERONOMER
ADVERSE	ADZ	AERIALITY	AERONOMIC
ADVERSELY	ADZE	AERIALLY	AERONOMY
ADVERSER	ADZED	AERIALS	AEROPAUSE
ADVERSEST	ADZES	AERIE	AEROPHAGY
ADVERSITY	ADZING	AERIED	AEROPHOBE
ADVERT	ADZUKI	AERIER	AEROPHONE
ADVERTED	ADZUKIS	AERIES	AEROPHORE
ADVERTENT	AE	AERIEST	AEROPHYTE
ADVERTING	AECIA	AERIFIED	AEROPLANE
ADVERTISE	AECIAL	AERIFIES	AEROPULSE
ADVERTIZE	AECIDIA	AERIFORM	AEROS
ADVERTS	AECIDIAL	AERIFY	AEROSAT
ADVEW	AECIDIUM	AERIFYING	AEROSATS
ADVEWED	AECIUM	AERILY	AEROSCOPE
ADVEWING	AEDES	AERO	AEROSHELL
ADVEWS	AEDICULE	AEROBAT	AEROSOL
ADVICE	AEDICULES	AEROBATIC	AEROSOLS
ADVICEFUL	AEDILE	AEROBATS	AEROSPACE
ADVICES	AEDILES	AEROBE	AEROSTAT
ADVISABLE	AEDINE	AEROBES	AEROSTATS
ADVISABLY	AEFALD	AEROBIA	AEROTAXES
ADVISE	AEFAULD	AEROBIC	AEROTAXIS
ADVISED	AEGIRINE	AEROBICS	AEROTONE
ADVISEDLY	AEGIRINES	AEROBIONT	AEROTONES

AEROTRAIN	AFFEERING	AFFORCED	AFRONT
AERUGO	AFFEERS	AFFORCES	AFROS
AERUGOS	AFFERENT	AFFORCING	AFT
AERY	AFFERENTS	AFFORD	AFTER
AESC	AFFIANCE	AFFORDED	AFTERBODY
AESCES	AFFIANCED	AFFORDING	AFTERCARE
AESCULIN	AFFIANCES	AFFORDS	AFTERCLAP
AESCULINS	AFFIANT	AFFOREST	AFTERDAMP
AESIR	AFFIANTS	AFFORESTS	AFTERDECK
AESTHESES	AFFICHE	AFFRAP	AFTEREYE
AESTHESIA	AFFICHES	AFFRAPPED	AFTEREYED
AESTHESIS	AFFIDAVIT	AFFRAPS	AFTEREYES
AESTHETE	AFFIED	AFFRAY	AFTERGAME
AESTHETES	AFFIES	AFFRAYED	AFTERGLOW
AESTHETIC	AFFILIATE	AFFRAYER	AFTERHEAT ·
AESTIVAL	AFFINAL	AFFRAYERS	AFTERINGS
AESTIVATE	AFFINE	AFFRAYING	AFTERLIFE
AETHER	AFFINED	AFFRAYS	AFTERMATH
AETHEREAL	AFFINELY	AFFRENDED	AFTERMOST
AETHERIC	AFFINES	AFFRET	AFTERNOON
AETHERS	AFFINITY	AFFRETS	AFTERPAIN
AETIOLOGY	AFFIRM	AFFRICATE	AFTERPEAK
AFALD	AFFIRMANT	AFFRIGHT	AFTERS
AFAR	AFFIRMED	AFFRIGHTS	AFTERSHOW
AFARA	AFFIRMER	AFFRONT	AFTERSUN
AFARAS	AFFIRMERS	AFFRONTE	AFTERSUNS
AFARS	AFFIRMING	AFFRONTED	AFTERTAX
AFAWLD	AFFIRMS	AFFRONTEE	AFTERTIME
AFEAR	AFFIX	AFFRONTS	AFTERWARD
AFEARD	AFFIXABLE	AFFUSION	AFTERWORD
AFEARED	AFFIXAL	AFFUSIONS	AFTMOST
AFEARING	AFFIXED	AFFY	AFTOSA
AFEARS	AFFIXER	AFFYDE	AFTOSAS
AFEBRILE	AFFIXERS	AFFYING	AG
AFF	AFFIXES	AFGHAN	AGA
AFFABLE	AFFIXIAL	AFGHANI	AGACANT
AFFABLY	AFFIXING	AFGHANIS	AGACANTE
AFFAIR	AFFIXMENT	AFGHANS	AGACERIE
AFFAIRE	AFFIXTURE	AFIELD	AGACERIES
AFFAIRES	AFFLATED	AFIRE	AGAIN
AFFAIRS	AFFLATION	AFLAJ	AGAINST
AFFEAR	AFFLATUS	AFLAME	AGALACTIA
AFFEARD	AFFLICT	AFLATOXIN	AGALLOCH
AFFEARE	AFFLICTED	AFLOAT	AGALLOCHS
AFFEARED	AFFLICTER	AFLUTTER	AGALWOOD
AFFEARES	AFFLICTS	AFOOT	AGALWOODS
AFFEARING	AFFLUENCE	AFORE	AGAMA
AFFEARS	AFFLUENCY	AFOREHAND	AGAMAS
AFFECT	AFFLUENT	AFORESAID	AGAMETE
AFFECTED	AFFLUENTS	AFORETIME	AGAMETES
AFFECTER	AFFLUENZA	AFOUL	AGAMI
AFFECTERS	AFFLUX	AFRAID	AGAMIC
AFFECTING	AFFLUXES	AFREET	AGAMID
AFFECTION	AFFLUXION	AFREETS	AGAMIDS
AFFECTIVE	AFFOORD	AFRESH	AGAMIS
AFFECTS	AFFOORDED	AFRIT	AGAMOGONY
AFFEER	AFFOORDS	AFRITS	AGAMOID
AFFEERED	AFFORCE	AFRO	AGAMOIDS

AGAMONT
AGAMONTS
AGAMOUS
AGAPAE
AGAPAI
AGAPE
AGAPEIC
AGAPES
AGAR
AGARIC
AGARICS
AGAROSE
AGAROSES
AGARS
AGAS
AGAST
AGATE
AGATES
AGATEWARE
AGATISE
AGATISED
AGATISES
AGATISING
AGATIZE
AGATIZED
AGATIZES
AGATIZING
AGATOID
AGAVE
AGAVES
AGAZE
AGAZED
AGE
AGED
AGEDLY
AGEDNESS
AGEE
AGEING
AGEINGS
AGEISM
AGEISMS
AGEIST
AGEISTS
AGELAST
AGELASTIC
AGELASTS
AGELESS
AGELESSLY
AGELONG
AGEMATE
AGEMATES
AGEN
AGENCIES
AGENCY
AGENDA
AGENDAS
AGENDUM
AGENDUMS

AGENE
AGENES
AGENESES
AGENESIA
AGENESIAS
AGENESIS
AGENETIC
AGENISE
AGENISED
AGENISES
AGENISING
AGENIZE
AGENIZED
AGENIZES
AGENIZING
AGENT
AGENTED
AGENTIAL
AGENTING
AGENTINGS
AGENTIVAL
AGENTIVE
AGENTIVES
AGENTRIES
AGENTRY
AGENTS
AGER
AGERATUM
AGERATUMS
AGERS
AGES
AGEUSIA
AGEUSIAS
AGGADA
AGGADAH
AGGADAHS
AGGADAS
AGGADIC
AGGADOT
AGGADOTH
AGGER
AGGERS
AGGIE
AGGIES
AGGRACE
AGGRACED
AGGRACES
AGGRACING
AGGRADE
AGGRADED
AGGRADES
AGGRADING
AGGRATE
AGGRATED
AGGRATES
AGGRATING
AGGRAVATE
AGGREGATE

AGGRESS
AGGRESSED
AGGRESSES
AGGRESSOR
AGGRI
AGGRIEVE
AGGRIEVED
AGGRIEVES
AGGRO
AGGROS
AGGRY
AGHA
AGHAS
AGHAST
AGILA
AGILAS
AGILE
AGILELY
AGILENESS
AGILER
AGILEST
AGILITIES
AGILITY
AGIN
AGING
AGINGS
AGINNER
AGINNERS
AGIO
AGIOS
AGIOTAGE
AGIOTAGES
AGISM
AGISMS
AGIST
AGISTED
AGISTER
AGISTERS
AGISTING
AGISTMENT
AGISTOR
AGISTORS
AGISTS
AGITA
AGITABLE
AGITANS
AGITAS
AGITATE
AGITATED
AGITATES
AGITATING
AGITATION
AGITATIVE
AGITATO
AGITATOR
AGITATORS
AGITPOP
AGITPOPS

AGITPROP
AGITPROPS
AGLARE
AGLEAM
AGLEE
AGLET
AGLETS
AGLEY
AGLIMMER
AGLITTER
AGLOO
AGLOOS
AGLOSSAL
AGLOSSATE
AGLOSSIA
AGLOSSIAS
AGLOW
AGLU
AGLUS
AGLY
AGLYCON
AGLYCONE
AGLYCONES
AGLYCONS
AGMA
AGMAS
AGMINATE
AGNAIL
AGNAILS
AGNAME
AGNAMED
AGNAMES
AGNATE
AGNATES
AGNATHAN
AGNATHANS
AGNATHOUS
AGNATIC
AGNATICAL
AGNATION
AGNATIONS
AGNISE
AGNISED
AGNISES
AGNISING
AGNIZE
AGNIZED
AGNIZES
AGNIZING
AGNOMEN
AGNOMENS
AGNOMINA
AGNOMINAL
AGNOSIA
AGNOSIAS
AGNOSIC
AGNOSTIC
AGNOSTICS

AGO	AGREES	AHCHOO	AIGUILLE
AGOG	AGREGE	AHEAD	AIGUILLES
AGOGE	AGREGES	AHEAP	AIKIDO
AGOGES	AGREMENS	AHED	AIKIDOS
AGOGIC	AGREMENT	AHEIGHT	AIKONA
AGOGICS	AGREMENTS	AHEM	AIL
AGOING	AGRESTAL	AHEMERAL	AILANTHIC
AGON	AGRESTIAL	AHENT	AILANTHUS
AGONAL	AGRESTIC	AHI	AILANTO
AGONE	AGRIA	AHIGH	AILANTOS
AGONES	AGRIAS	AHIMSA	AILED
AGONIC	AGRIMONY	AHIMSAS	AILERON
AGONIES	AGRIN	AHIND	AILERONS
AGONISE	AGRIOLOGY	AHING	AILETTE
AGONISED	AGRISE	AHINT	AILETTES
AGONISES	AGRISED	AHIS	AILING
AGONISING	AGRISES	AHISTORIC	AILMENT
AGONIST	AGRISING	AHOLD	AILMENTS
AGONISTES	AGRIZE	AHOLDS	AILS
AGONISTIC	AGRIZED	AHORSE	AIM
AGONISTS	AGRIZES	AHOY	AIMED
AGONIZE	AGRIZING	AHS	AIMER
AGONIZED	AGRODOLCE	AHULL	AIMERS
AGONIZES	AGROLOGIC	AHUNGERED	AIMFUL
AGONIZING	AGROLOGY	AHUNGRY	AIMFULLY
AGONS	AGRONOMIC	AHURU	AIMING
AGONY	AGRONOMY	AHURUHURU	AIMLESS
AGOOD	AGROUND	AI	AIMLESSLY
AGORA	AGRYPNIA	AIA	AIMS
AGORAE	AGRYPNIAS	AIAS	AIN
AGORAS	AGRYZE	AIBLINS	AINE
AGOROT	AGRYZED	AID	AINEE
AGOROTH	AGRYZES	AIDANCE	AINGA
AGOUTA	AGRYZING	AIDANCES	AINGAS
AGOUTAS	AGS	AIDANT	AINS
AGOUTI	AGTERSKOT	AIDE	AINSELL
AGOUTIES	AGUACATE	AIDED	AINSELLS
AGOUTIS	AGUACATES	AIDER	AIOLI
AGOUTY	AGUE	AIDERS	AIOLIS
AGRAFE	AGUED	AIDES	AIR
AGRAFES	AGUELIKE	AIDFUL	AIRBAG
AGRAFFE	AGUES	AIDING	AIRBAGS
AGRAFFES	AGUEWEED	AIDLESS	AIRBASE
AGRAPHA	AGUEWEEDS	AIDMAN	AIRBASES
AGRAPHIA	AGUISE	AIDMEN	AIRBOAT
AGRAPHIAS	AGUISED	AIDOI	AIRBOATS
AGRAPHIC	AGUISES	AIDOS	AIRBORNE
AGRAPHON	AGUISH	AIDS	AIRBOUND
AGRARIAN	AGUISHLY	AIERIES	AIRBRICK
AGRARIANS	AGUISING	AIERY	AIRBRICKS
AGRASTE	AGUIZE	AIGA	AIRBRUSH
AGRAVIC	AGUIZED	AIGAS	AIRBURST
AGREE	AGUIZES	AIGLET	AIRBURSTS
AGREEABLE	AGUIZING	AIGLETS	AIRBUS
AGREEABLY	AGUTI	AIGRET	AIRBUSES
AGREED	AGUTIS	AIGRETS	AIRBUSSES
AGREEING	AH	AIGRETTE	AIRCHECK
AGREEMENT	AHA	AIGRETTES	AIRCHECKS

AIRCOACH	AIRMOBILE	AIRWARD	AKELAS
AIRCRAFT	AIRN	AIRWARDS	AKENE
AIRCREW	AIRNED	AIRWAVE	AKENES
AIRCREWS	AIRNING	AIRWAVES	AKENIAL
AIRDATE	AIRNS	AIRWAY	AKES
AIRDATES	AIRPARK	AIRWAYS	AKHARA
AIRDRAWN	AIRPARKS	AIRWISE	AKHARAS
AIRDROME	AIRPLANE	AIRWOMAN	AKIMBO
AIRDROMES	AIRPLANES	AIRWOMEN	AKIN
AIRDROP	AIRPLAY	AIRWORTHY	AKINESES
AIRDROPS	AIRPLAYS	AIRY	AKINESIA
AIRED	AIRPORT	AIS	AKINESIAS
AIRER	AIRPORTS	AISLE	AKINESIS
AIRERS	AIRPOST	AISLED	AKINETIC
AIREST	AIRPOSTS	AISLELESS	AKING
AIRFARE	AIRPOWER	AISLES	AKIRAHO
AIRFARES	AIRPOWERS	AISLEWAY	AKITA
AIRFIELD	AIRPROOF	AISLEWAYS	AKITAS
AIRFIELDS	AIRPROOFS	AISLING	AKKAS
AIRFLOW	AIRS	AISLINGS	AKOLUTHOS
AIRFLOWS	AIRSCAPE	AIT	AKRASIA
AIRFOIL	AIRSCAPES	AITCH	AKRASIAS
AIRFOILS	AIRSCREW	AITCHBONE	AKRATIC
AIRFRAME	AIRSCREWS	AITCHES	AKVAVIT
AIRFRAMES	AIRSHAFT	AITS	AKVAVITS
AIRGAP	AIRSHAFTS	AITU	AL
AIRGAPS	AIRSHED	AITUS	ALA
AIRGLOW	AIRSHEDS	AIVER	ALAAP
AIRGLOWS	AIRSHIP	AIVERS	ALAAPS
AIRGRAPH	AIRSHIPS	AIZLE	ALABAMINE
AIRGRAPHS	AIRSHOT	AIZLES	ALABASTER
AIRHEAD	AIRSHOTS	AJAR	ALACHLOR
AIRHEADED	AIRSHOW	AJEE	ALACHLORS
AIRHEADS	AIRSHOWS	AJIVA	ALACK
AIRHOLE	AIRSICK	AJIVAS	ALACKADAY
AIRHOLES	AIRSIDE	AJOWAN	ALACRITY
AIRIER	AIRSIDES	AJOWANS	ALAE
AIRIEST	AIRSPACE	AJUGA	ALAIMENT
AIRILY	AIRSPACES	AJUGAS	ALAIMENTS
AIRINESS	AIRSPEED	AJUTAGE	ALALAGMOI
AIRING	AIRSPEEDS	AJUTAGES	ALALAGMOS
AIRINGS	AIRSTOP	AJWAN	ALALIA
AIRLESS	AIRSTOPS	AJWANS	ALALIAS
AIRLIFT	AIRSTREAM	AKA	ALAMEDA
AIRLIFTED	AIRSTRIKE	AKARYOTE	ALAMEDAS
AIRLIFTS	AIRSTRIP	AKARYOTES	ALAMO
AIRLIKE	AIRSTRIPS	AKARYOTIC	ALAMODE
AIRLINE	AIRT	AKATEA	ALAMODES
AIRLINER	AIRTED	AKATHISIA	ALAMORT
AIRLINERS	AIRTH	AKE	ALAMOS
AIRLINES	AIRTHED	AKEAKE	ALAN
AIRLOCK	AIRTHING	AKEAKES	ALAND
AIRLOCKS	AIRTHS	AKED	ALANDS
AIRMAIL	AIRTIGHT	AKEDAH	ALANE
AIRMAILED	AIRTIME	AKEDAHS	ALANG
AIRMAILS	AIRTIMES	AKEE	ALANGS
AIRMAN	AIRTING	AKEES	ALANIN
AIRMEN	AIRTS	AKELA	ALANINE

ALANINES	ALBEDOS	ALCAIDE	ALDOXIME
ALANINS	ALBEE	ALCAIDES	ALDOXIMES
ALANNAH	ALBEIT	ALCALDE	ALDRIN
ALANNAHS	ALBERGHI	ALCALDES	ALDRINS
ALANS	ALBERGO	ALCARRAZA	ALE
ALANT	ALBERT	ALCATRAS	ALEATORIC
ALANTS	ALBERTITE	ALCAYDE	ALEATORY
ALANYL	ALBERTS	ALCAYDES	ALEBENCH
ALANYLS	ALBESCENT	ALCAZAR	ALEC
ALAP	ALBESPINE	ALCAZARS	ALECITHAL
ALAPA	ALBESPYNE	ALCHEMIC	ALECK
ALAPAS	ALBICORE	ALCHEMIES	ALECKS
ALAPS	ALBICORES	ALCHEMISE	ALECOST
ALAR	ALBINAL	ALCHEMIST	ALECOSTS
ALARM	ALBINESS	ALCHEMIZE	ALECS
ALARMABLE	ALBINIC	ALCHEMY	ALECTRYON
ALARMED	ALBINISM	ALCHERA	ALEE
ALARMEDLY	ALBINISMS	ALCHERAS	ALEF
ALARMING	ALBINO	ALCHYMIES	ALEFS
ALARMISM	ALBINOISM	ALCHYMY	ALEFT
ALARMISMS	ALBINOS	ALCID	ALEGAR
ALARMIST	ALBINOTIC	ALCIDINE	ALEGARS
ALARMISTS	ALBITE	ALCIDS	ALEGGE
ALARMS	ALBITES	ALCO	ALEGGED
ALARUM	ALBITIC	ALCOHOL	ALEGGES
ALARUMED	ALBITICAL	ALCOHOLIC	ALEGGING
ALARUMING	ALBITISE	ALCOHOLS	ALEHOUSE
ALARUMS	ALBITISED	ALCOLOCK	ALEHOUSES
ALARY	ALBITISES	ALCOLOCKS	ALEMBIC
ALAS	ALBITIZE	ALCOOL	ALEMBICS
ALASKA	ALBITIZED	ALCOOLS	ALEMBROTH
ALASKAS	ALBITIZES	ALCOPOP	ALENCON
ALASTOR	ALBIZIA	ALCOPOPS	ALENCONS
ALASTORS	ALBIZIAS	ALCORZA	ALENGTH
ALASTRIM	ALBIZZIA	ALCORZAS	ALEPH
ALASTRIMS	ALBIZZIAS	ALCOS	ALEPHS
ALATE	ALBRICIAS	ALCOVE	ALEPINE
ALATED	ALBS	ALCOVED	ALEPINES
ALATES	ALBUGO	ALCOVES	ALERCE
ALATION	ALBUGOS	ALDEA	ALERCES
ALATIONS	ALBUM	ALDEAS	ALERION
ALAY	ALBUMEN	ALDEHYDE	ALERIONS
ALAYED	ALBUMENS	ALDEHYDES	ALERT
ALAYING	ALBUMIN	ALDEHYDIC	ALERTED
ALAYS	ALBUMINS	ALDER	ALERTER
ALB	ALBUMOSE	ALDERFLY	ALERTEST
ALBA	ALBUMOSES	ALDERMAN	ALERTING
ALBACORE	ALBUMS	ALDERMEN	ALERTLY
ALBACORES	ALBURNOUS	ALDERN	ALERTNESS
ALBARELLI	ALBURNUM	ALDERS	ALERTS
ALBARELLO	ALBURNUMS	ALDICARB	ALES
ALBAS	ALBUTEROL	ALDICARBS	ALETHIC
ALBATA	ALCADE	ALDOL	ALEURON
ALBATAS	ALCADES	ALDOLASE	ALEURONE
ALBATROSS	ALCAHEST	ALDOLASES	ALEURONES
ALBE	ALCAHESTS	ALDOLS	ALEURONIC
ALBEDO	ALCAIC	ALDOSE	ALEURONS
ALBEDOES	ALCAICS	ALDOSES	ALEVIN

ALEVINS	ALGESIC	ALIENERS	ALIVE
ALEW	ALGESIS	ALIENING	ALIVENESS
ALEWASHED	ALGETIC	ALIENISM	ALIYA
ALEWIFE	ALGICIDAL	ALIENISMS	ALIYAH
ALEWIVES	ALGICIDE	ALIENIST	ALIYAHS
ALEWS	ALGICIDES	ALIENISTS	ALIYAS
ALEXANDER	ALGID	ALIENLY	ALIYOS
ALEXIA	ALGIDITY	ALIENNESS	ALIYOT
ALEXIAS	ALGIDNESS	ALIENOR	ALIYOTH
ALEXIC	ALGIN	ALIENORS	ALIZARI
ALEXIN	ALGINATE	ALIENS	ALIZARIN
ALEXINE	ALGINATES	ALIF	ALIZARINE
ALEXINES	ALGINIC	ALIFORM	ALIZARINS
ALEXINIC	ALGINS	ALIFS	ALIZARIS
ALEXINS	ALGOID	ALIGARTA	ALKAHEST
ALEYE	ALGOLOGY	ALIGARTAS	ALKAHESTS
ALEYED	ALGOMETER	ALIGHT	ALKALI
ALEYES	ALGOMETRY	ALIGHTED	ALKALIC
ALEYING	ALGOR	ALIGHTING	ALKALIES
ALF	ALGORISM	ALIGHTS	ALKALIFY
ALFA	ALGORISMS	ALIGN	ALKALIN
ALFAKI	ALGORITHM	ALIGNED	ALKALINE
ALFAKIS	ALGORS	ALIGNER	ALKALIS
ALFALFA	ALGUACIL	ALIGNERS	ALKALISE
ALFALFAS	ALGUACILS	ALIGNING	ALKALISED
ALFAQUI	ALGUAZIL	ALIGNMENT	ALKALISER
ALFAQUIN	ALGUAZILS	ALIGNS	ALKALISES
ALFAQUINS	ALGUM	ALIKE	ALKALIZE
ALFAQUIS	ALGUMS	ALIKENESS	ALKALIZED
ALFAS	ALIAS	ALIMENT	ALKALIZER
ALFERECES	ALIASES	ALIMENTAL	ALKALIZES
ALFEREZ	ALIASING	ALIMENTED	ALKALOID
ALFILARIA	ALIASINGS	ALIMENTS	ALKALOIDS
ALFILERIA	ALIBI	ALIMONIED	ALKALOSES
ALFORJA	ALIBIED	ALIMONIES	ALKALOSIS
ALFORJAS	ALIBIES	ALIMONY	ALKALOTIC
ALFREDO	ALIBIING	ALINE	ALKANE
ALFRESCO	ALIBIS	ALINED	ALKANES
ALFS	ALIBLE	ALINEMENT	ALKANET
ALGA	ALICANT	ALINER	ALKANETS
ALGAE	ALICANTS	ALINERS	ALKANNIN
ALGAECIDE	ALICYCLIC	ALINES	ALKANNINS
ALGAL	ALIDAD	ALINING	ALKENE
ALGAROBA	ALIDADE	ALIPED	ALKENES
ALGAROBAS	ALIDADES	ALIPEDS	ALKIE
ALGARROBA	ALIDADS	ALIPHATIC	ALKIES
ALGARROBO	ALIEN	ALIQUANT	ALKINE
ALGAS	ALIENABLE	ALIQUOT	ALKINES
ALGATE	ALIENAGE	ALIQUOTS	ALKO
ALGATES	ALIENAGES	ALISMA	ALKOS
ALGEBRA	ALIENATE	ALISMAS	ALKOXIDE
ALGEBRAIC	ALIENATED	ALISON	ALKOXIDES
ALGEBRAS	ALIENATES	ALISONS	ALKOXY
ALGERINE	ALIENATOR	ALIST	ALKY
ALGERINES	ALIENED	ALIT	ALKYD
ALGESES	ALIENEE	ALITERACY	ALKYDS
ALGESIA	ALIENEES	ALITERATE	ALKYL
ALGESIAS	ALIENER	ALIUNDE	ALKYLATE

ALKYLATED	ALLERGEN	ALLODS	ALLOZYMES
ALKYLATES	ALLERGENS	ALLOGAMY	ALLS
ALKYLIC	ALLERGIC	ALLOGENIC	ALLSEED
ALKYLS	ALLERGICS	ALLOGRAFT	ALLSEEDS
ALKYNE	ALLERGIES	ALLOGRAPH	ALLSORTS
ALKYNES	ALLERGIN	ALLOMERIC	ALLSPICE
ALL	ALLERGINS	ALLOMETRY	ALLSPICES
ALLANITE	ALLERGIST	ALLOMONE	ALLUDE
ALLANITES	ALLERGY	ALLOMONES	ALLUDED
ALLANTOIC	ALLERION	ALLOMORPH	ALLUDES
ALLANTOID	ALLERIONS	ALLONGE	ALLUDING
ALLANTOIN	ALLETHRIN	ALLONGES	ALLURE
ALLANTOIS	ALLEVIANT	ALLONS	ALLURED
ALLATIVE	ALLEVIATE	ALLONYM	ALLURER
ALLATIVES	ALLEY	ALLONYMS	ALLURERS
ALLAY	ALLEYCAT	ALLOPATH	ALLURES
ALLAYED	ALLEYCATS	ALLOPATHS	ALLURING
ALLAYER	ALLEYED	ALLOPATHY	ALLUSION
ALLAYERS	ALLEYS	ALLOPATRY	ALLUSIONS
ALLAYING	ALLEYWAY	ALLOPHANE	ALLUSIVE
ALLAYINGS	ALLEYWAYS	ALLOPHONE	ALLUVIA
ALLAYMENT	ALLHEAL	ALLOPLASM	ALLUVIAL
ALLAYS	ALLHEALS	ALLOSAUR	ALLUVIALS
ALLCOMERS	ALLIABLE	ALLOSAURS	ALLUVION
ALLEDGE	ALLIANCE	ALLOSTERY	ALLUVIONS
ALLEDGED	ALLIANCES	ALLOT	ALLUVIUM
ALLEDGES	ALLICE	ALLOTMENT	ALLUVIUMS
ALLEDGING	ALLICES	ALLOTROPE	ALLY
ALLEE	ALLICHOLY	ALLOTROPY ·	ALLYING
ALLEES	ALLICIN	ALLOTS	ALLYL
ALLEGE	ALLICINS	ALLOTTED	ALLYLIC
ALLEGED	ALLIED	ALLOTTEE	ALLYLS
ALLEGEDLY	ALLIES	ALLOTTEES	ALLYOU
ALLEGER	ALLIGARTA	ALLOTTER	ALMA
ALLEGERS	ALLIGATE	ALLOTTERS	ALMAGEST
ALLEGES	ALLIGATED	ALLOTTERY	ALMAGESTS
ALLEGGE	ALLIGATES	ALLOTTING	ALMAH
ALLEGGED	ALLIGATOR	ALLOTYPE	ALMAHS
ALLEGGES	ALLIS	ALLOTYPES	ALMAIN
ALLEGGING	ALLISES	ALLOTYPIC	ALMAINS
ALLEGIANT	ALLIUM	ALLOTYPY	ALMANAC
ALLEGING	ALLIUMS	ALLOVER	ALMANACK
ALLEGORIC	ALLNESS	ALLOVERS	ALMANACKS
ALLEGORY	ALLNESSES	ALLOW	ALMANACS
ALLEGRO	ALLNIGHT	ALLOWABLE	ALMANDINE
ALLEGROS	ALLOBAR	ALLOWABLY	ALMANDITE
ALLEL	ALLOBARS	ALLOWANCE	ALMAS
ALLELE	ALLOCABLE	ALLOWED	ALME
ALLELES	ALLOCARPY	ALLOWEDLY	ALMEH
ALLELIC	ALLOCATE	ALLOWING	ALMEHS
ALLELISM	ALLOCATED	ALLOWS	ALMEMAR
ALLELISMS	ALLOCATES	ALLOXAN	ALMEMARS
ALLELS	ALLOCATOR	ALLOXANS	ALMERIES
ALLELUIA	ALLOD	ALLOY	ALMERY
ALLELUIAH	ALLODIA	ALLOYED	ALMES
ALLELUIAS	ALLODIAL	ALLOYING	ALMIGHTY
ALLEMANDE	ALLODIUM	ALLOYS	ALMIRAH
ALLENARLY	ALLODIUMS	ALLOZYME	ALMIRAHS

ALMNER	ALONGST	ALTERCATE	ALUMINIC
ALMNERS	ALOOF	ALTERED	ALUMINISE
ALMOND	ALOOFLY	ALTERER	ALUMINIUM
ALMONDS	ALOOFNESS	ALTERERS	ALUMINIZE
ALMONDY	ALOPECIA	ALTERING	ALUMINOUS
ALMONER	ALOPECIAS	ALTERITY	ALUMINS
ALMONERS	ALOPECIC	ALTERN	ALUMINUM
ALMONRIES	ALOPECOID	ALTERNANT	ALUMINUMS
ALMONRY	ALOUD	ALTERNAT	ALUMISH
ALMOST	ALOW	ALTERNATE	ALUMIUM
ALMOUS	ALOWE	ALTERNATS	ALUMIUMS
ALMS	ALP	ALTERNE	ALUMNA
ALMSGIVER	ALPACA	ALTERNES	ALUMNAE
ALMSHOUSE	ALPACAS	ALTERS	ALUMNI
ALMSMAN	ALPACCA	ALTESSE	ALUMNUS
ALMSMEN	ALPACCAS	ALTESSES	ALUMROOT
ALMSWOMAN	ALPARGATA	ALTEZA	ALUMROOTS
ALMSWOMEN	ALPEEN	ALTEZAS	ALUMS
ALMUCE	ALPEENS	ALTEZZA	ALUMSTONE
ALMUCES	ALPENGLOW	ALTEZZAS	ALUNITE
ALMUD	ALPENHORN	ALTHAEA	ALUNITES
ALMUDE	ALPHA	ALTHAEAS	ALURE
ALMUDES	ALPHABET	ALTHEA	ALURES
ALMUDS	ALPHABETS	ALTHEAS	ALVEARIES
ALMUG	ALPHAS	ALTHO	ALVEARY
ALMUGS	ALPHASORT	ALTHORN	ALVEATED
ALNAGE	ALPHORN	ALTHORNS	ALVEOLAR
ALNAGER	ALPHORNS	ALTHOUGH	ALVEOLARS
ALNAGERS	ALPHOSIS	ALTIGRAPH	ALVEOLATE
ALNAGES	ALPHYL	ALTIMETER	ALVEOLE
ALNICO	ALPHYLS	ALTIMETRY	ALVEOLES
ALNICOS	ALPINE	ALTIPLANO	ALVEOLI
ALOCASIA	ALPINELY	ALTISSIMO	ALVEOLUS
ALOCASIAS	ALPINES	ALTITUDE	ALVINE
ALOD	ALPINISM	ALTITUDES	ALWAY
ALODIA	ALPINISMS	ALTO	ALWAYS
ALODIAL	ALPINIST	ALTOIST	ALYSSUM
ALODIUM	ALPINISTS	ALTOISTS	ALYSSUMS
ALODIUMS	ALPS	ALTOS	AM
ALODS	ALREADY	ALTRICES	AMA
ALOE	ALRIGHT	ALTRICIAL	AMABILE
ALOED	ALS	ALTRUISM	AMADAVAT
ALOES	ALSIKE	ALTRUISMS	AMADAVATS
ALOETIC	ALSIKES	ALTRUIST	AMADODA
ALOETICS	ALSO	ALTRUISTS	AMADOU
ALOFT	ALSOON	ALTS	AMADOUS
ALOGIA	ALSOONE	ALUDEL	AMAH
ALOGIAS	ALT	ALUDELS	AMAHS
ALOGICAL	ALTAR	ALULA	AMAIN
ALOHA	ALTARAGE	ALULAE	AMALGAM
ALOHAS	ALTARAGES	ALULAR	AMALGAMS
ALOIN	ALTARS	ALUM	AMANDINE
ALOINS	ALTARWISE	ALUMIN	AMANDINES
ALONE	ALTER	ALUMINA	AMANDLA
ALONELY	ALTERABLE	ALUMINAS	AMANDLAS
ALONENESS	ALTERABLY	ALUMINATE	AMANITA
ALONG	ALTERANT	ALUMINE	AMANITAS
ALONGSIDE	ALTERANTS	ALUMINES	AMANITIN

AMANITINS	AMBACHES	AMBOINA	AMENAGE
AMARACUS	AMBAGE	AMBOINAS	AMENAGED
AMARANT	AMBAGES	AMBONES	AMENAGES
AMARANTH	AMBAGIOUS	AMBOS	AMENAGING
AMARANTHS	AMBAN	AMBOYNA	AMENAUNCE
AMARANTIN	AMBANS	AMBOYNAS	AMEND
AMARANTS	AMBARI	AMBRIES	AMENDABLE
AMARELLE	AMBARIES	AMBROID	AMENDE
AMARELLES	AMBARIS	AMBROIDS	AMENDED
AMARETTI	AMBARY	AMBROSIA	AMENDER
AMARETTO	AMBASSAGE	AMBROSIAL	AMENDERS
AMARETTOS	AMBASSIES	AMBROSIAN	AMENDES
AMARNA	AMBASSY	AMBROSIAS	AMENDING
AMARONE	AMBATCH	AMBROTYPE	AMENDMENT
AMARONES	AMBATCHES	AMBRY	AMENDS
AMARYLLID	AMBEER	AMBSACE	AMENE
AMARYLLIS	AMBEERS	AMBSACES	AMENED
AMAS	AMBER	AMBULACRA	AMENING
AMASS	AMBERED	AMBULANCE	AMENITIES
AMASSABLE	AMBERGRIS	AMBULANT	AMENITY
AMASSED	AMBERIES	AMBULANTS	AMENS
AMASSER	AMBERINA	AMBULATE	AMENT
AMASSERS	AMBERINAS	AMBULATED	AMENTA
AMASSES	AMBERITE	AMBULATES	AMENTAL
AMASSING	AMBERITES	AMBULATOR	AMENTIA
AMASSMENT	AMBERJACK	AMBULETTE	AMENTIAS
AMATE	AMBEROID	AMBUSCADE	AMENTS
AMATED	AMBEROIDS	AMBUSCADO	AMENTUM
AMATES	AMBEROUS	AMBUSH	AMERCE
AMATEUR	AMBERS	AMBUSHED	AMERCED
AMATEURS	AMBERY	AMBUSHER	AMERCER
AMATING	AMBIANCE	AMBUSHERS	AMERCERS
AMATION	AMBIANCES	AMBUSHES	AMERCES
AMATIONS	AMBIENCE	AMBUSHING	AMERCING
AMATIVE	AMBIENCES	AMEARST	AMERICIUM
AMATIVELY	AMBIENT	AMEBA	AMESACE
AMATOL	AMBIENTS	AMEBAE	AMESACES
AMATOLS	AMBIGUITY	AMEBAN	AMETHYST
AMATORIAL	AMBIGUOUS	AMEBAS	AMETHYSTS
AMATORIAN	AMBIPOLAR	AMEBEAN	AMETROPIA
AMATORY	AMBIT	AMEBIASES	AMETROPIC
AMAUROSES	AMBITION	AMEBIASIS	AMI
AMAUROSIS	AMBITIONS	AMEBIC	AMIA
AMAUROTIC	AMBITIOUS	AMEBOCYTE	AMIABLE
AMAUT	AMBITS	AMEBOID	AMIABLY
AMAUTS	AMBITTY	AMEER	AMIANTHUS
AMAZE	AMBIVERT	AMEERATE	AMIANTUS
AMAZED	AMBIVERTS	AMEERATES	AMIAS
AMAZEDLY	AMBLE	AMEERS	AMICABLE
AMAZEMENT	AMBLED	AMEIOSES	AMICABLY
AMAZES	AMBLER	AMEIOSIS	AMICE
AMAZING	AMBLERS	AMELCORN	AMICES
AMAZINGLY	AMBLES	AMELCORNS	AMICI
AMAZON	AMBLING	AMELIA	AMICUS
AMAZONIAN	AMBLINGS	AMELIAS	AMID
AMAZONITE	AMBLYOPIA	AMEN	AMIDASE
AMAZONS	AMBLYOPIC	AMENABLE	AMIDASES
AMBACH	AMBO	AMENABLY	AMIDE

AMIDES	AMMINES	AMOEBIC	AMOUNT
AMIDIC	AMMINO	AMOEBOID	AMOUNTED
AMIDIN	AMMIRAL	AMOK	AMOUNTING
AMIDINE	AMMIRALS	AMOKS	AMOUNTS
AMIDINES	AMMO	AMOKURA	AMOUR
AMIDINS	AMMOCETE	AMOLE	AMOURETTE
AMIDMOST	AMMOCETES	AMOLES	AMOURS
AMIDO	AMMOCOETE	AMOMUM	AMOVE
AMIDOGEN	AMMON	AMOMUMS	AMOVED
AMIDOGENS	AMMONAL	AMONG	AMOVES
AMIDOL	AMMONALS	AMONGST	AMOVING
AMIDOLS	AMMONATE	AMOOVE	AMOWT
AMIDONE	AMMONATES	AMOOVED	AMOWTS
AMIDONES	AMMONIA	AMOOVES	AMP
AMIDS	AMMONIAC	AMOOVING	AMPASSIES
AMIDSHIP	AMMONIACS	AMORAL	AMPASSY
AMIDSHIPS	AMMONIAS	AMORALISM	AMPED
AMIDST	AMMONIATE	AMORALIST	AMPERAGE
AMIE	AMMONIC	AMORALITY	AMPERAGES
AMIES	AMMONICAL	AMORALLY	AMPERE
AMIGA	AMMONIFY	AMORANCE	AMPERES
AMIGAS	AMMONITE	AMORANCES	AMPERSAND
AMIGO	AMMONITES	AMORANT	AMPERZAND
AMIGOS	AMMONITIC	AMORCE	AMPHIBIA
AMILDAR	AMMONIUM	AMORCES	AMPHIBIAN
AMILDARS	AMMONIUMS	AMORET	AMPHIBOLE
AMIN	AMMONO	AMORETS	AMPHIBOLY
AMINE	AMMONOID	AMORETTI	AMPHIGORY
AMINES	AMMONOIDS	AMORETTO	AMPHIOXI
AMINIC	AMMONS	AMORETTOS	AMPHIOXUS
AMINITIES	AMMOS	AMORINI	AMPHIPATH
AMINITY	AMNESIA	AMORINO	AMPHIPOD
AMINO	AMNESIAC	AMORISM	AMPHIPODS
AMINS	AMNESIACS	AMORISMS	AMPHOLYTE
AMIR	AMNESIAS	AMORIST	AMPHORA
AMIRATE	AMNESIC	AMORISTIC	AMPHORAE
AMIRATES	AMNESICS	AMORISTS	AMPHORAL
AMIRS	AMNESTIC	AMORNINGS	AMPHORAS
AMIS	AMNESTIED	AMOROSA	AMPHORIC
AMISES	AMNESTIES	AMOROSAS	AMPING
AMISS	AMNESTY	AMOROSITY	AMPLE
AMISSES	AMNIA	AMOROSO	AMPLENESS
AMISSIBLE	AMNIC	AMOROSOS	AMPLER
AMISSING	AMNIO	AMOROUS	AMPLEST
AMITIES	AMNION	AMOROUSLY	AMPLEXUS
AMITOSES	AMNIONIC	AMORPHISM	AMPLIDYNE
AMITOSIS	AMNIONS	AMORPHOUS	AMPLIFIED
AMITOTIC	AMNIOS	AMORT	AMPLIFIER
AMITROLE	AMNIOTE	AMORTISE	AMPLIFIES
AMITROLES	AMNIOTES	AMORTISED	AMPLIFY
AMITY	AMNIOTIC	AMORTISES	AMPLITUDE
AMLA	AMNIOTOMY	AMORTIZE	AMPLOSOME
AMLAS	AMOEBA	AMORTIZED	AMPLY
AMMAN	AMOEBAE	AMORTIZES	AMPOULE
AMMANS	AMOEBAEAN	AMOSITE	AMPOULES
AMMETER	AMOEBAN	AMOSITES	AMPS
AMMETERS	AMOEBAS	AMOTION	AMPUL
AMMINE	AMOEBEAN	AMOTIONS	AMPULE

AMPULES	AMYL	ANAGOGE	ANALYZER
AMPULLA	AMYLASE	ANAGOGES	ANALYZERS
AMPULLAE	AMYLASES	ANAGOGIC	ANALYZES
AMPULLAR	AMYLENE	ANAGOGIES	ANALYZING
AMPULLARY	AMYLENES	ANAGOGY	ANAMNESES
AMPULS	AMYLIC	ANAGRAM	ANAMNESIS
AMPUTATE	AMYLOGEN	ANAGRAMS	ANAMNIOTE
AMPUTATED	AMYLOGENS	ANAL	ANAN
AMPUTATES	AMYLOID	ANALCIME	ANANA
AMPUTATOR	AMYLOIDAL	ANALCIMES	ANANAS
AMPUTEE	AMYLOIDS	ANALCIMIC	ANANASES
AMPUTEES	AMYLOPSIN	ANALCITE	ANANDROUS
AMREETA	AMYLOSE	ANALCITES	ANANKE
AMREETAS	AMYLOSES	ANALECTA	ANANKES
AMRIT	AMYLS	ANALECTIC	ANANTHOUS
AMRITA	AMYLUM	ANALECTS	ANAPAEST
AMRITAS	AMYLUMS	ANALEMMA	ANAPAESTS
AMRITS	AMYOTONIA	ANALEMMAS	ANAPEST
AMSINCKIA	AMYTAL	ANALEPTIC	ANAPESTIC
AMTMAN	AMYTALS	ANALGESIA	ANAPESTS
AMTMANS	AN	ANALGESIC	ANAPHASE
AMTRAC	ANA	ANALGETIC	ANAPHASES
AMTRACK	ANABAENA	ANALGIA	ANAPHASIC
AMTRACKS	ANABAENAS	ANALGIAS	ANAPHOR
AMTRACS	ANABANTID	ANALITIES	ANAPHORA
AMU	ANABAS	ANALITY	ANAPHORAL
AMUCK	ANABASES	ANALLY	ANAPHORAS
AMUCKS	ANABASIS	ANALOG	ANAPHORIC
AMULET	ANABATIC	ANALOGA	ANAPHORS
AMULETIC	ANABIOSES	ANALOGIC	ANAPLASIA
AMULETS	ANABIOSIS	ANALOGIES	ANAPLASTY
AMUS	ANABIOTIC	ANALOGISE	ANAPTYXES
AMUSABLE	ANABLEPS	ANALOGISM	ANAPTYXIS
AMUSE	ANABOLIC	ANALOGIST	ANARCH
AMUSEABLE	ANABOLISM	ANALOGIZE	ANARCHAL
AMUSED	ANABOLITE	ANALOGON	ANARCHIAL
AMUSEDLY	ANABRANCH	ANALOGONS	ANARCHIC
AMUSEMENT	ANACHARIS	ANALOGOUS	ANARCHIES
AMUSER	ANACLINAL	ANALOGS	ANARCHISE
AMUSERS	ANACLISES	ANALOGUE	ANARCHISM
AMUSES	ANACLISIS	ANALOGUES	ANARCHIST
AMUSETTE	ANACLITIC	ANALOGY	ANARCHIZE
AMUSETTES	ANACONDA	ANALYSAND	ANARCHS
AMUSIA	ANACONDAS	ANALYSE	ANARCHY
AMUSIAS	ANACRUSES	ANALYSED	ANARTHRIA
AMUSING	ANACRUSIS	ANALYSER	ANARTHRIC
AMUSINGLY	ANADEM	ANALYSERS	ANAS
AMUSIVE	ANADEMS	ANALYSES	ANASARCA
AMYGDAL	ANAEMIA	ANALYSING	ANASARCAS
AMYGDALA	ANAEMIAS	ANALYSIS	ANASTASES
AMYGDALAE	ANAEMIC	ANALYST	ANASTASIS
AMYGDALAS	ANAEROBE	ANALYSTS	ANASTATIC
AMYGDALE	ANAEROBES	ANALYTE	ANATA
AMYGDALES	ANAEROBIA	ANALYTES	ANATAS
AMYGDALIN	ANAEROBIC	ANALYTIC	ANATASE
AMYGDALS	ANAGLYPH	ANALYTICS	ANATASES
AMYGDULE	ANAGLYPHS	ANALYZE	ANATHEMA
AMYGDULES	ANAGLYPHY	ANALYZED	ANATHEMAS

ANATMAN	ANCOME	ANELE	ANGELHOOD
ANATMANS	ANCOMES	ANELED	ANGELIC
ANATOMIC	ANCON	ANELES	ANGELICA
ANATOMIES	ANCONAL	ANELING	ANGELICAL
ANATOMISE	ANCONE	ANEMIA	ANGELICAS
ANATOMIST	ANCONEAL	ANEMIAS	ANGELING
ANATOMIZE	ANCONES	ANEMIC	ANGELS
ANATOMY	ANCONOID	ANEMOGRAM	ANGELUS
ANATOXIN	ANCORA	ANEMOLOGY	ANGELUSES
ANATOXINS	ANCRESS	ANEMONE	ANGER
ANATROPY	ANCRESSES	ANEMONES	ANGERED
ANATTA	AND	ANEMOSES	ANGERING
ANATTAS	ANDANTE	ANEMOSIS	ANGERLESS
ANATTO	ANDANTES	ANENST	ANGERLY
ANATTOS	ANDANTINI	ANENT	ANGERS
ANAXIAL	ANDANTINO	ANERGIA	ANGICO
ANBURIES	ANDESINE	ANERGIAS	ANGICOS
ANBURY	ANDESINES	ANERGIC	ANGINA
ANCE	ANDESITE	ANERGIES	ANGINAL
ANCESTOR	ANDESITES	ANERGY	ANGINAS
ANCESTORS	ANDESITIC	ANERLY	ANGINOSE
ANCESTRAL	ANDESYTE	ANEROID	ANGINOUS
ANCESTRY	ANDESYTES	ANEROIDS	ANGIOGRAM
ANCHO	ANDIRON	ANES	ANGIOLOGY
ANCHOR	ANDIRONS	ANESTRA	ANGIOMA
ANCHORAGE	ANDOUILLE	ANESTRI	ANGIOMAS
ANCHORED	ANDRADITE	ANESTROUS	ANGIOMATA
ANCHORESS	ANDRO	ANESTRUM	ANGKLUNG
ANCHORET	ANDROECIA	ANESTRUS	ANGKLUNGS
ANCHORETS	ANDROGEN	ANETHOL	ANGLE
ANCHORING	ANDROGENS	ANETHOLE	ANGLED
ANCHORITE	ANDROGYNE	ANETHOLES	ANGLEDUG
ANCHORMAN	ANDROGYNY	ANETHOLS	ANGLEDUGS
ANCHORMEN	ANDROID	ANETIC	ANGLEPOD
ANCHORS	ANDROIDS	ANEUPLOID	ANGLEPODS
ANCHOS	ANDROLOGY	ANEURIN	ANGLER
ANCHOVETA	ANDROMEDA	ANEURINS	ANGLERS
ANCHOVIES	ANDROS	ANEURISM	ANGLES
ANCHOVY	ANDS	ANEURISMS	ANGLESITE
ANCHUSA	ANDVILE	ANEURYSM	ANGLEWISE
ANCHUSAS	ANDVILES	ANEURYSMS	ANGLEWORM
ANCHUSIN	ANE	ANEW	ANGLICE
ANCHUSINS	ANEAR	ANGA	ANGLICISE
ANCHYLOSE	ANEARED	ANGAKOK	ANGLICISM
ANCIENT	ANEARING	ANGAKOKS	ANGLICIST
ANCIENTER	ANEARS	ANGARIA	ANGLICIZE
ANCIENTLY	ANEATH	ANGARIAS	ANGLIFIED
ANCIENTRY	ANECDOTA	ANGARIES	ANGLIFIES
ANCIENTS	ANECDOTAL	ANGARY	ANGLIFY
ANCILE	ANECDOTE	ANGAS	ANGLING
ANCILIA	ANECDOTES	ANGASHORE	ANGLINGS
ANCILLA	ANECDOTIC	ANGEKKOK	ANGLIST
ANCILLAE	ANECDYSES	ANGEKKOKS	ANGLISTS
ANCILLARY	ANECDYSIS	ANGEKOK	ANGLO
ANCILLAS	ANECHOIC	ANGEKOKS	ANGLOPHIL
ANCIPITAL	ANELACE	ANGEL	ANGLOS
ANCLE	ANELACES	ANGELED	ANGOLA
ANCLES	ANELASTIC	ANGELFISH	ANGOPHORA

ANGORA	ANILINS	ANISOLE	ANNEALERS
ANGORAS	ANILITIES	ANISOLES	ANNEALING
ANGOSTURA	ANILITY	ANKER	ANNEALS
ANGRIER	ANILS	ANKERITE	ANNECTENT
ANGRIES	ANIMA	ANKERITES	ANNELID
ANGRIEST	ANIMACIES	ANKERS	ANNELIDAN
ANGRILY	ANIMACY	ANKH	ANNELIDS
ANGRINESS	ANIMAL	ANKHS	ANNEX
ANGRY	ANIMALIAN	ANKLE	ANNEXABLE
ANGST	ANIMALIC	ANKLEBONE	ANNEXE
ANGSTIER	ANIMALIER	ANKLED	ANNEXED
ANGSTIEST	ANIMALISE	ANKLES	ANNEXES
ANGSTROM	ANIMALISM	ANKLET	ANNEXING
ANGSTROMS	ANIMALIST	ANKLETS	ANNEXION
ANGSTS	ANIMALITY	ANKLING	ANNEXIONS
ANGSTY	ANIMALIZE	ANKLONG	ANNEXMENT
ANGUIFORM	ANIMALLY	ANKLONGS	ANNEXURE
ANGUINE	ANIMALS	ANKLUNG	ANNEXURES
ANGUIPED	ANIMAS	ANKLUNGS	ANNICUT
ANGUIPEDE	ANIMATE	ANKUS	ANNICUTS
ANGUISH	ANIMATED	ANKUSES	ANNO
ANGUISHED	ANIMATELY	ANKUSH	ANNONA
ANGUISHES	ANIMATER	ANKUSHES	ANNONAS
ANGULAR	ANIMATERS	ANKYLOSE	ANNOTATE
ANGULARLY	ANIMATES	ANKYLOSED	ANNOTATED
ANGULATE	ANIMATIC	ANKYLOSES	ANNOTATES
ANGULATED	ANIMATICS	ANKYLOSIS	ANNOTATOR
ANGULATES	ANIMATING	ANKYLOTIC	ANNOUNCE
ANGULOSE	ANIMATION	ANLACE	ANNOUNCED
ANGULOUS	ANIMATISM	ANLACES	ANNOUNCER
ANHEDONIA	ANIMATIST	ANLAGE	ANNOUNCES
ANHEDONIC	ANIMATO	ANLAGEN	ANNOY
ANHEDRAL	ANIMATOR	ANLAGES	ANNOYANCE
ANHINGA	ANIMATORS	ANLAS	ANNOYED
ANHINGAS	ANIME	ANLASES	ANNOYER
ANHUNGRED	ANIMES	ANN	ANNOYERS
ANHYDRASE	ANIMI	ANNA	ANNOYING
ANHYDRIDE	ANIMIS	ANNAL	ANNOYS
ANHYDRITE	ANIMISM	ANNALISE	ANNS
ANHYDROUS	ANIMISMS	ANNALISED	ANNUAL
ANI	ANIMIST	ANNALISES	ANNUALISE
ANICCA	ANIMISTIC	ANNALIST	ANNUALIZE
ANICCAS	ANIMISTS	ANNALISTS	ANNUALLY
ANICONIC	ANIMOSITY	ANNALIZE	ANNUALS
ANICONISM	ANIMUS	ANNALIZED	ANNUITANT
ANICONIST	ANIMUSES	ANNALIZES	ANNUITIES
ANICUT	ANION	ANNALS	ANNUITY
ANICUTS	ANIONIC	ANNAS	ANNUL
ANIDROSES	ANIONS	ANNAT	ANNULAR
ANIDROSIS	ANIS	ANNATES	ANNULARLY
ANIGH	ANISE	ANNATS	ANNULARS
ANIGHT	ANISEED	ANNATTA	ANNULATE
ANIL	ANISEEDS	ANNATTAS	ANNULATED
ANILE	ANISES	ANNATTO	ANNULATES
ANILIN	ANISETTE	ANNATTOS	ANNULET
ANILINE	ANISETTES	ANNEAL	ANNULETS
ANILINES	ANISIC	ANNEALED	ANNULI
ANILINGUS	ANISOGAMY	ANNEALER	ANNULLED

ANNULLING	ANONYMOUS	ANTAE	ANTHEMIA
ANNULMENT	ANONYMS	ANTALGIC	ANTHEMIC
ANNULOSE	ANOOPSIA	ANTALGICS	ANTHEMING
ANNULS	ANOOPSIAS	ANTALKALI	ANTHEMION
ANNULUS	ANOPHELES	ANTAR	ANTHEMS
ANNULUSES	ANOPIA	ANTARA	ANTHER
ANOA	ANOPIAS	ANTARAS	ANTHERAL
ANOAS	ANOPSIA	ANTARCTIC	ANTHERID
ANOBIID	ANOPSIAS	ANTARS	ANTHERIDS
ANOBIIDS	ANORAK	ANTAS	ANTHERS
ANODAL	ANORAKS	ANTBEAR	ANTHESES
ANODALLY	ANORECTAL	ANTBEARS	ANTHESIS
ANODE	ANORECTIC	ANTBIRD	ANTHILL
ANODES	ANORETIC	ANTBIRDS	ANTHILLS
ANODIC	ANORETICS	ANTE	ANTHOCARP
ANODISE	ANOREXIA	ANTEATER	ANTHOCYAN
ANODISED	ANOREXIAS	ANTEATERS	ANTHODIA
ANODISES	ANOREXIC	ANTECEDE	ANTHODIUM
ANODISING	ANOREXICS	ANTECEDED	ANTHOID
ANODIZE	ANOREXIES	ANTECEDES	ANTHOLOGY
ANODIZED	ANOREXY	ANTECHOIR	ANTHOTAXY
ANODIZES	ANORTHIC	ANTED	ANTHOZOAN
ANODIZING	ANORTHITE	ANTEDATE	ANTHOZOIC
ANODONTIA	ANOSMATIC	ANTEDATED	ANTHRACES
ANODYNE	ANOSMIA	ANTEDATES	ANTHRACIC
ANODYNES	ANOSMIAS	ANTEED	ANTHRAX
ANODYNIC	ANOSMIC	ANTEFIX	ANTHRAXES
ANOESES	ANOTHER	ANTEFIXA	ANTHROPIC
ANOESIS	ANOUGH	ANTEFIXAE	ANTHURIUM
ANOESTRA	ANOUROUS	ANTEFIXAL	ANTI
ANOESTRI	ANOVULANT	ANTEFIXES	ANTIABUSE
ANOESTRUM	ANOVULAR	ANTEING	ANTIACNE
ANOESTRUS	ANOW	ANTELOPE	ANTIAGING
ANOETIC	ANOXAEMIA	ANTELOPES	ANTIAIR
ANOINT	ANOXAEMIC	ANTELUCAN	ANTIALIEN
ANOINTED	ANOXEMIA	ANTENATAL	ANTIAR
ANOINTER	ANOXEMIAS	ANTENATI	ANTIARIN
ANOINTERS	ANOXEMIC	ANTENNA	ANTIARINS
ANOINTING	ANOXIA	ANTENNAE	ANTIARMOR
ANOINTS	ANOXIAS	ANTENNAL	ANTIARS
ANOLE	ANOXIC	ANTENNARY	ANTIATOM
ANOLES	ANSA	ANTENNAS	ANTIATOMS
ANOLYTE	ANSAE	ANTENNULE	ANTIAUXIN
ANOLYTES	ANSATE	ANTEPAST	ANTIBIAS
ANOMALIES	ANSATED	ANTEPASTS	ANTIBLACK
ANOMALOUS	ANSERINE	ANTERIOR	ANTIBODY
ANOMALY	ANSERINES	ANTEROOM	ANTIBOSS
ANOMIC	ANSEROUS	ANTEROOMS	ANTIBUG
ANOMIE	ANSWER	ANTES	ANTIBUSER
ANOMIES	ANSWERED	ANTETYPE	ANTIC
ANOMY	ANSWERER	ANTETYPES	ANTICAL
ANON	ANSWERERS	ANTEVERT	ANTICALLY
ANONYM	ANSWERING	ANTEVERTS	ANTICAR
ANONYMA	ANSWERS	ANTHELIA	ANTICHLOR
ANONYMAS	ANT	ANTHELION	ANTICISE
ANONYMISE	ANTA	ANTHELIX	ANTICISED
ANONYMITY	ANTACID	ANTHEM	ANTICISES
ANONYMIZE	ANTACIDS	ANTHEMED	ANTICITY

ANTICIVIC	ANTILIFE	ANTIQUARK	ANTITUMOR
ANTICIZE	ANTILIFER	ANTIQUARY	ANTITYPAL
ANTICIZED	ANTILOCK	ANTIQUATE	ANTITYPE
ANTICIZES	ANTILOG	ANTIQUE	ANTITYPES
ANTICK	ANTILOGS	ANTIQUED	ANTITYPIC
ANTICKE	ANTILOGY	ANTIQUELY	ANTIULCER
ANTICKED	ANTIMACHO	ANTIQUER	ANTIUNION
ANTICKING	ANTIMALE	ANTIQUERS	ANTIURBAN
ANTICKS	ANTIMAN	ANTIQUES	ANTIVENIN
ANTICLINE	ANTIMASK	ANTIQUEY	ANTIVENOM
ANTICLING	ANTIMASKS	ANTIQUING	ANTIVIRAL
ANTICLY	ANTIMERE	ANTIQUITY	ANTIVIRUS
ANTICODON	ANTIMERES	ANTIRADAR	ANTIWAR
ANTICOLD	ANTIMERIC	ANTIRAPE	ANTIWEAR
ANTICOUS	ANTIMINE	ANTIRED	ANTIWEED
ANTICRACK	ANTIMONIC	ANTIRIOT	ANTIWHITE
ANTICRIME	ANTIMONY	ANTIROCK	ANTIWOMAN
ANTICS	ANTIMONYL	ANTIROLL	ANTIWORLD
ANTICULT	ANTIMUON	ANTIROYAL	ANTLER
ANTICULTS	ANTIMUONS	ANTIRUST	ANTLERED
ANTIDORA	ANTIMUSIC	ANTIRUSTS	ANTLERS
ANTIDOTAL	ANTIMYCIN	ANTIS	ANTLIA
ANTIDOTE	ANTING	ANTISAG	ANTLIAE
ANTIDOTED	ANTINGS	ANTISCIAN	ANTLIATE
ANTIDOTES	ANTINODAL	ANTISENSE	ANTLIKE
ANTIDRAFT	ANTINODE	ANTISERA	ANTLION
ANTIDRUG	ANTINODES	ANTISERUM	ANTLIONS
ANTIDUNE	ANTINOISE	ANTISEX	ANTONYM
ANTIDUNES	ANTINOME	ANTISHARK	ANTONYMIC
ANTIELITE	ANTINOMES	ANTISHIP	ANTONYMS
ANTIENT	ANTINOMIC	ANTISHOCK	ANTONYMY
ANTIENTS	ANTINOMY	ANTISKID	ANTRA
ANTIFAT	ANTINOVEL	ANTISLEEP	ANTRAL
ANTIFLU	ANTINUKE	ANTISLIP	ANTRE
ANTIFOAM	ANTINUKER	ANTISMOG	ANTRES
ANTIFOG	ANTINUKES	ANTISMOKE	ANTRORSE
ANTIFRAUD	ANTIPAPAL	ANTISMUT	ANTRUM
ANTIFUR	ANTIPARTY	ANTISNOB	ANTRUMS
ANTIGANG	ANTIPASTI	ANTISNOBS	ANTS
ANTIGAY	ANTIPASTO	ANTISOLAR	ANTSIER
ANTIGEN	ANTIPATHY	ANTISPAM	ANTSIEST
ANTIGENE	ANTIPHON	ANTISPAST	ANTSINESS
ANTIGENES	ANTIPHONS	ANTISTAT	ANTSY
ANTIGENIC	ANTIPHONY	ANTISTATE	ANTWACKIE
ANTIGENS	ANTIPILL	ANTISTATS	ANUCLEATE
ANTIGLARE	ANTIPODAL	ANTISTICK	ANURAL
ANTIGRAFT	ANTIPODE	ANTISTORY	ANURAN
ANTIGUN	ANTIPODES	ANTISTYLE	ANURANS
ANTIHELIX	ANTIPOLAR	ANTITANK	ANURESES
ANTIHERO	ANTIPOLE	ANTITAX	ANURESIS
ANTIHUMAN	ANTIPOLES	ANTITHEFT	ANURETIC
ANTIJAM	ANTIPOPE	ANTITHET	ANURIA
ANTIKING	ANTIPOPES	ANTITHETS	ANURIAS
ANTIKINGS	ANTIPORN	ANTITOXIC	ANURIC
ANTIKNOCK	ANTIPOT	ANTITOXIN	ANUROUS
ANTILABOR	ANTIPRESS	ANTITRADE	ANUS
ANTILEAK	ANTIPYIC	ANTITRAGI	ANUSES
ANTILEFT	ANTIPYICS	ANTITRUST	ANVIL

ANVILED	APART	APHAKIA	APHRODITE
ANVILING	APARTHEID	APHAKIAS	APHTHA
ANVILLED	APARTMENT	APHANITE	APHTHAE
ANVILLING	APARTNESS	APHANITES	APHTHOUS
ANVILS	APATETIC	APHANITIC	APHYLLIES
ANVILTOP	APATHATON	APHASIA	APHYLLOUS
ANVILTOPS	APATHETIC	APHASIAC	APHYLLY
ANXIETIES	APATHIES	APHASIACS	APIACEOUS
ANXIETY	APATHY	APHASIAS	APIAN
ANXIOUS	APATITE	APHASIC	APIARIAN
ANXIOUSLY	APATITES	APHASICS	APIARIANS
ANY	APATOSAUR	APHELIA	APIARIES
ANYBODIES	APAY	APHELIAN	APIARIST
ANYBODY	APAYD	APHELION	APIARISTS
ANYHOW	APAYING	APHELIONS	APIARY
ANYMORE	APAYS	APHERESES	APICAL
ANYON	APE	APHERESIS	APICALLY
ANYONE	APEAK	APHERETIC	APICALS
ANYONES	APED	APHESES	APICES
ANYONS	APEDOM	APHESIS	APICIAN
ANYPLACE	APEDOMS	APHETIC	APICULATE
ANYROAD	APEEK	APHETISE	APICULI
ANYTHING	APEHOOD	APHETISED	APICULUS
ANYTHINGS	APEHOODS	APHETISES	APIECE
ANYTIME	APELIKE	APHETIZE	APIMANIA
ANYWAY	APEMAN	APHETIZED	APIMANIAS
ANYWAYS	APEMEN	APHETIZES	APING
ANYWHEN	APEPSIA	APHICIDE	APIOL
ANYWHERE	APEPSIAS	APHICIDES	APIOLOGY
ANYWHERES	APEPSIES	APHID	APIOLS
ANYWISE	APEPSY	APHIDES	APISH
ANZIANI	APER	APHIDIAN	APISHLY
AORIST	APERCU	APHIDIANS	APISHNESS
AORISTIC	APERCUS	APHIDIOUS	APISM
AORISTS	APERIENT	APHIDS	APISMS
AORTA	APERIENTS	APHIS	APIVOROUS
AORTAE	APERIES	APHOLATE	APLANAT
AORTAL	APERIODIC	APHOLATES	APLANATIC
AORTAS	APERITIF	APHONIA	APLANATS
AORTIC	APERITIFS	APHONIAS	APLANETIC
AORTITIS	APERITIVE	APHONIC	APLASIA
AOUDAD	APERS	APHONICS	APLASIAS
AOUDADS	APERT	APHONIES	APLASTIC
APACE	APERTNESS	APHONOUS	APLENTY
APACHE	APERTURAL	APHONY	APLITE
APACHES	APERTURE	APHORISE	APLITES
APADANA	APERTURED	APHORISED	APLITIC
APADANAS	APERTURES	APHORISER	APLOMB
APAGE	APERY	APHORISES	APLOMBS
APAGOGE	APES	APHORISM	APLUSTRE
APAGOGES	APETALIES	APHORISMS	APLUSTRES
APAGOGIC	APETALOUS	APHORIST	APNEA
APAID	APETALY	APHORISTS	APNEAL
APANAGE	APEX	APHORIZE	APNEAS
APANAGED	APEXES	APHORIZED	APNEIC
APANAGES	APGAR	APHORIZER	APNEUSES
APAREJO	APHAGIA	APHORIZES	APNEUSIS
APAREJOS	APHAGIAS	APHOTIC	APNEUSTIC

APNOEA	APOMIXES	APPALLED	APPENDING
APNOEAL	APOMIXIS	APPALLING	APPENDIX
APNOEAS	APOOP	APPALLS	APPENDS
APNOEIC	APOPHASES	APPALOOSA	APPERIL
APO	APOPHASIS	APPALS	APPERILL
APOAPSES	APOPHATIC	APPALTI	APPERILLS
APOAPSIS	APOPHONY	APPALTO	APPERILS
APOCARP	APOPHYGE	APPANAGE	APPERTAIN
APOCARPS	APOPHYGES	APPANAGED	APPESTAT
APOCARPY	APOPHYSES	APPANAGES	APPESTATS
APOCOPATE	APOPHYSIS	APPARAT	APPETENCE
APOCOPE	APOPLAST	APPARATS	APPETENCY
APOCOPES	APOPLASTS	APPARATUS	APPETENT
APOCOPIC	APOPLEX	APPAREL	APPETIBLE
APOCRINE	APOPLEXED	APPARELED	APPETISE
APOCRYPHA	APOPLEXES	APPARELS	APPETISED
APOD	APOPLEXY	APPARENCY	APPETISER
APODAL	APOPTOSES	APPARENT	APPETISES
APODE	APOPTOSIS	APPARENTS	APPETITE
APODES	APOPTOTIC	APPARITOR	APPETITES
APODICTIC	APORETIC	APPAY	APPETIZE
APODOSES	APORIA	APPAYD	APPETIZED
APODOSIS	APORIAS	APPAYING	APPETIZER
APODOUS	APORT	APPAYS	APPETIZES
APODS	APOS	APPEACH	APPLAUD
APOENZYME	APOSITIA	APPEACHED	APPLAUDED
APOGAEIC	APOSITIAS	APPEACHES	APPLAUDER
APOGAMIC	APOSITIC	APPEAL	APPLAUDS
APOGAMIES	APOSPORIC	APPEALED	APPLAUSE
APOGAMOUS	APOSPORY	APPEALER	APPLAUSES
APOGAMY	APOSTACY	APPEALERS	APPLE
APOGEAL	APOSTASY	APPEALING	APPLECART
APOGEAN	APOSTATE	APPEALS	APPLEJACK
APOGEE	APOSTATES	APPEAR	APPLES
APOGEES	APOSTATIC	APPEARED	APPLET
APOGEIC	APOSTIL	APPEARER	APPLETS
APOGRAPH	APOSTILLE	APPEARERS	APPLEY
APOGRAPHS	APOSTILS	APPEARING	APPLIABLE
APOLLO	APOSTLE	APPEARS	APPLIANCE
APOLLOS	APOSTLES	APPEASE	APPLICANT
APOLOG	APOSTOLIC	APPEASED	APPLICATE
APOLOGAL	APOTHECE	APPEASER	APPLIED
APOLOGIA	APOTHECES	APPEASERS	APPLIER
APOLOGIAE	APOTHECIA	APPEASES	APPLIERS
APOLOGIAS	APOTHEGM	APPEASING	APPLIES
APOLOGIES	APOTHEGMS	APPEL	APPLIQUE
APOLOGISE	APOTHEM	APPELLANT	APPLIQUED
APOLOGIST	APOTHEMS	APPELLATE	APPLIQUES
APOLOGIZE	APOZEM	APPELLEE	APPLY
APOLOGS	APOZEMS	APPELLEES	APPLYING
APOLOGUE	APP	APPELLOR	APPOINT
APOLOGUES	APPAID	APPELLORS	APPOINTED
APOLOGY	APPAIR	APPELS	APPOINTEE
APOLUNE	APPAIRED	APPEND	APPOINTER
APOLUNES	APPAIRING	APPENDAGE	APPOINTOR
APOMICT	APPAIRS	APPENDANT	APPOINTS
APOMICTIC	APPAL	APPENDED	APPORT
APOMICTS	APPALL	APPENDENT	APPORTION

APPORTS	APRAXIAS	APYREXIAS	ARABESK
APPOSABLE	APRAXIC	AQUA	ARABESKS
APPOSE	APRES	AQUABATIC	ARABESQUE
APPOSED	APRICATE	AQUABOARD	ARABIC
APPOSER	APRICATED	AQUACADE	ARABICA
APPOSERS	APRICATES	AQUACADES	ARABICAS
APPOSES	APRICOCK	AQUADROME	ARABICISE
APPOSING	APRICOCKS	AQUAE	ARABICIZE
APPOSITE	APRICOT	AQUAFARM	ARABILITY
APPRAISAL	APRICOTS	AQUAFARMS	ARABIN
APPRAISE	APRIORISM	AQUAFER	ARABINOSE
APPRAISED	APRIORIST	AQUAFERS	ARABINS
APPRAISEE	APRIORITY	AQUALUNG	ARABIS
APPRAISER	APRON	AQUALUNGS	ARABISE
APPRAISES	APRONED	AQUANAUT	ARABISED
APPREHEND	APRONFUL	AQUANAUTS	ARABISES
APPRESS	APRONFULS	AQUAPHOBE	ARABISING
APPRESSED	APRONING	AQUAPLANE	ARABIZE
APPRESSES	APRONLIKE	AQUAPORIN	ARABIZED
APPRISE	APRONS	AQUARELLE	ARABIZES
APPRISED	APROPOS	AQUARIA	ARABIZING
APPRISER	APROTIC	AQUARIAL	ARABLE
APPRISERS	APSARAS	AQUARIAN	ARABLES
APPRISES	APSARASES	AQUARIANS	ARACEOUS
APPRISING	APSE	AQUARIIST	ARACHIS
APPRIZE	APSES	AQUARIST	ARACHISES
APPRIZED	APSIDAL	AQUARISTS	ARACHNID
APPRIZER	APSIDES	AQUARIUM	ARACHNIDS
APPRIZERS	APSIDIOLE	AQUARIUMS	ARACHNOID
APPRIZES	APSIS	AQUAROBIC	ARAGONITE
APPRIZING	APSO	AQUAS	ARAISE
APPRO	APSOS	AQUASHOW	ARAISED
APPROACH	APT	AQUASHOWS	ARAISES
APPROBATE	APTED	AQUATIC	ARAISING
APPROOF	APTER	AQUATICS	ARAK
APPROOFS	APTERAL	AQUATINT	ARAKS
APPROS	APTERIA	AQUATINTA	ARALIA
APPROVAL	APTERISM	AQUATINTS	ARALIAS
APPROVALS	APTERISMS	AQUATONE	ARAME
APPROVE	APTERIUM	AQUATONES	ARAMES
APPROVED	APTEROUS	AQUAVIT	ARAMID
APPROVER	APTERYX	AQUAVITS	ARAMIDS
APPROVERS	APTERYXES	AQUEDUCT	ARANEID
APPROVES	APTEST	AQUEDUCTS	ARANEIDAN
APPROVING	APTING	AQUEOUS	ARANEIDS
APPS	APTITUDE	AQUEOUSLY	ARANEOUS
APPUI	APTITUDES	AQUIFER	ARAPAIMA
APPUIED	APTLY	AQUIFERS	ARAPAIMAS
APPUIS	APTNESS	AQUILEGIA	ARAPONGA
APPULSE	APTNESSES	AQUILINE	ARAPONGAS
APPULSES	APTOTE	AQUILON	ARAPUNGA
APPULSIVE	APTOTES	AQUILONS	ARAPUNGAS
APPUY	APTOTIC	AQUIVER	ARAR
APPUYED	APTS	AR	ARAROBA
APPUYING	APYRASE	ARAARA	ARAROBAS
APPUYS	APYRASES	ARAARAS	ARARS
APRACTIC	APYRETIC	ARABA	ARAUCARIA
APRAXIA	APYREXIA	ARABAS	ARAYSE

ARAYSED
ARAYSES
ARAYSING
ARB
ARBA
ARBALEST
ARBALESTS
ARBALIST
ARBALISTS
ARBAS
ARBELEST
ARBELESTS
ARBITER
ARBITERS
ARBITRAGE
ARBITRAL
ARBITRARY
ARBITRATE
ARBITRESS
ARBITRIUM
ARBLAST
ARBLASTER
ARBLASTS
ARBOR
ARBOREAL
ARBORED
ARBOREOUS
ARBORES
ARBORET
ARBORETA
ARBORETS
ARBORETUM
ARBORIO
ARBORISE
ARBORISED
ARBORISES
ARBORIST
ARBORISTS
ARBORIZE
ARBORIZED
ARBORIZES
ARBOROUS
ARBORS
ARBOUR
ARBOURED
ARBOURS
ARBOVIRAL
ARBOVIRUS
ARBS
ARBUSCLE
ARBUSCLES
ARBUTE
ARBUTEAN
ARBUTES
ARBUTUS
ARBUTUSES
ARC
ARCADE

ARCADED
ARCADES
ARCADIA
ARCADIAN
ARCADIANS
ARCADIAS
ARCADING
ARCADINGS
ARCANA
ARCANAS
ARCANE
ARCANELY
ARCANIST
ARCANISTS
ARCANUM
ARCANUMS
ARCATURE
ARCATURES
ARCCOS
ARCCOSES
ARCCOSINE
ARCED
ARCH
ARCHAEA
ARCHAEAL
ARCHAEAN
ARCHAEANS
ARCHAEI
ARCHAEON
ARCHAEUS
ARCHAIC
ARCHAICAL
ARCHAISE
ARCHAISED
ARCHAISER
ARCHAISES
ARCHAISM
ARCHAISMS
ARCHAIST
ARCHAISTS
ARCHAIZE
ARCHAIZED
ARCHAIZER
ARCHAIZES
ARCHANGEL
ARCHDUCAL
ARCHDUCHY
ARCHDUKE
ARCHDUKES
ARCHEAN
ARCHED
ARCHEI
ARCHENEMY
ARCHER
ARCHERESS
ARCHERIES
ARCHERS
ARCHERY

ARCHES
ARCHEST
ARCHETYPE
ARCHEUS
ARCHFIEND
ARCHFOE
ARCHFOES
ARCHICARP
ARCHIL
ARCHILOWE
ARCHILS
ARCHIMAGE
ARCHINE
ARCHINES
ARCHING
ARCHINGS
ARCHITECT
ARCHITYPE
ARCHIVAL
ARCHIVE
ARCHIVED
ARCHIVES
ARCHIVING
ARCHIVIST
ARCHIVOLT
ARCHLET
ARCHLETS
ARCHLUTE
ARCHLUTES
ARCHLY
ARCHNESS
ARCHOLOGY
ARCHON
ARCHONS
ARCHONTIC
ARCHOSAUR
ARCHRIVAL
ARCHWAY
ARCHWAYS
ARCHWISE
ARCIFORM
ARCING
ARCINGS
ARCKED
ARCKING
ARCKINGS
ARCMIN
ARCMINS
ARCO
ARCOGRAPH
ARCOLOGY
ARCS
ARCSEC
ARCSECOND
ARCSECS
ARCSIN
ARCSINE
ARCSINES

ARCSINS
ARCTAN
ARCTANS
ARCTIC
ARCTICS
ARCTIID
ARCTIIDS
ARCTOID
ARCTOPHIL
ARCUATE
ARCUATED
ARCUATELY
ARCUATION
ARCUS
ARCUSES
ARD
ARDEB
ARDEBS
ARDENCIES
ARDENCY
ARDENT
ARDENTLY
ARDOR
ARDORS
ARDOUR
ARDOURS
ARDRI
ARDRIGH
ARDRIGHS
ARDRIS
ARDS
ARDUOUS
ARDUOUSLY
ARE
AREA
AREACH
AREACHED
AREACHES
AREACHING
AREAD
AREADING
AREADS
AREAE
AREAL
AREALLY
AREAR
AREAS
AREAWAY
AREAWAYS
ARECA
ARECAS
ARECOLINE
ARED
AREDD
AREDE
AREDES
AREDING
AREFIED

AREFIES	ARGENTINE	ARGYLLS	ARISTOTLE
AREFY	ARGENTITE	ARGYRIA	ARK
AREFYING	ARGENTOUS	ARGYRIAS	ARKED
AREG	ARGENTS	ARGYRITE	ARKING
AREIC	ARGENTUM	ARGYRITES	ARKITE
ARENA	ARGENTUMS	ARHAT	ARKITES
ARENAS	ARGHAN	ARHATS	ARKOSE
ARENATION	ARGHANS	ARHATSHIP	ARKOSES
ARENE	ARGIL	ARHYTHMIA	ARKOSIC
ARENES	ARGILLITE	ARHYTHMIC	ARKS
ARENITE	ARGILS	ARIA	ARLE
ARENITES	ARGINASE	ARIARY	ARLED
ARENITIC	ARGINASES	ARIAS	ARLES
ARENOSE	ARGININE	ARID	ARLING
ARENOUS	ARGININES	ARIDER	ARM
AREOLA	ARGLE	ARIDEST	ARMADA
AREOLAE	ARGLED	ARIDITIES	ARMADAS
AREOLAR	ARGLES	ARIDITY	ARMADILLO
AREOLAS	ARGLING	ARIDLY	ARMAGNAC
AREOLATE	ARGOL	ARIDNESS	ARMAGNACS
AREOLATED	ARGOLS	ARIEL	ARMAMENT
AREOLE	ARGON	ARIELS	ARMAMENTS
AREOLES	ARGONAUT	ARIETTA	ARMATURE
AREOLOGY	ARGONAUTS	ARIETTAS	ARMATURED
AREOMETER	ARGONON	ARIETTE	ARMATURES
AREOSTYLE	ARGONONS	ARIETTES	ARMBAND
AREPA	ARGONS	ARIGHT	ARMBANDS
AREPAS	ARGOSIES	ARIKI	ARMCHAIR
ARERE	ARGOSY	ARIL	ARMCHAIRS
ARES	ARGOT	ARILED	ARMED
ARET	ARGOTIC	ARILLARY	ARMER
ARETE	ARGOTS	ARILLATE	ARMERS
ARETES	ARGUABLE	ARILLATED	ARMET
ARETHUSA	ARGUABLY	ARILLI	ARMETS
ARETHUSAS	ARGUE	ARILLODE	ARMFUL
ARETS	ARGUED	ARILLODES	ARMFULS
ARETT	ARGUER	ARILLOID	ARMGAUNT
ARETTED	ARGUERS	ARILLUS	ARMHOLE
ARETTING	ARGUES	ARILS	ARMHOLES
ARETTS	ARGUFIED	ARIOSE	ARMIES
AREW	ARGUFIER	ARIOSI	ARMIGER
ARF	ARGUFIERS	ARIOSO	ARMIGERAL
ARFS	ARGUFIES	ARIOSOS	ARMIGERO
ARGAL	ARGUFY	ARIOT	ARMIGEROS
ARGALA	ARGUFYING	ARIPPLE	ARMIGERS
ARGALAS	ARGUING	ARIS	ARMIL
ARGALI	ARGULI	ARISE	ARMILLA
ARGALIS	ARGULUS	ARISEN	ARMILLAE
ARGALS	ARGUMENT	ARISES	ARMILLARY
ARGAN	ARGUMENTA	ARISH	ARMILLAS
ARGAND	ARGUMENTS	ARISHES	ARMILS
ARGANDS	ARGUS	ARISING	ARMING
ARGANS	ARGUSES	ARISTA	ARMINGS
ARGEMONE	ARGUTE	ARISTAE	ARMISTICE
ARGEMONES	ARGUTELY	ARISTAS	ARMLESS
ARGENT	ARGYLE	ARISTATE	ARMLET
ARGENTAL	ARGYLES	ARISTO	ARMLETS
ARGENTIC	ARGYLL	ARISTOS	ARMLIKE

ARMLOAD	AROHAS	ARRASENE	ARRIVING
ARMLOADS	AROID	ARRASENES	ARRIVISME
ARMLOCK	AROIDS	ARRASES	ARRIVISTE
ARMLOCKED	AROINT	ARRAUGHT	ARROBA
ARMLOCKS	AROINTED	ARRAY	ARROBAS
ARMOIRE	AROINTING	ARRAYAL	ARROGANCE
ARMOIRES	AROINTS	ARRAYALS	ARROGANCY
ARMONICA	AROLLA	ARRAYED	ARROGANT
ARMONICAS	AROLLAS	ARRAYER	ARROGATE
ARMOR	AROMA	ARRAYERS	ARROGATED
ARMORED	AROMAS	ARRAYING	ARROGATES
ARMORER	AROMATASE	ARRAYMENT	ARROGATOR
ARMORERS	AROMATIC	ARRAYS	ARROW
ARMORIAL	AROMATICS	ARREAR	ARROWED
ARMORIALS	AROMATISE	ARREARAGE	ARROWHEAD
ARMORIES	AROMATIZE	ARREARS	ARROWING
ARMORING	AROSE	ARRECT	ARROWLESS
ARMORIST	AROUND	ARREEDE	ARROWLIKE
ARMORISTS	AROUSABLE	ARREEDES	ARROWROOT
ARMORLESS	AROUSAL	ARREEDING	ARROWS
ARMORS	AROUSALS	ARREST	ARROWWOOD
ARMORY	AROUSE	ARRESTANT	ARROWWORM
ARMOUR	AROUSED	ARRESTED	ARROWY
ARMOURED	AROUSER	ARRESTEE	ARROYO
ARMOURER	AROUSERS	ARRESTEES	ARROYOS
ARMOURERS	AROUSES	ARRESTER	ARS
ARMOURIES	AROUSING	ARRESTERS	ARSE
ARMOURING	AROW	ARRESTING	ARSED
ARMOURS	AROYNT	ARRESTIVE	ARSEHOLE
ARMOURY	AROYNTED	ARRESTOR	ARSEHOLES
ARMOZEEN	AROYNTING	ARRESTORS	ARSENAL
ARMOZEENS	AROYNTS	ARRESTS	ARSENALS
ARMOZINE	ARPEGGIO	ARRET	ARSENATE
ARMOZINES	ARPEGGIOS	ARRETS	ARSENATES
ARMPIT	ARPEN	ARRHIZAL	ARSENIATE
ARMPITS	ARPENS	ARRIAGE	ARSENIC
ARMREST	ARPENT	ARRIAGES	ARSENICAL
ARMRESTS	ARPENTS	ARRIBA	ARSENICS
ARMS	ARPILLERA	ARRIDE	ARSENIDE
ARMSFUL	ARQUEBUS	ARRIDED	ARSENIDES
ARMURE	ARRACACHA	ARRIDES	ARSENIOUS
ARMURES	ARRACK	ARRIDING	ARSENITE
ARMY	ARRACKS	ARRIERE	ARSENITES
ARMYWORM	ARRAH	ARRIERO	ARSENO
ARMYWORMS	ARRAIGN	ARRIEROS	ARSENOUS
ARNA	ARRAIGNED	ARRIS	ARSES
ARNAS	ARRAIGNER	ARRISES	ARSEY
ARNATTO	ARRAIGNS	ARRISH	ARSHEEN
ARNATTOS	ARRANGE	ARRISHES	ARSHEENS
ARNICA	ARRANGED	ARRIVAL	ARSHIN
ARNICAS	ARRANGER	ARRIVALS	ARSHINE
ARNOTTO	ARRANGERS	ARRIVANCE	ARSHINES
ARNOTTOS	ARRANGES	ARRIVANCY	ARSHINS
ARNUT	ARRANGING	ARRIVE	ARSIER
ARNUTS	ARRANT	ARRIVED	ARSIEST
AROBA	ARRANTLY	ARRIVER	ARSINE
AROBAS	ARRAS	ARRIVERS	ARSINES
AROHA	ARRASED	ARRIVES	ARSING

ARSINO

ARSINO	ARTISTES	ASCENDANT	ASEXUALLY
ARSIS	ARTISTIC	ASCENDED	ASH
ARSON	ARTISTRY	ASCENDENT	ASHAKE
ARSONIST	ARTISTS	ASCENDER	ASHAME
ARSONISTS	ARTLESS	ASCENDERS	ASHAMED
ARSONITE	ARTLESSLY	ASCENDEUR	ASHAMEDLY
ARSONITES	ARTS	ASCENDING	ASHAMES
ARSONOUS	ARTSIER	ASCENDS	ASHAMING
ARSONS	ARTSIES	ASCENSION	ASHCAKE
ARSY	ARTSIEST	ASCENSIVE	ASHCAKES
ART	ARTSINESS	ASCENT	ASHCAN
ARTAL	ARTSMAN	ASCENTS	ASHCANS
ARTEFACT	ARTSMEN	ASCERTAIN	ASHED
ARTEFACTS	ARTSY	ASCESES	ASHEN
ARTEL	ARTWORK	ASCESIS	ASHERIES
ARTELS	ARTWORKS	ASCETIC	ASHERY
ARTEMISIA	ARTY	ASCETICAL	ASHES
ARTERIAL	ARUGOLA	ASCETICS	ASHET
ARTERIALS	ARUGOLAS	ASCI	ASHETS
ARTERIES	ARUGULA	ASCIAN	ASHFALL
ARTERIOLE	ARUGULAS	ASCIANS	ASHFALLS
ARTERITIS	ARUHE	ASCIDIA	ASHIER
ARTERY	ARUM	ASCIDIAN	ASHIEST
ARTESIAN	ARUMS	ASCIDIANS	ASHINE
ARTFUL	ARUSPEX	ASCIDIATE	ASHINESS
ARTFULLY	ARUSPICES	ASCIDIUM	ASHING
ARTHRITIC	ARVAL	ASCITES	ASHIVER
ARTHRITIS	ARVICOLE	ASCITIC	ASHKEY
ARTHRODIA	ARVICOLES	ASCITICAL	ASHKEYS
ARTHROPOD	ARVO	ASCLEPIAD	ASHLAR
ARTHROSES	ARVOS	ASCLEPIAS	ASHLARED
ARTHROSIS	ARY	ASCOCARP	ASHLARING
ARTI	ARYBALLOS	ASCOCARPS	ASHLARS
ARTIC	ARYL	ASCOGONIA	ASHLER
ARTICHOKE	ARYLS	ASCONCE	ASHLERED
ARTICLE	ARYTENOID	ASCORBATE	ASHLERING
ARTICLED	ARYTHMIA	ASCORBIC	ASHLERS
ARTICLES	ARYTHMIAS	ASCOSPORE	ASHLESS
ARTICLING	ARYTHMIC	ASCOT	ASHMAN
ARTICS	AS	ASCOTS	ASHMEN
ARTICULAR	ASAFETIDA	ASCRIBE	ASHORE
ARTIER	ASANA	ASCRIBED	ASHPLANT
ARTIES	ASANAS	ASCRIBES	ASHPLANTS
ARTIEST	ASAR	ASCRIBING	ASHRAF
ARTIFACT	ASARUM	ASCUS	ASHRAM
ARTIFACTS	ASARUMS	ASDIC	ASHRAMA
ARTIFICE	ASBESTIC	ASDICS	ASHRAMAS
ARTIFICER	ASBESTINE	ASEA	ASHRAMITE
ARTIFICES	ASBESTOS	ASEISMIC	ASHRAMS
ARTILLERY	ASBESTOUS	ASEITIES	ASHTRAY
ARTILY	ASBESTUS	ASEITY	ASHTRAYS
ARTINESS	ASCARED	ASEPALOUS	ASHY
ARTIS	ASCARID	ASEPSES	ASIAGO
ARTISAN	ASCARIDES	ASEPSIS	ASIAGOS
ARTISANAL	ASCARIDS	ASEPTATE	ASIDE
ARTISANS	ASCARIS	ASEPTIC	ASIDES
ARTIST	ASCAUNT	ASEPTICS	ASINICO
ARTISTE	ASCEND	ASEXUAL	ASINICOS

ASININE	ASPERGER	ASPIRIN	ASSEGAI
ASININELY	ASPERGERS	ASPIRING	ASSEGAIED
ASININITY	ASPERGES	ASPIRINS	ASSEGAIS
ASK	ASPERGILL	ASPIS	ASSEMBLE
ASKANCE	ASPERGING	ASPISES	ASSEMBLED
ASKANCED	ASPERITY	ASPISH	ASSEMBLER
ASKANCES	ASPERMIA	ASPLENIUM	ASSEMBLES
ASKANCING	ASPERMIAS	ASPORT	ASSEMBLY
ASKANT	ASPEROUS	ASPORTED	ASSENT
ASKANTED	ASPERS	ASPORTING	ASSENTED
ASKANTING	ASPERSE	ASPORTS	ASSENTER
ASKANTS	ASPERSED	ASPOUT	ASSENTERS
ASKARI	ASPERSER	ASPRAWL	ASSENTING
ASKARIS	ASPERSERS	ASPREAD	ASSENTIVE
ASKED	ASPERSES	ASPRO	ASSENTOR
ASKER	ASPERSING	ASPROS	ASSENTORS
ASKERS	ASPERSION	ASPROUT	ASSENTS
ASKESES	ASPERSIVE	ASPS	ASSERT
ASKESIS	ASPERSOIR	ASQUAT	ASSERTED
ASKEW	ASPERSOR	ASQUINT	ASSERTER
ASKEWNESS	ASPERSORS	ASRAMA	ASSERTERS
ASKING	ASPERSORY	ASRAMAS	ASSERTING
ASKINGS	ASPHALT	ASS	ASSERTION
ASKLENT	ASPHALTED	ASSAGAI	ASSERTIVE
ASKOI	ASPHALTER	ASSAGAIED	ASSERTOR
ASKOS	ASPHALTIC	ASSAGAIS	ASSERTORS
ASKS	ASPHALTS	ASSAI	ASSERTORY
ASLAKE	ASPHALTUM	ASSAIL	ASSERTS
ASLAKED	ASPHERIC	ASSAILANT	ASSES
ASLAKES	ASPHODEL	ASSAILED	ASSESS
ASLAKING	ASPHODELS	ASSAILER	ASSESSED
ASLANT	ASPHYXIA	ASSAILERS	ASSESSES
ASLEEP	ASPHYXIAL	ASSAILING	ASSESSING
ASLOPE	ASPHYXIAS	ASSAILS	ASSESSOR
ASLOSH	ASPHYXIES	ASSAIS	ASSESSORS
ASMEAR	ASPHYXY	ASSAM	ASSET
ASMOULDER	ASPIC	ASSAMS	ASSETLESS
ASOCIAL	ASPICK	ASSART	ASSETS
ASOCIALS	ASPICKS	ASSARTED	ASSEVER
ASP	ASPICS	ASSARTING	ASSEVERED
ASPARAGUS	ASPIDIA	ASSARTS	ASSEVERS
ASPARKLE	ASPIDIOID	ASSASSIN	ASSEZ
ASPARTAME	ASPIDIUM	ASSASSINS	ASSHOLE
ASPARTATE	ASPINE	ASSAULT	ASSHOLES
ASPARTIC	ASPINES	ASSAULTED	ASSIDUITY
ASPECT	ASPIRANT	ASSAULTER	ASSIDUOUS
ASPECTED	ASPIRANTS	ASSAULTS	ASSIEGE
ASPECTING	ASPIRATA	ASSAY	ASSIEGED
ASPECTS	ASPIRATAE	ASSAYABLE	ASSIEGES
ASPECTUAL	ASPIRATE	ASSAYED	ASSIEGING
ASPEN	ASPIRATED	ASSAYER	ASSIENTO
ASPENS	ASPIRATES	ASSAYERS	ASSIENTOS
ASPER	ASPIRATOR	ASSAYING	ASSIGN
ASPERATE	ASPIRE	ASSAYINGS	ASSIGNAT
ASPERATED	ASPIRED	ASSAYS	ASSIGNATS
ASPERATES	ASPIRER	ASSED	ASSIGNED
ASPERGE	ASPIRERS	ASSEGAAI	ASSIGNEE
ASPERGED	ASPIRES	ASSEGAAIS	ASSIGNEES

ASSIGNER	ASSUMED	ASTERS	ASTRODOME
ASSIGNERS	ASSUMEDLY	ASTERT	ASTROFELL
ASSIGNING	ASSUMER	ASTERTED	ASTROID
ASSIGNOR	ASSUMERS	ASTERTING	ASTROIDS
ASSIGNORS	ASSUMES	ASTERTS	ASTROLABE
ASSIGNS	ASSUMING	ASTHENIA	ASTROLOGY
ASSIST	ASSUMINGS	ASTHENIAS	ASTRONAUT
ASSISTANT	ASSUMPSIT	ASTHENIC	ASTRONOMY
ASSISTED	ASSURABLE	ASTHENICS	ASTROPHEL
ASSISTER	ASSURANCE	ASTHENIES	ASTRUT
ASSISTERS	ASSURE	ASTHENY	ASTUCIOUS
ASSISTING	ASSURED	ASTHMA	ASTUCITY
ASSISTIVE	ASSUREDLY	ASTHMAS	ASTUN
ASSISTOR	ASSUREDS	ASTHMATIC	ASTUNNED
ASSISTORS	ASSURER	ASTHORE	ASTUNNING
ASSISTS	ASSURERS	ASTHORES	ASTUNS
ASSIZE	ASSURES	ASTICHOUS	ASTUTE
ASSIZED	ASSURGENT	ASTIGMIA	ASTUTELY
ASSIZER	ASSURING	ASTIGMIAS	ASTUTER
ASSIZERS	ASSUROR	ASTILBE	ASTUTEST
ASSIZES	ASSURORS	ASTILBES	ASTYLAR
ASSIZING	ASSWAGE	ASTIR	ASUDDEN
ASSLIKE	ASSWAGED	ASTOMATAL	ASUNDER
ASSOCIATE	ASSWAGES	ASTOMOUS	ASWARM
ASSOIL	ASSWAGING	ASTONE	ASWAY
ASSOILED	ASTABLE	ASTONED	ASWIM
ASSOILING	ASTARE	ASTONES	ASWING
ASSOILS	ASTART	ASTONIED	ASWIRL
ASSOILZIE	ASTARTED	ASTONIES	ASWOON
ASSONANCE	ASTARTING	ASTONING	ASYLA
ASSONANT	ASTARTS	ASTONISH	ASYLLABIC
ASSONANTS	ASTASIA	ASTONY	ASYLUM
ASSONATE	ASTASIAS	ASTONYING	ASYLUMS
ASSONATED	ASTATIC	ASTOOP	ASYMMETRY
ASSONATES	ASTATIDE	ASTOUND	ASYMPTOTE
ASSORT	ASTATIDES	ASTOUNDED	ASYNAPSES
ASSORTED	ASTATINE	ASTOUNDS	ASYNAPSIS
ASSORTER	ASTATINES	ASTRACHAN	ASYNDETA
ASSORTERS	ASTATKI	ASTRADDLE	ASYNDETIC
ASSORTING	ASTATKIS	ASTRAGAL	ASYNDETON
ASSORTIVE	ASTEISM	ASTRAGALI	ASYNERGIA
ASSORTS	ASTEISMS	ASTRAGALS	ASYNERGY
ASSOT	ASTELIC	ASTRAKHAN	ASYSTOLE
ASSOTS	ASTELIES	ASTRAL	ASYSTOLES
ASSOTT	ASTELY	ASTRALLY	ASYSTOLIC
ASSOTTED	ASTER	ASTRALS	AT
ASSOTTING	ASTERIA	ASTRAND	ATAATA
ASSUAGE	ASTERIAS	ASTRANTIA	ATAATAS
ASSUAGED	ASTERID	ASTRAY	ATABAL
ASSUAGER	ASTERIDS	ASTRICT	ATABALS
ASSUAGERS	ASTERISK	ASTRICTED	ATABEG
ASSUAGES	ASTERISKS	ASTRICTS	ATABEGS
ASSUAGING	ASTERISM	ASTRIDE	ATABEK
ASSUASIVE	ASTERISMS	ASTRINGE	ATABEKS
ASSUETUDE	ASTERN	ASTRINGED	ATABRIN
ASSUMABLE	ASTERNAL	ASTRINGER	ATABRINE
ASSUMABLY	ASTEROID	ASTRINGES	ATABRINES
ASSUME	ASTEROIDS	ASTROCYTE	ATABRINS

ATACAMITE	ATHEIST	ATMA	ATONEABLE
ATACTIC	ATHEISTIC	ATMAN	ATONED
ATAGHAN	ATHEISTS	ATMANS	ATONEMENT
ATAGHANS	ATHEIZE	ATMAS	ATONER
ATALAYA	ATHEIZED	ATMOLOGY	ATONERS
ATALAYAS	ATHEIZES	ATMOLYSE	ATONES
ATAMAN	ATHEIZING	ATMOLYSED	ATONIA
ATAMANS	ATHELING	ATMOLYSES	ATONIAS
ATAMASCO	ATHELINGS	ATMOLYSIS	ATONIC
ATAMASCOS	ATHEMATIC	ATMOLYZE	ATONICITY
ATAP	ATHENAEUM	ATMOLYZED	ATONICS
ATAPS	ATHENEUM	ATMOLYZES	ATONIES
ATARACTIC	ATHENEUMS	ATMOMETER	ATONING
ATARAXIA	ATHEOLOGY	ATMOMETRY	ATONINGLY
ATARAXIAS	ATHEOUS	ATOC	ATONY
ATARAXIC	ATHERINE	ATOCIA	ATOP
ATARAXICS	ATHERINES	ATOCIAS	ATOPIC
ATARAXIES	ATHEROMA	ATOCS	ATOPIES
ATARAXY	ATHEROMAS	ATOK	ATOPY
ATAVIC	ATHETESES	ATOKAL	ATRAMENT
ATAVISM	ATHETESIS	ATOKE	ATRAMENTS
ATAVISMS	ATHETISE	ATOKES	ATRAZINE
ATAVIST	ATHETISED	ATOKOUS	ATRAZINES
ATAVISTIC	ATHETISES	ATOKS	ATREMBLE
ATAVISTS	ATHETIZE	ATOLL	ATRESIA
ATAXIA	ATHETIZED	ATOLLS	ATRESIAS
ATAXIAS	ATHETIZES	ATOM	ATRESIC
ATAXIC	ATHETOID	ATOMIC	ATRETIC
ATAXICS	ATHETOSES	ATOMICAL	ATRIA
ATAXIES	ATHETOSIC	ATOMICITY	ATRIAL
ATAXY	ATHETOSIS	ATOMICS	ATRIP
ATCHIEVE	ATHETOTIC	ATOMIES	ATRIUM
ATCHIEVED	ATHIRST	ATOMISE	ATRIUMS
ATCHIEVES	ATHLETA	ATOMISED	ATROCIOUS
ATE	ATHLETAS	ATOMISER	ATROCITY
ATEBRIN	ATHLETE	ATOMISERS	ATROPHIA
ATEBRINS	ATHLETES	ATOMISES	ATROPHIAS
ATECHNIC	ATHLETIC	ATOMISING	ATROPHIC
ATELIC	ATHLETICS	ATOMISM	ATROPHIED
ATELIER	ATHODYD	ATOMISMS	ATROPHIES
ATELIERS	ATHODYDS	ATOMIST	ATROPHY
ATEMOYA	ATHRILL	ATOMISTIC	ATROPIA
ATEMOYAS	ATHROB	ATOMISTS	ATROPIAS
ATEMPORAL	ATHROCYTE	ATOMIZE	ATROPIN
ATENOLOL	ATHWART	ATOMIZED	ATROPINE
ATENOLOLS	ATIGI	ATOMIZER	ATROPINES
ATES	ATIGIS	ATOMIZERS	ATROPINS
ATHAME	ATILT	ATOMIZES	ATROPISM
ATHAMES	ATIMIES	ATOMIZING	ATROPISMS
ATHANASY	ATIMY	ATOMS	ATROPOUS
ATHANOR	ATINGLE	ATOMY	ATT
ATHANORS	ATISHOO	ATONABLE	ATTABOY
ATHEISE	ATISHOOS	ATONAL	ATTACH
ATHEISED	ATLANTES	ATONALISM	ATTACHE
ATHEISES	ATLAS	ATONALIST	ATTACHED
ATHEISING	ATLASES	ATONALITY	ATTACHER
ATHEISM	ATLATL	ATONALLY	ATTACHERS
ATHEISMS	ATLATLS	ATONE	ATTACHES

ATTACHING	ATTESTERS	ATTRITTED	AUDILES
ATTACK	ATTESTING	ATTUENT	AUDING
ATTACKED	ATTESTOR	ATTUITE	AUDINGS
ATTACKER	ATTESTORS	ATTUITED	AUDIO
ATTACKERS	ATTESTS	ATTUITES	AUDIOBOOK
ATTACKING	ATTIC	ATTUITING	AUDIOGRAM
ATTACKMAN	ATTICISE	ATTUITION	AUDIOLOGY
ATTACKMEN	ATTICISED	ATTUITIVE	AUDIOPHIL
ATTACKS	ATTICISES	ATTUNE	AUDIOS
ATTAGIRL	ATTICISM	ATTUNED	AUDIOTAPE
ATTAIN	ATTICISMS	ATTUNES	AUDIPHONE
ATTAINDER	ATTICIST	ATTUNING	AUDIT
ATTAINED	ATTICISTS	ATUA	AUDITABLE
ATTAINER	ATTICIZE	ATUAS	AUDITED
ATTAINERS	ATTICIZED	ATWAIN	AUDITEE
ATTAINING	ATTICIZES	ATWEEL	AUDITEES
ATTAINS	ATTICS	ATWEEN	AUDITING
ATTAINT	ATTIRE	ATWITTER	AUDITION
ATTAINTED	ATTIRED	ATWIXT	AUDITIONS
ATTAINTS	ATTIRES	ATYPIC	AUDITIVE
ATTAP	ATTIRING	ATYPICAL	AUDITIVES
ATTAPS	ATTIRINGS	AUA	AUDITOR
ATTAR	ATTITUDE	AUBADE	AUDITORIA
ATTARS	ATTITUDES	AUBADES	AUDITORS
ATTASK	ATTOLASER	AUBERGE	AUDITORY
ATTASKED	ATTOLLENS	AUBERGES	AUDITRESS
ATTASKING	ATTOLLENT	AUBERGINE	AUDITS
ATTASKS	ATTONCE	AUBRETIA	AUE
ATTASKT	ATTONE	AUBRETIAS	AUF
ATTEMPER	ATTONES	AUBRIETA	AUFGABE
ATTEMPERS	ATTORN	AUBRIETAS	AUFGABES
ATTEMPT	ATTORNED	AUBRIETIA	AUFS
ATTEMPTED	ATTORNEY	AUBURN	AUGEND
ATTEMPTER	ATTORNEYS	AUBURNS	AUGENDS
ATTEMPTS	ATTORNING	AUCEPS	AUGER
ATTEND	ATTORNS	AUCEPSES	AUGERS
ATTENDANT	ATTRACT	AUCTION	AUGHT
ATTENDED	ATTRACTED	AUCTIONED	AUGHTS
ATTENDEE	ATTRACTER	AUCTIONS	AUGITE
ATTENDEES	ATTRACTOR	AUCTORIAL	AUGITES
ATTENDER	ATTRACTS	AUCUBA	AUGITIC
ATTENDERS	ATTRAHENS	AUCUBAS	AUGMENT
ATTENDING	ATTRAHENT	AUDACIOUS	AUGMENTED
ATTENDS	ATTRAP	AUDACITY	AUGMENTER
ATTENT	ATTRAPPED	AUDAD	AUGMENTOR
ATTENTAT	ATTRAPS	AUDADS	AUGMENTS
ATTENTATS	ATTRIBUTE	AUDIAL	AUGUR
ATTENTION	ATTRIST	AUDIBLE	AUGURAL
ATTENTIVE	ATTRISTED	AUDIBLED	AUGURED
ATTENTS	ATTRISTS	AUDIBLES	AUGURER
ATTENUANT	ATTRIT	AUDIBLING	AUGURERS
ATTENUATE	ATTRITE	AUDIBLY	AUGURIES
ATTERCOP	ATTRITED	AUDIENCE	AUGURING
ATTERCOPS	ATTRITES	AUDIENCES	AUGURS
ATTEST	ATTRITING	AUDIENCIA	AUGURSHIP
ATTESTANT	ATTRITION	AUDIENT	AUGURY
ATTESTED	ATTRITIVE	AUDIENTS	AUGUST
ATTESTER	ATTRITS	AUDILE	AUGUSTE

AUGUSTER	AUREI	AUSTRAL	AUTOCRATS
AUGUSTES	AUREITIES	AUSTRALES	AUTOCRIME
AUGUSTEST	AUREITY	AUSTRALIS	AUTOCRINE
AUGUSTLY	AURELIA	AUSTRALS	AUTOCROSS
AUGUSTS	AURELIAN	AUSUBO	AUTOCUE
AUK	AURELIANS	AUSUBOS	AUTOCUES
AUKLET	AURELIAS	AUTACOID	AUTOCUTIE
AUKLETS	AUREOLA	AUTACOIDS	AUTOCYCLE
AUKS	AUREOLAE	AUTARCH	AUTODYNE
AULA	AUREOLAS	AUTARCHIC	AUTODYNES
AULARIAN	AUREOLE	AUTARCHS	AUTOECISM
AULARIANS	AUREOLED	AUTARCHY	AUTOED
AULAS	AUREOLES	AUTARKIC	AUTOFLARE
AULD	AUREOLING	AUTARKIES	AUTOFOCUS
AULDER	AURES	AUTARKIST	AUTOGAMIC
AULDEST	AUREUS	AUTARKY	AUTOGAMY
AULIC	AURIC	AUTECIOUS	AUTOGENIC
AULNAGE	AURICLE	AUTECISM	AUTOGENY
AULNAGER	AURICLED	AUTECISMS	AUTOGIRO
AULNAGERS	AURICLES	AUTEUR	AUTOGIROS
AULNAGES	AURICULA	AUTEURISM	AUTOGRAFT
AULOI	AURICULAE	AUTEURIST	AUTOGRAPH
AULOS	AURICULAR	AUTEURS	AUTOGUIDE
AUMAIL	AURICULAS	AUTHENTIC	AUTOGYRO
AUMAILED	AURIFIED	AUTHOR	AUTOGYROS
AUMAILING	AURIFIES	AUTHORED	AUTOHARP
AUMAILS	AURIFORM	AUTHORESS	AUTOHARPS
AUMBRIES	AURIFY	AUTHORIAL	AUTOICOUS
AUMBRY	AURIFYING	AUTHORING	AUTOING
AUMIL	AURIS	AUTHORISE	AUTOLATRY
AUMILS	AURISCOPE	AUTHORISH	AUTOLOGY
AUNE	AURIST	AUTHORISM	AUTOLYSE
AUNES	AURISTS	AUTHORITY	AUTOLYSED
AUNT	AUROCHS	AUTHORIZE	AUTOLYSES
AUNTER	AUROCHSES	AUTHORS	AUTOLYSIN
AUNTERS	AURORA	AUTISM	AUTOLYSIS
AUNTHOOD	AURORAE	AUTISMS	AUTOLYTIC
AUNTHOODS	AURORAL	AUTIST	AUTOLYZE
AUNTIE	AURORALLY	AUTISTIC	AUTOLYZED
AUNTIES	AURORAS	AUTISTICS	AUTOLYZES
AUNTLIER	AUROREAN	AUTISTS	AUTOMAKER
AUNTLIEST	AUROUS	AUTO	AUTOMAN
AUNTLIKE	AURUM	AUTOBAHN	AUTOMAT
AUNTLY	AURUMS	AUTOBAHNS	AUTOMATA
AUNTS	AUSFORM	AUTOBUS	AUTOMATE
AUNTY	AUSFORMED	AUTOBUSES	AUTOMATED
AURA	AUSFORMS	AUTOCADE	AUTOMATES
AURAE	AUSLANDER	AUTOCADES	AUTOMATIC
AURAL	AUSPEX	AUTOCAR	AUTOMATON
AURALITY	AUSPICATE	AUTOCARP	AUTOMATS
AURALLY	AUSPICE	AUTOCARPS	AUTOMEN
AURAR	AUSPICES	AUTOCARS	AUTOMETER
AURAS	AUSTENITE	AUTOCIDAL	AUTONOMIC
AURATE	AUSTERE	AUTOCLAVE	AUTONOMY
AURATED	AUSTERELY	AUTOCOID	AUTONYM
AURATES	AUSTERER	AUTOCOIDS	AUTONYMS
AUREATE	AUSTEREST	AUTOCRACY	AUTOPEN
AUREATELY	AUSTERITY	AUTOCRAT	AUTOPENS

AUTOPHAGY	AUXOMETER	AVENTRES	AVIATORS
AUTOPHOBY	AUXOSPORE	AVENTRING	AVIATRESS
AUTOPHONY	AUXOTONIC	AVENTURE	AVIATRICE
AUTOPHYTE	AUXOTROPH	AVENTURES	AVIATRIX
AUTOPILOT	AVA	AVENTURIN	AVICULAR
AUTOPISTA	AVADAVAT	AVENUE	AVID
AUTOPOINT	AVADAVATS	AVENUES	AVIDER
AUTOPSIA	AVAIL	AVER	AVIDEST
AUTOPSIAS	AVAILABLE	AVERAGE	AVIDIN
AUTOPSIC	AVAILABLY	AVERAGED	AVIDINS
AUTOPSIED	AVAILE	AVERAGELY	AVIDITIES
AUTOPSIES	AVAILED	AVERAGES	AVIDITY
AUTOPSIST	AVAILES	AVERAGING	AVIDLY
AUTOPSY	AVAILFUL	AVERMENT	AVIDNESS
AUTOPTIC	AVAILING	AVERMENTS	AVIETTE
AUTOPUT	AVAILS	AVERRABLE	AVIETTES
AUTOPUTS	AVAL	AVERRED	AVIFAUNA
AUTOROUTE	AVALANCHE	AVERRING	AVIFAUNAE
AUTOS	AVALE	AVERS	AVIFAUNAL
AUTOSCOPY	AVALED	AVERSE	AVIFAUNAS
AUTOSOMAL	AVALES	AVERSELY	AVIFORM
AUTOSOME	AVALING	AVERSION	AVIGATOR
AUTOSOMES	AVANT	AVERSIONS	AVIGATORS
AUTOSPORE	AVANTI	AVERSIVE	AVINE
AUTOTELIC	AVANTIST	AVERSIVES	AVION
AUTOTIMER	AVANTISTS	AVERT	AVIONIC
AUTOTOMIC	AVARICE	AVERTABLE	AVIONICS
AUTOTOMY	AVARICES	AVERTED	AVIONS
AUTOTOXIC	AVAS	AVERTEDLY	AVIRULENT
AUTOTOXIN	AVASCULAR	AVERTER	AVISANDUM
AUTOTROPH	AVAST	AVERTERS	AVISE
AUTOTUNE	AVATAR	AVERTIBLE	AVISED
AUTOTUNES	AVATARS	AVERTING	AVISEMENT
AUTOTYPE	AVAUNT	AVERTS	AVISES
AUTOTYPED	AVAUNTED	AVES	AVISING
AUTOTYPES	AVAUNTING	AVGAS	AVISO
AUTOTYPIC	AVAUNTS	AVGASES	AVISOS
AUTOTYPY	AVE	AVGASSES	AVITAL
AUTOVAC	AVEL	AVIAN	AVIZANDUM
AUTOVACS	AVELLAN	AVIANISE	AVIZE
AUTUMN	AVELLANE	AVIANISED	AVIZED
AUTUMNAL	AVELS	AVIANISES	AVIZEFULL
AUTUMNS	AVENGE	AVIANIZE	AVIZES
AUTUMNY	AVENGED	AVIANIZED	AVIZING
AUTUNITE	AVENGEFUL	AVIANIZES	AVO
AUTUNITES	AVENGER	AVIANS	AVOCADO
AUXESES	AVENGERS	AVIARIES	AVOCADOES
AUXESIS	AVENGES	AVIARIST	AVOCADOS
AUXETIC	AVENGING	AVIARISTS	AVOCATION
AUXETICS	AVENIR	AVIARY	AVOCET
AUXILIAR	AVENIRS	AVIATE	AVOCETS
AUXILIARS	AVENS	AVIATED	AVODIRE
AUXILIARY	AVENSES	AVIATES	AVODIRES
AUXIN	AVENTAIL	AVIATIC	AVOID
AUXINIC	AVENTAILE	AVIATING	AVOIDABLE
AUXINS	AVENTAILS	AVIATION	AVOIDABLY
AUXOCYTE	AVENTRE	AVIATIONS	AVOIDANCE
AUXOCYTES	AVENTRED	AVIATOR	AVOIDANT

AVOIDED	AWAITS	AWETOS	AXEL
AVOIDER	AWAKE	AWFUL	AXELS
AVOIDERS	AWAKED	AWFULLER	AXEMAN
AVOIDING	AWAKEN	AWFULLEST	AXEMEN
AVOIDS	AWAKENED	AWFULLY	AXENIC
AVOISION	AWAKENER	AWFULNESS	AXES
AVOISIONS	AWAKENERS	AWHAPE	AXIAL
AVOS	AWAKENING	AWHAPED	AXIALITY
AVOSET	AWAKENS	AWHAPES	AXIALLY
AVOSETS	AWAKES	AWHAPING	AXIL
AVOUCH	AWAKING	AWHATO	AXILE
AVOUCHED	AWAKINGS	AWHEEL	AXILEMMA
AVOUCHER	AWANTING	AWHEELS	AXILEMMAS
AVOUCHERS	AWARD	AWHETO	AXILLA
AVOUCHES	AWARDABLE	AWHILE	AXILLAE
AVOUCHING	AWARDED	AWHIRL	AXILLAR
AVOURE	AWARDEE	AWING	AXILLARS
AVOURES	AWARDEES	AWKWARD	AXILLARY
AVOUTERER	AWARDER	AWKWARDER	AXILLAS
AVOUTRER	AWARDERS	AWKWARDLY	AXILS
AVOUTRERS	AWARDING	AWL	AXING
AVOUTRIES	AWARDS	AWLBIRD	AXINITE
AVOUTRY	AWARE	AWLBIRDS	AXINITES
AVOW	AWARENESS	AWLESS	AXIOLOGY
AVOWABLE	AWARER	AWLS	AXIOM
AVOWABLY	AWAREST	AWLWORT	AXIOMATIC
AVOWAL	AWARN	AWLWORTS	AXIOMS
AVOWALS	AWARNED	AWMOUS	AXION
AVOWED	AWARNING	AWMRIE	AXIONS
AVOWEDLY	AWARNS	AWMRIES	AXIS
AVOWER	AWASH	AWMRY	AXISED
AVOWERS	AWATCH	AWN	AXISES
AVOWING	AWATO	AWNED	AXITE
AVOWRIES	AWAVE	AWNER	AXITES
AVOWRY	AWAY	AWNERS	AXLE
AVOWS	AWAYDAY	AWNIER	AXLED
AVOYER	AWAYDAYS	AWNIEST	AXLES
AVOYERS	AWAYES	AWNING	AXLETREE
AVRUGA	AWAYNESS	AWNINGED	AXLETREES
AVRUGAS	AWAYS	AWNINGS	AXLIKE
AVULSE	AWDL	AWNLESS	AXMAN
AVULSED	AWDLS	AWNS	AXMEN
AVULSES	AWE	AWNY	AXOID
AVULSING	AWEARIED	AWOKE	AXOIDS
AVULSION	AWEARY	AWOKEN	AXOLEMMA
AVULSIONS	AWEATHER	AWOL	AXOLEMMAS
AVUNCULAR	AWED	AWOLS	AXOLOTL
AVYZE	AWEE	AWORK	AXOLOTLS
AVYZED	AWEEL	AWRACK	AXON
AVYZES	AWEIGH	AWRONG	AXONAL
AVYZING	AWEING	AWRY	AXONE
AW	AWELESS	AWSOME	AXONEMAL
AWA	AWES	AX	AXONEME·
AWAIT	AWESOME	AXAL	AXONEMES
AWAITED	AWESOMELY	AXE	AXONES
AWAITER	AWESTRIKE	AXEBIRD	AXONIC
AWAITERS	AWESTRUCK	AXEBIRDS	AXONS
AWAITING	AWETO	AXED	AXOPLASM

AXOPLASMS
AXSEED
AXSEEDS
AY
AYAH
AYAHS
AYAHUASCA
AYAHUASCO
AYATOLLAH
AYE
AYELP
AYENBITE
AYENBITES
AYES
AYGRE
AYIN
AYINS
AYONT
AYRE
AYRES
AYRIE
AYRIES
AYS
AYU
AYURVEDA
AYURVEDAS
AYURVEDIC
AYUS
AYWORD
AYWORDS
AZALEA
AZALEAS
AZAN
AZANS
AZEDARACH
AZEOTROPE
AZEOTROPY
AZERTY
AZIDE
AZIDES
AZIDO
AZIMUTH
AZIMUTHAL
AZIMUTHS
AZINE
AZINES
AZIONE
AZIONES
AZLON
AZLONS
AZO
AZOIC
AZOLE
AZOLES
AZOLLA
AZOLLAS
AZON
AZONAL

AZONIC
AZONS
AZOTAEMIA
AZOTAEMIC
AZOTE
AZOTED
AZOTEMIA
AZOTEMIAS
AZOTEMIC
AZOTES
AZOTH
AZOTHS
AZOTIC
AZOTISE
AZOTISED
AZOTISES
AZOTISING
AZOTIZE
AZOTIZED
AZOTIZES
AZOTIZING
AZOTOUS
AZOTURIA
AZOTURIAS
AZUKI
AZUKIS
AZULEJO
AZULEJOS
AZURE
AZUREAN
AZURES
AZURINE
AZURINES
AZURITE
AZURITES
AZURN
AZURY
AZYGIES
AZYGOS
AZYGOSES
AZYGOUS
AZYGY
AZYM
AZYME
AZYMES
AZYMITE
AZYMITES
AZYMOUS
AZYMS

B

BA
BAA
BAAED
BAAING
BAAINGS
BAAL
BAALEBOS
BAALIM
BAALISM
BAALISMS
BAALS
BAAS
BAASES
BAASKAAP
BAASKAAPS
BAASKAP
BAASKAPS
BAASSKAP
BAASSKAPS
BABA
BABACO
BABACOOTE
BABACOS
BABALAS
BABAS
BABASSU
BABASSUS
BABBELAS
BABBITRY
BABBITT
BABBITTED
BABBITTRY
BABBITTS
BABBLE
BABBLED
BABBLER
BABBLERS
BABBLES
BABBLIER
BABBLIEST
BABBLING
BABBLINGS
BABBLY
BABE
BABEL
BABELDOM
BABELDOMS
BABELISH
BABELISM
BABELISMS
BABELS
BABES
BABESIA

BABESIAS
BABICHE
BABICHES
BABIED
BABIER
BABIES
BABIEST
BABIRUSA
BABIRUSAS
BABIRUSSA
BABKA
BABKAS
BABLAH
BABLAHS
BABOO
BABOOL
BABOOLS
BABOON
BABOONERY
BABOONISH
BABOONS
BABOOS
BABOOSH
BABOOSHES
BABOUCHE
BABOUCHES
BABU
BABUCHE
BABUCHES
BABUDOM
BABUDOMS
BABUISM
BABUISMS
BABUL
BABULS
BABUS
BABUSHKA
BABUSHKAS
BABY
BABYDOLL
BABYDOLLS
BABYFOOD
BABYFOODS
BABYHOOD
BABYHOODS
BABYING
BABYISH
BABYISHLY
BABYPROOF
BABYSAT
BABYSIT
BABYSITS
BAC

BACALAO
BACALAOS
BACCA
BACCAE
BACCARA
BACCARAS
BACCARAT
BACCARATS
BACCARE
BACCAS
BACCATE
BACCATED
BACCHANAL
BACCHANT
BACCHANTE
BACCHANTS
BACCHIAC
BACCHIAN
BACCHIC
BACCHII
BACCHIUS
BACCIES
BACCIFORM
BACCO
BACCOES
BACCOS
BACCY
BACH
BACHA
BACHARACH
BACHAS
BACHCHA
BACHCHAS
BACHED
BACHELOR
BACHELORS
BACHES
BACHING
BACHS
BACILLAR
BACILLARY
BACILLI
BACILLUS
BACK
BACKACHE
BACKACHES
BACKARE
BACKBAND
BACKBANDS
BACKBEAT
BACKBEATS
BACKBENCH
BACKBEND

BACKBENDS
BACKBIT
BACKBITE
BACKBITER
BACKBITES
BACKBLOCK
BACKBOARD
BACKBOND
BACKBONDS
BACKBONE
BACKBONED
BACKBONES
BACKBURN
BACKBURNS
BACKCAST
BACKCASTS
BACKCHAT
BACKCHATS
BACKCHECK
BACKCLOTH
BACKCOMB
BACKCOMBS
BACKCOURT
BACKCROSS
BACKDATE
BACKDATED
BACKDATES
BACKDOOR
BACKDOWN
BACKDOWNS
BACKDRAFT
BACKDROP
BACKDROPS
BACKDROPT
BACKED
BACKER
BACKERS
BACKET
BACKETS
BACKFALL
BACKFALLS
BACKFIELD
BACKFILE
BACKFILES
BACKFILL
BACKFILLS
BACKFIRE
BACKFIRED
BACKFIRES
BACKFISCH
BACKFIT
BACKFITS
BACKFLIP

BACKFLIPS	BACKSIDE	BACTERIAS	BAFFED
BACKFLOW	BACKSIDES	BACTERIC	BAFFIES
BACKFLOWS	BACKSIGHT	BACTERIN	BAFFING
BACKHAND	BACKSLAP	BACTERINS	BAFFLE
BACKHANDS	BACKSLAPS	BACTERISE	BAFFLED
BACKHAUL	BACKSLASH	BACTERIUM	BAFFLEGAB
BACKHAULS	BACKSLID	BACTERIZE	BAFFLER
BACKHOE	BACKSLIDE	BACTEROID	BAFFLERS
BACKHOED	BACKSPACE	BACULA	BAFFLES
BACKHOES	BACKSPEER	BACULINE	BAFFLING
BACKHOUSE	BACKSPEIR	BACULITE	BAFFS
BACKIE	BACKSPIN	BACULITES	BAFFY
BACKIES	BACKSPINS	BACULUM	BAFT
BACKING	BACKSTAB	BACULUMS	BAFTS
BACKINGS	BACKSTABS	BAD	BAG
BACKLAND	BACKSTAGE	BADASS	BAGARRE
BACKLANDS	BACKSTAIR	BADASSED	BAGARRES
BACKLASH	BACKSTALL	BADASSES	BAGASS
BACKLESS	BACKSTAMP	BADDER	BAGASSE
BACKLIFT	BACKSTAY	BADDEST	BAGASSES
BACKLIFTS	BACKSTAYS	BADDIE	BAGATELLE
BACKLIGHT	BACKSTOP	BADDIES	BAGEL
BACKLIST	BACKSTOPS	BADDISH	BAGELS
BACKLISTS	BACKSTORY	BADDY	BAGFUL
BACKLIT	BACKSWEPT	BADE	BAGFULS
BACKLOAD	BACKSWING	BADGE	BAGGAGE
BACKLOADS	BACKSWORD	BADGED	BAGGAGES
BACKLOG	BACKTRACK	BADGELESS	BAGGED
BACKLOGS	BACKUP	BADGER	BAGGER
BACKLOT	BACKUPS	BADGERED	BAGGERS
BACKLOTS	BACKVELD	BADGERING	BAGGIE
BACKMOST	BACKVELDS	BADGERLY	BAGGIER
BACKOUT	BACKWARD	BADGERS	BAGGIES
BACKOUTS	BACKWARDS	BADGES	BAGGIEST
BACKPACK	BACKWASH	BADGING	BAGGILY
BACKPACKS	BACKWATER	BADINAGE	BAGGINESS
BACKPAY	BACKWOOD	BADINAGED	BAGGING
BACKPAYS	BACKWOODS	BADINAGES	BAGGINGS
BACKPEDAL	BACKWORD	BADINERIE	BAGGIT
BACKPIECE	BACKWORDS	BADIOUS	BAGGITS
BACKRA	BACKWORK	BADLAND	BAGGY
BACKRAS	BACKWORKS	BADLANDS	BAGH
BACKREST	BACKWRAP	BADLY	BAGHOUSE
BACKRESTS	BACKWRAPS	BADMAN	BAGHOUSES
BACKROOM	BACKYARD	BADMASH	BAGHS
BACKROOMS	BACKYARDS	BADMASHES	BAGIE
BACKRUSH	BACLAVA	BADMEN	BAGIES
BACKS	BACLAVAS	BADMINTON	BAGLESS
BACKSAW	BACLOFEN	BADMOUTH	BAGLIKE
BACKSAWS	BACLOFENS	BADMOUTHS	BAGMAN
BACKSEAT	BACON	BADNESS	BAGMEN
BACKSEATS	BACONER	BADNESSES	BAGNETTE
BACKSET	BACONERS	BADS	BAGNETTES
BACKSETS	BACONS	BAEL	BAGNIO
BACKSEY	BACS	BAELS	BAGNIOS
BACKSEYS	BACTERIA	BAETYL	BAGPIPE
BACKSHISH	BACTERIAL	BAETYLS	BAGPIPED
BACKSHORE	BACTERIAN	BAFF	BAGPIPER

BAGPIPERS	BAILS	BAKESTONE	BALDNESS
BAGPIPES	BAILSMAN	BAKEWARE	BALDPATE
BAGPIPING	BAILSMEN	BAKEWARES	BALDPATED
BAGS	BAININ	BAKHSHISH	BALDPATES
BAGSFUL	BAININS	BAKING	BALDRIC
BAGUET	BAINITE	BAKINGS	BALDRICK
BAGUETS	BAINITES	BAKKIE	BALDRICKS
BAGUETTE	BAIRN	BAKKIES	BALDRICS
BAGUETTES	BAIRNISH	BAKLAVA	BALDS
BAGUIO	BAIRNLIER	BAKLAVAS	BALDY
BAGUIOS	BAIRNLIKE	BAKLAWA	BALE
BAGWASH	BAIRNLY	BAKLAWAS	BALECTION
BAGWASHES	BAIRNS	BAKRA	BALED
BAGWIG	BAISEMAIN	BAKRAS	BALEEN
BAGWIGS	BAIT	BAKSHEESH	BALEENS
BAGWORM	BAITED	BAKSHISH	BALEFIRE
BAGWORMS	BAITER	BAL	BALEFIRES
BAH	BAITERS	BALACLAVA	BALEFUL
BAHADA	BAITFISH	BALADIN	BALEFULLY
BAHADAS	BAITH	BALADINE	BALER
BAHADUR	BAITING	BALADINES	BALERS
BAHADURS	BAITINGS	BALADINS	BALES
BAHT	BAITS	BALALAIKA	BALING
BAHTS	BAIZA	BALANCE	BALISAUR
BAHUT	BAIZAS	BALANCED	BALISAURS
BAHUTS	BAIZE	BALANCER	BALISTA
BAHUVRIHI	BAIZED	BALANCERS	BALISTAE
BAIDARKA	BAIZES	BALANCES	BALISTAS
BAIDARKAS	BAIZING	BALANCING	BALK
BAIGNOIRE	BAJADA	BALANITIS	BALKANISE
BAIL	BAJADAS	BALAS	BALKANIZE
BAILABLE	BAJAN	BALASES	BALKED
BAILBOND	BAJANS	BALATA	BALKER
BAILBONDS	BAJRA	BALATAS	BALKERS
BAILED	BAJRAS	BALBOA	BALKIER
BAILEE	BAJREE	BALBOAS	BALKIEST
BAILEES	BAJREES	BALCONET	BALKILY
BAILER	BAJRI	BALCONETS	BALKINESS
BAILERS	BAJRIS	BALCONIED	BALKING
BAILEY	BAJU	BALCONIES	BALKINGLY
BAILEYS	BAJUS	BALCONY	BALKINGS
BAILIE	BAKE	BALD	BALKLINE
BAILIES	BAKEAPPLE	BALDACHIN	BALKLINES
BAILIFF	BAKEBOARD	BALDAQUIN	BALKS
BAILIFFS	BAKED	BALDED	BALKY
BAILING	BAKEHOUSE	BALDER	BALL
BAILIWICK	BAKELITE	BALDEST	BALLABILE
BAILLI	BAKELITES	BALDFACED	BALLABILI
BAILLIAGE	BAKEMEAT	BALDHEAD	BALLAD
BAILLIE	BAKEMEATS	BALDHEADS	BALLADE
BAILLIES	BAKEN	BALDICOOT	BALLADED
BAILLIS	BAKER	BALDIER	BALLADEER
BAILMENT	BAKERIES	BALDIES	BALLADES
BAILMENTS	BAKERS	BALDIEST	BALLADIC
BAILOR	BAKERY	BALDING	BALLADIN
BAILORS	BAKES	BALDISH	BALLADINE
BAILOUT	BAKESHOP	BALDLY	BALLADING
BAILOUTS	BAKESHOPS	BALDMONEY	BALLADINS

BALLADIST	BALLOTERS	BALTIS	BANDANNA
BALLADRY	BALLOTING	BALU	BANDANNAS
BALLADS	BALLOTINI	BALUN	BANDAR
BALLAN	BALLOTS	BALUNS	BANDARI
BALLANS	BALLOW	BALUS	BANDARIS
BALLANT	BALLOWS	BALUSTER	BANDARS
BALLANTED	BALLPARK	BALUSTERS	BANDAS
BALLANTS	BALLPARKS	BALZARINE	BANDBOX
BALLAST	BALLPOINT	BAM	BANDBOXES
BALLASTED	BALLROOM	BAMBI	BANDBRAKE
BALLASTER	BALLROOMS	BAMBINI	BANDEAU
BALLASTS	BALLS	BAMBINO	BANDEAUS
BALLAT	BALLSIER	BAMBINOS	BANDEAUX
BALLATED	BALLSIEST	BAMBIS	BANDED
BALLATING	BALLSY	BAMBOO	BANDELET
BALLATS	BALLUP	BAMBOOS	BANDELETS
BALLCLAY	BALLUPS	BAMBOOZLE	BANDELIER
BALLCLAYS	BALLUTE	BAMMED	BANDER
BALLCOCK	BALLUTES	BAMMER	BANDEROL
BALLCOCKS	BALLY	BAMMERS	BANDEROLE
BALLED	BALLYARD	BAMMING	BANDEROLS
BALLER	BALLYARDS	BAMPOT	BANDERS
BALLERINA	BALLYHOO	BAMPOTS	BANDH
BALLERINE	BALLYHOOS	BAMS	BANDHS
BALLERS	BALLYRAG	BAN	BANDICOOT
BALLET	BALLYRAGS	BANAK	BANDIED
BALLETED	BALM	BANAKS	BANDIER
BALLETIC	BALMACAAN	BANAL	BANDIES
BALLETING	BALMED	BANALER	BANDIEST
BALLETS	BALMIER	BANALEST	BANDINESS
BALLGAME	BALMIEST	BANALISE	BANDING
BALLGAMES	BALMILY	BANALISED	BANDINGS
BALLHAWK	BALMINESS	BANALISES	BANDIT
BALLHAWKS	BALMING	BANALITY	BANDITO
BALLIES	BALMLIKE	BANALIZE	BANDITOS
BALLING	BALMORAL	BANALIZED	BANDITRY
BALLINGS	BALMORALS	BANALIZES	BANDITS
BALLISTA	BALMS	BANALLY	BANDITTI
BALLISTAE	BALMY	BANANA	BANDITTIS
BALLISTAS	BALNEAL	BANANAS	BANDMATE
BALLISTIC	BALNEARY	BANAUSIAN	BANDMATES
BALLIUM	BALONEY	BANAUSIC	BANDOBAST
BALLIUMS	BALONEYS	BANC	BANDOBUST
BALLOCKS	BALOO	BANCO	BANDOG
BALLON	BALOOS	BANCOS	BANDOGS
BALLONET	BALS	BANCS	BANDOLEER
BALLONETS	BALSA	BAND	BANDOLEON
BALLONNE	BALSAM	BANDA	BANDOLERO
BALLONNES	BALSAMED	BANDAGE	BANDOLIER
BALLONS	BALSAMIC	BANDAGED	BANDOLINE
BALLOON	BALSAMING	BANDAGER	BANDONEON
BALLOONED	BALSAMS	BANDAGERS	BANDONION
BALLOONS	BALSAMY	BANDAGES	BANDOOK
BALLOT	BALSAS	BANDAGING	BANDOOKS
BALLOTED	BALSAWOOD	BANDAID	BANDORA
BALLOTEE	BALTHASAR	BANDALORE	BANDORAS
BALLOTEES	BALTHAZAR	BANDANA	BANDORE
BALLOTER	BALTI	BANDANAS	BANDORES

BANDROL	BANISHES	BANNING	BAPTISIAS
BANDROLS	BANISHING	BANNISTER	BAPTISING
BANDS	BANISTER	BANNOCK	BAPTISM
BANDSAW	BANISTERS	BANNOCKS	BAPTISMAL
BANDSAWS	BANJAX	BANNS	BAPTISMS
BANDSHELL	BANJAXED	BANOFFEE	BAPTIST
BANDSMAN	BANJAXES	BANOFFEES	BAPTISTRY
BANDSMEN	BANJAXING	BANOFFI	BAPTISTS
BANDSTAND	BANJO	BANOFFIS	BAPTIZE
BANDSTER	BANJOES	BANQUET	BAPTIZED
BANDSTERS	BANJOIST	BANQUETED	BAPTIZER
BANDURA	BANJOISTS	BANQUETER	BAPTIZERS
BANDURAS	BANJOS	BANQUETS	BAPTIZES
BANDWAGON	BANJULELE	BANQUETTE	BAPTIZING
BANDWIDTH	BANK	BANS	BAPU
BANDY	BANKABLE	BANSELA	BAPUS
BANDYING	BANKBOOK	BANSELAS	BAR
BANDYINGS	BANKBOOKS	BANSHEE	BARACAN
BANDYMAN	BANKCARD	BANSHEES	BARACANS
BANDYMEN	BANKCARDS	BANSHIE	BARACHOIS
BANE	BANKED	BANSHIES	BARAGOUIN
BANEBERRY	BANKER	BANT	BARASINGA
BANED	BANKERLY	BANTAM	BARATHEA
BANEFUL	BANKERS	BANTAMS	BARATHEAS
BANEFULLY	BANKET	BANTED	BARATHRUM
BANES	BANKETS	BANTENG	BARAZA
BANG	BANKING	BANTENGS	BARAZAS
BANGALAY	BANKINGS	BANTER	BARB
BANGALAYS	BANKIT	BANTERED	BARBAL
BANGALORE	BANKITS	BANTERER	BARBARIAN
BANGALOW	BANKNOTE	BANTERERS	BARBARIC
BANGALOWS	BANKNOTES	BANTERING	BARBARISE
BANGED	BANKROLL	BANTERS	BARBARISM
BANGER	BANKROLLS	BANTIES	BARBARITY
BANGERS	BANKRUPT	BANTING	BARBARIZE
BANGING	BANKRUPTS	BANTINGS	BARBAROUS
BANGINGS	BANKS	BANTLING	BARBASCO
BANGKOK	BANKSIA	BANTLINGS	BARBASCOS
BANGKOKS	BANKSIAS	BANTS	BARBASTEL
BANGLE	BANKSIDE	BANTU	BARBATE
BANGLED	BANKSIDES	BANTUS	BARBATED
BANGLES	BANKSMAN	BANTY	BARBE
BANGS	BANKSMEN	BANXRING	BARBECUE
BANGSRING	BANLIEUE	BANXRINGS	BARBECUED
BANGSTER	BANLIEUES	BANYAN	BARBECUER
BANGSTERS	BANNABLE	BANYANS	BARBECUES
BANGTAIL	BANNED	BANZAI	BARBED
BANGTAILS	BANNER	BANZAIS	BARBEL
BANI	BANNERALL	BAOBAB	BARBELL
BANIA	BANNERED	BAOBABS	BARBELLS
BANIAN	BANNERET	BAP	BARBELS
BANIANS	BANNERETS	BAPS	BARBEQUE
BANIAS	BANNERING	BAPTISE	BARBEQUED
BANING	BANNEROL	BAPTISED	BARBEQUES
BANISH	BANNEROLS	BAPTISER	BARBER
BANISHED	BANNERS	BAPTISERS	BARBERED
BANISHER	BANNET	BAPTISES	BARBERING
BANISHERS	BANNETS	BAPTISIA	BARBERRY

BARBERS

BARBERS	BAREBACK	BARHOPPED	BARMY
BARBES	BAREBOAT	BARHOPS	BARN
BARBET	BAREBOATS	BARIATRIC	BARNACLE
BARBETS	BAREBONE	BARIC	BARNACLED
BARBETTE	BAREBONED	BARILLA	BARNACLES
BARBETTES	BAREBONES	BARILLAS	BARNBRACK
BARBICAN	BARED	BARING	BARNED
BARBICANS	BAREFACED	BARISH	BARNET
BARBICEL	BAREFIT	BARISTA	BARNETS
BARBICELS	BAREFOOT	BARISTAS	BARNEY
BARBIE	BAREGE	BARITE	BARNEYED
BARBIES	BAREGES	BARITES	BARNEYING
BARBING	BAREGINE	BARITONAL	BARNEYS
BARBITAL	BAREGINES	BARITONE	BARNIER
BARBITALS	BAREHAND	BARITONES	BARNIEST
BARBITONE	BAREHANDS	BARIUM	BARNING
BARBLESS	BAREHEAD	BARIUMS	BARNLIKE
BARBOLA	BARELY	BARK	BARNS
BARBOLAS	BARENESS	BARKAN	BARNSTORM
BARBOTINE	BARER	BARKANS	BARNY
BARBS	BARES	BARKED	BARNYARD
BARBULE	BARESARK	BARKEEP	BARNYARDS
BARBULES	BARESARKS	BARKEEPER	BAROCCO
BARBUT	BAREST	BARKEEPS	BAROCCOS
BARBUTS	BARF	BARKEN	BAROCK
BARBWIRE	BARFED	BARKENED	BAROCKS
BARBWIRES	BARFING	BARKENING	BAROGRAM
BARBY	BARFLIES	BARKENS	BAROGRAMS
BARCA	BARFLY	BARKER	BAROGRAPH
BARCAROLE	BARFS	BARKERS	BAROLO
BARCAS	BARFUL	BARKHAN	BAROLOS
BARCHAN	BARGAIN	BARKHANS	BAROMETER
BARCHANE	BARGAINED	BARKIER	BAROMETRY
BARCHANES	BARGAINER	BARKIEST	BAROMETZ
BARCHANS	BARGAINS	BARKING	BARON
BARD	BARGANDER	BARKLESS	BARONAGE
BARDASH	BARGE	BARKS	BARONAGES
BARDASHES	BARGED	BARKY	BARONESS
BARDE	BARGEE	BARLEDUC	BARONET
BARDED	BARGEES	BARLEDUCS	BARONETCY
BARDES	BARGEESE	BARLESS	BARONETS
BARDIC	BARGELLO	BARLEY	BARONG
BARDIE	BARGELLOS	BARLEYS	BARONGS
BARDIER	BARGEMAN	BARLOW	BARONIAL
BARDIES	BARGEMEN	BARLOWS	BARONIES
BARDIEST	BARGEPOLE	BARM	BARONNE
BARDING	BARGES	BARMAID	BARONNES
BARDISM	BARGEST	BARMAIDS	BARONS
BARDISMS	BARGESTS	BARMAN	BARONY
BARDLING	BARGHEST	BARMBRACK	BAROPHILE
BARDLINGS	BARGHESTS	BARMEN	BAROQUE
BARDO	BARGING	BARMIE	BAROQUELY
BARDOS	BARGOON	BARMIER	BAROQUES
BARDS	BARGOONS	BARMIEST	BAROSAUR
BARDSHIP	BARGOOSE	BARMINESS	BAROSAURS
BARDSHIPS	BARGUEST	BARMKIN	BAROSCOPE
BARDY	BARGUESTS	BARMKINS	BAROSTAT
BARE	BARHOP	BARMS	BAROSTATS

BAROUCHE
BAROUCHES
BARP
BARPERSON
BARPS
BARQUE
BARQUES
BARQUETTE
BARRA
BARRABLE
BARRACAN
BARRACANS
BARRACE
BARRACES
BARRACK
BARRACKED
BARRACKER
BARRACKS
BARRACOON
BARRACUDA
BARRAGE
BARRAGED
BARRAGES
BARRAGING
BARRANCA
BARRANCAS
BARRANCO
BARRANCOS
BARRAS
BARRAT
BARRATER
BARRATERS
BARRATOR
BARRATORS
BARRATRY
BARRATS
BARRE
BARRED
BARREED
BARREFULL
BARREING
BARREL
BARRELAGE
BARRELED
BARRELFUL
BARRELING
BARRELLED
BARRELS
BARREN
BARRENER
BARRENEST
BARRENLY
BARRENS
BARRES
BARRET
BARRETOR
BARRETORS
BARRETRY

BARRETS
BARRETTE
BARRETTER
BARRETTES
BARRICADE
BARRICADO
BARRICO
BARRICOES
BARRICOS
BARRIE
BARRIER
BARRIERED
BARRIERS
BARRIES
BARRIEST
BARRING
BARRINGS
BARRIO
BARRIOS
BARRISTER
BARRO
BARROOM
BARROOMS
BARROW
BARROWFUL
BARROWS
BARRULET
BARRULETS
BARRY
BARS
BARSTOOL
BARSTOOLS
BARTEND
BARTENDED
BARTENDER
BARTENDS
BARTER
BARTERED
BARTERER
BARTERERS
BARTERING
BARTERS
BARTISAN
BARTISANS
BARTIZAN
BARTIZANS
BARTON
BARTONS
BARTSIA
BARTSIAS
BARWARE
BARWARES
BARWOOD
BARWOODS
BARYE
BARYES
BARYON
BARYONIC

BARYONS
BARYTA
BARYTAS
BARYTE
BARYTES
BARYTIC
BARYTON
BARYTONE
BARYTONES
BARYTONS
BAS
BASAL
BASALLY
BASALT
BASALTES
BASALTIC
BASALTINE
BASALTS
BASAN
BASANITE
BASANITES
BASANS
BASCINET
BASCINETS
BASCULE
BASCULES
BASE
BASEBALL
BASEBALLS
BASEBAND
BASEBANDS
BASEBOARD
BASEBORN
BASED
BASELARD
BASELARDS
BASELESS
BASELINE
BASELINER
BASELINES
BASELY
BASEMAN
BASEMEN
BASEMENT
BASEMENTS
BASENESS
BASENJI
BASENJIS
BASEPLATE
BASER
BASES
BASEST
BASH
BASHAW
BASHAWISM
BASHAWS
BASHED
BASHER

BASHERS
BASHES
BASHFUL
BASHFULLY
BASHING
BASHINGS
BASHLESS
BASHLIK
BASHLIKS
BASHLYK
BASHLYKS
BASHO
BASIC
BASICALLY
BASICITY
BASICS
BASIDIA
BASIDIAL
BASIDIUM
BASIFIED
BASIFIER
BASIFIERS
BASIFIES
BASIFIXED
BASIFUGAL
BASIFY
BASIFYING
BASIL
BASILAR
BASILARY
BASILECT
BASILECTS
BASILIC
BASILICA
BASILICAE
BASILICAL
BASILICAN
BASILICAS
BASILICON
BASILISK
BASILISKS
BASILS
BASIN
BASINAL
BASINED
BASINET
BASINETS
BASINFUL
BASINFULS
BASING
BASINLIKE
BASINS
BASION
BASIONS
BASIPETAL
BASIS
BASK
BASKED

BASKET	BASTARDY	BATFOWLS	BATOONED
BASKETFUL	BASTE	BATGIRL	BATOONING
BASKETRY	BASTED	BATGIRLS	BATOONS
BASKETS	BASTER	BATH	BATRACHIA
BASKING	BASTERS	BATHCUBE	BATS
BASKS	BASTES	BATHCUBES	BATSMAN
BASMATI	BASTI	BATHE	BATSMEN
BASMATIS	BASTIDE	BATHED	BATSWING
BASNET	BASTIDES	BATHER	BATSWOMAN
BASNETS	BASTILE	BATHERS	BATSWOMEN
BASOCHE	BASTILES	BATHES	BATT
BASOCHES	BASTILLE	BATHETIC	BATTA
BASON	BASTILLES	BATHHOUSE	BATTALIA
BASONS	BASTINADE	BATHING	BATTALIAS
BASOPHIL	BASTINADO	BATHLESS	BATTALION
BASOPHILE	BASTING	BATHMAT	BATTAS
BASOPHILS	BASTINGS	BATHMATS	BATTEAU
BASQUE	BASTION	BATHMIC	BATTEAUX
BASQUED	BASTIONED	BATHMISM	BATTED
BASQUES	BASTIONS	BATHMISMS	BATTEL
BASQUINE	BASTIS	BATHOLITE	BATTELED
BASQUINES	BASTLE	BATHOLITH	BATTELER
BASS	BASTLES	BATHORSE	BATTELERS
BASSE	BASTO	BATHORSES	BATTELING
BASSED	BASTOS	BATHOS	BATTELLED
BASSER	BASTS	BATHOSES	BATTELS
BASSES	BASUCO	BATHROBE	BATTEMENT
BASSEST	BASUCOS	BATHROBES	BATTEN
BASSET	BAT	BATHROOM	BATTENED
BASSETED	BATABLE	BATHROOMS	BATTENER
BASSETING	BATATA	BATHS	BATTENERS
BASSETS	BATATAS	BATHTUB	BATTENING
BASSETT	BATAVIA	BATHTUBS	BATTENS
BASSETTED	BATAVIAS	BATHWATER	BATTER
BASSETTS	BATBOY	BATHYAL	BATTERED
BASSI	BATBOYS	BATHYBIUS	BATTERER
BASSIER	BATCH	BATHYLITE	BATTERERS
BASSIEST	BATCHED	BATHYLITH	BATTERIE
BASSINET	BATCHER	BATIK	BATTERIES
BASSINETS	BATCHERS	BATIKED	BATTERING
BASSING	BATCHES	BATIKING	BATTERO
BASSIST	BATCHING	BATIKS	BATTEROS
BASSISTS	BATCHINGS	BATING	BATTERS
BASSLY	BATE	BATISTE	BATTERY
BASSNESS	BATEAU	BATISTES	BATTIER
BASSO	BATEAUX	BATLER	BATTIEST
BASSOON	BATED	BATLERS	BATTIK
BASSOONS	BATELESS	BATLET	BATTIKS
BASSOS	BATELEUR	BATLETS	BATTILL
BASSWOOD	BATELEURS	BATLIKE	BATTILLED
BASSWOODS	BATEMENT	BATMAN	BATTILLS
BASSY	BATEMENTS	BATMEN	BATTINESS
BAST	BATES	BATOLOGY	BATTING
BASTA	BATFISH	BATON	BATTINGS
BASTARD	BATFISHES	BATONED	BATTLE
BASTARDLY	BATFOWL	BATONING	BATTLEBUS
BASTARDRY	BATFOWLED	BATONS	BATTLED
BASTARDS	BATFOWLER	BATOON	BATTLER

BATTLERS	BAVAROIS	BAYLE	BEADERS
BATTLES	BAVIN	BAYLES	BEADHOUSE
BATTLING	BAVINS	BAYMAN	BEADIER
BATTOLOGY	BAWBEE	BAYMEN	BEADIEST
BATTS	BAWBEES	BAYONET	BEADILY
BATTU	BAWBLE	BAYONETED	BEADINESS
BATTUE	BAWBLES	BAYONETS	BEADING
BATTUES	BAWCOCK	BAYOU	BEADINGS
BATTUTA	BAWCOCKS	BAYOUS	BEADLE
BATTUTAS	BAWD	BAYS	BEADLEDOM
BATTY	BAWDIER	BAYT	BEADLES
BATWING	BAWDIES	BAYTED	BEADLIKE
BATWOMAN	BAWDIEST	BAYTING	BEADMAN
BATWOMEN	BAWDILY	BAYTS	BEADMEN
BAUBEE	BAWDINESS	BAYWOOD	BEADROLL
BAUBEES	BAWDKIN	BAYWOODS	BEADROLLS
BAUBLE	BAWDKINS	BAYYAN	BEADS
BAUBLES	BAWDRIC	BAYYANS	BEADSMAN
BAUBLING	BAWDRICS	BAZAAR	BEADSMEN
BAUCHLE	BAWDRIES	BAZAARS	BEADWORK
BAUCHLED	BAWDRY	BAZAR	BEADWORKS
BAUCHLES	BAWDS	BAZARS	BEADY
BAUCHLING	BAWDY	BAZAZZ	BEAGLE
BAUD	BAWL	BAZAZZES	BEAGLED
BAUDEKIN	BAWLED	BAZILLION	BEAGLER
BAUDEKINS	BAWLER	BAZOO	BEAGLERS
BAUDRIC	BAWLERS	BAZOOKA	BEAGLES
BAUDRICK	BAWLEY	BAZOOKAS	BEAGLING
BAUDRICKE	BAWLEYS	BAZOOMS	BEAGLINGS
BAUDRICKS	BAWLING	BAZOOS	BEAK
BAUDRICS	BAWLINGS	BAZOUKI	BEAKED
BAUDRONS	BAWLS	BAZOUKIS	BEAKER
BAUDS	BAWN	BDELLIUM	BEAKERS
BAUERA	BAWNEEN	BDELLIUMS	BEAKIER
BAUERAS	BAWNEENS	BE	BEAKIEST
BAUHINIA	BAWNS	BEACH	BEAKLESS
BAUHINIAS	BAWR	BEACHBALL	BEAKLIKE
BAUK	BAWRS	BEACHBOY	BEAKS
BAUKED	BAWSUNT	BEACHBOYS	BEAKY
BAUKING	BAWTIE	BEACHCOMB	BEAM
BAUKS	BAWTIES	BEACHED	BEAMED
BAULK	BAWTY	BEACHES	BEAMER
BAULKED	BAXTER	BEACHGOER	BEAMERS
BAULKER	BAXTERS	BEACHHEAD	BEAMIER
BAULKERS	BAY	BEACHIER	BEAMIEST
BAULKIER	BAYADEER	BEACHIEST	BEAMILY
BAULKIEST	BAYADEERS	BEACHING	BEAMINESS
BAULKILY	BAYADERE	BEACHSIDE	BEAMING
BAULKING	BAYADERES	BEACHWEAR	BEAMINGLY
BAULKS	BAYAMO	BEACHY	BEAMINGS
BAULKY	BAYAMOS	BEACON	BEAMISH
BAUR	BAYARD	BEACONED	BEAMISHLY
BAURS	BAYARDS	BEACONING	BEAMLESS
BAUSOND	BAYBERRY	BEACONS	BEAMLET
BAUXITE	BAYE	BEAD	BEAMLETS
BAUXITES	BAYED	BEADBLAST	BEAMLIKE
BAUXITIC	BAYES	BEADED	BEAMS
BAVARDAGE	BAYING	BEADER	BEAMY

BEAN	BEARWOODS	BEAUX	BECKET
BEANBAG	BEAST	BEAUXITE	BECKETS
BEANBAGS	BEASTHOOD	BEAUXITES	BECKING
BEANBALL	BEASTIE	BEAVER	BECKON
BEANBALLS	BEASTIES	BEAVERED	BECKONED
BEANED	BEASTILY	BEAVERIES	BECKONER
BEANERIES	BEASTINGS	BEAVERING	BECKONERS
BEANERY	BEASTLIER	BEAVERS	BECKONING
BEANFEAST	BEASTLIKE	BEAVERY	BECKONS
BEANIE	BEASTLY	BEBEERINE	BECKS
BEANIES	BEASTOID	BEBEERU	BECLAMOR
BEANING	BEASTOIDS	BEBEERUS	BECLAMORS
BEANLIKE	BEASTS	BEBLOOD	BECLASP
BEANO	BEAT	BEBLOODED	BECLASPED
BEANOS	BEATABLE	BEBLOODS	BECLASPS
BEANPOLE	BEATBOX	BEBOP	BECLOAK
BEANPOLES	BEATBOXES	BEBOPPED	BECLOAKED
BEANS	BEATEN	BEBOPPER	BECLOAKS
BEANSTALK	BEATER	BEBOPPERS	BECLOG
BEANY	BEATERS	BEBOPPING	BECLOGGED
BEAR	BEATH	BEBOPS	BECLOGS
BEARABLE	BEATHED	BEBUNG	BECLOTHE
BEARABLY	BEATHING	BEBUNGS	BECLOTHED
BEARBERRY	BEATHS	BECALL	BECLOTHES
BEARBINE	BEATIER	BECALLED	BECLOUD
BEARBINES	BEATIEST	BECALLING	BECLOUDED
BEARCAT	BEATIFIC	BECALLS	BECLOUDS
BEARCATS	BEATIFIED	BECALM	BECLOWN
BEARD	BEATIFIES	BECALMED	BECLOWNED
BEARDED	BEATIFY	BECALMING	BECLOWNS
BEARDIE	BEATING	BECALMS	BECOME
BEARDIER	BEATINGS	BECAME	BECOMES
BEARDIES	BEATITUDE	BECAP	BECOMING
BEARDIEST	BEATLESS	BECAPPED	BECOMINGS
BEARDING	BEATNIK	BECAPPING	BECOWARD
BEARDLESS	BEATNIKS	BECAPS	BECOWARDS
BEARDS	BEATS	BECARPET	BECQUEREL
BEARDY	BEATY	BECARPETS	BECRAWL
BEARE	BEAU	BECASSE	BECRAWLED
BEARED	BEAUCOUP	BECASSES	BECRAWLS
BEARER	BEAUCOUPS	BECAUSE	BECRIME
BEARERS	BEAUFET	BECCACCIA	BECRIMED
BEARES	BEAUFETS	BECCAFICO	BECRIMES
BEARGRASS	BEAUFFET	BECHALK	BECRIMING
BEARHUG	BEAUFFETS	BECHALKED	BECROWD
BEARHUGS	BEAUFIN	BECHALKS	BECROWDED
BEARING	BEAUFINS	BECHAMEL	BECROWDS
BEARINGS	BEAUISH	BECHAMELS	BECRUST
BEARISH	BEAUS	BECHANCE	BECRUSTED
BEARISHLY	BEAUT	BECHANCED	BECRUSTS
BEARLIKE	BEAUTEOUS	BECHANCES	BECUDGEL
BEARNAISE	BEAUTIED	BECHARM	BECUDGELS
BEARS	BEAUTIES	BECHARMED	BECURL
BEARSKIN	BEAUTIFUL	BECHARMS	BECURLED
BEARSKINS	BEAUTIFY	BECK	BECURLING
BEARWARD	BEAUTS	BECKE	BECURLS
BEARWARDS	BEAUTY	BECKED	BECURSE
BEARWOOD	BEAUTYING	BECKES	BECURSED

BECURSES	BEDEL	BEDOUINS	BEDSTRAW
BECURSING	BEDELL	BEDPAN	BEDSTRAWS
BECURST	BEDELLS	BEDPANS	BEDTICK
BED	BEDELS	BEDPLATE	BEDTICKS
BEDABBLE	BEDELSHIP	BEDPLATES	BEDTIME
BEDABBLED	BEDEMAN	BEDPOST	BEDTIMES
BEDABBLES	BEDEMEN	BEDPOSTS	BEDU
BEDAD	BEDERAL	BEDQUILT	BEDUCK
BEDAGGLE	BEDERALS	BEDQUILTS	BEDUCKED
BEDAGGLED	BEDES	BEDRAGGLE	BEDUCKING
BEDAGGLES	BEDESMAN	BEDRAIL	BEDUCKS
BEDAMN	BEDESMEN	BEDRAILS	BEDUIN
BEDAMNED	BEDEVIL	BEDRAL	BEDUINS
BEDAMNING	BEDEVILED	BEDRALS	BEDUMB
BEDAMNS	BEDEVILS	BEDRAPE	BEDUMBED
BEDARKEN	BEDEW	BEDRAPED	BEDUMBING
BEDARKENS	BEDEWED	BEDRAPES	BEDUMBS
BEDASH	BEDEWING	BEDRAPING	BEDUNCE
BEDASHED	BEDEWS	BEDRENCH	BEDUNCED
BEDASHES	BEDFAST	BEDRID	BEDUNCES
BEDASHING	BEDFELLOW	BEDRIDDEN	BEDUNCING
BEDAUB	BEDFRAME	BEDRIGHT	BEDUNG
BEDAUBED	BEDFRAMES	BEDRIGHTS	BEDUNGED
BEDAUBING	BEDGOWN	BEDRIVEL	BEDUNGING
BEDAUBS	BEDGOWNS	BEDRIVELS	BEDUNGS
BEDAWIN	BEDIAPER	BEDROCK	BEDUST
BEDAWINS	BEDIAPERS	BEDROCKS	BEDUSTED
BEDAZE	BEDIDE	BEDROLL	BEDUSTING
BEDAZED	BEDIGHT	BEDROLLS	BEDUSTS
BEDAZES	BEDIGHTED	BEDROOM	BEDWARD
BEDAZING	BEDIGHTS	BEDROOMED	BEDWARDS
BEDAZZLE	BEDIM	BEDROOMS	BEDWARF
BEDAZZLED	BEDIMMED	BEDROP	BEDWARFED
BEDAZZLES	BEDIMMING	BEDROPPED	BEDWARFS
BEDBOARD	BEDIMPLE	BEDROPS	BEDWARMER
BEDBOARDS	BEDIMPLED	BEDROPT	BEDWETTER
BEDBUG	BEDIMPLES	BEDRUG	BEDYDE
BEDBUGS	BEDIMS	BEDRUGGED	BEDYE
BEDCHAIR	BEDIRTIED	BEDRUGS	BEDYED
BEDCHAIRS	BEDIRTIES	BEDS	BEDYEING
BEDCOVER	BEDIRTY	BEDSHEET	BEDYES
BEDCOVERS	BEDIZEN	BEDSHEETS	BEE
BEDDABLE	BEDIZENED	BEDSIDE	BEEBEE
BEDDED	BEDIZENS	BEDSIDES	BEEBEES
BEDDER	BEDLAM	BEDSIT	BEEBREAD
BEDDERS	BEDLAMISM	BEDSITS	BEEBREADS
BEDDING	BEDLAMITE	BEDSITTER	BEECH
BEDDINGS	BEDLAMP	BEDSOCKS	BEECHEN
BEDE	BEDLAMPS	BEDSONIA	BEECHES
BEDEAFEN	BEDLAMS	BEDSONIAS	BEECHIER
BEDEAFENS	BEDLESS	BEDSORE	BEECHIEST
BEDECK	BEDLIKE	BEDSORES	BEECHMAST
BEDECKED	BEDMAKER	BEDSPREAD	BEECHNUT
BEDECKING	BEDMAKERS	BEDSPRING	BEECHNUTS
BEDECKS	BEDMATE	BEDSTAND	BEECHWOOD
BEDEGUAR	BEDMATES	BEDSTANDS	BEECHY
BEDEGUARS	BEDOTTED	BEDSTEAD	BEEDI
BEDEHOUSE	BEDOUIN	BEDSTEADS	BEEDIES

BEEF	BEESWINGS	BEFOGGING	BEGGINGLY
BEEFALO	BEET	BEFOGS	BEGGINGS
BEEFALOES	BEETED	BEFOOL	BEGHARD
BEEFALOS	BEETFLIES	BEFOOLED	BEGHARDS
BEEFCAKE	BEETFLY	BEFOOLING	BEGIFT
BEEFCAKES	BEETING	BEFOOLS	BEGIFTED
BEEFEATER	BEETLE	BEFORE	BEGIFTING
BEEFED	BEETLED	BEFORTUNE	BEGIFTS
BEEFIER	BEETLER	BEFOUL	BEGILD
BEEFIEST	BEETLERS	BEFOULED	BEGILDED
BEEFILY	BEETLES	BEFOULER	BEGILDING
BEEFINESS	BEETLING	BEFOULERS	BEGILDS
BEEFING	BEETROOT	BEFOULING	BEGILT
BEEFLESS	BEETROOTS	BEFOULS	BEGIN
BEEFS	BEETS	BEFRET	BEGINNE
BEEFSTEAK	BEEVES	BEFRETS	BEGINNER
BEEFWOOD	BEEYARD	BEFRETTED	BEGINNERS
BEEFWOODS	BEEYARDS	BEFRIEND	BEGINNES
BEEFY	BEEZER	BEFRIENDS	BEGINNING
BEEGAH	BEEZERS	BEFRINGE	BEGINS
BEEGAHS	BEFALL	BEFRINGED	BEGIRD
BEEHIVE	BEFALLEN	BEFRINGES	BEGIRDED
BEEHIVES	BEFALLING	BEFUDDLE	BEGIRDING
BEEKEEPER	BEFALLS	BEFUDDLED	BEGIRDLE
BEELIKE	BEFANA	BEFUDDLES	BEGIRDLED
BEELINE	BEFANAS	BEG	BEGIRDLES
BEELINED	BEFELD	BEGAD	BEGIRDS
BEELINES	BEFELL	BEGALL	BEGIRT
BEELINING	BEFFANA	BEGALLED	BEGLAD
BEEN	BEFFANAS	BEGALLING	BEGLADDED
BEENAH	BEFINGER	BEGALLS	BEGLADS
BEENAHS	BEFINGERS	BEGAN	BEGLAMOR
BEENTO	BEFINNED	BEGAR	BEGLAMORS
BEENTOS	BEFIT	BEGARS	BEGLAMOUR
BEEP	BEFITS	BEGAT	BEGLERBEG
BEEPED	BEFITTED	BEGAZE	BEGLOOM
BEEPER	BEFITTING	BEGAZED	BEGLOOMED
BEEPERS	BEFLAG	BEGAZES	BEGLOOMS
BEEPING	BEFLAGGED	BEGAZING	BEGNAW
BEEPS	BEFLAGS	BEGEM	BEGNAWED
BEER	BEFLEA	BEGEMMED	BEGNAWING
BEERAGE	BEFLEAED	BEGEMMING	BEGNAWS
BEERAGES	BEFLEAING	BEGEMS	BEGO
BEERHALL	BEFLEAS	BEGET	BEGOES
BEERHALLS	BEFLECK	BEGETS	BEGOGGLED
BEERIER	BEFLECKED	BEGETTER	BEGOING
BEERIEST	BEFLECKS	BEGETTERS	BEGONE
BEERILY	BEFLOWER	BEGETTING	BEGONIA
BEERINESS	BEFLOWERS	BEGGAR	BEGONIAS
BEERS	BEFLUM	BEGGARDOM	BEGORAH
BEERY	BEFLUMMED	BEGGARED	BEGORED
BEES	BEFLUMS	BEGGARIES	BEGORRA
BEESOME	BEFOAM	BEGGARING	BEGORRAH
BEESTINGS	BEFOAMED	BEGGARLY	BEGOT
BEESWAX	BEFOAMING	BEGGARS	BEGOTTEN
BEESWAXED	BEFOAMS	BEGGARY	BEGRIM
BEESWAXES	BEFOG	BEGGED	BEGRIME
BEESWING	BEFOGGED	BEGGING	BEGRIMED

BEGRIMES	BEHEMOTHS	BEJESUIT	BELAYERS
BEGRIMING	BEHEST	BEJESUITS	BELAYING
BEGRIMMED	BEHESTS	BEJESUS	BELAYS
BEGRIMS	BEHIGHT	BEJEWEL	BELCH
BEGROAN	BEHIGHTS	BEJEWELED	BELCHED
BEGROANED	BEHIND	BEJEWELS	BELCHER
BEGROANS	BEHINDS	BEJUMBLE	BELCHERS
BEGRUDGE	BEHOLD	BEJUMBLED	BELCHES
BEGRUDGED	BEHOLDEN	BEJUMBLES	BELCHING
BEGRUDGER	BEHOLDER	BEKAH	BELDAM
BEGRUDGES	BEHOLDERS	BEKAHS	BELDAME
BEGS	BEHOLDING	BEKISS	BELDAMES
BEGUILE	BEHOLDS	BEKISSED	BELDAMS
BEGUILED	BEHOOF	BEKISSES	BELEAGUER
BEGUILER	BEHOOFS	BEKISSING	BELEAP
BEGUILERS	BEHOOVE	BEKNAVE	BELEAPED
BEGUILES	BEHOOVED	BEKNAVED	BELEAPING
BEGUILING	BEHOOVES	BEKNAVES	BELEAPS
BEGUIN	BEHOOVING	BEKNAVING	BELEAPT
BEGUINAGE	BEHOTE	BEKNIGHT	BELEE
BEGUINE	BEHOTES	BEKNIGHTS	BELEED
BEGUINES	BEHOTING	BEKNOT	BELEEING
BEGUINS	BEHOVE	BEKNOTS	BELEES
BEGULF	BEHOVED	BEKNOTTED	BELEMNITE
BEGULFED	BEHOVEFUL	BEKNOWN	BELEMNOID
BEGULFING	BEHOVELY	BEL	BELFRIED
BEGULFS	BEHOVES	BELABOR	BELFRIES
BEGUM	BEHOVING	BELABORED	BELFRY
BEGUMS	BEHOWL	BELABORS	BELGA
BEGUN	BEHOWLED	BELABOUR	BELGARD
BEGUNK	BEHOWLING	BELABOURS	BELGARDS
BEGUNKED	BEHOWLS	BELACE	BELGAS
BEGUNKING	BEIGE	BELACED	BELIE
BEGUNKS	BEIGEL	BELACES	BELIED
BEHALF	BEIGELS	BELACING	BELIEF
BEHALVES	BEIGES	BELADIED	BELIEFS
BEHAPPEN	BEIGNE	BELADIES	BELIER
BEHAPPENS	BEIGNES	BELADY	BELIERS
BEHATTED	BEIGNET	BELADYING	BELIES
BEHAVE	BEIGNETS	BELAH	BELIEVE
BEHAVED	BEIGY	BELAHS	BELIEVED
BEHAVER	BEIN	BELAMIES	BELIEVER
BEHAVERS	BEING	BELAMOURE	BELIEVERS
BEHAVES	BEINGLESS	BELAMY	BELIEVES
BEHAVING	BEINGNESS	BELAR	BELIEVING
BEHAVIOR	BEINGS	BELARS	BELIKE
BEHAVIORS	BEINKED	BELATE	BELIQUOR
BEHAVIOUR	BEINNESS	BELATED	BELIQUORS
BEHEAD	BEJABBERS	BELATEDLY	BELITTLE
BEHEADAL	BEJABERS	BELATES	BELITTLED
BEHEADALS	BEJADE	BELATING	BELITTLER
BEHEADED	BEJADED	BELAUD	BELITTLES
BEHEADER	BEJADES	BELAUDED	BELIVE
BEHEADERS	BEJADING	BELAUDING	BELL
BEHEADING	BEJANT	BELAUDS	BELLBIND
BEHEADS	BEJANTS	BELAY	BELLBINDS
BEHELD	BEJEEBERS	BELAYED	BELLBIRD
BEHEMOTH	BEJEEZUS	BELAYER	BELLBIRDS

BELLBOY	BELOW	BEMIRED	BENCHED
BELLBOYS	BELOWS	BEMIRES	BENCHER
BELLCOTE	BELS	BEMIRING	BENCHERS
BELLCOTES	BELT	BEMIST	BENCHES
BELLE	BELTED	BEMISTED	BENCHIER
BELLED	BELTER	BEMISTING	BENCHIEST
BELLEEK	BELTERS	BEMISTS	BENCHING
BELLEEKS	BELTING	BEMIX	BENCHLAND
BELLES	BELTINGS	BEMIXED	BENCHLESS
BELLETER	BELTLESS	BEMIXES	BENCHMARK
BELLETERS	BELTLINE	BEMIXING	BENCHTOP
BELLHOP	BELTLINES	BEMIXT	BENCHY
BELLHOPS	BELTMAN	BEMOAN	BEND
BELLIBONE	BELTMEN	BEMOANED	BENDABLE
BELLICOSE	BELTS	BEMOANER	BENDAY
BELLIED	BELTWAY	BEMOANERS	BENDAYED
BELLIES	BELTWAYS	BEMOANING	BENDAYING
BELLING	BELUGA	BEMOANS	BENDAYS
BELLINGS	BELUGAS	BEMOCK	BENDED
BELLMAN	BELVEDERE	BEMOCKED	BENDEE
BELLMEN	BELYING	BEMOCKING	BENDEES
BELLOCK	BEMA	BEMOCKS	BENDER
BELLOCKED	BEMAD	BEMOIL	BENDERS
BELLOCKS	BEMADAM	BEMOILED	BENDIER
BELLOW	BEMADAMED	BEMOILING	BENDIEST
BELLOWED	BEMADAMS	BEMOILS	BENDING
BELLOWER	BEMADDED	BEMONSTER	BENDINGLY
BELLOWERS	BEMADDEN	BEMOUTH	BENDINGS
BELLOWING	BEMADDENS	BEMOUTHED	BENDLET
BELLOWS	BEMADDING	BEMOUTHS	BENDLETS
BELLPULL	BEMADS	BEMUD	BENDS
BELLPULLS	BEMAS	BEMUDDED	BENDWAYS
BELLPUSH	BEMATA	BEMUDDING	BENDWISE
BELLS	BEMAUL	BEMUDDLE	BENDY
BELLWORT	BEMAULED	BEMUDDLED	BENDYS
BELLWORTS	BEMAULING	BEMUDDLES	BENE
BELLY	BEMAULS	BEMUDS	BENEATH
BELLYACHE	BEMAZED	BEMUFFLE	BENEDICK
BELLYBAND	BEMBEX	BEMUFFLED	BENEDICKS
BELLYFUL	BEMBEXES	BEMUFFLES	BENEDICT
BELLYFULS	BEMBIX	BEMURMUR	BENEDICTS
BELLYING	BEMBIXES	BEMURMURS	BENEDIGHT
BELLYINGS	BEMEAN	BEMUSE	BENEFACT
BELLYLIKE	BEMEANED	BEMUSED	BENEFACTS
BELOMANCY	BEMEANING	BEMUSEDLY	BENEFIC
BELON	BEMEANS	BEMUSES	BENEFICE
BELONG	BEMEANT	BEMUSING	BENEFICED
BELONGED	BEMEDAL	BEMUZZLE	BENEFICES
BELONGER	BEMEDALED	BEMUZZLED	BENEFIT
BELONGERS	BEMEDALS	BEMUZZLES	BENEFITED
BELONGING	BEMETE	BEN	BENEFITER
BELONGS	BEMETED	BENADRYL	BENEFITS
BELONS	BEMETES	BENADRYLS	BENEMPT
BELOVE	BEMETING	BENAME	BENEMPTED
BELOVED	BEMINGLE	BENAMED	BENES
BELOVEDS	BEMINGLED	BENAMES	BENET
BELOVES	BEMINGLES	BENAMING	BENETS
BELOVING	BEMIRE	BENCH	BENETTED

BENETTING	BENUMBS	BEPOMMEL	BERET
BENGALINE	BENZAL	BEPOMMELS	BERETS
BENI	BENZALS	BEPOWDER	BERETTA
BENIGHT	BENZENE	BEPOWDERS	BERETTAS
BENIGHTED	BENZENES	BEPRAISE	BERG
BENIGHTEN	BENZENOID	BEPRAISED	BERGAMA
BENIGHTER	BENZIDIN	BEPRAISES	BERGAMAS
BENIGHTS	BENZIDINE	BEPROSE	BERGAMASK
BENIGN	BENZIDINS	BEPROSED	BERGAMOT
BENIGNANT	BENZIL	BEPROSES	BERGAMOTS
BENIGNER	BENZILS	BEPROSING	BERGANDER
BENIGNEST	BENZIN	BEPUFF	BERGEN
BENIGNITY	BENZINE	BEPUFFED	BERGENIA
BENIGNLY	BENZINES	BEPUFFING	BERGENIAS
BENIS	BENZINS	BEPUFFS	BERGENS
BENISEED	BENZOATE	BEQUEATH	BERGERE
BENISEEDS	BENZOATES	BEQUEATHS	BERGERES
BENISON	BENZOIC	BEQUEST	BERGFALL
BENISONS	BENZOIN	BEQUESTS	BERGFALLS
BENITIER	BENZOINS	BERAKE	BERGHAAN
BENITIERS	BENZOL	BERAKED	BERGHAANS
BENJ	BENZOLE	BERAKES	BERGMEHL
BENJAMIN	BENZOLES	BERAKING	BERGMEHLS
BENJAMINS	BENZOLINE	BERASCAL	BERGOMASK
BENJES	BENZOLS	BERASCALS	BERGS
BENNE	BENZOYL	BERATE	BERGYLT
BENNES	BENZOYLS	BERATED	BERGYLTS
BENNET	BENZYL	BERATES	BERHYME
BENNETS	BENZYLIC	BERATING	BERHYMED
BENNI	BENZYLS	BERAY	BERHYMES
BENNIES	BEPAINT	BERAYED	BERHYMING
BENNIS	BEPAINTED	BERAYING	BERIBERI
BENNY	BEPAINTS	BERAYS	BERIBERIS
BENOMYL	BEPAT	BERBERE	BERIMBAU
BENOMYLS	BEPATCHED	BERBERES	BERIMBAUS
BENS	BEPATS	BERBERIN	BERIME
BENT	BEPATTED	BERBERINE	BERIMED
BENTGRASS	BEPATTING	BERBERINS	BERIMES
BENTHAL	BEPEARL	BERBERIS	BERIMING
BENTHIC	BEPEARLED	BERBICE	BERINGED
BENTHOAL	BEPEARLS	BERCEAU	BERK
BENTHON	BEPELT	BERCEAUX	BERKELIUM
BENTHONIC	BEPELTED	BERCEUSE	BERKO
BENTHONS	BEPELTING	BERCEUSES	BERKS
BENTHOS	BEPELTS	BERDACHE	BERLEY
BENTHOSES	BEPEPPER	BERDACHES	BERLEYED
BENTIER	BEPEPPERS	BERDASH	BERLEYING
BENTIEST	BEPESTER	BERDASHES	BERLEYS
BENTO	BEPESTERS	BERE	BERLIN
BENTONITE	BEPIMPLE	BEREAVE	BERLINE
BENTOS	BEPIMPLED	BEREAVED	BERLINES
BENTS	BEPIMPLES	BEREAVEN	BERLINS
BENTWOOD	BEPITIED	BEREAVER	BERM
BENTWOODS	BEPITIES	BEREAVERS	BERME
BENTY	BEPITY	BEREAVES	BERMED
BENUMB	BEPITYING	BEREAVING	BERMES
BENUMBED	BEPLASTER	BEREFT	BERMING
BENUMBING	BEPLUMED	BERES	BERMS

BERMUDAS	BESCREEN	BESINGING	BESORTING
BERNICLE	BESCREENS	BESINGS	BESORTS
BERNICLES	BESEE	BESIT	BESOT
BEROB	BESEECH	BESITS	BESOTS
BEROBBED	BESEECHED	BESITTING	BESOTTED
BEROBBING	BESEECHER	BESLAVE	BESOTTING
BEROBED	BESEECHES	BESLAVED	BESOUGHT
BEROBS	BESEEING	BESLAVER	BESOULED
BEROUGED	BESEEKE	BESLAVERS	BESPAKE
BERRET	BESEEKES	BESLAVES	BESPANGLE
BERRETS	BESEEKING	BESLAVING	BESPAT
BERRETTA	BESEEM	BESLIME	BESPATE
BERRETTAS	BESEEMED	BESLIMED	BESPATTER
BERRIED	BESEEMING	BESLIMES	BESPEAK
BERRIES	BESEEMLY	BESLIMING	BESPEAKS
BERRIGAN	BESEEMS	BESLOBBER	BESPECKLE
BERRIGANS	BESEEN	BESLUBBER	BESPED
BERRY	BESEES	BESMEAR	BESPEED
BERRYING	BESES	BESMEARED	BESPEEDS
BERRYINGS	BESET	BESMEARER	BESPICE
BERRYLESS	BESETMENT	BESMEARS	BESPICED
BERRYLIKE	BESETS	BESMILE	BESPICES
BERSEEM	BESETTER	BESMILED	BESPICING
BERSEEMS	BESETTERS	BESMILES	BESPIT
BERSERK	BESETTING	BESMILING	BESPITS
BERSERKER	BESHADOW	BESMIRCH	BESPOKE
BERSERKLY	BESHADOWS	BESMOKE	BESPOKEN
BERSERKS	BESHAME	BESMOKED	BESPORT
BERTH	BESHAMED	BESMOKES	BESPORTED
BERTHA	BESHAMES	BESMOKING	BESPORTS
BERTHAGE	BESHAMING	BESMOOTH	BESPOT
BERTHAGES	BESHINE	BESMOOTHS	BESPOTS
BERTHAS	BESHINES	BESMUDGE	BESPOTTED
BERTHE	BESHINING	BESMUDGED	BESPOUSE
BERTHED	BESHIVER	BESMUDGES	BESPOUSED
BERTHES	BESHIVERS	BESMUT	BESPOUSES
BERTHING	BESHONE	BESMUTCH	BESPOUT
BERTHS	BESHOUT	BESMUTS	BESPOUTED
BERYL	BESHOUTED	BESMUTTED	BESPOUTS
BERYLINE	BESHOUTS	BESNOW	BESPREAD
BERYLLIA	BESHREW	BESNOWED	BESPREADS
BERYLLIAS	BESHREWED	BESNOWING	BESPRENT
BERYLLIUM	BESHREWS	BESNOWS	BEST
BERYLS	BESHROUD	BESOGNIO	BESTAD
BES	BESHROUDS	BESOGNIOS	BESTADDE
BESAINT	BESIDE	BESOIN	BESTAIN
BESAINTED	BESIDES	BESOINS	BESTAINED
BESAINTS	BESIEGE	BESOM	BESTAINS
BESANG	BESIEGED	BESOMED	BESTAR
BESAT	BESIEGER	BESOMING	BESTARRED
BESAW	BESIEGERS	BESOMS	BESTARS
BESCATTER	BESIEGES	BESONIAN	BESTEAD
BESCORCH	BESIEGING	BESONIANS	BESTEADED
BESCOUR	BESIGH	BESOOTHE	BESTEADS
BESCOURED	BESIGHED	BESOOTHED	BESTED
BESCOURS	BESIGHING	BESOOTHES	BESTI
BESCRAWL	BESIGHS	BESORT	BESTIAL
BESCRAWLS	BESING	BESORTED	BESTIALLY

BESTIALS	BETATOPIC	BETITLE	BETWIXT
BESTIARY	BETATRON	BETITLED	BEUNCLED
BESTICK	BETATRONS	BETITLES	BEURRE
BESTICKS	BETATTER	BETITLING	BEURRES
BESTILL	BETATTERS	BETOIL	BEVATRON
BESTILLED	BETAXED	BETOILED	BEVATRONS
BESTILLS	BETE	BETOILING	BEVEL
BESTING	BETED	BETOILS	BEVELED
BESTIR	BETEEM	BETOKEN	BEVELER
BESTIRRED	BETEEME	BETOKENED	BEVELERS
BESTIRS	BETEEMED	BETOKENS	BEVELING
BESTIS	BETEEMES	BETON	BEVELLED
BESTORM	BETEEMING	BETONIES	BEVELLER
BESTORMED	BETEEMS	BETONS	BEVELLERS
BESTORMS	BETEL	BETONY	BEVELLING
BESTOW	BETELNUT	BETOOK	BEVELMENT
BESTOWAL	BETELNUTS	BETOSS	BEVELS
BESTOWALS	BETELS	BETOSSED	BEVER
BESTOWED	BETES	BETOSSES	BEVERAGE
BESTOWER	BETH	BETOSSING	BEVERAGES
BESTOWERS	BETHANK	BETRAY	BEVERS
BESTOWING	BETHANKED	BETRAYAL	BEVIES
BESTOWS	BETHANKIT	BETRAYALS	BEVOMIT
BESTREAK	BETHANKS	BETRAYED	BEVOMITED
BESTREAKS	BETHEL	BETRAYER	BEVOMITS
BESTREW	BETHELS	BETRAYERS	BEVOR
BESTREWED	BETHESDA	BETRAYING	BEVORS
BESTREWN	BETHESDAS	BETRAYS	BEVUE
BESTREWS	BETHINK	BETREAD	BEVUES
BESTRID	BETHINKS	BETREADS	BEVVIED
BESTRIDE	BETHORN	BETRIM	BEVVIES
BESTRIDES	BETHORNED	BETRIMMED	BEVVY
BESTRODE	BETHORNS	BETRIMS	BEVVYING
BESTROW	BETHOUGHT	BETROD	BEVY
BESTROWED	BETHRALL	BETRODDEN	BEWAIL
BESTROWN	BETHRALLS	BETROTH	BEWAILED
BESTROWS	BETHS	BETROTHAL	BEWAILER
BESTS	BETHUMB	BETROTHED	BEWAILERS
BESTUCK	BETHUMBED	BETROTHS	BEWAILING
BESTUD	BETHUMBS	BETS	BEWAILS
BESTUDDED	BETHUMP	BETTA	BEWARE
BESTUDS	BETHUMPED	BETTAS	BEWARED
BESUITED	BETHUMPS	BETTED	BEWARES
BESUNG	BETHWACK	BETTER	BEWARING
BESWARM	BETHWACKS	BETTERED	BEWEARIED
BESWARMED	BETID	BETTERING	BEWEARIES
BESWARMS	BETIDE	BETTERS	BEWEARY
BET	BETIDED	BETTIES	BEWEEP
BETA	BETIDES	BETTING	BEWEEPING
BETACISM	BETIDING	BETTINGS	BEWEEPS
BETACISMS	BETIGHT	BETTONG	BEWENT
BETAINE	BETIME	BETTONGS	BEWEPT
BETAINES	BETIMED	BETTOR	BEWET
BETAKE	BETIMES	BETTORS	BEWETS
BETAKEN	BETIMING	BETTY	BEWETTED
BETAKES	BETING	BETUMBLED	BEWETTING
BETAKING	BETISE	BETWEEN	BEWHORE
BETAS	BETISES	BETWEENS	BEWHORED

BEWHORES	BEZZLED	BIANNUAL	BICEP
BEWHORING	BEZZLES	BIANNUALS	BICEPS
BEWIG	BEZZLING	BIAS	BICEPSES
BEWIGGED	BHAGEE	BIASED	BICES
BEWIGGING	BHAGEES	BIASEDLY	BICHORD
BEWIGS	BHAJAN	BIASES	BICHROME
BEWILDER	BHAJANS	BIASING	BICIPITAL
BEWILDERS	BHAJEE	BIASINGS	BICKER
BEWINGED	BHAJEES	BIASNESS	BICKERED
BEWITCH	BHAJI	BIASSED	BICKERER
BEWITCHED	BHAJIS	BIASSEDLY	BICKERERS
BEWITCHER	BHAKTA	BIASSES	BICKERING
BEWITCHES	BHAKTAS	BIASSING	BICKERS
BEWORM	BHAKTI	BIATHLETE	BICKIE
BEWORMED	BHAKTIS	BIATHLON	BICKIES
BEWORMING	BHANG	BIATHLONS	BICOASTAL
BEWORMS	BHANGRA	BIAXAL	BICOLOR
BEWORRIED	BHANGRAS	BIAXIAL	BICOLORED
BEWORRIES	BHANGS	BIAXIALLY	BICOLORS
BEWORRY	BHARAL	BIB	BICOLOUR
BEWRAP	BHARALS	BIBACIOUS	BICOLOURS
BEWRAPPED	BHAT	BIBASIC	BICONCAVE
BEWRAPS	BHAVAN	BIBATION	BICONVEX
BEWRAPT	BHAVANS	BIBATIONS	BICORN
BEWRAY	BHAWAN	BIBB	BICORNATE
BEWRAYED	BHAWANS	BIBBED	BICORNE
BEWRAYER	BHEESTIE	BIBBER	BICORNES
BEWRAYERS	BHEESTIES	BIBBERIES	BICORNS
BEWRAYING	BHEESTY	BIBBERS	BICRON
BEWRAYS	BHEL	BIBBERY	BICRONS
BEY	BHELS	BIBBING	BICUSPID
BEYLIC	BHIKHU	BIBBLE	BICUSPIDS
BEYLICS	BHIKHUS	BIBBLES	BICYCLE
BEYLIK	BHIKKHUNI	BIBBS	BICYCLED
BEYLIKS	BHINDI	BIBCOCK	BICYCLER
BEYOND	BHINDIS	BIBCOCKS	BICYCLERS
BEYONDS	BHISHTI	BIBELOT	BICYCLES
BEYS	BHISHTIS	BIBELOTS	BICYCLIC
BEZ	BHISTEE	BIBLE	BICYCLING
BEZANT	BHISTEES	BIBLES	BICYCLIST
BEZANTS	BHISTI	BIBLESS	BID
BEZAZZ	BHISTIE	BIBLICAL	BIDARKA
BEZAZZES	BHISTIES	BIBLICISM	BIDARKAS
BEZEL	BHISTIS	BIBLICIST	BIDARKEE
BEZELS	BHOOT	BIBLIKE	BIDARKEES
BEZES	BHOOTS	BIBLIOTIC	BIDDABLE
BEZIL	BHUNA	BIBLIST	BIDDABLY
BEZILS	BHUNAS	BIBLISTS	BIDDEN
BEZIQUE	BHUT	BIBS	BIDDER
BEZIQUES	BHUTS	BIBULOUS	BIDDERS
BEZOAR	BI	BICAMERAL	BIDDIES
BEZOARDIC	BIACETYL	BICARB	BIDDING
BEZOARS	BIACETYLS	BICARBS	BIDDINGS
BEZONIAN	BIALI	BICAUDAL	BIDDY
BEZONIANS	BIALIES	BICCIES	BIDE
BEZZANT	BIALIS	BICCY	BIDED
BEZZANTS	BIALY	BICE	BIDENT
BEZZLE	BIALYS	BICENTRIC	BIDENTAL

BIDENTALS	BIFOLD	BIGHTED	BILBERRY
BIDENTATE	BIFOLIATE	BIGHTING	BILBIES
BIDENTS	BIFORATE	BIGHTS	BILBO
BIDER	BIFORKED	BIGLY	BILBOA
BIDERS	BIFORM	BIGMOUTH	BILBOAS
BIDES	BIFORMED	BIGMOUTHS	BILBOES
BIDET	BIFTER	BIGNESS	BILBOS
BIDETS	BIFTERS	BIGNESSES	BILBY
BIDI	BIFURCATE	BIGNONIA	BILE
BIDING	BIG	BIGNONIAS	BILECTION
BIDINGS	BIGA	BIGOS	BILED
BIDIS	BIGAE	BIGOSES	BILES
BIDON	BIGAMIES	BIGOT	BILESTONE
BIDONS	BIGAMIST	BIGOTED	BILEVEL
BIDS	BIGAMISTS	BIGOTEDLY	BILEVELS
BIELD	BIGAMOUS	BIGOTRIES	BILGE
BIELDED	BIGAMY	BIGOTRY	BILGED
BIELDIER	BIGARADE	BIGOTS	BILGES
BIELDIEST	BIGARADES	BIGS	BILGIER
BIELDING	BIGAROON	BIGSTICK	BILGIEST
BIELDS	BIGAROONS	BIGTIME	BILGING
BIELDY	BIGARREAU	BIGUANIDE	BILGY
BIEN	BIGEMINAL	BIGWIG	BILHARZIA
BIENNALE	BIGEMINY	BIGWIGS	BILIAN
BIENNALES	BIGENER	BIHOURLY	BILIANS
BIENNIA	BIGENERIC	BIJECTION	BILIARIES
BIENNIAL	BIGENERS	BIJECTIVE	BILIARY
BIENNIALS	BIGEYE	BIJOU	BILIMBI
BIENNIUM	BIGEYES	BIJOUS	BILIMBING
BIENNIUMS	BIGFEET	BIJOUX	BILIMBIS
BIER	BIGFOOT	BIJUGATE	BILINEAR
BIERS	BIGFOOTED	BIJUGOUS	BILING
BIESTINGS	BIGFOOTS	BIJWONER	BILINGUAL
BIFACE	BIGG	BIJWONERS	BILIOUS
BIFACES	BIGGED	BIKE	BILIOUSLY
BIFACIAL	BIGGER	BIKED	BILIRUBIN
BIFARIOUS	BIGGEST	BIKER	BILITERAL
BIFF	BIGGETY	BIKERS	BILK
BIFFED	BIGGIE	BIKES	BILKED
BIFFER	BIGGIES	BIKEWAY	BILKER
BIFFERS	BIGGIN	BIKEWAYS	BILKERS
BIFFIES	BIGGING	BIKIE	BILKING
BIFFIN	BIGGINGS	BIKIES	BILKS
BIFFING	BIGGINS	BIKING	BILL
BIFFINS	BIGGISH	BIKINGS	BILLABLE
BIFFO	BIGGITY	BIKINI	BILLABONG
BIFFOS	BIGGON	BIKINIED	BILLBOARD
BIFFS	BIGGONS	BIKINIS	BILLBOOK
BIFFY	BIGGS	BIKKIE	BILLBOOKS
BIFID	BIGGY	BIKKIES	BILLBUG
BIFIDITY	BIGHA	BILABIAL	BILLBUGS
BIFIDLY	BIGHAS	BILABIALS	BILLED
BIFILAR	BIGHEAD	BILABIATE	BILLER
BIFILARLY	BIGHEADED	BILANDER	BILLERS
BIFLEX	BIGHEADS	BILANDERS	BILLET
BIFOCAL	BIGHORN	BILATERAL	BILLETED
BIFOCALED	BIGHORNS	BILAYER	BILLETEE
BIFOCALS	BIGHT	BILAYERS	BILLETEES

BILLETER	BIMBASHI	BINGHI	BIOETHIC
BILLETERS	BIMBASHIS	BINGHIS	BIOETHICS
BILLETING	BIMBETTE	BINGIES	BIOFACT
BILLETS	BIMBETTES	BINGING	BIOFACTS
BILLFISH	BIMBLE	BINGLE	BIOFILM
BILLFOLD	BIMBO	BINGLED	BIOFILMS
BILLFOLDS	BIMBOES	BINGLES	BIOFOULER
BILLHEAD	BIMBOS	BINGLING	BIOFUEL
BILLHEADS	BIMENSAL	BINGO	BIOFUELED
BILLHOOK	BIMESTER	BINGOES	BIOFUELS
BILLHOOKS	BIMESTERS	BINGOS	BIOG
BILLIARD	BIMETAL	BINGS	BIOGAS
BILLIARDS	BIMETALS	BINGY	BIOGASES
BILLIE	BIMETHYL	BINIOU	BIOGASSES
BILLIES	BIMETHYLS	BINIOUS	BIOGEN
BILLING	BIMODAL	BINIT	BIOGENIC
BILLINGS	BIMONTHLY	BINITS	BIOGENIES
BILLION	BIMORPH	BINK	BIOGENOUS
BILLIONS	BIMORPHS	BINKS	BIOGENS
BILLIONTH	BIN	BINMAN	BIOGENY
BILLMAN	BINAL	BINMEN	BIOGRAPH
BILLMEN	BINARIES	BINNACLE	BIOGRAPHS
BILLON	BINARISM	BINNACLES	BIOGRAPHY
BILLONS	BINARISMS	BINNED	BIOGS
BILLOW	BINARY	BINNING	BIOHAZARD
BILLOWED	BINATE	BINOCLE	BIOHERM
BILLOWIER	BINATELY	BINOCLES	BIOHERMS
BILLOWING	BINAURAL	BINOCS	BIOLOGIC
BILLOWS	BIND	BINOCULAR	BIOLOGICS
BILLOWY	BINDABLE	BINOMIAL	BIOLOGIES
BILLS	BINDER	BINOMIALS	BIOLOGISM
BILLY	BINDERIES	BINOMINAL	BIOLOGIST
BILLYBOY	BINDERS	BINOVULAR	BIOLOGY
BILLYBOYS	BINDERY	BINS	BIOLYSES
BILLYCAN	BINDHI	BINT	BIOLYSIS
BILLYCANS	BINDHIS	BINTS	BIOLYTIC
BILLYCOCK	BINDI	BINTURONG	BIOMARKER
BILLYO	BINDING	BINUCLEAR	BIOMASS
BILLYOH	BINDINGLY	BIO	BIOMASSES
BILLYOHS	BINDINGS	BIOACTIVE	BIOME
BILLYOS	BINDIS	BIOASSAY	BIOMES
BILOBAR	BINDLE	BIOASSAYS	BIOMETER
BILOBATE	BINDLES	BIOBLAST	BIOMETERS
BILOBATED	BINDS	BIOBLASTS	BIOMETRIC
BILOBED	BINDWEED	BIOCENOSE	BIOMETRY
BILOBULAR	BINDWEEDS	BIOCHEMIC	BIOMINING
BILOCULAR	BINE	BIOCHIP	BIOMORPH
BILSTED	BINER	BIOCHIPS	BIOMORPHS
BILSTEDS	BINERS	BIOCIDAL	BIONIC
BILTONG	BINERVATE	BIOCIDE	BIONICS
BILTONGS	BINES	BIOCIDES	BIONOMIC
BIMA	BING	BIOCLEAN	BIONOMICS
BIMAH	BINGE	BIOCYCLE	BIONOMIES
BIMAHS	BINGED	BIOCYCLES	BIONOMIST
BIMANAL	BINGEING	BIODATA	BIONOMY
BIMANOUS	BINGER	BIODIESEL	BIONT
BIMANUAL	BINGERS	BIODOT	BIONTIC
BIMAS	BINGES	BIODOTS	BIONTS

BIOPARENT	BIOTYPES	BIRDIES	BIRRS
BIOPHILIA	BIOTYPIC	BIRDING	BIRSE
BIOPHOR	BIOVULAR	BIRDINGS	BIRSES
BIOPHORE	BIOWEAPON	BIRDLIFE	BIRSIER
BIOPHORES	BIPACK	BIRDLIKE	BIRSIEST
BIOPHORS	BIPACKS	BIRDLIME	BIRSLE
BIOPIC	BIPAROUS	BIRDLIMED	BIRSLED
BIOPICS	BIPARTED	BIRDLIMES	BIRSLES
BIOPIRACY	BIPARTITE	BIRDMAN	BIRSLING
BIOPIRATE	BIPARTY	BIRDMEN	BIRSY
BIOPLASM	BIPED	BIRDS	BIRTH
BIOPLASMS	BIPEDAL	BIRDSEED	BIRTHDAY
BIOPLAST	BIPEDALLY	BIRDSEEDS	BIRTHDAYS
BIOPLASTS	BIPEDS	BIRDSEYE	BIRTHDOM
BIOPSIC	BIPHASIC	BIRDSEYES	BIRTHDOMS
BIOPSIED	BIPHENYL	BIRDSHOT	BIRTHED
BIOPSIES	BIPHENYLS	BIRDSHOTS	BIRTHING
BIOPSY	BIPINNATE	BIRDSONG	BIRTHINGS
BIOPSYING	BIPLANE	BIRDSONGS	BIRTHMARK
BIOPTIC	BIPLANES	BIRDWATCH	BIRTHNAME
BIOREGION	BIPOD	BIRDWING	BIRTHRATE
BIORHYTHM	BIPODS	BIRDWINGS	BIRTHROOT
BIOS	BIPOLAR	BIREME	BIRTHS
BIOSAFETY	BIPRISM	BIREMES	BIRTHWORT
BIOSCOPE	BIPRISMS	BIRETTA	BIRYANI
BIOSCOPES	BIPYRAMID	BIRETTAS	BIRYANIS
BIOSCOPY	BIRACIAL	BIRIANI	BIS
BIOSENSOR	BIRADIAL	BIRIANIS	BISCACHA
BIOSOCIAL	BIRADICAL	BIRIYANI	BISCACHAS
BIOSOLID	BIRAMOSE	BIRIYANIS	BISCOTTI
BIOSOLIDS	BIRAMOUS	BIRK	BISCOTTO
BIOSPHERE	BIRCH	BIRKEN	BISCUIT
BIOSTABLE	BIRCHBARK	BIRKIE	BISCUITS
BIOSTATIC	BIRCHED	BIRKIER	BISCUITY
BIOSTROME	BIRCHEN	BIRKIES	BISE
BIOTA	BIRCHES	BIRKIEST	BISECT
BIOTAS	BIRCHING	BIRKS	BISECTED
BIOTECH	BIRD	BIRL	BISECTING
BIOTECHS	BIRDBATH	BIRLE	BISECTION
BIOTERROR	BIRDBATHS	BIRLED	BISECTOR
BIOTIC	BIRDBRAIN	BIRLER	BISECTORS
BIOTICAL	BIRDCAGE	BIRLERS	BISECTRIX
BIOTICS	BIRDCAGES	BIRLES	BISECTS
BIOTIN	BIRDCALL	BIRLIEMAN	BISERIAL
BIOTINS	BIRDCALLS	BIRLIEMEN	BISERIATE
BIOTITE	BIRDDOG	BIRLING	BISERRATE
BIOTITES	BIRDDOGS	BIRLINGS	BISES
BIOTITIC	BIRDED	BIRLINN	BISEXUAL
BIOTOPE	BIRDER	BIRLINNS	BISEXUALS
BIOTOPES	BIRDERS	BIRLS	BISH
BIOTOXIN	BIRDFARM	BIRO	BISHES
BIOTOXINS	BIRDFARMS	BIROS	BISHOP
BIOTRON	BIRDFEED	BIRR	BISHOPDOM
BIOTRONS	BIRDFEEDS	BIRRED	BISHOPED
BIOTROPH	BIRDHOUSE	BIRRETTA	BISHOPESS
BIOTROPHS	BIRDIE	BIRRETTAS	BISHOPING
BIOTURBED	BIRDIED	BIRRING	BISHOPRIC
BIOTYPE	BIRDIEING	BIRROTCH	BISHOPS

BISK
BISKS
BISMAR
BISMARS
BISMILLAH
BISMUTH
BISMUTHAL
BISMUTHIC
BISMUTHS
BISNAGA
BISNAGAS
BISON
BISONS
BISONTINE
BISQUE
BISQUES
BISSON
BIST
BISTABLE
BISTABLES
BISTATE
BISTER
BISTERED
BISTERS
BISTORT
BISTORTS
BISTOURY
BISTRE
BISTRED
BISTRES
BISTRO
BISTROIC
BISTROS
BISULCATE
BISULFATE
BISULFIDE
BISULFITE
BIT
BITABLE
BITCH
BITCHED
BITCHEN
BITCHERY
BITCHES
BITCHFEST
BITCHIER
BITCHIEST
BITCHILY
BITCHING
BITCHY
BITE
BITEABLE
BITEPLATE
BITER
BITERS
BITES
BITESIZE
BITEWING

BITEWINGS
BITING
BITINGLY
BITINGS
BITLESS
BITMAP
BITMAPPED
BITMAPS
BITO
BITONAL
BITOS
BITOU
BITS
BITSER
BITSERS
BITSIER
BITSIEST
BITSTOCK
BITSTOCKS
BITSTREAM
BITSY
BITT
BITTACLE
BITTACLES
BITTE
BITTED
BITTEN
BITTER
BITTERED
BITTERER
BITTEREST
BITTERING
BITTERISH
BITTERLY
BITTERN
BITTERNS
BITTERNUT
BITTERS
BITTIE
BITTIER
BITTIES
BITTIEST
BITTINESS
BITTING
BITTINGS
BITTOCK
BITTOCKS
BITTOR
BITTORS
BITTOUR
BITTOURS
BITTS
BITTUR
BITTURS
BITTY
BITUMED
BITUMEN
BITUMENS

BIUNIQUE
BIVALENCE
BIVALENCY
BIVALENT
BIVALENTS
BIVALVATE
BIVALVE
BIVALVED
BIVALVES
BIVARIANT
BIVARIATE
BIVIA
BIVINYL
BIVINYLS
BIVIOUS
BIVIUM
BIVOUAC
BIVOUACKS
BIVOUACS
BIVVIED
BIVVIES
BIVVY
BIVVYING
BIWEEKLY
BIYEARLY
BIZ
BIZARRE
BIZARRELY
BIZARRES
BIZARRO
BIZARROS
BIZAZZ
BIZAZZES
BIZCACHA
BIZCACHAS
BIZE
BIZES
BIZNAGA
BIZNAGAS
BIZONAL
BIZONE
BIZONES
BIZZES
BIZZIES
BIZZO
BIZZOS
BIZZY
BLAB
BLABBED
BLABBER
BLABBERED
BLABBERS
BLABBING
BLABBINGS
BLABBY
BLABS
BLACK
BLACKBALL

BLACKBAND
BLACKBIRD
BLACKBODY
BLACKBOY
BLACKBOYS
BLACKBUCK
BLACKBUTT
BLACKCAP
BLACKCAPS
BLACKCOCK
BLACKDAMP
BLACKED
BLACKEN
BLACKENED
BLACKENER
BLACKENS
BLACKER
BLACKEST
BLACKFACE
BLACKFIN
BLACKFINS
BLACKFISH
BLACKFLY
BLACKGAME
BLACKGUM
BLACKGUMS
BLACKHEAD
BLACKING
BLACKINGS
BLACKISH
BLACKJACK
BLACKLAND
BLACKLEAD
BLACKLEG
BLACKLEGS
BLACKLIST
BLACKLY
BLACKMAIL
BLACKNESS
BLACKOUT
BLACKOUTS
BLACKPOLL
BLACKS
BLACKTAIL
BLACKTOP
BLACKTOPS
BLACKWASH
BLACKWOOD
BLAD
BLADDED
BLADDER
BLADDERED
BLADDERS
BLADDERY
BLADDING
BLADE
BLADED
BLADELESS

BLADELIKE	BLANCOED	BLASTING	BLAZINGLY
BLADER	BLANCOING	BLASTINGS	BLAZON
BLADERS	BLANCOS	BLASTMENT	BLAZONED
BLADES	BLAND	BLASTOFF	BLAZONER
BLADEWORK	BLANDER	BLASTOFFS	BLAZONERS
BLADING	BLANDEST	BLASTOID	BLAZONING
BLADINGS	BLANDISH	BLASTOIDS	BLAZONRY
BLADS	BLANDLY	BLASTOMA	BLAZONS
BLADY	BLANDNESS	BLASTOMAS	BLEACH
BLAE	BLANDS	BLASTOPOR	BLEACHED
BLAEBERRY	BLANK	BLASTS	BLEACHER
BLAER	BLANKED	BLASTULA	BLEACHERS
BLAES	BLANKER	BLASTULAE	BLEACHERY
BLAEST	BLANKEST	BLASTULAR	BLEACHES
BLAFF	BLANKET	BLASTULAS	BLEACHING
BLAFFS	BLANKETED	BLASTY	BLEAK
BLAG	BLANKETS	BLAT	BLEAKER
BLAGGED	BLANKETY	BLATANCY	BLEAKEST
BLAGGER	BLANKIES	BLATANT	BLEAKISH
BLAGGERS	BLANKING	BLATANTLY	BLEAKLY
BLAGGING	BLANKINGS	BLATE	BLEAKNESS
BLAGGINGS	BLANKLY	BLATER	BLEAKS
BLAGS	BLANKNESS	BLATEST	BLEAKY
BLAGUE	BLANKS	BLATHER	BLEAR
BLAGUER	BLANKY	BLATHERED	BLEARED
BLAGUERS	BLANQUET	BLATHERER	BLEARER
BLAGUES	BLANQUETS	BLATHERS	BLEAREST
BLAGUEUR	BLARE	BLATS	BLEAREYED
BLAGUEURS	BLARED	BLATT	BLEARIER
BLAH	BLARES	BLATTANT	BLEARIEST
BLAHED	BLARING	BLATTED	BLEARILY
BLAHING	BLARNEY	BLATTER	BLEARING
BLAHS	BLARNEYED	BLATTERED	BLEARS
BLAIN	BLARNEYS	BLATTERS	BLEARY
BLAINS	BLART	BLATTING	BLEAT
BLAISE	BLARTED	BLATTS	BLEATED
BLAIZE	BLARTING	BLAUBOK	BLEATER
BLAM	BLARTS	BLAUBOKS	BLEATERS
BLAMABLE	BLASE	BLAUD	BLEATING
BLAMABLY	BLASH	BLAUDED	BLEATINGS
BLAME	BLASHES	BLAUDING	BLEATS
BLAMEABLE	BLASHIER	BLAUDS	BLEB
BLAMEABLY	BLASHIEST	BLAW	BLEBBING
BLAMED	BLASHY	BLAWED	BLEBBINGS
BLAMEFUL	BLASPHEME	BLAWING	BLEBBY
BLAMELESS	BLASPHEMY	BLAWN	BLEBS
BLAMER	BLAST	BLAWORT	BLED
BLAMERS	BLASTED	BLAWORTS	BLEE
BLAMES	BLASTEMA	BLAWS	BLEED
BLAMING	BLASTEMAL	BLAY	BLEEDER
BLAMS	BLASTEMAS	BLAYS	BLEEDERS
BLANCH	BLASTEMIC	BLAZE	BLEEDING
BLANCHED	BLASTER	BLAZED	BLEEDINGS
BLANCHER	BLASTERS	BLAZER	BLEEDS
BLANCHERS	BLASTIE	BLAZERED	BLEEP
BLANCHES	BLASTIER	BLAZERS	BLEEPED
BLANCHING	BLASTIES	BLAZES	BLEEPER
BLANCO	BLASTIEST	BLAZING	BLEEPERS

BLEEPING	BLEY	BLINTZ	BLOCKADE
BLEEPS	BLEYS	BLINTZE	BLOCKADED
BLEES	BLIGHT	BLINTZES	BLOCKADER
BLELLUM	BLIGHTED	BLINY	BLOCKADES
BLELLUMS	BLIGHTER	BLIP	BLOCKAGE
BLEMISH	BLIGHTERS	BLIPPED	BLOCKAGES
BLEMISHED	BLIGHTIES	BLIPPING	BLOCKBUST
BLEMISHER	BLIGHTING	BLIPS	BLOCKED
BLEMISHES	BLIGHTS	BLIPVERT	BLOCKER
BLENCH	BLIGHTY	BLIPVERTS	BLOCKERS
BLENCHED	BLIKSEM	BLISS	BLOCKHEAD
BLENCHER	BLIMBING	BLISSED	BLOCKHOLE
BLENCHERS	BLIMBINGS	BLISSES	BLOCKIE
BLENCHES	BLIMEY	BLISSFUL	BLOCKIER
BLENCHING	BLIMP	BLISSING	BLOCKIES
BLEND	BLIMPISH	BLISSLESS	BLOCKIEST
BLENDE	BLIMPS	BLIST	BLOCKING
BLENDED	BLIMY	BLISTER	BLOCKINGS
BLENDER	BLIN	BLISTERED	BLOCKISH
BLENDERS	BLIND	BLISTERS	BLOCKS
BLENDES	BLINDAGE	BLISTERY	BLOCKWORK
BLENDING	BLINDAGES	BLITE	BLOCKY
BLENDINGS	BLINDED	BLITES	BLOCS
BLENDS	BLINDER	BLITHE	BLOG
BLENNIES	BLINDERS	BLITHEFUL	BLOGGER
BLENNIOID	BLINDEST	BLITHELY	BLOGGERS
BLENNY	BLINDFISH	BLITHER	BLOGGING
BLENT	BLINDFOLD	BLITHERED	BLOGGINGS
BLERT	BLINDGUT	BLITHERS	BLOGS
BLERTS	BLINDGUTS	BLITHEST	BLOKE
BLESBOK	BLINDING	BLITZ	BLOKEDOM
BLESBOKS	BLINDINGS	BLITZED	BLOKEDOMS
BLESBUCK	BLINDLESS	BLITZER	BLOKEISH
BLESBUCKS	BLINDLY	BLITZERS	BLOKES
BLESS	BLINDNESS	BLITZES	BLOKEY
BLESSED	BLINDS	BLITZING	BLOKIER
BLESSEDER	BLINDSIDE	BLIVE	BLOKIEST
BLESSEDLY	BLINDWORM	BLIZZARD	BLOKISH
BLESSER	BLING	BLIZZARDS	BLONCKET
BLESSERS	BLINGER	BLIZZARDY	BLOND
BLESSES	BLINGEST	BLOAT	BLONDE
BLESSING	BLINGING	BLOATED	BLONDER
BLESSINGS	BLINGLISH	BLOATER	BLONDES
BLEST	BLINGS	BLOATERS	BLONDEST
BLET	BLINI	BLOATING	BLONDINE
BLETHER	BLINIS	BLOATINGS	BLONDINED
BLETHERED	BLINK	BLOATS	BLONDINES
BLETHERER	BLINKARD	BLOATWARE	BLONDING
BLETHERS	BLINKARDS	BLOB	BLONDINGS
BLETS	BLINKED	BLOBBED	BLONDISH
BLETTED	BLINKER	BLOBBIER	BLONDNESS
BLETTING	BLINKERED	BLOBBIEST	BLONDS
BLEUATRE	BLINKERS	BLOBBING	BLOOD
BLEW	BLINKING	BLOBBY	BLOODBATH
BLEWART	BLINKS	BLOBS	BLOODED
BLEWARTS	BLINNED	BLOC	BLOODFIN
BLEWITS	BLINNING	BLOCK	BLOODFINS
BLEWITSES	BLINS	BLOCKABLE	BLOODHEAT

BLOODIED	BLOTCHY	BLOWLAMP	BLUEBALL
BLOODIER	BLOTLESS	BLOWLAMPS	BLUEBALLS
BLOODIES	BLOTS	BLOWN	BLUEBEARD
BLOODIEST	BLOTTED	BLOWOFF	BLUEBEAT
BLOODILY	BLOTTER	BLOWOFFS	BLUEBEATS
BLOODING	BLOTTERS	BLOWOUT	BLUEBELL
BLOODINGS	BLOTTIER	BLOWOUTS	BLUEBELLS
BLOODLESS	BLOTTIEST	BLOWPIPE	BLUEBERRY
BLOODLIKE	BLOTTING	BLOWPIPES	BLUEBILL
BLOODLINE	BLOTTINGS	BLOWS	BLUEBILLS
BLOODLUST	BLOTTO	BLOWSE	BLUEBIRD
BLOODRED	BLOTTY	BLOWSED	BLUEBIRDS
BLOODROOT	BLOUBOK	BLOWSES	BLUEBLOOD
BLOODS	BLOUBOKS	BLOWSIER	BLUEBOOK
BLOODSHED	BLOUSE	BLOWSIEST	BLUEBOOKS
BLOODSHOT	BLOUSED	BLOWSILY	BLUEBUCK
BLOODWOOD	BLOUSES	BLOWSY	BLUEBUCKS
BLOODWORM	BLOUSIER	BLOWTORCH	BLUEBUSH
BLOODWORT	BLOUSIEST	BLOWTUBE	BLUECAP
BLOODY	BLOUSILY	BLOWTUBES	BLUECAPS
BLOODYING	BLOUSING	BLOWUP	BLUECOAT
BLOOEY	BLOUSON	BLOWUPS	BLUECOATS
BLOOIE	BLOUSONS	BLOWY	BLUECURLS
BLOOM	BLOUSY	BLOWZE	BLUED
BLOOMED	BLOVIATE	BLOWZED	BLUEFIN
BLOOMER	BLOVIATED	BLOWZES	BLUEFINS
BLOOMERS	BLOVIATES	BLOWZIER	BLUEFISH
BLOOMERY	BLOW	BLOWZIEST	BLUEGILL
BLOOMIER	BLOWBACK	BLOWZILY	BLUEGILLS
BLOOMIEST	BLOWBACKS	BLOWZY	BLUEGOWN
BLOOMING	BLOWBALL	BLUB	BLUEGOWNS
BLOOMLESS	BLOWBALLS	BLUBBED	BLUEGRASS
BLOOMS	BLOWBY	BLUBBER	BLUEGUM
BLOOMY	BLOWBYS	BLUBBERED	BLUEGUMS
BLOOP	BLOWDOWN	BLUBBERER	BLUEHEAD
BLOOPED	BLOWDOWNS	BLUBBERS	BLUEHEADS
BLOOPER	BLOWED	BLUBBERY	BLUEING
BLOOPERS	BLOWER	BLUBBING	BLUEINGS
BLOOPING	BLOWERS	BLUBS	BLUEISH
BLOOPS	BLOWFISH	BLUCHER	BLUEJACK
BLOOSME	BLOWFLIES	BLUCHERS	BLUEJACKS
BLOOSMED	BLOWFLY	BLUDE	BLUEJAY
BLOOSMES	BLOWGUN	BLUDES	BLUEJAYS
BLOOSMING	BLOWGUNS	BLUDGE	BLUEJEANS
BLOQUISTE	BLOWHARD	BLUDGED	BLUELINE
BLORE	BLOWHARDS	BLUDGEON	BLUELINER
BLORES	BLOWHOLE	BLUDGEONS	BLUELINES
BLOSSOM	BLOWHOLES	BLUDGER	BLUELY
BLOSSOMED	BLOWIE	BLUDGERS	BLUENESS
BLOSSOMS	BLOWIER	BLUDGES	BLUENOSE
BLOSSOMY	BLOWIES	BLUDGING	BLUENOSED
BLOT	BLOWIEST	BLUDIE	BLUENOSES
BLOTCH	BLOWINESS	BLUDIER	BLUEPOINT
BLOTCHED	BLOWING	BLUDIEST	BLUEPRINT
BLOTCHES	BLOWJOB	BLUDY	BLUER
BLOTCHIER	BLOWJOBS	BLUE	BLUES
BLOTCHILY	BLOWKART	BLUEBACK	BLUESHIFT
BLOTCHING	BLOWKARTS	BLUEBACKS	BLUESIER

BLUESIEST	BLUNGERS	BLUTWURST	BOATING
BLUESMAN	BLUNGES	BLYPE	BOATINGS
BLUESMEN	BLUNGING	BLYPES	BOATLIFT
BLUEST	BLUNK	BO	BOATLIFTS
BLUESTEM	BLUNKED	BOA	BOATLIKE
BLUESTEMS	BLUNKER	BOAB	BOATLOAD
BLUESTONE	BLUNKERS	BOABS	BOATLOADS
BLUESY	BLUNKING	BOAK	BOATMAN
BLUET	BLUNKS	BOAKED	BOATMEN
BLUETICK	BLUNT	BOAKING	BOATNECK
BLUETICKS	BLUNTED	BOAKS	BOATNECKS
BLUETIT	BLUNTER	BOAR	BOATS
BLUETITS	BLUNTEST	BOARD	BOATSMAN
BLUETS	BLUNTHEAD	BOARDABLE	BOATSMEN
BLUETTE	BLUNTING	BOARDED	BOATSWAIN
BLUETTES	BLUNTISH	BOARDER	BOATTAIL
BLUEWEED	BLUNTLY	BOARDERS	BOATTAILS
BLUEWEEDS	BLUNTNESS	BOARDING	BOATYARD
BLUEWING	BLUNTS	BOARDINGS	BOATYARDS
BLUEWINGS	BLUR	BOARDLIKE	BOB
BLUEWOOD	BLURB	BOARDMAN	BOBA
BLUEWOODS	BLURBED	BOARDMEN	BOBAC
BLUEY	BLURBING	BOARDROOM	BOBACS
BLUEYS	BLURBIST	BOARDS	BOBAK
BLUFF	BLURBISTS	BOARDWALK	BOBAKS
BLUFFABLE	BLURBS	BOARFISH	BOBAS
BLUFFED	BLURRED	BOARHOUND	BOBBED
BLUFFER	BLURREDLY	BOARISH	BOBBEJAAN
BLUFFERS	BLURRIER	BOARISHLY	BOBBER
BLUFFEST	BLURRIEST	BOARS	BOBBERIES
BLUFFING	BLURRILY	BOART	BOBBERS
BLUFFLY	BLURRING	BOARTS	BOBBERY
BLUFFNESS	BLURRY	BOAS	BOBBIES
BLUFFS	BLURS	BOAST	BOBBIN
BLUGGIER	BLURT	BOASTED	BOBBINET
BLUGGIEST	BLURTED	BOASTER	BOBBINETS
BLUGGY	BLURTER	BOASTERS	BOBBING
BLUID	BLURTERS	BOASTFUL	BOBBINS
BLUIDIER	BLURTING	BOASTING	BOBBISH
BLUIDIEST	BLURTINGS	BOASTINGS	BOBBITT
BLUIDS	BLURTS	BOASTLESS	BOBBITTED
BLUIDY	BLUSH	BOASTS	BOBBITTS
BLUIER	BLUSHED	BOAT	BOBBLE
BLUIEST	BLUSHER	BOATABLE	BOBBLED
BLUING	BLUSHERS	BOATBILL	BOBBLES
BLUINGS	BLUSHES	BOATBILLS	BOBBLIER
BLUISH	BLUSHET	BOATED	BOBBLIEST
BLUME	BLUSHETS	BOATEL	BOBBLING
BLUMED	BLUSHFUL	BOATELS	BOBBLY
BLUMES	BLUSHING	BOATER	BOBBY
BLUMING	BLUSHINGS	BOATERS	BOBBYSOCK
BLUNDER	BLUSHLESS	BOATFUL	BOBBYSOX
BLUNDERED	BLUSTER	BOATFULS	BOBCAT
BLUNDERER	BLUSTERED	BOATHOOK	BOBCATS
BLUNDERS	BLUSTERER	BOATHOOKS	BOBECHE
BLUNGE	BLUSTERS	BOATHOUSE	BOBECHES
BLUNGED	BLUSTERY	BOATIE	BOBFLOAT
BLUNGER	BLUSTROUS	BOATIES	BOBFLOATS

BOBLET	BODEFUL	BOERTJIE	BOGLES
BOBLETS	BODEGA	BOERTJIES	BOGMAN
BOBOL	BODEGAS	BOET	BOGMEN
BOBOLINK	BODEGUERO	BOETS	BOGOAK
BOBOLINKS	BODEMENT	BOEUF	BOGOAKS
BOBOLLED	BODEMENTS	BOFF	BOGONG
BOBOLLING	BODES	BOFFED	BOGONGS
BOBOLS	BODGE	BOFFIN	BOGS
BOBOTIE	BODGED	BOFFING	BOGUS
BOBOTIES	BODGER	BOFFINS	BOGUSLY
BOBOWLER	BODGERS	BOFFO	BOGUSNESS
BOBOWLERS	BODGES	BOFFOLA	BOGWOOD
BOBS	BODGIE	BOFFOLAS	BOGWOODS
BOBSLED	BODGIER	BOFFOS	BOGY
BOBSLEDS	BODGIES	BOFFS	BOGYISM
BOBSLEIGH	BODGIEST	BOG	BOGYISMS
BOBSTAY	BODGING	BOGAN	BOGYMAN
BOBSTAYS	BODHRAN	BOGANS	BOGYMEN
BOBTAIL	BODHRANS	BOGART	BOH
BOBTAILED	BODICE	BOGARTED	BOHEA
BOBTAILS	BODICES	BOGARTING	BOHEAS
BOBWEIGHT	BODIED	BOGARTS	BOHEMIA
BOBWHEEL	BODIES	BOGBEAN	BOHEMIAN
BOBWHEELS	BODIKIN	BOGBEANS	BOHEMIANS
BOBWHITE	BODIKINS	BOGEY	BOHEMIAS
BOBWHITES	BODILESS	BOGEYED	BOHO
BOBWIG	BODILY	BOGEYING	BOHOS
BOBWIGS	BODING	BOGEYISM	BOHRIUM
BOCACCIO	BODINGLY	BOGEYISMS	BOHRIUMS
BOCACCIOS	BODINGS	BOGEYMAN	BOHS
BOCAGE	BODKIN	BOGEYMEN	BOHUNK
BOCAGES	BODKINS	BOGEYS	BOHUNKS
BOCCA	BODLE	BOGGARD	BOI
BOCCAS	BODLES	BOGGARDS	BOIL
BOCCE	BODRAG	BOGGART	BOILABLE
BOCCES	BODRAGS	BOGGARTS	BOILED
BOCCI	BODS	BOGGED	BOILER
BOCCIA	BODY	BOGGER	BOILERIES
BOCCIAS	BODYBOARD	BOGGERS	BOILERS
BOCCIE	BODYCHECK	BOGGIER	BOILERY
BOCCIES	BODYGUARD	BOGGIEST	BOILING
BOCCIS	BODYING	BOGGINESS	BOILINGLY
BOCHE	BODYLINE	BOGGING	BOILINGS
BOCHES	BODYLINES	BOGGISH	BOILOFF
BOCK	BODYSHELL	BOGGLE	BOILOFFS
BOCKED	BODYSUIT	BOGGLED	BOILOVER
BOCKEDY	BODYSUITS	BOGGLER	BOILOVERS
BOCKING	BODYSURF	BOGGLERS	BOILS
BOCKS	BODYSURFS	BOGGLES	BOING
BOCONCINI	BODYWORK	BOGGLING	BOINGED
BOD	BODYWORKS	BOGGY	BOINGING
BODACH	BOEHMITE	BOGIE	BOINGS
BODACHS	BOEHMITES	BOGIED	BOINK
BODACIOUS	BOEP	BOGIEING	BOINKED
BODDLE	BOEPS	BOGIES	BOINKING
BODDLES	BOERBUL	BOGLAND	BOINKS
BODE	BOERBULS	BOGLANDS	BOIS
BODED	BOEREWORS	BOGLE	BOISERIE

BOISERIES	BOLLING	BOMBABLE	BONANZAS
BOITE	BOLLIX	BOMBARD	BONASSUS
BOITES	BOLLIXED	BOMBARDE	BONASUS
BOK	BOLLIXES	BOMBARDED	BONASUSES
BOKE	BOLLIXING	BOMBARDER	BONBON
BOKED	BOLLOCK	BOMBARDES	BONBONS
BOKES	BOLLOCKED	BOMBARDON	BONCE
BOKING	BOLLOCKS	BOMBARDS	BONCES
BOKO	BOLLOX	BOMBASINE	BOND
BOKOS	BOLLOXED	BOMBAST	BONDABLE
BOKS	BOLLOXES	BOMBASTED	BONDAGE
BOLA	BOLLOXING	BOMBASTER	BONDAGER
BOLAR	BOLLS	BOMBASTIC	BONDAGERS
BOLAS	BOLLWORM	BOMBASTS	BONDAGES
BOLASES	BOLLWORMS	BOMBAX	BONDED
BOLD	BOLO	BOMBAXES	BONDER
BOLDEN	BOLOGNA	BOMBAZINE	BONDERS
BOLDENED	BOLOGNAS	BOMBE	BONDING
BOLDENING	BOLOGRAPH	BOMBED	BONDINGS
BOLDENS	BOLOMETER	BOMBER	BONDLESS
BOLDER	BOLOMETRY	BOMBERS	BONDMAID
BOLDEST	BOLONEY	BOMBES	BONDMAIDS
BOLDFACE	BOLONEYS	BOMBESIN	BONDMAN
BOLDFACED	BOLOS	BOMBESINS	BONDMEN
BOLDFACES	BOLSHEVIK	BOMBILATE	BONDS
BOLDLY	BOLSHIE	BOMBINATE	BONDSMAN
BOLDNESS	BOLSHIER	BOMBING	BONDSMEN
BOLDS	BOLSHIES	BOMBINGS	BONDSTONE
BOLE	BOLSHIEST	BOMBLET	BONDUC
BOLECTION	BOLSHY	BOMBLETS	BONDUCS
BOLERO	BOLSON	BOMBLOAD	BONDWOMAN
BOLEROS	BOLSONS	BOMBLOADS	BONDWOMEN
BOLES	BOLSTER	BOMBO	BONE
BOLETE	BOLSTERED	BOMBORA	BONEBLACK
BOLETES	BOLSTERER	BOMBORAS	BONED
BOLETI	BOLSTERS	BOMBOS	BONEFISH
BOLETUS	BOLT	BOMBPROOF	BONEHEAD
BOLETUSES	BOLTED	BOMBS	BONEHEADS
BOLIDE	BOLTER	BOMBSHELL	BONELESS
BOLIDES	BOLTERS	BOMBSIGHT	BONEMEAL
BOLINE	BOLTHEAD	BOMBSITE	BONEMEALS
BOLINES	BOLTHEADS	BOMBSITES	BONER
BOLIVAR	BOLTHOLE	BOMBYCID	BONERS
BOLIVARES	BOLTHOLES	BOMBYCIDS	BONES
BOLIVARS	BOLTING	BOMBYCOID	BONESET
BOLIVIA	BOLTINGS	BOMBYX	BONESETS
BOLIVIANO	BOLTLESS	BOMBYXES	BONEY
BOLIVIAS	BOLTLIKE	BOMMIE	BONEYARD
BOLIX	BOLTONIA	BOMMIES	BONEYARDS
BOLIXED	BOLTONIAS	BON	BONEYER
BOLIXES	BOLTROPE	BONA	BONEYEST
BOLIXING	BOLTROPES	BONACI	BONFIRE
BOLL	BOLTS	BONACIS	BONFIRES
BOLLARD	BOLUS	BONAMANI	BONG
BOLLARDS	BOLUSES	BONAMANO	BONGED
BOLLED	BOMA	BONAMIA	BONGING
BOLLEN	BOMAS	BONAMIAS	BONGO
BOLLETRIE	BOMB	BONANZA	BONGOES

BONGOIST	BONOBOS	BOOED	BOOKLAND
BONGOISTS	BONSAI	BOOFHEAD	BOOKLANDS
BONGOS	BONSAIS	BOOFHEADS	BOOKLESS
BONGRACE	BONSELA	BOOFIER	BOOKLET
BONGRACES	BONSELAS	BOOFIEST	BOOKLETS
BONGS	BONSELLA	BOOFY	BOOKLICE
BONHAM	BONSELLAS	BOOGER	BOOKLIGHT
BONHAMS	BONSOIR	BOOGERMAN	BOOKLORE
BONHOMIE	BONSPELL	BOOGERMEN	BOOKLORES
BONHOMIES	BONSPELLS	BOOGERS	BOOKLOUSE
BONHOMMIE	BONSPIEL	BOOGEY	BOOKMAKER
BONHOMOUS	BONSPIELS	BOOGEYED	BOOKMAN
BONIATO	BONTEBOK	BOOGEYING	BOOKMARK
BONIATOS	BONTEBOKS	BOOGEYMAN	BOOKMARKS
BONIBELL	BONUS	BOOGEYMEN	BOOKMEN
BONIBELLS	BONUSES	BOOGEYS	BOOKOO
BONIE	BONXIE	BOOGIE	BOOKOOS
BONIER	BONXIES	BOOGIED	BOOKPLATE
BONIEST	BONY	BOOGIEING	BOOKRACK
BONIFACE	BONZA	BOOGIEMAN	BOOKRACKS
BONIFACES	BONZE	BOOGIEMEN	BOOKREST
BONILASSE	BONZER	BOOGIES	BOOKRESTS
BONINESS	BONZES	BOOGY	BOOKS
BONING	BOO	BOOGYING	BOOKSHELF
BONINGS	BOOB	BOOGYMAN	BOOKSHOP
BONISM	BOOBED	BOOGYMEN	BOOKSHOPS
BONISMS	BOOBHEAD	BOOH	BOOKSIE
BONIST	BOOBHEADS	BOOHAI	BOOKSIER
BONISTS	BOOBIALLA	BOOHAIS	BOOKSIEST
BONITA	BOOBIE	BOOHED	BOOKSTALL
BONITAS	BOOBIES	BOOHING	BOOKSTAND
BONITO	BOOBING	BOOHOO	BOOKSTORE
BONITOES	BOOBIRD	BOOHOOED	BOOKSY
BONITOS	BOOBIRDS	BOOHOOING	BOOKWORK
BONJOUR	BOOBISH	BOOHOOS	BOOKWORKS
BONK	BOOBOISIE	BOOHS	BOOKWORM
BONKED	BOOBOO	BOOING	BOOKWORMS
BONKERS	BOOBOOK	BOOJUM	BOOKY
BONKING	BOOBOOKS	BOOJUMS	BOOL
BONKINGS	BOOBOOS	BOOK	BOOLED
BONKS	BOOBS	BOOKABLE	BOOLING
BONNE	BOOBY	BOOKCASE	BOOLS
BONNES	BOOBYISH	BOOKCASES	BOOM
BONNET	BOOBYISM	BOOKED	BOOMBOX
BONNETED	BOOBYISMS	BOOKEND	BOOMBOXES
BONNETING	BOOCOO	BOOKENDS	BOOMED
BONNETS	BOOCOOS	BOOKER	BOOMER
BONNIBELL	BOODIE	BOOKERS	BOOMERANG
BONNIE	BOODIED	BOOKFUL	BOOMERS
BONNIER	BOODIES	BOOKFULS	BOOMIER
BONNIES	BOODLE	BOOKIE	BOOMIEST
BONNIEST	BOODLED	BOOKIER	BOOMING
BONNILY	BOODLER	BOOKIES	BOOMINGLY
BONNINESS	BOODLERS	BOOKIEST	BOOMINGS
BONNOCK	BOODLES	BOOKING	BOOMKIN
BONNOCKS	BOODLING	BOOKINGS	BOOMKINS
BONNY	BOODY	BOOKISH	BOOMLET
BONOBO	BOODYING	BOOKISHLY	BOOMLETS

BOOMS	BOOTJACK	BORAZON	BORM
BOOMSLANG	BOOTJACKS	BORAZONS	BORMED
BOOMTOWN	BOOTLACE	BORD	BORMING
BOOMTOWNS	BOOTLACES	BORDAR	BORMS
BOOMY	BOOTLAST	BORDARS	BORN
BOON	BOOTLASTS	BORDE	BORNA
BOONDOCK	BOOTLEG	BORDEAUX	BORNE
BOONDOCKS	BOOTLEGS	BORDEL	BORNEOL
BOONER	BOOTLESS	BORDELLO	BORNEOLS
BOONERS	BOOTLICK	BORDELLOS	BORNITE
BOONG	BOOTLICKS	BORDELS	BORNITES
BOONGA	BOOTMAKER	BORDER	BORNITIC
BOONGARY	BOOTS	BORDEREAU	BORNYL
BOONGAS	BOOTSTRAP	BORDERED	BORNYLS
BOONGS	BOOTY	BORDERER	BORON
BOONIES	BOOZE	BORDERERS	BORONIA
BOONLESS	BOOZED	BORDERING	BORONIAS
BOONS	BOOZER	BORDERS	BORONIC
BOOR	BOOZERS	BORDES	BORONS
BOORD	BOOZES	BORDS	BOROUGH
BOORDE	BOOZEY	BORDURE	BOROUGHS
BOORDES	BOOZIER	BORDURES	BORREL
BOORDS	BOOZIEST	BORE	BORRELIA
BOORISH	BOOZILY	BOREAL	BORRELIAS
BOORISHLY	BOOZINESS	BOREALIS	BORRELL
BOORKA	BOOZING	BOREAS	BORROW
BOORKAS	BOOZY	BOREASES	BORROWED
BOORS	BOP	BORECOLE	BORROWER
BOORTREE	BOPEEP	BORECOLES	BORROWERS
BOORTREES	BOPEEPS	BORED	BORROWING
BOOS	BOPPED	BOREDOM	BORROWS
BOOSE	BOPPER	BOREDOMS	BORS
BOOSED	BOPPERS	BOREE	BORSCH
BOOSES	BOPPING	BOREEN	BORSCHES
BOOSHIT	BOPS	BOREENS	BORSCHT
BOOSING	BOR	BOREES	BORSCHTS
BOOST	BORA	BOREHOLE	BORSHCH
BOOSTED	BORACES	BOREHOLES	BORSHCHES
BOOSTER	BORACHIO	BOREL	BORSHT
BOOSTERS	BORACHIOS	BORER	BORSHTS
BOOSTING	BORACIC	BORERS	BORSIC
BOOSTS	BORACITE	BORES	BORSICS
BOOT	BORACITES	BORESCOPE	BORSTAL
BOOTABLE	BORAGE	BORESOME	BORSTALL
BOOTBLACK	BORAGES	BORGHETTO	BORSTALLS
BOOTED	BORAK	BORGO	BORSTALS
BOOTEE	BORAKS	BORGOS	BORT
BOOTEES	BORAL	BORIC	BORTIER
BOOTERIES	BORALS	BORIDE	BORTIEST
BOOTERY	BORANE	BORIDES	BORTS
BOOTH	BORANES	BORING	BORTSCH
BOOTHOSE	BORAS	BORINGLY	BORTSCHES
BOOTHS	BORATE	BORINGS	BORTY
BOOTIE	BORATED	BORK	BORTZ
BOOTIES	BORATES	BORKED	BORTZES
BOOTIKIN	BORATING	BORKING	BORZOI
BOOTIKINS	BORAX	BORKS	BORZOIS
BOOTING	BORAXES	BORLOTTI	BOS

BOSBERAAD	BOSSILY	BOTHANS	BOTULISM
BOSBOK	BOSSINESS	BOTHER	BOTULISMS
BOSBOKS	BOSSING	BOTHERED	BOUBOU
BOSCAGE	BOSSISM	BOTHERING	BOUBOUS
BOSCAGES	BOSSISMS	BOTHERS	BOUCHE
BOSCHBOK	BOSSY	BOTHIE	BOUCHEE
BOSCHBOKS	BOSTANGI	BOTHIES	BOUCHEES
BOSCHE	BOSTANGIS	BOTHOLE	BOUCHES
BOSCHES	BOSTHOON	BOTHOLES	BOUCLE
BOSCHVARK	BOSTHOONS	BOTHRIA	BOUCLEE
BOSCHVELD	BOSTON	BOTHRIUM	BOUCLEES
BOSH	BOSTONS	BOTHRIUMS	BOUCLES
BOSHBOK	BOSTRYX	BOTHY	BOUDERIE
BOSHBOKS	BOSTRYXES	BOTHYMAN	BOUDERIES
BOSHES	BOSUN	BOTHYMEN	BOUDIN
BOSHTA	BOSUNS	BOTNET	BOUDINS
BOSHTER	BOT	BOTNETS	BOUDOIR
BOSHVARK	BOTA	BOTONE	BOUDOIRS
BOSHVARKS	BOTANIC	BOTONEE	BOUFFANT
BOSK	BOTANICA	BOTONNEE	BOUFFANTS
BOSKAGE	BOTANICAL	BOTRYOID	BOUFFE
BOSKAGES	BOTANICAS	BOTRYOSE	BOUFFES
BOSKER	BOTANICS	BOTRYTIS	BOUGE
BOSKET	BOTANIES	BOTS	BOUGED
BOSKETS	BOTANISE	BOTT	BOUGES
BOSKIER	BOTANISED	BOTTE	BOUGET
BOSKIEST	BOTANISER	BOTTED	BOUGETS
BOSKINESS	BOTANISES	BOTTEGA	BOUGH
BOSKS	BOTANIST	BOTTEGAS	BOUGHED
BOSKY	BOTANISTS	BOTTES	BOUGHLESS
BOSOM	BOTANIZE	BOTTIES	BOUGHPOT
BOSOMED	BOTANIZED	BOTTINE	BOUGHPOTS
BOSOMIER	BOTANIZER	BOTTINES	BOUGHS
BOSOMIEST	BOTANIZES	BOTTING	BOUGHT
BOSOMING	BOTANY	BOTTLE	BOUGHTEN
BOSOMS	BOTARGO	BOTTLED	BOUGHTS
BOSOMY	BOTARGOES	BOTTLEFUL	BOUGIE
BOSON	BOTARGOS	BOTTLER	BOUGIES
BOSONIC	BOTAS	BOTTLERS	BOUGING
BOSONS	BOTCH	BOTTLES	BOUILLI
BOSQUE	BOTCHED	BOTTLING	BOUILLIS
BOSQUES	BOTCHEDLY	BOTTLINGS	BOUILLON
BOSQUET	BOTCHER	BOTTOM	BOUILLONS
BOSQUETS	BOTCHERS	BOTTOMED	BOUK
BOSS	BOTCHERY	BOTTOMER	BOUKS
BOSSBOY	BOTCHES	BOTTOMERS	BOULDER
BOSSBOYS	BOTCHIER	BOTTOMING	BOULDERED
BOSSDOM	BOTCHIEST	BOTTOMRY	BOULDERER
BOSSDOMS	BOTCHILY	BOTTOMS	BOULDERS
BOSSED	BOTCHING	BOTTOMSET	BOULDERY
BOSSER	BOTCHINGS	BOTTONY	BOULE
BOSSES	BOTCHY	BOTTS	BOULES
BOSSEST	BOTEL	BOTTY	BOULEVARD
BOSSET	BOTELS	BOTULIN	BOULLE
BOSSETS	BOTFLIES	BOTULINAL	BOULLES
BOSSIER	BOTFLY	BOTULINS	BOULT
BOSSIES	BOTH	BOTULINUM	BOULTED
BOSSIEST	BOTHAN	BOTULINUS	BOULTER

BOULTERS	BOURNE	BOWELED	BOWRS
BOULTING	BOURNES	BOWELING	BOWS
BOULTINGS	BOURNS	BOWELLED	BOWSAW
BOULTS	BOURREE	BOWELLESS	BOWSAWS
BOUN	BOURREES	BOWELLING	BOWSE
BOUNCE	BOURRIDE	BOWELS	BOWSED
BOUNCED	BOURRIDES	BOWER	BOWSER
BOUNCER	BOURSE	BOWERBIRD	BOWSERS
BOUNCERS	BOURSES	BOWERED	BOWSES
BOUNCES	BOURSIER	BOWERIES	BOWSEY
BOUNCIER	BOURSIERS	BOWERING	BOWSEYS
BOUNCIEST	BOURSIN	BOWERS	BOWSHOT
BOUNCILY	BOURSINS	BOWERY	BOWSHOTS
BOUNCING	BOURTREE	BOWES	BOWSIE
BOUNCY	BOURTREES	BOWET	BOWSIES
BOUND	BOUSE	BOWETS	BOWSING
BOUNDABLE	BOUSED	BOWFIN	BOWSPRIT
BOUNDARY	BOUSES	BOWFINS	BOWSPRITS
BOUNDED	BOUSIER	BOWFRONT	BOWSTRING
BOUNDEN	BOUSIEST	BOWGET	BOWSTRUNG
BOUNDER	BOUSING	BOWGETS	BOWWOW
BOUNDERS	BOUSOUKI	BOWHEAD	BOWWOWED
BOUNDING	BOUSOUKIA	BOWHEADS	BOWWOWING
BOUNDLESS	BOUSOUKIS	BOWHUNTER	BOWWOWS
BOUNDNESS	BOUSY	BOWIE	BOWYANG
BOUNDS	BOUT	BOWING	BOWYANGS
BOUNED	BOUTADE	BOWINGLY	BOWYER
BOUNING	BOUTADES	BOWINGS	BOWYERS
BOUNS	BOUTIQUE	BOWKNOT	BOX
BOUNTEOUS	BOUTIQUES	BOWKNOTS	BOXBALL
BOUNTIED	BOUTIQUEY	BOWL	BOXBALLS
BOUNTIES	BOUTON	BOWLDER	BOXBERRY
BOUNTIFUL	BOUTONNE	BOWLDERS	BOXBOARD
BOUNTREE	BOUTONNEE	BOWLED	BOXBOARDS
BOUNTREES	BOUTONS	BOWLEG	BOXCAR
BOUNTY	BOUTS	BOWLEGGED	BOXCARS
BOUNTYHED	BOUVARDIA	BOWLEGS	BOXED
BOUQUET	BOUVIER	BOWLER	BOXEN
BOUQUETS	BOUVIERS	BOWLERS	BOXER
BOURASQUE	BOUZOUKI	BOWLESS	BOXERCISE
BOURBON	BOUZOUKIA	BOWLFUL	BOXERS
BOURBONS	BOUZOUKIS	BOWLFULS	BOXES
BOURD	BOVATE	BOWLIKE	BOXFISH
BOURDER	BOVATES	BOWLINE	BOXFISHES
BOURDERS	BOVID	BOWLINES	BOXFUL
BOURDON	BOVIDS	BOWLING	BOXFULS
BOURDONS	BOVINE	BOWLINGS	BOXHAUL
BOURDS	BOVINELY	BOWLLIKE	BOXHAULED
BOURG	BOVINES	BOWLS	BOXHAULS
BOURGEOIS	BOVINITY	BOWMAN	BOXIER
BOURGEON	BOVVER	BOWMEN	BOXIEST
BOURGEONS	BOVVERS	BOWNE	BOXILY
BOURGS	BOW	BOWNED	BOXINESS
BOURKHA	BOWAT	BOWNES	BOXING
BOURKHAS	BOWATS	BOWNING	BOXINGS
BOURLAW	BOWBENT	BOWPOT	BOXKEEPER
BOURLAWS	BOWED	BOWPOTS	BOXLIKE
BOURN	BOWEL	BOWR	BOXROOM

BOXROOMS	BRABBLERS	BRADOON	BRAINIEST
BOXTHORN	BRABBLES	BRADOONS	BRAINILY
BOXTHORNS	BRABBLING	BRADS	BRAINING
BOXWALLAH	BRACCATE	BRAE	BRAINISH
BOXWOOD	BRACCIA	BRAEHEID	BRAINLESS
BOXWOODS	BRACCIO	BRAEHEIDS	BRAINPAN
BOXY	BRACE	BRAES	BRAINPANS
BOY	BRACED	BRAG	BRAINS
BOYAR	BRACELET	BRAGGART	BRAINSICK
BOYARD	BRACELETS	BRAGGARTS	BRAINSTEM
BOYARDS	BRACER	BRAGGED	BRAINWASH
BOYARISM	BRACERO	BRAGGER	BRAINWAVE
BOYARISMS	BRACEROS	BRAGGERS	BRAINY
BOYARS	BRACERS	BRAGGEST	BRAIRD
BOYAU	BRACES	BRAGGIER	BRAIRDED
BOYAUX	BRACH	BRAGGIEST	BRAIRDING
BOYCHICK	BRACHAH	BRAGGING	BRAIRDS
BOYCHICKS	BRACHAHS	BRAGGINGS	BRAISE
BOYCHIK	BRACHES	BRAGGY	BRAISED
BOYCHIKS	BRACHET	BRAGLY	BRAISES
BOYCOTT	BRACHETS	BRAGS	BRAISING
BOYCOTTED	BRACHIA	BRAHMA	BRAIZE
BOYCOTTER	BRACHIAL	BRAHMAN	BRAIZES
BOYCOTTS	BRACHIALS	BRAHMANI	BRAK
BOYED	BRACHIATE	BRAHMANIS	BRAKE
BOYF	BRACHIUM	BRAHMANS	BRAKEAGE
BOYFRIEND	BRACHS	BRAHMAS	BRAKEAGES
BOYFS	BRACING	BRAHMIN	BRAKED
BOYG	BRACINGLY	BRAHMINS	BRAKELESS
BOYGS	BRACINGS	BRAID	BRAKEMAN
BOYHOOD	BRACIOLA	BRAIDE	BRAKEMEN
BOYHOODS	BRACIOLAS	BRAIDED	BRAKES
BOYING	BRACIOLE	BRAIDER	BRAKESMAN
BOYISH	BRACIOLES	BRAIDERS	BRAKESMEN
BOYISHLY	BRACK	BRAIDEST	BRAKIER
BOYLA	BRACKEN	BRAIDING	BRAKIEST
BOYLAS	BRACKENS	BRAIDINGS	BRAKING
BOYO	BRACKET	BRAIDS	BRAKS
BOYOS	BRACKETED	BRAIL	BRAKY
BOYS	BRACKETS	BRAILED	BRALESS
BOYSIER	BRACKISH	BRAILING	BRAMBLE
BOYSIEST	BRACKS	BRAILLE	BRAMBLED
BOYSY	BRACONID	BRAILLED	BRAMBLES
BOZO	BRACONIDS	BRAILLER	BRAMBLIER
BOZOS	BRACT	BRAILLERS	BRAMBLING
BOZZETTI	BRACTEAL	BRAILLES	BRAMBLY
BOZZETTO	BRACTEATE	BRAILLING	BRAME
BRA	BRACTED	BRAILLIST	BRAMES
BRAAI	BRACTEOLE	BRAILS	BRAN
BRAAIED	BRACTLESS	BRAIN	BRANCARD
BRAAIING	BRACTLET	BRAINBOX	BRANCARDS
BRAAIS	BRACTLETS	BRAINCASE	BRANCH
BRAATA	BRACTS	BRAINDEAD	BRANCHED
BRAATAS	BRAD	BRAINED	BRANCHER
BRAATASES	BRADAWL	BRAINFART	BRANCHERS
BRABBLE	BRADAWLS	BRAINIAC	BRANCHERY
BRABBLED	BRADDED	BRAINIACS	BRANCHES
BRABBLER	BRADDING	BRAINIER	BRANCHIA

71

BRANCHIAE	BRASCOS	BRATTICED	BRAWNIER
BRANCHIAL	BRASERO	BRATTICES	BRAWNIEST
BRANCHIER	BRASEROS	BRATTIER	BRAWNILY
BRANCHING	BRASES	BRATTIEST	BRAWNS
BRANCHLET	BRASH	BRATTISH	BRAWNY
BRANCHY	BRASHED	BRATTLE	BRAWS
BRAND	BRASHER	BRATTLED	BRAXIES
BRANDADE	BRASHES	BRATTLES	BRAXY
BRANDADES	BRASHEST	BRATTLING	BRAY
BRANDED	BRASHIER	BRATTY	BRAYED
BRANDER	BRASHIEST	BRATWURST	BRAYER
BRANDERED	BRASHING	BRAUNCH	BRAYERS
BRANDERS	BRASHLY	BRAUNCHED	BRAYING
BRANDIED	BRASHNESS	BRAUNCHES	BRAYS
BRANDIES	BRASHY	BRAUNITE	BRAZA
BRANDING	BRASIER	BRAUNITES	BRAZAS
BRANDINGS	BRASIERS	BRAVA	BRAZE
BRANDISE	BRASIL	BRAVADO	BRAZED
BRANDISES	BRASILEIN	BRAVADOED	BRAZELESS
BRANDISH	BRASILIN	BRAVADOES	BRAZEN
BRANDLESS	BRASILINS	BRAVADOS	BRAZENED
BRANDLING	BRASILS	BRAVAS	BRAZENING
BRANDRETH	BRASS	BRAVE	BRAZENLY
BRANDS	BRASSAGE	BRAVED	BRAZENRY
BRANDY	BRASSAGES	BRAVELY	BRAZENS
BRANDYING	BRASSARD	BRAVENESS	BRAZER
BRANGLE	BRASSARDS	BRAVER	BRAZERS
BRANGLED	BRASSART	BRAVERIES	BRAZES
BRANGLES	BRASSARTS	BRAVERS	BRAZIER
BRANGLING	BRASSED	BRAVERY	BRAZIERS
BRANK	BRASSERIE	BRAVES	BRAZIERY
BRANKED	BRASSES	BRAVEST	BRAZIL
BRANKIER	BRASSET	BRAVI	BRAZILEIN
BRANKIEST	BRASSETS	BRAVING	BRAZILIN
BRANKING	BRASSICA	BRAVO	BRAZILINS
BRANKS	BRASSICAS	BRAVOED	BRAZILS
BRANKY	BRASSIE	BRAVOES	BRAZING
BRANLE	BRASSIER	BRAVOING	BREACH
BRANLES	BRASSIERE	BRAVOS	BREACHED
BRANNED	BRASSIES	BRAVURA	BREACHER
BRANNER	BRASSIEST	BRAVURAS	BREACHERS
BRANNERS	BRASSILY	BRAVURE	BREACHES
BRANNIER	BRASSING	BRAW	BREACHING
BRANNIEST	BRASSISH	BRAWER	BREAD
BRANNIGAN	BRASSWARE	BRAWEST	BREADBOX
BRANNING	BRASSY	BRAWL	BREADED
BRANNY	BRAST	BRAWLED	BREADHEAD
BRANS	BRASTING	BRAWLER	BREADING
BRANSLE	BRASTS	BRAWLERS	BREADLESS
BRANSLES	BRAT	BRAWLIE	BREADLINE
BRANT	BRATCHET	BRAWLIER	BREADNUT
BRANTAIL	BRATCHETS	BRAWLIEST	BREADNUTS
BRANTAILS	BRATLING	BRAWLING	BREADROOM
BRANTLE	BRATLINGS	BRAWLINGS	BREADROOT
BRANTLES	BRATPACK	BRAWLS	BREADS
BRANTS	BRATPACKS	BRAWLY	BREADTH
BRAS	BRATS	BRAWN	BREADTHS
BRASCO	BRATTICE	BRAWNED	BREADY

BREAK
BREAKABLE
BREAKAGE
BREAKAGES
BREAKAWAY
BREAKBACK
BREAKBEAT
BREAKBONE
BREAKDOWN
BREAKER
BREAKERS
BREAKEVEN
BREAKFAST
BREAKING
BREAKINGS
BREAKNECK
BREAKOFF
BREAKOFFS
BREAKOUT
BREAKOUTS
BREAKS
BREAKTIME
BREAKUP
BREAKUPS
BREAKWALL
BREAM
BREAMED
BREAMING
BREAMS
BREARE
BREARES
BREASKIT
BREASKITS
BREAST
BREASTED
BREASTFED
BREASTING
BREASTPIN
BREASTS
BREATH
BREATHE
BREATHED
BREATHER
BREATHERS
BREATHES
BREATHFUL
BREATHIER
BREATHILY
BREATHING
BREATHS
BREATHY
BRECCIA
BRECCIAL
BRECCIAS
BRECCIATE
BRECHAM
BRECHAMS
BRECHAN

BRECHANS
BRED
BREDE
BREDED
BREDES
BREDIE
BREDIES
BREDING
BREE
BREECH
BREECHED
BREECHES
BREECHING
BREED
BREEDER
BREEDERS
BREEDING
BREEDINGS
BREEDS
BREEKS
BREEM
BREENGE
BREENGED
BREENGES
BREENGING
BREER
BREERED
BREERING
BREERS
BREES
BREESE
BREESES
BREEST
BREESTS
BREEZE
BREEZED
BREEZES
BREEZEWAY
BREEZIER
BREEZIEST
BREEZILY
BREEZING
BREEZY
BREGMA
BREGMATA
BREGMATE
BREGMATIC
BREHON
BREHONS
BREI
BREID
BREIDS
BREIING
BREINGE
BREINGED
BREINGES
BREINGING
BREIS

BREIST
BREISTS
BREKKIES
BREKKY
BRELOQUE
BRELOQUES
BREME
BREN
BRENNE
BRENNES
BRENNING
BRENS
BRENT
BRENTER
BRENTEST
BRENTS
BRER
BRERE
BRERES
BRERS
BRETASCHE
BRETESSE
BRETESSES
BRETHREN
BRETON
BRETONS
BRETTICE
BRETTICED
BRETTICES
BREVE
BREVES
BREVET
BREVETCY
BREVETE
BREVETED
BREVETING
BREVETS
BREVETTED
BREVIARY
BREVIATE
BREVIATES
BREVIER
BREVIERS
BREVIS
BREVISES
BREVITIES
BREVITY
BREW
BREWAGE
BREWAGES
BREWED
BREWER
BREWERIES
BREWERS
BREWERY
BREWING
BREWINGS
BREWIS

BREWISES
BREWPUB
BREWPUBS
BREWS
BREWSKI
BREWSKIES
BREWSKIS
BREWSTER
BREWSTERS
BREY
BREYED
BREYING
BREYS
BRIAR
BRIARD
BRIARDS
BRIARED
BRIARROOT
BRIARS
BRIARWOOD
BRIARY
BRIBABLE
BRIBE
BRIBEABLE
BRIBED
BRIBEE
BRIBEES
BRIBER
BRIBERIES
BRIBERS
BRIBERY
BRIBES
BRIBING
BRICABRAC
BRICHT
BRICHTER
BRICHTEST
BRICK
BRICKBAT
BRICKBATS
BRICKCLAY
BRICKED
BRICKEN
BRICKIE
BRICKIER
BRICKIES
BRICKIEST
BRICKING
BRICKINGS
BRICKKILN
BRICKLE
BRICKLES
BRICKLIKE
BRICKS
BRICKWALL
BRICKWORK
BRICKY
BRICKYARD

BRICOLAGE	BRIGADED	BRINES	BRISLINGS
BRICOLE	BRIGADES	BRING	BRISS
BRICOLES	BRIGADIER	BRINGDOWN	BRISSES
BRIDAL	BRIGADING	BRINGER	BRISTLE
BRIDALLY	BRIGALOW	BRINGERS	BRISTLED
BRIDALS	BRIGALOWS	BRINGING	BRISTLES
BRIDE	BRIGAND	BRINGINGS	BRISTLIER
BRIDECAKE	BRIGANDRY	BRINGS	BRISTLING
BRIDED	BRIGANDS	BRINIER	BRISTLY
BRIDEMAID	BRIGHT	BRINIES	BRISTOL
BRIDEMAN	BRIGHTEN	BRINIEST	BRISTOLS
BRIDEMEN	BRIGHTENS	BRININESS	BRISURE
BRIDES	BRIGHTER	BRINING	BRISURES
BRIDESMAN	BRIGHTEST	BRINISH	BRIT
BRIDESMEN	BRIGHTISH	BRINJAL	BRITANNIA
BRIDEWELL	BRIGHTLY	BRINJALS	BRITCHES
BRIDGABLE	BRIGHTS	BRINJARRY	BRITH
BRIDGE	BRIGS	BRINK	BRITHS
BRIDGED	BRIGUE	BRINKMAN	BRITS
BRIDGES	BRIGUED	BRINKMEN	BRITSCHKA
BRIDGING	BRIGUES	BRINKS	BRITSKA
BRIDGINGS	BRIGUING	BRINNIES	BRITSKAS
BRIDIE	BRIGUINGS	BRINNY	BRITT
BRIDIES	BRIK	BRINS	BRITTANIA
BRIDING	BRIKS	BRINY	BRITTLE
BRIDLE	BRILL	BRIO	BRITTLED
BRIDLED	BRILLER	BRIOCHE	BRITTLELY
BRIDLER	BRILLEST	BRIOCHES	BRITTLER
BRIDLERS	BRILLIANT	BRIOLETTE	BRITTLES
BRIDLES	BRILLO	BRIONIES	BRITTLEST
BRIDLEWAY	BRILLOS	BRIONY	BRITTLING
BRIDLING	BRILLS	BRIOS	BRITTLY
BRIDOON	BRIM	BRIQUET	BRITTS
BRIDOONS	BRIMFUL	BRIQUETED	BRITZKA
BRIE	BRIMFULL	BRIQUETS	BRITZKAS
BRIEF	BRIMFULLY	BRIQUETTE	BRITZSKA
BRIEFCASE	BRIMING	BRIS	BRITZSKAS
BRIEFED	BRIMINGS	BRISANCE	BRIZE
BRIEFER	BRIMLESS	BRISANCES	BRIZES
BRIEFERS	BRIMMED	BRISANT	BRO
BRIEFEST	BRIMMER	BRISE	BROACH
BRIEFING	BRIMMERS	BRISES	BROACHED
BRIEFINGS	BRIMMING	BRISK	BROACHER
BRIEFLESS	BRIMS	BRISKED	BROACHERS
BRIEFLY	BRIMSTONE	BRISKEN	BROACHES
BRIEFNESS	BRIMSTONY	BRISKENED	BROACHING
BRIEFS	BRIN	BRISKENS	BROAD
BRIER	BRINDED	BRISKER	BROADAX
BRIERED	BRINDISI	BRISKEST	BROADAXE
BRIERIER	BRINDISIS	BRISKET	BROADAXES
BRIERIEST	BRINDLE	BRISKETS	BROADBAND
BRIERROOT	BRINDLED	BRISKING	BROADBEAN
BRIERS	BRINDLES	BRISKISH	BROADBILL
BRIERWOOD	BRINE	BRISKLY	BROADBRIM
BRIERY	BRINED	BRISKNESS	BROADCAST
BRIES	BRINELESS	BRISKS	BROADEN
BRIG	BRINER	BRISKY	BROADENED
BRIGADE	BRINERS	BRISLING	BROADENER

BROADENS	BRODDLING	BROMELAIN	BRONZING
BROADER	BRODEKIN	BROMELIA	BRONZINGS
BROADEST	BRODEKINS	BROMELIAD	BRONZITE
BROADISH	BRODKIN	BROMELIAS	BRONZITES
BROADLEAF	BRODKINS	BROMELIN	BRONZY
BROADLINE	BRODS	BROMELINS	BROO
BROADLOOM	BROEKIES	BROMEOSIN	BROOCH
BROADLY	BROG	BROMES	BROOCHED
BROADNESS	BROGAN	BROMIC	BROOCHES
BROADS	BROGANS	BROMID	BROOCHING
BROADSIDE	BROGGED	BROMIDE	BROOD
BROADTAIL	BROGGING	BROMIDES	BROODED
BROADWAY	BROGH	BROMIDIC	BROODER
BROADWAYS	BROGHS	BROMIDS	BROODERS
BROADWISE	BROGS	BROMIN	BROODIER
BROCADE	BROGUE	BROMINATE	BROODIEST
BROCADED	BROGUEISH	BROMINE	BROODILY
BROCADES	BROGUERY	BROMINES	BROODING
BROCADING	BROGUES	BROMINISM	BROODINGS
BROCAGE	BROGUISH	BROMINS	BROODLESS
BROCAGES	BROIDER	BROMISE	BROODMARE
BROCARD	BROIDERED	BROMISED	BROODS
BROCARDS	BROIDERER	BROMISES	BROODY
BROCATEL	BROIDERS	BROMISING	BROOK
BROCATELS	BROIDERY	BROMISM	BROOKABLE
BROCCOLI	BROIL	BROMISMS	BROOKED
BROCCOLIS	BROILED	BROMIZE	BROOKIE
BROCH	BROILER	BROMIZED	BROOKIES
BROCHAN	BROILERS	BROMIZES	BROOKING
BROCHANS	BROILING	BROMIZING	BROOKITE
BROCHE	BROILS	BROMMER	BROOKITES
BROCHED	BROKAGE	BROMMERS	BROOKLET
BROCHES	BROKAGES	BROMO	BROOKLETS
BROCHETTE	BROKE	BROMOFORM	BROOKLIKE
BROCHING	BROKED	BROMOS	BROOKLIME
BROCHO	BROKEN	BRONC	BROOKS
BROCHOS	BROKENLY	BRONCHI	BROOKWEED
BROCHS	BROKER	BRONCHIA	BROOL
BROCHURE	BROKERAGE	BRONCHIAL	BROOLS
BROCHURES	BROKERED	BRONCHIUM	BROOM
BROCK	BROKERIES	BRONCHO	BROOMBALL
BROCKAGE	BROKERING	BRONCHOS	BROOMCORN
BROCKAGES	BROKERS	BRONCHUS	BROOMED
BROCKED	BROKERY	BRONCO	BROOMIER
BROCKET	BROKES	BRONCOS	BROOMIEST
BROCKETS	BROKING	BRONCS	BROOMING
BROCKIT	BROKINGS	BROND	BROOMRAPE
BROCKRAM	BROLGA	BRONDS	BROOMS
BROCKRAMS	BROLGAS	BRONDYRON	BROOMY
BROCKS	BROLLIES	BRONZE	BROOS
BROCOLI	BROLLY	BRONZED	BROOSE
BROCOLIS	BROMAL	BRONZEN	BROOSES
BROD	BROMALS	BRONZER	BROS
BRODDED	BROMATE	BRONZERS	BROSE
BRODDING	BROMATED	BRONZES	BROSES
BRODDLE	BROMATES	BRONZIER	BROSY
BRODDLED	BROMATING	BRONZIEST	BROTH
BRODDLES	BROME	BRONZIFY	BROTHEL

BROTHELS	BRR	BRUNCHING	BRUTENESS
BROTHER	BRRR	BRUNET	BRUTER
BROTHERED	BRU	BRUNETS	BRUTERS
BROTHERLY	BRUCELLA	BRUNETTE	BRUTES
BROTHERS	BRUCELLAE	BRUNETTES	BRUTIFIED
BROTHS	BRUCELLAS	BRUNG	BRUTIFIES
BROTHY	BRUCHID	BRUNIZEM	BRUTIFY
BROUGH	BRUCHIDS	BRUNIZEMS	BRUTING
BROUGHAM	BRUCIN	BRUNT	BRUTINGS
BROUGHAMS	BRUCINE	BRUNTED	BRUTISH
BROUGHS	BRUCINES	BRUNTING	BRUTISHLY
BROUGHT	BRUCINS	BRUNTS	BRUTISM
BROUGHTA	BRUCITE	BRUS	BRUTISMS
BROUGHTAS	BRUCITES	BRUSH	BRUTS
BROUHAHA	BRUCKLE	BRUSHBACK	BRUX
BROUHAHAS	BRUGH	BRUSHED	BRUXED
BROUZE	BRUGHS	BRUSHER	BRUXES
BROUZES	BRUHAHA	BRUSHERS	BRUXING
BROW	BRUHAHAS	BRUSHES	BRUXISM
BROWALLIA	BRUILZIE	BRUSHFIRE	BRUXISMS
BROWBAND	BRUILZIES	BRUSHIER	BRYOLOGY
BROWBANDS	BRUIN	BRUSHIEST	BRYONIES
BROWBEAT	BRUINS	BRUSHING	BRYONY
BROWBEATS	BRUISE	BRUSHINGS	BRYOPHYTE
BROWED	BRUISED	BRUSHLAND	BRYOZOAN
BROWLESS	BRUISER	BRUSHLESS	BRYOZOANS
BROWN	BRUISERS	BRUSHLIKE	BUAT
BROWNED	BRUISES	BRUSHMARK	BUATS
BROWNER	BRUISING	BRUSHOFF	BUAZE
BROWNEST	BRUISINGS	BRUSHOFFS	BUAZES
BROWNIE	BRUIT	BRUSHUP	BUB
BROWNIER	BRUITED	BRUSHUPS	BUBA
BROWNIES	BRUITER	BRUSHWOOD	BUBAL
BROWNIEST	BRUITERS	BRUSHWORK	BUBALE
BROWNING	BRUITING	BRUSHY	BUBALES
BROWNINGS	BRUITS	BRUSK	BUBALINE
BROWNISH	BRULE	BRUSKER	BUBALIS
BROWNNESS	BRULES	BRUSKEST	BUBALISES
BROWNNOSE	BRULOT	BRUSQUE	BUBALS
BROWNOUT	BRULOTS	BRUSQUELY	BUBAS
BROWNOUTS	BRULYIE	BRUSQUER	BUBBA
BROWNS	BRULYIES	BRUSQUEST	BUBBAS
BROWNY	BRULZIE	BRUSSEN	BUBBIES
BROWRIDGE	BRULZIES	BRUST	BUBBLE
BROWS	BRUMAL	BRUSTING	BUBBLED
BROWSABLE	BRUMBIES	BRUSTS	BUBBLEGUM
BROWSE	BRUMBY	BRUT	BUBBLER
BROWSED	BRUME	BRUTAL	BUBBLERS
BROWSER	BRUMES	BRUTALISE	BUBBLES
BROWSERS	BRUMMAGEM	BRUTALISM	BUBBLIER
BROWSES	BRUMMER	BRUTALIST	BUBBLIES
BROWSIER	BRUMMERS	BRUTALITY	BUBBLIEST
BROWSIEST	BRUMOUS	BRUTALIZE	BUBBLING
BROWSING	BRUNCH	BRUTALLY	BUBBLY
BROWSINGS	BRUNCHED	BRUTE	BUBBY
BROWST	BRUNCHER	BRUTED	BUBINGA
BROWSTS	BRUNCHERS	BRUTELIKE	BUBINGAS
BROWSY	BRUNCHES	BRUTELY	BUBKES

BUBO	BUCKLINGS	BUDGED	BUFFOON
BUBOED	BUCKO	BUDGER	BUFFOONS
BUBOES	BUCKOES	BUDGEREE	BUFFOS
BUBONIC	BUCKOS	BUDGERO	BUFFS
BUBS	BUCKRA	BUDGEROS	BUFFY
BUBU	BUCKRAKE	BUDGEROW	BUFO
BUBUKLE	BUCKRAKES	BUDGEROWS	BUFOS
BUBUKLES	BUCKRAM	BUDGERS	BUFOTALIN
BUBUS	BUCKRAMED	BUDGES	BUG
BUCCAL	BUCKRAMS	BUDGET	BUGABOO
BUCCALLY	BUCKRAS	BUDGETARY	BUGABOOS
BUCCANEER	BUCKS	BUDGETED	BUGBANE
BUCCANIER	BUCKSAW	BUDGETEER	BUGBANES
BUCCINA	BUCKSAWS	BUDGETER	BUGBEAR
BUCCINAS	BUCKSHEE	BUDGETERS	BUGBEARS
BUCELLAS	BUCKSHEES	BUDGETING	BUGEYE
BUCENTAUR	BUCKSHISH	BUDGETS	BUGEYES
BUCHU	BUCKSHOT	BUDGIE	BUGGAN
BUCHUS	BUCKSHOTS	BUDGIES	BUGGANE
BUCK	BUCKSKIN	BUDGING	BUGGANES
BUCKAROO	BUCKSKINS	BUDI	BUGGANS
BUCKAROOS	BUCKSOM	BUDIS	BUGGED
BUCKAYRO	BUCKTAIL	BUDLESS	BUGGER
BUCKAYROS	BUCKTAILS	BUDLIKE	BUGGERED
BUCKBEAN	BUCKTEETH	BUDMASH	BUGGERIES
BUCKBEANS	BUCKTHORN	BUDMASHES	BUGGERING
BUCKBOARD	BUCKTOOTH	BUDO	BUGGERS
BUCKBRUSH	BUCKU	BUDOS	BUGGERY
BUCKED	BUCKUS	BUDS	BUGGIER
BUCKEEN	BUCKWHEAT	BUDWORM	BUGGIES
BUCKEENS	BUCKYBALL	BUDWORMS	BUGGIEST
BUCKER	BUCKYTUBE	BUFF	BUGGIN
BUCKEROO	BUCOLIC	BUFFA	BUGGINESS
BUCKEROOS	BUCOLICAL	BUFFABLE	BUGGING
BUCKERS	BUCOLICS	BUFFALO	BUGGINGS
BUCKET	BUD	BUFFALOED	BUGGINS
BUCKETED	BUDA	BUFFALOES	BUGGY
BUCKETFUL	BUDAS	BUFFALOS	BUGHOUSE
BUCKETING	BUDDED	BUFFE	BUGHOUSES
BUCKETS	BUDDER	BUFFED	BUGLE
BUCKEYE	BUDDERS	BUFFEL	BUGLED
BUCKEYES	BUDDHA	BUFFER	BUGLER
BUCKHORN	BUDDHAS	BUFFERED	BUGLERS
BUCKHORNS	BUDDIED	BUFFERING	BUGLES
BUCKHOUND	BUDDIER	BUFFERS	BUGLET
BUCKIE	BUDDIES	BUFFEST	BUGLETS
BUCKIES	BUDDIEST	BUFFET	BUGLEWEED
BUCKING	BUDDING	BUFFETED	BUGLING
BUCKINGS	BUDDINGS	BUFFETER	BUGLOSS
BUCKISH	BUDDLE	BUFFETERS	BUGLOSSES
BUCKISHLY	BUDDLED	BUFFETING	BUGONG
BUCKLE	BUDDLEIA	BUFFETS	BUGONGS
BUCKLED	BUDDLEIAS	BUFFI	BUGOUT
BUCKLER	BUDDLES	BUFFIER	BUGOUTS
BUCKLERED	BUDDLING	BUFFIEST	BUGS
BUCKLERS	BUDDY	BUFFING	BUGSEED
BUCKLES	BUDDYING	BUFFINGS	BUGSEEDS
BUCKLING	BUDGE	BUFFO	BUGSHA

BUGSHAS	BULGE	BULLDOZER	BULLSHITS
BUGWORT	BULGED	BULLDOZES	BULLSHOT
BUGWORTS	BULGER	BULLDUST	BULLSHOTS
BUHL	BULGERS	BULLDUSTS	BULLSNAKE
BUHLS	BULGES	BULLDYKE	BULLWADDY
BUHLWORK	BULGHUR	BULLDYKES	BULLWEED
BUHLWORKS	BULGHURS	BULLED	BULLWEEDS
BUHR	BULGIER	BULLER	BULLWHACK
BUHRS	BULGIEST	BULLERED	BULLWHIP
BUHRSTONE	BULGINE	BULLERING	BULLWHIPS
BUHUND	BULGINES	BULLERS	BULLY
BUHUNDS	BULGINESS	BULLET	BULLYBOY
BUIBUI	BULGING	BULLETED	BULLYBOYS
BUIBUIS	BULGINGLY	BULLETIN	BULLYING
BUIK	BULGUR	BULLETING	BULLYISM
BUIKS	BULGURS	BULLETINS	BULLYISMS
BUILD	BULGY	BULLETRIE	BULLYRAG
BUILDABLE	BULIMIA	BULLETS	BULLYRAGS
BUILDDOWN	BULIMIAC	BULLFIGHT	BULNBULN
BUILDED	BULIMIAS	BULLFINCH	BULNBULNS
BUILDER	BULIMIC	BULLFROG	BULRUSH
BUILDERS	BULIMICS	BULLFROGS	BULRUSHES
BUILDING	BULIMIES	BULLGINE	BULRUSHY
BUILDINGS .	BULIMUS	BULLGINES	BULSE
BUILDS	BULIMUSES	BULLHEAD	BULSES
BUILDUP	BULIMY	BULLHEADS	BULWADDEE
BUILDUPS	BULK	BULLHORN	BULWADDY
BUILT	BULKAGE	BULLHORNS	BULWARK
BUIRDLIER	BULKAGES	BULLIED	BULWARKED
BUIRDLY	BULKED	BULLIER	BULWARKS
BUIST	BULKER	BULLIES	BUM
BUISTED	BULKERS	BULLIEST	BUMALO
BUISTING	BULKHEAD	BULLING	BUMALOTI
BUISTS	BULKHEADS	BULLINGS	BUMALOTIS
BUKE	BULKIER	BULLION	BUMBAG
BUKES	BULKIEST	BULLIONS	BUMBAGS
BUKKAKE	BULKILY	BULLISH	BUMBAZE
BUKKAKES	BULKINESS	BULLISHLY	BUMBAZED
BUKSHEE	BULKING	BULLNECK	BUMBAZES
BUKSHEES	BULKS	BULLNECKS	BUMBAZING
BUKSHI	BULKY	BULLNOSE	BUMBLE
BUKSHIS	BULL	BULLNOSES	BUMBLEBEE
BULB	BULLA	BULLOCK	BUMBLED
BULBAR	BULLACE	BULLOCKED	BUMBLEDOM
BULBED	BULLACES	BULLOCKS	BUMBLER
BULBEL	BULLAE	BULLOCKY	BUMBLERS
BULBELS	BULLARIES	BULLOSA	BUMBLES
BULBIL	BULLARY	BULLOUS	BUMBLING
BULBILS	BULLATE	BULLPEN	BUMBLINGS
BULBING	BULLBAR	BULLPENS	BUMBO
BULBLET	BULLBARS	BULLPOUT	BUMBOAT
BULBLETS	BULLBAT	BULLPOUTS	BUMBOATS
BULBOSITY	BULLBATS	BULLRING	BUMBOS
BULBOUS	BULLBRIER	BULLRINGS	BUMELIA
BULBOUSLY	BULLDOG	BULLRUSH	BUMELIAS
BULBS	BULLDOGS	BULLS	BUMF
BULBUL	BULLDOZE	BULLSHAT	BUMFLUFF
BULBULS	BULLDOZED	BULLSHIT	BUMFLUFFS

BUMFS	BUNCHING	BUNGLERS	BUNTING
BUMFUZZLE	BUNCHINGS	BUNGLES	BUNTINGS
BUMKIN	BUNCHY	BUNGLING	BUNTLINE
BUMKINS	BUNCING	BUNGLINGS	BUNTLINES
BUMMALO	BUNCO	BUNGS	BUNTS
BUMMALOS	BUNCOED	BUNGWALL	BUNTY
BUMMALOTI	BUNCOING	BUNGWALLS	BUNYA
BUMMAREE	BUNCOMBE	BUNGY	BUNYAS
BUMMAREES	BUNCOMBES	BUNIA	BUNYIP
BUMMED	BUNCOS	BUNIAS	BUNYIPS
BUMMEL	BUND	BUNION	BUOY
BUMMELS	BUNDE	BUNIONS	BUOYAGE
BUMMER	BUNDED	BUNJE	BUOYAGES
BUMMERS	BUNDH	BUNJEE	BUOYANCE
BUMMEST	BUNDHS	BUNJEES	BUOYANCES
BUMMING	BUNDIES	BUNJES	BUOYANCY
BUMMLE	BUNDING	BUNJIE	BUOYANT
BUMMLED	BUNDIST	BUNJIES	BUOYANTLY
BUMMLES	BUNDISTS	BUNJY	BUOYED
BUMMLING	BUNDLE	BUNK	BUOYING
BUMMOCK	BUNDLED	BUNKED	BUOYS
BUMMOCKS	BUNDLER	BUNKER	BUPKES
BUMP	BUNDLERS	BUNKERED	BUPKUS
BUMPED	BUNDLES	BUNKERING	BUPLEVER
BUMPER	BUNDLING	BUNKERS	BUPLEVERS
BUMPERED	BUNDLINGS	BUNKHOUSE	BUPPIE
BUMPERING	BUNDOBUST	BUNKING	BUPPIES
BUMPERS	BUNDOOK	BUNKMATE	BUPPY
BUMPH	BUNDOOKS	BUNKMATES	BUPRESTID
BUMPHS	BUNDS	BUNKO	BUQSHA
BUMPIER	BUNDT	BUNKOED	BUQSHAS
BUMPIEST	BUNDTS	BUNKOING	BUR
BUMPILY	BUNDU	BUNKOS	BURA
BUMPINESS	BUNDUS	BUNKS	BURAN
BUMPING	BUNDWALL	BUNKUM	BURANS
BUMPINGS	BUNDWALLS	BUNKUMS	BURAS
BUMPKIN	BUNDY	BUNN	BURB
BUMPKINLY	BUNFIGHT	BUNNET	BURBLE
BUMPKINS	BUNFIGHTS	BUNNETS	BURBLED
BUMPOLOGY	BUNG	BUNNIA	BURBLER
BUMPS	BUNGALOID	BUNNIAS	BURBLERS
BUMPTIOUS	BUNGALOW	BUNNIES	BURBLES
BUMPY	BUNGALOWS	BUNNS	BURBLIER
BUMS	BUNGED	BUNNY	BURBLIEST
BUMSTERS	BUNGEE	BUNODONT	BURBLING
BUMSUCKER	BUNGEES	BUNRAKU	BURBLINGS
BUN	BUNGER	BUNRAKUS	BURBLY
BUNA	BUNGERS	BUNS	BURBOT
BUNAS	BUNGEY	BUNSEN	BURBOTS
BUNCE	BUNGEYS	BUNSENS	BURBS
BUNCED	BUNGHOLE	BUNT	BURD
BUNCES	BUNGHOLES	BUNTAL	BURDASH
BUNCH	BUNGIE	BUNTALS	BURDASHES
BUNCHED	BUNGIES	BUNTED	BURDEN
BUNCHES	BUNGING	BUNTER	BURDENED
BUNCHIER	BUNGLE	BUNTERS	BURDENER
BUNCHIEST	BUNGLED	BUNTIER	BURDENERS
BUNCHILY	BUNGLER	BUNTIEST	BURDENING

BURDENOUS
BURDENS
BURDIE
BURDIES
BURDIZZO
BURDIZZOS
BURDOCK
BURDOCKS
BURDS
BUREAU
BUREAUS
BUREAUX
BURET
BURETS
BURETTE
BURETTES
BURG
BURGAGE
BURGAGES
BURGANET
BURGANETS
BURGEE
BURGEES
BURGEON
BURGEONED
BURGEONS
BURGER
BURGERS
BURGESS
BURGESSES
BURGH
BURGHAL
BURGHER
BURGHERS
BURGHS
BURGHUL
BURGHULS
BURGLAR
BURGLARED
BURGLARS
BURGLARY
BURGLE
BURGLED
BURGLES
BURGLING
BURGONET
BURGONETS
BURGOO
BURGOOS
BURGOUT
BURGOUTS
BURGRAVE
BURGRAVES
BURGS
BURGUNDY
BURHEL
BURHELS
BURIAL

BURIALS
BURIED
BURIER
BURIERS
BURIES
BURIN
BURINIST
BURINISTS
BURINS
BURITI
BURITIS
BURK
BURKA
BURKAS
BURKE
BURKED
BURKER
BURKERS
BURKES
BURKING
BURKITE
BURKITES
BURKS
BURL
BURLADERO
BURLAP
BURLAPS
BURLED
BURLER
BURLERS
BURLESK
BURLESKS
BURLESQUE
BURLETTA
BURLETTAS
BURLEY
BURLEYCUE
BURLEYED
BURLEYING
BURLEYS
BURLIER
BURLIEST
BURLILY
BURLINESS
BURLING
BURLS
BURLY
BURN
BURNABLE
BURNABLES
BURNED
BURNER
BURNERS
BURNET
BURNETS
BURNIE
BURNIES
BURNING

BURNINGLY
BURNINGS
BURNISH
BURNISHED
BURNISHER
BURNISHES
BURNOOSE
BURNOOSED
BURNOOSES
BURNOUS
BURNOUSE
BURNOUSED
BURNOUSES
BURNOUT
BURNOUTS
BURNS
BURNSIDE
BURNSIDES
BURNT
BUROO
BUROOS
BURP
BURPED
BURPEE
BURPEES
BURPING
BURPS
BURQA
BURQAS
BURR
BURRAMYS
BURRAWANG
BURRED
BURREL
BURRELL
BURRELLS
BURRELS
BURRER
BURRERS
BURRHEL
BURRHELS
BURRIER
BURRIEST
BURRING
BURRITO
BURRITOS
BURRO
BURROS
BURROW
BURROWED
BURROWER
BURROWERS
BURROWING
BURROWS
BURRS
BURRSTONE
BURRY
BURS

BURSA
BURSAE
BURSAL
BURSAR
BURSARIAL
BURSARIES
BURSARS
BURSARY
BURSAS
BURSATE
BURSE
BURSEED
BURSEEDS
BURSERA
BURSES
BURSICON
BURSICONS
BURSIFORM
BURSITIS
BURST
BURSTED
BURSTEN
BURSTER
BURSTERS
BURSTING
BURSTONE
BURSTONES
BURSTS
BURTHEN
BURTHENED
BURTHENS
BURTON
BURTONS
BURWEED
BURWEEDS
BURY
BURYING
BUS
BUSBAR
BUSBARS
BUSBIES
BUSBOY
BUSBOYS
BUSBY
BUSED
BUSERA
BUSERAS
BUSES
BUSGIRL
BUSGIRLS
BUSH
BUSHBABY
BUSHBUCK
BUSHBUCKS
BUSHCRAFT
BUSHED
BUSHEL
BUSHELED

BUSHELER
BUSHELERS
BUSHELING
BUSHELLED
BUSHELLER
BUSHELMAN
BUSHELMEN
BUSHELS
BUSHER
BUSHERS
BUSHES
BUSHFIRE
BUSHFIRES
BUSHFLIES
BUSHFLY
BUSHGOAT
BUSHGOATS
BUSHIDO
BUSHIDOS
BUSHIE
BUSHIER
BUSHIES
BUSHIEST
BUSHILY
BUSHINESS
BUSHING
BUSHINGS
BUSHLAND
BUSHLANDS
BUSHLESS
BUSHLIKE
BUSHMAN
BUSHMEAT
BUSHMEATS
BUSHMEN
BUSHPIG
BUSHPIGS
BUSHTIT
BUSHTITS
BUSHVELD
BUSHVELDS
BUSHWA
BUSHWAH
BUSHWAHS
BUSHWALK
BUSHWALKS
BUSHWAS
BUSHWHACK
BUSHWOMAN
BUSHWOMEN
BUSHY
BUSIED
BUSIER
BUSIES
BUSIEST
BUSILY
BUSINESS
BUSINESSY

BUSING
BUSINGS
BUSK
BUSKED
BUSKER
BUSKERS
BUSKET
BUSKETS
BUSKIN
BUSKINED
BUSKING
BUSKINGS
BUSKINS
BUSKS
BUSKY
BUSLOAD
BUSLOADS
BUSMAN
BUSMEN
BUSS
BUSSED
BUSSES
BUSSING
BUSSINGS
BUSSU
BUSSUS
BUST
BUSTARD
BUSTARDS
BUSTED
BUSTEE
BUSTEES
BUSTER
BUSTERS
BUSTI
BUSTIC
BUSTICATE
BUSTICS
BUSTIER
BUSTIERS
BUSTIEST
BUSTINESS
BUSTING
BUSTINGS
BUSTIS
BUSTLE
BUSTLED
BUSTLER
BUSTLERS
BUSTLES
BUSTLINE
BUSTLINES
BUSTLING
BUSTS
BUSTY
BUSULFAN
BUSULFANS
BUSUUTI

BUSUUTIS
BUSY
BUSYBODY
BUSYING
BUSYNESS
BUSYWORK
BUSYWORKS
BUT
BUTADIENE
BUTANE
BUTANES
BUTANOL
BUTANOLS
BUTANONE
BUTANONES
BUTCH
BUTCHER
BUTCHERED
BUTCHERER
BUTCHERLY
BUTCHERS
BUTCHERY
BUTCHES
BUTCHEST
BUTCHING
BUTCHINGS
BUTCHNESS
BUTE
BUTENE
BUTENES
BUTEO
BUTEONINE
BUTEOS
BUTES
BUTLE
BUTLED
BUTLER
BUTLERAGE
BUTLERED
BUTLERIES
BUTLERING
BUTLERS
BUTLERY
BUTLES
BUTLING
BUTMENT
BUTMENTS
BUTS
BUTSUDAN
BUTSUDANS
BUTT
BUTTALS
BUTTE
BUTTED
BUTTER
BUTTERBUR
BUTTERCUP
BUTTERED

BUTTERFAT
BUTTERFLY
BUTTERIER
BUTTERIES
BUTTERINE
BUTTERING
BUTTERNUT
BUTTERS
BUTTERY
BUTTES
BUTTHEAD
BUTTHEADS
BUTTIES
BUTTING
BUTTINSKI
BUTTINSKY
BUTTLE
BUTTLED
BUTTLES
BUTTLING
BUTTOCK
BUTTOCKED
BUTTOCKS
BUTTON
BUTTONED
BUTTONER
BUTTONERS
BUTTONING
BUTTONS
BUTTONY
BUTTRESS
BUTTS
BUTTSTOCK
BUTTY
BUTTYMAN
BUTTYMEN
BUTUT
BUTUTS
BUTYL
BUTYLATE
BUTYLATED
BUTYLATES
BUTYLENE
BUTYLENES
BUTYLS
BUTYRAL
BUTYRALS
BUTYRATE
BUTYRATES
BUTYRIC
BUTYRIN
BUTYRINS
BUTYROUS
BUTYRYL
BUTYRYLS
BUVETTE
BUVETTES
BUXOM

BUXOMER
BUXOMEST
BUXOMLY
BUXOMNESS
BUY
BUYABLE
BUYABLES
BUYBACK
BUYBACKS
BUYER
BUYERS
BUYING
BUYOFF
BUYOFFS
BUYOUT
BUYOUTS
BUYS
BUZKASHI
BUZKASHIS
BUZUKI
BUZUKIA
BUZUKIS
BUZZ
BUZZARD
BUZZARDS
BUZZCUT
BUZZCUTS
BUZZED
BUZZER
BUZZERS
BUZZES
BUZZIER
BUZZIEST
BUZZING
BUZZINGLY
BUZZINGS
BUZZWIG
BUZZWIGS
BUZZWORD
BUZZWORDS
BUZZY
BWANA
BWANAS
BWAZI
BWAZIS
BY
BYCATCH
BYCATCHES
BYCOKET
BYCOKETS
BYDE
BYDED
BYDES
BYDING
BYE
BYELAW
BYELAWS
BYES

BYGONE
BYGONES
BYKE
BYKED
BYKES
BYKING
BYLANDER
BYLANDERS
BYLANE
BYLANES
BYLAW
BYLAWS
BYLINE
BYLINED
BYLINER
BYLINERS
BYLINES
BYLINING
BYLIVE
BYNAME
BYNAMES
BYNEMPT
BYPASS
BYPASSED
BYPASSES
BYPASSING
BYPAST
BYPATH
BYPATHS
BYPLACE
BYPLACES
BYPLAY
BYPLAYS
BYPRODUCT
BYRE
BYREMAN
BYREMEN
BYRES
BYREWOMAN
BYREWOMEN
BYRL
BYRLADY
BYRLAKIN
BYRLAW
BYRLAWS
BYRLED
BYRLING
BYRLS
BYRNIE
BYRNIES
BYROAD
BYROADS
BYROOM
BYROOMS
BYS
BYSSAL
BYSSI
BYSSINE

BYSSOID
BYSSUS
BYSSUSES
BYSTANDER
BYSTREET
BYSTREETS
BYTALK
BYTALKS
BYTE
BYTES
BYTOWNITE
BYWAY
BYWAYS
BYWONER
BYWONERS
BYWORD
BYWORDS
BYWORK
BYWORKS
BYZANT
BYZANTINE
BYZANTS

C

CAA
CAAED
CAAING
CAAS
CAATINGA
CAATINGAS
CAB
CABA
CABAL
CABALA
CABALAS
CABALETTA
CABALETTE
CABALISM
CABALISMS
CABALIST
CABALISTS
CABALLED
CABALLER
CABALLERO
CABALLERS
CABALLINE
CABALLING
CABALS
CABANA
CABANAS
CABARET
CABARETS
CABAS
CABBAGE
CABBAGED
CABBAGES
CABBAGEY
CABBAGING
CABBAGY
CABBALA
CABBALAH
CABBALAHS
CABBALAS
CABBALISM
CABBALIST
CABBED
CABBIE
CABBIES
CABBING
CABBY
CABDRIVER
CABER
CABERNET
CABERNETS
CABERS
CABESTRO
CABESTROS

CABEZON
CABEZONE
CABEZONES
CABEZONS
CABILDO
CABILDOS
CABIN
CABINED
CABINET
CABINETRY
CABINETS
CABINMATE
CABINS
CABLE
CABLECAST
CABLED
CABLEGRAM
CABLER
CABLERS
CABLES
CABLET
CABLETS
CABLEWAY
CABLEWAYS
CABLING
CABLINGS
CABMAN
CABMEN
CABOB
CABOBBED
CABOBBING
CABOBS
CABOC
CABOCEER
CABOCEERS
CABOCHED
CABOCHON
CABOCHONS
CABOCS
CABOMBA
CABOMBAS
CABOODLE
CABOODLES
CABOOSE
CABOOSES
CABOSHED
CABOTAGE
CABOTAGES
CABOVER
CABRE
CABRESTA
CABRESTAS

CABRESTO
CABRESTOS
CABRETTA
CABRETTAS
CABRIE
CABRIES
CABRILLA
CABRILLAS
CABRIO
CABRIOLE
CABRIOLES
CABRIOLET
CABRIOS
CABRIT
CABRITS
CABS
CABSTAND
CABSTANDS
CACA
CACAFOGO
CACAFOGOS
CACAFUEGO
CACAO
CACAOS
CACAS
CACHAEMIA
CACHAEMIC
CACHALOT
CACHALOTS
CACHE
CACHECTIC
CACHED
CACHEPOT
CACHEPOTS
CACHES
CACHET
CACHETED
CACHETING
CACHETS
CACHEXIA
CACHEXIAS
CACHEXIC
CACHEXIES
CACHEXY
CACHING
CACHOLONG
CACHOLOT
CACHOLOTS
CACHOU
CACHOUS
CACHUCHA
CACHUCHAS
CACIQUE

CACIQUES
CACIQUISM
CACKIER
CACKIEST
CACKLE
CACKLED
CACKLER
CACKLERS
CACKLES
CACKLING
CACKY
CACODEMON
CACODOXY
CACODYL
CACODYLIC
CACODYLS
CACOEPIES
CACOEPY
CACOETHES
CACOETHIC
CACOGENIC
CACOLET
CACOLETS
CACOLOGY
CACOMIXL
CACOMIXLE
CACOMIXLS
CACONYM
CACONYMS
CACONYMY
CACOON
CACOONS
CACOPHONY
CACOTOPIA
CACTI
CACTIFORM
CACTOID
CACTUS
CACTUSES
CACUMEN
CACUMINA
CACUMINAL
CAD
CADAGA
CADAGAS
CADAGI
CADAGIS
CADASTER
CADASTERS
CADASTRAL
CADASTRE
CADASTRES
CADAVER

CADAVERIC	CADS	CAGANER	CAIQUES
CADAVERS	CADUAC	CAGANERS	CAIRD
CADDICE	CADUACS	CAGE	CAIRDS
CADDICES	CADUCEAN	CAGEBIRD	CAIRN
CADDIE	CADUCEI	CAGEBIRDS	CAIRNED
CADDIED	CADUCEUS	CAGED	CAIRNGORM
CADDIES	CADUCITY	CAGEFUL	CAIRNS
CADDIS	CADUCOUS	CAGEFULS	CAIRNY
CADDISED	CAECA	CAGELIKE	CAISSON
CADDISES	CAECAL	CAGELING	CAISSONS
CADDISFLY	CAECALLY	CAGELINGS	CAITIFF
CADDISH	CAECILIAN	CAGER	CAITIFFS
CADDISHLY	CAECITIS	CAGERS	CAITIVE
CADDY	CAECUM	CAGES	CAITIVES
CADDYING	CAEOMA	CAGEWORK	CAJAPUT
CADDYSS	CAEOMAS	CAGEWORKS	CAJAPUTS
CADDYSSES	CAERULE	CAGEY	CAJEPUT
CADE	CAERULEAN	CAGEYNESS	CAJEPUTS
CADEAU	CAESAR	CAGIER	CAJOLE
CADEAUX	CAESAREAN	CAGIEST	CAJOLED
CADEE	CAESARIAN	CAGILY	CAJOLER
CADEES	CAESARISM	CAGINESS	CAJOLERS
CADELLE	CAESARS	CAGING	CAJOLERY
CADELLES	CAESE	CAGMAG	CAJOLES
CADENCE	CAESIOUS	CAGMAGGED	CAJOLING
CADENCED	CAESIUM	CAGMAGS	CAJON
CADENCES	CAESIUMS	CAGOT	CAJONES
CADENCIES	CAESTUS	CAGOTS	CAJUN
CADENCING	CAESTUSES	CAGOUL	CAJUPUT
CADENCY	CAESURA	CAGOULE	CAJUPUTS
CADENT	CAESURAE	CAGOULES	CAKE
CADENTIAL	CAESURAL	CAGOULS	CAKED
CADENZA	CAESURAS	CAGS	CAKES
CADENZAS	CAESURIC	CAGY	CAKEWALK
CADES	CAFARD	CAGYNESS	CAKEWALKS
CADET	CAFARDS	CAHIER	CAKEY
CADETS	CAFE	CAHIERS	CAKIER
CADETSHIP	CAFES	CAHOOT	CAKIEST
CADGE	CAFETERIA	CAHOOTS	CAKINESS
CADGED	CAFETIERE	CAHOW	CAKING
CADGER	CAFETORIA	CAHOWS	CAKINGS
CADGERS	CAFF	CAID	CAKY
CADGES	CAFFEIN	CAIDS	CALABASH
CADGIER	CAFFEINE	CAILLACH	CALABAZA
CADGIEST	CAFFEINES	CAILLACHS	CALABAZAS
CADGING	CAFFEINIC	CAILLE	CALABOGUS
CADGY	CAFFEINS	CAILLEACH	CALABOOSE
CADI	CAFFEISM	CAILLES	CALABRESE
CADIE	CAFFEISMS	CAILLIACH	CALADIUM
CADIES	CAFFILA	CAIMAC	CALADIUMS
CADIS	CAFFILAS	CAIMACAM	CALALOO
CADMIC	CAFFS	CAIMACAMS	CALALOOS
CADMIUM	CAFILA	CAIMACS	CALALU
CADMIUMS	CAFILAS	CAIMAN	CALALUS
CADRANS	CAFTAN	CAIMANS	CALAMANCO
CADRANSES	CAFTANED	CAIN	CALAMAR
CADRE	CAFTANS	CAINS	CALAMARI
CADRES	CAG	CAIQUE	CALAMARIS

CALAMARS
CALAMARY
CALAMATA
CALAMATAS
CALAMI
CALAMINE
CALAMINED
CALAMINES
CALAMINT
CALAMINTS
CALAMITE
CALAMITES
CALAMITY
CALAMUS
CALANDO
CALANDRIA
CALANTHE
CALANTHES
CALASH
CALASHES
CALATHEA
CALATHEAS
CALATHI
CALATHOS
CALATHUS
CALAVANCE
CALCANEA
CALCANEAL
CALCANEAN
CALCANEI
CALCANEUM
CALCANEUS
CALCAR
CALCARATE
CALCARIA
CALCARINE
CALCARS
CALCEATE
CALCEATED
CALCEATES
CALCED
CALCEDONY
CALCES
CALCIC
CALCICOLE
CALCIFIC
CALCIFIED
CALCIFIES
CALCIFUGE
CALCIFY
CALCIMINE
CALCINE
CALCINED
CALCINES
CALCINING
CALCITE
CALCITES
CALCITIC

CALCIUM
CALCIUMS
CALCRETE
CALCRETES
CALCSPAR
CALCSPARS
CALCTUFA
CALCTUFAS
CALCTUFF
CALCTUFFS
CALCULAR
CALCULARY
CALCULATE
CALCULI
CALCULOSE
CALCULOUS
CALCULUS
CALDARIA
CALDARIUM
CALDERA
CALDERAS
CALDRON
CALDRONS
CALECHE
CALECHES
CALEFIED
CALEFIES
CALEFY
CALEFYING
CALEMBOUR
CALENDAL
CALENDAR
CALENDARS
CALENDER
CALENDERS
CALENDRER
CALENDRIC
CALENDRY
CALENDS
CALENDULA
CALENTURE
CALESA
CALESAS
CALESCENT
CALF
CALFDOZER
CALFLESS
CALFLICK
CALFLICKS
CALFLIKE
CALFS
CALFSKIN
CALFSKINS
CALIATOUR
CALIBER
CALIBERED
CALIBERS
CALIBRATE

CALIBRE
CALIBRED
CALIBRES
CALICES
CALICHE
CALICHES
CALICLE
CALICLES
CALICO
CALICOES
CALICOS
CALICULAR
CALID
CALIDITY
CALIF
CALIFATE
CALIFATES
CALIFONT
CALIFONTS
CALIFS
CALIGO
CALIGOES
CALIGOS
CALIMA
CALIMAS
CALIOLOGY
CALIPASH
CALIPEE
CALIPEES
CALIPER
CALIPERED
CALIPERS
CALIPH
CALIPHAL
CALIPHATE
CALIPHS
CALISAYA
CALISAYAS
CALIVER
CALIVERS
CALIX
CALK
CALKED
CALKER
CALKERS
CALKIN
CALKING
CALKINGS
CALKINS
CALKS
CALL
CALLA
CALLABLE
CALLAIDES
CALLAIS
CALLALOO
CALLALOOS
CALLAN

CALLANS
CALLANT
CALLANTS
CALLAS
CALLBACK
CALLBACKS
CALLBOARD
CALLBOY
CALLBOYS
CALLED
CALLEE
CALLEES
CALLER
CALLERS
CALLET
CALLETS
CALLID
CALLIDITY
CALLIGRAM
CALLING
CALLINGS
CALLIOPE
CALLIOPES
CALLIPASH
CALLIPEE
CALLIPEES
CALLIPER
CALLIPERS
CALLOP
CALLOPS
CALLOSE
CALLOSES
CALLOSITY
CALLOUS
CALLOUSED
CALLOUSES
CALLOUSLY
CALLOW
CALLOWER
CALLOWEST
CALLOWS
CALLS
CALLUNA
CALLUNAS
CALLUS
CALLUSED
CALLUSES
CALLUSING
CALM
CALMANT
CALMANTS
CALMATIVE
CALMED
CALMER
CALMEST
CALMIER
CALMIEST
CALMING

CALMINGLY
CALMINGS
CALMLY
CALMNESS
CALMS
CALMSTONE
CALMY
CALO
CALOMEL
CALOMELS
CALORIC
CALORICS
CALORIE
CALORIES
CALORIFIC
CALORISE
CALORISED
CALORISES
CALORIST
CALORISTS
CALORIZE
CALORIZED
CALORIZES
CALORY
CALOS
CALOTTE
CALOTTES
CALOTYPE
CALOTYPES
CALOYER
CALOYERS
CALP
CALPA
CALPAC
CALPACK
CALPACKS
CALPACS
CALPAIN
CALPAINS
CALPAS
CALPS
CALQUE
CALQUED
CALQUES
CALQUING
CALTHA
CALTHAS
CALTHROP
CALTHROPS
CALTRAP
CALTRAPS
CALTROP
CALTROPS
CALUMBA
CALUMBAS
CALUMET
CALUMETS
CALUMNIES

CALUMNY
CALUTRON
CALUTRONS
CALVADOS
CALVARIA
CALVARIAL
CALVARIAN
CALVARIAS
CALVARIES
CALVARIUM
CALVARY
CALVE
CALVED
CALVER
CALVERED
CALVERING
CALVERS
CALVES
CALVING
CALVITIES
CALX
CALXES
CALYCATE
CALYCEAL
CALYCES
CALYCINAL
CALYCINE
CALYCLE
CALYCLED
CALYCLES
CALYCOID
CALYCULAR
CALYCULE
CALYCULES
CALYCULI
CALYCULUS
CALYPSO
CALYPSOES
CALYPSOS
CALYPTER
CALYPTERA
CALYPTERS
CALYPTRA
CALYPTRAS
CALYX
CALYXES
CALZONE
CALZONES
CALZONI
CAM
CAMA
CAMAIEU
CAMAIEUX
CAMAIL
CAMAILED
CAMAILS
CAMAN
CAMANACHD

CAMANS
CAMARILLA
CAMARON
CAMARONS
CAMAS
CAMASES
CAMASH
CAMASHES
CAMASS
CAMASSES
CAMBER
CAMBERED
CAMBERING
CAMBERS
CAMBIA
CAMBIAL
CAMBIFORM
CAMBISM
CAMBISMS
CAMBIST
CAMBISTRY
CAMBISTS
CAMBIUM
CAMBIUMS
CAMBOGE
CAMBOGES
CAMBOGIA
CAMBOGIAS
CAMBOOSE
CAMBOOSES
CAMBREL
CAMBRELS
CAMBRIC
CAMBRICS
CAMCORDER
CAME
CAMEL
CAMELBACK
CAMELEER
CAMELEERS
CAMELEON
CAMELEONS
CAMELHAIR
CAMELIA
CAMELIAS
CAMELID
CAMELIDS
CAMELINE
CAMELINES
CAMELISH
CAMELLIA
CAMELLIAS
CAMELLIKE
CAMELOID
CAMELOIDS
CAMELOT
CAMELOTS
CAMELRIES

CAMELRY
CAMELS
CAMEO
CAMEOED
CAMEOING
CAMEOS
CAMERA
CAMERAE
CAMERAL
CAMERAMAN
CAMERAMEN
CAMERAS
CAMERATED
CAMES
CAMESE
CAMESES
CAMION
CAMIONS
CAMIS
CAMISA
CAMISADE
CAMISADES
CAMISADO
CAMISADOS
CAMISAS
CAMISE
CAMISES
CAMISIA
CAMISIAS
CAMISOLE
CAMISOLES
CAMLET
CAMLETS
CAMMED
CAMMIE
CAMMIES
CAMMING
CAMO
CAMOGIE
CAMOGIES
CAMOMILE
CAMOMILES
CAMOODI
CAMOODIS
CAMORRA
CAMORRAS
CAMORRIST
CAMOS
CAMOTE
CAMOTES
CAMOUFLET
CAMP
CAMPAGNA
CAMPAGNAS
CAMPAGNE
CAMPAIGN
CAMPAIGNS
CAMPANA

CAMPANAS	CAMPUSED	CANCANS	CANEBRAKE
CAMPANERO	CAMPUSES	CANCEL	CANED
CAMPANILE	CAMPUSING	CANCELED	CANEFRUIT
CAMPANILI	CAMPY	CANCELEER	CANEH
CAMPANIST	CAMS	CANCELER	CANEHS
CAMPANULA	CAMSHAFT	CANCELERS	CANELLA
CAMPCRAFT	CAMSHAFTS	CANCELIER	CANELLAS
CAMPEADOR	CAMSHO	CANCELING	CANELLINI
CAMPED	CAMSHOCH	CANCELLED	CANEPHOR
CAMPER	CAMSTAIRY	CANCELLER	CANEPHORA
CAMPERS	CAMSTANE	CANCELLI	CANEPHORE
CAMPESINO	CAMSTANES	CANCELS	CANEPHORS
CAMPEST	CAMSTEARY	CANCER	CANER
CAMPFIRE	CAMSTONE	CANCERATE	CANERS
CAMPFIRES	CAMSTONES	CANCERED	CANES
CAMPHANE	CAMUS	CANCEROUS	CANESCENT
CAMPHANES	CAMUSES	CANCERS	CANEWARE
CAMPHENE	CAMWOOD	CANCHA	CANEWARES
CAMPHENES	CAMWOODS	CANCHAS	CANFIELD
CAMPHINE	CAN	CANCRINE	CANFIELDS
CAMPHINES	CANADA	CANCROID	CANFUL
CAMPHIRE	CANADAS	CANCROIDS	CANFULS
CAMPHIRES	CANAIGRE	CANDELA	CANG
CAMPHOL	CANAIGRES	CANDELAS	CANGLE
CAMPHOLS	CANAILLE	CANDENT	CANGLED
CAMPHOR	CANAILLES	CANDID	CANGLES
CAMPHORIC	CANAKIN	CANDIDA	CANGLING
CAMPHORS	CANAKINS	CANDIDACY	CANGS
CAMPI	CANAL	CANDIDAL	CANGUE
CAMPIER	CANALBOAT	CANDIDAS	CANGUES
CAMPIEST	CANALED	CANDIDATE	CANICULAR
CAMPILY	CANALING	CANDIDER	CANID
CAMPINESS	CANALISE	CANDIDEST	CANIDS
CAMPING	CANALISED	CANDIDLY	CANIER
CAMPINGS	CANALISES	CANDIDS	CANIEST
CAMPION	CANALIZE	CANDIE	CANIKIN
CAMPIONS	CANALIZED	CANDIED	CANIKINS
CAMPLE	CANALIZES	CANDIES	CANINE
CAMPLED	CANALLED	CANDLE	CANINES
CAMPLES	CANALLER	CANDLED	CANING
CAMPLING	CANALLERS	CANDLELIT	CANINGS
CAMPLY	CANALLING	CANDLENUT	CANINITY
CAMPNESS	CANALS	CANDLEPIN	CANISTEL
CAMPO	CANAPE	CANDLER	CANISTELS
CAMPODEID	CANAPES	CANDLERS	CANISTER
CAMPONG	CANARD	CANDLES	CANISTERS
CAMPONGS	CANARDS	CANDLING	CANITIES
CAMPOREE	CANARIED	CANDOCK	CANKER
CAMPOREES	CANARIES	CANDOCKS	CANKERED
CAMPOS	CANARY	CANDOR	CANKERING
CAMPOUT	CANARYING	CANDORS	CANKEROUS
CAMPOUTS	CANASTA	CANDOUR	CANKERS
CAMPS	CANASTAS	CANDOURS	CANKERY
CAMPSHIRT	CANASTER	CANDY	CANN
CAMPSITE	CANASTERS	CANDYGRAM	CANNA
CAMPSITES	CANBANK	CANDYING	CANNABIC
CAMPSTOOL	CANBANKS	CANDYTUFT	CANNABIN
CAMPUS	CANCAN	CANE	CANNABINS

CANNABIS
CANNACH
CANNACHS
CANNAE
CANNAS
CANNED
CANNEL
CANNELON
CANNELONI
CANNELONS
CANNELS
CANNELURE
CANNER
CANNERIES
CANNERS
CANNERY
CANNIBAL
CANNIBALS
CANNIE
CANNIER
CANNIEST
CANNIKIN
CANNIKINS
CANNILY
CANNINESS
CANNING
CANNINGS
CANNISTER
CANNOLI
CANNOLIS
CANNON
CANNONADE
CANNONED
CANNONEER
CANNONIER
CANNONING
CANNONRY
CANNONS
CANNOT
CANNS
CANNULA
CANNULAE
CANNULAR
CANNULAS
CANNULATE
CANNY
CANOE
CANOEABLE
CANOED
CANOEING
CANOEINGS
CANOEIST
CANOEISTS
CANOER
CANOERS
CANOES
CANOEWOOD
CANOLA

CANOLAS
CANON
CANONESS
CANONIC
CANONICAL
CANONISE
CANONISED
CANONISER
CANONISES
CANONIST
CANONISTS
CANONIZE
CANONIZED
CANONIZER
CANONIZES
CANONRIES
CANONRY
CANONS
CANOODLE
CANOODLED
CANOODLER
CANOODLES
CANOPIC
CANOPIED
CANOPIES
CANOPY
CANOPYING
CANOROUS
CANS
CANSFUL
CANSO
CANSOS
CANST
CANSTICK
CANSTICKS
CANT
CANTABANK
CANTABILE
CANTAL
CANTALA
CANTALAS
CANTALOUP
CANTALS
CANTAR
CANTARS
CANTATA
CANTATAS
CANTATE
CANTATES
CANTDOG
CANTDOGS
CANTED
CANTEEN
CANTEENS
CANTER
CANTERED
CANTERING
CANTERS

CANTEST
CANTHAL
CANTHARI
CANTHARID
CANTHARIS
CANTHARUS
CANTHI
CANTHITIS
CANTHOOK
CANTHOOKS
CANTHUS
CANTIC
CANTICLE
CANTICLES
CANTICO
CANTICOED
CANTICOS
CANTICOY
CANTICOYS
CANTICUM
CANTICUMS
CANTIER
CANTIEST
CANTILENA
CANTILY
CANTINA
CANTINAS
CANTINESS
CANTING
CANTINGLY
CANTINGS
CANTION
CANTIONS
CANTLE
CANTLED
CANTLES
CANTLET
CANTLETS
CANTLING
CANTO
CANTON
CANTONAL
CANTONED
CANTONING
CANTONISE
CANTONIZE
CANTONS
CANTOR
CANTORIAL
CANTORIS
CANTORS
CANTOS
CANTRAIP
CANTRAIPS
CANTRAP
CANTRAPS
CANTRED
CANTREDS

CANTREF
CANTREFS
CANTRIP
CANTRIPS
CANTS
CANTUS
CANTY
CANULA
CANULAE
CANULAR
CANULAS
CANULATE
CANULATED
CANULATES
CANVAS
CANVASED
CANVASER
CANVASERS
CANVASES
CANVASING
CANVASS
CANVASSED
CANVASSER
CANVASSES
CANY
CANYON
CANYONEER
CANYONING
CANYONS
CANZONA
CANZONAS
CANZONE
CANZONES
CANZONET
CANZONETS
CANZONI
CAP
CAPA
CAPABLE
CAPABLER
CAPABLEST
CAPABLY
CAPACIOUS
CAPACITOR
CAPACITY
CAPARISON
CAPAS
CAPE
CAPED
CAPELAN
CAPELANS
CAPELET
CAPELETS
CAPELIN
CAPELINE
CAPELINES
CAPELINS
CAPELLET

CAPELLETS
CAPELLINE
CAPELLINI
CAPER
CAPERED
CAPERER
CAPERERS
CAPERING
CAPERS
CAPES
CAPESKIN
CAPESKINS
CAPEWORK
CAPEWORKS
CAPFUL
CAPFULS
CAPH
CAPHS
CAPI
CAPIAS
CAPIASES
CAPILLARY
CAPING
CAPITA
CAPITAL
CAPITALLY
CAPITALS
CAPITAN
CAPITANI
CAPITANO
CAPITANOS
CAPITANS
CAPITATE
CAPITATED
CAPITAYN
CAPITAYNS
CAPITELLA
CAPITOL
CAPITOLS
CAPITULA
CAPITULAR
CAPITULUM
CAPIZ
CAPIZES
CAPLE
CAPLES
CAPLESS
CAPLET
CAPLETS
CAPLIN
CAPLINS
CAPMAKER
CAPMAKERS
CAPO
CAPOCCHIA
CAPOEIRA
CAPOEIRAS
CAPON

CAPONATA
CAPONATAS
CAPONIER
CAPONIERE
CAPONIERS
CAPONISE
CAPONISED
CAPONISES
CAPONIZE
CAPONIZED
CAPONIZES
CAPONS
CAPORAL
CAPORALS
CAPOS
CAPOT
CAPOTASTO
CAPOTE
CAPOTES
CAPOTS
CAPOTTED
CAPOTTING
CAPOUCH
CAPOUCHES
CAPPED
CAPPER
CAPPERS
CAPPING
CAPPINGS
CAPRATE
CAPRATES
CAPRIC
CAPRICCI
CAPRICCIO
CAPRICE
CAPRICES
CAPRID
CAPRIDS
CAPRIFIED
CAPRIFIES
CAPRIFIG
CAPRIFIGS
CAPRIFOIL
CAPRIFOLE
CAPRIFORM
CAPRIFY
CAPRINE
CAPRIOLE
CAPRIOLED
CAPRIOLES
CAPRIS
CAPROATE
CAPROATES
CAPROCK
CAPROCKS
CAPROIC
CAPRYLATE
CAPRYLIC

CAPS
CAPSAICIN
CAPSICIN
CAPSICINS
CAPSICUM
CAPSICUMS
CAPSID
CAPSIDAL
CAPSIDS
CAPSIZAL
CAPSIZALS
CAPSIZE
CAPSIZED
CAPSIZES
CAPSIZING
CAPSOMER
CAPSOMERE
CAPSOMERS
CAPSTAN
CAPSTANS
CAPSTONE
CAPSTONES
CAPSULAR
CAPSULARY
CAPSULATE
CAPSULE
CAPSULED
CAPSULES
CAPSULING
CAPSULISE
CAPSULIZE
CAPTAIN
CAPTAINCY
CAPTAINED
CAPTAINRY
CAPTAINS
CAPTAN
CAPTANS
CAPTION
CAPTIONED
CAPTIONS
CAPTIOUS
CAPTIVATE
CAPTIVE
CAPTIVED
CAPTIVES
CAPTIVING
CAPTIVITY
CAPTOPRIL
CAPTOR
CAPTORS
CAPTURE
CAPTURED
CAPTURER
CAPTURERS
CAPTURES
CAPTURING
CAPUCCIO

CAPUCCIOS
CAPUCHE
CAPUCHED
CAPUCHES
CAPUCHIN
CAPUCHINS
CAPUERA
CAPUERAS
CAPUL
CAPULS
CAPUT
CAPYBARA
CAPYBARAS
CAR
CARABAO
CARABAOS
CARABID
CARABIDS
CARABIN
CARABINE
CARABINER
CARABINES
CARABINS
CARACAL
CARACALS
CARACARA
CARACARAS
CARACK
CARACKS
CARACOL
CARACOLE
CARACOLED
CARACOLER
CARACOLES
CARACOLS
CARACT
CARACTS
CARACUL
CARACULS
CARAFE
CARAFES
CARAGANA
CARAGANAS
CARAGEEN
CARAGEENS
CARAMBA
CARAMBOLA
CARAMBOLE
CARAMEL
CARAMELS
CARANGID
CARANGIDS
CARANGOID
CARANNA
CARANNAS
CARAP
CARAPACE
CARAPACED

CARAPACES	CARBONARA	CARDECUES	CAREGIVER
CARAPAX	CARBONATE	CARDECUS	CARELESS
CARAPAXES	CARBONIC	CARDED	CARELINE
CARAPS	CARBONISE	CARDER	CARELINES
CARASSOW	CARBONIUM	CARDERS	CAREME
CARASSOWS	CARBONIZE	CARDI	CAREMES
CARAT	CARBONOUS	CARDIA	CARER
CARATE	CARBONS	CARDIAC	CARERS
CARATES	CARBONYL	CARDIACAL	CARES
CARATS	CARBONYLS	CARDIACS	CARESS
CARAUNA	CARBORA	CARDIAE	CARESSED
CARAUNAS	CARBORAS	CARDIALGY	CARESSER
CARAVAN	CARBOS	CARDIAS	CARESSERS
CARAVANCE	CARBOXYL	CARDIE	CARESSES
CARAVANED	CARBOXYLS	CARDIES	CARESSING
CARAVANER	CARBOY	CARDIGAN	CARESSIVE
CARAVANS	CARBOYED	CARDIGANS	CARET
CARAVEL	CARBOYS	CARDINAL	CARETAKE
CARAVELLE	CARBS	CARDINALS	CARETAKEN
CARAVELS	CARBUNCLE	CARDING	CARETAKER
CARAWAY	CARBURATE	CARDINGS	CARETAKES
CARAWAYS	CARBURET	CARDIO	CARETOOK
CARB	CARBURETS	CARDIOID	CARETS
CARBACHOL	CARBURISE	CARDIOIDS	CAREWORN
CARBAMATE	CARBURIZE	CARDIS	CAREX
CARBAMIC	CARBY	CARDITIC	CARFARE
CARBAMIDE	CARCAJOU	CARDITIS	CARFARES
CARBAMINO	CARCAJOUS	CARDON	CARFAX
CARBAMOYL	CARCAKE	CARDONS	CARFAXES
CARBAMYL	CARCAKES	CARDOON	CARFOX
CARBAMYLS	CARCANET	CARDOONS	CARFOXES
CARBANION	CARCANETS	CARDPHONE	CARFUFFLE
CARBARN	CARCASE	CARDPUNCH	CARFUL
CARBARNS	CARCASED	CARDS	CARFULS
CARBARYL	CARCASES	CARDSHARP	CARGEESE
CARBARYLS	CARCASING	CARDUUS	CARGO
CARBAZOLE	CARCASS	CARDUUSES	CARGOED
CARBEEN	CARCASSED	CARDY	CARGOES
CARBEENS	CARCASSES	CARE	CARGOING
CARBENE	CARCEL	CARED	CARGOOSE
CARBENES	CARCELS	CAREEN	CARGOS
CARBIDE	CARCERAL	CAREENAGE	CARHOP
CARBIDES	CARCINOID	CAREENED	CARHOPPED
CARBIES	CARCINOMA	CAREENER	CARHOPS
CARBINE	CARD	CAREENERS	CARIACOU
CARBINEER	CARDAMINE	CAREENING	CARIACOUS
CARBINES	CARDAMOM	CAREENS	CARIAMA
CARBINIER	CARDAMOMS	CAREER	CARIAMAS
CARBINOL	CARDAMON	CAREERED	CARIBE
CARBINOLS	CARDAMONS	CAREERER	CARIBES
CARBO	CARDAMUM	CAREERERS	CARIBOU
CARBOLIC	CARDAMUMS	CAREERING	CARIBOUS
CARBOLICS	CARDAN	CAREERISM	CARICES
CARBOLISE	CARDBOARD	CAREERIST	CARIED
CARBOLIZE	CARDCASE	CAREERS	CARIERE
CARBON	CARDCASES	CAREFREE	CARIERES
CARBONADE	CARDECU	CAREFUL	CARIES
CARBONADO	CARDECUE	CAREFULLY	CARILLON

CARILLONS
CARINA
CARINAE
CARINAL
CARINAS
CARINATE
CARINATED
CARING
CARIOCA
CARIOCAS
CARIOLE
CARIOLES
CARIOSE
CARIOSITY
CARIOUS
CARITAS
CARITASES
CARITATES
CARJACK
CARJACKED
CARJACKER
CARJACKS
CARJACOU
CARJACOUS
CARK
CARKED
CARKING
CARKS
CARL
CARLE
CARLES
CARLESS
CARLIN
CARLINE
CARLINES
CARLING
CARLINGS
CARLINS
CARLISH
CARLOAD
CARLOADS
CARLOCK
CARLOCKS
CARLOT
CARLOTS
CARLS
CARMAKER
CARMAKERS
CARMAN
CARMELITE
CARMEN
CARMINE
CARMINES
CARN
CARNAGE
CARNAGES
CARNAHUBA
CARNAL

CARNALISE
CARNALISM
CARNALIST
CARNALITY
CARNALIZE
CARNALLED
CARNALLY
CARNALS
CARNAROLI
CARNATION
CARNAUBA
CARNAUBAS
CARNELIAN
CARNEOUS
CARNET
CARNETS
CARNEY
CARNEYED
CARNEYING
CARNEYS
CARNIE
CARNIED
CARNIER
CARNIES
CARNIEST
CARNIFEX
CARNIFIED
CARNIFIES
CARNIFY
CARNITINE
CARNIVAL
CARNIVALS
CARNIVORA
CARNIVORE
CARNIVORY
CARNOSAUR
CARNOSE
CARNOSITY
CARNOTITE
CARNS
CARNY
CARNYING
CAROACH
CAROACHES
CAROB
CAROBS
CAROCH
CAROCHE
CAROCHES
CAROL
CAROLED
CAROLER
CAROLERS
CAROLI
CAROLING
CAROLINGS
CAROLLED
CAROLLER

CAROLLERS
CAROLLING
CAROLS
CAROLUS
CAROLUSES
CAROM
CAROMED
CAROMEL
CAROMELS
CAROMING
CAROMS
CAROTENE
CAROTENES
CAROTID
CAROTIDAL
CAROTIDS
CAROTIN
CAROTINS
CAROUSAL
CAROUSALS
CAROUSE
CAROUSED
CAROUSEL
CAROUSELS
CAROUSER
CAROUSERS
CAROUSES
CAROUSING
CARP
CARPACCIO
CARPAL
CARPALE
CARPALES
CARPALIA
CARPALS
CARPARK
CARPARKS
CARPED
CARPEL
CARPELS
CARPENTER
CARPENTRY
CARPER
CARPERS
CARPET
CARPETBAG
CARPETED
CARPETING
CARPETS
CARPI
CARPING
CARPINGLY
CARPINGS
CARPOLOGY
CARPOOL
CARPOOLED
CARPOOLER
CARPOOLS

CARPORT
CARPORTS
CARPS
CARPUS
CARR
CARRACK
CARRACKS
CARRACT
CARRACTS
CARRAGEEN
CARRAT
CARRATS
CARRAWAY
CARRAWAYS
CARRECT
CARRECTS
CARREFOUR
CARREL
CARRELL
CARRELLS
CARRELS
CARRIAGE
CARRIAGES
CARRICK
CARRIED
CARRIER
CARRIERS
CARRIES
CARRIOLE
CARRIOLES
CARRION
CARRIONS
CARRITCH
CARROCH
CARROCHES
CARROM
CARROMED
CARROMING
CARROMS
CARRON
CARRONADE
CARROT
CARROTIER
CARROTIN
CARROTINS
CARROTS
CARROTTOP
CARROTY
CARROUSEL
CARRS
CARRY
CARRYALL
CARRYALLS
CARRYBACK
CARRYCOT
CARRYCOTS
CARRYING
CARRYON

CARRYONS	CARUCAGE	CASEATES	CASHLESS
CARRYOUT	CARUCAGES	CASEATING	CASHMERE
CARRYOUTS	CARUCATE	CASEATION	CASHMERES
CARRYOVER	CARUCATES	CASEBOOK	CASHOO
CARRYTALE	CARUNCLE	CASEBOOKS	CASHOOS
CARS	CARUNCLES	CASEBOUND	CASHPOINT
CARSE	CARVACROL	CASED	CASIMERE
CARSES	CARVE	CASEFIED	CASIMERES
CARSEY	CARVED	CASEFIES	CASIMIRE
CARSEYS	CARVEL	CASEFY	CASIMIRES
CARSICK	CARVELS	CASEFYING	CASING
CART	CARVEN	CASEIC	CASINGS
CARTA	CARVER	CASEIN	CASINI
CARTABLE	CARVERIES	CASEINATE	CASINO
CARTAGE	CARVERS	CASEINS	CASINOS
CARTAGES	CARVERY	CASELOAD	CASITA
CARTAS	CARVES	CASELOADS	CASITAS
CARTE	CARVIES	CASEMAKER	CASK
CARTED	CARVING	CASEMAN	CASKED
CARTEL	CARVINGS	CASEMATE	CASKET
CARTELISE	CARVY	CASEMATED	CASKETED
CARTELISM	CARWASH	CASEMATES	CASKETING
CARTELIST	CARWASHES	CASEMEN	CASKETS
CARTELIZE	CARYATIC	CASEMENT	CASKING
CARTELS	CARYATID	CASEMENTS	CASKS
CARTER	CARYATIDS	CASEOSE	CASKSTAND
CARTERS	CARYOPSES	CASEOSES	CASKY
CARTES	CARYOPSIS	CASEOUS	CASQUE
CARTFUL	CARYOTIN	CASERN	CASQUED
CARTFULS	CARYOTINS	CASERNE	CASQUES
CARTHORSE	CASA	CASERNES	CASSABA
CARTILAGE	CASABA	CASERNS	CASSABAS
CARTING	CASABAS	CASES	CASSAREEP
CARTLOAD	CASAS	CASETTE	CASSATA
CARTLOADS	CASAVA	CASETTES	CASSATAS
CARTOGRAM	CASAVAS	CASEWORK	CASSATION
CARTOLOGY	CASBAH	CASEWORKS	CASSAVA
CARTON	CASBAHS	CASEWORM	CASSAVAS
CARTONAGE	CASCABEL	CASEWORMS	CASSENA
CARTONED	CASCABELS	CASH	CASSENAS
CARTONING	CASCABLE	CASHABLE	CASSENE
CARTONS	CASCABLES	CASHAW	CASSENES
CARTOON	CASCADE	CASHAWS	CASSEROLE
CARTOONED	CASCADED	CASHBACK	CASSETTE
CARTOONS	CASCADES	CASHBACKS	CASSETTES
CARTOONY	CASCADING	CASHBOOK	CASSIA
CARTOP	CASCADURA	CASHBOOKS	CASSIAS
CARTOPPER	CASCARA	CASHBOX	CASSIMERE
CARTOUCH	CASCARAS	CASHBOXES	CASSINA
CARTOUCHE	CASCHROM	CASHED	CASSINAS
CARTRIDGE	CASCHROMS	CASHES	CASSINE
CARTROAD	CASCO	CASHEW	CASSINES
CARTROADS	CASCOS	CASHEWS	CASSINGLE
CARTS	CASE	CASHIER	CASSINO
CARTULARY	CASEASE	CASHIERED	CASSINOS
CARTWAY	CASEASES	CASHIERER	CASSIS
CARTWAYS	CASEATE	CASHIERS	CASSISES
CARTWHEEL	CASEATED	CASHING	CASSOCK

CASSOCKED	CASUALTY	CATAPULTS	CATECHOLS
CASSOCKS	CASUARINA	CATARACT	CATECHU
CASSONADE	CASUIST	CATARACTS	CATECHUS
CASSONE	CASUISTIC	CATARHINE	CATEGORIC
CASSONES	CASUISTRY	CATARRH	CATEGORY
CASSOULET	CASUISTS	CATARRHAL	CATELOG
CASSOWARY	CASUS	CATARRHS	CATELOGS
CASSPIR	CAT	CATASTA	CATENA
CASSPIRS	CATABASES	CATASTAS	CATENAE
CAST	CATABASIS	CATATONIA	CATENANE
CASTABLE	CATABATIC	CATATONIC	CATENANES
CASTANET	CATABOLIC	CATATONY	CATENARY
CASTANETS	CATACLASM	CATAWBA	CATENAS
CASTAWAY	CATACLYSM	CATAWBAS	CATENATE
CASTAWAYS	CATACOMB	CATBIRD	CATENATED
CASTE	CATACOMBS	CATBIRDS	CATENATES
CASTED	CATAFALCO	CATBOAT	CATENOID
CASTEISM	CATALASE	CATBOATS	CATENOIDS
CASTEISMS	CATALASES	CATBRIER	CATER
CASTELESS	CATALATIC	CATBRIERS	CATERAN
CASTELLA	CATALEPSY	CATCALL	CATERANS
CASTELLAN	CATALEXES	CATCALLED	CATERED
CASTELLUM	CATALEXIS	CATCALLER	CATERER
CASTER	CATALO	CATCALLS	CATERERS
CASTERS	CATALOES	CATCH	CATERESS
CASTES	CATALOG	CATCHABLE	CATERING
CASTIGATE	CATALOGED	CATCHALL	CATERINGS
CASTING	CATALOGER	CATCHALLS	CATERS
CASTINGS	CATALOGIC	CATCHCRY	CATERWAUL
CASTLE	CATALOGS	CATCHED	CATES
CASTLED	CATALOGUE	CATCHEN	CATFACE
CASTLES	CATALOS	CATCHER	CATFACES
CASTLING	CATALPA	CATCHERS	CATFACING
CASTOCK	CATALPAS	CATCHES	CATFALL
CASTOCKS	CATALYSE	CATCHFLY	CATFALLS
CASTOFF	CATALYSED	CATCHIER	CATFIGHT
CASTOFFS	CATALYSER	CATCHIEST	CATFIGHTS
CASTOR	CATALYSES	CATCHING	CATFISH
CASTOREUM	CATALYSIS	CATCHINGS	CATFISHES
CASTORIES	CATALYST	CATCHMENT	CATGUT
CASTORS	CATALYSTS	CATCHPOLE	CATGUTS
CASTORY	CATALYTIC	CATCHPOLL	CATHARISE
CASTRAL	CATALYZE	CATCHT	CATHARIZE
CASTRATE	CATALYZED	CATCHUP	CATHARSES
CASTRATED	CATALYZER	CATCHUPS	CATHARSIS
CASTRATER	CATALYZES	CATCHWEED	CATHARTIC
CASTRATES	CATAMARAN	CATCHWORD	CATHEAD
CASTRATI	CATAMENIA	CATCHY	CATHEADS
CASTRATO	CATAMITE	CATCLAW	CATHECT
CASTRATOR	CATAMITES	CATCLAWS	CATHECTED
CASTRATOS	CATAMOUNT	CATE	CATHECTIC
CASTS	CATAPAN	CATECHIN	CATHECTS
CASUAL	CATAPANS	CATECHINS	CATHEDRA
CASUALISE	CATAPHORA	CATECHISE	CATHEDRAE
CASUALISM	CATAPHYLL	CATECHISM	CATHEDRAL
CASUALIZE	CATAPLASM	CATECHIST	CATHEDRAS
CASUALLY	CATAPLEXY	CATECHIZE	CATHEPSIN
CASUALS	CATAPULT	CATECHOL	CATHEPTIC

CATHETER	CATTABU	CAUDRONS	CAUSERS
CATHETERS	CATTABUS	CAUF	CAUSES
CATHETUS	CATTAIL	CAUGHT	CAUSEWAY
CATHEXES	CATTAILS	CAUK	CAUSEWAYS
CATHEXIS	CATTALO	CAUKER	CAUSEY
CATHISMA	CATTALOES	CAUKERS	CAUSEYED
CATHISMAS	CATTALOS	CAUKS	CAUSEYS
CATHODAL	CATTED	CAUL	CAUSING
CATHODE	CATTERIES	CAULD	CAUSTIC
CATHODES	CATTERY	CAULDER	CAUSTICAL
CATHODIC	CATTIE	CAULDEST	CAUSTICS
CATHOLE	CATTIER	CAULDRIFE	CAUTEL
CATHOLES	CATTIES	CAULDRON	CAUTELOUS
CATHOLIC	CATTIEST	CAULDRONS	CAUTELS
CATHOLICS	CATTILY	CAULDS	CAUTER
CATHOLYTE	CATTINESS	CAULES	CAUTERANT
CATHOOD	CATTING	CAULICLE	CAUTERIES
CATHOODS	CATTISH	CAULICLES	CAUTERISE
CATHOUSE	CATTISHLY	CAULICULI	CAUTERISM
CATHOUSES	CATTLE	CAULIFORM	CAUTERIZE
CATION	CATTLEMAN	CAULINARY	CAUTERS
CATIONIC	CATTLEMEN	CAULINE	CAUTERY
CATIONS	CATTLEYA	CAULIS	CAUTION
CATJANG	CATTLEYAS	CAULK	CAUTIONED
CATJANGS	CATTY	CAULKED	CAUTIONER
CATKIN	CATWALK	CAULKER	CAUTIONRY
CATKINATE	CATWALKS	CAULKERS	CAUTIONS
CATKINS	CATWORKS	CAULKING	CAUTIOUS
CATLIKE	CATWORM	CAULKINGS	CAUVES
CATLIN	CATWORMS	CAULKS	CAVA
CATLING	CAUCHEMAR	CAULOME	CAVALCADE
CATLINGS	CAUCUS	CAULOMES	CAVALERO
CATLINS	CAUCUSED	CAULS	CAVALEROS
CATMINT	CAUCUSES	CAUM	CAVALETTI
CATMINTS	CAUCUSING	CAUMED	CAVALIER
CATNAP	CAUCUSSED	CAUMING	CAVALIERS
CATNAPER	CAUCUSSES	CAUMS	CAVALLA
CATNAPERS	CAUDA	CAUMSTONE	CAVALLAS
CATNAPPED	CAUDAD	CAUP	CAVALLIES
CATNAPPER	CAUDAE	CAUPS	CAVALLY
CATNAPS	CAUDAL	CAUSA	CAVALRIES
CATNEP	CAUDALLY	CAUSABLE	CAVALRY
CATNEPS	CAUDATE	CAUSAE	CAVAS
CATNIP	CAUDATED	CAUSAL	CAVASS
CATNIPS	CAUDATES	CAUSALGIA	CAVASSES
CATOLYTE	CAUDATION	CAUSALGIC	CAVATINA
CATOLYTES	CAUDEX	CAUSALITY	CAVATINAS
CATOPTRIC	CAUDEXES	CAUSALLY	CAVATINE
CATRIGGED	CAUDICES	CAUSALS	CAVE
CATS	CAUDICLE	CAUSATION	CAVEAT
CATSKIN	CAUDICLES	CAUSATIVE	CAVEATED
CATSKINS	CAUDILLO	CAUSE	CAVEATING
CATSPAW	CAUDILLOS	CAUSED	CAVEATOR
CATSPAWS	CAUDLE	CAUSELESS	CAVEATORS
CATSUIT	CAUDLED	CAUSEN	CAVEATS
CATSUITS	CAUDLES	CAUSER	CAVED
CATSUP	CAUDLING	CAUSERIE	CAVEFISH
CATSUPS	CAUDRON	CAUSERIES	CAVEL

CAVELIKE	CAWING	CEDED	CELIBATIC
CAVELS	CAWINGS	CEDER	CELL
CAVEMAN	CAWK	CEDERS	CELLA
CAVEMEN	CAWKER	CEDES	CELLAE
CAVENDISH	CAWKERS	CEDI	CELLAR
CAVER	CAWKS	CEDILLA	CELLARAGE
CAVERN	CAWS	CEDILLAS	CELLARED
CAVERNED	CAXON	CEDING	CELLARER
CAVERNING	CAXONS	CEDIS	CELLARERS
CAVERNOUS	CAY	CEDRATE	CELLARET
CAVERNS	CAYENNE	CEDRATES	CELLARETS
CAVERS	CAYENNED	CEDRINE	CELLARING
CAVES	CAYENNES	CEDULA	CELLARIST
CAVESSON	CAYMAN	CEDULAS	CELLARMAN
CAVESSONS	CAYMANS	CEE	CELLARMEN
CAVETTI	CAYS	CEES	CELLAROUS
CAVETTO	CAYUSE	CEIBA	CELLARS
CAVETTOS	CAYUSES	CEIBAS	CELLARWAY
CAVIAR	CAZ	CEIL	CELLBLOCK
CAVIARE	CAZIQUE	CEILED	CELLED
CAVIARES	CAZIQUES	CEILER	CELLI
CAVIARIE	CEANOTHUS	CEILERS	CELLING
CAVIARIES	CEAS	CEILI	CELLIST
CAVIARS	CEASE	CEILIDH	CELLISTS
CAVICORN	CEASED	CEILIDHS	CELLMATE
CAVICORNS	CEASEFIRE	CEILING	CELLMATES
CAVIE	CEASELESS	CEILINGED	CELLO
CAVIER	CEASES	CEILINGS	CELLOIDIN
CAVIERS	CEASING	CEILIS	CELLOS
CAVIES	CEASINGS	CEILS	CELLOSE
CAVIL	CEAZE	CEINTURE	CELLOSES
CAVILED	CEAZED	CEINTURES	CELLPHONE
CAVILER	CEAZES	CEL	CELLS
CAVILERS	CEAZING	CELADON	CELLULAR
CAVILING	CEBADILLA	CELADONS	CELLULARS
CAVILLED	CEBID	CELANDINE	CELLULASE
CAVILLER	CEBIDS	CELEB	CELLULE
CAVILLERS	CEBOID	CELEBRANT	CELLULES
CAVILLING	CEBOIDS	CELEBRATE	CELLULITE
CAVILS	CECA	CELEBRITY	CELLULOID
CAVING	CECAL	CELEBS	CELLULOSE
CAVINGS	CECALLY	CELERIAC	CELLULOUS
CAVITARY	CECILS	CELERIACS	CELOM
CAVITATE	CECITIES	CELERIES	CELOMATA
CAVITATED	CECITIS	CELERITY	CELOMIC
CAVITATES	CECITISES	CELERY	CELOMS
CAVITIED	CECITY	CELESTA	CELOSIA
CAVITIES	CECROPIA	CELESTAS	CELOSIAS
CAVITY	CECROPIAS	CELESTE	CELOTEX
CAVORT	CECUM	CELESTES	CELOTEXES
CAVORTED	CEDAR	CELESTIAL	CELS
CAVORTER	CEDARBIRD	CELESTINE	CELSITUDE
CAVORTERS	CEDARED	CELESTITE	CELT
CAVORTING	CEDARN	CELIAC	CELTS
CAVORTS	CEDARS	CELIACS	CEMBALI
CAVY	CEDARWOOD	CELIBACY	CEMBALIST
CAW	CEDARY	CELIBATE	CEMBALO
CAWED	CEDE	CELIBATES	CEMBALOS

CEMBRA	CENTAS	CENTRISM	CERATITIS
CEMBRAS	CENTAUR	CENTRISMS	CERATODUS
CEMENT	CENTAUREA	CENTRIST	CERATOID
CEMENTA	CENTAURIC	CENTRISTS	CERBEREAN
CEMENTED	CENTAURS	CENTRODE	CERBERIAN
CEMENTER	CENTAURY	CENTRODES	CERCAL
CEMENTERS	CENTAVO	CENTROID	CERCARIA
CEMENTING	CENTAVOS	CENTROIDS	CERCARIAE
CEMENTITE	CENTENARY	CENTRUM	CERCARIAL
CEMENTS	CENTENIER	CENTRUMS	CERCARIAN
CEMENTUM	CENTER	CENTRY	CERCARIAS
CEMENTUMS	CENTERED	CENTS	CERCI
CEMETERY	CENTERING	CENTU	CERCIS
CEMITARE	CENTERS	CENTUM	CERCISES
CEMITARES	CENTESES	CENTUMS	CERCUS
CENACLE	CENTESIMI	CENTUMVIR	CERE
CENACLES	CENTESIMO	CENTUPLE	CEREAL
CENDRE	CENTESIS	CENTUPLED	CEREALIST
CENOBITE	CENTIARE	CENTUPLES	CEREALS
CENOBITES	CENTIARES	CENTURIAL	CEREBELLA
CENOBITIC	CENTIGRAM	CENTURIES	CEREBRA
CENOTAPH	CENTILE	CENTURION	CEREBRAL
CENOTAPHS	CENTILES	CENTURY	CEREBRALS
CENOTE	CENTIME	CEORL	CEREBRATE
CENOTES	CENTIMES	CEORLISH	CEREBRIC
CENOZOIC	CENTIMO	CEORLS	CEREBROID
CENS	CENTIMOS	CEP	CEREBRUM
CENSE	CENTINEL	CEPACEOUS	CEREBRUMS
CENSED	CENTINELL	CEPE	CERECLOTH
CENSER	CENTINELS	CEPES	CERED
CENSERS	CENTIPEDE	CEPHALAD	CEREMENT
CENSES	CENTNER	CEPHALATE	CEREMENTS
CENSING	CENTNERS	CEPHALIC	CEREMONY
CENSOR	CENTO	CEPHALICS	CEREOUS
CENSORED	CENTOIST	CEPHALIN	CERES
CENSORIAL	CENTOISTS	CEPHALINS	CERESIN
CENSORIAN	CENTONATE	CEPHALOUS	CERESINE
CENSORING	CENTONEL	CEPHEID	CERESINES
CENSORS	CENTONELL	CEPHEIDS	CERESINS
CENSUAL	CENTONELS	CEPS	CEREUS
CENSURE	CENTONES	CERACEOUS	CEREUSES
CENSURED	CENTONIST	CERAMAL	CERGE
CENSURER	CENTOS	CERAMALS	CERGES
CENSURERS	CENTRA	CERAMIC	CERIA
CENSURES	CENTRAL	CERAMICS	CERIAS
CENSURING	CENTRALER	CERAMIDE	CERIC
CENSUS	CENTRALLY	CERAMIDES	CERING
CENSUSED	CENTRALS	CERAMIST	CERIPH
CENSUSES	CENTRE	CERAMISTS	CERIPHS
CENSUSING	CENTRED	CERASIN	CERISE
CENT	CENTREING	CERASINS	CERISES
CENTAGE	CENTRES	CERASTES	CERITE
CENTAGES	CENTRIC	CERASTIUM	CERITES
CENTAI	CENTRICAL	CERATE	CERIUM
CENTAL	CENTRIES	CERATED	CERIUMS
CENTALS	CENTRING	CERATES	CERMET
CENTARE	CENTRINGS	CERATIN	CERMETS
CENTARES	CENTRIOLE	CERATINS	CERNE

CERNED	CESAREVNA	CEVICHE	CHAFFER
CERNES	CESARIAN	CEVICHES	CHAFFERED
CERNING	CESARIANS	CEYLANITE	CHAFFERER
CERNUOUS	CESIOUS	CEYLONITE	CHAFFERS
CERO	CESIUM	CH	CHAFFERY
CEROGRAPH	CESIUMS	CHA	CHAFFIER
CEROMANCY	CESPITOSE	CHABAZITE	CHAFFIEST
CEROON	CESS	CHABLIS	CHAFFINCH
CEROONS	CESSATION	CHABOUK	CHAFFING
CEROS	CESSE	CHABOUKS	CHAFFINGS
CEROTIC	CESSED	CHABUK	CHAFFRON
CEROTYPE	CESSER	CHABUKS	CHAFFRONS
CEROTYPES	CESSERS	CHACE	CHAFFS
CEROUS	CESSES	CHACED	CHAFFY
CERRIAL	CESSING	CHACES	CHAFING
CERRIS	CESSION	CHACHKA	CHAFT
CERRISES	CESSIONS	CHACHKAS	CHAFTS
CERT	CESSPIT	CHACING	CHAGAN
CERTAIN	CESSPITS	CHACK	CHAGANS
CERTAINER	CESSPOOL	CHACKED	CHAGRIN
CERTAINLY	CESSPOOLS	CHACKING	CHAGRINED
CERTAINTY	CESTA	CHACKS	CHAGRINS
CERTES	CESTAS	CHACMA	CHAI
CERTIFIED	CESTI	CHACMAS	CHAIN
CERTIFIER	CESTODE	CHACO	CHAINE
CERTIFIES	CESTODES	CHACOES	CHAINED
CERTIFY	CESTOI	CHACONNE	CHAINES
CERTITUDE	CESTOID	CHACONNES	CHAINFALL
CERTS	CESTOIDS	CHACOS	CHAINING
CERULE	CESTOS	CHAD	CHAINLESS
CERULEAN	CESTOSES	CHADAR	CHAINLET
CERULEANS	CESTUI	CHADARIM	CHAINLETS
CERULEIN	CESTUIS	CHADARS	CHAINMAN
CERULEINS	CESTUS	CHADDAR	CHAINMEN
CERULEOUS	CESTUSES	CHADDARS	CHAINS
CERUMEN	CESURA	CHADDOR	CHAINSAW
CERUMENS	CESURAE	CHADDORS	CHAINSAWS
CERUSE	CESURAL	CHADLESS	CHAINSHOT
CERUSES	CESURAS	CHADO	CHAINWORK
CERUSITE	CESURE	CHADOR	CHAIR
CERUSITES	CESURES	CHADORS	CHAIRDAYS
CERUSSITE	CETACEAN	CHADOS	CHAIRED
CERVELAS	CETACEANS	CHADRI	CHAIRING
CERVELAT	CETACEOUS	CHADS	CHAIRLIFT
CERVELATS	CETANE	CHAEBOL	CHAIRMAN
CERVEZA	CETANES	CHAEBOLS	CHAIRMANS
CERVEZAS	CETE	CHAETA	CHAIRMEN
CERVICAL	CETERACH	CHAETAE	CHAIRS
CERVICES	CETERACHS	CHAETAL	CHAIS
CERVICUM	CETES	CHAETODON	CHAISE
CERVICUMS	CETOLOGY	CHAETOPOD	CHAISES
CERVID	CETRIMIDE	CHAFE	CHAKALAKA
CERVIDS	CETYL	CHAFED	CHAKRA
CERVINE	CETYLS	CHAFER	CHAKRAS
CERVIX	CETYWALL	CHAFERS	CHAL
CERVIXES	CETYWALLS	CHAFES	CHALAH
CESAREAN	CEVADILLA	CHAFF	CHALAHS
CESAREANS	CEVAPCICI	CHAFFED	CHALAN

CHALANED	CHALUTZ	CHAMPER	CHANOYUS
CHALANING	CHALUTZES	CHAMPERS	CHANSON
CHALANS	CHALUTZIM	CHAMPERTY	CHANSONS
CHALAZA	CHALYBEAN	CHAMPING	CHANT
CHALAZAE	CHALYBITE	CHAMPION	CHANTABLE
CHALAZAL	CHAM	CHAMPIONS	CHANTAGE
CHALAZAS	CHAMADE	CHAMPLEVE	CHANTAGES
CHALAZIA	CHAMADES	CHAMPS	CHANTED
CHALAZION	CHAMBER	CHAMPY	CHANTER
CHALCID	CHAMBERED	CHAMS	CHANTERS
CHALCIDS	CHAMBERER	CHANCE	CHANTEUSE
CHALCOGEN	CHAMBERS	CHANCED	CHANTEY
CHALDER	CHAMBRAY	CHANCEFUL	CHANTEYS
CHALDERS	CHAMBRAYS	CHANCEL	CHANTIE
CHALDRON	CHAMBRE	CHANCELS	CHANTIES
CHALDRONS	CHAMELEON	CHANCER	CHANTILLY
CHALEH	CHAMELOT	CHANCERS	CHANTING
CHALEHS	CHAMELOTS	CHANCERY	CHANTOR
CHALET	CHAMETZ	CHANCES	CHANTORS
CHALETS	CHAMETZES	CHANCEY	CHANTRESS
CHALICE	CHAMFER	CHANCIER	CHANTRIES
CHALICED	CHAMFERED	CHANCIEST	CHANTRY
CHALICES	CHAMFERER	CHANCILY	CHANTS
CHALK	CHAMFERS	CHANCING	CHANTY
CHALKED	CHAMFRAIN	CHANCRE	CHANUKIAH
CHALKFACE	CHAMFRON	CHANCRES	CHAO
CHALKIER	CHAMFRONS	CHANCROID	CHAOLOGY
CHALKIEST	CHAMISA	CHANCROUS	CHAORDIC
CHALKING	CHAMISAL	CHANCY	CHAOS
CHALKLIKE	CHAMISALS	CHANDELLE	CHAOSES
CHALKPIT	CHAMISAS	CHANDLER	CHAOTIC
CHALKPITS	CHAMISE	CHANDLERS	CHAP
CHALKS	CHAMISES	CHANDLERY	CHAPARRAL
CHALKY	CHAMISO	CHANFRON	CHAPATI
CHALLA	CHAMISOS	CHANFRONS	CHAPATIES
CHALLAH	CHAMLET	CHANG	CHAPATIS
CHALLAHS	CHAMLETS	CHANGA	CHAPATTI
CHALLAN	CHAMMIED	CHANGE	CHAPATTIS
CHALLANED	CHAMMIES	CHANGED	CHAPBOOK
CHALLANS	CHAMMY	CHANGEFUL	CHAPBOOKS
CHALLAS	CHAMMYING	CHANGER	CHAPE
CHALLENGE	CHAMOIS	CHANGERS	CHAPEAU
CHALLIE	CHAMOISED	CHANGES	CHAPEAUS
CHALLIES	CHAMOISES	CHANGEUP	CHAPEAUX
CHALLIS	CHAMOIX	CHANGEUPS	CHAPEL
CHALLISES	CHAMOMILE	CHANGING	CHAPELESS
CHALLOT	CHAMP	CHANGS	CHAPELRY
CHALLOTH	CHAMPAC	CHANK	CHAPELS
CHALLY	CHAMPACA	CHANKS	CHAPERON
CHALONE	CHAMPACAS	CHANNEL	CHAPERONE
CHALONES	CHAMPACS	CHANNELED	CHAPERONS
CHALONIC	CHAMPAGNE	CHANNELER	CHAPES
CHALOT	CHAMPAIGN	CHANNELS	CHAPESS
CHALOTH	CHAMPAK	CHANNER	CHAPESSES
CHALS	CHAMPAKS	CHANNERS	CHAPITER
CHALUMEAU	CHAMPART	CHANOYO	CHAPITERS
CHALUPA	CHAMPARTS	CHANOYOS	CHAPKA
CHALUPAS	CHAMPED	CHANOYU	CHAPKAS

CHAPLAIN
CHAPLAINS
CHAPLESS
CHAPLET
CHAPLETED
CHAPLETS
CHAPMAN
CHAPMEN
CHAPPAL
CHAPPALS
CHAPPATI
CHAPPATIS
CHAPPED
CHAPPESS
CHAPPIE
CHAPPIER
CHAPPIES
CHAPPIEST
CHAPPING
CHAPPY
CHAPRASSI
CHAPS
CHAPSTICK
CHAPT
CHAPTER
CHAPTERAL
CHAPTERED
CHAPTERS
CHAPTREL
CHAPTRELS
CHAQUETA
CHAQUETAS
CHAR
CHARA
CHARABANC
CHARACID
CHARACIDS
CHARACIN
CHARACINS
CHARACT
CHARACTER
CHARACTS
CHARADE
CHARADES
CHARANGA
CHARANGAS
CHARANGO
CHARANGOS
CHARAS
CHARASES
CHARBROIL
CHARCOAL
CHARCOALS
CHARCOALY
CHARD
CHARDS
CHARE
CHARED

CHARES
CHARET
CHARETS
CHARGE
CHARGED
CHARGEFUL
CHARGER
CHARGERS
CHARGES
CHARGING
CHARGRILL
CHARIDEE
CHARIDEES
CHARIER
CHARIEST
CHARILY
CHARINESS
CHARING
CHARIOT
CHARIOTED
CHARIOTS
CHARISM
CHARISMA
CHARISMAS
CHARISMS
CHARITIES
CHARITY
CHARIVARI
CHARK
CHARKA
CHARKAS
CHARKED
CHARKHA
CHARKHAS
CHARKING
CHARKS
CHARLADY
CHARLATAN
CHARLEY
CHARLEYS
CHARLIE
CHARLIER
CHARLIES
CHARLOCK
CHARLOCKS
CHARLOTTE
CHARM
CHARMED
CHARMER
CHARMERS
CHARMEUSE
CHARMFUL
CHARMING
CHARMLESS
CHARMONIA
CHARMS
CHARNECO
CHARNECOS

CHARNEL
CHARNELS
CHAROSET
CHAROSETH
CHAROSETS
CHARPAI
CHARPAIS
CHARPIE
CHARPIES
CHARPOY
CHARPOYS
CHARQUI
CHARQUID
CHARQUIS
CHARR
CHARRED
CHARRIER
CHARRIEST
CHARRING
CHARRO
CHARROS
CHARRS
CHARRY
CHARS
CHART
CHARTA
CHARTABLE
CHARTAS
CHARTED
CHARTER
CHARTERED
CHARTERER
CHARTERS
CHARTING
CHARTISM
CHARTISMS
CHARTIST
CHARTISTS
CHARTLESS
CHARTS
CHARVER
CHARVERS
CHARWOMAN
CHARWOMEN
CHARY
CHAS
CHASE
CHASEABLE
CHASED
CHASEPORT
CHASER
CHASERS
CHASES
CHASING
CHASINGS
CHASM
CHASMAL
CHASMED

CHASMIC
CHASMIER
CHASMIEST
CHASMS
CHASMY
CHASSE
CHASSED
CHASSEED
CHASSEING
CHASSEPOT
CHASSES
CHASSEUR
CHASSEURS
CHASSIS
CHASTE
CHASTELY
CHASTEN
CHASTENED
CHASTENER
CHASTENS
CHASTER
CHASTEST
CHASTISE
CHASTISED
CHASTISER
CHASTISES
CHASTITY
CHASUBLE
CHASUBLES
CHAT
CHATBOT
CHATBOTS
CHATCHKA
CHATCHKAS
CHATCHKE
CHATCHKES
CHATEAU
CHATEAUS
CHATEAUX
CHATELAIN
CHATLINE
CHATLINES
CHATON
CHATONS
CHATOYANT
CHATROOM
CHATROOMS
CHATS
CHATTA
CHATTAS
CHATTED
CHATTEL
CHATTELS
CHATTER
CHATTERED
CHATTERER
CHATTERS
CHATTERY

CHATTI	CHAWKS	CHECKED	CHEERIEST
CHATTIER	CHAWS	CHECKER	CHEERILY
CHATTIES	CHAY	CHECKERED	CHEERING
CHATTIEST	CHAYA	CHECKERS	CHEERIO
CHATTILY	CHAYAS	CHECKING	CHEERIOS
CHATTING	CHAYOTE	CHECKLESS	CHEERLEAD
CHATTIS	CHAYOTES	CHECKLIST	CHEERLED
CHATTY	CHAYROOT	CHECKMARK	CHEERLESS
CHAUFE	CHAYROOTS	CHECKMATE	CHEERLY
CHAUFED	CHAYS	CHECKOFF	CHEERO
CHAUFER	CHAZAN	CHECKOFFS	CHEEROS
CHAUFERS	CHAZANIM	CHECKOUT	CHEERS
CHAUFES	CHAZANS	CHECKOUTS	CHEERY
CHAUFF	CHAZZAN	CHECKRAIL	CHEESE
CHAUFFED	CHAZZANIM	CHECKREIN	CHEESED
CHAUFFER	CHAZZANS	CHECKROOM	CHEESES
CHAUFFERS	CHAZZEN	CHECKROW	CHEESEVAT
CHAUFFEUR	CHAZZENIM	CHECKROWS	CHEESIER
CHAUFFING	CHAZZENS	CHECKS	CHEESIEST
CHAUFFS	CHE	CHECKSUM	CHEESILY
CHAUFING	CHEAP	CHECKSUMS	CHEESING
CHAUMER	CHEAPED	CHECKUP	CHEESY
CHAUMERS	CHEAPEN	CHECKUPS	CHEETAH
CHAUNCE	CHEAPENED	CHECKY	CHEETAHS
CHAUNCED	CHEAPENER	CHEDDAR	CHEEWINK
CHAUNCES	CHEAPENS	CHEDDARS	CHEEWINKS
CHAUNCING	CHEAPER	CHEDDARY	CHEF
CHAUNGE	CHEAPEST	CHEDDITE	CHEFDOM
CHAUNGED	CHEAPIE	CHEDDITES	CHEFDOMS
CHAUNGES	CHEAPIES	CHEDER	CHEFED
CHAUNGING	CHEAPING	CHEDERS	CHEFFED
CHAUNT	CHEAPISH	CHEDITE	CHEFFING
CHAUNTED	CHEAPJACK	CHEDITES	CHEFING
CHAUNTER	CHEAPLY	CHEECHAKO	CHEFS
CHAUNTERS	CHEAPNESS	CHEEK	CHEGOE
CHAUNTING	CHEAPO	CHEEKBONE	CHEGOES
CHAUNTRY	CHEAPOS	CHEEKED	CHEILITIS
CHAUNTS	CHEAPS	CHEEKFUL	CHEKA
CHAUSSES	CHEAPY	CHEEKFULS	CHEKAS
CHAUSSURE	CHEAT	CHEEKIER	CHEKIST
CHAUVIN	CHEATABLE	CHEEKIEST	CHEKISTS
CHAUVINS	CHEATED	CHEEKILY	CHELA
CHAV	CHEATER	CHEEKING	CHELAE
CHAVE	CHEATERS	CHEEKLESS	CHELAS
CHAVENDER	CHEATERY	CHEEKS	CHELASHIP
CHAVETTE	CHEATING	CHEEKY	CHELATE
CHAVETTES	CHEATINGS	CHEEP	CHELATED
CHAVISH	CHEATS	CHEEPED	CHELATES
CHAVS	CHEBEC	CHEEPER	CHELATING
CHAW	CHEBECS	CHEEPERS	CHELATION
CHAWBACON	CHECHAKO	CHEEPING	CHELATOR
CHAWDRON	CHECHAKOS	CHEEPS	CHELATORS
CHAWDRONS	CHECHAQUO	CHEER	CHELICERA
CHAWED	CHECHIA	CHEERED	CHELIFORM
CHAWER	CHECHIAS	CHEERER	CHELIPED
CHAWERS	CHECK	CHEERERS	CHELIPEDS
CHAWING	CHECKABLE	CHEERFUL	CHELLUP
CHAWK	CHECKBOOK	CHEERIER	CHELLUPS

CHELOID
CHELOIDAL
CHELOIDS
CHELONE
CHELONES
CHELONIAN
CHELP
CHELPED
CHELPING
CHELPS
CHEMIC
CHEMICAL
CHEMICALS
CHEMICKED
CHEMICS
CHEMISE
CHEMISES
CHEMISM
CHEMISMS
CHEMISORB
CHEMIST
CHEMISTRY
CHEMISTS
CHEMITYPE
CHEMITYPY
CHEMMIES
CHEMMY
CHEMO
CHEMOKINE
CHEMOS
CHEMOSORB
CHEMOSTAT
CHEMPADUK
CHEMURGIC
CHEMURGY
CHENAR
CHENARS
CHENET
CHENETS
CHENILLE
CHENILLES
CHENIX
CHENIXES
CHENOPOD
CHENOPODS
CHEONGSAM
CHEQUE
CHEQUER
CHEQUERED
CHEQUERS
CHEQUES
CHEQUING
CHEQUY
CHER
CHERALITE
CHERE
CHERIMOYA
CHERISH

CHERISHED
CHERISHER
CHERISHES
CHERNOZEM
CHEROOT
CHEROOTS
CHERRIED
CHERRIER
CHERRIES
CHERRIEST
CHERRY
CHERRYING
CHERT
CHERTIER
CHERTIEST
CHERTS
CHERTY
CHERUB
CHERUBIC
CHERUBIM
CHERUBIMS
CHERUBIN
CHERUBINS
CHERUBS
CHERUP
CHERUPED
CHERUPING
CHERUPS
CHERVIL
CHERVILS
CHESHIRE
CHESHIRES
CHESIL
CHESILS
CHESNUT
CHESNUTS
CHESS
CHESSEL
CHESSELS
CHESSES
CHESSMAN
CHESSMEN
CHEST
CHESTED
CHESTFUL
CHESTFULS
CHESTIER
CHESTIEST
CHESTILY
CHESTING
CHESTNUT
CHESTNUTS
CHESTS
CHESTY
CHETAH
CHETAHS
CHETH
CHETHS

CHETNIK
CHETNIKS
CHETRUM
CHETRUMS
CHEVAL
CHEVALET
CHEVALETS
CHEVALIER
CHEVELURE
CHEVEN
CHEVENS
CHEVEREL
CHEVERELS
CHEVERIL
CHEVERILS
CHEVERON
CHEVERONS
CHEVERYE
CHEVERYES
CHEVET
CHEVETS
CHEVIED
CHEVIES
CHEVILLE
CHEVILLES
CHEVIN
CHEVINS
CHEVIOT
CHEVIOTS
CHEVRE
CHEVRES
CHEVRET
CHEVRETS
CHEVRETTE
CHEVRON
CHEVRONED
CHEVRONS
CHEVRONY
CHEVY
CHEVYING
CHEW
CHEWABLE
CHEWED
CHEWER
CHEWERS
CHEWET
CHEWETS
CHEWIE
CHEWIER
CHEWIES
CHEWIEST
CHEWINESS
CHEWING
CHEWINK
CHEWINKS
CHEWS
CHEWY
CHEZ

CHI
CHIA
CHIACK
CHIACKED
CHTACKING
CHIACKS
CHIANTI
CHIANTIS
CHIAO
CHIAREZZA
CHIAREZZE
CHIAS
CHIASM
CHIASMA
CHIASMAL
CHIASMAS
CHIASMATA
CHIASMI
CHIASMIC
CHIASMS
CHIASMUS
CHIASTIC
CHIAUS
CHIAUSED
CHIAUSES
CHIAUSING
CHIB
CHIBBED
CHIBBING
CHIBOL
CHIBOLS
CHIBOUK
CHIBOUKS
CHIBOUQUE
CHIBS
CHIC
CHICA
CHICALOTE
CHICANA
CHICANAS
CHICANE
CHICANED
CHICANER
CHICANERS
CHICANERY
CHICANES
CHICANING
CHICANO
CHICANOS
CHICAS
CHICCORY
CHICER
CHICEST
CHICH
CHICHA
CHICHAS
CHICHES
CHICHI

CHICHIER	CHIFFON	CHILIDOGS	CHIMNEYED
CHICHIEST	CHIFFONS	CHILIES	CHIMNEYS
CHICHIS	CHIFFONY	CHILIOI	CHIMO
CHICK	CHIGETAI	CHILIOIS	CHIMP
CHICKADEE	CHIGETAIS	CHILIS	CHIMPS
CHICKAREE	CHIGGA	CHILL	CHIN
CHICKEE	CHIGGAS	CHILLADA	CHINA
CHICKEES	CHIGGER	CHILLADAS	CHINAMAN
CHICKEN	CHIGGERS	CHILLED	CHINAMEN
CHICKENED	CHIGNON	CHILLER	CHINAMPA
CHICKENS	CHIGNONED	CHILLERS	CHINAMPAS
CHICKLING	CHIGNONS	CHILLEST	CHINAR
CHICKORY	CHIGOE	CHILLI	CHINAROOT
CHICKPEA	CHIGOES	CHILLIER	CHINARS
CHICKPEAS	CHIGRE	CHILLIES	CHINAS
CHICKS	CHIGRES	CHILLIEST	CHINAWARE
CHICKWEED	CHIHUAHUA	CHILLILY	CHINBONE
CHICLE	CHIK	CHILLING	CHINBONES
CHICLES	CHIKARA	CHILLINGS	CHINCAPIN
CHICLY	CHIKARAS	CHILLIS	CHINCH
CHICNESS	CHIKHOR	CHILLNESS	CHINCHES
CHICO	CHIKHORS	CHILLS	CHINCHIER
CHICON	CHIKOR	CHILLUM	CHINCHY
CHICONS	CHIKORS	CHILLUMS	CHINCOUGH
CHICORIES	CHIKS	CHILLY	CHINDIT
CHICORY	CHILBLAIN	CHILOPOD	CHINDITS
CHICOS	CHILD	CHILOPODS	CHINE
CHICS	CHILDBED	CHILTEPIN	CHINED
CHID	CHILDBEDS	CHIMAERA	CHINES
CHIDDEN	CHILDCARE	CHIMAERAS	CHINESE
CHIDE	CHILDE	CHIMAERIC	CHINING
CHIDED	CHILDED	CHIMAR	CHINK
CHIDER	CHILDER	CHIMARS	CHINKAPIN
CHIDERS	CHILDES	CHIMB	CHINKARA
CHIDES	CHILDHOOD	CHIMBLEY	CHINKARAS
CHIDING	CHILDING	CHIMBLEYS	CHINKED
CHIDINGLY	CHILDISH	CHIMBLIES	CHINKIE
CHIDINGS	CHILDLESS	CHIMBLY	CHINKIER
CHIDLINGS	CHILDLIER	CHIMBS	CHINKIES
CHIEF	CHILDLIKE	CHIME	CHINKIEST
CHIEFDOM	CHILDLY	CHIMED	CHINKING
CHIEFDOMS	CHILDNESS	CHIMER	CHINKS
CHIEFER	CHILDREN	CHIMERA	CHINKY
CHIEFERY	CHILDS	CHIMERAS	CHINLESS
CHIEFESS	CHILE	CHIMERE	CHINNED
CHIEFEST	CHILES	CHIMERES	CHINNING
CHIEFLESS	CHILI	CHIMERIC	CHINO
CHIEFLING	CHILIAD	CHIMERID	CHINONE
CHIEFLY	CHILIADAL	CHIMERIDS	CHINONES
CHIEFRIES	CHILIADIC	CHIMERISM	CHINOOK
CHIEFRY	CHILIADS	CHIMERS	CHINOOKS
CHIEFS	CHILIAGON	CHIMES	CHINOS
CHIEFSHIP	CHILIARCH	CHIMING	CHINOVNIK
CHIEFTAIN	CHILIASM	CHIMLA	CHINS
CHIEL	CHILIASMS	CHIMLAS	CHINSTRAP
CHIELD	CHILIAST	CHIMLEY	CHINTS
CHIELDS	CHILIASTS	CHIMLEYS	CHINTSES
CHIELS	CHILIDOG	CHIMNEY	CHINTZ

CHINTZES
CHINTZIER
CHINTZY
CHINWAG
CHINWAGS
CHIP
CHIPBOARD
CHIPMUCK
CHIPMUCKS
CHIPMUNK
CHIPMUNKS
CHIPOCHIA
CHIPOLATA
CHIPOTLE
CHIPOTLES
CHIPPABLE
CHIPPED
CHIPPER
CHIPPERED
CHIPPERS
CHIPPIE
CHIPPIER
CHIPPIES
CHIPPIEST
CHIPPING
CHIPPINGS
CHIPPY
CHIPS
CHIPSET
CHIPSETS
CHIRAGRA
CHIRAGRAS
CHIRAGRIC
CHIRAL
CHIRALITY
CHIRIMOYA
CHIRK
CHIRKED
CHIRKER
CHIRKEST
CHIRKING
CHIRKS
CHIRL
CHIRLED
CHIRLING
CHIRLS
CHIRM
CHIRMED
CHIRMING
CHIRMS
CHIRO
CHIROLOGY
CHIRONOMY
CHIROPODY
CHIROPTER
CHIROS
CHIRP
CHIRPED

CHIRPER
CHIRPERS
CHIRPIER
CHIRPIEST
CHIRPILY
CHIRPING
CHIRPS
CHIRPY
CHIRR
CHIRRE
CHIRRED
CHIRREN
CHIRRES
CHIRRING
CHIRRS
CHIRRUP
CHIRRUPED
CHIRRUPER
CHIRRUPS
CHIRRUPY
CHIRT
CHIRTED
CHIRTING
CHIRTS
CHIRU
CHIRUS
CHIS
CHISEL
CHISELED
CHISELER
CHISELERS
CHISELING
CHISELLED
CHISELLER
CHISELS
CHIT
CHITAL
CHITALS
CHITCHAT
CHITCHATS
CHITIN
CHITINOID
CHITINOUS
CHITINS
CHITLIN
CHITLING
CHITLINGS
CHITLINS
CHITON
CHITONS
CHITOSAN
CHITOSANS
CHITS
CHITTED
CHITTER
CHITTERED
CHITTERS
CHITTIER

CHITTIES
CHITTIEST
CHITTING
CHITTY
CHIV
CHIVALRIC
CHIVALRY
CHIVAREE
CHIVAREED
CHIVAREES
CHIVARI
CHIVARIED
CHIVARIES
CHIVE
CHIVED
CHIVES
CHIVIED
CHIVIES
CHIVING
CHIVS
CHIVVED
CHIVVIED
CHIVVIES
CHIVVING
CHIVVY
CHIVVYING
CHIVY
CHIVYING
CHIYOGAMI
CHIZ
CHIZZ
CHIZZED
CHIZZES
CHIZZING
CHLAMYDES
CHLAMYDIA
CHLAMYS
CHLAMYSES
CHLOASMA
CHLOASMAS
CHLORACNE
CHLORAL
CHLORALS
CHLORATE
CHLORATES
CHLORDAN
CHLORDANE
CHLORDANS
CHLORELLA
CHLORIC
CHLORID
CHLORIDE
CHLORIDES
CHLORIDIC
CHLORIDS
CHLORIN
CHLORINE
CHLORINES

CHLORINS
CHLORITE
CHLORITES
CHLORITIC
CHLOROSES
CHLOROSIS
CHLOROTIC
CHLOROUS
CHOANA
CHOANAE
CHOBDAR
CHOBDARS
CHOC
CHOCCIER
CHOCCIES
CHOCCIEST
CHOCCY
CHOCHO
CHOCHOS
CHOCK
CHOCKED
CHOCKER
CHOCKFUL
CHOCKFULL
CHOCKING
CHOCKO
CHOCKOS
CHOCKS
CHOCO
CHOCOLATE
CHOCOLATY
CHOCOS
CHOCS
CHOCTAW
CHOCTAWS
CHODE
CHOENIX
CHOENIXES
CHOG
CHOGS
CHOICE
CHOICEFUL
CHOICELY
CHOICER
CHOICES
CHOICEST
CHOIR
CHOIRBOY
CHOIRBOYS
CHOIRED
CHOIRGIRL
CHOIRING
CHOIRLIKE
CHOIRMAN
CHOIRMEN
CHOIRS
CHOKE
CHOKEABLE

CHOKEBORE
CHOKECOIL
CHOKED
CHOKEDAMP
CHOKEHOLD
CHOKER
CHOKERS
CHOKES
CHOKEY
CHOKEYS
CHOKIDAR
CHOKIDARS
CHOKIER
CHOKIES
CHOKIEST
CHOKING
CHOKINGLY
CHOKO
CHOKOS
CHOKRA
CHOKRAS
CHOKRI
CHOKRIS
CHOKY
CHOLA
CHOLAEMIA
CHOLAEMIC
CHOLAS
CHOLATE
CHOLATES
CHOLECYST
CHOLELITH
CHOLEMIA
CHOLEMIAS
CHOLENT
CHOLENTS
CHOLER
CHOLERA
CHOLERAIC
CHOLERAS
CHOLERIC
CHOLEROID
CHOLERS
CHOLI
CHOLIAMB
CHOLIAMBS
CHOLIC
CHOLINE
CHOLINES
CHOLIS
CHOLLA
CHOLLAS
CHOLLERS
CHOLO
CHOLOS
CHOLTRIES
CHOLTRY
CHOMA

CHOMAS
CHOMETZ
CHOMETZES
CHOMMIE
CHOMMIES
CHOMP
CHOMPED
CHOMPER
CHOMPERS
CHOMPING
CHOMPS
CHON
CHONDRAL
CHONDRE
CHONDRES
CHONDRI
CHONDRIFY
CHONDRIN
CHONDRINS
CHONDRITE
CHONDROID
CHONDROMA
CHONDRULE
CHONDRUS
CHONS
CHOOF
CHOOFED
CHOOFING
CHOOFS
CHOOK
CHOOKED
CHOOKIE
CHOOKIES
CHOOKING
CHOOKS
CHOOM
CHOOMS
CHOOSE
CHOOSER
CHOOSERS
CHOOSES
CHOOSEY
CHOOSIER
CHOOSIEST
CHOOSING
CHOOSY
CHOP
CHOPHOUSE
CHOPIN
CHOPINE
CHOPINES
CHOPINS
CHOPLOGIC
CHOPPED
CHOPPER
CHOPPERED
CHOPPERS
CHOPPIER

CHOPPIEST
CHOPPILY
CHOPPING
CHOPPINGS
CHOPPY
CHOPS
CHOPSOCKY
CHOPSTICK
CHORAGI
CHORAGIC
CHORAGUS
CHORAL
CHORALE
CHORALES
CHORALIST
CHORALLY
CHORALS
CHORD
CHORDA
CHORDAE
CHORDAL
CHORDATE
CHORDATES
CHORDED
CHORDEE
CHORDEES
CHORDING
CHORDINGS
CHORDS
CHORDWISE
CHORE
CHOREA
CHOREAL
CHOREAS
CHOREATIC
CHORED
CHOREE
CHOREES
CHOREGI
CHOREGIC
CHOREGUS
CHOREIC
CHOREMAN
CHOREMEN
CHOREOID
CHORES
CHOREUS
CHOREUSES
CHORIA
CHORIAL
CHORIAMB
CHORIAMBI
CHORIAMBS
CHORIC
CHORINE
CHORINES
CHORING
CHORIOID

CHORIOIDS
CHORION
CHORIONIC
CHORIONS
CHORISES
CHORISIS
CHORISM
CHORISMS
CHORIST
CHORISTER
CHORISTS
CHORIZO
CHORIZONT
CHORIZOS
CHOROID
CHOROIDAL
CHOROIDS
CHOROLOGY
CHORRIE
CHORRIES
CHORTEN
CHORTENS
CHORTLE
CHORTLED
CHORTLER
CHORTLERS
CHORTLES
CHORTLING
CHORUS
CHORUSED
CHORUSES
CHORUSING
CHORUSSED
CHORUSSES
CHOSE
CHOSEN
CHOSES
CHOTA
CHOTT
CHOTTS
CHOU
CHOUGH
CHOUGHS
CHOULTRY
CHOUNTER
CHOUNTERS
CHOUSE
CHOUSED
CHOUSER
CHOUSERS
CHOUSES
CHOUSH
CHOUSHES
CHOUSING
CHOUT
CHOUTS
CHOUX
CHOW

CHOWCHOW	CHROMIDES	CHUCKS	CHUMS
CHOWCHOWS	CHROMIDIA	CHUCKY	CHUMSHIP
CHOWDER	CHROMIER	CHUDDAH	CHUMSHIPS
CHOWDERED	CHROMIEST	CHUDDAHS	CHUNDER
CHOWDERS	CHROMING	CHUDDAR	CHUNDERED
CHOWED	CHROMINGS	CHUDDARS	CHUNDERS
CHOWHOUND	CHROMISE	CHUDDER	CHUNK
CHOWING	CHROMISED	CHUDDERS	CHUNKED
CHOWK	CHROMISES	CHUDDIES	CHUNKIER
CHOWKIDAR	CHROMITE	CHUDDY	CHUNKIEST
CHOWKS	CHROMITES	CHUFA	CHUNKILY
CHOWRI	CHROMIUM	CHUFAS	CHUNKING
CHOWRIES	CHROMIUMS	CHUFF	CHUNKINGS
CHOWRIS	CHROMIZE	CHUFFED	CHUNKS
CHOWRY	CHROMIZED	CHUFFER	CHUNKY
CHOWS	CHROMIZES	CHUFFEST	CHUNNEL
CHOWSE	CHROMO	CHUFFIER	CHUNNELS
CHOWSED	CHROMOGEN	CHUFFIEST	CHUNNER
CHOWSES	CHROMOS	CHUFFING	CHUNNERED
CHOWSING	CHROMOUS	CHUFFS	CHUNNERS
CHOWTIME	CHROMY	CHUFFY	CHUNTER
CHOWTIMES	CHROMYL	CHUG	CHUNTERED
CHRESARD	CHROMYLS	CHUGALUG	CHUNTERS
CHRESARDS	CHRONAXIE	CHUGALUGS	CHUPATI
CHRISM	CHRONAXY	CHUGGED	CHUPATIS
CHRISMA	CHRONIC	CHUGGER	CHUPATTI
CHRISMAL	CHRONICAL	CHUGGERS	CHUPATTIS
CHRISMALS	CHRONICLE	CHUGGING	CHUPATTY
CHRISMON	CHRONICS	CHUGS	CHUPPA
CHRISMONS	CHRONON	CHUKAR	CHUPPAH
CHRISMS	CHRONONS	CHUKARS	CHUPPAHS
CHRISOM	CHRYSALID	CHUKKA	CHUPPAS
CHRISOMS	CHRYSALIS	CHUKKAR	CHUPRASSY
CHRISTEN	CHRYSANTH	CHUKKARS	CHURCH
CHRISTENS	CHTHONIAN	CHUKKAS	CHURCHED
CHRISTIAN	CHTHONIC	CHUKKER	CHURCHES
CHRISTIE	CHUB	CHUKKERS	CHURCHIER
CHRISTIES	CHUBASCO	CHUKOR	CHURCHING
CHRISTOM	CHUBASCOS	CHUKORS	CHURCHISM
CHRISTOMS	CHUBBIER	CHUM	CHURCHLY
CHRISTY	CHUBBIEST	CHUMASH	CHURCHMAN
CHROMA	CHUBBILY	CHUMASHES	CHURCHMEN
CHROMAKEY	CHUBBY	CHUMLEY	CHURCHWAY
CHROMAS	CHUBS	CHUMLEYS	CHURCHY
CHROMATE	CHUCK	CHUMMAGE	CHURIDAR
CHROMATES	CHUCKED	CHUMMAGES	CHURIDARS
CHROMATIC	CHUCKER	CHUMMED	CHURINGA
CHROMATID	CHUCKERS	CHUMMIER	CHURINGAS
CHROMATIN	CHUCKHOLE	CHUMMIES	CHURL
CHROME	CHUCKIE	CHUMMIEST	CHURLISH
CHROMED	CHUCKIES	CHUMMILY	CHURLS
CHROMEL	CHUCKING	CHUMMING	CHURN
CHROMELS	CHUCKLE	CHUMMY	CHURNED
CHROMENE	CHUCKLED	CHUMP	CHURNER
CHROMENES	CHUCKLER	CHUMPED	CHURNERS
CHROMES	CHUCKLERS	CHUMPING	CHURNING
CHROMIC	CHUCKLES	CHUMPINGS	CHURNINGS
CHROMIDE	CHUCKLING	CHUMPS	CHURNMILK

CHURNS	CIABATTA	CIDES	CINCHONA
CHURR	CIABATTAS	CIDING	CINCHONAS
CHURRED	CIABATTE	CIDS	CINCHONIC
CHURRING	CIAO	CIEL	CINCINNUS
CHURRO	CIAOS	CIELED	CINCT
CHURROS	CIBATION	CIELING	CINCTURE
CHURRS	CIBATIONS	CIELINGS	CINCTURED
CHURRUS	CIBOL	CIELS	CINCTURES
CHURRUSES	CIBOLS	CIERGE	CINDER
CHUSE	CIBORIA	CIERGES	CINDERED
CHUSES	CIBORIUM	CIG	CINDERING
CHUSING	CIBOULE	CIGAR	CINDEROUS
CHUT	CIBOULES	CIGARET	CINDERS
CHUTE	CICADA	CIGARETS	CINDERY
CHUTED	CICADAE	CIGARETTE	CINE
CHUTES	CICADAS	CIGARILLO	CINEAST
CHUTING	CICALA	CIGARLIKE	CINEASTE
CHUTIST	CICALAS	CIGARS	CINEASTES
CHUTISTS	CICALE	CIGGIE	CINEASTS
CHUTNEE	CICATRICE	CIGGIES	CINEMA
CHUTNEES	CICATRISE	CIGGY	CINEMAS
CHUTNEY	CICATRIX	CIGS	CINEMATIC
CHUTNEYS	CICATRIZE	CIGUATERA	CINEOL
CHUTZPA	CICELIES	CILANTRO	CINEOLE
CHUTZPAH	CICELY	CILANTROS	CINEOLES
CHUTZPAHS	CICERO	CILIA	CINEOLS
CHUTZPAS	CICERONE	CILIARY	CINEPHILE
CHYACK	CICERONED	CILIATE	CINEPLEX
CHYACKED	CICERONES	CILIATED	CINERAMIC
CHYACKING	CICERONI	CILIATELY	CINERARIA
CHYACKS	CICEROS	CILIATES	CINERARY
CHYLDE	CICHLID	CILIATION	CINERATOR
CHYLE	CICHLIDAE	CILICE	CINEREA
CHYLES	CICHLIDS	CILICES	CINEREAL
CHYLIFIED	CICHLOID	CILICIOUS	CINEREAS
CHYLIFIES	CICINNUS	CILIOLATE	CINEREOUS
CHYLIFY	CICISBEI	CILIUM	CINERIN
CHYLOUS	CICISBEO	CILL	CINERINS
CHYLURIA	CICISBEOS	CILLS	CINES
CHYLURIAS	CICLATON	CIMAR	CINGULA
CHYME	CICLATONS	CIMARS	CINGULAR
CHYMES	CICLATOUN	CIMBALOM	CINGULATE
CHYMIC	CICOREE	CIMBALOMS	CINGULUM
CHYMICS	CICOREES	CIMELIA	CINNABAR
CHYMIFIED	CICUTA	CIMEX	CINNABARS
CHYMIFIES	CICUTAS	CIMICES	CINNAMIC
CHYMIFY	CICUTINE	CIMIER	CINNAMON
CHYMIST	CICUTINES	CIMIERS	CINNAMONS
CHYMISTRY	CID	CIMINITE	CINNAMONY
CHYMISTS	CIDARIS	CIMINITES	CINNAMYL
CHYMOSIN	CIDARISES	CIMMERIAN	CINNAMYLS
CHYMOSINS	CIDE	CIMOLITE	CINQUAIN
CHYMOUS	CIDED	CIMOLITES	CINQUAINS
CHYND	CIDER	CINCH	CINQUE
CHYPRE	CIDERKIN	CINCHED	CINQUES
CHYPRES	CIDERKINS	CINCHES	CION
CHYTRID	CIDERS	CINCHING	CIONS
CHYTRIDS	CIDERY	CINCHINGS	CIOPPINO

CIOPPINOS	CIRRIPED	CITEABLE	CITY
CIPHER	CIRRIPEDE	CITED	CITYFIED
CIPHERED	CIRRIPEDS	CITER	CITYFIES
CIPHERER	CIRROSE	CITERS	CITYFY
CIPHERERS	CIRROUS	CITES	CITYFYING
CIPHERING	CIRRUS	CITESS	CITYSCAPE
CIPHERS	CIRSOID	CITESSES	CITYWARD
CIPHONIES	CIS	CITHARA	CITYWIDE
CIPHONY	CISALPINE	CITHARAS	CIVE
CIPOLIN	CISCO	CITHARIST	CIVES
CIPOLINS	CISCOES	CITHER	CIVET
CIPOLLINO	CISCOS	CITHERN	CIVETLIKE
CIPPI	CISELEUR	CITHERNS	CIVETS
CIPPUS	CISELEURS	CITHERS	CIVIC
CIRCA	CISELURE	CITHREN	CIVICALLY
CIRCADIAN	CISELURES	CITHRENS	CIVICISM
CIRCAR	CISLUNAR	CITIED	CIVICISMS
CIRCARS	CISPADANE	CITIES	CIVICS
CIRCINATE	CISPLATIN	CITIFIED	CIVIE
CIRCITER	CISSIER	CITIFIES	CIVIES
CIRCLE	CISSIES	CITIFY	CIVIL
CIRCLED	CISSIEST	CITIFYING	CIVILIAN
CIRCLER	CISSIFIED	CITIGRADE	CIVILIANS
CIRCLERS	CISSING	CITING	CIVILISE
CIRCLES	CISSINGS	CITIZEN	CIVILISED
CIRCLET	CISSOID	CITIZENLY	CIVILISER
CIRCLETS	CISSOIDS	CITIZENRY	CIVILISES
CIRCLING	CISSUS	CITIZENS	CIVILIST
CIRCLINGS	CISSUSES	CITO	CIVILISTS
CIRCLIP	CISSY	CITOLA	CIVILITY
CIRCLIPS	CIST	CITOLAS	CIVILIZE
CIRCS	CISTED	CITOLE	CIVILIZED
CIRCUIT	CISTERN	CITOLES	CIVILIZER
CIRCUITAL	CISTERNA	CITRAL	CIVILIZES
CIRCUITED	CISTERNAE	CITRALS	CIVILLY
CIRCUITRY	CISTERNAL	CITRANGE	CIVILNESS
CIRCUITS	CISTERNS	CITRANGES	CIVISM
CIRCUITY	CISTIC	CITRATE	CIVISMS
CIRCULAR	CISTRON	CITRATED	CIVVIES
CIRCULARS	CISTRONIC	CITRATES	CIVVY
CIRCULATE	CISTRONS	CITREOUS	CIZERS
CIRCUS	CISTS	CITRIC	CLABBER
CIRCUSES	CISTUS	CITRIN	CLABBERED
CIRCUSSY	CISTUSES	CITRINE	CLABBERS
CIRCUSY	CISTVAEN	CITRINES	CLACH
CIRE	CISTVAENS	CITRININ	CLACHAN
CIRES	CIT	CITRININS	CLACHANS
CIRL	CITABLE	CITRINS	CLACHS
CIRLS	CITADEL	CITRON	CLACK
CIRQUE	CITADELS	CITRONS	CLACKBOX
CIRQUES	CITAL	CITROUS	CLACKDISH
CIRRATE	CITALS	CITRUS	CLACKED
CIRRHOSED	CITATION	CITRUSES	CLACKER
CIRRHOSES	CITATIONS	CITRUSSY	CLACKERS
CIRRHOSIS	CITATOR	CITRUSY	CLACKING
CIRRHOTIC	CITATORS	CITS	CLACKS
CIRRI	CITATORY	CITTERN	CLAD
CIRRIFORM	CITE	CITTERNS	CLADDAGH

CLADDAGHS	CLAMMILY	CLAPNET	CLARY
CLADDED	CLAMMING	CLAPNETS	CLASH
CLADDER	CLAMMY	CLAPPED	CLASHED
CLADDERS	CLAMOR	CLAPPER	CLASHER
CLADDIE	CLAMORED	CLAPPERED	CLASHERS
CLADDIES	CLAMORER	CLAPPERS	CLASHES
CLADDING	CLAMORERS	CLAPPING	CLASHING
CLADDINGS	CLAMORING	CLAPPINGS	CLASHINGS
CLADE	CLAMOROUS	CLAPS	CLASP
CLADES	CLAMORS	CLAPT	CLASPED
CLADISM	CLAMOUR	CLAPTRAP	CLASPER
CLADISMS	CLAMOURED	CLAPTRAPS	CLASPERS
CLADIST	CLAMOURER	CLAQUE	CLASPING
CLADISTIC	CLAMOURS	CLAQUER	CLASPINGS
CLADISTS	CLAMP	CLAQUERS	CLASPS
CLADODE	CLAMPDOWN	CLAQUES	CLASPT
CLADODES	CLAMPED	CLAQUEUR	CLASS
CLADODIAL	CLAMPER	CLAQUEURS	CLASSABLE
CLADOGRAM	CLAMPERED	CLARAIN	CLASSED
CLADS	CLAMPERS	CLARAINS	CLASSER
CLAES	CLAMPING	CLARENCE	CLASSERS
CLAFOUTI	CLAMPS	CLARENCES	CLASSES
CLAFOUTIS	CLAMS	CLARENDON	CLASSIBLE
CLAG	CLAMSHELL	CLARET	CLASSIC
CLAGGED	CLAMWORM	CLARETED	CLASSICAL
CLAGGIER	CLAMWORMS	CLARETING	CLASSICO
CLAGGIEST	CLAN	CLARETS	CLASSICS
CLAGGING	CLANG	CLARIES	CLASSIER
CLAGGY	CLANGBOX	CLARIFIED	CLASSIEST
CLAGS	CLANGED	CLARIFIER	CLASSIFIC
CLAIM	CLANGER	CLARIFIES	CLASSIFY
CLAIMABLE	CLANGERS	CLARIFY	CLASSILY
CLAIMANT	CLANGING	CLARINET	CLASSING
CLAIMANTS	CLANGINGS	CLARINETS	CLASSINGS
CLAIMED	CLANGOR	CLARINI	CLASSIS
CLAIMER	CLANGORED	CLARINO	CLASSISM
CLAIMERS	CLANGORS	CLARINOS	CLASSISMS
CLAIMING	CLANGOUR	CLARION	CLASSIST
CLAIMS	CLANGOURS	CLARIONED	CLASSISTS
CLAM	CLANGS	CLARIONET	CLASSLESS
CLAMANCY	CLANK	CLARIONS	CLASSMAN
CLAMANT	CLANKED	CLARITIES	CLASSMATE
CLAMANTLY	CLANKIER	CLARITY	CLASSMEN
CLAMBAKE	CLANKIEST	CLARKIA	CLASSON
CLAMBAKES	CLANKING	CLARKIAS	CLASSONS
CLAMBE	CLANKINGS	CLARO	CLASSROOM
CLAMBER	CLANKS	CLAROES	CLASSWORK
CLAMBERED	CLANKY	CLAROS	CLASSY
CLAMBERER	CLANNISH	CLARSACH	CLAST
CLAMBERS	CLANS	CLARSACHS	CLASTIC
CLAME	CLANSHIP	CLART	CLASTICS
CLAMES	CLANSHIPS	CLARTED	CLASTS
CLAMLIKE	CLANSMAN	CLARTHEAD	CLAT
CLAMMED	CLANSMEN	CLARTIER	CLATCH
CLAMMER	CLAP	CLARTIEST	CLATCHED
CLAMMERS	CLAPBOARD	CLARTING	CLATCHES
CLAMMIER	CLAPBREAD	CLARTS	CLATCHING
CLAMMIEST	CLAPDISH	CLARTY	CLATHRATE

CLATS
CLATTED
CLATTER
CLATTERED
CLATTERER
CLATTERS
CLATTERY
CLATTING
CLAUCHT
CLAUCHTED
CLAUCHTS
CLAUGHT
CLAUGHTED
CLAUGHTS
CLAUSAL
CLAUSE
CLAUSES
CLAUSTRA
CLAUSTRAL
CLAUSTRUM
CLAUSULA
CLAUSULAE
CLAUSULAR
CLAUT
CLAUTED
CLAUTING
CLAUTS
CLAVATE
CLAVATED
CLAVATELY
CLAVATION
CLAVE
CLAVECIN
CLAVECINS
CLAVER
CLAVERED
CLAVERING
CLAVERS
CLAVES
CLAVI
CLAVICLE
CLAVICLES
CLAVICORN
CLAVICULA
CLAVIE
CLAVIER
CLAVIERS
CLAVIES
CLAVIFORM
CLAVIGER
CLAVIGERS
CLAVIS
CLAVULATE
CLAVUS
CLAW
CLAWBACK
CLAWBACKS
CLAWED

CLAWER
CLAWERS
CLAWING
CLAWLESS
CLAWLIKE
CLAWS
CLAXON
CLAXONS
CLAY
CLAYBANK
CLAYBANKS
CLAYED
CLAYEY
CLAYIER
CLAYIEST
CLAYING
CLAYISH
CLAYLIKE
CLAYMORE
CLAYMORES
CLAYPAN
CLAYPANS
CLAYS
CLAYSTONE
CLAYTONIA
CLAYWARE
CLAYWARES
CLEAN
CLEANABLE
CLEANED
CLEANER
CLEANERS
CLEANEST
CLEANING
CLEANINGS
CLEANLIER
CLEANLILY
CLEANLY
CLEANNESS
CLEANS
CLEANSE
CLEANSED
CLEANSER
CLEANSERS
CLEANSES
CLEANSING
CLEANSKIN
CLEANUP
CLEANUPS
CLEAR
CLEARABLE
CLEARAGE
CLEARAGES
CLEARANCE
CLEARCOLE
CLEARCUT
CLEARCUTS
CLEARED

CLEARER
CLEARERS
CLEAREST
CLEAREYED
CLEARING
CLEARINGS
CLEARLY
CLEARNESS
CLEARS
CLEARSKIN
CLEARWAY
CLEARWAYS
CLEARWEED
CLEARWING
CLEAT
CLEATED
CLEATING
CLEATS
CLEAVABLE
CLEAVAGE
CLEAVAGES
CLEAVE
CLEAVED
CLEAVER
CLEAVERS
CLEAVES
CLEAVING
CLEAVINGS
CLECHE
CLECK
CLECKED
CLECKIER
CLECKIEST
CLECKING
CLECKINGS
CLECKS
CLECKY
CLEEK
CLEEKED
CLEEKING
CLEEKIT
CLEEKS
CLEEP
CLEEPED
CLEEPING
CLEEPS
CLEEVE
CLEEVES
CLEF
CLEFS
CLEFT
CLEFTED
CLEFTING
CLEFTS
CLEG
CLEGS
CLEIDOIC
CLEIK

CLEIKS
CLEITHRAL
CLEM
CLEMATIS
CLEMENCY
CLEMENT
CLEMENTLY
CLEMMED
CLEMMING
CLEMS
CLENCH
CLENCHED
CLENCHER
CLENCHERS
CLENCHES
CLENCHING
CLEOME
CLEOMES
CLEOPATRA
CLEPE
CLEPED
CLEPES
CLEPING
CLEPSYDRA
CLEPT
CLERGIES
CLERGY
CLERGYMAN
CLERGYMEN
CLERIC
CLERICAL
CLERICALS
CLERICATE
CLERICITY
CLERICS
CLERID
CLERIDS
CLERIHEW
CLERIHEWS
CLERISIES
CLERISY
CLERK
CLERKDOM
CLERKDOMS
CLERKED
CLERKESS
CLERKING
CLERKISH
CLERKLIER
CLERKLIKE
CLERKLING
CLERKLY
CLERKS
CLERKSHIP
CLERUCH
CLERUCHIA
CLERUCHS
CLERUCHY

CLEUCH
CLEUCHS
CLEUGH
CLEUGHS
CLEVE
CLEVEITE
CLEVEITES
CLEVER
CLEVERER
CLEVEREST
CLEVERISH
CLEVERLY
CLEVES
CLEVIS
CLEVISES
CLEW
CLEWED
CLEWING
CLEWS
CLIANTHUS
CLICHE
CLICHED
CLICHEED
CLICHES
CLICK
CLICKABLE
CLICKED
CLICKER
CLICKERS
CLICKET
CLICKETED
CLICKETS
CLICKING
CLICKINGS
CLICKLESS
CLICKS
CLICKWRAP
CLIED
CLIENT
CLIENTAGE
CLIENTAL
CLIENTELE
CLIENTS
CLIES
CLIFF
CLIFFED
CLIFFHANG
CLIFFHUNG
CLIFFIER
CLIFFIEST
CLIFFLIKE
CLIFFS
CLIFFY
CLIFT
CLIFTED
CLIFTIER
CLIFTIEST
CLIFTS

CLIFTY
CLIMACTIC
CLIMATAL
CLIMATE
CLIMATED
CLIMATES
CLIMATIC
CLIMATING
CLIMATISE
CLIMATIZE
CLIMATURE
CLIMAX
CLIMAXED
CLIMAXES
CLIMAXING
CLIMB
CLIMBABLE
CLIMBDOWN
CLIMBED
CLIMBER
CLIMBERS
CLIMBING
CLIMBINGS
CLIMBS
CLIME
CLIMES
CLINAL
CLINALLY
CLINAMEN
CLINAMENS
CLINCH
CLINCHED
CLINCHER
CLINCHERS
CLINCHES
CLINCHING
CLINE
CLINES
CLING
CLINGED
CLINGER
CLINGERS
CLINGFILM
CLINGFISH
CLINGIER
CLINGIEST
CLINGING
CLINGS
CLINGY
CLINIC
CLINICAL
CLINICIAN
CLINICS
CLINIQUE
CLINIQUES
CLINK
CLINKED
CLINKER

CLINKERED
CLINKERS
CLINKING
CLINKS
CLINOAXES
CLINOAXIS
CLINOSTAT
CLINQUANT
CLINT
CLINTONIA
CLINTS
CLIP
CLIPART
CLIPARTS
CLIPBOARD
CLIPE
CLIPED
CLIPES
CLIPING
CLIPPABLE
CLIPPED
CLIPPER
CLIPPERS
CLIPPIE
CLIPPIES
CLIPPING
CLIPPINGS
CLIPS
CLIPSHEAR
CLIPSHEET
CLIPT
CLIQUE
CLIQUED
CLIQUES
CLIQUEY
CLIQUIER
CLIQUIEST
CLIQUING
CLIQUISH
CLIQUISM
CLIQUISMS
CLIQUY
CLITELLA
CLITELLAR
CLITELLUM
CLITHRAL
CLITIC
CLITICISE
CLITICIZE
CLITICS
CLITORAL
CLITORIC
CLITORIS
CLITTER
CLITTERED
CLITTERS
CLIVERS
CLIVIA

CLIVIAS
CLOACA
CLOACAE
CLOACAL
CLOACAS
CLOACINAL
CLOACITIS
CLOAK
CLOAKED
CLOAKING
CLOAKROOM
CLOAKS
CLOAM
CLOAMS
CLOBBER
CLOBBERED
CLOBBERS
CLOCHARD
CLOCHARDS
CLOCHE
CLOCHES
CLOCK
CLOCKED
CLOCKER
CLOCKERS
CLOCKING
CLOCKINGS
CLOCKLIKE
CLOCKS
CLOCKWISE
CLOCKWORK
CLOD
CLODDED
CLODDIER
CLODDIEST
CLODDING
CLODDISH
CLODDY
CLODLY
CLODPATE
CLODPATED
CLODPATES
CLODPOLE
CLODPOLES
CLODPOLL
CLODPOLLS
CLODS
CLOFF
CLOFFS
CLOG
CLOGDANCE
CLOGGED
CLOGGER
CLOGGERS
CLOGGIER
CLOGGIEST
CLOGGILY
CLOGGING

CLOGGY	CLOSEOUTS	CLOUDING	CLUB
CLOGS	CLOSER	CLOUDINGS	CLUBABLE
CLOISON	CLOSERS	CLOUDLAND	CLUBBABLE
CLOISONNE	CLOSES	CLOUDLESS	CLUBBED
CLOISONS	CLOSEST	CLOUDLET	CLUBBER
CLOISTER	CLOSET	CLOUDLETS	CLUBBERS
CLOISTERS	CLOSETED	CLOUDLIKE	CLUBBIER
CLOISTRAL	CLOSETFUL	CLOUDS	CLUBBIEST
CLOKE	CLOSETING	CLOUDTOWN	CLUBBILY
CLOKED	CLOSETS	CLOUDY	CLUBBING
CLOKES	CLOSEUP	CLOUGH	CLUBBINGS
CLOKING	CLOSEUPS	CLOUGHS	CLUBBISH
CLOMB	CLOSING	CLOUR	CLUBBISM
CLOMP	CLOSINGS	CLOURED	CLUBBISMS
CLOMPED	CLOSURE	CLOURING	CLUBBIST
CLOMPING	CLOSURED	CLOURS	CLUBBISTS
CLOMPS	CLOSURES	CLOUS	CLUBBY
CLON	CLOSURING	CLOUT	CLUBFACE
CLONAL	CLOT	CLOUTED	CLUBFACES
CLONALLY	CLOTBUR	CLOUTER	CLUBFEET
CLONE	CLOTBURS	CLOUTERLY	CLUBFOOT
CLONED	CLOTE	CLOUTERS	CLUBHAND
CLONER	CLOTES	CLOUTING	CLUBHANDS
CLONERS	CLOTH	CLOUTS	CLUBHAUL
CLONES	CLOTHE	CLOVE	CLUBHAULS
CLONIC	CLOTHED	CLOVEN	CLUBHEAD
CLONICITY	CLOTHES	CLOVEPINK	CLUBHEADS
CLONIDINE	CLOTHIER	CLOVER	CLUBHOUSE
CLONING	CLOTHIERS	CLOVERED	CLUBLAND
CLONINGS	CLOTHING	CLOVERS	CLUBLANDS
CLONISM	CLOTHINGS	CLOVERY	CLUBMAN
CLONISMS	CLOTHLIKE	CLOVES	CLUBMEN
CLONK	CLOTHS	CLOVIS	CLUBROOM
CLONKED	CLOTPOLL	CLOW	CLUBROOMS
CLONKING	CLOTPOLLS	CLOWDER	CLUBROOT
CLONKS	CLOTS	CLOWDERS	CLUBROOTS
CLONS	CLOTTED	CLOWN	CLUBRUSH
CLONUS	CLOTTER	CLOWNED	CLUBS
CLONUSES	CLOTTERED	CLOWNERY	CLUBWOMAN
CLOOP	CLOTTERS	CLOWNING	CLUBWOMEN
CLOOPS	CLOTTIER	CLOWNINGS	CLUCK
CLOOT	CLOTTIEST	CLOWNISH	CLUCKED
CLOOTS	CLOTTING	CLOWNS	CLUCKIER
CLOP	CLOTTINGS	CLOWS	CLUCKIEST
CLOPPED	CLOTTISH	CLOY	CLUCKING
CLOPPING	CLOTTY	CLOYE	CLUCKS
CLOPS	CLOTURE	CLOYED	CLUCKY
CLOQUE	CLOTURED	CLOYES	CLUDGIE
CLOQUES	CLOTURES	CLOYING	CLUDGIES
CLOSABLE	CLOTURING	CLOYINGLY	CLUE
CLOSE	CLOU	CLOYLESS	CLUED
CLOSEABLE	CLOUD	CLOYMENT	CLUEING
CLOSED	CLOUDAGE	CLOYMENTS	CLUELESS
CLOSEDOWN	CLOUDAGES	CLOYS	CLUES
CLOSEHEAD	CLOUDED	CLOYSOME	CLUING
CLOSELY	CLOUDIER	CLOZAPINE	CLUMBER
CLOSENESS	CLOUDIEST	CLOZE	CLUMBERS
CLOSEOUT	CLOUDILY	CLOZES	CLUMP

CLUMPED	CNEMIDES	COALAS	COANNEXED
CLUMPER	CNEMIS	COALBALL	COANNEXES
CLUMPERS	CNIDA	COALBALLS	COAPPEAR
CLUMPIER	CNIDAE	COALBIN	COAPPEARS
CLUMPIEST	CNIDARIAN	COALBINS	COAPT
CLUMPING	COACH	COALBOX	COAPTED
CLUMPISH	COACHABLE	COALBOXES	COAPTING
CLUMPLIKE	COACHDOG	COALED	COAPTS
CLUMPS	COACHDOGS	COALER	COARB
CLUMPY	COACHED	COALERS	COARBS
CLUMSIER	COACHEE	COALESCE	COARCTATE
CLUMSIEST	COACHEES	COALESCED	COARSE
CLUMSILY	COACHER	COALESCES	COARSELY
CLUMSY	COACHERS	COALFACE	COARSEN
CLUNCH	COACHES	COALFACES	COARSENED
CLUNCHES	COACHIES	COALFIELD	COARSENS
CLUNG	COACHING	COALFISH	COARSER
CLUNK	COACHINGS	COALHOLE	COARSEST
CLUNKED	COACHLINE	COALHOLES	COARSISH
CLUNKER	COACHLOAD	COALHOUSE	COASSIST
CLUNKERS	COACHMAN	COALIER	COASSISTS
CLUNKIER	COACHMEN	COALIEST	COASSUME
CLUNKIEST	COACHWHIP	COALIFIED	COASSUMED
CLUNKING	COACHWOOD	COALIFIES	COASSUMES
CLUNKS	COACHWORK	COALIFY	COAST
CLUNKY	COACHY	COALING	COASTAL
CLUPEID	COACT	COALISE	COASTALLY
CLUPEIDS	COACTED	COALISED	COASTED
CLUPEOID	COACTING	COALISES	COASTER
CLUPEOIDS	COACTION	COALISING	COASTERS
CLUSIA	COACTIONS	COALITION	COASTING
CLUSIAS	COACTIVE	COALIZE	COASTINGS
CLUSTER	COACTOR	COALIZED	COASTLAND
CLUSTERED	COACTORS	COALIZES	COASTLINE
CLUSTERS	COACTS	COALIZING	COASTS
CLUSTERY	COADAPTED	COALLESS	COASTWARD
CLUTCH	COADJUTOR	COALMAN	COASTWISE
CLUTCHED	COADMIRE	COALMEN	COAT
CLUTCHES	COADMIRED	COALMINE	COATDRESS
CLUTCHING	COADMIRES	COALMINER	COATE
CLUTCHY	COADMIT	COALMINES	COATED
CLUTTER	COADMITS	COALPIT	COATEE
CLUTTERED	COADUNATE	COALPITS	COATEES
CLUTTERS	COAEVAL	COALS	COATER
CLUTTERY	COAEVALS	COALSACK	COATERS
CLY	COAGENCY	COALSACKS	COATES
CLYING	COAGENT	COALSHED	COATI
CLYPE	COAGENTS	COALSHEDS	COATING
CLYPEAL	COAGULA	COALTAR	COATINGS
CLYPEATE	COAGULANT	COALTARS	COATIS
CLYPED	COAGULASE	COALY	COATLESS
CLYPEI	COAGULATE	COALYARD	COATRACK
CLYPES	COAGULUM	COALYARDS	COATRACKS
CLYPEUS	COAGULUMS	COAMING	COATROOM
CLYPING	COAITA	COAMINGS	COATROOMS
CLYSTER	COAITAS	COANCHOR	COATS
CLYSTERS	COAL	COANCHORS	COATSTAND
CNEMIAL	COALA	COANNEX	COATTAIL

COATTAILS	COBURGS	COCKADED	COCKROACH
COATTEND	COBWEB	COCKADES	COCKS
COATTENDS	COBWEBBED	COCKAMAMY	COCKSCOMB
COATTEST	COBWEBBY	COCKAPOO	COCKSFOOT
COATTESTS	COBWEBS	COCKAPOOS	COCKSHIES
COAUTHOR	COBZA	COCKATEEL	COCKSHOT
COAUTHORS	COBZAS	COCKATIEL	COCKSHOTS
COAX	COCA	COCKATOO	COCKSHUT
COAXAL	COCAIN	COCKATOOS	COCKSHUTS
COAXED	COCAINE	COCKBILL	COCKSHY
COAXER	COCAINES	COCKBILLS	COCKSIER
COAXERS	COCAINISE	COCKBIRD	COCKSIEST
COAXES	COCAINISM	COCKBIRDS	COCKSPUR
COAXIAL	COCAINIST	COCKBOAT	COCKSPURS
COAXIALLY	COCAINIZE	COCKBOATS	COCKSURE
COAXING	COCAINS	COCKCROW	COCKSWAIN
COAXINGLY	COCAPTAIN	COCKCROWS	COCKSY
COB	COCAS	COCKED	COCKTAIL
COBAEA	COCCAL	COCKER	COCKTAILS
COBAEAS	COCCI	COCKERED	COCKUP
COBALAMIN	COCCIC	COCKEREL	COCKUPS
COBALT	COCCID	COCKERELS	COCKY
COBALTIC	COCCIDIA	COCKERING	COCO
COBALTINE	COCCIDIUM	COCKERS	COCOA
COBALTITE	COCCIDS	COCKET	COCOANUT
COBALTOUS	COCCO	COCKETS	COCOANUTS
COBALTS	COCCOID	COCKEYE	COCOAS
COBB	COCCOIDAL	COCKEYED	COCOBOLA
COBBED	COCCOIDS	COCKEYES	COCOBOLAS
COBBER	COCCOLITE	COCKFIGHT	COCOBOLO
COBBERS	COCCOLITH	COCKHORSE	COCOBOLOS
COBBIER	COCCOS	COCKIER	COCOMAT
COBBIEST	COCCOUS	COCKIES	COCOMATS
COBBING	COCCUS	COCKIEST	COCONUT
COBBLE	COCCYGEAL	COCKILY	COCONUTS
COBBLED	COCCYGES	COCKINESS	COCOON
COBBLER	COCCYGIAN	COCKING	COCOONED
COBBLERS	COCCYX	COCKISH	COCOONERY
COBBLERY	COCCYXES	COCKLE	COCOONING
COBBLES	COCH	COCKLEBUR	COCOONS
COBBLING	COCHAIR	COCKLED	COCOPAN
COBBLINGS	COCHAIRED	COCKLEERT	COCOPANS
COBBS	COCHAIRS	COCKLEMAN	COCOPLUM
COBBY	COCHES	COCKLEMEN	COCOPLUMS
COBIA	COCHIN	COCKLER	COCOS
COBIAS	COCHINEAL	COCKLERS	COCOTTE
COBLE	COCHINS	COCKLES	COCOTTES
COBLES	COCHLEA	COCKLIKE	COCOUNSEL
COBLOAF	COCHLEAE	COCKLING	COCOYAM
COBLOAVES	COCHLEAR	COCKLOFT	COCOYAMS
COBNUT	COCHLEARE	COCKLOFTS	COCOZELLE
COBNUTS	COCHLEARS	COCKMATCH	COCREATE
COBRA	COCHLEAS	COCKNEY	COCREATED
COBRAS	COCHLEATE	COCKNEYFY	COCREATES
COBRIC	COCINERA	COCKNEYS	COCREATOR
COBRIFORM	COCINERAS	COCKNIFY	COCTILE
COBS	COCK	COCKPIT	COCTION
COBURG	COCKADE	COCKPITS	COCTIONS

COCULTURE	CODICILS	COEMBODY	COEVOLVES
COCURATOR	CODIFIED	COEMPLOY	COEXERT
COCUSWOOD	CODIFIER	COEMPLOYS	COEXERTED
COD	CODIFIERS	COEMPT	COEXERTS
CODA	CODIFIES	COEMPTED	COEXIST
CODABLE	CODIFY	COEMPTING	COEXISTED
CODAS	CODIFYING	COEMPTION	COEXISTS
CODDED	CODILLA	COEMPTS	COEXTEND
CODDER	CODILLAS	COENACLE	COEXTENDS
CODDERS	CODILLE	COENACLES	COFACTOR
CODDING	CODILLES	COENACT	COFACTORS
CODDLE	CODING	COENACTED	COFEATURE
CODDLED	CODINGS	COENACTS	COFF
CODDLER	CODIRECT	COENAMOR	COFFED
CODDLERS	CODIRECTS	COENAMORS	COFFEE
CODDLES	CODIST	COENDURE	COFFEEPOT
CODDLING	CODISTS	COENDURED	COFFEES
CODE	CODLIN	COENDURES	COFFER
CODEBOOK	CODLING	COENOBIA	COFFERDAM
CODEBOOKS	CODLINGS	COENOBITE	COFFERED
CODEBTOR	CODLINS	COENOBIUM	COFFERING
CODEBTORS	CODOLOGY	COENOCYTE	COFFERS
CODEC	CODOMAIN	COENOSARC	COFFIN
CODECS	CODOMAINS	COENURE	COFFINED
CODED	CODON	COENURES	COFFING
CODEIA	CODONS	COENURI	COFFINING
CODEIAS	CODPIECE	COENURUS	COFFINITE
CODEIN	CODPIECES	COENZYME	COFFINS
CODEINA	CODRIVE	COENZYMES	COFFLE
CODEINAS	CODRIVEN	COEQUAL	COFFLED
CODEINE	CODRIVER	COEQUALLY	COFFLES
CODEINES	CODRIVERS	COEQUALS	COFFLING
CODEINS	CODRIVES	COEQUATE	COFFRET
CODELESS	CODRIVING	COEQUATED	COFFRETS
CODEN	CODROVE	COEQUATES	COFFS
CODENAME	CODS	COERCE	COFINANCE
CODENAMES	COED	COERCED	COFOUND
CODENS	COEDIT	COERCER	COFOUNDED
CODER	COEDITED	COERCERS	COFOUNDER
CODERIVE	COEDITING	COERCES	COFOUNDS
CODERIVED	COEDITOR	COERCIBLE	COFT
CODERIVES	COEDITORS	COERCIBLY	COG
CODERS	COEDITS	COERCING	COGENCE
CODES	COEDS	COERCION	COGENCES
CODESIGN	COEFFECT	COERCIONS	COGENCIES
CODESIGNS	COEFFECTS	COERCIVE	COGENCY
CODETTA	COEHORN	COERECT	COGENER
CODETTAS	COEHORNS	COERECTED	COGENERS
CODEVELOP	COELIAC	COERECTS	COGENT
CODEWORD	COELIACS	COESITE	COGENTLY
CODEWORDS	COELOM	COESITES	COGGED
CODEX	COELOMATA	COETERNAL	COGGER
CODFISH	COELOMATE	COEVAL	COGGERS
CODFISHES	COELOME	COEVALITY	COGGIE
CODGER	COELOMES	COEVALLY	COGGIES
CODGERS	COELOMIC	COEVALS	COGGING
CODICES	COELOMS	COEVOLVE	COGGINGS
CODICIL	COELOSTAT	COEVOLVED	COGGLE

COGGLED	COHABITER	COIFFES	COISTRILS
COGGLES	COHABITOR	COIFFEUR	COIT
COGGLIER	COHABITS	COIFFEURS	COITAL
COGGLIEST	COHABS	COIFFEUSE	COITALLY
COGGLING	COHEAD	COIFFING	COITION
COGGLY	COHEADED	COIFFURE	COITIONAL
COGIE	COHEADING	COIFFURED	COITIONS
COGIES	COHEADS	COIFFURES	COITS
COGITABLE	COHEIR	COIFING	COITUS
COGITATE	COHEIRESS	COIFS	COITUSES
COGITATED	COHEIRS	COIGN	COJOIN
COGITATES	COHERE	COIGNE	COJOINED
COGITATOR	COHERED	COIGNED	COJOINING
COGITO	COHERENCE	COIGNES	COJOINS
COGITOS	COHERENCY	COIGNING	COJONES
COGNAC	COHERENT	COIGNS	COKE
COGNACS	COHERER	COIL	COKED
COGNATE	COHERERS	COILED	COKEHEAD
COGNATELY	COHERES	COILER	COKEHEADS
COGNATES	COHERING	COILERS	COKELIKE
COGNATION	COHERITOR	COILING	COKERNUT
COGNISANT	COHESIBLE	COILS	COKERNUTS
COGNISE	COHESION	COIN	COKES
COGNISED	COHESIONS	COINABLE	COKESES
COGNISER	COHESIVE	COINAGE	COKIER
COGNISERS	COHIBIT	COINAGES	COKIEST
COGNISES	COHIBITED	COINCIDE	COKING
COGNISING	COHIBITS	COINCIDED	COKULORIS
COGNITION	COHO	COINCIDES	COKY
COGNITIVE	COHOBATE	COINED	COL
COGNIZANT	COHOBATED	COINER	COLA
COGNIZE	COHOBATES	COINERS	COLANDER
COGNIZED	COHOE	COINFECT	COLANDERS
COGNIZER	COHOES	COINFECTS	COLAS
COGNIZERS	COHOG	COINFER	COLBIES
COGNIZES	COHOGS	COINFERS	COLBY
COGNIZING	COHOLDER	COINHERE	COLBYS
COGNOMEN	COHOLDERS	COINHERED	COLCANNON
COGNOMENS	COHORN	COINHERES	COLCHICA
COGNOMINA	COHORNS	COINING	COLCHICUM
COGNOSCE	COHORT	COININGS	COLCOTHAR
COGNOSCED	COHORTS	COINMATE	COLD
COGNOSCES	COHOS	COINMATES	COLDBLOOD
COGNOVIT	COHOSH	COINS	COLDCOCK
COGNOVITS	COHOSHES	COINSURE	COLDCOCKS
COGON	COHOST	COINSURED	COLDER
COGONS	COHOSTED	COINSURER	COLDEST
COGS	COHOSTESS	COINSURES	COLDHOUSE
COGUE	COHOSTING	COINTER	COLDIE
COGUES	COHOSTS	COINTERS	COLDIES
COGWAY	COHOUSING	COINTREAU	COLDISH
COGWAYS	COHUNE	COINVENT	COLDLY
COGWHEEL	COHUNES	COINVENTS	COLDNESS
COGWHEELS	COHYPONYM	COIR	COLDS
COHAB	COIF	COIRS	COLE
COHABIT	COIFED	COISTREL	COLEAD
COHABITED	COIFFE	COISTRELS	COLEADER
COHABITEE	COIFFED	COISTRIL	COLEADERS

COLEADING	COLLAPSED	COLLINSIA	COLONES
COLEADS	COLLAPSES	COLLISION	COLONI
COLECTOMY	COLLAR	COLLOCATE	COLONIAL
COLED	COLLARD	COLLODION	COLONIALS
COLEOPTER	COLLARDS	COLLODIUM	COLONIC
COLES	COLLARED	COLLOGUE	COLONICS
COLESEED	COLLARET	COLLOGUED	COLONIES
COLESEEDS	COLLARETS	COLLOGUES	COLONISE
COLESLAW	COLLARING	COLLOID	COLONISED
COLESLAWS	COLLARS	COLLOIDAL	COLONISER
COLESSEE	COLLATE	COLLOIDS	COLONISES
COLESSEES	COLLATED	COLLOP	COLONIST
COLESSOR	COLLATES	COLLOPS	COLONISTS
COLESSORS	COLLATING	COLLOQUE	COLONITIS
COLETIT	COLLATION	COLLOQUED	COLONIZE
COLETITS	COLLATIVE	COLLOQUES	COLONIZED
COLEUS	COLLATOR	COLLOQUIA	COLONIZER
COLEUSES	COLLATORS	COLLOQUY	COLONIZES
COLEWORT	COLLEAGUE	COLLOTYPE	COLONNADE
COLEWORTS	COLLECT	COLLOTYPY	COLONS
COLEY	COLLECTED	COLLS	COLONUS
COLEYS	COLLECTOR	COLLUDE	COLONY
COLIBRI	COLLECTS	COLLUDED	COLOPHON
COLIBRIS	COLLED	COLLUDER	COLOPHONS
COLIC	COLLEEN	COLLUDERS	COLOPHONY
COLICIN	COLLEENS	COLLUDES	COLOR
COLICINE	COLLEGE	COLLUDING	COLORABLE
COLICINES	COLLEGER	COLLUSION	COLORABLY
COLICINS	COLLEGERS	COLLUSIVE	COLORADO
COLICKIER	COLLEGES	COLLUVIA	COLORANT
COLICKY	COLLEGIA	COLLUVIAL	COLORANTS
COLICROOT	COLLEGIAL	COLLUVIES	COLORBRED
COLICS	COLLEGIAN	COLLUVIUM	COLORCAST
COLICWEED	COLLEGIUM	COLLY	COLORED
COLIES	COLLET	COLLYING	COLOREDS
COLIFORM	COLLETED	COLLYRIA	COLORER
COLIFORMS	COLLETING	COLLYRIUM	COLORERS
COLIN	COLLETS	COLOBI	COLORFAST
COLINEAR	COLLICULI	COLOBID	COLORFUL
COLINS	COLLIDE	COLOBOMA	COLORIFIC
COLIPHAGE	COLLIDED	COLOBOMAS	COLORING
COLISEUM	COLLIDER	COLOBUS	COLORINGS
COLISEUMS	COLLIDERS	COLOBUSES	COLORISE
COLISTIN	COLLIDES	COLOCATE	COLORISED
COLISTINS	COLLIDING	COLOCATED	COLORISER
COLITIC	COLLIE	COLOCATES	COLORISES
COLITIS	COLLIED	COLOCYNTH	COLORISM
COLITISES	COLLIER	COLOG	COLORISMS
COLL	COLLIERS	COLOGNE	COLORIST
COLLAGE	COLLIERY	COLOGNED	COLORISTS
COLLAGED	COLLIES	COLOGNES	COLORIZE
COLLAGEN	COLLIGATE	COLOGS	COLORIZED
COLLAGENS	COLLIMATE	COLOMBARD	COLORIZER
COLLAGES	COLLINEAR	COLON	COLORIZES
COLLAGING	COLLING	COLONE	COLORLESS
COLLAGIST	COLLINGS	COLONEL	COLORMAN
COLLAPSAR	COLLINS	COLONELCY	COLORMEN
COLLAPSE	COLLINSES	COLONELS	COLORS

COLORWAY	COLUMELLA	COMBIER	COMETHER
COLORWAYS	COLUMELS	COMBIES	COMETHERS
COLORY	COLUMN	COMBIEST	COMETIC
COLOSSAL	COLUMNAL	COMBINATE	COMETS
COLOSSEUM	COLUMNAR	COMBINE	COMFIER
COLOSSI	COLUMNEA	COMBINED	COMFIEST
COLOSSUS	COLUMNEAS	COMBINEDS	COMFINESS
COLOSTOMY	COLUMNED	COMBINER	COMFIT
COLOSTRAL	COLUMNIST	COMBINERS	COMFITS
COLOSTRIC	COLUMNS	COMBINES	COMFITURE
COLOSTRUM	COLURE	COMBING	COMFORT
COLOTOMY	COLURES	COMBINGS	COMFORTED
COLOUR	COLY	COMBINING	COMFORTER
COLOURANT	COLZA	COMBIS	COMFORTS
COLOURED	COLZAS	COMBLE	COMFREY
COLOUREDS	COMA	COMBLES	COMFREYS
COLOURER	COMADE	COMBLESS	COMFY
COLOURERS	COMAE	COMBLIKE	COMIC
COLOURFUL	COMAKE	COMBO	COMICAL
COLOURING	COMAKER	COMBOS	COMICALLY
COLOURISE	COMAKERS	COMBRETUM	COMICE
COLOURIST	COMAKES	COMBS	COMICES
COLOURIZE	COMAKING	COMBUST	COMICS
COLOURMAN	COMAL	COMBUSTED	COMING
COLOURMEN	COMANAGE	COMBUSTOR	COMINGLE
COLOURS	COMANAGED	COMBUSTS	COMINGLED
COLOURWAY	COMANAGER	COMBWISE	COMINGLES
COLOURY	COMANAGES	COMBY	COMINGS
COLPITIS	COMARB	COME	COMIQUE
COLPOTOMY	COMARBS	COMEBACK	COMIQUES
COLS	COMART	COMEBACKS	COMITADJI
COLT	COMARTS	COMEDDLE	COMITAL
COLTAN	COMAS	COMEDDLED	COMITATUS
COLTANS	COMATE	COMEDDLES	COMITIA
COLTED	COMATES	COMEDIAN	COMITIAL
COLTER	COMATIC	COMEDIANS	COMITIAS
COLTERS	COMATIK	COMEDIC	COMITIES
COLTING	COMATIKS	COMEDIES	COMITY
COLTISH	COMATOSE	COMEDO	COMIX
COLTISHLY	COMATULA	COMEDONES	COMM
COLTS	COMATULAE	COMEDOS	COMMA
COLTSFOOT	COMATULID	COMEDOWN	COMMAND
COLTWOOD	COMB	COMEDOWNS	COMMANDED
COLTWOODS	COMBAT	COMEDY	COMMANDER
COLUBRIAD	COMBATANT	COMELIER	COMMANDO
COLUBRID	COMBATED	COMELIEST	COMMANDOS
COLUBRIDS	COMBATER	COMELILY	COMMANDS
COLUBRINE	COMBATERS	COMELY	COMMAS
COLUGO	COMBATING	COMEMBER	COMMATA
COLUGOS	COMBATIVE	COMEMBERS	COMMENCE
COLUMBARY	COMBATS	COMEOVER	COMMENCED
COLUMBATE	COMBATTED	COMEOVERS	COMMENCER
COLUMBIC	COMBE	COMER	COMMENCES
COLUMBINE	COMBED	COMERS	COMMEND
COLUMBITE	COMBER	COMES	COMMENDAM
COLUMBIUM	COMBERS	COMET	COMMENDED
COLUMBOUS	COMBES	COMETARY	COMMENDER
COLUMEL	COMBI	COMETH	COMMENDS

COMMENSAL
COMMENT
COMMENTED
COMMENTER
COMMENTOR
COMMENTS
COMMER
COMMERCE
COMMERCED
COMMERCES
COMMERE
COMMERES
COMMERGE
COMMERGED
COMMERGES
COMMERS
COMMIE
COMMIES
COMMINATE
COMMINGLE
COMMINUTE
COMMIS
COMMISSAR
COMMIT
COMMITS
COMMITTAL
COMMITTED
COMMITTEE
COMMITTER
COMMIX
COMMIXED
COMMIXES
COMMIXING
COMMIXT
COMMO
COMMODE
COMMODES
COMMODIFY
COMMODITY
COMMODO
COMMODORE
COMMON
COMMONAGE
COMMONED
COMMONER
COMMONERS
COMMONEST
COMMONEY
COMMONEYS
COMMONING
COMMONLY
COMMONS
COMMORANT
COMMOS
COMMOT
COMMOTE
COMMOTES
COMMOTION

COMMOTS
COMMOVE
COMMOVED
COMMOVES
COMMOVING
COMMS
COMMUNAL
COMMUNARD
COMMUNE
COMMUNED
COMMUNER
COMMUNERS
COMMUNES
COMMUNING
COMMUNION
COMMUNISE
COMMUNISM
COMMUNIST
COMMUNITY
COMMUNIZE
COMMUTATE
COMMUTE
COMMUTED
COMMUTER
COMMUTERS
COMMUTES
COMMUTING
COMMUTUAL
COMMY
COMODO
COMONOMER
COMORBID
COMOSE
COMOUS
COMP
COMPACT
COMPACTED
COMPACTER
COMPACTLY
COMPACTOR
COMPACTS
COMPADRE
COMPADRES
COMPAGE
COMPAGES
COMPAND
COMPANDED
COMPANDER
COMPANDOR
COMPANDS
COMPANIED
COMPANIES
COMPANING
COMPANION
COMPANY
COMPARE
COMPARED
COMPARER

COMPARERS
COMPARES
COMPARING
COMPART
COMPARTED
COMPARTS
COMPAS
COMPASS
COMPASSED
COMPASSES
COMPAST
COMPEAR
COMPEARED
COMPEARS
COMPED
COMPEER
COMPEERED
COMPEERS
COMPEL
COMPELLED
COMPELLER
COMPELS
COMPEND
COMPENDIA
COMPENDS
COMPER
COMPERE
COMPERED
COMPERES
COMPERING
COMPERS
COMPESCE
COMPESCED
COMPESCES
COMPETE
COMPETED
COMPETENT
COMPETES
COMPETING
COMPILE
COMPILED
COMPILER
COMPILERS
COMPILES
COMPILING
COMPING
COMPINGS
COMPITAL
COMPLAIN
COMPLAINS
COMPLAINT
COMPLEAT
COMPLECT
COMPLECTS
COMPLETE
COMPLETED
COMPLETER
COMPLETES

COMPLEX
COMPLEXED
COMPLEXER
COMPLEXES
COMPLEXLY
COMPLEXUS
COMPLIANT
COMPLICE
COMPLICES
COMPLICIT
COMPLIED
COMPLIER
COMPLIERS
COMPLIES
COMPLIN
COMPLINE
COMPLINES
COMPLINS
COMPLISH
COMPLOT
COMPLOTS
COMPLUVIA
COMPLY
COMPLYING
COMPO
COMPONE
COMPONENT
COMPONY
COMPORT
COMPORTED
COMPORTS
COMPOS
COMPOSE
COMPOSED
COMPOSER
COMPOSERS
COMPOSES
COMPOSING
COMPOSITE
COMPOST
COMPOSTED
COMPOSTER
COMPOSTS
COMPOSURE
COMPOT
COMPOTE
COMPOTES
COMPOTIER
COMPOTS
COMPOUND
COMPOUNDS
COMPRADOR
COMPRESS
COMPRINT
COMPRINTS
COMPRISAL
COMPRISE
COMPRISED

COMPRISES	CONCEALER	CONCISE	CONDIES
COMPRIZE	CONCEALS	CONCISED	CONDIGN
COMPRIZED	CONCEDE	CONCISELY	CONDIGNLY
COMPRIZES	CONCEDED	CONCISER	CONDIMENT
COMPS	CONCEDER	CONCISES	CONDITION
COMPT	CONCEDERS	CONCISEST	CONDO
COMPTABLE	CONCEDES	CONCISING	CONDOES
COMPTED	CONCEDING	CONCISION	CONDOLE
COMPTER	CONCEDO	CONCLAVE	CONDOLED
COMPTERS	CONCEIT	CONCLAVES	CONDOLENT
COMPTIBLE	CONCEITED	CONCLUDE	CONDOLER
COMPTING	CONCEITS	CONCLUDED	CONDOLERS
COMPTROLL	CONCEITY	CONCLUDER	CONDOLES
COMPTS	CONCEIVE	CONCLUDES	CONDOLING
COMPULSE	CONCEIVED	CONCOCT	CONDOM
COMPULSED	CONCEIVER	CONCOCTED	CONDOMS
COMPULSES	CONCEIVES	CONCOCTER	CONDONE
COMPUTANT	CONCENT	CONCOCTOR	CONDONED
COMPUTE	CONCENTER	CONCOCTS	CONDONER
COMPUTED	CONCENTRE	CONCOLOR	CONDONERS
COMPUTER	CONCENTS	CONCORD	CONDONES
COMPUTERS	CONCENTUS	CONCORDAL	CONDONING
COMPUTES	CONCEPT	CONCORDAT	CONDOR
COMPUTING	CONCEPTI	CONCORDED	CONDORES
COMPUTIST	CONCEPTS	CONCORDS	CONDORS
COMRADE	CONCEPTUS	CONCOURS	CONDOS
COMRADELY	CONCERN	CONCOURSE	CONDUCE
COMRADERY	CONCERNED	CONCREATE	CONDUCED
COMRADES	CONCERNS	CONCRETE	CONDUCER
COMS	CONCERT	CONCRETED	CONDUCERS
COMSYMP	CONCERTED	CONCRETES	CONDUCES
COMSYMPS	CONCERTI	CONCREW	CONDUCING
COMTE	CONCERTO	CONCREWED	CONDUCIVE
COMTES	CONCERTOS	CONCREWS	CONDUCT
COMUS	CONCERTS	CONCUBINE	CONDUCTED
COMUSES	CONCETTI	CONCUPIES	CONDUCTI
CON	CONCETTO	CONCUPY	CONDUCTOR
CONACRE	CONCH	CONCUR	CONDUCTS
CONACRED	CONCHA	CONCURRED	CONDUCTUS
CONACRES	CONCHAE	CONCURS	CONDUIT
CONACRING	CONCHAL	CONCUSS	CONDUITS
CONARIA	CONCHAS	CONCUSSED	CONDYLAR
CONARIAL	CONCHATE	CONCUSSES	CONDYLE
CONARIUM	CONCHE	CONCYCLIC	CONDYLES
CONATION	CONCHED	COND	CONDYLOID
CONATIONS	CONCHES	CONDEMN	CONDYLOMA
CONATIVE	CONCHIE	CONDEMNED	CONE
CONATUS	CONCHIES	CONDEMNER	CONED
CONCAUSE	CONCHING	CONDEMNOR	CONELRAD
CONCAUSES	CONCHITIS	CONDEMNS	CONELRADS
CONCAVE	CONCHO	CONDENSE	CONENOSE
CONCAVED	CONCHOID	CONDENSED	CONENOSES
CONCAVELY	CONCHOIDS	CONDENSER	CONEPATE
CONCAVES	CONCHOS	CONDENSES	CONEPATES
CONCAVING	CONCHS	CONDER	CONEPATL
CONCAVITY	CONCHY	CONDERS	CONEPATLS
CONCEAL	CONCIERGE	CONDIDDLE	CONES
CONCEALED	CONCILIAR	CONDIE	CONEY

CONEYS	CONFLATE	CONGESTED	CONIUMS
CONF	CONFLATED	CONGESTS	CONJECT
CONFAB	CONFLATES	CONGIARY	CONJECTED
CONFABBED	CONFLICT	CONGII	CONJECTS
CONFABS	CONFLICTS	CONGIUS	CONJEE
CONFECT	CONFLUENT	CONGLOBE	CONJEED
CONFECTED	CONFLUX	CONGLOBED	CONJEEING
CONFECTS	CONFLUXES	CONGLOBES	CONJEES
CONFER	CONFOCAL	CONGO	CONJOIN
CONFEREE	CONFORM	CONGOES	CONJOINED
CONFEREES	CONFORMAL	CONGOS	CONJOINER
CONFERRAL	CONFORMED	CONGOU	CONJOINS
CONFERRED	CONFORMER	CONGOUS	CONJOINT
CONFERREE	CONFORMS	CONGRATS	CONJUGAL
CONFERRER	CONFOUND	CONGREE	CONJUGANT
CONFERS	CONFOUNDS	CONGREED	CONJUGATE
CONFERVA	CONFRERE	CONGREES	CONJUNCT
CONFERVAE	CONFRERES	CONGREET	CONJUNCTS
CONFERVAL	CONFRERIE	CONGREETS	CONJUNTO
CONFERVAS	CONFRONT	CONGRESS	CONJUNTOS
CONFESS	CONFRONTE	CONGRUE	CONJURE
CONFESSED	CONFRONTS	CONGRUED	CONJURED
CONFESSES	CONFS	CONGRUENT	CONJURER
CONFESSOR	CONFUSE	CONGRUES	CONJURERS
CONFEST	CONFUSED	CONGRUING	CONJURES
CONFESTLY	CONFUSES	CONGRUITY	CONJURIES
CONFETTI	CONFUSING	CONGRUOUS	CONJURING
CONFETTO	CONFUSION	CONI	CONJUROR
CONFIDANT	CONFUTE	CONIA	CONJURORS
CONFIDE	CONFUTED	CONIAS	CONJURY
CONFIDED	CONFUTER	CONIC	CONK
CONFIDENT	CONFUTERS	CONICAL	CONKED
CONFIDER	CONFUTES	CONICALLY	CONKER
CONFIDERS	CONFUTING	CONICINE	CONKERS
CONFIDES	CONGA	CONICINES	CONKIER
CONFIDING	CONGAED	CONICITY	CONKIEST
CONFIGURE	CONGAING	CONICS	CONKING
CONFINE	CONGAS	CONIDIA	CONKS
CONFINED	CONGE	CONIDIAL	CONKY
CONFINER	CONGEAL	CONIDIAN	CONN
CONFINERS	CONGEALED	CONIDIUM	CONNATE
CONFINES	CONGEALER	CONIES	CONNATELY
CONFINING	CONGEALS	CONIFER	CONNATION
CONFIRM	CONGED	CONIFERS	CONNATURE
CONFIRMED	CONGEE	CONIFORM	CONNE
CONFIRMEE	CONGEED	CONIINE	CONNECT
CONFIRMER	CONGEEING	CONIINES	CONNECTED
CONFIRMOR	CONGEES	CONIMA	CONNECTER
CONFIRMS	CONGEING	CONIMAS	CONNECTOR
CONFISEUR	CONGENER	CONIN	CONNECTS
CONFIT	CONGENERS	CONINE	CONNED
CONFITEOR	CONGENIAL	CONINES	CONNER
CONFITS	CONGENIC	CONING	CONNERS
CONFITURE	CONGER	CONINS	CONNES
CONFIX	CONGERIES	CONIOLOGY	CONNEXION
CONFIXED	CONGERS	CONIOSES	CONNEXIVE
CONFIXES	CONGES	CONIOSIS	CONNING
CONFIXING	CONGEST	CONIUM	CONNINGS·

CONNIVE	CONSISTS	CONSUMED	CONTINUE
CONNIVED	CONSOCIES	CONSUMER	CONTINUED
CONNIVENT	CONSOL	CONSUMERS	CONTINUER
CONNIVER	CONSOLATE	CONSUMES	CONTINUES
CONNIVERS	CONSOLE	CONSUMING	CONTINUO
CONNIVERY	CONSOLED	CONSUMPT	CONTINUOS
CONNIVES	CONSOLER	CONSUMPTS	CONTINUUM
CONNIVING	CONSOLERS	CONTACT	CONTLINE
CONNOTATE	CONSOLES	CONTACTED	CONTLINES
CONNOTE	CONSOLING	CONTACTEE	CONTO
CONNOTED	CONSOLS	CONTACTOR	CONTORNO
CONNOTES	CONSOLUTE	CONTACTS	CONTORNOS
CONNOTING	CONSOMME	CONTADINA	CONTORT
CONNOTIVE	CONSOMMES	CONTADINE	CONTORTED
CONNS	CONSONANT	CONTADINI	CONTORTS
CONNUBIAL	CONSONOUS	CONTADINO	CONTOS
CONODONT	CONSORT	CONTAGIA	CONTOUR
CONODONTS	CONSORTED	CONTAGION	CONTOURED
CONOID	CONSORTER	CONTAGIUM	CONTOURS
CONOIDAL	CONSORTIA	CONTAIN	CONTRA
CONOIDIC	CONSORTS	CONTAINED	CONTRACT
CONOIDS	CONSPIRE	CONTAINER	CONTRACTS
CONOMINEE	CONSPIRED	CONTAINS	CONTRAIL
CONQUER	CONSPIRER	CONTANGO	CONTRAILS
CONQUERED	CONSPIRES	CONTANGOS	CONTRAIR
CONQUERER	CONSTABLE	CONTE	CONTRALTI
CONQUEROR	CONSTANCY	CONTECK	CONTRALTO
CONQUERS	CONSTANT	CONTECKS	CONTRARY
CONQUEST	CONSTANTS	CONTEMN	CONTRAS
CONQUESTS	CONSTATE	CONTEMNED	CONTRAST
CONQUIAN	CONSTATED	CONTEMNER	CONTRASTS
CONQUIANS	CONSTATES	CONTEMNOR	CONTRASTY
CONS	CONSTER	CONTEMNS	CONTRAT
CONSCIENT	CONSTERED	CONTEMPER	CONTRATE
CONSCIOUS	CONSTERS	CONTEMPO	CONTRATS
CONSCRIBE	CONSTRAIN	CONTEMPT	CONTRIST
CONSCRIPT	CONSTRICT	CONTEMPTS	CONTRISTS
CONSEIL	CONSTRUAL	CONTEND	CONTRITE
CONSEILS	CONSTRUCT	CONTENDED	CONTRIVE
CONSENSUS	CONSTRUE	CONTENDER	CONTRIVED
CONSENT	CONSTRUED	CONTENDS	CONTRIVER
CONSENTED	CONSTRUER	CONTENT	CONTRIVES
CONSENTER	CONSTRUES	CONTENTED	CONTROL
CONSENTS	CONSUL	CONTENTLY	CONTROLE
CONSERVE	CONSULAGE	CONTENTS	CONTROLS
CONSERVED	CONSULAR	CONTES	CONTROUL
CONSERVER	CONSULARS	CONTESSA	CONTROULS
CONSERVES	CONSULATE	CONTESSAS	CONTUMACY
CONSIDER	CONSULS	CONTEST	CONTUMELY
CONSIDERS	CONSULT	CONTESTED	CONTUND
CONSIGN	CONSULTA	CONTESTER	CONTUNDED
CONSIGNED	CONSULTAS	CONTESTS	CONTUNDS
CONSIGNEE	CONSULTED	CONTEXT	CONTUSE
CONSIGNER	CONSULTEE	CONTEXTS	CONTUSED
CONSIGNOR	CONSULTER	CONTICENT	CONTUSES
CONSIGNS	CONSULTOR	CONTINENT	CONTUSING
CONSIST	CONSULTS	CONTINUA	CONTUSION
CONSISTED	CONSUME	CONTINUAL	CONTUSIVE

CONUNDRUM	CONVINCES	COOKHOUSE	COOMED
CONURBAN	CONVIVE	COOKIE	COOMIER
CONURBIA	CONVIVED	COOKIES	COOMIEST
CONURBIAS	CONVIVES	COOKING	COOMING
CONURE	CONVIVIAL	COOKINGS	COOMS
CONURES	CONVIVING	COOKLESS	COOMY
CONUS	CONVO	COOKMAID	COON
CONVECT	CONVOCATE	COOKMAIDS	COONCAN
CONVECTED	CONVOKE	COOKOFF	COONCANS
CONVECTOR	CONVOKED	COOKOFFS	COONDOG
CONVECTS	CONVOKER	COOKOUT	COONDOGS
CONVENE	CONVOKERS	COOKOUTS	COONHOUND
CONVENED	CONVOKES	COOKROOM	COONS
CONVENER	CONVOKING	COOKROOMS	COONSKIN
CONVENERS	CONVOLUTE	COOKS	COONSKINS
CONVENES	CONVOLVE	COOKSHACK	COONTIE
CONVENING	CONVOLVED	COOKSHOP	COONTIES
CONVENOR	CONVOLVES	COOKSHOPS	COONTY
CONVENORS	CONVOS	COOKSTOVE	COOP
CONVENT	CONVOY	COOKTOP	COOPED
CONVENTED	CONVOYED	COOKTOPS	COOPER
CONVENTS	CONVOYING	COOKWARE	COOPERAGE
CONVERGE	CONVOYS	COOKWARES	COOPERATE
CONVERGED	CONVULSE	COOKY	COOPERED
CONVERGES	CONVULSED	COOL	COOPERIES
CONVERSE	CONVULSES	COOLABAH	COOPERING
CONVERSED	CONY	COOLABAHS	COOPERS
CONVERSER	COO	COOLAMON	COOPERY
CONVERSES	COOCH	COOLAMONS	COOPING
CONVERSO	COOCHES	COOLANT	COOPS
CONVERSOS	COOCOO	COOLANTS	COOPT
CONVERT	COOED	COOLDOWN	COOPTED
CONVERTED	COOEE	COOLDOWNS	COOPTING
CONVERTER	COOEED	COOLED	COOPTION
CONVERTOR	COOEEING	COOLER	COOPTIONS
CONVERTS	COOEES	COOLERS	COOPTS
CONVEX	COOER	COOLEST	COORDINAL
CONVEXED	COOERS	COOLHOUSE	COORIE
CONVEXES	COOEY	COOLIBAH	COORIED
CONVEXING	COOEYED	COOLIBAHS	COORIEING
CONVEXITY	COOEYING	COOLIBAR	COORIES
CONVEXLY	COOEYS	COOLIBARS	COOS
CONVEY	COOF	COOLIE	COOSEN
CONVEYAL	COOFS	COOLIES	COOSENED
CONVEYALS	COOING	COOLING	COOSENING
CONVEYED	COOINGLY	COOLINGLY	COOSENS
CONVEYER	COOINGS	COOLISH	COOSER
CONVEYERS	COOK	COOLLY	COOSERS
CONVEYING	COOKABLE	COOLNESS	COOSIN
CONVEYOR	COOKBOOK	COOLS	COOSINED
CONVEYORS	COOKBOOKS	COOLTH	COOSINING
CONVEYS	COOKED	COOLTHS	COOSINS
CONVICT	COOKER	COOLY	COOST
CONVICTED	COOKERIES	COOM	COOT
CONVICTS	COOKERS	COOMB	COOTCH
CONVINCE	COOKERY	COOMBE	COOTCHED
CONVINCED	COOKEY	COOMBES	COOTCHES
CONVINCER	COOKEYS	COOMBS	COOTCHING

COOTER
COOTERS
COOTIE
COOTIES
COOTIKIN
COOTIKINS
COOTS
COOZE
COOZES
COP
COPACETIC
COPAIBA
COPAIBAS
COPAIVA
COPAIVAS
COPAL
COPALM
COPALMS
COPALS
COPARCENY
COPARENT
COPARENTS
COPARTNER
COPASETIC
COPASTOR
COPASTORS
COPATAINE
COPATRIOT
COPATRON
COPATRONS
COPAY
COPAYMENT
COPAYS
COPE
COPECK
COPECKS
COPED
COPEMATE
COPEMATES
COPEN
COPENS
COPEPOD
COPEPODS
COPER
COPERED
COPERING
COPERS
COPES
COPESETIC
COPESTONE
COPIED
COPIER
COPIERS
COPIES
COPIHUE
COPIHUES
COPILOT
COPILOTS

COPING
COPINGS
COPIOUS
COPIOUSLY
COPITA
COPITAS
COPLANAR
COPLOT
COPLOTS
COPLOTTED
COPOLYMER
COPOUT
COPOUTS
COPPED
COPPER
COPPERAH
COPPERAHS
COPPERAS
COPPERED
COPPERING
COPPERISH
COPPERS
COPPERY
COPPICE
COPPICED
COPPICES
COPPICING
COPPIES
COPPIN
COPPING
COPPINS
COPPLE
COPPLES
COPPRA
COPPRAS
COPPY
COPRA
COPRAH
COPRAHS
COPRAS
COPREMIA
COPREMIAS
COPREMIC
COPRESENT
COPRINCE
COPRINCES
COPRODUCE
COPRODUCT
COPROLITE
COPROLITH
COPROLOGY
COPROSMA
COPROSMAS
COPROZOIC
COPS
COPSE
COPSED
COPSES

COPSEWOOD
COPSHOP
COPSHOPS
COPSIER
COPSIEST
COPSING
COPSY
COPTER
COPTERS
COPUBLISH
COPULA
COPULAE
COPULAR
COPULAS
COPULATE
COPULATED
COPULATES
COPURIFY
COPY
COPYABLE
COPYBOOK
COPYBOOKS
COPYBOY
COPYBOYS
COPYCAT
COPYCATS
COPYDESK
COPYDESKS
COPYEDIT
COPYEDITS
COPYGIRL
COPYGIRLS
COPYGRAPH
COPYHOLD
COPYHOLDS
COPYING
COPYISM
COPYISMS
COPYIST
COPYISTS
COPYLEFT
COPYLEFTS
COPYREAD
COPYREADS
COPYRIGHT
COPYTAKER
COQUET
COQUETRY
COQUETS
COQUETTE
COQUETTED
COQUETTES
COQUILLA
COQUILLAS
COQUILLE
COQUILLES
COQUINA
COQUINAS

COQUITO
COQUITOS
COR
CORACLE
CORACLES
CORACOID
CORACOIDS
CORAGGIO
CORAGGIOS
CORAL
CORALLA
CORALLINE
CORALLITE
CORALLOID
CORALLUM
CORALROOT
CORALS
CORALWORT
CORAM
CORAMINE
CORAMINES
CORANACH
CORANACHS
CORANTO
CORANTOES
CORANTOS
CORBAN
CORBANS
CORBE
CORBEAU
CORBEAUS
CORBEIL
CORBEILLE
CORBEILS
CORBEL
CORBELED
CORBELING
CORBELLED
CORBELS
CORBES
CORBICULA
CORBIE
CORBIES
CORBINA
CORBINAS
CORBY
CORCASS
CORCASSES
CORD
CORDAGE
CORDAGES
CORDATE
CORDATELY
CORDED
CORDELLE
CORDELLED
CORDELLES
CORDER

CORDERS	CORIA	CORNBREAD	CORNIFIES
CORDGRASS	CORIANDER	CORNCAKE	CORNIFORM
CORDIAL	CORIES	CORNCAKES	CORNIFY
CORDIALLY	CORING	CORNCOB	CORNILY
CORDIALS	CORIOUS	CORNCOBS	CORNINESS
CORDIFORM	CORIUM	CORNCRAKE	CORNING
CORDINER	CORIUMS	CORNCRIB	CORNIST
CORDINERS	CORIVAL	CORNCRIBS	CORNISTS
CORDING	CORIVALRY	CORNEA	CORNLAND
CORDINGS	CORIVALS	CORNEAE	CORNLANDS
CORDITE	CORIXID	CORNEAL	CORNLOFT
CORDITES	CORIXIDS	CORNEAS	CORNLOFTS
CORDLESS	CORK	CORNED	CORNMEAL
CORDLIKE	CORKAGE	CORNEITIS	CORNMEALS
CORDOBA	CORKAGES	CORNEL	CORNMILL
CORDOBAS	CORKBOARD	CORNELIAN	CORNMILLS
CORDON	CORKBORER	CORNELS	CORNMOTH
CORDONED	CORKED	CORNEMUSE	CORNMOTHS
CORDONING	CORKER	CORNEOUS	CORNO
CORDONNET	CORKERS	CORNER	CORNOPEAN
CORDONS	CORKIER	CORNERED	CORNPIPE
CORDOTOMY	CORKIEST	CORNERING	CORNPIPES
CORDOVAN	CORKINESS	CORNERMAN	CORNPONE
CORDOVANS	CORKING	CORNERMEN	CORNPONES
CORDS	CORKIR	CORNERS	CORNRENT
CORDUROY	CORKIRS	CORNET	CORNRENTS
CORDUROYS	CORKLIKE	CORNETCY	CORNROW
CORDWAIN	CORKS	CORNETIST	CORNROWED
CORDWAINS	CORKSCREW	CORNETS	CORNROWS
CORDWOOD	CORKTREE	CORNETT	CORNS
CORDWOODS	CORKTREES	CORNETTI	CORNSTALK
CORDYLINE	CORKWING	CORNETTO	CORNSTONE
CORE	CORKWINGS	CORNETTS	CORNU
CORED	CORKWOOD	CORNFED	CORNUA
COREDEEM	CORKWOODS	CORNFIELD	CORNUAL
COREDEEMS	CORKY	CORNFLAG	CORNUS
COREGENT	CORM	CORNFLAGS	CORNUSES
COREGENTS	CORMEL	CORNFLAKE	CORNUTE
COREIGN	CORMELS	CORNFLIES	CORNUTED
COREIGNS	CORMIDIA	CORNFLOUR	CORNUTES
CORELATE	CORMIDIUM	CORNFLY	CORNUTING
CORELATED	CORMLIKE	CORNHUSK	CORNUTO
CORELATES	CORMOID	CORNHUSKS	CORNUTOS
CORELESS	CORMORANT	CORNI	CORNWORM
CORELLA	CORMOUS	CORNICE	CORNWORMS
CORELLAS	CORMS	CORNICED	CORNY
COREMIA	CORMUS	CORNICES	COROCORE
COREMIUM	CORMUSES	CORNICHE	COROCORES
COREOPSIS	CORN	CORNICHES	COROCORO
CORER	CORNACRE	CORNICHON	COROCOROS
CORERS	CORNACRES	CORNICING	CORODIES
CORES	CORNAGE	CORNICLE	CORODY
COREY	CORNAGES	CORNICLES	COROLLA
COREYS	CORNBALL	CORNICULA	COROLLARY
CORF	CORNBALLS	CORNIER	COROLLAS
CORFHOUSE	CORNBORER	CORNIEST	COROLLATE
CORGI	CORNBRAID	CORNIFIC	COROLLINE
CORGIS	CORNBRASH	CORNIFIED	CORONA

CORONACH	CORREAS	CORSLETED	CORYPHAEI
CORONACHS	CORRECT	CORSLETS	CORYPHE
CORONAE	CORRECTED	CORSNED	CORYPHEE
CORONAL	CORRECTER	CORSNEDS	CORYPHEES
CORONALLY	CORRECTLY	CORSO	CORYPHENE
CORONALS	CORRECTOR	CORSOS	CORYPHES
CORONARY	CORRECTS	CORTEGE	CORYZA
CORONAS	CORRELATE	CORTEGES	CORYZAL
CORONATE	CORRIDA	CORTEX	CORYZAS
CORONATED	CORRIDAS	CORTEXES	COS
CORONATES	CORRIDOR	CORTICAL	COSCRIPT
CORONEL	CORRIDORS	CORTICATE	COSCRIPTS
CORONELS	CORRIE	CORTICES	COSE
CORONER	CORRIES	CORTICOID	COSEC
CORONERS	CORRIGENT	CORTICOSE	COSECANT
CORONET	CORRIVAL	CORTILE	COSECANTS
CORONETED	CORRIVALS	CORTILI	COSECH
CORONETS	CORRODANT	CORTIN	COSECHS
CORONIS	CORRODE	CORTINA	COSECS
CORONISES	CORRODED	CORTINAS	COSED
CORONIUM	CORRODENT	CORTINS	COSEISMAL
CORONIUMS	CORRODER	CORTISOL	COSEISMIC
CORONOID	CORRODERS	CORTISOLS	COSES
COROTATE	CORRODES	CORTISONE	COSET
COROTATED	CORRODIES	CORULER	COSETS
COROTATES	CORRODING	CORULERS	COSEY
COROZO	CORRODY	CORUNDUM	COSEYS
COROZOS	CORROSION	CORUNDUMS	COSH
CORPORA	CORROSIVE	CORUSCANT	COSHED
CORPORAL	CORRUGATE	CORUSCATE	COSHER
CORPORALE	CORRUPT	CORVEE	COSHERED
CORPORALS	CORRUPTED	CORVEES	COSHERER
CORPORAS	CORRUPTER	CORVES	COSHERERS
CORPORATE	CORRUPTLY	CORVET	COSHERIES
CORPOREAL	CORRUPTOR	CORVETED	COSHERING
CORPORIFY	CORRUPTS	CORVETING	COSHERS
CORPOSANT	CORS	CORVETS	COSHERY
CORPS	CORSAC	CORVETTE	COSHES
CORPSE	CORSACS	CORVETTED	COSHING
CORPSED	CORSAGE	CORVETTES	COSIE
CORPSES	CORSAGES	CORVID	COSIED
CORPSING	CORSAIR	CORVIDS	COSIER
CORPSMAN	CORSAIRS	CORVINA	COSIERS
CORPSMEN	CORSE	CORVINAS	COSIES
CORPULENT	CORSELET	CORVINE	COSIEST
CORPUS	CORSELETS	CORVUS	COSIGN
CORPUSCLE	CORSES	CORVUSES	COSIGNED
CORPUSES	CORSET	CORY	COSIGNER
CORRADE	CORSETED	CORYBANT	COSIGNERS
CORRADED	CORSETIER	CORYBANTS	COSIGNING
CORRADES	CORSETING	CORYDALIS	COSIGNS
CORRADING	CORSETRY	CORYLUS	COSILY
CORRAL	CORSETS	CORYLUSES	COSINE
CORRALLED	CORSEY	CORYMB	COSINES
CORRALS	CORSEYS	CORYMBED	COSINESS
CORRASION	CORSIVE	CORYMBOSE	COSING
CORRASIVE	CORSIVES	CORYMBOUS	COSMEA
CORREA	CORSLET	CORYMBS	COSMEAS

COSMESES	COSTER	COTINGA	COTYLE
COSMESIS	COSTERS	COTINGAS	COTYLEDON
COSMETIC	COSTES	COTININE	COTYLES
COSMETICS	COSTING	COTININES	COTYLOID
COSMIC	COSTIVE	COTISE	COTYLOIDS
COSMICAL	COSTIVELY	COTISED	COTYPE
COSMID	COSTLESS	COTISES	COTYPES
COSMIDS	COSTLIER	COTISING	COUCAL
COSMIN	COSTLIEST	COTLAND	COUCALS
COSMINE	COSTLY	COTLANDS	COUCH
COSMINES	COSTMARY	COTQUEAN	COUCHANT
COSMINS	COSTOTOMY	COTQUEANS	COUCHE
COSMISM	COSTREL	COTRUSTEE	COUCHED
COSMISMS	COSTRELS	COTS	COUCHEE
COSMIST	COSTS	COTT	COUCHEES
COSMISTS	COSTUME	COTTA	COUCHER
COSMOCRAT	COSTUMED	COTTABUS	COUCHERS
COSMOGENY	COSTUMER	COTTAE	COUCHES
COSMOGONY	COSTUMERS	COTTAGE	COUCHETTE
COSMOID	COSTUMERY	COTTAGED	COUCHING
COSMOLINE	COSTUMES	COTTAGER	COUCHINGS
COSMOLOGY	COSTUMEY	COTTAGERS	COUDE
COSMONAUT	COSTUMIER	COTTAGES	COUGAN
COSMORAMA	COSTUMING	COTTAGEY	COUGANS
COSMOS	COSTUS	COTTAGING	COUGAR
COSMOSES	COSTUSES	COTTAR	COUGARS
COSMOTRON	COSY	COTTARS	COUGH
COSPHERED	COSYING	COTTAS	COUGHED
COSPONSOR	COT	COTTED	COUGHER
COSS	COTAN	COTTER	COUGHERS
COSSACK	COTANGENT	COTTERED	COUGHING
COSSACKS	COTANS	COTTERING	COUGHINGS
COSSES	COTE	COTTERS	COUGHS
COSSET	COTEAU	COTTID	COUGUAR
COSSETED	COTEAUX	COTTIDS	COUGUARS
COSSETING	COTED	COTTIER	COULD
COSSETS	COTELETTE	COTTIERS	COULDEST
COSSIE	COTELINE	COTTING	COULDST
COSSIES	COTELINES	COTTISE	COULEE
COST	COTENANCY	COTTISED	COULEES
COSTA	COTENANT	COTTISES	COULIBIAC
COSTAE	COTENANTS	COTTISING	COULIS
COSTAL	COTERIE	COTTOID	COULISSE
COSTALGIA	COTERIES	COTTON	COULISSES
COSTALLY	COTES	COTTONADE	COULOIR
COSTALS	COTH	COTTONED	COULOIRS
COSTAR	COTHS	COTTONING	COULOMB
COSTARD	COTHURN	COTTONS	COULOMBIC
COSTARDS	COTHURNAL	COTTONY	COULOMBS
COSTARRED	COTHURNI	COTTOWN	COULTER
COSTARS	COTHURNS	COTTOWNS	COULTERS
COSTATE	COTHURNUS	COTTS	COUMARIC
COSTATED	COTICULAR	COTTUS	COUMARIN
COSTE	COTIDAL	COTTUSES	COUMARINS
COSTEAN	COTILLION	COTURNIX	COUMARONE
COSTEANED	COTILLON	COTWAL	COUMAROU
COSTEANS	COTILLONS	COTWALS	COUMAROUS
COSTED	COTING	COTYLAE	COUNCIL

COUNCILOR	COURANT	COUSCOUS	COVERED
COUNCILS	COURANTE	COUSIN	COVERER
COUNSEL	COURANTES	COUSINAGE	COVERERS
COUNSELED	COURANTO	COUSINLY	COVERING
COUNSELEE	COURANTOS	COUSINRY	COVERINGS
COUNSELOR	COURANTS	COUSINS	COVERLESS
COUNSELS	COURB	COUTEAU	COVERLET
COUNT	COURBARIL	COUTEAUX	COVERLETS
COUNTABLE	COURBED	COUTER	COVERLID
COUNTABLY	COURBETTE	COUTERS	COVERLIDS
COUNTBACK	COURBING	COUTH	COVERS
COUNTDOWN	COURBS	COUTHER	COVERSED
COUNTED	COURD	COUTHEST	COVERSINE
COUNTER	COURE	COUTHIE	COVERSLIP
COUNTERED	COURED	COUTHIER	COVERT
COUNTERS	COURES	COUTHIEST	COVERTLY
COUNTESS	COURGETTE	COUTHS	COVERTS
COUNTIAN	COURIE	COUTHY	COVERTURE
COUNTIANS	COURIED	COUTIL	COVERUP
COUNTIES	COURIEING	COUTILLE	COVERUPS
COUNTING	COURIER	COUTILLES	COVES
COUNTLESS	COURIERED	COUTILS	COVET
COUNTLINE	COURIERS	COUTURE	COVETABLE
COUNTRIES	COURIES	COUTURES	COVETED
COUNTROL	COURING	COUTURIER	COVETER
COUNTROLS	COURLAN	COUVADE	COVETERS
COUNTRY	COURLANS	COUVADES	COVETING
COUNTS	COURS	COUVERT	COVETISE
COUNTSHIP	COURSE	COUVERTS	COVETISES
COUNTY	COURSED	COUZIN	COVETOUS
COUP	COURSER	COUZINS	COVETS
COUPE	COURSERS	COVALENCE	COVEY
COUPED	COURSES	COVALENCY	COVEYS
COUPEE	COURSING	COVALENT	COVIN
COUPEES	COURSINGS	COVARIANT	COVING
COUPER	COURT	COVARIATE	COVINGS
COUPERS	COURTED	COVARIED	COVINOUS
COUPES	COURTEOUS	COVARIES	COVINS
COUPING	COURTER	COVARY	COVYNE
COUPLE	COURTERS	COVARYING	COVYNES
COUPLED	COURTESAN	COVE	COW
COUPLEDOM	COURTESY	COVED	COWAGE
COUPLER	COURTEZAN	COVELET	COWAGES
COUPLERS	COURTIER	COVELETS	COWAL
COUPLES	COURTIERS	COVELLINE	COWALS
COUPLET	COURTING	COVELLITE	COWAN
COUPLETS	COURTINGS	COVEN	COWANS
COUPLING	COURTLET	COVENANT	COWARD
COUPLINGS	COURTLETS	COVENANTS	COWARDED
COUPON	COURTLIER	COVENS	COWARDICE
COUPONING	COURTLIKE	COVENT	COWARDING
COUPONS	COURTLING	COVENTS	COWARDLY
COUPS	COURTLY	COVER	COWARDRY
COUPURE	COURTROOM	COVERABLE	COWARDS
COUPURES	COURTS	COVERAGE	COWBANE
COUR	COURTSHIP	COVERAGES	COWBANES
COURAGE	COURTSIDE	COVERALL	COWBELL
COURAGES	COURTYARD	COVERALLS	COWBELLS

COWBERRY
COWBIND
COWBINDS
COWBIRD
COWBIRDS
COWBOY
COWBOYED
COWBOYING
COWBOYS
COWED
COWEDLY
COWER
COWERED
COWERING
COWERS
COWFEEDER
COWFISH
COWFISHES
COWFLAP
COWFLAPS
COWFLOP
COWFLOPS
COWGIRL
COWGIRLS
COWGRASS
COWHAGE
COWHAGES
COWHAND
COWHANDS
COWHEARD
COWHEARDS
COWHEEL
COWHEELS
COWHERB
COWHERBS
COWHERD
COWHERDS
COWHIDE
COWHIDED
COWHIDES
COWHIDING
COWHOUSE
COWHOUSES
COWIER
COWIEST
COWING
COWINNER
COWINNERS
COWISH
COWITCH
COWITCHES
COWK
COWKED
COWKING
COWKS
COWL
COWLED
COWLICK

COWLICKS
COWLING
COWLINGS
COWLS
COWLSTAFF
COWMAN
COWMEN
COWORKER
COWORKERS
COWP
COWPAT
COWPATS
COWPEA
COWPEAS
COWPED
COWPIE
COWPIES
COWPING
COWPLOP
COWPLOPS
COWPOKE
COWPOKES
COWPOX
COWPOXES
COWPS
COWRIE
COWRIES
COWRITE
COWRITER
COWRITERS
COWRITES
COWRITING
COWRITTEN
COWROTE
COWRY
COWS
COWSHED
COWSHEDS
COWSKIN
COWSKINS
COWSLIP
COWSLIPS
COWTREE
COWTREES
COWY
COX
COXA
COXAE
COXAL
COXALGIA
COXALGIAS
COXALGIC
COXALGIES
COXALGY
COXCOMB
COXCOMBIC
COXCOMBRY
COXCOMBS

COXED
COXES
COXIER
COXIEST
COXINESS
COXING
COXITIDES
COXITIS
COXLESS
COXSWAIN
COXSWAINS
COXY
COY
COYDOG
COYDOGS
COYED
COYER
COYEST
COYING
COYISH
COYISHLY
COYLY
COYNESS
COYNESSES
COYOTE
COYOTES
COYOTILLO
COYPOU
COYPOUS
COYPU
COYPUS
COYS
COYSTREL
COYSTRELS
COYSTRIL
COYSTRILS
COZ
COZE
COZED
COZEN
COZENAGE
COZENAGES
COZENED
COZENER
COZENERS
COZENING
COZENS
COZES
COZEY
COZEYS
COZIE
COZIED
COZIER
COZIERS
COZIES
COZIEST
COZILY
COZINESS

COZING
COZY
COZYING
COZZES
CRAAL
CRAALED
CRAALING
CRAALS
CRAB
CRABABBLE
CRABBED
CRABBEDLY
CRABBER
CRABBERS
CRABBIER
CRABBIEST
CRABBILY
CRABBING
CRABBY
CRABEATER
CRABGRASS
CRABLIKE
CRABMEAT
CRABMEATS
CRABS
CRABSTICK
CRABWISE
CRABWOOD
CRABWOODS
CRACK
CRACKA
CRACKAS
CRACKBACK
CRACKDOWN
CRACKED
CRACKER
CRACKERS
CRACKET
CRACKETS
CRACKHEAD
CRACKING
CRACKINGS
CRACKJAW
CRACKJAWS
CRACKLE
CRACKLED
CRACKLES
CRACKLIER
CRACKLING
CRACKLY
CRACKNEL
CRACKNELS
CRACKPOT
CRACKPOTS
CRACKS
CRACKSMAN
CRACKSMEN
CRACKUP

CRACKUPS	CRAMOISIE	CRANKNESS	CRASIS
CRACKY	CRAMOISY	CRANKOUS	CRASS
CRACOWE	CRAMP	CRANKPIN	CRASSER
CRACOWES	CRAMPBARK	CRANKPINS	CRASSEST
CRADLE	CRAMPED	CRANKS	CRASSLY
CRADLED	CRAMPER	CRANKY	CRASSNESS
CRADLER	CRAMPERS	CRANNIED	CRATCH
CRADLERS	CRAMPET	CRANNIES	CRATCHES
CRADLES	CRAMPETS	CRANNOG	CRATE
CRADLING	CRAMPFISH	CRANNOGE	CRATED
CRADLINGS	CRAMPIER	CRANNOGES	CRATEFUL
CRAFT	CRAMPIEST	CRANNOGS	CRATEFULS
CRAFTED	CRAMPING	CRANNY	CRATER
CRAFTER	CRAMPIT	CRANNYING	CRATERED
CRAFTERS	CRAMPITS	CRANREUCH	CRATERING
CRAFTIER	CRAMPON	CRANS	CRATERLET
CRAFTIEST	CRAMPONED	CRANTS	CRATEROUS
CRAFTILY	CRAMPONS	CRANTSES	CRATERS
CRAFTING	CRAMPOON	CRAP	CRATES
CRAFTLESS	CRAMPOONS	CRAPAUD	CRATING
CRAFTS	CRAMPS	CRAPAUDS	CRATON
CRAFTSMAN	CRAMPY	CRAPE	CRATONIC
CRAFTSMEN	CRAMS	CRAPED	CRATONS
CRAFTWORK	CRAN	CRAPELIKE	CRATUR
CRAFTY	CRANAGE	CRAPES	CRATURS
CRAG	CRANAGES	CRAPIER	CRAUNCH
CRAGFAST	CRANBERRY	CRAPIEST	CRAUNCHED
CRAGGED	CRANCH	CRAPING	CRAUNCHES
CRAGGIER	CRANCHED	CRAPLE	CRAUNCHY
CRAGGIEST	CRANCHES	CRAPLES	CRAVAT
CRAGGILY	CRANCHING	CRAPOLA	CRAVATS
CRAGGY	CRANE	CRAPOLAS	CRAVATTED
CRAGS	CRANED	CRAPPED	CRAVE
CRAGSMAN	CRANEFLY	CRAPPER	CRAVED
CRAGSMEN	CRANES	CRAPPERS	CRAVEN
CRAIC	CRANIA	CRAPPIE	CRAVENED
CRAICS	CRANIAL	CRAPPIER	CRAVENING
CRAIG	CRANIALLY	CRAPPIES	CRAVENLY
CRAIGS	CRANIATE	CRAPPIEST	CRAVENS
CRAKE	CRANIATES	CRAPPING	CRAVER
CRAKED	CRANING	CRAPPY	CRAVERS
CRAKES	CRANIUM	CRAPS	CRAVES
CRAKING	CRANIUMS	CRAPSHOOT	CRAVING
CRAM	CRANK	CRAPULENT	CRAVINGS
CRAMBE	CRANKCASE	CRAPULOUS	CRAW
CRAMBES	CRANKED	CRAPY	CRAWDAD
CRAMBO	CRANKER	CRARE	CRAWDADDY
CRAMBOES	CRANKEST	CRARES	CRAWDADS
CRAMBOS	CRANKIER	CRASES	CRAWFISH
CRAME	CRANKIEST	CRASH	CRAWL
CRAMES	CRANKILY	CRASHED	CRAWLED
CRAMESIES	CRANKING	CRASHER	CRAWLER
CRAMESY	CRANKISH	CRASHERS	CRAWLERS
CRAMMABLE	CRANKLE	CRASHES	CRAWLIER
CRAMMED	CRANKLED	CRASHING	CRAWLIEST
CRAMMER	CRANKLES	CRASHLAND	CRAWLING
CRAMMERS	CRANKLING	CRASHPAD	CRAWLINGS
CRAMMING	CRANKLY	CRASHPADS	CRAWLS

CRAWLWAY	CREANCE	CREDULITY	CREMOCARP
CRAWLWAYS	CREANCES	CREDULOUS	CREMONA
CRAWLY	CREANT	CREE	CREMONAS
CRAWS	CREASE	CREED	CREMOR
CRAY	CREASED	CREEDAL	CREMORNE
CRAYER	CREASER	CREEDS	CREMORNES
CRAYERS	CREASERS	CREEING	CREMORS
CRAYFISH	CREASES	CREEK	CREMOSIN
CRAYON	CREASIER	CREEKIER	CREMS
CRAYONED	CREASIEST	CREEKIEST	CREMSIN
CRAYONER	CREASING	CREEKS	CRENA
CRAYONERS	CREASOTE	CREEKY	CRENAS
CRAYONING	CREASOTED	CREEL	CRENATE
CRAYONIST	CREASOTES	CREELED	CRENATED
CRAYONS	CREASY	CREELING	CRENATELY
CRAYS	CREATABLE	CREELS	CRENATION
CRAYTHUR	CREATE	CREEP	CRENATURE
CRAYTHURS	CREATED	CREEPAGE	CRENEL
CRAZE	CREATES	CREEPAGES	CRENELATE
CRAZED	CREATIC	CREEPED	CRENELED
CRAZES	CREATIN	CREEPER	CRENELING
CRAZIER	CREATINE	CREEPERED	CRENELLE
CRAZIES	CREATINES	CREEPERS	CRENELLED
CRAZIEST	CREATING	CREEPIE	CRENELLES
CRAZILY	CREATINS	CREEPIER	CRENELS
CRAZINESS	CREATION	CREEPIES	CRENSHAW
CRAZING	CREATIONS	CREEPIEST	CRENSHAWS
CRAZY	CREATIVE	CREEPILY	CRENULATE
CRAZYWEED	CREATIVES	CREEPING	CREODONT
CREACH	CREATOR	CREEPS	CREODONTS
CREACHS	CREATORS	CREEPY	CREOLE
CREAGH	CREATRESS	CREES	CREOLES
CREAGHS	CREATRIX	CREESE	CREOLIAN
CREAK	CREATURAL	CREESED	CREOLIANS
CREAKED	CREATURE	CREESES	CREOLISE
CREAKIER	CREATURES	CREESH	CREOLISED
CREAKIEST	CRECHE	CREESHED	CREOLISES
CREAKILY	CRECHES	CREESHES	CREOLIST
CREAKING	CRED	CREESHIER	CREOLISTS
CREAKS	CREDAL	CREESHING	CREOLIZE
CREAKY	CREDENCE	CREESHY	CREOLIZED
CREAM	CREDENCES	CREESING	CREOLIZES
CREAMCUPS	CREDENDA	CREM	CREOPHAGY
CREAMED	CREDENDUM	CREMAINS	CREOSOL
CREAMER	CREDENT	CREMANT	CREOSOLS
CREAMERS	CREDENZA	CREMASTER	CREOSOTE
CREAMERY	CREDENZAS	CREMATE	CREOSOTED
CREAMIER	CREDIBLE	CREMATED	CREOSOTES
CREAMIEST	CREDIBLY	CREMATES	CREOSOTIC
CREAMILY	CREDIT	CREMATING	CREPANCE
CREAMING	CREDITED	CREMATION	CREPANCES
CREAMLAID	CREDITING	CREMATOR	CREPE
CREAMLIKE	CREDITOR	CREMATORS	CREPED
CREAMPUFF	CREDITORS	CREMATORY	CREPERIE
CREAMS	CREDITS	CREME	CREPERIES
CREAMWARE	CREDO	CREMES	CREPES
CREAMWOVE	CREDOS	CREMINI	CREPEY
CREAMY	CREDS	CREMINIS	CREPIER

CREPIEST	CREVETTES	CRICOID	CRINGLES
CREPINESS	CREVICE	CRICOIDS	CRINING
CREPING	CREVICED	CRIED	CRINITE
CREPITANT	CREVICES	CRIER	CRINITES
CREPITATE	CREW	CRIERS	CRINKLE
CREPITUS	CREWCUT	CRIES	CRINKLED
CREPOLINE	CREWCUTS	CRIKEY	CRINKLES
CREPON	CREWE	CRIM	CRINKLIER
CREPONS	CREWED	CRIME	CRINKLIES
CREPT	CREWEL	CRIMED	CRINKLING
CREPUSCLE	CREWELIST	CRIMEFUL	CRINKLY
CREPY	CREWELLED	CRIMELESS	CRINOID
CRESCENDI	CREWELS	CRIMEN	CRINOIDAL
CRESCENDO	CREWES	CRIMES	CRINOIDS
CRESCENT	CREWING	CRIMEWAVE	CRINOLINE
CRESCENTS	CREWLESS	CRIMINA	CRINOSE
CRESCIVE	CREWMAN	CRIMINAL	CRINUM
CRESOL	CREWMATE	CRIMINALS	CRINUMS
CRESOLS	CREWMATES	CRIMINATE	CRIOLLO
CRESS	CREWMEN	CRIMINE	CRIOLLOS
CRESSES	CREWNECK	CRIMING	CRIOS
CRESSET	CREWNECKS	CRIMINI	CRIOSES
CRESSETS	CREWS	CRIMINIS	CRIPE
CRESSY	CRIANT	CRIMINOUS	CRIPES
CREST	CRIB	CRIMINY	CRIPPLE
CRESTA	CRIBBAGE	CRIMMER	CRIPPLED
CRESTAL	CRIBBAGES	CRIMMERS	CRIPPLER
CRESTED	CRIBBED	CRIMP	CRIPPLERS
CRESTING	CRIBBER	CRIMPED	CRIPPLES
CRESTINGS	CRIBBERS	CRIMPER	CRIPPLING
CRESTLESS	CRIBBING	CRIMPERS	CRIS
CRESTON	CRIBBINGS	CRIMPIER	CRISE
CRESTONS	CRIBBLE	CRIMPIEST	CRISES
CRESTS	CRIBBLED	CRIMPING	CRISIC
CRESYL	CRIBBLES	CRIMPLE	CRISIS
CRESYLIC	CRIBBLING	CRIMPLED	CRISP
CRESYLS	CRIBELLA	CRIMPLES	CRISPATE
CRETIC	CRIBELLAR	CRIMPLING	CRISPATED
CRETICS	CRIBELLUM	CRIMPS	CRISPED
CRETIN	CRIBLE	CRIMPY	CRISPEN
CRETINISE	CRIBRATE	CRIMS	CRISPENED
CRETINISM	CRIBROSE	CRIMSON	CRISPENS
CRETINIZE	CRIBROUS	CRIMSONED	CRISPER
CRETINOID	CRIBS	CRIMSONS	CRISPERS
CRETINOUS	CRIBWORK	CRINAL	CRISPEST
CRETINS	CRIBWORKS	CRINATE	CRISPHEAD
CRETISM	CRICETID	CRINATED	CRISPIER
CRETISMS	CRICETIDS	CRINE	CRISPIEST
CRETONNE	CRICK	CRINED	CRISPILY
CRETONNES	CRICKED	CRINES	CRISPIN
CREUTZER	CRICKET	CRINGE	CRISPING
CREUTZERS	CRICKETED	CRINGED	CRISPINS
CREVALLE	CRICKETER	CRINGER	CRISPLY
CREVALLES	CRICKETS	CRINGERS	CRISPNESS
CREVASSE	CRICKEY	CRINGES	CRISPS
CREVASSED	CRICKING	CRINGING	CRISPY
CREVASSES	CRICKS	CRINGINGS	CRISSA
CREVETTE	CRICKY	CRINGLE	CRISSAL

CRISSUM	CROCKETED	CRONYISMS	CROSS
CRISTA	CROCKETS	CROODLE	CROSSABLE
CRISTAE	CROCKING	CROODLED	CROSSARM
CRISTATE	CROCKPOT	CROODLES	CROSSARMS
CRISTATED	CROCKPOTS	CROODLING	CROSSBAND
CRIT	CROCKS	CROOK	CROSSBAR
CRITERIA	CROCODILE	CROOKBACK	CROSSBARS
CRITERIAL	CROCOITE	CROOKED	CROSSBEAM
CRITERION	CROCOITES	CROOKEDER	CROSSBILL
CRITERIUM	CROCOSMIA	CROOKEDLY	CROSSBIT
CRITH	CROCS	CROOKER	CROSSBITE
CRITHS	CROCUS	CROOKERY	CROSSBOW
CRITIC	CROCUSES	CROOKEST	CROSSBOWS
CRITICAL	CROFT	CROOKING	CROSSBRED
CRITICISE	CROFTER	CROOKNECK	CROSSBUCK
CRITICISM	CROFTERS	CROOKS	CROSSCUT
CRITICIZE	CROFTING	CROOL	CROSSCUTS
CRITICS	CROFTINGS	CROOLED	CROSSE
CRITIQUE	CROFTS	CROOLING	CROSSED
CRITIQUED	CROG	CROOLS	CROSSER
CRITIQUES	CROGGED	CROON	CROSSERS
CRITS	CROGGIES	CROONED	CROSSES
CRITTER	CROGGING	CROONER	CROSSEST
CRITTERS	CROGGY	CROONERS	CROSSETTE
CRITTUR	CROGS	CROONING	CROSSFALL
CRITTURS	CROISSANT	CROONINGS	CROSSFIRE
CRIVENS	CROJIK	CROONS	CROSSFISH
CRIVVENS	CROJIKS	CROOVE	CROSSHAIR
CROAK	CROKINOLE	CROOVES	CROSSHEAD
CROAKED	CROMACK	CROP	CROSSING
CROAKER	CROMACKS	CROPBOUND	CROSSINGS
CROAKERS	CROMB	CROPFUL	CROSSISH
CROAKIER	CROMBEC	CROPFULL	CROSSJACK
CROAKIEST	CROMBECS	CROPFULS	CROSSLET
CROAKILY	CROMBED	CROPLAND	CROSSLETS
CROAKING	CROMBING	CROPLANDS	CROSSLY
CROAKINGS	CROMBS	CROPLESS	CROSSNESS
CROAKS	CROME	CROPPED	CROSSOVER
CROAKY	CROMED	CROPPER	CROSSROAD
CROC	CROMES	CROPPERS	CROSSRUFF
CROCEATE	CROMING	CROPPIE	CROSSTALK
CROCEIN	CROMLECH	CROPPIES	CROSSTIE
CROCEINE	CROMLECHS	CROPPING	CROSSTIED
CROCEINES	CROMORNA	CROPPINGS	CROSSTIES
CROCEINS	CROMORNAS	CROPPY	CROSSTOWN
CROCEOUS	CROMORNE	CROPS	CROSSTREE
CROCHE	CROMORNES	CROPSICK	CROSSWALK
CROCHES	CRONE	CROQUANTE	CROSSWAY
CROCHET	CRONES	CROQUET	CROSSWAYS
CROCHETED	CRONET	CROQUETED	CROSSWIND
CROCHETER	CRONETS	CROQUETS	CROSSWISE
CROCHETS	CRONIES	CROQUETTE	CROSSWORD
CROCI	CRONISH	CROQUIS	CROSSWORT
CROCINE	CRONK	CRORE	CROST
CROCK	CRONKER	CRORES	CROSTINI
CROCKED	CRONKEST	CROSIER	CROSTINIS
CROCKERY	CRONY	CROSIERED	CROSTINO
CROCKET	CRONYISM	CROSIERS	CROTAL

CROTALA	CROWDERS	CRUCIFIX	CRUMBED
CROTALINE	CROWDIE	CRUCIFORM	CRUMBER
CROTALISM	CROWDIES	CRUCIFY	CRUMBERS
CROTALS	CROWDING	CRUCK	CRUMBIER
CROTALUM	CROWDS	CRUCKS	CRUMBIEST
CROTCH	CROWDY	CRUD	CRUMBING
CROTCHED	CROWEA	CRUDDED	CRUMBLE
CROTCHES	CROWEAS	CRUDDIER	CRUMBLED
CROTCHET	CROWED	CRUDDIEST	CRUMBLES
CROTCHETS	CROWER	CRUDDING	CRUMBLIER
CROTCHETY	CROWERS	CRUDDLE	CRUMBLIES
CROTON	CROWFEET	CRUDDLED	CRUMBLING
CROTONBUG	CROWFOOT	CRUDDLES	CRUMBLY
CROTONIC	CROWFOOTS	CRUDDLING	CRUMBS
CROTONS	CROWING	CRUDDY	CRUMBUM
CROTTLE	CROWINGLY	CRUDE	CRUMBUMS
CROTTLES	CROWN	CRUDELY	CRUMBY
CROUCH	CROWNED	CRUDENESS	CRUMEN
CROUCHED	CROWNER	CRUDER	CRUMENAL
CROUCHES	CROWNERS	CRUDES	CRUMENALS
CROUCHING	CROWNET	CRUDEST	CRUMENS
CROUP	CROWNETS	CRUDITES	CRUMHORN
CROUPADE	CROWNING	CRUDITIES	CRUMHORNS
CROUPADES	CROWNINGS	CRUDITY	CRUMMACK
CROUPE	CROWNLAND	CRUDS	CRUMMACKS
CROUPED	CROWNLESS	CRUDY	CRUMMIE
CROUPER	CROWNLET	CRUE	CRUMMIER
CROUPERS	CROWNLETS	CRUEL	CRUMMIES
CROUPES	CROWNS	CRUELER	CRUMMIEST
CROUPIER	CROWNWORK	CRUELEST	CRUMMOCK
CROUPIERS	CROWS	CRUELLER	CRUMMOCKS
CROUPIEST	CROWSFEET	CRUELLEST	CRUMMY
CROUPILY	CROWSFOOT	CRUELLS	CRUMP
CROUPING	CROWSTEP	CRUELLY	CRUMPED
CROUPON	CROWSTEPS	CRUELNESS	CRUMPER
CROUPONS	CROZE	CRUELS	CRUMPEST
CROUPOUS	CROZER	CRUELTIES	CRUMPET
CROUPS	CROZERS	CRUELTY	CRUMPETS
CROUPY	CROZES	CRUES	CRUMPIER
CROUSE	CROZIER	CRUET	CRUMPIEST
CROUSELY	CROZIERS	CRUETS	CRUMPING
CROUSTADE	CROZZLED	CRUISE	CRUMPLE
CROUT	CRU	CRUISED	CRUMPLED
CROUTE	CRUBEEN	CRUISER	CRUMPLES
CROUTES	CRUBEENS	CRUISERS	CRUMPLIER
CROUTON	CRUCES	CRUISES	CRUMPLING
CROUTONS	CRUCIAL	CRUISEWAY	CRUMPLY
CROUTS	CRUCIALLY	CRUISIE	CRUMPS
CROW	CRUCIAN	CRUISIES	CRUMPY
CROWBAR	CRUCIANS	CRUISING	CRUNCH
CROWBARS	CRUCIATE	CRUISINGS	CRUNCHED
CROWBERRY	CRUCIBLE	CRUIVE	CRUNCHER
CROWBOOT	CRUCIBLES	CRUIVES	CRUNCHERS
CROWBOOTS	CRUCIFER	CRUIZIE	CRUNCHES
CROWD	CRUCIFERS	CRUIZIES	CRUNCHIE
CROWDED	CRUCIFIED	CRULLER	CRUNCHIER
CROWDEDLY	CRUCIFIER	CRULLERS	CRUNCHIES
CROWDER	CRUCIFIES	CRUMB	CRUNCHILY

CRUNCHING	CRUSTY	CRYSTAL	CUBITAL
CRUNCHY	CRUSY	CRYSTALS	CUBITI
CRUNKLE	CRUTCH	CSARDAS	CUBITS
CRUNKLED	CRUTCHED	CSARDASES	CUBITUS
CRUNKLES	CRUTCHES	CTENE	CUBITUSES
CRUNKLING	CRUTCHING	CTENES	CUBLESS
CRUNODAL	CRUVE	CTENIDIA	CUBOID
CRUNODE	CRUVES	CTENIDIUM	CUBOIDAL
CRUNODES	CRUX	CTENIFORM	CUBOIDS
CRUOR	CRUXES	CTENOID	CUBS
CRUORES	CRUZADO	CUADRILLA	CUCKING
CRUORS	CRUZADOES	CUATRO	CUCKOLD
CRUPPER	CRUZADOS	CUATROS	CUCKOLDED
CRUPPERS	CRUZEIRO	CUB	CUCKOLDLY
CRURA	CRUZEIROS	CUBAGE	CUCKOLDOM
CRURAL	CRUZIE	CUBAGES	CUCKOLDRY
CRUS	CRUZIES	CUBANE	CUCKOLDS
CRUSADE	CRWTH	CUBANELLE	CUCKOO
CRUSADED	CRWTHS	CUBANES	CUCKOOED
CRUSADER	CRY	CUBATURE	CUCKOOING
CRUSADERS	CRYBABIES	CUBATURES	CUCKOOS
CRUSADES	CRYBABY	CUBBED	CUCULLATE
CRUSADING	CRYING	CUBBIES	CUCUMBER
CRUSADO	CRYINGLY	CUBBING	CUCUMBERS
CRUSADOES	CRYINGS	CUBBINGS	CUCURBIT
CRUSADOS	CRYOBANK	CUBBISH	CUCURBITS
CRUSE	CRYOBANKS	CUBBISHLY	CUD
CRUSES	CRYOCABLE	CUBBY	CUDBEAR
CRUSET	CRYOGEN	CUBBYHOLE	CUDBEARS
CRUSETS	CRYOGENIC	CUBE	CUDDEN
CRUSH	CRYOGENS	CUBEB	CUDDENS
CRUSHABLE	CRYOGENY	CUBEBS	CUDDIE
CRUSHED	CRYOLITE	CUBED	CUDDIES
CRUSHER	CRYOLITES	CUBER	CUDDIN
CRUSHERS	CRYOMETER	CUBERS	CUDDINS
CRUSHES	CRYOMETRY	CUBES	CUDDLE
CRUSHING	CRYONIC	CUBHOOD	CUDDLED
CRUSIAN	CRYONICS	CUBHOODS	CUDDLER
CRUSIANS	CRYOPHYTE	CUBIC	CUDDLERS
CRUSIE	CRYOPROBE	CUBICA	CUDDLES
CRUSIES	CRYOSCOPE	CUBICAL	CUDDLIER
CRUSILY	CRYOSCOPY	CUBICALLY	CUDDLIEST
CRUST	CRYOSTAT	CUBICAS	CUDDLING
CRUSTA	CRYOSTATS	CUBICITY	CUDDLY
CRUSTACEA	CRYOTRON	CUBICLE	CUDDY
CRUSTAE	CRYOTRONS	CUBICLES	CUDGEL
CRUSTAL	CRYPT	CUBICLY	CUDGELED
CRUSTATE	CRYPTADIA	CUBICS	CUDGELER
CRUSTATED	CRYPTAL	CUBICULA	CUDGELERS
CRUSTED	CRYPTIC	CUBICULUM	CUDGELING
CRUSTIER	CRYPTICAL	CUBIFORM	CUDGELLED
CRUSTIES	CRYPTO	CUBING	CUDGELLER
CRUSTIEST	CRYPTOGAM	CUBISM	CUDGELS
CRUSTILY	CRYPTON	CUBISMS	CUDGERIE
CRUSTING	CRYPTONS	CUBIST	CUDGERIES
CRUSTLESS	CRYPTONYM	CUBISTIC	CUDS
CRUSTOSE	CRYPTOS	CUBISTS	CUDWEED
CRUSTS	CRYPTS	CUBIT	CUDWEEDS

CUE	CULETS	CULTIGEN	CUMMIN
CUED	CULEX	CULTIGENS	CUMMINS
CUEING	CULEXES	CULTISH	CUMQUAT
CUEIST	CULICES	CULTISHLY	CUMQUATS
CUEISTS	CULICID	CULTISM	CUMSHAW
CUES	CULICIDS	CULTISMS	CUMSHAWS
CUESTA	CULICINE	CULTIST	CUMULATE
CUESTAS	CULICINES	CULTISTS	CUMULATED
CUFF	CULINARY	CULTIVAR	CUMULATES
CUFFED	CULL	CULTIVARS	CUMULET
CUFFIN	CULLAY	CULTIVATE	CUMULETS
CUFFING	CULLAYS	CULTLIKE	CUMULI
CUFFINS	CULLED	CULTRATE	CUMULOSE
CUFFLE	CULLENDER	CULTRATED	CUMULOUS
CUFFLED	CULLER	CULTS	CUMULUS
CUFFLES	CULLERS	CULTURAL	CUNABULA
CUFFLESS	CULLET	CULTURATI	CUNCTATOR
CUFFLING	CULLETS	CULTURE	CUNDIES
CUFFLINK	CULLIED	CULTURED	CUNDUM
CUFFLINKS	CULLIES	CULTURES	CUNDUMS
CUFFO	CULLING	CULTURING	CUNDY
CUFFS	CULLINGS	CULTURIST	CUNEAL
CUFFUFFLE	CULLION	CULTUS	CUNEATE
CUIF	CULLIONLY	CULTUSES	CUNEATED
CUIFS	CULLIONS	CULTY	CUNEATELY
CUING	CULLIS	CULVER	CUNEATIC
CUIRASS	CULLISES	CULVERIN	CUNEI
CUIRASSED	CULLS	CULVERINS	CUNEIFORM
CUIRASSES	CULLY	CULVERS	CUNETTE
CUISH	CULLYING	CULVERT	CUNETTES
CUISHES	CULLYISM	CULVERTS	CUNEUS
CUISINART	CULLYISMS	CUM	CUNIFORM
CUISINE	CULM	CUMACEAN	CUNIFORMS
CUISINES	CULMED	CUMACEANS	CUNJEVOI
CUISINIER	CULMEN	CUMARIC	CUNJEVOIS
CUISSE	CULMENS	CUMARIN	CUNNER
CUISSER	CULMINANT	CUMARINS	CUNNERS
CUISSERS	CULMINATE	CUMARONE	CUNNING
CUISSES	CULMING	CUMARONES	CUNNINGER
CUIT	CULMS	CUMBENT	CUNNINGLY
CUITER	CULOTTE	CUMBER	CUNNINGS
CUITERED	CULOTTES	CUMBERED	CUNT
CUITERING	CULPA	CUMBERER	CUNTS
CUITERS	CULPABLE	CUMBERERS	CUP
CUITIKIN	CULPABLY	CUMBERING	CUPBEARER
CUITIKINS	CULPAE	CUMBERS	CUPBOARD
CUITS	CULPATORY	CUMBIA	CUPBOARDS
CUITTLE	CULPRIT	CUMBIAS	CUPCAKE
CUITTLED	CULPRITS	CUMBRANCE	CUPCAKES
CUITTLES	CULT	CUMBROUS	CUPEL
CUITTLING	CULTCH	CUMBUNGI	CUPELED
CUKE	CULTCHES	CUMBUNGIS	CUPELER
CUKES	CULTER	CUMEC	CUPELERS
CULCH	CULTERS	CUMECS	CUPELING
CULCHES	CULTI	CUMIN	CUPELLED
CULCHIE	CULTIC	CUMINS	CUPELLER
CULCHIES	CULTIER	CUMMER	CUPELLERS
CULET	CULTIEST	CUMMERS	CUPELLING

CUPELS	CURANDERO	CURDLE	CURLIER
CUPFERRON	CURARA	CURDLED	CURLIEST
CUPFUL	CURARAS	CURDLER	CURLILY
CUPFULS	CURARE	CURDLERS	CURLINESS
CUPGALL	CURARES	CURDLES	CURLING
CUPGALLS	CURARI	CURDLING	CURLINGS
CUPHEAD	CURARINE	CURDS	CURLPAPER
CUPHEADS	CURARINES	CURDY	CURLS
CUPID	CURARIS	CURE	CURLY
CUPIDITY	CURARISE	CURED	CURLYCUE
CUPIDS	CURARISED	CURELESS	CURLYCUES
CUPLIKE	CURARISES	CURER	CURN
CUPMAN	CURARIZE	CURERS	CURNEY
CUPMEN	CURARIZED	CURES	CURNIER
CUPOLA	CURARIZES	CURET	CURNIEST
CUPOLAED	CURASSOW	CURETS	CURNS
CUPOLAING	CURASSOWS	CURETTAGE	CURNY
CUPOLAR	CURAT	CURETTE	CURPEL
CUPOLAS	CURATE	CURETTED	CURPELS
CUPOLATED	CURATED	CURETTES	CURR
CUPPA	CURATES	CURETTING	CURRACH
CUPPAS	CURATING	CURF	CURRACHS
CUPPED	CURATIVE	CURFEW	CURRAGH
CUPPER	CURATIVES	CURFEWS	CURRAGHS
CUPPERS	CURATOR	CURFS	CURRAJONG
CUPPIER	CURATORS	CURFUFFLE	CURRAN
CUPPIEST	CURATORY	CURIA	CURRANS
CUPPING	CURATRIX	CURIAE	CURRANT
CUPPINGS	CURATS	CURIAL	CURRANTS
CUPPY	CURB	CURIALISM	CURRANTY
CUPREOUS	CURBABLE	CURIALIST	CURRAWONG
CUPRESSUS	CURBED	CURIAS	CURRED
CUPRIC	CURBER	CURIE	CURREJONG
CUPRITE	CURBERS	CURIES	CURRENCY
CUPRITES	CURBING	CURIET	CURRENT
CUPROUS	CURBINGS	CURIETS	CURRENTLY
CUPRUM	CURBLESS	CURING	CURRENTS
CUPRUMS	CURBS	CURIO	CURRICLE
CUPS	CURBSIDE	CURIOS	CURRICLES
CUPSFUL	CURBSIDES	CURIOSA	CURRICULA
CUPULA	CURBSTONE	CURIOSITY	CURRIE
CUPULAE	CURCH	CURIOUS	CURRIED
CUPULAR	CURCHEF	CURIOUSER	CURRIER
CUPULATE	CURCHEFS	CURIOUSLY	CURRIERS
CUPULE	CURCHES	CURITE	CURRIERY
CUPULES	CURCULIO	CURITES	CURRIES
CUR	CURCULIOS	CURIUM	CURRIJONG
CURABLE	CURCUMA	CURIUMS	CURRING
CURABLY	CURCUMAS	CURL	CURRISH
CURACAO	CURCUMIN	CURLED	CURRISHLY
CURACAOS	CURCUMINE	CURLER	CURRS
CURACIES	CURCUMINS	CURLERS	CURRY
CURACOA	CURD	CURLEW	CURRYCOMB
CURACOAS	CURDED	CURLEWS	CURRYING
CURACY	CURDIER	CURLI	CURRYINGS
CURAGH	CURDIEST	CURLICUE	CURS
CURAGHS	CURDINESS	CURLICUED	CURSAL
CURANDERA	CURDING	CURLICUES	CURSE

CURSED	CURTSYING	CUSPIDAL	CUTCHES
CURSEDER	CURULE	CUSPIDATE	CUTDOWN
CURSEDEST	CURVATE	CUSPIDES	CUTDOWNS
CURSEDLY	CURVATED	CUSPIDOR	CUTE
CURSENARY	CURVATION	CUSPIDORE	CUTELY
CURSER	CURVATIVE	CUSPIDORS	CUTENESS
CURSERS	CURVATURE	CUSPIDS	CUTER
CURSES	CURVE	CUSPIS	CUTES
CURSI	CURVEBALL	CUSPS	CUTESIE
CURSING	CURVED	CUSS	CUTESIER
CURSINGS	CURVEDLY	CUSSED	CUTESIEST
CURSITOR	CURVES	CUSSEDLY	CUTEST
CURSITORS	CURVESOME	CUSSER	CUTESY
CURSITORY	CURVET	CUSSERS	CUTEY
CURSIVE	CURVETED	CUSSES	CUTEYS
CURSIVELY	CURVETING	CUSSING	CUTGLASS
CURSIVES	CURVETS	CUSSO	CUTGRASS
CURSOR	CURVETTED	CUSSOS	CUTICLE
CURSORARY	CURVEY	CUSSWORD	CUTICLES
CURSORES	CURVIER	CUSSWORDS	CUTICULA
CURSORIAL	CURVIEST	CUSTARD	CUTICULAE
CURSORILY	CURVIFORM	CUSTARDS	CUTICULAR
CURSORS	CURVING	CUSTARDY	CUTIE
CURSORY	CURVITAL	CUSTOCK	CUTIES
CURST	CURVITIES	CUSTOCKS	CUTIKIN
CURSTNESS	CURVITY	CUSTODE	CUTIKINS
CURSUS	CURVY	CUSTODES	CUTIN
CURT	CUSCUS	CUSTODIAL	CUTINISE
CURTAIL	CUSCUSES	CUSTODIAN	CUTINISED
CURTAILED	CUSEC	CUSTODIER	CUTINISES
CURTAILER	CUSECS	CUSTODIES	CUTINIZE
CURTAILS	CUSH	CUSTODY	CUTINIZED
CURTAIN	CUSHAT	CUSTOM	CUTINIZES
CURTAINED	CUSHATS	CUSTOMARY	CUTINS
CURTAINS	CUSHAW	CUSTOMED	CUTIS
CURTAL	CUSHAWS	CUSTOMER	CUTISES
CURTALAX	CUSHES	CUSTOMERS	CUTLAS
CURTALAXE	CUSHIE	CUSTOMISE	CUTLASES
CURTALS	CUSHIER	CUSTOMIZE	CUTLASS
CURTANA	CUSHIES	CUSTOMS	CUTLASSES
CURTANAS	CUSHIEST	CUSTOS	CUTLER
CURTATE	CUSHILY	CUSTREL	CUTLERIES
CURTATION	CUSHINESS	CUSTRELS	CUTLERS
CURTAXE	CUSHION	CUSTUMAL	CUTLERY
CURTAXES	CUSHIONED	CUSTUMALS	CUTLET
CURTER	CUSHIONET	CUSTUMARY	CUTLETS
CURTESIES	CUSHIONS	CUT	CUTLINE
CURTEST	CUSHIONY	CUTANEOUS	CUTLINES
CURTESY	CUSHTY	CUTAWAY	CUTOFF
CURTILAGE	CUSHY	CUTAWAYS	CUTOFFS
CURTLY	CUSK	CUTBACK	CUTOUT
CURTNESS	CUSKS	CUTBACKS	CUTOUTS
CURTSEY	CUSP	CUTBANK	CUTOVER
CURTSEYED	CUSPAL	CUTBANKS	CUTOVERS
CURTSEYS	CUSPATE	CUTCH	CUTPURSE
CURTSIED	CUSPATED	CUTCHA	CUTPURSES
CURTSIES	CUSPED	CUTCHERRY	CUTS
CURTSY	CUSPID	CUTCHERY	CUTTABLE

CUTTAGE	CYANISES	CYCLER	CYGNETS
CUTTAGES	CYANISING	CYCLERIES	CYLICES
CUTTER	CYANITE	CYCLERS	CYLINDER
CUTTERS	CYANITES	CYCLERY	CYLINDERS
CUTTHROAT	CYANITIC	CYCLES	CYLINDRIC
CUTTIER	CYANIZE	CYCLEWAY	CYLIX
CUTTIES	CYANIZED	CYCLEWAYS	CYMA
CUTTIEST	CYANIZES	CYCLIC	CYMAE
CUTTING	CYANIZING	CYCLICAL	CYMAGRAPH
CUTTINGLY	CYANO	CYCLICALS	CYMAR
CUTTINGS	CYANOGEN	CYCLICISM	CYMARS
CUTTLE	CYANOGENS	CYCLICITY	CYMAS
CUTTLED	CYANOSED	CYCLICLY	CYMATIA
CUTTLES	CYANOSES	CYCLIN	CYMATICS
CUTTLING	CYANOSIS	CYCLING	CYMATIUM
CUTTO	CYANOTIC	CYCLINGS	CYMBAL
CUTTOE	CYANOTYPE	CYCLINS	CYMBALEER
CUTTOES	CYANS	CYCLISE	CYMBALER
CUTTY	CYANURATE	CYCLISED	CYMBALERS
CUTUP	CYANURET	CYCLISES	CYMBALIST
CUTUPS	CYANURETS	CYCLISING	CYMBALO
CUTWATER	CYATHI	CYCLIST	CYMBALOES
CUTWATERS	CYATHIA	CYCLISTS	CYMBALOM
CUTWORK	CYATHIUM	CYCLITOL	CYMBALOMS
CUTWORKS	CYATHUS	CYCLITOLS	CYMBALOS
CUTWORM	CYBER	CYCLIZE	CYMBALS
CUTWORMS	CYBERCAFE	CYCLIZED	CYMBIDIA
CUVEE	CYBERCAST	CYCLIZES	CYMBIDIUM
CUVEES	CYBERNATE	CYCLIZINE	CYMBIFORM
CUVETTE	CYBERNAUT	CYCLIZING	CYMBLING
CUVETTES	CYBERPET	CYCLO	CYMBLINGS
CUZ	CYBERPETS	CYCLOGIRO	CYME
CUZZES	CYBERPORN	CYCLOID	CYMENE
CWM	CYBERPUNK	CYCLOIDAL	CYMENES
CWMS	CYBERSEX	CYCLOIDS	CYMES
CWTCH	CYBERWAR	CYCLOLITH	CYMLIN
CWTCHED	CYBERWARS	CYCLONAL	CYMLING
CWTCHES	CYBORG	CYCLONE	CYMLINGS
CWTCHING	CYBORGS	CYCLONES	CYMLINS
CYAN	CYBRARIAN	CYCLONIC	CYMOGENE
CYANAMID	CYBRID	CYCLONITE	CYMOGENES
CYANAMIDE	CYBRIDS	CYCLOPEAN	CYMOGRAPH
CYANAMIDS	CYCAD	CYCLOPES	CYMOID
CYANATE	CYCADEOID	CYCLOPIAN	CYMOL
CYANATES	CYCADS	CYCLOPIC	CYMOLS
CYANIC	CYCAS	CYCLOPS	CYMOPHANE
CYANID	CYCASES	CYCLORAMA	CYMOSE
CYANIDE	CYCASIN	CYCLOS	CYMOSELY
CYANIDED	CYCASINS	CYCLOSES	CYMOUS
CYANIDES	CYCLAMATE	CYCLOSIS	CYNANCHE
CYANIDING	CYCLAMEN	CYCLOTRON	CYNANCHES
CYANIDS	CYCLAMENS	CYCLUS	CYNEGETIC
CYANIN	CYCLASE	CYCLUSES	CYNIC
CYANINE	CYCLASES	CYDER	CYNICAL
CYANINES	CYCLE	CYDERS	CYNICALLY
CYANINS	CYCLECAR	CYESES	CYNICISM
CYANISE	CYCLECARS	CYESIS	CYNICISMS
CYANISED	CYCLED	CYGNET	CYNICS

CYNODONT
CYNODONTS
CYNOMOLGI
CYNOSURAL
CYNOSURE
CYNOSURES
CYPHER
CYPHERED
CYPHERING
CYPHERS
CYPRES
CYPRESES
CYPRESS
CYPRESSES
CYPRIAN
CYPRIANS
CYPRID
CYPRIDES
CYPRIDS
CYPRINE
CYPRINID
CYPRINIDS
CYPRINOID
CYPRIS
CYPRUS
CYPRUSES
CYPSELA
CYPSELAE
CYST
CYSTEIN
CYSTEINE
CYSTEINES
CYSTEINIC
CYSTEINS
CYSTIC
CYSTID
CYSTIDEAN
CYSTIDS
CYSTIFORM
CYSTINE
CYSTINES
CYSTITIS
CYSTOCARP
CYSTOCELE
CYSTOID
CYSTOIDS
CYSTOLITH
CYSTOTOMY
CYSTS
CYTASE
CYTASES
CYTASTER
CYTASTERS
CYTE
CYTES
CYTIDINE
CYTIDINES
CYTIDYLIC

CYTISI
CYTISINE
CYTISINES
CYTISUS
CYTODE
CYTODES
CYTOGENY
CYTOID
CYTOKINE
CYTOKINES
CYTOKININ
CYTOLOGIC
CYTOLOGY
CYTOLYSES
CYTOLYSIN
CYTOLYSIS
CYTOLYTIC
CYTOMETER
CYTOMETRY
CYTON
CYTONS
CYTOPENIA
CYTOPLASM
CYTOPLAST
CYTOSINE
CYTOSINES
CYTOSOL
CYTOSOLIC
CYTOSOLS
CYTOSOME
CYTOSOMES
CYTOTAXES
CYTOTAXIS
CYTOTOXIC
CYTOTOXIN
CZAPKA
CZAPKAS
CZAR
CZARDAS
CZARDASES
CZARDOM
CZARDOMS
CZAREVICH
CZAREVNA
CZAREVNAS
CZARINA
CZARINAS
CZARISM
CZARISMS
CZARIST
CZARISTS
CZARITSA
CZARITSAS
CZARITZA
CZARITZAS
CZARS

D

DA
DAB
DABBA
DABBAS
DABBED
DABBER
DABBERS
DABBING
DABBITIES
DABBITY
DABBLE
DABBLED
DABBLER
DABBLERS
DABBLES
DABBLING
DABBLINGS
DABCHICK
DABCHICKS
DABS
DABSTER
DABSTERS
DACE
DACES
DACHA
DACHAS
DACHSHUND
DACITE
DACITES
DACK
DACKED
DACKER
DACKERED
DACKERING
DACKERS
DACKING
DACKS
DACOIT
DACOITAGE
DACOITIES
DACOITS
DACOITY
DACQUOISE
DACRON
DACRONS
DACTYL
DACTYLAR
DACTYLI
DACTYLIC
DACTYLICS
DACTYLIST
DACTYLS
DACTYLUS

DAD
DADA
DADAH
DADAHS
DADAISM
DADAISMS
DADAIST
DADAISTIC
DADAISTS
DADAS
DADDED
DADDIES
DADDING
DADDLE
DADDLED
DADDLES
DADDLING
DADDOCK
DADDOCKS
DADDY
DADGUM
DADO
DADOED
DADOES
DADOING
DADOS
DADS
DAE
DAEDAL
DAEDALEAN
DAEDALIAN
DAEDALIC
DAEING
DAEMON
DAEMONES
DAEMONIC
DAEMONS
DAES
DAFF
DAFFED
DAFFIER
DAFFIES
DAFFIEST
DAFFILY
DAFFINESS
DAFFING
DAFFINGS
DAFFODIL
DAFFODILS
DAFFS
DAFFY
DAFT
DAFTAR

DAFTARS
DAFTER
DAFTEST
DAFTIE
DAFTIES
DAFTLY
DAFTNESS
DAG
DAGABA
DAGABAS
DAGGA
DAGGAS
DAGGED
DAGGER
DAGGERED
DAGGERING
DAGGERS
DAGGIER
DAGGIEST
DAGGING
DAGGINGS
DAGGLE
DAGGLED
DAGGLES
DAGGLING
DAGGY
DAGLOCK
DAGLOCKS
DAGO
DAGOBA
DAGOBAS
DAGOES
DAGOS
DAGS
DAGWOOD
DAGWOODS
DAH
DAHABEAH
DAHABEAHS
DAHABEEAH
DAHABIAH
DAHABIAHS
DAHABIEH
DAHABIEHS
DAHABIYA
DAHABIYAH
DAHABIYAS
DAHABIYEH
DAHL
DAHLIA
DAHLIAS
DAHLS
DAHOON

DAHOONS
DAHS
DAIDLE
DAIDLED
DAIDLES
DAIDLING
DAIDZEIN
DAIDZEINS
DAIKER
DAIKERED
DAIKERING
DAIKERS
DAIKON
DAIKONS
DAILIES
DAILINESS
DAILY
DAILYNESS
DAIMEN
DAIMIO
DAIMIOS
DAIMOKU
DAIMOKUS
DAIMON
DAIMONES
DAIMONIC
DAIMONS
DAIMYO
DAIMYOS
DAINE
DAINED
DAINES
DAINING
DAINT
DAINTIER
DAINTIES
DAINTIEST
DAINTILY
DAINTY
DAIQUIRI
DAIQUIRIS
DAIRIES
DAIRY
DAIRYING
DAIRYINGS
DAIRYMAID
DAIRYMAN
DAIRYMEN
DAIS
DAISES
DAISHIKI
DAISHIKIS
DAISIED

DAISIES	DALTS	DAMNINGLY	DANDIACAL
DAISY	DAM	DAMNS	DANDIER
DAK	DAMAGE	DAMOISEL	DANDIES
DAKER	DAMAGED	DAMOISELS	DANDIEST
DAKERED	DAMAGER	DAMOSEL	DANDIFIED
DAKERHEN	DAMAGERS	DAMOSELS	DANDIFIES
DAKERHENS	DAMAGES	DAMOZEL	DANDIFY
DAKERING	DAMAGING	DAMOZELS	DANDILY
DAKERS	DAMAN	DAMP	DANDIPRAT
DAKOIT	DAMANS	DAMPED	DANDLE
DAKOITI	DAMAR	DAMPEN	DANDLED
DAKOITIES	DAMARS	DAMPENED	DANDLER
DAKOITIS	DAMASCENE	DAMPENER	DANDLERS
DAKOITS	DAMASK	DAMPENERS	DANDLES
DAKOITY	DAMASKED	DAMPENING	DANDLING
DAKS	DAMASKEEN	DAMPENS	DANDRIFF
DAL	DAMASKIN	DAMPER	DANDRIFFS
DALAPON	DAMASKING	DAMPERS	DANDRUFF
DALAPONS	DAMASKINS	DAMPEST	DANDRUFFS
DALASI	DAMASKS	DAMPIER	DANDRUFFY
DALASIS	DAMASQUIN	DAMPIEST	DANDY
DALE	DAMASSIN	DAMPING	DANDYFUNK
DALED	DAMASSINS	DAMPINGS	DANDYISH
DALEDH	DAMBOARD	DAMPISH	DANDYISM
DALEDHS	DAMBOARDS	DAMPLY	DANDYISMS
DALEDS	DAMBROD	DAMPNESS	DANDYPRAT
DALES	DAMBRODS	DAMPS	DANEGELD
DALESMAN	DAME	DAMPY	DANEGELDS
DALESMEN	DAMES	DAMS	DANEGELT
DALETH	DAMEWORT	DAMSEL	DANEGELTS
DALETHS	DAMEWORTS	DAMSELFLY	DANELAGH
DALGYTE	DAMFOOL	DAMSELS	DANELAGHS
DALGYTES	DAMIANA	DAMSON	DANELAW
DALI	DAMIANAS	DAMSONS	DANELAWS
DALIS	DAMMAR	DAN	DANEWEED
DALLE	DAMMARS	DANAZOL	DANEWEEDS
DALLES	DAMME	DANAZOLS	DANEWORT
DALLIANCE	DAMMED	DANCE	DANEWORTS
DALLIED	DAMMER	DANCEABLE	DANG
DALLIER	DAMMERS	DANCED	DANGED
DALLIERS	DAMMING	DANCEHALL	DANGER
DALLIES	DAMMIT	DANCER	DANGERED
DALLOP	DAMN	DANCERS	DANGERING
DALLOPS	DAMNABLE	DANCES	DANGEROUS
DALLY	DAMNABLY	DANCETTE	DANGERS
DALLYING	DAMNATION	DANCETTEE	DANGING
DALMAHOY	DAMNATORY	DANCETTES	DANGLE
DALMAHOYS	DAMNDEST	DANCETTY	DANGLED
DALMATIAN	DAMNDESTS	DANCEY	DANGLER
DALMATIC	DAMNED	DANCIER	DANGLERS
DALMATICS	DAMNEDER	DANCIEST	DANGLES
DALS	DAMNEDEST	DANCING	DANGLIER
DALT	DAMNER	DANCINGS	DANGLIEST
DALTON	DAMNERS	DANDELION	DANGLING
DALTONIAN	DAMNIFIED	DANDER	DANGLINGS
DALTONIC	DAMNIFIES	DANDERED	DANGLY
DALTONISM	DAMNIFY	DANDERING	DANGS
DALTONS	DAMNING	DANDERS	DANIO

DANIOS	DARCY	DARLING	DASHEENS
DANISH	DARCYS	DARLINGLY	DASHEKI
DANISHES	DARE	DARLINGS	DASHEKIS
DANK	DARED	DARN	DASHER
DANKER	DAREDEVIL	DARNATION	DASHERS
DANKEST	DAREFUL	DARNDEST	DASHES
DANKISH	DARER	DARNDESTS	DASHI
DANKLY	DARERS	DARNED	DASHIER
DANKNESS	DARES	DARNEDER	DASHIEST
DANKS	DARESAY	DARNEDEST	DASHIKI
DANNEBROG	DARG	DARNEL	DASHIKIS
DANNIES	DARGA	DARNELS	DASHING
DANNY	DARGAH	DARNER	DASHINGLY
DANS	DARGAHS	DARNERS	DASHIS
DANSEUR	DARGAS	DARNING	DASHPOT
DANSEURS	DARGLE	DARNINGS	DASHPOTS
DANSEUSE	DARGLES	DARNS	DASHY
DANSEUSES	DARGS	DAROGHA	DASSIE
DANT	DARI	DAROGHAS	DASSIES
DANTED	DARIC	DARRAIGN	DASTARD
DANTHONIA	DARICS	DARRAIGNE	DASTARDLY
DANTING	DARING	DARRAIGNS	DASTARDS
DANTON	DARINGLY	DARRAIN	DASTARDY
DANTONED	DARINGS	DARRAINE	DASYMETER
DANTONING	DARIOLE	DARRAINED	DASYPOD
DANTONS	DARIOLES	DARRAINES	DASYPODS
DANTS	DARIS	DARRAINS	DASYURE
DAP	DARK	DARRAYN	DASYURES
DAPHNE	DARKED	DARRAYNED	DATA
DAPHNES	DARKEN	DARRAYNS	DATABANK
DAPHNIA	DARKENED	DARRE	DATABANKS
DAPHNIAS	DARKENER	DARRED	DATABASE
DAPHNID	DARKENERS	DARRES	DATABASED
DAPHNIDS	DARKENING	DARRING	DATABASES
DAPPED	DARKENS	DARSHAN	DATABLE
DAPPER	DARKER	DARSHANS	DATABUS
DAPPERER	DARKEST	DART	DATABUSES
DAPPEREST	DARKEY	DARTBOARD	DATACARD
DAPPERLY	DARKEYS	DARTED	DATACARDS
DAPPERS	DARKIE	DARTER	DATACOMMS
DAPPING	DARKIES	DARTERS	DATAFLOW
DAPPLE	DARKING	DARTING	DATAGLOVE
DAPPLED	DARKISH	DARTINGLY	DATAL
DAPPLES	DARKLE	DARTLE	DATALLER
DAPPLING	DARKLED	DARTLED	DATALLERS
DAPS	DARKLES	DARTLES	DATALS
DAPSONE	DARKLIER	DARTLING	DATARIA
DAPSONES	DARKLIEST	DARTRE	DATARIAS
DAQUIRI	DARKLING	DARTRES	DATARIES
DAQUIRIS	DARKLINGS	DARTROUS	DATARY
DARAF	DARKLY	DARTS	DATCHA
DARAFS	DARKMANS	DARZI	DATCHAS
DARB	DARKNESS	DARZIS	DATE
DARBAR	DARKROOM	DAS	DATEABLE
DARBARS	DARKROOMS	DASH	DATEBOOK
DARBIES	DARKS	DASHBOARD	DATEBOOKS
DARBS	DARKSOME	DASHED	DATED
DARCIES	DARKY	DASHEEN	DATEDLY

DATEDNESS
DATELESS
DATELINE
DATELINED
DATELINES
DATER
DATERS
DATES
DATING
DATINGS
DATIVAL
DATIVE
DATIVELY
DATIVES
DATO
DATOLITE
DATOLITES
DATOS
DATTO
DATTOS
DATUM
DATUMS
DATURA
DATURAS
DATURIC
DATURINE
DATURINES
DAUB
DAUBE
DAUBED
DAUBER
DAUBERIES
DAUBERS
DAUBERY
DAUBES
DAUBIER
DAUBIEST
DAUBING
DAUBINGLY
DAUBINGS
DAUBRIES
DAUBRY
DAUBS
DAUBY
DAUD
DAUDED
DAUDING
DAUDS
DAUGHTER
DAUGHTERS
DAULT
DAULTS
DAUNDER
DAUNDERED
DAUNDERS
DAUNER
DAUNERED
DAUNERING

DAUNERS
DAUNT
DAUNTED
DAUNTER
DAUNTERS
DAUNTING
DAUNTLESS
DAUNTON
DAUNTONED
DAUNTONS
DAUNTS
DAUPHIN
DAUPHINE
DAUPHINES
DAUPHINS
DAUR
DAURED
DAURING
DAURS
DAUT
DAUTED
DAUTIE
DAUTIES
DAUTING
DAUTS
DAVEN
DAVENED
DAVENING
DAVENPORT
DAVENS
DAVIDIA
DAVIDIAS
DAVIES
DAVIT
DAVITS
DAVY
DAW
DAWAH
DAWAHS
DAWBAKE
DAWBAKES
DAWBRIES
DAWBRY
DAWCOCK
DAWCOCKS
DAWD
DAWDED
DAWDING
DAWDLE
DAWDLED
DAWDLER
DAWDLERS
DAWDLES
DAWDLING
DAWDS
DAWED
DAWEN
DAWING

DAWISH
DAWK
DAWKS
DAWN
DAWNED
DAWNER
DAWNERED
DAWNERING
DAWNERS
DAWNEY
DAWNING
DAWNINGS
DAWNLIKE
DAWNS
DAWS
DAWSONITE
DAWT
DAWTED
DAWTIE
DAWTIES
DAWTING
DAWTS
DAY
DAYAN
DAYANIM
DAYANS
DAYBED
DAYBEDS
DAYBOOK
DAYBOOKS
DAYBOY
DAYBOYS
DAYBREAK
DAYBREAKS
DAYCARE
DAYCARES
DAYCENTRE
DAYCH
DAYCHED
DAYCHES
DAYCHING
DAYDREAM
DAYDREAMS
DAYDREAMT
DAYDREAMY
DAYFLIES
DAYFLOWER
DAYFLY
DAYGLO
DAYGLOW
DAYGLOWS
DAYLIGHT
DAYLIGHTS
DAYLILIES
DAYLILY
DAYLIT
DAYLONG
DAYMARE

DAYMARES
DAYMARK
DAYMARKS
DAYNT
DAYROOM
DAYROOMS
DAYS
DAYSACK
DAYSACKS
DAYSHELL
DAYSHELLS
DAYSIDE
DAYSIDES
DAYSMAN
DAYSMEN
DAYSPRING
DAYSTAR
DAYSTARS
DAYTALE
DAYTALER
DAYTALERS
DAYTALES
DAYTIME
DAYTIMES
DAYWORK
DAYWORKER
DAYWORKS
DAZE
DAZED
DAZEDLY
DAZEDNESS
DAZER
DAZERS
DAZES
DAZING
DAZZLE
DAZZLED
DAZZLER
DAZZLERS
DAZZLES
DAZZLING
DAZZLINGS
DE
DEACIDIFY
DEACON
DEACONED
DEACONESS
DEACONING
DEACONRY
DEACONS
DEAD
DEADBEAT
DEADBEATS
DEADBOLT
DEADBOLTS
DEADBOY
DEADBOYS
DEADED

DEADEN	DEALATED	DEATHBEDS	DEBATING
DEADENED	DEALATES	DEATHBLOW	DEBAUCH
DEADENER	DEALATION	DEATHCUP	DEBAUCHED
DEADENERS	DEALBATE	DEATHCUPS	DEBAUCHEE
DEADENING	DEALER	DEATHFUL	DEBAUCHER
DEADENS	DEALERS	DEATHIER	DEBAUCHES
DEADER	DEALFISH	DEATHIEST	DEBBIER
DEADERS	DEALING	DEATHLESS	DEBBIES
DEADEST	DEALINGS	DEATHLIER	DEBBIEST
DEADEYE	DEALS	DEATHLIKE	DEBBY
DEADEYES	DEALT	DEATHLY	DEBE
DEADFALL	DEAMINASE	DEATHS	DEBEAK
DEADFALLS	DEAMINATE	DEATHSMAN	DEBEAKED
DEADHEAD	DEAMINISE	DEATHSMEN	DEBEAKING
DEADHEADS	DEAMINIZE	DEATHTRAP	DEBEAKS
DEADHOUSE	DEAN	DEATHWARD	DEBEARD
DEADING	DEANED	DEATHY	DEBEARDED
DEADLIER	DEANER	DEAVE	DEBEARDS
DEADLIEST	DEANERIES	DEAVED	DEBEL
DEADLIFT	DEANERS	DEAVES	DEBELLED
DEADLIFTS	DEANERY	DEAVING	DEBELLING
DEADLIGHT	DEANING	DEAW	DEBELS
DEADLINE	DEANS	DEAWIE	DEBENTURE
DEADLINED	DEANSHIP	DEAWS	DEBES
DEADLINES	DEANSHIPS	DEAWY	DEBILE
DEADLOCK	DEAR	DEB	DEBILITY
DEADLOCKS	DEARE	DEBACLE	DEBIT
DEADLY	DEARED	DEBACLES	DEBITED
DEADMAN	DEARER	DEBAG	DEBITING
DEADMEN	DEARES	DEBAGGED	DEBITOR
DEADNESS	DEAREST	DEBAGGING	DEBITORS
DEADPAN	DEARIE	DEBAGS	DEBITS
DEADPANS	DEARIES	DEBAR	DEBONAIR
DEADS	DEARING	DEBARK	DEBONAIRE
DEADSTOCK	DEARLING	DEBARKED	DEBONE
DEADWOOD	DEARLINGS	DEBARKER	DEBONED
DEADWOODS	DEARLY	DEBARKERS	DEBONER
DEAERATE	DEARN	DEBARKING	DEBONERS
DEAERATED	DEARNESS	DEBARKS	DEBONES
DEAERATES	DEARNFUL	DEBARMENT	DEBONING
DEAERATOR	DEARNLY	DEBARRASS	DEBOSH
DEAF	DEARNS	DEBARRED	DEBOSHED
DEAFBLIND	DEARS	DEBARRING	DEBOSHES
DEAFEN	DEARTH	DEBARS	DEBOSHING
DEAFENED	DEARTHS	DEBASE	DEBOSS
DEAFENING	DEARY	DEBASED	DEBOSSED
DEAFENS	DEASH	DEBASER	DEBOSSES
DEAFER	DEASHED	DEBASERS	DEBOSSING
DEAFEST	DEASHES	DEBASES	DEBOUCH
DEAFISH	DEASHING	DEBASING	DEBOUCHE
DEAFLY	DEASIL	DEBATABLE	DEBOUCHED
DEAFNESS	DEASILS	DEBATABLY	DEBOUCHES
DEAIR	DEASIUL	DEBATE	DEBRIDE
DEAIRED	DEASIULS	DEBATED	DEBRIDED
DEAIRING	DEASOIL	DEBATEFUL	DEBRIDES
DEAIRS	DEASOILS	DEBATER	DEBRIDING
DEAL	DEATH	DEBATERS	DEBRIEF
DEALATE	DEATHBED	DEBATES	DEBRIEFED

DEBRIEFER	DECADENTS	DECAUDATE	DECIBELS
DEBRIEFS	DECADES	DECAY	DECIDABLE
DEBRIS	DECADS	DECAYABLE	DECIDE
DEBRUISE	DECAF	DECAYED	DECIDED
DEBRUISED	DECAFF	DECAYER	DECIDEDLY
DEBRUISES	DECAFFS	DECAYERS	DECIDER
DEBS	DECAFS	DECAYING	DECIDERS
DEBT	DECAGON	DECAYLESS	DECIDES
DEBTED	DECAGONAL	DECAYS	DECIDING
DEBTEE	DECAGONS	DECCIE	DECIDUA
DEBTEES	DECAGRAM	DECCIES	DECIDUAE
DEBTLESS	DECAGRAMS	DECEASE	DECIDUAL
DEBTOR	DECAHEDRA	DECEASED	DECIDUAS
DEBTORS	DECAL	DECEASES	DECIDUATE
DEBTS	DECALCIFY	DECEASING	DECIDUOUS
DEBUD	DECALED	DECEDENT	DECIGRAM
DEBUDDED	DECALING	DECEDENTS	DECIGRAMS
DEBUDDING	DECALITER	DECEIT	DECILE
DEBUDS	DECALITRE	DECEITFUL	DECILES
DEBUG	DECALLED	DECEITS	DECILITER
DEBUGGED	DECALLING	DECEIVE	DECILITRE
DEBUGGER	DECALOG	DECEIVED	DECILLION
DEBUGGERS	DECALOGS	DECEIVER	DECIMAL
DEBUGGING	DECALOGUE	DECEIVERS	DECIMALLY
DEBUGS	DECALS	DECEIVES	DECIMALS
DEBUNK	DECAMETER	DECEIVING	DECIMATE
DEBUNKED	DECAMETRE	DECELERON	DECIMATED
DEBUNKER	DECAMP	DECEMVIR	DECIMATES
DEBUNKERS	DECAMPED	DECEMVIRI	DECIMATOR
DEBUNKING	DECAMPING	DECEMVIRS	DECIME
DEBUNKS	DECAMPS	DECENARY	DECIMES
DEBURR	DECANAL	DECENCIES	DECIMETER
DEBURRED	DECANALLY	DECENCY	DECIMETRE
DEBURRING	DECANE	DECENNARY	DECIPHER
DEBURRS	DECANES	DECENNIA	DECIPHERS
DEBUS	DECANI	DECENNIAL	DECISION
DEBUSED	DECANOIC	DECENNIUM	DECISIONS
DEBUSES	DECANT	DECENT	DECISIVE
DEBUSING	DECANTATE	DECENTER	DECISORY
DEBUSSED	DECANTED	DECENTERS	DECISTERE
DEBUSSES	DECANTER	DECENTEST	DECK
DEBUSSING	DECANTERS	DECENTLY	DECKCHAIR
DEBUT	DECANTING	DECENTRE	DECKED
DEBUTANT	DECANTS	DECENTRED	DECKEL
DEBUTANTE	DECAPOD	DECENTRES	DECKELS
DEBUTANTS	DECAPODAL	DECEPTION	DECKER
DEBUTED	DECAPODAN	DECEPTIVE	DECKERS
DEBUTING	DECAPODS	DECEPTORY	DECKHAND
DEBUTS	DECARB	DECERN	DECKHANDS
DEBYE	DECARBED	DECERNED	DECKHOUSE
DEBYES	DECARBING	DECERNING	DECKING
DECACHORD	DECARBS	DECERNS	DECKINGS
DECAD	DECARE	DECERTIFY	DECKLE
DECADAL	DECARES	DECESSION	DECKLED
DECADE	DECASTERE	DECHEANCE	DECKLES
DECADENCE	DECASTICH	DECIARE	DECKO
DECADENCY	DECASTYLE	DECIARES	DECKOED
DECADENT	DECATHLON	DECIBEL	DECKOING

DECKOS	DECOLORED	DECRIES	DEDUCTS
DECKS	DECOLORS	DECROWN	DEE
DECLAIM	DECOLOUR	DECROWNED	DEED
DECLAIMED	DECOLOURS	DECROWNS	DEEDED
DECLAIMER	DECOMMIT	DECRY	DEEDER
DECLAIMS	DECOMMITS	DECRYING	DEEDEST
DECLARANT	DECOMPLEX	DECRYPT	DEEDFUL
DECLARE	DECOMPOSE	DECRYPTED	DEEDIER
DECLARED	DECONGEST	DECRYPTS	DEEDIEST
DECLARER	DECONTROL	DECTET	DEEDILY
DECLARERS	DECOR	DECTETS	DEEDING
DECLARES	DECORATE	DECUBITAL	DEEDLESS
DECLARING	DECORATED	DECUBITI	DEEDS
DECLASS	DECORATES	DECUBITUS	DEEDY
DECLASSE	DECORATOR	DECUMAN	DEEING
DECLASSED	DECOROUS	DECUMANS	DEEJAY
DECLASSEE	DECORS	DECUMBENT	DEEJAYED
DECLASSES	DECORUM	DECUPLE	DEEJAYING
DECLAW	DECORUMS	DECUPLED	DEEJAYS
DECLAWED	DECOS	DECUPLES	DEEK
DECLAWING	DECOUPAGE	DECUPLING	DEELY
DECLAWS	DECOUPLE	DECURIA	DEEM
DECLINAL	DECOUPLED	DECURIAS	DEEMED
DECLINANT	DECOUPLER	DECURIES	DEEMING
DECLINATE	DECOUPLES	DECURION	DEEMS
DECLINE	DECOY	DECURIONS	DEEMSTER
DECLINED	DECOYED	DECURRENT	DEEMSTERS
DECLINER	DECOYER	DECURSION	DEEN
DECLINERS	DECOYERS	DECURSIVE	DEENS
DECLINES	DECOYING	DECURVE	DEEP
DECLINING	DECOYS	DECURVED	DEEPEN
DECLINIST	DECREASE	DECURVES	DEEPENED
DECLIVITY	DECREASED	DECURVING	DEEPENER
DECLIVOUS	DECREASES	DECURY	DEEPENERS
DECLUTCH	DECREE	DECUSSATE	DEEPENING
DECLUTTER	DECREED	DEDAL	DEEPENS
DECO	DECREEING	DEDALIAN	DEEPER
DECOCT	DECREER	DEDANS	DEEPEST
DECOCTED	DECREERS	DEDICANT	DEEPFELT
DECOCTING	DECREES	DEDICANTS	DEEPFROZE
DECOCTION	DECREET	DEDICATE	DEEPIE
DECOCTIVE	DECREETS	DEDICATED	DEEPIES
DECOCTS	DECREMENT	DEDICATEE	DEEPLY
DECOCTURE	DECREPIT	DEDICATES	DEEPMOST
DECODE	DECRETAL	DEDICATOR	DEEPNESS
DECODED	DECRETALS	DEDIMUS	DEEPS
DECODER	DECRETIST	DEDIMUSES	DEEPWATER
DECODERS	DECRETIVE	DEDUCE	DEER
DECODES	DECRETORY	DEDUCED	DEERBERRY
DECODING	DECREW	DEDUCES	DEERE
DECOHERER	DECREWED	DEDUCIBLE	DEERFLIES
DECOKE	DECREWING	DEDUCIBLY	DEERFLY
DECOKED	DECREWS	DEDUCING	DEERGRASS
DECOKES	DECRIAL	DEDUCT	DEERHORN
DECOKING	DECRIALS	DEDUCTED	DEERHORNS
DECOLLATE	DECRIED	DEDUCTING	DEERHOUND
DECOLLETE	DECRIER	DEDUCTION	DEERLET
DECOLOR	DECRIERS	DEDUCTIVE	DEERLETS

DEERLIKE	DEFECATE	DEFILADED	DEFOGGER
DEERS	DEFECATED	DEFILADES	DEFOGGERS
DEERSKIN	DEFECATES	DEFILE	DEFOGGING
DEERSKINS	DEFECATOR	DEFILED	DEFOGS
DEERWEED	DEFECT	DEFILER	DEFOLIANT
DEERWEEDS	DEFECTED	DEFILERS	DEFOLIATE
DEERYARD	DEFECTING	DEFILES	DEFORCE
DEERYARDS	DEFECTION	DEFILING	DEFORCED
DEES	DEFECTIVE	DEFINABLE	DEFORCER
DEET	DEFECTOR	DEFINABLY	DEFORCERS
DEETS	DEFECTORS	DEFINE	DEFORCES
DEEV	DEFECTS	DEFINED	DEFORCING
DEEVE	DEFENCE	DEFINER	DEFOREST
DEEVED	DEFENCED	DEFINERS	DEFORESTS
DEEVES	DEFENCES	DEFINES	DEFORM
DEEVING	DEFENCING	DEFINIENS	DEFORMED
DEEVS	DEFEND	DEFINING	DEFORMER
DEEWAN	DEFENDANT	DEFINITE	DEFORMERS
DEEWANS	DEFENDED	DEFIS	DEFORMING
DEF	DEFENDER	DEFLATE	DEFORMITY
DEFACE	DEFENDERS	DEFLATED	DEFORMS
DEFACED	DEFENDING	DEFLATER	DEFOUL
DEFACER	DEFENDS	DEFLATERS	DEFOULED
DEFACERS	DEFENSE	DEFLATES	DEFOULING
DEFACES	DEFENSED	DEFLATING	DEFOULS
DEFACING	DEFENSES	DEFLATION	DEFRAG
DEFAECATE	DEFENSING	DEFLATOR	DEFRAGGED
DEFALCATE	DEFENSIVE	DEFLATORS	DEFRAGGER
DEFAME	DEFER	DEFLEA	DEFRAGS
DEFAMED	DEFERABLE	DEFLEAED	DEFRAUD
DEFAMER	DEFERENCE	DEFLEAING	DEFRAUDED
DEFAMERS	DEFERENT	DEFLEAS	DEFRAUDER
DEFAMES	DEFERENTS	DEFLECT	DEFRAUDS
DEFAMING	DEFERMENT	DEFLECTED	DEFRAY
DEFAMINGS	DEFERRAL	DEFLECTOR	DEFRAYAL
DEFANG	DEFERRALS	DEFLECTS	DEFRAYALS
DEFANGED	DEFERRED	DEFLEX	DEFRAYED
DEFANGING	DEFERRER	DEFLEXED	DEFRAYER
DEFANGS	DEFERRERS	DEFLEXES	DEFRAYERS
DEFAST	DEFERRING	DEFLEXING	DEFRAYING
DEFASTE	DEFERS	DEFLEXION	DEFRAYS
DEFAT	DEFFER	DEFLEXURE	DEFREEZE
DEFATS	DEFFEST	DEFLORATE	DEFREEZES
DEFATTED	DEFFLY	DEFLOWER	DEFROCK
DEFATTING	DEFFO	DEFLOWERS	DEFROCKED
DEFAULT	DEFI	DEFLUENT	DEFROCKS
DEFAULTED	DEFIANCE	DEFLUXION	DEFROST
DEFAULTER	DEFIANCES	DEFOAM	DEFROSTED
DEFAULTS	DEFIANT	DEFOAMED	DEFROSTER
DEFEAT	DEFIANTLY	DEFOAMER	DEFROSTS
DEFEATED	DEFICIENT	DEFOAMERS	DEFROZE
DEFEATER	DEFICIT	DEFOAMING	DEFROZEN
DEFEATERS	DEFICITS	DEFOAMS	DEFT
DEFEATING	DEFIED	DEFOCUS	DEFTER
DEFEATISM	DEFIER	DEFOCUSED	DEFTEST
DEFEATIST	DEFIERS	DEFOCUSES	DEFTLY
DEFEATS	DEFIES	DEFOG	DEFTNESS
DEFEATURE	DEFILADE	DEFOGGED	DEFUEL

DEFUELED	DEGRADERS	DEIFIC	DEKALOGY
DEFUELING	DEGRADES	DEIFICAL	DEKAMETER
DEFUELLED	DEGRADING	DEIFIED	DEKAMETRE
DEFUELS	DEGRAS	DEIFIER	DEKARE
DEFUNCT	DEGREASE	DEIFIERS	DEKARES
DEFUNCTS	DEGREASED	DEIFIES	DEKE
DEFUND	DEGREASER	DEIFORM	DEKED
DEFUNDED	DEGREASES	DEIFY	DEKEING
DEFUNDING	DEGREE	DEIFYING	DEKES
DEFUNDS	DEGREED	DEIGN	DEKING
DEFUSE	DEGREES	DEIGNED	DEKKO
DEFUSED	DEGS	DEIGNING	DEKKOED
DEFUSER	DEGUM	DEIGNS	DEKKOING
DEFUSERS	DEGUMMED	DEIL	DEKKOS
DEFUSES	DEGUMMING	DEILS	DEL
DEFUSING	DEGUMS	DEINDEX	DELAINE
DEFUZE	DEGUST	DEINDEXED	DELAINES
DEFUZED	DEGUSTATE	DEINDEXES	DELAPSE
DEFUZES	DEGUSTED	DEINOSAUR	DELAPSED
DEFUZING	DEGUSTING	DEIONISE	DELAPSES
DEFY	DEGUSTS	DEIONISED	DELAPSING
DEFYING	DEHISCE	DEIONISER	DELAPSION
DEG	DEHISCED	DEIONISES	DELATE
DEGAGE	DEHISCENT	DEIONIZE	DELATED
DEGAME	DEHISCES	DEIONIZED	DELATES
DEGAMES	DEHISCING	DEIONIZER	DELATING
DEGAMI	DEHORN	DEIONIZES	DELATION
DEGAMIS	DEHORNED	DEIPAROUS	DELATIONS
DEGARNISH	DEHORNER	DEISEAL	DELATOR
DEGAS	DEHORNERS	DEISEALS	DELATORS
DEGASES	DEHORNING	DEISHEAL	DELAY
DEGASSED	DEHORNS	DEISHEALS	DELAYABLE
DEGASSER	DEHORT	DEISM	DELAYED
DEGASSERS	DEHORTED	DEISMS	DELAYER
DEGASSES	DEHORTER	DEIST	DELAYERS
DEGASSING	DEHORTERS	DEISTIC	DELAYING
DEGAUSS	DEHORTING	DEISTICAL	DELAYS
DEGAUSSED	DEHORTS	DEISTS	DELE
DEGAUSSER	DEHYDRATE	DEITIES	DELEAD
DEGAUSSES	DEI	DEITY	DELEADED
DEGEARING	DEICE	DEIXES	DELEADING
DEGENDER	DEICED	DEIXIS	DELEADS
DEGENDERS	DEICER	DEIXISES	DELEAVE
DEGERM	DEICERS	DEJECT	DELEAVED
DEGERMED	DEICES	DEJECTA	DELEAVES
DEGERMING	DEICIDAL	DEJECTED	DELEAVING
DEGERMS	DEICIDE	DEJECTING	DELEBLE
DEGGED	DEICIDES	DEJECTION	DELECTATE
DEGGING	DEICING	DEJECTORY	DELED
DEGLAZE	DEICTIC	DEJECTS	DELEGABLE
DEGLAZED	DEICTICS	DEJEUNE	DELEGACY
DEGLAZES	DEID	DEJEUNER	DELEGATE
DEGLAZING	DEIDER	DEJEUNERS	DELEGATED
DEGOUT	DEIDEST	DEJEUNES	DELEGATEE
DEGOUTS	DEIDS	DEKAGRAM	DELEGATES
DEGRADE	DEIF	DEKAGRAMS	DELEGATOR
DEGRADED	DEIFER	DEKALITER	DELEING
DEGRADER	DEIFEST	DEKALITRE	DELENDA

DELES	DELIVERY	DELVING	DEMERARA
DELETABLE	DELL	DEMAGOG	DEMERARAN
DELETE	DELLIES	DEMAGOGED	DEMERARAS
DELETED	DELLS	DEMAGOGIC	DEMERGE
DELETES	DELLY	DEMAGOGS	DEMERGED
DELETING	DELO	DEMAGOGUE	DEMERGER
DELETION	DELOPE	DEMAGOGY	DEMERGERS
DELETIONS	DELOPED	DEMAIN	DEMERGES
DELETIVE	DELOPES	DEMAINE	DEMERGING
DELETORY	DELOPING	DEMAINES	DEMERIT
DELF	DELOS	DEMAINS	DEMERITED
DELFS	DELOUSE	DEMAN	DEMERITS
DELFT	DELOUSED	DEMAND	DEMERSAL
DELFTS	DELOUSER	DEMANDANT	DEMERSE
DELFTWARE	DELOUSERS	DEMANDED	DEMERSED
DELI	DELOUSES	DEMANDER	DEMERSES
DELIBATE	DELOUSING	DEMANDERS	DEMERSING
DELIBATED	DELPH	DEMANDING	DEMERSION
DELIBATES	DELPHIC	DEMANDS	DEMES
DELIBLE	DELPHIN	DEMANNED	DEMESNE
DELICACY	DELPHINIA	DEMANNING	DEMESNES
DELICATE	DELPHS	DEMANS	DEMETON
DELICATES	DELS	DEMANTOID	DEMETONS
DELICE	DELT	DEMARCATE	DEMIC
DELICES	DELTA	DEMARCHE	DEMIES
DELICIOUS	DELTAIC	DEMARCHES	DEMIGOD
DELICT	DELTAS	DEMARK	DEMIGODS
DELICTS	DELTIC	DEMARKED	DEMIJOHN
DELIGHT	DELTOID	DEMARKET	DEMIJOHNS
DELIGHTED	DELTOIDEI	DEMARKETS	DEMILUNE
DELIGHTER	DELTOIDS	DEMARKING	DEMILUNES
DELIGHTS	DELTS	DEMARKS	DEMIMONDE
DELIME	DELUBRUM	DEMAST	DEMIPIQUE
DELIMED	DELUBRUMS	DEMASTED	DEMIREP
DELIMES	DELUDABLE	DEMASTING	DEMIREPS
DELIMING	DELUDE	DEMASTS	DEMISABLE
DELIMIT	DELUDED	DEMAYNE	DEMISE
DELIMITED	DELUDER	DEMAYNES	DEMISED
DELIMITER	DELUDERS	DEME	DEMISES
DELIMITS	DELUDES	DEMEAN	DEMISING
DELINEATE	DELUDING	DEMEANE	DEMISS
DELIQUIUM	DELUGE	DEMEANED	DEMISSION
DELIRIA	DELUGED	DEMEANES	DEMISSIVE
DELIRIANT	DELUGES	DEMEANING	DEMISSLY
DELIRIOUS	DELUGING	DEMEANOR	DEMIST
DELIRIUM	DELUNDUNG	DEMEANORS	DEMISTED
DELIRIUMS	DELUSION	DEMEANOUR	DEMISTER
DELIS	DELUSIONS	DEMEANS	DEMISTERS
DELISH	DELUSIVE	DEMENT	DEMISTING
DELIST	DELUSORY	DEMENTATE	DEMISTS
DELISTED	DELUSTER	DEMENTED	DEMIT
DELISTING	DELUSTERS	DEMENTI	DEMITASSE
DELISTS	DELUXE	DEMENTIA	DEMITS
DELIVER	DELVE	DEMENTIAL	DEMITTED
DELIVERED	DELVED	DEMENTIAS	DEMITTING
DELIVERER	DELVER	DEMENTING	DEMIURGE
DELIVERLY	DELVERS	DEMENTIS	DEMIURGES
DELIVERS	DELVES	DEMENTS	DEMIURGIC

DEMIURGUS	DEMPSTERS	DENIABLY	DENTATE
DEMIVEG	DEMPT	DENIAL	DENTATED
DEMIVEGES	DEMULCENT	DENIALS	DENTATELY
DEMIVOLT	DEMULSIFY	DENIED	DENTATION
DEMIVOLTE	DEMUR	DENIER	DENTED
DEMIVOLTS	DEMURE	DENIERS	DENTEL
DEMIWORLD	DEMURED	DENIES	DENTELLE
DEMO	DEMURELY	DENIGRATE	DENTELLES
DEMOB	DEMURER	DENIM	DENTELS
DEMOBBED	DEMURES	DENIMED	DENTEX
DEMOBBING	DEMUREST	DENIMS	DENTEXES
DEMOBS	DEMURING	DENIS	DENTICLE
DEMOCRACY	DEMURRAGE	DENITRATE	DENTICLES
DEMOCRAT	DEMURRAL	DENITRIFY	DENTIFORM
DEMOCRATS	DEMURRALS	DENIZEN	DENTIL
DEMOCRATY	DEMURRED	DENIZENED	DENTILED
DEMODE	DEMURRER	DENIZENS	DENTILS
DEMODED	DEMURRERS	DENNED	DENTIN
DEMOED	DEMURRING	DENNET	DENTINAL
DEMOING	DEMURS	DENNETS	DENTINE
DEMOLISH	DEMY	DENNING	DENTINES
DEMOLOGY	DEMYSHIP	DENOMINAL	DENTING
DEMON	DEMYSHIPS	DENOTABLE	DENTINS
DEMONESS	DEMYSTIFY	DENOTATE	DENTIST
DEMONIAC	DEN	DENOTATED	DENTISTRY
DEMONIACS	DENAR	DENOTATES	DENTISTS
DEMONIAN	DENARI	DENOTE	DENTITION
DEMONIC	DENARIES	DENOTED	DENTOID
DEMONICAL	DENARII	DENOTES	DENTS
DEMONISE	DENARIUS	DENOTING	DENTULOUS
DEMONISED	DENARS	DENOTIVE	DENTURAL
DEMONISES	DENARY	DENOUNCE	DENTURE
DEMONISM	DENATURE	DENOUNCED	DENTURES
DEMONISMS	DENATURED	DENOUNCER	DENTURIST
DEMONIST	DENATURES	DENOUNCES	DENUDATE
DEMONISTS	DENAY	DENS	DENUDATED
DEMONIZE	DENAYED	DENSE	DENUDATES
DEMONIZED	DENAYING	DENSELY	DENUDE
DEMONIZES	DENAYS	DENSENESS	DENUDED
DEMONRIES	DENAZIFY	DENSER	DENUDER
DEMONRY	DENDRIMER	DENSEST	DENUDERS
DEMONS	DENDRITE	DENSIFIED	DENUDES
DEMOS	DENDRITES	DENSIFIER	DENUDING
DEMOSES	DENDRITIC	DENSIFIES	DENY
DEMOTE	DENDROID	DENSIFY	DENYING
DEMOTED	DENDRON	DENSITIES	DENYINGLY
DEMOTES	DENDRONS	DENSITY	DEODAND
DEMOTIC	DENE	DENT	DEODANDS
DEMOTICS	DENERVATE	DENTAL	DEODAR
DEMOTING	DENES	DENTALIA	DEODARA
DEMOTION	DENET	DENTALITY	DEODARAS
DEMOTIONS	DENETS	DENTALIUM	DEODARS
DEMOTIST	DENETTED	DENTALLY	DEODATE
DEMOTISTS	DENETTING	DENTALS	DEODATES
DEMOUNT	DENGUE	DENTARIA	DEODORANT
DEMOUNTED	DENGUES	DENTARIAS	DEODORISE
DEMOUNTS	DENI	DENTARIES	DEODORIZE
DEMPSTER	DENIABLE	DENTARY	DEONTIC

DEONTICS
DEORBIT
DEORBITED
DEORBITS
DEOXIDATE
DEOXIDISE
DEOXIDIZE
DEOXY
DEPAINT
DEPAINTED
DEPAINTS
DEPANNEUR
DEPART
DEPARTED
DEPARTEE
DEPARTEES
DEPARTER
DEPARTERS
DEPARTING
DEPARTS
DEPARTURE
DEPASTURE
DEPECHE
DEPECHES
DEPEINCT
DEPEINCTS
DEPEND
DEPENDANT
DEPENDED
DEPENDENT
DEPENDING
DEPENDS
DEPEOPLE
DEPEOPLED
DEPEOPLES
DEPERM
DEPERMED
DEPERMING
DEPERMS
DEPICT
DEPICTED
DEPICTER
DEPICTERS
DEPICTING
DEPICTION
DEPICTIVE
DEPICTOR
DEPICTORS
DEPICTS
DEPICTURE
DEPILATE
DEPILATED
DEPILATES
DEPILATOR
DEPLANE
DEPLANED
DEPLANES
DEPLANING

DEPLETE
DEPLETED
DEPLETER
DEPLETERS
DEPLETES
DEPLETING
DEPLETION
DEPLETIVE
DEPLETORY
DEPLORE
DEPLORED
DEPLORER
DEPLORERS
DEPLORES
DEPLORING
DEPLOY
DEPLOYED
DEPLOYER
DEPLOYERS
DEPLOYING
DEPLOYS
DEPLUME
DEPLUMED
DEPLUMES
DEPLUMING
DEPOLISH
DEPONE
DEPONED
DEPONENT
DEPONENTS
DEPONES
DEPONING
DEPORT
DEPORTED
DEPORTEE
DEPORTEES
DEPORTER
DEPORTERS
DEPORTING
DEPORTS
DEPOSABLE
DEPOSAL
DEPOSALS
DEPOSE
DEPOSED
DEPOSER
DEPOSERS
DEPOSES
DEPOSING
DEPOSIT
DEPOSITED
DEPOSITOR
DEPOSITS
DEPOT
DEPOTS
DEPRAVE
DEPRAVED
DEPRAVER

DEPRAVERS
DEPRAVES
DEPRAVING
DEPRAVITY
DEPRECATE
DEPREDATE
DEPREHEND
DEPRENYL
DEPRENYLS
DEPRESS
DEPRESSED
DEPRESSES
DEPRESSOR
DEPRIVAL
DEPRIVALS
DEPRIVE
DEPRIVED
DEPRIVER
DEPRIVERS
DEPRIVES
DEPRIVING
DEPROGRAM
DEPSIDE
DEPSIDES
DEPTH
DEPTHLESS
DEPTHS
DEPURANT
DEPURANTS
DEPURATE
DEPURATED
DEPURATES
DEPURATOR
DEPUTABLE
DEPUTE
DEPUTED
DEPUTES
DEPUTIES
DEPUTING
DEPUTISE
DEPUTISED
DEPUTISES
DEPUTIZE
DEPUTIZED
DEPUTIZES
DEPUTY
DERACINE
DERAIGN
DERAIGNED
DERAIGNS
DERAIL
DERAILED
DERAILER
DERAILERS
DERAILING
DERAILS
DERANGE
DERANGED

DERANGER
DERANGERS
DERANGES
DERANGING
DERAT
DERATE
DERATED
DERATES
DERATING
DERATINGS
DERATION
DERATIONS
DERATS
DERATTED
DERATTING
DERAY
DERAYED
DERAYING
DERAYS
DERBIES
DERBY
DERE
DERED
DERELICT
DERELICTS
DEREPRESS
DERES
DERHAM
DERHAMS
DERIDE
DERIDED
DERIDER
DERIDERS
DERIDES
DERIDING
DERIG
DERIGGED
DERIGGING
DERIGS
DERING
DERINGER
DERINGERS
DERISIBLE
DERISION
DERISIONS
DERISIVE
DERISORY
DERIVABLE
DERIVABLY
DERIVATE
DERIVATES
DERIVE
DERIVED
DERIVER
DERIVERS
DERIVES
DERIVING
DERM

DERMA	DESCANTS	DESILVER	DESORBING
DERMAL	DESCEND	DESILVERS	DESORBS
DERMAS	DESCENDED	DESINE	DESOXY
DERMATIC	DESCENDER	DESINED	DESPAIR
DERMATOID	DESCENDS	DESINENCE	DESPAIRED
DERMATOME	DESCENT	DESINENT	DESPAIRER
DERMESTID	DESCENTS	DESINES	DESPAIRS
DERMIC	DESCHOOL	DESINING	DESPATCH
DERMIS	DESCHOOLS	DESIPIENT	DESPERADO
DERMISES	DESCRIBE	DESIRABLE	DESPERATE
DERMOID	DESCRIBED	DESIRABLY	DESPIGHT
DERMOIDS	DESCRIBER	DESIRE	DESPIGHTS
DERMS	DESCRIBES	DESIRED	DESPISAL
DERN	DESCRIED	DESIRER	DESPISALS
DERNFUL	DESCRIER	DESIRERS	DESPISE
DERNIER	DESCRIERS	DESIRES	DESPISED
DERNLY	DESCRIES	DESIRING	DESPISER
DERNS	DESCRIVE	DESIROUS	DESPISERS
DERO	DESCRIVED	DESIST	DESPISES
DEROGATE	DESCRIVES	DESISTED	DESPISING
DEROGATED	DESCRY	DESISTING	DESPITE
DEROGATES	DESCRYING	DESISTS	DESPITED
DEROS	DESECRATE	DESK	DESPITES
DERRICK	DESELECT	DESKBOUND	DESPITING
DERRICKED	DESELECTS	DESKFAST	DESPOIL
DERRICKS	DESERT	DESKFASTS	DESPOILED
DERRIERE	DESERTED	DESKILL	DESPOILER
DERRIERES	DESERTER	DESKILLED	DESPOILS
DERRIES	DESERTERS	DESKILLS	DESPOND
DERRINGER	DESERTIC	DESKMAN	DESPONDED
DERRIS	DESERTIFY	DESKMEN	DESPONDS
DERRISES	DESERTING	DESKNOTE	DESPOT
DERRO	DESERTION	DESKNOTES	DESPOTAT
DERROS	DESERTS	DESKS	DESPOTATE
DERRY	DESERVE	DESKTOP	DESPOTATS
DERTH	DESERVED	DESKTOPS	DESPOTIC
DERTHS	DESERVER	DESMAN	DESPOTISM
DERV	DESERVERS	DESMANS	DESPOTS
DERVISH	DESERVES	DESMID	DESPUMATE
DERVISHES	DESERVING	DESMIDIAN	DESSE
DERVS	DESEX	DESMIDS	DESSERT
DESALT	DESEXED	DESMINE	DESSERTS
DESALTED	DESEXES	DESMINES	DESSES
DESALTER	DESEXING	DESMODIUM	DESTAIN
DESALTERS	DESHI	DESMOID	DESTAINED
DESALTING	DESI	DESMOIDS	DESTAINS
DESALTS	DESICCANT	DESMOSOME	DESTEMPER
DESAND	DESICCATE	DESNOOD	DESTINATE
DESANDED	DESIGN	DESNOODED	DESTINE
DESANDING	DESIGNATE	DESNOODS	DESTINED
DESANDS	DESIGNED	DESOEUVRE	DESTINES
DESCALE	DESIGNEE	DESOLATE	DESTINIES
DESCALED	DESIGNEES	DESOLATED	DESTINING
DESCALES	DESIGNER	DESOLATER	DESTINY
DESCALING	DESIGNERS	DESOLATES	DESTITUTE
DESCANT	DESIGNFUL	DESOLATOR	DESTOCK
DESCANTED	DESIGNING	DESORB	DESTOCKED
DESCANTER	DESIGNS	DESORBED	DESTOCKS

DESTRIER	DETENTION	DETOURS	DEVAS
DESTRIERS	DETENTIST	DETOX	DEVASTATE
DESTROY	DETENTS	DETOXED	DEVEIN
DESTROYED	DETENU	DETOXES	DEVEINED
DESTROYER	DETENUE	DETOXIFY	DEVEINING
DESTROYS	DETENUES	DETOXING	DEVEINS
DESTRUCT	DETENUS	DETRACT	DEVEL
DESTRUCTO	DETER	DETRACTED	DEVELED
DESTRUCTS	DETERGE	DETRACTOR	DEVELING
DESUETUDE	DETERGED	DETRACTS	DEVELLED
DESUGAR	DETERGENT	DETRAIN	DEVELLING
DESUGARED	DETERGER	DETRAINED	DEVELOP
DESUGARS	DETERGERS	DETRAINS	DEVELOPE
DESULFUR	DETERGES	DETRAQUE	DEVELOPED
DESULFURS	DETERGING	DETRAQUEE	DEVELOPER
DESULPHUR	DETERMENT	DETRAQUES	DEVELOPES
DESULTORY	DETERMINE	DETRIMENT	DEVELOPPE
DESYATIN	DETERRED	DETRITAL	DEVELOPS
DESYATINS	DETERRENT	DETRITION	DEVELS
DESYNE	DETERRER	DETRITUS	DEVERBAL
DESYNED	DETERRERS	DETRUDE	DEVERBALS
DESYNES	DETERRING	DETRUDED	DEVEST
DESYNING	DETERS	DETRUDES	DEVESTED
DETACH	DETERSION	DETRUDING	DEVESTING
DETACHED	DETERSIVE	DETRUSION	DEVESTS
DETACHER	DETEST	DETUNE	DEVIANCE
DETACHERS	DETESTED	DETUNED	DEVIANCES
DETACHES	DETESTER	DETUNES	DEVIANCY
DETACHING	DETESTERS	DETUNING	DEVIANT
DETAIL	DETESTING	DEUCE	DEVIANTS
DETAILED	DETESTS	DEUCED	DEVIATE
DETAILER	DETHATCH	DEUCEDLY	DEVIATED
DETAILERS	DETHRONE	DEUCES	DEVIATES
DETAILING	DETHRONED	DEUCING	DEVIATING
DETAILS	DETHRONER	DEUDDARN	DEVIATION
DETAIN	DETHRONES	DEUDDARNS	DEVIATIVE
DETAINED	DETICK	DEUS	DEVIATOR
DETAINEE	DETICKED	DEUTERATE	DEVIATORS
DETAINEES	DETICKER	DEUTERIC	DEVIATORY
DETAINER	DETICKERS	DEUTERIDE	DEVICE
DETAINERS	DETICKING	DEUTERIUM	DEVICEFUL
DETAINING	DETICKS	DEUTERON	DEVICES
DETAINS	DETINUE	DEUTERONS	DEVIL
DETASSEL	DETINUES	DEUTON	DEVILDOM
DETASSELS	DETONABLE	DEUTONS	DEVILDOMS
DETECT	DETONATE	DEUTZIA	DEVILED
DETECTED	DETONATED	DEUTZIAS	DEVILESS
DETECTER	DETONATES	DEV	DEVILET
DETECTERS	DETONATOR	DEVA	DEVILETS
DETECTING	DETORSION	DEVALL	DEVILFISH
DETECTION	DETORT	DEVALLED	DEVILING
DETECTIVE	DETORTED	DEVALLING	DEVILINGS
DETECTOR	DETORTING	DEVALLS	DEVILISH
DETECTORS	DETORTION	DEVALUATE	DEVILISM
DETECTS	DETORTS	DEVALUE	DEVILISMS
DETENT	DETOUR	DEVALUED	DEVILKIN
DETENTE	DETOURED	DEVALUES	DEVILKINS
DETENTES	DETOURING	DEVALUING	DEVILLED

DEVILLING
DEVILMENT
DEVILRIES
DEVILRY
DEVILS
DEVILSHIP
DEVILTRY
DEVILWOOD
DEVIOUS
DEVIOUSLY
DEVISABLE
DEVISAL
DEVISALS
DEVISE
DEVISED
DEVISEE
DEVISEES
DEVISER
DEVISERS
DEVISES
DEVISING
DEVISOR
DEVISORS
DEVITRIFY
DEVLING
DEVLINGS
DEVOICE
DEVOICED
DEVOICES
DEVOICING
DEVOID
DEVOIR
DEVOIRS
DEVOLVE
DEVOLVED
DEVOLVES
DEVOLVING
DEVON
DEVONIAN
DEVONPORT
DEVONS
DEVORE
DEVORES
DEVOT
DEVOTE
DEVOTED
DEVOTEDLY
DEVOTEE
DEVOTEES
DEVOTES
DEVOTING
DEVOTION
DEVOTIONS
DEVOTS
DEVOUR
DEVOURED
DEVOURER
DEVOURERS

DEVOURING
DEVOURS
DEVOUT
DEVOUTER
DEVOUTEST
DEVOUTLY
DEVS
DEVVEL
DEVVELLED
DEVVELS
DEW
DEWAN
DEWANI
DEWANIS
DEWANNIES
DEWANNY
DEWANS
DEWAR
DEWARS
DEWATER
DEWATERED
DEWATERER
DEWATERS
DEWAX
DEWAXED
DEWAXES
DEWAXING
DEWBERRY
DEWCLAW
DEWCLAWED
DEWCLAWS
DEWDROP
DEWDROPS
DEWED
DEWFALL
DEWFALLS
DEWFULL
DEWIER
DEWIEST
DEWILY
DEWINESS
DEWING
DEWITT
DEWITTED
DEWITTING
DEWITTS
DEWLAP
DEWLAPPED
DEWLAPS
DEWLAPT
DEWLESS
DEWOOL
DEWOOLED
DEWOOLING
DEWOOLS
DEWORM
DEWORMED
DEWORMER

DEWORMERS
DEWORMING
DEWORMS
DEWPOINT
DEWPOINTS
DEWS
DEWY
DEX
DEXES
DEXIE
DEXIES
DEXTER
DEXTERITY
DEXTEROUS
DEXTERS
DEXTRAL
DEXTRALLY
DEXTRAN
DEXTRANS
DEXTRIN
DEXTRINE
DEXTRINES
DEXTRINS
DEXTRO
DEXTRORSE
DEXTROSE
DEXTROSES
DEXTROUS
DEXY
DEY
DEYS
DEZINC
DEZINCED
DEZINCING
DEZINCKED
DEZINCS
DHAK
DHAKS
DHAL
DHALS
DHAMMA
DHAMMAS
DHANSAK
DHANSAKS
DHARMA
DHARMAS
DHARMIC
DHARMSALA
DHARNA
DHARNAS
DHOBI
DHOBIS
DHOL
DHOLE
DHOLES
DHOLL
DHOLLS
DHOLS

DHOOLIES
DHOOLY
DHOORA
DHOORAS
DHOOTI
DHOOTIE
DHOOTIES
DHOOTIS
DHOTI
DHOTIS
DHOURRA
DHOURRAS
DHOW
DHOWS
DHURNA
DHURNAS
DHURRA
DHURRAS
DHURRIE
DHURRIES
DHUTI
DHUTIS
DI
DIABASE
DIABASES
DIABASIC
DIABETES
DIABETIC
DIABETICS
DIABLE
DIABLERIE
DIABLERY
DIABLES
DIABOLIC
DIABOLISE
DIABOLISM
DIABOLIST
DIABOLIZE
DIABOLO
DIABOLOGY
DIABOLOS
DIACETYL
DIACETYLS
DIACHRONY
DIACHYLON
DIACHYLUM
DIACID
DIACIDIC
DIACIDS
DIACODION
DIACODIUM
DIACONAL
DIACONATE
DIACRITIC
DIACT
DIACTINAL
DIACTINE
DIACTINIC

DIADEM	DIALOGITE	DIAPER	DIASTEMA
DIADEMED	DIALOGIZE	DIAPERED	DIASTEMAS
DIADEMING	DIALOGS	DIAPERING	DIASTEMS
DIADEMS	DIALOGUE	DIAPERS	DIASTER
DIADOCHI	DIALOGUED	DIAPHONE	DIASTERS
DIADOCHY	DIALOGUER	DIAPHONES	DIASTOLE
DIADROM	DIALOGUES	DIAPHONIC	DIASTOLES
DIADROMS	DIALS	DIAPHONY	DIASTOLIC
DIAERESES	DIALYSATE	DIAPHRAGM	DIASTRAL
DIAERESIS	DIALYSE	DIAPHYSES	DIASTYLE
DIAERETIC	DIALYSED	DIAPHYSIS	DIASTYLES
DIAGLYPH	DIALYSER	DIAPIR	DIATHERMY
DIAGLYPHS	DIALYSERS	DIAPIRIC	DIATHESES
DIAGNOSE	DIALYSES	DIAPIRISM	DIATHESIS
DIAGNOSED	DIALYSING	DIAPIRS	DIATHETIC
DIAGNOSES	DIALYSIS	DIAPSID	DIATOM
DIAGNOSIS	DIALYTIC	DIAPSIDS	DIATOMIC
DIAGONAL	DIALYZATE	DIAPYESES	DIATOMIST
DIAGONALS	DIALYZE	DIAPYESIS	DIATOMITE
DIAGRAM	DIALYZED	DIAPYETIC	DIATOMS
DIAGRAMED	DIALYZER	DIARCH	DIATONIC
DIAGRAMS	DIALYZERS	DIARCHAL	DIATRETUM
DIAGRAPH	DIALYZES	DIARCHIC	DIATRIBE
DIAGRAPHS	DIALYZING	DIARCHIES	DIATRIBES
DIAGRID	DIAMAGNET	DIARCHY	DIATRON
DIAGRIDS	DIAMANTE	DIARIAL	DIATRONS
DIAL	DIAMANTES	DIARIAN	DIATROPIC
DIALECT	DIAMETER	DIARIES	DIAXON
DIALECTAL	DIAMETERS	DIARISE	DIAXONS
DIALECTIC	DIAMETRAL	DIARISED	DIAZEPAM
DIALECTS	DIAMETRIC	DIARISES	DIAZEPAMS
DIALED	DIAMIDE	DIARISING	DIAZEUXES
DIALER	DIAMIDES	DIARIST	DIAZEUXIS
DIALERS	DIAMIN	DIARISTIC	DIAZIN
DIALING	DIAMINE	DIARISTS	DIAZINE
DIALINGS	DIAMINES	DIARIZE	DIAZINES
DIALIST	DIAMINS	DIARIZED	DIAZINON
DIALISTS	DIAMOND	DIARIZES	DIAZINONS
DIALLAGE	DIAMONDED	DIARIZING	DIAZINS
DIALLAGES	DIAMONDS	DIARRHEA	DIAZO
DIALLAGIC	DIAMYL	DIARRHEAL	DIAZOES
DIALLED	DIANDRIES	DIARRHEAS	DIAZOLE
DIALLEL	DIANDROUS	DIARRHEIC	DIAZOLES
DIALLER	DIANDRY	DIARRHOEA	DIAZONIUM
DIALLERS	DIANODAL	DIARY	DIAZOS
DIALLING	DIANOETIC	DIASCOPE	DIAZOTISE
DIALLINGS	DIANOIA	DIASCOPES	DIAZOTIZE
DIALLIST	DIANOIAS	DIASPORA	DIB
DIALLISTS	DIANTHUS	DIASPORAS	DIBASIC
DIALOG	DIAPASE	DIASPORE	DIBBED
DIALOGED	DIAPASES	DIASPORES	DIBBER
DIALOGER	DIAPASON	DIASPORIC	DIBBERED
DIALOGERS	DIAPASONS	DIASTASE	DIBBERING
DIALOGIC	DIAPAUSE	DIASTASES	DIBBERS
DIALOGING	DIAPAUSED	DIASTASIC	DIBBING
DIALOGISE	DIAPAUSES	DIASTASIS	DIBBLE
DIALOGISM	DIAPENTE	DIASTATIC	DIBBLED
DIALOGIST	DIAPENTES	DIASTEM	DIBBLER

DIBBLERS

DIBBLERS
DIBBLES
DIBBLING
DIBBS
DIBBUK
DIBBUKIM
DIBBUKKIM
DIBBUKS
DIBROMIDE
DIBS
DIBUTYL
DICACIOUS
DICACITY
DICACODYL
DICAMBA
DICAMBAS
DICAST
DICASTERY
DICASTIC
DICASTS
DICE
DICED
DICENTRA
DICENTRAS
DICENTRIC
DICER
DICERS
DICES
DICEY
DICH
DICHASIA
DICHASIAL
DICHASIUM
DICHOGAMY
DICHONDRA
DICHOPTIC
DICHORD
DICHORDS
DICHOTIC
DICHOTOMY
DICHROIC
DICHROISM
DICHROITE
DICHROMAT
DICHROMIC
DICHT
DICHTED
DICHTING
DICHTS
DICIER
DICIEST
DICING
DICINGS
DICK
DICKED
DICKENS
DICKENSES
DICKER

DICKERED
DICKERING
DICKERS
DICKEY
DICKEYS
DICKHEAD
DICKHEADS
DICKIE
DICKIER
DICKIES
DICKIEST
DICKING
DICKS
DICKTIER
DICKTIEST
DICKTY
DICKY
DICKYBIRD
DICLINIES
DICLINISM
DICLINOUS
DICLINY
DICOT
DICOTS
DICOTYL
DICOTYLS
DICROTAL
DICROTIC
DICROTISM
DICROTOUS
DICT
DICTA
DICTATE
DICTATED
DICTATES
DICTATING
DICTATION
DICTATOR
DICTATORS
DICTATORY
DICTATRIX
DICTATURE
DICTED
DICTIER
DICTIEST
DICTING
DICTION
DICTIONAL
DICTIONS
DICTS
DICTUM
DICTUMS
DICTY
DICTYOGEN
DICUMAROL
DICYCLIC
DICYCLIES
DICYCLY

DID
DIDACT
DIDACTIC
DIDACTICS
DIDACTS
DIDACTYL
DIDACTYLS
DIDAKAI
DIDAKAIS
DIDAKEI
DIDAKEIS
DIDAPPER
DIDAPPERS
DIDDER
DIDDERED
DIDDERING
DIDDERS
DIDDICOY
DIDDICOYS
DIDDIER
DIDDIES
DIDDIEST
DIDDLE
DIDDLED
DIDDLER
DIDDLERS
DIDDLES
DIDDLEY
DIDDLEYS
DIDDLIES
DIDDLING
DIDDLY
DIDDY
DIDELPHIC
DIDELPHID
DIDICOI
DIDICOIS
DIDICOY
DIDICOYS
DIDIE
DIDIES
DIDJERIDU
DIDO
DIDOES
DIDOS
DIDRACHM
DIDRACHMA
DIDRACHMS
DIDST
DIDY
DIDYMIUM
DIDYMIUMS
DIDYMOUS
DIDYNAMY
DIE
DIEB
DIEBACK
DIEBACKS

DIEBS
DIECIOUS
DIED
DIEDRAL
DIEDRALS
DIEDRE
DIEDRES
DIEGESES
DIEGESIS
DIEHARD
DIEHARDS
DIEING
DIEL
DIELDRIN
DIELDRINS
DIELYTRA
DIELYTRAS
DIEMAKER
DIEMAKERS
DIENE
DIENES
DIEOFF
DIEOFFS
DIERESES
DIERESIS
DIERETIC
DIES
DIESEL
DIESELED
DIESELING
DIESELISE
DIESELIZE
DIESELS
DIESES
DIESINKER
DIESIS
DIESTER
DIESTERS
DIESTOCK
DIESTOCKS
DIESTROUS
DIESTRUM
DIESTRUMS
DIESTRUS
DIET
DIETARIAN
DIETARIES
DIETARILY
DIETARY
DIETED
DIETER
DIETERS
DIETETIC
DIETETICS
DIETHER
DIETHERS
DIETHYL
DIETHYLS

DIETICIAN	DIGESTIVE	DIGRESS	DILEMMAS
DIETINE	DIGESTOR	DIGRESSED	DILEMMIC
DIETINES	DIGESTORS	DIGRESSER	DILIGENCE
DIETING	DIGESTS	DIGRESSES	DILIGENT
DIETINGS	DIGGABLE	DIGS	DILL
DIETIST	DIGGED	DIGYNIAN	DILLED
DIETISTS	DIGGER	DIGYNOUS	DILLI
DIETITIAN	DIGGERS	DIHEDRA	DILLIER
DIETS	DIGGING	DIHEDRAL	DILLIES
DIF	DIGGINGS	DIHEDRALS	DILLIEST
DIFF	DIGHT	DIHEDRON	DILLING
DIFFER	DIGHTED	DIHEDRONS	DILLINGS
DIFFERED	DIGHTING	DIHYBRID	DILLIS
DIFFERENT	DIGHTS	DIHYBRIDS	DILLS
DIFFERING	DIGICAM	DIHYDRIC	DILLY
DIFFERS	DIGICAMS	DIKA	DILTIAZEM
DIFFICILE	DIGIT	DIKAS	DILUENT
DIFFICULT	DIGITAL	DIKAST	DILUENTS
DIFFIDENT	DIGITALIN	DIKASTS	DILUTABLE
DIFFLUENT	DIGITALIS	DIKDIK	DILUTE
DIFFORM	DIGITALLY	DIKDIKS	DILUTED
DIFFRACT	DIGITALS	DIKE	DILUTEE
DIFFRACTS	DIGITATE	DIKED	DILUTEES
DIFFS	DIGITATED	DIKER	DILUTER
DIFFUSE	DIGITISE	DIKERS	DILUTERS
DIFFUSED	DIGITISED	DIKES	DILUTES
DIFFUSELY	DIGITISER	DIKEY	DILUTING
DIFFUSER	DIGITISES	DIKIER	DILUTION
DIFFUSERS	DIGITIZE	DIKIEST	DILUTIONS
DIFFUSES	DIGITIZED	DIKING	DILUTIVE
DIFFUSING	DIGITIZER	DIKKOP	DILUTOR
DIFFUSION	DIGITIZES	DIKKOPS	DILUTORS
DIFFUSIVE	DIGITONIN	DIKTAT	DILUVIA
DIFFUSOR	DIGITOXIN	DIKTATS	DILUVIAL
DIFFUSORS	DIGITRON	DILATABLE	DILUVIAN
DIFS	DIGITRONS	DILATABLY	DILUVION
DIG	DIGITS	DILATANCY	DILUVIONS
DIGAMIES	DIGITULE	DILATANT	DILUVIUM
DIGAMIST	DIGITULES	DILATANTS	DILUVIUMS
DIGAMISTS	DIGLOSSIA	DILATATE	DIM
DIGAMMA	DIGLOSSIC	DILATATOR	DIMBLE
DIGAMMAS	DIGLOT	DILATE	DIMBLES
DIGAMOUS	DIGLOTS	DILATED	DIME
DIGAMY	DIGLOTTIC	DILATER	DIMENSION
DIGASTRIC	DIGLYPH	DILATERS	DIMER
DIGENESES	DIGLYPHS	DILATES	DIMERIC
DIGENESIS	DIGNIFIED	DILATING	DIMERISE
DIGENETIC	DIGNIFIES	DILATION	DIMERISED
DIGERATI	DIGNIFY	DILATIONS	DIMERISES
DIGEST	DIGNITARY	DILATIVE	DIMERISM
DIGESTANT	DIGNITIES	DILATOR	DIMERISMS
DIGESTED	DIGNITY	DILATORS	DIMERIZE
DIGESTER	DIGONAL	DILATORY	DIMERIZED
DIGESTERS	DIGOXIN	DILDO	DIMERIZES
DIGESTIF	DIGOXINS	DILDOE	DIMEROUS
DIGESTIFS	DIGRAPH	DILDOES	DIMERS
DIGESTING	DIGRAPHIC	DILDOS	DIMES
DIGESTION	DIGRAPHS	DILEMMA	DIMETER

DIMETERS	DINFUL	DINNERING	DIORAMIC
DIMETHYL	DING	DINNERS	DIORISM
DIMETHYLS	DINGBAT	DINNING	DIORISMS
DIMETRIC	DINGBATS	DINNLE	DIORISTIC
DIMIDIATE	DINGDONG	DINNLED	DIORITE
DIMINISH	DINGDONGS	DINNLES	DIORITES
DIMISSORY	DINGE	DINNLING	DIORITIC
DIMITIES	DINGED	DINO	DIOSGENIN
DIMITY	DINGER	DINOCERAS	DIOTA
DIMLY	DINGERS	DINOMANIA	DIOTAS
DIMMABLE	DINGES	DINOS	DIOXAN
DIMMED	DINGESES	DINOSAUR	DIOXANE
DIMMER	DINGEY	DINOSAURS	DIOXANES
DIMMERS	DINGEYS	DINOTHERE	DIOXANS
DIMMEST	DINGHIES	DINS	DIOXID
DIMMING	DINGHY	DINT	DIOXIDE
DIMMISH	DINGIER	DINTED	DIOXIDES
DIMNESS	DINGIES	DINTING	DIOXIDS
DIMNESSES	DINGIEST	DINTLESS	DIOXIN
DIMORPH	DINGILY	DINTS	DIOXINS
DIMORPHIC	DINGINESS	DIOBOL	DIP
DIMORPHS	DINGING	DIOBOLON	DIPCHICK
DIMOUT	DINGLE	DIOBOLONS	DIPCHICKS
DIMOUTS	DINGLES	DIOBOLS	DIPEPTIDE
DIMP	DINGO	DIOCESAN	DIPHASE
DIMPLE	DINGOED	DIOCESANS	DIPHASIC
DIMPLED	DINGOES	DIOCESE	DIPHENYL
DIMPLES	DINGOING	DIOCESES	DIPHENYLS
DIMPLIER	DINGS	DIODE	DIPHONE
DIMPLIEST	DINGUS	DIODES	DIPHONES
DIMPLING	DINGUSES	DIOECIES	DIPHTHONG
DIMPLY	DINGY	DIOECIOUS	DIPHYSITE
DIMPS	DINIC	DIOECISM	DIPLEGIA
DIMPSIES	DINICS	DIOECISMS	DIPLEGIAS
DIMPSY	DINING	DIOECY	DIPLEGIC
DIMS	DINITRO	DIOESTRUS	DIPLEX
DIMWIT	DINK	DIOICOUS	DIPLEXER
DIMWITS	DINKED	DIOL	DIPLEXERS
DIMWITTED	DINKER	DIOLEFIN	DIPLOE
DIMYARIAN	DINKEST	DIOLEFINS	DIPLOES
DIN	DINKEY	DIOLS	DIPLOGEN
DINAR	DINKEYS	DIONYSIAC	DIPLOGENS
DINARCHY	DINKIE	DIONYSIAN	DIPLOIC
DINARS	DINKIER	DIOPSIDE	DIPLOID
DINDLE	DINKIES	DIOPSIDES	DIPLOIDIC
DINDLED	DINKIEST	DIOPSIDIC	DIPLOIDS
DINDLES	DINKING	DIOPTASE	DIPLOIDY
DINDLING	DINKLY	DIOPTASES	DIPLOMA
DINE	DINKS	DIOPTER	DIPLOMACY
DINED	DINKUM	DIOPTERS	DIPLOMAED
DINER	DINKUMS	DIOPTRAL	DIPLOMAS
DINERIC	DINKY	DIOPTRATE	DIPLOMAT
DINERO	DINMONT	DIOPTRE	DIPLOMATA
DINEROS	DINMONTS	DIOPTRES	DIPLOMATE
DINERS	DINNA	DIOPTRIC	DIPLOMATS
DINES	DINNED	DIOPTRICS	DIPLON
DINETTE	DINNER	DIORAMA	DIPLONEMA
DINETTES	DINNERED	DIORAMAS	DIPLONS

DIPLONT	DIPTEROUS	DIRKES	DISARMERS
DIPLONTIC	DIPTYCA	DIRKING	DISARMING
DIPLONTS	DIPTYCAS	DIRKS	DISARMS
DIPLOPIA	DIPTYCH	DIRL	DISARRAY
DIPLOPIAS	DIPTYCHS	DIRLED	DISARRAYS
DIPLOPIC	DIQUARK	DIRLING	DISAS
DIPLOPOD	DIQUARKS	DIRLS	DISASTER
DIPLOPODS	DIQUAT	DIRNDL	DISASTERS
DIPLOSES	DIQUATS	DIRNDLS	DISATTIRE
DIPLOSIS	DIRAM	DIRT	DISATTUNE
DIPLOTENE	DIRAMS	DIRTBAG	DISAVOUCH
DIPLOZOA	DIRDAM	DIRTBAGS	DISAVOW
DIPLOZOIC	DIRDAMS	DIRTED	DISAVOWAL
DIPLOZOON	DIRDUM	DIRTIED	DISAVOWED
DIPNET	DIRDUMS	DIRTIER	DISAVOWER
DIPNETS	DIRE	DIRTIES	DISAVOWS
DIPNETTED	DIRECT	DIRTIEST	DISBAND
DIPNOAN	DIRECTED	DIRTILY	DISBANDED
DIPNOANS	DIRECTER	DIRTINESS	DISBANDS
DIPNOOUS	DIRECTEST	DIRTING	DISBAR
DIPODIC	DIRECTING	DIRTS	DISBARK
DIPODIES	DIRECTION	DIRTY	DISBARKED
DIPODY	DIRECTIVE	DIRTYING	DISBARKS
DIPOLAR	DIRECTLY	DIS	DISBARRED
DIPOLE	DIRECTOR	DISA	DISBARS
DIPOLES	DIRECTORS	DISABLE	DISBELIEF
DIPPABLE	DIRECTORY	DISABLED	DISBENCH
DIPPED	DIRECTRIX	DISABLER	DISBODIED
DIPPER	DIRECTS	DISABLERS	DISBOSOM
DIPPERFUL	DIREFUL	DISABLES	DISBOSOMS
DIPPERS	DIREFULLY	DISABLING	DISBOUND
DIPPIER	DIRELY	DISABUSAL	DISBOWEL
DIPPIEST	DIREMPT	DISABUSE	DISBOWELS
DIPPINESS	DIREMPTED	DISABUSED	DISBRANCH
DIPPING	DIREMPTS	DISABUSES	DISBUD
DIPPINGS	DIRENESS	DISACCORD	DISBUDDED
DIPPY	DIRER	DISADORN	DISBUDS
DIPROTIC	DIREST	DISADORNS	DISBURDEN
DIPS	DIRGE	DISAFFECT	DISBURSAL
DIPSADES	DIRGEFUL	DISAFFIRM	DISBURSE
DIPSAS	DIRGELIKE	DISAGREE	DISBURSED
DIPSHIT	DIRGES	DISAGREED	DISBURSER
DIPSHITS	DIRHAM	DISAGREES	DISBURSES
DIPSO	DIRHAMS	DISALLIED	DISC
DIPSOS	DIRHEM	DISALLIES	DISCAGE
DIPSTICK	DIRHEMS	DISALLOW	DISCAGED
DIPSTICKS	DIRIGE	DISALLOWS	DISCAGES
DIPT	DIRIGENT	DISALLY	DISCAGING
DIPTERA	DIRIGES	DISANCHOR	DISCAL
DIPTERAL	DIRIGIBLE	DISANNEX	DISCALCED
DIPTERAN	DIRIGISM	DISANNUL	DISCANDIE
DIPTERANS	DIRIGISME	DISANNULS	DISCANDY
DIPTERAS	DIRIGISMS	DISANOINT	DISCANT
DIPTERIST	DIRIGISTE	DISAPPEAR	DISCANTED
DIPTEROI	DIRIMENT	DISAPPLY	DISCANTER
DIPTERON	DIRK	DISARM	DISCANTS
DIPTERONS	DIRKE	DISARMED	DISCARD
DIPTEROS	DIRKED	DISARMER	DISCARDED

DISCARDER	DISCOUNT	DISFAVOR	DISHFUL
DISCARDS	DISCOUNTS	DISFAVORS	DISHFULS
DISCASE	DISCOURE	DISFAVOUR	DISHIER
DISCASED	DISCOURED	DISFIGURE	DISHIEST
DISCASES	DISCOURES	DISFLESH	DISHING
DISCASING	DISCOURSE	DISFLUENT	DISHINGS
DISCED	DISCOVER	DISFOREST	DISHLIKE
DISCEPT	DISCOVERS	DISFORM	DISHOME
DISCEPTED	DISCOVERT	DISFORMED	DISHOMED
DISCEPTS	DISCOVERY	DISFORMS	DISHOMES
DISCERN	DISCREDIT	DISFROCK	DISHOMING
DISCERNED	DISCREET	DISFROCKS	DISHONEST
DISCERNER	DISCRETE	DISGAVEL	DISHONOR
DISCERNS	DISCRETER	DISGAVELS	DISHONORS
DISCERP	DISCROWN	DISGEST	DISHONOUR
DISCERPED	DISCROWNS	DISGESTED	DISHORN
DISCERPS	DISCS	DISGESTS	DISHORNED
DISCHARGE	DISCUMBER	DISGODDED	DISHORNS
DISCHURCH	DISCURE	DISGORGE	DISHORSE
DISCI	DISCURED	DISGORGED	DISHORSED
DISCIDE	DISCURES	DISGORGER	DISHORSES
DISCIDED	DISCURING	DISGORGES	DISHOUSE
DISCIDES	DISCURSUS	DISGOWN	DISHOUSED
DISCIDING	DISCUS	DISGOWNED	DISHOUSES
DISCIFORM	DISCUSES	DISGOWNS	DISHPAN
DISCINCT	DISCUSS	DISGRACE	DISHPANS
DISCING	DISCUSSED	DISGRACED	DISHRAG
DISCIPLE	DISCUSSER	DISGRACER	DISHRAGS
DISCIPLED	DISCUSSES	DISGRACES	DISHTOWEL
DISCIPLES	DISDAIN	DISGRADE	DISHUMOUR
DISCLAIM	DISDAINED	DISGRADED	DISHWARE
DISCLAIMS	DISDAINS	DISGRADES	DISHWARES
DISCLIKE	DISEASE	DISGUISE	DISHWATER
DISCLIMAX	DISEASED	DISGUISED	DISHY
DISCLOSE	DISEASES	DISGUISER	DISILLUDE
DISCLOSED	DISEASING	DISGUISES	DISIMMURE
DISCLOSER	DISEDGE	DISGUST	DISINFECT
DISCLOSES	DISEDGED	DISGUSTED	DISINFEST
DISCLOST	DISEDGES	DISGUSTS	DISINFORM
DISCO	DISEDGING	DISH	DISINHUME
DISCOBOLI	DISEMBARK	DISHABIT	DISINTER
DISCOED	DISEMBODY	DISHABITS	DISINTERS
DISCOER	DISEMPLOY	DISHABLE	DISINURE
DISCOERS	DISENABLE	DISHABLED	DISINURED
DISCOID	DISENDOW	DISHABLES	DISINURES
DISCOIDAL	DISENDOWS	DISHALLOW	DISINVEST
DISCOIDS	DISENGAGE	DISHCLOTH	DISINVITE
DISCOING	DISENROL	DISHCLOUT	DISJASKIT
DISCOLOGY	DISENROLS	DISHDASHA	DISJECT
DISCOLOR	DISENTAIL	DISHED	DISJECTED
DISCOLORS	DISENTOMB	DISHELM	DISJECTS
DISCOLOUR	DISESTEEM	DISHELMED	DISJOIN
DISCOMFIT	DISEUR	DISHELMS	DISJOINED
DISCOMMON	DISEURS	DISHERIT	DISJOINS
DISCORD	DISEUSE	DISHERITS	DISJOINT
DISCORDED	DISEUSES	DISHES	DISJOINTS
DISCORDS	DISFAME	DISHEVEL	DISJUNCT
DISCOS	DISFAMES	DISHEVELS	DISJUNCTS

DISJUNE	DISMASKS	DISPATHY	DISPONING
DISJUNES	DISMAST	DISPAUPER	DISPORT
DISK	DISMASTED	DISPEACE	DISPORTED
DISKED	DISMASTS	DISPEACES	DISPORTS
DISKETTE	DISMAY	DISPEL	DISPOSAL
DISKETTES	DISMAYD	DISPELLED	DISPOSALS
DISKING	DISMAYED	DISPELLER	DISPOSE
DISKLESS	DISMAYFUL	DISPELS	DISPOSED
DISKLIKE	DISMAYING	DISPENCE	DISPOSER
DISKS	DISMAYL	DISPENCED	DISPOSERS
DISLEAF	DISMAYLED	DISPENCES	DISPOSES
DISLEAFED	DISMAYLS	DISPEND	DISPOSING
DISLEAFS	DISMAYS	DISPENDED	DISPOST
DISLEAL	DISME	DISPENDS	DISPOSTED
DISLEAVE	DISMEMBER	DISPENSE	DISPOSTS
DISLEAVED	DISMES	DISPENSED	DISPOSURE
DISLEAVES	DISMISS	DISPENSER	DISPRAD
DISLIKE	DISMISSAL	DISPENSES	DISPRAISE
DISLIKED	DISMISSED	DISPEOPLE	DISPREAD
DISLIKEN	DISMISSES	DISPERSAL	DISPREADS
DISLIKENS	DISMODED	DISPERSE	DISPRED
DISLIKER	DISMOUNT	DISPERSED	DISPREDS
DISLIKERS	DISMOUNTS	DISPERSER	DISPRISON
DISLIKES	DISNEST	DISPERSES	DISPRIZE
DISLIKING	DISNESTED	DISPIRIT	DISPRIZED
DISLIMB	DISNESTS	DISPIRITS	DISPRIZES
DISLIMBED	DISOBEY	DISPLACE	DISPROFIT
DISLIMBS	DISOBEYED	DISPLACED	DISPROOF
DISLIMN	DISOBEYER	DISPLACER	DISPROOFS
DISLIMNED	DISOBEYS	DISPLACES	DISPROOVE
DISLIMNS	DISOBLIGE	DISPLANT	DISPROVAL
DISLINK	DISOMIC	DISPLANTS	DISPROVE
DISLINKED	DISOMIES	DISPLAY	DISPROVED
DISLINKS	DISOMY	DISPLAYED	DISPROVEN
DISLOAD	DISORBED	DISPLAYER	DISPROVER
DISLOADED	DISORDER	DISPLAYS	DISPROVES
DISLOADS	DISORDERS	DISPLE	DISPUNGE
DISLOCATE	DISORIENT	DISPLEASE	DISPUNGED
DISLODGE	DISOWN	DISPLED	DISPUNGES
DISLODGED	DISOWNED	DISPLES	DISPURSE
DISLODGES	DISOWNER	DISPLING	DISPURSED
DISLOIGN	DISOWNERS	DISPLODE	DISPURSES
DISLOIGNS	DISOWNING	DISPLODED	DISPURVEY
DISLOYAL	DISOWNS	DISPLODES	DISPUTANT
DISLUSTRE	DISPACE	DISPLUME	DISPUTE
DISMAL	DISPACED	DISPLUMED	DISPUTED
DISMALER	DISPACES	DISPLUMES	DISPUTER
DISMALEST	DISPACING	DISPONDEE	DISPUTERS
DISMALITY	DISPARAGE	DISPONE	DISPUTES
DISMALLER	DISPARATE	DISPONED	DISPUTING
DISMALLY	DISPARITY	DISPONEE	DISQUIET
DISMALS	DISPARK	DISPONEES	DISQUIETS
DISMAN	DISPARKED	DISPONER	DISRANK
DISMANNED	DISPARKS	DISPONERS	DISRANKED
DISMANS	DISPART	DISPONES	DISRANKS
DISMANTLE	DISPARTED	DISPONGE	DISRATE
DISMASK	DISPARTS	DISPONGED	DISRATED
DISMASKED	DISPATCH	DISPONGES	DISRATES

DISRATING	DISSEVER	DISTOMES	DITAL
DISREGARD	DISSEVERS	DISTORT	DITALS
DISRELISH	DISSHIVER	DISTORTED	DITAS
DISREPAIR	DISSIDENT	DISTORTER	DITCH
DISREPUTE	DISSIGHT	DISTORTS	DITCHED
DISROBE	DISSIGHTS	DISTRACT	DITCHER
DISROBED	DISSIMILE	DISTRACTS	DITCHERS
DISROBER	DISSING	DISTRAIL	DITCHES
DISROBERS	DISSIPATE	DISTRAILS	DITCHING
DISROBES	DISSOCIAL	DISTRAIN	DITCHLESS
DISROBING	DISSOLUTE	DISTRAINS	DITE
DISROOT	DISSOLVE	DISTRAINT	DITED
DISROOTED	DISSOLVED	DISTRAIT	DITES
DISROOTS	DISSOLVER	DISTRAITE	DITHECAL
DISRUPT	DISSOLVES	DISTRESS	DITHECOUS
DISRUPTED	DISSONANT	DISTRICT	DITHEISM
DISRUPTER	DISSUADE	DISTRICTS	DITHEISMS
DISRUPTOR	DISSUADED	DISTRIX	DITHEIST
DISRUPTS	DISSUADER	DISTRIXES	DITHEISTS
DISS	DISSUADES	DISTRUST	DITHELETE
DISSAVE	DISSUNDER	DISTRUSTS	DITHELISM
DISSAVED	DISTAFF	DISTUNE	DITHER
DISSAVES	DISTAFFS	DISTUNED	DITHERED
DISSAVING	DISTAIN	DISTUNES	DITHERER
DISSEAT	DISTAINED	DISTUNING	DITHERERS
DISSEATED	DISTAINS	DISTURB	DITHERIER
DISSEATS	DISTAL	DISTURBED	DITHERING
DISSECT	DISTALLY	DISTURBER	DITHERS
DISSECTED	DISTANCE	DISTURBS	DITHERY
DISSECTOR	DISTANCED	DISTYLE	DITHIOL
DISSECTS	DISTANCES	DISTYLES	DITHYRAMB
DISSED	DISTANT	DISULFATE	DITING
DISSEISE	DISTANTLY	DISULFID	DITOKOUS
DISSEISED	DISTASTE	DISULFIDE	DITONE
DISSEISEE	DISTASTED	DISULFIDS	DITONES
DISSEISES	DISTASTES	DISUNION	DITROCHEE
DISSEISIN	DISTAVES	DISUNIONS	DITS
DISSEISOR	DISTEMPER	DISUNITE	DITSIER
DISSEIZE	DISTEND	DISUNITED	DITSIEST
DISSEIZED	DISTENDED	DISUNITER	DITSINESS
DISSEIZEE	DISTENDER	DISUNITES	DITSY
DISSEIZES	DISTENDS	DISUNITY	DITT
DISSEIZIN	DISTENT	DISUSAGE	DITTANDER
DISSEIZOR	DISTHENE	DISUSAGES	DITTANIES
DISSEMBLE	DISTHENES	DISUSE	DITTANY
DISSEMBLY	DISTHRONE	DISUSED	DITTAY
DISSENSUS	DISTICH	DISUSES	DITTAYS
DISSENT	DISTICHAL	DISUSING	DITTED
DISSENTED	DISTICHS	DISVALUE	DITTIED
DISSENTER	DISTIL	DISVALUED	DITTIES
DISSENTS	DISTILL	DISVALUES	DITTING
DISSERT	DISTILLED	DISVOUCH	DITTIT
DISSERTED	DISTILLER	DISYOKE	DITTO
DISSERTS	DISTILLS	DISYOKED	DITTOED
DISSERVE	DISTILS	DISYOKES	DITTOING
DISSERVED	DISTINCT	DISYOKING	DITTOLOGY
DISSERVES	DISTINGUE	DIT	DITTOS
DISSES	DISTOME	DITA	DITTS

DITTY	DIVES	DIVORCES	DJIBBAHS
DITTYING	DIVEST	DIVORCING	DJIN
DITZ	DIVESTED	DIVORCIVE	DJINN
DITZES	DIVESTING	DIVOT	DJINNI
DITZIER	DIVESTS	DTVOTS	DJINNS
DITZIEST	DIVESTURE	DIVS	DJINNY
DITZINESS	DIVI	DIVULGATE	DJINS
DITZY	DIVIDABLE	DIVULGE	DO
DIURESES	DIVIDANT	DIVULGED	DOAB
DIURESIS	DIVIDE	DIVULGER	DOABLE
DIURETIC	DIVIDED	DIVULGERS	DOABS
DIURETICS	DIVIDEDLY	DIVULGES	DOAT
DIURNAL	DIVIDEND	DIVULGING	DOATED
DIURNALLY	DIVIDENDS	DIVULSE	DOATER
DIURNALS	DIVIDER	DIVULSED	DOATERS
DIURON	DIVIDERS	DIVULSES	DOATING
DIURONS	DIVIDES	DIVULSING	DOATINGS
DIUTURNAL	DIVIDING	DIVULSION	DOATS
DIV	DIVIDINGS	DIVULSIVE	DOB
DIVA	DIVIDIVI	DIVVIED	DOBBED
DIVAGATE	DIVIDIVIS	DIVVIES	DOBBER
DIVAGATED	DIVIDUAL	DIVVY	DOBBERS
DIVAGATES	DIVIDUOUS	DIVVYING	DOBBIE
DIVALENCE	DIVINABLE	DIWAN	DOBBIES
DIVALENCY	DIVINATOR	DIWANS	DOBBIN
DIVALENT	DIVINE	DIXI	DOBBING
DIVALENTS	DIVINED	DIXIE	DOBBINS
DIVAN	DIVINELY	DIXIES	DOBBY
DIVANS	DIVINER	DIXIT	DOBCHICK
DIVAS	DIVINERS	DIXITS	DOBCHICKS
DIVE	DIVINES	DIXY	DOBHASH
DIVEBOMB	DIVINEST	DIZAIN	DOBHASHES
DIVEBOMBS	DIVING	DIZAINS	DOBIE
DIVED	DIVINGS	DIZEN	DOBIES
DIVELLENT	DIVINIFY	DIZENED	DOBLA
DIVER	DIVINING	DIZENING	DOBLAS
DIVERGE	DIVINISE	DIZENMENT	DOBLON
DIVERGED	DIVINISED	DIZENS	DOBLONES
DIVERGENT	DIVINISES	DIZYGOTIC	DOBLONS
DIVERGES	DIVINITY	DIZYGOUS	DOBRA
DIVERGING	DIVINIZE	DIZZARD	DOBRAS
DIVERS	DIVINIZED	DIZZARDS	DOBRO
DIVERSE	DIVINIZES	DIZZIED	DOBROS
DIVERSED	DIVIS	DIZZIER	DOBS
DIVERSELY	DIVISIBLE	DIZZIES	DOBSON
DIVERSES	DIVISIBLY	DIZZIEST	DOBSONFLY
DIVERSIFY	DIVISIM	DIZZILY	DOBSONS
DIVERSING	DIVISION	DIZZINESS	DOBY
DIVERSION	DIVISIONS	DIZZY	DOC
DIVERSITY	DIVISIVE	DIZZYING	DOCENT
DIVERSLY	DIVISOR	DJEBEL	DOCENTS
DIVERT	DIVISORS	DJEBELS	DOCETIC
DIVERTED	DIVORCE	DJELLABA	DOCHMIAC
DIVERTER	DIVORCED	DJELLABAH	DOCHMII
DIVERTERS	DIVORCEE	DJELLABAS	DOCHMIUS
DIVERTING	DIVORCEES	DJEMBE	DOCHT
DIVERTIVE	DIVORCER	DJEMBES	DOCIBLE
DIVERTS	DIVORCERS	DJIBBAH	DOCILE

DOCILELY
DOCILER
DOCILEST
DOCILITY
DOCIMASY
DOCK
DOCKAGE
DOCKAGES
DOCKED
DOCKEN
DOCKENS
DOCKER
DOCKERS
DOCKET
DOCKETED
DOCKETING
DOCKETS
DOCKHAND
DOCKHANDS
DOCKING
DOCKINGS
DOCKISE
DOCKISED
DOCKISES
DOCKISING
DOCKIZE
DOCKIZED
DOCKIZES
DOCKIZING
DOCKLAND
DOCKLANDS
DOCKS
DOCKSIDE
DOCKSIDES
DOCKYARD
DOCKYARDS
DOCO
DOCOS
DOCQUET
DOCQUETED
DOCQUETS
DOCS
DOCTOR
DOCTORAL
DOCTORAND
DOCTORATE
DOCTORED
DOCTORESS
DOCTORIAL
DOCTORING
DOCTORLY
DOCTORS
DOCTRESS
DOCTRINAL
DOCTRINE
DOCTRINES
DOCUDRAMA
DOCUMENT

DOCUMENTS
DOD
DODDARD
DODDED
DODDER
DODDERED
DODDERER
DODDERERS
DODDERIER
DODDERING
DODDERS
DODDERY
DODDIER
DODDIES
DODDIEST
DODDING
DODDIPOLL
DODDLE
DODDLES
DODDY
DODDYPOLL
DODECAGON
DODGE
DODGEBALL
DODGED
DODGEM
DODGEMS
DODGER
DODGERIES
DODGERS
DODGERY
DODGES
DODGIER
DODGIEST
DODGINESS
DODGING
DODGINGS
DODGY
DODKIN
DODKINS
DODMAN
DODMANS
DODO
DODOES
DODOISM
DODOISMS
DODOS
DODS
DOE
DOEK
DOEKS
DOEN
DOER
DOERS
DOES
DOESKIN
DOESKINS
DOEST

DOETH
DOF
DOFF
DOFFED
DOFFER
DOFFERS
DOFFING
DOFFS
DOG
DOGARESSA
DOGATE
DOGATES
DOGBANE
DOGBANES
DOGBERRY
DOGBOLT
DOGBOLTS
DOGCART
DOGCARTS
DOGDAYS
DOGDOM
DOGDOMS
DOGE
DOGEAR
DOGEARED
DOGEARING
DOGEARS
DOGEATE
DOGEATES
DOGEDOM
DOGEDOMS
DOGES
DOGESHIP
DOGESHIPS
DOGEY
DOGEYS
DOGFACE
DOGFACES
DOGFIGHT
DOGFIGHTS
DOGFISH
DOGFISHES
DOGFOUGHT
DOGFOX
DOGFOXES
DOGGED
DOGGEDER
DOGGEDEST
DOGGEDLY
DOGGER
DOGGEREL
DOGGERELS
DOGGERIES
DOGGERMAN
DOGGERMEN
DOGGERS
DOGGERY
DOGGESS

DOGGESSES
DOGGIE
DOGGIER
DOGGIES
DOGGIEST
DOGGINESS
DOGGING
DOGGINGS
DOGGISH
DOGGISHLY
DOGGO
DOGGONE
DOGGONED
DOGGONER
DOGGONES
DOGGONEST
DOGGONING
DOGGREL
DOGGRELS
DOGGY
DOGHANGED
DOGHOLE
DOGHOLES
DOGHOUSE
DOGHOUSES
DOGIE
DOGIES
DOGLEG
DOGLEGGED
DOGLEGS
DOGLIKE
DOGMA
DOGMAN
DOGMAS
DOGMATA
DOGMATIC
DOGMATICS
DOGMATISE
DOGMATISM
DOGMATIST
DOGMATIZE
DOGMATORY
DOGMEN
DOGNAP
DOGNAPED
DOGNAPER
DOGNAPERS
DOGNAPING
DOGNAPPED
DOGNAPPER
DOGNAPS
DOGROBBER
DOGS
DOGSBODY
DOGSHIP
DOGSHIPS
DOGSHORES
DOGSKIN

DOGSKINS	DOLICHURI	DOLPHINS	DOMINIQUE
DOGSLED	DOLINA	DOLS	DOMINIUM
DOGSLEDS	DOLINAS	DOLT	DOMINIUMS
DOGSLEEP	DOLINE	DOLTISH	DOMINO
DOGSLEEPS	DOLINES	DOLTISHLY	DOMINOES
DOGTEETH	DOLING	DOLTS	DOMINOS
DOGTOOTH	DOLIUM	DOM	DOMS
DOGTOWN	DOLL	DOMAIN	DOMY
DOGTOWNS	DOLLAR	DOMAINAL	DON
DOGTROT	DOLLARED	DOMAINE	DONA
DOGTROTS	DOLLARISE	DOMAINES	DONAH
DOGVANE	DOLLARIZE	DOMAINS	DONAHS
DOGVANES	DOLLARS	DOMAL	DONARIES
DOGWATCH	DOLLDOM	DOMANIAL	DONARY
DOGWOOD	DOLLDOMS	DOMATIA	DONAS
DOGWOODS	DOLLED	DOMATIUM	DONATARY
DOGY	DOLLHOOD	DOME	DONATE
DOH	DOLLHOODS	DOMED	DONATED
DOHS	DOLLHOUSE	DOMELIKE	DONATES
DOHYO	DOLLIED	DOMES	DONATING
DOHYOS	DOLLIER	DOMESDAY	DONATION
DOILED	DOLLIERS	DOMESDAYS	DONATIONS
DOILIES	DOLLIES	DOMESTIC	DONATISM
DOILT	DOLLINESS	DOMESTICS	DONATISMS
DOILTER	DOLLING	DOMETT	DONATIVE
DOILTEST	DOLLISH	DOMETTS	DONATIVES
DOILY	DOLLISHLY	DOMIC	DONATOR
DOING	DOLLOP	DOMICAL	DONATORS
DOINGS	DOLLOPED	DOMICALLY	DONATORY
DOIT	DOLLOPING	DOMICIL	DONDER
DOITED	DOLLOPS	DOMICILE	DONDERED
DOITIT	DOLLS	DOMICILED	DONDERING
DOITKIN	DOLLY	DOMICILES	DONDERS
DOITKINS	DOLLYBIRD	DOMICILS	DONE
DOITS	DOLLYING	DOMIER	DONEE
DOJO	DOLMA	DOMIEST	DONEES
DOJOS	DOLMADES	DOMINANCE	DONENESS
DOL	DOLMAN	DOMINANCY	DONER
DOLABRATE	DOLMANS	DOMINANT	DONG
DOLCE	DOLMAS	DOMINANTS	DONGA
DOLCES	DOLMEN	DOMINATE	DONGAS
DOLCETTO	DOLMENIC	DOMINATED	DONGED
DOLCETTOS	DOLMENS	DOMINATES	DONGING
DOLCI	DOLOMITE	DOMINATOR	DONGLE
DOLDRUMS	DOLOMITES	DOMINE	DONGLES
DOLE	DOLOMITIC	DOMINEE	DONGOLA
DOLED	DOLOR	DOMINEER	DONGOLAS
DOLEFUL	DOLORIFIC	DOMINEERS	DONGS
DOLEFULLY	DOLOROSO	DOMINEES	DONING
DOLENT	DOLOROUS	DOMINES	DONINGS
DOLENTE	DOLORS	DOMING	DONJON
DOLERITE	DOLOS	DOMINICAL	DONJONS
DOLERITES	DOLOSSE	DOMINICK	DONKEY
DOLERITIC	DOLOSTONE	DOMINICKS	DONKEYS
DOLES	DOLOUR	DOMINIE	DONKO
DOLESOME	DOLOURS	DOMINIES	DONKOS
DOLIA	DOLPHIN	DOMINION	DONNA
DOLICHOS	DOLPHINET	DOMINIONS	DONNARD

DONNART	DOODLES	DOORKNOBS	DOPESTERS
DONNAS	DOODLING	DOORKNOCK	DOPEY
DONNAT	DOODOO	DOORLESS	DOPEYNESS
DONNATS	DOODOOS	DOORMAN	DOPIAZA
DONNE	DOODY	DOORMAT	DOPIAZAS
DONNED	DOOFER	DOORMATS	DOPIER
DONNEE	DOOFERS	DOORMEN	DOPIEST
DONNEES	DOOFUS	DOORN	DOPILY
DONNERD	DOOFUSES	DOORNAIL	DOPINESS
DONNERED	DOOHICKEY	DOORNAILS	DOPING
DONNERT	DOOK	DOORNS	DOPINGS
DONNES	DOOKED	DOORPLATE	DOPPED
DONNICKER	DOOKET	DOORPOST	DOPPER
DONNIES	DOOKETS	DOORPOSTS	DOPPERS
DONNIKER	DOOKING	DOORS	DOPPIE
DONNIKERS	DOOKS	DOORSILL	DOPPIES
DONNING	DOOL	DOORSILLS	DOPPING
DONNISH	DOOLALLY	DOORSMAN	DOPPINGS
DONNISHLY	DOOLAN	DOORSMEN	DOPPIO
DONNISM	DOOLANS	DOORSTEP	DOPPIOS
DONNISMS	DOOLE	DOORSTEPS	DOPS
DONNOT	DOOLEE	DOORSTONE	DOPY
DONNOTS	DOOLEES	DOORSTOP	DOR
DONNY	DOOLES	DOORSTOPS	DORAD
DONOR	DOOLIE	DOORWAY	DORADO
DONORS	DOOLIES	DOORWAYS	DORADOS
DONORSHIP	DOOLS	DOORWOMAN	DORADS
DONS	DOOLY	DOORWOMEN	DORB
DONSHIP	DOOM	DOORYARD	DORBA
DONSHIPS	DOOMED	DOORYARDS	DORBAS
DONSIE	DOOMFUL	DOOS	DORBEETLE
DONSIER	DOOMFULLY	DOOSRA	DORBS
DONSIEST	DOOMIER	DOOSRAS	DORBUG
DONSY	DOOMIEST	DOOWOP	DORBUGS
DONUT	DOOMILY	DOOWOPS	DORE
DONUTS	DOOMING	DOOZER	DOREE
DONUTTED	DOOMS	DOOZERS	DOREES
DONUTTING	DOOMSAYER	DOOZIE	DORHAWK
DONZEL	DOOMSDAY	DOOZIES	DORHAWKS
DONZELS	DOOMSDAYS	DOOZY	DORIC
DOO	DOOMSMAN	DOP	DORIDOID
DOOB	DOOMSMEN	DOPA	DORIDOIDS
DOOBIE	DOOMSTER	DOPAMINE	DORIES
DOOBIES	DOOMSTERS	DOPAMINES	DORIS
DOOBS	DOOMWATCH	DOPANT	DORISE
DOOCED	DOOMY	DOPANTS	DORISED
DOOCOT	DOON	DOPAS	DORISES
DOOCOTS	DOONA	DOPATTA	DORISING
DOODAD	DOONAS	DOPATTAS	DORIZE
DOODADS	DOOR	DOPE	DORIZED
DOODAH	DOORBELL	DOPED	DORIZES
DOODAHS	DOORBELLS	DOPEHEAD	DORIZING
DOODIES	DOORCASE	DOPEHEADS	DORK
DOODLE	DOORCASES	DOPER	DORKIER
DOODLEBUG	DOORFRAME	DOPERS	DORKIEST
DOODLED	DOORJAMB	DOPES	DORKINESS
DOODLER	DOORJAMBS	DOPESHEET	DORKS
DOODLERS	DOORKNOB	DOPESTER	DORKY

DORLACH	DORTOURS	DOTES	DOUBTFULS
DORLACHS	DORTS	DOTH	DOUBTING
DORM	DORTY	DOTIER	DOUBTINGS
DORMANCY	DORY	DOTIEST	DOUBTLESS
DORMANT	DOS	DOTING	DOUBTS
DORMANTS	DOSAGE	DOTINGLY	DOUC
DORMER	DOSAGES	DOTINGS	DOUCE
DORMERED	DOSE	DOTISH	DOUCELY
DORMERS	DOSED	DOTS	DOUCENESS
DORMICE	DOSEH	DOTTED	DOUCEPERE
DORMIE	DOSEHS	DOTTEL	DOUCER
DORMIENT	DOSEMETER	DOTTELS	DOUCEST
DORMIN	DOSER	DOTTER	DOUCET
DORMINS	DOSERS	DOTTEREL	DOUCETS
DORMITION	DOSES	DOTTERELS	DOUCEUR
DORMITIVE	DOSH	DOTTERS	DOUCEURS
DORMITORY	DOSHES	DOTTIER	DOUCHE
DORMOUSE	DOSIMETER	DOTTIEST	DOUCHEBAG
DORMS	DOSIMETRY	DOTTILY	DOUCHED
DORMY	DOSING	DOTTINESS	DOUCHES
DORNECK	DOSIOLOGY	DOTTING	DOUCHING
DORNECKS	DOSOLOGY	DOTTLE	DOUCINE
DORNICK	DOSS	DOTTLED	DOUCINES
DORNICKS	DOSSAL	DOTTLER	DOUCS
DORNOCK	DOSSALS	DOTTLES	DOUGH
DORNOCKS	DOSSED	DOTTLEST	DOUGHBOY
DORONICUM	DOSSEL	DOTTREL	DOUGHBOYS
DORP	DOSSELS	DOTTRELS	DOUGHFACE
DORPER	DOSSER	DOTTY	DOUGHIER
DORPERS	DOSSERET	DOTY	DOUGHIEST
DORPS	DOSSERETS	DOUANE	DOUGHLIKE
DORR	DOSSERS	DOUANES	DOUGHNUT
DORRED	DOSSES	DOUANIER	DOUGHNUTS
DORRING	DOSSHOUSE	DOUANIERS	DOUGHS
DORRS	DOSSIER	DOUAR	DOUGHT
DORS	DOSSIERS	DOUARS	DOUGHTIER
DORSA	DOSSIL	DOUBLE	DOUGHTILY
DORSAD	DOSSILS	DOUBLED	DOUGHTY
DORSAL	DOSSING	DOUBLER	DOUGHY
DORSALLY	DOST	DOUBLERS	DOUK
DORSALS	DOT	DOUBLES	DOUKED
DORSE	DOTAGE	DOUBLET	DOUKING
DORSEL	DOTAGES	DOUBLETON	DOUKS
DORSELS	DOTAL	DOUBLETS	DOULA
DORSER	DOTANT	DOUBLING	DOULAS
DORSERS	DOTANTS	DOUBLINGS	DOULEIA
DORSES	DOTARD	DOUBLOON	DOULEIAS
DORSIFLEX	DOTARDLY	DOUBLOONS	DOUM
DORSUM	DOTARDS	DOUBLURE	DOUMA
DORT	DOTATION	DOUBLURES	DOUMAS
DORTED	DOTATIONS	DOUBLY	DOUMS
DORTER	DOTCOM	DOUBT	DOUN
DORTERS	DOTCOMMER	DOUBTABLE	DOUP
DORTIER	DOTCOMS	DOUBTABLY	DOUPIONI
DORTIEST	DOTE	DOUBTED	DOUPIONIS
DORTINESS	DOTED	DOUBTER	DOUPPIONI
DORTING	DOTER	DOUBTERS	DOUPS
DORTOUR	DOTERS	DOUBTFUL	DOUR

DOURA	DOWAGERS	DOWNCOMES	DOWNSWING
DOURAH	DOWAR	DOWNCOURT	DOWNTHROW
DOURAHS	DOWARS	DOWNDRAFT	DOWNTICK
DOURAS	DOWD	DOWNED	DOWNTICKS
DOURER	DOWDIER	DOWNER	DOWNTIME
DOUREST	DOWDIES	DOWNERS	DOWNTIMES
DOURINE	DOWDIEST	DOWNFALL	DOWNTOWN
DOURINES	DOWDILY	DOWNFALLS	DOWNTOWNS
DOURLY	DOWDINESS	DOWNFIELD	DOWNTREND
DOURNESS	DOWDS	DOWNFLOW	DOWNTROD
DOUSE	DOWDY	DOWNFLOWS	DOWNTURN
DOUSED	DOWDYISH	DOWNFORCE	DOWNTURNS
DOUSER	DOWDYISM	DOWNGRADE	DOWNWARD
DOUSERS	DOWDYISMS	DOWNHAUL	DOWNWARDS
DOUSES	DOWED	DOWNHAULS	DOWNWASH
DOUSING	DOWEL	DOWNHILL	DOWNWIND
DOUT	DOWELED	DOWNHILLS	DOWNY
DOUTED	DOWELING	DOWNHOLE	DOWNZONE
DOUTER	DOWELLED	DOWNIER	DOWNZONED
DOUTERS	DOWELLING	DOWNIEST	DOWNZONES
DOUTING	DOWELS	DOWNINESS	DOWP
DOUTS	DOWER	DOWNING	DOWPS
DOUX	DOWERED	DOWNLAND	DOWRIES
DOUZEPER	DOWERIES	DOWNLANDS	DOWRY
DOUZEPERS	DOWERING	DOWNLESS	DOWS
DOVE	DOWERLESS	DOWNLIGHT	DOWSABEL
DOVECOT	DOWERS	DOWNLIKE	DOWSABELS
DOVECOTE	DOWERY	DOWNLINK	DOWSE
DOVECOTES	DOWF	DOWNLINKS	DOWSED
DOVECOTS	DOWFNESS	DOWNLOAD	DOWSER
DOVED	DOWIE	DOWNLOADS	DOWSERS
DOVEISH	DOWIER	DOWNMOST	DOWSES
DOVEKEY	DOWIEST	DOWNPIPE	DOWSET
DOVEKEYS	DOWING	DOWNPIPES	DOWSETS
DOVEKIE	DOWITCHER	DOWNPLAY	DOWSING
DOVEKIES	DOWL	DOWNPLAYS	DOWT
DOVELET	DOWLAS	DOWNPOUR	DOWTS
DOVELETS	DOWLASES	DOWNPOURS	DOXASTIC
DOVELIKE	DOWLE	DOWNRANGE	DOXIE
DOVEN	DOWLES	DOWNRIGHT	DOXIES
DOVENED	DOWLIER	DOWNRIVER	DOXOLOGY
DOVENING	DOWLIEST	DOWNRUSH	DOXY
DOVENS	DOWLNE	DOWNS	DOY
DOVER	DOWLNES	DOWNSCALE	DOYEN
DOVERED	DOWLNEY	DOWNSHIFT	DOYENNE
DOVERING	DOWLS	DOWNSIDE	DOYENNES
DOVERS	DOWLY	DOWNSIDES	DOYENS
DOVES	DOWN	DOWNSIZE	DOYLEY
DOVETAIL	DOWNA	DOWNSIZED	DOYLEYS
DOVETAILS	DOWNBEAT	DOWNSIZES	DOYLIES
DOVIE	DOWNBEATS	DOWNSLIDE	DOYLY
DOVIER	DOWNBOW	DOWNSLOPE	DOYS
DOVIEST	DOWNBOWS	DOWNSPIN	DOZE
DOVING	DOWNBURST	DOWNSPINS	DOZED
DOVISH	DOWNCAST	DOWNSPOUT	DOZEN
DOW	DOWNCASTS	DOWNSTAGE	DOZENED
DOWABLE	DOWNCOME	DOWNSTAIR	DOZENING
DOWAGER	DOWNCOMER	DOWNSTATE	DOZENS

DOZENTH	DRAFFIER	DRAGROPES	DRAPE
DOZENTHS	DRAFFIEST	DRAGS	DRAPEABLE
DOZER	DRAFFISH	DRAGSMAN	DRAPED
DOZERS	DRAFFS	DRAGSMEN	DRAPER
DOZES	DRAFFY	DRAGSTER	DRAPERIED
DOZIER	DRAFT	DRAGSTERS	DRAPERIES
DOZIEST	DRAFTABLE	DRAGSTRIP	DRAPERS
DOZILY	DRAFTED	DRAIL	DRAPERY
DOZINESS	DRAFTEE	DRAILED	DRAPES
DOZING	DRAFTEES	DRAILING	DRAPET
DOZINGS	DRAFTER	DRAILS	DRAPETS
DOZY	DRAFTERS	DRAIN	DRAPEY
DRAB	DRAFTIER	DRAINABLE	DRAPIER
DRABBED	DRAFTIEST	DRAINAGE	DRAPIERS
DRABBER	DRAFTILY	DRAINAGES	DRAPING
DRABBERS	DRAFTING	DRAINED	DRAPPED
DRABBEST	DRAFTINGS	DRAINER	DRAPPIE
DRABBET	DRAFTS	DRAINERS	DRAPPIES
DRABBETS	DRAFTSMAN	DRAINING	DRAPPING
DRABBIER	DRAFTSMEN	DRAINPIPE	DRAPPY
DRABBIEST	DRAFTY	DRAINS	DRAPS
DRABBING	DRAG	DRAISENE	DRASTIC
DRABBISH	DRAGEE	DRAISENES	DRASTICS
DRABBLE	DRAGEES	DRAISINE	DRAT
DRABBLED	DRAGGED	DRAISINES	DRATCHELL
DRABBLER	DRAGGER	DRAKE	DRATS
DRABBLERS	DRAGGERS	DRAKES	DRATTED
DRABBLES	DRAGGIER	DRAM	DRATTING
DRABBLING	DRAGGIEST	DRAMA	DRAUGHT
DRABBY	DRAGGING	DRAMADIES	DRAUGHTED
DRABETTE	DRAGGLE	DRAMADY	DRAUGHTER
DRABETTES	DRAGGLED	DRAMAS	DRAUGHTS
DRABLER	DRAGGLES	DRAMATIC	DRAUGHTY
DRABLERS	DRAGGLING	DRAMATICS	DRAUNT
DRABLY	DRAGGY	DRAMATISE	DRAUNTED
DRABNESS	DRAGHOUND	DRAMATIST	DRAUNTING
DRABS	DRAGLINE	DRAMATIZE	DRAUNTS
DRAC	DRAGLINES	DRAMATURG	DRAVE
DRACAENA	DRAGNET	DRAMEDIES	DRAW
DRACAENAS	DRAGNETS	DRAMEDY	DRAWABLE
DRACENA	DRAGOMAN	DRAMMACH	DRAWBACK
DRACENAS	DRAGOMANS	DRAMMACHS	DRAWBACKS
DRACHM	DRAGOMEN	DRAMMED	DRAWBAR
DRACHMA	DRAGON	DRAMMING	DRAWBARS
DRACHMAE	DRAGONESS	DRAMMOCK	DRAWBORE
DRACHMAI	DRAGONET	DRAMMOCKS	DRAWBORES
DRACHMAS	DRAGONETS	DRAMS	DRAWDOWN
DRACHMS	DRAGONFLY	DRAMSHOP	DRAWDOWNS
DRACK	DRAGONISE	DRAMSHOPS	DRAWEE
DRACO	DRAGONISH	DRANGWAY	DRAWEES
DRACONE	DRAGONISM	DRANGWAYS	DRAWER
DRACONES	DRAGONIZE	DRANK	DRAWERFUL
DRACONIAN	DRAGONNE	DRANT	DRAWERS
DRACONIC	DRAGONNE	DRANTED	DRAWING
DRACONISM	DRAGONS	DRANTING	DRAWINGS
DRACONTIC	DRAGOON	DRANTS	DRAWKNIFE
DRAD	DRAGOONED	DRAP	DRAWL
DRAFF	DRAGOONS	DRAPABLE	DRAWLED
	DRAGROPE		

DRAWLER	DREARER	DRESSAGE	DRIFTPIN
DRAWLERS	DREARES	DRESSAGES	DRIFTPINS
DRAWLIER	DREAREST	DRESSED	DRIFTS
DRAWLIEST	DREARIER	DRESSER	DRIFTWOOD
DRAWLING	DREARIES	DRESSERS	DRIFTY
DRAWLS	DREARIEST	DRESSES	DRILL
DRAWLY	DREARILY	DRESSIER	DRILLABLE
DRAWN	DREARING	DRESSIEST	DRILLED
DRAWNWORK	DREARINGS	DRESSILY	DRILLER
DRAWPLATE	DREARS	DRESSING	DRILLERS
DRAWS	DREARY	DRESSINGS	DRILLING
DRAWSHAVE	DRECK	DRESSMADE	DRILLINGS
DRAWTUBE	DRECKIER	DRESSMAKE	DRILLS
DRAWTUBES	DRECKIEST	DRESSY	DRILLSHIP
DRAY	DRECKS	DREST	DRILY
DRAYAGE	DRECKSILL	DREVILL	DRINK
DRAYAGES	DRECKY	DREVILLS	DRINKABLE
DRAYED	DREDGE	DREW	DRINKABLY
DRAYHORSE	DREDGED	DREY	DRINKER
DRAYING	DREDGER	DREYS	DRINKERS
DRAYMAN	DREDGERS	DRIB	DRINKING
DRAYMEN	DREDGES	DRIBBED	DRINKINGS
DRAYS	DREDGING	DRIBBER	DRINKS
DRAZEL	DREDGINGS	DRIBBERS	DRIP
DRAZELS	DREE	DRIBBING	DRIPLESS
DREAD	DREED	DRIBBLE	DRIPPED
DREADED	DREEING	DRIBBLED	DRIPPER
DREADER	DREES	DRIBBLER	DRIPPERS
DREADERS	DREG	DRIBBLERS	DRIPPIER
DREADFUL	DREGGIER	DRIBBLES	DRIPPIEST
DREADFULS	DREGGIEST	DRIBBLET	DRIPPILY
DREADING	DREGGISH	DRIBBLETS	DRIPPING
DREADLESS	DREGGY	DRIBBLIER	DRIPPINGS
DREADLOCK	DREGS	DRIBBLING	DRIPPY
DREADLY	DREICH	DRIBBLY	DRIPS
DREADS	DREICHER	DRIBLET	DRIPSTONE
DREAM	DREICHEST	DRIBLETS	DRIPT
DREAMBOAT	DREIDEL	DRIBS	DRISHEEN
DREAMED	DREIDELS	DRICE	DRISHEENS
DREAMER	DREIDL	DRICES	DRIVABLE
DREAMERS	DREIDLS	DRICKSIE	DRIVE
DREAMERY	DREIGH	DRICKSIER	DRIVEABLE
DREAMFUL	DREK	DRIED	DRIVEL
DREAMHOLE	DREKS	DRIEGH	DRIVELED
DREAMIER	DRENCH	DRIER	DRIVELER
DREAMIEST	DRENCHED	DRIERS	DRIVELERS
DREAMILY	DRENCHER	DRIES	DRIVELINE
DREAMING	DRENCHERS	DRIEST	DRIVELING
DREAMINGS	DRENCHES	DRIFT	DRIVELLED
DREAMLAND	DRENCHING	DRIFTAGE	DRIVELLER
DREAMLESS	DRENT	DRIFTAGES	DRIVELS
DREAMLIKE	DREPANID	DRIFTED	DRIVEN
DREAMS	DREPANIDS	DRIFTER	DRIVER
DREAMT	DREPANIUM	DRIFTERS	DRIVERS
DREAMTIME	DRERE	DRIFTIER	DRIVES
DREAMY	DRERES	DRIFTIEST	DRIVEWAY
DREAR	DRERIHEAD	DRIFTING	DRIVEWAYS
DREARE	DRESS	DRIFTLESS	DRIVING

DRIVINGLY	DRONERS	DROPPER	DROWNDS
DRIVINGS	DRONES	DROPPERS	DROWNED
DRIZZLE	DRONGO	DROPPING	DROWNER
DRIZZLED	DRONGOES	DROPPINGS	DROWNERS
DRIZZLES	DRONGOS	DROPPLE	DROWNING
DRIZZLIER	DRONIER	DROPPLES	DROWNINGS
DRIZZLING	DRONIEST	DROPS	DROWNS
DRIZZLY	DRONING	DROPSHOT	DROWS
DROGER	DRONINGLY	DROPSHOTS	DROWSE
DROGERS	DRONISH	DROPSICAL	DROWSED
DROGHER	DRONISHLY	DROPSIED	DROWSES
DROGHERS	DRONKLAP	DROPSIES	DROWSIER
DROGUE	DRONKLAPS	DROPSONDE	DROWSIEST
DROGUES	DRONY	DROPSTONE	DROWSIHED
DROGUET	DROOB	DROPSY	DROWSILY
DROGUETS	DROOBS	DROPT	DROWSING
DROICH	DROOG	DROPWISE	DROWSY
DROICHIER	DROOGISH	DROPWORT	DRUB
DROICHS	DROOGS	DROPWORTS	DRUBBED
DROICHY	DROOK	DROSERA	DRUBBER
DROID	DROOKED	DROSERAS	DRUBBERS
DROIDS	DROOKING	DROSHKIES	DRUBBING
DROIL	DROOKINGS	DROSHKY	DRUBBINGS
DROILED	DROOKIT	DROSKIES	DRUBS
DROILING	DROOKS	DROSKY	DRUCKEN
DROILS	DROOL	DROSS	DRUDGE
DROIT	DROOLED	DROSSES	DRUDGED
DROITS	DROOLIER	DROSSIER	DRUDGER
DROLE	DROOLIEST	DROSSIEST	DRUDGERS
DROLER	DROOLING	DROSSY	DRUDGERY
DROLES	DROOLS	DROSTDIES	DRUDGES
DROLEST	DROOLY	DROSTDY	DRUDGING
DROLL	DROOME	DROSTDYS	DRUDGISM
DROLLED	DROOMES	DROUGHT	DRUDGISMS
DROLLER	DROOP	DROUGHTS	DRUG
DROLLERY	DROOPED	DROUGHTY	DRUGGED
DROLLEST	DROOPIER	DROUK	DRUGGER
DROLLING	DROOPIEST	DROUKED	DRUGGERS
DROLLINGS	DROOPILY	DROUKING	DRUGGET
DROLLISH	DROOPING	DROUKINGS	DRUGGETS
DROLLNESS	DROOPS	DROUKIT	DRUGGIE
DROLLS	DROOPY	DROUKS	DRUGGIER
DROLLY	DROP	DROUTH	DRUGGIES
DROME	DROPCLOTH	DROUTHIER	DRUGGIEST
DROMEDARE	DROPFLIES	DROUTHS	DRUGGING
DROMEDARY	DROPFLY	DROUTHY	DRUGGIST
DROMES	DROPFORGE	DROVE	DRUGGISTS
DROMIC	DROPHEAD	DROVED	DRUGGY
DROMICAL	DROPHEADS	DROVER	DRUGLORD
DROMOI	DROPKICK	DROVERS	DRUGLORDS
DROMON	DROPKICKS	DROVES	DRUGMAKER
DROMOND	DROPLET	DROVING	DRUGS
DROMONDS	DROPLETS	DROVINGS	DRUGSTORE
DROMONS	DROPLIGHT	DROW	DRUID
DROMOS	DROPOUT	DROWN	DRUIDESS
DRONE	DROPOUTS	DROWND	DRUIDIC
DRONED	DROPPABLE	DROWNDED	DRUIDICAL
DRONER	DROPPED	DROWNDING	DRUIDISM

DRUIDISMS	DRYABLE	DUALIZING	DUCKBOARD
DRUIDRIES	DRYAD	DUALLED	DUCKED
DRUIDRY	DRYADES	DUALLING	DUCKER
DRUIDS	DRYADIC	DUALLY	DUCKERS
DRUM	DRYADS	DUALS	DUCKFOOT
DRUMBEAT	DRYASDUST	DUAN	DUCKIE
DRUMBEATS	DRYBEAT	DUANS	DUCKIER
DRUMBLE	DRYBEATEN	DUAR	DUCKIES
DRUMBLED	DRYBEATS	DUARCHIES	DUCKIEST
DRUMBLES	DRYER	DUARCHY	DUCKING
DRUMBLING	DRYERS	DUARS	DUCKINGS
DRUMFIRE	DRYEST	DUATHLON	DUCKLING
DRUMFIRES	DRYING	DUATHLONS	DUCKLINGS
DRUMFISH	DRYINGS	DUB	DUCKMOLE
DRUMHEAD	DRYISH	DUBBED	DUCKMOLES
DRUMHEADS	DRYLAND	DUBBER	DUCKPIN
DRUMLIER	DRYLOT	DUBBERS	DUCKPINS
DRUMLIEST	DRYLOTS	DUBBIN	DUCKS
DRUMLIKE	DRYLY	DUBBING	DUCKSHOVE
DRUMLIN	DRYMOUTH	DUBBINGS	DUCKTAIL
DRUMLINS	DRYMOUTHS	DUBBINS	DUCKTAILS
DRUMLY	DRYNESS	DUBBO	DUCKWALK
DRUMMED	DRYNESSES	DUBBOS	DUCKWALKS
DRUMMER	DRYPOINT	DUBIETIES	DUCKWEED
DRUMMERS	DRYPOINTS	DUBIETY	DUCKWEEDS
DRUMMIES	DRYS	DUBIOSITY	DUCKY
DRUMMING	DRYSALTER	DUBIOUS	DUCT
DRUMMOCK	DRYSTONE	DUBIOUSLY	DUCTAL
DRUMMOCKS	DRYWALL	DUBITABLE	DUCTED
DRUMMY	DRYWALLED	DUBITABLY	DUCTILE
DRUMROLL	DRYWALLS	DUBITANCY	DUCTILELY
DRUMROLLS	DRYWELL	DUBITATE	DUCTILITY
DRUMS	DRYWELLS	DUBITATED	DUCTING
DRUMSTICK	DSO	DUBITATES	DUCTINGS
DRUNK	DSOBO	DUBNIUM	DUCTLESS
DRUNKARD	DSOBOS	DUBNIUMS	DUCTS
DRUNKARDS	DSOMO	DUBONNET	DUCTULE
DRUNKEN	DSOMOS	DUBONNETS	DUCTULES
DRUNKENLY	DSOS	DUBS	DUCTWORK
DRUNKER	DUAD	DUCAL	DUCTWORKS
DRUNKEST	DUADS	DUCALLY	DUD
DRUNKS	DUAL	DUCAT	DUDDER
DRUPE	DUALIN	DUCATOON	DUDDERIES
DRUPEL	DUALINS	DUCATOONS	DUDDERS
DRUPELET	DUALISE	DUCATS	DUDDERY
DRUPELETS	DUALISED	DUCDAME	DUDDIE
DRUPELS	DUALISES	DUCE	DUDDIER
DRUPES	DUALISING	DUCES	DUDDIEST
DRUSE	DUALISM	DUCHESS	DUDDY
DRUSES	DUALISMS	DUCHESSE	DUDE
DRUSIER	DUALIST	DUCHESSED	DUDED
DRUSIEST	DUALISTIC	DUCHESSES	DUDEEN
DRUSY	DUALISTS	DUCHIES	DUDEENS
DRUTHERS	DUALITIES	DUCHY	DUDES
DRUXIER	DUALITY	DUCI	DUDGEON
DRUXIEST	DUALIZE	DUCK	DUDGEONS
DRUXY	DUALIZED	DUCKBILL	DUDHEEN
DRY	DUALIZES	DUCKBILLS	DUDHEENS

DUDING	DUFFERISM	DULCIFY	DUMBO
DUDISH	DUFFERS	DULCIMER	DUMBOS
DUDISHLY	DUFFEST	DULCIMERS	DUMBS
DUDISM	DUFFING	DULCIMORE	DUMBSHIT
DUDISMS	DUFFINGS	DULCINEA	DUMBSHITS
DUDS	DUFFLE	DULCINEAS	DUMDUM
DUE	DUFFLES	DULCITE	DUMDUMS
DUECENTO	DUFFS	DULCITES	DUMELA
DUECENTOS	DUFUS	DULCITOL	DUMFOUND
DUED	DUFUSES	DULCITOLS	DUMFOUNDS
DUEFUL	DUG	DULCITUDE	DUMKA
DUEL	DUGITE	DULCOSE	DUMKY
DUELED	DUGITES	DULCOSES	DUMMERER
DUELER	DUGONG	DULE	DUMMERERS
DUELERS	DUGONGS	DULES	DUMMIED
DUELING	DUGOUT	DULIA	DUMMIER
DUELIST	DUGOUTS	DULIAS	DUMMIES
DUELISTS	DUGS	DULL	DUMMIEST
DUELLED	DUH	DULLARD	DUMMINESS
DUELLER	DUHKHA	DULLARDS	DUMMKOPF
DUELLERS	DUHKHAS	DULLED	DUMMKOPFS
DUELLI	DUI	DULLER	DUMMY
DUELLING	DUIKER	DULLEST	DUMMYING
DUELLINGS	DUIKERBOK	DULLIER	DUMOSE
DUELLIST	DUIKERS	DULLIEST	DUMOSITY
DUELLISTS	DUING	DULLING	DUMOUS
DUELLO	DUIT	DULLISH	DUMP
DUELLOS	DUITS	DULLISHLY	DUMPBIN
DUELS	DUKA	DULLNESS	DUMPBINS
DUELSOME	DUKAS	DULLS	DUMPCART
DUENDE	DUKE	DULLY	DUMPCARTS
DUENDES	DUKED	DULNESS	DUMPED
DUENESS	DUKEDOM	DULNESSES	DUMPER
DUENESSES	DUKEDOMS	DULOCRACY	DUMPERS
DUENNA	DUKELING	DULOSES	DUMPIER
DUENNAS	DUKELINGS	DULOSIS	DUMPIES
DUES	DUKERIES	DULOTIC	DUMPIEST
DUET	DUKERY	DULSE	DUMPILY
DUETED	DUKES	DULSES	DUMPINESS
DUETING	DUKESHIP	DULY	DUMPING
DUETS	DUKESHIPS	DUMA	DUMPINGS
DUETT	DUKING	DUMAIST	DUMPISH
DUETTED	DUKKA	DUMAISTS	DUMPISHLY
DUETTI	DUKKAH	DUMAS	DUMPLE
DUETTING	DUKKAHS	DUMB	DUMPLED
DUETTINO	DUKKAS	DUMBBELL	DUMPLES
DUETTINOS	DUKKHA	DUMBBELLS	DUMPLING
DUETTIST	DUKKHAS	DUMBCANE	DUMPLINGS
DUETTISTS	DULCAMARA	DUMBCANES	DUMPS
DUETTO	DULCET	DUMBED	DUMPSITE
DUETTOS	DULCETLY	DUMBER	DUMPSITES
DUETTS	DULCETS	DUMBEST	DUMPSTER
DUFF	DULCIAN	DUMBFOUND	DUMPSTERS
DUFFED	DULCIANA	DUMBHEAD	DUMPTRUCK
DUFFEL	DULCIANAS	DUMBHEADS	DUMPY
DUFFELS	DULCIANS	DUMBING	DUN
DUFFER	DULCIFIED	DUMBLY	DUNAM
DUFFERDOM	DULCIFIES	DUMBNESS	DUNAMS

DUNCE	DUNNED	DUPING	DURGAN
DUNCEDOM	DUNNER	DUPION	DURGANS
DUNCEDOMS	DUNNESS	DUPIONS	DURGIER
DUNCELIKE	DUNNESSES	DUPLE	DURGIEST
DUNCERIES	DUNNEST	DUPLET	DURGY
DUNCERY	DUNNIER	DUPLETS	DURIAN
DUNCES	DUNNIES	DUPLEX	DURIANS
DUNCH	DUNNIEST	DUPLEXED	DURICRUST
DUNCHED	DUNNING	DUPLEXER	DURING
DUNCHES	DUNNINGS	DUPLEXERS	DURION
DUNCHING	DUNNISH	DUPLEXES	DURIONS
DUNCICAL	DUNNITE	DUPLEXING	DURMAST
DUNCISH	DUNNITES	DUPLEXITY	DURMASTS
DUNCISHLY	DUNNO	DUPLICAND	DURN
DUNDER	DUNNOCK	DUPLICATE	DURNDEST
DUNDERS	DUNNOCKS	DUPLICITY	DURNED
DUNE	DUNNY	DUPLIED	DURNEDER
DUNELAND	DUNS	DUPLIES	DURNEDEST
DUNELANDS	DUNSH	DUPLY	DURNING
DUNELIKE	DUNSHED	DUPLYING	DURNS
DUNES	DUNSHES	DUPONDII	DURO
DUNG	DUNSHING	DUPONDIUS	DUROC
DUNGAREE	DUNT	DUPPED	DUROCS
DUNGAREED	DUNTED	DUPPIES	DUROMETER
DUNGAREES	DUNTING	DUPPING	DUROS
DUNGED	DUNTS	DUPPY	DUROY
DUNGEON	DUO	DUPS	DUROYS
DUNGEONED	DUOBINARY	DURA	DURR
DUNGEONER	DUODECIMO	DURABLE	DURRA
DUNGEONS	DUODENA	DURABLES	DURRAS
DUNGER	DUODENAL	DURABLY	DURRIE
DUNGERS	DUODENARY	DURAL	DURRIES
DUNGHILL	DUODENUM	DURALS	DURRS
DUNGHILLS	DUODENUMS	DURALUMIN	DURRY
DUNGIER	DUOLOG	DURAMEN	DURST
DUNGIEST	DUOLOGS	DURAMENS	DURUKULI
DUNGING	DUOLOGUE	DURANCE	DURUKULIS
DUNGMERE	DUOLOGUES	DURANCES	DURUM
DUNGMERES	DUOMI	DURANT	DURUMS
DUNGS	DUOMO	DURANTS	DURZI
DUNGY	DUOMOS	DURAS	DURZIS
DUNITE	DUOPOLIES	DURATION	DUSH
DUNITES	DUOPOLY	DURATIONS	DUSHED
DUNITIC	DUOPSONY	DURATIVE	DUSHES
DUNK	DUOS	DURATIVES	DUSHING
DUNKED	DUOTONE	DURBAR	DUSK
DUNKER	DUOTONES	DURBARS	DUSKED
DUNKERS	DUP	DURDUM	DUSKEN
DUNKING	DUPABLE	DURDUMS	DUSKENED
DUNKS	DUPATTA	DURE	DUSKENING
DUNLIN	DUPATTAS	DURED	DUSKENS
DUNLINS	DUPE	DUREFUL	DUSKER
DUNNAGE	DUPED	DURES	DUSKEST
DUNNAGES	DUPER	DURESS	DUSKIER
DUNNAKIN	DUPERIES	DURESSE	DUSKIEST
DUNNAKINS	DUPERS	DURESSES	DUSKILY
DUNNART	DUPERY	DURGAH	DUSKINESS
DUNNARTS	DUPES	DURGAHS	DUSKING

DUSKISH
DUSKISHLY
DUSKLY
DUSKNESS
DUSKS
DUSKY
DUST
DUSTBIN
DUSTBINS
DUSTCART
DUSTCARTS
DUSTCOVER
DUSTED
DUSTER
DUSTERS
DUSTHEAP
DUSTHEAPS
DUSTIER
DUSTIEST
DUSTILY
DUSTINESS
DUSTING
DUSTINGS
DUSTLESS
DUSTLIKE
DUSTMAN
DUSTMEN
DUSTOFF
DUSTOFFS
DUSTPAN
DUSTPANS
DUSTPROOF
DUSTRAG
DUSTRAGS
DUSTS
DUSTSHEET
DUSTSTORM
DUSTUP
DUSTUPS
DUSTY
DUTCH
DUTCHES
DUTCHMAN
DUTCHMEN
DUTEOUS
DUTEOUSLY
DUTIABLE
DUTIED
DUTIES
DUTIFUL
DUTIFULLY
DUTY
DUUMVIR
DUUMVIRAL
DUUMVIRI
DUUMVIRS
DUVET
DUVETINE

DUVETINES
DUVETS
DUVETYN
DUVETYNE
DUVETYNES
DUVETYNS
DUX
DUXELLES
DUXES
DUYKER
DUYKERS
DVANDVA
DVANDVAS
DVORNIK
DVORNIKS
DWAAL
DWAALS
DWALE
DWALES
DWALM
DWALMED
DWALMING
DWALMS
DWAM
DWAMMED
DWAMMING
DWAMS
DWANG
DWANGS
DWARF
DWARFED
DWARFER
DWARFEST
DWARFING
DWARFISH
DWARFISM
DWARFISMS
DWARFLIKE
DWARFNESS
DWARFS
DWARVES
DWAUM
DWAUMED
DWAUMING
DWAUMS
DWEEB
DWEEBIER
DWEEBIEST
DWEEBISH
DWEEBS
DWEEBY
DWELL
DWELLED
DWELLER
DWELLERS
DWELLING
DWELLINGS
DWELLS

DWELT
DWILE
DWILES
DWINDLE
DWINDLED
DWINDLES
DWINDLING
DWINE
DWINED
DWINES
DWINING
DYABLE
DYAD
DYADIC
DYADICS
DYADS
DYARCHAL
DYARCHIC
DYARCHIES
DYARCHY
DYBBUK
DYBBUKIM
DYBBUKKIM
DYBBUKS
DYE
DYEABLE
DYED
DYEING
DYEINGS
DYELINE
DYELINES
DYER
DYERS
DYES
DYESTER
DYESTERS
DYESTUFF
DYESTUFFS
DYEWEED
DYEWEEDS
DYEWOOD
DYEWOODS
DYING
DYINGLY
DYINGNESS
DYINGS
DYKE
DYKED
DYKES
DYKEY
DYKIER
DYKIEST
DYKING
DYNAMETER
DYNAMIC
DYNAMICAL
DYNAMICS
DYNAMISE

DYNAMISED
DYNAMISES
DYNAMISM
DYNAMISMS
DYNAMIST
DYNAMISTS
DYNAMITE
DYNAMITED
DYNAMITER
DYNAMITES
DYNAMITIC
DYNAMIZE
DYNAMIZED
DYNAMIZES
DYNAMO
DYNAMOS
DYNAMOTOR
DYNAST
DYNASTIC
DYNASTIES
DYNASTS
DYNASTY
DYNATRON
DYNATRONS
DYNE
DYNEIN
DYNEINS
DYNEL
DYNELS
DYNES
DYNODE
DYNODES
DYNORPHIN
DYSBINDIN
DYSCHROA
DYSCHROAS
DYSCHROIA
DYSCRASIA
DYSCRASIC
DYSCRATIC
DYSENTERY
DYSGENIC
DYSGENICS
DYSLALIA
DYSLALIAS
DYSLECTIC
DYSLEXIA
DYSLEXIAS
DYSLEXIC
DYSLEXICS
DYSLOGIES
DYSLOGY
DYSMELIA
DYSMELIAS
DYSMELIC
DYSODIL
DYSODILE
DYSODILES

DYSODILS
DYSODYLE
DYSODYLES
DYSPATHY
DYSPEPSIA
DYSPEPSY
DYSPEPTIC
DYSPHAGIA
DYSPHAGIC
DYSPHAGY
DYSPHASIA
DYSPHASIC
DYSPHONIA
DYSPHONIC
DYSPHORIA
DYSPHORIC
DYSPLASIA
DYSPNEA
DYSPNEAL
DYSPNEAS
DYSPNEIC
DYSPNOEA
DYSPNOEAL
DYSPNOEAS
DYSPNOEIC
DYSPNOIC
DYSPRAXIA
DYSTAXIA
DYSTAXIAS
DYSTECTIC
DYSTHESIA
DYSTHETIC
DYSTHYMIA
DYSTHYMIC
DYSTOCIA
DYSTOCIAL
DYSTOCIAS
DYSTONIA
DYSTONIAS
DYSTONIC
DYSTOPIA
DYSTOPIAN
DYSTOPIAS
DYSTROPHY
DYSURIA
DYSURIAS
DYSURIC
DYSURIES
DYSURY
DYTISCID
DYTISCIDS
DYVOUR
DYVOURIES
DYVOURS
DYVOURY
DZEREN
DZERENS
DZHO

DZHOS
DZIGGETAI
DZO
DZOS

E

EA	EARED	EARS	EASELED
EACH	EARFLAP	EARSHOT	EASELESS
EACHWHERE	EARFLAPS	EARSHOTS	EASELS
EADISH	EARFUL	EARST	EASEMENT
EADISHES	EARFULS	EARSTONE	EASEMENTS
EAGER	EARING	EARSTONES	EASER
EAGERER	EARINGS	EARTH	EASERS
EAGEREST	EARL	EARTHBORN	EASES
EAGERLY	EARLAP	EARTHED	EASIED
EAGERNESS	EARLAPS	EARTHEN	EASIER
EAGERS	EARLDOM	EARTHFALL	EASIES
EAGLE	EARLDOMS	EARTHFAST	EASIEST
EAGLED	EARLESS	EARTHFLAX	EASILY
EAGLES	EARLIER	EARTHIER	EASINESS
EAGLET	EARLIES	EARTHIEST	EASING
EAGLETS	EARLIEST	EARTHILY	EASLE
EAGLEWOOD	EARLIKE	EARTHING	EASLES
EAGLING	EARLINESS	EARTHLIER	EASSEL
EAGRE	EARLOBE	EARTHLIES	EASSIL
EAGRES	EARLOBES	EARTHLIKE	EAST
EALDORMAN	EARLOCK	EARTHLING	EASTBOUND
EALDORMEN	EARLOCKS	EARTHLY	EASTED
EALE	EARLS	EARTHMAN	EASTER
EALES	EARLSHIP	EARTHMEN	EASTERLY
EAN	EARLSHIPS	EARTHNUT	EASTERN
EANED	EARLY	EARTHNUTS	EASTERNER
EANING	EARLYWOOD	EARTHPEA	EASTERS
EANLING	EARMARK	EARTHPEAS	EASTING
EANLINGS	EARMARKED	EARTHRISE	EASTINGS
EANS	EARMARKS	EARTHS	EASTLAND
EAR	EARMUFF	EARTHSET	EASTLANDS
EARACHE	EARMUFFS	EARTHSETS	EASTLIN
EARACHES	EARN	EARTHSTAR	EASTLING
EARBALL	EARNED	EARTHWARD	EASTLINGS
EARBALLS	EARNER	EARTHWAX	EASTLINS
EARBASH	EARNERS	EARTHWOLF	EASTMOST
EARBASHED	EARNEST	EARTHWORK	EASTS
EARBASHER	EARNESTLY	EARTHWORM	EASTWARD
EARBASHES	EARNESTS	EARTHY	EASTWARDS
EARBOB	EARNING	EARWAX	EASY
EARBOBS	EARNINGS	EARWAXES	EASYGOING
EARBUD	EARNS	EARWIG	EASYING
EARBUDS	EARPHONE	EARWIGGED	EAT
EARCON	EARPHONES	EARWIGGY	EATABLE
EARCONS	EARPICK	EARWIGS	EATABLES
EARD	EARPICKS	EARWORM	EATAGE
EARDED	EARPIECE	EARWORMS	EATAGES
EARDING	EARPIECES	EAS	EATCHE
EARDROP	EARPLUG	EASE	EATCHES
EARDROPS	EARPLUGS	EASED	EATEN
EARDRUM	EARRING	EASEFUL	EATER
EARDRUMS	EARRINGED	EASEFULLY	EATERIE
EARDS	EARRINGS	EASEL	EATERIES

EATERS	EBONIZES	ECHELON	ECLIPSE
EATERY	EBONIZING	ECHELONED	ECLIPSED
EATH	EBONS	ECHELONS	ECLIPSER
EATHE	EBONY	ECHES	ECLIPSERS
EATHLY	EBOOK	ECHEVERIA	ECLIPSES
EATING	EBOOKS	ECHIDNA	ECLIPSING
EATINGS	EBRIATE	ECHIDNAE	ECLIPSIS
EATS	EBRIATED	ECHIDNAS	ECLIPTIC
EAU	EBRIETIES	ECHIDNINE	ECLIPTICS
EAUS	EBRIETY	ECHINACEA	ECLOGITE
EAUX	EBRILLADE	ECHINATE	ECLOGITES
EAVE	EBRIOSE	ECHINATED	ECLOGUE
EAVED	EBRIOSITY	ECHING	ECLOGUES
EAVES	EBULLIENT	ECHINI	ECLOSE
EAVESDRIP	EBURNEAN	ECHINOID	ECLOSED
EAVESDROP	EBURNEOUS	ECHINOIDS	ECLOSES
EAVING	ECAD	ECHINUS	ECLOSING
EBAUCHE	ECADS	ECHINUSES	ECLOSION
EBAUCHES	ECARINATE	ECHIUM	ECLOSIONS
EBAYER	ECARTE	ECHIUMS	ECO
EBAYERS	ECARTES	ECHIUROID	ECOCIDAL
EBAYING	ECAUDATE	ECHO	ECOCIDE
EBAYINGS	ECBOLE	ECHOED	ECOCIDES
EBB	ECBOLES	ECHOER	ECOD
EBBED	ECBOLIC	ECHOERS	ECOFREAK
EBBET	ECBOLICS	ECHOES	ECOFREAKS
EBBETS	ECCE	ECHOEY	ECOLOGIC
EBBING	ECCENTRIC	ECHOGRAM	ECOLOGIES
EBBLESS	ECCLESIA	ECHOGRAMS	ECOLOGIST
EBBS	ECCLESIAE	ECHOIC	ECOLOGY
EBBTIDE	ECCLESIAL	ECHOING	ECOMMERCE
EBBTIDES	ECCO	ECHOISE	ECONOBOX
EBENEZER	ECCRINE	ECHOISED	ECONOMIC
EBENEZERS	ECCRISES	ECHOISES	ECONOMICS
EBENISTE	ECCRISIS	ECHOISING	ECONOMIES
EBENISTES	ECCRITIC	ECHOISM	ECONOMISE
EBIONISE	ECCRITICS	ECHOISMS	ECONOMISM
EBIONISED	ECDEMIC	ECHOIST	ECONOMIST
EBIONISES	ECDYSES	ECHOISTS	ECONOMIZE
EBIONISM	ECDYSIAL	ECHOIZE	ECONOMY
EBIONISMS	ECDYSIAST	ECHOIZED	ECONUT
EBIONITIC	ECDYSIS	ECHOIZES	ECONUTS
EBIONIZE	ECDYSON	ECHOIZING	ECOPHOBIA
EBIONIZED	ECDYSONE	ECHOLALIA	ECORCHE
EBIONIZES	ECDYSONES	ECHOLALIC	ECORCHES
EBON	ECDYSONS	ECHOLESS	ECOREGION
EBONICS	ECESIC	ECHOS	ECOS
EBONIES	ECESIS	ECHOVIRUS	ECOSPHERE
EBONISE	ECESISES	ECHT	ECOSSAISE
EBONISED	ECH	ECLAIR	ECOSTATE
EBONISES	ECHAPPE	ECLAIRS	ECOSYSTEM
EBONISING	ECHAPPES	ECLAMPSIA	ECOTAGE
EBONIST	ECHARD	ECLAMPSY	ECOTAGES
EBONISTS	ECHARDS	ECLAMPTIC	ECOTONAL
EBONITE	ECHE	ECLAT	ECOTONE
EBONITES	ECHED	ECLATS	ECOTONES
EBONIZE	ECHELLE	ECLECTIC	ECOTOUR
EBONIZED	ECHELLES	ECLECTICS	ECOTOURS

ECOTOXIC	ECU	EDICTAL	EECHED
ECOTYPE	ECUELLE	EDICTALLY	EECHES
ECOTYPES	ECUELLES	EDICTS	EECHING
ECOTYPIC	ECUMENIC	EDIFICE	EEJIT
ECRASEUR	ECUMENICS	EDIFICES	EEJITS
ECRASEURS	ECUMENISM	EDIFICIAL	EEK
ECRITOIRE	ECUMENIST	EDIFIED	EEL
ECRU	ECURIE	EDIFIER	EELFARE
ECRUS	ECURIES	EDIFIERS	EELFARES
ECSTASES	ECUS	EDIFIES	EELGRASS
ECSTASIED	ECZEMA	EDIFY	EELIER
ECSTASIES	ECZEMAS	EDIFYING	EELIEST
ECSTASIS	ED	EDILE	EELLIKE
ECSTASISE	EDACIOUS	EDILES	EELPOUT
ECSTASIZE	EDACITIES	EDIT	EELPOUTS
ECSTASY	EDACITY	EDITABLE	EELS
ECSTATIC	EDAPHIC	EDITED	EELWORM
ECSTATICS	EDDIED	EDITING	EELWORMS
ECTASES	EDDIES	EDITINGS	EELWRACK
ECTASIA	EDDISH	EDITION	EELWRACKS
ECTASIAS	EDDISHES	EDITIONED	EELY
ECTASIS	EDDO	EDITIONS	EEN
ECTATIC	EDDOES	EDITOR	EERIE
ECTHYMA	EDDY	EDITORIAL	EERIER
ECTHYMAS	EDDYING	EDITORS	EERIEST
ECTHYMATA	EDELWEISS	EDITRESS	EERILY
ECTOBLAST	EDEMA	EDITRICES	EERINESS
ECTOCRINE	EDEMAS	EDITRIX	EERY
ECTODERM	EDEMATA	EDITRIXES	EEVEN
ECTODERMS	EDEMATOSE	EDITS	EEVENS
ECTOGENIC	EDEMATOUS	EDS	EEVN
ECTOGENY	EDENIC	EDUCABLE	EEVNING
ECTOMERE	EDENTAL	EDUCABLES	EEVNINGS
ECTOMERES	EDENTATE	EDUCATE	EEVNS
ECTOMERIC	EDENTATES	EDUCATED	EF
ECTOMORPH	EDGE	EDUCATES	EFF
ECTOPHYTE	EDGEBONE	EDUCATING	EFFABLE
ECTOPIA	EDGEBONES	EDUCATION	EFFACE
ECTOPIAS	EDGED	EDUCATIVE	EFFACED
ECTOPIC	EDGELESS	EDUCATOR	EFFACER
ECTOPIES	EDGER	EDUCATORS	EFFACERS
ECTOPLASM	EDGERS	EDUCATORY	EFFACES
ECTOPROCT	EDGES	EDUCE	EFFACING
ECTOPY	EDGEWAYS	EDUCED	EFFECT
ECTOSARC	EDGEWISE	EDUCEMENT	EFFECTED
ECTOSARCS	EDGIER	EDUCES	EFFECTER
ECTOTHERM	EDGIEST	EDUCIBLE	EFFECTERS
ECTOZOA	EDGILY	EDUCING	EFFECTING
ECTOZOAN	EDGINESS	EDUCT	EFFECTIVE
ECTOZOANS	EDGING	EDUCTION	EFFECTOR
ECTOZOIC	EDGINGS	EDUCTIONS	EFFECTORS
ECTOZOON	EDGY	EDUCTIVE	EFFECTS
ECTROPIC	EDH	EDUCTOR	EFFECTUAL
ECTROPION	EDHS	EDUCTORS	EFFED
ECTROPIUM	EDIBILITY	EDUCTS	EFFEIR
ECTYPAL	EDIBLE	EDUSKUNTA	EFFEIRED
ECTYPE	EDIBLES	EE	EFFEIRING
ECTYPES	EDICT	EECH	EFFEIRS

EFFENDI	EFTSOONS	EGGWHISKS	EIDOGRAPH
EFFENDIS	EGAD	EGGY	EIDOLA
EFFERE	EGADS	EGIS	EIDOLIC
EFFERED	EGAL	EGISES	EIDOLON
EFFERENCE	EGALITE	EGLANTINE	EIDOLONS
EFFERENT	EGALITES	EGLATERE	EIDOS
EFFERENTS	EGALITIES	EGLATERES	EIGENMODE
EFFERES	EGALITY	EGLOMISE	EIGENTONE
EFFERING	EGALLY	EGMA	EIGHT
EFFETE	EGAREMENT	EGMAS	EIGHTBALL
EFFETELY	EGENCE	EGO	EIGHTEEN
EFFICACY	EGENCES	EGOISM	EIGHTEENS
EFFICIENT	EGENCIES	EGOISMS	EIGHTFOIL
EFFIERCE	EGENCY	EGOIST	EIGHTFOLD
EFFIERCED	EGER	EGOISTIC	EIGHTFOOT
EFFIERCES	EGERS	EGOISTS	EIGHTH
EFFIGIAL	EGEST	EGOITIES	EIGHTHLY
EFFIGIES	EGESTA	EGOITY	EIGHTHS
EFFIGY	EGESTED	EGOLESS	EIGHTIES
EFFING	EGESTING	EGOMANIA	EIGHTIETH
EFFINGS	EGESTION	EGOMANIAC	EIGHTS
EFFLUENCE	EGESTIONS	EGOMANIAS	EIGHTSMAN
EFFLUENT	EGESTIVE	EGOS	EIGHTSMEN
EFFLUENTS	EGESTS	EGOTHEISM	EIGHTSOME
EFFLUVIA	EGG	EGOTISE	EIGHTVO
EFFLUVIAL	EGGAR	EGOTISED	EIGHTVOS
EFFLUVIUM	EGGARS	EGOTISES	EIGHTY
EFFLUX	EGGBEATER	EGOTISING	EIGNE
EFFLUXES	EGGCUP	EGOTISM	EIK
EFFLUXION	EGGCUPS	EGOTISMS	EIKED
EFFORCE	EGGED	EGOTIST	EIKING
EFFORCED	EGGER	EGOTISTIC	EIKON
EFFORCES	EGGERIES	EGOTISTS	EIKONES
EFFORCING	EGGERS	EGOTIZE	EIKONS
EFFORT	EGGERY	EGOTIZED	EIKS
EFFORTFUL	EGGFRUIT	EGOTIZES	EILD
EFFORTS	EGGFRUITS	EGOTIZING	EILDING
EFFRAIDE	EGGHEAD	EGREGIOUS	EILDINGS
EFFRAY	EGGHEADED	EGRESS	EILDS
EFFRAYS	EGGHEADS	EGRESSED	EINA
EFFS	EGGIER	EGRESSES	EINE
EFFULGE	EGGIEST	EGRESSING	EINKORN
EFFULGED	EGGING	EGRESSION	EINKORNS
EFFULGENT	EGGLER	EGRET	EINSTEIN
EFFULGES	EGGLERS	EGRETS	EINSTEINS
EFFULGING	EGGLESS	EGYPTIAN	EIRACK
EFFUSE	EGGMASS	EGYPTIANS	EIRACKS
EFFUSED	EGGMASSES	EH	EIRENIC
EFFUSES	EGGNOG	EHED	EIRENICAL
EFFUSING	EGGNOGS	EHING	EIRENICON
EFFUSION	EGGPLANT	EHS	EISEGESES
EFFUSIONS	EGGPLANTS	EIDE	EISEGESIS
EFFUSIVE	EGGS	EIDENT	EISEL
EFS	EGGSHELL	EIDER	EISELL
EFT	EGGSHELLS	EIDERDOWN	EISELLS
EFTEST	EGGWASH	EIDERS	EISELS
EFTS	EGGWASHES	EIDETIC	EISH
EFTSOON	EGGWHISK	EIDETICS	EISWEIN

EISWEINS	ELASTANCE	ELECTEE	ELENCH
EITHER	ELASTANE	ELECTEES	ELENCHI
EJACULATE	ELASTANES	ELECTING	ELENCHIC
EJECT	ELASTASE	ELECTION	ELENCHS
EJECTA	ELASTASES	ELECTIONS	ELENCHTIC
EJECTABLE	ELASTIC	ELECTIVE	ELENCHUS
EJECTED	ELASTICS	ELECTIVES	ELENCTIC
EJECTING	ELASTIN	ELECTOR	ELEOPTENE
EJECTION	ELASTINS	ELECTORAL	ELEPHANT
EJECTIONS	ELASTOMER	ELECTORS	ELEPHANTS
EJECTIVE	ELATE	ELECTRESS	ELEUTHERI
EJECTIVES	ELATED	ELECTRET	ELEVATE
EJECTMENT	ELATEDLY	ELECTRETS	ELEVATED
EJECTOR	ELATER	ELECTRIC	ELEVATEDS
EJECTORS	ELATERID	ELECTRICS	ELEVATES
EJECTS	ELATERIDS	ELECTRIFY	ELEVATING
EKE	ELATERIN	ELECTRISE	ELEVATION
EKED	ELATERINS	ELECTRIZE	ELEVATOR
EKES	ELATERITE	ELECTRO	ELEVATORS
EKING	ELATERIUM	ELECTRODE	ELEVATORY
EKISTIC	ELATERS	ELECTROED	ELEVEN
EKISTICAL	ELATES	ELECTRON	ELEVENS
EKISTICS	ELATING	ELECTRONS	ELEVENSES
EKKA	ELATION	ELECTROS	ELEVENTH
EKKAS	ELATIONS	ELECTRUM	ELEVENTHS
EKLOGITE	ELATIVE	ELECTRUMS	ELEVON
EKLOGITES	ELATIVES	ELECTS	ELEVONS
EKPHRASES	ELBOW	ELECTUARY	ELF
EKPHRASIS	ELBOWED	ELEDOISIN	ELFED
EKPWELE	ELBOWING	ELEGANCE	ELFHOOD
EKPWELES	ELBOWROOM	ELEGANCES	ELFHOODS
EKTEXINE	ELBOWS	ELEGANCY	ELFIN
EKTEXINES	ELCHEE	ELEGANT	ELFING
EKUELE	ELCHEES	ELEGANTLY	ELFINS
EL	ELCHI	ELEGIAC	ELFISH
ELABORATE	ELCHIS	ELEGIACAL	ELFISHLY
ELAEOLITE	ELD	ELEGIACS	ELFLAND
ELAIN	ELDER	ELEGIAST	ELFLANDS
ELAINS	ELDERCARE	ELEGIASTS	ELFLIKE
ELAIOSOME	ELDERLIES	ELEGIES	ELFLOCK
ELAN	ELDERLY	ELEGISE	ELFLOCKS
ELANCE	ELDERS	ELEGISED	ELFS
ELANCED	ELDERSHIP	ELEGISES	ELHI
ELANCES	ELDEST	ELEGISING	ELIAD
ELANCING	ELDIN	ELEGIST	ELIADS
ELAND	ELDING	ELEGISTS	ELICHE
ELANDS	ELDINGS	ELEGIT	ELICHES
ELANET	ELDINS	ELEGITS	ELICIT
ELANETS	ELDORADO	ELEGIZE	ELICITED
ELANS	ELDORADOS	ELEGIZED	ELICITING
ELAPHINE	ELDRESS	ELEGIZES	ELICITOR
ELAPID	ELDRESSES	ELEGIZING	ELICITORS
ELAPIDS	ELDRICH	ELEGY	ELICITS
ELAPINE	ELDRITCH	ELEMENT	ELIDE
ELAPSE	ELDS	ELEMENTAL	ELIDED
ELAPSED	ELECT	ELEMENTS	ELIDES
ELAPSES	ELECTABLE	ELEMI	ELIDIBLE
ELAPSING	ELECTED	ELEMIS	ELIDING

ELIGIBLE	ELOIGNED	ELUSORY	EMBAIL
ELIGIBLES	ELOIGNER	ELUTE	EMBAILED
ELIGIBLY	ELOIGNERS	ELUTED	EMBAILING
ELIMINANT	ELOIGNING	ELUTES	EMBAILS
ELIMINATE	ELOIGNS	ELUTING	EMBALE
ELINT	ELOIN	ELUTION	EMBALED
ELINTS	ELOINED	ELUTIONS	EMBALES
ELISION	ELOINER	ELUTOR	EMBALING
ELISIONS	ELOINERS	ELUTORS	EMBALL
ELITE	ELOINING	ELUTRIATE	EMBALLED
ELITES	ELOINMENT	ELUVIA	EMBALLING
ELITISM	ELOINS	ELUVIAL	EMBALLS
ELITISMS	ELONGATE	ELUVIATE	EMBALM
ELITIST	ELONGATED	ELUVIATED	EMBALMED
ELITISTS	ELONGATES	ELUVIATES	EMBALMER
ELIXIR	ELOPE	ELUVIUM	EMBALMERS
ELIXIRS	ELOPED	ELUVIUMS	EMBALMING
ELK	ELOPEMENT	ELVAN	EMBALMS
ELKHOUND	ELOPER	ELVANITE	EMBANK
ELKHOUNDS	ELOPERS	ELVANITES	EMBANKED
ELKS	ELOPES	ELVANS	EMBANKER
ELL	ELOPING	ELVER	EMBANKERS
ELLAGIC	ELOPS	ELVERS	EMBANKING
ELLIPSE	ELOPSES	ELVES	EMBANKS
ELLIPSES	ELOQUENCE	ELVISH	EMBAR
ELLIPSIS	ELOQUENT	ELVISHLY	EMBARGO
ELLIPSOID	ELPEE	ELYSIAN	EMBARGOED
ELLIPTIC	ELPEES	ELYTRA	EMBARGOES
ELLOPS	ELS	ELYTRAL	EMBARK
ELLOPSES	ELSE	ELYTROID	EMBARKED
ELLS	ELSEWHERE	ELYTRON	EMBARKING
ELLWAND	ELSEWISE	ELYTROUS	EMBARKS
ELLWANDS	ELSHIN	ELYTRUM	EMBARRASS
ELM	ELSHINS	EM	EMBARRED
ELMEN	ELSIN	EMACIATE	EMBARRING
ELMIER	ELSINS	EMACIATED	EMBARS
ELMIEST	ELT	EMACIATES	EMBASE
ELMS	ELTCHI	EMACS	EMBASED
ELMWOOD	ELTCHIS	EMACSEN	EMBASES
ELMWOODS	ELTS	EMAIL	EMBASING
ELMY	ELUANT	EMAILED	EMBASSADE
ELOCUTE	ELUANTS	EMAILING	EMBASSAGE
ELOCUTED	ELUATE	EMAILS	EMBASSIES
ELOCUTES	ELUATES	EMANANT	EMBASSY
ELOCUTING	ELUCIDATE	EMANATE	EMBASTE
ELOCUTION	ELUDE	EMANATED	EMBATHE
ELOCUTORY	ELUDED	EMANATES	EMBATHED
ELODEA	ELUDER	EMANATING	EMBATHES
ELODEAS	ELUDERS	EMANATION	EMBATHING
ELOGE	ELUDES	EMANATIST	EMBATTLE
ELOGES	ELUDIBLE	EMANATIVE	EMBATTLED
ELOGIES	ELUDING	EMANATOR	EMBATTLES
ELOGIST	ELUENT	EMANATORS	EMBAY
ELOGISTS	ELUENTS	EMANATORY	EMBAYED
ELOGIUM	ELUSION	EMBACE	EMBAYING
ELOGIUMS	ELUSIONS	EMBACED	EMBAYLD
ELOGY	ELUSIVE	EMBACES	EMBAYMENT
ELOIGN	ELUSIVELY	EMBACING	EMBAYS

EMBED	EMBOLIES	EMBRAIDS	EMCEES
EMBEDDED	EMBOLISE	EMBRANGLE	EMDASH
EMBEDDING	EMBOLISED	EMBRASOR	EMDASHES
EMBEDMENT	EMBOLISES	EMBRASORS	EME
EMBEDS	EMBOLISM	EMBRASURE	EMEER
EMBELLISH	EMBOLISMS	EMBRAVE	EMEERATE
EMBER	EMBOLIZE	EMBRAVED	EMEERATES
EMBERS	EMBOLIZED	EMBRAVES	EMEERS
EMBEZZLE	EMBOLIZES	EMBRAVING	EMEND
EMBEZZLED	EMBOLUS	EMBRAZURE	EMENDABLE
EMBEZZLER	EMBOLUSES	EMBREAD	EMENDALS
EMBEZZLES	EMBOLY	EMBREADED	EMENDATE
EMBITTER	EMBORDER	EMBREADS	EMENDATED
EMBITTERS	EMBORDERS	EMBREATHE	EMENDATES
EMBLAZE	EMBOSCATA	EMBRITTLE	EMENDATOR
EMBLAZED	EMBOSK	EMBROCATE	EMENDED
EMBLAZER	EMBOSKED	EMBROGLIO	EMENDER
EMBLAZERS	EMBOSKING	EMBROIDER	EMENDERS
EMBLAZES	EMBOSKS	EMBROIL	EMENDING
EMBLAZING	EMBOSOM	EMBROILED	EMENDS
EMBLAZON	EMBOSOMED	EMBROILER	EMERALD
EMBLAZONS	EMBOSOMS	EMBROILS	EMERALDS
EMBLEM	EMBOSS	EMBROWN	EMERAUDE
EMBLEMA	EMBOSSED	EMBROWNED	EMERAUDES
EMBLEMATA	EMBOSSER	EMBROWNS	EMERGE
EMBLEMED	EMBOSSERS	EMBRUE	EMERGED
EMBLEMING	EMBOSSES	EMBRUED	EMERGENCE
EMBLEMISE	EMBOSSING	EMBRUES	EMERGENCY
EMBLEMIZE	EMBOST	EMBRUING	EMERGENT
EMBLEMS	EMBOUND	EMBRUTE	EMERGENTS
EMBLIC	EMBOUNDED	EMBRUTED	EMERGES
EMBLICS	EMBOUNDS	EMBRUTES	EMERGING
EMBLOOM	EMBOW	EMBRUTING	EMERIED
EMBLOOMED	EMBOWED	EMBRYO	EMERIES
EMBLOOMS	EMBOWEL	EMBRYOID	EMERITA
EMBLOSSOM	EMBOWELED	EMBRYOIDS	EMERITAE
EMBODIED	EMBOWELS	EMBRYON	EMERITAS
EMBODIER	EMBOWER	EMBRYONAL	EMERITI
EMBODIERS	EMBOWERED	EMBRYONIC	EMERITUS
EMBODIES	EMBOWERS	EMBRYONS	EMEROD
EMBODY	EMBOWING	EMBRYOS	EMERODS
EMBODYING	EMBOWMENT	EMBRYOTIC	EMEROID
EMBOG	EMBOWS	EMBUS	EMEROIDS
EMBOGGED	EMBOX	EMBUSED	EMERSED
EMBOGGING	EMBOXED	EMBUSES	EMERSION
EMBOGS	EMBOXES	EMBUSIED	EMERSIONS
EMBOGUE	EMBOXING	EMBUSIES	EMERY
EMBOGUED	EMBRACE	EMBUSING	EMERYING
EMBOGUES	EMBRACED	EMBUSQUE	EMES
EMBOGUING	EMBRACEOR	EMBUSQUES	EMESES
EMBOIL	EMBRACER	EMBUSSED	EMESIS
EMBOILED	EMBRACERS	EMBUSSES	EMETIC
EMBOILING	EMBRACERY	EMBUSSING	EMETICAL
EMBOILS	EMBRACES	EMBUSY	EMETICS
EMBOLDEN	EMBRACING	EMBUSYING	EMETIN
EMBOLDENS	EMBRACIVE	EMCEE	EMETINE
EMBOLI	EMBRAID	EMCEED	EMETINES
EMBOLIC	EMBRAIDED	EMCEEING	EMETINS

EMEU	EMMEWED	EMPARE	EMPIGHT
EMEUS	EMMEWING	EMPARED	EMPIRE
EMEUTE	EMMEWS	EMPARES	EMPIRES
EMEUTES	EMMOVE	EMPARING	EMPIRIC
EMIC	EMMOVED	EMPARL	EMPIRICAL
EMICANT	EMMOVES	EMPARLED	EMPIRICS
EMICATE	EMMOVING	EMPARLING	EMPLACE
EMICATED	EMMY	EMPARLS	EMPLACED
EMICATES	EMMYS	EMPART	EMPLACES
EMICATING	EMO	EMPARTED	EMPLACING
EMICATION	EMODIN	EMPARTING	EMPLANE
EMICTION	EMODINS	EMPARTS	EMPLANED
EMICTIONS	EMOLLIATE	EMPATHIC	EMPLANES
EMICTORY	EMOLLIENT	EMPATHIES	EMPLANING
EMIGRANT	EMOLUMENT	EMPATHISE	EMPLASTER
EMIGRANTS	EMONG	EMPATHIST	EMPLASTIC
EMIGRATE	EMONGES	EMPATHIZE	EMPLEACH
EMIGRATED	EMONGEST	EMPATHY	EMPLECTON
EMIGRATES	EMONGST	EMPATRON	EMPLECTUM
EMIGRE	EMOS	EMPATRONS	EMPLONGE
EMIGRES	EMOTE	EMPAYRE	EMPLONGED
EMINENCE	EMOTED	EMPAYRED	EMPLONGES
EMINENCES	EMOTER	EMPAYRES	EMPLOY
EMINENCY	EMOTERS	EMPAYRING	EMPLOYE
EMINENT	EMOTES	EMPEACH	EMPLOYED
EMINENTLY	EMOTICON	EMPEACHED	EMPLOYEE
EMIR	EMOTICONS	EMPEACHES	EMPLOYEES
EMIRATE	EMOTING	EMPENNAGE	EMPLOYER
EMIRATES	EMOTION	EMPEOPLE	EMPLOYERS
EMIRS	EMOTIONAL	EMPEOPLED	EMPLOYES
EMISSARY	EMOTIONS	EMPEOPLES	EMPLOYING
EMISSILE	EMOTIVE	EMPERCE	EMPLOYS
EMISSION	EMOTIVELY	EMPERCED	EMPLUME
EMISSIONS	EMOTIVISM	EMPERCES	EMPLUMED
EMISSIVE	EMOTIVITY	EMPERCING	EMPLUMES
EMIT	EMOVE	EMPERIES	EMPLUMING
EMITS	EMOVED	EMPERISE	EMPOISON
EMITTANCE	EMOVES	EMPERISED	EMPOISONS
EMITTED	EMOVING	EMPERISES	EMPOLDER
EMITTER	EMPACKET	EMPERISH	EMPOLDERS
EMITTERS	EMPACKETS	EMPERIZE	EMPORIA
EMITTING	EMPAESTIC	EMPERIZED	EMPORIUM
EMLETS	EMPAIRE	EMPERIZES	EMPORIUMS
EMMA	EMPAIRED	EMPEROR	EMPOWER
EMMARBLE	EMPAIRES	EMPERORS	EMPOWERED
EMMARBLED	EMPAIRING	EMPERY	EMPOWERS
EMMARBLES	EMPALE	EMPHASES	EMPRESS
EMMAS	EMPALED	EMPHASIS	EMPRESSE
EMMER	EMPALER	EMPHASISE	EMPRESSES
EMMERS	EMPALERS	EMPHASIZE	EMPRISE
EMMESH	EMPALES	EMPHATIC	EMPRISES
EMMESHED	EMPALING	EMPHATICS	EMPRIZE
EMMESHES	EMPANADA	EMPHLYSES	EMPRIZES
EMMESHING	EMPANADAS	EMPHLYSIS	EMPT
EMMET	EMPANEL	EMPHYSEMA	EMPTED
EMMETROPE	EMPANELED	EMPIERCE	EMPTIABLE
EMMETS	EMPANELS	EMPIERCED	EMPTIED
EMMEW	EMPANOPLY	EMPIERCES	EMPTIER

EMPTIERS	EMULSIN	ENAMINE	ENCHAFE
EMPTIES	EMULSINS	ENAMINES	ENCHAFED
EMPTIEST	EMULSION	ENAMOR	ENCHAFES
EMPTILY	EMULSIONS	ENAMORADO	ENCHAFING
EMPTINESS	EMULSIVE	ENAMORED	ENCHAIN
EMPTING	EMULSOID	ENAMORING	ENCHAINED
EMPTINGS	EMULSOIDS	ENAMORS	ENCHAINS
EMPTINS	EMULSOR	ENAMOUR	ENCHANT
EMPTION	EMULSORS	ENAMOURED	ENCHANTED
EMPTIONAL	EMUNCTION	ENAMOURS	ENCHANTER
EMPTIONS	EMUNCTORY	ENARCH	ENCHANTS
EMPTS	EMUNGE	ENARCHED	ENCHARGE
EMPTY	EMUNGED	ENARCHES	ENCHARGED
EMPTYING	EMUNGES	ENARCHING	ENCHARGES
EMPTYINGS	EMUNGING	ENARM	ENCHARM
EMPTYSES	EMURE	ENARMED	ENCHARMED
EMPTYSIS	EMURED	ENARMING	ENCHARMS
EMPURPLE	EMURES	ENARMS	ENCHASE
EMPURPLED	EMURING	ENATE	ENCHASED
EMPURPLES	EMUS	ENATES	ENCHASER
EMPUSA	EMYD	ENATIC	ENCHASERS
EMPUSAS	EMYDE	ENATION	ENCHASES
EMPUSE	EMYDES	ENATIONS	ENCHASING
EMPUSES	EMYDS	ENAUNTER	ENCHEASON
EMPYEMA	EMYS	ENCAENIA	ENCHEER
EMPYEMAS	EN	ENCAENIAS	ENCHEERED
EMPYEMATA	ENABLE	ENCAGE	ENCHEERS
EMPYEMIC	ENABLED	ENCAGED	ENCHILADA
EMPYESES	ENABLER	ENCAGES	ENCHORIAL
EMPYESIS	ENABLERS	ENCAGING	ENCHORIC
EMPYREAL	ENABLES	ENCALM	ENCIERRO
EMPYREAN	ENABLING	ENCALMED	ENCIERROS
EMPYREANS	ENACT	ENCALMING	ENCINA
EMPYREUMA	ENACTABLE	ENCALMS	ENCINAL
EMS	ENACTED	ENCAMP	ENCINAS
EMU	ENACTING	ENCAMPED	ENCIPHER
EMULATE	ENACTION	ENCAMPING	ENCIPHERS
EMULATED	ENACTIONS	ENCAMPS	ENCIRCLE
EMULATES	ENACTIVE	ENCANTHIS	ENCIRCLED
EMULATING	ENACTMENT	ENCAPSULE	ENCIRCLES
EMULATION	ENACTOR	ENCARPUS	ENCLASP
EMULATIVE	ENACTORS	ENCASE	ENCLASPED
EMULATOR	ENACTORY	ENCASED	ENCLASPS
EMULATORS	ENACTS	ENCASES	ENCLAVE
EMULE	ENACTURE	ENCASH	ENCLAVED
EMULED	ENACTURES	ENCASHED	ENCLAVES
EMULES	ENALAPRIL	ENCASHES	ENCLAVING
EMULGE	ENALLAGE	ENCASHING	ENCLISES
EMULGED	ENALLAGES	ENCASING	ENCLISIS
EMULGENCE	ENAMEL	ENCASTRE	ENCLITIC
EMULGENT	ENAMELED	ENCAUSTIC	ENCLITICS
EMULGES	ENAMELER	ENCAVE	ENCLOSE
EMULGING	ENAMELERS	ENCAVED	ENCLOSED
EMULING	ENAMELING	ENCAVES	ENCLOSER
EMULOUS	ENAMELIST	ENCAVING	ENCLOSERS
EMULOUSLY	ENAMELLED	ENCEINTE	ENCLOSES
EMULSIBLE	ENAMELLER	ENCEINTES	ENCLOSING
EMULSIFY	ENAMELS	ENCEPHALA	ENCLOSURE

ENCLOTHE	ENCYSTS	ENDITE	ENDOSCOPY
ENCLOTHED	END	ENDITED	ENDOSMOS
ENCLOTHES	ENDAMAGE	ENDITES	ENDOSMOSE
ENCLOUD	ENDAMAGED	ENDITING	ENDOSOME
ENCLOUDED	ENDAMAGES	ENDIVE	ENDOSOMES
ENCLOUDS	ENDAMEBA	ENDIVES	ENDOSPERM
ENCODABLE	ENDAMEBAE	ENDLANG	ENDOSPORE
ENCODE	ENDAMEBAS	ENDLEAF	ENDOSS
ENCODED	ENDAMEBIC	ENDLEAFS	ENDOSSED
ENCODER	ENDAMOEBA	ENDLEAVES	ENDOSSES
ENCODERS	ENDANGER	ENDLESS	ENDOSSING
ENCODES	ENDANGERS	ENDLESSLY	ENDOSTEA
ENCODING	ENDARCH	ENDLONG	ENDOSTEAL
ENCOLOUR	ENDARCHY	ENDMOST	ENDOSTEUM
ENCOLOURS	ENDART	ENDNOTE	ENDOSTYLE
ENCOLPION	ENDARTED	ENDNOTES	ENDOTHERM
ENCOLPIUM	ENDARTING	ENDOBLAST	ENDOTOXIC
ENCOLURE	ENDARTS	ENDOCARP	ENDOTOXIN
ENCOLURES	ENDASH	ENDOCARPS	ENDOW
ENCOMIA	ENDASHES	ENDOCAST	ENDOWED
ENCOMIAST	ENDBRAIN	ENDOCASTS	ENDOWER
ENCOMION	ENDBRAINS	ENDOCRINE	ENDOWERS
ENCOMIUM	ENDEAR	ENDOCYTIC	ENDOWING
ENCOMIUMS	ENDEARED	ENDODERM	ENDOWMENT
ENCOMPASS	ENDEARING	ENDODERMS	ENDOWS
ENCORE	ENDEARS	ENDODYNE	ENDOZOA
ENCORED	ENDEAVOR	ENDOERGIC	ENDOZOIC
ENCORES	ENDEAVORS	ENDOGAMIC	ENDOZOON
ENCORING	ENDEAVOUR	ENDOGAMY	ENDPAPER
ENCOUNTER	ENDECAGON	ENDOGEN	ENDPAPERS
ENCOURAGE	ENDED	ENDOGENIC	ENDPLATE
ENCRADLE	ENDEICTIC	ENDOGENS	ENDPLATES
ENCRADLED	ENDEIXES	ENDOGENY	ENDPLAY
ENCRADLES	ENDEIXIS	ENDOLYMPH	ENDPLAYED
ENCRATIES	ENDEMIAL	ENDOMIXES	ENDPLAYS
ENCRATY	ENDEMIC	ENDOMIXIS	ENDPOINT
ENCREASE	ENDEMICAL	ENDOMORPH	ENDPOINTS
ENCREASED	ENDEMICS	ENDOPHAGY	ENDRIN
ENCREASES	ENDEMISM	ENDOPHYTE	ENDRINS
ENCRIMSON	ENDEMISMS	ENDOPLASM	ENDS
ENCRINAL	ENDENIZEN	ENDOPOD	ENDSHIP
ENCRINIC	ENDER	ENDOPODS	ENDSHIPS
ENCRINITE	ENDERMIC	ENDOPROCT	ENDUE
ENCROACH	ENDERON	ENDORPHIN	ENDUED
ENCRUST	ENDERONS	ENDORSE	ENDUES
ENCRUSTED	ENDERS	ENDORSED	ENDUING
ENCRUSTS	ENDEW	ENDORSEE	ENDUNGEON
ENCRYPT	ENDEWED	ENDORSEES	ENDURABLE
ENCRYPTED	ENDEWING	ENDORSER	ENDURABLY
ENCRYPTS	ENDEWS	ENDORSERS	ENDURANCE
ENCUMBER	ENDEXINE	ENDORSES	ENDURE
ENCUMBERS	ENDEXINES	ENDORSING	ENDURED
ENCURTAIN	ENDGAME	ENDORSIVE	ENDURER
ENCYCLIC	ENDGAMES	ENDORSOR	ENDURERS
ENCYCLICS	ENDING	ENDORSORS	ENDURES
ENCYST	ENDINGS	ENDOSARC	ENDURING
ENCYSTED	ENDIRON	ENDOSARCS	ENDURO
ENCYSTING	ENDIRONS	ENDOSCOPE	ENDUROS

ENDWAYS	ENFEVERED	ENG	ENGORED
ENDWISE	ENFEVERS	ENGAGE	ENGORES
ENDYSES	ENFIERCE	ENGAGED	ENGORGE
ENDYSIS	ENFIERCED	ENGAGEDLY	ENGORGED
FNF	ENFIERCES	ENGAGEE	ENGORGES
ENEMA	ENFILADE	ENGAGER	ENGORGING
ENEMAS	ENFILADED	ENGAGERS	ENGORING
ENEMATA	ENFILADES	ENGAGES	ENGOULED
ENEMIES	ENFILED	ENGAGING	ENGOUMENT
ENEMY	ENFIRE	ENGAOL	ENGRACE
ENERGETIC	ENFIRED	ENGAOLED	ENGRACED
ENERGIC	ENFIRES	ENGAOLING	ENGRACES
ENERGID	ENFIRING	ENGAOLS	ENGRACING
ENERGIDS	ENFIX	ENGARLAND	ENGRAFF
ENERGIES	ENFIXED	ENGENDER	ENGRAFFED
ENERGISE	ENFIXES	ENGENDERS	ENGRAFFS
ENERGISED	ENFIXING	ENGENDURE	ENGRAFT
ENERGISER	ENFLAME	ENGILD	ENGRAFTED
ENERGISES	ENFLAMED	ENGILDED	ENGRAFTS
ENERGIZE	ENFLAMES	ENGILDING	ENGRAIL
ENERGIZED	ENFLAMING	ENGILDS	ENGRAILED
ENERGIZER	ENFLESH	ENGILT	ENGRAILS
ENERGIZES	ENFLESHED	ENGINE	ENGRAIN
ENERGUMEN	ENFLESHES	ENGINED	ENGRAINED
ENERGY	ENFLOWER	ENGINEER	ENGRAINER
ENERVATE	ENFLOWERS	ENGINEERS	ENGRAINS
ENERVATED	ENFOLD	ENGINER	ENGRAM
ENERVATES	ENFOLDED	ENGINERS	ENGRAMMA
ENERVATOR	ENFOLDER	ENGINERY	ENGRAMMAS
ENERVE	ENFOLDERS	ENGINES	ENGRAMME
ENERVED	ENFOLDING	ENGINING	ENGRAMMES
ENERVES	ENFOLDS	ENGINOUS	ENGRAMMIC
ENERVING	ENFORCE	ENGIRD	ENGRAMS
ENES	ENFORCED	ENGIRDED	ENGRASP
ENEW	ENFORCER	ENGIRDING	ENGRASPED
ENEWED	ENFORCERS	ENGIRDLE	ENGRASPS
ENEWING	ENFORCES	ENGIRDLED	ENGRAVE
ENEWS	ENFORCING	ENGIRDLES	ENGRAVED
ENFACE	ENFOREST	ENGIRDS	ENGRAVEN
ENFACED	ENFORESTS	ENGIRT	ENGRAVER
ENFACES	ENFORM	ENGISCOPE	ENGRAVERS
ENFACING	ENFORMED	ENGLACIAL	ENGRAVERY
ENFANT	ENFORMING	ENGLISH	ENGRAVES
ENFANTS	ENFORMS	ENGLISHED	ENGRAVING
ENFEEBLE	ENFRAME	ENGLISHES	ENGRENAGE
ENFEEBLED	ENFRAMED	ENGLOBE	ENGRIEVE
ENFEEBLER	ENFRAMES	ENGLOBED	ENGRIEVED
ENFEEBLES	ENFRAMING	ENGLOBES	ENGRIEVES
ENFELON	ENFREE	ENGLOBING	ENGROOVE
ENFELONED	ENFREED	ENGLOOM	ENGROOVED
ENFELONS	ENFREEDOM	ENGLOOMED	ENGROOVES
ENFEOFF	ENFREEING	ENGLOOMS	ENGROSS
ENFEOFFED	ENFREES	ENGLUT	ENGROSSED
ENFEOFFS	ENFREEZE	ENGLUTS	ENGROSSER
ENFESTED	ENFREEZES	ENGLUTTED	ENGROSSES
ENFETTER	ENFROSEN	ENGOBE	ENGS
ENFETTERS	ENFROZE	ENGOBES	ENGUARD
ENFEVER	ENFROZEN	ENGORE	ENGUARDED

ENGUARDS	ENJOYMENT	ENMEWED	ENOUNCED
ENGULF	ENJOYS	ENMEWING	ENOUNCES
ENGULFED	ENKERNEL	ENMEWS	ENOUNCING
ENGULFING	ENKERNELS	ENMITIES	ENOW
ENGULFS	ENKINDLE	ENMITY	ENOWS
ENGULPH	ENKINDLED	ENMOSSED	ENPLANE
ENGULPHED	ENKINDLER	ENMOVE	ENPLANED
ENGULPHS	ENKINDLES	ENMOVED	ENPLANES
ENGYSCOPE	ENLACE	ENMOVES	ENPLANING
ENHALO	ENLACED	ENMOVING	ENPRINT
ENHALOED	ENLACES	ENNAGE	ENPRINTS
ENHALOES	ENLACING	ENNAGES	ENQUIRE
ENHALOING	ENLARD	ENNEAD	ENQUIRED
ENHALOS	ENLARDED	ENNEADIC	ENQUIRER
ENHANCE	ENLARDING	ENNEADS	ENQUIRERS
ENHANCED	ENLARDS	ENNEAGON	ENQUIRES
ENHANCER	ENLARGE	ENNEAGONS	ENQUIRIES
ENHANCERS	ENLARGED	ENNOBLE	ENQUIRING
ENHANCES	ENLARGEN	ENNOBLED	ENQUIRY
ENHANCING	ENLARGENS	ENNOBLER	ENRACE
ENHANCIVE	ENLARGER	ENNOBLERS	ENRACED
ENHEARSE	ENLARGERS	ENNOBLES	ENRACES
ENHEARSED	ENLARGES	ENNOBLING	ENRACING
ENHEARSES	ENLARGING	ENNOG	ENRAGE
ENHEARTEN	ENLEVE	ENNOGS	ENRAGED
ENHUNGER	ENLIGHT	ENNUI	ENRAGEDLY
ENHUNGERS	ENLIGHTED	ENNUIED	ENRAGES
ENHYDRITE	ENLIGHTEN	ENNUIS	ENRAGING
ENHYDROS	ENLIGHTS	ENNUYE	ENRANCKLE
ENHYDROUS	ENLINK	ENNUYED	ENRANGE
ENIAC	ENLINKED	ENNUYEE	ENRANGED
ENIACS	ENLINKING	ENNUYING	ENRANGES
ENIGMA	ENLINKS	ENODAL	ENRANGING
ENIGMAS	ENLIST	ENOKI	ENRANK
ENIGMATA	ENLISTED	ENOKIDAKE	ENRANKED
ENIGMATIC	ENLISTEE	ENOKIS	ENRANKING
ENISLE	ENLISTEES	ENOKITAKE	ENRANKS
ENISLED	ENLISTER	ENOL	ENRAPT
ENISLES	ENLISTERS	ENOLASE	ENRAPTURE
ENISLING	ENLISTING	ENOLASES	ENRAUNGE
ENJAMB	ENLISTS	ENOLIC	ENRAUNGED
ENJAMBED	ENLIT	ENOLOGIES	ENRAUNGES
ENJAMBING	ENLIVEN	ENOLOGIST	ENRAVISH
ENJAMBS	ENLIVENED	ENOLOGY	ENRHEUM
ENJOIN	ENLIVENER	ENOLS	ENRHEUMED
ENJOINDER	ENLIVENS	ENOMOTIES	ENRHEUMS
ENJOINED	ENLOCK	ENOMOTY	ENRICH
ENJOINER	ENLOCKED	ENOPHILE	ENRICHED
ENJOINERS	ENLOCKING	ENOPHILES	ENRICHER
ENJOINING	ENLOCKS	ENORM	ENRICHERS
ENJOINS	ENLUMINE	ENORMITY	ENRICHES
ENJOY	ENLUMINED	ENORMOUS	ENRICHING
ENJOYABLE	ENLUMINES	ENOSES	ENRIDGED
ENJOYABLY	ENMESH	ENOSIS	ENRING
ENJOYED	ENMESHED	ENOSISES	ENRINGED
ENJOYER	ENMESHES	ENOUGH	ENRINGING
ENJOYERS	ENMESHING	ENOUGHS	ENRINGS
ENJOYING	ENMEW	ENOUNCE	ENRIVEN

ENROBE
ENROBED
ENROBER
ENROBERS
ENROBES
ENROBING
ENROL
ENROLL
ENROLLED
ENROLLEE
ENROLLEES
ENROLLER
ENROLLERS
ENROLLING
ENROLLS
ENROLMENT
ENROLS
ENROOT
ENROOTED
ENROOTING
ENROOTS
ENROUGH
ENROUGHED
ENROUGHS
ENROUND
ENROUNDED
ENROUNDS
ENS
ENSAMPLE
ENSAMPLED
ENSAMPLES
ENSATE
ENSCONCE
ENSCONCED
ENSCONCES
ENSCROLL
ENSCROLLS
ENSEAL
ENSEALED
ENSEALING
ENSEALS
ENSEAM
ENSEAMED
ENSEAMING
ENSEAMS
ENSEAR
ENSEARED
ENSEARING
ENSEARS
ENSEMBLE
ENSEMBLES
ENSERF
ENSERFED
ENSERFING
ENSERFS
ENSEW
ENSEWED
ENSEWING

ENSEWS
ENSHEATH
ENSHEATHE
ENSHEATHS
ENSHELL
ENSHELLED
ENSHELLS
ENSHELTER
ENSHIELD
ENSHIELDS
ENSHRINE
ENSHRINED
ENSHRINEE
ENSHRINES
ENSHROUD
ENSHROUDS
ENSIFORM
ENSIGN
ENSIGNCY
ENSIGNED
ENSIGNING
ENSIGNS
ENSILAGE
ENSILAGED
ENSILAGES
ENSILE
ENSILED
ENSILES
ENSILING
ENSKIED
ENSKIES
ENSKY
ENSKYED
ENSKYING
ENSLAVE
ENSLAVED
ENSLAVER
ENSLAVERS
ENSLAVES
ENSLAVING
ENSNARE
ENSNARED
ENSNARER
ENSNARERS
ENSNARES
ENSNARING
ENSNARL
ENSNARLED
ENSNARLS
ENSORCEL
ENSORCELL
ENSORCELS
ENSOUL
ENSOULED
ENSOULING
ENSOULS
ENSPHERE
ENSPHERED

ENSPHERES
ENSTAMP
ENSTAMPED
ENSTAMPS
ENSTATITE
ENSTEEP
ENSTEEPED
ENSTEEPS
ENSTYLE
ENSTYLED
ENSTYLES
ENSTYLING
ENSUE
ENSUED
ENSUES
ENSUING
ENSURE
ENSURED
ENSURER
ENSURERS
ENSURES
ENSURING
ENSWATHE
ENSWATHED
ENSWATHES
ENSWEEP
ENSWEEPS
ENSWEPT
ENTAIL
ENTAILED
ENTAILER
ENTAILERS
ENTAILING
ENTAILS
ENTAME
ENTAMEBA
ENTAMEBAE
ENTAMEBAS
ENTAMED
ENTAMES
ENTAMING
ENTAMOEBA
ENTANGLE
ENTANGLED
ENTANGLER
ENTANGLES
ENTASES
ENTASIA
ENTASIAS
ENTASIS
ENTASTIC
ENTAYLE
ENTAYLED
ENTAYLES
ENTAYLING
ENTELECHY
ENTELLUS
ENTENDER

ENTENDERS
ENTENTE
ENTENTES
ENTER
ENTERA
ENTERABLE
ENTERAL
ENTERALLY
ENTERATE
ENTERED
ENTERER
ENTERERS
ENTERIC
ENTERICS
ENTERING
ENTERINGS
ENTERITIS
ENTERON
ENTERONS
ENTERS
ENTERTAIN
ENTERTAKE
ENTERTOOK
ENTETE
ENTETEE
ENTHALPY
ENTHETIC
ENTHRAL
ENTHRALL
ENTHRALLS
ENTHRALS
ENTHRONE
ENTHRONED
ENTHRONES
ENTHUSE
ENTHUSED
ENTHUSES
ENTHUSING
ENTHYMEME
ENTIA
ENTICE
ENTICED
ENTICER
ENTICERS
ENTICES
ENTICING
ENTICINGS
ENTIRE
ENTIRELY
ENTIRES
ENTIRETY
ENTITIES
ENTITLE
ENTITLED
ENTITLES
ENTITLING
ENTITY
ENTOBLAST

ENTODERM	ENTREZ	ENVENOMS	ENZOOTIC
ENTODERMS	ENTRIES	ENVERMEIL	ENZOOTICS
ENTOIL	ENTRISM	ENVIABLE	ENZYM
ENTOILED	ENTRISMS	ENVIABLY	ENZYMATIC
ENTOILING	ENTRIST	ENVIED	ENZYME
ENTOILS	ENTRISTS	ENVIER	ENZYMES
ENTOMB	ENTROLD	ENVIERS	ENZYMIC
ENTOMBED	ENTROPIC	ENVIES	ENZYMS
ENTOMBING	ENTROPIES	ENVIOUS	EOAN
ENTOMBS	ENTROPION	ENVIOUSLY	EOBIONT
ENTOMIC	ENTROPIUM	ENVIRO	EOBIONTS
ENTOPHYTE	ENTROPY	ENVIRON	EOCENE
ENTOPIC	ENTRUST	ENVIRONED	EOHIPPUS
ENTOPROCT	ENTRUSTED	ENVIRONS	EOLIAN
ENTOPTIC	ENTRUSTS	ENVIROS	EOLIENNE
ENTOPTICS	ENTRY	ENVISAGE	EOLIENNES
ENTOTIC	ENTRYISM	ENVISAGED	EOLIPILE
ENTOURAGE	ENTRYISMS	ENVISAGES	EOLIPILES
ENTOZOA	ENTRYIST	ENVISION	EOLITH
ENTOZOAL	ENTRYISTS	ENVISIONS	EOLITHIC
ENTOZOAN	ENTRYWAY	ENVOI	EOLITHS
ENTOZOANS	ENTRYWAYS	ENVOIS	EOLOPILE
ENTOZOIC	ENTWINE	ENVOY	EOLOPILES
ENTOZOON	ENTWINED	ENVOYS	EON
ENTRAIL	ENTWINES	ENVOYSHIP	EONIAN
ENTRAILED	ENTWINING	ENVY	EONISM
ENTRAILS	ENTWIST	ENVYING	EONISMS
ENTRAIN	ENTWISTED	ENVYINGLY	EONS
ENTRAINED	ENTWISTS	ENVYINGS	EORL
ENTRAINER	ENUCLEATE	ENWALL	EORLS
ENTRAINS	ENUF	ENWALLED	EOSIN
ENTRALL	ENUMERATE	ENWALLING	EOSINE
ENTRALLES	ENUNCIATE	ENWALLOW	EOSINES
ENTRAMMEL	ENURE	ENWALLOWS	EOSINIC
ENTRANCE	ENURED	ENWALLS	EOSINS
ENTRANCED	ENUREMENT	ENWHEEL	EOTHEN
ENTRANCES	ENURES	ENWHEELED	EPACRID
ENTRANT	ENURESES	ENWHEELS	EPACRIDS
ENTRANTS	ENURESIS	ENWIND	EPACRIS
ENTRAP	ENURETIC	ENWINDING	EPACRISES
ENTRAPPED	ENURETICS	ENWINDS	EPACT
ENTRAPPER	ENURING	ENWOMB	EPACTS
ENTRAPS	ENVASSAL	ENWOMBED	EPAENETIC
ENTREAT	ENVASSALS	ENWOMBING	EPAGOGE
ENTREATED	ENVAULT	ENWOMBS	EPAGOGES
ENTREATS	ENVAULTED	ENWOUND	EPAGOGIC
ENTREATY	ENVAULTS	ENWRAP	EPANODOS
ENTRECHAT	ENVEIGLE	ENWRAPPED	EPARCH
ENTRECOTE	ENVEIGLED	ENWRAPS	EPARCHATE
ENTREE	ENVEIGLES	ENWREATH	EPARCHIAL
ENTREES	ENVELOP	ENWREATHE	EPARCHIES
ENTREMES	ENVELOPE	ENWREATHS	EPARCHS
ENTREMETS	ENVELOPED	ENZIAN	EPARCHY
ENTRENCH	ENVELOPER	ENZIANS	EPATANT
ENTREPOT	ENVELOPES	ENZONE	EPAULE
ENTREPOTS	ENVELOPS	ENZONED	EPAULES
ENTRESOL	ENVENOM	ENZONES	EPAULET
ENTRESOLS	ENVENOMED	ENZONING	EPAULETS

EPAULETTE	EPIBIOSIS	EPIDERMIC	EPILOGISE
EPAXIAL	EPIBIOTIC	EPIDERMIS	EPILOGIST
EPAZOTE	EPIBLAST	EPIDERMS	EPILOGIZE
EPAZOTES	EPIBLASTS	EPIDICTIC	EPILOGS
EPEDAPHIC	EPIBLEM	EPIDOSITE	EPILOGUE
EPEE	EPIBLEMS	EPIDOTE	EPILOGUED
EPEEIST	EPIBOLIC	EPIDOTES	EPILOGUES
EPEEISTS	EPIBOLIES	EPIDOTIC	EPIMER
EPEES	EPIBOLY	EPIDURAL	EPIMERASE
EPEIRA	EPIC	EPIDURALS	EPIMERE
EPEIRAS	EPICAL	EPIFAUNA	EPIMERES
EPEIRIC	EPICALLY	EPIFAUNAE	EPIMERIC
EPEIRID	EPICALYX	EPIFAUNAL	EPIMERISM
EPEIRIDS	EPICANTHI	EPIFAUNAS	EPIMERS
EPENDYMA	EPICARDIA	EPIFOCAL	EPIMYSIA
EPENDYMAL	EPICARP	EPIGAEAL	EPIMYSIUM
EPENDYMAS	EPICARPS	EPIGAEAN	EPINAOI
EPEOLATRY	EPICEDE	EPIGAEOUS	EPINAOS
EPERDU	EPICEDES	EPIGAMIC	EPINASTIC
EPERDUE	EPICEDIA	EPIGEAL	EPINASTY
EPERGNE	EPICEDIAL	EPIGEAN	EPINEURAL
EPERGNES	EPICEDIAN	EPIGEIC	EPINEURIA
EPHA	EPICEDIUM	EPIGENE	EPINICIAN
EPHAH	EPICENE	EPIGENIC	EPINICION
EPHAHS	EPICENES	EPIGENIST	EPINIKIAN
EPHAS	EPICENISM	EPIGENOUS	EPINIKION
EPHEBE	EPICENTER	EPIGEOUS	EPINOSIC
EPHEBES	EPICENTRA	EPIGON	EPIPHANIC
EPHEBI	EPICENTRE	EPIGONE	EPIPHANY
EPHEBIC	EPICIER	EPIGONES	EPIPHRAGM
EPHEBOI	EPICIERS	EPIGONI	EPIPHYSES
EPHEBOS	EPICISM	EPIGONIC	EPIPHYSIS
EPHEBUS	EPICISMS	EPIGONISM	EPIPHYTAL
EPHEDRA	EPICIST	EPIGONOUS	EPIPHYTE
EPHEDRAS	EPICISTS	EPIGONS	EPIPHYTES
EPHEDRIN	EPICLESES	EPIGONUS	EPIPHYTIC
EPHEDRINE	EPICLESIS	EPIGRAM	EPIPLOIC
EPHEDRINS	EPICLIKE	EPIGRAMS	EPIPLOON
EPHELIDES	EPICOTYL	EPIGRAPH	EPIPLOONS
EPHELIS	EPICOTYLS	EPIGRAPHS	EPIPOLIC
EPHEMERA	EPICRANIA	EPIGRAPHY	EPIPOLISM
EPHEMERAE	EPICRISES	EPIGYNIES	EPIROGENY
EPHEMERAL	EPICRISIS	EPIGYNOUS	EPIRRHEMA
EPHEMERAS	EPICRITIC	EPIGYNY	EPISCIA
EPHEMERID	EPICS	EPILATE	EPISCIAS
EPHEMERIS	EPICURE	EPILATED	EPISCOPAL
EPHEMERON	EPICUREAN	EPILATES	EPISCOPE
EPHIALTES	EPICURES	EPILATING	EPISCOPES
EPHOD	EPICURISE	EPILATION	EPISCOPY
EPHODS	EPICURISM	EPILATOR	EPISEMON
EPHOR	EPICURIZE	EPILATORS	EPISEMONS
EPHORAL	EPICYCLE	EPILEPSY	EPISODAL
EPHORALTY	EPICYCLES	EPILEPTIC	EPISODE
EPHORATE	EPICYCLIC	EPILIMNIA	EPISODES
EPHORATES	EPIDEMIC	EPILITHIC	EPISODIAL
EPHORI	EPIDEMICS	EPILOBIUM	EPISODIC
EPHORS	EPIDERM	EPILOG	EPISOMAL
EPIBIOSES	EPIDERMAL	EPILOGIC	EPISOME

EPISOMES

EPISOMES	EPITONIC	EPSOMITES	EQUINES
EPISPERM	EPITOPE	EPUISE	EQUINIA
EPISPERMS	EPITOPES	EPUISEE	EQUINIAS
EPISPORE	EPITRITE	EPULARY	EQUINITY
EPISPORES	EPITRITES	EPULATION	EQUINOX
EPISTASES	EPIZEUXES	EPULIDES	EQUINOXES
EPISTASIS	EPIZEUXIS	EPULIS	EQUIP
EPISTASY	EPIZOA	EPULISES	EQUIPAGE
EPISTATIC	EPIZOAN	EPULOTIC	EQUIPAGED
EPISTAXES	EPIZOANS	EPULOTICS	EQUIPAGES
EPISTAXIS	EPIZOIC	EPURATE	EQUIPE
EPISTEMIC	EPIZOISM	EPURATED	EQUIPES
EPISTERNA	EPIZOISMS	EPURATES	EQUIPMENT
EPISTLE	EPIZOITE	EPURATING	EQUIPOISE
EPISTLED	EPIZOITES	EPURATION	EQUIPPED
EPISTLER	EPIZOON	EPYLLIA	EQUIPPER
EPISTLERS	EPIZOOTIC	EPYLLION	EQUIPPERS
EPISTLES	EPIZOOTY	EPYLLIONS	EQUIPPING
EPISTLING	EPOCH	EQUABLE	EQUIPS
EPISTOLER	EPOCHA	EQUABLY	EQUISETA
EPISTOLET	EPOCHAL	EQUAL	EQUISETIC
EPISTOLIC	EPOCHALLY	EQUALED	EQUISETUM
EPISTOME	EPOCHAS	EQUALI	EQUITABLE
EPISTOMES	EPOCHS	EQUALING	EQUITABLY
EPISTYLE	EPODE	EQUALISE	EQUITANT
EPISTYLES	EPODES	EQUALISED	EQUITES
EPITAPH	EPODIC	EQUALISER	EQUITIES
EPITAPHED	EPONYM	EQUALISES	EQUITY
EPITAPHER	EPONYMIC	EQUALITY	EQUIVALVE
EPITAPHIC	EPONYMIES	EQUALIZE	EQUIVOCAL
EPITAPHS	EPONYMOUS	EQUALIZED	EQUIVOKE
EPITASES	EPONYMS	EQUALIZER	EQUIVOKES
EPITASIS	EPONYMY	EQUALIZES	EQUIVOQUE
EPITAXES	EPOPEE	EQUALLED	ER
EPITAXIAL	EPOPEES	EQUALLING	ERA
EPITAXIC	EPOPOEIA	EQUALLY	ERADIATE
EPITAXIES	EPOPOEIAS	EQUALNESS	ERADIATED
EPITAXIS	EPOPT	EQUALS	ERADIATES
EPITAXY	EPOPTS	EQUANT	ERADICANT
EPITHECA	EPOS	EQUANTS	ERADICATE
EPITHECAE	EPOSES	EQUATABLE	ERAS
EPITHELIA	EPOXIDE	EQUATE	ERASABLE
EPITHEM	EPOXIDES	EQUATED	ERASE
EPITHEMA	EPOXIDISE	EQUATES	ERASED
EPITHEMS	EPOXIDIZE	EQUATING	ERASEMENT
EPITHESES	EPOXIED	EQUATION	ERASER
EPITHESIS	EPOXIES	EQUATIONS	ERASERS
EPITHET	EPOXY	EQUATOR	ERASES
EPITHETED	EPOXYED	EQUATORS	ERASING
EPITHETIC	EPOXYING	EQUERRIES	ERASION
EPITHETON	EPRIS	EQUERRY	ERASIONS
EPITHETS	EPRISE	EQUID	ERASURE
EPITOME	EPROM	EQUIDS	ERASURES
EPITOMES	EPROMS	EQUIMOLAL	ERATHEM
EPITOMIC	EPSILON	EQUIMOLAR	ERATHEMS
EPITOMISE	EPSILONIC	EQUINAL	ERBIA
EPITOMIST	EPSILONS	EQUINE	ERBIAS
EPITOMIZE	EPSOMITE	EQUINELY	ERBIUM

ERBIUMS	ERGON	ERNS	ERRANTRY
ERE	ERGONOMIC	ERODABLE	ERRANTS
ERECT	ERGONS	ERODE	ERRATA
ERECTABLE	ERGOS	ERODED	ERRATAS
ERECTED	ERGOT	ERODENT	ERRATIC
ERECTER	ERGOTIC	ERODENTS	ERRATICAL
ERECTERS	ERGOTISE	ERODES	ERRATICS
ERECTILE	ERGOTISED	ERODIBLE	ERRATUM
ERECTING	ERGOTISES	ERODING	ERRED
ERECTION	ERGOTISM	ERODIUM	ERRHINE
ERECTIONS	ERGOTISMS	ERODIUMS	ERRHINES
ERECTIVE	ERGOTIZE	EROGENIC	ERRING
ERECTLY	ERGOTIZED	EROGENOUS	ERRINGLY
ERECTNESS	ERGOTIZES	EROS	ERRINGS
ERECTOR	ERGOTS	EROSE	ERRONEOUS
ERECTORS	ERGS	EROSELY	ERROR
ERECTS	ERIACH	EROSES	ERRORIST
ERED	ERIACHS	EROSIBLE	ERRORISTS
ERELONG	ERIC	EROSION	ERRORLESS
EREMIC	ERICA	EROSIONAL	ERRORS
EREMITAL	ERICAS	EROSIONS	ERRS
EREMITE	ERICK	EROSIVE	ERS
EREMITES	ERICKS	EROSIVITY	ERSATZ
EREMITIC	ERICOID	EROSTRATE	ERSATZES
EREMITISH	ERICS	EROTEMA	ERSES
EREMITISM	ERIGERON	EROTEMAS	ERST
EREMURI	ERIGERONS	EROTEME	ERSTWHILE
EREMURUS	ERING	EROTEMES	ERUCIC
ERENOW	ERINGO	EROTESES	ERUCIFORM
EREPSIN	ERINGOES	EROTESIS	ERUCT
EREPSINS	ERINGOS	EROTETIC	ERUCTATE
ERES	ERINITE	EROTIC	ERUCTATED
ERETHIC	ERINITES	EROTICA	ERUCTATES
ERETHISM	ERINUS	EROTICAL	ERUCTED
ERETHISMS	ERINUSES	EROTICISE	ERUCTING
ERETHITIC	ERIOMETER	EROTICISM	ERUCTS
EREV	ERIONITE	EROTICIST	ERUDITE
EREVS	ERIONITES	EROTICIZE	ERUDITELY
EREWHILE	ERIOPHYID	EROTICS	ERUDITES
EREWHILES	ERISTIC	EROTISE	ERUDITION
ERF	ERISTICAL	EROTISED	ERUGO
ERG	ERISTICS	EROTISES	ERUGOS
ERGASTIC	ERK	EROTISING	ERUMPENT
ERGATANER	ERKS	EROTISM	ERUPT
ERGATE	ERLANG	EROTISMS	ERUPTED
ERGATES	ERLANGS	EROTIZE	ERUPTIBLE
ERGATIVE	ERLKING	EROTIZED	ERUPTING
ERGATIVES	ERLKINGS	EROTIZES	ERUPTION
ERGATOID	ERMELIN	EROTIZING	ERUPTIONS
ERGO	ERMELINS	EROTOLOGY	ERUPTIVE
ERGODIC	ERMINE	ERR	ERUPTIVES
ERGOGENIC	ERMINED	ERRABLE	ERUPTS
ERGOGRAM	ERMINES	ERRANCIES	ERUV
ERGOGRAMS	ERN	ERRANCY	ERUVIM
ERGOGRAPH	ERNE	ERRAND	ERUVIN
ERGOMANIA	ERNED	ERRANDS	ERUVS
ERGOMETER	ERNES	ERRANT	ERVALENTA
ERGOMETRY	ERNING	ERRANTLY	ERVEN

ERVIL
ERVILS
ERYNGIUM
ERYNGIUMS
ERYNGO
ERYNGOES
ERYNGOS
ERYTHEMA
ERYTHEMAL
ERYTHEMAS
ERYTHEMIC
ERYTHRINA
ERYTHRISM
ERYTHRITE
ERYTHROID
ERYTHRON
ERYTHRONS
ES
ESCALADE
ESCALADED
ESCALADER
ESCALADES
ESCALADO
ESCALATE
ESCALATED
ESCALATES
ESCALATOR
ESCALIER
ESCALIERS
ESCALLOP
ESCALLOPS
ESCALOP
ESCALOPE
ESCALOPED
ESCALOPES
ESCALOPS
ESCAPABLE
ESCAPADE
ESCAPADES
ESCAPADO
ESCAPE
ESCAPED
ESCAPEE
ESCAPEES
ESCAPER
ESCAPERS
ESCAPES
ESCAPING
ESCAPISM
ESCAPISMS
ESCAPIST
ESCAPISTS
ESCAR
ESCARGOT
ESCARGOTS
ESCAROLE
ESCAROLES
ESCARP

ESCARPED
ESCARPING
ESCARPS
ESCARS
ESCHALOT
ESCHALOTS
ESCHAR
ESCHARS
ESCHEAT
ESCHEATED
ESCHEATOR
ESCHEATS
ESCHEW
ESCHEWAL
ESCHEWALS
ESCHEWED
ESCHEWER
ESCHEWERS
ESCHEWING
ESCHEWS
ESCLANDRE
ESCOLAR
ESCOLARS
ESCOPETTE
ESCORT
ESCORTAGE
ESCORTED
ESCORTING
ESCORTS
ESCOT
ESCOTED
ESCOTING
ESCOTS
ESCOTTED
ESCOTTING
ESCRIBANO
ESCRIBE
ESCRIBED
ESCRIBES
ESCRIBING
ESCROC
ESCROCS
ESCROL
ESCROLL
ESCROLLS
ESCROLS
ESCROW
ESCROWED
ESCROWING
ESCROWS
ESCUAGE
ESCUAGES
ESCUDO
ESCUDOS
ESCULENT
ESCULENTS
ESEMPLASY
ESERINE

ESERINES
ESES
ESILE
ESILES
ESKAR
ESKARS
ESKER
ESKERS
ESKIES
ESKY
ESLOIN
ESLOINED
ESLOINING
ESLOINS
ESLOYNE
ESLOYNED
ESLOYNES
ESLOYNING
ESNE
ESNECIES
ESNECY
ESNES
ESOPHAGI
ESOPHAGUS
ESOTERIC
ESOTERICA
ESOTERIES
ESOTERISM
ESOTERY
ESOTROPIA
ESOTROPIC
ESPADA
ESPADAS
ESPAGNOLE
ESPALIER
ESPALIERS
ESPANOL
ESPANOLES
ESPARTO
ESPARTOS
ESPECIAL
ESPERANCE
ESPIAL
ESPIALS
ESPIED
ESPIEGLE
ESPIER
ESPIERS
ESPIES
ESPIONAGE
ESPLANADE
ESPOUSAL
ESPOUSALS
ESPOUSE
ESPOUSED
ESPOUSER
ESPOUSERS
ESPOUSES

ESPOUSING
ESPRESSO
ESPRESSOS
ESPRIT
ESPRITS
ESPUMOSO
ESPUMOSOS
ESPY
ESPYING
ESQUIRE
ESQUIRED
ESQUIRES
ESQUIRESS
ESQUIRING
ESQUISSE
ESQUISSES
ESS
ESSAY
ESSAYED
ESSAYER
ESSAYERS
ESSAYETTE
ESSAYING
ESSAYISH
ESSAYIST
ESSAYISTS
ESSAYS
ESSE
ESSENCE
ESSENCES
ESSENTIAL
ESSES
ESSIVE
ESSIVES
ESSOIN
ESSOINER
ESSOINERS
ESSOINS
ESSONITE
ESSONITES
ESSOYNE
ESSOYNES
EST
ESTABLISH
ESTACADE
ESTACADES
ESTAFETTE
ESTAMINET
ESTANCIA
ESTANCIAS
ESTATE
ESTATED
ESTATES
ESTATING
ESTEEM
ESTEEMED
ESTEEMING
ESTEEMS

ESTER	ESTREPING	ETATISTE	ETHERISE
ESTERASE	ESTRICH	ETATISTES	ETHERISED
ESTERASES	ESTRICHES	ETATS	ETHERISER
ESTERIFY	ESTRIDGE	ETCETERA	ETHERISES
ESTERS	ESTRIDGES	ETCETERAS	ETHERISH
ESTHESES	ESTRILDID	ETCH	ETHERISM
ESTHESIA	ESTRIN	ETCHANT	ETHERISMS
ESTHESIAS	ESTRINS	ETCHANTS	ETHERIST
ESTHESIS	ESTRIOL	ETCHED	ETHERISTS
ESTHETE	ESTRIOLS	ETCHER	ETHERIZE
ESTHETES	ESTRO	ETCHERS	ETHERIZED
ESTHETIC	ESTROGEN	ETCHES	ETHERIZER
ESTHETICS	ESTROGENS	ETCHING	ETHERIZES
ESTIMABLE	ESTRONE	ETCHINGS	ETHERS
ESTIMABLY	ESTRONES	ETEN	ETHIC
ESTIMATE	ESTROS	ETENS	ETHICAL
ESTIMATED	ESTROUS	ETERNAL	ETHICALLY
ESTIMATES	ESTRUAL	ETERNALLY	ETHICALS
ESTIMATOR	ESTRUM	ETERNALS	ETHICIAN
ESTIVAL	ESTRUMS	ETERNE	ETHICIANS
ESTIVATE	ESTRUS	ETERNISE	ETHICISE
ESTIVATED	ESTRUSES	ETERNISED	ETHICISED
ESTIVATES	ESTS	ETERNISES	ETHICISES
ESTIVATOR	ESTUARIAL	ETERNITY	ETHICISM
ESTOC	ESTUARIAN	ETERNIZE	ETHICISMS
ESTOCS	ESTUARIES	ETERNIZED	ETHICIST
ESTOILE	ESTUARINE	ETERNIZES	ETHICISTS
ESTOILES	ESTUARY	ETESIAN	ETHICIZE
ESTOP	ESURIENCE	ETESIANS	ETHICIZED
ESTOPPAGE	ESURIENCY	ETH	ETHICIZES
ESTOPPED	ESURIENT	ETHAL	ETHICS
ESTOPPEL	ET	ETHALS	ETHINYL
ESTOPPELS	ETA	ETHANAL	ETHINYLS
ESTOPPING	ETACISM	ETHANALS	ETHION
ESTOPS	ETACISMS	ETHANE	ETHIONINE
ESTOVER	ETAERIO	ETHANES	ETHIONS
ESTOVERS	ETAERIOS	ETHANOATE	ETHIOPS
ESTRADE	ETAGE	ETHANOIC	ETHIOPSES
ESTRADES	ETAGERE	ETHANOL	ETHMOID
ESTRADIOL	ETAGERES	ETHANOLS	ETHMOIDAL
ESTRAGON	ETAGES	ETHANOYL	ETHMOIDS
ESTRAGONS	ETALAGE	ETHANOYLS	ETHNARCH
ESTRAL	ETALAGES	ETHE	ETHNARCHS
ESTRANGE	ETALON	ETHENE	ETHNARCHY
ESTRANGED	ETALONS	ETHENES	ETHNIC
ESTRANGER	ETAMIN	ETHEPHON	ETHNICAL
ESTRANGES	ETAMINE	ETHEPHONS	ETHNICISM
ESTRAPADE	ETAMINES	ETHER	ETHNICITY
ESTRAY	ETAMINS	ETHERCAP	ETHNICS
ESTRAYED	ETAPE	ETHERCAPS	ETHNOCIDE
ESTRAYING	ETAPES	ETHEREAL	ETHNOGENY
ESTRAYS	ETAS	ETHEREOUS	ETHNOLOGY
ESTREAT	ETAT	ETHERIAL	ETHNONYM
ESTREATED	ETATISM	ETHERIC	ETHNONYMS
ESTREATS	ETATISME	ETHERICAL	ETHNOS
ESTREPE	ETATISMES	ETHERIFY	ETHNOSES
ESTREPED	ETATISMS	ETHERION	ETHOGRAM
ESTREPES	ETATIST	ETHERIONS	ETHOGRAMS

ETHOLOGIC	ETUDE	EUGENICAL	EUNUCHS
ETHOLOGY	ETUDES	EUGENICS	EUOI
ETHONONE	ETUI	EUGENISM	EUONYMIN
ETHONONES	ETUIS	EUGENISMS	EUONYMINS
ETHOS	ETWEE	EUGENIST	EUONYMUS
ETHOSES	ETWEES	EUGENISTS	EUOUAE
ETHOXIDE	ETYMA	EUGENOL	EUOUAES
ETHOXIDES	ETYMIC	EUGENOLS	EUPAD
ETHOXIES	ETYMOLOGY	EUGH	EUPADS
ETHOXY	ETYMON	EUGHEN	EUPATRID
ETHOXYL	ETYMONS	EUGHS	EUPATRIDS
ETHOXYLS	ETYPIC	EUGLENA	EUPEPSIA
ETHS	ETYPICAL	EUGLENAS	EUPEPSIAS
ETHYL	EUCAIN	EUGLENID	EUPEPSIES
ETHYLATE	EUCAINE	EUGLENIDS	EUPEPSY
ETHYLATED	EUCAINES	EUGLENOID	EUPEPTIC
ETHYLATES	EUCAINS	EUK	EUPHAUSID
ETHYLENE	EUCALYPT	EUKARYON	EUPHEMISE
ETHYLENES	EUCALYPTI	EUKARYONS	EUPHEMISM
ETHYLENIC	EUCALYPTS	EUKARYOT	EUPHEMIST
ETHYLIC	EUCARYON	EUKARYOTE	EUPHEMIZE
ETHYLS	EUCARYONS	EUKARYOTS	EUPHENIC
ETHYNE	EUCARYOT	EUKED	EUPHENICS
ETHYNES	EUCARYOTE	EUKING	EUPHOBIA
ETHYNYL	EUCARYOTS	EUKS	EUPHOBIAS
ETHYNYLS	EUCHARIS	EULACHAN	EUPHON
ETIC	EUCHLORIC	EULACHANS	EUPHONIA
ETIOLATE	EUCHLORIN	EULACHON	EUPHONIAS
ETIOLATED	EUCHOLOGY	EULACHONS	EUPHONIC
ETIOLATES	EUCHRE	EULOGIA	EUPHONIES
ETIOLIN	EUCHRED	EULOGIAE	EUPHONISE
ETIOLINS	EUCHRES	EULOGIAS	EUPHONISM
ETIOLOGIC	EUCHRING	EULOGIES	EUPHONIUM
ETIOLOGY	EUCLASE	EULOGISE	EUPHONIZE
ETIQUETTE	EUCLASES	EULOGISED	EUPHONS
ETNA	EUCLIDEAN	EULOGISER	EUPHONY
ETNAS	EUCLIDIAN	EULOGISES	EUPHORBIA
ETOILE	EUCRITE	EULOGIST	EUPHORIA
ETOILES	EUCRITES	EULOGISTS	EUPHORIAS
ETOUFFEE	EUCRITIC	EULOGIUM	EUPHORIC
ETOUFFEES	EUCRYPHIA	EULOGIUMS	EUPHORIES
ETOURDI	EUCYCLIC	EULOGIZE	EUPHORY
ETOURDIE	EUDAEMON	EULOGIZED	EUPHOTIC
ETRANGER	EUDAEMONS	EULOGIZER	EUPHRASY
ETRANGERE	EUDAEMONY	EULOGIZES	EUPHROE
ETRANGERS	EUDAIMON	EULOGY	EUPHROES
ETRENNE	EUDAIMONS	EUMELANIN	EUPHUISE
ETRENNES	EUDEMON	EUMERISM	EUPHUISED
ETRIER	EUDEMONIA	EUMERISMS	EUPHUISES
ETRIERS	EUDEMONIC	EUMONG	EUPHUISM
ETTERCAP	EUDEMONS	EUMONGS	EUPHUISMS
ETTERCAPS	EUDIALYTE	EUMUNG	EUPHUIST
ETTIN	EUGARIE	EUMUNGS	EUPHUISTS
ETTINS	EUGARIES	EUNUCH	EUPHUIZE
ETTLE	EUGE	EUNUCHISE	EUPHUIZED
ETTLED	EUGENIA	EUNUCHISM	EUPHUIZES
ETTLES	EUGENIAS	EUNUCHIZE	EUPLASTIC
ETTLING	EUGENIC	EUNUCHOID	EUPLOID

EUPLOIDS	EUTECTICS	EVAPORITE	EVERTING
EUPLOIDY	EUTECTOID	EVASIBLE	EVERTOR
EUPNEA	EUTEXIA	EVASION	EVERTORS
EUPNEAS	EUTEXIAS	EVASIONAL	EVERTS
EUPNEIC	EUTHANASY	EVASIONS	EVERWHERE
EUPNOEA	EUTHANISE	EVASIVE	EVERWHICH
EUPNOEAS	EUTHANIZE	EVASIVELY	EVERY
EUPNOEIC	EUTHENICS	EVE	EVERYBODY
EUREKA	EUTHENIST	EVECTION	EVERYDAY
EUREKAS	EUTHERIAN	EVECTIONS	EVERYDAYS
EURHYTHMY	EUTHYMIA	EVEJAR	EVERYMAN
EURIPI	EUTHYMIAS	EVEJARS	EVERYMEN
EURIPUS	EUTHYROID	EVEN	EVERYONE
EURIPUSES	EUTRAPELY	EVENED	EVERYWAY
EURO	EUTROPHIC	EVENEMENT	EVERYWHEN
EUROBOND	EUTROPHY	EVENER	EVES
EUROBONDS	EUTROPIC	EVENERS	EVET
EUROCRAT	EUTROPIES	EVENEST	EVETS
EUROCRATS	EUTROPOUS	EVENFALL	EVHOE
EUROCREEP	EUTROPY	EVENFALLS	EVICT
EUROKIES	EUXENITE	EVENING	EVICTED
EUROKOUS	EUXENITES	EVENINGS	EVICTEE
EUROKY	EVACUANT	EVENLY	EVICTEES
EURONOTE	EVACUANTS	EVENNESS	EVICTING
EURONOTES	EVACUATE	EVENS	EVICTION
EUROPHILE	EVACUATED	EVENSONG	EVICTIONS
EUROPIUM	EVACUATES	EVENSONGS	EVICTOR
EUROPIUMS	EVACUATOR	EVENT	EVICTORS
EUROS	EVACUEE	EVENTED	EVICTS
EURYBATH	EVACUEES	EVENTER	EVIDENCE
EURYBATHS	EVADABLE	EVENTERS	EVIDENCED
EURYOKIES	EVADE	EVENTFUL	EVIDENCES
EURYOKOUS	EVADED	EVENTIDE	EVIDENT
EURYOKY	EVADER	EVENTIDES	EVIDENTLY
EURYTHERM	EVADERS	EVENTING	EVIDENTS
EURYTHMIC	EVADES	EVENTINGS	EVIL
EURYTHMY	EVADIBLE	EVENTISE	EVILDOER
EURYTOPIC	EVADING	EVENTISED	EVILDOERS
EUSOCIAL	EVADINGLY	EVENTISES	EVILDOING
EUSOL	EVAGATION	EVENTIZE	EVILER
EUSOLS	EVAGINATE	EVENTIZED	EVILEST
EUSTACIES	EVALUABLE	EVENTIZES	EVILLER
EUSTACY	EVALUATE	EVENTLESS	EVILLEST
EUSTASIES	EVALUATED	EVENTRATE	EVILLY
EUSTASY	EVALUATES	EVENTS	EVILNESS
EUSTATIC	EVALUATOR	EVENTUAL	EVILS
EUSTELE	EVANESCE	EVENTUATE	EVINCE
EUSTELES	EVANESCED	EVER	EVINCED
EUSTYLE	EVANESCES	EVERGLADE	EVINCES
EUSTYLES	EVANGEL	EVERGREEN	EVINCIBLE
EUTAXIA	EVANGELIC	EVERMORE	EVINCIBLY
EUTAXIAS	EVANGELS	EVERNET	EVINCING
EUTAXIES	EVANGELY	EVERNETS	EVINCIVE
EUTAXITE	EVANISH	EVERSIBLE	EVIRATE
EUTAXITES	EVANISHED	EVERSION	EVIRATED
EUTAXITIC	EVANISHES	EVERSIONS	EVIRATES
EUTAXY	EVANITION	EVERT	EVIRATING
EUTECTIC	EVAPORATE	EVERTED	EVITABLE

EVITATE	EVZONE	EXAMINES	EXCERPT
EVITATED	EVZONES	EXAMINING	EXCERPTA
EVITATES	EWE	EXAMPLAR	EXCERPTED
EVITATING	EWER	EXAMPLARS	EXCERPTER
EVITATION	EWERS	EXAMPLE	EXCERPTOR
EVITE	EWES	EXAMPLED	EXCERPTS
EVITED	EWEST	EXAMPLES	EXCERPTUM
EVITERNAL	EWFTES	EXAMPLING	EXCESS
EVITES	EWGHEN	EXAMS	EXCESSED
EVITING	EWHOW	EXANIMATE	EXCESSES
EVO	EWK	EXANTHEM	EXCESSING
EVOCABLE	EWKED	EXANTHEMA	EXCESSIVE
EVOCATE	EWKING	EXANTHEMS	EXCHANGE
EVOCATED	EWKS	EXAPTED	EXCHANGED
EVOCATES	EWT	EXAPTIVE	EXCHANGER
EVOCATING	EWTS	EXARATE	EXCHANGES
EVOCATION	EX	EXARATION	EXCHEAT
EVOCATIVE	EXABYTE	EXARCH	EXCHEATS
EVOCATOR	EXABYTES	EXARCHAL	EXCHEQUER
EVOCATORS	EXACT	EXARCHATE	EXCIDE
EVOCATORY	EXACTA	EXARCHIES	EXCIDED
EVOE	EXACTABLE	EXARCHIST	EXCIDES
EVOHE	EXACTAS	EXARCHS	EXCIDING
EVOKE	EXACTED	EXARCHY	EXCIMER
EVOKED	EXACTER	EXCAMB	EXCIMERS
EVOKER	EXACTERS	EXCAMBED	EXCIPIENT
EVOKERS	EXACTEST	EXCAMBING	EXCIPLE
EVOKES	EXACTING	EXCAMBION	EXCIPLES
EVOKING	EXACTION	EXCAMBIUM	EXCISABLE
EVOLUE	EXACTIONS	EXCAMBS	EXCISE
EVOLUES	EXACTLY	EXCARNATE	EXCISED
EVOLUTE	EXACTMENT	EXCAUDATE	EXCISEMAN
EVOLUTED	EXACTNESS	EXCAVATE	EXCISEMEN
EVOLUTES	EXACTOR	EXCAVATED	EXCISES
EVOLUTING	EXACTORS	EXCAVATES	EXCISING
EVOLUTION	EXACTRESS	EXCAVATOR	EXCISION
EVOLUTIVE	EXACTS	EXCEED	EXCISIONS
EVOLVABLE	EXACUM	EXCEEDED	EXCITABLE
EVOLVE	EXACUMS	EXCEEDER	EXCITABLY
EVOLVED	EXAHERTZ	EXCEEDERS	EXCITANCY
EVOLVENT	EXALT	EXCEEDING	EXCITANT
EVOLVER	EXALTED	EXCEEDS	EXCITANTS
EVOLVERS	EXALTEDLY	EXCEL	EXCITE
EVOLVES	EXALTER	EXCELLED	EXCITED
EVOLVING	EXALTERS	EXCELLENT	EXCITEDLY
EVONYMUS	EXALTING	EXCELLING	EXCITER
EVOS	EXALTS	EXCELS	EXCITERS
EVOVAE	EXAM	EXCELSIOR	EXCITES
EVOVAES	EXAMEN	EXCENTRIC	EXCITING
EVULGATE	EXAMENS	EXCEPT	EXCITON
EVULGATED	EXAMINANT	EXCEPTANT	EXCITONIC
EVULGATES	EXAMINATE	EXCEPTED	EXCITONS
EVULSE	EXAMINE	EXCEPTING	EXCITOR
EVULSED	EXAMINED	EXCEPTION	EXCITORS
EVULSES	EXAMINEE	EXCEPTIVE	EXCLAIM
EVULSING	EXAMINEES	EXCEPTOR	EXCLAIMED
EVULSION	EXAMINER	EXCEPTORS	EXCLAIMER
EVULSIONS	EXAMINERS	EXCEPTS	EXCLAIMS

EXCLAVE
EXCLAVES
EXCLOSURE
EXCLUDE
EXCLUDED
EXCLUDEE
EXCLUDEES
EXCLUDER
EXCLUDERS
EXCLUDES
EXCLUDING
EXCLUSION
EXCLUSIVE
EXCLUSORY
EXCORIATE
EXCREMENT
EXCRETA
EXCRETAL
EXCRETE
EXCRETED
EXCRETER
EXCRETERS
EXCRETES
EXCRETING
EXCRETION
EXCRETIVE
EXCRETORY
EXCUBANT
EXCUDIT
EXCULPATE
EXCURRENT
EXCURSE
EXCURSED
EXCURSES
EXCURSING
EXCURSION
EXCURSIVE
EXCURSUS
EXCUSABLE
EXCUSABLY
EXCUSAL
EXCUSALS
EXCUSE
EXCUSED
EXCUSER
EXCUSERS
EXCUSES
EXCUSING
EXCUSIVE
EXEAT
EXEATS
EXEC
EXECRABLE
EXECRABLY
EXECRATE
EXECRATED
EXECRATES
EXECRATOR

EXECS
EXECUTANT
EXECUTARY
EXECUTE
EXECUTED
EXECUTER
EXECUTERS
EXECUTES
EXECUTING
EXECUTION
EXECUTIVE
EXECUTOR
EXECUTORS
EXECUTORY
EXECUTRIX
EXECUTRY
EXED
EXEDRA
EXEDRAE
EXEEM
EXEEMED
EXEEMING
EXEEMS
EXEGESES
EXEGESIS
EXEGETE
EXEGETES
EXEGETIC
EXEGETICS
EXEGETIST
EXEME
EXEMED
EXEMES
EXEMING
EXEMPLA
EXEMPLAR
EXEMPLARS
EXEMPLARY
EXEMPLE
EXEMPLES
EXEMPLIFY
EXEMPLUM
EXEMPT
EXEMPTED
EXEMPTING
EXEMPTION
EXEMPTIVE
EXEMPTS
EXEQUATUR
EXEQUIAL
EXEQUIES
EXEQUY
EXERCISE
EXERCISED
EXERCISER
EXERCISES
EXERCYCLE
EXERGONIC

EXERGUAL
EXERGUE
EXERGUES
EXERT
EXERTED
EXERTING
EXERTION
EXERTIONS
EXERTIVE
EXERTS
EXES
EXEUNT
EXFOLIANT
EXFOLIATE
EXHALABLE
EXHALANT
EXHALANTS
EXHALE
EXHALED
EXHALENT
EXHALENTS
EXHALES
EXHALING
EXHAUST
EXHAUSTED
EXHAUSTER
EXHAUSTS
EXHEDRA
EXHEDRAE
EXHIBIT
EXHIBITED
EXHIBITER
EXHIBITOR
EXHIBITS
EXHORT
EXHORTED
EXHORTER
EXHORTERS
EXHORTING
EXHORTS
EXHUMATE
EXHUMATED
EXHUMATES
EXHUME
EXHUMED
EXHUMER
EXHUMERS
EXHUMES
EXHUMING
EXIES
EXIGEANT
EXIGEANTE
EXIGENCE
EXIGENCES
EXIGENCY
EXIGENT
EXIGENTLY
EXIGENTS

EXIGIBLE
EXIGUITY
EXIGUOUS
EXILABLE
EXILE
EXILED
EXILEMENT
EXILER
EXILERS
EXILES
EXILIAN
EXILIC
EXILING
EXILITIES
EXILITY
EXIMIOUS
EXINE
EXINES
EXING
EXIST
EXISTED
EXISTENCE
EXISTENT
EXISTENTS
EXISTING
EXISTS
EXIT
EXITANCE
EXITANCES
EXITED
EXITING
EXITLESS
EXITS
EXO
EXOCARP
EXOCARPS
EXOCRINE
EXOCRINES
EXOCYCLIC
EXOCYTIC
EXOCYTOSE
EXODE
EXODERM
EXODERMAL
EXODERMIS
EXODERMS
EXODES
EXODIC
EXODIST
EXODISTS
EXODOI
EXODONTIA
EXODOS
EXODUS
EXODUSES
EXOENZYME
EXOERGIC
EXOGAMIC

EXOGAMIES	EXOTIC	EXPENSED	EXPLORERS
EXOGAMOUS	EXOTICA	EXPENSES	EXPLORES
EXOGAMY	EXOTICISM	EXPENSING	EXPLORING
EXOGEN	EXOTICIST	EXPENSIVE	EXPLOSION
EXOGENISM	EXOTICS	EXPERT	EXPLOSIVE
EXOGENOUS	EXOTISM	EXPERTED	EXPO
EXOGENS	EXOTISMS	EXPERTING	EXPONENT
EXOMION	EXOTOXIC	EXPERTISE	EXPONENTS
EXOMIONS	EXOTOXIN	EXPERTISM	EXPONIBLE
EXOMIS	EXOTOXINS	EXPERTIZE	EXPORT
EXOMISES	EXOTROPIA	EXPERTLY	EXPORTED
EXON	EXOTROPIC	EXPERTS	EXPORTER
EXONERATE	EXPAND	EXPIABLE	EXPORTERS
EXONIC	EXPANDED	EXPIATE	EXPORTING
EXONS	EXPANDER	EXPIATED	EXPORTS
EXONUMIA	EXPANDERS	EXPIATES	EXPOS
EXONUMIST	EXPANDING	EXPIATING	EXPOSABLE
EXONYM	EXPANDOR	EXPIATION	EXPOSAL
EXONYMS	EXPANDORS	EXPIATOR	EXPOSALS
EXOPHAGY	EXPANDS	EXPIATORS	EXPOSE
EXOPHORIC	EXPANSE	EXPIATORY	EXPOSED
EXOPLANET	EXPANSES	EXPIRABLE	EXPOSER
EXOPLASM	EXPANSILE	EXPIRANT	EXPOSERS
EXOPLASMS	EXPANSION	EXPIRANTS	EXPOSES
EXOPOD	EXPANSIVE	EXPIRE	EXPOSING
EXOPODITE	EXPAT	EXPIRED	EXPOSIT
EXOPODS	EXPATIATE	EXPIRER	EXPOSITED
EXORABLE	EXPATS	EXPIRERS	EXPOSITOR
EXORATION	EXPECT	EXPIRES	EXPOSITS
EXORCISE	EXPECTANT	EXPIRIES	EXPOSTURE
EXORCISED	EXPECTED	EXPIRING	EXPOSURE
EXORCISER	EXPECTER	EXPIRY	EXPOSURES
EXORCISES	EXPECTERS	EXPISCATE	EXPOUND
EXORCISM	EXPECTING	EXPLAIN	EXPOUNDED
EXORCISMS	EXPECTS	EXPLAINED	EXPOUNDER
EXORCIST	EXPEDIENT	EXPLAINER	EXPOUNDS
EXORCISTS	EXPEDITE	EXPLAINS	EXPRESS
EXORCIZE	EXPEDITED	EXPLANT	EXPRESSED
EXORCIZED	EXPEDITER	EXPLANTED	EXPRESSER
EXORCIZER	EXPEDITES	EXPLANTS	EXPRESSES
EXORCIZES	EXPEDITOR	EXPLETIVE	EXPRESSLY
EXORDIA	EXPEL	EXPLETORY	EXPRESSO
EXORDIAL	EXPELLANT	EXPLICATE	EXPRESSOS
EXORDIUM	EXPELLED	EXPLICIT	EXPUGN
EXORDIUMS	EXPELLEE	EXPLICITS	EXPUGNED
EXOSMIC	EXPELLEES	EXPLODE	EXPUGNING
EXOSMOSE	EXPELLENT	EXPLODED	EXPUGNS
EXOSMOSES	EXPELLER	EXPLODER	EXPULSE
EXOSMOSIS	EXPELLERS	EXPLODERS	EXPULSED
EXOSMOTIC	EXPELLING	EXPLODES	EXPULSES
EXOSPHERE	EXPELS	EXPLODING	EXPULSING
EXOSPORAL	EXPEND	EXPLOIT	EXPULSION
EXOSPORE	EXPENDED	EXPLOITED	EXPULSIVE
EXOSPORES	EXPENDER	EXPLOITER	EXPUNCT
EXOSPORIA	EXPENDERS	EXPLOITS	EXPUNCTED
EXOSTOSES	EXPENDING	EXPLORE	EXPUNCTS
EXOSTOSIS	EXPENDS	EXPLORED	EXPUNGE
EXOTERIC	EXPENSE	EXPLORER	EXPUNGED

EXPUNGER
EXPUNGERS
EXPUNGES
EXPUNGING
EXPURGATE
EXPURGE
EXPURGED
EXPURGES
EXPURGING
EXQUISITE
EXSCIND
EXSCINDED
EXSCINDS
EXSECANT
EXSECANTS
EXSECT
EXSECTED
EXSECTING
EXSECTION
EXSECTS
EXSERT
EXSERTED
EXSERTILE
EXSERTING
EXSERTION
EXSERTS
EXSICCANT
EXSICCATE
EXSTROPHY
EXSUCCOUS
EXTANT
EXTASIES
EXTASY
EXTATIC
EXTEMPORE
EXTEND
EXTENDANT
EXTENDED
EXTENDER
EXTENDERS
EXTENDING
EXTENDS
EXTENSE
EXTENSILE
EXTENSION
EXTENSITY
EXTENSIVE
EXTENSOR
EXTENSORS
EXTENT
EXTENTS
EXTENUATE
EXTERIOR
EXTERIORS
EXTERMINE
EXTERN
EXTERNAL
EXTERNALS

EXTERNAT
EXTERNATS
EXTERNE
EXTERNES
EXTERNS
EXTINCT
EXTINCTED
EXTINCTS
EXTINE
EXTINES
EXTIRP
EXTIRPATE
EXTIRPED
EXTIRPING
EXTIRPS
EXTOL
EXTOLD
EXTOLL
EXTOLLED
EXTOLLER
EXTOLLERS
EXTOLLING
EXTOLLS
EXTOLMENT
EXTOLS
EXTORSIVE
EXTORT
EXTORTED
EXTORTER
EXTORTERS
EXTORTING
EXTORTION
EXTORTIVE
EXTORTS
EXTRA
EXTRABOLD
EXTRACT
EXTRACTED
EXTRACTOR
EXTRACTS
EXTRADITE
EXTRADOS
EXTRAIT
EXTRAITS
EXTRALITY
EXTRANET
EXTRANETS
EXTRAPOSE
EXTRAS
EXTRAUGHT
EXTRAVERT
EXTREAT
EXTREATS
EXTREMA
EXTREMAL
EXTREMALS
EXTREME
EXTREMELY

EXTREMER
EXTREMES
EXTREMEST
EXTREMISM
EXTREMIST
EXTREMITY
EXTREMUM
EXTRICATE
EXTRINSIC
EXTRORSAL
EXTRORSE
EXTROVERT
EXTRUDE
EXTRUDED
EXTRUDER
EXTRUDERS
EXTRUDES
EXTRUDING
EXTRUSION
EXTRUSIVE
EXTRUSORY
EXTUBATE
EXTUBATED
EXTUBATES
EXUBERANT
EXUBERATE
EXUDATE
EXUDATES
EXUDATION
EXUDATIVE
EXUDE
EXUDED
EXUDES
EXUDING
EXUL
EXULS
EXULT
EXULTANCE
EXULTANCY
EXULTANT
EXULTED
EXULTING
EXULTS
EXURB
EXURBAN
EXURBIA
EXURBIAS
EXURBS
EXUVIA
EXUVIAE
EXUVIAL
EXUVIATE
EXUVIATED
EXUVIATES
EXUVIUM
EYALET
EYALETS
EYAS

EYASES
EYASS
EYASSES
EYE
EYEABLE
EYEBALL
EYEBALLED
EYEBALLS
EYEBANK
EYEBANKS
EYEBAR
EYEBARS
EYEBATH
EYEBATHS
EYEBEAM
EYEBEAMS
EYEBLACK
EYEBLACKS
EYEBLINK
EYEBLINKS
EYEBOLT
EYEBOLTS
EYEBRIGHT
EYEBROW
EYEBROWED
EYEBROWS
EYECUP
EYECUPS
EYED
EYEDNESS
EYEDROPS
EYEFOLD
EYEFOLDS
EYEFUL
EYEFULS
EYEGLASS
EYEHOLE
EYEHOLES
EYEHOOK
EYEHOOKS
EYEING
EYELASH
EYELASHES
EYELESS
EYELET
EYELETED
EYELETEER
EYELETING
EYELETS
EYELETTED
EYELEVEL
EYELIAD
EYELIADS
EYELID
EYELIDS
EYELIFT
EYELIFTS
EYELIKE

EYELINER

EYELINER
EYELINERS
EYEN
EYEOPENER
EYEPIECE
EYEPIECES
EYEPOINT
EYEPOINTS
EYEPOPPER
EYER
EYERS
EYES
EYESHADE
EYESHADES
EYESHADOW
EYESHINE
EYESHINES
EYESHOT
EYESHOTS
EYESIGHT
EYESIGHTS
EYESOME
EYESORE
EYESORES
EYESPOT
EYESPOTS
EYESTALK
EYESTALKS
EYESTONE
EYESTONES
EYESTRAIN
EYESTRING
EYETEETH
EYETOOTH
EYEWASH
EYEWASHES
EYEWATER
EYEWATERS
EYEWEAR
EYEWINK
EYEWINKS
EYING
EYLIAD
EYLIADS
EYNE
EYOT
EYOTS
EYRA
EYRAS
EYRE
EYRES
EYRIE
EYRIES
EYRIR
EYRY

F

FA
FAA
FAAN
FAAS
FAB
FABACEOUS
FABBER
FABBEST
FABLE
FABLED
FABLER
FABLERS
FABLES
FABLIAU
FABLIAUX
FABLING
FABLINGS
FABRIC
FABRICANT
FABRICATE
FABRICKED
FABRICS
FABS
FABULAR
FABULATE
FABULATED
FABULATES
FABULATOR
FABULISE
FABULISED
FABULISES
FABULIST
FABULISTS
FABULIZE
FABULIZED
FABULIZES
FABULOUS
FABURDEN
FABURDENS
FACADE
FACADES
FACE
FACEABLE
FACEBAR
FACEBARS
FACECLOTH
FACED
FACEDOWN
FACEDOWNS
FACELESS
FACELIFT
FACELIFTS
FACEMAIL

FACEMAILS
FACEMAN
FACEMASK
FACEMASKS
FACEMEN
FACEPLATE
FACEPRINT
FACER
FACERS
FACES
FACET
FACETE
FACETED
FACETELY
FACETIAE
FACETING
FACETIOUS
FACETS
FACETTED
FACETTING
FACEUP
FACIA
FACIAE
FACIAL
FACIALLY
FACIALS
FACIAS
FACIEND
FACIENDS
FACIES
FACILE
FACILELY
FACILITY
FACING
FACINGS
FACONNE
FACONNES
FACSIMILE
FACT
FACTFUL
FACTICE
FACTICES
FACTICITY
FACTION
FACTIONAL
FACTIONS
FACTIOUS
FACTIS
FACTISES
FACTITIVE
FACTIVE
FACTOID
FACTOIDAL

FACTOIDS
FACTOR
FACTORAGE
FACTORED
FACTORIAL
FACTORIES
FACTORING
FACTORISE
FACTORIZE
FACTORS
FACTORY
FACTOTUM
FACTOTUMS
FACTS
FACTSHEET
FACTUAL
FACTUALLY
FACTUM
FACTUMS
FACTURE
FACTURES
FACULA
FACULAE
FACULAR
FACULTIES
FACULTY
FACUNDITY
FAD
FADABLE
FADAISE
FADAISES
FADDIER
FADDIEST
FADDINESS
FADDISH
FADDISHLY
FADDISM
FADDISMS
FADDIST
FADDISTS
FADDLE
FADDLED
FADDLES
FADDLING
FADDY
FADE
FADEAWAY
FADEAWAYS
FADED
FADEDLY
FADEDNESS
FADEIN
FADEINS

FADELESS
FADEOUT
FADEOUTS
FADER
FADERS
FADES
FADEUR
FADEURS
FADGE
FADGED
FADGES
FADGING
FADIER
FADIEST
FADING
FADINGS
FADLIKE
FADO
FADOMETER
FADOS
FADS
FADY
FAE
FAECAL
FAECES
FAENA
FAENAS
FAERIE
FAERIES
FAERY
FAFF
FAFFED
FAFFING
FAFFS
FAG
FAGACEOUS
FAGGED
FAGGERIES
FAGGERY
FAGGIER
FAGGIEST
FAGGING
FAGGINGS
FAGGOT
FAGGOTED
FAGGOTING
FAGGOTRY
FAGGOTS
FAGGOTY
FAGGY
FAGIN
FAGINS
FAGOT

FAGOTED
FAGOTER
FAGOTERS
FAGOTING
FAGOTINGS
FAGOTS
FAGOTTI
FAGOTTIST
FAGOTTO
FAGS
FAH
FAHLBAND
FAHLBANDS
FAHLERZ
FAHLERZES
FAHLORE
FAHLORES
FAHS
FAIBLE
FAIBLES
FAIENCE
FAIENCES
FAIK
FAIKED
FAIKES
FAIKING
FAIKS
FAIL
FAILED
FAILING
FAILINGLY
FAILINGS
FAILLE
FAILLES
FAILS
FAILURE
FAILURES
FAIN
FAINE
FAINEANCE
FAINEANCY
FAINEANT
FAINEANTS
FAINED
FAINER
FAINES
FAINEST
FAINING
FAINITES
FAINLY
FAINNE
FAINNES
FAINNESS
FAINS
FAINT
FAINTED
FAINTER
FAINTERS

FAINTEST
FAINTIER
FAINTIEST
FAINTING
FAINTINGS
FAINTISH
FAINTLY
FAINTNESS
FAINTS
FAINTY
FAIR
FAIRED
FAIRER
FAIREST
FAIRFACED
FAIRGOER
FAIRGOERS
FAIRIES
FAIRILY
FAIRING
FAIRINGS
FAIRISH
FAIRISHLY
FAIRLEAD
FAIRLEADS
FAIRLY
FAIRNESS
FAIRS
FAIRWAY
FAIRWAYS
FAIRY
FAIRYDOM
FAIRYDOMS
FAIRYHOOD
FAIRYISM
FAIRYISMS
FAIRYLAND
FAIRYLIKE
FAIRYTALE
FAITH
FAITHCURE
FAITHED
FAITHER
FAITHERS
FAITHFUL
FAITHFULS
FAITHING
FAITHLESS
FAITHS
FAITOR
FAITORS
FAITOUR
FAITOURS
FAIX
FAJITA
FAJITAS
FAKE
FAKED

FAKEER
FAKEERS
FAKEMENT
FAKEMENTS
FAKER
FAKERIES
FAKERS
FAKERY
FAKES
FAKEY
FAKING
FAKIR
FAKIRISM
FAKIRISMS
FAKIRS
FALAFEL
FALAFELS
FALAJ
FALANGISM
FALANGIST
FALBALA
FALBALAS
FALCADE
FALCADES
FALCATE
FALCATED
FALCATION
FALCES
FALCHION
FALCHIONS
FALCIFORM
FALCON
FALCONER
FALCONERS
FALCONET
FALCONETS
FALCONINE
FALCONOID
FALCONRY
FALCONS
FALCULA
FALCULAE
FALCULAS
FALCULATE
FALDAGE
FALDAGES
FALDERAL
FALDERALS
FALDEROL
FALDEROLS
FALDETTA
FALDETTAS
FALDSTOOL
FALL
FALLACIES
FALLACY
FALLAL
FALLALERY

FALLALS
FALLAWAY
FALLAWAYS
FALLBACK
FALLBACKS
FALLBOARD
FALLEN
FALLER
FALLERS
FALLFISH
FALLIBLE
FALLIBLY
FALLING
FALLINGS
FALLOFF
FALLOFFS
FALLOUT
FALLOUTS
FALLOW
FALLOWED
FALLOWER
FALLOWEST
FALLOWING
FALLOWS
FALLS
FALSE
FALSED
FALSEFACE
FALSEHOOD
FALSELY
FALSENESS
FALSER
FALSERS
FALSES
FALSEST
FALSETTO
FALSETTOS
FALSEWORK
FALSIE
FALSIES
FALSIFIED
FALSIFIER
FALSIFIES
FALSIFY
FALSING
FALSISH
FALSISM
FALSISMS
FALSITIES
FALSITY
FALTBOAT
FALTBOATS
FALTER
FALTERED
FALTERER
FALTERERS
FALTERING
FALTERS

FALX
FAME
FAMED
FAMELESS
FAMES
FAMILIAL
FAMILIAR
FAMILIARS
FAMILIES
FAMILISM
FAMILISMS
FAMILLE
FAMILLES
FAMILY
FAMINE
FAMINES
FAMING
FAMISH
FAMISHED
FAMISHES
FAMISHING
FAMOUS
FAMOUSED
FAMOUSES
FAMOUSING
FAMOUSLY
FAMULI
FAMULUS
FAMULUSES
FAN
FANAL
FANALS
FANATIC
FANATICAL
FANATICS
FANBASE
FANBASES
FANCIABLE
FANCIED
FANCIER
FANCIERS
FANCIES
FANCIEST
FANCIFIED
FANCIFIES
FANCIFUL
FANCIFY
FANCILESS
FANCILY
FANCINESS
FANCY
FANCYING
FANCYWORK
FAND
FANDANGLE
FANDANGO
FANDANGOS
FANDED

FANDING
FANDOM
FANDOMS
FANDS
FANE
FANEGA
FANEGADA
FANEGADAS
FANEGAS
FANES
FANFARADE
FANFARE
FANFARED
FANFARES
FANFARING
FANFARON
FANFARONA
FANFARONS
FANFIC
FANFICS
FANFOLD
FANFOLDED
FANFOLDS
FANG
FANGA
FANGAS
FANGED
FANGING
FANGLE
FANGLED
FANGLES
FANGLESS
FANGLIKE
FANGLING
FANGO
FANGOS
FANGS
FANION
FANIONS
FANJET
FANJETS
FANK
FANKLE
FANKLED
FANKLES
FANKLING
FANKS
FANLIGHT
FANLIGHTS
FANLIKE
FANNED
FANNEL
FANNELL
FANNELLS
FANNELS
FANNER
FANNERS
FANNIES

FANNING
FANNINGS
FANNY
FANO
FANON
FANONS
FANOS
FANS
FANTAD
FANTADS
FANTAIL
FANTAILED
FANTAILS
FANTASIA
FANTASIAS
FANTASIE
FANTASIED
FANTASIES
FANTASISE
FANTASIST
FANTASIZE
FANTASM
FANTASMAL
FANTASMIC
FANTASMS
FANTASQUE
FANTAST
FANTASTIC
FANTASTRY
FANTASTS
FANTASY
FANTEEG
FANTEEGS
FANTIGUE
FANTIGUES
FANTOD
FANTODS
FANTOM
FANTOMS
FANTOOSH
FANUM
FANUMS
FANWISE
FANWORT
FANWORTS
FANZINE
FANZINES
FAP
FAQIR
FAQIRS
FAQUIR
FAQUIRS
FAR
FARAD
FARADAIC
FARADAY
FARADAYS
FARADIC

FARADISE
FARADISED
FARADISER
FARADISES
FARADISM
FARADISMS
FARADIZE
FARADIZED
FARADIZER
FARADIZES
FARADS
FARAND
FARANDINE
FARANDOLE
FARAWAY
FARAWAYS
FARCE
FARCED
FARCEMEAT
FARCER
FARCERS
FARCES
FARCEUR
FARCEURS
FARCEUSE
FARCEUSES
FARCI
FARCICAL
FARCIE
FARCIED
FARCIES
FARCIFIED
FARCIFIES
FARCIFY
FARCIN
FARCING
FARCINGS
FARCINS
FARCY
FARD
FARDAGE
FARDAGES
FARDED
FARDEL
FARDELS
FARDEN
FARDENS
FARDING
FARDINGS
FARDS
FARE
FAREBOX
FAREBOXES
FARED
FARER
FARERS
FARES
FAREWELL

FAREWELLS	FARRENS	FASCISMS	FATE
FARFAL	FARRIER	FASCIST	FATED
FARFALLE	FARRIERS	FASCISTA	FATEFUL
FARFALS	FARRIERY	FASCISTI	FATEFULLY
FARFEL	FARRING	FASCISTIC	FATES
FARFELS	FARROW	FASCISTS	FATHEAD
FARFET	FARROWED	FASCITIS	FATHEADED
FARINA	FARROWING	FASH	FATHEADS
FARINAS	FARROWS	FASHED	FATHER
FARING	FARRUCA	FASHERIES	FATHERED
FARINHA	FARRUCAS	FASHERY	FATHERING
FARINHAS	FARS	FASHES	FATHERLY
FARINOSE	FARSE	FASHING	FATHERS
FARL	FARSED	FASHION	FATHOM
FARLE	FARSEEING	FASHIONED	FATHOMED
FARLES	FARSES	FASHIONER	FATHOMER
FARLS	FARSIDE	FASHIONS	FATHOMERS
FARM	FARSIDES	FASHIONY	FATHOMING
FARMABLE	FARSING	FASHIOUS	FATHOMS
FARMED	FART	FAST	FATIDIC
FARMER	FARTED	FASTBACK	FATIDICAL
FARMERESS	FARTHEL	FASTBACKS	FATIGABLE
FARMERIES	FARTHELS	FASTBALL	FATIGATE
FARMERS	FARTHER	FASTBALLS	FATIGATED
FARMERY	FARTHEST	FASTED	FATIGATES
FARMHAND	FARTHING	FASTEN	FATIGUE
FARMHANDS	FARTHINGS	FASTENED	FATIGUED
FARMHOUSE	FARTING	FASTENER	FATIGUES
FARMING	FARTLEK	FASTENERS	FATIGUING
FARMINGS	FARTLEKS	FASTENING	FATING
FARMLAND	FARTS	FASTENS	FATISCENT
FARMLANDS	FAS	FASTER	FATLESS
FARMOST	FASCES	FASTERS	FATLIKE
FARMS	FASCI	FASTEST	FATLING
FARMSTEAD	FASCIA	FASTI	FATLINGS
FARMWIFE	FASCIAE	FASTIE	FATLY
FARMWIVES	FASCIAL	FASTIES	FATNESS
FARMWORK	FASCIAS	FASTIGIUM	FATNESSES
FARMWORKS	FASCIATE	FASTING	FATS
FARMYARD	FASCIATED	FASTINGS	FATSIA
FARMYARDS	FASCICLE	FASTISH	FATSIAS
FARNARKEL	FASCICLED	FASTLY	FATSO
FARNESOL	FASCICLES	FASTNESS	FATSOES
FARNESOLS	FASCICULE	FASTS	FATSOS
FARNESS	FASCICULI	FASTUOUS	FATSTOCK
FARNESSES	FASCIITIS	FAT	FATSTOCKS
FARO	FASCINATE	FATAL	FATTED
FAROLITO	FASCINE	FATALISM	FATTEN
FAROLITOS	FASCINES	FATALISMS	FATTENED
FAROS	FASCIO	FATALIST	FATTENER
FAROUCHE	FASCIOLA	FATALISTS	FATTENERS
FARRAGO	FASCIOLAS	FATALITY	FATTENING
FARRAGOES	FASCIOLE	FATALLY	FATTENS
FARRAGOS	FASCIOLES	FATALNESS	FATTER
FARRAND	FASCIS	FATBACK	FATTEST
FARRANT	FASCISM	FATBACKS	FATTIER
FARRED	FASCISMI	FATBIRD	FATTIES
FARREN	FASCISMO	FATBIRDS	FATTIEST

FATTILY	FAUNISTIC	FAVOUR	FEALED
FATTINESS	FAUNISTS	FAVOURED	FEALING
FATTING	FAUNLIKE	FAVOURER	FEALS
FATTISH	FAUNS	FAVOURERS	FEALTIES
FATTISM	FAUNULA	FAVOURING	FEALTY
FATTISMS	FAUNULAE	FAVOURITE	FEAR
FATTIST	FAUNULE	FAVOURS	FEARE
FATTISTS	FAUNULES	FAVOUS	FEARED
FATTRELS	FAUR	FAVRILE	FEARER
FATTY	FAURD	FAVRILES	FEARERS
FATUITIES	FAURER	FAVUS	FEARES
FATUITOUS	FAUREST	FAVUSES	FEARFUL
FATUITY	FAUSTIAN	FAW	FEARFULLY
FATUOUS	FAUT	FAWN	FEARING
FATUOUSLY	FAUTED	FAWNED	FEARLESS
FATWA	FAUTEUIL	FAWNER	FEARS
FATWAED	FAUTEUILS	FAWNERS	FEARSOME
FATWAH	FAUTING	FAWNIER	FEASANCE
FATWAHED	FAUTOR	FAWNIEST	FEASANCES
FATWAHING	FAUTORS	FAWNING	FEASE
FATWAHS	FAUTS	FAWNINGLY	FEASED
FATWAING	FAUVE	FAWNINGS	FEASES
FATWAS	FAUVES	FAWNLIKE	FEASIBLE
FATWOOD	FAUVETTE	FAWNS	FEASIBLY
FATWOODS	FAUVETTES	FAWNY	FEASING
FAUBOURG	FAUVISM	FAWS	FEAST
FAUBOURGS	FAUVISMS	FAX	FEASTED
FAUCAL	FAUVIST	FAXED	FEASTER
FAUCALS	FAUVISTS	FAXES	FEASTERS
FAUCES	FAUX	FAXING	FEASTFUL
FAUCET	FAVA	FAY	FEASTING
FAUCETS	FAVAS	FAYALITE	FEASTINGS
FAUCHION	FAVE	FAYALITES	FEASTLESS
FAUCHIONS	FAVEL	FAYED	FEASTS
FAUCHON	FAVELA	FAYENCE	FEAT
FAUCHONS	FAVELAS	FAYENCES	FEATED
FAUCIAL	FAVELL	FAYER	FEATEOUS
FAUGH	FAVELLA	FAYEST	FEATER
FAULCHION	FAVELLAS	FAYING	FEATEST
FAULD	FAVEOLATE	FAYNE	FEATHER
FAULDS	FAVER	FAYNED	FEATHERED
FAULT	FAVES	FAYNES	FEATHERS
FAULTED	FAVEST	FAYNING	FEATHERY
FAULTFUL	FAVISM	FAYRE	FEATING
FAULTIER	FAVISMS	FAYRES	FEATLIER
FAULTIEST	FAVONIAN	FAYS	FEATLIEST
FAULTILY	FAVOR	FAZE	FEATLY
FAULTING	FAVORABLE	FAZED	FEATOUS
FAULTLESS	FAVORABLY	FAZENDA	FEATS
FAULTS	FAVORED	FAZENDAS	FEATUOUS
FAULTY	FAVORER	FAZES	FEATURE
FAUN	FAVORERS	FAZING	FEATURED
FAUNA	FAVORING	FE	FEATURELY
FAUNAE	FAVORITE	FEAGUE	FEATURES
FAUNAL	FAVORITES	FEAGUED	FEATURING
FAUNALLY	FAVORLESS	FEAGUES	FEAZE
FAUNAS	FAVORS	FEAGUING	FEAZED
FAUNIST	FAVOSE	FEAL	FEAZES

FEAZING	FEDS	FEERS	FELICIA
FEBLESSE	FEE	FEES	FELICIAS
FEBLESSES	FEEB	FEESE	FELICIFIC
FEBRICITY	FEEBLE	FEESED	FELICITER
FEBRICULA	FEEBLED	FEESES	FELICITY
FEBRICULE	FEEBLER	FEESING	FELID
FEBRIFIC	FEEBLES	FEET	FELIDS
FEBRIFUGE	FEEBLEST	FEETFIRST	FELINE
FEBRILE	FEEBLING	FEETLESS	FELINELY
FEBRILITY	FEEBLISH	FEEZE	FELINES
FECAL	FEEBLY	FEEZED	FELINITY
FECES	FEEBS	FEEZES	FELL
FECHT	FEED	FEEZING	FELLA
FECHTER	FEEDABLE	FEG	FELLABLE
FECHTERS	FEEDBACK	FEGARIES	FELLAH
FECHTING	FEEDBACKS	FEGARY	FELLAHEEN
FECHTS	FEEDBAG	FEGS	FELLAHIN
FECIAL	FEEDBAGS	FEH	FELLAHS
FECIALS	FEEDBOX	FEHM	FELLAS
FECIT	FEEDBOXES	FEHME	FELLATE
FECK	FEEDER	FEHMIC	FELLATED
FECKIN	FEEDERS	FEHS	FELLATES
FECKING	FEEDGRAIN	FEIGN	FELLATING
FECKLESS	FEEDHOLE	FEIGNED	FELLATIO
FECKLY	FEEDHOLES	FEIGNEDLY	FELLATION
FECKS	FEEDING	FEIGNER	FELLATIOS
FECULA	FEEDINGS	FEIGNERS	FELLATOR
FECULAE	FEEDLOT	FEIGNING	FELLATORS
FECULAS	FEEDLOTS	FEIGNINGS	FELLATRIX
FECULENCE	FEEDS	FEIGNS	FELLED
FECULENCY	FEEDSTOCK	FEIJOA	FELLER
FECULENT	FEEDSTUFF	FEIJOAS	FELLERS
FECUND	FEEDWATER	FEINT	FELLEST
FECUNDATE	FEEDYARD	FEINTED	FELLIES
FECUNDITY	FEEDYARDS	FEINTER	FELLING
FED	FEEING	FEINTEST	FELLNESS
FEDARIE	FEEL	FEINTING	FELLOE
FEDARIES	FEELBAD	FEINTS	FELLOES
FEDAYEE	FEELBADS	FEIRIE	FELLOW
FEDAYEEN	FEELER	FEIS	FELLOWED
FEDELINI	FEELERS	FEISEANNA	FELLOWING
FEDELINIS	FEELESS	FEIST	FELLOWLY
FEDERACY	FEELGOOD	FEISTIER	FELLOWMAN
FEDERAL	FEELGOODS	FEISTIEST	FELLOWMEN
FEDERALLY	FEELING	FEISTILY	FELLOWS
FEDERALS	FEELINGLY	FEISTS	FELLS
FEDERARIE	FEELINGS	FEISTY	FELLY
FEDERARY	FEELS	FELAFEL	FELON
FEDERATE	FEEN	FELAFELS	FELONIES
FEDERATED	FEENS	FELDGRAU	FELONIOUS
FEDERATES	FEER	FELDGRAUS	FELONOUS
FEDERATOR	FEERED	FELDSCHAR	FELONRIES
FEDEX	FEERIE	FELDSCHER	FELONRY
FEDEXED	FEERIES	FELDSHER	FELONS
FEDEXES	FEERIN	FELDSHERS	FELONY
FEDEXING	FEERING	FELDSPAR	FELSIC
FEDORA	FEERINGS	FELDSPARS	FELSITE
FEDORAS	FEERINS	FELDSPATH	FELSITES

FELSITIC	FEMMY	FENTANYL	FERMENTER
FELSPAR	FEMORA	FENTANYLS	FERMENTOR
FELSPARS	FEMORAL	FENTHION	FERMENTS
FELSTONE	FEMS	FENTHIONS	FERMI
FELSTONES	FEMUR	FENTS	FERMION
FELT	FEMURS	FENUGREEK	FERMIONIC
FELTED	FEN	FENURON	FERMIONS
FELTER	FENAGLE	FENURONS	FERMIS
FELTERED	FENAGLED	FEOD	FERMIUM
FELTERING	FENAGLES	FEODAL	FERMIUMS
FELTERS	FENAGLING	FEODARIES	FERMS
FELTIER	FENCE	FEODARY	FERN
FELTIEST	FENCED	FEODS	FERNBIRD
FELTING	FENCELESS	FEOFF	FERNBIRDS
FELTINGS	FENCELIKE	FEOFFED	FERNERIES
FELTLIKE	FENCER	FEOFFEE	FERNERY
FELTS	FENCEROW	FEOFFEES	FERNIER
FELTY	FENCEROWS	FEOFFER	FERNIEST
FELUCCA	FENCERS	FEOFFERS	FERNING
FELUCCAS	FENCES	FEOFFING	FERNINGS
FELWORT	FENCIBLE	FEOFFMENT	FERNINST
FELWORTS	FENCIBLES	FEOFFOR	FERNLESS
FEM	FENCING	FEOFFORS	FERNLIKE
FEMAL	FENCINGS	FEOFFS	FERNS
FEMALE	FEND	FER	FERNSHAW
FEMALES	FENDED	FERACIOUS	FERNSHAWS
FEMALITY	FENDER	FERACITY	FERNTICLE
FEMALS	FENDERED	FERAL	FERNY
FEME	FENDERS	FERALISED	FEROCIOUS
FEMERALL	FENDIER	FERALIZED	FEROCITY
FEMERALLS	FENDIEST	FERALS	FERRATE
FEMES	FENDING	FERBAM	FERRATES
FEMETARY	FENDS	FERBAMS	FERREL
FEMINACY	FENDY	FERE	FERRELED
FEMINAL	FENESTRA	FERER	FERRELING
FEMINAZI	FENESTRAE	FERES	FERRELLED
FEMINAZIS	FENESTRAL	FEREST	FERRELS
FEMINEITY	FENESTRAS	FERETORY	FERREOUS
FEMINIE	FENI	FERIA	FERRET
FEMININE	FENIS	FERIAE	FERRETED
FEMININES	FENITAR	FERIAL	FERRETER
FEMINISE	FENITARS	FERIAS	FERRETERS
FEMINISED	FENKS	FERINE	FERRETING
FEMINISES	FENLAND	FERITIES	FERRETS
FEMINISM	FENLANDS	FERITY	FERRETY
FEMINISMS	FENMAN	FERLIE	FERRIAGE
FEMINIST	FENMEN	FERLIED	FERRIAGES
FEMINISTS	FENNEC	FERLIER	FERRIC
FEMINITY	FENNECS	FERLIES	FERRIED
FEMINIZE	FENNEL	FERLIEST	FERRIES
FEMINIZED	FENNELS	FERLY	FERRITE
FEMINIZES	FENNIER	FERLYING	FERRITES
FEMITER	FENNIES	FERM	FERRITIC
FEMITERS	FENNIEST	FERMATA	FERRITIN
FEMME	FENNISH	FERMATAS	FERRITINS
FEMMES	FENNY	FERMATE	FERROCENE
FEMMIER	FENS	FERMENT	FERROTYPE
FEMMIEST	FENT	FERMENTED	FERROUS

FERRUGO	FESTERED	FETISHES	FEUDS
FERRUGOS	FESTERING	FETISHISE	FEUED
FERRULE	FESTERS	FETISHISM	FEUILLETE
FERRULED	FESTIER	FETISHIST	FEUING
FERRULES	FESTIEST	FETISHIZE	FEUS
FERRULING	FESTILOGY	FETLOCK	FEUTRE
FERRUM	FESTINATE	FETLOCKED	FEUTRED
FERRUMS	FESTIVAL	FETLOCKS	FEUTRES
FERRY	FESTIVALS	FETOLOGY	FEUTRING
FERRYBOAT	FESTIVE	FETOR	FEVER
FERRYING	FESTIVELY	FETORS	FEVERED
FERRYMAN	FESTIVITY	FETOSCOPE	FEVERFEW
FERRYMEN	FESTIVOUS	FETOSCOPY	FEVERFEWS
FERTIGATE	FESTOLOGY	FETS	FEVERING
FERTILE	FESTOON	FETT	FEVERISH
FERTILELY	FESTOONED	FETTA	FEVERLESS
FERTILER	FESTOONS	FETTAS	FEVEROUS
FERTILEST	FESTS	FETTED	FEVERROOT
FERTILISE	FESTY	FETTER	FEVERS
FERTILITY	FET	FETTERED	FEVERWEED
FERTILIZE	FETA	FETTERER	FEVERWORT
FERULA	FETAL	FETTERERS	FEW
FERULAE	FETAS	FETTERING	FEWER
FERULAS	FETATION	FETTERS	FEWEST
FERULE	FETATIONS	FETTING	FEWMET
FERULED	FETCH	FETTLE	FEWMETS
FERULES	FETCHED	FETTLED	FEWNESS
FERULING	FETCHER	FETTLER	FEWNESSES
FERVENCY	FETCHERS	FETTLERS	FEWTER
FERVENT	FETCHES	FETTLES	FEWTERED
FERVENTER	FETCHING	FETTLING	FEWTERING
FERVENTLY	FETE	FETTLINGS	FEWTERS
FERVID	FETED	FETTS	FEWTRILS
FERVIDER	FETERITA	FETTUCINE	FEY
FERVIDEST	FETERITAS	FETTUCINI	FEYED
FERVIDITY	FETES	FETUS	FEYER
FERVIDLY	FETIAL	FETUSES	FEYEST
FERVOR	FETIALES	FETWA	FEYING
FERVOROUS	FETIALIS	FETWAS	FEYLY
FERVORS	FETIALS	FEU	FEYNESS
FERVOUR	FETICH	FEUAR	FEYNESSES
FERVOURS	FETICHE	FEUARS	FEYS
FES	FETICHES	FEUD	FEZ
FESCUE	FETICHISE	FEUDAL	FEZES
FESCUES	FETICHISM	FEUDALISE	FEZZED
FESS	FETICHIST	FEUDALISM	FEZZES
FESSE	FETICHIZE	FEUDALIST	FEZZY
FESSED	FETICIDAL	FEUDALITY	FIACRE
FESSES	FETICIDE	FEUDALIZE	FIACRES
FESSING	FETICIDES	FEUDALLY	FIANCE
FESSWISE	FETID	FEUDARIES	FIANCEE
FEST	FETIDER	FEUDARY	FIANCEES
FESTA	FETIDEST	FEUDATORY	FIANCES
FESTAL	FETIDITY	FEUDED	FIAR
FESTALLY	FETIDLY	FEUDING	FIARS
FESTALS	FETIDNESS	FEUDINGS	FIASCHI
FESTAS	FETING	FEUDIST	FIASCO
FESTER	FETISH	FEUDISTS	FIASCOES

FIASCOS	FIBROSED	FIDEISTIC	FIERILY
FIAT	FIBROSES	FIDEISTS	FIERINESS
FIATED	FIBROSING	FIDELISMO	FIERS
FIATING	FIBROSIS	FIDELISTA	FIERY
FIATS	FIBROTIC	FIDELITY	FTEST
FIAUNT	FIBROUS	FIDGE	FIESTA
FIAUNTS	FIBROUSLY	FIDGED	FIESTAS
FIB	FIBS	FIDGES	FIFE
FIBBED	FIBSTER	FIDGET	FIFED
FIBBER	FIBSTERS	FIDGETED	FIFER
FIBBERIES	FIBULA	FIDGETER	FIFERS
FIBBERS	FIBULAE	FIDGETERS	FIFES
FIBBERY	FIBULAR	FIDGETIER	FIFI
FIBBING	FIBULAS	FIDGETING	FIFING
FIBER	FICE	FIDGETS	FIFTEEN
FIBERED	FICES	FIDGETY	FIFTEENER
FIBERFILL	FICHE	FIDGING	FIFTEENS
FIBERISE	FICHES	FIDIBUS	FIFTEENTH
FIBERISED	FICHU	FIDIBUSES	FIFTH
FIBERISES	FICHUS	FIDO	FIFTHLY
FIBERIZE	FICIN	FIDOS	FIFTHS
FIBERIZED	FICINS	FIDS	FIFTIES
FIBERIZES	FICKLE	FIDUCIAL	FIFTIETH
FIBERLESS	FICKLED	FIDUCIARY	FIFTIETHS
FIBERLIKE	FICKLER	FIE	FIFTY
FIBERS	FICKLES	FIEF	FIFTYISH
FIBRANNE	FICKLEST	FIEFDOM	FIG
FIBRANNES	FICKLING	FIEFDOMS	FIGEATER
FIBRE	FICKLY	FIEFS	FIGEATERS
FIBRED	FICO	FIELD	FIGGED
FIBREFILL	FICOES	FIELDED	FIGGERIES
FIBRELESS	FICOS	FIELDER	FIGGERY
FIBRES	FICTILE	FIELDERS	FIGGING
FIBRIFORM	FICTION	FIELDFARE	FIGHT
FIBRIL	FICTIONAL	FIELDING	FIGHTABLE
FIBRILAR	FICTIONS	FIELDINGS	FIGHTBACK
FIBRILLA	FICTIVE	FIELDMICE	FIGHTER
FIBRILLAE	FICTIVELY	FIELDS	FIGHTERS
FIBRILLAR	FICTOR	FIELDSMAN	FIGHTING
FIBRILLIN	FICTORS	FIELDSMEN	FIGHTINGS
FIBRILS	FICUS	FIELDVOLE	FIGHTS
FIBRIN	FICUSES	FIELDWARD	FIGJAM
FIBRINOID	FID	FIELDWORK	FIGJAMS
FIBRINOUS	FIDDIOUS	FIEND	FIGMENT
FIBRINS	FIDDLE	FIENDISH	FIGMENTS
FIBRO	FIDDLED	FIENDLIKE	FIGO
FIBROCYTE	FIDDLER	FIENDS	FIGOS
FIBROID	FIDDLERS	FIENT	FIGS
FIBROIDS	FIDDLES	FIENTS	FIGULINE
FIBROIN	FIDDLEY	FIER	FIGULINES
FIBROINS	FIDDLEYS	FIERCE	FIGURABLE
FIBROLINE	FIDDLIER	FIERCELY	FIGURAL
FIBROLITE	FIDDLIEST	FIERCER	FIGURALLY
FIBROMA	FIDDLING	FIERCEST	FIGURANT
FIBROMAS	FIDDLY	FIERE	FIGURANTE
FIBROMATA	FIDEISM	FIERES	FIGURANTS
FIBROS	FIDEISMS	FIERIER	FIGURATE
FIBROSE	FIDEIST	FIERIEST	FIGURE

FIGURED	FILCHED	FILLET	FILTER
FIGUREDLY	FILCHER	FILLETED	FILTERED
FIGURER	FILCHERS	FILLETING	FILTERER
FIGURERS	FILCHES	FILLETS	FILTERERS
FIGURES	FILCHING	FILLIBEG	FILTERING
FIGURINE	FILCHINGS	FILLIBEGS	FILTERS
FIGURINES	FILE	FILLIES	FILTH
FIGURING	FILEABLE	FILLING	FILTHIER
FIGURIST	FILECARD	FILLINGS	FILTHIEST
FIGURISTS	FILECARDS	FILLIP	FILTHILY
FIGWORT	FILED	FILLIPED	FILTHS
FIGWORTS	FILEFISH	FILLIPEEN	FILTHY
FIKE	FILEMOT	FILLIPING	FILTRABLE
FIKED	FILEMOTS	FILLIPS	FILTRATE
FIKERIES	FILENAME	FILLISTER	FILTRATED
FIKERY	FILENAMES	FILLO	FILTRATES
FIKES	FILER	FILLOS	FILUM
FIKIER	FILERS	FILLS	FIMBLE
FIKIEST	FILES	FILLY	FIMBLES
FIKING	FILET	FILM	FIMBRIA
FIKISH	FILETED	FILMABLE	FIMBRIAE
FIKY	FILETING	FILMCARD	FIMBRIAL
FIL	FILETS	FILMCARDS	FIMBRIATE
FILA	FILFOT	FILMDOM	FIN
FILABEG	FILFOTS	FILMDOMS	FINABLE
FILABEGS	FILIAL	FILMED	FINAGLE
FILACEOUS	FILIALLY	FILMER	FINAGLED
FILACER	FILIATE	FILMERS	FINAGLER
FILACERS	FILIATED	FILMGOER	FINAGLERS
FILAGREE	FILIATES	FILMGOERS	FINAGLES
FILAGREED	FILIATING	FILMGOING	FINAGLING
FILAGREES	FILIATION	FILMI	FINAL
FILAMENT	FILIBEG	FILMIC	FINALE
FILAMENTS	FILIBEGS	FILMIER	FINALES
FILANDER	FILICIDAL	FILMIEST	FINALIS
FILANDERS	FILICIDE	FILMILY	FINALISE
FILAR	FILICIDES	FILMINESS	FINALISED
FILAREE	FILIFORM	FILMING	FINALISER
FILAREES	FILIGRAIN	FILMIS	FINALISES
FILARIA	FILIGRANE	FILMISH	FINALISM
FILARIAE	FILIGREE	FILMLAND	FINALISMS
FILARIAL	FILIGREED	FILMLANDS	FINALIST
FILARIAN	FILIGREES	FILMLESS	FINALISTS
FILARIAS	FILING	FILMLIKE	FINALITY
FILARIID	FILINGS	FILMMAKER	FINALIZE
FILARIIDS	FILIOQUE	FILMS	FINALIZED
FILASSE	FILIOQUES	FILMSET	FINALIZER
FILASSES	FILISTER	FILMSETS	FINALIZES
FILATORY	FILISTERS	FILMSTRIP	FINALLY
FILATURE	FILL	FILMY	FINALS
FILATURES	FILLABLE	FILO	FINANCE
FILAZER	FILLAGREE	FILOPLUME	FINANCED
FILAZERS	FILLE	FILOPODIA	FINANCES
FILBERD	FILLED	FILOS	FINANCIAL
FILBERDS	FILLER	FILOSE	FINANCIER
FILBERT	FILLERS	FILOSELLE	FINANCING
FILBERTS	FILLES	FILOVIRUS	FINBACK
FILCH	FILLESTER	FILS	FINBACKS

FINCA	FINICKIER	FINOCHIOS	FIREFLIES
FINCAS	FINICKIN	FINOS	FIREFLOAT
FINCH	FINICKING	FINS	FIREFLOOD
FINCHED	FINICKY	FINSKO	FIREFLY
FINCHES	FINIKIN	FIORATURA	FIREGUARD
FIND	FINIKING	FIORD	FIREHALL
FINDABLE	FINING	FIORDS	FIREHALLS
FINDER	FININGS	FIORIN	FIREHOUSE
FINDERS	FINIS	FIORINS	FIRELESS
FINDING	FINISES	FIORITURA	FIRELIGHT
FINDINGS	FINISH	FIORITURE	FIRELIT
FINDRAM	FINISHED	FIPPENCE	FIRELOCK
FINDRAMS	FINISHER	FIPPENCES	FIRELOCKS
FINDS	FINISHERS	FIPPLE	FIREMAN
FINE	FINISHES	FIPPLES	FIREMANIC
FINEABLE	FINISHING	FIQUE	FIREMARK
FINED	FINITE	FIQUES	FIREMARKS
FINEER	FINITELY	FIR	FIREMEN
FINEERED	FINITES	FIRE	FIREPAN
FINEERING	FINITISM	FIREABLE	FIREPANS
FINEERS	FINITISMS	FIREARM	FIREPINK
FINEISH	FINITO	FIREARMED	FIREPINKS
FINELESS	FINITUDE	FIREARMS	FIREPLACE
FINELY	FINITUDES	FIREBACK	FIREPLUG
FINENESS	FINJAN	FIREBACKS	FIREPLUGS
FINER	FINJANS	FIREBALL	FIREPOT
FINERIES	FINK	FIREBALLS	FIREPOTS
FINERS	FINKED	FIREBASE	FIREPOWER
FINERY	FINKING	FIREBASES	FIREPROOF
FINES	FINKS	FIREBIRD	FIRER
FINESPUN	FINLESS	FIREBIRDS	FIREROOM
FINESSE	FINLIKE	FIREBOARD	FIREROOMS
FINESSED	FINMARK	FIREBOAT	FIRERS
FINESSER	FINMARKS	FIREBOATS	FIRES
FINESSERS	FINNAC	FIREBOMB	FIRESHIP
FINESSES	FINNACK	FIREBOMBS	FIRESHIPS
FINESSING	FINNACKS	FIREBOX	FIRESIDE
FINEST	FINNACS	FIREBOXES	FIRESIDES
FINFISH	FINNAN	FIREBRAND	FIRESTONE
FINFISHES	FINNANS	FIREBRAT	FIRESTORM
FINFOOT	FINNED	FIREBRATS	FIRETHORN
FINFOOTS	FINNER	FIREBREAK	FIRETRAP
FINGAN	FINNERS	FIREBRICK	FIRETRAPS
FINGANS	FINNESKO	FIREBUG	FIRETRUCK
FINGER	FINNICKY	FIREBUGS	FIREWALL
FINGERED	FINNIER	FIREBUSH	FIREWALLS
FINGERER	FINNIEST	FIRECLAY	FIREWATER
FINGERERS	FINNING	FIRECLAYS	FIREWEED
FINGERING	FINNMARK	FIRECREST	FIREWEEDS
FINGERS	FINNMARKS	FIRED	FIREWOMAN
FINGERTIP	FINNOCHIO	FIREDAMP	FIREWOMEN
FINI	FINNOCK	FIREDAMPS	FIREWOOD
FINIAL	FINNOCKS	FIREDOG	FIREWOODS
FINIALED	FINNSKO	FIREDOGS	FIREWORK
FINIALS	FINNY	FIREDRAKE	FIREWORKS
FINICAL	FINO	FIREFANG	FIREWORM
FINICALLY	FINOCCHIO	FIREFANGS	FIREWORMS
FINICKETY	FINOCHIO	FIREFIGHT	FIRIE

FIRIES
FIRING
FIRINGS
FIRK
FIRKED
FIRKIN
FIRKING
FIRKINS
FIRKS
FIRLOT
FIRLOTS
FIRM
FIRMAMENT
FIRMAN
FIRMANS
FIRMED
FIRMER
FIRMERS
FIRMEST
FIRMING
FIRMLESS
FIRMLY
FIRMNESS
FIRMS
FIRMWARE
FIRMWARES
FIRN
FIRNS
FIRRIER
FIRRIEST
FIRRING
FIRRINGS
FIRRY
FIRS
FIRST
FIRSTBORN
FIRSTHAND
FIRSTLING
FIRSTLY
FIRSTNESS
FIRSTS
FIRTH
FIRTHS
FISC
FISCAL
FISCALIST
FISCALLY
FISCALS
FISCS
FISGIG
FISGIGS
FISH
FISHABLE
FISHBALL
FISHBALLS
FISHBOLT
FISHBOLTS
FISHBONE

FISHBONES
FISHBOWL
FISHBOWLS
FISHCAKE
FISHCAKES
FISHED
FISHER
FISHERIES
FISHERMAN
FISHERMEN
FISHERS
FISHERY
FISHES
FISHEYE
FISHEYES
FISHFUL
FISHGIG
FISHGIGS
FISHHOOK
FISHHOOKS
FISHIER
FISHIEST
FISHIFIED
FISHIFIES
FISHIFY
FISHILY
FISHINESS
FISHING
FISHINGS
FISHKILL
FISHKILLS
FISHLESS
FISHLIKE
FISHLINE
FISHLINES
FISHMEAL
FISHMEALS
FISHNET
FISHNETS
FISHPLATE
FISHPOLE
FISHPOLES
FISHPOND
FISHPONDS
FISHSKIN
FISHSKINS
FISHTAIL
FISHTAILS
FISHWAY
FISHWAYS
FISHWIFE
FISHWIVES
FISHWORM
FISHWORMS
FISHY
FISHYBACK
FISK
FISKED

FISKING
FISKS
FISNOMIE
FISNOMIES
FISSATE
FISSILE
FISSILITY
FISSION
FISSIONAL
FISSIONED
FISSIONS
FISSIPED
FISSIPEDE
FISSIPEDS
FISSIVE
FISSLE
FISSLED
FISSLES ·
FISSLING
FISSURAL
FISSURE
FISSURED
FISSURES
FISSURING
FIST
FISTED
FISTFIGHT
FISTFUL
FISTFULS
FISTIANA
FISTIC
FISTICAL
FISTICUFF
FISTIER
FISTIEST
FISTING
FISTMELE
FISTMELES
FISTNOTE
FISTNOTES
FISTS
FISTULA
FISTULAE
FISTULAR
FISTULAS
FISTULATE
FISTULOSE
FISTULOUS
FISTY
FIT
FITCH
FITCHE
FITCHEE
FITCHES
FITCHET
FITCHETS
FITCHEW
FITCHEWS

FITCHY
FITFUL
FITFULLY
FITLIER
FITLIEST
FITLY
FITMENT
FITMENTS
FITNA
FITNAS
FITNESS
FITNESSES
FITS
FITT
FITTABLE
FITTE
FITTED
FITTER
FITTERS
FITTES
FITTEST
FITTING
FITTINGLY
FITTINGS
FITTS
FIVE
FIVEFOLD
FIVEPENCE
FIVEPENNY
FIVEPIN
FIVEPINS
FIVER
FIVERS
FIVES
FIX
FIXABLE
FIXATE
FIXATED
FIXATES
FIXATIF
FIXATIFS
FIXATING
FIXATION
FIXATIONS
FIXATIVE
FIXATIVES
FIXATURE
FIXATURES
FIXED
FIXEDLY
FIXEDNESS
FIXER
FIXERS
FIXES
FIXING
FIXINGS
FIXIT
FIXITIES

FIXITY	FLAFFED	FLAM	FLANGERS
FIXIVE	FLAFFER	FLAMBE	FLANGES
FIXT	FLAFFERED	FLAMBEAU	FLANGING
FIXTURE	FLAFFERS	FLAMBEAUS	FLANK
FIXTURES	FLAFFING	FLAMBEAUX	FLANKED
FIXURE	FLAFFS	FLAMBEE	FLANKEN
FIXURES	FLAG	FLAMBEED	FLANKER
FIZ	FLAGELLA	FLAMBEES	FLANKERED
FIZGIG	FLAGELLAR	FLAMBEING	FLANKERS
FIZGIGS	FLAGELLIN	FLAMBES	FLANKING
FIZZ	FLAGELLUM	FLAME	FLANKS
FIZZED	FLAGEOLET	FLAMED	FLANNEL
FIZZEN	FLAGGED	FLAMELESS	FLANNELED
FIZZENS	FLAGGER	FLAMELET	FLANNELET
FIZZER	FLAGGERS	FLAMELETS	FLANNELLY
FIZZERS	FLAGGIER	FLAMELIKE	FLANNELS
FIZZES	FLAGGIEST	FLAMEN	FLANNEN
FIZZGIG	FLAGGING	FLAMENCO	FLANNENS
FIZZGIGS	FLAGGINGS	FLAMENCOS	FLANS
FIZZIER	FLAGGY	FLAMENS	FLAP
FIZZIEST	FLAGITATE	FLAMEOUT	FLAPERON
FIZZINESS	FLAGLESS	FLAMEOUTS	FLAPERONS
FIZZING	FLAGMAN	FLAMER	FLAPJACK
FIZZINGS	FLAGMEN	FLAMERS	FLAPJACKS
FIZZLE	FLAGON	FLAMES	FLAPLESS
FIZZLED	FLAGONS	FLAMFEW	FLAPPABLE
FIZZLES	FLAGPOLE	FLAMFEWS	FLAPPED
FIZZLING	FLAGPOLES	FLAMIER	FLAPPER
FIZZY	FLAGRANCE	FLAMIEST	FLAPPERS
FJELD	FLAGRANCY	FLAMINES	FLAPPIER
FJELDS	FLAGRANT	FLAMING	FLAPPIEST
FJORD	FLAGS	FLAMINGLY	FLAPPING
FJORDIC	FLAGSHIP	FLAMINGO	FLAPPINGS
FJORDS	FLAGSHIPS	FLAMINGOS	FLAPPY
FLAB	FLAGSTAFF	FLAMM	FLAPS
FLABBIER	FLAGSTICK	FLAMMABLE	FLAPTRACK
FLABBIEST	FLAGSTONE	FLAMMED	FLARE
FLABBILY	FLAIL	FLAMMING	FLAREBACK
FLABBY	FLAILED	FLAMMS	FLARED
FLABELLA	FLAILING	FLAMMULE	FLARES
FLABELLUM	FLAILS	FLAMMULES	FLAREUP
FLABS	FLAIR	FLAMS	FLAREUPS
FLACCID	FLAIRS	FLAMY	FLARIER
FLACCIDER	FLAK	FLAN	FLARIEST
FLACCIDLY	FLAKE	FLANCARD	FLARING
FLACK	FLAKED	FLANCARDS	FLARINGLY
FLACKED	FLAKER	FLANCH	FLARY
FLACKER	FLAKERS	FLANCHED	FLASER
FLACKERED	FLAKES	FLANCHES	FLASERS
FLACKERS	FLAKEY	FLANCHING	FLASH
FLACKERY	FLAKIER	FLANERIE	FLASHBACK
FLACKET	FLAKIES	FLANERIES	FLASHBULB
FLACKETS	FLAKIEST	FLANES	FLASHCARD
FLACKING	FLAKILY	FLANEUR	FLASHCUBE
FLACKS	FLAKINESS	FLANEURS	FLASHED
FLACON	FLAKING	FLANGE	FLASHER
FLACONS	FLAKS	FLANGED	FLASHERS
FLAFF	FLAKY	FLANGER	FLASHES

FLASHEST	FLATTEN	FLAVINES	FLEAS
FLASHGUN	FLATTENED	FLAVINS	FLEASOME
FLASHGUNS	FLATTENER	FLAVONE	FLEAWORT
FLASHIER	FLATTENS	FLAVONES	FLEAWORTS
FLASHIEST	FLATTER	FLAVONOID	FLECHE
FLASHILY	FLATTERED	FLAVONOL	FLECHES
FLASHING	FLATTERER	FLAVONOLS	FLECHETTE
FLASHINGS	FLATTERS	FLAVOR	FLECK
FLASHLAMP	FLATTERY	FLAVORED	FLECKED
FLASHOVER	FLATTEST	FLAVORER	FLECKER
FLASHTUBE	FLATTIE	FLAVORERS	FLECKERED
FLASHY	FLATTIES	FLAVORFUL	FLECKERS
FLASK	FLATTING	FLAVORING	FLECKING
FLASKET	FLATTINGS	FLAVORIST	FLECKLESS
FLASKETS	FLATTISH	FLAVOROUS	FLECKS
FLASKS	FLATTOP	FLAVORS	FLECKY
FLAT	FLATTOPS	FLAVORY	FLECTION
FLATBACK	FLATTY	FLAVOUR	FLECTIONS
FLATBACKS	FLATULENT	FLAVOURED	FLED
FLATBED	FLATUOUS	FLAVOURER	FLEDGE
FLATBEDS	FLATUS	FLAVOURS	FLEDGED
FLATBOAT	FLATUSES	FLAVOURY	FLEDGES
FLATBOATS	FLATWARE	FLAW	FLEDGIER
FLATBREAD	FLATWARES	FLAWED	FLEDGIEST
FLATCAP	FLATWASH	FLAWIER	FLEDGING
FLATCAPS	FLATWAYS	FLAWIEST	FLEDGLING
FLATCAR	FLATWISE	FLAWING	FLEDGY
FLATCARS	FLATWORK	FLAWLESS	FLEE
FLATETTE	FLATWORKS	FLAWN	FLEECE
FLATETTES	FLATWORM	FLAWNS	FLEECED
FLATFEET	FLATWORMS	FLAWS	FLEECER
FLATFISH	FLAUGHT	FLAWY	FLEECERS
FLATFOOT	FLAUGHTED	FLAX	FLEECES
FLATFOOTS	FLAUGHTER	FLAXEN	FLEECH
FLATHEAD	FLAUGHTS	FLAXES	FLEECHED
FLATHEADS	FLAUNCH	FLAXIER	FLEECHES
FLATIRON	FLAUNCHED	FLAXIEST	FLEECHING
FLATIRONS	FLAUNCHES	FLAXSEED	FLEECIE
FLATLAND	FLAUNE	FLAXSEEDS	FLEECIER
FLATLANDS	FLAUNES	FLAXY	FLEECIES
FLATLET	FLAUNT	FLAY	FLEECIEST
FLATLETS	FLAUNTED	FLAYED	FLEECILY
FLATLINE	FLAUNTER	FLAYER	FLEECING
FLATLINED	FLAUNTERS	FLAYERS	FLEECY
FLATLINER	FLAUNTIER	FLAYING	FLEEIN
FLATLINES	FLAUNTILY	FLAYS	FLEEING
FLATLING	FLAUNTING	FLAYSOME	FLEER
FLATLINGS	FLAUNTS	FLEA	FLEERED
FLATLONG	FLAUNTY	FLEABAG	FLEERER
FLATLY	FLAUTA	FLEABAGS	FLEERERS
FLATMATE	FLAUTAS	FLEABANE	FLEERING
FLATMATES	FLAUTIST	FLEABANES	FLEERINGS
FLATNESS	FLAUTISTS	FLEABITE	FLEERS
FLATPACK	FLAVANOL	FLEABITES	FLEES
FLATPACKS	FLAVANOLS	FLEAM	FLEET
FLATS	FLAVANONE	FLEAMS	FLEETED
FLATSHARE	FLAVIN	FLEAPIT	FLEETER
FLATTED	FLAVINE	FLEAPITS	FLEETEST

FLEETING	FLETTON	FLIES	FLIPPERS
FLEETLY	FLETTONS	FLIEST	FLIPPEST
FLEETNESS	FLEURET	FLIGHT	FLIPPING
FLEETS	FLEURETS	FLIGHTED	FLIPPY
FLEG	FLEURETTE	FLIGHTTER	FLIPS
FLEGGED	FLEURON	FLIGHTILY	FLIR
FLEGGING	FLEURONS	FLIGHTING	FLIRS
FLEGS	FLEURY	FLIGHTS	FLIRT
FLEHMEN	FLEW	FLIGHTY	FLIRTED
FLEHMENED	FLEWED	FLIM	FLIRTER
FLEHMENS	FLEWS	FLIMFLAM	FLIRTERS
FLEISHIG	FLEX	FLIMFLAMS	FLIRTIER
FLEISHIK	FLEXAGON	FLIMP	FLIRTIEST
FLEME	FLEXAGONS	FLIMPED	FLIRTING
FLEMES	FLEXED	FLIMPING	FLIRTINGS
FLEMING	FLEXES	FLIMPS	FLIRTISH
FLEMISH	FLEXIBLE	FLIMS	FLIRTS
FLEMISHED	FLEXIBLY	FLIMSIER	FLIRTY
FLEMISHES	FLEXILE	FLIMSIES	FLISK
FLEMIT	FLEXING	FLIMSIEST	FLISKED
FLENCH	FLEXION	FLIMSILY	FLISKIER
FLENCHED	FLEXIONAL	FLIMSY	FLISKIEST
FLENCHER	FLEXIONS	FLINCH	FLISKING
FLENCHERS	FLEXITIME	FLINCHED	FLISKS
FLENCHES	FLEXO	FLINCHER	FLISKY
FLENCHING	FLEXOR	FLINCHERS	FLIT
FLENSE	FLEXORS	FLINCHES	FLITCH
FLENSED	FLEXOS	FLINCHING	FLITCHED
FLENSER	FLEXTIME	FLINDER	FLITCHES
FLENSERS	FLEXTIMER	FLINDERS	FLITCHING
FLENSES	FLEXTIMES	FLING	FLITE
FLENSING	FLEXUOSE	FLINGER	FLITED
FLESH	FLEXUOUS	FLINGERS	FLITES
FLESHED	FLEXURAL	FLINGING	FLITING
FLESHER	FLEXURE	FLINGS	FLITS
FLESHERS	FLEXURES	FLINKITE	FLITT
FLESHES	FLEY	FLINKITES	FLITTED
FLESHHOOD	FLEYED	FLINT	FLITTER
FLESHIER	FLEYING	FLINTED	FLITTERED
FLESHIEST	FLEYS	FLINTHEAD	FLITTERN
FLESHILY	FLIBBERT	FLINTIER	FLITTERNS
FLESHING	FLIBBERTS	FLINTIEST	FLITTERS
FLESHINGS	FLIC	FLINTIFY	FLITTING
FLESHLESS	FLICHTER	FLINTILY	FLITTINGS
FLESHLIER	FLICHTERS	FLINTING	FLIVVER
FLESHLING	FLICK	FLINTLIKE	FLIVVERS
FLESHLY	FLICKABLE	FLINTLOCK	FLIX
FLESHMENT	FLICKED	FLINTS	FLIXED
FLESHPOT	FLICKER	FLINTY	FLIXES
FLESHPOTS	FLICKERED	FLIP	FLIXING
FLESHWORM	FLICKERS	FLIPBOOK	FLOAT
FLESHY	FLICKERY	FLIPBOOKS	FLOATABLE
FLETCH	FLICKING	FLIPFLOP	FLOATAGE
FLETCHED	FLICKS	FLIPFLOPS	FLOATAGES
FLETCHER	FLICS	FLIPPANCY	FLOATANT
FLETCHERS	FLIED	FLIPPANT	FLOATANTS
FLETCHES	FLIER	FLIPPED	FLOATCUT
FLETCHING	FLIERS	FLIPPER	FLOATED

FLOATEL
FLOATELS
FLOATER
FLOATERS
FLOATIER
FLOATIEST
FLOATING
FLOATINGS
FLOATS
FLOATY
FLOC
FLOCCED
FLOCCI
FLOCCING
FLOCCOSE
FLOCCULAR
FLOCCULE
FLOCCULES
FLOCCULI
FLOCCULUS
FLOCCUS
FLOCK
FLOCKED
FLOCKIER
FLOCKIEST
FLOCKING
FLOCKINGS
FLOCKLESS
FLOCKS
FLOCKY
FLOCS
FLOE
FLOES
FLOG
FLOGGABLE
FLOGGED
FLOGGER
FLOGGERS
FLOGGING
FLOGGINGS
FLOGS
FLOKATI
FLOKATIS
FLONG
FLONGS
FLOOD
FLOODABLE
FLOODED
FLOODER
FLOODERS
FLOODGATE
FLOODING
FLOODINGS
FLOODLESS
FLOODLIT
FLOODMARK
FLOODS
FLOODTIDE

FLOODWALL
FLOODWAY
FLOODWAYS
FLOOEY
FLOOIE
FLOOR
FLOORAGE
FLOORAGES
FLOORED
FLOORER
FLOORERS
FLOORHEAD
FLOORING
FLOORINGS
FLOORLESS
FLOORS
FLOORSHOW
FLOOSIE
FLOOSIES
FLOOSY
FLOOZIE
FLOOZIES
FLOOZY
FLOP
FLOPHOUSE
FLOPOVER
FLOPOVERS
FLOPPED
FLOPPER
FLOPPERS
FLOPPIER
FLOPPIES
FLOPPIEST
FLOPPILY
FLOPPING
FLOPPY
FLOPS
FLOPTICAL
FLOR
FLORA
FLORAE
FLORAL
FLORALLY
FLORALS
FLORAS
FLOREANT
FLOREAT
FLOREATED
FLORENCE
FLORENCES
FLORET
FLORETS
FLORIATED
FLORICANE
FLORID
FLORIDEAN
FLORIDER
FLORIDEST

FLORIDITY
FLORIDLY
FLORIER
FLORIEST
FLORIFORM
FLORIGEN
FLORIGENS
FLORIN
FLORINS
FLORIST
FLORISTIC
FLORISTRY
FLORISTS
FLORS
FLORUIT
FLORUITS
FLORULA
FLORULAE
FLORULE
FLORULES
FLORY
FLOSCULAR
FLOSCULE
FLOSCULES
FLOSH
FLOSHES
FLOSS
FLOSSED
FLOSSER
FLOSSERS
FLOSSES
FLOSSIE
FLOSSIER
FLOSSIES
FLOSSIEST
FLOSSILY
FLOSSING
FLOSSINGS
FLOSSY
FLOTA
FLOTAGE
FLOTAGES
FLOTANT
FLOTAS
FLOTATION
FLOTE
FLOTEL
FLOTELS
FLOTES
FLOTILLA
FLOTILLAS
FLOTSAM
FLOTSAMS
FLOUNCE
FLOUNCED
FLOUNCES
FLOUNCIER
FLOUNCING

FLOUNCY
FLOUNDER
FLOUNDERS
FLOUR
FLOURED
FLOURIER
FLOURIEST
FLOURING
FLOURISH
FLOURISHY
FLOURLESS
FLOURS
FLOURY
FLOUSE
FLOUSED
FLOUSES
FLOUSH
FLOUSHED
FLOUSHES
FLOUSHING
FLOUSING
FLOUT
FLOUTED
FLOUTER
FLOUTERS
FLOUTING
FLOUTS
FLOW
FLOWAGE
FLOWAGES
FLOWCHART
FLOWED
FLOWER
FLOWERAGE
FLOWERBED
FLOWERED
FLOWERER
FLOWERERS
FLOWERET
FLOWERETS
FLOWERFUL
FLOWERIER
FLOWERILY
FLOWERING
FLOWERPOT
FLOWERS
FLOWERY
FLOWING
FLOWINGLY
FLOWMETER
FLOWN
FLOWS
FLOWSTONE
FLU
FLUATE
FLUATES
FLUB
FLUBBED

FLUBBER	FLUIDNESS	FLUOROSIS	FLUXGATE
FLUBBERS	FLUIDRAM	FLUOROTIC	FLUXGATES
FLUBBING	FLUIDRAMS	FLUORS	FLUXING
FLUBDUB	FLUIDS	FLUORSPAR	FLUXION
FLUBDUBS	FLUIER	FLURR	FLUXIONAL
FLUBS	FLUIEST	FLURRED	FLUXIONS
FLUCTUANT	FLUISH	FLURRIED	FLUXIVE
FLUCTUATE	FLUKE	FLURRIES	FLUXMETER
FLUE	FLUKED	FLURRING	FLUYT
FLUED	FLUKES	FLURRS	FLUYTS
FLUELLEN	FLUKEY	FLURRY	FLY
FLUELLENS	FLUKIER	FLURRYING	FLYABLE
FLUELLIN	FLUKIEST	FLUS	FLYAWAY
FLUELLINS	FLUKILY	FLUSH	FLYAWAYS
FLUENCE	FLUKINESS	FLUSHABLE	FLYBACK
FLUENCES	FLUKING	FLUSHED	FLYBACKS
FLUENCIES	FLUKY	FLUSHER	FLYBANE
FLUENCY	FLUME	FLUSHERS	FLYBANES
FLUENT	FLUMED	FLUSHES	FLYBELT
FLUENTLY	FLUMES	FLUSHEST	FLYBELTS
FLUENTS	FLUMING	FLUSHIER	FLYBLEW
FLUERIC	FLUMMERY	FLUSHIEST	FLYBLOW
FLUERICS	FLUMMOX	FLUSHING	FLYBLOWN
FLUES	FLUMMOXED	FLUSHINGS	FLYBLOWS
FLUEWORK	FLUMMOXES	FLUSHNESS	FLYBOAT
FLUEWORKS	FLUMP	FLUSHWORK	FLYBOATS
FLUEY	FLUMPED	FLUSHY	FLYBOOK
FLUFF	FLUMPING	FLUSTER	FLYBOOKS
FLUFFED	FLUMPS	FLUSTERED	FLYBOY
FLUFFER	FLUNG	FLUSTERS	FLYBOYS
FLUFFERS	FLUNK	FLUSTERY	FLYBRIDGE
FLUFFIER	FLUNKED	FLUSTRATE	FLYBY
FLUFFIEST	FLUNKER	FLUTE	FLYBYS
FLUFFILY	FLUNKERS	FLUTED	FLYER
FLUFFING	FLUNKEY	FLUTELIKE	FLYERS
FLUFFS	FLUNKEYS	FLUTER	FLYEST
FLUFFY	FLUNKIE	FLUTERS	FLYHAND
FLUGEL	FLUNKIES	FLUTES	FLYHANDS
FLUGELMAN	FLUNKING	FLUTEY	FLYING
FLUGELMEN	FLUNKS	FLUTIER	FLYINGS
FLUGELS	FLUNKY	FLUTIEST	FLYLEAF
FLUID	FLUNKYISM	FLUTINA	FLYLEAVES
FLUIDAL	FLUOR	FLUTINAS	FLYLESS
FLUIDALLY	FLUORENE	FLUTING	FLYMAKER
FLUIDIC	FLUORENES	FLUTINGS	FLYMAKERS
FLUIDICS	FLUORESCE	FLUTIST	FLYMAN
FLUIDIFY	FLUORIC	FLUTISTS	FLYMEN
FLUIDISE	FLUORID	FLUTTER	FLYOFF
FLUIDISED	FLUORIDE	FLUTTERED	FLYOFFS
FLUIDISER	FLUORIDES	FLUTTERER	FLYOVER
FLUIDISES	FLUORIDS	FLUTTERS	FLYOVERS
FLUIDITY	FLUORIN	FLUTTERY	FLYPAPER
FLUIDIZE	FLUORINE	FLUTY	FLYPAPERS
FLUIDIZED	FLUORINES	FLUVIAL	FLYPAST
FLUIDIZER	FLUORINS	FLUVIATIC	FLYPASTS
FLUIDIZES	FLUORITE	FLUX	FLYPE
FLUIDLIKE	FLUORITES	FLUXED	FLYPED
FLUIDLY	FLUOROSES	FLUXES	FLYPES

FLYPING
FLYPITCH
FLYRODDER
FLYSCH
FLYSCHES
FLYSCREEN
FLYSHEET
FLYSHEETS
FLYSPECK
FLYSPECKS
FLYSTRIKE
FLYTE
FLYTED
FLYTES
FLYTIER
FLYTIERS
FLYTING
FLYTINGS
FLYTRAP
FLYTRAPS
FLYWAY
FLYWAYS
FLYWEIGHT
FLYWHEEL
FLYWHEELS
FOAL
FOALED
FOALFOOT
FOALFOOTS
FOALING
FOALS
FOAM
FOAMABLE
FOAMED
FOAMER
FOAMERS
FOAMIER
FOAMIEST
FOAMILY
FOAMINESS
FOAMING
FOAMINGLY
FOAMINGS
FOAMLESS
FOAMLIKE
FOAMS
FOAMY
FOB
FOBBED
FOBBING
FOBS
FOCACCIA
FOCACCIAS
FOCAL
FOCALISE
FOCALISED
FOCALISES
FOCALIZE

FOCALIZED
FOCALIZES
FOCALLY
FOCI
FOCIMETER
FOCOMETER
FOCUS
FOCUSABLE
FOCUSED
FOCUSER
FOCUSERS
FOCUSES
FOCUSING
FOCUSINGS
FOCUSLESS
FOCUSSED
FOCUSSES
FOCUSSING
FODDER
FODDERED
FODDERER
FODDERERS
FODDERING
FODDERS
FODGEL
FOE
FOEDARIE
FOEDARIES
FOEDERATI
FOEHN
FOEHNS
FOEMAN
FOEMEN
FOEN
FOES
FOETAL
FOETATION
FOETICIDE
FOETID
FOETIDER
FOETIDEST
FOETIDLY
FOETOR
FOETORS
FOETUS
FOETUSES
FOG
FOGASH
FOGASHES
FOGBOUND
FOGBOW
FOGBOWS
FOGDOG
FOGDOGS
FOGEY
FOGEYDOM
FOGEYDOMS
FOGEYISH

FOGEYISM
FOGEYISMS
FOGEYS
FOGFRUIT
FOGFRUITS
FOGGAGE
FOGGAGES
FOGGED
FOGGER
FOGGERS
FOGGIER
FOGGIEST
FOGGILY
FOGGINESS
FOGGING
FOGGY
FOGHORN
FOGHORNS
FOGIE
FOGIES
FOGLE
FOGLES
FOGLESS
FOGMAN
FOGMEN
FOGRAM
FOGRAMITE
FOGRAMITY
FOGRAMS
FOGS
FOGY
FOGYDOM
FOGYDOMS
FOGYISH
FOGYISM
FOGYISMS
FOH
FOHN
FOHNS
FOHS
FOIBLE
FOIBLES
FOID
FOIDS
FOIL
FOILABLE
FOILBORNE
FOILED
FOILING
FOILINGS
FOILS
FOILSMAN
FOILSMEN
FOIN
FOINED
FOINING
FOININGLY
FOINS

FOISON
FOISONS
FOIST
FOISTED
FOISTER
FOISTERS
FOISTING
FOISTS
FOLACIN
FOLACINS
FOLATE
FOLATES
FOLD
FOLDABLE
FOLDAWAY
FOLDAWAYS
FOLDBACK
FOLDBACKS
FOLDBOAT
FOLDBOATS
FOLDED
FOLDER
FOLDEROL
FOLDEROLS
FOLDERS
FOLDING
FOLDINGS
FOLDOUT
FOLDOUTS
FOLDS
FOLDUP
FOLDUPS
FOLEY
FOLEYS
FOLIA
FOLIAGE
FOLIAGED
FOLIAGES
FOLIAR
FOLIATE
FOLIATED
FOLIATES
FOLIATING
FOLIATION
FOLIATURE
FOLIC
FOLIE
FOLIES
FOLIO
FOLIOED
FOLIOING
FOLIOLATE
FOLIOLE
FOLIOLES
FOLIOLOSE
FOLIOS
FOLIOSE
FOLIOUS

FOLIUM	FOMITES	FOOFARAWS	FOOTLESS
FOLIUMS	FON	FOOL	FOOTLIGHT
FOLK	FOND	FOOLED	FOOTLIKE
FOLKIE	FONDA	FOOLERIES	FOOTLING
FOLKIER	FONDANT	FOOLERY	FOOTLINGS
FOLKIES	FONDANTS	FOOLFISH	FOOTLOOSE
FOLKIEST	FONDAS	FOOLHARDY	FOOTMAN
FOLKISH	FONDED	FOOLING	FOOTMARK
FOLKLAND	FONDER	FOOLINGS	FOOTMARKS
FOLKLANDS	FONDEST	FOOLISH	FOOTMEN
FOLKLIFE	FONDING	FOOLISHER	FOOTMUFF
FOLKLIKE	FONDLE	FOOLISHLY	FOOTMUFFS
FOLKLIVES	FONDLED	FOOLPROOF	FOOTNOTE
FOLKLORE	FONDLER	FOOLS	FOOTNOTED
FOLKLORES	FONDLERS	FOOLSCAP	FOOTNOTES
FOLKLORIC	FONDLES	FOOLSCAPS	FOOTPACE
FOLKMOOT	FONDLING	FOOSBALL	FOOTPACES
FOLKMOOTS	FONDLINGS	FOOSBALLS	FOOTPAD
FOLKMOT	FONDLY	FOOT	FOOTPADS
FOLKMOTE	FONDNESS	FOOTAGE	FOOTPAGE
FOLKMOTES	FONDS	FOOTAGES	FOOTPAGES
FOLKMOTS	FONDU	FOOTBAG	FOOTPATH
FOLKS	FONDUE	FOOTBAGS	FOOTPATHS
FOLKSIER	FONDUED	FOOTBALL	FOOTPLATE
FOLKSIEST	FONDUEING	FOOTBALLS	FOOTPOST
FOLKSILY	FONDUES	FOOTBAR	FOOTPOSTS
FOLKSONG	FONDUING	FOOTBARS	FOOTPRINT
FOLKSONGS	FONDUS	FOOTBATH	FOOTRA
FOLKSY	FONE	FOOTBATHS	FOOTRACE
FOLKTALE	FONLY	FOOTBOARD	FOOTRACES
FOLKTALES	FONNED	FOOTBOY	FOOTRAS
FOLKWAY	FONNING	FOOTBOYS	FOOTREST
FOLKWAYS	FONS	FOOTCLOTH	FOOTRESTS
FOLKY	FONT	FOOTED	FOOTROPE
FOLLES	FONTAL	FOOTER	FOOTROPES
FOLLICLE	FONTANEL	FOOTERED	FOOTROT
FOLLICLES	FONTANELS	FOOTERING	FOOTROTS
FOLLIED	FONTANGE	FOOTERS	FOOTRULE
FOLLIES	FONTANGES	FOOTFALL	FOOTRULES
FOLLIS	FONTICULI	FOOTFALLS	FOOTS
FOLLOW	FONTINA	FOOTFAULT	FOOTSIE
FOLLOWED	FONTINAS	FOOTGEAR	FOOTSIES
FOLLOWER	FONTLET	FOOTGEARS	FOOTSLOG
FOLLOWERS	FONTLETS	FOOTHILL	FOOTSLOGS
FOLLOWING	FONTS	FOOTHILLS	FOOTSORE
FOLLOWS	FOOBAR	FOOTHOLD	FOOTSTALK
FOLLOWUP	FOOD	FOOTHOLDS	FOOTSTALL
FOLLOWUPS	FOODFUL	FOOTIE	FOOTSTEP
FOLLY	FOODIE	FOOTIER	FOOTSTEPS
FOLLYING	FOODIES	FOOTIES	FOOTSTOCK
FOMENT	FOODISM	FOOTIEST	FOOTSTONE
FOMENTED	FOODISMS	FOOTING	FOOTSTOOL
FOMENTER	FOODLESS	FOOTINGS	FOOTSY
FOMENTERS	FOODS	FOOTLE	FOOTWALL
FOMENTING	FOODSTUFF	FOOTLED	FOOTWALLS
FOMENTS	FOODWAYS	FOOTLER	FOOTWAY
FOMES	FOODY	FOOTLERS	FOOTWAYS
FOMITE	FOOFARAW	FOOTLES	FOOTWEAR

FOOTWEARS	FORBIDDEN	FOREBODY	FOREIGNLY
FOOTWEARY	FORBIDDER	FOREBOOM	FOREJUDGE
FOOTWELL	FORBIDS	FOREBOOMS	FOREKING
FOOTWELLS	FORBODE	FOREBRAIN	FOREKINGS
FOOTWORK	FORBODED	FOREBY	FOREKNEW
FOOTWORKS	FORBODES	FOREBYE	FOREKNOW
FOOTWORN	FORBODING	FORECABIN	FOREKNOWN
FOOTY	FORBORE	FORECAR	FOREKNOWS
FOOZLE	FORBORNE	FORECARS	FOREL
FOOZLED	FORBS	FORECAST	FORELADY
FOOZLER	FORBY	FORECASTS	FORELAID
FOOZLERS	FORBYE	FORECHECK	FORELAIN
FOOZLES	FORCAT	FORECLOSE	FORELAND
FOOZLING	FORCATS	FORECLOTH	FORELANDS
FOOZLINGS	FORCE	FORECOURT	FORELAY
FOP	FORCEABLE	FOREDATE	FORELAYS
FOPLING	FORCED	FOREDATED	FORELEG
FOPLINGS	FORCEDLY	FOREDATES	FORELEGS
FOPPED	FORCEFUL	FOREDECK	FORELEND
FOPPERIES	FORCELESS	FOREDECKS	FORELENDS
FOPPERY	FORCEMEAT	FOREDID	FORELENT
FOPPING	FORCEPS	FOREDO	FORELIE
FOPPISH	FORCEPSES	FOREDOES	FORELIES
FOPPISHLY	FORCER	FOREDOING	FORELIFT
FOPS	FORCERS	FOREDONE	FORELIFTS
FOR	FORCES	FOREDOOM	FORELIMB
FORA	FORCIBLE	FOREDOOMS	FORELIMBS
FORAGE	FORCIBLY	FOREFACE	FORELOCK
FORAGED	FORCING	FOREFACES	FORELOCKS
FORAGER	FORCINGLY	FOREFEEL	FORELS
FORAGERS	FORCIPATE	FOREFEELS	FORELYING
FORAGES	FORCIPES	FOREFEET	FOREMAN
FORAGING	FORD	FOREFELT	FOREMAST
FORAM	FORDABLE	FOREFEND	FOREMASTS
FORAMEN	FORDED	FOREFENDS	FOREMEAN
FORAMENS	FORDID	FOREFOOT	FOREMEANS
FORAMINA	FORDING	FOREFRONT	FOREMEANT
FORAMINAL	FORDLESS	FOREGLEAM	FOREMEN
FORAMS	FORDO	FOREGO	FOREMILK
FORANE	FORDOES	FOREGOER	FOREMILKS
FORASMUCH	FORDOING	FOREGOERS	FOREMOST
FORAY	FORDONE	FOREGOES	FORENAME
FORAYED	FORDS	FOREGOING	FORENAMED
FORAYER	FORE	FOREGONE	FORENAMES
FORAYERS	FOREANENT	FOREGUT	FORENIGHT
FORAYING	FOREARM	FOREGUTS	FORENOON
FORAYS	FOREARMED	FOREHAND	FORENOONS
FORB	FOREARMS	FOREHANDS	FORENSIC
FORBAD	FOREBAY	FOREHEAD	FORENSICS
FORBADE	FOREBAYS	FOREHEADS	FOREPART
FORBARE	FOREBEAR	FOREHENT	FOREPARTS
FORBEAR	FOREBEARS	FOREHENTS	FOREPAST
FORBEARER	FOREBITT	FOREHOCK	FOREPAW
FORBEARS	FOREBITTS	FOREHOCKS	FOREPAWS
FORBID	FOREBODE	FOREHOOF	FOREPEAK
FORBIDAL	FOREBODED	FOREHOOFS	FOREPEAKS
FORBIDALS	FOREBODER	FOREIGN	FOREPLAN
FORBIDDAL	FOREBODES	FOREIGNER	FOREPLANS

FOREPLAY	FORESTER	FORFEX	FORJESKIT
FOREPLAYS	FORESTERS	FORFEXES	FORJUDGE
FOREPOINT	FORESTIAL	FORFICATE	FORJUDGED
FORERAN	FORESTINE	FORFOCHEN	FORJUDGES
FORERANK	FORESTING	FORGAT	FORK
FORERANKS	FORESTRY	FORGATHER	FORKBALL
FOREREACH	FORESTS	FORGAVE	FORKBALLS
FOREREAD	FORESWEAR	FORGE	FORKED
FOREREADS	FORESWORE	FORGEABLE	FORKEDLY
FORERUN	FORESWORN	FORGED	FORKER
FORERUNS	FORETASTE	FORGEMAN	FORKERS
FORES	FORETEACH	FORGEMEN	FORKFUL
FORESAID	FORETEETH	FORGER	FORKFULS
FORESAIL	FORETELL	FORGERIES	FORKHEAD
FORESAILS	FORETELLS	FORGERS	FORKHEADS
FORESAW	FORETHINK	FORGERY	FORKIER
FORESAY	FORETIME	FORGES	FORKIEST
FORESAYS	FORETIMES	FORGET	FORKINESS
FORESEE	FORETOKEN	FORGETFUL	FORKING
FORESEEN	FORETOLD	FORGETIVE	FORKLESS
FORESEER	FORETOOTH	FORGETS	FORKLIFT
FORESEERS	FORETOP	FORGETTER	FORKLIFTS
FORESEES	FORETOPS	FORGING	FORKLIKE
FORESHANK	FOREVER	FORGINGS	FORKS
FORESHEET	FOREVERS	FORGIVE	FORKSFUL
FORESHEW	FOREWARD	FORGIVEN	FORKTAIL
FORESHEWN	FOREWARDS	FORGIVER	FORKTAILS
FORESHEWS	FOREWARN	FORGIVERS	FORKY
FORESHIP	FOREWARNS	FORGIVES	FORLANA
FORESHIPS	FOREWEIGH	FORGIVING	FORLANAS
FORESHOCK	FOREWENT	FORGO	FORLEND
FORESHORE	FOREWIND	FORGOER	FORLENDS
FORESHOW	FOREWINDS	FORGOERS	FORLENT
FORESHOWN	FOREWING	FORGOES	FORLESE
FORESHOWS	FOREWINGS	FORGOING	FORLESES
FORESIDE	FOREWOMAN	FORGONE	FORLESING
FORESIDES	FOREWOMEN	FORGOT	FORLORE
FORESIGHT	FOREWORD	FORGOTTEN	FORLORN
FORESKIN	FOREWORDS	FORHAILE	FORLORNER
FORESKINS	FOREWORN	FORHAILED	FORLORNLY
FORESKIRT	FOREX	FORHAILES	FORLORNS
FORESLACK	FOREXES	FORHENT	FORM
FORESLOW	FOREYARD	FORHENTS	FORMABLE
FORESLOWS	FOREYARDS	FORHOO	FORMABLY
FORESPAKE	FORFAIR	FORHOOED	FORMAL
FORESPEAK	FORFAIRED	FORHOOIE	FORMALIN
FORESPEND	FORFAIRN	FORHOOIED	FORMALINS
FORESPENT	FORFAIRS	FORHOOIES	FORMALISE
FORESPOKE	FORFAITER	FORHOOING	FORMALISM
FOREST	FORFAULT	FORHOOS	FORMALIST
FORESTAGE	FORFAULTS	FORHOW	FORMALITY
FORESTAIR	FORFEIT	FORHOWED	FORMALIZE
FORESTAL	FORFEITED	FORHOWING	FORMALLY
FORESTALL	FORFEITER	FORHOWS	FORMALS
FORESTAY	FORFEITS	FORINSEC	FORMAMIDE
FORESTAYS	FORFEND	FORINT	FORMANT
FORESTEAL	FORFENDED	FORINTS	FORMANTS
FORESTED	FORFENDS	FORJASKIT	FORMAT

FORMATE
FORMATED
FORMATES
FORMATING
FORMATION
FORMATIVE
FORMATS
FORMATTED
FORMATTER
FORME
FORMED
FORMEE
FORMER
FORMERLY
FORMERS
FORMES
FORMFUL
FORMIATE
FORMIATES
FORMIC
FORMICA
FORMICANT
FORMICARY
FORMICAS
FORMICATE
FORMING
FORMINGS
FORMLESS
FORMOL
FORMOLS
FORMS
FORMULA
FORMULAE
FORMULAIC
FORMULAR
FORMULARY
FORMULAS
FORMULATE
FORMULISE
FORMULISM
FORMULIST
FORMULIZE
FORMWORK
FORMWORKS
FORMYL
FORMYLS
FORNENST
FORNENT
FORNICAL
FORNICATE
FORNICES
FORNIX
FORPET
FORPETS
FORPINE
FORPINED
FORPINES
FORPINING

FORPIT
FORPITS
FORRAD
FORRADER
FORRARDER
FORRAY
FORRAYED
FORRAYING
FORRAYS
FORREN
FORRIT
FORSAID
FORSAKE
FORSAKEN
FORSAKER
FORSAKERS
FORSAKES
FORSAKING
FORSAY
FORSAYING
FORSAYS
FORSLACK
FORSLACKS
FORSLOE
FORSLOED
FORSLOES
FORSLOW
FORSLOWED
FORSLOWS
FORSOOK
FORSOOTH
FORSPEAK
FORSPEAKS
FORSPEND
FORSPENDS
FORSPENT
FORSPOKE
FORSPOKEN
FORSWATT
FORSWEAR
FORSWEARS
FORSWINK
FORSWINKS
FORSWONCK
FORSWORE
FORSWORN
FORSWUNK
FORSYTHIA
FORT
FORTALICE
FORTE
FORTED
FORTES
FORTH
FORTHCAME
FORTHCOME
FORTHINK
FORTHINKS

FORTHWITH
FORTHY
FORTIES
FORTIETH
FORTIETHS
FORTIFIED
FORTIFIER
FORTIFIES
FORTIFY
FORTILAGE
FORTING
FORTIS
FORTITUDE
FORTLET
FORTLETS
FORTNIGHT
FORTRESS
FORTS
FORTUITY
FORTUNATE
FORTUNE
FORTUNED
FORTUNES
FORTUNING
FORTUNISE
FORTUNIZE
FORTY
FORTYISH
FORUM
FORUMS
FORWANDER
FORWARD
FORWARDED
FORWARDER
FORWARDLY
FORWARDS
FORWARN
FORWARNED
FORWARNS
FORWASTE
FORWASTED
FORWASTES
FORWEARY
FORWENT
FORWHY
FORWORN
FORZA
FORZANDI
FORZANDO
FORZANDOS
FORZAS
FORZATI
FORZATO
FORZATOS
FOSCARNET
FOSS
FOSSA
FOSSAE

FOSSAS
FOSSATE
FOSSE
FOSSED
FOSSES
FOSSETTE
FOSSETTES
FOSSICK
FOSSICKED
FOSSICKER
FOSSICKS
FOSSIL
FOSSILISE
FOSSILIZE
FOSSILS
FOSSOR
FOSSORIAL
FOSSORS
FOSSULA
FOSSULAE
FOSSULATE
FOSTER
FOSTERAGE
FOSTERED
FOSTERER
FOSTERERS
FOSTERING
FOSTERS
FOSTRESS
FOTHER
FOTHERED
FOTHERING
FOTHERS
FOU
FOUAT
FOUATS
FOUD
FOUDRIE
FOUDRIES
FOUDS
FOUER
FOUEST
FOUET
FOUETS
FOUETTE
FOUETTES
FOUGADE
FOUGADES
FOUGASSE
FOUGASSES
FOUGHT
FOUGHTEN
FOUGHTIER
FOUGHTY
FOUL
FOULARD
FOULARDS
FOULBROOD

FOULDER	FOUSSA	FOXHUNT	FRACTI
FOULDERED	FOUSSAS	FOXHUNTED	FRACTING
FOULDERS	FOUSTIER	FOXHUNTER	FRACTION
FOULE	FOUSTIEST	FOXHUNTS	FRACTIONS
FOULED	FOUSTY	FOXIE	FRACTIOUS
FOULER	FOUTER	FOXIER	FRACTS
FOULES	FOUTERED	FOXIES	FRACTUR
FOULEST	FOUTERING	FOXIEST	FRACTURAL
FOULIE	FOUTERS	FOXILY	FRACTURE
FOULIES	FOUTH	FOXINESS	FRACTURED
FOULING	FOUTHS	FOXING	FRACTURER
FOULINGS	FOUTRA	FOXINGS	FRACTURES
FOULLY	FOUTRAS	FOXLIKE	FRACTURS
FOULMART	FOUTRE	FOXSHARK	FRACTUS
FOULMARTS	FOUTRED	FOXSHARKS	FRAE
FOULNESS	FOUTRES	FOXSHIP	FRAENA
FOULS	FOUTRING	FOXSHIPS	FRAENUM
FOUMART	FOVEA	FOXSKIN	FRAENUMS
FOUMARTS	FOVEAE	FOXSKINS	FRAG
FOUND	FOVEAL	FOXTAIL	FRAGGED
FOUNDED	FOVEAS	FOXTAILS	FRAGGING
FOUNDER	FOVEATE	FOXTROT	FRAGGINGS
FOUNDERED	FOVEATED	FOXTROTS	FRAGILE
FOUNDERS	FOVEIFORM	FOXY	FRAGILELY
FOUNDING	FOVEOLA	FOY	FRAGILER
FOUNDINGS	FOVEOLAE	FOYBOAT	FRAGILEST
FOUNDLING	FOVEOLAR	FOYBOATS	FRAGILITY
FOUNDRESS	FOVEOLAS	FOYER	FRAGMENT
FOUNDRIES	FOVEOLATE	FOYERS	FRAGMENTS
FOUNDRY	FOVEOLE	FOYLE	FRAGOR
FOUNDS	FOVEOLES	FOYLED	FRAGORS
FOUNT	FOVEOLET	FOYLES	FRAGRANCE
FOUNTAIN	FOVEOLETS	FOYLING	FRAGRANCY
FOUNTAINS	FOWL	FOYNE	FRAGRANT
FOUNTFUL	FOWLED	FOYNED	FRAGS
FOUNTS	FOWLER	FOYNES	FRAICHEUR
FOUR	FOWLERS	FOYNING	FRAIL
FOURBALL	FOWLING	FOYS	FRAILER
FOURBALLS	FOWLINGS	FOZIER	FRAILEST
FOURCHEE	FOWLPOX	FOZIEST	FRAILISH
FOUREYED	FOWLPOXES	FOZINESS	FRAILLY
FOURFOLD	FOWLS	FOZY	FRAILNESS
FOURGON	FOWTH	FRA	FRAILS
FOURGONS	FOWTHS	FRAB	FRAILTEE
FOURPENCE	FOX	FRABBED	FRAILTEES
FOURPENNY	FOXBERRY	FRABBING	FRAILTIES
FOURPLEX	FOXED	FRABBIT	FRAILTY
FOURS	FOXES	FRABJOUS	FRAIM
FOURSCORE	FOXFIRE	FRABS	FRAIMS
FOURSES	FOXFIRES	FRACAS	FRAISE
FOURSOME	FOXFISH	FRACASES	FRAISED
FOURSOMES	FOXFISHES	FRACK	FRAISES
FOURTEEN	FOXGLOVE	FRACKING	FRAISING
FOURTEENS	FOXGLOVES	FRACKINGS	FRAKTUR
FOURTH	FOXHOLE	FRACT	FRAKTURS
FOURTHLY	FOXHOLES	FRACTAL	FRAMABLE
FOURTHS	FOXHOUND	FRACTALS	FRAMBESIA
FOUS	FOXHOUNDS	FRACTED	FRAMBOISE

FRAME
FRAMEABLE
FRAMED
FRAMELESS
FRAMER
FRAMERS
FRAMES
FRAMEWORK
FRAMING
FRAMINGS
FRAMPAL
FRAMPLER
FRAMPLERS
FRAMPOLD
FRANC
FRANCHISE
FRANCISE
FRANCISED
FRANCISES
FRANCIUM
FRANCIUMS
FRANCIZE
FRANCIZED
FRANCIZES
FRANCO
FRANCOLIN
FRANCS
FRANGER
FRANGERS
FRANGIBLE
FRANGLAIS
FRANION
FRANIONS
FRANK
FRANKABLE
FRANKED
FRANKER
FRANKERS
FRANKEST
FRANKFORT
FRANKFURT
FRANKING
FRANKLIN
FRANKLINS
FRANKLY
FRANKNESS
FRANKS
FRANSERIA
FRANTIC
FRANTICLY
FRANZIER
FRANZIEST
FRANZY
FRAP
FRAPE
FRAPPANT
FRAPPE
FRAPPED

FRAPPEE
FRAPPES
FRAPPING
FRAPS
FRAS
FRASCATI
FRASCATIS
FRASS
FRASSES
FRAT
FRATCH
FRATCHES
FRATCHETY
FRATCHIER
FRATCHING
FRATCHY
FRATE
FRATER
FRATERIES
FRATERNAL
FRATERS
FRATERY
FRATI
FRATRIES
FRATRY
FRATS
FRAU
FRAUD
FRAUDFUL
FRAUDS
FRAUDSMAN
FRAUDSMEN
FRAUDSTER
FRAUGHAN
FRAUGHANS
FRAUGHT
FRAUGHTED
FRAUGHTER
FRAUGHTS
FRAULEIN
FRAULEINS
FRAUS
FRAUTAGE
FRAUTAGES
FRAWZEY
FRAWZEYS
FRAY
FRAYED
FRAYING
FRAYINGS
FRAYS
FRAZIL
FRAZILS
FRAZZLE
FRAZZLED
FRAZZLES
FRAZZLING
FREAK

FREAKED
FREAKERY
FREAKFUL
FREAKIER
FREAKIEST
FREAKILY
FREAKING
FREAKISH
FREAKOUT
FREAKOUTS
FREAKS
FREAKY
FRECKLE
FRECKLED
FRECKLES
FRECKLIER
FRECKLING
FRECKLY
FREDAINE
FREDAINES
FREE
FREEBASE
FREEBASED
FREEBASER
FREEBASES
FREEBEE
FREEBEES
FREEBIE
FREEBIES
FREEBOARD
FREEBOOT
FREEBOOTS
FREEBOOTY
FREEBORN
FREED
FREEDMAN
FREEDMEN
FREEDOM
FREEDOMS
FREEFORM
FREEGAN
FREEGANS
FREEHAND
FREEHOLD
FREEHOLDS
FREEING
FREELANCE
FREELOAD
FREELOADS
FREELY
FREEMAN
FREEMASON
FREEMEN
FREENESS
FREEPHONE
FREER
FREERS
FREES

FREESHEET
FREESIA
FREESIAS
FREEST
FREESTONE
FREESTYLE
FREET
FREETIER
FREETIEST
FREETS
FREETY
FREEWARE
FREEWARES
FREEWAY
FREEWAYS
FREEWHEEL
FREEWILL
FREEWOMAN
FREEWOMEN
FREEWRITE
FREEWROTE
FREEZABLE
FREEZE
FREEZER
FREEZERS
FREEZES
FREEZING
FREEZINGS
FREIGHT
FREIGHTED
FREIGHTER
FREIGHTS
FREIT
FREITIER
FREITIEST
FREITS
FREITY
FREMD
FREMDS
FREMIT
FREMITS
FREMITUS
FRENA
FRENCH
FRENCHED
FRENCHES
FRENCHIFY
FRENCHING
FRENETIC
FRENETICS
FRENNE
FRENULA
FRENULAR
FRENULUM
FRENULUMS
FRENUM
FRENUMS
FRENZICAL

FRENZIED
FRENZIES
FRENZILY
FRENZY
FRENZYING
FREON
FREONS
FREQUENCE
FREQUENCY
FREQUENT
FREQUENTS
FRERE
FRERES
FRESCADE
FRESCADES
FRESCO
FRESCOED
FRESCOER
FRESCOERS
FRESCOES
FRESCOING
FRESCOIST
FRESCOS
FRESH
FRESHED
FRESHEN
FRESHENED
FRESHENER
FRESHENS
FRESHER
FRESHERS
FRESHES
FRESHEST
FRESHET
FRESHETS
FRESHIE
FRESHIES
FRESHING
FRESHISH
FRESHLY
FRESHMAN
FRESHMEN
FRESHNESS
FRESNEL
FRESNELS
FRET
FRETBOARD
FRETFUL
FRETFULLY
FRETLESS
FRETS
FRETSAW
FRETSAWS
FRETSOME
FRETTED
FRETTER
FRETTERS
FRETTIER

FRETTIEST
FRETTING
FRETTINGS
FRETTY
FRETWORK
FRETWORKS
FRIABLE
FRIAND
FRIANDE
FRIANDES
FRIANDS
FRIAR
FRIARBIRD
FRIARIES
FRIARLY
FRIARS
FRIARY
FRIB
FRIBBLE
FRIBBLED
FRIBBLER
FRIBBLERS
FRIBBLES
FRIBBLING
FRIBBLISH
FRIBS
FRICADEL
FRICADELS
FRICANDO
FRICASSEE
FRICATIVE
FRICHT
FRICHTED
FRICHTING
FRICHTS
FRICKING
FRICTION
FRICTIONS
FRIDGE
FRIDGED
FRIDGES
FRIDGING
FRIED
FRIEDCAKE
FRIEND
FRIENDED
FRIENDING
FRIENDLY
FRIENDS
FRIER
FRIERS
FRIES
FRIEZE
FRIEZED
FRIEZES
FRIEZING
FRIG
FRIGATE

FRIGATES
FRIGATOON
FRIGES
FRIGGED
FRIGGER
FRIGGERS
FRIGGING
FRIGGINGS
FRIGHT
FRIGHTED
FRIGHTEN
FRIGHTENS
FRIGHTFUL
FRIGHTING
FRIGHTS
FRIGID
FRIGIDER
FRIGIDEST
FRIGIDITY
FRIGIDLY
FRIGOT
FRIGOTS
FRIGS
FRIJOL
FRIJOLE
FRIJOLES
FRIKKADEL
FRILL
FRILLED
FRILLER
FRILLERS
FRILLIER
FRILLIES
FRILLIEST
FRILLING
FRILLINGS
FRILLS
FRILLY
FRINGE
FRINGED
FRINGES
FRINGIER
FRINGIEST
FRINGING
FRINGY
FRIPON
FRIPONS
FRIPPER
FRIPPERER
FRIPPERS
FRIPPERY
FRIPPET
FRIPPETS
FRIS
FRISBEE
FRISBEES
FRISE
FRISEE

FRISEES
FRISES
FRISETTE
FRISETTES
FRISEUR
FRISEURS
FRISK
FRISKA
FRISKAS
FRISKED
FRISKER
FRISKERS
FRISKET
FRISKETS
FRISKFUL
FRISKIER
FRISKIEST
FRISKILY
FRISKING
FRISKINGS
FRISKS
FRISKY
FRISSON
FRISSONS
FRIST
FRISTED
FRISTING
FRISTS
FRISURE
FRISURES
FRIT
FRITES
FRITFLIES
FRITFLY
FRITH
FRITHBORH
FRITHS
FRITS
FRITT
FRITTATA
FRITTATAS
FRITTED
FRITTER
FRITTERED
FRITTERER
FRITTERS
FRITTING
FRITTS
FRITURE
FRITURES
FRITZ
FRITZES
FRIVOL
FRIVOLED
FRIVOLER
FRIVOLERS
FRIVOLING
FRIVOLITY

FRIVOLLED	FROGLING	FRONTOONS	FROUZILY
FRIVOLLER	FROGLINGS	FRONTPAGE	FROUZY
FRIVOLOUS	FROGMAN	FRONTS	FROW
FRIVOLS	FROGMARCH	FRONTWARD	FROWARD
FRIZ	FROGMEN	FRONTWAYS	FROWARDLY
FRIZE	FROGMOUTH	FRONTWISE	FROWARDS
FRIZED	FROGS	FRORE	FROWIE
FRIZER	FROGSPAWN	FROREN	FROWIER
FRIZERS	FROIDEUR	FRORN	FROWIEST
FRIZES	FROIDEURS	FRORNE	FROWN
FRIZETTE	FROING	FRORY	FROWNED
FRIZETTES	FROINGS	FROS	FROWNER
FRIZING	FROISE	FROSH	FROWNERS
FRIZZ	FROISES	FROSHES	FROWNING
FRIZZANTE	FROLIC	FROST	FROWNS
FRIZZED	FROLICKED	FROSTBIT	FROWS
FRIZZER	FROLICKER	FROSTBITE	FROWSIER
FRIZZERS	FROLICKY	FROSTED	FROWSIEST
FRIZZES	FROLICS	FROSTEDS	FROWST
FRIZZIER	FROM	FROSTFISH	FROWSTED
FRIZZIES	FROMAGE	FROSTIER	FROWSTER
FRIZZIEST	FROMAGES	FROSTIEST	FROWSTERS
FRIZZILY	FROMENTY	FROSTILY	FROWSTIER
FRIZZING	FROND	FROSTING	FROWSTING
FRIZZLE	FRONDAGE	FROSTINGS	FROWSTS
FRIZZLED	FRONDAGES	FROSTLESS	FROWSTY
FRIZZLER	FRONDED	FROSTLIKE	FROWSY
FRIZZLERS	FRONDENT	FROSTLINE	FROWY
FRIZZLES	FRONDEUR	FROSTNIP	FROWZIER
FRIZZLIER	FRONDEURS	FROSTNIPS	FROWZIEST
FRIZZLING	FRONDLESS	FROSTS	FROWZILY
FRIZZLY	FRONDOSE	FROSTWORK	FROWZY
FRIZZY	FRONDOUS	FROSTY	FROZE
FRO	FRONDS	FROTH	FROZEN
FROCK	FRONS	FROTHED	FROZENLY
FROCKED	FRONT	FROTHER	FRUCTAN
FROCKING	FRONTAGE	FROTHERS	FRUCTANS
FROCKINGS	FRONTAGER	FROTHERY	FRUCTED
FROCKLESS	FRONTAGES	FROTHIER	FRUCTIFY
FROCKS	FRONTAL	FROTHIEST	FRUCTIVE
FROE	FRONTALLY	FROTHILY	FRUCTOSE
FROES	FRONTALS	FROTHING	FRUCTOSES
FROG	FRONTED	FROTHLESS	FRUCTUARY
FROGBIT	FRONTENIS	FROTHS	FRUCTUATE
FROGBITS	FRONTER	FROTHY	FRUCTUOUS
FROGEYE	FRONTES	FROTTAGE	FRUG
FROGEYED	FRONTIER	FROTTAGES	FRUGAL
FROGEYES	FRONTIERS	FROTTEUR	FRUGALIST
FROGFISH	FRONTING	FROTTEURS	FRUGALITY
FROGGED	FRONTLESS	FROUFROU	FRUGALLY
FROGGERY	FRONTLET	FROUFROUS	FRUGGED
FROGGIER	FRONTLETS	FROUGHIER	FRUGGING
FROGGIEST	FRONTLINE	FROUGHY	FRUGIVORE
FROGGING	FRONTLIST	FROUNCE	FRUGS
FROGGINGS	FRONTMAN	FROUNCED	FRUICT
FROGGY	FRONTMEN	FROUNCES	FRUICTS
FROGLET	FRONTON	FROUNCING	FRUIT
FROGLETS	FRONTONS	FROUZIER	FRUITAGE
FROGLIKE	FRONTOON	FROUZIEST	FRUITAGES

FRUITCAKE
FRUITED
FRUITER
FRUITERER
FRUTTERS
FRUITERY
FRUITFUL
FRUITIER
FRUITIEST
FRUITILY
FRUITING
FRUITINGS
FRUITION
FRUITIONS
FRUITIVE
FRUITLESS
FRUITLET
FRUITLETS
FRUITLIKE
FRUITS
FRUITWOOD
FRUITY
FRUMENTY
FRUMP
FRUMPED
FRUMPIER
FRUMPIEST
FRUMPILY
FRUMPING
FRUMPISH
FRUMPLE
FRUMPLED
FRUMPLES
FRUMPLING
FRUMPS
FRUMPY
FRUSEMIDE
FRUSH
FRUSHED
FRUSHES
FRUSHING
FRUST
FRUSTA
FRUSTRATE
FRUSTS
FRUSTULE
FRUSTULES
FRUSTUM
FRUSTUMS
FRUTEX
FRUTICES
FRUTICOSE
FRUTIFIED
FRUTIFIES
FRUTIFY
FRY
FRYABLE
FRYBREAD
FRYBREADS

FRYER
FRYERS
FRYING
FRYINGS
FRYPAN
FRYPANS
FUB
FUBAR
FUBBED
FUBBERIES
FUBBERY
FUBBIER
FUBBIEST
FUBBING
FUBBY
FUBS
FUBSIER
FUBSIEST
FUBSY
FUCHSIA
FUCHSIAS
FUCHSIN
FUCHSINE
FUCHSINES
FUCHSINS
FUCHSITE
FUCHSITES
FUCI
FUCK
FUCKED
FUCKER
FUCKERS
FUCKING
FUCKINGS
FUCKOFF
FUCKOFFS
FUCKS
FUCKUP
FUCKUPS
FUCKWIT
FUCKWITS
FUCOID
FUCOIDAL
FUCOIDS
FUCOSE
FUCOSES
FUCOUS
FUCUS
FUCUSED
FUCUSES
FUD
FUDDIES
FUDDLE
FUDDLED
FUDDLER
FUDDLERS
FUDDLES
FUDDLING
FUDDLINGS

FUDDY
FUDGE
FUDGED
FUDGES
FUDGING
FUDS
FUEHRER
FUEHRERS
FUEL
FUELED
FUELER
FUELERS
FUELING
FUELLED
FUELLER
FUELLERS
FUELLING
FUELS
FUELWOOD
FUELWOODS
FUERO
FUEROS
FUFF
FUFFED
FUFFIER
FUFFIEST
FUFFING
FUFFS
FUFFY
FUG
FUGACIOUS
FUGACITY
FUGAL
FUGALLY
FUGATO
FUGATOS
FUGGED
FUGGIER
FUGGIEST
FUGGILY
FUGGING
FUGGY
FUGHETTA
FUGHETTAS
FUGIE
FUGIES
FUGIO
FUGIOS
FUGITIVE
FUGITIVES
FUGLE
FUGLED
FUGLEMAN
FUGLEMEN
FUGLES
FUGLIER
FUGLIEST
FUGLING
FUGLY

FUGS
FUGU
FUGUE
FUGUED
FUGUELIKE
FUGUES
FUGUING
FUGUIST
FUGUISTS
FUGUS
FUHRER
FUHRERS
FUJI
FUJIS
FULCRA
FULCRATE
FULCRUM
FULCRUMS
FULFIL
FULFILL
FULFILLED
FULFILLER
FULFILLS
FULFILS
FULGENCY
FULGENT
FULGENTLY
FULGID
FULGOR
FULGOROUS
FULGORS
FULGOUR
FULGOURS
FULGURAL
FULGURANT
FULGURATE
FULGURITE
FULGUROUS
FULHAM
FULHAMS
FULL
FULLAGE
FULLAGES
FULLAM
FULLAMS
FULLAN
FULLANS
FULLBACK
FULLBACKS
FULLBLOOD
FULLED
FULLER
FULLERED
FULLERENE
FULLERIDE
FULLERIES
FULLERING
FULLERITE
FULLERS

FULLERY	FUMETS	FUNG	FUNNYMAN
FULLEST	FUMETTE	FUNGAL	FUNNYMEN
FULLFACE	FUMETTES	FUNGALS	FUNPLEX
FULLFACES	FUMETTI	FUNGI	FUNPLEXES
FULLING	FUMETTO	FUNGIBLE	FUNS
FULLISH	FUMIER	FUNGIBLES	FUNSTER
FULLNESS	FUMIEST	FUNGIC	FUNSTERS
FULLS	FUMIGANT	FUNGICIDE	FUR
FULLY	FUMIGANTS	FUNGIFORM	FURACIOUS
FULMAR	FUMIGATE	FUNGISTAT	FURACITY
FULMARS	FUMIGATED	FUNGO	FURAL
FULMINANT	FUMIGATES	FUNGOES	FURALS
FULMINATE	FUMIGATOR	FUNGOID	FURAN
FULMINE	FUMING	FUNGOIDAL	FURANE
FULMINED	FUMINGLY	FUNGOIDS	FURANES
FULMINES	FUMITORY	FUNGOSITY	FURANOSE
FULMINIC	FUMOSITY	FUNGOUS	FURANOSES
FULMINING	FUMOUS	FUNGS	FURANS
FULMINOUS	FUMS	FUNGUS	FURBEARER
FULNESS	FUMULI	FUNGUSES	FURBELOW
FULNESSES	FUMULUS	FUNHOUSE	FURBELOWS
FULSOME	FUMY	FUNHOUSES	FURBISH
FULSOMELY	FUN	FUNICLE	FURBISHED
FULSOMER	FUNBOARD	FUNICLES	FURBISHER
FULSOMEST	FUNBOARDS	FUNICULAR	FURBISHES
FULVID	FUNCTION	FUNICULI	FURCA
FULVOUS	FUNCTIONS	FUNICULUS	FURCAE
FUM	FUNCTOR	FUNK	FURCAL
FUMADO	FUNCTORS	FUNKED	FURCATE
FUMADOES	FUND	FUNKER	FURCATED
FUMADOS	FUNDABLE	FUNKERS	FURCATELY
FUMAGE	FUNDAMENT	FUNKHOLE	FURCATES
FUMAGES	FUNDED	FUNKHOLES	FURCATING
FUMARASE	FUNDER	FUNKIA	FURCATION
FUMARASES	FUNDERS	FUNKIAS	FURCRAEA
FUMARATE	FUNDI	FUNKIER	FURCRAEAS
FUMARATES	FUNDIC	FUNKIEST	FURCULA
FUMARIC	FUNDIE	FUNKILY	FURCULAE
FUMAROLE	FUNDIES	FUNKINESS	FURCULAR
FUMAROLES	FUNDING	FUNKING	FURCULUM
FUMAROLIC	FUNDINGS	FUNKS	FURDER
FUMATORIA	FUNDIS	FUNKSTER	FUREUR
FUMATORY	FUNDLESS	FUNKSTERS	FUREURS
FUMBLE	FUNDRAISE	FUNKY	FURFAIR
FUMBLED	FUNDS	FUNNED	FURFAIRS
FUMBLER	FUNDUS	FUNNEL	FURFUR
FUMBLERS	FUNDY	FUNNELED	FURFURAL
FUMBLES	FUNEBRAL	FUNNELING	FURFURALS
FUMBLING	FUNEBRE	FUNNELLED	FURFURAN
FUME	FUNEBRIAL	FUNNELS	FURFURANS
FUMED	FUNERAL	FUNNER	FURFURES
FUMELESS	FUNERALS	FUNNEST	FURFUROL
FUMELIKE	FUNERARY	FUNNIER	FURFUROLE
FUMER	FUNEREAL	FUNNIES	FURFUROLS
FUMEROLE	FUNEST	FUNNIEST	FURFUROUS
FUMEROLES	FUNFAIR	FUNNILY	FURFURS
FUMERS	FUNFAIRS	FUNNINESS	FURIBUND
FUMES	FUNFEST	FUNNING	FURIES
FUMET	FUNFESTS	FUNNY	FURIOSITY

FURIOSO
FURIOSOS
FURIOUS
FURIOUSLY
FURKTD
FURKIDS
FURL
FURLABLE
FURLANA
FURLANAS
FURLED
FURLER
FURLERS
FURLESS
FURLING
FURLONG
FURLONGS
FURLOUGH
FURLOUGHS
FURLS
FURMENTY
FURMETIES
FURMETY
FURMITIES
FURMITY
FURNACE
FURNACED
FURNACES
FURNACING
FURNIMENT
FURNISH
FURNISHED
FURNISHER
FURNISHES
FURNITURE
FUROL
FUROLE
FUROLES
FUROLS
FUROR
FURORE
FURORES
FURORS
FURPHIES
FURPHY
FURR
FURRED
FURRIER
FURRIERS
FURRIERY
FURRIES
FURRIEST
FURRILY
FURRINER
FURRINERS
FURRINESS
FURRING
FURRINGS
FURROW

FURROWED
FURROWER
FURROWERS
FURROWING
FURROWS
FURROWY
FURRS
FURRY
FURS
FURTH
FURTHER
FURTHERED
FURTHERER
FURTHERS
FURTHEST
FURTIVE
FURTIVELY
FURUNCLE
FURUNCLES
FURY
FURZE
FURZES
FURZIER
FURZIEST
FURZY
FUSAIN
FUSAINS
FUSARIA
FUSARIUM
FUSAROL
FUSAROLE
FUSAROLES
FUSAROLS
FUSC
FUSCOUS
FUSE
FUSED
FUSEE
FUSEES
FUSEL
FUSELAGE
FUSELAGES
FUSELESS
FUSELIKE
FUSELS
FUSES
FUSHION
FUSHIONS
FUSIBLE
FUSIBLY
FUSIFORM
FUSIL
FUSILE
FUSILEER
FUSILEERS
FUSILIER
FUSILIERS
FUSILLADE
FUSILLI

FUSILLIS
FUSILS
FUSING
FUSION
FUSIONAL
FUSIONISM
FUSIONIST
FUSIONS
FUSS
FUSSED
FUSSER
FUSSERS
FUSSES
FUSSIER
FUSSIEST
FUSSILY
FUSSINESS
FUSSING
FUSSPOT
FUSSPOTS
FUSSY
FUST
FUSTED
FUSTET
FUSTETS
FUSTIAN
FUSTIANS
FUSTIC
FUSTICS
FUSTIER
FUSTIEST
FUSTIGATE
FUSTILUGS
FUSTILY
FUSTINESS
FUSTING
FUSTOC
FUSTOCS
FUSTS
FUSTY
FUSULINID
FUSUMA
FUTCHEL
FUTCHELS
FUTHARC
FUTHARCS
FUTHARK
FUTHARKS
FUTHORC
FUTHORCS
FUTHORK
FUTHORKS
FUTILE
FUTILELY
FUTILER
FUTILEST
FUTILITY
FUTON
FUTONS

FUTSAL
FUTSALS
FUTTOCK
FUTTOCKS
FUTURAL
FUTURE
FUTURES
FUTURISM
FUTURISMS
FUTURIST
FUTURISTS
FUTURITY
FUTZ
FUTZED
FUTZES
FUTZING
FUZE
FUZED
FUZEE
FUZEES
FUZES
FUZIL
FUZILS
FUZING
FUZZ
FUZZED
FUZZES
FUZZIER
FUZZIEST
FUZZILY
FUZZINESS
FUZZING
FUZZLE
FUZZLED
FUZZLES
FUZZLING
FUZZTONE
FUZZTONES
FUZZY
FY
FYCE
FYCES
FYKE
FYKED
FYKES
FYKING
FYLE
FYLES
FYLFOT
FYLFOTS
FYNBOS
FYNBOSES
FYRD
FYRDS
FYTTE
FYTTES

G

GAB
GABARDINE
GABBARD
GABBARDS
GABBART
GABBARTS
GABBED
GABBER
GABBERS
GABBIER
GABBIEST
GABBINESS
GABBING
GABBLE
GABBLED
GABBLER
GABBLERS
GABBLES
GABBLING
GABBLINGS
GABBRO
GABBROIC
GABBROID
GABBROS
GABBY
GABELLE
GABELLED
GABELLER
GABELLERS
GABELLES
GABERDINE
GABFEST
GABFESTS
GABIES
GABION
GABIONADE
GABIONAGE
GABIONED
GABIONS
GABLE
GABLED
GABLELIKE
GABLES
GABLET
GABLETS
GABLING
GABNASH
GABNASHES
GABOON
GABOONS
GABS
GABY
GAD

GADABOUT
GADABOUTS
GADARENE
GADDED
GADDER
GADDERS
GADDI
GADDING
GADDIS
GADE
GADES
GADFLIES
GADFLY
GADGE
GADGES
GADGET
GADGETEER
GADGETRY
GADGETS
GADGETY
GADGIE
GADGIES
GADI
GADID
GADIDS
GADIS
GADJE
GADJES
GADJO
GADLING
GADLINGS
GADOID
GADOIDS
GADOLINIC
GADROON
GADROONED
GADROONS
GADS
GADSMAN
GADSMEN
GADSO
GADSOS
GADWALL
GADWALLS
GADZOOKS
GAE
GAED
GAEING
GAELICISE
GAELICISM
GAELICIZE
GAEN
GAES

GAFF
GAFFE
GAFFED
GAFFER
GAFFERS
GAFFES
GAFFING
GAFFINGS
GAFFS
GAFFSAIL
GAFFSAILS
GAG
GAGA
GAGAKU
GAGAKUS
GAGE
GAGEABLE
GAGEABLY
GAGED
GAGER
GAGERS
GAGES
GAGGED
GAGGER
GAGGERIES
GAGGERS
GAGGERY
GAGGING
GAGGLE
GAGGLED
GAGGLES
GAGGLING
GAGGLINGS
GAGING
GAGMAN
GAGMEN
GAGS
GAGSTER
GAGSTERS
GAHNITE
GAHNITES
GAID
GAIDS
GAIETIES
GAIETY
GAIJIN
GAILLARD
GAILLARDE
GAILY
GAIN
GAINABLE
GAINED
GAINER

GAINERS
GAINEST
GAINFUL
GAINFULLY
GAINING
GAININGS
GAINLESS
GAINLIER
GAINLIEST
GAINLY
GAINS
GAINSAID
GAINSAY
GAINSAYER
GAINSAYS
GAINST
GAIR
GAIRFOWL
GAIRFOWLS
GAIRS
GAIT
GAITED
GAITER
GAITERS
GAITING
GAITS
GAITT
GAITTS
GAJO
GAJOS
GAL
GALA
GALABEA
GALABEAH
GALABEAHS
GALABEAS
GALABIA
GALABIAH
GALABIAHS
GALABIAS
GALABIEH
GALABIEHS
GALABIYA
GALABIYAH
GALABIYAS
GALACTIC
GALACTOSE
GALAGE
GALAGES
GALAGO
GALAGOS
GALAH
GALAHS

GALANGA	GALLABIEH	GALLISIZE	GALOPPING
GALANGAL	GALLABIYA	GALLIUM	GALOPS
GALANGALS	GALLAMINE	GALLIUMS	GALORE
GALANGAS	GALLANT	GALLIVANT	GALORES
GALANT	GALLANTED	GALLIVAT	GALOSH
GALANTINE	GALLANTER	GALLIVATS	GALOSHE
GALANTY	GALLANTLY	GALLIWASP	GALOSHED
GALAPAGO	GALLANTRY	GALLIZE	GALOSHES
GALAPAGOS	GALLANTS	GALLIZED	GALOSHING
GALAS	GALLATE	GALLIZES	GALOWSES
GALATEA	GALLATES	GALLIZING	GALRAVAGE
GALATEAS	GALLEASS	GALLNUT	GALS
GALAVANT	GALLED	GALLNUTS	GALTONIA
GALAVANTS	GALLEIN	GALLOCK	GALTONIAS
GALAX	GALLEINS	GALLON	GALUMPH
GALAXES	GALLEON	GALLONAGE	GALUMPHED
GALAXIES	GALLEONS	GALLONS	GALUMPHER
GALAXY	GALLERIA	GALLOON	GALUMPHS
GALBANUM	GALLERIAS	GALLOONED	GALUT
GALBANUMS	GALLERIED	GALLOONS	GALUTH
GALDRAGON	GALLERIES	GALLOOT	GALUTHS
GALE	GALLERIST	GALLOOTS	GALUTS
GALEA	GALLERY	GALLOP	GALVANIC
GALEAE	GALLET	GALLOPADE	GALVANISE
GALEAS	GALLETA	GALLOPED	GALVANISM
GALEATE	GALLETAS	GALLOPER	GALVANIST
GALEATED	GALLETED	GALLOPERS	GALVANIZE
GALEIFORM	GALLETING	GALLOPING	GALVO
GALENA	GALLETS	GALLOPS	GALVOS
GALENAS	GALLEY	GALLOUS	GALYAC
GALENGALE	GALLEYS	GALLOW	GALYACS
GALENIC	GALLFLIES	GALLOWED	GALYAK
GALENICAL	GALLFLY	GALLOWING	GALYAKS
GALENITE	GALLIARD	GALLOWS	GAM
GALENITES	GALLIARDS	GALLOWSES	GAMA
GALENOID	GALLIASS	GALLS	GAMAHUCHE
GALERE	GALLIC	GALLSTONE	GAMARUCHE
GALERES	GALLICA	GALLUMPH	GAMAS
GALES	GALLICAN	GALLUMPHS	GAMASH
GALETTE	GALLICAS	GALLUS	GAMASHES
GALETTES	GALLICISE	GALLUSED	GAMAY
GALILEE	GALLICISM	GALLUSES	GAMAYS
GALILEES	GALLICIZE	GALLY	GAMB
GALINGALE	GALLIED	GALLYING	GAMBA
GALIONGEE	GALLIES	GALOCHE	GAMBADE
GALIOT	GALLINAZO	GALOCHED	GAMBADES
GALIOTS	GALLING	GALOCHES	GAMBADO
GALIPOT	GALLINGLY	GALOCHING	GAMBADOED
GALIPOTS	GALLINULE	GALOOT	GAMBADOES
GALIVANT	GALLIOT	GALOOTS	GAMBADOS
GALIVANTS	GALLIOTS	GALOP	GAMBAS
GALL	GALLIPOT	GALOPADE	GAMBE
GALLABEA	GALLIPOTS	GALOPADES	GAMBES
GALLABEAH	GALLISE	GALOPED	GAMBESON
GALLABEAS	GALLISED	GALOPIN	GAMBESONS
GALLABIA	GALLISES	GALOPING	GAMBET
GALLABIAH	GALLISING	GALOPINS	GAMBETS
GALLABIAS	GALLISISE	GALOPPED	GAMBETTA

GAMBETTAS
GAMBIA
GAMBIAS
GAMBIER
GAMBIERS
GAMBIR
GAMBIRS
GAMBIST
GAMBISTS
GAMBIT
GAMBITED
GAMBITING
GAMBITS
GAMBLE
GAMBLED
GAMBLER
GAMBLERS
GAMBLES
GAMBLING
GAMBLINGS
GAMBO
GAMBOGE
GAMBOGES
GAMBOGIAN
GAMBOGIC
GAMBOL
GAMBOLED
GAMBOLING
GAMBOLLED
GAMBOLS
GAMBOS
GAMBREL
GAMBRELS
GAMBROON
GAMBROONS
GAMBS
GAMBUSIA
GAMBUSIAS
GAME
GAMECOCK
GAMECOCKS
GAMED
GAMELAN
GAMELANS
GAMELIKE
GAMELY
GAMENESS
GAMEPLAY
GAMEPLAYS
GAMER
GAMERS
GAMES
GAMESIER
GAMESIEST
GAMESMAN
GAMESMEN
GAMESOME
GAMEST

GAMESTER
GAMESTERS
GAMESY
GAMETAL
GAMETE
GAMETES
GAMETIC
GAMEY
GAMIC
GAMIER
GAMIEST
GAMILY
GAMIN
GAMINE
GAMINERIE
GAMINES
GAMINESS
GAMING
GAMINGS
GAMINS
GAMMA
GAMMADIA
GAMMADION
GAMMAS
GAMMAT
GAMMATIA
GAMMATION
GAMMATS
GAMME
GAMMED
GAMMER
GAMMERS
GAMMES
GAMMIER
GAMMIEST
GAMMING
GAMMOCK
GAMMOCKED
GAMMOCKS
GAMMON
GAMMONED
GAMMONER
GAMMONERS
GAMMONING
GAMMONS
GAMMY
GAMODEME
GAMODEMES
GAMONE
GAMONES
GAMP
GAMPISH
GAMPS
GAMS
GAMUT
GAMUTS
GAMY
GAMYNESS

GAN
GANACHE
GANACHES
GANCH
GANCHED
GANCHES
GANCHING
GANDER
GANDERED
GANDERING
GANDERISM
GANDERS
GANDY
GANE
GANEF
GANEFS
GANEV
GANEVS
GANG
GANGBANG
GANGBANGS
GANGBOARD
GANGED
GANGER
GANGERS
GANGING
GANGINGS
GANGLAND
GANGLANDS
GANGLIA
GANGLIAL
GANGLIAR
GANGLIATE
GANGLIER
GANGLIEST
GANGLING
GANGLION
GANGLIONS
GANGLY
GANGPLANK
GANGPLOW
GANGPLOWS
GANGREL
GANGRELS
GANGRENE
GANGRENED
GANGRENES
GANGS
GANGSHAG
GANGSHAGS
GANGSMAN
GANGSMEN
GANGSTA
GANGSTAS
GANGSTER
GANGSTERS
GANGUE
GANGUES

GANGWAY
GANGWAYS
GANISTER
GANISTERS
GANJA
GANJAH
GANJAHS
GANJAS
GANNED
GANNET
GANNETRY
GANNETS
GANNING
GANNISTER
GANOF
GANOFS
GANOID
GANOIDS
GANOIN
GANOINE
GANOINES
GANOINS
GANS
GANSEY
GANSEYS
GANT
GANTED
GANTELOPE
GANTING
GANTLET
GANTLETED
GANTLETS
GANTLINE
GANTLINES
GANTLOPE
GANTLOPES
GANTRIES
GANTRY
GANTS
GANYMEDE
GANYMEDES
GAOL
GAOLBIRD
GAOLBIRDS
GAOLBREAK
GAOLED
GAOLER
GAOLERESS
GAOLERS
GAOLING
GAOLLESS
GAOLS
GAP
GAPE
GAPED
GAPER
GAPERS
GAPES

GAPESEED
GAPESEEDS
GAPEWORM
GAPEWORMS
GAPING
GAPINGLY
GAPINGS
GAPLESS
GAPO
GAPOS
GAPOSIS
GAPOSISES
GAPPED
GAPPER
GAPPERS
GAPPIER
GAPPIEST
GAPPING
GAPPY
GAPS
GAPY
GAR
GARAGE
GARAGED
GARAGEMAN
GARAGEMEN
GARAGES
GARAGING
GARAGINGS
GARAGIST
GARAGISTE
GARAGISTS
GARB
GARBAGE
GARBAGES
GARBAGEY
GARBAGY
GARBANZO
GARBANZOS
GARBE
GARBED
GARBES
GARBING
GARBLE
GARBLED
GARBLER
GARBLERS
GARBLES
GARBLESS
GARBLING
GARBLINGS
GARBO
GARBOARD
GARBOARDS
GARBOIL
GARBOILS
GARBOLOGY
GARBOS

GARBS
GARBURE
GARBURES
GARCINIA
GARCINIAS
GARCON
GARCONS
GARDA
GARDAI
GARDANT
GARDANTS
GARDEN
GARDENED
GARDENER
GARDENERS
GARDENFUL
GARDENIA
GARDENIAS
GARDENING
GARDENS
GARDEROBE
GARDYLOO
GARDYLOOS
GARE
GAREFOWL
GAREFOWLS
GARFISH
GARFISHES
GARGANEY
GARGANEYS
GARGANTUA
GARGARISE
GARGARISM
GARGARIZE
GARGET
GARGETS
GARGETY
GARGLE
GARGLED
GARGLER
GARGLERS
GARGLES
GARGLING
GARGOYLE
GARGOYLED
GARGOYLES
GARI
GARIAL
GARIALS
GARIBALDI
GARIGUE
GARIGUES
GARIS
GARISH
GARISHED
GARISHES
GARISHING
GARISHLY

GARJAN
GARJANS
GARLAND
GARLANDED
GARLANDRY
GARLANDS
GARLIC
GARLICKED
GARLICKY
GARLICS
GARMENT
GARMENTED
GARMENTS
GARNER
GARNERED
GARNERING
GARNERS
GARNET
GARNETS
GARNI
GARNISH
GARNISHED
GARNISHEE
GARNISHER
GARNISHES
GARNISHRY
GARNITURE
GAROTE
GAROTED
GAROTES
GAROTING
GAROTTE
GAROTTED
GAROTTER
GAROTTERS
GAROTTES
GAROTTING
GAROUPA
GAROUPAS
GARPIKE
GARPIKES
GARRAN
GARRANS
GARRE
GARRED
GARRES
GARRET
GARRETED
GARRETEER
GARRETS
GARRIGUE
GARRIGUES
GARRING
GARRISON
GARRISONS
GARRON
GARRONS
GARROT

GARROTE
GARROTED
GARROTER
GARROTERS
GARROTES
GARROTING
GARROTS
GARROTTE
GARROTTED
GARROTTER
GARROTTES
GARRULITY
GARRULOUS
GARRYA
GARRYAS
GARRYOWEN
GARS
GART
GARTER
GARTERED
GARTERING
GARTERS
GARTH
GARTHS
GARUDA
GARUDAS
GARUM
GARUMS
GARVEY
GARVEYS
GARVIE
GARVIES
GARVOCK
GARVOCKS
GAS
GASAHOL
GASAHOLS
GASALIER
GASALIERS
GASBAG
GASBAGGED
GASBAGS
GASCON
GASCONADE
GASCONISM
GASCONS
GASEITIES
GASEITY
GASELIER
GASELIERS
GASEOUS
GASES
GASFIELD
GASFIELDS
GASH
GASHED
GASHER
GASHES

GASHEST	GASSILY	GATHERERS	GAULTER
GASHFUL	GASSINESS	GATHERING	GAULTERS
GASHING	GASSING	GATHERS	GAULTS
GASHLY	GASSINGS	GATHS	GAUM
GASHOLDER	GASSY	GATING	GAUMED
GASHOUSE	GAST	GATINGS	GAUMIER
GASHOUSES	GASTED	GATOR	GAUMIEST
GASIFIED	GASTER	GATORS	GAUMING
GASIFIER	GASTERS	GATS	GAUMLESS
GASIFIERS	GASTFULL	GATVOL	GAUMS
GASIFIES	GASTIGHT	GAU	GAUMY
GASIFORM	GASTING	GAUCHE	GAUN
GASIFY	GASTNESS	GAUCHELY	GAUNCH
GASIFYING	GASTNESSE	GAUCHER	GAUNCHED
GASKET	GASTRAEA	GAUCHERIE	GAUNCHES
GASKETS	GASTRAEAS	GAUCHESCO	GAUNCHING
GASKIN	GASTRAEUM	GAUCHEST	GAUNT
GASKING	GASTRAL	GAUCHO	GAUNTED
GASKINGS	GASTREA	GAUCHOS	GAUNTER
GASKINS	GASTREAS	GAUCIE	GAUNTEST
GASLESS	GASTRIC	GAUCIER	GAUNTING
GASLIGHT	GASTRIN	GAUCIEST	GAUNTLET
GASLIGHTS	GASTRINS	GAUCY	GAUNTLETS
GASLIT	GASTRITIC	GAUD	GAUNTLY
GASMAN	GASTRITIS	GAUDEAMUS	GAUNTNESS
GASMEN	GASTROPOD	GAUDED	GAUNTREE
GASOGENE	GASTRULA	GAUDERIES	GAUNTREES
GASOGENES	GASTRULAE	GAUDERY	GAUNTRIES
GASOHOL	GASTRULAR	GAUDGIE	GAUNTRY
GASOHOLS	GASTRULAS	GAUDGIES	GAUNTS
GASOLENE	GASTS	GAUDIER	GAUP
GASOLENES	GASWORKS	GAUDIES	GAUPED
GASOLIER	GAT	GAUDIEST	GAUPER
GASOLIERS	GATE	GAUDILY	GAUPERS
GASOLINE	GATEAU	GAUDINESS	GAUPING
GASOLINES	GATEAUS	GAUDING	GAUPS
GASOLINIC	GATEAUX	GAUDS	GAUPUS
GASOMETER	GATECRASH	GAUDY	GAUPUSES
GASOMETRY	GATED	GAUFER	GAUR
GASP	GATEFOLD	GAUFERS	GAURS
GASPED	GATEFOLDS	GAUFFER	GAUS
GASPER	GATEHOUSE	GAUFFERED	GAUSS
GASPEREAU	GATELEG	GAUFFERS	GAUSSES
GASPERS	GATELESS	GAUFRE	GAUSSIAN
GASPIER	GATELIKE	GAUFRES	GAUZE
GASPIEST	GATEMAN	GAUGE	GAUZELIKE
GASPINESS	GATEMEN	GAUGEABLE	GAUZES
GASPING	GATEPOST	GAUGEABLY	GAUZIER
GASPINGLY	GATEPOSTS	GAUGED	GAUZIEST
GASPINGS	GATER	GAUGER	GAUZILY
GASPS	GATERS	GAUGERS	GAUZINESS
GASPY	GATES	GAUGES	GAUZY
GASSED	GATEWAY	GAUGING	GAVAGE
GASSER	GATEWAYS	GAUGINGS	GAVAGES
GASSERS	GATH	GAUJE	GAVE
GASSES	GATHER	GAUJES	GAVEL
GASSIER	GATHERED	GAULEITER	GAVELED
GASSIEST	GATHERER	GAULT	GAVELING

GAVELKIND
GAVELLED
GAVELLING
GAVELMAN
GAVELMEN
GAVELOCK
GAVELOCKS
GAVELS
GAVIAL
GAVIALOID
GAVIALS
GAVOT
GAVOTS
GAVOTTE
GAVOTTED
GAVOTTES
GAVOTTING
GAWCIER
GAWCIEST
GAWCY
GAWD
GAWDS
GAWK
GAWKED
GAWKER
GAWKERS
GAWKIER
GAWKIES
GAWKIEST
GAWKIHOOD
GAWKILY
GAWKINESS
GAWKING
GAWKISH
GAWKISHLY
GAWKS
GAWKY
GAWP
GAWPED
GAWPER
GAWPERS
GAWPING
GAWPS
GAWPUS
GAWPUSES
GAWSIE
GAWSIER
GAWSIEST
GAWSY
GAY
GAYAL
GAYALS
GAYDAR
GAYDARS
GAYER
GAYEST
GAYETIES
GAYETY

GAYLY
GAYNESS
GAYNESSES
GAYS
GAYSOME
GAYWINGS
GAZABO
GAZABOES
GAZABOS
GAZAL
GAZALS
GAZANIA
GAZANIAS
GAZAR
GAZARS
GAZE
GAZEBO
GAZEBOES
GAZEBOS
GAZED
GAZEFUL
GAZEHOUND
GAZELLE
GAZELLES
GAZEMENT
GAZEMENTS
GAZER
GAZERS
GAZES
GAZETTE
GAZETTED
GAZETTEER
GAZETTES
GAZETTING
GAZIER
GAZIEST
GAZILLION
GAZING
GAZINGS
GAZOGENE
GAZOGENES
GAZON
GAZONS
GAZOO
GAZOOKA
GAZOOKAS
GAZOON
GAZOONS
GAZOOS
GAZPACHO
GAZPACHOS
GAZUMP
GAZUMPED
GAZUMPER
GAZUMPERS
GAZUMPING
GAZUMPS
GAZUNDER

GAZUNDERS
GAZY
GEAL
GEALED
GEALING
GEALOUS
GEALOUSY
GEALS
GEAN
GEANS
GEAR
GEARBOX
GEARBOXES
GEARCASE
GEARCASES
GEARE
GEARED
GEARES
GEARHEAD
GEARHEADS
GEARING
GEARINGS
GEARLESS
GEARS
GEARSHIFT
GEARWHEEL
GEASON
GEAT
GEATS
GEBUR
GEBURS
GECK
GECKED
GECKING
GECKO
GECKOES
GECKOS
GECKS
GED
GEDACT
GEDACTS
GEDDIT
GEDECKT
GEDECKTS
GEDS
GEE
GEEBAG
GEEBAGS
GEEBUNG
GEEBUNGS
GEECHEE
GEECHEES
GEED
GEEGAW
GEEGAWS
GEEING
GEEK
GEEKDOM

GEEKDOMS
GEEKED
GEEKIER
GEEKIEST
GEEKINESS
GEEKS
GEEKSPEAK
GEEKY
GEELBEK
GEELBEKS
GEEP
GEEPOUND
GEEPOUNDS
GEEPS
GEES
GEESE
GEEST
GEESTS
GEEZ
GEEZAH
GEEZAHS
GEEZER
GEEZERS
GEFILTE
GEFUFFLE
GEFUFFLED
GEFUFFLES
GEFULLTE
GEGGIE
GEGGIES
GEHLENITE
GEISHA
GEISHAS
GEIST
GEISTS
GEIT
GEITS
GEL
GELABLE
GELADA
GELADAS
GELANDE
GELANT
GELANTS
GELASTIC
GELATE
GELATED
GELATES
GELATI
GELATIN
GELATINE
GELATINES
GELATING
GELATINS
GELATION
GELATIONS
GELATIS
GELATO

237

GELATOS
GELCAP
GELCAPS
GELD
GELDED
GELDER
GELDERS
GELDING
GELDINGS
GELDS
GELEE
GELEES
GELID
GELIDER
GELIDEST
GELIDITY
GELIDLY
GELIDNESS
GELIGNITE
GELLANT
GELLANTS
GELLED
GELLIES
GELLING
GELLY
GELOSIES
GELOSY
GELS
GELSEMIA
GELSEMINE
GELSEMIUM
GELT
GELTS
GEM
GEMATRIA
GEMATRIAS
GEMCLIP
GEMCLIPS
GEMEL
GEMELS
GEMFISH
GEMFISHES
GEMINAL
GEMINALLY
GEMINATE
GEMINATED
GEMINATES
GEMINI
GEMINIES
GEMINOUS
GEMINY
GEMLIKE
GEMMA
GEMMAE
GEMMAN
GEMMATE
GEMMATED
GEMMATES

GEMMATING
GEMMATION
GEMMATIVE
GEMMED
GEMMEN
GEMMEOUS
GEMMERIES
GEMMERY
GEMMIER
GEMMIEST
GEMMILY
GEMMINESS
GEMMING
GEMMOLOGY
GEMMULE
GEMMULES
GEMMY
GEMOLOGY
GEMONY
GEMOT
GEMOTE
GEMOTES
GEMOTS
GEMS
GEMSBOK
GEMSBOKS
GEMSBUCK
GEMSBUCKS
GEMSHORN
GEMSHORNS
GEMSTONE
GEMSTONES
GEMUTLICH
GEN
GENA
GENAL
GENAPPE
GENAPPES
GENAS
GENDARME
GENDARMES
GENDER
GENDERED
GENDERING
GENDERISE
GENDERIZE
GENDERS
GENE
GENEALOGY
GENERA
GENERABLE
GENERAL
GENERALCY
GENERALE
GENERALIA
GENERALLY
GENERALS
GENERANT

GENERANTS
GENERATE
GENERATED
GENERATES
GENERATOR
GENERIC
GENERICAL
GENERICS
GENEROUS
GENES
GENESES
GENESIS
GENET
GENETIC
GENETICAL
GENETICS
GENETRIX
GENETS
GENETTE
GENETTES
GENEVA
GENEVAS
GENIAL
GENIALISE
GENIALITY
GENIALIZE
GENIALLY
GENIC
GENICALLY
GENICULAR
GENIE
GENIES
GENII
GENIP
GENIPAP
GENIPAPS
GENIPS
GENISTA
GENISTAS
GENISTEIN
GENITAL
GENITALIA
GENITALIC
GENITALLY
GENITALS
GENITIVAL
GENITIVE
GENITIVES
GENITOR
GENITORS
GENITRIX
GENITURE
GENITURES
GENIUS
GENIUSES
GENIZAH
GENIZAHS
GENLOCK

GENLOCKS
GENNAKER
GENNAKERS
GENNED
GENNEL
GENNELS
GENNET
GENNETS
GENNIES
GENNING
GENNY
GENOA
GENOAS
GENOCIDAL
GENOCIDE
GENOCIDES
GENOGRAM
GENOGRAMS
GENOISE
GENOISES
GENOM
GENOME
GENOMES
GENOMIC
GENOMICS
GENOMS
GENOTYPE
GENOTYPES
GENOTYPIC
GENRE
GENRES
GENRO
GENROS
GENS
GENSENG
GENSENGS
GENT
GENTEEL
GENTEELER
GENTEELLY
GENTES
GENTIAN
GENTIANS
GENTIER
GENTIEST
GENTIL
GENTILE
GENTILES
GENTILIC
GENTILISE
GENTILISH
GENTILISM
GENTILITY
GENTILIZE
GENTLE
GENTLED
GENTLEMAN
GENTLEMEN

GENTLER
GENTLES
GENTLEST
GENTLING
GENTLY
GENTOO
GENTOOS
GENTRICE
GENTRICES
GENTRIES
GENTRIFY
GENTRY
GENTS
GENTY
GENU
GENUA
GENUFLECT
GENUINE
GENUINELY
GENUS
GENUSES
GEO
GEOBOTANY
GEOCARPIC
GEOCARPY
GEOCORONA
GEODE
GEODES
GEODESIC
GEODESICS
GEODESIES
GEODESIST
GEODESY
GEODETIC
GEODETICS
GEODIC
GEODUCK
GEODUCKS
GEOFACT
GEOFACTS
GEOGENIES
GEOGENY
GEOGNOSES
GEOGNOSIS
GEOGNOST
GEOGNOSTS
GEOGNOSY
GEOGONIC
GEOGONIES
GEOGONY
GEOGRAPHY
GEOID
GEOIDAL
GEOIDS
GEOLATRY
GEOLOGER
GEOLOGERS
GEOLOGIAN

GEOLOGIC
GEOLOGIES
GEOLOGISE
GEOLOGIST
GEOLOGTZE
GEOLOGY
GEOMANCER
GEOMANCY
GEOMANT
GEOMANTIC
GEOMANTS
GEOMETER
GEOMETERS
GEOMETRIC
GEOMETRID
GEOMETRY
GEOMYOID
GEOPHAGIA
GEOPHAGY
GEOPHILIC
GEOPHONE
GEOPHONES
GEOPHYTE
GEOPHYTES
GEOPHYTIC
GEOPONIC
GEOPONICS
GEOPROBE
GEOPROBES
GEORGETTE
GEORGIC
GEORGICAL
GEORGICS
GEOS
GEOSPHERE
GEOSTATIC
GEOTACTIC
GEOTAXES
GEOTAXIS
GEOTHERM
GEOTHERMS
GEOTROPIC
GERAH
GERAHS
GERANIAL
GERANIALS
GERANIOL
GERANIOLS
GERANIUM
GERANIUMS
GERARDIA
GERARDIAS
GERBE
GERBERA
GERBERAS
GERBES
GERBIL
GERBTLLE

GERBILLES
GERBILS
GERE
GERENT
GERENTS
GERENUK
GERENUKS
GERES
GERFALCON
GERIATRIC
GERLE
GERLES
GERM
GERMAIN
GERMAINE
GERMAINES
GERMAINS
GERMAN
GERMANDER
GERMANE
GERMANELY
GERMANIC
GERMANISE
GERMANITE
GERMANIUM
GERMANIZE
GERMANOUS
GERMANS
GERMED
GERMEN
GERMENS
GERMFREE
GERMICIDE
GERMIER
GERMIEST
GERMIN
GERMINA
GERMINAL
GERMINANT
GERMINATE
GERMINESS
GERMING
GERMINS
GERMLIKE
GERMPLASM
GERMPROOF
GERMS
GERMY
GERNE
GERNED
GERNES
GERNING
GERONIMO
GERONTIC
GEROPIGA
GEROPIGAS
GERT
GERTCHA

GERUND
GERUNDIAL
GERUNDIVE
GERUNDS
GESNERIA
GESNERIAD
GESNERIAS
GESSAMINE
GESSE
GESSED
GESSES
GESSING
GESSO
GESSOED
GESSOES
GEST
GESTALT
GESTALTEN
GESTALTS
GESTANT
GESTAPO
GESTAPOS
GESTATE
GESTATED
GESTATES
GESTATING
GESTATION
GESTATIVE
GESTATORY
GESTE
GESTES
GESTIC
GESTICAL
GESTS
GESTURAL
GESTURE
GESTURED
GESTURER
GESTURERS
GESTURES
GESTURING
GET
GETA
GETABLE
GETAS
GETATABLE
GETAWAY
GETAWAYS
GETS
GETTABLE
GETTER
GETTERED
GETTERING
GETTERS
GETTING
GETTINGS
GETUP
GETUPS

GEUM	GHI	GIBBING	GIFTEES
GEUMS	GHIBLI	GIBBON	GIFTING
GEWGAW	GHIBLIS	GIBBONS	GIFTLESS
GEWGAWED	GHILGAI	GIBBOSE	GIFTS
GEWGAWS	GHILGAIS	GIBBOSITY	GIFTSHOP
GEY	GHILLIE	GIBBOUS	GIFTSHOPS
GEYAN	GHILLIED	GIBBOUSLY	GIFTWARE
GEYER	GHILLIES	GIBBSITE	GIFTWARES
GEYEST	GHILLYING	GIBBSITES	GIFTWRAP
GEYSER	GHIS	GIBE	GIFTWRAPS
GEYSERITE	GHOST	GIBED	GIG
GEYSERS	GHOSTED	GIBEL	GIGA
GHARIAL	GHOSTIER	GIBELS	GIGABIT
GHARIALS	GHOSTIEST	GIBER	GIGABITS
GHARRI	GHOSTING	GIBERS	GIGABYTE
GHARRIES	GHOSTINGS	GIBES	GIGABYTES
GHARRIS	GHOSTLIER	GIBING	GIGACYCLE
GHARRY	GHOSTLIKE	GIBINGLY	GIGAFLOP
GHAST	GHOSTLY	GIBLET	GIGAFLOPS
GHASTED	GHOSTS	GIBLETS	GIGAHERTZ
GHASTFUL	GHOSTY	GIBLI	GIGANTEAN
GHASTING	GHOUL	GIBLIS	GIGANTIC
GHASTLIER	GHOULIE	GIBS	GIGANTISM
GHASTLY	GHOULIES	GIBSON	GIGAS
GHASTNESS	GHOULISH	GIBSONS	GIGATON
GHASTS	GHOULS	GIBUS	GIGATONS
GHAT	GHYLL	GIBUSES	GIGAWATT
GHATS	GHYLLS	GID	GIGAWATTS
GHAUT	GI	GIDDAP	GIGGED
GHAUTS	GIAMBEUX	GIDDAY	GIGGING
GHAZAL	GIANT	GIDDIED	GIGGIT
GHAZALS	GIANTESS	GIDDIER	GIGGITED
GHAZEL	GIANTHOOD	GIDDIES	GIGGITING
GHAZELS	GIANTISM	GIDDIEST	GIGGITS
GHAZI	GIANTISMS	GIDDILY	GIGGLE
GHAZIES	GIANTLIER	GIDDINESS	GIGGLED
GHAZIS	GIANTLIKE	GIDDUP	GIGGLER
GHEE	GIANTLY	GIDDY	GIGGLERS
GHEES	GIANTRIES	GIDDYAP	GIGGLES
GHERAO	GIANTRY	GIDDYING	GIGGLIER
GHERAOED	GIANTS	GIDDYUP	GIGGLIEST
GHERAOES	GIANTSHIP	GIDGEE	GIGGLING
GHERAOING	GIAOUR	GIDGEES	GIGGLINGS
GHERAOS	GIAOURS	GIDJEE	GIGGLY
GHERKIN	GIARDIA	GIDJEES	GIGHE
GHERKINS	GIARDIAS	GIDS	GIGLET
GHESSE	GIB	GIE	GIGLETS
GHESSED	GIBBED	GIED	GIGLOT
GHESSES	GIBBER	GIEING	GIGLOTS
GHESSING	GIBBERED	GIEN	GIGMAN
GHEST	GIBBERING	GIES	GIGMANITY
GHETTO	GIBBERISH	GIF	GIGMEN
GHETTOED	GIBBERS	GIFT	GIGOLO
GHETTOES	GIBBET	GIFTABLE	GIGOLOS
GHETTOING	GIBBETED	GIFTABLES	GIGOT
GHETTOISE	GIBBETING	GIFTED	GIGOTS
GHETTOIZE	GIBBETS	GIFTEDLY	GIGS
GHETTOS	GIBBETTED	GIFTEE	GIGUE

GIGUES	GILTS	GINGERLY	GIPPERS
GILA	GILTWOOD	GINGEROUS	GIPPIES
GILAS	GIMBAL	GINGERS	GIPPING
GILBERT	GIMBALED	GINGERY	GIPPO
GILBERTS	GIMBALING	GINGES	GIPPOES
GILCUP	GIMBALLED	GINGHAM	GIPPOS
GILCUPS	GIMBALS	GINGHAMS	GIPPY
GILD	GIMCRACK	GINGILI	GIPS
GILDED	GIMCRACKS	GINGILIS	GIPSEN
GILDEN	GIMEL	GINGILLI	GIPSENS
GILDER	GIMELS	GINGILLIS	GIPSIED
GILDERS	GIMLET	GINGIVA	GIPSIES
GILDHALL	GIMLETED	GINGIVAE	GIPSY
GILDHALLS	GIMLETING	GINGIVAL	GIPSYDOM
GILDING	GIMLETS	GINGKO	GIPSYDOMS
GILDINGS	GIMMAL	GINGKOES	GIPSYHOOD
GILDS	GIMMALLED	GINGKOS	GIPSYING
GILDSMAN	GIMMALS	GINGLE	GIPSYISH
GILDSMEN	GIMME	GINGLES	GIPSYWORT
GILET	GIMMER	GINGLYMI	GIRAFFE
GILETS	GIMMERS	GINGLYMUS	GIRAFFES
GILGAI	GIMMES	GINGS	GIRAFFID
GILGAIS	GIMMICK	GINHOUSE	GIRAFFINE
GILGIE	GIMMICKED	GINHOUSES	GIRAFFISH
GILGIES	GIMMICKRY	GINK	GIRAFFOID
GILL	GIMMICKS	GINKGO	GIRANDOLA
GILLAROO	GIMMICKY	GINKGOES	GIRANDOLE
GILLAROOS	GIMMIE	GINKGOS	GIRASOL
GILLED	GIMMIES	GINKS	GIRASOLE
GILLER	GIMMOR	GINN	GIRASOLES
GILLERS	GIMMORS	GINNED	GIRASOLS
GILLET	GIMP	GINNEL	GIRD
GILLETS	GIMPED	GINNELS	GIRDED
GILLFLIRT	GIMPIER	GINNER	GIRDER
GILLIE	GIMPIEST	GINNERIES	GIRDERS
GILLIED	GIMPING	GINNERS	GIRDING
GILLIES	GIMPS	GINNERY	GIRDINGLY
GILLING	GIMPY	GINNIER	GIRDINGS
GILLION	GIN	GINNIEST	GIRDLE
GILLIONS	GING	GINNING	GIRDLED
GILLNET	GINGAL	GINNINGS	GIRDLER
GILLNETS	GINGALL	GINNY	GIRDLERS
GILLS	GINGALLS	GINORMOUS	GIRDLES
GILLY	GINGALS	GINS	GIRDLING
GILLYING	GINGE	GINSENG	GIRDS
GILLYVOR	GINGELEY	GINSENGS	GIRKIN
GILLYVORS	GINGELEYS	GINSHOP	GIRKINS
GILPEY	GINGELI	GINSHOPS	GIRL
GILPEYS	GINGELIES	GINZO	GIRLHOOD
GILPIES	GINGELIS	GINZOES	GIRLHOODS
GILPY	GINGELLI	GIO	GIRLIE
GILRAVAGE	GINGELLIS	GIOCOSO	GIRLIER
GILSONITE	GINGELLY	GIOS	GIRLIES
GILT	GINGELY	GIP	GIRLIEST
GILTCUP	GINGER	GIPON	GIRLISH
GILTCUPS	GINGERADE	GIPONS	GIRLISHLY
GILTHEAD	GINGERED	GIPPED	GIRLOND
GILTHEADS	GINGERING	GIPPER	GIRLONDS

GIRLS	GITTERN	GLACIERS	GLAIRS
GIRLY	GITTERNED	GLACIS	GLAIRY
GIRN	GITTERNS	GLACISES	GLAIVE
GIRNED	GITTIN	GLAD	GLAIVED
GIRNEL	GITTING	GLADDED	GLAIVES
GIRNELS	GIUST	GLADDEN	GLAM
GIRNER	GIUSTED	GLADDENED	GLAMOR
GIRNERS	GIUSTING	GLADDENER	GLAMORED
GIRNIE	GIUSTO	GLADDENS	GLAMORING
GIRNIER	GIUSTS	GLADDER	GLAMORISE
GIRNIEST	GIVABLE	GLADDEST	GLAMORIZE
GIRNING	GIVE	GLADDIE	GLAMOROUS
GIRNS	GIVEABLE	GLADDIES	GLAMORS
GIRO	GIVEAWAY	GLADDING	GLAMOUR
GIROLLE	GIVEAWAYS	GLADDON	GLAMOURED
GIROLLES	GIVEBACK	GLADDONS	GLAMOURS
GIRON	GIVEBACKS	GLADE	GLAMS
GIRONIC	GIVED	GLADELIKE	GLANCE
GIRONNY	GIVEN	GLADES	GLANCED
GIRONS	GIVENNESS	GLADFUL	GLANCER
GIROS	GIVENS	GLADIATE	GLANCERS
GIROSOL	GIVER	GLADIATOR	GLANCES
GIROSOLS	GIVERS	GLADIER	GLANCING
GIRR	GIVES	GLADIEST	GLANCINGS
GIRRS	GIVING	GLADIOLA	GLAND
GIRSH	GIVINGS	GLADIOLAR	GLANDERED
GIRSHES	GIZMO	GLADIOLAS	GLANDERS
GIRT	GIZMOLOGY	GLADIOLE	GLANDES
GIRTED	GIZMOS	GLADIOLES	GLANDLESS
GIRTH	GIZZ	GLADIOLI	GLANDLIKE
GIRTHED	GIZZARD	GLADIOLUS	GLANDS
GIRTHING	GIZZARDS	GLADIUS	GLANDULAR
GIRTHLINE	GIZZEN	GLADIUSES	GLANDULE
GIRTHS	GIZZENED	GLADLIER	GLANDULES
GIRTING	GIZZENING	GLADLIEST	GLANS
GIRTLINE	GIZZENS	GLADLY	GLARE
GIRTLINES	GIZZES	GLADNESS	GLAREAL
GIRTS	GJETOST	GLADS	GLARED
GIS	GJETOSTS	GLADSOME	GLARELESS
GISARME	GJU	GLADSOMER	GLAREOUS
GISARMES	GJUS	GLADSTONE	GLARES
GISM	GLABELLA	GLADWRAP	GLARIER
GISMO	GLABELLAE	GLADWRAPS	GLARIEST
GISMOLOGY	GLABELLAR	GLADY	GLARINESS
GISMOS	GLABRATE	GLAIK	GLARING
GISMS	GLABROUS	GLAIKET	GLARINGLY
GIST	GLACE	GLAIKIT	GLARY
GISTS	GLACEED	GLAIKS	GLASNOST
GIT	GLACEING	GLAIR	GLASNOSTS
GITANA	GLACES	GLAIRE	GLASS
GITANAS	GLACIAL	GLAIRED	GLASSED
GITANO	GLACIALLY	GLAIREOUS	GLASSEN
GITANOS	GLACIALS	GLAIRES	GLASSES
GITE	GLACIATE	GLAIRIER	GLASSFUL
GITES	GLACIATED	GLAIRIEST	GLASSFULS
GITS	GLACIATES	GLAIRIN	GLASSIE
GITTARONE	GLACIER	GLAIRING	GLASSIER
GITTED	GLACIERED	GLAIRINS	GLASSIES

GLASSIEST	GLEANINGS	GLENTING	GLIMPSING
GLASSIFY	GLEANS	GLENTS	GLIMS
GLASSILY	GLEAVE	GLEY	GLINT
GLASSINE	GLEAVES	GLEYED	GLINTED
GLASSINES	GLEBA	GLEYING	GLINTIER
GLASSING	GLEBAE	GLEYINGS	GLINTIEST
GLASSLESS	GLEBE	GLEYS	GLINTING
GLASSLIKE	GLEBELESS	GLIA	GLINTS
GLASSMAN	GLEBES	GLIADIN	GLINTY
GLASSMEN	GLEBOUS	GLIADINE	GLIOMA
GLASSWARE	GLEBY	GLIADINES	GLIOMAS
GLASSWORK	GLED	GLIADINS	GLIOMATA
GLASSWORM	GLEDE	GLIAL	GLIOSES
GLASSWORT	GLEDES	GLIAS	GLIOSIS
GLASSY	GLEDGE	GLIB	GLISK
GLAUCOMA	GLEDGED	GLIBBED	GLISKS
GLAUCOMAS	GLEDGES	GLIBBER	GLISSADE
GLAUCOUS	GLEDGING	GLIBBERY	GLISSADED
GLAUM	GLEDS	GLIBBEST	GLISSADER
GLAUMED	GLEE	GLIBBING	GLISSADES
GLAUMING	GLEED	GLIBLY	GLISSANDI
GLAUMS	GLEEDS	GLIBNESS	GLISSANDO
GLAUR	GLEEFUL	GLIBS	GLISTEN
GLAURIER	GLEEFULLY	GLID	GLISTENED
GLAURIEST	GLEEING	GLIDDER	GLISTENS
GLAURS	GLEEK	GLIDDERY	GLISTER
GLAURY	GLEEKED	GLIDDEST	GLISTERED
GLAZE	GLEEKING	GLIDE	GLISTERS
GLAZED	GLEEKS	GLIDED	GLIT
GLAZEN	GLEEMAN	GLIDEPATH	GLITCH
GLAZER	GLEEMEN	GLIDER	GLITCHES
GLAZERS	GLEENIE	GLIDERS	GLITCHIER
GLAZES	GLEENIES	GLIDES	GLITCHY
GLAZIER	GLEES	GLIDING	GLITS
GLAZIERS	GLEESOME	GLIDINGLY	GLITTER
GLAZIERY	GLEET	GLIDINGS	GLITTERED
GLAZIEST	GLEETED	GLIFF	GLITTERS
GLAZILY	GLEETIER	GLIFFING	GLITTERY
GLAZINESS	GLEETIEST	GLIFFINGS	GLITZ
GLAZING	GLEETING	GLIFFS	GLITZED
GLAZINGS	GLEETS	GLIFT	GLITZES
GLAZY	GLEETY	GLIFTS	GLITZIER
GLEAM	GLEG	GLIKE	GLITZIEST
GLEAMED	GLEGGER	GLIKES	GLITZILY
GLEAMER	GLEGGEST	GLIM	GLITZING
GLEAMERS	GLEGLY	GLIME	GLITZY
GLEAMIER	GLEGNESS	GLIMED	GLOAM
GLEAMIEST	GLEI	GLIMES	GLOAMING
GLEAMING	GLEIS	GLIMING	GLOAMINGS
GLEAMINGS	GLEN	GLIMMER	GLOAMS
GLEAMS	GLENGARRY	GLIMMERED	GLOAT
GLEAMY	GLENLIKE	GLIMMERS	GLOATED
GLEAN	GLENOID	GLIMMERY	GLOATER
GLEANABLE	GLENOIDAL	GLIMPSE	GLOATERS
GLEANED	GLENOIDS	GLIMPSED	GLOATING
GLEANER	GLENS	GLIMPSER	GLOATS
GLEANERS	GLENT	GLIMPSERS	GLOB
GLEANING	GLENTED	GLIMPSES	GLOBAL

GLOBALISE
GLOBALISM
GLOBALIST
GLOBALIZE
GLOBALLY
GLOBATE
GLOBATED
GLOBBIER
GLOBBIEST
GLOBBY
GLOBE
GLOBED
GLOBEFISH
GLOBELIKE
GLOBES
GLOBESITY
GLOBETROT
GLOBI
GLOBIN
GLOBING
GLOBINS
GLOBOID
GLOBOIDS
GLOBOSE
GLOBOSELY
GLOBOSES
GLOBOSITY
GLOBOUS
GLOBS
GLOBULAR
GLOBULARS
GLOBULE
GLOBULES
GLOBULET
GLOBULETS
GLOBULIN
GLOBULINS
GLOBULITE
GLOBULOUS
GLOBUS
GLOBY
GLOCHID
GLOCHIDIA
GLOCHIDS
GLODE
GLOGG
GLOGGS
GLOIRE
GLOIRES
GLOM
GLOMERA
GLOMERATE
GLOMERULE
GLOMERULI
GLOMMED
GLOMMING
GLOMS
GLOMUS

GLONOIN
GLONOINS
GLOOM
GLOOMED
GLOOMFUL
GLOOMIER
GLOOMIEST
GLOOMILY
GLOOMING
GLOOMINGS
GLOOMLESS
GLOOMS
GLOOMY
GLOOP
GLOOPED
GLOOPIER
GLOOPIEST
GLOOPING
GLOOPS
GLOOPY
GLOP
GLOPPED
GLOPPIER
GLOPPIEST
GLOPPING
GLOPPY
GLOPS
GLORIA
GLORIAS
GLORIED
GLORIES
GLORIFIED
GLORIFIER
GLORIFIES
GLORIFY
GLORIOLE
GLORIOLES
GLORIOSA
GLORIOSAS
GLORIOUS
GLORY
GLORYING
GLOSS
GLOSSA
GLOSSAE
GLOSSAL
GLOSSARY
GLOSSAS
GLOSSATOR
GLOSSED
GLOSSEME
GLOSSEMES
GLOSSER
GLOSSERS
GLOSSES
GLOSSIER
GLOSSIES
GLOSSIEST

GLOSSILY
GLOSSINA
GLOSSINAS
GLOSSING
GLOSSIST
GLOSSISTS
GLOSSITIC
GLOSSITIS
GLOSSLESS
GLOSSY
GLOST
GLOSTS
GLOTTAL
GLOTTIC
GLOTTIDES
GLOTTIS
GLOTTISES
GLOUT
GLOUTED
GLOUTING
GLOUTS
GLOVE
GLOVED
GLOVELESS
GLOVER
GLOVERS
GLOVES
GLOVING
GLOVINGS
GLOW
GLOWED
GLOWER
GLOWERED
GLOWERING
GLOWERS
GLOWFLIES
GLOWFLY
GLOWING
GLOWINGLY
GLOWLAMP
GLOWLAMPS
GLOWS
GLOWSTICK
GLOWWORM
GLOWWORMS
GLOXINIA
GLOXINIAS
GLOZE
GLOZED
GLOZES
GLOZING
GLOZINGS
GLUCAGON
GLUCAGONS
GLUCAN
GLUCANS
GLUCINA
GLUCINAS

GLUCINIC
GLUCINIUM
GLUCINUM
GLUCINUMS
GLUCONATE
GLUCOSE
GLUCOSES
GLUCOSIC
GLUCOSIDE
GLUE
GLUED
GLUEING
GLUELIKE
GLUEPOT
GLUEPOTS
GLUER
GLUERS
GLUES
GLUEY
GLUEYNESS
GLUG
GLUGGABLE
GLUGGED
GLUGGING
GLUGS
GLUHWEIN
GLUHWEINS
GLUIER
GLUIEST
GLUILY
GLUINESS
GLUING
GLUISH
GLUM
GLUME
GLUMELIKE
GLUMELLA
GLUMELLAS
GLUMES
GLUMLY
GLUMMER
GLUMMEST
GLUMNESS
GLUMPIER
GLUMPIEST
GLUMPILY
GLUMPISH
GLUMPS
GLUMPY
GLUMS
GLUNCH
GLUNCHED
GLUNCHES
GLUNCHING
GLUON
GLUONS
GLURGE
GLURGES

GLUT
GLUTAEAL
GLUTAEI
GLUTAEUS
GLUTAMATE
GLUTAMIC
GLUTAMINE
GLUTE
GLUTEAL
GLUTEI
GLUTELIN
GLUTELINS
GLUTEN
GLUTENIN
GLUTENINS
GLUTENOUS
GLUTENS
GLUTES
GLUTEUS
GLUTINOUS
GLUTS
GLUTTED
GLUTTING
GLUTTON
GLUTTONS
GLUTTONY
GLYCAEMIA
GLYCAEMIC
GLYCAN
GLYCANS
GLYCEMIA
GLYCEMIAS
GLYCEMIC
GLYCERIA
GLYCERIAS
GLYCERIC
GLYCERIDE
GLYCERIN
GLYCERINE
GLYCERINS
GLYCEROL
GLYCEROLS
GLYCERYL
GLYCERYLS
GLYCIN
GLYCINE
GLYCINES
GLYCINS
GLYCOCOLL
GLYCOGEN
GLYCOGENS
GLYCOL
GLYCOLIC
GLYCOLLIC
GLYCOLS
GLYCONIC
GLYCONICS
GLYCOSE

GLYCOSES
GLYCOSIDE
GLYCOSYL
GLYCOSYLS
GLYCYL
GLYCYLS
GLYPH
GLYPHIC
GLYPHS
GLYPTAL
GLYPTALS
GLYPTIC
GLYPTICS
GMELINITE
GNAMMA
GNAR
GNARL
GNARLED
GNARLIER
GNARLIEST
GNARLING
GNARLS
GNARLY
GNARR
GNARRED
GNARRING
GNARRS
GNARS
GNASH
GNASHED
GNASHER
GNASHERS
GNASHES
GNASHING
GNAT
GNATHAL
GNATHIC
GNATHION
GNATHIONS
GNATHITE
GNATHITES
GNATHONIC
GNATLIKE
GNATLING
GNATLINGS
GNATS
GNATTIER
GNATTIEST
GNATTY
GNAW
GNAWABLE
GNAWED
GNAWER
GNAWERS
GNAWING
GNAWINGLY
GNAWINGS
GNAWN

GNAWS
GNEISS
GNEISSES
GNEISSIC
GNEISSOID
GNEISSOSE
GNOCCHI
GNOCCHIS
GNOMAE
GNOME
GNOMELIKE
GNOMES
GNOMIC
GNOMICAL
GNOMISH
GNOMIST
GNOMISTS
GNOMON
GNOMONIC
GNOMONICS
GNOMONS
GNOSES
GNOSIS
GNOSTIC
GNOSTICAL
GNOSTICS
GNOW
GNOWS
GNU
GNUS
GO
GOA
GOAD
GOADED
GOADING
GOADLIKE
GOADS
GOADSMAN
GOADSMEN
GOADSTER
GOADSTERS
GOAF
GOAFS
GOAL
GOALBALL
GOALBALLS
GOALED
GOALIE
GOALIES
GOALING
GOALLESS
GOALMOUTH
GOALPOST
GOALPOSTS
GOALS
GOALWARD
GOANNA
GOANNAS

GOARY
GOAS
GOAT
GOATEE
GOATEED
GOATEES
GOATFISH
GOATHERD
GOATHERDS
GOATIER
GOATIEST
GOATISH
GOATISHLY
GOATLIKE
GOATLING
GOATLINGS
GOATS
GOATSKIN
GOATSKINS
GOATWEED
GOATWEEDS
GOATY
GOB
GOBAN
GOBANG
GOBANGS
GOBANS
GOBBED
GOBBELINE
GOBBET
GOBBETS
GOBBI
GOBBIER
GOBBIEST
GOBBING
GOBBLE
GOBBLED
GOBBLER
GOBBLERS
GOBBLES
GOBBLING
GOBBO
GOBBY
GOBIES
GOBIID
GOBIIDS
GOBIOID
GOBIOIDS
GOBLET
GOBLETS
GOBLIN
GOBLINS
GOBO
GOBOES
GOBONEE
GOBONY
GOBOS
GOBS

GOBSHITE
GOBSHITES
GOBURRA
GOBURRAS
GOBY
GOD
GODCHILD
GODDAM
GODDAMMED
GODDAMN
GODDAMNED
GODDAMNS
GODDAMS
GODDED
GODDEN
GODDENS
GODDESS
GODDESSES
GODDING
GODET
GODETIA
GODETIAS
GODETS
GODFATHER
GODHEAD
GODHEADS
GODHOOD
GODHOODS
GODLESS
GODLESSLY
GODLIER
GODLIEST
GODLIKE
GODLILY
GODLINESS
GODLING
GODLINGS
GODLY
GODMOTHER
GODOWN
GODOWNS
GODPARENT
GODROON
GODROONED
GODROONS
GODS
GODSEND
GODSENDS
GODSHIP
GODSHIPS
GODSLOT
GODSLOTS
GODSO
GODSON
GODSONS
GODSOS
GODSPEED
GODSPEEDS

GODSQUAD
GODSQUADS
GODWARD
GODWARDS
GODWIT
GODWITS
GOE
GOEL
GOELS
GOER
GOERS
GOES
GOETHITE
GOETHITES
GOETIC
GOETIES
GOETY
GOEY
GOFER
GOFERS
GOFF
GOFFED
GOFFER
GOFFERED
GOFFERING
GOFFERS
GOFFING
GOFFS
GOGGA
GOGGAS
GOGGLE
GOGGLEBOX
GOGGLED
GOGGLER
GOGGLERS
GOGGLES
GOGGLIER
GOGGLIEST
GOGGLING
GOGGLINGS
GOGGLY
GOGLET
GOGLETS
GOGO
GOGOS
GOHONZON
GOHONZONS
GOIER
GOIEST
GOING
GOINGS
GOITER
GOITERED
GOITERS
GOITRE
GOITRED
GOITRES
GOITROGEN

GOITROUS
GOLCONDA
GOLCONDAS
GOLD
GOLDARN
GOLDARNS
GOLDBRICK
GOLDBUG
GOLDBUGS
GOLDCREST
GOLDEN
GOLDENED
GOLDENER
GOLDENEST
GOLDENEYE
GOLDENING
GOLDENLY
GOLDENROD
GOLDENS
GOLDER
GOLDEST
GOLDEYE
GOLDEYES
GOLDFIELD
GOLDFINCH
GOLDFINNY
GOLDFISH
GOLDIER
GOLDIEST
GOLDISH
GOLDLESS
GOLDMINER
GOLDS
GOLDSINNY
GOLDSIZE
GOLDSIZES
GOLDSMITH
GOLDSPINK
GOLDSTICK
GOLDSTONE
GOLDTAIL
GOLDTONE
GOLDURN
GOLDURNS
GOLDY
GOLE
GOLEM
GOLEMS
GOLES
GOLF
GOLFED
GOLFER
GOLFERS
GOLFIANA
GOLFIANAS
GOLFING
GOLFINGS
GOLFS

GOLGOTHA
GOLGOTHAS
GOLIARD
GOLIARDIC
GOLIARDS
GOLIARDY
GOLIAS
GOLIASED
GOLIASES
GOLIASING
GOLIATH
GOLIATHS
GOLLAN
GOLLAND
GOLLANDS
GOLLANS
GOLLAR
GOLLARED
GOLLARING
GOLLARS
GOLLER
GOLLERED
GOLLERING
GOLLERS
GOLLIED
GOLLIES
GOLLIWOG
GOLLIWOGG
GOLLIWOGS
GOLLOP
GOLLOPED
GOLLOPER
GOLLOPERS
GOLLOPING
GOLLOPS
GOLLY
GOLLYING
GOLLYWOG
GOLLYWOGS
GOLOMYNKA
GOLOSH
GOLOSHE
GOLOSHED
GOLOSHES
GOLOSHING
GOLOSHOES
GOLP
GOLPE
GOLPES
GOLPS
GOMBEEN
GOMBEENS
GOMBO
GOMBOS
GOMBRO
GOMBROON
GOMBROONS
GOMBROS

GOMER
GOMERAL
GOMERALS
GOMEREL
GOMERELS
GOMERIL
GOMERILS
GOMERS
GOMOKU
GOMOKUS
GOMPA
GOMPAS
GOMPHOSES
GOMPHOSIS
GOMUTI
GOMUTIS
GOMUTO
GOMUTOS
GON
GONAD
GONADAL
GONADIAL
GONADIC
GONADS
GONDELAY
GONDELAYS
GONDOLA
GONDOLAS
GONDOLIER
GONE
GONEF
GONEFS
GONENESS
GONER
GONERS
GONFALON
GONFALONS
GONFANON
GONFANONS
GONG
GONGED
GONGING
GONGLIKE
GONGS
GONGSTER
GONGSTERS
GONGYO
GONGYOS
GONIA
GONIATITE
GONIDIA
GONIDIAL
GONIDIC
GONIDIUM
GONIF
GONIFF
GONIFFS
GONIFS

GONION
GONIUM
GONK
GONKS
GONNA
GONOCOCCI
GONOCYTE
GONOCYTES
GONODUCT
GONODUCTS
GONOF
GONOFS
GONOPH
GONOPHORE
GONOPHS
GONOPOD
GONOPODS
GONOPORE
GONOPORES
GONORRHEA
GONOSOME
GONOSOMES
GONS
GONYS
GONYSES
GONZO
GOO
GOOBER
GOOBERS
GOOBIES
GOOBY
GOOD
GOODBY
GOODBYE
GOODBYES
GOODBYS
GOODFACED
GOODIE
GOODIER
GOODIES
GOODIEST
GOODINESS
GOODISH
GOODLIER
GOODLIEST
GOODLY
GOODMAN
GOODMEN
GOODNESS
GOODNIGHT
GOODS
GOODSIRE
GOODSIRES
GOODTIME
GOODWIFE
GOODWILL
GOODWILLS
GOODWIVES

GOODY
GOODYEAR
GOODYEARS
GOOEY
GOOEYNESS
GOOF
GOOFBALL
GOOFBALLS
GOOFED
GOOFIER
GOOFIEST
GOOFILY
GOOFINESS
GOOFING
GOOFS
GOOFY
GOOG
GOOGLE
GOOGLED
GOOGLES
GOOGLIES
GOOGLING
GOOGLY
GOOGOL
GOOGOLS
GOOGS
GOOIER
GOOIEST
GOOILY
GOOK
GOOKS
GOOKY
GOOL
GOOLD
GOOLDS
GOOLEY
GOOLEYS
GOOLIE
GOOLIES
GOOLS
GOOLY
GOOMBAH
GOOMBAHS
GOOMBAY
GOOMBAYS
GOON
GOONDA
GOONDAS
GOONEY
GOONEYS
GOONIE
GOONIER
GOONIES
GOONIEST
GOONS
GOONY
GOOP
GOOPIER

GOOPIEST
GOOPS
GOOPY
GOOR
GOORAL
GOORALS
GOORIE
GOORIES
GOOROO
GOOROOS
GOORS
GOORY
GOOS
GOOSANDER
GOOSE
GOOSED
GOOSEFISH
GOOSEFOOT
GOOSEGOB
GOOSEGOBS
GOOSEGOG
GOOSEGOGS
GOOSEHERD
GOOSENECK
GOOSERIES
GOOSERY
GOOSES
GOOSEY
GOOSEYS
GOOSIER
GOOSIES
GOOSIEST
GOOSINESS
GOOSING
GOOSY
GOPAK
GOPAKS
GOPHER
GOPHERED
GOPHERING
GOPHERS
GOPIK
GOPURA
GOPURAM
GOPURAMS
GOPURAS
GOR
GORA
GORAL
GORALS
GORAMIES
GORAMY
GORAS
GORBELLY
GORBLIMEY
GORBLIMY
GORCOCK
GORCOCKS

247

GORCROW
GORCROWS
GORDITA
GORDITAS
GORE
GORED
GOREHOUND
GORES
GORGE
GORGEABLE
GORGED
GORGEDLY
GORGEOUS
GORGER
GORGERIN
GORGERINS
GORGERS
GORGES
GORGET
GORGETED
GORGETS
GORGIA
GORGIAS
GORGING
GORGIO
GORGIOS
GORGON
GORGONEIA
GORGONIAN
GORGONISE
GORGONIZE
GORGONS
GORHEN
GORHENS
GORI
GORIER
GORIEST
GORILLA
GORILLAS
GORILLIAN
GORILLINE
GORILLOID
GORILY
GORINESS
GORING
GORINGS
GORIS
GORM
GORMAND
GORMANDS
GORMED
GORMIER
GORMIEST
GORMING
GORMLESS
GORMS
GORMY
GORP

GORPED
GORPING
GORPS
GORSE
GORSEDD
GORSEDDS
GORSES
GORSIER
GORSIEST
GORSOON
GORSOONS
GORSY
GORY
GOS
GOSH
GOSHAWK
GOSHAWKS
GOSHT
GOSHTS
GOSLARITE
GOSLET
GOSLETS
GOSLING
GOSLINGS
GOSPEL
GOSPELER
GOSPELERS
GOSPELISE
GOSPELIZE
GOSPELLED
GOSPELLER
GOSPELLY
GOSPELS
GOSPODA
GOSPODAR
GOSPODARS
GOSPODIN
GOSPORT
GOSPORTS
GOSS
GOSSAMER
GOSSAMERS
GOSSAMERY
GOSSAN
GOSSANS
GOSSE
GOSSED
GOSSES
GOSSIB
GOSSIBS
GOSSING
GOSSIP
GOSSIPED
GOSSIPER
GOSSIPERS
GOSSIPING
GOSSIPPED
GOSSIPPER

GOSSIPRY
GOSSIPS
GOSSIPY
GOSSOON
GOSSOONS
GOSSYPINE
GOSSYPOL
GOSSYPOLS
GOSTER
GOSTERED
GOSTERING
GOSTERS
GOT
GOTCHA
GOTCHAS
GOTH
GOTHIC
GOTHICISE
GOTHICISM
GOTHICIZE
GOTHICS
GOTHITE
GOTHITES
GOTHS
GOTTA
GOTTEN
GOUACHE
GOUACHES
GOUGE
GOUGED
GOUGER
GOUGERE
GOUGERES
GOUGERS
GOUGES
GOUGING
GOUJEERS
GOUJON
GOUJONS
GOUK
GOUKS
GOULASH
GOULASHES
GOURA
GOURAMI
GOURAMIES
GOURAMIS
GOURAS
GOURD
GOURDE
GOURDES
GOURDIER
GOURDIEST
GOURDLIKE
GOURDS
GOURDY
GOURMAND
GOURMANDS

GOURMET
GOURMETS
GOUSTIER
GOUSTIEST
GOUSTROUS
GOUSTY
GOUT
GOUTFLIES
GOUTFLY
GOUTIER
GOUTIEST
GOUTILY
GOUTINESS
GOUTS
GOUTTE
GOUTTES
GOUTWEED
GOUTWEEDS
GOUTWORT
GOUTWORTS
GOUTY
GOV
GOVERN
GOVERNALL
GOVERNED
GOVERNESS
GOVERNING
GOVERNOR
GOVERNORS
GOVERNS
GOVS
GOWAN
GOWANED
GOWANS
GOWANY
GOWD
GOWDER
GOWDEST
GOWDS
GOWDSPINK
GOWF
GOWFED
GOWFER
GOWFERS
GOWFING
GOWFS
GOWK
GOWKS
GOWL
GOWLAN
GOWLAND
GOWLANDS
GOWLANS
GOWLED
GOWLING
GOWLS
GOWN
GOWNBOY

GOWNBOYS	GRADATE	GRAFTING	GRAMP
GOWNED	GRADATED	GRAFTINGS	GRAMPA
GOWNING	GRADATES	GRAFTS	GRAMPAS
GOWNMAN	GRADATIM	GRAHAM	GRAMPS
GOWNMEN	GRADATING	GRAHAMS	GRAMPUS
GOWNS	GRADATION	GRAIL	GRAMPUSES
GOWNSMAN	GRADATORY	GRAILE	GRAMS
GOWNSMEN	GRADDAN	GRAILES	GRAN
GOWPEN	GRADDANED	GRAILS	GRANA
GOWPENFUL	GRADDANS	GRAIN	GRANARIES
GOWPENS	GRADE	GRAINAGE	GRANARY
GOX	GRADED	GRAINAGES	GRAND
GOXES	GRADELESS	GRAINE	GRANDAD
GOY	GRADELIER	GRAINED	GRANDADDY
GOYIM	GRADELY	GRAINER	GRANDADS
GOYISCH	GRADER	GRAINERS	GRANDAM
GOYISH	GRADERS	GRAINES	GRANDAME
GOYS	GRADES	GRAINIER	GRANDAMES
GOZZAN	GRADIENT	GRAINIEST	GRANDAMS
GOZZANS	GRADIENTS	GRAINING	GRANDAUNT
GRAAL	GRADIN	GRAININGS	GRANDBABY
GRAALS	GRADINE	GRAINLESS	GRANDDAD
GRAB	GRADINES	GRAINS	GRANDDADS
GRABBABLE	GRADING	GRAINY	GRANDDAM
GRABBED	GRADINI	GRAIP	GRANDDAMS
GRABBER	GRADINO	GRAIPS	GRANDE
GRABBERS	GRADINS	GRAITH	GRANDEE
GRABBIER	GRADS	GRAITHED	GRANDEES
GRABBIEST	GRADUAL	GRAITHING	GRANDER
GRABBING	GRADUALLY	GRAITHLY	GRANDEST
GRABBLE	GRADUALS	GRAITHS	GRANDEUR
GRABBLED	GRADUAND	GRAKLE	GRANDEURS
GRABBLER	GRADUANDS	GRAKLES	GRANDIOSE
GRABBLERS	GRADUATE	GRALLOCH	GRANDIOSO
GRABBLES	GRADUATED	GRALLOCHS	GRANDKID
GRABBLING	GRADUATES	GRAM	GRANDKIDS
GRABBY	GRADUATOR	GRAMA	GRANDLY
GRABEN	GRADUS	GRAMARIES	GRANDMA
GRABENS	GRADUSES	GRAMARY	GRANDMAMA
GRABS	GRAECISE	GRAMARYE	GRANDMAS
GRACE	GRAECISED	GRAMARYES	GRANDNESS
GRACED	GRAECISES	GRAMAS	GRANDPA
GRACEFUL	GRAECIZE	GRAMASH	GRANDPAPA
GRACELESS	GRAECIZED	GRAMASHES	GRANDPAS
GRACES	GRAECIZES	GRAME	GRANDS
GRACILE	GRAFF	GRAMERCY	GRANDSIR
GRACILES	GRAFFED	GRAMES	GRANDSIRE
GRACILIS	GRAFFING	GRAMMA	GRANDSIRS
GRACILITY	GRAFFITI	GRAMMAGE	GRANDSON
GRACING	GRAFFITIS	GRAMMAGES	GRANDSONS
GRACIOSO	GRAFFITO	GRAMMAR	GRANFER
GRACIOSOS	GRAFFS	GRAMMARS	GRANFERS
GRACIOUS	GRAFT	GRAMMAS	GRANGE
GRACKLE	GRAFTAGE	GRAMMATIC	GRANGER
GRACKLES	GRAFTAGES	GRAMME	GRANGERS
GRAD	GRAFTED	GRAMMES	GRANGES
GRADABLE	GRAFTER	GRAMOCHE	GRANITA
GRADABLES	GRAFTERS	GRAMOCHES	GRANITAS

GRANITE
GRANITES
GRANITIC
GRANITISE
GRANITITE
GRANITIZE
GRANITOID
GRANIVORE
GRANNAM
GRANNAMS
GRANNIE
GRANNIED
GRANNIES
GRANNOM
GRANNOMS
GRANNY
GRANNYING
GRANNYISH
GRANOLA
GRANOLAS
GRANOLITH
GRANS
GRANT
GRANTABLE
GRANTED
GRANTEE
GRANTEES
GRANTER
GRANTERS
GRANTING
GRANTOR
GRANTORS
GRANTS
GRANTSMAN
GRANTSMEN
GRANULAR
GRANULARY
GRANULATE
GRANULE
GRANULES
GRANULITE
GRANULOMA
GRANULOSE
GRANULOUS
GRANUM
GRAPE
GRAPED
GRAPELESS
GRAPELIKE
GRAPERIES
GRAPERY
GRAPES
GRAPESEED
GRAPESHOT
GRAPETREE
GRAPEVINE
GRAPEY
GRAPH

GRAPHED
GRAPHEME
GRAPHEMES
GRAPHEMIC
GRAPHIC
GRAPHICAL
GRAPHICLY
GRAPHICS
GRAPHING
GRAPHITE
GRAPHITES
GRAPHITIC
GRAPHIUM
GRAPHIUMS
GRAPHS
GRAPIER
GRAPIEST
GRAPINESS
GRAPING
GRAPLE
GRAPLES
GRAPLIN
GRAPLINE
GRAPLINES
GRAPLINS
GRAPNEL
GRAPNELS
GRAPPA
GRAPPAS
GRAPPLE
GRAPPLED
GRAPPLER
GRAPPLERS
GRAPPLES
GRAPPLING
GRAPY
GRASP
GRASPABLE
GRASPED
GRASPER
GRASPERS
GRASPING
GRASPLESS
GRASPS
GRASS
GRASSED
GRASSER
GRASSERS
GRASSES
GRASSHOOK
GRASSIER
GRASSIEST
GRASSILY
GRASSING
GRASSINGS
GRASSLAND
GRASSLESS
GRASSLIKE

GRASSPLOT
GRASSQUIT
GRASSROOT
GRASSUM
GRASSUMS
GRASSY
GRASTE
GRAT
GRATE
GRATED
GRATEFUL
GRATELESS
GRATER
GRATERS
GRATES
GRATICULE
GRATIFIED
GRATIFIER
GRATIFIES
GRATIFY
GRATIN
GRATINATE
GRATINE
GRATINEE
GRATINEED
GRATINEES
GRATING
GRATINGLY
GRATINGS
GRATINS
GRATIS
GRATITUDE
GRATTOIR
GRATTOIRS
GRATUITY
GRATULANT
GRATULATE
GRAUNCH
GRAUNCHED
GRAUNCHER
GRAUNCHES
GRAUPEL
GRAUPELS
GRAV
GRAVADLAX
GRAVAMEN
GRAVAMENS
GRAVAMINA
GRAVE
GRAVED
GRAVEL
GRAVELED
GRAVELESS
GRAVELIKE
GRAVELING
GRAVELISH
GRAVELLED
GRAVELLY

GRAVELS
GRAVELY
GRAVEN
GRAVENESS
GRAVER
GRAVERS
GRAVES
GRAVESIDE
GRAVESITE
GRAVEST
GRAVEWARD
GRAVEYARD
GRAVID
GRAVIDA
GRAVIDAE
GRAVIDAS
GRAVIDITY
GRAVIDLY
GRAVIES
GRAVING
GRAVINGS
GRAVIS
GRAVITAS
GRAVITATE
GRAVITIES
GRAVITINO
GRAVITON
GRAVITONS
GRAVITY
GRAVLAKS
GRAVLAX
GRAVLAXES
GRAVS
GRAVURE
GRAVURES
GRAVY
GRAY
GRAYBACK
GRAYBACKS
GRAYBEARD
GRAYED
GRAYER
GRAYEST
GRAYFISH
GRAYFLIES
GRAYFLY
GRAYHOUND
GRAYING
GRAYISH
GRAYLAG
GRAYLAGS
GRAYLE
GRAYLES
GRAYLING
GRAYLINGS
GRAYLY
GRAYMAIL
GRAYMAILS

GRAYNESS
GRAYOUT
GRAYOUTS
GRAYS
GRAYSCALE
GRAYWACKE
GRAYWATER
GRAZABLE
GRAZE
GRAZEABLE
GRAZED
GRAZER
GRAZERS
GRAZES
GRAZIER
GRAZIERS
GRAZING
GRAZINGLY
GRAZINGS
GRAZIOSO
GREASE
GREASED
GREASER
GREASERS
GREASES
GREASIER
GREASIES
GREASIEST
GREASILY
GREASING
GREASY
GREAT
GREATCOAT
GREATEN
GREATENED
GREATENS
GREATER
GREATEST
GREATESTS
GREATLY
GREATNESS
GREATS
GREAVE
GREAVED
GREAVES
GREAVING
GREBE
GREBES
GRECE
GRECES
GRECIAN
GRECIANS
GRECISE
GRECISED
GRECISES
GRECISING
GRECIZE
GRECIZED

GRECIZES
GRECIZING
GRECQUE
GRECQUES
GREE
GREEBO
GREEBOES
GREECE
GREECES
GREED
GREEDIER
GREEDIEST
GREEDILY
GREEDLESS
GREEDS
GREEDSOME
GREEDY
GREEGREE
GREEGREES
GREEING
GREEK
GREEKED
GREEKING
GREEKINGS
GREEN
GREENBACK
GREENBELT
GREENBONE
GREENBUG
GREENBUGS
GREENED
GREENER
GREENERS
GREENERY
GREENEST
GREENFLY
GREENGAGE
GREENHAND
GREENHEAD
GREENHORN
GREENIE
GREENIER
GREENIES
GREENIEST
GREENING
GREENINGS
GREENISH
GREENLET
GREENLETS
GREENLING
GREENLIT
GREENLY
GREENMAIL
GREENNESS
GREENROOM
GREENS
GREENSAND
GREENSICK

GREENSOME
GREENTH
GREENTHS
GREENWASH
GREENWAY
GREENWAYS
GREENWEED
GREENWING
GREENWOOD
GREENY
GREES
GREESE
GREESES
GREESING
GREESINGS
GREET
GREETE
GREETED
GREETER
GREETERS
GREETES
GREETING
GREETINGS
GREETS
GREFFIER
GREFFIERS
GREGALE
GREGALES
GREGARIAN
GREGARINE
GREGATIM
GREGE
GREGO
GREGOS
GREIGE
GREIGES
GREIN
GREINED
GREINING
GREINS
GREISEN
GREISENS
GREISLY
GREMIAL
GREMIALS
GREMLIN
GREMLINS
GREMMIE
GREMMIES
GREMMY
GREMOLATA
GREN
GRENADE
GRENADES
GRENADIER
GRENADINE
GRENNED
GRENNING

GRENS
GRENZ
GRESE
GRESES
GRESSING
GRESSINGS
GREVE
GREVES
GREVILLEA
GREW
GREWED
GREWHOUND
GREWING
GREWS
GREWSOME
GREWSOMER
GREX
GREXES
GREY
GREYBACK
GREYBACKS
GREYBEARD
GREYED
GREYER
GREYEST
GREYHEN
GREYHENS
GREYHOUND
GREYING
GREYINGS
GREYISH
GREYLAG
GREYLAGS
GREYLIST
GREYLISTS
GREYLY
GREYNESS
GREYS
GREYSTONE
GREYWACKE
GRIBBLE
GRIBBLES
GRICE
GRICED
GRICER
GRICERS
GRICES
GRICING
GRICINGS
GRID
GRIDDED
GRIDDER
GRIDDERS
GRIDDLE
GRIDDLED
GRIDDLES
GRIDDLING
GRIDE

GRIDED	GRILLAGE	GRINNERS	GRIST
GRIDELIN	GRILLAGES	GRINNING	GRISTER
GRIDELINS	GRILLE	GRINS	GRISTERS
GRIDES	GRILLED	GRIOT	GRISTLE
GRIDING	GRILLER	GRIOTS	GRISTLES
GRIDIRON	GRILLERS	GRIP	GRISTLIER
GRIDIRONS	GRILLERY	GRIPE	GRISTLY
GRIDLOCK	GRILLES	GRIPED	GRISTMILL
GRIDLOCKS	GRILLING	GRIPER	GRISTS
GRIDS	GRILLINGS	GRIPERS	GRISY
GRIECE	GRILLION	GRIPES	GRIT
GRIECED	GRILLIONS	GRIPEY	GRITH
GRIECES	GRILLROOM	GRIPIER	GRITHS
GRIEF	GRILLS	GRIPIEST	GRITLESS
GRIEFER	GRILLWORK	GRIPING	GRITS
GRIEFERS	GRILSE	GRIPINGLY	GRITSTONE
GRIEFFUL	GRILSES	GRIPLE	GRITTED
GRIEFLESS	GRIM	GRIPMAN	GRITTER
GRIEFS	GRIMACE	GRIPMEN	GRITTERS
GRIESIE	GRIMACED	GRIPPE	GRITTEST
GRIESLY	GRIMACER	GRIPPED	GRITTIER
GRIESY	GRIMACERS	GRIPPER	GRITTIEST
GRIEVANCE	GRIMACES	GRIPPERS	GRITTILY
GRIEVANT	GRIMACING	GRIPPES	GRITTING
GRIEVANTS	GRIMALKIN	GRIPPIER	GRITTY
GRIEVE	GRIME	GRIPPIEST	GRIVATION
GRIEVED	GRIMED	GRIPPING	GRIVET
GRIEVER	GRIMES	GRIPPLE	GRIVETS
GRIEVERS	GRIMIER	GRIPPLES	GRIZE
GRIEVES	GRIMIEST	GRIPPY	GRIZES
GRIEVING	GRIMILY	GRIPS	GRIZZLE
GRIEVINGS	GRIMINESS	GRIPSACK	GRIZZLED
GRIEVOUS	GRIMING	GRIPSACKS	GRIZZLER
GRIFF	GRIMLY	GRIPT	GRIZZLERS
GRIFFE	GRIMMER	GRIPTAPE	GRIZZLES
GRIFFES	GRIMMEST	GRIPTAPES	GRIZZLIER
GRIFFIN	GRIMNESS	GRIPY	GRIZZLIES
GRIFFINS	GRIMOIRE	GRIS	GRIZZLING
GRIFFON	GRIMOIRES	GRISAILLE	GRIZZLY
GRIFFONS	GRIMY	GRISE	GROAN
GRIFFS	GRIN	GRISED	GROANED
GRIFT	GRINCH	GRISELY	GROANER
GRIFTED	GRINCHES	GRISEOUS	GROANERS
GRIFTER	GRIND	GRISES	GROANFUL
GRIFTERS	GRINDED	GRISETTE	GROANING
GRIFTING	GRINDELIA	GRISETTES	GROANINGS
GRIFTS	GRINDER	GRISGRIS	GROANS
GRIG	GRINDERS	GRISING	GROAT
GRIGGED	GRINDERY	GRISKIN	GROATS
GRIGGING	GRINDING	GRISKINS	GROCER
GRIGRI	GRINDINGS	GRISLED	GROCERIES
GRIGRIS	GRINDS	GRISLIER	GROCERS
GRIGS	GRINGA	GRISLIES	GROCERY
GRIKE	GRINGAS	GRISLIEST	GROCKLE
GRIKES	GRINGO	GRISLY	GROCKLES
GRILL	GRINGOS	GRISON	GRODIER
GRILLADE	GRINNED	GRISONS	GRODIEST
GRILLADES	GRINNER	GRISSINI	GRODY

GROG	GROOVY	GROUNDEN	GROVELS
GROGGED	GROPE	GROUNDER	GROVES
GROGGERY	GROPED	GROUNDERS	GROVET
GROGGIER	GROPER	GROUNDHOG	GROVETS
GROGGIEST	GROPERS	GROUNDING	GROW
GROGGILY	GROPES	GROUNDMAN	GROWABLE
GROGGING	GROPING	GROUNDMEN	GROWER
GROGGY	GROPINGLY	GROUNDNUT	GROWERS
GROGRAM	GROSBEAK	GROUNDOUT	GROWING
GROGRAMS	GROSBEAKS	GROUNDS	GROWINGLY
GROGS	GROSCHEN	GROUNDSEL	GROWINGS
GROGSHOP	GROSCHENS	GROUP	GROWL
GROGSHOPS	GROSER	GROUPABLE	GROWLED
GROIN	GROSERS	GROUPAGE	GROWLER
GROINED	GROSERT	GROUPAGES	GROWLERS
GROINING	GROSERTS	GROUPED	GROWLERY
GROININGS	GROSET	GROUPER	GROWLIER
GROINS	GROSETS	GROUPERS	GROWLIEST
GROK	GROSGRAIN	GROUPIE	GROWLING
GROKKED	GROSS	GROUPIES	GROWLINGS
GROKKING	GROSSART	GROUPING	GROWLS
GROKS	GROSSARTS	GROUPINGS	GROWLY
GROMA	GROSSED	GROUPIST	GROWN
GROMAS	GROSSER	GROUPISTS	GROWNUP
GROMET	GROSSERS	GROUPLET	GROWNUPS
GROMETS	GROSSES	GROUPLETS	GROWS
GROMMET	GROSSEST	GROUPOID	GROWTH
GROMMETED	GROSSING	GROUPOIDS	GROWTHIER
GROMMETS	GROSSLY	GROUPS	GROWTHIST
GROMWELL	GROSSNESS	GROUPWARE	GROWTHS
GROMWELLS	GROSSULAR	GROUPY	GROWTHY
GRONE	GROSZ	GROUSE	GROYNE
GRONED	GROSZE	GROUSED	GROYNES
GRONEFULL	GROSZY	GROUSER	GROZING
GRONES	GROT	GROUSERS	GRUB
GRONING	GROTESQUE	GROUSES	GRUBBED
GROOF	GROTS	GROUSEST	GRUBBER
GROOFS	GROTTIER	GROUSING	GRUBBERS
GROOLIER	GROTTIEST	GROUT	GRUBBIER
GROOLIEST	GROTTO	GROUTED	GRUBBIEST
GROOLY	GROTTOED	GROUTER	GRUBBILY
GROOM	GROTTOES	GROUTERS	GRUBBING
GROOMED	GROTTOS	GROUTIER	GRUBBLE
GROOMER	GROTTY	GROUTIEST	GRUBBLED
GROOMERS	GROUCH	GROUTING	GRUBBLES
GROOMING	GROUCHED	GROUTINGS	GRUBBLING
GROOMINGS	GROUCHES	GROUTS	GRUBBY
GROOMS	GROUCHIER	GROUTY	GRUBS
GROOMSMAN	GROUCHILY	GROVE	GRUBSTAKE
GROOMSMEN	GROUCHING	GROVED	GRUBWORM
GROOVE	GROUCHY	GROVEL	GRUBWORMS
GROOVED	GROUF	GROVELED	GRUDGE
GROOVER	GROUFS	GROVELER	GRUDGED
GROOVERS	GROUGH	GROVELERS	GRUDGEFUL
GROOVES	GROUGHS	GROVELESS	GRUDGER
GROOVIER	GROUND	GROVELING	GRUDGERS
GROOVIEST	GROUNDAGE	GROVELLED	GRUDGES
GROOVING	GROUNDED	GROVELLER	GRUDGING

GRUDGINGS
GRUE
GRUED
GRUEING
GRUEL
GRUELED
GRUELER
GRUELERS
GRUELING
GRUELINGS
GRUELLED
GRUELLER
GRUELLERS
GRUELLING
GRUELS
GRUES
GRUESOME
GRUESOMER
GRUFE
GRUFES
GRUFF
GRUFFED
GRUFFER
GRUFFEST
GRUFFIER
GRUFFIEST
GRUFFILY
GRUFFING
GRUFFISH
GRUFFLY
GRUFFNESS
GRUFFS
GRUFFY
GRUFTED
GRUGRU
GRUGRUS
GRUIFORM
GRUING
GRUM
GRUMBLE
GRUMBLED
GRUMBLER
GRUMBLERS
GRUMBLES
GRUMBLIER
GRUMBLING
GRUMBLY
GRUME
GRUMES
GRUMLY
GRUMMER
GRUMMEST
GRUMMET
GRUMMETED
GRUMMETS
GRUMNESS
GRUMOSE
GRUMOUS
GRUMP

GRUMPED
GRUMPH
GRUMPHED
GRUMPHIE
GRUMPHIES
GRUMPHING
GRUMPHS
GRUMPHY
GRUMPIER
GRUMPIEST
GRUMPILY
GRUMPING
GRUMPISH
GRUMPS
GRUMPY
GRUNDIES
GRUNGE
GRUNGER
GRUNGERS
GRUNGES
GRUNGIER
GRUNGIEST
GRUNGY
GRUNION
GRUNIONS
GRUNT
GRUNTED
GRUNTER
GRUNTERS
GRUNTING
GRUNTINGS
GRUNTLE
GRUNTLED
GRUNTLES
GRUNTLING
GRUNTS
GRUPPETTI
GRUPPETTO
GRUSHIE
GRUTCH
GRUTCHED
GRUTCHES
GRUTCHING
GRUTTEN
GRUYERE
GRUYERES
GRYCE
GRYCES
GRYDE
GRYDED
GRYDES
GRYDING
GRYESY
GRYFON
GRYFONS
GRYKE
GRYKES
GRYPE
GRYPES

GRYPHON
GRYPHONS
GRYPT
GRYSBOK
GRYSBOKS
GRYSELY
GRYSIE
GU
GUACAMOLE
GUACHARO
GUACHAROS
GUACO
GUACOS
GUAIAC
GUAIACOL
GUAIACOLS
GUAIACS
GUAIACUM
GUAIACUMS
GUAIOCUM
GUAIOCUMS
GUAN
GUANA
GUANABANA
GUANACO
GUANACOS
GUANAS
GUANASE
GUANASES
GUANAY
GUANAYS
GUANAZOLO
GUANGO
GUANGOS
GUANIDIN
GUANIDINE
GUANIDINS
GUANIN
GUANINE
GUANINES
GUANINS
GUANO
GUANOS
GUANOSINE
GUANS
GUANXI
GUANXIS
GUANYLIC
GUAR
GUARANA
GUARANAS
GUARANI
GUARANIES
GUARANIS
GUARANTEE
GUARANTOR
GUARANTY
GUARD
GUARDABLE

GUARDAGE
GUARDAGES
GUARDANT
GUARDANTS
GUARDDOG
GUARDDOGS
GUARDED
GUARDEDLY
GUARDEE
GUARDEES
GUARDER
GUARDERS
GUARDIAN
GUARDIANS
GUARDING
GUARDLESS
GUARDLIKE
GUARDRAIL
GUARDROOM
GUARDS
GUARDSHIP
GUARDSMAN
GUARDSMEN
GUARISH
GUARISHED
GUARISHES
GUARS
GUAVA
GUAVAS
GUAYABERA
GUAYULE
GUAYULES
GUB
GUBBAH
GUBBAHS
GUBBINS
GUBBINSES
GUBERNIYA
GUBS
GUCK
GUCKIER
GUCKIEST
GUCKS
GUCKY
GUDDLE
GUDDLED
GUDDLES
GUDDLING
GUDE
GUDEMAN
GUDEMEN
GUDES
GUDESIRE
GUDESIRES
GUDEWIFE
GUDEWIVES
GUDGEON
GUDGEONED
GUDGEONS

GUE	GUIDANCES	GUIRO	GULLIES
GUENON	GUIDE	GUIROS	GULLING
GUENONS	GUIDEBOOK	GUISARD	GULLISH
GUERDON	GUIDED	GUISARDS	GULLS
GUERDONED	GUIDELESS	GUISE	GULLWING
GUERDONER	GUIDELINE	GUISED	GULLY
GUERDONS	GUIDEPOST	GUISER	GULLYING
GUEREZA	GUIDER	GUISERS	GULOSITY
GUEREZAS	GUIDERS	GUISES	GULP
GUERIDON	GUIDES	GUISING	GULPED
GUERIDONS	GUIDESHIP	GUISINGS	GULPER
GUERILLA	GUIDEWAY	GUITAR	GULPERS
GUERILLAS	GUIDEWAYS	GUITARIST	GULPH
GUERITE	GUIDEWORD	GUITARS	GULPHS
GUERITES	GUIDING	GUITGUIT	GULPIER
GUERNSEY	GUIDINGS	GUITGUITS	GULPIEST
GUERNSEYS	GUIDON	GUIZER	GULPING
GUERRILLA	GUIDONS	GUIZERS	GULPINGLY
GUES	GUIDS	GUL	GULPS
GUESS	GUILD	GULA	GULPY
GUESSABLE	GUILDER	GULAG	GULS
GUESSED	GUILDERS	GULAGS	GULY
GUESSER	GUILDHALL	GULAR	GUM
GUESSERS	GUILDRIES	GULAS	GUMBALL
GUESSES	GUILDRY	GULCH	GUMBALLS
GUESSING	GUILDS	GULCHED	GUMBO
GUESSINGS	GUILDSHIP	GULCHES	GUMBOIL
GUESSWORK	GUILDSMAN	GULCHING	GUMBOILS
GUEST	GUILDSMEN	GULDEN	GUMBOOT
GUESTED	GUILE	GULDENS	GUMBOOTS
GUESTEN	GUILED	GULE	GUMBOS
GUESTENED	GUILEFUL	GULES	GUMBOTIL
GUESTENS	GUILELESS	GULF	GUMBOTILS
GUESTING	GUILER	GULFED	GUMDROP
GUESTS	GUILERS	GULFIER	GUMDROPS
GUESTWISE	GUILES	GULFIEST	GUMLANDS
GUFF	GUILING	GULFING	GUMLESS
GUFFAW	GUILLEMET	GULFLIKE	GUMLIKE
GUFFAWED	GUILLEMOT	GULFS	GUMLINE
GUFFAWING	GUILLOCHE	GULFWEED	GUMLINES
GUFFAWS	GUILT	GULFWEEDS	GUMMA
GUFFIE	GUILTIER	GULFY	GUMMAS
GUFFIES	GUILTIEST	GULL	GUMMATA
GUFFS	GUILTILY	GULLABLE	GUMMATOUS
GUGA	GUILTLESS	GULLABLY	GUMMED
GUGAS	GUILTS	GULLED	GUMMER
GUGGLE	GUILTY	GULLER	GUMMERS
GUGGLED	GUIMBARD	GULLERIES	GUMMIER
GUGGLES	GUIMBARDS	GULLERS	GUMMIES
GUGGLING	GUIMP	GULLERY	GUMMIEST
GUGLET	GUIMPE	GULLET	GUMMILY
GUGLETS	GUIMPED	GULLETS	GUMMINESS
GUICHET	GUIMPES	GULLEY	GUMMING
GUICHETS	GUIMPING	GULLEYED	GUMMINGS
GUID	GUIMPS	GULLEYING	GUMMITE
GUIDABLE	GUINEA	GULLEYS	GUMMITES
GUIDAGE	GUINEAS	GULLIBLE	GUMMOSE
GUIDAGES	GUIPURE	GULLIBLY	GUMMOSES
GUIDANCE	GUIPURES	GULLIED	GUMMOSIS

GUMMOSITY	GUNKS	GUNTER	GURUDOMS
GUMMOUS	GUNKY	GUNTERS	GURUISM
GUMMY	GUNLAYER	GUNWALE	GURUISMS
GUMNUT	GUNLAYERS	GUNWALES	GURUS
GUMNUTS	GUNLESS	GUNYAH	GURUSHIP
GUMP	GUNLOCK	GUNYAHS	GURUSHIPS
GUMPED	GUNLOCKS	GUP	GUS
GUMPHION	GUNMAKER	GUPPIES	GUSH
GUMPHIONS	GUNMAKERS	GUPPY	GUSHED
GUMPING	GUNMAN	GUPS	GUSHER
GUMPS	GUNMEN	GUR	GUSHERS
GUMPTION	GUNMETAL	GURAMI	GUSHES
GUMPTIONS	GUNMETALS	GURAMIS	GUSHIER
GUMPTIOUS	GUNNAGE	GURDWARA	GUSHIEST
GUMS	GUNNAGES	GURDWARAS	GUSHILY
GUMSHIELD	GUNNED	GURGE	GUSHINESS
GUMSHOE	GUNNEL	GURGED	GUSHING
GUMSHOED	GUNNELS	GURGES	GUSHINGLY
GUMSHOES	GUNNEN	GURGING	GUSHY
GUMSUCKER	GUNNER	GURGLE	GUSLA
GUMTREE	GUNNERA	GURGLED	GUSLAR
GUMTREES	GUNNERAS	GURGLES	GUSLARS
GUMWEED	GUNNERIES	GURGLET	GUSLAS
GUMWEEDS	GUNNERS	GURGLETS	GUSLE
GUMWOOD	GUNNERY	GURGLING	GUSLES
GUMWOODS	GUNNIES	GURGOYLE	GUSLI
GUN	GUNNING	GURGOYLES	GUSLIS
GUNBOAT	GUNNINGS	GURJUN	GUSSET
GUNBOATS	GUNNY	GURJUNS	GUSSETED
GUNCOTTON	GUNNYBAG	GURL	GUSSETING
GUNDIES	GUNNYBAGS	GURLED	GUSSETS
GUNDOG	GUNNYSACK	GURLET	GUSSIE
GUNDOGS	GUNPAPER	GURLETS	GUSSIED
GUNDY	GUNPAPERS	GURLIER	GUSSIES
GUNFIGHT	GUNPLAY	GURLIEST	GUSSY
GUNFIGHTS	GUNPLAYS	GURLING	GUSSYING
GUNFIRE	GUNPOINT	GURLS	GUST
GUNFIRES	GUNPOINTS	GURLY	GUSTABLE
GUNFLINT	GUNPORT	GURN	GUSTABLES
GUNFLINTS	GUNPORTS	GURNARD	GUSTATION
GUNFOUGHT	GUNPOWDER	GURNARDS	GUSTATIVE
GUNG	GUNROOM	GURNED	GUSTATORY
GUNGE	GUNROOMS	GURNET	GUSTED
GUNGED	GUNRUNNER	GURNETS	GUSTFUL
GUNGES	GUNS	GURNEY	GUSTIE
GUNGIER	GUNSEL	GURNEYS	GUSTIER
GUNGIEST	GUNSELS	GURNING	GUSTIEST
GUNGING	GUNSHIP	GURNS	GUSTILY
GUNGY	GUNSHIPS	GURRAH	GUSTINESS
GUNHOUSE	GUNSHOT	GURRAHS	GUSTING
GUNHOUSES	GUNSHOTS	GURRIER	GUSTLESS
GUNITE	GUNSMITH	GURRIERS	GUSTO
GUNITES	GUNSMITHS	GURRIES	GUSTOES
GUNK	GUNSTICK	GURRY	GUSTOS
GUNKHOLE	GUNSTICKS	GURS	GUSTS
GUNKHOLED	GUNSTOCK	GURSH	GUSTY
GUNKHOLES	GUNSTOCKS	GURSHES	GUT
GUNKIER	GUNSTONE	GURU	GUTBUCKET
GUNKIEST	GUNSTONES	GURUDOM	GUTCHER

GUTCHERS
GUTFUL
GUTFULS
GUTLESS
GUTLIKE
GUTROT
GUTROTS
GUTS
GUTSED
GUTSER
GUTSERS
GUTSES
GUTSFUL
GUTSFULS
GUTSIER
GUTSIEST
GUTSILY
GUTSINESS
GUTSING
GUTSY
GUTTA
GUTTAE
GUTTAS
GUTTATE
GUTTATED
GUTTATES
GUTTATING
GUTTATION
GUTTED
GUTTER
GUTTERED
GUTTERING
GUTTERS
GUTTERY
GUTTIER
GUTTIES
GUTTIEST
GUTTING
GUTTLE
GUTTLED
GUTTLER
GUTTLERS
GUTTLES
GUTTLING
GUTTURAL
GUTTURALS
GUTTY
GUTZER
GUTZERS
GUV
GUVS
GUY
GUYED
GUYING
GUYLE
GUYLED
GUYLER
GUYLERS
GUYLES

GUYLINE
GUYLINES
GUYLING
GUYOT
GUYOTS
GUYS
GUYSE
GUYSES
GUZZLE
GUZZLED
GUZZLER
GUZZLERS
GUZZLES
GUZZLING
GWEDUC
GWEDUCK
GWEDUCKS
GWEDUCS
GWINE
GWINIAD
GWINIADS
GWYNIAD
GWYNIADS
GYAL
GYALS
GYBE
GYBED
GYBES
GYBING
GYELD
GYELDS
GYLDEN
GYM
GYMBAL
GYMBALS
GYMKHANA
GYMKHANAS
GYMMAL
GYMMALS
GYMNASIA
GYMNASIAL
GYMNASIC
GYMNASIEN
GYMNASIUM
GYMNAST
GYMNASTIC
GYMNASTS
GYMNIC
GYMNOSOPH
GYMP
GYMPED
GYMPIE
GYMPIES
GYMPING
GYMPS
GYMS
GYMSLIP
GYMSLIPS
GYNAE

GYNAECEA
GYNAECEUM
GYNAECIA
GYNAECIUM
GYNAECOID
GYNAES
GYNANDRY
GYNARCHIC
GYNARCHY
GYNECIA
GYNECIC
GYNECIUM
GYNECOID
GYNIATRY
GYNIE
GYNIES
GYNNEY
GYNNEYS
GYNNIES
GYNNY
GYNOCRACY
GYNOECIA
GYNOECIUM
GYNOPHOBE
GYNOPHORE
GYNY
GYOZA
GYOZAS
GYP
GYPLURE
GYPLURES
GYPPED
GYPPER
GYPPERS
GYPPIE
GYPPIES
GYPPING
GYPPO
GYPPOS
GYPPY
GYPS
GYPSEIAN
GYPSEOUS
GYPSIED
GYPSIES
GYPSTER
GYPSTERS
GYPSUM
GYPSUMS
GYPSY
GYPSYDOM
GYPSYDOMS
GYPSYHOOD
GYPSYING
GYPSYISH
GYPSYISM
GYPSYISMS
GYPSYWORT
GYRAL

GYRALLY
GYRANT
GYRASE
GYRASES
GYRATE
GYRATED
GYRATES
GYRATING
GYRATION
GYRATIONS
GYRATOR
GYRATORS
GYRATORY
GYRE
GYRED
GYRENE
GYRENES
GYRES
GYRFALCON
GYRI
GYRING
GYRO
GYROCAR
GYROCARS
GYRODYNE
GYRODYNES
GYROIDAL
GYROLITE
GYROLITES
GYROMANCY
GYRON
GYRONIC
GYRONNY
GYRONS
GYROPILOT
GYROPLANE
GYROS
GYROSCOPE
GYROSE
GYROSTAT
GYROSTATS
GYROUS
GYROVAGUE
GYRUS
GYRUSES
GYTE
GYTES
GYTRASH
GYTRASHES
GYTTJA
GYTTJAS
GYVE
GYVED
GYVES
GYVING

H

HA
HAAF
HAAFS
HAANEPOOT
HAAR
HAARS
HABANERA
HABANERAS
HABANERO
HABANEROS
HABDABS
HABDALAH
HABDALAHS
HABERDINE
HABERGEON
HABILABLE
HABILE
HABIT
HABITABLE
HABITABLY
HABITAN
HABITANS
HABITANT
HABITANTS
HABITAT
HABITATS
HABITED
HABITING
HABITS
HABITUAL
HABITUALS
HABITUATE
HABITUDE
HABITUDES
HABITUE
HABITUES
HABITUS
HABLE
HABOOB
HABOOBS
HABU
HABUS
HACEK
HACEKS
HACENDADO
HACHIS
HACHURE
HACHURED
HACHURES
HACHURING
HACIENDA
HACIENDAS
HACK

HACKABLE
HACKAMORE
HACKBERRY
HACKBOLT
HACKBOLTS
HACKBUT
HACKBUTS
HACKED
HACKEE
HACKEES
HACKER
HACKERIES
HACKERS
HACKERY
HACKETTE
HACKETTES
HACKIE
HACKIES
HACKING
HACKINGS
HACKLE
HACKLED
HACKLER
HACKLERS
HACKLES
HACKLET
HACKLETS
HACKLIER
HACKLIEST
HACKLING
HACKLY
HACKMAN
HACKMEN
HACKNEY
HACKNEYED
HACKNEYS
HACKS
HACKSAW
HACKSAWED
HACKSAWN
HACKSAWS
HACKWORK
HACKWORKS
HACQUETON
HAD
HADAL
HADARIM
HADAWAY
HADDEN
HADDEST
HADDIE
HADDIES
HADDING

HADDOCK
HADDOCKS
HADE
HADED
HADEDAH
HADEDAHS
HADES
HADING
HADITH
HADITHS
HADJ
HADJEE
HADJEES
HADJES
HADJI
HADJIS
HADROME
HADROMES
HADRON
HADRONIC
HADRONS
HADROSAUR
HADS
HADST
HAE
HAECCEITY
HAED
HAEING
HAEM
HAEMAL
HAEMATAL
HAEMATEIN
HAEMATIC
HAEMATICS
HAEMATIN
HAEMATINS
HAEMATITE
HAEMATOID
HAEMATOMA
HAEMIC
HAEMIN
HAEMINS
HAEMOCOEL
HAEMOCYTE
HAEMOID
HAEMONIES
HAEMONY
HAEMOSTAT
HAEMS
HAEN
HAEREDES
HAEREMAI
HAERES

HAES
HAET
HAETS
HAFF
HAFFET
HAFFETS
HAFFIT
HAFFITS
HAFFLIN
HAFFLINS
HAFFS
HAFIZ
HAFIZES
HAFNIUM
HAFNIUMS
HAFT
HAFTARA
HAFTARAH
HAFTARAHS
HAFTARAS
HAFTAROT
HAFTAROTH
HAFTED
HAFTER
HAFTERS
HAFTING
HAFTORAH
HAFTORAHS
HAFTOROS
HAFTOROT
HAFTOROTH
HAFTS
HAG
HAGADIC
HAGADIST
HAGADISTS
HAGBERRY
HAGBOLT
HAGBOLTS
HAGBORN
HAGBUSH
HAGBUSHES
HAGBUT
HAGBUTEER
HAGBUTS
HAGBUTTER
HAGDEN
HAGDENS
HAGDON
HAGDONS
HAGDOWN
HAGDOWNS
HAGFISH

HAGFISHES	HAILERS	HAIRPIECE	HALAKHOT
HAGG	HAILIER	HAIRPIN	HALAKHOTH
HAGGADA	HAILIEST	HAIRPINS	HALAKIC
HAGGADAH	HAILING	HAIRS	HALAKIST
HAGGADAHS	HAILS	HAIRSPRAY	HALAKISTS
HAGGADIC	HAILSHOT	HAIRST	HALAKOTH
HAGGADIST	HAILSHOTS	HAIRSTED	HALAL
HAGGADOT	HAILSTONE	HAIRSTING	HALALA
HAGGADOTH	HAILSTORM	HAIRSTS	HALALAH
HAGGARD	HAILY	HAIRSTYLE	HALALAHS
HAGGARDLY	HAIMISH	HAIRTAIL	HALALAS
HAGGARDS	HAIN	HAIRTAILS	HALALLED
HAGGED	HAINCH	HAIRWORK	HALALLING
HAGGING	HAINCHED	HAIRWORKS	HALALS
HAGGIS	HAINCHES	HAIRWORM	HALATION
HAGGISES	HAINCHING	HAIRWORMS	HALATIONS
HAGGISH	HAINED	HAIRY	HALAVAH
HAGGISHLY	HAINING	HAIRYBACK	HALAVAHS
HAGGLE	HAININGS	HAITH	HALAZONE
HAGGLED	HAINS	HAJ	HALAZONES
HAGGLER	HAINT	HAJES	HALBERD
HAGGLERS	HAINTS	HAJI	HALBERDS
HAGGLES	HAIQUE	HAJIS	HALBERT
HAGGLING	HAIQUES	HAJJ	HALBERTS
HAGGS	HAIR	HAJJAH	HALCYON
HAGIARCHY	HAIRBALL	HAJJAHS	HALCYONIC
HAGIOLOGY	HAIRBALLS	HAJJES	HALCYONS
HAGLET	HAIRBAND	HAJJI	HALE
HAGLETS	HAIRBANDS	HAJJIS	HALED
HAGLIKE	HAIRBELL	HAKA	HALENESS
HAGRIDDEN	HAIRBELLS	HAKAM	HALER
HAGRIDE	HAIRBRUSH	HAKAMS	HALERS
HAGRIDER	HAIRCAP	HAKARI	HALERU
HAGRIDERS	HAIRCAPS	HAKAS	HALES
HAGRIDES	HAIRCLOTH	HAKE	HALEST
HAGRIDING	HAIRCUT	HAKEA	HALF
HAGRODE	HAIRCUTS	HAKEAS	HALFA
HAGS	HAIRDO	HAKEEM	HALFAS
HAH	HAIRDOS	HAKEEMS	HALFBACK
HAHA	HAIRDRIER	HAKES	HALFBACKS
HAHAS	HAIRDRYER	HAKIM	HALFBEAK
HAHNIUM	HAIRED	HAKIMS	HALFBEAKS
HAHNIUMS	HAIRGRIP	HAKU	HALFEN
HAHS	HAIRGRIPS	HAKUS	HALFLIFE
HAICK	HAIRIER	HALACHA	HALFLIN
HAICKS	HAIRIEST	HALACHAS	HALFLING
HAIDUK	HAIRIF	HALACHIC	HALFLINGS
HAIDUKS	HAIRIFS	HALACHIST	HALFLINS
HAIK	HAIRINESS	HALACHOT	HALFLIVES
HAIKA	HAIRING	HALACHOTH	HALFNESS
HAIKAI	HAIRLESS	HALAKAH	HALFPACE
HAIKS	HAIRLIKE	HALAKAHS	HALFPACES
HAIKU	HAIRLINE	HALAKHA	HALFPENCE
HAIKUS	HAIRLINES	HALAKHAH	HALFPENNY
HAIL	HAIRLOCK	HALAKHAHS	HALFPIPE
HAILED	HAIRLOCKS	HALAKHAS	HALFPIPES
HAILER	HAIRNET	HALAKHIC	HALFS
	HATRNETS	HALAKHIST	HALFTIME

HALFTIMES	HALLO	HALOUMI	HAMBURG
HALFTONE	HALLOA	HALOUMIS	HAMBURGER
HALFTONES	HALLOAED	HALSE	HAMBURGS
HALFTRACK	HALLOAING	HALSED	HAME
HALFWAY	HALLOAS	HALSER	HAMED
HALFWIT	HALLOED	HALSERS	HAMES
HALFWITS	HALLOES	HALSES	HAMEWITH
HALIBUT	HALLOING	HALSING	HAMFATTER
HALIBUTS	HALLOO	HALT	HAMING
HALICORE	HALLOOED	HALTED	HAMLET
HALICORES	HALLOOING	HALTER	HAMLETS
HALID	HALLOOS	HALTERE	HAMMADA
HALIDE	HALLOS	HALTERED	HAMMADAS
HALIDES	HALLOT	HALTERES	HAMMAL
HALIDOM	HALLOTH	HALTERING	HAMMALS
HALIDOME	HALLOUMI	HALTERS	HAMMAM
HALIDOMES	HALLOUMIS	HALTING	HAMMAMS
HALIDOMS	HALLOW	HALTINGLY	HAMMED
HALIDS	HALLOWED	HALTINGS	HAMMER
HALIEUTIC	HALLOWER	HALTLESS	HAMMERED
HALIMOT	HALLOWERS	HALTS	HAMMERER
HALIMOTE	HALLOWING	HALUTZ	HAMMERERS
HALIMOTES	HALLOWS	HALUTZIM	HAMMERING
HALIMOTS	HALLS	HALVA	HAMMERKOP
HALING	HALLSTAND	HALVAH	HAMMERMAN
HALIOTIS	HALLUCAL	HALVAHS	HAMMERMEN
HALITE	HALLUCES	HALVAS	HAMMERS
HALITES	HALLUX	HALVE	HAMMERTOE
HALITOSES	HALLWAY	HALVED	HAMMIER
HALITOSIS	HALLWAYS	HALVER	HAMMIEST
HALITOTIC	HALLYON	HALVERS	HAMMILY
HALITOUS	HALLYONS	HALVES	HAMMINESS
HALITUS	HALM	HALVING	HAMMING
HALITUSES	HALMA	HALYARD	HAMMOCK
HALL	HALMAS	HALYARDS	HAMMOCKS
HALLAH	HALMS	HAM	HAMMY
HALLAHS	HALO	HAMADA	HAMOSE
HALLAL	HALOBIONT	HAMADAS	HAMOUS
HALLALI	HALOCLINE	HAMADRYAD	HAMPER
HALLALIS	HALOED	HAMADRYAS	HAMPERED
HALLALLED	HALOES	HAMAL	HAMPERER
HALLALOO	HALOGEN	HAMALS	HAMPERERS
HALLALOOS	HALOGENS	HAMAMELIS	HAMPERING
HALLALS	HALOGETON	HAMARTIA	HAMPERS
HALLAN	HALOID	HAMARTIAS	HAMPSTER
HALLANS	HALOIDS	HAMATE	HAMPSTERS
HALLEL	HALOING	HAMATES	HAMS
HALLELS	HALOLIKE	HAMAUL	HAMSTER
HALLIAN	HALON	HAMAULS	HAMSTERS
HALLIANS	HALONS	HAMBA	HAMSTRING
HALLIARD	HALOPHILE	HAMBLE	HAMSTRUNG
HALLIARDS	HALOPHILY	HAMBLED	HAMULAR
HALLING	HALOPHOBE	HAMBLES	HAMULATE
HALLINGS	HALOPHYTE	HAMBLING	HAMULI
HALLION	HALOS	HAMBONE	HAMULOSE
HALLIONS	HALOSERE	HAMBONED	HAMULOUS
HALLMARK	HALOSERES	HAMBONES	HAMULUS
HALLMARKS	HALOTHANE	HAMBONING	HAMZA

HAMZAH
HAMZAHS
HAMZAS
HAN
HANAP
HANAPER
HANAPERS
HANAPS
HANCE
HANCES
HANCH
HANCHED
HANCHES
HANCHING
HAND
HANDAX
HANDAXES
HANDBAG
HANDBAGS
HANDBALL
HANDBALLS
HANDBELL
HANDBELLS
HANDBILL
HANDBILLS
HANDBLOWN
HANDBOOK
HANDBOOKS
HANDBRAKE
HANDCAR
HANDCARS
HANDCART
HANDCARTS
HANDCLAP
HANDCLAPS
HANDCLASP
HANDCRAFT
HANDCUFF
HANDCUFFS
HANDED
HANDER
HANDERS
HANDFAST
HANDFASTS
HANDFED
HANDFEED
HANDFEEDS
HANDFUL
HANDFULS
HANDGRIP
HANDGRIPS
HANDGUN
HANDGUNS
HANDHELD
HANDHELDS
HANDHOLD
HANDHOLDS
HANDICAP

HANDICAPS
HANDIER
HANDIEST
HANDILY
HANDINESS
HANDING
HANDISM
HANDISMS
HANDIWORK
HANDJAR
HANDJARS
HANDLE
HANDLEBAR
HANDLED
HANDLER
HANDLERS
HANDLES
HANDLESS
HANDLIKE
HANDLING
HANDLINGS
HANDLIST
HANDLISTS
HANDLOOM
HANDLOOMS
HANDMADE
HANDMAID
HANDMAIDS
HANDOFF
HANDOFFS
HANDOUT
HANDOUTS
HANDOVER
HANDOVERS
HANDPHONE
HANDPICK
HANDPICKS
HANDPLAY
HANDPLAYS
HANDPRESS
HANDPRINT
HANDRAIL
HANDRAILS
HANDROLL
HANDROLLS
HANDS
HANDSAW
HANDSAWS
HANDSEL
HANDSELED
HANDSELS
HANDSET
HANDSETS
HANDSEWN
HANDSFUL
HANDSHAKE
HANDSOME
HANDSOMER

HANDSPIKE
HANDSTAFF
HANDSTAMP
HANDSTAND
HANDSTURN
HANDTOWEL
HANDWHEEL
HANDWORK
HANDWORKS
HANDWOVEN
HANDWRIT
HANDWRITE
HANDWROTE
HANDY
HANDYMAN
HANDYMEN
HANDYWORK
HANEPOOT
HANEPOOTS
HANG
HANGABLE
HANGAR
HANGARED
HANGARING
HANGARS
HANGBIRD
HANGBIRDS
HANGDOG
HANGDOGS
HANGED
HANGER
HANGERS
HANGFIRE
HANGFIRES
HANGI
HANGING
HANGINGS
HANGIS
HANGMAN
HANGMEN
HANGNAIL
HANGNAILS
HANGNEST
HANGNESTS
HANGOUT
HANGOUTS
HANGOVER
HANGOVERS
HANGS
HANGTAG
HANGTAGS
HANGUL
HANGUP
HANGUPS
HANIWA
HANJAR
HANJARS
HANK

HANKED
HANKER
HANKERED
HANKERER
HANKERERS
HANKERING
HANKERS
HANKIE
HANKIES
HANKING
HANKS
HANKY
HANSA
HANSAS
HANSE
HANSEATIC
HANSEL
HANSELED
HANSELING
HANSELLED
HANSELS
HANSES
HANSOM
HANSOMS
HANT
HANTED
HANTING
HANTLE
HANTLES
HANTS
HANUKIAH
HANUKIAHS
HANUMAN
HANUMANS
HAO
HAOLE
HAOLES
HAOMA
HAOMAS
HAP
HAPAX
HAPAXES
HAPHAZARD
HAPHTARA
HAPHTARAH
HAPHTARAS
HAPHTAROT
HAPKIDO
HAPKIDOS
HAPLESS
HAPLESSLY
HAPLITE
HAPLITES
HAPLITIC
HAPLOID
HAPLOIDIC
HAPLOIDS
HAPLOIDY

HAPLOLOGY	HARANGUES	HARDHACKS	HARELIKE
HAPLONT	HARASS	HARDHAT	HARELIP
HAPLONTIC	HARASSED	HARDHATS	HARELIPS
HAPLONTS	HARASSER	HARDHEAD	HAREM
HAPLOPIA	HARASSERS	HARDHEADS	HAREMS
HAPLOPIAS	HARASSES	HARDIER	HARES
HAPLOSES	HARASSING	HARDIES	HARESTAIL
HAPLOSIS	HARBINGER	HARDIEST	HAREWOOD
HAPLOTYPE	HARBOR	HARDIHEAD	HAREWOODS
HAPLY	HARBORAGE	HARDIHOOD	HARIANA
HAPPED	HARBORED	HARDILY	HARIANAS
HAPPEN	HARBORER	HARDIMENT	HARICOT
HAPPENED	HARBORERS	HARDINESS	HARICOTS
HAPPENING	HARBORFUL	HARDISH	HARIGALDS
HAPPENS	HARBORING	HARDLINE	HARIGALS
HAPPIED	HARBOROUS	HARDLINER	HARIJAN
HAPPIER	HARBORS	HARDLY	HARIJANS
HAPPIES	HARBOUR	HARDMAN	HARIM
HAPPIEST	HARBOURED	HARDMEN	HARIMS
HAPPILY	HARBOURER	HARDNESS	HARING
HAPPINESS	HARBOURS	HARDNOSE	HARIOLATE
HAPPING	HARD	HARDNOSED	HARIRA
HAPPY	HARDASS	HARDNOSES	HARIRAS
HAPPYING	HARDASSES	HARDOKE	HARISH
HAPS	HARDBACK	HARDOKES	HARISSA
HAPTEN	HARDBACKS	HARDPACK	HARISSAS
HAPTENE	HARDBAG	HARDPACKS	HARK
HAPTENES	HARDBAGS	HARDPAN	HARKED
HAPTENIC	HARDBAKE	HARDPANS	HARKEN
HAPTENS	HARDBAKES	HARDPARTS	HARKENED
HAPTERON	HARDBALL	HARDROCK	HARKENER
HAPTERONS	HARDBALLS	HARDROCKS	HARKENERS
HAPTIC	HARDBEAM	HARDS	HARKENING
HAPTICAL	HARDBEAMS	HARDSET	HARKENS
HAPTICS	HARDBOARD	HARDSHELL	HARKING
HAPU	HARDBOOT	HARDSHIP	HARKS
HAPUKA	HARDBOOTS	HARDSHIPS	HARL
HAPUKAS	HARDBOUND	HARDSTAND	HARLED
HAPUKU	HARDCASE	HARDTACK	HARLEQUIN
HAPUKUS	HARDCORE	HARDTACKS	HARLING
HAPUS	HARDCORES	HARDTOP	HARLINGS
HAQUETON	HARDCOURT	HARDTOPS	HARLOT
HAQUETONS	HARDCOVER	HARDWARE	HARLOTRY
HARAKEKE	HARDEDGE	HARDWARES	HARLOTS
HARAKEKES	HARDEDGES	HARDWIRE	HARLS
HARAM	HARDEN	HARDWIRED	HARM
HARAMBEE	HARDENED	HARDWIRES	HARMALA
HARAMBEES	HARDENER	HARDWOOD	HARMALAS
HARAMDA	HARDENERS	HARDWOODS	HARMALIN
HARAMDAS	HARDENING	HARDY	HARMALINE
HARAMDI	HARDENS	HARE	HARMALINS
HARAMDIS	HARDER	HAREBELL	HARMAN
HARAMS	HARDEST	HAREBELLS	HARMANS
HARAMZADA	HARDFACE	HARED	HARMATTAN
HARAMZADI	HARDFACES	HAREEM	HARMDOING
HARANGUE	HARDGOODS	HAREEMS	HARMED
HARANGUED	HARDGRASS	HARELD	HARMEL
HARANGUER	HARDHACK	HARELDS	HARMELS

HARMER	HARRIER	HASHISHES	HATCHECKS
HARMERS	HARRIERS	HASHMARK	HATCHED
HARMFUL	HARRIES	HASHMARKS	HATCHEL
HARMFULLY	HARROW	HASHY	HATCHELED
HARMIN	HARROWED	HASK	HATCHELS
HARMINE	HARROWER	HASKS	HATCHER
HARMINES	HARROWERS	HASLET	HATCHERS
HARMING	HARROWING	HASLETS	HATCHERY
HARMINS	HARROWS	HASP	HATCHES
HARMLESS	HARRUMPH	HASPED	HATCHET
HARMONIC	HARRUMPHS	HASPING	HATCHETS
HARMONICA	HARRY	HASPS	HATCHETY
HARMONICS	HARRYING	HASSAR	HATCHING
HARMONIES	HARSH	HASSARS	HATCHINGS
HARMONISE	HARSHEN	HASSEL	HATCHLING
HARMONIST	HARSHENED	HASSELS	HATCHMENT
HARMONIUM	HARSHENS	HASSIUM	HATCHWAY
HARMONIZE	HARSHER	HASSIUMS	HATCHWAYS
HARMONY	HARSHEST	HASSLE	HATE
HARMOST	HARSHLY	HASSLED	HATEABLE
HARMOSTS	HARSHNESS	HASSLES	HATED
HARMOSTY	HARSLET	HASSLING	HATEFUL
HARMOTOME	HARSLETS	HASSOCK	HATEFULLY
HARMS	HART	HASSOCKS	HATELESS
HARN	HARTAL	HASSOCKY	HATER
HARNESS	HARTALS	HAST	HATERENT
HARNESSED	HARTBEES	HASTA	HATERENTS
HARNESSER	HARTBEEST	HASTATE	HATERS
HARNESSES	HARTELY	HASTATED	HATES
HARNS	HARTEN	HASTATELY	HATFUL
HARO	HARTENED	HASTE	HATFULS
HAROS	HARTENING	HASTED	HATGUARD
HAROSET	HARTENS	HASTEFUL	HATGUARDS
HAROSETH	HARTLESSE	HASTEN	HATH
HAROSETHS	HARTS	HASTENED	HATHA
HAROSETS	HARTSHORN	HASTENER	HATING
HARP	HARUMPH	HASTENERS	HATLESS
HARPED	HARUMPHED	HASTENING	HATLIKE
HARPER	HARUMPHS	HASTENS	HATMAKER
HARPERS	HARUSPEX	HASTES	HATMAKERS
HARPIES	HARUSPICY	HASTIER	HATPEG
HARPIN	HARVEST	HASTIEST	HATPEGS
HARPING	HARVESTED	HASTILY	HATPIN
HARPINGS	HARVESTER	HASTINESS	HATPINS
HARPINS	HARVESTS	HASTING	HATRACK
HARPIST	HAS	HASTINGS	HATRACKS
HARPISTS	HASBIAN	HASTY	HATRED
HARPOON	HASBIANS	HAT	HATREDS
HARPOONED	HASH	HATABLE	HATS
HARPOONER	HASHED	HATBAND	HATSFUL
HARPOONS	HASHEESH	HATBANDS	HATSTAND
HARPS	HASHES	HATBOX	HATSTANDS
HARPY	HASHHEAD	HATBOXES	HATTED
HARPYLIKE	HASHHEADS	HATBRUSH	HATTER
HARQUEBUS	HASHIER	HATCH	HATTERED
HARRIDAN	HASHIEST	HATCHABLE	HATTERIA
HARRIDANS	HASHING	HATCHBACK	HATTERIAS
HARRTED	HASHISH	HATCHECK	HATTERING

HATTERS	HAUSES	HAWBUCK	HAYCOCKS
HATTING	HAUSFRAU	HAWBUCKS	HAYED
HATTINGS	HAUSFRAUS	HAWED	HAYER
HATTOCK	HAUSING	HAWFINCH	HAYERS
HATTOCKS	HAUSTELLA	HAWING	HAYEY
HAUBERK	HAUSTORIA	HAWK	HAYFIELD
HAUBERKS	HAUT	HAWKBELL	HAYFIELDS
HAUBOIS	HAUTBOIS	HAWKBELLS	HAYFORK
HAUD	HAUTBOY	HAWKBILL	HAYFORKS
HAUDEN	HAUTBOYS	HAWKBILLS	HAYING
HAUDING	HAUTE	HAWKBIT	HAYINGS
HAUDS	HAUTEUR	HAWKBITS	HAYLAGE
HAUF	HAUTEURS	HAWKED	HAYLAGES
HAUFS	HAUYNE	HAWKER	HAYLE
HAUGH	HAUYNES	HAWKERS	HAYLES
HAUGHS	HAVARTI	HAWKEY	HAYLOFT
HAUGHT	HAVARTIS	HAWKEYED	HAYLOFTS
HAUGHTIER	HAVDALAH	HAWKEYS	HAYMAKER
HAUGHTILY	HAVDALAHS	HAWKIE	HAYMAKERS
HAUGHTY	HAVDOLOH	HAWKIES	HAYMAKING
HAUL	HAVDOLOHS	HAWKING	HAYMOW
HAULAGE	HAVE	HAWKINGS	HAYMOWS
HAULAGES	HAVELOCK	HAWKISH	HAYRACK
HAULD	HAVELOCKS	HAWKISHLY	HAYRACKS
HAULDS	HAVEN	HAWKIT	HAYRICK
HAULED	HAVENED	HAWKLIKE	HAYRICKS
HAULER	HAVENING	HAWKMOTH	HAYRIDE
HAULERS	HAVENLESS	HAWKMOTHS	HAYRIDES
HAULIER	HAVENS	HAWKNOSE	HAYS
HAULIERS	HAVEOUR	HAWKNOSES	HAYSEED
HAULING	HAVEOURS	HAWKS	HAYSEEDS
HAULM	HAVER	HAWKSBILL	HAYSEL
HAULMIER	HAVERED	HAWKSHAW	HAYSELS
HAULMIEST	HAVEREL	HAWKSHAWS	HAYSTACK
HAULMS	HAVERELS	HAWKWEED	HAYSTACKS
HAULMY	HAVERING	HAWKWEEDS	HAYWARD
HAULS	HAVERINGS	HAWM	HAYWARDS
HAULST	HAVERS	HAWMED	HAYWIRE
HAULT	HAVERSACK	HAWMING	HAYWIRES
HAULYARD	HAVERSINE	HAWMS	HAZAN
HAULYARDS	HAVES	HAWS	HAZANIM
HAUNCH	HAVILDAR	HAWSE	HAZANS
HAUNCHED	HAVILDARS	HAWSED	HAZARD
HAUNCHES	HAVING	HAWSEHOLE	HAZARDED
HAUNCHING	HAVINGS	HAWSEPIPE	HAZARDER
HAUNT	HAVIOR	HAWSER	HAZARDERS
HAUNTED	HAVIORS	HAWSERS	HAZARDING
HAUNTER	HAVIOUR	HAWSES	HAZARDIZE
HAUNTERS	HAVIOURS	HAWSING	HAZARDOUS
HAUNTING	HAVOC	HAWTHORN	HAZARDRY
HAUNTINGS	HAVOCKED	HAWTHORNS	HAZARDS
HAUNTS	HAVOCKER	HAWTHORNY	HAZE
HAURIANT	HAVOCKERS	HAY	HAZED
HAURIENT	HAVOCKING	HAYBAND	HAZEL
HAUSE	HAVOCS	HAYBANDS	HAZELHEN
HAUSED	HAW	HAYBOX	HAZELHENS
HAUSEN	HAWALA	HAYBOXES	HAZELLY
HAUSENS	HAWALAS	HAYCOCK	HAZELNUT

HAZELNUTS	HEADIEST	HEADSMAN	HEARD
HAZELS	HEADILY	HEADSMEN	HEARDS
HAZER	HEADINESS	HEADSPACE	HEARE
HAZERS	HEADING	HEADSTALL	HEARER
HAZES	HEADINGS	HEADSTAND	HEARERS
HAZIER	HEADLAMP	HEADSTAY	HEARES
HAZIEST	HEADLAMPS	HEADSTAYS	HEARIE
HAZILY	HEADLAND	HEADSTICK	HEARING
HAZINESS	HEADLANDS	HEADSTOCK	HEARINGS
HAZING	HEADLEASE	HEADSTONE	HEARKEN
HAZINGS	HEADLESS	HEADWARD	HEARKENED
HAZMAT	HEADLIGHT	HEADWARDS	HEARKENER
HAZMATS	HEADLIKE	HEADWATER	HEARKENS
HAZY	HEADLINE	HEADWAY	HEARS
HAZZAN	HEADLINED	HEADWAYS	HEARSAY
HAZZANIM	HEADLINER	HEADWIND	HEARSAYS
HAZZANS	HEADLINES	HEADWINDS	HEARSE
HE	HEADLOCK	HEADWORD	HEARSED
HEAD	HEADLOCKS	HEADWORDS	HEARSES
HEADACHE	HEADLONG	HEADWORK	HEARSIER
HEADACHES	HEADMAN	HEADWORKS	HEARSIEST
HEADACHEY	HEADMARK	HEADY	HEARSING
HEADACHY	HEADMARKS	HEAL	HEARSY
HEADAGE	HEADMEN	HEALABLE	HEART
HEADAGES	HEADMOST	HEALD	HEARTACHE
HEADBAND	HEADNOTE	HEALDED	HEARTBEAT
HEADBANDS	HEADNOTES	HEALDING	HEARTBURN
HEADBANG	HEADPEACE	HEALDS	HEARTED
HEADBANGS	HEADPHONE	HEALED	HEARTEN
HEADBOARD	HEADPIECE	HEALEE	HEARTENED
HEADCASE	HEADPIN	HEALEES	HEARTENER
HEADCASES	HEADPINS	HEALER	HEARTENS
HEADCHAIR	HEADRACE	HEALERS	HEARTFELT
HEADCLOTH	HEADRACES	HEALING	HEARTFREE
HEADCOUNT	HEADRAIL	HEALINGLY	HEARTH
HEADDRESS	HEADRAILS	HEALINGS	HEARTHRUG
HEADED	HEADREACH	HEALS	HEARTHS
HEADEND	HEADREST	HEALSOME	HEARTIER
HEADENDS	HEADRESTS	HEALTH	HEARTIES
HEADER	HEADRIG	HEALTHFUL	HEARTIEST
HEADERS	HEADRIGS	HEALTHIER	HEARTIKIN
HEADFAST	HEADRING	HEALTHILY	HEARTILY
HEADFASTS	HEADRINGS	HEALTHISM	HEARTING
HEADFIRST	HEADROOM	HEALTHS	HEARTLAND
HEADFISH	HEADROOMS	HEALTHY	HEARTLESS
HEADFRAME	HEADROPE	HEAME	HEARTLET
HEADFUCK	HEADROPES	HEAP	HEARTLETS
HEADFUCKS	HEADS	HEAPED	HEARTLING
HEADFUL	HEADSAIL	HEAPER	HEARTLY
HEADFULS	HEADSAILS	HEAPERS	HEARTPEA
HEADGATE	HEADSCARF	HEAPIER	HEARTPEAS
HEADGATES	HEADSET	HEAPIEST	HEARTS
HEADGEAR	HEADSETS	HEAPING	HEARTSEED
HEADGEARS	HEADSHAKE	HEAPS	HEARTSICK
HEADGUARD	HEADSHIP	HEAPSTEAD	HEARTSOME
HEADHUNT	HEADSHIPS	HEAPY	HEARTSORE
HEADHUNTS	HEADSHOT	HEAR	HEARTWOOD
HEADIER	HEADSHOTS	HEARABLE	HEARTWORM

HEARTY
HEAST
HEASTE
HEASTES
HEASTS
HEAT
HEATABLE
HEATED
HEATEDLY
HEATER
HEATERS
HEATH
HEATHBIRD
HEATHCOCK
HEATHEN
HEATHENRY
HEATHENS
HEATHER
HEATHERED
HEATHERS
HEATHERY
HEATHFOWL
HEATHIER
HEATHIEST
HEATHLAND
HEATHLESS
HEATHLIKE
HEATHS
HEATHY
HEATING
HEATINGS
HEATLESS
HEATPROOF
HEATS
HEATSPOT
HEATSPOTS
HEAUME
HEAUMES
HEAVE
HEAVED
HEAVEN
HEAVENLY
HEAVENS
HEAVER
HEAVERS
HEAVES
HEAVIER
HEAVIES
HEAVIEST
HEAVILY
HEAVINESS
HEAVING
HEAVINGS
HEAVY
HEAVYSET
HEBDOMAD
HEBDOMADS
HEBE

HEBEN
HEBENON
HEBENONS
HEBENS
HEBES
HEBETANT
HEBETATE
HEBETATED
HEBETATES
HEBETIC
HEBETUDE
HEBETUDES
HEBONA
HEBONAS
HEBRAISE
HEBRAISED
HEBRAISES
HEBRAIZE
HEBRAIZED
HEBRAIZES
HECATOMB
HECATOMBS
HECH
HECHT
HECHTING
HECHTS
HECK
HECKLE
HECKLED
HECKLER
HECKLERS
HECKLES
HECKLING
HECKLINGS
HECKS
HECOGENIN
HECTARE
HECTARES
HECTIC
HECTICAL
HECTICLY
HECTICS
HECTOGRAM
HECTOR
HECTORED
HECTORER
HECTORERS
HECTORING
HECTORISM
HECTORLY
HECTORS
HEDDLE
HEDDLED
HEDDLES
HEDDLING
HEDER
HEDERA
HEDERAL

HEDERAS
HEDERATED
HEDERS
HEDGE
HEDGEBILL
HEDGED
HEDGEHOG
HEDGEHOGS
HEDGEHOP
HEDGEHOPS
HEDGEPIG
HEDGEPIGS
HEDGER
HEDGEROW
HEDGEROWS
HEDGERS
HEDGES
HEDGIER
HEDGIEST
HEDGING
HEDGINGLY
HEDGINGS
HEDGY
HEDONIC
HEDONICS
HEDONISM
HEDONISMS
HEDONIST
HEDONISTS
HEDYPHANE
HEED
HEEDED
HEEDER
HEEDERS
HEEDFUL
HEEDFULLY
HEEDINESS
HEEDING
HEEDLESS
HEEDS
HEEDY
HEEHAW
HEEHAWED
HEEHAWING
HEEHAWS
HEEL
HEELBALL
HEELBALLS
HEELED
HEELER
HEELERS
HEELING
HEELINGS
HEELLESS
HEELPIECE
HEELPLATE
HEELPOST
HEELPOSTS

HEELS
HEELTAP
HEELTAPS
HEEZE
HEEZED
HEEZES
HEEZIE
HEEZIES
HEEZING
HEFT
HEFTE
HEFTED
HEFTER
HEFTERS
HEFTIER
HEFTIEST
HEFTILY
HEFTINESS
HEFTING
HEFTS
HEFTY
HEGARI
HEGARIS
HEGEMON
HEGEMONIC
HEGEMONS
HEGEMONY
HEGIRA
HEGIRAS
HEGUMEN
HEGUMENE
HEGUMENES
HEGUMENOI
HEGUMENOS
HEGUMENS
HEGUMENY
HEH
HEHS
HEID
HEIDS
HEIFER
HEIFERS
HEIGH
HEIGHT
HEIGHTEN
HEIGHTENS
HEIGHTH
HEIGHTHS
HEIGHTISM
HEIGHTS
HEIL
HEILED
HEILING
HEILS
HEIMISH
HEINIE
HEINIES
HEINOUS

HEINOUSLY	HELICOPT	HELLICAT	HELPLESS
HEIR	HELICOPTS	HELLICATS	HELPLINE
HEIRDOM	HELICTITE	HELLIER	HELPLINES
HEIRDOMS	HELIDECK	HELLIERS	HELPMATE
HEIRED	HELIDECKS	HELLING	HELPMATES
HEIRESS	HELIDROME	HELLION	HELPMEET
HEIRESSES	HELILIFT	HELLIONS	HELPMEETS
HEIRING	HELILIFTS	HELLISH	HELPS
HEIRLESS	HELIMAN	HELLISHLY	HELVE
HEIRLOOM	HELIMEN	HELLKITE	HELVED
HEIRLOOMS	HELING	HELLKITES	HELVES
HEIRS	HELIO	HELLO	HELVETIUM
HEIRSHIP	HELIODOR	HELLOED	HELVING
HEIRSHIPS	HELIODORS	HELLOES	HEM
HEISHI	HELIOGRAM	HELLOING	HEMAGOG
HEIST	HELIOLOGY	HELLOS	HEMAGOGS
HEISTED	HELIOS	HELLOVA	HEMAGOGUE
HEISTER	HELIOSES	HELLS	HEMAL
HEISTERS	HELIOSIS	HELLUVA	HEMATAL
HEISTING	HELIOSTAT	HELLWARD	HEMATEIN
HEISTS	HELIOTYPE	HELLWARDS	HEMATEINS
HEITIKI	HELIOTYPY	HELM	HEMATIC
HEITIKIS	HELIOZOAN	HELMED	HEMATICS
HEJAB	HELIOZOIC	HELMER	HEMATIN
HEJABS	HELIPAD	HELMERS	HEMATINE
HEJIRA	HELIPADS	HELMET	HEMATINES
HEJIRAS	HELIPILOT	HELMETED	HEMATINIC
HEJRA	HELIPORT	HELMETING	HEMATINS
HEJRAS	HELIPORTS	HELMETS	HEMATITE
HEKETARA	HELISTOP	HELMING	HEMATITES
HEKETARAS	HELISTOPS	HELMINTH	HEMATITIC
HEKTARE	HELIUM	HELMINTHS	HEMATOID
HEKTARES	HELIUMS	HELMLESS	HEMATOMA
HEKTOGRAM	HELIX	HELMS	HEMATOMAS
HELCOID	HELIXES	HELMSMAN	HEMATOSES
HELD	HELL	HELMSMEN	HEMATOSIS
HELE	HELLBENT	HELO	HEMATOZOA
HELED	HELLBOX	HELOPHYTE	HEMATURIA
HELENIUM	HELLBOXES	HELOS	HEMATURIC
HELENIUMS	HELLBROTH	HELOT	HEME
HELES	HELLCAT	HELOTAGE	HEMELYTRA
HELIAC	HELLCATS	HELOTAGES	HEMES
HELIACAL	HELLDIVER	HELOTISM	HEMIALGIA
HELIAST	HELLEBORE	HELOTISMS	HEMIC
HELIASTS	HELLED	HELOTRIES	HEMICYCLE
HELIBORNE	HELLENISE	HELOTRY	HEMIHEDRY
HELIBUS	HELLENIZE	HELOTS	HEMIN
HELIBUSES	HELLER	HELP	HEMINA
HELICAL	HELLERI	HELPABLE	HEMINAS
HELICALLY	HELLERIES	HELPDESK	HEMINS
HELICES	HELLERIS	HELPDESKS	HEMIOLA
HELICITY	HELLERS	HELPED	HEMIOLAS
HELICLINE	HELLERY	HELPER	HEMIOLIA
HELICOID	HELLFIRE	HELPERS	HEMIOLIAS
HELICOIDS	HELLFIRES	HELPFUL	HEMIOLIC
HELICON	HELLHOLE	HELPFULLY	HEMIONE
HELICONIA	HELLHOLES	HELPING	HEMIONES
HELICONS	HELLHOUND	HELPINGS	HEMIONUS

HEMIOPIA	HENBANE	HENTS	HERBALIST
HEMIOPIAS	HENBANES	HEP	HERBALS
HEMIOPIC	HENBIT	HEPAR	HERBAR
HEMIOPSIA	HENBITS	HEPARIN	HERBARIA
HEMIPOD	HENCE	HEPARINS	HERBARIAL
HEMIPODE	HENCHMAN	HEPARS	HERBARIAN
HEMIPODES	HENCHMEN	HEPATIC	HERBARIES
HEMIPODS	HENCOOP	HEPATICA	HERBARIUM
HEMIPTER	HENCOOPS	HEPATICAE	HERBARS
HEMIPTERS	HEND	HEPATICAL	HERBARY
HEMISPACE	HENDED	HEPATICAS	HERBED
HEMISTICH	HENDIADYS	HEPATICS	HERBELET
HEMITROPE	HENDING	HEPATISE	HERBELETS
HEMITROPY	HENDS	HEPATISED	HERBICIDE
HEMLINE	HENEQUEN	HEPATISES	HERBIER
HEMLINES	HENEQUENS	HEPATITE	HERBIEST
HEMLOCK	HENEQUIN	HEPATITES	HERBIST
HEMLOCKS	HENEQUINS	HEPATITIS	HERBISTS
HEMMED	HENGE	HEPATIZE	HERBIVORA
HEMMER	HENGES	HEPATIZED	HERBIVORE
HEMMERS	HENHOUSE	HEPATIZES	HERBIVORY
HEMMING	HENHOUSES	HEPATOMA	HERBLESS
HEMOCOEL	HENIQUEN	HEPATOMAS	HERBLET
HEMOCOELS	HENIQUENS	HEPCAT	HERBLETS
HEMOCYTE	HENIQUIN	HEPCATS	HERBLIKE
HEMOCYTES	HENIQUINS	HEPPER	HERBOLOGY
HEMOID	HENLEY	HEPPEST	HERBORISE
HEMOLYMPH	HENLEYS	HEPS	HERBORIST
HEMOLYSE	HENLIKE	HEPSTER	HERBORIZE
HEMOLYSED	HENNA	HEPSTERS	HERBOSE
HEMOLYSES	HENNAED	HEPT	HERBOUS
HEMOLYSIN	HENNAING	HEPTAD	HERBS
HEMOLYSIS	HENNAS	HEPTADS	HERBY
HEMOLYTIC	HENNED	HEPTAGLOT	HERCOGAMY
HEMOLYZE	HENNER	HEPTAGON	HERCULEAN
HEMOLYZED	HENNERIES	HEPTAGONS	HERCULES
HEMOLYZES	HENNERS	HEPTANE	HERCYNITE
HEMOPHILE	HENNERY	HEPTANES	HERD
HEMOSTAT	HENNIER	HEPTAPODY	HERDBOY
HEMOSTATS	HENNIES	HEPTARCH	HERDBOYS
HEMOTOXIC	HENNIEST	HEPTARCHS	HERDED
HEMOTOXIN	HENNIN	HEPTARCHY	HERDEN
HEMP	HENNING	HEPTOSE	HERDENS
HEMPEN	HENNINS	HEPTOSES	HERDER
HEMPIE	HENNISH	HER	HERDERS
HEMPIER	HENNISHLY	HERALD	HERDESS
HEMPIES	HENNY	HERALDED	HERDESSES
HEMPIEST	HENOTIC	HERALDIC	HERDIC
HEMPLIKE	HENPECK	HERALDING	HERDICS
HEMPS	HENPECKED	HERALDIST	HERDING
HEMPSEED	HENPECKS	HERALDRY	HERDLIKE
HEMPSEEDS	HENRIES	HERALDS	HERDMAN
HEMPWEED	HENRY	HERB	HERDMEN
HEMPWEEDS	HENRYS	HERBAGE	HERDS
HEMPY	HENS	HERBAGED	HERDSMAN
HEMS	HENT	HERBAGES	HERDSMEN
HEMSTITCH	HENTED	HERBAL	HERDWICK
HEN	HENTING	HERBALISM	HERDWICKS

HERE	HERMITAGE	HERPETOID	HETAIRA
HEREABOUT	HERMITESS	HERPTILE	HETAIRAI
HEREAFTER	HERMITIC	HERRIED	HETAIRAS
HEREAT	HERMITISM	HERRIES	HETAIRIA
HEREAWAY	HERMITRY	HERRIMENT	HETAIRIAS
HEREAWAYS	HERMITS	HERRING	HETAIRIC
HEREBY	HERMS	HERRINGER	HETAIRISM
HEREDES	HERN	HERRINGS	HETAIRIST
HEREDITY	HERNIA	HERRY	HETE
HEREFROM	HERNIAE	HERRYING	HETERO
HEREIN	HERNIAL	HERRYMENT	HETERODOX
HEREINTO	HERNIAS	HERS	HETERONYM
HERENESS	HERNIATE	HERSALL	HETEROPOD
HEREOF	HERNIATED	HERSALLS	HETEROS
HEREON	HERNIATES	HERSE	HETEROSES
HERES	HERNS	HERSED	HETEROSIS
HERESIES	HERNSHAW	HERSELF	HETEROTIC
HERESY	HERNSHAWS	HERSES	HETES
HERETIC	HERO	HERSHIP	HETH
HERETICAL	HEROE	HERSHIPS	HETHER
HERETICS	HEROES	HERSTORY	HETHS
HERETO	HEROIC	HERTZ	HETING
HERETRIX	HEROICAL	HERTZES	HETMAN
HEREUNDER	HEROICISE	HERY	HETMANATE
HEREUNTO	HEROICIZE	HERYE	HETMANS
HEREUPON	HEROICLY	HERYED	HETS
HEREWITH	HEROICS	HERYES	HEUCH
HERIED	HEROIN	HERYING	HEUCHERA
HERIES	HEROINE	HES	HEUCHERAS
HERIOT	HEROINES	HESITANCE	HEUCHS
HERIOTS	HEROINISM	HESITANCY	HEUGH
HERISSE	HEROINS	HESITANT	HEUGHS
HERISSON	HEROISE	HESITATE	HEUREKA
HERISSONS	HEROISED	HESITATED	HEUREKAS
HERITABLE	HEROISES	HESITATER	HEURETIC
HERITABLY	HEROISING	HESITATES	HEURETICS
HERITAGE	HEROISM	HESITATOR	HEURISM
HERITAGES	HEROISMS	HESP	HEURISMS
HERITOR	HEROIZE	HESPED	HEURISTIC
HERITORS	HEROIZED	HESPERID	HEVEA
HERITRESS	HEROIZES	HESPERIDS	HEVEAS
HERITRIX	HEROIZING	HESPING	HEW
HERKOGAMY	HERON	HESPS	HEWABLE
HERL	HERONRIES	HESSIAN	HEWED
HERLING	HERONRY	HESSIANS	HEWER
HERLINGS	HERONS	HESSITE	HEWERS
HERLS	HERONSEW	HESSITES	HEWGH
HERM	HERONSEWS	HESSONITE	HEWING
HERMA	HERONSHAW	HEST	HEWINGS
HERMAE	HEROON	HESTERNAL	HEWN
HERMAEAN	HEROONS	HESTS	HEWS
HERMAI	HEROS	HET	HEX
HERMANDAD	HEROSHIP	HETAERA	HEXACHORD
HERMETIC	HEROSHIPS	HETAERAE	HEXACT
HERMETICS	HERPES	HETAERAS	HEXACTS
HERMETISM	HERPESES	HETAERIC	HEXAD
HERMETIST	HERPETIC	HETAERISM	HEXADE
HERMIT	HERPETICS	HETAERIST	HEXADES

HEXADIC	HEYED	HIDEBOUND	HIGHCHAIR
HEXADS	HEYING	HIDED	HIGHED
HEXAFOIL	HEYS	HIDELESS	HIGHER
HEXAFOILS	HI	HIDEOSITY	HIGHERED
HEXAGLOT	HIANT	HIDEOUS	HIGHERING
HEXAGON	HIATAL	HIDEOUSLY	HIGHERS
HEXAGONAL	HIATUS	HIDEOUT	HIGHEST
HEXAGONS	HIATUSES	HIDEOUTS	HIGHFLIER
HEXAGRAM	HIBACHI	HIDER	HIGHFLYER
HEXAGRAMS	HIBACHIS	HIDERS	HIGHING
HEXAHEDRA	HIBAKUSHA	HIDES	HIGHISH
HEXAMERAL	HIBERNAL	HIDING	HIGHJACK
HEXAMETER	HIBERNATE	HIDINGS	HIGHJACKS
HEXAMINE	HIBERNISE	HIDLING	HIGHLAND
HEXAMINES	HIBERNIZE	HIDLINGS	HIGHLANDS
HEXANE	HIBISCUS	HIDLINS	HIGHLIFE
HEXANES	HIC	HIDROSES	HIGHLIFES
HEXANOIC	HICATEE	HIDROSIS	HIGHLIGHT
HEXAPLA	HICATEES	HIDROTIC	HIGHLY
HEXAPLAR	HICCATEE	HIDROTICS	HIGHMAN
HEXAPLAS	HICCATEES	HIE	HIGHMEN
HEXAPLOID	HICCOUGH	HIED	HIGHMOST
HEXAPOD	HICCOUGHS	HIEING	HIGHNESS
HEXAPODIC	HICCUP	HIELAMAN	HIGHRISE
HEXAPODS	HICCUPED	HIELAMANS	HIGHRISES
HEXAPODY	HICCUPING	HIELAND	HIGHROAD
HEXARCH	HICCUPPED	HIEMAL	HIGHROADS
HEXARCHY	HICCUPS	HIEMS	HIGHS
HEXASTICH	HICCUPY	HIERACIUM	HIGHSPOT
HEXASTYLE	HICK	HIERARCH	HIGHSPOTS
HEXED	HICKEY	HIERARCHS	HIGHT
HEXENE	HICKEYS	HIERARCHY	HIGHTAIL
HEXENES	HICKIE	HIERATIC	HIGHTAILS
HEXER	HICKIES	HIERATICA	HIGHTED
HEXEREI	HICKISH	HIEROCRAT	HIGHTH
HEXEREIS	HICKORIES	HIERODULE	HIGHTHS
HEXERS	HICKORY	HIEROGRAM	HIGHTING
HEXES	HICKS	HIEROLOGY	HIGHTOP
HEXING	HICKWALL	HIERURGY	HIGHTOPS
HEXINGS	HICKWALLS	HIES	HIGHTS
HEXONE	HICKYMAL	HIFALUTIN	HIGHVELD
HEXONES	HICKYMALS	HIGGLE	HIGHVELDS
HEXOSAN	HID	HIGGLED	HIGHWAY
HEXOSANS	HIDABLE	HIGGLER	HIGHWAYS
HEXOSE	HIDAGE	HIGGLERS	HIJAB
HEXOSES	HIDAGES	HIGGLES	HIJABS
HEXYL	HIDALGA	HIGGLING	HIJACK
HEXYLENE	HIDALGAS	HIGGLINGS	HIJACKED
HEXYLENES	HIDALGO	HIGH	HIJACKER
HEXYLIC	HIDALGOS	HIGHBALL	HIJACKERS
HEXYLS	HIDDEN	HIGHBALLS	HIJACKING
HEY	HIDDENITE	HIGHBORN	HIJACKS
HEYDAY	HIDDENLY	HIGHBOY	HIJINKS
HEYDAYS	HIDDER	HIGHBOYS	HIJRA
HEYDEY	HIDDERS	HIGHBRED	HIJRAH
HEYDEYS	HIDE	HIGHBROW	HIJRAHS
HEYDUCK	HIDEAWAY	HIGHBROWS	HIJRAS
HEYDUCKS	HIDEAWAYS	HIGHBUSH	HIKE

HIKED	HILTLESS	HINT	HIPT
HIKER	HILTS	HINTED	HIRABLE
HIKERS	HILUM	HINTER	HIRAGANA
HIKES	HILUS	HINTERS	HIRAGANAS
HIKING	HIM	HINTING	HIRAGE
HIKOI	HIMATIA	HINTINGLY	HIRAGES
HIKOIED	HIMATION	HINTINGS	HIRCINE
HIKOIING	HIMATIONS	HINTS	HIRCOSITY
HIKOIS	HIMBO	HIOI	HIRE
HILA	HIMBOS	HIOIS	HIREABLE
HILAR	HIMS	HIP	HIREAGE
HILARIOUS	HIMSELF	HIPBONE	HIREAGES
HILARITY	HIN	HIPBONES	HIRED
HILCH	HINAHINA	HIPHUGGER	HIREE
HILCHED	HINAU	HIPLESS	HIREES
HILCHES	HIND	HIPLIKE	HIRELING
HILCHING	HINDBERRY	HIPLINE	HIRELINGS
HILD	HINDBRAIN	HIPLINES	HIRER
HILDING	HINDER	HIPLY	HIRERS
HILDINGS	HINDERED	HIPNESS	HIRES
HILI	HINDERER	HIPNESSES	HIRING
HILL	HINDERERS	HIPPARCH	HIRINGS
HILLBILLY	HINDERING	HIPPARCHS	HIRLING
HILLCREST	HINDERS	HIPPED	HIRLINGS
HILLED	HINDFEET	HIPPEN	HIRPLE
HILLER	HINDFOOT	HIPPENS	HIRPLED
HILLERS	HINDGUT	HIPPER	HIRPLES
HILLFOLK	HINDGUTS	HIPPEST	HIRPLING
HILLFORT	HINDHEAD	HIPPIATRY	HIRRIENT
HILLFORTS	HINDHEADS	HIPPIC	HIRRIENTS
HILLIER	HINDLEG	HIPPIE	HIRSEL
HILLIEST	HINDLEGS	HIPPIEDOM	HIRSELED
HILLINESS	HINDMOST	HIPPIEISH	HIRSELING
HILLING	HINDRANCE	HIPPIER	HIRSELLED
HILLMEN	HINDS	HIPPIES	HIRSELS
HILLO	HINDSHANK	HIPPIEST	HIRSLE
HILLOA	HINDSIGHT	HIPPIN	HIRSLED
HILLOAED	HINDWARD	HIPPINESS	HIRSLES
HILLOAING	HINDWING	HIPPING	HIRSLING
HILLOAS	HINDWINGS	HIPPINGS	HIRSTIE
HILLOCK	HING	HIPPINS	HIRSUTE
HILLOCKED	HINGE	HIPPISH	HIRSUTISM
HILLOCKS	HINGED	HIPPO	HIRUDIN
HILLOCKY	HINGELESS	HIPPOCRAS	HIRUDINS
HILLOED	HINGELIKE	HIPPODAME	HIRUNDINE
HILLOES	HINGER	HIPPOLOGY	HIS
HILLOING	HINGERS	HIPPOS	HISH
HILLOS	HINGES	HIPPURIC	HISHED
HILLS	HINGING	HIPPURITE	HISHES
HILLSIDE	HINGS	HIPPUS	HISHING
HILLSIDES	HINKIER	HIPPUSES	HISN
HILLSLOPE	HINKIEST	HIPPY	HISPANISM
HILLTOP	HINKY	HIPPYDOM	HISPID
HILLTOPS	HINNIED	HIPPYDOMS	HISPIDITY
HILLY	HINNIES	HIPS	HISS
HILT	HINNY	HIPSHOT	HISSED
HILTED	HINNYING	HIPSTER	HISSELF
HILTING	HINS	HIPSTERS	HISSER

HISSERS	HITHES	HOARSE	HOBNAIL
HISSES	HITLESS	HOARSELY	HOBNAILED
HISSIER	HITMAN	HOARSEN	HOBNAILS
HISSIES	HITMEN	HOARSENED	HOBNOB
HISSIEST	HITS	HOARSENS	HOBNOBBED
HISSING	HITTABLE	HOARSER	HOBNOBBER
HISSINGLY	HITTER	HOARSEST	HOBNOBBY
HISSINGS	HITTERS	HOARY	HOBNOBS
HISSY	HITTING	HOAS	HOBO
HIST	HIVE	HOAST	HOBODOM
HISTAMIN	HIVED	HOASTED	HOBODOMS
HISTAMINE	HIVELESS	HOASTING	HOBOED
HISTAMINS	HIVELIKE	HOASTMAN	HOBOES
HISTED	HIVER	HOASTMEN	HOBOING
HISTIDIN	HIVERS	HOASTS	HOBOISM
HISTIDINE	HIVES	HOATCHING	HOBOISMS
HISTIDINS	HIVEWARD	HOATZIN	HOBOS
HISTIE	HIVEWARDS	HOATZINES	HOBS
HISTING	HIVING	HOATZINS	HOC
HISTIOID	HIYA	HOAX	HOCK
HISTOGEN	HIZEN	HOAXED	HOCKED
HISTOGENS	HIZENS	HOAXER	HOCKER
HISTOGENY	HIZZ	HOAXERS	HOCKERS
HISTOGRAM	HIZZED	HOAXES	HOCKEY
HISTOID	HIZZES	HOAXING	HOCKEYS
HISTOLOGY	HIZZING	HOB	HOCKING
HISTONE	HIZZONER	HOBBED	HOCKLE
HISTONES	HIZZONERS	HOBBER	HOCKLED
HISTORIAN	HM	HOBBERS	HOCKLES
HISTORIC	HMM	HOBBIES	HOCKLING
HISTORIED	HO	HOBBING	HOCKS
HISTORIES	HOA	HOBBISH	HOCKSHOP
HISTORIFY	HOACTZIN	HOBBIT	HOCKSHOPS
HISTORISM	HOACTZINS	HOBBITRY	HOCUS
HISTORY	HOAED	HOBBITS	HOCUSED
HISTRIO	HOAGIE	HOBBLE	HOCUSES
HISTRION	HOAGIES	HOBBLED	HOCUSING
HISTRIONS	HOAGY	HOBBLER	HOCUSSED
HISTRIOS	HOAING	HOBBLERS	HOCUSSES
HISTS	HOAR	HOBBLES	HOCUSSING
HIT	HOARD	HOBBLING	HOD
HITCH	HOARDED	HOBBLINGS	HODAD
HITCHED	HOARDER	HOBBY	HODADDIES
HITCHER	HOARDERS	HOBBYISM	HODADDY
HITCHERS	HOARDING	HOBBYISMS	HODADS
HITCHES	HOARDINGS	HOBBYIST	HODDED
HITCHHIKE	HOARDS	HOBBYISTS	HODDEN
HITCHIER	HOARED	HOBBYLESS	HODDENS
HITCHIEST	HOARFROST	HOBDAY	HODDIN
HITCHILY	HOARHEAD	HOBDAYED	HODDING
HITCHING	HOARHEADS	HOBDAYING	HODDINS
HITCHY	HOARHOUND	HOBDAYS	HODDLE
HITHE	HOARIER	HOBGOBLIN	HODDLED
HITHER	HOARIEST	HOBJOB	HODDLES
HITHERED	HOARILY	HOBJOBBED	HODDLING
HITHERING	HOARINESS	HOBJOBBER	HODIERNAL
HITHERS	HOARING	HOBJOBS	HODJA
HITHERTO	HOARS	HOBLIKE	HODJAS

HODMAN	HOGNOSES	HOKE	HOLIDAYER
HODMANDOD	HOGNUT	HOKED	HOLIDAYS
HODMEN	HOGNUTS	HOKES	HOLIER
HODOGRAPH	HOGS	HOKEY	HOLIES
HODOMETER	HOGSHEAD	HOKEYNESS	HOLIEST
HODOMETRY	HOGSHEADS	HOKI	HOLILY
HODOSCOPE	HOGTIE	HOKIER	HOLINESS
HODS	HOGTIED	HOKIEST	HOLING
HOE	HOGTIEING	HOKILY	HOLINGS
HOECAKE	HOGTIES	HOKINESS	HOLISM
HOECAKES	HOGTYING	HOKING	HOLISMS
HOED	HOGWARD	HOKIS	HOLIST
HOEDOWN	HOGWARDS	HOKKU	HOLISTIC
HOEDOWNS	HOGWASH	HOKONUI	HOLISTS
HOEING	HOGWASHES	HOKONUIS	HOLK
HOELIKE	HOGWEED	HOKUM	HOLKED
HOER	HOGWEEDS	HOKUMS	HOLKING
HOERS	HOH	HOKYPOKY	HOLKS
HOES	HOHA	HOLANDRIC	HOLLA
HOG	HOHED	HOLARCHY	HOLLAED
HOGAN	HOHING	HOLARD	HOLLAING
HOGANS	HOHS	HOLARDS	HOLLAND
HOGBACK	HOI	HOLD	HOLLANDS
HOGBACKS	HOICK	HOLDABLE	HOLLAS
HOGEN	HOICKED	HOLDALL	HOLLER
HOGENS	HOICKING	HOLDALLS	HOLLERED
HOGFISH	HOICKS	HOLDBACK	HOLLERING
HOGFISHES	HOICKSED	HOLDBACKS	HOLLERS
HOGG	HOICKSES	HOLDDOWN	HOLLIDAM
HOGGED	HOICKSING	HOLDDOWNS	HOLLIDAMS
HOGGER	HOIDEN	HOLDEN	HOLLIES
HOGGEREL	HOIDENED	HOLDER	HOLLO
HOGGERELS	HOIDENING	HOLDERBAT	HOLLOA
HOGGERIES	HOIDENISH	HOLDERS	HOLLOAED
HOGGERS	HOIDENS	HOLDFAST	HOLLOAING
HOGGERY	HOIK	HOLDFASTS	HOLLOAS
HOGGET	HOIKED	HOLDING	HOLLOED
HOGGETS	HOIKING	HOLDINGS	HOLLOES
HOGGIN	HOIKS	HOLDOUT	HOLLOING
HOGGING	HOING	HOLDOUTS	HOLLOO
HOGGINGS	HOISE	HOLDOVER	HOLLOOED
HOGGINS	HOISED	HOLDOVERS	HOLLOOING
HOGGISH	HOISES	HOLDS	HOLLOOS
HOGGISHLY	HOISIN	HOLDUP	HOLLOS
HOGGS	HOISING	HOLDUPS	HOLLOW
HOGH	HOISINS	HOLE	HOLLOWARE
HOGHOOD	HOIST	HOLED	HOLLOWED
HOGHOODS	HOISTED	HOLELESS	HOLLOWER
HOGHS	HOISTER	HOLES	HOLLOWEST
HOGLIKE	HOISTERS	HOLESOM	HOLLOWING
HOGMANAY	HOISTING	HOLESOME	HOLLOWLY
HOGMANAYS	HOISTINGS	HOLEY	HOLLOWS
HOGMANE	HOISTMAN	HOLEYER	HOLLY
HOGMANES	HOISTMEN	HOLEYEST	HOLLYHOCK
HOGMENAY	HOISTS	HOLIBUT	HOLM
HOGMENAYS	HOISTWAY	HOLIBUTS	HOLMIA
HOGNOSE	HOISTWAYS	HOLIDAY	HOLMIAS
HOGNOSED	HOKA	HOLIDAYED	HOLMIC

HOLMIUM	HOME	HOMESTAY	HOMOEOTIC
HOLMIUMS	HOMEBIRTH	HOMESTAYS	HOMOGAMIC
HOLMS	HOMEBODY	HOMESTEAD	HOMOGAMY
HOLOCAUST	HOMEBOUND	HOMETOWN	HOMOGENY
HOLOCENE	HOMEBOY	HOMETOWNS	HOMOGONY
HOLOCRINE	HOMEBOYS	HOMEWARD	HOMOGRAFT
HOLOGAMY	HOMEBRED	HOMEWARDS	HOMOGRAPH
HOLOGRAM	HOMEBREDS	HOMEWARE	HOMOLOG
HOLOGRAMS	HOMEBREW	HOMEWARES	HOMOLOGIC
HOLOGRAPH	HOMEBREWS	HOMEWORK	HOMOLOGS
HOLOGYNIC	HOMEBUILT	HOMEWORKS	HOMOLOGUE
HOLOGYNY	HOMEBUYER	HOMEY	HOMOLOGY
HOLOHEDRA	HOMECOMER	HOMEYNESS	HOMOLYSES
HOLON	HOMECRAFT	HOMEYS	HOMOLYSIS
HOLONIC	HOMED	HOMICIDAL	HOMOLYTIC
HOLONS	HOMEFELT	HOMICIDE	HOMOMORPH
HOLOPHOTE	HOMEGIRL	HOMICIDES	HOMONYM
HOLOPHYTE	HOMEGIRLS	HOMIE	HOMONYMIC
HOLOPTIC	HOMEGROWN	HOMIER	HOMONYMS
HOLOTYPE	HOMELAND	HOMIES	HOMONYMY
HOLOTYPES	HOMELANDS	HOMIEST	HOMOPHILE
HOLOTYPIC	HOMELESS	HOMILETIC	HOMOPHOBE
HOLOZOIC	HOMELIER	HOMILIES	HOMOPHONE
HOLP	HOMELIEST	HOMILIST	HOMOPHONY
HOLPEN	HOMELIKE	HOMILISTS	HOMOPHYLY
HOLS	HOMELILY	HOMILY	HOMOPLASY
HOLSTEIN	HOMELY	HOMINES	HOMOPOLAR
HOLSTEINS	HOMELYN	HOMINESS	HOMOS
HOLSTER	HOMELYNS	HOMING	HOMOSEX
HOLSTERED	HOMEMADE	HOMINGS	HOMOSEXES
HOLSTERS	HOMEMAKER	HOMINIAN	HOMOSPORY
HOLT	HOMEOBOX	HOMINIANS	HOMOSTYLY
HOLTS	HOMEOMERY	HOMINID	HOMOTAXES
HOLY	HOMEOPATH	HOMINIDS	HOMOTAXIC
HOLYDAM	HOMEOSES	HOMINIES	HOMOTAXIS
HOLYDAME	HOMEOSIS	HOMININE	HOMOTONIC
HOLYDAMES	HOMEOTIC	HOMINISE	HOMOTONY
HOLYDAMS	HOMEOWNER	HOMINISED	HOMOTYPAL
HOLYDAY	HOMEPAGE	HOMINISES	HOMOTYPE
HOLYDAYS	HOMEPAGES	HOMINIZE	HOMOTYPES
HOLYSTONE	HOMEPLACE	HOMINIZED	HOMOTYPIC
HOLYTIDE	HOMEPORT	HOMINIZES	HOMOTYPY
HOLYTIDES	HOMEPORTS	HOMINOID	HOMOUSIAN
HOM	HOMER	HOMINOIDS	HOMS
HOMA	HOMERED	HOMINY	HOMUNCLE
HOMAGE	HOMERIC	HOMME	HOMUNCLES
HOMAGED	HOMERING	HOMMES	HOMUNCULE
HOMAGER	HOMEROOM	HOMMOCK	HOMUNCULI
HOMAGERS	HOMEROOMS	HOMMOCKS	HOMY
HOMAGES	HOMERS	HOMMOS	HON
HOMAGING	HOMES	HOMMOSES	HONAN
HOMALOID	HOMESICK	HOMO	HONANS
HOMALOIDS	HOMESITE	HOMOCERCY	HONCHO
HOMAS	HOMESITES	HOMODONT	HONCHOED
HOMBRE	HOMESPUN	HOMODYNE	HONCHOING
HOMBRES	HOMESPUNS	HOMOEOBOX	HONCHOS
HOMBURG	HOMESTALL	HOMOEOSES	HOND
HOMBURGS	HOMESTAND	HOMOEOSIS	HONDA

HONDAS	HONKY	HOOFBEAT	HOOPED
HONDLE	HONOR	HOOFBEATS	HOOPER
HONDLED	HONORABLE	HOOFBOUND	HOOPERS
HONDLES	HONORABLY	HOOFED	HOOPING
HONDLING	HONORAND	HOOFER	HOOPLA
HONDS	HONORANDS	HOOFERS	HOOPLAS
HONE	HONORARIA	HOOFING	HOOPLESS
HONED	HONORARY	HOOFLESS	HOOPLIKE
HONER	HONORED	HOOFLIKE	HOOPOE
HONERS	HONOREE	HOOFPRINT	HOOPOES
HONES	HONOREES	HOOFROT	HOOPOO
HONEST	HONORER	HOOFROTS	HOOPOOS
HONESTER	HONORERS	HOOFS	HOOPS
HONESTEST	HONORIFIC	HOOK	HOOPSKIRT
HONESTIES	HONORING	HOOKA	HOOPSTER
HONESTLY	HONORLESS	HOOKAH	HOOPSTERS
HONESTY	HONORS	HOOKAHS	HOORAH
HONEWORT	HONOUR	HOOKAS	HOORAHED
HONEWORTS	HONOURED	HOOKCHECK	HOORAHING
HONEY	HONOURER	HOOKED	HOORAHS
HONEYBEE	HONOURERS	HOOKER	HOORAY
HONEYBEES	HONOURING	HOOKERS	HOORAYED
HONEYBUN	HONOURS	HOOKEY	HOORAYING
HONEYBUNS	HONS	HOOKEYS	HOORAYS
HONEYCOMB	HOO	HOOKIER	HOORD
HONEYDEW	HOOCH	HOOKIES	HOORDS
HONEYDEWS	HOOCHES	HOOKIEST	HOOROO
HONEYED	HOOCHIE	HOOKING	HOOSEGOW
HONEYEDLY	HOOCHIES	HOOKLESS	HOOSEGOWS
HONEYFUL	HOOD	HOOKLET	HOOSGOW
HONEYING	HOODED	HOOKLETS	HOOSGOWS
HONEYLESS	HOODIA	HOOKLIKE	HOOSH
HONEYMOON	HOODIAS	HOOKNOSE	HOOSHED
HONEYPOT	HOODIE	HOOKNOSED	HOOSHES
HONEYPOTS	HOODIER	HOOKNOSES	HOOSHING
HONEYS	HOODIES	HOOKS	HOOT
HONEYTRAP	HOODIEST	HOOKUP	HOOTCH
HONG	HOODING	HOOKUPS	HOOTCHES
HONGI	HOODLESS	HOOKWORM	HOOTED
HONGIED	HOODLIKE	HOOKWORMS	HOOTER
HONGIES	HOODLUM	HOOKY	HOOTERS
HONGIING	HOODLUMS	HOOLACHAN	HOOTIER
HONGING	HOODMAN	HOOLEY	HOOTIEST
HONGIS	HOODMEN	HOOLEYS	HOOTING
HONGS	HOODMOLD	HOOLICAN	HOOTNANNY
HONIED	HOODMOLDS	HOOLICANS	HOOTS
HONIEDLY	HOODOO	HOOLIE	HOOTY
HONING	HOODOOED	HOOLIER	HOOVE
HONK	HOODOOING	HOOLIES	HOOVED
HONKED	HOODOOISM	HOOLIEST	HOOVEN
HONKER	HOODOOS	HOOLIGAN	HOOVER
HONKERS	HOODS	HOOLIGANS	HOOVERED
HONKEY	HOODWINK	HOOLOCK	HOOVERING
HONKEYS	HOODWINKS	HOOLOCKS	HOOVERS
HONKIE	HOODY	HOOLY	HOOVES
HONKIES	HOOEY	HOON	HOOVING
HONKING	HOOEYS	HOONS	HOP
HONKS	HOOF	HOOP	HOPBIND

HOPBINDS	HORDOCKS	HORNPIPES	HORSELIKE
HOPBINE	HORE	HORNPOUT	HORSEMAN
HOPBINES	HOREHOUND	HORNPOUTS	HORSEMEAT
HOPDOG	HORI	HORNS	HORSEMEN
HOPDOGS	HORIATIKI	HORNSTONE	HORSEMINT
HOPE	HORIS	HORNTAIL	HORSEPLAY
HOPED	HORIZON	HORNTAILS	HORSEPOND
HOPEFUL	HORIZONAL	HORNWORK	HORSEPOX
HOPEFULLY	HORIZONS	HORNWORKS	HORSERACE
HOPEFULS	HORKEY	HORNWORM	HORSES
HOPELESS	HORKEYS	HORNWORMS	HORSESHIT
HOPER	HORLICKS	HORNWORT	HORSESHOD
HOPERS	HORME	HORNWORTS	HORSESHOE
HOPES	HORMES	HORNWRACK	HORSETAIL
HOPHEAD	HORMIC	HORNY	HORSEWAY
HOPHEADS	HORMONAL	HORNYHEAD	HORSEWAYS
HOPING	HORMONE	HORNYWINK	HORSEWEED
HOPINGLY	HORMONES	HOROEKA	HORSEWHIP
HOPLITE	HORMONIC	HOROKAKA	HORSEY
HOPLITES	HORN	HOROLOGE	HORSIER
HOPLITIC	HORNBAG	HOROLOGER	HORSIEST
HOPLOLOGY	HORNBAGS	HOROLOGES	HORSILY
HOPPED	HORNBEAK	HOROLOGIA	HORSINESS
HOPPER	HORNBEAKS	HOROLOGIC	HORSING
HOPPERCAR	HORNBEAM	HOROLOGY	HORSINGS
HOPPERS	HORNBEAMS	HOROMETRY	HORSON
HOPPIER	HORNBILL	HOROPITO	HORSONS
HOPPIEST	HORNBILLS	HOROPITOS	HORST
HOPPING	HORNBOOK	HOROPTER	HORSTE
HOPPINGS	HORNBOOKS	HOROPTERS	HORSTES
HOPPLE	HORNBUG	HOROSCOPE	HORSTS
HOPPLED	HORNBUGS	HOROSCOPY	HORSY
HOPPLER	HORNED	HORRENT	HORTATION
HOPPLERS	HORNER	HORRIBLE	HORTATIVE
HOPPLES	HORNERS	HORRIBLES	HORTATORY
HOPPLING	HORNET	HORRIBLY	HOS
HOPPY	HORNETS	HORRID	HOSANNA
HOPS	HORNFELS	HORRIDER	HOSANNAED
HOPSACK	HORNFUL	HORRIDEST	HOSANNAH
HOPSACKS	HORNFULS	HORRIDLY	HOSANNAHS
HOPSCOTCH	HORNGELD	HORRIFIC	HOSANNAS
HOPTOAD	HORNGELDS	HORRIFIED	HOSE
HOPTOADS	HORNIER	HORRIFIES	HOSED
HORA	HORNIEST	HORRIFY	HOSEL
HORAH	HORNILY	HORROR	HOSELIKE
HORAHS	HORNINESS	HORRORS	HOSELS
HORAL	HORNING	HORS	HOSEMAN
HORARY	HORNINGS	HORSE	HOSEMEN
HORAS	HORNISH	HORSEBACK	HOSEN
HORDE	HORNIST	HORSEBEAN	HOSEPIPE
HORDED	HORNISTS	HORSEBOX	HOSEPIPES
HORDEIN	HORNITO	HORSECAR	HOSER
HORDEINS	HORNITOS	HORSECARS	HOSERS
HORDEOLA	HORNLESS	HORSED	HOSES
HORDEOLUM	HORNLET	HORSEFLY	HOSEY
HORDES	HORNLETS	HORSEHAIR	HOSEYED
HORDING	HORNLIKE	HORSEHIDE	HOSEYING
HORDOCK	HORNPIPE	HORSELESS	HOSEYS

HOSIER	HOTCAKES	HOTTIE	HOUSEKEEP
HOSIERIES	HOTCH	HOTTIES	HOUSEKEPT
HOSIERS	HOTCHED	HOTTING	HOUSEL
HOSIERY	HOTCHES	HOTTINGS	HOUSELED
HOSING	HOTCHING	HOTTISH	HOUSELEEK
HOSPICE	HOTCHPOT	HOTTY	HOUSELESS
HOSPICES	HOTCHPOTS	HOUDAH	HOUSELINE
HOSPITAGE	HOTDOG	HOUDAHS	HOUSELING
HOSPITAL	HOTDOGGED	HOUDAN	HOUSELLED
HOSPITALE	HOTDOGGER	HOUDANS	HOUSELS
HOSPITALS	HOTDOGS	HOUF	HOUSEMAID
HOSPITIA	HOTE	HOUFED	HOUSEMAN
HOSPITIUM	HOTEL	HOUFF	HOUSEMATE
HOSPODAR	HOTELDOM	HOUFFED	HOUSEMEN
HOSPODARS	HOTELDOMS	HOUFFING	HOUSER
HOSS	HOTELIER	HOUFFS	HOUSEROOM
HOSSES	HOTELIERS	HOUFING	HOUSERS
HOST	HOTELMAN	HOUFS	HOUSES
HOSTA	HOTELMEN	HOUGH	HOUSESAT
HOSTAGE	HOTELS	HOUGHED	HOUSESIT
HOSTAGES	HOTEN	HOUGHING	HOUSESITS
HOSTAS	HOTFOOT	HOUGHS	HOUSETOP
HOSTED	HOTFOOTED	HOUHERE	HOUSETOPS
HOSTEL	HOTFOOTS	HOUMMOS	HOUSEWIFE
HOSTELED	HOTHEAD	HOUMMOSES	HOUSEWORK
HOSTELER	HOTHEADED	HOUMOUS	HOUSEY
HOSTELERS	HOTHEADS	HOUMOUSES	HOUSIER
HOSTELING	HOTHOUSE	HOUMUS	HOUSIEST
HOSTELLED	HOTHOUSED	HOUMUSES	HOUSING
HOSTELLER	HOTHOUSES	HOUND	HOUSINGS
HOSTELRY	HOTLINE	HOUNDED	HOUSLING
HOSTELS	HOTLINES	HOUNDER	HOUSTONIA
HOSTESS	HOTLINK	HOUNDERS	HOUT
HOSTESSED	HOTLINKS	HOUNDFISH	HOUTED
HOSTESSES	HOTLY	HOUNDING	HOUTING
HOSTIE	HOTNESS	HOUNDS	HOUTINGS
HOSTIES	HOTNESSES	HOUNGAN	HOUTS
HOSTILE	HOTPLATE	HOUNGANS	HOVE
HOSTILELY	HOTPLATES	HOUR	HOVEA
HOSTILES	HOTPOT	HOURGLASS	HOVEAS
HOSTILITY	HOTPOTS	HOURI	HOVED
HOSTING	HOTPRESS	HOURIS	HOVEL
HOSTINGS	HOTROD	HOURLIES	HOVELED
HOSTLER	HOTRODS	HOURLONG	HOVELING
HOSTLERS	HOTS	HOURLY	HOVELLED
HOSTLESSE	HOTSHOT	HOURPLATE	HOVELLER
HOSTLY	HOTSHOTS	HOURS	HOVELLERS
HOSTRIES	HOTSPOT	HOUSE	HOVELLING
HOSTRY	HOTSPOTS	HOUSEBOAT	HOVELS
HOSTS	HOTSPUR	HOUSEBOY	HOVEN
HOT	HOTSPURS	HOUSEBOYS	HOVER
HOTBED	HOTTED	HOUSECARL	HOVERED
HOTBEDS	HOTTENTOT	HOUSECOAT	HOVERER
HOTBLOOD	HOTTER	HOUSED	HOVERERS
HOTBLOODS	HOTTERED	HOUSEFLY	HOVERFLY
HOTBOX	HOTTERING	HOUSEFUL	HOVERING
HOTBOXES	HOTTERS	HOUSEFULS	HOVERPORT
HOTCAKE	HOTTEST	HOUSEHOLD	HOVERS

HOVES
HOVING
HOW
HOWBE
HOWBEIT
HOWDAH
HOWDAHS
HOWDIE
HOWDIED
HOWDIES
HOWDY
HOWDYING
HOWE
HOWES
HOWEVER
HOWF
HOWFED
HOWFF
HOWFFED
HOWFFING
HOWFFS
HOWFING
HOWFS
HOWITZER
HOWITZERS
HOWK
HOWKED
HOWKER
HOWKERS
HOWKING
HOWKS
HOWL
HOWLBACK
HOWLBACKS
HOWLED
HOWLER
HOWLERS
HOWLET
HOWLETS
HOWLING
HOWLINGLY
HOWLINGS
HOWLROUND
HOWLS
HOWRE
HOWRES
HOWS
HOWSO
HOWSOEVER
HOWTOWDIE
HOWZAT
HOWZIT
HOX
HOXED
HOXES
HOXING
HOY
HOYA

HOYAS
HOYDEN
HOYDENED
HOYDENING
HOYDENISH
HOYDENISM
HOYDENS
HOYED
HOYING
HOYLE
HOYLES
HOYS
HRYVNA
HRYVNAS
HRYVNIA
HRYVNIAS
HRYVNYA
HRYVNYAS
HUANACO
HUANACOS
HUAQUERO
HUAQUEROS
HUARACHE
HUARACHES
HUARACHO
HUARACHOS
HUB
HUBBIES
HUBBLY
HUBBUB
HUBBUBOO
HUBBUBOOS
HUBBUBS
HUBBY
HUBCAP
HUBCAPS
HUBRIS
HUBRISES
HUBRISTIC
HUBS
HUCK
HUCKABACK
HUCKERY
HUCKLE
HUCKLES
HUCKS
HUCKSTER
HUCKSTERS
HUCKSTERY
HUDDEN
HUDDLE
HUDDLED
HUDDLER
HUDDLERS
HUDDLES
HUDDLING
HUDDUP
HUDNA

HUDNAS
HUDUD
HUDUDS
HUE
HUED
HUELESS
HUER
HUERS
HUES
HUFF
HUFFED
HUFFER
HUFFERS
HUFFIER
HUFFIEST
HUFFILY
HUFFINESS
HUFFING
HUFFINGS
HUFFISH
HUFFISHLY
HUFFKIN
HUFFKINS
HUFFS
HUFFY
HUG
HUGE
HUGELY
HUGENESS
HUGEOUS
HUGEOUSLY
HUGER
HUGEST
HUGGABLE
HUGGED
HUGGER
HUGGERS
HUGGIER
HUGGIEST
HUGGING
HUGGY
HUGS
HUGY
HUH
HUHU
HUHUS
HUI
HUIA
HUIAS
HUIC
HUIPIL
HUIPILES
HUIPILS
HUIS
HUISACHE
HUISACHES
HUISSIER
HUISSIERS

HUITAIN
HUITAINS
HULA
HULAS
HULE
HULES
HULK
HULKED
HULKIER
HULKIEST
HULKING
HULKS
HULKY
HULL
HULLED
HULLER
HULLERS
HULLIER
HULLIEST
HULLING
HULLO
HULLOA
HULLOAED
HULLOAING
HULLOAS
HULLOED
HULLOES
HULLOING
HULLOO
HULLOOED
HULLOOING
HULLOOS
HULLOS
HULLS
HULLY
HUM
HUMA
HUMAN
HUMANE
HUMANELY
HUMANER
HUMANEST
HUMANHOOD
HUMANISE
HUMANISED
HUMANISER
HUMANISES
HUMANISM
HUMANISMS
HUMANIST
HUMANISTS
HUMANITY
HUMANIZE
HUMANIZED
HUMANIZER
HUMANIZES
HUMANKIND
HUMANLIKE

HUMANLY	HUMIDICES	HUMORSOME	HUNGERS
HUMANNESS	HUMIDIFY	HUMOUR	HUNGOVER
HUMANOID	HUMIDITY	HUMOURED	HUNGRIER
HUMANOIDS	HUMIDLY	HUMOURFUL	HUNGRIEST
HUMANS	HUMIDNESS	HUMOURING	HUNGRILY
HUMAS	HUMIDOR	HUMOURS	HUNGRY
HUMATE	HUMIDORS	HUMOUS	HUNH
HUMATES	HUMIFIED	HUMP	HUNK
HUMBLE	HUMIFIES	HUMPBACK	HUNKER
HUMBLEBEE	HUMIFY	HUMPBACKS	HUNKERED
HUMBLED	HUMIFYING	HUMPED	HUNKERING
HUMBLER	HUMILIANT	HUMPEN	HUNKERS
HUMBLERS	HUMILIATE	HUMPENS	HUNKEY
HUMBLES	HUMILITY	HUMPER	HUNKEYS
HUMBLESSE	HUMINT	HUMPERS	HUNKIE
HUMBLEST	HUMINTS	HUMPH	HUNKIER
HUMBLING	HUMITE	HUMPHED	HUNKIES
HUMBLINGS	HUMITES	HUMPHING	HUNKIEST
HUMBLY	HUMITURE	HUMPHS	HUNKS
HUMBUCKER	HUMITURES	HUMPIER	HUNKSES
HUMBUG	HUMLIE	HUMPIES	HUNKY
HUMBUGGED	HUMLIES	HUMPIEST	HUNNISH
HUMBUGGER	HUMMABLE	HUMPINESS	HUNS
HUMBUGS	HUMMAUM	HUMPING	HUNT
HUMBUZZ	HUMMAUMS	HUMPLESS	HUNTABLE
HUMBUZZES	HUMMED	HUMPLIKE	HUNTAWAY
HUMDINGER	HUMMEL	HUMPS	HUNTAWAYS
HUMDRUM	HUMMELLED	HUMPTIES	HUNTED
HUMDRUMS	HUMMELLER	HUMPTY	HUNTEDLY
HUMECT	HUMMELS	HUMPY	HUNTER
HUMECTANT	HUMMER	HUMS	HUNTERS
HUMECTATE	HUMMERS	HUMSTRUM	HUNTING
HUMECTED	HUMMING	HUMSTRUMS	HUNTINGS
HUMECTING	HUMMINGS	HUMUNGOUS	HUNTRESS
HUMECTIVE	HUMMOCK	HUMUS	HUNTS
HUMECTS	HUMMOCKED	HUMUSES	HUNTSMAN
HUMEFIED	HUMMOCKS	HUMUSY	HUNTSMEN
HUMEFIES	HUMMOCKY	HUMVEE	HUP
HUMEFY	HUMMUM	HUMVEES	HUPIRO
HUMEFYING	HUMMUMS	HUN	HUPPAH
HUMERAL	HUMMUS	HUNCH	HUPPAHS
HUMERALS	HUMMUSES	HUNCHBACK	HUPPED
HUMERI	HUMOGEN	HUNCHED	HUPPING
HUMERUS	HUMOGENS	HUNCHES	HUPS
HUMF	HUMONGOUS	HUNCHING	HURCHEON
HUMFED	HUMOR	HUNDRED	HURCHEONS
HUMFING	HUMORAL	HUNDREDER	HURDEN
HUMFS	HUMORALLY	HUNDREDOR	HURDENS
HUMHUM	HUMORED	HUNDREDS	HURDIES
HUMHUMS	HUMORESK	HUNDREDTH	HURDLE
HUMIC	HUMORESKS	HUNG	HURDLED
HUMICOLE	HUMORFUL	HUNGAN	HURDLER
HUMICOLES	HUMORING	HUNGANS	HURDLERS
HUMID	HUMORIST	HUNGER	HURDLES
HUMIDER	HUMORISTS	HUNGERED	HURDLING
HUMIDEST	HUMORLESS	HUNGERFUL	HURDLINGS
HUMIDEX	HUMOROUS	HUNGERING	HURDS
HUMIDEXES	HUMORS	HUNGERLY	HURL

HURLBAT
HURLBATS
HURLED
HURLER
HURLERS
HURLEY
HURLEYS
HURLIES
HURLING
HURLINGS
HURLS
HURLY
HURRA
HURRAED
HURRAH
HURRAHED
HURRAHING
HURRAHS
HURRAING
HURRAS
HURRAY
HURRAYED
HURRAYING
HURRAYS
HURRICANE
HURRICANO
HURRIED
HURRIEDLY
HURRIER
HURRIERS
HURRIES
HURRY
HURRYING
HURRYINGS
HURST
HURSTS
HURT
HURTER
HURTERS
HURTFUL
HURTFULLY
HURTING
HURTLE
HURTLED
HURTLES
HURTLESS
HURTLING
HURTS
HUSBAND
HUSBANDED
HUSBANDER
HUSBANDLY
HUSBANDRY
HUSBANDS
HUSH
HUSHABIED
HUSHABIES
HUSHABY

HUSHED
HUSHEDLY
HUSHER
HUSHERED
HUSHERING
HUSHERS
HUSHES
HUSHFUL
HUSHIER
HUSHIEST
HUSHING
HUSHPUPPY
HUSHY
HUSK
HUSKED
HUSKER
HUSKERS
HUSKIER
HUSKIES
HUSKIEST
HUSKILY
HUSKINESS
HUSKING
HUSKINGS
HUSKLIKE
HUSKS
HUSKY
HUSO
HUSOS
HUSS
HUSSAR
HUSSARS
HUSSES
HUSSIES
HUSSIF
HUSSIFS
HUSSY
HUSTINGS
HUSTLE
HUSTLED
HUSTLER
HUSTLERS
HUSTLES
HUSTLING
HUSTLINGS
HUSWIFE
HUSWIFES
HUSWIVES
HUT
HUTCH
HUTCHED
HUTCHES
HUTCHIE
HUTCHIES
HUTCHING
HUTIA
HUTIAS
HUTLIKE

HUTMENT
HUTMENTS
HUTS
HUTTED
HUTTING
HUTTINGS
HUTZPA
HUTZPAH
HUTZPAHS
HUTZPAS
HUZOOR
HUZOORS
HUZZA
HUZZAED
HUZZAH
HUZZAHED
HUZZAHING
HUZZAHS
HUZZAING
HUZZAS
HUZZIES
HUZZY
HWAN
HWYL
HWYLS
HYACINE
HYACINES
HYACINTH
HYACINTHS
HYAENA
HYAENAS
HYAENIC
HYALIN
HYALINE
HYALINES
HYALINISE
HYALINIZE
HYALINS
HYALITE
HYALITES
HYALOGEN
HYALOGENS
HYALOID
HYALOIDS
HYALONEMA
HYBRID
HYBRIDISE
HYBRIDISM
HYBRIDIST
HYBRIDITY
HYBRIDIZE
HYBRIDOMA
HYBRIDOUS
HYBRIDS
HYBRIS
HYBRISES
HYBRISTIC
HYDANTOIN

HYDATHODE
HYDATID
HYDATIDS
HYDATOID
HYDRA
HYDRACID
HYDRACIDS
HYDRAE
HYDRAEMIA
HYDRAGOG
HYDRAGOGS
HYDRANGEA
HYDRANT
HYDRANTH
HYDRANTHS
HYDRANTS
HYDRAS
HYDRASE
HYDRASES
HYDRASTIS
HYDRATE
HYDRATED
HYDRATES
HYDRATING
HYDRATION
HYDRATOR
HYDRATORS
HYDRAULIC
HYDRAZIDE
HYDRAZINE
HYDRAZOIC
HYDREMIA
HYDREMIAS
HYDRIA
HYDRIAE
HYDRIC
HYDRID
HYDRIDE
HYDRIDES
HYDRIDS
HYDRILLA
HYDRILLAS
HYDRIODIC
HYDRO
HYDROCAST
HYDROCELE
HYDROFOIL
HYDROGEL
HYDROGELS
HYDROGEN
HYDROGENS
HYDROID
HYDROIDS
HYDROLASE
HYDROLOGY
HYDROLYSE
HYDROLYTE
HYDROLYZE

HYDROMA	HYGRODEIK	HYMNISTS	HYPETHRAL
HYDROMAS	HYGROLOGY	HYMNLESS	HYPHA
HYDROMATA	HYGROMA	HYMNLIKE	HYPHAE
HYDROMEL	HYGROMAS	HYMNODIES	HYPHAL
HYDROMELS	HYGROMATA	HYMNODIST	HYPHEMIA
HYDRONAUT	HYGROPHIL	HYMNODY	HYPHEMIAS
HYDRONIC	HYGROSTAT	HYMNOLOGY	HYPHEN
HYDRONIUM	HYING	HYMNS	HYPHENATE
HYDROPATH	HYKE	HYNDE	HYPHENED
HYDROPIC	HYKES	HYNDES	HYPHENIC
HYDROPS	HYLA	HYOID	HYPHENING
HYDROPSES	HYLAS	HYOIDAL	HYPHENISE
HYDROPSY	HYLDING	HYOIDEAN	HYPHENISM
HYDROPTIC	HYLDINGS	HYOIDS	HYPHENIZE
HYDROPULT	HYLE	HYOSCINE	HYPHENS
HYDROS	HYLEG	HYOSCINES	HYPING
HYDROSERE	HYLEGS	HYP	HYPINOSES
HYDROSKI	HYLES	HYPALGIA	HYPINOSIS
HYDROSKIS	HYLIC	HYPALGIAS	HYPNIC
HYDROSOL	HYLICISM	HYPALLAGE	HYPNICS
HYDROSOLS	HYLICISMS	HYPANTHIA	HYPNOGENY
HYDROSOMA	HYLICIST	HYPATE	HYPNOID
HYDROSOME	HYLICISTS	HYPATES	HYPNOIDAL
HYDROSTAT	HYLISM	HYPE	HYPNOLOGY
HYDROUS	HYLISMS	HYPED	HYPNONE
HYDROVANE	HYLIST	HYPER	HYPNONES
HYDROXIDE	HYLISTS	HYPERACID	HYPNOSES
HYDROXY	HYLOBATE	HYPERARID	HYPNOSIS
HYDROXYL	HYLOBATES	HYPERBOLA	HYPNOTEE
HYDROXYLS	HYLOIST	HYPERBOLE	HYPNOTEES
HYDROZOA	HYLOISTS	HYPERCUBE	HYPNOTIC
HYDROZOAN	HYLOPHYTE	HYPEREMIA	HYPNOTICS
HYDROZOON	HYLOZOIC	HYPEREMIC	HYPNOTISE
HYDYNE	HYLOZOISM	HYPERFINE	HYPNOTISM
HYDYNES	HYLOZOIST	HYPERGAMY	HYPNOTIST
HYE	HYMEN	HYPERGOL	HYPNOTIZE
HYED	HYMENAEAL	HYPERGOLS	HYPNOTOID
HYEING	HYMENAEAN	HYPERICUM	HYPNUM
HYEN	HYMENAL	HYPERLINK	HYPNUMS
HYENA	HYMENEAL	HYPERMART	HYPO
HYENAS	HYMENEALS	HYPERNOVA	HYPOACID
HYENIC	HYMENEAN	HYPERNYM	HYPOBARIC
HYENINE	HYMENIA	HYPERNYMS	HYPOBLAST
HYENOID	HYMENIAL	HYPERNYMY	HYPOBOLE
HYENS	HYMENIUM	HYPERON	HYPOBOLES
HYES	HYMENIUMS	HYPERONS	HYPOCAUST
HYETAL	HYMENS	HYPEROPE	HYPOCIST
HYETOLOGY	HYMN	HYPEROPES	HYPOCISTS
HYGEIST	HYMNAL	HYPEROPIA	HYPOCOTYL
HYGEISTS	HYMNALS	HYPEROPIC	HYPOCRISY
HYGIEIST	HYMNARIES	HYPERPNEA	HYPOCRITE
HYGIEISTS	HYMNARY	HYPERPURE	HYPODERM
HYGIENE	HYMNBOOK	HYPERREAL	HYPODERMA
HYGIENES	HYMNBOOKS	HYPERS	HYPODERMS
HYGIENIC	HYMNED	HYPERTEXT	HYPOED
HYGIENICS	HYMNIC	HYPES	HYPOGAEA
HYGIENIST	HYMNING	HYPESTER	HYPOGAEAL
HYGRISTOR	HYMNIST	HYPESTERS	HYPOGAEAN

HYPOGAEUM
HYPOGEA
HYPOGEAL
HYPOGEAN
HYPOGENE
HYPOGENIC
HYPOGEOUS
HYPOGEUM
HYPOGYNY
HYPOID
HYPOING
HYPOMANIA
HYPOMANIC
HYPOMORPH
HYPONASTY
HYPONEA
HYPONEAS
HYPONOIA
HYPONOIAS
HYPONYM
HYPONYMS
HYPONYMY
HYPOPHYGE
HYPOPLOID
HYPOPNEA
HYPOPNEAS
HYPOPNEIC
HYPOPNOEA
HYPOPYON
HYPOPYONS
HYPOS
HYPOSTOME
HYPOSTYLE
HYPOTAXES
HYPOTAXIS
HYPOTHEC
HYPOTHECA
HYPOTHECS
HYPOTONIA
HYPOTONIC
HYPOXEMIA
HYPOXEMIC
HYPOXIA
HYPOXIAS
HYPOXIC
HYPPED
HYPPING
HYPS
HYPURAL
HYRACES
HYRACOID
HYRACOIDS
HYRAX
HYRAXES
HYSON
HYSONS
HYSSOP
HYSSOPS

HYSTERIA
HYSTERIAS
HYSTERIC
HYSTERICS
HYSTEROID
HYTE
HYTHE
HYTHES

I

IAMB	ICEMAN	ICONIC	IDEALNESS
IAMBI	ICEMEN	ICONICAL	IDEALOGUE
IAMBIC	ICEPACK	ICONICITY	IDEALOGY
IAMBICS	ICEPACKS	ICONIFIED	IDEALS
IAMBIST	ICER	ICONIFIES	IDEAS
IAMBISTS	ICERS	ICONIFY	IDEATA
IAMBS	ICES	ICONISE	IDEATE
IAMBUS	ICESTONE	ICONISED	IDEATED
IAMBUSES	ICESTONES	ICONISES	IDEATES
IANTHINE	ICEWINE	ICONISING	IDEATING
IATRIC	ICEWINES	ICONIZE	IDEATION
IATRICAL	ICH	ICONIZED	IDEATIONS
IATROGENY	ICHABOD	ICONIZES	IDEATIVE
IBERIS	ICHED	ICONIZING	IDEATUM
IBERISES	ICHES	ICONOLOGY	IDEE
IBEX	ICHING	ICONOSTAS	IDEES
IBEXES	ICHNEUMON	ICONS	IDEM
IBICES	ICHNITE	ICTAL	IDENT
IBIDEM	ICHNITES	ICTERIC	IDENTIC
IBIS	ICHNOLITE	ICTERICAL	IDENTICAL
IBISES	ICHNOLOGY	ICTERICS	IDENTIFY
IBOGAINE	ICHOR	ICTERID	IDENTIKIT
IBOGAINES	ICHOROUS	ICTERIDS	IDENTITY
IBUPROFEN	ICHORS	ICTERINE	IDENTS
ICE	ICHS	ICTERUS	IDEOGRAM
ICEBALL	ICHTHIC	ICTERUSES	IDEOGRAMS
ICEBALLS	ICHTHYIC	ICTIC	IDEOGRAPH
ICEBERG	ICHTHYOID	ICTUS	IDEOLOGIC
ICEBERGS	ICHTHYS	ICTUSES	IDEOLOGUE
ICEBLINK	ICHTHYSES	ICY	IDEOLOGY
ICEBLINKS	ICICLE	ID	IDEOMOTOR
ICEBOAT	ICICLED	IDANT	IDEOPHONE
ICEBOATER	ICICLES	IDANTS	IDES
ICEBOATS	ICIER	IDE	IDIOBLAST
ICEBOUND	ICIEST	IDEA	IDIOCIES
ICEBOX	ICILY	IDEAED	IDIOCY
ICEBOXES	ICINESS	IDEAL	IDIOGRAM
ICECAP	ICINESSES	IDEALESS	IDIOGRAMS
ICECAPPED	ICING	IDEALISE	IDIOGRAPH
ICECAPS	ICINGS	IDEALISED	IDIOLECT
ICED	ICK	IDEALISER	IDIOLECTS
ICEFALL	ICKER	IDEALISES	IDIOM
ICEFALLS	ICKERS	IDEALISM	IDIOMATIC
ICEFIELD	ICKIER	IDEALISMS	IDIOMS
ICEFIELDS	ICKIEST	IDEALIST	IDIOPATHY
ICEHOUSE	ICKILY	IDEALISTS	IDIOPHONE
ICEHOUSES	ICKINESS	IDEALITY	IDIOPLASM
ICEKHANA	ICKLE	IDEALIZE	IDIOT
ICEKHANAS	ICKLER	IDEALIZED	IDIOTCIES
ICELESS	ICKLEST	IDEALIZER	IDIOTCY
ICELIKE	ICKY	IDEALIZES	IDIOTIC
ICEMAKER	ICON	IDEALLESS	IDIOTICAL
ICEMAKERS	ICONES	IDEALLY	IDIOTICON

IDIOTISH	IDYLLS	IGNORAMUS	ILLAPSES
IDIOTISM	IDYLS	IGNORANCE	ILLAPSING
IDIOTISMS	IF	IGNORANT	ILLATION
IDIOTS	IFF	IGNORANTS	ILLATIONS
IDIOTYPE	IFFIER	IGNORE	ILLATIVE
IDIOTYPES	IFFIEST	IGNORED	ILLATIVES
IDIOTYPIC	IFFINESS	IGNORER	ILLEGAL
IDLE	IFFY	IGNORERS	ILLEGALLY
IDLED	IFS	IGNORES	ILLEGALS
IDLEHOOD	IFTAR	IGNORING	ILLEGIBLE
IDLEHOODS	IFTARS	IGUANA	ILLEGIBLY
IDLENESS	IGAD	IGUANAS	ILLER
IDLER	IGAPO	IGUANIAN	ILLEST
IDLERS	IGAPOS	IGUANIANS	ILLIAD
IDLES	IGARAPE	IGUANID	ILLIADS
IDLESSE	IGARAPES	IGUANIDS	ILLIBERAL
IDLESSES	IGG	IGUANODON	ILLICIT
IDLEST	IGGED	IHRAM	ILLICITLY
IDLING	IGGING	IHRAMS	ILLIMITED
IDLY	IGGS	IJTIHAD	ILLINIUM
IDOCRASE	IGLOO	IJTIHADS	ILLINIUMS
IDOCRASES	IGLOOS	IKAN	ILLIPE
IDOL	IGLU	IKANS	ILLIPES
IDOLA	IGLUS	IKAT	ILLIQUID
IDOLATER	IGNARO	IKATS	ILLISION
IDOLATERS	IGNAROES	IKEBANA	ILLISIONS
IDOLATOR	IGNAROS	IKEBANAS	ILLITE
IDOLATORS	IGNATIA	IKON	ILLITES
IDOLATRY	IGNATIAS	IKONS	ILLITIC
IDOLISE	IGNEOUS	ILEA	ILLNESS
IDOLISED	IGNESCENT	ILEAC	ILLNESSES
IDOLISER	IGNIFIED	ILEAL	ILLOGIC
IDOLISERS	IGNIFIES	ILEITIDES	ILLOGICAL
IDOLISES	IGNIFY	ILEITIS	ILLOGICS
IDOLISING	IGNIFYING	ILEITISES	ILLS
IDOLISM	IGNITABLE	ILEOSTOMY	ILLTH
IDOLISMS	IGNITE	ILEUM	ILLTHS
IDOLIST	IGNITED	ILEUS	ILLUDE
IDOLISTS	IGNITER	ILEUSES	ILLUDED
IDOLIZE	IGNITERS	ILEX	ILLUDES
IDOLIZED	IGNITES	ILEXES	ILLUDING
IDOLIZER	IGNITIBLE	ILIA	ILLUME
IDOLIZERS	IGNITING	ILIAC	ILLUMED
IDOLIZES	IGNITION	ILIACUS	ILLUMES
IDOLIZING	IGNITIONS	ILIACUSES	ILLUMINE
IDOLS	IGNITOR	ILIAD	ILLUMINED
IDOLUM	IGNITORS	ILIADS	ILLUMINER
IDONEITY	IGNITRON	ILIAL	ILLUMINES
IDONEOUS	IGNITRONS	ILICES	ILLUMING
IDS	IGNOBLE	ILIUM	ILLUPI
IDYL	IGNOBLER	ILK	ILLUPIS
IDYLIST	IGNOBLEST	ILKA	ILLUSION
IDYLISTS	IGNOBLY	ILKADAY	ILLUSIONS
IDYLL	IGNOMIES	ILKADAYS	ILLUSIVE
IDYLLIAN	IGNOMINY	ILKS	ILLUSORY
IDYLLIC	IGNOMY	ILL	ILLUVIA
IDYLLIST	IGNORABLE	ILLAPSE	ILLUVIAL
IDYLLISTS	IGNORAMI	ILLAPSED	ILLUVIATE

ILLUVIUM
ILLUVIUMS
ILLY
ILMENITE
ILMENITES
IMAGE
IMAGEABLE
IMAGED
IMAGELESS
IMAGER
IMAGERIES
IMAGERS
IMAGERY
IMAGES
IMAGINAL
IMAGINARY
IMAGINE
IMAGINED
IMAGINER
IMAGINERS
IMAGINES
IMAGING
IMAGINGS
IMAGINING
IMAGINIST
IMAGISM
IMAGISMS
IMAGIST
IMAGISTIC
IMAGISTS
IMAGO
IMAGOES
IMAGOS
IMAM
IMAMATE
IMAMATES
IMAMS
IMARET
IMARETS
IMARI
IMARIS
IMAUM
IMAUMS
IMBALANCE
IMBALM
IMBALMED
IMBALMER
IMBALMERS
IMBALMING
IMBALMS
IMBAR
IMBARK
IMBARKED
IMBARKING
IMBARKS
IMBARRED
IMBARRING
IMBARS

IMBASE
IMBASED
IMBASES
IMBASING
IMBATHE
IMBATHED
IMBATHES
IMBATHING
IMBECILE
IMBECILES
IMBECILIC
IMBED
IMBEDDED
IMBEDDING
IMBEDS
IMBIBE
IMBIBED
IMBIBER
IMBIBERS
IMBIBES
IMBIBING
IMBITTER
IMBITTERS
IMBIZO
IMBIZOS
IMBLAZE
IMBLAZED
IMBLAZES
IMBLAZING
IMBODIED
IMBODIES
IMBODY
IMBODYING
IMBOLDEN
IMBOLDENS
IMBORDER
IMBORDERS
IMBOSK
IMBOSKED
IMBOSKING
IMBOSKS
IMBOSOM
IMBOSOMED
IMBOSOMS
IMBOSS
IMBOSSED
IMBOSSES
IMBOSSING
IMBOWER
IMBOWERED
IMBOWERS
IMBRANGLE
IMBRAST
IMBREX
IMBRICATE
IMBRICES
IMBROGLIO
IMBROWN

IMBROWNED
IMBROWNS
IMBRUE
IMBRUED
IMBRUES
IMBRUING
IMBRUTE
IMBRUTED
IMBRUTES
IMBRUTING
IMBUE
IMBUED
IMBUEMENT
IMBUES
IMBUING
IMBURSE
IMBURSED
IMBURSES
IMBURSING
IMID
IMIDAZOLE
IMIDE
IMIDES
IMIDIC
IMIDO
IMIDS
IMINAZOLE
IMINE
IMINES
IMINO
IMINOUREA
IMITABLE
IMITANCY
IMITANT
IMITANTS
IMITATE
IMITATED
IMITATES
IMITATING
IMITATION
IMITATIVE
IMITATOR
IMITATORS
IMMANACLE
IMMANE
IMMANELY
IMMANENCE
IMMANENCY
IMMANENT
IMMANITY
IMMANTLE
IMMANTLED
IMMANTLES
IMMASK
IMMASKED
IMMASKING
IMMASKS
IMMATURE

IMMATURES
IMMEDIACY
IMMEDIATE
IMMENSE
IMMENSELY
IMMENSER
IMMENSEST
IMMENSITY
IMMERGE
IMMERGED
IMMERGES
IMMERGING
IMMERSE
IMMERSED
IMMERSER
IMMERSERS
IMMERSES
IMMERSING
IMMERSION
IMMERSIVE
IMMESH
IMMESHED
IMMESHES
IMMESHING
IMMEW
IMMEWED
IMMEWING
IMMEWS
IMMIES
IMMIGRANT
IMMIGRATE
IMMINENCE
IMMINENCY
IMMINENT
IMMINGLE
IMMINGLED
IMMINGLES
IMMINUTE
IMMISSION
IMMIT
IMMITS
IMMITTED
IMMITTING
IMMIX
IMMIXED
IMMIXES
IMMIXING
IMMIXTURE
IMMOBILE
IMMODEST
IMMODESTY
IMMOLATE
IMMOLATED
IMMOLATES
IMMOLATOR
IMMOMENT
IMMORAL
IMMORALLY

285

IMMORTAL
IMMORTALS
IMMOTILE
IMMOVABLE
IMMOVABLY
IMMUNE
IMMUNES
IMMUNISE
IMMUNISED
IMMUNISER
IMMUNISES
IMMUNITY
IMMUNIZE
IMMUNIZED
IMMUNIZER
IMMUNIZES
IMMUNOGEN
IMMURE
IMMURED
IMMURES
IMMURING
IMMUTABLE
IMMUTABLY
IMMY
IMP
IMPACABLE
IMPACT
IMPACTED
IMPACTER
IMPACTERS
IMPACTFUL
IMPACTING
IMPACTION
IMPACTITE
IMPACTIVE
IMPACTOR
IMPACTORS
IMPACTS
IMPAINT
IMPAINTED
IMPAINTS
IMPAIR
IMPAIRED
IMPAIRER
IMPAIRERS
IMPAIRING
IMPAIRS
IMPALA
IMPALAS
IMPALE
IMPALED
IMPALER
IMPALERS
IMPALES
IMPALING
IMPANATE
IMPANEL
IMPANELED

IMPANELS
IMPANNEL
IMPANNELS
IMPARITY
IMPARK
IMPARKED
IMPARKING
IMPARKS
IMPARL
IMPARLED
IMPARLING
IMPARLS
IMPART
IMPARTED
IMPARTER
IMPARTERS
IMPARTIAL
IMPARTING
IMPARTS
IMPASSE
IMPASSES
IMPASSION
IMPASSIVE
IMPASTE
IMPASTED
IMPASTES
IMPASTING
IMPASTO
IMPASTOED
IMPASTOS
IMPATIENS
IMPATIENT
IMPAVE
IMPAVED
IMPAVES
IMPAVID
IMPAVIDLY
IMPAVING
IMPAWN
IMPAWNED
IMPAWNING
IMPAWNS
IMPEACH
IMPEACHED
IMPEACHER
IMPEACHES
IMPEARL
IMPEARLED
IMPEARLS
IMPECCANT
IMPED
IMPEDANCE
IMPEDE
IMPEDED
IMPEDER
IMPEDERS
IMPEDES
IMPEDING

IMPEDOR
IMPEDORS
IMPEL
IMPELLED
IMPELLENT
IMPELLER
IMPELLERS
IMPELLING
IMPELLOR
IMPELLORS
IMPELS
IMPEND
IMPENDED
IMPENDENT
IMPENDING
IMPENDS
IMPENNATE
IMPERATOR
IMPERFECT
IMPERIA
IMPERIAL
IMPERIALS
IMPERIL
IMPERILED
IMPERILS
IMPERIOUS
IMPERIUM
IMPERIUMS
IMPETICOS
IMPETIGO
IMPETIGOS
IMPETRATE
IMPETUOUS
IMPETUS
IMPETUSES
IMPHEE
IMPHEES
IMPI
IMPIES
IMPIETIES
IMPIETY
IMPING
IMPINGE
IMPINGED
IMPINGENT
IMPINGER
IMPINGERS
IMPINGES
IMPINGING
IMPINGS
IMPIOUS
IMPIOUSLY
IMPIS
IMPISH
IMPISHLY
IMPLANT
IMPLANTED
IMPLANTER

IMPLANTS
IMPLATE
IMPLATED
IMPLATES
IMPLATING
IMPLEACH
IMPLEAD
IMPLEADED
IMPLEADER
IMPLEADS
IMPLED
IMPLEDGE
IMPLEDGED
IMPLEDGES
IMPLEMENT
IMPLETE
IMPLETED
IMPLETES
IMPLETING
IMPLETION
IMPLEX
IMPLEXES
IMPLEXION
IMPLICATE
IMPLICIT
IMPLICITY
IMPLIED
IMPLIEDLY
IMPLIES
IMPLODE
IMPLODED
IMPLODENT
IMPLODES
IMPLODING
IMPLORE
IMPLORED
IMPLORER
IMPLORERS
IMPLORES
IMPLORING
IMPLOSION
IMPLOSIVE
IMPLUNGE
IMPLUNGED
IMPLUNGES
IMPLUVIA
IMPLUVIUM
IMPLY
IMPLYING
IMPOCKET
IMPOCKETS
IMPOLDER
IMPOLDERS
IMPOLICY
IMPOLITE
IMPOLITER
IMPOLITIC
IMPONE

IMPONED	IMPRESSES	IMSHI	INBROUGHT
IMPONENT	IMPREST	IMSHY	INBUILT
IMPONENTS	IMPRESTS	IN	INBURNING
IMPONES	IMPRIMIS	INABILITY	INBURST
IMPONING	IMPRINT	INACTION	INBURSTS
IMPOROUS	IMPRINTED	INACTIONS	INBY
IMPORT	IMPRINTER	INACTIVE	INBYE
IMPORTANT	IMPRINTS	INAIDABLE	INCAGE
IMPORTED	IMPRISON	INAMORATA	INCAGED
IMPORTER	IMPRISONS	INAMORATO	INCAGES
IMPORTERS	IMPROBITY	INANE	INCAGING
IMPORTING	IMPROMPTU	INANELY	INCANT
IMPORTS	IMPROPER	INANENESS	INCANTED
IMPORTUNE	IMPROV	INANER	INCANTING
IMPOSABLE	IMPROVE	INANES	INCANTS
IMPOSE	IMPROVED	INANEST	INCAPABLE
IMPOSED	IMPROVER	INANGA	INCAPABLY
IMPOSER	IMPROVERS	INANGAS	INCARNATE
IMPOSERS	IMPROVES	INANIMATE	INCASE
IMPOSES	IMPROVING	INANITIES	INCASED
IMPOSING	IMPROVISE	INANITION	INCASES
IMPOST	IMPROVS	INANITY	INCASING
IMPOSTED	IMPRUDENT	INAPT	INCAUTION
IMPOSTER	IMPS	INAPTLY	INCAVE
IMPOSTERS	IMPSONITE	INAPTNESS	INCAVED
IMPOSTING	IMPUDENCE	INARABLE	INCAVES
IMPOSTOR	IMPUDENCY	INARCH	INCAVI
IMPOSTORS	IMPUDENT	INARCHED	INCAVING
IMPOSTS	IMPUGN	INARCHES	INCAVO
IMPOSTUME	IMPUGNED	INARCHING	INCEDE
IMPOSTURE	IMPUGNER	INARM	INCEDED
IMPOT	IMPUGNERS	INARMED	INCEDES
IMPOTENCE	IMPUGNING	INARMING	INCEDING
IMPOTENCY	IMPUGNS	INARMS	INCENSE
IMPOTENT	IMPULSE	INASMUCH	INCENSED
IMPOTENTS	IMPULSED	INAUDIBLE	INCENSER
IMPOTS	IMPULSES	INAUDIBLY	INCENSERS
IMPOUND	IMPULSING	INAUGURAL	INCENSES
IMPOUNDED	IMPULSION	INAURATE	INCENSING
IMPOUNDER	IMPULSIVE	INBEING	INCENSOR
IMPOUNDS	IMPUNDULU	INBEINGS	INCENSORS
IMPOWER	IMPUNITY	INBENT	INCENSORY
IMPOWERED	IMPURE	INBOARD	INCENT
IMPOWERS	IMPURELY	INBOARDS	INCENTED
IMPRECATE	IMPURER	INBORN	INCENTER
IMPRECISE	IMPUREST	INBOUND	INCENTERS
IMPREGN	IMPURITY	INBOUNDED	INCENTING
IMPREGNED	IMPURPLE	INBOUNDS	INCENTIVE
IMPREGNS	IMPURPLED	INBREAK	INCENTRE
IMPRESA	IMPURPLES	INBREAKS	INCENTRES
IMPRESARI	IMPUTABLE	INBREATHE	INCENTS
IMPRESAS	IMPUTABLY	INBRED	INCEPT
IMPRESE	IMPUTE	INBREDS	INCEPTED
IMPRESES	IMPUTED	INBREED	INCEPTING
IMPRESS	IMPUTER	INBREEDER	INCEPTION
IMPRESSE	IMPUTERS	INBREEDS	INCEPTIVE
IMPRESSED	IMPUTES	INBRING	INCEPTOR
IMPRESSER	IMPUTING	INBRINGS	INCEPTORS

INCEPTS	INCLE	INCROSS	INDARTING
INCERTAIN	INCLEMENT	INCROSSED	INDARTS
INCESSANT	INCLES	INCROSSES	INDEBTED
INCEST	INCLINE	INCRUST	INDECENCY
INCESTS	INCLINED	INCRUSTED	INDECENT
INCH	INCLINER	INCRUSTS	INDECORUM
INCHASE	INCLINERS	INCUBATE	INDEED
INCHASED	INCLINES	INCUBATED	INDELIBLE
INCHASES	INCLINING	INCUBATES	INDELIBLY
INCHASING	INCLIP	INCUBATOR	INDEMNIFY
INCHED	INCLIPPED	INCUBI	INDEMNITY
INCHER	INCLIPS	INCUBOUS	INDENE
INCHERS	INCLOSE	INCUBUS	INDENES
INCHES	INCLOSED	INCUBUSES	INDENT
INCHING	INCLOSER	INCUDAL	INDENTED
INCHMEAL	INCLOSERS	INCUDATE	INDENTER
INCHOATE	INCLOSES	INCUDES	INDENTERS
INCHOATED	INCLOSING	INCULCATE	INDENTING
INCHOATES	INCLOSURE	INCULPATE	INDENTION
INCHPIN	INCLUDE	INCULT	INDENTOR
INCHPINS	INCLUDED	INCUMBENT	INDENTORS
INCHWORM	INCLUDES	INCUMBER	INDENTS
INCHWORMS	INCLUDING	INCUMBERS	INDENTURE
INCIDENCE	INCLUSION	INCUNABLE	INDEVOUT
INCIDENT	INCLUSIVE	INCUR	INDEW
INCIDENTS	INCOG	INCURABLE	INDEWED
INCIPIENT	INCOGNITA	INCURABLY	INDEWING
INCIPIT	INCOGNITO	INCURIOUS	INDEWS
INCIPITS	INCOGS	INCURRED	INDEX
INCISAL	INCOME	INCURRENT	INDEXABLE
INCISE	INCOMER	INCURRING	INDEXAL
INCISED	INCOMERS	INCURS	INDEXED
INCISES	INCOMES	INCURSION	INDEXER
INCISING	INCOMING	INCURSIVE	INDEXERS
INCISION	INCOMINGS	INCURVATE	INDEXES
INCISIONS	INCOMMODE	INCURVE	INDEXICAL
INCISIVE	INCOMPACT	INCURVED	INDEXING
INCISOR	INCONDITE	INCURVES	INDEXINGS
INCISORS	INCONIE	INCURVING	INDEXLESS
INCISORY	INCONNU	INCURVITY	INDICAN
INCISURAL	INCONNUE	INCUS	INDICANS
INCISURE	INCONNUES	INCUSE	INDICANT
INCISURES	INCONNUS	INCUSED	INDICANTS
INCITABLE	INCONY	INCUSES	INDICATE
INCITANT	INCORPSE	INCUSING	INDICATED
INCITANTS	INCORPSED	INCUT	INDICATES
INCITE	INCORPSES	INDABA	INDICATOR
INCITED	INCORRECT	INDABAS	INDICES
INCITER	INCORRUPT	INDAGATE	INDICIA
INCITERS	INCREASE	INDAGATED	INDICIAL
INCITES	INCREASED	INDAGATES	INDICIAS
INCITING	INCREASER	INDAGATOR	INDICIUM
INCIVIL	INCREASES	INDAMIN	INDICIUMS
INCIVISM	INCREATE	INDAMINE	INDICT
INCIVISMS	INCREMATE	INDAMINES	INDICTED
INCLASP	INCREMENT	INDAMINS	INDICTEE
INCLASPED	INCRETION	INDART	INDICTEES
INCLASPS	INCRETORY	INDARTED	INDICTER

INDICTERS	INDORSER	INDUNA	INEXACT
INDICTING	INDORSERS	INDUNAS	INEXACTLY
INDICTION	INDORSES	INDURATE	INEXPERT
INDICTOR	INDORSING	INDURATED	INEXPERTS
INDICTORS	INDORSOR	INDURATES	INFALL
INDICTS	INDORSORS	INDUSIA	INFALLING
INDIE	INDOW	INDUSIAL	INFALLS
INDIES	INDOWED	INDUSIATE	INFAME
INDIGEN	INDOWING	INDUSIUM	INFAMED
INDIGENCE	INDOWS	INDUSTRY	INFAMES
INDIGENCY	INDOXYL	INDUVIAE	INFAMIES
INDIGENE	INDOXYLS	INDUVIAL	INFAMING
INDIGENES	INDRAFT	INDUVIATE	INFAMISE
INDIGENS	INDRAFTS	INDWELL	INFAMISED
INDIGENT	INDRAUGHT	INDWELLER	INFAMISES
INDIGENTS	INDRAWN	INDWELLS	INFAMIZE
INDIGEST	INDRENCH	INDWELT	INFAMIZED
INDIGESTS	INDRI	INEARTH	INFAMIZES
INDIGN	INDRIS	INEARTHED	INFAMOUS
INDIGNANT	INDRISES	INEARTHS	INFAMY
INDIGNIFY	INDUBIOUS	INEBRIANT	INFANCIES
INDIGNITY	INDUCE	INEBRIATE	INFANCY
INDIGNLY	INDUCED	INEBRIETY	INFANT
INDIGO	INDUCER	INEBRIOUS	INFANTA
INDIGOES	INDUCERS	INEDIBLE	INFANTAS
INDIGOID	INDUCES	INEDIBLY	INFANTE
INDIGOIDS	INDUCIAE	INEDITA	INFANTES
INDIGOS	INDUCIBLE	INEDITED	INFANTILE
INDIGOTIC	INDUCING	INEFFABLE	INFANTINE
INDIGOTIN	INDUCT	INEFFABLY	INFANTRY
INDINAVIR	INDUCTED	INELASTIC	INFANTS
INDIRECT	INDUCTEE	INELEGANT	INFARCT
INDIRUBIN	INDUCTEES	INEPT	INFARCTED
INDISPOSE	INDUCTILE	INEPTER	INFARCTS
INDITE	INDUCTING	INEPTEST	INFARE
INDITED	INDUCTION	INEPTLY	INFARES
INDITER	INDUCTIVE	INEPTNESS	INFATUATE
INDITERS	INDUCTOR	INEQUABLE	INFAUNA
INDITES	INDUCTORS	INEQUITY	INFAUNAE
INDITING	INDUCTS	INERM	INFAUNAL
INDIUM	INDUE	INERMOUS	INFAUNAS
INDIUMS	INDUED	INERRABLE	INFAUST
INDIVIDUA	INDUES	INERRABLY	INFECT
INDOCIBLE	INDUING	INERRANCY	INFECTANT
INDOCILE	INDULGE	INERRANT	INFECTED
INDOL	INDULGED	INERT	INFECTER
INDOLE	INDULGENT	INERTER	INFECTERS
INDOLENCE	INDULGER	INERTEST	INFECTING
INDOLENCY	INDULGERS	INERTIA	INFECTION
INDOLENT	INDULGES	INERTIAE	INFECTIVE
INDOLES	INDULGING	INERTIAL	INFECTOR
INDOLS	INDULIN	INERTIAS	INFECTORS
INDOOR	INDULINE	INERTLY	INFECTS
INDOORS	INDULINES	INERTNESS	INFECUND
INDORSE	INDULINS	INERTS	INFEFT
INDORSED	INDULT	INERUDITE	INFEFTED
INDORSEE	INDULTS	INESSIVE	INFEFTING
INDORSEES	INDUMENTA	INESSIVES	INFEFTS

INFELT	INFIX	INFORCES	INGEST
INFEOFF	INFIXED	INFORCING	INGESTA
INFEOFFED	INFIXES	INFORM	INGESTED
INFEOFFS	INFIXING	INFORMAL	INGESTING
INFER	INFIXION	INFORMANT	INGESTION
INFERABLE	INFIXIONS	INFORMED	INGESTIVE
INFERABLY	INFLAME	INFORMER	INGESTS
INFERE	INFLAMED	INFORMERS	INGINE
INFERENCE	INFLAMER	INFORMING	INGINES
INFERIAE	INFLAMERS	INFORMS	INGLE
INFERIBLE	INFLAMES	INFORTUNE	INGLENEUK
INFERIOR	INFLAMING	INFOS	INGLENOOK
INFERIORS	INFLATE	INFOUGHT	INGLES
INFERNAL	INFLATED	INFRA	INGLOBE
INFERNO	INFLATER	INFRACT	INGLOBED
INFERNOS	INFLATERS	INFRACTED	INGLOBES
INFERRED	INFLATES	INFRACTOR	INGLOBING
INFERRER	INFLATING	INFRACTS	INGLUVIAL
INFERRERS	INFLATION	INFRARED	INGLUVIES
INFERRING	INFLATIVE	INFRAREDS	INGO
INFERS	INFLATOR	INFRINGE	INGOES
INFERTILE	INFLATORS	INFRINGED	INGOING
INFEST	INFLATUS	INFRINGER	INGOINGS
INFESTANT	INFLECT	INFRINGES	INGOT
INFESTED	INFLECTED	INFRUGAL	INGOTED
INFESTER	INFLECTOR	INFULA	INGOTING
INFESTERS	INFLECTS	INFULAE	INGOTS
INFESTING	INFLEXED	INFURIATE	INGRAFT
INFESTS	INFLEXION	INFUSCATE	INGRAFTED
INFICETE	INFLEXURE	INFUSE	INGRAFTS
INFIDEL	INFLICT	INFUSED	INGRAIN
INFIDELIC	INFLICTED	INFUSER	INGRAINED
INFIDELS	INFLICTER	INFUSERS	INGRAINS
INFIELD	INFLICTOR	INFUSES	INGRAM
INFIELDER	INFLICTS	INFUSIBLE	INGRATE
INFIELDS	INFLIGHT	INFUSING	INGRATELY
INFIGHT	INFLOW	INFUSION	INGRATES
INFIGHTER	INFLOWING	INFUSIONS	INGRESS
INFIGHTS	INFLOWS	INFUSIVE	INGRESSES
INFILL	INFLUENCE	INFUSORIA	INGROOVE
INFILLED	INFLUENT	INFUSORY	INGROOVED
INFILLING	INFLUENTS	INGAN	INGROOVES
INFILLS	INFLUENZA	INGANS	INGROSS
INFIMA	INFLUX	INGATE	INGROSSED
INFIMUM	INFLUXES	INGATES	INGROSSES
INFIMUMS	INFLUXION	INGATHER	INGROUND
INFINITE	INFO	INGATHERS	INGROUP
INFINITES	INFOBAHN	INGENER	INGROUPS
INFINITY	INFOBAHNS	INGENERS	INGROWING
INFIRM	INFOLD	INGENIOUS	INGROWN
INFIRMARY	INFOLDED	INGENIUM	INGROWTH
INFIRMED	INFOLDER	INGENIUMS	INGROWTHS
INFIRMER	INFOLDERS	INGENU	INGRUM
INFIRMEST	INFOLDING	INGENUE	INGUINAL
INFIRMING	INFOLDS	INGENUES	INGULF
INFIRMITY	INFOMANIA	INGENUITY	INGULFED
INFIRMLY	INFORCE	INGENUOUS	INGULFING
INFIRMS	INFORCED	INGENUS	INGULFS

INGULPH
INGULPHED
INGULPHS
INHABIT
INHABITED
INHABITER
INHABITOR
INHABITS
INHALANT
INHALANTS
INHALATOR
INHALE
INHALED
INHALER
INHALERS
INHALES
INHALING
INHARMONY
INHAUL
INHAULER
INHAULERS
INHAULS
INHAUST
INHAUSTED
INHAUSTS
INHEARSE
INHEARSED
INHEARSES
INHERCE
INHERCED
INHERCES
INHERCING
INHERE
INHERED
INHERENCE
INHERENCY
INHERENT
INHERES
INHERING
INHERIT
INHERITED
INHERITOR
INHERITS
INHESION
INHESIONS
INHIBIN
INHIBINS
INHIBIT
INHIBITED
INHIBITER
INHIBITOR
INHIBITS
INHOLDER
INHOLDERS
INHOLDING
INHOOP
INHOOPED
INHOOPING

INHOOPS
INHUMAN
INHUMANE
INHUMANLY
INHUMATE
INHUMATED
INHUMATES
INHUME
INHUMED
INHUMER
INHUMERS
INHUMES
INHUMING
INIA
INIMICAL
INION
INIONS
INIQUITY
INISLE
INISLED
INISLES
INISLING
INITIAL
INITIALED
INITIALER
INITIALLY
INITIALS
INITIATE
INITIATED
INITIATES
INITIATOR
INJECT
INJECTANT
INJECTED
INJECTING
INJECTION
INJECTIVE
INJECTOR
INJECTORS
INJECTS
INJELLIED
INJELLIES
INJELLY
INJERA
INJERAS
INJOINT
INJOINTED
INJOINTS
INJUNCT
INJUNCTED
INJUNCTS
INJURABLE
INJURE
INJURED
INJURER
INJURERS
INJURES
INJURIES

INJURING
INJURIOUS
INJURY
INJUSTICE
INK
INKBERRY
INKBLOT
INKBLOTS
INKED
INKER
INKERS
INKHOLDER
INKHORN
INKHORNS
INKIER
INKIEST
INKINESS
INKING
INKJET
INKLE
INKLED
INKLES
INKLESS
INKLIKE
INKLING
INKLINGS
INKPOT
INKPOTS
INKS
INKSPOT
INKSPOTS
INKSTAND
INKSTANDS
INKSTONE
INKSTONES
INKWELL
INKWELLS
INKWOOD
INKWOODS
INKY
INLACE
INLACED
INLACES
INLACING
INLAID
INLAND
INLANDER
INLANDERS
INLANDS
INLAY
INLAYER
INLAYERS
INLAYING
INLAYINGS
INLAYS
INLET
INLETS
INLETTING

INLIER
INLIERS
INLOCK
INLOCKED
INLOCKING
INLOCKS
INLY
INLYING
INMATE
INMATES
INMESH
INMESHED
INMESHES
INMESHING
INMIGRANT
INMOST
INN
INNAGE
INNAGES
INNARDS
INNATE
INNATELY
INNATIVE
INNED
INNER
INNERLY
INNERMOST
INNERNESS
INNERS
INNERSOLE
INNERVATE
INNERVE
INNERVED
INNERVES
INNERVING
INNERWEAR
INNING
INNINGS
INNKEEPER
INNLESS
INNOCENCE
INNOCENCY
INNOCENT
INNOCENTS
INNOCUITY
INNOCUOUS
INNOVATE
INNOVATED
INNOVATES
INNOVATOR
INNOXIOUS
INNS
INNUENDO
INNUENDOS
INNYARD
INNYARDS
INOCULA
INOCULANT

INOCULATE	INRUNS	INSETTED	INSOLES
INOCULUM	INRUSH	INSETTER	INSOLUBLE
INOCULUMS	INRUSHES	INSETTERS	INSOLUBLY
INODOROUS	INRUSHING	INSETTING	INSOLVENT
INOPINATE	INS	INSHALLAH	INSOMNIA
INORB	INSANE	INSHEATH	INSOMNIAC
INORBED	INSANELY	INSHEATHE	INSOMNIAS
INORBING	INSANER	INSHEATHS	INSOMUCH
INORBS	INSANEST	INSHELL	INSOOTH
INORGANIC	INSANIE	INSHELLED	INSOUL
INORNATE	INSANIES	INSHELLS	INSOULED
INOSINE	INSANITY	INSHELTER	INSOULING
INOSINES	INSATIATE	INSHIP	INSOULS
INOSITE	INSATIETY	INSHIPPED	INSPAN
INOSITES	INSCAPE	INSHIPS	INSPANNED
INOSITOL	INSCAPES	INSHORE	INSPANS
INOSITOLS	INSCIENCE	INSHRINE	INSPECT
INOTROPIC	INSCIENT	INSHRINED	INSPECTED
INPATIENT	INSCONCE	INSHRINES	INSPECTOR
INPAYMENT	INSCONCED	INSIDE	INSPECTS
INPHASE	INSCONCES	INSIDER	INSPHERE
INPOUR	INSCRIBE	INSIDERS	INSPHERED
INPOURED	INSCRIBED	INSIDES	INSPHERES
INPOURING	INSCRIBER	INSIDIOUS	INSPIRE
INPOURS	INSCRIBES	INSIGHT	INSPIRED
INPUT	INSCROLL	INSIGHTS	INSPIRER
INPUTS	INSCROLLS	INSIGNE	INSPIRERS
INPUTTED	INSCULP	INSIGNIA	INSPIRES
INPUTTER	INSCULPED	INSIGNIAS	INSPIRING
INPUTTERS	INSCULPS	INSINCERE	INSPIRIT
INPUTTING	INSCULPT	INSINEW	INSPIRITS
INQILAB	INSEAM	INSINEWED	INSTABLE
INQILABS	INSEAMED	INSINEWS	INSTAL
INQUERE	INSEAMING	INSINUATE	INSTALL
INQUERED	INSEAMS	INSIPID	INSTALLED
INQUERES	INSECT	INSIPIDLY	INSTALLER
INQUERING	INSECTAN	INSIPIENT	INSTALLS
INQUEST	INSECTARY	INSIST	INSTALS
INQUESTS	INSECTEAN	INSISTED	INSTANCE
INQUIET	INSECTILE	INSISTENT	INSTANCED
INQUIETED	INSECTION	INSISTER	INSTANCES
INQUIETLY	INSECTS	INSISTERS	INSTANCY
INQUIETS	INSECURE	INSISTING	INSTANT
INQUILINE	INSEEM	INSISTS	INSTANTER
INQUINATE	INSEEMED	INSNARE	INSTANTLY
INQUIRE	INSEEMING	INSNARED	INSTANTS
INQUIRED	INSEEMS	INSNARER	INSTAR
INQUIRER	INSELBERG	INSNARERS	INSTARRED
INQUIRERS	INSENSATE	INSNARES	INSTARS
INQUIRES	INSERT	INSNARING	INSTATE
INQUIRIES	INSERTED	INSOFAR	INSTATED
INQUIRING	INSERTER	INSOLATE	INSTATES
INQUIRY	INSERTERS	INSOLATED	INSTATING
INQUORATE	INSERTING	INSOLATES	INSTEAD
INRO	INSERTION	INSOLE	INSTEP
INROAD	INSERTS	INSOLENCE	INSTEPS
INROADS	INSET	INSOLENT	INSTIGATE
INRUN	INSETS	INSOLENTS	INSTIL

INSTILL	INTAGLI	INTERCOMS	INTERNAL
INSTILLED	INTAGLIO	INTERCROP	INTERNALS
INSTILLER	INTAGLIOS	INTERCUT	INTERNE
INSTILLS	INTAKE	INTERCUTS	INTERNED
INSTILS	INTAKES	INTERDASH	INTERNEE
INSTINCT	INTARSIA	INTERDEAL	INTERNEES
INSTINCTS	INTARSIAS	INTERDICT	INTERNES
INSTITUTE	INTEGER	INTERDINE	INTERNET
INSTRESS	INTEGERS	INTERESS	INTERNETS
INSTROKE	INTEGRAL	INTERESSE	INTERNING
INSTROKES	INTEGRALS	INTEREST	INTERNIST
INSTRUCT	INTEGRAND	INTERESTS	INTERNODE
INSTRUCTS	INTEGRANT	INTERFACE	INTERNS
INSUCKEN	INTEGRATE	INTERFERE	INTERPAGE
INSULA	INTEGRITY	INTERFILE	INTERPLAY
INSULAE	INTEL	INTERFIRM	INTERPLED
INSULANT	INTELLECT	INTERFLOW	INTERPONE
INSULANTS	INTELS	INTERFOLD	INTERPOSE
INSULAR	INTENABLE	INTERFUSE	INTERPRET
INSULARLY	INTEND	INTERGANG	INTERRACE
INSULARS	INTENDANT	INTERGREW	INTERRAIL
INSULAS	INTENDED	INTERGROW	INTERRED
INSULATE	INTENDEDS	INTERIM	INTERREX
INSULATED	INTENDER	INTERIMS	INTERRING
INSULATES	INTENDERS	INTERIOR	INTERROW
INSULATOR	INTENDING	INTERIORS	INTERRUPT
INSULIN	INTENDS	INTERJECT	INTERS
INSULINS	INTENIBLE	INTERJOIN	INTERSECT
INSULSE	INTENSATE	INTERKNIT	INTERSERT
INSULSITY	INTENSE	INTERKNOT	INTERSEX
INSULT	INTENSELY	INTERLACE	INTERTERM
INSULTANT	INTENSER	INTERLAID	INTERTEXT
INSULTED	INTENSEST	INTERLAP	INTERTIE
INSULTER	INTENSIFY	INTERLAPS	INTERTIES
INSULTERS	INTENSION	INTERLARD	INTERTILL
INSULTING	INTENSITY	INTERLAY	INTERUNIT
INSULTS	INTENSIVE	INTERLAYS	INTERVAL
INSURABLE	INTENT	INTERLEAF	INTERVALE
INSURANCE	INTENTION	INTERLEND	INTERVALS
INSURANT	INTENTIVE	INTERLENT	INTERVEIN
INSURANTS	INTENTLY	INTERLINE	INTERVENE
INSURE	INTENTS	INTERLINK	INTERVIEW
INSURED	INTER	INTERLOAN	INTERWAR
INSUREDS	INTERACT	INTERLOCK	INTERWIND
INSURER	INTERACTS	INTERLOOP	INTERWORK
INSURERS	INTERAGE	INTERLOPE	INTERWOVE
INSURES	INTERARCH	INTERLUDE	INTERZONE
INSURGENT	INTERBANK	INTERMALE	INTESTACY
INSURING	INTERBED	INTERMAT	INTESTATE
INSWATHE	INTERBEDS	INTERMATS	INTESTINE
INSWATHED	INTERBRED	INTERMENT	INTHRAL
INSWATHES	INTERCEDE	INTERMESH	INTHRALL
INSWEPT	INTERCELL	INTERMIT	INTHRALLS
INSWING	INTERCEPT	INTERMITS	INTHRALS
INSWINGER	INTERCITY	INTERMIX	INTHRONE
INSWINGS	INTERCLAN	INTERMONT	INTHRONED
INTACT	INTERCLUB	INTERMURE	INTHRONES
TNTACTLY	INTERCOM	INTERN	INTI

INTIFADA
INTIFADAH
INTIFADAS
INTIFADEH
INTIL
INTIMA
INTIMACY
INTIMAE
INTIMAL
INTIMAS
INTIMATE
INTIMATED
INTIMATER
INTIMATES
INTIME
INTIMISM
INTIMISMS
INTIMIST
INTIMISTE
INTIMISTS
INTIMITY
INTINE
INTINES
INTIRE
INTIS
INTITLE
INTITLED
INTITLES
INTITLING
INTITULE
INTITULED
INTITULES
INTO
INTOED
INTOMB
INTOMBED
INTOMBING
INTOMBS
INTONACO
INTONACOS
INTONATE
INTONATED
INTONATES
INTONATOR
INTONE
INTONED
INTONER
INTONERS
INTONES
INTONING
INTONINGS
INTORSION
INTORT
INTORTED
INTORTING
INTORTION
INTORTS
INTOWN
INTRA

INTRACITY
INTRADA
INTRADAS
INTRADAY
INTRADOS
INTRANET
INTRANETS
INTRANT
INTRANTS
INTREAT
INTREATED
INTREATS
INTRENCH
INTREPID
INTRICACY
INTRICATE
INTRIGANT
INTRIGUE
INTRIGUED
INTRIGUER
INTRIGUES
INTRINCE
INTRINSIC
INTRO
INTRODUCE
INTROFIED
INTROFIES
INTROFY
INTROIT
INTROITAL
INTROITS
INTROITUS
INTROJECT
INTROLD
INTROMIT
INTROMITS
INTRON
INTRONS
INTRORSE
INTROS
INTROVERT
INTRUDE
INTRUDED
INTRUDER
INTRUDERS
INTRUDES
INTRUDING
INTRUSION
INTRUSIVE
INTRUST
INTRUSTED
INTRUSTS
INTUBATE
INTUBATED
INTUBATES
INTUIT
INTUITED
INTUITING
INTUITION

INTUITIVE
INTUITS
INTUMESCE
INTURN
INTURNED
INTURNS
INTUSE
INTUSES
INTWINE
INTWINED
INTWINES
INTWINING
INTWIST
INTWISTED
INTWISTS
INUKSHUIT
INUKSHUK
INUKSHUKS
INULA
INULAS
INULASE
INULASES
INULIN
INULINS
INUMBRATE
INUNCTION
INUNDANT
INUNDATE
INUNDATED
INUNDATES
INUNDATOR
INURBANE
INURE
INURED
INUREMENT
INURES
INURING
INURN
INURNED
INURNING
INURNMENT
INURNS
INUSITATE
INUST
INUSTION
INUSTIONS
INUTILE
INUTILELY
INUTILITY
INVADABLE
INVADE
INVADED
INVADER
INVADERS
INVADES
INVADING
INVALID
INVALIDED
INVALIDLY

INVALIDS
INVAR
INVARIANT
INVARS
INVASION
INVASIONS
INVASIVE
INVEAGLE
INVEAGLED
INVEAGLES
INVECKED
INVECTED
INVECTIVE
INVEIGH
INVEIGHED
INVEIGHER
INVEIGHS
INVEIGLE
INVEIGLED
INVEIGLER
INVEIGLES
INVENIT
INVENT
INVENTED
INVENTER
INVENTERS
INVENTING
INVENTION
INVENTIVE
INVENTOR
INVENTORS
INVENTORY
INVENTS
INVERITY
INVERNESS
INVERSE
INVERSED
INVERSELY
INVERSES
INVERSING
INVERSION
INVERSIVE
INVERT
INVERTASE
INVERTED
INVERTER
INVERTERS
INVERTIN
INVERTING
INVERTINS
INVERTOR
INVERTORS
INVERTS
INVEST
INVESTED
INVESTING
INVESTOR
INVESTORS
INVESTS

INVEXED	INWICK	IODOFORMS	IRADE
INVIABLE	INWICKED	IODOMETRY	IRADES
INVIABLY	INWICKING	IODOPHILE	IRASCIBLE
INVIDIOUS	INWICKS	IODOPHOR	IRASCIBLY
INVIOLACY	INWIND	IODOPHORS	IRATE
INVIOLATE	INWINDING	IODOPSIN	IRATELY
INVIOUS	INWINDS	IODOPSINS	IRATENESS
INVIRILE	INWIT	IODOUS	IRATER
INVISCID	INWITH	IODURET	IRATEST
INVISIBLE	INWITS	IODURETS	IRE
INVISIBLY	INWORK	IODYRITE	IRED
INVITAL	INWORKED	IODYRITES	IREFUL
INVITE	INWORKING	IOLITE	IREFULLY
INVITED	INWORKS	IOLITES	IRELESS
INVITEE	INWORN	ION	IRENIC
INVITEES	INWOUND	IONIC	IRENICAL
INVITER	INWOVE	IONICITY	IRENICISM
INVITERS	INWOVEN	IONICS	IRENICON
INVITES	INWRAP	IONISABLE	IRENICONS
INVITING	INWRAPPED	IONISE	IRENICS
INVITINGS	INWRAPS	IONISED	IRENOLOGY
INVOCABLE	INWREATHE	IONISER	IRES
INVOCATE	INWROUGHT	IONISERS	IRID
INVOCATED	INYALA	IONISES	IRIDAL
INVOCATES	INYALAS	IONISING	IRIDEAL
INVOCATOR	IO	IONIUM	IRIDES
INVOICE	IODATE	IONIUMS	IRIDIAL
INVOICED	IODATED	IONIZABLE	IRIDIAN
INVOICES	IODATES	IONIZE	IRIDIC
INVOICING	IODATING	IONIZED	IRIDISE
INVOKE	IODATION	IONIZER	IRIDISED
INVOKED	IODATIONS	IONIZERS	IRIDISES
INVOKER	IODIC	IONIZES	IRIDISING
INVOKERS	IODID	IONIZING	IRIDIUM
INVOKES	IODIDE	IONOGEN	IRIDIUMS
INVOKING	IODIDES	IONOGENIC	IRIDIZE
INVOLUCEL	IODIDS	IONOGENS	IRIDIZED
INVOLUCRA	IODIN	IONOMER	IRIDIZES
INVOLUCRE	IODINATE	IONOMERS	IRIDIZING
INVOLUTE	IODINATED	IONONE	IRIDOCYTE
INVOLUTED	IODINATES	IONONES	IRIDOLOGY
INVOLUTES	IODINE	IONOPAUSE	IRIDOTOMY
INVOLVE	IODINES	IONOPHORE	IRIDS
INVOLVED	IODINS	IONOSONDE	IRING
INVOLVER	IODISE	IONOTROPY	IRIS
INVOLVERS	IODISED	IONS	IRISATE
INVOLVES	IODISER	IOS	IRISATED
INVOLVING	IODISERS	IOTA	IRISATES
INWALL	IODISES	IOTACISM	IRISATING
INWALLED	IODISING	IOTACISMS	IRISATION
INWALLING	IODISM	IOTAS	IRISCOPE
INWALLS	IODISMS	IPECAC	IRISCOPES
INWARD	IODIZE	IPECACS	IRISED
INWARDLY	IODIZED	IPOMOEA	IRISES
INWARDS	IODIZER	IPOMOEAS	IRISING
INWEAVE	IODIZERS	IPPON	IRITIC
INWEAVED	IODIZES	IPPONS	IRITIS
INWEAVES	IODIZING	IPRINDOLE	IRITISES
INWEAVING	IODOFORM	IRACUND	IRK

IRKED	IRREALITY	ISCHURIA	ISOCHIME
IRKING	IRREDENTA	ISCHURIAS	ISOCHIMES
IRKS	IRREGULAR	ISEIKONIA	ISOCHOR
IRKSOME	IRRELATED	ISEIKONIC	ISOCHORE
IRKSOMELY	IRRIDENTA	ISENERGIC	ISOCHORES
IROKO	IRRIGABLE	ISH	ISOCHORIC
IROKOS	IRRIGABLY	ISHES	ISOCHORS
IRON	IRRIGATE	ISINGLASS	ISOCHRON
IRONBARK	IRRIGATED	ISIT	ISOCHRONE
IRONBARKS	IRRIGATES	ISLAND	ISOCHRONS
IRONBOUND	IRRIGATOR	ISLANDED	ISOCLINAL
IRONCLAD	IRRIGUOUS	ISLANDER	ISOCLINE
IRONCLADS	IRRISION	ISLANDERS	ISOCLINES
IRONE	IRRISIONS	ISLANDING	ISOCLINIC
IRONED	IRRISORY	ISLANDS	ISOCRACY
IRONER	IRRITABLE	ISLE	ISOCRATIC
IRONERS	IRRITABLY	ISLED	ISOCRYMAL
IRONES	IRRITANCY	ISLELESS	ISOCRYME
IRONIC	IRRITANT	ISLEMAN	ISOCRYMES
IRONICAL	IRRITANTS	ISLEMEN	ISOCYANIC
IRONIER	IRRITATE	ISLES	ISOCYCLIC
IRONIES	IRRITATED	ISLESMAN	ISODICA
IRONIEST	IRRITATES	ISLESMEN	ISODICON
IRONING	IRRITATOR	ISLET	ISODOMA
IRONINGS	IRRUPT	ISLETED	ISODOMON
IRONISE	IRRUPTED	ISLETS	ISODOMONS
IRONISED	IRRUPTING	ISLING	ISODOMOUS
IRONISES	IRRUPTION	ISLOMANIA	ISODOMUM
IRONISING	IRRUPTIVE	ISM	ISODONT
IRONIST	IRRUPTS	ISMATIC	ISODONTAL
IRONISTS	IS	ISMATICAL	ISODONTS
IRONIZE	ISABEL	ISMS	ISODOSE
IRONIZED	ISABELLA	ISNA	ISODOSES
IRONIZES	ISABELLAS	ISNAE	ISOENZYME
IRONIZING	ISABELS	ISO	ISOETES
IRONLESS	ISAGOGE	ISOAMYL	ISOFORM
IRONLIKE	ISAGOGES	ISOAMYLS	ISOFORMS
IRONMAN	ISAGOGIC	ISOBAR	ISOGAMETE
IRONMEN	ISAGOGICS	ISOBARE	ISOGAMIC
IRONNESS	ISALLOBAR	ISOBARES	ISOGAMIES
IRONS	ISARITHM	ISOBARIC	ISOGAMOUS
IRONSIDE	ISARITHMS	ISOBARISM	ISOGAMY
IRONSIDES	ISATIN	ISOBARS	ISOGENEIC
IRONSMITH	ISATINE	ISOBASE	ISOGENIC
IRONSTONE	ISATINES	ISOBASES	ISOGENIES
IRONWARE	ISATINIC	ISOBATH	ISOGENOUS
IRONWARES	ISATINS	ISOBATHIC	ISOGENY
IRONWEED	ISBA	ISOBATHS	ISOGLOSS
IRONWEEDS	ISBAS	ISOBRONT	ISOGON
IRONWOMAN	ISCHAEMIA	ISOBRONTS	ISOGONAL
IRONWOMEN	ISCHAEMIC	ISOBUTANE	ISOGONALS
IRONWOOD	ISCHEMIA	ISOBUTENE	ISOGONE
IRONWOODS	ISCHEMIAS	ISOBUTYL	ISOGONES
IRONWORK	ISCHEMIC	ISOBUTYLS	ISOGONIC
IRONWORKS	ISCHIA	ISOCHASM	ISOGONICS
IRONY	ISCHIADIC	ISOCHASMS	ISOGONIES
IRRADIANT	ISCHIAL	ISOCHEIM	ISOGONS
IRRADIATE	ISCHIATIC	ISOCHEIMS	ISOGONY
IRREAL	ISCHIUM	ISOCHIMAL	ISOGRAFT

ISOGRAFTS	ISOPACHS	ISSUABLY	ITEMS
ISOGRAM	ISOPHONE	ISSUANCE	ITERANCE
ISOGRAMS	ISOPHONES	ISSUANCES	ITERANCES
ISOGRAPH	ISOPHOTAL	ISSUANT	ITERANT
ISOGRAPHS	ISOPHOTE	ISSUE	ITERATE
ISOGRIV	ISOPHOTES	ISSUED	ITERATED
ISOGRIVS	ISOPLETH	ISSUELESS	ITERATES
ISOHEL	ISOPLETHS	ISSUER	ITERATING
ISOHELS	ISOPOD	ISSUERS	ITERATION
ISOHYDRIC	ISOPODAN	ISSUES	ITERATIVE
ISOHYET	ISOPODANS	ISSUING	ITERUM
ISOHYETAL	ISOPODOUS	ISTANA	ITHER
ISOHYETS	ISOPODS	ISTANAS	ITINERACY
ISOKONT	ISOPOLITY	ISTHMI	ITINERANT
ISOKONTAN	ISOPRENE	ISTHMIAN	ITINERARY
ISOKONTS	ISOPRENES	ISTHMIANS	ITINERATE
ISOLABLE	ISOPROPYL	ISTHMIC	ITS
ISOLATE	ISOPYCNAL	ISTHMOID	ITSELF
ISOLATED	ISOPYCNIC	ISTHMUS	IURE
ISOLATES	ISOS	ISTHMUSES	IVIED
ISOLATING	ISOSCELES	ISTLE	IVIES
ISOLATION	ISOSMOTIC	ISTLES	IVORIED
ISOLATIVE	ISOSPIN	IT	IVORIES
ISOLATOR	ISOSPINS	ITA	IVORIST
ISOLATORS	ISOSPORY	ITACISM	IVORISTS
ISOLEAD	ISOSTACY	ITACISMS	IVORY
ISOLEADS	ISOSTASY	ITACONIC	IVORYBILL
ISOLEX	ISOSTATIC	ITALIC	IVORYLIKE
ISOLEXES	ISOSTERIC	ITALICISE	IVORYWOOD
ISOLINE	ISOTACH	ITALICIZE	IVRESSE
ISOLINES	ISOTACHS	ITALICS	IVRESSES
ISOLOG	ISOTACTIC	ITAS	IVY
ISOLOGOUS	ISOTHERAL	ITCH	IVYLIKE
ISOLOGS	ISOTHERE	ITCHED	IWI
ISOLOGUE	ISOTHERES	ITCHES	IWIS
ISOLOGUES	ISOTHERM	ITCHIER	IXIA
ISOMER	ISOTHERMS	ITCHIEST	IXIAS
ISOMERASE	ISOTONE	ITCHILY	IXODIASES
ISOMERE	ISOTONES	ITCHINESS	IXODIASIS
ISOMERES	ISOTONIC	ITCHING	IXODID
ISOMERIC	ISOTOPE	ITCHINGS	IXODIDS
ISOMERISE	ISOTOPES	ITCHWEED	IXORA
ISOMERISM	ISOTOPIC	ITCHWEEDS	IXORAS
ISOMERIZE	ISOTOPIES	ITCHY	IXTLE
ISOMEROUS	ISOTOPY	ITEM	IXTLES
ISOMERS	ISOTRON	ITEMED	IZAR
ISOMETRIC	ISOTRONS	ITEMING	IZARD
ISOMETRY	ISOTROPIC	ITEMISE	IZARDS
ISOMORPH	ISOTROPY	ITEMISED	IZARS
ISOMORPHS	ISOTYPE	ITEMISER	IZVESTIA
ISONIAZID	ISOTYPES	ITEMISERS	IZVESTIAS
ISONOME	ISOTYPIC	ITEMISES	IZVESTIYA
ISONOMES	ISOZYME	ITEMISING	IZZARD
ISONOMIC	ISOZYMES	ITEMIZE	IZZARDS
ISONOMIES	ISOZYMIC	ITEMIZED	IZZAT
ISONOMOUS	ISPAGHULA	ITEMIZER	IZZATS
ISONOMY	ISSEI	ITEMIZERS	
ISOOCTANE	ISSEIS	ITEMIZES	
ISOPACH	ISSUABLE	ITEMIZING	

J

JA
JAAP
JAAPS
JAB
JABBED
JABBER
JABBERED
JABBERER
JABBERERS
JABBERING
JABBERS
JABBING
JABBINGLY
JABBLE
JABBLED
JABBLES
JABBLING
JABERS
JABIRU
JABIRUS
JABORANDI
JABOT
JABOTS
JABS
JACAL
JACALES
JACALS
JACAMAR
JACAMARS
JACANA
JACANAS
JACARANDA
JACARE
JACARES
JACCHUS
JACCHUSES
JACENT
JACINTH
JACINTHE
JACINTHES
JACINTHS
JACK
JACKAL
JACKALLED
JACKALS
JACKAROO
JACKAROOS
JACKASS
JACKASSES
JACKBOOT
JACKBOOTS
JACKDAW
JACKDAWS

JACKED
JACKEEN
JACKEENS
JACKER
JACKEROO
JACKEROOS
JACKERS
JACKET
JACKETED
JACKETING
JACKETS
JACKFISH
JACKFRUIT
JACKIES
JACKING
JACKINGS
JACKKNIFE
JACKLEG
JACKLEGS
JACKLIGHT
JACKMAN
JACKMEN
JACKPLANE
JACKPOT
JACKPOTS
JACKROLL
JACKROLLS
JACKS
JACKSCREW
JACKSHAFT
JACKSIE
JACKSIES
JACKSMELT
JACKSMITH
JACKSNIPE
JACKSTAY
JACKSTAYS
JACKSTONE
JACKSTRAW
JACKSY
JACKY
JACOBIN
JACOBINS
JACOBUS
JACOBUSES
JACONET
JACONETS
JACQUARD
JACQUARDS
JACQUERIE
JACTATION
JACULATE
JACULATED

JACULATES
JACULATOR
JACUZZI
JACUZZIS
JADE
JADED
JADEDLY
JADEDNESS
JADEITE
JADEITES
JADELIKE
JADERIES
JADERY
JADES
JADING
JADISH
JADISHLY
JADITIC
JAEGER
JAEGERS
JAFA
JAFAS
JAG
JAGA
JAGAED
JAGAING
JAGAS
JAGER
JAGERS
JAGG
JAGGARIES
JAGGARY
JAGGED
JAGGEDER
JAGGEDEST
JAGGEDLY
JAGGER
JAGGERIES
JAGGERS
JAGGERY
JAGGHERY
JAGGIER
JAGGIES
JAGGIEST
JAGGING
JAGGS
JAGGY
JAGHIR
JAGHIRDAR
JAGHIRE
JAGHIRES
JAGHIRS
JAGIR

JAGIRS
JAGLESS
JAGRA
JAGRAS
JAGS
JAGUAR
JAGUARS
JAI
JAIL
JAILABLE
JAILBAIT
JAILBIRD
JAILBIRDS
JAILBREAK
JAILED
JAILER
JAILERESS
JAILERS
JAILHOUSE
JAILING
JAILLESS
JAILOR
JAILORESS
JAILORS
JAILS
JAIS
JAK
JAKE
JAKES
JAKESES
JAKEY
JAKEYS
JAKFRUIT
JAKFRUITS
JAKS
JAL
JALAP
JALAPENO
JALAPENOS
JALAPIC
JALAPIN
JALAPINS
JALAPS
JALOP
JALOPIES
JALOPPIES
JALOPPY
JALOPS
JALOPY
JALOUSE
JALOUSED
JALOUSES
JALOUSIE

JALOUSIED	JAMMIES	JAPANISES	JAROOL
JALOUSIES	JAMMIEST	JAPANIZE	JAROOLS
JALOUSING	JAMMING	JAPANIZED	JAROSITE
JAM	JAMMINGS	JAPANIZES	JAROSITES
JAMADAR	JAMMY	JAPANNED	JAROVISE
JAMADARS	JAMPACKED	JAPANNER	JAROVISED
JAMB	JAMPAN	JAPANNERS	JAROVISES
JAMBALAYA	JAMPANEE	JAPANNING	JAROVIZE
JAMBART	JAMPANEES	JAPANS	JAROVIZED
JAMBARTS	JAMPANI	JAPE	JAROVIZES
JAMBE	JAMPANIS	JAPED	JARP
JAMBEAU	JAMPANS	JAPER	JARPED
JAMBEAUX	JAMPOT	JAPERIES	JARPING
JAMBED	JAMPOTS	JAPERS	JARPS
JAMBEE	JAMS	JAPERY	JARRAH
JAMBEES	JANDAL	JAPES	JARRAHS
JAMBER	JANDALS	JAPING	JARRED
JAMBERS	JANE	JAPINGLY	JARRING
JAMBES	JANES	JAPINGS	JARRINGLY
JAMBEUX	JANGLE	JAPONICA	JARRINGS
JAMBIER	JANGLED	JAPONICAS	JARS
JAMBIERS	JANGLER	JAPPED	JARSFUL
JAMBING	JANGLERS	JAPPING	JARTA
JAMBIYA	JANGLES	JAPS	JARTAS
JAMBIYAH	JANGLIER	JAR	JARUL
JAMBIYAHS	JANGLIEST	JARARACA	JARULS
JAMBIYAS	JANGLING	JARARACAS	JARVEY
JAMBO	JANGLINGS	JARARAKA	JARVEYS
JAMBOK	JANGLY	JARARAKAS	JARVIE
JAMBOKKED	JANIFORM	JARFUL	JARVIES
JAMBOKS	JANISARY	JARFULS	JASEY
JAMBOLAN	JANISSARY	JARGON	JASEYS
JAMBOLANA	JANITOR	JARGONED	JASIES
JAMBOLANS	JANITORS	JARGONEER	JASMIN
JAMBONE	JANITRESS	JARGONEL	JASMINE
JAMBONES	JANITRIX	JARGONELS	JASMINES
JAMBOOL	JANIZAR	JARGONING	JASMINS
JAMBOOLS	JANIZARS	JARGONISE	JASP
JAMBOREE	JANIZARY	JARGONISH	JASPE
JAMBOREES	JANKER	JARGONIST	JASPER
JAMBOS	JANKERS	JARGONIZE	JASPERISE
JAMBS	JANN	JARGONS	JASPERIZE
JAMBU	JANNIES	JARGONY	JASPEROUS
JAMBUL	JANNOCK	JARGOON	JASPERS
JAMBULS	JANNOCKS	JARGOONS	JASPERY
JAMBUS	JANNS	JARHEAD	JASPES
JAMDANI	JANNY	JARHEADS	JASPIDEAN
JAMDANIS	JANSKY	JARINA	JASPILITE
JAMES	JANSKYS	JARINAS	JASPIS
JAMESES	JANTEE	JARK	JASPISES
JAMJAR	JANTIER	JARKMAN	JASPS
JAMJARS	JANTIES	JARKMEN	JASS
JAMLIKE	JANTIEST	JARKS	JASSES
JAMMABLE	JANTY	JARL	JASSID
JAMMED	JAP	JARLDOM	JASSIDS
JAMMER	JAPAN	JARLDOMS	JASY
JAMMERS	JAPANISE	JARLS	JATAKA
JAMMIER	JAPANISED	JARLSBERG	JATAKAS

JATO	JAWHOLE	JEBEL	JELL
JATOS	JAWHOLES	JEBELS	JELLABA
JAUK	JAWING	JEDI	JELLABAH
JAUKED	JAWINGS	JEDIS	JELLABAHS
JAUKING	JAWLESS	JEE	JELLABAS
JAUKS	JAWLIKE	JEED	JELLED
JAUNCE	JAWLINE	JEEING	JELLIED
JAUNCED	JAWLINES	JEEL	JELLIES
JAUNCES	JAWS	JEELED	JELLIFIED
JAUNCING	JAXIE	JEELIE	JELLIFIES
JAUNDICE	JAXIES	JEELIED	JELLIFY
JAUNDICED	JAXY	JEELIEING	JELLING
JAUNDICES	JAY	JEELIES	JELLO
JAUNSE	JAYBIRD	JEELING	JELLOS
JAUNSED	JAYBIRDS	JEELS	JELLS
JAUNSES	JAYGEE	JEELY	JELLY
JAUNSING	JAYGEES	JEELYING	JELLYBEAN
JAUNT	JAYHAWKER	JEEP	JELLYFISH
JAUNTED	JAYS	JEEPED	JELLYING
JAUNTEE	JAYVEE	JEEPERS	JELLYLIKE
JAUNTIE	JAYVEES	JEEPING	JELLYROLL
JAUNTIER	JAYWALK	JEEPNEY	JELUTONG
JAUNTIES	JAYWALKED	JEEPNEYS	JELUTONGS
JAUNTIEST	JAYWALKER	JEEPS	JEMADAR
JAUNTILY	JAYWALKS	JEER	JEMADARS
JAUNTING	JAZERANT	JEERED	JEMBE
JAUNTS	JAZERANTS	JEERER	JEMBES
JAUNTY	JAZIES	JEERERS	JEMIDAR
JAUP	JAZY	JEERING	JEMIDARS
JAUPED	JAZZ	JEERINGLY	JEMIMA
JAUPING	JAZZBO	JEERINGS	JEMIMAS
JAUPS	JAZZBOS	JEERS	JEMMIED
JAVA	JAZZED	JEES	JEMMIER
JAVAS	JAZZER	JEEZ	JEMMIES
JAVEL	JAZZERS	JEFE	JEMMIEST
JAVELIN	JAZZES	JEFES	JEMMINESS
JAVELINA	JAZZIER	JEFF	JEMMY
JAVELINAS	JAZZIEST	JEFFED	JEMMYING
JAVELINED	JAZZILY	JEFFING	JENNET
JAVELINS	JAZZINESS	JEFFS	JENNETING
JAVELS	JAZZING	JEHAD	JENNETS
JAW	JAZZLIKE	JEHADI	JENNIES
JAWAN	JAZZMAN	JEHADIS	JENNY
JAWANS	JAZZMEN	JEHADISM	JEOFAIL
JAWARI	JAZZY	JEHADISMS	JEOFAILS
JAWARIS	JEALOUS	JEHADIST	JEON
JAWBATION	JEALOUSE	JEHADISTS	JEOPARD
JAWBONE	JEALOUSED	JEHADS	JEOPARDED
JAWBONED	JEALOUSES	JEHU	JEOPARDER
JAWBONER	JEALOUSLY	JEHUS	JEOPARDS
JAWBONERS	JEALOUSY	JEJUNA	JEOPARDY
JAWBONES	JEAN	JEJUNAL	JEQUERITY
JAWBONING	JEANED	JEJUNE	JEQUIRITY
JAWBOX	JEANETTE	JEJUNELY	JERBIL
JAWBOXES	JEANETTES	JEJUNITY	JERBILS
JAWED	JEANS	JEJUNUM	JERBOA
JAWFALL	JEAT	JELAB	JERBOAS
JAWFALLS	JEATS	JELABS	JEREED

JEREEDS
JEREMIAD
JEREMIADS
JEREPIGO
JEREPIGOS
JERFALCON
JERID
JERIDS
JERK
JERKED
JERKER
JERKERS
JERKIER
JERKIES
JERKIEST
JERKILY
JERKIN
JERKINESS
JERKING
JERKINGLY
JERKINGS
JERKINS
JERKS
JERKWATER
JERKY
JEROBOAM
JEROBOAMS
JERQUE
JERQUED
JERQUER
JERQUERS
JERQUES
JERQUING
JERQUINGS
JERREED
JERREEDS
JERRICAN
JERRICANS
JERRID
JERRIDS
JERRIES
JERRY
JERRYCAN
JERRYCANS
JERSEY
JERSEYED
JERSEYING
JERSEYS
JESS
JESSAMIES
JESSAMINE
JESSAMY
JESSANT
JESSE
JESSED
JESSERANT
JESSES
JESSIE

JESSIES
JESSING
JEST
JESTBOOK
JESTBOOKS
JESTED
JESTEE
JESTEES
JESTER
JESTERS
JESTFUL
JESTING
JESTINGLY
JESTINGS
JESTS
JESUIT
JESUITIC
JESUITISM
JESUITRY
JESUITS
JESUS
JET
JETBEAD
JETBEADS
JETE
JETES
JETFOIL
JETFOILS
JETLAG
JETLAGS
JETLIKE
JETLINER
JETLINERS
JETON
JETONS
JETPLANE
JETPLANES
JETPORT
JETPORTS
JETS
JETSAM
JETSAMS
JETSOM
JETSOMS
JETSON
JETSONS
JETSTREAM
JETTATURA
JETTED
JETTIED
JETTIER
JETTIES
JETTIEST
JETTINESS
JETTING
JETTISON
JETTISONS
JETTON

JETTONS
JETTY
JETTYING
JETWAY
JETWAYS
JEU
JEUNE
JEUX
JEW
JEWED
JEWEL
JEWELED
JEWELER
JEWELERS
JEWELFISH
JEWELING
JEWELLED
JEWELLER
JEWELLERS
JEWELLERY
JEWELLIKE
JEWELLING
JEWELRIES
JEWELRY
JEWELS
JEWELWEED
JEWFISH
JEWFISHES
JEWIE
JEWIES
JEWING
JEWS
JEZAIL
JEZAILS
JEZEBEL
JEZEBELS
JHALA
JHALAS
JHATKA
JHATKAS
JIAO
JIAOS
JIB
JIBB
JIBBAH
JIBBAHS
JIBBED
JIBBER
JIBBERED
JIBBERING
JIBBERS
JIBBING
JIBBINGS
JIBBONS
JIBBOOM
JIBBOOMS
JIBBS
JIBE

JIBED
JIBER
JIBERS
JIBES
JIBING
JIBINGLY
JIBS
JICAMA
JICAMAS
JICKAJOG
JICKAJOGS
JIFF
JIFFIES
JIFFS
JIFFY
JIG
JIGABOO
JIGABOOS
JIGAJIG
JIGAJIGS
JIGAJOG
JIGAJOGS
JIGAMAREE
JIGGED
JIGGER
JIGGERED
JIGGERING
JIGGERS
JIGGIER
JIGGIEST
JIGGING
JIGGINGS
JIGGISH
JIGGLE
JIGGLED
JIGGLES
JIGGLIER
JIGGLIEST
JIGGLING
JIGGLY
JIGGUMBOB
JIGGY
JIGJIG
JIGJIGGED
JIGJIGS
JIGLIKE
JIGOT
JIGOTS
JIGS
JIGSAW
JIGSAWED
JIGSAWING
JIGSAWN
JIGSAWS
JIHAD
JIHADI
JIHADIS
JIHADISM

JIHADISMS
JIHADIST
JIHADISTS
JIHADS
JILBAB
JILBABS
JILGIE
JILGIES
JILL
JILLAROO
JILLAROOS
JILLET
JILLETS
JILLFLIRT
JILLION
JILLIONS
JILLIONTH
JILLS
JILT
JILTED
JILTER
JILTERS
JILTING
JILTS
JIMCRACK
JIMCRACKS
JIMINY
JIMJAM
JIMJAMS
JIMMIE
JIMMIED
JIMMIES
JIMMINY
JIMMY
JIMMYING
JIMP
JIMPER
JIMPEST
JIMPIER
JIMPIEST
JIMPLY
JIMPNESS
JIMPY
JIMSON
JIN
JINGAL
JINGALL
JINGALLS
JINGALS
JINGBANG
JINGBANGS
JINGKO
JINGKOES
JINGLE
JINGLED
JINGLER
JINGLERS
JINGLES

JINGLET
JINGLETS
JINGLIER
JINGLIEST
JINGLING
JINGLY
JINGO
JINGOES
JINGOISH
JINGOISM
JINGOISMS
JINGOIST
JINGOISTS
JINJILI
JINJILIS
JINK
JINKED
JINKER
JINKERS
JINKING
JINKS
JINN
JINNE
JINNEE
JINNI
JINNIS
JINNS
JINRIKSHA
JINS
JINX
JINXED
JINXES
JINXING
JIPIJAPA
JIPIJAPAS
JIPYAPA
JIPYAPAS
JIRBLE
JIRBLED
JIRBLES
JIRBLING
JIRD
JIRDS
JIRGA
JIRGAS
JIRKINET
JIRKINETS
JIRRE
JISM
JISMS
JISSOM
JISSOMS
JITNEY
JITNEYS
JITTER
JITTERBUG
JITTERED
JITTERIER

JITTERING
JITTERS
JITTERY
JIUJITSU
JIUJITSUS
JIUJUTSU
JIUJUTSUS
JIVE
JIVEASS
JIVED
JIVER
JIVERS
JIVES
JIVEY
JIVIER
JIVIEST
JIVING
JIVY
JIZ
JIZZ
JIZZES
JNANA
JNANAS
JO
JOANNA
JOANNAS
JOANNES
JOANNESES
JOB
JOBATION
JOBATIONS
JOBBED
JOBBER
JOBBERIES
JOBBERS
JOBBERY
JOBBIE
JOBBIES
JOBBING
JOBBINGS
JOBCENTRE
JOBE
JOBED
JOBERNOWL
JOBES
JOBHOLDER
JOBING
JOBLESS
JOBNAME
JOBNAMES
JOBS
JOBSEEKER
JOBSHARE
JOBSHARES
JOBSWORTH
JOCK
JOCKETTE
JOCKETTES

JOCKEY
JOCKEYED
JOCKEYING
JOCKEYISH
JOCKEYISM
JOCKEYS
JOCKNEY
JOCKNEYS
JOCKO
JOCKOS
JOCKS
JOCKSTRAP
JOCKTELEG
JOCO
JOCOSE
JOCOSELY
JOCOSITY
JOCULAR
JOCULARLY
JOCULATOR
JOCUND
JOCUNDITY
JOCUNDLY
JODEL
JODELLED
JODELLING
JODELS
JODHPUR
JODHPURS
JOE
JOES
JOEY
JOEYS
JOG
JOGGED
JOGGER
JOGGERS
JOGGING
JOGGINGS
JOGGLE
JOGGLED
JOGGLER
JOGGLERS
JOGGLES
JOGGLING
JOGPANTS
JOGS
JOGTROT
JOGTROTS
JOHANNES
JOHN
JOHNBOAT
JOHNBOATS
JOHNNIE
JOHNNIES
JOHNNY
JOHNS
JOHNSON

JOHNSONS
JOIN
JOINABLE
JOINDER
JOINDERS
JOINED
JOINER
JOINERIES
JOINERS
JOINERY
JOINING
JOININGS
JOINS
JOINT
JOINTED
JOINTEDLY
JOINTER
JOINTERS
JOINTING
JOINTLESS
JOINTLY
JOINTNESS
JOINTRESS
JOINTS
JOINTURE
JOINTURED
JOINTURES
JOINTWEED
JOINTWORM
JOIST
JOISTED
JOISTING
JOISTS
JOJOBA
JOJOBAS
JOKE
JOKED
JOKER
JOKERS
JOKES
JOKESMITH
JOKESOME
JOKESTER
JOKESTERS
JOKEY
JOKIER
JOKIEST
JOKILY
JOKINESS
JOKING
JOKINGLY
JOKOL
JOKY
JOL
JOLE
JOLED
JOLES
JOLING

JOLL
JOLLED
JOLLEY
JOLLEYER
JOLLEYERS
JOLLEYING
JOLLEYS
JOLLIED
JOLLIER
JOLLIERS
JOLLIES
JOLLIEST
JOLLIFIED
JOLLIFIES
JOLLIFY
JOLLILY
JOLLIMENT
JOLLINESS
JOLLING
JOLLITIES
JOLLITY
JOLLOP
JOLLOPS
JOLLS
JOLLY
JOLLYBOAT
JOLLYER
JOLLYERS
JOLLYHEAD
JOLLYING
JOLLYINGS
JOLS
JOLT
JOLTED
JOLTER
JOLTERS
JOLTHEAD
JOLTHEADS
JOLTIER
JOLTIEST
JOLTILY
JOLTING
JOLTINGLY
JOLTS
JOLTY
JOMO
JOMON
JOMOS
JONCANOE
JONCANOES
JONES
JONESED
JONESES
JONESING
JONG
JONGLEUR
JONGLEURS
JONGS

JONNOCK
JONNYCAKE
JONQUIL
JONQUILS
JONTIES
JONTY
JOOK
JOOKED
JOOKERIES
JOOKERY
JOOKING
JOOKS
JOR
JORAM
JORAMS
JORDAN
JORDANS
JORDELOO
JORDELOOS
JORS
JORUM
JORUMS
JOSEPH
JOSEPHS
JOSH
JOSHED
JOSHER
JOSHERS
JOSHES
JOSHING
JOSHINGLY
JOSKIN
JOSKINS
JOSS
JOSSER
JOSSERS
JOSSES
JOSTLE
JOSTLED
JOSTLER
JOSTLERS
JOSTLES
JOSTLING
JOSTLINGS
JOT
JOTA
JOTAS
JOTS
JOTTED
JOTTER
JOTTERS
JOTTING
JOTTINGS
JOTTY
JOTUN
JOTUNN
JOTUNNS
JOTUNS

JOUAL
JOUALS
JOUGS
JOUISANCE
JOUK
JOUKED
JOUKERIES
JOUKERY
JOUKING
JOUKS
JOULE
JOULED
JOULES
JOULING
JOUNCE
JOUNCED
JOUNCES
JOUNCIER
JOUNCIEST
JOUNCING
JOUNCY
JOUR
JOURNAL
JOURNALED
JOURNALS
JOURNEY
JOURNEYED
JOURNEYER
JOURNEYS
JOURNO
JOURNOS
JOURS
JOUST
JOUSTED
JOUSTER
JOUSTERS
JOUSTING
JOUSTS
JOVIAL
JOVIALITY
JOVIALLY
JOVIALTY
JOW
JOWAR
JOWARI
JOWARIS
JOWARS
JOWED
JOWING
JOWL
JOWLED
JOWLER
JOWLERS
JOWLIER
JOWLIEST
JOWLINESS
JOWLING
JOWLS

JOWLY	JUDGED	JUGULATE	JUMBLE
JOWS	JUDGELESS	JUGULATED	JUMBLED
JOY	JUDGELIKE	JUGULATES	JUMBLER
JOYANCE	JUDGEMENT	JUGULUM	JUMBLERS
JOYANCES	JUDGER	JUGUM	JUMBLES
JOYED	JUDGERS	JUGUMS	JUMBLIER
JOYFUL	JUDGES	JUICE	JUMBLIEST
JOYFULLER	JUDGESHIP	JUICED	JUMBLING
JOYFULLY	JUDGING	JUICEHEAD	JUMBLY
JOYING	JUDGINGLY	JUICELESS	JUMBO
JOYLESS	JUDGMATIC	JUICER	JUMBOISE
JOYLESSLY	JUDGMENT	JUICERS	JUMBOISED
JOYOUS	JUDGMENTS	JUICES	JUMBOISES
JOYOUSLY	JUDICABLE	JUICIER	JUMBOIZE
JOYPOP	JUDICATOR	JUICIEST	JUMBOIZED
JOYPOPPED	JUDICIAL	JUICILY	JUMBOIZES
JOYPOPPER	JUDICIARY	JUICINESS	JUMBOS
JOYPOPS	JUDICIOUS	JUICING	JUMBUCK
JOYRIDDEN	JUDIES	JUICY	JUMBUCKS
JOYRIDE	JUDO	JUJITSU	JUMBY
JOYRIDER	JUDOGI	JUJITSUS	JUMELLE
JOYRIDERS	JUDOGIS	JUJU	JUMELLES
JOYRIDES	JUDOIST	JUJUBE	JUMP
JOYRIDING	JUDOISTS	JUJUBES	JUMPABLE
JOYRODE	JUDOKA	JUJUISM	JUMPED
JOYS	JUDOKAS	JUJUISMS	JUMPER
JOYSTICK	JUDOS	JUJUIST	JUMPERS
JOYSTICKS	JUDS	JUJUISTS	JUMPIER
JUBA	JUDY	JUJUS	JUMPIEST
JUBAS	JUG	JUJUTSU	JUMPILY
JUBATE	JUGA	JUJUTSUS	JUMPINESS
JUBBAH	JUGAL	JUKE	JUMPING
JUBBAHS	JUGALS	JUKEBOX	JUMPINGLY
JUBE	JUGATE	JUKEBOXES	JUMPINGS
JUBES	JUGFUL	JUKED	JUMPOFF
JUBHAH	JUGFULS	JUKES	JUMPOFFS
JUBHAHS	JUGGED	JUKING	JUMPS
JUBILANCE	JUGGING	JUKSKEI	JUMPSUIT
JUBILANCY	JUGGINGS	JUKSKEIS	JUMPSUITS
JUBILANT	JUGGINS	JUKU	JUMPY
JUBILATE	JUGGINSES	JUKUS	JUN
JUBILATED	JUGGLE	JULEP	JUNCATE
JUBILATES	JUGGLED	JULEPS	JUNCATES
JUBILE	JUGGLER	JULIENNE	JUNCO
JUBILEE	JUGGLERS	JULIENNED	JUNCOES
JUBILEES	JUGGLERY	JULIENNES	JUNCOS
JUBILES	JUGGLES	JUMAR	JUNCTION
JUCO	JUGGLING	JUMARED	JUNCTIONS
JUCOS	JUGGLINGS	JUMARING	JUNCTURAL
JUD	JUGHEAD	JUMARRED	JUNCTURE
JUDAS	JUGHEADS	JUMARRING	JUNCTURES
JUDASES	JUGLET	JUMARS	JUNCUS
JUDDER	JUGLETS	JUMART	JUNCUSES
JUDDERED	JUGS	JUMARTS	JUNEATING
JUDDERING	JUGSFUL	JUMBAL	JUNGLE
JUDDERS	JUGULA	JUMBALS	JUNGLED
JUDGE	JUGULAR	JUMBIE	JUNGLEGYM
JUDGEABLE	JUGULARS	JUMBIES	JUNGLES

JUNGLI
JUNGLIER
JUNGLIEST
JUNGLIS
JUNGLIST
JUNGLISTS
JUNGLY
JUNIOR
JUNIORATE
JUNIORITY
JUNIORS
JUNIPER
JUNIPERS
JUNK
JUNKANOO
JUNKANOOS
JUNKED
JUNKER
JUNKERS
JUNKET
JUNKETED
JUNKETEER
JUNKETER
JUNKETERS
JUNKETING
JUNKETS
JUNKETTED
JUNKETTER
JUNKIE
JUNKIER
JUNKIES
JUNKIEST
JUNKINESS
JUNKING
JUNKMAN
JUNKMEN
JUNKS
JUNKY
JUNKYARD
JUNKYARDS
JUNTA
JUNTAS
JUNTO
JUNTOS
JUPATI
JUPATIS
JUPE
JUPES
JUPON
JUPONS
JURA
JURAL
JURALLY
JURANT
JURANTS
JURASSIC
JURAT
JURATORY

JURATS
JURE
JUREL
JURELS
JURIDIC
JURIDICAL
JURIED
JURIES
JURIST
JURISTIC
JURISTS
JUROR
JURORS
JURY
JURYING
JURYLESS
JURYMAN
JURYMAST
JURYMASTS
JURYMEN
JURYWOMAN
JURYWOMEN
JUS
JUSSIVE
JUSSIVES
JUST
JUSTED
JUSTER
JUSTERS
JUSTEST
JUSTICE
JUSTICER
JUSTICERS
JUSTICES
JUSTICIAR
JUSTIFIED
JUSTIFIER
JUSTIFIES
JUSTIFY
JUSTING
JUSTLE
JUSTLED
JUSTLES
JUSTLING
JUSTLY
JUSTNESS
JUSTS
JUT
JUTE
JUTELIKE
JUTES
JUTS
JUTTED
JUTTIED
JUTTIES
JUTTING
JUTTINGLY
JUTTY

JUTTYING
JUVE
JUVENAL
JUVENALS
JUVENILE
JUVENILES
JUVENILIA
JUVES
JUXTAPOSE
JYMOLD
JYMOLDS
JYNX
JYNXES

K

KA
KAAL
KAAMA
KAAMAS
KAAS
KAB
KABAB
KABABBED
KABABBING
KABABS
KABADDI
KABADDIS
KABAKA
KABAKAS
KABALA
KABALAS
KABALISM
KABALISMS
KABALIST
KABALISTS
KABAR
KABARS
KABAYA
KABAYAS
KABBALA
KABBALAH
KABBALAHS
KABBALAS
KABBALISM
KABBALIST
KABELE
KABELES
KABELJOU
KABELJOUS
KABELJOUW
KABIKI
KABIKIS
KABOB
KABOBBED
KABOBBING
KABOBS
KABS
KABUKI
KABUKIS
KACCHA
KACCHAS
KACHA
KACHAHRI
KACHAHRIS
KACHAS
KACHCHA
KACHCHAS
KACHERA

KACHERAS
KACHERI
KACHERIS
KACHINA
KACHINAS
KADAITCHA
KADDISH
KADDISHES
KADDISHIM
KADE
KADES
KADI
KADIS
KAE
KAED
KAEING
KAES
KAF
KAFFIR
KAFFIRS
KAFFIYAH
KAFFIYAHS
KAFFIYEH
KAFFIYEHS
KAFILA
KAFILAS
KAFIR
KAFIRS
KAFS
KAFTAN
KAFTANS
KAGO
KAGOOL
KAGOOLS
KAGOS
KAGOUL
KAGOULE
KAGOULES
KAGOULS
KAGU
KAGUS
KAHAL
KAHALS
KAHAWAI
KAHAWAIS
KAHIKATEA
KAHIKATOA
KAHUNA
KAHUNAS
KAI
KAIAK
KAIAKED
KAIAKING

KAIAKS
KAID
KAIDS
KAIE
KAIES
KAIF
KAIFS
KAIK
KAIKA
KAIKAI
KAIKAIS
KAIKAS
KAIKAWAKA
KAIKOMAKO
KAIKS
KAIL
KAILS
KAILYAIRD
KAILYARD
KAILYARDS
KAIM
KAIMAKAM
KAIMAKAMS
KAIMS
KAIN
KAING
KAINGA
KAINGAS
KAINIT
KAINITE
KAINITES
KAINITS
KAINS
KAIROMONE
KAIS
KAISER
KAISERDOM
KAISERIN
KAISERINS
KAISERISM
KAISERS
KAIZEN
KAIZENS
KAJAWAH
KAJAWAHS
KAJEPUT
KAJEPUTS
KAK
KAKA
KAKAPO
KAKAPOS
KAKARIKI
KAKAS

KAKEMONO
KAKEMONOS
KAKI
KAKIEMON
KAKIEMONS
KAKIS
KAKODYL
KAKODYLS
KAKS
KALAM
KALAMATA
KALAMATAS
KALAMDAN
KALAMDANS
KALAMKARI
KALAMS
KALANCHOE
KALE
KALENDAR
KALENDARS
KALENDS
KALES
KALEWIFE
KALEWIVES
KALEYARD
KALEYARDS
KALI
KALIAN
KALIANS
KALIF
KALIFATE
KALIFATES
KALIFS
KALIMBA
KALIMBAS
KALINITE
KALINITES
KALIPH
KALIPHATE
KALIPHS
KALIS
KALIUM
KALIUMS
KALLIDIN
KALLIDINS
KALLITYPE
KALMIA
KALMIAS
KALONG
KALONGS
KALOTYPE
KALOTYPES
KALPA

KALPAC
KALPACS
KALPAK
KALPAKS
KALPAS
KALPIS
KALPISES
KALSOMINE
KALUMPIT
KALUMPITS
KALYPTRA
KALYPTRAS
KAM
KAMA
KAMAAINA
KAMAAINAS
KAMACITE
KAMACITES
KAMAHI
KAMALA
KAMALAS
KAMAS
KAME
KAMEES
KAMEESES
KAMEEZ
KAMEEZES
KAMELA
KAMELAS
KAMERAD
KAMERADED
KAMERADS
KAMES
KAMI
KAMICHI
KAMICHIS
KAMIK
KAMIKAZE
KAMIKAZES
KAMIKS
KAMILA
KAMILAS
KAMIS
KAMISES
KAMME
KAMOKAMO
KAMPONG
KAMPONGS
KAMSEEN
KAMSEENS
KAMSIN
KAMSINS
KANA
KANAE
KANAKA
KANAKAS
KANAMYCIN
KANAS

KANBAN
KANBANS
KANDIES
KANDY
KANE
KANEH
KANEHS
KANES
KANG
KANGA
KANGAROO
KANGAROOS
KANGAS
KANGHA
KANGHAS
KANGS
KANJI
KANJIS
KANS
KANSES
KANT
KANTAR
KANTARS
KANTED
KANTELA
KANTELAS
KANTELE
KANTELES
KANTEN
KANTENS
KANTHA
KANTHAS
KANTIKOY
KANTIKOYS
KANTING
KANTS
KANUKA
KANZU
KANZUS
KAOLIANG
KAOLIANGS
KAOLIN
KAOLINE
KAOLINES
KAOLINIC
KAOLINISE
KAOLINITE
KAOLINIZE
KAOLINS
KAON
KAONIC
KAONS
KAPA
KAPAS
KAPH
KAPHS
KAPOK
KAPOKS

KAPPA
KAPPAS
KAPUKA
KAPUT
KAPUTT
KARA
KARABINER
KARAISM
KARAISMS
KARAIT
KARAITS
KARAKA
KARAKAS
KARAKIA
KARAKIAS
KARAKUL
KARAKULS
KARAMU
KARAMUS
KARANGA
KARANGAED
KARANGAS
KARAOKE
KARAOKES
KARAS
KARAT
KARATE
KARATEIST
KARATEKA
KARATEKAS
KARATES
KARATS
KAREAREA
KARENGO
KARENGOS
KARITE
KARITES
KARK
KARKED
KARKING
KARKS
KARMA
KARMAS
KARMIC
KARN
KARNS
KARO
KAROO
KAROOS
KARORO
KAROROS
KAROSHI
KAROSHIS
KAROSS
KAROSSES
KARRI
KARRIS
KARROO

KARROOS
KARSEY
KARSEYS
KARSIES
KARST
KARSTIC
KARSTIFY
KARSTS
KARSY
KART
KARTER
KARTERS
KARTING
KARTINGS
KARTS
KARYOGAMY
KARYOGRAM
KARYOLOGY
KARYON
KARYONS
KARYOSOME
KARYOTIN
KARYOTINS
KARYOTYPE
KARZIES
KARZY
KAS
KASBAH
KASBAHS
KASHA
KASHAS
KASHER
KASHERED
KASHERING
KASHERS
KASHMIR
KASHMIRS
KASHRUS
KASHRUSES
KASHRUT
KASHRUTH
KASHRUTHS
KASHRUTS
KASME
KAT
KATA
KATABASES
KATABASIS
KATABATIC
KATABOLIC
KATAKANA
KATAKANAS
KATANA
KATANAS
KATAS
KATCHINA
KATCHINAS
KATCINA

KATCINAS	KAYAKS	KECKLED	KEEN
KATHAK	KAYLE	KECKLES	KEENED
KATHAKALI	KAYLES	KECKLING	KEENER
KATHAKS	KAYLIED	KECKLINGS	KEENERS
KATHARSES	KAYO	KECKS	KEENEST
KATHARSIS	KAYOED	KECKSES	KEENING
KATHODAL	KAYOES	KECKSIES	KEENINGS
KATHODE	KAYOING	KECKSY	KEENLY
KATHODES	KAYOINGS	KED	KEENNESS
KATHODIC	KAYOS	KEDDAH	KEENO
KATI	KAYS	KEDDAHS	KEENOS
KATION	KAZACHKI	KEDGE	KEENS
KATIONS	KAZACHOK	KEDGED	KEEP
KATIPO	KAZATSKI	KEDGER	KEEPABLE
KATIPOS	KAZATSKY	KEDGEREE	KEEPER
KATIS	KAZATZKA	KEDGEREES	KEEPERS
KATORGA	KAZATZKAS	KEDGERS	KEEPING
KATORGAS	KAZI	KEDGES	KEEPINGS
KATS	KAZILLION	KEDGIER	KEEPNET
KATSURA	KAZIS	KEDGIEST	KEEPNETS
KATSURAS	KAZOO	KEDGING	KEEPS
KATTI	KAZOOS	KEDGY	KEEPSAKE
KATTIS	KBAR	KEDS	KEEPSAKES
KATYDID	KBARS	KEECH	KEEPSAKY
KATYDIDS	KEA	KEECHES	KEESHOND
KAUGH	KEAS	KEEF	KEESHONDS
KAUGHS	KEASAR	KEEFS	KEESTER
KAUMATUA	KEASARS	KEEK	KEESTERS
KAUMATUAS	KEAVIE	KEEKED	KEET
KAUPAPA	KEAVIES	KEEKER	KEETS
KAUPAPAS	KEB	KEEKERS	KEEVE
KAURI	KEBAB	KEEKING	KEEVES
KAURIES	KEBABBED	KEEKS	KEF
KAURIS	KEBABBING	KEEL	KEFFEL
KAURU	KEBABS	KEELAGE	KEFFELS
KAURY	KEBAR	KEELAGES	KEFFIYAH
KAVA	KEBARS	KEELBOAT	KEFFIYAHS
KAVAKAVA	KEBBED	KEELBOATS	KEFFIYEH
KAVAKAVAS	KEBBIE	KEELED	KEFFIYEHS
KAVAS	KEBBIES	KEELER	KEFIR
KAVASS	KEBBING	KEELERS	KEFIRS
KAVASSES	KEBBOCK	KEELHALE	KEFS
KAW	KEBBOCKS	KEELHALED	KEFTEDES
KAWA	KEBBUCK	KEELHALES	KEFUFFLE
KAWAKAWA	KEBBUCKS	KEELHAUL	KEFUFFLED
KAWAKAWAS	KEBELE	KEELHAULS	KEFUFFLES
KAWAS	KEBELES	KEELIE	KEG
KAWAU	KEBLAH	KEELIES	KEGELER
KAWED	KEBLAHS	KEELING	KEGELERS
KAWING	KEBOB	KEELINGS	KEGGED
KAWS	KEBOBBED	KEELIVINE	KEGGER
KAY	KEBOBBING	KEELLESS	KEGGERS
KAYAK	KEBOBS	KEELMAN	KEGGING
KAYAKED	KEBS	KEELMEN	KEGLER
KAYAKER	KECK	KEELS	KEGLERS
KAYAKERS	KECKED	KEELSON	KEGLING
KAYAKING	KECKING	KEELSONS	KEGLINGS
KAYAKINGS	KECKLE	KEELYVINE	KEGS

KEHUA
KEHUAS
KEIGHT
KEIR
KEIRETSU
KEIRETSUS
KEIRS
KEISTER
KEISTERS
KEITLOA
KEITLOAS
KEKENO
KEKERENGU
KEKS
KEKSYE
KEKSYES
KELEP
KELEPS
KELIM
KELIMS
KELL
KELLAUT
KELLAUTS
KELLIES
KELLS
KELLY
KELOID
KELOIDAL
KELOIDS
KELP
KELPED
KELPER
KELPERS
KELPIE
KELPIES
KELPING
KELPS
KELPY
KELSON
KELSONS
KELT
KELTER
KELTERS
KELTIE
KELTIES
KELTS
KELTY
KELVIN
KELVINS
KEMB
KEMBED
KEMBING
KEMBLA
KEMBLAS
KEMBO
KEMBOED
KEMBOING
KEMBOS

KEMBS
KEMP
KEMPED
KEMPER
KEMPERS
KEMPIER
KEMPIEST
KEMPING
KEMPINGS
KEMPLE
KEMPLES
KEMPS
KEMPT
KEMPY
KEN
KENAF
KENAFS
KENCH
KENCHES
KENDO
KENDOS
KENNED
KENNEL
KENNELED
KENNELING
KENNELLED
KENNELS
KENNER
KENNERS
KENNET
KENNETS
KENNETT
KENNETTED
KENNETTS
KENNING
KENNINGS
KENO
KENOS
KENOSES
KENOSIS
KENOSISES
KENOTIC
KENOTRON
KENOTRONS
KENS
KENSPECK
KENT
KENTE
KENTED
KENTES
KENTIA
KENTIAS
KENTING
KENTLEDGE
KENTS
KEP
KEPHALIC
KEPHALICS

KEPHALIN
KEPHALINS
KEPHIR
KEPHIRS
KEPI
KEPIS
KEPPED
KEPPEN
KEPPING
KEPPIT
KEPS
KEPT
KERAMIC
KERAMICS
KERATIN
KERATINS
KERATITIS
KERATOID
KERATOMA
KERATOMAS
KERATOSE
KERATOSES
KERATOSIC
KERATOSIS
KERATOTIC
KERB
KERBAYA
KERBAYAS
KERBED
KERBING
KERBINGS
KERBS
KERBSIDE
KERBSIDES
KERBSTONE
KERCHIEF
KERCHIEFS
KERCHOO
KEREL
KERELS
KERERU
KERF
KERFED
KERFING
KERFLOOEY
KERFS
KERFUFFLE
KERKIER
KERKIEST
KERKY
KERMA
KERMAS
KERMES
KERMESITE
KERMESS
KERMESSE
KERMESSES
KERMIS

KERMISES
KERN
KERNE
KERNED
KERNEL
KERNELED
KERNELING
KERNELLED
KERNELLY
KERNELS
KERNES
KERNING
KERNINGS
KERNISH
KERNITE
KERNITES
KERNS
KERO
KEROGEN
KEROGENS
KEROS
KEROSENE
KEROSENES
KEROSINE
KEROSINES
KERPLUNK
KERPLUNKS
KERRIA
KERRIAS
KERRIES
KERRY
KERSEY
KERSEYS
KERVE
KERVED
KERVES
KERVING
KERYGMA
KERYGMAS
KERYGMATA
KESAR
KESARS
KESH
KESHES
KEST
KESTING
KESTREL
KESTRELS
KESTS
KET
KETA
KETAMINE
KETAMINES
KETAS
KETCH
KETCHES
KETCHING
KETCHUP

KETCHUPS
KETE
KETENE
KETENES
KETMIA
KETMIAS
KETO
KETOGENIC
KETOL
KETOLS
KETONE
KETONEMIA
KETONES
KETONIC
KETONURIA
KETOSE
KETOSES
KETOSIS
KETOTIC
KETOXIME
KETOXIMES
KETS
KETTLE
KETTLEFUL
KETTLES
KETUBAH
KETUBAHS
KETUBOT
KETUBOTH
KEVEL
KEVELS
KEVIL
KEVILS
KEWL
KEWLER
KEWLEST
KEWPIE
KEWPIES
KEX
KEXES
KEY
KEYBOARD
KEYBOARDS
KEYBUGLE
KEYBUGLES
KEYBUTTON
KEYCARD
KEYCARDS
KEYED
KEYHOLE
KEYHOLES
KEYING
KEYINGS
KEYLESS
KEYLINE
KEYLINES
KEYLOGGER
KEYNOTE

KEYNOTED
KEYNOTER
KEYNOTERS
KEYNOTES
KEYNOTING
KEYPAD
KEYPADS
KEYPAL
KEYPALS
KEYPUNCH
KEYRING
KEYS
KEYSET
KEYSETS
KEYSTER
KEYSTERS
KEYSTONE
KEYSTONED
KEYSTONES
KEYSTROKE
KEYWAY
KEYWAYS
KEYWORD
KEYWORDS
KGOTLA
KGOTLAS
KHADDAR
KHADDARS
KHADI
KHADIS
KHAF
KHAFS
KHAKI
KHAKILIKE
KHAKIS
KHALAT
KHALATS
KHALIF
KHALIFA
KHALIFAH
KHALIFAHS
KHALIFAS
KHALIFAT
KHALIFATE
KHALIFATS
KHALIFS
KHAMSEEN
KHAMSEENS
KHAMSIN
KHAMSINS
KHAN
KHANATE
KHANATES
KHANDA
KHANDAS
KHANGA
KHANGAS
KHANJAR

KHANJARS
KHANS
KHANSAMA
KHANSAMAH
KHANSAMAS
KHANUM
KHANUMS
KHAPH
KHAPHS
KHARIF
KHARIFS
KHAT
KHATS
KHAYA
KHAYAL
KHAYALS
KHAYAS
KHAZEN
KHAZENIM
KHAZENS
KHAZI
KHAZIS
KHEDA
KHEDAH
KHEDAHS
KHEDAS
KHEDIVA
KHEDIVAL
KHEDIVAS
KHEDIVATE
KHEDIVE
KHEDIVES
KHEDIVIAL
KHET
KHETH
KHETHS
KHETS
KHI
KHILAFAT
KHILAFATS
KHILAT
KHILATS
KHILIM
KHILIMS
KHIRKAH
KHIRKAHS
KHIS
KHODJA
KHODJAS
KHOJA
KHOJAS
KHOR
KHORS
KHOTBAH
KHOTBAHS
KHOTBEH
KHOTBEHS
KHOUM

KHOUMS
KHUD
KHUDS
KHURTA
KHURTAS
KHUSKHUS
KHUTBAH
KHUTBAHS
KI
KIAAT
KIAATS
KIANG
KIANGS
KIAUGH
KIAUGHS
KIBBE
KIBBEH
KIBBEHS
KIBBES
KIBBI
KIBBIS
KIBBITZ
KIBBITZED
KIBBITZER
KIBBITZES
KIBBLE
KIBBLED
KIBBLES
KIBBLING
KIBBUTZ
KIBBUTZIM
KIBE
KIBEI
KIBEIS
KIBES
KIBITKA
KIBITKAS
KIBITZ
KIBITZED
KIBITZER
KIBITZERS
KIBITZES
KIBITZING
KIBLA
KIBLAH
KIBLAHS
KIBLAS
KIBOSH
KIBOSHED
KIBOSHES
KIBOSHING
KICK
KICKABLE
KICKABOUT
KICKBACK
KICKBACKS
KICKBALL
KICKBALLS

KICKBOARD
KICKBOX
KICKBOXED
KICKBOXER
KICKBOXES
KICKDOWN
KICKDOWNS
KICKED
KICKER
KICKERS
KICKIER
KICKIEST
KICKING
KICKOFF
KICKOFFS
KICKS
KICKSHAW
KICKSHAWS
KICKSTAND
KICKSTART
KICKUP
KICKUPS
KICKY
KID
KIDDED
KIDDER
KIDDERS
KIDDIE
KIDDIED
KIDDIER
KIDDIERS
KIDDIES
KIDDING
KIDDINGLY
KIDDISH
KIDDLE
KIDDLES
KIDDO
KIDDOES
KIDDOS
KIDDUSH
KIDDUSHES
KIDDY
KIDDYING
KIDDYWINK
KIDEL
KIDELS
KIDGE
KIDGIE
KIDGIER
KIDGIEST
KIDGLOVE
KIDLET
KIDLETS
KIDLIKE
KIDLING
KIDLINGS
KIDNAP

KIDNAPED
KIDNAPEE
KIDNAPEES
KIDNAPER
KIDNAPERS
KIDNAPING
KIDNAPPED
KIDNAPPEE
KIDNAPPER
KIDNAPS
KIDNEY
KIDNEYS
KIDOLOGY
KIDS
KIDSKIN
KIDSKINS
KIDSTAKES
KIDULT
KIDULTS
KIDVID
KIDVIDS
KIEF
KIEFS
KIEKIE
KIEKIES
KIELBASA
KIELBASAS
KIELBASI
KIELBASY
KIER
KIERIE
KIERIES
KIERS
KIESELGUR
KIESERITE
KIESTER
KIESTERS
KIEVE
KIEVES
KIF
KIFF
KIFS
KIGHT
KIGHTS
KIKE
KIKES
KIKOI
KIKOIS
KIKUMON
KIKUMONS
KIKUYU
KIKUYUS
KILD
KILDERKIN
KILERG
KILERGS
KILEY
KILEYS

KILIM
KILIMS
KILL
KILLABLE
KILLADAR
KILLADARS
KILLAS
KILLASES
KTLLCOW
KILLCOWS
KILLCROP
KILLCROPS
KILLDEE
KILLDEER
KILLDEERS
KILLDEES
KILLED
KILLER
KILLERS
KILLICK
KILLICKS
KILLIE
KILLIES
KILLIFISH
KILLING
KILLINGLY
KILLINGS
KILLJOY
KILLJOYS
KILLOCK
KILLOCKS
KILLOGIE
KILLOGIES
KILLS
KILLUT
KILLUTS
KILN
KILNED
KILNING
KILNS
KILO
KILOBAR
KILOBARS
KILOBASE
KILOBASES
KILOBAUD
KILOBAUDS
KILOBIT
KILOBITS
KILOBYTE
KILOBYTES
KILOCURIE
KILOCYCLE
KILOGAUSS
KILOGRAM
KILOGRAMS
KILOGRAY
KILOGRAYS

KILOHERTZ
KILOJOULE
KILOLITER
KILOLITRE
KILOMETER
KILOMETRE
KILOMOLE
KILOMOLES
KILORAD
KILORADS
KILOS
KILOTON
KILOTONS
KILOVOLT
KILOVOLTS
KILOWATT
KILOWATTS
KILP
KILPS
KILT
KILTED
KILTER
KILTERS
KILTIE
KILTIES
KILTING
KILTINGS
KILTLIKE
KILTS
KILTY
KIMBO
KIMBOED
KIMBOING
KIMBOS
KIMCHEE
KIMCHEES
KIMCHI
KIMCHIS
KIMMER
KIMMERS
KIMONO
KIMONOED
KIMONOS
KIN
KINA
KINAKINA
KINAKINAS
KINARA
KINARAS
KINAS
KINASE
KINASES
KINCHIN
KINCHINS
KINCOB
KINCOBS
KIND
KINDA

KINDED	KINGKLIPS	KIOSKS	KIRTANS
KINDER	KINGLE	KIP	KIRTLE
KINDERS	KINGLES	KIPE	KIRTLED
KINDEST	KINGLESS	KIPES	KIRTLES
KINDIE	KINGLET	KIPP	KIS
KINDIES	KINGLETS	KIPPA	KISAN
KINDING	KINGLIER	KIPPAGE	KISANS
KINDLE	KINGLIEST	KIPPAGES	KISH
KINDLED	KINGLIKE	KIPPAS	KISHES
KINDLER	KINGLING	KIPPED	KISHKA
KINDLERS	KINGLINGS	KIPPEN	KISHKAS
KINDLES	KINGLY	KIPPER	KISHKE
KINDLESS	KINGMAKER	KIPPERED	KISHKES
KINDLIER	KINGPIN	KIPPERER	KISMAT
KINDLIEST	KINGPINS	KIPPERERS	KISMATS
KINDLILY	KINGPOST	KIPPERING	KISMET
KINDLING	KINGPOSTS	KIPPERS	KISMETIC
KINDLINGS	KINGS	KIPPING	KISMETS
KINDLY	KINGSHIP	KIPPS	KISS
KINDNESS	KINGSHIPS	KIPS	KISSABLE
KINDRED	KINGSIDE	KIPSKIN	KISSABLY
KINDREDS	KINGSIDES	KIPSKINS	KISSAGRAM
KINDS	KINGSNAKE	KIR	KISSED
KINDY	KINGWOOD	KIRBEH	KISSEL
KINE	KINGWOODS	KIRBEHS	KISSELS
KINEMA	KININ	KIRBIGRIP	KISSER
KINEMAS	KININS	KIRBY	KISSERS
KINEMATIC	KINK	KIRIGAMI	KISSES
KINES	KINKAJOU	KIRIGAMIS	KISSING
KINESCOPE	KINKAJOUS	KIRIMON	KISSOGRAM
KINESES	KINKED	KIRIMONS	KISSY
KINESIC	KINKIER	KIRK	KIST
KINESICS	KINKIEST	KIRKED	KISTED
KINESIS	KINKILY	KIRKING	KISTFUL
KINETIC	KINKINESS	KIRKINGS	KISTFULS
KINETICAL	KINKING	KIRKMAN	KISTING
KINETICS	KINKLE	KIRKMEN	KISTS
KINETIN	KINKLES	KIRKS	KISTVAEN
KINETINS	KINKS	KIRKTON	KISTVAENS
KINFOLK	KINKY	KIRKTONS	KIT
KINFOLKS	KINLESS	KIRKWARD	KITBAG
KING	KINO	KIRKYAIRD	KITBAGS
KINGBIRD	KINONE	KIRKYARD	KITCHEN
KINGBIRDS	KINONES	KIRKYARDS	KITCHENED
KINGBOLT	KINOS	KIRMESS	KITCHENER
KINGBOLTS	KINRED	KIRMESSES	KITCHENET
KINGCRAFT	KINREDS	KIRN	KITCHENS
KINGCUP	KINS	KIRNED	KITE
KINGCUPS	KINSFOLK	KIRNING	KITED
KINGDOM	KINSFOLKS	KIRNS	KITELIKE
KINGDOMED	KINSHIP	KIRPAN	KITENGE
KINGDOMS	KINSHIPS	KIRPANS	KITENGES
KINGED	KINSMAN	KIRRI	KITER
KINGFISH	KINSMEN	KIRRIS	KITERS
KINGHOOD	KINSWOMAN	KIRS	KITES
KINGHOODS	KINSWOMEN	KIRSCH	KITH
KINGING	KIORE	KIRSCHES	KITHARA
KINGKLIP	KIOSK	KIRTAN	KITHARAS

KITHE	KLAVERNS	KLUDGIEST	KNAVERIES
KITHED	KLAVIER	KLUDGING	KNAVERY
KITHES	KLAVIERS	KLUDGY	KNAVES
KITHING	KLAXON	KLUGE	KNAVESHIP
KITHS	KLAXONED	KLUGED	KNAVISH
KITING	KLAXONING	KLUGES	KNAVISHLY
KITINGS	KLAXONS	KLUGING	KNAWE
KITLING	KLEAGLE	KLUTZ	KNAWEL
KITLINGS	KLEAGLES	KLUTZES	KNAWELS
KITS	KLEENEX	KLUTZIER	KNAWES
KITSCH	KLEENEXES	KLUTZIEST	KNEAD
KITSCHES	KLENDUSIC	KLUTZY	KNEADABLE
KITSCHIER	KLEPHT	KLYSTRON	KNEADED
KITSCHIFY	KLEPHTIC	KLYSTRONS	KNEADER
KITSCHILY	KLEPHTISM	KNACK	KNEADERS
KITSCHY	KLEPHTS	KNACKED	KNEADING
KITSET	KLEPTO	KNACKER	KNEADS
KITSETS	KLEPTOS	KNACKERED	KNEE
KITTED	KLETT	KNACKERS	KNEECAP
KITTEL	KLETTS	KNACKERY	KNEECAPS
KITTELS	KLEZMER	KNACKIER	KNEED
KITTEN	KLEZMERS	KNACKIEST	KNEEHOLE
KITTENED	KLEZMORIM	KNACKING	KNEEHOLES
KITTENING	KLICK	KNACKISH	KNEEING
KITTENISH	KLICKS	KNACKS	KNEEJERK
KITTENS	KLIEG	KNACKY	KNEEL
KITTENY	KLIK	KNAG	KNEELED
KITTIES	KLIKS	KNAGGIER	KNEELER
KITTING	KLINKER	KNAGGIEST	KNEELERS
KITTIWAKE	KLINKERS	KNAGGY	KNEELING
KITTLE	KLINOSTAT	KNAGS	KNEELS
KITTLED	KLIPDAS	KNAIDEL	KNEEPAD
KITTLER	KLIPDASES	KNAIDLACH	KNEEPADS
KITTLES	KLISTER	KNAP	KNEEPAN
KITTLEST	KLISTERS	KNAPPED	KNEEPANS
KITTLIER	KLONDIKE	KNAPPER	KNEEPIECE
KITTLIEST	KLONDIKED	KNAPPERS	KNEES
KITTLING	KLONDIKER	KNAPPING	KNEESIES
KITTLY	KLONDIKES	KNAPPLE	KNEESOCK
KITTUL	KLONDYKE	KNAPPLED	KNEESOCKS
KITTULS	KLONDYKED	KNAPPLES	KNEIDEL
KITTY	KLONDYKER	KNAPPLING	KNEIDLACH
KIVA	KLONDYKES	KNAPS	KNELL
KIVAS	KLONG	KNAPSACK	KNELLED
KIWI	KLONGS	KNAPSACKS	KNELLING
KIWIFRUIT	KLOOCH	KNAPWEED	KNELLS
KIWIS	KLOOCHES	KNAPWEEDS	KNELT
KLANG	KLOOCHMAN	KNAR	KNESSET
KLANGS	KLOOCHMEN	KNARL	KNESSETS
KLAP	KLOOF	KNARLS	KNEVELL
KLAPPED	KLOOFS	KNARLY	KNEVELLED
KLAPPING	KLOOTCH	KNARRED	KNEVELLS
KLAPS	KLOOTCHES	KNARRING	KNEW
KLATCH	KLUDGE	KNARRY	KNICKER
KLATCHES	KLUDGED	KNARS	KNICKERED
KLATSCH	KLUDGES	KNAUR	KNICKERS
KLATSCHES	KLUDGEY	KNAURS	KNICKS
KLAVERN	KLUDGIER	KNAVE	KNIFE

KNIFED	KNOCKDOWN	KNOWINGLY	KOCHIA
KNIFELESS	KNOCKED	KNOWINGS	KOCHIAS
KNIFELIKE	KNOCKER	KNOWLEDGE	KOEKOEA
KNIFEMAN	KNOCKERS	KNOWN	KOEL
KNIFEMEN	KNOCKING	KNOWNS	KOELS
KNIFER	KNOCKINGS	KNOWS	KOFF
KNIFEREST	KNOCKLESS	KNUB	KOFFS
KNIFERS	KNOCKOFF	KNUBBIER	KOFTA
KNIFES	KNOCKOFFS	KNUBBIEST	KOFTAS
KNIFING	KNOCKOUT	KNUBBLE	KOFTGAR
KNIFINGS	KNOCKOUTS	KNUBBLED	KOFTGARI
KNIGHT	KNOCKS	KNUBBLES	KOFTGARIS
KNIGHTAGE	KNOLL	KNUBBLIER	KOFTGARS
KNIGHTED	KNOLLED	KNUBBLING	KOFTWORK
KNIGHTING	KNOLLER	KNUBBLY	KOFTWORKS
KNIGHTLY	KNOLLERS	KNUBBY	KOHA
KNIGHTS	KNOLLING	KNUBS	KOHAS
KNIPHOFIA	KNOLLS	KNUCKLE	KOHEKOHE
KNISH	KNOLLY	KNUCKLED	KOHL
KNISHES	KNOP	KNUCKLER	KOHLRABI
KNIT	KNOPPED	KNUCKLERS	KOHLRABIS
KNITCH	KNOPS	KNUCKLES	KOHLS
KNITCHES	KNOSP	KNUCKLIER	KOI
KNITS	KNOSPS	KNUCKLING	KOINE
KNITTABLE	KNOT	KNUCKLY	KOINES
KNITTED	KNOTGRASS	KNUR	KOIS
KNITTER	KNOTHOLE	KNURL	KOJI
KNITTERS	KNOTHOLES	KNURLED	KOJIS
KNITTING	KNOTLESS	KNURLIER	KOKAKO
KNITTINGS	KNOTLIKE	KNURLIEST	KOKAKOS
KNITTLE	KNOTS	KNURLING	KOKANEE
KNITTLES	KNOTTED	KNURLINGS	KOKANEES
KNITWEAR	KNOTTER	KNURLS	KOKER
KNITWEARS	KNOTTERS	KNURLY	KOKERS
KNIVE	KNOTTIER	KNURR	KOKIRI
KNIVED	KNOTTIEST	KNURRS	KOKOBEH
KNIVES	KNOTTILY	KNURS	KOKOPU
KNIVING	KNOTTING	KNUT	KOKOWAI
KNOB	KNOTTINGS	KNUTS	KOKOWAIS
KNOBBED	KNOTTY	KO	KOKRA
KNOBBER	KNOTWEED	KOA	KOKRAS
KNOBBERS	KNOTWEEDS	KOALA	KOKUM
KNOBBIER	KNOTWORK	KOALAS	KOKUMS
KNOBBIEST	KNOTWORKS	KOAN	KOLA
KNOBBING	KNOUT	KOANS	KOLACKY
KNOBBLE	KNOUTED	KOAP	KOLAS
KNOBBLED	KNOUTING	KOAPS	KOLBASI
KNOBBLES	KNOUTS	KOAS	KOLBASIS
KNOBBLIER	KNOW	KOB	KOLBASSI
KNOBBLING	KNOWABLE	KOBAN	KOLBASSIS
KNOBBLY	KNOWE	KOBANG	KOLHOZ
KNOBBY	KNOWER	KOBANGS	KOLHOZES
KNOBHEAD	KNOWERS	KOBANS	KOLHOZY
KNOBHEADS	KNOWES	KOBO	KOLINSKI
KNOBLIKE	KNOWHOW	KOBOLD	KOLINSKY
KNOBS	KNOWHOWS	KOBOLDS	KOLKHOS
KNOBSTICK	KNOWING	KOBOS	KOLKHOSES
KNOCK	KNOWINGER	KOBS	KOLKHOSY

KOLKHOZ	KOPECKS	KOTCHED	KRAMERIAS
KOLKHOZES	KOPEK	KOTCHES	KRANG
KOLKHOZY	KOPEKS	KOTCHING	KRANGS
KOLKOZ	KOPH	KOTO	KRANS
KOLKOZES	KOPHS	KOTOS	KRANSES
KOLKOZY	KOPIYKA	KOTOW	KRANTZ
KOLO	KOPIYKAS	KOTOWED	KRANTZES
KOLOS	KOPJE	KOTOWER	KRANZ
KOMATIK	KOPJES	KOTOWERS	KRANZES
KOMATIKS	KOPPA	KOTOWING	KRATER
KOMBU	KOPPAS	KOTOWS	KRATERS
KOMBUS	KOPPIE	KOTTABOS	KRAUT
KOMISSAR	KOPPIES	KOTUKU	KRAUTS
KOMISSARS	KOPS	KOTWAL	KREASOTE
KOMITAJI	KOR	KOTWALS	KREASOTED
KOMITAJIS	KORA	KOULAN	KREASOTES
KOMONDOR	KORAI	KOULANS	KREATINE
KOMONDORS	KORARI	KOUMIS	KREATINES
KON	KORAS	KOUMISES	KREEP
KONAKI	KORAT	KOUMISS	KREEPS
KONBU	KORATS	KOUMISSES	KREESE
KONBUS	KORE	KOUMYS	KREESED
KOND	KORERO	KOUMYSES	KREESES
KONDO	KOREROED	KOUMYSS	KREESING
KONDOS	KOREROING	KOUMYSSES	KREMLIN
KONEKE	KOREROS	KOUPREY	KREMLINS
KONFYT	KORES	KOUPREYS	KRENG
KONFYTS	KORFBALL	KOURA	KRENGS
KONGONI	KORFBALLS	KOURBASH	KREOSOTE
KONIMETER	KORIMAKO	KOUROI	KREOSOTED
KONINI	KORKIR	KOUROS	KREOSOTES
KONIOLOGY	KORKIRS	KOUSKOUS	KREPLACH
KONISCOPE	KORMA	KOUSSO	KREPLECH
KONK	KORMAS	KOUSSOS	KREUTZER
KONKED	KORO	KOW	KREUTZERS
KONKING	KOROMIKO	KOWHAI	KREUZER
KONKS	KORORA	KOWHAIS	KREUZERS
KONNING	KORORAS	KOWS	KREWE
KONS	KOROWAI	KOWTOW	KREWES
KOODOO	KORS	KOWTOWED	KRILL
KOODOOS	KORU	KOWTOWER	KRILLS
KOOK	KORUN	KOWTOWERS	KRIMMER
KOOKED	KORUNA	KOWTOWING	KRIMMERS
KOOKIE	KORUNAS	KOWTOWS	KRIS
KOOKIER	KORUNY	KRAAL	KRISED
KOOKIEST	KORUS	KRAALED	KRISES
KOOKINESS	KOS	KRAALING	KRISING
KOOKING	KOSES	KRAALS	KROMESKY
KOOKS	KOSHER	KRAB	KRONA
KOOKY	KOSHERED	KRABS	KRONE
KOOLAH	KOSHERING	KRAFT	KRONEN
KOOLAHS	KOSHERS	KRAFTS	KRONER
KOORI	KOSMOS	KRAIT	KRONOR
KOORIES	KOSMOSES	KRAITS	KRONUR
KOORIS	KOSS	KRAKEN	KROON
KOP	KOSSES	KRAKENS	KROONI
KOPASETIC	KOTARE	KRAKOWIAK	KROONS
KOPECK	KOTCH	KRAMERIA	KRUBI

KRUBIS
KRUBUT
KRUBUTS
KRULLER
KRULLERS
KRUMHORN
KRUMHORNS
KRUMKAKE
KRUMKAKES
KRUMMHOLZ
KRUMMHORN
KRYOLITE
KRYOLITES
KRYOLITH
KRYOLITHS
KRYOMETER
KRYPSES
KRYPSIS
KRYPTON
KRYPTONS
KRYTRON
KRYTRONS
KSAR
KSARS
KUCHCHA
KUCHEN
KUCHENS
KUDLIK
KUDLIKS
KUDO
KUDOS
KUDOSES
KUDU
KUDUS
KUDZU
KUDZUS
KUE
KUEH
KUES
KUFI
KUFIS
KUFIYAH
KUFIYAHS
KUGEL
KUGELS
KUIA
KUIAS
KUKRI
KUKRIS
KUKU
KUKUS
KULA
KULAK
KULAKI
KULAKS
KULAN
KULANS
KULAS

KULFI
KULFIS
KULTUR
KULTURS
KUMARA
KUMARAHOU
KUMARAS
KUMARI
KUMARIS
KUMBALOI
KUMERA
KUMERAS
KUMIKUMI
KUMISS
KUMISSES
KUMITE
KUMITES
KUMMEL
KUMMELS
KUMQUAT
KUMQUATS
KUMYS
KUMYSES
KUNA
KUNDALINI
KUNE
KUNJOOS
KUNKAR
KUNKARS
KUNKUR
KUNKURS
KUNZITE
KUNZITES
KURBASH
KURBASHED
KURBASHES
KURFUFFLE
KURGAN
KURGANS
KURI
KURIS
KURRAJONG
KURRE
KURRES
KURSAAL
KURSAALS
KURTA
KURTAS
KURTOSES
KURTOSIS
KURU
KURUS
KURVEY
KURVEYED
KURVEYING
KURVEYOR
KURVEYORS
KURVEYS

KUSSO
KUSSOS
KUTA
KUTAS
KUTCH
KUTCHA
KUTCHES
KUTI
KUTIS
KUTU
KUTUS
KUVASZ
KUVASZOK
KUZU
KUZUS
KVAS
KVASES
KVASS
KVASSES
KVELL
KVELLED
KVELLING
KVELLS
KVETCH
KVETCHED
KVETCHER
KVETCHERS
KVETCHES
KVETCHIER
KVETCHILY
KVETCHING
KVETCHY
KWACHA
KWACHAS
KWAITO
KWAITOS
KWANZA
KWANZAS
KWELA
KWELAS
KY
KYACK
KYACKS
KYAK
KYAKS
KYANG
KYANGS
KYANISE
KYANISED
KYANISES
KYANISING
KYANITE
KYANITES
KYANITIC
KYANIZE
KYANIZED
KYANIZES
KYANIZING

KYAR
KYARS
KYAT
KYATS
KYBO
KYBOS
KYBOSH
KYBOSHED
KYBOSHES
KYBOSHING
KYDST
KYE
KYES
KYLE
KYLES
KYLICES
KYLIE
KYLIES
KYLIKES
KYLIN
KYLINS
KYLIX
KYLLOSES
KYLLOSIS
KYLOE
KYLOES
KYMOGRAM
KYMOGRAMS
KYMOGRAPH
KYND
KYNDE
KYNDED
KYNDES
KYNDING
KYNDS
KYNE
KYOGEN
KYOGENS
KYPE
KYPES
KYPHOSES
KYPHOSIS
KYPHOTIC
KYRIE
KYRIELLE
KYRIELLES
KYRIES
KYTE
KYTES
KYTHE
KYTHED
KYTHES
KYTHING
KYU
KYUS

L

LA
LAAGER
LAAGERED
LAAGERING
LAAGERS
LAARI
LAARIS
LAB
LABARA
LABARUM
LABARUMS
LABDA
LABDACISM
LABDANUM
LABDANUMS
LABDAS
LABEL
LABELABLE
LABELED
LABELER
LABELERS
LABELING
LABELLA
LABELLATE
LABELLED
LABELLER
LABELLERS
LABELLING
LABELLIST
LABELLOID
LABELLUM
LABELS
LABIA
LABIAL
LABIALISE
LABIALISM
LABIALITY
LABIALIZE
LABIALLY
LABIALS
LABIATE
LABIATED
LABIATES
LABILE
LABILITY
LABIS
LABISES
LABIUM
LABLAB
LABLABS
LABOR
LABORED
LABOREDLY

LABORER
LABORERS
LABORING
LABORIOUS
LABORISM
LABORISMS
LABORIST
LABORISTS
LABORITE
LABORITES
LABORS
LABOUR
LABOURED
LABOURER
LABOURERS
LABOURING
LABOURISM
LABOURIST
LABOURS
LABRA
LABRADOR
LABRADORS
LABRET
LABRETS
LABRID
LABRIDS
LABROID
LABROIDS
LABROSE
LABRUM
LABRUMS
LABRUSCA
LABRYS
LABRYSES
LABS
LABURNUM
LABURNUMS
LABYRINTH
LAC
LACCOLITE
LACCOLITH
LACE
LACEBARK
LACEBARKS
LACED
LACELESS
LACELIKE
LACER
LACERABLE
LACERANT
LACERATE
LACERATED
LACERATES

LACERS
LACERTIAN
LACERTID
LACERTIDS
LACERTINE
LACES
LACET
LACETS
LACEWING
LACEWINGS
LACEWOOD
LACEWOODS
LACEWORK
LACEWORKS
LACEY
LACHES
LACHESES
LACHRYMAL
LACIER
LACIEST
LACILY
LACINESS
LACING
LACINGS
LACINIA
LACINIAE
LACINIATE
LACK
LACKADAY
LACKED
LACKER
LACKERED
LACKERING
LACKERS
LACKEY
LACKEYED
LACKEYING
LACKEYS
LACKING
LACKLAND
LACKLANDS
LACKS
LACMUS
LACMUSES
LACONIC
LACONICAL
LACONISM
LACONISMS
LACQUER
LACQUERED
LACQUERER
LACQUERS
LACQUEY

LACQUEYED
LACQUEYS
LACRIMAL
LACRIMALS
LACRIMOSO
LACROSSE
LACROSSES
LACRYMAL
LACRYMALS
LACS
LACTAM
LACTAMS
LACTARIAN
LACTARY
LACTASE
LACTASES
LACTATE
LACTATED
LACTATES
LACTATING
LACTATION
LACTEAL
LACTEALLY
LACTEALS
LACTEAN
LACTEOUS
LACTIC
LACTIFIC
LACTONE
LACTONES
LACTONIC
LACTOSE
LACTOSES
LACUNA
LACUNAE
LACUNAL
LACUNAR
LACUNARIA
LACUNARS
LACUNARY
LACUNAS
LACUNATE
LACUNE
LACUNES
LACUNOSE
LACY
LAD
LADANUM
LADANUMS
LADDER
LADDERED
LADDERING
LADDERS

LADDERY	LADYISM	LAGUNA	LAIRING
LADDIE	LADYISMS	LAGUNAS	LAIRISE
LADDIES	LADYKIN	LAGUNE	LAIRISED
LADDISH	LADYKINS	LAGUNES	LAIRISES
LADE	LADYLIKE	LAH	LAIRISING
LADED	LADYLOVE	LAHAR	LAIRIZE
LADEN	LADYLOVES	LAHARS	LAIRIZED
LADENED	LADYPALM	LAHS	LAIRIZES
LADENING	LADYPALMS	LAIC	LAIRIZING
LADENS	LADYSHIP	LAICAL	LAIRS
LADER	LADYSHIPS	LAICALLY	LAIRY
LADERS	LAER	LAICH	LAISSE
LADES	LAERED	LAICHS	LAISSES
LADETTE	LAERING	LAICISE	LAITANCE
LADETTES	LAERS	LAICISED	LAITANCES
LADHOOD	LAESIE	LAICISES	LAITH
LADHOODS	LAETARE	LAICISING	LAITHLY
LADIES	LAETARES	LAICISM	LAITIES
LADIFIED	LAETRILE	LAICISMS	LAITY
LADIFIES	LAETRILES	LAICITIES	LAKE
LADIFY	LAEVIGATE	LAICITY	LAKEBED
LADIFYING	LAEVO	LAICIZE	LAKEBEDS
LADING	LAEVULIN	LAICIZED	LAKED
LADINGS	LAEVULINS	LAICIZES	LAKEFRONT
LADINO	LAEVULOSE	LAICIZING	LAKELAND
LADINOS	LAG	LAICS	LAKELANDS
LADLE	LAGAN	LAID	LAKELET
LADLED	LAGANS	LAIDED	LAKELETS
LADLEFUL	LAGENA	LAIDING	LAKELIKE
LADLEFULS	LAGENAS	LAIDLY	LAKEPORT
LADLER	LAGEND	LAIDS	LAKEPORTS
LADLERS	LAGENDS	LAIGH	LAKER
LADLES	LAGER	LAIGHER	LAKERS
LADLING	LAGERED	LAIGHEST	LAKES
LADRON	LAGERING	LAIGHS	LAKESHORE
LADRONE	LAGERS	LAIK	LAKESIDE
LADRONES	LAGGARD	LAIKA	LAKESIDES
LADRONS	LAGGARDLY	LAIKAS	LAKH
LADS	LAGGARDS	LAIKED	LAKHS
LADY	LAGGED	LAIKER	LAKIER
LADYBIRD	LAGGEN	LAIKERS	LAKIEST
LADYBIRDS	LAGGENS	LAIKING	LAKIN
LADYBOY	LAGGER	LAIKS	LAKING
LADYBOYS	LAGGERS	LAIN	LAKINGS
LADYBUG	LAGGIN	LAIPSE	LAKINS
LADYBUGS	LAGGING	LAIPSED	LAKISH
LADYCOW	LAGGINGLY	LAIPSES	LAKSA
LADYCOWS	LAGGINGS	LAIPSING	LAKSAS
LADYFIED	LAGGINS	LAIR	LAKY
LADYFIES	LAGNAPPE	LAIRAGE	LALANG
LADYFISH	LAGNAPPES	LAIRAGES	LALANGS
LADYFLIES	LAGNIAPPE	LAIRD	LALDIE
LADYFLY	LAGOMORPH	LAIRDLY	LALDIES
LADYFY	LAGOON	LAIRDS	LALDY
LADYFYING	LAGOONAL	LAIRDSHIP	LALIQUE
LADYHOOD	LAGOONS	LAIRED	LALIQUES
LADYHOODS	LAGRIMOSO	LAIRIER	LALL
LADYISH	LAGS	LAIRIEST	LALLAN

LALLAND
LALLANDS
LALLANS
LALLATION
LALLED
LALLING
LALLINGS
LALLS
LALLYGAG
LALLYGAGS
LAM
LAMA
LAMAISTIC
LAMANTIN
LAMANTINS
LAMAS
LAMASERAI
LAMASERY
LAMB
LAMBADA
LAMBADAS
LAMBAST
LAMBASTE
LAMBASTED
LAMBASTES
LAMBASTS
LAMBDA
LAMBDAS
LAMBDOID
LAMBED
LAMBENCY
LAMBENT
LAMBENTLY
LAMBER
LAMBERS
LAMBERT
LAMBERTS
LAMBIE
LAMBIER
LAMBIES
LAMBIEST
LAMBING
LAMBINGS
LAMBITIVE
LAMBKILL
LAMBKILLS
LAMBKIN
LAMBKINS
LAMBLIKE
LAMBLING
LAMBLINGS
LAMBOYS
LAMBRUSCO
LAMBS
LAMBSKIN
LAMBSKINS
LAMBY
LAME

LAMEBRAIN
LAMED
LAMEDH
LAMEDHS
LAMEDS
LAMELLA
LAMELLAE
LAMELLAR
LAMELLAS
LAMELLATE
LAMELLOID
LAMELLOSE
LAMELY
LAMENESS
LAMENT
LAMENTED
LAMENTER
LAMENTERS
LAMENTING
LAMENTS
LAMER
LAMES
LAMEST
LAMETER
LAMETERS
LAMIA
LAMIAE
LAMIAS
LAMIGER
LAMIGERS
LAMINA
LAMINABLE
LAMINAE
LAMINAL
LAMINALS
LAMINAR
LAMINARIA
LAMINARIN
LAMINARY
LAMINAS
LAMINATE
LAMINATED
LAMINATES
LAMINATOR
LAMING
LAMINGTON
LAMININ
LAMININS
LAMINITIS
LAMINOSE
LAMINOUS
LAMISH
LAMISTER
LAMISTERS
LAMITER
LAMITERS
LAMMED
LAMMER

LAMMERS
LAMMIE
LAMMIES
LAMMIGER
LAMMIGERS
LAMMING
LAMMINGS
LAMMY
LAMP
LAMPAD
LAMPADARY
LAMPADIST
LAMPADS
LAMPAS
LAMPASES
LAMPASSE
LAMPASSES
LAMPBLACK
LAMPED
LAMPER
LAMPERN
LAMPERNS
LAMPERS
LAMPERSES
LAMPHOLE
LAMPHOLES
LAMPING
LAMPINGS
LAMPION
LAMPIONS
LAMPLIGHT
LAMPOON
LAMPOONED
LAMPOONER
LAMPOONS
LAMPPOST
LAMPPOSTS
LAMPREY
LAMPREYS
LAMPS
LAMPSHADE
LAMPSHELL
LAMPUKA
LAMPUKAS
LAMPUKI
LAMPUKIS
LAMPYRID
LAMPYRIDS
LAMS
LAMSTER
LAMSTERS
LANA
LANAI
LANAIS
LANAS
LANATE
LANATED
LANCE

LANCED
LANCEGAY
LANCEGAYS
LANCEJACK
LANCELET
LANCELETS
LANCEOLAR
LANCER
LANCERS
LANCES
LANCET
LANCETED
LANCETS
LANCEWOOD
LANCH
LANCHED
LANCHES
LANCHING
LANCIERS
LANCIFORM
LANCINATE
LANCING
LAND
LANDAMMAN
LANDAU
LANDAULET
LANDAUS
LANDBOARD
LANDDAMNE
LANDDROS
LANDDROST
LANDE
LANDED
LANDER
LANDERS
LANDES
LANDFALL
LANDFALLS
LANDFILL
LANDFILLS
LANDFORCE
LANDFORM
LANDFORMS
LANDGRAB
LANDGRABS
LANDGRAVE
LANDING
LANDINGS
LANDLADY
LANDLER
LANDLERS
LANDLESS
LANDLINE
LANDLINES
LANDLOPER
LANDLORD
LANDLORDS
LANDMAN

LANDMARK	LANGUAGE	LANTSKIP	LAPSE
LANDMARKS	LANGUAGED	LANTSKIPS	LAPSED
LANDMASS	LANGUAGES	LANUGO	LAPSER
LANDMEN	LANGUE	LANUGOS	LAPSERS
LANDOWNER	LANGUED	LANX	LAPSES
LANDRACE	LANGUES	LANYARD	LAPSIBLE
LANDRACES	LANGUET	LANYARDS	LAPSING
LANDRAIL	LANGUETS	LAODICEAN	LAPSTONE
LANDRAILS	LANGUETTE	LAOGAI	LAPSTONES
LANDS	LANGUID	LAOGAIS	LAPSTRAKE
LANDSCAPE	LANGUIDLY	LAP	LAPSTREAK
LANDSHARK	LANGUISH	LAPBOARD	LAPSUS
LANDSIDE	LANGUOR	LAPBOARDS	LAPTOP
LANDSIDES	LANGUORS	LAPDOG	LAPTOPS
LANDSKIP	LANGUR	LAPDOGS	LAPTRAY
LANDSKIPS	LANGURS	LAPEL	LAPTRAYS
LANDSLEIT	LANIARD	LAPELED	LAPWING
LANDSLID	LANIARDS	LAPELLED	LAPWINGS
LANDSLIDE	LANIARIES	LAPELS	LAPWORK
LANDSLIP	LANIARY	LAPFUL	LAPWORKS
LANDSLIPS	LANITAL	LAPFULS	LAQUEARIA
LANDSMAN	LANITALS	LAPHELD	LAR
LANDSMEN	LANK	LAPIDARY	LARBOARD
LANDWARD	LANKED	LAPIDATE	LARBOARDS
LANDWARDS	LANKER	LAPIDATED	LARCENER
LANDWIND	LANKEST	LAPIDATES	LARCENERS
LANDWINDS	LANKIER	LAPIDEOUS	LARCENIES
LANE	LANKIEST	LAPIDES	LARCENIST
LANELY	LANKILY	LAPIDIFIC	LARCENOUS
LANES	LANKINESS	LAPIDIFY	LARCENY
LANEWAY	LANKING	LAPIDIST	LARCH
LANEWAYS	LANKLY	LAPIDISTS	LARCHEN
LANG	LANKNESS	LAPILLI	LARCHES
LANGAHA	LANKS	LAPILLUS	LARD
LANGAHAS	LANKY	LAPIN	LARDALITE
LANGAR	LANNER	LAPINS	LARDED
LANGARS	LANNERET	LAPIS	LARDER
LANGER	LANNERETS	LAPISES	LARDERER
LANGERED	LANNERS	LAPJE	LARDERERS
LANGERS	LANOLATED	LAPJES	LARDERS
LANGEST	LANOLIN	LAPPED	LARDIER
LANGLAUF	LANOLINE	LAPPEL	LARDIEST
LANGLAUFS	LANOLINES	LAPPELS	LARDING
LANGLEY	LANOLINS	LAPPER	LARDLIKE
LANGLEYS	LANOSE	LAPPERED	LARDON
LANGOUSTE	LANOSITY	LAPPERING	LARDONS
LANGRAGE	LANT	LAPPERS	LARDOON
LANGRAGES	LANTANA	LAPPET	LARDOONS
LANGREL	LANTANAS	LAPPETED	LARDS
LANGRELS	LANTERLOO	LAPPETS	LARDY
LANGRIDGE	LANTERN	LAPPIE	LARE
LANGSHAN	LANTERNED	LAPPIES	LAREE
LANGSHANS	LANTERNS	LAPPING	LAREES
LANGSPEL	LANTHANON	LAPPINGS	LARES
LANGSPELS	LANTHANUM	LAPS	LARGANDO
LANGSPIEL	LANTHORN	LAPSABLE	LARGE
LANGSYNE	LANTHORNS	LAPSANG	LARGELY
LANGSYNES	LANTS	LAPSANGS	LARGEN

LARGENED	LARRUPPED	LASSITUDE	LATENTS
LARGENESS	LARRUPS	LASSLORN	LATER
LARGENING	LARS	LASSO	LATERA
LARGENS	LARUM	LASSOCK	LATERAD
LARGER	LARUMS	LASSOCKS	LATERAL
LARGES	LARVA	LASSOED	LATERALED
LARGESS	LARVAE	LASSOER	LATERALLY
LARGESSE	LARVAL	LASSOERS	LATERALS
LARGESSES	LARVAS	LASSOES	LATERBORN
LARGEST	LARVATE	LASSOING	LATERISE
LARGHETTO	LARVATED	LASSOS	LATERISED
LARGISH	LARVICIDE	LASSU	LATERISES
LARGITION	LARVIFORM	LASSUS	LATERITE
LARGO	LARVIKITE	LAST	LATERITES
LARGOS	LARYNGAL	LASTAGE	LATERITIC
LARI	LARYNGALS	LASTAGES	LATERIZE
LARIAT	LARYNGEAL	LASTBORN	LATERIZED
LARIATED	LARYNGES	LASTBORNS	LATERIZES
LARIATING	LARYNX	LASTED	LATESCENT
LARIATS	LARYNXES	LASTER	LATEST
LARINE	LAS	LASTERS	LATESTS
LARIS	LASAGNA	LASTING	LATEWAKE
LARK	LASAGNAS	LASTINGLY	LATEWAKES
LARKED	LASAGNE	LASTINGS	LATEWOOD
LARKER	LASAGNES	LASTLY	LATEWOODS
LARKERS	LASCAR	LASTS	LATEX
LARKIER	LASCARS	LAT	LATEXES
LARKIEST	LASE	LATAH	LATH
LARKINESS	LASED	LATAHS	LATHE
LARKING	LASER	LATAKIA	LATHED
LARKISH	LASERDISC	LATAKIAS	LATHEE
LARKS	LASERDISK	LATCH	LATHEES
LARKSOME	LASERS	LATCHED	LATHEN
LARKSPUR	LASERWORT	LATCHES	LATHER
LARKSPURS	LASES	LATCHET	LATHERED
LARKY	LASH	LATCHETS	LATHERER
LARMIER	LASHED	LATCHING	LATHERERS
LARMIERS	LASHER	LATCHKEY	LATHERIER
LARN	LASHERS	LATCHKEYS	LATHERING
LARNAKES	LASHES	LATE	LATHERS
LARNAX	LASHING	LATECOMER	LATHERY
LARNED	LASHINGLY	LATED	LATHES
LARNEY	LASHINGS	LATEEN	LATHI
LARNEYS	LASHINS	LATEENER	LATHIER
LARNIER	LASHKAR	LATEENERS	LATHIEST
LARNIEST	LASHKARS	LATEENS	LATHING
LARNING	LASING	LATELY	LATHINGS
LARNS	LASINGS	LATEN	LATHIS
LAROID	LASKET	LATENCE	LATHLIKE
LARRIGAN	LASKETS	LATENCES	LATHS
LARRIGANS	LASQUE	LATENCIES	LATHWORK
LARRIKIN	LASQUES	LATENCY	LATHWORKS
LARRIKINS	LASS	LATENED	LATHY
LARRUP	LASSES	LATENESS	LATHYRISM
LARRUPED	LASSI	LATENING	LATHYRUS
LARRUPER	LASSIE	LATENS	LATI
LARRUPERS	LASSIES	LATENT	LATICES
LARRUPING	LASSIS	LATENTLY	LATICIFER

LATICLAVE	LAUANS	LAURA	LAVISHES
LATIFONDI	LAUCH	LAURAE	LAVISHEST
LATIGO	LAUCHING	LAURAS	LAVISHING
LATIGOES	LAUCHS	LAUREATE	LAVISHLY
LATIGOS	LAUD	LAUREATED	LAVOLT
LATILLA	LAUDABLE	LAUREATES	LAVOLTA
LATILLAS	LAUDABLY	LAUREL	LAVOLTAED
LATIMERIA	LAUDANUM	LAURELED	LAVOLTAS
LATINA	LAUDANUMS	LAURELING	LAVOLTED
LATINAS	LAUDATION	LAURELLED	LAVOLTING
LATINISE	LAUDATIVE	LAURELS	LAVOLTS
LATINISED	LAUDATOR	LAURIC	LAVRA
LATINISES	LAUDATORS	LAURYL	LAVRAS
LATINITY	LAUDATORY	LAURYLS	LAVROCK
LATINIZE	LAUDED	LAUWINE	LAVROCKS
LATINIZED	LAUDER	LAUWINES	LAVS
LATINIZES	LAUDERS	LAV	LAW
LATINO	LAUDING	LAVA	LAWBOOK
LATINOS	LAUDS	LAVABO	LAWBOOKS
LATISH	LAUF	LAVABOES	LAWED
LATITANCY	LAUFS	LAVABOS	LAWER
LATITANT	LAUGH	LAVAFORM	LAWEST
LATITAT	LAUGHABLE	LAVAGE	LAWFUL
LATITATS	LAUGHABLY	LAVAGES	LAWFULLY
LATITUDE	LAUGHED	LAVALAVA	LAWGIVER
LATITUDES	LAUGHER	LAVALAVAS	LAWGIVERS
LATKE	LAUGHERS	LAVALIER	LAWGIVING
LATKES	LAUGHFUL	LAVALIERE	LAWIN
LATOSOL	LAUGHIER	LAVALIERS	LAWINE
LATOSOLIC	LAUGHIEST	LAVALIKE	LAWINES
LATOSOLS	LAUGHING	LAVAS	LAWING
LATRANT	LAUGHINGS	LAVASH	LAWINGS
LATRATION	LAUGHLINE	LAVASHES	LAWINS
LATRIA	LAUGHS	LAVATERA	LAWK
LATRIAS	LAUGHSOME	LAVATERAS	LAWKS
LATRINE	LAUGHTER	LAVATION	LAWLAND
LATRINES	LAUGHTERS	LAVATIONS	LAWLANDS
LATROCINY	LAUGHY	LAVATORY	LAWLESS
LATRON	LAUNCE	LAVE	LAWLESSLY
LATRONS	LAUNCED	LAVED	LAWLIKE
LATS	LAUNCES	LAVEER	LAWMAKER
LATTE	LAUNCH	LAVEERED	LAWMAKERS
LATTEN	LAUNCHED	LAVEERING	LAWMAKING
LATTENS	LAUNCHER	LAVEERS	LAWMAN
LATTER	LAUNCHERS	LAVEMENT	LAWMEN
LATTERLY	LAUNCHES	LAVEMENTS	LAWMONGER
LATTES	LAUNCHING	LAVENDER	LAWN
LATTICE	LAUNCHPAD	LAVENDERS	LAWNIER
LATTICED	LAUNCING	LAVER	LAWNIEST
LATTICES	LAUND	LAVEROCK	LAWNMOWER
LATTICING	LAUNDER	LAVEROCKS	LAWNS
LATTICINI	LAUNDERED	LAVERS	LAWNY
LATTICINO	LAUNDERER	LAVES	LAWS
LATTIN	LAUNDERS	LAVING	LAWSUIT
LATTINS	LAUNDRESS	LAVISH	LAWSUITS
LATU	LAUNDRIES	LAVISHED	LAWYER
LATUS	LAUNDRY	LAVISHER	LAWYERED
LAUAN	LAUNDS	LAVISHERS	LAWYERING

LAWYERLY	LAYSHAFTS	LEACHOURS	LEAGUERED
LAWYERS	LAYSTALL	LEACHY	LEAGUERS
LAX	LAYSTALLS	LEAD	LEAGUES
LAXATION	LAYTIME	LEADED	LEAGUING
LAXATIONS	LAYTIMES	LEADEN	LEAK
LAXATIVE	LAYUP	LEADENED	LEAKAGE
LAXATIVES	LAYUPS	LEADENING	LEAKAGES
LAXATOR	LAYWOMAN	LEADENLY	LEAKED
LAXATORS	LAYWOMEN	LEADENS	LEAKER
LAXER	LAZAR	LEADER	LEAKERS
LAXES	LAZARET	LEADERENE	LEAKIER
LAXEST	LAZARETS	LEADERS	LEAKIEST
LAXISM	LAZARETTE	LEADIER	LEAKILY
LAXISMS	LAZARETTO	LEADIEST	LEAKINESS
LAXIST	LAZARS	LEADING	LEAKING
LAXISTS	LAZE	LEADINGLY	LEAKLESS
LAXITIES	LAZED	LEADINGS	LEAKPROOF
LAXITY	LAZES	LEADLESS	LEAKS
LAXLY	LAZIED	LEADMAN	LEAKY
LAXNESS	LAZIER	LEADMEN	LEAL
LAXNESSES	LAZIES	LEADOFF	LEALER
LAY	LAZIEST	LEADOFFS	LEALEST
LAYABOUT	LAZILY	LEADPLANT	LEALLY
LAYABOUTS	LAZINESS	LEADS	LEALTIES
LAYAWAY	LAZING	LEADSCREW	LEALTY
LAYAWAYS	LAZO	LEADSMAN	LEAM
LAYBACK	LAZOED	LEADSMEN	LEAMED
LAYBACKED	LAZOES	LEADWORK	LEAMING
LAYBACKS	LAZOING	LEADWORKS	LEAMS
LAYDEEZ	LAZOS	LEADWORT	LEAN
LAYED	LAZULI	LEADWORTS	LEANED
LAYER	LAZULIS	LEADY	LEANER
LAYERAGE	LAZULITE	LEAF	LEANERS
LAYERAGES	LAZULITES	LEAFAGE	LEANEST
LAYERED	LAZURITE	LEAFAGES	LEANING
LAYERING	LAZURITES	LEAFBUD	LEANINGS
LAYERINGS	LAZY	LEAFBUDS	LEANLY
LAYERS	LAZYBONES	LEAFED	LEANNESS
LAYETTE	LAZYING	LEAFERIES	LEANS
LAYETTES	LAZYISH	LEAFERY	LEANT
LAYIN	LAZZARONE	LEAFIER	LEANY
LAYING	LAZZARONI	LEAFIEST	LEAP
LAYINGS	LAZZI	LEAFINESS	LEAPED
LAYINS	LAZZO	LEAFING	LEAPER
LAYLOCK	LEA	LEAFLESS	LEAPEROUS
LAYLOCKS	LEACH	LEAFLET	LEAPERS
LAYMAN	LEACHABLE	LEAFLETED	LEAPFROG
LAYMEN	LEACHATE	LEAFLETER	LEAPFROGS
LAYOFF	LEACHATES	LEAFLETS	LEAPING
LAYOFFS	LEACHED	LEAFLIKE	LEAPOROUS
LAYOUT	LEACHER	LEAFS	LEAPROUS
LAYOUTS	LEACHERS	LEAFSTALK	LEAPS
LAYOVER	LEACHES	LEAFWORM	LEAPT
LAYOVERS	LEACHIER	LEAFWORMS	LEAR
LAYPEOPLE	LEACHIEST	LEAFY	LEARE
LAYPERSON	LEACHING	LEAGUE	LEARED
LAYS	LEACHINGS	LEAGUED	LEARES
LAYSHAFT	LEACHOUR	LEAGUER	LEARIER

LEARIEST	LEAVES	LED	LEEWAY
LEARINESS	LEAVIER	LEDDEN	LEEWAYS
LEARING	LEAVIEST	LEDDENS	LEFT
LEARN	LEAVING	LEDGE	LEFTE
LEARNABLE	LEAVINGS	LEDGED	LEFTER
LEARNED	LEAVY	LEDGER	LEFTEST
LEARNEDLY	LEAZE	LEDGERED	LEFTIE
LEARNER	LEAZES	LEDGERING	LEFTIES
LEARNERS	LEBBEK	LEDGERS	LEFTISH
LEARNING	LEBBEKS	LEDGES	LEFTISM
LEARNINGS	LEBEN	LEDGIER	LEFTISMS
LEARNS	LEBENS	LEDGIEST	LEFTIST
LEARNT	LEBKUCHEN	LEDGY	LEFTISTS
LEARS	LECANORA	LEDUM	LEFTMOST
LEARY	LECANORAS	LEDUMS	LEFTMOSTS
LEAS	LECCIES	LEE	LEFTOVER
LEASABLE	LECCY	LEEAR	LEFTOVERS
LEASE	LECH	LEEARS	LEFTS
LEASEBACK	LECHAIM	LEEBOARD	LEFTWARD
LEASED	LECHAIMS	LEEBOARDS	LEFTWARDS
LEASEHOLD	LECHAYIM	LEECH	LEFTWING
LEASER	LECHAYIMS	LEECHDOM	LEFTY
LEASERS	LECHED	LEECHDOMS	LEG
LEASES	LECHER	LEECHED	LEGACIES
LEASH	LECHERED	LEECHEE	LEGACY
LEASHED	LECHERIES	LEECHEES	LEGAL
LEASHES	LECHERING	LEECHES	LEGALESE
LEASHING	LECHEROUS	LEECHING	LEGALESES
LEASING	LECHERS	LEECHLIKE	LEGALISE
LEASINGS	LECHERY	LEED	LEGALISED
LEASOW	LECHES	LEEING	LEGALISER
LEASOWE	LECHING	LEEK	LEGALISES
LEASOWED	LECHWE	LEEKS	LEGALISM
LEASOWES	LECHWES	LEEP	LEGALISMS
LEASOWING	LECITHIN	LEEPED	LEGALIST
LEASOWS	LECITHINS	LEEPING	LEGALISTS
LEAST	LECTERN	LEEPS	LEGALITY
LEASTS	LECTERNS	LEER	LEGALIZE
LEASTWAYS	LECTIN	LEERED	LEGALIZED
LEASTWISE	LECTINS	LEERIER	LEGALIZER
LEASURE	LECTION	LEERIEST	LEGALIZES
LEASURES	LECTIONS	LEERILY	LEGALLY
LEAT	LECTOR	LEERINESS	LEGALS
LEATHER	LECTORATE	LEERING	LEGATARY
LEATHERED	LECTORS	LEERINGLY	LEGATE
LEATHERN	LECTOTYPE	LEERINGS	LEGATED
LEATHERS	LECTRESS	LEERS	LEGATEE
LEATHERY	LECTURE	LEERY	LEGATEES
LEATS	LECTURED	LEES	LEGATES
LEAVE	LECTURER	LEESE	LEGATINE
LEAVED	LECTURERS	LEESES	LEGATING
LEAVEN	LECTURES	LEESING	LEGATION
LEAVENED	LECTURING	LEET	LEGATIONS
LEAVENING	LECTURN	LEETLE	LEGATO
LEAVENOUS	LECTURNS	LEETS	LEGATOR
LEAVENS	LECYTHI	LEEWARD	LEGATORS
LEAVER	LECYTHIS	LEEWARDLY	LEGATOS
LEAVERS	LECYTHUS	LEEWARDS	LEGEND

LEGENDARY	LEGROOM	LEKKINGS	LENDS
LEGENDISE	LEGROOMS	LEKS	LENES
LEGENDIST	LEGS	LEKU	LENG
LEGENDIZE	LEGUAAN	LEKVAR	LENGED
LEGENDRY	LEGUAANS	LEKVARS	LENGER
LEGENDS	LEGUME	LEKYTHI	LENGEST
LEGER	LEGUMES	LEKYTHOI	LENGING
LEGERING	LEGUMIN	LEKYTHOS	LENGS
LEGERINGS	LEGUMINS	LEKYTHUS	LENGTH
LEGERITY	LEGWARMER	LEMAN	LENGTHEN
LEGERS	LEGWEAR	LEMANS	LENGTHENS
LEGES	LEGWEARS	LEME	LENGTHFUL
LEGGE	LEGWORK	LEMED	LENGTHIER
LEGGED	LEGWORKS	LEMEL	LENGTHILY
LEGGER	LEHAIM	LEMELS	LENGTHMAN
LEGGERS	LEHAIMS	LEMES	LENGTHMEN
LEGGES	LEHAYIM	LEMING	LENGTHS
LEGGIER	LEHAYIMS	LEMMA	LENGTHY
LEGGIERO	LEHR	LEMMAS	LENIENCE
LEGGIEST	LEHRJAHRE	LEMMATA	LENIENCES
LEGGIN	LEHRS	LEMMATISE	LENIENCY
LEGGINESS	LEHUA	LEMMATIZE	LENIENT
LEGGING	LEHUAS	LEMMING	LENIENTLY
LEGGINGED	LEI	LEMMINGS	LENIENTS
LEGGINGS	LEIDGER	LEMNISCAL	LENIFIED
LEGGINS	LEIDGERS	LEMNISCI	LENIFIES
LEGGISM	LEIGER	LEMNISCUS	LENIFY
LEGGISMS	LEIGERS	LEMON	LENIFYING
LEGGY	LEIOMYOMA	LEMONADE	LENIS
LEGHORN	LEIPOA	LEMONADES	LENITE
LEGHORNS	LEIPOAS	LEMONED	LENITED
LEGIBLE	LEIR	LEMONFISH	LENITES
LEGIBLY	LEIRED	LEMONIER	LENITIES
LEGION	LEIRING	LEMONIEST	LENITING
LEGIONARY	LEIRS	LEMONING	LENITION
LEGIONED	LEIS	LEMONISH	LENITIONS
LEGIONS	LEISH	LEMONLIKE	LENITIVE
LEGISLATE	LEISHER	LEMONS	LENITIVES
LEGIST	LEISHEST	LEMONWOOD	LENITY
LEGISTS	LEISLER	LEMONY	LENO
LEGIT	LEISLERS	LEMPIRA	LENOS
LEGITIM	LEISTER	LEMPIRAS	LENS
LEGITIMS	LEISTERED	LEMUR	LENSE
LEGITS	LEISTERS	LEMURES	LENSED
LEGLAN	LEISURE	LEMURIAN	LENSES
LEGLANS	LEISURED	LEMURIANS	LENSING
LEGLEN	LEISURELY	LEMURINE	LENSLESS
LEGLENS	LEISURES	LEMURINES	LENSMAN
LEGLESS	LEISURING	LEMURLIKE	LENSMEN
LEGLET	LEITMOTIF	LEMUROID	LENT
LEGLETS	LEITMOTIV	LEMUROIDS	LENTANDO
LEGLIKE	LEK	LEMURS	LENTEN
LEGLIN	LEKE	LEND	LENTI
LEGLINS	LEKGOTLA	LENDABLE	LENTIC
LEGMAN	LEKGOTLAS	LENDER	LENTICEL
LEGMEN	LEKKED	LENDERS	LENTICELS
LEGONG	LEKKER	LENDING	LENTICLE
LEGONGS	LEKKING	LENDINGS	LENTICLES

LENTICULE	LEPTOTENE	LETHEE	LEUKEMIC
LENTIFORM	LEQUEAR	LETHEES	LEUKEMICS
LENTIGO	LEQUEARS	LETHES	LEUKEMOID
LENTIL	LERE	LETHIED	LEUKOCYTE
LENTILS	LERED	LETS	LEUKOMA
LENTISK	LERES	LETTABLE	LEUKOMAS
LENTISKS	LERING	LETTED	LEUKON
LENTO	LERNAEAN	LETTER	LEUKONS
LENTOID	LERNEAN	LETTERBOX	LEUKOSES
LENTOIDS	LERP	LETTERED	LEUKOSIS
LENTOR	LERPS	LETTERER	LEUKOTIC
LENTORS	LES	LETTERERS	LEUKOTOMY
LENTOS	LESBIAN	LETTERING	LEV
LENTOUS	LESBIANS	LETTERMAN	LEVA
LENVOY	LESBIC	LETTERMEN	LEVANT
LENVOYS	LESBO	LETTERN	LEVANTED
LEONE	LESBOS	LETTERNS	LEVANTER
LEONES	LESES	LETTERS	LEVANTERS
LEONINE	LESION	LETTERSET	LEVANTINE
LEOPARD	LESIONED	LETTING	LEVANTING
LEOPARDS	LESIONING	LETTINGS	LEVANTS
LEOTARD	LESIONS	LETTRE	LEVATOR
LEOTARDED	LESPEDEZA	LETTRES	LEVATORES
LEOTARDS	LESS	LETTUCE	LEVATORS
LEP	LESSEE	LETTUCES	LEVE
LEPER	LESSEES	LETUP	LEVEE
LEPERS	LESSEN	LETUPS	LEVEED
LEPID	LESSENED	LEU	LEVEEING
LEPIDOTE	LESSENING	LEUCAEMIA	LEVEES
LEPIDOTES	LESSENS	LEUCAEMIC	LEVEL
LEPORID	LESSER	LEUCEMIA	LEVELED
LEPORIDAE	LESSES	LEUCEMIAS	LEVELER
LEPORIDS	LESSON	LEUCEMIC	LEVELERS
LEPORINE	LESSONED	LEUCH	LEVELING
LEPPED	LESSONING	LEUCHEN	LEVELLED
LEPPING	LESSONS	LEUCIN	LEVELLER
LEPRA	LESSOR	LEUCINE	LEVELLERS
LEPRAS	LESSORS	LEUCINES	LEVELLEST
LEPROSE	LEST	LEUCINS	LEVELLING
LEPROSERY	LESTED	LEUCITE	LEVELLY
LEPROSIES	LESTING	LEUCITES	LEVELNESS
LEPROSITY	LESTS	LEUCITIC	LEVELS
LEPROSY	LET	LEUCO	LEVER
LEPROTIC	LETCH	LEUCOCYTE	LEVERAGE
LEPROUS	LETCHED	LEUCOMA	LEVERAGED
LEPROUSLY	LETCHES	LEUCOMAS	LEVERAGES
LEPS	LETCHING	LEUCOSIN	LEVERED
LEPT	LETCHINGS	LEUCOSINS	LEVERET
LEPTA	LETDOWN	LEUCOTOME	LEVERETS
LEPTIN	LETDOWNS	LEUCOTOMY	LEVERING
LEPTINS	LETHAL	LEUD	LEVERS
LEPTOME	LETHALITY	LEUDES	LEVIABLE
LEPTOMES	LETHALLY	LEUDS	LEVIATHAN
LEPTON	LETHALS	LEUGH	LEVIED
LEPTONIC	LETHARGIC	LEUGHEN	LEVIER
LEPTONS	LETHARGY	LEUKAEMIA	LEVIERS
LEPTOPHOS	LETHE	LEUKEMIA	LEVIES
LEPTOSOME	LETHEAN	LEUKEMIAS	LEVIGABLE

LEVIGATE	LEXIGRAM	LIBECCHIO	LIBRATING
LEVIGATED	LEXIGRAMS	LIBECCIO	LIBRATION
LEVIGATES	LEXIS	LIBECCIOS	LIBRATORY
LEVIGATOR	LEXISES	LIBEL	LIBRETTI
LEVIN	LEY	LIBELANT	LIBRETTO
LEVINS	LEYLANDI	LIBELANTS	LIBRETTOS
LEVIRATE	LEYLANDII	LIBELED	LIBRI
LEVIRATES	LEYLANDIS	LIBELEE	LIBRIFORM
LEVIRATIC	LEYS	LIBELEES	LIBS
LEVIS	LEZ	LIBELER	LICE
LEVITATE	LEZES	LIBELERS	LICENCE
LEVITATED	LEZZ	LIBELING	LICENCED
LEVITATES	LEZZA	LIBELINGS	LICENCEE
LEVITATOR	LEZZAS	LIBELIST	LICENCEES
LEVITE	LEZZES	LIBELISTS	LICENCER
LEVITES	LEZZIE	LIBELLANT	LICENCERS
LEVITIC	LEZZIES	LIBELLED	LICENCES
LEVITICAL	LEZZY	LIBELLEE	LICENCING
LEVITIES	LI	LIBELLEES	LICENSE
LEVITY	LIABILITY	LIBELLER	LICENSED
LEVO	LIABLE	LIBELLERS	LICENSEE
LEVODOPA	LIAISE	LIBELLING	LICENSEES
LEVODOPAS	LIAISED	LIBELLOUS	LICENSER
LEVOGYRE	LIAISES	LIBELOUS	LICENSERS
LEVULIN	LIAISING	LIBELS	LICENSES
LEVULINS	LIAISON	LIBER	LICENSING
LEVULOSE	LIAISONS	LIBERAL	LICENSOR
LEVULOSES	LIANA	LIBERALLY	LICENSORS
LEVY	LIANAS	LIBERALS	LICENSURE
LEVYING	LIANE	LIBERATE	LICENTE
LEW	LIANES	LIBERATED	LICH
LEWD	LIANG	LIBERATES	LICHANOS
LEWDER	LIANGS	LIBERATOR	LICHEE
LEWDEST	LIANOID	LIBERO	LICHEES
LEWDLY	LIAR	LIBEROS	LICHEN
LEWDNESS	LIARD	LIBERS	LICHENED
LEWDSBIES	LIARDS	LIBERTIES	LICHENIN
LEWDSBY	LIARS	LIBERTINE	LICHENING
LEWDSTER	LIART	LIBERTY	LICHENINS
LEWDSTERS	LIAS	LIBIDINAL	LICHENISM
LEWIS	LIASES	LIBIDO	LICHENIST
LEWISES	LIATRIS	LIBIDOS	LICHENOID
LEWISIA	LIATRISES	LIBKEN	LICHENOSE
LEWISIAS	LIB	LIBKENS	LICHENOUS
LEWISITE	LIBANT	LIBLAB	LICHENS
LEWISITES	LIBATE	LIBLABS	LICHES
LEWISSON	LIBATED	LIBRA	LICHGATE
LEWISSONS	LIBATES	LIBRAE	LICHGATES
LEX	LIBATING	LIBRAIRE	LICHI
LEXEME	LIBATION	LIBRAIRES	LICHIS
LEXEMES	LIBATIONS	LIBRAIRIE	LICHT
LEXEMIC	LIBATORY	LIBRARIAN	LICHTED
LEXES	LIBBARD	LIBRARIES	LICHTER
LEXICA	LIBBARDS	LIBRARY	LICHTEST
LEXICAL	LIBBED	LIBRAS	LICHTING
LEXICALLY	LIBBER	LIBRATE	LICHTLIED
LEXICON	LIBBERS	LIBRATED	LICHTLIES
LEXICONS	LIBBING	LIBRATES	LICHTLY

LICHTS
LICHWAKE
LICHWAKES
LICHWAY
LICHWAYS
LICIT
LICITLY
LICITNESS
LICK
LICKED
LICKER
LICKERISH
LICKERS
LICKING
LICKINGS
LICKPENNY
LICKS
LICKSPIT
LICKSPITS
LICORICE
LICORICES
LICTOR
LICTORIAN
LICTORS
LID
LIDAR
LIDARS
LIDDED
LIDDING
LIDGER
LIDGERS
LIDLESS
LIDO
LIDOCAINE
LIDOS
LIDS
LIE
LIED
LIEDER
LIEF
LIEFER
LIEFEST
LIEFLY
LIEFS
LIEGE
LIEGEDOM
LIEGEDOMS
LIEGELESS
LIEGEMAN
LIEGEMEN
LIEGER
LIEGERS
LIEGES
LIEN
LIENABLE
LIENAL
LIENS
LIENTERIC

LIENTERY
LIER
LIERNE
LIERNES
LIERS
LIES
LIEU
LIEUS
LIEVE
LIEVER
LIEVEST
LIFE
LIFEBELT
LIFEBELTS
LIFEBLOOD
LIFEBOAT
LIFEBOATS
LIFEBUOY
LIFEBUOYS
LIFECARE
LIFECARES
LIFEFUL
LIFEGUARD
LIFEHOLD
LIFELESS
LIFELIKE
LIFELINE
LIFELINES
LIFELONG
LIFER
LIFERS
LIFES
LIFESAVER
LIFESOME
LIFESPAN
LIFESPANS
LIFESTYLE
LIFETIME
LIFETIMES
LIFEWAY
LIFEWAYS
LIFEWORK
LIFEWORKS
LIFEWORLD
LIFT
LIFTABLE
LIFTBACK
LIFTBACKS
LIFTBOY
LIFTBOYS
LIFTED
LIFTER
LIFTERS
LIFTGATE
LIFTGATES
LIFTING
LIFTMAN
LIFTMEN

LIFTOFF
LIFTOFFS
LIFTS
LIFULL
LIG
LIGAMENT
LIGAMENTS
LIGAN
LIGAND
LIGANDS
LIGANS
LIGASE
LIGASES
LIGATE
LIGATED
LIGATES
LIGATING
LIGATION
LIGATIONS
LIGATIVE
LIGATURE
LIGATURED
LIGATURES
LIGER
LIGERS
LIGGE
LIGGED
LIGGEN
LIGGER
LIGGERS
LIGGES
LIGGING
LIGGINGS
LIGHT
LIGHTBULB
LIGHTED
LIGHTEN
LIGHTENED
LIGHTENER
LIGHTENS
LIGHTER
LIGHTERED
LIGHTERS
LIGHTEST
LIGHTFACE
LIGHTFAST
LIGHTFUL
LIGHTING
LIGHTINGS
LIGHTISH
LIGHTLESS
LIGHTLIED
LIGHTLIES
LIGHTLY
LIGHTNESS
LIGHTNING
LIGHTS
LIGHTSHIP

LIGHTSOME
LIGHTWAVE
LIGHTWOOD
LIGNAGE
LIGNAGES
LIGNALOES
LIGNAN
LIGNANS
LIGNE
LIGNEOUS
LIGNES
LIGNICOLE
LIGNIFIED
LIGNIFIES
LIGNIFORM
LIGNIFY
LIGNIN
LIGNINS
LIGNITE
LIGNITES
LIGNITIC
LIGNOSE
LIGNOSES
LIGNUM
LIGNUMS
LIGROIN
LIGROINE
LIGROINES
LIGROINS
LIGS
LIGULA
LIGULAE
LIGULAR
LIGULAS
LIGULATE
LIGULATED
LIGULE
LIGULES
LIGULOID
LIGURE
LIGURES
LIKABLE
LIKE
LIKEABLE
LIKED
LIKELIER
LIKELIEST
LIKELY
LIKEN
LIKENED
LIKENESS
LIKENING
LIKENS
LIKER
LIKERS
LIKES
LIKEST
LIKEWAKE

LIKEWAKES
LIKEWALK
LIKEWALKS
LIKEWISE
LIKTN
LIKING
LIKINGS
LIKINS
LIKUTA
LILAC
LILACS
LILANGENI
LILIED
LILIES
LILL
LILLED
LILLING
LILLIPUT
LILLIPUTS
LILLS
LILO
LILOS
LILT
LILTED
LILTING
LILTINGLY
LILTS
LILY
LILYLIKE
LIMA
LIMACEL
LIMACELS
LIMACEOUS
LIMACES
LIMACINE
LIMACON
LIMACONS
LIMAIL
LIMAILS
LIMAN
LIMANS
LIMAS
LIMATION
LIMATIONS
LIMAX
LIMB
LIMBA
LIMBAS
LIMBATE
LIMBEC
LIMBECK
LIMBECKS
LIMBECS
LIMBED
LIMBER
LIMBERED
LIMBERER
LIMBEREST

LIMBERING
LIMBERLY
LIMBERS
LIMBI
LIMBIC
LIMBIER
LIMBIEST
LIMBING
LIMBLESS
LIMBMEAL
LIMBO
LIMBOS
LIMBOUS
LIMBS
LIMBUS
LIMBUSES
LIMBY
LIME
LIMEADE
LIMEADES
LIMED
LIMEKILN
LIMEKILNS
LIMELESS
LIMELIGHT
LIMELIT
LIMEN
LIMENS
LIMEPIT
LIMEPITS
LIMERICK
LIMERICKS
LIMES
LIMESCALE
LIMESTONE
LIMEWASH
LIMEWATER
LIMEY
LIMEYS
LIMIER
LIMIEST
LIMINA
LIMINAL
LIMINESS
LIMING
LIMINGS
LIMIT
LIMITABLE
LIMITARY
LIMITED
LIMITEDLY
LIMITEDS
LIMITER
LIMITERS
LIMITES
LIMITING
LIMITINGS
LIMITLESS

LIMITS
LIMMA
LIMMAS
LIMMER
LIMMERS
LIMN
LIMNAEID
LIMNAEIDS
LIMNED
LIMNER
LIMNERS
LIMNETIC
LIMNIC
LIMNING
LIMNOLOGY
LIMNS
LIMO
LIMONENE
LIMONENES
LIMONITE
LIMONITES
LIMONITIC
LIMOS
LIMOSES
LIMOSIS
LIMOUS
LIMOUSINE
LIMP
LIMPA
LIMPAS
LIMPED
LIMPER
LIMPERS
LIMPEST
LIMPET
LIMPETS
LIMPID
LIMPIDITY
LIMPIDLY
LIMPING
LIMPINGLY
LIMPINGS
LIMPKIN
LIMPKINS
LIMPLY
LIMPNESS
LIMPS
LIMPSEY
LIMPSIER
LIMPSIEST
LIMPSY
LIMULI
LIMULOID
LIMULOIDS
LIMULUS
LIMULUSES
LIMY
LIN

LINABLE
LINAC
LINACS
LINAGE
LINAGES
LINALOL
LINALOLS
LINALOOL
LINALOOLS
LINCH
LINCHES
LINCHET
LINCHETS
LINCHPIN
LINCHPINS
LINCRUSTA
LINCTURE
LINCTURES
LINCTUS
LINCTUSES
LIND
LINDANE
LINDANES
LINDEN
LINDENS
LINDIES
LINDS
LINDWORM
LINDWORMS
LINDY
LINE
LINEABLE
LINEAGE
LINEAGES
LINEAL
LINEALITY
LINEALLY
LINEAMENT
LINEAR
LINEARISE
LINEARITY
LINEARIZE
LINEARLY
LINEATE
LINEATED
LINEATION
LINEBRED
LINECUT
LINECUTS
LINED
LINELESS
LINELIKE
LINEMAN
LINEMEN
LINEN
LINENS
LINENY
LINEOLATE

LINER	LINGULATE	LINOLEUMS	LIONISES
LINERLESS	LINGY	LINOS	LIONISING
LINERS	LINHAY	LINOTYPE	LIONISM
LINES	LINHAYS	LINOTYPED	LIONISMS
LINESMAN	LINIER	LINOTYPER	LIONIZE
LINESMEN	LINIEST	LINOTYPES	LIONIZED
LINEUP	LINIMENT	LINS	LIONIZER
LINEUPS	LINIMENTS	LINSANG	LIONIZERS
LINEY	LININ	LINSANGS	LIONIZES
LING	LINING	LINSEED	LIONIZING
LINGA	LININGS	LINSEEDS	LIONLIKE
LINGAM	LININS	LINSEY	LIONLY
LINGAMS	LINISH	LINSEYS	LIONS
LINGAS	LINISHED	LINSTOCK	LIP
LINGBERRY	LINISHER	LINSTOCKS	LIPA
LINGCOD	LINISHERS	LINT	LIPAEMIA
LINGCODS	LINISHES	LINTED	LIPAEMIAS
LINGEL	LINISHING	LINTEL	LIPARITE
LINGELS	LINK	LINTELLED	LIPARITES
LINGER	LINKABLE	LINTELS	LIPASE
LINGERED	LINKAGE	LINTER	LIPASES
LINGERER	LINKAGES	LINTERS	LIPE
LINGERERS	LINKBOY	LINTIE	LIPECTOMY
LINGERIE	LINKBOYS	LINTIER	LIPEMIA
LINGERIES	LINKED	LINTIES	LIPEMIAS
LINGERING	LINKER	LINTIEST	LIPID
LINGERS	LINKERS	LINTING	LIPIDE
LINGIER	LINKING	LINTLESS	LIPIDES
LINGIEST	LINKMAN	LINTOL	LIPIDIC
LINGLE	LINKMEN	LINTOLS	LIPIDS
LINGLES	LINKS	LINTS	LIPIN
LINGO	LINKSLAND	LINTSEED	LIPINS
LINGOES	LINKSMAN	LINTSEEDS	LIPLESS
LINGOT	LINKSMEN	LINTSTOCK	LIPLIKE
LINGOTS	LINKSTER	LINTWHITE	LIPO
LINGS	LINKSTERS	LINTY	LIPOCYTE
LINGSTER	LINKUP	LINUM	LIPOCYTES
LINGSTERS	LINKUPS	LINUMS	LIPOGRAM
LINGUA	LINKWORK	LINURON	LIPOGRAMS
LINGUAE	LINKWORKS	LINURONS	LIPOIC
LINGUAL	LINKY	LINUX	LIPOID
LINGUALLY	LINN	LINUXES	LIPOIDAL
LINGUALS	LINNED	LINY	LIPOIDS
LINGUAS	LINNET	LION	LIPOLITIC
LINGUICA	LINNETS	LIONCEL	LIPOLYSES
LINGUICAS	LINNEY	LIONCELLE	LIPOLYSIS
LINGUINE	LINNEYS	LIONCELS	LIPOLYTIC
LINGUINES	LINNIES	LIONEL	LIPOMA
LINGUINI	LINNING	LIONELS	LIPOMAS
LINGUINIS	LINNS	LIONESS	LIPOMATA
LINGUISA	LINNY	LIONESSES	LIPOPLAST
LINGUISAS	LINO	LIONET	LIPOS
LINGUIST	LINOCUT	LIONETS	LIPOSOMAL
LINGUISTS	LINOCUTS	LIONFISH	LIPOSOME
LINGULA	LINOLEATE	LIONISE	LIPOSOMES
LINGULAE	LINOLEIC	LIONISED	LIPOSUCK
LINGULAR	LINOLENIC	LIONISER	LIPOSUCKS
LINGULAS	LINOLEUM	LIONISERS	LIPOTROPY

LIPPED	LIQUORS	LISTETH	LITHIFY
LIPPEN	LIRA	LISTFUL	LITHING
LIPPENED	LIRAS	LISTING	LITHISTID
LIPPENING	LIRE	LISTINGS	LITHITE
LIPPENS	LIRI	LISTLESS	LITHITES
LIPPER	LIRIOPE	LISTS	LITHIUM
LIPPERED	LIRIOPES	LISTSERV	LITHIUMS
LIPPERING	LIRIPIPE	LISTSERVS	LITHO
LIPPERS	LIRIPIPES	LIT	LITHOCYST
LIPPIE	LIRIPOOP	LITAI	LITHOED
LIPPIER	LIRIPOOPS	LITANIES	LITHOID
LIPPIES	LIRK	LITANY	LITHOIDAL
LIPPIEST	LIRKED	LITAS	LITHOING
LIPPINESS	LIRKING	LITCHI	LITHOLOGY
LIPPING	LIRKS	LITCHIS	LITHOPONE
LIPPINGS	LIROT	LITE	LITHOPS
LIPPITUDE	LIROTH	LITED	LITHOS
LIPPY	LIS	LITENESS	LITHOSOL
LIPREAD	LISENTE	LITER	LITHOSOLS
LIPREADER	LISK	LITERACY	LITHOTOME
LIPREADS	LISKS	LITERAL	LITHOTOMY
LIPS	LISLE	LITERALLY	LITHS
LIPSTICK	LISLES	LITERALS	LITIGABLE
LIPSTICKS	LISP	LITERARY	LITIGANT
LIPURIA	LISPED	LITERATE	LITIGANTS
LIPURIAS	LISPER	LITERATES	LITIGATE
LIQUABLE	LISPERS	LITERATI	LITIGATED
LIQUATE	LISPING	LITERATIM	LITIGATES
LIQUATED	LISPINGLY	LITERATO	LITIGATOR
LIQUATES	LISPINGS	LITERATOR	LITIGIOUS
LIQUATING	LISPOUND	LITERATUS	LITING
LIQUATION	LISPOUNDS	LITEROSE	LITMUS
LIQUEFIED	LISPS	LITERS	LITMUSES
LIQUEFIER	LISPUND	LITES	LITORAL
LIQUEFIES	LISPUNDS	LITH	LITOTES
LIQUEFY	LISSES	LITHARGE	LITOTIC
LIQUESCE	LISSOM	LITHARGES	LITRE
LIQUESCED	LISSOME	LITHATE	LITRES
LIQUESCES	LISSOMELY	LITHATES	LITS
LIQUEUR	LISSOMLY	LITHE	LITTEN
LIQUEURED	LIST	LITHED	LITTER
LIQUEURS	LISTABLE	LITHELY	LITTERBAG
LIQUID	LISTED	LITHEMIA	LITTERBUG
LIQUIDATE	LISTEE	LITHEMIAS	LITTERED
LIQUIDISE	LISTEES	LITHEMIC	LITTERER
LIQUIDITY	LISTEL	LITHENESS	LITTERERS
LIQUIDIZE	LISTELS	LITHER	LITTERING
LIQUIDLY	LISTEN	LITHERLY	LITTERS
LIQUIDS	LISTENED	LITHES	LITTERY
LIQUIDUS	LISTENER	LITHESOME	LITTLE
LIQUIFIED	LISTENERS	LITHEST	LITTLER
LIQUIFIES	LISTENING	LITHIA	LITTLES
LIQUIFY	LISTENS	LITHIAS	LITTLEST
LIQUOR	LISTER	LITHIASES	LITTLIE
LIQUORED	LISTERIA	LITHIASIS	LITTLIES
LIQUORICE	LISTERIAL	LITHIC	LITTLIN
LIQUORING	LISTERIAS	LITHIFIED	LITTLING
LIQUORISH	LISTERS	LITHIFIES	LITTLINGS

LITTLINS	LIVEYERES	LOAFERS	LOBBY
LITTLISH	LIVEYERS	LOAFING	LOBBYER
LITTORAL	LIVID	LOAFINGS	LOBBYERS
LITTORALS	LIVIDER	LOAFS	LOBBYGOW
LITU	LIVIDEST	LOAM	LOBBYGOWS
LITURGIC	LIVIDITY	LOAMED	LOBBYING
LITURGICS	LIVIDLY	LOAMIER	LOBBYINGS
LITURGIES	LIVIDNESS	LOAMIEST	LOBBYISM
LITURGISM	LIVIER	LOAMINESS	LOBBYISMS
LITURGIST	LIVIERS	LOAMING	LOBBYIST
LITURGY	LIVING	LOAMLESS	LOBBYISTS
LITUUS	LIVINGLY	LOAMS	LOBE
LITUUSES	LIVINGS	LOAMY	LOBECTOMY
LIVABLE	LIVOR	LOAN	LOBED
LIVE	LIVORS	LOANABLE	LOBEFIN
LIVEABLE	LIVRAISON	LOANBACK	LOBEFINS
LIVED	LIVRE	LOANBACKS	LOBELET
LIVEDO	LIVRES	LOANED	LOBELETS
LIVEDOS	LIVYER	LOANER	LOBELIA
LIVELIER	LIVYERS	LOANERS	LOBELIAS
LIVELIEST	LIXIVIA	LOANING	LOBELINE
LIVELILY	LIXIVIAL	LOANINGS	LOBELINES
LIVELOD	LIXIVIATE	LOANS	LOBES
LIVELODS	LIXIVIOUS	LOANSHIFT	LOBI
LIVELONG	LIXIVIUM	LOANWORD	LOBING
LIVELONGS	LIXIVIUMS	LOANWORDS	LOBINGS
LIVELOOD	LIZARD	LOAST	LOBIPED
LIVELOODS	LIZARDS	LOATH	LOBLOLLY
LIVELY	LIZZIE	LOATHE	LOBO
LIVEN	LIZZIES	LOATHED	LOBOLA
LIVENED	LLAMA	LOATHER	LOBOLAS
LIVENER	LLAMAS	LOATHERS	LOBOLO
LIVENERS	LLANERO	LOATHES	LOBOLOS
LIVENESS	LLANEROS	LOATHEST	LOBOS
LIVENING	LLANO	LOATHFUL	LOBOSE
LIVENS	LLANOS	LOATHING	LOBOTOMY
LIVER	LO	LOATHINGS	LOBS
LIVERED	LOACH	LOATHLY	LOBSCOUSE
LIVERIED	LOACHES	LOATHNESS	LOBSTER
LIVERIES	LOAD	LOATHSOME	LOBSTERED
LIVERING	LOADED	LOATHY	LOBSTERER
LIVERISH	LOADEN	LOAVE	LOBSTERS
LIVERLEAF	LOADENED	LOAVED	LOBSTICK
LIVERLESS	LOADENING	LOAVES	LOBSTICKS
LIVERS	LOADENS	LOAVING	LOBULAR
LIVERWORT	LOADER	LOB	LOBULARLY
LIVERY	LOADERS	LOBAR	LOBULATE
LIVERYMAN	LOADING	LOBATE	LOBULATED
LIVERYMEN	LOADINGS	LOBATED	LOBULE
LIVES	LOADS	LOBATELY	LOBULES
LIVEST	LOADSPACE	LOBATION	LOBULI
LIVESTOCK	LOADSTAR	LOBATIONS	LOBULOSE
LIVETRAP	LOADSTARS	LOBBED	LOBULUS
LIVETRAPS	LOADSTONE	LOBBER	LOBUS
LIVEWARE	LOAF	LOBBERS	LOBWORM
LIVEWARES	LOAFED	LOBBIED	LOBWORMS
LIVEYER	LOAFER	LOBBIES	LOCA
LIVEYERE	LOAFERISH	LOBBING	LOCAL

LOCALE	LOCKFULS	LOCUSTA	LOGAN
LOCALES	LOCKHOUSE	LOCUSTAE	LOGANIA
LOCALISE	LOCKING	LOCUSTAL	LOGANIAS
LOCALISED	LOCKINGS	LOCUSTED	LOGANS
LOCALISER	LOCKJAW	LOCUSTING	LOGAOEDIC
LOCALISES	LOCKJAWS	LOCUSTS	LOGARITHM
LOCALISM	LOCKMAKER	LOCUTION	LOGBOARD
LOCALISMS	LOCKMAN	LOCUTIONS	LOGBOARDS
LOCALIST	LOCKMEN	LOCUTORY	LOGBOOK
LOCALISTS	LOCKNUT	LOD	LOGBOOKS
LOCALITE	LOCKNUTS	LODE	LOGE
LOCALITES	LOCKOUT	LODEN	LOGES
LOCALITY	LOCKOUTS	LODENS	LOGGAT
LOCALIZE	LOCKPICK	LODES	LOGGATS
LOCALIZED	LOCKPICKS	LODESMAN	LOGGED
LOCALIZER	LOCKRAM	LODESMEN	LOGGER
LOCALIZES	LOCKRAMS	LODESTAR	LOGGERS
LOCALLY	LOCKS	LODESTARS	LOGGETS
LOCALNESS	LOCKSET	LODESTONE	LOGGIA
LOCALS	LOCKSETS	LODGE	LOGGIAS
LOCATABLE	LOCKSMAN	LODGEABLE	LOGGIE
LOCATE	LOCKSMEN	LODGED	LOGGIER
LOCATED	LOCKSMITH	LODGEMENT	LOGGIEST
LOCATER	LOCKSTEP	LODGEPOLE	LOGGING
LOCATERS	LOCKSTEPS	LODGER	LOGGINGS
LOCATES	LOCKUP	LODGERS	LOGGISH
LOCATING	LOCKUPS	LODGES	LOGGY
LOCATION	LOCO	LODGING	LOGIA
LOCATIONS	LOCOED	LODGINGS	LOGIC
LOCATIVE	LOCOES	LODGMENT	LOGICAL
LOCATIVES	LOCOFOCO	LODGMENTS	LOGICALLY
LOCATOR	LOCOFOCOS	LODICULA	LOGICIAN
LOCATORS	LOCOING	LODICULAE	LOGICIANS
LOCELLATE	LOCOISM	LODICULE	LOGICISE
LOCH	LOCOISMS	LODICULES	LOGICISED
LOCHAN	LOCOMAN	LODS	LOGICISES
LOCHANS	LOCOMEN	LOERIE	LOGICISM
LOCHIA	LOCOMOTE	LOERIES	LOGICISMS
LOCHIAL	LOCOMOTED	LOESS	LOGICIST
LOCHS	LOCOMOTES	LOESSAL	LOGICISTS
LOCI	LOCOMOTOR	LOESSES	LOGICIZE
LOCK	LOCOPLANT	LOESSIAL	LOGICIZED
LOCKABLE	LOCOS	LOFT	LOGICIZES
LOCKAGE	LOCOWEED	LOFTED	LOGICLESS
LOCKAGES	LOCOWEEDS	LOFTER	LOGICS
LOCKAWAY	LOCULAR	LOFTERS	LOGIE
LOCKAWAYS	LOCULATE	LOFTIER	LOGIER
LOCKBOX	LOCULATED	LOFTIEST	LOGIES
LOCKBOXES	LOCULE	LOFTILY	LOGIEST
LOCKDOWN	LOCULED	LOFTINESS	LOGILY
LOCKDOWNS	LOCULES	LOFTING	LOGIN
LOCKED	LOCULI	LOFTLESS	LOGINESS
LOCKER	LOCULUS	LOFTLIKE	LOGINS
LOCKERS	LOCUM	LOFTS	LOGION
LOCKET	LOCUMS	LOFTSMAN	LOGIONS
LOCKETS	LOCUPLETE	LOFTSMEN	LOGISTIC
LOCKFAST	LOCUS	LOFTY	LOGISTICS
LOCKFUL	LOCUST	LOG	LOGJAM

LOGJAMMED
LOGJAMS
LOGJUICE
LOGJUICES
LOGLINE
LOGLINES
LOGLOG
LOGLOGS
LOGNORMAL
LOGO
LOGOFF
LOGOFFS
LOGOGRAM
LOGOGRAMS
LOGOGRAPH
LOGOGRIPH
LOGOI
LOGOMACH
LOGOMACHS
LOGOMACHY
LOGON
LOGONS
LOGOPEDIC
LOGOPHILE
LOGORRHEA
LOGOS
LOGOTHETE
LOGOTYPE
LOGOTYPES
LOGOTYPY
LOGOUT
LOGOUTS
LOGROLL
LOGROLLED
LOGROLLER
LOGROLLS
LOGS
LOGWAY
LOGWAYS
LOGWOOD
LOGWOODS
LOGY
LOHAN
LOHANS
LOID
LOIDED
LOIDING
LOIDS
LOIN
LOINCLOTH
LOINS
LOIPE
LOIPEN
LOIR
LOIRS
LOITER
LOITERED
LOITERER

LOITERERS
LOITERING
LOITERS
LOKE
LOKES
LOKSHEN
LOLIGO
LOLIGOS
LOLIUM
LOLIUMS
LOLL
LOLLED
LOLLER
LOLLERS
LOLLIES
LOLLING
LOLLINGLY
LOLLIPOP
LOLLIPOPS
LOLLOP
LOLLOPED
LOLLOPING
LOLLOPS
LOLLOPY
LOLLS
LOLLY
LOLLYGAG
LOLLYGAGS
LOLLYPOP
LOLLYPOPS
LOLOG
LOLOGS
LOMA
LOMAS
LOMATA
LOME
LOMED
LOMEIN
LOMEINS
LOMENT
LOMENTA
LOMENTS
LOMENTUM
LOMENTUMS
LOMES
LOMING
LOMPISH
LONE
LONELIER
LONELIEST
LONELILY
LONELY
LONENESS
LONER
LONERS
LONESOME
LONESOMES
LONG

LONGA
LONGAEVAL
LONGAN
LONGANS
LONGAS
LONGBOARD
LONGBOAT
LONGBOATS
LONGBOW
LONGBOWS
LONGCASE
LONGCLOTH
LONGE
LONGED
LONGEING
LONGER
LONGERON
LONGERONS
LONGERS
LONGES
LONGEST
LONGEVAL
LONGEVITY
LONGEVOUS
LONGHAIR
LONGHAIRS
LONGHAND
LONGHANDS
LONGHEAD
LONGHEADS
LONGHORN
LONGHORNS
LONGHOUSE
LONGICORN
LONGIES
LONGING
LONGINGLY
LONGINGS
LONGISH
LONGITUDE
LONGJUMP
LONGJUMPS
LONGLEAF
LONGLINE
LONGLINES
LONGLY
LONGNECK
LONGNECKS
LONGNESS
LONGS
LONGSHIP
LONGSHIPS
LONGSHORE
LONGSOME
LONGSPUR
LONGSPURS
LONGTIME
LONGUEUR

LONGUEURS
LONGWALL
LONGWALLS
LONGWAYS
LONGWISE
LONICERA
LONICERAS
LOO
LOOBIER
LOOBIES
LOOBIEST
LOOBILY
LOOBY
LOOED
LOOEY
LOOEYS
LOOF
LOOFA
LOOFAH
LOOFAHS
LOOFAS
LOOFFUL
LOOFFULS
LOOFS
LOOIE
LOOIES
LOOING
LOOK
LOOKALIKE
LOOKDOWN
LOOKDOWNS
LOOKED
LOOKER
LOOKERS
LOOKING
LOOKISM
LOOKISMS
LOOKIST
LOOKISTS
LOOKOUT
LOOKOUTS
LOOKOVER
LOOKOVERS
LOOKS
LOOKSISM
LOOKSISMS
LOOKUP
LOOKUPS
LOOM
LOOMED
LOOMING
LOOMS
LOON
LOONEY
LOONEYS
LOONIE
LOONIER
LOONIES

LOONIEST	LOPES	LORELS	LOSTNESS
LOONILY	LOPGRASS	LORES	LOT
LOONINESS	LOPHODONT	LORETTE	LOTA
LOONING	LOPING	LORETTES	LOTAH
LOONINGS	LOPOLITH	LORGNETTE	LOTAHS
LOONS	LOPOLITHS	LORGNON	LOTAS
LOONY	LOPPED	LORGNONS	LOTE
LOOP	LOPPER	LORIC	LOTES
LOOPED	LOPPERED	LORICA	LOTH
LOOPER	LOPPERING	LORICAE	LOTHARIO
LOOPERS	LOPPERS	LORICATE	LOTHARIOS
LOOPHOLE	LOPPIER	LORICATED	LOTHEFULL
LOOPHOLED	LOPPIES	LORICATES	LOTHER
LOOPHOLES	LOPPIEST	LORICS	LOTHEST
LOOPIER	LOPPING	LORIES	LOTHFULL
LOOPIEST	LOPPINGS	LORIKEET	LOTHNESS
LOOPILY	LOPPY	LORIKEETS	LOTHSOME
LOOPINESS	LOPS	LORIMER	LOTI
LOOPING	LOPSIDED	LORIMERS	LOTIC
LOOPINGS	LOPSTICK	LORINER	LOTION
LOOPS	LOPSTICKS	LORINERS	LOTIONS
LOOPY	LOQUACITY	LORING	LOTO
LOOR	LOQUAT	LORINGS	LOTOS
LOORD	LOQUATS	LORIOT	LOTOSES
LOORDS	LOQUITUR	LORIOTS	LOTS
LOOS	LOR	LORIS	LOTTE
LOOSE	LORAL	LORISES	LOTTED
LOOSEBOX	LORAN	LORN	LOTTER
LOOSED	LORANS	LORNNESS	LOTTERIES
LOOSELY	LORATE	LORRELL	LOTTERS
LOOSEN	LORAZEPAM	LORRELLS	LOTTERY
LOOSENED	LORCHA	LORRIES	LOTTES
LOOSENER	LORCHAS	LORRY	LOTTING
LOOSENERS	LORD	LORY	LOTTO
LOOSENESS	LORDED	LOS	LOTTOS
LOOSENING	LORDING	LOSABLE	LOTUS
LOOSENS	LORDINGS	LOSE	LOTUSES
LOOSER	LORDKIN	LOSED	LOTUSLAND
LOOSES	LORDKINS	LOSEL	LOU
LOOSEST	LORDLESS	LOSELS	LOUCHE
LOOSIE	LORDLIER	LOSEN	LOUCHELY
LOOSIES	LORDLIEST	LOSER	LOUD
LOOSING	LORDLIKE	LOSERS	LOUDEN
LOOSINGS	LORDLING	LOSES	LOUDENED
LOOT	LORDLINGS	LOSH	LOUDENING
LOOTED	LORDLY	LOSING	LOUDENS
LOOTEN	LORDOMA	LOSINGLY	LOUDER
LOOTER	LORDOMAS	LOSINGS	LOUDEST
LOOTERS	LORDOSES	LOSLYF	LOUDISH
LOOTING	LORDOSIS	LOSLYFS	LOUDLIER
LOOTINGS	LORDOTIC	LOSS	LOUDLIEST
LOOTS	LORDS	LOSSES	LOUDLY
LOOVES	LORDSHIP	LOSSIER	LOUDMOUTH
LOP	LORDSHIPS	LOSSIEST	LOUDNESS
LOPE	LORDY	LOSSLESS	LOUED
LOPED	LORE	LOSSMAKER	LOUGH
LOPER	LOREAL	LOSSY	LOUGHS
LOPERS	LOREL	LOST	LOUIE

LOUIES
LOUING
LOUIS
LOUMA
LOUMAS
LOUN
LOUND
LOUNDED
LOUNDER
LOUNDERED
LOUNDERS
LOUNDING
LOUNDS
LOUNED
LOUNGE
LOUNGED
LOUNGER
LOUNGERS
LOUNGES
LOUNGING
LOUNGINGS
LOUNGY
LOUNING
LOUNS
LOUP
LOUPE
LOUPED
LOUPEN
LOUPES
LOUPING
LOUPIT
LOUPS
LOUR
LOURE
LOURED
LOURES
LOURIE
LOURIER
LOURIES
LOURIEST
LOURING
LOURINGLY
LOURINGS
LOURS
LOURY
LOUS
LOUSE
LOUSED
LOUSER
LOUSERS
LOUSES
LOUSEWORT
LOUSIER
LOUSIEST
LOUSILY
LOUSINESS
LOUSING
LOUSY

LOUT
LOUTED
LOUTING
LOUTISH
LOUTISHLY
LOUTS
LOUVAR
LOUVARS
LOUVER
LOUVERED
LOUVERS
LOUVRE
LOUVRED
LOUVRES
LOVABLE
LOVABLY
LOVAGE
LOVAGES
LOVAT
LOVATS
LOVE
LOVEABLE
LOVEABLY
LOVEBIRD
LOVEBIRDS
LOVEBITE
LOVEBITES
LOVEBUG
LOVEBUGS
LOVED
LOVEFEST
LOVEFESTS
LOVELESS
LOVELIER
LOVELIES
LOVELIEST
LOVELIGHT
LOVELILY
LOVELOCK
LOVELOCKS
LOVELORN
LOVELY
LOVEMAKER
LOVER
LOVERED
LOVERLESS
LOVERLY
LOVERS
LOVES
LOVESEAT
LOVESEATS
LOVESICK
LOVESOME
LOVEVINE
LOVEVINES
LOVEY
LOVEYS
LOVIES

LOVING
LOVINGLY
LOVINGS
LOW
LOWAN
LOWANS
LOWBALL
LOWBALLED
LOWBALLS
LOWBORN
LOWBOY
LOWBOYS
LOWBRED
LOWBROW
LOWBROWED
LOWBROWS
LOWDOWN
LOWDOWNS
LOWE
LOWED
LOWER
LOWERABLE
LOWERCASE
LOWERED
LOWERIER
LOWERIEST
LOWERING
LOWERINGS
LOWERMOST
LOWERS
LOWERY
LOWES
LOWEST
LOWING
LOWINGS
LOWISH
LOWLAND
LOWLANDER
LOWLANDS
LOWLIER
LOWLIEST
LOWLIFE
LOWLIFER
LOWLIFERS
LOWLIFES
LOWLIGHT
LOWLIGHTS
LOWLIHEAD
LOWLILY
LOWLINESS
LOWLIVES
LOWLY
LOWN
LOWND
LOWNDED
LOWNDING
LOWNDS
LOWNE

LOWNED
LOWNES
LOWNESS
LOWNESSES
LOWNING
LOWNS
LOWP
LOWPED
LOWPING
LOWPS
LOWRIDER
LOWRIDERS
LOWRIE
LOWRIES
LOWRY
LOWS
LOWSE
LOWSED
LOWSENING
LOWSER
LOWSES
LOWSEST
LOWSING
LOWSIT
LOWT
LOWTED
LOWTING
LOWTS
LOWVELD
LOWVELDS
LOX
LOXED
LOXES
LOXING
LOXODROME
LOXODROMY
LOXYGEN
LOXYGENS
LOY
LOYAL
LOYALER
LOYALEST
LOYALISM
LOYALISMS
LOYALIST
LOYALISTS
LOYALLER
LOYALLEST
LOYALLY
LOYALNESS
LOYALTIES
LOYALTY
LOYS
LOZELL
LOZELLS
LOZEN
LOZENGE
LOZENGED

LOZENGES	LUCKIER	LUGGIE	LUMINANTS
LOZENGY	LUCKIES	LUGGIES	LUMINARIA
LOZENS	LUCKIEST	LUGGING	LUMINARY
LUACH	LUCKILY	LUGHOLE	LUMINE
LUAU	LUCKINESS	LUGHOLES	LUMINED
LUAUS	LUCKING	LUGING	LUMINES
LUBBARD	LUCKLESS	LUGINGS	LUMINESCE
LUBBARDS	LUCKPENNY	LUGS	LUMINING
LUBBER	LUCKS	LUGSAIL	LUMINISM
LUBBERLY	LUCKY	LUGSAILS	LUMINISMS
LUBBERS	LUCRATIVE	LUGWORM	LUMINIST
LUBE	LUCRE	LUGWORMS	LUMINISTS
LUBED	LUCRES	LUIT	LUMINOUS
LUBES	LUCTATION	LUITEN	LUMME
LUBFISH	LUCUBRATE	LUKE	LUMMIER
LUBFISHES	LUCULENT	LUKEWARM	LUMMIEST
LUBING	LUCUMA	LULIBUB	LUMMOX
LUBRA	LUCUMAS	LULIBUBS	LUMMOXES
LUBRAS	LUCUMO	LULL	LUMMY
LUBRIC	LUCUMONES	LULLABIED	LUMP
LUBRICAL	LUCUMOS	LULLABIES	LUMPED
LUBRICANT	LUD	LULLABY	LUMPEN
LUBRICATE	LUDE	LULLED	LUMPENLY
LUBRICITY	LUDERICK	LULLER	LUMPENS
LUBRICOUS	LUDERICKS	LULLERS	LUMPER
LUCARNE	LUDES	LULLING	LUMPERS
LUCARNES	LUDIC	LULLS	LUMPFISH
LUCE	LUDICALLY	LULU	LUMPIER
LUCENCE	LUDICROUS	LULUS	LUMPIEST
LUCENCES	LUDO	LUM	LUMPILY
LUCENCIES	LUDOS	LUMA	LUMPINESS
LUCENCY	LUDS	LUMAS	LUMPING
LUCENT	LUDSHIP	LUMBAGO	LUMPINGLY
LUCENTLY	LUDSHIPS	LUMBAGOS	LUMPISH
LUCERN	LUES	LUMBANG	LUMPISHLY
LUCERNE	LUETIC	LUMBANGS	LUMPKIN
LUCERNES	LUETICS	LUMBAR	LUMPKINS
LUCERNS	LUFF	LUMBARS	LUMPS
LUCES	LUFFA	LUMBER	LUMPY
LUCHOT	LUFFAS	LUMBERED	LUMS
LUCHOTH	LUFFED	LUMBERER	LUNA
LUCID	LUFFING	LUMBERERS	LUNACIES
LUCIDER	LUFFS	LUMBERING	LUNACY
LUCIDEST	LUG	LUMBERLY	LUNANAUT
LUCIDITY	LUGE	LUMBERMAN	LUNANAUTS
LUCIDLY	LUGED	LUMBERMEN	LUNAR
LUCIDNESS	LUGEING	LUMBERS	LUNARIAN
LUCIFER	LUGEINGS	LUMBRICAL	LUNARIANS
LUCIFERIN	LUGER	LUMBRICI	LUNARIES
LUCIFERS	LUGERS	LUMBRICUS	LUNARIST
LUCIGEN	LUGES	LUMEN	LUNARISTS
LUCIGENS	LUGGABLE	LUMENAL	LUNARNAUT
LUCITE	LUGGABLES	LUMENS	LUNARS
LUCITES	LUGGAGE	LUMINA	LUNARY
LUCK	LUGGAGES	LUMINAIRE	LUNAS
LUCKED	LUGGED	LUMINAL	LUNATE
LUCKEN	LUGGER	LUMINANCE	LUNATED
LUCKIE	LUGGERS	LUMINANT	LUNATELY

LUNATES	LUNKERS	LURIDEST	LUSTRATE
LUNATIC	LUNKHEAD	LURIDLY	LUSTRATED
LUNATICAL	LUNKHEADS	LURIDNESS	LUSTRATES
LUNATICS	LUNKS	LURING	LUSTRE
LUNATION	LUNT	LURINGLY	LUSTRED
LUNATIONS	LUNTED	LURK	LUSTRES
LUNCH	LUNTING	LURKED	LUSTRINE
LUNCHBOX	LUNTS	LURKER	LUSTRINES
LUNCHED	LUNULA	LURKERS	LUSTRING
LUNCHEON	LUNULAE	LURKING	LUSTRINGS
LUNCHEONS	LUNULAR	LURKINGLY	LUSTROUS
LUNCHER	LUNULATE	LURKINGS	LUSTRUM
LUNCHERS	LUNULATED	LURKS	LUSTRUMS
LUNCHES	LUNULE	LURRIES	LUSTS
LUNCHING	LUNULES	LURRY	LUSTY
LUNCHMEAT	LUNY	LURS	LUSUS
LUNCHROOM	LUNYIE	LURVE	LUSUSES
LUNCHTIME	LUNYIES	LURVES	LUTANIST
LUNE	LUPANAR	LUSCIOUS	LUTANISTS
LUNES	LUPANARS	LUSER	LUTE
LUNET	LUPIN	LUSERS	LUTEA
LUNETS	LUPINE	LUSH	LUTEAL
LUNETTE	LUPINES	LUSHED	LUTECIUM
LUNETTES	LUPINS	LUSHER	LUTECIUMS
LUNG	LUPOUS	LUSHERS	LUTED
LUNGAN	LUPPEN	LUSHES	LUTEFISK
LUNGANS	LUPULIN	LUSHEST	LUTEFISKS
LUNGE	LUPULINE	LUSHIER	LUTEIN
LUNGED	LUPULINIC	LUSHIEST	LUTEINISE
LUNGEE	LUPULINS	LUSHING	LUTEINIZE
LUNGEES	LUPUS	LUSHLY	LUTEINS
LUNGEING	LUPUSES	LUSHNESS	LUTENIST
LUNGER	LUR	LUSHY	LUTENISTS
LUNGERS	LURCH	LUSK	LUTEOLIN
LUNGES	LURCHED	LUSKED	LUTEOLINS
LUNGFISH	LURCHER	LUSKING	LUTEOLOUS
LUNGFUL	LURCHERS	LUSKISH	LUTEOUS
LUNGFULS	LURCHES	LUSKS	LUTER
LUNGI	LURCHING	LUST	LUTERS
LUNGIE	LURDAN	LUSTED	LUTES
LUNGIES	LURDANE	LUSTER	LUTESCENT
LUNGING	LURDANES	LUSTERED	LUTETIUM
LUNGIS	LURDANS	LUSTERING	LUTETIUMS
LUNGS	LURDEN	LUSTERS	LUTEUM
LUNGWORM	LURDENS	LUSTFUL	LUTFISK
LUNGWORMS	LURE	LUSTFULLY	LUTFISKS
LUNGWORT	LURED	LUSTICK	LUTHERN
LUNGWORTS	LURER	LUSTIER	LUTHERNS
LUNGYI	LURERS	LUSTIEST	LUTHIER
LUNGYIS	LURES	LUSTIHEAD	LUTHIERS
LUNIER	LUREX	LUSTIHOOD	LUTING
LUNIES	LUREXES	LUSTILY	LUTINGS
LUNIEST	LURGI	LUSTINESS	LUTIST
LUNINESS	LURGIES	LUSTING	LUTISTS
LUNISOLAR	LURGIS	LUSTIQUE	LUTITE
LUNITIDAL	LURGY	LUSTLESS	LUTITES
LUNK	LURID	LUSTRA	LUTTEN
LUNKER	LURIDER	LUSTRAL	LUTZ

LUTZES
LUV
LUVS
LUVVIE
LUVVIES
LUVVY
LUX
LUXATE
LUXATED
LUXATES
LUXATING
LUXATION
LUXATIONS
LUXE
LUXES
LUXMETER
LUXMETERS
LUXURIANT
LUXURIATE
LUXURIES
LUXURIOUS
LUXURIST
LUXURISTS
LUXURY
LUZ
LUZERN
LUZERNS
LUZZES
LWEI
LWEIS
LYAM
LYAMS
LYARD
LYART
LYASE
LYASES
LYCEA
LYCEE
LYCEES
LYCEUM
LYCEUMS
LYCH
LYCHEE
LYCHEES
LYCHES
LYCHGATE
LYCHGATES
LYCHNIS
LYCHNISES
LYCOPENE
LYCOPENES
LYCOPOD
LYCOPODS
LYCRA
LYCRAS
LYDDITE
LYDDITES
LYE

LYES
LYFULL
LYING
LYINGLY
LYTNGS
LYKEWAKE
LYKEWAKES
LYKEWALK
LYKEWALKS
LYM
LYME
LYMES
LYMITER
LYMITERS
LYMPH
LYMPHAD
LYMPHADS
LYMPHATIC
LYMPHOID
LYMPHOMA
LYMPHOMAS
LYMPHS
LYMS
LYNAGE
LYNAGES
LYNCEAN
LYNCH
LYNCHED
LYNCHER
LYNCHERS
LYNCHES
LYNCHET
LYNCHETS
LYNCHING
LYNCHINGS
LYNCHPIN
LYNCHPINS
LYNE
LYNES
LYNX
LYNXES
LYNXLIKE
LYOLYSES
LYOLYSIS
LYOMEROUS
LYONNAISE
LYOPHIL
LYOPHILE
LYOPHILED
LYOPHILIC
LYOPHOBE
LYOPHOBIC
LYRA
LYRATE
LYRATED
LYRATELY
LYRE
LYREBIRD

LYREBIRDS
LYRES
LYRIC
LYRICAL
LYRICALLY
LYRICISE
LYRICISED
LYRICISES
LYRICISM
LYRICISMS
LYRICIST
LYRICISTS
LYRICIZE
LYRICIZED
LYRICIZES
LYRICON
LYRICONS
LYRICS
LYRIFORM
LYRISM
LYRISMS
LYRIST
LYRISTS
LYSATE
LYSATES
LYSE
LYSED
LYSERGIC
LYSERGIDE
LYSES
LYSIGENIC
LYSIMETER
LYSIN
LYSINE
LYSINES
LYSING
LYSINS
LYSIS
LYSOGEN
LYSOGENIC
LYSOGENS
LYSOGENY
LYSOL
LYSOLS
LYSOSOMAL
LYSOSOME
LYSOSOMES
LYSOZYME
LYSOZYMES
LYSSA
LYSSAS
LYTE
LYTED
LYTES
LYTHE
LYTHES
LYTIC
LYTICALLY

LYTING
LYTTA
LYTTAE
LYTTAS

M

MA
MAA
MAAED
MAAING
MAAR
MAARE
MAARS
MAAS
MAASES
MAATJES
MABE
MABELA
MABELAS
MABES
MAC
MACABER
MACABRE
MACABRELY
MACACO
MACACOS
MACADAM
MACADAMIA
MACADAMS
MACAHUBA
MACAHUBAS
MACALLUM
MACALLUMS
MACAQUE
MACAQUES
MACARISE
MACARISED
MACARISES
MACARISM
MACARISMS
MACARIZE
MACARIZED
MACARIZES
MACARONI
MACARONIC
MACARONIS
MACAROON
MACAROONS
MACASSAR
MACASSARS
MACAW
MACAWS
MACCABAW
MACCABAWS
MACCABOY
MACCABOYS
MACCARONI
MACCHIA
MACCHIATO

MACCHIE
MACCOBOY
MACCOBOYS
MACE
MACED
MACEDOINE
MACER
MACERAL
MACERALS
MACERATE
MACERATED
MACERATER
MACERATES
MACERATOR
MACERS
MACES
MACH
MACHAIR
MACHAIRS
MACHAN
MACHANS
MACHE
MACHER
MACHERS
MACHES
MACHETE
MACHETES
MACHI
MACHINATE
MACHINE
MACHINED
MACHINERY
MACHINES
MACHINING
MACHINIST
MACHISMO
MACHISMOS
MACHMETER
MACHO
MACHOISM
MACHOISMS
MACHOS
MACHREE
MACHREES
MACHS
MACHZOR
MACHZORIM
MACHZORS
MACING
MACINTOSH
MACK
MACKEREL
MACKERELS

MACKINAW
MACKINAWS
MACKLE
MACKLED
MACKLES
MACKLING
MACKS
MACLE
MACLED
MACLES
MACON
MACONS
MACOYA
MACOYAS
MACRAME
MACRAMES
MACRAMI
MACRAMIS
MACRO
MACROBIAN
MACROCODE
MACROCOPY
MACROCOSM
MACROCYST
MACROCYTE
MACRODOME
MACRODONT
MACROGLIA
MACROLOGY
MACROMERE
MACROMOLE
MACRON
MACRONS
MACROPOD
MACROPODS
MACROPSIA
MACROS
MACROTOUS
MACRURAL
MACRURAN
MACRURANS
MACRUROID
MACRUROUS
MACS
MACTATION
MACULA
MACULAE
MACULAR
MACULAS
MACULATE
MACULATED
MACULATES
MACULE

MACULED
MACULES
MACULING
MACULOSE
MACUMBA
MACUMBAS
MAD
MADAFU
MADAFUS
MADAM
MADAME
MADAMED
MADAMES
MADAMING
MADAMS
MADAROSES
MADAROSIS
MADBRAIN
MADCAP
MADCAPS
MADDED
MADDEN
MADDENED
MADDENING
MADDENS
MADDER
MADDERS
MADDEST
MADDING
MADDINGLY
MADDISH
MADDOCK
MADDOCKS
MADE
MADEFIED
MADEFIES
MADEFY
MADEFYING
MADEIRA
MADEIRAS
MADELEINE
MADERISE
MADERISED
MADERISES
MADERIZE
MADERIZED
MADERIZES
MADGE
MADGES
MADHOUSE
MADHOUSES
MADID
MADISON

MADISONS	MAESTROS	MAGICKED	MAGNOXES
MADLING	MAFFIA	MAGICKING	MAGNUM
MADLINGS	MAFFIAS	MAGICS	MAGNUMS
MADLY	MAFFICK	MAGILP	MAGNUS
MADMAN	MAFFICKED	MAGILPS	MAGOT
MADMEN	MAFFICKER	MAGISM	MAGOTS
MADNESS	MAFFICKS	MAGISMS	MAGPIE
MADNESSES	MAFFLED	MAGISTER	MAGPIES
MADONNA	MAFFLIN	MAGISTERS	MAGS
MADONNAS	MAFFLING	MAGISTERY	MAGSMAN
MADOQUA	MAFFLINGS	MAGISTRAL	MAGSMEN
MADOQUAS	MAFFLINS	MAGLEV	MAGUEY
MADRAS	MAFIA	MAGLEVS	MAGUEYS
MADRASA	MAFIAS	MAGMA	MAGUS
MADRASAH	MAFIC	MAGMAS	MAGYAR
MADRASAHS	MAFICS	MAGMATA	MAHARAJA
MADRASAS	MAFIOSI	MAGMATIC	MAHARAJAH
MADRASES	MAFIOSO	MAGMATISM	MAHARAJAS
MADRASSA	MAFIOSOS	MAGNALIUM	MAHARANEE
MADRASSAH	MAFTED	MAGNATE	MAHARANI
MADRASSAS	MAFTIR	MAGNATES	MAHARANIS
MADRE	MAFTIRS	MAGNES	MAHARISHI
MADREPORE	MAG	MAGNESES	MAHATMA
MADRES	MAGAININ	MAGNESIA	MAHATMAS
MADRIGAL	MAGAININS	MAGNESIAL	MAHEWU
MADRIGALS	MAGALOG	MAGNESIAN	MAHEWUS
MADRILENE	MAGALOGS	MAGNESIAS	MAHIMAHI
MADRONA	MAGALOGUE	MAGNESIC	MAHIMAHIS
MADRONAS	MAGAZINE	MAGNESITE	MAHJONG
MADRONE	MAGAZINES	MAGNESIUM	MAHJONGG
MADRONES	MAGDALEN	MAGNET	MAHJONGGS
MADRONO	MAGDALENE	MAGNETAR	MAHJONGS
MADRONOS	MAGDALENS	MAGNETARS	MAHLSTICK
MADS	MAGE	MAGNETIC	MAHMAL
MADTOM	MAGENTA	MAGNETICS	MAHMALS
MADTOMS	MAGENTAS	MAGNETISE	MAHOE
MADURO	MAGES	MAGNETISM	MAHOES
MADUROS	MAGESHIP	MAGNETIST	MAHOGANY
MADWOMAN	MAGESHIPS	MAGNETITE	MAHONIA
MADWOMEN	MAGG	MAGNETIZE	MAHONIAS
MADWORT	MAGGED	MAGNETO	MAHOUT
MADWORTS	MAGGIE	MAGNETON	MAHOUTS
MADZOON	MAGGIES	MAGNETONS	MAHSEER
MADZOONS	MAGGING	MAGNETOS	MAHSEERS
MAE	MAGGOT	MAGNETRON	MAHSIR
MAELID	MAGGOTIER	MAGNETS	MAHSIRS
MAELIDS	MAGGOTS	MAGNIFIC	MAHUA
MAELSTROM	MAGGOTY	MAGNIFICO	MAHUANG
MAENAD	MAGGS	MAGNIFIED	MAHUANGS
MAENADES	MAGI	MAGNIFIER	MAHUAS
MAENADIC	MAGIAN	MAGNIFIES	MAHWA
MAENADISM	MAGIANISM	MAGNIFY	MAHWAS
MAENADS	MAGIANS	MAGNITUDE	MAHZOR
MAES	MAGIC	MAGNOLIA	MAHZORIM
MAESTOSO	MAGICAL	MAGNOLIAS	MAHZORS
MAESTOSOS	MAGICALLY	MAGNON	MAIASAUR
MAESTRI	MAGICIAN	MAGNONS	MAIASAURA
MAESTRO	MAGICIANS	MAGNOX	MAIASAURS

MAID	MAILSHOT	MAIST	MAKOS
MAIDAN	MAILSHOTS	MAISTER	MAKS
MAIDANS	MAILVAN	MAISTERED	MAKUTA
MAIDED	MAILVANS	MAISTERS	MAKUTU
MAIDEN	MAIM	MAISTRIES	MAKUTUED
MAIDENISH	MAIMED	MAISTRING	MAKUTUING
MAIDENLY	MAIMER	MAISTRY	MAKUTUS
MAIDENS	MAIMERS	MAISTS	MAL
MAIDHOOD	MAIMING	MAIZE	MALA
MAIDHOODS	MAIMINGS	MAIZES	MALACCA
MAIDING	MAIMS	MAJAGUA	MALACCAS
MAIDISH	MAIN	MAJAGUAS	MALACHITE
MAIDISM	MAINBOOM	MAJESTIC	MALACIA
MAIDISMS	MAINBOOMS	MAJESTIES	MALACIAS
MAIDLESS	MAINBRACE	MAJESTY	MALADIES
MAIDS	MAINDOOR	MAJLIS	MALADROIT
MAIEUTIC	MAINDOORS	MAJLISES	MALADY
MAIEUTICS	MAINED	MAJOLICA	MALAGUENA
MAIGRE	MAINER	MAJOLICAS	MALAISE
MAIGRES	MAINEST	MAJOR	MALAISES
MAIHEM	MAINFRAME	MAJORAT	MALAM
MAIHEMS	MAINING	MAJORATS	MALAMS
MAIK	MAINLAND	MAJORDOMO	MALAMUTE
MAIKO	MAINLANDS	MAJORED	MALAMUTES
MAIKOS	MAINLINE	MAJORETTE	MALANDER
MAIKS	MAINLINED	MAJORING	MALANDERS
MAIL	MAINLINER	MAJORITY	MALANGA
MAILABLE	MAINLINES	MAJORLY	MALANGAS
MAILBAG	MAINLY	MAJORS	MALAPERT
MAILBAGS	MAINMAST	MAJORSHIP	MALAPERTS
MAILBOX	MAINMASTS	MAJUSCULE	MALAPROP
MAILBOXES	MAINOR	MAK	MALAPROPS
MAILCAR	MAINORS	MAKABLE	MALAR
MAILCARS	MAINOUR	MAKAR	MALARIA
MAILCOACH	MAINOURS	MAKARS	MALARIAL
MAILE	MAINPRISE	MAKE	MALARIAN
MAILED	MAINS	MAKEABLE	MALARIAS
MAILER	MAINSAIL	MAKEBATE	MALARIOUS
MAILERS	MAINSAILS	MAKEBATES	MALARKEY
MAILES	MAINSHEET	MAKEFAST	MALARKEYS
MAILGRAM	MAINSTAY	MAKEFASTS	MALARKIES
MAILGRAMS	MAINSTAYS	MAKELESS	MALARKY
MAILING	MAINTAIN	MAKEOVER	MALAROMA
MAILINGS	MAINTAINS	MAKEOVERS	MALAROMAS
MAILL	MAINTOP	MAKER	MALARS
MAILLESS	MAINTOPS	MAKEREADY	MALAS
MAILLOT	MAINYARD	MAKERS	MALATE
MAILLOTS	MAINYARDS	MAKES	MALATES
MAILLS	MAIOLICA	MAKESHIFT	MALATHION
MAILMAN	MAIOLICAS	MAKEUP	MALAX
MAILMEN	MAIR	MAKEUPS	MALAXAGE
MAILMERGE	MAIRE	MAKI	MALAXAGES
MAILPOUCH	MAIREHAU	MAKIMONO	MALAXATE
MAILROOM	MAIREHAUS	MAKIMONOS	MALAXATED
MAILROOMS	MAIRES	MAKING	MALAXATES
MAILS	MAIRS	MAKINGS	MALAXATOR
MAILSACK	MAISE	MAKIS	MALAXED
MAILSACKS	MAISES	MAKO	MALAXES

MALAXING	MALIST	MALTALENT	MAMELON
MALE	MALKIN	MALTASE	MAMELONS
MALEATE	MALKINS	MALTASES	MAMELUCO
MALEATES	MALL	MALTED	MAMELUCOS
MALEDICT	MALLAM	MALTEDS	MAMELUKE
MALEDICTS	MALLAMS	MALTHA	MAMELUKES
MALEFFECT	MALLANDER	MALTHAS	MAMEY
MALEFIC	MALLARD	MALTIER	MAMEYES
MALEFICE	MALLARDS	MALTIEST	MAMEYS
MALEFICES	MALLEABLE	MALTINESS	MAMIE
MALEIC	MALLEABLY	MALTING	MAMIES
MALEMIUT	MALLEATE	MALTINGS	MAMILLA
MALEMIUTS	MALLEATED	MALTMAN	MAMILLAE
MALEMUTE	MALLEATES	MALTMEN	MAMILLAR
MALEMUTES	MALLECHO	MALTOL	MAMILLARY
MALENESS	MALLECHOS	MALTOLS	MAMILLATE
MALENGINE	MALLED	MALTOSE	MAMLUK
MALES	MALLEE	MALTOSES	MAMLUKS
MALFED	MALLEES	MALTREAT	MAMMA
MALFORMED	MALLEI	MALTREATS	MAMMAE
MALGRADO	MALLEMUCK	MALTS	MAMMAL
MALGRE	MALLENDER	MALTSTER	MAMMALIAN
MALGRED	MALLEOLAR	MALTSTERS	MAMMALITY
MALGRES	MALLEOLI	MALTWORM	MAMMALOGY
MALGRING	MALLEOLUS	MALTWORMS	MAMMALS
MALI	MALLET	MALTY	MAMMARY
MALIBU	MALLETS	MALVA	MAMMAS
MALIC	MALLEUS	MALVAS	MAMMATE
MALICE	MALLEUSES	MALVASIA	MAMMATI
MALICED	MALLING	MALVASIAN	MAMMATUS
MALICES	MALLINGS	MALVASIAS	MAMMEE
MALICHO	MALLOW	MALVESIE	MAMMEES
MALICHOS	MALLOWS	MALVESIES	MAMMER
MALICING	MALLS	MALVOISIE	MAMMERED
MALICIOUS	MALM	MALWA	MAMMERING
MALIGN	MALMAG	MALWARE	MAMMERS
MALIGNANT	MALMAGS	MALWARES	MAMMET
MALIGNED	MALMIER	MALWAS	MAMMETRY
MALIGNER	MALMIEST	MAM	MAMMETS
MALIGNERS	MALMS	MAMA	MAMMEY
MALIGNING	MALMSEY	MAMAGUY	MAMMEYS
MALIGNITY	MALMSEYS	MAMAGUYED	MAMMIE
MALIGNLY	MALMSTONE	MAMAGUYS	MAMMIES
MALIGNS	MALMY	MAMAKAU	MAMMIFER
MALIHINI	MALODOR	MAMAKO	MAMMIFERS
MALIHINIS	MALODORS	MAMAKU	MAMMIFORM
MALIK	MALODOUR	MAMALIGA	MAMMILLA
MALIKS	MALODOURS	MAMALIGAS	MAMMILLAE
MALINE	MALONATE	MAMAS	MAMMITIS
MALINES	MALONATES	MAMBA	MAMMOCK
MALINGER	MALONIC	MAMBAS	MAMMOCKED
MALINGERS	MALOTI	MAMBO	MAMMOCKS
MALINGERY	MALPIGHIA	MAMBOED	MAMMOGRAM
MALIS	MALPOSED	MAMBOES	MAMMON
MALISM	MALS	MAMBOING	MAMMONISH
MALISMS	MALSTICK	MAMBOS	MAMMONISM
MALISON	MALSTICKS	MAMEE	MAMMONIST
MALISONS	MALT	MAMEES	MAMMONITE

MAMMONS	MANDAMUS	MANET	MANHOLE
MAMMOTH	MANDARIN	MANEUVER	MANHOLES
MAMMOTHS	MANDARINE	MANEUVERS	MANHOOD
MAMMY	MANDARINS	MANFUL	MANHOODS
MAMPARA	MANDATARY	MANFULLY	MANHUNT
MAMPARAS	MANDATE	MANG	MANHUNTER
MAMPOER	MANDATED	MANGA	MANHUNTS
MAMPOERS	MANDATES	MANGABEY	MANI
MAMS	MANDATING	MANGABEYS	MANIA
MAMSELLE	MANDATOR	MANGABIES	MANIAC
MAMSELLES	MANDATORS	MANGABY	MANIACAL
MAMZER	MANDATORY	MANGAL	MANIACS
MAMZERIM	MANDI	MANGALS	MANIAS
MAMZERS	MANDIBLE	MANGANATE	MANIC
MAN	MANDIBLES	MANGANESE	MANICALLY
MANA	MANDILION	MANGANIC	MANICOTTI
MANACLE	MANDIOC	MANGANIN	MANICS
MANACLED	MANDIOCA	MANGANINS	MANICURE
MANACLES	MANDIOCAS	MANGANITE	MANICURED
MANACLING	MANDIOCCA	MANGANOUS	MANICURES
MANAGE	MANDIOCS	MANGAS	MANIES
MANAGED	MANDIR	MANGE	MANIFEST
MANAGER	MANDIRA	MANGEAO	MANIFESTO
MANAGERS	MANDIRAS	MANGED	MANIFESTS
MANAGES	MANDIRS	MANGEL	MANIFOLD
MANAGING	MANDIS	MANGELS	MANIFOLDS
MANAIA	MANDOLA	MANGER	MANIFORM
MANAKIN	MANDOLAS	MANGERS	MANIHOC
MANAKINS	MANDOLIN	MANGES	MANIHOCS
MANANA	MANDOLINE	MANGETOUT	MANIHOT
MANANAS	MANDOLINS	MANGEY	MANIHOTS
MANAS	MANDOM	MANGIER	MANIKIN
MANAT	MANDOMS	MANGIEST	MANIKINS
MANATEE	MANDORA	MANGILY	MANILA
MANATEES	MANDORAS	MANGINESS	MANILAS
MANATI	MANDORLA	MANGING	MANILLA
MANATIS	MANDORLAS	MANGLE	MANILLAS
MANATOID	MANDRAKE	MANGLED	MANILLE
MANATS	MANDRAKES	MANGLER	MANILLES
MANATU	MANDREL	MANGLERS	MANIOC
MANAWA	MANDRELS	MANGLES	MANIOCA
MANAWAS	MANDRIL	MANGLING	MANIOCAS
MANCALA	MANDRILL	MANGO	MANIOCS
MANCALAS	MANDRILLS	MANGOES	MANIPLE
MANCANDO	MANDRILS	MANGOLD	MANIPLES
MANCHE	MANDUCATE	MANGOLDS	MANIPLIES
MANCHES	MANDYLION	MANGONEL	MANIPULAR
MANCHET	MANE	MANGONELS	MANIS
MANCHETS	MANED	MANGOS	MANITO
MANCIPATE	MANEGE	MANGOSTAN	MANITOS
MANCIPLE	MANEGED	MANGOUSTE	MANITOU
MANCIPLES	MANEGES	MANGROVE	MANITOUS
MANCUS	MANEGING	MANGROVES	MANITU
MANCUSES	MANEH	MANGS	MANITUS
MAND	MANEHS	MANGULATE	MANJACK
MANDALA	MANELESS	MANGY	MANJACKS
MANDALAS	MANENT	MANHANDLE	MANKIER
MANDALIC	MANES	MANHATTAN	MANKIEST

MANKIND	MANRIDING	MANTUA	MAPPEMOND
MANKINDS	MANROPE	MANTUAS	MAPPER
MANKY	MANROPES	MANTY	MAPPERIES
MANLESS	MANS	MANUAL	MAPPERS
MANLIER	MANSARD	MANUALLY	MAPPERY
MANLIEST	MANSARDED	MANUALS	MAPPING
MANLIKE	MANSARDS	MANUARY	MAPPINGS
MANLIKELY	MANSE	MANUBRIA	MAPPIST
MANLILY	MANSES	MANUBRIAL	MAPPISTS
MANLINESS	MANSHIFT	MANUBRIUM	MAPS
MANLY	MANSHIFTS	MANUHIRI	MAPSTICK
MANMADE	MANSION	MANUHIRIS	MAPSTICKS
MANNA	MANSIONS	MANUKA	MAPWISE
MANNAN	MANSLAYER	MANUKAS	MAQUETTE
MANNANS	MANSONRY	MANUL	MAQUETTES
MANNAS	MANSUETE	MANULS	MAQUI
MANNED	MANSWORN	MANUMEA	MAQUILA
MANNEQUIN	MANTA	MANUMEAS	MAQUILAS
MANNER	MANTAS	MANUMIT	MAQUIS
MANNERED	MANTEAU	MANUMITS	MAQUISARD
MANNERISM	MANTEAUS	MANURANCE	MAR
MANNERIST	MANTEAUX	MANURE	MARA
MANNERLY	MANTEEL	MANURED	MARABI
MANNERS	MANTEELS	MANURER	MARABIS
MANNIKIN	MANTEL	MANURERS	MARABOU
MANNIKINS	MANTELET	MANURES	MARABOUS
MANNING	MANTELETS	MANURIAL	MARABOUT
MANNISH	MANTELS	MANURING	MARABOUTS
MANNISHLY	MANTES	MANURINGS	MARABUNTA
MANNITE	MANTIC	MANUS	MARACA
MANNITES	MANTICORA	MANWARD	MARACAS
MANNITIC	MANTICORE	MANWARDS	MARAE
MANNITOL	MANTID	MANWISE	MARAES
MANNITOLS	MANTIDS	MANY	MARAGING
MANNOSE	MANTIES	MANYATA	MARAGINGS
MANNOSES	MANTILLA	MANYATAS	MARAH
MANO	MANTILLAS	MANYATTA	MARAHS
MANOAO	MANTIS	MANYATTAS	MARANATHA
MANOAOS	MANTISES	MANYFOLD	MARANTA
MANOEUVRE	MANTISSA	MANYPLIES	MARANTAS
MANOMETER	MANTISSAS	MANZANITA	MARARI
MANOMETRY	MANTLE	MANZELLO	MARARIS
MANOR	MANTLED	MANZELLOS	MARAS
MANORIAL	MANTLES	MAOMAO	MARASCA
MANORS	MANTLET	MAORMOR	MARASCAS
MANOS	MANTLETS	MAORMORS	MARASMIC
MANOSCOPY	MANTLING	MAP	MARASMOID
MANPACK	MANTLINGS	MAPAU	MARASMUS
MANPACKS	MANTO	MAPLE	MARATHON
MANPOWER	MANTOES	MAPLELIKE	MARATHONS
MANPOWERS	MANTOS	MAPLES	MARAUD
MANQUE	MANTRA	MAPLESS	MARAUDED
MANRED	MANTRAM	MAPLIKE	MARAUDER
MANREDS	MANTRAMS	MAPMAKER	MARAUDERS
MANRENT	MANTRAP	MAPMAKERS	MARAUDING
MANRENTS	MANTRAPS	MAPMAKING	MARAUDS
MANRIDER	MANTRAS	MAPPABLE	MARAVEDI
MANRIDERS	MANTRIC	MAPPED	MARAVEDIS

MARBELISE	MARESCHAL	MARINERS	MARLINS
MARBELIZE	MARG	MARINES	MARLITE
MARBLE	MARGARIC	MARINIERE	MARLITES
MARBLED	MARGARIN	MARIPOSA	MARLITIC
MARBLEISE	MARGARINE	MARIPOSAS	MARLS
MARBLEIZE	MARGARINS	MARISCHAL	MARLSTONE
MARBLER	MARGARITA	MARISH	MARLY
MARBLERS	MARGARITE	MARISHES	MARM
MARBLES	MARGAY	MARITAGE	MARMALADE
MARBLIER	MARGAYS	MARITAGES	MARMALISE
MARBLIEST	MARGE	MARITAL	MARMALIZE
MARBLING	MARGENT	MARITALLY	MARMARISE
MARBLINGS	MARGENTED	MARITIME	MARMARIZE
MARBLY	MARGENTS	MARJORAM	MARMELISE
MARC	MARGES	MARJORAMS	MARMELIZE
MARCASITE	MARGIN	MARK	MARMITE
MARCATO	MARGINAL	MARKA	MARMITES
MARCATOS	MARGINALS	MARKAS	MARMOREAL
MARCEL	MARGINATE	MARKDOWN	MARMOREAN
MARCELLA	MARGINED	MARKDOWNS	MARMOSE
MARCELLAS	MARGINING	MARKED	MARMOSES
MARCELLED	MARGINS	MARKEDLY	MARMOSET
MARCELLER	MARGOSA	MARKER	MARMOSETS
MARCELS	MARGOSAS	MARKERS	MARMOT
MARCH	MARGRAVE	MARKET	MARMOTS
MARCHED	MARGRAVES	MARKETED	MARMS
MARCHEN	MARGS	MARKETEER	MAROCAIN
MARCHER	MARIA	MARKETER	MAROCAINS
MARCHERS	MARIACHI	MARKETERS	MARON
MARCHES	MARIACHIS	MARKETING	MARONS
MARCHESA	MARIALITE	MARKETS	MAROON
MARCHESAS	MARID	MARKHOOR	MAROONED
MARCHESE	MARIDS	MARKHOORS	MAROONER
MARCHESES	MARIES	MARKHOR	MAROONERS
MARCHESI	MARIGOLD	MARKHORS	MAROONING
MARCHING	MARIGOLDS	MARKING	MAROONS
MARCHLAND	MARIGRAM	MARKINGS	MAROQUIN
MARCHLIKE	MARIGRAMS	MARKKA	MAROQUINS
MARCHMAN	MARIGRAPH	MARKKAA	MAROR
MARCHMEN	MARIHUANA	MARKKAS	MARORS
MARCHPANE	MARIJUANA	MARKMAN	MARPLOT
MARCONI	MARIMBA	MARKMEN	MARPLOTS
MARCONIED	MARIMBAS	MARKS	MARQUE
MARCONIS	MARIMBIST	MARKSMAN	MARQUEE
MARCS	MARINA	MARKSMEN	MARQUEES
MARD	MARINADE	MARKUP	MARQUES
MARDIED	MARINADED	MARKUPS	MARQUESS
MARDIER	MARINADES	MARL	MARQUETRY
MARDIES	MARINARA	MARLE	MARQUIS
MARDIEST	MARINARAS	MARLED	MARQUISE
MARDY	MARINAS	MARLES	MARQUISES
MARDYING	MARINATE	MARLIER	MARRAM
MARE	MARINATED	MARLIEST	MARRAMS
MAREMMA	MARINATES	MARLIN	MARRANO
MAREMMAS	MARINE	MARLINE	MARRANOS
MAREMME	MARINER	MARLINES	MARRED
MARENGO	MARINERA	MARLING	MARRELS
MARES	MARINERAS	MARLINGS	MARRER

MARRERS	MARTED	MASALA	MASJID
MARRI	MARTEL	MASALAS	MASJIDS
MARRIAGE	MARTELLED	MASAS	MASK
MARRIAGES	MARTELLO	MASCARA	MASKABLE
MARRIED	MARTELLOS	MASCARAED	MASKED
MARRIEDS	MARTELS	MASCARAS	MASKEG
MARRIER	MARTEN	MASCARON	MASKEGS
MARRIERS	MARTENS	MASCARONS	MASKER
MARRIES	MARTEXT	MASCLE	MASKERS
MARRING	MARTEXTS	MASCLED	MASKING
MARRIS	MARTIAL	MASCLES	MASKINGS
MARRON	MARTIALLY	MASCON	MASKLIKE
MARRONS	MARTIAN	MASCONS	MASKS
MARROW	MARTIANS	MASCOT	MASLIN
MARROWED	MARTIN	MASCOTS	MASLINS
MARROWFAT	MARTINET	MASCULINE	MASOCHISM
MARROWING	MARTINETS	MASCULIST	MASOCHIST
MARROWISH	MARTING	MASCULY	MASON
MARROWS	MARTINGAL	MASE	MASONED
MARROWSKY	MARTINI	MASED	MASONIC
MARROWY	MARTINIS	MASER	MASONING
MARRUM	MARTINS	MASERS	MASONITE
MARRUMS	MARTLET	MASES	MASONITES
MARRY	MARTLETS	MASH	MASONRIED
MARRYING	MARTS	MASHALLAH	MASONRIES
MARRYINGS	MARTYR	MASHED	MASONRY
MARS	MARTYRDOM	MASHER	MASONS
MARSALA	MARTYRED	MASHERS	MASOOLAH
MARSALAS	MARTYRIA	MASHES	MASOOLAHS
MARSE	MARTYRIES	MASHGIACH	MASQUE
MARSEILLE	MARTYRING	MASHGIAH	MASQUER
MARSES	MARTYRISE	MASHGIHIM	MASQUERS
MARSH	MARTYRIUM	MASHIACH	MASQUES
MARSHAL	MARTYRIZE	MASHIACHS	MASS
MARSHALCY	MARTYRLY	MASHIE	MASSA
MARSHALED	MARTYRS	MASHIER	MASSACRE
MARSHALER	MARTYRY	MASHIES	MASSACRED
MARSHALL	MARVEL	MASHIEST	MASSACRER
MARSHALLS	MARVELED	MASHING	MASSACRES
MARSHALS	MARVELING	MASHINGS	MASSAGE
MARSHBUCK	MARVELLED	MASHLAM	MASSAGED
MARSHES	MARVELOUS	MASHLAMS	MASSAGER
MARSHIER	MARVELS	MASHLIM	MASSAGERS
MARSHIEST	MARVER	MASHLIMS	MASSAGES
MARSHLAND	MARVERED	MASHLIN	MASSAGING
MARSHLIKE	MARVERING	MASHLINS	MASSAGIST
MARSHWORT	MARVERS	MASHLOCH	MASSAS
MARSHY	MARVY	MASHLOCHS	MASSCULT
MARSPORT	MARXISANT	MASHLUM	MASSCULTS
MARSPORTS	MARY	MASHLUMS	MASSE
MARSQUAKE	MARYBUD	MASHMAN	MASSED
MARSUPIA	MARYBUDS	MASHMEN	MASSEDLY
MARSUPIAL	MARYJANE	MASHUA	MASSES
MARSUPIAN	MARYJANES	MASHUAS	MASSETER
MARSUPIUM	MARZIPAN	MASHUP	MASSETERS
MART	MARZIPANS	MASHUPS	MASSEUR
MARTAGON	MAS	MASHY	MASSEURS
MARTAGONS	MASA	MASING	MASSEUSE

MASSEUSES	MASTODONT	MATELOTTE	MATRICS
MASSICOT	MASTOID	MATER	MATRICULA
MASSICOTS	MASTOIDAL	MATERIAL	MATRILINY
MASSIER	MASTOIDS	MATERIALS	MATRIMONY
MASSIEST	MASTOPEXY	MATERIEL	MATRIX
MASSIF	MASTS	MATERIELS	MATRIXES
MASSIFS	MASTY	MATERNAL	MATRON
MASSINESS	MASU	MATERNITY	MATRONAGE
MASSING	MASULA	MATERS	MATRONAL
MASSIVE	MASULAS	MATES	MATRONISE
MASSIVELY	MASURIUM	MATESHIP	MATRONIZE
MASSLESS	MASURIUMS	MATESHIPS	MATRONLY
MASSOOLA	MASUS	MATEY	MATRONS
MASSOOLAS	MAT	MATEYNESS	MATROSS
MASSY	MATACHIN	MATEYS	MATROSSES
MASSYMORE	MATACHINA	MATFELON	MATS
MAST	MATACHINI	MATFELONS	MATSAH
MASTABA	MATADOR	MATGRASS	MATSAHS
MASTABAH	MATADORA	MATH	MATSURI
MASTABAHS	MATADORAS	MATHESES	MATSURIS
MASTABAS	MATADORE	MATHESIS	MATSUTAKE
MASTED	MATADORES	MATHS	MATT
MASTER	MATADORS	MATICO	MATTAMORE
MASTERATE	MATAGOURI	MATICOS	MATTE
MASTERDOM	MATAI	MATIER	MATTED
MASTERED	MATAIS	MATIES	MATTEDLY
MASTERFUL	MATAMATA	MATIEST	MATTER
MASTERIES	MATAMATAS	MATILDA	MATTERED
MASTERING	MATAMBALA	MATILDAS	MATTERFUL
MASTERLY	MATATA	MATILY	MATTERING
MASTERS	MATCH	MATIN	MATTERS
MASTERY	MATCHABLE	MATINAL	MATTERY
MASTFUL	MATCHBOOK	MATINEE	MATTES
MASTHEAD	MATCHBOX	MATINEES	MATTIE
MASTHEADS	MATCHED	MATINESS	MATTIES
MASTHOUSE	MATCHER	MATING	MATTIFIED
MASTIC	MATCHERS	MATINGS	MATTIFIES
MASTICATE	MATCHES	MATINS	MATTIFY
MASTICH	MATCHET	MATIPO	MATTIN
MASTICHE	MATCHETS	MATIPOS	MATTING
MASTICHES	MATCHING	MATJES	MATTINGS
MASTICHS	MATCHLESS	MATLESS	MATTINS
MASTICOT	MATCHLOCK	MATLO	MATTOCK
MASTICOTS	MATCHMADE	MATLOS	MATTOCKS
MASTICS	MATCHMAKE	MATLOW	MATTOID
MASTIER	MATCHMARK	MATLOWS	MATTOIDS
MASTIEST	MATCHPLAY	MATOKE	MATTRASS
MASTIFF	MATCHUP	MATOKES	MATTRESS
MASTIFFS	MATCHUPS	MATOOKE	MATTS
MASTING	MATCHWOOD	MATOOKES	MATURABLE
MASTITIC	MATE	MATRASS	MATURATE
MASTITIS	MATED	MATRASSES	MATURATED
MASTIX	MATELASSE	MATRES	MATURATES
MASTIXES	MATELESS	MATRIARCH	MATURE
MASTLESS	MATELOT	MATRIC	MATURED
MASTLIKE	MATELOTE	MATRICE	MATURELY
MASTODON	MATELOTES	MATRICES	MATURER
MASTODONS	MATELOTS	MATRICIDE	MATURERS

MATURES	MAUNDY	MAWPUSES	MAYBES
MATUREST	MAUNGIER	MAWR	MAYBIRD
MATURING	MAUNGIEST	MAWRS	MAYBIRDS
MATURITY	MAUNGY	MAWS	MAYBUSH
MATUTINAL	MAUNNA	MAWSEED	MAYBUSHES
MATUTINE	MAURI	MAWSEEDS	MAYDAY
MATWEED	MAURIS	MAWTHER	MAYDAYS
MATWEEDS	MAUSOLEA	MAWTHERS	MAYED
MATY	MAUSOLEAN	MAX	MAYEST
MATZA	MAUSOLEUM	MAXED	MAYFLIES
MATZAH	MAUT	MAXES	MAYFLOWER
MATZAHS	MAUTHER	MAXI	MAYFLY
MATZAS	MAUTHERS	MAXICOAT	MAYHAP
MATZO	MAUTS	MAXICOATS	MAYHAPPEN
MATZOH	MAUVAIS	MAXILLA	MAYHEM
MATZOHS	MAUVAISE	MAXILLAE	MAYHEMS
MATZOON	MAUVE	MAXILLAR	MAYING
MATZOONS	MAUVEIN	MAXILLARY	MAYINGS
MATZOS	MAUVEINE	MAXILLAS	MAYO
MATZOT	MAUVEINES	MAXILLULA	MAYOR
MATZOTH	MAUVEINS	MAXIM	MAYORAL
MAUBIES	MAUVER	MAXIMA	MAYORALTY
MAUBY	MAUVES	MAXIMAL	MAYORESS
MAUD	MAUVEST	MAXIMALLY	MAYORS
MAUDLIN	MAUVIN	MAXIMALS	MAYORSHIP
MAUDLINLY	MAUVINE	MAXIMIN	MAYOS
MAUDS	MAUVINES	MAXIMINS	MAYPOLE
MAUGER	MAUVINS	MAXIMISE	MAYPOLES
MAUGRE	MAVEN	MAXIMISED	MAYPOP
MAUGRED	MAVENS	MAXIMISER	MAYPOPS
MAUGRES	MAVERICK	MAXIMISES	MAYS
MAUGRING	MAVERICKS	MAXIMIST	MAYST
MAUL	MAVIE	MAXIMISTS	MAYSTER
MAULED	MAVIES	MAXIMITE	MAYSTERS
MAULER	MAVIN	MAXIMITES	MAYVIN
MAULERS	MAVINS	MAXIMIZE	MAYVINS
MAULGRE	MAVIS	MAXIMIZED	MAYWEED
MAULGRED	MAVISES	MAXIMIZER	MAYWEEDS
MAULGRES	MAVOURNIN	MAXIMIZES	MAZAEDIA
MAULGRING	MAW	MAXIMS	MAZAEDIUM
MAULING	MAWBOUND	MAXIMUM	MAZARD
MAULS	MAWED	MAXTMUMLY	MAZARDS
MAULSTICK	MAWGER	MAXIMUMS	MAZARINE
MAULVI	MAWING	MAXIMUS	MAZARINES
MAULVIS	MAWK	MAXIMUSES	MAZE
MAUMET	MAWKIER	MAXING	MAZED
MAUMETRY	MAWKIEST	MAXIS	MAZEDLY
MAUMETS	MAWKIN	MAXIXE	MAZEDNESS
MAUN	MAWKINS	MAXIXES	MAZEFUL
MAUND	MAWKISH	MAXWELL	MAZELIKE
MAUNDED	MAWKISHLY	MAXWELLS	MAZELTOV
MAUNDER	MAWKS	MAY	MAZEMENT
MAUNDERED	MAWKY	MAYA	MAZEMENTS
MAUNDERER	MAWMET	MAYAN	MAZER
MAUNDERS	MAWMETRY	MAYAPPLE	MAZERS
MAUNDIES	MAWMETS	MAYAPPLES	MAZES
MAUNDING	MAWN	MAYAS	MAZEY
MAUNDS	MAWPUS	MAYBE	MAZHBI

MAZHBIS	MEANDER	MEATIER	MEDCINAL
MAZIER	MEANDERED	MEATIEST	MEDDLE
MAZIEST	MEANDERER	MEATILY	MEDDLED
MAZILY	MEANDERS	MEATINESS	MEDDLER
MAZINESS	MEANDRIAN	MEATLESS	MEDDLERS
MAZING	MEANDROUS	MEATLOAF	MEDDLES
MAZOURKA	MEANE	MEATMAN	MEDDLING
MAZOURKAS	MEANED	MEATMEN	MEDDLINGS
MAZOUT	MEANER	MEATS	MEDEVAC
MAZOUTS	MEANERS	MEATSPACE	MEDEVACED
MAZUMA	MEANES	MEATUS	MEDEVACS
MAZUMAS	MEANEST	MEATUSES	MEDFLIES
MAZURKA	MEANIE	MEATY	MEDFLY
MAZURKAS	MEANIES	MEAWES	MEDIA
MAZUT	MEANING	MEAZEL	MEDIACIES
MAZUTS	MEANINGLY	MEAZELS	MEDIACY
MAZY	MEANINGS	MEBOS	MEDIAD
MAZZARD	MEANLY	MEBOSES	MEDIAE
MAZZARDS	MEANNESS	MECCA	MEDIAEVAL
MBAQANGA	MEANS	MECCAS	MEDIAL
MBAQANGAS	MEANT	MECHANIC	MEDIALLY
MBIRA	MEANTIME	MECHANICS	MEDIALS
MBIRAS	MEANTIMES	MECHANISE	MEDIAN
ME	MEANWHILE	MECHANISM	MEDIANLY
MEACOCK	MEANY	MECHANIST	MEDIANS
MEACOCKS	MEARE	MECHANIZE	MEDIANT
MEAD	MEARES	MECHITZA	MEDIANTS
MEADOW	MEARING	MECHITZAS	MEDIAS
MEADOWS	MEASE	MECHITZOT	MEDIATE
MEADOWY	MEASED	MECK	MEDIATED
MEADS	MEASES	MECKS	MEDIATELY
MEAGER	MEASING	MECLIZINE	MEDIATES
MEAGERLY	MEASLE	MECONATE	MEDIATING
MEAGRE	MEASLED	MECONATES	MEDIATION
MEAGRELY	MEASLES	MECONIC	MEDIATISE
MEAGRER	MEASLIER	MECONIN	MEDIATIVE
MEAGRES	MEASLIEST	MECONINS	MEDIATIZE
MEAGREST	MEASLING	MECONIUM	MEDIATOR
MEAL	MEASLY	MECONIUMS	MEDIATORS
MEALED	MEASURE	MED	MEDIATORY
MEALER	MEASURED	MEDACCA	MEDIATRIX
MEALERS	MEASURER	MEDACCAS	MEDIC
MEALIE	MEASURERS	MEDAILLON	MEDICABLE
MEALIER	MEASURES	MEDAKA	MEDICABLY
MEALIES	MEASURING	MEDAKAS	MEDICAID
MEALIEST	MEAT	MEDAL	MEDICAIDS
MEALINESS	MEATAL	MEDALED	MEDICAL
MEALING	MEATAXE	MEDALET	MEDICALLY
MEALLESS	MEATAXES	MEDALETS	MEDICALS
MEALS	MEATBALL	MEDALING	MEDICANT
MEALTIME	MEATBALLS	MEDALIST	MEDICANTS
MEALTIMES	MEATED	MEDALISTS	MEDICARE
MEALWORM	MEATH	MEDALLED	MEDICARES
MEALWORMS	MEATHE	MEDALLIC	MEDICATE
MEALY	MEATHEAD	MEDALLING	MEDICATED
MEALYBUG	MEATHEADS	MEDALLION	MEDICATES
MEALYBUGS	MEATHES	MEDALLIST	MEDICIDE
MEAN	MEATHS	MEDALS	MEDICIDES

MEDICINAL	MEEK	MEGAGAUSS	MEINED
MEDICINE	MEEKEN	MEGAHERTZ	MEINEY
MEDICINED	MEEKENED	MEGAHIT	MEINEYS
MEDICINER	MEEKENING	MEGAHITS	MEINIE
MEDICINES	MEEKENS	MEGAJOULE	MEINIES
MEDICK	MEEKER	MEGALITH	MEINING
MEDICKS	MEEKEST	MEGALITHS	MEINS
MEDICO	MEEKLY	MEGALITRE	MEINT
MEDICOS	MEEKNESS	MEGALOPIC	MEINY
MEDICS	MEEMIE	MEGALOPS	MEIOCYTE
MEDIEVAL	MEEMIES	MEGAPHONE	MEIOCYTES
MEDIEVALS	MEER	MEGAPHYLL	MEIOFAUNA
MEDIGAP	MEERCAT	MEGAPIXEL	MEIONITE
MEDIGAPS	MEERCATS	MEGAPLEX	MEIONITES
MEDII	MEERED	MEGAPOD	MEIOSES
MEDINA	MEERING	MEGAPODE	MEIOSIS
MEDINAS	MEERKAT	MEGAPODES	MEIOSPORE
MEDIOCRE	MEERKATS	MEGAPODS	MEIOTIC
MEDITATE	MEERS	MEGARA	MEISHI
MEDITATED	MEES	MEGARAD	MEISHIS
MEDITATES	MEET	MEGARADS	MEISTER
MEDITATOR	MEETER	MEGARON	MEISTERS
MEDIUM	MEETERS	MEGARONS	MEITH
MEDIUMS	MEETEST	MEGASCOPE	MEITHS
MEDIUS	MEETING	MEGASPORE	MEJLIS
MEDIUSES	MEETINGS	MEGASS	MEJLISES
MEDIVAC	MEETLY	MEGASSE	MEKKA
MEDIVACED	MEETNESS	MEGASSES	MEKKAS
MEDIVACS	MEETS	MEGASTAR	MEKOMETER
MEDLAR	MEFF	MEGASTARS	MEL
MEDLARS	MEFFS	MEGASTORE	MELA
MEDLE	MEG	MEGATHERE	MELALEUCA
MEDLED	MEGA	MEGATON	MELAMDIM
MEDLES	MEGABAR	MEGATONIC	MELAMED
MEDLEY	MEGABARS	MEGATONS	MELAMINE
MEDLEYS	MEGABIT	MEGAVOLT	MELAMINES
MEDLING	MEGABITS	MEGAVOLTS	MELAMPODE
MEDRESE	MEGABUCK	MEGAWATT	MELANGE
MEDRESES	MEGABUCKS	MEGAWATTS	MELANGES
MEDRESSEH	MEGABYTE	MEGILLA	MELANIAN
MEDS	MEGABYTES	MEGILLAH	MELANIC
MEDULLA	MEGACITY	MEGILLAHS	MELANICS
MEDULLAE	MEGACURIE	MEGILLAS	MELANIN
MEDULLAR	MEGACYCLE	MEGILLOTH	MELANINS
MEDULLARY	MEGADEAL	MEGILP	MELANISE
MEDULLAS	MEGADEALS	MEGILPH	MELANISED
MEDULLATE	MEGADEATH	MEGILPHS	MELANISES
MEDUSA	MEGADOSE	MEGILPS	MELANISM
MEDUSAE	MEGADOSES	MEGOHM	MELANISMS
MEDUSAL	MEGADYNE	MEGOHMS	MELANIST
MEDUSAN	MEGADYNES	MEGRIM	MELANISTS
MEDUSANS	MEGAFARAD	MEGRIMS	MELANITE
MEDUSAS	MEGAFAUNA	MEGS	MELANITES
MEDUSOID	MEGAFLOP	MEHNDI	MELANITIC
MEDUSOIDS	MEGAFLOPS	MEHNDIS	MELANIZE
MEE	MEGAFLORA	MEIBOMIAN	MELANIZED
MEED	MEGAFOG	MEIKLE	MELANIZES
MEEDS	MEGAFOGS	MEIN	MELANO

MELANOID	MELLOWING	MELTON	MENAGERIE
MELANOIDS	MELLOWLY	MELTONS	MENAGES
MELANOMA	MELLOWS	MELTS	MENACING
MELANOMAS	MELLOWY	MELTWATER	MENARCHE
MELANOS	MELLS	MELTY	MENARCHES
MELANOSES	MELOCOTON	MELUNGEON	MENAZON
MELANOSIS	MELODEON	MEM	MENAZONS
MELANOTIC	MELODEONS	MEMBER	MEND
MELANOUS	MELODIA	MEMBERED	MENDABLE
MELANURIA	MELODIAS	MEMBERS	MENDACITY
MELANURIC	MELODIC	MEMBRAL	MENDED
MELAPHYRE	MELODICA	MEMBRANAL	MENDER
MELAS	MELODICAS	MEMBRANE	MENDERS
MELASTOME	MELODICS	MEMBRANED	MENDICANT
MELATONIN	MELODIES	MEMBRANES	MENDICITY
MELD	MELODION	MEME	MENDIGO
MELDED	MELODIONS	MEMENTO	MENDIGOS
MELDER	MELODIOUS	MEMENTOES	MENDING
MELDERS	MELODISE	MEMENTOS	MENDINGS
MELDING	MELODISED	MEMES	MENDS
MELDS	MELODISER	MEMETICS	MENE
MELEE	MELODISES	MEMO	MENED
MELEES	MELODIST	MEMOIR	MENEER
MELENA	MELODISTS	MEMOIRISM	MENEERS
MELENAS	MELODIZE	MEMOIRIST	MENES
MELIC	MELODIZED	MEMOIRS	MENFOLK
MELICK	MELODIZER	MEMORABLE	MENFOLKS
MELICKS	MELODIZES	MEMORABLY	MENG
MELICS	MELODRAMA	MEMORANDA	MENGE
MELIK	MELODRAME	MEMORIAL	MENGED
MELIKS	MELODY	MEMORIALS	MENGES
MELILITE	MELOID	MEMORIES	MENGING
MELILITES	MELOIDS	MEMORISE	MENGS
MELILOT	MELOMANIA	MEMORISED	MENHADEN
MELILOTS	MELOMANIC	MEMORISER	MENHADENS
MELINITE	MELON	MEMORISES	MENHIR
MELINITES	MELONGENE	MEMORITER	MENHIRS
MELIORATE	MELONS	MEMORIZE	MENIAL
MELIORISM	MELPHALAN	MEMORIZED	MENIALLY
MELIORIST	MELS	MEMORIZER	MENIALS
MELIORITY	MELT	MEMORIZES	MENILITE
MELISMA	MELTABLE	MEMORY	MENILITES
MELISMAS	MELTAGE	MEMOS	MENING
MELISMATA	MELTAGES	MEMS	MENINGEAL
MELL	MELTDOWN	MEMSAHIB	MENINGES
MELLAY	MELTDOWNS	MEMSAHIBS	MENINX
MELLAYS	MELTED	MEN	MENISCAL
MELLED	MELTEMI	MENACE	MENISCATE
MELLIFIC	MELTEMIS	MENACED	MENISCI
MELLING	MELTER	MENACER	MENISCOID
MELLITE	MELTERS	MENACERS	MENISCUS
MELLITES	MELTIER	MENACES	MENO
MELLITIC	MELTIEST	MENACING	MENOLOGY
MELLOTRON	MELTING	MENAD	MENOMINEE
MELLOW	MELTINGLY	MENADIONE	MENOMINI
MELLOWED	MELTINGS	MENADS	MENOMINIS
MELLOWER	MELTITH	MENAGE	MENOPAUSE
MELLOWEST	MELTITHS	MENAGED	MENOPOLIS

MENOPOME	MENTUM	MERCUROUS	MERIT
MENOPOMES	MENU	MERCURY	MERITED
MENORAH	MENUDO	MERCY	MERITING
MENORAHS	MENUDOS	MERDE	MERITLESS
MENORRHEA	MENUISIER	MERDES	MERITS
MENSA	MENUS	MERE	MERK
MENSAE	MENYIE	MERED	MERKIN
MENSAL	MENYIES	MEREL	MERKINS
MENSAS	MEOU	MERELL	MERKS
MENSCH	MEOUED	MERELLS	MERL
MENSCHEN	MEOUING	MERELS	MERLE
MENSCHES	MEOUS	MERELY	MERLES
MENSCHY	MEOW	MERENGUE	MERLIN
MENSE	MEOWED	MERENGUES	MERLING
MENSED	MEOWING	MEREOLOGY	MERLINGS
MENSEFUL	MEOWS	MERER	MERLINS
MENSELESS	MEPACRINE	MERES	MERLON
MENSES	MEPHITIC	MERESMAN	MERLONS
MENSH	MEPHITIS	MERESMEN	MERLOT
MENSHED	MEPHITISM	MEREST	MERLOTS
MENSHEN	MERANTI	MERESTONE	MERLS
MENSHES	MERANTIS	MERFOLK	MERMAID
MENSHING	MERBROMIN	MERFOLKS	MERMAIDEN
MENSING	MERC	MERGANSER	MERMAIDS
MENSTRUA	MERCAPTAN	MERGE	MERMAN
MENSTRUAL	MERCAPTO	MERGED	MERMEN
MENSTRUUM	MERCAT	MERGEE	MEROCRINE
MENSUAL	MERCATS	MERGEES	MEROGONY
MENSURAL	MERCENARY	MERGENCE	MEROISTIC
MENSWEAR	MERCER	MERGENCES	MEROME
MENSWEARS	MERCERIES	MERGER	MEROMES
MENT	MERCERISE	MERGERS	MERONYM
MENTA	MERCERIZE	MERGES	MERONYMS
MENTAL	MERCERS	MERGING	MERONYMY
MENTALESE	MERCERY	MERGINGS	MEROPIA
MENTALISM	MERCES	MERI	MEROPIAS
MENTALIST	MERCH	MERICARP	MEROPIC
MENTALITY	MERCHANT	MERICARPS	MEROPIDAN
MENTALLY	MERCHANTS	MERIDIAN	MEROSOME
MENTATION	MERCHES	MERIDIANS	MEROSOMES
MENTEE	MERCHET	MERIL	MEROZOITE
MENTEES	MERCHETS	MERILS	MERPEOPLE
MENTHENE	MERCHILD	MERIMAKE	MERRIER
MENTHENES	MERCIABLE	MERIMAKES	MERRIES
MENTHOL	MERCIES	MERING	MERRIEST
MENTHOLS	MERCIFIDE	MERINGS	MERRILY
MENTICIDE	MERCIFIED	MERINGUE	MERRIMENT
MENTION	MERCIFIES	MERINGUES	MERRINESS
MENTIONED	MERCIFUL	MERINO	MERRY
MENTIONER	MERCIFY	MERINOS	MERRYMAN
MENTIONS	MERCILESS	MERIS	MERRYMEN
MENTO	MERCS	MERISES	MERSALYL
MENTOR	MERCURATE	MERISIS	MERSALYLS
MENTORED	MERCURIAL	MERISM	MERSE
MENTORIAL	MERCURIC	MERISMS	MERSES
MENTORING	MERCURIES	MERISTEM	MERSION
MENTORS	MERCURISE	MERISTEMS	MERSIONS
MENTOS	MERCURIZE	MERISTIC	MERYCISM

MERYCISMS	MESMERISM	MESSES	METALISED
MES	MESMERIST	MESSIAH	METALISES
MESA	MESMERIZE	MESSIAHS	METALIST
MESAIL	MESNALTY	MESSIANIC	METALISTS
MESAILS	MESNE	MESSIAS	METALIZE
MESAL	MESNES	MESSIASES	METALIZED
MESALLY	MESOBLAST	MESSIER	METALIZES
MESARAIC	MESOCARP	MESSIEST	METALLED
MESARCH	MESOCARPS	MESSIEURS	METALLIC
MESAS	MESOCRANY	MESSILY	METALLICS
MESCAL	MESODERM	MESSINESS	METALLIKE
MESCALIN	MESODERMS	MESSING	METALLINE
MESCALINE	MESOGLEA	MESSMAN	METALLING
MESCALINS	MESOGLEAL	MESSMATE	METALLISE
MESCALISM	MESOGLEAS	MESSMATES	METALLIST
MESCALS	MESOGLOEA	MESSMEN	METALLIZE
MESCLUM	MESOLITE	MESSUAGE	METALLOID
MESCLUMS	MESOLITES	MESSUAGES	METALLY
MESCLUN	MESOMERE	MESSY	METALMARK
MESCLUNS	MESOMERES	MESTEE	METALS
MESDAMES	MESOMORPH	MESTEES	METALWARE
MESE	MESON	MESTER	METALWORK
MESEEMED	MESONIC	MESTERS	METAMALE
MESEEMETH	MESONS	MESTESO	METAMALES
MESEEMS	MESOPAUSE	MESTESOES	METAMER
MESEL	MESOPHILE	MESTESOS	METAMERAL
MESELED	MESOPHYL	MESTINO	METAMERE
MESELS	MESOPHYLL	MESTINOES	METAMERES
MESENTERA	MESOPHYLS	MESTINOS	METAMERIC
MESENTERY	MESOPHYTE	MESTIZA	METAMERS
MESES	MESOSCALE	MESTIZAS	METAMICT
MESETA	MESOSOME	MESTIZO	METANOIA
MESETAS	MESOSOMES	MESTIZOES	METANOIAS
MESH	MESOTRON	MESTIZOS	METAPELET
MESHED	MESOTRONS	MESTO	METAPHASE
MESHES	MESOZOAN	MESTOM	METAPHOR
MESHIER	MESOZOANS	MESTOME	METAPHORS
MESHIEST	MESOZOIC	MESTOMES	METAPLASM
MESHING	MESPRISE	MESTOMS	METAPLOT
MESHINGS	MESPRISES	MESTRANOL	METARCHON
MESHUGA	MESPRIZE	MET	METASOMA
MESHUGAAS	MESPRIZES	META	METASOMAS
MESHUGAH	MESQUIN	METABASES	METATAG
MESHUGAS	MESQUINE	METABASIS	METATAGS
MESHUGGA	MESQUIT	METABATIC	METATARSI
MESHUGGAH	MESQUITE	METABOLIC	METATE
MESHUGGE	MESQUITES	METABOLY	METATES
MESHWORK	MESQUITS	METACARPI	METAXYLEM
MESHWORKS	MESS	METAGE	METAYAGE
MESHY	MESSAGE	METAGENIC	METAYAGES
MESIAD	MESSAGED	METAGES	METAYER
MESIAL	MESSAGES	METAIRIE	METAYERS
MESIALLY	MESSAGING	METAIRIES	METAZOA
MESIAN	MESSALINE	METAL	METAZOAL
MESIC	MESSAN	METALED	METAZOAN
MESICALLY	MESSANS	METALHEAD	METAZOANS
MESMERIC	MESSED	METALING	METAZOIC
MESMERISE	MESSENGER	METALISE	METAZOON

METCAST	METHYLALS	METRIST	MEZUZAHS
METCASTS	METHYLASE	METRISTS	MEZUZAS
METE	METHYLATE	METRITIS	MEZUZOT
METED	METHYLENE	METRO	MEZUZOTH
METEOR	METHYLIC	METROLOGY	MEZZ
METEORIC	METHYLS	METRONOME	MEZZALUNA
METEORISM	METHYSES	METROPLEX	MEZZANINE
METEORIST	METHYSIS	METROS	MEZZE
METEORITE	METHYSTIC	METS	MEZZES
METEOROID	METIC	METTLE	MEZZO
METEOROUS	METICAIS	METTLED	MEZZOS
METEORS	METICAL	METTLES	MEZZOTINT
METEPA	METICALS	METUMP	MGANGA
METEPAS	METICS	METUMPS	MGANGAS
METER	METIER	MEU	MHO
METERAGE	METIERS	MEUNIERE	MHORR
METERAGES	METIF	MEUS	MHORRS
METERED	METIFS	MEUSE	MHOS
METERING	METING	MEUSED	MI
METERS	METIS	MEUSES	MIAOU
METES	METISSE	MEUSING	MIAOUED
METESTICK	METISSES	MEVE	MIAOUING
METESTRUS	METOL	MEVED	MIAOUS
METEWAND	METOLS	MEVES	MIAOW
METEWANDS	METONYM	MEVING	MIAOWED
METEYARD	METONYMIC	MEVROU	MIAOWING
METEYARDS	METONYMS	MEVROUS	MIAOWS
METFORMIN	METONYMY	MEW	MIASM
METH	METOPAE	MEWED	MIASMA
METHADON	METOPE	MEWING	MIASMAL
METHADONE	METOPES	MEWL	MIASMAS
METHADONS	METOPIC	MEWLED	MIASMATA
METHANAL	METOPISM	MEWLER	MIASMATIC
METHANALS	METOPISMS	MEWLERS	MIASMIC
METHANE	METOPON	MEWLING	MIASMOUS
METHANES	METOPONS	MEWLS	MIASMS
METHANOIC	METOPRYL	MEWS	MIAUL
METHANOL	METOPRYLS	MEWSED	MIAULED
METHANOLS	METRALGIA	MEWSES	MIAULING
METHEGLIN	METRAZOL	MEWSING	MIAULS
METHINK	METRAZOLS	MEYNT	MIB
METHINKS	METRE	MEZAIL	MIBS
METHO	METRED	MEZAILS	MIC
METHOD	METRES	MEZCAL	MICA
METHODIC	METRIC	MEZCALINE	MICACEOUS
METHODISE	METRICAL	MEZCALS	MICAS
METHODISM	METRICATE	MEZE	MICATE
METHODIST	METRICIAN	MEZEREON	MICATED
METHODIZE	METRICISE	MEZEREONS	MICATES
METHODS	METRICISM	MEZEREUM	MICATING
METHOS	METRICIST	MEZEREUMS	MICAWBER
METHOUGHT	METRICIZE	MEZES	MICAWBERS
METHOXIDE	METRICS	MEZQUIT	MICE
METHOXY	METRIFIED	MEZQUITE	MICELL
METHOXYL	METRIFIER	MEZQUITES	MICELLA
METHS	METRIFIES	MEZQUITS	MICELLAE
METHYL	METRIFY	MEZUZA	MICELLAR
METHYLAL	METRING	MEZUZAH	MICELLAS

MICELLE	MICROGLIA	MIDDLED	MIDRIFFS
MICELLES	MICROGRAM	MIDDLEMAN	MIDS
MICELLS	MICROHM	MIDDLEMEN	MIDSHIP
MICH	MICROHMS	MIDDLER	MIDSHIPS
MICHE	MICROINCH	MIDDLERS	MIDSIZE
MICHED	MICROJET	MIDDLES	MIDSIZED
MICHER	MICROJETS	MIDDLING	MIDSOLE
MICHERS	MICROLITE	MIDDLINGS	MIDSOLES
MICHES	MICROLITH	MIDDORSAL	MIDSPACE
MICHIGAN	MICROLOAN	MIDDY	MIDSPACES
MICHIGANS	MICROLOGY	MIDFIELD	MIDST
MICHING	MICROLUX	MIDFIELDS	MIDSTORY
MICHINGS	MICROMERE	MIDGE	MIDSTREAM
MICHT	MICROMESH	MIDGES	MIDSTS
MICHTS	MICROMHO	MIDGET	MIDSUMMER
MICK	MICROMHOS	MIDGETS	MIDTERM
MICKEY	MICROMINI	MIDGIE	MIDTERMS
MICKEYED	MICROMOLE	MIDGIES	MIDTOWN
MICKEYING	MICRON	MIDGUT	MIDTOWNS
MICKEYS	MICRONISE	MIDGUTS	MIDWATCH
MICKIES	MICRONIZE	MIDGY	MIDWAY
MICKLE	MICRONS	MIDI	MIDWAYS
MICKLER	MICROPORE	MIDINETTE	MIDWEEK
MICKLES	MICROPSIA	MIDIRON	MIDWEEKLY
MICKLEST	MICROPUMP	MIDIRONS	MIDWEEKS
MICKS	MICROPYLE	MIDIS	MIDWIFE
MICKY	MICROS	MIDISKIRT	MIDWIFED
MICO	MICROSITE	MIDLAND	MIDWIFERY
MICOS	MICROSOME	MIDLANDS	MIDWIFES
MICRA	MICROTOME	MIDLEG	MIDWIFING
MICRIFIED	MICROTOMY	MIDLEGS	MIDWINTER
MICRIFIES	MICROTONE	MIDLIFE	MIDWIVE
MICRIFY	MICROVOLT	MIDLIFER	MIDWIVED
MICRO	MICROWATT	MIDLIFERS	MIDWIVES
MICROBAR	MICROWAVE	MIDLINE	MIDWIVING
MICROBARS	MICROWIRE	MIDLINES	MIDYEAR
MICROBE	MICRURGY	MIDLIST	MIDYEARS
MICROBEAM	MICS	MIDLISTS	MIELIE
MICROBES	MICTION	MIDLIVES	MIELIES
MICROBIAL	MICTIONS	MIDMONTH	MIEN
MICROBIAN	MICTURATE	MIDMONTHS	MIENS
MICROBIC	MID	MIDMOST	MIEVE
MICROBREW	MIDAIR	MIDMOSTS	MIEVED
MICROBUS	MIDAIRS	MIDNIGHT	MIEVES
MICROCAP	MIDBRAIN	MIDNIGHTS	MIEVING
MICROCAR	MIDBRAINS	MIDNOON	MIFF
MICROCARD	MIDCAP	MIDNOONS	MIFFED
MICROCARS	MIDCOURSE	MIDPOINT	MIFFIER
MICROCHIP	MIDCULT	MIDPOINTS	MIFFIEST
MICROCODE	MIDCULTS	MIDRANGE	MIFFILY
MICROCOPY	MIDDAY	MIDRANGES	MIFFINESS
MICROCOSM	MIDDAYS	MIDRASH	MIFFING
MICROCYTE	MIDDEN	MIDRASHIC	MIFFS
MICRODONT	MIDDENS	MIDRASHIM	MIFFY
MICRODOT	MIDDEST	MIDRASHOT	MIFTY
MICRODOTS	MIDDIE	MIDRIB	MIG
MICROFILM	MIDDIES	MIDRIBS	MIGG
MICROFORM	MIDDLE	MIDRIFF	MIGGLE

MIGGLES	MILAGE	MILKED	MILLIARD
MIGGS	MILAGES	MILKEN	MILLIARDS
MIGHT	MILCH	MILKER	MILLIARE
MIGHTEST	MILCHIG	MILKERS	MILLIARES
MIGHTFUL	MILCHIK	MILKFISH	MILLIARY
MIGHTIER	MILD	MILKIER	MILLIBAR
MIGHTIEST	MILDED	MILKIEST	MILLIBARS
MIGHTILY	MILDEN	MILKILY	MILLIE
MIGHTS	MILDENED	MILKINESS	MILLIEME
MIGHTST	MILDENING	MILKING	MILLIEMES
MIGHTY	MILDENS	MILKINGS	MILLIER
MIGMATITE	MILDER	MILKLESS	MILLIERS
MIGNON	MILDEST	MILKLIKE	MILLIES
MIGNONNE	MILDEW	MILKMAID	MILLIGAL
MIGNONS	MILDEWED	MILKMAIDS	MILLIGALS
MIGRAINE	MILDEWING	MILKMAN	MILLIGRAM
MIGRAINES	MILDEWS	MILKMEN	MILLILUX
MIGRANT	MILDEWY	MILKO	MILLIME
MIGRANTS	MILDING	MILKOS	MILLIMES
MIGRATE	MILDLY	MILKS	MILLIMHO
MIGRATED	MILDNESS	MILKSHAKE	MILLIMHOS
MIGRATES	MILDS	MILKSHED	MILLIMOLE
MIGRATING	MILE	MILKSHEDS	MILLINE
MIGRATION	MILEAGE	MILKSOP	MILLINER
MIGRATOR	MILEAGES	MILKSOPPY	MILLINERS
MIGRATORS	MILEPOST	MILKSOPS	MILLINERY
MIGRATORY	MILEPOSTS	MILKTOAST	MILLINES
MIGS	MILER	MILKWEED	MILLING
MIHA	MILERS	MILKWEEDS	MILLINGS
MIHI	MILES	MILKWOOD	MILLIOHM
MIHIED	MILESIAN	MILKWOODS	MILLIOHMS
MIHIING	MILESIMO	MILKWORT	MILLION
MIHIS	MILESIMOS	MILKWORTS	MILLIONS
MIHRAB	MILESTONE	MILKY	MILLIONTH
MIHRABS	MILFOIL	MILL	MILLIPED
MIJNHEER	MILFOILS	MILLABLE	MILLIPEDE
MIJNHEERS	MILIA	MILLAGE	MILLIPEDS
MIKADO	MILIARIA	MILLAGES	MILLIREM
MIKADOS	MILIARIAL	MILLBOARD	MILLIREMS
MIKE	MILIARIAS	MILLCAKE	MILLIVOLT
MIKED	MILIARY	MILLCAKES	MILLIWATT
MIKES	MILIEU	MILLDAM	MILLOCRAT
MIKING	MILIEUS	MILLDAMS	MILLPOND
MIKRA	MILIEUX	MILLE	MILLPONDS
MIKRON	MILITANCE	MILLED	MILLRACE
MIKRONS	MILITANCY	MILLENARY	MILLRACES
MIKVAH	MILITANT	MILLENNIA	MILLRIND
MIKVAHS	MILITANTS	MILLEPED	MILLRINDS
MIKVEH	MILITAR	MILLEPEDE	MILLRUN
MIKVEHS	MILITARIA	MILLEPEDS	MILLRUNS
MIKVOS	MILITARY	MILLEPORE	MILLS
MIKVOT	MILITATE	MILLER	MILLSCALE
MIKVOTH	MILITATED	MILLERITE	MILLSTONE
MIL	MILITATES	MILLERS	MILLTAIL
MILADI	MILITIA	MILLES	MILLTAILS
MILADIES	MILITIAS	MILLET	MILLWHEEL
MILADIS	MILIUM	MILLETS	MILLWORK
MILADY	MILK	MILLHOUSE	MILLWORKS

MILNEB
MILNEBS
MILO
MILOMETER
MILOR
MILORD
MILORDS
MILORS
MILOS
MILPA
MILPAS
MILREIS
MILS
MILSEY
MILSEYS
MILT
MILTED
MILTER
MILTERS
MILTIER
MILTIEST
MILTING
MILTONIA
MILTONIAS
MILTS
MILTY
MILTZ
MILTZES
MILVINE
MIM
MIMBAR
MIMBARS
MIME
MIMED
MIMEO
MIMEOED
MIMEOING
MIMEOS
MIMER
MIMERS
MIMES
MIMESES
MIMESIS
MIMESISES
MIMESTER
MIMESTERS
MIMETIC
MIMETICAL
MIMETITE
MIMETITES
MIMIC
MIMICAL
MIMICKED
MIMICKER
MIMICKERS
MIMICKING
MIMICRIES
MIMICRY

MIMICS
MIMING
MIMMER
MIMMEST
MIMMICK
MIMMICKED
MIMMICKS
MIMOSA
MIMOSAS
MIMSEY
MIMSIER
MIMSIEST
MIMSY
MIMULUS
MIMULUSES
MINA
MINABLE
MINACIOUS
MINACITY
MINAE
MINAR
MINARET
MINARETED
MINARETS
MINARS
MINAS
MINATORY
MINBAR
MINBARS
MINCE
MINCED
MINCEMEAT
MINCER
MINCERS
MINCES
MINCEUR
MINCIER
MINCIEST
MINCING
MINCINGLY
MINCINGS
MINCY
MIND
MINDED
MINDER
MINDERS
MINDFUCK
MINDFUCKS
MINDFUL
MINDFULLY
MINDING
MINDINGS
MINDLESS
MINDS
MINDSET
MINDSETS
MINDSHARE
MINE

MINEABLE
MINED
MINEFIELD
MINELAYER
MINEOLA
MINEOLAS
MINER
MINERAL
MINERALS
MINERS
MINES
MINESHAFT
MINESTONE
MINETTE
MINETTES
MINEVER
MINEVERS
MING
MINGE
MINGED
MINGER
MINGERS
MINGES
MINGIER
MINGIEST
MINGIN
MINGINESS
MINGING
MINGLE
MINGLED
MINGLER
MINGLERS
MINGLES
MINGLING
MINGLINGS
MINGS
MINGY
MINI
MINIATE
MINIATED
MINIATES
MINIATING
MINIATION
MINIATURE
MINIBAR
MINIBARS
MINIBIKE
MINIBIKER
MINIBIKES
MINIBREAK
MINIBUS
MINIBUSES
MINICAB
MINICABS
MINICAM
MINICAMP
MINICAMPS
MINICAMS

MINICAR
MINICARS
MINICOM
MINICOMS
MINIDISC
MINIDISCS
MINIDISH
MINIDISK
MINIDISKS
MINIDRESS
MINIER
MINIEST
MINIFIED
MINIFIES
MINIFY
MINIFYING
MINIKIN
MINIKINS
MINILAB
MINILABS
MINIM
MINIMA
MINIMAL
MINIMALLY
MINIMALS
MINIMAX
MINIMAXED
MINIMAXES
MINIMENT
MINIMENTS
MINIMILL
MINIMILLS
MINIMISE
MINIMISED
MINIMISER
MINIMISES
MINIMISM
MINIMISMS
MINIMIST
MINIMISTS
MINIMIZE
MINIMIZED
MINIMIZER
MINIMIZES
MINIMOTO
MINIMOTOS
MINIMS
MINIMUM
MINIMUMS
MINIMUS
MINIMUSES
MINING
MININGS
MINION
MINIONS
MINIPARK
MINIPARKS
MINIPILL

MINIPILLS	MINSTRELS	MIRADORS	MIS
MINIRUGBY	MINT	MIRAGE	MISACT
MINIS	MINTAGE	MIRAGES	MISACTED
MINISCULE	MINTAGES	MIRANDISE	MISACTING
MINISH	MINTED	MIRANDIZE	MISACTS
MINISHED	MINTER	MIRBANE	MISADAPT
MINISHES	MINTERS	MIRBANES	MISADAPTS
MINISHING	MINTIER	MIRCHI	MISADD
MINISKI	MINTIEST	MIRE	MISADDED
MINISKIRT	MINTING	MIRED	MISADDING
MINISKIS	MINTS	MIREPOIX	MISADDS
MINISTATE	MINTY	MIRES	MISADJUST
MINISTER	MINUEND	MIREX	MISADVICE
MINISTERS	MINUENDS	MIREXES	MISADVISE
MINISTRY	MINUET	MIRI	MISAGENT
MINITOWER	MINUETS	MIRIER	MISAGENTS
MINITRACK	MINUS	MIRIEST	MISAIM
MINIUM	MINUSCULE	MIRIFIC	MISAIMED
MINIUMS	MINUSES	MIRIFICAL	MISAIMING
MINIVAN	MINUTE	MIRIN	MISAIMS
MINIVANS	MINUTED	MIRINESS	MISALIGN
MINIVER	MINUTELY	MIRING	MISALIGNS
MINIVERS	MINUTEMAN	MIRINS	MISALLEGE
MINIVET	MINUTEMEN	MIRITI	MISALLIED
MINIVETS	MINUTER	MIRITIS	MISALLIES
MINK	MINUTES	MIRK	MISALLOT
MINKE	MINUTEST	MIRKER	MISALLOTS
MINKES	MINUTIA	MIRKEST	MISALLY
MINKS	MINUTIAE	MIRKIER	MISALTER
MINNEOLA	MINUTIAL	MIRKIEST	MISALTERS
MINNEOLAS	MINUTING	MIRKILY	MISANDRY
MINNICK	MINUTIOSE	MIRKINESS	MISAPPLY
MINNICKED	MINX	MIRKS	MISARRAY
MINNICKS	MINXES	MIRKY	MISARRAYS
MINNIE	MINXISH	MIRLIER	MISASSAY
MINNIES	MINY	MIRLIEST	MISASSAYS
MINNOCK	MINYAN	MIRLIGOES	MISASSIGN
MINNOCKED	MINYANIM	MIRLITON	MISATE
MINNOCKS	MINYANS	MIRLITONS	MISATONE
MINNOW	MIOCENE	MIRLY	MISATONED
MINNOWS	MIOMBO	MIRO	MISATONES
MINNY	MIOMBOS	MIROMIRO	MISAUNTER
MINO	MIOSES	MIRROR	MISAVER
MINOR	MIOSIS	MIRRORED	MISAVERS
MINORCA	MIOTIC	MIRRORING	MISAVISED
MINORCAS	MIOTICS	MIRRORS	MISAWARD
MINORED	MIPS	MIRS	MISAWARDS
MINORING	MIQUELET	MIRTH	MISBECAME
MINORITY	MIQUELETS	MIRTHFUL	MISBECOME
MINORS	MIR	MIRTHLESS	MISBEGAN
MINORSHIP	MIRABELLE	MIRTHS	MISBEGIN
MINOS	MIRABILIA	MIRV	MISBEGINS
MINOXIDIL	MIRABILIS	MIRVED	MISBEGOT
MINSHUKU	MIRABLE	MIRVING	MISBEGUN
MINSHUKUS	MIRACIDIA	MIRVS	MISBEHAVE
MINSTER	MIRACLE	MIRY	MISBELIEF
MINSTERS	MIRACLES	MIRZA	MISBESEEM
MINSTREL	MIRADOR	MIRZAS	MISBESTOW

MISBIAS	MISCOOKED	MISDREAD	MISFIELDS
MISBIASED	MISCOOKS	MISDREADS	MISFILE
MISBIASES	MISCOPIED	MISDREW	MISFILED
MISBILL	MISCOPIES	MISDRIVE	MISFILES
MISBILLED	MISCOPY	MISDRIVEN	MISFILING
MISBILLS	MISCOUNT	MISDRIVES	MISFIRE
MISBIND	MISCOUNTS	MISDROVE	MISFIRED
MISBINDS	MISCREANT	MISE	MISFIRES
MISBIRTH	MISCREATE	MISEASE	MISFIRING
MISBIRTHS	MISCREDIT	MISEASES	MISFIT
MISBORN	MISCREED	MISEAT	MISFITS
MISBOUND	MISCREEDS	MISEATEN	MISFITTED
MISBRAND	MISCUE	MISEATING	MISFOCUS
MISBRANDS	MISCUED	MISEATS	MISFORM
MISBUILD	MISCUEING	MISEDIT	MISFORMED
MISBUILDS	MISCUES	MISEDITED	MISFORMS
MISBUILT	MISCUING	MISEDITS	MISFRAME
MISBUTTON	MISCUT	MISEMPLOY	MISFRAMED
MISCALL	MISCUTS	MISENROL	MISFRAMES
MISCALLED	MISDATE	MISENROLL	MISGAUGE
MISCALLER	MISDATED	MISENROLS	MISGAUGED
MISCALLS	MISDATES	MISENTER	MISGAUGES
MISCARRY	MISDATING	MISENTERS	MISGAVE
MISCAST	MISDEAL	MISENTRY	MISGIVE
MISCASTS	MISDEALER	MISER	MISGIVEN
MISCEGEN	MISDEALS	MISERABLE	MISGIVES
MISCEGENE	MISDEALT	MISERABLY	MISGIVING
MISCEGENS	MISDEED	MISERE	MISGO
MISCEGINE	MISDEEDS	MISERERE	MISGOES
MISCH	MISDEEM	MISERERES	MISGOING
MISCHANCE	MISDEEMED	MISERES	MISGONE
MISCHANCY	MISDEEMS	MISERIES	MISGOTTEN
MISCHARGE	MISDEFINE	MISERLIER	MISGOVERN
MISCHIEF	MISDEMEAN	MISERLY	MISGRADE
MISCHIEFS	MISDEMPT	MISERS	MISGRADED
MISCHOICE	MISDESERT	MISERY	MISGRADES
MISCHOOSE	MISDIAL	MISES	MISGRAFF
MISCHOSE	MISDIALED	MISESTEEM	MISGRAFT
MISCHOSEN	MISDIALS	MISEVENT	MISGRAFTS
MISCIBLE	MISDID	MISEVENTS	MISGREW
MISCITE	MISDIET	MISFAITH	MISGROW
MISCITED	MISDIETS	MISFAITHS	MISGROWN
MISCITES	MISDIGHT	MISFALL	MISGROWS
MISCITING	MISDIRECT	MISFALLEN	MISGROWTH
MISCLAIM	MISDIVIDE	MISFALLS	MISGUESS
MISCLAIMS	MISDO	MISFALNE	MISGUGGLE
MISCLASS	MISDOER	MISFARE	MISGUIDE
MISCODE	MISDOERS	MISFARED	MISGUIDED
MISCODED	MISDOES	MISFARES	MISGUIDER
MISCODES	MISDOING	MISFARING	MISGUIDES
MISCODING	MISDOINGS	MISFEASOR	MISHANDLE
MISCOIN	MISDONE	MISFED	MISHANTER
MISCOINED	MISDONNE	MISFEED	MISHAP
MISCOINS	MISDOUBT	MISFEEDS	MISHAPPED
MISCOLOR	MISDOUBTS	MISFEIGN	MISHAPPEN
MISCOLORS	MISDRAW	MISFEIGNS	MISHAPS
MISCOLOUR	MISDRAWN	MISFELL	MISHAPT
MISCOOK	MISDRAWS	MISFIELD	MISHEAR

MISHEARD	MISLEADS	MISMOVING	MISPRAISE
MISHEARS	MISLEARED	MISNAME	MISPRICE
MISHEGAAS	MISLEARN	MISNAMED	MISPRICED
MISHEGOSS	MISLEARNS	MISNAMES	MISPRICES
MISHIT	MISLEARNT	MISNAMING	MISPRINT
MISHITS	MISLED	MISNOMER	MISPRINTS
MISHMASH	MISLEEKE	MISNOMERS	MISPRISE
MISHMEE	MISLEEKED	MISNUMBER	MISPRISED
MISHMEES	MISLEEKES	MISO	MISPRISER
MISHMI	MISLETOE	MISOCLERE	MISPRISES
MISHMIS	MISLETOES	MISOGAMIC	MISPRIZE
MISHMOSH	MISLIE	MISOGAMY	MISPRIZED
MISINFER	MISLIES	MISOGYNIC	MISPRIZER
MISINFERS	MISLIGHT	MISOGYNY	MISPRIZES
MISINFORM	MISLIGHTS	MISOLOGY	MISPROUD
MISINTEND	MISLIKE	MISONEISM	MISQUOTE
MISINTER	MISLIKED	MISONEIST	MISQUOTED
MISINTERS	MISLIKER	MISORDER	MISQUOTER
MISJOIN	MISLIKERS	MISORDERS	MISQUOTES
MISJOINED	MISLIKES	MISORIENT	MISRAISE
MISJOINS	MISLIKING	MISOS	MISRAISED
MISJUDGE	MISLIPPEN	MISPAGE	MISRAISES
MISJUDGED	MISLIT	MISPAGED	MISRATE
MISJUDGER	MISLIVE	MISPAGES	MISRATED
MISJUDGES	MISLIVED	MISPAGING	MISRATES
MISKAL	MISLIVES	MISPAINT	MISRATING
MISKALS	MISLIVING	MISPAINTS	MISREAD
MISKEEP	MISLOCATE	MISPARSE	MISREADS
MISKEEPS	MISLODGE	MISPARSED	MISRECKON
MISKEN	MISLODGED	MISPARSES	MISRECORD
MISKENNED	MISLODGES	MISPART	MISREFER
MISKENS	MISLUCK	MISPARTED	MISREFERS
MISKENT	MISLUCKED	MISPARTS	MISREGARD
MISKEPT	MISLUCKS	MISPATCH	MISRELATE
MISKEY	MISLYING	MISPEN	MISRELIED
MISKEYED	MISMADE	MISPENNED	MISRELIES
MISKEYING	MISMAKE	MISPENS	MISRELY
MISKEYS	MISMAKES	MISPHRASE	MISRENDER
MISKICK	MISMAKING	MISPICKEL	MISREPORT
MISKICKED	MISMANAGE	MISPLACE	MISRHYMED
MISKICKS	MISMARK	MISPLACED	MISROUTE
MISKNEW	MISMARKED	MISPLACES	MISROUTED
MISKNOW	MISMARKS	MISPLAN	MISROUTES
MISKNOWN	MISMARRY	MISPLANS	MISRULE
MISKNOWS	MISMATCH	MISPLANT	MISRULED
MISLABEL	MISMATE	MISPLANTS	MISRULES
MISLABELS	MISMATED	MISPLAY	MISRULING
MISLABOR	MISMATES	MISPLAYED	MISS
MISLABORS	MISMATING	MISPLAYS	MISSA
MISLAID	MTSMEET	MISPLEAD	MISSABLE
MISLAIN	MISMEETS	MISPLEADS	MISSAE
MISLAY	MISMET	MISPLEASE	MISSAID
MISLAYER	MISMETRE	MISPLED	MISSAL
MISLAYERS	MISMETRED	MISPOINT	MISSALS
MISLAYING	MISMETRES	MISPOINTS	MISSAW
MISLAYS	MISMOVE	MISPOISE	MISSAY
MISLEAD	MISMOVED	MISPOISED	MISSAYING
MISLEADER	MISMOVES	MISPOISES	MISSAYS

MISSEAT	MISSPACES	MISTERING	MISTUNED
MISSEATED	MISSPEAK	MISTERM	MISTUNES
MISSEATS	MISSPEAKS	MISTERMED	MISTUNING
MISSED	MISSPELL	MISTERMS	MISTUTOR
MISSEE	MISSPELLS	MISTERS	MISTUTORS
MISSEEING	MISSPELT	MISTERY	MISTY
MISSEEM	MISSPEND	MISTEUK	MISTYPE
MISSEEMED	MISSPENDS	MISTFUL	MISTYPED
MISSEEMS	MISSPENT	MISTHINK	MISTYPES
MISSEEN	MISSPOKE	MISTHINKS	MISTYPING
MISSEES	MISSPOKEN	MISTHREW	MISUNION
MISSEL	MISSTAMP	MISTHROW	MISUNIONS
MISSELS	MISSTAMPS	MISTHROWN	MISUSAGE
MISSEND	MISSTART	MISTHROWS	MISUSAGES
MISSENDS	MISSTARTS	MISTICO	MISUSE
MISSENSE	MISSTATE	MISTICOS	MISUSED
MISSENSES	MISSTATED	MISTIER	MISUSER
MISSENT	MISSTATES	MISTIEST	MISUSERS
MISSES	MISSTEER	MISTIGRIS	MISUSES
MISSET	MISSTEERS	MISTILY	MISUSING
MISSETS	MISSTEP	MISTIME	MISUST
MISSHAPE	MISSTEPS	MISTIMED	MISVALUE
MISSHAPED	MISSTOP	MISTIMES	MISVALUED
MISSHAPEN	MISSTOPS	MISTIMING	MISVALUES
MISSHAPER	MISSTRIKE	MISTINESS	MISWEEN
MISSHAPES	MISSTRUCK	MISTING	MISWEENED
MISSHOD	MISSTYLE	MISTINGS	MISWEENS
MISSHOOD	MISSTYLED	MISTITLE	MISWEND
MISSHOODS	MISSTYLES	MISTITLED	MISWENDS
MISSIER	MISSUIT	MISTITLES	MISWENT
MISSIES	MISSUITED	MISTLE	MISWORD
MISSIEST	MISSUITS	MISTLED	MISWORDED
MISSILE	MISSUS	MISTLES	MISWORDS
MISSILEER	MISSUSES	MISTLETOE	MISWRIT
MISSILERY	MISSY	MISTLING	MISWRITE
MISSILES	MIST	MISTOLD	MISWRITES
MISSILRY	MISTAKE	MISTOOK	MISWROTE
MISSING	MISTAKEN	MISTOUCH	MISYOKE
MISSINGLY	MISTAKER	MISTRACE	MISYOKED
MISSION	MISTAKERS	MISTRACED	MISYOKES
MISSIONAL	MISTAKES	MISTRACES	MISYOKING
MISSIONED	MISTAKING	MISTRAIN	MITCH
MISSIONER	MISTAL	MISTRAINS	MITCHED
MISSIONS	MISTALS	MISTRAL	MITCHES
MISSIS	MISTAUGHT	MISTRALS	MITCHING
MISSISES	MISTBOW	MISTREAT	MITE
MISSISH	MISTBOWS	MISTREATS	MITER
MISSIVE	MISTEACH	MISTRESS	MITERED
MISSIVES	MISTED	MISTRIAL	MITERER
MISSORT	MISTELL	MISTRIALS	MITERERS
MISSORTED	MISTELLS	MISTRUST	MITERING
MISSORTS	MISTEMPER	MISTRUSTS	MITERS
MISSOUND	MISTEND	MISTRUTH	MITERWORT
MISSOUNDS	MISTENDED	MISTRUTHS	MITES
MISSOUT	MISTENDS	MISTRYST	MITHER
MISSOUTS	MISTER	MISTRYSTS	MITHERED
MISSPACE	MISTERED	MISTS	MITHERING
MISSPACED	MISTERIES	MISTUNE	MITHERS

MITICIDAL	MIXIER	MOANS	MOCASSIN
MITICIDE	MIXIEST	MOAS	MOCASSINS
MITICIDES	MIXING	MOAT	MOCCASIN
MITIER	MIXMASTER	MOATED	MOCCASINS
MITIEST	MIXOLOGY	MOATING	MOCCIES
MITIGABLE	MIXT	MOATLIKE	MOCH
MITIGANT	MIXTE	MOATS	MOCHA
MITIGATE	MIXTION	MOB	MOCHAS
MITIGATED	MIXTIONS	MOBBED	MOCHELL
MITIGATES	MIXTURE	MOBBER	MOCHELLS
MITIGATOR	MIXTURES	MOBBERS	MOCHIE
MITIS	MIXUP	MOBBIE	MOCHIER
MITISES	MIXUPS	MOBBIES	MOCHIEST
MITOGEN	MIXY	MOBBING	MOCHILA
MITOGENIC	MIZ	MOBBINGS	MOCHILAS
MITOGENS	MIZEN	MOBBISH	MOCHINESS
MITOMYCIN	MIZENMAST	MOBBISHLY	MOCHS
MITOSES	MIZENS	MOBBISM	MOCHY
MITOSIS	MIZMAZE	MOBBISMS	MOCK
MITOTIC	MIZMAZES	MOBBLE	MOCKABLE
MITRAILLE	MIZUNA	MOBBLED	MOCKADO
MITRAL	MIZUNAS	MOBBLES	MOCKADOES
MITRE	MIZZ	MOBBLING	MOCKAGE
MITRED	MIZZEN	MOBBY	MOCKAGES
MITRES	MIZZENS	MOBCAP	MOCKED
MITREWORT	MIZZES	MOBCAPS	MOCKER
MITRIFORM	MIZZLE	MOBE	MOCKERIES
MITRING	MIZZLED	MOBES	MOCKERNUT
MITSVAH	MIZZLES	MOBIE	MOCKERS
MITSVAHS	MIZZLIER	MOBIES	MOCKERY
MITSVOTH	MIZZLIEST	MOBILE	MOCKING
MITT	MIZZLING	MOBILES	MOCKINGLY
MITTEN	MIZZLINGS	MOBILISE	MOCKINGS
MITTENED	MIZZLY	MOBILISED	MOCKNEY
MITTENS	MIZZONITE	MOBILISER	MOCKNEYS
MITTIMUS	MIZZY	MOBILISES	MOCKS
MITTS	MM	MOBILITY	MOCKTAIL
MITUMBA	MNA	MOBILIZE	MOCKTAILS
MITUMBAS	MNAS	MOBILIZED	MOCKUP
MITY	MNEME	MOBILIZER	MOCKUPS
MITZVAH	MNEMES	MOBILIZES	MOCOCK
MITZVAHS	MNEMIC	MOBLE	MOCOCKS
MITZVOTH	MNEMON	MOBLED	MOCS
MIURUS	MNEMONIC	MOBLES	MOCUCK
MIURUSES	MNEMONICS	MOBLING	MOCUCKS
MIX	MNEMONIST	MOBLOG	MOCUDDUM
MIXABLE	MNEMONS	MOBLOGGER	MOCUDDUMS
MIXDOWN	MO	MOBLOGS	MOD
MIXDOWNS	MOA	MOBOCRACY	MODAL
MIXED	MOAT	MOBOCRAT	MODALISM
MIXEDLY	MOAN	MOBOCRATS	MODALISMS
MIXEDNESS	MOANED	MOBS	MODALIST
MIXEN	MOANER	MOBSMAN	MODALISTS
MIXENS	MOANERS	MOBSMEN	MODALITY
MIXER	MOANFUL	MOBSTER	MODALLY
MIXERS	MOANFULLY	MOBSTERS	MODALS
MIXES	MOANING	MOBY	MODE
MIXIBLE	MOANINGLY	MOC	MODEL

363

MODELED	MODIFIERS	MOGHUL	MOISTS
MODELER	MODIFIES	MOGHULS	MOISTURE
MODELERS	MODIFY	MOGS	MOISTURES
MODELING	MODIFYING	MOGUL	MOIT
MODELINGS	MODII	MOGULED	MOITHER
MODELIST	MODILLION	MOGULS	MOITHERED
MODELISTS	MODIOLAR	MOHAIR	MOITHERS
MODELLED	MODIOLI	MOHAIRS	MOITS
MODELLER	MODIOLUS	MOHALIM	MOJARRA
MODELLERS	MODISH	MOHAWK	MOJARRAS
MODELLI	MODISHLY	MOHAWKS	MOJO
MODELLING	MODIST	MOHEL	MOJOES
MODELLO	MODISTE	MOHELIM	MOJOS
MODELLOS	MODISTES	MOHELS	MOKADDAM
MODELS	MODISTS	MOHICAN	MOKADDAMS
MODEM	MODIUS	MOHICANS	MOKE
MODEMED	MODIWORT	MOHR	MOKES
MODEMING	MODIWORTS	MOHRS	MOKI
MODEMS	MODS	MOHUA	MOKIHI
MODENA	MODULAR	MOHUR	MOKIS
MODENAS	MODULARLY	MOHURS	MOKO
MODER	MODULARS	MOI	MOKOMOKO
MODERATE	MODULATE	MOIDER	MOKOPUNA
MODERATED	MODULATED	MOIDERED	MOKOPUNAS
MODERATES	MODULATES	MOIDERING	MOKORO
MODERATO	MODULATOR	MOIDERS	MOKOROS
MODERATOR	MODULE	MOIDORE	MOKOS
MODERATOS	MODULES	MOIDORES	MOKSHA
MODERN	MODULI	MOIETIES	MOKSHAS
MODERNE	MODULO	MOIETY	MOL
MODERNER	MODULUS	MOIL	MOLA
MODERNES	MODUS	MOILED	MOLAL
MODERNEST	MOE	MOILER	MOLALITY
MODERNISE	MOELLON	MOILERS	MOLAR
MODERNISM	MOELLONS	MOILING	MOLARITY
MODERNIST	MOER	MOILINGLY	MOLARS
MODERNITY	MOERED	MOILS	MOLAS
MODERNIZE	MOERING	MOINEAU	MOLASSE
MODERNLY	MOERS	MOINEAUS	MOLASSES
MODERNS	MOES	MOIRA	MOLD
MODERS	MOFETTE	MOIRAI	MOLDABLE
MODES	MOFETTES	MOIRE	MOLDAVITE
MODEST	MOFFETTE	MOIRES	MOLDBOARD
MODESTER	MOFFETTES	MOISER	MOLDED
MODESTEST	MOFFIE	MOISERS	MOLDER
MODESTIES	MOFFIES	MOIST	MOLDERED
MODESTLY	MOFO	MOISTED	MOLDERING
MODESTY	MOFOS	MOISTEN	MOLDERS
MODGE	MOFUSSIL	MOISTENED	MOLDIER
MODGED	MOFUSSILS	MOISTENER	MOLDIEST
MODGES	MOG	MOISTENS	MOLDINESS
MODGING	MOGGAN	MOISTER	MOLDING
MODI	MOGGANS	MOISTEST	MOLDINGS
MODICA	MOGGED	MOISTFUL	MOLDS
MODICUM	MOGGIE	MOISTIFY	MOLDWARP
MODICUMS	MOGGIES	MOISTING	MOLDWARPS
MODIFIED	MOGGING	MOISTLY	MOLDY
MODIFIER	MOGGY	MOISTNESS	MOLE

MOLECAST
MOLECASTS
MOLECULAR
MOLECULE
MOLECULES
MOLEHILL
MOLEHILLS
MOLEHUNT
MOLEHUNTS
MOLERAT
MOLERATS
MOLES
MOLESKIN
MOLESKINS
MOLEST
MOLESTED
MOLESTER
MOLESTERS
MOLESTFUL
MOLESTING
MOLESTS
MOLIES
MOLIMEN
MOLIMENS
MOLINE
MOLINES
MOLINET
MOLINETS
MOLL
MOLLA
MOLLAH
MOLLAHS
MOLLAS
MOLLIE
MOLLIES
MOLLIFIED
MOLLIFIER
MOLLIFIES
MOLLIFY
MOLLITIES
MOLLS
MOLLUSC
MOLLUSCA
MOLLUSCAN
MOLLUSCS
MOLLUSCUM
MOLLUSK
MOLLUSKAN
MOLLUSKS
MOLLY
MOLLYHAWK
MOLLYMAWK
MOLOCH
MOLOCHISE
MOLOCHIZE
MOLOCHS
MOLOSSI
MOLOSSUS

MOLS
MOLT
MOLTED
MOLTEN
MOLTENLY
MOLTER
MOLTERS
MOLTING
MOLTO
MOLTS
MOLY
MOLYBDATE
MOLYBDIC
MOLYBDOUS
MOM
MOME
MOMENT
MOMENTA
MOMENTANY
MOMENTARY
MOMENTLY
MOMENTO
MOMENTOES
MOMENTOS
MOMENTOUS
MOMENTS
MOMENTUM
MOMENTUMS
MOMES
MOMI
MOMISM
MOMISMS
MOMMA
MOMMAS
MOMMET
MOMMETS
MOMMIES
MOMMY
MOMS
MOMSER
MOMSERS
MOMUS
MOMUSES
MOMZER
MOMZERIM
MOMZERS
MON
MONA
MONACHAL
MONACHISM
MONACHIST
MONACID
MONACIDIC
MONACIDS
MONACT
MONACTINE
MONAD
MONADAL

MONADES
MONADIC
MONADICAL
MONADISM
MONADISMS
MONADNOCK
MONADS
MONAL
MONALS
MONANDRY
MONARCH
MONARCHAL
MONARCHIC
MONARCHS
MONARCHY
MONARDA
MONARDAS
MONAS
MONASES
MONASTERY
MONASTIC
MONASTICS
MONATOMIC
MONAUL
MONAULS
MONAURAL
MONAXIAL
MONAXON
MONAXONIC
MONAXONS
MONAZITE
MONAZITES
MONDAIN
MONDAINE
MONDAINES
MONDAINS
MONDE
MONDES
MONDIAL
MONDO
MONDOS
MONECIAN
MONECIOUS
MONELLIN
MONELLINS
MONEME
MONEMES
MONER
MONERA
MONERAN
MONERANS
MONERGISM
MONERON
MONETARY
MONETH
MONETHS
MONETISE
MONETISED

MONETISES
MONETIZE
MONETIZED
MONETIZES
MONEY
MONEYBAG
MONEYBAGS
MONEYED
MONEYER
MONEYERS
MONEYLESS
MONEYMAN
MONEYMEN
MONEYS
MONEYWORT
MONG
MONGCORN
MONGCORNS
MONGED
MONGEESE
MONGER
MONGERED
MONGERIES
MONGERING
MONGERS
MONGERY
MONGO
MONGOE
MONGOES
MONGOL
MONGOLIAN
MONGOLISM
MONGOLOID
MONGOLS
MONGOOSE
MONGOOSES
MONGOS
MONGREL
MONGRELLY
MONGRELS
MONGS
MONGST
MONIAL
MONIALS
MONICKER
MONICKERS
MONIE
MONIED
MONIES
MONIKER
MONIKERS
MONILIA
MONILIAL
MONILIAS
MONIMENT
MONIMENTS
MONIPLIES
MONISH

MONISHED	MONOCYCLE	MONOMIALS	MONOTYPIC
MONISHES	MONOCYTE	MONOMODE	MONOVULAR
MONISHING	MONOCYTES	MONONYM	MONOXIDE
MONISM	MONOCYTIC	MONONYMS	MONOXIDES
MONISMS	MONODIC	MONOPHAGY	MONOXYLON
MONIST	MONODICAL	MONOPHASE	MONS
MONISTIC	MONODIES	MONOPHONY	MONSIEUR
MONISTS	MONODIST	MONOPHYLY	MONSIGNOR
MONITION	MONODISTS	MONOPITCH	MONSOON
MONITIONS	MONODONT	MONOPLANE	MONSOONAL
MONITIVE	MONODRAMA	MONOPLOID	MONSOONS
MONITOR	MONODY	MONOPOD	MONSTER
MONITORED	MONOECIES	MONOPODE	MONSTERA
MONITORS	MONOECISM	MONOPODES	MONSTERAS
MONITORY	MONOECY	MONOPODIA	MONSTERED
MONITRESS	MONOESTER	MONOPODS	MONSTERS
MONK	MONOFIL	MONOPODY	MONSTROUS
MONKERIES	MONOFILS	MONOPOLE	MONTADALE
MONKERY	MONOFUEL	MONOPOLES	MONTAGE
MONKEY	MONOFUELS	MONOPOLY	MONTAGED
MONKEYED	MONOGAMIC	MONOPSONY	MONTAGES
MONKEYING	MONOGAMY	MONOPTERA	MONTAGING
MONKEYISH	MONOGENIC	MONOPTOTE	MONTAN
MONKEYISM	MONOGENY	MONOPULSE	MONTANE
MONKEYPOD	MONOGERM	MONORAIL	MONTANES
MONKEYPOT	MONOGLOT	MONORAILS	MONTANT
MONKEYS	MONOGLOTS	MONORCHID	MONTANTO
MONKFISH	MONOGONY	MONORHINE	MONTANTOS
MONKHOOD	MONOGRAM	MONORHYME	MONTANTS
MONKHOODS	MONOGRAMS	MONOS	MONTARIA
MONKISH	MONOGRAPH	MONOSEMY	MONTARIAS
MONKISHLY	MONOGYNY	MONOSES	MONTE
MONKS	MONOHULL	MONOSIES	MONTEITH
MONKSHOOD	MONOHULLS	MONOSIS	MONTEITHS
MONO	MONOICOUS	MONOSKI	MONTEM
MONOACID	MONOKINE	MONOSKIER	MONTEMS
MONOACIDS	MONOKINES	MONOSKIS	MONTERO
MONOAMINE	MONOKINI	MONOSOME	MONTEROS
MONOAO	MONOKINIS	MONOSOMES	MONTES
MONOBASIC	MONOLATER	MONOSOMIC	MONTH
MONOBROW	MONOLATRY	MONOSOMY	MONTHLIES
MONOBROWS	MONOLAYER	MONOSTELE	MONTHLING
MONOCARP	MONOLITH	MONOSTELY	MONTHLONG
MONOCARPS	MONOLITHS	MONOSTICH	MONTHLY
MONOCEROS	MONOLOG	MONOSTOME	MONTHS
MONOCHORD	MONOLOGIC	MONOSTYLE	MONTICLE
MONOCLE	MONOLOGS	MONOSY	MONTICLES
MONOCLED	MONOLOGUE	MONOTINT	MONTICULE
MONOCLES	MONOLOGY	MONOTINTS	MONTIES
MONOCLINE	MONOMACHY	MONOTONE	MONTRE
MONOCOQUE	MONOMANIA	MONOTONED	MONTRES
MONOCOT	MONOMARK	MONOTONES	MONTURE
MONOCOTS	MONOMARKS	MONOTONIC	MONTURES
MONOCOTYL	MONOMER	MONOTONY	MONTY
MONOCRACY	MONOMERIC	MONOTREME	MONUMENT
MONOCRAT	MONOMERS	MONOTROCH	MONUMENTS
MONOCRATS	MONOMETER	MONOTYPE	MONURON
MONOCULAR	MONOMIAL	MONOTYPES	MONURONS

MONY	MOONER	MOOPS	MOPBOARD
MONYPLIES	MOONERS	MOOR	MOPBOARDS
MONZONITE	MOONEYE	MOORAGE	MOPE
MOO	MOONEYES	MOORAGES	MOPED
MOOCH	MOONFACE	MOORBURN	MOPEDS
MOOCHED	MOONFACED	MOORBURNS	MOPEHAWK
MOOCHER	MOONFACES	MOORCOCK	MOPEHAWKS
MOOCHERS	MOONFISH	MOORCOCKS	MOPER
MOOCHES	MOONIER	MOORED	MOPERIES
MOOCHING	MOONIES	MOORFOWL	MOPERS
MOOD	MOONIEST	MOORFOWLS	MOPERY
MOODIED	MOONILY	MOORHEN	MOPES
MOODIER	MOONINESS	MOORHENS	MOPEY
MOODIES	MOONING	MOORIER	MOPHEAD
MOODIEST	MOONISH	MOORIEST	MOPHEADS
MOODILY	MOONISHLY	MOORILL	MOPIER
MOODINESS	MOONLESS	MOORILLS	MOPIEST
MOODS	MOONLET	MOORING	MOPINESS
MOODY	MOONLETS	MOORINGS	MOPING
MOODYING	MOONLIGHT	MOORISH	MOPINGLY
MOOED	MOONLIKE	MOORLAND	MOPISH
MOOI	MOONLIT	MOORLANDS	MOPISHLY
MOOING	MOONPHASE	MOORLOG	MOPOKE
MOOK	MOONPORT	MOORLOGS	MOPOKES
MOOKS	MOONPORTS	MOORMAN	MOPPED
MOOKTAR	MOONQUAKE	MOORMEN	MOPPER
MOOKTARS	MOONRAKER	MOORS	MOPPERS
MOOL	MOONRISE	MOORVA	MOPPET
MOOLA	MOONRISES	MOORVAS	MOPPETS
MOOLAH	MOONROCK	MOORWORT	MOPPIER
MOOLAHS	MOONROCKS	MOORWORTS	MOPPIEST
MOOLAS	MOONROOF	MOORY	MOPPING
MOOLED	MOONROOFS	MOOS	MOPPY
MOOLEY	MOONS	MOOSE	MOPS
MOOLEYS	MOONSAIL	MOOSEBIRD	MOPSIES
MOOLI	MOONSAILS	MOOSEWOOD	MOPSTICK
MOOLIES	MOONSCAPE	MOOSEYARD	MOPSTICKS
MOOLING	MOONSEED	MOOT	MOPSY
MOOLIS	MOONSEEDS	MOOTABLE	MOPUS
MOOLOO	MOONSET	MOOTED	MOPUSES
MOOLOOS	MOONSETS	MOOTER	MOPY
MOOLS	MOONSHEE	MOOTERS	MOQUETTE
MOOLVI	MOONSHEES	MOOTEST	MOQUETTES
MOOLVIE	MOONSHINE	MOOTING	MOR
MOOLVIES	MOONSHINY	MOOTINGS	MORA
MOOLVIS	MOONSHOT	MOOTMAN	MORACEOUS
MOOLY	MOONSHOTS	MOOTMEN	MORAE
MOON	MOONSTONE	MOOTNESS	MORAINAL
MOONBEAM	MOONWALK	MOOTS	MORAINE
MOONBEAMS	MOONWALKS	MOOVE	MORAINES
MOONBLIND	MOONWARD	MOOVED	MORAINIC
MOONBOW	MOONWARDS	MOOVES	MORAL
MOONBOWS	MOONWORT	MOOVING	MORALE
MOONCALF	MOONWORTS	MOP	MORALES
MOONCHILD	MOONY	MOPANE	MORALISE
MOONDUST	MOOP	MOPANES	MORALISED
MOONDUSTS	MOOPED	MOPANI	MORALISER
MOONED	MOOPING	MOPANIS	MORALISES

MORALISM	MORENDO	MORPHED	MORTALLY
MORALISMS	MORENESS	MORPHEME	MORTALS
MORALIST	MOREOVER	MORPHEMES	MORTAR
MORALISTS	MOREPORK	MORPHEMIC	MORTARED
MORALITY	MOREPORKS	MORPHETIC	MORTARING
MORALIZE	MORES	MORPHEW	MORTARMAN
MORALIZED	MORESQUE	MORPHEWS	MORTARMEN
MORALIZER	MORESQUES	MORPHIA	MORTARS
MORALIZES	MORGAN	MORPHIAS	MORTARY
MORALL	MORGANITE	MORPHIC	MORTBELL
MORALLED	MORGANS	MORPHIN	MORTBELLS
MORALLER	MORGAY	MORPHINE	MORTCLOTH
MORALLERS	MORGAYS	MORPHINES	MORTGAGE
MORALLING	MORGEN	MORPHING	MORTGAGED
MORALLS	MORGENS	MORPHINGS	MORTGAGEE
MORALLY	MORGUE	MORPHINIC	MORTGAGER
MORALS	MORGUES	MORPHINS	MORTGAGES
MORAS	MORIA	MORPHO	MORTGAGOR
MORASS	MORIAS	MORPHOGEN	MORTICE
MORASSES	MORIBUND	MORPHOS	MORTICED
MORASSY	MORICHE	MORPHOSES	MORTICER
MORAT	MORICHES	MORPHOSIS	MORTICERS
MORATORIA	MORION	MORPHOTIC	MORTICES
MORATORY	MORIONS	MORPHS	MORTICIAN
MORATS	MORISCO	MORRA	MORTICING
MORAY	MORISCOES	MORRAS	MORTIFIC
MORAYS	MORISCOS	MORRELL	MORTIFIED
MORBID	MORISH	MORRELLS	MORTIFIER
MORBIDER	MORKIN	MORRHUA	MORTIFIES
MORBIDEST	MORKINS	MORRHUAS	MORTIFY
MORBIDITY	MORLING	MORRICE	MORTISE
MORBIDLY	MORLINGS	MORRICES	MORTISED
MORBIFIC	MORMAOR	MORRION	MORTISER
MORBILLI	MORMAORS	MORRIONS	MORTISERS
MORBUS	MORN	MORRIS	MORTISES
MORBUSES	MORNAY	MORRISED	MORTISING
MORCEAU	MORNAYS	MORRISES	MORTLING
MORCEAUX	MORNE	MORRISING	MORTLINGS
MORCHA	MORNED	MORRO	MORTMAIN
MORCHAS	MORNES	MORROS	MORTMAINS
MORDACITY	MORNING	MORROW	MORTS
MORDANCY	MORNINGS	MORROWS	MORTSAFE
MORDANT	MORNS	MORS	MORTSAFES
MORDANTED	MOROCCO	MORSAL	MORTUARY
MORDANTLY	MOROCCOS	MORSE	MORULA
MORDANTS	MORON	MORSEL	MORULAE
MORDENT	MORONIC	MORSELED	MORULAR
MORDENTS	MORONISM	MORSELING	MORULAS
MORE	MORONISMS	MORSELLED	MORWONG
MOREEN	MORONITY	MORSELS	MORWONGS
MOREENS	MORONS	MORSES	MORYAH
MOREISH	MOROSE	MORSURE	MOS
MOREL	MOROSELY	MORSURES	MOSAIC
MORELLE	MOROSER	MORT	MOSAICISM
MORELLES	MOROSEST	MORTAL	MOSAICIST
MORELLO	MOROSITY	MORTALISE	MOSAICKED
MORELLOS	MORPH	MORTALITY	MOSAICS
MORELS	MORPHEAN	MORTALIZE	MOSASAUR

MOSASAURI	MOSTS	MOTIVES	MOTTIES
MOSASAURS	MOSTWHAT	MOTIVIC	MOTTIEST
MOSCHATE	MOT	MOTIVING	MOTTLE
MOSCHATEL	MOTE	MOTIVITY	MOTTLED
MOSE	MOTED	MOTLEY	MOTTLER
MOSED	MOTEL	MOTLEYER	MOTTLERS
MOSELLE	MOTELIER	MOTLEYEST	MOTTLES
MOSELLES	MOTELIERS	MOTLEYS	MOTTLING
MOSES	MOTELS	MOTLIER	MOTTLINGS
MOSEY	MOTEN	MOTLIEST	MOTTO
MOSEYED	MOTES	MOTMOT	MOTTOED
MOSEYING	MOTET	MOTMOTS	MOTTOES
MOSEYS	MOTETS	MOTOCROSS	MOTTOS
MOSH	MOTETT	MOTOR	MOTTS
MOSHAV	MOTETTIST	MOTORABLE	MOTTY
MOSHAVIM	MOTETTS	MOTORAIL	MOTU
MOSHED	MOTEY	MOTORAILS	MOTUCA
MOSHER	MOTH	MOTORBIKE	MOTUCAS
MOSHERS	MOTHBALL	MOTORBOAT	MOTUS
MOSHES	MOTHBALLS	MOTORBUS	MOTZA
MOSHING	MOTHED	MOTORCADE	MOTZAS
MOSHINGS	MOTHER	MOTORCAR	MOU
MOSHPIT	MOTHERED	MOTORCARS	MOUCH
MOSHPITS	MOTHERESE	MOTORDOM	MOUCHARD
MOSING	MOTHERING	MOTORDOMS	MOUCHARDS
MOSK	MOTHERLY	MOTORED	MOUCHED
MOSKONFYT	MOTHERS	MOTORHOME	MOUCHER
MOSKS	MOTHERY	MOTORIAL	MOUCHERS
MOSLINGS	MOTHIER	MOTORIC	MOUCHES
MOSQUE	MOTHIEST	MOTORING	MOUCHING
MOSQUES	MOTHLIKE	MOTORINGS	MOUCHOIR
MOSQUITO	MOTHPROOF	MOTORISE	MOUCHOIRS
MOSQUITOS	MOTHS	MOTORISED	MOUDIWART
MOSS	MOTHY	MOTORISES	MOUDIWORT
MOSSBACK	MOTI	MOTORIST	MOUE
MOSSBACKS	MOTIER	MOTORISTS	MOUES
MOSSED	MOTIEST	MOTORIUM	MOUFFLON
MOSSER	MOTIF	MOTORIUMS	MOUFFLONS
MOSSERS	MOTIFIC	MOTORIZE	MOUFLON
MOSSES	MOTIFS	MOTORIZED	MOUFLONS
MOSSGROWN	MOTILE	MOTORIZES	MOUGHT
MOSSIE	MOTILES	MOTORLESS	MOUILLE
MOSSIER	MOTILITY	MOTORMAN	MOUJIK
MOSSIES	MOTION	MOTORMEN	MOUJIKS
MOSSIEST	MOTIONAL	MOTORS	MOULAGE
MOSSINESS	MOTIONED	MOTORSHIP	MOULAGES
MOSSING	MOTIONER	MOTORWAY	MOULD
MOSSLAND	MOTIONERS	MOTORWAYS	MOULDABLE
MOSSLANDS	MOTIONING	MOTORY	MOULDED
MOSSLIKE	MOTIONIST	MOTOSCAFI	MOULDER
MOSSO	MOTIONS	MOTOSCAFO	MOULDERED
MOSSPLANT	MOTIS	MOTS	MOULDERS
MOSSY	MOTIVATE	MOTSER	MOULDIER
MOST	MOTIVATED	MOTSERS	MOULDIEST
MOSTE	MOTIVATES	MOTT	MOULDING
MOSTEST	MOTIVATOR	MOTTE	MOULDINGS
MOSTESTS	MOTIVE	MOTTES	MOULDS
MOSTLY	MOTIVED	MOTTIER	MOULDWARP

MOULDY	MOUSEOVER	MOUTHING	MOXIE
MOULIN	MOUSEPAD	MOUTHLESS	MOXIES
MOULINET	MOUSEPADS	MOUTHLIKE	MOY
MOULINETS	MOUSER	MOUTHPART	MOYA
MOULINS	MOUSERIES	MOUTHS	MOYAS
MOULS	MOUSERS	MOUTHWASH	MOYGASHEL
MOULT	MOUSERY	MOUTHY	MOYITIES
MOULTED	MOUSES	MOUTON	MOYITY
MOULTEN	MOUSETAIL	MOUTONNEE	MOYL
MOULTER	MOUSETRAP	MOUTONS	MOYLE
MOULTERS	MOUSEY	MOVABLE	MOYLED
MOULTING	MOUSIE	MOVABLES	MOYLES
MOULTINGS	MOUSIER	MOVABLY	MOYLING
MOULTS	MOUSIES	MOVE	MOYLS
MOUND	MOUSIEST	MOVEABLE	MOYS
MOUNDBIRD	MOUSILY	MOVEABLES	MOZ
MOUNDED	MOUSINESS	MOVEABLY	MOZE
MOUNDING	MOUSING	MOVED	MOZED
MOUNDS	MOUSINGS	MOVELESS	MOZES
MOUNSEER	MOUSLE	MOVEMENT	MOZETTA
MOUNSEERS	MOUSLED	MOVEMENTS	MOZETTAS
MOUNT	MOUSLES	MOVER	MOZETTE
MOUNTABLE	MOUSLING	MOVERS	MOZING
MOUNTAIN	MOUSME	MOVES	MOZO
MOUNTAINS	MOUSMEE	MOVIE	MOZOS
MOUNTAINY	MOUSMEES	MOVIEDOM	MOZZ
MOUNTANT	MOUSMES	MOVIEDOMS	MOZZES
MOUNTANTS	MOUSSAKA	MOVIEGOER	MOZZETTA
MOUNTED	MOUSSAKAS	MOVIELAND	MOZZETTAS
MOUNTER	MOUSSE	MOVIEOKE	MOZZETTE
MOUNTERS	MOUSSED	MOVIEOKES	MOZZIE
MOUNTING	MOUSSES	MOVIEOLA	MOZZIES
MOUNTINGS	MOUSSING	MOVIEOLAS	MOZZLE
MOUNTS	MOUST	MOVIES	MOZZLES
MOUP	MOUSTACHE	MOVING	MPRET
MOUPED	MOUSTED	MOVINGLY	MPRETS
MOUPING	MOUSTING	MOVIOLA	MRIDAMGAM
MOUPS	MOUSTS	MOVIOLAS	MRIDANG
MOURN	MOUSY	MOW	MRIDANGA
MOURNED	MOUTAN	MOWA	MRIDANGAM
MOURNER	MOUTANS	MOWAS	MRIDANGAS
MOURNERS	MOUTER	MOWBURN	MRIDANGS
MOURNFUL	MOUTERED	MOWBURNED	MU
MOURNING	MOUTERER	MOWBURNS	MUCATE
MOURNINGS	MOUTERERS	MOWBURNT	MUCATES
MOURNIVAL	MOUTERING	MOWDIE	MUCH
MOURNS	MOUTERS	MOWDIES	MUCHACHO
MOUS	MOUTH	MOWED	MUCHACHOS
MOUSAKA	MOUTHABLE	MOWER	MUCHEL
MOUSAKAS	MOUTHED	MOWERS	MUCHELL
MOUSE	MOUTHER	MOWING	MUCHELLS
MOUSEBIRD	MOUTHERS	MOWINGS	MUCHELS
MOUSED	MOUTHFEEL	MOWN	MUCHES
MOUSEKIN	MOUTHFUL	MOWRA	MUCHLY
MOUSEKINS	MOUTHFULS	MOWRAS	MUCHNESS
MOUSELIKE	MOUTHIER	MOWS	MUCHO
MOUSEMAT	MOUTHIEST	MOXA	MUCIC
MOUSEMATS	MOUTHILY	MOXAS	MUCID

MUCIDITY	MUCROS	MUDHOOKS	MUG
MUCIDNESS	MUCULENT	MUDIR	MUGEARITE
MUCIGEN	MUCUS	MUDIRIA	MUGFUL
MUCIGENS	MUCUSES	MUDIRIAS	MUGFULS
MUCILAGE	MUD	MUDIRIEH	MUGG
MUCILAGES	MUDBATH	MUDIRIEHS	MUGGA
MUCIN	MUDBATHS	MUDIRS	MUGGAR
MUCINOGEN	MUDBUG	MUDLARK	MUGGARS
MUCINOID	MUDBUGS	MUDLARKED	MUGGAS
MUCINOUS	MUDCAP	MUDLARKS	MUGGED
MUCINS	MUDCAPPED	MUDLOGGER	MUGGEE
MUCK	MUDCAPS	MUDPACK	MUGGEES
MUCKAMUCK	MUDCAT	MUDPACKS	MUGGER
MUCKED	MUDCATS	MUDPUPPY	MUGGERS
MUCKENDER	MUDDED	MUDRA	MUGGIER
MUCKER	MUDDER	MUDRAS	MUGGIEST
MUCKERED	MUDDERS	MUDROCK	MUGGILY
MUCKERING	MUDDIED	MUDROCKS	MUGGINESS
MUCKERISH	MUDDIER	MUDROOM	MUGGING
MUCKERS	MUDDIES	MUDROOMS	MUGGINGS
MUCKHEAP	MUDDIEST	MUDS	MUGGINS
MUCKHEAPS	MUDDILY	MUDSCOW	MUGGINSES
MUCKIER	MUDDINESS	MUDSCOWS	MUGGISH
MUCKIEST	MUDDING	MUDSILL	MUGGS
MUCKILY	MUDDLE	MUDSILLS	MUGGUR
MUCKINESS	MUDDLED	MUDSLIDE	MUGGURS
MUCKING	MUDDLER	MUDSLIDES	MUGGY
MUCKLE	MUDDLERS	MUDSTONE	MUGHAL
MUCKLES	MUDDLES	MUDSTONES	MUGHALS
MUCKLUCK	MUDDLING	MUDWORT	MUGS
MUCKLUCKS	MUDDLY	MUDWORTS	MUGSHOT
MUCKRAKE	MUDDY	MUEDDIN	MUGSHOTS
MUCKRAKED	MUDDYING	MUEDDINS	MUGWORT
MUCKRAKER	MUDEJAR	MUENSTER	MUGWORTS
MUCKRAKES	MUDEJARES	MUENSTERS	MUGWUMP
MUCKS	MUDEYE	MUESLI	MUGWUMPS
MUCKSWEAT	MUDEYES	MUESLIS	MUHLIES
MUCKWORM	MUDFISH	MUEZZIN	MUHLY
MUCKWORMS	MUDFISHES	MUEZZINS	MUID
MUCKY	MUDFLAP	MUFF	MUIDS
MUCLUC	MUDFLAPS	MUFFED	MUIL
MUCLUCS	MUDFLAT	MUFFIN	MUILS
MUCOID	MUDFLATS	MUFFINEER	MUIR
MUCOIDAL	MUDFLOW	MUFFING	MUIRBURN
MUCOIDS	MUDFLOWS	MUFFINS	MUIRBURNS
MUCOLYTIC	MUDGE	MUFFISH	MUIRS
MUCOR	MUDGED	MUFFLE	MUIST
MUCORS	MUDGER	MUFFLED	MUISTED
MUCOSA	MUDGERS	MUFFLER	MUISTING
MUCOSAE	MUDGES	MUFFLERED	MUISTS
MUCOSAL	MUDGING	MUFFLERS	MUJAHEDIN
MUCOSAS	MUDGUARD	MUFFLES	MUJAHIDIN
MUCOSE	MUDGUARDS	MUFFLING	MUJIK
MUCOSITY	MUDHEN	MUFFS	MUJIKS
MUCOUS	MUDHENS	MUFLON	MUKHTAR
MUCRO	MUDHOLE	MUFLONS	MUKHTARS
MUCRONATE	MUDHOLES	MUFTI	MUKLUK
MUCRONES	MUDHOOK	MUFTIS	MUKLUKS

MUKTUK
MUKTUKS
MULATTA
MULATTAS
MULATTO
MULATTOES
MULATTOS
MULBERRY
MULCH
MULCHED
MULCHES
MULCHING
MULCT
MULCTED
MULCTING
MULCTS
MULE
MULED
MULES
MULESED
MULESES
MULESING
MULETA
MULETAS
MULETEER
MULETEERS
MULEY
MULEYS
MULGA
MULGAS
MULING
MULISH
MULISHLY
MULL
MULLA
MULLAH
MULLAHISM
MULLAHS
MULLARKY
MULLAS
MULLED
MULLEIN
MULLEINS
MULLEN
MULLENS
MULLER
MULLERED
MULLERS
MULLET
MULLETS
MULLEY
MULLEYS
MULLIGAN
MULLIGANS
MULLING
MULLION
MULLIONED
MULLIONS

MULLITE
MULLITES
MULLOCK
MULLOCKS
MULLOCKY
MULLOWAY
MULLOWAYS
MULLS
MULMUL
MULMULL
MULMULLS
MULMULS
MULSE
MULSES
MULSH
MULSHED
MULSHES
MULSHING
MULTEITY
MULTIAGE
MULTIATOM
MULTIBAND
MULTIBANK
MULTICAR
MULTICAST
MULTICELL
MULTICIDE
MULTICITY
MULTICOPY
MULTIDAY
MULTIDISC
MULTIDRUG
MULTIFID
MULTIFIL
MULTIFILS
MULTIFOIL
MULTIFOLD
MULTIFORM
MULTIGERM
MULTIGRID
MULTIGYM
MULTIGYMS
MULTIHUED
MULTIHULL
MULTIJET
MULTILANE
MULTILINE
MULTILOBE
MULTIMODE
MULTIPACK
MULTIPAGE
MULTIPARA
MULTIPART
MULTIPATH
MULTIPED
MULTIPEDE
MULTIPEDS
MULTIPION

MULTIPLE
MULTIPLES
MULTIPLET
MULTIPLEX
MULTIPLY
MULTIPOLE
MULTIPORT
MULTIROLE
MULTIROOM
MULTISITE
MULTISIZE
MULTISTEP
MULTITASK
MULTITON
MULTITONE
MULTITUDE
MULTIUNIT
MULTIUSE
MULTIUSER
MULTIWALL
MULTIYEAR
MULTUM
MULTUMS
MULTURE
MULTURED
MULTURER
MULTURERS
MULTURES
MULTURING
MUM
MUMBLE
MUMBLED
MUMBLER
MUMBLERS
MUMBLES
MUMBLING
MUMBLINGS
MUMBLY
MUMCHANCE
MUMM
MUMMED
MUMMER
MUMMERIES
MUMMERS
MUMMERY
MUMMIA
MUMMIAS
MUMMICHOG
MUMMIED
MUMMIES
MUMMIFIED
MUMMIFIES
MUMMIFORM
MUMMIFY
MUMMING
MUMMINGS
MUMMOCK
MUMMOCKS

MUMMS
MUMMY
MUMMYING
MUMP
MUMPED
MUMPER
MUMPERS
MUMPING
MUMPISH
MUMPISHLY
MUMPS
MUMPSIMUS
MUMS
MUMSIER
MUMSIEST
MUMSY
MUMU
MUMUS
MUN
MUNCH
MUNCHABLE
MUNCHED
MUNCHER
MUNCHERS
MUNCHES
MUNCHIES
MUNCHING
MUNCHKIN
MUNCHKINS
MUNDANE
MUNDANELY
MUNDANER
MUNDANEST
MUNDANITY
MUNDIC
MUNDICS
MUNDIFIED
MUNDIFIES
MUNDIFY
MUNDUNGO
MUNDUNGOS
MUNDUNGUS
MUNG
MUNGA
MUNGAS
MUNGCORN
MUNGCORNS
MUNGED
MUNGING
MUNGO
MUNGOES
MUNGOOSE
MUNGOOSES
MUNGOS
MUNGS
MUNI
MUNICIPAL
MUNIFIED

MUNIFIES
MUNIFY
MUNIFYING
MUNIMENT
MUNIMENTS
MUNIS
MUNITE
MUNITED
MUNITES
MUNITING
MUNITION
MUNITIONS
MUNNION
MUNNIONS
MUNS
MUNSHI
MUNSHIS
MUNSTER
MUNSTERS
MUNT
MUNTER
MUNTERS
MUNTIN
MUNTING
MUNTINGS
MUNTINS
MUNTJAC
MUNTJACS
MUNTJAK
MUNTJAKS
MUNTRIE
MUNTRIES
MUNTS
MUNTU
MUNTUS
MUON
MUONIC
MUONIUM
MUONIUMS
MUONS
MUPPET
MUPPETS
MUQADDAM
MUQADDAMS
MURA
MURAENA
MURAENAS
MURAENID
MURAENIDS
MURAGE
MURAGES
MURAL
MURALED
MURALIST
MURALISTS
MURALLED
MURALS
MURAS

MURDABAD
MURDER
MURDERED
MURDEREE
MURDEREES
MURDERER
MURDERERS
MURDERESS
MURDERING
MURDEROUS
MURDERS
MURE
MURED
MUREIN
MUREINS
MURENA
MURENAS
MURES
MUREX
MUREXES
MURGEON
MURGEONED
MURGEONS
MURIATE
MURIATED
MURIATES
MURIATIC
MURICATE
MURICATED
MURICES
MURID
MURIDS
MURIFORM
MURINE
MURINES
MURING
MURK
MURKER
MURKEST
MURKIER
MURKIEST
MURKILY
MURKINESS
MURKISH
MURKLY
MURKS
MURKSOME
MURKY
MURL
MURLAIN
MURLAINS
MURLAN
MURLANS
MURLED
MURLIER
MURLIEST
MURLIN
MURLING

MURLINS
MURLS
MURLY
MURMUR
MURMURED
MURMURER
MURMURERS
MURMURING
MURMUROUS
MURMURS
MURPHIES
MURPHY
MURR
MURRA
MURRAGH
MURRAGHS
MURRAIN
MURRAINED
MURRAINS
MURRAM
MURRAMS
MURRAS
MURRAY
MURRAYS
MURRE
MURREE
MURREES
MURRELET
MURRELETS
MURREN
MURRENS
MURRES
MURREY
MURREYS
MURRHA
MURRHAS
MURRHINE
MURRI
MURRIES
MURRIN
MURRINE
MURRINS
MURRION
MURRIONS
MURRIS
MURRS
MURRY
MURTHER
MURTHERED
MURTHERER
MURTHERS
MURTI
MURTIS
MURVA
MURVAS
MUS
MUSACEOUS
MUSANG

MUSANGS
MUSAR
MUSARS
MUSCA
MUSCADEL
MUSCADELS
MUSCADET
MUSCADETS
MUSCADIN
MUSCADINE
MUSCADINS
MUSCAE
MUSCARINE
MUSCAT
MUSCATEL
MUSCATELS
MUSCATS
MUSCAVADO
MUSCID
MUSCIDS
MUSCLE
MUSCLED
MUSCLEMAN
MUSCLEMEN
MUSCLES
MUSCLIER
MUSCLIEST
MUSCLING
MUSCLINGS
MUSCLY
MUSCOID
MUSCOLOGY
MUSCONE
MUSCONES
MUSCOSE
MUSCOVADO
MUSCOVITE
MUSCULAR
MUSCULOUS
MUSE
MUSED
MUSEFUL
MUSEFULLY
MUSEOLOGY
MUSER
MUSERS
MUSES
MUSET
MUSETS
MUSETTE
MUSETTES
MUSEUM
MUSEUMS
MUSH
MUSHA
MUSHED
MUSHER
MUSHERS

MUSHES	MUSKONES	MUSTERS	MUTING
MUSHIER	MUSKOX	MUSTH	MUTINIED
MUSHIEST	MUSKOXEN	MUSTHS	MUTINIES
MUSHILY	MUSKRAT	MUSTIER	MUTINING
MUSHINESS	MUSKRATS	MUSTIEST	MUTINOUS
MUSHING	MUSKROOT	MUSTILY	MUTINY
MUSHMOUTH	MUSKROOTS	MUSTINESS	MUTINYING
MUSHROOM	MUSKS	MUSTING	MUTIS
MUSHROOMS	MUSKY	MUSTS	MUTISM
MUSHY	MUSLIN	MUSTY	MUTISMS
MUSIC	MUSLINED	MUT	MUTON
MUSICAL	MUSLINET	MUTABLE	MUTONS
MUSICALE	MUSLINETS	MUTABLY	MUTOSCOPE
MUSICALES	MUSLINS	MUTAGEN	MUTS
MUSICALLY	MUSMON	MUTAGENIC	MUTT
MUSICALS	MUSMONS	MUTAGENS	MUTTER
MUSICIAN	MUSO	MUTANDA	MUTTERED
MUSICIANS	MUSOS	MUTANDUM	MUTTERER
MUSICK	MUSPIKE	MUTANT	MUTTERERS
MUSICKED	MUSPIKES	MUTANTS	MUTTERING
MUSICKER	MUSQUASH	MUTASE	MUTTERS
MUSICKERS	MUSROL	MUTASES	MUTTON
MUSICKING	MUSROLS	MUTATE	MUTTONS
MUSICKS	MUSS	MUTATED	MUTTONY
MUSICLESS	MUSSE	MUTATES	MUTTS
MUSICS	MUSSED	MUTATING	MUTUAL
MUSIMON	MUSSEL	MUTATION	MUTUALISE
MUSIMONS	MUSSELLED	MUTATIONS	MUTUALISM
MUSING	MUSSELS	MUTATIVE	MUTUALIST
MUSINGLY	MUSSES	MUTATORY	MUTUALITY
MUSINGS	MUSSIER	MUTCH	MUTUALIZE
MUSIT	MUSSIEST	MUTCHED	MUTUALLY
MUSITS	MUSSILY	MUTCHES	MUTUALS
MUSIVE	MUSSINESS	MUTCHING	MUTUCA
MUSJID	MUSSING	MUTCHKIN	MUTUCAS
MUSJIDS	MUSSITATE	MUTCHKINS	MUTUEL
MUSK	MUSSY	MUTE	MUTUELS
MUSKED	MUST	MUTED	MUTULAR
MUSKEG	MUSTACHE	MUTEDLY	MUTULE
MUSKEGS	MUSTACHED	MUTELY	MUTULES
MUSKET	MUSTACHES	MUTENESS	MUTUUM
MUSKETEER	MUSTACHIO	MUTER	MUTUUMS
MUSKETOON	MUSTANG	MUTES	MUUMUU
MUSKETRY	MUSTANGS	MUTEST	MUUMUUS
MUSKETS	MUSTARD	MUTHA	MUX
MUSKIE	MUSTARDS	MUTHAS	MUXED
MUSKIER	MUSTARDY	MUTI	MUXES
MUSKIES	MUSTED	MUTICATE	MUXING
MUSKIEST	MUSTEE	MUTICOUS	MUZAKY
MUSKILY	MUSTEES	MUTILATE	MUZHIK
MUSKINESS	MUSTELID	MUTILATED	MUZHIKS
MUSKING	MUSTELIDS	MUTILATES	MUZJIK
MUSKIT	MUSTELINE	MUTILATOR	MUZJIKS
MUSKITS	MUSTER	MUTINE	MUZZ
MUSKLE	MUSTERED	MUTINED	MUZZED
MUSKLES	MUSTERER	MUTINEER	MUZZES
MUSKMELON	MUSTERERS	MUTINEERS	MUZZIER
MUSKONE	MUSTERING	MUTINES	MUZZIEST

MUZZILY	MYELINES	MYOMATOUS	MYRRHOLS
MUZZINESS	MYELINIC	MYONEURAL	MYRRHS
MUZZING	MYELINS	MYOPATHIC	MYRTLE
MUZZLE	MYELITIS	MYOPATHY	MYRTLES
MUZZLED	MYELOCYTE	MYOPE	MYSELF
MUZZLER	MYELOGRAM	MYOPES	MYSID
MUZZLERS	MYELOID	MYOPHILY	MYSIDS
MUZZLES	MYELOMA	MYOPIA	MYSOST
MUZZLING	MYELOMAS	MYOPIAS	MYSOSTS
MUZZY	MYELOMATA	MYOPIC	MYSTAGOG
MVULE	MYELON	MYOPICS	MYSTAGOGS
MVULES	MYELONS	MYOPIES	MYSTAGOGY
MWALIMU	MYGALE	MYOPS	MYSTERIES
MWALIMUS	MYGALES	MYOPSES	MYSTERY
MY	MYIASES	MYOPY	MYSTIC
MYAL	MYIASIS	MYOSCOPE	MYSTICAL
MYALGIA	MYIOPHILY	MYOSCOPES	MYSTICETE
MYALGIAS	MYLAR	MYOSES	MYSTICISM
MYALGIC	MYLARS	MYOSIN	MYSTICLY
MYALISM	MYLODON	MYOSINS	MYSTICS
MYALISMS	MYLODONS	MYOSIS	MYSTIFIED
MYALIST	MYLODONT	MYOSITIS	MYSTIFIER
MYALISTS	MYLODONTS	MYOSOTE	MYSTIFIES
MYALL	MYLOHYOID	MYOSOTES	MYSTIFY
MYALLS	MYLONITE	MYOSOTIS	MYSTIQUE
MYASES	MYLONITES	MYOTIC	MYSTIQUES
MYASIS	MYLONITIC	MYOTICS	MYTH
MYC	MYNA	MYOTOME	MYTHI
MYCELE	MYNAH	MYOTOMES	MYTHIC
MYCELES	MYNAHS	MYOTONIA	MYTHICAL
MYCELIA	MYNAS	MYOTONIAS	MYTHICISE
MYCELIAL	MYNHEER	MYOTONIC	MYTHICISM
MYCELIAN	MYNHEERS	MYOTUBE	MYTHICIST
MYCELIUM	MYOBLAST	MYOTUBES	MYTHICIZE
MYCELLA	MYOBLASTS	MYRBANE	MYTHIER
MYCELLAS	MYOCARDIA	MYRBANES	MYTHIEST
MYCELOID	MYOCLONIC	MYRIAD	MYTHISE
MYCETES	MYOCLONUS	MYRIADS	MYTHISED
MYCETOMA	MYOFIBRIL	MYRIADTH	MYTHISES
MYCETOMAS	MYOGEN	MYRIADTHS	MYTHISING
MYCOBIONT	MYOGENIC	MYRIAPOD	MYTHISM
MYCOFLORA	MYOGENS	MYRIAPODS	MYTHISMS
MYCOLOGIC	MYOGLOBIN	MYRICA	MYTHIST
MYCOLOGY	MYOGRAM	MYRICAS	MYTHISTS
MYCOPHAGY	MYOGRAMS	MYRINGA	MYTHIZE
MYCOPHILE	MYOGRAPH	MYRINGAS	MYTHIZED
MYCORHIZA	MYOGRAPHS	MYRIOPOD	MYTHIZES
MYCOSES	MYOGRAPHY	MYRIOPODS	MYTHIZING
MYCOSIS	MYOID	MYRIORAMA	MYTHMAKER
MYCOTIC	MYOLOGIC	MYRISTIC	MYTHOI
MYCOTOXIN	MYOLOGIES	MYRMECOID	MYTHOLOGY
MYCOVIRUS	MYOLOGIST	MYRMIDON	MYTHOMANE
MYCS	MYOLOGY	MYRMIDONS	MYTHOPEIC
MYDRIASES	MYOMA	MYROBALAN	MYTHOPOET
MYDRIASIS	MYOMANCY	MYRRH	MYTHOS
MYDRIATIC	MYOMANTIC	MYRRHIC	MYTHS
MYELIN	MYOMAS	MYRRHINE	MYTHUS
MYELINE	MYOMATA	MYRRHOL	MYTHY

MYTILOID

MYTILOID
MYXAMEBA
MYXAMEBAE
MYXAMEBAS
MYXAMOEBA
MYXEDEMA
MYXEDEMAS
MYXEDEMIC
MYXO
MYXOCYTE
MYXOCYTES
MYXOEDEMA
MYXOID
MYXOMA
MYXOMAS
MYXOMATA
MYXOS
MYXOVIRAL
MYXOVIRUS
MZEE
MZEES
MZUNGU
MZUNGUS

N

NA
NAAM
NAAMS
NAAN
NAANS
NAARTJE
NAARTJES
NAARTJIE
NAARTJIES
NAB
NABBED
NABBER
NABBERS
NABBING
NABE
NABES
NABIS
NABK
NABKS
NABLA
NABLAS
NABOB
NABOBERY
NABOBESS
NABOBISH
NABOBISM
NABOBISMS
NABOBS
NABS
NACARAT
NACARATS
NACELLE
NACELLES
NACH
NACHAS
NACHE
NACHES
NACHO
NACHOS
NACHTMAAL
NACKET
NACKETS
NACRE
NACRED
NACREOUS
NACRES
NACRITE
NACRITES
NACROUS
NADA
NADAS
NADIR
NADIRAL

NADIRS
NADORS
NADS
NAE
NAEBODIES
NAEBODY
NAETHING
NAETHINGS
NAEVE
NAEVES
NAEVI
NAEVOID
NAEVUS
NAFF
NAFFED
NAFFER
NAFFEST
NAFFING
NAFFLY
NAFFNESS
NAFFS
NAG
NAGA
NAGANA
NAGANAS
NAGAPIE
NAGAPIES
NAGARI
NAGARIS
NAGAS
NAGGED
NAGGER
NAGGERS
NAGGIER
NAGGIEST
NAGGING
NAGGINGLY
NAGGY
NAGMAAL
NAGMAALS
NAGOR
NAGORS
NAGS
NAH
NAHAL
NAHALS
NAIAD
NAIADES
NAIADS
NAIANT
NAIF
NAIFER
NAIFEST

NAIFLY
NAIFNESS
NAIFS
NAIK
NAIKS
NAIL
NAILBITER
NAILBRUSH
NAILED
NAILER
NAILERIES
NAILERS
NAILERY
NAILFILE
NAILFILES
NAILFOLD
NAILFOLDS
NAILHEAD
NAILHEADS
NAILING
NAILINGS
NAILLESS
NAILS
NAILSET
NAILSETS
NAIN
NAINSELL
NAINSELLS
NAINSOOK
NAINSOOKS
NAIRA
NAIRAS
NAIRU
NAIRUS
NAISSANCE
NAISSANT
NAIVE
NAIVELY
NAIVENESS
NAIVER
NAIVES
NAIVEST
NAIVETE
NAIVETES
NAIVETIES
NAIVETY
NAIVIST
NAKED
NAKEDER
NAKEDEST
NAKEDLY
NAKEDNESS
NAKER

NAKERS
NAKFA
NAKFAS
NALA
NALAS
NALED
NALEDS
NALLA
NALLAH
NALLAHS
NALLAS
NALOXONE
NALOXONES
NAM
NAMABLE
NAMASKAR
NAMASKARS
NAMASTE
NAMASTES
NAMAYCUSH
NAME
NAMEABLE
NAMECHECK
NAMED
NAMELESS
NAMELY
NAMEPLATE
NAMER
NAMERS
NAMES
NAMESAKE
NAMESAKES
NAMETAG
NAMETAGS
NAMETAPE
NAMETAPES
NAMING
NAMINGS
NAMMA
NAMS
NAMU
NAN
NANA
NANAS
NANCE
NANCES
NANCIES
NANCIFIED
NANCY
NANDIN
NANDINA
NANDINAS
NANDINE

NANDINES	NAPES	NARCOMA	NARRATOR
NANDINS	NAPHTHA	NARCOMAS	NARRATORS
NANDOO	NAPHTHAS	NARCOMATA	NARRATORY
NANDOOS	NAPHTHENE	NARCOS	NARRE
NANDU	NAPHTHOL	NARCOSE	NARROW
NANDUS	NAPHTHOLS	NARCOSES	NARROWED
NANE	NAPHTHOUS	NARCOSIS	NARROWER
NANISM	NAPHTHYL	NARCOTIC	NARROWEST
NANISMS	NAPHTHYLS	NARCOTICS	NARROWING
NANKEEN	NAPHTOL	NARCOTINE	NARROWISH
NANKEENS	NAPHTOLS	NARCOTISE	NARROWLY
NANKIN	NAPIFORM	NARCOTISM	NARROWS
NANKINS	NAPING	NARCOTIST	NARTHEX
NANNA	NAPKIN	NARCOTIZE	NARTHEXES
NANNAS	NAPKINS	NARCS	NARTJIE
NANNIE	NAPLESS	NARD	NARTJIES
NANNIED	NAPOLEON	NARDED	NARWAL
NANNIES	NAPOLEONS	NARDINE	NARWALS
NANNY	NAPOO	NARDING	NARWHAL
NANNYGAI	NAPOOED	NARDOO	NARWHALE
NANNYGAIS	NAPOOING	NARDOOS	NARWHALES
NANNYING	NAPOOS	NARDS	NARWHALS
NANNYISH	NAPPA	NARE	NARY
NANOBE	NAPPAS	NARES	NAS
NANOBES	NAPPE	NARGHILE	NASAL
NANODOT	NAPPED	NARGHILES	NASALISE
NANODOTS	NAPPER	NARGHILLY	NASALISED
NANOGRAM	NAPPERS	NARGHILY	NASALISES
NANOGRAMS	NAPPES	NARGILE	NASALISM
NANOMETER	NAPPIE	NARGILEH	NASALISMS
NANOMETRE	NAPPIER	NARGILEHS	NASALITY
NANOOK	NAPPIES	NARGILES	NASALIZE
NANOOKS	NAPPIEST	NARGILIES	NASALIZED
NANOSCALE	NAPPINESS	NARGILY	NASALIZES
NANOTECH	NAPPING	NARIAL	NASALLY
NANOTECHS	NAPPY	NARIC	NASALS
NANOTESLA	NAPRON	NARICORN	NASARD
NANOTUBE	NAPRONS	NARICORNS	NASARDS
NANOTUBES	NAPROXEN	NARINE	NASCENCE
NANOWATT	NAPROXENS	NARIS	NASCENCES
NANOWATTS	NAPS	NARK	NASCENCY
NANOWORLD	NARAS	NARKED	NASCENT
NANS	NARASES	NARKIER	NASEBERRY
NANUA	NARC	NARKIEST	NASHGAB
NAOI	NARCEEN	NARKING	NASHGABS
NAOS	NARCEENS	NARKS	NASHI
NAOSES	NARCEIN	NARKY	NASHIS
NAP	NARCEINE	NARQUOIS	NASIAL
NAPA	NARCEINES	NARRAS	NASION
NAPALM	NARCEINS	NARRASES	NASIONS
NAPALMED	NARCISM	NARRATE	NASSELLA
NAPALMING	NARCISMS	NARRATED	NASTALIK
NAPALMS	NARCISSI	NARRATER	NASTALIKS
NAPAS	NARCISSUS	NARRATERS	NASTIC
NAPE	NARCIST	NARRATES	NASTIER
NAPED	NARCISTIC	NARRATING	NASTIES
NAPERIES	NARCISTS	NARRATION	NASTIEST
NAPERY	NARCO	NARRATIVE	NASTILY

NASTINESS	NATURED	NAVELWORT	NEANIC
NASTY	NATURES	NAVES	NEAP
NASUTE	NATURING	NAVETTE	NEAPED
NASUTES	NATURISM	NAVETTES	NEAPING
NAT	NATURISMS	NAVEW	NEAPS
NATAL	NATURIST	NAVEWS	NEAR
NATALITY	NATURISTS	NAVICERT	NEARBY
NATANT	NAUCH	NAVICERTS	NEARED
NATANTLY	NAUCHES	NAVICULA	NEARER
NATATION	NAUGAHYDE	NAVICULAR	NEAREST
NATATIONS	NAUGHT	NAVICULAS	NEARING
NATATORIA	NAUGHTIER	NAVIES	NEARLIER
NATATORY	NAUGHTIES	NAVIGABLE	NEARLIEST
NATCH	NAUGHTILY	NAVIGABLY	NEARLY
NATCHES	NAUGHTS	NAVIGATE	NEARNESS
NATES	NAUGHTY	NAVIGATED	NEARS
NATHELESS	NAUMACHIA	NAVIGATES	NEARSHORE
NATHEMO	NAUMACHY	NAVIGATOR	NEARSIDE
NATHEMORE	NAUNT	NAVVIED	NEARSIDES
NATHLESS	NAUNTS	NAVVIES	NEAT
NATIFORM	NAUPLIAL	NAVVY	NEATEN
NATION	NAUPLII	NAVVYING	NEATENED
NATIONAL	NAUPLIOID	NAVY	NEATENING
NATIONALS	NAUPLIUS	NAW	NEATENS
NATIONS	NAUSEA	NAWAB	NEATER
NATIS	NAUSEANT	NAWABS	NEATEST
NATIVE	NAUSEANTS	NAY	NEATH
NATIVELY	NAUSEAS	NAYS	NEATHERD
NATIVES	NAUSEATE	NAYSAID	NEATHERDS
NATIVISM	NAUSEATED	NAYSAY	NEATLY
NATIVISMS	NAUSEATES	NAYSAYER	NEATNESS
NATIVIST	NAUSEOUS	NAYSAYERS	NEATNIK
NATIVISTS	NAUTCH	NAYSAYING	NEATNIKS
NATIVITY	NAUTCHES	NAYSAYS	NEATS
NATRIUM	NAUTIC	NAYTHLES	NEB
NATRIUMS	NAUTICAL	NAYWARD	NEBBED
NATROLITE	NAUTICS	NAYWARDS	NEBBICH
NATRON	NAUTILI	NAYWORD	NEBBICHS
NATRONS	NAUTILOID	NAYWORDS	NEBBING
NATS	NAUTILUS	NAZE	NEBBISH
NATTER	NAVAID	NAZES	NEBBISHE
NATTERED	NAVAIDS	NAZI	NEBBISHER
NATTERER	NAVAL	NAZIFIED	NEBBISHES
NATTERERS	NAVALISM	NAZIFIES	NEBBISHY
NATTERING	NAVALISMS	NAZIFY	NEBBUK
NATTERS	NAVALLY	NAZIFYING	NEBBUKS
NATTERY	NAVAR	NAZIR	NEBECK
NATTIER	NAVARCH	NAZIRS	NEBECKS
NATTIEST	NAVARCHS	NAZIS	NEBEK
NATTILY	NAVARCHY	NE	NEBEKS
NATTINESS	NAVARHO	NEAFE	NEBEL
NATTY	NAVARHOS	NEAFES	NEBELS
NATURA	NAVARIN	NEAFFE	NEBENKERN
NATURAE	NAVARINS	NEAFFES	NEBISH
NATURAL	NAVARS	NEAL	NEBISHES
NATURALLY	NAVE	NEALED	NEBRIS
NATURALS	NAVEL	NEALING	NEBRISES
NATURE	NAVELS	NEALS	NEBS

NEBULA	NECROSE	NEEDS	NEGRESS
NEBULAE	NECROSED	NEEDY	NEGRESSES
NEBULAR	NECROSES	NEELD	NEGRITUDE
NEBULAS	NECROSING	NEELDS	NEGRO
NEBULE	NECROSIS	NEELE	NEGROES
NEBULES	NECROTIC	NEELES	NEGROHEAD
NEBULISE	NECROTISE	NEEM	NEGROID
NEBULISED	NECROTIZE	NEEMB	NEGROIDAL
NEBULISER	NECROTOMY	NEEMBS	NEGROIDS
NEBULISES	NECTAR	NEEMS	NEGROISM
NEBULIUM	NECTAREAL	NEEP	NEGROISMS
NEBULIUMS	NECTAREAN	NEEPS	NEGRONI
NEBULIZE	NECTARED	NEESBERRY	NEGRONIS
NEBULIZED	NECTARIAL	NEESE	NEGROPHIL
NEBULIZER	NECTARIED	NEESED	NEGS
NEBULIZES	NECTARIES	NEESES	NEGUS
NEBULOSE	NECTARINE	NEESING	NEGUSES
NEBULOUS	NECTAROUS	NEEZE	NEIF
NEBULY	NECTARS	NEEZED	NEIFS
NECESSARY	NECTARY	NEEZES	NEIGH
NECESSITY	NED	NEEZING	NEIGHBOR
NECK	NEDDIER	NEF	NEIGHBORS
NECKATEE	NEDDIES	NEFANDOUS	NEIGHBOUR
NECKATEES	NEDDIEST	NEFARIOUS	NEIGHED
NECKBAND	NEDDISH	NEFAST	NEIGHING
NECKBANDS	NEDDY	NEFS	NEIGHS
NECKBEEF	NEDETTE	NEG	NEINEI
NECKBEEFS	NEDETTES	NEGATE	NEINEIS
NECKCLOTH	NEDS	NEGATED	NEIST
NECKED	NEE	NEGATER	NEITHER
NECKER	NEED	NEGATERS	NEIVE
NECKERS	NEEDED	NEGATES	NEIVES
NECKGEAR	NEEDER	NEGATING	NEK
NECKGEARS	NEEDERS	NEGATION	NEKS
NECKING	NEEDFIRE	NEGATIONS	NEKTON
NECKINGS	NEEDFIRES	NEGATIVE	NEKTONIC
NECKLACE	NEEDFUL	NEGATIVED	NEKTONS
NECKLACED	NEEDFULLY	NEGATIVES	NELIES
NECKLACES	NEEDFULS	NEGATON	NELIS
NECKLESS	NEEDIER	NEGATONS	NELLIE
NECKLET	NEEDIEST	NEGATOR	NELLIES
NECKLETS	NEEDILY	NEGATORS	NELLY
NECKLIKE	NEEDINESS	NEGATORY	NELSON
NECKLINE	NEEDING	NEGATRON	NELSONS
NECKLINES	NEEDLE	NEGATRONS	NELUMBIUM
NECKPIECE	NEEDLED	NEGLECT	NELUMBO
NECKS	NEEDLEFUL	NEGLECTED	NELUMBOS
NECKTIE	NEEDLER	NEGLECTER	NEMA
NECKTIES	NEEDLERS	NEGLECTOR	NEMAS
NECKVERSE	NEEDLES	NEGLECTS	NEMATIC
NECKWEAR	NEEDLESS	NEGLIGE	NEMATODE
NECKWEARS	NEEDLIER	NEGLIGEE	NEMATODES
NECKWEED	NEEDLIEST	NEGLIGEES	NEMATOID
NECKWEEDS	NEEDLING	NEGLIGENT	NEMERTEAN
NECROLOGY	NEEDLINGS	NEGLIGES	NEMERTIAN
NECROPHIL	NEEDLY	NEGOCIANT	NEMERTINE
NECROPOLI	NEEDMENT	NEGOTIANT	NEMESES
NECROPSY	NEEDMENTS	NEGOTIATE	NEMESIA

NEMESIAS	NEOPILINA	NEPOTISMS	NERVULES
NEMESIS	NEOPLASIA	NEPOTIST	NERVURE
NEMN	NEOPLASM	NEPOTISTS	NERVURES
NEMNED	NEOPLASMS	NEPS	NERVY
NEMNING	NEOPLASTY	NEPTUNIUM	NESCIENCE
NEMNS	NEOPRENE	NERAL	NESCIENT
NEMOPHILA	NEOPRENES	NERALS	NESCIENTS
NEMORAL	NEOTEINIA	NERD	NESH
NEMOROUS	NEOTENIC	NERDIER	NESHER
NEMPT	NEOTENIES	NERDIEST	NESHEST
NENE	NEOTENOUS	NERDINESS	NESHNESS
NENES	NEOTENY	NERDISH	NESS
NENNIGAI	NEOTERIC	NERDS	NESSES
NENNIGAIS	NEOTERICS	NERDY	NEST
NENUPHAR	NEOTERISE	NEREID	NESTABLE
NENUPHARS	NEOTERISM	NEREIDES	NESTED
NEOBLAST	NEOTERIST	NEREIDS	NESTER
NEOBLASTS	NEOTERIZE	NEREIS	NESTERS
NEOCON	NEOTOXIN	NERINE	NESTFUL
NEOCONS	NEOTOXINS	NERINES	NESTFULS
NEOCORTEX	NEOTROPIC	NERITE	NESTING
NEODYMIUM	NEOTYPE	NERITES	NESTINGS
NEOGENE	NEOTYPES	NERITIC	NESTLE
NEOGOTHIC	NEP	NERK	NESTLED
NEOLITH	NEPENTHE	NERKA	NESTLER
NEOLITHIC	NEPENTHES	NERKAS	NESTLERS
NEOLITHS	NEPER	NERKS	NESTLES
NEOLOGIAN	NEPERS	NEROL	NESTLIKE
NEOLOGIC	NEPETA	NEROLI	NESTLING
NEOLOGIES	NEPETAS	NEROLIS	NESTLINGS
NEOLOGISE	NEPHALISM	NEROLS	NESTOR
NEOLOGISM	NEPHALIST	NERTS	NESTORS
NEOLOGIST	NEPHELINE	NERTZ	NESTS
NEOLOGIZE	NEPHELITE	NERVAL	NET
NEOLOGY	NEPHEW	NERVATE	NETBALL
NEOMORPH	NEPHEWS	NERVATION	NETBALLER
NEOMORPHS	NEPHOGRAM	NERVATURE	NETBALLS
NEOMYCIN	NEPHOLOGY	NERVE	NETE
NEOMYCINS	NEPHRALGY	NERVED	NETES
NEON	NEPHRIC	NERVELESS	NETFUL
NEONATAL	NEPHRIDIA	NERVELET	NETFULS
NEONATE	NEPHRISM	NERVELETS	NETHEAD
NEONATES	NEPHRISMS	NERVER	NETHEADS
NEONED	NEPHRITE	NERVERS	NETHELESS
NEONOMIAN	NEPHRITES	NERVES	NETHER
NEONS	NEPHRITIC	NERVIER	NETIZEN
NEOPAGAN	NEPHRITIS	NERVIEST	NETIZENS
NEOPAGANS	NEPHROID	NERVILY	NETLESS
NEOPHILE	NEPHRON	NERVINE	NETLIKE
NEOPHILES	NEPHRONS	NERVINES	NETMINDER
NEOPHILIA	NEPHROSES	NERVINESS	NETOP
NEOPHOBE	NEPHROSIS	NERVING	NETOPS
NEOPHOBES	NEPHROTIC	NERVINGS	NETS
NEOPHOBIA	NEPIONIC	NERVOSITY	NETSPEAK
NEOPHOBIC	NEPIT	NERVOUS	NETSPEAKS
NEOPHYTE	NEPITS	NERVOUSLY	NETSUKE
NEOPHYTES	NEPOTIC	NERVULAR	NETSUKES
NEOPHYTIC	NEPOTISM	NERVULE	NETT

NETTABLE	NEUROMAST	NEWED	NEWSROOM
NETTED	NEUROMATA	NEWEL	NEWSROOMS
NETTER	NEURON	NEWELL	NEWSSTAND
NETTERS	NEURONAL	NEWELLED	NEWSTRADE
NETTIE	NEURONE	NEWELLS	NEWSWIRE
NETTIER	NEURONES	NEWELS	NEWSWIRES
NETTIES	NEURONIC	NEWER	NEWSWOMAN
NETTIEST	NEURONS	NEWEST	NEWSWOMEN
NETTING	NEUROPATH	NEWFANGLE	NEWSY
NETTINGS	NEUROPIL	NEWFOUND	NEWT
NETTLE	NEUROPILS	NEWIE	NEWTON
NETTLED	NEUROSAL	NEWIES	NEWTONS
NETTLER	NEUROSES	NEWING	NEWTS
NETTLERS	NEUROSIS	NEWISH	NEWWAVER
NETTLES	NEUROTIC	NEWISHLY	NEWWAVERS
NETTLIER	NEUROTICS	NEWLY	NEXT
NETTLIEST	NEUROTOMY	NEWLYWED	NEXTDOOR
NETTLING	NEURULA	NEWLYWEDS	NEXTLY
NETTLY	NEURULAE	NEWMARKET	NEXTNESS
NETTS	NEURULAR	NEWMOWN	NEXTS
NETTY	NEURULAS	NEWNESS	NEXUS
NETWORK	NEUSTIC	NEWNESSES	NEXUSES
NETWORKED	NEUSTON	NEWS	NGAIO
NETWORKER	NEUSTONIC	NEWSAGENT	NGAIOS
NETWORKS	NEUSTONS	NEWSBEAT	NGANA
NEUK	NEUTER	NEWSBEATS	NGANAS
NEUKS	NEUTERED	NEWSBOY	NGARARA
NEUM	NEUTERING	NEWSBOYS	NGATI
NEUMATIC	NEUTERS	NEWSBREAK	NGATIS
NEUME	NEUTRAL	NEWSCAST	NGOMA
NEUMES	NEUTRALLY	NEWSCASTS	NGOMAS
NEUMIC	NEUTRALS	NEWSDESK	NGULTRUM
NEUMS	NEUTRETTO	NEWSDESKS	NGULTRUMS
NEURAL	NEUTRINO	NEWSED	NGWEE
NEURALGIA	NEUTRINOS	NEWSES	NHANDU
NEURALGIC	NEUTRON	NEWSFLASH	NHANDUS
NEURALLY	NEUTRONIC	NEWSGIRL	NIACIN
NEURATION	NEUTRONS	NEWSGIRLS	NIACINS
NEURAXON	NEVE	NEWSGROUP	NIAISERIE
NEURAXONS	NEVEL	NEWSHAWK	NIALAMIDE
NEURILITY	NEVELLED	NEWSHAWKS	NIB
NEURINE	NEVELLING	NEWSHOUND	NIBBED
NEURINES	NEVELS	NEWSIE	NIBBING
NEURISM	NEVER	NEWSIER	NIBBLE
NEURISMS	NEVERMIND	NEWSIES	NIBBLED
NEURITE	NEVERMORE	NEWSIEST	NIBBLER
NEURITES	NEVES	NEWSINESS	NIBBLERS
NEURITIC	NEVI	NEWSING	NIBBLES
NEURITICS	NEVOID	NEWSLESS	NIBBLING
NEURITIS	NEVUS	NEWSMAKER	NIBBLINGS
NEUROCHIP	NEW	NEWSMAN	NIBLICK
NEUROCOEL	NEWBIE	NEWSMEN	NIBLICKS
NEUROGLIA	NEWBIES	NEWSPAPER	NIBLIKE
NEUROGRAM	NEWBORN	NEWSPEAK	NIBS
NEUROID	NEWBORNS	NEWSPEAKS	NICAD
NEUROLOGY	NEWCOME	NEWSPRINT	NICADS
NEUROMA	NEWCOMER	NEWSREEL	NICCOLITE
NEUROMAS	NEWCOMERS	NEWSREELS	NICE

NICEISH	NICOTIANS	NIELLOED	NIGHEST
NICELY	NICOTIN	NIELLOING	NIGHING
NICENESS	NICOTINE	NIELLOS	NIGHLY
NICER	NICOTINED	NIES	NIGHNESS
NICEST	NICOTINES	NIEVE	NIGHS
NICETIES	NICOTINIC	NIEVEFUL	NIGHT
NICETY	NICOTINS	NIEVEFULS	NIGHTBIRD
NICHE	NICTATE	NIEVES	NIGHTCAP
NICHED	NICTATED	NIFE	NIGHTCAPS
NICHER	NICTATES	NIFES	NIGHTCLUB
NICHERED	NICTATING	NIFF	NIGHTED
NICHERING	NICTATION	NIFFED	NIGHTFALL
NICHERS	NICTITANT	NIFFER	NIGHTFIRE
NICHES	NICTITATE	NIFFERED	NIGHTGEAR
NICHING	NID	NIFFERING	NIGHTGLOW
NICHT	NIDAL	NIFFERS	NIGHTGOWN
NICHTS	NIDAMENTA	NIFFIER	NIGHTHAWK
NICISH	NIDATE	NIFFIEST	NIGHTIE
NICK	NIDATED	NIFFING	NIGHTIES
NICKAR	NIDATES	NIFFNAFF	NIGHTJAR
NICKARS	NIDATING	NIFFNAFFS	NIGHTJARS
NICKED	NIDATION	NIFFS	NIGHTLESS
NICKEL	NIDATIONS	NIFFY	NIGHTLIFE
NICKELED	NIDDERING	NIFTIER	NIGHTLIKE
NICKELIC	NIDDICK	NIFTIES	NIGHTLONG
NICKELINE	NIDDICKS	NIFTIEST	NIGHTLY
NICKELING	NIDE	NIFTILY	NIGHTMARE
NICKELISE	NIDED	NIFTINESS	NIGHTMARY
NICKELIZE	NIDERING	NIFTY	NIGHTS
NICKELLED	NIDERINGS	NIGELLA	NIGHTSIDE
NICKELOUS	NIDERLING	NIGELLAS	NIGHTSPOT
NICKELS	NIDES	NIGER	NIGHTTIDE
NICKER	NIDGET	NIGERS	NIGHTTIME
NICKERED	NIDGETS	NIGGARD	NIGHTWARD
NICKERING	NIDI	NIGGARDED	NIGHTWEAR
NICKERS	NIDIFIED	NIGGARDLY	NIGHTY
NICKING	NIDIFIES	NIGGARDS	NIGIRI
NICKLE	NIDIFY	NIGGER	NIGIRIS
NICKLED	NIDIFYING	NIGGERDOM	NIGRICANT
NICKLES	NIDING	NIGGERED	NIGRIFIED
NICKLING	NIDINGS	NIGGERING	NIGRIFIES
NICKNACK	NIDOR	NIGGERISH	NIGRIFY
NICKNACKS	NIDOROUS	NIGGERISM	NIGRITUDE
NICKNAME	NIDORS	NIGGERS	NIGROSIN
NICKNAMED	NIDS	NIGGERY	NIGROSINE
NICKNAMER	NIDUS	NIGGLE	NIGROSINS
NICKNAMES	NIDUSES	NIGGLED	NIHIL
NICKPOINT	NIE	NIGGLER	NIHILISM
NICKS	NIECE	NIGGLERS	NIHILISMS
NICKSTICK	NIECES	NIGGLES	NIHILIST
NICKUM	NIED	NIGGLIER	NIHILISTS
NICKUMS	NIEF	NIGGLIEST	NIHILITY
NICOISE	NIEFS	NIGGLING	NIHILS
NICOL	NIELLATED	NIGGLINGS	NIHONGA
NICOLS	NIELLI	NIGGLY	NIHONGAS
NICOMPOOP	NIELLIST	NIGH	NIKAU
NICOTIAN	NIELLISTS	NIGHED	NIKAUS
NICOTIANA	NIELLO	NIGHER	NIL

NILGAI	NINETEEN	NIRLIE	NITREOUS
NILGAIS	NINETEENS	NIRLIER	NITRES
NILGAU	NINETIES	NIRLIEST	NITRIC
NILGAUS	NINETIETH	NIRLING	NITRID
NILGHAI	NINETY	NIRLIT	NITRIDE
NILGHAIS	NINHYDRIN	NIRLS	NITRIDED
NILGHAU	NINJA	NIRLY	NITRIDES
NILGHAUS	NINJAS	NIRVANA	NITRIDING
NILL	NINJITSU	NIRVANAS	NITRIDS
NILLED	NINJITSUS	NIRVANIC	NITRIFIED
NILLING	NINJUTSU	NIS	NITRIFIER
NILLS	NINJUTSUS	NISBERRY	NITRIFIES
NILPOTENT	NINNIES	NISEI	NITRIFY
NILS	NINNY	NISEIS	NITRIL
NIM	NINNYISH	NISGUL	NITRILE
NIMB	NINON	NISGULS	NITRILES
NIMBED	NINONS	NISH	NITRILS
NIMBI	NINTH	NISHES	NITRITE
NIMBLE	NINTHLY	NISI	NITRITES
NIMBLER	NINTHS	NISSE	NITRO
NIMBLESSE	NIOBATE	NISSES	NITROGEN
NIMBLEST	NIOBATES	NISUS	NITROGENS
NIMBLEWIT	NIOBIC	NIT	NITROLIC
NIMBLY	NIOBITE	NITCHIE	NITROS
NIMBS	NIOBITES	NITCHIES	NITROSO
NIMBUS	NIOBIUM	NITE	NITROSYL
NIMBUSED	NIOBIUMS	NITER	NITROSYLS
NIMBUSES	NIOBOUS	NITERIE	NITROUS
NIMBYISM	NIP	NITERIES	NITROXYL
NIMBYISMS	NIPA	NITERS	NITROXYLS
NIMBYNESS	NIPAS	NITERY	NITRY
NIMIETIES	NIPCHEESE	NITES	NITRYL
NIMIETY	NIPPED	NITHER	NITRYLS
NIMIOUS	NIPPER	NITHERED	NITS
NIMMED	NIPPERED	NITHERING	NITTIER
NIMMER	NIPPERING	NITHERS	NITTIEST
NIMMERS	NIPPERKIN	NITHING	NITTY
NIMMING	NIPPERS	NITHINGS	NITWIT
NIMONIC	NIPPIER	NITID	NITWITS
NIMPS	NIPPIEST	NITINOL	NITWITTED
NIMROD	NIPPILY	NITINOLS	NIVAL
NIMRODS	NIPPINESS	NITON	NIVATION
NIMS	NIPPING	NITONS	NIVATIONS
NINCOM	NIPPINGLY	NITPICK	NIVEOUS
NINCOMS	NIPPLE	NITPICKED	NIX
NINCUM	NIPPLED	NITPICKER	NIXE
NINCUMS	NIPPLES	NITPICKS	NIXED
NINE	NIPPLING	NITPICKY	NIXER
NINEBARK	NIPPY	NITRAMINE	NIXERS
NINEBARKS	NIPS	NITRATE	NIXES
NINEFOLD	NIPTER	NITRATED	NIXIE
NINEHOLES	NIPTERS	NITRATES	NIXIES
NINEPENCE	NIQAB	NITRATINE	NIXING
NINEPENNY	NIQABS	NITRATING	NIXY
NINEPIN	NIRAMIAI	NITRATION	NIZAM
NINEPINS	NIRAMIAIS	NITRATOR	NIZAMATE
NINES	NIRL	NITRATORS	NIZAMATES
NINESCORE	NIRLED	NITRE	NIZAMS

NKOSI	NOCTULE	NOESISES	NOMADIES
NKOSIS	NOCTULES	NOETIC	NOMADISE
NO	NOCTUOID	NOG	NOMADISED
NOAH	NOCTURIA	NOGAKU	NOMADISES
NOAHS	NOCTURIAS	NOGG	NOMADISM
NOB	NOCTURN	NOGGED	NOMADISMS
NOBBIER	NOCTURNAL	NOGGIN	NOMADIZE
NOBBIEST	NOCTURNE	NOGGING	NOMADIZED
NOBBILY	NOCTURNES	NOGGINGS	NOMADIZES
NOBBINESS	NOCTURNS	NOGGINS	NOMADS
NOBBLE	NOCUOUS	NOGGS	NOMADY
NOBBLED	NOCUOUSLY	NOGS	NOMARCH
NOBBLER	NOD	NOH	NOMARCHS
NOBBLERS	NODAL	NOHOW	NOMARCHY
NOBBLES	NODALISE	NOHOWISH	NOMAS
NOBBLING	NODALISED	NOIL	NOMBLES
NOBBUT	NODALISES	NOILS	NOMBRIL
NOBBY	NODALITY	NOILY	NOMBRILS
NOBELIUM	NODALIZE	NOINT	NOME
NOBELIUMS	NODALIZED	NOINTED	NOMEN
NOBILESSE	NODALIZES	NOINTER	NOMES
NOBILIARY	NODALLY	NOINTERS	NOMIC
NOBILITY	NODATED	NOINTING	NOMINA
NOBLE	NODATION	NOINTS	NOMINABLE
NOBLEMAN	NODATIONS	NOIR	NOMINAL
NOBLEMEN	NODDED	NOIRISH	NOMINALLY
NOBLENESS	NODDER	NOIRS	NOMINALS
NOBLER	NODDERS	NOISE	NOMINATE
NOBLES	NODDIES	NOISED	NOMINATED
NOBLESSE	NODDING	NOISEFUL	NOMINATES
NOBLESSES	NODDINGLY	NOISELESS	NOMINATOR
NOBLEST	NODDINGS	NOISENIK	NOMINEE
NOBLY	NODDLE	NOISENIKS	NOMINEES
NOBODIES	NODDLED	NOISES	NOMISM
NOBODY	NODDLES	NOISETTE	NOMISMS
NOBS	NODDLING	NOISETTES	NOMISTIC
NOCAKE	NODDY	NOISIER	NOMOCRACY
NOCAKES	NODE	NOISIEST	NOMOGENY
NOCENT	NODES	NOISILY	NOMOGRAM
NOCENTLY	NODI	NOISINESS	NOMOGRAMS
NOCENTS	NODICAL	NOISING	NOMOGRAPH
NOCHEL	NODOSE	NOISOME	NOMOI
NOCHELLED	NODOSITY	NOISOMELY	NOMOLOGIC
NOCHELS	NODOUS	NOISY	NOMOLOGY
NOCK	NODS	NOLE	NOMOS
NOCKED	NODULAR	NOLES	NOMOTHETE
NOCKET	NODULATED	NOLITION	NOMS
NOCKETS	NODULE	NOLITIONS	NON
NOCKING	NODULED	NOLL	NONA
NOCKS	NODULES	NOLLS	NONACID
NOCTILIO	NODULOSE	NOLO	NONACIDIC
NOCTILIOS	NODULOUS	NOLOS	NONACIDS
NOCTILUCA	NODUS	NOM	NONACTING
NOCTUA	NOEL	NOMA	NONACTION
NOCTUARY	NOELS	NOMAD	NONACTIVE
NOCTUAS	NOES	NOMADE	NONACTOR
NOCTUID	NOESES	NOMADES	NONACTORS
NOCTUIDS	NOESIS	NOMADIC	NONADDICT

NONADULT	NONCOMBAT	NONFAMILY	NONINERT
NONADULTS	NONCOMS	NONFAN	NONINJURY
NONAGE	NONCONCUR	NONFANS	NONINSECT
NONAGED	NONCORE	NONFARM	NONIONIC
NONAGES	NONCOUNTY	NONFARMER	NONIRON
NONAGON	NONCREDIT	NONFAT	NONIS
NONAGONAL	NONCRIME	NONFATAL	NONISSUE
NONAGONS	NONCRIMES	NONFATTY	NONISSUES
NONANE	NONCRISES	NONFEUDAL	NONJOINER
NONANES	NONCRISIS	NONFILIAL	NONJURIES
NONANIMAL	NONCYCLIC	NONFINAL	NONJURING
NONANOIC	NONDAIRY	NONFINITE	NONJUROR
NONANSWER	NONDANCE	NONFISCAL	NONJURORS
NONARABLE	NONDANCER	NONFLUID	NONJURY
NONART	NONDANCES	NONFLUIDS	NONKOSHER
NONARTIST	NONDEGREE	NONFLYING	NONLABOR
NONARTS	NONDEMAND	NONFOCAL	NONLAWYER
NONARY	NONDESERT	NONFOOD	NONLEADED
NONAS	NONDOCTOR	NONFORMAL	NONLEAFY
NONATOMIC	NONDOLLAR	NONFOSSIL	NONLEAGUE
NONAUTHOR	NONDRIP	NONFROZEN	NONLEGAL
NONBANK	NONDRIVER	NONFUEL	NONLEGUME
NONBANKS	NONDRUG	NONFUNDED	NONLETHAL
NONBASIC	NONDRYING	NONG	NONLEVEL
NONBEING	NONE	NONGAME	NONLIABLE
NONBEINGS	NONEDIBLE	NONGAY	NONLIFE
NONBELIEF	NONEGO	NONGAYS	NONLINEAL
NONBINARY	NONEGOS	NONGHETTO	NONLINEAR
NONBITING	NONELECT	NONGLARE	NONLIQUID
NONBLACK	NONELITE	NONGLARES	NONLIVES
NONBLACKS	NONEMPTY	NONGLAZED	NONLIVING
NONBODIES	NONENDING	NONGLOSSY	NONLOCAL
NONBODY	NONENERGY	NONGOLFER	NONLOCALS
NONBONDED	NONENTITY	NONGRADED	NONLOVING
NONBOOK	NONENTRY	NONGREASY	NONLOYAL
NONBOOKS	NONEQUAL	NONGREEN	NONLYRIC
NONBRAND	NONEQUALS	NONGROWTH	NONMAJOR
NONBUYING	NONEROTIC	NONGS	NONMAJORS
NONCAKING	NONES	NONGUEST	NONMAN
NONCAMPUS	NONESUCH	NONGUESTS	NONMANUAL
NONCAREER	NONET	NONGUILT	NONMARKET
NONCASH	NONETHNIC	NONGUILTS	NONMATURE
NONCASUAL	NONETS	NONHARDY	NONMEAT
NONCAUSAL	NONETTE	NONHEME	NONMEMBER
NONCE	NONETTES	NONHERO	NONMEN
NONCEREAL	NONETTI	NONHEROES	NONMENTAL
NONCES	NONETTO	NONHEROIC	NONMETAL
NONCHURCH	NONETTOS	NONHOME	NONMETALS
NONCLASS	NONEVENT	NONHUMAN	NONMETRIC
NONCLING	NONEVENTS	NONHUMANS	NONMETRO
NONCODING	NONEXEMPT	NONHUNTER	NONMOBILE
NONCOITAL	NONEXOTIC	NONI	NONMODAL
NONCOKING	NONEXPERT	NONIDEAL	NONMODERN
NONCOLA	NONEXTANT	NONILLION	NONMONEY
NONCOLAS	NONFACT	NONIMAGE	NONMORAL
NONCOLOR	NONFACTOR	NONIMAGES	NONMORTAL
NONCOLORS	NONFACTS	NONIMMUNE	NONMOTILE
NONCOM	NONFADING	NONIMPACT	NONMOVING

NONMUSIC	NONQUOTA	NONSUITS	NONWOOL
NONMUSICS	NONRACIAL	NONSYSTEM	NONWORD
NONMUTANT	NONRANDOM	NONTALKER	NONWORDS
NONMUTUAL	NONRATED	NONTARGET	NONWORK
NONNASAL	NONREADER	NONTARIFF	NONWORKER
NONNATIVE	NONRETURN	NONTAX	NONWOVEN
NONNAVAL	NONRHOTIC	NONTAXES	NONWOVENS
NONNEURAL	NONRIGID	NONTHEIST	NONWRITER
NONNEWS	NONRIOTER	NONTIDAL	NONYL
NONNIES	NONRIVAL	NONTITLE	NONYLS
NONNOBLE	NONRIVALS	NONTONAL	NONZERO
NONNORMAL	NONROYAL	NONTONIC	NOO
NONNOVEL	NONRUBBER	NONTOXIC	NOODGE
NONNOVELS	NONRULING	NONTRAGIC	NOODGED
NONNY	NONRURAL	NONTRIBAL	NOODGES
NONOBESE	NONSACRED	NONTRUMP	NOODGING
NONOHMIC	NONSALINE	NONTRUTH	NOODLE
NONOILY	NONSCHOOL	NONTRUTHS	NOODLED
NONORAL	NONSECRET	NONUNION	NOODLEDOM
NONORALLY	NONSECURE	NONUNIONS	NOODLES
NONOWNER	NONSELF	NONUNIQUE	NOODLING
NONOWNERS	NONSELVES	NONUPLE	NOODLINGS
NONPAGAN	NONSENSE	NONUPLES	NOOGIE
NONPAGANS	NONSENSES	NONUPLET	NOOGIES
NONPAID	NONSERIAL	NONUPLETS	NOOIT
NONPAPAL	NONSEXIST	NONURBAN	NOOK
NONPAPIST	NONSEXUAL	NONURGENT	NOOKIE
NONPAR	NONSHRINK	NONUSABLE	NOOKIER
NONPAREIL	NONSIGNER	NONUSE	NOOKIES
NONPARENT	NONSKATER	NONUSER	NOOKIEST
NONPARITY	NONSKED	NONUSERS	NOOKLIKE
NONPAROUS	NONSKEDS	NONUSES	NOOKS
NONPARTY	NONSKID	NONUSING	NOOKY
NONPAST	NONSKIER	NONVACANT	NOOLOGIES
NONPASTS	NONSKIERS	NONVALID	NOOLOGY
NONPAYING	NONSLIP	NONVECTOR	NOOMETRY
NONPEAK	NONSMOKER	NONVENOUS	NOON
NONPERSON	NONSOCIAL	NONVERBAL	NOONDAY
NONPLANAR	NONSOLAR	NONVESTED	NOONDAYS
NONPLAY	NONSOLID	NONVIABLE	NOONED
NONPLAYER	NONSOLIDS	NONVIEWER	NOONER
NONPLAYS	NONSPEECH	NONVIRAL	NOONERS
NONPLIANT	NONSTAPLE	NONVIRGIN	NOONING
NONPLUS	NONSTATIC	NONVIRILE	NOONINGS
NONPLUSED	NONSTEADY	NONVISUAL	NOONS
NONPLUSES	NONSTICK	NONVITAL	NOONTIDE
NONPOETIC	NONSTICKY	NONVOCAL	NOONTIDES
NONPOINT	NONSTOP	NONVOCALS	NOONTIME
NONPOLAR	NONSTOPS	NONVOTER	NOONTIMES
NONPOLICE	NONSTORY	NONVOTERS	NOOP
NONPOOR	NONSTYLE	NONVOTING	NOOPS
NONPOROUS	NONSTYLES	NONWAGE	NOOSE
NONPOSTAL	NONSUCH	NONWAR	NOOSED
NONPRINT	NONSUCHES	NONWARS	NOOSER
NONPROFIT	NONSUGAR	NONWHITE	NOOSERS
NONPROS	NONSUGARS	NONWHITES	NOOSES
NONPROVEN	NONSUIT	NONWINGED	NOOSING
NONPUBLIC	NONSUITED	NONWOODY	NOOSPHERE

NOOTROPIC	NORTHINGS	NOSTOC	NOTED
NOPAL	NORTHLAND	NOSTOCS	NOTEDLY
NOPALES	NORTHMOST	NOSTOI	NOTEDNESS
NOPALITO	NORTHS	NOSTOLOGY	NOTELESS
NOPALITOS	NORTHWARD	NOSTOS	NOTELET
NOPALS	NORTHWEST	NOSTRIL	NOTELETS
NOPE	NORWARD	NOSTRILS	NOTEPAD
NOPLACE	NORWARDS	NOSTRO	NOTEPADS
NOR	NOS	NOSTRUM	NOTEPAPER
NORDIC	NOSE	NOSTRUMS	NOTER
NORI	NOSEAN	NOSY	NOTERS
NORIA	NOSEANS	NOT	NOTES
NORIAS	NOSEBAG	NOTA	NOTHER
NORIMON	NOSEBAGS	NOTABILIA	NOTHING
NORIMONS	NOSEBAND	NOTABLE	NOTHINGS
NORIS	NOSEBANDS	NOTABLES	NOTICE
NORITE	NOSEBLEED	NOTABLY	NOTICED
NORITES	NOSED	NOTAEUM	NOTICER
NORITIC	NOSEDIVE	NOTAEUMS	NOTICERS
NORK	NOSEDIVED	NOTAL	NOTICES
NORKS	NOSEDIVES	NOTANDA	NOTICING
NORLAND	NOSEDOVE	NOTANDUM	NOTIFIED
NORLANDS	NOSEGAY	NOTAPHILY	NOTIFIER
NORM	NOSEGAYS	NOTARIAL	NOTIFIERS
NORMA	NOSEGUARD	NOTARIES	NOTIFIES
NORMAL	NOSELESS	NOTARISE	NOTIFY
NORMALCY	NOSELIKE	NOTARISED	NOTIFYING
NORMALISE	NOSELITE	NOTARISES	NOTING
NORMALITY	NOSELITES	NOTARIZE	NOTION
NORMALIZE	NOSEPIECE	NOTARIZED	NOTIONAL
NORMALLY	NOSER	NOTARIZES	NOTIONIST
NORMALS	NOSERS	NOTARY	NOTIONS
NORMAN	NOSES	NOTATE	NOTITIA
NORMANDE	NOSEWHEEL	NOTATED	NOTITIAE
NORMANS	NOSEY	NOTATES	NOTITIAS
NORMAS	NOSEYS	NOTATING	NOTOCHORD
NORMATIVE	NOSH	NOTATION	NOTORIETY
NORMED	NOSHED	NOTATIONS	NOTORIOUS
NORMLESS	NOSHER	NOTCH	NOTORNIS
NORMS	NOSHERIE	NOTCHBACK	NOTOUR
NORSEL	NOSHERIES	NOTCHED	NOTT
NORSELLED	NOSHERS	NOTCHEL	NOTTURNI
NORSELLER	NOSHERY	NOTCHELS	NOTTURNO
NORSELS	NOSHES	NOTCHER	NOTUM
NORTENA	NOSHING	NOTCHERS	NOUGAT
NORTENAS	NOSIER	NOTCHES	NOUGATS
NORTENO	NOSIES	NOTCHIER	NOUGHT
NORTENOS	NOSIEST	NOTCHIEST	NOUGHTIES
NORTH	NOSILY	NOTCHING	NOUGHTS
NORTHEAST	NOSINESS	NOTCHINGS	NOUL
NORTHED	NOSING	NOTCHY	NOULD
NORTHER	NOSINGS	NOTE	NOULDE
NORTHERED	NOSODE	NOTEBOOK	NOULE
NORTHERLY	NOSODES	NOTEBOOKS	NOULES
NORTHERN	NOSOLOGIC	NOTECARD	NOULS
NORTHERNS	NOSOLOGY	NOTECARDS	NOUMENA
NORTHERS	NOSTALGIA	NOTECASE	NOUMENAL
NORTHING	NOSTALGIC	NOTECASES	NOUMENON

NOUN	NOVELIZE	NOYADE	NUCLEAL
NOUNAL	NOVELIZED	NOYADES	NUCLEAR
NOUNALLY	NOVELIZER	NOYANCE	NUCLEASE
NOUNIER	NOVELIZES	NOYANCES	NUCLEASES
NOUNTEST	NOVELLA	NOYAU	NUCLEATE
NOUNLESS	NOVELLAE	NOYAUS	NUCLEATED
NOUNS	NOVELLAS	NOYED	NUCLEATES
NOUNY	NOVELLE	NOYES	NUCLEATOR
NOUP	NOVELLY	NOYESES	NUCLEI
NOUPS	NOVELS	NOYING	NUCLEIC
NOURICE	NOVELTIES	NOYOUS	NUCLEIDE
NOURICES	NOVELTY	NOYS	NUCLEIDES
NOURISH	NOVENA	NOYSOME	NUCLEIN
NOURISHED	NOVENAE	NOZZER	NUCLEINIC
NOURISHER	NOVENARY	NOZZERS	NUCLEINS
NOURISHES	NOVENAS	NOZZLE	NUCLEOID
NOURITURE	NOVENNIAL	NOZZLES	NUCLEOIDS
NOURSLE	NOVERCAL	NTH	NUCLEOLAR
NOURSLED	NOVERINT	NU	NUCLEOLE
NOURSLES	NOVERINTS	NUANCE	NUCLEOLES
NOURSLING	NOVICE	NUANCED	NUCLEOLI
NOUS	NOVICES	NUANCES	NUCLEOLUS
NOUSELL	NOVICIATE	NUANCING	NUCLEON
NOUSELLED	NOVITIATE	NUB	NUCLEONIC
NOUSELLS	NOVITIES	NUBBED	NUCLEONS
NOUSES	NOVITY	NUBBIER	NUCLEUS
NOUSLE	NOVOCAINE	NUBBIEST	NUCLEUSES
NOUSLED	NOVODAMUS	NUBBIN	NUCLIDE
NOUSLES	NOVUM	NUBBINESS	NUCLIDES
NOUSLING	NOVUMS	NUBBING	NUCLIDIC
NOUT	NOW	NUBBINS	NUCULE
NOUVEAU	NOWADAYS	NUBBLE	NUCULES
NOUVEAUX	NOWAY	NUBBLED	NUDATION
NOUVELLE	NOWAYS	NUBBLES	NUDATIONS
NOUVELLES	NOWED	NUBBLIER	NUDDIES
NOVA	NOWHENCE	NUBBLIEST	NUDDY
NOVAE	NOWHERE	NUBBLING	NUDE
NOVALIA	NOWHERES	NUBBLY	NUDELY
NOVALIKE	NOWHITHER	NUBBY	NUDENESS
NOVAS	NOWISE	NUBECULA	NUDER
NOVATED	NOWL	NUBECULAE	NUDES
NOVATION	NOWLS	NUBIA	NUDEST
NOVATIONS	NOWN	NUBIAS	NUDGE
NOVEL	NOWNESS	NUBIFORM	NUDGED
NOVELDOM	NOWNESSES	NUBILE	NUDGER
NOVELDOMS	NOWS	NUBILITY	NUDGERS
NOVELESE	NOWT	NUBILOSE	NUDGES
NOVELESES	NOWTIER	NUBILOUS	NUDGING
NOVELETTE	NOWTIEST	NUBS	NUDICAUL
NOVELISE	NOWTS	NUBUCK	NUDIE
NOVELISED	NOWTY	NUBUCKS	NUDIES
NOVELISER	NOWY	NUCELLAR	NUDISM
NOVELISES	NOX	NUCELLI	NUDISMS
NOVELISH	NOXAL	NUCELLUS	NUDIST
NOVELISM	NOXES	NUCHA	NUDISTS
NOVELISMS	NOXIOUS	NUCHAE	NUDITIES
NOVELIST	NOXIOUSLY	NUCHAL	NUDITY
NOVELISTS	NOY	NUCHALS	NUDNICK

NUDNICKS	NUMBING	NUNHOODS	NURTURERS
NUDNIK	NUMBINGLY	NUNLIKE	NURTURES
NUDNIKS	NUMBLES	NUNNATION	NURTURING
NUDZH	NUMBLY	NUNNERIES	NUS
NUDZHED	NUMBNESS	NUNNERY	NUT
NUDZHES	NUMBS	NUNNISH	NUTANT
NUDZHING	NUMBSKULL	NUNNY	NUTARIAN
NUFF	NUMCHUCK	NUNS	NUTARIANS
NUFFIN	NUMCHUCKS	NUNSHIP	NUTATE
NUFFINS	NUMDAH	NUNSHIPS	NUTATED
NUFFS	NUMDAHS	NUPTIAL	NUTATES
NUGAE	NUMEN	NUPTIALLY	NUTATING
NUGATORY	NUMERABLE	NUPTIALS	NUTATION
NUGGAR	NUMERABLY	NUR	NUTATIONS
NUGGARS	NUMERACY	NURAGHE	NUTBROWN
NUGGET	NUMERAIRE	NURAGHI	NUTBUTTER
NUGGETED	NUMERAL	NURAGHIC	NUTCASE
NUGGETING	NUMERALLY	NURD	NUTCASES
NUGGETS	NUMERALS	NURDIER	NUTGALL
NUGGETTED	NUMERARY	NURDIEST	NUTGALLS
NUGGETY	NUMERATE	NURDISH	NUTGRASS
NUISANCE	NUMERATED	NURDLE	NUTHATCH
NUISANCER	NUMERATES	NURDLED	NUTHOUSE
NUISANCES	NUMERATOR	NURDLES	NUTHOUSES
NUKE	NUMERIC	NURDLING	NUTJOBBER
NUKED	NUMERICAL	NURDS	NUTLET
NUKES	NUMERICS	NURDY	NUTLETS
NUKING	NUMEROUS	NURHAG	NUTLIKE
NULL	NUMINA	NURHAGS	NUTMEAL
NULLA	NUMINOUS	NURL	NUTMEALS
NULLAH	NUMMARY	NURLED	NUTMEAT
NULLAHS	NUMMULAR	NURLING	NUTMEATS
NULLAS	NUMMULARY	NURLS	NUTMEG
NULLED	NUMMULINE	NURR	NUTMEGGED
NULLIFIED	NUMMULITE	NURRS	NUTMEGGY
NULLIFIER	NUMNAH	NURS	NUTMEGS
NULLIFIES	NUMNAHS	NURSE	NUTPECKER
NULLIFY	NUMPTIES	NURSED	NUTPICK
NULLING	NUMPTY	NURSELIKE	NUTPICKS
NULLINGS	NUMSKULL	NURSELING	NUTRIA
NULLIPARA	NUMSKULLS	NURSEMAID	NUTRIAS
NULLIPORE	NUN	NURSER	NUTRIENT
NULLITIES	NUNATAK	NURSERIES	NUTRIENTS
NULLITY	NUNATAKER	NURSERS	NUTRIMENT
NULLNESS	NUNATAKS	NURSERY	NUTRITION
NULLS	NUNCHAKU	NURSES	NUTRITIVE
NUMB	NUNCHAKUS	NURSING	NUTS
NUMBAT	NUNCHEON	NURSINGS	NUTSEDGE
NUMBATS	NUNCHEONS	NURSLE	NUTSEDGES
NUMBED	NUNCIO	NURSLED	NUTSHELL
NUMBER	NUNCIOS	NURSLES	NUTSHELLS
NUMBERED	NUNCLE	NURSLING	NUTSIER
NUMBERER	NUNCLES	NURSLINGS	NUTSIEST
NUMBERERS	NUNCUPATE	NURTURAL	NUTSO
NUMBERING	NUNDINAL	NURTURANT	NUTSY
NUMBERS	NUNDINE	NURTURE	NUTTED
NUMBEST	NUNDINES	NURTURED	NUTTER
NUMBFISH	NUNHOOD	NURTURER	NUTTERIES

NUTTERS
NUTTERY
NUTTIER
NUTTIEST
NUTTILY
NUTTINESS
NUTTING
NUTTINGS
NUTTY
NUTWOOD
NUTWOODS
NUZZER
NUZZERS
NUZZLE
NUZZLED
NUZZLER
NUZZLERS
NUZZLES
NUZZLING
NY
NYAFF
NYAFFED
NYAFFING
NYAFFS
NYALA
NYALAS
NYANZA
NYANZAS
NYAS
NYASES
NYBBLE
NYBBLES
NYCTALOPS
NYE
NYED
NYES
NYING
NYLGHAI
NYLGHAIS
NYLGHAU
NYLGHAUS
NYLON
NYLONS
NYMPH
NYMPHA
NYMPHAE
NYMPHAEA
NYMPHAEUM
NYMPHAL
NYMPHALID
NYMPHEAN
NYMPHET
NYMPHETIC
NYMPHETS
NYMPHETTE
NYMPHIC
NYMPHICAL
NYMPHISH

NYMPHLIKE
NYMPHLY
NYMPHO
NYMPHOS
NYMPHS
NYS
NYSSA
NYSSAS
NYSTAGMIC
NYSTAGMUS
NYSTATIN
NYSTATINS

O

OAF
OAFISH
OAFISHLY
OAFS
OAK
OAKED
OAKEN
OAKENSHAW
OAKER
OAKERS
OAKIER
OAKIES
OAKIEST
OAKLEAF
OAKLEAVES
OAKLIKE
OAKLING
OAKLINGS
OAKMOSS
OAKMOSSES
OAKS
OAKUM
OAKUMS
OAKY
OANSHAGH
OANSHAGHS
OAR
OARAGE
OARAGES
OARED
OARFISH
OARFISHES
OARIER
OARIEST
OARING
OARLESS
OARLIKE
OARLOCK
OARLOCKS
OARS
OARSMAN
OARSMEN
OARSWOMAN
OARSWOMEN
OARWEED
OARWEEDS
OARY
OASES
OASIS
OAST
OASTHOUSE
OASTS
OAT

OATCAKE
OATCAKES
OATEN
OATER
OATERS
OATH
OATHABLE
OATHS
OATLIKE
OATMEAL
OATMEALS
OATS
OAVES
OB
OBA
OBANG
OBANGS
OBAS
OBBLIGATI
OBBLIGATO
OBCONIC
OBCONICAL
OBCORDATE
OBDURACY
OBDURATE
OBDURATED
OBDURATES
OBDURE
OBDURED
OBDURES
OBDURING
OBE
OBEAH
OBEAHED
OBEAHING
OBEAHISM
OBEAHISMS
OBEAHS
OBECHE
OBECHES
OBEDIENCE
OBEDIENT
OBEISANCE
OBEISANT
OBEISM
OBEISMS
OBELI
OBELIA
OBELIAS
OBELION
OBELISCAL
OBELISE
OBELISED

OBELISES
OBELISING
OBELISK
OBELISKS
OBELISM
OBELISMS
OBELIZE
OBELIZED
OBELIZES
OBELIZING
OBELUS
OBENTO
OBENTOS
OBES
OBESE
OBESELY
OBESENESS
OBESER
OBESEST
OBESITIES
OBESITY
OBEY
OBEYABLE
OBEYED
OBEYER
OBEYERS
OBEYING
OBEYS
OBFUSCATE
OBI
OBIA
OBIAS
OBIED
OBIING
OBIISM
OBIISMS
OBIIT
OBIS
OBIT
OBITAL
OBITER
OBITS
OBITUAL
OBITUARY
OBJECT
OBJECTED
OBJECTIFY
OBJECTING
OBJECTION
OBJECTIVE
OBJECTOR
OBJECTORS
OBJECTS

OBJET
OBJETS
OBJURE
OBJURED
OBJURES
OBJURGATE
OBJURING
OBLAST
OBLASTI
OBLASTS
OBLATE
OBLATELY
OBLATES
OBLATION
OBLATIONS
OBLATORY
OBLIGABLE
OBLIGANT
OBLIGANTS
OBLIGATE
OBLIGATED
OBLIGATES
OBLIGATI
OBLIGATO
OBLIGATOR
OBLIGATOS
OBLIGE
OBLIGED
OBLIGEE
OBLIGEES
OBLIGER
OBLIGERS
OBLIGES
OBLIGING
OBLIGOR
OBLIGORS
OBLIQUE
OBLIQUED
OBLIQUELY
OBLIQUER
OBLIQUES
OBLIQUEST
OBLIQUID
OBLIQUING
OBLIQUITY
OBLIVION
OBLIVIONS
OBLIVIOUS
OBLONG
OBLONGLY
OBLONGS
OBLOQUIAL
OBLOQUIES

OBLOQUY	OBSIGN	OBTUSITY	OCCULTISM
OBNOXIOUS	OBSIGNATE	OBUMBRATE	OCCULTIST
OBO	OBSIGNED	OBVENTION	OCCULTLY
OBOE	OBSIGNING	OBVERSE	OCCULTS
OBOES	OBSIGNS	OBVERSELY	OCCUPANCE
OBOIST	OBSOLESCE	OBVERSES	OCCUPANCY
OBOISTS	OBSOLETE	OBVERSION	OCCUPANT
OBOL	OBSOLETED	OBVERT	OCCUPANTS
OBOLARY	OBSOLETES	OBVERTED	OCCUPATE
OBOLE	OBSTACLE	OBVERTING	OCCUPATED
OBOLES	OBSTACLES	OBVERTS	OCCUPATES
OBOLI	OBSTETRIC	OBVIABLE	OCCUPIED
OBOLS	OBSTINACY	OBVIATE	OCCUPIER
OBOLUS	OBSTINATE	OBVIATED	OCCUPIERS
OBOS	OBSTRUCT	OBVIATES	OCCUPIES
OBOVATE	OBSTRUCTS	OBVIATING	OCCUPY
OBOVATELY	OBSTRUENT	OBVIATION	OCCUPYING
OBOVOID	OBTAIN	OBVIATOR	OCCUR
OBREPTION	OBTAINED	OBVIATORS	OCCURRED
OBS	OBTAINER	OBVIOUS	OCCURRENT
OBSCENE	OBTAINERS	OBVIOUSLY	OCCURRING
OBSCENELY	OBTAINING	OBVOLUTE	OCCURS
OBSCENER	OBTAINS	OBVOLUTED	OCCY
OBSCENEST	OBTECT	OBVOLVENT	OCEAN
OBSCENITY	OBTECTED	OCA	OCEANARIA
OBSCURANT	OBTEMPER	OCARINA	OCEANAUT
OBSCURE	OBTEMPERS	OCARINAS	OCEANAUTS
OBSCURED	OBTEND	OCAS	OCEANIC
OBSCURELY	OBTENDED	OCCAM	OCEANID
OBSCURER	OBTENDING	OCCAMIES	OCEANIDES
OBSCURERS	OBTENDS	OCCAMS	OCEANIDS
OBSCURES	OBTENTION	OCCAMY	OCEANS
OBSCUREST	OBTEST	OCCASION	OCELLAR
OBSCURING	OBTESTED	OCCASIONS	OCELLATE
OBSCURITY	OBTESTING	OCCIDENT	OCELLATED
OBSECRATE	OBTESTS	OCCIDENTS	OCELLI
OBSEQUENT	OBTRUDE	OCCIES	OCELLUS
OBSEQUIAL	OBTRUDED	OCCIPITA	OCELOID
OBSEQUIE	OBTRUDER	OCCIPITAL	OCELOT
OBSEQUIES	OBTRUDERS	OCCIPUT	OCELOTS
OBSEQUY	OBTRUDES	OCCIPUTS	OCH
OBSERVANT	OBTRUDING	OCCLUDE	OCHE
OBSERVE	OBTRUSION	OCCLUDED	OCHER
OBSERVED	OBTRUSIVE	OCCLUDENT	OCHERED
OBSERVER	OBTUND	OCCLUDER	OCHERING
OBSERVERS	OBTUNDED	OCCLUDERS	OCHEROUS
OBSERVES	OBTUNDENT	OCCLUDES	OCHERS
OBSERVING	OBTUNDING	OCCLUDING	OCHERY
OBSESS	OBTUNDITY	OCCLUSAL	OCHES
OBSESSED	OBTUNDS	OCCLUSION	OCHIDORE
OBSESSES	OBTURATE	OCCLUSIVE	OCHIDORES
OBSESSING	OBTURATED	OCCLUSOR	OCHLOCRAT
OBSESSION	OBTURATES	OCCLUSORS	OCHONE
OBSESSIVE	OBTURATOR	OCCULT	OCHRE
OBSESSOR	OBTUSE	OCCULTED	OCHREA
OBSESSORS	OBTUSELY	OCCULTER	OCHREAE
OBSIDIAN	OBTUSER	OCCULTERS	OCHREATE
OBSIDIANS	OBTUSEST	OCCULTING	OCHRED

OCHREOUS	OCTENNIAL	ODALISQUE	ODORATE
OCHRES	OCTET	ODALLER	ODORED
OCHREY	OCTETS	ODALLERS	ODORFUL
OCHRING	OCTETT	ODALS	ODORISE
OCHROID	OCTETTE	ODAS	ODORISED
OCHROUS	OCTETTES	ODD	ODORISES
OCHRY	OCTETTS	ODDBALL	ODORISING
OCICAT	OCTILLION	ODDBALLS	ODORIZE
OCICATS	OCTOFID	ODDER	ODORIZED
OCKER	OCTOHEDRA	ODDEST	ODORIZES
OCKERISM	OCTONARII	ODDISH	ODORIZING
OCKERISMS	OCTONARY	ODDITIES	ODORLESS
OCKERS	OCTOPI	ODDITY	ODOROUS
OCKODOLS	OCTOPLOID	ODDLY	ODOROUSLY
OCOTILLO	OCTOPOD	ODDMENT	ODORS
OCOTILLOS	OCTOPODAN	ODDMENTS	ODOUR
OCREA	OCTOPODES	ODDNESS	ODOURED
OCREAE	OCTOPODS	ODDNESSES	ODOURFUL
OCREATE	OCTOPUS	ODDS	ODOURLESS
OCTA	OCTOPUSES	ODDSMAKER	ODOURS
OCTACHORD	OCTOPUSH	ODDSMAN	ODS
OCTAD	OCTOROON	ODDSMEN	ODSO
OCTADIC	OCTOROONS	ODE	ODSOS
OCTADS	OCTOSTYLE	ODEA	ODYL
OCTAGON	OCTOTHORP	ODEON	ODYLE
OCTAGONAL	OCTROI	ODEONS	ODYLES
OCTAGONS	OCTROIS	ODES	ODYLISM
OCTAHEDRA	OCTUOR	ODEUM	ODYLISMS
OCTAL	OCTUORS	ODEUMS	ODYLS
OCTALS	OCTUPLE	ODIC	ODYSSEY
OCTAMETER	OCTUPLED	ODIFEROUS	ODYSSEYS
OCTAN	OCTUPLES	ODIOUS	ODZOOKS
OCTANE	OCTUPLET	ODIOUSLY	OE
OCTANES	OCTUPLETS	ODISM	OECIST
OCTANGLE	OCTUPLEX	ODISMS	OECISTS
OCTANGLES	OCTUPLING	ODIST	OECOLOGY
OCTANOL	OCTUPLY	ODISTS	OECUMENIC
OCTANOLS	OCTYL	ODIUM	OEDEMA
OCTANS	OCTYLS	ODIUMS	OEDEMAS
OCTANT	OCULAR	ODOGRAPH	OEDEMATA
OCTANTAL	OCULARIST	ODOGRAPHS	OEDIPAL
OCTANTS	OCULARLY	ODOMETER	OEDIPALLY
OCTAPLA	OCULARS	ODOMETERS	OEDIPEAN
OCTAPLAS	OCULATE	ODOMETRY	OEDOMETER
OCTAPLOID	OCULATED	ODONATE	OEILLADE
OCTAPODIC	OCULI	ODONATES	OEILLADES
OCTAPODY	OCULIST	ODONATIST	OENANTHIC
OCTARCHY	OCULISTS	ODONTALGY	OENOLOGY
OCTAROON	OCULUS	ODONTIC	OENOMANCY
OCTAROONS	OD	ODONTIST	OENOMANIA
OCTAS	ODA	ODONTISTS	OENOMEL
OCTASTICH	ODAH	ODONTOID	OENOMELS
OCTASTYLE	ODAHS	ODONTOIDS	OENOMETER
OCTAVAL	ODAL	ODONTOMA	OENOPHIL
OCTAVE	ODALIQUE	ODONTOMAS	OENOPHILE
OCTAVES	ODALIQUES	ODOR	OENOPHILS
OCTAVO	ODALISK	ODORANT	OENOPHILY
OCTAVOS	ODALISKS	ODORANTS	OENOTHERA

OERLIKON
OERLIKONS
OERSTED
OERSTEDS
OES
OESOPHAGI
OESTRAL
OESTRIN
OESTRINS
OESTRIOL
OESTRIOLS
OESTROGEN
OESTRONE
OESTRONES
OESTROUS
OESTRUM
OESTRUMS
OESTRUS
OESTRUSES
OEUVRE
OEUVRES
OF
OFAY
OFAYS
OFF
OFFAL
OFFALS
OFFBEAT
OFFBEATS
OFFCAST
OFFCASTS
OFFCUT
OFFCUTS
OFFED
OFFENCE
OFFENCES
OFFEND
OFFENDED
OFFENDER
OFFENDERS
OFFENDING
OFFENDS
OFFENSE
OFFENSES
OFFENSIVE
OFFER
OFFERABLE
OFFERED
OFFEREE
OFFEREES
OFFERER
OFFERERS
OFFERING
OFFERINGS
OFFEROR
OFFERORS
OFFERS
OFFERTORY

OFFHAND
OFFHANDED
OFFICE
OFFICER
OFFICERED
OFFICERS
OFFICES
OFFICIAL
OFFICIALS
OFFICIANT
OFFICIARY
OFFICIATE
OFFICINAL
OFFICIOUS
OFFING
OFFINGS
OFFISH
OFFISHLY
OFFKEY
OFFLINE
OFFLOAD
OFFLOADED
OFFLOADS
OFFPEAK
OFFPRINT
OFFPRINTS
OFFPUT
OFFPUTS
OFFRAMP
OFFRAMPS
OFFS
OFFSADDLE
OFFSCREEN
OFFSCUM
OFFSCUMS
OFFSEASON
OFFSET
OFFSETS
OFFSHOOT
OFFSHOOTS
OFFSHORE
OFFSHORES
OFFSIDE
OFFSIDER
OFFSIDERS
OFFSIDES
OFFSPRING
OFFSTAGE
OFFSTAGES
OFFTAKE
OFFTAKES
OFFTRACK
OFLAG
OFLAGS
OFT
OFTEN
OFTENER
OFTENEST

OFTENNESS
OFTER
OFTEST
OFTTIMES
OGAM
OGAMIC
OGAMS
OGDOAD
OGDOADS
OGEE
OGEES
OGGIN
OGGINS
OGHAM
OGHAMIC
OGHAMIST
OGHAMISTS
OGHAMS
OGIVAL
OGIVE
OGIVES
OGLE
OGLED
OGLER
OGLERS
OGLES
OGLING
OGLINGS
OGMIC
OGRE
OGREISH
OGREISHLY
OGREISM
OGREISMS
OGRES
OGRESS
OGRESSES
OGRISH
OGRISHLY
OGRISM
OGRISMS
OH
OHED
OHIA
OHIAS
OHING
OHM
OHMAGE
OHMAGES
OHMIC
OHMICALLY
OHMMETER
OHMMETERS
OHMS
OHO
OHONE
OHOS
OHS

OI
OIDIA
OIDIOID
OIDIUM
OIK
OIKIST
OIKISTS
OIKS
OIL
OILBIRD
OILBIRDS
OILCAMP
OILCAMPS
OILCAN
OILCANS
OILCLOTH
OILCLOTHS
OILCUP
OILCUPS
OILED
OILER
OILERIES
OILERS
OILERY
OILFIELD
OILFIELDS
OILFIRED
OILGAS
OILGASES
OILHOLE
OILHOLES
OILIER
OILIEST
OILILY
OILINESS
OILING
OILLET
OILLETS
OILMAN
OILMEN
OILNUT
OILNUTS
OILPAPER
OILPAPERS
OILPROOF
OILS
OILSEED
OILSEEDS
OILSKIN
OILSKINS
OILSTONE
OILSTONES
OILTIGHT
OILWAY
OILWAYS
OILY
OINK
OINKED

OINKING	OLEA	OLIGOMERS	OMASA
OINKS	OLEACEOUS	OLIGOPOLY	OMASAL
OINOLOGY	OLEANDER	OLIGURIA	OMASUM
OINOMEL	OLEANDERS	OLIGURIAS	OMBER
OINOMELS	OLEARIA	OLINGO	OMBERS
OINT	OLEARIAS	OLINGOS	OMBRE
OINTED	OLEASTER	OLIO	OMBRELLA
OINTING	OLEASTERS	OLIOS	OMBRELLAS
OINTMENT	OLEATE	OLIPHANT	OMBRES
OINTMENTS	OLEATES	OLIPHANTS	OMBROPHIL
OINTS	OLECRANAL	OLITORIES	OMBU
OITICICA	OLECRANON	OLITORY	OMBUDSMAN
OITICICAS	OLEFIANT	OLIVARY	OMBUDSMEN
OJIME	OLEFIN	OLIVE	OMBUS
OJIMES	OLEFINE	OLIVENITE	OMEGA
OKA	OLEFINES	OLIVER	OMEGAS
OKAPI	OLEFINIC	OLIVERS	OMELET
OKAPIS	OLEFINS	OLIVES	OMELETS
OKAS	OLEIC	OLIVET	OMELETTE
OKAY	OLEIN	OLIVETS	OMELETTES
OKAYED	OLEINE	OLIVINE	OMEN
OKAYING	OLEINES	OLIVINES	OMENED
OKAYS	OLEINS	OLIVINIC	OMENING
OKE	OLENT	OLLA	OMENS
OKEH	OLEO	OLLAMH	OMENTA
OKEHS	OLEOGRAPH	OLLAMHS	OMENTAL
OKES	OLEORESIN	OLLAS	OMENTUM
OKEYDOKE	OLEOS	OLLAV	OMENTUMS
OKEYDOKEY	OLES	OLLAVS	OMER
OKIMONO	OLESTRA	OLLER	OMERS
OKIMONOS	OLESTRAS	OLLERS	OMERTA
OKRA	OLEUM	OLLIE	OMERTAS
OKRAS	OLEUMS	OLLIES	OMICRON
OKTA	OLFACT	OLM	OMICRONS
OKTAS	OLFACTED	OLMS	OMIGOD
OLD	OLFACTING	OLOGIES	OMIKRON
OLDEN	OLFACTION	OLOGIST	OMIKRONS
OLDENED	OLFACTIVE	OLOGISTS	OMINOUS
OLDENING	OLFACTORY	OLOGOAN	OMINOUSLY
OLDENS	OLFACTS	OLOGOANED	OMISSIBLE
OLDER	OLIBANUM	OLOGOANS	OMISSION
OLDEST	OLIBANUMS	OLOGY	OMISSIONS
OLDIE	OLICOOK	OLOLIUQUI	OMISSIVE
OLDIES	OLICOOKS	OLOROSO	OMIT
OLDISH	OLID	OLOROSOS	OMITS
OLDNESS	OLIGAEMIA	OLPAE	OMITTANCE
OLDNESSES	OLIGAEMIC	OLPE	OMITTED
OLDS	OLIGARCH	OLPES	OMITTER
OLDSQUAW	OLIGARCHS	OLYCOOK	OMITTERS
OLDSQUAWS	OLIGARCHY	OLYCOOKS	OMITTING
OLDSTER	OLIGEMIA	OLYKOEK	OMLAH
OLDSTERS	OLIGEMIAS	OLYKOEKS	OMLAHS
OLDSTYLE	OLIGEMIC	OLYMPIAD	OMMATEA
OLDSTYLES	OLIGIST	OLYMPIADS	OMMATEUM
OLDWIFE	OLIGISTS	OLYMPICS	OMMATIDIA
OLDWIVES	OLIGOCENE	OM	OMNEITIES
OLDY	OLIGOGENE	OMADHAUN	OMNEITY
OLE	OLIGOMER	OMADHAUNS	OMNIANA

OMNIARCH	ONCOGENE	ONGOING	ONTOGENIC
OMNIARCHS	ONCOGENES	ONGOINGS	ONTOGENY
OMNIBUS	ONCOGENIC	ONIE	ONTOLOGIC
OMNIBUSES	ONCOGENS	ONION	ONTOLOGY
OMNIETIES	ONCOLOGIC	ONIONED	ONUS
OMNIETY	ONCOLOGY	ONIONIER	ONUSES
OMNIFIC	ONCOLYSES	ONIONIEST	ONWARD
OMNIFIED	ONCOLYSIS	ONIONING	ONWARDLY
OMNIFIES	ONCOLYTIC	ONIONS	ONWARDS
OMNIFORM	ONCOME	ONIONSKIN	ONY
OMNIFY	ONCOMES	ONIONY	ONYCHA
OMNIFYING	ONCOMETER	ONIRIC	ONYCHAS
OMNIMODE	ONCOMICE	ONISCOID	ONYCHIA
OMNIRANGE	ONCOMING	ONIUM	ONYCHIAS
OMNIUM	ONCOMINGS	ONIUMS	ONYCHITE
OMNIUMS	ONCOMOUSE	ONKUS	ONYCHITES
OMNIVORA	ONCOST	ONLAY	ONYCHITIS
OMNIVORE	ONCOSTMAN	ONLAYS	ONYCHIUM
OMNIVORES	ONCOSTMEN	ONLIEST	ONYCHIUMS
OMNIVORY	ONCOSTS	ONLINE	ONYMOUS
OMOHYOID	ONCOTOMY	ONLINER	ONYX
OMOHYOIDS	ONCOVIRUS	ONLINERS	ONYXES
OMOPHAGIA	ONCUS	ONLOAD	OO
OMOPHAGIC	ONDATRA	ONLOADED	OOBIT
OMOPHAGY	ONDATRAS	ONLOADING	OOBITS
OMOPHORIA	ONDINE	ONLOADS	OOCYST
OMOPLATE	ONDINES	ONLOOKER	OOCYSTS
OMOPLATES	ONDING	ONLOOKERS	OOCYTE
OMOV	ONDINGS	ONLOOKING	OOCYTES
OMOVS	ONDOGRAM	ONLY	OODLES
OMPHACITE	ONDOGRAMS	ONNED	OODLINS
OMPHALI	ONDOGRAPH	ONNING	OOF
OMPHALIC	ONE	ONO	OOFIER
OMPHALOID	ONEFOLD	ONOMASTIC	OOFIEST
OMPHALOS	ONEIRIC	ONOS	OOFS
OMRAH	ONELY	ONRUSH	OOFTISH
OMRAHS	ONENESS	ONRUSHES	OOFTISHES
OMS	ONENESSES	ONRUSHING	OOFY
ON	ONER	ONS	OOGAMETE
ONAGER	ONERIER	ONSCREEN	OOGAMETES
ONAGERS	ONERIEST	ONSET	OOGAMIES
ONAGRI	ONEROUS	ONSETS	OOGAMOUS
ONANISM	ONEROUSLY	ONSETTER	OOGAMY
ONANISMS	ONERS	ONSETTERS	OOGENESES
ONANIST	ONERY	ONSETTING	OOGENESIS
ONANISTIC	ONES	ONSHORE	OOGENETIC
ONANISTS	ONESELF	ONSHORING	OOGENIES
ONBEAT	ONETIME	ONSIDE	OOGENY
ONBEATS	ONEYER	ONSIDES	OOGONIA
ONBOARD	ONEYERS	ONSLAUGHT	OOGONIAL
ONCE	ONEYRE	ONST	OOGONIUM
ONCER	ONEYRES	ONSTAGE	OOGONIUMS
ONCERS	ONFALL	ONSTEAD	OOH
ONCES	ONFALLS	ONSTEADS	OOHED
ONCET	ONFLOW	ONSTREAM	OOHING
ONCIDIUM	ONFLOWS	ONTIC	OOHS
ONCIDIUMS	ONGAONGA	ONTICALLY	OOIDAL
ONCOGEN	ONGAONGAS	ONTO	OOLACHAN

OOLACHANS	OOSPERM	OPENCAST	OPHITE
OOLAKAN	OOSPERMS	OPENED	OPHITES
OOLAKANS	OOSPHERE	OPENER	OPHITIC
OOLITE	OOSPHERES	OPENERS	OPHIURA
OOLITES	OOSPORE	OPENEST	OPHIURAN
OOLITH	OOSPORES	OPENING	OPHIURANS
OOLITHS	OOSPORIC	OPENINGS	OPHIURAS
OOLITIC	OOSPOROUS	OPENLY	OPHIURID
OOLOGIC	OOSY	OPENNESS	OPHIURIDS
OOLOGICAL	OOT	OPENS	OPHIUROID
OOLOGIES	OOTHECA	OPENSIDE	OPIATE
OOLOGIST	OOTHECAE	OPENSIDES	OPIATED
OOLOGISTS	OOTHECAL	OPENWORK	OPIATES
OOLOGY	OOTID	OPENWORKS	OPIATING
OOLONG	OOTIDS	OPEPE	OPIFICER
OOLONGS	OOTS	OPEPES	OPIFICERS
OOM	OOZE	OPERA	OPINABLE
OOMIAC	OOZED	OPERABLE	OPINE
OOMIACK	OOZES	OPERABLY	OPINED
OOMIACKS	OOZIER	OPERAGOER	OPINES
OOMIACS	OOZIEST	OPERAND	OPING
OOMIAK	OOZILY	OPERANDS	OPINICUS
OOMIAKS	OOZINESS	OPERANT	OPINING
OOMPAH	OOZING	OPERANTLY	OPINION
OOMPAHED	OOZY	OPERANTS	OPINIONED
OOMPAHING	OP	OPERAS	OPINIONS
OOMPAHS	OPACIFIED	OPERATE	OPIOID
OOMPH	OPACIFIER	OPERATED	OPIOIDS
OOMPHS	OPACIFIES	OPERATES	OPIUM
OOMS	OPACIFY	OPERATIC	OPIUMISM
OOMYCETE	OPACITIES	OPERATICS	OPIUMISMS
OOMYCETES	OPACITY	OPERATING	OPIUMS
OON	OPACOUS	OPERATION	OPOBALSAM
OONS	OPAH	OPERATISE	OPODELDOC
OONT	OPAHS	OPERATIVE	OPOPANAX
OONTS	OPAL	OPERATIZE	OPORICE
OOP	OPALED	OPERATOR	OPORICES
OOPED	OPALESCE	OPERATORS	OPOSSUM
OOPHORON	OPALESCED	OPERCELE	OPOSSUMS
OOPHORONS	OPALESCES	OPERCELES	OPPIDAN
OOPHYTE	OPALINE	OPERCULA	OPPIDANS
OOPHYTES	OPALINES	OPERCULAR	OPPILANT
OOPHYTIC	OPALISED	OPERCULE	OPPILATE
OOPING	OPALIZED	OPERCULES	OPPILATED
OOPS	OPALS	OPERCULUM	OPPILATES
OOR	OPAQUE	OPERETTA	OPPO
OORALI	OPAQUED	OPERETTAS	OPPONENCY
OORALIS	OPAQUELY	OPERON	OPPONENT
OORIAL	OPAQUER	OPERONS	OPPONENTS
OORIALS	OPAQUES	OPEROSE	OPPORTUNE
OORIE	OPAQUEST	OPEROSELY	OPPOS
OORIER	OPAQUING	OPEROSITY	OPPOSABLE
OORIEST	OPCODE	OPES	OPPOSABLY
OOS	OPCODES	OPGEFOK	OPPOSE
OOSE	OPE	OPHIDIAN	OPPOSED
OOSES	OPED	OPHIDIANS	OPPOSER
OOSIER	OPEN	OPHIOLITE	OPPOSERS
OOSIEST	OPENABLE	OPHIOLOGY	OPPOSES

OPPOSING	OPTIMISER	ORACULOUS	ORBIER
OPPOSITE	OPTIMISES	ORACY	ORBIEST
OPPOSITES	OPTIMISM	ORAD	ORBING
OPPRESS	OPTIMISMS	ORAGIOUS	ORBIT
OPPRESSED	OPTIMIST	ORAL	ORBITA
OPPRESSES	OPTIMISTS	ORALISM	ORBITAL
OPPRESSOR	OPTIMIZE	ORALISMS	ORBITALLY
OPPUGN	OPTIMIZED	ORALIST	ORBITALS
OPPUGNANT	OPTIMIZER	ORALISTS	ORBITAS
OPPUGNED	OPTIMIZES	ORALITIES	ORBITED
OPPUGNER	OPTIMUM	ORALITY	ORBITER
OPPUGNERS	OPTIMUMS	ORALLY	ORBITERS
OPPUGNING	OPTING	ORALS	ORBITIES
OPPUGNS	OPTION	ORANG	ORBITING
OPS	OPTIONAL	ORANGE	ORBITS
OPSIMATH	OPTIONALS	ORANGEADE	ORBITY
OPSIMATHS	OPTIONED	ORANGER	ORBLESS
OPSIMATHY	OPTIONEE	ORANGERIE	ORBS
OPSIN	OPTIONEES	ORANGERY	ORBY
OPSINS	OPTIONING	ORANGES	ORC
OPSOMANIA	OPTIONS	ORANGEST	ORCA
OPSONIC	OPTOLOGY	ORANGEY	ORCAS
OPSONIFY	OPTOMETER	ORANGIER	ORCEIN
OPSONIN	OPTOMETRY	ORANGIEST	ORCEINS
OPSONINS	OPTOPHONE	ORANGISH	ORCHARD
OPSONISE	OPTRONICS	ORANGS	ORCHARDS
OPSONISED	OPTS	ORANGUTAN	ORCHAT
OPSONISES	OPULENCE	ORANGY	ORCHATS
OPSONIUM	OPULENCES	ORANT	ORCHEL
OPSONIUMS	OPULENCY	ORANTS	ORCHELLA
OPSONIZE	OPULENT	ORARIA	ORCHELLAS
OPSONIZED	OPULENTLY	ORARIAN	ORCHELS
OPSONIZES	OPULUS	ORARIANS	ORCHESES
OPT	OPULUSES	ORARION	ORCHESIS
OPTANT	OPUNTIA	ORARIONS	ORCHESTIC
OPTANTS	OPUNTIAS	ORARIUM	ORCHESTRA
OPTATIVE	OPUS	ORARIUMS	ORCHID
OPTATIVES	OPUSCLE	ORATE	ORCHIDIST
OPTED	OPUSCLES	ORATED	ORCHIDS
OPTER	OPUSCULA	ORATES	ORCHIL
OPTERS	OPUSCULAR	ORATING	ORCHILLA
OPTIC	OPUSCULE	ORATION	ORCHILLAS
OPTICAL	OPUSCULES	ORATIONS	ORCHILS
OPTICALLY	OPUSCULUM	ORATOR	ORCHIS
OPTICIAN	OPUSES	ORATORIAL	ORCHISES
OPTICIANS	OQUASSA	ORATORIAN	ORCHITIC
OPTICIST	OQUASSAS	ORATORIES	ORCHITIS
OPTICISTS	OR	ORATORIO	ORCIN
OPTICS	ORA	ORATORIOS	ORCINE
OPTIMA	ORACH	ORATORS	ORCINES
OPTIMAL	ORACHE	ORATORY	ORCINOL
OPTIMALLY	ORACHES	ORATRESS	ORCINOLS
OPTIMATE	ORACIES	ORATRICES	ORCINS
OPTIMATES	ORACLE	ORATRIX	ORCS
OPTIME	ORACLED	ORATRIXES	ORD
OPTIMES	ORACLES	ORB	ORDAIN
OPTIMISE	ORACLING	ORBED	ORDAINED
OPTIMISED	ORACULAR	ORBICULAR	ORDAINER

ORDAINERS	OREPEARCH	ORGIASTS	ORISHA
ORDAINING	ORES	ORGIC	ORISHAS
ORDAINS	ORESTUNCK	ORGIES	ORISON
ORDALIAN	OREWEED	ORGILLOUS	ORISONS
ORDALIUM	OREWEEDS	ORGONE	ORIXA
ORDALIUMS	OREXIS	ORGONES	ORIXAS
ORDEAL	OREXISES	ORGUE	ORLE
ORDEALS	ORF	ORGUES	ORLEANS
ORDER	ORFE	ORGULOUS	ORLEANSES
ORDERABLE	ORFES	ORGY	ORLES
ORDERED	ORFRAY	ORIBATID	ORLON
ORDERER	ORFRAYS	ORIBATIDS	ORLONS
ORDERERS	ORFS	ORIBI	ORLOP
ORDERING	ORGAN	ORIBIS	ORLOPS
ORDERINGS	ORGANA	ORICALCHE	ORMER
ORDERLESS	ORGANDIE	ORICHALC	ORMERS
ORDERLIES	ORGANDIES	ORICHALCS	ORMOLU
ORDERLY	ORGANDY	ORIEL	ORMOLUS
ORDERS	ORGANELLE	ORIELLED	ORNAMENT
ORDINAIRE	ORGANIC	ORIELS	ORNAMENTS
ORDINAL	ORGANICAL	ORIENCIES	ORNATE
ORDINALLY	ORGANICS	ORIENCY	ORNATELY
ORDINALS	ORGANISE	ORIENT	ORNATER
ORDINANCE	ORGANISED	ORIENTAL	ORNATEST
ORDINAND	ORGANISER	ORIENTALS	ORNERIER
ORDINANDS	ORGANISES	ORIENTATE	ORNERIEST
ORDINANT	ORGANISM	ORIENTED	ORNERY
ORDINANTS	ORGANISMS	ORIENTEER	ORNIS
ORDINAR	ORGANIST	ORIENTER	ORNISES
ORDINARS	ORGANISTS	ORIENTERS	ORNITHES
ORDINARY	ORGANITY	ORIENTING	ORNITHIC
ORDINATE	ORGANIZE	ORIENTS	ORNITHINE
ORDINATED	ORGANIZED	ORIFEX	ORNITHOID
ORDINATES	ORGANIZER	ORIFEXES	OROGEN
ORDINEE	ORGANIZES	ORIFICE	OROGENIC
ORDINEES	ORGANON	ORIFICES	OROGENIES
ORDINES	ORGANONS	ORIFICIAL	OROGENS
ORDNANCE	ORGANOSOL	ORIFLAMME	OROGENY
ORDNANCES	ORGANOTIN	ORIGAMI	OROGRAPHY
ORDO	ORGANS	ORIGAMIS	OROIDE
ORDOS	ORGANUM	ORIGAN	OROIDES
ORDS	ORGANUMS	ORIGANE	OROLOGIES
ORDURE	ORGANZA	ORIGANES	OROLOGIST
ORDURES	ORGANZAS	ORIGANS	OROLOGY
ORDUROUS	ORGANZINE	ORIGANUM	OROMETER
ORE	ORGASM	ORIGANUMS	OROMETERS
OREAD	ORGASMED	ORIGIN	ORONASAL
OREADES	ORGASMIC	ORIGINAL	OROPESA
OREADS	ORGASMING	ORIGINALS	OROPESAS
ORECTIC	ORGASMS	ORIGINATE	OROTUND
ORECTIVE	ORGASTIC	ORIGINS	ORPHAN
OREGANO	ORGEAT	ORIHOU	ORPHANAGE
OREGANOS	ORGEATS	ORILLION	ORPHANED
OREIDE	ORGIA	ORILLIONS	ORPHANING
OREIDES	ORGIAC	ORINASAL	ORPHANISM
OREODONT	ORGIAS	ORINASALS	ORPHANS
OREODONTS	ORGIAST	ORIOLE	ORPHARION
OREOLOGY	ORGIASTIC	ORIOLES	ORPHIC

ORPHICAL	ORYXES	OSMOSE	OSTEOID
ORPHISM	ORZO	OSMOSED	OSTEOIDS
ORPHISMS	ORZOS	OSMOSES	OSTEOLOGY
ORPHREY	OS	OSMOSING	OSTEOMA
ORPHREYED	OSAR	OSMOSIS	OSTEOMAS
ORPHREYS	OSCAR	OSMOTIC	OSTEOMATA
ORPIMENT	OSCARS	OSMOUS	OSTEOPATH
ORPIMENTS	OSCHEAL	OSMUND	OSTEOSES
ORPIN	OSCILLATE	OSMUNDA	OSTEOSIS
ORPINE	OSCINE	OSMUNDAS	OSTEOTOME
ORPINES	OSCINES	OSMUNDINE	OSTEOTOMY
ORPINS	OSCININE	OSMUNDS	OSTIA
ORRA	OSCITANCE	OSNABURG	OSTIAL
ORRAMAN	OSCITANCY	OSNABURGS	OSTIARIES
ORRAMEN	OSCITANT	OSPREY	OSTIARY
ORRERIES	OSCITATE	OSPREYS	OSTIATE
ORRERY	OSCITATED	OSSA	OSTINATI
ORRICE	OSCITATES	OSSARIUM	OSTINATO
ORRICES	OSCULA	OSSARIUMS	OSTINATOS
ORRIS	OSCULANT	OSSATURE	OSTIOLAR
ORRISES	OSCULAR	OSSATURES	OSTIOLATE
ORRISROOT	OSCULATE	OSSEIN	OSTIOLE
ORS	OSCULATED	OSSEINS	OSTIOLES
ORSEILLE	OSCULATES	OSSELET	OSTIUM
ORSEILLES	OSCULE	OSSELETS	OSTLER
ORSELLIC	OSCULES	OSSEOUS	OSTLERESS
ORT	OSCULUM	OSSEOUSLY	OSTLERS
ORTANIQUE	OSE	OSSETER	OSTMARK
ORTHIAN	OSES	OSSETERS	OSTMARKS
ORTHICON	OSETRA	OSSETRA	OSTOMATE
ORTHICONS	OSETRAS	OSSETRAS	OSTOMATES
ORTHO	OSHAC	OSSIA	OSTOMIES
ORTHOAXES	OSHACS	OSSICLE	OSTOMY
ORTHOAXIS	OSIER	OSSICLES	OSTOSES
ORTHODOX	OSIERED	OSSICULAR	OSTOSIS
ORTHODOXY	OSIERIES	OSSIFIC	OSTOSISES
ORTHOEPIC	OSIERS	OSSIFIED	OSTRACA
ORTHOEPY	OSIERY	OSSIFIER	OSTRACEAN
ORTHOPEDY	OSMATE	OSSIFIERS	OSTRACISE
ORTHOPOD	OSMATES	OSSIFIES	OSTRACISM
ORTHOPODS	OSMATIC	OSSIFRAGA	OSTRACIZE
ORTHOPTER	OSMETERIA	OSSIFRAGE	OSTRACOD
ORTHOPTIC	OSMIATE	OSSIFY	OSTRACODE
ORTHOS	OSMIATES	OSSIFYING	OSTRACODS
ORTHOSES	OSMIC	OSSUARIES	OSTRACON
ORTHOSIS	OSMICALLY	OSSUARY	OSTRACONS
ORTHOTIC	OSMICS	OSTEAL	OSTRAKA
ORTHOTICS	OSMIOUS	OSTEITIC	OSTRAKON
ORTHOTIST	OSMIUM	OSTEITIS	OSTREGER
ORTHOTONE	OSMIUMS	OSTENSIVE	OSTREGERS
ORTHROS	OSMOL	OSTENSORY	OSTRICH
ORTHROSES	OSMOLAL	OSTENT	OSTRICHES
ORTOLAN	OSMOLAR	OSTENTS	OTAKU
ORTOLANS	OSMOLE	OSTEOCYTE	OTALGIA
ORTS	OSMOLES	OSTEODERM	OTALGIAS
ORVAL	OSMOLS	OSTEOGEN	OTALGIC
ORVALS	OSMOMETER	OSTEOGENS	OTALGIES
ORYX	OSMOMETRY	OSTEOGENY	OTALGY

OTARIES	OUCHES	OURARI	OUTBAWL
OTARINE	OUCHING	OURARIS	OUTBAWLED
OTARY	OUCHT	OUREBI	OUTBAWLS
OTHER	OUCHTS	OUREBIS	OUTBEAM
OTHERNESS	OUD	OURIE	OUTBEAMED
OTHERS	OUDS	OURIER	OUTBEAMS
OTHERWISE	OUGHLIED	OURIEST	OUTBEG
OTIC	OUGHLIES	OURN	OUTBEGGED
OTIOSE	OUGHLY	OUROBOROS	OUTBEGS
OTIOSELY	OUGHLYING	OUROLOGY	OUTBID
OTIOSITY	OUGHT	OUROSCOPY	OUTBIDDEN
OTITIC	OUGHTED	OURS	OUTBIDDER
OTITIDES	OUGHTING	OURSELF	OUTBIDS
OTITIS	OUGHTNESS	OURSELVES	OUTBITCH
OTITISES	OUGHTS	OUS	OUTBLAZE
OTOCYST	OUGLIE	OUSEL	OUTBLAZED
OTOCYSTIC	OUGLIED	OUSELS	OUTBLAZES
OTOCYSTS	OUGLIEING	OUST	OUTBLEAT
OTOLITH	OUGLIES	OUSTED	OUTBLEATS
OTOLITHIC	OUGUIYA	OUSTER	OUTBLESS
OTOLITHS	OUGUIYAS	OUSTERS	OUTBLOOM
OTOLOGIES	OUIJA	OUSTING	OUTBLOOMS
OTOLOGIST	OUIJAS	OUSTITI	OUTBLUFF
OTOLOGY	OUISTITI	OUSTITIS	OUTBLUFFS
OTOPLASTY	OUISTITIS	OUSTS	OUTBLUSH
OTORRHOEA	OUK	OUT	OUTBOARD
OTOSCOPE	OUKS	OUTACT	OUTBOARDS
OTOSCOPES	OULACHON	OUTACTED	OUTBOAST
OTOSCOPIC	OULACHONS	OUTACTING	OUTBOASTS
OTOSCOPY	OULAKAN	OUTACTS	OUTBOUGHT
OTOTOXIC	OULAKANS	OUTADD	OUTBOUND
OTTAR	OULD	OUTADDED	OUTBOUNDS
OTTARS	OULDER	OUTADDING	OUTBOX
OTTAVA	OULDEST	OUTADDS	OUTBOXED
OTTAVAS	OULK	OUTAGE	OUTBOXES
OTTAVINO	OULKS	OUTAGES	OUTBOXING
OTTAVINOS	OULONG	OUTARGUE	OUTBRAG
OTTER	OULONGS	OUTARGUED	OUTBRAGS
OTTERED	OUMA	OUTARGUES	OUTBRAVE
OTTERING	OUMAS	OUTASIGHT	OUTBRAVED
OTTERS	OUNCE	OUTASK	OUTBRAVES
OTTO	OUNCES	OUTASKED	OUTBRAWL
OTTOMAN	OUNDY	OUTASKING	OUTBRAWLS
OTTOMANS	OUP	OUTASKS	OUTBRAZEN
OTTOS	OUPA	OUTATE	OUTBREAK
OTTRELITE	OUPAS	OUTBACK	OUTBREAKS
OU	OUPED	OUTBACKER	OUTBRED
OUABAIN	OUPH	OUTBACKS	OUTBREED
OUABAINS	OUPHE	OUTBAKE	OUTBREEDS
OUAKARI	OUPHES	OUTBAKED	OUTBRIBE
OUAKARIS	OUPHS	OUTBAKES	OUTBRIBED
OUBAAS	OUPING	OUTBAKING	OUTBRIBES
OUBAASES	OUPS	OUTBAR	OUTBROKE
OUBIT	OUR	OUTBARK	OUTBROKEN
OUBITS	OURALI	OUTBARKED	OUTBUILD
OUBLIETTE	OURALIS	OUTBARKS	OUTBUILDS
OUCH	OURANG	OUTBARRED	OUTBUILT
OUCHED	OURANGS	OUTBARS	OUTBULGE

OUTBULGED	OUTCROP	OUTDROP	OUTFIGHTS
OUTBULGES	OUTCROPS	OUTDROPS	OUTFIGURE
OUTBULK	OUTCROSS	OUTDROVE	OUTFIND
OUTBULKED	OUTCROW	OUTDRUNK	OUTFINDS
OUTBULKS	OUTCROWD	OUTDUEL	OUTFIRE
OUTBULLY	OUTCROWDS	OUTDUELED	OUTFIRED
OUTBURN	OUTCROWED	OUTDUELS	OUTFIRES
OUTBURNED	OUTCROWS	OUTDURE	OUTFIRING
OUTBURNS	OUTCRY	OUTDURED	OUTFISH
OUTBURNT	OUTCRYING	OUTDURES	OUTFISHED
OUTBURST	OUTCURSE	OUTDURING	OUTFISHES
OUTBURSTS	OUTCURSED	OUTDWELL	OUTFIT
OUTBUY	OUTCURSES	OUTDWELLS	OUTFITS
OUTBUYING	OUTCURVE	OUTDWELT	OUTFITTED
OUTBUYS	OUTCURVES	OUTEARN	OUTFITTER
OUTBY	OUTDANCE	OUTEARNED	OUTFLANK
OUTBYE	OUTDANCED	OUTEARNS	OUTFLANKS
OUTCALL	OUTDANCES	OUTEAT	OUTFLASH
OUTCALLS	OUTDARE	OUTEATEN	OUTFLEW
OUTCAPER	OUTDARED	OUTEATING	OUTFLIES
OUTCAPERS	OUTDARES	OUTEATS	OUTFLING
OUTCAST	OUTDARING	OUTECHO	OUTFLINGS
OUTCASTE	OUTDATE	OUTECHOED	OUTFLOAT
OUTCASTED	OUTDATED	OUTECHOES	OUTFLOATS
OUTCASTES	OUTDATES	OUTED	OUTFLOW
OUTCASTS	OUTDATING	OUTEDGE	OUTFLOWED
OUTCATCH	OUTDAZZLE	OUTEDGES	OUTFLOWN
OUTCAUGHT	OUTDEBATE	OUTER	OUTFLOWS
OUTCAVIL	OUTDESIGN	OUTERCOAT	OUTFLUSH
OUTCAVILS	OUTDID	OUTERMOST	OUTFLY
OUTCHARGE	OUTDO	OUTERS	OUTFLYING
OUTCHARM	OUTDODGE	OUTERWEAR	OUTFOOL
OUTCHARMS	OUTDODGED	OUTFABLE	OUTFOOLED
OUTCHEAT	OUTDODGES	OUTFABLED	OUTFOOLS
OUTCHEATS	OUTDOER	OUTFABLES	OUTFOOT
OUTCHID	OUTDOERS	OUTFACE	OUTFOOTED
OUTCHIDE	OUTDOES	OUTFACED	OUTFOOTS
OUTCHIDED	OUTDOING	OUTFACES	OUTFOUGHT
OUTCHIDES	OUTDONE	OUTFACING	OUTFOUND
OUTCITIES	OUTDOOR	OUTFALL	OUTFOX
OUTCITY	OUTDOORS	OUTFALLS	OUTFOXED
OUTCLASS	OUTDOORSY	OUTFAST	OUTFOXES
OUTCLIMB	OUTDRAG	OUTFASTED	OUTFOXING
OUTCLIMBS	OUTDRAGS	OUTFASTS	OUTFROWN
OUTCLOMB	OUTDRANK	OUTFAWN	OUTFROWNS
OUTCOACH	OUTDRAW	OUTFAWNED	OUTFUMBLE
OUTCOME	OUTDRAWN	OUTFAWNS	OUTGAIN
OUTCOMES	OUTDRAWS	OUTFEAST	OUTGAINED
OUTCOOK	OUTDREAM	OUTFEASTS	OUTGAINS
OUTCOOKED	OUTDREAMS	OUTFEEL	OUTGALLOP
OUTCOOKS	OUTDREAMT	OUTFEELS	OUTGAMBLE
OUTCOUNT	OUTDRESS	OUTFELT	OUTGAS
OUTCOUNTS	OUTDREW	OUTFENCE	OUTGASES
OUTCRAFTY	OUTDRINK	OUTFENCED	OUTGASSED
OUTCRAWL	OUTDRINKS	OUTFENCES	OUTGASSES
OUTCRAWLS	OUTDRIVE	OUTFIELD	OUTGATE
OUTCRIED	OUTDRIVEN	OUTFIELDS	OUTGATES
OUTCRIES	OUTDRIVES	OUTFIGHT	OUTGAVE

OUTGAZE	OUTHIRED	OUTLASHES	OUTMANNED
OUTGAZED	OUTHIRES	OUTLAST	OUTMANS
OUTGAZES	OUTHIRING	OUTLASTED	OUTMANTLE
OUTGAZING	OUTHIT	OUTLASTS	OUTMARCH
OUTGIVE	OUTHITS	OUTLAUGH	OUTMASTER
OUTGIVEN	OUTHOMER	OUTLAUGHS	OUTMATCH
OUTGIVES	OUTHOMERS	OUTLAUNCE	OUTMODE
OUTGIVING	OUTHOUSE	OUTLAUNCH	OUTMODED
OUTGLARE	OUTHOUSES	OUTLAW	OUTMODES
OUTGLARED	OUTHOWL	OUTLAWED	OUTMODING
OUTGLARES	OUTHOWLED	OUTLAWING	OUTMOST
OUTGLEAM	OUTHOWLS	OUTLAWRY	OUTMOVE
OUTGLEAMS	OUTHUMOR	OUTLAWS	OUTMOVED
OUTGLOW	OUTHUMORS	OUTLAY	OUTMOVES
OUTGLOWED	OUTHUNT	OUTLAYING	OUTMOVING
OUTGLOWS	OUTHUNTED	OUTLAYS	OUTMUSCLE
OUTGNAW	OUTHUNTS	OUTLEAD	OUTNAME
OUTGNAWED	OUTHUSTLE	OUTLEADS	OUTNAMED
OUTGNAWN	OUTHYRE	OUTLEAP	OUTNAMES
OUTGNAWS	OUTHYRED	OUTLEAPED	OUTNAMING
OUTGO	OUTHYRES	OUTLEAPS	OUTNESS
OUTGOER	OUTHYRING	OUTLEAPT	OUTNESSES
OUTGOERS	OUTING	OUTLEARN	OUTNIGHT
OUTGOES	OUTINGS	OUTLEARNS	OUTNIGHTS
OUTGOING	OUTJEST	OUTLEARNT	OUTNUMBER
OUTGOINGS	OUTJESTED	OUTLED	OUTOFFICE
OUTGONE	OUTJESTS	OUTLER	OUTPACE
OUTGREW	OUTJET	OUTLERS	OUTPACED
OUTGRIN	OUTJETS	OUTLET	OUTPACES
OUTGRINS	OUTJINX	OUTLETS	OUTPACING
OUTGROSS	OUTJINXED	OUTLIE	OUTPAINT
OUTGROUP	OUTJINXES	OUTLIED	OUTPAINTS
OUTGROUPS	OUTJOCKEY	OUTLIER	OUTPART
OUTGROW	OUTJUGGLE	OUTLIERS	OUTPARTS
OUTGROWN	OUTJUMP	OUTLIES	OUTPASS
OUTGROWS	OUTJUMPED	OUTLINE	OUTPASSED
OUTGROWTH	OUTJUMPS	OUTLINEAR	OUTPASSES
OUTGUARD	OUTJUT	OUTLINED	OUTPEEP
OUTGUARDS	OUTJUTS	OUTLINER	OUTPEEPED
OUTGUESS	OUTJUTTED	OUTLINERS	OUTPEEPS
OUTGUIDE	OUTKEEP	OUTLINES	OUTPEER
OUTGUIDED	OUTKEEPS	OUTLINING	OUTPEERED
OUTGUIDES	OUTKEPT	OUTLIVE	OUTPEERS
OUTGUN	OUTKICK	OUTLIVED	OUTPEOPLE
OUTGUNNED	OUTKICKED	OUTLIVER	OUTPITCH
OUTGUNS	OUTKICKS	OUTLIVERS	OUTPITIED
OUTGUSH	OUTKILL	OUTLIVES	OUTPITIES
OUTGUSHED	OUTKILLED	OUTLIVING	OUTPITY
OUTGUSHES	OUTKILLS	OUTLOOK	OUTPLACE
OUTHANDLE	OUTKISS	OUTLOOKED	OUTPLACED
OUTHAUL	OUTKISSED	OUTLOOKS	OUTPLACER
OUTHAULER	OUTKISSES	OUTLOVE	OUTPLACES
OUTHAULS	OUTLAID	OUTLOVED	OUTPLAN
OUTHEAR	OUTLAIN	OUTLOVES	OUTPLANS
OUTHEARD	OUTLAND	OUTLOVING	OUTPLAY
OUTHEARS	OUTLANDER	OUTLUSTRE	OUTPLAYED
OUTHER	OUTLANDS	OUTLYING	OUTPLAYS
OUTHIRE	OUTLASH	OUTMAN	OUTPLOD

OUTPLODS	OUTRAISES	OUTROLLED	OUTSERVES
OUTPLOT	OUTRAN	OUTROLLS	OUTSET
OUTPLOTS	OUTRANCE	OUTROOP	OUTSETS
OUTPOINT	OUTRANCES	OUTROOPER	OUTSHAME
OUTPOINTS	OUTRANG	OUTROOPS	OUTSHAMED
OUTPOLL	OUTRANGE	OUTROOT	OUTSHAMES
OUTPOLLED	OUTRANGED	OUTROOTED	OUTSHINE
OUTPOLLS	OUTRANGES	OUTROOTS	OUTSHINED
OUTPORT	OUTRANK	OUTROPE	OUTSHINES
OUTPORTER	OUTRANKED	OUTROPER	OUTSHONE
OUTPORTS	OUTRANKS	OUTROPERS	OUTSHOOT
OUTPOST	OUTRATE	OUTROPES	OUTSHOOTS
OUTPOSTS	OUTRATED	OUTROS	OUTSHOT
OUTPOUR	OUTRATES	OUTROW	OUTSHOTS
OUTPOURED	OUTRATING	OUTROWED	OUTSHOUT
OUTPOURER	OUTRAVE	OUTROWING	OUTSHOUTS
OUTPOURS	OUTRAVED	OUTROWS	OUTSIDE
OUTPOWER	OUTRAVES	OUTRUN	OUTSIDER
OUTPOWERS	OUTRAVING	OUTRUNG	OUTSIDERS
OUTPRAY	OUTRE	OUTRUNNER	OUTSIDES
OUTPRAYED	OUTREACH	OUTRUNS	OUTSIGHT
OUTPRAYS	OUTREAD	OUTRUSH	OUTSIGHTS
OUTPREACH	OUTREADS	OUTRUSHED	OUTSIN
OUTPREEN	OUTREASON	OUTRUSHES	OUTSING
OUTPREENS	OUTRECKON	OUTS	OUTSINGS
OUTPRESS	OUTRED	OUTSAID	OUTSINNED
OUTPRICE	OUTREDDED	OUTSAIL	OUTSINS
OUTPRICED	OUTREDDEN	OUTSAILED	OUTSIT
OUTPRICES	OUTREDS	OUTSAILS	OUTSITS
OUTPRIZE	OUTREIGN	OUTSANG	OUTSIZE
OUTPRIZED	OUTREIGNS	OUTSAT	OUTSIZED
OUTPRIZES	OUTRELIEF	OUTSAVOR	OUTSIZES
OUTPULL	OUTREMER	OUTSAVORS	OUTSKATE
OUTPULLED	OUTREMERS	OUTSAW	OUTSKATED
OUTPULLS	OUTRIDDEN	OUTSAY	OUTSKATES
OUTPUNCH	OUTRIDE	OUTSAYING	OUTSKIRT
OUTPUPIL	OUTRIDER	OUTSAYS	OUTSKIRTS
OUTPUPILS	OUTRIDERS	OUTSCHEME	OUTSLEEP
OUTPURSUE	OUTRIDES	OUTSCOLD	OUTSLEEPS
OUTPUSH	OUTRIDING	OUTSCOLDS	OUTSLEPT
OUTPUSHED	OUTRIG	OUTSCOOP	OUTSLICK
OUTPUSHES	OUTRIGGED	OUTSCOOPS	OUTSLICKS
OUTPUT	OUTRIGGER	OUTSCORE	OUTSMART
OUTPUTS	OUTRIGHT	OUTSCORED	OUTSMARTS
OUTPUTTED	OUTRIGS	OUTSCORES	OUTSMELL
OUTQUOTE	OUTRING	OUTSCORN	OUTSMELLS
OUTQUOTED	OUTRINGS	OUTSCORNS	OUTSMELT
OUTQUOTES	OUTRIVAL	OUTSCREAM	OUTSMILE
OUTRACE	OUTRIVALS	OUTSEE	OUTSMILED
OUTRACED	OUTRO	OUTSEEING	OUTSMILES
OUTRACES	OUTROAR	OUTSEEN	OUTSMOKE
OUTRACING	OUTROARED	OUTSEES	OUTSMOKED
OUTRAGE	OUTROARS	OUTSELL	OUTSMOKES
OUTRAGED	OUTROCK	OUTSELLS	OUTSNORE
OUTRAGES	OUTROCKED	OUTSERT	OUTSNORED
OUTRAGING	OUTROCKS	OUTSERTS	OUTSNORES
OUTRAISE	OUTRODE	OUTSERVE	OUTSOAR
OUTRAISED	OUTROLL	OUTSERVED	OUTSOARED

OUTSOARS	OUTSULK	OUTTRADES	OUTWELL
OUTSOLD	OUTSULKED	OUTTRAVEL	OUTWELLED
OUTSOLE	OUTSULKS	OUTTRICK	OUTWELLS
OUTSOLES	OUTSUM	OUTTRICKS	OUTWENT
OUTSOURCE	OUTSUMMED	OUTTROT	OUTWEPT
OUTSPAN	OUTSUMS	OUTTROTS	OUTWHIRL
OUTSPANS	OUTSUNG	OUTTRUMP	OUTWHIRLS
OUTSPEAK	OUTSWAM	OUTTRUMPS	OUTWICK
OUTSPEAKS	OUTSWARE	OUTTURN	OUTWICKED
OUTSPED	OUTSWEAR	OUTTURNS	OUTWICKS
OUTSPEED	OUTSWEARS	OUTVALUE	OUTWILE
OUTSPEEDS	OUTSWEEP	OUTVALUED	OUTWILED
OUTSPELL	OUTSWEEPS	OUTVALUES	OUTWILES
OUTSPELLS	OUTSWELL	OUTVAUNT	OUTWILING
OUTSPELT	OUTSWELLS	OUTVAUNTS	OUTWILL
OUTSPEND	OUTSWEPT	OUTVENOM	OUTWILLED
OUTSPENDS	OUTSWIM	OUTVENOMS	OUTWILLS
OUTSPENT	OUTSWIMS	OUTVIE	OUTWIN
OUTSPOKE	OUTSWING	OUTVIED	OUTWIND
OUTSPOKEN	OUTSWINGS	OUTVIES	OUTWINDED
OUTSPORT	OUTSWORE	OUTVOICE	OUTWINDS
OUTSPORTS	OUTSWORN	OUTVOICED	OUTWING
OUTSPRANG	OUTSWUM	OUTVOICES	OUTWINGED
OUTSPREAD	OUTSWUNG	OUTVOTE	OUTWINGS
OUTSPRING	OUTTAKE	OUTVOTED	OUTWINS
OUTSPRINT	OUTTAKEN	OUTVOTER	OUTWISH
OUTSPRUNG	OUTTAKES	OUTVOTERS	OUTWISHED
OUTSTAND	OUTTAKING	OUTVOTES	OUTWISHES
OUTSTANDS	OUTTALK	OUTVOTING	OUTWIT
OUTSTARE	OUTTALKED	OUTVYING	OUTWITH
OUTSTARED	OUTTALKS	OUTWAIT	OUTWITS
OUTSTARES	OUTTASK	OUTWAITED	OUTWITTED
OUTSTART	OUTTASKED	OUTWAITS	OUTWON
OUTSTARTS	OUTTASKS	OUTWALK	OUTWORE
OUTSTATE	OUTTELL	OUTWALKED	OUTWORK
OUTSTATED	OUTTELLS	OUTWALKS	OUTWORKED
OUTSTATES	OUTTHANK	OUTWAR	OUTWORKER
OUTSTAY	OUTTHANKS	OUTWARD	OUTWORKS
OUTSTAYED	OUTTHIEVE	OUTWARDLY	OUTWORN
OUTSTAYS	OUTTHINK	OUTWARDS	OUTWORTH
OUTSTEER	OUTTHINKS	OUTWARRED	OUTWORTHS
OUTSTEERS	OUTTHREW	OUTWARS	OUTWOUND
OUTSTEP	OUTTHROB	OUTWASH	OUTWREST
OUTSTEPS	OUTTHROBS	OUTWASHES	OUTWRESTS
OUTSTOOD	OUTTHROW	OUTWASTE	OUTWRIT
OUTSTRAIN	OUTTHROWN	OUTWASTED	OUTWRITE
OUTSTRIDE	OUTTHROWS	OUTWASTES	OUTWRITES
OUTSTRIKE	OUTTHRUST	OUTWATCH	OUTWROTE
OUTSTRIP	OUTTOLD	OUTWEAR	OUTYELL
OUTSTRIPS	OUTTONGUE	OUTWEARS	OUTYELLED
OUTSTRIVE	OUTTOOK	OUTWEARY	OUTYELLS
OUTSTRODE	OUTTOP	OUTWEED	OUTYELP
OUTSTROKE	OUTTOPPED	OUTWEEDED	OUTYELPED
OUTSTROVE	OUTTOPS	OUTWEEDS	OUTYELPS
OUTSTRUCK	OUTTOWER	OUTWEEP	OUTYIELD
OUTSTUDY	OUTTOWERS	OUTWEEPS	OUTYIELDS
OUTSTUNT	OUTTRADE	OUTWEIGH	OUVERT
OUTSTUNTS	OUTTRADED	OUTWEIGHS	OUVERTE

OUVRAGE	OVERAGED	OVERBUILD	OVERCUT
OUVRAGES	OVERAGES	OVERBUILT	OVERCUTS
OUVRIER	OVERALERT	OVERBULK	OVERDARE
OUVRIERE	OVERALL	OVERBULKS	OVERDARED
OUVRIERES	OVERALLED	OVERBURN	OVERDARES
OUVRIERS	OVERALLS	OVERBURNS	OVERDATED
OUZEL	OVERAPT	OVERBURNT	OVERDEAR
OUZELS	OVERARCH	OVERBUSY	OVERDECK
OUZO	OVERARM	OVERBUY	OVERDECKS
OUZOS	OVERARMED	OVERBUYS	OVERDID
OVA	OVERARMS	OVERBY	OVERDIGHT
OVAL	OVERATE	OVERCALL	OVERDO
OVALBUMIN	OVERAWE	OVERCALLS	OVERDOER
OVALITIES	OVERAWED	OVERCAME	OVERDOERS
OVALITY	OVERAWES	OVERCARRY	OVERDOES
OVALLY	OVERAWING	OVERCAST	OVERDOG
OVALNESS	OVERBAKE	OVERCASTS	OVERDOGS
OVALS	OVERBAKED	OVERCATCH	OVERDOING
OVARIAL	OVERBAKES	OVERCHEAP	OVERDONE
OVARIAN	OVERBEAR	OVERCHECK	OVERDOSE
OVARIES	OVERBEARS	OVERCHILL	OVERDOSED
OVARIOLE	OVERBEAT	OVERCIVIL	OVERDOSES
OVARIOLES	OVERBEATS	OVERCLAD	OVERDRAFT
OVARIOUS	OVERBED	OVERCLAIM	OVERDRANK
OVARITIS	OVERBET	OVERCLASS	OVERDRAW
OVARY	OVERBETS	OVERCLEAN	OVERDRAWN
OVATE	OVERBID	OVERCLEAR	OVERDRAWS
OVATED	OVERBIDS	OVERCLOSE	OVERDRESS
OVATELY	OVERBIG	OVERCLOUD	OVERDREW
OVATES	OVERBILL	OVERCLOY	OVERDRIED
OVATING	OVERBILLS	OVERCLOYS	OVERDRIES
OVATION	OVERBITE	OVERCOACH	OVERDRINK
OVATIONAL	OVERBITES	OVERCOAT	OVERDRIVE
OVATIONS	OVERBLEW	OVERCOATS	OVERDROVE
OVATOR	OVERBLOW	OVERCOLD	OVERDRUNK
OVATORS	OVERBLOWN	OVERCOLOR	OVERDRY
OVEL	OVERBLOWS	OVERCOME	OVERDUB
OVELS	OVERBOARD	OVERCOMER	OVERDUBS
OVEN	OVERBOIL	OVERCOMES	OVERDUE
OVENABLE	OVERBOILS	OVERCOOK	OVERDUST
OVENBIRD	OVERBOLD	OVERCOOKS	OVERDUSTS
OVENBIRDS	OVERBOOK	OVERCOOL	OVERDYE
OVENED	OVERBOOKS	OVERCOOLS	OVERDYED
OVENING	OVERBOOT	OVERCOUNT	OVERDYER
OVENLIKE	OVERBOOTS	OVERCOVER	OVERDYERS
OVENPROOF	OVERBORE	OVERCOY	OVERDYES
OVENS	OVERBORN	OVERCRAM	OVEREAGER
OVENWARE	OVERBORNE	OVERCRAMS	OVEREASY
OVENWARES	OVERBOUND	OVERCRAW	OVEREAT
OVENWOOD	OVERBRAKE	OVERCRAWS	OVEREATEN
OVENWOODS	OVERBRED	OVERCROP	OVEREATER
OVER	OVERBREED	OVERCROPS	OVEREATS
OVERABLE	OVERBRIEF	OVERCROW	OVERED
OVERACT	OVERBRIM	OVERCROWD	OVEREDIT
OVERACTED	OVERBRIMS	OVERCROWS	OVEREDITS
OVERACTS	OVERBROAD	OVERCURE	OVEREGG
OVERACUTE	OVERBROW	OVERCURED	OVEREGGED
OVERAGE	OVERBROWS	OVERCURES	OVEREGGS

OVEREMOTE	OVERGIVEN	OVERHOLDS	OVERLENDS
OVEREXERT	OVERGIVES	OVERHOLY	OVERLENT
OVEREYE	OVERGLAD	OVERHONOR	OVERLET
OVEREYED	OVERGLAZE	OVERHOPE	OVERLETS
OVEREYES	OVERGLOOM	OVERHOPED	OVERLEWD
OVEREYING	OVERGO	OVERHOPES	OVERLIE
OVERFALL	OVERGOAD	OVERHOT	OVERLIER
OVERFALLS	OVERGOADS	OVERHUNG	OVERLIERS
OVERFAR	OVERGOES	OVERHUNT	OVERLIES
OVERFAST	OVERGOING	OVERHUNTS	OVERLIGHT
OVERFAT	OVERGONE	OVERHYPE	OVERLIT
OVERFAVOR	OVERGORGE	OVERHYPED	OVERLIVE
OVERFEAR	OVERGOT	OVERHYPES	OVERLIVED
OVERFEARS	OVERGRADE	OVERIDLE	OVERLIVES
OVERFED	OVERGRAIN	OVERING	OVERLOAD
OVERFEED	OVERGRASS	OVERINKED	OVERLOADS
OVERFEEDS	OVERGRAZE	OVERISSUE	OVERLOCK
OVERFELL	OVERGREAT	OVERJOY	OVERLOCKS
OVERFILL	OVERGREEN	OVERJOYED	OVERLONG
OVERFILLS	OVERGREW	OVERJOYS	OVERLOOK
OVERFINE	OVERGROW	OVERJUMP	OVERLOOKS
OVERFISH	OVERGROWN	OVERJUMPS	OVERLORD
OVERFIT	OVERGROWS	OVERJUST	OVERLORDS
OVERFLEW	OVERHAILE	OVERKEEN	OVERLOUD
OVERFLIES	OVERHAIR	OVERKEEP	OVERLOVE
OVERFLOOD	OVERHAIRS	OVERKEEPS	OVERLOVED
OVERFLOW	OVERHALE	OVERKEPT	OVERLOVES
OVERFLOWN	OVERHALED	OVERKEST	OVERLUSH
OVERFLOWS	OVERHALES	OVERKILL	OVERLUSTY
OVERFLUSH	OVERHAND	OVERKILLS	OVERLY
OVERFLY	OVERHANDS	OVERKIND	OVERLYING
OVERFOCUS	OVERHANG	OVERKING	OVERMAN
OVERFOLD	OVERHANGS	OVERKINGS	OVERMANS
OVERFOLDS	OVERHAPPY	OVERKNEE	OVERMANY
OVERFOND	OVERHARD	OVERLABOR	OVERMAST
OVERFOUL	OVERHASTE	OVERLADE	OVERMASTS
OVERFRANK	OVERHASTY	OVERLADED	OVERMATCH
OVERFREE	OVERHATE	OVERLADEN	OVERMEEK
OVERFULL	OVERHATED	OVERLADES	OVERMELT
OVERFUND	OVERHATES	OVERLAID	OVERMELTS
OVERFUNDS	OVERHAUL	OVERLAIN	OVERMEN
OVERFUSSY	OVERHAULS	OVERLAND	OVERMERRY
OVERGALL	OVERHEAD	OVERLANDS	OVERMILD
OVERGALLS	OVERHEADS	OVERLAP	OVERMILK
OVERGANG	OVERHEAP	OVERLAPS	OVERMILKS
OVERGANGS	OVERHEAPS	OVERLARD	OVERMINE
OVERGAVE	OVERHEAR	OVERLARDS	OVERMINED
OVERGEAR	OVERHEARD	OVERLARGE	OVERMINES
OVERGEARS	OVERHEARS	OVERLATE	OVERMIX
OVERGET	OVERHEAT	OVERLAX	OVERMIXED
OVERGETS	OVERHEATS	OVERLAY	OVERMIXES
OVERGILD	OVERHELD	OVERLAYS	OVERMOUNT
OVERGILDS	OVERHENT	OVERLEAF	OVERMUCH
OVERGILT	OVERHENTS	OVERLEAP	OVERNAME
OVERGIRD	OVERHIGH	OVERLEAPS	OVERNAMED
OVERGIRDS	OVERHIT	OVERLEAPT	OVERNAMES
OVERGIRT	OVERHITS	OVERLEARN	OVERNEAR
OVERGIVE	OVERHOLD	OVERLEND	OVERNEAT

OVERNET	OVERRATES	OVERSEWN	OVERSTEER
OVERNETS	OVERREACH	OVERSEWS	OVERSTEP
OVERNEW	OVERREACT	OVERSEXED	OVERSTEPS
OVERNICE	OVERREAD	OVERSHADE	OVERSTINK
OVERNIGHT	OVERREADS	OVERSHARP	OVERSTIR
OVERPACK	OVERRED	OVERSHINE	OVERSTIRS
OVERPACKS	OVERREDS	OVERSHIRT	OVERSTOCK
OVERPAGE	OVERREN	OVERSHOE	OVERSTOOD
OVERPAID	OVERRENS	OVERSHOES	OVERSTORY
OVERPAINT	OVERRICH	OVERSHONE	OVERSTREW
OVERPART	OVERRIDE	OVERSHOOT	OVERSTUDY
OVERPARTS	OVERRIDER	OVERSHOT	OVERSTUFF
OVERPASS	OVERRIDES	OVERSHOTS	OVERSTUNK
OVERPAST	OVERRIFE	OVERSICK	OVERSUDS
OVERPAY	OVERRIGID	OVERSIDE	OVERSUP
OVERPAYS	OVERRIPE	OVERSIDES	OVERSUPS
OVERPEDAL	OVERRIPEN	OVERSIGHT	OVERSURE
OVERPEER	OVERROAST	OVERSIZE	OVERSWAM
OVERPEERS	OVERRODE	OVERSIZED	OVERSWAY
OVERPERCH	OVERRUDE	OVERSIZES	OVERSWAYS
OVERPERT	OVERRUFF	OVERSKIP	OVERSWEAR
OVERPITCH	OVERRUFFS	OVERSKIPS	OVERSWEET
OVERPLAID	OVERRULE	OVERSKIRT	OVERSWELL
OVERPLAN	OVERRULED	OVERSLEEP	OVERSWIM
OVERPLANS	OVERRULER	OVERSLEPT	OVERSWIMS
OVERPLANT	OVERRULES	OVERSLIP	OVERSWING
OVERPLAST	OVERRUN	OVERSLIPS	OVERSWORE
OVERPLAY	OVERRUNS	OVERSLIPT	OVERSWORN
OVERPLAYS	OVERS	OVERSLOW	OVERSWUM
OVERPLIED	OVERSAD	OVERSMAN	OVERSWUNG
OVERPLIES	OVERSAIL	OVERSMEN	OVERT
OVERPLOT	OVERSAILS	OVERSMOKE	OVERTAKE
OVERPLOTS	OVERSALE	OVERSOAK	OVERTAKEN
OVERPLUS	OVERSALES	OVERSOAKS	OVERTAKES
OVERPLY	OVERSALT	OVERSOFT	OVERTALK
OVERPOISE	OVERSALTS	OVERSOLD	OVERTALKS
OVERPOST	OVERSAUCE	OVERSOON	OVERTAME
OVERPOSTS	OVERSAVE	OVERSOUL	OVERTART
OVERPOWER	OVERSAVED	OVERSOULS	OVERTASK
OVERPRESS	OVERSAVES	OVERSOW	OVERTASKS
OVERPRICE	OVERSAW	OVERSOWED	OVERTAX
OVERPRINT	OVERSCALE	OVERSOWN	OVERTAXED
OVERPRIZE	OVERSCORE	OVERSOWS	OVERTAXES
OVERPROOF	OVERSEA	OVERSPEND	OVERTEACH
OVERPROUD	OVERSEAS	OVERSPENT	OVERTEEM
OVERPUMP	OVERSEE	OVERSPICE	OVERTEEMS
OVERPUMPS	OVERSEED	OVERSPILL	OVERTHICK
OVERQUICK	OVERSEEDS	OVERSPILT	OVERTHIN
OVERRACK	OVERSEEN	OVERSPIN	OVERTHINK
OVERRACKS	OVERSEER	OVERSPINS	OVERTHREW
OVERRAKE	OVERSEERS	OVERSTAFF	OVERTHROW
OVERRAKED	OVERSEES	OVERSTAIN	OVERTIGHT
OVERRAKES	OVERSELL	OVERSTAND	OVERTIME
OVERRAN	OVERSELLS	OVERSTANK	OVERTIMED
OVERRANK	OVERSET	OVERSTARE	OVERTIMER
OVERRASH	OVERSETS	OVERSTATE	OVERTIMES
OVERRATE	OVERSEW	OVERSTAY	OVERTIMID
OVERRATED	OVERSEWED	OVERSTAYS	OVERTIP

OVERTIPS	OVERWEEN	OVOLO	OWRELAY
OVERTIRE	OVERWEENS	OVOLOS	OWRELAYS
OVERTIRED	OVERWEIGH	OVONIC	OWRES
OVERTIRES	OVERWENT	OVONICS	OWREWORD
OVERTLY	OVERWET	OVOTESTES	OWREWORDS
OVERTNESS	OVERWETS	OVOTESTIS	OWRIE
OVERTOIL	OVERWHELM	OVULAR	OWRIER
OVERTOILS	OVERWIDE	OVULARY	OWRIEST
OVERTONE	OVERWILY	OVULATE	OWSE
OVERTONES	OVERWIND	OVULATED	OWSEN
OVERTOOK	OVERWINDS	OVULATES	OWT
OVERTOP	OVERWING	OVULATING	OWTS
OVERTOPS	OVERWINGS	OVULATION	OX
OVERTOWER	OVERWISE	OVULATORY	OXACILLIN
OVERTRADE	OVERWORD	OVULE	OXALATE
OVERTRAIN	OVERWORDS	OVULES	OXALATED
OVERTREAT	OVERWORE	OVUM	OXALATES
OVERTRICK	OVERWORK	OW	OXALATING
OVERTRIM	OVERWORKS	OWCHE	OXALIC
OVERTRIMS	OVERWORN	OWCHES	OXALIS
OVERTRIP	OVERWOUND	OWE	OXALISES
OVERTRIPS	OVERWREST	OWED	OXAZEPAM
OVERTRUMP	OVERWRITE	OWELTIES	OXAZEPAMS
OVERTRUST	OVERWROTE	OWELTY	OXAZINE
OVERTURE	OVERYEAR	OWER	OXAZINES
OVERTURED	OVERYEARS	OWERBY	OXBLOOD
OVERTURES	OVERZEAL	OWERLOUP	OXBLOODS
OVERTURN	OVERZEALS	OWERLOUPS	OXBOW
OVERTURNS	OVIBOS	OWES	OXBOWS
OVERTYPE	OVIBOSES	OWING	OXCART
OVERTYPED	OVIBOVINE	OWL	OXCARTS
OVERTYPES	OVICIDAL	OWLED	OXEN
OVERURGE	OVICIDE	OWLER	OXER
OVERURGED	OVICIDES	OWLERIES	OXERS
OVERURGES	OVIDUCAL	OWLERS	OXES
OVERUSE	OVIDUCT	OWLERY	OXEYE
OVERUSED	OVIDUCTAL	OWLET	OXEYES
OVERUSES	OVIDUCTS	OWLETS	OXFORD
OVERUSING	OVIFEROUS	OWLIER	OXFORDS
OVERVALUE	OVIFORM	OWLIEST	OXGANG
OVERVEIL	OVIGEROUS	OWLING	OXGANGS
OVERVEILS	OVINE	OWLISH	OXGATE
OVERVIEW	OVINES	OWLISHLY	OXGATES
OVERVIEWS	OVIPARA	OWLLIKE	OXHEAD
OVERVIVID	OVIPARITY	OWLS	OXHEADS
OVERVOTE	OVIPAROUS	OWLY	OXHEART
OVERVOTED	OVIPOSIT	OWN	OXHEARTS
OVERVOTES	OVIPOSITS	OWNABLE	OXHIDE
OVERWARM	OVIRAPTOR	OWNED	OXHIDES
OVERWARMS	OVISAC	OWNER	OXID
OVERWARY	OVISACS	OWNERLESS	OXIDABLE
OVERWASH	OVIST	OWNERS	OXIDANT
OVERWATCH	OVISTS	OWNERSHIP	OXIDANTS
OVERWATER	OVOID	OWNING	OXIDASE
OVERWEAK	OVOIDAL	OWNS	OXIDASES
OVERWEAR	OVOIDALS	OWRE	OXIDASIC
OVERWEARS	OVOIDS	OWRECOME	OXIDATE
OVERWEARY	OVOLI	OWRECOMES	OXIDATED

OXIDATES
OXIDATING
OXIDATION
OXIDATIVE
OXIDE
OXIDES
OXIDIC
OXIDISE
OXIDISED
OXIDISER
OXIDISERS
OXIDISES
OXIDISING
OXIDIZE
OXIDIZED
OXIDIZER
OXIDIZERS
OXIDIZES
OXIDIZING
OXIDS
OXIM
OXIME
OXIMES
OXIMETER
OXIMETERS
OXIMETRY
OXIMS
OXLAND
OXLANDS
OXLIKE
OXLIP
OXLIPS
OXO
OXONIUM
OXONIUMS
OXPECKER
OXPECKERS
OXSLIP
OXSLIPS
OXTAIL
OXTAILS
OXTER
OXTERED
OXTERING
OXTERS
OXTONGUE
OXTONGUES
OXY
OXYACID
OXYACIDS
OXYCODONE
OXYGEN
OXYGENASE
OXYGENATE
OXYGENIC
OXYGENISE
OXYGENIZE
OXYGENOUS

OXYGENS
OXYMEL
OXYMELS
OXYMORA
OXYMORON
OXYMORONS
OXYNTIC
OXYPHIL
OXYPHILE
OXYPHILES
OXYPHILIC
OXYPHILS
OXYSALT
OXYSALTS
OXYSOME
OXYSOMES
OXYTOCIC
OXYTOCICS
OXYTOCIN
OXYTOCINS
OXYTONE
OXYTONES
OY
OYE
OYER
OYERS
OYES
OYESES
OYESSES
OYEZ
OYEZES
OYS
OYSTER
OYSTERED
OYSTERER
OYSTERERS
OYSTERING
OYSTERMAN
OYSTERMEN
OYSTERS
OYSTRIGE
OYSTRIGES
OZAENA
OZAENAS
OZALID
OZALIDS
OZEKI
OZEKIS
OZOCERITE
OZOKERITE
OZONATE
OZONATED
OZONATES
OZONATING
OZONATION
OZONE
OZONES
OZONIC

OZONIDE
OZONIDES
OZONISE
OZONISED
OZONISER
OZONISERS
OZONISES
OZONISING
OZONIZE
OZONIZED
OZONIZER
OZONIZERS
OZONIZES
OZONIZING
OZONOUS
OZZIE
OZZIES

P

PA
PAAL
PAALS
PABLUM
PABLUMS
PABOUCHE
PABOUCHES
PABULAR
PABULOUS
PABULUM
PABULUMS
PAC
PACA
PACABLE
PACAS
PACATION
PACATIONS
PACE
PACED
PACEMAKER
PACER
PACERS
PACES
PACEWAY
PACEWAYS
PACEY
PACHA
PACHADOM
PACHADOMS
PACHAK
PACHAKS
PACHALIC
PACHALICS
PACHAS
PACHINKO
PACHINKOS
PACHISI
PACHISIS
PACHOULI
PACHOULIS
PACHUCO
PACHUCOS
PACHYDERM
PACHYTENE
PACIER
PACIEST
PACIFIC
PACIFICAL
PACIFIED
PACIFIER
PACIFIERS
PACIFIES
PACIFISM

PACIFISMS
PACIFIST
PACIFISTS
PACIFY
PACIFYING
PACING
PACK
PACKABLE
PACKAGE
PACKAGED
PACKAGER
PACKAGERS
PACKAGES
PACKAGING
PACKBOARD
PACKED
PACKER
PACKERS
PACKET
PACKETED
PACKETING
PACKETS
PACKFONG
PACKFONGS
PACKFRAME
PACKHORSE
PACKING
PACKINGS
PACKLY
PACKMAN
PACKMEN
PACKNESS
PACKS
PACKSACK
PACKSACKS
PACKSHEET
PACKSTAFF
PACKWAX
PACKWAXES
PACKWAY
PACKWAYS
PACO
PACOS
PACS
PACT
PACTA
PACTION
PACTIONAL
PACTIONED
PACTIONS
PACTS
PACTUM
PACY

PAD
PADANG
PADANGS
PADAUK
PADAUKS
PADDED
PADDER
PADDERS
PADDIES
PADDING
PADDINGS
PADDLE
PADDLED
PADDLER
PADDLERS
PADDLES
PADDLING
PADDLINGS
PADDOCK
PADDOCKED
PADDOCKS
PADDY
PADDYWACK
PADELLA
PADELLAS
PADEMELON
PADERERO
PADEREROS
PADI
PADIS
PADISHAH
PADISHAHS
PADKOS
PADLE
PADLES
PADLOCK
PADLOCKED
PADLOCKS
PADMA
PADMAS
PADNAG
PADNAGS
PADOUK
PADOUKS
PADRE
PADRES
PADRI
PADRONE
PADRONES
PADRONI
PADRONISM
PADS
PADSAW

PADSAWS
PADSHAH
PADSHAHS
PADUASOY
PADUASOYS
PADYMELON
PAEAN
PAEANISM
PAEANISMS
PAEANS
PAEDERAST
PAEDEUTIC
PAEDIATRY
PAEDOLOGY
PAELLA
PAELLAS
PAENULA
PAENULAE
PAENULAS
PAEON
PAEONIC
PAEONICS
PAEONIES
PAEONS
PAEONY
PAESAN
PAESANI
PAESANO
PAESANOS
PAESANS
PAGAN
PAGANDOM
PAGANDOMS
PAGANISE
PAGANISED
PAGANISER
PAGANISES
PAGANISH
PAGANISM
PAGANISMS
PAGANIST
PAGANISTS
PAGANIZE
PAGANIZED
PAGANIZER
PAGANIZES
PAGANS
PAGE
PAGEANT
PAGEANTRY
PAGEANTS
PAGEBOY
PAGEBOYS

PAGED	PAIN	PAITRICKS	PALATED
PAGEFUL	PAINCH	PAJAMA	PALATES
PAGEFULS	PAINCHES	PAJAMAED	PALATIAL
PAGEHOOD	PAINED	PAJAMAS	PALATINE
PAGEHOODS	PAINFUL	PAJOCK	PALATINES
PAGER	PAINFULLY	PAJOCKE	PALATING
PAGERS	PAINIM	PAJOCKES	PALAVER
PAGES	PAINIMS	PAJOCKS	PALAVERED
PAGEVIEW	PAINING	PAKAHI	PALAVERER
PAGEVIEWS	PAINLESS	PAKAHIS	PALAVERS
PAGINAL	PAINS	PAKAPOO	PALAY
PAGINATE	PAINT	PAKAPOOS	PALAYS
PAGINATED	PAINTABLE	PAKEHA	PALAZZI
PAGINATES	PAINTBALL	PAKEHAS	PALAZZO
PAGING	PAINTBOX	PAKFONG	PALAZZOS
PAGINGS	PAINTED	PAKFONGS	PALE
PAGLE	PAINTER	PAKIHI	PALEA
PAGLES	PAINTERLY	PAKIHIS	PALEAE
PAGOD	PAINTERS	PAKKA	PALEAL
PAGODA	PAINTIER	PAKOKO	PALEATE
PAGODAS	PAINTIEST	PAKOKOS	PALEBUCK
PAGODS	PAINTING	PAKORA	PALEBUCKS
PAGRI	PAINTINGS	PAKORAS	PALED
PAGRIS	PAINTRESS	PAKTHONG	PALEFACE
PAGURIAN	PAINTS	PAKTHONGS	PALEFACES
PAGURIANS	PAINTURE	PAKTONG	PALELY
PAGURID	PAINTURES	PAKTONGS	PALEMPORE
PAGURIDS	PAINTWORK	PAL	PALENESS
PAH	PAINTY	PALABRA	PALEOCENE
PAHAUTEA	PAIOCK	PALABRAS	PALEOGENE
PAHLAVI	PAIOCKE	PALACE	PALEOLITH
PAHLAVIS	PAIOCKES	PALACED	PALEOLOGY
PAHOEHOE	PAIOCKS	PALACES	PALEOSOL
PAHOEHOES	PAIR	PALADIN	PALEOSOLS
PAHS	PATRE	PALADINS	PALEOZOIC
PAID	PAIRED	PALAESTRA	PALER
PAIDEUTIC	PAIRER	PALAFITTE	PALES
PAIDLE	PAIRES	PALAGI	PALEST
PAIDLED	PAIREST	PALAGIS	PALESTRA
PAIDLES	PAIRIAL	PALAIS	PALESTRAE
PAIDLING	PAIRIALS	PALAMA	PALESTRAL
PAIGLE	PAIRING	PALAMAE	PALESTRAS
PAIGLES	PAIRINGS	PALAMATE	PALET
PAIK	PAIRS	PALAMINO	PALETOT
PAIKED	PAIRWISE	PALAMINOS	PALETOTS
PAIKING	PAIS	PALAMPORE	PALETS
PAIKS	PAISA	PALANKEEN	PALETTE
PAIL	PAISAN	PALANQUIN	PALETTES
PAILFUL	PAISANA	PALAPA	PALEWAYS
PAILFULS	PAISANAS	PALAPAS	PALEWISE
PAILLARD	PAISANO	PALAS	PALFREY
PAILLARDS	PAISANOS	PALASES	PALFREYED
PAILLASSE	PAISANS	PALATABLE	PALFREYS
PAILLETTE	PAISAS	PALATABLY	PALIER
PAILLON	PAISE	PALATAL	PALIEST
PAILLONS	PAISLEY	PALATALLY	PALIFORM
PAILS	PAISLEYS	PALATALS	PALIKAR
PAILSFUL	PAITRICK	PALATE	PALIKARS

PALILALIA	PALLONES	PALPAL	PAMPAS
PALILLOGY	PALLOR	PALPATE	PAMPASES
PALIMONY	PALLORS	PALPATED	PAMPEAN
PALING	PALLS	PALPATES	PAMPEANS
PALINGS	PALLY	PALPATING	PAMPER
PALINKA	PALM	PALPATION	PAMPERED
PALINKAS	PALMAR	PALPATOR	PAMPERER
PALINODE	PALMARIAN	PALPATORS	PAMPERERS
PALINODES	PALMARY	PALPATORY	PAMPERING
PALINODY	PALMATE	PALPEBRA	PAMPERO
PALINOPIA	PALMATED	PALPEBRAE	PAMPEROS
PALISADE	PALMATELY	PALPEBRAL	PAMPERS
PALISADED	PALMATION	PALPEBRAS	PAMPHLET
PALISADES	PALMED	PALPED	PAMPHLETS
PALISADO	PALMER	PALPI	PAMPHREY
PALISH	PALMERS	PALPING	PAMPHREYS
PALKEE	PALMETTE	PALPITANT	PAMPOEN
PALKEES	PALMETTES	PALPITATE	PAMPOENS
PALKI	PALMETTO	PALPS	PAMPOOTIE
PALKIS	PALMETTOS	PALPUS	PAMS
PALL	PALMFUL	PALS	PAN
PALLA	PALMFULS	PALSGRAVE	PANACEA
PALLADIA	PALMHOUSE	PALSHIP	PANACEAN
PALLADIC	PALMIE	PALSHIPS	PANACEAS
PALLADIUM	PALMIER	PALSIED	PANACHAEA
PALLADOUS	PALMIES	PALSIER	PANACHE
PALLAE	PALMIEST	PALSIES	PANACHES
PALLAH	PALMIET	PALSIEST	PANADA
PALLAHS	PALMIETS	PALSTAFF	PANADAS
PALLED	PALMING	PALSTAFFS	PANAMA
PALLET	PALMIPED	PALSTAVE	PANAMAS
PALLETED	PALMIPEDE	PALSTAVES	PANARIES
PALLETING	PALMIPEDS	PALSY	PANARY
PALLETISE	PALMIST	PALSYING	PANATELA
PALLETIZE	PALMISTER	PALSYLIKE	PANATELAS
PALLETS	PALMISTRY	PALTER	PANATELLA
PALLETTE	PALMISTS	PALTERED	PANAX
PALLETTES	PALMITATE	PALTERER	PANAXES
PALLIA	PALMITIC	PALTERERS	PANBROIL
PALLIAL	PALMITIN	PALTERING	PANBROILS
PALLIARD	PALMITINS	PALTERS	PANCAKE
PALLIARDS	PALMLIKE	PALTRIER	PANCAKED
PALLIASSE	PALMS	PALTRIEST	PANCAKES
PALLIATE	PALMTOP	PALTRILY	PANCAKING
PALLIATED	PALMTOPS	PALTRY	PANCE
PALLIATES	PALMY	PALUDAL	PANCES
PALLIATOR	PALMYRA	PALUDIC	PANCETTA
PALLID	PALMYRAS	PALUDINAL	PANCETTAS
PALLIDER	PALOLO	PALUDINE	PANCHAX
PALLIDEST	PALOLOS	PALUDISM	PANCHAXES
PALLIDITY	PALOMINO	PALUDISMS	PANCHAYAT
PALLIDLY	PALOMINOS	PALUDOSE	PANCHEON
PALLIER	PALOOKA	PALUDOUS	PANCHEONS
PALLIEST	PALOOKAS	PALUS	PANCHION
PALLING	PALOVERDE	PALUSTRAL	PANCHIONS
PALLIUM	PALP	PALY	PANCOSMIC
PALLIUMS	PALPABLE	PAM	PANCRATIA
PALLONE	PALPABLY	PAMPA	PANCRATIC

PANCREAS	PANELESS	PANICUMS	PANPIPE
PAND	PANELING	PANIER	PANPIPES
PANDA	PANELINGS	PANIERS	PANS
PANDANI	PANELISED	PANIM	PANSEXUAL
PANDANUS	PANELIST	PANIMS	PANSIED
PANDAR	PANELISTS	PANING	PANSIES
PANDARED	PANELIZED	PANINI	PANSOPHIC
PANDARING	PANELLED	PANINO	PANSOPHY
PANDARS	PANELLING	PANISC	PANSPERMY
PANDAS	PANELLIST	PANISCS	PANSY
PANDATION	PANELS	PANISK	PANT
PANDECT	PANES	PANISKS	PANTABLE
PANDECTS	PANETELA	PANISLAM	PANTABLES
PANDEMIA	PANETELAS	PANISLAMS	PANTAGAMY
PANDEMIAN	PANETELLA	PANJANDRA	PANTALEON
PANDEMIAS	PANETTONE	PANLOGISM	PANTALET
PANDEMIC	PANETTONI	PANMICTIC	PANTALETS
PANDEMICS	PANFISH	PANMIXES	PANTALON
PANDER	PANFISHES	PANMIXIA	PANTALONE
PANDERED	PANFRIED	PANMIXIAS	PANTALONS
PANDERER	PANFRIES	PANMIXIS	PANTALOON
PANDERERS	PANFRY	PANNAGE	PANTDRESS
PANDERESS	PANFRYING	PANNAGES	PANTED
PANDERING	PANFUL	PANNE	PANTER
PANDERISM	PANFULS	PANNED	PANTERS
PANDERLY	PANG	PANNELLED	PANTHEISM
PANDEROUS	PANGA	PANNER	PANTHEIST
PANDERS	PANGAMIC	PANNERS	PANTHENOL
PANDIED	PANGAMIES	PANNES	PANTHEON
PANDIES	PANGAMY	PANNICK	PANTHEONS
PANDIT	PANGAS	PANNICKS	PANTHER
PANDITS	PANGED	PANNICLE	PANTHERS
PANDOOR	PANGEN	PANNICLES	PANTIE
PANDOORS	PANGENE	PANNIER	PANTIES
PANDORA	PANGENES	PANNIERED	PANTIHOSE
PANDORAS	PANGENS	PANNIERS	PANTILE
PANDORE	PANGING	PANNIKEL	PANTILED
PANDORES	PANGLESS	PANNIKELL	PANTILES
PANDOUR	PANGOLIN	PANNIKELS	PANTILING
PANDOURS	PANGOLINS	PANNIKIN	PANTINE
PANDOWDY	PANGRAM	PANNIKINS	PANTINES
PANDS	PANGRAMS	PANNING	PANTING
PANDURA	PANGS	PANNINGS	PANTINGLY
PANDURAS	PANHANDLE	PANNOSE	PANTINGS
PANDURATE	PANHUMAN	PANNUS	PANTLER
PANDY	PANIC	PANNUSES	PANTLERS
PANDYING	PANICALLY	PANOCHA	PANTO
PANE	PANICK	PANOCHAS	PANTOFFLE
PANED	PANICKED	PANOCHE	PANTOFLE
PANEER	PANICKIER	PANOCHES	PANTOFLES
PANEERS	PANICKING	PANOISTIC	PANTOMIME
PANEGOISM	PANICKS	PANOPLIED	PANTON
PANEGYRIC	PANICKY	PANOPLIES	PANTONS
PANEGYRY	PANICLE	PANOPLY	PANTOS
PANEITIES	PANICLED	PANOPTIC	PANTOUFLE
PANEITY	PANICLES	PANORAMA	PANTOUM
PANEL	PANICS	PANORAMAS	PANTOUMS
PANELED	PANICUM	PANORAMIC	PANTRIES

PANTROPIC
PANTRY
PANTRYMAN
PANTRYMEN
PANTS
PANTSUIT
PANTSUITS
PANTUN
PANTUNS
PANTY
PANTYHOSE
PANZER
PANZERS
PANZOOTIC
PAOLI
PAOLO
PAP
PAPA
PAPABLE
PAPACIES
PAPACY
PAPADAM
PAPADAMS
PAPADOM
PAPADOMS
PAPADUM
PAPADUMS
PAPAIN
PAPAINS
PAPAL
PAPALISE
PAPALISED
PAPALISES
PAPALISM
PAPALISMS
PAPALIST
PAPALISTS
PAPALIZE
PAPALIZED
PAPALIZES
PAPALLY
PAPARAZZI
PAPARAZZO
PAPAS
PAPAUMA
PAPAW
PAPAWS
PAPAYA
PAPAYAN
PAPAYAS
PAPE
PAPER
PAPERBACK
PAPERBARK
PAPERBOY
PAPERBOYS
PAPERCLIP
PAPERED

PAPERER
PAPERERS
PAPERGIRL
PAPERIER
PAPERIEST
PAPERING
PAPERINGS
PAPERLESS
PAPERS
PAPERWARE
PAPERWORK
PAPERY
PAPES
PAPETERIE
PAPHIAN
PAPHIANS
PAPILIO
PAPILIOS
PAPILLA
PAPILLAE
PAPILLAR
PAPILLARY
PAPILLATE
PAPILLOMA
PAPILLON
PAPILLONS
PAPILLOSE
PAPILLOTE
PAPILLOUS
PAPILLULE
PAPISH
PAPISHER
PAPISHERS
PAPISHES
PAPISM
PAPISMS
PAPIST
PAPISTIC
PAPISTRY
PAPISTS
PAPOOSE
PAPOOSES
PAPPADAM
PAPPADAMS
PAPPADOM
PAPPADOMS
PAPPED
PAPPI
PAPPIER
PAPPIES
PAPPIEST
PAPPING
PAPPOOSE
PAPPOOSES
PAPPOSE
PAPPOUS
PAPPUS
PAPPUSES

PAPPY
PAPRICA
PAPRICAS
PAPRIKA
PAPRIKAS
PAPS
PAPULA
PAPULAE
PAPULAR
PAPULE
PAPULES
PAPULOSE
PAPULOUS
PAPYRAL
PAPYRI
PAPYRIAN
PAPYRINE
PAPYRUS
PAPYRUSES
PAR
PARA
PARABASES
PARABASIS
PARABEMA
PARABLAST
PARABLE
PARABLED
PARABLES
PARABLING
PARABOLA
PARABOLAS
PARABOLE
PARABOLES
PARABOLIC
PARABRAKE
PARACHOR
PARACHORS
PARACHUTE
PARACLETE
PARACME
PARACMES
PARACRINE
PARACUSES
PARACUSIS
PARADE
PARADED
PARADER
PARADERS
PARADES
PARADIGM
PARADIGMS
PARADING
PARADISAL
PARADISE
PARADISES
PARADISIC
PARADOR
PARADORES

PARADORS
PARADOS
PARADOSES
PARADOX
PARADOXAL
PARADOXER
PARADOXES
PARADOXY
PARADROP
PARADROPS
PARAE
PARAFFIN
PARAFFINE
PARAFFINS
PARAFFINY
PARAFFLE
PARAFFLES
PARAFLE
PARAFLES
PARAFOIL
PARAFOILS
PARAFORM
PARAFORMS
PARAGE
PARAGES
PARAGLIDE
PARAGOGE
PARAGOGES
PARAGOGIC
PARAGOGUE
PARAGON
PARAGONED
PARAGONS
PARAGRAM
PARAGRAMS
PARAGRAPH
PARAKEET
PARAKEETS
PARAKELIA
PARAKITE
PARAKITES
PARALALIA
PARALEGAL
PARALEXIA
PARALEXIC
PARALLAX
PARALLEL
PARALLELS
PARALOGIA
PARALOGY
PARALYSE
PARALYSED
PARALYSER
PARALYSES
PARALYSIS
PARALYTIC
PARALYZE
PARALYZED

PARALYZER	PARASHAHS	PARCLOSE	PARETICS
PARALYZES	PARASHOT	PARCLOSES	PAREU
PARAMATTA	PARASHOTH	PARD	PAREUS
PARAMECIA	PARASITE	PARDAH	PAREV
PARAMEDIC	PARASITES	PARDAHS	PAREVE
PARAMENT	PARASITIC	PARDAL	PARFAIT
PARAMENTA	PARASOL	PARDALE	PARFAITS
PARAMENTS	PARASOLED	PARDALES	PARFLECHE
PARAMESE	PARASOLS	PARDALIS	PARFLESH
PARAMESES	PARATAXES	PARDALOTE	PARFOCAL
PARAMETER	PARATAXIS	PARDALS	PARGANA
PARAMO	PARATHA	PARDED	PARGANAS
PARAMORPH	PARATHAS	PARDEE	PARGASITE
PARAMOS	PARATHION	PARDI	PARGE
PARAMOUNT	PARATONIC	PARDIE	PARGED
PARAMOUR	PARATROOP	PARDINE	PARGES
PARAMOURS	PARAVAIL	PARDING	PARGET
PARAMYLUM	PARAVANE	PARDNER	PARGETED
PARANETE	PARAVANES	PARDNERS	PARGETER
PARANETES	PARAVANT	PARDON	PARGETERS
PARANG	PARAVAUNT	PARDONED	PARGETING
PARANGS	PARAWING	PARDONER	PARGETS
PARANOEA	PARAWINGS	PARDONERS	PARGETTED
PARANOEAS	PARAXIAL	PARDONING	PARGING
PARANOEIC	PARAZOA	PARDONS	PARGINGS
PARANOIA	PARAZOAN	PARDS	PARGO
PARANOIAC	PARAZOANS	PARDY	PARGOS
PARANOIAS	PARAZOON	PARE	PARGYLINE
PARANOIC	PARBAKE	PARECIOUS	PARHELIA
PARANOICS	PARBAKED	PARECISM	PARHELIC
PARANOID	PARBAKES	PARECISMS	PARHELION
PARANOIDS	PARBAKING	PARED	PARHYPATE
PARANYM	PARBOIL	PAREGORIC	PARIAH
PARANYMPH	PARBOILED	PAREIRA	PARIAHS
PARANYMS	PARBOILS	PAREIRAS	PARIAL
PARAPARA	PARBREAK	PARELLA	PARIALS
PARAPENTE	PARBREAKS	PARELLAS	PARIAN
PARAPET	PARBUCKLE	PARELLE	PARIANS
PARAPETED	PARCEL	PARELLES	PARIES
PARAPETS	PARCELED	PARENESES	PARIETAL
PARAPH	PARCELING	PARENESIS	PARIETALS
PARAPHED	PARCELLED	PARENT	PARIETES
PARAPHING	PARCELS	PARENTAGE	PARING
PARAPHS	PARCENARY	PARENTAL	PARINGS
PARAPODIA	PARCENER	PARENTED	PARIS
PARAQUAT	PARCENERS	PARENTING	PARISCHAN
PARAQUATS	PARCH	PARENTS	PARISES
PARAQUET	PARCHED	PAREO	PARISH
PARAQUETS	PARCHEDLY	PAREOS	PARISHAD
PARAQUITO	PARCHEESI	PARER	PARISHADS
PARARHYME	PARCHES	PARERA	PARISHEN
PARAS	PARCHESI	PARERGA	PARISHENS
PARASAIL	PARCHESIS	PARERGON	PARISHES
PARASAILS	PARCHING	PARERS	PARISON
PARASANG	PARCHISI	PARES	PARISONS
PARASANGS	PARCHISIS	PARESES	PARITIES
PARASCEVE	PARCHMENT	PARESIS	PARITOR
PARASHAH	PARCIMONY	PARETIC	PARITORS

PARITY	PARLORS	PAROXYSMS	PARSEC
PARK	PARLOUR	PARP	PARSECS
PARKA	PARLOURS	PARPANE	PARSED
PARKADE	PARLOUS	PARPANES	PARSER
PARKADES	PARLOUSLY	PARPED	PARSERS
PARKAS	PARLY	PARPEN	PARSES
PARKED	PARMESAN	PARPEND	PARSIMONY
PARKEE	PARMESANS	PARPENDS	PARSING
PARKEES	PAROCHIAL	PARPENS	PARSINGS
PARKER	PAROCHIN	PARPENT	PARSLEY
PARKERS	PAROCHINE	PARPENTS	PARSLEYED
PARKETTE	PAROCHINS	PARPING	PARSLEYS
PARKETTES	PARODIC	PARPOINT	PARSLIED
PARKI	PARODICAL	PARPOINTS	PARSNEP
PARKIE	PARODIED	PARPS	PARSNEPS
PARKIER	PARODIES	PARQUET	PARSNIP
PARKIES	PARODIST	PARQUETED	PARSNIPS
PARKIEST	PARODISTS	PARQUETRY	PARSON
PARKIN	PARODOI	PARQUETS	PARSONAGE
PARKING	PARODOS	PARR	PARSONIC
PARKINGS	PARODY	PARRA	PARSONISH
PARKINS	PARODYING	PARRAKEET	PARSONS
PARKIS	PAROEMIA	PARRAL	PART
PARKISH	PAROEMIAC	PARRALS	PARTAKE
PARKLAND	PAROEMIAL	PARRAS	PARTAKEN
PARKLANDS	PAROEMIAS	PARRED	PARTAKER
PARKLIKE	PAROICOUS	PARREL	PARTAKERS
PARKLY	PAROL	PARRELS	PARTAKES
PARKOUR	PAROLABLE	PARRHESIA	PARTAKING
PARKOURS	PAROLE	PARRICIDE	PARTAN
PARKS	PAROLED	PARRIDGE	PARTANS
PARKWARD	PAROLEE	PARRIDGES	PARTED
PARKWARDS	PAROLEES	PARRIED	PARTER
PARKWAY	PAROLES	PARRIER	PARTERRE
PARKWAYS	PAROLING	PARRIERS	PARTERRES
PARKY	PAROLS	PARRIES	PARTERS
PARLANCE	PARONYM	PARRING	PARTI
PARLANCES	PARONYMIC	PARRITCH	PARTIAL
PARLANDO	PARONYMS	PARROCK	PARTIALLY
PARLANTE	PARONYMY	PARROCKED	PARTIALS
PARLAY	PAROQUET	PARROCKS	PARTIBLE
PARLAYED	PAROQUETS	PARROKET	PARTICLE
PARLAYING	PARORE	PARROKETS	PARTICLES
PARLAYS	PAROSMIA	PARROQUET	PARTIED
PARLE	PAROSMIAS	PARROT	PARTIER
PARLED	PAROTIC	PARROTED	PARTIERS
PARLEMENT	PAROTID	PARROTER	PARTIES
PARLES	PAROTIDS	PARROTERS	PARTIM
PARLEY	PAROTIS	PARROTING	PARTING
PARLEYED	PAROTISES	PARROTRY	PARTINGS
PARLEYER	PAROTITIC	PARROTS	PARTIS
PARLEYERS	PAROTITIS	PARROTY	PARTISAN
PARLEYING	PAROTOID	PARRS	PARTISANS
PARLEYS	PAROTOIDS	PARRY	PARTITA
PARLEYVOO	PAROUS	PARRYING	PARTITAS
PARLIES	PAROUSIA	PARS	PARTITE
PARLING	PAROUSIAS	PARSABLE	PARTITION
PARLOR	PAROXYSM	PARSE	PARTITIVE

PARTITURA	PASEOS	PASSENGER	PASTES
PARTIZAN	PASES	PASSEPIED	PASTEUP
PARTIZANS	PASH	PASSER	PASTEUPS
PARTLET	PASHA	PASSERBY	PASTICCI
PARTLETS	PASHADOM	PASSERINE	PASTICCIO
PARTLY	PASHADOMS	PASSERS	PASTICHE
PARTNER	PASHALIC	PASSERSBY	PASTICHES
PARTNERED	PASHALICS	PASSES	PASTIE
PARTNERS	PASHALIK	PASSIBLE	PASTIER
PARTON	PASHALIKS	PASSIBLY	PASTIES
PARTONS	PASHAS	PASSIM	PASTIEST
PARTOOK	PASHED	PASSING	PASTIL
PARTRIDGE	PASHES	PASSINGLY	PASTILLE
PARTS	PASHIM	PASSINGS	PASTILLES
PARTURE	PASHIMS	PASSION	PASTILS
PARTURES	PASHING	PASSIONAL	PASTILY
PARTWAY	PASHKA	PASSIONED	PASTIME
PARTWORK	PASHKAS	PASSIONS	PASTIMES
PARTWORKS	PASHM	PASSIVATE	PASTINA
PARTY	PASHMINA	PASSIVE	PASTINAS
PARTYER	PASHMINAS	PASSIVELY	PASTINESS
PARTYERS	PASHMS	PASSIVES	PASTING
PARTYGOER	PASODOBLE	PASSIVISM	PASTINGS
PARTYING	PASPALUM	PASSIVIST	PASTIS
PARTYISM	PASPALUMS	PASSIVITY	PASTISES
PARTYISMS	PASPIES	PASSKEY	PASTITSIO
PARULIDES	PASPY	PASSKEYS	PASTITSO
PARULIS	PASQUIL	PASSLESS	PASTITSOS
PARULISES	PASQUILER	PASSMAN	PASTLESS
PARURA	PASQUILS	PASSMEN	PASTNESS
PARURAS	PASS	PASSMENT	PASTOR
PARURE	PASSABLE	PASSMENTS	PASTORAL
PARURES	PASSABLY	PASSOUT	PASTORALE
PARVE	PASSADE	PASSOUTS	PASTORALI
PARVENU	PASSADES	PASSOVER	PASTORALS
PARVENUE	PASSADO	PASSOVERS	PASTORATE
PARVENUES	PASSADOES	PASSPORT	PASTORED
PARVENUS	PASSADOS	PASSPORTS	PASTORING
PARVIS	PASSAGE	PASSUS	PASTORIUM
PARVISE	PASSAGED	PASSUSES	PASTORLY
PARVISES	PASSAGER	PASSWORD	PASTORS
PARVO	PASSAGES	PASSWORDS	PASTRAMI
PARVOLIN	PASSAGING	PAST	PASTRAMIS
PARVOLINE	PASSALONG	PASTA	PASTRIES
PARVOLINS	PASSAMENT	PASTALIKE	PASTROMI
PARVOS	PASSANT	PASTANCE	PASTROMIS
PAS	PASSATA	PASTANCES	PASTRY
PASCAL	PASSATAS	PASTAS	PASTS
PASCALS	PASSBAND	PASTE	PASTURAGE
PASCHAL	PASSBANDS	PASTED	PASTURAL
PASCHALS	PASSBOOK	PASTEDOWN	PASTURE
PASCUAL	PASSBOOKS	PASTEL	PASTURED
PASE	PASSE	PASTELIST	PASTURER
PASEAR	PASSED	PASTELS	PASTURERS
PASEARED	PASSEE	PASTER	PASTURES
PASEARING	PASSEL	PASTERN	PASTURING
PASEARS	PASSELS	PASTERNS	PASTY
PASEO	PASSEMENT	PASTERS	PAT

PATACA
PATACAS
PATAGIA
PATAGIAL
PATAGIUM
PATAKA
PATAMAR
PATAMARS
PATBALL
PATBALLS
PATCH
PATCHABLE
PATCHED
PATCHER
PATCHERS
PATCHERY
PATCHES
PATCHIER
PATCHIEST
PATCHILY
PATCHING
PATCHINGS
PATCHOCKE
PATCHOULI
PATCHOULY
PATCHWORK
PATCHY
PATE
PATED
PATELA
PATELAS
PATELLA
PATELLAE
PATELLAR
PATELLAS
PATELLATE
PATEN
PATENCIES
PATENCY
PATENS
PATENT
PATENTED
PATENTEE
PATENTEES
PATENTING
PATENTLY
PATENTOR
PATENTORS
PATENTS
PATER
PATERA
PATERAE
PATERCOVE
PATERERO
PATEREROS
PATERNAL
PATERNITY
PATERS

PATES
PATH
PATHED
PATHETIC
PATHETICS
PATHIC
PATHICS
PATHING
PATHLESS
PATHNAME
PATHNAMES
PATHOGEN
PATHOGENE
PATHOGENS
PATHOGENY
PATHOLOGY
PATHOS
PATHOSES
PATHS
PATHWAY
PATHWAYS
PATIBLE
PATIENCE
PATIENCES
PATIENT
PATIENTED
PATIENTER
PATIENTLY
PATIENTS
PATIKI
PATIN
PATINA
PATINAE
PATINAED
PATINAS
PATINATE
PATINATED
PATINATES
PATINE
PATINED
PATINES
PATINING
PATINISE
PATINISED
PATINISES
PATINIZE
PATINIZED
PATINIZES
PATINS
PATIO
PATIOS
PATISSIER
PATLY
PATNESS
PATNESSES
PATOIS
PATONCE
PATOOTIE

PATOOTIES
PATRIAL
PATRIALS
PATRIARCH
PATRIATE
PATRIATED
PATRIATES
PATRICIAN
PATRICIDE
PATRICK
PATRICKS
PATRICO
PATRICOES
PATRILINY
PATRIMONY
PATRIOT
PATRIOTIC
PATRIOTS
PATRISTIC
PATROL
PATROLLED
PATROLLER
PATROLMAN
PATROLMEN
PATROLOGY
PATROLS
PATRON
PATRONAGE
PATRONAL
PATRONESS
PATRONISE
PATRONIZE
PATRONLY
PATRONNE
PATRONNES
PATRONS
PATROON
PATROONS
PATS
PATSIES
PATSY
PATTAMAR
PATTAMARS
PATTE
PATTED
PATTEE
PATTEN
PATTENED
PATTENING
PATTENS
PATTER
PATTERED
PATTERER
PATTERERS
PATTERING
PATTERN
PATTERNED
PATTERNS

PATTERS
PATTES
PATTIE
PATTIES
PATTING
PATTLE
PATTLES
PATTY
PATTYPAN
PATTYPANS
PATU
PATULENT
PATULIN
PATULINS
PATULOUS
PATUS
PATUTUKI
PATUTUKIS
PATY
PATZER
PATZERS
PAUA
PAUAS
PAUCAL
PAUCALS
PAUCITIES
PAUCITY
PAUGHTIER
PAUGHTY
PAUL
PAULDRON
PAULDRONS
PAULIN
PAULINS
PAULOWNIA
PAULS
PAUNCE
PAUNCES
PAUNCH
PAUNCHED
PAUNCHES
PAUNCHIER
PAUNCHING
PAUNCHY
PAUPER
PAUPERED
PAUPERESS
PAUPERING
PAUPERISE
PAUPERISM
PAUPERIZE
PAUPERS
PAUPIETTE
PAUROPOD
PAUROPODS
PAUSAL
PAUSE
PAUSED

PAUSEFUL
PAUSELESS
PAUSER
PAUSERS
PAUSES
PAUSING
PAUSINGLY
PAUSINGS
PAV
PAVAGE
PAVAGES
PAVAN
PAVANE
PAVANES
PAVANS
PAVE
PAVED
PAVEED
PAVEMENT
PAVEMENTS
PAVEN
PAVENS
PAVER
PAVERS
PAVES
PAVID
PAVILION
PAVILIONS
PAVILLON
PAVILLONS
PAVIN
PAVING
PAVINGS
PAVINS
PAVIOR
PAVIORS
PAVIOUR
PAVIOURS
PAVIS
PAVISE
PAVISER
PAVISERS
PAVISES
PAVISSE
PAVISSES
PAVLOVA
PAVLOVAS
PAVONAZZO
PAVONE
PAVONES
PAVONIAN
PAVONINE
PAVS
PAW
PAWA
PAWAS
PAWAW
PAWAWED

PAWAWING
PAWAWS
PAWED
PAWER
PAWERS
PAWING
PAWK
PAWKIER
PAWKIEST
PAWKILY
PAWKINESS
PAWKS
PAWKY
PAWL
PAWLS
PAWN
PAWNABLE
PAWNAGE
PAWNAGES
PAWNCE
PAWNCES
PAWNED
PAWNEE
PAWNEES
PAWNER
PAWNERS
PAWNING
PAWNOR
PAWNORS
PAWNS
PAWNSHOP
PAWNSHOPS
PAWPAW
PAWPAWS
PAWS
PAX
PAXES
PAXIUBA
PAXIUBAS
PAXWAX
PAXWAXES
PAY
PAYABLE
PAYABLES
PAYABLY
PAYBACK
PAYBACKS
PAYCHECK
PAYCHECKS
PAYDAY
PAYDAYS
PAYED
PAYEE
PAYEES
PAYER
PAYERS
PAYFONE
PAYFONES

PAYGRADE
PAYGRADES
PAYING
PAYINGS
PAYLOAD
PAYLOADS
PAYMASTER
PAYMENT
PAYMENTS
PAYNIM
PAYNIMRY
PAYNIMS
PAYOFF
PAYOFFS
PAYOLA
PAYOLAS
PAYOR
PAYORS
PAYOUT
PAYOUTS
PAYPHONE
PAYPHONES
PAYROLL
PAYROLLED
PAYROLLS
PAYS
PAYSAGE
PAYSAGES
PAYSAGIST
PAYSD
PAYSLIP
PAYSLIPS
PAZAZZ
PAZAZZES
PAZZAZZ
PAZZAZZES
PE
PEA
PEABERRY
PEACE
PEACEABLE
PEACEABLY
PEACED
PEACEFUL
PEACELESS
PEACENIK
PEACENIKS
PEACES
PEACETIME
PEACH
PEACHBLOW
PEACHED
PEACHER
PEACHERS
PEACHES
PEACHIER
PEACHIEST
PEACHILY

PEACHING
PEACHY
PEACING
PEACOAT
PEACOATS
PEACOCK
PEACOCKED
PEACOCKS
PEACOCKY
PEACOD
PEACODS
PEAFOWL
PEAFOWLS
PEAG
PEAGE
PEAGES
PEAGS
PEAHEN
PEAHENS
PEAK
PEAKED
PEAKIER
PEAKIEST
PEAKING
PEAKISH
PEAKLESS
PEAKLIKE
PEAKS
PEAKY
PEAL
PEALED
PEALIKE
PEALING
PEALS
PEAN
PEANED
PEANING
PEANS
PEANUT
PEANUTS
PEAPOD
PEAPODS
PEAR
PEARCE
PEARCED
PEARCES
PEARCING
PEARE
PEARES
PEARL
PEARLASH
PEARLED
PEARLER
PEARLERS
PEARLIER
PEARLIES
PEARLIEST
PEARLIN

PEARLING	PEAZED	PECTINAL	PEDANTS
PEARLINGS	PEAZES	PECTINATE	PEDATE
PEARLINS	PEAZING	PECTINEAL	PEDATELY
PEARLISED	PEBA	PECTINES	PEDATIFID
PEARLITE	PEBAS	PECTINOUS	PEDDER
PEARLITES	PEBBLE	PECTINS	PEDDERS
PEARLITIC	PEBBLED	PECTISE	PEDDLE
PEARLIZED	PEBBLES	PECTISED	PEDDLED
PEARLS	PEBBLIER	PECTISES	PEDDLER
PEARLWORT	PEBBLIEST	PECTISING	PEDDLERS
PEARLY	PEBBLING	PECTIZE	PEDDLERY
PEARMAIN	PEBBLINGS	PECTIZED	PEDDLES
PEARMAINS	PEBBLY	PECTIZES	PEDDLING
PEARS	PEBRINE	PECTIZING	PEDDLINGS
PEARST	PEBRINES	PECTOLITE	PEDERAST
PEART	PEC	PECTORAL	PEDERASTS
PEARTER	PECAN	PECTORALS	PEDERASTY
PEARTEST	PECANS	PECTOSE	PEDERERO
PEARTLY	PECCABLE	PECTOSES	PEDEREROS
PEARTNESS	PECCANCY	PECULATE	PEDES
PEARWOOD	PECCANT	PECULATED	PEDESES
PEARWOODS	PECCANTLY	PECULATES	PEDESIS
PEAS	PECCARIES	PECULATOR	PEDESTAL
PEASANT	PECCARY	PECULIA	PEDESTALS
PEASANTRY	PECCAVI	PECULIAR	PEDETIC
PEASANTS	PECCAVIS	PECULIARS	PEDIATRIC
PEASANTY	PECH	PECULIUM	PEDICAB
PEASCOD	PECHAN	PECUNIARY	PEDICABS
PEASCODS	PECHANS	PECUNIOUS	PEDICEL
PEASE	PECHED	PED	PEDICELS
PEASECOD	PECHING	PEDAGOG	PEDICLE
PEASECODS	PECHS	PEDAGOGIC	PEDICLED
PEASED	PECK	PEDAGOGS	PEDICLES
PEASEN	PECKE	PEDAGOGUE	PEDICULAR
PEASES	PECKED	PEDAGOGY	PEDICULI
PEASING	PECKER	PEDAL	PEDICULUS
PEASON	PECKERS	PEDALED	PEDICURE
PEASOUPER	PECKES	PEDALER	PEDICURED
PEAT	PECKIER	PEDALERS	PEDICURES
PEATARIES	PECKIEST	PEDALFER	PEDIFORM
PEATARY	PECKING	PEDALFERS	PEDIGREE
PEATERIES	PECKINGS	PEDALIER	PEDIGREED
PEATERY	PECKISH	PEDALIERS	PEDIGREES
PEATIER	PECKISHLY	PEDALING	PEDIMENT
PEATIEST	PECKS	PEDALLED	PEDIMENTS
PEATLAND	PECKY	PEDALLER	PEDIPALP
PEATLANDS	PECORINI	PEDALLERS	PEDIPALPI
PEATMAN	PECORINO	PEDALLING	PEDIPALPS
PEATMEN	PECORINOS	PEDALO	PEDLAR
PEATS	PECS	PEDALOES	PEDLARIES
PEATSHIP	PECTASE	PEDALOS	PEDLARS
PEATSHIPS	PECTASES	PEDALS	PEDLARY
PEATY	PECTATE	PEDANT	PEDLER
PEAVEY	PECTATES	PEDANTIC	PEDLERIES
PEAVEYS	PECTEN	PEDANTISE	PEDLERS
PEAVIES	PECTENS	PEDANTISM	PEDLERY
PEAVY	PECTIC	PEDANTIZE	PEDOCAL
PEAZE	PECTIN	PEDANTRY	PEDOCALIC

PEDOCALS	PEEPED	PEGHS	PELF
PEDOGENIC	PEEPER	PEGLEGGED	PELFS
PEDOLOGIC	PEEPERS	PEGLESS	PELHAM
PEDOLOGY	PEEPES	PEGLIKE	PELHAMS
PEDOMETER	PEEPHOLE	PEGMATITE	PELICAN
PEDOPHILE	PEEPHOLES	PEGS	PELICANS
PEDORTHIC	PEEPING	PEH	PELISSE
PEDRAIL	PEEPS	PEHS	PELISSES
PEDRAILS	PEEPSHOW	PEIGNOIR	PELITE
PEDRERO	PEEPSHOWS	PEIGNOIRS	PELITES
PEDREROES	PEEPUL	PEIN	PELITIC
PEDREROS	PEEPULS	PEINCT	PELL
PEDRO	PEER	PEINCTED	PELLACH
PEDROS	PEERAGE	PEINCTING	PELLACHS
PEDS	PEERAGES	PEINCTS	PELLACK
PEDUNCLE	PEERED	PEINED	PELLACKS
PEDUNCLED	PEERESS	PEINING	PELLAGRA
PEDUNCLES	PEERESSES	PEINS	PELLAGRAS
PEE	PEERIE	PEIRASTIC	PELLAGRIN
PEEBEEN	PEERIER	PEISE	PELLED
PEEBEENS	PEERIES	PEISED	PELLET
PEECE	PEERIEST	PEISES	PELLETAL
PEECED	PEERING	PEISHWA	PELLETED
PEECES	PEERLESS	PEISHWAH	PELLETIFY
PEECING	PEERS	PEISHWAHS	PELLETING
PEED	PEERY	PEISHWAS	PELLETISE
PEEING	PEES	PEISING	PELLETIZE
PEEK	PEESWEEP	PEIZE	PELLETS
PEEKABO	PEESWEEPS	PEIZED	PELLICLE
PEEKABOO	PEETWEET	PEIZES	PELLICLES
PEEKABOOS	PEETWEETS	PEIZING	PELLING
PEEKABOS	PEEVE	PEJORATE	PELLITORY
PEEKAPOO	PEEVED	PEJORATED	PELLMELL
PEEKAPOOS	PEEVER	PEJORATES	PELLMELLS
PEEKED	PEEVERS	PEKAN	PELLOCK
PEEKING	PEEVES	PEKANS	PELLOCKS
PEEKS	PEEVING	PEKE	PELLS
PEEL	PEEVISH	PEKEPOO	PELLUCID
PEELABLE	PEEVISHLY	PEKEPOOS	PELLUM
PEELED	PEEWEE	PEKES	PELLUMS
PEELER	PEEWEES	PEKIN	PELMA
PEELERS	PEEWIT	PEKINS	PELMANISM
PEELING	PEEWITS	PEKOE	PELMAS
PEELINGS	PEG	PEKOES	PELMATIC
PEELS	PEGASUS	PELA	PELMET
PEEN	PEGASUSES	PELAGE	PELMETS
PEENED	PEGBOARD	PELAGES	PELOID
PEENGE	PEGBOARDS	PELAGIAL	PELOIDS
PEENGED	PEGBOX	PELAGIAN	PELOLOGY
PEENGEING	PEGBOXES	PELAGIANS	PELON
PEENGES	PEGGED	PELAGIC	PELORIA
PEENGING	PEGGIES	PELAGICS	PELORIAN
PEENING	PEGGING	PELAS	PELORIAS
PEENS	PEGGINGS	PELE	PELORIC
PEEOY	PEGGY	PELECYPOD	PELORIES
PEEOYS	PEGH	PELERINE	PELORISED
PEEP	PEGHED	PELERINES	PELORISM
PEEPE	PEGHING	PELES	PELORISMS

PELORIZED	PENALTIES	PENFUL	PENNIA
PELORUS	PENALTY	PENFULS	PENNIED
PELORUSES	PENANCE	PENGO	PENNIES
PELORY	PENANCED	PENGOS	PENNIFORM
PELOTA	PENANCES	PENGUIN	PENNILESS
PELOTAS	PENANCING	PENGUINRY	PENNILL
PELOTON	PENANG	PENGUINS	PENNINE
PELOTONS	PENANGS	PENHOLDER	PENNINES
PELT	PENATES	PENI	PENNING
PELTA	PENCE	PENIAL	PENNINITE
PELTAE	PENCEL	PENICIL	PENNIS
PELTAS	PENCELS	PENICILS	PENNON
PELTAST	PENCES	PENIE	PENNONCEL
PELTASTS	PENCHANT	PENIES	PENNONED
PELTATE	PENCHANTS	PENILE	PENNONS
PELTATELY	PENCIL	PENILL	PENNY
PELTATION	PENCILED	PENILLION	PENNYBOY
PELTED	PENCILER	PENING	PENNYBOYS
PELTER	PENCILERS	PENINSULA	PENNYFEE
PELTERED	PENCILING	PENIS	PENNYFEES
PELTERING	PENCILLED	PENISES	PENNYLAND
PELTERS	PENCILLER	PENISTONE	PENNYWISE
PELTING	PENCILS	PENITENCE	PENNYWORT
PELTINGLY	PENCRAFT	PENITENCY	PENOCHE
PELTINGS	PENCRAFTS	PENITENT	PENOCHES
PELTLESS	PEND	PENITENTS	PENOLOGY
PELTRIES	PENDANT	PENK	PENONCEL
PELTRY	PENDANTLY	PENKNIFE	PENONCELS
PELTS	PENDANTS	PENKNIVES	PENPOINT
PELVES	PENDED	PENKS	PENPOINTS
PELVIC	PENDENCY	PENLIGHT	PENPUSHER
PELVICS	PENDENT	PENLIGHTS	PENS
PELVIFORM	PENDENTLY	PENLITE	PENSEE
PELVIS	PENDENTS	PENLITES	PENSEES
PELVISES	PENDICLE	PENMAN	PENSEL
PEMBINA	PENDICLER	PENMEN	PENSELS
PEMBINAS	PENDICLES	PENNA	PENSIL
PEMBROKE	PENDING	PENNAE	PENSILE
PEMBROKES	PENDRAGON	PENNAL	PENSILITY
PEMICAN	PENDS	PENNALISM	PENSILS
PEMICANS	PENDU	PENNALS	PENSION
PEMMICAN	PENDULAR	PENNAME	PENSIONE
PEMMICANS	PENDULATE	PENNAMES	PENSIONED
PEMOLINE	PENDULE	PENNANT	PENSIONER
PEMOLINES	PENDULES	PENNANTS	PENSIONES
PEMPHIGUS	PENDULINE	PENNATE	PENSIONS
PEMPHIX	PENDULOUS	PENNATED	PENSIVE
PEMPHIXES	PENDULUM	PENNATULA	PENSIVELY
PEN	PENDULUMS	PENNE	PENSTEMON
PENAL	PENE	PENNED	PENSTER
PENALISE	PENED	PENNEECH	PENSTERS
PENALISED	PENEPLAIN	PENNEECHS	PENSTOCK
PENALISES	PENEPLANE	PENNEECK	PENSTOCKS
PENALITY	PENES	PENNEECKS	PENSUM
PENALIZE	PENETRANT	PENNER	PENSUMS
PENALIZED	PENETRATE	PENNERS	PENT
PENALIZES	PENFOLD	PENNES	PENTACLE
PENALLY	PENFOLDS	PENNI	PENTACLES

PENTACT	PENUCHIS	PEPPERED	PERAEOPOD
PENTACTS	PENUCHLE	PEPPERER	PERAI
PENTAD	PENUCHLES	PEPPERERS	PERAIS
PENTADIC	PENUCKLE	PEPPERIER	PERBORATE
PENTADS	PENUCKLES	PEPPERING	PERCALE
PENTAGON	PENULT	PEPPERONI	PERCALES
PENTAGONS	PENULTIMA	PEPPERS	PERCALINE
PENTAGRAM	PENULTS	PEPPERY	PERCASE
PENTALOGY	PENUMBRA	PEPPIER	PERCE
PENTALPHA	PENUMBRAE	PEPPIEST	PERCEABLE
PENTAMERY	PENUMBRAL	PEPPILY	PERCEANT
PENTANE	PENUMBRAS	PEPPINESS	PERCED
PENTANES	PENURIES	PEPPING	PERCEIVE
PENTANGLE	PENURIOUS	PEPPY	PERCEIVED
PENTANOIC	PENURY	PEPS	PERCEIVER
PENTANOL	PENWOMAN	PEPSIN	PERCEIVES
PENTANOLS	PENWOMEN	PEPSINATE	PERCEN
PENTAPODY	PEON	PEPSINE	PERCENT
PENTARCH	PEONAGE	PEPSINES	PERCENTAL
PENTARCHS	PEONAGES	PEPSINS	PERCENTS
PENTARCHY	PEONES	PEPTALK	PERCEPT
PENTATHLA	PEONIES	PEPTALKED	PERCEPTS
PENTEL	PEONISM	PEPTALKS	PERCES
PENTELS	PEONISMS	PEPTIC	PERCH
PENTENE	PEONS	PEPTICITY	PERCHANCE
PENTENES	PEONY	PEPTICS	PERCHED
PENTHIA	PEOPLE	PEPTID	PERCHER
PENTHIAS	PEOPLED	PEPTIDASE	PERCHERON
PENTHOUSE	PEOPLER	PEPTIDE	PERCHERS
PENTICE	PEOPLERS	PEPTIDES	PERCHERY
PENTICED	PEOPLES	PEPTIDIC	PERCHES
PENTICES	PEOPLING	PEPTIDS	PERCHING
PENTICING	PEP	PEPTISE	PERCHINGS
PENTISE	PEPERINO	PEPTISED	PERCIFORM
PENTISED	PEPERINOS	PEPTISER	PERCINE
PENTISES	PEPEROMIA	PEPTISERS	PERCING
PENTISING	PEPERONI	PEPTISES	PERCOCT
PENTITI	PEPERONIS	PEPTISING	PERCOID
PENTITO	PEPFUL	PEPTIZE	PERCOIDS
PENTODE	PEPINO	PEPTIZED	PERCOLATE
PENTODES	PEPINOS	PEPTIZER	PERCOLIN
PENTOMIC	PEPLA	PEPTIZERS	PERCOLINS
PENTOSAN	PEPLOS	PEPTIZES	PERCUSS
PENTOSANE	PEPLOSES	PEPTIZING	PERCUSSED
PENTOSANS	PEPLUM	PEPTONE	PERCUSSES
PENTOSE	PEPLUMED	PEPTONES	PERCUSSOR
PENTOSES	PEPLUMS	PEPTONIC	PERDENDO
PENTOSIDE	PEPLUS	PEPTONISE	PERDIE
PENTOXIDE	PEPLUSES	PEPTONIZE	PERDITION
PENTROOF	PEPO	PEQUISTE	PERDU
PENTROOFS	PEPONIDA	PEQUISTES	PERDUE
PENTS	PEPONIDAS	PER	PERDUES
PENTYL	PEPONIUM	PERACID	PERDURE
PENTYLENE	PEPONIUMS	PERACIDS	PERDURED
PENTYLS	PEPOS	PERACUTE	PERDURES
PENUCHE	PEPPED	PERAEA	PERDURING
PENUCHES	PEPPER	PERAEON	PERDUS
PENUCHI	PEPPERBOX	PERAEONS	PERDY

PERE
PEREA
PEREGAL
PEREGALS
PEREGRIN
PEREGRINE
PEREGRINS
PEREIA
PEREION
PEREIONS
PEREIOPOD
PEREIRA
PEREIRAS
PERENNATE
PERENNIAL
PERENNITY
PERENTIE
PERENTIES
PERENTY
PEREON
PEREONS
PEREOPOD
PEREOPODS
PERES
PERFAY
PERFECT
PERFECTA
PERFECTAS
PERFECTED
PERFECTER
PERFECTI
PERFECTLY
PERFECTO
PERFECTOR
PERFECTOS
PERFECTS
PERFERVID
PERFERVOR
PERFET
PERFIDIES
PERFIDY
PERFIN
PERFING
PERFINGS
PERFINS
PERFORANS
PERFORANT
PERFORATE
PERFORCE
PERFORM
PERFORMED
PERFORMER
PERFORMS
PERFUME
PERFUMED
PERFUMER
PERFUMERS
PERFUMERY

PERFUMES
PERFUMIER
PERFUMING
PERFUMY
PERFUSATE
PERFUSE
PERFUSED
PERFUSES
PERFUSING
PERFUSION
PERFUSIVE
PERGOLA
PERGOLAS
PERGUNNAH
PERHAPS
PERHAPSES
PERI
PERIAGUA
PERIAGUAS
PERIAKTOI
PERIAKTOS
PERIANTH
PERIANTHS
PERIAPSES
PERIAPSIS
PERIAPT
PERIAPTS
PERIBLAST
PERIBLEM
PERIBLEMS
PERIBOLI
PERIBOLOI
PERIBOLOS
PERIBOLUS
PERICARP
PERICARPS
PERICLASE
PERICLINE
PERICON
PERICONES
PERICOPAE
PERICOPAL
PERICOPE
PERICOPES
PERICOPIC
PERICYCLE
PERIDERM
PERIDERMS
PERIDIA
PERIDIAL
PERIDINIA
PERIDIUM
PERIDIUMS
PERIDOT
PERIDOTE
PERIDOTES
PERIDOTIC
PERIDOTS

PERIDROME
PERIGEAL
PERIGEAN
PERIGEE
PERIGEES
PERIGON
PERIGONE
PERIGONES
PERIGONIA
PERIGONS
PERIGYNY
PERIHELIA
PERIKARYA
PERIL
PERILED
PERILING
PERILLA`
PERILLAS
PERILLED
PERILLING
PERILOUS
PERILS
PERILUNE
PERILUNES
PERILYMPH
PERIMETER
PERIMETRY
PERIMORPH
PERIMYSIA
PERINAEUM
PERINATAL
PERINEA
PERINEAL
PERINEUM
PERINEUMS
PERIOD
PERIODATE
PERIODED
PERIODIC
PERIODID
PERIODIDE
PERIODIDS
PERIODING
PERIODS
PERIOST
PERIOSTEA
PERIOSTS
PERIOTIC
PERIOTICS
PERIPATUS
PERIPETIA
PERIPETY
PERIPHERY
PERIPLASM
PERIPLAST
PERIPLUS
PERIPROCT
PERIPTER

PERIPTERS
PERIPTERY
PERIQUE
PERIQUES
PERIS
PERISARC
PERISARCS
PERISCIAN
PERISCOPE
PERISH
PERISHED
PERISHER
PERISHERS
PERISHES
PERISHING
PERISPERM
PERISTOME
PERISTYLE
PERITI
PERITONEA
PERITRACK
PERITRICH
PERITUS
PERIWIG
PERIWIGS
PERJINK
PERJURE
PERJURED
PERJURER
PERJURERS
PERJURES
PERJURIES
PERJURING
PERJUROUS
PERJURY
PERK
PERKED
PERKIER
PERKIEST
PERKILY
PERKIN
PERKINESS
PERKING
PERKINS
PERKISH
PERKS
PERKY
PERLEMOEN
PERLITE
PERLITES
PERLITIC
PERLOUS
PERM
PERMALLOY
PERMANENT
PERMEABLE
PERMEABLY
PERMEANCE

PERMEANT	PERPLEX	PERSUADE	PERVADING
PERMEASE	PERPLEXED	PERSUADED	PERVASION
PERMEASES	PERPLEXER	PERSUADER	PERVASIVE
PERMEATE	PERPLEXES	PERSUADES	PERVE
PERMEATED	PERPS	PERSUE	PERVED
PERMEATES	PERRADIAL	PERSUED	PERVERSE
PERMEATOR	PERRADII	PERSUES	PERVERSER
PERMED	PERRADIUS	PERSUING	PERVERT
PERMIAN	PERRIER	PERSWADE	PERVERTED
PERMIE	PERRIERS	PERSWADED	PERVERTER
PERMIES	PERRIES	PERSWADES	PERVERTS
PERMING	PERRON	PERT	PERVES
PERMIT	PERRONS	PERTAIN	PERVIATE
PERMITS	PERRUQUE	PERTAINED	PERVIATED
PERMITTED	PERRUQUES	PERTAINS	PERVIATES
PERMITTEE	PERRY	PERTAKE	PERVICACY
PERMITTER	PERSALT	PERTAKEN	PERVING
PERMS	PERSALTS	PERTAKES	PERVIOUS
PERMUTATE	PERSANT	PERTAKING	PERVS
PERMUTE	PERSAUNT	PERTER	PES
PERMUTED	PERSE	PERTEST	PESADE
PERMUTES	PERSECUTE	PERTHITE	PESADES
PERMUTING	PERSEITY	PERTHITES	PESANT
PERN	PERSELINE	PERTHITIC	PESANTE
PERNANCY	PERSES	PERTINENT	PESANTS
PERNED	PERSEVERE	PERTLY	PESAUNT
PERNING	PERSICO	PERTNESS	PESAUNTS
PERNIO	PERSICOS	PERTOOK	PESETA
PERNIONES	PERSICOT	PERTS	PESETAS
PERNOD	PERSICOTS	PERTURB	PESEWA
PERNODS	PERSIENNE	PERTURBED	PESEWAS
PERNS	PERSIMMON	PERTURBER	PESHWA
PERONE	PERSING	PERTURBS	PESHWAS
PERONEAL	PERSIST	PERTUSATE	PESKIER
PERONES	PERSISTED	PERTUSE	PESKIEST
PERONEUS	PERSISTER	PERTUSED	PESKILY
PERORAL	PERSISTS	PERTUSION	PESKINESS
PERORALLY	PERSON	PERTUSSAL	PESKY
PERORATE	PERSONA	PERTUSSES	PESO
PERORATED	PERSONAE	PERTUSSIS	PESOS
PERORATES	PERSONAGE	PERUKE	PESSARIES
PERORATOR	PERSONAL	PERUKED	PESSARY
PEROVSKIA	PERSONALS	PERUKES	PESSIMA
PEROXID	PERSONAS	PERUSABLE	PESSIMAL
PEROXIDE	PERSONATE	PERUSAL	PESSIMISM
PEROXIDED	PERSONIFY	PERUSALS	PESSIMIST
PEROXIDES	PERSONISE	PERUSE	PESSIMUM
PEROXIDIC	PERSONIZE	PERUSED	PEST
PEROXIDS	PERSONNED	PERUSER	PESTER
PEROXO	PERSONNEL	PERUSERS	PESTERED
PEROXY	PERSONS	PERUSES	PESTERER
PERP	PERSPEX	PERUSING	PESTERERS
PERPEND	PERSPEXES	PERV	PESTERING
PERPENDED	PERSPIRE	PERVADE	PESTEROUS
PERPENDS	PERSPIRED	PERVADED	PESTERS
PERPENT	PERSPIRES	PERVADER	PESTFUL
PERPENTS	PERSPIRY	PERVADERS	PESTHOLE
PERPETUAL	PERST	PERVADES	PESTHOLES

PESTHOUSE	PETERSHAM	PETTEDLY	PEYTRELS
PESTICIDE	PETHER	PETTER	PEZANT
PESTIER	PETHERS	PETTERS	PEZANTS
PESTIEST	PETHIDINE	PETTI	PEZIZOID
PESTILENT	PETILLANT	PETTICOAT	PFENNIG
PESTLE	PETIOLAR	PETTIER	PFENNIGE
PESTLED	PETIOLATE	PETTIES	PFENNIGS
PESTLES	PETIOLE	PETTIEST	PFENNING
PESTLING	PETIOLED	PETTIFOG	PFENNINGS
PESTO	PETIOLES	PETTIFOGS	PFFT
PESTOLOGY	PETIOLULE	PETTILY	PFUI
PESTOS	PETIT	PETTINESS	PHACELIA
PESTS	PETITE	PETTING	PHACELIAS
PESTY	PETITES	PETTINGS	PHACOID
PET	PETITIO	PETTISH	PHACOIDAL
PETABYTE	PETITION	PETTISHLY	PHACOLITE
PETABYTES	PETITIONS	PETTITOES	PHACOLITH
PETAHERTZ	PETITORY	PETTLE	PHAEIC
PETAL	PETNAP	PETTLED	PHAEISM
PETALED	PETNAPER	PETTLES	PHAEISMS
PETALINE	PETNAPERS	PETTLING	PHAENOGAM
PETALISM	PETNAPING	PETTO	PHAETON
PETALISMS	PETNAPPED	PETTY	PHAETONS
PETALLED	PETNAPPER	PETULANCE	PHAGE
PETALLIKE	PETNAPS	PETULANCY	PHAGEDENA
PETALODIC	PETRALE	PETULANT	PHAGES
PETALODY	PETRALES	PETUNIA	PHAGOCYTE
PETALOID	PETRARIES	PETUNIAS	PHAGOSOME
PETALOUS	PETRARY	PETUNTSE	PHALANGAL
PETALS	PETRE	PETUNTSES	PHALANGE
PETANQUE	PETREL	PETUNTZE	PHALANGER
PETANQUES	PETRELS	PETUNTZES	PHALANGES
PETAR	PETRES	PEW	PHALANGID
PETARA	PETRIFIC	PEWEE	PHALANX
PETARAS	PETRIFIED	PEWEES	PHALANXES
PETARD	PETRIFIER	PEWHOLDER	PHALAROPE
PETARDS	PETRIFIES	PEWIT	PHALLI
PETARIES	PETRIFY	PEWITS	PHALLIC
PETARS	PETROGENY	PEWS	PHALLIN
PETARY	PETROGRAM	PEWTER	PHALLINS
PETASOS	PETROL	PEWTERER	PHALLISM
PETASOSES	PETROLAGE	PEWTERERS	PHALLISMS
PETASUS	PETROLEUM	PEWTERS	PHALLIST
PETASUSES	PETROLEUR	PEYOTE	PHALLISTS
PETAURINE	PETROLIC	PEYOTES	PHALLOID
PETAURIST	PETROLLED	PEYOTISM	PHALLUS
PETCHARY	PETROLOGY	PEYOTISMS	PHALLUSES
PETCOCK	PETROLS	PEYOTIST	PHANG
PETCOCKS	PETRONEL	PEYOTISTS	PHANGED
PETECHIA	PETRONELS	PEYOTL	PHANGING
PETECHIAE	PETROSAL	PEYOTLS	PHANGS
PETECHIAL	PETROSALS	PEYSE	PHANSIGAR
PETER	PETROUS	PEYSED	PHANTASIM
PETERED	PETS	PEYSES	PHANTASM
PETERING	PETSAI	PEYSING	PHANTASMA
PETERMAN	PETSAIS	PEYTRAL	PHANTASMS
PETERMEN	PETTABLE	PEYTRALS	PHANTAST
PETERS	PETTED	PEYTREL	PHANTASTS

PHANTASY	PHEEZED	PHEW	PHLEGMY
PHANTOM	PHEEZES	PHI	PHLOEM
PHANTOMS	PHEEZING	PHIAL	PHLOEMS
PHANTOMY	PHELLEM	PHIALLED	PHLOMIS
PHANTOSME	PHELLEMS	PHIALLING	PHLOMISES
PHARAOH	PHELLOGEN	PHIALS	PHLORIZIN
PHARAOHS	PHELLOID	PHILABEG	PHLOX
PHARAONIC	PHELONIA	PHILABEGS	PHLOXES
PHARE	PHELONION	PHILAMOT	PHLYCTENA
PHARES	PHENACITE	PHILAMOTS	PHO
PHARISAIC	PHENAKISM	PHILANDER	PHOBIA
PHARISEE	PHENAKITE	PHILATELY	PHOBIAS
PHARISEES	PHENATE	PHILHORSE	PHOBIC
PHARMA	PHENATES	PHILIBEG	PHOBICS
PHARMACY	PHENAZIN	PHILIBEGS	PHOBISM
PHARMAS	PHENAZINE	PHILIPPIC	PHOBISMS
PHARMING	PHENAZINS	PHILISTIA	PHOBIST
PHARMINGS	PHENE	PHILLABEG	PHOBISTS
PHAROS	PHENES	PHILLIBEG	PHOCA
PHAROSES	PHENETIC	PHILOGYNY	PHOCAE
PHARYNGAL	PHENETICS	PHILOLOGY	PHOCAS
PHARYNGES	PHENETOL	PHILOMATH	PHOCINE
PHARYNX	PHENETOLE	PHILOMEL	PHOCOMELY
PHARYNXES	PHENETOLS	PHILOMELA	PHOEBE
PHASE	PHENGITE	PHILOMELS	PHOEBES
PHASEAL	PHENGITES	PHILOMOT	PHOEBUS
PHASED	PHENIC	PHILOMOTS	PHOEBUSES
PHASEDOWN	PHENIX	PHILOPENA	PHOENIX
PHASELESS	PHENIXES	PHILTER	PHOENIXES
PHASEOLIN	PHENOCOPY	PHILTERED	PHOH
PHASEOUT	PHENOGAM	PHILTERS	PHOHS
PHASEOUTS	PHENOGAMS	PHILTRA	PHOLADES
PHASES	PHENOL	PHILTRE	PHOLAS
PHASIC	PHENOLATE	PHILTRED	PHON
PHASING	PHENOLIC	PHILTRES	PHONAL
PHASINGS	PHENOLICS	PHILTRING	PHONATE
PHASIS	PHENOLOGY	PHILTRUM	PHONATED
PHASMID	PHENOLS	PHIMOSES	PHONATES
PHASMIDS	PHENOM	PHIMOSIS	PHONATHON
PHASOR	PHENOMENA	PHIMOTIC	PHONATING
PHASORS	PHENOMS	PHINNOCK	PHONATION
PHAT	PHENOTYPE	PHINNOCKS	PHONATORY
PHATIC	PHENOXIDE	PHIS	PHONE
PHATTER	PHENOXY	PHISHING	PHONECAM
PHATTEST	PHENYL	PHISHINGS	PHONECAMS
PHEASANT	PHENYLENE	PHISNOMY	PHONECARD
PHEASANTS	PHENYLIC	PHIZ	PHONED
PHEAZAR	PHENYLS	PHIZES	PHONEME
PHEAZARS	PHENYTOIN	PHIZOG	PHONEMES
PHEER	PHEON	PHIZOGS	PHONEMIC
PHEERE	PHEONS	PHIZZES	PHONEMICS
PHEERES	PHERESES	PHLEBITIC	PHONER
PHEERS	PHERESIS	PHLEBITIS	PHONERS
PHEESE	PHEROMONE	PHLEGM	PHONES
PHEESED	PHESE	PHLEGMIER	PHONETIC
PHEESES	PHESED	PHLEGMON	PHONETICS
PHEESING	PHESES	PHLEGMONS	PHONETISE
PHEEZE	PHESING	PHLEGMS	PHONETISM

PHONETIST
PHONETIZE
PHONEY
PHONEYED
PHONEYING
PHONEYS
PHONIC
PHONICS
PHONIED
PHONIER
PHONIES
PHONIEST
PHONILY
PHONINESS
PHONING
PHONMETER
PHONO
PHONOGRAM
PHONOLITE
PHONOLOGY
PHONON
PHONONS
PHONOPORE
PHONOS
PHONOTYPE
PHONOTYPY
PHONS
PHONY
PHONYING
PHOOEY
PHORATE
PHORATES
PHORESIES
PHORESY
PHORMINX
PHORMIUM
PHORMIUMS
PHORONID
PHORONIDS
PHOS
PHOSGENE
PHOSGENES
PHOSPHATE
PHOSPHENE
PHOSPHID
PHOSPHIDE
PHOSPHIDS
PHOSPHIN
PHOSPHINE
PHOSPHINS
PHOSPHITE
PHOSPHOR
PHOSPHORE
PHOSPHORI
PHOSPHORS
PHOSSY
PHOT
PHOTIC

PHOTICS
PHOTINIA
PHOTINIAS
PHOTISM
PHOTISMS
PHOTO
PHOTOCELL
PHOTOCOPY
PHOTOED
PHOTOFIT
PHOTOFITS
PHOTOG
PHOTOGEN
PHOTOGENE
PHOTOGENS
PHOTOGENY
PHOTOGRAM
PHOTOGS
PHOTOING
PHOTOLYSE
PHOTOLYZE
PHOTOMAP
PHOTOMAPS
PHOTOMASK
PHOTON
PHOTONIC
PHOTONICS
PHOTONS
PHOTOPHIL
PHOTOPIA
PHOTOPIAS
PHOTOPIC
PHOTOPLAY
PHOTOPSIA
PHOTOPSY
PHOTOS
PHOTOSCAN
PHOTOSET
PHOTOSETS
PHOTOSTAT
PHOTOTAXY
PHOTOTUBE
PHOTOTYPE
PHOTOTYPY
PHOTS
PHPHT
PHRASAL
PHRASALLY
PHRASE
PHRASED
PHRASEMAN
PHRASEMEN
PHRASER
PHRASERS
PHRASES
PHRASIER
PHRASIEST
PHRASING

PHRASINGS
PHRASY
PHRATRAL
PHRATRIC
PHRATRIES
PHRATRY
PHREAK
PHREAKED
PHREAKER
PHREAKERS
PHREAKING
PHREAKS
PHREATIC
PHRENESES
PHRENESIS
PHRENETIC
PHRENIC
PHRENISM
PHRENISMS
PHRENITIC
PHRENITIS
PHRENSIED
PHRENSIES
PHRENSY
PHRENTICK
PHRYGANA
PHRYGANAS
PHT
PHTHALATE
PHTHALEIN
PHTHALIC
PHTHALIN
PHTHALINS
PHTHISES
PHTHISIC
PHTHISICS
PHTHISIS
PHUT
PHUTS
PHUTTED
PHUTTING
PHYCOCYAN
PHYCOLOGY
PHYLA
PHYLAE
PHYLAR
PHYLARCH
PHYLARCHS
PHYLARCHY
PHYLAXIS
PHYLE
PHYLESES
PHYLESIS
PHYLETIC
PHYLETICS
PHYLIC
PHYLLARY
PHYLLID

PHYLLIDS
PHYLLITE
PHYLLITES
PHYLLITIC
PHYLLO
PHYLLODE
PHYLLODES
PHYLLODIA
PHYLLODY
PHYLLOID
PHYLLOIDS
PHYLLOME
PHYLLOMES
PHYLLOMIC
PHYLLOPOD
PHYLLOS
PHYLOGENY
PHYLON
PHYLONS
PHYLUM
PHYSALIA
PHYSALIAS
PHYSALIS
PHYSED
PHYSEDS
PHYSES
PHYSETER
PHYSETERS
PHYSIATRY
PHYSIC
PHYSICAL
PHYSICALS
PHYSICIAN
PHYSICISM
PHYSICIST
PHYSICKED
PHYSICKY
PHYSICS
PHYSIO
PHYSIOS
PHYSIQUE
PHYSIQUED
PHYSIQUES
PHYSIS
PHYTANE
PHYTANES
PHYTIN
PHYTINS
PHYTOGENY
PHYTOID
PHYTOL
PHYTOLITH
PHYTOLOGY
PHYTOLS
PHYTON
PHYTONIC
PHYTONS
PHYTOSES

PHYTOSIS
PHYTOTOMY
PHYTOTRON
PI
PIA
PIACEVOLE
PIACULAR
PIAFFE
PIAFFED
PIAFFER
PIAFFERS
PIAFFES
PIAFFING
PIAL
PIAN
PIANETTE
PIANETTES
PIANIC
PIANINO
PIANINOS
PIANISM
PIANISMS
PIANIST
PIANISTE
PIANISTES
PIANISTIC
PIANISTS
PIANO
PIANOLIST
PIANOS
PIANS
PIARIST
PIARISTS
PIAS
PIASABA
PIASABAS
PIASAVA
PIASAVAS
PIASSABA
PIASSABAS
PIASSAVA
PIASSAVAS
PIASTER
PIASTERS
PIASTRE
PIASTRES
PIAZZA
PIAZZAS
PIAZZE
PIAZZIAN
PIBAL
PIBALS
PIBROCH
PIBROCHS
PIC
PICA
PICACHO
PICACHOS

PICADILLO
PICADOR
PICADORES
PICADORS
PICAL
PICAMAR
PICAMARS
PICANINNY
PICANTE
PICARA
PICARAS
PICARIAN
PICARIANS
PICARO
PICAROON
PICAROONS
PICAROS
PICAS
PICAYUNE
PICAYUNES
PICCADILL
PICCANIN
PICCANINS
PICCATA
PICCIES
PICCOLO
PICCOLOS
PICCY
PICE
PICENE
PICENES
PICEOUS
PICHOLINE
PICHURIM
PICHURIMS
PICIFORM
PICINE
PICK
PICKABACK
PICKABLE
PICKADIL
PTCKADILL
PICKADILS
PICKAPACK
PICKAROON
PICKAX
PICKAXE
PICKAXED
PICKAXES
PICKAXING
PICKBACK
PICKBACKS
PICKED
PICKEER
PICKEERED
PICKEERER
PICKEERS
PICKER

PICKEREL
PICKERELS
PICKERIES
PICKERS
PICKERY
PICKET
PICKETED
PICKETER
PICKETERS
PICKETING
PICKETS
PICKIER
PICKIEST
PICKILY
PICKIN
PICKINESS
PICKING
PICKINGS
PICKINS
PICKLE
PICKLED
PICKLER
PICKLERS
PICKLES
PICKLING
PICKLOCK
PICKLOCKS
PICKMAW
PICKMAWS
PICKOFF
PICKOFFS
PICKPROOF
PICKS
PICKTHANK
PICKUP
PICKUPS
PICKWICK
PICKWICKS
PICKY
PICLORAM
PICLORAMS
PICNIC
PICNICKED
PICNICKER
PICNICKY
PICNICS
PICOCURIE
PICOFARAD
PICOGRAM
PICOGRAMS
PICOLIN
PICOLINE
PICOLINES
PICOLINIC
PICOLINS
PICOMETER
PICOMETRE
PICOMOLE

PICOMOLES
PICONG
PICONGS
PICOT
PICOTE
PICOTED
PICOTEE
PICOTEES
PICOTING
PICOTITE
PICOTITES
PICOTS
PICOWAVE
PICOWAVED
PICOWAVES
PICQUET
PICQUETED
PICQUETS
PICRA
PICRAS
PICRATE
PICRATED
PICRATES
PICRIC
PICRITE
PICRITES
PICRITIC
PICS
PICTARNIE
PICTOGRAM
PICTORIAL
PICTURAL
PICTURALS
PICTURE
PICTURED
PICTURES
PICTURING
PICTURISE
PICTURIZE
PICUL
PICULS
PIDDLE
PIDDLED
PIDDLER
PIDDLERS
PIDDLES
PIDDLING
PIDDLY
PIDDOCK
PIDDOCKS
PIDGEON
PIDGEONS
PIDGIN
PIDGINISE
PIDGINIZE
PIDGINS
PIE
PIEBALD

PIEBALDS	PIEROGIES	PIGGISH	PIGTAIL
PIECE	PIERRETTE	PIGGISHLY	PIGTAILED
PIECED	PIERROT	PIGGY	PIGTAILS
PIECELESS	PIERROTS	PIGGYBACK	PIGWASH
PIECEMEAL	PIERS	PIGHEADED	PIGWASHES
PIECEN	PIERST	PIGHT	PIGWEED
PIECENED	PIERT	PIGHTED	PIGWEEDS
PIECENER	PIERTS	PIGHTING	PIHOIHOI
PIECENERS	PIES	PIGHTLE	PIING
PIECENING	PIET	PIGHTLES	PIKA
PIECENS	PIETA	PIGHTS	PIKAKE
PIECER	PIETAS	PIGLET	PIKAKES
PIECERS	PIETIES	PIGLETS	PIKAS
PIECES	PIETISM	PIGLIKE	PIKAU
PIECEWISE	PIETISMS	PIGLING	PIKAUS
PIECEWORK	PIETIST	PIGLINGS	PIKE
PIECING	PIETISTIC	PIGMAEAN	PIKED
PIECINGS	PIETISTS	PIGMEAN	PIKELET
PIECRUST	PIETS	PIGMEAT	PIKELETS
PIECRUSTS	PIETY	PIGMEATS	PIKEMAN
PIED	PIEZO	PIGMENT	PIKEMEN
PIEDFORT	PIFFERARI	PIGMENTAL	PIKEPERCH
PIEDFORTS	PIFFERARO	PIGMENTED	PIKER
PIEDISH	PIFFERO	PIGMENTS	PIKERS
PIEDISHES	PIFFEROS	PIGMIES	PIKES
PIEDMONT	PIFFLE	PIGMOID	PIKESTAFF
PIEDMONTS	PIFFLED	PIGMY	PIKEY
PIEDNESS	PIFFLER	PIGNERATE	PIKEYS
PIEFORT	PIFFLERS	PIGNOLI	PIKI
PIEFORTS	PIFFLES	PIGNOLIA	PIKING
PIEHOLE	PIFFLING	PIGNOLIAS	PIKINGS
PIEHOLES	PIG	PIGNOLIS	PIKIS
PIEING	PIGBOAT	PIGNORA	PIKUL
PIEMAN	PIGBOATS	PIGNORATE	PIKULS
PIEMEN	PIGEON	PIGNUS	PILA
PIEND	PIGEONED	PIGNUT	PILAE
PIENDED	PIGEONING	PIGNUTS	PILAF
PIENDING	PIGEONITE	PIGOUT	PILAFF
PIENDS	PIGEONRY	PIGOUTS	PILAFFS
PIEPLANT	PIGEONS	PIGPEN	PILAFS
PIEPLANTS	PIGFACE	PIGPENS	PILAO
PIEPOWDER	PIGFACES	PIGS	PILAOS
PIER	PIGFEED	PIGSCONCE	PILAR
PIERAGE	PIGFEEDS	PIGSKIN	PILASTER
PIERAGES	PIGFISH	PIGSKINS	PILASTERS
PIERCE	PIGFISHES	PIGSNEY	PILAU
PIERCED	PIGGED	PIGSNEYS	PILAUS
PIERCER	PIGGERIES	PIGSNIE	PILAW
PIERCERS	PIGGERY	PIGSNIES	PILAWS
PIERCES	PIGGIE	PIGSNY	PILCH
PIERCING	PIGGIER	PIGSNYS	PILCHARD
PIERCINGS	PIGGIES	PIGSTICK	PILCHARDS
PIERID	PIGGIEST	PIGSTICKS	PILCHER
PIERIDINE	PIGGIN	PIGSTIES	PILCHERS
PIERIDS	PIGGINESS	PIGSTUCK	PILCHES
PIERIS	PIGGING	PIGSTY	PILCORN
PIERISES	PIGGINGS	PIGSWILL	PILCORNS
PIEROGI	PIGGINS	PIGSWILLS	PILCROW

PILCROWS	PILLICOCK	PIMA	PINCHERS
PILE	PILLIE	PIMAS	PINCHES
PILEA	PILLIES	PIMENT	PINCHFIST
PILEAS	PILLING	PIMENTO	PINCHGUT
PILEATE	PILLINGS	PIMENTON	PINCHGUTS
PILEATED	PILLION	PIMENTONS	PINCHING
PILED	PILLIONED	PIMENTOS	PINCHINGS
PILEI	PILLIONS	PIMENTS	PINDAN
PILELESS	PILLOCK	PIMIENTO	PINDANS
PILEOUS	PILLOCKS	PIMIENTOS	PINDAREE
PILER	PILLORIED	PIMP	PINDAREES
PILERS	PILLORIES	PIMPED	PINDARI
PILES	PILLORISE	PIMPERNEL	PINDARIS
PILEUM	PILLORIZE	PIMPING	PINDER
PILEUP	PILLORY	PIMPLE	PINDERS
PILEUPS	PILLOW	PIMPLED	PINDLING
PILEUS	PILLOWED	PIMPLES	PINDOWN
PILEWORK	PILLOWING	PIMPLIER	PINDOWNS
PILEWORKS	PILLOWS	PIMPLIEST	PINE
PILEWORT	PILLOWY	PIMPLY	PINEAL
PILEWORTS	PILLS	PIMPS	PINEALS
PILFER	PILLWORM	PIN	PINEAPPLE
PILFERAGE	PILLWORMS	PINA	PINECONE
PILFERED	PILLWORT	PINACEOUS	PINECONES
PILFERER	PILLWORTS	PINACOID	PINED
PILFERERS	PILOMOTOR	PINACOIDS	PINEDROPS
PILFERIES	PILONIDAL	PINAFORE	PINELAND
PILFERING	PILOSE	PINAFORED	PINELANDS
PILFERS	PILOSITY	PINAFORES	PINELIKE
PILFERY	PILOT	PINAKOID	PINENE
PILGARLIC	PILOTAGE	PINAKOIDS	PINENES
PILGRIM	PILOTAGES	PINANG	PINERIES
PILGRIMER	PILOTED	PINANGS	PINERY
PILGRIMS	PILOTFISH	PINAS	PINES
PILI	PILOTI	PINASTER	PINESAP
PILIFORM	PILOTING	PINASTERS	PINESAPS
PILING	PILOTINGS	PINATA	PINETA
PILINGS	PILOTIS	PINATAS	PINETUM
PILIS	PILOTLESS	PINBALL	PINEWOOD
PILL	PILOTMAN	PINBALLED	PINEWOODS
PILLAGE	PILOTMEN	PINBALLS	PINEY
PILLAGED	PILOTS	PINBONE	PINFALL
PILLAGER	PILOUS	PINBONES	PINFALLS
PILLAGERS	PILOW	PINCASE	PINFISH
PILLAGES	PILOWS	PINCASES	PINFISHES
PILLAGING	PILSENER	PINCER	PINFOLD
PILLAR	PILSENERS	PINCERED	PINFOLDED
PILLARED	PILSNER	PINCERING	PINFOLDS
PILLARING	PILSNERS	PINCERS	PING
PILLARIST	PILULA	PINCH	PINGED
PILLARS	PILULAE	PINCHBECK	PINGER
PILLAU	PILULAR	PINCHBUG	PINGERS
PILLAUS	PILULAS	PINCHBUGS	PINGING
PILLBOX	PILULE	PINCHCOCK	PINGLE
PILLBOXES	PILULES	PINCHECK	PINGLED
PILLED	PILUM	PINCHECKS	PINGLER
PILLHEAD	PILUS	PINCHED	PINGLERS
PILLHEADS	PILY	PINCHER	PINGLES

PINGLING
PINGO
PINGOES
PINGOS
PINGPONG
PINGPONGS
PINGRASS
PINGS
PINGUEFY
PINGUID
PINGUIN
PINGUINS
PINHEAD
PINHEADED
PINHEADS
PINHOLE
PINHOLES
PINHOOKER
PINIER
PINIES
PINIEST
PINING
PINION
PINIONED
PINIONING
PINIONS
PINITE
PINITES
PINITOL
PINITOLS
PINK
PINKED
PINKEN
PINKENED
PINKENING
PINKENS
PINKER
PINKERS
PINKERTON
PINKEST
PINKEY
PINKEYE
PINKEYES
PINKEYS
PINKIE
PINKIER
PINKIES
PINKIEST
PINKINESS
PINKING
PINKINGS
PINKISH
PINKLY
PINKNESS
PINKO
PINKOES
PINKOS
PINKROOT

PINKROOTS
PINKS
PINKY
PINNA
PINNACE
PINNACES
PINNACLE
PINNACLED
PINNACLES
PINNAE
PINNAL
PINNAS
PINNATE
PINNATED
PINNATELY
PINNATION
PINNED
PINNER
PINNERS
PINNET
PINNETS
PINNIE
PINNIES
PINNING
PINNINGS
PINNIPED
PINNIPEDE
PINNIPEDS
PINNOCK
PINNOCKS
PINNOED
PINNULA
PINNULAE
PINNULAR
PINNULAS
PINNULATE
PINNULE
PINNULES
PINNY
PINOCHLE
PINOCHLES
PINOCLE
PINOCLES
PINOCYTIC
PINOLE
PINOLES
PINON
PINONES
PINONS
PINOT
PINOTAGE
PINOTAGES
PINOTS
PINPOINT
PINPOINTS
PINPRICK
PINPRICKS
PINS

PINSCHER
PINSCHERS
PINSETTER
PINSTRIPE
PINSWELL
PINSWELLS
PINT
PINTA
PINTABLE
PINTABLES
PINTADA
PINTADAS
PINTADERA
PINTADO
PINTADOES
PINTADOS
PINTAIL
PINTAILED
PINTAILS
PINTANO
PINTANOS
PINTAS
PINTLE
PINTLES
PINTO
PINTOES
PINTOS
PINTS
PINTSIZE
PINTSIZED
PINUP
PINUPS
PINWALE
PINWALES
PINWEED
PINWEEDS
PINWHEEL
PINWHEELS
PINWORK
PINWORKS
PINWORM
PINWORMS
PINWRENCH
PINXIT
PINY
PINYIN
PINYON
PINYONS
PIOLET
PIOLETS
PION
PIONED
PIONEER
PIONEERED
PIONEERS
PIONER
PIONERS
PIONEY

PIONEYS
PIONIC
PIONIES
PIONING
PIONINGS
PIONS
PIONY
PIOPIO
PIOSITIES
PIOSITY
PIOTED
PIOUS
PIOUSLY
PIOUSNESS
PIOY
PIOYE
PIOYES
PIOYS
PIP
PIPA
PIPAGE
PIPAGES
PIPAL
PIPALS
PIPAS
PIPE
PIPEAGE
PIPEAGES
PIPECLAY
PIPECLAYS
PIPED
PIPEFISH
PIPEFUL
PIPEFULS
PIPELESS
PIPELIKE
PIPELINE
PIPELINED
PIPELINES
PIPER
PIPERIC
PIPERINE
PIPERINES
PIPERONAL
PIPERS
PIPES
PIPESTEM
PIPESTEMS
PIPESTONE
PIPET
PIPETED
PIPETING
PIPETS
PIPETTE
PIPETTED
PIPETTES
PIPETTING
PIPEWORK

PIPEWORKS	PIRATE	PISHER	PITA
PIPEWORT	PIRATED	PISHERS	PITAHAYA
PIPEWORTS	PIRATES	PISHES	PITAHAYAS
PIPI	PIRATIC	PISHING	PITAPAT
PIPIER	PIRATICAL	PISHOGE	PITAPATS
PIPIEST	PIRATING	PISHOGES	PITARA
PIPINESS	PIRAYA	PISHOGUE	PITARAH
PIPING	PIRAYAS	PISHOGUES	PITARAHS
PIPINGLY	PIRIFORM	PISIFORM	PITARAS
PIPINGS	PIRL	PISIFORMS	PITAS
PIPIS	PIRLED	PISKIES	PITAYA
PIPISTREL	PIRLICUE	PISKY	PITAYAS
PIPIT	PIRLICUED	PISMIRE	PITCH
PIPITS	PIRLICUES	PISMIRES	PITCHBEND
PIPKIN	PIRLING	PISO	PITCHED
PIPKINS	PIRLS	PISOLITE	PITCHER
PIPLESS	PIRN	PISOLITES	PITCHERS
PIPPED	PIRNIF	PISOLITH	PITCHES
PIPPIER	PIRNIES	PISOLITHS	PITCHFORK
PIPPIEST	PIRNIT	PISOLITIC	PITCHIER
PIPPIN	PIRNS	PISOS	PITCHIEST
PIPPING	PIROG	PISS	PITCHILY
PIPPINS	PIROGEN	PISSANT	PITCHING
PIPPY	PIROGHI	PISSANTS	PITCHINGS
PIPS	PIROGI	PISSED	PITCHMAN
PIPSQUEAK	PIROGIES	PISSER	PITCHMEN
PIPUL	PIROGUE	PISSERS	PITCHOUT
PIPULS	PIROGUES	PISSES	PITCHOUTS
PIPY	PIROJKI	PISSHEAD	PITCHPINE
PIQUANCE	PIROPLASM	PISSHEADS	PITCHPIPE
PIQUANCES	PIROQUE	PISSING	PITCHPOLE
PIQUANCY	PIROQUES	PISSOIR	PITCHY
PIQUANT	PIROSHKI	PISSOIRS	PITEOUS
PIQUANTLY	PIROUETTE	PISTACHE	PITEOUSLY
PIQUE	PIROZHKI	PISTACHES	PITFALL
PIQUED	PIROZHOK	PISTACHIO	PITFALLS
PIQUES	PIRS	PISTAREEN	PITH
PIQUET	PIS	PISTE	PITHBALL
PIQUETED	PISCARIES	PISTES	PITHBALLS
PIQUETING	PISCARY	PISTIL	PITHEAD
PIQUETS	PISCATOR	PISTILS	PITHEADS
PIQUILLO	PISCATORS	PISTOL	PITHECOID
PIQUILLOS	PISCATORY	PISTOLE	PITHED
PIQUING	PISCATRIX	PISTOLED	PITHFUL
PIR	PISCIFORM	PISTOLEER	PITHIER
PIRACETAM	PISCINA	PISTOLERO	PITHIEST
PIRACIES	PISCINAE	PISTOLES	PITHILY
PIRACY	PISCINAL	PISTOLET	PITHINESS
PIRAGUA	PISCINAS	PISTOLETS	PITHING
PIRAGUAS	PISCINE	PISTOLIER	PITHLESS
PIRAI	PISCINES	PISTOLING	PITHLIKE
PIRAIS	PISCIVORE	PISTOLLED	PITHOI
PIRANA	PISCO	PISTOLS	PITHOS
PIRANAS	PISCOS	PISTON	PITHS
PIRANHA	PISE	PISTONS	PITHY
PIRANHAS	PISES	PISTOU	PITIABLE
PIRARUCU	PISH	PISTOUS	PITIABLY
PIRARUCUS	PISHED	PIT	PITIED

PITIER	PIVOTS	PLACEBO	PLAICES
PITIERS	PIX	PLACEBOES	PLAID
PITIES	PIXEL	PLACEBOS	PLAIDED
PITIFUL	PIXELS	PLACED	PLAIDING
PITIFULLY	PIXES	PLACEKICK	PLAIDINGS
PITILESS	PIXIE	PLACELESS	PLAIDMAN
PITMAN	PIXIEISH	PLACEMAN	PLAIDMEN
PITMANS	PIXIES	PLACEMEN	PLAIDS
PITMEN	PIXILATED	PLACEMENT	PLAIN
PITON	PIXINESS	PLACENTA	PLAINANT
PITONS	PIXY	PLACENTAE	PLAINANTS
PITPROP	PIXYISH	PLACENTAL	PLAINED
PITPROPS	PIZAZZ	PLACENTAS	PLAINER
PITS	PIZAZZES	PLACER	PLAINEST
PITSAW	PIZAZZY	PLACERS	PLAINFUL
PITSAWS	PIZE	PLACES	PLAINING
PITTA	PIZED	PLACET	PLAININGS
PITTANCE	PIZES	PLACETS	PLAINISH
PITTANCES	PIZING	PLACID	PLAINLY
PITTAS	PIZZA	PLACIDER	PLAINNESS
PITTED	PIZZAIOLA	PLACIDEST	PLAINS
PITTEN	PIZZALIKE	PLACIDITY	PLAINSMAN
PITTER	PIZZAS	PLACIDLY	PLAINSMEN
PITTERED	PIZZAZ	PLACING	PLAINSONG
PITTERING	PIZZAZES	PLACINGS	PLAINT
PITTERS	PIZZAZZ	PLACIT	PLAINTEXT
PITTING	PIZZAZZES	PLACITA	PLAINTFUL
PITTINGS	PIZZAZZY	PLACITORY	PLAINTIFF
PITTITE	PIZZELLE	PLACITS	PLAINTIVE
PITTITES	PIZZELLES	PLACITUM	PLAINTS
PITUITA	PIZZERIA	PLACK	PLAINWORK
PITUITARY	PIZZERIAS	PLACKET	PLAISTER
PITUITAS	PIZZICATI	PLACKETS	PLAISTERS
PITUITE	PIZZICATO	PLACKLESS	PLAIT
PITUITES	PIZZLE	PLACKS	PLAITED
PITUITRIN	PIZZLES	PLACODERM	PLAITER
PITURI	PLAAS	PLACOID	PLAITERS
PITURIS	PLAASES	PLACOIDS	PLAITING
PITY	PLACABLE	PLAFOND	PLAITINGS
PITYING	PLACABLY	PLAFONDS	PLAITS
PITYINGLY	PLACARD	PLAGAL	PLAN
PITYROID	PLACARDED	PLAGE	PLANAR
PIU	PLACARDS	PLAGES	PLANARIA
PIUM	PLACATE	PLAGIARY	PLANARIAN
PIUMS	PLACATED	PLAGIUM	PLANARIAS
PIUPIU	PLACATER	PLAGIUMS	PLANARITY
PIUPIUS	PLACATERS	PLAGUE	PLANATE
PIVOT	PLACATES	PLAGUED	PLANATION
PIVOTABLE	PLACATING	PLAGUER	PLANCH
PIVOTAL	PLACATION	PLAGUERS	PLANCHE
PIVOTALLY	PLACATIVE	PLAGUES	PLANCHED
PIVOTED	PLACATORY	PLAGUEY	PLANCHES
PIVOTER	PLACCAT	PLAGUIER	PLANCHET
PIVOTERS	PLACCATE	PLAGUIEST	PLANCHETS
PIVOTING	PLACCATES	PLAGUILY	PLANCHING
PIVOTINGS	PLACCATS	PLAGUING	PLANE
PIVOTMAN	PLACE	PLAGUY	PLANED
PIVOTMEN	PLACEABLE	PLAICE	PLANELOAD

PLANENESS	PLANTSMAN	PLASTIC	PLATINUM
PLANER	PLANTSMEN	PLASTICKY	PLATINUMS
PLANERS	PLANTULE	PLASTICLY	PLATITUDE
PLANES	PLANTULES	PLASTICS	PLATONIC
PLANESIDE	PLANULA	PLASTID	PLATONICS
PLANET	PLANULAE	PLASTIDS	PLATONISM
PLANETARY	PLANULAR	PLASTIQUE	PLATOON
PLANETIC	PLANULATE	PLASTISOL	PLATOONED
PLANETOID	PLANULOID	PLASTRAL	PLATOONS
PLANETS	PLANURIA	PLASTRON	PLATS
PLANFORM	PLANURIAS	PLASTRONS	PLATTED
PLANFORMS	PLANURIES	PLASTRUM	PLATTER
PLANGENCY	PLANURY	PLASTRUMS	PLATTERS
PLANGENT	PLANXTIES	PLAT	PLATTING
PLANING	PLANXTY	PLATAN	PLATTINGS
PLANISH	PLAP	PLATANE	PLATY
PLANISHED	PLAPPED	PLATANES	PLATYFISH
PLANISHER	PLAPPING	PLATANNA	PLATYPI
PLANISHES	PLAPS	PLATANNAS	PLATYPUS
PLANK	PLAQUE	PLATANS	PLATYS
PLANKED	PLAQUES	PLATBAND	PLATYSMA
PLANKING	PLAQUETTE	PLATBANDS	PLATYSMAS
PLANKINGS	PLASH	PLATE	PLAUDIT
PLANKS	PLASHED	PLATEASM	PLAUDITE
PLANKTER	PLASHER	PLATEASMS	PLAUDITS
PLANKTERS	PLASHERS	PLATEAU	PLAUSIBLE
PLANKTON	PLASHES	PLATEAUED	PLAUSIBLY
PLANKTONS	PLASHET	PLATEAUS	PLAUSIVE
PLANLESS	PLASHETS	PLATEAUX	PLAUSTRAL
PLANNED	PLASHIER	PLATED	PLAY
PLANNER	PLASHIEST	PLATEFUL	PLAYA
PLANNERS	PLASHING	PLATEFULS	PLAYABLE
PLANNING	PLASHINGS	PLATELET	PLAYACT
PLANNINGS	PLASHY	PLATELETS	PLAYACTED
PLANOSOL	PLASM	PLATELIKE	PLAYACTOR
PLANOSOLS	PLASMA	PLATEMAN	PLAYACTS
PLANS	PLASMAGEL	PLATEMARK	PLAYAS
PLANT	PLASMAS	PLATEMEN	PLAYBACK
PLANTA	PLASMASOL	PLATEN	PLAYBACKS
PLANTABLE	PLASMATIC	PLATENS	PLAYBILL
PLANTAE	PLASMIC	PLATER	PLAYBILLS
PLANTAGE	PLASMID	PLATERS	PLAYBOOK
PLANTAGES	PLASMIDS	PLATES	PLAYBOOKS
PLANTAIN	PLASMIN	PLATESFUL	PLAYBOY
PLANTAINS	PLASMINS	PLATFORM	PLAYBOYS
PLANTAR	PLASMODIA	PLATFORMS	PLAYBUS
PLANTAS	PLASMOID	PLATIER	PLAYBUSES
PLANTED	PLASMOIDS	PLATIES	PLAYDATE
PLANTER	PLASMON	PLATIEST	PLAYDATES
PLANTERS	PLASMONS	PLATINA	PLAYDAY
PLANTING	PLASMS	PLATINAS	PLAYDAYS
PLANTINGS	PLAST	PLATING	PLAYDOWN
PLANTLESS	PLASTE	PLATINGS	PLAYDOWNS
PLANTLET	PLASTER	PLATINIC	PLAYED
PLANTLETS	PLASTERED	PLATINISE	PLAYER
PLANTLIKE	PLASTERER	PLATINIZE	PLAYERS
PLANTLING	PLASTERS	PLATINOID	PLAYFIELD
PLANTS	PLASTERY	PLATINOUS	PLAYFUL

PLAYFULLY	PLEASEMAN	PLEIADES	PLEUCHING
PLAYGIRL	PLEASEMEN	PLEIADS	PLEUCHS
PLAYGIRLS	PLEASER	PLEIOCENE	PLEUGH
PLAYGOER	PLEASERS	PLEIOMERY	PLEUGHED
PLAYGOERS	PLEASES	PLEIOTAXY	PLEUGHING
PLAYGOING	PLEASETH	PLENA	PLEUGHS
PLAYGROUP	PLEASING	PLENARIES	PLEURA
PLAYHOUSE	PLEASINGS	PLENARILY	PLEURAE
PLAYING	PLEASURE	PLENARTY	PLEURAL
PLAYLAND	PLEASURED	PLENARY	PLEURAS
PLAYLANDS	PLEASURER	PLENCH	PLEURISY
PLAYLESS	PLEASURES	PLENCHES	PLEURITIC
PLAYLET	PLEAT	PLENILUNE	PLEURITIS
PLAYLETS	PLEATED	PLENIPO	PLEURON
PLAYLIKE	PLEATER	PLENIPOES	PLEUSTON
PLAYLIST	PLEATERS	PLENIPOS	PLEUSTONS
PLAYLISTS	PLEATHER	PLENISH	PLEW
PLAYMAKER	PLEATHERS	PLENISHED	PLEWS
PLAYMATE	PLEATING	PLENISHER	PLEX
PLAYMATES	PLEATLESS	PLENISHES	PLEXAL
PLAYOFF	PLEATS	PLENISM	PLEXES
PLAYOFFS	PLEB	PLENISMS	PLEXIFORM
PLAYPEN	PLEBBIER	PLENIST	PLEXOR
PLAYPENS	PLEBBIEST	PLENISTS	PLEXORS
PLAYROOM	PLEBBY	PLENITUDE	PLEXURE
PLAYROOMS	PLEBE	PLENTEOUS	PLEXURES
PLAYS	PLEBEAN	PLENTIES	PLEXUS
PLAYSOME	PLEBEIAN	PLENTIFUL	PLEXUSES
PLAYSUIT	PLEBEIANS	PLENTY	PLIABLE
PLAYSUITS	PLEBES	PLENUM	PLIABLY
PLAYTHING	PLEBIFIED	PLENUMS	PLIANCIES
PLAYTIME	PLEBIFIES	PLEON	PLIANCY
PLAYTIMES	PLEBIFY	PLEONAL	PLIANT
PLAYWEAR	PLEBS	PLEONASM	PLIANTLY
PLAZA	PLECTRA	PLEONASMS	PLICA
PLAZAS	PLECTRE	PLEONAST	PLICAE
PLEA	PLECTRES	PLEONASTE	PLICAL
PLEACH	PLECTRON	PLEONASTS	PLICATE
PLEACHED	PLECTRONS	PLEONEXIA	PLICATED
PLEACHES	PLECTRUM	PLEONIC	PLICATELY
PLEACHING	PLECTRUMS	PLEONS	PLICATES
PLEAD	PLED	PLEOPOD	PLICATING
PLEADABLE	PLEDGABLE	PLEOPODS	PLICATION
PLEADED	PLEDGE	PLERION	PLICATURE
PLEADER	PLEDGED	PLERIONS	PLIE
PLEADERS	PLEDGEE	PLEROMA	PLIED
PLEADING	PLEDGEES	PLEROMAS	PLIER
PLEADINGS	PLEDGEOR	PLEROME	PLIERS
PLEADS	PLEDGEORS	PLEROMES	PLIES
PLEAED	PLEDGER	PLESH	PLIGHT
PLEAING	PLEDGERS	PLESHES	PLIGHTED
PLEAS	PLEDGES	PLESSOR	PLIGHTER
PLEASABLE	PLEDGET	PLESSORS	PLIGHTERS
PLEASANCE	PLEDGETS	PLETHORA	PLIGHTFUL
PLEASANT	PLEDGING	PLETHORAS	PLIGHTING
PLEASE	PLEDGOR	PLETHORIC	PLIGHTS
PLEASED	PLEDGORS	PLEUCH	PLIM
PLEASEDLY	PLEIAD	PLEUCHED	PLIMMED

PLIMMING	PLONKERS	PLOUKIEST	PLUGGER
PLIMS	PLONKIER	PLOUKS	PLUGGERS
PLIMSOL	PLONKIEST	PLOUKY	PLUGGING
PLIMSOLE	PLONKING	PLOUTER	PLUGGINGS
PLIMSOLES	PLONKINGS	PLOUTERED	PLUGHOLE
PLIMSOLL	PLONKO	PLOUTERS	PLUGHOLES
PLIMSOLLS	PLONKOS	PLOVER	PLUGLESS
PLIMSOLS	PLONKS	PLOVERS	PLUGOLA
PLING	PLONKY	PLOVERY	PLUGOLAS
PLINGS	PLOOK	PLOW	PLUGS
PLINK	PLOOKIE	PLOWABLE	PLUGUGLY
PLINKED	PLOOKIER	PLOWBACK	PLUM
PLINKER	PLOOKIEST	PLOWBACKS	PLUMAGE
PLINKERS	PLOOKS	PLOWBOY	PLUMAGED
PLINKING	PLOOKY	PLOWBOYS	PLUMAGES
PLINKINGS	PLOP	PLOWED	PLUMATE
PLINKS	PLOPPED	PLOWER	PLUMB
PLINTH	PLOPPING	PLOWERS	PLUMBABLE
PLINTHS	PLOPS	PLOWHEAD	PLUMBAGO
PLIOCENE	PLOSION	PLOWHEADS	PLUMBAGOS
PLIOFILM	PLOSIONS	PLOWING	PLUMBATE
PLIOFILMS	PLOSIVE	PLOWLAND	PLUMBATES
PLIOSAUR	PLOSIVES	PLOWLANDS	PLUMBED
PLIOSAURS	PLOT	PLOWMAN	PLUMBEOUS
PLIOTRON	PLOTFUL	PLOWMEN	PLUMBER
PLIOTRONS	PLOTLESS	PLOWS	PLUMBERS
PLISKIE	PLOTLINE	PLOWSHARE	PLUMBERY
PLISKIES	PLOTLINES	PLOWSTAFF	PLUMBIC
PLISKY	PLOTS	PLOWTER	PLUMBING
PLISSE	PLOTTAGE	PLOWTERED	PLUMBINGS
PLISSES	PLOTTAGES	PLOWTERS	PLUMBISM
PLOAT	PLOTTED	PLOY	PLUMBISMS
PLOATED	PLOTTER	PLOYED	PLUMBITE
PLOATING	PLOTTERED	PLOYING	PLUMBITES
PLOATS	PLOTTERS	PLOYS	PLUMBLESS
PLOD	PLOTTIE	PLU	PLUMBNESS
PLODDED	PLOTTIER	PLUCK	PLUMBOUS
PLODDER	PLOTTIES	PLUCKED	PLUMBS
PLODDERS	PLOTTIEST	PLUCKER	PLUMBUM
PLODDING	PLOTTING	PLUCKERS	PLUMBUMS
PLODDINGS	PLOTTINGS	PLUCKIER	PLUMCOT
PLODGE	PLOTTY	PLUCKIEST	PLUMCOTS
PLODGED	PLOTZ	PLUCKILY	PLUMDAMAS
PLODGES	PLOTZED	PLUCKING	PLUME
PLODGING	PLOTZES	PLUCKS	PLUMED
PLODS	PLOTZING	PLUCKY	PLUMELESS
PLOIDIES	PLOUGH	PLUE	PLUMELET
PLOIDY	PLOUGHBOY	PLUES	PLUMELETS
PLONG	PLOUGHED	PLUFF	PLUMELIKE
PLONGD	PLOUGHER	PLUFFED	PLUMERIA
PLONGE	PLOUGHERS	PLUFFIER	PLUMERIAS
PLONGED	PLOUGHING	PLUFFIEST	PLUMERIES
PLONGES	PLOUGHMAN	PLUFFING	PLUMERY
PLONGING	PLOUGHMEN	PLUFFS	PLUMES
PLONGS	PLOUGHS	PLUFFY	PLUMIER
PLONK	PLOUK	PLUG	PLUMIEST
PLONKED	PLOUKIE	PLUGBOARD	PLUMING
PLONKER	PLOUKIER	PLUGGED	PLUMIPED

PLUMIPEDS	PLUNKIEST	PLYING	POCKMARKS
PLUMIST	PLUNKING	PLYINGLY	POCKPIT
PLUMISTS	PLUNKS	PLYWOOD	POCKPITS
PLUMLIKE	PLUNKY	PLYWOODS	POCKS
PLUMMER	PLURAL	PNEUMA	POCKY
PLUMMEST	PLURALISE	PNEUMAS	POCO
PLUMMET	PLURALISM	PNEUMATIC	POCOSEN
PLUMMETED	PLURALIST	PNEUMONIA	POCOSENS
PLUMMETS	PLURALITY	PNEUMONIC	POCOSIN
PLUMMIER	PLURALIZE	PO	POCOSINS
PLUMMIEST	PLURALLY	POA	POCOSON
PLUMMY	PLURALS	POACEOUS	POCOSONS
PLUMOSE	PLURIPARA	POACH	POD
PLUMOSELY	PLURISIE	POACHABLE	PODAGRA
PLUMOSITY	PLURISIES	POACHED	PODAGRAL
PLUMOUS	PLURRY	POACHER	PODAGRAS
PLUMP	PLUS	POACHERS	PODAGRIC
PLUMPED	PLUSAGE	POACHES	PODAGROUS
PLUMPEN	PLUSAGES	POACHIER	PODAL
PLUMPENED	PLUSED	POACHIEST	PODALIC
PLUMPENS	PLUSES	POACHING	PODARGUS
PLUMPER	PLUSH	POACHINGS	PODCAST
PLUMPERS	PLUSHER	POACHY	PODCASTED
PLUMPEST	PLUSHES	POAKA	PODCASTER
PLUMPIE	PLUSHEST	POAKAS	PODCASTS
PLUMPIER	PLUSHIER	POAKE	PODDED
PLUMPIEST	PLUSHIEST	POAKES	PODDIE
PLUMPING	PLUSHILY	POAS	PODDIER
PLUMPISH	PLUSHLY	POBLANO	PODDIES
PLUMPLY	PLUSHNESS	POBLANOS	PODDIEST
PLUMPNESS	PLUSHY	POBOY	PODDING
PLUMPS	PLUSING	POBOYS	PODDLE
PLUMPY	PLUSSAGE	POCHARD	PODDLED
PLUMS	PLUSSAGES	POCHARDS	PODDLES
PLUMULA	PLUSSED	POCHAY	PODDLING
PLUMULAE	PLUSSES	POCHAYS	PODDY
PLUMULAR	PLUSSING	POCHETTE	PODESTA
PLUMULATE	PLUTEAL	POCHETTES	PODESTAS
PLUMULE	PLUTEI	POCHOIR	PODEX
PLUMULES	PLUTEUS	POCHOIRS	PODEXES
PLUMULOSE	PLUTEUSES	POCK	PODGE
PLUMY	PLUTOCRAT	POCKARD	PODGES
PLUNDER	PLUTOLOGY	POCKARDS	PODGIER
PLUNDERED	PLUTON	POCKED	PODGIEST
PLUNDERER	PLUTONIAN	POCKET	PODGILY
PLUNDERS	PLUTONIC	POCKETED	PODGINESS
PLUNGE	PLUTONISM	POCKETER	PODGY
PLUNGED	PLUTONIUM	POCKETERS	PODIA
PLUNGER	PLUTONOMY	POCKETFUL	PODIAL
PLUNGERS	PLUTONS	POCKETING	PODIATRIC
PLUNGES	PLUVIAL	POCKETS	PODIATRY
PLUNGING	PLUVIALS	POCKIER	PODITE
PLUNGINGS	PLUVIAN	POCKIES	PODITES
PLUNK	PLUVIOSE	POCKIEST	PODITIC
PLUNKED	PLUVIOUS	POCKILY	PODITICS
PLUNKER	PLY	POCKING	PODIUM
PLUNKERS	PLYER	POCKMANKY	PODIUMS
PLUNKIER	PLYERS	POCKMARK	PODLEY

PODLEYS	POETLESS	POINTELS	POKEYS
PODLIKE	POETLIKE	POINTER	POKIE
PODOCARP	POETRESSE	POINTERS	POKIER
PODOCARPS	POETRIES	POINTES	POKIES
PODOLOGY	POETRY	POINTIER	POKIEST
PODOMERE	POETS	POINTIEST	POKILY
PODOMERES	POETSHIP	POINTILLE	POKINESS
PODS	POETSHIPS	POINTING	POKING
PODSOL	POFFLE	POINTINGS	POKY
PODSOLIC	POFFLES	POINTLESS	POL
PODSOLISE	POGEY	POINTMAN	POLACCA
PODSOLIZE	POGEYS	POINTMEN	POLACCAS
PODSOLS	POGGE	POINTS	POLACRE
PODZOL	POGGES	POINTSMAN	POLACRES
PODZOLIC	POGIES	POINTSMEN	POLAR
PODZOLISE	POGO	POINTY	POLARISE
PODZOLIZE	POGOED	POIS	POLARISED
PODZOLS	POGOER	POISE	POLARISER
POECHORE	POGOERS	POISED	POLARISES
POECHORES	POGOING	POISER	POLARITY
POEM	POGONIA	POISERS	POLARIZE
POEMATIC	POGONIAS	POISES	POLARIZED
POEMS	POGONIP	POISHA	POLARIZER
POENOLOGY	POGONIPS	POISING	POLARIZES
POEP	POGOS	POISON	POLARON
POEPOL	POGROM	POISONED	POLARONS
POEPOLS	POGROMED	POISONER	POLARS
POEPS	POGROMING	POISONERS	POLDER
POESIED	POGROMIST	POISONING	POLDERED
POESIES	POGROMS	POISONOUS	POLDERING
POESY	POGY	POISONS	POLDERS
POESYING	POH	POISSON	POLE
POET	POHIRI	POISSONS	POLEAX
POETASTER	POHIRIS	POITIN	POLEAXE
POETASTRY	POI	POITINS	POLEAXED
POETESS	POIGNADO	POITREL	POLEAXES
POETESSES	POIGNANCE	POITRELS	POLEAXING
POETIC	POIGNANCY	POITRINE	POLECAT
POETICAL	POIGNANT	POITRINES	POLECATS
POETICALS	POILU	POKABLE	POLED
POETICISE	POILUS	POKAL	POLEIS
POETICISM	POINADO	POKALS	POLELESS
POETICIZE	POINADOES	POKE	POLEMARCH
POETICIZM	POINCIANA	POKEBERRY	POLEMIC
POETICS	POIND	POKED	POLEMICAL
POETICULE	POINDED	POKEFUL	POLEMICS
POETISE	POINDER	POKEFULS	POLEMISE
POETISED	POINDERS	POKELOGAN	POLEMISED
POETISER	POINDING	POKER	POLEMISES
POETISERS	POINDINGS	POKERISH	POLEMIST
POETISES	POINDS	POKEROOT	POLEMISTS
POETISING	POINT	POKEROOTS	POLEMIZE
POETIZE	POINTABLE	POKERS	POLEMIZED
POETIZED	POINTE	POKERWORK	POLEMIZES
POETIZER	POINTED	POKES	POLENTA
POETIZERS	POINTEDLY	POKEWEED	POLENTAS
POETIZES	POINTEL	POKEWEEDS	POLER
POETIZING	POINTELLE	POKEY	POLERS

POLES	POLKS	POLLUTION	POLYCOT
POLESTAR	POLL	POLLUTIVE	POLYCOTS
POLESTARS	POLLACK	POLLY	POLYDEMIC
POLEWARD	POLLACKS	POLLYANNA	POLYENE
POLEY	POLLAN	POLLYWIG	POLYENES
POLEYN	POLLANS	POLLYWIGS	POLYENIC
POLEYNS	POLLARD	POLLYWOG	POLYESTER
POLEYS	POLLARDED	POLLYWOGS	POLYGALA
POLIANITE	POLLARDS	POLO	POLYGALAS
POLICE	POLLED	POLOIDAL	POLYGAM
POLICED	POLLEE	POLOIST	POLYGAMIC
POLICEMAN	POLLEES	POLOISTS	POLYGAMS
POLICEMEN	POLLEN	POLONAISE	POLYGAMY
POLICER	POLLENATE	POLONIE	POLYGENE
POLICERS	POLLENED	POLONIES	POLYGENES
POLICES	POLLENING	POLONISE	POLYGENIC
POLICIES	POLLENS	POLONISED	POLYGENY
POLICING	POLLENT	POLONISES	POLYGLOT
POLICINGS	POLLER	POLONISM	POLYGLOTS
POLICY	POLLERS	POLONISMS	POLYGLOTT
POLIES	POLLEX	POLONIUM	POLYGON
POLING	POLLICAL	POLONIUMS	POLYGONAL
POLINGS	POLLICES	POLONIZE	POLYGONS
POLIO	POLLICIE	POLONIZED	POLYGONUM
POLIOS	POLLICIES	POLONIZES	POLYGONY
POLIS	POLLICY	POLONY	POLYGRAPH
POLISH	POLLIES	POLOS	POLYGYNY
POLISHED	POLLINATE	POLS	POLYHEDRA
POLISHER	POLLING	POLT	POLYIMIDE
POLISHERS	POLLINGS	POLTED	POLYLEMMA
POLISHES	POLLINIA	POLTFEET	POLYMASTY
POLISHING	POLLINIC	POLTFOOT	POLYMATH
POLITBURO	POLLINISE	POLTING	POLYMATHS
POLITE	POLLINIUM	POLTROON	POLYMATHY
POLITELY	POLLINIZE	POLTROONS	POLYMER
POLITER	POLLIST	POLTS	POLYMERIC
POLITESSE	POLLISTS	POLVERINE	POLYMERS
POLITEST	POLLIWIG	POLY	POLYMERY
POLITIC	POLLIWIGS	POLYACID	POLYMORPH
POLITICAL	POLLIWOG	POLYACIDS	POLYMYXIN
POLITICK	POLLIWOGS	POLYACT	POLYNIA
POLITICKS	POLLMAN	POLYADIC	POLYNIAS
POLITICLY	POLLMEN	POLYAMIDE	POLYNYA
POLITICO	POLLOCK	POLYAMINE	POLYNYAS
POLITICOS	POLLOCKS	POLYANDRY	POLYNYI
POLITICS	POLLS	POLYANTHA	POLYOL
POLITIES	POLLSTER	POLYANTHI	POLYOLS
POLITIQUE	POLLSTERS	POLYARCH	POLYOMA
POLITY	POLLTAKER	POLYARCHY	POLYOMAS
POLJE	POLLUCITE	POLYAXIAL	POLYOMINO
POLJES	POLLUSION	POLYAXON	POLYONYM
POLK	POLLUTANT	POLYAXONS	POLYONYMS
POLKA	POLLUTE	POLYBASIC	POLYONYMY
POLKAED	POLLUTED	POLYBRID	POLYP
POLKAING	POLLUTER	POLYBRIDS	POLYPARIA
POLKAS	POLLUTERS	POLYCARPY	POLYPARY
POLKED	POLLUTES	POLYCHETE	POLYPE
POLKING	POLLUTING	POLYCONIC	POLYPED

POLYPEDS	POLYZOANS	POMPILIDS	PONG
POLYPES	POLYZOARY	POMPION	PONGA
POLYPHAGY	POLYZOIC	POMPIONS	PONGAS
POLYPHASE	POLYZONAL	POMPOM	PONGED
POLYPHON	POLYZOOTD	POMPOMS	PONGEE
POLYPHONE	POLYZOON	POMPON	PONGEES
POLYPHONS	POM	POMPONS	PONGID
POLYPHONY	POMACE	POMPOON	PONGIDS
POLYPI	POMACEOUS	POMPOONS	PONGIER
POLYPIDE	POMACES	POMPOSITY	PONGIEST
POLYPIDES	POMADE	POMPOUS	PONGING
POLYPIDOM	POMADED	POMPOUSLY	PONGO
POLYPILL	POMADES	POMPS	PONGOES
POLYPILLS	POMADING	POMROY	PONGOS
POLYPINE	POMANDER	POMROYS	PONGS
POLYPITE	POMANDERS	POMS	PONGY
POLYPITES	POMATO	POMWATER	PONIARD
POLYPLOID	POMATOES	POMWATERS	PONIARDED
POLYPNEA	POMATUM	PONCE	PONIARDS
POLYPNEAS	POMATUMS	PONCEAU	PONIED
POLYPNEIC	POMBE	PONCEAUS	PONIES
POLYPOD	POMBES	PONCEAUX	PONK
POLYPODS	POME	PONCED	PONKED
POLYPODY	POMELO	PONCES	PONKING
POLYPOID	POMELOS	PONCEY	PONKS
POLYPORE	POMEROY	PONCHO	PONS
POLYPORES	POMEROYS	PONCHOED	PONT
POLYPOSES	POMES	PONCHOS	PONTAGE
POLYPOSIS	POMFRET	PONCIER	PONTAGES
POLYPOUS	POMFRETS	PONCIEST	PONTAL
POLYPS	POMMEE	PONCING	PONTES
POLYPTYCH	POMMEL	PONCY	PONTIANAC
POLYPUS	POMMELE	POND	PONTIANAK
POLYPUSES	POMMELED	PONDAGE	PONTIC
POLYS	POMMELING	PONDAGES	PONTIE
POLYSEME	POMMELLED	PONDED	PONTIES
POLYSEMES	POMMELS	PONDER	PONTIFEX
POLYSEMIC	POMMETTY	PONDERAL	PONTIFF
POLYSEMY	POMMIE	PONDERATE	PONTIFFS
POLYSOME	POMMIES	PONDERED	PONTIFIC
POLYSOMES	POMMY	PONDERER	PONTIFICE
POLYSOMIC	POMO	PONDERERS	PONTIFIED
POLYSOMY	POMOERIUM	PONDERING	PONTIFIES
POLYSTYLE	POMOLOGY	PONDEROSA	PONTIFY
POLYTENE	POMOS	PONDEROUS	PONTIL
POLYTENY	POMP	PONDERS	PONTILE
POLYTHENE	POMPADOUR	PONDING	PONTILES
POLYTONAL	POMPANO	PONDOK	PONTILS
POLYTYPE	POMPANOS	PONDOKKIE	PONTINE
POLYTYPES	POMPELO	PONDOKS	PONTLEVIS
POLYTYPIC	POMPELOS	PONDS	PONTON
POLYURIA	POMPEY	PONDWEED	PONTONEER
POLYURIAS	POMPEYED	PONDWEEDS	PONTONIER
POLYURIC	POMPEYING	PONE	PONTONS
POLYVINYL	POMPEYS	PONENT	PONTOON
POLYWATER	POMPHOLYX	PONES	PONTOONED
POLYZOA	POMPIER	PONEY	PONTOONER
POLYZOAN	POMPILID	PONEYS	PONTOONS

PONTS
PONTY
PONY
PONYING
PONYSKIN
PONYSKINS
PONYTAIL
PONYTAILS
PONZU
PONZUS
POO
POOCH
POOCHED
POOCHES
POOCHING
POOD
POODLE
POODLES
POODS
POOED
POOF
POOFIER
POOFIEST
POOFS
POOFTAH
POOFTAHS
POOFTER
POOFTERS
POOFY
POOGYE
POOGYES
POOH
POOHED
POOHING
POOHS
POOING
POOJA
POOJAH
POOJAHS
POOJAS
POOK
POOKA
POOKAS
POOKING
POOKIT
POOKS
POOL
POOLED
POOLER
POOLERS
POOLHALL
POOLHALLS
POOLING
POOLROOM
POOLROOMS
POOLS
POOLSIDE
POOLSIDES

POON
POONAC
POONACS
POONCE
POONCED
POONCES
POONCING
POONS
POONTANG
POONTANGS
POOP
POOPED
POOPER
POOPERS
POOPING
POOPS
POOR
POORER
POOREST
POORHOUSE
POORI
POORIS
POORISH
POORLIER
POORLIEST
POORLY
POORMOUTH
POORNESS
POORT
POORTITH
POORTITHS
POORTS
POORWILL
POORWILLS
POOS
POOT
POOTED
POOTER
POOTERS
POOTING
POOTLE
POOTLED
POOTLES
POOTLING
POOTS
POOVE
POOVERIES
POOVERY
POOVES
POOVIER
POOVIEST
POOVY
POP
POPADUM
POPADUMS
POPCORN
POPCORNS
POPE

POPEDOM
POPEDOMS
POPEHOOD
POPEHOODS
POPELESS
POPELIKE
POPELING
POPELINGS
POPERA
POPERAS
POPERIES
POPERIN
POPERINS
POPERY
POPES
POPESEYE
POPESHIP
POPESHIPS
POPETTE
POPETTES
POPEYED
POPGUN
POPGUNS
POPINJAY
POPINJAYS
POPISH
POPISHLY
POPJOY
POPJOYED
POPJOYING
POPJOYS
POPLAR
POPLARS
POPLIN
POPLINS
POPLITEAL
POPLITEI
POPLITEUS
POPLITIC
POPOVER
POPOVERS
POPPA
POPPADOM
POPPADOMS
POPPADUM
POPPADUMS
POPPAS
POPPED
POPPER
POPPERING
POPPERS
POPPET
POPPETS
POPPIED
POPPIER
POPPIES
POPPIEST
POPPING

POPPISH
POPPIT
POPPITS
POPPLE
POPPLED
POPPLES
POPPLIER
POPPLIEST
POPPLING
POPPLY
POPPY
POPPYCOCK
POPPYHEAD
POPRIN
POPRINS
POPS
POPSICLE
POPSICLES
POPSIE
POPSIES
POPSTER
POPSTERS
POPSY
POPULACE
POPULACES
POPULAR
POPULARLY
POPULARS
POPULATE
POPULATED
POPULATES
POPULISM
POPULISMS
POPULIST
POPULISTS
POPULOUS
PORAE
PORAES
PORAL
PORANGI
PORBEAGLE
PORCELAIN
PORCH
PORCHES
PORCINE
PORCINI
PORCINIS
PORCINO
PORCUPINE
PORCUPINY
PORE
PORED
PORER
PORERS
PORES
PORGE
PORGED
PORGES

PORGIE	PORPHYRIC	PORTESS	PORTULAN
PORGIES	PORPHYRIN	PORTESSE	PORTULANS
PORGING	PORPHYRIO	PORTESSES	PORTY
PORGY	PORPHYRY	PORTFIRE	PORWIGGLE
PORIER	PORPOISE	PORTFIRES	PORY
PORIEST	PORPOISED	PORTFOLIO	POS
PORIFER	PORPOISES	PORTHOLE	POSABLE
PORIFERAL	PORPORATE	PORTHOLES	POSADA
PORIFERAN	PORRECT	PORTHORS	POSADAS
PORIFERS	PORRECTED	PORTHOS	POSAUNE
PORINA	PORRECTS	PORTHOSES	POSAUNES
PORINAS	PORRENGER	PORTHOUSE	POSE
PORINESS	PORRIDGE	PORTICO	POSEABLE
PORING	PORRIDGES	PORTICOED	POSED
PORISM	PORRIDGY	PORTICOES	POSER
PORISMS	PORRIGO	PORTICOS	POSERISH
PORISTIC	PORRIGOS	PORTIER	POSERS
PORK	PORRINGER	PORTIERE	POSES
PORKED	PORT	PORTIERED	POSEUR
PORKER	PORTA	PORTIERES	POSEURS
PORKERS	PORTABLE	PORTIEST	POSEUSE
PORKIER	PORTABLES	PORTIGUE	POSEUSES
PORKIES	PORTABLY	PORTIGUES	POSEY
PORKIEST	PORTAGE	PORTING	POSH
PORKINESS	PORTAGED	PORTION	POSHED
PORKING	PORTAGES	PORTIONED	POSHER
PORKLING	PORTAGING	PORTIONER	POSHES
PORKLINGS	PORTAGUE	PORTIONS	POSHEST
PORKPIE	PORTAGUES	PORTLAND	POSHING
PORKPIES	PORTAL	PORTLANDS	POSHLY
PORKS	PORTALED	PORTLAST	POSHNESS
PORKWOOD	PORTALING	PORTLASTS	POSHO
PORKWOODS	PORTALLED	PORTLESS	POSHOS
PORKY	PORTALS	PORTLIER	POSHTEEN
PORN	PORTANCE	PORTLIEST	POSHTEENS
PORNIER	PORTANCES	PORTLY	POSIER
PORNIEST	PORTAPACK	PORTMAN	POSIES
PORNO	PORTAPAK	PORTMEN	POSIEST
PORNOMAG	PORTAPAKS	PORTOISE	POSIGRADE
PORNOMAGS	PORTAS	PORTOISES	POSING
PORNOS	PORTASES	PORTOLAN	POSINGLY
PORNS	PORTATE	PORTOLANI	POSINGS
PORNY	PORTATILE	PORTOLANO	POSIT
POROGAMIC	PORTATIVE	PORTOLANS	POSITED
POROGAMY	PORTED	PORTOUS	POSITIF
POROMERIC	PORTEND	PORTOUSES	POSITIFS
POROSCOPE	PORTENDED	PORTRAIT	POSITING
POROSCOPY	PORTENDS	PORTRAITS	POSITION
POROSE	PORTENT	PORTRAY	POSITIONS
POROSES	PORTENTS	PORTRAYAL	POSITIVE
POROSIS	PORTEOUS	PORTRAYED	POSITIVER
POROSITY	PORTER	PORTRAYER	POSITIVES
POROUS	PORTERAGE	PORTRAYS	POSITON
POROUSLY	PORTERED	PORTREEVE	POSITONS
PORPESS	PORTERESS	PORTRESS	POSITRON
PORPESSE	PORTERING	PORTS	POSITRONS
PORPESSES	PORTERLY	PORTSIDE	POSITS
PORPHYRIA	PORTERS	PORTULACA	POSNET

POSNETS	POSTCRASH	POSTLUDE	POTAGER
POSOLE	POSTDATE	POSTLUDES	POTAGERS
POSOLES	POSTDATED	POSTMAN	POTAGES
POSOLOGIC	POSTDATES	POSTMARK	POTAMIC
POSOLOGY	POSTDIVE	POSTMARKS	POTASH
POSS	POSTDOC	POSTMEN	POTASHED
POSSE	POSTDOCS	POSTNASAL	POTASHES
POSSED	POSTDRUG	POSTNATAL	POTASHING
POSSER	POSTED	POSTNATI	POTASS
POSSERS	POSTEEN	POSTOP	POTASSA
POSSES	POSTEENS	POSTOPS	POTASSAS
POSSESS	POSTER	POSTORAL	POTASSES
POSSESSED	POSTERED	POSTPAID	POTASSIC
POSSESSES	POSTERING	POSTPONE	POTASSIUM
POSSESSOR	POSTERIOR	POSTPONED	POTATION
POSSET	POSTERITY	POSTPONER	POTATIONS
POSSETED	POSTERN	POSTPONES	POTATO
POSSETING	POSTERNS	POSTPOSE	POTATOBUG
POSSETS	POSTERS	POSTPOSED	POTATOES
POSSIBLE	POSTFACE	POSTPOSES	POTATORY
POSSIBLER	POSTFACES	POSTPUNK	POTBELLY
POSSIBLES	POSTFAULT	POSTRACE	POTBOIL
POSSIBLY	POSTFIRE	POSTRIDER	POTBOILED
POSSIE	POSTFIX	POSTRIOT	POTBOILER
POSSIES	POSTFIXAL	POSTS	POTBOILS
POSSING	POSTFIXED	POSTSHOW	POTBOUND
POSSUM	POSTFIXES	POSTSYNC	POTBOY
POSSUMED	POSTFORM	POSTSYNCS	POTBOYS
POSSUMING	POSTFORMS	POSTTAX	POTCH
POSSUMS	POSTGAME	POSTTEEN	POTCHE
POST	POSTGRAD	POSTTEENS	POTCHED
POSTAGE	POSTGRADS	POSTTEST	POTCHER
POSTAGES	POSTHASTE	POSTTESTS	POTCHERS
POSTAL	POSTHEAT	POSTTRIAL	POTCHES
POSTALLY	POSTHEATS	POSTULANT	POTCHING
POSTALS	POSTHOLE	POSTULATA	POTE
POSTANAL	POSTHOLES	POSTULATE	POTED
POSTAXIAL	POSTHORSE	POSTURAL	POTEEN
POSTBAG	POSTHOUSE	POSTURE	POTEENS
POSTBAGS	POSTICAL	POSTURED	POTENCE
POSTBASE	POSTICHE	POSTURER	POTENCES
POSTBOX	POSTICHES	POSTURERS	POTENCIES
POSTBOXES	POSTICOUS	POSTURES	POTENCY
POSTBOY	POSTIE	POSTURING	POTENT
POSTBOYS	POSTIES	POSTURISE	POTENTATE
POSTBURN	POSTIL	POSTURIST	POTENTIAL
POSTBUS	POSTILED	POSTURIZE	POTENTISE
POSTBUSES	POSTILING	POSTVIRAL	POTENTIZE
POSTCARD	POSTILION	POSTWAR	POTENTLY
POSTCARDS	POSTILLED	POSTWOMAN	POTENTS
POSTCAVA	POSTILLER	POSTWOMEN	POTES
POSTCAVAE	POSTILS	POSY	POTFUL
POSTCAVAL	POSTIN	POT	POTFULS
POSTCAVAS	POSTING	POTABLE	POTGUN
POSTCODE	POSTINGS	POTABLES	POTGUNS
POSTCODED	POSTINS	POTAE	POTHEAD
POSTCODES	POSTIQUE	POTAES	POTHEADS
POSTCOUP	POSTIQUES	POTAGE	POTHECARY

POTHEEN	POTSHOT	POUFFY	POUNDED
POTHEENS	POTSHOTS	POUFING	POUNDER
POTHER	POTSIE	POUFS	POUNDERS
POTHERB	POTSIES	POUFTAH	POUNDING
POTHERBS	POTSTONE	POUFTAHS	POUNDS
POTHERED	POTSTONES	POUFTER	POUPE
POTHERING	POTSY	POUFTERS	POUPED
POTHERS	POTT	POUK	POUPES
POTHERY	POTTAGE	POUKE	POUPING
POTHOLDER	POTTAGES	POUKED	POUPT
POTHOLE	POTTED	POUKES	POUR
POTHOLED	POTTEEN	POUKING	POURABLE
POTHOLER	POTTEENS	POUKIT	POURBOIRE
POTHOLERS	POTTER	POUKS	POURED
POTHOLES	POTTERED	POULAINE	POURER
POTHOLING	POTTERER	POULAINES	POURERS
POTHOOK	POTTERERS	POULARD	POURIE
POTHOOKS	POTTERIES	POULARDE	POURIES
POTHOS	POTTERING	POULARDES	POURING
POTHOUSE	POTTERS	POULARDS	POURINGLY
POTHOUSES	POTTERY	POULDER	POURINGS
POTHUNTER	POTTIER	POULDERED	POURPOINT
POTICARY	POTTIES	POULDERS	POURS
POTICHE	POTTIEST	POULDRE	POURSEW
POTICHES	POTTINESS	POULDRES	POURSEWED
POTIN	POTTING	POULDRON	POURSEWS
POTING	POTTINGAR	POULDRONS	POURSUE
POTINS	POTTINGER	POULE	POURSUED
POTION	POTTLE	POULES	POURSUES
POTIONS	POTTLES	POULP	POURSUING
POTLACH	POTTO	POULPE	POURSUIT
POTLACHE	POTTOS	POULPES	POURSUITS
POTLACHES	POTTS	POULPS	POURTRAY
POTLATCH	POTTY	POULT	POURTRAYD
POTLIKE	POTWALLER	POULTER	POURTRAYS
POTLINE	POTZER	POULTERER	POUSOWDIE
POTLINES	POTZERS	POULTERS	POUSSE
POTLUCK	POUCH	POULTICE	POUSSES
POTLUCKS	POUCHED	POULTICED	POUSSETTE
POTMAN	POUCHES	POULTICES	POUSSIE
POTMEN	POUCHFUL	POULTRIES	POUSSIES
POTOMETER	POUCHFULS	POULTRY	POUSSIN
POTOO	POUCHIER	POULTS	POUSSINS
POTOOS	POUCHIEST	POUNCE	POUT
POTOROO	POUCHING	POUNCED	POUTED
POTOROOS	POUCHY	POUNCER	POUTER
POTPIE	POUDER	POUNCERS	POUTERS
POTPIES	POUDERS	POUNCES	POUTFUL
POTPOURRI	POUDRE	POUNCET	POUTHER
POTS	POUDRES	POUNCETS	POUTHERED
POTSHARD	POUF	POUNCHING	POUTHERS
POTSHARDS	POUFED	POUNCING	POUTIER
POTSHARE	POUFF	POUND	POUTIEST
POTSHARES	POUFFE	POUNDAGE	POUTINE
POTSHERD	POUFFED	POUNDAGES	POUTINES
POTSHERDS	POUFFES	POUNDAL	POUTING
POTSHOP	POUFFING	POUNDALS	POUTINGLY
POTSHOPS	POUFFS	POUNDCAKE	POUTINGS

POUTS	POX	PRAECIPES	PRANKFUL
POUTY	POXED	PRAECOCES	PRANKIER
POVERTIES	POXES	PRAEDIAL	PRANKIEST
POVERTY	POXIER	PRAEDIALS	PRANKING
POW	POXIEST	PRAEFECT	PRANKINGS
POWAN	POXING	PRAEFECTS	PRANKISH
POWANS	POXVIRUS	PRAELECT	PRANKLE
POWDER	POXY	PRAELECTS	PRANKLED
POWDERED	POYNANT	PRAELUDIA	PRANKLES
POWDERER	POYNT	PRAENOMEN	PRANKLING
POWDERERS	POYNTED	PRAESES	PRANKS
POWDERIER	POYNTING	PRAESIDIA	PRANKSOME
POWDERING	POYNTS	PRAETOR	PRANKSTER
POWDERS	POYOU	PRAETORS	PRANKY
POWDERY	POYOUS	PRAGMATIC	PRAO
POWELLISE	POYSE	PRAHU	PRAOS
POWELLITE	POYSED	PRAHUS	PRASE
POWELLIZE	POYSES	PRAIRIE	PRASES
POWER	POYSING	PRAIRIED	PRAT
POWERBOAT	POYSON	PRAIRIES	PRATE
POWERED	POYSONED	PRAISE	PRATED
POWERFUL	POYSONING	PRAISEACH	PRATER
POWERING	POYSONS	PRAISED	PRATERS
POWERLESS	POZ	PRAISEFUL	PRATES
POWERPLAY	POZOLE	PRAISER	PRATFALL
POWERS	POZOLES	PRAISERS	PRATFALLS
POWFAGGED	POZZ	PRAISES	PRATFELL
POWHIRI	POZZIES	PRAISING	PRATIE
POWHIRIS	POZZOLAN	PRAISINGS	PRATIES
POWIN	POZZOLANA	PRAJNA	PRATING
POWINS	POZZOLANS	PRAJNAS	PRATINGLY
POWN	POZZY	PRALINE	PRATINGS
POWND	PRAAM	PRALINES	PRATIQUE
POWNDED	PRAAMS	PRAM	PRATIQUES
POWNDING	PRABBLE	PRAMS	PRATS
POWNDS	PRABBLES	PRANA	PRATT
POWNEY	PRACHARAK	PRANAS	PRATTED
POWNEYS	PRACTIC	PRANAYAMA	PRATTING
POWNIE	PRACTICAL	PRANCE	PRATTLE
POWNIES	PRACTICE	PRANCED	PRATTLED
POWNS	PRACTICED	PRANCER	PRATTLER
POWNY	PRACTICER	PRANCERS	PRATTLERS
POWRE	PRACTICES	PRANCES	PRATTLES
POWRED	PRACTICK	PRANCING	PRATTLING
POWRES	PRACTICKS	PRANCINGS	PRATTS
POWRING	PRACTICS	PRANCK	PRATY
POWS	PRACTICUM	PRANCKE	PRAU
POWSOWDY	PRACTIQUE	PRANCKED	PRAUNCE
POWTER	PRACTISE	PRANCKES	PRAUNCED
POWTERED	PRACTISED	PRANCKING	PRAUNCES
POWTERING	PRACTISER	PRANCKS	PRAUNCING
POWTERS	PRACTISES	PRANDIAL	PRAUS
POWWAW	PRACTIVE	PRANG	PRAVITIES
POWWAWS	PRACTOLOL	PRANGED	PRAVITY
POWWOW	PRAD	PRANGING	PRAWLE
POWWOWED	PRADS	PRANGS	PRAWLES
POWWOWING	PRAEAMBLE	PRANK	PRAWLIN
POWWOWS	PRAECIPE	PRANKED	PRAWLINS

PRAWN	PREAMPS	PREBOUND	PRECISER
PRAWNED	PREANAL	PREBUDGET	PRECISES
PRAWNER	PREAPPLY	PREBUILD	PRECISEST
PRAWNERS	PREARM	PREBUILDS	PRECISIAN
PRAWNING	PREARMED	PREBUILT	PRECISING
PRAWNS	PREARMING	PREBUTTAL	PRECISION
PRAXES	PREARMS	PREBUY	PRECISIVE
PRAXIS	PREASE	PREBUYING	PRECITED
PRAXISES	PREASED	PREBUYS	PRECLEAN
PRAY	PREASES	PRECANCEL	PRECLEANS
PRAYED	PREASING	PRECANCER	PRECLEAR
PRAYER	PREASSE	PRECAST	PRECLEARS
PRAYERFUL	PREASSED	PRECASTS	PRECLUDE
PRAYERS	PREASSES	PRECATIVE	PRECLUDED
PRAYING	PREASSIGN	PRECATORY	PRECLUDES
PRAYINGLY	PREASSING	PRECAUDAL	PRECOCIAL
PRAYINGS	PREASSURE	PRECAVA	PRECOCITY
PRAYS	PREATOMIC	PRECAVAE	PRECODE
PRE	PREATTUNE	PRECAVAL	PRECODED
PREABSORB	PREAUDIT	PRECEDE	PRECODES
PREACCUSE	PREAUDITS	PRECEDED	PRECODING
PREACE	PREAVER	PRECEDENT	PRECOITAL
PREACED	PREAVERS	PRECEDES	PRECONISE
PREACES	PREAXIAL	PRECEDING	PRECONIZE
PREACH	PREBADE	PRECEESE	PRECOOK
PREACHED	PREBAKE	PRECENSOR	PRECOOKED
PREACHER	PREBAKED	PRECENT	PRECOOKER
PREACHERS	PREBAKES	PRECENTED	PRECOOKS
PREACHES	PREBAKING	PRECENTOR	PRECOOL
PREACHIER	PREBASAL	PRECENTS	PRECOOLED
PREACHIFY	PREBASE	PRECEPIT	PRECOOLS
PREACHILY	PREBATTLE	PRECEPITS	PRECOUP
PREACHING	PREBEND	PRECEPT	PRECRASH
PREACHY	PREBENDAL	PRECEPTOR	PRECREASE
PREACING	PREBENDS	PRECEPTS	PRECRISIS
PREACT	PREBID	PRECESS	PRECURE
PREACTED	PREBIDDEN	PRECESSED	PRECURED
PREACTING	PREBIDS	PRECESSES	PRECURES
PREACTS	PREBILL	PRECHARGE	PRECURING
PREADAMIC	PREBILLED	PRECHECK	PRECURRER
PREADAPT	PREBILLS	PRECHECKS	PRECURSE
PREADAPTS	PREBIND	PRECHILL	PRECURSES
PREADJUST	PREBINDS	PRECHILLS	PRECURSOR
PREADMIT	PREBIOTIC	PRECHOOSE	PRECUT
PREADMITS	PREBIRTH	PRECHOSE	PRECUTS
PREADOPT	PREBIRTHS	PRECHOSEN	PREDACITY
PREADOPTS	PREBLESS	PRECIEUSE	PREDATE
PREADULT	PREBOARD	PRECIEUX	PREDATED
PREADULTS	PREBOARDS	PRECINCT	PREDATES
PREAGED	PREBOIL	PRECINCTS	PREDATING
PREALLOT	PREBOILED	PRECIOUS	PREDATION
PREALLOTS	PREBOILS	PRECIPE	PREDATISM
PREALTER	PREBOOK	PRECIPES	PREDATIVE
PREALTERS	PREBOOKED	PRECIPICE	PREDATOR
PREAMBLE	PREBOOKS	PRECIS	PREDATORS
PREAMBLED	PREBOOM	PRECISE	PREDATORY
PREAMBLES	PREBORN	PRECISED	PREDAWN
PREAMP	PREBOUGHT	PRECISELY	PREDAWNS

PREDEATH	PREEMPTS	PREFIX	PREINVITE
PREDEATHS	PREEN	PREFIXAL	PREJINK
PREDEBATE	PREENACT	PREFIXED	PREJUDGE
PREDEDUCT	PREENACTS	PREFIXES	PREJUDGED
PREDEFINE	PREENED	PREFIXING	PREJUDGER
PREDELLA	PREENER	PREFIXION	PREJUDGES
PREDELLAS	PREENERS	PREFLAME	PREJUDICE
PREDELLE	PREENING	PREFLIGHT	PREJUDIZE
PREDESIGN	PREENS	PREFOCUS	PRELACIES
PREDEVOTE	PREERECT	PREFORM	PRELACY
PREDIAL	PREERECTS	PREFORMAT	PRELATE
PREDIALS	PREES	PREFORMED	PRELATES
PREDICANT	PREEVE	PREFORMS	PRELATESS
PREDICATE	PREEVED	PREFRANK	PRELATIAL
PREDICT	PREEVES	PREFRANKS	PRELATIC
PREDICTED	PREEVING	PREFREEZE	PRELATIES
PREDICTER	PREEXCITE	PREFROZE	PRELATION
PREDICTOR	PREEXEMPT	PREFROZEN	PRELATISE
PREDICTS	PREEXILIC	PREFUND	PRELATISH
PREDIED	PREEXIST	PREFUNDED	PRELATISM
PREDIES	PREEXISTS	PREFUNDS	PRELATIST
PREDIGEST	PREEXPOSE	PREGAME	PRELATIZE
PREDIKANT	PREFAB	PREGAMES	PRELATURE
PREDILECT	PREFABBED	PREGGERS	PRELATY
PREDINNER	PREFABS	PREGGIER	PRELAUNCH
PREDIVE	PREFACE	PREGGIEST	PRELAW
PREDIVES	PREFACED	PREGGY	PRELECT
PREDOOM	PREFACER	PREGNABLE	PRELECTED
PREDOOMED	PREFACERS	PREGNANCE	PRELECTOR
PREDOOMS	PREFACES	PREGNANCY	PRELECTS
PREDRAFT	PREFACIAL	PREGNANT	PRELEGAL
PREDRIED	PREFACING	PREGROWTH	PRELIFE
PREDRIES	PREFADE	PREGUIDE	PRELIM
PREDRILL	PREFADED	PREGUIDED	PRELIMIT
PREDRILLS	PREFADES	PREGUIDES	PRELIMITS
PREDRY	PREFADING	PREHALLUX	PRELIMS
PREDRYING	PREFARD	PREHANDLE	PRELIVES
PREDUSK	PREFATORY	PREHARDEN	PRELOAD
PREDUSKS	PREFECT	PREHEAT	PRELOADED
PREDY	PREFECTS	PREHEATED	PRELOADS
PREDYE	PREFER	PREHEATER	PRELOCATE
PREDYED	PREFERRED	PREHEATS	PRELOVED
PREDYEING	PREFERRER	PREHEND	PRELUDE
PREDYES	PREFERS	PREHENDED	PRELUDED
PREDYING	PREFEUDAL	PREHENDS	PRELUDER
PREE	PREFIGHT	PREHENSOR	PRELUDERS
PREED	PREFIGURE	PREHIRING	PRELUDES
PREEDIT	PREFILE	PREHNITE	PRELUDI
PREEDITED	PREFILED	PREHNITES	PRELUDIAL
PREEDITS	PREFILES	PREHUMAN	PRELUDING
PREEING	PREFILING	PREHUMANS	PRELUDIO
PREELECT	PREFILL	PREIF	PRELUNCH
PREELECTS	PREFILLED	PREIFE	PRELUSION
PREEMIE	PREFILLS	PREIFES	PRELUSIVE
PREEMIES	PREFIRE	PREIFS	PRELUSORY
PREEMPT	PREFIRED	PREIMPOSE	PREM
PREEMPTED	PREFIRES	PREINFORM	PREMADE
PREEMPTOR	PREFIRING	PREINSERT	PREMAN

PREMARKET	PRENATALS	PREPLAN	PRERUPT
PREMATURE	PRENOMEN	PREPLANS	PRESA
PREMEAL	PRENOMENS	PREPLANT	PRESAGE
PREMED	PRENOMINA	PREPLANTS	PRESAGED
PREMEDIC	PRENOON	PREPOLLEX	PRESAGER
PREMEDICS	PRENOTIFY	PREPONE	PRESAGERS
PREMEDS	PRENOTION	PREPONED	PRESAGES
PREMEET	PRENT	PREPONES	PRESAGING
PREMEETS	PRENTED	PREPONING	PRESALE
PREMEN	PRENTICE	PREPOSE	PRESALES
PREMERGER	PRENTICED	PREPOSED	PRESBYOPE
PREMIA	PRENTICES	PREPOSES	PRESBYOPY
PREMIE	PRENTING	PREPOSING	PRESBYTE
PREMIER	PRENTS	PREPOSTOR	PRESBYTER
PREMIERE	PRENUBILE	PREPOTENT	PRESBYTES
PREMIERED	PRENUMBER	PREPPED	PRESBYTIC
PREMIERES	PRENUP	PREPPIE	PRESCHOOL
PREMIERS	PRENUPS	PREPPIER	PRESCIENT
PREMIES	PRENZIE	PREPPIES	PRESCIND
PREMISE	PREOBTAIN	PREPPIEST	PRESCINDS
PREMISED	PREOCCUPY	PREPPILY	PRESCIOUS
PREMISES	PREOCULAR	PREPPING	PRESCORE
PREMISING	PREOP	PREPPY	PRESCORED
PREMISS	PREOPS	PREPREG	PRESCORES
PREMISSES	PREOPTION	PREPREGS	PRESCREEN
PREMIUM	PREORAL	PREPRESS	PRESCRIBE
PREMIUMS	PREORDAIN	PREPRICE	PRESCRIPT
PREMIX	PREORDER	PREPRICED	PRESCUTA
PREMIXED	PREORDERS	PREPRICES	PRESCUTUM
PREMIXES	PREOWNED	PREPRINT	PRESE
PREMIXING	PREP	PREPRINTS	PRESEASON
PREMIXT	PREPACK	PREPS	PRESELECT
PREMODERN	PREPACKED	PREPUBES	PRESELL
PREMODIFY	PREPACKS	PREPUBIS	PRESELLS
PREMOLAR	PREPAID	PREPUCE	PRESENCE
PREMOLARS	PREPARE	PREPUCES	PRESENCES
PREMOLD	PREPARED	PREPUEBLO	PRESENILE
PREMOLDED	PREPARER	PREPUNCH	PRESENT
PREMOLDS	PREPARERS	PREPUPA	PRESENTED
PREMOLT	PREPARES	PREPUPAE	PRESENTEE
PREMOLTS	PREPARING	PREPUPAL	PRESENTER
PREMONISH	PREPASTE	PREPUPAS	PRESENTLY
PREMORAL	PREPASTED	PREPUTIAL	PRESENTS
PREMORSE	PREPASTES	PREQUEL	PRESERVE
PREMOSAIC	PREPAVE	PREQUELS	PRESERVED
PREMOTION	PREPAVED	PRERACE	PRESERVER
PREMOVE	PREPAVES	PRERADIO	PRESERVES
PREMOVED	PREPAVING	PRERECORD	PRESES
PREMOVES	PREPAY	PRERECTAL	PRESET
PREMOVING	PREPAYING	PREREFORM	PRESETS
PREMS	PREPAYS	PRERENAL	PRESETTLE
PREMUNE	PREPENSE	PRERETURN	PRESHAPE
PREMY	PREPENSED	PREREVIEW	PRESHAPED
PRENAME	PREPENSES	PRERINSE	PRESHAPES
PRENAMES	PREPILL	PRERINSED	PRESHIP
PRENASAL	PREPLACE	PRERINSES	PRESHIPS
PRENASALS	PREPLACED	PRERIOT	PRESHOW
PRENATAL	PREPLACES	PREROCK	PRESHOWED

PRESHOWN	PRESSROOM	PRETERMIT	PREVENT
PRESHOWS	PRESSRUN	PRETERMS	PREVENTED
PRESHRANK	PRESSRUNS	PRETEST	PREVENTER
PRESHRINK	PRESSURE	PRETESTED	PREVENTS
PRESHRUNK	PRESSURED	PRETESTS	PREVERB
PRESIDE	PRESSURES	PRETEXT	PREVERBAL
PRESIDED	PRESSWORK	PRETEXTED	PREVERBS
PRESIDENT	PREST	PRETEXTS	PREVES
PRESIDER	PRESTAMP	PRETOLD	PREVIABLE
PRESIDERS	PRESTAMPS	PRETONIC	PREVIEW
PRESIDES	PRESTED	PRETOR	PREVIEWED
PRESIDIA	PRESTER	PRETORIAL	PREVIEWER
PRESIDIAL	PRESTERNA	PRETORIAN	PREVIEWS
PRESIDING	PRESTERS	PRETORS	PREVING
PRESIDIO	PRESTIGE	PRETRAIN	PREVIOUS
PRESIDIOS	PRESTIGES	PRETRAINS	PREVISE
PRESIDIUM	PRESTING	PRETRAVEL	PREVISED
PRESIFT	PRESTO	PRETREAT	PREVISES
PRESIFTED	PRESTORE	PRETREATS	PREVISING
PRESIFTS	PRESTORED	PRETRIAL	PREVISION
PRESIGNAL	PRESTORES	PRETRIALS	PREVISIT
PRESLEEP	PRESTOS	PRETRIM	PREVISITS
PRESLICE	PRESTRESS	PRETRIMS	PREVISOR
PRESLICED	PRESTRIKE	PRETTIED	PREVISORS
PRESLICES	PRESTS	PRETTIER	PREVUE
PRESOAK	PRESUME	PRETTIES	PREVUED
PRESOAKED	PRESUMED	PRETTIEST	PREVUES
PRESOAKS	PRESUMER	PRETTIFY	PREVUING
PRESOLD	PRESUMERS	PRETTILY	PREWAR
PRESOLVE	PRESUMES	PRETTY	PREWARM
PRESOLVED	PRESUMING	PRETTYING	PREWARMED
PRESOLVES	PRESUMMIT	PRETTYISH	PREWARMS
PRESONG	PRESURVEY	PRETTYISM	PREWARN
PRESORT	PRETAPE	PRETYPE	PREWARNED
PRESORTED	PRETAPED	PRETYPED	PREWARNS
PRESORTS	PRETAPES	PRETYPES	PREWASH
PRESPLIT	PRETAPING	PRETYPING	PREWASHED
PRESS	PRETASTE	PRETZEL	PREWASHES
PRESSED	PRETASTED	PRETZELS	PREWEIGH
PRESSER	PRETASTES	PREUNION	PREWEIGHS
PRESSERS	PRETAX	PREUNIONS	PREWIRE
PRESSES	PRETEEN	PREUNITE	PREWIRED
PRESSFAT	PRETEENS	PREUNITED	PREWIRES
PRESSFATS	PRETELL	PREUNITES	PREWIRING
PRESSFUL	PRETELLS	PREVAIL	PREWORK
PRESSFULS	PRETENCE	PREVAILED	PREWORKED
PRESSGANG	PRETENCES	PREVAILER	PREWORKS
PRESSIE	PRETEND	PREVAILS	PREWORN
PRESSIES	PRETENDED	PREVALENT	PREWRAP
PRESSING	PRETENDER	PREVALUE	PREWRAPS
PRESSINGS	PRETENDS	PREVALUED	PREWYN
PRESSION	PRETENSE	PREVALUES	PREWYNS
PRESSIONS	PRETENSES	PREVE	PREX
PRESSMAN	PRETERIST	PREVED	PREXES
PRESSMARK	PRETERIT	PREVENE	PREXIES
PRESSMEN	PRETERITE	PREVENED	PREXY
PRESSOR	PRETERITS	PREVENES	PREY
PRESSORS	PRETERM	PREVENING	PREYED

PREYER	PRIDELESS	PRIMATE	PRINCED
PREYERS	PRIDES	PRIMATES	PRINCEDOM
PREYFUL	PRIDIAN	PRIMATIAL	PRINCEKIN
PREYING	PRIDING	PRIMATIC	PRINCELET
PREYS	PRIED	PRIMAVERA	PRINCELY
PREZ	PRIEDIEU	PRIME	PRINCES
PREZES	PRIEDIEUS	PRIMED	PRINCESS
PREZZES	PRIEDIEUX	PRIMELY	PRINCESSE
PREZZIE	PRIEF	PRIMENESS	PRINCING
PREZZIES	PRIEFE	PRIMER	PRINCIPAL
PRIAL	PRIEFED	PRIMERO	PRINCIPE
PRIALS	PRIEFES	PRIMEROS	PRINCIPI
PRIAPEAN	PRIEFING	PRIMERS	PRINCIPIA
PRIAPI	PRIEFS	PRIMES	PRINCIPLE
PRIAPIC	PRIER	PRIMETIME	PRINCOCK
PRIAPISM	PRIERS	PRIMEUR	PRINCOCKS
PRIAPISMS	PRIES	PRIMEURS	PRINCOX
PRIAPUS	PRIEST	PRIMEVAL	PRINCOXES
PRIAPUSES	PRIESTED	PRIMI	PRINK
PRIBBLE	PRIESTESS	PRIMINE	PRINKED
PRIBBLES	PRIESTING	PRIMINES	PRINKER
PRICE	PRIESTLY	PRIMING	PRINKERS
PRICEABLE	PRIESTS	PRIMINGS	PRINKING
PRICED	PRIEVE	PRIMIPARA	PRINKS
PRICELESS	PRIEVED	PRIMITIA	PRINT
PRICER	PRIEVES	PRIMITIAE	PRINTABLE
PRICERS	PRIEVING	PRIMITIAL	PRINTED
PRICES	PRIG	PRIMITIAS	PRINTER
PRICEY	PRIGGED	PRIMITIVE	PRINTERS
PRICIER	PRIGGER	PRIMLY	PRINTERY
PRICIEST	PRIGGERS	PRIMMED	PRINTHEAD
PRICILY	PRIGGERY	PRIMMER	PRINTING
PRICINESS	PRIGGING	PRIMMERS	PRINTINGS
PRICING	PRIGGINGS	PRIMMEST	PRINTLESS
PRICINGS	PRIGGISH	PRIMMING	PRINTOUT
PRICK	PRIGGISM	PRIMNESS	PRINTOUTS
PRICKED	PRIGGISMS	PRIMO	PRINTS
PRICKER	PRIGS	PRIMORDIA	PRION
PRICKERS	PRILL	PRIMOS	PRIONS
PRICKET	PRILLED	PRIMP	PRIOR
PRICKETS	PRILLING	PRIMPED	PRIORATE
PRICKIER	PRILLS	PRIMPING	PRIORATES
PRICKIEST	PRIM	PRIMPS	PRIORESS
PRICKING	PRIMA	PRIMROSE	PRIORIES
PRICKINGS	PRIMACIES	PRIMROSED	PRIORITY
PRICKLE	PRIMACY	PRIMROSES	PRIORLY
PRICKLED	PRIMAEVAL	PRIMROSY	PRIORS
PRICKLES	PRIMAGE	PRIMS	PRIORSHIP
PRICKLIER	PRIMAGES	PRIMSIE	PRIORY
PRICKLING	PRIMAL	PRIMSIER	PRISAGE
PRICKLY	PRIMALITY	PRIMSIEST	PRISAGES
PRICKS	PRIMALLY	PRIMULA	PRISE
PRICKWOOD	PRIMARIES	PRIMULAS	PRISED
PRICKY	PRIMARILY	PRIMULINE	PRISER
PRICY	PRIMARY	PRIMUS	PRISERE
PRIDE	PRIMAS	PRIMUSES	PRISERES
PRIDED	PRIMATAL	PRIMY	PRISERS
PRIDEFUL	PRIMATALS	PRINCE	PRISES

PRISING	PRIZEMEN	PROCESSER	PRODRUGS
PRISM	PRIZER	PROCESSES	PRODS
PRISMATIC	PRIZERS	PROCESSOR	PRODUCE
PRISMOID	PRIZES	PROCHAIN	PRODUCED
PRISMOIDS	PRIZING	PROCHEIN	PRODUCER
PRISMS	PRO	PROCHOICE	PRODUCERS
PRISMY	PROA	PROCHURCH	PRODUCES
PRISON	PROACTION	PROCIDENT	PRODUCING
PRISONED	PROACTIVE	PROCINCT	PRODUCT
PRISONER	PROAS	PROCINCTS	PRODUCTS
PRISONERS	PROB	PROCLAIM	PROEM
PRISONING	PROBABLE	PROCLAIMS	PROEMBRYO
PRISONOUS	PROBABLES	PROCLISES	PROEMIAL
PRISONS	PROBABLY	PROCLISIS	PROEMS
PRISS	PROBALL	PROCLITIC	PROENZYME
PRISSED	PROBAND	PROCLIVE	PROESTRUS
PRISSES	PROBANDS	PROCONSUL	PROETTE
PRISSIER	PROBANG	PROCREANT	PROETTES
PRISSIES	PROBANGS	PROCREATE	PROF
PRISSIEST	PROBATE	PROCTAL	PROFACE
PRISSILY	PROBATED	PROCTITIS	PROFAMILY
PRISSING	PROBATES	PROCTODEA	PROFANE
PRISSY	PROBATING	PROCTOR	PROFANED
PRISTANE	PROBATION	PROCTORED	PROFANELY
PRISTANES	PROBATIVE	PROCTORS	PROFANER
PRISTINE	PROBATORY	PROCURACY	PROFANERS
PRITHEE	PROBE	PROCURAL	PROFANES
PRIVACIES	PROBEABLE	PROCURALS	PROFANING
PRIVACY	PROBED	PROCURE	PROFANITY
PRIVADO	PROBER	PROCURED	PROFESS
PRIVADOES	PROBERS	PROCURER	PROFESSED
PRIVADOS	PROBES	PROCURERS	PROFESSES
PRIVATE	PROBING	PROCURES	PROFESSOR
PRIVATEER	PROBINGLY	PROCURESS	PROFFER
PRIVATELY	PROBIOTIC	PROCUREUR	PROFFERED
PRIVATER	PROBIT	PROCURING	PROFFERER
PRIVATES	PROBITIES	PROD	PROFFERS
PRIVATEST	PROBITS	PRODDED	PROFILE
PRIVATION	PROBITY	PRODDER	PROFILED
PRIVATISE	PROBLEM	PRODDERS	PROFILER
PRIVATISM	PROBLEMS	PRODDING	PROFILERS
PRIVATIST	PROBOSCIS	PRODIGAL	PROFILES
PRIVATIVE	PROBS	PRODIGALS	PROFILING
PRIVATIZE	PROCACITY	PRODIGIES	PROFILIST
PRIVET	PROCAINE	PRODIGY	PROFIT
PRIVETS	PROCAINES	PRODITOR	PROFITED
PRIVIER	PROCAMBIA	PRODITORS	PROFITEER
PRIVIES	PROCARP	PRODITORY	PROFITER
PRIVIEST	PROCARPS	PRODNOSE	PROFITERS
PRIVILEGE	PROCARYON	PRODNOSED	PROFITING
PRIVILY	PROCEDURE	PRODNOSES	PROFITS
PRIVITIES	PROCEED	PRODROMAL	PROFLUENT
PRIVITY	PROCEEDED	PRODROME	PROFORMA
PRIVY	PROCEEDER	PRODROMES	PROFORMAS
PRIZABLE	PROCEEDS	PRODROMI	PROFOUND
PRIZE	PROCERITY	PRODROMIC	PROFOUNDS
PRIZED	PROCESS	PRODROMUS	PROFS
PRIZEMAN	PROCESSED	PRODRUG	PROFUSE

PROFUSELY	PROLACTIN	PROLUSION	PRONATES
PROFUSER	PROLAMIN	PROLUSORY	PRONATING
PROFUSERS	PROLAMINE	PROM	PRONATION
PROFUSION	PROLAMINS	PROMACHOS	PRONATOR
PROFUSIVE	PROLAN	PROMENADE	PRONATORS
PROG	PROLANS	PROMETAL	PRONE
PROGENIES	PROLAPSE	PROMETALS	PRONELY
PROGENY	PROLAPSED	PROMETRIC	PRONENESS
PROGERIA	PROLAPSES	PROMINE	PRONEPHRA
PROGERIAS	PROLAPSUS	PROMINENT	PRONER
PROGESTIN	PROLATE	PROMINES	PRONES
PROGGED	PROLATED	PROMISE	PRONEST
PROGGER	PROLATELY	PROMISED	PRONEUR
PROGGERS	PROLATES	PROMISEE	PRONEURS
PROGGING	PROLATING	PROMISEES	PRONG
PROGGINS	PROLATION	PROMISER	PRONGBUCK
PROGNOSE	PROLATIVE	PROMISERS	PRONGED
PROGNOSED	PROLE	PROMISES	PRONGHORN
PROGNOSES	PROLED	PROMISING	PRONGING
PROGNOSIS	PROLEG	PROMISOR	PRONGS
PROGRADE	PROLEGS	PROMISORS	PRONK
PROGRADED	PROLEPSES	PROMISSOR	PRONKED
PROGRADES	PROLEPSIS	PROMMER	PRONKING
PROGRAM	PROLEPTIC	PROMMERS	PRONKS
PROGRAMED	PROLER	PROMO	PRONOTA
PROGRAMER	PROLERS	PROMODERN	PRONOTAL
PROGRAMME	PROLES	PROMOED	PRONOTUM
PROGRAMS	PROLETARY	PROMOING	PRONOUN
PROGRESS	PROLICIDE	PROMOS	PRONOUNCE
PROGS	PROLIFIC	PROMOTE	PRONOUNS
PROGUN	PROLINE	PROMOTED	PRONTO
PROHIBIT	PROLINES	PROMOTER	PRONUCLEI
PROHIBITS	PROLING	PROMOTERS	PRONUNCIO
PROIGN	PROLIX	PROMOTES	PROO
PROIGNED	PROLIXITY	PROMOTING	PROOEMION
PROIGNING	PROLIXLY	PROMOTION	PROOEMIUM
PROIGNS	PROLL	PROMOTIVE	PROOF
PROIN	PROLLED	PROMOTOR	PROOFED
PROINE	PROLLER	PROMOTORS	PROOFER
PROINED	PROLLERS	PROMPT	PROOFERS
PROINES	PROLLING	PROMPTED	PROOFING
PROINING	PROLLS	PROMPTER	PROOFINGS
PROINS	PROLOG	PROMPTERS	PROOFLESS
PROJECT	PROLOGED	PROMPTEST	PROOFREAD
PROJECTED	PROLOGING	PROMPTING	PROOFROOM
PROJECTOR	PROLOGISE	PROMPTLY	PROOFS
PROJECTS	PROLOGIST	PROMPTS	PROOTIC
PROJET	PROLOGIZE	PROMPTURE	PROOTICS
PROJETS	PROLOGS	PROMS	PROP
PROKARYON	PROLOGUE	PROMULGE	PROPAGATE
PROKARYOT	PROLOGUED	PROMULGED	PROPAGE
PROKE	PROLOGUES	PROMULGES	PROPAGED
PROKED	PROLONG	PROMUSCES	PROPAGES
PROKER	PROLONGE	PROMUSCIS	PROPAGING
PROKERS	PROLONGED	PRONAOI	PROPAGULA
PROKES	PROLONGER	PRONAOS	PROPAGULE
PROKING	PROLONGES	PRONATE	PROPALE
PROLABOR	PROLONGS	PRONATED	PROPALED

PROPALES	PROPONING	PROSE	PROSTRATE
PROPALING	PROPOSAL	PROSECT	PROSTYLE
PROPANE	PROPOSALS	PROSECTED	PROSTYLES
PROPANES	PROPOSE	PROSECTOR	PROSUMER
PROPANOIC	PROPOSED	PROSECTS	PROSUMERS
PROPANOL	PROPOSER	PROSECUTE	PROSY
PROPANOLS	PROPOSERS	PROSED	PROTAMIN
PROPANONE	PROPOSES	PROSELIKE	PROTAMINE
PROPEL	PROPOSING	PROSELYTE	PROTAMINS
PROPELLED	PROPOSITA	PROSEMAN	PROTANDRY
PROPELLER	PROPOSITI	PROSEMEN	PROTANOPE
PROPELLOR	PROPOUND	PROSER	PROTASES
PROPELS	PROPOUNDS	PROSERS	PROTASIS
PROPEND	PROPPANT	PROSES	PROTATIC
PROPENDED	PROPPANTS	PROSEUCHA	PROTEA
PROPENDS	PROPPED	PROSEUCHE	PROTEAN
PROPENE	PROPPING	PROSIER	PROTEANS
PROPENES	PROPRETOR	PROSIEST	PROTEAS
PROPENOIC	PROPRIA	PROSIFIED	PROTEASE
PROPENOL	PROPRIETY	PROSIFIES	PROTEASES
PROPENOLS	PROPRIUM	PROSIFY	PROTECT
PROPENSE	PROPS	PROSILY	PROTECTED
PROPENYL	PROPTOSES	PROSIMIAN	PROTECTER
PROPER	PROPTOSIS	PROSINESS	PROTECTOR
PROPERDIN	PROPULSOR	PROSING	PROTECTS
PROPERER	PROPYL	PROSINGS	PROTEGE
PROPEREST	PROPYLA	PROSIT	PROTEGEE
PROPERLY	PROPYLAEA	PROSO	PROTEGEES
PROPERS	PROPYLENE	PROSODIAL	PROTEGES
PROPERTY	PROPYLIC	PROSODIAN	PROTEI
PROPHAGE	PROPYLITE	PROSODIC	PROTEID
PROPHAGES	PROPYLON	PROSODIES	PROTEIDE
PROPHASE	PROPYLONS	PROSODIST	PROTEIDES
PROPHASES	PROPYLS	PROSODY	PROTEIDS
PROPHASIC	PRORATE	PROSOMA	PROTEIN
PROPHECY	PRORATED	PROSOMAL	PROTEINIC
PROPHESY	PRORATES	PROSOMAS	PROTEINS
PROPHET	PRORATING	PROSOMATA	PROTEND
PROPHETIC	PRORATION	PROSOPON	PROTENDED
PROPHETS	PRORE	PROSOPONS	PROTENDS
PROPHYLL	PRORECTOR	PROSOS	PROTENSE
PROPHYLLS	PROREFORM	PROSPECT	PROTENSES
PROPINE	PRORES	PROSPECTS	PROTEOME
PROPINED	PROROGATE	PROSPER	PROTEOMES
PROPINES	PROROGUE	PROSPERED	PROTEOMIC
PROPINING	PROROGUED	PROSPERS	PROTEOSE
PROPIONIC	PROROGUES	PROSS	PROTEOSES
PROPJET	PROS	PROSSES	PROTEST
PROPJETS	PROSAIC	PROSSIE	PROTESTED
PROPMAN	PROSAICAL	PROSSIES	PROTESTER
PROPMEN	PROSAISM	PROST	PROTESTOR
PROPODEON	PROSAISMS	PROSTATE	PROTESTS
PROPODEUM	PROSAIST	PROSTATES	PROTEUS
PROPOLIS	PROSAISTS	PROSTATIC	PROTEUSES
PROPONE	PROSATEUR	PROSTERNA	PROTHALLI
PROPONED	PROSCENIA	PROSTIE	PROTHESES
PROPONENT	PROSCRIBE	PROSTIES	PROTHESIS
PROPONES	PROSCRIPT	PROSTOMIA	PROTHETIC

PROTHORAX	PROUSTITE	PROVOKERS	PRUNELLE
PROTHYL	PROVABLE	PROVOKES	PRUNELLES
PROTHYLS	PROVABLY	PROVOKING	PRUNELLO
PROTIST	PROVAND	PROVOLONE	PRUNELLOS
PROTISTAN	PROVANDS	PROVOST	PRUNER
PROTISTIC	PROVANT	PROVOSTRY	PRUNERS
PROTISTS	PROVANTED	PROVOSTS	PRUNES
PROTIUM	PROVANTS	PROW	PRUNING
PROTIUMS	PROVE	PROWAR	PRUNINGS
PROTOAVIS	PROVEABLE	PROWER	PRUNT
PROTOCOL	PROVEABLY	PROWESS	PRUNTED
PROTOCOLS	PROVED	PROWESSED	PRUNTS
PROTODERM	PROVEDOR	PROWESSES	PRUNUS
PROTOGINE	PROVEDORE	PROWEST	PRUNUSES
PROTOGYNY	PROVEDORS	PROWL	PRURIENCE
PROTON	PROVEN	PROWLED	PRURIENCY
PROTONATE	PROVEND	PROWLER	PRURIENT
PROTONEMA	PROVENDER	PROWLERS	PRURIGO
PROTONIC	PROVENDS	PROWLING	PRURIGOS
PROTONS	PROVENLY	PROWLINGS	PRURITIC
PROTOPOD	PROVER	PROWLS	PRURITUS
PROTOPODS	PROVERB	PROWS	PRUSIK
PROTORE	PROVERBED	PROXEMIC	PRUSIKED
PROTORES	PROVERBS	PROXEMICS	PRUSIKING
PROTOSTAR	PROVERS	PROXIES	PRUSIKS
PROTOTYPE	PROVES	PROXIMAL	PRUSSIATE
PROTOXID	PROVIANT	PROXIMATE	PRUSSIC
PROTOXIDE	PROVIANTS	PROXIMITY	PRUTA
PROTOXIDS	PROVIDE	PROXIMO	PRUTAH
PROTOZOA	PROVIDED	PROXY	PRUTOT
PROTOZOAL	PROVIDENT	PROYN	PRUTOTH
PROTOZOAN	PROVIDER	PROYNE	PRY
PROTOZOIC	PROVIDERS	PROYNED	PRYER
PROTOZOON	PROVIDES	PROYNES	PRYERS
PROTRACT	PROVIDING	PROYNING	PRYING
PROTRACTS	PROVIDOR	PROYNS	PRYINGLY
PROTRADE	PROVIDORS	PROZYMITE	PRYINGS
PROTRUDE	PROVINCE	PRUDE	PRYS
PROTRUDED	PROVINCES	PRUDENCE	PRYSE
PROTRUDES	PROVINE	PRUDENCES	PRYSED
PROTYL	PROVINED	PRUDENT	PRYSES
PROTYLE	PROVINES	PRUDENTLY	PRYSING
PROTYLES	PROVING	PRUDERIES	PRYTANEA
PROTYLS	PROVINGS	PRUDERY	PRYTANEUM
PROUD	PROVINING	PRUDES	PRYTHEE
PROUDER	PROVIRAL	PRUDISH	PSALM
PROUDEST	PROVIRUS	PRUDISHLY	PSALMBOOK
PROUDFUL	PROVISION	PRUH	PSALMED
PROUDISH	PROVISO	PRUINA	PSALMIC
PROUDLY	PROVISOES	PRUINAS	PSALMING
PROUDNESS	PROVISOR	PRUINE	PSALMIST
PROUL	PROVISORS	PRUINES	PSALMISTS
PROULED	PROVISORY	PRUINOSE	PSALMODIC
PROULER	PROVISOS	PRUNABLE	PSALMODY
PROULERS	PROVOCANT	PRUNE	PSALMS
PROULING	PROVOKE	PRUNED	PSALTER
PROULS	PROVOKED	PRUNELLA	PSALTERIA
PROUNION	PROVOKER	PRUNELLAS	PSALTERS

PSALTERY	PSORIATIC	PTOMAINES	PUCES
PSALTRESS	PSORIC	PTOMAINIC	PUCEST
PSALTRIES	PSST	PTOMAINS	PUCK
PSALTRY	PST	PTOOEY	PUCKA
PSAMMITE	PSYCH	PTOSES	PUCKED
PSAMMITES	PSYCHE	PTOSIS	PUCKER
PSAMMITIC	PSYCHED	PTOTIC	PUCKERED
PSAMMON	PSYCHES	PTUI	PUCKERER
PSAMMONS	PSYCHIC	PTYALIN	PUCKERERS
PSCHENT	PSYCHICAL	PTYALINS	PUCKERIER
PSCHENTS	PSYCHICS	PTYALISE	PUCKERING
PSELLISM	PSYCHING	PTYALISED	PUCKEROOD
PSELLISMS	PSYCHISM	PTYALISES	PUCKEROOS
PSEPHISM	PSYCHISMS	PTYALISM	PUCKERY
PSEPHISMS	PSYCHIST	PTYALISMS	PUCKFIST
PSEPHITE	PSYCHISTS	PTYALIZE	PUCKFISTS
PSEPHITES	PSYCHO	PTYALIZED	PUCKING
PSEPHITIC	PSYCHOGAS	PTYALIZES	PUCKISH
PSEUD	PSYCHOID	PTYXES	PUCKISHLY
PSEUDAXES	PSYCHOIDS	PTYXIS	PUCKLE
PSEUDAXIS	PSYCHOS	PTYXISES	PUCKLES
PSEUDERY	PSYCHOSES	PUB	PUCKS
PSEUDISH	PSYCHOSIS	PUBBED	PUD
PSEUDO	PSYCHOTIC	PUBBING	PUDDEN
PSEUDONYM	PSYCHS	PUBE	PUDDENING
PSEUDOPOD	PSYLLA	PUBERAL	PUDDENS
PSEUDOS	PSYLLAS	PUBERTAL	PUDDER
PSEUDS	PSYLLID	PUBERTIES	PUDDERED
PSHAW	PSYLLIDS	PUBERTY	PUDDERING
PSHAWED	PSYLLIUM	PUBES	PUDDERS
PSHAWING	PSYLLIUMS	PUBESCENT	PUDDIES
PSHAWS	PSYOP	PUBIC	PUDDING
PSI	PSYOPS	PUBIS	PUDDINGS
PSILOCIN	PSYWAR	PUBISES	PUDDINGY
PSILOCINS	PSYWARS	PUBLIC	PUDDLE
PSILOSES	PTARMIC	PUBLICAN	PUDDLED
PSILOSIS	PTARMICS	PUBLICANS	PUDDLER
PSILOTIC	PTARMIGAN	PUBLICISE	PUDDLERS
PSION	PTERIA	PUBLICIST	PUDDLES
PSIONIC	PTERIDINE	PUBLICITY	PUDDLIER
PSIONICS	PTERIN	PUBLICIZE	PUDDLIEST
PSIONS	PTERINS	PUBLICLY	PUDDLING
PSIS	PTERION	PUBLICS	PUDDLINGS
PSOAE	PTEROPOD	PUBLISH	PUDDLY
PSOAI	PTEROPODS	PUBLISHED	PUDDOCK
PSOAS	PTEROSAUR	PUBLISHER	PUDDOCKS
PSOASES	PTERYGIA	PUBLISHES	PUDDY
PSOATIC	PTERYGIAL	PUBS	PUDENCIES
PSOCID	PTERYGIUM	PUCAN	PUDENCY
PSOCIDS	PTERYGOID	PUCANS	PUDENDA
PSORA	PTERYLA	PUCCOON	PUDENDAL
PSORALEA	PTERYLAE	PUCCOONS	PUDENDOUS
PSORALEAS	PTILOSES	PUCE	PUDENDUM
PSORALEN	PTILOSIS	PUCELAGE	PUDENT
PSORALENS	PTISAN	PUCELAGES	PUDGE
PSORAS	PTISANS	PUCELLE	PUDGES
PSORIASES	PTOMAIN	PUCELLES	PUDGIER
PSORIASIS	PTOMAINE	PUCER	PUDGIEST

PUDGILY	PUGGERY	PUKERS	PULLUS
PUDGINESS	PUGGIE	PUKES	PULMO
PUDGY	PUGGIER	PUKING	PULMONARY
PUDIBUND	PUGGIES	PUKKA	PULMONATE
PUDIC	PUGGIEST	PUKU	PULMONES
PUDICITY	PUGGINESS	PUKUS	PULMONIC
PUDOR	PUGGING	PUL	PULMONICS
PUDORS	PUGGINGS	PULA	PULMOTOR
PUDS	PUGGISH	PULAO	PULMOTORS
PUDSEY	PUGGLE	PULAOS	PULP
PUDSIER	PUGGLED	PULAS	PULPAL
PUDSIEST	PUGGLES	PULDRON	PULPALLY
PUDSY	PUGGLING	PULDRONS	PULPBOARD
PUDU	PUGGREE	PULE	PULPED
PUDUS	PUGGREES	PULED	PULPER
PUEBLO	PUGGRIES	PULER	PULPERS
PUEBLOS	PUGGRY	PULERS	PULPIER
PUER	PUGGY	PULES	PULPIEST
PUERED	PUGH	PULI	PULPIFIED
PUERILE	PUGHS	PULICENE	PULPIFIES
PUERILELY	PUGIL	PULICIDE	PULPIFY
PUERILISM	PUGILISM	PULICIDES	PULPILY
PUERILITY	PUGILISMS	PULIER	PULPINESS
PUERING	PUGILIST	PULIEST	PULPING
PUERPERA	PUGILISTS	PULIK	PULPIT
PUERPERAE	PUGILS	PULING	PULPITAL
PUERPERAL	PUGMARK	PULINGLY	PULPITED
PUERPERIA	PUGMARKS	PULINGS	PULPITEER
PUERS	PUGNACITY	PULIS	PULPITER
PUFF	PUGREE	PULK	PULPITERS
PUFFBALL	PUGREES	PULKA	PULPITING
PUFFBALLS	PUGS	PULKAS	PULPITRY
PUFFBIRD	PUH	PULKHA	PULPITS
PUFFBIRDS	PUHA	PULKHAS	PULPITUM
PUFFED	PUHAS	PULKS	PULPITUMS
PUFFER	PUIR	PULL	PULPLESS
PUFFERIES	PUIRER	PULLBACK	PULPMILL
PUFFERS	PUIREST	PULLBACKS	PULPMILLS
PUFFERY	PUIRTITH	PULLED	PULPOUS
PUFFIER	PUIRTITHS	PULLER	PULPS
PUFFIEST	PUISNE	PULLERS	PULPSTONE
PUFFILY	PUISNES	PULLET	PULPWOOD
PUFFIN	PUISNY	PULLETS	PULPWOODS
PUFFINESS	PUISSANCE	PULLEY	PULPY
PUFFING	PUISSANT	PULLEYS	PULQUE
PUFFINGLY	PUISSAUNT	PULLI	PULQUES
PUFFINGS	PUJA	PULLING	PULS
PUFFINS	PUJAH	PULLMAN	PULSANT
PUFFS	PUJAHS	PULLMANS	PULSAR
PUFFY	PUJAS	PULLORUM	PULSARS
PUFTALOON	PUKA	PULLOUT	PULSATE
PUG	PUKATEA	PULLOUTS	PULSATED
PUGAREE	PUKATEAS	PULLOVER	PULSATES
PUGAREES	PUKE	PULLOVERS	PULSATILE
PUGGAREE	PUKED	PULLS	PULSATING
PUGGAREES	PUKEKO	PULLULATE	PULSATION
PUGGED	PUKEKOS	PULLUP	PULSATIVE
PUGGERIES	PUKER	PULLUPS	PULSATOR

PULSATORS	PULWARS	PUNCHED	PUNITIONS
PULSATORY	PULY	PUNCHEON	PUNITIVE
PULSE	PUMA	PUNCHEONS	PUNITORY
PULSED	PUMAS	PUNCHER	PUNJI
PULSEJET	PUMELO	PUNCHERS	PUNJIS
PULSEJETS	PUMELOS	PUNCHES	PUNK
PULSELESS	PUMICATE	PUNCHIER	PUNKA
PULSER	PUMICATED	PUNCHIEST	PUNKAH
PULSERS	PUMICATES	PUNCHILY	PUNKAHS
PULSES	PUMICE	PUNCHING	PUNKAS
PULSIDGE	PUMICED	PUNCHLESS	PUNKER
PULSIDGES	PUMICEOUS	PUNCHY	PUNKERS
PULSIFIC	PUMICER	PUNCING	PUNKEST
PULSING	PUMICERS	PUNCTA	PUNKEY
PULSION	PUMICES	PUNCTATE	PUNKEYS
PULSIONS	PUMICING	PUNCTATED	PUNKIE
PULSOJET	PUMICITE	PUNCTATOR	PUNKIER
PULSOJETS	PUMICITES	PUNCTILIO	PUNKIES
PULTAN	PUMIE	PUNCTO	PUNKIEST
PULTANS	PUMIES	PUNCTOS	PUNKIN
PULTON	PUMMEL	PUNCTUAL	PUNKINESS
PULTONS	PUMMELED	PUNCTUATE	PUNKINS
PULTOON	PUMMELING	PUNCTULE	PUNKISH
PULTOONS	PUMMELLED	PUNCTULES	PUNKS
PULTUN	PUMMELO	PUNCTUM	PUNKY
PULTUNS	PUMMELOS	PUNCTURE	PUNNED
PULTURE	PUMMELS	PUNCTURED	PUNNER
PULTURES	PUMP	PUNCTURER	PUNNERS
PULU	PUMPED	PUNCTURES	PUNNET
PULUS	PUMPER	PUNDIT	PUNNETS
PULVER	PUMPERS	PUNDITIC	PUNNIER
PULVERED	PUMPHOOD	PUNDITRY	PUNNIEST
PULVERINE	PUMPHOODS	PUNDITS	PUNNING
PULVERING	PUMPING	PUNDONOR	PUNNINGLY
PULVERISE	PUMPION	PUNG	PUNNINGS
PULVERIZE	PUMPIONS	PUNGA	PUNNY
PULVEROUS	PUMPKIN	PUNGAS	PUNS
PULVERS	PUMPKING	PUNGENCE	PUNSTER
PULVIL	PUMPKINGS	PUNGENCES	PUNSTERS
PULVILIO	PUMPKINS	PUNGENCY	PUNT
PULVILIOS	PUMPLESS	PUNGENT	PUNTED
PULVILLAR	PUMPLIKE	PUNGENTLY	PUNTEE
PULVILLE	PUMPS	PUNGLE	PUNTEES
PULVILLED	PUMY	PUNGLED	PUNTER
PULVILLES	PUN	PUNGLES	PUNTERS
PULVILLI	PUNA	PUNGLING	PUNTIES
PULVILLIO	PUNALUA	PUNGS	PUNTING
PULVILLO	PUNALUAN	PUNIER	PUNTO
PULVILLOS	PUNALUAS	PUNIEST	PUNTOS
PULVILLUS	PUNAS	PUNILY	PUNTS
PULVILS	PUNCE	PUNINESS	PUNTSMAN
PULVINAR	PUNCED	PUNISH	PUNTSMEN
PULVINARS	PUNCES	PUNISHED	PUNTY
PULVINATE	PUNCH	PUNISHER	PUNY
PULVINI	PUNCHBAG	PUNISHERS	PUP
PULVINULE	PUNCHBAGS	PUNISHES	PUPA
PULVINUS	PUNCHBALL	PUNISHING	PUPAE
PULWAR	PUNCHBOWL	PUNITION	PUPAL

PUPARIA	PURDAHED	PURISTS	PURRED
PUPARIAL	PURDAHS	PURITAN	PURRING
PUPARIUM	PURDAS	PURITANIC	PURRINGLY
PUPAS	PURDONIUM	PURITANS	PURRINGS
PUPATE	PURE	PURITIES	PURRS
PUPATED	PUREBLOOD	PURITY	PURS
PUPATES	PUREBRED	PURL	PURSE
PUPATING	PUREBREDS	PURLED	PURSED
PUPATION	PURED	PURLER	PURSEFUL
PUPATIONS	PUREE	PURLERS	PURSEFULS
PUPFISH	PUREED	PURLICUE	PURSELIKE
PUPFISHES	PUREEING	PURLICUED	PURSER
PUPIL	PUREES	PURLICUES	PURSERS
PUPILAGE	PURELY	PURLIEU	PURSES
PUPILAGES	PURENESS	PURLIEUS	PURSEW
PUPILAR	PURER	PURLIN	PURSEWED
PUPILARY	PURES	PURLINE	PURSEWING
PUPILLAGE	PUREST	PURLINES	PURSEWS
PUPILLAR	PURFLE	PURLING	PURSIER
PUPILLARY	PURFLED	PURLINGS	PURSIEST
PUPILLATE	PURFLER	PURLINS	PURSILY
PUPILS	PURFLERS	PURLOIN	PURSINESS
PUPILSHIP	PURFLES	PURLOINED	PURSING
PUPPED	PURFLING	PURLOINER	PURSLAIN
PUPPET	PURFLINGS	PURLOINS	PURSLAINS
PUPPETEER	PURFLY	PURLS	PURSLANE
PUPPETRY	PURGATION	PUROMYCIN	PURSLANES
PUPPETS	PURGATIVE	PURPIE	PURSUABLE
PUPPIED	PURGATORY	PURPIES	PURSUAL
PUPPIES	PURGE	PURPLE	PURSUALS
PUPPING	PURGEABLE	PURPLED	PURSUANCE
PUPPODUM	PURGED	PURPLER	PURSUANT
PUPPODUMS	PURGER	PURPLES	PURSUE
PUPPY	PURGERS	PURPLEST	PURSUED
PUPPYDOM	PURGES	PURPLIER	PURSUER
PUPPYDOMS	PURGING	PURPLIEST	PURSUERS
PUPPYHOOD	PURGINGS	PURPLING	PURSUES
PUPPYING	PURI	PURPLISH	PURSUING
PUPPYISH	PURIFIED	PURPLY	PURSUINGS
PUPPYISM	PURIFIER	PURPORT	PURSUIT
PUPPYISMS	PURIFIERS	PURPORTED	PURSUITS
PUPPYLIKE	PURIFIES	PURPORTS	PURSY
PUPS	PURIFY	PURPOSE	PURTIER
PUPU	PURIFYING	PURPOSED	PURTIEST
PUPUNHA	PURIM	PURPOSELY	PURTRAID
PUPUNHAS	PURIMS	PURPOSES	PURTRAY
PUPUS	PURIN	PURPOSING	PURTRAYD
PUR	PURINE	PURPOSIVE	PURTRAYS
PURANA	PURINES	PURPURA	PURTY
PURANAS	PURING	PURPURAS	PURULENCE
PURANIC	PURINS	PURPURE	PURULENCY
PURBLIND	PURIRI	PURPUREAL	PURULENT
PURCHASE	PURIRIS	PURPURES	PURVEY
PURCHASED	PURIS	PURPURIC	PURVEYED
PURCHASER	PURISM	PURPURIN	PURVEYING
PURCHASES	PURISMS	PURPURINS	PURVEYOR
PURDA	PURIST	PURPY	PURVEYORS
PURDAH	PURISTIC	PURR	PURVEYS

PURVIEW	PUSSYTOES	PUTTER	PYCNON
PURVIEWS	PUSTULANT	PUTTERED	PYCNONS
PUS	PUSTULAR	PUTTERER	PYCNOSES
PUSES	PUSTULATE	PUTTERERS	PYCNOSIS
PUSH	PUSTULE	PUTTERING	PYCNOTIC
PUSHBALL	PUSTULED	PUTTERS	PYE
PUSHBALLS	PUSTULES	PUTTI	PYEBALD
PUSHCART	PUSTULOUS	PUTTIE	PYEBALDS
PUSHCARTS	PUT	PUTTIED	PYEING
PUSHCHAIR	PUTAMEN	PUTTIER	PYELITIC
PUSHDOWN	PUTAMINA	PUTTIERS	PYELITIS
PUSHDOWNS	PUTATIVE	PUTTIES	PYELOGRAM
PUSHED	PUTCHEON	PUTTING	PYEMIA
PUSHER	PUTCHEONS	PUTTINGS	PYEMIAS
PUSHERS	PUTCHER	PUTTO	PYEMIC
PUSHES	PUTCHERS	PUTTOCK	PYENGADU
PUSHFUL	PUTCHOCK	PUTTOCKS	PYENGADUS
PUSHFULLY	PUTCHOCKS	PUTTS	PYES
PUSHIER	PUTCHUK	PUTTY	PYET
PUSHIEST	PUTCHUKS	PUTTYING	PYETS
PUSHILY	PUTDOWN	PUTTYLESS	PYGAL
PUSHINESS	PUTDOWNS	PUTTYLIKE	PYGALS
PUSHING	PUTEAL	PUTTYROOT	PYGARG
PUSHINGLY	PUTEALS	PUTURE	PYGARGS
PUSHOVER	PUTELI	PUTURES	PYGIDIA
PUSHOVERS	PUTELIS	PUTZ	PYGIDIAL
PUSHPIN	PUTID	PUTZED	PYGIDIUM
PUSHPINS	PUTLOCK	PUTZES	PYGIDIUMS
PUSHROD	PUTLOCKS	PUTZING	PYGMAEAN
PUSHRODS	PUTLOG	PUY	PYGMEAN
PUSHUP	PUTLOGS	PUYS	PYGMIES
PUSHUPS	PUTOFF	PUZEL	PYGMOID
PUSHY	PUTOFFS	PUZELS	PYGMY
PUSLE	PUTOIS	PUZZEL	PYGMYISH
PUSLED	PUTOISES	PUZZELS	PYGMYISM
PUSLES	PUTON	PUZZLE	PYGMYISMS
PUSLEY	PUTONGHUA	PUZZLED	PYGOSTYLE
PUSLEYS	PUTONS	PUZZLEDLY	PYIC
PUSLIKE	PUTOUT	PUZZLEDOM	PYIN
PUSLING	PUTOUTS	PUZZLER	PYINKADO
PUSS	PUTREFIED	PUZZLERS	PYINKADOS
PUSSEL	PUTREFIER	PUZZLES	PYINS
PUSSELS	PUTREFIES	PUZZLING	PYJAMA
PUSSER	PUTREFY	PUZZOLANA	PYJAMAED
PUSSERS	PUTRID	PYA	PYJAMAS
PUSSES	PUTRIDER	PYAEMIA	PYKNIC
PUSSIER	PUTRIDEST	PYAEMIAS	PYKNICS
PUSSIES	PUTRIDITY	PYAEMIC	PYKNOSES
PUSSIEST	PUTRIDLY	PYAS	PYKNOSIS
PUSSLEY	PUTS	PYAT	PYKNOSOME
PUSSLEYS	PUTSCH	PYATS	PYKNOTIC
PUSSLIES	PUTSCHES	PYCNIC	PYLON
PUSSLIKE	PUTSCHIST	PYCNICS	PYLONS
PUSSLY	PUTT	PYCNIDIA	PYLORI
PUSSY	PUTTED	PYCNIDIAL	PYLORIC
PUSSYCAT	PUTTEE	PYCNIDIUM	PYLORUS
PUSSYCATS	PUTTEES	PYCNITE	PYLORUSES
PUSSYFOOT	PUTTEN	PYCNITES	PYNE

PYNED
PYNES
PYNING
PYODERMA
PYODERMAS
PYODERMIC
PYOGENIC
PYOID
PYONER
PYONERS
PYONINGS
PYORRHEA
PYORRHEAL
PYORRHEAS
PYORRHEIC
PYORRHOEA
PYOSES
PYOSIS
PYOT
PYOTS
PYRACANTH
PYRAL
PYRALID
PYRALIDID
PYRALIDS
PYRALIS
PYRALISES
PYRAMID
PYRAMIDAL
PYRAMIDED
PYRAMIDES
PYRAMIDIA
PYRAMIDIC
PYRAMIDON
PYRAMIDS
PYRAMIS
PYRAMISES
PYRAN
PYRANOID
PYRANOSE
PYRANOSES
PYRANS
PYRAZOLE
PYRAZOLES
PYRE
PYRENE
PYRENEITE
PYRENES
PYRENOID
PYRENOIDS
PYRES
PYRETHRIN
PYRETHRUM
PYRETIC
PYREX
PYREXES
PYREXIA
PYREXIAL

PYREXIAS
PYREXIC
PYRIC
PYRIDIC
PYRIDINE
PYRIDINES
PYRIDOXAL
PYRIDOXIN
PYRIFORM
PYRITE
PYRITES
PYRITIC
PYRITICAL
PYRITISE
PYRITISED
PYRITISES
PYRITIZE
PYRITIZED
PYRITIZES
PYRITOUS
PYRO
PYROCERAM
PYROCLAST
PYROGEN
PYROGENIC
PYROGENS
PYROLA
PYROLAS
PYROLATER
PYROLATRY
PYROLISE
PYROLISED
PYROLISES
PYROLIZE
PYROLIZED
PYROLIZES
PYROLOGY
PYROLYSE
PYROLYSED
PYROLYSER
PYROLYSES
PYROLYSIS
PYROLYTIC
PYROLYZE
PYROLYZED
PYROLYZER
PYROLYZES
PYROMANCY
PYROMANIA
PYROMETER
PYROMETRY
PYRONE
PYRONES
PYRONINE
PYRONINES
PYROPE
PYROPES
PYROPHONE

PYROPUS
PYROPUSES
PYROS
PYROSCOPE
PYROSES
PYROSIS
PYROSISES
PYROSOME
PYROSOMES
PYROSTAT
PYROSTATS
PYROXENE
PYROXENES
PYROXENIC
PYROXYLE
PYROXYLES
PYROXYLIC
PYROXYLIN
PYRRHIC
PYRRHICS
PYRRHOUS
PYRROL
PYRROLE
PYRROLES
PYRROLIC
PYRROLS
PYRUVATE
PYRUVATES
PYRUVIC
PYTHIUM
PYTHIUMS
PYTHON
PYTHONESS
PYTHONIC
PYTHONS
PYURIA
PYURIAS
PYX
PYXED
PYXES
PYXIDES
PYXIDIA
PYXIDIUM
PYXIE
PYXIES
PYXING
PYXIS
PZAZZ
PZAZZES

Q

QABALA
QABALAH
QABALAHS
QABALAS
QABALISM
QABALISMS
QABALIST
QABALISTS
QADI
QADIS
QAID
QAIDS
QAIMAQAM
QAIMAQAMS
QALAMDAN
QALAMDANS
QANAT
QANATS
QASIDA
QASIDAS
QAT
QATS
QAWWAL
QAWWALI
QAWWALIS
QAWWALS
QI
QIBLA
QIBLAS
QIGONG
QIGONGS
QINDAR
QINDARKA
QINDARS
QINGHAOSU
QINTAR
QINTARS
QIS
QIVIUT
QIVIUTS
QOPH
QOPHS
QORMA
QORMAS
QUA
QUAALUDE
QUAALUDES
QUACK
QUACKED
QUACKER
QUACKERS
QUACKERY
QUACKIER

QUACKIEST
QUACKING
QUACKISH
QUACKISM
QUACKISMS
QUACKLE
QUACKLED
QUACKLES
QUACKLING
QUACKS
QUACKY
QUAD
QUADDED
QUADDING
QUADPLEX
QUADRANS
QUADRANT
QUADRANTS
QUADRAT
QUADRATE
QUADRATED
QUADRATES
QUADRATIC
QUADRATS
QUADRATUS
QUADRELLA
QUADRIC
QUADRICEP
QUADRICS
QUADRIFID
QUADRIGA
QUADRIGAE
QUADRIGAS
QUADRILLE
QUADRIVIA
QUADROON
QUADROONS
QUADRUMAN
QUADRUPED
QUADRUPLE
QUADRUPLY
QUADS
QUAERE
QUAERED
QUAEREING
QUAERES
QUAERITUR
QUAESITUM
QUAESTOR
QUAESTORS
QUAFF
QUAFFABLE
QUAFFED

QUAFFER
QUAFFERS
QUAFFING
QUAFFS
QUAG
QUAGGA
QUAGGAS
QUAGGIER
QUAGGIEST
QUAGGY
QUAGMIRE
QUAGMIRED
QUAGMIRES
QUAGMIRY
QUAGS
QUAHAUG
QUAHAUGS
QUAHOG
QUAHOGS
QUAI
QUAICH
QUAICHES
QUAICHS
QUAIGH
QUAIGHS
QUAIL
QUAILED
QUAILING
QUAILINGS
QUAILS
QUAINT
QUAINTER
QUAINTEST
QUAINTLY
QUAIR
QUAIRS
QUAIS
QUAKE
QUAKED
QUAKER
QUAKERS
QUAKES
QUAKIER
QUAKIEST
QUAKILY
QUAKINESS
QUAKING
QUAKINGLY
QUAKINGS
QUAKY
QUALE
QUALIA
QUALIFIED

QUALIFIER
QUALIFIES
QUALIFY
QUALITIED
QUALITIES
QUALITY
QUALM
QUALMIER
QUALMIEST
QUALMING
QUALMISH
QUALMLESS
QUALMS
QUALMY
QUAMASH
QUAMASHES
QUANDANG
QUANDANGS
QUANDARY
QUANDONG
QUANDONGS
QUANGO
QUANGOS
QUANNET
QUANNETS
QUANT
QUANTA
QUANTAL
QUANTALLY
QUANTED
QUANTIC
QUANTICAL
QUANTICS
QUANTIFY
QUANTILE
QUANTILES
QUANTING
QUANTISE
QUANTISED
QUANTISER
QUANTISES
QUANTITY
QUANTIZE
QUANTIZED
QUANTIZER
QUANTIZES
QUANTONG
QUANTONGS
QUANTS
QUANTUM
QUARE
QUARENDEN
QUARENDER

QUARER
QUAREST
QUARK
QUARKS
QUARREL
QUARRELED
QUARRELER
QUARRELS
QUARRIAN
QUARRIANS
QUARRIED
QUARRIER
QUARRIERS
QUARRIES
QUARRION
QUARRIONS
QUARRY
QUARRYING
QUARRYMAN
QUARRYMEN
QUART
QUARTAN
QUARTANS
QUARTE
QUARTER
QUARTERED
QUARTERER
QUARTERLY
QUARTERN
QUARTERNS
QUARTERS
QUARTES
QUARTET
QUARTETS
QUARTETT
QUARTETTE
QUARTETTI
QUARTETTO
QUARTETTS
QUARTIC
QUARTICS
QUARTIER
QUARTIERS
QUARTILE
QUARTILES
QUARTO
QUARTOS
QUARTS
QUARTZ
QUARTZES
QUARTZIER
QUARTZITE
QUARTZOSE
QUARTZOUS
QUARTZY
QUASAR
QUASARS
QUASH

QUASHED
QUASHEE
QUASHEES
QUASHER
QUASHERS
QUASHES
QUASHIE
QUASHIES
QUASHING
QUASI
QUASS
QUASSES
QUASSIA
QUASSIAS
QUASSIN
QUASSINS
QUAT
QUATCH
QUATCHED
QUATCHES
QUATCHING
QUATE
QUATORZE
QUATORZES
QUATRAIN
QUATRAINS
QUATRE
QUATRES
QUATS
QUAVER
QUAVERED
QUAVERER
QUAVERERS
QUAVERIER
QUAVERING
QUAVERS
QUAVERY
QUAY
QUAYAGE
QUAYAGES
QUAYD
QUAYLIKE
QUAYS
QUAYSIDE
QUAYSIDES
QUAZZIER
QUAZZIEST
QUAZZY
QUBIT
QUBITS
QUBYTE
QUBYTES
QUEACH
QUEACHES
QUEACHIER
QUEACHY
QUEAN
QUEANS

QUEASIER
QUEASIEST
QUEASILY
QUEASY
QUEAZIER
QUEAZIEST
QUEAZY
QUEBRACHO
QUEECHIER
QUEECHY
QUEEN
QUEENCAKE
QUEENDOM
QUEENDOMS
QUEENED
QUEENHOOD
QUEENIE
QUEENIER
QUEENIES
QUEENIEST
QUEENING
QUEENINGS
QUEENITE
QUEENITES
QUEENLESS
QUEENLET
QUEENLETS
QUEENLIER
QUEENLY
QUEENS
QUEENSHIP
QUEENSIDE
QUEENY
QUEER
QUEERCORE
QUEERDOM
QUEERDOMS
QUEERED
QUEERER
QUEEREST
QUEERING
QUEERISH
QUEERITY
QUEERLY
QUEERNESS
QUEERS
QUEEST
QUEESTS
QUEINT
QUELCH
QUELCHED
QUELCHES
QUELCHING
QUELEA
QUELEAS
QUELL
QUELLABLE
QUELLED

QUELLER
QUELLERS
QUELLING
QUELLS
QUEME
QUEMED
QUEMES
QUEMING
QUENA
QUENAS
QUENCH
QUENCHED
QUENCHER
QUENCHERS
QUENCHES
QUENCHING
QUENELLE
QUENELLES
QUEP
QUERCETIC
QUERCETIN
QUERCETUM
QUERCINE
QUERCITIN
QUERIDA
QUERIDAS
QUERIED
QUERIER
QUERIERS
QUERIES
QUERIMONY
QUERIST
QUERISTS
QUERN
QUERNS
QUERULOUS
QUERY
QUERYING
QUERYINGS
QUEST
QUESTANT
QUESTANTS
QUESTED
QUESTER
QUESTERS
QUESTING
QUESTINGS
QUESTION
QUESTIONS
QUESTOR
QUESTORS
QUESTRIST
QUESTS
QUETCH
QUETCHED
QUETCHES
QUETCHING
QUETHE

QUETHES	QUIDAMS	QUILLBACK	QUINOID
QUETHING	QUIDDANY	QUILLED	QUINOIDAL
QUETSCH	QUIDDIT	QUILLET	QUINOIDS
QUETSCHES	QUIDDITCH	QUILLETS	QUINOL
QUETZAL	QUIDDITS	QUILLING	QUINOLIN
QUETZALES	QUIDDITY	QUILLINGS	QUINOLINE
QUETZALS	QUIDDLE	QUILLMAN	QUINOLINS
QUEUE	QUIDDLED	QUILLMEN	QUINOLONE
QUEUED	QUIDDLER	QUILLON	QUINOLS
QUEUEING	QUIDDLERS	QUILLONS	QUINONE
QUEUEINGS	QUIDDLES	QUILLS	QUINONES
QUEUER	QUIDDLING	QUILLWORK	QUINONOID
QUEUERS	QUIDNUNC	QUILLWORT	QUINOS
QUEUES	QUIDNUNCS	QUILT	QUINQUINA
QUEUING	QUIDS	QUILTED	QUINS
QUEUINGS	QUIESCE	QUILTER	QUINSIED
QUEY	QUIESCED	QUILTERS	QUINSIES
QUEYN	QUIESCENT	QUILTING	QUINSY
QUEYNIE	QUIESCES	QUILTINGS	QUINT
QUEYNIES	QUIESCING	QUILTS	QUINTA
QUEYNS	QUIET	QUIM	QUINTAIN
QUEYS	QUIETED	QUIMS	QUINTAINS
QUEZAL	QUIETEN	QUIN	QUINTAL
QUEZALES	QUIETENED	QUINA	QUINTALS
QUEZALS	QUIETENER	QUINARIES	QUINTAN
QUIBBLE	QUIETENS	QUINARY	QUINTANS
QUIBBLED	QUIETER	QUINAS	QUINTAR
QUIBBLER	QUIETERS	QUINATE	QUINTARS
QUIBBLERS	QUIETEST	QUINCE	QUINTAS
QUIBBLES	QUIETING	QUINCES	QUINTE
QUIBBLING	QUIETINGS	QUINCHE	QUINTES
QUIBLIN	QUIETISM	QUINCHED	QUINTET
QUIBLINS	QUIETISMS	QUINCHES	QUINTETS
QUICH	QUIETIST	QUINCHING	QUINTETT
QUICHE	QUIETISTS	QUINCUNX	QUINTETTE
QUICHED	QUIETIVE	QUINE	QUINTETTI
QUICHES	QUIETIVES	QUINELA	QUINTETTO
QUICHING	QUIETLY	QUINELAS	QUINTETTS
QUICK	QUIETNESS	QUINELLA	QUINTIC
QUICKBEAM	QUIETS	QUINELLAS	QUINTICS
QUICKEN	QUIETSOME	QUINES	QUINTILE
QUICKENED	QUIETUDE	QUINIC	QUINTILES
QUICKENER	QUIETUDES	QUINIDINE	QUINTIN
QUICKENS	QUIETUS	QUINIE	QUINTINS
QUICKER	QUIETUSES	QUINIELA	QUINTROON
QUICKEST	QUIFF	QUINIELAS	QUINTS
QUICKIE	QUIFFS	QUINIES	QUINTUPLE
QUICKIES	QUIGHT	QUININ	QUINTUPLY
QUICKLIME	QUIGHTED	QUININA	QUINZE
QUICKLY	QUIGHTING	QUININAS	QUINZES
QUICKNESS	QUIGHTS	QUININE	QUIP
QUICKS	QUILL	QUININES	QUIPO
QUICKSAND	QUILLAI	QUININS	QUIPOS
QUICKSET	QUILLAIA	QUINNAT	QUIPPED
QUICKSETS	QUILLAIAS	QUINNATS	QUIPPER
QUICKSTEP	QUILLAIS	QUINO	QUIPPERS
QUID	QUILLAJA	QUINOA	QUIPPIER
QUIDAM	QUILLAJAS	QUINOAS	QUIPPIEST

QUIPPING
QUIPPISH
QUIPPU
QUIPPUS
QUIPPY
QUIPS
QUIPSTER
QUIPSTERS
QUIPU
QUIPUS
QUIRE
QUIRED
QUIRES
QUIRING
QUIRISTER
QUIRK
QUIRKED
QUIRKIER
QUIRKIEST
QUIRKILY
QUIRKING
QUIRKISH
QUIRKS
QUIRKY
QUIRT
QUIRTED
QUIRTING
QUIRTS
QUISLING
QUISLINGS
QUIST
QUISTS
QUIT
QUITCH
QUITCHED
QUITCHES
QUITCHING
QUITCLAIM
QUITE
QUITED
QUITES
QUITING
QUITRENT
QUITRENTS
QUITS
QUITTAL
QUITTALS
QUITTANCE
QUITTED
QUITTER
QUITTERS
QUITTING
QUITTOR
QUITTORS
QUIVER
QUIVERED
QUIVERER
QUIVERERS

QUIVERFUL
QUIVERIER
QUIVERING
QUIVERISH
QUIVERS
QUIVERY
QUIXOTE
QUIXOTES
QUIXOTIC
QUIXOTISM
QUIXOTRY
QUIZ
QUIZZED
QUIZZER
QUIZZERS
QUIZZERY
QUIZZES
QUIZZICAL
QUIZZIFY
QUIZZING
QUIZZINGS
QUOAD
QUOD
QUODDED
QUODDING
QUODLIBET
QUODLIN
QUODLINS
QUODS
QUOHOG
QUOHOGS
QUOIF
QUOIFED
QUOIFING
QUOIFS
QUOIN
QUOINED
QUOINING
QUOINS
QUOIST
QUOISTS
QUOIT
QUOITED
QUOITER
QUOITERS
QUOITING
QUOITS
QUOKKA
QUOKKAS
QUOLL
QUOLLS
QUOMODO
QUOMODOS
QUONDAM
QUONK
QUONKED
QUONKING
QUONKS

QUOOKE
QUOP
QUOPPED
QUOPPING
QUOPS
QUORATE
QUORUM
QUORUMS
QUOTA
QUOTABLE
QUOTABLY
QUOTAS
QUOTATION
QUOTATIVE
QUOTE
QUOTED
QUOTER
QUOTERS
QUOTES
QUOTH
QUOTHA
QUOTIDIAN
QUOTIENT
QUOTIENTS
QUOTING
QUOTITION
QUOTUM
QUOTUMS
QURSH
QURSHES
QURUSH
QURUSHES
QUYTE
QUYTED
QUYTES
QUYTING
QWERTIES
QWERTY
QWERTYS

R

RABANNA
RABANNAS
RABAT
RABATINE
RABATINES
RABATMENT
RABATO
RABATOES
RABATOS
RABATS
RABATTE
RABATTED
RABATTES
RABATTING
RABBET
RABBETED
RABBETING
RABBETS
RABBI
RABBIES
RABBIN
RABBINATE
RABBINIC
RABBINICS
RABBINISM
RABBINIST
RABBINITE
RABBINS
RABBIS
RABBIT
RABBITED
RABBITER
RABBITERS
RABBITING
RABBITO
RABBITOH
RABBITOHS
RABBITOS
RABBITRY
RABBITS
RABBITY
RABBLE
RABBLED
RABBLER
RABBLERS
RABBLES
RABBLING
RABBLINGS
RABBONI
RABBONIS
RABI
RABIC
RABID

RABIDER
RABIDEST
RABIDITY
RABIDLY
RABIDNESS
RABIES
RABIETIC
RABIS
RACA
RACAHOUT
RACAHOUTS
RACCAHOUT
RACCOON
RACCOONS
RACE
RACECARD
RACECARDS
RACED
RACEGOER
RACEGOERS
RACEGOING
RACEHORSE
RACEMATE
RACEMATES
RACEME
RACEMED
RACEMES
RACEMIC
RACEMISE
RACEMISED
RACEMISES
RACEMISM
RACEMISMS
RACEMIZE
RACEMIZED
RACEMIZES
RACEMOID
RACEMOSE
RACEMOUS
RACEPATH
RACEPATHS
RACER
RACERS
RACES
RACETRACK
RACEWALK
RACEWALKS
RACEWAY
RACEWAYS
RACH
RACHE
RACHES
RACHET

RACHETED
RACHETING
RACHETS
RACHIAL
RACHIDES
RACHIDIAL
RACHIDIAN
RACHILLA
RACHILLAE
RACHILLAS
RACHIS
RACHISES
RACHITIC
RACHITIS
RACIAL
RACIALISE
RACIALISM
RACIALIST
RACIALIZE
RACIALLY
RACIATION
RACIER
RACIEST
RACILY
RACINESS
RACING
RACINGS
RACISM
RACISMS
RACIST
RACISTS
RACK
RACKED
RACKER
RACKERS
RACKET
RACKETED
RACKETEER
RACKETER
RACKETERS
RACKETIER
RACKETING
RACKETRY
RACKETS
RACKETT
RACKETTS
RACKETY
RACKFUL
RACKFULS
RACKING
RACKINGLY
RACKINGS
RACKLE

RACKS
RACKWORK
RACKWORKS
RACLETTE
RACLETTES
RACLOIR
RACLOIRS
RACON
RACONS
RACONTEUR
RACOON
RACOONS
RACQUET
RACQUETED
RACQUETS
RACY
RAD
RADAR
RADARS
RADDED
RADDER
RADDEST
RADDING
RADDLE
RADDLED
RADDLEMAN
RADDLEMEN
RADDLES
RADDLING
RADDOCKE
RADDOCKES
RADE
RADGE
RADGER
RADGES
RADGEST
RADIABLE
RADIAL
RADIALE
RADIALIA
RADIALISE
RADIALITY
RADIALIZE
RADIALLY
RADIALS
RADIAN
RADIANCE
RADIANCES
RADIANCY
RADIANS
RADIANT
RADIANTLY
RADIANTS

RADIATA	RADULATE	RAGGEE	RAGWORTS
RADIATAS	RADWASTE	RAGGEES	RAH
RADIATE	RADWASTES	RAGGERIES	RAHED
RADIATED	RAFALE	RAGGERY	RAHING
RADIATELY	RAFALES	RAGGIER	RAHS
RADIATES	RAFF	RAGGIES	RAHUI
RADIATING	RAFFIA	RAGGIEST	RAHUIS
RADIATION	RAFFIAS	RAGGING	RAI
RADIATIVE	RAFFINATE	RAGGINGS	RAIA
RADIATOR	RAFFINOSE	RAGGLE	RAIAS
RADIATORS	RAFFISH	RAGGLED	RAID
RADIATORY	RAFFISHLY	RAGGLES	RAIDED
RADICAL	RAFFLE	RAGGLING	RAIDER
RADICALLY	RAFFLED	RAGGS	RAIDERS
RADICALS	RAFFLER	RAGGY	RAIDING
RADICAND	RAFFLERS	RAGHEAD	RAIDINGS
RADICANDS	RAFFLES	RAGHEADS	RAIDS
RADICANT	RAFFLESIA	RAGI	RAIK
RADICATE	RAFFLING	RAGING	RAIKED
RADICATED	RAFFS	RAGINGLY	RAIKING
RADICATES	RAFT	RAGINGS	RAIKS
RADICCHIO	RAFTED	RAGINI	RAIL
RADICEL	RAFTER	RAGINIS	RAILBED
RADICELS	RAFTERED	RAGIS	RAILBEDS
RADICES	RAFTERING	RAGLAN	RAILBIRD
RADICLE	RAFTERS	RAGLANS	RAILBIRDS
RADICLES	RAFTING	RAGMAN	RAILBUS
RADICULAR	RAFTINGS	RAGMANS	RAILBUSES
RADICULE	RAFTMAN	RAGMEN	RAILCAR
RADICULES	RAFTMEN	RAGMENT	RAILCARD
RADII	RAFTS	RAGMENTS	RAILCARDS
RADIO	RAFTSMAN	RAGOUT	RAILCARS
RADIOED	RAFTSMEN	RAGOUTED	RAILE
RADIOGRAM	RAG	RAGOUTING	RAILED
RADIOING	RAGA	RAGOUTS	RAILER
RADIOLOGY	RAGAS	RAGPICKER	RAILERS
RADIOMAN	RAGBAG	RAGS	RAILES
RADIOMEN	RAGBAGS	RAGSTONE	RAILHEAD
RADIONICS	RAGBOLT	RAGSTONES	RAILHEADS
RADIOS	RAGBOLTS	RAGTAG	RAILING
RADIOTHON	RAGDE	RAGTAGS	RAILINGLY
RADISH	RAGE	RAGTIME	RAILINGS
RADISHES	RAGED	RAGTIMER	RAILLERY
RADIUM	RAGEE	RAGTIMERS	RAILLESS
RADIUMS	RAGEES	RAGTIMES	RAILLIES
RADIUS	RAGEFUL	RAGTOP	RAILLY
RADIUSES	RAGER	RAGTOPS	RAILMAN
RADIX	RAGERS	RAGULED	RAILMEN
RADIXES	RAGES	RAGULY	RAILROAD
RADOME	RAGG	RAGWEED	RAILROADS
RADOMES	RAGGA	RAGWEEDS	RAILS
RADON	RAGGAS	RAGWHEEL	RAILWAY
RADONS	RAGGED	RAGWHEELS	RAILWAYS
RADS	RAGGEDER	RAGWORK	RAILWOMAN
RADULA	RAGGEDEST	RAGWORKS	RAILWOMEN
RADULAE	RAGGEDIER	RAGWORM	RAIMENT
RADULAR	RAGGEDLY	RAGWORMS	RAIMENTS
RADULAS	RAGGEDY	RAGWORT	RAIN

RAINBAND	RAITED	RALPHING	RAMMIER
RAINBANDS	RAITING	RALPHS	RAMMIES
RAINBIRD	RAITS	RAM	RAMMIEST
RAINBIRDS	RAIYAT	RAMADA	RAMMING
RAINBOW	RAIYATS	RAMADAS	RAMMISH
RAINBOWED	RAJ	RAMAKIN	RAMMISHLY
RAINBOWS	RAJA	RAMAKINS	RAMMLE
RAINBOWY	RAJAH	RAMAL	RAMMLES
RAINCHECK	RAJAHS	RAMATE	RAMMY
RAINCOAT	RAJAHSHIP	RAMBLA	RAMONA
RAINCOATS	RAJAS	RAMBLAS	RAMONAS
RAINDATE	RAJASHIP	RAMBLE	RAMOSE
RAINDATES	RAJASHIPS	RAMBLED	RAMOSELY
RAINDROP	RAJES	RAMBLER	RAMOSITY
RAINDROPS	RAKE	RAMBLERS	RAMOUS
RAINE	RAKED	RAMBLES	RAMOUSLY
RAINED	RAKEE	RAMBLING	RAMP
RAINES	RAKEES	RAMBLINGS	RAMPAGE
RAINFALL	RAKEHELL	RAMBUTAN	RAMPAGED
RAINFALLS	RAKEHELLS	RAMBUTANS	RAMPAGER
RAINIER	RAKEHELLY	RAMCAT	RAMPAGERS
RAINIEST	RAKEOFF	RAMCATS	RAMPAGES
RAINILY	RAKEOFFS	RAMEAL	RAMPAGING
RAININESS	RAKER	RAMEE	RAMPANCY
RAINING	RAKERIES	RAMEES	RAMPANT
RAINLESS	RAKERS	RAMEKIN	RAMPANTLY
RAINMAKER	RAKERY	RAMEKINS	RAMPART
RAINOUT	RAKES	RAMEN	RAMPARTED
RAINOUTS	RAKESHAME	RAMENS	RAMPARTS
RAINPROOF	RAKI	RAMENTA	RAMPAUGE
RAINS	RAKING	RAMENTUM	RAMPAUGED
RAINSPOUT	RAKINGS	RAMEOUS	RAMPAUGES
RAINSTORM	RAKIS	RAMEQUIN	RAMPED
RAINTIGHT	RAKISH	RAMEQUINS	RAMPER
RAINWASH	RAKISHLY	RAMET	RAMPERS
RAINWATER	RAKSHAS	RAMETS	RAMPICK
RAINWEAR	RAKSHASA	RAMI	RAMPICKED
RAINWEARS	RAKSHASAS	RAMIE	RAMPICKS
RAINY	RAKSHASES	RAMIES	RAMPIKE
RAIRD	RAKU	RAMIFIED	RAMPIKES
RAIRDS	RAKUS	RAMIFIES	RAMPING
RAIS	RALE	RAMIFORM	RAMPINGS
RAISABLE	RALES	RAMIFY	RAMPION
RAISE	RALLIED	RAMIFYING	RAMPIONS
RAISEABLE	RALLIER	RAMILIE	RAMPIRE
RAISED	RALLIERS	RAMILIES	RAMPIRED
RAISER	RALLIES	RAMILLIE	RAMPIRES
RAISERS	RALLIFORM	RAMILLIES	RAMPOLE
RAISES	RALLINE	RAMIN	RAMPOLES
RAISIN	RALLY	RAMINS	RAMPS
RAISING	RALLYE	RAMIS	RAMPSMAN
RAISINGS	RALLYES	RAMJET	RAMPSMEN
RAISINS	RALLYING	RAMJETS	RAMROD
RAISINY	RALLYINGS	RAMMED	RAMRODDED
RAISONNE	RALLYIST	RAMMEL	RAMRODS
RAIT	RALLYISTS	RAMMELS	RAMS
RAITA	RALPH	RAMMER	RAMSHORN
RAITAS	RALPHED	RAMMERS	RAMSHORNS

RAMSON	RANDEM	RANKISH	RAPHANIA
RAMSONS	RANDEMS	RANKISM	RAPHANIAS
RAMSTAM	RANDIE	RANKISMS	RAPHE
RAMTIL	RANDIER	RANKLE	RAPHES
RAMTILLA	RANDIES	RANKLED	RAPHIA
RAMTILLAS	RANDIEST	RANKLES	RAPHIAS
RAMTILS	RANDILY	RANKLESS	RAPHIDE
RAMULAR	RANDINESS	RANKLING	RAPHIDES
RAMULI	RANDING	RANKLY	RAPHIS
RAMULOSE	RANDLORD	RANKNESS	RAPID
RAMULOUS	RANDLORDS	RANKS	RAPIDER
RAMULUS	RANDOM	RANKSHIFT	RAPIDEST
RAMUS	RANDOMISE	RANPIKE	RAPIDITY
RAN	RANDOMIZE	RANPIKES	RAPIDLY
RANA	RANDOMLY	RANSACK	RAPIDNESS
RANARIAN	RANDOMS	RANSACKED	RAPIDS
RANARIUM	RANDON	RANSACKER	RAPIER
RANARIUMS	RANDONS	RANSACKS	RAPIERED
RANAS	RANDS	RANSEL	RAPIERS
RANCE	RANDY	RANSELS	RAPINE
RANCED	RANEE	RANSHAKLE	RAPINES
RANCEL	RANEES	RANSOM	RAPING
RANCELS	RANG	RANSOMED	RAPINI
RANCES	RANGATIRA	RANSOMER	RAPIST
RANCH	RANGE	RANSOMERS	RAPISTS
RANCHED	RANGED	RANSOMING	RAPLOCH
RANCHER	RANGELAND	RANSOMS	RAPLOCHS
RANCHERIA	RANGER	RANT	RAPPAREE
RANCHERIE	RANGERS	RANTED	RAPPAREES
RANCHERO	RANGES	RANTER	RAPPE
RANCHEROS	RANGI	RANTERISM	RAPPED
RANCHERS	RANGIER	RANTERS	RAPPEE
RANCHES	RANGIEST	RANTING	RAPPEES
RANCHING	RANGILY	RANTINGLY	RAPPEL
RANCHINGS	RANGINESS	RANTINGS	RAPPELED
RANCHLESS	RANGING	RANTIPOLE	RAPPELING
RANCHLIKE	RANGINGS	RANTS	RAPPELLED
RANCHMAN	RANGIORA	RANULA	RAPPELS
RANCHMEN	RANGIORAS	RANULAR	RAPPEN
RANCHO	RANGIS	RANULAS	RAPPER
RANCHOS	RANGOLI	RANUNCULI	RAPPERS
RANCID	RANGOLIS	RANZEL	RAPPES
RANCIDER	RANGY	RANZELMAN	RAPPING
RANCIDEST	RANI	RANZELMEN	RAPPINGS
RANCIDITY	RANID	RANZELS	RAPPINI
RANCIDLY	RANIDS	RAOULIA	RAPPORT
RANCING	RANIFORM	RAOULIAS	RAPPORTS
RANCOR	RANINE	RAP	RAPS
RANCORED	RANIS	RAPACIOUS	RAPT
RANCOROUS	RANK	RAPACITY	RAPTLY
RANCORS	RANKE	RAPE	RAPTNESS
RANCOUR	RANKED	RAPED	RAPTOR
RANCOURED	RANKER	RAPER	RAPTORIAL
RANCOURS	RANKERS	RAPERS	RAPTORS
RAND	RANKES	RAPES	RAPTURE
RANDAN	RANKEST	RAPESEED	RAPTURED
RANDANS	RANKING	RAPESEEDS	RAPTURES
RANDED	RANKINGS	RAPHAE	RAPTURING

RAPTURISE
RAPTURIST
RAPTURIZE
RAPTUROUS
RARE
RAREBIT
RAREBITS
RARED
RAREE
RAREFIED
RAREFIER
RAREFIERS
RAREFIES
RAREFY
RAREFYING
RARELY
RARENESS
RARER
RARERIPE
RARERIPES
RARES
RAREST
RARIFIED
RARIFIES
RARIFY
RARIFYING
RARING
RARITIES
RARITY
RARK
RARKED
RARKING
RARKS
RAS
RASBORA
RASBORAS
RASCAILLE
RASCAL
RASCALDOM
RASCALISM
RASCALITY
RASCALLY
RASCALS
RASCASSE
RASCASSES
RASCHEL
RASCHELS
RASE
RASED
RASER
RASERS
RASES
RASH
RASHED
RASHER
RASHERS
RASHES
RASHEST

RASHIE
RASHIES
RASHING
RASHLIKE
RASHLY
RASHNESS
RASING
RASMALAI
RASMALAIS
RASORIAL
RASP
RASPATORY
RASPBERRY
RASPED
RASPER
RASPERS
RASPIER
RASPIEST
RASPINESS
RASPING
RASPINGLY
RASPINGS
RASPISH
RASPS
RASPY
RASSE
RASSES
RASSLE
RASSLED
RASSLES
RASSLING
RAST
RASTA
RASTAFARI
RASTER
RASTERED
RASTERING
RASTERISE
RASTERIZE
RASTERS
RASTRUM
RASTRUMS
RASURE
RASURES
RAT
RATA
RATABLE
RATABLES
RATABLY
RATAFEE
RATAFEES
RATAFIA
RATAFIAS
RATAL
RATALS
RATAN
RATANIES
RATANS

RATANY
RATAPLAN
RATAPLANS
RATAS
RATATAT
RATATATS
RATBAG
RATBAGS
RATBITE
RATCH
RATCHED
RATCHES
RATCHET
RATCHETED
RATCHETS
RATCHING
RATE
RATEABLE
RATEABLY
RATED
RATEEN
RATEENS
RATEL
RATELS
RATEMETER
RATEPAYER
RATER
RATERS
RATES
RATFINK
RATFINKS
RATFISH
RATFISHES
RATH
RATHA
RATHAS
RATHE
RATHER
RATHEREST
RATHERIPE
RATHERISH
RATHEST
RATHOLE
RATHOLES
RATHOUSE
RATHOUSES
RATHRIPE
RATHRIPES
RATHS
RATICIDE
RATICIDES
RATIFIED
RATIFIER
RATIFIERS
RATIFIES
RATIFY
RATIFYING
RATINE

RATINES
RATING
RATINGS
RATIO
RATION
RATIONAL
RATIONALE
RATIONALS
RATIONED
RATIONING
RATIONS
RATIOS
RATITE
RATITES
RATLIKE
RATLIN
RATLINE
RATLINES
RATLING
RATLINGS
RATLINS
RATO
RATOO
RATOON
RATOONED
RATOONER
RATOONERS
RATOONING
RATOONS
RATOOS
RATOS
RATPACK
RATPACKS
RATPROOF
RATS
RATSBANE
RATSBANES
RATTAIL
RATTAILED
RATTAILS
RATTAN
RATTANS
RATTED
RATTEEN
RATTEENS
RATTEN
RATTENED
RATTENER
RATTENERS
RATTENING
RATTENS
RATTER
RATTERIES
RATTERS
RATTERY
RATTIER
RATTIEST
RATTILY

RATTINESS	RAVAGE	RAWBONED	RAZOO
RATTING	RAVAGED	RAWER	RAZOOS
RATTINGS	RAVAGER	RAWEST	RAZOR
RATTISH	RAVAGERS	RAWHEAD	RAZORABLE
RATTLE	RAVAGES	RAWHEADS	RAZORBACK
RATTLEBAG	RAVAGING	RAWHIDE	RAZORBILL
RATTLEBOX	RAVE	RAWHIDED	RAZORED
RATTLED	RAVED	RAWHIDES	RAZORING
RATTLER	RAVEL	RAWHIDING	RAZORS
RATTLERS	RAVELED	RAWIN	RAZURE
RATTLES	RAVELER	RAWING	RAZURES
RATTLIER	RAVELERS	RAWINGS	RAZZ
RATTLIEST	RAVELIN	RAWINS	RAZZBERRY
RATTLIN	RAVELING	RAWISH	RAZZED
RATTLINE	RAVELINGS	RAWLY	RAZZES
RATTLINES	RAVELINS	RAWMAISH	RAZZIA
RATTLING	RAVELLED	RAWN	RAZZIAS
RATTLINGS	RAVELLER	RAWNESS	RAZZING
RATTLINS	RAVELLERS	RAWNESSES	RAZZLE
RATTLY	RAVELLING	RAWNS	RAZZLES
RATTON	RAVELLY	RAWS	RE
RATTONS	RAVELMENT	RAX	REABSORB
RATTOON	RAVELS	RAXED	REABSORBS
RATTOONED	RAVEN	RAXES	REACCEDE
RATTOONS	RAVENED	RAXING	REACCEDED
RATTRAP	RAVENER	RAY	REACCEDES
RATTRAPS	RAVENERS	RAYA	REACCENT
RATTY	RAVENING	RAYAH	REACCENTS
RATU	RAVENINGS	RAYAHS	REACCEPT
RATUS	RAVENLIKE	RAYAS	REACCEPTS
RAUCID	RAVENOUS	RAYED	REACCLAIM
RAUCITIES	RAVENS	RAYGRASS	REACCUSE
RAUCITY	RAVER	RAYING	REACCUSED
RAUCLE	RAVERS	RAYLE	REACCUSES
RAUCLER	RAVES	RAYLED	REACH
RAUCLEST	RAVIGOTE	RAYLES	REACHABLE
RAUCOUS	RAVIGOTES	RAYLESS	REACHED
RAUCOUSLY	RAVIGOTTE	RAYLESSLY	REACHER
RAUGHT	RAVIN	RAYLET	REACHERS
RAUN	RAVINE	RAYLETS	REACHES
RAUNCH	RAVINED	RAYLIKE	REACHING
RAUNCHED	RAVINES	RAYLING	REACHLESS
RAUNCHES	RAVING	RAYNE	REACQUIRE
RAUNCHIER	RAVINGLY	RAYNES	REACT
RAUNCHILY	RAVINGS	RAYON	REACTANCE
RAUNCHING	RAVINING	RAYONS	REACTANT
RAUNCHY	RAVINS	RAYS	REACTANTS
RAUNGE	RAVIOLI	RAZE	REACTED
RAUNGED	RAVIOLIS	RAZED	REACTING
RAUNGES	RAVISH	RAZEE	REACTION
RAUNGING	RAVISHED	RAZEED	REACTIONS
RAUNS	RAVISHER	RAZEEING	REACTIVE
RAUPATU	RAVISHERS	RAZEES	REACTOR
RAUPATUS	RAVISHES	RAZER	REACTORS
RAUPO	RAVISHING	RAZERS	REACTS
RAURIKI	RAW	RAZES	REACTUATE
RAURIKIS	RAWARU	RAZING	READ
RAUWOLFIA	RAWBONE	RAZMATAZ	READABLE

READABLY	REAKS	REAMENDS	REARMOST
READAPT	REAL	REAMER	REARMOUSE
READAPTED	REALER	REAMERS	REARMS
READAPTS	REALES	REAMES	REAROSE
READD	REALEST	REAMIER	REAROUSAL
READDED	REALGAR	REAMIEST	REAROUSE
READDICT	REALGARS	REAMING	REAROUSED
READDICTS	REALIA	REAMS	REAROUSES
READDING	REALIGN	REAMY	REARRANGE
READDRESS	REALIGNED	REAN	REARREST
READDS	REALIGNS	REANALYSE	REARRESTS
READER	REALISE	REANALYZE	REARS
READERLY	REALISED	REANIMATE	REARWARD
READERS	REALISER	REANNEX	REARWARDS
READIED	REALISERS	REANNEXED	REASCEND
READIER	REALISES	REANNEXES	REASCENDS
READIES	REALISING	REANOINT	REASCENT
READIEST	REALISM	REANOINTS	REASCENTS
READILY	REALISMS	REANS	REASON
READINESS	REALIST	REANSWER	REASONED
READING	REALISTIC	REANSWERS	REASONER
READINGS	REALISTS	REAP	REASONERS
READJUST	REALITIES	REAPABLE	REASONING
READJUSTS	REALITY	REAPED	REASONS
READMIT	REALIZE	REAPER	REASSAIL
READMITS	REALIZED	REAPERS	REASSAILS
READOPT	REALIZER	REAPHOOK	REASSERT
READOPTED	REALIZERS	REAPHOOKS	REASSERTS
READOPTS	REALIZES	REAPING	REASSESS
READORN	REALIZING	REAPPAREL	REASSIGN
READORNED	REALLIE	REAPPEAR	REASSIGNS
READORNS	REALLIED	REAPPEARS	REASSORT
READOUT	REALLIES	REAPPLIED	REASSORTS
READOUTS	REALLOT	REAPPLIES	REASSUME
READS	REALLOTS	REAPPLY	REASSUMED
READVANCE	REALLY	REAPPOINT	REASSUMES
READVISE	REALLYING	REAPPROVE	REASSURE
READVISED	REALM	REAPS	REASSURED
READVISES	REALMLESS	REAR	REASSURER
READY	REALMS	REARED	REASSURES
READYING	REALNESS	REARER	REAST
READYMADE	REALO	REARERS	REASTED
REAEDIFY	REALOS	REARGUARD	REASTIER
REAEDIFYE	REALS	REARGUE	REASTIEST
REAFFIRM	REALTER	REARGUED	REASTING
REAFFIRMS	REALTERED	REARGUES	REASTS
REAFFIX	REALTERS	REARGUING	REASTY
REAFFIXED	REALTIE	REARHORSE	REATA
REAFFIXES	REALTIES	REARING	REATAS
REAGENCY	REALTIME	REARISE	REATE
REAGENT	REALTOR	REARISEN	REATES
REAGENTS	REALTORS	REARISES	REATTACH
REAGIN	REALTY	REARISING	REATTACK
REAGINIC	REAM	REARLY	REATTACKS
REAGINS	REAME	REARM	REATTAIN
REAK	REAMED	REARMED	REATTAINS
REAKED	REAMEND	REARMICE	REATTEMPT
REAKING	REAMENDED	REARMING	REAVAIL

REAVAILED	REBEGINS	REBOOTING	REBUTMENT
REAVAILS	REBEGUN	REBOOTS	REBUTS
REAVE	REBEL	REBOP	REBUTTAL
REAVED	REBELDOM	REBOPS	REBUTTALS
REAVER	REBELDOMS	REBORE	REBUTTED
REAVERS	REBELLED	REBORED	REBUTTER
REAVES	REBELLER	REBORES	REBUTTERS
REAVING	REBELLERS	REBORING	REBUTTING
REAVOW	REBELLING	REBORN	REBUTTON
REAVOWED	REBELLION	REBORROW	REBUTTONS
REAVOWING	REBELLOW	REBORROWS	REBUY
REAVOWS	REBELLOWS	REBOTTLE	REBUYING
REAWAKE	REBELS	REBOTTLED	REBUYS
REAWAKED	REBID	REBOTTLES	REC
REAWAKEN	REBIDDEN	REBOUGHT	RECAL
REAWAKENS	REBIDDING	REBOUND	RECALESCE
REAWAKES	REBIDS	REBOUNDED	RECALL
REAWAKING	REBILL	REBOUNDER	RECALLED
REAWOKE	REBILLED	REBOUNDS	RECALLER
REAWOKEN	REBILLING	REBOZO	RECALLERS
REB	REBILLS	REBOZOS	RECALLING
REBACK	REBIND	REBRACE	RECALLS
REBACKED	REBINDING	REBRACED	RECALMENT
REBACKING	REBINDS	REBRACES	RECALS
REBACKS	REBIRTH	REBRACING	RECAMIER
REBADGE	REBIRTHS	REBRANCH	RECAMIERS
REBADGED	REBIT	REBRAND	RECANE
REBADGES	REBITE	REBRANDED	RECANED
REBADGING	REBITES	REBRANDS	RECANES
REBAIT	REBITING	REBRED	RECANING
REBAITED	REBITTEN	REBREED	RECANT
REBAITING	REBLEND	REBREEDS	RECANTED
REBAITS	REBLENDED	REBS	RECANTER
REBALANCE	REBLENDS	REBUFF	RECANTERS
REBAPTISE	REBLENT	REBUFFED	RECANTING
REBAPTISM	REBLOOM	REBUFFING	RECANTS
REBAPTIZE	REBLOOMED	REBUFFS	RECAP
REBAR	REBLOOMS	REBUILD	RECAPPED
REBARS	REBLOSSOM	REBUILDED	RECAPPING
REBATABLE	REBOANT	REBUILDS	RECAPS
REBATE	REBOARD	REBUILT	RECAPTION
REBATED	REBOARDED	REBUKABLE	RECAPTOR
REBATER	REBOARDS	REBUKE	RECAPTORS
REBATERS	REBOATION	REBUKED	RECAPTURE
REBATES	REBODIED	REBUKEFUL	RECARPET
REBATING	REBODIES	REBUKER	RECARPETS
REBATO	REBODY	REBUKERS	RECARRIED
REBATOES	REBODYING	REBUKES	RECARRIES
REBATOS	REBOIL	REBUKING	RECARRY
REBBE	REBOILED	REBURIAL	RECAST
REBBES	REBOILING	REBURIALS	RECASTING
REBBETZIN	REBOILS	REBURIED	RECASTS
REBEC	REBOOK	REBURIES	RECATALOG
REBECK	REBOOKED	REBURY	RECATCH
REBECKS	REBOOKING	REBURYING	RECATCHES
REBECS	REBOOKS	REBUS	RECAUGHT
REBEGAN	REBOOT	REBUSES	RECAUTION
REBEGIN	REBOOTED	REBUT	RECCE

RECCED
RECCEED
RECCEING
RECCES
RECCIED
RECCIES
RECCO
RECCOS
RECCY
RECCYING
RECEDE
RECEDED
RECEDES
RECEDING
RECEIPT
RECEIPTED
RECEIPTOR
RECEIPTS
RECEIVAL
RECEIVALS
RECEIVE
RECEIVED
RECEIVER
RECEIVERS
RECEIVES
RECEIVING
RECEMENT
RECEMENTS
RECENCIES
RECENCY
RECENSE
RECENSED
RECENSES
RECENSING
RECENSION
RECENSOR
RECENSORS
RECENT
RECENTER
RECENTEST
RECENTLY
RECENTRE
RECENTRED
RECENTRES
RECEPT
RECEPTION
RECEPTIVE
RECEPTOR
RECEPTORS
RECEPTS
RECERTIFY
RECESS
RECESSED
RECESSES
RECESSING
RECESSION
RECESSIVE
RECHANGE

RECHANGED
RECHANGES
RECHANNEL
RECHARGE
RECHARGED
RECHARGER
RECHARGES
RECHART
RECHARTED
RECHARTER
RECHARTS
RECHATE
RECHATES
RECHAUFFE
RECHEAT
RECHEATED
RECHEATS
RECHECK
RECHECKED
RECHECKS
RECHERCHE
RECHEW
RECHEWED
RECHEWING
RECHEWS
RECHIE
RECHLESSE
RECHOOSE
RECHOOSES
RECHOSE
RECHOSEN
RECIPE
RECIPES
RECIPIENT
RECIRCLE
RECIRCLED
RECIRCLES
RECISION
RECISIONS
RECIT
RECITABLE
RECITAL
RECITALS
RECITE
RECITED
RECITER
RECITERS
RECITES
RECITING
RECITS
RECK
RECKAN
RECKED
RECKING
RECKLESS
RECKLING
RECKLINGS
RECKON

RECKONED
RECKONER
RECKONERS
RECKONING
RECKONS
RECKS
RECLAD
RECLADDED
RECLADS
RECLAIM
RECLAIMED
RECLAIMER
RECLAIMS
RECLAME
RECLAMES
RECLASP
RECLASPED
RECLASPS
RECLEAN
RECLEANED
RECLEANS
RECLIMB
RECLIMBED
RECLIMBS
RECLINATE
RECLINE
RECLINED
RECLINER
RECLINERS
RECLINES
RECLINING
RECLOSE
RECLOSED
RECLOSES
RECLOSING
RECLOTHE
RECLOTHED
RECLOTHES
RECLUSE
RECLUSELY
RECLUSES
RECLUSION
RECLUSIVE
RECLUSORY
RECOAL
RECOALED
RECOALING
RECOALS
RECOAT
RECOATED
RECOATING
RECOATS
RECOCK
RECOCKED
RECOCKING
RECOCKS
RECODE
RECODED

RECODES
RECODIFY
RECODING
RECOGNISE
RECOGNIZE
RECOIL
RECOILED
RECOILER
RECOILERS
RECOILING
RECOILS
RECOIN
RECOINAGE
RECOINED
RECOINING
RECOINS
RECOLLECT
RECOLLET
RECOLLETS
RECOLOR
RECOLORED
RECOLORS
RECOMB
RECOMBED
RECOMBINE
RECOMBING
RECOMBS
RECOMFORT
RECOMMEND
RECOMMIT
RECOMMITS
RECOMPACT
RECOMPILE
RECOMPOSE
RECOMPUTE
RECON
RECONCILE
RECONDITE
RECONDUCT
RECONFER
RECONFERS
RECONFINE
RECONFIRM
RECONNECT
RECONNED
RECONNING
RECONQUER
RECONS
RECONSIGN
RECONSOLE
RECONSULT
RECONTACT
RECONTOUR
RECONVENE
RECONVERT
RECONVEY
RECONVEYS
RECONVICT

RECOOK	RECREANCY	RECULING	REDATING
RECOOKED	RECREANT	RECUMBENT	REDBACK
RECOOKING	RECREANTS	RECUR	REDBACKS
RECOOKS	RECREATE	RECURE	REDBAIT
RECOPTED	RECREATED	RECURED	REDBAITED
RECOPIES	RECREATES	RECURES	REDBAITER
RECOPY	RECREATOR	RECURING	REDBAITS
RECOPYING	RECREMENT	RECURRED	REDBAY
RECORD	RECROSS	RECURRENT	REDBAYS
RECORDED	RECROSSED	RECURRING	REDBELLY
RECORDER	RECROSSES	RECURS	REDBIRD
RECORDERS	RECROWN	RECURSION	REDBIRDS
RECORDING	RECROWNED	RECURSIVE	REDBONE
RECORDIST	RECROWNS	RECURVATE	REDBONES
RECORDS	RECRUIT	RECURVE	REDBREAST
RECORK	RECRUITAL	RECURVED	REDBRICK
RECORKED	RECRUITED	RECURVES	REDBRICKS
RECORKING	RECRUITER	RECURVING	REDBUD
RECORKS	RECRUITS	RECUSAL	REDBUDS
RECOUNT	RECS	RECUSALS	REDBUG
RECOUNTAL	RECTA	RECUSANCE	REDBUGS
RECOUNTED	RECTAL	RECUSANCY	REDCAP
RECOUNTER	RECTALLY	RECUSANT	REDCAPS
RECOUNTS	RECTANGLE	RECUSANTS	REDCOAT
RECOUP	RECTI	RECUSE	REDCOATS
RECOUPE	RECTIFIED	RECUSED	REDD
RECOUPED	RECTIFIER	RECUSES	REDDED
RECOUPING	RECTIFIES	RECUSING	REDDEN
RECOUPLE	RECTIFY	RECUT	REDDENDA
RECOUPLED	RECTION	RECUTS	REDDENDO
RECOUPLES	RECTIONS	RECUTTING	REDDENDOS
RECOUPS	RECTITIC	RECYCLATE	REDDENDUM
RECOURE	RECTITIS	RECYCLE	REDDENED
RECOURED	RECTITUDE	RECYCLED	REDDENING
RECOURES	RECTO	RECYCLER	REDDENS
RECOURING	RECTOCELE	RECYCLERS	REDDER
RECOURSE	RECTOR	RECYCLES	REDDERS
RECOURSED	RECTORAL	RECYCLING	REDDEST
RECOURSES	RECTORATE	RECYCLIST	REDDIER
RECOVER	RECTORESS	RED	REDDIEST
RECOVERED	RECTORIAL	REDACT	REDDING
RECOVEREE	RECTORIES	REDACTED	REDDINGS
RECOVERER	RECTORS	REDACTING	REDDISH
RECOVEROR	RECTORY	REDACTION	REDDISHLY
RECOVERS	RECTOS	REDACTOR	REDDLE
RECOVERY	RECTRESS	REDACTORS	REDDLED
RECOWER	RECTRICES	REDACTS	REDDLEMAN
RECOWERED	RECTRIX	REDAMAGE	REDDLEMEN
RECOWERS	RECTUM	REDAMAGED	REDDLES
RECOYLE	RECTUMS	REDAMAGES	REDDLING
RECOYLED	RECTUS	REDAN	REDDS
RECOYLES	RECUILE	REDANS	REDDY
RECOYLING	RECUILED	REDARGUE	REDE
RECRATE	RECUILES	REDARGUED	REDEAL
RECRATED	RECUILING	REDARGUES	REDEALING
RECRATES	RECULE	REDATE	REDEALS
RECRATING	RECULED	REDATED	REDEALT
RECREANCE	RECULES	REDATES	REDEAR

REDEARS
REDECIDE
REDECIDED
REDECIDES
REDECRAFT
REDED
REDEEM
REDEEMED
REDEEMER
REDEEMERS
REDEEMING
REDEEMS
REDEFEAT
REDEFEATS
REDEFECT
REDEFECTS
REDEFIED
REDEFIES
REDEFINE
REDEFINED
REDEFINES
REDEFY
REDEFYING
REDELESS
REDELIVER
REDEMAND
REDEMANDS
REDENIED
REDENIES
REDENY
REDENYING
REDEPLOY
REDEPLOYS
REDEPOSIT
REDES
REDESCEND
REDESIGN
REDESIGNS
REDEVELOP
REDEYE
REDEYES
REDFIN
REDFINS
REDFISH
REDFISHES
REDFOOT
REDFOOTS
REDHANDED
REDHEAD
REDHEADED
REDHEADS
REDHORSE
REDHORSES
REDIA
REDIAE
REDIAL
REDIALED
REDIALING

REDIALLED
REDIALS
REDIAS
REDICTATE
REDID
REDIGEST
REDIGESTS
REDIGRESS
REDING
REDINGOTE
REDIP
REDIPPED
REDIPPING
REDIPS
REDIPT
REDIRECT
REDIRECTS
REDISCUSS
REDISPLAY
REDISPOSE
REDISTIL
REDISTILL
REDISTILS
REDIVIDE
REDIVIDED
REDIVIDES
REDIVIVUS
REDIVORCE
REDLEG
REDLEGS
REDLINE
REDLINED
REDLINER
REDLINERS
REDLINES
REDLINING
REDLY
REDNECK
REDNECKED
REDNECKS
REDNESS
REDNESSES
REDO
REDOCK
REDOCKED
REDOCKING
REDOCKS
REDOES
REDOING
REDOLENCE
REDOLENCY
REDOLENT
REDON
REDONE
REDONNED
REDONNING
REDONS
REDOS

REDOUBLE
REDOUBLED
REDOUBLER
REDOUBLES
REDOUBT
REDOUBTED
REDOUBTS
REDOUND
REDOUNDED
REDOUNDS
REDOUT
REDOUTS
REDOWA
REDOWAS
REDOX
REDOXES
REDPOLL
REDPOLLS
REDRAFT
REDRAFTED
REDRAFTS
REDRAW
REDRAWER
REDRAWERS
REDRAWING
REDRAWN
REDRAWS
REDREAM
REDREAMED
REDREAMS
REDREAMT
REDRESS
REDRESSED
REDRESSER
REDRESSES
REDRESSOR
REDREW
REDRIED
REDRIES
REDRILL
REDRILLED
REDRILLS
REDRIVE
REDRIVEN
REDRIVES
REDRIVING
REDROOT
REDROOTS
REDROVE
REDRY
REDRYING
REDS
REDSEAR
REDSHANK
REDSHANKS
REDSHARE
REDSHIFT
REDSHIFTS

REDSHIRE
REDSHIRT
REDSHIRTS
REDSHORT
REDSKIN
REDSKINS
REDSTART
REDSTARTS
REDSTREAK
REDTAIL
REDTAILS
REDTOP
REDTOPS
REDUB
REDUBBED
REDUBBING
REDUBS
REDUCE
REDUCED
REDUCER
REDUCERS
REDUCES
REDUCIBLE
REDUCIBLY
REDUCING
REDUCTANT
REDUCTASE
REDUCTION
REDUCTIVE
REDUCTOR
REDUCTORS
REDUIT
REDUITS
REDUNDANT
REDUVIID
REDUVIIDS
REDUX
REDWARE
REDWARES
REDWATER
REDWATERS
REDWING
REDWINGS
REDWOOD
REDWOODS
REDYE
REDYED
REDYEING
REDYES
REE
REEARN
REEARNED
REEARNING
REEARNS
REEBOK
REEBOKS
REECH
REECHED

REECHES	REEFS	REENJOYS	REFASTEN
REECHIE	REEFY	REENLARGE	REFASTENS
REECHIER	REEJECT	REENLIST	REFECT
REECHIEST	REEJECTED	REENLISTS	REFECTED
REECHTNG	REEJECTS	REENROLL	REFECTING
REECHO	REEK	REENROLLS	REFECTION
REECHOED	REEKED	REENS	REFECTIVE
REECHOES	REEKER	REENSLAVE	REFECTORY
REECHOING	REEKERS	REENTER	REFECTS
REECHY	REEKIE	REENTERED	REFED
REED	REEKIER	REENTERS	REFEED
REEDBED	REEKIEST	REENTRANT	REFEEDING
REEDBEDS	REEKING	REENTRIES	REFEEDS
REEDBIRD	REEKINGLY	REENTRY	REFEEL
REEDBIRDS	REEKS	REEQUIP	REFEELING
REEDBUCK	REEKY	REEQUIPS	REFEELS
REEDBUCKS	REEL	REERECT	REFEL
REEDE	REELABLE	REERECTED	REFELL
REEDED	REELECT	REERECTS	REFELLED
REEDEN	REELECTED	REES	REFELLING
REEDER	REELECTS	REEST	REFELS
REEDERS	REELED	REESTED	REFELT
REEDES	REELER	REESTIER	REFENCE
REEDIER	REELERS	REESTIEST	REFENCED
REEDIEST	REELEVATE	REESTING	REFENCES
REEDIFIED	REELING	REESTS	REFENCING
REEDIFIES	REELINGLY	REESTY	REFER
REEDIFY	REELINGS	REEVE	REFERABLE
REEDILY	REELMAN	REEVED	REFEREE
REEDINESS	REELMEN	REEVES	REFEREED
REEDING	REELS	REEVING	REFEREES
REEDINGS	REEMBARK	REEVOKE	REFERENCE
REEDIT	REEMBARKS	REEVOKED	REFERENDA
REEDITED	REEMBODY	REEVOKES	REFERENT
REEDITING	REEMBRACE	REEVOKING	REFERENTS
REEDITION	REEMERGE	REEXAMINE	REFERRAL
REEDITS	REEMERGED	REEXECUTE	REFERRALS
REEDLIKE	REEMERGES	REEXHIBIT	REFERRED
REEDLING	REEMIT	REEXPEL	REFERRER
REEDLINGS	REEMITS	REEXPELS	REFERRERS
REEDMACE	REEMITTED	REEXPLAIN	REFERRING
REEDMACES	REEMPLOY	REEXPLORF	REFERS
REEDMAN	REEMPLOYS	REEXPORT	REFFED
REEDMEN	REEN	REEXPORTS	REFFING
REEDS	REENACT	REEXPOSE	REFFO
REEDSTOP	REENACTED	REEXPOSED	REFFOS
REEDSTOPS	REENACTOR	REEXPOSES	REFIGHT
REEDUCATE	REENACTS	REEXPRESS	REFIGHTS
REEDY	REENDOW	REF	REFIGURE
REEF	REENDOWED	REFACE	REFIGURED
REEFABLE	REENDOWS	REFACED	REFIGURES
REEFED	REENFORCE	REFACES	REFILE
REEFER	REENGAGE	REFACING	REFILED
REEFERS	REENGAGED	REFALL	REFILES
REEFIER	REENGAGES	REFALLEN	REFILING
REEFIEST	REENGRAVE	REFALLING	REFILL
REEFING	REENJOY	REFALLS	REFILLED
REEFINGS	REENJOYED	REFASHION	REFILLING

REFILLS	REFLIES	REFRACT	REFUSE
REFILM	REFLOAT	REFRACTED	REFUSED
REFILMED	REFLOATED	REFRACTOR	REFUSENIK
REFILMING	REFLOATS	REFRACTS	REFUSER
REFILMS	REFLOOD	REFRAIN	REFUSERS
REFILTER	REFLOODED	REFRAINED	REFUSES
REFILTERS	REFLOODS	REFRAINER	REFUSING
REFINABLE	REFLOW	REFRAINS	REFUSION
REFINANCE	REFLOWED	REFRAME	REFUSIONS
REFIND	REFLOWER	REFRAMED	REFUSNIK
REFINDING	REFLOWERS	REFRAMES	REFUSNIKS
REFINDS	REFLOWING	REFRAMING	REFUTABLE
REFINE	REFLOWN	REFREEZE	REFUTABLY
REFINED	REFLOWS	REFREEZES	REFUTAL
REFINEDLY	REFLUENCE	REFRESH	REFUTALS
REFINER	REFLUENT	REFRESHED	REFUTE
REFINERS	REFLUX	REFRESHEN	REFUTED
REFINERY	REFLUXED	REFRESHER	REFUTER
REFINES	REFLUXES	REFRESHES	REFUTERS
REFINING	REFLUXING	REFRIED	REFUTES
REFININGS	REFLY	REFRIES	REFUTING
REFINISH	REFLYING	REFRINGE	REG
REFIRE	REFOCUS	REFRINGED	REGAIN
REFIRED	REFOCUSED	REFRINGES	REGAINED
REFIRES	REFOCUSES	REFRONT	REGAINER
REFIRING	REFOLD	REFRONTED	REGAINERS
REFIT	REFOLDED	REFRONTS	REGAINING
REFITMENT	REFOLDING	REFROZE	REGAINS
REFITS	REFOLDS	REFROZEN	REGAL
REFITTED	REFOOT	REFRY	REGALE
REFITTING	REFOOTED	REFRYING	REGALED
REFIX	REFOOTING	REFS	REGALER
REFIXED	REFOOTS	REFT	REGALERS
REFIXES	REFOREST	REFUEL	REGALES
REFIXING	REFORESTS	REFUELED	REGALIA
REFLAG	REFORGE	REFUELING	REGALIAN
REFLAGGED	REFORGED	REFUELLED	REGALIAS
REFLAGS	REFORGES	REFUELS	REGALING
REFLATE	REFORGING	REFUGE	REGALISM
REFLATED	REFORM	REFUGED	REGALISMS
REFLATES	REFORMADE	REFUGEE	REGALIST
REFLATING	REFORMADO	REFUGEES	REGALISTS
REFLATION	REFORMAT	REFUGES	REGALITY
REFLECT	REFORMATE	REFUGIA	REGALLY
REFLECTED	REFORMATS	REFUGING	REGALNESS
REFLECTER	REFORMED	REFUGIUM	REGALS
REFLECTOR	REFORMER	REFULGENT	REGAR
REFLECTS	REFORMERS	REFUND	REGARD
REFLET	REFORMING	REFUNDED	REGARDANT
REFLETS	REFORMISM	REFUNDER	REGARDED
REFLEW	REFORMIST	REFUNDERS	REGARDER
REFLEX	REFORMS	REFUNDING	REGARDERS
REFLEXED	REFORTIFY	REFUNDS	REGARDFUL
REFLEXES	REFOUGHT	REFURBISH	REGARDING
REFLEXING	REFOUND	REFURNISH	REGARDS
REFLEXION	REFOUNDED	REFUSABLE	REGARS
REFLEXIVE	REFOUNDER	REFUSAL	REGATHER
REFLEXLY	REFOUNDS	REFUSALS	REGATHERS

REGATTA	REGISTRY	REGRATING	REGULIZE
REGATTAS	REGIUS	REGRATOR	REGULIZED
REGAUGE	REGIVE	REGRATORS	REGULIZES
REGAUGED	REGIVEN	REGREDE	REGULO
REGAUGES	REGIVES	REGREDED	REGULOS
REGAUGING	REGIVING	REGREDES	REGULUS
REGAVE	REGLAZE	REGREDING	REGULUSES
REGEAR	REGLAZED	REGREEN	REGUR
REGEARED	REGLAZES	REGREENED	REGURS
REGEARING	REGLAZING	REGREENS	REH
REGEARS	REGLET	REGREET	REHAB
REGELATE	REGLETS	REGREETED	REHABBED
REGELATED	REGLORIFY	REGREETS	REHABBER
REGELATES	REGLOSS	REGRESS	REHABBERS
REGENCE	REGLOSSED	REGRESSED	REHABBING
REGENCES	REGLOSSES	REGRESSES	REHABS
REGENCIES	REGLOW	REGRESSOR	REHAMMER
REGENCY	REGLOWED	REGRET	REHAMMERS
REGENT	REGLOWING	REGRETFUL	REHANDLE
REGENTAL	REGLOWS	REGRETS	REHANDLED
REGENTS	REGLUE	REGRETTED	REHANDLES
REGES	REGLUED	REGRETTER	REHANG
REGEST	REGLUES	REGREW	REHANGED
REGESTS	REGLUING	REGRIND	REHANGING
REGGAE	REGMA	REGRINDS	REHANGS
REGGAES	REGMAKER	REGROOM	REHARDEN
REGGO	REGMAKERS	REGROOMED	REHARDENS
REGGOS	REGMATA	REGROOMS	REHASH
REGICIDAL	REGNA	REGROOVE	REHASHED
REGICIDE	REGNAL	REGROOVED	REHASHES
REGICIDES	REGNANCY	REGROOVES	REHASHING
REGIE	REGNANT	REGROUND	REHEAR
REGIES	REGNUM	REGROUP	REHEARD
REGILD	REGO	REGROUPED	REHEARING
REGILDED	REGOLITH	REGROUPS	REHEARS
REGILDING	REGOLITHS	REGROW	REHEARSAL
REGILDS	REGORGE	REGROWING	REHEARSE
REGILT	REGORGED	REGROWN	REHEARSED
REGIME	REGORGES	REGROWS	REHEARSER
REGIMEN	REGORGING	REGROWTH	REHEARSES
REGIMENS	REGOS	REGROWTHS	REHEAT
REGIMENT	REGOSOL	REGS	REHEATED
REGIMENTS	REGOSOLS	REGUERDON	REHEATER
REGIMES	REGRADE	REGULA	REHEATERS
REGIMINAL	REGRADED	REGULABLE	REHEATING
REGINA	REGRADES	REGULAE	REHEATS
REGINAE	REGRADING	REGULAR	REHEEL
REGINAL	REGRAFT	REGULARLY	REHEELED
REGINAS	REGRAFTED	REGULARS	REHEELING
REGION	REGRAFTS	REGULATE	REHEELS
REGIONAL	REGRANT	REGULATED	REHEM
REGIONALS	REGRANTED	REGULATES	REHEMMED
REGIONARY	REGRANTS	REGULATOR	REHEMMING
REGIONS	REGRATE	REGULI	REHEMS
REGISSEUR	REGRATED	REGULINE	REHINGE
REGISTER	REGRATER	REGULISE	REHINGED
REGISTERS	REGRATERS	REGULISED	REHINGES
REGISTRAR	REGRATES	REGULISES	REHINGING

REHIRE
REHIRED
REHIRES
REHIRING
REHOBOAM
REHOBOAMS
REHOUSE
REHOUSED
REHOUSES
REHOUSING
REHS
REHUNG
REHYDRATE
REI
REIF
REIFIED
REIFIER
REIFIERS
REIFIES
REIFS
REIFY
REIFYING
REIGN
REIGNED
REIGNING
REIGNITE
REIGNITED
REIGNITES
REIGNS
REIK
REIKI
REIKIS
REIKS
REILLUME
REILLUMED
REILLUMES
REIMAGE
REIMAGED
REIMAGES
REIMAGINE
REIMAGING
REIMBURSE
REIMMERSE
REIMPLANT
REIMPORT
REIMPORTS
REIMPOSE
REIMPOSED
REIMPOSES
REIN
REINCITE
REINCITED
REINCITES
REINCUR
REINCURS
REINDEER
REINDEERS
REINDEX

REINDEXED
REINDEXES
REINDICT
REINDICTS
REINDUCE
REINDUCED
REINDUCES
REINDUCT
REINDUCTS
REINED
REINETTE
REINETTES
REINFECT
REINFECTS
REINFLAME
REINFLATE
REINFORCE
REINFORM
REINFORMS
REINFUND
REINFUNDS
REINFUSE
REINFUSED
REINFUSES
REINHABIT
REINING
REINJECT
REINJECTS
REINJURE
REINJURED
REINJURES
REINJURY
REINK
REINKED
REINKING
REINKS
REINLESS
REINS
REINSERT
REINSERTS
REINSMAN
REINSMEN
REINSPECT
REINSPIRE
REINSTAL
REINSTALL
REINSTALS
REINSTATE
REINSURE
REINSURED
REINSURER
REINSURES
REINTER
REINTERS
REINVADE
REINVADED
REINVADES
REINVENT

REINVENTS
REINVEST
REINVESTS
REINVITE
REINVITED
REINVITES
REINVOKE
REINVOKED
REINVOKES
REINVOLVE
REIRD
REIRDS
REIS
REISES
REISSUE
REISSUED
REISSUER
REISSUERS
REISSUES
REISSUING
REIST
REISTAFEL
REISTED
REISTING
REISTS
REITBOK
REITBOKS
REITER
REITERANT
REITERATE
REITERS
REIVE
REIVED
REIVER
REIVERS
REIVES
REIVING
REJACKET
REJACKETS
REJECT
REJECTED
REJECTEE
REJECTEES
REJECTER
REJECTERS
REJECTING
REJECTION
REJECTIVE
REJECTOR
REJECTORS
REJECTS
REJIG
REJIGGED
REJIGGER
REJIGGERS
REJIGGING
REJIGS
REJOICE

REJOICED
REJOICER
REJOICERS
REJOICES
REJOICING
REJOIN
REJOINDER
REJOINED
REJOINING
REJOINS
REJON
REJONEO
REJONEOS
REJONES
REJOURN
REJOURNED
REJOURNS
REJUDGE
REJUDGED
REJUDGES
REJUDGING
REJUGGLE
REJUGGLED
REJUGGLES
REJUSTIFY
REKE
REKED
REKES
REKEY
REKEYED
REKEYING
REKEYS
REKINDLE
REKINDLED
REKINDLES
REKING
REKNIT
REKNITS
REKNITTED
REKNOT
REKNOTS
REKNOTTED
RELABEL
RELABELED
RELABELS
RELACE
RELACED
RELACES
RELACHE
RELACHES
RELACING
RELACQUER
RELAID
RELAND
RELANDED
RELANDING
RELANDS
RELAPSE

RELAPSED	RELEND	RELINING	RELUCTANT
RELAPSER	RELENDING	RELINK	RELUCTATE
RELAPSERS	RELENDS	RELINKED	RELUCTED
RELAPSES	RELENT	RELINKING	RELUCTING
RELAPSING	RELENTED	RELINKS	RELUCTS
RELATA	RELENTING	RELIQUARY	RELUME
RELATABLE	RELENTS	RELIQUE	RELUMED
RELATE	RELET	RELIQUEFY	RELUMES
RELATED	RELETS	RELIQUES	RELUMINE
RELATEDLY	RELETTER	RELIQUIAE	RELUMINED
RELATER	RELETTERS	RELISH	RELUMINES
RELATERS	RELETTING	RELISHED	RELUMING
RELATES	RELEVANCE	RELISHES	RELY
RELATING	RELEVANCY	RELISHING	RELYING
RELATION	RELEVANT	RELIST	REM
RELATIONS	RELEVE	RELISTED	REMADE
RELATIVAL	RELEVES	RELISTING	REMADES
RELATIVE	RELIABLE	RELISTS	REMAIL
RELATIVES	RELIABLES	RELIT	REMAILED
RELATOR	RELIABLY	RELIVABLE	REMAILING
RELATORS	RELIANCE	RELIVE	REMAILS
RELATUM	RELIANCES	RELIVED	REMAIN
RELAUNCH	RELIANT	RELIVER	REMAINDER
RELAUNDER	RELIANTLY	RELIVERED	REMAINED
RELAX	RELIC	RELIVERS	REMAINING
RELAXABLE	RELICENSE	RELIVES	REMAINS
RELAXANT	RELICS	RELIVING	REMAKE
RELAXANTS	RELICT	RELLENO	REMAKER
RELAXED	RELICTION	RELLENOS	REMAKERS
RELAXEDLY	RELICTS	RELLIES	REMAKES
RELAXER	RELIDE	RELLISH	REMAKING
RELAXERS	RELIE	RELLISHED	REMAN
RELAXES	RELIED	RELLISHES	REMAND
RELAXIN	RELIEF	RELOAD	REMANDED
RELAXING	RELIEFS	RELOADED	REMANDING
RELAXINS	RELIER	RELOADER	REMANDS
RELAY	RELIERS	RELOADERS	REMANENCE
RELAYED	RELIES	RELOADING	REMANENCY
RELAYING	RELIEVE	RELOADS	REMANENT
RELAYS	RELIEVED	RELOAN	REMANENTS
RELEARN	RELIEVER	RELOANED	REMANET
RELEARNED	RELIEVERS	RELOANING	REMANETS
RELEARNS	RELIEVES	RELOANS	REMANIE
RELEARNT	RELIEVING	RELOCATE	REMANIES
RELEASE	RELIEVO	RELOCATED	REMANNED
RELEASED	RELIEVOS	RELOCATEE	REMANNING
RELEASEE	RELIGHT	RELOCATES	REMANS
RELEASEES	RELIGHTED	RELOCATOR	REMAP
RELEASER	RELIGHTS	RELOCK	REMAPPED
RELEASERS	RELIGIEUX	RELOCKED	REMAPPING
RELEASES	RELIGION	RELOCKING	REMAPS
RELEASING	RELIGIONS	RELOCKS	REMARK
RELEASOR	RELIGIOSE	RELOOK	REMARKED
RELEASORS	RELIGIOSO	RELOOKED	REMARKER
RELEGABLE	RELIGIOUS	RELOOKING	REMARKERS
RELEGATE	RELINE	RELOOKS	REMARKET
RELEGATED	RELINED	RELUCENT	REMARKETS
RELEGATES	RELINES	RELUCT	REMARKING

REMARKS
REMARQUE
REMARQUED
REMARQUES
REMARRIED
REMARRIES
REMARRY
REMASTER
REMASTERS
REMATCH
REMATCHED
REMATCHES
REMATE
REMATED
REMATES
REMATING
REMBLAI
REMBLAIS
REMBLE
REMBLED
REMBLES
REMBLING
REMEAD
REMEADED
REMEADING
REMEADS
REMEASURE
REMEDE
REMEDED
REMEDES
REMEDIAL
REMEDIAT
REMEDIATE
REMEDIED
REMEDIES
REMEDING
REMEDY
REMEDYING
REMEET
REMEETING
REMEETS
REMEID
REMEIDED
REMEIDING
REMEIDS
REMELT
REMELTED
REMELTING
REMELTS
REMEMBER
REMEMBERS
REMEN
REMEND
REMENDED
REMENDING
REMENDS
REMENS
REMERCIED

REMERCIES
REMERCY
REMERGE
REMERGED
REMERGES
REMERGING
REMET
REMEX
REMIGATE
REMIGATED
REMIGATES
REMIGES
REMIGIAL
REMIGRATE
REMIND
REMINDED
REMINDER
REMINDERS
REMINDFUL
REMINDING
REMINDS
REMINISCE
REMINT
REMINTED
REMINTING
REMINTS
REMISE
REMISED
REMISES
REMISING
REMISS
REMISSION
REMISSIVE
REMISSLY
REMISSORY
REMIT
REMITMENT
REMITS
REMITTAL
REMITTALS
REMITTED
REMITTEE
REMITTEES
REMITTENT
REMITTER
REMITTERS
REMITTING
REMITTOR
REMITTORS
REMIX
REMIXED
REMIXES
REMIXING
REMIXT
REMIXTURE
REMNANT
REMNANTAL
REMNANTS

REMODEL
REMODELED
REMODELER
REMODELS
REMODIFY
REMOISTEN
REMOLADE
REMOLADES
REMOLD
REMOLDED
REMOLDING
REMOLDS
REMONTANT
REMONTOIR
REMORA
REMORAS
REMORID
REMORSE
REMORSES
REMOTE
REMOTELY
REMOTER
REMOTES
REMOTEST
REMOTION
REMOTIONS
REMOUD
REMOULADE
REMOULD
REMOULDED
REMOULDS
REMOUNT
REMOUNTED
REMOUNTS
REMOVABLE
REMOVABLY
REMOVAL
REMOVALS
REMOVE
REMOVED
REMOVEDLY
REMOVER
REMOVERS
REMOVES
REMOVING
REMS
REMUAGE
REMUAGES
REMUDA
REMUDAS
REMUEUR
REMUEURS
REMURMUR
REMURMURS
REN
RENAGUE
RENAGUED
RENAGUES

RENAGUING
RENAIL
RENAILED
RENAILING
RENAILS
RENAL
RENAME
RENAMED
RENAMES
RENAMING
RENASCENT
RENATURE
RENATURED
RENATURES
RENAY
RENAYED
RENAYING
RENAYS
RENCONTRE
REND
RENDED
RENDER
RENDERED
RENDERER
RENDERERS
RENDERING
RENDERS
RENDIBLE
RENDING
RENDITION
RENDS
RENDZINA
RENDZINAS
RENEGADE
RENEGADED
RENEGADES
RENEGADO
RENEGADOS
RENEGATE
RENEGATES
RENEGE
RENEGED
RENEGER
RENEGERS
RENEGES
RENEGING
RENEGUE
RENEGUED
RENEGUER
RENEGUERS
RENEGUES
RENEGUING
RENEST
RENESTED
RENESTING
RENESTS
RENEW
RENEWABLE

RENEWABLY	RENOVATES	REOPENING	REPASSES
RENEWAL	RENOVATOR	REOPENS	REPASSING
RENEWALS	RENOWN	REOPERATE	REPAST
RENEWED	RENOWNED	REOPPOSE	REPASTED
RENEWEDLY	RENOWNER	REOPPOSED	REPASTING
RENEWER	RENOWNERS	REOPPOSES	REPASTS
RENEWERS	RENOWNING	REORDAIN	REPASTURE
RENEWING	RENOWNS	REORDAINS	REPATCH
RENEWINGS	RENS	REORDER	REPATCHED
RENEWS	RENT	REORDERED	REPATCHES
RENEY	RENTABLE	REORDERS	REPATTERN
RENEYED	RENTAL	REORIENT	REPAVE
RENEYING	RENTALLER	REORIENTS	REPAVED
RENEYS	RENTALS	REOS	REPAVES
RENFIERST	RENTE	REOUTFIT	REPAVING
RENFORCE	RENTED	REOUTFITS	REPAY
RENFORCED	RENTER	REOVIRUS	REPAYABLE
RENFORCES	RENTERS	REOXIDISE	REPAYING
RENFORST	RENTES	REOXIDIZE	REPAYMENT
RENGA	RENTIER	REP	REPAYS
RENGAS	RENTIERS	REPACIFY	REPEAL
RENIED	RENTING	REPACK	REPEALED
RENIES	RENTINGS	REPACKAGE	REPEALER
RENIFORM	RENTS	REPACKED	REPEALERS
RENIG	RENUMBER	REPACKING	REPEALING
RENIGGED	RENUMBERS	REPACKS	REPEALS
RENIGGING	RENVERSE	REPAID	REPEAT
RENIGS	RENVERSED	REPAINT	REPEATED
RENIN	RENVERSES	REPAINTED	REPEATER
RENINS	RENVERST	REPAINTS	REPEATERS
RENITENCE	RENVOI	REPAIR	REPEATING
RENITENCY	RENVOIS	REPAIRED	REPEATS
RENITENT	RENVOY	REPAIRER	REPECHAGE
RENK	RENVOYS	REPAIRERS	REPEG
RENKER	RENY	REPAIRING	REPEGGED
RENKEST	RENYING	REPAIRMAN	REPEGGING
RENMINBI	REO	REPAIRMEN	REPEGS
RENMINBIS	REOBJECT	REPAIRS	REPEL
RENNASE	REOBJECTS	REPAND	REPELLANT
RENNASES	REOBSERVE	REPANDLY	REPELLED
RENNE	REOBTAIN	REPANEL	REPELLENT
RENNED	REOBTAINS	REPANELED	REPELLER
RENNES	REOCCUPY	REPANELS	REPELLERS
RENNET	REOCCUR	REPAPER	REPELLING
RENNETS	REOCCURS	REPAPERED	REPELS
RENNIN	REOFFEND	REPAPERS	REPENT
RENNING	REOFFENDS	REPARABLE	REPENTANT
RENNINGS	REOFFER	REPARABLY	REPENTED
RENNINS	REOFFERED	REPARK	REPENTER
RENOGRAM	REOFFERS	REPARKED	REPENTERS
RENOGRAMS	REOIL	REPARKING	REPENTING
RENOTIFY	REOILED	REPARKS	REPENTS
RENOUNCE	REOILING	REPARTEE	REPEOPLE
RENOUNCED	REOILS	REPARTEED	REPEOPLED
RENOUNCER	REOPEN	REPARTEES	REPEOPLES
RENOUNCES	REOPENED	REPASS	REPERCUSS
RENOVATE	REOPENER	REPASSAGE	REPEREPE
RENOVATED	REOPENERS	REPASSED	REPERK

485

REPERKED	REPLEDGES	REPORTERS	REPRICING
REPERKING	REPLENISH	REPORTING	REPRIEFE
REPERKS	REPLETE	REPORTS	REPRIEFES
REPERTORY	REPLETED	REPOS	REPRIEVAL
REPERUSAL	REPLETELY	REPOSAL	REPRIEVE
REPERUSE	REPLETES	REPOSALL	REPRIEVED
REPERUSED	REPLETING	REPOSALLS	REPRIEVER
REPERUSES	REPLETION	REPOSALS	REPRIEVES
REPETEND	REPLEVIED	REPOSE	REPRIMAND
REPETENDS	REPLEVIES	REPOSED	REPRIME
REPHRASE	REPLEVIN	REPOSEDLY	REPRIMED
REPHRASED	REPLEVINS	REPOSEFUL	REPRIMES
REPHRASES	REPLEVY	REPOSER	REPRIMING
REPIGMENT	REPLICA	REPOSERS	REPRINT
REPIN	REPLICAS	REPOSES	REPRINTED
REPINE	REPLICASE	REPOSING	REPRINTER
REPINED	REPLICATE	REPOSIT	REPRINTS
REPINER	REPLICON	REPOSITED	REPRISAL
REPINERS	REPLICONS	REPOSITOR	REPRISALS
REPINES	REPLIED	REPOSITS	REPRISE
REPINING	REPLIER	REPOSSESS	REPRISED
REPININGS	REPLIERS	REPOST	REPRISES
REPINNED	REPLIES	REPOSTED	REPRISING
REPINNING	REPLOT	REPOSTING	REPRIVE
REPINS	REPLOTS	REPOSTS	REPRIVED
REPIQUE	REPLOTTED	REPOSURE	REPRIVES
REPIQUED	REPLOW	REPOSURES	REPRIVING
REPIQUES	REPLOWED	REPOT	REPRIZE
REPIQUING	REPLOWING	REPOTS	REPRIZED
REPLA	REPLOWS	REPOTTED	REPRIZES
REPLACE	REPLUM	REPOTTING	REPRIZING
REPLACED	REPLUMB	REPOUR	REPRO
REPLACER	REPLUMBED	REPOURED	REPROACH
REPLACERS	REPLUMBS	REPOURING	REPROBACY
REPLACES	REPLUNGE	REPOURS	REPROBATE
REPLACING	REPLUNGED	REPOUSSE	REPROBE
REPLAN	REPLUNGES	REPOUSSES	REPROBED
REPLANNED	REPLY	REPOWER	REPROBES
REPLANS	REPLYING	REPOWERED	REPROBING
REPLANT	REPO	REPOWERS	REPROCESS
REPLANTED	REPOINT	REPP	REPRODUCE
REPLANTS	REPOINTED	REPPED	REPROGRAM
REPLASTER	REPOINTS	REPPING	REPROOF
REPLATE	REPOLISH	REPPINGS	REPROOFED
REPLATED	REPOLL	REPPS	REPROOFS
REPLATES	REPOLLED	REPREEVE	REPROS
REPLATING	REPOLLING	REPREEVED	REPROVAL
REPLAY	REPOLLS	REPREEVES	REPROVALS
REPLAYED	REPOMAN	REPREHEND	REPROVE
REPLAYING	REPOMEN	REPRESENT	REPROVED
REPLAYS	REPONE	REPRESS	REPROVER
REPLEAD	REPONED	REPRESSED	REPROVERS
REPLEADED	REPONES	REPRESSER	REPROVES
REPLEADER	REPONING	REPRESSES	REPROVING
REPLEADS	REPORT	REPRESSOR	REPRYVE
REPLED	REPORTAGE	REPRICE	REPRYVED
REPLEDGE	REPORTED	REPRICED	REPRYVES
REPLEDGED	REPORTER	REPRICES	REPRYVING

REPS
REPTANT
REPTATION
REPTILE
REPTILES
REPTILIA
REPTILIAN
REPTILIUM
REPTILOID
REPUBLIC
REPUBLICS
REPUBLISH
REPUDIATE
REPUGN
REPUGNANT
REPUGNED
REPUGNING
REPUGNS
REPULP
REPULPED
REPULPING
REPULPS
REPULSE
REPULSED
REPULSER
REPULSERS
REPULSES
REPULSING
REPULSION
REPULSIVE
REPUMP
REPUMPED
REPUMPING
REPUMPS
REPUNIT
REPUNITS
REPURE
REPURED
REPURES
REPURIFY
REPURING
REPURPOSE
REPURSUE
REPURSUED
REPURSUES
REPUTABLE
REPUTABLY
REPUTE
REPUTED
REPUTEDLY
REPUTES
REPUTING
REPUTINGS
REQUALIFY
REQUERE
REQUERED
REQUERES
REQUERING

REQUEST
REQUESTED
REQUESTER
REQUESTOR
REQUESTS
REQUICKEN
REQUIEM
REQUIEMS
REQUIGHT
REQUIGHTS
REQUIN
REQUINS
REQUIRE
REQUIRED
REQUIRER
REQUIRERS
REQUIRES
REQUIRING
REQUISITE
REQUIT
REQUITAL
REQUITALS
REQUITE
REQUITED
REQUITER
REQUITERS
REQUITES
REQUITING
REQUITS
REQUITTED
REQUOTE
REQUOTED
REQUOTES
REQUOTING
REQUOYLE
REQUOYLED
REQUOYLES
RERACK
RERACKED
RERACKING
RERACKS
RERADIATE
RERAIL
RERAILED
RERAILING
RERAILS
RERAISE
RERAISED
RERAISES
RERAISING
RERAN
REREAD
REREADING
REREADS
REREBRACE
RERECORD
RERECORDS
REREDOS

REREDOSES
REREDOSSE
RERELEASE
REREMAI
REREMICE
REREMIND
REREMINDS
REREMOUSE
RERENT
RERENTED
RERENTING
RERENTS
REREPEAT
REREPEATS
REREVIEW
REREVIEWS
REREVISE
REREVISED
REREVISES
REREWARD
REREWARDS
RERIG
RERIGGED
RERIGGING
RERIGS
RERISE
RERISEN
RERISES
RERISING
REROLL
REROLLED
REROLLER
REROLLERS
REROLLING
REROLLS
REROOF
REROOFED
REROOFING
REROOFS
REROSE
REROUTE
REROUTED
REROUTES
REROUTING
RERUN
RERUNNING
RERUNS
RES
RESADDLE
RESADDLED
RESADDLES
RESAID
RESAIL
RESAILED
RESAILING
RESAILS
RESALABLE
RESALE

RESALES
RESALGAR
RESALGARS
RESALUTE
RESALUTED
RESALUTES
RESAMPLE
RESAMPLED
RESAMPLES
RESAT
RESAW
RESAWED
RESAWING
RESAWN
RESAWS
RESAY
RESAYING
RESAYS
RESCALE
RESCALED
RESCALES
RESCALING
RESCHOOL
RESCHOOLS
RESCIND
RESCINDED
RESCINDER
RESCINDS
RESCORE
RESCORED
RESCORES
RESCORING
RESCREEN
RESCREENS
RESCRIPT
RESCRIPTS
RESCUABLE
RESCUE
RESCUED
RESCUER
RESCUERS
RESCUES
RESCUING
RESCULPT
RESCULPTS
RESEAL
RESEALED
RESEALING
RESEALS
RESEARCH
RESEASON
RESEASONS
RESEAT
RESEATED
RESEATING
RESEATS
RESEAU
RESEAUS

RESEAUX
RESECT
RESECTED
RESECTING
RESECTION
RESECTS
RESECURE
RESECURED
RESECURES
RESEDA
RESEDAS
RESEE
RESEED
RESEEDED
RESEEDING
RESEEDS
RESEEING
RESEEK
RESEEKING
RESEEKS
RESEEN
RESEES
RESEIZE
RESEIZED
RESEIZES
RESEIZING
RESEIZURE
RESELECT
RESELECTS
RESELL
RESELLER
RESELLERS
RESELLING
RESELLS
RESEMBLE
RESEMBLED
RESEMBLER
RESEMBLES
RESEND
RESENDING
RESENDS
RESENT
RESENTED
RESENTER
RESENTERS
RESENTFUL
RESENTING
RESENTIVE
RESENTS
RESERPINE
RESERVE
RESERVED
RESERVER
RESERVERS
RESERVES
RESERVICE
RESERVING
RESERVIST

RESERVOIR
RESES
RESET
RESETS
RESETTED
RESETTER
RESETTERS
RESETTING
RESETTLE
RESETTLED
RESETTLES
RESEW
RESEWED
RESEWING
RESEWN
RESEWS
RESH
RESHAPE
RESHAPED
RESHAPER
RESHAPERS
RESHAPES
RESHAPING
RESHARPEN
RESHAVE
RESHAVED
RESHAVEN
RESHAVES
RESHAVING
RESHES
RESHINE
RESHINED
RESHINES
RESHINGLE
RESHINING
RESHIP
RESHIPPED
RESHIPPER
RESHIPS
RESHOD
RESHOE
RESHOED
RESHOEING
RESHOES
RESHONE
RESHOOT
RESHOOTS
RESHOT
RESHOW
RESHOWED
RESHOWER
RESHOWERS
RESHOWING
RESHOWN
RESHOWS
RESHUFFLE
RESIANCE
RESIANCES

RESIANT
RESIANTS
RESID
RESIDE
RESIDED
RESIDENCE
RESIDENCY
RESIDENT
RESIDENTS
RESIDER
RESIDERS
RESIDES
RESIDING
RESIDS
RESIDUA
RESIDUAL
RESIDUALS
RESIDUARY
RESIDUE
RESIDUES
RESIDUOUS
RESIDUUM
RESIDUUMS
RESIFT
RESIFTED
RESIFTING
RESIFTS
RESIGHT
RESIGHTED
RESIGHTS
RESIGN
RESIGNED
RESIGNER
RESIGNERS
RESIGNING
RESIGNS
RESILE
RESILED
RESILES
RESILIENT
RESILIN
RESILING
RESILINS
RESILVER
RESILVERS
RESIN
RESINATA
RESINATAS
RESINATE
RESINATED
RESINATES
RESINED
RESINER
RESINERS
RESINIFY
RESINING
RESINISE
RESINISED

RESINISES
RESINIZE
RESINIZED
RESINIZES
RESINLIKE
RESINOID
RESINOIDS
RESINOSES
RESINOSIS
RESINOUS
RESINS
RESINY
RESIST
RESISTANT
RESISTED
RESISTENT
RESISTER
RESISTERS
RESISTING
RESISTIVE
RESISTOR
RESISTORS
RESISTS
RESIT
RESITE
RESITED
RESITES
RESITING
RESITS
RESITTING
RESITUATE
RESIZE
RESIZED
RESIZES
RESIZING
RESKETCH
RESKEW
RESKEWED
RESKEWING
RESKEWS
RESKILL
RESKILLED
RESKILLS
RESKUE
RESKUED
RESKUES
RESKUING
RESLATE
RESLATED
RESLATES
RESLATING
RESMELT
RESMELTED
RESMELTS
RESMOOTH
RESMOOTHS
RESNATRON
RESOAK

RESOAKED	RESOWING	RESPRAYS	RESTOKE
RESOAKING	RESOWN	RESPREAD	RESTOKED
RESOAKS	RESOWS	RESPREADS	RESTOKES
RESOD	RESPACE	RESPRING	RESTOKING
RESODDED	RESPACED	RESPRINGS	RESTORAL
RESODDING	RESPACES	RESPROUT	RESTORALS
RESODS	RESPACING	RESPROUTS	RESTORE
RESOFTEN	RESPADE	RESPRUNG	RESTORED
RESOFTENS	RESPADED	RESSALDAR	RESTORER
RESOJET	RESPADES	REST	RESTORERS
RESOJETS	RESPADING	RESTABLE	RESTORES
RESOLD	RESPEAK	RESTABLED	RESTORING
RESOLDER	RESPEAKS	RESTABLES	RESTOS
RESOLDERS	RESPECIFY	RESTACK	RESTRAIN
RESOLE	RESPECT	RESTACKED	RESTRAINS
RESOLED	RESPECTED	RESTACKS	RESTRAINT
RESOLES	RESPECTER	RESTAFF	RESTRESS
RESOLING	RESPECTS	RESTAFFED	RESTRETCH
RESOLUBLE	RESPELL	RESTAFFS	RESTRICT
RESOLUTE	RESPELLED	RESTAGE	RESTRICTS
RESOLUTER	RESPELLS	RESTAGED	RESTRIKE
RESOLUTES	RESPELT	RESTAGES	RESTRIKES
RESOLVE	RESPIRE	RESTAGING	RESTRING
RESOLVED	RESPIRED	RESTAMP	RESTRINGE
RESOLVENT	RESPIRES	RESTAMPED	RESTRINGS
RESOLVER	RESPIRING	RESTAMPS	RESTRIVE
RESOLVERS	RESPITE	RESTART	RESTRIVEN
RESOLVES	RESPITED	RESTARTED	RESTRIVES
RESOLVING	RESPITES	RESTARTER	RESTROOM
RESONANCE	RESPITING	RESTARTS	RESTROOMS
RESONANT	RESPLEND	RESTATE	RESTROVE
RESONANTS	RESPLENDS	RESTATED	RESTRUCK
RESONATE	RESPLICE	RESTATES	RESTRUNG
RESONATED	RESPLICED	RESTATING	RESTS
RESONATES	RESPLICES	RESTATION	RESTUDIED
RESONATOR	RESPLIT	RESTED	RESTUDIES
RESORB	RESPLITS	RESTEM	RESTUDY
RESORBED	RESPOKE	RESTEMMED	RESTUFF
RESORBENT	RESPOKEN	RESTEMS	RESTUFFED
RESORBING	RESPOND	RESTER	RESTUFFS
RESORBS	RESPONDED	RESTERS	RESTUMP
RESORCIN	RESPONDER	RESTFUL	RESTUMPED
RESORCINS	RESPONDS	RESTFULLY	RESTUMPS
RESORT	RESPONSA	RESTIER	RESTY
RESORTED	RESPONSE	RESTIEST	RESTYLE
RESORTER	RESPONSER	RESTIFF	RESTYLED
RESORTERS	RESPONSES	RESTIFORM	RESTYLES
RESORTING	RESPONSOR	RESTING	RESTYLING
RESORTS	RESPONSUM	RESTINGS	RESUBJECT
RESOUGHT	RESPOOL	RESTITCH	RESUBMIT
RESOUND	RESPOOLED	RESTITUTE	RESUBMITS
RESOUNDED	RESPOOLS	RESTIVE	RESULT
RESOUNDS	RESPOT	RESTIVELY	RESULTANT
RESOURCE	RESPOTS	RESTLESS	RESULTED
RESOURCED	RESPOTTED	RESTO	RESULTFUL
RESOURCES	RESPRANG	RESTOCK	RESULTING
RESOW	RESPRAY	RESTOCKED	RESULTS
RESOWED	RESPRAYED	RESTOCKS	RESUMABLE

RESUME	RETALLIES	RETESTIFY	RETINTING
RESUMED	RETALLY	RETESTING	RETINTS
RESUMER	RETAMA	RETESTS	RETINUE
RESUMERS	RETAMAS	RETEXTURE	RETINUED
RESUMES	RETAPE	RETHINK	RETINUES
RESUMING	RETAPED	RETHINKER	RETINULA
RESUMMON	RETAPES	RETHINKS	RETINULAE
RESUMMONS	RETAPING	RETHOUGHT	RETINULAR
RESUPINE	RETARD	RETHREAD	RETINULAS
RESUPPLY	RETARDANT	RETHREADS	RETIRACY
RESURFACE	RETARDATE	RETIA	RETIRAL
RESURGE	RETARDED	RETIAL	RETIRALS
RESURGED	RETARDER	RETIARII	RETIRANT
RESURGENT	RETARDERS	RETIARIUS	RETIRANTS
RESURGES	RETARDING	RETIARY	RETIRE
RESURGING	RETARDS	RETICELLA	RETIRED
RESURRECT	RETARGET	RETICENCE	RETIREDLY
RESURVEY	RETARGETS	RETICENCY	RETIREE
RESURVEYS	RETASTE	RETICENT	RETIREES
RESUSPEND	RETASTED	RETICLE	RETIRER
RESWALLOW	RETASTES	RETICLES	RETIRERS
RET	RETASTING	RETICULA	RETIRES
RETABLE	RETAUGHT	RETICULAR	RETIRING
RETABLES	RETAX	RETICULE	RETITLE
RETACK	RETAXED	RETICULES	RETITLED
RETACKED	RETAXES	RETICULUM	RETITLES
RETACKING	RETAXING	RETIE	RETITLING
RETACKLE	RETCH	RETIED	RETOLD
RETACKLED	RETCHED	RETIEING	RETOOK
RETACKLES	RETCHES	RETIES	RETOOL
RETACKS	RETCHING	RETIFORM	RETOOLED
RETAG	RETCHLESS	RETIGHTEN	RETOOLING
RETAGGED	RETE	RETILE	RETOOLS
RETAGGING	RETEACH	RETILED	RETORE
RETAGS	RETEACHES	RETILES	RETORN
RETAIL	RETEAM	RETILING	RETORSION
RETAILED	RETEAMED	RETIME	RETORT
RETAILER	RETEAMING	RETIMED	RETORTED
RETAILERS	RETEAMS	RETIMES	RETORTER
RETAILING	RETEAR	RETIMING	RETORTERS
RETAILOR	RETEARING	RETINA	RETORTING
RETAILORS	RETEARS	RETINAE	RETORTION
RETAILS	RETELL	RETINAL	RETORTIVE
RETAIN	RETELLER	RETINALS	RETORTS
RETAINED	RETELLERS	RETINAS	RETOTAL
RETAINER	RETELLING	RETINE	RETOTALED
RETAINERS	RETELLS	RETINENE	RETOTALS
RETAINING	RETEM	RETINENES	RETOUCH
RETAINS	RETEMPER	RETINES	RETOUCHED
RETAKE	RETEMPERS	RETINITE	RETOUCHER
RETAKEN	RETEMS	RETINITES	RETOUCHES
RETAKER	RETENE	RETINITIS	RETOUR
RETAKERS	RETENES	RETINOID	RETOURED
RETAKES	RETENTION	RETINOIDS	RETOURING
RETAKING	RETENTIVE	RETINOL	RETOURS
RETAKINGS	RETES	RETINOLS	RETRACE
RETALIATE	RETEST	RETINT	RETRACED
RETALLIED	RETESTED	RETINTED	RETRACER

RETRACERS
RETRACES
RETRACING
RETRACK
RETRACKED
RETRACKS
RETRACT
RETRACTED
RETRACTOR
RETRACTS
RETRAICT
RETRAICTS
RETRAIN
RETRAINED
RETRAINEE
RETRAINS
RETRAIT
RETRAITE
RETRAITES
RETRAITS
RETRAITT
RETRAITTS
RETRAL
RETRALLY
RETRATE
RETRATED
RETRATES
RETRATING
RETREAD
RETREADED
RETREADS
RETREAT
RETREATED
RETREATER
RETREATS
RETREE
RETREES
RETRENCH
RETRIAL
RETRIALS
RETRIBUTE
RETRIED
RETRIES
RETRIEVAL
RETRIEVE
RETRIEVED
RETRIEVER
RETRIEVES
RETRIM
RETRIMMED
RETRIMS
RETRO
RETROACT
RETROACTS
RETROCEDE
RETROD
RETRODDEN
RETRODICT

RETROFIRE
RETROFIT
RETROFITS
RETROFLEX
RETROJECT
RETRONYM
RETRONYMS
RETROPACK
RETRORSE
RETROS
RETROUSSE
RETROVERT
RETRY
RETRYING
RETS
RETSINA
RETSINAS
RETTED
RETTERIES
RETTERY
RETTING
RETUND
RETUNDED
RETUNDING
RETUNDS
RETUNE
RETUNED
RETUNES
RETUNING
RETURF
RETURFED
RETURFING
RETURFS
RETURN
RETURNED
RETURNEE
RETURNEES
RETURNER
RETURNERS
RETURNIK
RETURNIKS
RETURNING
RETURNS
RETUSE
RETWIST
RETWISTED
RETWISTS
RETYING
RETYPE
RETYPED
RETYPES
RETYPING
REUNIFIED
REUNIFIES
REUNIFY
REUNION
REUNIONS
REUNITE

REUNITED
REUNITER
REUNITERS
REUNITES
REUNITING
REUPTAKE
REUPTAKES
REURGE
REURGED
REURGES
REURGING
REUSABLE
REUSABLES
REUSE
REUSED
REUSES
REUSING
REUTILISE
REUTILIZE
REUTTER
REUTTERED
REUTTERS
REV
REVALENTA
REVALUATE
REVALUE
REVALUED
REVALUES
REVALUING
REVAMP
REVAMPED
REVAMPER
REVAMPERS
REVAMPING
REVAMPS
REVANCHE
REVANCHES
REVARNISH
REVEAL
REVEALED
REVEALER
REVEALERS
REVEALING
REVEALS
REVEHENT
REVEILLE
REVEILLES
REVEL
REVELATOR
REVELED
REVELER
REVELERS
REVELING
REVELLED
REVELLER
REVELLERS
REVELLING
REVELMENT

REVELRIES
REVELROUS
REVELRY
REVELS
REVENANT
REVENANTS
REVENGE
REVENGED
REVENGER
REVENGERS
REVENGES
REVENGING
REVENGIVE
REVENUAL
REVENUE
REVENUED
REVENUER
REVENUERS
REVENUES
REVERABLE
REVERB
REVERBED
REVERBING
REVERBS
REVERE
REVERED
REVERENCE
REVEREND
REVERENDS
REVERENT
REVERER
REVERERS
REVERES
REVERIE
REVERIES
REVERIFY
REVERING
REVERIST
REVERISTS
REVERS
REVERSAL
REVERSALS
REVERSE
REVERSED
REVERSELY
REVERSER
REVERSERS
REVERSES
REVERSI
REVERSING
REVERSION
REVERSIS
REVERSO
REVERSOS
REVERT
REVERTANT
REVERTED
REVERTER

REVERTERS
REVERTING
REVERTIVE
REVERTS
REVERY
REVEST
REVESTED
REVESTING
REVESTRY
REVESTS
REVET
REVETMENT
REVETS
REVETTED
REVETTING
REVEUR
REVEURS
REVEUSE
REVEUSES
REVIBRATE
REVICTUAL
REVIE
REVIED
REVIES
REVIEW
REVIEWAL
REVIEWALS
REVIEWED
REVIEWER
REVIEWERS
REVIEWING
REVIEWS
REVILE
REVILED
REVILER
REVILERS
REVILES
REVILING
REVILINGS
REVIOLATE
REVISABLE
REVISAL
REVISALS
REVISE
REVISED
REVISER
REVISERS
REVISES
REVISING
REVISION
REVISIONS
REVISIT
REVISITED
REVISITS
REVISOR
REVISORS
REVISORY
REVIVABLE

REVIVABLY
REVIVAL
REVIVALS
REVIVE
REVIVED
REVIVER
REVIVERS
REVIVES
REVIVIFY
REVIVING
REVIVINGS
REVIVOR
REVIVORS
REVOCABLE
REVOCABLY
REVOICE
REVOICED
REVOICES
REVOICING
REVOKABLE
REVOKABLY
REVOKE
REVOKED
REVOKER
REVOKERS
REVOKES
REVOKING
REVOLT
REVOLTED
REVOLTER
REVOLTERS
REVOLTING
REVOLTS
REVOLUTE
REVOLVE
REVOLVED
REVOLVER
REVOLVERS
REVOLVES
REVOLVING
REVOTE
REVOTED
REVOTES
REVOTING
REVS
REVUE
REVUES
REVUIST
REVUISTS
REVULSED
REVULSION
REVULSIVE
REVVED
REVVING
REVYING
REW
REWAKE
REWAKED

REWAKEN
REWAKENED
REWAKENS
REWAKES
REWAKING
REWAN
REWARD
REWARDED
REWARDER
REWARDERS
REWARDFUL
REWARDING
REWARDS
REWAREWA
REWAREWAS
REWARM
REWARMED
REWARMING
REWARMS
REWASH
REWASHED
REWASHES
REWASHING
REWAX
REWAXED
REWAXES
REWAXING
REWEAR
REWEARING
REWEARS
REWEAVE
REWEAVED
REWEAVES
REWEAVING
REWED
REWEDDED
REWEDDING
REWEDS
REWEIGH
REWEIGHED
REWEIGHS
REWELD
REWELDED
REWELDING
REWELDS
REWET
REWETS
REWETTED
REWETTING
REWIDEN
REWIDENED
REWIDENS
REWIN
REWIND
REWINDED
REWINDER
REWINDERS
REWINDING

REWINDS
REWINNING
REWINS
REWIRABLE
REWIRE
REWIRED
REWIRES
REWIRING
REWOKE
REWOKEN
REWON
REWORD
REWORDED
REWORDING
REWORDS
REWORE
REWORK
REWORKED
REWORKING
REWORKS
REWORN
REWOUND
REWOVE
REWOVEN
REWRAP
REWRAPPED
REWRAPS
REWRAPT
REWRITE
REWRITER
REWRITERS
REWRITES
REWRITING
REWRITTEN
REWROTE
REWROUGHT
REWS
REWTH
REWTHS
REX
REXES
REXINE
REXINES
REYNARD
REYNARDS
REZ
REZERO
REZEROED
REZEROES
REZEROING
REZEROS
REZONE
REZONED
REZONES
REZONING
REZZES
RHABDOID
RHABDOIDS

RHABDOM
RHABDOMAL
RHABDOME
RHABDOMES
RHABDOMS
RHABDUS
RHABDUSES
RHACHIAL
RHACHIDES
RHACHILLA
RHACHIS
RHACHISES
RHACHITIS
RHAGADES
RHAMNOSE
RHAMNOSES
RHAMNUS
RHAMNUSES
RHAMPHOID
RHANJA
RHANJAS
RHAPHAE
RHAPHE
RHAPHES
RHAPHIDE
RHAPHIDES
RHAPHIS
RHAPONTIC
RHAPSODE
RHAPSODES
RHAPSODIC
RHAPSODY
RHATANIES
RHATANY
RHEA
RHEAS
RHEBOK
RHEBOKS
RHEMATIC
RHEME
RHEMES
RHENIUM
RHENIUMS
RHEOBASE
RHEOBASES
RHEOBASIC
RHEOCHORD
RHEOCORD
RHEOCORDS
RHEOLOGIC
RHEOLOGY
RHEOMETER
RHEOMETRY
RHEOPHIL
RHEOPHILE
RHEOSTAT
RHEOSTATS
RHEOTAXES

RHEOTAXIS
RHEOTOME
RHEOTOMES
RHEOTROPE
RHESUS
RHESUSES
RHETOR
RHETORIC
RHETORICS
RHETORISE
RHETORIZE
RHETORS
RHEUM
RHEUMATIC
RHEUMATIZ
RHEUMED
RHEUMIC
RHEUMIER
RHEUMIEST
RHEUMS
RHEUMY
RHEXES
RHEXIS
RHEXISES
RHIES
RHIGOLENE
RHIME
RHIMES
RHINAL
RHINE
RHINES
RHINITIC
RHINITIS
RHINO
RHINOCERI
RHINOLITH
RHINOLOGY
RHINOS
RHIPIDATE
RHIPIDION
RHIPIDIUM
RHIZIC
RHIZINE
RHIZINES
RHIZOBIA
RHIZOBIAL
RHIZOBIUM
RHIZOCARP
RHIZOCAUL
RHIZOID
RHIZOIDAL
RHIZOIDS
RHIZOMA
RHIZOMATA
RHIZOME
RHIZOMES
RHIZOMIC
RHIZOPI

RHIZOPOD
RHIZOPODS
RHIZOPUS
RHIZOTOMY
RHO
RHODAMIN
RHODAMINE
RHODAMINS
RHODANATE
RHODANIC
RHODANISE
RHODANIZE
RHODIC
RHODIE
RHODIES
RHODINAL
RHODINALS
RHODIUM
RHODIUMS
RHODOLITE
RHODONITE
RHODOPSIN
RHODORA
RHODORAS
RHODOUS
RHODY
RHOEADINE
RHOMB
RHOMBI
RHOMBIC
RHOMBICAL
RHOMBOI
RHOMBOID
RHOMBOIDS
RHOMBOS
RHOMBS
RHOMBUS
RHOMBUSES
RHONCHAL
RHONCHI
RHONCHIAL
RHONCHUS
RHONE
RHONES
RHOPALIC
RHOPALISM
RHOS
RHOTACISE
RHOTACISM
RHOTACIST
RHOTACIZE
RHOTIC
RHOTICITY
RHUBARB
RHUBARBED
RHUBARBS
RHUBARBY
RHUMB

RHUMBA
RHUMBAED
RHUMBAING
RHUMBAS
RHUMBS
RHUS
RHUSES
RHY
RHYME
RHYMED
RHYMELESS
RHYMER
RHYMERS
RHYMES
RHYMESTER
RHYMING
RHYMIST
RHYMISTS
RHYNE
RHYNES
RHYOLITE
RHYOLITES
RHYOLITIC
RHYTA
RHYTHM
RHYTHMAL
RHYTHMED
RHYTHMI
RHYTHMIC
RHYTHMICS
RHYTHMISE
RHYTHMIST
RHYTHMIZE
RHYTHMS
RHYTHMUS
RHYTIDOME
RHYTINA
RHYTINAS
RHYTON
RHYTONS
RIA
RIAL
RIALS
RIALTO
RIALTOS
RIANCIES
RIANCY
RIANT
RIANTLY
RIAS
RIATA
RIATAS
RIB
RIBA
RIBALD
RIBALDLY
RIBALDRY
RIBALDS

RIBAND	RICEBIRDS	RICKSHA	RIDGEWAY
RIBANDS	RICED	RICKSHAS	RIDGEWAYS
RIBAS	RICER	RICKSHAW	RIDGIER
RIBATTUTA	RICERCAR	RICKSHAWS	RIDGIEST
RIBAUD	RICERCARE	RICKSTAND	RIDGIL
RIBAUDRED	RICERCARI	RICKSTICK	RIDGILS
RIBAUDRY	RICERCARS	RICKYARD	RIDGING
RIBAUDS	RICERCATA	RICKYARDS	RIDGINGS
RIBAVIRIN	RICERS	RICOCHET	RIDGLING
RIBBAND	RICES	RICOCHETS	RIDGLINGS
RIBBANDS	RICEY	RICOTTA	RIDGY
RIBBED	RICH	RICOTTAS	RIDICULE
RIBBER	RICHED	RICRAC	RIDICULED
RIBBERS	RICHEN	RICRACS	RIDICULER
RIBBIER	RICHENED	RICTAL	RIDICULES
RIBBIEST	RICHENING	RICTUS	RIDING
RIBBING	RICHENS	RICTUSES	RIDINGS
RIBBINGS	RICHER	RICY	RIDLEY
RIBBON	RICHES	RID	RIDLEYS
RIBBONED	RICHESSE	RIDABLE	RIDOTTO
RIBBONING	RICHESSES	RIDDANCE	RIDOTTOS
RIBBONRY	RICHEST	RIDDANCES	RIDS
RIBBONS	RICHING	RIDDED	RIEL
RIBBONY	RICHLY	RIDDEN	RIELS
RIBBY	RICHNESS	RIDDER	RIEM
RIBCAGE	RICHT	RIDDERS	RIEMPIE
RIBCAGES	RICHTED	RIDDING	RIEMPIES
RIBES	RICHTER	RIDDLE	RIEMS
RIBGRASS	RICHTEST	RIDDLED	RIESLING
RIBIBE	RICHTING	RIDDLER	RIESLINGS
RIBIBES	RICHTS	RIDDLERS	RIEVE
RIBIBLE	RICHWEED	RIDDLES	RIEVER
RIBIBLES	RICHWEEDS	RIDDLING	RIEVERS
RIBIER	RICIER	RIDDLINGS	RIEVES
RIBIERS	RICIEST	RIDE	RIEVING
RIBLESS	RICIN	RIDEABLE	RIF
RIBLET	RICING	RIDENT	RIFAMPIN
RIBLETS	RICINS	RIDER	RIFAMPINS
RIBLIKE	RICINUS	RIDERED	RIFAMYCIN
RIBOSE	RICINUSES	RIDERLESS	RIFE
RIBOSES	RICK	RIDERS	RIFELY
RIBOSOMAL	RICKED	RIDERSHIP	RIFENESS
RIBOSOME	RICKER	RIDES	RIFER
RIBOSOMES	RICKERS	RIDGE	RIFEST
RIBOZYMAL	RICKETIER	RIDGEBACK	RIFF
RIBOZYME	RICKETILY	RIDGED	RIFFAGE
RIBOZYMES	RICKETS	RIDGEL	RIFFAGES
RIBS	RICKETTY	RIDGELIKE	RIFFED
RIBSTON	RICKETY	RIDGELINE	RIFFING
RIBSTONE	RICKEY	RIDGELING	RIFFLE
RIBSTONES	RICKEYS	RIDGELS	RIFFLED
RIBSTONS	RICKING	RIDGEPOLE	RIFFLER
RIBWORK	RICKLE	RIDGER	RIFFLERS
RIBWORKS	RICKLES	RIDGERS	RIFFLES
RIBWORT	RICKLY	RIDGES	RIFFLING
RIBWORTS	RICKRACK	RIDGETOP	RIFFOLA
RICE	RICKRACKS	RIDGETOPS	RIFFOLAS
RICEBIRD	RICKS	RIDGETREE	RIFFRAFF

RIFFRAFFS
RIFFS
RIFLE
RIFLEBIRD
RIFLED
RIFLEMAN
RIFLEMEN
RIFLER
RIFLERIES
RIFLERS
RIFLERY
RIFLES
RIFLING
RIFLINGS
RIFLIP
RIFLIPS
RIFS
RIFT
RIFTE
RIFTED
RIFTIER
RIFTIEST
RIFTING
RIFTLESS
RIFTS
RIFTY
RIG
RIGADOON
RIGADOONS
RIGATONI
RIGATONIS
RIGAUDON
RIGAUDONS
RIGG
RIGGALD
RIGGALDS
RIGGED
RIGGER
RIGGERS
RIGGING
RIGGINGS
RIGGISH
RIGGS
RIGHT
RIGHTABLE
RIGHTABLY
RIGHTED
RIGHTEN
RIGHTENED
RIGHTENS
RIGHTEOUS
RIGHTER
RIGHTERS
RIGHTEST
RIGHTFUL
RIGHTIES
RIGHTING
RIGHTINGS

RIGHTISH
RIGHTISM
RIGHTISMS
RIGHTIST
RIGHTTSTS
RIGHTLESS
RIGHTLY
RIGHTMOST
RIGHTNESS
RIGHTO
RIGHTOS
RIGHTS
RIGHTSIZE
RIGHTWARD
RIGHTY
RIGID
RIGIDER
RIGIDEST
RIGIDIFY
RIGIDISE
RIGIDISED
RIGIDISES
RIGIDITY
RIGIDIZE
RIGIDIZED
RIGIDIZES
RIGIDLY
RIGIDNESS
RIGIDS
RIGLIN
RIGLING
RIGLINGS
RIGLINS
RIGMAROLE
RIGOL
RIGOLL
RIGOLLS
RIGOLS
RIGOR
RIGORISM
RIGORISMS
RIGORIST
RIGORISTS
RIGOROUS
RIGORS
RIGOUR
RIGOURS
RIGOUT
RIGOUTS
RIGS
RIGSDALER
RIGWIDDIE
RIGWOODIE
RIJSTAFEL
RIKISHA
RIKISHAS
RIKISHI
RIKSHAW

RIKSHAWS
RILE
RILED
RILES
RILEY
RILIER
RILIEST
RILIEVI
RILIEVO
RILING
RILL
RILLE
RILLED
RILLES
RILLET
RILLETS
RILLETTES
RILLING
RILLMARK
RILLMARKS
RILLS
RIM
RIMA
RIMAE
RIMAYE
RIMAYES
RIME
RIMED
RIMELESS
RIMER
RIMERS
RIMES
RIMESTER
RIMESTERS
RIMFIRE
RIMFIRES
RIMIER
RIMIEST
RIMINESS
RIMING
RIMLAND
RIMLANDS
RIMLESS
RIMMED
RIMMER
RIMMERS
RIMMING
RIMMINGS
RIMOSE
RIMOSELY
RIMOSITY
RIMOUS
RIMPLE
RIMPLED
RIMPLES
RIMPLING
RIMROCK
RIMROCKS

RIMS
RIMSHOT
RIMSHOTS
RIMU
RIMUS
RIMY
RIN
RIND
RINDED
RINDIER
RINDIEST
RINDING
RINDLESS
RINDS
RINDY
RINE
RINES
RING
RINGBARK
RINGBARKS
RINGBIT
RINGBITS
RINGBOLT
RINGBOLTS
RINGBONE
RINGBONES
RINGDOVE
RINGDOVES
RINGED
RINGENT
RINGER
RINGERS
RINGGIT
RINGGITS
RINGHALS
RINGING
RINGINGLY
RINGINGS
RINGLESS
RINGLET
RINGLETED
RINGLETS
RINGLIKE
RINGMAN
RINGMEN
RINGNECK
RINGNECKS
RINGS
RINGSIDE
RINGSIDER
RINGSIDES
RINGSTAND
RINGSTER
RINGSTERS
RINGTAIL
RINGTAILS
RINGTAW
RINGTAWS

RINGTONE	RIPENED	RIPTIDES	RITORNELL
RINGTONES	RIPENER	RIRORIRO	RITORNELS
RINGTOSS	RIPENERS	RIRORIROS	RITS
RINGWAY	RIPENESS	RISALDAR	RITT
RINGWAYS	RIPENING	RISALDARS	RITTED
RINGWISE	RIPENS	RISE	RITTER
RINGWOMB	RIPER	RISEN	RITTERS
RINGWOMBS	RIPERS	RISER	RITTING
RINGWORK	RIPES	RISERS	RITTS
RINGWORKS	RIPEST	RISES	RITUAL
RINGWORM	RIPIENI	RISHI	RITUALISE
RINGWORMS	RIPIENIST	RISHIS	RITUALISM
RINK	RIPIENO	RISIBLE	RITUALIST
RINKED	RIPIENOS	RISIBLES	RITUALIZE
RINKHALS	RIPING	RISIBLY	RITUALLY
RINKING	RIPOFF	RISING	RITUALS
RINKS	RIPOFFS	RISINGS	RITZ
RINNING	RIPOST	RISK	RITZES
RINS	RIPOSTE	RISKED	RITZIER
RINSABLE	RIPOSTED	RISKER	RITZIEST
RINSE	RIPOSTES	RISKERS	RITZILY
RINSEABLE	RIPOSTING	RISKFUL	RITZINESS
RINSED	RIPOSTS	RISKIER	RITZY
RINSER	RIPP	RISKIEST	RIVA
RINSERS	RIPPABLE	RISKILY	RIVAGE
RINSES	RIPPED	RISKINESS	RIVAGES
RINSIBLE	RIPPER	RISKING	RIVAL
RINSING	RIPPERS	RISKLESS	RIVALED
RINSINGS	RIPPIER	RISKS	RIVALESS
RIOJA	RIPPIERS	RISKY	RIVALING
RIOJAS	RIPPING	RISOLUTO	RIVALISE
RIOT	RIPPINGLY	RISOTTO	RIVALISED
RIOTED	RIPPLE	RISOTTOS	RIVALISES
RIOTER	RIPPLED	RISP	RIVALITY
RIOTERS	RIPPLER	RISPED	RIVALIZE
RIOTING	RIPPLERS	RISPETTI	RIVALIZED
RIOTINGS	RIPPLES	RISPETTO	RIVALIZES
RIOTISE	RIPPLET	RISPING	RIVALLED
RIOTISES	RIPPLETS	RISPINGS	RIVALLESS
RIOTIZE	RIPPLIER	RISPS	RIVALLING
RIOTIZES	RIPPLIEST	RISQUE	RIVALRIES
RIOTOUS	RIPPLING	RISQUES	RIVALROUS
RIOTOUSLY	RIPPLINGS	RISSOLE	RIVALRY
RIOTRIES	RIPPLY	RISSOLES	RIVALS
RIOTRY	RIPPS	RISTRA	RIVALSHIP
RIOTS	RIPRAP	RISTRAS	RIVAS
RIP	RIPRAPPED	RISUS	RIVE
RIPARIAL	RIPRAPS	RISUSES	RIVED
RIPARIAN	RIPS	RIT	RIVEL
RIPARIANS	RIPSAW	RITARD	RIVELLED
RIPCORD	RIPSAWED	RITARDS	RIVELLING
RIPCORDS	RIPSAWING	RITE	RIVELS
RIPE	RIPSAWN	RITELESS	RIVEN
RIPECK	RIPSAWS	RITENUTO	RIVER
RIPECKS	RIPSTOP	RITENUTOS	RIVERAIN
RIPED	RIPSTOPS	RITES	RIVERAINS
RIPELY	RIPT	RITONAVIR	RIVERBANK
RIPEN	RIPTIDE	RITORNEL	RIVERBED

RIVERBEDS	RIZZORED	ROARS	ROBUSTAS
RIVERBOAT	RIZZORING	ROARY	ROBUSTER
RIVERED	RIZZORS	ROAST	ROBUSTEST
RIVERET	ROACH	ROASTED	ROBUSTLY
RIVERETS	ROACHED	ROASTER	ROC
RIVERHEAD	ROACHES	ROASTERS	ROCAILLE
RIVERINE	ROACHING	ROASTING	ROCAILLES
RIVERLESS	ROAD	ROASTINGS	ROCAMBOLE
RIVERLIKE	ROADBED	ROASTS	ROCH
RIVERMAN	ROADBEDS	ROATE	ROCHES
RIVERMEN	ROADBLOCK	ROATED	ROCHET
RIVERS	ROADCRAFT	ROATES	ROCHETS
RIVERSIDE	ROADEO	ROATING	ROCK
RIVERWARD	ROADEOS	ROB	ROCKABIES
RIVERWAY	ROADHOUSE	ROBALO	ROCKABLE
RIVERWAYS	ROADIE	ROBALOS	ROCKABY
RIVERWEED	ROADIES	ROBAND	ROCKABYE
RIVERY	ROADING	ROBANDS	ROCKABYES
RIVES	ROADINGS	ROBBED	ROCKAWAY
RIVET	ROADKILL	ROBBER	ROCKAWAYS
RIVETED	ROADKILLS	ROBBERIES	ROCKBOUND
RIVETER	ROADLESS	ROBBERS	ROCKCRESS
RIVETERS	ROADMAN	ROBBERY	ROCKED
RIVETING	ROADMEN	ROBBIN	ROCKER
RIVETINGS	ROADS	ROBBING	ROCKERIES
RIVETS	ROADSHOW	ROBBINS	ROCKERS
RIVETTED	ROADSHOWS	ROBE	ROCKERY
RIVETTING	ROADSIDE	ROBED	ROCKET
RIVIERA	ROADSIDES	ROBES	ROCKETED
RIVIERAS	ROADSMAN	ROBIN	ROCKETEER
RIVIERE	ROADSMEN	ROBING	ROCKETER
RIVIERES	ROADSTEAD	ROBINGS	ROCKETERS
RIVING	ROADSTER	ROBINIA	ROCKETING
RIVLIN	ROADSTERS	ROBINIAS	ROCKETRY
RIVLINS	ROADWAY	ROBINS	ROCKETS
RIVO	ROADWAYS	ROBLE	ROCKFALL
RIVOS	ROADWORK	ROBLES	ROCKFALLS
RIVULET	ROADWORKS	ROBORANT	ROCKFISH
RIVULETS	ROAM	ROBORANTS	ROCKHOUND
RIVULOSE	ROAMED	ROBOT	ROCKIER
RIYAL	ROAMER	ROBOTIC	ROCKIERS
RIYALS	ROAMERS	ROBOTICS	ROCKIEST
RIZ	ROAMING	ROBOTISE	ROCKILY
RIZA	ROAMINGS	ROBOTISED	ROCKINESS
RIZARD	ROAMS	ROBOTISES	ROCKING
RIZARDS	ROAN	ROBOTISM	ROCKINGLY
RIZAS	ROANS	ROBOTISMS	ROCKINGS
RIZZAR	ROAR	ROBOTIZE	ROCKLAY
RIZZARED	ROARED	ROBOTIZED	ROCKLAYS
RIZZARING	ROARER	ROBOTIZES	ROCKLESS
RIZZARS	ROARERS	ROBOTRIES	ROCKLIKE
RIZZART	ROARIE	ROBOTRY	ROCKLING
RIZZARTS	ROARIER	ROBOTS	ROCKLINGS
RIZZER	ROARIEST	ROBS	ROCKOON
RIZZERED	ROARING	ROBURITE	ROCKOONS
RIZZERING	ROARINGLY	ROBURITES	ROCKROSE
RIZZERS	ROARINGS	ROBUST	ROCKROSES
RIZZOR	ROARMING	ROBUSTA	ROCKS

ROCKSHAFT	ROGERED	ROLAMITES	ROMANCES
ROCKSLIDE	ROGERING	ROLE	ROMANCING
ROCKWATER	ROGERINGS	ROLES	ROMANISE
ROCKWEED	ROGERS	ROLF	ROMANISED
ROCKWEEDS	ROGNON	ROLFED	ROMANISES
ROCKWORK	ROGNONS	ROLFER	ROMANIZE
ROCKWORKS	ROGUE	ROLFERS	ROMANIZED
ROCKY	ROGUED	ROLFING	ROMANIZES
ROCOCO	ROGUEING	ROLFINGS	ROMANO
ROCOCOS	ROGUERIES	ROLFS	ROMANOS
ROCQUET	ROGUERY	ROLL	ROMANS
ROCQUETS	ROGUES	ROLLABLE	ROMANTIC
ROCS	ROGUESHIP	ROLLAWAY	ROMANTICS
ROD	ROGUING	ROLLAWAYS	ROMANZA
RODDED	ROGUISH	ROLLBACK	ROMANZAS
RODDING	ROGUISHLY	ROLLBACKS	ROMAS
RODDINGS	ROGUY	ROLLBAR	ROMAUNT
RODE	ROIL	ROLLBARS	ROMAUNTS
RODED	ROILED	ROLLED	ROMCOM
RODENT	ROILIER	ROLLER	ROMCOMS
RODENTS	ROILIEST	ROLLERS	ROMELDALE
RODEO	ROILING	ROLLICK	ROMEO
RODEOED	ROILS	ROLLICKED	ROMEOS
RODEOING	ROILY	ROLLICKS	ROMNEYA
RODEOS	ROIN	ROLLICKY	ROMNEYAS
RODES	ROINED	ROLLING	ROMP
RODEWAY	ROINING	ROLLINGS	ROMPED
RODEWAYS	ROINISH	ROLLMOP	ROMPER
RODFISHER	ROINS	ROLLMOPS	ROMPERS
RODGERSIA	ROIST	ROLLNECK	ROMPING
RODING	ROISTED	ROLLNECKS	ROMPINGLY
RODINGS	ROISTER	ROLLOCK	ROMPISH
RODLESS	ROISTERED	ROLLOCKS	ROMPISHLY
RODLIKE	ROISTERER	ROLLOUT	ROMPS
RODMAN	ROISTERS	ROLLOUTS	ROMS
RODMEN	ROISTING	ROLLOVER	RONCADOR
RODS	ROISTS	ROLLOVERS	RONCADORS
RODSMAN	ROJAK	ROLLS	RONDACHE
RODSMEN	ROJAKS	ROLLTOP	RONDACHES
RODSTER	ROJI	ROLLWAY	RONDAVEL
RODSTERS	ROJIS	ROLLWAYS	RONDAVELS
ROE	ROK	ROM	RONDE
ROEBUCK	ROKE	ROMA	RONDEAU
ROEBUCKS	ROKED	ROMAGE	RONDEAUX
ROED	ROKELAY	ROMAGES	RONDEL
ROEMER	ROKELAYS	ROMAIKA	RONDELET
ROEMERS	ROKER	ROMAIKAS	RONDELETS
ROENTGEN	ROKERS	ROMAINE	RONDELLE
ROENTGENS	ROKES	ROMAINES	RONDELLES
ROES	ROKIER	ROMAJI	RONDELS
ROESTONE	ROKIEST	ROMAJIS	RONDES
ROESTONES	ROKING	ROMAL	RONDINO
ROGALLO	ROKKAKU	ROMALS	RONDINOS
ROGALLOS	ROKS	ROMAN	RONDO
ROGATION	ROKY	ROMANCE	RONDOS
ROGATIONS	ROLAG	ROMANCED	RONDURE
ROGATORY	ROLAGS	ROMANCER	RONDURES
ROGER	ROLAMITE	ROMANCERS	RONE

RONEO
RONEOED
RONEOING
RONEOS
RONEPTPE
RONEPIPES
RONES
RONG
RONGGENG
RONGGENGS
RONIN
RONINS
RONION
RONIONS
RONNE
RONNEL
RONNELS
RONNIE
RONNIES
RONNING
RONT
RONTE
RONTES
RONTGEN
RONTGENS
RONTS
RONYON
RONYONS
RONZER
RONZERS
ROO
ROOD
ROODS
ROOF
ROOFED
ROOFER
ROOFERS
ROOFIE
ROOFIER
ROOFIES
ROOFIEST
ROOFING
ROOFINGS
ROOFLESS
ROOFLIKE
ROOFLINE
ROOFLINES
ROOFS
ROOFSCAPE
ROOFTOP
ROOFTOPS
ROOFTREE
ROOFTREES
ROOFY
ROOIBOS
ROOIKAT
ROOIKATS
ROOINEK

ROOINEKS
ROOK
ROOKED
ROOKERIES
ROOKERY
ROOKIE
ROOKIER
ROOKIES
ROOKIEST
ROOKING
ROOKISH
ROOKS
ROOKY
ROOM
ROOMED
ROOMER
ROOMERS
ROOMETTE
ROOMETTES
ROOMFUL
ROOMFULS
ROOMIE
ROOMIER
ROOMIES
ROOMIEST
ROOMILY
ROOMINESS
ROOMING
ROOMMATE
ROOMMATES
ROOMS
ROOMSOME
ROOMY
ROON
ROONS
ROOP
ROOPED
ROOPIER
ROOPIEST
ROOPING
ROOPIT
ROOPS
ROOPY
ROORBACH
ROORBACHS
ROORBACK
ROORBACKS
ROOS
ROOSA
ROOSAS
ROOSE
ROOSED
ROOSER
ROOSERS
ROOSES
ROOSING
ROOST
ROOSTED

ROOSTER
ROOSTERS
ROOSTING
ROOSTS
ROOT
ROOTAGE
ROOTAGES
ROOTCAP
ROOTCAPS
ROOTED
ROOTEDLY
ROOTER
ROOTERS
ROOTHOLD
ROOTHOLDS
ROOTIER
ROOTIES
ROOTIEST
ROOTINESS
ROOTING
ROOTINGS
ROOTLE
ROOTLED
ROOTLES
ROOTLESS
ROOTLET
ROOTLETS
ROOTLIKE
ROOTLING
ROOTS
ROOTSIER
ROOTSIEST
ROOTSTALK
ROOTSTOCK
ROOTSY
ROOTWORM
ROOTWORMS
ROOTY
ROPABLE
ROPE
ROPEABLE
ROPED
ROPELIKE
ROPER
ROPERIES
ROPERS
ROPERY
ROPES
ROPEWALK
ROPEWALKS
ROPEWAY
ROPEWAYS
ROPEWORK
ROPEWORKS
ROPEY
ROPIER
ROPIEST
ROPILY

ROPINESS
ROPING
ROPINGS
ROPY
ROQUE
ROQUES
ROQUET
ROQUETED
ROQUETING
ROQUETS
ROQUETTE
ROQUETTES
RORAL
RORE
RORES
RORIC
RORID
RORIE
RORIER
RORIEST
RORQUAL
RORQUALS
RORT
RORTED
RORTER
RORTERS
RORTIER
RORTIEST
RORTING
RORTS
RORTY
RORY
ROSACE
ROSACEA
ROSACEAS
ROSACEOUS
ROSACES
ROSAKER
ROSAKERS
ROSALIA
ROSALIAS
ROSANILIN
ROSARIA
ROSARIAN
ROSARIANS
ROSARIES
ROSARIUM
ROSARIUMS
ROSARY
ROSBIF
ROSBIFS
ROSCID
ROSCOE
ROSCOES
ROSE
ROSEAL
ROSEATE
ROSEATELY

ROSEBAY	ROSING	ROTATES	ROTTED
ROSEBAYS	ROSINING	ROTATING	ROTTEN
ROSEBOWL	ROSINOL	ROTATION	ROTTENER
ROSEBOWLS	ROSINOLS	ROTATIONS	ROTTENEST
ROSEBUD	ROSINOUS	ROTATIVE	ROTTENLY
ROSEBUDS	ROSINS	ROTATOR	ROTTENS
ROSEBUSH	ROSINWEED	ROTATORES	ROTTER
ROSED	ROSINY	ROTATORS	ROTTERS
ROSEFINCH	ROSIT	ROTATORY	ROTTES
ROSEFISH	ROSITED	ROTAVATE	ROTTING
ROSEHIP	ROSITING	ROTAVATED	ROTULA
ROSEHIPS	ROSITS	ROTAVATES	ROTULAE
ROSELESS	ROSMARINE	ROTAVATOR	ROTULAS
ROSELIKE	ROSOGLIO	ROTAVIRUS	ROTUND
ROSELLA	ROSOGLIOS	ROTCH	ROTUNDA
ROSELLAS	ROSOLIO	ROTCHE	ROTUNDAS
ROSELLE	ROSOLIOS	ROTCHES	ROTUNDATE
ROSELLES	ROSSER	ROTCHIE	ROTUNDED
ROSEMARY	ROSSERS	ROTCHIES	ROTUNDER
ROSEOLA	ROST	ROTE	ROTUNDEST
ROSEOLAR	ROSTED	ROTED	ROTUNDING
ROSEOLAS	ROSTELLA	ROTENONE	ROTUNDITY
ROSERIES	ROSTELLAR	ROTENONES	ROTUNDLY
ROSEROOT	ROSTELLUM	ROTES	ROTUNDS
ROSEROOTS	ROSTER	ROTGRASS	ROTURIER
ROSERY	ROSTERED	ROTGUT	ROTURIERS
ROSES	ROSTERING	ROTGUTS	ROUBLE
ROSESLUG	ROSTERS	ROTHER	ROUBLES
ROSESLUGS	ROSTI	ROTHERS	ROUCHE
ROSET	ROSTING	ROTI	ROUCHES
ROSETED	ROSTIS	ROTIFER	ROUCOU
ROSETING	ROSTRA	ROTIFERAL	ROUCOUS
ROSETS	ROSTRAL	ROTIFERAN	ROUE
ROSETTE	ROSTRALLY	ROTIFERS	ROUEN
ROSETTED	ROSTRATE	ROTIFORM	ROUENS
ROSETTES	ROSTRATED	ROTING	ROUES
ROSETTY	ROSTRUM	ROTIS	ROUGE
ROSETY	ROSTRUMS	ROTL	ROUGED
ROSEWATER	ROSTS	ROTLS	ROUGES
ROSEWOOD	ROSULA	ROTO	ROUGH
ROSEWOODS	ROSULAS	ROTOGRAPH	ROUGHAGE
ROSHI	ROSULATE	ROTOLO	ROUGHAGES
ROSHIS	ROSY	ROTOLOS	ROUGHBACK
ROSIED	ROSYING	ROTON	ROUGHCAST
ROSIER	ROT	ROTONS	ROUGHDRY
ROSIERE	ROTA	ROTOR	ROUGHED
ROSIERES	ROTACHUTE	ROTORS	ROUGHEN
ROSIERS	ROTAL	ROTOS	ROUGHENED
ROSIES	ROTAMETER	ROTOTILL	ROUGHENS
ROSIEST	ROTAN	ROTOTILLS	ROUGHER
ROSILY	ROTANS	ROTOVATE	ROUGHERS
ROSIN	ROTAPLANE	ROTOVATED	ROUGHEST
ROSINATE	ROTARIES	ROTOVATES	ROUGHHEW
ROSINATES	ROTARY	ROTOVATOR	ROUGHHEWN
ROSINED	ROTAS	ROTS	ROUGHHEWS
ROSINER	ROTATABLE	ROTTAN	ROUGHIE
ROSINERS	ROTATE	ROTTANS	ROUGHIES
ROSINESS	ROTATED	ROTTE	ROUGHING

ROUGHISH	ROUNDSMEN	ROUTINISE	ROWNDS
ROUGHLEG	ROUNDTRIP	ROUTINISM	ROWOVER
ROUGHLEGS	ROUNDUP	ROUTINIST	ROWOVERS
ROUGHLY	ROUNDUPS	ROUTINIZE	ROWS
ROUGHNECK	ROUNDURE	ROUTOUS	ROWT
ROUGHNESS	ROUNDURES	ROUTOUSLY	ROWTED
ROUGHS	ROUNDWOOD	ROUTS	ROWTH
ROUGHSHOD	ROUNDWORM	ROUX	ROWTHS
ROUGHT	ROUP	ROVE	ROWTING
ROUGHY	ROUPED	ROVED	ROWTS
ROUGING	ROUPET	ROVEN	ROYAL
ROUILLE	ROUPIER	ROVER	ROYALET
ROUILLES	ROUPIEST	ROVERS	ROYALETS
ROUL	ROUPILY	ROVES	ROYALISE
ROULADE	ROUPING	ROVING	ROYALISED
ROULADES	ROUPIT	ROVINGLY	ROYALISES
ROULE	ROUPS	ROVINGS	ROYALISM
ROULEAU	ROUPY	ROW	ROYALISMS
ROULEAUS	ROUSANT	ROWABLE	ROYALIST
ROULEAUX	ROUSE	ROWAN	ROYALISTS
ROULES	ROUSED	ROWANS	ROYALIZE
ROULETTE	ROUSEMENT	ROWBOAT	ROYALIZED
ROULETTED	ROUSER	ROWBOATS	ROYALIZES
ROULETTES	ROUSERS	ROWDEDOW	ROYALLER
ROULS	ROUSES	ROWDEDOWS	ROYALLEST
ROUM	ROUSING	ROWDIER	ROYALLY
ROUMING	ROUSINGLY	ROWDIES	ROYALMAST
ROUMINGS	ROUSSEAU	ROWDIEST	ROYALS
ROUMS	ROUSSEAUS	ROWDILY	ROYALTIES
ROUNCE	ROUSSETTE	ROWDINESS	ROYALTY
ROUNCES	ROUST	ROWDY	ROYNE
ROUNCEVAL	ROUSTED	ROWDYDOW	ROYNED
ROUNCIES	ROUSTER	ROWDYDOWS	ROYNES
ROUNCY	ROUSTERS	ROWDYISH	ROYNING
ROUND	ROUSTING	ROWDYISM	ROYNISH
ROUNDARCH	ROUSTS	ROWDYISMS	ROYST
ROUNDBALL	ROUT	ROWED	ROYSTED
ROUNDED	ROUTE	ROWEL	ROYSTER
ROUNDEDLY	ROUTED	ROWELED	ROYSTERED
ROUNDEL	ROUTEING	ROWELING	ROYSTERER
ROUNDELAY	ROUTEMAN	ROWELLED	ROYSTERS
ROUNDELS	ROUTEMEN	ROWELLING	ROYSTING
ROUNDER	ROUTER	ROWELS	ROYSTS
ROUNDERS	ROUTERS	ROWEN	ROZELLE
ROUNDEST	ROUTES	ROWENS	ROZELLES
ROUNDHAND	ROUTEWAY	ROWER	ROZET
ROUNDHEEL	ROUTEWAYS	ROWERS	ROZETED
ROUNDING	ROUTH	ROWING	ROZETING
ROUNDINGS	ROUTHIE	ROWINGS	ROZETS
ROUNDISH	ROUTHIER	ROWLOCK	ROZIT
ROUNDLE	ROUTHIEST	ROWLOCKS	ROZITED
ROUNDLES	ROUTHS	ROWME	ROZITING
ROUNDLET	ROUTINE	ROWMES	ROZITS
ROUNDLETS	ROUTINEER	ROWND	ROZZER
ROUNDLY	ROUTINELY	ROWNDED	ROZZERS
ROUNDNESS	ROUTINES	ROWNDELL	RUANA
ROUNDS	ROUTING	ROWNDELLS	RUANAS
ROUNDSMAN	ROUTINGS	ROWNDING	RUB

RUBABOO
RUBABOOS
RUBACE
RUBACES
RUBAI
RUBAIYAT
RUBASSE
RUBASSES
RUBATI
RUBATO
RUBATOS
RUBBABOO
RUBBABOOS
RUBBED
RUBBER
RUBBERED
RUBBERIER
RUBBERING
RUBBERISE
RUBBERIZE
RUBBERS
RUBBERY
RUBBET
RUBBIDIES
RUBBIDY
RUBBIES
RUBBING
RUBBINGS
RUBBISH
RUBBISHED
RUBBISHES
RUBBISHLY
RUBBISHY
RUBBIT
RUBBITIES
RUBBITY
RUBBLE
RUBBLED
RUBBLES
RUBBLIER
RUBBLIEST
RUBBLING
RUBBLY
RUBBOARD
RUBBOARDS
RUBBY
RUBDOWN
RUBDOWNS
RUBE
RUBEFIED
RUBEFIES
RUBEFY
RUBEFYING
RUBEL
RUBELLA
RUBELLAN
RUBELLANS
RUBELLAS

RUBELLITE
RUBELS
RUBEOLA
RUBEOLAR
RUBEOLAS
RUBES
RUBESCENT
RUBICELLE
RUBICON
RUBICONED
RUBICONS
RUBICUND
RUBIDIC
RUBIDIUM
RUBIDIUMS
RUBIED
RUBIER
RUBIES
RUBIEST
RUBIFIED
RUBIFIES
RUBIFY
RUBIFYING
RUBIGO
RUBIGOS
RUBIN
RUBINE
RUBINEOUS
RUBINES
RUBINS
RUBIOUS
RUBLE
RUBLES
RUBOFF
RUBOFFS
RUBOUT
RUBOUTS
RUBRIC
RUBRICAL
RUBRICATE
RUBRICIAN
RUBRICS
RUBS
RUBSTONE
RUBSTONES
RUBUS
RUBY
RUBYING
RUBYLIKE
RUC
RUCHE
RUCHED
RUCHES
RUCHING
RUCHINGS
RUCK
RUCKED
RUCKING

RUCKLE
RUCKLED
RUCKLES
RUCKLING
RUCKMAN
RUCKMEN
RUCKS
RUCKSACK
RUCKSACKS
RUCKSEAT
RUCKSEATS
RUCKUS
RUCKUSES
RUCOLA
RUCOLAS
RUCS
RUCTATION
RUCTION
RUCTIONS
RUCTIOUS
RUD
RUDACEOUS
RUDAS
RUDASES
RUDBECKIA
RUDD
RUDDED
RUDDER
RUDDERS
RUDDIED
RUDDIER
RUDDIES
RUDDIEST
RUDDILY
RUDDINESS
RUDDING
RUDDLE
RUDDLED
RUDDLEMAN
RUDDLEMEN
RUDDLES
RUDDLING
RUDDOCK
RUDDOCKS
RUDDS
RUDDY
RUDDYING
RUDE
RUDELY
RUDENESS
RUDER
RUDERAL
RUDERALS
RUDERIES
RUDERY
RUDES
RUDESBIES
RUDESBY

RUDEST
RUDIE
RUDIES
RUDIMENT
RUDIMENTS
RUDISH
RUDS
RUE
RUED
RUEFUL
RUEFULLY
RUEING
RUEINGS
RUELLE
RUELLES
RUELLIA
RUELLIAS
RUER
RUERS
RUES
RUFESCENT
RUFF
RUFFE
RUFFED
RUFFES
RUFFIAN
RUFFIANED
RUFFIANLY
RUFFIANS
RUFFIN
RUFFING
RUFFINS
RUFFLE
RUFFLED
RUFFLER
RUFFLERS
RUFFLES
RUFFLIER
RUFFLIEST
RUFFLIKE
RUFFLING
RUFFLINGS
RUFFLY
RUFFS
RUFIYAA
RUFIYAAS
RUFOUS
RUG
RUGA
RUGAE
RUGAL
RUGALACH
RUGATE
RUGBIES
RUGBY
RUGELACH
RUGGED
RUGGEDER

RUGGEDEST	RULLIONS	RUMNESS	RUNDS
RUGGEDISE	RULLOCK	RUMNESSES	RUNE
RUGGEDIZE	RULLOCKS	RUMOR	RUNECRAFT
RUGGEDLY	RULY	RUMORED	RUNED
RUGGELACH	RUM	RUMORING	RUNELIKE
RUGGER	RUMAKI	RUMOROUS	RUNES
RUGGERS	RUMAKIS	RUMORS	RUNFLAT
RUGGIER	RUMAL	RUMOUR	RUNG
RUGGIEST	RUMALS	RUMOURED	RUNGLESS
RUGGING	RUMBA	RUMOURER	RUNGS
RUGGINGS	RUMBAED	RUMOURERS	RUNIC
RUGGY	RUMBAING	RUMOURING	RUNKLE
RUGLIKE	RUMBAS	RUMOURS	RUNKLED
RUGOLA	RUMBELOW	RUMP	RUNKLES
RUGOLAS	RUMBELOWS	RUMPED	RUNKLING
RUGOSA	RUMBLE	RUMPIES	RUNLESS
RUGOSAS	RUMBLED	RUMPING	RUNLET
RUGOSE	RUMBLER	RUMPLE	RUNLETS
RUGOSELY	RUMBLERS	RUMPLED	RUNNABLE
RUGOSITY	RUMBLES	RUMPLES	RUNNEL
RUGOUS	RUMBLIER	RUMPLESS	RUNNELS
RUGS	RUMBLIEST	RUMPLIER	RUNNER
RUGULOSE	RUMBLING	RUMPLIEST	RUNNERS
RUIN	RUMBLINGS	RUMPLING	RUNNET
RUINABLE	RUMBLY	RUMPLY	RUNNETS
RUINATE	RUMBO	RUMPO	RUNNIER
RUINATED	RUMBOS	RUMPOS	RUNNIEST
RUINATES	RUME	RUMPS	RUNNINESS
RUINATING	RUMEN	RUMPUS	RUNNING
RUINATION	RUMENS	RUMPUSES	RUNNINGLY
RUINED	RUMES	RUMPY	RUNNINGS
RUINER	RUMINA	RUMRUNNER	RUNNION
RUINERS	RUMINAL	RUMS	RUNNIONS
RUING	RUMINANT	RUN	RUNNY
RUINGS	RUMINANTS	RUNABOUT	RUNOFF
RUINING	RUMINATE	RUNABOUTS	RUNOFFS
RUININGS	RUMINATED	RUNAGATE	RUNOUT
RUINOUS	RUMINATES	RUNAGATES	RUNOUTS
RUINOUSLY	RUMINATOR	RUNANGA	RUNOVER
RUINS	RUMKIN	RUNAROUND	RUNOVERS
RUKH	RUMKINS	RUNAWAY	RUNRIG
RUKHS	RUMLY	RUNAWAYS	RUNRIGS
RULABLE	RUMMAGE	RUNBACK	RUNROUND
RULE	RUMMAGED	RUNBACKS	RUNROUNDS
RULED	RUMMAGER	RUNCH	RUNS
RULELESS	RUMMAGERS	RUNCHES	RUNT
RULER	RUMMAGES	RUNCIBLE	RUNTED
RULERED	RUMMAGING	RUNCINATE	RUNTIER
RULERING	RUMMER	RUND	RUNTIEST
RULERS	RUMMERS	RUNDALE	RUNTINESS
RULERSHIP	RUMMEST	RUNDALES	RUNTISH
RULES	RUMMIER	RUNDLE	RUNTISHLY
RULESSE	RUMMIES	RUNDLED	RUNTS
RULIER	RUMMIEST	RUNDLES	RUNTY
RULIEST	RUMMILY	RUNDLET	RUNWAY
RULING	RUMMINESS	RUNDLETS	RUNWAYS
RULINGS	RUMMISH	RUNDOWN	RUPEE
RULLION	RUMMY	RUNDOWNS	RUPEES

RUPIA
RUPIAH
RUPIAHS
RUPIAS
RUPTURE
RUPTURED
RUPTURES
RUPTURING
RURAL
RURALISE
RURALISED
RURALISES
RURALISM
RURALISMS
RURALIST
RURALISTS
RURALITE
RURALITES
RURALITY
RURALIZE
RURALIZED
RURALIZES
RURALLY
RURALNESS
RURALS
RURBAN
RURP
RURPS
RURU
RURUS
RUSA
RUSALKA
RUSALKAS
RUSAS
RUSCUS
RUSCUSES
RUSE
RUSES
RUSH
RUSHED
RUSHEE
RUSHEES
RUSHEN
RUSHER
RUSHERS
RUSHES
RUSHIER
RUSHIEST
RUSHINESS
RUSHING
RUSHINGS
RUSHLIGHT
RUSHLIKE
RUSHY
RUSINE
RUSK
RUSKS
RUSMA

RUSMAS
RUSSE
RUSSEL
RUSSELS
RUSSET
RUSSETED
RUSSETING
RUSSETS
RUSSETY
RUSSIA
RUSSIAS
RUSSIFIED
RUSSIFIES
RUSSIFY
RUSSULA
RUSSULAE
RUSSULAS
RUST
RUSTABLE
RUSTED
RUSTIC
RUSTICAL
RUSTICALS
RUSTICANA
RUSTICATE
RUSTICIAL
RUSTICISE
RUSTICISM
RUSTICITY
RUSTICIZE
RUSTICLY
RUSTICS
RUSTIER
RUSTIEST
RUSTILY
RUSTINESS
RUSTING
RUSTINGS
RUSTLE
RUSTLED
RUSTLER
RUSTLERS
RUSTLES
RUSTLESS
RUSTLING
RUSTLINGS
RUSTPROOF
RUSTRE
RUSTRED
RUSTRES
RUSTS
RUSTY
RUT
RUTABAGA
RUTABAGAS
RUTACEOUS
RUTH
RUTHENIC

RUTHENIUM
RUTHFUL
RUTHFULLY
RUTHLESS
RUTHS
RUTILANT
RUTILATED
RUTILE
RUTILES
RUTIN
RUTINS
RUTS
RUTTED
RUTTER
RUTTERS
RUTTIER
RUTTIEST
RUTTILY
RUTTINESS
RUTTING
RUTTINGS
RUTTISH
RUTTISHLY
RUTTY
RYA
RYAL
RYALS
RYAS
RYBAT
RYBATS
RYBAUDRYE
RYE
RYEBREAD
RYEBREADS
RYEFLOUR
RYEFLOURS
RYEGRASS
RYEPECK
RYEPECKS
RYES
RYFE
RYKE
RYKED
RYKES
RYKING
RYMME
RYMMED
RYMMES
RYMMING
RYND
RYNDS
RYOKAN
RYOKANS
RYOT
RYOTS
RYOTWARI
RYOTWARIS
RYPE

RYPECK
RYPECKS
RYPER

S

SAB
SABADILLA
SABAL
SABALS
SABATON
SABATONS
SABAYON
SABAYONS
SABBAT
SABBATH
SABBATHS
SABBATIC
SABBATICS
SABBATINE
SABBATISE
SABBATISM
SABBATIZE
SABBATS
SABBED
SABBING
SABE
SABED
SABEING
SABELLA
SABELLAS
SABER
SABERED
SABERING
SABERLIKE
SABERS
SABES
SABIN
SABINE
SABINES
SABINS
SABIR
SABIRS
SABKHA
SABKHAH
SABKHAHS
SABKHAS
SABKHAT
SABKHATS
SABLE
SABLED
SABLEFISH
SABLES
SABLING
SABOT
SABOTAGE
SABOTAGED
SABOTAGES
SABOTEUR

SABOTEURS
SABOTIER
SABOTIERS
SABOTS
SABRA
SABRAS
SABRE
SABRED
SABRES
SABREUR
SABREURS
SABRING
SABS
SABULINE
SABULOSE
SABULOUS
SABURRA
SABURRAL
SABURRAS
SAC
SACATON
SACATONS
SACBUT
SACBUTS
SACCADE
SACCADES
SACCADIC
SACCATE
SACCHARIC
SACCHARIN
SACCHARUM
SACCIFORM
SACCOI
SACCOS
SACCOSES
SACCULAR
SACCULATE
SACCULE
SACCULES
SACCULI
SACCULUS
SACELLA
SACELLUM
SACHEM
SACHEMDOM
SACHEMIC
SACHEMS
SACHET
SACHETED
SACHETS
SACK
SACKABLE
SACKAGE

SACKAGES
SACKBUT
SACKBUTS
SACKCLOTH
SACKED
SACKER
SACKERS
SACKFUL
SACKFULS
SACKING
SACKINGS
SACKLESS
SACKLIKE
SACKS
SACKSFUL
SACLESS
SACLIKE
SACQUE
SACQUES
SACRA
SACRAL
SACRALGIA
SACRALISE
SACRALIZE
SACRALS
SACRAMENT
SACRARIA
SACRARIAL
SACRARIUM
SACRED
SACREDLY
SACRIFICE
SACRIFIDE
SACRIFIED
SACRIFIES
SACRIFY
SACRILEGE
SACRING
SACRINGS
SACRIST
SACRISTAN
SACRISTS
SACRISTY
SACRUM
SACRUMS
SACS
SAD
SADDEN
SADDENED
SADDENING
SADDENS
SADDER
SADDEST

SADDHU
SADDHUS
SADDISH
SADDLE
SADDLEBAG
SADDLEBOW
SADDLED
SADDLER
SADDLERS
SADDLERY
SADDLES
SADDLING
SADDO
SADDOES
SADDOS
SADE
SADES
SADHANA
SADHANAS
SADHE
SADHES
SADHU
SADHUS
SADI
SADIRON
SADIRONS
SADIS
SADISM
SADISMS
SADIST
SADISTIC
SADISTS
SADLY
SADNESS
SADNESSES
SADO
SADOS
SADZA
SADZAS
SAE
SAECULUM
SAECULUMS
SAETER
SAETERS
SAFARI
SAFARIED
SAFARIING
SAFARIS
SAFARIST
SAFARISTS
SAFE
SAFED
SAFEGUARD

SAFELIGHT	SAGEST	SAICES	SAINTISMS
SAFELY	SAGGAR	SAICK	SAINTLESS
SAFENESS	SAGGARD	SAICKS	SAINTLIER
SAFER	SAGGARDS	SAICS	SAINTLIKE
SAFES	SAGGARED	SAID	SAINTLILY
SAFEST	SAGGARING	SAIDEST	SAINTLING
SAFETIED	SAGGARS	SAIDS	SAINTLY
SAFETIES	SAGGED	SAIDST	SAINTS
SAFETY	SAGGER	SAIGA	SAINTSHIP
SAFETYING	SAGGERED	SAIGAS	SAIQUE
SAFETYMAN	SAGGERING	SAIKEI	SAIQUES
SAFETYMEN	SAGGERS	SAIKEIS	SAIR
SAFFIAN	SAGGIER	SAIKLESS	SAIRED
SAFFIANS	SAGGIEST	SAIL	SAIRER
SAFFLOWER	SAGGING	SAILABLE	SAIREST
SAFFRON	SAGGINGS	SAILBOARD	SAIRING
SAFFRONED	SAGGY	SAILBOAT	SAIRS
SAFFRONS	SAGIER	SAILBOATS	SAIS
SAFFRONY	SAGIEST	SAILCLOTH	SAIST
SAFING	SAGINATE	SAILED	SAITH
SAFRANIN	SAGINATED	SAILER	SAITHE
SAFRANINE	SAGINATES	SAILERS	SAITHES
SAFRANINS	SAGITTA	SAILFISH	SAITHS
SAFROL	SAGITTAL	SAILING	SAIYID
SAFROLE	SAGITTARY	SAILINGS	SAIYIDS
SAFROLES	SAGITTAS	SAILLESS	SAJOU
SAFROLS	SAGITTATE	SAILMAKER	SAJOUS
SAFRONAL	SAGO	SAILOR	SAKAI
SAFRONALS	SAGOIN	SAILORING	SAKAIS
SAFT	SAGOINS	SAILORLY	SAKE
SAFTER	SAGOS	SAILORS	SAKER
SAFTEST	SAGOUIN	SAILPLANE	SAKERET
SAG	SAGOUINS	SAILROOM	SAKERETS
SAGA	SAGRADA	SAILROOMS	SAKERS
SAGACIOUS	SAGS	SAILS	SAKES
SAGACITY	SAGUARO	SAIM	SAKI
SAGAMAN	SAGUAROS	SAIMIN	SAKIA
SAGAMEN	SAGUIN	SAIMINS	SAKIAS
SAGAMORE	SAGUINS	SAIMIRI	SAKIEH
SAGAMORES	SAGUM	SAIMIRIS	SAKIEHS
SAGANASH	SAGY	SAIMS	SAKIS
SAGAPENUM	SAHEB	SAIN	SAKIYEH
SAGAS	SAHEBS	SAINE	SAKIYEHS
SAGATHIES	SAHIB	SAINED	SAKKOI
SAGATHY	SAHIBA	SAINFOIN	SAKKOS
SAGBUT	SAHIBAH	SAINFOINS	SAKKOSES
SAGBUTS	SAHIBAHS	SAINING	SAKSAUL
SAGE	SAHIBAS	SAINS	SAKSAULS
SAGEBRUSH	SAHIBS	SAINT	SAL
SAGELY	SAHIWAL	SAINTDOM	SALAAM
SAGENE	SAHIWALS	SAINTDOMS	SALAAMED
SAGENES	SAHUARO	SAINTED	SALAAMING
SAGENESS	SAHUAROS	SAINTESS	SALAAMS
SAGENITE	SAI	SAINTFOIN	SALABLE
SAGENITES	SAIBLING	SAINTHOOD	SALABLY
SAGENITIC	SAIBLINGS	SAINTING	SALACIOUS
SAGER	SAIC	SAINTISH	SALACITY
SAGES	SAICE	SAINTISM	SALAD

SALADANG
SALADANGS
SALADE
SALADES
SALADING
SALADINGS
SALADS
SALAL
SALALS
SALAMI
SALAMIS
SALAMON
SALAMONS
SALANGANE
SALARIAT
SALARIATS
SALARIED
SALARIES
SALARY
SALARYING
SALARYMAN
SALARYMEN
SALBAND
SALBANDS
SALCHOW
SALCHOWS
SALE
SALEABLE
SALEABLY
SALEP
SALEPS
SALERATUS
SALERING
SALERINGS
SALEROOM
SALEROOMS
SALES
SALESGIRL
SALESLADY
SALESMAN
SALESMEN
SALESROOM
SALET
SALETS
SALEWD
SALEYARD
SALEYARDS
SALFERN
SALFERNS
SALIAUNCE
SALIC
SALICES
SALICET
SALICETA
SALICETS
SALICETUM
SALICIN
SALICINE

SALICINES
SALICINS
SALICYLIC
SALIENCE
SALIENCES
SALIENCY
SALIENT
SALIENTLY
SALIENTS
SALIFIED
SALIFIES
SALIFY
SALIFYING
SALIGOT
SALIGOTS
SALIMETER
SALIMETRY
SALINA
SALINAS
SALINE
SALINES
SALINISE
SALINISED
SALINISES
SALINITY
SALINIZE
SALINIZED
SALINIZES
SALIVA
SALIVAL
SALIVARY
SALIVAS
SALIVATE
SALIVATED
SALIVATES
SALIVATOR
SALIX
SALL
SALLAD
SALLADS
SALLAL
SALLALS
SALLE
SALLEE
SALLEES
SALLES
SALLET
SALLETS
SALLIED
SALLIER
SALLIERS
SALLIES
SALLOW
SALLOWED
SALLOWER
SALLOWEST
SALLOWING
SALLOWISH

SALLOWLY
SALLOWS
SALLOWY
SALLY
SALLYING
SALLYPORT
SALMI
SALMIS
SALMON
SALMONET
SALMONETS
SALMONID
SALMONIDS
SALMONOID
SALMONS
SALOL
SALOLS
SALOMETER
SALON
SALONS
SALOON
SALOONS
SALOOP
SALOOPS
SALOP
SALOPIAN
SALOPS
SALP
SALPA
SALPAE
SALPAS
SALPIAN
SALPIANS
SALPICON
SALPICONS
SALPID
SALPIDS
SALPIFORM
SALPINGES
SALPINX
SALPINXES
SALPS
SALS
SALSA
SALSAED
SALSAING
SALSAS
SALSE
SALSES
SALSIFIES
SALSIFY
SALSILLA
SALSILLAS
SALT
SALTANDO
SALTANT
SALTANTS
SALTATE

SALTATED
SALTATES
SALTATING
SALTATION
SALTATO
SALTATORY
SALTBOX
SALTBOXES
SALTBUSH
SALTCAT
SALTCATS
SALTCHUCK
SALTED
SALTER
SALTERN
SALTERNS
SALTERS
SALTEST
SALTFISH
SALTIE
SALTIER
SALTIERS
SALTIES
SALTIEST
SALTILY
SALTINE
SALTINES
SALTINESS
SALTING
SALTINGS
SALTIRE
SALTIRES
SALTISH
SALTISHLY
SALTLESS
SALTLIKE
SALTLY
SALTNESS
SALTO
SALTOED
SALTOING
SALTOS
SALTPAN
SALTPANS
SALTPETER
SALTPETRE
SALTS
SALTUS
SALTUSES
SALTWATER
SALTWORK
SALTWORKS
SALTWORT
SALTWORTS
SALTY
SALUBRITY
SALUE
SALUED

SALUES	SAMAS	SAMMING	SANDALLED
SALUING	SAMBA	SAMMY	SANDALS
SALUKI	SAMBAED	SAMNITIS	SANDARAC
SALUKIS	SAMBAING	SAMOSA	SANDARACH
SALURETIC	SAMBAL	SAMOSAS	SANDARACS
SALUTARY	SAMBALS	SAMOVAR	SANDBAG
SALUTE	SAMBAR	SAMOVARS	SANDBAGS
SALUTED	SAMBARS	SAMOYED	SANDBANK
SALUTER	SAMBAS	SAMOYEDS	SANDBANKS
SALUTERS	SAMBHAR	SAMP	SANDBAR
SALUTES	SAMBHARS	SAMPAN	SANDBARS
SALUTING	SAMBHUR	SAMPANS	SANDBLAST
SALVABLE	SAMBHURS	SAMPHIRE	SANDBOX
SALVABLY	SAMBO	SAMPHIRES	SANDBOXES
SALVAGE	SAMBOS	SAMPI	SANDBOY
SALVAGED	SAMBUCA	SAMPIRE	SANDBOYS
SALVAGEE	SAMBUCAS	SAMPIRES	SANDBUR
SALVAGEES	SAMBUKE	SAMPIS	SANDBURR
SALVAGER	SAMBUKES	SAMPLE	SANDBURRS
SALVAGERS	SAMBUR	SAMPLED	SANDBURS
SALVAGES	SAMBURS	SAMPLER	SANDCRACK
SALVAGING	SAME	SAMPLERS	SANDDAB
SALVARSAN	SAMECH	SAMPLERY	SANDDABS
SALVATION	SAMECHS	SAMPLES	SANDED
SALVATORY	SAMEK	SAMPLING	SANDEK
SALVE	SAMEKH	SAMPLINGS	SANDEKS
SALVED	SAMEKHS	SAMPS	SANDER
SALVER	SAMEKS	SAMS	SANDERS
SALVERS	SAMEL	SAMSARA	SANDERSES
SALVES	SAMELY	SAMSARAS	SANDFISH
SALVETE	SAMEN	SAMSHOO	SANDFLIES
SALVETES	SAMENESS	SAMSHOOS	SANDFLY
SALVIA	SAMES	SAMSHU	SANDGLASS
SALVIAS	SAMEY	SAMSHUS	SANDHEAP
SALVIFIC	SAMFOO	SAMURAI	SANDHEAPS
SALVING	SAMFOOS	SAMURAIS	SANDHI
SALVINGS	SAMFU	SAN	SANDHILL
SALVO	SAMFUS	SANATIVE	SANDHILLS
SALVOED	SAMIEL	SANATORIA	SANDHIS
SALVOES	SAMIELS	SANATORY	SANDHOG
SALVOING	SAMIER	SANBENITO	SANDHOGS
SALVOR	SAMIEST	SANCAI	SANDIER
SALVORS	SAMISEN	SANCAIS	SANDIEST
SALVOS	SAMISENS	SANCHO	SANDINESS
SALWAR	SAMITE	SANCHOS	SANDING
SAM	SAMITES	SANCTA	SANDINGS
SAMA	SAMITHI	SANCTIFY	SANDIVER
SAMAAN	SAMITHIS	SANCTION	SANDIVERS
SAMAANS	SAMITI	SANCTIONS	SANDLESS
SAMADHI	SAMITIS	SANCTITY	SANDLIKE
SAMADHIS	SAMIZDAT	SANCTUARY	SANDLING
SAMAN	SAMIZDATS	SANCTUM	SANDLINGS
SAMANS	SAMLET	SANCTUMS	SANDLOT
SAMARA	SAMLETS	SAND	SANDLOTS
SAMARAS	SAMLOR	SANDABLE	SANDMAN
SAMARITAN	SAMLORS	SANDAL	SANDMEN
SAMARIUM	SAMMED	SANDALED	SANDPAPER
SAMARIUMS	SAMMIES	SANDALING	SANDPEEP

SANDPEEPS	SANICLE	SANTALINS	SAPIENCE
SANDPILE	SANICLES	SANTALOL	SAPIENCES
SANDPILES	SANIDINE	SANTALOLS	SAPIENCY
SANDPIPER	SANIDINES	SANTALS	SAPIENS
SANDPIT	SANIES	SANTERA	SAPIENT
SANDPITS	SANIFIED	SANTERAS	SAPIENTLY
SANDPUMP	SANIFIES	SANTERIA	SAPIENTS
SANDPUMPS	SANIFY	SANTERIAS	SAPLESS
SANDS	SANIFYING	SANTERO	SAPLING
SANDSHOE	SANING	SANTEROS	SAPLINGS
SANDSHOES	SANIOUS	SANTIMI	SAPODILLA
SANDSOAP	SANITARIA	SANTIMS	SAPOGENIN
SANDSOAPS	SANITARY	SANTIMU	SAPONARIA
SANDSPOUT	SANITATE	SANTIR	SAPONATED
SANDSPUR	SANITATED	SANTIRS	SAPONIFY
SANDSPURS	SANITATES	SANTO	SAPONIN
SANDSTONE	SANITIES	SANTOL	SAPONINE
SANDSTORM	SANITISE	SANTOLINA	SAPONINES
SANDWICH	SANITISED	SANTOLS	SAPONINS
SANDWORM	SANITISER	SANTON	SAPONITE
SANDWORMS	SANITISES	SANTONICA	SAPONITES
SANDWORT	SANITIZE	SANTONIN	SAPOR
SANDWORTS	SANITIZED	SANTONINS	SAPORIFIC
SANDY	SANITIZER	SANTONS	SAPOROUS
SANE	SANITIZES	SANTOOR	SAPORS
SANED	SANITORIA	SANTOORS	SAPOTA
SANELY	SANITY	SANTOS	SAPOTAS
SANENESS	SANJAK	SANTOUR	SAPOTE
SANER	SANJAKS	SANTOURS	SAPOTES
SANES	SANK	SANTS	SAPOUR
SANEST	SANKO	SANTUR	SAPOURS
SANG	SANKOS	SANTURS	SAPPAN
SANGA	SANNIE	SANYASI	SAPPANS
SANGAR	SANNIES	SANYASIS	SAPPED
SANGAREE	SANNOP	SAOUARI	SAPPER
SANGAREES	SANNOPS	SAOUARIS	SAPPERS
SANGARS	SANNUP	SAP	SAPPHIC
SANGAS	SANNUPS	SAPAJOU	SAPPHICS
SANGER	SANNYASI	SAPAJOUS	SAPPHIRE
SANGERS	SANNYASIN	SAPAN	SAPPHIRED
SANGFROID	SANNYASIS	SAPANS	SAPPHIRES
SANGH	SANPAN	SAPANWOOD	SAPPHISM
SANGHAT	SANPANS	SAPEGO	SAPPHISMS
SANGHATS	SANPRO	SAPEGOES	SAPPHIST
SANGHS	SANPROS	SAPELE	SAPPHISTS
SANGLIER	SANS	SAPELES	SAPPIER
SANGLIERS	SANSA	SAPFUL	SAPPIEST
SANGO	SANSAR	SAPHEAD	SAPPILY
SANGOMA	SANSARS	SAPHEADED	SAPPINESS
SANGOMAS	SANSAS	SAPHEADS	SAPPING
SANGOS	SANSEI	SAPHENA	SAPPLE
SANGRIA	SANSEIS	SAPHENAE	SAPPLED
SANGRIAS	SANSERIF	SAPHENAS	SAPPLES
SANGS	SANSERIFS	SAPHENOUS	SAPPLING
SANGUIFY	SANT	SAPID	SAPPY
SANGUINE	SANTAL	SAPIDITY	SAPRAEMIA
SANGUINED	SANTALIC	SAPIDLESS	SAPRAEMIC
SANGUINES	SANTALIN	SAPIDNESS	SAPREMIA

SAPREMIAS	SARDAR	SARONGS	SASSIES
SAPREMIC	SARDARS	SARONIC	SASSIEST
SAPROBE	SARDEL	SAROS	SASSILY
SAPROBES	SARDELLE	SAROSES	SASSINESS
SAPROBIAL	SARDELLES	SARPANCH	SASSING
SAPROBIC	SARDELS	SARRASIN	SASSOLIN
SAPROLITE	SARDINE	SARRASINS	SASSOLINS
SAPROPEL	SARDINED	SARRAZIN	SASSOLITE
SAPROPELS	SARDINES	SARRAZINS	SASSWOOD
SAPROZOIC	SARDINING	SARS	SASSWOODS
SAPS	SARDIUS	SARSAR	SASSY
SAPSAGO	SARDIUSES	SARSARS	SASSYWOOD
SAPSAGOS	SARDONIAN	SARSDEN	SASTRA
SAPSUCKER	SARDONIC	SARSDENS	SASTRAS
SAPUCAIA	SARDONYX	SARSEN	SASTRUGA
SAPUCAIAS	SARDS	SARSENET	SASTRUGI
SAPWOOD	SARED	SARSENETS	SAT
SAPWOODS	SAREE	SARSENS	SATAI
SAR	SAREES	SARSNET	SATAIS
SARABAND	SARGASSO	SARSNETS	SATANG
SARABANDE	SARGASSOS	SARTOR	SATANGS
SARABANDS	SARGASSUM	SARTORIAL	SATANIC
SARAFAN	SARGE	SARTORIAN	SATANICAL
SARAFANS	SARGES	SARTORII	SATANISM
SARAN	SARGO	SARTORIUS	SATANISMS
SARANGI	SARGOS	SARTORS	SATANIST
SARANGIS	SARGOSES	SARUS	SATANISTS
SARANS	SARGUS	SARUSES	SATANITY
SARAPE	SARGUSES	SASARARA	SATARA
SARAPES	SARI	SASARARAS	SATARAS
SARBACANE	SARIN	SASER	SATAY
SARCASM	SARING	SASERS	SATAYS
SARCASMS	SARINS	SASH	SATCHEL
SARCASTIC	SARIS	SASHAY	SATCHELED
SARCENET	SARK	SASHAYED	SATCHELS
SARCENETS	SARKIER	SASHAYING	SATE
SARCINA	SARKIEST	SASHAYS	SATED
SARCINAE	SARKING	SASHED	SATEDNESS
SARCINAS	SARKINGS	SASHES	SATEEN
SARCOCARP	SARKS	SASHIMI	SATEENS
SARCODE	SARKY	SASHIMIS	SATELESS
SARCODES	SARMENT	SASHING	SATELLES
SARCODIC	SARMENTA	SASHLESS	SATELLITE
SARCOID	SARMENTS	SASIN	SATEM
SARCOIDS	SARMENTUM	SASINE	SATES
SARCOLOGY	SARMIE	SASINES	SATI
SARCOMA	SARMIES	SASINS	SATIABLE
SARCOMAS	SARNEY	SASKATOON	SATIABLY
SARCOMATA	SARNEYS	SASQUATCH	SATIATE
SARCOMERE	SARNIE	SASS	SATIATED
SARCONET	SARNIES	SASSABIES	SATIATES
SARCONETS	SAROD	SASSABY	SATIATING
SARCOPTIC	SARODE	SASSAFRAS	SATIATION
SARCOSOME	SARODES	SASSARARA	SATIETIES
SARCOUS	SARODIST	SASSE	SATIETY
SARD	SARODISTS	SASSED	SATIN
SARDANA	SARODS	SASSES	SATINED
SARDANAS	SARONG	SASSIER	SATINET

SATINETS	SATYRESS	SAUNTER	SAVE
SATINETTA	SATYRIC	SAUNTERED	SAVEABLE
SATINETTE	SATYRICAL	SAUNTERER	SAVED
SATING	SATYRID	SAUNTERS	SAVEGARD
SATINING	SATYRIDS	SAUNTING	SAVEGARDS
SATINPOD	SATYRISK	SAUNTS	SAVELOY
SATINPODS	SATYRISKS	SAUREL	SAVELOYS
SATINS	SATYRLIKE	SAURELS	SAVER
SATINWOOD	SATYRS	SAURIAN	SAVERS
SATINY	SAU	SAURIANS	SAVES
SATIRE	SAUBA	SAURIES	SAVEY
SATIRES	SAUBAS	SAUROID	SAVEYED
SATIRIC	SAUCE	SAUROPOD	SAVEYING
SATIRICAL	SAUCEBOAT	SAUROPODS	SAVEYS
SATIRISE	SAUCEBOX	SAURY	SAVIN
SATIRISED	SAUCED	SAUSAGE	SAVINE
SATIRISER	SAUCELESS	SAUSAGES	SAVINES
SATIRISES	SAUCEPAN	SAUT	SAVING
SATIRIST	SAUCEPANS	SAUTE	SAVINGLY
SATIRISTS	SAUCEPOT	SAUTED	SAVINGS
SATIRIZE	SAUCEPOTS	SAUTEED	SAVINS
SATIRIZED	SAUCER	SAUTEEING	SAVIOR
SATIRIZER	SAUCERFUL	SAUTEES	SAVIORS
SATIRIZES	SAUCERS	SAUTEING	SAVIOUR
SATIS	SAUCES	SAUTERNE	SAVIOURS
SATISFICE	SAUCH	SAUTERNES	SAVOR
SATISFIED	SAUCHS	SAUTES	SAVORED
SATISFIER	SAUCIER	SAUTING	SAVORER
SATISFIES	SAUCIERS	SAUTOIR	SAVORERS
SATISFY	SAUCIEST	SAUTOIRE	SAVORIER
SATIVE	SAUCILY	SAUTOIRES	SAVORIES
SATORI	SAUCINESS	SAUTOIRS	SAVORIEST
SATORIS	SAUCING	SAUTS	SAVORILY
SATRAP	SAUCISSE	SAV	SAVORING
SATRAPAL	SAUCISSES	SAVABLE	SAVORLESS
SATRAPIES	SAUCISSON	SAVAGE	SAVOROUS
SATRAPS	SAUCY	SAVAGED	SAVORS
SATRAPY	SAUFGARD	SAVAGEDOM	SAVORY
SATSUMA	SAUFGARDS	SAVAGELY	SAVOUR
SATSUMAS	SAUGER	SAVAGER	SAVOURED
SATURABLE	SAUGERS	SAVAGERY	SAVOURER
SATURANT	SAUGH	SAVAGES	SAVOURERS
SATURANTS	SAUGHS	SAVAGEST	SAVOURIER
SATURATE	SAUGHY	SAVAGING	SAVOURIES
SATURATED	SAUL	SAVAGISM	SAVOURILY
SATURATER	SAULGE	SAVAGISMS	SAVOURING
SATURATES	SAULGES	SAVANNA	SAVOURLY
SATURATOR	SAULIE	SAVANNAH	SAVOURS
SATURNIC	SAULIES	SAVANNAHS	SAVOURY
SATURNIID	SAULS	SAVANNAS	SAVOY
SATURNINE	SAULT	SAVANT	SAVOYARD
SATURNISM	SAULTS	SAVANTE	SAVOYARDS
SATURNIST	SAUNA	SAVANTES	SAVOYS
SATYR	SAUNAED	SAVANTS	SAVS
SATYRA	SAUNAING	SAVARIN	SAVVEY
SATYRAL	SAUNAS	SAVARINS	SAVVEYED
SATYRALS	SAUNT	SAVATE	SAVVEYING
SATYRAS	SAUNTED	SAVATES	SAVVEYS

SAVVIED	SAXAULS	SCABIETIC	SCALDINGS
SAVVIER	SAXE	SCABIOSA	SCALDINI
SAVVIES	SAXES	SCABIOSAS	SCALDINO
SAVVIEST	SAXHORN	SCABIOUS	SCALDS
SAVVILY	SAXHORNS	SCABLAND	SCALDSHIP
SAVVINESS	SAXICOLE	SCABLANDS	SCALE
SAVVY	SAXIFRAGE	SCABLIKE	SCALED
SAVVYING	SAXITOXIN	SCABRID	SCALELESS
SAW	SAXONIES	SCABROUS	SCALELIKE
SAWAH	SAXONITE	SCABS	SCALENE
SAWAHS	SAXONITES	SCAD	SCALENI
SAWBILL	SAXONY	SCADS	SCALENUS
SAWBILLS	SAXOPHONE	SCAFF	SCALEPAN
SAWBLADE	SAXTUBA	SCAFFIE	SCALEPANS
SAWBLADES	SAXTUBAS	SCAFFIES	SCALER
SAWBONES	SAY	SCAFFOLD	SCALERS
SAWBUCK	SAYABLE	SCAFFOLDS	SCALES
SAWBUCKS	SAYED	SCAFFS	SCALETAIL
SAWDER	SAYEDS	SCAG	SCALEUP
SAWDERED	SAYER	SCAGGED	SCALEUPS
SAWDERING	SAYERS	SCAGGING	SCALEWORK
SAWDERS	SAYEST	SCAGLIA	SCALIER
SAWDUST	SAYID	SCAGLIAS	SCALIEST
SAWDUSTED	SAYIDS	SCAGLIOLA	SCALINESS
SAWDUSTS	SAYING	SCAGS	SCALING
SAWDUSTY	SAYINGS	SCAIL	SCALINGS
SAWED	SAYNE	SCAILED	SCALL
SAWER	SAYON	SCAILING	SCALLAWAG
SAWERS	SAYONARA	SCAILS	SCALLED
SAWFISH	SAYONARAS	SCAITH	SCALLIES
SAWFISHES	SAYONS	SCAITHED	SCALLION
SAWFLIES	SAYS	SCAITHING	SCALLIONS
SAWFLY	SAYST	SCAITHS	SCALLOP
SAWHORSE	SAYYID	SCALA	SCALLOPED
SAWHORSES	SAYYIDS	SCALABLE	SCALLOPER
SAWING	SAZ	SCALABLY	SCALLOPS
SAWINGS	SAZERAC	SCALADE	SCALLS
SAWLIKE	SAZERACS	SCALADES	SCALLY
SAWLOG	SAZES	SCALADO	SCALLYWAG
SAWLOGS	SAZHEN	SCALADOS	SCALOGRAM
SAWMILL	SAZHENS	SCALAE	SCALP
SAWMILLS	SAZZES	SCALAGE	SCALPED
SAWN	SBIRRI	SCALAGES	SCALPEL
SAWNEY	SBIRRO	SCALAR	SCALPELS
SAWNEYS	SCAB	SCALARE	SCALPER
SAWPIT	SCABBARD	SCALARES	SCALPERS
SAWPITS	SCABBARDS	SCALARS	SCALPING
SAWS	SCABBED	SCALATION	SCALPINGS
SAWSHARK	SCABBIER	SCALAWAG	SCALPINS
SAWSHARKS	SCABBIEST	SCALAWAGS	SCALPLESS
SAWTEETH	SCABBILY	SCALD	SCALPRUM
SAWTIMBER	SCABBING	SCALDED	SCALPRUMS
SAWTOOTH	SCABBLE	SCALDER	SCALPS
SAWYER	SCABBLED	SCALDERS	SCALY
SAWYERS	SCABBLES	SCALDFISH	SCAM
SAX	SCABBLING	SCALDHEAD	SCAMBLE
SAXATILE	SCABBY	SCALDIC	SCAMBLED
SAXAUL	SCABIES	SCALDING	SCAMBLER

SCAMBLERS	SCANTLE	SCARF	SCARTED
SCAMBLES	SCANTLED	SCARFED	SCARTH
SCAMBLING	SCANTLES	SCARFER	SCARTHS
SCAMEL	SCANTLING	SCARFERS	SCARTING
SCAMELS	SCANTLY	SCARFING	SCARTS
SCAMMED	SCANTNESS	SCARFINGS	SCARVES
SCAMMER	SCANTS	SCARFISH	SCARY
SCAMMERS	SCANTY	SCARFPIN	SCAT
SCAMMING	SCAPA	SCARFPINS	SCATBACK
SCAMMONY	SCAPAED	SCARFS	SCATBACKS
SCAMP	SCAPAING	SCARFSKIN	SCATCH
SCAMPED	SCAPAS	SCARFWISE	SCATCHES
SCAMPER	SCAPE	SCARIER	SCATH
SCAMPERED	SCAPED	SCARIEST	SCATHE
SCAMPERER	SCAPEGOAT	SCARIFIED	SCATHED
SCAMPERS	SCAPELESS	SCARIFIER	SCATHEFUL
SCAMPI	SCAPEMENT	SCARIFIES	SCATHES
SCAMPIES	SCAPES	SCARIFY	SCATHING
SCAMPING	SCAPHOID	SCARILY	SCATHS
SCAMPINGS	SCAPHOIDS	SCARINESS	SCATOLE
SCAMPIS	SCAPHOPOD	SCARING	SCATOLES
SCAMPISH	SCAPI	SCARIOSE	SCATOLOGY
SCAMPS	SCAPING	SCARIOUS	SCATS
SCAMS	SCAPOLITE	SCARLESS	SCATT
SCAMSTER	SCAPOSE	SCARLET	SCATTED
SCAMSTERS	SCAPPLE	SCARLETED	SCATTER
SCAMTO	SCAPPLED	SCARLETS	SCATTERED
SCAMTOS	SCAPPLES	SCARMOGE	SCATTERER
SCAN	SCAPPLING	SCARMOGES	SCATTERS
SCAND	SCAPULA	SCARP	SCATTERY
SCANDAL	SCAPULAE	SCARPA	SCATTIER
SCANDALED	SCAPULAR	SCARPAED	SCATTIEST
SCANDALS	SCAPULARS	SCARPAING	SCATTILY
SCANDENT	SCAPULARY	SCARPAS	SCATTING
SCANDIA	SCAPULAS	SCARPED	SCATTINGS
SCANDIAS	SCAPUS	SCARPER	SCATTS
SCANDIC	SCAR	SCARPERED	SCATTY
SCANDIUM	SCARAB	SCARPERS	SCAUD
SCANDIUMS	SCARABAEI	SCARPETTI	SCAUDED
SCANNABLE	SCARABEE	SCARPETTO	SCAUDING
SCANNED	SCARABEES	SCARPH	SCAUDS
SCANNER	SCARABOID	SCARPHED	SCAUP
SCANNERS	SCARABS	SCARPHING	SCAUPED
SCANNING	SCARCE	SCARPHS	SCAUPER
SCANNINGS	SCARCELY	SCARPINES	SCAUPERS
SCANS	SCARCER	SCARPING	SCAUPING
SCANSION	SCARCEST	SCARPINGS	SCAUPS
SCANSIONS	SCARCITY	SCARPS	SCAUR
SCANT	SCARE	SCARRE	SCAURED
SCANTED	SCARECROW	SCARRED	SCAURIES
SCANTER	SCARED	SCARRES	SCAURING
SCANTEST	SCAREDER	SCARRIER	SCAURS
SCANTIER	SCAREDEST	SCARRIEST	SCAURY
SCANTIES	SCAREHEAD	SCARRING	SCAVAGE
SCANTIEST	SCARER	SCARRINGS	SCAVAGER
SCANTILY	SCARERS	SCARRY	SCAVAGERS
SCANTING	SCARES	SCARS	SCAVAGES
SCANTITY	SCAREY	SCART	SCAVENGE

SCAVENGED	SCEPTICAL	SCHILLING	SCHMATTE
SCAVENGER	SCEPTICS	SCHIMMEL	SCHMATTES
SCAVENGES	SCEPTRAL	SCHIMMELS	SCHMEAR
SCAW	SCEPTRE	SCHISM	SCHMEARED
SCAWS	SCEPTRED	SCHISMA	SCHMEARS
SCAWTITE	SCEPTRES	SCHISMAS	SCHMECK
SCAWTITES	SCEPTRING	SCHISMS	SCHMECKS
SCAZON	SCEPTRY	SCHIST	SCHMEER
SCAZONS	SCERNE	SCHISTOSE	SCHMEERED
SCAZONTES	SCERNED	SCHISTOUS	SCHMEERS
SCAZONTIC	SCERNES	SCHISTS	SCHMELZ
SCEAT	SCERNING	SCHIZIER	SCHMELZE
SCEATT	SCHANSE	SCHIZIEST	SCHMELZES
SCEATTAS	SCHANSES	SCHIZO	SCHMICK
SCEDULE	SCHANTZE	SCHIZOID	SCHMO
SCEDULED	SCHANTZES	SCHIZOIDS	SCHMOCK
SCEDULES	SCHANZE	SCHIZONT	SCHMOCKS
SCEDULING	SCHANZES	SCHIZONTS	SCHMOE
SCELERAT	SCHAPPE	SCHIZOPOD	SCHMOES
SCELERATE	SCHAPPED	SCHIZOS	SCHMOOS
SCELERATS	SCHAPPES	SCHIZY	SCHMOOSE
SCENA	SCHAPSKA	SCHIZZIER	SCHMOOSED
SCENARIES	SCHAPSKAS	SCHIZZY	SCHMOOSES
SCENARIO	SCHATCHEN	SCHLAGER	SCHMOOZ
SCENARIOS	SCHAV	SCHLAGERS	SCHMOOZE
SCENARISE	SCHAVS	SCHLEMIEL	SCHMOOZED
SCENARIST	SCHECHITA	SCHLEMIHL	SCHMOOZER
SCENARIZE	SCHEDULAR	SCHLEP	SCHMOOZES
SCENARY	SCHEDULE	SCHLEPP	SCHMOOZY
SCENAS	SCHEDULED	SCHLEPPED	SCHMOS
SCEND	SCHEDULER	SCHLEPPER	SCHMUCK
SCENDED	SCHEDULES	SCHLEPPS	SCHMUCKS
SCENDING	SCHEELITE	SCHLEPPY	SCHMUTTER
SCENDS	SCHELLUM	SCHLEPS	SCHNAPPER
SCENE	SCHELLUMS	SCHLICH	SCHNAPPS
SCENED	SCHELM	SCHLICHS	SCHNAPS
SCENEMAN	SCHELMS	SCHLIERE	SCHNAPSES
SCENEMEN	SCHEMA	SCHLIEREN	SCHNAUZER
SCENERIES	SCHEMAS	SCHLIERIC	SCHNECKE
SCENERY	SCHEMATA	SCHLOCK	SCHNECKEN
SCENES	SCHEMATIC	SCHLOCKER	SCHNELL
SCENIC	SCHEME	SCHLOCKS	SCHNITZEL
SCENICAL	SCHEMED	SCHLOCKY	SCHNOOK
SCENICS	SCHEMER	SCHLONG	SCHNOOKS
SCENING	SCHEMERS	SCHLONGS	SCHNORKEL
SCENT	SCHEMES	SCHLOSS	SCHNORR
SCENTED	SCHEMIE	SCHLOSSES	SCHNORRED
SCENTFUL	SCHEMIES	SCHLUB	SCHNORRER
SCENTING	SCHEMING	SCHLUBS	SCHNORRS
SCENTINGS	SCHEMINGS	SCHLUMP	SCHNOZ
SCENTLESS	SCHERZI	SCHLUMPED	SCHNOZES
SCENTS	SCHERZO	SCHLUMPS	SCHNOZZ
SCEPSIS	SCHERZOS	SCHLUMPY	SCHNOZZES
SCEPSISES	SCHIAVONE	SCHMALTZ	SCHNOZZLE
SCEPTER	SCHIEDAM	SCHMALTZY	SCHOLAR
SCEPTERED	SCHIEDAMS	SCHMALZ	SCHOLARCH
SCEPTERS	SCHILLER	SCHMALZES	SCHOLARLY
SCEPTIC	SCHILLERS	SCHMALZY	SCHOLARS

SCHOLIA	SCIAENOID	SCISSOR	SCODIER
SCHOLIAST	SCIAMACHY	SCISSORED	SCODIEST
SCHOLION	SCIARID	SCISSORER	SCODY
SCHOLIUM	SCIARIDS	SCISSORS	SCOFF
SCHOLIUMS	SCIATIC	SCISSURE	SCOFFED
SCHOOL	SCIATICA	SCISSURES	SCOFFER
SCHOOLBAG	SCIATICAL	SCIURID	SCOFFERS
SCHOOLBOY	SCIATICAS	SCIURIDS	SCOFFING
SCHOOLDAY	SCIATICS	SCIURINE	SCOFFINGS
SCHOOLE	SCIENCE	SCIURINES	SCOFFLAW
SCHOOLED	SCIENCED	SCIUROID	SCOFFLAWS
SCHOOLERY	SCIENCES	SCLAFF	SCOFFS
SCHOOLES	SCIENT	SCLAFFED	SCOG
SCHOOLIE	SCIENTER	SCLAFFER	SCOGGED
SCHOOLIES	SCIENTIAL	SCLAFFERS	SCOGGING
SCHOOLING	SCIENTISE	SCLAFFING	SCOGS
SCHOOLKID	SCIENTISM	SCLAFFS	SCOINSON
SCHOOLMAN	SCIENTIST	SCLATE	SCOINSONS
SCHOOLMEN	SCIENTIZE	SCLATED	SCOLD
SCHOOLS	SCILICET	SCLATES	SCOLDABLE
SCHOONER	SCILLA	SCLATING	SCOLDED
SCHOONERS	SCILLAS	SCLAUNDER	SCOLDER
SCHORL	SCIMETAR	SCLAVE	SCOLDERS
SCHORLS	SCIMETARS	SCLAVES	SCOLDING
SCHOUT	SCIMITAR	SCLERA	SCOLDINGS
SCHOUTS	SCIMITARS	SCLERAE	SCOLDS
SCHRIK	SCIMITER	SCLERAL	SCOLECES
SCHRIKS	SCIMITERS	SCLERAS	SCOLECID
SCHROD	SCINCOID	SCLERE	SCOLECIDS
SCHRODS	SCINCOIDS	SCLEREID	SCOLECITE
SCHTICK	SCINTILLA	SCLEREIDE	SCOLECOID
SCHTICKS	SCIOLISM	SCLEREIDS	SCOLEX
SCHTIK	SCIOLISMS	SCLEREMA	SCOLIA
SCHTIKS	SCIOLIST	SCLEREMAS	SCOLICES
SCHTOOK	SCIOLISTS	SCLERES	SCOLIOMA
SCHTOOKS	SCIOLOUS	SCLERITE	SCOLIOMAS
SCHTOOM	SCIOLTO	SCLERITES	SCOLION
SCHTUCK	SCIOMACHY	SCLERITIC	SCOLIOSES
SCHTUCKS	SCIOMANCY	SCLERITIS	SCOLIOSIS
SCHUIT	SCION	SCLEROID	SCOLIOTIC
SCHUITS	SCIONS	SCLEROMA	SCOLLOP
SCHUL	SCIOPHYTE	SCLEROMAS	SCOLLOPED
SCHULN	SCIOSOPHY	SCLEROSAL	SCOLLOPS
SCHULS	SCIROC	SCLEROSE	SCOLYTID
SCHUSS	SCIROCCO	SCLEROSED	SCOLYTIDS
SCHUSSED	SCIROCCOS	SCLEROSES	SCOLYTOID
SCHUSSER	SCIROCS	SCLEROSIS	SCOMBRID
SCHUSSERS	SCIRRHI	SCLEROTAL	SCOMBRIDS
SCHUSSES	SCIRRHOID	SCLEROTIA	SCOMBROID
SCHUSSING	SCIRRHOUS	SCLEROTIC	SCOMFISH
SCHUYT	SCIRRHUS	SCLEROTIN	SCONCE
SCHUYTS	SCISSEL	SCLEROUS	SCONCED
SCHVARTZE	SCISSELS	SCLIFF	SCONCES
SCHWA	SCISSIL	SCLIFFS	SCONCHEON
SCHWARTZE	SCISSILE	SCLIM	SCONCING
SCHWAS	SCISSILS	SCLIMMED	SCONE
SCIAENID	SCISSION	SCLIMMING	SCONES
SCIAENIDS	SCISSIONS	SCLIMS	SCONTION

SCONTIONS
SCOOBIES
SCOOBY
SCOOCH
SCOOCHED
SCOOCHES
SCOOCHING
SCOOG
SCOOGED
SCOOGING
SCOOGS
SCOOP
SCOOPABLE
SCOOPED
SCOOPER
SCOOPERS
SCOOPFUL
SCOOPFULS
SCOOPING
SCOOPINGS
SCOOPS
SCOOPSFUL
SCOOSH
SCOOSHED
SCOOSHES
SCOOSHING
SCOOT
SCOOTCH
SCOOTCHED
SCOOTCHES
SCOOTED
SCOOTER
SCOOTERS
SCOOTING
SCOOTS
SCOP
SCOPA
SCOPAE
SCOPAS
SCOPATE
SCOPE
SCOPED
SCOPELID
SCOPELIDS
SCOPELOID
SCOPES
SCOPING
SCOPOLINE
SCOPS
SCOPULA
SCOPULAE
SCOPULAS
SCOPULATE
SCORBUTIC
SCORCH
SCORCHED
SCORCHER
SCORCHERS

SCORCHES
SCORCHING
SCORDATO
SCORE
SCORECARD
SCORED
SCORELESS
SCORELINE
SCOREPAD
SCOREPADS
SCORER
SCORERS
SCORES
SCORIA
SCORIAC
SCORIAE
SCORIFIED
SCORIFIER
SCORIFIES
SCORIFY
SCORING
SCORINGS
SCORIOUS
SCORN
SCORNED
SCORNER
SCORNERS
SCORNFUL
SCORNING
SCORNINGS
SCORNS
SCORODITE
SCORPER
SCORPERS
SCORPIOID
SCORPION
SCORPIONS
SCORRENDO
SCORSE
SCORSED
SCORSER
SCORSERS
SCORSES
SCORSING
SCOT
SCOTCH
SCOTCHED
SCOTCHES
SCOTCHING
SCOTER
SCOTERS
SCOTIA
SCOTIAS
SCOTOMA
SCOTOMAS
SCOTOMATA
SCOTOMIA
SCOTOMIAS

SCOTOMIES
SCOTOMY
SCOTOPHIL
SCOTOPIA
SCOTOPIAS
SCOTOPIC
SCOTS
SCOTTIE
SCOTTIES
SCOUG
SCOUGED
SCOUGING
SCOUGS
SCOUNDREL
SCOUP
SCOUPED
SCOUPING
SCOUPS
SCOUR
SCOURED
SCOURER
SCOURERS
SCOURGE
SCOURGED
SCOURGER
SCOURGERS
SCOURGES
SCOURGING
SCOURIE
SCOURIES
SCOURING
SCOURINGS
SCOURS
SCOURSE
SCOURSED
SCOURSES
SCOURSING
SCOUSE
SCOUSER
SCOUSERS
SCOUSES
SCOUT
SCOUTED
SCOUTER
SCOUTERS
SCOUTH
SCOUTHER
SCOUTHERS
SCOUTHERY
SCOUTHS
SCOUTING
SCOUTINGS
SCOUTS
SCOW
SCOWDER
SCOWDERED
SCOWDERS
SCOWED

SCOWING
SCOWL
SCOWLED
SCOWLER
SCOWLERS
SCOWLING
SCOWLS
SCOWP
SCOWPED
SCOWPING
SCOWPS
SCOWRER
SCOWRERS
SCOWRIE
SCOWRIES
SCOWS
SCOWTH
SCOWTHER
SCOWTHERS
SCOWTHS
SCOZZA
SCOZZAS
SCRAB
SCRABBED
SCRABBING
SCRABBLE
SCRABBLED
SCRABBLER
SCRABBLES
SCRABBLY
SCRABS
SCRAE
SCRAES
SCRAG
SCRAGGED
SCRAGGIER
SCRAGGILY
SCRAGGING
SCRAGGLY
SCRAGGY
SCRAGS
SCRAICH
SCRAICHED
SCRAICHS
SCRAIGH
SCRAIGHED
SCRAIGHS
SCRAM
SCRAMB
SCRAMBED
SCRAMBING
SCRAMBLE
SCRAMBLED
SCRAMBLER
SCRAMBLES
SCRAMBS
SCRAMJET
SCRAMJETS

SCRAMMED	SCRAWL	SCREET	SCRIES
SCRAMMING	SCRAWLED	SCREETED	SCRIEVE
SCRAMS	SCRAWLER	SCREETING	SCRIEVED
SCRAN	SCRAWLERS	SCREETS	SCRIEVES
SCRANCH	SCRAWLIER	SCREEVE	SCRIEVING
SCRANCHED	SCRAWLING	SCREEVED	SCRIGGLE
SCRANCHES	SCRAWLS	SCREEVER	SCRIGGLED
SCRANNEL	SCRAWLY	SCREEVERS	SCRIGGLES
SCRANNELS	SCRAWM	SCREEVES	SCRIGGLY
SCRANNIER	SCRAWMED	SCREEVING	SCRIKE
SCRANNY	SCRAWMING	SCREICH	SCRIKED
SCRANS	SCRAWMS	SCREICHED	SCRIKES
SCRAP	SCRAWNIER	SCREICHES	SCRIKING
SCRAPABLE	SCRAWNILY	SCREICHS	SCRIM
SCRAPBOOK	SCRAWNY	SCREIGH	SCRIMMAGE
SCRAPE	SCRAWP	SCREIGHED	SCRIMP
SCRAPED	SCRAWPED	SCREIGHS	SCRIMPED
SCRAPEGUT	SCRAWPING	SCREW	SCRIMPER
SCRAPER	SCRAWPS	SCREWABLE	SCRIMPERS
SCRAPERS	SCRAWS	SCREWBALL	SCRIMPIER
SCRAPES	SCRAY	SCREWBEAN	SCRIMPILY
SCRAPHEAP	SCRAYE	SCREWED	SCRIMPING
SCRAPIE	SCRAYES	SCREWER	SCRIMPIT
SCRAPIES	SCRAYS	SCREWERS	SCRIMPLY
SCRAPING	SCREAK	SCREWIER	SCRIMPS
SCRAPINGS	SCREAKED	SCREWIEST	SCRIMPY
SCRAPPAGE	SCREAKIER	SCREWING	SCRIMS
SCRAPPED	SCREAKING	SCREWINGS	SCRIMSHAW
SCRAPPER	SCREAKS	SCREWLIKE	SCRIMURE
SCRAPPERS	SCREAKY	SCREWS	SCRIMURES
SCRAPPIER	SCREAM	SCREWTOP	SCRINE
SCRAPPILY	SCREAMED	SCREWTOPS	SCRINES
SCRAPPING	SCREAMER	SCREWUP	SCRIP
SCRAPPLE	SCREAMERS	SCREWUPS	SCRIPPAGE
SCRAPPLES	SCREAMING	SCREWWORM	SCRIPS
SCRAPPY	SCREAMS	SCREWY	SCRIPT
SCRAPS	SCREE	SCRIBABLE	SCRIPTED
SCRAPYARD	SCREECH	SCRIBAL	SCRIPTER
SCRAT	SCREECHED	SCRIBBLE	SCRIPTERS
SCRATCH	SCREECHER	SCRIBBLED	SCRIPTING
SCRATCHED	SCREECHES	SCRIBBLER	SCRIPTORY
SCRATCHER	SCREECHY	SCRIBBLES	SCRIPTS
SCRATCHES	SCREED	SCRIBBLY	SCRIPTURE
SCRATCHIE	SCREEDED	SCRIBE	SCRITCH
SCRATCHY	SCREEDER	SCRIBED	SCRITCHED
SCRATS	SCREEDERS	SCRIBER	SCRITCHES
SCRATTED	SCREEDING	SCRIBERS	SCRIVE
SCRATTING	SCREEDS	SCRIBES	SCRIVED
SCRATTLE	SCREEN	SCRIBING	SCRIVENER
SCRATTLED	SCREENED	SCRIBINGS	SCRIVES
SCRATTLES	SCREENER	SCRIBISM	SCRIVING
SCRAUCH	SCREENERS	SCRIBISMS	SCROBE
SCRAUCHED	SCREENFUL	SCRIECH	SCROBES
SCRAUCHS	SCREENIE	SCRIECHED	SCROD
SCRAUGH	SCREENIES	SCRIECHS	SCRODDLED
SCRAUGHED	SCREENING	SCRIED	SCRODS
SCRAUGHS	SCREENS	SCRIENE	SCROFULA
SCRAW	SCREES	SCRIENES	SCROFULAS

SCROG
SCROGGIE
SCROGGIER
SCROGGIN
SCROGGINS
SCROGGY
SCROGS
SCROLL
SCROLLED
SCROLLING
SCROLLS
SCROME
SCROMED
SCROMES
SCROMING
SCROOCH
SCROOCHED
SCROOCHES
SCROOGE
SCROOGED
SCROOGES
SCROOGING
SCROOP
SCROOPED
SCROOPING
SCROOPS
SCROOTCH
SCRORP
SCRORPS
SCROTA
SCROTAL
SCROTE
SCROTES
SCROTUM
SCROTUMS
SCROUGE
SCROUGED
SCROUGER
SCROUGERS
SCROUGES
SCROUGING
SCROUNGE
SCROUNGED
SCROUNGER
SCROUNGES
SCROUNGY
SCROW
SCROWDGE
SCROWDGED
SCROWDGES
SCROWL
SCROWLE
SCROWLED
SCROWLES
SCROWLING
SCROWLS
SCROWS
SCROYLE

SCROYLES
SCRUB
SCRUBBED
SCRUBBER
SCRUBBERS
SCRUBBIER
SCRUBBILY
SCRUBBING
SCRUBBY
SCRUBLAND
SCRUBS
SCRUFF
SCRUFFIER
SCRUFFILY
SCRUFFS
SCRUFFY
SCRUM
SCRUMDOWN
SCRUMMAGE
SCRUMMED
SCRUMMIE
SCRUMMIER
SCRUMMIES
SCRUMMING
SCRUMMY
SCRUMP
SCRUMPED
SCRUMPIES
SCRUMPING
SCRUMPLE
SCRUMPLED
SCRUMPLES
SCRUMPOX
SCRUMPS
SCRUMPY
SCRUMS
SCRUNCH
SCRUNCHED
SCRUNCHES
SCRUNCHIE
SCRUNCHY
SCRUNT
SCRUNTIER
SCRUNTS
SCRUNTY
SCRUPLE
SCRUPLED
SCRUPLER
SCRUPLERS
SCRUPLES
SCRUPLING
SCRUTABLE
SCRUTATOR
SCRUTINY
SCRUTO
SCRUTOIRE
SCRUTOS
SCRUZE

SCRUZED
SCRUZES
SCRUZING
SCRY
SCRYDE
SCRYER
SCRYERS
SCRYING
SCRYINGS
SCRYNE
SCRYNES
SCUBA
SCUBAED
SCUBAING
SCUBAS
SCUCHIN
SCUCHINS
SCUD
SCUDDALER
SCUDDED
SCUDDER
SCUDDERS
SCUDDING
SCUDDLE
SCUDDLED
SCUDDLES
SCUDDLING
SCUDI
SCUDLER
SCUDLERS
SCUDO
SCUDS
SCUFF
SCUFFED
SCUFFER
SCUFFERS
SCUFFING
SCUFFLE
SCUFFLED
SCUFFLER
SCUFFLERS
SCUFFLES
SCUFFLING
SCUFFS
SCUFT
SCUFTS
SCUG
SCUGGED
SCUGGING
SCUGS
SCUL
SCULCH
SCULCHES
SCULK
SCULKED
SCULKER
SCULKERS
SCULKING

SCULKS
SCULL
SCULLE
SCULLED
SCULLER
SCULLERS
SCULLERY
SCULLES
SCULLING
SCULLINGS
SCULLION
SCULLIONS
SCULLS
SCULP
SCULPED
SCULPIN
SCULPING
SCULPINS
SCULPS
SCULPSIT
SCULPT
SCULPTED
SCULPTING
SCULPTOR
SCULPTORS
SCULPTS
SCULPTURE
SCULS
SCULTCH
SCULTCHES
SCUM
SCUMBAG
SCUMBAGS
SCUMBER
SCUMBERED
SCUMBERS
SCUMBLE
SCUMBLED
SCUMBLES
SCUMBLING
SCUMFISH
SCUMLESS
SCUMLIKE
SCUMMED
SCUMMER
SCUMMERS
SCUMMIER
SCUMMIEST
SCUMMILY
SCUMMING
SCUMMINGS
SCUMMY
SCUMS
SCUNCHEON
SCUNDERED
SCUNGE
SCUNGED
SCUNGES

SCUNGIER	SCUTELLAR	SDEINED	SEAKALES
SCUNGIEST	SCUTELLUM	SDEINING	SEAL
SCUNGILLI	SCUTES	SDEINS	SEALABLE
SCUNGING	SCUTIFORM	SEA	SEALANT
SCUNGY	SCUTIGER	SEABAG	SEALANTS
SCUNNER	SCUTIGERS	SEABAGS	SEALCH
SCUNNERED	SCUTS	SEABANK	SEALCHS
SCUNNERS	SCUTTER	SEABANKS	SEALED
SCUP	SCUTTERED	SEABEACH	SEALER
SCUPPAUG	SCUTTERS	SEABED	SEALERIES
SCUPPAUGS	SCUTTLE	SEABEDS	SEALERS
SCUPPER	SCUTTLED	SEABIRD	SEALERY
SCUPPERED	SCUTTLER	SEABIRDS	SEALGH
SCUPPERS	SCUTTLERS	SEABLITE	SEALGHS
SCUPS	SCUTTLES	SEABLITES	SEALIFT
SCUR	SCUTTLING	SEABOARD	SEALIFTED
SCURF	SCUTUM	SEABOARDS	SEALIFTS
SCURFIER	SCUTWORK	SEABOOT	SEALINE
SCURFIEST	SCUTWORKS	SEABOOTS	SEALINES
SCURFS	SCUZZ	SEABORNE	SEALING
SCURFY	SCUZZBALL	SEABOTTLE	SEALINGS
SCURRED	SCUZZES	SEACOAST	SEALLIKE
SCURRIED	SCUZZIER	SEACOASTS	SEALPOINT
SCURRIER	SCUZZIEST	SEACOCK	SEALS
SCURRIERS	SCUZZY	SEACOCKS	SEALSKIN
SCURRIES	SCYBALA	SEACRAFT	SEALSKINS
SCURRIL	SCYBALOUS	SEACRAFTS	SEALWAX
SCURRILE	SCYBALUM	SEACUNNY	SEALWAXES
SCURRING	SCYE	SEADOG	SEALYHAM
SCURRIOUR	SCYES	SEADOGS	SEALYHAMS
SCURRY	SCYPHATE	SEADROME	SEAM
SCURRYING	SCYPHI	SEADROMES	SEAMAID
SCURS	SCYPHUS	SEAFARER	SEAMAIDS
SCURVIER	SCYTALE	SEAFARERS	SEAMAN
SCURVIES	SCYTALES	SEAFARING	SEAMANLY
SCURVIEST	SCYTHE	SEAFLOOR	SEAMARK
SCURVILY	SCYTHED	SEAFLOORS	SEAMARKS
SCURVY	SCYTHEMAN	SEAFOLK	SEAME
SCUSE	SCYTHEMEN	SEAFOLKS	SEAMED
SCUSED	SCYTHER	SEAFOOD	SEAMEN
SCUSES	SCYTHERS	SEAFOODS	SEAMER
SCUSING	SCYTHES	SEAFOWL	SEAMERS
SCUT	SCYTHING	SEAFOWLS	SEAMES
SCUTA	SDAINE	SEAFRONT	SEAMIER
SCUTAGE	SDAINED	SEAFRONTS	SEAMIEST
SCUTAGES	SDAINES	SEAGIRT	SEAMINESS
SCUTAL	SDAINING	SEAGOING	SEAMING
SCUTATE	SDAYN	SEAGULL	SEAMLESS
SCUTATION	SDAYNED	SEAGULLS	SEAMLIKE
SCUTCH	SDAYNING	SEAHAWK	SEAMOUNT
SCUTCHED	SDAYNS	SEAHAWKS	SEAMOUNTS
SCUTCHEON	SDEIGN	SEAHOG	SEAMS
SCUTCHER	SDEIGNE	SEAHOGS	SEAMSET
SCUTCHERS	SDEIGNED	SEAHORSE	SEAMSETS
SCUTCHES	SDEIGNES	SEAHORSES	SEAMSTER
SCUTCHING	SDEIGNING	SEAHOUND	SEAMSTERS
SCUTE	SDEIGNS	SEAHOUNDS	SEAMY
SCUTELLA	SDEIN	SEAKALE	SEAN

SEANCE
SEANCES
SEANED
SEANING
SEANS
SEAPIECE
SEAPIECES
SEAPLANE
SEAPLANES
SEAPORT
SEAPORTS
SEAQUAKE
SEAQUAKES
SEAQUARIA
SEAR
SEARAT
SEARATS
SEARCE
SEARCED
SEARCES
SEARCH
SEARCHED
SEARCHER
SEARCHERS
SEARCHES
SEARCHING
SEARCING
SEARE
SEARED
SEARER
SEAREST
SEARING
SEARINGLY
SEARINGS
SEARNESS
SEAROBIN
SEAROBINS
SEARS
SEAS
SEASCAPE
SEASCAPES
SEASCOUT
SEASCOUTS
SEASE
SEASED
SEASES
SEASHELL
SEASHELLS
SEASHORE
SEASHORES
SEASICK
SEASICKER
SEASIDE
SEASIDES
SEASING
SEASON
SEASONAL
SEASONALS

SEASONED
SEASONER
SEASONERS
SEASONING
SEASONS
SEASPEAK
SEASPEAKS
SEASTRAND
SEASURE
SEASURES
SEAT
SEATBACK
SEATBACKS
SEATBELT
SEATBELTS
SEATED
SEATER
SEATERS
SEATING
SEATINGS
SEATLESS
SEATMATE
SEATMATES
SEATRAIN
SEATRAINS
SEATROUT
SEATROUTS
SEATS
SEATWORK
SEATWORKS
SEAWALL
SEAWALLS
SEAWAN
SEAWANS
SEAWANT
SEAWANTS
SEAWARD
SEAWARDLY
SEAWARDS
SEAWARE
SEAWARES
SEAWATER
SEAWATERS
SEAWAY
SEAWAYS
SEAWEED
SEAWEEDS
SEAWIFE
SEAWIVES
SEAWOMAN
SEAWOMEN
SEAWORM
SEAWORMS
SEAWORTHY
SEAZE
SEAZED
SEAZES
SEAZING

SEBACEOUS
SEBACIC
SEBASIC
SEBATE
SEBATES
SEBESTEN
SEBESTENS
SEBIFIC
SEBORRHEA
SEBUM
SEBUMS
SEBUNDIES
SEBUNDY
SEC
SECALOSE
SECALOSES
SECANT
SECANTLY
SECANTS
SECATEUR
SECATEURS
SECCO
SECCOS
SECEDE
SECEDED
SECEDER
SECEDERS
SECEDES
SECEDING
SECERN
SECERNED
SECERNENT
SECERNING
SECERNS
SECESH
SECESHER
SECESHERS
SECESHES
SECESSION
SECH
SECHS
SECKEL
SECKELS
SECKLE
SECKLES
SECLUDE
SECLUDED
SECLUDES
SECLUDING
SECLUSION
SECLUSIVE
SECO
SECODONT
SECODONTS
SECONAL
SECONALS
SECOND
SECONDARY

SECONDE
SECONDED
SECONDEE
SECONDEES
SECONDER
SECONDERS
SECONDES
SECONDI
SECONDING
SECONDLY
SECONDO
SECONDS
SECPAR
SECPARS
SECRECIES
SECRECY
SECRET
SECRETA
SECRETAGE
SECRETARY
SECRETE
SECRETED
SECRETER
SECRETES
SECRETEST
SECRETIN
SECRETING
SECRETINS
SECRETION
SECRETIVE
SECRETLY
SECRETOR
SECRETORS
SECRETORY
SECRETS
SECS
SECT
SECTARIAL
SECTARIAN
SECTARIES
SECTARY
SECTATOR
SECTATORS
SECTILE
SECTILITY
SECTION
SECTIONAL
SECTIONED
SECTIONS
SECTOR
SECTORAL
SECTORED
SECTORIAL
SECTORING
SECTORISE
SECTORIZE
SECTORS
SECTS

SECULAR	SEDUCE	SEEINGS	SEG
SECULARLY	SEDUCED	SEEK	SEGAR
SECULARS	SEDUCER	SEEKER	SEGARS
SECULUM	SEDUCERS	SEEKERS	SEGETAL
SECULUMS	SEDUCES	SEEKING	SEGGAR
SECUND	SEDUCIBLE	SEEKS	SEGGARS
SECUNDINE	SEDUCING	SEEL	SEGHOL
SECUNDLY	SEDUCINGS	SEELD	SEGHOLATE
SECUNDUM	SEDUCIVE	SEELED	SEGHOLS
SECURABLE	SEDUCTION	SEELIE	SEGMENT
SECURANCE	SEDUCTIVE	SEELIER	SEGMENTAL
SECURE	SEDUCTOR	SEELIEST	SEGMENTED
SECURED	SEDUCTORS	SEELING	SEGMENTS
SECURELY	SEDULITY	SEELINGS	SEGNI
SECURER	SEDULOUS	SEELS	SEGNO
SECURERS	SEDUM	SEELY	SEGNOS
SECURES	SEDUMS	SEEM	SEGO
SECUREST	SEE	SEEMED	SEGOL
SECURING	SEEABLE	SEEMER	SEGOLATE
SECURITAN	SEECATCH	SEEMERS	SEGOLATES
SECURITY	SEED	SEEMING	SEGOLS
SED	SEEDBED	SEEMINGLY	SEGOS
SEDAN	SEEDBEDS	SEEMINGS	SEGREANT
SEDANS	SEEDBOX	SEEMLESS	SEGREGANT
SEDARIM	SEEDBOXES	SEEMLIER	SEGREGATE
SEDATE	SEEDCAKE	SEEMLIEST	SEGS
SEDATED	SEEDCAKES	SEEMLIHED	SEGUE
SEDATELY	SEEDCASE	SEEMLY	SEGUED
SEDATER	SEEDCASES	SEEMLYHED	SEGUEING
SEDATES	SEEDEATER	SEEMS	SEGUES
SEDATEST	SEEDED	SEEN	SEI
SEDATING	SEEDER	SEEP	SEICENTO
SEDATION	SEEDERS	SEEPAGE	SEICENTOS
SEDATIONS	SEEDIER	SEEPAGES	SEICHE
SEDATIVE	SEEDIEST	SEEPED	SEICHES
SEDATIVES	SEEDILY	SEEPIER	SEIDEL
SEDENT	SEEDINESS	SEEPIEST	SEIDELS
SEDENTARY	SEEDING	SEEPING	SEIF
SEDER	SEEDINGS	SEEPS	SEIFS
SEDERS	SEEDLESS	SEEPY	SEIGNEUR
SEDERUNT	SEEDLIKE	SEER	SEIGNEURS
SEDERUNTS	SEEDLING	SEERESS	SEIGNEURY
SEDES	SEEDLINGS	SEERESSES	SEIGNIOR
SEDGE	SEEDLIP	SEERS	SEIGNIORS
SEDGED	SEEDLIPS	SEES	SEIGNIORY
SEDGELAND	SEEDMAN	SEESAW	SEIGNORAL
SEDGES	SEEDMEN	SEESAWED	SEIGNORY
SEDGIER	SEEDNESS	SEESAWING	SEIK
SEDGIEST	SEEDPOD	SEESAWS	SEIKER
SEDGY	SEEDPODS	SEETHE	SEIKEST
SEDILE	SEEDS	SEETHED	SEIL
SEDILIA	SEEDSMAN	SEETHER	SEILED
SEDILIUM	SEEDSMEN	SEETHERS	SEILING
SEDIMENT	SEEDSTOCK	SEETHES	SEILS
SEDIMENTS	SEEDTIME	SEETHING	SEINE
SEDITION	SEEDTIMES	SEETHINGS	SEINED
SEDITIONS	SEEDY	SEEWING	SEINER
SEDITIOUS	SEEING	SEFER	SEINERS

SEINES	SELAHS	SELFNESS	SEMBLES
SEINING	SELAMLIK	SELFS	SEMBLING
SEININGS	SELAMLIKS	SELFSAME	SEME
SEIR	SELCOUTH	SELFWARD	SEMEE
SEIRS	SELD	SELFWARDS	SEMEED
SEIS	SELDOM	SELICTAR	SEMEIA
SEISABLE	SELDOMLY	SELICTARS	SEMEION
SEISE	SELDSEEN	SELKIE	SEMEIOTIC
SEISED	SELDSHOWN	SELKIES	SEMEME
SEISER	SELE	SELL	SEMEMES
SEISERS	SELECT	SELLA	SEMEMIC
SEISES	SELECTA	SELLABLE	SEMEN
SEISIN	SELECTAS	SELLAE	SEMENS
SEISING	SELECTED	SELLAS	SEMES
SEISINGS	SELECTEE	SELLE	SEMESTER
SEISINS	SELECTEES	SELLER	SEMESTERS
SEISM	SELECTING	SELLERS	SEMESTRAL
SEISMAL	SELECTION	SELLES	SEMI
SEISMIC	SELECTIVE	SELLING	SEMIANGLE
SEISMICAL	SELECTLY	SELLOFF	SEMIARID
SEISMISM	SELECTMAN	SELLOFFS	SEMIBALD
SEISMISMS	SELECTMEN	SELLOTAPE	SEMIBOLD
SEISMS	SELECTOR	SELLOUT	SEMIBOLDS
SEISOR	SELECTORS	SELLOUTS	SEMIBREVE
SEISORS	SELECTS	SELLS	SEMIBULL
SEISURE	SELENATE	SELS	SEMIBULLS
SEISURES	SELENATES	SELSYN	SEMICOLON
SEITAN	SELENIAN	SELSYNS	SEMICOMA
SEITANS	SELENIC	SELTZER	SEMICOMAS
SEITEN	SELENIDE	SELTZERS	SEMICURED
SEITENS	SELENIDES	SELVA	SEMIDEAF
SEITIES	SELENIOUS	SELVAGE	SEMIDEIFY
SEITY	SELENITE	SELVAGED	SEMIDOME
SEIZABLE	SELENITES	SELVAGEE	SEMIDOMED
SEIZE	SELENITIC	SELVAGEES	SEMIDOMES
SEIZED	SELENIUM	SELVAGES	SEMIDRY
SEIZER	SELENIUMS	SELVAGING	SEMIDWARF
SEIZERS	SELENOSES	SELVAS	SEMIE
SEIZES	SELENOSIS	SELVEDGE	SEMIERECT
SEIZIN	SELENOUS	SELVEDGED	SEMIES
SEIZING	SELES	SELVEDGES	SEMIFINAL
SEIZINGS	SELF	SELVES	SEMIFIT
SEIZINS	SELFDOM	SEMAINIER	SEMIFLUID
SEIZOR	SELFDOMS	SEMANTEME	SEMIGALA
SEIZORS	SELFED	SEMANTIC	SEMIGLOSS
SEIZURE	SELFHEAL	SEMANTICS	SEMIGROUP
SEIZURES	SELFHEALS	SEMANTIDE	SEMIHARD
SEJANT	SELFHOOD	SEMANTRA	SEMIHIGH
SEJEANT	SELFHOODS	SEMANTRON	SEMIHOBO
SEKOS	SELFING	SEMAPHORE	SEMIHOBOS
SEKOSES	SELFINGS	SEMATIC	SEMILLON
SEKT	SELFISH	SEMBLABLE	SEMILLONS
SEKTS	SELFISHLY	SEMBLABLY	SEMILOG
SEL	SELFISM	SEMBLANCE	SEMILUNAR
SELACHIAN	SELFISMS	SEMBLANT	SEMILUNE
SELADANG	SELFIST	SEMBLANTS	SEMILUNES
SELADANGS	SELFISTS	SEMBLE	SEMIMAT
SELAH	SELFLESS	SEMBLED	SEMIMATT

SEMIMATTE	SEMIWILD	SENHORA	SENSIS
SEMIMETAL	SEMIWORKS	SENHORAS	SENSISM
SEMIMICRO	SEMMIT	SENHORES	SENSISMS
SEMIMILD	SEMMITS	SENHORITA	SENSIST
SEMIMOIST	SEMOLINA	SENHORS	SENSISTS
SEMIMUTE	SEMOLINAS	SENILE	SENSITISE
SEMINA	SEMPER	SENILELY	SENSITIVE
SEMINAL	SEMPLE	SENILES	SENSITIZE
SEMINALLY	SEMPLER	SENILITY	SENSOR
SEMINAR	SEMPLEST	SENIOR	SENSORIA
SEMINARS	SEMPLICE	SENIORITY	SENSORIAL
SEMINARY	SEMPRE	SENIORS	SENSORILY
SEMINATE	SEMPSTER	SENITI	SENSORIUM
SEMINATED	SEMPSTERS	SENNA	SENSORS
SEMINATES	SEMSEM	SENNACHIE	SENSORY
SEMINOMA	SEMSEMS	SENNAS	SENSUAL
SEMINOMAD	SEMUNCIA	SENNET	SENSUALLY
SEMINOMAS	SEMUNCIAE	SENNETS	SENSUM
SEMINUDE	SEMUNCIAL	SENNIGHT	SENSUOUS
SEMIOLOGY	SEMUNCIAS	SENNIGHTS	SENT
SEMIOPEN	SEN	SENNIT	SENTE
SEMIOSES	SENA	SENNITS	SENTED
SEMIOSIS	SENARIES	SENOPIA	SENTENCE
SEMIOTIC	SENARII	SENOPIAS	SENTENCED
SEMIOTICS	SENARIUS	SENOR	SENTENCER
SEMIOVAL	SENARY	SENORA	SENTENCES
SEMIPED	SENAS	SENORAS	SENTENTIA
SEMIPEDS	SENATE	SENORES	SENTI
SEMIPIOUS	SENATES	SENORITA	SENTIENCE
SEMIPLUME	SENATOR	SENORITAS	SENTIENCY
SEMIPOLAR	SENATORS	SENORS	SENTIENT
SEMIPRO	SEND	SENRYU	SENTIENTS
SEMIPROS	SENDABLE	SENS	SENTIMENT
SEMIRAW	SENDAL	SENSA	SENTIMO
SEMIRIGID	SENDALS	SENSATE	SENTIMOS
SEMIROUND	SENDED	SENSATED	SENTINEL
SEMIRURAL	SENDER	SENSATELY	SENTINELS
SEMIS	SENDERS	SENSATES	SENTING
SEMISES	SENDING	SENSATING	SENTRIES
SEMISOFT	SENDINGS	SENSATION	SENTRY
SEMISOLID	SENDOFF	SENSE	SENTS
SEMISOLUS	SENDOFFS	SENSED	SENVIES
SEMISTIFF	SENDS	SENSEFUL	SENVY
SEMISWEET	SENDUP	SENSEI	SENZA
SEMITAR	SENDUPS	SENSEIS	SEPAD
SEMITARS	SENE	SENSELESS	SEPADDED
SEMITAUR	SENECA	SENSES	SEPADDING
SEMITAURS	SENECAS	SENSI	SEPADS
SEMITIST	SENECIO	SENSIBLE	SEPAL
SEMITISTS	SENECIOS	SENSIBLER	SEPALED
SEMITONAL	SENEGA	SENSIBLES	SEPALINE
SEMITONE	SENEGAS	SENSIBLY	SEPALLED
SEMITONES	SENESCENT	SENSILE	SEPALODY
SEMITONIC	SENESCHAL	SENSILLA	SEPALOID
SEMITRUCK	SENGI	SENSILLAE	SEPALOUS
SEMIURBAN	SENGREEN	SENSILLUM	SEPALS
SEMIVOCAL	SENGREENS	SENSING	SEPARABLE
SEMIVOWEL	SENHOR	SENSINGS	SEPARABLY

SEPARATA	SEPTUOR	SERAPHIN	SERIALIZE
SEPARATE	SEPTUORS	SERAPHINE	SERIALLY
SEPARATED	SEPTUPLE	SERAPHINS	SERIALS
SEPARATES	SEPTUPLED	SERAPHS	SERIATE
SEPARATOR	SEPTUPLES	SERASKIER	SERIATED
SEPARATUM	SEPTUPLET	SERDAB	SERIATELY
SEPHEN	SEPULCHER	SERDABS	SERIATES
SEPHENS	SEPULCHRE	SERE	SERIATIM
SEPIA	SEPULTURE	SERED	SERIATING
SEPIAS	SEQUACITY	SEREIN	SERIATION
SEPIC	SEQUEL	SEREINS	SERIC
SEPIMENT	SEQUELA	SERENADE	SERICEOUS
SEPIMENTS	SEQUELAE	SERENADED	SERICIN
SEPIOLITE	SEQUELISE	SERENADER	SERICINS
SEPIOST	SEQUELIZE	SERENADES	SERICITE
SEPIOSTS	SEQUELS	SERENATA	SERICITES
SEPIUM	SEQUENCE	SERENATAS	SERICITIC
SEPIUMS	SEQUENCED	SERENATE	SERICON
SEPMAG	SEQUENCER	SERENATES	SERICONS
SEPOY	SEQUENCES	SERENE	SERIEMA
SEPOYS	SEQUENCY	SERENED	SERIEMAS
SEPPUKU	SEQUENT	SERENELY	SERIES
SEPPUKUS	SEQUENTLY	SERENER	SERIF
SEPS	SEQUENTS	SERENES	SERIFED
SEPSES	SEQUESTER	SERENEST	SERIFFED
SEPSIS	SEQUESTRA	SERENING	SERIFS
SEPT	SEQUIN	SERENITY	SERIGRAPH
SEPTA	SEQUINED	SERER	SERIN
SEPTAGE	SEQUINING	SERES	SERINE
SEPTAGES	SEQUINNED	SEREST	SERINES
SEPTAL	SEQUINS	SERF	SERINETTE
SEPTARIA	SEQUITUR	SERFAGE	SERING
SEPTARIAN	SEQUITURS	SERFAGES	SERINGA
SEPTARIUM	SEQUOIA	SERFDOM	SERINGAS
SEPTATE	SEQUOIAS	SERFDOMS	SERINS
SEPTATION	SER	SERFHOOD	SERIOUS
SEPTEMFID	SERA	SERFHOODS	SERIOUSLY
SEPTEMVIR	SERAC	SERFISH	SERIPH
SEPTENARY	SERACS	SERFLIKE	SERIPHS
SEPTENNIA	SERAFILE	SERFS	SERJEANCY
SEPTET	SERAFILES	SERFSHIP	SERJEANT
SEPTETS	SERAFIN	SERFSHIPS	SERJEANTS
SEPTETTE	SERAFINS	SERGE	SERJEANTY
SEPTETTES	SERAGLIO	SERGEANCY	SERK
SEPTIC	SERAGLIOS	SERGEANT	SERKALI
SEPTICAL	SERAI	SERGEANTS	SERKALIS
SEPTICITY	SERAIL	SERGEANTY	SERKS
SEPTICS	SERAILS	SERGED	SERMON
SEPTIFORM	SERAIS	SERGER	SERMONED
SEPTIMAL	SERAL	SERGERS	SERMONEER
SEPTIME	SERANG	SERGES	SERMONER
SEPTIMES	SERANGS	SERGING	SERMONERS
SEPTIMOLE	SERAPE	SERGINGS	SERMONET
SEPTLEVA	SERAPES	SERIAL	SERMONETS
SEPTLEVAS	SERAPH	SERIALISE	SERMONIC
SEPTS	SERAPHIC	SERIALISM	SERMONING
SEPTUM	SERAPHIM	SERIALIST	SERMONISE
SEPTUMS	SERAPHIMS	SERIALITY	SERMONIZE

SERMONS	SERRED	SERVLET	SETOFF
SEROLOGIC	SERREFILE	SERVLETS	SETOFFS
SEROLOGY	SERRES	SERVO	SETON
SERON	SERRICORN	SERVOS	SETONS
SERONS	SERRTED	SERVQUAL	SETOSE
SEROON	SERRIEDLY	SERVQUALS	SETOUS
SEROONS	SERRIES	SESAME	SETOUT
SEROPUS	SERRIFORM	SESAMES	SETOUTS
SEROPUSES	SERRING	SESAMOID	SETS
SEROSA	SERRS	SESAMOIDS	SETSCREW
SEROSAE	SERRULATE	SESE	SETSCREWS
SEROSAL	SERRY	SESELI	SETT
SEROSAS	SERRYING	SESELIS	SETTEE
SEROSITY	SERS	SESEY	SETTEES
SEROTINAL	SERUEWE	SESH	SETTER
SEROTINE	SERUEWED	SESHES	SETTERED
SEROTINES	SERUEWES	SESS	SETTERING
SEROTINY	SERUEWING	SESSA	SETTERS
SEROTONIN	SERUM	SESSES	SETTING
SEROTYPE	SERUMAL	SESSILE	SETTINGS
SEROTYPED	SERUMS	SESSILITY	SETTLE
SEROTYPES	SERVABLE	SESSION	SETTLED
SEROUS	SERVAL	SESSIONAL	SETTLER
SEROVAR	SERVALS	SESSIONS	SETTLERS
SEROVARS	SERVANT	SESSPOOL	SETTLES
SEROW	SERVANTED	SESSPOOLS	SETTLING
SEROWS	SERVANTRY	SESTERCE	SETTLINGS
SERPENT	SERVANTS	SESTERCES	SETTLOR
SERPENTRY	SERVE	SESTERTIA	SETTLORS
SERPENTS	SERVEABLE	SESTERTII	SETTS
SERPIGO	SERVED	SESTET	SETUALE
SERPIGOES	SERVER	SESTETS	SETUALES
SERPIGOS	SERVERIES	SESTETT	SETULE
SERPULA	SERVERS	SESTETTE	SETULES
SERPULAE	SERVERY	SESTETTES	SETULOSE
SERPULID	SERVES	SESTETTO	SETULOUS
SERPULIDS	SERVEWE	SESTETTOS	SETUP
SERPULITE	SERVEWED	SESTETTS	SETUPS
SERR	SERVEWES	SESTINA	SETWALL
SERRA	SERVEWING	SESTINAS	SETWALLS
SERRAE	SERVICE	SESTINE	SEVEN
SERRAN	SERVICED	SESTINES	SEVENFOLD
SERRANID	SERVICER	SESTON	SEVENS
SERRANIDS	SERVICERS	SESTONS	SEVENTEEN
SERRANO	SERVICES	SET	SEVENTH
SERRANOID	SERVICING	SETA	SEVENTHLY
SERRANOS	SERVIENT	SETACEOUS	SEVENTHS
SERRANS	SERVIETTE	SETAE	SEVENTIES
SERRAS	SERVILE	SETAL	SEVENTY
SERRATE	SERVILELY	SETBACK	SEVER
SERRATED	SERVILES	SETBACKS	SEVERABLE
SERRATES	SERVILISM	SETENANT	SEVERAL
SERRATI	SERVILITY	SETENANTS	SEVERALLY
SERRATING	SERVING	SETIFORM	SEVERALS
SERRATION	SERVINGS	SETLINE	SEVERALTY
SERRATURE	SERVITOR	SETLINES	SEVERANCE
SERRATUS	SERVITORS	SETNESS	SEVERE
SERRE	SERVITUDE	SETNESSES	SEVERED

SEVERELY	SEXISM	SEYENS	SHADIEST
SEVERER	SEXISMS	SEYS	SHADILY
SEVEREST	SEXIST	SEYSURE	SHADINESS
SEVERIES	SEXISTS	SEYSURES	SHADING
SEVERING	SEXLESS	SEZ	SHADINGS
SEVERITY	SEXLESSLY	SFERICS	SHADKHAN
SEVERS	SEXLINKED	SFORZANDI	SHADKHANS
SEVERY	SEXOLOGIC	SFORZANDO	SHADOOF
SEVICHE	SEXOLOGY	SFORZATI	SHADOOFS
SEVICHES	SEXPERT	SFORZATO	SHADOW
SEVRUGA	SEXPERTS	SFORZATOS	SHADOWBOX
SEVRUGAS	SEXPOT	SFUMATO	SHADOWED
SEW	SEXPOTS	SFUMATOS	SHADOWER
SEWABLE	SEXT	SGRAFFITI	SHADOWERS
SEWAGE	SEXTAIN	SGRAFFITO	SHADOWIER
SEWAGES	SEXTAINS	SH	SHADOWILY
SEWAN	SEXTAN	SHA	SHADOWING
SEWANS	SEXTANS	SHABASH	SHADOWS
SEWAR	SEXTANSES	SHABBATOT	SHADOWY
SEWARS	SEXTANT	SHABBIER	SHADRACH
SEWED	SEXTANTAL	SHABBIEST	SHADRACHS
SEWEL	SEXTANTS	SHABBILY	SHADS
SEWELLEL	SEXTARII	SHABBLE	SHADUF
SEWELLELS	SEXTARIUS	SHABBLES	SHADUFS
SEWELS	SEXTET	SHABBY	SHADY
SEWEN	SEXTETS	SHABRACK	SHAFT
SEWENS	SEXTETT	SHABRACKS	SHAFTED
SEWER	SEXTETTE	SHACK	SHAFTER
SEWERAGE	SEXTETTES	SHACKED	SHAFTERS
SEWERAGES	SEXTETTS	SHACKING	SHAFTING
SEWERED	SEXTILE	SHACKLE	SHAFTINGS
SEWERING	SEXTILES	SHACKLED	SHAFTLESS
SEWERINGS	SEXTO	SHACKLER	SHAFTS
SEWERLESS	SEXTOLET	SHACKLERS	SHAG
SEWERLIKE	SEXTOLETS	SHACKLES	SHAGBARK
SEWERS	SEXTON	SHACKLING	SHAGBARKS
SEWIN	SEXTONESS	SHACKO	SHAGGABLE
SEWING	SEXTONS	SHACKOES	SHAGGED
SEWINGS	SEXTOS	SHACKOS	SHAGGIER
SEWINS	SEXTS	SHACKS	SHAGGIEST
SEWN	SEXTUOR	SHAD	SHAGGILY
SEWS	SEXTUORS	SHADBERRY	SHAGGING
SEX	SEXTUPLE	SHADBLOW	SHAGGY
SEXAHOLIC	SEXTUPLED	SHADBLOWS	SHAGPILE
SEXED	SEXTUPLES	SHADBUSH	SHAGREEN
SEXENNIAL	SEXTUPLET	SHADCHAN	SHAGREENS
SEXER	SEXTUPLY	SHADCHANS	SHAGROON
SEXERCISE	SEXUAL	SHADDOCK	SHAGROONS
SEXERS	SEXUALISE	SHADDOCKS	SHAGS
SEXES	SEXUALISM	SHADE	SHAH
SEXFID	SEXUALIST	SHADED	SHAHADA
SEXFOIL	SEXUALITY	SHADELESS	SHAHADAS
SEXFOILS	SEXUALIZE	SHADER	SHAHDOM
SEXIER	SEXUALLY	SHADERS	SHAHDOMS
SEXIEST	SEXVALENT	SHADES	SHAHS
SEXILY	SEXY	SHADFLIES	SHAHTOOSH
SEXINESS	SEY	SHADFLY	SHAIKH
SEXING	SEYEN	SHADIER	SHAIKHS

SHAIRD	SHALOM	SHAMMY	SHAPES
SHAIRDS	SHALOMS	SHAMMYING	SHAPEUP
SHAIRN	SHALOT	SHAMOIS	SHAPEUPS
SHAIRNS	SHALOTS	SHAMOS	SHAPEWEAR
SHAITAN	SHALT	SHAMOSIM	SHAPING
SHAITANS	SHALWAR	SHAMOY	SHAPINGS
SHAKABLE	SHALWARS	SHAMOYED	SHAPS
SHAKE	SHALY	SHAMOYING	SHARABLE
SHAKEABLE	SHAM	SHAMOYS	SHARD
SHAKED	SHAMA	SHAMPOO	SHARDED
SHAKEDOWN	SHAMABLE	SHAMPOOED	SHARDS
SHAKEN	SHAMABLY	SHAMPOOER	SHARE
SHAKEOUT	SHAMAN	SHAMPOOS	SHAREABLE
SHAKEOUTS	SHAMANIC	SHAMROCK	SHARECROP
SHAKER	SHAMANISM	SHAMROCKS	SHARED
SHAKERS	SHAMANIST	SHAMS	SHAREMAN
SHAKES	SHAMANS	SHAMUS	SHAREMEN
SHAKEUP	SHAMAS	SHAMUSES	SHARER
SHAKEUPS	SHAMATEUR	SHAN	SHARERS
SHAKIER	SHAMBA	SHANACHIE	SHARES
SHAKIEST	SHAMBAS	SHAND	SHARESMAN
SHAKILY	SHAMBLE	SHANDIES	SHARESMEN
SHAKINESS	SHAMBLED	SHANDRIES	SHAREWARE
SHAKING	SHAMBLES	SHANDRY	SHARIA
SHAKINGS	SHAMBLIER	SHANDS	SHARIAH
SHAKO	SHAMBLING	SHANDY	SHARIAHS
SHAKOES	SHAMBLY	SHANGHAI	SHARIAS
SHAKOS	SHAMBOLIC	SHANGHAIS	SHARIAT
SHAKT	SHAME	SHANK	SHARIATS
SHAKUDO	SHAMEABLE	SHANKBONE	SHARIF
SHAKUDOS	SHAMEABLY	SHANKED	SHARIFIAN
SHAKY	SHAMED	SHANKING	SHARIFS
SHALE	SHAMEFAST	SHANKS	SHARING
SHALED	SHAMEFUL	SHANNIES	SHARINGS
SHALELIKE	SHAMELESS	SHANNY	SHARK
SHALES	SHAMER	SHANS	SHARKED
SHALEY	SHAMERS	SHANTEY	SHARKER
SHALIER	SHAMES	SHANTEYS	SHARKERS
SHALIEST	SHAMIANA	SHANTI	SHARKING
SHALING	SHAMIANAH	SHANTIES	SHARKINGS
SHALL	SHAMIANAS	SHANTIH	SHARKLIKE
SHALLI	SHAMINA	SHANTIHS	SHARKS
SHALLIS	SHAMINAS	SHANTIS	SHARKSKIN
SHALLON	SHAMING	SHANTUNG	SHARN
SHALLONS	SHAMISEN	SHANTUNGS	SHARNIER
SHALLOON	SHAMISENS	SHANTY	SHARNIEST
SHALLOONS	SHAMMAS	SHANTYMAN	SHARNS
SHALLOP	SHAMMASH	SHANTYMEN	SHARNY
SHALLOPS	SHAMMASIM	SHAPABLE	SHARON
SHALLOT	SHAMMED	SHAPE	SHARP
SHALLOTS	SHAMMER	SHAPEABLE	SHARPED
SHALLOW	SHAMMERS	SHAPED	SHARPEN
SHALLOWED	SHAMMES	SHAPELESS	SHARPENED
SHALLOWER	SHAMMIED	SHAPELIER	SHARPENER
SHALLOWLY	SHAMMIES	SHAPELY	SHARPENS
SHALLOWS	SHAMMING	SHAPEN	SHARPER
SHALM	SHAMMOS	SHAPER	SHARPERS
SHALMS	SHAMMOSIM	SHAPERS	SHARPEST

SHARPIE	SHAWLEYS	SHEATHY	SHEEPLIKE
SHARPIES	SHAWLIE	SHEAVE	SHEEPMAN
SHARPING	SHAWLIES	SHEAVED	SHEEPMEN
SHARPINGS	SHAWLING	SHEAVES	SHEEPO
SHARPISH	SHAWLINGS	SHEAVING	SHEEPOS
SHARPLY	SHAWLLESS	SHEBANG	SHEEPSKIN
SHARPNESS	SHAWLS	SHEBANGS	SHEEPWALK
SHARPS	SHAWM	SHEBEAN	SHEEPY
SHARPY	SHAWMS	SHEBEANS	SHEER
SHASH	SHAWN	SHEBEEN	SHEERED
SHASHED	SHAWS	SHEBEENED	SHEERER
SHASHES	SHAY	SHEBEENER	SHEEREST
SHASHING	SHAYA	SHEBEENS	SHEERING
SHASHLICK	SHAYAS	SHECHITA	SHEERLEG
SHASHLIK	SHAYS	SHECHITAH	SHEERLEGS
SHASHLIKS	SHAZAM	SHECHITAS	SHEERLY
SHASLIK	SHCHI	SHED	SHEERNESS
SHASLIKS	SHCHIS	SHEDABLE	SHEERS
SHASTER	SHE	SHEDDABLE	SHEESH
SHASTERS	SHEA	SHEDDED	SHEET
SHASTRA	SHEADING	SHEDDER	SHEETED
SHASTRAS	SHEADINGS	SHEDDERS	SHEETER
SHAT	SHEAF	SHEDDING	SHEETERS
SHATTER	SHEAFED	SHEDDINGS	SHEETFED
SHATTERED	SHEAFIER	SHEDFUL	SHEETIER
SHATTERER	SHEAFIEST	SHEDFULS	SHEETIEST
SHATTERS	SHEAFING	SHEDLIKE	SHEETING
SHATTERY	SHEAFLIKE	SHEDLOAD	SHEETINGS
SHAUCHLE	SHEAFS	SHEDLOADS	SHEETLESS
SHAUCHLED	SHEAFY	SHEDS	SHEETLIKE
SHAUCHLES	SHEAL	SHEEL	SHEETROCK
SHAUCHLY	SHEALED	SHEELED	SHEETS
SHAUGH	SHEALING	SHEELING	SHEETY
SHAUGHS	SHEALINGS	SHEELS	SHEEVE
SHAUL	SHEALS	SHEEN	SHEEVES
SHAULED	SHEAR	SHEENED	SHEGETZ
SHAULING	SHEARED	SHEENEY	SHEHITA
SHAULS	SHEARER	SHEENEYS	SHEHITAH
SHAVABLE	SHEARERS	SHEENFUL	SHEHITAHS
SHAVE	SHEARING	SHEENIE	SHEHITAS
SHAVEABLE	SHEARINGS	SHEENIER	SHEIK
SHAVED	SHEARLEG	SHEENIES	SHEIKDOM
SHAVELING	SHEARLEGS	SHEENIEST	SHEIKDOMS
SHAVEN	SHEARLING	SHEENING	SHEIKH
SHAVER	SHEARMAN	SHEENS	SHEIKHA
SHAVERS	SHEARMEN	SHEENY	SHEIKHAS
SHAVES	SHEARS	SHEEP	SHEIKHDOM
SHAVETAIL	SHEAS	SHEEPCOT	SHEIKHS
SHAVIE	SHEATFISH	SHEEPCOTE	SHEIKS
SHAVIES	SHEATH	SHEEPCOTS	SHEILA
SHAVING	SHEATHE	SHEEPDOG	SHEILAS
SHAVINGS	SHEATHED	SHEEPDOGS	SHEILING
SHAW	SHEATHER	SHEEPFOLD	SHEILINGS
SHAWED	SHEATHERS	SHEEPHEAD	SHEITAN
SHAWING	SHEATHES	SHEEPIER	SHEITANS
SHAWL	SHEATHIER	SHEEPIEST	SHEKALIM
SHAWLED	SHEATHING	SHEEPISH	SHEKEL
SHAWLEY	SHEATHS	SHEEPLE	SHEKELIM

SHEKELS	SHEMOZZLE	SHEVA	SHIFTWORK
SHELDDUCK	SHEND	SHEVAS	SHIFTY
SHELDRAKE	SHENDING	SHEW	SHIGELLA
SHELDUCK	SHENDS	SHEWBREAD	SHIGELLAE
SHELDUCKS	SHENT	SHEWED	SHIGELLAS
SHELF	SHEOL	SHEWEL	SHIITAKE
SHELFED	SHEOLS	SHEWELS	SHIITAKES
SHELFFUL	SHEPHERD	SHEWER	SHIKAR
SHELFFULS	SHEPHERDS	SHEWERS	SHIKAREE
SHELFIER	SHEQALIM	SHEWING	SHIKAREES
SHELFIEST	SHEQEL	SHEWN	SHIKARI
SHELFING	SHEQELS	SHEWS	SHIKARIS
SHELFLIKE	SHERANG	SHH	SHIKARRED
SHELFROOM	SHERANGS	SHIAI	SHIKARS
SHELFS	SHERBERT	SHIAIS	SHIKKER
SHELFY	SHERBERTS	SHIATSU	SHIKKERS
SHELL	SHERBET	SHIATSUS	SHIKSA
SHELLAC	SHERBETS	SHIATZU	SHIKSAS
SHELLACK	SHERD	SHIATZUS	SHIKSE
SHELLACKS	SHERDS	SHIBAH	SHIKSEH
SHELLACS	SHERE	SHIBAHS	SHIKSEHS
SHELLBACK	SHEREEF	SHIBUICHI	SHIKSES
SHELLBARK	SHEREEFS	SHICKER	SHILINGI
SHELLDUCK	SHERIA	SHICKERED	SHILL
SHELLED	SHERIAS	SHICKERS	SHILLABER
SHELLER	SHERIAT	SHICKSA	SHILLALA
SHELLERS	SHERIATS	SHICKSAS	SHILLALAH
SHELLFIRE	SHERIF	SHIDDER	SHILLALAS
SHELLFISH	SHERIFF	SHIDDERS	SHILLED
SHELLFUL	SHERIFFS	SHIDDUCH	SHILLELAH
SHELLFULS	SHERIFIAN	SHIED	SHILLING
SHELLIER	SHERIFS	SHIEL	SHILLINGS
SHELLIEST	SHERLOCK	SHIELD	SHILLS
SHELLING	SHERLOCKS	SHIELDED	SHILPIT
SHELLINGS	SHEROOT	SHIELDER	SHILY
SHELLS	SHEROOTS	SHIELDERS	SHIM
SHELLWORK	SHERPA	SHIELDING	SHIMAAL
SHELLY	SHERPAS	SHIELDS	SHIMAALS
SHELTA	SHERRIES	SHIELED	SHIMMED
SHELTAS	SHERRIS	SHIELING	SHIMMER
SHELTER	SHERRISES	SHIELINGS	SHIMMERED
SHELTERED	SHERRY	SHIELS	SHIMMERS
SHELTERER	SHERWANI	SHIER	SHIMMERY
SHELTERS	SHERWANIS	SHIERS	SHIMMEY
SHELTERY	SHES	SHIES	SHIMMEYS
SHELTIE	SHET	SHIEST	SHIMMIED
SHELTIES	SHETLAND	SHIFT	SHIMMIES
SHELTY	SHETLANDS	SHIFTABLE	SHIMMING
SHELVE	SHETS	SHIFTED	SHIMMY
SHELVED	SHETTING	SHIFTER	SHIMMYING
SHELVER	SHEUCH	SHIFTERS	SHIMOZZLE
SHELVERS	SHEUCHED	SHIFTIER	SHIMS
SHELVES	SHEUCHING	SHIFTIEST	SHIN
SHELVIER	SHEUCHS	SHIFTILY	SHINBONE
SHELVIEST	SHEUGH	SHIFTING	SHINBONES
SHELVING	SHEUGHED	SHIFTINGS	SHINDIES
SHELVINGS	SHEUGHING	SHIFTLESS	SHINDIG
SHELVY	SHEUGHS	SHIFTS	SHINDIGS

SHINDY
SHINDYS
SHINE
SHINED
SHINELESS
SHINER
SHINERS
SHINES
SHINESS
SHINESSES
SHINGLE
SHINGLED
SHINGLER
SHINGLERS
SHINGLES
SHINGLIER
SHINGLING
SHINGLY
SHINGUARD
SHINIER
SHINIES
SHINIEST
SHINILY
SHININESS
SHINING
SHININGLY
SHINJU
SHINJUS
SHINKIN
SHINKINS
SHINLEAF
SHINLEAFS
SHINNE
SHINNED
SHINNERY
SHINNES
SHINNEY
SHINNEYED
SHINNEYS
SHINNIED
SHINNIES
SHINNING
SHINNY
SHINNYING
SHINS
SHINTIED
SHINTIES
SHINTY
SHINTYING
SHINY
SHIP
SHIPBOARD
SHIPBORNE
SHIPFUL
SHIPFULS
SHIPLAP
SHIPLAPS
SHIPLESS

SHIPLOAD
SHIPLOADS
SHIPMAN
SHIPMATE
SHIPMATES
SHIPMEN
SHIPMENT
SHIPMENTS
SHIPOWNER
SHIPPABLE
SHIPPED
SHIPPEN
SHIPPENS
SHIPPER
SHIPPERS
SHIPPIE
SHIPPIES
SHIPPING
SHIPPINGS
SHIPPO
SHIPPON
SHIPPONS
SHIPPOS
SHIPPOUND
SHIPS
SHIPSHAPE
SHIPSIDE
SHIPSIDES
SHIPWAY
SHIPWAYS
SHIPWORM
SHIPWORMS
SHIPWRECK
SHIPYARD
SHIPYARDS
SHIR
SHIRALEE
SHIRALEES
SHIRE
SHIRED
SHIREMAN
SHIREMEN
SHIRES
SHIRING
SHIRK
SHIRKED
SHIRKER
SHIRKERS
SHIRKING
SHIRKS
SHIRR
SHIRRA
SHIRRALEE
SHIRRAS
SHIRRED
SHIRRING
SHIRRINGS
SHIRRS

SHIRS
SHIRT
SHIRTBAND
SHIRTED
SHIRTIER
SHIRTIEST
SHIRTILY
SHIRTING
SHIRTINGS
SHIRTLESS
SHIRTS
SHIRTTAIL
SHIRTY
SHISH
SHISHA
SHISHAS
SHISO
SHISOS
SHIST
SHISTS
SHIT
SHITAKE
SHITAKES
SHITE
SHITED
SHITES
SHITFACED
SHITHEAD
SHITHEADS
SHITHOLE
SHITHOLES
SHITING
SHITLESS
SHITLIST
SHITLISTS
SHITLOAD
SHITLOADS
SHITS
SHITTAH
SHITTAHS
SHITTED
SHITTIER
SHITTIEST
SHITTILY
SHITTIM
SHITTIMS
SHITTING
SHITTY
SHIUR
SHIURIM
SHIV
SHIVA
SHIVAH
SHIVAHS
SHIVAREE
SHIVAREED
SHIVAREES
SHIVAS

SHIVE
SHIVER
SHIVERED
SHIVERER
SHIVERERS
SHIVERIER
SHIVERING
SHIVERS
SHIVERY
SHIVES
SHIVITI
SHIVITIS
SHIVOO
SHIVOOS
SHIVS
SHIVVED
SHIVVING
SHKOTZIM
SHLEMIEHL
SHLEMIEL
SHLEMIELS
SHLEP
SHLEPP
SHLEPPED
SHLEPPER
SHLEPPERS
SHLEPPING
SHLEPPS
SHLEPS
SHLIMAZEL
SHLOCK
SHLOCKIER
SHLOCKS
SHLOCKY
SHLOSHIM
SHLOSHIMS
SHLUB
SHLUBS
SHLUMP
SHLUMPED
SHLUMPING
SHLUMPS
SHLUMPY
SHMALTZ
SHMALTZES
SHMALTZY
SHMATTE
SHMATTES
SHMEAR
SHMEARS
SHMEK
SHMEKS
SHMO
SHMOCK
SHMOCKS
SHMOES
SHMOOSE
SHMOOSED

SHMOOSES	SHOELACE	SHOOING	SHORE
SHMOOSING	SHOELACES	SHOOK	SHOREBIRD
SHMOOZE	SHOELESS	SHOOKS	SHORED
SHMOOZED	SHOEMAKER	SHOOL	SHORELESS
SHMOOZES	SHOEPAC	SHOOLE	SHORELINE
SHMOOZING	SHOEPACK	SHOOLED	SHOREMAN
SHMUCK	SHOEPACKS	SHOOLES	SHOREMEN
SHMUCKS	SHOEPACS	SHOOLING	SHORER
SHNAPPS	SHOER	SHOOLS	SHORERS
SHNAPS	SHOERS	SHOON	SHORES
SHNOOK	SHOES	SHOORA	SHORESIDE
SHNOOKS	SHOESHINE	SHOORAS	SHORESMAN
SHNORRER	SHOETREE	SHOOS	SHORESMEN
SHNORRERS	SHOETREES	SHOOT	SHOREWARD
SHOAL	SHOFAR	SHOOTABLE	SHOREWEED
SHOALED	SHOFARS	SHOOTDOWN	SHORING
SHOALER	SHOFROTH	SHOOTER	SHORINGS
SHOALEST	SHOG	SHOOTERS	SHORL
SHOALIER	SHOGGED	SHOOTING	SHORLS
SHOALIEST	SHOGGING	SHOOTINGS	SHORN
SHOALING	SHOGGLE	SHOOTIST	SHORT
SHOALINGS	SHOGGLED	SHOOTISTS	SHORTAGE
SHOALNESS	SHOGGLES	SHOOTOUT	SHORTAGES
SHOALS	SHOGGLIER	SHOOTOUTS	SHORTARM
SHOALWISE	SHOGGLING	SHOOTS	SHORTCAKE
SHOALY	SHOGGLY	SHOP	SHORTCUT
SHOAT	SHOGI	SHOPBOARD	SHORTCUTS
SHOATS	SHOGIS	SHOPBOY	SHORTED
SHOCHET	SHOGS	SHOPBOYS	SHORTEN
SHOCHETIM	SHOGUN	SHOPE	SHORTENED
SHOCHETS	SHOGUNAL	SHOPFRONT	SHORTENER
SHOCK	SHOGUNATE	SHOPFUL	SHORTENS
SHOCKABLE	SHOGUNS	SHOPFULS	SHORTER
SHOCKED	SHOJI	SHOPGIRL	SHORTEST
SHOCKER	SHOJIS	SHOPGIRLS	SHORTFALL
SHOCKERS	SHOLA	SHOPHAR	SHORTGOWN
SHOCKING	SHOLAS	SHOPHARS	SHORTHAIR
SHOCKS	SHOLOM	SHOPHROTH	SHORTHAND
SHOD	SHOLOMS	SHOPLIFT	SHORTHEAD
SHODDEN	SHONE	SHOPLIFTS	SHORTHOLD
SHODDIER	SHONEEN	SHOPMAN	SHORTHORN
SHODDIES	SHONEENS	SHOPMEN	SHORTIA
SHODDIEST	SHONKIER	SHOPPE	SHORTIAS
SHODDILY	SHONKIEST	SHOPPED	SHORTIE
SHODDY	SHONKY	SHOPPER	SHORTIES
SHODER	SHOO	SHOPPERS	SHORTING
SHODERS	SHOOED	SHOPPES	SHORTISH
SHOE	SHOOFLIES	SHOPPIER	SHORTLIST
SHOEBILL	SHOOFLY	SHOPPIEST	SHORTLY
SHOEBILLS	SHOOGIE	SHOPPING	SHORTNESS
SHOEBLACK	SHOOGIED	SHOPPINGS	SHORTS
SHOEBOX	SHOOGIES	SHOPPY	SHORTSTOP
SHOEBOXES	SHOOGLE	SHOPS	SHORTWAVE
SHOED	SHOOGLED	SHOPTALK	SHORTY
SHOEHORN	SHOOGLES	SHOPTALKS	SHOT
SHOEHORNS	SHOOGLIER	SHOPWORN	SHOTE
SHOEING	SHOOGLING	SHORAN	SHOTES
SHOEINGS	SHOOGLY	SHORANS	SHOTFIRER

SHOTGUN	SHOWBIZ	SHRANK	SHRILL
SHOTGUNS	SHOWBIZZY	SHRAPNEL	SHRILLED
SHOTHOLE	SHOWBOAT	SHRAPNELS	SHRILLER
SHOTHOLES	SHOWBOATS	SHRED	SHRILLEST
SHOTMAKER	SHOWBOX	SHREDDED	SHRILLIER
SHOTPROOF	SHOWBOXES	SHREDDER	SHRILLING
SHOTPUT	SHOWBREAD	SHREDDERS	SHRILLS
SHOTPUTS	SHOWCASE	SHREDDIER	SHRILLY
SHOTS	SHOWCASED	SHREDDING	SHRIMP
SHOTT	SHOWCASES	SHREDDY	SHRIMPED
SHOTTE	SHOWD	SHREDLESS	SHRIMPER
SHOTTED	SHOWDED	SHREDS	SHRIMPERS
SHOTTEN	SHOWDING	SHREEK	SHRIMPIER
SHOTTES	SHOWDOWN	SHREEKED	SHRIMPING
SHOTTING	SHOWDOWNS	SHREEKING	SHRIMPS
SHOTTLE	SHOWDS	SHREEKS	SHRIMPY
SHOTTLES	SHOWED	SHREIK	SHRINAL
SHOTTS	SHOWER	SHREIKED	SHRINE
SHOUGH	SHOWERED	SHREIKING	SHRINED
SHOUGHS	SHOWERER	SHREIKS	SHRINES
SHOULD	SHOWERERS	SHREW	SHRINING
SHOULDER	SHOWERFUL	SHREWD	SHRINK
SHOULDERS	SHOWERIER	SHREWDER	SHRINKAGE
SHOULDEST	SHOWERING	SHREWDEST	SHRINKER
SHOULDST	SHOWERS	SHREWDIE	SHRINKERS
SHOUSE	SHOWERY	SHREWDIES	SHRINKING
SHOUSES	SHOWGHE	SHREWDLY	SHRINKS
SHOUT	SHOWGHES	SHREWED	SHRIS
SHOUTED	SHOWGIRL	SHREWING	SHRITCH
SHOUTER	SHOWGIRLS	SHREWISH	SHRITCHED
SHOUTERS	SHOWIER	SHREWLIKE	SHRITCHES
SHOUTHER	SHOWIEST	SHREWMICE	SHRIVE
SHOUTHERS	SHOWILY	SHREWS	SHRIVED
SHOUTIER	SHOWINESS	SHRI	SHRIVEL
SHOUTIEST	SHOWING	SHRIECH	SHRIVELED
SHOUTING	SHOWINGS	SHRIECHED	SHRIVELS
SHOUTINGS	SHOWMAN	SHRIECHES	SHRIVEN
SHOUTLINE	SHOWMANLY	SHRIEK	SHRIVER
SHOUTS	SHOWMEN	SHRIEKED	SHRIVERS
SHOUTY	SHOWN	SHRIEKER	SHRIVES
SHOVE	SHOWOFF	SHRIEKERS	SHRIVING
SHOVED	SHOWOFFS	SHRIEKIER	SHRIVINGS
SHOVEL	SHOWPIECE	SHRIEKING	SHROFF
SHOVELED	SHOWPLACE	SHRIEKS	SHROFFAGE
SHOVELER	SHOWRING	SHRIEKY	SHROFFED
SHOVELERS	SHOWRINGS	SHRIEVAL	SHROFFING
SHOVELFUL	SHOWROOM	SHRIEVE	SHROFFS
SHOVELING	SHOWROOMS	SHRIEVED	SHROOM
SHOVELLED	SHOWS	SHRIEVES	SHROOMED
SHOVELLER	SHOWTIME	SHRIEVING	SHROOMER
SHOVELS	SHOWTIMES	SHRIFT	SHROOMERS
SHOVER	SHOWY	SHRIFTS	SHROOMING
SHOVERS	SHOWYARD	SHRIGHT	SHROOMS
SHOVES	SHOWYARDS	SHRIGHTS	SHROUD
SHOVING	SHOYU	SHRIKE	SHROUDED
SHOVINGS	SHOYUS	SHRIKED	SHROUDIER
SHOW	SHRADDHA	SHRIKES	SHROUDING
SHOWABLE	SHRADDHAS	SHRIKING	SHROUDS

SHROUDY	SHUDDER	SHUTING	SIAMESING
SHROVE	SHUDDERED	SHUTOFF	SIAMEZE
SHROVED	SHUDDERS	SHUTOFFS	SIAMEZED
SHROVES	SHUDDERY	SHUTOUT	SIAMEZES
SHROVING	SHUFFLE	SHUTOUTS	SIAMEZING
SHROW	SHUFFLED	SHUTS	SIB
SHROWD	SHUFFLER	SHUTTER	SIBB
SHROWED	SHUFFLERS	SHUTTERED	SIBBS
SHROWING	SHUFFLES	SHUTTERS	SIBILANCE
SHROWS	SHUFFLING	SHUTTING	SIBILANCY
SHRUB	SHUFTI	SHUTTLE	SIBILANT
SHRUBBED	SHUFTIES	SHUTTLED	SIBILANTS
SHRUBBERY	SHUFTIS	SHUTTLER	SIBILATE
SHRUBBIER	SHUFTY	SHUTTLERS	SIBILATED
SHRUBBING	SHUGGIES	SHUTTLES	SIBILATES
SHRUBBY	SHUGGY	SHUTTLING	SIBILATOR
SHRUBLAND	SHUL	SHVARTZE	SIBILOUS
SHRUBLESS	SHULE	SHVARTZES	SIBLING
SHRUBLIKE	SHULED	SHWA	SIBLINGS
SHRUBS	SHULES	SHWANPAN	SIBS
SHRUG	SHULING	SHWANPANS	SIBSHIP
SHRUGGED	SHULN	SHWAS	SIBSHIPS
SHRUGGING	SHULS	SHWESHWE	SIBYL
SHRUGS	SHUN	SHWESHWES	SIBYLIC
SHRUNK	SHUNLESS	SHY	SIBYLLIC
SHRUNKEN	SHUNNABLE	SHYER	SIBYLLINE
SHTCHI	SHUNNED	SHYERS	SIBYLS
SHTCHIS	SHUNNER	SHYEST	SIC
SHTETEL	SHUNNERS	SHYING	SICCAN
SHTETELS	SHUNNING	SHYISH	SICCAR
SHTETL	SHUNPIKE	SHYLOCK	SICCATIVE
SHTETLACH	SHUNPIKED	SHYLOCKED	SICCED
SHTETLS	SHUNPIKER	SHYLOCKS	SICCING
SHTICK	SHUNPIKES	SHYLY	SICCITIES
SHTICKIER	SHUNS	SHYNESS	SICCITY
SHTICKS	SHUNT	SHYNESSES	SICE
SHTICKY	SHUNTED	SHYPOO	SICES
SHTIK	SHUNTER	SHYPOOS	SICH
SHTIKS	SHUNTERS	SHYSTER	SICHT
SHTOOK	SHUNTING	SHYSTERS	SICHTED
SHTOOKS	SHUNTINGS	SI	SICHTING
SHTOOM	SHUNTS	SIAL	SICHTS
SHTUCK	SHURA	SIALIC	SICILIANA
SHTUCKS	SHURAS	SIALID	SICILIANE
SHTUM	SHUSH	SIALIDAN	SICILIANO
SHTUMM	SHUSHED	SIALIDANS	SICK
SHTUP	SHUSHER	SIALIDS	SICKBAY
SHTUPPED	SHUSHERS	SIALOGRAM	SICKBAYS
SHTUPPING	SHUSHES	SIALOID	SICKBED
SHTUPS	SHUSHING	SIALOLITH	SICKBEDS
SHUBUNKIN	SHUT	SIALON	SICKED
SHUCK	SHUTDOWN	SIALONS	SICKEE
SHUCKED	SHUTDOWNS	SIALS	SICKEES
SHUCKER	SHUTE	SIAMANG	SICKEN
SHUCKERS	SHUTED	SIAMANGS	SICKENED
SHUCKING	SHUTES	SIAMESE	SICKENER
SHUCKINGS	SHUTEYE	SIAMESED	SICKENERS
SHUCKS	SHUTEYES	SIAMESES	SICKENING

SICKENS	SIDECARS	SIDEWARD	SIFAKAS
SICKER	SIDECHECK	SIDEWARDS	SIFFLE
SICKERLY	SIDED	SIDEWAY	SIFFLED
SICKEST	SIDEDNESS	SIDEWAYS	SIFFLES
SICKIE	SIDEDRESS	SIDEWHEEL	SIFFLEUR
SICKIES	SIDEHILL	SIDEWISE	SIFFLEURS
SICKING	SIDEHILLS	SIDH	SIFFLEUSE
SICKISH	SIDEKICK	SIDHA	SIFFLING
SICKISHLY	SIDEKICKS	SIDHAS	SIFREI
SICKLE	SIDELIGHT	SIDHE	SIFT
SICKLED	SIDELINE	SIDING	SIFTED
SICKLEMAN	SIDELINED	SIDINGS	SIFTER
SICKLEMEN	SIDELINER	SIDLE	SIFTERS
SICKLEMIA	SIDELINES	SIDLED	SIFTING
SICKLEMIC	SIDELING	SIDLER	SIFTINGLY
SICKLES	SIDELOCK	SIDLERS	SIFTINGS
SICKLIED	SIDELOCKS	SIDLES	SIFTS
SICKLIER	SIDELONG	SIDLING	SIGANID
SICKLIES	SIDEMAN	SIDLINGLY	SIGANIDS
SICKLIEST	SIDEMEN	SIECLE	SIGH
SICKLILY	SIDENOTE	SIECLES	SIGHED
SICKLING	SIDENOTES	SIEGE	SIGHER
SICKLY	SIDEPATH	SIEGED	SIGHERS
SICKLYING	SIDEPATHS	SIEGER	SIGHFUL
SICKNESS	SIDEPIECE	SIEGERS	SIGHING
SICKNURSE	SIDER	SIEGES	SIGHINGLY
SICKO	SIDERAL	SIEGING	SIGHLESS
SICKOS	SIDERATE	SIELD	SIGHLIKE
SICKOUT	SIDERATED	SIEMENS	SIGHS
SICKOUTS	SIDERATES	SIEN	SIGHT
SICKROOM	SIDEREAL	SIENITE	SIGHTABLE
SICKROOMS	SIDERITE	SIENITES	SIGHTED
SICKS	SIDERITES	SIENNA	SIGHTER
SICLIKE	SIDERITIC	SIENNAS	SIGHTERS
SICS	SIDEROAD	SIENS	SIGHTING
SIDA	SIDEROADS	SIENT	SIGHTINGS
SIDALCEA	SIDEROSES	SIENTS	SIGHTLESS
SIDALCEAS	SIDEROSIS	SIEROZEM	SIGHTLIER
SIDAS	SIDEROTIC	SIEROZEMS	SIGHTLINE
SIDDHA	SIDERS	SIERRA	SIGHTLY
SIDDHAS	SIDES	SIERRAN	SIGHTS
SIDDHI	SIDESHOOT	SIERRAS	SIGHTSAW
SIDDHIS	SIDESHOW	SIES	SIGHTSEE
SIDDHUISM	SIDESHOWS	SIESTA	SIGHTSEEN
SIDDUR	SIDESLIP	SIESTAS	SIGHTSEER
SIDDURIM	SIDESLIPS	SIETH	SIGHTSEES
SIDDURS	SIDESMAN	SIETHS	SIGHTSMAN
SIDE	SIDESMEN	SIEUR	SIGHTSMEN
SIDEARM	SIDESPIN	SIEURS	SIGIL
SIDEARMS	SIDESPINS	SIEVE	SIGILLARY
SIDEBAND	SIDESTEP	SIEVED	SIGILLATE
SIDEBANDS	SIDESTEPS	SIEVELIKE	SIGILS
SIDEBAR	SIDESWIPE	SIEVERT	SIGISBEI
SIDEBARS	SIDETRACK	SIEVERTS	SIGISBEO
SIDEBOARD	SIDEWALK	SIEVES	SIGLA
SIDEBONES	SIDEWALKS	SIEVING	SIGLAS
SIDEBURNS	SIDEWALL	SIF	SIGLOI
SIDECAR	SIDEWALLS	SIFAKA	SIGLOS

SIGLUM
SIGMA
SIGMAS
SIGMATE
SIGMATED
SIGMATES
SIGMATIC
SIGMATING
SIGMATION
SIGMATISM
SIGMATRON
SIGMOID
SIGMOIDAL
SIGMOIDS
SIGN
SIGNA
SIGNABLE
SIGNAGE
SIGNAGES
SIGNAL
SIGNALED
SIGNALER
SIGNALERS
SIGNALING
SIGNALISE
SIGNALIZE
SIGNALLED
SIGNALLER
SIGNALLY
SIGNALMAN
SIGNALMEN
SIGNALS
SIGNARIES
SIGNARY
SIGNATORY
SIGNATURE
SIGNBOARD
SIGNED
SIGNEE
SIGNEES
SIGNER
SIGNERS
SIGNET
SIGNETED
SIGNETING
SIGNETS
SIGNEUR
SIGNEURIE
SIGNIEUR
SIGNIEURS
SIGNIFICS
SIGNIFIED
SIGNIFIER
SIGNIFIES
SIGNIFY
SIGNING
SIGNINGS
SIGNIOR

SIGNIORI
SIGNIORS
SIGNIORY
SIGNLESS
SIGNOR
SIGNORA
SIGNORAS
SIGNORE
SIGNORES
SIGNORI
SIGNORIA
SIGNORIAL
SIGNORIAS
SIGNORIES
SIGNORINA
SIGNORINE
SIGNORINI
SIGNORINO
SIGNORS
SIGNORY
SIGNPOST
SIGNPOSTS
SIGNS
SIJO
SIJOS
SIK
SIKA
SIKAS
SIKE
SIKER
SIKES
SIKORSKY
SILAGE
SILAGED
SILAGEING
SILAGES
SILAGING
SILANE
SILANES
SILASTIC
SILASTICS
SILD
SILDS
SILE
SILED
SILEN
SILENCE
SILENCED
SILENCER
SILENCERS
SILENCES
SILENCING
SILENE
SILENES
SILENI
SILENS
SILENT
SILENTER

SILENTEST
SILENTLY
SILENTS
SILENUS
SILER
SILERS
SILES
SILESIA
SILESIAS
SILEX
SILEXES
SILICA
SILICAS
SILICATE
SILICATED
SILICATES
SILICEOUS
SILICIC
SILICIDE
SILICIDES
SILICIFY
SILICIOUS
SILICIUM
SILICIUMS
SILICLE
SILICLES
SILICON
SILICONE
SILICONES
SILICONS
SILICOSES
SILICOSIS
SILICOTIC
SILICULA
SILICULAE
SILICULAS
SILICULE
SILICULES
SILING
SILIQUA
SILIQUAE
SILIQUAS
SILIQUE
SILIQUES
SILIQUOSE
SILIQUOUS
SILK
SILKALENE
SILKALINE
SILKED
SILKEN
SILKENED
SILKENING
SILKENS
SILKIE
SILKIER
SILKIES
SILKIEST

SILKILY
SILKINESS
SILKING
SILKLIKE
SILKOLINE
SILKS
SILKTAIL
SILKTAILS
SILKWEED
SILKWEEDS
SILKWORM
SILKWORMS
SILKY
SILL
SILLABUB
SILLABUBS
SILLADAR
SILLADARS
SILLER
SILLERS
SILLIBUB
SILLIBUBS
SILLIER
SILLIES
SILLIEST
SILLILY
SILLINESS
SILLOCK
SILLOCKS
SILLS
SILLY
SILO
SILOED
SILOING
SILOS
SILOXANE
SILOXANES
SILPHIA
SILPHIUM
SILPHIUMS
SILT
SILTATION
SILTED
SILTIER
SILTIEST
SILTING
SILTS
SILTSTONE
SILTY
SILURIAN
SILURID
SILURIDS
SILURIST
SILURISTS
SILUROID
SILUROIDS
SILVA
SILVAE

SILVAN	SIMKINS	SIMPLISMS	SINFONIA
SILVANS	SIMLIN	SIMPLIST	SINFONIAS
SILVAS	SIMLINS	SIMPLISTE	SINFONIE
SILVATIC	SIMMER	SIMPLISTS	SINFUL
SILVER	SIMMERED	SIMPLY	SINFULLY
SILVERED	SIMMERING	SIMPS	SING
SILVERER	SIMMERS	SIMS	SINGABLE
SILVERERS	SIMNEL	SIMUL	SINGALONG
SILVEREYE	SIMNELS	SIMULACRA	SINGE
SILVERIER	SIMOLEON	SIMULACRE	SINGED
SILVERING	SIMOLEONS	SIMULANT	SINGEING
SILVERISE	SIMONIAC	SIMULANTS	SINGER
SILVERIZE	SIMONIACS	SIMULAR	SINGERS
SILVERLY	SIMONIES	SIMULARS	SINGES
SILVERN	SIMONIOUS	SIMULATE	SINGING
SILVERS	SIMONISE	SIMULATED	SINGINGLY
SILVERY	SIMONISED	SIMULATES	SINGINGS
SILVEX	SIMONISES	SIMULATOR	SINGLE
SILVEXES	SIMONIST	SIMULCAST	SINGLED
SILVICAL	SIMONISTS	SIMULIUM	SINGLEDOM
SILVICS	SIMONIZE	SIMULIUMS	SINGLES
SIM	SIMONIZED	SIMULS	SINGLET
SIMA	SIMONIZES	SIMURG	SINGLETON
SIMAR	SIMONY	SIMURGH	SINGLETS
SIMAROUBA	SIMOOM	SIMURGHS	SINGLING
SIMARRE	SIMOOMS	SIMURGS	SINGLINGS
SIMARRES	SIMOON	SIN	SINGLY
SIMARS	SIMOONS	SINAPISM	SINGS
SIMARUBA	SIMORG	SINAPISMS	SINGSONG
SIMARUBAS	SIMORGS	SINCE	SINGSONGS
SIMAS	SIMP	SINCERE	SINGSONGY
SIMATIC	SIMPAI	SINCERELY	SINGSPIEL
SIMAZINE	SIMPAIS	SINCERER	SINGULAR
SIMAZINES	SIMPATICO	SINCEREST	SINGULARS
SIMBA	SIMPER	SINCERITY	SINGULARY
SIMBAS	SIMPERED	SINCIPITA	SINGULT
SIMI	SIMPERER	SINCIPUT	SINGULTS
SIMIAL	SIMPERERS	SINCIPUTS	SINGULTUS
SIMIAN	SIMPERING	SIND	SINH
SIMIANS	SIMPERS	SINDED	SINHS
SIMILAR	SIMPKIN	SINDING	SINICAL
SIMILARLY	SIMPKINS	SINDINGS	SINICISE
SIMILE	SIMPLE	SINDON	SINICISED
SIMILES	SIMPLED	SINDONS	SINICISES
SIMILISE	SIMPLER	SINDS	SINICIZE
SIMILISED	SIMPLERS	SINE	SINICIZED
SIMILISES	SIMPLES	SINECURE	SINICIZES
SIMILIZE	SIMPLESSE	SINECURES	SINING
SIMILIZED	SIMPLEST	SINED	SINISTER
SIMILIZES	SIMPLETON	SINES	SINISTRAL
SIMILOR	SIMPLEX	SINEW	SINK
SIMILORS	SIMPLEXES	SINEWED	SINKABLE
SIMIOID	SIMPLICES	SINEWIER	SINKAGE
SIMIOUS	SIMPLICIA	SINEWIEST	SINKAGES
SIMIS	SIMPLIFY	SINEWING	SINKER
SIMITAR	SIMPLING	SINEWLESS	SINKERS
SIMITARS	SIMPLINGS	SINEWS	SINKHOLE
SIMKIN	SIMPLISM	SINEWY	SINKHOLES

SINKIER	SIPHONED	SIROC	SISTRUM
SINKIEST	SIPHONET	SIROCCO	SISTRUMS
SINKING	SIPHONETS	SIROCCOS	SISTS
SINKINGS	SIPHONIC	SIROCS	SIT
SINKS	SIPHONING	SIRONISE	SITAR
SINKY	SIPHONS	SIRONISED	SITARIST
SINLESS	SIPHUNCLE	SIRONISES	SITARISTS
SINLESSLY	SIPING	SIRONIZE	SITARS
SINNED	SIPPED	SIRONIZED	SITATUNGA
SINNER	SIPPER	SIRONIZES	SITCOM
SINNERED	SIPPERS	SIROSET	SITCOMS
SINNERING	SIPPET	SIRRA	SITE
SINNERS	SIPPETS	SIRRAH	SITED
SINNET	SIPPING	SIRRAHS	SITELLA
SINNETS	SIPPLE	SIRRAS	SITELLAS
SINNING	SIPPLED	SIRRED	SITES
SINNINGIA	SIPPLES	SIRREE	SITFAST
SINOLOGUE	SIPPLING	SIRREES	SITFASTS
SINOLOGY	SIPPY	SIRRING	SITH
SINOPIA	SIPS	SIRS	SITHE
SINOPIAS	SIR	SIRUP	SITHED
SINOPIE	SIRCAR	SIRUPED	SITHEE
SINOPIS	SIRCARS	SIRUPIER	SITHEN
SINOPISES	SIRDAR	SIRUPIEST	SITHENCE
SINOPITE	SIRDARS	SIRUPING	SITHENS
SINOPITES	SIRE	SIRUPS	SITHES
SINS	SIRED	SIRUPY	SITHING
SINSYNE	SIREE	SIRVENTE	SITING
SINTER	SIREES	SIRVENTES	SITIOLOGY
SINTERED	SIREN	SIS	SITKA
SINTERING	SIRENIAN	SISAL	SITKAMER
SINTERS	SIRENIANS	SISALS	SITKAMERS
SINTERY	SIRENIC	SISERARY	SITOLOGY
SINUATE	SIRENISE	SISES	SITREP
SINUATED	SIRENISED	SISKIN	SITREPS
SINUATELY	SIRENISES	SISKINS	SITS
SINUATES	SIRENIZE	SISS	SITTAR
SINUATING	SIRENIZED	SISSES	SITTARS
SINUATION	SIRENIZES	SISSIER	SITTELLA
SINUITIS	SIRENS	SISSIES	SITTELLAS
SINUOSE	SIRES	SISSIEST	SITTEN
SINUOSITY	SIRGANG	SISSIFIED	SITTER
SINUOUS	SIRGANGS	SISSINESS	SITTERS
SINUOUSLY	SIRI	SISSOO	SITTINE
SINUS	SIRIASES	SISSOOS	SITTING
SINUSES	SIRIASIS	SISSY	SITTINGS
SINUSITIS	SIRIH	SISSYISH	SITUATE
SINUSLIKE	SIRIHS	SISSYNESS	SITUATED
SINUSOID	SIRING	SIST	SITUATES
SINUSOIDS	SIRIS	SISTED	SITUATING
SIP	SIRKAR	SISTER	SITUATION
SIPE	SIRKARS	SISTERED	SITULA
SIPED	SIRLOIN	SISTERING	SITULAE
SIPES	SIRLOINS	SISTERLY	SITUP
SIPHON	SIRNAME	SISTERS	SITUPS
SIPHONAGE	SIRNAMED	SISTING	SITUS
SIPHONAL	SIRNAMES	SISTRA	SITUSES
SIPHONATE	SIRNAMING	SISTROID	SITUTUNGA

SITZ	SIZES	SKATER	SKEIGHEST
SITZKRIEG	SIZIER	SKATERS	SKEIN
SITZMARK	SIZIEST	SKATES	SKEINED
SITZMARKS	SIZINESS	SKATING	SKEINING
SIVER	SIZING	SKATINGS	SKEINS
SIVERS	SIZINGS	SKATOL	SKELDER
SIWASH	SIZISM	SKATOLE	SKELDERED
SIWASHED	SIZISMS	SKATOLES	SKELDERS
SIWASHES	SIZIST	SKATOLS	SKELETAL
SIWASHING	SIZISTS	SKATS	SKELETON
SIX	SIZY	SKATT	SKELETONS
SIXAIN	SIZZLE	SKATTS	SKELF
SIXAINE	SIZZLED	SKAW	SKELFS
SIXAINES	SIZZLER	SKAWS	SKELL
SIXAINS	SIZZLERS	SKEAN	SKELLIE
SIXER	SIZZLES	SKEANE	SKELLIED
SIXERS	SIZZLING	SKEANES	SKELLIER
SIXES	SIZZLINGS	SKEANS	SKELLIES
SIXFOLD	SJAMBOK	SKEAR	SKELLIEST
SIXMO	SJAMBOKED	SKEARED	SKELLOCH
SIXMOS	SJAMBOKS	SKEARIER	SKELLOCHS
SIXPENCE	SJOE	SKEARIEST	SKELLS
SIXPENCES	SKA	SKEARING	SKELLUM
SIXPENNY	SKAG	SKEARS	SKELLUMS
SIXSCORE	SKAGS	SKEARY	SKELLY
SIXSCORES	SKAIL	SKEDADDLE	SKELLYING
SIXTE	SKAILED	SKEE	SKELM
SIXTEEN	SKAILING	SKEECHAN	SKELMS
SIXTEENER	SKAILS	SKEECHANS	SKELP
SIXTEENMO	SKAITH	SKEED	SKELPED
SIXTEENS	SKAITHED	SKEEF	SKELPING
SIXTEENTH	SKAITHING	SKEEING	SKELPINGS
SIXTES	SKAITHS	SKEELIER	SKELPIT
SIXTH	SKALD	SKEELIEST	SKELPS
SIXTHLY	SKALDIC	SKEELY	SKELTER
SIXTHS	SKALDS	SKEEN	SKELTERED
SIXTIES	SKALDSHIP	SKEENS	SKELTERS
SIXTIETH	SKANGER	SKEER	SKELUM
SIXTIETHS	SKANGERS	SKEERED	SKELUMS
SIXTY	SKANK	SKEERIER	SKEN
SIXTYISH	SKANKED	SKEERIEST	SKENE
SIZABLE	SKANKER	SKEERING	SKENES
SIZABLY	SKANKERS	SKEERS	SKENNED
SIZAR	SKANKIER	SKEERY	SKENNING
SIZARS	SKANKIEST	SKEES	SKENS
SIZARSHIP	SKANKING	SKEESICKS	SKEO
SIZE	SKANKINGS	SKEET	SKEOS
SIZEABLE	SKANKS	SKEETER	SKEP
SIZEABLY	SKANKY	SKEETERS	SKEPFUL
SIZED	SKART	SKEETS	SKEPFULS
SIZEISM	SKARTH	SKEG	SKEPPED
SIZEISMS	SKARTHS	SKEGG	SKEPPING
SIZEIST	SKARTS	SKEGGER	SKEPS
SIZEISTS	SKAS	SKEGGERS	SKEPSIS
SIZEL	SKAT	SKEGGS	SKEPSISES
SIZELS	SKATE	SKEGS	SKEPTIC
SIZER	SKATED	SKEIGH	SKEPTICAL
SIZERS	SKATEPARK	SKEIGHER	SKEPTICS

SKER	SKIDDOO	SKIMMERS	SKIPPED
SKERRED	SKIDDOOED	SKIMMIA	SKIPPER
SKERRICK	SKIDDOOS	SKIMMIAS	SKIPPERED
SKERRICKS	SKIDDY	SKIMMING	SKIPPERS
SKERRIES	SKIDLID	SKIMMINGS	SKIPPET
SKERRING	SKIDLIDS	SKIMO	SKIPPETS
SKERRY	SKIDOO	SKIMOBILE	SKIPPIER
SKERS	SKIDOOED	SKIMOS	SKIPPIEST
SKET	SKIDOOING	SKIMP	SKIPPING
SKETCH	SKIDOOS	SKIMPED	SKIPPINGS
SKETCHED	SKIDPAN	SKIMPIER	SKIPPY
SKETCHER	SKIDPANS	SKIMPIEST	SKIPS
SKETCHERS	SKIDPROOF	SKIMPILY	SKIRL
SKETCHES	SKIDS	SKIMPING	SKIRLED
SKETCHIER	SKIDWAY	SKIMPS	SKIRLING
SKETCHILY	SKIDWAYS	SKIMPY	SKIRLINGS
SKETCHING	SKIED	SKIMS	SKIRLS
SKETCHPAD	SKIER	SKIN	SKIRMISH
SKETCHY	SKIERS	SKINCARE	SKIRR
SKETS	SKIES	SKINCARES	SKIRRED
SKETTED	SKIEY	SKINFLICK	SKIRRET
SKETTING	SKIEYER	SKINFLINT	SKIRRETS
SKEW	SKIEYEST	SKINFOOD	SKIRRING
SKEWBACK	SKIFF	SKINFOODS	SKIRRS
SKEWBACKS	SKIFFED	SKINFUL	SKIRT
SKEWBALD	SKIFFING	SKINFULS	SKIRTED
SKEWBALDS	SKIFFLE	SKINHEAD	SKIRTER
SKEWED	SKIFFLED	SKINHEADS	SKIRTERS
SKEWER	SKIFFLES	SKINK	SKIRTING
SKEWERED	SKIFFLESS	SKINKED	SKIRTINGS
SKEWERING	SKIFFLING	SKINKER	SKIRTLESS
SKEWERS	SKIFFS	SKINKERS	SKIRTLIKE
SKEWEST	SKIING	SKINKING	SKIRTS
SKEWING	SKIINGS	SKINKS	SKIS
SKEWNESS	SKIJORER	SKINLESS	SKIT
SKEWS	SKIJORERS	SKINLIKE	SKITCH
SKEWWHIFF	SKIJORING	SKINNED	SKITCHED
SKI	SKILFUL	SKINNER	SKITCHES
SKIABLE	SKILFULLY	SKINNERS	SKITCHING
SKIAGRAM	SKILL	SKINNIER	SKITE
SKIAGRAMS	SKILLED	SKINNIEST	SKITED
SKIAGRAPH	SKILLESS	SKINNING	SKITES
SKIAMACHY	SKILLET	SKINNY	SKITING
SKIASCOPE	SKILLETS	SKINS	SKITS
SKIASCOPY	SKILLFUL	SKINT	SKITTER
SKIATRON	SKILLIER	SKINTER	SKITTERED
SKIATRONS	SKILLIES	SKINTEST	SKITTERS
SKIBOB	SKILLIEST	SKINTIGHT	SKITTERY
SKIBOBBED	SKILLING	SKIO	SKITTISH
SKIBOBBER	SKILLINGS	SKIORING	SKITTLE
SKIBOBS	SKILLION	SKIORINGS	SKITTLED
SKID	SKILLIONS	SKIOS	SKITTLES
SKIDDED	SKILLS	SKIP	SKITTLING
SKIDDER	SKILLY	SKIPJACK	SKIVE
SKIDDERS	SKIM	SKIPJACKS	SKIVED
SKIDDIER	SKIMBOARD	SKIPLANE	SKIVER
SKIDDIEST	SKIMMED	SKIPLANES	SKIVERED
SKIDDING	SKIMMER	SKIPPABLE	SKIVERING

SKIVERS	SKRANS	SKULPINS	SKYJACKS
SKIVES	SKREEGH	SKUMMER	SKYLAB
SKIVIE	SKREEGHED	SKUMMERED	SKYLABS
SKIVIER	SKREEGHS	SKUMMERS	SKYLARK
SKIVIEST	SKREEN	SKUNK	SKYLARKED
SKIVING	SKREENS	SKUNKBIRD	SKYLARKER
SKIVINGS	SKREIGH	SKUNKED	SKYLARKS
SKIVVIED	SKREIGHED	SKUNKIER	SKYLIGHT
SKIVVIES	SKREIGHS	SKUNKIEST	SKYLIGHTS
SKIVVY	SKRIECH	SKUNKING	SKYLIKE
SKIVVYING	SKRIECHED	SKUNKS	SKYLINE
SKIVY	SKRIECHS	SKUNKWEED	SKYLINES
SKIWEAR	SKRIED	SKUNKY	SKYLIT
SKLATE	SKRIEGH	SKURRIED	SKYMAN
SKLATED	SKRIEGHED	SKURRIES	SKYMEN
SKLATES	SKRIEGHS	SKURRY	SKYPHOI
SKLATING	SKRIES	SKURRYING	SKYPHOS
SKLENT	SKRIK	SKUTTLE	SKYR
SKLENTED	SKRIKE	SKUTTLED	SKYRE
SKLENTING	SKRIKED	SKUTTLES	SKYRED
SKLENTS	SKRIKES	SKUTTLING	SKYRES
SKLIFF	SKRIKING	SKY	SKYRING
SKLIFFS	SKRIKS	SKYBOARD	SKYROCKET
SKLIM	SKRIMMAGE	SKYBOARDS	SKYRS
SKLIMMED	SKRIMP	SKYBORN	SKYSAIL
SKLIMMING	SKRIMPED	SKYBORNE	SKYSAILS
SKLIMS	SKRIMPING	SKYBOX	SKYSCAPE
SKOAL	SKRIMPS	SKYBOXES	SKYSCAPES
SKOALED	SKRUMP	SKYBRIDGE	SKYSURF
SKOALING	SKRUMPED	SKYCAP	SKYSURFED
SKOALS	SKRUMPING	SKYCAPS	SKYSURFER
SKOFF	SKRUMPS	SKYCLAD	SKYSURFS
SKOFFED	SKRY	SKYDIVE	SKYTE
SKOFFING	SKRYER	SKYDIVED	SKYTED
SKOFFS	SKRYERS	SKYDIVER	SKYTES
SKOKIAAN	SKRYING	SKYDIVERS	SKYTING
SKOKIAANS	SKUA	SKYDIVES	SKYWALK
SKOL	SKUAS	SKYDIVING	SKYWALKS
SKOLIA	SKUDLER	SKYDOVE	SKYWARD
SKOLION	SKUDLERS	SKYED	SKYWARDS
SKOLLED	SKUG	SKYER	SKYWAY
SKOLLIE	SKUGGED	SKYERS	SKYWAYS
SKOLLIES	SKUGGING	SKYEY	SKYWRITE
SKOLLING	SKUGS	SKYF	SKYWRITER
SKOLLY	SKULK	SKYFED	SKYWRITES
SKOLS	SKULKED	SKYFING	SKYWROTE
SKOOKUM	SKULKER	SKYFS	SLAB
SKOOL	SKULKERS	SKYHOME	SLABBED
SKOOLS	SKULKING	SKYHOMES	SLABBER
SKOOSH	SKULKINGS	SKYHOOK	SLABBERED
SKOOSHED	SKULKS	SKYHOOKS	SLABBERER
SKOOSHES	SKULL	SKYIER	SLABBERS
SKOOSHING	SKULLCAP	SKYIEST	SLABBERY
SKORT	SKULLCAPS	SKYING	SLABBIER
SKORTS	SKULLED	SKYISH	SLABBIEST
SKOSH	SKULLING	SKYJACK	SLABBING
SKOSHES	SKULLS	SKYJACKED	SLABBY
SKRAN	SKULPIN	SKYJACKER	SLABLIKE

SLABS
SLABSTONE
SLACK
SLACKED
SLACKEN
SLACKENED
SLACKENER
SLACKENS
SLACKER
SLACKERS
SLACKEST
SLACKING
SLACKLY
SLACKNESS
SLACKS
SLADANG
SLADANGS
SLADE
SLADES
SLAE
SLAES
SLAG
SLAGGED
SLAGGIER
SLAGGIEST
SLAGGING
SLAGGINGS
SLAGGY
SLAGS
SLAID
SLAIN
SLAINTE
SLAIRG
SLAIRGED
SLAIRGING
SLAIRGS
SLAISTER
SLAISTERS
SLAISTERY
SLAKABLE
SLAKE
SLAKEABLE
SLAKED
SLAKELESS
SLAKER
SLAKERS
SLAKES
SLAKING
SLALOM
SLALOMED
SLALOMER
SLALOMERS
SLALOMING
SLALOMIST
SLALOMS
SLAM
SLAMDANCE
SLAMMAKIN

SLAMMED
SLAMMER
SLAMMERS
SLAMMING
SLAMMINGS
SLAMS
SLANDER
SLANDERED
SLANDERER
SLANDERS
SLANE
SLANES
SLANG
SLANGED
SLANGER
SLANGERS
SLANGIER
SLANGIEST
SLANGILY
SLANGING
SLANGINGS
SLANGISH
SLANGS
SLANGUAGE
SLANGULAR
SLANGY
SLANK
SLANT
SLANTED
SLANTER
SLANTERS
SLANTING
SLANTLY
SLANTS
SLANTWAYS
SLANTWISE
SLANTY
SLAP
SLAPDASH
SLAPHAPPY
SLAPHEAD
SLAPHEADS
SLAPJACK
SLAPJACKS
SLAPPED
SLAPPER
SLAPPERS
SLAPPING
SLAPS
SLAPSHOT
SLAPSHOTS
SLAPSTICK
SLART
SLARTED
SLARTING
SLARTS
SLASH
SLASHED

SLASHER
SLASHERS
SLASHES
SLASHFEST
SLASHING
SLASHINGS
SLAT
SLATCH
SLATCHES
SLATE
SLATED
SLATELIKE
SLATER
SLATERS
SLATES
SLATEY
SLATHER
SLATHERED
SLATHERS
SLATIER
SLATIEST
SLATINESS
SLATING
SLATINGS
SLATS
SLATTED
SLATTER
SLATTERED
SLATTERN
SLATTERNS
SLATTERS
SLATTERY
SLATTING
SLATTINGS
SLATY
SLAUGHTER
SLAVE
SLAVED
SLAVER
SLAVERED
SLAVERER
SLAVERERS
SLAVERIES
SLAVERING
SLAVERS
SLAVERY
SLAVES
SLAVEY
SLAVEYS
SLAVING
SLAVISH
SLAVISHLY
SLAVOCRAT
SLAVOPHIL
SLAW
SLAWS
SLAY
SLAYABLE

SLAYED
SLAYER
SLAYERS
SLAYING
SLAYS
SLEAVE
SLEAVED
SLEAVES
SLEAVING
SLEAZE
SLEAZEBAG
SLEAZES
SLEAZIER
SLEAZIEST
SLEAZILY
SLEAZO
SLEAZOID
SLEAZOIDS
SLEAZY
SLED
SLEDDED
SLEDDER
SLEDDERS
SLEDDING
SLEDDINGS
SLEDED
SLEDGE
SLEDGED
SLEDGER
SLEDGERS
SLEDGES
SLEDGING
SLEDGINGS
SLEDS
SLEE
SLEECH
SLEECHES
SLEECHIER
SLEECHY
SLEEK
SLEEKED
SLEEKEN
SLEEKENED
SLEEKENS
SLEEKER
SLEEKERS
SLEEKEST
SLEEKIER
SLEEKIEST
SLEEKING
SLEEKINGS
SLEEKIT
SLEEKLY
SLEEKNESS
SLEEKS
SLEEKY
SLEEP
SLEEPAWAY

SLEEPER
SLEEPERS
SLEEPERY
SLEEPIER
SLEEPIEST
SLEEPILY
SLEEPING
SLEEPINGS
SLEEPLESS
SLEEPLIKE
SLEEPOUT
SLEEPOUTS
SLEEPOVER
SLEEPRY
SLEEPS
SLEEPSUIT
SLEEPWALK
SLEEPWEAR
SLEEPY
SLEER
SLEEST
SLEET
SLEETED
SLEETIER
SLEETIEST
SLEETING
SLEETS
SLEETY
SLEEVE
SLEEVED
SLEEVEEN
SLEEVEENS
SLEEVELET
SLEEVER
SLEEVERS
SLEEVES
SLEEVING
SLEEVINGS
SLEEZIER
SLEEZIEST
SLEEZY
SLEIDED
SLEIGH
SLEIGHED
SLEIGHER
SLEIGHERS
SLEIGHING
SLEIGHS
SLEIGHT
SLEIGHTS
SLENDER
SLENDERER
SLENDERLY
SLENTER
SLENTERS
SLEPT
SLEUTH
SLEUTHED

SLEUTHING
SLEUTHS
SLEW
SLEWED
SLEWING
SLEWS
SLEY
SLEYS
SLICE
SLICEABLE
SLICED
SLICER
SLICERS
SLICES
SLICING
SLICINGS
SLICK
SLICKED
SLICKEN
SLICKENED
SLICKENER
SLICKENS
SLICKER
SLICKERED
SLICKERS
SLICKEST
SLICKING
SLICKINGS
SLICKLY
SLICKNESS
SLICKROCK
SLICKS
SLICKSTER
SLID
SLIDABLE
SLIDDEN
SLIDDER
SLIDDERED
SLIDDERS
SLIDDERY
SLIDE
SLIDED
SLIDER
SLIDERS
SLIDES
SLIDEWAY
SLIDEWAYS
SLIDING
SLIDINGLY
SLIDINGS
SLIER
SLIEST
SLIEVE
SLIEVES
SLIGHT
SLIGHTED
SLIGHTER
SLIGHTERS

SLIGHTEST
SLIGHTING
SLIGHTISH
SLIGHTLY
SLIGHTS
SLILY
SLIM
SLIMDOWN
SLIMDOWNS
SLIME
SLIMEBALL
SLIMED
SLIMES
SLIMIER
SLIMIEST
SLIMILY
SLIMINESS
SLIMING
SLIMLINE
SLIMLY
SLIMMED
SLIMMER
SLIMMERS
SLIMMEST
SLIMMING
SLIMMINGS
SLIMMISH
SLIMNESS
SLIMPSIER
SLIMPSY
SLIMS
SLIMSIER
SLIMSIEST
SLIMSY
SLIMY
SLING
SLINGBACK
SLINGER
SLINGERS
SLINGING
SLINGS
SLINGSHOT
SLINK
SLINKED
SLINKER
SLINKERS
SLINKIER
SLINKIEST
SLINKILY
SLINKING
SLINKS
SLINKSKIN
SLINKWEED
SLINKY
SLINTER
SLINTERS
SLIOTAR
SLIOTARS

SLIP
SLIPCASE
SLIPCASED
SLIPCASES
SLIPCOVER
SLIPDRESS
SLIPE
SLIPED
SLIPES
SLIPFORM
SLIPFORMS
SLIPING
SLIPKNOT
SLIPKNOTS
SLIPLESS
SLIPNOOSE
SLIPOUT
SLIPOUTS
SLIPOVER
SLIPOVERS
SLIPPAGE
SLIPPAGES
SLIPPED
SLIPPER
SLIPPERED
SLIPPERS
SLIPPERY
SLIPPIER
SLIPPIEST
SLIPPILY
SLIPPING
SLIPPY
SLIPRAIL
SLIPRAILS
SLIPS
SLIPSHEET
SLIPSHOD
SLIPSLOP
SLIPSLOPS
SLIPSOLE
SLIPSOLES
SLIPT
SLIPUP
SLIPUPS
SLIPWARE
SLIPWARES
SLIPWAY
SLIPWAYS
SLISH
SLISHES
SLIT
SLITHER
SLITHERED
SLITHERS
SLITHERY
SLITLESS
SLITLIKE
SLITS

SLITTED	SLOIDS	SLOTBACK	SLUBBERS
SLITTER	SLOJD	SLOTBACKS	SLUBBIER
SLITTERS	SLOJDS	SLOTH	SLUBBIEST
SLITTIER	SLOKEN	SLOTHED	SLUBBING
SLITTTEST	SLOKENED	SLOTHFUL	SLUBBINGS
SLITTING	SLOKENING	SLOTHING	SLUBBS
SLITTY	SLOKENS	SLOTHS	SLUBBY
SLIVE	SLOMMOCK	SLOTS	SLUBS
SLIVED	SLOMMOCKS	SLOTTED	SLUDGE
SLIVEN	SLOOM	SLOTTER	SLUDGED
SLIVER	SLOOMED	SLOTTERS	SLUDGES
SLIVERED	SLOOMIER	SLOTTING	SLUDGIER
SLIVERER	SLOOMIEST	SLOUCH	SLUDGIEST
SLIVERERS	SLOOMING	SLOUCHED	SLUDGING
SLIVERING	SLOOMS	SLOUCHER	SLUDGY
SLIVERS	SLOOMY	SLOUCHERS	SLUE
SLIVES	SLOOP	SLOUCHES	SLUED
SLIVING	SLOOPS	SLOUCHIER	SLUEING
SLIVOVIC	SLOOSH	SLOUCHILY	SLUES
SLIVOVICA	SLOOSHED	SLOUCHING	SLUFF
SLIVOVITZ	SLOOSHES	SLOUCHY	SLUFFED
SLIVOWITZ	SLOOSHING	SLOUGH	SLUFFING
SLOAN	SLOOT	SLOUGHED	SLUFFS
SLOANS	SLOOTS	SLOUGHIER	SLUG
SLOB	SLOP	SLOUGHING	SLUGABED
SLOBBER	SLOPE	SLOUGHS	SLUGABEDS
SLOBBERED	SLOPED	SLOUGHY	SLUGFEST
SLOBBERER	SLOPER	SLOVE	SLUGFESTS
SLOBBERS	SLOPERS	SLOVEN	SLUGGABED
SLOBBERY	SLOPES	SLOVENLY	SLUGGARD
SLOBBIER	SLOPEWISE	SLOVENRY	SLUGGARDS
SLOBBIEST	SLOPIER	SLOVENS	SLUGGED
SLOBBISH	SLOPIEST	SLOW	SLUGGER
SLOBBY	SLOPING	SLOWBACK	SLUGGERS
SLOBLAND	SLOPINGLY	SLOWBACKS	SLUGGING
SLOBLANDS	SLOPPED	SLOWCOACH	SLUGGISH
SLOBS	SLOPPIER	SLOWDOWN	SLUGHORN
SLOCKEN	SLOPPIEST	SLOWDOWNS	SLUGHORNE
SLOCKENED	SLOPPILY	SLOWED	SLUGHORNS
SLOCKENS	SLOPPING	SLOWER	SLUGS
SLOE	SLOPPY	SLOWEST	SLUICE
SLOEBUSH	SLOPS	SLOWING	SLUICED
SLOES	SLOPWORK	SLOWINGS	SLUICES
SLOETHORN	SLOPWORKS	SLOWISH	SLUICEWAY
SLOETREE	SLOPY	SLOWLY	SLUICIER
SLOETREES	SLORM	SLOWNESS	SLUICIEST
SLOG	SLORMED	SLOWPOKE	SLUICING
SLOGAN	SLORMING	SLOWPOKES	SLUICY
SLOGANEER	SLORMS	SLOWS	SLUING
SLOGANISE	SLOSH	SLOWWORM	SLUIT
SLOGANIZE	SLOSHED	SLOWWORMS	SLUITS
SLOGANS	SLOSHES	SLOYD	SLUM
SLOGGED	SLOSHIER	SLOYDS	SLUMBER
SLOGGER	SLOSHIEST	SLUB	SLUMBERED
SLOGGERS	SLOSHING	SLUBB	SLUMBERER
SLOGGING	SLOSHINGS	SLUBBED	SLUMBERS
SLOGS	SLOSHY	SLUBBER	SLUMBERY
SLOID	SLOT	SLUBBERED	SLUMBROUS

SLUMBRY	SLUTCHES	SMALTINE	SMEAR
SLUMGUM	SLUTCHIER	SMALTINES	SMEARCASE
SLUMGUMS	SLUTCHY	SMALTITE	SMEARED
SLUMISM	SLUTS	SMALTITES	SMEARER
SLUMISMS	SLUTTERY	SMALTO	SMEARERS
SLUMLORD	SLUTTIER	SMALTOS	SMEARIER
SLUMLORDS	SLUTTIEST	SMALTS	SMEARIEST
SLUMMED	SLUTTISH	SMARAGD	SMEARILY
SLUMMER	SLUTTY	SMARAGDE	SMEARING
SLUMMERS	SLY	SMARAGDES	SMEARS
SLUMMIER	SLYBOOTS	SMARAGDS	SMEARY
SLUMMIEST	SLYER	SMARM	SMEATH
SLUMMING	SLYEST	SMARMED	SMEATHS
SLUMMINGS	SLYISH	SMARMIER	SMECTIC
SLUMMOCK	SLYLY	SMARMIEST	SMECTITE
SLUMMOCKS	SLYNESS	SMARMILY	SMECTITES
SLUMMY	SLYNESSES	SMARMING	SMECTITIC
SLUMP	SLYPE	SMARMS	SMEDDUM
SLUMPED	SLYPES	SMARMY	SMEDDUMS
SLUMPIER	SMA	SMART	SMEE
SLUMPIEST	SMAAK	SMARTARSE	SMEECH
SLUMPING	SMAAKED	SMARTASS	SMEECHED
SLUMPS	SMAAKING	SMARTED	SMEECHES
SLUMPY	SMAAKS	SMARTEN	SMEECHING
SLUMS	SMACK	SMARTENED	SMEEK
SLUNG	SMACKED	SMARTENS	SMEEKED
SLUNGSHOT	SMACKER	SMARTER	SMEEKING
SLUNK	SMACKERS	SMARTEST	SMEEKS
SLUR	SMACKHEAD	SMARTIE	SMEES
SLURB	SMACKING	SMARTIES	SMEETH
SLURBAN	SMACKINGS	SMARTING	SMEETHS
SLURBS	SMACKS	SMARTISH	SMEGMA
SLURP	SMAIK	SMARTLY	SMEGMAS
SLURPED	SMAIKS	SMARTNESS	SMELL
SLURPER	SMALL	SMARTS	SMELLED
SLURPERS	SMALLAGE	SMARTWEED	SMELLER
SLURPING	SMALLAGES	SMARTY	SMELLERS
SLURPS	SMALLBOY	SMASH	SMELLIER
SLURRED	SMALLBOYS	SMASHABLE	SMELLIES
SLURRIED	SMALLED	SMASHED	SMELLIEST
SLURRIES	SMALLER	SMASHER	SMELLING
SLURRING	SMALLEST	SMASHEROO	SMELLINGS
SLURRY	SMALLING	SMASHERS	SMELLS
SLURRYING	SMALLISH	SMASHES	SMELLY
SLURS	SMALLNESS	SMASHING	SMELT
SLUSE	SMALLPOX	SMASHINGS	SMELTED
SLUSES	SMALLS	SMASHUP	SMELTER
SLUSH	SMALLSAT	SMASHUPS	SMELTERS
SLUSHED	SMALLSATS	SMATCH	SMELTERY
SLUSHES	SMALLTIME	SMATCHED	SMELTING
SLUSHIER	SMALM	SMATCHES	SMELTINGS
SLUSHIES	SMALMED	SMATCHING	SMELTS
SLUSHIEST	SMALMILY	SMATTER	SMERK
SLUSHILY	SMALMING	SMATTERED	SMERKED
SLUSHING	SMALMS	SMATTERER	SMERKING
SLUSHY	SMALMY	SMATTERS	SMERKS
SLUT	SMALT	SMAZE	SMEUSE
SLUTCH	SMALTI	SMAZES	SMEUSES

SMEW	SMIRKY	SMOKELIKE	SMOOTHING
SMEWS	SMIRR	SMOKEPOT	SMOOTHISH
SMICKER	SMIRRED	SMOKEPOTS	SMOOTHLY
SMICKERED	SMIRRIER	SMOKER	SMOOTHS
SMICKERS	SMIRRIEST	SMOKERS	SMOOTHY
SMICKET	SMIRRING	SMOKES	SMOOTING
SMICKETS	SMIRRS	SMOKETREE	SMOOTS
SMICKLY	SMIRRY	SMOKEY	SMORBROD
SMIDDIED	SMIRS	SMOKIER	SMORBRODS
SMIDDIES	SMIRTING	SMOKIES	SMORE
SMIDDY	SMIRTINGS	SMOKIEST	SMORED
SMIDDYING	SMIT	SMOKILY	SMORES
SMIDGE	SMITE	SMOKINESS	SMORING
SMIDGEN	SMITER	SMOKING	SMORZANDO
SMIDGENS	SMITERS	SMOKINGS	SMORZATO
SMIDGEON	SMITES	SMOKO	SMOTE
SMIDGEONS	SMITH	SMOKOS	SMOTHER
SMIDGES	SMITHED	SMOKY	SMOTHERED
SMIDGIN	SMITHERS	SMOLDER	SMOTHERER
SMIDGINS	SMITHERY	SMOLDERED	SMOTHERS
SMIERCASE	SMITHIED	SMOLDERS	SMOTHERY
SMIGHT	SMITHIES	SMOLT	SMOUCH
SMIGHTING	SMITHING	SMOLTS	SMOUCHED
SMIGHTS	SMITHS	SMOOCH	SMOUCHES
SMILAX	SMITHY	SMOOCHED	SMOUCHING
SMILAXES	SMITHYING	SMOOCHER	SMOULDER
SMILE	SMITING	SMOOCHERS	SMOULDERS
SMILED	SMITS	SMOOCHES	SMOULDRY
SMILEFUL	SMITTED	SMOOCHING	SMOUSE
SMILELESS	SMITTEN	SMOOCHY	SMOUSED
SMILER	SMITTING	SMOODGE	SMOUSER
SMILERS	SMITTLE	SMOODGED	SMOUSERS
SMILES	SMOCK	SMOODGES	SMOUSES
SMILET	SMOCKED	SMOODGING	SMOUSING
SMILETS	SMOCKING	SMOOGE	SMOUT
SMILEY	SMOCKINGS	SMOOGED	SMOUTED
SMILEYS	SMOCKLIKE	SMOOGES	SMOUTING
SMILING	SMOCKS	SMOOGING	SMOUTS
SMILINGLY	SMOG	SMOOR	SMOWT
SMILINGS	SMOGGIER	SMOORED	SMOWTS
SMILODON	SMOGGIEST	SMOORING	SMOYLE
SMILODONS	SMOGGY	SMOORS	SMOYLED
SMIR	SMOGLESS	SMOOSH	SMOYLES
SMIRCH	SMOGS	SMOOSHED	SMOYLING
SMIRCHED	SMOILE	SMOOSHES	SMRITI
SMIRCHER	SMOILED	SMOOSHING	SMRITIS
SMIRCHERS	SMOILES	SMOOT	SMUDGE
SMIRCHES	SMOILING	SMOOTED	SMUDGED
SMIRCHING	SMOKABLE	SMOOTH	SMUDGEDLY
SMIRK	SMOKE	SMOOTHED	SMUDGER
SMIRKED	SMOKEABLE	SMOOTHEN	SMUDGERS
SMIRKER	SMOKEBUSH	SMOOTHENS	SMUDGES
SMIRKERS	SMOKED	SMOOTHER	SMUDGIER
SMIRKIER	SMOKEHO	SMOOTHERS	SMUDGIEST
SMIRKIEST	SMOKEHOOD	SMOOTHES	SMUDGILY
SMIRKILY	SMOKEHOS	SMOOTHEST	SMUDGING
SMIRKING	SMOKEJACK	SMOOTHIE	SMUDGINGS
SMIRKS	SMOKELESS	SMOOTHIES	SMUDGY

SMUG	SNAFFLED	SNAPPER	SNATCH
SMUGGED	SNAFFLES	SNAPPERED	SNATCHED
SMUGGER	SNAFFLING	SNAPPERS	SNATCHER
SMUGGERY	SNAFU	SNAPPIER	SNATCHERS
SMUGGEST	SNAFUED	SNAPPIEST	SNATCHES
SMUGGING	SNAFUING	SNAPPILY	SNATCHIER
SMUGGLE	SNAFUS	SNAPPING	SNATCHILY
SMUGGLED	SNAG	SNAPPINGS	SNATCHING
SMUGGLER	SNAGGED	SNAPPISH	SNATCHY
SMUGGLERS	SNAGGIER	SNAPPY	SNATH
SMUGGLES	SNAGGIEST	SNAPS	SNATHE
SMUGGLING	SNAGGING	SNAPSHOT	SNATHES
SMUGLY	SNAGGY	SNAPSHOTS	SNATHS
SMUGNESS	SNAGLIKE	SNAPTIN	SNAW
SMUGS	SNAGS	SNAPTINS	SNAWED
SMUR	SNAIL	SNAPWEED	SNAWING
SMURFING	SNAILED	SNAPWEEDS	SNAWS
SMURFINGS	SNAILERY	SNAR	SNAZZIER
SMURRED	SNAILFISH	SNARE	SNAZZIEST
SMURRIER	SNAILIER	SNARED	SNAZZILY
SMURRIEST	SNAILIEST	SNARELESS	SNAZZY
SMURRING	SNAILING	SNARER	SNEAD
SMURRY	SNAILLIKE	SNARERS	SNEADS
SMURS	SNAILS	SNARES	SNEAK
SMUSH	SNAILY	SNARF	SNEAKED
SMUSHED	SNAKE	SNARFED	SNEAKER
SMUSHES	SNAKEBIRD	SNARFING	SNEAKERED
SMUSHING	SNAKEBIT	SNARFS	SNEAKERS
SMUT	SNAKEBITE	SNARIER	SNEAKEUP
SMUTCH	SNAKED	SNARIEST	SNEAKEUPS
SMUTCHED	SNAKEFISH	SNARING	SNEAKIER
SMUTCHES	SNAKEHEAD	SNARINGS	SNEAKIEST
SMUTCHIER	SNAKELIKE	SNARK	SNEAKILY
SMUTCHING	SNAKEPIT	SNARKIER	SNEAKING
SMUTCHY	SNAKEPITS	SNARKIEST	SNEAKISH
SMUTS	SNAKEROOT	SNARKILY	SNEAKS
SMUTTED	SNAKES	SNARKS	SNEAKSBY
SMUTTIER	SNAKESKIN	SNARKY	SNEAKY
SMUTTIEST	SNAKEWEED	SNARL	SNEAP
SMUTTILY	SNAKEWISE	SNARLED	SNEAPED
SMUTTING	SNAKEWOOD	SNARLER	SNEAPING
SMUTTY	SNAKEY	SNARLERS	SNEAPS
SMYTRIE	SNAKIER	SNARLIER	SNEATH
SMYTRIES	SNAKIEST	SNARLIEST	SNEATHS
SNAB	SNAKILY	SNARLING	SNEB
SNABBLE	SNAKINESS	SNARLINGS	SNEBBE
SNABBLED	SNAKING	SNARLS	SNEBBED
SNABBLES	SNAKISH	SNARLY	SNEBBES
SNABBLING	SNAKY	SNARRED	SNEBBING
SNABS	SNAP	SNARRING	SNEBS
SNACK	SNAPBACK	SNARS	SNECK
SNACKED	SNAPBACKS	SNARY	SNECKED
SNACKER	SNAPHANCE	SNASH	SNECKING
SNACKERS	SNAPLESS	SNASHED	SNECKS
SNACKETTE	SNAPLINK	SNASHES	SNED
SNACKING	SNAPLINKS	SNASHING	SNEDDED
SNACKS	SNAPPABLE	SNASTE	SNEDDING
SNAFFLE	SNAPPED	SNASTES	SNEDS

SNEE	SNIDER	SNIPEFISH	SNOBLINGS
SNEED	SNIDES	SNIPELIKE	SNOBS
SNEEING	SNIDEST	SNIPER	SNOD
SNEER	SNIDEY	SNIPERS	SNODDED
SNEERED	SNIDIER	SNIPES	SNODDER
SNEERER	SNIDIEST	SNIPIER	SNODDEST
SNEERERS	SNIDING	SNIPIEST	SNODDING
SNEERFUL	SNIES	SNIPING	SNODDIT
SNEERIER	SNIFF	SNIPINGS	SNODS
SNEERIEST	SNIFFABLE	SNIPPED	SNOEK
SNEERING	SNIFFED	SNIPPER	SNOEKS
SNEERINGS	SNIFFER	SNIPPERS	SNOEP
SNEERS	SNIFFERS	SNIPPET	SNOG
SNEERY	SNIFFIER	SNIPPETS	SNOGGED
SNEES	SNIFFIEST	SNIPPETY	SNOGGING
SNEESH	SNIFFILY	SNIPPIER	SNOGS
SNEESHAN	SNIFFING	SNIPPIEST	SNOKE
SNEESHANS	SNIFFINGS	SNIPPILY	SNOKED
SNEESHES	SNIFFISH	SNIPPING	SNOKES
SNEESHIN	SNIFFLE	SNIPPINGS	SNOKING
SNEESHING	SNIFFLED	SNIPPY	SNOOD
SNEESHINS	SNIFFLER	SNIPS	SNOODED
SNEEZE	SNIFFLERS	SNIPY	SNOODING
SNEEZED	SNIFFLES	SNIRT	SNOODS
SNEEZER	SNIFFLIER	SNIRTLE	SNOOK
SNEEZERS	SNIFFLING	SNIRTLED	SNOOKED
SNEEZES	SNIFFLY	SNIRTLES	SNOOKER
SNEEZIER	SNIFFS	SNIRTLING	SNOOKERED
SNEEZIEST	SNIFFY	SNIRTS	SNOOKERS
SNEEZING	SNIFT	SNIT	SNOOKING
SNEEZINGS	SNIFTED	SNITCH	SNOOKS
SNEEZY	SNIFTER	SNITCHED	SNOOL
SNELL	SNIFTERED	SNITCHER	SNOOLED
SNELLED	SNIFTERS	SNITCHERS	SNOOLING
SNELLER	SNIFTIER	SNITCHES	SNOOLS
SNELLEST	SNIFTIEST	SNITCHIER	SNOOP
SNELLING	SNIFTING	SNITCHING	SNOOPED
SNELLS	SNIFTS	SNITCHY	SNOOPER
SNELLY	SNIFTY	SNITS	SNOOPERS
SNIB	SNIG	SNIVEL	SNOOPIER
SNIBBED	SNIGGED	SNIVELED	SNOOPIEST
SNIBBING	SNIGGER	SNIVELER	SNOOPILY
SNIBS	SNIGGERED	SNIVELERS	SNOOPING
SNICK	SNIGGERER	SNIVELING	SNOOPS
SNICKED	SNIGGERS	SNIVELLED	SNOOPY
SNICKER	SNIGGING	SNIVELLER	SNOOT
SNICKERED	SNIGGLE	SNIVELLY	SNOOTED
SNICKERER	SNIGGLED	SNIVELS	SNOOTFUL
SNICKERS	SNIGGLER	SNOB	SNOOTFULS
SNICKERY	SNIGGLERS	SNOBBERY	SNOOTIER
SNICKET	SNIGGLES	SNOBBIER	SNOOTIEST
SNICKETS	SNIGGLING	SNOBBIEST	SNOOTILY
SNICKING	SNIGLET	SNOBBILY	SNOOTING
SNICKS	SNIGLETS	SNOBBISH	SNOOTS
SNIDE	SNIGS	SNOBBISM	SNOOTY
SNIDED	SNIP	SNOBBISMS	SNOOZE
SNIDELY	SNIPE	SNOBBY	SNOOZED
SNIDENESS	SNIPED	SNOBLING	SNOOZER

SNOOZERS	SNOWBANK	SNOWSCAPE	SNUGGEST
SNOOZES	SNOWBANKS	SNOWSHED	SNUGGIES
SNOOZIER	SNOWBELL	SNOWSHEDS	SNUGGING
SNOOZIEST	SNOWBELLS	SNOWSHOE	SNUGGLE
SNOOZING	SNOWBELT	SNOWSHOED	SNUGGLED
SNOOZLE	SNOWBELTS	SNOWSHOER	SNUGGLES
SNOOZLED	SNOWBERRY	SNOWSHOES	SNUGGLING
SNOOZLES	SNOWBIRD	SNOWSLIDE	SNUGLY
SNOOZLING	SNOWBIRDS	SNOWSLIP	SNUGNESS
SNOOZY	SNOWBLINK	SNOWSLIPS	SNUGS
SNORE	SNOWBOARD	SNOWSTORM	SNUSH
SNORED	SNOWBOOT	SNOWSUIT	SNUSHED
SNORER	SNOWBOOTS	SNOWSUITS	SNUSHES
SNORERS	SNOWBOUND	SNOWY	SNUSHING
SNORES	SNOWBRUSH	SNUB	SNUZZLE
SNORING	SNOWBUSH	SNUBBE	SNUZZLED
SNORINGS	SNOWCAP	SNUBBED	SNUZZLES
SNORKEL	SNOWCAPS	SNUBBER	SNUZZLING
SNORKELED	SNOWCAT	SNUBBERS	SNY
SNORKELER	SNOWCATS	SNUBBES	SNYE
SNORKELS	SNOWDRIFT	SNUBBIER	SNYES
SNORT	SNOWDROP	SNUBBIEST	SO
SNORTED	SNOWDROPS	SNUBBING	SOAK
SNORTER	SNOWED	SNUBBINGS	SOAKAGE
SNORTERS	SNOWFALL	SNUBBISH	SOAKAGES
SNORTIER	SNOWFALLS	SNUBBY	SOAKAWAY
SNORTIEST	SNOWFIELD	SNUBNESS	SOAKAWAYS
SNORTING	SNOWFLAKE	SNUBS	SOAKED
SNORTINGS	SNOWFLECK	SNUCK	SOAKEN
SNORTS	SNOWFLICK	SNUDGE	SOAKER
SNORTY	SNOWIER	SNUDGED	SOAKERS
SNOT	SNOWIEST	SNUDGES	SOAKING
SNOTS	SNOWILY	SNUDGING	SOAKINGLY
SNOTTED	SNOWINESS	SNUFF	SOAKINGS
SNOTTER	SNOWING	SNUFFBOX	SOAKS
SNOTTERED	SNOWISH	SNUFFED	SOAP
SNOTTERS	SNOWK	SNUFFER	SOAPBARK
SNOTTERY	SNOWKED	SNUFFERS	SOAPBARKS
SNOTTIE	SNOWKING	SNUFFIER	SOAPBERRY
SNOTTIER	SNOWKS	SNUFFIEST	SOAPBOX
SNOTTIES	SNOWLAND	SNUFFILY	SOAPBOXED
SNOTTIEST	SNOWLANDS	SNUFFING	SOAPBOXES
SNOTTILY	SNOWLESS	SNUFFINGS	SOAPED
SNOTTING	SNOWLIKE	SNUFFLE	SOAPER
SNOTTY	SNOWLINE	SNUFFLED	SOAPERS
SNOUT	SNOWLINES	SNUFFLER	SOAPIE
SNOUTED	SNOWMAKER	SNUFFLERS	SOAPIER
SNOUTIER	SNOWMAN	SNUFFLES	SOAPIES
SNOUTIEST	SNOWMELT	SNUFFLIER	SOAPIEST
SNOUTING	SNOWMELTS	SNUFFLING	SOAPILY
SNOUTISH	SNOWMEN	SNUFFLY	SOAPINESS
SNOUTLESS	SNOWMOLD	SNUFFS	SOAPING
SNOUTLIKE	SNOWMOLDS	SNUFFY	SOAPLAND
SNOUTS	SNOWPACK	SNUG	SOAPLANDS
SNOUTY	SNOWPACKS	SNUGGED	SOAPLESS
SNOW	SNOWPLOW	SNUGGER	SOAPLIKE
SNOWBALL	SNOWPLOWS	SNUGGERIE	SOAPROOT
SNOWBALLS	SNOWS	SNUGGERY	SOAPROOTS

SOAPS	SOCCAGES	SODAMIDE	SOFTCOVER
SOAPSTONE	SOCCER	SODAMIDES	SOFTED
SOAPSUDS	SOCCERS	SODAS	SOFTEN
SOAPSUDSY	SOCIABLE	SODBUSTER	SOFTENED
SOAPWORT	SOCIABLES	SODDED	SOFTENER
SOAPWORTS	SOCIABLY	SODDEN	SOFTENERS
SOAPY	SOCIAL	SODDENED	SOFTENING
SOAR	SOCIALISE	SODDENING	SOFTENS
SOARAWAY	SOCIALISM	SODDENLY	SOFTER
SOARE	SOCIALIST	SODDENS	SOFTEST
SOARED	SOCIALITE	SODDIER	SOFTGOODS
SOARER	SOCIALITY	SODDIES	SOFTHEAD
SOARERS	SOCIALIZE	SODDIEST	SOFTHEADS
SOARES	SOCIALLY	SODDING	SOFTIE
SOARING	SOCIALS	SODDY	SOFTIES
SOARINGLY	SOCIATE	SODGER	SOFTING
SOARINGS	SOCIATES	SODGERED	SOFTISH
SOARS	SOCIATION	SODGERING	SOFTLING
SOAVE	SOCIATIVE	SODGERS	SOFTLINGS
SOAVES	SOCIETAL	SODIC	SOFTLY
SOB	SOCIETIES	SODICITY	SOFTNESS
SOBA	SOCIETY	SODIUM	SOFTPASTE
SOBAS	SOCIOGRAM	SODIUMS	SOFTS
SOBBED	SOCIOLECT	SODOM	SOFTSHELL
SOBBER	SOCIOLOGY	SODOMIES	SOFTWARE
SOBBERS	SOCIOPATH	SODOMISE	SOFTWARES
SOBBING	SOCK	SODOMISED	SOFTWOOD
SOBBINGLY	SOCKED	SODOMISES	SOFTWOODS
SOBBINGS	SOCKET	SODOMIST	SOFTY
SOBEIT	SOCKETED	SODOMISTS	SOG
SOBER	SOCKETING	SODOMITE	SOGER
SOBERED	SOCKETS	SODOMITES	SOGERS
SOBERER	SOCKETTE	SODOMITIC	SOGGED
SOBEREST	SOCKETTES	SODOMIZE	SOGGIER
SOBERING	SOCKEYE	SODOMIZED	SOGGIEST
SOBERISE	SOCKEYES	SODOMIZES	SOGGILY
SOBERISED	SOCKING	SODOMS	SOGGINESS
SOBERISES	SOCKLESS	SODOMY	SOGGING
SOBERIZE	SOCKMAN	SODS	SOGGINGS
SOBERIZED	SOCKMEN	SOEVER	SOGGY
SOBERIZES	SOCKO	SOFA	SOGS
SOBERLY	SOCKS	SOFABED	SOH
SOBERNESS	SOCLE	SOFABEDS	SOHO
SOBERS	SOCLES	SOFAR	SOHS
SOBFUL	SOCMAN	SOFARS	SOIGNE
SOBOLE	SOCMEN	SOFAS	SOIGNEE
SOBOLES	SOCS	SOFFIONI	SOIL
SOBRIETY	SOD	SOFFIT	SOILAGE
SOBRIQUET	SODA	SOFFITS	SOILAGES
SOBS	SODAIC	SOFT	SOILBORNE
SOC	SODAIN	SOFTA	SOILED
SOCA	SODAINE	SOFTAS	SOILIER
SOCAGE	SODALESS	SOFTBACK	SOILIEST
SOCAGER	SODALIST	SOFTBACKS	SOILINESS
SOCAGERS	SODALISTS	SOFTBALL	SOILING
SOCAGES	SODALITE	SOFTBALLS	SOILINGS
SOCAS	SODALITES	SOFTBOUND	SOILLESS
SOCCAGE	SODALITY	SOFTCORE	SOILS

SOILURE	SOLARIUMS	SOLEMNIZE	SOLION
SOILURES	SOLARIZE	SOLEMNLY	SOLIONS
SOILY	SOLARIZED	SOLENESS	SOLIPED
SOIREE	SOLARIZES	SOLENETTE	SOLIPEDS
SOIREES	SOLARS	SOLENODON	SOLIPSISM
SOJA	SOLAS	SOLENOID	SOLIPSIST
SOJAS	SOLATE	SOLENOIDS	SOLIQUID
SOJOURN	SOLATED	SOLEPLATE	SOLIQUIDS
SOJOURNED	SOLATES	SOLEPRINT	SOLITAIRE
SOJOURNER	SOLATIA	SOLER	SOLITARY
SOJOURNS	SOLATING	SOLERA	SOLITO
SOKAH	SOLATION	SOLERAS	SOLITON
SOKAHS	SOLATIONS	SOLERET	SOLITONS
SOKAIYA	SOLATIUM	SOLERETS	SOLITUDE
SOKE	SOLD	SOLERS	SOLITUDES
SOKEMAN	SOLDADO	SOLES	SOLIVE
SOKEMANRY	SOLDADOS	SOLEUS	SOLIVES
SOKEMEN	SOLDAN	SOLEUSES	SOLLAR
SOKEN	SOLDANS	SOLFATARA	SOLLARS
SOKENS	SOLDE	SOLFEGE	SOLLER
SOKES	SOLDER	SOLFEGES	SOLLERET
SOKOL	SOLDERED	SOLFEGGI	SOLLERETS
SOKOLS	SOLDERER	SOLFEGGIO	SOLLERS
SOL	SOLDERERS	SOLFERINO	SOLLICKER
SOLA	SOLDERING	SOLGEL	SOLO
SOLACE	SOLDERS	SOLI	SOLOED
SOLACED	SOLDES	SOLICIT	SOLOING
SOLACER	SOLDI	SOLICITED	SOLOIST
SOLACERS	SOLDIER	SOLICITOR	SOLOISTIC
SOLACES	SOLDIERED	SOLICITS	SOLOISTS
SOLACING	SOLDIERLY	SOLICITY	SOLON
SOLACIOUS	SOLDIERS	SOLID	SOLONCHAK
SOLAH	SOLDIERY	SOLIDAGO	SOLONETS
SOLAHS	SOLDO	SOLIDAGOS	SOLONETZ
SOLAN	SOLDS	SOLIDARE	SOLONS
SOLAND	SOLE	SOLIDARES	SOLOS
SOLANDER	SOLECISE	SOLIDARY	SOLPUGID
SOLANDERS	SOLECISED	SOLIDATE	SOLPUGIDS
SOLANDS	SOLECISES	SOLIDATED	SOLS
SOLANIN	SOLECISM	SOLIDATES	SOLSTICE
SOLANINE	SOLECISMS	SOLIDER	SOLSTICES
SOLANINES	SOLECIST	SOLIDEST	SOLUBLE
SOLANINS	SOLECISTS	SOLIDI	SOLUBLES
SOLANO	SOLECIZE	SOLIDIFY	SOLUBLY
SOLANOS	SOLECIZED	SOLIDISH	SOLUM
SOLANS	SOLECIZES	SOLIDISM	SOLUMS
SOLANUM	SOLED	SOLIDISMS	SOLUNAR
SOLANUMS	SOLEI	SOLIDIST	SOLUS
SOLAR	SOLEIN	SOLIDISTS	SOLUTE
SOLARIA	SOLELESS	SOLIDITY	SOLUTES
SOLARISE	SOLELY	SOLIDLY	SOLUTION
SOLARISED	SOLEMN	SOLIDNESS	SOLUTIONS
SOLARISES	SOLEMNER	SOLIDS	SOLUTIVE
SOLARISM	SOLEMNESS	SOLIDUM	SOLVABLE
SOLARISMS	SOLEMNEST	SOLIDUMS	SOLVATE
SOLARIST	SOLEMNIFY	SOLIDUS	SOLVATED
SOLARISTS	SOLEMNISE	SOLILOQUY	SOLVATES
SOLARIUM	SOLEMNITY	SOLING	SOLVATING

SOLVATION
SOLVE
SOLVED
SOLVENCY
SOLVENT
SOLVENTLY
SOLVENTS
SOLVER
SOLVERS
SOLVES
SOLVING
SOM
SOMA
SOMAN
SOMANS
SOMAS
SOMASCOPE
SOMATA
SOMATIC
SOMATISM
SOMATISMS
SOMATIST
SOMATISTS
SOMBER
SOMBERED
SOMBERER
SOMBEREST
SOMBERING
SOMBERLY
SOMBERS
SOMBRE
SOMBRED
SOMBRELY
SOMBRER
SOMBRERO
SOMBREROS
SOMBRES
SOMBREST
SOMBRING
SOMBROUS
SOME
SOMEBODY
SOMEDAY
SOMEDEAL
SOMEDELE
SOMEGATE
SOMEHOW
SOMEONE
SOMEONES
SOMEPLACE
SOMERSET
SOMERSETS
SOMETHING
SOMETIME
SOMETIMES
SOMEWAY
SOMEWAYS
SOMEWHAT

SOMEWHATS
SOMEWHEN
SOMEWHERE
SOMEWHILE
SOMEWHY
SOMEWISE
SOMITAL
SOMITE
SOMITES
SOMITIC
SOMMELIER
SOMNIAL
SOMNIATE
SOMNIATED
SOMNIATES
SOMNIFIC
SOMNOLENT
SOMONI
SOMS
SOMY
SON
SONANCE
SONANCES
SONANCIES
SONANCY
SONANT
SONANTAL
SONANTIC
SONANTS
SONAR
SONARMAN
SONARMEN
SONARS
SONATA
SONATAS
SONATINA
SONATINAS
SONATINE
SONCE
SONCES
SONDAGE
SONDAGES
SONDE
SONDELI
SONDELIS
SONDER
SONDERS
SONDES
SONE
SONERI
SONERIS
SONES
SONG
SONGBIRD
SONGBIRDS
SONGBOOK
SONGBOOKS
SONGCRAFT

SONGFEST
SONGFESTS
SONGFUL
SONGFULLY
SONGKOK
SONGKOKS
SONGLESS
SONGLIKE
SONGMAN
SONGMEN
SONGOLOLO
SONGS
SONGSMITH
SONGSTER
SONGSTERS
SONHOOD
SONHOODS
SONIC
SONICALLY
SONICATE
SONICATED
SONICATES
SONICATOR
SONICS
SONLESS
SONLIKE
SONLY
SONNE
SONNES
SONNET
SONNETARY
SONNETED
SONNETEER
SONNETING
SONNETISE
SONNETIZE
SONNETS
SONNETTED
SONNIES
SONNY
SONOBUOY
SONOBUOYS
SONOGRAM
SONOGRAMS
SONOGRAPH
SONOMETER
SONORANT
SONORANTS
SONORITY
SONOROUS
SONOVOX
SONOVOXES
SONS
SONSE
SONSES
SONSHIP
SONSHIPS
SONSIE

SONSIER
SONSIEST
SONSY
SONTAG
SONTAGS
SONTIES
SOOCHONG
SOOCHONGS
SOOEY
SOOGEE
SOOGEED
SOOGEEING
SOOGEES
SOOGIE
SOOGIED
SOOGIEING
SOOGIES
SOOJEY
SOOJEYS
SOOK
SOOKED
SOOKING
SOOKS
SOOL
SOOLE
SOOLED
SOOLES
SOOLING
SOOLS
SOOM
SOOMED
SOOMING
SOOMS
SOON
SOONER
SOONERS
SOONEST
SOOP
SOOPED
SOOPING
SOOPINGS
SOOPS
SOOPSTAKE
SOOT
SOOTE
SOOTED
SOOTERKIN
SOOTES
SOOTFLAKE
SOOTH
SOOTHE
SOOTHED
SOOTHER
SOOTHERED
SOOTHERS
SOOTHES
SOOTHEST
SOOTHFAST

SOOTHFUL	SORA	SOREE	SORPTIONS
SOOTHING	SORAGE	SOREES	SORPTIVE
SOOTHINGS	SORAGES	SOREHEAD	SORRA
SOOTHLICH	SORAL	SOREHEADS	SORRAS
SOOTHLY	SORAS	SOREHON	SORREL
SOOTHS	SORB	SOREHONS	SORRELS
SOOTHSAID	SORBABLE	SOREL	SORRIER
SOOTHSAY	SORBARIA	SORELL	SORRIEST
SOOTHSAYS	SORBARIAS	SORELLS	SORRILY
SOOTIER	SORBATE	SORELS	SORRINESS
SOOTIEST	SORBATES	SORELY	SORROW
SOOTILY	SORBED	SORENESS	SORROWED
SOOTINESS	SORBENT	SORER	SORROWER
SOOTING	SORBENTS	SORES	SORROWERS
SOOTLESS	SORBET	SOREST	SORROWFUL
SOOTS	SORBETS	SOREX	SORROWING
SOOTY	SORBIC	SOREXES	SORROWS
SOP	SORBING	SORGHO	SORRY
SOPAPILLA	SORBITE	SORGHOS	SORRYISH
SOPH	SORBITES	SORGHUM	SORT
SOPHERIC	SORBITIC	SORGHUMS	SORTA
SOPHERIM	SORBITISE	SORGO	SORTABLE
SOPHIES	SORBITIZE	SORGOS	SORTABLY
SOPHISM	SORBITOL	SORI	SORTAL
SOPHISMS	SORBITOLS	SORICINE	SORTALS
SOPHIST	SORBO	SORICOID	SORTANCE
SOPHISTER	SORBOSE	SORING	SORTANCES
SOPHISTIC	SORBOSES	SORINGS	SORTATION
SOPHISTRY	SORBS	SORITES	SORTED
SOPHISTS	SORBUS	SORITIC	SORTER
SOPHOMORE	SORBUSES	SORITICAL	SORTERS
SOPHS	SORCERER	SORN	SORTES
SOPHY	SORCERERS	SORNED	SORTIE
SOPITE	SORCERESS	SORNER	SORTIED
SOPITED	SORCERIES	SORNERS	SORTIEING
SOPITES	SORCEROUS	SORNING	SORTIES
SOPITING	SORCERY	SORNINGS	SORTILEGE
SOPOR	SORD	SORNS	SORTILEGY
SOPORIFIC	SORDA	SOROBAN	SORTING
SOPOROSE	SORDES	SOROBANS	SORTINGS
SOPOROUS	SORDID	SOROCHE	SORTITION
SOPORS	SORDIDER	SOROCHES	SORTMENT
SOPPED	SORDIDEST	SORORAL	SORTMENTS
SOPPIER	SORDIDLY	SORORALLY	SORTS
SOPPIEST	SORDINE	SORORATE	SORUS
SOPPILY	SORDINES	SORORATES	SOS
SOPPINESS	SORDINI	SORORIAL	SOSATIE
SOPPING	SORDINO	SORORISE	SOSATIES
SOPPINGS	SORDO	SORORISED	SOSS
SOPPY	SORDOR	SORORISES	SOSSED
SOPRA	SORDORS	SORORITY	SOSSES
SOPRANI	SORDS	SORORIZE	SOSSING
SOPRANINI	SORE	SORORIZED	SOSSINGS
SOPRANINO	SORED	SORORIZES	SOSTENUTI
SOPRANIST	SOREDIA	SOROSES	SOSTENUTO
SOPRANO	SOREDIAL	SOROSIS	SOT
SOPRANOS	SOREDIATE	SOROSISES	SOTERIAL
SOPS	SOREDIUM	SORPTION	SOTH

SOTHS	SOUMING	SOURISH	SOUTPIEL
SOTOL	SOUMINGS	SOURISHLY	SOUTPIELS
SOTOLS	SOUMS	SOURLY	SOUTS
SOTS	SOUND	SOURNESS	SOUVENIR
SOTTED	SOUNDABLE	SOUROCK	SOUVENIRS
SOTTEDLY	SOUNDBITE	SOUROCKS	SOUVLAKI
SOTTING	SOUNDBOX	SOURPUSS	SOUVLAKIA
SOTTINGS	SOUNDCARD	SOURS	SOUVLAKIS
SOTTISH	SOUNDED	SOURSE	SOV
SOTTISHLY	SOUNDER	SOURSES	SOVENANCE
SOTTISIER	SOUNDERS	SOURSOP	SOVEREIGN
SOU	SOUNDEST	SOURSOPS	SOVIET
SOUARI	SOUNDING	SOURWOOD	SOVIETIC
SOUARIS	SOUNDINGS	SOURWOODS	SOVIETISE
SOUBISE	SOUNDLESS	SOUS	SOVIETISM
SOUBISES	SOUNDLY	SOUSE	SOVIETIST
SOUBRETTE	SOUNDMAN	SOUSED	SOVIETIZE
SOUCAR	SOUNDMEN	SOUSES	SOVIETS
SOUCARS	SOUNDNESS	SOUSING	SOVKHOZ
SOUCE	SOUNDPOST	SOUSINGS	SOVKHOZES
SOUCED	SOUNDS	SOUSLIK	SOVKHOZY
SOUCES	SOUP	SOUSLIKS	SOVRAN
SOUCHONG	SOUPCON	SOUT	SOVRANLY
SOUCHONGS	SOUPCONS	SOUTACHE	SOVRANS
SOUCING	SOUPED	SOUTACHES	SOVRANTY
SOUCT	SOUPER	SOUTANE	SOVS
SOUDAN	SOUPERS	SOUTANES	SOW
SOUDANS	SOUPFIN	SOUTAR	SOWABLE
SOUFFLE	SOUPFINS	SOUTARS	SOWANS
SOUFFLED	SOUPIER	SOUTENEUR	SOWAR
SOUFFLEED	SOUPIEST	SOUTER	SOWARREE
SOUFFLES	SOUPING	SOUTERLY	SOWARREES
SOUGH	SOUPLE	SOUTERS	SOWARRIES
SOUGHED	SOUPLED	SOUTH	SOWARRY
SOUGHING	SOUPLES	SOUTHEAST	SOWARS
SOUGHS	SOUPLESS	SOUTHED	SOWBACK
SOUGHT	SOUPLIKE	SOUTHER	SOWBACKS
SOUK	SOUPLING	SOUTHERED	SOWBELLY
SOUKED	SOUPS	SOUTHERLY	SOWBREAD
SOUKING	SOUPSPOON	SOUTHERN	SOWBREADS
SOUKOUS	SOUPY	SOUTHERNS	SOWCAR
SOUKOUSES	SOUR	SOUTHERS	SOWCARS
SOUKS	SOURBALL	SOUTHING	SOWCE
SOUL	SOURBALLS	SOUTHINGS	SOWCED
SOULDAN	SOURCE	SOUTHLAND	SOWCES
SOULDANS	SOURCED	SOUTHMOST	SOWCING
SOULDIER	SOURCEFUL	SOUTHPAW	SOWED
SOULDIERS	SOURCES	SOUTHPAWS	SOWENS
SOULED	SOURCING	SOUTHRON	SOWER
SOULFUL	SOURCINGS	SOUTHRONS	SOWERS
SOULFULLY	SOURDINE	SOUTHS	SOWF
SOULLESS	SOURDINES	SOUTHSAID	SOWFED
SOULLIKE	SOURDOUGH	SOUTHSAY	SOWFF
SOULMATE	SOURED	SOUTHSAYS	SOWFFED
SOULMATES	SOURER	SOUTHWARD	SOWFFING
SOULS	SOUREST	SOUTHWEST	SOWFFS
SOUM	SOURING	SOUTIE	SOWFING
SOUMED	SOURINGS	SOUTIES	SOWFS

SOWING	SOZZLING	SPADIXES	SPALES
SOWINGS	SOZZLY	SPADO	SPALL
SOWL	SPA	SPADOES	SPALLABLE
SOWLE	SPACE	SPADONES	SPALLE
SOWLED	SPACEBAND	SPADOS	SPALLED
SOWLES	SPACED	SPADROON	SPALLER
SOWLING	SPACELAB	SPADROONS	SPALLERS
SOWLS	SPACELABS	SPAE	SPALLES
SOWM	SPACELESS	SPAED	SPALLING
SOWMED	SPACEMAN	SPAEING	SPALLINGS
SOWMING	SPACEMEN	SPAEINGS	SPALLS
SOWMS	SPACEPORT	SPAEMAN	SPALPEEN
SOWN	SPACER	SPAEMEN	SPALPEENS
SOWND	SPACERS	SPAER	SPALT
SOWNDED	SPACES	SPAERS	SPALTED
SOWNDING	SPACESHIP	SPAES	SPALTING
SOWNDS	SPACESUIT	SPAETZLE	SPALTS
SOWNE	SPACEWALK	SPAETZLES	SPAM
SOWNES	SPACEWARD	SPAEWIFE	SPAMBOT
SOWP	SPACEY	SPAEWIVES	SPAMBOTS
SOWPS	SPACIAL	SPAG	SPAMMED
SOWS	SPACIALLY	SPAGERIC	SPAMMER
SOWSE	SPACIER	SPAGERICS	SPAMMERS
SOWSED	SPACIEST	SPAGERIST	SPAMMIE
SOWSES	SPACINESS	SPAGGED	SPAMMIER
SOWSING	SPACING	SPAGGING	SPAMMIES
SOWSSE	SPACINGS	SPAGHETTI	SPAMMIEST
SOWSSED	SPACIOUS	SPAGIRIC	SPAMMING
SOWSSES	SPACKLE	SPAGIRICS	SPAMMINGS
SOWSSING	SPACKLED	SPAGIRIST	SPAMMY
SOWTER	SPACKLES	SPAGS	SPAMS
SOWTERS	SPACKLING	SPAGYRIC	SPAN
SOWTH	SPACY	SPAGYRICS	SPANAEMIA
SOWTHED	SPADASSIN	SPAGYRIST	SPANAEMIC
SOWTHING	SPADE	SPAHEE	SPANCEL
SOWTHS	SPADED	SPAHEES	SPANCELED
SOX	SPADEFISH	SPAHI	SPANCELS
SOY	SPADEFUL	SPAHIS	SPANDEX
SOYA	SPADEFULS	SPAIL	SPANDEXES
SOYAS	SPADELIKE	SPAILS	SPANDREL
SOYBEAN	SPADEMAN	SPAIN	SPANDRELS
SOYBEANS	SPADEMEN	SPAINED	SPANDRIL
SOYLE	SPADER	SPAING	SPANDRILS
SOYLES	SPADERS	SPAINGS	SPANE
SOYMILK	SPADES	SPAINING	SPANED
SOYMILKS	SPADESMAN	SPAINS	SPANES
SOYS	SPADESMEN	SPAIRGE	SPANG
SOYUZ	SPADEWORK	SPAIRGED	SPANGED
SOYUZES	SPADGER	SPAIRGES	SPANGHEW
SOZIN	SPADGERS	SPAIRGING	SPANGHEWS
SOZINE	SPADICES	SPAIT	SPANGING
SOZINES	SPADILLE	SPAITS	SPANGLE
SOZINS	SPADILLES	SPAKE	SPANGLED
SOZZLE	SPADILLIO	SPALD	SPANGLER
SOZZLED	SPADILLO	SPALDEEN	SPANGLERS
SOZZLES	SPADILLOS	SPALDEENS	SPANGLES
SOZZLIER	SPADING	SPALDS	SPANGLET
SOZZLIEST	SPADIX	SPALE	SPANGLETS

SPANGLIER
SPANGLING
SPANGLY
SPANGS
SPANIEL
SPANIELS
SPANING
SPANK
SPANKED
SPANKER
SPANKERS
SPANKING
SPANKINGS
SPANKS
SPANLESS
SPANNED
SPANNER
SPANNERS
SPANNING
SPANS
SPANSPEK
SPANSPEKS
SPANSULE
SPANSULES
SPANWORM
SPANWORMS
SPAR
SPARABLE
SPARABLES
SPARAXIS
SPARD
SPARE
SPAREABLE
SPARED
SPARELESS
SPARELY
SPARENESS
SPARER
SPARERIB
SPARERIBS
SPARERS
SPARES
SPAREST
SPARGE
SPARGED
SPARGER
SPARGERS
SPARGES
SPARGING
SPARID
SPARIDS
SPARING
SPARINGLY
SPARK
SPARKE
SPARKED
SPARKER
SPARKERS

SPARKES
SPARKIE
SPARKIER
SPARKIES
SPARKIEST
SPARKILY
SPARKING
SPARKISH
SPARKLE
SPARKLED
SPARKLER
SPARKLERS
SPARKLES
SPARKLESS
SPARKLET
SPARKLETS
SPARKLIER
SPARKLIES
SPARKLING
SPARKLY
SPARKPLUG
SPARKS
SPARKY
SPARLIKE
SPARLING
SPARLINGS
SPAROID
SPAROIDS
SPARRE
SPARRED
SPARRER
SPARRERS
SPARRES
SPARRIER
SPARRIEST
SPARRING
SPARRINGS
SPARROW
SPARROWS
SPARRY
SPARS
SPARSE
SPARSEDLY
SPARSELY
SPARSER
SPARSEST
SPARSITY
SPART
SPARTAN
SPARTANS
SPARTEINE
SPARTERIE
SPARTH
SPARTHE
SPARTHES
SPARTHS
SPARTINA
SPARTINAS

SPARTS
SPAS
SPASM
SPASMATIC
SPASMED
SPASMIC
SPASMING
SPASMODIC
SPASMS
SPASTIC
SPASTICS
SPAT
SPATE
SPATES
SPATFALL
SPATFALLS
SPATHAL
SPATHE
SPATHED
SPATHES
SPATHIC
SPATHOSE
SPATIAL
SPATIALLY
SPATLESE
SPATLESEN
SPATLESES
SPATS
SPATTED
SPATTEE
SPATTEES
SPATTER
SPATTERED
SPATTERS
SPATTING
SPATULA
SPATULAR
SPATULAS
SPATULATE
SPATULE
SPATULES
SPATZLE
SPATZLES
SPAUL
SPAULD
SPAULDS
SPAULS
SPAVIE
SPAVIES
SPAVIET
SPAVIN
SPAVINED
SPAVINS
SPAW
SPAWL
SPAWLED
SPAWLING
SPAWLS

SPAWN
SPAWNED
SPAWNER
SPAWNERS
SPAWNIER
SPAWNIEST
SPAWNING
SPAWNINGS
SPAWNS
SPAWNY
SPAWS
SPAY
SPAYAD
SPAYADS
SPAYD
SPAYDS
SPAYED
SPAYING
SPAYS
SPAZ
SPAZA
SPAZZ
SPAZZED
SPAZZES
SPAZZING
SPEAK
SPEAKABLE
SPEAKEASY
SPEAKER
SPEAKERS
SPEAKING
SPEAKINGS
SPEAKOUT
SPEAKOUTS
SPEAKS
SPEAL
SPEALS
SPEAN
SPEANED
SPEANING
SPEANS
SPEAR
SPEARED
SPEARER
SPEARERS
SPEARFISH
SPEARGUN
SPEARGUNS
SPEARHEAD
SPEARIER
SPEARIEST
SPEARING
SPEARLIKE
SPEARMAN
SPEARMEN
SPEARMINT
SPEARS
SPEARWORT

SPEARY	SPECULUM	SPEKBOOM	SPENSE
SPEAT	SPECULUMS	SPEKBOOMS	SPENSES
SPEATS	SPED	SPEKS	SPENT
SPEC	SPEECH	SPELAEAN	SPEOS
SPECCED	SPEECHED	SPELD	SPEOSES
SPECCIES	SPEECHES	SPELDED	SPERLING
SPECCING	SPEECHFUL	SPELDER	SPERLINGS
SPECCY	SPEECHIFY	SPELDERED	SPERM
SPECIAL	SPEECHING	SPELDERS	SPERMARIA
SPECIALER	SPEED	SPELDIN	SPERMARY
SPECIALLY	SPEEDBALL	SPELDING	SPERMATIA
SPECIALS	SPEEDBOAT	SPELDINGS	SPERMATIC
SPECIALTY	SPEEDED	SPELDINS	SPERMATID
SPECIATE	SPEEDER	SPELDRIN	SPERMIC
SPECIATED	SPEEDERS	SPELDRING	SPERMINE
SPECIATES	SPEEDFUL	SPELDRINS	SPERMINES
SPECIE	SPEEDIER	SPELDS	SPERMOUS
SPECIES	SPEEDIEST	SPELEAN	SPERMS
SPECIFIC	SPEEDILY	SPELK	SPERRE
SPECIFICS	SPEEDING	SPELKS	SPERRED
SPECIFIED	SPEEDINGS	SPELL	SPERRES
SPECIFIER	SPEEDLESS	SPELLABLE	SPERRING
SPECIFIES	SPEEDO	SPELLBIND	SPERSE
SPECIFY	SPEEDOS	SPELLDOWN	SPERSED
SPECIMEN	SPEEDREAD	SPELLED	SPERSES
SPECIMENS	SPEEDS	SPELLER	SPERSING
SPECIOUS	SPEEDSTER	SPELLERS	SPERST
SPECK	SPEEDUP	SPELLFUL	SPERTHE
SPECKED	SPEEDUPS	SPELLICAN	SPERTHES
SPECKIER	SPEEDWAY	SPELLING	SPET
SPECKIEST	SPEEDWAYS	SPELLINGS	SPETCH
SPECKING	SPEEDWELL	SPELLS	SPETCHES
SPECKLE	SPEEDY	SPELT	SPETS
SPECKLED	SPEEL	SPELTER	SPETSNAZ
SPECKLES	SPEELED	SPELTERS	SPETTING
SPECKLESS	SPEELER	SPELTS	SPETZNAZ
SPECKLING	SPEELERS	SPELTZ	SPEUG
SPECKS	SPEELING	SPELTZES	SPEUGS
SPECKY	SPEELS	SPELUNK	SPEW
SPECS	SPEER	SPELUNKED	SPEWED
SPECTACLE	SPEERED	SPELUNKER	SPEWER
SPECTATE	SPEERING	SPELUNKS	SPEWERS
SPECTATED	SPEERINGS	SPENCE	SPEWIER
SPECTATES	SPEERS	SPENCER	SPEWIEST
SPECTATOR	SPEIL	SPENCERS	SPEWINESS
SPECTER	SPEILED	SPENCES	SPEWING
SPECTERS	SPEILING	SPEND	SPEWS
SPECTRA	SPEILS	SPENDABLE	SPEWY
SPECTRAL	SPEIR	SPENDALL	SPHACELUS
SPECTRE	SPEIRED	SPENDALLS	SPHAER
SPECTRES	SPEIRING	SPENDER	SPHAERE
SPECTRIN	SPEIRINGS	SPENDERS	SPHAERES
SPECTRINS	SPEIRS	SPENDIER	SPHAERITE
SPECTRUM	SPEISE	SPENDIEST	SPHAERS
SPECTRUMS	SPEISES	SPENDING	SPHAGNOUS
SPECULA	SPEISS	SPENDINGS	SPHAGNUM
SPECULAR	SPEISSES	SPENDS	SPHAGNUMS
SPECULATE	SPEK	SPENDY	SPHAIREE

SPHAIREES	SPICEY	SPIFFYING	SPILTHS
SPHEAR	SPICIER	SPIFS	SPIM
SPHEARE	SPICIEST	SPIGHT	SPIMS
SPHEARES	SPICILEGE	SPIGHTED	SPIN
SPHEARS	SPICILY	SPIGHTING	SPINA
SPHENDONE	SPICINESS	SPIGHTS	SPINACENE
SPHENE	SPICING	SPIGNEL	SPINACH
SPHENES	SPICK	SPIGNELS	SPINACHES
SPHENIC	SPICKER	SPIGOT	SPINACHY
SPHENODON	SPICKEST	SPIGOTS	SPINAE
SPHENOID	SPICKNEL	SPIK	SPINAGE
SPHENOIDS	SPICKNELS	SPIKE	SPINAGES
SPHERAL	SPICKS	SPIKED	SPINAL
SPHERE	SPICS	SPIKEFISH	SPINALLY
SPHERED	SPICULA	SPIKELET	SPINALS
SPHERES	SPICULAE	SPIKELETS	SPINAR
SPHERIC	SPICULAR	SPIKELIKE	SPINARS
SPHERICAL	SPICULATE	SPIKENARD	SPINAS
SPHERICS	SPICULE	SPIKER	SPINATE
SPHERIER	SPICULES	SPIKERIES	SPINDLE
SPHERIEST	SPICULUM	SPIKERS	SPINDLED
SPHERING	SPICY	SPIKERY	SPINDLER
SPHEROID	SPIDE	SPIKES	SPINDLERS
SPHEROIDS	SPIDER	SPIKEY	SPINDLES
SPHERULAR	SPIDERIER	SPIKIER	SPINDLIER
SPHERULE	SPIDERISH	SPIKIEST	SPINDLING
SPHERULES	SPIDERMAN	SPIKILY	SPINDLY
SPHERY	SPIDERMEN	SPIKINESS	SPINDRIFT
SPHINCTER	SPIDERS	SPIKING	SPINE
SPHINGES	SPIDERWEB	SPIKS	SPINED
SPHINGID	SPIDERY	SPIKY	SPINEL
SPHINGIDS	SPIDES	SPILE	SPINELESS
SPHINX	SPIE	SPILED	SPINELIKE
SPHINXES	SPIED	SPILES	SPINELLE
SPHYGMIC	SPIEGEL	SPILIKIN	SPINELLES
SPHYGMOID	SPIEGELS	SPILIKINS	SPINELS
SPHYGMUS	SPIEL	SPILING	SPINES
SPHYNX	SPIELED	SPILINGS	SPINET
SPHYNXES	SPIELER	SPILITE	SPINETS
SPIAL	SPIELERS	SPILITES	SPINETTE
SPIALS	SPIELING	SPILITIC	SPINETTES
SPIC	SPIELS	SPILL	SPINIER
SPICA	SPIER	SPILLABLE	SPINIEST
SPICAE	SPIERED	SPILLAGE	SPINIFEX
SPICAS	SPIERING	SPILLAGES	SPINIFORM
SPICATE	SPIERS	SPILLED	SPININESS
SPICATED	SPIES	SPILLER	SPINK
SPICCATO	SPIF	SPILLERS	SPINKS
SPICCATOS	SPIFF	SPILLIKIN	SPINLESS
SPICE	SPIFFED	SPILLING	SPINNAKER
SPICEBUSH	SPIFFIED	SPILLINGS	SPINNER
SPICED	SPIFFIER	SPILLOVER	SPINNERET
SPICELESS	SPIFFIES	SPILLS	SPINNERS
SPICER	SPIFFIEST	SPILLWAY	SPINNERY
SPICERIES	SPIFFILY	SPILLWAYS	SPINNET
SPICERS	SPIFFING	SPILOSITE	SPINNETS
SPICERY	SPIFFS	SPILT	SPINNEY
SPICES	SPIFFY	SPILTH	SPINNEYS

SPINNIES
SPINNING
SPINNINGS
SPINNY
SPINODE
SPINODES
SPINOFF
SPINOFFS
SPINONE
SPINONI
SPINOR
SPINORS
SPINOSE
SPINOSELY
SPINOSITY
SPINOUS
SPINOUT
SPINOUTS
SPINS
SPINSTER
SPINSTERS
SPINTEXT
SPINTEXTS
SPINTO
SPINTOS
SPINULA
SPINULAE
SPINULATE
SPINULE
SPINULES
SPINULOSE
SPINULOUS
SPINY
SPIRACLE
SPIRACLES
SPIRACULA
SPIRAEA
SPIRAEAS
SPIRAL
SPIRALED
SPIRALING
SPIRALISM
SPIRALIST
SPIRALITY
SPIRALLED
SPIRALLY
SPIRALS
SPIRANT
SPIRANTS
SPIRASTER
SPIRATED
SPIRATION
SPIRE
SPIREA
SPIREAS
SPIRED
SPIRELESS
SPIRELET

SPIRELETS
SPIREM
SPIREME
SPIREMES
SPIREMS
SPIRES
SPIREWISE
SPIRIC
SPIRICS
SPIRIER
SPIRIEST
SPIRILLA
SPIRILLAR
SPIRILLUM
SPIRING
SPIRIT
SPIRITED
SPIRITFUL
SPIRITING
SPIRITISM
SPIRITIST
SPIRITOSO
SPIRITOUS
SPIRITS
SPIRITUAL
SPIRITUEL
SPIRITUS
SPIRITY
SPIRLING
SPIRLINGS
SPIROGRAM
SPIROGYRA
SPIROID
SPIRT
SPIRTED
SPIRTING
SPIRTLE
SPIRTLES
SPIRTS
SPIRULA
SPIRULAE
SPIRULAS
SPIRULINA
SPIRY
SPIT
SPITAL
SPITALS
SPITBALL
SPITBALLS
SPITCHER
SPITE
SPITED
SPITEFUL
SPITES
SPITFIRE
SPITFIRES
SPITING
SPITS

SPITTED
SPITTEN
SPITTER
SPITTERS
SPITTING
SPITTINGS
SPITTLE
SPITTLES
SPITTOON
SPITTOONS
SPITZ
SPITZES
SPIV
SPIVS
SPIVVERY
SPIVVIER
SPIVVIEST
SPIVVY
SPLAKE
SPLAKES
SPLASH
SPLASHED
SPLASHER
SPLASHERS
SPLASHES
SPLASHIER
SPLASHILY
SPLASHING
SPLASHY
SPLAT
SPLATCH
SPLATCHED
SPLATCHES
SPLATS
SPLATTED
SPLATTER
SPLATTERS
SPLATTING
SPLAY
SPLAYED
SPLAYFEET
SPLAYFOOT
SPLAYING
SPLAYS
SPLEEN
SPLEENFUL
SPLEENIER
SPLEENISH
SPLEENS
SPLEENY
SPLENDENT
SPLENDID
SPLENDOR
SPLENDORS
SPLENDOUR
SPLENETIC
SPLENIA
SPLENIAL

SPLENIC
SPLENII
SPLENITIS
SPLENIUM
SPLENIUMS
SPLENIUS
SPLENT
SPLENTS
SPLEUCHAN
SPLICE
SPLICED
SPLICER
SPLICERS
SPLICES
SPLICING
SPLIFF
SPLIFFS
SPLINE
SPLINED
SPLINES
SPLINING
SPLINT
SPLINTED
SPLINTER
SPLINTERS
SPLINTERY
SPLINTING
SPLINTS
SPLIT
SPLITS
SPLITTED
SPLITTER
SPLITTERS
SPLITTING
SPLODGE
SPLODGED
SPLODGES
SPLODGIER
SPLODGILY
SPLODGING
SPLODGY
SPLOOSH
SPLOOSHED
SPLOOSHES
SPLORE
SPLORES
SPLOSH
SPLOSHED
SPLOSHES
SPLOSHING
SPLOTCH
SPLOTCHED
SPLOTCHES
SPLOTCHY
SPLURGE
SPLURGED
SPLURGER
SPLURGERS

SPLURGES	SPONGEOUS	SPOON	SPORTERS
SPLURGIER	SPONGER	SPOONBAIT	SPORTFUL
SPLURGING	SPONGERS	SPOONBILL	SPORTIER
SPLURGY	SPONGES	SPOONED	SPORTIES
SPLUTTER	SPONGIER	SPOONEY	SPORTIEST
SPLUTTERS	SPONGIEST	SPOONEYS	SPORTIF
SPLUTTERY	SPONGILY	SPOONFED	SPORTILY
SPOD	SPONGIN	SPOONFUL	SPORTING
SPODDIER	SPONGING	SPOONFULS	SPORTIVE
SPODDIEST	SPONGINS	SPOONIER	SPORTLESS
SPODDY	SPONGIOSE	SPOONIES	SPORTS
SPODE	SPONGIOUS	SPOONIEST	SPORTSMAN
SPODES	SPONGOID	SPOONILY	SPORTSMEN
SPODIUM	SPONGY	SPOONING	SPORTY
SPODIUMS	SPONSAL	SPOONS	SPORULAR
SPODOGRAM	SPONSALIA	SPOONSFUL	SPORULATE
SPODOSOL	SPONSIBLE	SPOONWAYS	SPORULE
SPODOSOLS	SPONSING	SPOONWISE	SPORULES
SPODS	SPONSINGS	SPOONY	SPOSH
SPODUMENE	SPONSION	SPOOR	SPOSHES
SPOFFISH	SPONSIONS	SPOORED	SPOSHIER
SPOFFY	SPONSON	SPOORER	SPOSHIEST
SPOIL	SPONSONS	SPOORERS	SPOSHY
SPOILABLE	SPONSOR	SPOORING	SPOT
SPOILAGE	SPONSORED	SPOORS	SPOTLESS
SPOILAGES	SPONSORS	SPOOT	SPOTLIGHT
SPOILED	SPONTOON	SPOOTS	SPOTLIT
SPOILER	SPONTOONS	SPORADIC	SPOTS
SPOILERS	SPOOF	SPORAL	SPOTTABLE
SPOILFIVE	SPOOFED	SPORANGIA	SPOTTED
SPOILFUL	SPOOFER	SPORE	SPOTTER
SPOILING	SPOOFERS	SPORED	SPOTTERS
SPOILS	SPOOFERY	SPORES	SPOTTIE
SPOILSMAN	SPOOFING	SPORICIDE	SPOTTIER
SPOILSMEN	SPOOFINGS	SPORIDESM	SPOTTIES
SPOILT	SPOOFS	SPORIDIA	SPOTTIEST
SPOKE	SPOOFY	SPORIDIAL	SPOTTILY
SPOKED	SPOOK	SPORIDIUM	SPOTTING
SPOKEN	SPOOKED	SPORING	SPOTTINGS
SPOKES	SPOOKERY	SPOROCARP	SPOTTY
SPOKESMAN	SPOOKIER	SPOROCYST	SPOUSAGE
SPOKESMEN	SPOOKIEST	SPOROCYTE	SPOUSAGES
SPOKEWISE	SPOOKILY	SPOROGENY	SPOUSAL
SPOKING	SPOOKING	SPOROGONY	SPOUSALLY
SPOLIATE	SPOOKISH	SPOROID	SPOUSALS
SPOLIATED	SPOOKS	SPOROPHYL	SPOUSE
SPOLIATES	SPOOKY	SPOROZOA	SPOUSED
SPOLIATOR	SPOOL	SPOROZOAL	SPOUSES
SPONDAIC	SPOOLED	SPOROZOAN	SPOUSING
SPONDAICS	SPOOLER	SPOROZOIC	SPOUT
SPONDEE	SPOOLERS	SPOROZOON	SPOUTED
SPONDEES	SPOOLING	SPORRAN	SPOUTER
SPONDULIX	SPOOLINGS	SPORRANS	SPOUTERS
SPONDYL	SPOOLS	SPORT	SPOUTIER
SPONDYLS	SPOOM	SPORTABLE	SPOUTIEST
SPONGE	SPOOMED	SPORTANCE	SPOUTING
SPONGEBAG	SPOOMING	SPORTED	SPOUTINGS
SPONGED	SPOOMS	SPORTER	SPOUTLESS

SPOUTS	SPREATHE	SPRINGILY	SPRUIKED
SPOUTY	SPREATHED	SPRINGING	SPRUIKER
SPRACK	SPREATHES	SPRINGLE	SPRUIKERS
SPRACKLE	SPREAZE	SPRINGLES	SPRUIKING
SPRACKLED	SPREAZED	SPRINGLET	SPRUIKS
SPRACKLES	SPREAZES	SPRINGS	SPRUIT
SPRAD	SPREAZING	SPRINGY	SPRUITS
SPRADDLE	SPRECHERY	SPRINKLE	SPRUNG
SPRADDLED	SPRECKLED	SPRINKLED	SPRUSH
SPRADDLES	SPRED	SPRINKLER	SPRUSHED
SPRAG	SPREDD	SPRINKLES	SPRUSHES
SPRAGGED	SPREDDE	SPRINT	SPRUSHING
SPRAGGING	SPREDDEN	SPRINTED	SPRY
SPRAGS	SPREDDES	SPRINTER	SPRYER
SPRAID	SPREDDING	SPRINTERS	SPRYEST
SPRAIN	SPREDDS	SPRINTING	SPRYLY
SPRAINED	SPREDS	SPRINTS	SPRYNESS
SPRAINING	SPREE	SPRIT	SPUD
SPRAINS	SPREED	SPRITE	SPUDDED
SPRAINT	SPREEING	SPRITEFUL	SPUDDER
SPRAINTS	SPREES	SPRITELY	SPUDDERS
SPRANG	SPREETHE	SPRITES	SPUDDIER
SPRANGLE	SPREETHED	SPRITS	SPUDDIEST
SPRANGLED	SPREETHES	SPRITSAIL	SPUDDING
SPRANGLES	SPREEZE	SPRITZ	SPUDDINGS
SPRANGS	SPREEZED	SPRITZED	SPUDDLE
SPRAT	SPREEZES	SPRITZER	SPUDDLES
SPRATS	SPREEZING	SPRITZERS	SPUDDY
SPRATTLE	SPREKELIA	SPRITZES	SPUDS
SPRATTLED	SPRENT	SPRITZIG	SPUE
SPRATTLES	SPREW	SPRITZIGS	SPUED
SPRAUCHLE	SPREWS	SPRITZING	SPUEING
SPRAUNCY	SPRIER	SPROCKET	SPUER
SPRAWL	SPRIEST	SPROCKETS	SPUERS
SPRAWLED	SPRIG	SPROD	SPUES
SPRAWLER	SPRIGGED	SPRODS	SPUG
SPRAWLERS	SPRIGGER	SPROG	SPUGGIES
SPRAWLIER	SPRIGGERS	SPROGS	SPUGGY
SPRAWLING	SPRIGGIER	SPRONG	SPUGS
SPRAWLS	SPRIGGING	SPROUT	SPUILZIE
SPRAWLY	SPRIGGY	SPROUTED	SPUILZIED
SPRAY	SPRIGHT	SPROUTING	SPUILZIES
SPRAYED	SPRIGHTED	SPROUTS	SPUING
SPRAYER	SPRIGHTLY	SPRUCE	SPULE
SPRAYERS	SPRIGHTS	SPRUCED	SPULES
SPRAYEY	SPRIGS	SPRUCELY	SPULYE
SPRAYIER	SPRIGTAIL	SPRUCER	SPULYED
SPRAYIEST	SPRING	SPRUCES	SPULYEING
SPRAYING	SPRINGAL	SPRUCEST	SPULYES
SPRAYINGS	SPRINGALD	SPRUCIER	SPULYIE
SPRAYS	SPRINGALS	SPRUCIEST	SPULYIED
SPREAD	SPRINGBOK	SPRUCING	SPULYIES
SPREADER	SPRINGE	SPRUCY	SPULZIE
SPREADERS	SPRINGED	SPRUE	SPULZIED
SPREADING	SPRINGER	SPRUES	SPULZIES
SPREADS	SPRINGERS	SPRUG	SPUMANTE
SPREAGH	SPRINGES	SPRUGS	SPUMANTES
SPREAGHS	SPRINGIER	SPRUIK	SPUME

SPUMED	SPURT	SQUADRONS	SQUASH
SPUMES	SPURTED	SQUADS	SQUASHED
SPUMIER	SPURTER	SQUAIL	SQUASHER
SPUMIEST	SPURTERS	SQUAILED	SQUASHERS
SPUMING	SPURTING	SQUAILER	SQUASHES
SPUMONE	SPURTLE	SQUAILERS	SQUASHIER
SPUMONES	SPURTLES	SQUAILING	SQUASHILY
SPUMONI	SPURTS	SQUAILS	SQUASHING
SPUMONIS	SPURWAY	SQUALENE	SQUASHY
SPUMOUS	SPURWAYS	SQUALENES	SQUAT
SPUMY	SPUTA	SQUALID	SQUATLY
SPUN	SPUTNIK	SQUALIDER	SQUATNESS
SPUNGE	SPUTNIKS	SQUALIDLY	SQUATS
SPUNGES	SPUTTER	SQUALL	SQUATTED
SPUNK	SPUTTERED	SQUALLED	SQUATTER
SPUNKED	SPUTTERER	SQUALLER	SQUATTERS
SPUNKIE	SPUTTERS	SQUALLERS	SQUATTEST
SPUNKIER	SPUTTERY	SQUALLIER	SQUATTIER
SPUNKIES	SPUTUM	SQUALLING	SQUATTILY
SPUNKIEST	SPY	SQUALLISH	SQUATTING
SPUNKILY	SPYAL	SQUALLS	SQUATTLE
SPUNKING	SPYALS	SQUALLY	SQUATTLED
SPUNKS	SPYGLASS	SQUALOID	SQUATTLES
SPUNKY	SPYHOLE	SQUALOR	SQUATTY
SPUNYARN	SPYHOLES	SQUALORS	SQUAW
SPUNYARNS	SPYING	SQUAMA	SQUAWBUSH
SPUR	SPYINGS	SQUAMAE	SQUAWFISH
SPURGALL	SPYMASTER	SQUAMATE	SQUAWK
SPURGALLS	SPYPLANE	SQUAMATES	SQUAWKED
SPURGE	SPYPLANES	SQUAME	SQUAWKER
SPURGES	SPYRE	SQUAMELLA	SQUAWKERS
SPURIAE	SPYRES	SQUAMES	SQUAWKIER
SPURIOUS	SPYWARE	SQUAMOSAL	SQUAWKING
SPURLESS	SPYWARES	SQUAMOSE	SQUAWKS
SPURLING	SQUAB	SQUAMOUS	SQUAWKY
SPURLINGS	SQUABASH	SQUAMULA	SQUAWMAN
SPURN	SQUABBED	SQUAMULAS	SQUAWMEN
SPURNE	SQUABBER	SQUAMULE	SQUAWROOT
SPURNED	SQUABBEST	SQUAMULES	SQUAWS
SPURNER	SQUABBIER	SQUANDER	SQUEAK
SPURNERS	SQUABBING	SQUANDERS	SQUEAKED
SPURNES	SQUABBISH	SQUARE	SQUEAKER
SPURNING	SQUABBLE	SQUARED	SQUEAKERS
SPURNINGS	SQUABBLED	SQUARELY	SQUEAKERY
SPURNS	SQUABBLER	SQUARER	SQUEAKIER
SPURRED	SQUABBLES	SQUARERS	SQUEAKILY
SPURRER	SQUABBY	SQUARES	SQUEAKING
SPURRERS	SQUABS	SQUAREST	SQUEAKS
SPURREY	SQUACCO	SQUARIAL	SQUEAKY
SPURREYS	SQUACCOS	SQUARIALS	SQUEAL
SPURRIER	SQUAD	SQUARING	SQUEALED
SPURRIERS	SQUADDED	SQUARINGS	SQUEALER
SPURRIES	SQUADDIE	SQUARISH	SQUEALERS
SPURRIEST	SQUADDIES	SQUARK	SQUEALING
SPURRING	SQUADDING	SQUARKS	SQUEALS
SPURRINGS	SQUADDY	SQUARROSE	SQUEAMISH
SPURRY	SQUADRON	SQUARSON	SQUEEGEE
SPURS	SQUADRONE	SQUARSONS	SQUEEGEED

SQUEEGEES	SQUINCHED	SQUISHIER	STACKER
SQUEEZE	SQUINCHES	SQUISHING	STACKERS
SQUEEZED	SQUINIED	SQUISHY	STACKET
SQUEEZER	SQUINIES	SQUIT	STACKETS
SQUEEZERS	SQUINNIED	SQUITCH	STACKING
SQUEEZES	SQUINNIER	SQUITCHES	STACKINGS
SQUEEZIER	SQUINNIES	SQUITS	STACKLESS
SQUEEZING	SQUINNY	SQUIZ	STACKROOM
SQUEEZY	SQUINT	SQUIZZES	STACKS
SQUEG	SQUINTED	SQUOOSH	STACKUP
SQUEGGED	SQUINTER	SQUOOSHED	STACKUPS
SQUEGGER	SQUINTERS	SQUOOSHES	STACKYARD
SQUEGGERS	SQUINTEST	SQUOOSHY	STACTE
SQUEGGING	SQUINTIER	SQUUSH	STACTES
SQUEGS	SQUINTING	SQUUSHED	STADDA
SQUELCH	SQUINTS	SQUUSHES	STADDAS
SQUELCHED	SQUINTY	SQUUSHING	STADDLE
SQUELCHER	SQUINY	SRADDHA	STADDLES
SQUELCHES	SQUINYING	SRADDHAS	STADE
SQUELCHY	SQUIRAGE	SRADHA	STADES
SQUIB	SQUIRAGES	SRADHAS	STADIA
SQUIBBED	SQUIRALTY	SRI	STADIAL
SQUIBBING	SQUIRARCH	SRIS	STADIALS
SQUIBS	SQUIRE	ST	STADIAS
SQUID	SQUIREAGE	STAB	STADIUM
SQUIDDED	SQUIRED	STABBED	STADIUMS
SQUIDDING	SQUIREDOM	STABBER	STAFF
SQUIDGE	SQUIREEN	STABBERS	STAFFAGE
SQUIDGED	SQUIREENS	STABBING	STAFFAGES
SQUIDGES	SQUIRELY	STABBINGS	STAFFED
SQUIDGIER	SQUIRES	STABILATE	STAFFER
SQUIDGING	SQUIRESS	STABILE	STAFFERS
SQUIDGY	SQUIRING	STABILES	STAFFING
SQUIDS	SQUIRISH	STABILISE	STAFFMAN
SQUIER	SQUIRM	STABILITY	STAFFMEN
SQUIERS	SQUIRMED	STABILIZE	STAFFROOM
SQUIFF	SQUIRMER	STABLE	STAFFS
SQUIFFED	SQUIRMERS	STABLEBOY	STAG
SQUIFFER	SQUIRMIER	STABLED	STAGE
SQUIFFERS	SQUIRMING	STABLEMAN	STAGEABLE
SQUIFFIER	SQUIRMS	STABLEMEN	STAGED
SQUIFFY	SQUIRMY	STABLER	STAGEFUL
SQUIGGLE	SQUIRR	STABLERS	STAGEFULS
SQUIGGLED	SQUIRRED	STABLES	STAGEHAND
SQUIGGLER	SQUIRREL	STABLEST	STAGELIKE
SQUIGGLES	SQUIRRELS	STABLING	STAGER
SQUIGGLY	SQUIRRELY	STABLINGS	STAGERIES
SQUILGEE	SQUIRRING	STABLISH	STAGERS
SQUILGEED	SQUIRRS	STABLY	STAGERY
SQUILGEES	SQUIRT	STABS	STAGES
SQUILL	SQUIRTED	STACCATI	STAGEY
SQUILLA	SQUIRTER	STACCATO	STAGGARD
SQUILLAE	SQUIRTERS	STACCATOS	STAGGARDS
SQUILLAS	SQUIRTING	STACHYS	STAGGART
SQUILLION	SQUIRTS	STACHYSES	STAGGARTS
SQUILLS	SQUISH	STACK	STAGGED
SQUINANCY	SQUISHED	STACKABLE	STAGGER
SQUINCH	SQUISHES	STACKED	STAGGERED

STAGGERER	STAITHE	STAMINODE	STANDOUT
STAGGERS	STAITHES	STAMINODY	STANDOUTS
STAGGERY	STAITHS	STAMINOID	STANDOVER
STAGGIE	STAKE	STAMMEL	STANDPAT
STAGGIER	STAKED	STAMMELS	STANDPIPE
STAGGIES	STAKEOUT	STAMMER	STANDS
STAGGIEST	STAKEOUTS	STAMMERED	STANDUP
STAGGING	STAKES	STAMMERER	STANDUPS
STAGGY	STAKING	STAMMERS	STANE
STAGHORN	STALACTIC	STAMNOI	STANED
STAGHORNS	STALAG	STAMNOS	STANES
STAGHOUND	STALAGS	STAMP	STANG
STAGIER	STALE	STAMPED	STANGED
STAGIEST	STALED	STAMPEDE	STANGING
STAGILY	STALELY	STAMPEDED	STANGS
STAGINESS	STALEMATE	STAMPEDER	STANHOPE
STAGING	STALENESS	STAMPEDES	STANHOPES
STAGINGS	STALER	STAMPEDO	STANIEL
STAGNANCE	STALES	STAMPEDOS	STANIELS
STAGNANCY	STALEST	STAMPER	STANINE
STAGNANT	STALING	STAMPERS	STANINES
STAGNATE	STALK	STAMPING	STANING
STAGNATED	STALKED	STAMPINGS	STANK
STAGNATES	STALKER	STAMPLESS	STANKED
STAGS	STALKERS	STAMPS	STANKING
STAGY	STALKIER	STANCE	STANKS
STAID	STALKIEST	STANCES	STANNARY
STAIDER	STALKILY	STANCH	STANNATE
STAIDEST	STALKING	STANCHED	STANNATES
STAIDLY	STALKINGS	STANCHEL	STANNATOR
STAIDNESS	STALKLESS	STANCHELS	STANNEL
STAIG	STALKLIKE	STANCHER	STANNELS
STAIGS	STALKO	STANCHERS	STANNIC
STAIN	STALKOES	STANCHES	STANNITE
STAINABLE	STALKS	STANCHEST	STANNITES
STAINED	STALKY	STANCHING	STANNOUS
STAINER	STALL	STANCHION	STANNUM
STAINERS	STALLAGE	STANCHLY	STANNUMS
STAINING	STALLAGES	STANCK	STANOL
STAININGS	STALLED	STAND	STANOLS
STAINLESS	STALLING	STANDARD	STANYEL
STAINS	STALLINGS	STANDARDS	STANYELS
STAIR	STALLION	STANDAWAY	STANZA
STAIRCASE	STALLIONS	STANDBY	STANZAED
STAIRED	STALLMAN	STANDBYS	STANZAIC
STAIRFOOT	STALLMEN	STANDDOWN	STANZAS
STAIRHEAD	STALLS	STANDEE	STANZE
STAIRLESS	STALWART	STANDEES	STANZES
STAIRLIFT	STALWARTS	STANDEN	STANZO
STAIRLIKE	STALWORTH	STANDER	STANZOES
STAIRS	STAMEN	STANDERS	STANZOS
STAIRSTEP	STAMENED	STANDFAST	STAP
STAIRWAY	STAMENS	STANDGALE	STAPEDES
STAIRWAYS	STAMINA	STANDING	STAPEDIAL
STAIRWELL	STAMINAL	STANDINGS	STAPEDII
STAIRWISE	STAMINAS	STANDISH	STAPEDIUS
STAIRWORK	STAMINATE	STANDOFF	STAPELIA
STAITH	STAMINEAL	STANDOFFS	STAPELIAS

STAPES	STARKEST	STARTUP	STATIONED
STAPH	STARKING	STARTUPS	STATIONER
STAPHS	STARKLY	STARVE	STATIONS
STAPLE	STARKNESS	STARVED	STATISM
STAPLED	STARKS	STARVER	STATISMS
STAPLER	STARLESS	STARVERS	STATIST
STAPLERS	STARLET	STARVES	STATISTIC
STAPLES	STARLETS	STARVING	STATISTS
STAPLING	STARLIGHT	STARVINGS	STATIVE
STAPPED	STARLIKE	STARWORT	STATIVES
STAPPING	STARLING	STARWORTS	STATOCYST
STAPPLE	STARLINGS	STASES	STATOLITH
STAPPLES	STARLIT	STASH	STATOR
STAPS	STARN	STASHED	STATORS
STAR	STARNED	STASHES	STATS
STARAGEN	STARNIE	STASHIE	STATUA
STARAGENS	STARNIES	STASHIES	STATUARY
STARBOARD	STARNING	STASHING	STATUAS
STARBURST	STARNOSE	STASIDION	STATUE
STARCH	STARNOSES	STASIMA	STATUED
STARCHED	STARNS	STASIMON	STATUES
STARCHER	STAROSTA	STASIS	STATUETTE
STARCHERS	STAROSTAS	STAT	STATURE
STARCHES	STAROSTY	STATABLE	STATURED
STARCHIER	STARR	STATAL	STATURES
STARCHILY	STARRED	STATANT	STATUS
STARCHING	STARRIER	STATE	STATUSES
STARCHY	STARRIEST	STATEABLE	STATUSY
STARDOM	STARRILY	STATED	STATUTE
STARDOMS	STARRING	STATEDLY	STATUTES
STARDRIFT	STARRINGS	STATEHOOD	STATUTORY
STARDUST	STARRS	STATELESS	STAUMREL
STARDUSTS	STARRY	STATELET	STAUMRELS
STARE	STARS	STATELETS	STAUN
STARED	STARSHINE	STATELIER	STAUNCH
STARER	STARSHIP	STATELILY	STAUNCHED
STARERS	STARSHIPS	STATELY	STAUNCHER
STARES	STARSPOT	STATEMENT	STAUNCHES
STARETS	STARSPOTS	STATER	STAUNCHLY
STARETSES	STARSTONE	STATEROOM	STAUNING
STARETZ	START	STATERS	STAUNS
STARETZES	STARTED	STATES	STAVE
STARFISH	STARTER	STATESIDE	STAVED
STARFRUIT	STARTERS	STATESMAN	STAVES
STARGAZE	STARTFUL	STATESMEN	STAVING
STARGAZED	STARTING	STATEWIDE	STAVUDINE
STARGAZER	STARTINGS	STATIC	STAW
STARGAZES	STARTISH	STATICAL	STAWED
STARING	STARTLE	STATICE	STAWING
STARINGLY	STARTLED	STATICES	STAWS
STARINGS	STARTLER	STATICKY	STAY
STARK	STARTLERS	STATICS	STAYAWAY
STARKED	STARTLES	STATIM	STAYAWAYS
STARKEN	STARTLING	STATIN	STAYED
STARKENED	STARTLISH	STATING	STAYER
STARKENS	STARTLY	STATINS	STAYERS
STARKER	STARTS	STATION	STAYING
STARKERS	STARTSY	STATIONAL	STAYLESS

STAYMAKER	STEAMS	STEEDING	STEEPLES
STAYNE	STEAMSHIP	STEEDLIKE	STEEPLY
STAYNED	STEAMY	STEEDS	STEEPNESS
STAYNES	STEAN	STEEDY	STEEPS
STAYNING	STEANE	STEEDYING	STEEPUP
STAYRE	STEANED	STEEK	STEEPY
STAYRES	STEANES	STEEKED	STEER
STAYS	STEANING	STEEKING	STEERABLE
STAYSAIL	STEANINGS	STEEKIT	STEERAGE
STAYSAILS	STEANS	STEEKS	STEERAGES
STEAD	STEAPSIN	STEEL	STEERED
STEADED	STEAPSINS	STEELBOW	STEERER
STEADFAST	STEAR	STEELBOWS	STEERERS
STEADICAM	STEARAGE	STEELD	STEERIES
STEADIED	STEARAGES	STEELED	STEERING
STEADIER	STEARATE	STEELHEAD	STEERINGS
STEADIERS	STEARATES	STEELIE	STEERLING
STEADIES	STEARD	STEELIER	STEERS
STEADIEST	STEARE	STEELIES	STEERSMAN
STEADILY	STEARED	STEELIEST	STEERSMEN
STEADING	STEARES	STEELING	STEERY
STEADINGS	STEARIC	STEELINGS	STEEVE
STEADS	STEARIN	STEELMAN	STEEVED
STEADY	STEARINE	STEELMEN	STEEVELY
STEADYING	STEARINES	STEELS	STEEVER
STEAK	STEARING	STEELWARE	STEEVES
STEAKS	STEARINS	STEELWORK	STEEVEST
STEAL	STEARS	STEELY	STEEVING
STEALABLE	STEARSMAN	STEELYARD	STEEVINGS
STEALAGE	STEARSMEN	STEEM	STEGNOSES
STEALAGES	STEATITE	STEEMED	STEGNOSIS
STEALE	STEATITES	STEEMING	STEGNOTIC
STEALED	STEATITIC	STEEMS	STEGODON
STEALER	STEATOMA	STEEN	STEGODONS
STEALERS	STEATOMAS	STEENBOK	STEGODONT
STEALES	STEATOSES	STEENBOKS	STEGOMYIA
STEALING	STEATOSIS	STEENBRAS	STEGOSAUR
STEALINGS	STED	STEENBUCK	STEIL
STEALS	STEDD	STEENED	STEILS
STEALT	STEDDE	STEENING	STEIN
STEALTH	STEDDED	STEENINGS	STEINBOCK
STEALTHED	STEDDES	STEENKIRK	STEINBOK
STEALTHS	STEDDIED	STEENS	STEINBOKS
STEALTHY	STEDDIES	STEEP	STEINED
STEAM	STEDDING	STEEPED	STEINING
STEAMBOAT	STEDDS	STEEPEN	STEININGS
STEAMED	STEDDY	STEEPENED	STEINKIRK
STEAMER	STEDDYING	STEEPENS	STEINS
STEAMERED	STEDE	STEEPER	STELA
STEAMERS	STEDED	STEEPERS	STELAE
STEAMIE	STEDES	STEEPEST	STELAI
STEAMIER	STEDFAST	STEEPEUP	STELAR
STEAMIES	STEDING	STEEPIER	STELE
STEAMIEST	STEDS	STEEPIEST	STELENE
STEAMILY	STEED	STEEPING	STELES
STEAMING	STEEDED	STEEPISH	STELIC
STEAMINGS	STEEDIED	STEEPLE	STELL
STEAMROLL	STEEDIES	STEEPLED	STELLA

STELLAR	STENCHIER	STEPSTOOL	STEROL
STELLAS	STENCHING	STEPT	STEROLS
STELLATE	STENCHY	STEPWISE	STERTOR
STELLATED	STENCIL	STERADIAN	STERTORS
STELLED	STENCILED	STERCORAL	STERVE
STELLERID	STENCILER	STERCULIA	STERVED
STELLIFY	STENCILS	STERE	STERVES
STELLING	STEND	STEREO	STERVING
STELLION	STENDED	STEREOED	STET
STELLIONS	STENDING	STEREOING	STETS
STELLITE	STENDS	STEREOME	STETSON
STELLITES	STENGAH	STEREOMES	STETSONS
STELLS	STENGAHS	STEREOS	STETTED
STELLULAR	STENLOCK	STERES	STETTING
STEM	STENLOCKS	STERIC	STEVEDORE
STEMBOK	STENNED	STERICAL	STEVEN
STEMBOKS	STENNING	STERIGMA	STEVENS
STEMBUCK	STENO	STERIGMAS	STEW
STEMBUCKS	STENOBATH	STERILANT	STEWABLE
STEME	STENOKIES	STERILE	STEWARD
STEMED	STENOKOUS	STERILELY	STEWARDED
STEMES	STENOKY	STERILISE	STEWARDRY
STEMHEAD	STENOPAIC	STERILITY	STEWARDS
STEMHEADS	STENOS	STERILIZE	STEWARTRY
STEMING	STENOSED	STERLET	STEWBUM
STEMLESS	STENOSES	STERLETS	STEWBUMS
STEMLET	STENOSIS	STERLING	STEWED
STEMLETS	STENOTIC	STERLINGS	STEWER
STEMLIKE	STENOTYPE	STERN	STEWERS
STEMMA	STENOTYPY	STERNA	STEWIER
STEMMAS	STENS	STERNAGE	STEWIEST
STEMMATA	STENT	STERNAGES	STEWING
STEMMATIC	STENTED	STERNAL	STEWINGS
STEMME	STENTING	STERNEBRA	STEWPAN
STEMMED	STENTOR	STERNED	STEWPANS
STEMMER	STENTORS	STERNER	STEWPOND
STEMMERS	STENTOUR	STERNEST	STEWPONDS
STEMMERY	STENTOURS	STERNFAST	STEWPOT
STEMMES	STENTS	STERNING	STEWPOTS
STEMMIER	STEP	STERNITE	STEWS
STEMMIEST	STEPBAIRN	STERNITES	STEWY
STEMMING	STEPCHILD	STERNITIC	STEY
STEMMINGS	STEPDAME	STERNLY	STEYER
STEMMY	STEPDAMES	STERNMOST	STEYEST
STEMPEL	STEPHANE	STERNNESS	STHENIA
STEMPELS	STEPHANES	STERNPORT	STHENIAS
STEMPLE	STEPLIKE	STERNPOST	STHENIC
STEMPLES	STEPNEY	STERNS	STIBBLE
STEMS	STEPNEYS	STERNSON	STIBBLER
STEMSON	STEPPE	STERNSONS	STIBBLERS
STEMSONS	STEPPED	STERNUM	STIBBLES
STEMWARE	STEPPER	STERNUMS	STIBIAL
STEMWARES	STEPPERS	STERNWARD	STIBINE
STEN	STEPPES	STERNWAY	STIBINES
STENCH	STEPPING	STERNWAYS	STIBIUM
STENCHED	STEPS	STEROID	STIBIUMS
STENCHES	STEPSON	STEROIDAL	STIBNITE
STENCHFUL	STEPSONS	STEROIDS	STIBNITES

STICCADO	STIDDIED	STILLED	STINGO
STICCADOS	STIDDIES	STILLER	STINGOS
STICCATO	STIE	STILLERS	STINGRAY
STICCATOS	STIED	STILLEST	STINGRAYS
STICH	STIES	STILLIER	STINGS
STICHARIA	STIEVE	STILLIEST	STINGY
STICHERA	STIEVELY	STILLING	STINK
STICHERON	STIEVER	STILLINGS	STINKARD
STICHIC	STIEVEST	STILLION	STINKARDS
STICHIDIA	STIFF	STILLIONS	STINKBUG
STICHOI	STIFFED	STILLMAN	STINKBUGS
STICHOS	STIFFEN	STILLMEN	STINKER
STICHS	STIFFENED	STILLNESS	STINKEROO
STICK	STIFFENER	STILLROOM	STINKERS
STICKABLE	STIFFENS	STILLS	STINKHORN
STICKBALL	STIFFER	STILLY	STINKIER
STICKED	STIFFEST	STILT	STINKIEST
STICKER	STIFFIE	STILTBIRD	STINKING
STICKERED	STIFFIES	STILTED	STINKINGS
STICKERS	STIFFING	STILTEDLY	STINKO
STICKFUL	STIFFISH	STILTER	STINKPOT
STICKFULS	STIFFLY	STILTERS	STINKPOTS
STICKIED	STIFFNESS	STILTIER	STINKS
STICKIER	STIFFS	STILTIEST	STINKWEED
STICKIES	STIFFWARE	STILTING	STINKWOOD
STICKIEST	STIFFY	STILTINGS	STINKY
STICKILY	STIFLE	STILTISH	STINT
STICKING	STIFLED	STILTS	STINTED
STICKINGS	STIFLER	STILTY	STINTEDLY
STICKIT	STIFLERS	STIM	STINTER
STICKJAW	STIFLES	STIME	STINTERS
STICKJAWS	STIFLING	STIMED	STINTIER
STICKLE	STIFLINGS	STIMES	STINTIEST
STICKLED	STIGMA	STIMIE	STINTING
STICKLER	STIGMAL	STIMIED	STINTINGS
STICKLERS	STIGMAS	STIMIES	STINTLESS
STICKLES	STIGMATA	STIMING	STINTS
STICKLIKE	STIGMATIC	STIMS	STINTY
STICKLING	STIGME	STIMULANT	STIPA
STICKMAN	STIGMES	STIMULATE	STIPAS
STICKMEN	STILB	STIMULI	STIPE
STICKOUT	STILBENE	STIMULUS	STIPED
STICKOUTS	STILBENES	STIMY	STIPEL
STICKPIN	STILBITE	STIMYING	STIPELS
STICKPINS	STILBITES	STING	STIPEND
STICKS	STILBS	STINGAREE	STIPENDS
STICKSEED	STILE	STINGBULL	STIPES
STICKUM	STILED	STINGED	STIPIFORM
STICKUMS	STILES	STINGER	STIPITATE
STICKUP	STILET	STINGERS	STIPITES
STICKUPS	STILETS	STINGFISH	STIPPLE
STICKWEED	STILETTO	STINGIER	STIPPLED
STICKWORK	STILETTOS	STINGIES	STIPPLER
STICKY	STILING	STINGIEST	STIPPLERS
STICKYING	STILL	STINGILY	STIPPLES
STICTION	STILLAGE	STINGING	STIPPLING
STICTIONS	STILLAGES	STINGINGS	STIPULAR
STIDDIE	STILLBORN	STINGLESS	STIPULARY

STIPULATE	STOATS	STOEPS	STOMACKS
STIPULE	STOB	STOGEY	STOMAL
STIPULED	STOBBED	STOGEYS	STOMAS
STIPULES	STOBBING	STOGIE	STOMATA
STIR	STOBS	STOGIES	STOMATAL
STIRABOUT	STOCCADO	STOGY	STOMATE
STIRE	STOCCADOS	STOIC	STOMATES
STIRED	STOCCATA	STOICAL	STOMATIC
STIRES	STOCCATAS	STOICALLY	STOMATOUS
STIRING	STOCIOUS	STOICISM	STOMIA
STIRK	STOCK	STOICISMS	STOMIUM
STIRKS	STOCKADE	STOICS	STOMIUMS
STIRLESS	STOCKADED	STOIT	STOMODAEA
STIRP	STOCKADES	STOITED	STOMODEA
STIRPES	STOCKAGE	STOITER	STOMODEAL
STIRPS	STOCKAGES	STOITERED	STOMODEUM
STIRRA	STOCKCAR	STOITERS	STOMP
STIRRABLE	STOCKCARS	STOITING	STOMPED
STIRRAH	STOCKED	STOITS	STOMPER
STIRRAHS	STOCKER	STOKE	STOMPERS
STIRRAS	STOCKERS	STOKED	STOMPIE
STIRRE	STOCKFISH	STOKEHOLD	STOMPIES
STIRRED	STOCKHORN	STOKEHOLE	STOMPING
STIRRER	STOCKIER	STOKER	STOMPS
STIRRERS	STOCKIEST	STOKERS	STONABLE
STIRRES	STOCKILY	STOKES	STOND
STIRRING	STOCKINET	STOKESIA	STONDS
STIRRINGS	STOCKING	STOKESIAS	STONE
STIRRUP	STOCKINGS	STOKING	STONEABLE
STIRRUPS	STOCKISH	STOKVEL	STONEBOAT
STIRS	STOCKIST	STOKVELS	STONECAST
STISHIE	STOCKISTS	STOLE	STONECHAT
STISHIES	STOCKLESS	STOLED	STONECROP
STITCH	STOCKLIST	STOLEN	STONED
STITCHED	STOCKLOCK	STOLES	STONEFISH
STITCHER	STOCKMAN	STOLID	STONEFLY
STITCHERS	STOCKMEN	STOLIDER	STONEHAND
STITCHERY	STOCKPILE	STOLIDEST	STONELESS
STITCHES	STOCKPOT	STOLIDITY	STONELIKE
STITCHING	STOCKPOTS	STOLIDLY	STONEN
STITHIED	STOCKROOM	STOLLEN	STONER
STITHIES	STOCKS	STOLLENS	STONERAG
STITHY	STOCKTAKE	STOLN	STONERAGS
STITHYING	STOCKTOOK	STOLON	STONERAW
STIVE	STOCKWORK	STOLONATE	STONERAWS
STIVED	STOCKY	STOLONIC	STONERN
STIVER	STOCKYARD	STOLONS	STONERS
STIVERS	STODGE	STOLPORT	STONES
STIVES	STODGED	STOLPORTS	STONESHOT
STIVIER	STODGER	STOMA	STONEWALL
STIVIEST	STODGERS	STOMACH	STONEWARE
STIVING	STODGES	STOMACHAL	STONEWASH
STIVY	STODGIER	STOMACHED	STONEWORK
STOA	STODGIEST	STOMACHER	STONEWORT
STOAE	STODGILY	STOMACHIC	STONEY
STOAI	STODGING	STOMACHS	STONG
STOAS	STODGY	STOMACHY	STONIED
STOAT	STOEP	STOMACK	STONIER

STONIES	STOP	STORGES	STOUPS
STONIEST	STOPBANK	STORIATED	STOUR
STONILY	STOPBANKS	STORIED	STOURE
STONINESS	STOPCOCK	STORIES	STOURES
STONING	STOPCOCKS	STORIETTE	STOURIE
STONINGS	STOPE	STORING	STOURIER
STONISH	STOPED	STORK	STOURIEST
STONISHED	STOPER	STORKS	STOURS
STONISHES	STOPERS	STORM	STOURY
STONK	STOPES	STORMBIRD	STOUSH
STONKED	STOPGAP	STORMED	STOUSHED
STONKER	STOPGAPS	STORMER	STOUSHES
STONKERED	STOPING	STORMERS	STOUSHIE
STONKERS	STOPINGS	STORMFUL	STOUSHIES
STONKING	STOPLESS	STORMIER	STOUSHING
STONKS	STOPLIGHT	STORMIEST	STOUT
STONN	STOPOFF	STORMILY	STOUTEN
STONNE	STOPOFFS	STORMING	STOUTENED
STONNED	STOPOVER	STORMINGS	STOUTENS
STONNES	STOPOVERS	STORMLESS	STOUTER
STONNING	STOPPABLE	STORMLIKE	STOUTEST
STONNS	STOPPAGE	STORMS	STOUTH
STONY	STOPPAGES	STORMY	STOUTHS
STONYING	STOPPED	STORNELLI	STOUTISH
STOOD	STOPPER	STORNELLO	STOUTLY
STOODEN	STOPPERED	STORY	STOUTNESS
STOOGE	STOPPERS	STORYBOOK	STOUTS
STOOGED	STOPPING	STORYETTE	STOVAINE
STOOGES	STOPPINGS	STORYING	STOVAINES
STOOGING	STOPPLE	STORYINGS	STOVE
STOOK	STOPPLED	STORYLINE	STOVED
STOOKED	STOPPLES	STOSS	STOVEPIPE
STOOKER	STOPPLING	STOSSES	STOVER
STOOKERS	STOPS	STOT	STOVERS
STOOKIE	STOPT	STOTIN	STOVES
STOOKIES	STOPWATCH	STOTINKA	STOVETOP
STOOKING	STOPWORD	STOTINKI	STOVETOPS
STOOKS	STOPWORDS	STOTINOV	STOVIES
STOOL	STORABLE	STOTINS	STOVING
STOOLBALL	STORABLES	STOTIOUS	STOVINGS
STOOLED	STORAGE	STOTS	STOW
STOOLIE	STORAGES	STOTT	STOWABLE
STOOLIES	STORAX	STOTTED	STOWAGE
STOOLING	STORAXES	STOTTER	STOWAGES
STOOLS	STORE	STOTTERED	STOWAWAY
STOOP	STORED	STOTTERS	STOWAWAYS
STOOPBALL	STOREMAN	STOTTIE	STOWDOWN
STOOPE	STOREMEN	STOTTIES	STOWDOWNS
STOOPED	STORER	STOTTING	STOWED
STOOPER	STOREROOM	STOTTS	STOWER
STOOPERS	STORERS	STOUN	STOWERS
STOOPES	STORES	STOUND	STOWING
STOOPING	STORESHIP	STOUNDED	STOWINGS
STOOPS	STOREWIDE	STOUNDING	STOWLINS
STOOR	STOREY	STOUNDS	STOWN
STOORS	STOREYED	STOUNING	STOWND
STOOSHIE	STOREYS	STOUNS	STOWNDED
STOOSHIES	STORGE	STOUP	STOWNDING

STOWNDS	STRAITLY	STRATIFY	STREAMLET
STOWNLINS	STRAITS	STRATONIC	STREAMS
STOWP	STRAKE	STRATOSE	STREAMY
STOWPS	STRAKED	STRATOUS	STREEK
STOWRE	STRAKES	STRATUM	STREEKED
STOWRES	STRAMACON	STRATUMS	STREEKER
STOWS	STRAMASH	STRATUS	STREEKERS
STRABISM	STRAMAZON	STRAUCHT	STREEKING
STRABISMS	STRAMMEL	STRAUCHTS	STREEKS
STRAD	STRAMMELS	STRAUGHT	STREEL
STRADDLE	STRAMONY	STRAUGHTS	STREELED
STRADDLED	STRAMP	STRAUNGE	STREELING
STRADDLER	STRAMPED	STRAVAGE	STREELS
STRADDLES	STRAMPING	STRAVAGED	STREET
STRADIOT	STRAMPS	STRAVAGES	STREETAGE
STRADIOTS	STRAND	STRAVAIG	STREETBOY
STRADS	STRANDED	STRAVAIGS	STREETCAR
STRAE	STRANDER	STRAW	STREETED
STRAES	STRANDERS	STRAWED	STREETFUL
STRAFE	STRANDING	STRAWEN	STREETIER
STRAFED	STRANDS	STRAWHAT	STREETING
STRAFER	STRANG	STRAWIER	STREETS
STRAFERS	STRANGE	STRAWIEST	STREETY
STRAFES	STRANGELY	STRAWING	STREIGHT
STRAFF	STRANGER	STRAWLESS	STREIGHTS
STRAFFED	STRANGERS	STRAWLIKE	STREIGNE
STRAFFING	STRANGES	STRAWN	STREIGNED
STRAFFS	STRANGEST	STRAWS	STREIGNES
STRAFING	STRANGLE	STRAWWORM	STRELITZ
STRAG	STRANGLED	STRAWY	STRELITZI
STRAGGLE	STRANGLER	STRAY	STRENE
STRAGGLED	STRANGLES	STRAYED	STRENES
STRAGGLER	STRANGURY	STRAYER	STRENGTH
STRAGGLES	STRAP	STRAYERS	STRENGTHS
STRAGGLY	STRAPHANG	STRAYING	STRENUITY
STRAGS	STRAPHUNG	STRAYINGS	STRENUOUS
STRAICHT	STRAPLESS	STRAYLING	STREP
STRAIGHT	STRAPLINE	STRAYS	STREPENT
STRAIGHTS	STRAPPADO	STRAYVE	STREPS
STRAIK	STRAPPED	STRAYVED	STRESS
STRAIKED	STRAPPER	STRAYVES	STRESSED
STRAIKING	STRAPPERS	STRAYVING	STRESSES
STRAIKS	STRAPPIER	STREAK	STRESSFUL
STRAIN	STRAPPING	STREAKED	STRESSING
STRAINED	STRAPPY	STREAKER	STRESSOR
STRAINER	STRAPS	STREAKERS	STRESSORS
STRAINERS	STRAPWORT	STREAKIER	STRETCH
STRAINING	STRASS	STREAKILY	STRETCHED
STRAINS	STRASSES	STREAKING	STRETCHER
STRAINT	STRATA	STREAKS	STRETCHES
STRAINTS	STRATAGEM	STREAKY	STRETCHY
STRAIT	STRATAL	STREAM	STRETTA
STRAITED	STRATAS	STREAMBED	STRETTAS
STRAITEN	STRATEGIC	STREAMED	STRETTE
STRAITENS	STRATEGY	STREAMER	STRETTI
STRAITER	STRATH	STREAMERS	STRETTO
STRAITEST	STRATHS	STREAMIER	STRETTOS
STRAITING	STRATI	STREAMING	STREUSEL

STREUSELS	STRIFTS	STRIVINGS	STRONGMAN
STREW	STRIG	STROAM	STRONGMEN
STREWAGE	STRIGA	STROAMED	STRONGYL
STREWAGES	STRIGAE	STROAMING	STRONGYLE
STREWED	STRIGATE	STROAMS	STRONGYLS
STREWER	STRIGGED	STROBE	STRONTIA
STREWERS	STRIGGING	STROBED	STRONTIAN
STREWING	STRIGIL	STROBES	STRONTIAS
STREWINGS	STRIGILS	STROBIC	STRONTIC
STREWMENT	STRIGINE	STROBIL	STRONTIUM
STREWN	STRIGOSE	STROBILA	STROOK
STREWS	STRIGS	STROBILAE	STROOKE
STREWTH	STRIKE	STROBILAR	STROOKEN
STRIA	STRIKEOUT	STROBILE	STROOKES
STRIAE	STRIKER	STROBILES	STROP
STRIATA	STRIKERS	STROBILI	STROPHE
STRIATE	STRIKES	STROBILS	STROPHES
STRIATED	STRIKING	STROBILUS	STROPHIC
STRIATES	STRIKINGS	STROBING	STROPHOID
STRIATING	STRING	STROBINGS	STROPHULI
STRIATION	STRINGED	STRODDLE	STROPPED
STRIATUM	STRINGENT	STRODDLED	STROPPER
STRIATUMS	STRINGER	STRODDLES	STROPPERS
STRIATURE	STRINGERS	STRODE	STROPPIER
STRICH	STRINGIER	STRODLE	STROPPILY
STRICHES	STRINGILY	STRODLED	STROPPING
STRICK	STRINGING	STRODLES	STROPPY
STRICKEN	STRINGS	STRODLING	STROPS
STRICKLE	STRINGY	STROKE	STROSSERS
STRICKLED	STRINKLE	STROKED	STROUD
STRICKLES	STRINKLED	STROKEN	STROUDING
STRICKS	STRINKLES	STROKER	STROUDS
STRICT	STRIP	STROKERS	STROUP
STRICTER	STRIPE	STROKES	STROUPACH
STRICTEST	STRIPED	STROKING	STROUPAN
STRICTION	STRIPER	STROKINGS	STROUPANS
STRICTISH	STRIPERS	STROLL	STROUPS
STRICTLY	STRIPES	STROLLED	STROUT
STRICTURE	STRIPEY	STROLLER	STROUTED
STRIDDEN	STRIPIER	STROLLERS	STROUTING
STRIDDLE	STRIPIEST	STROLLING	STROUTS
STRIDDLED	STRIPING	STROLLS	STROVE
STRIDDLES	STRIPINGS	STROMA	STROW
STRIDE	STRIPLING	STROMAL	STROWED
STRIDENCE	STRIPPED	STROMATA	STROWER
STRIDENCY	STRIPPER	STROMATIC	STROWERS
STRIDENT	STRIPPERS	STROMB	STROWING
STRIDER	STRIPPING	STROMBS	STROWINGS
STRIDERS	STRIPS	STROMBUS	STROWN
STRIDES	STRIPT	STROND	STROWS
STRIDING	STRIPY	STRONDS	STROY
STRIDLING	STRIVE	STRONG	STROYED
STRIDOR	STRIVED	STRONGARM	STROYER
STRIDORS	STRIVEN	STRONGBOX	STROYERS
STRIFE	STRIVER	STRONGER	STROYING
STRIFEFUL	STRIVERS	STRONGEST	STROYS
STRIFES	STRIVES	STRONGISH	STRUCK
STRIFT	STRIVING	STRONGLY	STRUCKEN

STRUCTURE	STUCCOES	STULL	STUPEFIED
STRUDEL	STUCCOING	STULLS	STUPEFIER
STRUDELS	STUCCOS	STULM	STUPEFIES
STRUGGLE	STUCK	STULMS	STUPEFY
STRUGGLED	STUCKS	STULTIFY	STUPENT
STRUGGLER	STUD	STUM	STUPES
STRUGGLES	STUDBOOK	STUMBLE	STUPID
STRUM	STUDBOOKS	STUMBLED	STUPIDER
STRUMA	STUDDED	STUMBLER	STUPIDEST
STRUMAE	STUDDEN	STUMBLERS	STUPIDITY
STRUMAS	STUDDIE	STUMBLES	STUPIDLY
STRUMATIC	STUDDIES	STUMBLIER	STUPIDS
STRUMITIS	STUDDING	STUMBLING	STUPING
STRUMMED	STUDDINGS	STUMBLY	STUPOR
STRUMMEL	STUDDLE	STUMER	STUPOROUS
STRUMMELS	STUDDLES	STUMERS	STUPORS
STRUMMER	STUDENT	STUMM	STUPRATE
STRUMMERS	STUDENTRY	STUMMED	STUPRATED
STRUMMING	STUDENTS	STUMMEL	STUPRATES
STRUMOSE	STUDENTY	STUMMELS	STURDIED
STRUMOUS	STUDFARM	STUMMING	STURDIER
STRUMPET	STUDFARMS	STUMP	STURDIES
STRUMPETS	STUDFISH	STUMPAGE	STURDIEST
STRUMS	STUDHORSE	STUMPAGES	STURDILY
STRUNG	STUDIED	STUMPED	STURDY
STRUNT	STUDIEDLY	STUMPER	STURE
STRUNTED	STUDIER	STUMPERS	STURGEON
STRUNTING	STUDIERS	STUMPIER	STURGEONS
STRUNTS	STUDIES	STUMPIES	STURMER
STRUT	STUDIO	STUMPIEST	STURMERS
STRUTS	STUDIOS	STUMPILY	STURNINE
STRUTTED	STUDIOUS	STUMPING	STURNOID
STRUTTER	STUDLIER	STUMPS	STURNUS
STRUTTERS	STUDLIEST	STUMPWORK	STURNUSES
STRUTTING	STUDLY	STUMPY	STURT
STRYCHNIA	STUDS	STUMS	STURTED
STRYCHNIC	STUDWORK	STUN	STURTING
STUB	STUDWORKS	STUNG	STURTS
STUBBED	STUDY	STUNK	STUSHIE
STUBBIE	STUDYING	STUNKARD	STUSHIES
STUBBIER	STUFF	STUNNED	STUTTER
STUBBIES	STUFFED	STUNNER	STUTTERED
STUBBIEST	STUFFER	STUNNERS	STUTTERER
STUBBILY	STUFFERS	STUNNING	STUTTERS
STUBBING	STUFFIER	STUNNINGS	STY
STUBBLE	STUFFIEST	STUNS	STYE
STUBBLED	STUFFILY	STUNSAIL	STYED
STUBBLES	STUFFING	STUNSAILS	STYES
STUBBLIER	STUFFINGS	STUNT	STYGIAN
STUBBLY	STUFFLESS	STUNTED	STYING
STUBBORN	STUFFS	STUNTING	STYLAR
STUBBORNS	STUFFY	STUNTMAN	STYLATE
STUBBY	STUGGIER	STUNTMEN	STYLE
STUBS	STUGGIEST	STUNTS	STYLEBOOK
STUCCO	STUGGY	STUPA	STYLED
STUCCOED	STUIVER	STUPAS	STYLELESS
STUCCOER	STUIVERS	STUPE	STYLER
STUCCOERS	STUKKEND	STUPED	STYLERS

STYLES	STYRAX	SUBALTERN	SUBCLIMAX
STYLET	STYRAXES	SUBAPICAL	SUBCODE
STYLETS	STYRE	SUBAQUA	SUBCODES
STYLI	STYRED	SUBARCTIC	SUBCOLONY
STYLIE	STYRENE	SUBAREA	SUBCONSUL
STYLIER	STYRENES	SUBAREAS	SUBCOOL
STYLIEST	STYRES	SUBARID	SUBCOOLED
STYLIFORM	STYRING	SUBAS	SUBCOOLS
STYLING	STYROFOAM	SUBASTRAL	SUBCORTEX
STYLINGS	STYTE	SUBATOM	SUBCOSTA
STYLISE	STYTED	SUBATOMIC	SUBCOSTAE
STYLISED	STYTES	SUBATOMS	SUBCOSTAL
STYLISER	STYTING	SUBAUDIO	SUBCOUNTY
STYLISERS	SUABILITY	SUBAURAL	SUBCRUST
STYLISES	SUABLE	SUBAXIAL	SUBCRUSTS
STYLISH	SUABLY	SUBBASAL	SUBCULT
STYLISHLY	SUASIBLE	SUBBASE	SUBCULTS
STYLISING	SUASION	SUBBASES	SUBCUTES
STYLIST	SUASIONS	SUBBASIN	SUBCUTIS
STYLISTIC	SUASIVE	SUBBASINS	SUBDEACON
STYLISTS	SUASIVELY	SUBBASS	SUBDEALER
STYLITE	SUASORY	SUBBASSES	SUBDEAN
STYLITES	SUAVE	SUBBED	SUBDEANS
STYLITIC	SUAVELY	SUBBIE	SUBDEB
STYLITISM	SUAVENESS	SUBBIES	SUBDEBS
STYLIZE	SUAVER	SUBBING	SUBDEPOT
STYLIZED	SUAVEST	SUBBINGS	SUBDEPOTS
STYLIZER	SUAVITIES	SUBBLOCK	SUBDEPUTY
STYLIZERS	SUAVITY	SUBBLOCKS	SUBDERMAL
STYLIZES	SUB	SUBBRANCH	SUBDEW
STYLIZING	SUBA	SUBBREED	SUBDEWED
STYLO	SUBABBOT	SUBBREEDS	SUBDEWING
STYLOBATE	SUBABBOTS	SUBBUREAU	SUBDEWS
STYLOID	SUBACID	SUBBY	SUBDIVIDE
STYLOIDS	SUBACIDLY	SUBCANTOR	SUBDOLOUS
STYLOLITE	SUBACRID	SUBCASTE	SUBDORSAL
STYLOPES	SUBACT	SUBCASTES	SUBDUABLE
STYLOPISE	SUBACTED	SUBCAUDAL	SUBDUABLY
STYLOPIZE	SUBACTING	SUBCAUSE	SUBDUAL
STYLOPS	SUBACTION	SUBCAUSES	SUBDUALS
STYLOS	SUBACTS	SUBCAVITY	SUBDUCE
STYLUS	SUBACUTE	SUBCELL	SUBDUCED
STYLUSES	SUBADAR	SUBCELLAR	SUBDUCES
STYME	SUBADARS	SUBCELLS	SUBDUCING
STYMED	SUBADULT	SUBCENTER	SUBDUCT
STYMES	SUBADULTS	SUBCHASER	SUBDUCTED
STYMIE	SUBAERIAL	SUBCHIEF	SUBDUCTS
STYMIED	SUBAGENCY	SUBCHIEFS	SUBDUE
STYMIEING	SUBAGENT	SUBCHORD	SUBDUED
STYMIES	SUBAGENTS	SUBCHORDS	SUBDUEDLY
STYMING	SUBAH	SUBCLAIM	SUBDUER
STYMY	SUBAHDAR	SUBCLAIMS	SUBDUERS
STYMYING	SUBAHDARS	SUBCLAN	SUBDUES
STYPSIS	SUBAHDARY	SUBCLANS	SUBDUING
STYPSISES	SUBAHS	SUBCLASS	SUBDUPLE
STYPTIC	SUBAHSHIP	SUBCLAUSE	SUBDURAL
STYPTICAL	SUBALAR	SUBCLERK	SUBDWARF
STYPTICS	SUBALPINE	SUBCLERKS	SUBDWARFS

SUBECHO	SUBGRADES	SUBLIMELY	SUBOCTAVE
SUBECHOES	SUBGRAPH	SUBLIMER	SUBOCULAR
SUBEDAR	SUBGRAPHS	SUBLIMERS	SUBOFFICE
SUBEDARS	SUBGROUP	SUBLIMES	SUBOPTIC
SUBEDIT	SUBGROUPS	SUBLIMEST	SUBORAL
SUBEDITED	SUBGUM	SUBLIMING	SUBORDER
SUBEDITOR	SUBGUMS	SUBLIMISE	SUBORDERS
SUBEDITS	SUBHA	SUBLIMIT	SUBORN
SUBENTIRE	SUBHAS	SUBLIMITS	SUBORNED
SUBENTRY	SUBHEAD	SUBLIMITY	SUBORNER
SUBEPOCH	SUBHEADS	SUBLIMIZE	SUBORNERS
SUBEPOCHS	SUBHEDRAL	SUBLINE	SUBORNING
SUBEQUAL	SUBHUMAN	SUBLINEAR	SUBORNS
SUBER	SUBHUMANS	SUBLINES	SUBOSCINE
SUBERATE	SUBHUMID	SUBLOT	SUBOVAL
SUBERATES	SUBIDEA	SUBLOTS	SUBOVATE
SUBERECT	SUBIDEAS	SUBLUNAR	SUBOXIDE
SUBEREOUS	SUBIMAGO	SUBLUNARY	SUBOXIDES
SUBERIC	SUBIMAGOS	SUBLUNATE	SUBPANEL
SUBERIN	SUBINCISE	SUBLUXATE	SUBPANELS
SUBERINS	SUBINDEX	SUBMAN	SUBPAR
SUBERISE	SUBINFEUD	SUBMARINE	SUBPART
SUBERISED	SUBITEM	SUBMARKET	SUBPARTS
SUBERISES	SUBITEMS	SUBMATRIX	SUBPENA
SUBERIZE	SUBITISE	SUBMEN	SUBPENAED
SUBERIZED	SUBITISED	SUBMENTA	SUBPENAS
SUBERIZES	SUBITISES	SUBMENTAL	SUBPERIOD
SUBEROSE	SUBITIZE	SUBMENTUM	SUBPHASE
SUBEROUS	SUBITIZED	SUBMENU	SUBPHASES
SUBERS	SUBITIZES	SUBMENUS	SUBPHYLA
SUBFAMILY	SUBITO	SUBMERGE	SUBPHYLAR
SUBFEU	SUBJACENT	SUBMERGED	SUBPHYLUM
SUBFEUED	SUBJECT	SUBMERGES	SUBPLOT
SUBFEUING	SUBJECTED	SUBMERSE	SUBPLOTS
SUBFEUS	SUBJECTS	SUBMERSED	SUBPOENA
SUBFIELD	SUBJOIN	SUBMERSES	SUBPOENAS
SUBFIELDS	SUBJOINED	SUBMICRON	SUBPOLAR
SUBFILE	SUBJOINS	SUBMISS	SUBPOTENT
SUBFILES	SUBJUGATE	SUBMISSLY	SUBPRIOR
SUBFIX	SUBLATE	SUBMIT	SUBPRIORS
SUBFIXES	SUBLATED	SUBMITS	SUBPUBIC
SUBFLOOR	SUBLATES	SUBMITTAL	SUBRACE
SUBFLOORS	SUBLATING	SUBMITTED	SUBRACES
SUBFLUID	SUBLATION	SUBMITTER	SUBREGION
SUBFOSSIL	SUBLEASE	SUBMUCOSA	SUBRENT
SUBFRAME	SUBLEASED	SUBMUCOUS	SUBRENTS
SUBFRAMES	SUBLEASES	SUBNASAL	SUBRING
SUBFUSC	SUBLESSEE	SUBNET	SUBRINGS
SUBFUSCS	SUBLESSOR	SUBNETS	SUBROGATE
SUBFUSK	SUBLET	SUBNEURAL	SUBRULE
SUBFUSKS	SUBLETHAL	SUBNICHE	SUBRULES
SUBGENERA	SUBLETS	SUBNICHES	SUBS
SUBGENRE	SUBLETTER	SUBNIVEAL	SUBSACRAL
SUBGENRES	SUBLEVEL	SUBNIVEAN	SUBSALE
SUBGENUS	SUBLEVELS	SUBNODAL	SUBSALES
SUBGOAL	SUBLIMATE	SUBNORMAL	SUBSAMPLE
SUBGOALS	SUBLIME	SUBNUCLEI	SUBSCALE
SUBGRADE	SUBLIMED	SUBOCEAN	SUBSCALES

SUBSCHEMA	SUBSTANCE	SUBTONE	SUBVISUAL
SUBSCRIBE	SUBSTATE	SUBTONES	SUBVOCAL
SUBSCRIPT	SUBSTATES	SUBTONIC	SUBWARDEN
SUBSEA	SUBSTRACT	SUBTONICS	SUBWAY
SUBSECIVE	SUBSTRATA	SUBTOPIA	SUBWAYED
SUBSECT	SUBSTRATE	SUBTOPIAN	SUBWAYING
SUBSECTOR	SUBSTRUCT	SUBTOPIAS	SUBWAYS
SUBSECTS	SUBSTYLAR	SUBTOPIC	SUBWOOFER
SUBSELLIA	SUBSTYLE	SUBTOPICS	SUBWORLD
SUBSENSE	SUBSTYLES	SUBTORRID	SUBWORLDS
SUBSENSES	SUBSULTUS	SUBTOTAL	SUBWRITER
SUBSERE	SUBSUME	SUBTOTALS	SUBZERO
SUBSERES	SUBSUMED	SUBTRACT	SUBZONAL
SUBSERIES	SUBSUMES	SUBTRACTS	SUBZONE
SUBSERVE	SUBSUMING	SUBTREND	SUBZONES
SUBSERVED	SUBSYSTEM	SUBTRENDS	SUCCADE
SUBSERVES	SUBTACK	SUBTRIBE	SUCCADES
SUBSET	SUBTACKS	SUBTRIBES	SUCCAH
SUBSETS	SUBTASK	SUBTRIST	SUCCAHS
SUBSHAFT	SUBTASKS	SUBTROPIC	SUCCEDENT
SUBSHAFTS	SUBTAXA	SUBTRUDE	SUCCEED
SUBSHELL	SUBTAXON	SUBTRUDED	SUCCEEDED
SUBSHELLS	SUBTAXONS	SUBTRUDES	SUCCEEDER
SUBSHRUB	SUBTEEN	SUBTUNIC	SUCCEEDS
SUBSHRUBS	SUBTEENS	SUBTUNICS	SUCCENTOR
SUBSIDE	SUBTENANT	SUBTYPE	SUCCES
SUBSIDED	SUBTEND	SUBTYPES	SUCCESS
SUBSIDER	SUBTENDED	SUBUCULA	SUCCESSES
SUBSIDERS	SUBTENDS	SUBUCULAS	SUCCESSOR
SUBSIDES	SUBTENSE	SUBULATE	SUCCI
SUBSIDIES	SUBTENSES	SUBUNIT	SUCCINATE
SUBSIDING	SUBTENURE	SUBUNITS	SUCCINCT
SUBSIDISE	SUBTEST	SUBURB	SUCCINIC
SUBSIDIZE	SUBTESTS	SUBURBAN	SUCCINITE
SUBSIDY	SUBTEXT	SUBURBANS	SUCCINYL
SUBSIST	SUBTEXTS	SUBURBED	SUCCINYLS
SUBSISTED	SUBTHEME	SUBURBIA	SUCCISE
SUBSISTER	SUBTHEMES	SUBURBIAS	SUCCOR
SUBSISTS	SUBTIDAL	SUBURBS	SUCCORED
SUBSITE	SUBTIL	SUBURSINE	SUCCORER
SUBSITES	SUBTILE	SUBVASSAL	SUCCORERS
SUBSIZAR	SUBTILELY	SUBVENE	SUCCORIES
SUBSIZARS	SUBTILER	SUBVENED	SUCCORING
SUBSKILL	SUBTILEST	SUBVENES	SUCCORS
SUBSKILLS	SUBTILIN	SUBVENING	SUCCORY
SUBSOCIAL	SUBTILINS	SUBVERSAL	SUCCOS
SUBSOIL	SUBTILISE	SUBVERSE	SUCCOSE
SUBSOILED	SUBTILITY	SUBVERSED	SUCCOT
SUBSOILER	SUBTILIZE	SUBVERSES	SUCCOTASH
SUBSOILS	SUBTILTY	SUBVERST	SUCCOTH
SUBSOLAR	SUBTITLE	SUBVERT	SUCCOUR
SUBSONG	SUBTITLED	SUBVERTED	SUCCOURED
SUBSONGS	SUBTITLES	SUBVERTER	SUCCOURER
SUBSONIC	SUBTLE	SUBVERTS	SUCCOURS
SUBSPACE	SUBTLER	SUBVICAR	SUCCOUS
SUBSPACES	SUBTLEST	SUBVICARS	SUCCUBA
SUBSTAGE	SUBTLETY	SUBVIRAL	SUCCUBAE
SUBSTAGES	SUBTLY	SUBVIRUS	SUCCUBAS

SUCCUBI	SUCTORIAL	SUETIEST	SUGARLOAF
SUCCUBINE	SUCTORIAN	SUETS	SUGARPLUM
SUCCUBOUS	SUCURUJU	SUETTIER	SUGARS
SUCCUBUS	SUCURUJUS	SUETTIEST	SUGARY
SUCCULENT	SUD	SUETTY	SUGGEST
SUCCUMB	SUDAMEN	SUETY	SUGGESTED
SUCCUMBED	SUDAMINA	SUFFARI	SUGGESTER
SUCCUMBER	SUDAMINAL	SUFFARIS	SUGGESTS
SUCCUMBS	SUDARIA	SUFFECT	SUGGING
SUCCURSAL	SUDARIES	SUFFER	SUGGINGS
SUCCUS	SUDARIUM	SUFFERED	SUGH
SUCCUSS	SUDARY	SUFFERER	SUGHED
SUCCUSSED	SUDATE	SUFFERERS	SUGHING
SUCCUSSES	SUDATED	SUFFERING	SUGHS
SUCH	SUDATES	SUFFERS	SUI
SUCHLIKE	SUDATING	SUFFETE	SUICIDAL
SUCHNESS	SUDATION	SUFFETES	SUICIDE
SUCHWISE	SUDATIONS	SUFFICE	SUICIDED
SUCK	SUDATORIA	SUFFICED	SUICIDES
SUCKED	SUDATORY	SUFFICER	SUICIDING
SUCKEN	SUDD	SUFFICERS	SUID
SUCKENER	SUDDEN	SUFFICES	SUIDIAN
SUCKENERS	SUDDENLY	SUFFICING	SUIDIANS
SUCKENS	SUDDENS	SUFFIX	SUIDS
SUCKER	SUDDENTY	SUFFIXAL	SUILLINE
SUCKERED	SUDDER	SUFFIXED	SUING
SUCKERING	SUDDERS	SUFFIXES	SUINGS
SUCKERS	SUDDS	SUFFIXING	SUINT
SUCKET	SUDOR	SUFFIXION	SUINTS
SUCKETS	SUDORAL	SUFFLATE	SUIPLAP
SUCKFISH	SUDORIFIC	SUFFLATED	SUIPLAPS
SUCKIER	SUDOROUS	SUFFLATES	SUIT
SUCKIEST	SUDORS	SUFFOCATE	SUITABLE
SUCKING	SUDS	SUFFRAGAN	SUITABLY
SUCKINGS	SUDSED	SUFFRAGE	SUITCASE
SUCKLE	SUDSER	SUFFRAGES	SUITCASES
SUCKLED	SUDSERS	SUFFUSE	SUITE
SUCKLER	SUDSES	SUFFUSED	SUITED
SUCKLERS	SUDSIER	SUFFUSES	SUITER
SUCKLES	SUDSIEST	SUFFUSING	SUITERS
SUCKLESS	SUDSING	SUFFUSION	SUITES
SUCKLING	SUDSLESS	SUFFUSIVE	SUITING
SUCKLINGS	SUDSY	SUGAN	SUITINGS
SUCKS	SUE	SUGANS	SUITLIKE
SUCKY	SUEABLE	SUGAR	SUITOR
SUCRALOSE	SUED	SUGARALLY	SUITORED
SUCRASE	SUEDE	SUGARBUSH	SUITORING
SUCRASES	SUEDED	SUGARCANE	SUITORS
SUCRE	SUEDES	SUGARCOAT	SUITRESS
SUCRES	SUEDETTE	SUGARED	SUITS
SUCRIER	SUEDETTES	SUGARER	SUIVANTE
SUCRIERS	SUEDING	SUGARERS	SUIVANTES
SUCROSE	SUENT	SUGARIER	SUIVEZ
SUCROSES	SUER	SUGARIEST	SUJEE
SUCTION	SUERS	SUGARING	SUJEES
SUCTIONAL	SUES	SUGARINGS	SUK
SUCTIONED	SUET	SUGARLESS	SUKH
SUCTIONS	SUETIER	SUGARLIKE	SUKHS

SUKIYAKI	SULFURYLS	SULTRIEST	SUMMONING
SUKIYAKIS	SULK	SULTRILY	SUMMONS
SUKKAH	SULKED	SULTRY	SUMMONSED
SUKKAHS	SULKER	SULU	SUMMONSES
SUKKOS	SULKERS	SULUS	SUMO
SUKKOT	SULKIER	SUM	SUMOIST
SUKKOTH	SULKIES	SUMAC	SUMOISTS
SUKS	SULKIEST	SUMACH	SUMOS
SULCAL	SULKILY	SUMACHS	SUMOTORI
SULCALISE	SULKINESS	SUMACS	SUMOTORIS
SULCALIZE	SULKING	SUMATRA	SUMP
SULCATE	SULKS	SUMATRAS	SUMPH
SULCATED	SULKY	SUMLESS	SUMPHISH
SULCATION	SULLAGE	SUMMA	SUMPHS
SULCI	SULLAGES	SUMMABLE	SUMPIT
SULCUS	SULLEN	SUMMAE	SUMPITAN
SULDAN	SULLENER	SUMMAND	SUMPITANS
SULDANS	SULLENEST	SUMMANDS	SUMPITS
SULFA	SULLENLY	SUMMAR	SUMPS
SULFAS	SULLENS	SUMMARIES	SUMPSIMUS
SULFATASE	SULLIABLE	SUMMARILY	SUMPTER
SULFATE	SULLIED	SUMMARISE	SUMPTERS
SULFATED	SULLIES	SUMMARIST	SUMPTUARY
SULFATES	SULLY	SUMMARIZE	SUMPTUOUS
SULFATIC	SULLYING	SUMMARY	SUMPWEED
SULFATING	SULPHA	SUMMAS	SUMPWEEDS
SULFATION	SULPHAS	SUMMAT	SUMS
SULFID	SULPHATE	SUMMATE	SUN
SULFIDE	SULPHATED	SUMMATED	SUNBACK
SULFIDES	SULPHATES	SUMMATES	SUNBAKE
SULFIDS	SULPHATIC	SUMMATING	SUNBAKED
SULFINYL	SULPHID	SUMMATION	SUNBAKES
SULFINYLS	SULPHIDE	SUMMATIVE	SUNBAKING
SULFITE	SULPHIDES	SUMMATS	SUNBATH
SULFITES	SULPHIDS	SUMMED	SUNBATHE
SULFITIC	SULPHINYL	SUMMER	SUNBATHED
SULFO	SULPHITE	SUMMERED	SUNBATHER
SULFONATE	SULPHITES	SUMMERIER	SUNBATHES
SULFONE	SULPHITIC	SUMMERING	SUNBATHS
SULFONES	SULPHONE	SUMMERLY	SUNBEAM
SULFONIC	SULPHONES	SUMMERS	SUNBEAMED
SULFONIUM	SULPHONIC	SUMMERSET	SUNBEAMS
SULFONYL	SULPHONYL	SUMMERY	SUNBEAMY
SULFONYLS	SULPHUR	SUMMING	SUNBEAT
SULFOXIDE	SULPHURED	SUMMINGS	SUNBEATEN
SULFUR	SULPHURET	SUMMIST	SUNBED
SULFURATE	SULPHURIC	SUMMISTS	SUNBEDS
SULFURED	SULPHURS	SUMMIT	SUNBELT
SULFURET	SULPHURY	SUMMITAL	SUNBELTS
SULFURETS	SULPHURYL	SUMMITED	SUNBERRY
SULFURIC	SULTAN	SUMMITEER	SUNBIRD
SULFURING	SULTANA	SUMMITING	SUNBIRDS
SULFURISE	SULTANAS	SUMMITRY	SUNBLIND
SULFURIZE	SULTANATE	SUMMITS	SUNBLINDS
SULFUROUS	SULTANESS	SUMMON	SUNBLOCK
SULFURS	SULTANIC	SUMMONED	SUNBLOCKS
SULFURY	SULTANS	SUMMONER	SUNBONNET
SULFURYL	SULTRIER	SUMMONERS	SUNBOW

SUNBOWS
SUNBRIGHT
SUNBURN
SUNBURNED
SUNBURNS
SUNBURNT
SUNBURST
SUNBURSTS
SUNCHOKE
SUNCHOKES
SUNDAE
SUNDAES
SUNDARI
SUNDARIS
SUNDECK
SUNDECKS
SUNDER
SUNDERED
SUNDERER
SUNDERERS
SUNDERING
SUNDERS
SUNDEW
SUNDEWS
SUNDIAL
SUNDIALS
SUNDOG
SUNDOGS
SUNDOWN
SUNDOWNED
SUNDOWNER
SUNDOWNS
SUNDRA
SUNDRAS
SUNDRESS
SUNDRI
SUNDRIES
SUNDRILY
SUNDRIS
SUNDROPS
SUNDRY
SUNFAST
SUNFISH
SUNFISHES
SUNFLOWER
SUNG
SUNGAR
SUNGARS
SUNGLASS
SUNGLOW
SUNGLOWS
SUNGREBE
SUNGREBES
SUNHAT
SUNHATS
SUNK
SUNKEN
SUNKET

SUNKETS
SUNKIE
SUNKIES
SUNKS
SUNLAMP
SUNLAMPS
SUNLAND
SUNLANDS
SUNLESS
SUNLESSLY
SUNLIGHT
SUNLIGHTS
SUNLIKE
SUNLIT
SUNN
SUNNA
SUNNAH
SUNNAHS
SUNNAS
SUNNED
SUNNIER
SUNNIES
SUNNIEST
SUNNILY
SUNNINESS
SUNNING
SUNNS
SUNNY
SUNPORCH
SUNPROOF
SUNRAY
SUNRAYS
SUNRISE
SUNRISES
SUNRISING
SUNROOF
SUNROOFS
SUNROOM
SUNROOMS
SUNS
SUNSCALD
SUNSCALDS
SUNSCREEN
SUNSEEKER
SUNSET
SUNSETS
SUNSHADE
SUNSHADES
SUNSHINE
SUNSHINES
SUNSHINY
SUNSPOT
SUNSPOTS
SUNSTAR
SUNSTARS
SUNSTONE
SUNSTONES
SUNSTROKE

SUNSTRUCK
SUNSUIT
SUNSUITS
SUNTAN
SUNTANNED
SUNTANS
SUNTRAP
SUNTRAPS
SUNUP
SUNUPS
SUNWARD
SUNWARDS
SUNWISE
SUP
SUPAWN
SUPAWNS
SUPE
SUPER
SUPERABLE
SUPERABLY
SUPERADD
SUPERADDS
SUPERATE
SUPERATED
SUPERATES
SUPERATOM
SUPERB
SUPERBAD
SUPERBANK
SUPERBER
SUPERBEST
SUPERBIKE
SUPERBITY
SUPERBLY
SUPERBOLD
SUPERBOMB
SUPERBRAT
SUPERBUG
SUPERBUGS
SUPERCAR
SUPERCARS
SUPERCEDE
SUPERCHIC
SUPERCITY
SUPERCLUB
SUPERCOIL
SUPERCOLD
SUPERCOOL
SUPERCOP
SUPERCOPS
SUPERCOW
SUPERCOWS
SUPERCUTE
SUPERED
SUPEREGO
SUPEREGOS
SUPERETTE
SUPERFAN

SUPERFANS
SUPERFARM
SUPERFAST
SUPERFINE
SUPERFIRM
SUPERFIT
SUPERFIX
SUPERFLUX
SUPERFUND
SUPERFUSE
SUPERGENE
SUPERGLUE
SUPERGOOD
SUPERGUN
SUPERGUNS
SUPERHEAT
SUPERHERO
SUPERHET
SUPERHETS
SUPERHIGH
SUPERHIT
SUPERHITS
SUPERHIVE
SUPERHOT
SUPERHYPE
SUPERING
SUPERIOR
SUPERIORS
SUPERJET
SUPERJETS
SUPERJOCK
SUPERLAIN
SUPERLAY
SUPERLIE
SUPERLIES
SUPERLOAD
SUPERLONG
SUPERLOO
SUPERLOOS
SUPERMALE
SUPERMAN
SUPERMART
SUPERMAX
SUPERMEN
SUPERMIND
SUPERMINI
SUPERMOM
SUPERMOMS
SUPERMOTO
SUPERNAL
SUPERNATE
SUPERNOVA
SUPERPIMP
SUPERPLUS
SUPERPORT
SUPERPOSE
SUPERPRO
SUPERPROS

SUPERRACE	SUPPLICAT	SURBEDS	SURFMEN
SUPERREAL	SUPPLIED	SURBET	SURFPERCH
SUPERRICH	SUPPLIER	SURCEASE	SURFRIDER
SUPERROAD	SUPPLIERS	SURCEASED	SURFS
SUPERS	SUPPLIES	SURCEASES	SURFSIDE
SUPERSAFE	SUPPLING	SURCHARGE	SURFY
SUPERSALE	SUPPLY	SURCINGLE	SURGE
SUPERSALT	SUPPLYING	SURCOAT	SURGED
SUPERSAUR	SUPPORT	SURCOATS	SURGEFUL
SUPERSEDE	SUPPORTED	SURCULI	SURGELESS
SUPERSELL	SUPPORTER	SURCULOSE	SURGENT
SUPERSEX	SUPPORTS	SURCULUS	SURGEON
SUPERSHOW	SUPPOSAL	SURD	SURGEONCY
SUPERSIZE	SUPPOSALS	SURDITIES	SURGEONS
SUPERSOFT	SUPPOSE	SURDITY	SURGER
SUPERSOLD	SUPPOSED	SURDS	SURGERIES
SUPERSPY	SUPPOSER	SURE	SURGERS
SUPERSTAR	SUPPOSERS	SURED	SURGERY
SUPERSTUD	SUPPOSES	SUREFIRE	SURGES
SUPERTAX	SUPPOSING	SURELY	SURGICAL
SUPERTHIN	SUPPRESS	SURENESS	SURGIER
SUPERVENE	SUPPURATE	SURER	SURGIEST
SUPERVISE	SUPRA	SURES	SURGING
SUPERWAIF	SUPREMACY	SUREST	SURGINGS
SUPERWAVE	SUPREME	SURETIED	SURGY
SUPERWEED	SUPREMELY	SURETIES	SURICATE
SUPERWIDE	SUPREMER	SURETY	SURICATES
SUPERWIFE	SUPREMES	SURETYING	SURIMI
SUPES	SUPREMEST	SURF	SURIMIS
SUPINATE	SUPREMITY	SURFABLE	SURING
SUPINATED	SUPREMO	SURFACE	SURLIER
SUPINATES	SUPREMOS	SURFACED	SURLIEST
SUPINATOR	SUPS	SURFACER	SURLILY
SUPINE	SUQ	SURFACERS	SURLINESS
SUPINELY	SUQS	SURFACES	SURLOIN
SUPINES	SUR	SURFACING	SURLOINS
SUPLEX	SURA	SURFBIRD	SURLY
SUPLEXES	SURAH	SURFBIRDS	SURMASTER
SUPPAWN	SURAHS	SURFBOARD	SURMISAL
SUPPAWNS	SURAL	SURFBOAT	SURMISALS
SUPPEAGO	SURAMIN	SURFBOATS	SURMISE
SUPPED	SURAMINS	SURFED	SURMISED
SUPPER	SURANCE	SURFEIT	SURMISER
SUPPERED	SURANCES	SURFEITED	SURMISERS
SUPPERING	SURAS	SURFEITER	SURMISES
SUPPERS	SURAT	SURFEITS	SURMISING
SUPPING	SURATS	SURFER	SURMOUNT
SUPPLANT	SURBAHAR	SURFERS	SURMOUNTS
SUPPLANTS	SURBAHARS	SURFFISH	SURMULLET
SUPPLE	SURBASE	SURFICIAL	SURNAME
SUPPLED	SURBASED	SURFIE	SURNAMED
SUPPLELY	SURBASES	SURFIER	SURNAMER
SUPPLER	SURBATE	SURFIES	SURNAMERS
SUPPLES	SURBATED	SURFIEST	SURNAMES
SUPPLEST	SURBATES	SURFING	SURNAMING
SUPPLIAL	SURBATING	SURFINGS	SURPASS
SUPPLIALS	SURBED	SURFLIKE	SURPASSED
SUPPLIANT	SURBEDDED	SURFMAN	SURPASSER

SURPASSES	SURVEYS	SUTLERIES	SWADDY
SURPLICE	SURVIEW	SUTLERS	SWADS
SURPLICED	SURVIEWED	SUTLERY	SWAG
SURPLICES	SURVIEWS	SUTOR	SWAGE
SURPLUS	SURVIVAL	SUTORIAL	SWAGED
SURPLUSED	SURVIVALS	SUTORIAN	SWAGER
SURPLUSES	SURVIVE	SUTORS	SWAGERS
SURPRINT	SURVIVED	SUTRA	SWAGES
SURPRINTS	SURVIVER	SUTRAS	SWAGGED
SURPRISAL	SURVIVERS	SUTTA	SWAGGER
SURPRISE	SURVIVES	SUTTAS	SWAGGERED
SURPRISED	SURVIVING	SUTTEE	SWAGGERER
SURPRISER	SURVIVOR	SUTTEEISM	SWAGGERS
SURPRISES	SURVIVORS	SUTTEES	SWAGGIE
SURPRIZE	SUS	SUTTLE	SWAGGIES
SURPRIZED	SUSCEPTOR	SUTTLED	SWAGGING
SURPRIZES	SUSCITATE	SUTTLES	SWAGING
SURQUEDRY	SUSES	SUTTLETIE	SWAGMAN
SURQUEDY	SUSHI	SUTTLING	SWAGMEN
SURRA	SUSHIS	SUTTLY	SWAGS
SURRAS	SUSLIK	SUTURAL	SWAGSHOP
SURREAL	SUSLIKS	SUTURALLY	SWAGSHOPS
SURREALLY	SUSPECT	SUTURE	SWAGSMAN
SURREBUT	SUSPECTED	SUTURED	SWAGSMEN
SURREBUTS	SUSPECTER	SUTURES	SWAIL
SURREINED	SUSPECTS	SUTURING	SWAILS
SURREJOIN	SUSPENCE	SUZERAIN	SWAIN
SURRENDER	SUSPEND	SUZERAINS	SWAINING
SURRENDRY	SUSPENDED	SVARAJ	SWAININGS
SURREY	SUSPENDER	SVARAJES	SWAINISH
SURREYS	SUSPENDS	SVASTIKA	SWAINS
SURROGACY	SUSPENS	SVASTIKAS	SWALE
SURROGATE	SUSPENSE	SVEDBERG	SWALED
SURROUND	SUSPENSER	SVEDBERGS	SWALES
SURROUNDS	SUSPENSES	SVELTE	SWALIER
SURROYAL	SUSPENSOR	SVELTELY	SWALIEST
SURROYALS	SUSPICION	SVELTER	SWALING
SURTAX	SUSPIRE	SVELTEST	SWALINGS
SURTAXED	SUSPIRED	SWAB	SWALLET
SURTAXES	SUSPIRES	SWABBED	SWALLETS
SURTAXING	SUSPIRING	SWABBER	SWALLOW
SURTITLE	SUSS	SWABBERS	SWALLOWED
SURTITLES	SUSSED	SWABBIE	SWALLOWER
SURTOUT	SUSSES	SWABBIES	SWALLOWS
SURTOUTS	SUSSING	SWABBING	SWALY
SURUCUCU	SUSTAIN	SWABBY	SWAM
SURUCUCUS	SUSTAINED	SWABS	SWAMI
SURVEIL	SUSTAINER	SWACK	SWAMIES
SURVEILED	SUSTAINS	SWACKED	SWAMIS
SURVEILLE	SUSTINENT	SWAD	SWAMP
SURVEILS	SUSU	SWADDIE	SWAMPED
SURVEY	SUSURRANT	SWADDIES	SWAMPER
SURVEYAL	SUSURRATE	SWADDLE	SWAMPERS
SURVEYALS	SUSURROUS	SWADDLED	SWAMPIER
SURVEYED	SUSURRUS	SWADDLER	SWAMPIEST
SURVEYING	SUSUS	SWADDLERS	SWAMPING
SURVEYOR	SUTILE	SWADDLES	SWAMPISH
SURVEYORS	SUTLER	SWADDLING	SWAMPLAND

SWAMPLESS	SWARDIEST	SWATS	SWEDGERS
SWAMPS	SWARDING	SWATTED	SWEE
SWAMPY	SWARDS	SWATTER	SWEED
SWAMY	SWARDY	SWATTERED	SWEEING
SWAN	SWARE	SWATTERS	SWEEL
SWANG	SWARF	SWATTING	SWEELED
SWANHERD	SWARFED	SWATTINGS	SWEELING
SWANHERDS	SWARFING	SWAY	SWEELS
SWANK	SWARFS	SWAYABLE	SWEENEY
SWANKED	SWARM	SWAYBACK	SWEENEYS
SWANKER	SWARMED	SWAYBACKS	SWEENIES
SWANKERS	SWARMER	SWAYED	SWEENY
SWANKEST	SWARMERS	SWAYER	SWEEP
SWANKEY	SWARMING	SWAYERS	SWEEPBACK
SWANKEYS	SWARMINGS	SWAYFUL	SWEEPER
SWANKIE	SWARMS	SWAYING	SWEEPERS
SWANKIER	SWART	SWAYINGS	SWEEPIER
SWANKIES	SWARTH	SWAYL	SWEEPIEST
SWANKIEST	SWARTHIER	SWAYLED	SWEEPING
SWANKILY	SWARTHILY	SWAYLING	SWEEPINGS
SWANKING	SWARTHS	SWAYLINGS	SWEEPS
SWANKPOT	SWARTHY	SWAYLS	SWEEPY
SWANKPOTS	SWARTNESS	SWAYS	SWEER
SWANKS	SWARTY	SWAZZLE	SWEERED
SWANKY	SWARVE	SWAZZLES	SWEERER
SWANLIKE	SWARVED	SWEAL	SWEEREST
SWANNED	SWARVES	SWEALED	SWEERING
SWANNERY	SWARVING	SWEALING	SWEERS
SWANNIE	SWASH	SWEALINGS	SWEERT
SWANNIER	SWASHED	SWEALS	SWEES
SWANNIES	SWASHER	SWEAR	SWEET
SWANNIEST	SWASHERS	SWEARD	SWEETCORN
SWANNING	SWASHES	SWEARDS	SWEETED
SWANNINGS	SWASHIER	SWEARER	SWEETEN
SWANNY	SWASHIEST	SWEARERS	SWEETENED
SWANPAN	SWASHING	SWEARING	SWEETENER
SWANPANS	SWASHINGS	SWEARINGS	SWEETENS
SWANS	SWASHWORK	SWEARS	SWEETER
SWANSDOWN	SWASHY	SWEARWORD	SWEETEST
SWANSKIN	SWASTICA	SWEAT	SWEETFISH
SWANSKINS	SWASTICAS	SWEATBAND	SWEETIE
SWAP	SWASTIKA	SWEATBOX	SWEETIES
SWAPPED	SWASTIKAS	SWEATED	SWEETING
SWAPPER	SWAT	SWEATER	SWEETINGS
SWAPPERS	SWATCH	SWEATERS	SWEETISH
SWAPPING	SWATCHES	SWEATIER	SWEETLY
SWAPPINGS	SWATH	SWEATIEST	SWEETMAN
SWAPS	SWATHABLE	SWEATILY	SWEETMEAL
SWAPT	SWATHE	SWEATING	SWEETMEAT
SWAPTION	SWATHED	SWEATINGS	SWEETMEN
SWAPTIONS	SWATHER	SWEATLESS	SWEETNESS
SWARAJ	SWATHERS	SWEATS	SWEETPEA
SWARAJES	SWATHES	SWEATSHOP	SWEETPEAS
SWARAJISM	SWATHIER	SWEATSUIT	SWEETS
SWARAJIST	SWATHIEST	SWEATY	SWEETSHOP
SWARD	SWATHING	SWEDE	SWEETSOP
SWARDED	SWATHS	SWEDES	SWEETSOPS
SWARDIER	SWATHY	SWEDGER	SWEETWOOD

SWEETY	SWIFTED	SWINEPOX	SWIRLIEST
SWEIR	SWIFTER	SWINERIES	SWIRLING
SWEIRED	SWIFTERS	SWINERY	SWIRLS
SWEIRER	SWIFTEST	SWINES	SWIRLY
SWEIREST	SWIFTIE	SWING	SWISH
SWEIRING	SWIFTIES	SWINGBEAT	SWISHED
SWEIRNESS	SWIFTING	SWINGBOAT	SWISHER
SWEIRS	SWIFTLET	SWINGBY	SWISHERS
SWEIRT	SWIFTLETS	SWINGBYS	SWISHES
SWELCHIE	SWIFTLY	SWINGE	SWISHEST
SWELCHIES	SWIFTNESS	SWINGED	SWISHIER
SWELL	SWIFTS	SWINGEING	SWISHIEST
SWELLDOM	SWIFTY	SWINGER	SWISHING
SWELLDOMS	SWIG	SWINGERS	SWISHINGS
SWELLED	SWIGGED	SWINGES	SWISHY
SWELLER	SWIGGER	SWINGIER	SWISS
SWELLERS	SWIGGERS	SWINGIEST	SWISSES
SWELLEST	SWIGGING	SWINGING	SWISSING
SWELLFISH	SWIGS	SWINGINGS	SWISSINGS
SWELLHEAD	SWILER	SWINGISM	SWITCH
SWELLING	SWILERS	SWINGISMS	SWITCHED
SWELLINGS	SWILL	SWINGLE	SWITCHEL
SWELLISH	SWILLED	SWINGLED	SWITCHELS
SWELLS	SWILLER	SWINGLES	SWITCHER
SWELT	SWILLERS	SWINGLING	SWITCHERS
SWELTED	SWILLING	SWINGMAN	SWITCHES
SWELTER	SWILLINGS	SWINGMEN	SWITCHIER
SWELTERED	SWILLS	SWINGS	SWITCHING
SWELTERS	SWIM	SWINGTREE	SWITCHMAN
SWELTING	SWIMMABLE	SWINGY	SWITCHMEN
SWELTRIER	SWIMMER	SWINISH	SWITCHY
SWELTRY	SWIMMERET	SWINISHLY	SWITH
SWELTS	SWIMMERS	SWINK	SWITHE
SWEPT	SWIMMIER	SWINKED	SWITHER
SWEPTBACK	SWIMMIEST	SWINKER	SWITHERED
SWEPTWING	SWIMMILY	SWINKERS	SWITHERS
SWERF	SWIMMING	SWINKING	SWITHLY
SWERFED	SWIMMINGS	SWINKS	SWITS
SWERFING	SWIMMY	SWINNEY	SWITSES
SWERFS	SWIMS	SWINNEYS	SWIVE
SWERVABLE	SWIMSUIT	SWIPE	SWIVED
SWERVE	SWIMSUITS	SWIPED	SWIVEL
SWERVED	SWIMWEAR	SWIPER	SWIVELED
SWERVER	SWIMWEARS	SWIPERS	SWIVELING
SWERVERS	SWINDGE	SWIPES	SWIVELLED
SWERVES	SWINDGED	SWIPEY	SWIVELS
SWERVING	SWINDGES	SWIPIER	SWIVES
SWERVINGS	SWINDGING	SWIPIEST	SWIVET
SWEVEN	SWINDLE	SWIPING	SWIVETS
SWEVENS	SWINDLED	SWIPLE	SWIVING
SWEY	SWINDLER	SWIPLES	SWIZ
SWEYED	SWINDLERS	SWIPPLE	SWIZZ
SWEYING	SWINDLES	SWIPPLES	SWIZZED
SWEYS	SWINDLING	SWIRE	SWIZZES
SWIDDEN	SWINE	SWIRES	SWIZZING
SWIDDENS	SWINEHERD	SWIRL	SWIZZLE
SWIES	SWINEHOOD	SWIRLED	SWIZZLED
SWIFT	SWINELIKE	SWIRLIER	SWIZZLER

SWIZZLERS	SWORDMAN	SYCEE	SYLVA
SWIZZLES	SWORDMEN	SYCEES	SYLVAE
SWIZZLING	SWORDPLAY	SYCES	SYLVAN
SWOB	SWORDS	SYCOMORE	SYLVANER
SWOBBED	SWORDSMAN	SYCOMORES	SYLVANERS
SWOBBER	SWORDSMEN	SYCONIA	SYLVANITE
SWOBBERS	SWORDTAIL	SYCONIUM	SYLVANS
SWOBBING	SWORE	SYCOPHANT	SYLVAS
SWOBS	SWORN	SYCOSES	SYLVATIC
SWOFFER	SWOT	SYCOSIS	SYLVIA
SWOFFERS	SWOTS	SYE	SYLVIAS
SWOFFING	SWOTTED	SYED	SYLVIINE
SWOFFINGS	SWOTTER	SYEING	SYLVIN
SWOLLEN	SWOTTERS	SYEN	SYLVINE
SWOLLENLY	SWOTTIER	SYENITE	SYLVINES
SWOLN	SWOTTIEST	SYENITES	SYLVINITE
SWONE	SWOTTING	SYENITIC	SYLVINS
SWONES	SWOTTINGS	SYENS	SYLVITE
SWOON	SWOTTY	SYES	SYLVITES
SWOONED	SWOUN	SYKE	SYMAR
SWOONER	SWOUND	SYKER	SYMARS
SWOONERS	SWOUNDED	SYKES	SYMBION
SWOONIER	SWOUNDING	SYLI	SYMBIONS
SWOONIEST	SWOUNDS	SYLIS	SYMBIONT
SWOONING	SWOUNE	SYLLABARY	SYMBIONTS
SWOONINGS	SWOUNED	SYLLABI	SYMBIOSES
SWOONS	SWOUNES	SYLLABIC	SYMBIOSIS
SWOONY	SWOUNING	SYLLABICS	SYMBIOT
SWOOP	SWOUNS	SYLLABIFY	SYMBIOTE
SWOOPED	SWOWND	SYLLABISE	SYMBIOTES
SWOOPER	SWOWNDS	SYLLABISM	SYMBIOTIC
SWOOPERS	SWOWNE	SYLLABIZE	SYMBIOTS
SWOOPIER	SWOWNES	SYLLABLE	SYMBOL
SWOOPIEST	SWOZZLE	SYLLABLED	SYMBOLE
SWOOPING	SWOZZLES	SYLLABLES	SYMBOLED
SWOOPS	SWUM	SYLLABUB	SYMBOLES
SWOOPY	SWUNG	SYLLABUBS	SYMBOLIC
SWOOSH	SWY	SYLLABUS	SYMBOLICS
SWOOSHED	SYBARITE	SYLLEPSES	SYMBOLING
SWOOSHES	SYBARITES	SYLLEPSIS	SYMBOLISE
SWOOSHING	SYBARITIC	SYLLEPTIC	SYMBOLISM
SWOP	SYBBE	SYLLOGISE	SYMBOLIST
SWOPPED	SYBBES	SYLLOGISM	SYMBOLIZE
SWOPPER	SYBIL	SYLLOGIST	SYMBOLLED
SWOPPERS	SYBILS	SYLLOGIZE	SYMBOLOGY
SWOPPING	SYBO	SYLPH	SYMBOLS
SWOPPINGS	SYBOE	SYLPHIC	SYMITAR
SWOPS	SYBOES	SYLPHID	SYMITARE
SWOPT	SYBOTIC	SYLPHIDE	SYMITARES
SWORD	SYBOTISM	SYLPHIDES	SYMITARS
SWORDBILL	SYBOTISMS	SYLPHIDS	SYMMETRAL
SWORDED	SYBOW	SYLPHIER	SYMMETRIC
SWORDER	SYBOWS	SYLPHIEST	SYMMETRY
SWORDERS	SYCAMINE	SYLPHINE	SYMPATHIN
SWORDFISH	SYCAMINES	SYLPHISH	SYMPATHY
SWORDING	SYCAMORE	SYLPHLIKE	SYMPATICO
SWORDLESS	SYCAMORES	SYLPHS	SYMPATRIC
SWORDLIKE	SYCE	SYLPHY	SYMPATRY

SYMPETALY	SYNCARP	SYNEDRIAL	SYNOPSES
SYMPHILE	SYNCARPS	SYNEDRION	SYNOPSIS
SYMPHILES	SYNCARPY	SYNEDRIUM	SYNOPSISE
SYMPHILY	SYNCED	SYNERESES	SYNOPSIZE
SYMPHONIC	SYNCH	SYNERESIS	SYNOPTIC
SYMPHONY	SYNCHED	SYNERGIA	SYNOPTICS
SYMPHYSES	SYNCHING	SYNERGIAS	SYNOPTIST
SYMPHYSIS	SYNCHRO	SYNERGIC	SYNOVIA
SYMPHYTIC	SYNCHRONY	SYNERGID	SYNOVIAL
SYMPLAST	SYNCHROS	SYNERGIDS	SYNOVIAS
SYMPLASTS	SYNCHS	SYNERGIES	SYNOVITIC
SYMPLOCE	SYNCHYSES	SYNERGISE	SYNOVITIS
SYMPLOCES	SYNCHYSIS	SYNERGISM	SYNROC
SYMPODIA	SYNCING	SYNERGIST	SYNROCS
SYMPODIAL	SYNCLINAL	SYNERGIZE	SYNTACTIC
SYMPODIUM	SYNCLINE	SYNERGY	SYNTAGM
SYMPOSIA	SYNCLINES	SYNES	SYNTAGMA
SYMPOSIAC	SYNCOM	SYNESES	SYNTAGMAS
SYMPOSIAL	SYNCOMS	SYNESIS	SYNTAGMIC
SYMPOSIUM	SYNCOPAL	SYNESISES	SYNTAGMS
SYMPTOM	SYNCOPATE	SYNFUEL	SYNTAN
SYMPTOMS	SYNCOPE	SYNFUELS	SYNTANS
SYMPTOSES	SYNCOPES	SYNGAMIC	SYNTAX
SYMPTOSIS	SYNCOPIC	SYNGAMIES	SYNTAXES
SYMPTOTIC	SYNCOPTIC	SYNGAMOUS	SYNTECTIC
SYN	SYNCRETIC	SYNGAMY	SYNTENIC
SYNAGOG	SYNCS	SYNGAS	SYNTENIES
SYNAGOGAL	SYNCYTIA	SYNGASES	SYNTENY
SYNAGOGS	SYNCYTIAL	SYNGASSES	SYNTEXIS
SYNAGOGUE	SYNCYTIUM	SYNGENEIC	SYNTH
SYNALEPHA	SYND	SYNGENIC	SYNTHESES
SYNANDRIA	SYNDACTYL	SYNGRAPH	SYNTHESIS
SYNANGIA	SYNDED	SYNGRAPHS	SYNTHETIC
SYNANGIUM	SYNDESES	SYNING	SYNTHON
SYNANON	SYNDESIS	SYNIZESES	SYNTHONS
SYNANONS	SYNDET	SYNIZESIS	SYNTHPOP
SYNANTHIC	SYNDETIC	SYNKARYA	SYNTHPOPS
SYNANTHY	SYNDETON	SYNKARYON	SYNTHRONI
SYNAPHEA	SYNDETONS	SYNOD	SYNTHS
SYNAPHEAS	SYNDETS	SYNODAL	SYNTONIC
SYNAPHEIA	SYNDIC	SYNODALS	SYNTONIES
SYNAPSE	SYNDICAL	SYNODIC	SYNTONIN
SYNAPSED	SYNDICATE	SYNODICAL	SYNTONINS
SYNAPSES	SYNDICS	SYNODS	SYNTONISE
SYNAPSID	SYNDING	SYNODSMAN	SYNTONIZE
SYNAPSIDS	SYNDINGS	SYNODSMEN	SYNTONOUS
SYNAPSING	SYNDROME	SYNOECETE	SYNTONY
SYNAPSIS	SYNDROMES	SYNOECISE	SYNURA
SYNAPTASE	SYNDROMIC	SYNOECISM	SYNURAE
SYNAPTE	SYNDS	SYNOECIZE	SYPE
SYNAPTES	SYNE	SYNOEKETE	SYPED
SYNAPTIC	SYNECHIA	SYNOICOUS	SYPES
SYNARCHY	SYNECHIAS	SYNONYM	SYPH
SYNASTRY	SYNECIOUS	SYNONYME	SYPHER
SYNAXARIA	SYNECTIC	SYNONYMES	SYPHERED
SYNAXES	SYNECTICS	SYNONYMIC	SYPHERING
SYNAXIS	SYNED	SYNONYMS	SYPHERS
SYNC	SYNEDRIA	SYNONYMY	SYPHILIS

SYPHILISE
SYPHILIZE
SYPHILOID
SYPHILOMA
SYPHON
SYPHONED
SYPHONING
SYPHONS
SYPHS
SYPING
SYRAH
SYRAHS
SYREN
SYRENS
SYRETTE
SYRETTES
SYRINGA
SYRINGAS
SYRINGE
SYRINGEAL
SYRINGED
SYRINGES
SYRINGING
SYRINX
SYRINXES
SYRPHIAN
SYRPHIANS
SYRPHID
SYRPHIDS
SYRTES
SYRTIS
SYRUP
SYRUPED
SYRUPIER
SYRUPIEST
SYRUPING
SYRUPLIKE
SYRUPS
SYRUPY
SYSADMIN
SYSADMINS
SYSOP
SYSOPS
SYSSITIA
SYSSITIAS
SYSTALTIC
SYSTEM
SYSTEMED
SYSTEMIC
SYSTEMICS
SYSTEMISE
SYSTEMIZE
SYSTEMS
SYSTOLE
SYSTOLES
SYSTOLIC
SYSTYLE
SYSTYLES

SYTHE
SYTHES
SYVER
SYVERS
SYZYGAL
SYZYGETIC
SYZYGIAL
SYZYGIES
SYZYGY

T

TA	TABLAS	TABOULIS	TACHISMS
TAAL	TABLATURE	TABOUR	TACHIST
TAALS	TABLE	TABOURED	TACHISTE
TAATA	TABLEAU	TABOURER	TACHISTES
TAATAS	TABLEAUS	TABOURERS	TACHISTS
TAB	TABLEAUX	TABOURET	TACHO
TABANID	TABLED	TABOURETS	TACHOGRAM
TABANIDS	TABLEFUL	TABOURIN	TACHOS
TABARD	TABLEFULS	TABOURING	TACHS
TABARDED	TABLELAND	TABOURINS	TACHYLITE
TABARDS	TABLELESS	TABOURS	TACHYLYTE
TABARET	TABLEMATE	TABRERE	TACHYON
TABARETS	TABLES	TABRERES	TACHYONIC
TABASHEER	TABLESFUL	TABRET	TACHYONS
TABASHIR	TABLET	TABRETS	TACHYPNEA
TABASHIRS	TABLETED	TABS	TACIT
TABBED	TABLETING	TABU	TACITLY
TABBIED	TABLETOP	TABUED	TACITNESS
TABBIES	TABLETOPS	TABUING	TACITURN
TABBINET	TABLETS	TABULA	TACK
TABBINETS	TABLETTED	TABULABLE	TACKBOARD
TABBING	TABLEWARE	TABULAE	TACKED
TABBIS	TABLEWISE	TABULAR	TACKER
TABBISES	TABLIER	TABULARLY	TACKERS
TABBOULEH	TABLIERS	TABULATE	TACKET
TABBOULI	TABLING	TABULATED	TACKETS
TABBOULIS	TABLINGS	TABULATES	TACKETY
TABBY	TABLOID	TABULATOR	TACKEY
TABBYHOOD	TABLOIDS	TABULI	TACKIER
TABBYING	TABLOIDY	TABULIS	TACKIES
TABEFIED	TABOGGAN	TABUN	TACKIEST
TABEFIES	TABOGGANS	TABUNS	TACKIFIED
TABEFY	TABOO	TABUS	TACKIFIER
TABEFYING	TABOOED	TACAHOUT	TACKIFIES
TABELLION	TABOOING	TACAHOUTS	TACKIFY
TABER	TABOOLEY	TACAMAHAC	TACKILY
TABERD	TABOOLEYS	TACAN	TACKINESS
TABERDAR	TABOOS	TACANS	TACKING
TABERDARS	TABOR	TACE	TACKINGS
TABERDS	TABORED	TACES	TACKLE
TABERED	TABORER	TACET	TACKLED
TABERING	TABORERS	TACETED	TACKLER
TABERS	TABORET	TACETING	TACKLERS
TABES	TABORETS	TACETS	TACKLES
TABESCENT	TABORIN	TACH	TACKLESS
TABETIC	TABORINE	TACHE	TACKLING
TABETICS	TABORINES	TACHES	TACKLINGS
TABI	TABORING	TACHINA	TACKS
TABID	TABORINS	TACHINID	TACKSMAN
TABINET	TABORS	TACHINIDS	TACKSMEN
TABINETS	TABOULEH	TACHISM	TACKY
TABIS	TABOULEHS	TACHISME	TACMAHACK
TABLA	TABOULI	TACHISMES	TACNODE

TACNODES	TAFFIA	TAHSIL	TAILORESS
TACO	TAFFIAS	TAHSILDAR	TAILORING
TACONITE	TAFFIES	TAHSILS	TAILORS
TACONITES	TAFFRAIL	TAI	TAILPIECE
TACOS	TAFFRAILS	TAIAHA	TAILPIPE
TACRINE	TAFFY	TAIAHAS	TAILPIPED
TACRINES	TAFIA	TAIG	TAILPIPES
TACT	TAFIAS	TAIGA	TAILPLANE
TACTFUL	TAG	TAIGAS	TAILRACE
TACTFULLY	TAGALONG	TAIGLACH	TAILRACES
TACTIC	TAGALONGS	TAIGLE	TAILS
TACTICAL	TAGAREEN	TAIGLED	TAILSKID
TACTICIAN	TAGAREENS	TAIGLES	TAILSKIDS
TACTICITY	TAGBOARD	TAIGLING	TAILSLIDE
TACTICS	TAGBOARDS	TAIGS	TAILSPIN
TACTILE	TAGETES	TAIHOA	TAILSPINS
TACTILELY	TAGGANT	TAIKONAUT	TAILSTOCK
TACTILIST	TAGGANTS	TAIL	TAILWATER
TACTILITY	TAGGED	TAILARD	TAILWHEEL
TACTION	TAGGEE	TAILARDS	TAILWIND
TACTIONS	TAGGEES	TAILBACK	TAILWINDS
TACTISM	TAGGER	TAILBACKS	TAILYE
TACTISMS	TAGGERS	TAILBOARD	TAILYES
TACTLESS	TAGGIER	TAILBONE	TAILZIE
TACTS	TAGGIEST	TAILBONES	TAILZIES
TACTUAL	TAGGING	TAILCOAT	TAIN
TACTUALLY	TAGGINGS	TAILCOATS	TAINS
TAD	TAGGY	TAILED	TAINT
TADDIE	TAGHAIRM	TAILENDER	TAINTED
TADDIES	TAGHAIRMS	TAILER	TAINTING
TADPOLE	TAGINE	TAILERON	TAINTLESS
TADPOLES	TAGINES	TAILERONS	TAINTS
TADS	TAGLIKE	TAILERS	TAINTURE
TADVANCE	TAGLINE	TAILFAN	TAINTURES
TAE	TAGLINES	TAILFANS	TAIPAN
TAED	TAGLIONI	TAILFIN	TAIPANS
TAEDIUM	TAGLIONIS	TAILFINS	TAIRA
TAEDIUMS	TAGMA	TAILFLIES	TAIRAS
TAEING	TAGMATA	TAILFLY	TAIS
TAEKWONDO	TAGMEME	TAILGATE	TAISCH
TAEL	TAGMEMES	TAILGATED	TAISCHES
TAELS	TAGMEMIC	TAILGATER	TAISH
TAENIA	TAGMEMICS	TAILGATES	TAISHES
TAENIAE	TAGRAG	TAILING	TAIT
TAENIAS	TAGRAGS	TAILINGS	TAITS
TAENIASES	TAGS	TAILLAMP	TAIVER
TAENIASIS	TAGUAN	TAILLAMPS	TAIVERED
TAENIATE	TAGUANS	TAILLE	TAIVERING
TAENIOID	TAHA	TAILLES	TAIVERS
TAES	TAHAS	TAILLESS	TAIVERT
TAFFAREL	TAHINA	TAILLEUR	TAJ
TAFFARELS	TAHINAS	TAILLEURS	TAJES
TAFFEREL	TAHINI	TAILLIE	TAJINE
TAFFERELS	TAHINIS	TAILLIES	TAJINES
TAFFETA	TAHOU	TAILLIGHT	TAK
TAFFETAS	TAHOUS	TAILLIKE	TAKA
TAFFETIES	TAHR	TAILOR	TAKABLE
TAFFETY	TAHRS	TAILORED	TAKAHE

587

TAKAHES	TALCIER	TALKIER	TALLS
TAKAMAKA	TALCIEST	TALKIES	TALLY
TAKAMAKAS	TALCING	TALKIEST	TALLYHO
TAKAS	TALCKED	TALKINESS	TALLYHOED
TAKE	TALCKIER	TALKING	TALLYHOS
TAKEABLE	TALCKIEST	TALKINGS	TALLYING
TAKEAWAY	TALCKING	TALKS	TALLYMAN
TAKEAWAYS	TALCKY	TALKY	TALLYMEN
TAKEDOWN	TALCOSE	TALL	TALLYSHOP
TAKEDOWNS	TALCOUS	TALLAGE	TALMA
TAKEN	TALCS	TALLAGED	TALMAS
TAKEOFF	TALCUM	TALLAGES	TALMUD
TAKEOFFS	TALCUMS	TALLAGING	TALMUDIC
TAKEOUT	TALCY	TALLAISIM	TALMUDISM
TAKEOUTS	TALE	TALLAT	TALMUDS
TAKEOVER	TALEA	TALLATS	TALON
TAKEOVERS	TALEAE	TALLBOY	TALONED
TAKER	TALEFUL	TALLBOYS	TALONS
TAKERS	TALEGALLA	TALLENT	TALOOKA
TAKES	TALEGGIO	TALLENTS	TALOOKAS
TAKEUP	TALEGGIOS	TALLER	TALPA
TAKEUPS	TALENT	TALLEST	TALPAE
TAKHI	TALENTED	TALLET	TALPAS
TAKHIS	TALENTS	TALLETS	TALUK
TAKI	TALER	TALLGRASS	TALUKA
TAKIER	TALERS	TALLIABLE	TALUKAS
TAKIEST	TALES	TALLIATE	TALUKDAR
TAKIN	TALESMAN	TALLIATED	TALUKDARS
TAKING	TALESMEN	TALLIATES	TALUKS
TAKINGLY	TALEYSIM	TALLIED	TALUS
TAKINGS	TALI	TALLIER	TALUSES
TAKINS	TALIGRADE	TALLIERS	TALWEG
TAKIS	TALION	TALLIES	TALWEGS
TAKKIES	TALIONIC	TALLIS	TAM
TAKS	TALIONS	TALLISES	TAMABLE
TAKY	TALIPAT	TALLISH	TAMAL
TALA	TALIPATS	TALLISIM	TAMALE
TALAK	TALIPED	TALLIT	TAMALES
TALAKS	TALIPEDS	TALLITES	TAMALS
TALANT	TALIPES	TALLITH	TAMANDU
TALANTS	TALIPOT	TALLITHES	TAMANDUA
TALAPOIN	TALIPOTS	TALLITHIM	TAMANDUAS
TALAPOINS	TALISMAN	TALLITHS	TAMANDUS
TALAQ	TALISMANS	TALLITIM	TAMANOIR
TALAQS	TALK	TALLITOT	TAMANOIRS
TALAR	TALKABLE	TALLITOTH	TAMANU
TALARIA	TALKATHON	TALLITS	TAMANUS
TALARS	TALKATIVE	TALLNESS	TAMARA
TALAS	TALKBACK	TALLOL	TAMARACK
TALAUNT	TALKBACKS	TALLOLS	TAMARACKS
TALAUNTS	TALKBOX	TALLOT	TAMARAO
TALAYOT	TALKBOXES	TALLOTS	TAMARAOS
TALAYOTS	TALKED	TALLOW	TAMARAS
TALBOT	TALKER	TALLOWED	TAMARAU
TALBOTS	TALKERS	TALLOWING	TAMARAUS
TALBOTYPE	TALKFEST	TALLOWISH	TAMARI
TALC	TALKFESTS	TALLOWS	TAMARILLO
TALCED	TALKIE	TALLOWY	TAMARIN

TAMARIND	TAMP	TANGENT	TANKERS
TAMARINDS	TAMPALA	TANGENTAL	TANKFUL
TAMARINS	TAMPALAS	TANGENTS	TANKFULS
TAMARIS	TAMPAN	TANGERINE	TANKIA
TAMARISK	TAMPANS	TANGHIN	TANKIAS
TAMARISKS	TAMPED	TANGHININ	TANKIES
TAMASHA	TAMPER	TANGHINS	TANKING
TAMASHAS	TAMPERED	TANGI	TANKINGS
TAMBAC	TAMPERER	TANGIBLE	TANKINI
TAMBACS	TAMPERERS	TANGIBLES	TANKINIS
TAMBAK	TAMPERING	TANGIBLY	TANKLESS
TAMBAKS	TAMPERS	TANGIE	TANKLIKE
TAMBALA	TAMPING	TANGIER	TANKS
TAMBALAS	TAMPINGS	TANGIES	TANKSHIP
TAMBER	TAMPION	TANGIEST	TANKSHIPS
TAMBERS	TAMPIONS	TANGINESS	TANKY
TAMBOUR	TAMPON	TANGING	TANLING
TAMBOURA	TAMPONADE	TANGIS	TANLINGS
TAMBOURAS	TAMPONAGE	TANGLE	TANNA
TAMBOURED	TAMPONED	TANGLED	TANNABLE
TAMBOURER	TAMPONING	TANGLER	TANNAGE
TAMBOURIN	TAMPONS	TANGLERS	TANNAGES
TAMBOURS	TAMPS	TANGLES	TANNAH
TAMBUR	TAMS	TANGLIER	TANNAHS
TAMBURA	TAMWORTH	TANGLIEST	TANNAS
TAMBURAS	TAMWORTHS	TANGLING	TANNATE
TAMBURIN	TAN	TANGLINGS	TANNATES
TAMBURINS	TANA	TANGLY	TANNED
TAMBURS	TANADAR	TANGO	TANNER
TAME	TANADARS	TANGOED	TANNERIES
TAMEABLE	TANAGER	TANGOES	TANNERS
TAMED	TANAGERS	TANGOING	TANNERY
TAMEIN	TANAGRA	TANGOIST	TANNEST
TAMEINS	TANAGRAS	TANGOISTS	TANNIC
TAMELESS	TANAGRINE	TANGOLIKE	TANNIE
TAMELY	TANAISTE	TANGOS	TANNIES
TAMENESS	TANAISTES	TANGRAM	TANNIN
TAMER	TANALISED	TANGRAMS	TANNING
TAMERS	TANALIZED	TANGS	TANNINGS
TAMES	TANAS	TANGUN	TANNINS
TAMEST	TANBARK	TANGUNS	TANNISH
TAMIN	TANBARKS	TANGY	TANNOY
TAMINE	TANDEM	TANH	TANNOYED
TAMINES	TANDEMS	TANHS	TANNOYING
TAMING	TANDOOR	TANIST	TANNOYS
TAMINGS	TANDOORI	TANISTRY	TANREC
TAMINS	TANDOORIS	TANISTS	TANRECS
TAMIS	TANDOORS	TANIWHA	TANS
TAMISE	TANE	TANIWHAS	TANSIES
TAMISES	TANG	TANK	TANSY
TAMMAR	TANGA	TANKA	TANTALATE
TAMMARS	TANGAS	TANKAGE	TANTALIC
TAMMIE	TANGED	TANKAGES	TANTALISE
TAMMIED	TANGELO	TANKARD	TANTALISM
TAMMIES	TANGELOS	TANKARDS	TANTALITE
TAMMY	TANGENCE	TANKAS	TANTALIZE
TAMMYING	TANGENCES	TANKED	TANTALOUS
TAMOXIFEN	TANGENCY	TANKER	TANTALUM

TANTALUMS	TAPERS	TAPUED	TARIFF
TANTALUS	TAPERWISE	TAPUING	TARIFFED
TANTARA	TAPES	TAPUS	TARIFFING
TANTARARA	TAPESTRY	TAQUERIA	TARIFFS
TANTARAS	TAPET	TAQUERIAS	TARING
TANTI	TAPETA	TAR	TARINGS
TANTIVIES	TAPETAL	TARA	TARLATAN
TANTIVY	TAPETI	TARAIRE	TARLATANS
TANTO	TAPETIS	TARAKIHI	TARLETAN
TANTONIES	TAPETS	TARAKIHIS	TARLETANS
TANTONY	TAPETUM	TARAMA	TARMAC
TANTRA	TAPEWORM	TARAMAS	TARMACKED
TANTRAS	TAPEWORMS	TARAMEA	TARMACS
TANTRIC	TAPHOLE	TARAMEAS	TARN
TANTRISM	TAPHOLES	TARAND	TARNAL
TANTRISMS	TAPHONOMY	TARANDS	TARNALLY
TANTRUM	TAPHOUSE	TARANTARA	TARNATION
TANTRUMS	TAPHOUSES	TARANTAS	TARNISH
TANUKI	TAPING	TARANTASS	TARNISHED
TANUKIS	TAPIOCA	TARANTISM	TARNISHER
TANYARD	TAPIOCAS	TARANTIST	TARNISHES
TANYARDS	TAPIR	TARANTULA	TARNS
TANZANITE	TAPIROID	TARAS	TARO
TAO	TAPIRS	TARAXACUM	TAROC
TAOISEACH	TAPIS	TARBOGGIN	TAROCS
TAONGA	TAPISES	TARBOOSH	TAROK
TAONGAS	TAPIST	TARBOUCHE	TAROKS
TAOS	TAPISTS	TARBOUSH	TAROS
TAP	TAPLASH	TARBOY	TAROT
TAPA	TAPLASHES	TARBOYS	TAROTS
TAPACOLO	TAPPA	TARBUSH	TARP
TAPACOLOS	TAPPABLE	TARBUSHES	TARPAN
TAPACULO	TAPPAS	TARCEL	TARPANS
TAPACULOS	TAPPED	TARCELS	TARPAPER
TAPADERA	TAPPER	TARDIED	TARPAPERS
TAPADERAS	TAPPERS	TARDIER	TARPAULIN
TAPADERO	TAPPET	TARDIES	TARPON
TAPADEROS	TAPPETS	TARDIEST	TARPONS
TAPALO	TAPPICE	TARDILY	TARPS
TAPALOS	TAPPICED	TARDINESS	TARRAGON
TAPAS	TAPPICES	TARDIVE	TARRAGONS
TAPE	TAPPICING	TARDO	TARRAS
TAPEABLE	TAPPING	TARDY	TARRASES
TAPED	TAPPINGS	TARDYING	TARRE
TAPELESS	TAPPIT	TARDYON	TARRED
TAPELIKE	TAPROOM	TARDYONS	TARRES
TAPELINE	TAPROOMS	TARE	TARRIANCE
TAPELINES	TAPROOT	TARED	TARRIED
TAPEN	TAPROOTED	TARES	TARRIER
TAPENADE	TAPROOTS	TARGE	TARRIERS
TAPENADES	TAPS	TARGED	TARRIES
TAPER	TAPSMAN	TARGES	TARRIEST
TAPERED	TAPSMEN	TARGET	TARRINESS
TAPERER	TAPSTER	TARGETED	TARRING
TAPERERS	TAPSTERS	TARGETEER	TARRINGS
TAPERING	TAPSTRESS	TARGETING	TARROCK
TAPERINGS	TAPSTRY	TARGETS	TARROCKS
TAPERNESS	TAPU	TARGING	TARROW

TARROWED	TARTRATES	TASTEABLE	TATTLER
TARROWING	TARTS	TASTED	TATTLERS
TARROWS	TARTUFE	TASTEFUL	TATTLES
TARRY	TARTUFES	TASTELESS	TATTLING
TARRYING	TARTUFFE	TASTER	TATTLINGS
TARS	TARTUFFES	TASTERS	TATTOO
TARSAL	TARTY	TASTES	TATTOOED
TARSALGIA	TARWEED	TASTEVIN	TATTOOER
TARSALS	TARWEEDS	TASTEVINS	TATTOOERS
TARSEAL	TARWHINE	TASTIER	TATTOOING
TARSEALS	TARWHINES	TASTIEST	TATTOOIST
TARSEL	TARZAN	TASTILY	TATTOOS
TARSELS	TARZANS	TASTINESS	TATTOW
TARSI	TAS	TASTING	TATTOWED
TARSIA	TASAR	TASTINGS	TATTOWING
TARSIAS	TASARS	TASTY	TATTOWS
TARSIER	TASER	TAT	TATTS
TARSIERS	TASERED	TATAHASH	TATTY
TARSIOID	TASERING	TATAMI	TATU
TARSIPED	TASERS	TATAMIS	TATUED
TARSIPEDS	TASH	TATAR	TATUING
TARSUS	TASHED	TATARS	TATUS
TART	TASHES	TATE	TAU
TARTAN	TASHING	TATER	TAUBE
TARTANA	TASIMETER	TATERS	TAUBES
TARTANAS	TASIMETRY	TATES	TAUGHT
TARTANE	TASK	TATH	TAUHINU
TARTANED	TASKBAR	TATHED	TAUHINUS
TARTANES	TASKBARS	TATHING	TAUHOU
TARTANRY	TASKED	TATHS	TAUIWI
TARTANS	TASKER	TATIE	TAUIWIS
TARTAR	TASKERS	TATIES	TAULD
TARTARE	TASKING	TATLER	TAUNT
TARTARES	TASKINGS	TATLERS	TAUNTED
TARTARIC	TASKLESS	TATOU	TAUNTER
TARTARISE	TASKS	TATOUAY	TAUNTERS
TARTARIZE	TASKWORK	TATOUAYS	TAUNTING
TARTARLY	TASKWORKS	TATOUS	TAUNTINGS
TARTAROUS	TASLET	TATS	TAUNTS
TARTARS	TASLETS	TATSOI	TAUON
TARTED	TASS	TATSOIS	TAUONS
TARTER	TASSE	TATT	TAUPATA
TARTEST	TASSEL	TATTED	TAUPE
TARTIER	TASSELED	TATTER	TAUPES
TARTIEST	TASSELING	TATTERED	TAUPIE
TARTILY	TASSELL	TATTERING	TAUPIES
TARTINE	TASSELLED	TATTERS	TAUREAN
TARTINES	TASSELLS	TATTERY	TAURIC
TARTINESS	TASSELLY	TATTIE	TAURIFORM
TARTING	TASSELS	TATTIER	TAURINE
TARTISH	TASSES	TATTIES	TAURINES
TARTISHLY	TASSET	TATTIEST	TAUS
TARTLET	TASSETS	TATTILY	TAUT
TARTLETS	TASSIE	TATTINESS	TAUTAUG
TARTLY	TASSIES	TATTING	TAUTAUGS
TARTNESS	TASSWAGE	TATTINGS	TAUTED
TARTRATE	TASTABLE	TATTLE	TAUTEN
TARTRATED	TASTE	TATTLED	TAUTENED

TAUTENING
TAUTENS
TAUTER
TAUTEST
TAUTING
TAUTIT
TAUTLY
TAUTNESS
TAUTOG
TAUTOGS
TAUTOLOGY
TAUTOMER
TAUTOMERS
TAUTONYM
TAUTONYMS
TAUTONYMY
TAUTS
TAV
TAVA
TAVAH
TAVAHS
TAVAS
TAVER
TAVERED
TAVERING
TAVERN
TAVERNA
TAVERNAS
TAVERNER
TAVERNERS
TAVERNS
TAVERS
TAVERT
TAVS
TAW
TAWA
TAWAI
TAWAIS
TAWAS
TAWDRIER
TAWDRIES
TAWDRIEST
TAWDRILY
TAWDRY
TAWED
TAWER
TAWERIES
TAWERS
TAWERY
TAWHAI
TAWHAIS
TAWHIRI
TAWIE
TAWIER
TAWIEST
TAWING
TAWINGS
TAWNEY

TAWNEYS
TAWNIER
TAWNIES
TAWNIEST
TAWNILY
TAWNINESS
TAWNY
TAWPIE
TAWPIES
TAWS
TAWSE
TAWSED
TAWSES
TAWSING
TAWT
TAWTED
TAWTIE
TAWTIER
TAWTIEST
TAWTING
TAWTS
TAX
TAXA
TAXABLE
TAXABLES
TAXABLY
TAXACEOUS
TAXAMETER
TAXATION
TAXATIONS
TAXATIVE
TAXED
TAXEME
TAXEMES
TAXEMIC
TAXER
TAXERS
TAXES
TAXI
TAXIARCH
TAXIARCHS
TAXICAB
TAXICABS
TAXIDERMY
TAXIED
TAXIES
TAXIING
TAXIMAN
TAXIMEN
TAXIMETER
TAXING
TAXINGLY
TAXINGS
TAXIPLANE
TAXIS
TAXITE
TAXITES
TAXITIC

TAXIWAY
TAXIWAYS
TAXLESS
TAXMAN
TAXMEN
TAXOL
TAXOLS
TAXON
TAXONOMER
TAXONOMIC
TAXONOMY
TAXONS
TAXOR
TAXORS
TAXPAID
TAXPAYER
TAXPAYERS
TAXPAYING
TAXUS
TAXWISE
TAXYING
TAY
TAYASSUID
TAYBERRY
TAYRA
TAYRAS
TAYS
TAZZA
TAZZAS
TAZZE
TCHICK
TCHICKED
TCHICKING
TCHICKS
TCHOTCHKE
TE
TEA
TEABERRY
TEABOARD
TEABOARDS
TEABOWL
TEABOWLS
TEABOX
TEABOXES
TEABREAD
TEABREADS
TEACAKE
TEACAKES
TEACART
TEACARTS
TEACH
TEACHABLE
TEACHABLY
TEACHER
TEACHERLY
TEACHERS
TEACHES
TEACHIE

TEACHING
TEACHINGS
TEACHLESS
TEACUP
TEACUPFUL
TEACUPS
TEAD
TEADE
TEADES
TEADS
TEAED
TEAGLE
TEAGLED
TEAGLES
TEAGLING
TEAHOUSE
TEAHOUSES
TEAING
TEAK
TEAKETTLE
TEAKS
TEAKWOOD
TEAKWOODS
TEAL
TEALIKE
TEALS
TEAM
TEAMAKER
TEAMAKERS
TEAMED
TEAMER
TEAMERS
TEAMING
TEAMINGS
TEAMMATE
TEAMMATES
TEAMS
TEAMSTER
TEAMSTERS
TEAMWISE
TEAMWORK
TEAMWORKS
TEAPOT
TEAPOTS
TEAPOY
TEAPOYS
TEAR
TEARABLE
TEARAWAY
TEARAWAYS
TEARDOWN
TEARDOWNS
TEARDROP
TEARDROPS
TEARED
TEARER
TEARERS
TEARFUL

TEARFULLY	TEAZLING	TEDIUM	TEETERS
TEARGAS	TEBBAD	TEDIUMS	TEETH
TEARGASES	TEBBADS	TEDS	TEETHE
TEARIER	TEC	TEDY	TEETHED
TEARIEST	TECH	TEE	TEETHER
TEARILY	TECHED	TEED	TEETHERS
TEARINESS	TECHIE	TEEING	TEETHES
TEARING	TECHIER	TEEK	TEETHING
TEARLESS	TECHIES	TEEL	TEETHINGS
TEAROOM	TECHIEST	TEELS	TEETHLESS
TEAROOMS	TECHILY	TEEM	TEETOTAL
TEARS	TECHINESS	TEEMED	TEETOTALS
TEARSHEET	TECHNIC	TEEMER	TEETOTUM
TEARSTAIN	TECHNICAL	TEEMERS	TEETOTUMS
TEARSTRIP	TECHNICS	TEEMFUL	TEF
TEARY	TECHNIKON	TEEMING	TEFF
TEAS	TECHNIQUE	TEEMINGLY	TEFFS
TEASABLE	TECHNO	TEEMLESS	TEFILLAH
TEASE	TECHNOPOP	TEEMS	TEFILLIN
TEASED	TECHNOS	TEEN	TEFLON
TEASEL	TECHS	TEENAGE	TEFLONS
TEASELED	TECHY	TEENAGED	TEFS
TEASELER	TECKEL	TEENAGER	TEG
TEASELERS	TECKELS	TEENAGERS	TEGG
TEASELING	TECS	TEEND	TEGGS
TEASELLED	TECTA	TEENDED	TEGMEN
TEASELLER	TECTAL	TEENDING	TEGMENTA
TEASELS	TECTIFORM	TEENDS	TEGMENTAL
TEASER	TECTITE	TEENE	TEGMENTUM
TEASERS	TECTITES	TEENED	TEGMINA
TEASES	TECTONIC	TEENER	TEGMINAL
TEASHOP	TECTONICS	TEENERS	TEGS
TEASHOPS	TECTONISM	TEENES	TEGU
TEASING	TECTORIAL	TEENFUL	TEGUA
TEASINGLY	TECTRICES	TEENIER	TEGUAS
TEASINGS	TECTRIX	TEENIEST	TEGUEXIN
TEASPOON	TECTUM	TEENING	TEGUEXINS
TEASPOONS	TECTUMS	TEENS	TEGULA
TEAT	TED	TEENSIER	TEGULAE
TEATASTER	TEDDED	TEENSIEST	TEGULAR
TEATED	TEDDER	TEENSY	TEGULARLY
TEATIME	TEDDERED	TEENTIER	TEGULATED
TEATIMES	TEDDERING	TEENTIEST	TEGUMEN
TEATS	TEDDERS	TEENTSIER	TEGUMENT
TEAWARE	TEDDIE	TEENTSY	TEGUMENTS
TEAWARES	TEDDIES	TEENTY	TEGUMINA
TEAZE	TEDDING	TEENY	TEGUS
TEAZED	TEDDY	TEENYBOP	TEHR
TEAZEL	TEDESCA	TEEPEE	TEHRS
TEAZELED	TEDESCHE	TEEPEES	TEIGLACH
TEAZELING	TEDESCHI	TEER	TEIID
TEAZELLED	TEDESCO	TEERED	TEIIDS
TEAZELS	TEDIER	TEERING	TEIL
TEAZES	TEDIEST	TEERS	TEILS
TEAZING	TEDIOSITY	TEES	TEIND
TEAZLE	TEDIOUS	TEETER	TEINDED
TEAZLED	TEDIOUSLY	TEETERED	TEINDING
TEAZLES	TEDISOME	TEETERING	TEINDS

TEKKIE	TELEPHOTO	TELIAL	TELPHERED
TEKKIES	TELEPLAY	TELIC	TELPHERIC
TEKNONYMY	TELEPLAYS	TELICALLY	TELPHERS
TEKTITE	TELEPOINT	TELIUM	TELS
TEKTITES	TELEPORT	TELL	TELSON
TEKTITIC	TELEPORTS	TELLABLE	TELSONIC
TEL	TELERAN	TELLAR	TELSONS
TELA	TELERANS	TELLARED	TELT
TELAE	TELERGIC	TELLARING	TEMAZEPAM
TELAMON	TELERGIES	TELLARS	TEMBLOR
TELAMONES	TELERGY	TELLEN	TEMBLORES
TELAMONS	TELES	TELLENS	TEMBLORS
TELARY	TELESALE	TELLER	TEME
TELCO	TELESALES	TELLERED	TEMED
TELCOS	TELESCOPE	TELLERING	TEMENE
TELD	TELESCOPY	TELLERS	TEMENOS
TELE	TELESEME	TELLIES	TEMERITY
TELECAST	TELESEMES	TELLIN	TEMEROUS
TELECASTS	TELESES	TELLING	TEMES
TELECHIR	TELESHOP	TELLINGLY	TEMP
TELECHIRS	TELESHOPS	TELLINGS	TEMPED
TELECINE	TELESIS	TELLINOID	TEMPEH
TELECINES	TELESM	TELLINS	TEMPEHS
TELECOM	TELESMS	TELLS	TEMPER
TELECOMS	TELESTIC	TELLTALE	TEMPERA
TELEDU	TELESTICH	TELLTALES	TEMPERAS
TELEDUS	TELESTICS	TELLURAL	TEMPERATE
TELEFAX	TELETEX	TELLURATE	TEMPERED
TELEFAXED	TELETEXES	TELLURIAN	TEMPERER
TELEFAXES	TELETEXT	TELLURIC	TEMPERERS
TELEFILM	TELETEXTS	TELLURIDE	TEMPERING
TELEFILMS	TELETHON	TELLURION	TEMPERS
TELEGA	TELETHONS	TELLURISE	TEMPEST
TELEGAS	TELETRON	TELLURITE	TEMPESTED
TELEGENIC	TELETRONS	TELLURIUM	TEMPESTS
TELEGONIC	TELETYPE	TELLURIZE	TEMPI
TELEGONY	TELETYPED	TELLUROUS	TEMPING
TELEGRAM	TELETYPES	TELLUS	TEMPLAR
TELEGRAMS	TELEVIEW	TELLUSES	TEMPLARS
TELEGRAPH	TELEVIEWS	TELLY	TEMPLATE
TELEMAN	TELEVISE	TELLYS	TEMPLATES
TELEMARK	TELEVISED	TELNET	TEMPLE
TELEMARKS	TELEVISER	TELNETED	TEMPLED
TELEMATIC	TELEVISES	TELNETING	TEMPLES
TELEMEN	TELEVISOR	TELNETS	TEMPLET
TELEMETER	TELEX	TELNETTED	TEMPLETS
TELEMETRY	TELEXED	TELOI	TEMPO
TELEOLOGY	TELEXES	TELOME	TEMPORAL
TELEONOMY	TELEXING	TELOMERE	TEMPORALS
TELEOSAUR	TELFER	TELOMERES	TEMPORARY
TELEOST	TELFERAGE	TELOMES	TEMPORE
TELEOSTS	TELFERED	TELOMIC	TEMPORISE
TELEPATH	TELFERIC	TELOPHASE	TEMPORIZE
TELEPATHS	TELFERING	TELOS	TEMPOS
TELEPATHY	TELFERS	TELOSES	TEMPS
TELEPHEME	TELFORD	TELOTAXES	TEMPT
TELEPHONE	TELFORDS	TELOTAXIS	TEMPTABLE
TELEPHONY	TELIA	TELPHER	TEMPTED

TEMPTER	TENDING	TENONED	TENTAGES
TEMPTERS	TENDINOUS	TENONER	TENTATION
TEMPTING	TENDON	TENONERS	TENTATIVE
TEMPTINGS	TENDONS	TENONING	TENTED
TEMPTRESS	TENDRE	TENONS	IENTER
TEMPTS	TENDRES	TENOR	TENTERED
TEMPURA	TENDRESSE	TENORIST	TENTERING
TEMPURAS	TENDRIL	TENORISTS	TENTERS
TEMS	TENDRILED	TENORITE	TENTFUL
TEMSE	TENDRILS	TENORITES	TENTFULS
TEMSED	TENDRON	TENORLESS	TENTH
TEMSES	TENDRONS	TENOROON	TENTHLY
TEMSING	TENDS	TENOROONS	TENTHS
TEMULENCE	TENDU	TENORS	TENTIE
TEMULENCY	TENDUS	TENOTOMY	TENTIER
TEMULENT	TENE	TENOUR	TENTIEST
TEN	TENEBRAE	TENOURS	TENTIGO
TENABLE	TENEBRIO	TENPENCE	TENTIGOS
TENABLY	TENEBRIOS	TENPENCES	TENTING
TENACE	TENEBRISM	TENPENNY	TENTINGS
TENACES	TENEBRIST	TENPIN	TENTLESS
TENACIOUS	TENEBRITY	TENPINS	TENTLIKE
TENACITY	TENEBROSE	TENREC	TENTMAKER
TENACULA	TENEBROUS	TENRECS	TENTORIA
TENACULUM	TENEMENT	TENS	TENTORIAL
TENAIL	TENEMENTS	TENSE	TENTORIUM
TENAILLE	TENENDUM	TENSED	TENTS
TENAILLES	TENENDUMS	TENSELESS	TENTWISE
TENAILLON	TENES	TENSELY	TENTY
TENAILS	TENESMIC	TENSENESS	TENUE
TENANCIES	TENESMUS	TENSER	TENUES
TENANCY	TENET	TENSES	TENUIOUS
TENANT	TENETS	TENSEST	TENUIS
TENANTED	TENFOLD	TENSIBLE	TENUITIES
TENANTING	TENFOLDS	TENSIBLY	TENUITY
TENANTRY	TENGE	TENSILE	TENUOUS
TENANTS	TENGES	TENSILELY	TENUOUSLY
TENCH	TENIA	TENSILITY	TENURABLE
TENCHES	TENIACIDE	TENSING	TENURE
TEND	TENIAE	TENSION	TENURED
TENDANCE	TENIAFUGE	TENSIONAL	TENURES
TENDANCES	TENIAS	TENSIONED	TENURIAL
TENDED	TENIASES	TENSIONER	TENURING
TENDENCE	TENIASIS	TENSIONS	TENUTI
TENDENCES	TENIOID	TENSITIES	TENUTO
TENDENCY	TENNE	TENSITY	TENUTOS
TENDENZ	TENNER	TENSIVE	TENZON
TENDENZEN	TENNERS	TENSON	TENZONS
TENDER	TENNES	TENSONS	TEOCALLI
TENDERED	TENNIES	TENSOR	TEOCALLIS
TENDERER	TENNIS	TENSORIAL	TEOPAN
TENDERERS	TENNISES	TENSORS	TEOPANS
TENDEREST	TENNIST	TENT	TEOSINTE
TENDERING	TENNISTS	TENTACLE	TEOSINTES
TENDERISE	TENNO	TENTACLED	TEPA
TENDERIZE	TENNOS	TENTACLES	TEPAL
TENDERLY	TENNY	TENTACULA	TEPALS
TENDERS	TENON	TENTAGE	TEPAS

TEPEE

TEPEE	TERBIUMS	TERMITES	TERRET
TEPEES	TERCE	TERMITIC	TERRETS
TEPEFIED	TERCEL	TERMLESS	TERRIBLE
TEPEFIES	TERCELET	TERMLIES	TERRIBLES
TEPEFY	TERCELETS	TERMLY	TERRIBLY
TEPEFYING	TERCELS	TERMOR	TERRICOLE
TEPHIGRAM	TERCES	TERMORS	TERRIER
TEPHILLAH	TERCET	TERMS	TERRIERS
TEPHILLIN	TERCETS	TERMTIME	TERRIES
TEPHRA	TERCIO	TERMTIMES	TERRIFIC
TEPHRAS	TERCIOS	TERN	TERRIFIED
TEPHRITE	TEREBENE	TERNAL	TERRIFIER
TEPHRITES	TEREBENES	TERNARIES	TERRIFIES
TEPHRITIC	TEREBIC	TERNARY	TERRIFY
TEPHROITE	TEREBINTH	TERNATE	TERRINE
TEPID	TEREBRA	TERNATELY	TERRINES
TEPIDARIA	TEREBRAE	TERNE	TERRIT
TEPIDER	TEREBRANT	TERNED	TERRITORY
TEPIDEST	TEREBRAS	TERNES	TERRITS
TEPIDITY	TEREBRATE	TERNING	TERROIR
TEPIDLY	TEREDINES	TERNION	TERROIRS
TEPIDNESS	TEREDO	TERNIONS	TERROR
TEPOY	TEREDOS	TERNS	TERRORFUL
TEPOYS	TEREFA	TERPENE	TERRORISE
TEQUILA	TEREFAH	TERPENES	TERRORISM
TEQUILAS	TEREK	TERPENIC	TERRORIST
TEQUILLA	TEREKS	TERPENOID	TERRORIZE
TEQUILLAS	TERES	TERPINEOL	TERRORS
TERABYTE	TERETE	TERPINOL	TERRY
TERABYTES	TERETES	TERPINOLS	TERSE
TERAFLOP	TERF	TERRA	TERSELY
TERAFLOPS	TERFE	TERRACE	TERSENESS
TERAGLIN	TERFES	TERRACED	TERSER
TERAGLINS	TERFS	TERRACES	TERSEST
TERAHERTZ	TERGA	TERRACING	TERSION
TERAI	TERGAL	TERRAE	TERSIONS
TERAIS	TERGITE	TERRAFORM	TERTIA
TERAKIHI	TERGITES	TERRAIN	TERTIAL
TERAKIHIS	TERGUM	TERRAINS	TERTIALS
TERAOHM	TERIYAKI	TERRAMARA	TERTIAN
TERAOHMS	TERIYAKIS	TERRAMARE	TERTIANS
TERAPH	TERM	TERRANE	TERTIARY
TERAPHIM	TERMAGANT	TERRANES	TERTIAS
TERAPHIMS	TERMED	TERRAPIN	TERTIUM
TERAS	TERMER	TERRAPINS	TERTIUS
TERATA	TERMERS	TERRARIA	TERTIUSES
TERATISM	TERMINAL	TERRARIUM	TERTS
TERATISMS	TERMINALS	TERRAS	TERVALENT
TERATOGEN	TERMINATE	TERRASES	TERYLENE
TERATOID	TERMINER	TERRAZZO	TERYLENES
TERATOMA	TERMINERS	TERRAZZOS	TERZETTA
TERATOMAS	TERMING	TERREEN	TERZETTAS
TERAWATT	TERMINI	TERREENS	TERZETTI
TERAWATTS	TERMINISM	TERRELLA	TERZETTO
TERBIA	TERMINIST	TERRELLAS	TERZETTOS
TERBIAS	TERMINUS	TERRENE	TES
TERBIC	TERMITARY	TERRENELY	TESLA
TERBIUM	TERMITE	TERRENES	TESLAS

TESSELATE	TESTRILL	TETRARCH	TEXTBOOKS
TESSELLA	TESTRILLS	TETRARCHS	TEXTED
TESSELLAE	TESTRILS	TETRARCHY	TEXTER
TESSELLAR	TESTS	TETRAS	TEXTERS
TESSERA	TESTUDO	TETRAXON	TEXTILE
TESSERACT	TESTUDOS	TETRAXONS	TEXTILES
TESSERAE	TESTY	TETRI	TEXTING
TESSERAL	TET	TETRIS	TEXTLESS
TESSITURA	TETANAL	TETRODE	TEXTORIAL
TESSITURE	TETANIC	TETRODES	TEXTPHONE
TEST	TETANICAL	TETRONAL	TEXTS
TESTA	TETANICS	TETRONALS	TEXTUAL
TESTABLE	TETANIES	TETROXID	TEXTUALLY
TESTACEAN	TETANISE	TETROXIDE	TEXTUARY
TESTACIES	TETANISED	TETROXIDS	TEXTURAL
TESTACY	TETANISES	TETRYL	TEXTURE
TESTAE	TETANIZE	TETRYLS	TEXTURED
TESTAMENT	TETANIZED	TETS	TEXTURES
TESTAMUR	TETANIZES	TETTER	TEXTURING
TESTAMURS	TETANOID	TETTERED	TEXTURISE
TESTATE	TETANUS	TETTERING	TEXTURIZE
TESTATES	TETANUSES	TETTEROUS	THACK
TESTATION	TETANY	TETTERS	THACKED
TESTATOR	TETCHED	TETTIX	THACKING
TESTATORS	TETCHIER	TETTIXES	THACKS
TESTATRIX	TETCHIEST	TEUCH	THAE
TESTATUM	TETCHILY	TEUCHAT	THAGI
TESTATUMS	TETCHY	TEUCHATS	THAGIS
TESTCROSS	TETE	TEUCHER	THAIM
TESTE	TETES	TEUCHEST	THAIRM
TESTED	TETH	TEUCHTER	THAIRMS
TESTEE	TETHER	TEUCHTERS	THALAMI
TESTEES	TETHERED	TEUGH	THALAMIC
TESTER	TETHERING	TEUGHER	THALAMUS
TESTERN	TETHERS	TEUGHEST	THALASSIC
TESTERNED	TETHS	TEUGHLY	THALER
TESTERNS	TETOTUM	TEUTONISE	THALERS
TESTERS	TETOTUMS	TEUTONIZE	THALI
TESTES	TETRA	TEVATRON	THALIAN
TESTICLE	TETRACID	TEVATRONS	THALIS
TESTICLES	TETRACIDS	TEW	THALLI
TESTIER	TETRACT	TEWART	THALLIC
TESTIEST	TETRACTS	TEWARTS	THALLINE
TESTIFIED	TETRAD	TEWED	THALLIOUS
TESTIFIER	TETRADIC	TEWEL	THALLIUM
TESTIFIES	TETRADITE	TEWELS	THALLIUMS
TESTIFY	TETRADS	TEWHIT	THALLOID
TESTILY	TETRAGON	TEWHITS	THALLOUS
TESTIMONY	TETRAGONS	TEWING	THALLUS
TESTINESS	TETRAGRAM	TEWIT	THALLUSES
TESTING	TETRALOGY	TEWITS	THALWEG
TESTINGS	TETRAMER	TEWS	THALWEGS
TESTIS	TETRAMERS	TEX	THAN
TESTON	TETRAPLA	TEXAS	THANA
TESTONS	TETRAPLAS	TEXASES	THANADAR
TESTOON	TETRAPOD	TEXES	THANADARS
TESTOONS	TETRAPODS	TEXT	THANAGE
TESTRIL	TETRAPODY	TEXTBOOK	THANAGES

THANAH
THANAHS
THANAS
THANATISM
THANATIST
THANATOID
THANATOS
THANE
THANEDOM
THANEDOMS
THANEHOOD
THANES
THANESHIP
THANGKA
THANGKAS
THANK
THANKED
THANKEE
THANKER
THANKERS
THANKFUL
THANKING
THANKINGS
THANKLESS
THANKS
THANKYOU
THANKYOUS
THANNA
THANNAH
THANNAHS
THANNAS
THANS
THAR
THARM
THARMS
THARS
THAT
THATAWAY
THATCH
THATCHED
THATCHER
THATCHERS
THATCHES
THATCHIER
THATCHING
THATCHT
THATCHY
THATNESS
THAUMATIN
THAW
THAWED
THAWER
THAWERS
THAWIER
THAWIEST
THAWING
THAWINGS
THAWLESS

THAWS
THAWY
THE
THEACEOUS
THEANDRIC
THEARCHIC
THEARCHY
THEATER
THEATERS
THEATRAL
THEATRE
THEATRES
THEATRIC
THEATRICS
THEAVE
THEAVES
THEBAINE
THEBAINES
THEBE
THEBES
THECA
THECAE
THECAL
THECATE
THECODONT
THEE
THEED
THEEING
THEEK
THEEKED
THEEKING
THEEKS
THEELIN
THEELINS
THEELOL
THEELOLS
THEES
THEFT
THEFTLESS
THEFTS
THEFTUOUS
THEGITHER
THEGN
THEGNLY
THEGNS
THEIC
THEICS
THEIN
THEINE
THEINES
THEINS
THEIR
THEIRS
THEIRSELF
THEISM
THEISMS
THEIST
THEISTIC

THEISTS
THELEMENT
THELF
THELITIS
THELVES
THELYTOKY
THEM
THEMA
THEMATA
THEMATIC
THEMATICS
THEME
THEMED
THEMELESS
THEMES
THEMING
THEMSELF
THEN
THENABOUT
THENAGE
THENAGES
THENAL
THENAR
THENARS
THENCE
THENS
THEOCRACY
THEOCRASY
THEOCRAT
THEOCRATS
THEODICY
THEOGONIC
THEOGONY
THEOLOG
THEOLOGER
THEOLOGIC
THEOLOGS
THEOLOGUE
THEOLOGY
THEOMACHY
THEOMANCY
THEOMANIA
THEONOMY
THEOPATHY
THEOPHAGY
THEOPHANY
THEORBIST
THEORBO
THEORBOS
THEOREM
THEOREMIC
THEOREMS
THEORETIC
THEORIC
THEORICS
THEORIES
THEORIQUE
THEORISE

THEORISED
THEORISER
THEORISES
THEORIST
THEORISTS
THEORIZE
THEORIZED
THEORIZER
THEORIZES
THEORY
THEOSOPH
THEOSOPHS
THEOSOPHY
THEOTOKOI
THEOTOKOS
THEOW
THEOWS
THERALITE
THERAPIES
THERAPIST
THERAPSID
THERAPY
THERBLIG
THERBLIGS
THERE
THEREAT
THEREAWAY
THEREBY
THEREFOR
THEREFORE
THEREFROM
THEREIN
THEREINTO
THEREMIN
THEREMINS
THERENESS
THEREOF
THEREON
THEREOUT
THERES
THERETO
THEREUNTO
THEREUPON
THEREWITH
THERIAC
THERIACA
THERIACAL
THERIACAS
THERIACS
THERIAN
THERIANS
THERM
THERMAE
THERMAL
THERMALLY
THERMALS
THERME
THERMEL

THERMELS	THIAMINS	THIGGIT	THIONINE
THERMES	THIASUS	THIGH	THIONINES
THERMETTE	THIASUSES	THIGHBONE	THIONINS
THERMIC	THIAZIDE	THIGHED	THIONYL
THERMICAL	THIAZIDES	THIGHS	THIONYLS
THERMIDOR	THIAZIN	THIGS	THIOPHEN
THERMION	THIAZINE	THILK	THIOPHENE
THERMIONS	THIAZINES	THILL	THIOPHENS
THERMIT	THIAZINS	THILLER	THIOPHIL
THERMITE	THIAZOL	THILLERS	THIOTEPA
THERMITES	THIAZOLE	THILLS	THIOTEPAS
THERMITS	THIAZOLES	THIMBLE	THIOUREA
THERMOS	THIAZOLS	THIMBLED	THIOUREAS
THERMOSES	THIBET	THIMBLES	THIR
THERMOSET	THIBETS	THIMBLING	THIRAM
THERMOTIC	THIBLE	THIN	THIRAMS
THERMS	THIBLES	THINCLAD	THIRD
THEROID	THICK	THTNCLADS	THIRDED
THEROLOGY	THICKED	THINDOWN	THIRDHAND
THEROPOD	THICKEN	THINDOWNS	THIRDING
THEROPODS	THICKENED	THINE	THIRDINGS
THESAURAL	THICKENER	THING	THIRDLY
THESAURI	THICKENS	THINGAMY	THIRDS
THESAURUS	THICKER	THINGHOOD	THIRDSMAN
THESE	THICKEST	THINGIER	THIRDSMEN
THESES	THICKET	THINGIES	THIRL
THESIS	THICKETED	THINGIEST	THIRLAGE
THESP	THICKETS	THINGNESS	THIRLAGES
THESPIAN	THICKETY	THINGS	THIRLED
THESPIANS	THICKHEAD	THINGUMMY	THIRLING
THESPS	THICKIE	THINGY	THIRLS
THETA	THICKIES	THINK	THIRST
THETAS	THICKING	THINKABLE	THIRSTED
THETCH	THICKISH	THINKABLY	THIRSTER
THETCHED	THICKLEAF	THINKER	THIRSTERS
THETCHES	THICKLY	THINKERS	THIRSTFUL
THETCHING	THICKNESS	THINKING	THIRSTIER
THETE	THICKO	THINKINGS	THIRSTILY
THETES	THICKOES	THINKS	THIRSTING
THETHER	THICKOS	THINLY	THIRSTS
THETIC	THICKS	THINNED	THIRSTY
THETICAL	THICKSET	THINNER	THIRTEEN
THEURGIC	THICKSETS	THINNERS	THIRTEENS
THEURGIES	THICKSKIN	THINNESS	THIRTIES
THEURGIST	THICKY	THINNEST	THIRTIETH
THEURGY	THIEF	THINNING	THIRTY
THEW	THIEVE	THINNINGS	THIRTYISH
THEWED	THIEVED	THINNISH	THIS
THEWES	THIEVERY	THINS	THISAWAY
THEWIER	THIEVES	THIO	THISNESS
THEWIEST	THIEVING	THIOFURAN	THISTLE
THEWLESS	THIEVINGS	THIOL	THISTLES
THEWS	THIEVISH	THIOLIC	THISTLIER
THEWY	THIG	THIOLS	THISTLY
THEY	THIGGER	THIONATE	THITHER
THIAMIN	THIGGERS	THIONATES	THITHERTO
THIAMINE	THIGGING	THIONIC	THIVEL
THIAMINES	THIGGINGS	THIONIN	THIVELS

THLIPSES	THOSE	THREADING	THRIDDING
THLIPSIS	THOTHER	THREADS	THRIDS
THO	THOU	THREADY	THRIFT
THOFT	THOUED	THREAP	THRIFTIER
THOFTS	THOUGH	THREAPED	THRIFTILY
THOLE	THOUGHT	THREAPER	THRIFTS
THOLED	THOUGHTED	THREAPERS	THRIFTY
THOLEIITE	THOUGHTEN	THREAPING	THRILL
THOLEPIN	THOUGHTS	THREAPIT	THRILLANT
THOLEPINS	THOUING	THREAPS	THRILLED
THOLES	THOUS	THREAT	THRILLER
THOLI	THOUSAND	THREATED	THRILLERS
THOLING	THOUSANDS	THREATEN	THRILLIER
THOLOBATE	THOWEL	THREATENS	THRILLING
THOLOI	THOWELS	THREATFUL	THRILLS
THOLOS	THOWL	THREATING	THRILLY
THOLUS	THOWLESS	THREATS	THRIMSA
THON	THOWLS	THREAVE	THRIMSAS
THONDER	THRAE	THREAVES	THRIP
THONG	THRAIPING	THREE	THRIPS
THONGED	THRALDOM	THREEFOLD	THRIPSES
THONGS	THRALDOMS	THREENESS	THRISSEL
THORACAL	THRALL	THREEP	THRISSELS
THORACES	THRALLDOM	THREEPED	THRIST
THORACIC	THRALLED	THREEPER	THRISTED
THORAX	THRALLING	THREEPERS	THRISTING
THORAXES	THRALLS	THREEPING	THRISTLE
THORIA	THRANG	THREEPIT	THRISTLES
THORIAS	THRANGED	THREEPS	THRISTS
THORIC	THRANGING	THREES	THRISTY
THORITE	THRANGS	THREESOME	THRIVE
THORITES	THRAPPLE	THRENE	THRIVED
THORIUM	THRAPPLED	THRENES	THRIVEN
THORIUMS	THRAPPLES	THRENETIC	THRIVER
THORN	THRASH	THRENODE	THRIVERS
THORNBACK	THRASHED	THRENODES	THRIVES
THORNBILL	THRASHER	THRENODIC	THRIVING
THORNBUSH	THRASHERS	THRENODY	THRIVINGS
THORNED	THRASHES	THRENOS	THRO
THORNIER	THRASHING	THRENOSES	THROAT
THORNIEST	THRASONIC	THREONINE	THROATED
THORNILY	THRAVE	THRESH	THROATIER
THORNING	THRAVES	THRESHED	THROATILY
THORNLESS	THRAW	THRESHEL	THROATING
THORNLIKE	THRAWARD	THRESHELS	THROATS
THORNS	THRAWART	THRESHER	THROATY
THORNSET	THRAWED	THRESHERS	THROB
THORNTREE	THRAWING	THRESHES	THROBBED
THORNY	THRAWN	THRESHING	THROBBER
THORO	THRAWNLY	THRESHOLD	THROBBERS
THORON	THRAWS	THRETTIES	THROBBING
THORONS	THREAD	THRETTY	THROBLESS
THOROUGH	THREADED	THREW	THROBS
THOROUGHS	THREADEN	THRICE	THROE
THORP	THREADER	THRID	THROED
THORPE	THREADERS	THRIDACE	THROEING
THORPES	THREADFIN	THRIDACES	THROES
THORPS	THREADIER	THRIDDED	THROMBI

THROMBIN	THRUSTING	THUNDER	THYMOCYTE
THROMBINS	THRUSTOR	THUNDERED	THYMOL
THROMBOSE	THRUSTORS	THUNDERER	THYMOLS
THROMBUS	THRUSTS	THUNDERS	THYMOSIN
THRONE	THRUTCH	THUNDERY	THYMOSINS
THRONED	THRUTCHED	THUNDROUS	THYMUS
THRONES	THRUTCHES	THUNK	THYMUSES
THRONG	THRUWAY	THUNKED	THYMY
THRONGED	THRUWAYS	THUNKING	THYRATRON
THRONGFUL	THRYMSA	THUNKS	THYREOID
THRONGING	THRYMSAS	THURIBLE	THYREOIDS
THRONGS	THUD	THURIBLES	THYRISTOR
THRONING	THUDDED	THURIFER	THYROID
THRONNER	THUDDING	THURIFERS	THYROIDAL
THRONNERS	THUDS	THURIFIED	THYROIDS
THROPPLE	THUG	THURIFIES	THYROXIN
THROPPLED	THUGGEE	THURIFY	THYROXINE
THROPPLES	THUGGEES	THURL	THYROXINS
THROSTLE	THUGGERY	THURLS	THYRSE
THROSTLES	THUGGISH	THUS	THYRSES
THROTTLE	THUGGISM	THUSES	THYRSI
THROTTLED	THUGGISMS	THUSLY	THYRSOID
THROTTLER	THUGGO	THUSNESS	THYRSUS
THROTTLES	THUGGOS	THUSWISE	THYSELF
THROUGH	THUGS	THUYA	TI
THROUGHLY	THUJA	THUYAS	TIAR
THROVE	THUJAS	THWACK	TIARA
THROW	THULIA	THWACKED	TIARAED
THROWAWAY	THULIAS	THWACKER	TIARAS
THROWBACK	THULITE	THWACKERS	TIARS
THROWE	THULITES	THWACKING	TIBIA
THROWER	THULIUM	THWACKS	TIBIAE
THROWERS	THULIUMS	THWAITE	TIBIAL
THROWES	THUMB	THWAITES	TIBIAS
THROWING	THUMBED	THWART	TIC
THROWINGS	THUMBHOLE	THWARTED	TICAL
THROWN	THUMBIER	THWARTER	TICALS
THROWS	THUMBIEST	THWARTERS	TICCA
THROWSTER	THUMBING	THWARTING	TICCED
THRU	THUMBKIN	THWARTLY	TICCING
THRUM	THUMBKINS	THWARTS	TICE
THRUMMED	THUMBLESS	THY	TICED
THRUMMER	THUMBLIKE	THYINE	TICES
THRUMMERS	THUMBLING	THYLACINE	TICH
THRUMMIER	THUMBNAIL	THYLAKOID	TICHES
THRUMMING	THUMBNUT	THYLOSE	TICHIER
THRUMMY	THUMBNUTS	THYLOSES	TICHIEST
THRUMS	THUMBPOT	THYLOSIS	TICHY
THRUPENNY	THUMBPOTS	THYME	TICING
THRUPUT	THUMBS	THYMES	TICK
THRUPUTS	THUMBTACK	THYMEY	TICKED
THRUSH	THUMBY	THYMI	TICKEN
THRUSHES	THUMP	THYMIC	TICKENS
THRUST	THUMPED	THYMIDINE	TICKER
THRUSTED	THUMPER	THYMIER	TICKERS
THRUSTER	THUMPERS	THYMIEST	TICKET
THRUSTERS	THUMPING	THYMINE	TICKETED
THRUSTFUL	THUMPS	THYMINES	TICKETING

TICKETS

TICKETS
TICKEY
TICKEYS
TICKIES
TICKING
TICKINGS
TICKLACE
TICKLACES
TICKLE
TICKLED
TICKLER
TICKLERS
TICKLES
TICKLIER
TICKLIEST
TICKLING
TICKLINGS
TICKLISH
TICKLY
TICKS
TICKSEED
TICKSEEDS
TICKTACK
TICKTACKS
TICKTOCK
TICKTOCKS
TICKY
TICS
TICTAC
TICTACKED
TICTACS
TICTOC
TICTOCKED
TICTOCS
TID
TIDAL
TIDALLY
TIDBIT
TIDBITS
TIDDIER
TIDDIES
TIDDIEST
TIDDLE
TIDDLED
TIDDLER
TIDDLERS
TIDDLES
TIDDLEY
TIDDLEYS
TIDDLIER
TIDDLIES
TIDDLIEST
TIDDLING
TIDDLY
TIDDY
TIDE
TIDED
TIDELAND

TIDELANDS
TIDELESS
TIDELIKE
TIDEMARK
TIDEMARKS
TIDEMILL
TIDEMILLS
TIDERIP
TIDES
TIDESMAN
TIDESMEN
TIDEWATER
TIDEWAVE
TIDEWAVES
TIDEWAY
TIDEWAYS
TIDIED
TIDIER
TIDIERS
TIDIES
TIDIEST
TIDILY
TIDINESS
TIDING
TIDINGS
TIDIVATE
TIDIVATED
TIDIVATES
TIDS
TIDY
TIDYING
TIDYTIPS
TIE
TIEBACK
TIEBACKS
TIEBREAK
TIEBREAKS
TIECLASP
TIECLASPS
TIED
TIEING
TIELESS
TIEPIN
TIEPINS
TIER
TIERCE
TIERCED
TIERCEL
TIERCELET
TIERCELS
TIERCERON
TIERCES
TIERCET
TIERCETS
TIERED
TIERING
TIEROD

TIERODS
TIERS
TIES
TIETAC
TIETACK
TIETACKS
TIETACS
TIFF
TIFFANIES
TIFFANY
TIFFED
TIFFIN
TIFFINED
TIFFING
TIFFINGS
TIFFINING
TIFFINS
TIFFS
TIFOSI
TIFOSO
TIFT
TIFTED
TIFTING
TIFTS
TIG
TIGE
TIGER
TIGEREYE
TIGEREYES
TIGERISH
TIGERISM
TIGERISMS
TIGERLIKE
TIGERLY
TIGERS
TIGERY
TIGES
TIGGED
TIGGING
TIGHT
TIGHTASS
TIGHTEN
TIGHTENED
TIGHTENER
TIGHTENS
TIGHTER
TIGHTEST
TIGHTISH
TIGHTKNIT
TIGHTLY
TIGHTNESS
TIGHTROPE
TIGHTS
TIGHTWAD
TIGHTWADS
TIGHTWIRE
TIGLIC
TIGLON

TIGLONS
TIGON
TIGONS
TIGRESS
TIGRESSES
TIGRIDIA
TIGRIDIAS
TIGRINE
TIGRISH
TIGRISHLY
TIGROID
TIGS
TIKA
TIKANGA
TIKANGAS
TIKAS
TIKE
TIKES
TIKI
TIKIED
TIKIING
TIKIS
TIKKA
TIKKAS
TIKOLOSHE
TIL
TILAK
TILAKS
TILAPIA
TILAPIAS
TILBURIES
TILBURY
TILDE
TILDES
TILE
TILED
TILEFISH
TILELIKE
TILER
TILERIES
TILERS
TILERY
TILES
TILING
TILINGS
TILL
TILLABLE
TILLAGE
TILLAGES
TILLED
TILLER
TILLERED
TILLERING
TILLERMAN
TILLERMEN
TILLERS
TILLICUM
TILLICUMS

TILLIER	TIMENOGUY	TINCTS	TINKERERS
TILLIEST	TIMEOUS	TINCTURE	TINKERING
TILLING	TIMEOUSLY	TINCTURED	TINKERS
TILLINGS	TIMEOUT	TINCTURES	TINKERTOY
TILLITE	TIMEOUTS	TIND	TINKING
TILLITES	TIMEPASS	TINDAL	TINKLE
TILLS	TIMEPIECE	TINDALS	TINKLED
TILLY	TIMER	TINDED	TINKLER
TILS	TIMERS	TINDER	TINKLERS
TILT	TIMES	TINDERBOX	TINKLES
TILTABLE	TIMESAVER	TINDERS	TINKLIER
TILTED	TIMESCALE	TINDERY	TINKLIEST
TILTER	TIMETABLE	TINDING	TINKLING
TILTERS	TIMEWORK	TINDS	TINKLINGS
TILTH	TIMEWORKS	TINE	TINKLY
TILTHS	TIMEWORN	TINEA	TINKS
TILTING	TIMID	TINEAL	TINLIKE
TILTINGS	TIMIDER	TINEAS	TINMAN
TILTMETER	TIMIDEST	TINED	TINMEN
TILTROTOR	TIMIDITY	TINEID	TINNED
TILTS	TIMIDLY	TINEIDS	TINNER
TILTYARD	TIMIDNESS	TINES	TINNERS
TILTYARDS	TIMING	TINFOIL	TINNIE
TIMARAU	TIMINGS	TINFOILS	TINNIER
TIMARAUS	TIMIST	TINFUL	TINNIES
TIMARIOT	TIMISTS	TINFULS	TINNIEST
TIMARIOTS	TIMOCRACY	TING	TINNILY
TIMBAL	TIMOLOL	TINGE	TINNINESS
TIMBALE	TIMOLOLS	TINGED	TINNING
TIMBALES	TIMON	TINGEING	TINNINGS
TIMBALS	TIMONEER	TINGES	TINNITUS
TIMBER	TIMONEERS	TINGING	TINNY
TIMBERED	TIMONS	TINGLE	TINPLATE
TIMBERING	TIMOROUS	TINGLED	TINPLATED
TIMBERMAN	TIMORSOME	TINGLER	TINPLATES
TIMBERMEN	TIMOTHIES	TINGLERS	TINPOT
TIMBERS	TIMOTHY	TINGLES	TINPOTS
TIMBERY	TIMOUS	TINGLIER	TINS
TIMBO	TIMOUSLY	TINGLIEST	TINSEL
TIMBOS	TIMPANA	TINGLING	TINSELED
TIMBRAL	TIMPANI	TINGLINGS	TINSELING
TIMBRE	TIMPANIST	TINGLISH	TINSELLED
TIMBREL	TIMPANO	TINGLY	TINSELLY
TIMBRELS	TIMPANUM	TINGS	TINSELRY
TIMBRES	TIMPANUMS	TINGUAITE	TINSELS
TIME	TIMPS	TINHORN	TINSEY
TIMEBOMB	TIN	TINHORNS	TINSEYS
TIMEBOMBS	TINAJA	TINIER	TINSMITH
TIMECARD	TINAJAS	TINIES	TINSMITHS
TIMECARDS	TINAMOU	TINIEST	TINSNIPS
TIMED	TINAMOUS	TINILY	TINSTONE
TIMEFRAME	TINCAL	TININESS	TINSTONES
TIMELESS	TINCALS	TINING	TINT
TIMELIER	TINCHEL	TINK	TINTACK
TIMELIEST	TINCHELS	TINKED	TINTACKS
TIMELINE	TINCT	TINKER	TINTED
TIMELINES	TINCTED	TINKERED	TINTER
TIMELY	TINCTING	TINKERER	TINTERS

TINTIER	TIPSTAFF	TIRRIVEE	TITHONIA
TINTIEST	TIPSTAFFS	TIRRIVEES	TITHONIAS
TINTINESS	TIPSTAVES	TIRRIVIE	TITI
TINTING	TIPSTER	TIRRIVIES	TITIAN
TINTINGS	TIPSTERS	TIRRS	TITIANS
TINTLESS	TIPSTOCK	TIS	TITILLATE
TINTOOKIE	TIPSTOCKS	TISANE	TITIS
TINTS	TIPSY	TISANES	TITIVATE
TINTY	TIPT	TISICK	TITIVATED
TINTYPE	TIPTOE	TISICKS	TITIVATES
TINTYPES	TIPTOED	TISSUAL	TITIVATOR
TINWARE	TIPTOEING	TISSUE	TITLARK
TINWARES	TIPTOES	TISSUED	TITLARKS
TINWORK	TIPTOP	TISSUES	TITLE
TINWORKS	TIPTOPS	TISSUEY	TITLED
TINY	TIPTRONIC	TISSUING	TITLELESS
TIP	TIPULA	TISSULAR	TITLER
TIPCART	TIPULAS	TISWAS	TITLERS
TIPCARTS	TIPUNA	TISWASES	TITLES
TIPCAT	TIPUNAS	TIT	TITLING
TIPCATS	TIRADE	TITAN	TITLINGS
TIPI	TIRADES	TITANATE	TITLIST
TIPIS	TIRAGE	TITANATES	TITLISTS
TIPLESS	TIRAGES	TITANESS	TITMAN
TIPOFF	TIRAMISU	TITANIA	TITMEN
TIPOFFS	TIRAMISUS	TITANIAS	TITMICE
TIPPABLE	TIRASSE	TITANIC	TITMOSE
TIPPED	TIRASSES	TITANIS	TITMOUSE
TIPPEE	TIRE	TITANISES	TITOKI
TIPPEES	TIRED	TITANISM	TITOKIS
TIPPER	TIREDER	TITANISMS	TITRABLE
TIPPERS	TIREDEST	TITANITE	TITRANT
TIPPET	TIREDLY	TITANITES	TITRANTS
TIPPETS	TIREDNESS	TITANIUM	TITRATE
TIPPIER	TIRELESS	TITANIUMS	TITRATED
TIPPIEST	TIRELING	TITANOUS	TITRATES
TIPPING	TIRELINGS	TITANS	TITRATING
TIPPINGS	TIRES	TITBIT	TITRATION
TIPPLE	TIRESOME	TITBITS	TITRATOR
TIPPLED	TIREWOMAN	TITCH	TITRATORS
TIPPLER	TIREWOMEN	TITCHES	TITRE
TIPPLERS	TIRING	TITCHIER	TITRES
TIPPLES	TIRINGS	TITCHIEST	TITS
TIPPLING	TIRITI	TITCHY	TITTED
TIPPY	TIRITIS	TITE	TITTER
TIPPYTOE	TIRL	TITELY	TITTERED
TIPPYTOED	TIRLED	TITER	TITTERER
TIPPYTOES	TIRLING	TITERS	TITTERERS
TIPS	TIRLS	TITFER	TITTERING
TIPSHEET	TIRO	TITFERS	TITTERS
TIPSHEETS	TIROES	TITHABLE	TITTIE
TIPSIER	TIRONIC	TITHE	TITTIES
TIPSIEST	TIROS	TITHED	TITTING
TIPSIFIED	TIRR	TITHER	TITTISH
TIPSIFIES	TIRRED	TITHERS	TITTIVATE
TIPSIFY	TIRRING	TITHES	TITTLE
TIPSILY	TIRRIT	TITHING	TITTLEBAT
TIPSINESS	TIRRITS	TITHINGS	TITTLED

TITTLES	TOADSTOOL	TODDE	TOFT
TITTLING	TOADY	TODDED	TOFTS
TITTUP	TOADYING	TODDES	TOFU
TITTUPED	TOADYISH	TODDIES	TOFUS
TITTUPING	TOADYISM	TODDING	TOFUTTI
TITTUPPED	TOADYISMS	TODDLE	TOFUTTIS
TITTUPPY	TOAST	TODDLED	TOG
TITTUPS	TOASTED	TODDLER	TOGA
TITTUPY	TOASTER	TODDLERS	TOGAE
TITTY	TOASTERS	TODDLES	TOGAED
TITUBANCY	TOASTIE	TODDLING	TOGAS
TITUBANT	TOASTIER	TODDY	TOGATE
TITUBATE	TOASTIES	TODIES	TOGATED
TITUBATED	TOASTIEST	TODS	TOGAVIRUS
TITUBATES	TOASTING	TODY	TOGE
TITULAR	TOASTINGS	TOE	TOGED
TITULARLY	TOASTS	TOEA	TOGES
TITULARS	TOASTY	TOEAS	TOGETHER
TITULARY	TOAZE	TOEBIE	TOGGED
TITULE	TOAZED	TOEBIES	TOGGER
TITULED	TOAZES	TOECAP	TOGGERED
TITULES	TOAZING	TOECAPS	TOGGERIES
TITULI	TOBACCO	TOECLIP	TOGGERING
TITULING	TOBACCOES	TOECLIPS	TOGGERS
TITULUS	TOBACCOS	TOED	TOGGERY
TITUP	TOBIES	TOEHOLD	TOGGING
TITUPED	TOBOGGAN	TOEHOLDS	TOGGLE
TITUPING	TOBOGGANS	TOEIER	TOGGLED
TITUPPED	TOBOGGIN	TOEIEST	TOGGLER
TITUPPING	TOBOGGINS	TOEING	TOGGLERS
TITUPS	TOBY	TOELESS	TOGGLES
TITUPY	TOC	TOELIKE	TOGGLING
TIVY	TOCCATA	TOENAIL	TOGS
TIX	TOCCATAS	TOENAILED	TOGUE
TIZWAS	TOCCATE	TOENAILS	TOGUES
TIZWASES	TOCCATINA	TOEPIECE	TOHEROA
TIZZ	TOCHER	TOEPIECES	TOHEROAS
TIZZES	TOCHERED	TOEPLATE	TOHO
TIZZIES	TOCHERING	TOEPLATES	TOHOS
TIZZY	TOCHERS	TOERAG	TOHUNGA
TJANTING	TOCK	TOERAGGER	TOHUNGAS
TJANTINGS	TOCKED	TOERAGS	TOIL
TMESES	TOCKIER	TOES	TOILE
TMESIS	TOCKIEST	TOESHOE	TOILED
TO	TOCKING	TOESHOES	TOILER
TOAD	TOCKLEY	TOETOE	TOILERS
TOADEATER	TOCKLEYS	TOETOES	TOILES
TOADFISH	TOCKS	TOEY	TOILET
TOADFLAX	TOCKY	TOFF	TOILETED
TOADGRASS	TOCO	TOFFEE	TOILETING
TOADIED	TOCOLOGY	TOFFEES	TOILETRY
TOADIES	TOCOS	TOFFIER	TOILETS
TOADISH	TOCS	TOFFIES	TOILETTE
TOADLESS	TOCSIN	TOFFIEST	TOILETTES
TOADLIKE	TOCSINS	TOFFISH	TOILFUL
TOADRUSH	TOD	TOFFS	TOILFULLY
TOADS	TODAY	TOFFY	TOILINET
TOADSTONE	TODAYS	TOFORE	TOILINETS

TOILING	TOLARS	TOLTERS	TOMBOYISH
TOILINGS	TOLAS	TOLTS	TOMBOYS
TOILLESS	TOLBOOTH	TOLU	TOMBS
TOILS	TOLBOOTHS	TOLUATE	TOMBSTONE
TOILSOME	TOLD	TOLUATES	TOMCAT
TOILWORN	TOLE	TOLUENE	TOMCATS
TOING	TOLED	TOLUENES	TOMCATTED
TOINGS	TOLEDO	TOLUIC	TOMCOD
TOISE	TOLEDOS	TOLUID	TOMCODS
TOISEACH	TOLERABLE	TOLUIDE	TOME
TOISEACHS	TOLERABLY	TOLUIDES	TOMENTA
TOISECH	TOLERANCE	TOLUIDIDE	TOMENTOSE
TOISECHS	TOLERANT	TOLUIDIN	TOMENTOUS
TOISES	TOLERATE	TOLUIDINE	TOMENTUM
TOISON	TOLERATED	TOLUIDINS	TOMES
TOISONS	TOLERATES	TOLUIDS	TOMFOOL
TOIT	TOLERATOR	TOLUOL	TOMFOOLED
TOITED	TOLES	TOLUOLE	TOMFOOLS
TOITING	TOLEWARE	TOLUOLES	TOMIA
TOITOI	TOLEWARES	TOLUOLS	TOMIAL
TOITOIS	TOLIDIN	TOLUS	TOMIUM
TOITS	TOLIDINE	TOLUYL	TOMMED
TOKAMAK	TOLIDINES	TOLUYLS	TOMMIED
TOKAMAKS	TOLIDINS	TOLYL	TOMMIES
TOKAY	TOLING	TOLYLS	TOMMING
TOKAYS	TOLINGS	TOLZEY	TOMMY
TOKE	TOLL	TOLZEYS	TOMMYING
TOKED	TOLLABLE	TOM	TOMMYROT
TOKEN	TOLLAGE	TOMAHAWK	TOMMYROTS
TOKENED	TOLLAGES	TOMAHAWKS	TOMO
TOKENING	TOLLBAR	TOMALLEY	TOMOGRAM
TOKENISM	TOLLBARS	TOMALLEYS	TOMOGRAMS
TOKENISMS	TOLLBOOTH	TOMAN	TOMOGRAPH
TOKENS	TOLLDISH	TOMANS	TOMORROW
TOKER	TOLLED	TOMATILLO	TOMORROWS
TOKERS	TOLLER	TOMATO	TOMOS
TOKES	TOLLERS	TOMATOES	TOMPION
TOKING	TOLLGATE	TOMATOEY	TOMPIONS
TOKO	TOLLGATES	TOMB	TOMPON
TOKOLOGY	TOLLHOUSE	TOMBAC	TOMPONED
TOKOLOSHE	TOLLIE	TOMBACK	TOMPONING
TOKOLOSHI	TOLLIES	TOMBACKS	TOMPONS
TOKOMAK	TOLLING	TOMBACS	TOMS
TOKOMAKS	TOLLINGS	TOMBAK	TOMTIT
TOKONOMA	TOLLMAN	TOMBAKS	TOMTITS
TOKONOMAS	TOLLMEN	TOMBAL	TON
TOKOS	TOLLS	TOMBED	TONAL
TOKOTOKO	TOLLWAY	TOMBIC	TONALITE
TOKOTOKOS	TOLLWAYS	TOMBING	TONALITES
TOKTOKKIE	TOLLY	TOMBLESS	TONALITY
TOLA	TOLSEL	TOMBLIKE	TONALLY
TOLAN	TOLSELS	TOMBOC	TONANT
TOLANE	TOLSEY	TOMBOCS	TONDI
TOLANES	TOLSEYS	TOMBOLA	TONDINI
TOLANS	TOLT	TOMBOLAS	TONDINO
TOLAR	TOLTER	TOMBOLO	TONDINOS
TOLARJEV	TOLTERED	TOMBOLOS	TONDO
TOLARJI	TOLTERING	TOMBOY	TONDOS

TONE	TONLET	TOOLKIT	TOOTSED
TONEARM	TONLETS	TOOLKITS	TOOTSES
TONEARMS	TONNAG	TOOLLESS	TOOTSIE
TONED	TONNAGE	TOOLMAKER	TOOTSIES
TONELESS	TONNAGES	TOOLMAN	TOOTSING
TONEME	TONNAGS	TOOLMEN	TOOTSY
TONEMES	TONNE	TOOLROOM	TOP
TONEMIC	TONNEAU	TOOLROOMS	TOPALGIA
TONEPAD	TONNEAUS	TOOLS	TOPALGIAS
TONEPADS	TONNEAUX	TOOLSET	TOPARCH
TONER	TONNELL	TOOLSETS	TOPARCHS
TONERS	TONNELLS	TOOLSHED	TOPARCHY
TONES	TONNER	TOOLSHEDS	TOPAZ
TONETIC	TONNERS	TOOM	TOPAZES
TONETICS	TONNES	TOOMED	TOPAZINE
TONETTE	TONNISH	TOOMER	TOPCOAT
TONETTES	TONNISHLY	TOOMEST	TOPCOATS
TONEY	TONOMETER	TOOMING	TOPCROSS
TONG	TONOMETRY	TOOMS	TOPE
TONGA	TONOPLAST	TOON	TOPECTOMY
TONGAS	TONS	TOONIE	TOPED
TONGED	TONSIL	TOONIES	TOPEE
TONGER	TONSILAR	TOONS	TOPEES
TONGERS	TONSILLAR	TOORIE	TOPEK
TONGING	TONSILS	TOORIES	TOPEKS
TONGMAN	TONSOR	TOOSHIE	TOPER
TONGMEN	TONSORIAL	TOOT	TOPERS
TONGS	TONSORS	TOOTED	TOPES
TONGSTER	TONSURE	TOOTER	TOPFLIGHT
TONGSTERS	TONSURED	TOOTERS	TOPFUL
TONGUE	TONSURES	TOOTH	TOPFULL
TONGUED	TONSURING	TOOTHACHE	TOPH
TONGUELET	TONTINE	TOOTHCOMB	TOPHE
TONGUES	TONTINER	TOOTHED	TOPHES
TONGUING	TONTINERS	TOOTHFISH	TOPHI
TONGUINGS	TONTINES	TOOTHFUL	TOPHS
TONIC	TONUS	TOOTHFULS	TOPHUS
TONICALLY	TONUSES	TOOTHIER	TOPI
TONICITY	TONY	TOOTHIEST	TOPIARIAN
TONICS	TOO	TOOTHILY	TOPIARIES
TONIER	TOOART	TOOTHING	TOPIARIST
TONIES	TOOARTS	TOOTHINGS	TOPIARY
TONIEST	TOOK	TOOTHLESS	TOPIC
TONIGHT	TOOL	TOOTHLIKE	TOPICAL
TONIGHTS	TOOLBAG	TOOTHPICK	TOPICALLY
TONING	TOOLBAGS	TOOTHS	TOPICS
TONINGS	TOOLBAR	TOOTHSOME	TOPING
TONISH	TOOLBARS	TOOTHWASH	TOPIS
TONISHLY	TOOLBOX	TOOTHWORT	TOPKICK
TONITE	TOOLBOXES	TOOTHY	TOPKICKS
TONITES	TOOLED	TOOTING	TOPKNOT
TONK	TOOLER	TOOTLE	TOPKNOTS
TONKA	TOOLERS	TOOTLED	TOPLESS
TONKED	TOOLHEAD	TOOTLER	TOPLINE
TONKER	TOOLHEADS	TOOTLERS	TOPLINED
TONKERS	TOOLHOUSE	TOOTLES	TOPLINER
TONKING	TOOLING	TOOTLING	TOPLINERS
TONKS	TOOLINGS	TOOTS	TOPLINES

TOPLINING	TOQUETS	TORMENTOR	TORRIDER
TOPLOFTY	TOQUILLA	TORMENTS	TORRIDEST
TOPMAKER	TOQUILLAS	TORMENTUM	TORRIDITY
TOPMAKERS	TOR	TORMINA	TORRIDLY
TOPMAKING	TORA	TORMINAL	TORRIFIED
TOPMAN	TORAH	TORMINOUS	TORRIFIES
TOPMAST	TORAHS	TORN	TORRIFY
TOPMASTS	TORAN	TORNADE	TORRS
TOPMEN	TORANA	TORNADES	TORS
TOPMINNOW	TORANAS	TORNADIC	TORSADE
TOPMOST	TORANS	TORNADO	TORSADES
TOPNOTCH	TORAS	TORNADOES	TORSE
TOPO	TORBANITE	TORNADOS	TORSEL
TOPOGRAPH	TORC	TORNILLO	TORSELS
TOPOI	TORCH	TORNILLOS	TORSES
TOPOLOGIC	TORCHABLE	TORO	TORSI
TOPOLOGY	TORCHED	TOROID	TORSION
TOPONYM	TORCHER	TOROIDAL	TORSIONAL
TOPONYMAL	TORCHERE	TOROIDS	TORSIONS
TOPONYMIC	TORCHERES	TOROS	TORSIVE
TOPONYMS	TORCHERS	TOROSE	TORSK
TOPONYMY	TORCHES	TOROSITY	TORSKS
TOPOS	TORCHIER	TOROT	TORSO
TOPOTYPE	TORCHIERE	TOROTH	TORSOS
TOPOTYPES	TORCHIERS	TOROUS	TORT
TOPPED	TORCHIEST	TORPEDO	TORTA
TOPPER	TORCHING	TORPEDOED	TORTAS
TOPPERS	TORCHINGS	TORPEDOER	TORTE
TOPPING	TORCHLIKE	TORPEDOES	TORTEN
TOPPINGLY	TORCHON	TORPEDOS	TORTES
TOPPINGS	TORCHONS	TORPEFIED	TORTILE
TOPPLE	TORCHWOOD	TORPEFIES	TORTILITY
TOPPLED	TORCHY	TORPEFY	TORTILLA
TOPPLES	TORCS	TORPID	TORTILLAS
TOPPLING	TORCULAR	TORPIDITY	TORTILLON
TOPS	TORCULARS	TORPIDLY	TORTIOUS
TOPSAIL	TORDION	TORPIDS	TORTIVE
TOPSAILS	TORDIONS	TORPITUDE	TORTOISE
TOPSIDE	TORE	TORPOR	TORTOISES
TOPSIDER	TOREADOR	TORPORS	TORTONI
TOPSIDERS	TOREADORS	TORQUATE	TORTONIS
TOPSIDES	TORERO	TORQUATED	TORTRICES
TOPSMAN	TOREROS	TORQUE	TORTRICID
TOPSMEN	TORES	TORQUED	TORTRIX
TOPSOIL	TOREUTIC	TORQUER	TORTRIXES
TOPSOILED	TOREUTICS	TORQUERS	TORTS
TOPSOILS	TORGOCH	TORQUES	TORTUOUS
TOPSPIN	TORGOCHS	TORQUESES	TORTURE
TOPSPINS	TORI	TORQUING	TORTURED
TOPSTITCH	TORIC	TORR	TORTURER
TOPSTONE	TORICS	TORREFIED	TORTURERS
TOPSTONES	TORIES	TORREFIES	TORTURES
TOPWORK	TORII	TORREFY	TORTURING
TOPWORKED	TORMENT	TORRENT	TORTUROUS
TOPWORKS	TORMENTA	TORRENTS	TORULA
TOQUE	TORMENTED	TORRET	TORULAE
TOQUES	TORMENTER	TORRETS	TORULAS
TOQUET	TORMENTIL	TORRID	TORULI

TORULIN	TOTALISTS	TOUCHBACK	TOURINGS
TORULINS	TOTALITY	TOUCHDOWN	TOURISM
TORULOSE	TOTALIZE	TOUCHE	TOURISMS
TORULOSES	TOTALIZED	TOUCHED	TOURIST
TORULOSIS	TOTALIZER	TOUCHER	TOURISTA
TORULUS	TOTALIZES	TOUCHERS	TOURISTAS
TORUS	TOTALLED	TOUCHES	TOURISTED
TORY	TOTALLING	TOUCHHOLE	TOURISTIC
TOSA	TOTALLY	TOUCHIER	TOURISTS
TOSAS	TOTALS	TOUCHIEST	TOURISTY
TOSE	TOTANUS	TOUCHILY	TOURNEDOS
TOSED	TOTANUSES	TOUCHING	TOURNEY
TOSES	TOTAQUINE	TOUCHINGS	TOURNEYED
TOSH	TOTARA	TOUCHLESS	TOURNEYER
TOSHACH	TOTARAS	TOUCHLINE	TOURNEYS
TOSHACHS	TOTE	TOUCHMARK	TOURNURE
TOSHED	TOTEABLE	TOUCHPAD	TOURNURES
TOSHER	TOTED	TOUCHPADS	TOURS
TOSHERS	TOTEM	TOUCHTONE	TOURTIERE
TOSHES	TOTEMIC	TOUCHUP	TOUSE
TOSHIER	TOTEMISM	TOUCHUPS	TOUSED
TOSHIEST	TOTEMISMS	TOUCHWOOD	TOUSER
TOSHING	TOTEMIST	TOUCHY	TOUSERS
TOSHY	TOTEMISTS	TOUGH	TOUSES
TOSING	TOTEMITE	TOUGHED	TOUSIER
TOSS	TOTEMITES	TOUGHEN	TOUSIEST
TOSSED	TOTEMS	TOUGHENED	TOUSING
TOSSEN	TOTER	TOUGHENER	TOUSINGS
TOSSER	TOTERS	TOUGHENS	TOUSLE
TOSSERS	TOTES	TOUGHER	TOUSLED
TOSSES	TOTHER	TOUGHEST	TOUSLES
TOSSIER	TOTIENT	TOUGHIE	TOUSLING
TOSSIEST	TOTIENTS	TOUGHIES	TOUSTIE
TOSSILY	TOTING	TOUGHING	TOUSTIER
TOSSING	TOTITIVE	TOUGHISH	TOUSTIEST
TOSSINGS	TOTITIVES	TOUGHLY	TOUSY
TOSSPOT	TOTS	TOUGHNESS	TOUT
TOSSPOTS	TOTTED	TOUGHS	TOUTED
TOSSUP	TOTTER	TOUGHY	TOUTER
TOSSUPS	TOTTERED	TOUK	TOUTERS
TOSSY	TOTTERER	TOUKED	TOUTIE
TOST	TOTTERERS	TOUKING	TOUTIER
TOSTADA	TOTTERING	TOUKS	TOUTIEST
TOSTADAS	TOTTERS	TOUN	TOUTING
TOSTADO	TOTTERY	TOUNS	TOUTS
TOSTADOS	TOTTIE	TOUPEE	TOUZE
TOT	TOTTIER	TOUPEES	TOUZED
TOTABLE	TOTTIES	TOUPET	TOUZES
TOTAL	TOTTIEST	TOUPETS	TOUZIER
TOTALED	TOTTING	TOUR	TOUZIEST
TOTALING	TOTTINGS	TOURACO	TOUZING
TOTALISE	TOTTY	TOURACOS	TOUZLE
TOTALISED	TOUCAN	TOURED	TOUZLED
TOTALISER	TOUCANET	TOURER	TOUZLES
TOTALISES	TOUCANETS	TOURERS	TOUZLING
TOTALISM	TOUCANS	TOURIE	TOUZY
TOTALISMS	TOUCH	TOURIES	TOVARICH
TOTALIST	TOUCHABLE	TOURING	TOVARISCH

TOVARISH	TOWNHALL	TOWZING	TOZING
TOW	TOWNHOME	TOWZY	TRABEATE
TOWABLE	TOWNHOMES	TOXAEMIA	TRABEATED
TOWAGE	TOWNHOUSE	TOXAEMIAS	TRABECULA
TOWAGES	TOWNIE	TOXAEMIC	TRABS
TOWARD	TOWNIER	TOXAPHENE	TRACE
TOWARDLY	TOWNIES	TOXEMIA	TRACEABLE
TOWARDS	TOWNIEST	TOXEMIAS	TRACEABLY
TOWAWAY	TOWNISH	TOXEMIC	TRACED
TOWAWAYS	TOWNLAND	TOXIC	TRACELESS
TOWBAR	TOWNLANDS	TOXICAL	TRACER
TOWBARS	TOWNLESS	TOXICALLY	TRACERIED
TOWBOAT	TOWNLET	TOXICANT	TRACERIES
TOWBOATS	TOWNLETS	TOXICANTS	TRACERS
TOWED	TOWNLIER	TOXICITY	TRACERY
TOWEL	TOWNLIEST	TOXICOSES	TRACES
TOWELED	TOWNLING	TOXICOSIS	TRACEUR
TOWELETTE	TOWNLINGS	TOXICS	TRACEURS
TOWELHEAD	TOWNLY	TOXIGENIC	TRACHEA
TOWELING	TOWNS	TOXIN	TRACHEAE
TOWELINGS	TOWNSCAPE	TOXINE	TRACHEAL
TOWELLED	TOWNSFOLK	TOXINES	TRACHEARY
TOWELLING	TOWNSHIP	TOXINS	TRACHEAS
TOWELS	TOWNSHIPS	TOXOCARA	TRACHEATE
TOWER	TOWNSKIP	TOXOCARAS	TRACHEID
TOWERED	TOWNSKIPS	TOXOID	TRACHEIDE
TOWERIER	TOWNSMAN	TOXOIDS	TRACHEIDS
TOWERIEST	TOWNSMEN	TOXOPHILY	TRACHEOLE
TOWERING	TOWNWEAR	TOY	TRACHINUS
TOWERLESS	TOWNY	TOYED	TRACHITIS
TOWERLIKE	TOWPATH	TOYER	TRACHLE
TOWERS	TOWPATHS	TOYERS	TRACHLED
TOWERY	TOWPLANE	TOYING	TRACHLES
TOWHEAD	TOWPLANES	TOYINGS	TRACHLING
TOWHEADED	TOWROPE	TOYISH	TRACHOMA
TOWHEADS	TOWROPES	TOYISHLY	TRACHOMAS
TOWHEE	TOWS	TOYLESOME	TRACHYTE
TOWHEES	TOWSACK	TOYLESS	TRACHYTES
TOWIE	TOWSACKS	TOYLIKE	TRACHYTIC
TOWIER	TOWSE	TOYLSOM	TRACING
TOWIES	TOWSED	TOYMAN	TRACINGS
TOWIEST	TOWSER	TOYMEN	TRACK
TOWING	TOWSERS	TOYO	TRACKABLE
TOWINGS	TOWSES	TOYON	TRACKAGE
TOWKAY	TOWSIER	TOYONS	TRACKAGES
TOWKAYS	TOWSIEST	TOYOS	TRACKBALL
TOWLINE	TOWSING	TOYS	TRACKED
TOWLINES	TOWSY	TOYSHOP	TRACKER
TOWMON	TOWT	TOYSHOPS	TRACKERS
TOWMOND	TOWTED	TOYSOME	TRACKING
TOWMONDS	TOWTING	TOYTOWN	TRACKINGS
TOWMONS	TOWTS	TOYWOMAN	TRACKLESS
TOWMONT	TOWY	TOYWOMEN	TRACKMAN
TOWMONTS	TOWZE	TOZE	TRACKMEN
TOWN	TOWZED	TOZED	TRACKPAD
TOWNEE	TOWZES	TOZES	TRACKPADS
TOWNEES	TOWZIER	TOZIE	TRACKROAD
TOWNFOLK	TOWZIEST	TOZIES	TRACKS

TRACKSIDE	TRAGEDY	TRAITS	TRANCHET
TRACKSUIT	TRAGELAPH	TRAJECT	TRANCHETS
TRACKWAY	TRAGI	TRAJECTED	TRANCING
TRACKWAYS	TRAGIC	TRAJECTS	TRANECT
TRACT	TRAGICAL	TRAM	TRANECTS
TRACTABLE	TRAGICS	TRAMCAR	TRANGAM
TRACTABLY	TRAGOPAN	TRAMCARS	TRANGAMS
TRACTATE	TRAGOPANS	TRAMEL	TRANGLE
TRACTATES	TRAGULE	TRAMELED	TRANGLES
TRACTATOR	TRAGULES	TRAMELING	TRANK
TRACTED	TRAGULINE	TRAMELL	TRANKS
TRACTILE	TRAGUS	TRAMELLED	TRANKUM
TRACTING	TRAHISON	TRAMELLS	TRANKUMS
TRACTION	TRAHISONS	TRAMELS	TRANNIE
TRACTIONS	TRAIK	TRAMLESS	TRANNIES
TRACTIVE	TRAIKED	TRAMLINE	TRANNY
TRACTOR	TRAIKING	TRAMLINED	TRANQ
TRACTORS	TRAIKIT	TRAMLINES	TRANQS
TRACTRIX	TRAIKS	TRAMMED	TRANQUIL
TRACTS	TRAIL	TRAMMEL	TRANS
TRACTUS	TRAILABLE	TRAMMELED	TRANSACT
TRACTUSES	TRAILED	TRAMMELER	TRANSACTS
TRAD	TRAILER	TRAMMELS	TRANSAXLE
TRADABLE	TRAILERED	TRAMMIE	TRANSCEND
TRADE	TRAILERS	TRAMMIES	TRANSDUCE
TRADEABLE	TRAILHEAD	TRAMMING	TRANSE
TRADED	TRAILING	TRAMP	TRANSECT
TRADEFUL	TRAILLESS	TRAMPED	TRANSECTS
TRADELESS	TRAILS	TRAMPER	TRANSENNA
TRADEMARK	TRAILSIDE	TRAMPERS	TRANSEPT
TRADENAME	TRAIN	TRAMPET	TRANSEPTS
TRADEOFF	TRAINABLE	TRAMPETS	TRANSES
TRADEOFFS	TRAINBAND	TRAMPETTE	TRANSEUNT
TRADER	TRAINED	TRAMPIER	TRANSFARD
TRADERS	TRAINEE	TRAMPIEST	TRANSFECT
TRADES	TRAINEES	TRAMPING	TRANSFER
TRADESMAN	TRAINER	TRAMPINGS	TRANSFERS
TRADESMEN	TRAINERS	TRAMPISH	TRANSFIX
TRADING	TRAINFUL	TRAMPLE	TRANSFIXT
TRADINGS	TRAINFULS	TRAMPLED	TRANSFORM
TRADITION	TRAINING	TRAMPLER	TRANSFUSE
TRADITIVE	TRAININGS	TRAMPLERS	TRANSGENE
TRADITOR	TRAINLESS	TRAMPLES	TRANSHIP
TRADITORS	TRAINLOAD	TRAMPLING	TRANSHIPS
TRADS	TRAINMAN	TRAMPOLIN	TRANSHUME
TRADUCE	TRAINMEN	TRAMPS	TRANSIENT
TRADUCED	TRAINS	TRAMPY	TRANSIRE
TRADUCER	TRAINWAY	TRAMROAD	TRANSIRES
TRADUCERS	TRAINWAYS	TRAMROADS	TRANSIT
TRADUCES	TRAIPSE	TRAMS	TRANSITED
TRADUCIAN	TRAIPSED	TRAMWAY	TRANSITS
TRADUCING	TRAIPSES	TRAMWAYS	TRANSLATE
TRAFFIC	TRAIPSING	TRANCE	TRANSMEW
TRAFFICKY	TRAIT	TRANCED	TRANSMEWS
TRAFFICS	TRAITOR	TRANCEDLY	TRANSMIT
TRAGAL	TRAITORLY	TRANCES	TRANSMITS
TRAGEDIAN	TRAITORS	TRANCHE	TRANSMOVE
TRAGEDIES	TRAITRESS	TRANCHES	TRANSMUTE

TRANSOM	TRAPPIER	TRAVERSAL	TREADMILL
TRANSOMED	TRAPPIEST	TRAVERSE	TREADS
TRANSOMS	TRAPPING	TRAVERSED	TREAGUE
TRANSONIC	TRAPPINGS	TRAVERSER	TREAGUES
TRANSPIRE	TRAPPOSE	TRAVERSES	TREASON
TRANSPORT	TRAPPOUS	TRAVERTIN	TREASONS
TRANSPOSE	TRAPPY	TRAVES	TREASURE
TRANSSHIP	TRAPROCK	TRAVESTY	TREASURED
TRANSUDE	TRAPROCKS	TRAVIS	TREASURER
TRANSUDED	TRAPS	TRAVISES	TREASURES
TRANSUDES	TRAPT	TRAVOIS	TREASURY
TRANSUME	TRAPUNTO	TRAVOISE	TREAT
TRANSUMED	TRAPUNTOS	TRAVOISES	TREATABLE
TRANSUMES	TRASH	TRAWL	TREATED
TRANSUMPT	TRASHCAN	TRAWLED	TREATER
TRANSVEST	TRASHCANS	TRAWLER	TREATERS
TRANT	TRASHED	TRAWLERS	TREATIES
TRANTED	TRASHER	TRAWLEY	TREATING
TRANTER	TRASHERS	TRAWLEYS	TREATINGS
TRANTERS	TRASHERY	TRAWLING	TREATISE
TRANTING	TRASHES	TRAWLINGS	TREATISES
TRANTS	TRASHIER	TRAWLNET	TREATMENT
TRAP	TRASHIEST	TRAWLNETS	TREATS
TRAPAN	TRASHILY	TRAWLS	TREATY
TRAPANNED	TRASHING	TRAY	TREBBIANO
TRAPANNER	TRASHMAN	TRAYBIT	TREBLE
TRAPANS	TRASHMEN	TRAYBITS	TREBLED
TRAPBALL	TRASHTRIE	TRAYFUL	TREBLES
TRAPBALLS	TRASHY	TRAYFULS	TREBLING
TRAPDOOR	TRASS	TRAYNE	TREBLY
TRAPDOORS	TRASSES	TRAYNED	TREBUCHET
TRAPE	TRAT	TRAYNES	TREBUCKET
TRAPED	TRATS	TRAYNING	TRECENTO
TRAPES	TRATT	TRAYS	TRECENTOS
TRAPESED	TRATTORIA	TRAZODONE	TRECK
TRAPESES	TRATTORIE	TREACHER	TRECKED
TRAPESING	TRATTS	TREACHERS	TRECKING
TRAPEZE	TRAUCHLE	TREACHERY	TRECKS
TRAPEZED	TRAUCHLED	TREACHOUR	TREDDLE
TRAPEZES	TRAUCHLES	TREACLE	TREDDLED
TRAPEZIA	TRAUMA	TREACLED	TREDDLES
TRAPEZIAL	TRAUMAS	TREACLES	TREDDLING
TRAPEZII	TRAUMATA	TREACLIER	TREDILLE
TRAPEZING	TRAUMATIC	TREACLING	TREDILLES
TRAPEZIST	TRAVAIL	TREACLY	TREDRILLE
TRAPEZIUM	TRAVAILED	TREAD	TREE
TRAPEZIUS	TRAVAILS	TREADED	TREED
TRAPEZOID	TRAVE	TREADER	TREEHOUSE
TRAPING	TRAVEL	TREADERS	TREEING
TRAPLIKE	TRAVELED	TREADING	TREELAWN
TRAPLINE	TRAVELER	TREADINGS	TREELAWNS
TRAPLINES	TRAVELERS	TREADLE	TREELESS
TRAPNEST	TRAVELING	TREADLED	TREELIKE
TRAPNESTS	TRAVELLED	TREADLER	TREEN
TRAPPEAN	TRAVELLER	TREADLERS	TREENAIL
TRAPPED	TRAVELOG	TREADLES	TREENAILS
TRAPPER	TRAVELOGS	TREADLESS	TREENS
TRAPPERS	TRAVELS	TREADLING	TREENWARE

TREES	TREMULANT	TRESSURED	TRIALWARE
TREESHIP	TREMULATE	TRESSURES	TRIANGLE
TREESHIPS	TREMULOUS	TRESSY	TRIANGLED
TREETOP	TRENAIL	TREST	TRIANGLES
TREETOPS	TRENAILS	TRESTLE	TRIAPSAL
TREEWARE	TRENCH	TRESTLES	TRIARCH
TREEWARES	TRENCHAND	TRESTS	TRIARCHS
TREEWAX	TRENCHANT	TRET	TRIARCHY
TREEWAXES	TRENCHARD	TRETINOIN	TRIASSIC
TREF	TRENCHED	TRETS	TRIATHLON
TREFA	TRENCHER	TREVALLY	TRIATIC
TREFAH	TRENCHERS	TREVALLYS	TRIATICS
TREFOIL	TRENCHES	TREVET	TRIATOMIC
TREFOILED	TRENCHING	TREVETS	TRIAXIAL
TREFOILS	TREND	TREVIS	TRIAXIALS
TREGETOUR	TRENDED	TREVISES	TRIAXON
TREHALA	TRENDIER	TREVISS	TRIAXONS
TREHALAS	TRENDIES	TREVISSES	TRIAZIN
TREHALOSE	TRENDIEST	TREW	TRIAZINE
TREIF	TRENDIFY	TREWS	TRIAZINES
TREIFA	TRENDILY	TREWSMAN	TRIAZINS
TREILLAGE	TRENDING	TREWSMEN	TRIAZOLE
TREILLE	TRENDOID	TREY	TRIAZOLES
TREILLES	TRENDOIDS	TREYBIT	TRIAZOLIC
TREK	TRENDS	TREYBITS	TRIBADE
TREKKED	TRENDY	TREYS	TRIBADES
TREKKER	TRENDYISM	TREZ	TRIBADIC
TREKKERS	TRENISE	TREZES	TRIBADIES
TREKKING	TRENISES	TRIABLE	TRIBADISM
TREKS	TRENTAL	TRIAC	TRIBADY
TRELLIS	TRENTALS	TRIACID	TRIBAL
TRELLISED	TREPAN	TRIACIDS	TRIBALISM
TRELLISES	TREPANG	TRIACS	TRIBALIST
TREMA	TREPANGS	TRIACT	TRIBALLY
TREMAS	TREPANNED	TRIACTINE	TRIBALS
TREMATIC	TREPANNER	TRIAD	TRIBASIC
TREMATODE	TREPANS	TRIADIC	TRIBBLE
TREMATOID	TREPHINE	TRIADICS	TRIBBLES
TREMBLANT	TREPHINED	TRIADISM	TRIBE
TREMBLE	TREPHINER	TRIADISMS	TRIBELESS
TREMBLED	TREPHINES	TRIADIST	TRIBES
TREMBLER	TREPID	TRIADISTS	TRIBESMAN
TREMBLERS	TREPIDANT	TRIADS	TRIBESMEN
TREMBLES	TREPONEMA	TRIAGE	TRIBLET
TREMBLIER	TREPONEME	TRIAGED	TRIBLETS
TREMBLING	TRES	TRIAGES	TRIBOLOGY
TREMBLY	TRESPASS	TRIAGING	TRIBRACH
TREMIE	TRESS	TRIAL	TRIBRACHS
TREMIES	TRESSED	TRIALISM	TRIBULATE
TREMOLANT	TRESSEL	TRIALISMS	TRIBUNAL
TREMOLITE	TRESSELS	TRIALIST	TRIBUNALS
TREMOLO	TRESSES	TRIALISTS	TRIBUNARY
TREMOLOS	TRESSIER	TRIALITY	TRIBUNATE
TREMOR	TRESSIEST	TRIALLED	TRIBUNE
TREMORED	TRESSING	TRIALLING	TRIBUNES
TREMORING	TRESSOUR	TRIALLIST	TRIBUTARY
TREMOROUS	TRESSOURS	TRIALOGUE	TRIBUTE
TREMORS	TRESSURE	TRIALS	TRIBUTER

TRIBUTERS	TRICLINIA	TRIFFER	TRIHEDRON
TRIBUTES	TRICLINIC	TRIFFEST	TRIHYBRID
TRICAR	TRICLOSAN	TRIFFIC	TRIHYDRIC
TRICARS	TRICOLOR	TRIFFID	TRIJET
TRICE	TRICOLORS	TRIFFIDS	TRIJETS
TRICED	TRICOLOUR	TRIFFIDY	TRIJUGATE
TRICEP	TRICORN	TRIFID	TRIJUGOUS
TRICEPS	TRICORNE	TRIFLE	TRIKE
TRICEPSES	TRICORNES	TRIFLED	TRIKES
TRICERION	TRICORNS	TRIFLER	TRILBIES
TRICES	TRICOT	TRIFLERS	TRILBY
TRICHINA	TRICOTINE	TRIFLES	TRILBYS
TRICHINAE	TRICOTS	TRIFLING	TRILD
TRICHINAL	TRICROTIC	TRIFLINGS	TRILEMMA
TRICHINAS	TRICTRAC	TRIFOCAL	TRILEMMAS
TRICHITE	TRICTRACS	TRIFOCALS	TRILINEAR
TRICHITES	TRICUSPID	TRIFOLD	TRILITH
TRICHITIC	TRICYCLE	TRIFOLIES	TRILITHIC
TRICHOID	TRICYCLED	TRIFOLIUM	TRILITHON
TRICHOME	TRICYCLER	TRIFOLY	TRILITHS
TRICHOMES	TRICYCLES	TRIFORIA	TRILL
TRICHOMIC	TRICYCLIC	TRIFORIAL	TRILLED
TRICHORD	TRIDACNA	TRIFORIUM	TRILLER
TRICHORDS	TRIDACNAS	TRIFORM	TRILLERS
TRICHOSES	TRIDACTYL	TRIFORMED	TRILLING
TRICHOSIS	TRIDARN	TRIG	TRILLINGS
TRICHROIC	TRIDARNS	TRIGAMIES	TRILLION
TRICHROME	TRIDE	TRIGAMIST	TRILLIONS
TRICING	TRIDENT	TRIGAMOUS	TRILLIUM
TRICK	TRIDENTAL	TRIGAMY	TRILLIUMS
TRICKED	TRIDENTED	TRIGGED	TRILLO
TRICKER	TRIDENTS	TRIGGER	TRILLOES
TRICKERS	TRIDUAN	TRIGGERED	TRILLS
TRICKERY	TRIDUUM	TRIGGERS	TRILOBAL
TRICKIE	TRIDUUMS	TRIGGEST	TRILOBATE
TRICKIER	TRIDYMITE	TRIGGING	TRILOBE
TRICKIEST	TRIE	TRIGLOT	TRILOBED
TRICKILY	TRIECIOUS	TRIGLOTS	TRILOBES
TRICKING	TRIED	TRIGLY	TRILOBITE
TRICKINGS	TRIELLA	TRIGLYPH	TRILOGIES
TRICKISH	TRIELLAS	TRIGLYPHS	TRILOGY
TRICKLE	TRIENE	TRIGNESS	TRIM
TRICKLED	TRIENES	TRIGO	TRIMARAN
TRICKLES	TRIENNIA	TRIGON	TRIMARANS
TRICKLESS	TRIENNIAL	TRIGONAL	TRIMER
TRICKLET	TRIENNIUM	TRIGONIC	TRIMERIC
TRICKLETS	TRIENS	TRIGONOUS	TRIMERISM
TRICKLIER	TRIENTES	TRIGONS	TRIMEROUS
TRICKLING	TRIER	TRIGOS	TRIMERS
TRICKLY	TRIERARCH	TRIGRAM	TRIMESTER
TRICKS	TRIERS	TRIGRAMS	TRIMETER
TRICKSIER	TRIES	TRIGRAPH	TRIMETERS
TRICKSOME	TRIETERIC	TRIGRAPHS	TRIMETHYL
TRICKSTER	TRIETHYL	TRIGS	TRIMETRIC
TRICKSY	TRIFACIAL	TRIGYNIAN	TRIMLY
TRICKY	TRIFECTA	TRIGYNOUS	TRIMMED
TRICLAD	TRIFECTAS	TRIHEDRA	TRIMMER
TRICLADS	TRIFF	TRIHEDRAL	TRIMMERS

TRIMMEST	TRIOXIDS	TRIPPINGS	TRISTATE
TRIMMING	TRIOXYGEN	TRIPPLE	TRISTE
TRIMMINGS	TRIP	TRIPPLED	TRISTESSE
TRIMNESS	TRIPACK	TRIPPLER	TRISTEZA
TRIMORPH	TRIPACKS	TRIPPLERS	TRISTEZAS
TRIMORPHS	TRIPART	TRIPPLES	TRISTFUL
TRIMOTOR	TRIPE	TRIPPLING	TRISTICH
TRIMOTORS	TRIPEDAL	TRIPPY	TRISTICHS
TRIMS	TRIPERIES	TRIPS	TRISUL
TRIMTAB	TRIPERY	TRIPSES	TRISULA
TRIMTABS	TRIPES	TRIPSIS	TRISULAS
TRIN	TRIPEY	TRIPTAN	TRISULS
TRINAL	TRIPHASE	TRIPTANE	TRITE
TRINARY	TRIPHONE	TRIPTANES	TRITELY
TRINDLE	TRIPHONES	TRIPTANS	TRITENESS
TRINDLED	TRIPIER	TRIPTOTE	TRITER
TRINDLES	TRIPIEST	TRIPTOTES	TRITES
TRINDLING	TRIPITAKA	TRIPTYCA	TRITEST
TRINE	TRIPLANE	TRIPTYCAS	TRITHEISM
TRINED	TRIPLANES	TRIPTYCH	TRITHEIST
TRINES	TRIPLE	TRIPTYCHS	TRITHING
TRINGLE	TRIPLED	TRIPTYQUE	TRITHINGS
TRINGLES	TRIPLES	TRIPUDIA	TRITIATE
TRINING	TRIPLET	TRIPUDIUM	TRITIATED
TRINITIES	TRIPLETS	TRIPWIRE	TRITIATES
TRINITRIN	TRIPLEX	TRIPWIRES	TRITICAL
TRINITY	TRIPLEXES	TRIPY	TRITICALE
TRINKET	TRIPLIED	TRIQUETRA	TRITICISM
TRINKETED	TRIPLIES	TRIRADIAL	TRITICUM
TRINKETER	TRIPLING	TRIREME	TRITICUMS
TRINKETRY	TRIPLINGS	TRIREMES	TRITIDE
TRINKETS	TRIPLITE	TRISAGION	TRITIDES
TRINKUM	TRIPLITES	TRISCELE	TRITIUM
TRINKUMS	TRIPLOID	TRISCELES	TRITIUMS
TRINODAL	TRIPLOIDS	TRISECT	TRITOMA
TRINOMIAL	TRIPLOIDY	TRISECTED	TRITOMAS
TRINS	TRIPLY	TRISECTOR	TRITON
TRIO	TRIPLYING	TRISECTS	TRITONE
TRIODE	TRIPOD	TRISEME	TRITONES
TRIODES	TRIPODAL	TRISEMES	TRITONIA
TRIOL	TRIPODIC	TRISEMIC	TRITONIAS
TRIOLEIN	TRIPODIES	TRISERIAL	TRITONS
TRIOLEINS	TRIPODS	TRISHAW	TRITURATE
TRIOLET	TRIPODY	TRISHAWS	TRIUMPH
TRIOLETS	TRIPOLI	TRISKELE	TRIUMPHAL
TRIOLS	TRIPOLIS	TRISKELES	TRIUMPHED
TRIONES	TRIPOS	TRISKELIA	TRIUMPHER
TRIONYM	TRIPOSES	TRISMIC	TRIUMPHS
TRIONYMAL	TRIPPANT	TRISMUS	TRIUMVIR
TRIONYMS	TRIPPED	TRISMUSES	TRIUMVIRI
TRIOR	TRIPPER	TRISODIUM	TRIUMVIRS
TRIORS	TRIPPERS	TRISOME	TRIUMVIRY
TRIOS	TRIPPERY	TRISOMES	TRIUNE
TRIOSE	TRIPPET	TRISOMIC	TRIUNES
TRIOSES	TRIPPETS	TRISOMICS	TRIUNITY
TRIOXID	TRIPPIER	TRISOMIES	TRIVALENT
TRIOXIDE	TRIPPIEST	TRISOMY	TRIVALVE
TRIOXIDES	TRIPPING	TRIST	TRIVALVED

TRIVALVES	TROD	TROMINOS	TROPIST
TRIVET	TRODDEN	TROMMEL	TROPISTIC
TRIVETS	TRODE	TROMMELS	TROPISTS
TRIVIA	TRODES	TROMP	TROPOLOGY
TRIVIAL	TRODS	TROMPE	TROPONIN
TRIVIALLY	TROELIE	TROMPED	TROPONINS
TRIVIUM	TROELIES	TROMPES	TROPPO
TRIVIUMS	TROELY	TROMPING	TROSSERS
TRIWEEKLY	TROFFER	TROMPS	TROT
TRIZONAL	TROFFERS	TRON	TROTH
TRIZONE	TROG	TRONA	TROTHED
TRIZONES	TROGGED	TRONAS	TROTHFUL
TROAD	TROGGING	TRONC	TROTHING
TROADE	TROGGS	TRONCS	TROTHLESS
TROADES	TROGON	TRONE	TROTHS
TROADS	TROGONS	TRONES	TROTLINE
TROAK	TROGS	TRONK	TROTLINES
TROAKED	TROIKA	TRONKS	TROTS
TROAKING	TROIKAS	TRONS	TROTTED
TROAKS	TROILISM	TROOLIE	TROTTER
TROAT	TROILISMS	TROOLIES	TROTTERS
TROATED	TROILIST	TROOP	TROTTING
TROATING	TROILISTS	TROOPED	TROTTINGS
TROATS	TROILITE	TROOPER	TROTTOIR
TROCAR	TROILITES	TROOPERS	TROTTOIRS
TROCARS	TROILUS	TROOPIAL	TROTYL
TROCHAIC	TROILUSES	TROOPIALS	TROTYLS
TROCHAICS	TROIS	TROOPING	TROUBLE
TROCHAL	TROKE	TROOPS	TROUBLED
TROCHAR	TROKED	TROOPSHIP	TROUBLER
TROCHARS	TROKES	TROOSTITE	TROUBLERS
TROCHE	TROKING	TROOZ	TROUBLES
TROCHEE	TROLAND	TROP	TROUBLING
TROCHEES	TROLANDS	TROPAEOLA	TROUBLOUS
TROCHES	TROLL	TROPARIA	TROUCH
TROCHI	TROLLED	TROPARION	TROUCHES
TROCHIL	TROLLER	TROPE	TROUGH
TROCHILI	TROLLERS	TROPED	TROUGHS
TROCHILIC	TROLLEY	TROPEOLIN	TROULE
TROCHILS	TROLLEYED	TROPES	TROULED
TROCHILUS	TROLLEYS	TROPHESY	TROULES
TROCHISK	TROLLIED	TROPHI	TROULING
TROCHISKS	TROLLIES	TROPHIC	TROUNCE
TROCHITE	TROLLING	TROPHIED	TROUNCED
TROCHITES	TROLLINGS	TROPHIES	TROUNCER
TROCHLEA	TROLLIUS	TROPHY	TROUNCERS
TROCHLEAE	TROLLOP	TROPHYING	TROUNCES
TROCHLEAR	TROLLOPED	TROPIC	TROUNCING
TROCHLEAS	TROLLOPEE	TROPICAL	TROUPE
TROCHOID	TROLLOPS	TROPICALS	TROUPED
TROCHOIDS	TROLLOPY	TROPICS	TROUPER
TROCHUS	TROLLS	TROPIN	TROUPERS
TROCHUSES	TROLLY	TROPINE	TROUPES
TROCK	TROLLYING	TROPINES	TROUPIAL
TROCKED	TROMBONE	TROPING	TROUPIALS
TROCKEN	TROMBONES	TROPINS	TROUPING
TROCKING	TROMINO	TROPISM	TROUSE
TROCKS	TROMINOES	TROPISMS	TROUSER

TROUSERED	TRUCHMANS	TRUFFES	TRUSSED
TROUSERS	TRUCHMEN	TRUFFLE	TRUSSER
TROUSES	TRUCIAL	TRUFFLED	TRUSSERS
TROUSSEAU	TRUCING	TRUFFLES	TRUSSES
TROUT	TRUCK	TRUFFLING	TRUSSING
TROUTER	TRUCKABLE	TRUG	TRUSSINGS
TROUTERS	TRUCKAGE	TRUGO	TRUST
TROUTFUL	TRUCKAGES	TRUGOS	TRUSTABLE
TROUTIER	TRUCKED	TRUGS	TRUSTED
TROUTIEST	TRUCKER	TRUING	TRUSTEE
TROUTING	TRUCKERS	TRUISM	TRUSTEED
TROUTINGS	TRUCKFUL	TRUISMS	TRUSTEES
TROUTLESS	TRUCKFULS	TRUISTIC	TRUSTER
TROUTLET	TRUCKIE	TRULL	TRUSTERS
TROUTLETS	TRUCKIES	TRULLS	TRUSTFUL
TROUTLING	TRUCKING	TRULY	TRUSTIER
TROUTS	TRUCKINGS	TRUMEAU	TRUSTIES
TROUTY	TRUCKLE	TRUMEAUX	TRUSTIEST
TROUVERE	TRUCKLED	TRUMP	TRUSTILY
TROUVERES	TRUCKLER	TRUMPED	TRUSTING
TROUVEUR	TRUCKLERS	TRUMPERY	TRUSTLESS
TROUVEURS	TRUCKLES	TRUMPET	TRUSTOR
TROVE	TRUCKLINE	TRUMPETED	TRUSTORS
TROVER	TRUCKLING	TRUMPETER	TRUSTS
TROVERS	TRUCKLOAD	TRUMPETS	TRUSTY
TROVES	TRUCKMAN	TRUMPING	TRUTH
TROW	TRUCKMEN	TRUMPINGS	TRUTHFUL
TROWED	TRUCKS	TRUMPLESS	TRUTHIER
TROWEL	TRUCKSTOP	TRUMPS	TRUTHIEST
TROWELED	TRUCULENT	TRUNCAL	TRUTHLESS
TROWELER	TRUDGE	TRUNCATE	TRUTHLIKE
TROWELERS	TRUDGED	TRUNCATED	TRUTHS
TROWELING	TRUDGEN	TRUNCATES	TRUTHY
TROWELLED	TRUDGENS	TRUNCHEON	TRY
TROWELLER	TRUDGEON	TRUNDLE	TRYE
TROWELS	TRUDGEONS	TRUNDLED	TRYER
TROWING	TRUDGER	TRUNDLER	TRYERS
TROWS	TRUDGERS	TRUNDLERS	TRYING
TROWSERS	TRUDGES	TRUNDLES	TRYINGLY
TROWTH	TRUDGING	TRUNDLING	TRYINGS
TROWTHS	TRUDGINGS	TRUNK	TRYKE
TROY	TRUE	TRUNKED	TRYKES
TROYS	TRUEBLUE	TRUNKFISH	TRYMA
TRUANCIES	TRUEBLUES	TRUNKFUL	TRYMATA
TRUANCY	TRUEBORN	TRUNKFULS	TRYOUT
TRUANT	TRUEBRED	TRUNKING	TRYOUTS
TRUANTED	TRUED	TRUNKINGS	TRYP
TRUANTING	TRUEING	TRUNKLESS	TRYPAN
TRUANTLY	TRUELOVE	TRUNKS	TRYPS
TRUANTRY	TRUELOVES	TRUNNEL	TRYPSIN
TRUANTS	TRUEMAN	TRUNNELS	TRYPSINS
TRUCAGE	TRUEMEN	TRUNNION	TRYPTIC
TRUCAGES	TRUENESS	TRUNNIONS	TRYSAIL
TRUCE	TRUEPENNY	TRUQUAGE	TRYSAILS
TRUCED	TRUER	TRUQUAGES	TRYST
TRUCELESS	TRUES	TRUQUEUR	TRYSTE
TRUCES	TRUEST	TRUQUEURS	TRYSTED
TRUCHMAN	TRUFFE	TRUSS	TRYSTER

TRYSTERS	TSOTSI	TUBERCLES	TUCKET
TRYSTES	TSOTSIS	TUBERCULA	TUCKETS
TRYSTING	TSOURIS	TUBERCULE	TUCKING
TRYSTS	TSOURISES	TUBEROID	TUCKS
TRYWORKS	TSUBA	TUBEROSE	TUCKSHOP
TSADDIK	TSUBAS	TUBEROSES	TUCKSHOPS
TSADDIKIM	TSUNAMI	TUBEROUS	TUCOTUCO
TSADDIKS	TSUNAMIC	TUBERS	TUCOTUCOS
TSADDIQ	TSUNAMIS	TUBES	TUCUTUCO
TSADDIQIM	TSURIS	TUBEWORK	TUCUTUCOS
TSADDIQS	TSURISES	TUBEWORKS	TUCUTUCU
TSADE	TSUTSUMU	TUBEWORM	TUCUTUCUS
TSADES	TSUTSUMUS	TUBEWORMS	TUFA
TSADI	TUAN	TUBFAST	TUFACEOUS
TSADIS	TUANS	TUBFASTS	TUFAS
TSAMBA	TUART	TUBFISH	TUFF
TSAMBAS	TUARTS	TUBFISHES	TUFFE
TSANTSA	TUATARA	TUBFUL	TUFFES
TSANTSAS	TUATARAS	TUBFULS	TUFFET
TSAR	TUATERA	TUBICOLAR	TUFFETS
TSARDOM	TUATERAS	TUBICOLE	TUFFS
TSARDOMS	TUATH	TUBICOLES	TUFOLI
TSAREVICH	TUATHS	TUBIFEX	TUFT
TSAREVNA	TUATUA	TUBIFEXES	TUFTED
TSAREVNAS	TUB	TUBIFICID	TUFTER
TSARINA	TUBA	TUBIFORM	TUFTERS
TSARINAS	TUBAE	TUBING	TUFTIER
TSARISM	TUBAGE	TUBINGS	TUFTIEST
TSARISMS	TUBAGES	TUBIST	TUFTILY
TSARIST	TUBAIST	TUBISTS	TUFTING
TSARISTS	TUBAISTS	TUBLIKE	TUFTINGS
TSARITSA	TUBAL	TUBS	TUFTS
TSARITSAS	TUBAR	TUBULAR	TUFTY
TSARITZA	TUBAS	TUBULARLY	TUG
TSARITZAS	TUBATE	TUBULATE	TUGBOAT
TSARS	TUBBABLE	TUBULATED	TUGBOATS
TSATSKE	TUBBED	TUBULATES	TUGGED
TSATSKES	TUBBER	TUBULATOR	TUGGER
TSESSEBE	TUBBERS	TUBULE	TUGGERS
TSESSEBES	TUBBIER	TUBULES	TUGGING
TSETSE	TUBBIEST	TUBULIN	TUGGINGLY
TSETSES	TUBBINESS	TUBULINS	TUGGINGS
TSIGANE	TUBBING	TUBULOSE	TUGHRA
TSIGANES	TUBBINGS	TUBULOUS	TUGHRAS
TSIMMES	TUBBISH	TUBULURE	TUGHRIK
TSITSITH	TUBBY	TUBULURES	TUGHRIKS
TSK	TUBE	TUCHUN	TUGLESS
TSKED	TUBECTOMY	TUCHUNS	TUGRA
TSKING	TUBED	TUCK	TUGRAS
TSKS	TUBEFUL	TUCKAHOE	TUGRIK
TSKTSK	TUBEFULS	TUCKAHOES	TUGRIKS
TSKTSKED	TUBELESS	TUCKED	TUGS
TSKTSKING	TUBELIKE	TUCKER	TUI
TSKTSKS	TUBENOSE	TUCKERBAG	TUILLE
TSOORIS	TUBENOSES	TUCKERBOX	TUILLES
TSORES	TUBER	TUCKERED	TUILLETTE
TSORIS	TUBERCLE	TUCKERING	TUILYIE
TSORRISS	TUBERCLED	TUCKERS	TUILYIED

TUILYIES	TUMESCE	TUNDS	TUPEK
TUILZIE	TUMESCED	TUNDUN	TUPEKS
TUILZIED	TUMESCENT	TUNDUNS	TUPELO
TUILZIES	TUMESCES	TUNE	TUPELOS
TUINA	TUMESCING	TUNEABLE	TUPIK
TUINAS	TUMID	TUNEABLY	TUPIKS
TUIS	TUMIDITY	TUNED	TUPLE
TUISM	TUMIDLY	TUNEFUL	TUPLES
TUISMS	TUMIDNESS	TUNEFULLY	TUPPED
TUITION	TUMMIES	TUNELESS	TUPPENCE
TUITIONAL	TUMMLER	TUNER	TUPPENCES
TUITIONS	TUMMLERS	TUNERS	TUPPENNY
TUKTOO	TUMMY	TUNES	TUPPING
TUKTOOS	TUMOR	TUNESMITH	TUPS
TUKTU	TUMORAL	TUNEUP	TUPTOWING
TUKTUS	TUMORLIKE	TUNEUPS	TUPUNA
TULADI	TUMOROUS	TUNG	TUPUNAS
TULADIS	TUMORS	TUNGS	TUQUE
TULAREMIA	TUMOUR	TUNGSTATE	TUQUES
TULAREMIC	TUMOURS	TUNGSTEN	TURACIN
TULBAN	TUMP	TUNGSTENS	TURACINS
TULBANS	TUMPED	TUNGSTIC	TURACO
TULCHAN	TUMPHIES	TUNGSTITE	TURACOS
TULCHANS	TUMPHY	TUNGSTOUS	TURACOU
TULE	TUMPIER	TUNIC	TURACOUS
TULES	TUMPIEST	TUNICA	TURBAN
TULIP	TUMPING	TUNICAE	TURBAND
TULIPANT	TUMPLINE	TUNICATE	TURBANDS
TULIPANTS	TUMPLINES	TUNICATED	TURBANED
TULIPLIKE	TUMPS	TUNICATES	TURBANNED
TULIPS	TUMPY	TUNICIN	TURBANS
TULIPWOOD	TUMS	TUNICINS	TURBANT
TULLE	TUMSHIE	TUNICKED	TURBANTS
TULLES	TUMSHIES	TUNICLE	TURBARIES
TULLIBEE	TUMULAR	TUNICLES	TURBARY
TULLIBEES	TUMULARY	TUNICS	TURBETH
TULPA	TUMULI	TUNIER	TURBETHS
TULPAS	TUMULOSE	TUNIEST	TURBID
TULWAR	TUMULOUS	TUNING	TURBIDITE
TULWARS	TUMULT	TUNINGS	TURBIDITY
TUM	TUMULTED	TUNNAGE	TURBIDLY
TUMBLE	TUMULTING	TUNNAGES	TURBINAL
TUMBLEBUG	TUMULTS	TUNNED	TURBINALS
TUMBLED	TUMULUS	TUNNEL	TURBINATE
TUMBLER	TUMULUSES	TUNNELED	TURBINE
TUMBLERS	TUN	TUNNELER	TURBINED
TUMBLES	TUNA	TUNNELERS	TURBINES
TUMBLESET	TUNABLE	TUNNELING	TURBIT
TUMBLING	TUNABLY	TUNNELLED	TURBITH
TUMBLINGS	TUNAS	TUNNELLER	TURBITHS
TUMBREL	TUNBELLY	TUNNELS	TURBITS
TUMBRELS	TUND	TUNNIES	TURBO
TUMBRIL	TUNDED	TUNNING	TURBOCAR
TUMBRILS	TUNDING	TUNNINGS	TURBOCARS
TUMEFIED	TUNDISH	TUNNY	TURBOFAN
TUMEFIES	TUNDISHES	TUNS	TURBOFANS
TUMEFY	TUNDRA	TUNY	TURBOJET
TUMEFYING	TUNDRAS	TUP	TURBOJETS

TURBOND	TURKOIS	TURNSOLES	TUSSAHS
TURBONDS	TURKOISES	TURNSPIT	TUSSAL
TURBOPROP	TURKS	TURNSPITS	TUSSAR
TURBOS	TURLOUGH	TURNSTILE	TUSSARS
TURBOT	TURLOUGHS	TURNSTONE	TUSSEH
TURBOTS	TURM	TURNTABLE	TUSSEHS
TURBULENT	TURME	TURNUP	TUSSER
TURCOPOLE	TURMERIC	TURNUPS	TUSSERS
TURD	TURMERICS	TUROPHILE	TUSSES
TURDINE	TURMES	TURPETH	TUSSIS
TURDION	TURMOIL	TURPETHS	TUSSISES
TURDIONS	TURMOILED	TURPITUDE	TUSSIVE
TURDOID	TURMOILS	TURPS	TUSSLE
TURDS	TURMS	TURQUOIS	TUSSLED
TUREEN	TURN	TURQUOISE	TUSSLES
TUREENS	TURNABLE	TURRET	TUSSLING
TURF	TURNABOUT	TURRETED	TUSSOCK
TURFED	TURNAGAIN	TURRETS	TUSSOCKED
TURFEN	TURNBACK	TURRIBANT	TUSSOCKS
TURFGRASS	TURNBACKS	TURRICAL	TUSSOCKY
TURFIER	TURNCOAT	TURTLE	TUSSOR
TURFIEST	TURNCOATS	TURTLED	TUSSORE
TURFINESS	TURNCOCK	TURTLER	TUSSORES
TURFING	TURNCOCKS	TURTLERS	TUSSORS
TURFINGS	TURNDOWN	TURTLES	TUSSUCK
TURFITE	TURNDOWNS	TURTLING	TUSSUCKS
TURFITES	TURNDUN	TURTLINGS	TUSSUR
TURFLESS	TURNDUNS	TURVES	TUSSURS
TURFLIKE	TURNED	TUSCHE	TUT
TURFMAN	TURNER	TUSCHES	TUTANIA
TURFMEN	TURNERIES	TUSH	TUTANIAS
TURFS	TURNERS	TUSHED	TUTEE
TURFSKI	TURNERY	TUSHERIES	TUTEES
TURFSKIS	TURNHALL	TUSHERY	TUTELAGE
TURFY	TURNHALLS	TUSHES	TUTELAGES
TURGENCY	TURNING	TUSHIE	TUTELAR
TURGENT	TURNINGS	TUSHIES	TUTELARS
TURGENTLY	TURNIP	TUSHING	TUTELARY
TURGID	TURNIPED	TUSHKAR	TUTENAG
TURGIDER	TURNIPING	TUSHKARS	TUTENAGS
TURGIDEST	TURNIPS	TUSHKER	TUTIORISM
TURGIDITY	TURNKEY	TUSHKERS	TUTIORIST
TURGIDLY	TURNKEYS	TUSHY	TUTMAN
TURGITE	TURNOFF	TUSK	TUTMEN
TURGITES	TURNOFFS	TUSKAR	TUTOR
TURGOR	TURNON	TUSKARS	TUTORAGE
TURGORS	TURNONS	TUSKED	TUTORAGES
TURION	TURNOUT	TUSKER	TUTORED
TURIONS	TURNOUTS	TUSKERS	TUTORESS
TURISTA	TURNOVER	TUSKIER	TUTORIAL
TURISTAS	TURNOVERS	TUSKIEST	TUTORIALS
TURK	TURNPIKE	TUSKING	TUTORING
TURKEY	TURNPIKES	TUSKINGS	TUTORINGS
TURKEYS	TURNROUND	TUSKLESS	TUTORISE
TURKIES	TURNS	TUSKLIKE	TUTORISED
TURKIESES	TURNSKIN	TUSKS	TUTORISES
TURKIS	TURNSKINS	TUSKY	TUTORISM
TURKISES	TURNSOLE	TUSSAH	TUTORISMS

TUTORIZE	TWAINS	TWEEDLER	TWICER
TUTORIZED	TWAITE	TWEEDLERS	TWICERS
TUTORIZES	TWAITES	TWEEDLES	TWICHILD
TUTORS	TWAL	TWEEDLING	TWIDDLE
TUTORSHIP	TWALPENNY	TWEEDS	TWIDDLED
TUTOYED	TWALS	TWEEDY	TWIDDLER
TUTOYER	TWANG	TWEEL	TWIDDLERS
TUTOYERED	TWANGED	TWEELED	TWIDDLES
TUTOYERS	TWANGER	TWEELING	TWIDDLIER
TUTRESS	TWANGERS	TWEELS	TWIDDLING
TUTRESSES	TWANGIER	TWEELY	TWIDDLY
TUTRICES	TWANGIEST	TWEEN	TWIER
TUTRIX	TWANGING	TWEENAGER	TWIERS
TUTRIXES	TWANGINGS	TWEENER	TWIFOLD
TUTS	TWANGLE	TWEENERS	TWIFORKED
TUTSAN	TWANGLED	TWEENESS	TWIFORMED
TUTSANS	TWANGLER	TWEENIE	TWIG
TUTSED	TWANGLERS	TWEENIES	TWIGGED
TUTSES	TWANGLES	TWEENS	TWIGGEN
TUTSING	TWANGLING	TWEENY	TWIGGER
TUTTED	TWANGS	TWEER	TWIGGERS
TUTTI	TWANGY	TWEERED	TWIGGIER
TUTTIES	TWANK	TWEERING	TWIGGIEST
TUTTING	TWANKAY	TWEERS	TWIGGING
TUTTINGS	TWANKAYS	TWEEST	TWIGGY
TUTTIS	TWANKIES	TWEET	TWIGHT
TUTTY	TWANKS	TWEETED	TWIGHTED
TUTU	TWANKY	TWEETER	TWIGHTING
TUTUED	TWAS	TWEETERS	TWIGHTS
TUTUS	TWASOME	TWEETING	TWIGLESS
TUTWORK	TWASOMES	TWEETS	TWIGLIKE
TUTWORKER	TWAT	TWEEZE	TWIGLOO
TUTWORKS	TWATS	TWEEZED	TWIGLOOS
TUX	TWATTLE	TWEEZER	TWIGS
TUXEDO	TWATTLED	TWEEZERS	TWIGSOME
TUXEDOED	TWATTLER	TWEEZES	TWILIGHT
TUXEDOES	TWATTLERS	TWEEZING	TWILIGHTS
TUXEDOS	TWATTLES	TWELFTH	TWILIT
TUXES	TWATTLING	TWELFTHLY	TWILL
TUYER	TWAY	TWELFTHS	TWILLED
TUYERE	TWAYBLADE	TWELVE	TWILLIES
TUYERES	TWAYS	TWELVEMO	TWILLING
TUYERS	TWEAK	TWELVEMOS	TWILLINGS
TUZZ	TWEAKED	TWELVES	TWILLS
TUZZES	TWEAKER	TWENTIES	TWILLY
TWA	TWEAKERS	TWENTIETH	TWILT
TWADDLE	TWEAKIER	TWENTY	TWILTED
TWADDLED	TWEAKIEST	TWENTYISH	TWILTING
TWADDLER	TWEAKING	TWERP	TWILTS
TWADDLERS	TWEAKINGS	TWERPIER	TWIN
TWADDLES	TWEAKS	TWERPIEST	TWINBERRY
TWADDLIER	TWEAKY	TWERPS	TWINBORN
TWADDLING	TWEE	TWERPY	TWINE
TWADDLY	TWEED	TWIBIL	TWINED
TWAE	TWEEDIER	TWIBILL	TWINER
TWAES	TWEEDIEST	TWIBILLS	TWINERS
TWAFALD	TWEEDLE	TWIBILS	TWINES
TWAIN	TWEEDLED	TWICE	TWINGE

TWINGED	TWIST	TWONIE	TYMPANI
TWINGEING	TWISTABLE	TWONIES	TYMPANIC
TWINGES	TWISTED	TWOONIE	TYMPANICS
TWINGING	TWISTER	TWOONIES	TYMPANIES
TWINIER	TWISTERS	TWOPENCE	TYMPANIST
TWINIEST	TWISTIER	TWOPENCES	TYMPANO
TWINIGHT	TWISTIEST	TWOPENNY	TYMPANS
TWINING	TWISTING	TWOS	TYMPANUM
TWININGLY	TWISTINGS	TWOSEATER	TYMPANUMS
TWININGS	TWISTOR	TWOSOME	TYMPANY
TWINJET	TWISTORS	TWOSOMES	TYMPS
TWINJETS	TWISTS	TWOSTROKE	TYND
TWINK	TWISTY	TWP	TYNDE
TWINKED	TWIT	TWYER	TYNE
TWINKIE	TWITCH	TWYERE	TYNED
TWINKIES	TWITCHED	TWYERES	TYNES
TWINKING	TWITCHER	TWYERS	TYNING
TWINKLE	TWITCHERS	TWYFOLD	TYPABLE
TWINKLED	TWITCHES	TYCHISM	TYPAL
TWINKLER	TWITCHIER	TYCHISMS	TYPE
TWINKLERS	TWITCHILY	TYCOON	TYPEABLE
TWINKLES	TWITCHING	TYCOONATE	TYPEBAR
TWINKLING	TWITCHY	TYCOONERY	TYPEBARS
TWINKLY	TWITE	TYCOONS	TYPECASE
TWINKS	TWITES	TYDE	TYPECASES
TWINLING	TWITS	TYE	TYPECAST
TWINLINGS	TWITTED	TYED	TYPECASTS
TWINNED	TWITTEN	TYEE	TYPED
TWINNING	TWITTENS	TYEES	TYPEFACE
TWINNINGS	TWITTER	TYEING	TYPEFACES
TWINS	TWITTERED	TYER	TYPES
TWINSET	TWITTERER	TYERS	TYPESET
TWINSETS	TWITTERS	TYES	TYPESETS
TWINSHIP	TWITTERY	TYG	TYPESTYLE
TWINSHIPS	TWITTING	TYGS	TYPEWRITE
TWINTER	TWITTINGS	TYIN	TYPEWROTE
TWINTERS	TWIXT	TYING	TYPEY
TWINY	TWIZZLE	TYIYN	TYPHLITIC
TWIRE	TWIZZLED	TYKE	TYPHLITIS
TWIRED	TWIZZLES	TYKES	TYPHOID
TWIRES	TWIZZLING	TYKISH	TYPHOIDAL
TWIRING	TWO	TYLECTOMY	TYPHOIDIN
TWIRL	TWOCCER	TYLER	TYPHOIDS
TWIRLED	TWOCCERS	TYLERS	TYPHON
TWIRLER	TWOCCING	TYLOPOD	TYPHONIAN
TWIRLERS	TWOCCINGS	TYLOPODS	TYPHONIC
TWIRLIER	TWOCKER	TYLOSES	TYPHONS
TWIRLIEST	TWOCKERS	TYLOSIN	TYPHOON
TWIRLING	TWOCKING	TYLOSINS	TYPHOONS
TWIRLS	TWOCKINGS	TYLOSIS	TYPHOSE
TWIRLY	TWOER	TYLOTE	TYPHOUS
TWIRP	TWOERS	TYLOTES	TYPHUS
TWIRPIER	TWOFER	TYMBAL	TYPHUSES
TWIRPIEST	TWOFERS	TYMBALS	TYPIC
TWIRPS	TWOFOLD	TYMP	TYPICAL
TWIRPY	TWOFOLDS	TYMPAN	TYPICALLY
TWISCAR	TWONESS	TYMPANA	TYPIER
TWISCARS	TWONESSES	TYMPANAL	TYPIEST

TYPIFIED
TYPIFIER
TYPIFIERS
TYPIFIES
TYPIFY
TYPIFYING
TYPING
TYPINGS
TYPIST
TYPISTS
TYPO
TYPOGRAPH
TYPOLOGIC
TYPOLOGY
TYPOMANIA
TYPOS
TYPP
TYPPS
TYPTO
TYPTOED
TYPTOING
TYPTOS
TYPY
TYRAMINE
TYRAMINES
TYRAN
TYRANED
TYRANING
TYRANNE
TYRANNED
TYRANNES
TYRANNESS
TYRANNIC
TYRANNIES
TYRANNING
TYRANNIS
TYRANNISE
TYRANNIZE
TYRANNOUS
TYRANNY
TYRANS
TYRANT
TYRANTED
TYRANTING
TYRANTS
TYRE
TYRED
TYRELESS
TYRES
TYRING
TYRO
TYROCIDIN
TYROES
TYRONES
TYRONIC
TYROPITTA
TYROS
TYROSINE

TYROSINES
TYSTIE
TYSTIES
TYTE
TYTHE
TYTHED
TYTHES
TYTHING
TZADDIK
TZADDIKIM
TZADDIKS
TZADDIQ
TZADDIQIM
TZADDIQS
TZAR
TZARDOM
TZARDOMS
TZAREVNA
TZAREVNAS
TZARINA
TZARINAS
TZARISM
TZARISMS
TZARIST
TZARISTS
TZARITZA
TZARITZAS
TZARS
TZATZIKI
TZATZIKIS
TZETSE
TZETSES
TZETZE
TZETZES
TZIGANE
TZIGANES
TZIGANIES
TZIGANY
TZIMMES
TZITZIS
TZITZIT
TZITZITH
TZURIS

U

UAKARI
UAKARIS
UBEROUS
UBERTIES
UBERTY
UBIETIES
UBIETY
UBIQUE
UBIQUITIN
UBIQUITY
UCKERS
UDAL
UDALLER
UDALLERS
UDALS
UDDER
UDDERED
UDDERFUL
UDDERLESS
UDDERS
UDO
UDOMETER
UDOMETERS
UDOMETRIC
UDOMETRY
UDON
UDONS
UDOS
UDS
UEY
UEYS
UFO
UFOLOGIES
UFOLOGIST
UFOLOGY
UFOS
UG
UGALI
UGALIS
UGGED
UGGING
UGH
UGHS
UGLIED
UGLIER
UGLIES
UGLIEST
UGLIFIED
UGLIFIER
UGLIFIERS
UGLIFIES
UGLIFY
UGLIFYING

UGLILY
UGLINESS
UGLY
UGLYING
UGS
UGSOME
UH
UHLAN
UHLANS
UHURU
UHURUS
UILLEAN
UINTAHITE
UINTAITE
UINTAITES
UITLANDER
UJAMAA
UJAMAAS
UKASE
UKASES
UKE
UKELELE
UKELELES
UKES
UKULELE
UKULELES
ULAMA
ULAMAS
ULAN
ULANS
ULCER
ULCERATE
ULCERATED
ULCERATES
ULCERED
ULCERING
ULCEROUS
ULCERS
ULE
ULEMA
ULEMAS
ULES
ULEX
ULEXES
ULEXITE
ULEXITES
ULICON
ULICONS
ULIGINOSE
ULIGINOUS
ULIKON
ULIKONS
ULITIS

ULITISES
ULLAGE
ULLAGED
ULLAGES
ULLAGING
ULLING
ULLINGS
ULMACEOUS
ULMIN
ULMINS
ULNA
ULNAD
ULNAE
ULNAR
ULNARE
ULNARIA
ULNAS
ULOSES
ULOSIS
ULOTRICHY
ULPAN
ULPANIM
ULSTER
ULSTERED
ULSTERS
ULTERIOR
ULTIMA
ULTIMACY
ULTIMAS
ULTIMATA
ULTIMATE
ULTIMATED
ULTIMATES
ULTIMATUM
ULTIMO
ULTION
ULTIONS
ULTRA
ULTRACHIC
ULTRACOLD
ULTRACOOL
ULTRADRY
ULTRAFAST
ULTRAFINE
ULTRAHEAT
ULTRAHIGH
ULTRAHIP
ULTRAHOT
ULTRAISM
ULTRAISMS
ULTRAIST
ULTRAISTS
ULTRALEFT

ULTRALOW
ULTRAPOSH
ULTRAPURE
ULTRARARE
ULTRARED
ULTRAREDS
ULTRARICH
ULTRAS
ULTRASAFE
ULTRASLOW
ULTRASOFT
ULTRATHIN
ULTRATINY
ULTRAWIDE
ULU
ULULANT
ULULATE
ULULATED
ULULATES
ULULATING
ULULATION
ULUS
ULVA
ULVAS
ULYIE
ULYIES
ULZIE
ULZIES
UM
UMAMI
UMAMIS
UMANGITE
UMANGITES
UMBEL
UMBELED
UMBELLAR
UMBELLATE
UMBELLED
UMBELLET
UMBELLETS
UMBELLULE
UMBELS
UMBER
UMBERED
UMBERING
UMBERS
UMBERY
UMBILICAL
UMBILICI
UMBILICUS
UMBLE
UMBLES
UMBO

UMBONAL	UMPIRAGE	UNAIMED	UNATTIRED
UMBONATE	UMPIRAGES	UNAIRED	UNATTUNED
UMBONES	UMPIRE	UNAIS	UNAU
UMBONIC	UMPIRED	UNAKIN	UNAUDITED
UMBOS	UMPIRES	UNAKING	UNAUS
UMBRA	UMPIRING	UNAKITE	UNAVENGED
UMBRACULA	UMPS	UNAKITES	UNAVERAGE
UMBRAE	UMPTEEN	UNALARMED	UNAVERTED
UMBRAGE	UMPTEENTH	UNALERTED	UNAVOIDED
UMBRAGED	UMPTIETH	UNALIGNED	UNAVOWED
UMBRAGES	UMPTY	UNALIKE	UNAWAKE
UMBRAGING	UMPY	UNALIST	UNAWAKED
UMBRAL	UMQUHILE	UNALISTS	UNAWARDED
UMBRAS	UMTEENTH	UNALIVE	UNAWARE
UMBRATED	UMU	UNALLAYED	UNAWARELY
UMBRATIC	UMWELT	UNALLEGED	UNAWARES
UMBRATILE	UMWELTS	UNALLIED	UNAWED
UMBRE	UMWHILE	UNALLOWED	UNAWESOME
UMBREL	UN	UNALLOYED	UNAXED
UMBRELLA	UNABASHED	UNALTERED	UNBACKED
UMBRELLAS	UNABATED	UNAMASSED	UNBAFFLED
UMBRELLO	UNABATING	UNAMAZED	UNBAG
UMBRELLOS	UNABETTED	UNAMENDED	UNBAGGED
UMBRELS	UNABIDING	UNAMERCED	UNBAGGING
UMBRERE	UNABJURED	UNAMIABLE	UNBAGS
UMBRERES	UNABLE	UNAMUSED	UNBAITED
UMBRES	UNABORTED	UNAMUSING	UNBAKED
UMBRETTE	UNABRADED	UNANCHOR	UNBALANCE
UMBRETTES	UNABUSED	UNANCHORS	UNBALE
UMBRIERE	UNABUSIVE	UNANELED	UNBALED
UMBRIERES	UNACCRUED	UNANIMITY	UNBALES
UMBRIL	UNACCUSED	UNANIMOUS	UNBALING
UMBRILS	UNACERBIC	UNANNEXED	UNBAN
UMBROSE	UNACHING	UNANNOYED	UNBANDAGE
UMBROUS	UNACIDIC	UNANXIOUS	UNBANDED
UMFAZI	UNACTABLE	UNAPPAREL	UNBANKED
UMFAZIS	UNACTED	UNAPPLIED	UNBANNED
UMIAC	UNACTIVE	UNAPT	UNBANNING
UMIACK	UNADAPTED	UNAPTLY	UNBANS
UMIACKS	UNADDED	UNAPTNESS	UNBAPTISE
UMIACS	UNADEPT	UNARCHED	UNBAPTIZE
UMIAK	UNADEPTLY	UNARGUED	UNBAR
UMIAKS	UNADMIRED	UNARISEN	UNBARBED
UMIAQ	UNADOPTED	UNARM	UNBARE
UMIAQS	UNADORED	UNARMED	UNBARED
UMLAUT	UNADORNED	UNARMING	UNBARES
UMLAUTED	UNADULT	UNARMORED	UNBARING
UMLAUTING	UNADVISED	UNARMS	UNBARK
UMLAUTS	UNAFRAID	UNAROUSED	UNBARKED
UMLUNGU	UNAGED	UNARRAYED	UNBARKING
UMLUNGUS	UNAGEING	UNARTFUL	UNBARKS
UMM	UNAGILE	UNARY	UNBARRED
UMP	UNAGING	UNASHAMED	UNBARRING
UMPED	UNAGREED	UNASKED	UNBARS
UMPH	UNAI	UNASSAYED	UNBASED
UMPIE	UNAIDABLE	UNASSUMED	UNBASHFUL
UMPIES	UNAIDED	UNASSURED	UNBASTED
UMPING	UNAIDEDLY	UNATONED	UNBATED

625

UNBATHED	UNBITT	UNBOUGHT	UNBURROW
UNBE	UNBITTED	UNBOUNCY	UNBURROWS
UNBEAR	UNBITTEN	UNBOUND	UNBURTHEN
UNBEARDED	UNBITTER	UNBOUNDED	UNBURY
UNBEARED	UNBITTING	UNBOWED	UNBURYING
UNBEARING	UNBITTS	UNBOWING	UNBUSTED
UNBEARS	UNBLAMED	UNBOX	UNBUSY
UNBEATEN	UNBLENDED	UNBOXED	UNBUTTON
UNBED	UNBLENT	UNBOXES	UNBUTTONS
UNBEDDED	UNBLESS	UNBOXING	UNCAGE
UNBEDDING	UNBLESSED	UNBRACE	UNCAGED
UNBEDS	UNBLESSES	UNBRACED	UNCAGES
UNBEEN	UNBLEST	UNBRACES	UNCAGING
UNBEGET	UNBLIND	UNBRACING	UNCAKE
UNBEGETS	UNBLINDED	UNBRAID	UNCAKED
UNBEGGED	UNBLINDS	UNBRAIDED	UNCAKES
UNBEGOT	UNBLOCK	UNBRAIDS	UNCAKING
UNBEGUILE	UNBLOCKED	UNBRAKE	UNCALLED
UNBEGUN	UNBLOCKS	UNBRAKED	UNCANDID
UNBEING	UNBLOODED	UNBRAKES	UNCANDLED
UNBEINGS	UNBLOODY	UNBRAKING	UNCANDOUR
UNBEKNOWN	UNBLOTTED	UNBRANDED	UNCANNED
UNBELIEF	UNBLOWED	UNBRASTE	UNCANNIER
UNBELIEFS	UNBLOWN	UNBRED	UNCANNILY
UNBELIEVE	UNBLUNTED	UNBREECH	UNCANNY
UNBELOVED	UNBLURRED	UNBRIDGED	UNCANONIC
UNBELT	UNBOARDED	UNBRIDLE	UNCAP
UNBELTED	UNBOBBED	UNBRIDLED	UNCAPABLE
UNBELTING	UNBODIED	UNBRIDLES	UNCAPE
UNBELTS	UNBODING	UNBRIEFED	UNCAPED
UNBEMUSED	UNBOILED	UNBRIGHT	UNCAPES
UNBEND	UNBOLT	UNBRIZZED	UNCAPING
UNBENDED	UNBOLTED	UNBROILED	UNCAPPED
UNBENDING	UNBOLTING	UNBROKE	UNCAPPING
UNBENDS	UNBOLTS	UNBROKEN	UNCAPS
UNBENIGN	UNBONDED	UNBROWNED	UNCARDED
UNBENT	UNBONE	UNBRUISED	UNCAREFUL
UNBEREFT	UNBONED	UNBRUSED	UNCARING
UNBERUFEN	UNBONES	UNBRUSHED	UNCART
UNBESEEM	UNBONING	UNBUCKLE	UNCARTED
UNBESEEMS	UNBONNET	UNBUCKLED	UNCARTING
UNBESPEAK	UNBONNETS	UNBUCKLES	UNCARTS
UNBESPOKE	UNBOOKED	UNBUDDED	UNCARVED
UNBIAS	UNBOOKISH	UNBUDGING	UNCASE
UNBIASED	UNBOOT	UNBUILD	UNCASED
UNBIASES	UNBOOTED	UNBUILDS	UNCASES
UNBIASING	UNBOOTING	UNBUILT	UNCASHED
UNBIASSED	UNBOOTS	UNBULKY	UNCASING
UNBIASSES	UNBORE	UNBUNDLE	UNCASKED
UNBID	UNBORN	UNBUNDLED	UNCAST
UNBIDDEN	UNBORNE	UNBUNDLER	UNCATCHY
UNBIGOTED	UNBOSOM	UNBUNDLES	UNCATE
UNBILLED	UNBOSOMED	UNBURDEN	UNCATERED
UNBIND	UNBOSOMER	UNBURDENS	UNCAUGHT
UNBINDING	UNBOSOMS	UNBURIED	UNCAUSED
UNBINDS	UNBOTTLE	UNBURIES	UNCE
UNBISHOP	UNBOTTLED	UNBURNED	UNCEASING
UNBISHOPS	UNBOTTLES	UNBURNT	UNCEDED

UNCERTAIN	UNCITED	UNCLOYED	UNCOUNTED
UNCES	UNCIVIL	UNCLOYING	UNCOUPLE
UNCESSANT	UNCIVILLY	UNCLUTCH	UNCOUPLED
UNCHAIN	UNCLAD	UNCLUTTER	UNCOUPLER
UNCHAINED	UNCLAIMED	UNCO	UNCOUPLES
UNCHAINS	UNCLAMP	UNCOATED	UNCOURTLY
UNCHAIR	UNCLAMPED	UNCOATING	UNCOUTH
UNCHAIRED	UNCLAMPS	UNCOBBLED	UNCOUTHER
UNCHAIRS	UNCLARITY	UNCOCK	UNCOUTHLY
UNCHANCY	UNCLASP	UNCOCKED	UNCOVER
UNCHANGED	UNCLASPED	UNCOCKING	UNCOVERED
UNCHARGE	UNCLASPS	UNCOCKS	UNCOVERS
UNCHARGED	UNCLASSED	UNCODED	UNCOWL
UNCHARGES	UNCLASSY	UNCOER	UNCOWLED
UNCHARITY	UNCLAWED	UNCOERCED	UNCOWLING
UNCHARM	UNCLE	UNCOES	UNCOWLS
UNCHARMED	UNCLEAN	UNCOEST	UNCOY
UNCHARMS	UNCLEANED	UNCOFFIN	UNCOYNED
UNCHARNEL	UNCLEANER	UNCOFFINS	UNCRACKED
UNCHARRED	UNCLEANLY	UNCOIL	UNCRATE
UNCHARTED	UNCLEAR	UNCOILED	UNCRATED
UNCHARY	UNCLEARED	UNCOILING	UNCRATES
UNCHASTE	UNCLEARER	UNCOILS	UNCRATING
UNCHASTER	UNCLEARLY	UNCOINED	UNCRAZY
UNCHECK	UNCLED	UNCOLORED	UNCREATE
UNCHECKED	UNCLEFT	UNCOLT	UNCREATED
UNCHECKS	UNCLENCH	UNCOLTED	UNCREATES
UNCHEERED	UNCLES	UNCOLTING	UNCREWED
UNCHEWED	UNCLESHIP	UNCOLTS	UNCROPPED
UNCHIC	UNCLEW	UNCOMBED	UNCROSS
UNCHICLY	UNCLEWED	UNCOMBINE	UNCROSSED
UNCHILD	UNCLEWING	UNCOMELY	UNCROSSES
UNCHILDED	UNCLEWS	UNCOMIC	UNCROWDED
UNCHILDS	UNCLICHED	UNCOMMON	UNCROWN
UNCHILLED	UNCLINCH	UNCONCERN	UNCROWNED
UNCHOKE	UNCLING	UNCONFINE	UNCROWNS
UNCHOKED	UNCLIP	UNCONFORM	UNCRUDDED
UNCHOKES	UNCLIPPED	UNCONFUSE	UNCRUMPLE
UNCHOKING	UNCLIPS	UNCONGEAL	UNCRUSHED
UNCHOSEN	UNCLIPT	UNCOOKED	UNCTION
UNCHRISOM	UNCLOAK	UNCOOL	UNCTIONS
UNCHURCH	UNCLOAKED	UNCOOLED	UNCTUOUS
UNCI	UNCLOAKS	UNCOPE	UNCUFF
UNCIA	UNCLOG	UNCOPED	UNCUFFED
UNCIAE	UNCLOGGED	UNCOPES	UNCUFFING
UNCIAL	UNCLOGS	UNCOPING	UNCUFFS
UNCIALLY	UNCLOSE	UNCORD	UNCULLED
UNCIALS	UNCLOSED	UNCORDED	UNCURABLE
UNCIFORM	UNCLOSES	UNCORDIAL	UNCURABLY
UNCIFORMS	UNCLOSING	UNCORDING	UNCURB
UNCINAL	UNCLOTHE	UNCORDS	UNCURBED
UNCINARIA	UNCLOTHED	UNCORK	UNCURBING
UNCINATE	UNCLOTHES	UNCORKED	UNCURBS
UNCINATED	UNCLOUD	UNCORKING	UNCURDLED
UNCINI	UNCLOUDED	UNCORKS	UNCURED
UNCINUS	UNCLOUDS	UNCORRUPT	UNCURIOUS
UNCIPHER	UNCLOUDY	UNCOS	UNCURL
UNCIPHERS	UNCLOVEN	UNCOSTLY	UNCURLED

UNCURLING	UNDEIFIES	UNDERFED	UNDERPAID
UNCURLS	UNDEIFY	UNDERFEED	UNDERPART
UNCURRENT	UNDELAYED	UNDERFELT	UNDERPASS
UNCURSE	UNDELETED	UNDERFIRE	UNDERPAY
UNCURSED	UNDELIGHT	UNDERFISH	UNDERPAYS
UNCURSES	UNDELUDED	UNDERFLOW	UNDERPEEP
UNCURSING	UNDENIED	UNDERFONG	UNDERPIN
UNCURTAIN	UNDENTED	UNDERFOOT	UNDERPINS
UNCURVED	UNDER	UNDERFUND	UNDERPLAY
UNCUS	UNDERACT	UNDERFUR	UNDERPLOT
UNCUT	UNDERACTS	UNDERFURS	UNDERPROP
UNCUTE	UNDERAGE	UNDERGIRD	UNDERRAN
UNCYNICAL	UNDERAGED	UNDERGIRT	UNDERRATE
UNDAM	UNDERAGES	UNDERGO	UNDERRIPE
UNDAMAGED	UNDERARM	UNDERGOD	UNDERRUN
UNDAMMED	UNDERARMS	UNDERGODS	UNDERRUNS
UNDAMMING	UNDERATE	UNDERGOER	UNDERSAID
UNDAMNED	UNDERBAKE	UNDERGOES	UNDERSAY
UNDAMPED	UNDERBEAR	UNDERGONE	UNDERSAYS
UNDAMS	UNDERBID	UNDERGOWN	UNDERSEA
UNDARING	UNDERBIDS	UNDERGRAD	UNDERSEAL
UNDASHED	UNDERBIT	UNDERHAIR	UNDERSEAS
UNDATABLE	UNDERBITE	UNDERHAND	UNDERSELF
UNDATE	UNDERBODY	UNDERHEAT	UNDERSELL
UNDATED	UNDERBORE	UNDERHUNG	UNDERSET
UNDAUNTED	UNDERBOSS	UNDERIVED	UNDERSETS
UNDAWNING	UNDERBRED	UNDERJAW	UNDERSHOT
UNDAZZLE	UNDERBRIM	UNDERJAWS	UNDERSIDE
UNDAZZLED	UNDERBUD	UNDERKEEP	UNDERSIGN
UNDAZZLES	UNDERBUDS	UNDERKEPT	UNDERSIZE
UNDE	UNDERBUSH	UNDERKILL	UNDERSKY
UNDEAD	UNDERBUY	UNDERKING	UNDERSOIL
UNDEAF	UNDERBUYS	UNDERLAID	UNDERSOLD
UNDEAFED	UNDERCARD	UNDERLAIN	UNDERSONG
UNDEAFING	UNDERCART	UNDERLAP	UNDERSPIN
UNDEAFS	UNDERCAST	UNDERLAPS	UNDERTAKE
UNDEALT	UNDERCLAD	UNDERLAY	UNDERTANE
UNDEAR	UNDERCLAY	UNDERLAYS	UNDERTAX
UNDEBASED	UNDERCLUB	UNDERLEAF	UNDERTIME
UNDEBATED	UNDERCOAT	UNDERLET	UNDERTINT
UNDECAGON	UNDERCOOK	UNDERLETS	UNDERTONE
UNDECAYED	UNDERCOOL	UNDERLIE	UNDERTOOK
UNDECEIVE	UNDERCUT	UNDERLIER	UNDERTOW
UNDECENT	UNDERCUTS	UNDERLIES	UNDERTOWS
UNDECIDED	UNDERDAKS	UNDERLINE	UNDERUSE
UNDECIMAL	UNDERDECK	UNDERLING	UNDERUSED
UNDECK	UNDERDID	UNDERLIP	UNDERUSES
UNDECKED	UNDERDO	UNDERLIPS	UNDERVEST
UNDECKING	UNDERDOER	UNDERLIT	UNDERVOTE
UNDECKS	UNDERDOES	UNDERLOAD	UNDERWAY
UNDEE	UNDERDOG	UNDERMAN	UNDERWEAR
UNDEEDED	UNDERDOGS	UNDERMANS	UNDERWENT
UNDEFACED	UNDERDONE	UNDERMEN	UNDERWING
UNDEFIDE	UNDERDOSE	UNDERMINE	UNDERWIRE
UNDEFIED	UNDERDRAW	UNDERMOST	UNDERWIT
UNDEFILED	UNDERDREW	UNDERN	UNDERWITS
UNDEFINED	UNDEREAT	UNDERNOTE	UNDERWOOD
UNDEIFIED	UNDEREATS	UNDERNS	UNDERWOOL

UNDERWORK	UNDRILLED	UNENGAGED	UNFASTEN
UNDESERT	UNDRIVEN	UNENJOYED	UNFASTENS
UNDESERTS	UNDROSSY	UNENSURED	UNFAULTY
UNDESERVE	UNDROWNED	UNENTERED	UNFAVORED
UNDESIRED	UNDRUNK	UNENVIED	UNFAZED
UNDEVOUT	UNDUBBED	UNENVIOUS	UNFEARED
UNDID	UNDUE	UNENVYING	UNFEARFUL
UNDIES	UNDUG	UNEQUABLE	UNFEARING
UNDIGHT	UNDULANCE	UNEQUAL	UNFED
UNDIGHTS	UNDULANCY	UNEQUALED	UNFEED
UNDIGNIFY	UNDULANT	UNEQUALLY	UNFEELING
UNDILUTED	UNDULAR	UNEQUALS	UNFEIGNED
UNDIMMED	UNDULATE	UNERASED	UNFELLED
UNDINE	UNDULATED	UNEROTIC	UNFELT
UNDINES	UNDULATES	UNERRING	UNFELTED
UNDINISM	UNDULATOR	UNESPIED	UNFENCE
UNDINISMS	UNDULLED	UNESSAYED	UNFENCED
UNDINTED	UNDULOSE	UNESSENCE	UNFENCES
UNDIPPED	UNDULOUS	UNETH	UNFENCING
UNDIVIDED	UNDULY	UNETHICAL	UNFERTILE
UNDIVINE	UNDUTEOUS	UNEVADED	UNFETTER
UNDO	UNDUTIFUL	UNEVEN	UNFETTERS
UNDOABLE	UNDY	UNEVENER	UNFEUDAL
UNDOCILE	UNDYED	UNEVENEST	UNFEUED
UNDOCK	UNDYING	UNEVENLY	UNFIGURED
UNDOCKED	UNDYINGLY	UNEVOLVED	UNFILDE
UNDOCKING	UNDYNAMIC	UNEXALTED	UNFILED
UNDOCKS	UNEAGER	UNEXCITED	UNFILIAL
UNDOER	UNEAGERLY	UNEXCUSED	UNFILLED
UNDOERS	UNEARED	UNEXOTIC	UNFILMED
UNDOES	UNEARNED	UNEXPERT	UNFINE
UNDOING	UNEARTH	UNEXPIRED	UNFIRED
UNDOINGS	UNEARTHED	UNEXPOSED	UNFIRM
UNDONE	UNEARTHLY	UNEXTINCT	UNFISHED
UNDOOMED	UNEARTHS	UNEXTREME	UNFIT
UNDOTTED	UNEASE	UNEYED	UNFITLY
UNDOUBLE	UNEASES	UNFABLED	UNFITNESS
UNDOUBLED	UNEASIER	UNFACT	UNFITS
UNDOUBLES	UNEASIEST	UNFACTS	UNFITTED
UNDOUBTED	UNEASILY	UNFADABLE	UNFITTER
UNDRAINED	UNEASY	UNFADED	UNFITTEST
UNDRAPE	UNEATABLE	UNFADING	UNFITTING
UNDRAPED	UNEATEN	UNFAILING	UNFIX
UNDRAPES	UNEATH	UNFAIR	UNFIXED
UNDRAPING	UNEATHES	UNFAIRED	UNFIXES
UNDRAW	UNEDGE	UNFAIRER	UNFIXING
UNDRAWING	UNEDGED	UNFAIREST	UNFIXITY
UNDRAWN	UNEDGES	UNFAIRING	UNFIXT
UNDRAWS	UNEDGING	UNFAIRLY	UNFLAPPED
UNDREADED	UNEDIBLE	UNFAIRS	UNFLASHY
UNDREAMED	UNEDITED	UNFAITH	UNFLAWED
UNDREAMT	UNEFFACED	UNFAITHS	UNFLEDGED
UNDRESS	UNELATED	UNFAKED	UNFLESH
UNDRESSED	UNELECTED	UNFALLEN	UNFLESHED
UNDRESSES	UNEMPTIED	UNFAMED	UNFLESHES
UNDREST	UNENDED	UNFAMOUS	UNFLESHLY
UNDREW	UNENDING	UNFANCY	UNFLEXED
UNDRIED	UNENDOWED	UNFANNED	UNFLOORED

UNFLUSH	UNFURLED	UNGLOVES	UNGUMMING
UNFLUSHED	UNFURLING	UNGLOVING	UNGUMS
UNFLUSHES	UNFURLS	UNGLUE	UNGYVE
UNFLUTED	UNFURNISH	UNGLUED	UNGYVED
UNFLYABLE	UNFURRED	UNGLUES	UNGYVES
UNFOCUSED	UNFUSED	UNGLUING	UNGYVING
UNFOILED	UNFUSSIER	UNGOD	UNHABLE
UNFOLD	UNFUSSILY	UNGODDED	UNHACKED
UNFOLDED	UNFUSSY	UNGODDING	UNHAILED
UNFOLDER	UNGAG	UNGODLIER	UNHAIR
UNFOLDERS	UNGAGGED	UNGODLIKE	UNHAIRED
UNFOLDING	UNGAGGING	UNGODLILY	UNHAIRER
UNFOLDS	UNGAGS	UNGODLY	UNHAIRERS
UNFOND	UNGAIN	UNGODS	UNHAIRING
UNFOOL	UNGAINFUL	UNGORD	UNHAIRS
UNFOOLED	UNGAINLY	UNGORED	UNHALLOW
UNFOOLING	UNGALLANT	UNGORGED	UNHALLOWS
UNFOOLS	UNGALLED	UNGOT	UNHALSED
UNFOOTED	UNGARBED	UNGOTTEN	UNHALVED
UNFORBID	UNGARBLED	UNGOWN	UNHAND
UNFORCED	UNGATED	UNGOWNED	UNHANDED
UNFORGED	UNGAUGED	UNGOWNING	UNHANDIER
UNFORGOT	UNGAZING	UNGOWNS	UNHANDILY
UNFORKED	UNGEAR	UNGRACED	UNHANDING
UNFORM	UNGEARED	UNGRADED	UNHANDLED
UNFORMAL	UNGEARING	UNGRASSED	UNHANDS
UNFORMED	UNGEARS	UNGRAVELY	UNHANDY
UNFORMING	UNGELDED	UNGRAZED	UNHANG
UNFORMS	UNGENIAL	UNGREASED	UNHANGED
UNFORTUNE	UNGENTEEL	UNGREEDY	UNHANGING
UNFOUGHT	UNGENTLE	UNGROOMED	UNHANGS
UNFOUND	UNGENTLY	UNGROUND	UNHAPPIED
UNFOUNDED	UNGENUINE	UNGROUPED	UNHAPPIER
UNFRAMED	UNGERMANE	UNGROWN	UNHAPPIES
UNFRANKED	UNGET	UNGRUDGED	UNHAPPILY
UNFRAUGHT	UNGETS	UNGUAL	UNHAPPY
UNFREE	UNGETTING	UNGUARD	UNHARBOUR
UNFREED	UNGHOSTLY	UNGUARDED	UNHARDY
UNFREEDOM	UNGIFTED	UNGUARDS	UNHARMED
UNFREEING	UNGILD	UNGUENT	UNHARMFUL
UNFREEMAN	UNGILDED	UNGUENTA	UNHARMING
UNFREEMEN	UNGILDING	UNGUENTS	UNHARNESS
UNFREES	UNGILDS	UNGUENTUM	UNHARRIED
UNFREEZE	UNGILT	UNGUES	UNHASP
UNFREEZES	UNGIRD	UNGUESSED	UNHASPED
UNFRETTED	UNGIRDED	UNGUIDED	UNHASPING
UNFRIEND	UNGIRDING	UNGUIFORM	UNHASPS
UNFRIENDS	UNGIRDS	UNGUILTY	UNHASTING
UNFROCK	UNGIRT	UNGUINOUS	UNHASTY
UNFROCKED	UNGIRTH	UNGUIS	UNHAT
UNFROCKS	UNGIRTHED	UNGULA	UNHATCHED
UNFROZE	UNGIRTHS	UNGULAE	UNHATS
UNFROZEN	UNGIVING	UNGULAR	UNHATTED
UNFUELLED	UNGLAD	UNGULATE	UNHATTING
UNFUMED	UNGLAZED	UNGULATES	UNHAUNTED
UNFUNDED	UNGLOSSED	UNGULED	UNHEAD
UNFUNNY	UNGLOVE	UNGUM	UNHEADED
UNFURL	UNGLOVED	UNGUMMED	UNHEADING

UNHEADS	UNHOLILY	UNIFACE	UNIQUER
UNHEAL	UNHOLPEN	UNIFACES	UNIQUES
UNHEALED	UNHOLY	UNIFIABLE	UNIQUEST
UNHEALING	UNHOMELY	UNIFIC	UNIRAMOSE
UNHEALS	UNHONEST	UNIFIED	UNIRAMOUS
UNHEALTH	UNHONORED	UNIFIER	UNIRONED
UNHEALTHS	UNHOOD	UNIFIERS	UNIRONIC
UNHEALTHY	UNHOODED	UNIFIES	UNIS
UNHEARD	UNHOODING	UNIFILAR	UNISERIAL
UNHEARSE	UNHOODS	UNIFORM	UNISEX
UNHEARSED	UNHOOK	UNIFORMED	UNISEXES
UNHEARSES	UNHOOKED	UNIFORMER	UNISEXUAL
UNHEART	UNHOOKING	UNIFORMLY	UNISIZE
UNHEARTED	UNHOOKS	UNIFORMS	UNISON
UNHEARTS	UNHOOP	UNIFY	UNISONAL
UNHEATED	UNHOOPED	UNIFYING	UNISONANT
UNHEDGED	UNHOOPING	UNIFYINGS	UNISONOUS
UNHEEDED	UNHOOPS	UNIJUGATE	UNISONS
UNHEEDFUL	UNHOPED	UNILINEAL	UNISSUED
UNHEEDILY	UNHOPEFUL	UNILINEAR	UNIT
UNHEEDING	UNHORSE	UNILLUMED	UNITAGE
UNHEEDY	UNHORSED	UNILOBAR	UNITAGES
UNHELE	UNHORSES	UNILOBED	UNITAL
UNHELED	UNHORSING	UNIMBUED	UNITARD
UNHELES	UNHOSTILE	UNIMPEDED	UNITARDS
UNHELING	UNHOUSE	UNIMPOSED	UNITARIAN
UNHELM	UNHOUSED	UNINCITED	UNITARILY
UNHELMED	UNHOUSES	UNINDEXED	UNITARY
UNHELMING	UNHOUSING	UNINJURED	UNITE
UNHELMS	UNHUMAN	UNINSTALL	UNITED
UNHELPED	UNHUMANLY	UNINSURED	UNITEDLY
UNHELPFUL	UNHUMBLED	UNINURED	UNITER
UNHEPPEN	UNHUNG	UNINVITED	UNITERS
UNHEROIC	UNHUNTED	UNINVOKED	UNITES
UNHERST	UNHURRIED	UNION	UNITIES
UNHEWN	UNHURT	UNIONISE	UNITING
UNHIDDEN	UNHURTFUL	UNIONISED	UNITINGS
UNHINGE	UNHUSK	UNIONISER	UNITION
UNHINGED	UNHUSKED	UNIONISES	UNITIONS
UNHINGES	UNHUSKING	UNIONISM	UNITISE
UNHINGING	UNHUSKS	UNIONISMS	UNITISED
UNHIP	UNI	UNIONIST	UNITISER
UNHIPPER	UNIALGAL	UNIONISTS	UNITISERS
UNHIPPEST	UNIAXIAL	UNIONIZE	UNITISES
UNHIRABLE	UNIBODY	UNIONIZED	UNITISING
UNHIRED	UNIBROW	UNIONIZER	UNITIVE
UNHITCH	UNIBROWS	UNIONIZES	UNITIVELY
UNHITCHED	UNICITIES	UNIONS	UNITIZE
UNHITCHES	UNICITY	UNIPAROUS	UNITIZED
UNHIVE	UNICOLOR	UNIPED	UNITIZER
UNHIVED	UNICOLOUR	UNIPEDS	UNITIZERS
UNHIVES	UNICORN	UNIPLANAR	UNITIZES
UNHIVING	UNICORNS	UNIPOD	UNITIZING
UNHOARD	UNICYCLE	UNIPODS	UNITRUST
UNHOARDED	UNICYCLED	UNIPOLAR	UNITRUSTS
UNHOARDS	UNICYCLES	UNIPOTENT	UNITS
UNHOLIER	UNIDEAED	UNIQUE	UNITY
UNHOLIEST	UNIDEAL	UNIQUELY	UNIVALENT

UNIVALVE	UNKNIT	UNLETTED	UNLOOSENS
UNIVALVED	UNKNITS	UNLEVEL	UNLOOSES
UNIVALVES	UNKNITTED	UNLEVELED	UNLOOSING
UNIVERSAL	UNKNOT	UNLEVELS	UNLOPPED
UNIVERSE	UNKNOTS	UNLEVIED	UNLORD
UNIVERSES	UNKNOTTED	UNLICH	UNLORDED
UNIVOCAL	UNKNOWING	UNLICKED	UNLORDING
UNIVOCALS	UNKNOWN	UNLID	UNLORDLY
UNJADED	UNKNOWNS	UNLIDDED	UNLORDS
UNJAM	UNKOSHER	UNLIDDING	UNLOSABLE
UNJAMMED	UNLABELED	UNLIDS	UNLOST
UNJAMMING	UNLABORED	UNLIGHTED	UNLOVABLE
UNJAMS	UNLACE	UNLIKABLE	UNLOVE
UNJEALOUS	UNLACED	UNLIKE	UNLOVED
UNJOINED	UNLACES	UNLIKED	UNLOVELY
UNJOINT	UNLACING	UNLIKELY	UNLOVES
UNJOINTED	UNLADE	UNLIKES	UNLOVING
UNJOINTS	UNLADED	UNLIMBER	UNLUCKIER
UNJOYFUL	UNLADEN	UNLIMBERS	UNLUCKILY
UNJOYOUS	UNLADES	UNLIME	UNLUCKY
UNJUDGED	UNLADING	UNLIMED	UNLYRICAL
UNJUST	UNLADINGS	UNLIMES	UNMACHO
UNJUSTER	UNLAID	UNLIMING	UNMADE
UNJUSTEST	UNLASH	UNLIMITED	UNMAILED
UNJUSTLY	UNLASHED	UNLINE	UNMAIMED
UNKED	UNLASHES	UNLINEAL	UNMAKABLE
UNKEELED	UNLASHING	UNLINED	UNMAKE
UNKEMPT	UNLAST	UNLINES	UNMAKER
UNKEMPTLY	UNLASTE	UNLINING	UNMAKERS
UNKEND	UNLATCH	UNLINK	UNMAKES
UNKENNED	UNLATCHED	UNLINKED	UNMAKING
UNKENNEL	UNLATCHES	UNLINKING	UNMAKINGS
UNKENNELS	UNLAW	UNLINKS	UNMAN
UNKENT	UNLAWED	UNLISTED	UNMANACLE
UNKEPT	UNLAWFUL	UNLIT	UNMANAGED
UNKET	UNLAWING	UNLIVABLE	UNMANFUL
UNKID	UNLAWS	UNLIVE	UNMANLIER
UNKIND	UNLAY	UNLIVED	UNMANLIKE
UNKINDER	UNLAYING	UNLIVELY	UNMANLY
UNKINDEST	UNLAYS	UNLIVES	UNMANNED
UNKINDLED	UNLEAD	UNLIVING	UNMANNING
UNKINDLY	UNLEADED	UNLOAD	UNMANNISH
UNKING	UNLEADEDS	UNLOADED	UNMANS
UNKINGED	UNLEADING	UNLOADER	UNMANTLE
UNKINGING	UNLEADS	UNLOADERS	UNMANTLED
UNKINGLY	UNLEAL	UNLOADING	UNMANTLES
UNKINGS	UNLEARN	UNLOADS	UNMANURED
UNKINK	UNLEARNED	UNLOBED	UNMAPPED
UNKINKED	UNLEARNS	UNLOCATED	UNMARD
UNKINKING	UNLEARNT	UNLOCK	UNMARKED
UNKINKS	UNLEASED	UNLOCKED	UNMARRED
UNKISS	UNLEASH	UNLOCKING	UNMARRIED
UNKISSED	UNLEASHED	UNLOCKS	UNMARRIES
UNKISSES	UNLEASHES	UNLOGICAL	UNMARRY
UNKISSING	UNLED	UNLOOKED	UNMASK
UNKNELLED	UNLESS	UNLOOSE	UNMASKED
UNKNIGHT	UNLET	UNLOOSED	UNMASKER
UNKNIGHTS	UNLETHAL	UNLOOSEN	UNMASKERS

UNMASKING	UNMONIED	UNNUANCED	UNPENNED
UNMASKS	UNMOOR	UNOBEYED	UNPENNIED
UNMATCHED	UNMOORED	UNOBVIOUS	UNPENNING
UNMATED	UNMOORING	UNOFFERED	UNPENS
UNMATTED	UNMOORS	UNOFTEN	UNPENT
UNMATURED	UNMORAL	UNOILED	UNPEOPLE
UNMEANING	UNMORALLY	UNOPEN	UNPEOPLED
UNMEANT	UNMORTISE	UNOPENED	UNPEOPLES
UNMEEK	UNMOTIVED	UNOPPOSED	UNPERCH
UNMEET	UNMOULD	UNORDER	UNPERCHED
UNMEETLY	UNMOULDED	UNORDERED	UNPERCHES
UNMELLOW	UNMOULDS	UNORDERLY	UNPERFECT
UNMELTED	UNMOUNT	UNORDERS	UNPERPLEX
UNMENDED	UNMOUNTED	UNORNATE	UNPERSON
UNMERITED	UNMOUNTS	UNOWED	UNPERSONS
UNMERRY	UNMOURNED	UNOWNED	UNPERVERT
UNMESH	UNMOVABLE	UNPACED	UNPICK
UNMESHED	UNMOVABLY	UNPACK	UNPICKED
UNMESHES	UNMOVED	UNPACKED	UNPICKING
UNMESHING	UNMOVEDLY	UNPACKER	UNPICKS
UNMET	UNMOVING	UNPACKERS	UNPIERCED
UNMETED	UNMOWN	UNPACKING	UNPILE
UNMEW	UNMUFFLE	UNPACKS	UNPILED
UNMEWED	UNMUFFLED	UNPADDED	UNPILES
UNMEWING	UNMUFFLES	UNPAGED	UNPILING
UNMEWS	UNMUSICAL	UNPAID	UNPILOTED
UNMILKED	UNMUZZLE	UNPAINED	UNPIN
UNMILLED	UNMUZZLED	UNPAINFUL	UNPINKED
UNMINDED	UNMUZZLES	UNPAINT	UNPINKT
UNMINDFUL	UNNAIL	UNPAINTED	UNPINNED
UNMINED	UNNAILED	UNPAINTS	UNPINNING
UNMINGLE	UNNAILING	UNPAIRED	UNPINS
UNMINGLED	UNNAILS	UNPALSIED	UNPITIED
UNMINGLES	UNNAMABLE	UNPANEL	UNPITIFUL
UNMIRY	UNNAMED	UNPANELS	UNPITTED
UNMISSED	UNNANELD	UNPANGED	UNPITYING
UNMITER	UNNATIVE	UNPANNEL	UNPLACE
UNMITERED	UNNATURAL	UNPANNELS	UNPLACED
UNMITERS	UNNEATH	UNPAPER	UNPLACES
UNMITRE	UNNEEDED	UNPAPERED	UNPLACING
UNMITRED	UNNEEDFUL	UNPAPERS	UNPLAGUED
UNMITRES	UNNERVE	UNPARED	UNPLAINED
UNMITRING	UNNERVED	UNPARTED	UNPLAIT
UNMIX	UNNERVES	UNPARTIAL	UNPLAITED
UNMIXABLE	UNNERVING	UNPATCHED	UNPLAITS
UNMIXED	UNNEST	UNPATHED	UNPLANKED
UNMIXEDLY	UNNESTED	UNPAVED	UNPLANNED
UNMIXES	UNNESTING	UNPAY	UNPLANTED
UNMIXING	UNNESTS	UNPAYABLE	UNPLAYED
UNMIXT	UNNETHES	UNPAYING	UNPLEASED
UNMOANED	UNNETTED	UNPAYS	UNPLEATED
UNMODISH	UNNOBLE	UNPEELED	UNPLEDGED
UNMOLD	UNNOBLED	UNPEERED	UNPLIABLE
UNMOLDED	UNNOBLES	UNPEG	UNPLIABLY
UNMOLDING	UNNOBLING	UNPEGGED	UNPLIANT
UNMOLDS	UNNOISY	UNPEGGING	UNPLOWED
UNMOLTEN	UNNOTED	UNPEGS	UNPLUCKED
UNMONEYED	UNNOTICED	UNPEN	UNPLUG

UNPLUGGED	UNPRUNED	UNREASON	UNRIFLED
UNPLUGS	UNPUCKER	UNREASONS	UNRIG
UNPLUMB	UNPUCKERS	UNREAVE	UNRIGGED
UNPLUMBED	UNPULLED	UNREAVED	UNRIGGING
UNPLUMBS	UNPURE	UNREAVES	UNRIGHT
UNPLUME	UNPURELY	UNREAVING	UNRIGHTS
UNPLUMED	UNPURGED	UNREBATED	UNRIGS
UNPLUMES	UNPURSE	UNREBUKED	UNRIMED
UNPLUMING	UNPURSED	UNRECKED	UNRINGED
UNPOETIC	UNPURSES	UNRED	UNRINSED
UNPOINTED	UNPURSING	UNREDREST	UNRIP
UNPOISED	UNPURSUED	UNREDUCED	UNRIPE
UNPOISON	UNPUZZLE	UNREDY	UNRIPELY
UNPOISONS	UNPUZZLED	UNREEL	UNRIPENED
UNPOLICED	UNPUZZLES	UNREELED	UNRIPER
UNPOLISH	UNQUAKING	UNREELER	UNRIPEST
UNPOLITE	UNQUALIFY	UNREELERS	UNRIPPED
UNPOLITIC	UNQUEEN	UNREELING	UNRIPPING
UNPOLLED	UNQUEENED	UNREELS	UNRIPS
UNPOPE	UNQUEENLY	UNREEVE	UNRISEN
UNPOPED	UNQUEENS	UNREEVED	UNRIVALED
UNPOPES	UNQUELLED	UNREEVES	UNRIVEN
UNPOPING	UNQUIET	UNREEVING	UNRIVET
UNPOPULAR	UNQUIETED	UNREFINED	UNRIVETED
UNPOSED	UNQUIETER	UNREFUTED	UNRIVETS
UNPOSTED	UNQUIETLY	UNREIN	UNROASTED
UNPOTABLE	UNQUIETS	UNREINED	UNROBE
UNPOTTED	UNQUOTE	UNREINING	UNROBED
UNPRAISE	UNQUOTED	UNREINS	UNROBES
UNPRAISED	UNQUOTES	UNRELATED	UNROBING
UNPRAISES	UNQUOTING	UNRELAXED	UNROLL
UNPRAY	UNRACED	UNREMOVED	UNROLLED
UNPRAYED	UNRACKED	UNRENEWED	UNROLLING
UNPRAYING	UNRAISED	UNRENT	UNROLLS
UNPRAYS	UNRAKE	UNRENTED	UNROOF
UNPREACH	UNRAKED	UNREPAID	UNROOFED
UNPRECISE	UNRAKES	UNREPAIR	UNROOFING
UNPREDICT	UNRAKING	UNREPAIRS	UNROOFS
UNPREPARE	UNRANKED	UNRESERVE	UNROOST
UNPRESSED	UNRATED	UNREST	UNROOSTED
UNPRETTY	UNRAVAGED	UNRESTED	UNROOSTS
UNPRICED	UNRAVEL	UNRESTFUL	UNROOT
UNPRIEST	UNRAVELED	UNRESTING	UNROOTED
UNPRIESTS	UNRAVELS	UNRESTS	UNROOTING
UNPRIMED	UNRAZED	UNRETIRE	UNROOTS
UNPRINTED	UNRAZORED	UNRETIRED	UNROPE
UNPRISON	UNREACHED	UNRETIRES	UNROPED
UNPRISONS	UNREAD	UNREVISED	UNROPES
UNPRIZED	UNREADIER	UNREVOKED	UNROPING
UNPROBED	UNREADILY	UNRHYMED	UNROSINED
UNPROP	UNREADY	UNRIBBED	UNROTTED
UNPROPER	UNREAL	UNRID	UNROTTEN
UNPROPPED	UNREALISE	UNRIDABLE	UNROUGED
UNPROPS	UNREALISM	UNRIDDEN	UNROUGH
UNPROVED	UNREALITY	UNRIDDLE	UNROUND
UNPROVEN	UNREALIZE	UNRIDDLED	UNROUNDED
UNPROVIDE	UNREALLY	UNRIDDLER	UNROUNDS
UNPROVOKE	UNREAPED	UNRIDDLES	UNROUSED

UNROVE	UNSCALING	UNSERIOUS	UNSHOE
UNROVEN	UNSCANNED	UNSERVED	UNSHOED
UNROYAL	UNSCARRED	UNSET	UNSHOEING
UNROYALLY	UNSCARY	UNSETS	UNSHOES
UNRUBBED	UNSCATHED	UNSETTING	UNSHOOT
UNRUDE	UNSCENTED	UNSETTLE	UNSHOOTED
UNRUFFE	UNSCOURED	UNSETTLED	UNSHOOTS
UNRUFFLE	UNSCREW	UNSETTLES	UNSHORN
UNRUFFLED	UNSCREWED	UNSEVERED	UNSHOT
UNRUFFLES	UNSCREWS	UNSEW	UNSHOUT
UNRULE	UNSCYTHED	UNSEWED	UNSHOUTED
UNRULED	UNSEAL	UNSEWING	UNSHOUTS
UNRULES	UNSEALED	UNSEWN	UNSHOWN
UNRULIER	UNSEALING	UNSEWS	UNSHOWY
UNRULIEST	UNSEALS	UNSEX	UNSHRIVED
UNRULY	UNSEAM	UNSEXED	UNSHRIVEN
UNRUMPLED	UNSEAMED	UNSEXES	UNSHROUD
UNRUSHED	UNSEAMING	UNSEXING	UNSHROUDS
UNRUSTED	UNSEAMS	UNSEXIST	UNSHRUBD
UNS	UNSEARED	UNSEXUAL	UNSHRUNK
UNSADDLE	UNSEASON	UNSEXY	UNSHUNNED
UNSADDLED	UNSEASONS	UNSHACKLE	UNSHUT
UNSADDLES	UNSEAT	UNSHADED	UNSHUTS
UNSAFE	UNSEATED	UNSHADOW	UNSHUTTER
UNSAFELY	UNSEATING	UNSHADOWS	UNSICKER
UNSAFER	UNSEATS	UNSHAKED	UNSICKLED
UNSAFEST	UNSECRET	UNSHAKEN	UNSIFTED
UNSAFETY	UNSECULAR	UNSHALE	UNSIGHING
UNSAID	UNSECURED	UNSHALED	UNSIGHT
UNSAILED	UNSEDUCED	UNSHALES	UNSIGHTED
UNSAINED	UNSEEABLE	UNSHALING	UNSIGHTLY
UNSAINT	UNSEEDED	UNSHAMED	UNSIGHTS
UNSAINTED	UNSEEING	UNSHAPE	UNSIGNED
UNSAINTLY	UNSEEL	UNSHAPED	UNSILENT
UNSAINTS	UNSEELED	UNSHAPELY	UNSIMILAR
UNSALABLE	UNSEELIE	UNSHAPEN	UNSINEW
UNSALABLY	UNSEELING	UNSHAPES	UNSINEWED
UNSALTED	UNSEELS	UNSHAPING	UNSINEWS
UNSALUTED	UNSEEMING	UNSHARED	UNSINFUL
UNSAMPLED	UNSEEMLY	UNSHARP	UNSISTING
UNSAPPED	UNSEEN	UNSHAVED	UNSIZABLE
UNSASHED	UNSEENS	UNSHAVEN	UNSIZED
UNSATABLE	UNSEIZED	UNSHEATHE	UNSKILFUL
UNSATED	UNSELDOM	UNSHED	UNSKILLED
UNSATIATE	UNSELF	UNSHELL	UNSKIMMED
UNSATING	UNSELFED	UNSHELLED	UNSKINNED
UNSAVED	UNSELFING	UNSHELLS	UNSLAIN
UNSAVORY	UNSELFISH	UNSHENT	UNSLAKED
UNSAVOURY	UNSELFS	UNSHEWN	UNSLICED
UNSAWED	UNSELL	UNSHIFT	UNSLICK
UNSAWN	UNSELLING	UNSHIFTED	UNSLING
UNSAY	UNSELLS	UNSHIFTS	UNSLINGS
UNSAYABLE	UNSELVES	UNSHIP	UNSLUICE
UNSAYING	UNSENSE	UNSHIPPED	UNSLUICED
UNSAYS	UNSENSED	UNSHIPS	UNSLUICES
UNSCALE	UNSENSES	UNSHIRTED	UNSLUNG
UNSCALED	UNSENSING	UNSHOCKED	UNSMART
UNSCALES	UNSENT	UNSHOD	UNSMILING

UNSMITTEN	UNSPARING	UNSTICK	UNSUSPECT
UNSMOKED	UNSPARRED	UNSTICKS	UNSWADDLE
UNSMOOTH	UNSPARS	UNSTIFLED	UNSWATHE
UNSMOOTHS	UNSPEAK	UNSTILLED	UNSWATHED
UNSMOTE	UNSPEAKS	UNSTINTED	UNSWATHES
UNSNAG	UNSPED	UNSTIRRED	UNSWAYED
UNSNAGGED	UNSPELL	UNSTITCH	UNSWEAR
UNSNAGS	UNSPELLED	UNSTOCK	UNSWEARS
UNSNAP	UNSPELLS	UNSTOCKED	UNSWEET
UNSNAPPED	UNSPENT	UNSTOCKS	UNSWEPT
UNSNAPS	UNSPHERE	UNSTONED	UNSWOLLEN
UNSNARL	UNSPHERED	UNSTOP	UNSWORE
UNSNARLED	UNSPHERES	UNSTOPPED	UNSWORN
UNSNARLS	UNSPIDE	UNSTOPPER	UNTACK
UNSNECK	UNSPIED	UNSTOPS	UNTACKED
UNSNECKED	UNSPILLED	UNSTOW	UNTACKING
UNSNECKS	UNSPILT	UNSTOWED	UNTACKLE
UNSNUFFED	UNSPLIT	UNSTOWING	UNTACKLED
UNSOAKED	UNSPOILED	UNSTOWS	UNTACKLES
UNSOAPED	UNSPOILT	UNSTRAP	UNTACKS
UNSOBER	UNSPOKE	UNSTRAPS	UNTACTFUL
UNSOBERLY	UNSPOKEN	UNSTRESS	UNTAGGED
UNSOCIAL	UNSPOOL	UNSTRING	UNTAILED
UNSOCKET	UNSPOOLED	UNSTRINGS	UNTAINTED
UNSOCKETS	UNSPOOLS	UNSTRIP	UNTAKEN
UNSOD	UNSPOTTED	UNSTRIPED	UNTAMABLE
UNSODDEN	UNSPRAYED	UNSTRIPS	UNTAMABLY
UNSOFT	UNSPRUNG	UNSTRUCK	UNTAME
UNSOILED	UNSPUN	UNSTRUNG	UNTAMED
UNSOLACED	UNSQUARED	UNSTUCK	UNTAMES
UNSOLD	UNSTABLE	UNSTUDIED	UNTAMING
UNSOLDER	UNSTABLER	UNSTUFFED	UNTANGLE
UNSOLDERS	UNSTABLY	UNSTUFFY	UNTANGLED
UNSOLEMN	UNSTACK	UNSTUFT	UNTANGLES
UNSOLID	UNSTACKED	UNSTUNG	UNTANNED
UNSOLIDLY	UNSTACKS	UNSTYLISH	UNTAPPED
UNSOLVED	UNSTAID	UNSUBDUED	UNTARRED
UNSONCY	UNSTAINED	UNSUBJECT	UNTASTED
UNSONSIE	UNSTALKED	UNSUBTLE	UNTAUGHT
UNSONSY	UNSTAMPED	UNSUBTLY	UNTAX
UNSOOTE	UNSTARCH	UNSUCCESS	UNTAXED
UNSOOTHED	UNSTARRED	UNSUCKED	UNTAXES
UNSORTED	UNSTARRY	UNSUIT	UNTAXING
UNSOUGHT	UNSTATE	UNSUITED	UNTEACH
UNSOUL	UNSTATED	UNSUITING	UNTEACHES
UNSOULED	UNSTATES	UNSUITS	UNTEAM
UNSOULING	UNSTATING	UNSULLIED	UNTEAMED
UNSOULS	UNSTAYED	UNSUMMED	UNTEAMING
UNSOUND	UNSTAYING	UNSUNG	UNTEAMS
UNSOUNDED	UNSTEADY	UNSUNK	UNTEMPER
UNSOUNDER	UNSTEEL	UNSUNNED	UNTEMPERS
UNSOUNDLY	UNSTEELED	UNSUNNY	UNTEMPTED
UNSOURCED	UNSTEELS	UNSUPPLE	UNTENABLE
UNSOURED	UNSTEMMED	UNSURE	UNTENABLY
UNSOWED	UNSTEP	UNSURED	UNTENANT
UNSOWN	UNSTEPPED	UNSURELY	UNTENANTS
UNSPAR	UNSTEPS	UNSURER	UNTENDED
UNSPARED	UNSTERILE	UNSUREST	UNTENDER

UNTENT	UNTOILING	UNTUNEFUL	UNVEXED
UNTENTED	UNTOLD	UNTUNES	UNVEXT
UNTENTING	UNTOMB	UNTUNING	UNVIABLE
UNTENTS	UNTOMBED	UNTURBID	UNVIEWED
UNTENTY	UNTOMBING	UNTURF	UNVIRTUE
UNTENURED	UNTOMBS	UNTURFED	UNVIRTUES
UNTESTED	UNTONED	UNTURFING	UNVISITED
UNTETHER	UNTORN	UNTURFS	UNVISOR
UNTETHERS	UNTOUCHED	UNTURN	UNVISORED
UNTHANKED	UNTOWARD	UNTURNED	UNVISORS
UNTHATCH	UNTRACE	UNTURNING	UNVITAL
UNTHAW	UNTRACED	UNTURNS	UNVIZARD
UNTHAWED	UNTRACES	UNTUTORED	UNVIZARDS
UNTHAWING	UNTRACING	UNTWILLED	UNVOCAL
UNTHAWS	UNTRACK	UNTWINE	UNVOICE
UNTHINK	UNTRACKED	UNTWINED	UNVOICED
UNTHINKS	UNTRACKS	UNTWINES	UNVOICES
UNTHOUGHT	UNTRADED	UNTWINING	UNVOICING
UNTHREAD	UNTRAINED	UNTWIST	UNVULGAR
UNTHREADS	UNTRAPPED	UNTWISTED	UNWAGED
UNTHRIFT	UNTREAD	UNTWISTS	UNWAKED
UNTHRIFTS	UNTREADED	UNTYING	UNWAKENED
UNTHRIFTY	UNTREADS	UNTYINGS	UNWALLED
UNTHRONE	UNTREATED	UNTYPABLE	UNWANING
UNTHRONED	UNTRENDY	UNTYPICAL	UNWANTED
UNTHRONES	UNTRESSED	UNUNBIUM	UNWARDED
UNTIDIED	UNTRIDE	UNUNBIUMS	UNWARE
UNTIDIER	UNTRIED	UNUNITED	UNWARELY
UNTIDIES	UNTRIM	UNUNUNIUM	UNWARES
UNTIDIEST	UNTRIMMED	UNURGED	UNWARIE
UNTIDILY	UNTRIMS	UNUSABLE	UNWARIER
UNTIDY	UNTROD	UNUSABLY	UNWARIEST
UNTIDYING	UNTRODDEN	UNUSED	UNWARILY
UNTIE	UNTRUE	UNUSEFUL	UNWARLIKE
UNTIED	UNTRUER	UNUSHERED	UNWARMED
UNTIEING	UNTRUEST	UNUSUAL	UNWARNED
UNTIES	UNTRUISM	UNUSUALLY	UNWARPED
UNTIL	UNTRUISMS	UNUTTERED	UNWARY
UNTILE	UNTRULY	UNVAIL	UNWASHED
UNTILED	UNTRUSS	UNVAILE	UNWASHEDS
UNTILES	UNTRUSSED	UNVAILED	UNWASHEN
UNTILLING	UNTRUSSER	UNVAILES	UNWASTED
UNTILLED	UNTRUSSES	UNVAILING	UNWASTING
UNTILTED	UNTRUST	UNVAILS	UNWATCHED
UNTIMED	UNTRUSTS	UNVALUED	UNWATER
UNTIMELY	UNTRUSTY	UNVARIED	UNWATERED
UNTIMEOUS	UNTRUTH	UNVARYING	UNWATERS
UNTIN	UNTRUTHS	UNVEIL	UNWATERY
UNTINGED	UNTUCK	UNVEILED	UNWAXED
UNTINNED	UNTUCKED	UNVEILER	UNWAYED
UNTINNING	UNTUCKING	UNVEILERS	UNWEAL
UNTINS	UNTUCKS	UNVEILING	UNWEALS
UNTIPPED	UNTUFTED	UNVEILS	UNWEANED
UNTIRABLE	UNTUMBLED	UNVEINED	UNWEAPON
UNTIRED	UNTUNABLE	UNVENTED	UNWEAPONS
UNTIRING	UNTUNABLY	UNVERSED	UNWEARIED
UNTITLED	UNTUNE	UNVESTED	UNWEARY
UNTO	UNTUNED	UNVETTED	UNWEAVE

UNWEAVES

UNWEAVES	UNWITS	UNZONED	UPCASTS
UNWEAVING	UNWITTED	UP	UPCATCH
UNWEBBED	UNWITTILY	UPADAISY	UPCATCHES
UNWED	UNWITTING	UPAITHRIC	UPCAUGHT
UNWEDDED	UNWITTY	UPAS	UPCHEER
UNWEEDED	UNWIVE	UPASES	UPCHEERED
UNWEENED	UNWIVED	UPBEAR	UPCHEERS
UNWEETING	UNWIVES	UPBEARER	UPCHUCK
UNWEIGHED	UNWIVING	UPBEARERS	UPCHUCKED
UNWEIGHT	UNWOMAN	UPBEARING	UPCHUCKS
UNWEIGHTS	UNWOMANED	UPBEARS	UPCLIMB
UNWELCOME	UNWOMANLY	UPBEAT	UPCLIMBED
UNWELDED	UNWOMANS	UPBEATS	UPCLIMBS
UNWELDY	UNWON	UPBIND	UPCLOSE
UNWELL	UNWONT	UPBINDING	UPCLOSED
UNWEPT	UNWONTED	UPBINDS	UPCLOSES
UNWET	UNWOODED	UPBLEW	UPCLOSING
UNWETTED	UNWOOED	UPBLOW	UPCOAST
UNWHIPPED	UNWORDED	UPBLOWING	UPCOIL
UNWHIPT	UNWORK	UPBLOWN	UPCOILED
UNWHITE	UNWORKED	UPBLOWS	UPCOILING
UNWIELDLY	UNWORKING	UPBOIL	UPCOILS
UNWIELDY	UNWORKS	UPBOILED	UPCOME
UNWIFELY	UNWORLDLY	UPBOILING	UPCOMES
UNWIGGED	UNWORMED	UPBOILS	UPCOMING
UNWILFUL	UNWORN	UPBORE	UPCOUNTRY
UNWILL	UNWORRIED	UPBORNE	UPCOURT
UNWILLED	UNWORTH	UPBOUND	UPCURL
UNWILLING	UNWORTHS	UPBOUNDEN	UPCURLED
UNWILLS	UNWORTHY	UPBOW	UPCURLING
UNWIND	UNWOUND	UPBOWS	UPCURLS
UNWINDER	UNWOUNDED	UPBRAID	UPCURVE
UNWINDERS	UNWOVE	UPBRAIDED	UPCURVED
UNWINDING	UNWOVEN	UPBRAIDER	UPCURVES
UNWINDS	UNWRAP	UPBRAIDS	UPCURVING
UNWINGED	UNWRAPPED	UPBRAST	UPDART
UNWINKING	UNWRAPS	UPBRAY	UPDARTED
UNWIPED	UNWREAKED	UPBRAYED	UPDARTING
UNWIRE	UNWREATHE	UPBRAYING	UPDARTS
UNWIRED	UNWRINKLE	UPBRAYS	UPDATE
UNWIRES	UNWRITE	UPBREAK	UPDATED
UNWIRING	UNWRITES	UPBREAKS	UPDATER
UNWISDOM	UNWRITING	UPBRING	UPDATERS
UNWISDOMS	UNWRITTEN	UPBRINGS	UPDATES
UNWISE	UNWROTE	UPBROKE	UPDATING
UNWISELY	UNWROUGHT	UPBROKEN	UPDIVE
UNWISER	UNWRUNG	UPBROUGHT	UPDIVED
UNWISEST	UNYEANED	UPBUILD	UPDIVES
UNWISH	UNYOKE	UPBUILDER	UPDIVING
UNWISHED	UNYOKED	UPBUILDS	UPDO
UNWISHES	UNYOKES	UPBUILT	UPDOS
UNWISHFUL	UNYOKING	UPBURNING	UPDOVE
UNWISHING	UNYOUNG	UPBURST	UPDRAFT
UNWIST	UNZEALOUS	UPBURSTS	UPDRAFTS
UNWIT	UNZIP	UPBY	UPDRAG
UNWITCH	UNZIPPED	UPBYE	UPDRAGGED
UNWITCHED	UNZIPPING	UPCAST	UPDRAGS
UNWITCHES	UNZIPS	UPCASTING	UPDRAUGHT

UPDRAW	UPGRADES	UPHURLING	UPLOOKED
UPDRAWING	UPGRADING	UPHURLS	UPLOOKING
UPDRAWN	UPGREW	UPJET	UPLOOKS
UPDRAWS	UPGROW	UPJETS	UPLYING
UPDREW	UPGROWING	UPJETTED	UPMAKE
UPDRIED	UPGROWN	UPJETTING	UPMAKER
UPDRIES	UPGROWS	UPKEEP	UPMAKERS
UPDRY	UPGROWTH	UPKEEPS	UPMAKES
UPDRYING	UPGROWTHS	UPKNIT	UPMAKING
UPEND	UPGUSH	UPKNITS	UPMAKINGS
UPENDED	UPGUSHED	UPKNITTED	UPMANSHIP
UPENDING	UPGUSHES	UPLAID	UPMARKET
UPENDS	UPGUSHING	UPLAND	UPMOST
UPFIELD	UPHAND	UPLANDER	UPO
UPFILL	UPHANG	UPLANDERS	UPON
UPFILLED	UPHANGING	UPLANDISH	UPPED
UPFILLING	UPHANGS	UPLANDS	UPPER
UPFILLS	UPHAUD	UPLAY	UPPERCASE
UPFLING	UPHAUDING	UPLAYING	UPPERCUT
UPFLINGS	UPHAUDS	UPLAYS	UPPERCUTS
UPFLOW	UPHEAP	UPLEAD	UPPERMOST
UPFLOWED	UPHEAPED	UPLEADING	UPPERPART
UPFLOWING	UPHEAPING	UPLEADS	UPPERS
UPFLOWS	UPHEAPS	UPLEAN	UPPILE
UPFLUNG	UPHEAVAL	UPLEANED	UPPILED
UPFOLD	UPHEAVALS	UPLEANING	UPPILES
UPFOLDED	UPHEAVE	UPLEANS	UPPILING
UPFOLDING	UPHEAVED	UPLEANT	UPPING
UPFOLDS	UPHEAVER	UPLEAP	UPPINGS
UPFOLLOW	UPHEAVERS	UPLEAPED	UPPISH
UPFOLLOWS	UPHEAVES	UPLEAPING	UPPISHLY
UPFRONT	UPHEAVING	UPLEAPS	UPPITY
UPFURL	UPHELD	UPLEAPT	UPPROP
UPFURLED	UPHILD	UPLED	UPPROPPED
UPFURLING	UPHILL	UPLIFT	UPPROPS
UPFURLS	UPHILLS	UPLIFTED	UPRAISE
UPGANG	UPHOARD	UPLIFTER	UPRAISED
UPGANGS	UPHOARDED	UPLIFTERS	UPRAISER
UPGATHER	UPHOARDS	UPLIFTING	UPRAISERS
UPGATHERS	UPHOIST	UPLIFTS	UPRAISES
UPGAZE	UPHOISTED	UPLIGHT	UPRAISING
UPGAZED	UPHOISTS	UPLIGHTED	UPRAN
UPGAZES	UPHOLD	UPLIGHTER	UPRATE
UPGAZING	UPHOLDER	UPLIGHTS	UPRATED
UPGIRD	UPHOLDERS	UPLINK	UPRATES
UPGIRDED	UPHOLDING	UPLINKED	UPRATING
UPGIRDING	UPHOLDS	UPLINKING	UPREACH
UPGIRDS	UPHOLSTER	UPLINKS	UPREACHED
UPGIRT	UPHOORD	UPLIT	UPREACHES
UPGO	UPHOORDED	UPLOAD	UPREAR
UPGOES	UPHOORDS	UPLOADED	UPREARED
UPGOING	UPHOVE	UPLOADING	UPREARING
UPGOINGS	UPHROE	UPLOADS	UPREARS
UPGONE	UPHROES	UPLOCK	UPREST
UPGRADE	UPHUDDEN	UPLOCKED	UPRESTS
UPGRADED	UPHUNG	UPLOCKING	UPRIGHT
UPGRADER	UPHURL	UPLOCKS	UPRIGHTED
UPGRADERS	UPHURLED	UPLOOK	UPRIGHTLY

UPRIGHTS	UPSETTERS	UPSTATE	UPTHREW
UPRISAL	UPSETTING	UPSTATER	UPTHROW
UPRISALS	UPSEY	UPSTATERS	UPTHROWN
UPRISE	UPSEYS	UPSTATES	UPTHROWS
UPRISEN	UPSHIFT	UPSTAY	UPTHRUST
UPRISER	UPSHIFTED	UPSTAYED	UPTHRUSTS
UPRISERS	UPSHIFTS	UPSTAYING	UPTHUNDER
UPRISES	UPSHOOT	UPSTAYS	UPTICK
UPRISING	UPSHOOTS	UPSTEP	UPTICKS
UPRISINGS	UPSHOT	UPSTEPPED	UPTIE
UPRIST	UPSHOTS	UPSTEPS	UPTIED
UPRISTS	UPSIDE	UPSTIR	UPTIES
UPRIVER	UPSIDES	UPSTIRRED	UPTIGHT
UPRIVERS	UPSIES	UPSTIRS	UPTIGHTER
UPROAR	UPSILON	UPSTOOD	UPTILT
UPROARED	UPSILONS	UPSTREAM	UPTILTED
UPROARING	UPSITTING	UPSTREAMS	UPTILTING
UPROARS	UPSIZE	UPSTROKE	UPTILTS
UPROLL	UPSIZED	UPSTROKES	UPTIME
UPROLLED	UPSIZES	UPSURGE	UPTIMES
UPROLLING	UPSIZING	UPSURGED	UPTITLING
UPROLLS	UPSKILL	UPSURGES	UPTOOK
UPROOT	UPSKILLED	UPSURGING	UPTORE
UPROOTAL	UPSKILLS	UPSWARM	UPTORN
UPROOTALS	UPSLOPE	UPSWARMED	UPTOSS
UPROOTED	UPSOAR	UPSWARMS	UPTOSSED
UPROOTER	UPSOARED	UPSWAY	UPTOSSES
UPROOTERS	UPSOARING	UPSWAYED	UPTOSSING
UPROOTING	UPSOARS	UPSWAYING	UPTOWN
UPROOTS	UPSPAKE	UPSWAYS	UPTOWNER
UPROSE	UPSPEAK	UPSWEEP	UPTOWNERS
UPROUSE	UPSPEAKS	UPSWEEPS	UPTOWNS
UPROUSED	UPSPEAR	UPSWELL	UPTRAIN
UPROUSES	UPSPEARED	UPSWELLED	UPTRAINED
UPROUSING	UPSPEARS	UPSWELLS	UPTRAINS
UPRUN	UPSPOKE	UPSWEPT	UPTREND
UPRUNNING	UPSPOKEN	UPSWING	UPTRENDS
UPRUNS	UPSPRANG	UPSWINGS	UPTRILLED
UPRUSH	UPSPRING	UPSWOLLEN	UPTURN
UPRUSHED	UPSPRINGS	UPSWUNG	UPTURNED
UPRUSHES	UPSPRUNG	UPSY	UPTURNING
UPRUSHING	UPSTAGE	UPTA	UPTURNS
UPRYST	UPSTAGED	UPTAK	UPTYING
UPS	UPSTAGER	UPTAKE	UPVALUE
UPSADAISY	UPSTAGERS	UPTAKEN	UPVALUED
UPSCALE	UPSTAGES	UPTAKES	UPVALUES
UPSCALED	UPSTAGING	UPTAKING	UPVALUING
UPSCALES	UPSTAIR	UPTAKS	UPWAFT
UPSCALING	UPSTAIRS	UPTALK	UPWAFTED
UPSEE	UPSTAND	UPTALKED	UPWAFTING
UPSEES	UPSTANDS	UPTALKING	UPWAFTS
UPSEND	UPSTARE	UPTALKS	UPWARD
UPSENDING	UPSTARED	UPTEAR	UPWARDLY
UPSENDS	UPSTARES	UPTEARING	UPWARDS
UPSENT	UPSTARING	UPTEARS	UPWELL
UPSET	UPSTART	UPTEMPO	UPWELLED
UPSETS	UPSTARTED	UPTEMPOS	UPWELLING
UPSETTER	UPSTARTS	UPTER	UPWELLS

UPWENT	URARIS	UREIDES	URINATORS
UPWHIRL	URASE	UREMIA	URINE
UPWHIRLED	URASES	UREMIAS	URINED
UPWHIRLS	URATE	UREMIC	URTNEMIA
UPWIND	URATES	URENA	URINEMIAS
UPWINDING	URATIC	URENAS	URINEMIC
UPWINDS	URB	URENT	URINES
UPWOUND	URBAN	UREOTELIC	URINING
UPWRAP	URBANE	URES	URINOLOGY
UPWRAPS	URBANELY	URESES	URINOSE
UPWROUGHT	URBANER	URESIS	URINOUS
UR	URBANEST	URETER	URITE
URACHI	URBANISE	URETERAL	URITES
URACHUS	URBANISED	URETERIC	URMAN
URACHUSES	URBANISES	URETERS	URMANS
URACIL	URBANISM	URETHAN	URN
URACILS	URBANISMS	URETHANE	URNAL
URAEI	URBANIST	URETHANES	URNED
URAEMIA	URBANISTS	URETHANS	URNFIELD
URAEMIAS	URBANITE	URETHRA	URNFIELDS
URAEMIC	URBANITES	URETHRAE	URNFUL
URAEUS	URBANITY	URETHRAL	URNFULS
URAEUSES	URBANIZE	URETHRAS	URNING
URALI	URBANIZED	URETIC	URNINGS
URALIS	URBANIZES	URGE	URNLIKE
URALITE	URBIA	URGED	URNS
URALITES	URBIAS	URGENCE	UROBILIN
URALITIC	URBS	URGENCES	UROBILINS
URALITISE	URCEOLATE	URGENCIES	UROCHORD
URALITIZE	URCEOLI	URGENCY	UROCHORDS
URANIA	URCEOLUS	URGENT	UROCHROME
URANIAN	URCHIN	URGENTLY	URODELAN
URANIAS	URCHINS	URGER	URODELANS
URANIC	URD	URGERS	URODELE
URANIDE	URDE	URGES	URODELES
URANIDES	URDEE	URGING	URODELOUS
URANIN	URDS	URGINGLY	UROGENOUS
URANINITE	URDY	URGINGS	UROGRAPHY
URANINS	URE	URIAL	UROKINASE
URANISCI	UREA	URIALS	UROLAGNIA
URANISCUS	UREAL	URIC	UROLITH
URANISM	UREAS	URICASE	UROLITHIC
URANISMS	UREASE	URICASES	UROLITHS
URANITE	UREASES	URIDINE	UROLOGIC
URANITES	UREDIA	URIDINES	UROLOGIES
URANITIC	UREDIAL	URIDYLIC	UROLOGIST
URANIUM	UREDINE	URINAL	UROLOGY
URANIUMS	UREDINES	URINALS	UROMERE
URANOLOGY	UREDINIA	URINANT	UROMERES
URANOUS	UREDINIAL	URINARIES	UROPOD
URANYL	UREDINIUM	URINARY	UROPODAL
URANYLIC	UREDINOUS	URINATE	UROPODOUS
URANYLS	UREDIUM	URINATED	UROPODS
URAO	UREDO	URINATES	UROPYGIA
URAOS	UREDOS	URINATING	UROPYGIAL
URARE	UREDOSORI	URINATION	UROPYGIUM
URARES	UREIC	URINATIVE	UROSCOPIC
URARI	UREIDE	URINATOR	UROSCOPY

UROSES
UROSIS
UROSOME
UROSOMES
UROSTEGE
UROSTEGES
UROSTOMY
UROSTYLE
UROSTYLES
URP
URPED
URPING
URPS
URSA
URSAE
URSID
URSIDS
URSIFORM
URSINE
URSON
URSONS
URTEXT
URTEXTS
URTICA
URTICANT
URTICANTS
URTICARIA
URTICAS
URTICATE
URTICATED
URTICATES
URUBU
URUBUS
URUS
URUSES
URUSHIOL
URUSHIOLS
URVA
URVAS
US
USABILITY
USABLE
USABLY
USAGE
USAGER
USAGERS
USAGES
USANCE
USANCES
USAUNCE
USAUNCES
USE
USEABLE
USEABLY
USED
USEFUL
USEFULLY
USEFULS

USELESS
USELESSLY
USER
USERNAME
USERNAMES
USERS
USES
USHER
USHERED
USHERESS
USHERETTE
USHERING
USHERINGS
USHERS
USHERSHIP
USING
USNEA
USNEAS
USQUABAE
USQUABAES
USQUE
USQUEBAE
USQUEBAES
USQUES
USTION
USTIONS
USTULATE
USUAL
USUALLY
USUALNESS
USUALS
USUCAPION
USUCAPT
USUCAPTED
USUCAPTS
USUFRUCT
USUFRUCTS
USURE
USURED
USURER
USURERS
USURES
USURESS
USURESSES
USURIES
USURING
USURIOUS
USUROUS
USURP
USURPED
USURPEDLY
USURPER
USURPERS
USURPING
USURPINGS
USURPS
USURY
USWARD

USWARDS
UT
UTA
UTAS
UTASES
UTE
UTENSIL
UTENSILS
UTERI
UTERINE
UTERITIS
UTEROTOMY
UTERUS
UTERUSES
UTES
UTILE
UTILIDOR
UTILIDORS
UTILISE
UTILISED
UTILISER
UTILISERS
UTILISES
UTILISING
UTILITIES
UTILITY
UTILIZE
UTILIZED
UTILIZER
UTILIZERS
UTILIZES
UTILIZING
UTIS
UTISES
UTMOST
UTMOSTS
UTOPIA
UTOPIAN
UTOPIANS
UTOPIAS
UTOPIAST
UTOPIASTS
UTOPISM
UTOPISMS
UTOPIST
UTOPISTIC
UTOPISTS
UTRICLE
UTRICLES
UTRICULAR
UTRICULI
UTRICULUS
UTS
UTTER
UTTERABLE
UTTERANCE
UTTERED
UTTERER

UTTERERS
UTTEREST
UTTERING
UTTERINGS
UTTERLESS
UTTERLY
UTTERMOST
UTTERNESS
UTTERS
UTU
UTUS
UVA
UVAE
UVAROVITE
UVAS
UVEA
UVEAL
UVEAS
UVEITIC
UVEITIS
UVEITISES
UVEOUS
UVULA
UVULAE
UVULAR
UVULARLY
UVULARS
UVULAS
UVULITIS
UXORIAL
UXORIALLY
UXORICIDE
UXORIOUS

— V —

VAC
VACANCE
VACANCES
VACANCIES
VACANCY
VACANT
VACANTLY
VACATABLE
VACATE
VACATED
VACATES
VACATING
VACATION
VACATIONS
VACATUR
VACATURS
VACCINA
VACCINAL
VACCINAS
VACCINATE
VACCINE
VACCINEE
VACCINEES
VACCINES
VACCINIA
VACCINIAL
VACCINIAS
VACCINIUM
VACHERIN
VACHERINS
VACILLANT
VACILLATE
VACKED
VACKING
VACS
VACUA
VACUATE
VACUATED
VACUATES
VACUATING
VACUATION
VACUIST
VACUISTS
VACUITIES
VACUITY
VACUOLAR
VACUOLATE
VACUOLE
VACUOLES
VACUOUS
VACUOUSLY
VACUUM
VACUUMED

VACUUMING
VACUUMS
VADE
VADED
VADES
VADING
VADOSE
VAE
VAES
VAG
VAGABOND
VAGABONDS
VAGAL
VAGALLY
VAGARIES
VAGARIOUS
VAGARISH
VAGARY
VAGGED
VAGGING
VAGI
VAGILE
VAGILITY
VAGINA
VAGINAE
VAGINAL
VAGINALLY
VAGINANT
VAGINAS
VAGINATE
VAGINATED
VAGINITIS
VAGINOSES
VAGINOSIS
VAGINULA
VAGINULAE
VAGTNULE
VAGINULES
VAGITUS
VAGITUSES
VAGOTOMY
VAGOTONIA
VAGOTONIC
VAGRANCY
VAGRANT
VAGRANTLY
VAGRANTS
VAGROM
VAGROMS
VAGS
VAGUE
VAGUED
VAGUELY

VAGUENESS
VAGUER
VAGUES
VAGUEST
VAGUING
VAGUS
VAHANA
VAHANAS
VAHINE
VAHINES
VAIL
VAILED
VAILING
VAILS
VAIN
VAINER
VAINESSE
VAINESSES
VAINEST
VAINGLORY
VAINLY
VAINNESS
VAIR
VAIRE
VAIRIER
VAIRIEST
VAIRS
VAIRY
VAIVODE
VAIVODES
VAKASS
VAKASSES
VAKEEL
VAKEELS
VAKIL
VAKILS
VALANCE
VALANCED
VALANCES
VALANCING
VALE
VALENCE
VALENCES
VALENCIA
VALENCIAS
VALENCIES
VALENCY
VALENTINE
VALERATE
VALERATES
VALERIAN
VALERIANS
VALERIC

VALES
VALET
VALETA
VALETAS
VALETE
VALETED
VALETES
VALETING
VALETINGS
VALETS
VALGOID
VALGOUS
VALGUS
VALGUSES
VALI
VALIANCE
VALIANCES
VALIANCY
VALIANT
VALIANTLY
VALIANTS
VALID
VALIDATE
VALIDATED
VALIDATES
VALIDER
VALIDEST
VALIDITY
VALIDLY
VALIDNESS
VALINE
VALINES
VALIS
VALISE
VALISES
VALKYR
VALKYRIE
VALKYRIES
VALKYRS
VALLAR
VALLARY
VALLATE
VALLATION
VALLECULA
VALLEY
VALLEYED
VALLEYS
VALLHUND
VALLHUNDS
VALLONIA
VALLONIAS
VALLUM
VALLUMS

VALONEA	VAMBRACED	VANES	VAPORETTI
VALONEAS	VAMBRACES	VANESSA	VAPORETTO
VALONIA	VAMOOSE	VANESSAS	VAPORIFIC
VALONIAS	VAMOOSED	VANESSID	VAPORING
VALOR	VAMOOSES	VANESSIDS	VAPORINGS
VALORISE	VAMOOSING	VANG	VAPORISE
VALORISED	VAMOSE	VANGS	VAPORISED
VALORISES	VAMOSED	VANGUARD	VAPORISER
VALORIZE	VAMOSES	VANGUARDS	VAPORISES
VALORIZED	VAMOSING	VANILLA	VAPORISH
VALORIZES	VAMP	VANILLAS	VAPORIZE
VALOROUS	VAMPED	VANILLIC	VAPORIZED
VALORS	VAMPER	VANILLIN	VAPORIZER
VALOUR	VAMPERS	VANILLINS	VAPORIZES
VALOURS	VAMPIER	VANISH	VAPORLESS
VALPROATE	VAMPIEST	VANISHED	VAPORLIKE
VALPROIC	VAMPING	VANISHER	VAPOROUS
VALSE	VAMPINGS	VANISHERS	VAPORS
VALSED	VAMPIRE	VANISHES	VAPORWARE
VALSES	VAMPIRED	VANISHING	VAPORY
VALSING	VAMPIRES	VANITAS	VAPOUR
VALUABLE	VAMPIRIC	VANITASES	VAPOURED
VALUABLES	VAMPIRING	VANITIED	VAPOURER
VALUABLY	VAMPIRISE	VANITIES	VAPOURERS
VALUATE	VAMPIRISH	VANITORY	VAPOURING
VALUATED	VAMPIRISM	VANITY	VAPOURISH
VALUATES	VAMPIRIZE	VANLOAD	VAPOURS
VALUATING	VAMPISH	VANLOADS	VAPOURY
VALUATION	VAMPISHLY	VANMAN	VAPULATE
VALUATOR	VAMPLATE	VANMEN	VAPULATED
VALUATORS	VAMPLATES	VANNED	VAPULATES
VALUE	VAMPS	VANNER	VAQUERO
VALUED	VAMPY	VANNERS	VAQUEROS
VALUELESS	VAN	VANNING	VAR
VALUER	VANADATE	VANNINGS	VARA
VALUERS	VANADATES	VANPOOL	VARACTOR
VALUES	VANADIATE	VANPOOLS	VARACTORS
VALUING	VANADIC	VANQUISH	VARAN
VALUTA	VANADIUM	VANS	VARANS
VALUTAS	VANADIUMS	VANT	VARAS
VALVAL	VANADOUS	VANTAGE	VARDIES
VALVAR	VANASPATI	VANTAGED	VARDY
VALVASSOR	VANDA	VANTAGES	VARE
VALVATE	VANDAL	VANTAGING	VAREC
VALVE	VANDALIC	VANTBRACE	VARECH
VALVED	VANDALISE	VANTS	VARECHS
VALVELESS	VANDALISH	VANWARD	VARECS
VALVELET	VANDALISM	VAPID	VARES
VALVELETS	VANDALIZE	VAPIDER	VAREUSE
VALVELIKE	VANDALS	VAPIDEST	VAREUSES
VALVES	VANDAS	VAPIDITY	VARGUENO
VALVING	VANDYKE	VAPIDLY	VARGUENOS
VALVULA	VANDYKED	VAPIDNESS	VARIA
VALVULAE	VANDYKES	VAPOR	VARIABLE
VALVULAR	VANDYKING	VAPORABLE	VARIABLES
VALVULE	VANE	VAPORED	VARIABLY
VALVULES	VANED	VAPORER	VARIANCE
VAMBRACE	VANELESS	VAPORERS	VARIANCES

VARIANT	VARMINTS	VASSALLED	VAUNCING
VARIANTS	VARNA	VASSALRY	VAUNT
VARIAS	VARNAS	VASSALS	VAUNTAGE
VARIATE	VARNISH	VAST	VAUNTAGES
VARIATED	VARNISHED	VASTER	VAUNTED
VARIATES	VARNISHER	VASTEST	VAUNTER
VARIATING	VARNISHES	VASTIDITY	VAUNTERS
VARIATION	VARNISHY	VASTIER	VAUNTERY
VARIATIVE	VAROOM	VASTIEST	VAUNTFUL
VARICELLA	VAROOMED	VASTITIES	VAUNTIE
VARICES	VAROOMING	VASTITUDE	VAUNTIER
VARICOID	VAROOMS	VASTITY	VAUNTIEST
VARICOSE	VARROA	VASTLY	VAUNTING
VARICOSED	VARROAS	VASTNESS	VAUNTINGS
VARICOSES	VARS	VASTS	VAUNTS
VARICOSIS	VARSAL	VASTY	VAUNTY
VARIED	VARSITIES '	VAT	VAURIEN
VARIEDLY	VARSITY	VATABLE	VAURIENS
VARIEGATE	VARTABED	VATFUL	VAUS
VARIER	VARTABEDS	VATFULS	VAUT
VARIERS	VARUS	VATIC	VAUTE
VARIES	VARUSES	VATICAL	VAUTED
VARIETAL	VARVE	VATICIDE	VAUTES
VARIETALS	VARVED	VATICIDES	VAUTING
VARIETIES	VARVEL	VATICINAL	VAUTS
VARIETY	VARVELLED	VATMAN	VAV
VARIFOCAL	VARVELS	VATMEN	VAVASOR
VARIFORM	VARVES	VATS	VAVASORS
VARIOLA	VARY	VATTED	VAVASORY
VARIOLAR	VARYING	VATTER	VAVASOUR
VARIOLAS	VARYINGLY	VATTERS	VAVASOURS
VARIOLATE	VARYINGS	VATTING	VAVASSOR
VARIOLE	VAS	VATU	VAVASSORS
VARIOLES	VASA	VATUS	VAVS
VARIOLITE	VASAL	VAU	VAW
VARIOLOID	VASCULA	VAUCH	VAWARD
VARIOLOUS	VASCULAR	VAUCHED	VAWARDS
VARIORUM	VASCULUM	VAUCHES	VAWNTIE
VARIORUMS	VASCULUMS	VAUCHING	VAWS
VARIOUS	VASE	VAUDOO	VAWTE
VARIOUSLY	VASECTOMY	VAUDOOS	VAWTED
VARTSCITE	VASELIKE	VAUDOUX	VAWTES
VARISIZED	VASELINE	VAULT	VAWTING
VARISTOR	VASELINES	VAULTAGE	VEAL
VARISTORS	VASES	VAULTAGES	VEALE
VARITYPE	VASIFORM	VAULTED	VEALED
VARITYPED	VASOMOTOR	VAULTER	VEALER
VARITYPES	VASOSPASM	VAULTERS	VEALERS
VARIX	VASOTOCIN	VAULTIER	VEALES
VARLET	VASOTOMY	VAULTIEST	VEALIER
VARLETESS	VASOVAGAL	VAULTING	VEALIEST
VARLETRY	VASSAIL	VAULTINGS	VEALING
VARLETS	VASSAILS	VAULTLIKE	VEALS
VARLETTO	VASSAL	VAULTS	VEALY
VARLETTOS	VASSALAGE	VAULTY	VECTOR
VARMENT	VASSALESS	VAUNCE	VECTORED
VARMENTS	VASSALISE	VAUNCED	VECTORIAL
VARMINT	VASSALIZE	VAUNCES	VECTORING

VECTORISE	VEGGIE	VELARIC	VELVETIER
VECTORIZE	VEGGIES	VELARISE	VELVETING
VECTORS	VEGGING	VELARISED	VELVETS
VEDALIA	VEGIE	VELARISES	VELVETY
VEDALIAS	VEGIES	VELARIUM	VENA
VEDETTE	VEGO	VELARIZE	VENAE
VEDETTES	VEGOS	VELARIZED	VENAL
VEDUTA	VEHEMENCE	VELARIZES	VENALITY
VEDUTE	VEHEMENCY	VELARS	VENALLY
VEDUTISTA	VEHEMENT	VELATE	VENATIC
VEDUTISTI	VEHICLE	VELATED	VENATICAL
VEE	VEHICLES	VELATURA	VENATION
VEEJAY	VEHICULAR	VELATURAS	VENATIONS
VEEJAYS	VEHM	VELCRO	VENATOR
VEENA	VEHME	VELCROS	VENATORS
VEENAS	VEHMIC	VELD	VEND
VEEP	VEHMIQUE	VELDS	VENDABLE
VEEPEE	VEIL	VELDSKOEN	VENDABLES
VEEPEES	VEILED	VELDT	VENDACE
VEEPS	VEILEDLY	VELDTS	VENDACES
VEER	VEILER	VELE	VENDAGE
VEERED	VEILERS	VELES	VENDAGES
VEERIES	VEILIER	VELETA	VENDANGE
VEERING	VEILIEST	VELETAS	VENDANGES
VEERINGLY	VEILING	VELIGER	VENDED
VEERINGS	VEILINGS	VELIGERS	VENDEE
VEERS	VEILLESS	VELITES	VENDEES
VEERY	VEILLEUSE	VELL	VENDER
VEES	VEILLIKE	VELLEITY	VENDERS
VEG	VEILS	VELLENAGE	VENDETTA
VEGA	VEILY	VELLET	VENDETTAS
VEGAN	VEIN	VELLETS	VENDEUSE
VEGANIC	VEINAL	VELLICATE	VENDEUSES
VEGANISM	VEINED	VELLON	VENDIBLE
VEGANISMS	VEINER	VELLONS	VENDIBLES
VEGANS	VEINERS	VELLS	VENDIBLY
VEGAS	VEINIER	VELLUM	VENDING
VEGELATE	VEINIEST	VELLUMS	VENDINGS
VEGELATES	VEINING	VELOCE	VENDIS
VEGEMITE	VEININGS	VELOCITY	VENDISES
VEGEMITES	VEINLESS	VELODROME	VENDISS
VEGES	VEINLET	VELOUR	VENDISSES
VEGETABLE	VEINLETS	VELOURS	VENDITION
VEGETABLY	VEINLIKE	VELOUTE	VENDOR
VEGETAL	VEINOUS	VELOUTES	VENDORS
VEGETALLY	VEINS	VELOUTINE	VENDS
VEGETALS	VEINSTONE	VELSKOEN	VENDUE
VEGETANT	VEINSTUFF	VELSKOENS	VENDUES
VEGETATE	VEINULE	VELUM	VENEER
VEGETATED	VEINULES	VELURE	VENEERED
VEGETATES	VEINULET	VELURED	VENEERER
VEGETE	VEINULETS	VELURES	VENEERERS
VEGETIST	VEINY	VELURING	VENEERING
VEGETISTS	VELA	VELVERET	VENEERS
VEGETIVE	VELAMEN	VELVERETS	VENEFIC
VEGETIVES	VELAMINA	VELVET	VENEFICAL
VEGGED	VELAR	VELVETED	VENENATE
VEGGES	VELARIA	VELVETEEN	VENENATED

VENENATES	VENOMED	VENTUROUS	VERBOSELY
VENENE	VENOMER	VENUE	VERBOSER
VENENES	VENOMERS	VENUES	VERBOSEST
VENENOSE	VENOMING	VENULAR	VERBOSITY
VENERABLE	VENOMLESS	VENULE	VERBOTEN
VENERABLY	VENOMOUS	VENULES	VERBS
VENERATE	VENOMS	VENULOSE	VERD
VENERATED	VENOSE	VENULOUS	VERDANCY
VENERATES	VENOSITY	VENUS	VERDANT
VENERATOR	VENOUS	VENUSES	VERDANTLY
VENEREAL	VENOUSLY	VENVILLE	VERDELHO
VENEREAN	VENT	VENVILLES	VERDELHOS
VENEREANS	VENTAGE	VERA	VERDERER
VENEREOUS	VENTAGES	VERACIOUS	VERDERERS
VENERER	VENTAIL	VERACITY	VERDEROR
VENERERS	VENTAILE	VERANDA	VERDERORS
VENERIES	VENTAILES	VERANDAED	VERDET
VENERY	VENTAILS	VERANDAH	VERDETS
VENETIAN	VENTANA	VERANDAHS	VERDICT
VENETIANS	VENTANAS	VERANDAS	VERDICTS
VENEWE	VENTAYLE	VERAPAMIL	VERDIGRIS
VENEWES	VENTAYLES	VERATRIA	VERDIN
VENEY	VENTED	VERATRIAS	VERDINS
VENEYS	VENTER	VERATRIN	VERDIT
VENGE	VENTERS	VERATRINE	VERDITE
VENGEABLE	VENTIDUCT	VERATRINS	VERDITER
VENGEABLY	VENTIFACT	VERATRUM	VERDITERS
VENGEANCE	VENTIGE	VERATRUMS	VERDITES
VENGED	VENTIGES	VERB	VERDITS
VENGEFUL	VENTIL	VERBAL	VERDOY
VENGEMENT	VENTILATE	VERBALISE	VERDURE
VENGER	VENTILS	VERBALISM	VERDURED
VENGERS	VENTING	VERBALIST	VERDURES
VENGES	VENTINGS	VERBALITY	VERDUROUS
VENGING	VENTLESS	VERBALIZE	VERECUND
VENIAL	VENTOSE	VERBALLED	VERGE
VENIALITY	VENTOSITY	VERBALLY	VERGED
VENIALLY	VENTOUSE	VERBALS	VERGENCE
VENIDIUM	VENTOUSES	VERBARIAN	VERGENCES
VENIDIUMS	VENTRAL	VERBASCUM	VERGENCY
VENIN	VENTRALLY	VERBATIM	VERGER
VENINE	VENTRALS	VERBENA	VERGERS
VENINES	VENTRE	VERBENAS	VERGES
VENINS	VENTRED	VERBERATE	VERGING
VENIRE	VENTRES	VERBIAGE	VERGLAS
VENIREMAN	VENTRICLE	VERBIAGES	VERGLASES
VENIREMEN	VENTRING	VERBICIDE	VERIDIC
VENIRES	VENTRINGS	VERBID	VERIDICAL
VENISON	VENTROUS	VERBIDS	VERIER
VENISONS	VENTS	VERBIFIED	VERIEST
VENITE	VENTURE	VERBIFIES	VERIFIED
VENITES	VENTURED	VERBIFY	VERIFIER
VENNEL	VENTURER	VERBILE	VERIFIERS
VENNELS	VENTURERS	VERBILES	VERIFIES
VENOGRAM	VENTURES	VERBING	VERIFY
VENOGRAMS	VENTURI	VERBINGS	VERIFYING
VENOLOGY	VENTURING	VERBLESS	VERILY
VENOM	VENTURIS	VERBOSE	VERISM

VERISMO	VERNALITY	VERSINES	VESICATE
VERISMOS	VERNALIZE	VERSING	VESICATED
VERISMS	VERNALLY	VERSINGS	VESICATES
VERIST	VERNANT	VERSINS	VESICLE
VERISTIC	VERNATION	VERSION	VESICLES
VERISTS	VERNICLE	VERSIONAL	VESICULA
VERITABLE	VERNICLES	VERSIONER	VESICULAE
VERITABLY	VERNIER	VERSIONS	VESICULAR
VERITAS	VERNIERS	VERSO	VESPA
VERITATES	VERNIX	VERSOS	VESPAS
VERITE	VERNIXES	VERST	VESPER
VERITES	VERONAL	VERSTE	VESPERAL
VERITIES	VERONALS	VERSTES	VESPERALS
VERITY	VERONICA	VERSTS	VESPERS
VERJUICE	VERONICAS	VERSUS	VESPIARY
VERJUICED	VERONIQUE	VERSUTE	VESPID
VERJUICES	VERQUERE	VERT	VESPIDS
VERKRAMP	VERQUERES	VERTEBRA	VESPINE
VERLAN	VERQUIRE	VERTEBRAE	VESPOID
VERLANS	VERQUIRES	VERTEBRAL	VESSAIL
VERLIG	VERRA	VERTEBRAS	VESSAILS
VERLIGTE	VERREL	VERTED	VESSEL
VERLIGTES	VERRELS	VERTEX	VESSELED
VERMAL	VERREY	VERTEXES	VESSELS
VERMEIL	VERRUCA	VERTICAL	VEST
VERMEILED	VERRUCAE	VERTICALS	VESTA
VERMEILLE	VERRUCAS	VERTICES	VESTAL
VERMEILS	VERRUCOSE	VERTICIL	VESTALLY
VERMELL	VERRUCOUS	VERTICILS	VESTALS
VERMELLS	VERRUGA	VERTICITY	VESTAS
VERMES	VERRUGAS	VERTIGO	VESTED
VERMIAN	VERRY	VERTIGOES	VESTEE
VERMICIDE	VERS	VERTIGOS	VESTEES
VERMICULE	VERSAL	VERTING	VESTIARY
VERMIFORM	VERSALS	VERTIPORT	VESTIBULA
VERMIFUGE	VERSANT	VERTS	VESTIBULE
VERMIL	VERSANTS	VERTU	VESTIGE
VERMILIES	VERSATILE	VERTUE	VESTIGES
VERMILION	VERSE	VERTUES	VESTIGIA
VERMILLED	VERSED	VERTUOUS	VESTIGIAL
VERMILS	VERSELET	VERTUS	VESTIGIUM
VERMILY	VERSELETS	VERVAIN	VESTIMENT
VERMIN	VERSEMAN	VERVAINS	VESTING
VERMINATE	VERSEMEN	VERVE	VESTINGS
VERMINED	VERSER	VERVEL	VESTITURE
VERMINOUS	VERSERS	VERVELLED	VESTLESS
VERMINS	VERSES	VERVELS	VESTLIKE
VERMINY	VERSET	VERVEN	VESTMENT
VERMIS	VERSETS	VERVENS	VESTMENTS
VERMOULU	VERSICLE	VERVES	VESTRAL
VERMOUTH	VERSICLES	VERVET	VESTRIES
VERMOUTHS	VERSIFIED	VERVETS	VESTRY
VERMUTH	VERSIFIER	VERY	VESTRYMAN
VERMUTHS	VERSIFIES	VESICA	VESTRYMEN
VERNACLE	VERSIFORM	VESICAE	VESTS
VERNACLES	VERSIFY	VESICAL	VESTURAL
VERNAL	VERSIN	VESICANT	VESTURE
VERNALISE	VERSINE	VESICANTS	VESTURED

VESTURER	VEXT	VIBRATOR	VICIOSITY
VESTURERS	VEZIR	VIBRATORS	VICIOUS
VESTURES	VEZIRS	VIBRATORY	VICIOUSLY
VESTURING	VIA	VIBRATOS	VICOMTE
VESUVIAN	VIABILITY	VIBRIO	VICOMTES
VESUVIANS	VIABLE	VIBRIOID	VICTIM
VET	VIABLY	VIBRION	VICTIMISE
VETCH	VIADUCT	VIBRIONIC	VICTIMIZE
VETCHES	VIADUCTS	VIBRIONS	VICTIMS
VETCHIER	VIAE	VIBRIOS	VICTOR
VETCHIEST	VIAL	VIBRIOSES	VICTORESS
VETCHLING	VIALED	VIBRIOSIS	VICTORIA
VETCHY	VIALFUL	VIBRISSA	VICTORIAS
VETERAN	VIALFULS	VIBRISSAE	VICTORIES
VETERANS	VIALING	VIBRISSAL	VICTORINE
VETIVER	VIALLED	VIBRONIC	VICTORS
VETIVERS	VIALLING	VIBS	VICTORY
VETIVERT	VIALS	VIBURNUM	VICTRESS
VETIVERTS	VIAMETER	VIBURNUMS	VICTRIX
VETKOEK	VIAMETERS	VICAR	VICTRIXES
VETKOEKS	VIAND	VICARAGE	VICTROLLA
VETO	VIANDS	VICARAGES	VICTUAL
VETOED	VIAS	VICARATE	VICTUALED
VETOER	VIATIC	VICARATES	VICTUALER
VETOERS	VIATICA	VICARESS	VICTUALS
VETOES	VIATICAL	VICARIAL	VICUGNA
VETOING	VIATICALS	VICARIANT	VICUGNAS
VETOLESS	VIATICUM	VICARIATE	VICUNA
VETS	VIATICUMS	VICARIES	VICUNAS
VETTED	VIATOR	VICARIOUS	VID
VETTER	VIATORES	VICARLY	VIDAME
VETTERS	VIATORIAL	VICARS	VIDAMES
VETTING	VIATORS	VICARSHIP	VIDE
VETTURA	VIBE	VICARY	VIDELICET
VETTURAS	VIBES	VICE	VIDENDA
VETTURINI	VIBEX	VICED	VIDENDUM
VETTURINO	VIBEY	VICEGERAL	VIDEO
VEX	VIBICES	VICELESS	VIDEODISC
VEXATION	VIBIER	VICELIKE	VIDEODISK
VEXATIONS	VIBIEST	VICENARY	VIDEOED
VEXATIOUS	VIBIST	VICENNIAL	VIDEOFIT
VEXATORY	VIBISTS	VICEREGAL	VIDEOFITS
VEXED	VIBRACULA	VICEREINE	VIDEOGRAM
VEXEDLY	VIBRAHARP	VICEROY	VIDEOING
VEXEDNESS	VIBRANCE	VICEROYS	VIDEOLAND
VEXER	VIBRANCES	VICES	VIDEOS
VEXERS	VIBRANCY	VICESIMAL	VIDEOTAPE
VEXES	VIBRANT	VICHIES	VIDEOTEX
VEXIL	VIBRANTLY	VICHY	VIDEOTEXT
VEXILLA	VIBRANTS	VICIATE	VIDETTE
VEXILLAR	VIBRATE	VICIATED	VIDETTES
VEXILLARY	VIBRATED	VICIATES	VIDICON
VEXILLATE	VIBRATES	VICIATING	VIDICONS
VEXILLUM	VIBRATILE	VICINAGE	VIDIMUS
VEXILS	VIBRATING	VICINAGES	VIDIMUSES
VEXING	VIBRATION	VICINAL	VIDS
VEXINGLY	VIBRATIVE	VICING	VIDUAGE
VEXINGS	VIBRATO	VICINITY	VIDUAGES

649

VIDUAL	VIHARA	VILLEINS	VINEYARDS
VIDUITIES	VIHARAS	VILLENAGE	VINIC
VIDUITY	VIHUELA	VILLI	VINIER
VIDUOUS	VIHUELAS	VILLIAGO	VINIEST
VIE	VIKING	VILLIAGOS	VINIFERA
VIED	VIKINGISM	VILLIFORM	VINIFERAS
VIELLE	VIKINGS	VILLOSE	VINIFIED
VIELLES	VILAYET	VILLOSITY	VINIFIES
VIER	VILAYETS	VILLOUS	VINIFY
VIERS	VILD	VILLOUSLY	VINIFYING
VIES	VILDE	VILLS	VINING
VIEW	VILDLY	VILLUS	VINO
VIEWABLE	VILDNESS	VIM	VINOLENT
VIEWDATA	VILE	VIMANA	VINOLOGY
VIEWDATAS	VILELY	VIMANAS	VINOS
VIEWED	VILENESS	VIMEN	VINOSITY
VIEWER	VILER	VIMINA	VINOUS
VIEWERS	VILEST	VIMINAL	VINOUSLY
VIEWIER	VILIACO	VIMINEOUS	VINS
VIEWIEST	VILIACOES	VIMS	VINT
VIEWINESS	VILIACOS	VIN	VINTAGE
VIEWING	VILIAGO	VINA	VINTAGED
VIEWINGS	VILIAGOES	VINACEOUS	VINTAGER
VIEWLESS	VILIAGOS	VINAL	VINTAGERS
VIEWLY	VILIFIED	VINALS	VINTAGES
VIEWPHONE	VILIFIER	VINAS	VINTAGING
VIEWPOINT	VILIFIERS	VINASSE	VINTED
VIEWS	VILIFIES	VINASSES	VINTING
VIEWY	VILIFY	VINCA	VINTNER
VIFDA	VILIFYING	VINCAS	VINTNERS
VIFDAS	VILIPEND	VINCIBLE	VINTRIES
VIG	VILIPENDS	VINCIBLY	VINTRY
VIGA	VILL	VINCULA	VINTS
VIGAS	VILLA	VINCULUM	VINY
VIGESIMAL	VILLADOM	VINCULUMS	VINYL
VIGIA	VILLADOMS	VINDALOO	VINYLIC
VIGIAS	VILLAE	VINDALOOS	VINYLS
VIGIL	VILLAGE	VINDEMIAL	VIOL
VIGILANCE	VILLAGER	VINDICATE	VIOLA
VIGILANT	VILLAGERS	VINE	VIOLABLE
VIGILANTE	VILLAGERY	VINEAL	VIOLABLY
VIGILS	VILLAGES	VINED	VIOLAS
VIGNERON	VILLAGIO	VINEGAR	VIOLATE
VIGNERONS	VILLAGIOS	VINEGARED	VIOLATED
VIGNETTE	VILLAGREE	VINEGARS	VIOLATER
VIGNETTED	VILLAIN	VINEGARY	VIOLATERS
VIGNETTER	VILLAINS	VINELESS	VIOLATES
VIGNETTES	VILLAINY	VINELIKE	VIOLATING
VIGOR	VILLAN	VINER	VIOLATION
VIGORISH	VILLANAGE	VINERIES	VIOLATIVE
VIGORO	VILLANIES	VINERS	VIOLATOR
VIGOROS	VILLANOUS	VINERY	VIOLATORS
VIGOROSO	VILLANS	VINES	VIOLD
VIGOROUS	VILLANY	VINEW	VIOLENCE
VIGORS	VILLAR	VINEWED	VIOLENCES
VIGOUR	VILLAS	VINEWING	VIOLENT
VIGOURS	VILLATIC	VINEWS	VIOLENTED
VIGS	VILLEIN	VINEYARD	VIOLENTLY

VIOLENTS	VIRGE	VIRTUALLY	VISCUM
VIOLER	VIRGER	VIRTUE	VISCUMS
VIOLERS	VIRGERS	VIRTUES	VISCUS
VIOLET	VIRGES	VIRTUOSA	VISE
VIOLETS	VIRGIN	VIRTUOSAS	VISED
VIOLIN	VIRGINAL	VIRTUOSE	VISEED
VIOLINIST	VIRGINALS	VIRTUOSI	VISEING
VIOLINS	VIRGINED	VIRTUOSIC	VISELIKE
VIOLIST	VIRGINIA	VIRTUOSO	VISES
VIOLISTS	VIRGINIAS	VIRTUOSOS	VISIBLE
VIOLONE	VIRGINING	VIRTUOUS	VISIBLES
VIOLONES	VIRGINITY	VIRTUS	VISIBLY
VIOLS	VIRGINIUM	VIRUCIDAL	VISIE
VIOMYCIN	VIRGINLY	VIRUCIDE	VISIED
VIOMYCINS	VIRGINS	VIRUCIDES	VISIEING
VIOSTEROL	VIRGULATE	VIRULENCE	VISIER
VIPER	VIRGULE	VIRULENCY	VISIERS
VIPERFISH	VIRGULES	VIRULENT	VISIES
VIPERINE	VIRICIDAL	VIRUS	VISILE
VIPERISH	VIRICIDE	VIRUSES	VISILES
VIPEROUS	VIRICIDES	VIRUSLIKE	VISING
VIPERS	VIRID	VIRUSOID	VISION
VIRAEMIA	VIRIDIAN	VIRUSOIDS	VISIONAL
VIRAEMIAS	VIRIDIANS	VIS	VISIONARY
VIRAEMIC	VIRIDITE	VISA	VISIONED
VIRAGO	VIRIDITES	VISAED	VISIONER
VIRAGOES	VIRIDITY	VISAGE	VISIONERS
VIRAGOISH	VIRILE	VISAGED	VISIONING
VIRAGOS	VIRILELY	VISAGES	VISIONIST
VIRAL	VIRILISE	VISAGIST	VISIONS
VIRALLY	VIRILISED	VISAGISTE	VISIT
VIRANDA	VIRILISES	VISAGISTS	VISITABLE
VIRANDAS	VIRILISM	VISAING	VISITANT
VIRANDO	VIRILISMS	VISARD	VISITANTS
VIRANDOS	VIRILITY	VISARDS	VISITATOR
VIRE	VIRILIZE	VISAS	VISITE
VIRED	VIRILIZED	VISCACHA	VISITED
VIRELAI	VIRILIZES	VISCACHAS	VISITEE
VIRELAIS	VIRILOCAL	VISCARIA	VISITEES
VIRELAY	VIRING	VISCARIAS	VISITER
VIRELAYS	VIRINO	VISCERA	VISITERS
VIREMENT	VIRINOS	VISCERAL	VISITES
VIREMENTS	VIRION	VISCERATE	VISITING
VIREMIA	VIRIONS	VISCID	VISITINGS
VIREMIAS	VIRL	VISCIDITY	VISITOR
VIREMIC	VIRLS	VISCIDLY	VISITORS
VIRENT	VIROGENE	VISCIN	VISITRESS
VIREO	VIROGENES	VISCINS	VISITS
VIREONINE	VIROID	VISCOID	VISIVE
VIREOS	VIROIDS	VISCOIDAL	VISNE
VIRES	VIROLOGIC	VISCOSE	VISNES
VIRESCENT	VIROLOGY	VISCOSES	VISNOMIE
VIRETOT	VIROSE	VISCOSITY	VISNOMIES
VIRETOTS	VIROSES	VISCOUNT	VISNOMY
VIRGA	VIROSIS	VISCOUNTS	VISON
VIRGAS	VIROUS	VISCOUNTY	VISONS
VIRGATE	VIRTU	VISCOUS	VISOR
VIRGATES	VIRTUAL	VISCOUSLY	VISORED

VISORING
VISORLESS
VISORS
VISTA
VISTAED
VISTAING
VISTAL
VISTALESS
VISTAS
VISTO
VISTOS
VISUAL
VISUALISE
VISUALIST
VISUALITY
VISUALIZE
VISUALLY
VISUALS
VITA
VITACEOUS
VITAE
VITAL
VITALISE
VITALISED
VITALISER
VITALISES
VITALISM
VITALISMS
VITALIST
VITALISTS
VITALITY
VITALIZE
VITALIZED
VITALIZER
VITALIZES
VITALLY
VITALNESS
VITALS
VITAMER
VITAMERS
VITAMIN
VITAMINE
VITAMINES
VITAMINIC
VITAMINS
VITAS
VITASCOPE
VITATIVE
VITE
VITELLARY
VITELLI
VITELLIN
VITELLINE
VITELLINS
VITELLUS
VITESSE
VITESSES
VITEX

VITEXES
VITIABLE
VITIATE
VITIATED
VITIATES
VITIATING
VITIATION
VITIATOR
VITIATORS
VITICETA
VITICETUM
VITICIDE
VITICIDES
VITILIGO
VITILIGOS
VITIOSITY
VITRAGE
VITRAGES
VITRAIL
VITRAIN
VITRAINS
VITRAUX
VITREOUS
VITREUM
VITREUMS
VITRIC
VITRICS
VITRIFIED
VITRIFIES
VITRIFORM
VITRIFY
VITRINE
VITRINES
VITRIOL
VITRIOLED
VITRIOLIC
VITRIOLS
VITTA
VITTAE
VITTATE
VITTLE
VITTLED
VITTLES
VITTLING
VITULAR
VITULINE
VIVA
VIVACE
VIVACES
VIVACIOUS
VIVACITY
VIVAED
VIVAING
VIVAMENTE
VIVANDIER
VIVARIA
VIVARIES
VIVARIUM

VIVARIUMS
VIVARY
VIVAS
VIVAT
VIVATS
VIVDA
VIVDAS
VIVE
VIVELY
VIVENCIES
VIVENCY
VIVER
VIVERRA
VIVERRAS
VIVERRID
VIVERRIDS
VIVERRINE
VIVERS
VIVES
VIVIANITE
VIVID
VIVIDER
VIVIDEST
VIVIDITY
VIVIDLY
VIVIDNESS
VIVIFIC
VIVIFIED
VIVIFIER
VIVIFIERS
VIVIFIES
VIVIFY
VIVIFYING
VIVIPARA
VIVIPARY
VIVISECT
VIVISECTS
VIVO
VIVRES
VIXEN
VIXENISH
VIXENLY
VIXENS
VIZAMENT
VIZAMENTS
VIZARD
VIZARDED
VIZARDING
VIZARDS
VIZCACHA
VIZCACHAS
VIZIED
VIZIER
VIZIERATE
VIZIERIAL
VIZIERS
VIZIES
VIZIR

VIZIRATE
VIZIRATES
VIZIRIAL
VIZIRS
VIZIRSHIP
VIZOR
VIZORED
VIZORING
VIZORLESS
VIZORS
VIZSLA
VIZSLAS
VIZY
VIZYING
VIZZIE
VIZZIED
VIZZIEING
VIZZIES
VLEI
VLEIS
VLIES
VLY
VOAR
VOARS
VOCAB
VOCABLE
VOCABLES
VOCABLY
VOCABS
VOCABULAR
VOCAL
VOCALESE
VOCALESES
VOCALIC
VOCALICS
VOCALION
VOCALIONS
VOCALISE
VOCALISED
VOCALISER
VOCALISES
VOCALISM
VOCALISMS
VOCALIST
VOCALISTS
VOCALITY
VOCALIZE
VOCALIZED
VOCALIZER
VOCALIZES
VOCALLY
VOCALNESS
VOCALS
VOCATION
VOCATIONS
VOCATIVE
VOCATIVES
VOCES

VOCODER	VOIDING	VOLKSRAAD	VOLUTIONS
VOCODERS	VOIDINGS	VOLLEY	VOLUTOID
VOCULAR	VOIDNESS	VOLLEYED	VOLVA
VOCULE	VOIDS	VOLLEYER	VOLVAE
VOCULES	VOILA	VOLLEYERS	VOLVAS
VODKA	VOILE	VOLLEYING	VOLVATE
VODKAS	VOILES	VOLLEYS	VOLVE
VODOU	VOISINAGE	VOLOST	VOLVED
VODOUN	VOITURE	VOLOSTS	VOLVES
VODOUNS	VOITURES	VOLPINO	VOLVING
VODOUS	VOITURIER	VOLPINOS	VOLVOX
VODUN	VOIVODE	VOLPLANE	VOLVOXES
VODUNS	VOIVODES	VOLPLANED	VOLVULI
VOE	VOL	VOLPLANES	VOLVULUS
VOEMA	VOLA	VOLS	VOMER
VOEMAS	VOLABLE	VOLT	VOMERINE
VOERTSAK	VOLAE	VOLTA	VOMERS
VOERTSEK	VOLAGE	VOLTAGE	VOMICA
VOES	VOLANT	VOLTAGES	VOMICAE
VOETSAK	VOLANTE	VOLTAIC	VOMICAS
VOETSEK	VOLANTES	VOLTAISM	VOMIT
VOGIE	VOLAR	VOLTAISMS	VOMITED
VOGIER	VOLARIES	VOLTE	VOMITER
VOGIEST	VOLARY	VOLTES	VOMITERS
VOGUE	VOLATIC	VOLTI	VOMITING
VOGUED	VOLATILE	VOLTIGEUR	VOMITINGS
VOGUEING	VOLATILES	VOLTINISM	VOMITIVE
VOGUEINGS	VOLCANIAN	VOLTMETER	VOMITIVES
VOGUER	VOLCANIC	VOLTS	VOMITO
VOGUERS	VOLCANICS	VOLUBIL	VOMITORIA
VOGUES	VOLCANISE	VOLUBLE	VOMITORY
VOGUEY	VOLCANISM	VOLUBLY	VOMITOS
VOGUIER	VOLCANIST	VOLUCRINE	VOMITOUS
VOGUIEST	VOLCANIZE	VOLUME	VOMITS
VOGUING	VOLCANO	VOLUMED	VOMITUS
VOGUINGS	VOLCANOES	VOLUMES	VOMITUSES
VOGUISH	VOLCANOS	VOLUMETER	VOODOO
VOGUISHLY	VOLE	VOLUMETRY	VOODOOED
VOICE	VOLED	VOLUMINAL	VOODOOING
VOICED	VOLENS	VOLUMING	VOODOOISM
VOICEFUL	VOLERIES	VOLUMISE	VOODOOIST
VOICELESS	VOLERY	VOLUMISED	VOODOOS
VOICEMAIL	VOLES	VOLUMISES	VOORKAMER
VOICEOVER	VOLET	VOLUMIST	VOORSKOT
VOICER	VOLETS	VOLUMISTS	VOORSKOTS
VOICERS	VOLING	VOLUMIZE	VOR
VOICES	VOLITANT	VOLUMIZED	VORACIOUS
VOICING	VOLITATE	VOLUMIZES	VORACITY
VOICINGS	VOLITATED	VOLUNTARY	VORAGO
VOID	VOLITATES	VOLUNTEER	VORAGOES
VOIDABLE	VOLITIENT	VOLUSPA	VORANT
VOIDANCE	VOLITION	VOLUSPAS	VORLAGE
VOIDANCES	VOLITIONS	VOLUTE	VORLAGES
VOIDED	VOLITIVE	VOLUTED	VORPAL
VOIDEE	VOLITIVES	VOLUTES	VORRED
VOIDEES	VOLK	VOLUTIN	VORRING
VOIDER	VOLKS	VOLUTINS	VORS
VOIDERS	VOLKSLIED	VOLUTION	VORTEX

VORTEXES
VORTICAL
VORTICES
VORTICISM
VORTICIST
VORTICITY
VORTICOSE
VOSTRO
VOTABLE
VOTARESS
VOTARIES
VOTARIST
VOTARISTS
VOTARY
VOTE
VOTEABLE
VOTED
VOTEEN
VOTEENS
VOTELESS
VOTER
VOTERS
VOTES
VOTING
VOTINGS
VOTIVE
VOTIVELY
VOTIVES
VOTRESS
VOTRESSES
VOUCH
VOUCHED
VOUCHEE
VOUCHEES
VOUCHER
VOUCHERED
VOUCHERS
VOUCHES
VOUCHING
VOUCHSAFE
VOUDON
VOUDONS
VOUDOU
VOUDOUED
VOUDOUING
VOUDOUN
VOUDOUNS
VOUDOUS
VOUGE
VOUGES
VOULGE
VOULGES
VOULU
VOUSSOIR
VOUSSOIRS
VOUTSAFE
VOUTSAFED
VOUTSAFES

VOUVRAY
VOUVRAYS
VOW
VOWED
VOWEL
VOWELISE
VOWELISED
VOWELISES
VOWELIZE
VOWELIZED
VOWELIZES
VOWELLED
VOWELLESS
VOWELLING
VOWELLY
VOWELS
VOWER
VOWERS
VOWESS
VOWESSES
VOWING
VOWLESS
VOWS
VOX
VOXEL
VOXELS
VOYAGE
VOYAGED
VOYAGER
VOYAGERS
VOYAGES
VOYAGEUR
VOYAGEURS
VOYAGING
VOYEUR
VOYEURISM
VOYEURS
VOZHD
VOZHDS
VRAIC
VRAICKER
VRAICKERS
VRAICKING
VRAICS
VRIL
VRILS
VROOM
VROOMED
VROOMING
VROOMS
VROT
VROU
VROUS
VROUW
VROUWS
VROW
VROWS
VUG

VUGG
VUGGIER
VUGGIEST
VUGGS
VUGGY
VUGH
VUGHIER
VUGHIEST
VUGHS
VUGHY
VUGS
VULCAN
VULCANIAN
VULCANIC
VULCANISE
VULCANISM
VULCANIST
VULCANITE
VULCANIZE
VULCANS
VULGAR
VULGARER
VULGAREST
VULGARIAN
VULGARISE
VULGARISM
VULGARITY
VULGARIZE
VULGARLY
VULGARS
VULGATE
VULGATES
VULGO
VULGUS
VULGUSES
VULN
VULNED
VULNERARY
VULNERATE
VULNING
VULNS
VULPICIDE
VULPINE
VULPINISM
VULPINITE
VULSELLA
VULSELLAE
VULSELLUM
VULTURE
VULTURES
VULTURINE
VULTURISH
VULTURISM
VULTURN
VULTURNS
VULTUROUS
VULVA
VULVAE

VULVAL
VULVAR
VULVAS
VULVATE
VULVIFORM
VULVITIS
VUM
VUMMED
VUMMING
VUMS
VUTTIER
VUTTIEST
VUTTY
VUVUZELA
VUVUZELAS
VYING
VYINGLY

W

WAAC	WADDY	WAFFLER	WAGGONER
WAACS	WADDYING	WAFFLERS	WAGGONERS
WAB	WADE	WAFFLES	WAGGONING
WABAIN	WADEABLE	WAFFLIER	WAGGONS
WABAINS	WADED	WAFFLIEST	WAGHALTER
WABBIT	WADER	WAFFLING	WAGING
WABBLE	WADERS	WAFFLINGS	WAGMOIRE
WABBLED	WADES	WAFFLY	WAGMOIRES
WABBLER	WADI	WAFFS	WAGON
WABBLERS	WADIES	WAFT	WAGONAGE
WABBLES	WADING	WAFTAGE	WAGONAGES
WABBLIER	WADINGS	WAFTAGES	WAGONED
WABBLIEST	WADIS	WAFTED	WAGONER
WABBLING	WADMAAL	WAFTER	WAGONERS
WABBLY	WADMAALS	WAFTERS	WAGONETTE
WABOOM	WADMAL	WAFTING	WAGONFUL
WABOOMS	WADMALS	WAFTINGS	WAGONFULS
WABS	WADMEL	WAFTS	WAGONING
WABSTER	WADMELS	WAFTURE	WAGONLESS
WABSTERS	WADMOL	WAFTURES	WAGONLOAD
WACK	WADMOLL	WAG	WAGONS
WACKE	WADMOLLS	WAGE	WAGS
WACKER	WADMOLS	WAGED	WAGSOME
WACKERS	WADS	WAGELESS	WAGTAIL
WACKES	WADSET	WAGENBOOM	WAGTAILS
WACKEST	WADSETS	WAGER	WAHCONDA
WACKIER	WADSETT	WAGERED	WAHCONDAS
WACKIEST	WADSETTED	WAGERER	WAHINE
WACKILY	WADSETTER	WAGERERS	WAHINES
WACKINESS	WADSETTS	WAGERING	WAHOO
WACKO	WADT	WAGERS	WAHOOS
WACKOS	WADTS	WAGES	WAI
WACKS	WADY	WAGGA	WAIATA
WACKY	WAE	WAGGAS	WAIATAS
WAD	WAEFUL	WAGGED	WAID
WADABLE	WAENESS	WAGGER	WAIDE
WADD	WAENESSES	WAGGERIES	WAIF
WADDED	WAES	WAGGERS	WAIFED
WADDER	WAESOME	WAGGERY	WAIFING
WADDERS	WAESUCK	WAGGING	WAIFISH
WADDIE	WAESUCKS	WAGGISH	WAIFLIKE
WADDIED	WAFER	WAGGISHLY	WAIFS
WADDIES	WAFERED	WAGGLE	WAIFT
WADDING	WAFERING	WAGGLED	WAIFTS
WADDINGS	WAFERS	WAGGLER	WAIL
WADDLE	WAFERY	WAGGLERS	WAILED
WADDLED	WAFF	WAGGLES	WAILER
WADDLER	WAFFED	WAGGLIER	WAILERS
WADDLERS	WAFFIE	WAGGLIEST	WAILFUL
WADDLES	WAFFIES	WAGGLING	WAILFULLY
WADDLING	WAFFING	WAGGLY	WAILING
WADDLY	WAFFLE	WAGGON	WAILINGLY
WADDS	WAFFLED	WAGGONED	WAILINGS

WAILS
WAILSOME
WAIN
WAINAGE
WAINAGES
WAINED
WAINING
WAINS
WAINSCOT
WAINSCOTS
WAIR
WAIRED
WAIRING
WAIRS
WAIRSH
WAIRSHER
WAIRSHEST
WAIRUA
WAIRUAS
WAIS
WAIST
WAISTBAND
WAISTBELT
WAISTCOAT
WAISTED
WAISTER
WAISTERS
WAISTING
WAISTINGS
WAISTLESS
WAISTLINE
WAISTS
WAIT
WAITE
WAITED
WAITER
WAITERAGE
WAITERED
WAITERING
WAITERS
WAITES
WAITING
WAITINGLY
WAITINGS
WAITLIST
WAITLISTS
WAITRESS
WAITRON
WAITRONS
WAITS
WAITSTAFF
WAIVE
WAIVED
WAIVER
WAIVERS
WAIVES
WAIVING
WAIVODE

WAIVODES
WAIWODE
WAIWODES
WAKA
WAKAME
WAKAMES
WAKANDA
WAKANDAS
WAKANE
WAKANES
WAKAS
WAKE
WAKEBOARD
WAKED
WAKEFUL
WAKEFULLY
WAKELESS
WAKEMAN
WAKEMEN
WAKEN
WAKENED
WAKENER
WAKENERS
WAKENING
WAKENINGS
WAKENS
WAKER
WAKERIFE
WAKERS
WAKES
WAKF
WAKFS
WAKIKI
WAKIKIS
WAKING
WAKINGS
WALD
WALDFLUTE
WALDGRAVE
WALDHORN
WALDHORNS
WALDO
WALDOES
WALDOS
WALDRAPP
WALDRAPPS
WALDS
WALE
WALED
WALER
WALERS
WALES
WALI
WALIER
WALIES
WALIEST
WALING
WALIS

WALISE
WALISES
WALK
WALKABLE
WALKABOUT
WALKATHON
WALKAWAY
WALKAWAYS
WALKED
WALKER
WALKERS
WALKING
WALKINGS
WALKMILL
WALKMILLS
WALKOUT
WALKOUTS
WALKOVER
WALKOVERS
WALKS
WALKUP
WALKUPS
WALKWAY
WALKWAYS
WALKYRIE
WALKYRIES
WALL
WALLA
WALLABA
WALLABAS
WALLABIES
WALLABY
WALLAH
WALLAHS
WALLAROO
WALLAROOS
WALLAS
WALLBOARD
WALLCHART
WALLED
WALLER
WALLERS
WALLET
WALLETS
WALLEYE
WALLEYED
WALLEYES
WALLFISH
WALLIE
WALLIER
WALLIES
WALLIEST
WALLING
WALLINGS
WALLOP
WALLOPED
WALLOPER
WALLOPERS

WALLOPING
WALLOPS
WALLOW
WALLOWED
WALLOWER
WALLOWERS
WALLOWING
WALLOWS
WALLPAPER
WALLS
WALLSEND
WALLSENDS
WALLWORT
WALLWORTS
WALLY
WALLYBALL
WALLYDRAG
WALNUT
WALNUTS
WALRUS
WALRUSES
WALTIER
WALTIEST
WALTY
WALTZ
WALTZED
WALTZER
WALTZERS
WALTZES
WALTZING
WALTZINGS
WALTZLIKE
WALY
WAMBENGER
WAMBLE
WAMBLED
WAMBLES
WAMBLIER
WAMBLIEST
WAMBLING
WAMBLINGS
WAMBLY
WAME
WAMED
WAMEFOU
WAMEFOUS
WAMEFUL
WAMEFULS
WAMES
WAMMUL
WAMMULS
WAMMUS
WAMMUSES
WAMPEE
WAMPEES
WAMPISH
WAMPISHED
WAMPISHES

WAMPUM	WANKSTA	WAPPED	WARDROP
WAMPUMS	WANKSTAS	WAPPEND	WARDROPS
WAMPUS	WANKY	WAPPER	WARDS
WAMPUSES	WANLE	WAPPERED	WARDSHIP
WAMUS	WANLY	WAPPERING	WARDSHIPS
WAMUSES	WANNA	WAPPERS	WARE
WAN	WANNABE	WAPPING	WARED
WANCHANCY	WANNABEE	WAPS	WAREHOU
WAND	WANNABEES	WAQF	WAREHOUSE
WANDER	WANNABES	WAQFS	WARELESS
WANDERED	WANNED	WAR	WAREROOM
WANDERER	WANNEL	WARAGI	WAREROOMS
WANDERERS	WANNER	WARAGIS	WARES
WANDERING	WANNESS	WARATAH	WAREZ
WANDEROO	WANNESSES	WARATAHS	WARFARE
WANDEROOS	WANNEST	WARB	WARFARED
WANDERS	WANNIGAN	WARBIER	WARFARER
WANDLE	WANNIGANS	WARBIEST	WARFARERS
WANDLIKE	WANNING	WARBLE	WARFARES
WANDOO	WANNISH	WARBLED	WARFARIN
WANDOOS	WANS	WARBLER	WARFARING
WANDS	WANT	WARBLERS	WARFARINS
WANE	WANTAGE	WARBLES	WARHABLE
WANED	WANTAGES	WARBLING	WARHEAD
WANES	WANTED	WARBLINGS	WARHEADS
WANEY	WANTER	WARBONNET	WARHORSE
WANG	WANTERS	WARBS	WARHORSES
WANGAN	WANTHILL	WARBY	WARIBASHI
WANGANS	WANTHILLS	WARCRAFT	WARIER
WANGLE	WANTIES	WARCRAFTS	WARIEST
WANGLED	WANTING	WARD	WARILY
WANGLER	WANTINGS	WARDCORN	WARIMENT
WANGLERS	WANTON	WARDCORNS	WARIMENTS
WANGLES	WANTONED	WARDED	WARINESS
WANGLING	WANTONER	WARDEN	WARING
WANGLINGS	WANTONERS	WARDENED	WARISON
WANGS	WANTONEST	WARDENING	WARISONS
WANGUN	WANTONING	WARDENRY	WARK
WANGUNS	WANTONISE	WARDENS	WARKED
WANHOPE	WANTONIZE	WARDER	WARKING
WANHOPES	WANTONLY	WARDERED	WARKS
WANIER	WANTONS	WARDERING	WARLESS
WANIEST	WANTS	WARDERS	WARLIKE
WANIGAN	WANTY	WARDIAN	WARLING
WANIGANS	WANWORDY	WARDING	WARLINGS
WANING	WANWORTH	WARDINGS	WARLOCK
WANINGS	WANWORTHS	WARDLESS	WARLOCKRY
WANION	WANY	WARDMOTE	WARLOCKS
WANIONS	WANZE	WARDMOTES	WARLORD
WANK	WANZED	WARDOG	WARLORDS
WANKED	WANZES	WARDOGS	WARM
WANKER	WANZING	WARDRESS	WARMAKER
WANKERS	WAP	WARDROBE	WARMAKERS
WANKIER	WAPENSHAW	WARDROBED	WARMAN
WANKIEST	WAPENTAKE	WARDROBER	WARMBLOOD
WANKING	WAPINSHAW	WARDROBES	WARMED
WANKLE	WAPITI	WARDROOM	WARMEN
WANKS	WAPITIS	WARDROOMS	WARMER

WARMERS	WARRANTY	WARWORK	WASHUP
WARMEST	WARRAY	WARWORKS	WASHUPS
WARMING	WARRAYED	WARWORN	WASHWIPE
WARMINGS	WARRAYING	WARY	WASHWIPES
WARMISH	WARRAYS	WARZONE	WASHWOMAN
WARMLY	WARRE	WARZONES	WASHWOMEN
WARMNESS	WARRED	WAS	WASHY
WARMONGER	WARREN	WASABI	WASM
WARMOUTH	WARRENER	WASABIS	WASMS
WARMOUTHS	WARRENERS	WASE	WASP
WARMS	WARRENS	WASES	WASPIE
WARMTH	WARREY	WASH	WASPIER
WARMTHS	WARREYED	WASHABLE	WASPIES
WARMUP	WARREYING	WASHABLES	WASPIEST
WARMUPS	WARREYS	WASHAWAY	WASPILY
WARN	WARRIGAL	WASHAWAYS	WASPINESS
WARNED	WARRIGALS	WASHBALL	WASPISH
WARNER	WARRING	WASHBALLS	WASPISHLY
WARNERS	WARRIOR	WASHBASIN	WASPLIKE
WARNING	WARRIORS	WASHBOARD	WASPNEST
WARNINGLY	WARRISON	WASHBOWL	WASPNESTS
WARNINGS	WARRISONS	WASHBOWLS	WASPS
WARNS	WARS	WASHCLOTH	WASPY
WARP	WARSAW	WASHDAY	WASSAIL
WARPAGE	WARSAWS	WASHDAYS	WASSAILED
WARPAGES	WARSHIP	WASHED	WASSAILER
WARPATH	WARSHIPS	WASHEN	WASSAILRY
WARPATHS	WARSLE	WASHER	WASSAILS
WARPED	WARSLED	WASHERED	WASSERMAN
WARPER	WARSLER	WASHERIES	WASSERMEN
WARPERS	WARSLERS	WASHERING	WASSUP
WARPING	WARSLES	WASHERMAN	WAST
WARPINGS	WARSLING	WASHERMEN	WASTABLE
WARPLANE	WARST	WASHERS	WASTAGE
WARPLANES	WARSTLE	WASHERY	WASTAGES
WARPOWER	WARSTLED	WASHES	WASTE
WARPOWERS	WARSTLER	WASHHOUSE	WASTED
WARPS	WARSTLERS	WASHIER	WASTEFUL
WARPWISE	WARSTLES	WASHIEST	WASTEL
WARRAGAL	WARSTLING	WASHILY	WASTELAND
WARRAGALS	WART	WASHIN	WASTELOT
WARRAGLE	WARTED	WASHINESS	WASTELOTS
WARRAGLES	WARTHOG	WASHING	WASTELS
WARRAGUL	WARTHOGS	WASHINGS	WASTENESS
WARRAGULS	WARTIER	WASHINS	WASTER
WARRAN	WARTIEST	WASHLAND	WASTERED
WARRAND	WARTIME	WASHLANDS	WASTERFUL
WARRANDED	WARTIMES	WASHOUT	WASTERIE
WARRANDS	WARTLESS	WASHOUTS	WASTERIES
WARRANED	WARTLIKE	WASHPOT	WASTERING
WARRANING	WARTS	WASHPOTS	WASTERS
WARRANS	WARTWEED	WASHRAG	WASTERY
WARRANT	WARTWEEDS	WASHRAGS	WASTES
WARRANTED	WARTWORT	WASHROOM	WASTEWAY
WARRANTEE	WARTWORTS	WASHROOMS	WASTEWAYS
WARRANTER	WARTY	WASHSTAND	WASTEWEIR
WARRANTOR	WARWOLF	WASHTUB	WASTFULL
WARRANTS	WARWOLVES	WASHTUBS	WASTING

WASTINGLY	WATERHENS	WAUFFS	WAVERINGS
WASTINGS	WATERIER	WAUGH	WAVEROUS
WASTNESS	WATERIEST	WAUGHED	WAVERS
WASTREL	WATERILY	WAUGHING	WAVERY
WASTRELS	WATERING	WAUGHS	WAVES
WASTRIE	WATERINGS	WAUGHT	WAVESHAPE
WASTRIES	WATERISH	WAUGHTED	WAVESON
WASTRIFE	WATERJET	WAUGHTING	WAVESONS
WASTRIFES	WATERJETS	WAUGHTS	WAVEY
WASTRY	WATERLEAF	WAUK	WAVEYS
WASTS	WATERLESS	WAUKED	WAVICLE
WAT	WATERLILY	WAUKER	WAVICLES
WATAP	WATERLINE	WAUKERS	WAVIER
WATAPE	WATERLOG	WAUKING	WAVIES
WATAPES	WATERLOGS	WAUKMILL	WAVIEST
WATAPS	WATERLOO	WAUKMILLS	WAVILY
WATCH	WATERLOOS	WAUKRIFE	WAVINESS
WATCHABLE	WATERMAN	WAUKS	WAVING
WATCHBAND	WATERMARK	WAUL	WAVINGS
WATCHBOX	WATERMEN	WAULED	WAVY
WATCHCASE	WATERPOX	WAULING	WAW
WATCHCRY	WATERS	WAULINGS	WAWA
WATCHDOG	WATERSHED	WAULK	WAWAED
WATCHDOGS	WATERSIDE	WAULKED	WAWAING
WATCHED	WATERSKI	WAULKER	WAWAS
WATCHER	WATERSKIS	WAULKERS	WAWE
WATCHERS	WATERWAY	WAULKING	WAWES
WATCHES	WATERWAYS	WAULKMILL	WAWL
WATCHET	WATERWEED	WAULKS	WAWLED
WATCHETS	WATERWORK	WAULS	WAWLING
WATCHEYE	WATERWORN	WAUR	WAWLINGS
WATCHEYES	WATERY	WAURED	WAWLS
WATCHFUL	WATERZOOI	WAURING	WAWS
WATCHING	WATS	WAURS	WAX
WATCHLIST	WATT	WAURST	WAXABLE
WATCHMAN	WATTAGE	WAVE	WAXBERRY
WATCHMEN	WATTAGES	WAVEBAND	WAXBILL
WATCHOUT	WATTAPE	WAVEBANDS	WAXBILLS
WATCHOUTS	WATTAPES	WAVED	WAXCLOTH
WATCHWORD	WATTER	WAVEFORM	WAXCLOTHS
WATE	WATTEST	WAVEFORMS	WAXED
WATER	WATTHOUR	WAVEFRONT	WAXEN
WATERAGE	WATTHOURS	WAVEGUIDE	WAXER
WATERAGES	WATTLE	WAVELESS	WAXERS
WATERBED	WATTLED	WAVELET	WAXES
WATERBEDS	WATTLES	WAVELETS	WAXEYE
WATERBIRD	WATTLESS	WAVELIKE	WAXEYES
WATERBUCK	WATTLING	WAVELLITE	WAXFLOWER
WATERBUS	WATTLINGS	WAVEMETER	WAXIER
WATERDOG	WATTMETER	WAVEOFF	WAXIEST
WATERDOGS	WATTS	WAVEOFFS	WAXILY
WATERED	WAUCHT	WAVER	WAXINESS
WATERER	WAUCHTED	WAVERED	WAXING
WATERERS	WAUCHTING	WAVERER	WAXINGS
WATERFALL	WAUCHTS	WAVERERS	WAXLIKE
WATERFOWL	WAUFF	WAVERIER	WAXPLANT
WATERHEAD	WAUFFED	WAVERIEST	WAXPLANTS
WATERHEN	WAUFFING	WAVERING	WAXWEED

WAXWEEDS	WAYWORN	WEAPONISE	WEAZENS
WAXWING	WAYZGOOSE	WEAPONIZE	WEB
WAXWINGS	WAZIR	WEAPONRY	WEBBED
WAXWORK	WAZIRS	WEAPONS	WEBBIE
WAXWORKER	WAZOO	WEAR	WEBBIER
WAXWORKS	WAZOOS	WEARABLE	WEBBIES
WAXWORM	WAZZOCK	WEARABLES	WEBBIEST
WAXWORMS	WAZZOCKS	WEARED	WEBBING
WAXY	WE	WEARER	WEBBINGS
WAY	WEAK	WEARERS	WEBBY
WAYBILL	WEAKEN	WEARIED	WEBCAM
WAYBILLS	WEAKENED	WEARIER	WEBCAMS
WAYBOARD	WEAKENER	WEARIES	WEBCAST
WAYBOARDS	WEAKENERS	WEARIEST	WEBCASTED
WAYBREAD	WEAKENING	WEARIFUL	WEBCASTER
WAYBREADS	WEAKENS	WEARILESS	WEBCASTS
WAYED	WEAKER	WEARILY	WEBER
WAYFARE	WEAKEST	WEARINESS	WEBERS
WAYFARED	WEAKFISH	WEARING	WEBFED
WAYFARER	WEAKISH	WEARINGLY	WEBFEET
WAYFARERS	WEAKISHLY	WEARINGS	WEBFOOT
WAYFARES	WEAKLIER	WEARISH	WEBFOOTED
WAYFARING	WEAKLIEST	WEARISOME	WEBINAR
WAYGOING	WEAKLING	WEARPROOF	WEBINARS
WAYGOINGS	WEAKLINGS	WEARS	WEBLESS
WAYGONE	WEAKLY	WEARY	WEBLIKE
WAYGOOSE	WEAKNESS	WEARYING	WEBLISH
WAYGOOSES	WEAKON	WEASAND	WEBLISHES
WAYING	WEAKONS	WEASANDS	WEBLOG
WAYLAID	WEAKSIDE	WEASEL	WEBLOGGER
WAYLAY	WEAKSIDES	WEASELED	WEBLOGS
WAYLAYER	WEAL	WEASELER	WEBMAIL
WAYLAYERS	WEALD	WEASELERS	WEBMAILS
WAYLAYING	WEALDS	WEASELING	WEBMASTER
WAYLAYS	WEALS	WEASELLED	WEBPAGE
WAYLEAVE	WEALSMAN	WEASELLER	WEBPAGES
WAYLEAVES	WEALSMEN	WEASELLY	WEBS
WAYLEGGO	WEALTH	WEASELS	WEBSITE
WAYLESS	WEALTHIER	WEASELY	WEBSITES
WAYMARK	WEALTHILY	WEASON	WEBSTER
WAYMARKED	WEALTHS	WEASONS	WEBSTERS
WAYMARKS	WEALTHY	WEATHER	WEBWHEEL
WAYMENT	WEAMB	WEATHERED	WEBWHEELS
WAYMENTED	WEAMBS	WEATHERER	WEBWORK
WAYMENTS	WEAN	WEATHERLY	WEBWORKS
WAYPOINT	WEANED	WEATHERS	WEBWORM
WAYPOINTS	WEANEL	WEAVE	WEBWORMS
WAYPOST	WEANELS	WEAVED	WECHT
WAYPOSTS	WEANER	WEAVER	WECHTS
WAYS	WEANERS	WEAVERS	WED
WAYSIDE	WEANING	WEAVES	WEDDED
WAYSIDES	WEANLING	WEAVING	WEDDER
WAYWARD	WEANLINGS	WEAVINGS	WEDDERED
WAYWARDLY	WEANS	WEAZAND	WEDDERING
WAYWISER	WEAPON	WEAZANDS	WEDDERS
WAYWISERS	WEAPONED	WEAZEN	WEDDING
WAYWODE	WEAPONEER	WEAZENED	WEDDINGS
WAYWODES	WEAPONING	WEAZENING	WEDEL

WEDELED	WEEMS	WEFTED	WEIZE
WEDELING	WEEN	WEFTES	WEIZED
WEDELN	WEENED	WEFTING	WEIZES
WEDELNED	WEENIE	WEFTS	WEIZING
WEDELNING	WEENIER	WEFTWISE	WEKA
WEDELNS	WEENIES	WEID	WEKAS
WEDELS	WEENIEST	WEIDS	WELAWAY
WEDGE	WEENING	WEIGELA	WELCH
WEDGED	WEENS	WEIGELAS	WELCHED
WEDGELIKE	WEENSIER	WEIGELIA	WELCHER
WEDGES	WEENSIEST	WEIGELIAS	WELCHERS
WEDGEWISE	WEENSY	WEIGH	WELCHES
WEDGIE	WEENY	WEIGHABLE	WELCHING
WEDGIER	WEEP	WEIGHAGE	WELCOME
WEDGIES	WEEPER	WEIGHAGES	WELCOMED
WEDGIEST	WEEPERS	WEIGHED	WELCOMELY
WEDGING	WEEPHOLE	WEIGHER	WELCOMER
WEDGINGS	WEEPHOLES	WEIGHERS	WELCOMERS
WEDGY	WEEPIE	WEIGHING	WELCOMES
WEDLOCK	WEEPIER	WEIGHINGS	WELCOMING
WEDLOCKS	WEEPIES	WEIGHMAN	WELD
WEDS	WEEPIEST	WEIGHMEN	WELDABLE
WEE	WEEPILY	WEIGHS	WELDED
WEED	WEEPINESS	WEIGHT	WELDER
WEEDED	WEEPING	WEIGHTED	WELDERS
WEEDER	WEEPINGLY	WEIGHTER	WELDING
WEEDERIES	WEEPINGS	WEIGHTERS	WELDINGS
WEEDERS	WEEPS	WEIGHTIER	WELDLESS
WEEDERY	WEEPY	WEIGHTILY	WELDMENT
WEEDICIDE	WEER	WEIGHTING	WELDMENTS
WEEDIER	WEES	WEIGHTS	WELDMESH
WEEDIEST	WEEST	WEIGHTY	WELDOR
WEEDILY	WEET	WEIL	WELDORS
WEEDINESS	WEETE	WEILS	WELDS
WEEDING	WEETED	WEINER	WELFARE
WEEDINGS	WEETEN	WEINERS	WELFARES
WEEDLESS	WEETER	WEIR	WELFARISM
WEEDLIKE	WEETEST	WEIRD	WELFARIST
WEEDS	WEETING	WEIRDED	WELK
WEEDY	WEETINGLY	WEIRDER	WELKE
WEEING	WEETLESS	WEIRDEST	WELKED
WEEK	WEETS	WEIRDIE	WELKES
WEEKDAY	WEEVER	WEIRDIES	WELKIN
WEEKDAYS	WEEVERS	WEIRDING	WELKING
WEEKE	WEEVIL	WEIRDLY	WELKINS
WEEKEND	WEEVILED	WEIRDNESS	WELKS
WEEKENDED	WEEVILLED	WEIRDO	WELKT
WEEKENDER	WEEVILLY	WEIRDOES	WELL
WEEKENDS	WEEVILS	WEIRDOS	WELLADAY
WEEKES	WEEVILY	WEIRDS	WELLADAYS
WEEKLIES	WEEWEE	WEIRDY	WELLANEAR
WEEKLONG	WEEWEED	WEIRED	WELLAWAY
WEEKLY	WEEWEEING	WEIRING	WELLAWAYS
WEEKNIGHT	WEEWEES	WEIRS	WELLBEING
WEEKS	WEFT	WEISE	WELLBORN
WEEL	WEFTAGE	WEISED	WELLCURB
WEELS	WEFTAGES	WEISES	WELLCURBS
WEEM	WEFTE	WEISING	WELLDOER

661

WELLDOERS	WEPT	WETLY	WHALEBOAT
WELLED	WERE	WETNESS	WHALEBONE
WELLHEAD	WEREGILD	WETNESSES	WHALED
WELLHEADS	WEREGILDS	WETPROOF	WHALELIKE
WELLHOLE	WEREWOLF	WETS	WHALEMAN
WELLHOLES	WERGELD	WETSUIT	WHALEMEN
WELLHOUSE	WERGELDS	WETSUITS	WHALER
WELLIE	WERGELT	WETTABLE	WHALERIES
WELLIES	WERGELTS	WETTED	WHALERS
WELLING	WERGILD	WETTER	WHALERY
WELLINGS	WERGILDS	WETTERS	WHALES
WELLNESS	WERNERITE	WETTEST	WHALING
WELLS	WERO	WETTIE	WHALINGS
WELLSITE	WEROS	WETTIES	WHALLY
WELLSITES	WERRIS	WETTING	WHAM
WELLY	WERRISES	WETTINGS	WHAMMED
WELSH	WERSH	WETTISH	WHAMMIES
WELSHED	WERSHER	WETWARE	WHAMMING
WELSHER	WERSHEST	WETWARES	WHAMMO
WELSHERS	WERT	WEX	WHAMMOS
WELSHES	WERWOLF	WEXE	WHAMMY
WELSHING	WERWOLVES	WEXED	WHAMO
WELT	WESAND	WEXES	WHAMPLE
WELTED	WESANDS	WEXING	WHAMPLES
WELTER	WESKIT	WEY	WHAMS
WELTERED	WESKITS	WEYARD	WHANAU
WELTERING	WESSAND	WEYS	WHANAUS
WELTERS	WESSANDS	WEYWARD	WHANG
WELTING	WEST	WEZAND	WHANGAM
WELTINGS	WESTBOUND	WEZANDS	WHANGAMS
WELTS	WESTED	WHA	WHANGED
WEM	WESTER	WHACK	WHANGEE
WEMB	WESTERED	WHACKED	WHANGEES
WEMBS	WESTERING	WHACKER	WHANGING
WEMS	WESTERLY	WHACKERS	WHANGS
WEN	WESTERN	WHACKIER	WHAP
WENA	WESTERNER	WHACKIEST	WHAPPED
WENCH	WESTERNS	WHACKING	WHAPPER
WENCHED	WESTERS	WHACKINGS	WHAPPERS
WENCHER	WESTIE	WHACKO	WHAPPING
WENCHERS	WESTIES	WHACKOES	WHAPS
WENCHES	WESTING	WHACKOS	WHARE
WENCHING	WESTINGS	WHACKS	WHARENUI
WEND	WESTLIN	WHACKY	WHARENUIS
WENDED	WESTLINS	WHAE	WHAREPUNI
WENDIGO	WESTMOST	WHAISLE	WHARES
WENDIGOS	WESTS	WHAISLED	WHARF
WENDING	WESTWARD	WHAISLES	WHARFAGE
WENDS	WESTWARDS	WHAISLING	WHARFAGES
WENGE	WET	WHAIZLE	WHARFED
WENGES	WETA	WHAIZLED	WHARFIE
WENNIER	WETAS	WHAIZLES	WHARFIES
WENNIEST	WETBACK	WHAIZLING	WHARFING
WENNISH	WETBACKS	WHAKAIRO	WHARFINGS
WENNY	WETHER	WHAKAIROS	WHARFS
WENS	WETHERS	WHAKAPAPA	WHARVE
WENT	WETLAND	WHALE	WHARVES
WENTS	WETLANDS	WHALEBACK	WHAT

WHATA	WHEELLESS	WHELPING	WHETTER
WHATAS	WHEELMAN	WHELPLESS	WHETTERS
WHATEN	WHEELMEN	WHELPS	WHETTING
WHATEVER	WHEELS	WHEMMLE	WHEUGH
WHATNA	WHEELSMAN	WHEMMLED	WHEUGHED
WHATNESS	WHEELSMEN	WHEMMLES	WHEUGHING
WHATNOT	WHEELWORK	WHEMMLING	WHEUGHS
WHATNOTS	WHEELY	WHEN	WHEW
WHATS	WHEEN	WHENAS	WHEWED
WHATSIS	WHEENGE	WHENCE	WHEWING
WHATSISES	WHEENGED	WHENCES	WHEWS
WHATSIT	WHEENGES	WHENCEVER	WHEY
WHATSITS	WHEENGING	WHENEVER	WHEYEY
WHATSO	WHEENS	WHENS	WHEYFACE
WHATTEN	WHEEP	WHENUA	WHEYFACED
WHAUP	WHEEPED	WHENUAS	WHEYFACES
WHAUPS	WHEEPING	WHENWE	WHEYIER
WHAUR	WHEEPLE	WHENWES	WHEYIEST
WHAURS	WHEEPLED	WHERE	WHEYISH
WHEAL	WHEEPLES	WHEREAS	WHEYLIKE
WHEALS	WHEEPLING	WHEREASES	WHEYS
WHEAR	WHEEPS	WHEREAT	WHICH
WHEARE	WHEESH	WHEREBY	WHICHEVER
WHEAT	WHEESHED	WHEREFOR	WHICKER
WHEATEAR	WHEESHES	WHEREFORE	WHICKERED
WHEATEARS	WHEESHING	WHEREFROM	WHICKERS
WHEATEN	WHEESHT	WHEREIN	WHID
WHEATENS	WHEESHTED	WHEREINTO	WHIDAH
WHEATIER	WHEESHTS	WHERENESS	WHIDAHS
WHEATIEST	WHEEZE	WHEREOF	WHIDDED
WHEATLAND	WHEEZED	WHEREON	WHIDDER
WHEATLESS	WHEEZER	WHEREOUT	WHIDDERED
WHEATMEAL	WHEEZERS	WHERES	WHIDDERS
WHEATS	WHEEZES	WHERESO	WHIDDING
WHEATWORM	WHEEZIER	WHERETO	WHIDS
WHEATY	WHEEZIEST	WHEREUNTO	WHIFF
WHEE	WHEEZILY	WHEREUPON	WHIFFED
WHEECH	WHEEZING	WHEREVER	WHIFFER
WHEECHED	WHEEZINGS	WHEREWITH	WHIFFERS
WHEECHING	WHEEZLE	WHERRET	WHIFFET
WHEECHS	WHEEZLED	WHERRETED	WHIFFETS
WHEEDLE	WHEEZLES	WHERRETS	WHIFFIER
WHEEDLED	WHEEZLING	WHERRIED	WHIFFIEST
WHEEDLER	WHEEZY	WHERRIES	WHIFFING
WHEEDLERS	WHEFT	WHERRIT	WHIFFINGS
WHEEDLES	WHEFTS	WHERRITED	WHIFFLE
WHEEDLING	WHELK	WHERRITS	WHIFFLED
WHEEL	WHELKED	WHERRY	WHIFFLER
WHEELBASE	WHELKIER	WHERRYING	WHIFFLERS
WHEELED	WHELKIEST	WHERRYMAN	WHIFFLERY
WHEELER	WHELKS	WHERRYMEN	WHIFFLES
WHEELERS	WHELKY	WHERVE	WHIFFLING
WHEELIE	WHELM	WHERVES	WHIFFS
WHEELIER	WHELMED	WHET	WHIFFY
WHEELIES	WHELMING	WHETHER	WHIFT
WHEELIEST	WHELMS	WHETS	WHIFTS
WHEELING	WHELP	WHETSTONE	WHIG
WHEELINGS	WHELPED	WHETTED	WHIGGED

WHIGGING	WHINGES	WHIPTAIL	WHISPER
WHIGS	WHINGING	WHIPTAILS	WHISPERED
WHILE	WHINIARD	WHIPWORM	WHISPERER
WHILED	WHINIARDS	WHIPWORMS	WHISPERS
WHILERE	WHINIER	WHIR	WHISPERY
WHILES	WHINIEST	WHIRL	WHISS
WHILING	WHININESS	WHIRLBAT	WHISSED
WHILK	WHINING	WHIRLBATS	WHISSES
WHILLIED	WHININGLY	WHIRLED	WHISSING
WHILLIES	WHININGS	WHIRLER	WHIST
WHILLY	WHINNIED	WHIRLERS	WHISTED
WHILLYING	WHINNIER	WHIRLIER	WHISTING
WHILLYWHA	WHINNIES	WHIRLIES	WHISTLE
WHILOM ·	WHINNIEST	WHIRLIEST	WHISTLED
WHILST	WHINNY	WHIRLIGIG	WHISTLER
WHIM	WHINNYING	WHIRLING	WHISTLERS
WHIMBERRY	WHINS	WHIRLINGS	WHISTLES
WHIMBREL	WHINSTONE	WHIRLPOOL	WHISTLING
WHIMBRELS	WHINY	WHIRLS	WHISTS
WHIMMED	WHINYARD	WHIRLWIND	WHIT
WHIMMIER	WHINYARDS	WHIRLY	WHITE
WHIMMIEST	WHIO	WHIRR	WHITEBAIT
WHIMMING	WHIP	WHIRRED	WHITEBASS
WHIMMY	WHIPBIRD	WHIRRET	WHITEBEAM
WHIMPER	WHIPBIRDS	WHIRRETED	WHITECAP
WHIMPERED	WHIPCAT	WHIRRETS	WHITECAPS
WHIMPERER	WHIPCATS	WHIRRIED	WHITECOAT
WHIMPERS	WHIPCORD	WHIRRIES	WHITECOMB
WHIMPLE	WHIPCORDS	WHIRRING	WHITED
WHIMPLED	WHIPCORDY	WHIRRINGS	WHITEDAMP
WHIMPLES	WHIPJACK	WHIRRS	WHITEFACE
WHIMPLING	WHIPJACKS	WHIRRY	WHITEFISH
WHIMS	WHIPLASH	WHIRRYING	WHITEFLY
WHIMSEY	WHIPLIKE	WHIRS	WHITEHEAD
WHIMSEYS	WHIPPED	WHIRTLE	WHITELY
WHIMSICAL	WHIPPER	WHIRTLES	WHITEN
WHIMSIED	WHIPPERS	WHISH	WHITENED
WHIMSIER	WHIPPET	WHISHED	WHITENER
WHIMSIES	WHIPPETS	WHISHES	WHITENERS
WHIMSIEST	WHIPPIER	WHISHING	WHITENESS
WHIMSILY	WHIPPIEST	WHISHT	WHITENING
WHIMSY	WHIPPING	WHISHTED	WHITENS
WHIN	WHIPPINGS	WHISHTING	WHITEOUT
WHINBERRY	WHIPPY	WHISHTS	WHITEOUTS
WHINCHAT	WHIPRAY	WHISK	WHITEPOT
WHINCHATS	WHIPRAYS	WHISKED	WHITEPOTS
WHINE	WHIPS	WHISKER	WHITER
WHINED	WHIPSAW	WHISKERED	WHITES
WHINER	WHIPSAWED	WHISKERS	WHITEST
WHINERS	WHIPSAWN	WHISKERY	WHITETAIL
WHINES	WHIPSAWS	WHISKET	WHITEWALL
WHINEY	WHIPSNAKE	WHISKETS	WHITEWARE
WHINGDING	WHIPSTAFF	WHISKEY	WHITEWASH
WHINGE	WHIPSTALL	WHISKEYS	WHITEWING
WHINGED	WHIPSTER	WHISKIES	WHITEWOOD
WHINGEING	WHIPSTERS	WHISKING	WHITEY
WHINGER	WHIPSTOCK	WHISKS	WHITEYS
WHINGERS	WHIPT	WHISKY	WHITHER

WHITHERED	WHOLEMEAL	WHOPPED	WICCA
WHITHERS	WHOLENESS	WHOPPER	WICCAN
WHITIER	WHOLES	WHOPPERS	WICCANS
WHITIES	WHOLESALE	WHOPPING	WICCAS
WHITIEST	WHOLESOME	WHOPPINGS	WICE
WHITING	WHOLISM	WHOPS	WICH
WHITINGS	WHOLISMS	WHORE	WICHES
WHITISH	WHOLIST	WHORED	WICK
WHITLING	WHOLISTIC	WHOREDOM	WICKAPE
WHITLINGS	WHOLISTS	WHOREDOMS	WICKAPES
WHITLOW	WHOLLY	WHORES	WICKED
WHITLOWS	WHOM	WHORESON	WICKEDER
WHITRACK	WHOMBLE	WHORESONS	WICKEDEST
WHITRACKS	WHOMBLED	WHORING	WICKEDLY
WHITRET	WHOMBLES	WHORISH	WICKEDS
WHITRETS	WHOMBLING	WHORISHLY	WICKEN
WHITRICK	WHOMEVER	WHORL	WICKENS
WHITRICKS	WHOMMLE	WHORLBAT	WICKER
WHITS	WHOMMLED	WHORLBATS	WICKERED
WHITSTER	WHOMMLES	WHORLED	WICKERS
WHITSTERS	WHOMMLING	WHORLS	WICKET
WHITTAW	WHOMP	WHORT	WICKETS
WHITTAWER	WHOMPED	WHORTLE	WICKIES
WHITTAWS	WHOMPING	WHORTLES	WICKING
WHITTER	WHOMPS	WHORTS	WICKINGS
WHITTERED	WHOMSO	WHOSE	WICKIUP
WHITTERS	WHOOBUB	WHOSEVER	WICKIUPS
WHITTLE	WHOOBUBS	WHOSIS	WICKLESS
WHITTLED	WHOOF	WHOSISES	WICKS
WHITTLER	WHOOFED	WHOSO	WICKTHING
WHITTLERS	WHOOFING	WHOSOEVER	WICKY
WHITTLES	WHOOFS	WHOT	WICKYUP
WHITTLING	WHOOP	WHOW	WICKYUPS
WHITTRET	WHOOPED	WHUMMLE	WICOPIES
WHITTRETS	WHOOPEE	WHUMMLED	WICOPY
WHITY	WHOOPEES	WHUMMLES	WIDDER
WHIZ	WHOOPER	WHUMMLING	WIDDERS
WHIZBANG	WHOOPERS	WHUMP	WIDDIE
WHIZBANGS	WHOOPIE	WHUMPED	WIDDIES
WHIZZ	WHOOPIES	WHUMPING	WIDDLE
WHIZZBANG	WHOOPING	WHUMPS	WIDDLED
WHIZZED	WHOOPINGS	WHUNSTANE	WIDDLES
WHIZZER	WHOOPLA	WHUP	WIDDLING
WHIZZERS	WHOOPLAS	WHUPPED	WIDDY
WHIZZES	WHOOPS	WHUPPING	WIDE
WHIZZIER	WHOOPSIE	WHUPS	WIDEAWAKE
WHIZZIEST	WHOOPSIES	WHY	WIDEBAND
WHIZZING	WHOOSH	WHYDAH	WIDEBODY
WHIZZINGS	WHOOSHED	WHYDAHS	WIDELY
WHIZZY	WHOOSHES	WHYDUNIT	WIDEN
WHO	WHOOSHING	WHYDUNITS	WIDENED
WHOA	WHOOSIS	WHYDUNNIT	WIDENER
WHODUNIT	WHOOSISES	WHYEVER	WIDENERS
WHODUNITS	WHOOT	WHYS	WIDENESS
WHODUNNIT	WHOOTED	WIBBLE	WIDENING
WHOEVER	WHOOTING	WIBBLED	WIDENS
WHOLE	WHOOTS	WIBBLES	WIDEOUT
WHOLEFOOD	WHOP	WIBBLING	WIDEOUTS

WIDER	WIFIES	WILDER	WILLIE
WIDES	WIFING	WILDERED	WILLIED
WIDEST	WIFTIER	WILDERING	WILLIES
WIDGEON	WIFTIEST	WILDERS	WILLING
WIDGEONS	WIFTY	WILDEST	WILLINGER
WIDGET	WIG	WILDFIRE	WILLINGLY
WIDGETS	WIGAN	WILDFIRES	WILLIWAU
WIDGIE	WIGANS	WILDFOWL	WILLIWAUS
WIDGIES	WIGEON	WILDFOWLS	WILLIWAW
WIDISH	WIGEONS	WILDGRAVE	WILLIWAWS
WIDOW	WIGGA	WILDING	WILLOW
WIDOWBIRD	WIGGAS	WILDINGS	WILLOWED
WIDOWED	WIGGED	WILDISH	WILLOWER
WIDOWER	WIGGER	WILDLAND	WILLOWERS
WIDOWERED	WIGGERIES	WILDLANDS	WILLOWIER
WIDOWERS	WIGGERS	WILDLIFE	WILLOWING
WIDOWHOOD	WIGGERY	WILDLIFES	WILLOWISH
WIDOWING	WIGGIER	WILDLING	WILLOWS
WIDOWMAN	WIGGIEST	WILDLINGS	WILLOWY
WIDOWMEN	WIGGING	WILDLY	WILLPOWER
WIDOWS	WIGGINGS	WILDNESS	WILLS
WIDTH	WIGGLE	WILDS	WILLY
WIDTHS	WIGGLED	WILDWOOD	WILLYARD
WIDTHWAY	WIGGLER	WILDWOODS	WILLYART
WIDTHWAYS	WIGGLERS	WILE	WILLYING
WIDTHWISE	WIGGLES	WILED	WILLYWAW
WIEL	WIGGLIER	WILEFUL	WILLYWAWS
WIELD	WIGGLIEST	WILES	WILT
WIELDABLE	WIGGLING	WILFUL	WILTED
WIELDED	WIGGLY	WILFULLY	WILTING
WIELDER	WIGGY	WILGA	WILTJA
WIELDERS	WIGHT	WILGAS	WILTJAS
WIELDIER	WIGHTED	WILI	WILTS
WIELDIEST	WIGHTING	WILIER	WILY
WIELDING	WIGHTLY	WILIEST	WIMBLE
WIELDLESS	WIGHTS	WILILY	WIMBLED
WIELDS	WIGLESS	WILINESS	WIMBLES
WIELDY	WIGLET	WILING	WIMBLING
WIELS	WIGLETS	WILIS	WIMBREL
WIENER	WIGLIKE	WILJA	WIMBRELS
WIENERS	WIGMAKER	WILJAS	WIMMIN
WIENIE	WIGMAKERS	WILL	WIMP
WIENIES	WIGS	WILLABLE	WIMPED
WIFE	WIGWAG	WILLED	WIMPIER
WIFED	WIGWAGGED	WILLEMITE	WIMPIEST
WIFEDOM	WIGWAGGER	WILLER	WIMPINESS
WIFEDOMS	WIGWAGS	WILLERS	WIMPING
WIFEHOOD	WIGWAM	WILLEST	WIMPISH
WIFEHOODS	WIGWAMS	WILLET	WIMPISHLY
WIFELESS	WIKIUP	WILLETS	WIMPLE
WIFELIER	WIKIUPS	WILLEY	WIMPLED
WIFELIEST	WILCO	WILLEYED	WIMPLES
WIFELIKE	WILD	WILLEYING	WIMPLING
WIFELY	WILDCARD	WILLEYS	WIMPS
WIFES	WILDCARDS	WILLFUL	WIMPY
WIFEY	WILDCAT	WILLFULLY	WIN
WIFEYS	WILDCATS	WILLIAM	WINCE
WIFIE	WILDED	WILLIAMS	WINCED

WINCER	WINDINESS	WINELESS	WINKERS
WINCERS	WINDING	WINEMAKER	WINKING
WINCES	WINDINGLY	WINEPRESS	WINKINGLY
WINCEY	WINDINGS	WINERIES	WINKINGS
WINCEYS	WINDLASS	WINERY	WINKLE
WINCH	WINDLE	WINES	WINKLED
WINCHED	WINDLED	WINESAP	WINKLER
WINCHER	WINDLES	WINESAPS	WINKLERS
WINCHERS	WINDLESS	WINESHOP	WINKLES
WINCHES	WINDLING	WINESHOPS	WINKLING
WINCHING	WINDLINGS	WINESKIN	WINKS
WINCHMAN	WINDMILL	WINESKINS	WINLESS
WINCHMEN	WINDMILLS	WINESOP	WINN
WINCING	WINDOCK	WINESOPS	WINNA
WINCINGS	WINDOCKS	WINEY	WINNABLE
WINCOPIPE	WINDORE	WING	WINNARD
WIND	WINDORES	WINGBACK	WINNARDS
WINDABLE	WINDOW	WINGBACKS	WINNED
WINDAC	WINDOWED	WINGBEAT	WINNER
WINDACS	WINDOWING	WINGBEATS	WINNERS
WINDAGE	WINDOWS	WINGBOW	WINNING
WINDAGES	WINDOWY	WINGBOWS	WINNINGLY
WINDAS	WINDPIPE	WINGCHAIR	WINNINGS
WINDASES	WINDPIPES	WINGDING	WINNLE
WINDBAG	WINDPROOF	WINGDINGS	WINNLES
WINDBAGS	WINDRING	WINGE	WINNOCK
WINDBELL	WINDROSE	WINGED	WINNOCKS
WINDBELLS	WINDROSES	WINGEDLY	WINNOW
WINDBILL	WINDROW	WINGEING	WINNOWED
WINDBILLS	WINDROWED	WINGER	WINNOWER
WINDBLAST	WINDROWER	WINGERS	WINNOWERS
WINDBLOW	WINDROWS	WINGES	WINNOWING
WINDBLOWN	WINDS	WINGIER	WINNOWS
WINDBLOWS	WINDSAIL	WINGIEST	WINNS
WINDBORNE	WINDSAILS	WINGING	WINO
WINDBOUND	WINDSES	WINGLESS	WINOES
WINDBREAK	WINDSHAKE	WINGLET	WINOS
WINDBURN	WINDSHIP	WINGLETS	WINS
WINDBURNS	WINDSHIPS	WINGLIKE	WINSEY
WINDBURNT	WINDSOCK	WINGMAN	WINSEYS
WINDCHILL	WINDSOCKS	WINGMEN	WINSOME
WINDED	WINDSTORM	WINGOVER	WINSOMELY
WINDER	WINDSURF	WINGOVERS	WINSOMER
WINDERS	WINDSURFS	WINGS	WINSOMEST
WINDFALL	WINDSWEPT	WINGSPAN	WINTER
WINDFALLS	WINDTHROW	WINGSPANS	WINTERED
WINDFLAW	WINDTIGHT	WINGSUIT	WINTERER
WINDFLAWS	WINDUP	WINGSUITS	WINTERERS
WINDGALL	WINDUPS	WINGTIP	WINTERFED
WINDGALLS	WINDWARD	WINGTIPS	WINTERIER
WINDGUN	WINDWARDS	WINGY	WINTERING
WINDGUNS	WINDWAY	WINIER	WINTERISE
WINDHOVER	WINDWAYS	WINIEST	WINTERISH
WINDIER	WINDY	WINING	WINTERIZE
WINDIEST	WINE	WINISH	WINTERLY
WINDIGO	WINEBERRY	WINK	WINTERS
WINDIGOS	WINED	WINKED	WINTERY
WINDILY	WINEGLASS	WINKER	WINTLE

WINTLED	WIRRAHS	WISPY	WITHEROD
WINTLES	WIRRICOW	WISS	WITHERODS
WINTLING	WIRRICOWS	WISSED	WITHERS
WINTRIER	WIRY	WISSES	WITHES
WINTRIEST	WIS	WISSING	WITHHAULT
WINTRILY	WISARD	WIST	WITHHELD
WINTRY	WISARDS	WISTARIA	WITHHOLD
WINY	WISDOM	WISTARIAS	WITHHOLDS
WINZE	WISDOMS	WISTED	WITHIER
WINZES	WISE	WISTERIA	WITHIES
WIPE	WISEACRE	WISTERIAS	WITHIEST
WIPED	WISEACRES	WISTFUL	WITHIN
WIPEOUT	WISEASS	WISTFULLY	WITHING
WIPEOUTS	WISEASSES	WISTING	WITHINS
WIPER	WISECRACK	WISTITI	WITHOUT
WIPERS	WISED	WISTITIS	WITHOUTEN
WIPES	WISEGUY	WISTLY	WITHOUTS
WIPING	WISEGUYS	WISTS	WITHS
WIPINGS	WISELIER	WIT	WITHSTAND
WIPPEN	WISELIEST	WITAN	WITHSTOOD
WIPPENS	WISELING	WITANS	WITHWIND
WIRABLE	WISELINGS	WITBLITS	WITHWINDS
WIRE	WISELY	WITCH	WITHY
WIRED	WISENESS	WITCHED	WITHYWIND
WIREDRAW	WISENT	WITCHEN	WITING
WIREDRAWN	WISENTS	WITCHENS	WITLESS
WIREDRAWS	WISER	WITCHERY	WITLESSLY
WIREDREW	WISES	WITCHES	WITLING
WIREGRASS	WISEST	WITCHETTY	WITLINGS
WIREHAIR	WISEWOMAN	WITCHHOOD	WITLOOF
WIREHAIRS	WISEWOMEN	WITCHIER	WITLOOFS
WIRELESS	WISH	WITCHIEST	WITNESS
WIRELIKE	WISHA	WITCHING	WITNESSED
WIREMAN	WISHBONE	WITCHINGS	WITNESSER
WIREMEN	WISHBONES	WITCHKNOT	WITNESSES
WIREPHOTO	WISHED	WITCHLIKE	WITNEY
WIRER	WISHER	WITCHWEED	WITNEYS
WIRERS	WISHERS	WITCHY	WITS
WIRES	WISHES	WITE	WITTED
WIRETAP	WISHFUL	WITED	WITTER
WIRETAPS	WISHFULLY	WITELESS	WITTERED
WIREWAY	WISHING	WITES	WITTERING
WIREWAYS	WISHINGS	WITGAT	WITTERS
WIREWORK	WISHLESS	WITGATS	WITTICISM
WIREWORKS	WISHT	WITH	WITTIER
WIREWORM	WISING	WITHAL	WITTIEST
WIREWORMS	WISKET	WITHDRAW	WITTILY
WIREWOVE	WISKETS	WITHDRAWN	WITTINESS
WIRIER	WISP	WITHDRAWS	WITTING
WIRIEST	WISPED	WITHDREW	WITTINGLY
WIRILDA	WISPIER	WITHE	WITTINGS
WIRILDAS	WISPIEST	WITHED	WITTOL
WIRILY	WISPILY	WITHER	WITTOLLY
WIRINESS	WISPINESS	WITHERED	WITTOLS
WIRING	WISPING	WITHERER	WITTY
WIRINGS	WISPISH	WITHERERS	WITWALL
WIRRA	WISPLIKE	WITHERING	WITWALLS
WIRRAH	WISPS	WITHERITE	WITWANTON

WIVE	WOES	WOMAN	WONGI
WIVED	WOESOME	WOMANED	WONGIED
WIVEHOOD	WOF	WOMANHOOD	WONGIING
WIVEHOODS	WOFS	WOMANING	WONGIS
WIVER	WOFUL	WOMANISE	WONING
WIVERN	WOFULLER	WOMANISED	WONINGS
WIVERNS	WOFULLEST	WOMANISER	WONK
WIVERS	WOFULLY	WOMANISES	WONKIER
WIVES	WOFULNESS	WOMANISH	WONKIEST
WIVING	WOG	WOMANISM	WONKS
WIZ	WOGGISH	WOMANISMS	WONKY
WIZARD	WOGGLE	WOMANIST	WONNED
WIZARDLY	WOGGLES	WOMANISTS	WONNER
WIZARDRY	WOGS	WOMANIZE	WONNERS
WIZARDS	WOIWODE	WOMANIZED	WONNING
WIZEN	WOIWODES	WOMANIZER	WONNINGS
WIZENED	WOK	WOMANIZES	WONS
WIZENING	WOKE	WOMANKIND	WONT
WIZENS	WOKEN	WOMANLESS	WONTED
WIZES	WOKKA	WOMANLIER	WONTEDLY
WIZIER	WOKS	WOMANLIKE	WONTING
WIZIERS	WOLD	WOMANLY	WONTLESS
WIZZEN	WOLDS	WOMANNESS	WONTON
WIZZENS	WOLF	WOMANS	WONTONS
WIZZES	WOLFBERRY	WOMB	WONTS
WO	WOLFED	WOMBAT	WOO
WOAD	WOLFER	WOMBATS	WOOBUT
WOADED	WOLFERS	WOMBED	WOOBUTS
WOADS	WOLFFISH	WOMBIER	WOOD
WOADWAX	WOLFHOUND	WOMBIEST	WOODBIN
WOADWAXEN	WOLFING	WOMBING	WOODBIND
WOADWAXES	WOLFINGS	WOMBLIKE	WOODBINDS
WOALD	WOLFISH	WOMBS	WOODBINE
WOALDS	WOLFISHLY	WOMBY	WOODBINES
WOBBEGONG	WOLFKIN	WOMEN	WOODBINS
WOBBLE	WOLFKINS	WOMENFOLK	WOODBLOCK
WOBBLED	WOLFLIKE	WOMENKIND	WOODBORER
WOBBLER	WOLFLING	WOMERA	WOODBOX
WOBBLERS	WOLFLINGS	WOMERAS	WOODBOXES
WOBBLES	WOLFRAM	WOMMERA	WOODCHAT
WOBBLIER	WOLFRAMS	WOMMERAS	WOODCHATS
WOBBLIES	WOLFS	WOMMIT	WOODCHIP
WOBBLIEST	WOLFSBANE	WOMMITS	WOODCHIPS
WOBBLING	WOLFSKIN	WOMYN	WOODCHOP
WOBBLINGS	WOLFSKINS	WON	WOODCHOPS
WOBBLY	WOLLIES	WONDER	WOODCHUCK
WOBEGONE	WOLLY	WONDERED	WOODCOCK
WOCK	WOLVE	WONDERER	WOODCOCKS
WOCKS	WOLVED	WONDERERS	WOODCRAFT
WODGE	WOLVER	WONDERFUL	WOODCUT
WODGES	WOLVERENE	WONDERING	WOODCUTS
WOE	WOLVERINE	WONDERKID	WOODED
WOEBEGONE	WOLVERS	WONDEROUS	WOODEN
WOEFUL	WOLVES	WONDERS	WOODENED
WOEFULLER	WOLVING	WONDRED	WOODENER
WOEFULLY	WOLVINGS	WONDROUS	WOODENEST
WOENESS	WOLVISH	WONGA	WOODENING
WOENESSES	WOLVISHLY	WONGAS	WOODENLY

WOODENS	WOODSPITE	WOOLHAT	WOOSES
WOODENTOP	WOODSTONE	WOOLHATS	WOOSH
WOODFREE	WOODSTOVE	WOOLIE	WOOSHED
WOODGRAIN	WOODSY	WOOLIER	WOOSHES
WOODHEN	WOODTONE	WOOLIES	WOOSHING
WOODHENS	WOODTONES	WOOLIEST	WOOT
WOODHOLE	WOODWALE	WOOLINESS	WOOTZ
WOODHOLES	WOODWALES	WOOLLED	WOOTZES
WOODHORSE	WOODWARD	WOOLLEN	WOOZIER
WOODHOUSE	WOODWARDS	WOOLLENS	WOOZIEST
WOODIE	WOODWAX	WOOLLIER	WOOZILY
WOODIER	WOODWAXEN	WOOLLIES	WOOZINESS
WOODIES	WOODWAXES	WOOLLIEST	WOOZY
WOODIEST	WOODWIND	WOOLLIKE	WOP
WOODINESS	WOODWINDS	WOOLLILY	WOPPED
WOODING	WOODWORK	WOOLLY	WOPPING
WOODLAND	WOODWORKS	WOOLMAN	WOPS
WOODLANDS	WOODWORM	WOOLMEN	WORCESTER
WOODLARK	WOODWORMS	WOOLPACK	WORD
WOODLARKS	WOODWOSE	WOOLPACKS	WORDAGE
WOODLESS	WOODWOSES	WOOLS	WORDAGES
WOODLICE	WOODY	WOOLSACK	WORDBOOK
WOODLORE	WOODYARD	WOOLSACKS	WORDBOOKS
WOODLORES	WOODYARDS	WOOLSEY	WORDBOUND
WOODLOT	WOOED	WOOLSEYS	WORDBREAK
WOODLOTS	WOOER	WOOLSHED	WORDED
WOODLOUSE	WOOERS	WOOLSHEDS	WORDGAME
WOODMAN	WOOF	WOOLSKIN	WORDGAMES
WOODMEAL	WOOFED	WOOLSKINS	WORDIER
WOODMEALS	WOOFER	WOOLWARD	WORDIEST
WOODMEN	WOOFERS	WOOLWORK	WORDILY
WOODMICE	WOOFIER	WOOLWORKS	WORDINESS
WOODMOUSE	WOOFIEST	WOOLY	WORDING
WOODNESS	WOOFING	WOOMERA	WORDINGS
WOODNOTE	WOOFS	WOOMERANG	WORDISH
WOODNOTES	WOOFTER	WOOMERAS	WORDLESS
WOODPILE	WOOFTERS	WOON	WORDLORE
WOODPILES	WOOFY	WOONED	WORDLORES
WOODPRINT	WOOING	WOONING	WORDPLAY
WOODREEVE	WOOINGLY	WOONS	WORDPLAYS
WOODROOF	WOOINGS	WOOPIE	WORDS
WOODROOFS	WOOL	WOOPIES	WORDSMITH
WOODRUFF	WOOLD	WOOPS	WORDY
WOODRUFFS	WOOLDED	WOOPSED	WORE
WOODRUSH	WOOLDER	WOOPSES	WORK
WOODS	WOOLDERS	WOOPSING	WORKABLE
WOODSCREW	WOOLDING	WOORALI	WORKABLY
WOODSHED	WOOLDINGS	WOORALIS	WORKADAY
WOODSHEDS	WOOLDS	WOORARA	WORKADAYS
WOODSHOCK	WOOLED	WOORARAS	WORKBAG
WOODSIA	WOOLEN	WOORARI	WORKBAGS
WOODSIAS	WOOLENS	WOORARIS	WORKBENCH
WOODSIER	WOOLER	WOOS	WORKBOAT
WOODSIEST	WOOLERS	WOOSE	WORKBOATS
WOODSKIN	WOOLFAT	WOOSEL	WORKBOOK
WOODSKINS	WOOLFATS	WOOSELL	WORKBOOKS
WOODSMAN	WOOLFELL	WOOSELLS	WORKBOX
WOODSMEN	WOOLFELLS	WOOSELS	WORKBOXES

WORKDAY	WORLDED	WORRYCOW	WOULDEST
WORKDAYS	WORLDLIER	WORRYCOWS	WOULDS
WORKED	WORLDLING	WORRYGUTS	WOULDST
WORKER	WORLDLY	WORRYING	WOUND
WORKERIST	WORLDS	WORRYINGS	WOUNDABLE
WORKERS	WORLDVIEW	WORRYWART	WOUNDED
WORKFARE	WORLDWIDE	WORSE	WOUNDEDLY
WORKFARES	WORM	WORSED	WOUNDER
WORKFLOW	WORMCAST	WORSEN	WOUNDERS
WORKFLOWS	WORMCASTS	WORSENED	WOUNDILY
WORKFOLK	WORMED	WORSENESS	WOUNDING
WORKFOLKS	WORMER	WORSENING	WOUNDINGS
WORKFORCE	WORMERIES	WORSENS	WOUNDLESS
WORKFUL	WORMERS	WORSER	WOUNDS
WORKGIRL	WORMERY	WORSES	WOUNDWORT
WORKGIRLS	WORMFLIES	WORSET	WOUNDY
WORKGROUP	WORMFLY	WORSETS	WOURALI
WORKHORSE	WORMGEAR	WORSHIP	WOURALIS
WORKHOUR	WORMGEARS	WORSHIPED	WOVE
WORKHOURS	WORMHOLE	WORSHIPER	WOVEN
WORKHOUSE	WORMHOLED	WORSHIPS	WOVENS
WORKING	WORMHOLES	WORSING	WOW
WORKINGS	WORMIER	WORST	WOWED
WORKLESS	WORMIEST	WORSTED	WOWEE
WORKLOAD	WORMIL	WORSTEDS	WOWF
WORKLOADS	WORMILS	WORSTING	WOWFER
WORKMAN	WORMINESS	WORSTS	WOWFEST
WORKMANLY	WORMING	WORT	WOWING
WORKMATE	WORMISH	WORTH	WOWS
WORKMATES	WORMLIKE	WORTHED	WOWSER
WORKMEN	WORMROOT	WORTHFUL	WOWSERS
WORKOUT	WORMROOTS	WORTHIED	WOX
WORKOUTS	WORMS	WORTHIER	WOXEN
WORKPIECE	WORMSEED	WORTHIES	WRACK
WORKPLACE	WORMSEEDS	WORTHIEST	WRACKED
WORKPRINT	WORMWOOD	WORTHILY	WRACKFUL
WORKROOM	WORMWOODS	WORTHING	WRACKING
WORKROOMS	WORMY	WORTHLESS	WRACKS
WORKS	WORN	WORTHS	WRAITH
WORKSHEET	WORNNESS	WORTHY	WRAITHS
WORKSHOP	WORRAL	WORTHYING	WRANG
WORKSHOPS	WORRALS	WORTLE	WRANGED
WORKSHY	WORREL	WORTLES	WRANGING
WORKSOME	WORRELS	WORTS	WRANGLE
WORKSPACE	WORRICOW	WOS	WRANGLED
WORKTABLE	WORRICOWS	WOSBIRD	WRANGLER
WORKTOP	WORRIED	WOSBIRDS	WRANGLERS
WORKTOPS	WORRIEDLY	WOST	WRANGLES
WORKUP	WORRIER	WOT	WRANGLING
WORKUPS	WORRIERS	WOTCHER	WRANGS
WORKWEAR	WORRIES	WOTS	WRAP
WORKWEARS	WORRIMENT	WOTTED	WRAPOVER
WORKWEEK	WORRISOME	WOTTEST	WRAPOVERS
WORKWEEKS	WORRIT	WOTTETH	WRAPPAGE
WORKWOMAN	WORRITED	WOTTING	WRAPPAGES
WORKWOMEN	WORRITING	WOUBIT	WRAPPED
WORLD	WORRITS	WOUBITS	WRAPPER
WORLDBEAT	WORRY	WOULD	WRAPPERED

WRAPPERS	WREATHY	WRINGED	WRONGLY
WRAPPING	WRECK	WRINGER	WRONGNESS
WRAPPINGS	WRECKAGE	WRINGERS	WRONGOUS
WRAPROUND	WRECKAGES	WRINGING	WRONGS
WRAPS	WRECKED	WRINGINGS	WROOT
WRAPT	WRECKER	WRINGS	WROOTED
WRASSE	WRECKERS	WRINKLE	WROOTING
WRASSES	WRECKFISH	WRINKLED	WROOTS
WRASSLE	WRECKFUL	WRINKLES	WROTE
WRASSLED	WRECKING	WRINKLIER	WROTH
WRASSLES	WRECKINGS	WRINKLIES	WROTHFUL
WRASSLING	WRECKS	WRINKLING	WROUGHT
WRAST	WREN	WRINKLY	WRUNG
WRASTED	WRENCH	WRIST	WRY
WRASTING	WRENCHED	WRISTBAND	WRYBILL
WRASTLE	WRENCHER	WRISTIER	WRYBILLS
WRASTLED	WRENCHERS	WRISTIEST	WRYER
WRASTLES	WRENCHES	WRISTLET	WRYEST
WRASTLING	WRENCHING	WRISTLETS	WRYING
WRASTS	WRENS	WRISTLOCK	WRYLY
WRATE	WREST	WRISTS	WRYNECK
WRATH	WRESTED	WRISTY	WRYNECKS
WRATHED	WRESTER	WRIT	WRYNESS
WRATHFUL	WRESTERS	WRITABLE	WRYNESSES
WRATHIER	WRESTING	WRITATIVE	WRYTHEN
WRATHIEST	WRESTLE	WRITE	WUD
WRATHILY	WRESTLED	WRITEABLE	WUDDED
WRATHING	WRESTLER	WRITER	WUDDING
WRATHLESS	WRESTLERS	WRITERESS	WUDJULA
WRATHS	WRESTLES	WRITERLY	WUDJULAS
WRATHY	WRESTLING	WRITERS	WUDS
WRAWL	WRESTS	WRITES	WUDU
WRAWLED	WRETCH	WRITHE	WUDUS
WRAWLING	WRETCHED	WRITHED	WUKKAS
WRAWLS	WRETCHES	WRITHEN	WULFENITE
WRAXLE	WRETHE	WRITHER	WULL
WRAXLED	WRETHED	WRITHERS	WULLED
WRAXLES	WRETHES	WRITHES	WULLING
WRAXLING	WRETHING	WRITHING	WULLS
WRAXLINGS	WRICK	WRITHINGS	WUNNER
WREAK	WRICKED	WRITHLED	WUNNERS
WREAKED	WRICKING	WRITING	WURLEY
WREAKER	WRICKS	WRITINGS	WURLEYS
WREAKERS	WRIED	WRITS	WURLIE
WREAKFUL	WRIER	WRITTEN	WURLIES
WREAKING	WRIES	WRIZLED	WURST
WREAKLESS	WRIEST	WROATH	WURSTS
WREAKS	WRIGGLE	WROATHS	WURTZITE
WREATH	WRIGGLED	WROKE	WURTZITES
WREATHE	WRIGGLER	WROKEN	WURZEL
WREATHED	WRIGGLERS	WRONG	WURZELS
WREATHEN	WRIGGLES	WRONGDOER	WUS
WREATHER	WRIGGLIER	WRONGED	WUSES
WREATHERS	WRIGGLING	WRONGER	WUSHU
WREATHES	WRIGGLY	WRONGERS	WUSHUS
WREATHIER	WRIGHT	WRONGEST	WUSS
WREATHING	WRIGHTS	WRONGFUL	WUSSES
WREATHS	WRING	WRONGING	WUSSIER

WUSSIES
WUSSIEST
WUSSY
WUTHER
WUTHERED
WUTHERING
WUTHERS
WUXIA
WUXIAS
WUZZLE
WUZZLED
WUZZLES
WUZZLING
WYANDOTTE
WYCH
WYCHES
WYE
WYES
WYLE
WYLED
WYLES
WYLIECOAT
WYLING
WYN
WYND
WYNDS
WYNN
WYNNS
WYNS
WYSIWYG
WYTE
WYTED
WYTES
WYTING
WYVERN
WYVERNS

X

XANTHAM
XANTHAMS
XANTHAN
XANTHANS
XANTHATE
XANTHATES
XANTHEIN
XANTHEINS
XANTHENE
XANTHENES
XANTHIC
XANTHIN
XANTHINE
XANTHINES
XANTHINS
XANTHISM
XANTHISMS
XANTHOMA
XANTHOMAS
XANTHONE
XANTHONES
XANTHOUS
XANTHOXYL
XEBEC
XEBECS
XENIA
XENIAL
XENIAS
XENIC
XENIUM
XENOBLAST
XENOCRYST
XENOGAMY
XENOGENIC
XENOGENY
XENOGRAFT
XENOLITH
XENOLITHS
XENOMANIA
XENOMENIA
XENON
XENONS
XENOPHILE
XENOPHOBE
XENOPHOBY
XENOPHYA
XENOPUS
XENOPUSES
XENOTIME
XENOTIMES
XENURINE
XENURINES
XERAFIN

XERAFINS
XERANSES
XERANSIS
XERANTIC
XERAPHIM
XERAPHIMS
XERARCH
XERASIA
XERASIAS
XERIC
XERICALLY
XERISCAPE
XEROCHASY
XERODERMA
XEROMA
XEROMAS
XEROMATA
XEROMORPH
XEROPHAGY
XEROPHILE
XEROPHILY
XEROPHYTE
XEROSERE
XEROSERES
XEROSES
XEROSIS
XEROSTOMA
XEROTES
XEROTIC
XEROX
XEROXED
XEROXES
XEROXING
XERUS
XERUSES
XI
XIPHOID
XIPHOIDAL
XIPHOIDS
XIPHOPAGI
XIS
XOANA
XOANON
XU
XYLAN
XYLANS
XYLEM
XYLEMS
XYLENE
XYLENES
XYLENOL
XYLENOLS
XYLIC

XYLIDIN
XYLIDINE
XYLIDINES
XYLIDINS
XYLITOL
XYLITOLS
XYLOCARP
XYLOCARPS
XYLOGEN
XYLOGENS
XYLOGRAPH
XYLOID
XYLOIDIN
XYLOIDINE
XYLOIDINS
XYLOL
XYLOLOGY
XYLOLS
XYLOMA
XYLOMAS
XYLOMATA
XYLOMETER
XYLONIC
XYLONITE
XYLONITES
XYLOPHAGE
XYLOPHONE
XYLORIMBA
XYLOSE
XYLOSES
XYLOTOMY
XYLYL
XYLYLS
XYST
XYSTER
XYSTERS
XYSTI
XYSTOI
XYSTOS
XYSTS
XYSTUS

Y

YA	YAGIS	YANKED	YARDINGS
YAAR	YAGS	YANKER	YARDLAND
YAARS	YAH	YANKERS	YARDLANDS
YABA	YAHOO	YANKIE	YARDMAN
YABBA	YAHOOISM	YANKIES	YARDMEN
YABBAS	YAHOOISMS	YANKING	YARDS
YABBER	YAHOOS	YANKS	YARDSTICK
YABBERED	YAHRZEIT	YANQUI	YARDWAND
YABBERING	YAHRZEITS	YANQUIS	YARDWANDS
YABBERS	YAHS	YANTRA	YARDWORK
YABBIE	YAIRD	YANTRAS	YARDWORKS
YABBIED	YAIRDS	YAOURT	YARE
YABBIES	YAK	YAOURTS	YARELY
YABBY	YAKHDAN	YAP	YARER
YABBYING	YAKHDANS	YAPOCK	YAREST
YACCA	YAKIMONO	YAPOCKS	YARFA
YACCAS	YAKIMONOS	YAPOK	YARFAS
YACHT	YAKITORI	YAPOKS	YARK
YACHTED	YAKITORIS	YAPON	YARKED
YACHTER	YAKKA	YAPONS	YARKING
YACHTERS	YAKKAS	YAPP	YARKS
YACHTIE	YAKKED	YAPPED	YARMELKE
YACHTIES	YAKKER	YAPPER	YARMELKES
YACHTING	YAKKERS	YAPPERS	YARMULKA
YACHTINGS	YAKKING	YAPPIE	YARMULKAS
YACHTMAN	YAKOW	YAPPIER	YARMULKE
YACHTMEN	YAKOWS	YAPPIES	YARMULKES
YACHTS	YAKS	YAPPIEST	YARN
YACHTSMAN	YAKUZA	YAPPING	YARNED
YACHTSMEN	YALD	YAPPINGLY	YARNER
YACK	YALE	YAPPS	YARNERS
YACKA	YALES	YAPPY	YARNING
YACKAS	YAM	YAPS	YARNS
YACKED	YAMALKA	YAPSTER	YARPHA
YACKER	YAMALKAS	YAPSTERS	YARPHAS
YACKERS	YAMEN	YAQONA	YARR
YACKING	YAMENS	YAQONAS	YARRAMAN
YACKS	YAMMER	YAR	YARRAMANS
YAD	YAMMERED	YARCO	YARRAMEN
YADS	YAMMERER	YARCOS	YARRAN
YAE	YAMMERERS	YARD	YARRANS
YAFF	YAMMERING	YARDAGE	YARROW
YAFFED	YAMMERS	YARDAGES	YARROWS
YAFFING	YAMPIES	YARDANG	YARRS
YAFFLE	YAMPY	YARDANGS	YARTA
YAFFLES	YAMS	YARDARM	YARTAS
YAFFS	YAMULKA	YARDARMS	YARTO
YAG	YAMULKAS	YARDBIRD	YARTOS
YAGER	YAMUN	YARDBIRDS	YASHMAC
YAGERS	YAMUNS	YARDED	YASHMACS
YAGGER	YANG	YARDER	YASHMAK
YAGGERS	YANGS	YARDERS	YASHMAKS
YAGI	YANK	YARDING	YASMAK

YASMAKS	YBORE	YEAS	YELLOWY
YATAGAN	YBOUND	YEASAYER	YELLS
YATAGANS	YBOUNDEN	YEASAYERS	YELM
YATAGHAN	YBRENT	YEAST	YELMED
YATAGHANS	YCLAD	YEASTED	YELMING
YATE	YCLED	YEASTIER	YELMS
YATES	YCLEEPE	YEASTIEST	YELP
YATTER	YCLEEPED	YEASTILY	YELPED
YATTERED	YCLEEPES	YEASTING	YELPER
YATTERING	YCLEEPING	YEASTLESS	YELPERS
YATTERS	YCLEPED	YEASTLIKE	YELPING
YAUD	YCLEPT	YEASTS	YELPINGS
YAUDS	YCOND	YEASTY	YELPS
YAULD	YDRAD	YEBO	YELT
YAUP	YDRED	YECCH	YELTS
YAUPED	YE	YECCHS	YEMMER
YAUPER	YEA	YECH	YEMMERS
YAUPERS	YEAD	YECHS	YEN
YAUPING	YEADING	YECHY	YENNED
YAUPON	YEADS	YEDE	YENNING
YAUPONS	YEAH	YEDES	YENS
YAUPS	YEAHS	YEDING	YENTA
YAUTIA	YEALDON	YEED	YENTAS
YAUTIAS	YEALDONS	YEEDING	YENTE
YAW	YEALING	YEEDS	YENTES
YAWED	YEALINGS	YEELIN	YEOMAN
YAWEY	YEALM	YEELINS	YEOMANLY
YAWING	YEALMED	YEGG	YEOMANRY
YAWL	YEALMING	YEGGMAN	YEOMEN
YAWLED	YEALMS	YEGGMEN	YEP
YAWLING	YEAN	YEGGS	YEPS
YAWLS	YEANED	YEH	YERBA
YAWMETER	YEANING	YELD	YERBAS
YAWMETERS	YEANLING	YELDRING	YERD
YAWN	YEANLINGS	YELDRINGS	YERDED
YAWNED	YEANS	YELDROCK	YERDING
YAWNER	YEAR	YELDROCKS	YERDS
YAWNERS	YEARBOOK	YELK	YERK
YAWNIER	YEARBOOKS	YELKS	YERKED
YAWNIEST	YEARD	YELL	YERKING
YAWNING	YEARDED	YELLED	YERKS
YAWNINGLY	YEARDING	YELLER	YERSINIA
YAWNINGS	YEARDS	YELLERS	YERSINIAE
YAWNS	YEAREND	YELLING	YERSINIAS
YAWNY	YEARENDS	YELLINGS	YES
YAWP	YEARLIES	YELLOCH	YESES
YAWPED	YEARLING	YELLOCHED	YESHIVA
YAWPER	YEARLINGS	YELLOCHS	YESHIVAH
YAWPERS	YEARLONG	YELLOW	YESHIVAHS
YAWPING	YEARLY	YELLOWED	YESHIVAS
YAWPINGS	YEARN	YELLOWER	YESHIVOT
YAWPS	YEARNED	YELLOWEST	YESHIVOTH
YAWS	YEARNER	YELLOWFIN	YESK
YAWY	YEARNERS	YELLOWIER	YESKED
YAY	YEARNING	YELLOWING	YESKING
YAYS	YEARNINGS	YELLOWISH	YESKS
YBET	YEARNS	YELLOWLY	YESSED
YBLENT	YEARS	YELLOWS	YESSES

YESSING	YIKKER	YOBBISHLY	YOICKING
YEST	YIKKERED	YOBBISM	YOICKS
YESTER	YIKKERING	YOBBISMS	YOICKSED
YESTERDAY	YIKKERS	YOBBO	YOICKSES
YESTEREVE	YILL	YOBBOES	YOICKSING
YESTERN	YILLS	YOBBOS	YOJAN
YESTREEN	YIN	YOBS	YOJANA
YESTREENS	YINCE	YOCK	YOJANAS
YESTS	YINS	YOCKED	YOJANS
YESTY	YIP	YOCKING	YOK
YET	YIPE	YOCKS	YOKE
YETI	YIPES	YOD	YOKED
YETIS	YIPPED	YODE	YOKEL
YETT	YIPPEE	YODEL	YOKELESS
YETTIE	YIPPER	YODELED	YOKELISH
YETTIES	YIPPERS	YODELER	YOKELS
YETTS	YIPPIE	YODELERS	YOKEMATE
YEUK	YIPPIES	YODELING	YOKEMATES
YEUKED	YIPPING	YODELLED	YOKER
YEUKING	YIPPY	YODELLER	YOKERS
YEUKS	YIPS	YODELLERS	YOKES
YEUKY	YIRD	YODELLING	YOKING
YEVE	YIRDED	YODELS	YOKINGS
YEVEN	YIRDING	YODH	YOKKED
YEVES	YIRDS	YODHS	YOKKING
YEVING	YIRK	YODLE	YOKOZUNA
YEW	YIRKED	YODLED	YOKOZUNAS
YEWEN	YIRKING	YODLER	YOKS
YEWS	YIRKS	YODLERS	YOKUL
YEX	YIRR	YODLES	YOLD
YEXED	YIRRED	YODLING	YOLDRING
YEXES	YIRRING	YODS	YOLDRINGS
YEXING	YIRRS	YOGA	YOLK
YFERE	YIRTH	YOGAS	YOLKED
YGLAUNST	YIRTHS	YOGEE	YOLKIER
YGO	YITE	YOGEES	YOLKIEST
YGOE	YITES	YOGH	YOLKLESS
YIBBLES	YITIE	YOGHOURT	YOLKS
YICKER	YITIES	YOGHOURTS	YOLKY
YICKERED	YITTEN	YOGHS	YOM
YICKERING	YLEM	YOGHURT	YOMIM
YICKERS	YLEMS	YOGHURTS	YOMP
YID	YLIKE	YOGI	YOMPED
YIDAKI	YLKE	YOGIC	YOMPING
YIDAKIS	YLKES	YOGIN	YOMPS
YIDS	YMOLT	YOGINI	YON
YIELD	YMOLTEN	YOGINIS	YOND
YIELDABLE	YMPE	YOGINS	YONDER
YIELDED	YMPES	YOGIS	YONDERLY
YIELDER	YMPING	YOGISM	YONDERS
YIELDERS	YMPT	YOGISMS	YONI
YIELDING	YNAMBU	YOGURT	YONIC
YIELDINGS	YNAMBUS	YOGURTS	YONIS
YIELDS	YO	YOHIMBE	YONKER
YIKE	YOB	YOHIMBES	YONKERS
YIKED	YOBBERIES	YOHIMBINE	YONKS
YIKES	YOBBERY	YOICK	YONNIE
YIKING	YOBBISH	YOICKED	YONNIES

YONT
YOOF
YOOFS
YOOP
YOOPS
YOPPER
YOPPERS
YORE
YORES
YORK
YORKED
YORKER
YORKERS
YORKIE
YORKIES
YORKING
YORKS
YORP
YORPED
YORPING
YORPS
YOS
YOTTABYTE
YOU
YOUK
YOUKED
YOUKING
YOUKS
YOUNG
YOUNGER
YOUNGERS
YOUNGEST
YOUNGISH
YOUNGLING
YOUNGLY
YOUNGNESS
YOUNGS
YOUNGSTER
YOUNGTH
YOUNGTHLY
YOUNGTHS
YOUNKER
YOUNKERS
YOUPON
YOUPONS
YOUR
YOURN
YOURS
YOURSELF
YOURT
YOURTS
YOUS
YOUSE
YOUTH
YOUTHEN
YOUTHENED
YOUTHENS
YOUTHFUL

YOUTHHEAD
YOUTHHOOD
YOUTHIER
YOUTHIEST
YOUTHLESS
YOUTHLY
YOUTHS
YOUTHSOME
YOUTHY
YOW
YOWE
YOWED
YOWES
YOWIE
YOWIES
YOWING
YOWL
YOWLED
YOWLER
YOWLERS
YOWLEY
YOWLEYS
YOWLING
YOWLINGS
YOWLS
YOWS
YPERITE
YPERITES
YPIGHT
YPLAST
YPLIGHT
YPSILOID
YPSILON
YPSILONS
YRAPT
YRAVISHED
YRENT
YRIVD
YRNEH
YRNEHS
YSAME
YSHEND
YSHENDING
YSHENDS
YSHENT
YSLAKED
YTOST
YTTERBIA
YTTERBIAS
YTTERBIC
YTTERBITE
YTTERBIUM
YTTERBOUS
YTTRIA
YTTRIAS
YTTRIC
YTTRIOUS
YTTRIUM

YTTRIUMS
YU
YUAN
YUANS
YUCA
YUCAS
YUCCA
YUCCAS
YUCCH
YUCH
YUCK
YUCKED
YUCKER
YUCKERS
YUCKIER
YUCKIEST
YUCKINESS
YUCKING
YUCKO
YUCKS
YUCKY
YUFT
YUFTS
YUG
YUGA
YUGARIE
YUGARIES
YUGAS
YUGS
YUK
YUKATA
YUKATAS
YUKE
YUKED
YUKES
YUKIER
YUKIEST
YUKING
YUKKED
YUKKIER
YUKKIEST
YUKKING
YUKKY
YUKO
YUKOS
YUKS
YUKY
YULAN
YULANS
YULE
YULES
YULETIDE
YULETIDES
YUM
YUMMIER
YUMMIES
YUMMIEST
YUMMINESS

YUMMO
YUMMY
YUMP
YUMPED
YUMPIE
YUMPIES
YUMPING
YUMPS
YUNX
YUNXES
YUP
YUPON
YUPONS
YUPPIE
YUPPIEDOM
YUPPIEISH
YUPPIES
YUPPIFIED
YUPPIFIES
YUPPIFY
YUPPY
YUPS
YURT
YURTA
YURTAS
YURTS
YUS
YUTZ
YUTZES
YUZU
YUZUS
YWIS
YWROKE

Z

ZA	ZAMBO	ZAPATEO	ZEALOTS
ZABAIONE	ZAMBOMBA	ZAPATEOS	ZEALOUS
ZABAIONES	ZAMBOMBAS	ZAPOTILLA	ZEALOUSLY
ZABAJONE	ZAMBOORAK	ZAPPED	ZEALS
ZABAJONES	ZAMBOS	ZAPPER	ZEAS
ZABETA	ZAMBUCK	ZAPPERS	ZEATIN
ZABETAS	ZAMBUCKS	ZAPPIER	ZEATINS
ZABRA	ZAMBUK	ZAPPIEST	ZEBEC
ZABRAS	ZAMBUKS	ZAPPING	ZEBECK
ZABTIEH	ZAMIA	ZAPPY	ZEBECKS
ZABTIEHS	ZAMIAS	ZAPS	ZEBECS
ZACATON	ZAMINDAR	ZAPTIAH	ZEBRA
ZACATONS	ZAMINDARI	ZAPTIAHS	ZEBRAFISH
ZACK	ZAMINDARS	ZAPTIEH	ZEBRAIC
ZACKS	ZAMINDARY ·	ZAPTIEHS	ZEBRANO
ZADDICK	ZAMOUSE	ZARAPE	ZEBRANOS
ZADDIK	ZAMOUSES	ZARAPES	ZEBRAS
ZADDIKIM	ZAMPOGNA	ZARATITE	ZEBRASS
ZADDIKS	ZAMPOGNAS	ZARATITES	ZEBRASSES
ZAFFAR	ZAMPONE	ZAREBA	ZEBRAWOOD
ZAFFARS	ZAMPONI	ZAREBAS	ZEBRINA
ZAFFER	ZAMZAWED	ZAREEBA	ZEBRINAS
ZAFFERS	ZANANA	ZAREEBAS	ZEBRINE
ZAFFIR	ZANANAS	ZARF	ZEBRINES
ZAFFIRS	ZANDER	ZARFS	ZEBRINNY
ZAFFRE	ZANDERS	ZARIBA	ZEBROID
ZAFFRES	ZANELLA	ZARIBAS	ZEBRULA
ZAFTIG	ZANELLAS	ZARNEC	ZEBRULAS
ZAG	ZANIED	ZARNECS	ZEBRULE
ZAGGED	ZANIER	ZARNICH	ZEBRULES
ZAGGING	ZANIES	ZARNICHS	ZEBU
ZAGS	ZANIEST	ZARZUELA	ZEBUB
ZAIBATSU	ZANILY	ZARZUELAS	ZEBUBS
ZAIKAI	ZANINESS	ZAS	ZEBUS
ZAIKAIS	ZANJA	ZASTRUGA	ZECCHIN
ZAIRE	ZANJAS	ZASTRUGI	ZECCHINE
ZAIRES	ZANJERO	ZATI	ZECCHINES
ZAITECH	ZANJEROS	ZATIS	ZECCHINI
ZAITECHS	ZANTE	ZAX	ZECCHINO
ZAKAT	ZANTES	ZAXES	ZECCHINOS
ZAKATS	ZANTHOXYL	ZAYIN	ZECCHINS
ZAKOUSKA	ZANY	ZAYINS	ZECHIN
ZAKOUSKI	ZANYING	ZAZEN	ZECHINS
ZAKUSKA	ZANYISH	ZAZENS	ZED
ZAKUSKI	ZANYISM	ZEA	ZEDOARIES
ZAMAN	ZANYISMS	ZEAL	ZEDOARY
ZAMANG	ZANZA	ZEALANT	ZEDS
ZAMANGS	ZANZAS	ZEALANTS	ZEE
ZAMANS	ZANZE	ZEALFUL	ZEES
ZAMARRA	ZANZES	ZEALLESS	ZEIN
ZAMARRAS	ZAP	ZEALOT	ZEINS
ZAMARRO	ZAPATA	ZEALOTISM	ZEITGEBER
ZAMARROS	ZAPATEADO	ZEALOTRY	ZEITGEIST

ZEK	ZEST	ZIKKURATS	ZING
ZEKS	ZESTED	ZIKURAT	ZINGANI
ZEL	ZESTER	ZIKURATS	ZINGANO
ZELANT	ZESTERS	ZILA	ZINGARA
ZELANTS	ZESTFUL	ZILAS	ZINGARE
ZELATOR	ZESTFULLY	ZILCH	ZINGARI
ZELATORS	ZESTIER	ZILCHES	ZINGARO
ZELATRICE	ZESTIEST	ZILL	ZINGED
ZELATRIX	ZESTILY	ZILLA	ZINGEL
ZELKOVA	ZESTING	ZILLAH	ZINGELS
ZELKOVAS	ZESTLESS	ZILLAHS	ZINGER
ZELOSO	ZESTS	ZILLAS	ZINGERS
ZELOTYPIA	ZESTY	ZILLION	ZINGIBER
ZELS	ZETA	ZILLIONS	ZINGIBERS
ZEMINDAR	ZETAS	ZILLIONTH	ZINGIER
ZEMINDARI	ZETETIC	ZILLS	ZINGIEST
ZEMINDARS	ZETETICS	ZIMB	ZINGING
ZEMINDARY	ZETTABYTE	ZIMBI	ZINGS
ZEMSTVA	ZEUGMA	ZIMBIS	ZINGY
ZEMSTVO	ZEUGMAS	ZIMBS	ZINKE
ZEMSTVOS	ZEUGMATIC	ZIMMER	ZINKED
ZENAIDA	ZEUXITE	ZIMMERS	ZINKENITE
ZENAIDAS	ZEUXITES	ZIMOCCA	ZINKES
ZENANA	ZEX	ZIMOCCAS	ZINKIER
ZENANAS	ZEXES	ZIN	ZINKIEST
ZENDIK	ZEZE	ZINC	ZINKIFIED
ZENDIKS	ZEZES	ZINCATE	ZINKIFIES
ZENITH	ZHO	ZINCATES	ZINKIFY
ZENITHAL	ZHOMO	ZINCED	ZINKING
ZENITHS	ZHOMOS	ZINCIC	ZINKY
ZEOLITE	ZHOS	ZINCIER	ZINNIA
ZEOLITES	ZIBELINE	ZINCIEST	ZINNIAS
ZEOLITIC	ZIBELINES	ZINCIFIED	ZINS
ZEP	ZIBELLINE	ZINCIFIES	ZIP
ZEPHYR	ZIBET	ZINCIFY	ZIPLESS
ZEPHYRS	ZIBETH	ZINCING	ZIPLOCK
ZEPPELIN	ZIBETHS	ZINCITE	ZIPPED
ZEPPELINS	ZIBETS	ZINCITES	ZIPPER
ZEPPOLE	ZIFF	ZINCKED	ZIPPERED
ZEPPOLES	ZIFFIUS	ZINCKIER	ZIPPERING
ZEPPOLI	ZIFFIUSES	ZINCKIEST	ZIPPERS
ZEPS	ZIFFS	ZINCKIFY	ZIPPIER
ZERDA	ZIG	ZINCKING	ZIPPIEST
ZERDAS	ZIGAN	ZINCKY	ZIPPING
ZEREBA	ZIGANKA	ZINCO	ZIPPO
ZEREBAS	ZIGANKAS	ZINCODE	ZIPPOS
ZERIBA	ZIGANS	ZINCODES	ZIPPY
ZERIBAS	ZIGGED	ZINCOID	ZIPS
ZERK	ZIGGING	ZINCOS	ZIPTOP
ZERKS	ZIGGURAT	ZINCOUS	ZIRAM
ZERO	ZIGGURATS	ZINCS	ZIRAMS
ZEROED	ZIGS	ZINCY	ZIRCALLOY
ZEROES	ZIGZAG	ZINDABAD	ZIRCALOY
ZEROING	ZIGZAGGED	ZINE	ZIRCALOYS
ZEROS	ZIGZAGGER	ZINEB	ZIRCON
ZEROTH	ZIGZAGGY	ZINEBS	ZIRCONIA
ZERUMBET	ZIGZAGS	ZINES	ZIRCONIAS
ZERUMBETS	ZIKKURAT	ZINFANDEL	ZIRCONIC

ZIRCONIUM	ZOECHROME	ZONULA	ZOOLATRIA
ZIRCONS	ZOECIA	ZONULAE	ZOOLATRY
ZIT	ZOECIUM	ZONULAR	ZOOLITE
ZITE	ZOEFORM	ZONULAS	ZOOLITES
ZITHER	ZOETIC	ZONULE	ZOOLITH
ZITHERIST	ZOETROPE	ZONULES	ZOOLITHIC
ZITHERN	ZOETROPES	ZONULET	ZOOLITHS
ZITHERNS	ZOETROPIC	ZONULETS	ZOOLITIC
ZITHERS	ZOFTIG	ZONURE	ZOOLOGIC
ZITI	ZOIATRIA	ZONURES	ZOOLOGIES
ZITIS	ZOIATRIAS	ZOO	ZOOLOGIST
ZITS	ZOIATRICS	ZOOBIOTIC	ZOOLOGY
ZIZ	ZOIC	ZOOBLAST	ZOOM
ZIZANIA	ZOISITE	ZOOBLASTS	ZOOMANCY
ZIZANIAS	ZOISITES	ZOOCHORE	ZOOMANIA
ZIZEL	ZOISM	ZOOCHORES	ZOOMANIAS
ZIZELS	ZOISMS	ZOOCHORY	ZOOMANTIC
ZIZIT	ZOIST	ZOOCYTIA	ZOOMED
ZIZITH	ZOISTS	ZOOCYTIUM	ZOOMETRIC
ZIZYPHUS	ZOL	ZOOEA	ZOOMETRY
ZIZZ	ZOLS	ZOOEAE	ZOOMING
ZIZZED	ZOMBI	ZOOEAL	ZOOMORPH
ZIZZES	ZOMBIE	ZOOEAS	ZOOMORPHS
ZIZZING	ZOMBIES	ZOOECIA	ZOOMORPHY
ZIZZLE	ZOMBIFIED	ZOOECIUM	ZOOMS
ZIZZLED	ZOMBIFIES	ZOOEY	ZOON
ZIZZLES	ZOMBIFY	ZOOGAMETE	ZOONAL
ZIZZLING	ZOMBIISM	ZOOGAMIES	ZOONED
ZLOTE	ZOMBIISMS	ZOOGAMOUS	ZOONIC
ZLOTIES	ZOMBIS	ZOOGAMY	ZOONING
ZLOTY	ZOMBORUK	ZOOGENIC	ZOONITE
ZLOTYCH	ZOMBORUKS	ZOOGENIES	ZOONITES
ZLOTYS	ZONA	ZOOGENOUS	ZOONITIC
ZO	ZONAE	ZOOGENY	ZOONOMIA
ZOA	ZONAL	ZOOGLEA	ZOONOMIAS
ZOAEA	ZONALLY	ZOOGLEAE	ZOONOMIC
ZOAEAE	ZONARY	ZOOGLEAL	ZOONOMIES
ZOAEAS	ZONATE	ZOOGLEAS	ZOONOMIST
ZOARIA	ZONATED	ZOOGLOEA	ZOONOMY
ZOARIAL	ZONATION	ZOOGLOEAE	ZOONOSES
ZOARIUM	ZONATIONS	ZOOGLOEAL	ZOONOSIS
ZOBO	ZONDA	ZOOGLOEAS	ZOONOTIC
ZOBOS	ZONDAS	ZOOGLOEIC	ZOONS
ZOBU	ZONE	ZOOGONIES	ZOOPATHY
ZOBUS	ZONED	ZOOGONOUS	ZOOPERAL
ZOCALO	ZONELESS	ZOOGONY	ZOOPERIES
ZOCALOS	ZONER	ZOOGRAFT	ZOOPERIST
ZOCCO	ZONERS	ZOOGRAFTS	ZOOPERY
ZOCCOLO	ZONES	ZOOGRAPHY	ZOOPHAGAN
ZOCCOLOS	ZONETIME	ZOOID	ZOOPHAGY
ZOCCOS	ZONETIMES	ZOOIDAL	ZOOPHILE
ZODIAC	ZONING	ZOOIDS	ZOOPHILES
ZODIACAL	ZONINGS	ZOOIER	ZOOPHILIA
ZODIACS	ZONK	ZOOIEST	ZOOPHILIC
ZOEA	ZONKED	ZOOKEEPER	ZOOPHILY
ZOEAE	ZONKING	ZOOKS	ZOOPHOBE
ZOEAL	ZONKS	ZOOLATER	ZOOPHOBES
ZOEAS	ZONOID	ZOOLATERS	ZOOPHOBIA

ZOOPHORI
ZOOPHORIC
ZOOPHORUS
ZOOPHYTE
ZOOPHYTES
ZOOPHYTIC
ZOOPLASTY
ZOOS
ZOOSCOPIC
ZOOSCOPY
ZOOSPERM
ZOOSPERMS
ZOOSPORE
ZOOSPORES
ZOOSPORIC
ZOOSTEROL
ZOOT
ZOOTAXIES
ZOOTAXY
ZOOTECHNY
ZOOTHECIA
ZOOTHEISM
ZOOTHOME
ZOOTHOMES
ZOOTIER
ZOOTIEST
ZOOTOMIC
ZOOTOMIES
ZOOTOMIST
ZOOTOMY
ZOOTOXIC
ZOOTOXIN
ZOOTOXINS
ZOOTROPE
ZOOTROPES
ZOOTROPHY
ZOOTY
ZOOTYPE
ZOOTYPES
ZOOTYPIC
ZOOZOO
ZOOZOOS
ZOPILOTE
ZOPILOTES
ZOPPA
ZOPPO
ZORBING
ZORBINGS
ZORBONAUT
ZORGITE
ZORGITES
ZORI
ZORIL
ZORILLA
ZORILLAS
ZORILLE
ZORILLES
ZORILLO

ZORILLOS
ZORILS
ZORINO
ZORINOS
ZORIS
ZORRO
ZORROS
ZOS
ZOSTER
ZOSTERS
ZOUAVE
ZOUAVES
ZOUK
ZOUKS
ZOUNDS
ZOWIE
ZOYSIA
ZOYSIAS
ZUCCHETTI
ZUCCHETTO
ZUCCHINI
ZUCCHINIS
ZUCHETTA
ZUCHETTAS
ZUCHETTO
ZUCHETTOS
ZUFFOLI
ZUFFOLO
ZUFOLI
ZUFOLO
ZUGZWANG
ZUGZWANGS
ZULU
ZULUS
ZUMBOORUK
ZUPA
ZUPAN
ZUPANS
ZUPAS
ZURF
ZURFS
ZUZ
ZUZIM
ZWIEBACK
ZWIEBACKS
ZYDECO
ZYDECOS
ZYGA
ZYGAENID
ZYGAENOID
ZYGAL
ZYGANTRA
ZYGANTRUM
ZYGOCACTI
ZYGODONT
ZYGOID
ZYGOMA
ZYGOMAS

ZYGOMATA
ZYGOMATIC
ZYGON
ZYGOPHYTE
ZYGOSE
ZYGOSES
ZYGOSIS
ZYGOSITY
ZYGOSPERM
ZYGOSPORE
ZYGOTE
ZYGOTENE
ZYGOTENES
ZYGOTES
ZYGOTIC
ZYLONITE
ZYLONITES
ZYMASE
ZYMASES
ZYME
ZYMES
ZYMIC
ZYMITE
ZYMITES
ZYMOGEN
ZYMOGENE
ZYMOGENES
ZYMOGENIC
ZYMOGENS
ZYMOGRAM
ZYMOGRAMS
ZYMOID
ZYMOLOGIC
ZYMOLOGY
ZYMOLYSES
ZYMOLYSIS
ZYMOLYTIC
ZYMOME
ZYMOMES
ZYMOMETER
ZYMOSAN
ZYMOSANS
ZYMOSES
ZYMOSIS
ZYMOTIC
ZYMOTICS
ZYMURGIES
ZYMURGY
ZYTHUM
ZYTHUMS
ZYZZYVA
ZYZZYVAS
ZZZ
ZZZS

COLLINS SCRABBLE WORDS

10-15 LETTER WORDS

A

AARDWOLVES	ABHORRENCE	ABOLISHERS	ABREACTING
ABACTERIAL	ABHORRENCES	ABOLISHING	ABREACTION
ABACTINALLY	ABHORRENCIES	ABOLISHMENT	ABREACTIONS
ABANDONEDLY	ABHORRENCY	ABOLISHMENTS	ABREACTIVE
ABANDONEES	ABHORRENTLY	ABOLITIONAL	ABRIDGABLE
ABANDONERS	ABHORRINGS	ABOLITIONARY	ABRIDGEABLE
ABANDONING	ABIOGENESES	ABOLITIONISM	ABRIDGEMENT
ABANDONMENT	ABIOGENESIS	ABOLITIONISMS	ABRIDGEMENTS
ABANDONMENTS	ABIOGENETIC	ABOLITIONIST	ABRIDGMENT
ABANDONWARE	ABIOGENETICALLY	ABOLITIONISTS	ABRIDGMENTS
ABANDONWARES	ABIOGENICALLY	ABOLITIONS	ABROGATING
ABASEMENTS	ABIOGENIST	ABOMASUSES	ABROGATION
ABASHMENTS	ABIOGENISTS	ABOMINABLE	ABROGATIONS
ABATEMENTS	ABIOLOGICAL	ABOMINABLENESS	ABROGATIVE
ABBOTSHIPS	ABIOTICALLY	ABOMINABLY	ABROGATORS
ABBREVIATE	ABIOTROPHIC	ABOMINATED	ABRUPTIONS
ABBREVIATED	ABIOTROPHIES	ABOMINATES	ABRUPTNESS
ABBREVIATES	ABIOTROPHY	ABOMINATING	ABRUPTNESSES
ABBREVIATING	ABIRRITANT	ABOMINATION	ABSCESSING
ABBREVIATION	ABIRRITANTS	ABOMINATIONS	ABSCINDING
ABBREVIATIONS	ABIRRITATE	ABOMINATOR	ABSCISSINS
ABBREVIATOR	ABIRRITATED	ABOMINATORS	ABSCISSION
ABBREVIATORS	ABIRRITATES	ABONDANCES	ABSCISSIONS
ABBREVIATORY	ABIRRITATING	ABONNEMENT	ABSCONDENCE
ABBREVIATURE	ABITURIENT	ABONNEMENTS	ABSCONDENCES
ABBREVIATURES	ABITURIENTS	ABORIGINAL	ABSCONDERS
ABCOULOMBS	ABJECTIONS	ABORIGINALISM	ABSCONDING
ABDICATING	ABJECTNESS	ABORIGINALISMS	ABSEILINGS
ABDICATION	ABJECTNESSES	ABORIGINALITIES	ABSENTEEISM
ABDICATIONS	ABJOINTING	ABORIGINALITY	ABSENTEEISMS
ABDICATIVE	ABJUNCTION	ABORIGINALLY	ABSENTMINDED
ABDICATORS	ABJUNCTIONS	ABORIGINALS	ABSENTMINDEDLY
ABDOMINALLY	ABJURATION	ABORIGINES	ABSINTHIATED
ABDOMINALS	ABJURATIONS	ABORTICIDE	ABSINTHISM
ABDOMINOPLASTY	ABLACTATION	ABORTICIDES	ABSINTHISMS
ABDOMINOUS	ABLACTATIONS	ABORTIFACIENT	ABSOLUTELY
ABDUCENTES	ABLATITIOUS	ABORTIFACIENTS	ABSOLUTENESS
ABDUCTIONS	ABLATIVELY	ABORTIONAL	ABSOLUTENESSES
ABDUCTORES	ABLUTIONARY	ABORTIONIST	ABSOLUTEST
ABECEDARIAN	ABLUTOMANE	ABORTIONISTS	ABSOLUTION
ABECEDARIANS	ABLUTOMANES	ABORTIVELY	ABSOLUTIONS
ABERDEVINE	ABNEGATING	ABORTIVENESS	ABSOLUTISE
ABERDEVINES	ABNEGATION	ABORTIVENESSES	ABSOLUTISED
ABERNETHIES	ABNEGATIONS	ABORTUARIES	ABSOLUTISES
ABERRANCES	ABNEGATORS	ABOVEBOARD	ABSOLUTISING
ABERRANCIES	ABNORMALISM	ABOVEGROUND	ABSOLUTISM
ABERRANTLY	ABNORMALISMS	ABRACADABRA	ABSOLUTISMS
ABERRATING	ABNORMALITIES	ABRACADABRAS	ABSOLUTIST
ABERRATION	ABNORMALITY	ABRANCHIAL	ABSOLUTISTIC
ABERRATIONAL	ABNORMALLY	ABRANCHIATE	ABSOLUTISTS
ABERRATIONS	ABNORMITIES	ABRASIVELY	ABSOLUTIVE
ABEYANCIES	ABODEMENTS	ABRASIVENESS	ABSOLUTIZE
ABHOMINABLE	ABOLISHABLE	ABRASIVENESSES	ABSOLUTIZED

ABSOLUTIZES	ABSTINENCIES	ACALCULIAS	ACCENTUATION
ABSOLUTIZING	ABSTINENCY	ACALEPHANS	ACCENTUATIONS
ABSOLUTORY	ABSTINENTLY	ACANACEOUS	ACCEPTABILITIES
ABSOLVABLE	ABSTRACTABLE	ACANTHACEOUS	ACCEPTABILITY
ABSOLVENTS	ABSTRACTED	ACANTHOCEPHALAN	ACCEPTABLE
ABSOLVITOR	ABSTRACTEDLY	ACANTHUSES	ACCEPTABLENESS
ABSOLVITORS	ABSTRACTEDNESS	ACARICIDAL	ACCEPTABLY
ABSORBABILITIES	ABSTRACTER	ACARICIDES	ACCEPTANCE
ABSORBABILITY	ABSTRACTERS	ACARIDEANS	ACCEPTANCES
ABSORBABLE	ABSTRACTEST	ACARIDIANS	ACCEPTANCIES
ABSORBANCE	ABSTRACTING	ACARIDOMATIA	ACCEPTANCY
ABSORBANCES	ABSTRACTION	ACARIDOMATIUM	ACCEPTANTS
ABSORBANCIES	ABSTRACTIONAL	ACARODOMATIA	ACCEPTATION
ABSORBANCY	ABSTRACTIONISM	ACARODOMATIUM	ACCEPTATIONS
ABSORBANTS	ABSTRACTIONISMS	ACAROLOGIES	ACCEPTEDLY
ABSORBATES	ABSTRACTIONIST	ACAROLOGIST	ACCEPTILATION
ABSORBEDLY	ABSTRACTIONISTS	ACAROLOGISTS	ACCEPTILATIONS
ABSORBEFACIENT	ABSTRACTIONS	ACAROPHILIES	ACCEPTINGLY
ABSORBEFACIENTS	ABSTRACTIVE	ACAROPHILY	ACCEPTINGNESS
ABSORBENCIES	ABSTRACTIVELY	ACARPELLOUS	ACCEPTINGNESSES
ABSORBENCY	ABSTRACTIVES	ACARPELOUS	ACCEPTIVITIES
ABSORBENTS	ABSTRACTLY	ACATALECTIC	ACCEPTIVITY
ABSORBINGLY	ABSTRACTNESS	ACATALECTICS	ACCESSARIES
ABSORPTANCE	ABSTRACTNESSES	ACATALEPSIES	ACCESSARILY
ABSORPTANCES	ABSTRACTOR	ACATALEPSY	ACCESSARINESS
ABSORPTIOMETER	ABSTRACTORS	ACATALEPTIC	ACCESSARINESSES
ABSORPTIOMETERS	ABSTRICTED	ACATALEPTICS	ACCESSIBILITIES
ABSORPTION	ABSTRICTING	ACATAMATHESIA	ACCESSIBILITY
ABSORPTIONS	ABSTRICTION	ACATAMATHESIAS	ACCESSIBLE
ABSORPTIVE	ABSTRICTIONS	ACAULESCENT	ACCESSIBLENESS
ABSORPTIVENESS	ABSTRUSELY	ACCEDENCES	ACCESSIBLY
ABSORPTIVITIES	ABSTRUSENESS	ACCELERABLE	ACCESSIONAL
ABSORPTIVITY	ABSTRUSENESSES	ACCELERANDO	ACCESSIONED
ABSQUATULATE	ABSTRUSEST	ACCELERANDOS	ACCESSIONING
ABSQUATULATED	ABSTRUSITIES	ACCELERANT	ACCESSIONS
ABSQUATULATES	ABSTRUSITY	ACCELERANTS	ACCESSORIAL
ABSQUATULATING	ABSURDISMS	ACCELERATE	ACCESSORIES
ABSTAINERS	ABSURDISTS	ACCELERATED	ACCESSORII
ABSTAINING	ABSURDITIES	ACCELERATES	ACCESSORILY
ABSTEMIOUS	ABSURDNESS	ACCELERATING	ACCESSORINESS
ABSTEMIOUSLY	ABSURDNESSES	ACCELERATINGLY	ACCESSORINESSES
ABSTEMIOUSNESS	ABUNDANCES	ACCELERATION	ACCESSORISE
ABSTENTION	ABUNDANCIES	ACCELERATIONS	ACCESSORISED
ABSTENTIONISM	ABUNDANTLY	ACCELERATIVE	ACCESSORISES
ABSTENTIONISMS	ABUSIVENESS	ACCELERATOR	ACCESSORISING
ABSTENTIONIST	ABUSIVENESSES	ACCELERATORS	ACCESSORIUS
ABSTENTIONISTS	ABYSSOPELAGIC	ACCELERATORY	ACCESSORIZE
ABSTENTIONS	ACADEMICAL	ACCELEROMETER	ACCESSORIZED
ABSTENTIOUS	ACADEMICALISM	ACCELEROMETERS	ACCESSORIZES
ABSTERGENT	ACADEMICALISMS	ACCENSIONS	ACCESSORIZING
ABSTERGENTS	ACADEMICALLY	ACCENTLESS	ACCIACCATURA
ABSTERGING	ACADEMICALS	ACCENTUALITIES	ACCIACCATURAS
ABSTERSION	ACADEMICIAN	ACCENTUALITY	ACCIACCATURE
ABSTERSIONS	ACADEMICIANS	ACCENTUALLY	ACCIDENCES
ABSTERSIVE	ACADEMICISM	ACCENTUATE	ACCIDENTAL
ABSTERSIVES	ACADEMICISMS	ACCENTUATED	ACCIDENTALISM
ABSTINENCE	ACADEMISMS	ACCENTUATES	ACCIDENTALISMS
ABSTINENCES	ACADEMISTS	ACCENTUATING	ACCIDENTALITIES

ACCIDENTALITY ACCOMMODATORS ACCOUPLEMENTS ACCUSATIONS
ACCIDENTALLY ACCOMPANIED ACCOURAGED ACCUSATIVAL
ACCIDENTALNESS ACCOMPANIER ACCOURAGES ACCUSATIVE
ACCIDENTALS ACCOMPANIERS ACCOURAGING ACCUSATIVELY
ACCIDENTED ACCOMPANIES ACCOURTING ACCUSATIVES
ACCIDENTLY ACCOMPANIMENT ACCOUSTREMENT ACCUSATORIAL
ACCIDENTOLOGIES ACCOMPANIMENTS ACCOUSTREMENTS ACCUSATORY
ACCIDENTOLOGIST ACCOMPANIST ACCOUTERED ACCUSEMENT
ACCIDENTOLOGY ACCOMPANISTS ACCOUTERING ACCUSEMENTS
ACCIPITERS ACCOMPANYING ACCOUTERMENT ACCUSINGLY
ACCIPITRAL ACCOMPANYIST ACCOUTERMENTS ACCUSTOMARY
ACCIPITRINE ACCOMPANYISTS ACCOUTREMENT ACCUSTOMATION
ACCIPITRINES ACCOMPLICE ACCOUTREMENTS ACCUSTOMATIONS
ACCLAIMERS ACCOMPLICES ACCOUTRING ACCUSTOMED
ACCLAIMING ACCOMPLISH ACCREDITABLE ACCUSTOMEDNESS
ACCLAMATION ACCOMPLISHABLE ACCREDITATION ACCUSTOMING
ACCLAMATIONS ACCOMPLISHED ACCREDITATIONS ACCUSTREMENT
ACCLAMATORY ACCOMPLISHER ACCREDITED ACCUSTREMENTS
ACCLIMATABILITY ACCOMPLISHERS ACCREDITING ACEPHALOUS
ACCLIMATABLE ACCOMPLISHES ACCRESCENCE ACERACEOUS
ACCLIMATATION ACCOMPLISHING ACCRESCENCES ACERBATING
ACCLIMATATIONS ACCOMPLISHMENT ACCRESCENT ACERBICALLY
ACCLIMATED ACCOMPLISHMENTS ACCRETIONARY ACERBITIES
ACCLIMATES ACCOMPTABLE ACCRETIONS ACERVATELY
ACCLIMATING ACCOMPTANT ACCRUEMENT ACERVATION
ACCLIMATION ACCOMPTANTS ACCRUEMENTS ACERVATIONS
ACCLIMATIONS ACCOMPTING ACCUBATION ACESCENCES
ACCLIMATISABLE ACCORAGING ACCUBATIONS ACESCENCIES
ACCLIMATISATION ACCORDABLE ACCULTURAL ACETABULAR
ACCLIMATISE ACCORDANCE ACCULTURATE ACETABULUM
ACCLIMATISED ACCORDANCES ACCULTURATED ACETABULUMS
ACCLIMATISER ACCORDANCIES ACCULTURATES ACETALDEHYDE
ACCLIMATISERS ACCORDANCY ACCULTURATING ACETALDEHYDES
ACCLIMATISES ACCORDANTLY ACCULTURATION ACETAMIDES
ACCLIMATISING ACCORDINGLY ACCULTURATIONAL ACETAMINOPHEN
ACCLIMATIZABLE ACCORDIONIST ACCULTURATIONS ACETAMINOPHENS
ACCLIMATIZATION ACCORDIONISTS ACCULTURATIVE ACETANILID
ACCLIMATIZE ACCORDIONS ACCUMBENCIES ACETANILIDE
ACCLIMATIZED ACCOSTABLE ACCUMBENCY ACETANILIDES
ACCLIMATIZER ACCOUCHEMENT ACCUMULABLE ACETANILIDS
ACCLIMATIZERS ACCOUCHEMENTS ACCUMULATE ACETAZOLAMIDE
ACCLIMATIZES ACCOUCHEUR ACCUMULATED ACETAZOLAMIDES
ACCLIMATIZING ACCOUCHEURS ACCUMULATES ACETIFICATION
ACCLIVITIES ACCOUCHEUSE ACCUMULATING ACETIFICATIONS
ACCLIVITOUS ACCOUCHEUSES ACCUMULATION ACETIFIERS
ACCOASTING ACCOUNTABILITY ACCUMULATIONS ACETIFYING
ACCOLADING ACCOUNTABLE ACCUMULATIVE ACETOMETER
ACCOMMODABLE ACCOUNTABLENESS ACCUMULATIVELY ACETOMETERS
ACCOMMODATE ACCOUNTABLY ACCUMULATOR ACETONAEMIA
ACCOMMODATED ACCOUNTANCIES ACCUMULATORS ACETONAEMIAS
ACCOMMODATES ACCOUNTANCY ACCURACIES ACETONEMIA
ACCOMMODATING ACCOUNTANT ACCURATELY ACETONEMIAS
ACCOMMODATINGLY ACCOUNTANTS ACCURATENESS ACETONITRILE
ACCOMMODATION ACCOUNTANTSHIP ACCURATENESSES ACETONITRILES
ACCOMMODATIONAL ACCOUNTANTSHIPS ACCURSEDLY ACETONURIA
ACCOMMODATIONS ACCOUNTING ACCURSEDNESS ACETONURIAS
ACCOMMODATIVE ACCOUNTINGS ACCURSEDNESSES ACETOPHENETIDIN
ACCOMMODATOR ACCOUPLEMENT ACCUSATION ACETYLATED

ACETYLATES	ACIDIFYING	ACQUAINTING	ACROLITHIC
ACETYLATING	ACIDIMETER	ACQUIESCED	ACROMEGALIC
ACETYLATION	ACIDIMETERS	ACQUIESCENCE	ACROMEGALICS
ACETYLATIONS	ACIDIMETRIC	ACQUIESCENCES	ACROMEGALIES
ACETYLATIVE	ACIDIMETRICAL	ACQUIESCENT	ACROMEGALY
ACETYLCHOLINE	ACIDIMETRICALLY	ACQUIESCENTLY	ACRONICALLY
ACETYLCHOLINES	ACIDIMETRIES	ACQUIESCENTS	ACRONYCALLY
ACETYLENES	ACIDIMETRY	ACQUIESCES	ACRONYCHAL
ACETYLENIC	ACIDNESSES	ACQUIESCING	ACRONYCHALLY
ACETYLIDES	ACIDOMETER	ACQUIESCINGLY	ACRONYMANIA
ACETYLSALICYLIC	ACIDOMETERS	ACQUIGHTING	ACRONYMANIAS
ACHAENIUMS	ACIDOPHILE	ACQUIRABILITIES	ACRONYMICALLY
ACHAENOCARP	ACIDOPHILES	ACQUIRABILITY	ACRONYMOUS
ACHAENOCARPS	ACIDOPHILIC	ACQUIRABLE	ACROPARESTHESIA
ACHALASIAS	ACIDOPHILOUS	ACQUIREMENT	ACROPETALLY
ACHIEVABLE	ACIDOPHILS	ACQUIREMENTS	ACROPHOBES
ACHIEVEMENT	ACIDOPHILUS	ACQUISITION	ACROPHOBIA
ACHIEVEMENTS	ACIDOPHILUSES	ACQUISITIONAL	ACROPHOBIAS
ACHINESSES	ACIDULATED	ACQUISITIONS	ACROPHOBIC
ACHLAMYDEOUS	ACIDULATES	ACQUISITIVE	ACROPHONETIC
ACHLORHYDRIA	ACIDULATING	ACQUISITIVELY	ACROPHONIC
ACHLORHYDRIAS	ACIDULATION	ACQUISITIVENESS	ACROPHONIES
ACHLORHYDRIC	ACIDULATIONS	ACQUISITOR	ACROPOLISES
ACHONDRITE	ACIERATING	ACQUISITORS	ACROSPIRES
ACHONDRITES	ACIERATION	ACQUITMENT	ACROSTICAL
ACHONDRITIC	ACIERATIONS	ACQUITMENTS	ACROSTICALLY
ACHONDROPLASIA	ACINACEOUS	ACQUITTALS	ACROTERIAL
ACHONDROPLASIAS	ACINACIFORM	ACQUITTANCE	ACROTERION
ACHONDROPLASTIC	ACKNOWLEDGE	ACQUITTANCED	ACROTERIUM
ACHROMATIC	ACKNOWLEDGEABLE	ACQUITTANCES	ACROTERIUMS
ACHROMATICALLY	ACKNOWLEDGEABLY	ACQUITTANCING	ACRYLAMIDE
ACHROMATICITIES	ACKNOWLEDGED	ACQUITTERS	ACRYLAMIDES
ACHROMATICITY	ACKNOWLEDGEDLY	ACQUITTING	ACRYLONITRILE
ACHROMATIN	ACKNOWLEDGEMENT	ACRIDITIES	ACRYLONITRILES
ACHROMATINS	ACKNOWLEDGER	ACRIDNESSES	ACTABILITIES
ACHROMATISATION	ACKNOWLEDGERS	ACRIFLAVIN	ACTABILITY
ACHROMATISE	ACKNOWLEDGES	ACRIFLAVINE	ACTINICALLY
ACHROMATISED	ACKNOWLEDGING	ACRIFLAVINES	ACTINIFORM
ACHROMATISES	ACKNOWLEDGMENT	ACRIFLAVINS	ACTINOBACILLI
ACHROMATISING	ACKNOWLEDGMENTS	ACRIMONIES	ACTINOBACILLUS
ACHROMATISM	ACOELOMATE	ACRIMONIOUS	ACTINOBIOLOGIES
ACHROMATISMS	ACOELOMATES	ACRIMONIOUSLY	ACTINOBIOLOGY
ACHROMATIZATION	ACOLOUTHIC	ACRIMONIOUSNESS	ACTINOCHEMISTRY
ACHROMATIZE	ACOLOUTHITE	ACRITARCHS	ACTINOLITE
ACHROMATIZED	ACOLOUTHITES	ACROAMATIC	ACTINOLITES
ACHROMATIZES	ACOLOUTHOS	ACROAMATICAL	ACTINOMERE
ACHROMATIZING	ACOLOUTHOSES	ACROBATICALLY	ACTINOMERES
ACHROMATOPSIA	ACONITINES	ACROBATICS	ACTINOMETER
ACHROMATOPSIAS	ACOTYLEDON	ACROBATISM	ACTINOMETERS
ACHROMATOUS	ACOTYLEDONOUS	ACROBATISMS	ACTINOMETRIC
ACICULATED	ACOTYLEDONS	ACROCARPOUS	ACTINOMETRICAL
ACIDANTHERA	ACOUSTICAL	ACROCENTRIC	ACTINOMETRIES
ACIDANTHERAS	ACOUSTICALLY	ACROCENTRICS	ACTINOMETRY
ACIDFREAKS	ACOUSTICIAN	ACROCYANOSES	ACTINOMORPHIC
ACIDIFIABLE	ACOUSTICIANS	ACROCYANOSIS	ACTINOMORPHIES
ACIDIFICATION	ACQUAINTANCE	ACRODROMOUS	ACTINOMORPHOUS
ACIDIFICATIONS	ACQUAINTANCES	ACROGENOUS	ACTINOMORPHY
ACIDIFIERS	ACQUAINTED	ACROGENOUSLY	ACTINOMYCES

ACTINOMYCETE	ACYCLOVIRS	ADENOHYPOPHYSES	ADJUDGMENTS
ACTINOMYCETES	ACYLATIONS	ADENOHYPOPHYSIS	ADJUDICATE
ACTINOMYCETOUS	ADACTYLOUS	ADENOIDECTOMIES	ADJUDICATED
ACTINOMYCIN	ADAMANCIES	ADENOIDECTOMY	ADJUDICATES
ACTINOMYCINS	ADAMANTEAN	ADENOMATOUS	ADJUDICATING
ACTINOMYCOSES	ADAMANTINE	ADENOPATHIES	ADJUDICATION
ACTINOMYCOSIS	ADAPTABILITIES	ADENOPATHY	ADJUDICATIONS
ACTINOMYCOTIC	ADAPTABILITY	ADENOSINES	ADJUDICATIVE
ACTINOPODS	ADAPTABLENESS	ADENOVIRAL	ADJUDICATOR
ACTINOTHERAPIES	ADAPTABLENESSES	ADENOVIRUS	ADJUDICATORS
ACTINOTHERAPY	ADAPTATION	ADENOVIRUSES	ADJUDICATORY
ACTINOURANIUM	ADAPTATIONAL	ADEPTNESSES	ADJUNCTION
ACTINOURANIUMS	ADAPTATIONALLY	ADEQUACIES	ADJUNCTIONS
ACTINOZOAN	ADAPTATIONS	ADEQUATELY	ADJUNCTIVE
ACTIONABLE	ADAPTATIVE	ADEQUATENESS	ADJUNCTIVELY
ACTIONABLY	ADAPTEDNESS	ADEQUATENESSES	ADJURATION
ACTIONISTS	ADAPTEDNESSES	ADEQUATIVE	ADJURATIONS
ACTIONLESS	ADAPTIVELY	ADHERENCES	ADJURATORY
ACTIVATING	ADAPTIVENESS	ADHERENTLY	ADJUSTABILITIES
ACTIVATION	ADAPTIVENESSES	ADHESIONAL	ADJUSTABILITY
ACTIVATIONS	ADAPTIVITIES	ADHESIVELY	ADJUSTABLE
ACTIVATORS	ADAPTIVITY	ADHESIVENESS	ADJUSTABLY
ACTIVENESS	ADAPTOGENIC	ADHESIVENESSES	ADJUSTMENT
ACTIVENESSES	ADAPTOGENS	ADHIBITING	ADJUSTMENTAL
ACTIVISING	ADDERSTONE	ADHIBITION	ADJUSTMENTS
ACTIVISTIC	ADDERSTONES	ADHIBITIONS	ADJUTANCIES
ACTIVITIES	ADDERWORTS	ADHOCRACIES	ADJUVANCIES
ACTIVIZING	ADDICTEDNESS	ADIABATICALLY	ADMEASURED
ACTOMYOSIN	ADDICTEDNESSES	ADIABATICS	ADMEASUREMENT
ACTOMYOSINS	ADDICTIONS	ADIACTINIC	ADMEASUREMENTS
ACTUALISATION	ADDITAMENT	ADIAPHORISM	ADMEASURES
ACTUALISATIONS	ADDITAMENTS	ADIAPHORISMS	ADMEASURING
ACTUALISED	ADDITIONAL	ADIAPHORIST	ADMINICLES
ACTUALISES	ADDITIONALITIES	ADIAPHORISTIC	ADMINICULAR
ACTUALISING	ADDITIONALITY	ADIAPHORISTS	ADMINICULATE
ACTUALISTS	ADDITIONALLY	ADIAPHORON	ADMINICULATED
ACTUALITES	ADDITITIOUS	ADIAPHOROUS	ADMINICULATES
ACTUALITIES	ADDITIVELY	ADIATHERMANCIES	ADMINICULATING
ACTUALIZATION	ADDITIVITIES	ADIATHERMANCY	ADMINISTER
ACTUALIZATIONS	ADDITIVITY	ADIATHERMANOUS	ADMINISTERED
ACTUALIZED	ADDLEMENTS	ADIATHERMIC	ADMINISTERING
ACTUALIZES	ADDLEPATED	ADIPOCERES	ADMINISTERS
ACTUALIZING	ADDRESSABILITY	ADIPOCEROUS	ADMINISTRABLE
ACTUARIALLY	ADDRESSABLE	ADIPOCYTES	ADMINISTRANT
ACTUATIONS	ADDRESSEES	ADIPOSITIES	ADMINISTRANTS
ACUMINATED	ADDRESSERS	ADJACENCES	ADMINISTRATE
ACUMINATES	ADDRESSING	ADJACENCIES	ADMINISTRATED
ACUMINATING	ADDRESSORS	ADJACENTLY	ADMINISTRATES
ACUMINATION	ADDUCEABLE	ADJECTIVAL	ADMINISTRATING
ACUMINATIONS	ADDUCTIONS	ADJECTIVALLY	ADMINISTRATION
ACUPRESSURE	ADELANTADO	ADJECTIVELY	ADMINISTRATIONS
ACUPRESSURES	ADELANTADOS	ADJECTIVES	ADMINISTRATIVE
ACUPUNCTURAL	ADEMPTIONS	ADJOURNING	ADMINISTRATOR
ACUPUNCTURE	ADENECTOMIES	ADJOURNMENT	ADMINISTRATORS
ACUPUNCTURES	ADENECTOMY	ADJOURNMENTS	ADMINISTRATRIX
ACUPUNCTURIST	ADENITISES	ADJUDGEMENT	ADMIRABILITIES
ACUPUNCTURISTS	ADENOCARCINOMA	ADJUDGEMENTS	ADMIRABILITY
ACUTENESSES	ADENOCARCINOMAS	ADJUDGMENT	ADMIRABLENESS

ADMIRABLENESSES	ADPRESSING	ADULTEROUSLY	ADVERSARIAL
ADMIRALSHIP	ADRENALECTOMIES	ADULTESCENT	ADVERSARIES
ADMIRALSHIPS	ADRENALECTOMY	ADULTESCENTS	ADVERSARINESS
ADMIRALTIES	ADRENALINE	ADULTHOODS	ADVERSARINESSES
ADMIRANCES	ADRENALINES	ADULTNESSES	ADVERSATIVE
ADMIRATION	ADRENALINS	ADULTRESSES	ADVERSATIVELY
ADMIRATIONS	ADRENALISED	ADUMBRATED	ADVERSATIVES
ADMIRATIVE	ADRENALIZED	ADUMBRATES	ADVERSENESS
ADMIRAUNCE	ADRENERGIC	ADUMBRATING	ADVERSENESSES
ADMIRAUNCES	ADRENERGICALLY	ADUMBRATION	ADVERSITIES
ADMIRINGLY	ADRENOCHROME	ADUMBRATIONS	ADVERTENCE
ADMISSIBILITIES	ADRENOCHROMES	ADUMBRATIVE	ADVERTENCES
ADMISSIBILITY	ADRENOCORTICAL	ADUMBRATIVELY	ADVERTENCIES
ADMISSIBLE	ADRIAMYCIN	ADUNCITIES	ADVERTENCY
ADMISSIBLENESS	ADRIAMYCINS	ADVANCEMENT	ADVERTENTLY
ADMISSIONS	ADROITNESS	ADVANCEMENTS	ADVERTISED
ADMITTABLE	ADROITNESSES	ADVANCINGLY	ADVERTISEMENT
ADMITTANCE	ADSCITITIOUS	ADVANTAGEABLE	ADVERTISEMENTS
ADMITTANCES	ADSCITITIOUSLY	ADVANTAGED	ADVERTISER
ADMITTEDLY	ADSCRIPTION	ADVANTAGEOUS	ADVERTISERS
ADMIXTURES	ADSCRIPTIONS	ADVANTAGEOUSLY	ADVERTISES
ADMONISHED	ADSORBABILITIES	ADVANTAGES	ADVERTISING
ADMONISHER	ADSORBABILITY	ADVANTAGING	ADVERTISINGS
ADMONISHERS	ADSORBABLE	ADVECTIONS	ADVERTIZED
ADMONISHES	ADSORBATES	ADVENTITIA	ADVERTIZEMENT
ADMONISHING	ADSORBENTS	ADVENTITIAL	ADVERTIZEMENTS
ADMONISHINGLY	ADSORPTION	ADVENTITIAS	ADVERTIZER
ADMONISHMENT	ADSORPTIONS	ADVENTITIOUS	ADVERTIZERS
ADMONISHMENTS	ADSORPTIVE	ADVENTITIOUSLY	ADVERTIZES
ADMONITION	ADULARESCENCE	ADVENTIVES	ADVERTIZING
ADMONITIONS	ADULARESCENCES	ADVENTURED	ADVERTORIAL
ADMONITIVE	ADULARESCENT	ADVENTUREFUL	ADVERTORIALS
ADMONITORILY	ADULATIONS	ADVENTURER	ADVISABILITIES
ADMONITORS	ADULTERANT	ADVENTURERS	ADVISABILITY
ADMONITORY	ADULTERANTS	ADVENTURES	ADVISABLENESS
ADNOMINALS	ADULTERATE	ADVENTURESOME	ADVISABLENESSES
ADOLESCENCE	ADULTERATED	ADVENTURESS	ADVISATORY
ADOLESCENCES	ADULTERATES	ADVENTURESSES	ADVISEDNESS
ADOLESCENT	ADULTERATING	ADVENTURING	ADVISEDNESSES
ADOLESCENTLY	ADULTERATION	ADVENTURISM	ADVISEMENT
ADOLESCENTS	ADULTERATIONS	ADVENTURISMS	ADVISEMENTS
ADOPTABILITIES	ADULTERATOR	ADVENTURIST	ADVISERSHIP
ADOPTABILITY	ADULTERATORS	ADVENTURISTIC	ADVISERSHIPS
ADOPTIANISM	ADULTERERS	ADVENTURISTS	ADVISORATE
ADOPTIANISMS	ADULTERESS	ADVENTUROUS	ADVISORATES
ADOPTIANIST	ADULTERESSES	ADVENTUROUSLY	ADVISORIES
ADOPTIANISTS	ADULTERIES	ADVENTUROUSNESS	ADVOCACIES
ADOPTIONISM	ADULTERINE	ADVERBIALISE	ADVOCATING
ADOPTIONISMS	ADULTERINES	ADVERBIALISED	ADVOCATION
ADOPTIONIST	ADULTERISE	ADVERBIALISES	ADVOCATIONS
ADOPTIONISTS	ADULTERISED	ADVERBIALISING	ADVOCATIVE
ADOPTIVELY	ADULTERISES	ADVERBIALIZE	ADVOCATORS
ADORABILITIES	ADULTERISING	ADVERBIALIZED	ADVOCATORY
ADORABILITY	ADULTERIZE	ADVERBIALIZES	ADVOUTRERS
ADORABLENESS	ADULTERIZED	ADVERBIALIZING	ADVOUTRIES
ADORABLENESSES	ADULTERIZES	ADVERBIALLY	AECIDIOSPORE
ADORATIONS	ADULTERIZING	ADVERBIALS	AECIDIOSPORES
ADORNMENTS	ADULTEROUS	ADVERSARIA	AECIDOSPORE

AECIDOSPORES	AEROELASTICIANS	AEROSHELLS	AESTIVATORS
AECIOSPORE	AEROELASTICITY	AEROSIDERITE	AETHEREALITIES
AECIOSPORES	AEROEMBOLISM	AEROSIDERITES	AETHEREALITY
AEDILESHIP	AEROEMBOLISMS	AEROSOLISATION	AETHEREALLY
AEDILESHIPS	AEROGENERATOR	AEROSOLISATIONS	AETHRIOSCOPE
AEOLIPILES	AEROGENERATORS	AEROSOLISE	AETHRIOSCOPES
AEOLIPYLES	AEROGRAMME	AEROSOLISED	AETIOLOGICAL
AEOLOTROPIC	AEROGRAMMES	AEROSOLISES	AETIOLOGICALLY
AEOLOTROPIES	AEROGRAPHIES	AEROSOLISING	AETIOLOGIES
AEOLOTROPY	AEROGRAPHS	AEROSOLIZATION	AETIOLOGIST
AEPYORNISES	AEROGRAPHY	AEROSOLIZATIONS	AETIOLOGISTS
AERENCHYMA	AEROHYDROPLANE	AEROSOLIZE	AFFABILITIES
AERENCHYMAS	AEROHYDROPLANES	AEROSOLIZED	AFFABILITY
AERENCHYMATOUS	AEROLITHOLOGIES	AEROSOLIZES	AFFECTABILITIES
AERIALISTS	AEROLITHOLOGY	AEROSOLIZING	AFFECTABILITY
AERIALITIES	AEROLOGICAL	AEROSPACES	AFFECTABLE
AERIFICATION	AEROLOGIES	AEROSPHERE	AFFECTATION
AERIFICATIONS	AEROLOGIST	AEROSPHERES	AFFECTATIONS
AEROACOUSTICS	AEROLOGISTS	AEROSTATIC	AFFECTEDLY
AEROBALLISTICS	AEROMAGNETIC	AEROSTATICAL	AFFECTEDNESS
AEROBATICS	AEROMANCIES	AEROSTATICS	AFFECTEDNESSES
AEROBICALLY	AEROMECHANIC	AEROSTATION	AFFECTINGLY
AEROBICISE	AEROMECHANICAL	AEROSTATIONS	AFFECTIONAL
AEROBICISED	AEROMECHANICS	AEROSTRUCTURE	AFFECTIONALLY
AEROBICISES	AEROMEDICAL	AEROSTRUCTURES	AFFECTIONATE
AEROBICISING	AEROMEDICINE	AEROTACTIC	AFFECTIONATELY
AEROBICIST	AEROMEDICINES	AEROTRAINS	AFFECTIONED
AEROBICISTS	AEROMETERS	AEROTROPIC	AFFECTIONING
AEROBICIZE	AEROMETRIC	AEROTROPISM	AFFECTIONLESS
AEROBICIZED	AEROMETRIES	AEROTROPISMS	AFFECTIONS
AEROBICIZES	AEROMOTORS	AERUGINOUS	AFFECTIVELY
AEROBICIZING	AERONAUTIC	AESTHESIAS	AFFECTIVENESS
AEROBIOLOGICAL	AERONAUTICAL	AESTHESIOGEN	AFFECTIVENESSES
AEROBIOLOGIES	AERONAUTICALLY	AESTHESIOGENIC	AFFECTIVITIES
AEROBIOLOGIST	AERONAUTICS	AESTHESIOGENS	AFFECTIVITY
AEROBIOLOGISTS	AERONEUROSES	AESTHETICAL	AFFECTLESS
AEROBIOLOGY	AERONEUROSIS	AESTHETICALLY	AFFECTLESSNESS
AEROBIONTS	AERONOMERS	AESTHETICIAN	AFFEERMENT
AEROBIOSES	AERONOMICAL	AESTHETICIANS	AFFEERMENTS
AEROBIOSIS	AERONOMIES	AESTHETICISE	AFFENPINSCHER
AEROBIOTIC	AERONOMIST	AESTHETICISED	AFFENPINSCHERS
AEROBIOTICALLY	AERONOMISTS	AESTHETICISES	AFFERENTLY
AEROBRAKED	AEROPAUSES	AESTHETICISING	AFFETTUOSO
AEROBRAKES	AEROPHAGIA	AESTHETICISM	AFFETTUOSOS
AEROBRAKING	AEROPHAGIAS	AESTHETICISMS	AFFIANCING
AEROBRAKINGS	AEROPHAGIES	AESTHETICIST	AFFICIONADO
AEROBUSSES	AEROPHOBES	AESTHETICISTS	AFFICIONADOS
AERODONETICALLY	AEROPHOBIA	AESTHETICIZE	AFFIDAVITS
AERODONETICS	AEROPHOBIAS	AESTHETICIZED	AFFILIABLE
AERODROMES	AEROPHOBIC	AESTHETICIZES	AFFILIATED
AERODYNAMIC	AEROPHONES	AESTHETICIZING	AFFILIATES
AERODYNAMICAL	AEROPHORES	AESTHETICS	AFFILIATING
AERODYNAMICALLY	AEROPHYTES	AESTIVATED	AFFILIATION
AERODYNAMICIST	AEROPLANES	AESTIVATES	AFFILIATIONS
AERODYNAMICISTS	AEROPLANKTON	AESTIVATING	AFFINITIES
AERODYNAMICS	AEROPLANKTONS	AESTIVATION	AFFINITIVE
AEROELASTIC	AEROPULSES	AESTIVATIONS	AFFIRMABLE
AEROELASTICIAN	AEROSCOPES	AESTIVATOR	AFFIRMANCE

AFFIRMANCES

AFFIRMANCES AFFRIGHTED AFTERPIECE AGGLUTINABLE
AFFIRMANTS AFFRIGHTEDLY AFTERPIECES AGGLUTINANT
AFFIRMATION AFFRIGHTEN AFTERSALES AGGLUTINANTS
AFFIRMATIONS AFFRIGHTENED AFTERSENSATION AGGLUTINATE
AFFIRMATIVE AFFRIGHTENING AFTERSENSATIONS AGGLUTINATED
AFFIRMATIVELY AFFRIGHTENS AFTERSHAFT AGGLUTINATES
AFFIRMATIVES AFFRIGHTFUL AFTERSHAFTS AGGLUTINATING
AFFIRMATORY AFFRIGHTING AFTERSHAVE AGGLUTINATION
AFFIRMINGLY AFFRIGHTMENT AFTERSHAVES AGGLUTINATIONS
AFFIXATION AFFRIGHTMENTS AFTERSHOCK AGGLUTINATIVE
AFFIXATIONS AFFRONTING AFTERSHOCKS AGGLUTININ
AFFIXMENTS AFFRONTINGLY AFTERSHOWS AGGLUTININS
AFFIXTURES AFFRONTINGS AFTERSUPPER AGGLUTINOGEN
AFFLATIONS AFFRONTIVE AFTERSUPPERS AGGLUTINOGENIC
AFFLATUSES AFICIONADA AFTERSWARM AGGLUTINOGENS
AFFLICTERS AFICIONADAS AFTERSWARMS AGGRADATION
AFFLICTING AFICIONADO AFTERTASTE AGGRADATIONS
AFFLICTINGS AFICIONADOS AFTERTASTES AGGRANDISE
AFFLICTION AFLATOXINS AFTERTHOUGHT AGGRANDISED
AFFLICTIONS AFOREMENTIONED AFTERTHOUGHTS AGGRANDISEMENT
AFFLICTIVE AFORETHOUGHT AFTERTIMES AGGRANDISEMENTS
AFFLICTIVELY AFORETHOUGHTS AFTERWARDS AGGRANDISER
AFFLUENCES AFRORMOSIA AFTERWORDS AGGRANDISERS
AFFLUENCIES AFRORMOSIAS AFTERWORLD AGGRANDISES
AFFLUENTIAL AFTERBIRTH AFTERWORLDS AGGRANDISING
AFFLUENTIALS AFTERBIRTHS AGALACTIAS AGGRANDIZE
AFFLUENTLY AFTERBODIES AGALMATOLITE AGGRANDIZED
AFFLUENTNESS AFTERBRAIN AGALMATOLITES AGGRANDIZEMENT
AFFLUENTNESSES AFTERBRAINS AGAMICALLY AGGRANDIZEMENTS
AFFLUENZAS AFTERBURNER AGAMOGENESES AGGRANDIZER
AFFLUXIONS AFTERBURNERS AGAMOGENESIS AGGRANDIZERS
AFFOORDING AFTERBURNING AGAMOGENETIC AGGRANDIZES
AFFORCEMENT AFTERBURNINGS AGAMOGONIES AGGRANDIZING
AFFORCEMENTS AFTERCARES AGAMOSPERMIES AGGRAVATED
AFFORDABILITIES AFTERCLAPS AGAMOSPERMY AGGRAVATES
AFFORDABILITY AFTERDAMPS AGAPANTHUS AGGRAVATING
AFFORDABLE AFTERDECKS AGAPANTHUSES AGGRAVATINGLY
AFFORDABLY AFTEREFFECT AGARICACEOUS AGGRAVATION
AFFORESTABLE AFTEREFFECTS AGATEWARES AGGRAVATIONS
AFFORESTATION AFTEREYEING AGATHODAIMON AGGREGATED
AFFORESTATIONS AFTEREYING AGATHODAIMONS AGGREGATELY
AFFORESTED AFTERGAMES AGEDNESSES AGGREGATENESS
AFFORESTING AFTERGLOWS AGELESSNESS AGGREGATENESSES
AFFRANCHISE AFTERGRASS AGELESSNESSES AGGREGATES
AFFRANCHISED AFTERGRASSES AGENDALESS AGGREGATING
AFFRANCHISEMENT AFTERGROWTH AGENTIVITIES AGGREGATION
AFFRANCHISES AFTERGROWTHS AGENTIVITY AGGREGATIONAL
AFFRANCHISING AFTERHEATS AGGIORNAMENTI AGGREGATIONS
AFFRAPPING AFTERIMAGE AGGIORNAMENTO AGGREGATIVE
AFFREIGHTMENT AFTERIMAGES AGGIORNAMENTOS AGGREGATIVELY
AFFREIGHTMENTS AFTERLIFES AGGLOMERATE AGGREGATOR
AFFRICATED AFTERLIVES AGGLOMERATED AGGREGATORS
AFFRICATES AFTERMARKET AGGLOMERATES AGGRESSING
AFFRICATING AFTERMARKETS AGGLOMERATING AGGRESSION
AFFRICATION AFTERMATHS AGGLOMERATION AGGRESSIONS
AFFRICATIONS AFTERNOONS AGGLOMERATIONS AGGRESSIVE
AFFRICATIVE AFTERPAINS AGGLOMERATIVE AGGRESSIVELY
AFFRICATIVES AFTERPEAKS AGGLUTINABILITY AGGRESSIVENESS

AGGRESSIVITIES
AGGRESSIVITY
AGGRESSORS
AGGRIEVEDLY
AGGRIEVEMENT
AGGRIEVEMENTS
AGGRIEVING
AGILENESSES
AGISTMENTS
AGITATEDLY
AGITATIONAL
AGITATIONS
AGNATICALLY
AGNOIOLOGICALLY
AGNOIOLOGIES
AGNOIOLOGY
AGNOSTICISM
AGNOSTICISMS
AGONISEDLY
AGONISINGLY
AGONISTICAL
AGONISTICALLY
AGONISTICS
AGONIZEDLY
AGONIZINGLY
AGONOTHETES
AGORAPHOBE
AGORAPHOBES
AGORAPHOBIA
AGORAPHOBIAS
AGORAPHOBIC
AGORAPHOBICS
AGRANULOCYTE
AGRANULOCYTES
AGRANULOCYTOSES
AGRANULOCYTOSIS
AGRANULOSES
AGRANULOSIS
AGRARIANISM
AGRARIANISMS
AGREEABILITIES
AGREEABILITY
AGREEABLENESS
AGREEABLENESSES
AGREEMENTS
AGREGATION
AGREGATIONS
AGRIBUSINESS
AGRIBUSINESSES
AGRIBUSINESSMAN
AGRIBUSINESSMEN
AGRICHEMICAL
AGRICHEMICALS
AGRICULTURAL
AGRICULTURALIST
AGRICULTURALLY
AGRICULTURE
AGRICULTURES

AGRICULTURIST
AGRICULTURISTS
AGRIMONIES
AGRIOLOGIES
AGRIPRODUCT
AGRIPRODUCTS
AGRITOURISM
AGRITOURISMS
AGRITOURIST
AGRITOURISTS
AGROBIOLOGICAL
AGROBIOLOGIES
AGROBIOLOGIST
AGROBIOLOGISTS
AGROBIOLOGY
AGROBUSINESS
AGROBUSINESSES
AGROCHEMICAL
AGROCHEMICALS
AGRODOLCES
AGROFORESTER
AGROFORESTERS
AGROFORESTRIES
AGROFORESTRY
AGROINDUSTRIAL
AGROINDUSTRIES
AGROINDUSTRY
AGROLOGICAL
AGROLOGIES
AGROLOGIST
AGROLOGISTS
AGRONOMIAL
AGRONOMICAL
AGRONOMICALLY
AGRONOMICS
AGRONOMIES
AGRONOMIST
AGRONOMISTS
AGROSTEMMA
AGROSTEMMAS
AGROSTEMMATA
AGROSTOLOGICAL
AGROSTOLOGIES
AGROSTOLOGIST
AGROSTOLOGISTS
AGROSTOLOGY
AGROTERRORISM
AGROTERRORISMS
AGROTOURISM
AGROTOURISMS
AGROTOURIST
AGROTOURISTS
AGRYPNOPTICALLY
AGRYPNOTIC
AGRYPNOTICS
AGTERSKOTS
AGUARDIENTE
AGUARDIENTES

AHISTORICAL
AHORSEBACK
AICHMOPHOBIA
AICHMOPHOBIAS
AIGUILLETTE
AIGUILLETTES
AILANTHUSES
AILOUROPHILE
AILOUROPHILES
AILOUROPHILIA
AILOUROPHILIAS
AILOUROPHILIC
AILOUROPHOBE
AILOUROPHOBES
AILOUROPHOBIA
AILOUROPHOBIAS
AILOUROPHOBIC
AILUROPHILE
AILUROPHILES
AILUROPHILIA
AILUROPHILIAS
AILUROPHILIC
AILUROPHOBE
AILUROPHOBES
AILUROPHOBIA
AILUROPHOBIAS
AILUROPHOBIC
AIMLESSNESS
AIMLESSNESSES
AIRBRUSHED
AIRBRUSHES
AIRBRUSHING
AIRCOACHES
AIRCRAFTMAN
AIRCRAFTMEN
AIRCRAFTSMAN
AIRCRAFTSMEN
AIRCRAFTSWOMAN
AIRCRAFTSWOMEN
AIRCRAFTWOMAN
AIRCRAFTWOMEN
AIRDROPPED
AIRDROPPING
AIRFREIGHT
AIRFREIGHTED
AIRFREIGHTING
AIRFREIGHTS
AIRINESSES
AIRLESSNESS
AIRLESSNESSES
AIRLIFTING
AIRMAILING
AIRMANSHIP
AIRMANSHIPS
AIRPROOFED
AIRPROOFING
AIRSICKNESS
AIRSICKNESSES

AIRSTREAMS
AIRSTRIKES
AIRTIGHTNESS
AIRTIGHTNESSES
AIRWORTHIER
AIRWORTHIEST
AIRWORTHINESS
AIRWORTHINESSES
AITCHBONES
AKATHISIAS
AKOLOUTHOS
AKOLOUTHOSES
AKOLUTHOSES
ALABAMINES
ALABANDINE
ALABANDINES
ALABANDITE
ALABANDITES
ALABASTERS
ALABASTRINE
ALABLASTER
ALABLASTERS
ALACRITIES
ALACRITOUS
ALARMINGLY
ALBARELLOS
ALBATROSSES
ALBERTITES
ALBESCENCE
ALBESCENCES
ALBESPINES
ALBESPYNES
ALBINESSES
ALBINISTIC
ALBINOISMS
ALBITISING
ALBITIZING
ALBUGINEOUS
ALBUMBLATT
ALBUMBLATTER
ALBUMBLATTS
ALBUMENISE
ALBUMENISED
ALBUMENISES
ALBUMENISING
ALBUMENIZE
ALBUMENIZED
ALBUMENIZES
ALBUMENIZING
ALBUMINATE
ALBUMINATES
ALBUMINISE
ALBUMINISED
ALBUMINISES
ALBUMINISING
ALBUMINIZE
ALBUMINIZED
ALBUMINIZES

ALBUMINIZING	ALDERMANSHIPS	ALGOMETERS	ALKALINIZE
ALBUMINOID	ALDERWOMAN	ALGOMETRICALLY	ALKALINIZED
ALBUMINOIDS	ALDERWOMEN	ALGOMETRIES	ALKALINIZES
ALBUMINOUS	ALDOHEXOSE	ALGOPHOBIA	ALKALINIZING
ALBUMINURIA	ALDOHEXOSES	ALGOPHOBIAS	ALKALISABLE
ALBUMINURIAS	ALDOLISATION	ALGORISMIC	ALKALISERS
ALBUMINURIC	ALDOLISATIONS	ALGORITHMIC	ALKALISING
ALBUTEROLS	ALDOLIZATION	ALGORITHMICALLY	ALKALIZABLE
ALCAICERIA	ALDOLIZATIONS	ALGORITHMS	ALKALIZERS
ALCAICERIAS	ALDOPENTOSE	ALIENABILITIES	ALKALIZING
ALCARRAZAS	ALDOPENTOSES	ALIENABILITY	ALKALOIDAL
ALCATRASES	ALDOSTERONE	ALIENATING	ALKYLATING
ALCHEMICAL	ALDOSTERONES	ALIENATION	ALKYLATION
ALCHEMICALLY	ALDOSTERONISM	ALIENATIONS	ALKYLATIONS
ALCHEMISED	ALDOSTERONISMS	ALIENATORS	ALLANTOIDAL
ALCHEMISES	ALEATORIES	ALIENNESSES	ALLANTOIDES
ALCHEMISING	ALEBENCHES	ALIGHTMENT	ALLANTOIDS
ALCHEMISTIC	ALECTRYONS	ALIGHTMENTS	ALLANTOINS
ALCHEMISTICAL	ALEGGEAUNCE	ALIGNMENTS	ALLANTOISES
ALCHEMISTS	ALEGGEAUNCES	ALIKENESSES	ALLARGANDO
ALCHEMIZED	ALEMBICATED	ALIMENTARY	ALLAYMENTS
ALCHEMIZES	ALEMBICATION	ALIMENTATION	ALLEGATION
ALCHEMIZING	ALEMBICATIONS	ALIMENTATIONS	ALLEGATIONS
ALCHERINGA	ALEMBROTHS	ALIMENTATIVE	ALLEGEANCE
ALCHERINGAS	ALERTNESSES	ALIMENTING	ALLEGEANCES
ALCOHOLICALLY	ALEXANDERS	ALIMENTIVENESS	ALLEGIANCE
ALCOHOLICITIES	ALEXANDERSES	ALINEATION	ALLEGIANCES
ALCOHOLICITY	ALEXANDRINE	ALINEATIONS	ALLEGIANTS
ALCOHOLICS	ALEXANDRINES	ALINEMENTS	ALLEGORICAL
ALCOHOLISATION	ALEXANDRITE	ALISMACEOUS	ALLEGORICALLY
ALCOHOLISATIONS	ALEXANDRITES	ALITERACIES	ALLEGORICALNESS
ALCOHOLISE	ALEXIPHARMAKON	ALITERATES	ALLEGORIES
ALCOHOLISED	ALEXIPHARMAKONS	ALIVENESSES	ALLEGORISATION
ALCOHOLISES	ALEXIPHARMIC	ALIZARINES	ALLEGORISATIONS
ALCOHOLISING	ALEXIPHARMICS	ALKAHESTIC	ALLEGORISE
ALCOHOLISM	ALFILARIAS	ALKALESCENCE	ALLEGORISED
ALCOHOLISMS	ALFILERIAS	ALKALESCENCES	ALLEGORISER
ALCOHOLIZATION	ALGAECIDES	ALKALESCENCIES	ALLEGORISERS
ALCOHOLIZATIONS	ALGARROBAS	ALKALESCENCY	ALLEGORISES
ALCOHOLIZE	ALGARROBOS	ALKALESCENT	ALLEGORISING
ALCOHOLIZED	ALGEBRAICAL	ALKALIFIED	ALLEGORIST
ALCOHOLIZES	ALGEBRAICALLY	ALKALIFIES	ALLEGORISTS
ALCOHOLIZING	ALGEBRAIST	ALKALIFYING	ALLEGORIZATION
ALCOHOLOMETER	ALGEBRAISTS	ALKALIMETER	ALLEGORIZATIONS
ALCOHOLOMETERS	ALGIDITIES	ALKALIMETERS	ALLEGORIZE
ALCOHOLOMETRIES	ALGIDNESSES	ALKALIMETRIC	ALLEGORIZED
ALCOHOLOMETRY	ALGOLAGNIA	ALKALIMETRIES	ALLEGORIZER
ALCYONARIAN	ALGOLAGNIAC	ALKALIMETRY	ALLEGORIZERS
ALCYONARIANS	ALGOLAGNIACS	ALKALINISATION	ALLEGORIZES
ALDERFLIES	ALGOLAGNIAS	ALKALINISATIONS	ALLEGORIZING
ALDERMANIC	ALGOLAGNIC	ALKALINISE	ALLEGRETTO
ALDERMANITIES	ALGOLAGNIST	ALKALINISED	ALLEGRETTOS
ALDERMANITY	ALGOLAGNISTS	ALKALINISES	ALLELOMORPH
ALDERMANLIKE	ALGOLOGICAL	ALKALINISING	ALLELOMORPHIC
ALDERMANLY	ALGOLOGICALLY	ALKALINITIES	ALLELOMORPHISM
ALDERMANRIES	ALGOLOGIES	ALKALINITY	ALLELOMORPHISMS
ALDERMANRY	ALGOLOGIST	ALKALINIZATION	ALLELOMORPHS
ALDERMANSHIP	ALGOLOGISTS	ALKALINIZATIONS	ALLELOPATHIC

ALLELOPATHIES	ALLOCUTIONS	ALLOTTERIES	ALPHABETISING
ALLELOPATHY	ALLOGAMIES	ALLOTYPICALLY	ALPHABETIZATION
ALLELUIAHS	ALLOGAMOUS	ALLOTYPIES	ALPHABETIZE
ALLEMANDES	ALLOGENEIC	ALLOWABILITIES	ALPHABETIZED
ALLERGENIC	ALLOGRAFTED	ALLOWABILITY	ALPHABETIZER
ALLERGENICITIES	ALLOGRAFTING	ALLOWABLENESS	ALPHABETIZERS
ALLERGENICITY	ALLOGRAFTS	ALLOWABLENESSES	ALPHABETIZES
ALLERGISTS	ALLOGRAPHIC	ALLOWABLES	ALPHABETIZING
ALLETHRINS	ALLOGRAPHS	ALLOWANCED	ALPHAMERIC
ALLEVIANTS	ALLOIOSTROPHOS	ALLOWANCES	ALPHAMERICAL
ALLEVIATED	ALLOMERISM	ALLOWANCING	ALPHAMERICALLY
ALLEVIATES	ALLOMERISMS	ALLUREMENT	ALPHAMETIC
ALLEVIATING	ALLOMEROUS	ALLUREMENTS	ALPHAMETICS
ALLEVIATION	ALLOMETRIC	ALLURINGLY	ALPHANUMERIC
ALLEVIATIONS	ALLOMETRIES	ALLUSIVELY	ALPHANUMERICAL
ALLEVIATIVE	ALLOMORPHIC	ALLUSIVENESS	ALPHANUMERICS
ALLEVIATOR	ALLOMORPHISM	ALLUSIVENESSES	ALPHASORTED
ALLEVIATORS	ALLOMORPHISMS	ALLYCHOLLIES	ALPHASORTING
ALLEVIATORY	ALLOMORPHS	ALLYCHOLLY	ALPHASORTS
ALLHALLOND	ALLONYMOUS	ALMACANTAR	ALPHOSISES
ALLHALLOWEN	ALLOPATHIC	ALMACANTARS	ALSTROEMERIA
ALLHALLOWN	ALLOPATHICALLY	ALMANDINES	ALSTROEMERIAS
ALLHOLLOWN	ALLOPATHIES	ALMANDITES	ALTALTISSIMO
ALLIACEOUS	ALLOPATHIST	ALMIGHTILY	ALTALTISSIMOS
ALLICHOLIES	ALLOPATHISTS	ALMIGHTINESS	ALTARPIECE
ALLIGARTAS	ALLOPATRIC	ALMIGHTINESSES	ALTARPIECES
ALLIGATING	ALLOPATRICALLY	ALMSGIVERS	ALTAZIMUTH
ALLIGATION	ALLOPATRIES	ALMSGIVING	ALTAZIMUTHS
ALLIGATIONS	ALLOPHANES	ALMSGIVINGS	ALTERABILITIES
ALLIGATORS	ALLOPHONES	ALMSHOUSES	ALTERABILITY
ALLINEATION	ALLOPHONIC	ALMUCANTAR	ALTERATION
ALLINEATIONS	ALLOPLASMIC	ALMUCANTARS	ALTERATIONS
ALLITERATE	ALLOPLASMS	ALOGICALLY	ALTERATIVE
ALLITERATED	ALLOPLASTIC	ALONENESSES	ALTERATIVES
ALLITERATES	ALLOPOLYPLOID	ALONGSHORE	ALTERCATED
ALLITERATING	ALLOPOLYPLOIDS	ALONGSHOREMAN	ALTERCATES
ALLITERATION	ALLOPOLYPLOIDY	ALONGSHOREMEN	ALTERCATING
ALLITERATIONS	ALLOPURINOL	ALOOFNESSES	ALTERCATION
ALLITERATIVE	ALLOPURINOLS	ALPARGATAS	ALTERCATIONS
ALLITERATIVELY	ALLOSAURUS	ALPENGLOWS	ALTERCATIVE
ALLNIGHTER	ALLOSAURUSES	ALPENHORNS	ALTERITIES
ALLNIGHTERS	ALLOSTERIC	ALPENSTOCK	ALTERNANCE
ALLOANTIBODIES	ALLOSTERICALLY	ALPENSTOCKS	ALTERNANCES
ALLOANTIBODY	ALLOSTERIES	ALPESTRINE	ALTERNANTS
ALLOANTIGEN	ALLOTETRAPLOID	ALPHABETARIAN	ALTERNATED
ALLOANTIGENS	ALLOTETRAPLOIDS	ALPHABETARIANS	ALTERNATELY
ALLOCARPIES	ALLOTETRAPLOIDY	ALPHABETED	ALTERNATES
ALLOCATABLE	ALLOTHEISM	ALPHABETIC	ALTERNATIM
ALLOCATING	ALLOTHEISMS	ALPHABETICAL	ALTERNATING
ALLOCATION	ALLOTMENTS	ALPHABETICALLY	ALTERNATION
ALLOCATIONS	ALLOTRIOMORPHIC	ALPHABETIFORM	ALTERNATIONS
ALLOCATORS	ALLOTROPES	ALPHABETING	ALTERNATIVE
ALLOCHEIRIA	ALLOTROPIC	ALPHABETISATION	ALTERNATIVELY
ALLOCHEIRIAS	ALLOTROPICALLY	ALPHABETISE	ALTERNATIVENESS
ALLOCHIRIA	ALLOTROPIES	ALPHABETISED	ALTERNATIVES
ALLOCHIRIAS	ALLOTROPISM	ALPHABETISER	ALTERNATOR
ALLOCHTHONOUS	ALLOTROPISMS	ALPHABETISERS	ALTERNATORS
ALLOCUTION	ALLOTROPOUS	ALPHABETISES	ALTIGRAPHS

695

ALTIMETERS	AMARANTACEOUS	AMBITIONED	AMELIORATORS
ALTIMETRICAL	AMARANTHACEOUS	AMBITIONING	AMELIORATORY
ALTIMETRICALLY	AMARANTHINE	AMBITIONLESS	AMELOBLAST
ALTIMETRIES	AMARANTINE	AMBITIOUSLY	AMELOBLASTS
ALTIPLANOS	AMARYLLIDACEOUS	AMBITIOUSNESS	AMELOGENESES
ALTISONANT	AMARYLLIDS	AMBITIOUSNESSES	AMELOGENESIS
ALTITONANT	AMARYLLISES	AMBIVALENCE	AMENABILITIES
ALTITUDINAL	AMASSMENTS	AMBIVALENCES	AMENABILITY
ALTITUDINARIAN	AMATEURISH	AMBIVALENCIES	AMENABLENESS
ALTITUDINARIANS	AMATEURISHLY	AMBIVALENCY	AMENABLENESSES
ALTITUDINOUS	AMATEURISHNESS	AMBIVALENT	AMENAUNCES
ALTOCUMULI	AMATEURISM	AMBIVALENTLY	AMENDATORY
ALTOCUMULUS	AMATEURISMS	AMBIVERSION	AMENDMENTS
ALTOGETHER	AMATEURSHIP	AMBIVERSIONS	AMENORRHEA
ALTOGETHERS	AMATEURSHIPS	AMBLYGONITE	AMENORRHEAS
ALTORUFFLED	AMATIVENESS	AMBLYGONITES	AMENORRHEIC
ALTOSTRATI	AMATIVENESSES	AMBLYOPIAS	AMENORRHOEA
ALTOSTRATUS	AMATORIALLY	AMBOCEPTOR	AMENORRHOEAS
ALTRICIALS	AMATORIOUS	AMBOCEPTORS	AMENTACEOUS
ALTRUISTIC	AMAZEDNESS	AMBOSEXUAL	AMENTIFEROUS
ALTRUISTICALLY	AMAZEDNESSES	AMBROSIALLY	AMERCEABLE
ALUMINATES	AMAZEMENTS	AMBROTYPES	AMERCEMENT
ALUMINIFEROUS	AMAZONIANS	AMBULACRAL	AMERCEMENTS
ALUMINISED	AMAZONITES	AMBULACRUM	AMERCIABLE
ALUMINISES	AMAZONSTONE	AMBULANCEMAN	AMERCIAMENT
ALUMINISING	AMAZONSTONES	AMBULANCEMEN	AMERCIAMENTS
ALUMINIUMS	AMBAGITORY	AMBULANCES	AMERICIUMS
ALUMINIZED	AMBASSADOR	AMBULANCEWOMAN	AMETABOLIC
ALUMINIZES	AMBASSADORIAL	AMBULANCEWOMEN	AMETABOLISM
ALUMINIZING	AMBASSADORS	AMBULATING	AMETABOLISMS
ALUMINOSILICATE	AMBASSADORSHIP	AMBULATION	AMETABOLOUS
ALUMINOSITIES	AMBASSADORSHIPS	AMBULATIONS	AMETHYSTINE
ALUMINOSITY	AMBASSADRESS	AMBULATORIES	AMETROPIAS
ALUMINOTHERMIES	AMBASSADRESSES	AMBULATORILY	AMIABILITIES
ALUMINOTHERMY	AMBASSAGES	AMBULATORS	AMIABILITY
ALUMSTONES	AMBERGRISES	AMBULATORY	AMIABLENESS
ALVEOLARLY	AMBERJACKS	AMBULETTES	AMIABLENESSES
ALVEOLATION	AMBIDENTATE	AMBUSCADED	AMIANTHINE
ALVEOLATIONS	AMBIDEXTER	AMBUSCADER	AMIANTHOID
ALVEOLITIS	AMBIDEXTERITIES	AMBUSCADERS	AMIANTHOIDAL
ALVEOLITISES	AMBIDEXTERITY	AMBUSCADES	AMIANTHUSES
ALYCOMPAINE	AMBIDEXTEROUS	AMBUSCADING	AMIANTUSES
ALYCOMPAINES	AMBIDEXTERS	AMBUSCADOES	AMICABILITIES
AMAKWEREKWERE	AMBIDEXTROUS	AMBUSCADOS	AMICABILITY
AMALGAMATE	AMBIDEXTROUSLY	AMBUSHMENT	AMICABLENESS
AMALGAMATED	AMBIGUITIES	AMBUSHMENTS	AMICABLENESSES
AMALGAMATES	AMBIGUOUSLY	AMEBOCYTES	AMINOACIDURIA
AMALGAMATING	AMBIGUOUSNESS	AMELIORABLE	AMINOACIDURIAS
AMALGAMATION	AMBIGUOUSNESSES	AMELIORANT	AMINOBENZOIC
AMALGAMATIONS	AMBILATERAL	AMELIORANTS	AMINOBUTENE
AMALGAMATIVE	AMBIOPHONICALLY	AMELIORATE	AMINOBUTENES
AMALGAMATOR	AMBIOPHONIES	AMELIORATED	AMINOPEPTIDASE
AMALGAMATORS	AMBIOPHONY	AMELIORATES	AMINOPEPTIDASES
AMANTADINE	AMBISEXUAL	AMELIORATING	AMINOPHENAZONE
AMANTADINES	AMBISEXUALITIES	AMELIORATION	AMINOPHENAZONES
AMANUENSES	AMBISEXUALITY	AMELIORATIONS	AMINOPHENOL
AMANUENSIS	AMBISEXUALS	AMELIORATIVE	AMINOPHENOLS
AMARACUSES	AMBISONICS	AMELIORATOR	AMINOPHYLLINE

AMINOPHYLLINES	AMORTISATIONS	AMPHICTYONY	AMPICILLINS
AMINOPTERIN	AMORTISEMENT	AMPHIDENTATE	AMPLENESSES
AMINOPTERINS	AMORTISEMENTS	AMPHIDIPLOID	AMPLEXICAUL
AMINOPYRINE	AMORTISING	AMPHIDIPLOIDIES	AMPLEXUSES
AMINOPYRINES	AMORTIZABLE	AMPHIDIPLOIDS	AMPLIATION
AMISSIBILITIES	AMORTIZATION	AMPHIDIPLOIDY	AMPLIATIONS
AMISSIBILITY	AMORTIZATIONS	AMPHIGASTRIA	AMPLIATIVE
AMITOTICALLY	AMORTIZEMENT	AMPHIGASTRIUM	AMPLIDYNES
AMITRIPTYLINE	AMORTIZEMENTS	AMPHIGORIC	AMPLIFIABLE
AMITRIPTYLINES	AMORTIZING	AMPHIGORIES	AMPLIFICATION
AMITRYPTYLINE	AMOURETTES	AMPHIGOURI	AMPLIFICATIONS
AMITRYPTYLINES	AMOXICILLIN	AMPHIGOURIS	AMPLIFIERS
AMMOCOETES	AMOXICILLINS	AMPHIMACER	AMPLIFYING
AMMONIACAL	AMOXYCILLIN	AMPHIMACERS	AMPLITUDES
AMMONIACUM	AMOXYCILLINS	AMPHIMICTIC	AMPLOSOMES
AMMONIACUMS	AMPELOGRAPHIES	AMPHIMIXES	AMPULLACEAL
AMMONIATED	AMPELOGRAPHY	AMPHIMIXIS	AMPULLACEOUS
AMMONIATES	AMPELOPSES	AMPHIOXUSES	AMPULLOSITIES
AMMONIATING	AMPELOPSIS	AMPHIPATHIC	AMPULLOSITY
AMMONIATION	AMPEROMETRIC	AMPHIPHILE	AMPUTATING
AMMONIATIONS	AMPERSANDS	AMPHIPHILES	AMPUTATION
AMMONIFICATION	AMPERZANDS	AMPHIPHILIC	AMPUTATIONS
AMMONIFICATIONS	AMPHETAMINE	AMPHIPLOID	AMPUTATORS
AMMONIFIED	AMPHETAMINES	AMPHIPLOIDIES	AMRITATTVA
AMMONIFIES	AMPHIARTHROSES	AMPHIPLOIDS	AMRITATTVAS
AMMONIFYING	AMPHIARTHROSIS	AMPHIPLOIDY	AMSINCKIAS
AMMONOLYSES	AMPHIASTER	AMPHIPODOUS	AMUSEMENTS
AMMONOLYSIS	AMPHIASTERS	AMPHIPROSTYLAR	AMUSINGNESS
AMMOPHILOUS	AMPHIBIANS	AMPHIPROSTYLE	AMUSINGNESSES
AMMUNITION	AMPHIBIOTIC	AMPHIPROSTYLES	AMUSIVENESS
AMMUNITIONED	AMPHIBIOTICALLY	AMPHIPROTIC	AMUSIVENESSES
AMMUNITIONING	AMPHIBIOUS	AMPHISBAENA	AMYGDALACEOUS
AMMUNITIONS	AMPHIBIOUSLY	AMPHISBAENAE	AMYGDALATE
AMNESTYING	AMPHIBIOUSNESS	AMPHISBAENAS	AMYGDALINE
AMNIOCENTESES	AMPHIBLASTIC	AMPHISBAENIC	AMYGDALINS
AMNIOCENTESIS	AMPHIBLASTULA	AMPHISCIAN	AMYGDALOID
AMNIOTOMIES	AMPHIBLASTULAE	AMPHISCIANS	AMYGDALOIDAL
AMOBARBITAL	AMPHIBOLES	AMPHISTOMATAL	AMYGDALOIDS
AMOBARBITALS	AMPHIBOLIC	AMPHISTOMATALLY	AMYLACEOUS
AMOEBIASES	AMPHIBOLIES	AMPHISTOMATIC	AMYLOIDOSES
AMOEBIASIS	AMPHIBOLITE	AMPHISTOMOUS	AMYLOIDOSIS
AMOEBIFORM	AMPHIBOLITES	AMPHISTYLAR	AMYLOLYSES
AMOEBOCYTE	AMPHIBOLOGICAL	AMPHISTYLARS	AMYLOLYSIS
AMOEBOCYTES	AMPHIBOLOGIES	AMPHITHEATER	AMYLOLYTIC
AMONTILLADO	AMPHIBOLOGY	AMPHITHEATERS	AMYLOPECTIN
AMONTILLADOS	AMPHIBOLOUS	AMPHITHEATRAL	AMYLOPECTINS
AMORALISMS	AMPHIBRACH	AMPHITHEATRE	AMYLOPLAST
AMORALISTS	AMPHIBRACHIC	AMPHITHEATRES	AMYLOPLASTS
AMORALITIES	AMPHIBRACHS	AMPHITHEATRIC	AMYLOPSINS
AMOROSITIES	AMPHICHROIC	AMPHITHEATRICAL	AMYOTONIAS
AMOROUSNESS	AMPHICHROICALLY	AMPHITHECIA	AMYOTROPHIC
AMOROUSNESSES	AMPHICHROMATIC	AMPHITHECIUM	AMYOTROPHIES
AMORPHISMS	AMPHICHROMATISM	AMPHITRICHA	AMYOTROPHY
AMORPHOUSLY	AMPHICOELOUS	AMPHITRICHOUS	ANABANTIDS
AMORPHOUSNESS	AMPHICTYON	AMPHITROPOUS	ANABAPTISE
AMORPHOUSNESSES	AMPHICTYONIC	AMPHOLYTES	ANABAPTISED
AMORTISABLE	AMPHICTYONIES	AMPHOTERIC	ANABAPTISES
AMORTISATION	AMPHICTYONS	AMPICILLIN	ANABAPTISING

ANABAPTISM	ANAESTHESIAS	ANALOGISTS	ANAPHYLAXY
ANABAPTISMS	ANAESTHESIOLOGY	ANALOGIZED	ANAPLASIAS
ANABAPTIST	ANAESTHESIS	ANALOGIZES	ANAPLASMOSES
ANABAPTISTIC	ANAESTHETIC	ANALOGIZING	ANAPLASMOSIS
ANABAPTISTS	ANAESTHETICALLY	ANALOGOUSLY	ANAPLASTIC
ANABAPTIZE	ANAESTHETICS	ANALOGOUSNESS	ANAPLASTIES
ANABAPTIZED	ANAESTHETISE	ANALOGOUSNESSES	ANAPLEROSES
ANABAPTIZES	ANAESTHETISED	ANALPHABET	ANAPLEROSIS
ANABAPTIZING	ANAESTHETISES	ANALPHABETE	ANAPLEROTIC
ANABLEPSES	ANAESTHETISING	ANALPHABETES	ANAPTYCTIC
ANABOLISMS	ANAESTHETIST	ANALPHABETIC	ANAPTYCTICAL
ANABOLITES	ANAESTHETISTS	ANALPHABETICS	ANARCHICAL
ANABOLITIC	ANAESTHETIZE	ANALPHABETISM	ANARCHICALLY
ANABRANCHES	ANAESTHETIZED	ANALPHABETISMS	ANARCHISED
ANACARDIACEOUS	ANAESTHETIZES	ANALPHABETS	ANARCHISES
ANACARDIUM	ANAESTHETIZING	ANALYSABLE	ANARCHISING
ANACARDIUMS	ANAGENESES	ANALYSANDS	ANARCHISMS
ANACATHARSES	ANAGENESIS	ANALYSATION	ANARCHISTIC
ANACATHARSIS	ANAGLYPHIC	ANALYSATIONS	ANARCHISTS
ANACATHARTIC	ANAGLYPHICAL	ANALYTICAL	ANARCHIZED
ANACATHARTICS	ANAGLYPHICALLY	ANALYTICALLY	ANARCHIZES
ANACHARISES	ANAGLYPHIES	ANALYTICITIES	ANARCHIZING
ANACHORISM	ANAGLYPTIC	ANALYTICITY	ANARTHRIAS
ANACHORISMS	ANAGLYPTICAL	ANALYZABILITIES	ANARTHROUS
ANACHRONIC	ANAGNORISES	ANALYZABILITY	ANARTHROUSLY
ANACHRONICAL	ANAGNORISIS	ANALYZABLE	ANARTHROUSNESS
ANACHRONICALLY	ANAGOGICAL	ANALYZATION	ANASARCOUS
ANACHRONISM	ANAGOGICALLY	ANALYZATIONS	ANASTIGMAT
ANACHRONISMS	ANAGRAMMATIC	ANAMNESTIC	ANASTIGMATIC
ANACHRONISTIC	ANAGRAMMATICAL	ANAMNESTICALLY	ANASTIGMATISM
ANACHRONOUS	ANAGRAMMATISE	ANAMNIOTES	ANASTIGMATISMS
ANACHRONOUSLY	ANAGRAMMATISED	ANAMNIOTIC	ANASTIGMATS
ANACLASTIC	ANAGRAMMATISES	ANAMORPHIC	ANASTOMOSE
ANACOLUTHA	ANAGRAMMATISING	ANAMORPHISM	ANASTOMOSED
ANACOLUTHIA	ANAGRAMMATISM	ANAMORPHISMS	ANASTOMOSES
ANACOLUTHIAS	ANAGRAMMATISMS	ANAMORPHOSCOPE	ANASTOMOSING
ANACOLUTHIC	ANAGRAMMATIST	ANAMORPHOSCOPES	ANASTOMOSIS
ANACOLUTHICALLY	ANAGRAMMATISTS	ANAMORPHOSES	ANASTOMOTIC
ANACOLUTHON	ANAGRAMMATIZE	ANAMORPHOSIS	ANASTROPHE
ANACOLUTHONS	ANAGRAMMATIZED	ANAMORPHOUS	ANASTROPHES
ANACOUSTIC	ANAGRAMMATIZES	ANANDAMIDE	ANASTROZOLE
ANACREONTIC	ANAGRAMMATIZING	ANANDAMIDES	ANASTROZOLES
ANACREONTICALLY	ANAGRAMMED	ANAPAESTIC	ANATHEMATA
ANACREONTICS	ANAGRAMMER	ANAPAESTICAL	ANATHEMATICAL
ANACRUSTIC	ANAGRAMMERS	ANAPESTICS	ANATHEMATISE
ANADIPLOSES	ANAGRAMMING	ANAPHORESES	ANATHEMATISED
ANADIPLOSIS	ANALEMMATA	ANAPHORESIS	ANATHEMATISES
ANADROMOUS	ANALEMMATIC	ANAPHORICAL	ANATHEMATISING
ANADYOMENE	ANALEPTICS	ANAPHORICALLY	ANATHEMATIZE
ANAEROBICALLY	ANALGESIAS	ANAPHRODISIA	ANATHEMATIZED
ANAEROBIONT	ANALGESICS	ANAPHRODISIAC	ANATHEMATIZES
ANAEROBIONTS	ANALGETICS	ANAPHRODISIACS	ANATHEMATIZING
ANAEROBIOSES	ANALOGICAL	ANAPHRODISIAS	ANATOMICAL
ANAEROBIOSIS	ANALOGICALLY	ANAPHYLACTIC	ANATOMICALLY
ANAEROBIOTIC	ANALOGISED	ANAPHYLACTOID	ANATOMISATION
ANAEROBIUM	ANALOGISES	ANAPHYLAXES	ANATOMISATIONS
ANAESTHESES	ANALOGISING	ANAPHYLAXIES	ANATOMISED
ANAESTHESIA	ANALOGISMS	ANAPHYLAXIS	ANATOMISER

ANATOMISERS
ANATOMISES
ANATOMISING
ANATOMISTS
ANATOMIZATION
ANATOMIZATIONS
ANATOMIZED
ANATOMIZER
ANATOMIZERS
ANATOMIZES
ANATOMIZING
ANATROPIES
ANATROPOUS
ANCESTORED
ANCESTORIAL
ANCESTORING
ANCESTRALLY
ANCESTRESS
ANCESTRESSES
ANCESTRIES
ANCHORAGES
ANCHORESSES
ANCHORETIC
ANCHORETICAL
ANCHORETTE
ANCHORETTES
ANCHORITES
ANCHORITIC
ANCHORITICAL
ANCHORITICALLY
ANCHORLESS
ANCHORPEOPLE
ANCHORPERSON
ANCHORPERSONS
ANCHORWOMAN
ANCHORWOMEN
ANCHOVETAS
ANCHOVETTA
ANCHOVETTAS
ANCHYLOSED
ANCHYLOSES
ANCHYLOSING
ANCHYLOSIS
ANCHYLOTIC
ANCIENTEST
ANCIENTNESS
ANCIENTNESSES
ANCIENTRIES
ANCILLARIES
ANCIPITOUS
ANCYLOSTOMIASES
ANCYLOSTOMIASIS
ANDALUSITE
ANDALUSITES
ANDANTINOS
ANDOUILLES
ANDOUILLETTE
ANDOUILLETTES

ANDRADITES
ANDROCENTRIC
ANDROCENTRISM
ANDROCENTRISMS
ANDROCEPHALOUS
ANDROCLINIA
ANDROCLINIUM
ANDRODIOECIOUS
ANDRODIOECISM
ANDRODIOECISMS
ANDROECIAL
ANDROECIUM
ANDROECIUMS
ANDROGENESES
ANDROGENESIS
ANDROGENETIC
ANDROGENIC
ANDROGENOUS
ANDROGYNES
ANDROGYNIES
ANDROGYNOPHORE
ANDROGYNOPHORES
ANDROGYNOUS
ANDROLOGIES
ANDROLOGIST
ANDROLOGISTS
ANDROMEDAS
ANDROMEDOTOXIN
ANDROMEDOTOXINS
ANDROMONOECIOUS
ANDROMONOECISM
ANDROMONOECISMS
ANDROPAUSE
ANDROPAUSES
ANDROPHORE
ANDROPHORES
ANDROSPHINGES
ANDROSPHINX
ANDROSPHINXES
ANDROSTERONE
ANDROSTERONES
ANECDOTAGE
ANECDOTAGES
ANECDOTALISM
ANECDOTALISMS
ANECDOTALIST
ANECDOTALISTS
ANECDOTALLY
ANECDOTICAL
ANECDOTICALLY
ANECDOTIST
ANECDOTISTS
ANELASTICITIES
ANELASTICITY
ANEMICALLY
ANEMOCHORE
ANEMOCHORES
ANEMOCHOROUS

ANEMOGRAMS
ANEMOGRAPH
ANEMOGRAPHIC
ANEMOGRAPHIES
ANEMOGRAPHS
ANEMOGRAPHY
ANEMOLOGIES
ANEMOMETER
ANEMOMETERS
ANEMOMETRIC
ANEMOMETRICAL
ANEMOMETRIES
ANEMOMETRY
ANEMOPHILIES
ANEMOPHILOUS
ANEMOPHILY
ANEMOPHOBIA
ANEMOPHOBIAS
ANEMOSCOPE
ANEMOSCOPES
ANEMOSCOPICALLY
ANENCEPHALIA
ANENCEPHALIAS
ANENCEPHALIC
ANENCEPHALIES
ANENCEPHALY
ANESTHESIA
ANESTHESIAS
ANESTHESIOLOGY
ANESTHETIC
ANESTHETICALLY
ANESTHETICS
ANESTHETISE
ANESTHETISED
ANESTHETISES
ANESTHETISING
ANESTHETIST
ANESTHETISTS
ANESTHETIZATION
ANESTHETIZE
ANESTHETIZED
ANESTHETIZES
ANESTHETIZING
ANEUPLOIDIES
ANEUPLOIDS
ANEUPLOIDY
ANEURISMAL
ANEURISMALLY
ANEURISMATIC
ANEURYSMAL
ANEURYSMALLY
ANEURYSMATIC
ANFRACTUOSITIES
ANFRACTUOSITY
ANFRACTUOUS
ANGASHORES
ANGELFISHES
ANGELHOODS

ANGELICALLY
ANGELOLATRIES
ANGELOLATRY
ANGELOLOGIES
ANGELOLOGIST
ANGELOLOGISTS
ANGELOLOGY
ANGELOPHANIES
ANGELOPHANY
ANGIOCARPOUS
ANGIOGENESES
ANGIOGENESIS
ANGIOGENIC
ANGIOGRAMS
ANGIOGRAPHIC
ANGIOGRAPHIES
ANGIOGRAPHY
ANGIOLOGIES
ANGIOMATOUS
ANGIOPLASTIES
ANGIOPLASTY
ANGIOSARCOMA
ANGIOSARCOMAS
ANGIOSARCOMATA
ANGIOSPERM
ANGIOSPERMAL
ANGIOSPERMOUS
ANGIOSPERMS
ANGIOSTOMATOUS
ANGIOSTOMOUS
ANGIOTENSIN
ANGIOTENSINS
ANGLEBERRIES
ANGLEBERRY
ANGLEDOZER
ANGLEDOZERS
ANGLERFISH
ANGLERFISHES
ANGLESITES
ANGLETWITCH
ANGLETWITCHES
ANGLEWORMS
ANGLICISATION
ANGLICISATIONS
ANGLICISED
ANGLICISES
ANGLICISING
ANGLICISMS
ANGLICISTS
ANGLICIZATION
ANGLICIZATIONS
ANGLICIZED
ANGLICIZES
ANGLICIZING
ANGLIFYING
ANGLISTICS
ANGLOMANIA
ANGLOMANIAC

ANGLOMANIACS	ANIMADVERTERS	ANISOPHYLLY	ANNUALISING
ANGLOMANIAS	ANIMADVERTING	ANISOTROPIC	ANNUALIZED
ANGLOPHILE	ANIMADVERTS	ANISOTROPICALLY	ANNUALIZES
ANGLOPHILES	ANIMALCULA	ANISOTROPIES	ANNUALIZING
ANGLOPHILIA	ANIMALCULAR	ANISOTROPISM	ANNUITANTS
ANGLOPHILIAS	ANIMALCULE	ANISOTROPISMS	ANNULARITIES
ANGLOPHILIC	ANIMALCULES	ANISOTROPY	ANNULARITY
ANGLOPHILS	ANIMALCULISM	ANKLEBONES	ANNULATION
ANGLOPHOBE	ANIMALCULISMS	ANKYLOSAUR	ANNULATIONS
ANGLOPHOBES	ANIMALCULIST	ANKYLOSAURS	ANNULLABLE
ANGLOPHOBIA	ANIMALCULISTS	ANKYLOSAURUS	ANNULMENTS
ANGLOPHOBIAC	ANIMALCULUM	ANKYLOSAURUSES	ANNUNCIATE
ANGLOPHOBIAS	ANIMALIERS	ANKYLOSING	ANNUNCIATED
ANGLOPHOBIC	ANIMALISATION	ANKYLOSTOMIASES	ANNUNCIATES
ANGLOPHONE	ANIMALISATIONS	ANKYLOSTOMIASIS	ANNUNCIATING
ANGLOPHONES	ANIMALISED	ANNABERGITE	ANNUNCIATION
ANGLOPHONIC	ANIMALISES	ANNABERGITES	ANNUNCIATIONS
ANGOPHORAS	ANIMALISING	ANNALISING	ANNUNCIATIVE
ANGOSTURAS	ANIMALISMS	ANNALISTIC	ANNUNCIATOR
ANGRINESSES	ANIMALISTIC	ANNALIZING	ANNUNCIATORS
ANGUIFAUNA	ANIMALISTS	ANNEALINGS	ANNUNCIATORY
ANGUIFAUNAE	ANIMALITIES	ANNELIDANS	ANNUNTIATE
ANGUIFAUNAS	ANIMALIZATION	ANNEXATION	ANNUNTIATED
ANGUILLIFORM	ANIMALIZATIONS	ANNEXATIONAL	ANNUNTIATES
ANGUISHING	ANIMALIZED	ANNEXATIONISM	ANNUNTIATING
ANGULARITIES	ANIMALIZES	ANNEXATIONISMS	ANODICALLY
ANGULARITY	ANIMALIZING	ANNEXATIONIST	ANODISATION
ANGULARNESS	ANIMALLIKE	ANNEXATIONISTS	ANODISATIONS
ANGULARNESSES	ANIMATEDLY	ANNEXATIONS	ANODIZATION
ANGULATING	ANIMATENESS	ANNEXMENTS	ANODIZATIONS
ANGULATION	ANIMATENESSES	ANNIHILABLE	ANODONTIAS
ANGULATIONS	ANIMATINGLY	ANNIHILATE	ANOESTROUS
ANGUSTIFOLIATE	ANIMATIONS	ANNIHILATED	ANOINTMENT
ANGUSTIROSTRATE	ANIMATISMS	ANNIHILATES	ANOINTMENTS
ANGWANTIBO	ANIMATISTS	ANNIHILATING	ANOMALISTIC
ANGWANTIBOS	ANIMATRONIC	ANNIHILATION	ANOMALISTICAL
ANHARMONIC	ANIMATRONICALLY	ANNIHILATIONISM	ANOMALISTICALLY
ANHEDONIAS	ANIMATRONICS	ANNIHILATIONS	ANOMALOUSLY
ANHELATION	ANIMOSITIES	ANNIHILATIVE	ANOMALOUSNESS
ANHELATIONS	ANISEIKONIA	ANNIHILATOR	ANOMALOUSNESSES
ANHIDROSES	ANISEIKONIAS	ANNIHILATORS	ANONACEOUS
ANHIDROSIS	ANISEIKONIC	ANNIHILATORY	ANONYMISED
ANHIDROTIC	ANISOCERCAL	ANNIVERSARIES	ANONYMISES
ANHIDROTICS	ANISODACTYL	ANNIVERSARY	ANONYMISING
ANHUNGERED	ANISODACTYLOUS	ANNOTATABLE	ANONYMITIES
ANHYDRASES	ANISODACTYLS	ANNOTATING	ANONYMIZED
ANHYDRIDES	ANISOGAMIES	ANNOTATION	ANONYMIZES
ANHYDRITES	ANISOGAMOUS	ANNOTATIONS	ANONYMIZING
ANICONISMS	ANISOMERIC	ANNOTATIVE	ANONYMOUSLY
ANICONISTS	ANISOMEROUS	ANNOTATORS	ANONYMOUSNESS
ANILINCTUS	ANISOMETRIC	ANNOUNCEMENT	ANONYMOUSNESSES
ANILINCTUSES	ANISOMETRICALLY	ANNOUNCEMENTS	ANOPHELESES
ANILINGUSES	ANISOMETROPIA	ANNOUNCERS	ANOPHELINE
ANIMADVERSION	ANISOMETROPIAS	ANNOUNCING	ANOPHELINES
ANIMADVERSIONS	ANISOMETROPIC	ANNOYANCES	ANORECTICS
ANIMADVERT	ANISOMORPHIC	ANNOYINGLY	ANOREXIGENIC
ANIMADVERTED	ANISOPHYLLIES	ANNUALISED	ANORTHITES
ANIMADVERTER	ANISOPHYLLOUS	ANNUALISES	ANORTHITIC

ANORTHOSITE
ANORTHOSITES
ANORTHOSITIC
ANOTHERGUESS
ANOVULANTS
ANOVULATORY
ANOXAEMIAS
ANSWERABILITIES
ANSWERABILITY
ANSWERABLE
ANSWERABLENESS
ANSWERABLY
ANSWERLESS
ANSWERPHONE
ANSWERPHONES
ANTAGONISABLE
ANTAGONISATION
ANTAGONISATIONS
ANTAGONISE
ANTAGONISED
ANTAGONISES
ANTAGONISING
ANTAGONISM
ANTAGONISMS
ANTAGONIST
ANTAGONISTIC
ANTAGONISTS
ANTAGONIZABLE
ANTAGONIZATION
ANTAGONIZATIONS
ANTAGONIZE
ANTAGONIZED
ANTAGONIZES
ANTAGONIZING
ANTALKALIES
ANTALKALINE
ANTALKALINES
ANTALKALIS
ANTAPHRODISIAC
ANTAPHRODISIACS
ANTARTHRITIC
ANTARTHRITICS
ANTASTHMATIC
ANTASTHMATICS
ANTEBELLUM
ANTECEDENCE
ANTECEDENCES
ANTECEDENT
ANTECEDENTLY
ANTECEDENTS
ANTECEDING
ANTECESSOR
ANTECESSORS
ANTECHAMBER
ANTECHAMBERS
ANTECHAPEL
ANTECHAPELS
ANTECHOIRS

ANTEDATING
ANTEDILUVIAL
ANTEDILUVIALLY
ANTEDILUVIAN
ANTEDILUVIANS
ANTEMERIDIAN
ANTEMORTEM
ANTEMUNDANE
ANTENATALLY
ANTENATALS
ANTENNIFEROUS
ANTENNIFORM
ANTENNULAR
ANTENNULES
ANTENUPTIAL
ANTEORBITAL
ANTEPENDIA
ANTEPENDIUM
ANTEPENDIUMS
ANTEPENULT
ANTEPENULTIMA
ANTEPENULTIMAS
ANTEPENULTIMATE
ANTEPENULTS
ANTEPOSITION
ANTEPOSITIONS
ANTEPRANDIAL
ANTERIORITIES
ANTERIORITY
ANTERIORLY
ANTEROGRADE
ANTEVERSION
ANTEVERSIONS
ANTEVERTED
ANTEVERTING
ANTHELICES
ANTHELIONS
ANTHELIXES
ANTHELMINTHIC
ANTHELMINTHICS
ANTHELMINTIC
ANTHELMINTICS
ANTHEMWISE
ANTHERIDIA
ANTHERIDIAL
ANTHERIDIUM
ANTHEROZOID
ANTHEROZOIDS
ANTHEROZOOID
ANTHEROZOOIDS
ANTHERSMUT
ANTHERSMUTS
ANTHOCARPOUS
ANTHOCARPS
ANTHOCHLORE
ANTHOCHLORES
ANTHOCYANIN
ANTHOCYANINS

ANTHOCYANS
ANTHOLOGICAL
ANTHOLOGIES
ANTHOLOGISE
ANTHOLOGISED
ANTHOLOGISER
ANTHOLOGISERS
ANTHOLOGISES
ANTHOLOGISING
ANTHOLOGIST
ANTHOLOGISTS
ANTHOLOGIZE
ANTHOLOGIZED
ANTHOLOGIZER
ANTHOLOGIZERS
ANTHOLOGIZES
ANTHOLOGIZING
ANTHOMANIA
ANTHOMANIAC
ANTHOMANIACS
ANTHOMANIAS
ANTHOPHILOUS
ANTHOPHORE
ANTHOPHORES
ANTHOPHYLLITE
ANTHOPHYLLITES
ANTHOTAXIES
ANTHOXANTHIN
ANTHOXANTHINS
ANTHOZOANS
ANTHRACENE
ANTHRACENES
ANTHRACITE
ANTHRACITES
ANTHRACITIC
ANTHRACNOSE
ANTHRACNOSES
ANTHRACOID
ANTHRACOSES
ANTHRACOSIS
ANTHRANILATE
ANTHRANILATES
ANTHRAQUINONE
ANTHRAQUINONES
ANTHROPICAL
ANTHROPOBIOLOGY
ANTHROPOCENTRIC
ANTHROPOGENESES
ANTHROPOGENESIS
ANTHROPOGENETIC
ANTHROPOGENIC
ANTHROPOGENIES
ANTHROPOGENY
ANTHROPOGONIES
ANTHROPOGONY
ANTHROPOGRAPHY
ANTHROPOID
ANTHROPOIDAL

ANTHROPOIDS
ANTHROPOLATRIES
ANTHROPOLATRY
ANTHROPOLOGICAL
ANTHROPOLOGIES
ANTHROPOLOGIST
ANTHROPOLOGISTS
ANTHROPOLOGY
ANTHROPOMETRIC
ANTHROPOMETRIES
ANTHROPOMETRIST
ANTHROPOMETRY
ANTHROPOMORPH
ANTHROPOMORPHIC
ANTHROPOMORPHS
ANTHROPOPATHIC
ANTHROPOPATHIES
ANTHROPOPATHISM
ANTHROPOPATHY
ANTHROPOPHAGI
ANTHROPOPHAGIC
ANTHROPOPHAGIES
ANTHROPOPHAGITE
ANTHROPOPHAGOUS
ANTHROPOPHAGUS
ANTHROPOPHAGY
ANTHROPOPHOBIA
ANTHROPOPHOBIAS
ANTHROPOPHOBIC
ANTHROPOPHOBICS
ANTHROPOPHUISM
ANTHROPOPHUISMS
ANTHROPOPHYTE
ANTHROPOPHYTES
ANTHROPOPSYCHIC
ANTHROPOSOPHIC
ANTHROPOSOPHIES
ANTHROPOSOPHIST
ANTHROPOSOPHY
ANTHROPOTOMIES
ANTHROPOTOMY
ANTHURIUMS
ANTIABORTION
ANTIABORTIONIST
ANTIACADEMIC
ANTIADITIS
ANTIADITISES
ANTIAGGRESSION
ANTIAIRCRAFT
ANTIAIRCRAFTS
ANTIALCOHOL
ANTIALCOHOLISM
ANTIALCOHOLISMS
ANTIALLERGENIC
ANTIANEMIA
ANTIANXIETY
ANTIAPARTHEID
ANTIAPHRODISIAC

ANTIARRHYTHMIC	ANTICHOICERS	ANTICOMMUNISMS	ANTIEPILEPTICS
ANTIARRHYTHMICS	ANTICHOLESTEROL	ANTICOMMUNIST	ANTIEROTIC
ANTIARTHRITIC	ANTICHOLINERGIC	ANTICOMMUNISTS	ANTIESTROGEN
ANTIARTHRITICS	ANTICHRIST	ANTICOMPETITIVE	ANTIESTROGENS
ANTIARTHRITIS	ANTICHRISTIAN	ANTICONSUMER	ANTIEVOLUTION
ANTIASTHMA	ANTICHRISTIANLY	ANTICONVULSANT	ANTIFAMILY
ANTIASTHMATIC	ANTICHRISTS	ANTICONVULSANTS	ANTIFASCISM
ANTIASTHMATICS	ANTICHTHONES	ANTICONVULSIVE	ANTIFASCISMS
ANTIAUTHORITY	ANTICHURCH	ANTICONVULSIVES	ANTIFASCIST
ANTIAUXINS	ANTICIGARETTE	ANTICORPORATE	ANTIFASCISTS
ANTIBACCHII	ANTICIPANT	ANTICORROSION	ANTIFASHION
ANTIBACCHIUS	ANTICIPANTS	ANTICORROSIVE	ANTIFASHIONABLE
ANTIBACKLASH	ANTICIPATABLE	ANTICORROSIVES	ANTIFASHIONS
ANTIBACTERIAL	ANTICIPATE	ANTICORRUPTION	ANTIFATIGUE
ANTIBACTERIALS	ANTICIPATED	ANTICREATIVE	ANTIFEBRILE
ANTIBALLISTIC	ANTICIPATES	ANTICRUELTY	ANTIFEBRILES
ANTIBARBARUS	ANTICIPATING	ANTICULTURAL	ANTIFEDERALIST
ANTIBARBARUSES	ANTICIPATION	ANTICYCLONE	ANTIFEDERALISTS
ANTIBARYON	ANTICIPATIONS	ANTICYCLONES	ANTIFEMALE
ANTIBARYONS	ANTICIPATIVE	ANTICYCLONIC	ANTIFEMININE
ANTIBILIOUS	ANTICIPATIVELY	ANTIDANDRUFF	ANTIFEMINISM
ANTIBILLBOARD	ANTICIPATOR	ANTIDAZZLE	ANTIFEMINISMS
ANTIBIOSES	ANTICIPATORILY	ANTIDEFAMATION	ANTIFEMINIST
ANTIBIOSIS	ANTICIPATORS	ANTIDEMOCRATIC	ANTIFEMINISTS
ANTIBIOTIC	ANTICIPATORY	ANTIDEPRESSANT	ANTIFERROMAGNET
ANTIBIOTICALLY	ANTICISING	ANTIDEPRESSANTS	ANTIFERTILITY
ANTIBIOTICS	ANTICIVISM	ANTIDEPRESSION	ANTIFILIBUSTER
ANTIBLACKISM	ANTICIVISMS	ANTIDERIVATIVE	ANTIFOAMING
ANTIBLACKISMS	ANTICIZING	ANTIDERIVATIVES	ANTIFOGGING
ANTIBODIES	ANTICLASSICAL	ANTIDESICCANT	ANTIFORECLOSURE
ANTIBOURGEOIS	ANTICLASTIC	ANTIDESICCANTS	ANTIFOREIGN
ANTIBOYCOTT	ANTICLASTICALLY	ANTIDEVELOPMENT	ANTIFOREIGNER
ANTIBURGLAR	ANTICLERICAL	ANTIDIABETIC	ANTIFORMALIST
ANTIBURGLARY	ANTICLERICALISM	ANTIDIARRHEAL	ANTIFOULING
ANTIBUSERS	ANTICLERICALS	ANTIDIARRHEALS	ANTIFOULINGS
ANTIBUSINESS	ANTICLIMACTIC	ANTIDILUTION	ANTIFREEZE
ANTIBUSING	ANTICLIMACTICAL	ANTIDIURETIC	ANTIFREEZES
ANTICAKING	ANTICLIMAX	ANTIDIURETICS	ANTIFRICTION
ANTICANCER	ANTICLIMAXES	ANTIDOGMATIC	ANTIFUNGAL
ANTICAPITALISM	ANTICLINAL	ANTIDOTALLY	ANTIFUNGALS
ANTICAPITALISMS	ANTICLINALS	ANTIDOTING	ANTIGAMBLING
ANTICAPITALIST	ANTICLINES	ANTIDROMIC	ANTIGENICALLY
ANTICAPITALISTS	ANTICLINORIA	ANTIDROMICALLY	ANTIGENICITIES
ANTICARCINOGEN	ANTICLINORIUM	ANTIDUMPING	ANTIGENICITY
ANTICARCINOGENS	ANTICLINORIUMS	ANTIECONOMIC	ANTIGLOBULIN
ANTICARIES	ANTICLOCKWISE	ANTIEDUCATIONAL	ANTIGLOBULINS
ANTICATALYST	ANTICLOTTING	ANTIEGALITARIAN	ANTIGOVERNMENT
ANTICATALYSTS	ANTICOAGULANT	ANTIELECTRON	ANTIGRAVITIES
ANTICATHODE	ANTICOAGULANTS	ANTIELECTRONS	ANTIGRAVITY
ANTICATHODES	ANTICOAGULATING	ANTIELITES	ANTIGROPELOES
ANTICATHOLIC	ANTICODONS	ANTIELITISM	ANTIGROPELOS
ANTICELLULITE	ANTICOINCIDENCE	ANTIELITISMS	ANTIGROWTH
ANTICENSORSHIP	ANTICOLLISION	ANTIELITIST	ANTIGUERRILLA
ANTICENSORSHIPS	ANTICOLONIAL	ANTIEMETIC	ANTIHALATION
ANTICHLORISTIC	ANTICOLONIALISM	ANTIEMETICS	ANTIHALATIONS
ANTICHLORS	ANTICOLONIALIST	ANTIENTROPIC	ANTIHELICES
ANTICHOICE	ANTICOMMERCIAL	ANTIEPILEPSY	ANTIHELIXES
ANTICHOICER	ANTICOMMUNISM	ANTIEPILEPTIC	ANTIHELMINTHIC

ANTIHEROES
ANTIHEROIC
ANTIHEROINE
ANTIHEROINES
ANTIHERPES
ANTIHIJACK
ANTIHISTAMINE
ANTIHISTAMINES
ANTIHISTAMINIC
ANTIHISTAMINICS
ANTIHISTORICAL
ANTIHOMOSEXUAL
ANTIHUMANISM
ANTIHUMANISMS
ANTIHUMANISTIC
ANTIHUNTER
ANTIHUNTING
ANTIHYDROGEN
ANTIHYDROGENS
ANTIHYSTERIC
ANTIHYSTERICS
ANTIJACOBIN
ANTIJACOBINS
ANTIJAMMING
ANTIJAMMINGS
ANTIKICKBACK
ANTIKNOCKS
ANTILEGOMENA
ANTILEPROSY
ANTILEPTON
ANTILEPTONS
ANTILEUKEMIC
ANTILIBERAL
ANTILIBERALISM
ANTILIBERALISMS
ANTILIBERALS
ANTILIBERTARIAN
ANTILIFERS
ANTILITERATE
ANTILITTER
ANTILITTERING
ANTILOGARITHM
ANTILOGARITHMIC
ANTILOGARITHMS
ANTILOGICAL
ANTILOGIES
ANTILOGOUS
ANTILOPINE
ANTILYNCHING
ANTIMACASSAR
ANTIMACASSARS
ANTIMAGNETIC
ANTIMALARIA
ANTIMALARIAL
ANTIMALARIALS
ANTIMANAGEMENT
ANTIMARIJUANA
ANTIMARKET

ANTIMASQUE
ANTIMASQUES
ANTIMATERIALISM
ANTIMATERIALIST
ANTIMATTER
ANTIMATTERS
ANTIMECHANIST
ANTIMECHANISTS
ANTIMERGER
ANTIMERISM
ANTIMERISMS
ANTIMETABOLE
ANTIMETABOLES
ANTIMETABOLIC
ANTIMETABOLITE
ANTIMETABOLITES
ANTIMETATHESES
ANTIMETATHESIS
ANTIMICROBIAL
ANTIMICROBIALS
ANTIMILITARISM
ANTIMILITARISMS
ANTIMILITARIST
ANTIMILITARISTS
ANTIMILITARY
ANTIMISSILE
ANTIMISSILES
ANTIMITOTIC
ANTIMITOTICS
ANTIMNEMONIC
ANTIMNEMONICS
ANTIMODERN
ANTIMODERNIST
ANTIMODERNISTS
ANTIMONARCHICAL
ANTIMONARCHIST
ANTIMONARCHISTS
ANTIMONATE
ANTIMONATES
ANTIMONIAL
ANTIMONIALS
ANTIMONIATE
ANTIMONIATES
ANTIMONIDE
ANTIMONIDES
ANTIMONIES
ANTIMONIOUS
ANTIMONITE
ANTIMONITES
ANTIMONOPOLIST
ANTIMONOPOLISTS
ANTIMONOPOLY
ANTIMONOUS
ANTIMONYLS
ANTIMOSQUITO
ANTIMUSICAL
ANTIMUSICS
ANTIMUTAGEN

ANTIMUTAGENS
ANTIMYCINS
ANTIMYCOTIC
ANTINARRATIVE
ANTINARRATIVES
ANTINATIONAL
ANTINATIONALIST
ANTINATURAL
ANTINATURE
ANTINAUSEA
ANTINEOPLASTIC
ANTINEPHRITIC
ANTINEPHRITICS
ANTINEPOTISM
ANTINEUTRINO
ANTINEUTRINOS
ANTINEUTRON
ANTINEUTRONS
ANTINOMIAN
ANTINOMIANISM
ANTINOMIANISMS
ANTINOMIANS
ANTINOMICAL
ANTINOMICALLY
ANTINOMIES
ANTINOVELIST
ANTINOVELISTS
ANTINOVELS
ANTINUCLEAR
ANTINUCLEARIST
ANTINUCLEARISTS
ANTINUCLEON
ANTINUCLEONS
ANTINUKERS
ANTIOBESITY
ANTIOBSCENITY
ANTIODONTALGIC
ANTIODONTALGICS
ANTIOXIDANT
ANTIOXIDANTS
ANTIOZONANT
ANTIOZONANTS
ANTIPARALLEL
ANTIPARALLELS
ANTIPARASITIC
ANTIPARTICLE
ANTIPARTICLES
ANTIPARTIES
ANTIPASTOS
ANTIPATHETIC
ANTIPATHETICAL
ANTIPATHIC
ANTIPATHIES
ANTIPATHIST
ANTIPATHISTS
ANTIPERIODIC
ANTIPERIODICS
ANTIPERISTALSES

ANTIPERISTALSIS
ANTIPERISTALTIC
ANTIPERISTASES
ANTIPERISTASIS
ANTIPERSONNEL
ANTIPERSPIRANT
ANTIPERSPIRANTS
ANTIPESTICIDE
ANTIPETALOUS
ANTIPHLOGISTIC
ANTIPHLOGISTICS
ANTIPHONAL
ANTIPHONALLY
ANTIPHONALS
ANTIPHONARIES
ANTIPHONARY
ANTIPHONER
ANTIPHONERS
ANTIPHONIC
ANTIPHONICAL
ANTIPHONICALLY
ANTIPHONIES
ANTIPHRASES
ANTIPHRASIS
ANTIPHRASTIC
ANTIPHRASTICAL
ANTIPIRACY
ANTIPLAGUE
ANTIPLAQUE
ANTIPLEASURE
ANTIPOACHING
ANTIPODALS
ANTIPODEAN
ANTIPODEANS
ANTIPOETIC
ANTIPOLICE
ANTIPOLITICAL
ANTIPOLITICS
ANTIPOLLUTION
ANTIPOLLUTIONS
ANTIPOPULAR
ANTIPORNOGRAPHY
ANTIPOVERTY
ANTIPREDATOR
ANTIPROGRESSIVE
ANTIPROHIBITION
ANTIPROTON
ANTIPROTONS
ANTIPRURITIC
ANTIPRURITICS
ANTIPSYCHIATRIC
ANTIPSYCHIATRY
ANTIPSYCHOTIC
ANTIPSYCHOTICS
ANTIPYRESES
ANTIPYRESIS
ANTIPYRETIC
ANTIPYRETICS

ANTIPYRINE	ANTIRRHINUMS	ANTISPENDING	ANTITUBERCULOUS
ANTIPYRINES	ANTISATELLITE	ANTISPIRITUAL	ANTITUMORAL
ANTIQUARIAN	ANTISCIANS	ANTISTATIC	ANTITUMORS
ANTIQUARIANISM	ANTISCIENCE	ANTISTATICS	ANTITUSSIVE
ANTIQUARIANISMS	ANTISCIENCES	ANTISTORIES	ANTITUSSIVES
ANTIQUARIANS	ANTISCIENTIFIC	ANTISTRESS	ANTITYPHOID
ANTIQUARIES	ANTISCORBUTIC	ANTISTRIKE	ANTITYPICAL
ANTIQUARKS	ANTISCORBUTICS	ANTISTROPHE	ANTITYPICALLY
ANTIQUATED	ANTISCRIPTURAL	ANTISTROPHES	ANTIUNIVERSITY
ANTIQUATEDNESS	ANTISECRECY	ANTISTROPHIC	ANTIVENENE
ANTIQUATES	ANTISEGREGATION	ANTISTROPHON	ANTIVENENES
ANTIQUATING	ANTISEIZURE	ANTISTROPHONS	ANTIVENINS
ANTIQUATION	ANTISENTIMENTAL	ANTISTUDENT	ANTIVENOMS
ANTIQUATIONS	ANTISEPALOUS	ANTISTYLES	ANTIVIOLENCE
ANTIQUENESS	ANTISEPARATIST	ANTISUBMARINE	ANTIVIRUSES
ANTIQUENESSES	ANTISEPARATISTS	ANTISUBSIDY	ANTIVITAMIN
ANTIQUITARIAN	ANTISEPSES	ANTISUBVERSION	ANTIVITAMINS
ANTIQUITARIANS	ANTISEPSIS	ANTISUBVERSIVE	ANTIVIVISECTION
ANTIQUITIES	ANTISEPTIC	ANTISUICIDE	ANTIWELFARE
ANTIRABIES	ANTISEPTICALLY	ANTISYMMETRIC	ANTIWHALING
ANTIRACHITIC	ANTISEPTICISE	ANTISYPHILITIC	ANTIWORLDS
ANTIRACHITICS	ANTISEPTICISED	ANTISYPHILITICS	ANTIWRINKLE
ANTIRACISM	ANTISEPTICISES	ANTISYZYGIES	ANTONINIANUS
ANTIRACISMS	ANTISEPTICISING	ANTISYZYGY	ANTONINIANUSES
ANTIRACIST	ANTISEPTICISM	ANTITAKEOVER	ANTONOMASIA
ANTIRACISTS	ANTISEPTICISMS	ANTITARNISH	ANTONOMASIAS
ANTIRADARS	ANTISEPTICIZE	ANTITECHNOLOGY	ANTONOMASTIC
ANTIRADICAL	ANTISEPTICIZED	ANTITERRORISM	ANTONYMIES
ANTIRADICALISM	ANTISEPTICIZES	ANTITERRORISMS	ANTONYMOUS
ANTIRADICALISMS	ANTISEPTICIZING	ANTITERRORIST	ANTRORSELY
ANTIRATIONAL	ANTISEPTICS	ANTITERRORISTS	ANTSINESSES
ANTIRATIONALISM	ANTISERUMS	ANTITHALIAN	ANUCLEATED
ANTIRATIONALIST	ANTISEXIST	ANTITHEISM	ANXIOLYTIC
ANTIRATIONALITY	ANTISEXISTS	ANTITHEISMS	ANXIOLYTICS
ANTIREALISM	ANTISEXUAL	ANTITHEIST	ANXIOUSNESS
ANTIREALISMS	ANTISEXUALITIES	ANTITHEISTIC	ANXIOUSNESSES
ANTIREALIST	ANTISEXUALITY	ANTITHEISTS	ANYTHINGARIAN
ANTIREALISTS	ANTISHOCKS	ANTITHEORETICAL	ANYTHINGARIANS
ANTIRECESSION	ANTISHOPLIFTING	ANTITHESES	ANYWHITHER
ANTIREFLECTION	ANTISLAVERY	ANTITHESIS	AORISTICALLY
ANTIREFLECTIVE	ANTISMOKER	ANTITHETIC	AORTITISES
ANTIREFORM	ANTISMOKERS	ANTITHETICAL	AORTOGRAPHIC
ANTIREGULATORY	ANTISMOKING	ANTITHETICALLY	AORTOGRAPHIES
ANTIREJECTION	ANTISMUGGLING	ANTITHROMBIN	AORTOGRAPHY
ANTIRELIGION	ANTISOCIAL	ANTITHROMBINS	APAGOGICAL
ANTIRELIGIOUS	ANTISOCIALISM	ANTITHROMBOTIC	APAGOGICALLY
ANTIREPUBLICAN	ANTISOCIALISMS	ANTITHROMBOTICS	APARTHEIDS
ANTIREPUBLICANS	ANTISOCIALIST	ANTITHYROID	APARTHOTEL
ANTIRHEUMATIC	ANTISOCIALISTS	ANTITOBACCO	APARTHOTELS
ANTIRHEUMATICS	ANTISOCIALITIES	ANTITOXINS	APARTMENTAL
ANTIRITUALISM	ANTISOCIALITY	ANTITRADES	APARTMENTS
ANTIRITUALISMS	ANTISOCIALLY	ANTITRADITIONAL	APARTNESSES
ANTIROMANTIC	ANTISPASMODIC	ANTITRAGUS	APATHATONS
ANTIROMANTICISM	ANTISPASMODICS	ANTITRANSPIRANT	APATHETICAL
ANTIROMANTICS	ANTISPASTIC	ANTITRINITARIAN	APATHETICALLY
ANTIROYALIST	ANTISPASTS	ANTITRUSTER	APATOSAURS
ANTIROYALISTS	ANTISPECULATION	ANTITRUSTERS	APATOSAURUS
ANTIRRHINUM	ANTISPECULATIVE	ANTITUBERCULAR	APATOSAURUSES

APERIODICALLY	APOCALYPTISM	APOLOGISING	APOSTLESHIP
APERIODICITIES	APOCALYPTISMS	APOLOGISTS	APOSTLESHIPS
APERIODICITY	APOCALYPTIST	APOLOGIZED	APOSTOLATE
APERITIVES	APOCALYPTISTS	APOLOGIZER	APOSTOLATES
APERTNESSES	APOCARPIES	APOLOGIZERS	APOSTOLICAL
APFELSTRUDEL	APOCARPOUS	APOLOGIZES	APOSTOLICALLY
APFELSTRUDELS	APOCATASTASES	APOLOGIZING	APOSTOLICISM
APHAERESES	APOCATASTASIS	APOMICTICAL	APOSTOLICISMS
APHAERESIS	APOCHROMAT	APOMICTICALLY	APOSTOLICITIES
APHAERETIC	APOCHROMATIC	APOMORPHIA	APOSTOLICITY
APHANIPTEROUS	APOCHROMATISM	APOMORPHIAS	APOSTOLISE
APHELANDRA	APOCHROMATISMS	APOMORPHINE	APOSTOLISED
APHELANDRAS	APOCHROMATS	APOMORPHINES	APOSTOLISES
APHELIOTROPIC	APOCOPATED	APONEUROSES	APOSTOLISING
APHELIOTROPISM	APOCOPATES	APONEUROSIS	APOSTOLIZE
APHELIOTROPISMS	APOCOPATING	APONEUROTIC	APOSTOLIZED
APHETICALLY	APOCOPATION	APOPEMPTIC	APOSTOLIZES
APHETISING	APOCOPATIONS	APOPHLEGMATIC	APOSTOLIZING
APHETIZING	APOCRYPHAL	APOPHLEGMATICS	APOSTROPHE
APHIDICIDE	APOCRYPHALLY	APOPHONIES	APOSTROPHES
APHIDICIDES	APOCRYPHALNESS	APOPHTHEGM	APOSTROPHIC
APHORISERS	APOCRYPHON	APOPHTHEGMATIC	APOSTROPHISE
APHORISING	APOCYNACEOUS	APOPHTHEGMATISE	APOSTROPHISED
APHORISTIC	APOCYNTHION	APOPHTHEGMATIST	APOSTROPHISES
APHORISTICALLY	APOCYNTHIONS	APOPHTHEGMATIZE	APOSTROPHISING
APHORIZERS	APODEICTIC	APOPHTHEGMS	APOSTROPHIZE
APHORIZING	APODEICTICAL	APOPHYLLITE	APOSTROPHIZED
APHRODISIA	APODEICTICALLY	APOPHYLLITES	APOSTROPHIZES
APHRODISIAC	APODICTICAL	APOPHYSATE	APOSTROPHIZING
APHRODISIACAL	APODICTICALLY	APOPHYSEAL	APOSTROPHUS
APHRODISIACS	APODYTERIUM	APOPHYSIAL	APOSTROPHUSES
APHRODISIAS	APODYTERIUMS	APOPLECTIC	APOTHECARIES
APHRODITES	APOENZYMES	APOPLECTICAL	APOTHECARY
APICULTURAL	APOGAMOUSLY	APOPLECTICALLY	APOTHECIAL
APICULTURE	APOGEOTROPIC	APOPLECTICS	APOTHECIUM
APICULTURES	APOGEOTROPISM	APOPLEXIES	APOTHEGMATIC
APICULTURIST	APOGEOTROPISMS	APOPLEXING	APOTHEGMATICAL
APICULTURISTS	APOLAUSTIC	APOPROTEIN	APOTHEGMATISE
APIOLOGIES	APOLAUSTICS	APOPROTEINS	APOTHEGMATISED
APISHNESSES	APOLIPOPROTEIN	APOSEMATIC	APOTHEGMATISES
APITHERAPIES	APOLIPOPROTEINS	APOSEMATICALLY	APOTHEGMATISING
APITHERAPY	APOLITICAL	APOSIOPESES	APOTHEGMATIST
APLACENTAL	APOLITICALITIES	APOSIOPESIS	APOTHEGMATISTS
APLANATICALLY	APOLITICALITY	APOSIOPETIC	APOTHEGMATIZE
APLANATISM	APOLITICALLY	APOSPORIES	APOTHEGMATIZED
APLANATISMS	APOLITICISM	APOSPOROUS	APOTHEGMATIZES
APLANOGAMETE	APOLITICISMS	APOSTACIES	APOTHEGMATIZING
APLANOGAMETES	APOLLONIAN	APOSTASIES	APOTHEOSES
APLANOSPORE	APOLLONICON	APOSTATICAL	APOTHEOSIS
APLANOSPORES	APOLLONICONS	APOSTATISE	APOTHEOSISE
APOAPSIDES	APOLOGETIC	APOSTATISED	APOTHEOSISED
APOCALYPSE	APOLOGETICAL	APOSTATISES	APOTHEOSISES
APOCALYPSES	APOLOGETICALLY	APOSTATISING	APOTHEOSISING
APOCALYPTIC	APOLOGETICS	APOSTATIZE	APOTHEOSIZE
APOCALYPTICAL	APOLOGISED	APOSTATIZED	APOTHEOSIZED
APOCALYPTICALLY	APOLOGISER	APOSTATIZES	APOTHEOSIZES
APOCALYPTICISM	APOLOGISERS	APOSTATIZING	APOTHEOSIZING
APOCALYPTICISMS	APOLOGISES	APOSTILLES	APOTROPAIC

APOTROPAICALLY	APPENDICLES	APPLICANTS	APPRECIATORS
APOTROPAISM	APPENDICULAR	APPLICATION	APPRECIATORY
APOTROPAISMS	APPENDICULARIAN	APPLICATIONS	APPREHENDED
APOTROPOUS	APPENDICULATE	APPLICATIVE	APPREHENDING
APPALLINGLY	APPENDIXES	APPLICATIVELY	APPREHENDS
APPALOOSAS	APPERCEIVE	APPLICATOR	APPREHENSIBLE
APPARATCHIK	APPERCEIVED	APPLICATORS	APPREHENSIBLY
APPARATCHIKI	APPERCEIVES	APPLICATORY	APPREHENSION
APPARATCHIKS	APPERCEIVING	APPLIQUEING	APPREHENSIONS
APPARATUSES	APPERCEPTION	APPOGGIATURA	APPREHENSIVE
APPARELING	APPERCEPTIONS	APPOGGIATURAS	APPREHENSIVELY
APPARELLED	APPERCEPTIVE	APPOGGIATURE	APPRENTICE
APPARELLING	APPERCIPIENT	APPOINTEES	APPRENTICED
APPARELMENT	APPERTAINANCE	APPOINTERS	APPRENTICEHOOD
APPARELMENTS	APPERTAINANCES	APPOINTING	APPRENTICEHOODS
APPARENCIES	APPERTAINED	APPOINTIVE	APPRENTICEMENT
APPARENTLY	APPERTAINING	APPOINTMENT	APPRENTICEMENTS
APPARENTNESS	APPERTAINMENT	APPOINTMENTS	APPRENTICES
APPARENTNESSES	APPERTAINMENTS	APPOINTORS	APPRENTICESHIP
APPARITION	APPERTAINS	APPORTIONABLE	APPRENTICESHIPS
APPARITIONAL	APPERTINENT	APPORTIONED	APPRENTICING
APPARITIONS	APPERTINENTS	APPORTIONER	APPRESSING
APPARITORS	APPETEEZEMENT	APPORTIONERS	APPRESSORIA
APPARTEMENT	APPETEEZEMENTS	APPORTIONING	APPRESSORIUM
APPARTEMENTS	APPETENCES	APPORTIONMENT	APPRISINGS
APPASSIONATO	APPETENCIES	APPORTIONMENTS	APPRIZINGS
APPEACHING	APPETISEMENT	APPORTIONS	APPROACHABILITY
APPEACHMENT	APPETISEMENTS	APPOSITELY	APPROACHABLE
APPEACHMENTS	APPETISERS	APPOSITENESS	APPROACHED
APPEALABILITIES	APPETISING	APPOSITENESSES	APPROACHES
APPEALABILITY	APPETISINGLY	APPOSITION	APPROACHING
APPEALABLE	APPETITION	APPOSITIONAL	APPROBATED
APPEALINGLY	APPETITIONS	APPOSITIONS	APPROBATES
APPEALINGNESS	APPETITIVE	APPOSITIVE	APPROBATING
APPEALINGNESSES	APPETIZERS	APPOSITIVELY	APPROBATION
APPEARANCE	APPETIZING	APPOSITIVES	APPROBATIONS
APPEARANCES	APPETIZINGLY	APPRAISABLE	APPROBATIVE
APPEASABLE	APPLAUDABLE	APPRAISALS	APPROBATORY
APPEASEMENT	APPLAUDABLY	APPRAISEES	APPROPINQUATE
APPEASEMENTS	APPLAUDERS	APPRAISEMENT	APPROPINQUATED
APPEASINGLY	APPLAUDING	APPRAISEMENTS	APPROPINQUATES
APPELLANTS	APPLAUDINGLY	APPRAISERS	APPROPINQUATING
APPELLATION	APPLAUSIVE	APPRAISING	APPROPINQUATION
APPELLATIONAL	APPLAUSIVELY	APPRAISINGLY	APPROPINQUE
APPELLATIONS	APPLECARTS	APPRAISIVE	APPROPINQUED
APPELLATIVE	APPLEDRAIN	APPRAISIVELY	APPROPINQUES
APPELLATIVELY	APPLEDRAINS	APPRECIABLE	APPROPINQUING
APPELLATIVES	APPLEJACKS	APPRECIABLY	APPROPINQUITIES
APPENDAGES	APPLERINGIE	APPRECIATE	APPROPINQUITY
APPENDANTS	APPLERINGIES	APPRECIATED	APPROPRIABLE
APPENDECTOMIES	APPLESAUCE	APPRECIATES	APPROPRIACIES
APPENDECTOMY	APPLESAUCES	APPRECIATING	APPROPRIACY
APPENDENTS	APPLIANCES	APPRECIATION	APPROPRIATE
APPENDICECTOMY	APPLICABILITIES	APPRECIATIONS	APPROPRIATED
APPENDICES	APPLICABILITY	APPRECIATIVE	APPROPRIATELY
APPENDICITIS	APPLICABLE	APPRECIATIVELY	APPROPRIATENESS
APPENDICITISES	APPLICABLENESS	APPRECIATOR	APPROPRIATES
APPENDICLE	APPLICABLY	APPRECIATORILY	APPROPRIATING

APPROPRIATION	AQUAMANILES	ARABIZATIONS	ARBITRATRICES
APPROPRIATIONS	AQUAMARINE	ARACHIDONIC	ARBITRATRIX
APPROPRIATIVE	AQUAMARINES	ARACHNIDAN	ARBITRATRIXES
APPROPRIATOR	AQUANAUTICS	ARACHNIDANS	ARBITREMENT
APPROPRIATORS	AQUAPHOBES	ARACHNOIDAL	ARBITREMENTS
APPROVABLE	AQUAPHOBIA	ARACHNOIDITIS	ARBITRESSES
APPROVABLY	AQUAPHOBIAS	ARACHNOIDITISES	ARBITRIUMS
APPROVANCE	AQUAPHOBIC	ARACHNOIDS	ARBLASTERS
APPROVANCES	AQUAPHOBICS	ARACHNOLOGICAL	ARBORACEOUS
APPROVINGLY	AQUAPLANED	ARACHNOLOGIES	ARBOREALLY
APPROXIMAL	AQUAPLANER	ARACHNOLOGIST	ARBORESCENCE
APPROXIMATE	AQUAPLANERS	ARACHNOLOGISTS	ARBORESCENCES
APPROXIMATED	AQUAPLANES	ARACHNOLOGY	ARBORESCENT
APPROXIMATELY	AQUAPLANING	ARACHNOPHOBE	ARBORETUMS
APPROXIMATES	AQUAPLANINGS	ARACHNOPHOBES	ARBORICULTURAL
APPROXIMATING	AQUAPORINS	ARACHNOPHOBIA	ARBORICULTURE
APPROXIMATION	AQUARELLES	ARACHNOPHOBIAS	ARBORICULTURES
APPROXIMATIONS	AQUARELLIST	ARAEOMETER	ARBORICULTURIST
APPROXIMATIVE	AQUARELLISTS	ARAEOMETERS	ARBORISATION
APPULSIVELY	AQUARIISTS	ARAEOMETRIC	ARBORISATIONS
APPURTENANCE	AQUAROBICS	ARAEOMETRICAL	ARBORISING
APPURTENANCES	AQUATICALLY	ARAEOMETRIES	ARBORIZATION
APPURTENANT	AQUATINTAS	ARAEOMETRY	ARBORIZATIONS
APPURTENANTS	AQUATINTED	ARAEOSTYLE	ARBORIZING
APRICATING	AQUATINTER	ARAEOSTYLES	ARBORVITAE
APRICATION	AQUATINTERS	ARAEOSYSTYLE	ARBORVITAES
APRICATIONS	AQUATINTING	ARAEOSYSTYLES	ARBOVIRUSES
APRIORISMS	AQUATINTIST	ARAGONITES	ARBUSCULAR
APRIORISTS	AQUATINTISTS	ARAGONITIC	ARCANENESS
APRIORITIES	AQUICULTURAL	ARALIACEOUS	ARCANENESSES
APSIDIOLES	AQUICULTURE	ARAUCARIAN	ARCCOSINES
APTERYGIAL	AQUICULTURES	ARAUCARIAS	ARCHAEBACTERIA
APTITUDINAL	AQUICULTURIST	ARBALESTER	ARCHAEBACTERIUM
APTITUDINALLY	AQUICULTURISTS	ARBALESTERS	ARCHAEOBOTANIES
AQUABATICS	AQUIFEROUS	ARBALISTER	ARCHAEOBOTANIST
AQUABOARDS	AQUIFOLIACEOUS	ARBALISTERS	ARCHAEOBOTANY
AQUACEUTICAL	AQUILEGIAS	ARBITRABLE	ARCHAEOLOGICAL
AQUACEUTICALS	AQUILINITIES	ARBITRAGED	ARCHAEOLOGIES
AQUACULTURAL	AQUILINITY	ARBITRAGER	ARCHAEOLOGIST
AQUACULTURE	ARABESQUED	ARBITRAGERS	ARCHAEOLOGISTS
AQUACULTURES	ARABESQUES	ARBITRAGES	ARCHAEOLOGY
AQUACULTURIST	ARABICISATION	ARBITRAGEUR	ARCHAEOMETRIC
AQUACULTURISTS	ARABICISATIONS	ARBITRAGEURS	ARCHAEOMETRIES
AQUADROMES	ARABICISED	ARBITRAGING	ARCHAEOMETRIST
AQUAEROBICS	ARABICISES	ARBITRAMENT	ARCHAEOMETRISTS
AQUAFARMED	ARABICISING	ARBITRAMENTS	ARCHAEOMETRY
AQUAFARMING	ARABICIZATION	ARBITRARILY	ARCHAEOPTERYX
AQUAFITNESS	ARABICIZATIONS	ARBITRARINESS	ARCHAEOPTERYXES
AQUAFITNESSES	ARABICIZED	ARBITRARINESSES	ARCHAEORNIS
AQUAFORTIS	ARABICIZES	ARBITRATED	ARCHAEORNISES
AQUAFORTISES	ARABICIZING	ARBITRATES	ARCHAEOZOOLOGY
AQUAFORTIST	ARABILITIES	ARBITRATING	ARCHAEZOOLOGIES
AQUAFORTISTS	ARABINOSES	ARBITRATION	ARCHAEZOOLOGY
AQUALEATHER	ARABINOSIDE	ARBITRATIONAL	ARCHAICALLY
AQUALEATHERS	ARABINOSIDES	ARBITRATIONS	ARCHAICISM
AQUAMANALE	ARABISATION	ARBITRATIVE	ARCHAICISMS
AQUAMANALES	ARABISATIONS	ARBITRATOR	ARCHAISERS
AQUAMANILE	ARABIZATION	ARBITRATORS	ARCHAISING

ARCHAISTIC	ARCHETYPALLY	ARCHPRIESTSHIP	ARGUTENESSES
ARCHAIZERS	ARCHETYPES	ARCHPRIESTSHIPS	ARGYRODITE
ARCHAIZING	ARCHETYPICAL	ARCHRIVALS	ARGYRODITES
ARCHANGELIC	ARCHETYPICALLY	ARCOGRAPHS	ARHATSHIPS
ARCHANGELS	ARCHFIENDS	ARCOLOGIES	ARHYTHMIAS
ARCHBISHOP	ARCHGENETHLIAC	ARCSECONDS	ARIBOFLAVINOSES
ARCHBISHOPRIC	ARCHGENETHLIACS	ARCTANGENT	ARIBOFLAVINOSIS
ARCHBISHOPRICS	ARCHICARPS	ARCTANGENTS	ARIDNESSES
ARCHBISHOPS	ARCHIDIACONAL	ARCTICALLY	ARISTOCRACIES
ARCHDEACON	ARCHIDIACONATE	ARCTOPHILE	ARISTOCRACY
ARCHDEACONRIES	ARCHIDIACONATES	ARCTOPHILES	ARISTOCRAT
ARCHDEACONRY	ARCHIEPISCOPACY	ARCTOPHILIA	ARISTOCRATIC
ARCHDEACONS	ARCHIEPISCOPAL	ARCTOPHILIAS	ARISTOCRATICAL
ARCHDIOCESAN	ARCHIEPISCOPATE	ARCTOPHILIES	ARISTOCRATISM
ARCHDIOCESE	ARCHILOWES	ARCTOPHILIST	ARISTOCRATISMS
ARCHDIOCESES	ARCHIMAGES	ARCTOPHILISTS	ARISTOCRATS
ARCHDUCHESS	ARCHIMANDRITE	ARCTOPHILS	ARISTOLOCHIA
ARCHDUCHESSES	ARCHIMANDRITES	ARCTOPHILY	ARISTOLOCHIAS
ARCHDUCHIES	ARCHIPELAGIAN	ARCUATIONS	ARISTOLOGIES
ARCHDUKEDOM	ARCHIPELAGIC	ARCUBALIST	ARISTOLOGY
ARCHDUKEDOMS	ARCHIPELAGO	ARCUBALISTS	ARISTOTLES
ARCHEGONIA	ARCHIPELAGOES	ARDUOUSNESS	ARITHMETIC
ARCHEGONIAL	ARCHIPELAGOS	ARDUOUSNESSES	ARITHMETICAL
ARCHEGONIATE	ARCHIPHONEME	ARECOLINES	ARITHMETICALLY
ARCHEGONIATES	ARCHIPHONEMES	AREFACTION	ARITHMETICIAN
ARCHEGONIUM	ARCHIPLASM	AREFACTIONS	ARITHMETICIANS
ARCHENEMIES	ARCHIPLASMIC	ARENACEOUS	ARITHMETICS
ARCHENTERA	ARCHIPLASMS	ARENATIONS	ARITHMOMANIA
ARCHENTERIC	ARCHITECTED	ARENICOLOUS	ARITHMOMANIAS
ARCHENTERON	ARCHITECTING	AREOCENTRIC	ARITHMOMETER
ARCHENTERONS	ARCHITECTONIC	AREOGRAPHIC	ARITHMOMETERS
ARCHEOASTRONOMY	ARCHITECTONICS	AREOGRAPHIES	ARITHMOPHOBIA
ARCHEOBOTANICAL	ARCHITECTS	AREOGRAPHY	ARITHMOPHOBIAS
ARCHEOBOTANIES	ARCHITECTURAL	AREOLATION	ARMADILLOS
ARCHEOBOTANIST	ARCHITECTURALLY	AREOLATIONS	ARMAMENTARIA
ARCHEOBOTANISTS	ARCHITECTURE	AREOLOGIES	ARMAMENTARIUM
ARCHEOBOTANY	ARCHITECTURES	AREOMETERS	ARMAMENTARIUMS
ARCHEOLOGICAL	ARCHITRAVE	AREOSTYLES	ARMATURING
ARCHEOLOGICALLY	ARCHITRAVED	AREOSYSTILE	ARMIGEROUS
ARCHEOLOGIES	ARCHITRAVES	AREOSYSTILES	ARMILLARIA
ARCHEOLOGIST	ARCHITYPES	ARFVEDSONITE	ARMILLARIAS
ARCHEOLOGISTS	ARCHIVISTS	ARFVEDSONITES	ARMIPOTENCE
ARCHEOLOGY	ARCHIVOLTS	ARGENTIFEROUS	ARMIPOTENCES
ARCHEOMAGNETISM	ARCHNESSES	ARGENTINES	ARMIPOTENT
ARCHEOMETRIES	ARCHOLOGIES	ARGENTITES	ARMISTICES
ARCHEOMETRY	ARCHONSHIP	ARGILLACEOUS	ARMLOCKING
ARCHEOZOOLOGIES	ARCHONSHIPS	ARGILLIFEROUS	ARMORIALLY
ARCHEOZOOLOGIST	ARCHONTATE	ARGILLITES	ARMOURLESS
ARCHEOZOOLOGY	ARCHONTATES	ARGILLITIC	AROMATASES
ARCHERESSES	ARCHOPLASM	ARGONAUTIC	AROMATHERAPIES
ARCHERFISH	ARCHOPLASMIC	ARGUMENTATION	AROMATHERAPIST
ARCHERFISHES	ARCHOPLASMS	ARGUMENTATIONS	AROMATHERAPISTS
ARCHESPORE	ARCHOSAURIAN	ARGUMENTATIVE	AROMATHERAPY
ARCHESPORES	ARCHOSAURS	ARGUMENTATIVELY	AROMATICALLY
ARCHESPORIA	ARCHPRIEST	ARGUMENTIVE	AROMATICITIES
ARCHESPORIAL	ARCHPRIESTHOOD	ARGUMENTUM	AROMATICITY
ARCHESPORIUM	ARCHPRIESTHOODS	ARGUMENTUMS	AROMATISATION
ARCHETYPAL	ARCHPRIESTS	ARGUTENESS	AROMATISATIONS

AROMATISED	ARROGATIVE	ARTHRODIAE	ARTILLERYMAN
AROMATISES	ARROGATORS	ARTHRODIAL	ARTILLERYMEN
AROMATISING	ARRONDISSEMENT	ARTHROGRAPHIES	ARTINESSES
AROMATIZATION	ARRONDISSEMENTS	ARTHROGRAPHY	ARTIODACTYL
AROMATIZATIONS	ARROWGRASS	ARTHROMERE	ARTIODACTYLOUS
AROMATIZED	ARROWGRASSES	ARTHROMERES	ARTIODACTYLS
AROMATIZES	ARROWHEADS	ARTHROMERIC	ARTISANSHIP
AROMATIZING	ARROWROOTS	ARTHROPATHIES	ARTISANSHIPS
ARPEGGIATE	ARROWWOODS	ARTHROPATHY	ARTISTICAL
ARPEGGIATED	ARROWWORMS	ARTHROPLASTIES	ARTISTICALLY
ARPEGGIATES	ARSENIATES	ARTHROPLASTY	ARTISTRIES
ARPEGGIATING	ARSENICALS	ARTHROPODAL	ARTLESSNESS
ARPEGGIATION	ARSENOPYRITE	ARTHROPODAN	ARTLESSNESSES
ARPEGGIATIONS	ARSENOPYRITES	ARTHROPODOUS	ARTOCARPUS
ARPEGGIONE	ARSMETRICK	ARTHROPODS	ARTOCARPUSES
ARPEGGIONES	ARSMETRICKS	ARTHROSCOPE	ARTSINESSES
ARPILLERAS	ARSPHENAMINE	ARTHROSCOPES	ARUNDINACEOUS
ARQUEBUSADE	ARSPHENAMINES	ARTHROSCOPIC	ARVICOLINE
ARQUEBUSADES	ARTEFACTUAL	ARTHROSCOPIES	ARYBALLOID
ARQUEBUSES	ARTEMISIAS	ARTHROSCOPY	ARYBALLOSES
ARQUEBUSIER	ARTEMISININ	ARTHROSPORE	ARYTAENOID
ARQUEBUSIERS	ARTEMISININS	ARTHROSPORES	ARYTAENOIDS
ARRACACHAS	ARTERIALISATION	ARTHROSPORIC	ARYTENOIDAL
ARRAGONITE	ARTERIALISE	ARTHROSPOROUS	ARYTENOIDS
ARRAGONITES	ARTERIALISED	ARTICHOKES	ASAFETIDAS
ARRAIGNERS	ARTERIALISES	ARTICULABLE	ASAFOETIDA
ARRAIGNING	ARTERIALISING	ARTICULACIES	ASAFOETIDAS
ARRAIGNINGS	ARTERIALIZATION	ARTICULACY	ASARABACCA
ARRAIGNMENT	ARTERIALIZE	ARTICULATE	ASARABACCAS
ARRAIGNMENTS	ARTERIALIZED	ARTICULATED	ASBESTIFORM
ARRANGEABLE	ARTERIALIZES	ARTICULATELY	ASBESTOSES
ARRANGEMENT	ARTERIALIZING	ARTICULATENESS	ASBESTOSIS
ARRANGEMENTS	ARTERIALLY	ARTICULATES	ASBESTUSES
ARRAYMENTS	ARTERIOGRAM	ARTICULATING	ASCARIASES
ARREARAGES	ARTERIOGRAMS	ARTICULATION	ASCARIASIS
ARRESTABLE	ARTERIOGRAPHIC	ARTICULATIONS	ASCENDABLE
ARRESTANTS	ARTERIOGRAPHIES	ARTICULATIVE	ASCENDANCE
ARRESTATION	ARTERIOGRAPHY	ARTICULATOR	ASCENDANCES
ARRESTATIONS	ARTERIOLAR	ARTICULATORS	ASCENDANCIES
ARRESTINGLY	ARTERIOLES	ARTICULATORY	ASCENDANCY
ARRESTMENT	ARTERIOTOMIES	ARTIFACTUAL	ASCENDANTLY
ARRESTMENTS	ARTERIOTOMY	ARTIFICERS	ASCENDANTS
ARRHENOTOKIES	ARTERIOVENOUS	ARTIFICIAL	ASCENDENCE
ARRHENOTOKY	ARTERITIDES	ARTIFICIALISE	ASCENDENCES
ARRHYTHMIA	ARTERITISES	ARTIFICIALISED	ASCENDENCIES
ARRHYTHMIAS	ARTFULNESS	ARTIFICIALISES	ASCENDENCY
ARRHYTHMIC	ARTFULNESSES	ARTIFICIALISING	ASCENDENTS
ARRIVANCES	ARTHRALGIA	ARTIFICIALITIES	ASCENDEURS
ARRIVANCIES	ARTHRALGIAS	ARTIFICIALITY	ASCENDIBLE
ARRIVEDERCI	ARTHRALGIC	ARTIFICIALIZE	ASCENSIONAL
ARRIVISMES	ARTHRECTOMIES	ARTIFICIALIZED	ASCENSIONIST
ARRIVISTES	ARTHRECTOMY	ARTIFICIALIZES	ASCENSIONISTS
ARROGANCES	ARTHRITICALLY	ARTIFICIALIZING	ASCENSIONS
ARROGANCIES	ARTHRITICS	ARTIFICIALLY	ASCERTAINABLE
ARROGANTLY	ARTHRITIDES	ARTIFICIALNESS	ASCERTAINABLY
ARROGATING	ARTHRITISES	ARTILLERIES	ASCERTAINED
ARROGATION	ARTHRODESES	ARTILLERIST	ASCERTAINING
ARROGATIONS	ARTHRODESIS	ARTILLERISTS	ASCERTAINMENT

ASCERTAINMENTS	ASPERGILLOSIS	ASSAGAIING	ASSESSORSHIP
ASCERTAINS	ASPERGILLS	ASSAILABLE	ASSESSORSHIPS
ASCETICALLY	ASPERGILLUM	ASSAILANTS	ASSEVERATE
ASCETICISM	ASPERGILLUMS	ASSAILMENT	ASSEVERATED
ASCETICISMS	ASPERGILLUS	ASSAILMENTS	ASSEVERATES
ASCITITIOUS	ASPERITIES	ASSASSINATE	ASSEVERATING
ASCLEPIADACEOUS	ASPERSIONS	ASSASSINATED	ASSEVERATINGLY
ASCLEPIADS	ASPERSIVELY	ASSASSINATES	ASSEVERATION
ASCLEPIASES	ASPERSOIRS	ASSASSINATING	ASSEVERATIONS
ASCOCARPIC	ASPERSORIA	ASSASSINATION	ASSEVERATIVE
ASCOGONIUM	ASPERSORIES	ASSASSINATIONS	ASSEVERING
ASCOMYCETE	ASPERSORIUM	ASSASSINATOR	ASSIBILATE
ASCOMYCETES	ASPERSORIUMS	ASSASSINATORS	ASSIBILATED
ASCOMYCETOUS	ASPHALTERS	ASSAULTERS	ASSIBILATES
ASCORBATES	ASPHALTING	ASSAULTING	ASSIBILATING
ASCOSPORES	ASPHALTITE	ASSAULTIVE	ASSIBILATION
ASCOSPORIC	ASPHALTITES	ASSAULTIVELY	ASSIBILATIONS
ASCRIBABLE	ASPHALTUMS	ASSAULTIVENESS	ASSIDUITIES
ASCRIPTION	ASPHERICAL	ASSEGAAIED	ASSIDUOUSLY
ASCRIPTIONS	ASPHETERISE	ASSEGAAIING	ASSIDUOUSNESS
ASCRIPTIVE	ASPHETERISED	ASSEGAIING	ASSIDUOUSNESSES
ASEPTICALLY	ASPHETERISES	ASSEMBLAGE	ASSIGNABILITIES
ASEPTICISE	ASPHETERISING	ASSEMBLAGES	ASSIGNABILITY
ASEPTICISED	ASPHETERISM	ASSEMBLAGIST	ASSIGNABLE
ASEPTICISES	ASPHETERISMS	ASSEMBLAGISTS	ASSIGNABLY
ASEPTICISING	ASPHETERIZE	ASSEMBLANCE	ASSIGNATION
ASEPTICISM	ASPHETERIZED	ASSEMBLANCES	ASSIGNATIONS
ASEPTICISMS	ASPHETERIZES	ASSEMBLAUNCE	ASSIGNMENT
ASEPTICIZE	ASPHETERIZING	ASSEMBLAUNCES	ASSIGNMENTS
ASEPTICIZED	ASPHYXIANT	ASSEMBLERS	ASSIMILABILITY
ASEPTICIZES	ASPHYXIANTS	ASSEMBLIES	ASSIMILABLE
ASEPTICIZING	ASPHYXIATE	ASSEMBLING	ASSIMILABLY
ASEXUALITIES	ASPHYXIATED	ASSEMBLYMAN	ASSIMILATE
ASEXUALITY	ASPHYXIATES	ASSEMBLYMEN	ASSIMILATED
ASHAMEDNESS	ASPHYXIATING	ASSEMBLYWOMAN	ASSIMILATES
ASHAMEDNESSES	ASPHYXIATION	ASSEMBLYWOMEN	ASSIMILATING
ASHINESSES	ASPHYXIATIONS	ASSENTANEOUS	ASSIMILATION
ASHLARINGS	ASPHYXIATOR	ASSENTATION	ASSIMILATIONISM
ASHLERINGS	ASPHYXIATORS	ASSENTATIONS	ASSIMILATIONIST
ASHRAMITES	ASPIDISTRA	ASSENTATOR	ASSIMILATIONS
ASININITIES	ASPIDISTRAS	ASSENTATORS	ASSIMILATIVE
ASKEWNESSES	ASPIRATING	ASSENTIENT	ASSIMILATIVELY
ASPARAGINASE	ASPIRATION	ASSENTIENTS	ASSIMILATOR
ASPARAGINASES	ASPIRATIONAL	ASSENTINGLY	ASSIMILATORS
ASPARAGINE	ASPIRATIONS	ASSENTIVENESS	ASSIMILATORY
ASPARAGINES	ASPIRATORS	ASSENTIVENESSES	ASSISTANCE
ASPARAGUSES	ASPIRATORY	ASSERTABLE	ASSISTANCES
ASPARTAMES	ASPIRINGLY	ASSERTEDLY	ASSISTANTS
ASPARTATES	ASPIRINGNESS	ASSERTIBLE	ASSISTANTSHIP
ASPECTABLE	ASPIRINGNESSES	ASSERTIONS	ASSISTANTSHIPS
ASPENDICITIS	ASPLANCHNIC	ASSERTIVELY	ASSOCIABILITIES
ASPENDICITISES	ASPLENIUMS	ASSERTIVENESS	ASSOCIABILITY
ASPERATING	ASPORTATION	ASSERTIVENESSES	ASSOCIABLE
ASPERGATION	ASPORTATIONS	ASSERTORIC	ASSOCIATED
ASPERGATIONS	ASSAFETIDA	ASSESSABLE	ASSOCIATES
ASPERGILLA	ASSAFETIDAS	ASSESSMENT	ASSOCIATESHIP
ASPERGILLI	ASSAFOETIDA	ASSESSMENTS	ASSOCIATESHIPS
ASPERGILLOSES	ASSAFOETIDAS	ASSESSORIAL	ASSOCIATING

ASSOCIATION	ASTARBOARD	ASTRINGENCY	ASTRONOMIC
ASSOCIATIONAL	ASTATICALLY	ASTRINGENT	ASTRONOMICAL
ASSOCIATIONISM	ASTATICISM	ASTRINGENTLY	ASTRONOMICALLY
ASSOCIATIONISMS	ASTATICISMS	ASTRINGENTS	ASTRONOMIES
ASSOCIATIONIST	ASTEREOGNOSES	ASTRINGERS	ASTRONOMISE
ASSOCIATIONISTS	ASTEREOGNOSIS	ASTRINGING	ASTRONOMISED
ASSOCIATIONS	ASTERIATED	ASTROBIOLOGIES	ASTRONOMISES
ASSOCIATIVE	ASTERIDIAN	ASTROBIOLOGIST	ASTRONOMISING
ASSOCIATIVELY	ASTERIDIANS	ASTROBIOLOGISTS	ASTRONOMIZE
ASSOCIATIVITIES	ASTERISKED	ASTROBIOLOGY	ASTRONOMIZED
ASSOCIATIVITY	ASTERISKING	ASTROBLEME	ASTRONOMIZES
ASSOCIATOR	ASTERISKLESS	ASTROBLEMES	ASTRONOMIZING
ASSOCIATORS	ASTEROIDAL	ASTROBOTANIES	ASTROPHELS
ASSOCIATORY	ASTEROIDEAN	ASTROBOTANY	ASTROPHOBIA
ASSOILMENT	ASTEROIDEANS	ASTROCHEMISTRY	ASTROPHOBIAS
ASSOILMENTS	ASTHENOPIA	ASTROCOMPASS	ASTROPHOBIC
ASSOILZIED	ASTHENOPIAS	ASTROCOMPASSES	ASTROPHOTOGRAPH
ASSOILZIEING	ASTHENOPIC	ASTROCYTES	ASTROPHYSICAL
ASSOILZIES	ASTHENOSPHERE	ASTROCYTIC	ASTROPHYSICALLY
ASSONANCES	ASTHENOSPHERES	ASTROCYTOMA	ASTROPHYSICIST
ASSONANTAL	ASTHENOSPHERIC	ASTROCYTOMAS	ASTROPHYSICISTS
ASSONATING	ASTHMATICAL	ASTROCYTOMATA	ASTROPHYSICS
ASSORTATIVE	ASTHMATICALLY	ASTRODOMES	ASTROSPHERE
ASSORTATIVELY	ASTHMATICS	ASTRODYNAMICIST	ASTROSPHERES
ASSORTEDNESS	ASTIGMATIC	ASTRODYNAMICS	ASTROTOURISM
ASSORTEDNESSES	ASTIGMATICALLY	ASTROFELLS	ASTROTOURISMS
ASSORTMENT	ASTIGMATICS	ASTROGEOLOGIES	ASTROTOURIST
ASSORTMENTS	ASTIGMATISM	ASTROGEOLOGIST	ASTROTOURISTS
ASSUAGEMENT	ASTIGMATISMS	ASTROGEOLOGISTS	ASTUCIOUSLY
ASSUAGEMENTS	ASTOMATOUS	ASTROGEOLOGY	ASTUCITIES
ASSUAGINGS	ASTONISHED	ASTROHATCH	ASTUTENESS
ASSUBJUGATE	ASTONISHES	ASTROHATCHES	ASTUTENESSES
ASSUBJUGATED	ASTONISHING	ASTROLABES	ASYMMETRIC
ASSUBJUGATES	ASTONISHINGLY	ASTROLATRIES	ASYMMETRICAL
ASSUBJUGATING	ASTONISHMENT	ASTROLATRY	ASYMMETRICALLY
ASSUEFACTION	ASTONISHMENTS	ASTROLOGER	ASYMMETRIES
ASSUEFACTIONS	ASTOUNDING	ASTROLOGERS	ASYMPTOMATIC
ASSUETUDES	ASTOUNDINGLY	ASTROLOGIC	ASYMPTOTES
ASSUMABILITIES	ASTOUNDMENT	ASTROLOGICAL	ASYMPTOTIC
ASSUMABILITY	ASTOUNDMENTS	ASTROLOGICALLY	ASYMPTOTICAL
ASSUMINGLY	ASTRACHANS	ASTROLOGIES	ASYMPTOTICALLY
ASSUMPSITS	ASTRAGALUS	ASTROLOGIST	ASYNARTETE
ASSUMPTION	ASTRAGALUSES	ASTROLOGISTS	ASYNARTETES
ASSUMPTIONS	ASTRAKHANS	ASTROMETRIC	ASYNARTETIC
ASSUMPTIVE	ASTRANTIAS	ASTROMETRICAL	ASYNCHRONIES
ASSUMPTIVELY	ASTRAPHOBIA	ASTROMETRICALLY	ASYNCHRONISM
ASSURANCES	ASTRAPHOBIAS	ASTROMETRIES	ASYNCHRONISMS
ASSUREDNESS	ASTRAPHOBIC	ASTROMETRY	ASYNCHRONOUS
ASSUREDNESSES	ASTRAPOPHOBIA	ASTRONAUTIC	ASYNCHRONOUSLY
ASSURGENCIES	ASTRAPOPHOBIAS	ASTRONAUTICAL	ASYNCHRONY
ASSURGENCY	ASTRICTING	ASTRONAUTICALLY	ASYNDETICALLY
ASSYTHMENT	ASTRICTION	ASTRONAUTICS	ASYNDETONS
ASSYTHMENTS	ASTRICTIONS	ASTRONAUTS	ASYNERGIAS
ASTACOLOGICAL	ASTRICTIVE	ASTRONAVIGATION	ASYNERGIES
ASTACOLOGIES	ASTRICTIVELY	ASTRONAVIGATOR	ASYNTACTIC
ASTACOLOGIST	ASTRINGENCE	ASTRONAVIGATORS	ASYSTOLISM
ASTACOLOGISTS	ASTRINGENCES	ASTRONOMER	ASYSTOLISMS
ASTACOLOGY	ASTRINGENCIES	ASTRONOMERS	ATACAMITES

ATARACTICS	ATOMIZATIONS	ATTENUATED	ATTRACTINGLY
ATAVISTICALLY	ATONALISMS	ATTENUATES	ATTRACTION
ATCHIEVING	ATONALISTS	ATTENUATING	ATTRACTIONS
ATELECTASES	ATONALITIES	ATTENUATION	ATTRACTIVE
ATELECTASIS	ATONEMENTS	ATTENUATIONS	ATTRACTIVELY
ATELECTATIC	ATONICITIES	ATTENUATOR	ATTRACTIVENESS
ATELEIOSES	ATRABILIAR	ATTENUATORS	ATTRACTORS
ATELEIOSIS	ATRABILIOUS	ATTESTABLE	ATTRAHENTS
ATHANASIES	ATRABILIOUSNESS	ATTESTANTS	ATTRAPPING
ATHEISTICAL	ATRACURIUM	ATTESTATION	ATTRIBUTABLE
ATHEISTICALLY	ATRACURIUMS	ATTESTATIONS	ATTRIBUTED
ATHEMATICALLY	ATRAMENTAL	ATTESTATIVE	ATTRIBUTER
ATHENAEUMS	ATRAMENTOUS	ATTESTATOR	ATTRIBUTERS
ATHEOLOGICAL	ATROCIOUSLY	ATTESTATORS	ATTRIBUTES
ATHEOLOGIES	ATROCIOUSNESS	ATTICISING	ATTRIBUTING
ATHEORETICAL	ATROCIOUSNESSES	ATTICIZING	ATTRIBUTION
ATHERMANCIES	ATROCITIES	ATTIREMENT	ATTRIBUTIONAL
ATHERMANCY	ATROPHYING	ATTIREMENTS	ATTRIBUTIONS
ATHERMANOUS	ATTACHABLE	ATTITUDINAL	ATTRIBUTIVE
ATHEROGENESES	ATTACHMENT	ATTITUDINALLY	ATTRIBUTIVELY
ATHEROGENESIS	ATTACHMENTS	ATTITUDINARIAN	ATTRIBUTIVENESS
ATHEROGENIC	ATTACKABLE	ATTITUDINARIANS	ATTRIBUTIVES.
ATHEROMATA	ATTAINABILITIES	ATTITUDINISE	ATTRIBUTOR
ATHEROMATOUS	ATTAINABILITY	ATTITUDINISED	ATTRIBUTORS
ATHEROSCLEROSES	ATTAINABLE	ATTITUDINISER	ATTRISTING
ATHEROSCLEROSIS	ATTAINABLENESS	ATTITUDINISERS	ATTRITIONAL
ATHEROSCLEROTIC	ATTAINDERS	ATTITUDINISES	ATTRITIONS
ATHETISING	ATTAINMENT	ATTITUDINISING	ATTRITTING
ATHETIZING	ATTAINMENTS	ATTITUDINISINGS	ATTUITIONAL
ATHLETICALLY	ATTAINTING	ATTITUDINIZE	ATTUITIONS
ATHLETICISM	ATTAINTMENT	ATTITUDINIZED	ATTUITIVELY
ATHLETICISMS	ATTAINTMENTS	ATTITUDINIZER	ATTUNEMENT
ATHROCYTES	ATTAINTURE	ATTITUDINIZERS	ATTUNEMENTS
ATHROCYTOSES	ATTAINTURES	ATTITUDINIZES	ATYPICALITIES
ATHROCYTOSIS	ATTEMPERED	ATTITUDINIZING	ATYPICALITY
ATHWARTSHIP	ATTEMPERING	ATTITUDINIZINGS	ATYPICALLY
ATHWARTSHIPS	ATTEMPERMENT	ATTOLASERS	AUBERGINES
ATMOLOGIES	ATTEMPERMENTS	ATTOLLENTS	AUBERGISTE
ATMOLOGIST	ATTEMPTABILITY	ATTOPHYSICS	AUBERGISTES
ATMOLOGISTS	ATTEMPTABLE	ATTORNEYDOM	AUBRIETIAS
ATMOLYSING	ATTEMPTERS	ATTORNEYDOMS	AUCTIONARY
ATMOLYZING	ATTEMPTING	ATTORNEYED	AUCTIONEER
ATMOMETERS	ATTENDANCE	ATTORNEYING	AUCTIONEERED
ATMOMETRIES	ATTENDANCES	ATTORNEYISM	AUCTIONEERING
ATMOSPHERE	ATTENDANCIES	ATTORNEYISMS	AUCTIONEERS
ATMOSPHERED	ATTENDANCY	ATTORNEYSHIP	AUCTIONING
ATMOSPHERES	ATTENDANTS	ATTORNEYSHIPS	AUDACIOUSLY
ATMOSPHERIC	ATTENDEMENT	ATTORNMENT	AUDACIOUSNESS
ATMOSPHERICAL	ATTENDEMENTS	ATTORNMENTS	AUDACIOUSNESSES
ATMOSPHERICALLY	ATTENDINGS	ATTRACTABLE	AUDACITIES
ATMOSPHERICS	ATTENDMENT	ATTRACTANCE	AUDIBILITIES
ATOMICALLY	ATTENDMENTS	ATTRACTANCES	AUDIBILITY
ATOMICITIES	ATTENTIONAL	ATTRACTANCIES	AUDIBLENESS
ATOMISATION	ATTENTIONS	ATTRACTANCY	AUDIBLENESSES
ATOMISATIONS	ATTENTIVELY	ATTRACTANT	AUDIENCIAS
ATOMISTICAL	ATTENTIVENESS	ATTRACTANTS	AUDIOBOOKS
ATOMISTICALLY	ATTENTIVENESSES	ATTRACTERS	AUDIOCASSETTE
ATOMIZATION	ATTENUANTS	ATTRACTING	AUDIOCASSETTES

AUDIOGENIC	AURALITIES	AUTHENTICATOR	AUTOCEPHALOUS
AUDIOGRAMS	AUREATENESS	AUTHENTICATORS	AUTOCEPHALY
AUDIOGRAPH	AUREATENESSES	AUTHENTICITIES	AUTOCHANGER
AUDIOGRAPHS	AURICULARLY	AUTHENTICITY	AUTOCHANGERS
AUDIOLOGIC	AURICULARS	AUTHIGENIC	AUTOCHTHON
AUDIOLOGICAL	AURICULATE	AUTHORCRAFT	AUTOCHTHONAL
AUDIOLOGICALLY	AURICULATED	AUTHORCRAFTS	AUTOCHTHONES
AUDIOLOGIES	AURICULATELY	AUTHORESSES	AUTOCHTHONIC
AUDIOLOGIST	AURIFEROUS	AUTHORINGS	AUTOCHTHONIES
AUDIOLOGISTS	AURISCOPES	AUTHORISABLE	AUTOCHTHONISM
AUDIOMETER	AURISCOPIC	AUTHORISATION	AUTOCHTHONISMS
AUDIOMETERS	AUSCULTATE	AUTHORISATIONS	AUTOCHTHONOUS
AUDIOMETRIC	AUSCULTATED	AUTHORISED	AUTOCHTHONOUSLY
AUDIOMETRICALLY	AUSCULTATES	AUTHORISER	AUTOCHTHONS
AUDIOMETRICIAN	AUSCULTATING	AUTHORISERS	AUTOCHTHONY
AUDIOMETRICIANS	AUSCULTATION	AUTHORISES	AUTOCLAVED
AUDIOMETRIES	AUSCULTATIONS	AUTHORISING	AUTOCLAVES
AUDIOMETRIST	AUSCULTATIVE	AUTHORISMS	AUTOCLAVING
AUDIOMETRISTS	AUSCULTATOR	AUTHORITARIAN	AUTOCOPROPHAGY
AUDIOMETRY	AUSCULTATORS	AUTHORITARIANS	AUTOCORRELATION
AUDIOPHILE	AUSCULTATORY	AUTHORITATIVE	AUTOCRACIES
AUDIOPHILES	AUSFORMING	AUTHORITATIVELY	AUTOCRATIC
AUDIOPHILS	AUSLANDERS	AUTHORITIES	AUTOCRATICAL
AUDIOTAPED	AUSPICATED	AUTHORIZABLE	AUTOCRATICALLY
AUDIOTAPES	AUSPICATES	AUTHORIZATION	AUTOCRIMES
AUDIOTAPING	AUSPICATING	AUTHORIZATIONS	AUTOCRITIQUE
AUDIOTYPING	AUSPICIOUS	AUTHORIZED	AUTOCRITIQUES
AUDIOTYPINGS	AUSPICIOUSLY	AUTHORIZER	AUTOCROSSES
AUDIOTYPIST	AUSPICIOUSNESS	AUTHORIZERS	AUTOCUTIES
AUDIOTYPISTS	AUSTENITES	AUTHORIZES	AUTOCYCLES
AUDIOVISUAL	AUSTENITIC	AUTHORIZING	AUTODESTRUCT
AUDIOVISUALLY	AUSTERENESS	AUTHORLESS	AUTODESTRUCTED
AUDIOVISUALS	AUSTERENESSES	AUTHORSHIP	AUTODESTRUCTING
AUDIPHONES	AUSTERITIES	AUTHORSHIPS	AUTODESTRUCTIVE
AUDITIONED	AUSTRALITE	AUTISTICALLY	AUTODESTRUCTS
AUDITIONER	AUSTRALITES	AUTOALLOGAMIES	AUTODIDACT
AUDITIONERS	AUSTRINGER	AUTOALLOGAMY	AUTODIDACTIC
AUDITIONING	AUSTRINGERS	AUTOANTIBODIES	AUTODIDACTICISM
AUDITORIAL	AUTARCHICAL	AUTOANTIBODY	AUTODIDACTS
AUDITORIES	AUTARCHIES	AUTOBAHNEN	AUTOECIOUS
AUDITORILY	AUTARCHIST	AUTOBIOGRAPHER	AUTOECIOUSLY
AUDITORIUM	AUTARCHISTS	AUTOBIOGRAPHERS	AUTOECISMS
AUDITORIUMS	AUTARKICAL	AUTOBIOGRAPHIC	AUTOEROTIC
AUDITORSHIP	AUTARKISTS	AUTOBIOGRAPHIES	AUTOEROTICISM
AUDITORSHIPS	AUTECOLOGIC	AUTOBIOGRAPHY	AUTOEROTICISMS
AUDITRESSES	AUTECOLOGICAL	AUTOBUSSES	AUTOEROTISM
AUGMENTABLE	AUTECOLOGIES	AUTOCATALYSE	AUTOEROTISMS
AUGMENTATION	AUTECOLOGY	AUTOCATALYSED	AUTOEXPOSURE
AUGMENTATIONS	AUTEURISMS	AUTOCATALYSES	AUTOEXPOSURES
AUGMENTATIVE	AUTEURISTS	AUTOCATALYSING	AUTOFLARES
AUGMENTATIVELY	AUTHENTICAL	AUTOCATALYSIS	AUTOFOCUSES
AUGMENTATIVES	AUTHENTICALLY	AUTOCATALYTIC	AUTOGAMIES
AUGMENTERS	AUTHENTICATE	AUTOCATALYZE	AUTOGAMOUS
AUGMENTING	AUTHENTICATED	AUTOCATALYZED	AUTOGENESES
AUGMENTORS	AUTHENTICATES	AUTOCATALYZES	AUTOGENESIS
AUGURSHIPS	AUTHENTICATING	AUTOCATALYZING	AUTOGENETIC
AUGUSTNESS	AUTHENTICATION	AUTOCEPHALIC	AUTOGENETICALLY
AUGUSTNESSES	AUTHENTICATIONS	AUTOCEPHALIES	AUTOGENICS

AUTOGENIES	AUTOMATISATIONS	AUTOPLASTY	AUTOTOMISE
AUTOGENOUS	AUTOMATISE	AUTOPOINTS	AUTOTOMISED
AUTOGENOUSLY	AUTOMATISED	AUTOPOLYPLOID	AUTOTOMISES
AUTOGRAFTED	AUTOMATISES	AUTOPOLYPLOIDS	AUTOTOMISING
AUTOGRAFTING	AUTOMATISING	AUTOPOLYPLOIDY	AUTOTOMIZE
AUTOGRAFTS	AUTOMATISM	AUTOPSISTS	AUTOTOMIZED
AUTOGRAPHED	AUTOMATISMS	AUTOPSYING	AUTOTOMIZES
AUTOGRAPHIC	AUTOMATIST	AUTOPTICAL	AUTOTOMIZING
AUTOGRAPHICAL	AUTOMATISTS	AUTOPTICALLY	AUTOTOMOUS
AUTOGRAPHICALLY	AUTOMATIZATION	AUTORADIOGRAM	AUTOTOXAEMIA
AUTOGRAPHIES	AUTOMATIZATIONS	AUTORADIOGRAMS	AUTOTOXAEMIAS
AUTOGRAPHING	AUTOMATIZE	AUTORADIOGRAPH	AUTOTOXEMIA
AUTOGRAPHS	AUTOMATIZED	AUTORADIOGRAPHS	AUTOTOXEMIAS
AUTOGRAPHY	AUTOMATIZES	AUTORADIOGRAPHY	AUTOTOXINS
AUTOGRAVURE	AUTOMATIZING	AUTORICKSHAW	AUTOTRANSFORMER
AUTOGRAVURES	AUTOMATONS	AUTORICKSHAWS	AUTOTRANSFUSION
AUTOGUIDES	AUTOMATOUS	AUTOROTATE	AUTOTROPHIC
AUTOHYPNOSES	AUTOMETERS	AUTOROTATED	AUTOTROPHICALLY
AUTOHYPNOSIS	AUTOMOBILE	AUTOROTATES	AUTOTROPHIES
AUTOHYPNOTIC	AUTOMOBILED	AUTOROTATING	AUTOTROPHS
AUTOIMMUNE	AUTOMOBILES	AUTOROTATION	AUTOTROPHY
AUTOIMMUNITIES	AUTOMOBILIA	AUTOROTATIONS	AUTOTYPIES
AUTOIMMUNITY	AUTOMOBILING	AUTOROUTES	AUTOTYPING
AUTOINFECTION	AUTOMOBILISM	AUTOSCHEDIASM	AUTOTYPOGRAPHY
AUTOINFECTIONS	AUTOMOBILISMS	AUTOSCHEDIASMS	AUTOWINDER
AUTOINOCULATION	AUTOMOBILIST	AUTOSCHEDIASTIC	AUTOWINDERS
AUTOINOCULATORY	AUTOMOBILISTS	AUTOSCHEDIAZE	AUTOWORKER
AUTOIONISATION	AUTOMOBILITIES	AUTOSCHEDIAZED	AUTOWORKERS
AUTOIONISATIONS	AUTOMOBILITY	AUTOSCHEDIAZES	AUTOXIDATION
AUTOIONIZATION	AUTOMORPHIC	AUTOSCHEDIAZING	AUTOXIDATIONS
AUTOIONIZATIONS	AUTOMORPHICALLY	AUTOSCOPIC	AUTUMNALLY
AUTOJUMBLE	AUTOMORPHISM	AUTOSCOPIES	AUXANOMETER
AUTOJUMBLES	AUTOMORPHISMS	AUTOSEXING	AUXANOMETERS
AUTOKINESES	AUTOMOTIVE	AUTOSOMALLY	AUXILIARIES
AUTOKINESIS	AUTONOMICAL	AUTOSPORES	AUXOCHROME
AUTOKINETIC	AUTONOMICALLY	AUTOSTABILITIES	AUXOCHROMES
AUTOLATRIES	AUTONOMICS	AUTOSTABILITY	AUXOMETERS
AUTOLOADING	AUTONOMIES	AUTOSTRADA	AUXOSPORES
AUTOLOGIES	AUTONOMIST	AUTOSTRADAS	AUXOTROPHIC
AUTOLOGOUS	AUTONOMISTS	AUTOSTRADE	AUXOTROPHIES
AUTOLYSATE	AUTONOMOUS	AUTOSUGGEST	AUXOTROPHS
AUTOLYSATES	AUTONOMOUSLY	AUTOSUGGESTED	AUXOTROPHY
AUTOLYSING	AUTOPHAGIA	AUTOSUGGESTING	AVAILABILITIES
AUTOLYSINS	AUTOPHAGIAS	AUTOSUGGESTION	AVAILABILITY
AUTOLYZATE	AUTOPHAGIES	AUTOSUGGESTIONS	AVAILABLENESS
AUTOLYZATES	AUTOPHAGOUS	AUTOSUGGESTIVE	AVAILABLENESSES
AUTOLYZING	AUTOPHANOUS	AUTOSUGGESTS	AVAILINGLY
AUTOMAKERS	AUTOPHOBIA	AUTOTELLER	AVALANCHED
AUTOMATABLE	AUTOPHOBIAS	AUTOTELLERS	AVALANCHES
AUTOMATICAL	AUTOPHOBIES	AUTOTETRAPLOID	AVALANCHING
AUTOMATICALLY	AUTOPHONIES	AUTOTETRAPLOIDS	AVANTURINE
AUTOMATICITIES	AUTOPHYTES	AUTOTETRAPLOIDY	AVANTURINES
AUTOMATICITY	AUTOPHYTIC	AUTOTHEISM	AVARICIOUS
AUTOMATICS	AUTOPHYTICALLY	AUTOTHEISMS	AVARICIOUSLY
AUTOMATING	AUTOPILOTS	AUTOTHEIST	AVARICIOUSNESS
AUTOMATION	AUTOPISTAS	AUTOTHEISTS	AVASCULARITIES
AUTOMATIONS	AUTOPLASTIC	AUTOTIMERS	AVASCULARITY
AUTOMATISATION	AUTOPLASTIES	AUTOTOMIES	AVENACEOUS

AVENGEMENT
AVENGEMENTS
AVENGERESS
AVENGERESSES
AVENTAILES
AVENTURINE
AVENTURINES
AVENTURINS
AVERAGENESS
AVERAGENESSES
AVERAGINGS
AVERRUNCATE
AVERRUNCATED
AVERRUNCATES
AVERRUNCATING
AVERRUNCATION
AVERRUNCATIONS
AVERRUNCATOR
AVERRUNCATORS
AVERSENESS
AVERSENESSES
AVERSIVELY
AVERSIVENESS
AVERSIVENESSES
AVERTIMENT
AVERTIMENTS
AVGOLEMONO
AVGOLEMONOS
AVIANISING
AVIANIZING
AVIATRESSES
AVIATRICES
AVIATRIXES
AVICULTURE
AVICULTURES
AVICULTURIST
AVICULTURISTS
AVIDNESSES
AVISANDUMS
AVISEMENTS
AVITAMINOSES
AVITAMINOSIS
AVITAMINOTIC
AVIZANDUMS
AVOCATIONAL
AVOCATIONALLY
AVOCATIONS
AVOIDANCES
AVOIRDUPOIS
AVOIRDUPOISES
AVOUCHABLE
AVOUCHMENT
AVOUCHMENTS
AVOUTERERS
AVOWABLENESS
AVOWABLENESSES
AVUNCULARITIES
AVUNCULARITY

AVUNCULARLY
AVUNCULATE
AVUNCULATES
AVVOGADORE
AVVOGADORES
AWAKENINGS
AWARENESSES
AWAYNESSES
AWELESSNESS
AWELESSNESSES
AWESOMENESS
AWESOMENESSES
AWESTRICKEN
AWESTRIKES
AWESTRIKING
AWFULNESSES
AWKWARDEST
AWKWARDISH
AWKWARDNESS
AWKWARDNESSES
AXENICALLY
AXEROPHTHOL
AXEROPHTHOLS
AXIALITIES
AXILLARIES
AXINOMANCIES
AXINOMANCY
AXIOLOGICAL
AXIOLOGICALLY
AXIOLOGIES
AXIOLOGIST
AXIOLOGISTS
AXIOMATICAL
AXIOMATICALLY
AXIOMATICS
AXIOMATISATION
AXIOMATISATIONS
AXIOMATISE
AXIOMATISED
AXIOMATISES
AXIOMATISING
AXIOMATIZATION
AXIOMATIZATIONS
AXIOMATIZE
AXIOMATIZED
AXIOMATIZES
AXIOMATIZING
AXISYMMETRIC
AXISYMMETRICAL
AXISYMMETRIES
AXISYMMETRY
AXOLEMMATA
AXONOMETRIC
AXONOMETRICALLY
AXONOMETRIES
AXONOMETRY
AXOPLASMIC
AYAHUASCAS

AYAHUASCOS
AYATOLLAHS
AYUNTAMIENTO
AYUNTAMIENTOS
AYURVEDICS
AZATHIOPRINE
AZATHIOPRINES
AZEDARACHS
AZEOTROPES
AZEOTROPIC
AZEOTROPIES
AZIDOTHYMIDINE
AZIDOTHYMIDINES
AZIMUTHALLY
AZOBENZENE
AZOBENZENES
AZOOSPERMIA
AZOOSPERMIAS
AZOOSPERMIC
AZOTAEMIAS
AZOTOBACTER
AZOTOBACTERS
AZYGOSPORE
AZYGOSPORES

B

BAALEBATIM
BABACOOTES
BABBITRIES
BABBITTING
BABBITTRIES
BABBLATIVE
BABBLEMENT
BABBLEMENTS
BABELESQUE
BABESIASES
BABESIASIS
BABESIOSES
BABESIOSIS
BABINGTONITE
BABINGTONITES
BABIROUSSA
BABIROUSSAS
BABIRUSSAS
BABOONERIES
BABYPROOFED
BABYPROOFING
BABYPROOFS
BABYSITTING
BACCALAUREAN
BACCALAUREATE
BACCALAUREATES
BACCHANALIA
BACCHANALIAN
BACCHANALIANISM
BACCHANALIANS
BACCHANALS
BACCHANTES
BACCIFEROUS
BACCIVOROUS
BACHARACHS
BACHELORDOM
BACHELORDOMS
BACHELORETTE
BACHELORETTES
BACHELORHOOD
BACHELORHOODS
BACHELORISM
BACHELORISMS
BACHELORSHIP
BACHELORSHIPS
BACILLAEMIA
BACILLAEMIAS
BACILLEMIA
BACILLEMIAS
BACILLICIDE
BACILLICIDES
BACILLIFORM
BACILLURIA

BACILLURIAS
BACITRACIN
BACITRACINS
BACKBENCHER
BACKBENCHERS
BACKBENCHES
BACKBITERS
BACKBITING
BACKBITINGS
BACKBITTEN
BACKBLOCKER
BACKBLOCKERS
BACKBLOCKS
BACKBOARDS
BACKBONELESS
BACKBREAKER
BACKBREAKERS
BACKBREAKING
BACKBURNED
BACKBURNING
BACKCHATTED
BACKCHATTING
BACKCHECKED
BACKCHECKING
BACKCHECKS
BACKCLOTHS
BACKCOMBED
BACKCOMBING
BACKCOUNTRIES
BACKCOUNTRY
BACKCOURTMAN
BACKCOURTMEN
BACKCOURTS
BACKCROSSED
BACKCROSSES
BACKCROSSING
BACKDATING
BACKDRAFTS
BACKDRAUGHT
BACKDRAUGHTS
BACKDROPPED
BACKDROPPING
BACKFIELDS
BACKFILLED
BACKFILLING
BACKFIRING
BACKFISCHES
BACKFITTED
BACKFITTING
BACKFITTINGS
BACKFLIPPED
BACKFLIPPING
BACKGAMMON

BACKGAMMONED
BACKGAMMONING
BACKGAMMONS
BACKGROUND
BACKGROUNDED
BACKGROUNDER
BACKGROUNDERS
BACKGROUNDING
BACKGROUNDS
BACKHANDED
BACKHANDEDLY
BACKHANDEDNESS
BACKHANDER
BACKHANDERS
BACKHANDING
BACKHAULED
BACKHAULING
BACKHOEING
BACKHOUSES
BACKLASHED
BACKLASHER
BACKLASHERS
BACKLASHES
BACKLASHING
BACKLIGHTED
BACKLIGHTING
BACKLIGHTS
BACKLISTED
BACKLISTING
BACKLOADED
BACKLOADING
BACKLOGGED
BACKLOGGING
BACKMARKER
BACKMARKERS
BACKPACKED
BACKPACKER
BACKPACKERS
BACKPACKING
BACKPACKINGS
BACKPEDALED
BACKPEDALING
BACKPEDALLED
BACKPEDALLING
BACKPEDALS
BACKPIECES
BACKRUSHES
BACKSCATTER
BACKSCATTERED
BACKSCATTERING
BACKSCATTERINGS
BACKSCATTERS
BACKSCRATCH

BACKSCRATCHED
BACKSCRATCHER
BACKSCRATCHERS
BACKSCRATCHES
BACKSCRATCHING
BACKSCRATCHINGS
BACKSHEESH
BACKSHEESHED
BACKSHEESHES
BACKSHEESHING
BACKSHISHED
BACKSHISHES
BACKSHISHING
BACKSHORES
BACKSIGHTS
BACKSLAPPED
BACKSLAPPER
BACKSLAPPERS
BACKSLAPPING
BACKSLASHES
BACKSLIDDEN
BACKSLIDER
BACKSLIDERS
BACKSLIDES
BACKSLIDING
BACKSLIDINGS
BACKSPACED
BACKSPACER
BACKSPACERS
BACKSPACES
BACKSPACING
BACKSPEERED
BACKSPEERING
BACKSPEERS
BACKSPEIRED
BACKSPEIRING
BACKSPEIRS
BACKSPLASH
BACKSPLASHES
BACKSTABBED
BACKSTABBER
BACKSTABBERS
BACKSTABBING
BACKSTABBINGS
BACKSTAGES
BACKSTAIRS
BACKSTALLS
BACKSTAMPED
BACKSTAMPING
BACKSTAMPS
BACKSTARTING
BACKSTITCH
BACKSTITCHED

BACKSTITCHES	BACTERIOLYSES	BAHUVRIHIS	BALKANIZATION
BACKSTITCHING	BACTERIOLYSIN	BAIGNOIRES	BALKANIZATIONS
BACKSTOPPED	BACTERIOLYSINS	BAILIESHIP	BALKANIZED
BACKSTOPPING	BACTERIOLYSIS	BAILIESHIPS	BALKANIZES
BACKSTORIES	BACTERIOLYTIC	BAILIFFSHIP	BALKANIZING
BACKSTREET	BACTERIOPHAGE	BAILIFFSHIPS	BALKINESSES
BACKSTREETS	BACTERIOPHAGES	BAILIWICKS	BALLABILES
BACKSTRETCH	BACTERIOPHAGIC	BAILLIAGES	BALLADEERED
BACKSTRETCHES	BACTERIOPHAGIES	BAILLIESHIP	BALLADEERING
BACKSTROKE	BACTERIOPHAGOUS	BAILLIESHIPS	BALLADEERS
BACKSTROKES	BACTERIOPHAGY	BAIRNLIEST	BALLADINES
BACKSWINGS	BACTERIOSES	BAISEMAINS	BALLADISTS
BACKSWORDMAN	BACTERIOSIS	BAITFISHES	BALLADMONGER
BACKSWORDMEN	BACTERIOSTASES	BAKEAPPLES	BALLADMONGERS
BACKSWORDS	BACTERIOSTASIS	BAKEBOARDS	BALLADRIES
BACKSWORDSMAN	BACTERIOSTAT	BAKEHOUSES	BALLANTING
BACKSWORDSMEN	BACTERIOSTATIC	BAKESTONES	BALLANWRASSE
BACKTRACKED	BACTERIOSTATS	BAKHSHISHED	BALLANWRASSES
BACKTRACKING	BACTERIOTOXIN	BAKHSHISHES	BALLASTERS
BACKTRACKINGS	BACTERIOTOXINS	BAKHSHISHING	BALLASTING
BACKTRACKS	BACTERISATION	BAKSHEESHED	BALLBREAKER
BACKVELDER	BACTERISATIONS	BAKSHEESHES	BALLBREAKERS
BACKVELDERS	BACTERISED	BAKSHEESHING	BALLCARRIER
BACKWARDATION	BACTERISES	BAKSHISHED	BALLCARRIERS
BACKWARDATIONS	BACTERISING	BAKSHISHES	BALLERINAS
BACKWARDLY	BACTERIURIA	BAKSHISHING	BALLETICALLY
BACKWARDNESS	BACTERIURIAS	BALACLAVAS	BALLETOMANE
BACKWARDNESSES	BACTERIZATION	BALALAIKAS	BALLETOMANES
BACKWASHED	BACTERIZATIONS	BALANCEABLE	BALLETOMANIA
BACKWASHES	BACTERIZED	BALANCINGS	BALLETOMANIAS
BACKWASHING	BACTERIZES	BALANITISES	BALLFLOWER
BACKWATERS	BACTERIZING	BALBRIGGAN	BALLFLOWERS
BACKWOODSMAN	BACTEROIDS	BALBRIGGANS	BALLHANDLING
BACKWOODSMEN	BACTERURIA	BALBUTIENT	BALLHANDLINGS
BACKWOODSY	BACTERURIAS	BALCONETTE	BALLICATTER
BACKWORKER	BACULIFORM	BALCONETTES	BALLICATTERS
BACKWORKERS	BACULOVIRUS	BALDACHINO	BALLISTICALLY
BACTERAEMIA	BACULOVIRUSES	BALDACHINOS	BALLISTICS
BACTERAEMIAS	BADDELEYITE	BALDACHINS	BALLISTITE
BACTEREMIA	BADDELEYITES	BALDAQUINS	BALLISTITES
BACTEREMIAS	BADDERLOCK	BALDERDASH	BALLISTOSPORE
BACTEREMIC	BADDERLOCKS	BALDERDASHES	BALLISTOSPORES
BACTERIALLY	BADINAGING	BALDERLOCKS	BALLOCKSED
BACTERIALS	BADINERIES	BALDERLOCKSES	BALLOCKSES
BACTERICIDAL	BADMINTONS	BALDHEADED	BALLOCKSING
BACTERICIDALLY	BADMOUTHED	BALDICOOTS	BALLOONING
BACTERICIDE	BADMOUTHING	BALDMONEYS	BALLOONINGS
BACTERICIDES	BAFFLEGABS	BALDNESSES	BALLOONIST
BACTERIOCIN	BAFFLEMENT	BALECTIONS	BALLOONISTS
BACTERIOCINS	BAFFLEMENTS	BALEFULNESS	BALLOTTEMENT
BACTERIOID	BAFFLINGLY	BALEFULNESSES	BALLOTTEMENTS
BACTERIOIDS	BAGASSOSES	BALIBUNTAL	BALLPLAYER
BACTERIOLOGIC	BAGASSOSIS	BALIBUNTALS	BALLPLAYERS
BACTERIOLOGICAL	BAGATELLES	BALKANISATION	BALLPOINTS
BACTERIOLOGIES	BAGGINESSES	BALKANISATIONS	BALLSINESS
BACTERIOLOGIST	BAGPIPINGS	BALKANISED	BALLSINESSES
BACTERIOLOGISTS	BAGSWINGER	BALKANISES	BALLYHOOED
BACTERIOLOGY	BAGSWINGERS	BALKANISING	BALLYHOOING

BALLYRAGGED	BANDICOOTS	BANTINGISM	BARDOLATRY
BALLYRAGGING	BANDINESSES	BANTINGISMS	BAREBACKED
BALMACAANS	BANDITRIES	BAPHOMETIC	BAREFACEDLY
BALMINESSES	BANDLEADER	BAPTISMALLY	BAREFACEDNESS
BALMORALITIES	BANDLEADERS	BAPTISTERIES	BAREFACEDNESSES
BALMORALITY	BANDMASTER	BAPTISTERY	BAREFOOTED
BALNEARIES	BANDMASTERS	BAPTISTRIES	BAREHANDED
BALNEATION	BANDOBASTS	BARACHOISES	BAREHANDING
BALNEATIONS	BANDOBUSTS	BARAESTHESIA	BAREHEADED
BALNEOLOGICAL	BANDOLEERED	BARAESTHESIAS	BARELEGGED
BALNEOLOGIES	BANDOLEERS	BARAGOUINS	BARENESSES
BALNEOLOGIST	BANDOLEONS	BARASINGAS	BARESTHESIA
BALNEOLOGISTS	BANDOLEROS	BARASINGHA	BARESTHESIAS
BALNEOLOGY	BANDOLIERED	BARASINGHAS	BARGAINERS
BALNEOTHERAPIES	BANDOLIERS	BARATHRUMS	BARGAINING
BALNEOTHERAPY	BANDOLINED	BARBARESQUE	BARGAININGS
BALSAMIFEROUS	BANDOLINES	BARBARIANISM	BARGANDERS
BALSAMINACEOUS	BANDOLINING	BARBARIANISMS	BARGEBOARD
BALSAWOODS	BANDONEONS	BARBARIANS	BARGEBOARDS
BALTHASARS	BANDONIONS	BARBARICALLY	BARGEMASTER
BALTHAZARS	BANDSHELLS	BARBARISATION	BARGEMASTERS
BALUSTERED	BANDSPREADING	BARBARISATIONS	BARGEPOLES
BALUSTRADE	BANDSPREADINGS	BARBARISED	BARHOPPING
BALUSTRADED	BANDSTANDS	BARBARISES	BARKANTINE
BALUSTRADES	BANDWAGONS	BARBARISING	BARKANTINES
BALZARINES	BANDWIDTHS	BARBARISMS	BARKEEPERS
BAMBOOZLED	BANEBERRIES	BARBARITIES	BARKENTINE
BAMBOOZLEMENT	BANEFULNESS	BARBARIZATION	BARKENTINES
BAMBOOZLEMENTS	BANEFULNESSES	BARBARIZATIONS	BARLEYCORN
BAMBOOZLER	BANGSRINGS	BARBARIZED	BARLEYCORNS
BAMBOOZLERS	BANISHMENT	BARBARIZES	BARMBRACKS
BAMBOOZLES	BANISHMENTS	BARBARIZING	BARMINESSES
BAMBOOZLING	BANISTERED	BARBAROUSLY	BARMITSVAH
BANALISATION	BANJULELES	BARBAROUSNESS	BARMITSVAHS
BANALISATIONS	BANKABILITIES	BARBAROUSNESSES	BARMITZVAH
BANALISING	BANKABILITY	BARBASCOES	BARMITZVAHS
BANALITIES	BANKROLLED	BARBASTELLE	BARNBRACKS
BANALIZATION	BANKROLLER	BARBASTELLES	BARNSBREAKING
BANALIZATIONS	BANKROLLERS	BARBASTELS	BARNSBREAKINGS
BANALIZING	BANKROLLING	BARBECUERS	BARNSTORMED
BANCASSURANCE	BANKRUPTCIES	BARBECUING	BARNSTORMER
BANCASSURANCES	BANKRUPTCY	BARBELLATE	BARNSTORMERS
BANCASSURER	BANKRUPTED	BARBEQUING	BARNSTORMING
BANCASSURERS	BANKRUPTING	BARBERRIES	BARNSTORMINGS
BANDALORES	BANNERALLS	BARBERSHOP	BARNSTORMS
BANDBRAKES	BANNERETTE	BARBERSHOPS	BAROCEPTOR
BANDEIRANTE	BANNERETTES	BARBITONES	BAROCEPTORS
BANDEIRANTES	BANNISTERS	BARBITURATE	BARODYNAMICS
BANDELIERS	BANQUETEER	BARBITURATES	BAROGNOSES
BANDERILLA	BANQUETEERS	BARBITURIC	BAROGNOSIS
BANDERILLAS	BANQUETERS	BARBOTINES	BAROGRAPHIC
BANDERILLERO	BANQUETING	BARCAROLES	BAROGRAPHS
BANDERILLEROS	BANQUETINGS	BARCAROLLE	BAROMETERS
BANDEROLES	BANQUETTES	BARCAROLLES	BAROMETRIC
BANDERSNATCH	BANTAMWEIGHT	BARDOLATER	BAROMETRICAL
BANDERSNATCHES	BANTAMWEIGHTS	BARDOLATERS	BAROMETRICALLY
BANDICOOTED	BANTERINGLY	BARDOLATRIES	BAROMETRIES
BANDICOOTING	BANTERINGS	BARDOLATROUS	BAROMETZES

BARONESSES
BARONETAGE
BARONETAGES
BARONETCIES
BARONETESS
BARONETESSES
BARONETICAL
BAROPHILES
BAROPHILIC
BAROPHORESES
BAROPHORESIS
BARORECEPTOR
BARORECEPTORS
BAROSCOPES
BAROSCOPIC
BAROTRAUMA
BAROTRAUMAS
BAROTRAUMATA
BARPERSONS
BARQUANTINE
BARQUANTINES
BARQUENTINE
BARQUENTINES
BARQUETTES
BARRACKERS
BARRACKING
BARRACKINGS
BARRACOONS
BARRACOOTA
BARRACOOTAS
BARRACOUTA
BARRACOUTAS
BARRACUDAS
BARRAMUNDA
BARRAMUNDAS
BARRAMUNDI
BARRAMUNDIES
BARRAMUNDIS
BARRATRIES
BARRATROUS
BARRATROUSLY
BARRELAGES
BARRELFULS
BARRELHEAD
BARRELHEADS
BARRELHOUSE
BARRELHOUSES
BARRELLING
BARRELSFUL
BARRENNESS
BARRENNESSES
BARRENWORT
BARRENWORTS
BARRETRIES
BARRETROUS
BARRETROUSLY
BARRETTERS
BARRICADED

BARRICADER
BARRICADERS
BARRICADES
BARRICADING
BARRICADOED
BARRICADOES
BARRICADOING
BARRICADOS
BARRIERING
BARRISTERIAL
BARRISTERS
BARRISTERSHIP
BARRISTERSHIPS
BARROWFULS
BARTENDERS
BARTENDING
BARTIZANED
BARYCENTRE
BARYCENTRES
BARYCENTRIC
BARYSPHERE
BARYSPHERES
BASALTWARE
BASALTWARES
BASEBALLER
BASEBALLERS
BASEBOARDS
BASEBURNER
BASEBURNERS
BASELESSLY
BASELESSNESS
BASELESSNESSES
BASELINERS
BASEMENTLESS
BASENESSES
BASEPLATES
BASERUNNER
BASERUNNERS
BASERUNNING
BASERUNNINGS
BASHAWISMS
BASHAWSHIP
BASHAWSHIPS
BASHFULNESS
BASHFULNESSES
BASHIBAZOUK
BASHIBAZOUKS
BASICITIES
BASICRANIAL
BASIDIOCARP
BASIDIOCARPS
BASIDIOMYCETE
BASIDIOMYCETES
BASIDIOMYCETOUS
BASIDIOSPORE
BASIDIOSPORES
BASIDIOSPOROUS
BASIFICATION

BASIFICATIONS
BASILICONS
BASIPETALLY
BASKETBALL
BASKETBALLS
BASKETFULS
BASKETLIKE
BASKETRIES
BASKETSFUL
BASKETWEAVE
BASKETWEAVER
BASKETWEAVERS
BASKETWEAVES
BASKETWORK
BASKETWORKS
BASMITZVAH
BASMITZVAHS
BASOPHILES
BASOPHILIA
BASOPHILIAS
BASOPHILIC
BASSETTING
BASSNESSES
BASSOONIST
BASSOONISTS
BASTARDIES
BASTARDISATION
BASTARDISATIONS
BASTARDISE
BASTARDISED
BASTARDISES
BASTARDISING
BASTARDISM
BASTARDISMS
BASTARDIZATION
BASTARDIZATIONS
BASTARDIZE
BASTARDIZED
BASTARDIZES
BASTARDIZING
BASTARDRIES
BASTINADED
BASTINADES
BASTINADING
BASTINADOED
BASTINADOES
BASTINADOING
BASTNAESITE
BASTNAESITES
BASTNASITE
BASTNASITES
BATFOWLERS
BATFOWLING
BATFOWLINGS
BATHETICALLY
BATHHOUSES
BATHMITSVAH
BATHMITSVAHS

BATHMITZVAH
BATHMITZVAHS
BATHMIZVAH
BATHMIZVAHS
BATHOCHROME
BATHOCHROMES
BATHOCHROMIC
BATHOLITES
BATHOLITHIC
BATHOLITHS
BATHOLITIC
BATHOMETER
BATHOMETERS
BATHOMETRIC
BATHOMETRICALLY
BATHOMETRIES
BATHOMETRY
BATHOPHILOUS
BATHOPHOBIA
BATHOPHOBIAS
BATHWATERS
BATHYBIUSES
BATHYGRAPHICAL
BATHYLIMNETIC
BATHYLITES
BATHYLITHIC
BATHYLITHS
BATHYLITIC
BATHYMETER
BATHYMETERS
BATHYMETRIC
BATHYMETRICAL
BATHYMETRICALLY
BATHYMETRIES
BATHYMETRY
BATHYPELAGIC
BATHYSCAPE
BATHYSCAPES
BATHYSCAPH
BATHYSCAPHE
BATHYSCAPHES
BATHYSCAPHS
BATHYSPHERE
BATHYSPHERES
BATMITZVAH
BATMITZVAHS
BATOLOGICAL
BATOLOGIES
BATOLOGIST
BATOLOGISTS
BATRACHIAN
BATRACHIANS
BATRACHOPHOBIA
BATRACHOPHOBIAS
BATRACHOPHOBIC
BATSMANSHIP
BATSMANSHIPS
BATTAILOUS

BATTALIONS	BEACHGOERS	BEAUTIFICATIONS	BEDEHOUSES
BATTEILANT	BEACHHEADS	BEAUTIFIED	BEDELLSHIP
BATTELLING	BEADBLASTED	BEAUTIFIER	BEDELLSHIPS
BATTEMENTS	BEADBLASTER	BEAUTIFIERS	BEDELSHIPS
BATTENINGS	BEADBLASTERS	BEAUTIFIES	BEDEVILING
BATTERINGS	BEADBLASTING	BEAUTIFULLER	BEDEVILLED
BATTILLING	BEADBLASTS	BEAUTIFULLEST	BEDEVILLING
BATTINESSES	BEADHOUSES	BEAUTIFULLY	BEDEVILMENT
BATTLEBUSES	BEADINESSES	BEAUTIFULNESS	BEDEVILMENTS
BATTLEBUSSES	BEADLEDOMS	BEAUTIFULNESSES	BEDFELLOWS
BATTLEDOOR	BEADLEHOOD	BEAUTIFYING	BEDIAPERED
BATTLEDOORS	BEADLEHOODS	BEAVERBOARD	BEDIAPERING
BATTLEDORE	BEADLESHIP	BEAVERBOARDS	BEDIGHTING
BATTLEDORES	BEADLESHIPS	BEBEERINES	BEDIMMINGS
BATTLEDRESS	BEADSWOMAN	BEBLOODING	BEDIMPLING
BATTLEDRESSES	BEADSWOMEN	BEBLUBBERED	BEDIRTYING
BATTLEFIELD	BEAMINESSES	BECARPETED	BEDIZENING
BATTLEFIELDS	BEANFEASTS	BECARPETING	BEDIZENMENT
BATTLEFRONT	BEANSTALKS	BECCACCIAS	BEDIZENMENTS
BATTLEFRONTS	BEARABILITIES	BECCAFICOS	BEDLAMISMS
BATTLEGROUND	BEARABILITY	BECHALKING	BEDLAMITES
BATTLEGROUNDS	BEARABLENESS	BECHANCING	BEDPRESSER
BATTLEMENT	BEARABLENESSES	BECHARMING	BEDPRESSERS
BATTLEMENTED	BEARBAITING	BECLAMORED	BEDRAGGLED
BATTLEMENTS	BEARBAITINGS	BECLAMORING	BEDRAGGLES
BATTLEPIECE	BEARBERRIES	BECLASPING	BEDRAGGLING
BATTLEPIECES	BEARDEDNESS	BECLOAKING	BEDRENCHED
BATTLEPLANE	BEARDEDNESSES	BECLOGGING	BEDRENCHES
BATTLEPLANES	BEARDLESSNESS	BECLOTHING	BEDRENCHING
BATTLESHIP	BEARDLESSNESSES	BECLOUDING	BEDRIVELED
BATTLESHIPS	BEARDTONGUE	BECLOWNING	BEDRIVELING
BATTLEWAGON	BEARDTONGUES	BECOMINGLY	BEDRIVELLED
BATTLEWAGONS	BEARGRASSES	BECOMINGNESS	BEDRIVELLING
BATTOLOGICAL	BEARISHNESS	BECOMINGNESSES	BEDROPPING
BATTOLOGIES	BEARISHNESSES	BECOWARDED	BEDRUGGING
BAUDRICKES	BEARNAISES	BECOWARDING	BEDSITTERS
BAUDRONSES	BEASTHOODS	BECQUERELS	BEDSITTING
BAULKINESS	BEASTLIEST	BECRAWLING	BEDSPREADS
BAULKINESSES	BEASTLINESS	BECROWDING	BEDSPRINGS
BAVARDAGES	BEASTLINESSES	BECRUSTING	BEDWARFING
BAVAROISES	BEATIFICAL	BECUDGELED	BEDWARMERS
BAWDINESSES	BEATIFICALLY	BECUDGELING	BEDWETTERS
BAWDYHOUSE	BEATIFICATION	BECUDGELLED	BEECHDROPS
BAWDYHOUSES	BEATIFICATIONS	BECUDGELLING	BEECHMASTS
BAYBERRIES	BEATIFYING	BEDABBLING	BEECHWOODS
BAYONETING	BEATITUDES	BEDAGGLING	BEEFBURGER
BAYONETTED	BEAUJOLAIS	BEDARKENED	BEEFBURGERS
BAYONETTING	BEAUJOLAISES	BEDARKENING	BEEFEATERS
BAZILLIONS	BEAUMONTAGE	BEDAZZLEMENT	BEEFINESSES
BEACHBALLS	BEAUMONTAGES	BEDAZZLEMENTS	BEEFSTEAKS
BEACHCOMBED	BEAUMONTAGUE	BEDAZZLING	BEEKEEPERS
BEACHCOMBER	BEAUMONTAGUES	BEDCHAMBER	BEEKEEPING
BEACHCOMBERS	BEAUTEOUSLY	BEDCHAMBERS	BEEKEEPINGS
BEACHCOMBING	BEAUTEOUSNESS	BEDCLOTHES	BEERINESSES
BEACHCOMBINGS	BEAUTEOUSNESSES	BEDCOVERING	BEESWAXING
BEACHCOMBS	BEAUTICIAN	BEDCOVERINGS	BEESWINGED
BEACHFRONT	BEAUTICIANS	BEDEAFENED	BEETLEBRAIN
BEACHFRONTS	BEAUTIFICATION	BEDEAFENING	BEETLEBRAINED

BEETLEBRAINS	BEGUILEMENTS	BELITTLING	BELTCOURSES
BEETLEHEAD	BEGUILINGLY	BELITTLINGLY	BELVEDERES
BEETLEHEADED	BEGUINAGES	BELLADONNA	BEMADAMING
BEETLEHEADS	BEHAPPENED	BELLADONNAS	BEMADDENED
BEETMASTER	BEHAPPENING	BELLAMOURE	BEMADDENING
BEETMASTERS	BEHAVIORAL	BELLAMOURES	BEMEDALLED
BEETMISTER	BEHAVIORALLY	BELLARMINE	BEMEDALLING
BEETMISTERS	BEHAVIORISM	BELLARMINES	BEMINGLING
BEFINGERED	BEHAVIORISMS	BELLETRISM	BEMOANINGS
BEFINGERING	BEHAVIORIST	BELLETRISMS	BEMONSTERED
BEFITTINGLY	BEHAVIORISTIC	BELLETRIST	BEMONSTERING
BEFLAGGING	BEHAVIORISTS	BELLETRISTIC	BEMONSTERS
BEFLECKING	BEHAVIOURAL	BELLETRISTICAL	BEMOUTHING
BEFLOWERED	BEHAVIOURALLY	BELLETRISTS	BEMUDDLING
BEFLOWERING	BEHAVIOURISM	BELLETTRIST	BEMUFFLING
BEFLUMMING	BEHAVIOURISMS	BELLETTRISTS	BEMURMURED
BEFOREHAND	BEHAVIOURIST	BELLFLOWER	BEMURMURING
BEFORETIME	BEHAVIOURISTIC	BELLFLOWERS	BEMUSEMENT
BEFORTUNED	BEHAVIOURISTS	BELLFOUNDER	BEMUSEMENTS
BEFORTUNES	BEHAVIOURS	BELLFOUNDERS	BEMUZZLING
BEFORTUNING	BEHEADINGS	BELLFOUNDRIES	BENCHERSHIP
BEFOULMENT	BEHIGHTING	BELLFOUNDRY	BENCHERSHIPS
BEFOULMENTS	BEHINDHAND	BELLHANGER	BENCHLANDS
BEFRETTING	BEHOLDINGS	BELLHANGERS	BENCHMARKED
BEFRIENDED	BEINGNESSES	BELLIBONES	BENCHMARKING
BEFRIENDER	BEINNESSES	BELLICOSELY	BENCHMARKINGS
BEFRIENDERS	BEJESUITED	BELLICOSITIES	BENCHMARKS
BEFRIENDING	BEJESUITING	BELLICOSITY	BENCHWARMER
BEFRINGING	BEJEWELING	BELLIGERATI	BENCHWARMERS
BEFUDDLEMENT	BEJEWELLED	BELLIGERENCE	BENEDICITE
BEFUDDLEMENTS	BEJEWELLING	BELLIGERENCES	BENEDICITES
BEFUDDLING	BEJUMBLING	BELLIGERENCIES	BENEDICTION
BEGGARDOMS	BEKNIGHTED	BELLIGERENCY	BENEDICTIONAL
BEGGARHOOD	BEKNIGHTING	BELLIGERENT	BENEDICTIONS
BEGGARHOODS	BEKNOTTING	BELLIGERENTLY	BENEDICTIVE
BEGGARLINESS	BELABORING	BELLIGERENTS	BENEDICTORY
BEGGARLINESSES	BELABOURED	BELLOCKING	BENEDICTUS
BEGGARWEED	BELABOURING	BELLPUSHES	BENEDICTUSES
BEGGARWEEDS	BELAMOURES	BELLWETHER	BENEFACTED
BEGINNINGLESS	BELATEDNESS	BELLWETHERS	BENEFACTING
BEGINNINGS	BELATEDNESSES	BELLYACHED	BENEFACTION
BEGIRDLING	BELEAGUERED	BELLYACHER	BENEFACTIONS
BEGLADDING	BELEAGUERING	BELLYACHERS	BENEFACTOR
BEGLAMORED	BELEAGUERMENT	BELLYACHES	BENEFACTORS
BEGLAMORING	BELEAGUERMENTS	BELLYACHING	BENEFACTORY
BEGLAMOURED	BELEAGUERS	BELLYBANDS	BENEFACTRESS
BEGLAMOURING	BELEMNITES	BELLYBUTTON	BENEFACTRESSES
BEGLAMOURS	BELIEFLESS	BELLYBUTTONS	BENEFICENCE
BEGLERBEGS	BELIEVABILITIES	BELOMANCIES	BENEFICENCES
BEGLOOMING	BELIEVABILITY	BELONGINGNESS	BENEFICENT
BEGRIMMING	BELIEVABLE	BELONGINGNESSES	BENEFICENTIAL
BEGROANING	BELIEVABLY	BELONGINGS	BENEFICENTLY
BEGRUDGERIES	BELIEVINGLY	BELOWDECKS	BENEFICIAL
BEGRUDGERS	BELIQUORED	BELOWGROUND	BENEFICIALLY
BEGRUDGERY	BELIQUORING	BELOWSTAIRS	BENEFICIALNESS
BEGRUDGING	BELITTLEMENT	BELSHAZZAR	BENEFICIALS
BEGRUDGINGLY	BELITTLEMENTS	BELSHAZZARS	BENEFICIARIES
BEGUILEMENT	BELITTLERS	BELTCOURSE	BENEFICIARY

BENEFICIATE
BENEFICIATED
BENEFICIATES
BENEFICIATING
BENEFICIATION
BENEFICIATIONS
BENEFICING
BENEFITERS
BENEFITING
BENEFITTED
BENEFITTING
BENEPLACITO
BENEVOLENCE
BENEVOLENCES
BENEVOLENT
BENEVOLENTLY
BENEVOLENTNESS
BENGALINES
BENIGHTEDLY
BENIGHTEDNESS
BENIGHTEDNESSES
BENIGHTENED
BENIGHTENING
BENIGHTENINGS
BENIGHTENS
BENIGHTERS
BENIGHTING
BENIGHTINGS
BENIGHTMENT
BENIGHTMENTS
BENIGNANCIES
BENIGNANCY
BENIGNANTLY
BENIGNITIES
BENTGRASSES
BENTHOPELAGIC
BENTHOSCOPE
BENTHOSCOPES
BENTONITES
BENTONITIC
BENUMBEDNESS
BENUMBEDNESSES
BENUMBINGLY
BENUMBMENT
BENUMBMENTS
BENZALDEHYDE
BENZALDEHYDES
BENZANTHRACENE
BENZANTHRACENES
BENZENECARBONYL
BENZENOIDS
BENZIDINES
BENZIMIDAZOLE
BENZIMIDAZOLES
BENZOAPYRENE
BENZOAPYRENES
BENZOCAINE
BENZOCAINES

BENZODIAZEPINE
BENZODIAZEPINES
BENZOFURAN
BENZOFURANS
BENZOLINES
BENZOPHENONE
BENZOPHENONES
BENZOQUINONE
BENZOQUINONES
BENZPYRENE
BENZPYRENES
BENZYLIDINE
BENZYLIDINES
BEPAINTING
BEPEARLING
BEPEPPERED
BEPEPPERING
BEPESTERED
BEPESTERING
BEPIMPLING
BEPLASTERED
BEPLASTERING
BEPLASTERS
BEPOMMELLED
BEPOMMELLING
BEPOWDERED
BEPOWDERING
BEPRAISING
BEQUEATHABLE
BEQUEATHAL
BEQUEATHALS
BEQUEATHED
BEQUEATHER
BEQUEATHERS
BEQUEATHING
BEQUEATHMENT
BEQUEATHMENTS
BERASCALED
BERASCALING
BERBERIDACEOUS
BERBERINES
BERBERISES
BEREAVEMENT
BEREAVEMENTS
BERGAMASKS
BERGANDERS
BERGOMASKS
BERGSCHRUND
BERGSCHRUNDS
BERIBBONED
BERKELIUMS
BERRYFRUIT
BERRYFRUITS
BERSAGLIERE
BERSAGLIERI
BERSERKERS
BERTILLONAGE
BERTILLONAGES

BERYLLIOSES
BERYLLIOSIS
BERYLLIUMS
BESAINTING
BESCATTERED
BESCATTERING
BESCATTERS
BESCORCHED
BESCORCHES
BESCORCHING
BESCOURING
BESCRAWLED
BESCRAWLING
BESCREENED
BESCREENING
BESCRIBBLE
BESCRIBBLED
BESCRIBBLES
BESCRIBBLING
BESEECHERS
BESEECHING
BESEECHINGLY
BESEECHINGNESS
BESEECHINGS
BESEEMINGLY
BESEEMINGNESS
BESEEMINGNESSES
BESEEMINGS
BESETMENTS
BESHADOWED
BESHADOWING
BESHIVERED
BESHIVERING
BESHOUTING
BESHREWING
BESHROUDED
BESHROUDING
BESIEGEMENT
BESIEGEMENTS
BESIEGINGLY
BESIEGINGS
BESLAVERED
BESLAVERING
BESLOBBERED
BESLOBBERING
BESLOBBERS
BESLUBBERED
BESLUBBERING
BESLUBBERS
BESMEARERS
BESMEARING
BESMIRCHED
BESMIRCHES
BESMIRCHING
BESMOOTHED
BESMOOTHING
BESMUDGING
BESMUTCHED

BESMUTCHES
BESMUTCHING
BESMUTTING
BESOOTHING
BESOTTEDLY
BESOTTEDNESS
BESOTTEDNESSES
BESPANGLED
BESPANGLES
BESPANGLING
BESPATTERED
BESPATTERING
BESPATTERS
BESPEAKING
BESPECKLED
BESPECKLES
BESPECKLING
BESPECTACLED
BESPEEDING
BESPITTING
BESPORTING
BESPOTTEDNESS
BESPOTTEDNESSES
BESPOTTING
BESPOUSING
BESPOUTING
BESPREADING
BESPRINKLE
BESPRINKLED
BESPRINKLES
BESPRINKLING
BESTAINING
BESTARRING
BESTEADING
BESTIALISE
BESTIALISED
BESTIALISES
BESTIALISING
BESTIALISM
BESTIALISMS
BESTIALITIES
BESTIALITY
BESTIALIZE
BESTIALIZED
BESTIALIZES
BESTIALIZING
BESTIARIES
BESTICKING
BESTILLING
BESTIRRING
BESTORMING
BESTOWMENT
BESTOWMENTS
BESTRADDLE
BESTRADDLED
BESTRADDLES
BESTRADDLING
BESTRAUGHT

BESTREAKED
BESTREAKING
BESTREWING
BESTRIDABLE
BESTRIDDEN
BESTRIDING
BESTROWING
BESTSELLER
BESTSELLERDOM
BESTSELLERDOMS
BESTSELLERS
BESTSELLING
BESTUDDING
BESWARMING
BETACAROTENE
BETACAROTENES
BETACYANIN
BETACYANINS
BETATTERED
BETATTERING
BETHANKING
BETHANKITS
BETHINKING
BETHORNING
BETHRALLED
BETHRALLING
BETHUMBING
BETHUMPING
BETHWACKED
BETHWACKING
BETOKENING
BETREADING
BETRIMMING
BETROTHALS
BETROTHEDS
BETROTHING
BETROTHMENT
BETROTHMENTS
BETTERINGS
BETTERMENT
BETTERMENTS
BETTERMOST
BETTERNESS
BETTERNESSES
BETULACEOUS
BETWEENBRAIN
BETWEENBRAINS
BETWEENITIES
BETWEENITY
BETWEENNESS
BETWEENNESSES
BETWEENTIME
BETWEENTIMES
BETWEENWHILES
BEVELLINGS
BEVELMENTS
BEVOMITING
BEWAILINGLY

BEWAILINGS
BEWEARYING
BEWELTERED
BEWHISKERED
BEWILDERED
BEWILDEREDLY
BEWILDEREDNESS
BEWILDERING
BEWILDERINGLY
BEWILDERMENT
BEWILDERMENTS
BEWITCHERIES
BEWITCHERS
BEWITCHERY
BEWITCHING
BEWITCHINGLY
BEWITCHMENT
BEWITCHMENTS
BEWORRYING
BEWRAPPING
BHIKKHUNIS
BIANNUALLY
BIANNULATE
BIASNESSES
BIATHLETES
BIAURICULAR
BIAURICULATE
BIBLICALLY
BIBLICISMS
BIBLICISTS
BIBLIOGRAPHER
BIBLIOGRAPHERS
BIBLIOGRAPHIC
BIBLIOGRAPHICAL
BIBLIOGRAPHIES
BIBLIOGRAPHY
BIBLIOLATER
BIBLIOLATERS
BIBLIOLATRIES
BIBLIOLATRIST
BIBLIOLATRISTS
BIBLIOLATROUS
BIBLIOLATRY
BIBLIOLOGICAL
BIBLIOLOGIES
BIBLIOLOGIST
BIBLIOLOGISTS
BIBLIOLOGY
BIBLIOMANCIES
BIBLIOMANCY
BIBLIOMANE
BIBLIOMANES
BIBLIOMANIA
BIBLIOMANIAC
BIBLIOMANIACAL
BIBLIOMANIACS
BIBLIOMANIAS
BIBLIOPEGIC

BIBLIOPEGIES
BIBLIOPEGIST
BIBLIOPEGISTS
BIBLIOPEGY
BIBLIOPHAGIST
BIBLIOPHAGISTS
BIBLIOPHIL
BIBLIOPHILE
BIBLIOPHILES
BIBLIOPHILIC
BIBLIOPHILIES
BIBLIOPHILISM
BIBLIOPHILISMS
BIBLIOPHILIST
BIBLIOPHILISTIC
BIBLIOPHILISTS
BIBLIOPHILS
BIBLIOPHILY
BIBLIOPHOBIA
BIBLIOPHOBIAS
BIBLIOPOLE
BIBLIOPOLES
BIBLIOPOLIC
BIBLIOPOLICAL
BIBLIOPOLIES
BIBLIOPOLIST
BIBLIOPOLISTS
BIBLIOPOLY
BIBLIOTHECA
BIBLIOTHECAE
BIBLIOTHECAL
BIBLIOTHECARIES
BIBLIOTHECARY
BIBLIOTHECAS
BIBLIOTHERAPIES
BIBLIOTHERAPY
BIBLIOTICS
BIBLIOTIST
BIBLIOTISTS
BIBULOUSLY
BIBULOUSNESS
BIBULOUSNESSES
BICAMERALISM
BICAMERALISMS
BICAMERALIST
BICAMERALISTS
BICAPSULAR
BICARBONATE
BICARBONATES
BICARPELLARY
BICENTENARIES
BICENTENARY
BICENTENNIAL
BICENTENNIALS
BICEPHALOUS
BICHLORIDE
BICHLORIDES
BICHROMATE

BICHROMATED
BICHROMATES
BICKERINGS
BICOLLATERAL
BICOLOURED
BICOMPONENT
BICONCAVITIES
BICONCAVITY
BICONDITIONAL
BICONDITIONALS
BICONVEXITIES
BICONVEXITY
BICORNUATE
BICORPORATE
BICULTURAL
BICULTURALISM
BICULTURALISMS
BICUSPIDATE
BICUSPIDATES
BICYCLICAL
BICYCLISTS
BIDDABILITIES
BIDDABILITY
BIDDABLENESS
BIDDABLENESSES
BIDENTATED
BIDIALECTAL
BIDIALECTALISM
BIDIALECTALISMS
BIDIRECTIONAL
BIDIRECTIONALLY
BIDONVILLE
BIDONVILLES
BIENNIALLY
BIENSEANCE
BIENSEANCES
BIERKELLER
BIERKELLERS
BIFACIALLY
BIFARIOUSLY
BIFIDITIES
BIFLAGELLATE
BIFOLIOLATE
BIFUNCTIONAL
BIFURCATED
BIFURCATES
BIFURCATING
BIFURCATION
BIFURCATIONS
BIGAMOUSLY
BIGARREAUS
BIGEMINIES
BIGFOOTING
BIGHEADEDLY
BIGHEADEDNESS
BIGHEADEDNESSES
BIGHEARTED
BIGHEARTEDLY

BIGHEARTEDNESS
BIGMOUTHED
BIGNONIACEOUS
BIGUANIDES
BIJECTIONS
BIJOUTERIE
BIJOUTERIES
BILATERALISM
BILATERALISMS
BILATERALLY
BILBERRIES
BILDUNGSROMAN
BILDUNGSROMANS
BILECTIONS
BILESTONES
BILGEWATER
BILGEWATERS
BILHARZIAL
BILHARZIAS
BILHARZIASES
BILHARZIASIS
BILHARZIOSES
BILHARZIOSIS
BILIMBINGS
BILINGUALISM
BILINGUALISMS
BILINGUALLY
BILINGUALS
BILINGUIST
BILINGUISTS
BILIOUSNESS
BILIOUSNESSES
BILIRUBINS
BILIVERDIN
BILIVERDINS
BILLABONGS
BILLBOARDED
BILLBOARDING
BILLBOARDS
BILLFISHES
BILLINGSGATE
BILLINGSGATES
BILLIONAIRE
BILLIONAIRES
BILLIONTHS
BILLOWIEST
BILLOWINESS
BILLOWINESSES
BILLPOSTER
BILLPOSTERS
BILLPOSTING
BILLPOSTINGS
BILLSTICKER
BILLSTICKERS
BILLSTICKING
BILLSTICKINGS
BILLYCOCKS
BILOCATION

BILOCATIONS
BILOCULATE
BIMANUALLY
BIMESTRIAL
BIMESTRIALLY
BIMETALLIC
BIMETALLICS
BIMETALLISM
BIMETALLISMS
BIMETALLIST
BIMETALLISTIC
BIMETALLISTS
BIMILLENARIES
BIMILLENARY
BIMILLENNIA
BIMILLENNIAL
BIMILLENNIALS
BIMILLENNIUM
BIMILLENNIUMS
BIMODALITIES
BIMODALITY
BIMOLECULAR
BIMOLECULARLY
BIMONTHLIES
BIMORPHEMIC
BINATIONAL
BINAURALLY
BINDINGNESS
BINDINGNESSES
BINOCULARITIES
BINOCULARITY
BINOCULARLY
BINOCULARS
BINOMIALLY
BINOMINALS
BINTURONGS
BINUCLEATE
BINUCLEATED
BIOACCUMULATE
BIOACCUMULATED
BIOACCUMULATES
BIOACCUMULATING
BIOACCUMULATION
BIOACOUSTICS
BIOACTIVITIES
BIOACTIVITY
BIOAERATION
BIOAERATIONS
BIOAERONAUTICS
BIOASSAYED
BIOASSAYING
BIOASTRONAUTICS
BIOAVAILABILITY
BIOAVAILABLE
BIOCATALYST
BIOCATALYSTS
BIOCATALYTIC
BIOCELLATE

BIOCENOLOGIES
BIOCENOLOGY
BIOCENOSES
BIOCENOSIS
BIOCENOTIC
BIOCHEMICAL
BIOCHEMICALLY
BIOCHEMICALS
BIOCHEMIST
BIOCHEMISTRIES
BIOCHEMISTRY
BIOCHEMISTS
BIOCLASTIC
BIOCLIMATIC
BIOCLIMATOLOGY
BIOCOENOLOGIES
BIOCOENOLOGY
BIOCOENOSES
BIOCOENOSIS
BIOCOENOTIC
BIOCOMPATIBLE
BIOCOMPUTING
BIOCOMPUTINGS
BIOCONTROL
BIOCONTROLS
BIOCONVERSION
BIOCONVERSIONS
BIODEGRADABLE
BIODEGRADATION
BIODEGRADATIONS
BIODEGRADE
BIODEGRADED
BIODEGRADES
BIODEGRADING
BIODESTRUCTIBLE
BIODIESELS
BIODIVERSITIES
BIODIVERSITY
BIODYNAMIC
BIODYNAMICAL
BIODYNAMICS
BIOECOLOGICAL
BIOECOLOGICALLY
BIOECOLOGIES
BIOECOLOGIST
BIOECOLOGISTS
BIOECOLOGY
BIOELECTRIC
BIOELECTRICAL
BIOELECTRICITY
BIOENERGETIC
BIOENERGETICS
BIOENGINEER
BIOENGINEERED
BIOENGINEERING
BIOENGINEERINGS
BIOENGINEERS
BIOETHICAL

BIOETHICIST
BIOETHICISTS
BIOFEEDBACK
BIOFEEDBACKS
BIOFLAVONOID
BIOFLAVONOIDS
BIOFOULERS
BIOFOULING
BIOFOULINGS
BIOGENESES
BIOGENESIS
BIOGENETIC
BIOGENETICAL
BIOGENETICALLY
BIOGENETICS
BIOGEOCHEMICAL
BIOGEOCHEMICALS
BIOGEOCHEMISTRY
BIOGEOGRAPHER
BIOGEOGRAPHERS
BIOGEOGRAPHIC
BIOGEOGRAPHICAL
BIOGEOGRAPHIES
BIOGEOGRAPHY
BIOGRAPHED
BIOGRAPHEE
BIOGRAPHEES
BIOGRAPHER
BIOGRAPHERS
BIOGRAPHIC
BIOGRAPHICAL
BIOGRAPHICALLY
BIOGRAPHIES
BIOGRAPHING
BIOGRAPHISE
BIOGRAPHISED
BIOGRAPHISES
BIOGRAPHISING
BIOGRAPHIZE
BIOGRAPHIZED
BIOGRAPHIZES
BIOGRAPHIZING
BIOHAZARDOUS
BIOHAZARDS
BIOINDUSTRIES
BIOINDUSTRY
BIOINFORMATICS
BIOLOGICAL
BIOLOGICALLY
BIOLOGICALS
BIOLOGISMS
BIOLOGISTIC
BIOLOGISTS
BIOLUMINESCENCE
BIOLUMINESCENT
BIOMAGNETICS
BIOMARKERS
BIOMATERIAL

BIOMATERIALS	BIOREMEDIATION	BIPEDALISM	BIRTHRATES
BIOMATHEMATICAL	BIOREMEDIATIONS	BIPEDALISMS	BIRTHRIGHT
BIOMATHEMATICS	BIORHYTHMIC	BIPEDALITIES	BIRTHRIGHTS
BIOMECHANICAL	BIORHYTHMICALLY	BIPEDALTTY	BIRTHROOTS
BIOMECHANICALLY	BIORHYTHMICS	BIPETALOUS	BIRTHSTONE
BIOMECHANICS	BIORHYTHMS	BIPINNARIA	BIRTHSTONES
BIOMEDICAL	BIOSAFETIES	BIPINNARIAS	BIRTHWORTS
BIOMEDICINE	BIOSATELLITE	BIPINNATELY	BISECTIONAL
BIOMEDICINES	BIOSATELLITES	BIPOLARISATION	BISECTIONALLY
BIOMETEOROLOGY	BIOSCIENCE	BIPOLARISATIONS	BISECTIONS
BIOMETRICAL	BIOSCIENCES	BIPOLARISE	BISECTRICES
BIOMETRICALLY	BIOSCIENTIFIC	BIPOLARISED	BISEXUALISM
BIOMETRICIAN	BIOSCIENTIST	BIPOLARISES	BISEXUALISMS
BIOMETRICIANS	BIOSCIENTISTS	BIPOLARISING	BISEXUALITIES
BIOMETRICS	BIOSCOPIES	BIPOLARITIES	BISEXUALITY
BIOMETRIES	BIOSENSORS	BIPOLARITY	BISEXUALLY
BIOMIMETIC	BIOSOCIALLY	BIPOLARIZATION	BISHOPBIRD
BIOMIMETICS	BIOSPHERES	BIPOLARIZATIONS	BISHOPBIRDS
BIOMIMICRIES	BIOSPHERIC	BIPOLARIZE	BISHOPDOMS
BIOMIMICRY	BIOSTATICALLY	BIPOLARIZED	BISHOPESSES
BIOMININGS	BIOSTATICS ·	BIPOLARIZES	BISHOPRICS
BIOMOLECULAR	BIOSTATISTICAL	BIPOLARIZING	BISHOPWEED
BIOMOLECULE	BIOSTATISTICIAN	BIPROPELLANT	BISHOPWEEDS
BIOMOLECULES	BIOSTATISTICS	BIPROPELLANTS	BISMUTHINITE
BIOMORPHIC	BIOSTRATIGRAPHY	BIPYRAMIDAL	BISMUTHINITES
BIONOMICALLY	BIOSTROMES	BIPYRAMIDS	BISMUTHOUS
BIONOMISTS	BIOSURGERIES	BIQUADRATE	BISOCIATION
BIOPARENTS	BIOSURGERY	BIQUADRATES	BISOCIATIONS
BIOPESTICIDAL	BIOSYNTHESES	BIQUADRATIC	BISOCIATIVE
BIOPESTICIDE	BIOSYNTHESIS	BIQUADRATICS	BISPHOSPHONATE
BIOPESTICIDES	BIOSYNTHETIC	BIQUARTERLY	BISPHOSPHONATES
BIOPHILIAS	BIOSYSTEMATIC	BIQUINTILE	BISSEXTILE
BIOPHYSICAL	BIOSYSTEMATICS	BIQUINTILES	BISSEXTILES
BIOPHYSICALLY	BIOSYSTEMATIST	BIRACIALISM	BISTOURIES
BIOPHYSICIST	BIOSYSTEMATISTS	BIRACIALISMS	BISULFATES
BIOPHYSICISTS	BIOTECHNICAL	BIRACIALLY	BISULFIDES
BIOPHYSICS	BIOTECHNOLOGIES	BIRADICALS	BISULFITES
BIOPIRACIES	BIOTECHNOLOGIST	BIRDBRAINED	BISULPHATE
BIOPIRATES	BIOTECHNOLOGY	BIRDBRAINS	BISULPHATES
BIOPLASMIC	BIOTELEMETRIC	BIRDDOGGED	BISULPHIDE
BIOPOIESES	BIOTELEMETRIES	BIRDDOGGING	BISULPHIDES
BIOPOIESIS	BIOTELEMETRY	BIRDHOUSES	BISULPHITE
BIOPOLYMER	BIOTERRORS	BIRDLIMING	BISULPHITES
BIOPOLYMERS	BIOTICALLY	BIRDWATCHED	BISYMMETRIC
BIOPROSPECTING	BIOTURBATION	BIRDWATCHER	BISYMMETRICAL
BIOPROSPECTINGS	BIOTURBATIONS	BIRDWATCHERS	BISYMMETRICALLY
BIOPSYCHOLOGIES	BIOWEAPONS	BIRDWATCHES	BISYMMETRIES
BIOPSYCHOLOGY	BIPARENTAL	BIRDWATCHING	BISYMMETRY
BIOREACTOR	BIPARENTALLY	BIREFRINGENCE	BITARTRATE
BIOREACTORS	BIPARIETAL	BIREFRINGENCES	BITARTRATES
BIOREAGENT	BIPARTISAN	BIREFRINGENT	BITCHERIES
BIOREAGENTS	BIPARTISANISM	BIROSTRATE	BITCHFESTS
BIOREGIONAL	BIPARTISANISMS	BIRTHMARKS	BITCHINESS
BIOREGIONALISM	BIPARTISANSHIP	BIRTHNAMES	BITCHINESSES
BIOREGIONALISMS	BIPARTISANSHIPS	BIRTHNIGHT	BITEPLATES
BIOREGIONALIST	BIPARTITELY	BIRTHNIGHTS	BITMAPPING
BIOREGIONALISTS	BIPARTITION	BIRTHPLACE	BITONALITIES
BIOREGIONS	BIPARTITIONS	BIRTHPLACES	BITONALITY

BITSTREAMS	BLACKAMOORS	BLACKLISTING	BLANDISHES
BITTERBARK	BLACKBALLED	BLACKLISTINGS	BLANDISHING
BITTERBARKS	BLACKBALLING	BLACKLISTS	BLANDISHMENT
BITTERBRUSH	BLACKBALLINGS	BLACKMAILED	BLANDISHMENTS
BITTERBRUSHES	BLACKBALLS	BLACKMAILER	BLANDNESSES
BITTERCRESS	BLACKBANDS	BLACKMAILERS	BLANKETFLOWER
BITTERCRESSES	BLACKBERRIED	BLACKMAILING	BLANKETFLOWERS
BITTERLING	BLACKBERRIES	BLACKMAILS	BLANKETIES
BITTERLINGS	BLACKBERRY	BLACKNESSES	BLANKETING
BITTERNESS	BLACKBERRYING	BLACKPOLLS	BLANKETINGS
BITTERNESSES	BLACKBERRYINGS	BLACKSMITH	BLANKETLIKE
BITTERNUTS	BLACKBIRDED	BLACKSMITHING	BLANKETWEED
BITTERROOT	BLACKBIRDER	BLACKSMITHINGS	BLANKETWEEDS
BITTERROOTS	BLACKBIRDERS	BLACKSMITHS	BLANKNESSES
BITTERSWEET	BLACKBIRDING	BLACKSNAKE	BLANQUETTE
BITTERSWEETLY	BLACKBIRDINGS	BLACKSNAKES	BLANQUETTES
BITTERSWEETNESS	BLACKBIRDS	BLACKSTRAP	BLARNEYING
BITTERSWEETS	BLACKBOARD	BLACKTAILS	BLASPHEMED
BITTERWEED	BLACKBOARDS	BLACKTHORN	BLASPHEMER
BITTERWEEDS	BLACKBODIES	BLACKTHORNS	BLASPHEMERS
BITTERWOOD	BLACKBUCKS	BLACKTOPPED	BLASPHEMES
BITTERWOODS	BLACKBUTTS	BLACKTOPPING	BLASPHEMIES
BITTINESSES	BLACKCOCKS	BLACKWASHED	BLASPHEMING
BITUMINATE	BLACKCURRANT	BLACKWASHES	BLASPHEMOUS
BITUMINATED	BLACKCURRANTS	BLACKWASHING	BLASPHEMOUSLY
BITUMINATES	BLACKDAMPS	BLACKWATER	BLASPHEMOUSNESS
BITUMINATING	BLACKENERS	BLACKWATERS	BLASTEMATA
BITUMINISATION	BLACKENING	BLACKWOODS	BLASTEMATIC
BITUMINISATIONS	BLACKENINGS	BLADDERLIKE	BLASTMENTS
BITUMINISE	BLACKFACED	BLADDERNOSE	BLASTOCHYLE
BITUMINISED	BLACKFACES	BLADDERNOSES	BLASTOCHYLES
BITUMINISES	BLACKFISHES	BLADDERNUT	BLASTOCOEL
BITUMINISING	BLACKFLIES	BLADDERNUTS	BLASTOCOELE
BITUMINIZATION	BLACKGAMES	BLADDERWORT	BLASTOCOELES
BITUMINIZATIONS	BLACKGUARD	BLADDERWORTS	BLASTOCOELIC
BITUMINIZE	BLACKGUARDED	BLADDERWRACK	BLASTOCOELS
BITUMINIZED	BLACKGUARDING	BLADDERWRACKS	BLASTOCYST
BITUMINIZES	BLACKGUARDISM	BLADEWORKS	BLASTOCYSTS
BITUMINIZING	BLACKGUARDISMS	BLAEBERRIES	BLASTODERM
BITUMINOUS	BLACKGUARDLY	BLAMABLENESS	BLASTODERMIC
BIUNIQUENESS	BLACKGUARDS	BLAMABLENESSES	BLASTODERMS
BIUNIQUENESSES	BLACKHANDER	BLAMEABLENESS	BLASTODISC
BIVALENCES	BLACKHANDERS	BLAMEABLENESSES	BLASTODISCS
BIVALENCIES	BLACKHEADED	BLAMEFULLY	BLASTOGENESES
BIVALVULAR	BLACKHEADS	BLAMEFULNESS	BLASTOGENESIS
BIVARIANTS	BLACKHEART	BLAMEFULNESSES	BLASTOGENETIC
BIVARIATES	BLACKHEARTS	BLAMELESSLY	BLASTOGENIC
BIVOUACKED	BLACKISHLY	BLAMELESSNESS	BLASTOMATA
BIVOUACKING	BLACKJACKED	BLAMELESSNESSES	BLASTOMERE
BIWEEKLIES	BLACKJACKING	BLAMEWORTHINESS	BLASTOMERES
BIZARRENESS	BLACKJACKS	BLAMEWORTHY	BLASTOMERIC
BIZARRENESSES	BLACKLANDS	BLANCHISSEUSE	BLASTOMYCOSES
BIZARRERIE	BLACKLEADS	BLANCHISSEUSES	BLASTOMYCOSIS
BIZARRERIES	BLACKLEGGED	BLANCMANGE	BLASTOPORAL
BLABBERING	BLACKLEGGING	BLANCMANGES	BLASTOPORE
BLABBERMOUTH	BLACKLISTED	BLANDISHED	BLASTOPORES
BLABBERMOUTHS	BLACKLISTER	BLANDISHER	BLASTOPORIC
BLACKAMOOR	BLACKLISTERS	BLANDISHERS	BLASTOPORS

BLASTOSPHERE	BLIMPISHNESS	BLOCKISHLY	BLOQUISTES
BLASTOSPHERES	BLIMPISHNESSES	BLOCKISHNESS	BLOSSOMING
BLASTOSPORE	BLINDFISHES	BLOCKISHNESSES	BLOSSOMINGS
BLASTOSPORES	BLINDFOLDED	BLOCKWORKS	BLOSSOMLESS
BLASTULATION	BLINDFOLDING	BLOKEISHNESS	BLOTCHIEST
BLASTULATIONS	BLINDFOLDS	BLOKEISHNESSES	BLOTCHINESS
BLATANCIES	BLINDINGLY	BLOKISHNESS	BLOTCHINESSES
BLATHERERS	BLINDNESSES	BLOKISHNESSES	BLOTCHINGS
BLATHERING	BLINDSIDED	BLONDENESS	BLOTTESQUE
BLATHERSKITE	BLINDSIDES	BLONDENESSES	BLOTTESQUES
BLATHERSKITES	BLINDSIDING	BLONDINING	BLOVIATING
BLATTERING	BLINDSIGHT	BLONDNESSES	BLOVIATION
BLAXPLOITATION	BLINDSIGHTS	BLOODBATHS	BLOVIATIONS
BLAXPLOITATIONS	BLINDSTOREY	BLOODCURDLING	BLOWFISHES
BLAZONINGS	BLINDSTOREYS	BLOODCURDLINGLY	BLOWINESSES
BLAZONRIES	BLINDSTORIES	BLOODGUILT	BLOWKARTING
BLEACHABLE	BLINDSTORY	BLOODGUILTINESS	BLOWKARTINGS
BLEACHERIES	BLINDWORMS	BLOODGUILTS	BLOWSINESS
BLEACHERITE	BLINGLISHES	BLOODGUILTY	BLOWSINESSES
BLEACHERITES	BLINKERING	BLOODHEATS	BLOWTORCHED
BLEACHINGS	BLISSFULLY	BLOODHOUND	BLOWTORCHES
BLEAKNESSES	BLISSFULNESS	BLOODHOUNDS	BLOWTORCHING
BLEARINESS	BLISSFULNESSES	BLOODINESS	BLOWZINESS
BLEARINESSES	BLISTERIER	BLOODINESSES	BLOWZINESSES
BLEMISHERS	BLISTERIEST	BLOODLESSLY	BLUBBERERS
BLEMISHING	BLISTERING	BLOODLESSNESS	BLUBBERIER
BLEMISHMENT	BLISTERINGLY	BLOODLESSNESSES	BLUBBERIEST
BLEMISHMENTS	BLITHENESS	BLOODLETTER	BLUBBERING
BLENNIOIDS	BLITHENESSES	BLOODLETTERS	BLUDGEONED
BLENNORRHEA	BLITHERING	BLOODLETTING	BLUDGEONER
BLENNORRHEAS	BLITHESOME	BLOODLETTINGS	BLUDGEONERS
BLENNORRHOEA	BLITHESOMELY	BLOODLINES	BLUDGEONING
BLENNORRHOEAS	BLITHESOMENESS	BLOODLUSTS	BLUEBEARDS
BLEPHARISM	BLITZKRIEG	BLOODMOBILE	BLUEBERRIES
BLEPHARISMS	BLITZKRIEGS	BLOODMOBILES	BLUEBLOODS
BLEPHARITIC	BLIZZARDLY	BLOODROOTS	BLUEBONNET
BLEPHARITIS	BLOATEDNESS	BLOODSHEDS	BLUEBONNETS
BLEPHARITISES	BLOATEDNESSES	BLOODSPRENT	BLUEBOTTLE
BLEPHAROPLAST	BLOATWARES	BLOODSTAIN	BLUEBOTTLES
BLEPHAROPLASTS	BLOCKADERS	BLOODSTAINED	BLUEBREAST
BLEPHAROPLASTY	BLOCKADING	BLOODSTAINS	BLUEBREASTS
BLEPHAROSPASM	BLOCKBOARD	BLOODSTOCK	BLUEBUSHES
BLEPHAROSPASMS	BLOCKBOARDS	BLOODSTOCKS	BLUEFISHES
BLESSEDEST	BLOCKBUSTED	BLOODSTONE	BLUEGRASSES
BLESSEDNESS	BLOCKBUSTER	BLOODSTONES	BLUEISHNESS
BLESSEDNESSES	BLOCKBUSTERS	BLOODSTREAM	BLUEISHNESSES
BLETHERANSKATE	BLOCKBUSTING	BLOODSTREAMS	BLUEJACKET
BLETHERANSKATES	BLOCKBUSTINGS	BLOODSUCKER	BLUEJACKETS
BLETHERATION	BLOCKBUSTS	BLOODSUCKERS	BLUEJACKING
BLETHERATIONS	BLOCKHEADED	BLOODSUCKING	BLUEJACKINGS
BLETHERERS	BLOCKHEADEDLY	BLOODTHIRSTIER	BLUELINERS
BLETHERING	BLOCKHEADEDNESS	BLOODTHIRSTIEST	BLUENESSES
BLETHERINGS	BLOCKHEADS	BLOODTHIRSTILY	BLUEPOINTS
BLETHERSKATE	BLOCKHOLES	BLOODTHIRSTY	BLUEPRINTED
BLETHERSKATES	BLOCKHOUSE	BLOODWOODS	BLUEPRINTING
BLIGHTINGLY	BLOCKHOUSES	BLOODWORMS	BLUEPRINTS
BLIGHTINGS	BLOCKINESS	BLOODWORTS	BLUESHIFTED
BLIMPISHLY	BLOCKINESSES	BLOOMERIES	BLUESHIFTS

BLUESNARFING	BOATLIFTING	BOILERPLATE	BOMBILATING
BLUESNARFINGS	BOATSWAINS	BOILERPLATED	BOMBILATION
BLUESTOCKING	BOBBEJAANS	BOILERPLATES	BOMBILATIONS
BLUESTOCKINGS	BOBBITTING	BOILERPLATING	BOMBINATED
BLUESTONES	BOBBYSOCKS	BOILERSUIT	BOMBINATES
BLUETHROAT	BOBBYSOXER	BOILERSUITS	BOMBINATING
BLUETHROATS	BOBBYSOXERS	BOISTEROUS	BOMBINATION
BLUETONGUE	BOBSLEDDED	BOISTEROUSLY	BOMBINATIONS
BLUETONGUES	BOBSLEDDER	BOISTEROUSNESS	BOMBPROOFED
BLUFFNESSES	BOBSLEDDERS	BOKMAKIERIE	BOMBPROOFING
BLUISHNESS	BOBSLEDDING	BOKMAKIERIES	BOMBPROOFS
BLUISHNESSES	BOBSLEDDINGS	BOLDFACING	BOMBSHELLS
BLUNDERBUSS	BOBSLEIGHED	BOLDNESSES	BOMBSIGHTS
BLUNDERBUSSES	BOBSLEIGHING	BOLECTIONS	BONAMIASES
BLUNDERERS	BOBSLEIGHS	BOLIVIANOS	BONAMIASIS
BLUNDERING	BOBTAILING	BOLLETRIES	BONASSUSES
BLUNDERINGLY	BOBWEIGHTS	BOLLOCKING	BONBONNIERE
BLUNDERINGS	BOCCONCINI	BOLLOCKINGS	BONBONNIERES
BLUNTHEADS	BODACIOUSLY	BOLLOCKSED	BONDHOLDER
BLUNTNESSES	BODDHISATTVA	BOLLOCKSES	BONDHOLDERS
BLURREDNESS	BODDHISATTVAS	BOLLOCKSING	BONDMANSHIP
BLURREDNESSES	BODEGUEROS	BOLOGRAPHS	BONDMANSHIPS
BLURRINESS	BODHISATTVA	BOLOMETERS	BONDSERVANT
BLURRINESSES	BODHISATTVAS	BOLOMETRIC	BONDSERVANTS
BLURRINGLY	BODYBOARDED	BOLOMETRICALLY	BONDSTONES
BLUSHINGLY	BODYBOARDING	BOLOMETRIES	BONDSWOMAN
BLUSHLESSLY	BODYBOARDINGS	BOLSHEVIKI	BONDSWOMEN
BLUSTERERS	BODYBOARDS	BOLSHEVIKS	BONEBLACKS
BLUSTERIER	BODYBUILDER	BOLSHEVISE	BONEFISHES
BLUSTERIEST	BODYBUILDERS	BOLSHEVISED	BONEFISHING
BLUSTERING	BODYBUILDING	BOLSHEVISES	BONEFISHINGS
BLUSTERINGLY	BODYBUILDINGS	BOLSHEVISING	BONEHEADED
BLUSTERINGS	BODYCHECKED	BOLSHEVISM	BONEHEADEDNESS
BLUSTEROUS	BODYCHECKING	BOLSHEVISMS	BONESETTER
BLUSTEROUSLY	BODYCHECKS	BOLSHEVIST	BONESETTERS
BLUTWURSTS	BODYGUARDED	BOLSHEVISTS	BONESHAKER
BOARDINGHOUSE	BODYGUARDING	BOLSHEVIZE	BONESHAKERS
BOARDINGHOUSES	BODYGUARDS	BOLSHEVIZED	BONHOMMIES
BOARDROOMS	BODYSHELLS	BOLSHEVIZES	BONILASSES
BOARDSAILING	BODYSURFED	BOLSHEVIZING	BONINESSES
BOARDSAILINGS	BODYSURFER	BOLSTERERS	BONKBUSTER
BOARDSAILOR	BODYSURFERS	BOLSTERING	BONKBUSTERS
BOARDSAILORS	BODYSURFING	BOLSTERINGS	BONNIBELLS
BOARDWALKS	BODYWORKER	BOMBACACEOUS	BONNILASSE
BOARFISHES	BODYWORKERS	BOMBARDERS	BONNILASSES
BOARHOUNDS	BOEREMUSIEK	BOMBARDIER	BONNINESSES
BOARISHNESS	BOEREMUSIEKS	BOMBARDIERS	BONNYCLABBER
BOARISHNESSES	BOEREWORSES	BOMBARDING	BONNYCLABBERS
BOASTFULLY	BOGGINESSES	BOMBARDMENT	BOOBIALLAS
BOASTFULNESS	BOGTROTTER	BOMBARDMENTS	BOOBOISIES
BOASTFULNESSES	BOGTROTTERS	BOMBARDONS	BOOKBINDER
BOASTINGLY	BOGTROTTING	BOMBASINES	BOOKBINDERIES
BOATBUILDER	BOGTROTTINGS	BOMBASTERS	BOOKBINDERS
BOATBUILDERS	BOGUSNESSES	BOMBASTICALLY	BOOKBINDERY
BOATBUILDING	BOHEMIANISM	BOMBASTING	BOOKBINDING
BOATBUILDINGS	BOHEMIANISMS	BOMBAZINES	BOOKBINDINGS
BOATHOUSES	BOILERMAKER	BOMBILATED	BOOKCROSSING
BOATLIFTED	BOILERMAKERS	BOMBILATES	BOOKCROSSINGS

BOOKISHNESS
BOOKISHNESSES
BOOKKEEPER
BOOKKEEPERS
BOOKKEEPING
BOOKKEEPINGS
BOOKLIGHTS
BOOKMAKERS
BOOKMAKING
BOOKMAKINGS
BOOKMARKED
BOOKMARKER
BOOKMARKERS
BOOKMARKING
BOOKMOBILE
BOOKMOBILES
BOOKPLATES
BOOKSELLER
BOOKSELLERS
BOOKSELLING
BOOKSELLINGS
BOOKSHELVES
BOOKSTALLS
BOOKSTANDS
BOOKSTORES
BOOMERANGED
BOOMERANGING
BOOMERANGS
BOOMSLANGS
BOONDOGGLE
BOONDOGGLED
BOONDOGGLER
BOONDOGGLERS
BOONDOGGLES
BOONDOGGLING
BOONGARIES
BOORISHNESS
BOORISHNESSES
BOOSTERISH
BOOSTERISM
BOOSTERISMS
BOOTBLACKS
BOOTLEGGED
BOOTLEGGER
BOOTLEGGERS
BOOTLEGGING
BOOTLEGGINGS
BOOTLESSLY
BOOTLESSNESS
BOOTLESSNESSES
BOOTLICKED
BOOTLICKER
BOOTLICKERS
BOOTLICKING
BOOTLICKINGS
BOOTLOADER
BOOTLOADERS
BOOTMAKERS

BOOTMAKING
BOOTMAKINGS
BOOTSTRAPPED
BOOTSTRAPPING
BOOTSTRAPS
BOOTYLICIOUS
BOOZINESSES
BORAGINACEOUS
BORBORYGMAL
BORBORYGMI
BORBORYGMIC
BORBORYGMUS
BORBORYGMUSES
BORDEREAUX
BORDERLAND
BORDERLANDS
BORDERLESS
BORDERLINE
BORDERLINES
BORDRAGING
BORDRAGINGS
BORESCOPES
BORGHETTOS
BORINGNESS
BORINGNESSES
BOROHYDRIDE
BOROHYDRIDES
BOROSILICATE
BOROSILICATES
BORROWINGS
BOSBERAADS
BOSCHVARKS
BOSCHVELDS
BOSKINESSES
BOSSINESSES
BOSSYBOOTS
BOTANICALLY
BOTANICALS
BOTANISERS
BOTANISING
BOTANIZERS
BOTANIZING
BOTANOMANCIES
BOTANOMANCY
BOTCHERIES
BOTCHINESS
BOTCHINESSES
BOTHERATION
BOTHERATIONS
BOTHERSOME
BOTRYOIDAL
BOTRYTISES
BOTTLEBRUSH
BOTTLEBRUSHES
BOTTLEFULS
BOTTLENECK
BOTTLENECKED
BOTTLENECKING

BOTTLENECKS
BOTTLENOSE
BOTTOMLAND
BOTTOMLANDS
BOTTOMLESS
BOTTOMLESSLY
BOTTOMLESSNESS
BOTTOMMOST
BOTTOMNESS
BOTTOMNESSES
BOTTOMRIES
BOTULINUMS
BOTULINUSES
BOUGAINVILIA
BOUGAINVILIAS
BOUGAINVILLAEA
BOUGAINVILLAEAS
BOUGAINVILLEA
BOUGAINVILLEAS
BOUILLABAISSE
BOUILLABAISSES
BOUILLOTTE
BOUILLOTTES
BOULDERERS
BOULDERING
BOULDERINGS
BOULEVARDIER
BOULEVARDIERS
BOULEVARDS
BOULEVERSEMENT
BOULEVERSEMENTS
BOULLEWORK
BOULLEWORKS
BOUNCINESS
BOUNCINESSES
BOUNCINGLY
BOUNDARIES
BOUNDEDNESS
BOUNDEDNESSES
BOUNDERISH
BOUNDLESSLY
BOUNDLESSNESS
BOUNDLESSNESSES
BOUNDNESSES
BOUNTEOUSLY
BOUNTEOUSNESS
BOUNTEOUSNESSES
BOUNTIFULLY
BOUNTIFULNESS
BOUNTIFULNESSES
BOUNTYHEDS
BOUQUETIERE
BOUQUETIERES
BOURASQUES
BOURBONISM
BOURBONISMS
BOURGEOISE
BOURGEOISES

BOURGEOISIE
BOURGEOISIES
BOURGEOISIFIED
BOURGEOISIFIES
BOURGEOISIFY
BOURGEOISIFYING
BOURGEONED
BOURGEONING
BOURGUIGNON
BOURGUIGNONNE
BOUSINGKEN
BOUSINGKENS
BOUSTROPHEDON
BOUSTROPHEDONIC
BOUSTROPHEDONS
BOUTONNIERE
BOUTONNIERES
BOUVARDIAS
BOVINITIES
BOWDLERISATION
BOWDLERISATIONS
BOWDLERISE
BOWDLERISED
BOWDLERISER
BOWDLERISERS
BOWDLERISES
BOWDLERISING
BOWDLERISM
BOWDLERISMS
BOWDLERIZATION
BOWDLERIZATIONS
BOWDLERIZE
BOWDLERIZED
BOWDLERIZER
BOWDLERIZERS
BOWDLERIZES
BOWDLERIZING
BOWERBIRDS
BOWERWOMAN
BOWERWOMEN
BOWHUNTERS
BOWSTRINGED
BOWSTRINGING
BOWSTRINGS
BOXBERRIES
BOXERCISES
BOXHAULING
BOXINESSES
BOXKEEPERS
BOXWALLAHS
BOYCOTTERS
BOYCOTTING
BOYFRIENDS
BOYISHNESS
BOYISHNESSES
BOYSENBERRIES
BOYSENBERRY
BRAAIVLEIS

BRAAIVLEISES	BRACKISHNESS	BRAINSTORMS	BRATTINESSES
BRABBLEMENT	BRACKISHNESSES	BRAINTEASER	BRATTISHED
BRABBLEMENTS	BRACTEATES	BRAINTEASERS	BRATTISHES
BRACHIATED	BRACTEOLATE	BRAINWASHED	BRATTISHING
BRACHIATES	BRACTEOLES	BRAINWASHER	BRATTISHINGS
BRACHIATING	BRADYCARDIA	BRAINWASHERS	BRATTLINGS
BRACHIATION	BRADYCARDIAC	BRAINWASHES	BRATWURSTS
BRACHIATIONS	BRADYCARDIAS	BRAINWASHING	BRAUNCHING
BRACHIATOR	BRADYKINESIA	BRAINWASHINGS	BRAUNSCHWEIGER
BRACHIATORS	BRADYKINESIAS	BRAINWAVES	BRAUNSCHWEIGERS
BRACHIOCEPHALIC	BRADYKININ	BRAMBLIEST	BRAVADOING
BRACHIOPOD	BRADYKININS	BRAMBLINGS	BRAVENESSES
BRACHIOPODS	BRADYPEPTIC	BRANCHERIES	BRAVISSIMO
BRACHIOSAURUS	BRADYPEPTICS	BRANCHIATE	BRAWNINESS
BRACHIOSAURUSES	BRADYSEISM	BRANCHIEST	BRAWNINESSES
BRACHISTOCHRONE	BRADYSEISMS	BRANCHINGS	BRAZENNESS
BRACHYAXES	BRAGADISME	BRANCHIOPOD	BRAZENNESSES
BRACHYAXIS	BRAGADISMES	BRANCHIOPODS	BRAZENRIES
BRACHYCEPHAL	BRAGGADOCIO	BRANCHIOSTEGAL	BRAZIERIES
BRACHYCEPHALIC	BRAGGADOCIOS	BRANCHLESS	BRAZILEINS
BRACHYCEPHALICS	BRAGGADOCIOUS	BRANCHLETS	BRAZILWOOD
BRACHYCEPHALIES	BRAGGARTISM	BRANCHLIKE	BRAZILWOODS
BRACHYCEPHALISM	BRAGGARTISMS	BRANCHLINE	BREADBASKET
BRACHYCEPHALOUS	BRAGGARTLY	BRANCHLINES	BREADBASKETS
BRACHYCEPHALS	BRAGGINGLY	BRANDERING	BREADBERRIES
BRACHYCEPHALY	BRAHMANISM	BRANDISHED	BREADBERRY
BRACHYCEROUS	BRAHMANISMS	BRANDISHER	BREADBOARD
BRACHYDACTYL	BRAHMANIST	BRANDISHERS	BREADBOARDED
BRACHYDACTYLIC	BRAHMANISTS	BRANDISHES	BREADBOARDING
BRACHYDACTYLIES	BRAHMINISM	BRANDISHING	BREADBOARDS
BRACHYDACTYLISM	BRAHMINISMS	BRANDLINGS	BREADBOXES
BRACHYDACTYLOUS	BRAHMINIST	BRANDRETHS	BREADCRUMB
BRACHYDACTYLY	BRAHMINISTS	BRANFULNESS	BREADCRUMBED
BRACHYDIAGONAL	BRAILLEWRITER	BRANFULNESSES	BREADCRUMBING
BRACHYDIAGONALS	BRAILLEWRITERS	BRANGLINGS	BREADCRUMBS
BRACHYDOME	BRAILLISTS	BRANKURSINE	BREADFRUIT
BRACHYDOMES	BRAINBOXES	BRANKURSINES	BREADFRUITS
BRACHYGRAPHIES	BRAINCASES	BRANNIGANS	BREADHEADS
BRACHYGRAPHY	BRAINCHILD	BRASHINESS	BREADLINES
BRACHYLOGIES	BRAINCHILDREN	BRASHINESSES	BREADROOMS
BRACHYLOGOUS	BRAINFARTS	BRASHNESSES	BREADROOTS
BRACHYLOGY	BRAININESS	BRASILEINS	BREADSTICKS
BRACHYODONT	BRAININESSES	BRASSBOUND	BREADSTUFF
BRACHYPINAKOID	BRAINLESSLY	BRASSERIES	BREADSTUFFS
BRACHYPINAKOIDS	BRAINLESSNESS	BRASSFOUNDER	BREADTHWAYS
BRACHYPRISM	BRAINLESSNESSES	BRASSFOUNDERS	BREADTHWISE
BRACHYPRISMS	BRAINPOWER	BRASSFOUNDING	BREADWINNER
BRACHYPTERISM	BRAINPOWERS	BRASSFOUNDINGS	BREADWINNERS
BRACHYPTERISMS	BRAINSICKLY	BRASSICACEOUS	BREADWINNING
BRACHYPTEROUS	BRAINSICKNESS	BRASSIERES	BREADWINNINGS
BRACHYTHERAPIES	BRAINSICKNESSES	BRASSINESS	BREAKABLENESS
BRACHYTHERAPY	BRAINSTEMS	BRASSINESSES	BREAKABLENESSES
BRACHYURAL	BRAINSTORM	BRASSWARES	BREAKABLES
BRACHYURAN	BRAINSTORMED	BRATPACKER	BREAKAWAYS
BRACHYURANS	BRAINSTORMER	BRATPACKERS	BREAKBEATS
BRACHYUROUS	BRAINSTORMERS	BRATTICING	BREAKDANCE
BRACKETING	BRAINSTORMING	BRATTICINGS	BREAKDANCED
BRACKETINGS	BRAINSTORMINGS	BRATTINESS	BREAKDANCER

BREAKDANCERS	BREATHARIANISMS	BRICKLAYINGS	BRILLIANTINE
BREAKDANCES	BREATHARIANS	BRICKMAKER	BRILLIANTINES
BREAKDANCING	BREATHIEST	BRICKMAKERS	BRILLIANTING
BREAKDANCINGS	BREATHINESS	BRICKMAKING	BRILLIANTLY
BREAKDOWNS	BREATHINESSES	BRICKMAKINGS	BRILLIANTNESS
BREAKEVENS	BREATHINGS	BRICKSHAPED	BRILLIANTNESSES
BREAKFASTED	BREATHLESS	BRICKWALLS	BRILLIANTS
BREAKFASTER	BREATHLESSLY	BRICKWORKS	BRIMFULLNESS
BREAKFASTERS	BREATHLESSNESS	BRICKYARDS	BRIMFULLNESSES
BREAKFASTING	BREATHTAKING	BRICOLAGES	BRIMFULNESS
BREAKFASTS	BREATHTAKINGLY	BRIDECAKES	BRIMFULNESSES
BREAKFRONT	BRECCIATED	BRIDEGROOM	BRIMSTONES
BREAKFRONTS	BRECCIATES	BRIDEGROOMS	BRINELLING
BREAKPOINT	BRECCIATING	BRIDEMAIDEN	BRINELLINGS
BREAKPOINTS	BRECCIATION	BRIDEMAIDENS	BRINGDOWNS
BREAKTHROUGH	BRECCIATIONS	BRIDEMAIDS	BRININESSES
BREAKTHROUGHS	BREECHBLOCK	BRIDESMAID	BRINJARRIES
BREAKTIMES	BREECHBLOCKS	BRIDESMAIDS	BRINKMANSHIP
BREAKWALLS	BREECHCLOTH	BRIDEWEALTH	BRINKMANSHIPS
BREAKWATER	BREECHCLOTHS	BRIDEWEALTHS	BRINKSMANSHIP
BREAKWATERS	BREECHCLOUT	BRIDEWELLS	BRINKSMANSHIPS
BREASTBONE	BREECHCLOUTS	BRIDGEABLE	BRIOLETTES
BREASTBONES	BREECHINGS	BRIDGEBOARD	BRIQUETING
BREASTFEED	BREECHLESS	BRIDGEBOARDS	BRIQUETTED
BREASTFEEDING	BREECHLOADER	BRIDGEHEAD	BRIQUETTES
BREASTFEEDS	BREECHLOADERS	BRIDGEHEADS	BRIQUETTING
BREASTPINS	BREEZELESS	BRIDGELESS	BRISKENING
BREASTPLATE	BREEZEWAYS	BRIDGEWORK	BRISKNESSES
BREASTPLATES	BREEZINESS	BRIDGEWORKS	BRISTLECONE
BREASTPLOUGH	BREEZINESSES	BRIDLEWAYS	BRISTLECONES
BREASTPLOUGHS	BREMSSTRAHLUNG	BRIDLEWISE	BRISTLELIKE
BREASTRAIL	BREMSSTRAHLUNGS	BRIEFCASES	BRISTLETAIL
BREASTRAILS	BRESSUMMER	BRIEFNESSES	BRISTLETAILS
BREASTSTROKE	BRESSUMMERS	BRIERROOTS	BRISTLIEST
BREASTSTROKER	BRETASCHES	BRIERWOODS	BRISTLINESS
BREASTSTROKERS	BRETTICING	BRIGADIERS	BRISTLINESSES
BREASTSTROKES	BREUNNERITE	BRIGANDAGE	BRITANNIAS
BREASTSUMMER	BREUNNERITES	BRIGANDAGES	BRITSCHKAS
BREASTSUMMERS	BREVETCIES	BRIGANDINE	BRITTANIAS
BREASTWORK	BREVETTING	BRIGANDINES	BRITTLENESS
BREASTWORKS	BREVIARIES	BRIGANDRIES	BRITTLENESSES
BREATHABILITIES	BREVIPENNATE	BRIGANTINE	BROADBANDS
BREATHABILITY	BREWMASTER	BRIGANTINES	BROADBEANS
BREATHABLE	BREWMASTERS	BRIGHTENED	BROADBILLS
BREATHALYSE	BRIARROOTS	BRIGHTENER	BROADBRIMS
BREATHALYSED	BRIARWOODS	BRIGHTENERS	BROADBRUSH
BREATHALYSER	BRICABRACS	BRIGHTENING	BROADCASTED
BREATHALYSERS	BRICKCLAYS	BRIGHTNESS	BROADCASTER
BREATHALYSES	BRICKEARTH	BRIGHTNESSES	BROADCASTERS
BREATHALYSING	BRICKEARTHS	BRIGHTSOME	BROADCASTING
BREATHALYZE	BRICKFIELD	BRIGHTWORK	BROADCASTINGS
BREATHALYZED	BRICKFIELDER	BRIGHTWORKS	BROADCASTS
BREATHALYZER	BRICKFIELDERS	BRILLIANCE	BROADCLOTH
BREATHALYZERS	BRICKFIELDS	BRILLIANCES	BROADCLOTHS
BREATHALYZES	BRICKKILNS	BRILLIANCIES	BROADENERS
BREATHALYZING	BRICKLAYER	BRILLIANCY	BROADENING
BREATHARIAN	BRICKLAYERS	BRILLIANTE	BROADLEAVES
BREATHARIANISM	BRICKLAYING	BRILLIANTED	BROADLINES

BROADLOOMS	BRONCHIOLITIS	BROWBEATER	BRYOLOGIES
BROADMINDED	BRONCHIOLITISES	BROWBEATERS	BRYOLOGIST
BROADMINDEDLY	BRONCHITIC	BROWBEATING	BRYOLOGISTS
BROADMINDEDNESS	BRONCHITICS	BROWBEATINGS	BRYOPHYLLUM
BROADNESSES	BRONCHITIS	BROWNFIELD	BRYOPHYLLUMS
BROADPIECE	BRONCHITISES	BROWNFIELDS	BRYOPHYTES
BROADPIECES	BRONCHODILATOR	BROWNNESSES	BRYOPHYTIC
BROADSCALE	BRONCHODILATORS	BROWNNOSED	BUBBLEGUMS
BROADSHEET	BRONCHOGENIC	BROWNNOSER	BUBBLEHEAD
BROADSHEETS	BRONCHOGRAPHIES	BROWNNOSERS	BUBBLEHEADED
BROADSIDED	BRONCHOGRAPHY	BROWNNOSES	BUBBLEHEADS
BROADSIDES	BRONCHOSCOPE	BROWNNOSING	BUBONOCELE
BROADSIDING	BRONCHOSCOPES	BROWNSHIRT	BUBONOCELES
BROADSWORD	BRONCHOSCOPIC	BROWNSHIRTS	BUCCANEERED
BROADSWORDS	BRONCHOSCOPICAL	BROWNSTONE	BUCCANEERING
BROADTAILS	BRONCHOSCOPIES	BROWNSTONES	BUCCANEERINGS
BROBDINGNAGIAN	BRONCHOSCOPIST	BROWRIDGES	BUCCANEERISH
BROCATELLE	BRONCHOSCOPISTS	BROWSABLES	BUCCANEERS
BROCATELLES	BRONCHOSCOPY	BRUCELLOSES	BUCCANIERED
BROCHETTES	BRONCHOSPASM	BRUCELLOSIS	BUCCANIERING
BROGUERIES	BRONCHOSPASMS	BRUGMANSIA	BUCCANIERS
BROIDERERS	BRONCHOSPASTIC	BRUGMANSIAS	BUCCINATOR
BROIDERIES	BRONCOBUSTER	BRUMMAGEMS	BUCCINATORS
BROIDERING	BRONCOBUSTERS	BRUSCHETTA	BUCCINATORY
BROIDERINGS	BRONDYRONS	BRUSCHETTAS	BUCELLASES
BROKENHEARTED	BRONTOBYTE	BRUSCHETTE	BUCENTAURS
BROKENHEARTEDLY	BRONTOBYTES	BRUSHABILITIES	BUCKBOARDS
BROKENNESS	BRONTOSAUR	BRUSHABILITY	BUCKBRUSHES
BROKENNESSES	BRONTOSAURS	BRUSHBACKS	BUCKETFULS
BROKERAGES	BRONTOSAURUS	BRUSHFIRES	BUCKETINGS
BROKERINGS	BRONTOSAURUSES	BRUSHLANDS	BUCKETSFUL
BROMEGRASS	BRONZIFIED	BRUSHMARKS	BUCKHOUNDS
BROMEGRASSES	BRONZIFIES	BRUSHWHEEL	BUCKJUMPER
BROMELAINS	BRONZIFYING	BRUSHWHEELS	BUCKJUMPERS
BROMELIACEOUS	BROODINESS	BRUSHWOODS	BUCKJUMPING
BROMELIADS	BROODINESSES	BRUSHWORKS	BUCKJUMPINGS
BROMEOSINS	BROODINGLY	BRUSQUENESS	BUCKLERING
BROMHIDROSES	BROODMARES	BRUSQUENESSES	BUCKRAMING
BROMHIDROSIS	BROOKLIMES	BRUSQUERIE	BUCKSHISHED
BROMIDROSES	BROOKWEEDS	BRUSQUERIES	BUCKSHISHES
BROMIDROSIS	BROOMBALLER	BRUTALISATION	BUCKSHISHING
BROMINATED	BROOMBALLERS	BRUTALISATIONS	BUCKSKINNED
BROMINATES	BROOMBALLS	BRUTALISED	BUCKTHORNS
BROMINATING	BROOMCORNS	BRUTALISES	BUCKTOOTHED
BROMINATION	BROOMRAPES	BRUTALISING	BUCKWHEATS
BROMINATIONS	BROOMSTAFF	BRUTALISMS	BUCKYBALLS
BROMINISMS	BROOMSTAFFS	BRUTALISTS	BUCKYTUBES
BROMOCRIPTINE	BROOMSTICK	BRUTALITIES	BUCOLICALLY
BROMOCRIPTINES	BROOMSTICKS	BRUTALIZATION	BUDGERIGAR
BROMOFORMS	BROTHERHOOD	BRUTALIZATIONS	BUDGERIGARS
BROMOURACIL	BROTHERHOODS	BRUTALIZED	BUDGETEERS
BROMOURACILS	BROTHERING	BRUTALIZES	BUFFALOBERRIES
BRONCHIALLY	BROTHERLIKE	BRUTALIZING	BUFFALOBERRY
BRONCHIECTASES	BROTHERLINESS	BRUTENESSES	BUFFALOFISH
BRONCHIECTASIS	BROTHERLINESSES	BRUTIFYING	BUFFALOFISHES
BRONCHIOLAR	BROUGHTASES	BRUTISHNESS	BUFFALOING
BRONCHIOLE	BROWALLIAS	BRUTISHNESSES	BUFFETINGS
BRONCHIOLES	BROWBEATEN	BRYOLOGICAL	BUFFLEHEAD

BUFFLEHEADS	BULLSHITTED	BUPIVACAINES	BURNISHABLE
BUFFOONERIES	BULLSHITTER	BUPRENORPHINE	BURNISHERS
BUFFOONERY	BULLSHITTERS	BUPRENORPHINES	BURNISHING
BUFFOONISH	BULLSHITTING	BUPRESTIDS	BURNISHINGS
BUFOTALINS	BULLSHITTINGS	BURDENSOME	BURNISHMENT
BUFOTENINE	BULLSNAKES	BUREAUCRACIES	BURNISHMENTS
BUFOTENINES	BULLTERRIER	BUREAUCRACY	BURRAMUNDI
BUGGINESSES	BULLTERRIERS	BUREAUCRAT	BURRAMUNDIS
BUGLEWEEDS	BULLWADDIE	BUREAUCRATESE	BURRAMYSES
BUHRSTONES	BULLWADDIES	BUREAUCRATESES	BURRAWANGS
BUILDDOWNS	BULLWHACKED	BUREAUCRATIC	BURROWSTOWN
BUIRDLIEST	BULLWHACKING	BUREAUCRATISE	BURROWSTOWNS
BULBIFEROUS	BULLWHACKS	BUREAUCRATISED	BURRSTONES
BULBOSITIES	BULLWHIPPED	BUREAUCRATISES	BURSARSHIP
BULBOUSNESS	BULLWHIPPING	BUREAUCRATISING	BURSARSHIPS
BULBOUSNESSES	BULLYRAGGED	BUREAUCRATISM	BURSERACEOUS
BULGINESSES	BULLYRAGGING	BUREAUCRATISMS	BURSICULATE
BULKINESSES	BULWADDEES	BUREAUCRATIST	BURSITISES
BULLBAITING	BULWADDIES	BUREAUCRATISTS	BURTHENING
BULLBAITINGS	BULWARKING	BUREAUCRATIZE	BURTHENSOME
BULLBRIERS	BUMBAILIFF	BUREAUCRATIZED	BUSHBABIES
BULLDOGGED	BUMBAILIFFS	BUREAUCRATIZES	BUSHBASHING
BULLDOGGER	BUMBERSHOOT	BUREAUCRATIZING	BUSHBASHINGS
BULLDOGGERS	BUMBERSHOOTS	BUREAUCRATS	BUSHCRAFTS
BULLDOGGING	BUMBLEBEES	BURGEONING	BUSHELLERS
BULLDOGGINGS	BUMBLEDOMS	BURGLARIES	BUSHELLING
BULLDOZERS	BUMBLINGLY	BURGLARING	BUSHELLINGS
BULLDOZING	BUMFREEZER	BURGLARIOUS	BUSHELWOMAN
BULLETINED	BUMFREEZERS	BURGLARIOUSLY	BUSHELWOMEN
BULLETINING	BUMFUZZLED	BURGLARISE	BUSHHAMMER
BULLETPROOF	BUMFUZZLES	BURGLARISED	BUSHHAMMERS
BULLETPROOFED	BUMFUZZLING	BURGLARISES	BUSHINESSES
BULLETPROOFING	BUMMALOTIS	BURGLARISING	BUSHMANSHIP
BULLETPROOFS	BUMPINESSES	BURGLARIZE	BUSHMANSHIPS
BULLETRIES	BUMPKINISH	BURGLARIZED	BUSHMASTER
BULLETWOOD	BUMPOLOGIES	BURGLARIZES	BUSHMASTERS
BULLETWOODS	BUMPSADAISY	BURGLARIZING	BUSHRANGER
BULLFIGHTER	BUMPTIOUSLY	BURGLARPROOF	BUSHRANGERS
BULLFIGHTERS	BUMPTIOUSNESS	BURGOMASTER	BUSHRANGING
BULLFIGHTING	BUMPTIOUSNESSES	BURGOMASTERS	BUSHRANGINGS
BULLFIGHTINGS	BUMSUCKERS	BURGUNDIES	BUSHWALKED
BULLFIGHTS	BUMSUCKING	BURLADEROS	BUSHWALKER
BULLFINCHES	BUMSUCKINGS	BURLESQUED	BUSHWALKERS
BULLHEADED	BUNCHBERRIES	BURLESQUELY	BUSHWALKING
BULLHEADEDLY	BUNCHBERRY	BURLESQUER	BUSHWALKINGS
BULLHEADEDNESS	BUNCHGRASS	BURLESQUERS	BUSHWHACKED
BULLIONIST	BUNCHGRASSES	BURLESQUES	BUSHWHACKER
BULLIONISTS	BUNCHINESS	BURLESQUING	BUSHWHACKERS
BULLISHNESS	BUNCHINESSES	BURLEYCUES	BUSHWHACKING
BULLISHNESSES	BUNDOBUSTS	BURLINESSES	BUSHWHACKINGS
BULLMASTIFF	BUNGALOIDS	BURNETTISE	BUSHWHACKS
BULLMASTIFFS	BUNGLESOME	BURNETTISED	BUSINESSES
BULLNECKED	BUNGLINGLY	BURNETTISES	BUSINESSLIKE
BULLOCKIES	BUNKHOUSES	BURNETTISING	BUSINESSMAN
BULLOCKING	BUOYANCIES	BURNETTIZE	BUSINESSMEN
BULLROARER	BUOYANTNESS	BURNETTIZED	BUSINESSPEOPLE
BULLROARERS	BUOYANTNESSES	BURNETTIZES	BUSINESSPERSON
BULLRUSHES	BUPIVACAINE	BURNETTIZING	BUSINESSPERSONS

BUSINESSWOMAN
BUSINESSWOMEN
BUSTICATED
BUSTICATES
BUSTICATING
BUSTINESSES
BUSTLINGLY
BUSYBODIED
BUSYBODIES
BUSYBODYING
BUSYNESSES
BUTADIENES
BUTCHERBIRD
BUTCHERBIRDS
BUTCHERERS
BUTCHERIES
BUTCHERING
BUTCHERINGS
BUTCHNESSES
BUTENEDIOIC
BUTEONINES
BUTLERAGES
BUTLERSHIP
BUTLERSHIPS
BUTTERBALL
BUTTERBALLS
BUTTERBURS
BUTTERCUPS
BUTTERDOCK
BUTTERDOCKS
BUTTERFATS
BUTTERFINGERED
BUTTERFINGERS
BUTTERFISH
BUTTERFISHES
BUTTERFLIED
BUTTERFLIES
BUTTERFLYER
BUTTERFLYERS
BUTTERFLYING
BUTTERIEST
BUTTERINES
BUTTERINESS
BUTTERINESSES
BUTTERLESS
BUTTERMILK
BUTTERMILKS
BUTTERNUTS
BUTTERSCOTCH
BUTTERSCOTCHES
BUTTERWEED
BUTTERWEEDS
BUTTERWORT
BUTTERWORTS
BUTTINSKIES
BUTTINSKIS
BUTTOCKING
BUTTONBALL

BUTTONBALLS
BUTTONBUSH
BUTTONBUSHES
BUTTONHELD
BUTTONHOLD
BUTTONHOLDING
BUTTONHOLDS
BUTTONHOLE
BUTTONHOLED
BUTTONHOLER
BUTTONHOLERS
BUTTONHOLES
BUTTONHOLING
BUTTONHOOK
BUTTONHOOKED
BUTTONHOOKING
BUTTONHOOKS
BUTTONLESS
BUTTONMOULD
BUTTONMOULDS
BUTTONWOOD
BUTTONWOODS
BUTTRESSED
BUTTRESSES
BUTTRESSING
BUTTSTOCKS
BUTYLATING
BUTYLATION
BUTYLATIONS
BUTYRACEOUS
BUTYRALDEHYDE
BUTYRALDEHYDES
BUTYROPHENONE
BUTYROPHENONES
BUXOMNESSES
BYPRODUCTS
BYSSACEOUS
BYSSINOSES
BYSSINOSIS
BYSTANDERS
BYTOWNITES

C

CABALETTAS
CABALISTIC
CABALISTICAL
CABALLEROS
CABBAGETOWN
CABBAGETOWNS
CABBAGEWORM
CABBAGEWORMS
CABBALISMS
CABBALISTIC
CABBALISTICAL
CABBALISTS
CABDRIVERS
CABINETMAKER
CABINETMAKERS
CABINETMAKING
CABINETMAKINGS
CABINETRIES
CABINETWORK
CABINETWORKS
CABINMATES
CABLECASTED
CABLECASTING
CABLECASTS
CABLEGRAMS
CABLEVISION
CABLEVISIONS
CABRIOLETS
CACAFUEGOS
CACCIATORA
CACCIATORE
CACHAEMIAS
CACHECTICAL
CACHINNATE
CACHINNATED
CACHINNATES
CACHINNATING
CACHINNATION
CACHINNATIONS
CACHINNATORY
CACHOLONGS
CACIQUISMS
CACKERMANDER
CACKERMANDERS
CACKLEBERRIES
CACKLEBERRY
CACODAEMON
CACODAEMONS
CACODEMONIC
CACODEMONS
CACODOXIES
CACOEPISTIC
CACOGASTRIC

CACOGENICS
CACOGRAPHER
CACOGRAPHERS
CACOGRAPHIC
CACOGRAPHICAL
CACOGRAPHIES
CACOGRAPHY
CACOLOGIES
CACOMISTLE
CACOMISTLES
CACOMIXLES
CACONYMIES
CACOPHONIC
CACOPHONICAL
CACOPHONICALLY
CACOPHONIES
CACOPHONIOUS
CACOPHONOUS
CACOPHONOUSLY
CACOTOPIAN
CACOTOPIAS
CACOTROPHIES
CACOTROPHY
CACTACEOUS
CACTOBLASTES
CACTOBLASTIS
CACUMINALS
CACUMINOUS
CADASTRALLY
CADAVERINE
CADAVERINES
CADAVEROUS
CADAVEROUSLY
CADAVEROUSNESS
CADDISFLIES
CADDISHNESS
CADDISHNESSES
CADDISWORM
CADDISWORMS
CADETSHIPS
CADUCITIES
CAECILIANS
CAECITISES
CAENOGENESES
CAENOGENESIS
CAENOGENETIC
CAESALPINOID
CAESAREANS
CAESARIANS
CAESARISMS
CAESAROPAPISM
CAESAROPAPISMS
CAESPITOSE

CAESPITOSELY
CAFETERIAS
CAFETIERES
CAFETORIUM
CAFETORIUMS
CAFFEINATED
CAFFEINISM
CAFFEINISMS
CAGEYNESSES
CAGINESSES
CAGMAGGING
CAGYNESSES
CAILLEACHS
CAILLIACHS
CAINOGENESES
CAINOGENESIS
CAINOGENETIC
CAIRNGORMS
CAJOLEMENT
CAJOLEMENTS
CAJOLERIES
CAJOLINGLY
CAKEWALKED
CAKEWALKER
CAKEWALKERS
CAKEWALKING
CAKINESSES
CALABASHES
CALABOGUSES
CALABOOSES
CALABRESES
CALAMANCOES
CALAMANCOS
CALAMANDER
CALAMANDERS
CALAMARIES
CALAMINING
CALAMITIES
CALAMITOUS
CALAMITOUSLY
CALAMITOUSNESS
CALAMONDIN
CALAMONDINS
CALANDRIAS
CALAVANCES
CALAVERITE
CALAVERITES
CALCAREOUS
CALCAREOUSLY
CALCARIFEROUS
CALCARIFORM
CALCEAMENTA
CALCEAMENTUM

CALCEATING
CALCEDONIES
CALCEDONIO
CALCEDONIOS
CALCEIFORM
CALCEOLARIA
CALCEOLARIAS
CALCEOLATE
CALCICOLES
CALCICOLOUS
CALCIFEROL
CALCIFEROLS
CALCIFEROUS
CALCIFICATION
CALCIFICATIONS
CALCIFUGAL
CALCIFUGES
CALCIFUGOUS
CALCIFYING
CALCIGEROUS
CALCIMINED
CALCIMINES
CALCIMINING
CALCINABLE
CALCINATION
CALCINATIONS
CALCINOSES
CALCINOSIS
CALCITONIN
CALCITONINS
CALCSINTER
CALCSINTERS
CALCULABILITIES
CALCULABILITY
CALCULABLE
CALCULABLY
CALCULATED
CALCULATEDLY
CALCULATEDNESS
CALCULATES
CALCULATING
CALCULATINGLY
CALCULATION
CALCULATIONAL
CALCULATIONS
CALCULATIVE
CALCULATOR
CALCULATORS
CALCULUSES
CALEFACIENT
CALEFACIENTS
CALEFACTION
CALEFACTIONS

CALEFACTIVE	CALLIATURE	CALOTYPIST	CAMORRISTI
CALEFACTOR	CALLIATURES	CALOTYPISTS	CAMORRISTS
CALEFACTORIES	CALLIDITIES	CALUMNIABLE	CAMOUFLAGE
CALEFACTORS	CALLIGRAMME	CALUMNIATE	CAMOUFLAGEABLE
CALEFACTORY	CALLIGRAMMES	CALUMNIATED	CAMOUFLAGED
CALEMBOURS	CALLIGRAMS	CALUMNIATES	CAMOUFLAGES
CALENDARED	CALLIGRAPHER	CALUMNIATING	CAMOUFLAGIC
CALENDARER	CALLIGRAPHERS	CALUMNIATION	CAMOUFLAGING
CALENDARERS	CALLIGRAPHIC	CALUMNIATIONS	CAMOUFLETS
CALENDARING	CALLIGRAPHICAL	CALUMNIATOR	CAMOUFLEUR
CALENDARISATION	CALLIGRAPHIES	CALUMNIATORS	CAMOUFLEURS
CALENDARISE	CALLIGRAPHIST	CALUMNIATORY	CAMPAIGNED
CALENDARISED	CALLIGRAPHISTS	CALUMNIOUS	CAMPAIGNER
CALENDARISES	CALLIGRAPHY	CALUMNIOUSLY	CAMPAIGNERS
CALENDARISING	CALLIOPSIS	CALVADOSES	CAMPAIGNING
CALENDARIST	CALLIPASHES	CALVARIUMS	CAMPANEROS
CALENDARISTS	CALLIPERED	CALYCANTHEMIES	CAMPANIFORM
CALENDARIZATION	CALLIPERING	CALYCANTHEMY	CAMPANILES
CALENDARIZE	CALLIPYGEAN	CALYCANTHUS	CAMPANISTS
CALENDARIZED	CALLIPYGIAN	CALYCANTHUSES	CAMPANOLOGER
CALENDARIZES	CALLIPYGOUS	CALYCIFORM	CAMPANOLOGERS
CALENDARIZING	CALLISTEMON	CALYCOIDEOUS	CAMPANOLOGICAL
CALENDERED	CALLISTEMONS	CALYCULATE	CAMPANOLOGIES
CALENDERER	CALLISTHENIC	CALYPSONIAN	CAMPANOLOGIST
CALENDERERS	CALLISTHENICS	CALYPSONIANS	CAMPANOLOGISTS
CALENDERING	CALLITHUMP	CALYPTERAS	CAMPANOLOGY
CALENDERINGS	CALLITHUMPIAN	CALYPTRATE	CAMPANULACEOUS
CALENDRERS	CALLITHUMPS	CALYPTROGEN	CAMPANULAR
CALENDRICAL	CALLOSITIES	CALYPTROGENS	CAMPANULAS
CALENDRIES	CALLOUSING	CAMANACHDS	CAMPANULATE
CALENDULAS	CALLOUSNESS	CAMARADERIE	CAMPCRAFTS
CALENTURES	CALLOUSNESSES	CAMARADERIES	CAMPEADORS
CALESCENCE	CALLOWNESS	CAMARILLAS	CAMPESINOS
CALESCENCES	CALLOWNESSES	CAMBERINGS	CAMPESTRAL
CALFDOZERS	CALMATIVES	CAMBISTRIES	CAMPESTRIAN
CALIATOURS	CALMNESSES	CAMCORDERS	CAMPGROUND
CALIBRATED	CALMODULIN	CAMELBACKS	CAMPGROUNDS
CALIBRATER	CALMODULINS	CAMELEOPARD	CAMPHORACEOUS
CALIBRATERS	CALMSTONES	CAMELEOPARDS	CAMPHORATE
CALIBRATES	CALORESCENCE	CAMELHAIRS	CAMPHORATED
CALIBRATING	CALORESCENCES	CAMELOPARD	CAMPHORATES
CALIBRATION	CALORESCENT	CAMELOPARDS	CAMPHORATING
CALIBRATIONS	CALORICALLY	CAMERAPERSON	CAMPIMETRIES
CALIBRATOR	CALORICITIES	CAMERAPERSONS	CAMPIMETRY
CALIBRATORS	CALORICITY	CAMERATION	CAMPINESSES
CALIDITIES	CALORIFICALLY	CAMERATIONS	CAMPNESSES
CALIFORNIUM	CALORIFICATION	CAMERAWOMAN	CAMPODEIDS
CALIFORNIUMS	CALORIFICATIONS	CAMERAWOMEN	CAMPODEIFORM
CALIGINOSITIES	CALORIFIER	CAMERAWORK	CAMPSHIRTS
CALIGINOSITY	CALORIFIERS	CAMERAWORKS	CAMPSTOOLS
CALIGINOUS	CALORIMETER	CAMERLENGO	CAMPYLOBACTER
CALIOLOGIES	CALORIMETERS	CAMERLENGOS	CAMPYLOBACTERS
CALIPASHES	CALORIMETRIC	CAMERLINGO	CAMPYLOTROPOUS
CALIPERING	CALORIMETRICAL	CAMERLINGOS	CAMSTEERIE
CALIPHATES	CALORIMETRIES	CAMIKNICKERS	CANALBOATS
CALISTHENIC	CALORIMETRY	CAMIKNICKS	CANALICULAR
CALISTHENICS	CALORISING	CAMISADOES	CANALICULATE
CALLBOARDS	CALORIZING	CAMORRISTA	CANALICULATED

CANALICULI	CANDIDATURES	CANNABINOID	CANOPHILIA
CANALICULUS	CANDIDIASES	CANNABINOIDS	CANOPHILIAS
CANALISATION	CANDIDIASIS	CANNABINOL	CANOPHILIST
CANALISATIONS	CANDIDNESS	CANNABINOLS	CANOPHILISTS
CANALISING	CANDIDNESSES	CANNABISES	CANOPHOBIA
CANALIZATION	CANDLEBERRIES	CANNELLINI	CANOPHOBIAS
CANALIZATIONS	CANDLEBERRY	CANNELLONI	CANOROUSLY
CANALIZING	CANDLEFISH	CANNELURES	CANOROUSNESS
CANCELABLE	CANDLEFISHES	CANNIBALISATION	CANOROUSNESSES
CANCELATION	CANDLEHOLDER	CANNIBALISE	CANTABANKS
CANCELATIONS	CANDLEHOLDERS	CANNIBALISED	CANTABILES
CANCELEERED	CANDLELIGHT	CANNIBALISES	CANTALOUPE
CANCELEERING	CANDLELIGHTED	CANNIBALISING	CANTALOUPES
CANCELEERS	CANDLELIGHTER	CANNIBALISM	CANTALOUPS
CANCELIERED	CANDLELIGHTERS	CANNIBALISMS	CANTANKEROUS
CANCELIERING	CANDLELIGHTS	CANNIBALISTIC	CANTANKEROUSLY
CANCELIERS	CANDLENUTS	CANNIBALIZATION	CANTATRICE
CANCELLABLE	CANDLEPINS	CANNIBALIZE	CANTATRICES
CANCELLARIAL	CANDLEPOWER	CANNIBALIZED	CANTATRICI
CANCELLARIAN	CANDLEPOWERS	CANNIBALIZES	CANTERBURIES
CANCELLARIATE	CANDLESNUFFER	CANNIBALIZING	CANTERBURY
CANCELLARIATES	CANDLESNUFFERS	CANNIBALLY	CANTERBURYS
CANCELLATE	CANDLESTICK	CANNINESSES	CANTHARIDAL
CANCELLATED	CANDLESTICKS	CANNISTERS	CANTHARIDES
CANCELLATION	CANDLEWICK	CANNONADED	CANTHARIDIAN
CANCELLATIONS	CANDLEWICKS	CANNONADES	CANTHARIDIC
CANCELLERS	CANDLEWOOD	CANNONADING	CANTHARIDIN
CANCELLING	CANDLEWOODS	CANNONBALL	CANTHARIDINE
CANCELLOUS	CANDYFLOSS	CANNONBALLED	CANTHARIDINES
CANCERATED	CANDYFLOSSES	CANNONBALLING	CANTHARIDINS
CANCERATES	CANDYGRAMS	CANNONBALLS	CANTHARIDS
CANCERATING	CANDYTUFTS	CANNONEERS	CANTHAXANTHIN
CANCERATION	CANEBRAKES	CANNONIERS	CANTHAXANTHINE
CANCERATIONS	CANEFRUITS	CANNONRIES	CANTHAXANTHINES
CANCEROPHOBIA	CANEPHORAS	CANNULATED	CANTHAXANTHINS
CANCEROPHOBIAS	CANEPHORES	CANNULATES	CANTHITISES
CANCEROUSLY	CANEPHORUS	CANNULATING	CANTICOING
CANCERPHOBIA	CANEPHORUSES	CANNULATION	CANTICOYED
CANCERPHOBIAS	CANESCENCE	CANNULATIONS	CANTICOYING
CANCIONERO	CANESCENCES	CANOEWOODS	CANTILENAS
CANCIONEROS	CANINITIES	CANONESSES	CANTILEVER
CANCRIFORM	CANISTERED	CANONICALLY	CANTILEVERED
CANCRIZANS	CANISTERING	CANONICALS	CANTILEVERING
CANDELABRA	CANISTERISATION	CANONICATE	CANTILEVERS
CANDELABRAS	CANISTERISE	CANONICATES	CANTILLATE
CANDELABRUM	CANISTERISED	CANONICITIES	CANTILLATED
CANDELABRUMS	CANISTERISES	CANONICITY	CANTILLATES
CANDELILLA	CANISTERISING	CANONISATION	CANTILLATING
CANDELILLAS	CANISTERIZATION	CANONISATIONS	CANTILLATION
CANDESCENCE	CANISTERIZE	CANONISERS	CANTILLATIONS
CANDESCENCES	CANISTERIZED	CANONISING	CANTILLATORY
CANDESCENT	CANISTERIZES	CANONISTIC	CANTINESSES
CANDESCENTLY	CANISTERIZING	CANONIZATION	CANTONISATION
CANDIDACIES	CANKEREDLY	CANONIZATIONS	CANTONISATIONS
CANDIDATES	CANKEREDNESS	CANONIZERS	CANTONISED
CANDIDATESHIP	CANKEREDNESSES	CANONIZING	CANTONISES
CANDIDATESHIPS	CANKERWORM	CANOODLERS	CANTONISING
CANDIDATURE	CANKERWORMS	CANOODLING	CANTONIZATION

CANTONIZATIONS	CAPILLARIES	CAPPUCCINOS	CARABINIER
CANTONIZED	CAPILLARITIES	CAPREOLATE	CARABINIERE
CANTONIZES	CAPILLARITY	CAPRICCIOS	CARABINIERI
CANTONIZING	CAPILLITIA	CAPRICCIOSO	CARABINIERS
CANTONMENT	CAPILLITIUM	CAPRICIOUS	CARACOLERS
CANTONMENTS	CAPILLITIUMS	CAPRICIOUSLY	CARACOLING
CANULATING	CAPITALISATION	CAPRICIOUSNESS	CARACOLLED
CANULATION	CAPITALISATIONS	CAPRIFICATION	CARACOLLING
CANULATIONS	CAPITALISE	CAPRIFICATIONS	CARAGEENAN
CANVASBACK	CAPITALISED	CAPRIFOILS	CARAGEENANS
CANVASBACKS	CAPITALISES	CAPRIFOLES	CARAMBOLAS
CANVASLIKE	CAPITALISING	CAPRIFOLIACEOUS	CARAMBOLED
CANVASSERS	CAPITALISM	CAPRIFYING	CARAMBOLES
CANVASSING	CAPITALISMS	CAPRIOLING	CARAMBOLING
CANYONEERS	CAPITALIST	CAPROLACTAM	CARAMELISATION
CANYONINGS	CAPITALISTIC	CAPROLACTAMS	CARAMELISATIONS
CANZONETTA	CAPITALISTS	CAPRYLATES	CARAMELISE
CANZONETTAS	CAPITALIZATION	CAPSAICINS	CARAMELISED
CANZONETTE	CAPITALIZATIONS	CAPSIZABLE	CARAMELISES
CAOUTCHOUC	CAPITALIZE	CAPSOMERES	CARAMELISING
CAOUTCHOUCS	CAPITALIZED	CAPSULATED	CARAMELIZATION
CAPABILITIES	CAPITALIZES	CAPSULATION	CARAMELIZATIONS
CAPABILITY	CAPITALIZING	CAPSULATIONS	CARAMELIZE
CAPABLENESS	CAPITATION	CAPSULISED	CARAMELIZED
CAPABLENESSES	CAPITATIONS	CAPSULISES	CARAMELIZES
CAPACIOUSLY	CAPITATIVE	CAPSULISING	CARAMELIZING
CAPACIOUSNESS	CAPITELLUM	CAPSULIZED	CARAMELLED
CAPACIOUSNESSES	CAPITOLIAN	CAPSULIZES	CARAMELLING
CAPACITANCE	CAPITOLINE	CAPSULIZING	CARANGOIDS
CAPACITANCES	CAPITULANT	CAPTAINCIES	CARAPACIAL
CAPACITATE	CAPITULANTS	CAPTAINING	CARAVANCES
CAPACITATED	CAPITULARIES	CAPTAINRIES	CARAVANEER
CAPACITATES	CAPITULARLY	CAPTAINSHIP	CARAVANEERS
CAPACITATING	CAPITULARS	CAPTAINSHIPS	CARAVANERS
CAPACITATION	CAPITULARY	CAPTIONING	CARAVANETTE
CAPACITATIONS	CAPITULATE	CAPTIONLESS	CARAVANETTES
CAPACITIES	CAPITULATED	CAPTIOUSLY	CARAVANING
CAPACITIVE	CAPITULATES	CAPTIOUSNESS	CARAVANINGS
CAPACITIVELY	CAPITULATING	CAPTIOUSNESSES	CARAVANNED
CAPACITORS	CAPITULATION	CAPTIVANCE	CARAVANNER
CAPARISONED	CAPITULATIONS	CAPTIVANCES	CARAVANNERS
CAPARISONING	CAPITULATOR	CAPTIVATED	CARAVANNING
CAPARISONS	CAPITULATORS	CAPTIVATES	CARAVANNINGS
CAPELLINES	CAPITULATORY	CAPTIVATING	CARAVANSARAI
CAPELLMEISTER	CAPNOMANCIES	CAPTIVATINGLY	CARAVANSARAIS
CAPELLMEISTERS	CAPNOMANCY	CAPTIVATION	CARAVANSARIES
CAPERCAILLIE	CAPOCCHIAS	CAPTIVATIONS	CARAVANSARY
CAPERCAILLIES	CAPODASTRO	CAPTIVATOR	CARAVANSERAI
CAPERCAILZIE	CAPODASTROS	CAPTIVATORS	CARAVANSERAIS
CAPERCAILZIES	CAPONIERES	CAPTIVAUNCE	CARAVELLES
CAPERINGLY	CAPONISING	CAPTIVAUNCES	CARBACHOLS
CAPERNOITED	CAPONIZING	CAPTIVITIES	CARBAMATES
CAPERNOITIE	CAPOTASTOS	CAPTOPRILS	CARBAMAZEPINE
CAPERNOITIES	CAPPARIDACEOUS	CARABINEER	CARBAMAZEPINES
CAPERNOITY	CAPPELLETTI	CARABINEERS	CARBAMIDES
CAPILLACEOUS	CAPPERNOITIES	CARABINERO	CARBAMIDINE
CAPILLAIRE	CAPPERNOITY	CARABINEROS	CARBAMIDINES
CAPILLAIRES	CAPPUCCINO	CARABINERS	CARBAMOYLS

CARBANIONS
CARBAZOLES
CARBIMAZOLE
CARBIMAZOLES
CARBINEERS
CARBINIERS
CARBOCYCLIC
CARBOHYDRASE
CARBOHYDRASES
CARBOHYDRATE
CARBOHYDRATES
CARBOLATED
CARBOLISED
CARBOLISES
CARBOLISING
CARBOLIZED
CARBOLIZES
CARBOLIZING
CARBONACEOUS
CARBONADES
CARBONADOED
CARBONADOES
CARBONADOING
CARBONADOS
CARBONARAS
CARBONATED
CARBONATES
CARBONATING
CARBONATION
CARBONATIONS
CARBONATITE
CARBONATITES
CARBONETTE
CARBONETTES
CARBONIFEROUS
CARBONISATION
CARBONISATIONS
CARBONISED
CARBONISER
CARBONISERS
CARBONISES
CARBONISING
CARBONIUMS
CARBONIZATION
CARBONIZATIONS
CARBONIZED
CARBONIZER
CARBONIZERS
CARBONIZES
CARBONIZING
CARBONLESS
CARBONNADE
CARBONNADES
CARBONYLATE
CARBONYLATED
CARBONYLATES
CARBONYLATING
CARBONYLATION

CARBONYLATIONS
CARBONYLIC
CARBOXYLASE
CARBOXYLASES
CARBOXYLATE
CARBOXYLATED
CARBOXYLATES
CARBOXYLATING
CARBOXYLATION
CARBOXYLATIONS
CARBOXYLIC
CARBUNCLED
CARBUNCLES
CARBUNCULAR
CARBURATED
CARBURATES
CARBURATING
CARBURATION
CARBURATIONS
CARBURETED
CARBURETER
CARBURETERS
CARBURETING
CARBURETION
CARBURETIONS
CARBURETOR
CARBURETORS
CARBURETTED
CARBURETTER
CARBURETTERS
CARBURETTING
CARBURETTOR
CARBURETTORS
CARBURISATION
CARBURISATIONS
CARBURISED
CARBURISES
CARBURISING
CARBURIZATION
CARBURIZATIONS
CARBURIZED
CARBURIZES
CARBURIZING
CARBYLAMINE
CARBYLAMINES
CARCASSING
CARCINOGEN
CARCINOGENESES
CARCINOGENESIS
CARCINOGENIC
CARCINOGENICITY
CARCINOGENS
CARCINOIDS
CARCINOLOGICAL
CARCINOLOGIES
CARCINOLOGIST
CARCINOLOGISTS
CARCINOLOGY

CARCINOMAS
CARCINOMATA
CARCINOMATOID
CARCINOMATOSES
CARCINOMATOSIS
CARCINOMATOUS
CARCINOSARCOMA
CARCINOSARCOMAS
CARCINOSES
CARCINOSIS
CARDAMINES
CARDBOARDS
CARDBOARDY
CARDCASTLE
CARDCASTLES
CARDHOLDER
CARDHOLDERS
CARDIALGIA
CARDIALGIAS
CARDIALGIC
CARDIALGIES
CARDIGANED
CARDINALATE
CARDINALATES
CARDINALATIAL
CARDINALITIAL
CARDINALITIES
CARDINALITY
CARDINALLY
CARDINALSHIP
CARDINALSHIPS
CARDIOCENTESES
CARDIOCENTESIS
CARDIOGENIC
CARDIOGRAM
CARDIOGRAMS
CARDIOGRAPH
CARDIOGRAPHER
CARDIOGRAPHERS
CARDIOGRAPHIC
CARDIOGRAPHICAL
CARDIOGRAPHIES
CARDIOGRAPHS
CARDIOGRAPHY
CARDIOLOGICAL
CARDIOLOGIES
CARDIOLOGIST
CARDIOLOGISTS
CARDIOLOGY
CARDIOMEGALIES
CARDIOMEGALY
CARDIOMOTOR
CARDIOMYOPATHY
CARDIOPATHIES
CARDIOPATHY
CARDIOPLEGIA
CARDIOPLEGIAS
CARDIOPULMONARY

CARDIOTHORACIC
CARDIOTONIC
CARDIOTONICS
CARDIOVASCULAR
CARDITISES
CARDOPHAGI
CARDOPHAGUS
CARDPHONES
CARDPLAYER
CARDPLAYERS
CARDPUNCHES
CARDSHARPER
CARDSHARPERS
CARDSHARPING
CARDSHARPINGS
CARDSHARPS
CARDUACEOUS
CAREENAGES
CAREERISMS
CAREERISTS
CAREFREENESS
CAREFREENESSES
CAREFULLER
CAREFULLEST
CAREFULNESS
CAREFULNESSES
CAREGIVERS
CAREGIVING
CAREGIVINGS
CARELESSLY
CARELESSNESS
CARELESSNESSES
CARESSINGLY
CARESSINGS
CARESSIVELY
CARETAKERS
CARETAKING
CARETAKINGS
CAREWORKER
CAREWORKERS
CARFUFFLED
CARFUFFLES
CARFUFFLING
CARHOPPING
CARICATURA
CARICATURAL
CARICATURAS
CARICATURE
CARICATURED
CARICATURES
CARICATURING
CARICATURIST
CARICATURISTS
CARILLONED
CARILLONING
CARILLONIST
CARILLONISTS
CARILLONNED

CARILLONNEUR	CARPACCIOS	CARRONADES	CARTOUCHES
CARILLONNEURS	CARPELLARY	CARROTIEST	CARTRIDGES
CARILLONNING	CARPELLATE	CARROTTOPPED	CARTULARIES
CARIOGENIC	CARPELLATES	CARROTTOPS	CARTWHEELED
CARIOSITIES	CARPENTARIA	CARROUSELS	CARTWHEELER
CARIOUSNESS	CARPENTARIAS	CARRYBACKS	CARTWHEELERS
CARIOUSNESSES	CARPENTERED	CARRYFORWARD	CARTWHEELING
CARJACKERS	CARPENTERING	CARRYFORWARDS	CARTWHEELS
CARJACKING	CARPENTERS	CARRYOVERS	CARTWRIGHT
CARJACKINGS	CARPENTRIES	CARRYTALES	CARTWRIGHTS
CARMAGNOLE	CARPETBAGGED	CARSICKNESS	CARUNCULAR
CARMAGNOLES	CARPETBAGGER	CARSICKNESSES	CARUNCULATE
CARMELITES	CARPETBAGGERIES	CARTELISATION	CARUNCULATED
CARMINATIVE	CARPETBAGGERS	CARTELISATIONS	CARUNCULOUS
CARMINATIVES	CARPETBAGGERY	CARTELISED	CARVACROLS
CARNAHUBAS	CARPETBAGGING	CARTELISES	CARYATIDAL
CARNALISED	CARPETBAGS	CARTELISING	CARYATIDEAN
CARNALISES	CARPETINGS	CARTELISMS	CARYATIDES
CARNALISING	CARPETMONGER	CARTELISTS	CARYATIDIC
CARNALISMS	CARPETMONGERS	CARTELIZATION	CARYOPSIDES
CARNALISTS	CARPETWEED	CARTELIZATIONS	CARYOPTERIS
CARNALITIES	CARPETWEEDS	CARTELIZED	CARYOPTERISES
CARNALIZED	CARPHOLOGIES	CARTELIZES	CASCADURAS
CARNALIZES	CARPHOLOGY	CARTELIZING	CASCARILLA
CARNALIZING	CARPOGONIA	CARTHAMINE	CASCARILLAS
CARNALLING	CARPOGONIAL	CARTHAMINES	CASEATIONS
CARNALLITE	CARPOGONIUM	CARTHORSES	CASEBEARER
CARNALLITES	CARPOLOGICAL	CARTILAGES	CASEBEARERS
CARNAPTIOUS	CARPOLOGIES	CARTILAGINOUS	CASEINATES
CARNAROLIS	CARPOLOGIST	CARTOGRAMS	CASEINOGEN
CARNASSIAL	CARPOLOGISTS	CARTOGRAPHER	CASEINOGENS
CARNASSIALS	CARPOMETACARPI	CARTOGRAPHERS	CASEMAKERS
CARNATIONED	CARPOMETACARPUS	CARTOGRAPHIC	CASEMENTED
CARNATIONS	CARPOOLERS	CARTOGRAPHICAL	CASEWORKER
CARNELIANS	CARPOOLING	CARTOGRAPHIES	CASEWORKERS
CARNIFEXES	CARPOPHAGOUS	CARTOGRAPHY	CASHIERERS
CARNIFICATION	CARPOPHORE	CARTOLOGICAL	CASHIERING
CARNIFICATIONS	CARPOPHORES	CARTOLOGIES	CASHIERINGS
CARNIFICIAL	CARPOSPORE	CARTOMANCIES	CASHIERMENT
CARNIFYING	CARPOSPORES	CARTOMANCY	CASHIERMENTS
CARNITINES	CARRAGEENAN	CARTONAGES	CASHPOINTS
CARNIVALESQUE	CARRAGEENANS	CARTONNAGE	CASINGHEAD
CARNIVORES	CARRAGEENIN	CARTONNAGES	CASINGHEADS
CARNIVORIES	CARRAGEENINS	CARTOONING	CASKSTANDS
CARNIVOROUS	CARRAGEENS	CARTOONINGS	CASSAREEPS
CARNIVOROUSLY	CARRAGHEEN	CARTOONISH	CASSATIONS
CARNIVOROUSNESS	CARRAGHEENAN	CARTOONISHLY	CASSEROLED
CARNOSAURS	CARRAGHEENANS	CARTOONIST	CASSEROLES
CARNOSITIES	CARRAGHEENIN	CARTOONISTS	CASSEROLING
CARNOTITES	CARRAGHEENINS	CARTOONLIKE	CASSIMERES
CAROLLINGS	CARRAGHEENS	CARTOPHILE	CASSINGLES
CAROMELLED	CARREFOURS	CARTOPHILES	CASSIOPEIUM
CAROMELLING	CARRIAGEABLE	CARTOPHILIC	CASSIOPEIUMS
CAROTENOID	CARRIAGEWAY	CARTOPHILIES	CASSITERITE
CAROTENOIDS	CARRIAGEWAYS	CARTOPHILIST	CASSITERITES
CAROTINOID	CARRITCHES	CARTOPHILISTS	CASSOLETTE
CAROTINOIDS	CARRIWITCHET	CARTOPHILY	CASSOLETTES
CAROUSINGLY	CARRIWITCHETS	CARTOPPERS	CASSONADES

CASSOULETS
CASSOWARIES
CASSUMUNAR
CASSUMUNARS
CASTABILITIES
CASTABILITY
CASTANOSPERMINE
CASTELLANS
CASTELLATED
CASTELLATION
CASTELLATIONS
CASTELLUMS
CASTIGATED
CASTIGATES
CASTIGATING
CASTIGATION
CASTIGATIONS
CASTIGATOR
CASTIGATORS
CASTIGATORY
CASTOREUMS
CASTRAMETATION
CASTRAMETATIONS
CASTRATERS
CASTRATING
CASTRATION
CASTRATIONS
CASTRATORS
CASTRATORY
CASUALISATION
CASUALISATIONS
CASUALISED
CASUALISES
CASUALISING
CASUALISMS
CASUALIZATION
CASUALIZATIONS
CASUALIZED
CASUALIZES
CASUALIZING
CASUALNESS
CASUALNESSES
CASUALTIES
CASUARINAS
CASUISTICAL
CASUISTICALLY
CASUISTRIES
CATABOLICALLY
CATABOLISE
CATABOLISED
CATABOLISES
CATABOLISING
CATABOLISM
CATABOLISMS
CATABOLITE
CATABOLITES
CATABOLIZE
CATABOLIZED

CATABOLIZES
CATABOLIZING
CATACAUSTIC
CATACAUSTICS
CATACHRESES
CATACHRESIS
CATACHRESTIC
CATACHRESTICAL
CATACLASES
CATACLASIS
CATACLASMIC
CATACLASMS
CATACLASTIC
CATACLINAL
CATACLYSMAL
CATACLYSMIC
CATACLYSMICALLY
CATACLYSMS
CATACOUSTICS
CATACUMBAL
CATADIOPTRIC
CATADIOPTRICAL
CATADROMOUS
CATAFALCOES
CATAFALQUE
CATAFALQUES
CATALECTIC
CATALECTICS
CATALEPSIES
CATALEPTIC
CATALEPTICALLY
CATALEPTICS
CATALLACTIC
CATALLACTICALLY
CATALLACTICS
CATALOGERS
CATALOGING
CATALOGISE
CATALOGISED
CATALOGISES
CATALOGISING
CATALOGIZE
CATALOGIZED
CATALOGIZES
CATALOGIZING
CATALOGUED
CATALOGUER
CATALOGUERS
CATALOGUES
CATALOGUING
CATALOGUISE
CATALOGUISED
CATALOGUISES
CATALOGUISING
CATALOGUIST
CATALOGUISTS
CATALOGUIZE
CATALOGUIZED

CATALOGUIZES
CATALOGUIZING
CATALYSERS
CATALYSING
CATALYTICAL
CATALYTICALLY
CATALYZERS
CATALYZING
CATAMARANS
CATAMENIAL
CATAMOUNTAIN
CATAMOUNTAINS
CATAMOUNTS
CATANANCHE
CATANANCHES
CATAPHONIC
CATAPHONICS
CATAPHORAS
CATAPHORESES
CATAPHORESIS
CATAPHORETIC
CATAPHORIC
CATAPHRACT
CATAPHRACTIC
CATAPHRACTS
CATAPHYLLARY
CATAPHYLLS
CATAPHYSICAL
CATAPLASIA
CATAPLASIAS
CATAPLASMS
CATAPLASTIC
CATAPLECTIC
CATAPLEXIES
CATAPULTED
CATAPULTIC
CATAPULTIER
CATAPULTIERS
CATAPULTING
CATARACTOUS
CATARRHALLY
CATARRHINE
CATARRHINES
CATARRHOUS
CATASTASES
CATASTASIS
CATASTROPHE
CATASTROPHES
CATASTROPHIC
CATASTROPHISM
CATASTROPHISMS
CATASTROPHIST
CATASTROPHISTS
CATATONIAS
CATATONICALLY
CATATONICS
CATATONIES
CATCALLERS

CATCALLING
CATCHCRIES
CATCHFLIES
CATCHINESS
CATCHINESSES
CATCHMENTS
CATCHPENNIES
CATCHPENNY
CATCHPHRASE
CATCHPHRASES
CATCHPOLES
CATCHPOLLS
CATCHWATER
CATCHWEEDS
CATCHWEIGHT
CATCHWORDS
CATECHESES
CATECHESIS
CATECHETIC
CATECHETICAL
CATECHETICALLY
CATECHETICS
CATECHISATION
CATECHISATIONS
CATECHISED
CATECHISER
CATECHISERS
CATECHISES
CATECHISING
CATECHISINGS
CATECHISMAL
CATECHISMS
CATECHISTIC
CATECHISTICAL
CATECHISTICALLY
CATECHISTS
CATECHIZATION
CATECHIZATIONS
CATECHIZED
CATECHIZER
CATECHIZERS
CATECHIZES
CATECHIZING
CATECHIZINGS
CATECHOLAMINE
CATECHOLAMINES
CATECHUMEN
CATECHUMENAL
CATECHUMENATE
CATECHUMENATES
CATECHUMENICAL
CATECHUMENISM
CATECHUMENISMS
CATECHUMENS
CATECHUMENSHIP
CATECHUMENSHIPS
CATEGOREMATIC
CATEGORIAL

CATEGORIALLY	CATHETERISMS	CAULICULATE	CAVALIERED
CATEGORICAL	CATHETERIZATION	CAULICULUS	CAVALIERING
CATEGORICALLY	CATHETERIZE	CAULICULUSES	CAVALIERISH
CATEGORICALNESS	CATHETERIZED	CAULIFLORIES	CAVALIERISM
CATEGORIES	CATHETERIZES	CAULIFLOROUS	CAVALIERISMS
CATEGORISATION	CATHETERIZING	CAULIFLORY	CAVALIERLY
CATEGORISATIONS	CATHETOMETER	CAULIFLOWER	CAVALLETTI
CATEGORISE	CATHETOMETERS	CAULIFLOWERET	CAVALRYMAN
CATEGORISED	CATHETUSES	CAULIFLOWERETS	CAVALRYMEN
CATEGORISES	CATHODALLY	CAULIFLOWERS	CAVEFISHES
CATEGORISING	CATHODICAL	CAULIGENOUS	CAVENDISHES
CATEGORIST	CATHODICALLY	CAUMSTONES	CAVERNICOLOUS
CATEGORISTS	CATHODOGRAPH	CAUSABILITIES	CAVERNOUSLY
CATEGORIZATION	CATHODOGRAPHER	CAUSABILITY	CAVERNULOUS
CATEGORIZATIONS	CATHODOGRAPHERS	CAUSALGIAS	CAVILLATION
CATEGORIZE	CATHODOGRAPHIES	CAUSALITIES	CAVILLATIONS
CATEGORIZED	CATHODOGRAPHS	CAUSATIONAL	CAVILLINGS
CATEGORIZES	CATHODOGRAPHY	CAUSATIONISM	CAVITATING
CATEGORIZING	CATHOLICALLY	CAUSATIONISMS	CAVITATION
CATENACCIO	CATHOLICATE	CAUSATIONIST	CAVITATIONS
CATENACCIOS	CATHOLICATES	CAUSATIONISTS	CEANOTHUSES
CATENARIAN	CATHOLICISATION	CAUSATIONS	CEASEFIRES
CATENARIES	CATHOLICISE	CAUSATIVELY	CEASELESSLY
CATENATING	CATHOLICISED	CAUSATIVENESS	CEASELESSNESS
CATENATION	CATHOLICISES	CAUSATIVENESSES	CEASELESSNESSES
CATENATIONS	CATHOLICISING	CAUSATIVES	CEBADILLAS
CATENULATE	CATHOLICISM	CAUSELESSLY	CECUTIENCIES
CATERCORNER	CATHOLICISMS	CAUSELESSNESS	CECUTIENCY
CATERCORNERED	CATHOLICITIES	CAUSELESSNESSES	CEDARBIRDS
CATERESSES	CATHOLICITY	CAUSEWAYED	CEDARWOODS
CATERPILLAR	CATHOLICIZATION	CAUSEWAYING	CEDRELACEOUS
CATERPILLARS	CATHOLICIZE	CAUSTICALLY	CEILOMETER
CATERWAULED	CATHOLICIZED	CAUSTICITIES	CEILOMETERS
CATERWAULER	CATHOLICIZES	CAUSTICITY	CELANDINES
CATERWAULERS	CATHOLICIZING	CAUSTICNESS	CELEBRANTS
CATERWAULING	CATHOLICLY	CAUSTICNESSES	CELEBRATED
CATERWAULINGS	CATHOLICOI	CAUTERANTS	CELEBRATEDNESS
CATERWAULS	CATHOLICON	CAUTERISATION	CELEBRATES
CATFACINGS	CATHOLICONS	CAUTERISATIONS	CELEBRATING
CATHARISED	CATHOLICOS	CAUTERISED	CELEBRATION
CATHARISES	CATHOLICOSES	CAUTERISES	CELEBRATIONS
CATHARISING	CATHOLYTES	CAUTERISING	CELEBRATIVE
CATHARIZED	CATILINARIAN	CAUTERISMS	CELEBRATOR
CATHARIZES	CATIONICALLY	CAUTERIZATION	CELEBRATORS
CATHARIZING	CATNAPPERS	CAUTERIZATIONS	CELEBRATORY
CATHARTICAL	CATNAPPING	CAUTERIZED	CELEBRITIES
CATHARTICALLY	CATOPTRICAL	CAUTERIZES	CELERITIES
CATHARTICS	CATOPTRICS	CAUTERIZING	CELESTIALLY
CATHECTING	CATTINESSES	CAUTIONARY	CELESTIALS
CATHEDRALS	CATTISHNESS	CAUTIONERS	CELESTINES
CATHEDRATIC	CATTISHNESSES	CAUTIONING	CELESTITES
CATHEPSINS	CAUCHEMARS	CAUTIONRIES	CELIBACIES
CATHETERISATION	CAUCUSSING	CAUTIOUSLY	CELIBATARIAN
CATHETERISE	CAUDATIONS	CAUTIOUSNESS	CELLARAGES
CATHETERISED	CAUDILLISMO	CAUTIOUSNESSES	CELLARETTE
CATHETERISES	CAUDILLISMOS	CAVALCADED	CELLARETTES
CATHETERISING	CAULESCENT	CAVALCADES	CELLARISTS
CATHETERISM	CAULICOLOUS	CAVALCADING	CELLARWAYS

CELLBLOCKS	CENTENARIANISM	CENTRALISM	CENTROSOME
CELLENTANI	CENTENARIANISMS	CENTRALISMS	CENTROSOMES
CELLENTANIS	CENTENARIANS	CENTRALIST	CENTROSOMIC
CELLIFEROUS	CENTENARIES	CENTRALISTIC	CENTROSPHERE
CELLOBIOSE	CENTENIERS	CENTRALISTS	CENTROSPHERES
CELLOBIOSES	CENTENNIAL	CENTRALITIES	CENTROSYMMETRIC
CELLOIDINS	CENTENNIALLY	CENTRALITY	CENTUMVIRATE
CELLOPHANE	CENTENNIALS	CENTRALIZATION	CENTUMVIRATES
CELLOPHANES	CENTERBOARD	CENTRALIZATIONS	CENTUMVIRI
CELLPHONES	CENTERBOARDS	CENTRALIZE	CENTUPLICATE
CELLULARITIES	CENTEREDNESS	CENTRALIZED	CENTUPLICATED
CELLULARITY	CENTEREDNESSES	CENTRALIZER	CENTUPLICATES
CELLULASES	CENTERFOLD	CENTRALIZERS	CENTUPLICATING
CELLULATED	CENTERFOLDS	CENTRALIZES	CENTUPLICATION
CELLULIFEROUS	CENTERINGS	CENTRALIZING	CENTUPLICATIONS
CELLULITES	CENTERLESS	CENTREBOARD	CENTUPLING
CELLULITIS	CENTERLINE	CENTREBOARDS	CENTURIATION
CELLULITISES	CENTERLINES	CENTREFOLD	CENTURIATIONS
CELLULOIDS	CENTERPIECE	CENTREFOLDS	CENTURIATOR
CELLULOLYTIC	CENTERPIECES	CENTREINGS	CENTURIATORS
CELLULOSES	CENTESIMAL	CENTRELINE	CENTURIONS
CELLULOSIC	CENTESIMALLY	CENTRELINES	CEPHALAGRA
CELLULOSICS	CENTESIMALS	CENTREPIECE	CEPHALAGRAS
CELSITUDES	CENTESIMOS	CENTREPIECES	CEPHALALGIA
CEMBALISTS	CENTIGRADE	CENTRICALLY	CEPHALALGIAS
CEMENTATION	CENTIGRAMME	CENTRICALNESS	CEPHALALGIC
CEMENTATIONS	CENTIGRAMMES	CENTRICALNESSES	CEPHALEXIN
CEMENTATORY	CENTIGRAMS	CENTRICITIES	CEPHALEXINS
CEMENTITES	CENTILITER	CENTRICITY	CEPHALICALLY
CEMENTITIOUS	CENTILITERS	CENTRIFUGAL	CEPHALISATION
CEMETERIES	CENTILITRE	CENTRIFUGALISE	CEPHALISATIONS
CENESTHESES	CENTILITRES	CENTRIFUGALISED	CEPHALITIS
CENESTHESIA	CENTILLION	CENTRIFUGALISES	CEPHALITISES
CENESTHESIAS	CENTILLIONS	CENTRIFUGALIZE	CEPHALIZATION
CENESTHESIS	CENTILLIONTH	CENTRIFUGALIZED	CEPHALIZATIONS
CENESTHETIC	CENTILLIONTHS	CENTRIFUGALIZES	CEPHALOCELE
CENOBITICAL	CENTIMETER	CENTRIFUGALLY	CEPHALOCELES
CENOGENESES	CENTIMETERS	CENTRIFUGALS	CEPHALOCHORDATE
CENOGENESIS	CENTIMETRE	CENTRIFUGATION	CEPHALOMETER
CENOGENETIC	CENTIMETRES	CENTRIFUGATIONS	CEPHALOMETERS
CENOGENETICALLY	CENTIMETRIC	CENTRIFUGE	CEPHALOMETRIC
CENOSPECIES	CENTIMORGAN	CENTRIFUGED	CEPHALOMETRIES
CENOTAPHIC	CENTIMORGANS	CENTRIFUGENCE	CEPHALOMETRY
CENSORABLE	CENTINELLS	CENTRIFUGENCES	CEPHALOPOD
CENSORIOUS	CENTIPEDES	CENTRIFUGES	CEPHALOPODAN
CENSORIOUSLY	CENTIPOISE	CENTRIFUGING	CEPHALOPODANS
CENSORIOUSNESS	CENTIPOISES	CENTRIOLES	CEPHALOPODIC
CENSORSHIP	CENTONELLS	CENTRIPETAL	CEPHALOPODOUS
CENSORSHIPS	CENTONISTS	CENTRIPETALISM	CEPHALOPODS
CENSURABILITIES	CENTRALEST	CENTRIPETALISMS	CEPHALORIDINE
CENSURABILITY	CENTRALISATION	CENTRIPETALLY	CEPHALORIDINES
CENSURABLE	CENTRALISATIONS	CENTROBARIC	CEPHALOSPORIN
CENSURABLENESS	CENTRALISE	CENTROCLINAL	CEPHALOSPORINS
CENSURABLY	CENTRALISED	CENTROIDAL	CEPHALOTHIN
CENTAUREAS	CENTRALISER	CENTROLECITHAL	CEPHALOTHINS
CENTAURIAN	CENTRALISERS	CENTROMERE	CEPHALOTHORACES
CENTAURIES	CENTRALISES	CENTROMERES	CEPHALOTHORACIC
CENTENARIAN	CENTRALISING	CENTROMERIC	CEPHALOTHORAX

CEPHALOTHORAXES
CEPHALOTOMIES
CEPHALOTOMY
CERAMICIST
CERAMICISTS
CERAMOGRAPHIES
CERAMOGRAPHY
CERARGYRITE
CERARGYRITES
CERASTIUMS
CERATITISES
CERATODUSES
CERATOPSIAN
CERATOPSIANS
CERATOPSID
CERATOPSIDS
CERCARIANS
CERCOPITHECID
CERCOPITHECIDS
CERCOPITHECOID
CERCOPITHECOIDS
CEREALISTS
CEREBELLAR
CEREBELLIC
CEREBELLOUS
CEREBELLUM
CEREBELLUMS
CEREBRALISM
CEREBRALISMS
CEREBRALIST
CEREBRALISTS
CEREBRALLY
CEREBRATED
CEREBRATES
CEREBRATING
CEREBRATION
CEREBRATIONS
CEREBRIFORM
CEREBRITIS
CEREBRITISES
CEREBROSIDE
CEREBROSIDES
CEREBROSPINAL
CEREBROTONIA
CEREBROTONIAS
CEREBROTONIC
CEREBROVASCULAR
CERECLOTHS
CEREMONIAL
CEREMONIALISM
CEREMONIALISMS
CEREMONIALIST
CEREMONIALISTS
CEREMONIALLY
CEREMONIALS
CEREMONIES
CEREMONIOUS
CEREMONIOUSLY

CEREMONIOUSNESS
CERIFEROUS
CEROGRAPHIC
CEROGRAPHICAL
CEROGRAPHIES
CEROGRAPHIST
CEROGRAPHISTS
CEROGRAPHS
CEROGRAPHY
CEROMANCIES
CEROPLASTIC
CEROPLASTICS
CERTAINEST
CERTAINTIES
CERTIFIABLE
CERTIFIABLY
CERTIFICATE
CERTIFICATED
CERTIFICATES
CERTIFICATING
CERTIFICATION
CERTIFICATIONS
CERTIFICATORIES
CERTIFICATORY
CERTIFIERS
CERTIFYING
CERTIORARI
CERTIORARIS
CERTITUDES
CERULOPLASMIN
CERULOPLASMINS
CERUMINOUS
CERUSSITES
CERVELASES
CERVICITIS
CERVICITISES
CERVICOGRAPHIES
CERVICOGRAPHY
CESAREVICH
CESAREVICHES
CESAREVITCH
CESAREVITCHES
CESAREVNAS
CESAREWICH
CESAREWICHES
CESAREWITCH
CESAREWITCHES
CESPITOSELY
CESSATIONS
CESSIONARIES
CESSIONARY
CESTOIDEAN
CESTOIDEANS
CETEOSAURUS
CETEOSAURUSES
CETOLOGICAL
CETOLOGIES
CETOLOGIST

CETOLOGISTS
CETRIMIDES
CEVADILLAS
CEYLANITES
CEYLONITES
CHABAZITES
CHAENOMELES
CHAENOMELESES
CHAETIFEROUS
CHAETODONS
CHAETOGNATH
CHAETOGNATHS
CHAETOPODS
CHAFFERERS
CHAFFERIES
CHAFFERING
CHAFFINCHES
CHAFFINGLY
CHAGRINING
CHAGRINNED
CHAGRINNING
CHAINBRAKE
CHAINBRAKES
CHAINFALLS
CHAINPLATE
CHAINPLATES
CHAINSAWED
CHAINSAWING
CHAINSHOTS
CHAINSTITCH
CHAINSTITCHES
CHAINWHEEL
CHAINWHEELS
CHAINWORKS
CHAIRBORNE
CHAIRBOUND
CHAIRLIFTS
CHAIRMANED
CHAIRMANING
CHAIRMANNED
CHAIRMANNING
CHAIRMANSHIP
CHAIRMANSHIPS
CHAIRPERSON
CHAIRPERSONS
CHAIRWOMAN
CHAIRWOMEN
CHAISELESS
CHAKALAKAS
CHALAZIONS
CHALAZOGAMIC
CHALAZOGAMIES
CHALAZOGAMY
CHALCANTHITE
CHALCANTHITES
CHALCEDONIC
CHALCEDONIES
CHALCEDONY

CHALCEDONYX
CHALCEDONYXES
CHALCOCITE
CHALCOCITES
CHALCOGENIDE
CHALCOGENIDES
CHALCOGENS
CHALCOGRAPHER
CHALCOGRAPHERS
CHALCOGRAPHIC
CHALCOGRAPHICAL
CHALCOGRAPHIES
CHALCOGRAPHIST
CHALCOGRAPHISTS
CHALCOGRAPHY
CHALCOLITHIC
CHALCOPYRITE
CHALCOPYRITES
CHALICOTHERE
CHALICOTHERES
CHALKBOARD
CHALKBOARDS
CHALKFACES
CHALKINESS
CHALKINESSES
CHALKSTONE
CHALKSTONES
CHALLANING
CHALLENGEABLE
CHALLENGED
CHALLENGER
CHALLENGERS
CHALLENGES
CHALLENGING
CHALLENGINGLY
CHALUMEAUS
CHALUMEAUX
CHALYBEATE
CHALYBEATES
CHALYBITES
CHAMAELEON
CHAMAELEONS
CHAMAEPHYTE
CHAMAEPHYTES
CHAMBERERS
CHAMBERHAND
CHAMBERHANDS
CHAMBERING
CHAMBERINGS
CHAMBERLAIN
CHAMBERLAINS
CHAMBERLAINSHIP
CHAMBERMAID
CHAMBERMAIDS
CHAMBERPOT
CHAMBERPOTS
CHAMBRANLE
CHAMBRANLES

CHAMELEONIC	CHANGEOVER	CHAPLAINSHIPS	CHARCUTERIES
CHAMELEONLIKE	CHANGEOVERS	CHAPMANSHIP	CHARDONNAY
CHAMELEONS	CHANGEROUND	CHAPMANSHIPS	CHARDONNAYS
CHAMFERERS	CHANGEROUNDS	CHAPPESSES	CHARGEABILITIES
CHAMFERING	CHANNELERS	CHAPRASSIES	CHARGEABILITY
CHAMFRAINS	CHANNELING	CHAPRASSTS	CHARGEABLE
CHAMOISING	CHANNELISATION	CHAPSTICKS	CHARGEABLENESS
CHAMOMILES	CHANNELISATIONS	CHAPTALISATION	CHARGEABLY
CHAMPAGNES	CHANNELISE	CHAPTALISATIONS	CHARGEHAND
CHAMPAIGNS	CHANNELISED	CHAPTALISE	CHARGEHANDS
CHAMPERTIES	CHANNELISES	CHAPTALISED	CHARGELESS
CHAMPERTOUS	CHANNELISING	CHAPTALISES	CHARGENURSE
CHAMPIGNON	CHANNELIZATION	CHAPTALISING	CHARGENURSES
CHAMPIGNONS	CHANNELIZATIONS	CHAPTALIZATION	CHARGESHEET
CHAMPIONED	CHANNELIZE	CHAPTALIZATIONS	CHARGESHEETS
CHAMPIONESS	CHANNELIZED	CHAPTALIZE	CHARGRILLED
CHAMPIONESSES	CHANNELIZES	CHAPTALIZED	CHARGRILLING
CHAMPIONING	CHANNELIZING	CHAPTALIZES	CHARGRILLS
CHAMPIONSHIP	CHANNELLED	CHAPTALIZING	CHARINESSES
CHAMPIONSHIPS	CHANNELLER	CHAPTERHOUSE	CHARIOTEER
CHAMPLEVES	CHANNELLERS	CHAPTERHOUSES	CHARIOTEERED
CHANCELESS	CHANNELLING	CHAPTERING	CHARIOTEERING
CHANCELLERIES	CHANSONETTE	CHARABANCS	CHARIOTEERS
CHANCELLERY	CHANSONETTES	CHARACINOID	CHARIOTING
CHANCELLOR	CHANSONNIER	CHARACTERED	CHARISMATA
CHANCELLORIES	CHANSONNIERS	CHARACTERFUL	CHARISMATIC
CHANCELLORS	CHANTARELLE	CHARACTERIES	CHARISMATICS
CHANCELLORSHIP	CHANTARELLES	CHARACTERING	CHARITABLE
CHANCELLORSHIPS	CHANTECLER	CHARACTERISABLE	CHARITABLENESS
CHANCELLORY	CHANTECLERS	CHARACTERISE	CHARITABLY
CHANCERIES	CHANTERELLE	CHARACTERISED	CHARIVARIED
CHANCINESS	CHANTERELLES	CHARACTERISER	CHARIVARIING
CHANCINESSES	CHANTEUSES	CHARACTERISERS	CHARIVARIS
CHANCROIDAL	CHANTICLEER	CHARACTERISES	CHARLADIES
CHANCROIDS	CHANTICLEERS	CHARACTERISING	CHARLATANIC
CHANDELIER	CHANTINGLY	CHARACTERISM	CHARLATANICAL
CHANDELIERED	CHANTRESSES	CHARACTERISMS	CHARLATANISM
CHANDELIERS	CHANUKIAHS	CHARACTERISTIC	CHARLATANISMS
CHANDELLED	CHAOLOGIES	CHARACTERISTICS	CHARLATANISTIC
CHANDELLES	CHAOLOGIST	CHARACTERIZABLE	CHARLATANRIES
CHANDELLING	CHAOLOGISTS	CHARACTERIZE	CHARLATANRY
CHANDLERIES	CHAOTICALLY	CHARACTERIZED	CHARLATANS
CHANDLERING	CHAPARAJOS	CHARACTERIZER	CHARLESTON
CHANDLERINGS	CHAPAREJOS	CHARACTERIZERS	CHARLESTONED
CHANDLERLY	CHAPARRALS	CHARACTERIZES	CHARLESTONING
CHANGEABILITIES	CHAPATTIES	CHARACTERIZING	CHARLESTONS
CHANGEABILITY	CHAPELRIES	CHARACTERLESS	CHARLOTTES
CHANGEABLE	CHAPERONAGE	CHARACTEROLOGY	CHARMEUSES
CHANGEABLENESS	CHAPERONAGES	CHARACTERS	CHARMINGER
CHANGEABLY	CHAPERONED	CHARACTERY	CHARMINGEST
CHANGEFULLY	CHAPERONES	CHARBROILED	CHARMINGLY
CHANGEFULNESS	CHAPERONING	CHARBROILER	CHARMLESSLY
CHANGEFULNESSES	CHAPFALLEN	CHARBROILERS	CHARMONIUM
CHANGELESS	CHAPLAINCIES	CHARBROILING	CHAROSETHS
CHANGELESSLY	CHAPLAINCY	CHARBROILS	CHARTACEOUS
CHANGELESSNESS	CHAPLAINRIES	CHARCOALED	CHARTERERS
CHANGELING	CHAPLAINRY	CHARCOALING	CHARTERING
CHANGELINGS	CHAPLAINSHIP	CHARCUTERIE	CHARTERPARTIES

CHARTERPARTY	CHAUFFEUSING	CHECKWEIGHER	CHEESEWIRE
CHARTHOUSE	CHAULMOOGRA	CHECKWEIGHERS	CHEESEWIRES
CHARTHOUSES	CHAULMOOGRAS	CHEECHAKOES	CHEESEWOOD
CHARTOGRAPHER	CHAULMUGRA	CHEECHAKOS	CHEESEWOODS
CHARTOGRAPHERS	CHAULMUGRAS	CHEECHALKO	CHEESEWRING
CHARTOGRAPHIC	CHAUNTRESS	CHEECHALKOES	CHEESEWRINGS
CHARTOGRAPHICAL	CHAUNTRESSES	CHEECHALKOS	CHEESINESS
CHARTOGRAPHIES	CHAUNTRIES	CHEEKBONES	CHEESINESSES
CHARTOGRAPHY	CHAUSSURES	CHEEKINESS	CHEILITISES
CHARTREUSE	CHAUTAUQUA	CHEEKINESSES	CHELASHIPS
CHARTREUSES	CHAUTAUQUAS	CHEEKPIECE	CHELATABLE
CHARTULARIES	CHAUVINISM	CHEEKPIECES	CHELATIONS
CHARTULARY	CHAUVINISMS	CHEEKPOUCH	CHELICERAE
CHASEPORTS	CHAUVINIST	CHEEKPOUCHES	CHELICERAL
CHASMOGAMIC	CHAUVINISTIC	CHEEKTEETH	CHELICERATE
CHASMOGAMIES	CHAUVINISTS	CHEEKTOOTH	CHELICERATES
CHASMOGAMOUS	CHAVENDERS	CHEERFULLER	CHELIFEROUS
CHASMOGAMY	CHAVTASTIC	CHEERFULLEST	CHELONIANS
CHASSEPOTS	CHAWBACONS	CHEERFULLY	CHELUVIATION
CHASTENERS	CHEAPENERS	CHEERFULNESS	CHELUVIATIONS
CHASTENESS	CHEAPENING	CHEERFULNESSES	CHEMAUTOTROPH
CHASTENESSES	CHEAPISHLY	CHEERINESS	CHEMAUTOTROPHIC
CHASTENING	CHEAPJACKS	CHEERINESSES	CHEMAUTOTROPHS
CHASTENINGLY	CHEAPNESSES	CHEERINGLY	CHEMIATRIC
CHASTENMENT	CHEAPSKATE	CHEERISHNESS	CHEMICALLY
CHASTENMENTS	CHEAPSKATES	CHEERISHNESSES	CHEMICKING
CHASTISABLE	CHEATERIES	CHEERLEADER	CHEMIOSMOSES
CHASTISEMENT	CHEATINGLY	CHEERLEADERS	CHEMIOSMOSIS
CHASTISEMENTS	CHECHAKOES	CHEERLEADING	CHEMIOSMOTIC
CHASTISERS	CHECHAQUOS	CHEERLEADS	CHEMISETTE
CHASTISING	CHECKBOOKS	CHEERLESSLY	CHEMISETTES
CHASTITIES	CHECKCLERK	CHEERLESSNESS	CHEMISORBED
CHATEAUBRIAND	CHECKCLERKS	CHEERLESSNESSES	CHEMISORBING
CHATEAUBRIANDS	CHECKERBERRIES	CHEESEBOARD	CHEMISORBS
CHATELAINE	CHECKERBERRY	CHEESEBOARDS	CHEMISORPTION
CHATELAINES	CHECKERBLOOM	CHEESEBURGER	CHEMISORPTIONS
CHATELAINS	CHECKERBLOOMS	CHEESEBURGERS	CHEMISTRIES
CHATOYANCE	CHECKERBOARD	CHEESECAKE	CHEMITYPES
CHATOYANCES	CHECKERBOARDS	CHEESECAKES	CHEMITYPIES
CHATOYANCIES	CHECKERING	CHEESECLOTH	CHEMOATTRACTANT
CHATOYANCY	CHECKLATON	CHEESECLOTHS	CHEMOAUTOTROPH
CHATOYANTS	CHECKLATONS	CHEESECUTTER	CHEMOAUTOTROPHS
CHATTERATI	CHECKLISTED	CHEESECUTTERS	CHEMOAUTOTROPHY
CHATTERBOX	CHECKLISTING	CHEESEHOPPER	CHEMOAUTROPH
CHATTERBOXES	CHECKLISTS	CHEESEHOPPERS	CHEMOAUTROPHS
CHATTERERS	CHECKMARKED	CHEESEMITE	CHEMOCEPTOR
CHATTERING	CHECKMARKING	CHEESEMITES	CHEMOCEPTORS
CHATTERINGS	CHECKMARKS	CHEESEMONGER	CHEMOKINES
CHATTINESS	CHECKMATED	CHEESEMONGERS	CHEMOKINESES
CHATTINESSES	CHECKMATES	CHEESEPARER	CHEMOKINESIS
CHAUDFROID	CHECKMATING	CHEESEPARERS	CHEMOLITHOTROPH
CHAUDFROIDS	CHECKPOINT	CHEESEPARING	CHEMONASTIES
CHAUFFEURED	CHECKPOINTS	CHEESEPARINGS	CHEMONASTY
CHAUFFEURING	CHECKRAILS	CHEESEPRESS	CHEMOPSYCHIATRY
CHAUFFEURS	CHECKREINS	CHEESEPRESSES	CHEMORECEPTION
CHAUFFEUSE	CHECKROOMS	CHEESETASTER	CHEMORECEPTIONS
CHAUFFEUSED	CHECKROWED	CHEESETASTERS	CHEMORECEPTIVE
CHAUFFEUSES	CHECKROWING	CHEESEVATS	CHEMORECEPTOR

CHEMORECEPTORS	CHERRYLIKE	CHICNESSES	CHILLINESSES
CHEMOSMOSES	CHERRYSTONE	CHIEFERIES	CHILLINGLY
CHEMOSMOSIS	CHERRYSTONES	CHIEFESSES	CHILLNESSES
CHEMOSMOTIC	CHERSONESE	CHIEFLINGS	CHILOPODAN
CHEMOSORBED	CHERSONESES	CHIEFSHIPS	CHILOPODANS
CHEMOSORBING	CHERUBICAL	CHIEFTAINCIES	CHILOPODOUS
CHEMOSORBS	CHERUBICALLY	CHIEFTAINCY	CHILTEPINS
CHEMOSPHERE	CHERUBIMIC	CHIEFTAINESS	CHIMAERISM
CHEMOSPHERES	CHERUBLIKE	CHIEFTAINESSES	CHIMAERISMS
CHEMOSPHERIC	CHERVONETS	CHIEFTAINRIES	CHIMERICAL
CHEMOSTATS	CHESSBOARD	CHIEFTAINRY	CHIMERICALLY
CHEMOSURGERIES	CHESSBOARDS	CHIEFTAINS	CHIMERICALNESS
CHEMOSURGERY	CHESSPIECE	CHIEFTAINSHIP	CHIMERISMS
CHEMOSURGICAL	CHESSPIECES	CHIEFTAINSHIPS	CHIMICHANGA
CHEMOSYNTHESES	CHESSYLITE	CHIFFCHAFF	CHIMICHANGAS
CHEMOSYNTHESIS	CHESSYLITES	CHIFFCHAFFS	CHIMNEYBOARD
CHEMOSYNTHETIC	CHESTERFIELD	CHIFFONADE	CHIMNEYBOARDS
CHEMOTACTIC	CHESTERFIELDS	CHIFFONADES	CHIMNEYBREAST
CHEMOTACTICALLY	CHESTINESS	CHIFFONIER	CHIMNEYBREASTS
CHEMOTAXES	CHESTINESSES	CHIFFONIERS	CHIMNEYING
CHEMOTAXIS	CHEVALIERS	CHIFFONNIER	CHIMNEYLIKE
CHEMOTAXONOMIC	CHEVELURES	CHIFFONNIERS	CHIMNEYPIECE
CHEMOTAXONOMIES	CHEVESAILE	CHIFFOROBE	CHIMNEYPIECES
CHEMOTAXONOMIST	CHEVESAILES	CHIFFOROBES	CHIMNEYPOT
CHEMOTAXONOMY	CHEVISANCE	CHIHUAHUAS	CHIMNEYPOTS
CHEMOTHERAPIES	CHEVISANCES	CHILBLAINED	CHIMPANZEE
CHEMOTHERAPIST	CHEVRETTES	CHILBLAINS	CHIMPANZEES
CHEMOTHERAPISTS	CHEVROTAIN	CHILDBEARING	CHINABERRIES
CHEMOTHERAPY	CHEVROTAINS	CHILDBEARINGS	CHINABERRY
CHEMOTROPIC	CHEWINESSES	CHILDBIRTH	CHINACHINA
CHEMOTROPICALLY	CHIACKINGS	CHILDBIRTHS	CHINACHINAS
CHEMOTROPISM	CHIAROSCURISM	CHILDCARES	CHINAROOTS
CHEMOTROPISMS	CHIAROSCURISMS	CHILDCROWING	CHINAWARES
CHEMPADUKS	CHIAROSCURIST	CHILDCROWINGS	CHINCAPINS
CHEMURGICAL	CHIAROSCURISTS	CHILDERMAS	CHINCHERINCHEE
CHEMURGIES	CHIAROSCURO	CHILDERMASES	CHINCHERINCHEES
CHENOPODIACEOUS	CHIAROSCUROS	CHILDHOODS	CHINCHIEST
CHEONGSAMS	CHIASMATIC	CHILDISHLY	CHINCHILLA
CHEQUEBOOK	CHIASTOLITE	CHILDISHNESS	CHINCHILLAS
CHEQUEBOOKS	CHIASTOLITES	CHILDISHNESSES	CHINCOUGHS
CHEQUERBOARD	CHIBOUQUES	CHILDLESSNESS	CHINKAPINS
CHEQUERBOARDS	CHICALOTES	CHILDLESSNESSES	CHINKERINCHEE
CHEQUERING	CHICANERIES	CHILDLIEST	CHINKERINCHEES
CHEQUERWISE	CHICANINGS	CHILDLIKENESS	CHINOISERIE
CHEQUERWORK	CHICCORIES	CHILDLIKENESSES	CHINOISERIES
CHEQUERWORKS	CHICKABIDDIES	CHILDMINDER	CHINOVNIKS
CHERALITES	CHICKABIDDY	CHILDMINDERS	CHINQUAPIN
CHERIMOYAS	CHICKADEES	CHILDNESSES	CHINQUAPINS
CHERIMOYER	CHICKAREES	CHILDPROOF	CHINSTRAPS
CHERIMOYERS	CHICKENHEARTED	CHILIAGONS	CHINTZIEST
CHERISHABLE	CHICKENING	CHILIAHEDRA	CHINWAGGED
CHERISHERS	CHICKENPOX	CHILIAHEDRON	CHINWAGGING
CHERISHING	CHICKENPOXES	CHILIAHEDRONS	CHIONODOXA
CHERISHINGLY	CHICKENSHIT	CHILIARCHIES	CHIONODOXAS
CHERISHMENT	CHICKENSHITS	CHILIARCHS	CHIPBOARDS
CHERISHMENTS	CHICKLINGS	CHILIARCHY	CHIPOCHIAS
CHERNOZEMIC	CHICKORIES	CHILIASTIC	CHIPOLATAS
CHERNOZEMS	CHICKWEEDS	CHILLINESS	CHIPPERING

CHIPPINESS	CHISELLERS	CHLORIDISES	CHLOROMETRIES
CHIPPINESSES	CHISELLING	CHLORIDISING	CHLOROMETRY
CHIQUICHIQUI	CHISELLINGS	CHLORIDIZE	CHLOROPHYL
CHIQUICHIQUIS	CHITARRONE	CHLORIDIZED	CHLOROPHYLL
CHIRAGRICAL	CHITARRONI	CHLORIDIZES	CHLOROPHYLLOID
CHIRALITIES	CHITCHATTED	CHLORIDIZING	CHLOROPHYLLOUS
CHIRIMOYAS	CHITCHATTING	CHLORIMETER	CHLOROPHYLLS
CHIROGNOMIES	CHITTAGONG	CHLORIMETERS	CHLOROPHYLS
CHIROGNOMY	CHITTAGONGS	CHLORIMETRIC	CHLOROPHYTUM
CHIROGRAPH	CHITTERING	CHLORIMETRIES	CHLOROPHYTUMS
CHIROGRAPHER	CHITTERINGS	CHLORIMETRY	CHLOROPICRIN
CHIROGRAPHERS	CHITTERLING	CHLORINATE	CHLOROPICRINS
CHIROGRAPHIC	CHITTERLINGS	CHLORINATED	CHLOROPLAST
CHIROGRAPHICAL	CHIVALRIES	CHLORINATES	CHLOROPLASTAL
CHIROGRAPHIES	CHIVALROUS	CHLORINATING	CHLOROPLASTIC
CHIROGRAPHIST	CHIVALROUSLY	CHLORINATION	CHLOROPLASTS
CHIROGRAPHISTS	CHIVALROUSNESS	CHLORINATIONS	CHLOROPRENE
CHIROGRAPHS	CHIVAREEING	CHLORINATOR	CHLOROPRENES
CHIROGRAPHY	CHIVARING	CHLORINATORS	CHLOROQUIN
CHIROLOGIES	CHIYOGAMIS	CHLORINISE	CHLOROQUINE
CHIROLOGIST	CHLAMYDATE	CHLORINISED	CHLOROQUINES
CHIROLOGISTS	CHLAMYDEOUS	CHLORINISES	CHLOROQUINS
CHIROMANCER	CHLAMYDIAE	CHLORINISING	CHLOROTHIAZIDE
CHIROMANCERS	CHLAMYDIAL	CHLORINITIES	CHLOROTHIAZIDES
CHIROMANCIES	CHLAMYDIAS	CHLORINITY	CHLORPICRIN
CHIROMANCY	CHLAMYDOMONADES	CHLORINIZE	CHLORPICRINS
CHIROMANTIC	CHLAMYDOMONAS	CHLORINIZED	CHLORPROMAZINE
CHIROMANTICAL	CHLAMYDOSPORE	CHLORINIZES	CHLORPROMAZINES
CHIRONOMER	CHLAMYDOSPORES	CHLORINIZING	CHLORPROPAMIDE
CHIRONOMERS	CHLOANTHITE	CHLORITISATION	CHLORPROPAMIDES
CHIRONOMIC	CHLOANTHITES	CHLORITISATIONS	CHLORTHALIDONE
CHIRONOMID	CHLOASMATA	CHLORITIZATION	CHLORTHALIDONES
CHIRONOMIDS	CHLORACETIC	CHLORITIZATIONS	CHOANOCYTE
CHIRONOMIES	CHLORACNES	CHLOROACETIC	CHOANOCYTES
CHIROPODIAL	CHLORALISM	CHLOROARGYRITE	CHOCAHOLIC
CHIROPODIES	CHLORALISMS	CHLOROBENZENE	CHOCAHOLICS
CHIROPODIST	CHLORALOSE	CHLOROBENZENES	CHOCKABLOCK
CHIROPODISTS	CHLORALOSED	CHLOROBROMIDE	CHOCKSTONE
CHIROPRACTIC	CHLORALOSES	CHLOROBROMIDES	CHOCKSTONES
CHIROPRACTICS	CHLORAMBUCIL	CHLOROCRUORIN	CHOCOHOLIC
CHIROPRACTOR	CHLORAMBUCILS	CHLOROCRUORINS	CHOCOHOLICS
CHIROPRACTORS	CHLORAMINE	CHLORODYNE	CHOCOLATES
CHIROPTERAN	CHLORAMINES	CHLORODYNES	CHOCOLATEY
CHIROPTERANS	CHLORAMPHENICOL	CHLOROFORM	CHOCOLATIER
CHIROPTEROUS	CHLORARGYRITE	CHLOROFORMED	CHOCOLATIERS
CHIROPTERS	CHLORARGYRITES	CHLOROFORMER	CHOCOLATIEST
CHIRPINESS	CHLORDANES	CHLOROFORMERS	CHOICENESS
CHIRPINESSES	CHLORELLAS	CHLOROFORMING	CHOICENESSES
CHIRRUPERS	CHLORENCHYMA	CHLOROFORMIST	CHOIRGIRLS
CHIRRUPING	CHLORENCHYMAS	CHLOROFORMISTS	CHOIRMASTER
CHIRRUPPED	CHLORHEXIDINE	CHLOROFORMS	CHOIRMASTERS
CHIRRUPPING	CHLORHEXIDINES	CHLOROHYDRIN	CHOIRSCREEN
CHIRURGEON	CHLORIDATE	CHLOROHYDRINS	CHOIRSCREENS
CHIRURGEONLY	CHLORIDATED	CHLOROMETER	CHOIRSTALLS
CHIRURGEONS	CHLORIDATES	CHLOROMETERS	CHOKEBERRIES
CHIRURGERIES	CHLORIDATING	CHLOROMETHANE	CHOKEBERRY
CHIRURGERY	CHLORIDISE	CHLOROMETHANES	CHOKEBORES
CHIRURGICAL	CHLORIDISED	CHLOROMETRIC	CHOKECHERRIES

CHOKECHERRY	CHONDROCRANIA	CHOREOLOGIST	CHRISMATORY
CHOKECOILS	CHONDROCRANIUM	CHOREOLOGISTS	CHRISTCROSS
CHOKEDAMPS	CHONDROCRANIUMS	CHOREOLOGY	CHRISTCROSSES
CHOKEHOLDS	CHONDROGENESES	CHOREPISCOPAL	CHRISTENED
CHOLAEMIAS	CHONDROGENESIS	CHORIAMBIC	CHRISTENER
CHOLAGOGIC	CHONDROITIN	CHORTAMBICS	CHRISTENERS
CHOLAGOGUE	CHONDROITINS	CHORIAMBUS	CHRISTENING
CHOLAGOGUES	CHONDROMAS	CHORIAMBUSES	CHRISTENINGS
CHOLANGIOGRAM	CHONDROMATA	CHORIOALLANTOIC	CHRISTIANIA
CHOLANGIOGRAMS	CHONDROMATOSES	CHORIOALLANTOIS	CHRISTIANIAS
CHOLANGIOGRAPHY	CHONDROMATOSIS	CHORIOCARCINOMA	CHRISTIANISE
CHOLECALCIFEROL	CHONDROMATOUS	CHORISATION	CHRISTIANISED
CHOLECYSTECTOMY	CHONDROPHORINE	CHORISATIONS	CHRISTIANISER
CHOLECYSTITIS	CHONDROPHORINES	CHORISTERS	CHRISTIANISERS
CHOLECYSTITISES	CHONDROSKELETON	CHORIZATION	CHRISTIANISES
CHOLECYSTOKININ	CHONDROSTIAN	CHORIZATIONS	CHRISTIANISING
CHOLECYSTOSTOMY	CHONDROSTIANS	CHORIZONTIST	CHRISTIANIZE
CHOLECYSTOTOMY	CHONDRULES	CHORIZONTISTS	CHRISTIANIZED
CHOLECYSTS	CHOPFALLEN	CHORIZONTS	CHRISTIANIZER
CHOLELITHIASES	CHOPHOUSES	CHOROGRAPHER	CHRISTIANIZERS
CHOLELITHIASIS	CHOPLOGICS	CHOROGRAPHERS	CHRISTIANIZES
CHOLELITHS	CHOPPERING	CHOROGRAPHIC	CHRISTIANIZING
CHOLERICALLY	CHOPPINESS	CHOROGRAPHICAL	CHRISTIANLY
CHOLERICLY	CHOPPINESSES	CHOROGRAPHIES	CHRISTIANS
CHOLESTASES	CHOPSOCKIES	CHOROGRAPHY	CHRISTINGLE
CHOLESTASIS	CHOPSTICKS	CHOROIDITIS	CHRISTINGLES
CHOLESTATIC	CHORAGUSES	CHOROIDITISES	CHRISTOPHANIES
CHOLESTERIC	CHORALISTS	CHOROLOGICAL	CHRISTOPHANY
CHOLESTERIN	CHORDAMESODERM	CHOROLOGIES	CHROMAFFIN
CHOLESTERINS	CHORDAMESODERMS	CHOROLOGIST	CHROMAKEYS
CHOLESTEROL	CHORDOPHONE	CHOROLOGISTS	CHROMATICALLY
CHOLESTEROLEMIA	CHORDOPHONES	CHOROPLETH	CHROMATICISM
CHOLESTEROLS	CHORDOPHONIC	CHOROPLETHS	CHROMATICISMS
CHOLESTYRAMINE	CHORDOTOMIES	CHORUSMASTER	CHROMATICITIES
CHOLESTYRAMINES	CHORDOTOMY	CHORUSMASTERS	CHROMATICITY
CHOLIAMBIC	CHOREGRAPH	CHORUSSING	CHROMATICNESS
CHOLIAMBICS	CHOREGRAPHED	CHOUCROUTE	CHROMATICNESSES
CHOLINERGIC	CHOREGRAPHER	CHOUCROUTES	CHROMATICS
CHOLINERGICALLY	CHOREGRAPHERS	CHOULTRIES	CHROMATIDS
CHOLINESTERASE	CHOREGRAPHIC	CHOUNTERED	CHROMATINIC
CHOLINESTERASES	CHOREGRAPHIES	CHOUNTERING	CHROMATINS
CHOMOPHYTE	CHOREGRAPHING	CHOWDERHEAD	CHROMATIST
CHOMOPHYTES	CHOREGRAPHS	CHOWDERHEADED	CHROMATISTS
CHONDRICHTHYAN	CHOREGRAPHY	CHOWDERHEADS	CHROMATOGRAM
CHONDRICHTHYANS	CHOREGUSES	CHOWDERING	CHROMATOGRAMS
CHONDRIFICATION	CHOREIFORM	CHOWHOUNDS	CHROMATOGRAPH
CHONDRIFIED	CHOREODRAMA	CHOWKIDARS	CHROMATOGRAPHED
CHONDRIFIES	CHOREODRAMAS	CHREMATIST	CHROMATOGRAPHER
CHONDRIFYING	CHOREOGRAPH	CHREMATISTIC	CHROMATOGRAPHIC
CHONDRIOSOMAL	CHOREOGRAPHED	CHREMATISTICS	CHROMATOGRAPHS
CHONDRIOSOME	CHOREOGRAPHER	CHREMATISTS	CHROMATOGRAPHY
CHONDRIOSOMES	CHOREOGRAPHERS	CHRESTOMATHIC	CHROMATOID
CHONDRITES	CHOREOGRAPHIC	CHRESTOMATHICAL	CHROMATOLOGIES
CHONDRITIC	CHOREOGRAPHIES	CHRESTOMATHIES	CHROMATOLOGIST
CHONDRITIS	CHOREOGRAPHING	CHRESTOMATHY	CHROMATOLOGISTS
CHONDRITISES	CHOREOGRAPHS	CHRISMATION	CHROMATOLOGY
CHONDROBLAST	CHOREOGRAPHY	CHRISMATIONS	CHROMATOLYSES
CHONDROBLASTS	CHOREOLOGIES	CHRISMATORIES	CHROMATOLYSIS

CHROMATOLYTIC	CHRONICALLY	CHRYSANTHS	CHURCHINGS
CHROMATOPHORE	CHRONICITIES	CHRYSAROBIN	CHURCHISMS
CHROMATOPHORES	CHRONICITY	CHRYSAROBINS	CHURCHLESS
CHROMATOPHORIC	CHRONICLED	CHRYSOBERYL	CHURCHLIER
CHROMATOPHOROUS	CHRONICLER	CHRYSOBERYLS	CHURCHLIEST
CHROMATOPSIA	CHRONICLERS	CHRYSOCOLLA	CHURCHLINESS
CHROMATOPSIAS	CHRONICLES	CHRYSOCOLLAS	CHURCHLINESSES
CHROMATOSPHERE	CHRONICLING	CHRYSOCRACIES	CHURCHMANLY
CHROMATOSPHERES	CHRONOBIOLOGIC	CHRYSOCRACY	CHURCHMANSHIP
CHROMATYPE	CHRONOBIOLOGIES	CHRYSOLITE	CHURCHMANSHIPS
CHROMATYPES	CHRONOBIOLOGIST	CHRYSOLITES	CHURCHPEOPLE
CHROMIDIUM	CHRONOBIOLOGY	CHRYSOLITIC	CHURCHWARD
CHROMINANCE	CHRONOGRAM	CHRYSOMELID	CHURCHWARDEN
CHROMINANCES	CHRONOGRAMMATIC	CHRYSOMELIDS	CHURCHWARDENS
CHROMISING	CHRONOGRAMS	CHRYSOPHAN	CHURCHWARDS
CHROMIZING	CHRONOGRAPH	CHRYSOPHANS	CHURCHWAYS
CHROMOCENTER	CHRONOGRAPHER	CHRYSOPHILITE	CHURCHWOMAN
CHROMOCENTERS	CHRONOGRAPHERS	CHRYSOPHILITES	CHURCHWOMEN
CHROMODYNAMICS	CHRONOGRAPHIC	CHRYSOPHYTE	CHURCHYARD
CHROMOGENIC	CHRONOGRAPHIES	CHRYSOPHYTES	CHURCHYARDS
CHROMOGENS	CHRONOGRAPHS	CHRYSOPRASE	CHURLISHLY
CHROMOGRAM	CHRONOGRAPHY	CHRYSOPRASES	CHURLISHNESS
CHROMOGRAMS	CHRONOLOGER	CHRYSOTILE	CHURLISHNESSES
CHROMOMERE	CHRONOLOGERS	CHRYSOTILES	CHURNMILKS
CHROMOMERES	CHRONOLOGIC	CHUBBINESS	CHURRIGUERESCO
CHROMOMERIC	CHRONOLOGICAL	CHUBBINESSES	CHURRIGUERESQUE
CHROMONEMA	CHRONOLOGICALLY	CHUCKAWALLA	CHYLACEOUS
CHROMONEMAL	CHRONOLOGIES	CHUCKAWALLAS	CHYLIFEROUS
CHROMONEMATA	CHRONOLOGISE	CHUCKHOLES	CHYLIFICATION
CHROMONEMATIC	CHRONOLOGISED	CHUCKLEHEAD	CHYLIFICATIONS
CHROMONEMIC	CHRONOLOGISES	CHUCKLEHEADED	CHYLIFYING
CHROMOPHIL	CHRONOLOGISING	CHUCKLEHEADS	CHYLOMICRON
CHROMOPHILIC	CHRONOLOGIST	CHUCKLESOME	CHYLOMICRONS
CHROMOPHOBE	CHRONOLOGISTS	CHUCKLINGLY	CHYMIFEROUS
CHROMOPHONIC	CHRONOLOGIZE	CHUCKLINGS	CHYMIFICATION
CHROMOPHORE	CHRONOLOGIZED	CHUCKWALLA	CHYMIFICATIONS
CHROMOPHORES	CHRONOLOGIZES	CHUCKWALLAS	CHYMIFYING
CHROMOPHORIC	CHRONOLOGIZING	CHUFFINESS	CHYMISTRIES
CHROMOPHOROUS	CHRONOLOGY	CHUFFINESSES	CHYMOTRYPSIN
CHROMOPLAST	CHRONOMETER	CHUGALUGGED	CHYMOTRYPSINS
CHROMOPLASTS	CHRONOMETERS	CHUGALUGGING	CHYMOTRYPTIC
CHROMOPROTEIN	CHRONOMETRIC	CHUMMINESS	CIBACHROME
CHROMOPROTEINS	CHRONOMETRICAL	CHUMMINESSES	CIBACHROMES
CHROMOSCOPE	CHRONOMETRIES	CHUNDERING	CICADELLID
CHROMOSCOPES	CHRONOMETRY	CHUNDEROUS	CICADELLIDS
CHROMOSOMAL	CHRONOSCOPE	CHUNKINESS	CICATRICES
CHROMOSOMALLY	CHRONOSCOPES	CHUNKINESSES	CICATRICHULE
CHROMOSOME	CHRONOSCOPIC	CHUNNERING	CICATRICHULES
CHROMOSOMES	CHRONOTHERAPIES	CHUNTERING	CICATRICIAL
CHROMOSPHERE	CHRONOTHERAPY	CHUPATTIES	CICATRICLE
CHROMOSPHERES	CHRONOTRON	CHUPRASSIES	CICATRICLES
CHROMOSPHERIC	CHRONOTRONS	CHURCHGOER	CICATRICOSE
CHROMOTHERAPIES	CHRYSALIDAL	CHURCHGOERS	CICATRICULA
CHROMOTHERAPY	CHRYSALIDES	CHURCHGOING	CICATRICULAS
CHROMOTYPE	CHRYSALIDS	CHURCHGOINGS	CICATRISANT
CHROMOTYPES	CHRYSALISES	CHURCHIANITIES	CICATRISATION
CHROMOXYLOGRAPH	CHRYSANTHEMUM	CHURCHIANITY	CICATRISATIONS
CHRONAXIES	CHRYSANTHEMUMS	CHURCHIEST	CICATRISED

CICATRISER	CINEMATISES	CIRCULARISER	CIRCUMDUCTED
CICATRISERS	CINEMATISING	CIRCULARISERS	CIRCUMDUCTING
CICATRISES	CINEMATIZE	CIRCULARISES	CIRCUMDUCTION
CICATRISING	CINEMATIZED	CIRCULARISTNG	CIRCUMDUCTIONS
CICATRIXES	CINEMATIZES	CIRCULARITIES	CIRCUMDUCTORY
CICATRIZANT	CINEMATIZING	CIRCULARTTY	CTRCUMDUCTS
CICATRIZATION	CINEMATOGRAPH	CIRCULARIZATION	CIRCUMFERENCE
CICATRIZATIONS	CINEMATOGRAPHED	CIRCULARIZE	CIRCUMFERENCES
CICATRIZED	CINEMATOGRAPHER	CIRCULARIZED	CIRCUMFERENTIAL
CICATRIZER	CINEMATOGRAPHIC	CIRCULARIZER	CIRCUMFERENTOR
CICATRIZERS	CINEMATOGRAPHS	CIRCULARIZERS	CIRCUMFERENTORS
CICATRIZES	CINEMATOGRAPHY	CIRCULARIZES	CIRCUMFLECT
CICATRIZING	CINEMICROGRAPHY	CIRCULARIZING	CIRCUMFLECTED
CICERONEING	CINEPHILES	CIRCULARLY	CIRCUMFLECTING
CICHORACEOUS	CINEPLEXES	CIRCULARNESS	CIRCUMFLECTS
CICINNUSES	CINERARIAS	CIRCULARNESSES	CIRCUMFLEX
CICISBEISM	CINERARIUM	CIRCULATABLE	CIRCUMFLEXES
CICISBEISMS	CINERATION	CIRCULATED	CIRCUMFLEXION
CICLATOUNS	CINERATIONS	CIRCULATES	CIRCUMFLEXIONS
CICLOSPORIN	CINERATORS	CIRCULATING	CIRCUMFLUENCE
CICLOSPORINS	CINERITIOUS	CIRCULATINGS	CIRCUMFLUENCES
CIGARETTES	CINGULATED	CIRCULATION	CIRCUMFLUENT
CIGARILLOS	CINNABARIC	CIRCULATIONS	CIRCUMFLUOUS
CIGUATERAS	CINNABARINE	CIRCULATIVE	CIRCUMFORANEAN
CILIATIONS	CINNAMONIC	CIRCULATOR	CIRCUMFORANEOUS
CIMETIDINE	CINNARIZINE	CIRCULATORS	CIRCUMFUSE
CIMETIDINES	CINNARIZINES	CIRCULATORY	CIRCUMFUSED
CINCHONACEOUS	CINQUECENTIST	CIRCUMAMBAGES	CIRCUMFUSES
CINCHONIDINE	CINQUECENTISTS	CIRCUMAMBAGIOUS	CIRCUMFUSILE
CINCHONIDINES	CINQUECENTO	CIRCUMAMBIENCE	CIRCUMFUSING
CINCHONINE	CINQUECENTOS	CIRCUMAMBIENCES	CIRCUMFUSION
CINCHONINES	CINQUEFOIL	CIRCUMAMBIENCY	CIRCUMFUSIONS
CINCHONINIC	CINQUEFOILS	CIRCUMAMBIENT	CIRCUMGYRATE
CINCHONISATION	CIPHERINGS	CIRCUMAMBIENTLY	CIRCUMGYRATED
CINCHONISATIONS	CIPHERTEXT	CIRCUMAMBULATE	CIRCUMGYRATES
CINCHONISE	CIPHERTEXTS	CIRCUMAMBULATED	CIRCUMGYRATING
CINCHONISED	CIPOLLINOS	CIRCUMAMBULATES	CIRCUMGYRATION
CINCHONISES	CIPROFLOXACIN	CIRCUMAMBULATOR	CIRCUMGYRATIONS
CINCHONISING	CIPROFLOXACINS	CIRCUMBENDIBUS	CIRCUMGYRATORY
CINCHONISM	CIRCASSIAN	CIRCUMCENTER	CIRCUMINCESSION
CINCHONISMS	CIRCASSIANS	CIRCUMCENTERS	CIRCUMINSESSION
CINCHONIZATION	CIRCASSIENNE	CIRCUMCENTRE	CIRCUMJACENCIES
CINCHONIZATIONS	CIRCASSIENNES	CIRCUMCENTRES	CIRCUMJACENCY
CINCHONIZE	CIRCENSIAL	CIRCUMCIRCLE	CIRCUMJACENT
CINCHONIZED	CIRCENSIAN	CIRCUMCIRCLES	CIRCUMLITTORAL
CINCHONIZES	CIRCINATELY	CIRCUMCISE	CIRCUMLOCUTE
CINCHONIZING	CIRCUITEER	CIRCUMCISED	CIRCUMLOCUTED
CINCINNATE	CIRCUITEERS	CIRCUMCISER	CIRCUMLOCUTES
CINCINNUSES	CIRCUITIES	CIRCUMCISERS	CIRCUMLOCUTING
CINCTURING	CIRCUITING	CIRCUMCISES	CIRCUMLOCUTION
CINEANGIOGRAPHY	CIRCUITOUS	CIRCUMCISING	CIRCUMLOCUTIONS
CINEMAGOER	CIRCUITOUSLY	CIRCUMCISION	CIRCUMLOCUTORY
CINEMAGOERS	CIRCUITOUSNESS	CIRCUMCISIONS	CIRCUMLUNAR
CINEMATHEQUE	CIRCUITRIES	CIRCUMDUCE	CIRCUMMURE
CINEMATHEQUES	CIRCULABLE	CIRCUMDUCED	CIRCUMMURED
CINEMATICALLY	CIRCULARISATION	CIRCUMDUCES	CIRCUMMURES
CINEMATISE	CIRCULARISE	CIRCUMDUCING	CIRCUMMURING
CINEMATISED	CIRCULARISED	CIRCUMDUCT	CIRCUMNAVIGABLE

CIRCUMNAVIGATE	CIRCUMVENTS	CIVILIANISES	CLAMJAMFRY
CIRCUMNAVIGATED	CIRCUMVOLUTION	CIVILIANISING	CLAMJAMPHRIE
CIRCUMNAVIGATES	CIRCUMVOLUTIONS	CIVILIANIZATION	CLAMJAMPHRIES
CIRCUMNAVIGATOR	CIRCUMVOLUTORY	CIVILIANIZE	CLAMMINESS
CIRCUMNUTATE	CIRCUMVOLVE	CIVILIANIZED	CLAMMINESSES
CIRCUMNUTATED	CIRCUMVOLVED	CIVILIANIZES	CLAMOROUSLY
CIRCUMNUTATES	CIRCUMVOLVES	CIVILIANIZING	CLAMOROUSNESS
CIRCUMNUTATING	CIRCUMVOLVING	CIVILISABLE	CLAMOROUSNESSES
CIRCUMNUTATION	CIRRHIPEDE	CIVILISATION	CLAMOURERS
CIRCUMNUTATIONS	CIRRHIPEDES	CIVILISATIONAL	CLAMOURING
CIRCUMNUTATORY	CIRRHOTICS	CIVILISATIONS	CLAMPDOWNS
CIRCUMPOLAR	CIRRIGRADE	CIVILISERS	CLAMPERING
CIRCUMPOSE	CIRRIPEDES	CIVILISING	CLAMSHELLS
CIRCUMPOSED	CIRROCUMULI	CIVILITIES	CLANDESTINE
CIRCUMPOSES	CIRROCUMULUS	CIVILIZABLE	CLANDESTINELY
CIRCUMPOSING	CIRROSTRATI	CIVILIZATION	CLANDESTINENESS
CIRCUMPOSITION	CIRROSTRATIVE	CIVILIZATIONAL	CLANDESTINITIES
CIRCUMPOSITIONS	CIRROSTRATUS	CIVILIZATIONS	CLANDESTINITY
CIRCUMSCISSILE	CISMONTANE	CIVILIZERS	CLANGBOXES
CIRCUMSCRIBABLE	CISPLATINS	CIVILIZING	CLANGORING
CIRCUMSCRIBE	CISPONTINE	CIVILNESSES	CLANGOROUS
CIRCUMSCRIBED	CISTACEOUS	CLABBERING	CLANGOROUSLY
CIRCUMSCRIBER	CITATIONAL	CLACKBOXES	CLANGOURED
CIRCUMSCRIBERS	CITHARISTIC	CLACKDISHES	CLANGOURING
CIRCUMSCRIBES	CITHARISTS	CLADISTICALLY	CLANJAMFRAY
CIRCUMSCRIBING	CITIFICATION	CLADISTICS	CLANJAMFRAYS
CIRCUMSCRIPTION	CITIFICATIONS	CLADOCERAN	CLANKINGLY
CIRCUMSCRIPTIVE	CITIZENESS	CLADOCERANS	CLANNISHLY
CIRCUMSOLAR	CITIZENESSES	CLADOGENESES	CLANNISHNESS
CIRCUMSPECT	CITIZENISE	CLADOGENESIS	CLANNISHNESSES
CIRCUMSPECTION	CITIZENISED	CLADOGENETIC	CLANSWOMAN
CIRCUMSPECTIONS	CITIZENISES	CLADOGRAMS	CLANSWOMEN
CIRCUMSPECTIVE	CITIZENISING	CLADOPHYLL	CLAPBOARDED
CIRCUMSPECTLY	CITIZENIZE	CLADOPHYLLS	CLAPBOARDING
CIRCUMSPECTNESS	CITIZENIZED	CLADOSPORIA	CLAPBOARDS
CIRCUMSTANCE	CITIZENIZES	CLADOSPORIUM	CLAPBREADS
CIRCUMSTANCED	CITIZENIZING	CLADOSPORIUMS	CLAPDISHES
CIRCUMSTANCES	CITIZENRIES	CLAIRAUDIENCE	CLAPOMETER
CIRCUMSTANCING	CITIZENSHIP	CLAIRAUDIENCES	CLAPOMETERS
CIRCUMSTANTIAL	CITIZENSHIPS	CLAIRAUDIENT	CLAPPERBOARD
CIRCUMSTANTIALS	CITRICULTURE	CLAIRAUDIENTLY	CLAPPERBOARDS
CIRCUMSTANTIATE	CITRICULTURES	CLAIRAUDIENTS	CLAPPERBOY
CIRCUMSTELLAR	CITRICULTURIST	CLAIRCOLLE	CLAPPERBOYS
CIRCUMVALLATE	CITRICULTURISTS	CLAIRCOLLES	CLAPPERCLAW
CIRCUMVALLATED	CITRONELLA	CLAIRSCHACH	CLAPPERCLAWED
CIRCUMVALLATES	CITRONELLAL	CLAIRSCHACHS	CLAPPERCLAWER
CIRCUMVALLATING	CITRONELLALS	CLAIRVOYANCE	CLAPPERCLAWERS
CIRCUMVALLATION	CITRONELLAS	CLAIRVOYANCES	CLAPPERCLAWING
CIRCUMVENT	CITRONELLOL	CLAIRVOYANCIES	CLAPPERCLAWS
CIRCUMVENTED	CITRONELLOLS	CLAIRVOYANCY	CLAPPERING
CIRCUMVENTER	CITRULLINE	CLAIRVOYANT	CLAPPERINGS
CIRCUMVENTERS	CITRULLINES	CLAIRVOYANTLY	CLAPTRAPPERIES
CIRCUMVENTING	CITYFICATION	CLAIRVOYANTS	CLAPTRAPPERY
CIRCUMVENTION	CITYFICATIONS	CLAMANCIES	CLARABELLA
CIRCUMVENTIONS	CITYSCAPES	CLAMATORIAL	CLARABELLAS
CIRCUMVENTIVE	CIVILIANISATION	CLAMBERERS	CLARENDONS
CIRCUMVENTOR	CIVILIANISE	CLAMBERING	CLARIBELLA
CIRCUMVENTORS	CIVILIANISED	CLAMJAMFRIES	CLARIBELLAS

CLARICHORD	CLAUDICATION	CLEARSTORY	CLIANTHUSES
CLARICHORDS	CLAUDICATIONS	CLEARWEEDS	CLICKETING
CLARIFICATION	CLAUGHTING	CLEARWINGS	CLICKSTREAM
CLARIFICATIONS	CLAUSTRATION	CLEAVABILITIES	CLICKSTREAMS
CLARIFIERS	CLAUSTRATIONS	CLEAVABILITY	CLIENTAGES
CLARIFYING	CLAUSTROPHOBE	CLEAVABLENESS	CLIENTELES
CLARINETIST	CLAUSTROPHOBES	CLEAVABLENESSES	CLIENTLESS
CLARINETISTS	CLAUSTROPHOBIA	CLEISTOGAMIC	CLIENTSHIP
CLARINETTIST	CLAUSTROPHOBIAS	CLEISTOGAMIES	CLIENTSHIPS
CLARINETTISTS	CLAUSTROPHOBIC	CLEISTOGAMOUS	CLIFFHANGER
CLARIONETS	CLAVATIONS	CLEISTOGAMOUSLY	CLIFFHANGERS
CLARIONING	CLAVECINIST	CLEISTOGAMY	CLIFFHANGING
CLARTHEADS	CLAVECINISTS	CLEMATISES	CLIFFHANGINGS
CLASHINGLY	CLAVICEMBALO	CLEMENCIES	CLIFFHANGS
CLASSICALISM	CLAVICEMBALOS	CLEMENTINE	CLIMACTERIC
CLASSICALISMS	CLAVICHORD	CLEMENTINES	CLIMACTERICAL
CLASSICALIST	CLAVICHORDIST	CLENBUTEROL	CLIMACTERICALLY
CLASSICALISTS	CLAVICHORDISTS	CLENBUTEROLS	CLIMACTERICS
CLASSICALITIES	CLAVICHORDS	CLEOPATRAS	CLIMACTICAL
CLASSICALITY	CLAVICORNS	CLEPSYDRAE	CLIMACTICALLY
CLASSICALLY	CLAVICULAE	CLEPSYDRAS	CLIMATICAL
CLASSICALNESS	CLAVICULAR	CLEPTOCRACIES	CLIMATICALLY
CLASSICALNESSES	CLAVICULATE	CLEPTOCRACY	CLIMATISED
CLASSICALS	CLAVICYTHERIA	CLEPTOMANIA	CLIMATISES
CLASSICISE	CLAVICYTHERIUM	CLEPTOMANIAC	CLIMATISING
CLASSICISED	CLAVIERIST	CLEPTOMANIACS	CLIMATIZED
CLASSICISES	CLAVIERISTIC	CLEPTOMANIAS	CLIMATIZES
CLASSICISING	CLAVIERISTS	CLERESTORIED	CLIMATIZING
CLASSICISM	CLAVIGEROUS	CLERESTORIES	CLIMATOGRAPHIES
CLASSICISMS	CLAWHAMMER	CLERESTORY	CLIMATOGRAPHY
CLASSICIST	CLAYMATION	CLERGIABLE	CLIMATOLOGIC
CLASSICISTIC	CLAYMATIONS	CLERGYABLE	CLIMATOLOGICAL
CLASSICISTS	CLAYSTONES	CLERGYWOMAN	CLIMATOLOGIES
CLASSICIZE	CLAYTONIAS	CLERGYWOMEN	CLIMATOLOGIST
CLASSICIZED	CLEANABILITIES	CLERICALISM	CLIMATOLOGISTS
CLASSICIZES	CLEANABILITY	CLERICALISMS	CLIMATOLOGY
CLASSICIZING	CLEANHANDED	CLERICALIST	CLIMATURES
CLASSIFIABLE	CLEANLIEST	CLERICALISTS	CLIMAXLESS
CLASSIFICATION	CLEANLINESS	CLERICALLY	CLIMBDOWNS
CLASSIFICATIONS	CLEANLINESSES	CLERICATES	CLINANDRIA
CLASSIFICATORY	CLEANNESSES	CLERICITIES	CLINANDRIUM
CLASSIFIED	CLEANSABLE	CLERKESSES	CLINCHINGLY
CLASSIFIER	CLEANSINGS	CLERKLIEST	CLINDAMYCIN
CLASSIFIERS	CLEANSKINS	CLERKLINESS	CLINDAMYCINS
CLASSIFIES	CLEARANCES	CLERKLINESSES	CLINGFILMS
CLASSIFYING	CLEARCOLED	CLERKLINGS	CLINGFISHES
CLASSINESS	CLEARCOLES	CLERKSHIPS	CLINGINESS
CLASSINESSES	CLEARCOLING	CLEROMANCIES	CLINGINESSES
CLASSLESSNESS	CLEARCUTTING	CLEROMANCY	CLINGINGLY
CLASSLESSNESSES	CLEARHEADED	CLERUCHIAL	CLINGINGNESS
CLASSMATES	CLEARHEADEDLY	CLERUCHIAS	CLINGINGNESSES
CLASSROOMS	CLEARHEADEDNESS	CLERUCHIES	CLINGSTONE
CLASSWORKS	CLEARINGHOUSE	CLEVERALITIES	CLINGSTONES
CLATHRATES	CLEARINGHOUSES	CLEVERALITY	CLINICALLY
CLATTERERS	CLEARNESSES	CLEVERDICK	CLINICALNESS
CLATTERING	CLEARSKINS	CLEVERDICKS	CLINICALNESSES
CLATTERINGLY	CLEARSTORIED	CLEVERNESS	CLINICIANS
CLAUCHTING	CLEARSTORIES	CLEVERNESSES	CLINKERING

CLINKSTONE	CLODDISHNESS	CLOUDLANDS	COACHLOADS
CLINKSTONES	CLODDISHNESSES	CLOUDLESSLY	COACHWHIPS
CLINOCHLORE	CLODHOPPER	CLOUDLESSNESS	COACHWOODS
CLINOCHLORES	CLODHOPPERS	CLOUDLESSNESSES	COACHWORKS
CLINODIAGONAL	CLODHOPPING	CLOUDSCAPE	COACTIVELY
CLINODIAGONALS	CLOFIBRATE	CLOUDSCAPES	COACTIVITIES
CLINOMETER	CLOFIBRATES	CLOUDTOWNS	COACTIVITY
CLINOMETERS	CLOGDANCES	CLOVEPINKS	COADAPTATION
CLINOMETRIC	CLOGGINESS	CLOVERGRASS	COADAPTATIONS
CLINOMETRICAL	CLOGGINESSES	CLOVERGRASSES	COADJACENCIES
CLINOMETRIES	CLOISONNAGE	CLOVERLEAF	COADJACENCY
CLINOMETRY	CLOISONNAGES	CLOVERLEAFS	COADJACENT
CLINOPINACOID	CLOISONNES	CLOVERLEAVES	COADJUTANT
CLINOPINACOIDS	CLOISTERED	CLOWNERIES	COADJUTANTS
CLINOPINAKOID	CLOISTERER	CLOWNISHLY	COADJUTORS
CLINOPINAKOIDS	CLOISTERERS	CLOWNISHNESS	COADJUTORSHIP
CLINOPYROXENE	CLOISTERING	CLOWNISHNESSES	COADJUTORSHIPS
CLINOPYROXENES	CLOISTRESS	CLOXACILLIN	COADJUTRESS
CLINOSTATS	CLOISTRESSES	CLOXACILLINS	COADJUTRESSES
CLINQUANTS	CLOMIPHENE	CLOZAPINES	COADJUTRICES
CLINTONIAS	CLOMIPHENES	CLUBABILITIES	COADJUTRIX
CLIOMETRIC	CLONAZEPAM	CLUBABILITY	COADJUTRIXES
CLIOMETRICAL	CLONAZEPAMS	CLUBBABILITIES	COADMIRING
CLIOMETRICIAN	CLONICITIES	CLUBBABILITY	COADMITTED
CLIOMETRICIANS	CLONIDINES	CLUBBINESS	COADMITTING
CLIOMETRICS	CLOSEDOWNS	CLUBBINESSES	COADUNATED
CLIPBOARDS	CLOSEFISTED	CLUBFOOTED	COADUNATES
CLIPSHEARS	CLOSEHEADS	CLUBHAULED	COADUNATING
CLIPSHEETS	CLOSEMOUTHED	CLUBHAULING	COADUNATION
CLIQUINESS	CLOSENESSES	CLUBHOUSES	COADUNATIONS
CLIQUINESSES	CLOSESTOOL	CLUBMANSHIP	COADUNATIVE
CLIQUISHLY	CLOSESTOOLS	CLUBMANSHIPS	COAGENCIES
CLIQUISHNESS	CLOSETFULS	CLUBMASTER	COAGULABILITIES
CLIQUISHNESSES	CLOSTRIDIA	CLUBMASTERS	COAGULABILITY
CLISHMACLAVER	CLOSTRIDIAL	CLUBRUSHES	COAGULABLE
CLISHMACLAVERS	CLOSTRIDIAN	CLUMPINESS	COAGULANTS
CLISTOGAMIES	CLOSTRIDIUM	CLUMPINESSES	COAGULASES
CLISTOGAMY	CLOSTRIDIUMS	CLUMSINESS	COAGULATED
CLITICISED	CLOTHBOUND	CLUMSINESSES	COAGULATES
CLITICISES	CLOTHESHORSE	CLUSTERING	COAGULATING
CLITICISING	CLOTHESHORSES	CLUSTERINGLY	COAGULATION
CLITICIZED	CLOTHESLINE	CLUTTERING	COAGULATIONS
CLITICIZES	CLOTHESLINED	CLYPEIFORM	COAGULATIVE
CLITICIZING	CLOTHESLINES	CNIDARIANS	COAGULATOR
CLITORECTOMIES	CLOTHESLINING	CNIDOBLAST	COAGULATORS
CLITORECTOMY	CLOTHESPIN	CNIDOBLASTS	COAGULATORY
CLITORIDECTOMY	CLOTHESPINS	COACERVATE	COALESCENCE
CLITORIDES	CLOTHESPRESS	COACERVATED	COALESCENCES
CLITORISES	CLOTHESPRESSES	COACERVATES	COALESCENT
CLITTERING	CLOTTERING	COACERVATING	COALESCING
CLOACALINE	CLOTTINESS	COACERVATION	COALFIELDS
CLOACITISES	CLOTTINESSES	COACERVATIONS	COALFISHES
CLOAKROOMS	CLOUDBERRIES	COACHBUILDER	COALHOUSES
CLOBBERING	CLOUDBERRY	COACHBUILDERS	COALIFICATION
CLOCKMAKER	CLOUDBURST	COACHBUILDING	COALIFICATIONS
CLOCKMAKERS	CLOUDBURSTS	COACHBUILDINGS	COALIFYING
CLOCKWORKS	CLOUDINESS	COACHBUILT	COALITIONAL
CLODDISHLY	CLOUDINESSES	COACHLINES	COALITIONER

COALITIONERS	COBBLESTONING	COCKATEELS	COCKTEASER
COALITIONISM	COBELLIGERENT	COCKATIELS	COCKTEASERS
COALITIONISMS	COBELLIGERENTS	COCKATRICE	COCKTHROWING
COALITIONIST	COBWEBBERIES	COCKATRICES	COCKTHROWINGS
COALITIONISTS	COBWEBBERY	COCKBILLED	COCKYLEEKIES
COALITIONS	COBWEBBIER	COCKBILLING	COCKYLEEKY
COALMASTER	COBWEBBIEST	COCKCHAFER	COCOMPOSER
COALMASTERS	COBWEBBING	COCKCHAFERS	COCOMPOSERS
COALMINERS	COCAINISATION	COCKCROWING	COCONSCIOUS
COANCHORED	COCAINISATIONS	COCKCROWINGS	COCONSCIOUSES
COANCHORING	COCAINISED	COCKERNONIES	COCONSCIOUSNESS
COANNEXING	COCAINISES	COCKERNONY	COCONSPIRATOR
COAPPEARED	COCAINISING	COCKEYEDLY	COCONSPIRATORS
COAPPEARING	COCAINISMS	COCKEYEDNESS	COCOONERIES
COAPTATION	COCAINISTS	COCKEYEDNESSES	COCOONINGS
COAPTATIONS	COCAINIZATION	COCKFIGHTING	COCOUNSELED
COARCTATED	COCAINIZATIONS	COCKFIGHTINGS	COCOUNSELING
COARCTATES	COCAINIZED	COCKFIGHTS	COCOUNSELLED
COARCTATING	COCAINIZES	COCKHORSES	COCOUNSELLING
COARCTATION	COCAINIZING	COCKIELEEKIE	COCOUNSELS
COARCTATIONS	COCAPTAINED	COCKIELEEKIES	COCOZELLES
COARSENESS	COCAPTAINING	COCKINESSES	COCREATING
COARSENESSES	COCAPTAINS	COCKLEBOAT	COCREATORS
COARSENING	COCARBOXYLASE	COCKLEBOATS	COCULTIVATE
COASSISTED	COCARBOXYLASES	COCKLEBURS	COCULTIVATED
COASSISTING	COCARCINOGEN	COCKLEERTS	COCULTIVATES
COASSUMING	COCARCINOGENIC	COCKLESHELL	COCULTIVATING
COASTEERING	COCARCINOGENS	COCKLESHELLS	COCULTIVATION
COASTEERINGS	COCATALYST	COCKMATCHES	COCULTIVATIONS
COASTGUARD	COCATALYSTS	COCKNEYDOM	COCULTURED
COASTGUARDMAN	COCCIDIOSES	COCKNEYDOMS	COCULTURES
COASTGUARDMEN	COCCIDIOSIS	COCKNEYFICATION	COCULTURING
COASTGUARDS	COCCIDIOSTAT	COCKNEYFIED	COCURATORS
COASTGUARDSMAN	COCCIDIOSTATS	COCKNEYFIES	COCURRICULAR
COASTGUARDSMEN	COCCIFEROUS	COCKNEYFYING	COCUSWOODS
COASTLANDS	COCCINEOUS	COCKNEYISH	CODECLINATION
COASTLINES	COCCOLITES	COCKNEYISM	CODECLINATIONS
COASTWARDS	COCCOLITHS	COCKNEYISMS	CODEFENDANT
COATDRESSES	COCHAIRING	COCKNIFICATION	CODEFENDANTS
COATIMUNDI	COCHAIRMAN	COCKNIFICATIONS	CODEPENDENCE
COATIMUNDIS	COCHAIRMEN	COCKNIFIED	CODEPENDENCES
COATSTANDS	COCHAIRPERSON	COCKNIFIES	CODEPENDENCIES
COATTENDED	COCHAIRPERSONS	COCKNIFYING	CODEPENDENCY
COATTENDING	COCHAIRWOMAN	COCKROACHES	CODEPENDENT
COATTESTED	COCHAIRWOMEN	COCKSCOMBS	CODEPENDENTS
COATTESTING	COCHAMPION	COCKSFOOTS	CODERIVING
COAUTHORED	COCHAMPIONS	COCKSINESS	CODESIGNED
COAUTHORING	COCHINEALS	COCKSINESSES	CODESIGNING
COAUTHORSHIP	COCHLEARES	COCKSUCKER	CODETERMINATION
COAUTHORSHIPS	COCHLEARIFORM	COCKSUCKERS	CODEVELOPED
COBALAMINS	COCHLEATED	COCKSURELY	CODEVELOPER
COBALTIFEROUS	COCKABULLIES	COCKSURENESS	CODEVELOPERS
COBALTINES	COCKABULLY	COCKSURENESSES	CODEVELOPING
COBALTITES	COCKALEEKIE	COCKSWAINED	CODEVELOPS
COBBLERIES	COCKALEEKIES	COCKSWAINING	CODICILLARY
COBBLESTONE	COCKALORUM	COCKSWAINS	CODICOLOGICAL
COBBLESTONED	COCKALORUMS	COCKTAILED	CODICOLOGIES
COBBLESTONES	COCKAMAMIE	COCKTAILING	CODICOLOGY

CODIFIABILITIES

CODIFIABILITIES
CODIFIABILITY
CODIFICATION
CODIFICATIONS
CODIRECTED
CODIRECTING
CODIRECTION
CODIRECTIONS
CODIRECTOR
CODIRECTORS
CODISCOVER
CODISCOVERED
CODISCOVERER
CODISCOVERERS
CODISCOVERING
CODISCOVERS
CODOLOGIES
CODOMINANCE
CODOMINANCES
CODOMINANT
CODOMINANTS
CODSWALLOP
CODSWALLOPS
COEDUCATION
COEDUCATIONAL
COEDUCATIONALLY
COEDUCATIONS
COEFFICIENT
COEFFICIENTS
COELACANTH
COELACANTHIC
COELACANTHS
COELANAGLYPHIC
COELENTERA
COELENTERATE
COELENTERATES
COELENTERIC
COELENTERON
COELOMATES
COELOMATIC
COELOSTATS
COELUROSAUR
COELUROSAURS
COEMBODIED
COEMBODIES
COEMBODYING
COEMPLOYED
COEMPLOYING
COEMPTIONS
COENACTING
COENAESTHESES
COENAESTHESIA
COENAESTHESIAS
COENAESTHESIS
COENAMORED
COENAMORING
COENDURING
COENENCHYMA

COENENCHYMAS
COENENCHYMATA
COENESTHESES
COENESTHESIA
COENESTHESIAS
COENESTHESIS
COENESTHETIC
COENOBITES
COENOBITIC
COENOBITICAL
COENOBITISM
COENOBITISMS
COENOCYTES
COENOCYTIC
COENOSARCS
COENOSPECIES
COENOSTEUM
COENOSTEUMS
COENZYMATIC
COENZYMATICALLY
COEQUALITIES
COEQUALITY
COEQUALNESS
COEQUALNESSES
COEQUATING
COERCIMETER
COERCIMETERS
COERCIONIST
COERCIONISTS
COERCIVELY
COERCIVENESS
COERCIVENESSES
COERCIVITIES
COERCIVITY
COERECTING
COESSENTIAL
COESSENTIALITY
COESSENTIALLY
COESSENTIALNESS
COETANEOUS
COETANEOUSLY
COETANEOUSNESS
COETERNALLY
COETERNITIES
COETERNITY
COEVALITIES
COEVOLUTION
COEVOLUTIONARY
COEVOLUTIONS
COEVOLVING
COEXECUTOR
COEXECUTORS
COEXECUTRICES
COEXECUTRIX
COEXECUTRIXES
COEXERTING
COEXISTENCE
COEXISTENCES

COEXISTENT
COEXISTING
COEXTENDED
COEXTENDING
COEXTENSION
COEXTENSIONS
COEXTENSIVE
COEXTENSIVELY
COFAVORITE
COFAVORITES
COFEATURED
COFEATURES
COFEATURING
COFFEEHOUSE
COFFEEHOUSES
COFFEEMAKER
COFFEEMAKERS
COFFEEPOTS
COFFERDAMS
COFFINITES
COFINANCED
COFINANCES
COFINANCING
COFOUNDERS
COFOUNDING
COFUNCTION
COFUNCTIONS
COGENERATION
COGENERATIONS
COGENERATOR
COGENERATORS
COGITATING
COGITATINGLY
COGITATION
COGITATIONS
COGITATIVE
COGITATIVELY
COGITATIVENESS
COGITATORS
COGNATENESS
COGNATENESSES
COGNATIONS
COGNISABLE
COGNISABLY
COGNISANCE
COGNISANCES
COGNITIONAL
COGNITIONS
COGNITIVELY
COGNITIVISM
COGNITIVISMS
COGNITIVITIES
COGNITIVITY
COGNIZABLE
COGNIZABLY
COGNIZANCE
COGNIZANCES
COGNOMINAL

COGNOMINALLY
COGNOMINATE
COGNOMINATED
COGNOMINATES
COGNOMINATING
COGNOMINATION
COGNOMINATIONS
COGNOSCENTE
COGNOSCENTI
COGNOSCIBLE
COGNOSCING
COHABITANT
COHABITANTS
COHABITATION
COHABITATIONS
COHABITEES
COHABITERS
COHABITING
COHABITORS
COHEIRESSES
COHERENCES
COHERENCIES
COHERENTLY
COHERITORS
COHESIBILITIES
COHESIBILITY
COHESIONLESS
COHESIVELY
COHESIVENESS
COHESIVENESSES
COHIBITING
COHIBITION
COHIBITIONS
COHIBITIVE
COHOBATING
COHOMOLOGICAL
COHOMOLOGIES
COHOMOLOGY
COHORTATIVE
COHORTATIVES
COHOSTESSED
COHOSTESSES
COHOSTESSING
COHOUSINGS
COHYPONYMS
COIFFEUSES
COIFFURING
COILABILITIES
COILABILITY
COINCIDENCE
COINCIDENCES
COINCIDENCIES
COINCIDENCY
COINCIDENT
COINCIDENTAL
COINCIDENTALLY
COINCIDENTLY
COINCIDING

COINFECTED	COLEOPTILES	COLLEAGUESHIP	COLLETERIAL
COINFECTING	COLEORHIZA	COLLEAGUESHIPS	COLLICULUS
COINFERRED	COLEORHIZAE	COLLEAGUING	COLLICULUSES
COINFERRING	COLEORHIZAS	COLLECTABLE	COLLTERIES
COINHERENCE	COLEORRHIZA	COLLECTABLES	COLLIESHANGIE
COINHERENCES	COLEORRHIZAS	COLLECTANEA	COLLTESHANGTES
COINHERING	COLESTIPOL	COLLECTEDLY	COLLIGATED
COINHERITANCE	COLESTIPOLS	COLLECTEDNESS	COLLIGATES
COINHERITANCES	COLICKIEST	COLLECTEDNESSES	COLLIGATING
COINHERITOR	COLICROOTS	COLLECTIBLE	COLLIGATION
COINHERITORS	COLICWEEDS	COLLECTIBLES	COLLIGATIONS
COINSTANTANEITY	COLINEARITIES	COLLECTING	COLLIGATIVE
COINSTANTANEOUS	COLINEARITY	COLLECTINGS	COLLIMATED
COINSURANCE	COLIPHAGES	COLLECTION	COLLIMATES
COINSURANCES	COLLABORATE	COLLECTIONS	COLLIMATING
COINSURERS	COLLABORATED	COLLECTIVE	COLLIMATION
COINSURING	COLLABORATES	COLLECTIVELY	COLLIMATIONS
COINTERRED	COLLABORATING	COLLECTIVENESS	COLLIMATOR
COINTERRING	COLLABORATION	COLLECTIVES	COLLIMATORS
COINTREAUS	COLLABORATIONS	COLLECTIVISE	COLLINEARITIES
COINVENTED	COLLABORATIVE	COLLECTIVISED	COLLINEARITY
COINVENTING	COLLABORATIVELY	COLLECTIVISES	COLLINEARLY
COINVENTOR	COLLABORATIVES	COLLECTIVISING	COLLINSIAS
COINVENTORS	COLLABORATOR	COLLECTIVISM	COLLIQUABLE
COINVESTIGATOR	COLLABORATORS	COLLECTIVISMS	COLLIQUANT
COINVESTIGATORS	COLLAGENASE	COLLECTIVIST	COLLIQUATE
COINVESTOR	COLLAGENASES	COLLECTIVISTIC	COLLIQUATED
COINVESTORS	COLLAGENIC	COLLECTIVISTS	COLLIQUATES
COKULORISES	COLLAGENOUS	COLLECTIVITIES	COLLIQUATING
COLATITUDE	COLLAGISTS	COLLECTIVITY	COLLIQUATION
COLATITUDES	COLLAPSABILITY	COLLECTIVIZE	COLLIQUATIONS
COLCANNONS	COLLAPSABLE	COLLECTIVIZED	COLLIQUATIVE
COLCHICINE	COLLAPSARS	COLLECTIVIZES	COLLIQUESCENCE
COLCHICINES	COLLAPSIBILITY	COLLECTIVIZING	COLLIQUESCENCES
COLCHICUMS	COLLAPSIBLE	COLLECTORATE	COLLISIONAL
COLCOTHARS	COLLAPSING	COLLECTORATES	COLLISIONALLY
COLDBLOODS	COLLARBONE	COLLECTORS	COLLISIONS
COLDCOCKED	COLLARBONES	COLLECTORSHIP	COLLOCATED
COLDCOCKING	COLLARETTE	COLLECTORSHIPS	COLLOCATES
COLDHEARTED	COLLARETTES	COLLEGIALISM	COLLOCATING
COLDHEARTEDLY	COLLARLESS	COLLEGIALISMS	COLLOCATION
COLDHEARTEDNESS	COLLATABLE	COLLEGIALITIES	COLLOCATIONAL
COLDHOUSES	COLLATERAL	COLLEGIALITY	COLLOCATIONS
COLDNESSES	COLLATERALISE	COLLEGIALLY	COLLOCUTOR
COLECTOMIES	COLLATERALISED	COLLEGIANER	COLLOCUTORS
COLEMANITE	COLLATERALISES	COLLEGIANERS	COLLOCUTORY
COLEMANITES	COLLATERALISING	COLLEGIANS	COLLODIONS
COLEOPTERA	COLLATERALITIES	COLLEGIATE	COLLODIUMS
COLEOPTERAL	COLLATERALITY	COLLEGIATELY	COLLOGUING
COLEOPTERAN	COLLATERALIZE	COLLEGIATES	COLLOIDALITIES
COLEOPTERANS	COLLATERALIZED	COLLEGIUMS	COLLOIDALITY
COLEOPTERIST	COLLATERALIZES	COLLEMBOLAN	COLLOIDALLY
COLEOPTERISTS	COLLATERALIZING	COLLEMBOLANS	COLLOQUIAL
COLEOPTERON	COLLATERALLY	COLLEMBOLOUS	COLLOQUIALISM
COLEOPTERONS	COLLATERALS	COLLENCHYMA	COLLOQUIALISMS
COLEOPTEROUS	COLLATIONS	COLLENCHYMAS	COLLOQUIALIST
COLEOPTERS	COLLEAGUED	COLLENCHYMATA	COLLOQUIALISTS
COLEOPTILE	COLLEAGUES	COLLENCHYMATOUS	COLLOQUIALITIES

COLLOQUIALITY	COLONISATION	COLORPOINT	COLTISHNESSES
COLLOQUIALLY	COLONISATIONIST	COLORPOINTS	COLTSFOOTS
COLLOQUIALNESS	COLONISATIONS	COLOSSALLY	COLUBRIADS
COLLOQUIALS	COLONISERS	COLOSSEUMS	COLUBRIFORM
COLLOQUIED	COLONISING	COLOSSUSES	COLUMBARIA
COLLOQUIES	COLONITISES	COLOSTOMIES	COLUMBARIES
COLLOQUING	COLONIZABLE	COLOSTROUS	COLUMBARIUM
COLLOQUISE	COLONIZATION	COLOSTRUMS	COLUMBATES
COLLOQUISED	COLONIZATIONIST	COLOTOMIES	COLUMBINES
COLLOQUISES	COLONIZATIONS	COLOURABILITIES	COLUMBITES
COLLOQUISING	COLONIZERS	COLOURABILITY	COLUMBIUMS
COLLOQUIST	COLONIZING	COLOURABLE	COLUMELLAE
COLLOQUISTS	COLONNADED	COLOURABLENESS	COLUMELLAR
COLLOQUIUM	COLONNADES	COLOURABLY	COLUMNARITIES
COLLOQUIUMS	COLONOSCOPE	COLOURANTS	COLUMNARITY
COLLOQUIZE	COLONOSCOPES	COLOURATION	COLUMNATED
COLLOQUIZED	COLONOSCOPIES	COLOURATIONS	COLUMNIATED
COLLOQUIZES	COLONOSCOPY	COLOURFAST	COLUMNIATION
COLLOQUIZING	COLOPHONIES	COLOURFASTNESS	COLUMNIATIONS
COLLOQUYING	COLOQUINTIDA	COLOURFULLY	COLUMNISTIC
COLLOTYPES	COLOQUINTIDAS	COLOURFULNESS	COLUMNISTS
COLLOTYPIC	COLORATION	COLOURFULNESSES	COMANAGEMENT
COLLOTYPIES	COLORATIONS	COLOURINGS	COMANAGEMENTS
COLLUCTATION	COLORATURA	COLOURISATION	COMANAGERS
COLLUCTATIONS	COLORATURAS	COLOURISATIONS	COMANAGING
COLLUSIONS	COLORATURE	COLOURISED	COMANCHERO
COLLUSIVELY	COLORATURES	COLOURISES	COMANCHEROS
COLLUVIUMS	COLORBREED	COLOURISING	COMATOSELY
COLLYRIUMS	COLORBREEDING	COLOURISTIC	COMATULIDS
COLLYWOBBLES	COLORBREEDS	COLOURISTS	COMBATABLE
COLOBOMATA	COLORCASTED	COLOURIZATION	COMBATANTS
COLOCATING	COLORCASTING	COLOURIZATIONS	COMBATIVELY
COLOCYNTHS	COLORCASTS	COLOURIZED	COMBATIVENESS
COLOGARITHM	COLORECTAL	COLOURIZES	COMBATIVENESSES
COLOGARITHMS	COLORFASTNESS	COLOURIZING	COMBATTING
COLOMBARDS	COLORFASTNESSES	COLOURLESS	COMBINABILITIES
COLONELCIES	COLORFULLY	COLOURLESSLY	COMBINABILITY
COLONELLING	COLORFULNESS	COLOURLESSNESS	COMBINABLE
COLONELLINGS	COLORFULNESSES	COLOURPOINT	COMBINATION
COLONELSHIP	COLORIMETER	COLOURPOINTS	COMBINATIONAL
COLONELSHIPS	COLORIMETERS	COLOURWASH	COMBINATIONS
COLONIALISE	COLORIMETRIC	COLOURWASHED	COMBINATIVE
COLONIALISED	COLORIMETRICAL	COLOURWASHES	COMBINATORIAL
COLONIALISES	COLORIMETRIES	COLOURWASHING	COMBINATORIALLY
COLONIALISING	COLORIMETRY	COLOURWAYS	COMBINATORICS
COLONIALISM	COLORISATION	COLPITISES	COMBINATORY
COLONIALISMS	COLORISATIONS	COLPORTAGE	COMBININGS
COLONIALIST	COLORISERS	COLPORTAGES	COMBRETUMS
COLONIALISTIC	COLORISING	COLPORTEUR	COMBURGESS
COLONIALISTS	COLORISTIC	COLPORTEURS	COMBURGESSES
COLONIALIZE	COLORISTICALLY	COLPOSCOPE	COMBUSTIBILITY
COLONIALIZED	COLORIZATION	COLPOSCOPES	COMBUSTIBLE
COLONIALIZES	COLORIZATIONS	COLPOSCOPICAL	COMBUSTIBLENESS
COLONIALIZING	COLORIZERS	COLPOSCOPICALLY	COMBUSTIBLES
COLONIALLY	COLORIZING	COLPOSCOPIES	COMBUSTIBLY
COLONIALNESS	COLORLESSLY	COLPOSCOPY	COMBUSTING
COLONIALNESSES	COLORLESSNESS	COLPOTOMIES	COMBUSTION
COLONISABLE	COLORLESSNESSES	COLTISHNESS	COMBUSTIONS

COMBUSTIOUS
COMBUSTIVE
COMBUSTIVES
COMBUSTORS
COMEDDLING
COMEDICALLY
COMEDIENNE
COMEDIENNES
COMEDIETTA
COMEDIETTAS
COMEDOGENIC
COMELINESS
COMELINESSES
COMESTIBLE
COMESTIBLES
COMETOGRAPHIES
COMETOGRAPHY
COMETOLOGIES
COMETOLOGY
COMEUPPANCE
COMEUPPANCES
COMFINESSES
COMFITURES
COMFORTABLE
COMFORTABLENESS
COMFORTABLY
COMFORTERS
COMFORTING
COMFORTINGLY
COMFORTLESS
COMFORTLESSLY
COMFORTLESSNESS
COMICALITIES
COMICALITY
COMICALNESS
COMICALNESSES
COMINGLING
COMITADJIS
COMITATIVE
COMITATIVES
COMITATUSES
COMMANDABLE
COMMANDANT
COMMANDANTS
COMMANDANTSHIP
COMMANDANTSHIPS
COMMANDEER
COMMANDEERED
COMMANDEERING
COMMANDEERS
COMMANDERIES
COMMANDERS
COMMANDERSHIP
COMMANDERSHIPS
COMMANDERY
COMMANDING
COMMANDINGLY
COMMANDMENT

COMMANDMENTS
COMMANDOES
COMMEASURABLE
COMMEASURE
COMMEASURED
COMMEASURES
COMMEASURING
COMMEMORABLE
COMMEMORATE
COMMEMORATED
COMMEMORATES
COMMEMORATING
COMMEMORATION
COMMEMORATIONAL
COMMEMORATIONS
COMMEMORATIVE
COMMEMORATIVELY
COMMEMORATIVES
COMMEMORATOR
COMMEMORATORS
COMMEMORATORY
COMMENCEMENT
COMMENCEMENTS
COMMENCERS
COMMENCING
COMMENDABLE
COMMENDABLENESS
COMMENDABLY
COMMENDAMS
COMMENDATION
COMMENDATIONS
COMMENDATOR
COMMENDATORS
COMMENDATORY
COMMENDERS
COMMENDING
COMMENSALISM
COMMENSALISMS
COMMENSALITIES
COMMENSALITY
COMMENSALLY
COMMENSALS
COMMENSURABLE
COMMENSURABLY
COMMENSURATE
COMMENSURATELY
COMMENSURATION
COMMENSURATIONS
COMMENTARIAL
COMMENTARIAT
COMMENTARIATS
COMMENTARIES
COMMENTARY
COMMENTATE
COMMENTATED
COMMENTATES
COMMENTATING
COMMENTATION

COMMENTATIONS
COMMENTATOR
COMMENTATORIAL
COMMENTATORS
COMMENTERS
COMMENTING
COMMENTORS
COMMERCIAL
COMMERCIALESE
COMMERCIALESES
COMMERCIALISE
COMMERCIALISED
COMMERCIALISES
COMMERCIALISING
COMMERCIALISM
COMMERCIALISMS
COMMERCIALIST
COMMERCIALISTIC
COMMERCIALISTS
COMMERCIALITIES
COMMERCIALITY
COMMERCIALIZE
COMMERCIALIZED
COMMERCIALIZES
COMMERCIALIZING
COMMERCIALLY
COMMERCIALS
COMMERCING
COMMERGING
COMMINATED
COMMINATES
COMMINATING
COMMINATION
COMMINATIONS
COMMINATIVE
COMMINATORY
COMMINGLED
COMMINGLES
COMMINGLING
COMMINUTED
COMMINUTES
COMMINUTING
COMMINUTION
COMMINUTIONS
COMMISERABLE
COMMISERATE
COMMISERATED
COMMISERATES
COMMISERATING
COMMISERATINGLY
COMMISERATION
COMMISERATIONS
COMMISERATIVE
COMMISERATIVELY
COMMISERATOR
COMMISERATORS
COMMISSAIRE
COMMISSAIRES

COMMISSARIAL
COMMISSARIAT
COMMISSARIATS
COMMISSARIES
COMMISSARS
COMMISSARY
COMMISSARYSHIP
COMMISSARYSHIPS
COMMISSION
COMMISSIONAIRE
COMMISSIONAIRES
COMMISSIONAL
COMMISSIONARY
COMMISSIONED
COMMISSIONER
COMMISSIONERS
COMMISSIONING
COMMISSIONS
COMMISSURAL
COMMISSURE
COMMISSURES
COMMITMENT
COMMITMENTS
COMMITTABLE
COMMITTALS
COMMITTEEMAN
COMMITTEEMEN
COMMITTEES
COMMITTEESHIP
COMMITTEESHIPS
COMMITTEEWOMAN
COMMITTEEWOMEN
COMMITTERS
COMMITTING
COMMIXTION
COMMIXTIONS
COMMIXTURE
COMMIXTURES
COMMODIFICATION
COMMODIFIED
COMMODIFIES
COMMODIFYING
COMMODIOUS
COMMODIOUSLY
COMMODIOUSNESS
COMMODITIES
COMMODITISE
COMMODITISED
COMMODITISES
COMMODITISING
COMMODITIZE
COMMODITIZED
COMMODITIZES
COMMODITIZING
COMMODORES
COMMONABLE
COMMONAGES
COMMONALITIES

759

COMMONALITY	COMMUNICATES	COMPACTIFIES	COMPARTMENTS
COMMONALTIES	COMMUNICATING	COMPACTIFY	COMPASSABLE
COMMONALTY	COMMUNICATION	COMPACTIFYING	COMPASSING
COMMONHOLD	COMMUNICATIONAL	COMPACTING	COMPASSINGS
COMMONHOLDS	COMMUNICATIONS	COMPACTION	COMPASSION
COMMONINGS	COMMUNICATIVE	COMPACTIONS	COMPASSIONABLE
COMMONNESS	COMMUNICATIVELY	COMPACTNESS	COMPASSIONATE
COMMONNESSES	COMMUNICATOR	COMPACTNESSES	COMPASSIONATED
COMMONPLACE	COMMUNICATORS	COMPACTORS	COMPASSIONATELY
COMMONPLACED	COMMUNICATORY	COMPACTURE	COMPASSIONATES
COMMONPLACENESS	COMMUNINGS	COMPACTURES	COMPASSIONATING
COMMONPLACES	COMMUNIONAL	COMPAGINATE	COMPASSIONED
COMMONPLACING	COMMUNIONALLY	COMPAGINATED	COMPASSIONING
COMMONSENSE	COMMUNIONS	COMPAGINATES	COMPASSIONLESS
COMMONSENSIBLE	COMMUNIQUE	COMPAGINATING	COMPASSIONS
COMMONSENSICAL	COMMUNIQUES	COMPAGINATION	COMPATIBILITIES
COMMONWEAL	COMMUNISATION	COMPAGINATIONS	COMPATIBILITY
COMMONWEALS	COMMUNISATIONS	COMPANDERS	COMPATIBLE
COMMONWEALTH	COMMUNISED	COMPANDING	COMPATIBLENESS
COMMONWEALTHS	COMMUNISES	COMPANDORS	COMPATIBLES
COMMORANTS	COMMUNISING	COMPANIABLE	COMPATIBLY
COMMORIENTES	COMMUNISMS	COMPANIONABLE	COMPATRIOT
COMMOTIONAL	COMMUNISTIC	COMPANIONABLY	COMPATRIOTIC
COMMOTIONS	COMMUNISTICALLY	COMPANIONATE	COMPATRIOTISM
COMMUNALISATION	COMMUNISTS	COMPANIONED	COMPATRIOTISMS
COMMUNALISE	COMMUNITAIRE	COMPANIONHOOD	COMPATRIOTS
COMMUNALISED	COMMUNITAIRES	COMPANIONHOODS	COMPEARANCE
COMMUNALISER	COMMUNITARIAN	COMPANIONING	COMPEARANCES
COMMUNALISERS	COMMUNITARIANS	COMPANIONLESS	COMPEARANT
COMMUNALISES	COMMUNITIES	COMPANIONS	COMPEARANTS
COMMUNALISING	COMMUNIZATION	COMPANIONSHIP	COMPEARING
COMMUNALISM	COMMUNIZATIONS	COMPANIONSHIPS	COMPEERING
COMMUNALISMS	COMMUNIZED	COMPANIONWAY	COMPELLABLE
COMMUNALIST	COMMUNIZES	COMPANIONWAYS	COMPELLABLY
COMMUNALISTIC	COMMUNIZING	COMPANYING	COMPELLATION
COMMUNALISTS	COMMUTABILITIES	COMPARABILITIES	COMPELLATIONS
COMMUNALITIES	COMMUTABILITY	COMPARABILITY	COMPELLATIVE
COMMUNALITY	COMMUTABLE	COMPARABLE	COMPELLATIVES
COMMUNALIZATION	COMMUTABLENESS	COMPARABLENESS	COMPELLERS
COMMUNALIZE	COMMUTATED	COMPARABLY	COMPELLING
COMMUNALIZED	COMMUTATES	COMPARATIST	COMPELLINGLY
COMMUNALIZER	COMMUTATING	COMPARATISTS	COMPENDIOUS
COMMUNALIZERS	COMMUTATION	COMPARATIVE	COMPENDIOUSLY
COMMUNALIZES	COMMUTATIONS	COMPARATIVELY	COMPENDIOUSNESS
COMMUNALIZING	COMMUTATIVE	COMPARATIVENESS	COMPENDIUM
COMMUNALLY	COMMUTATIVELY	COMPARATIVES	COMPENDIUMS
COMMUNARDS	COMMUTATIVITIES	COMPARATIVIST	COMPENSABILITY
COMMUNAUTAIRE	COMMUTATIVITY	COMPARATIVISTS	COMPENSABLE
COMMUNAUTAIRES	COMMUTATOR	COMPARATOR	COMPENSATE
COMMUNICABILITY	COMMUTATORS	COMPARATORS	COMPENSATED
COMMUNICABLE	COMONOMERS	COMPARISON	COMPENSATES
COMMUNICABLY	COMPACTEDLY	COMPARISONS	COMPENSATING
COMMUNICANT	COMPACTEDNESS	COMPARTING	COMPENSATION
COMMUNICANTS	COMPACTEDNESSES	COMPARTMENT	COMPENSATIONAL
COMMUNICATE	COMPACTERS	COMPARTMENTAL	COMPENSATIONS
COMMUNICATED	COMPACTEST	COMPARTMENTALLY	COMPENSATIVE
COMMUNICATEE	COMPACTIBLE	COMPARTMENTED	COMPENSATOR
COMMUNICATEES	COMPACTIFIED	COMPARTMENTING	COMPENSATORS

COMPENSATORY
COMPESCING
COMPETENCE
COMPETENCES
COMPETENCIES
COMPETENCY
COMPETENTLY
COMPETENTNESS
COMPETENTNESSES
COMPETITION
COMPETITIONS
COMPETITIVE
COMPETITIVELY
COMPETITIVENESS
COMPETITOR
COMPETITORS
COMPILATION
COMPILATIONS
COMPILATOR
COMPILATORS
COMPILATORY
COMPILEMENT
COMPILEMENTS
COMPLACENCE
COMPLACENCES
COMPLACENCIES
COMPLACENCY
COMPLACENT
COMPLACENTLY
COMPLAINANT
COMPLAINANTS
COMPLAINED
COMPLAINER
COMPLAINERS
COMPLAINING
COMPLAININGLY
COMPLAININGS
COMPLAINTS
COMPLAISANCE
COMPLAISANCES
COMPLAISANT
COMPLAISANTLY
COMPLANATE
COMPLANATION
COMPLANATIONS
COMPLECTED
COMPLECTING
COMPLEMENT
COMPLEMENTAL
COMPLEMENTALLY
COMPLEMENTARIES
COMPLEMENTARILY
COMPLEMENTARITY
COMPLEMENTARY
COMPLEMENTATION
COMPLEMENTED
COMPLEMENTING
COMPLEMENTISER

COMPLEMENTISERS
COMPLEMENTIZER
COMPLEMENTIZERS
COMPLEMENTS
COMPLETABLE
COMPLETELY
COMPLETENESS
COMPLETENESSES
COMPLETERS
COMPLETEST
COMPLETING
COMPLETION
COMPLETIONS
COMPLETIST
COMPLETISTS
COMPLETIVE
COMPLETORY
COMPLEXATION
COMPLEXATIONS
COMPLEXEDNESS
COMPLEXEDNESSES
COMPLEXEST
COMPLEXIFIED
COMPLEXIFIES
COMPLEXIFY
COMPLEXIFYING
COMPLEXING
COMPLEXION
COMPLEXIONAL
COMPLEXIONED
COMPLEXIONLESS
COMPLEXIONS
COMPLEXITIES
COMPLEXITY
COMPLEXNESS
COMPLEXNESSES
COMPLEXOMETRIC
COMPLEXONE
COMPLEXONES
COMPLEXUSES
COMPLIABLE
COMPLIABLENESS
COMPLIABLY
COMPLIANCE
COMPLIANCES
COMPLIANCIES
COMPLIANCY
COMPLIANTLY
COMPLIANTNESS
COMPLIANTNESSES
COMPLICACIES
COMPLICACY
COMPLICANT
COMPLICATE
COMPLICATED
COMPLICATEDLY
COMPLICATEDNESS
COMPLICATES

COMPLICATING
COMPLICATION
COMPLICATIONS
COMPLICATIVE
COMPLICITIES
COMPLICITY
COMPLICITY
COMPLIMENT
COMPLIMENTAL
COMPLIMENTARILY
COMPLIMENTARY
COMPLIMENTED
COMPLIMENTER
COMPLIMENTERS
COMPLIMENTING
COMPLIMENTS
COMPLISHED
COMPLISHES
COMPLISHING
COMPLOTTED
COMPLOTTER
COMPLOTTERS
COMPLOTTING
COMPLUVIUM
COMPLUVIUMS
COMPONENCIES
COMPONENCY
COMPONENTAL
COMPONENTIAL
COMPONENTS
COMPORTANCE
COMPORTANCES
COMPORTING
COMPORTMENT
COMPORTMENTS
COMPOSEDLY
COMPOSEDNESS
COMPOSEDNESSES
COMPOSITED
COMPOSITELY
COMPOSITENESS
COMPOSITENESSES
COMPOSITES
COMPOSITING
COMPOSITION
COMPOSITIONAL
COMPOSITIONALLY
COMPOSITIONS
COMPOSITIVE
COMPOSITOR
COMPOSITORIAL
COMPOSITORS
COMPOSITOUS
COMPOSSIBILITY
COMPOSSIBLE
COMPOSTABLE
COMPOSTERS
COMPOSTING

COMPOSTURE
COMPOSTURED
COMPOSTURES
COMPOSTURING
COMPOSURES
COMPOTATION
COMPOTATIONS
COMPOTATIONSHIP
COMPOTATOR
COMPOTATORS
COMPOTATORY
COMPOTIERS
COMPOUNDABLE
COMPOUNDED
COMPOUNDER
COMPOUNDERS
COMPOUNDING
COMPRADORE
COMPRADORES
COMPRADORS
COMPREHEND
COMPREHENDED
COMPREHENDIBLE
COMPREHENDING
COMPREHENDS
COMPREHENSIBLE
COMPREHENSIBLY
COMPREHENSION
COMPREHENSIONS
COMPREHENSIVE
COMPREHENSIVELY
COMPREHENSIVES
COMPREHENSIVISE
COMPREHENSIVIZE
COMPRESSED
COMPRESSEDLY
COMPRESSES
COMPRESSIBILITY
COMPRESSIBLE
COMPRESSIBLY
COMPRESSING
COMPRESSION
COMPRESSIONAL
COMPRESSIONS
COMPRESSIVE
COMPRESSIVELY
COMPRESSOR
COMPRESSORS
COMPRESSURE
COMPRESSURES
COMPRIMARIO
COMPRIMARIOS
COMPRINTED
COMPRINTING
COMPRISABLE
COMPRISALS
COMPRISING
COMPRIZING

COMPROMISE

COMPROMISE
COMPROMISED
COMPROMISER
COMPROMISERS
COMPROMISES
COMPROMISING
COMPROMISINGLY
COMPROVINCIAL
COMPTROLLED
COMPTROLLER
COMPTROLLERS
COMPTROLLERSHIP
COMPTROLLING
COMPTROLLS
COMPULSATIVE
COMPULSATORY
COMPULSING
COMPULSION
COMPULSIONIST
COMPULSIONISTS
COMPULSIONS
COMPULSITOR
COMPULSITORS
COMPULSIVE
COMPULSIVELY
COMPULSIVENESS
COMPULSIVES
COMPULSIVITIES
COMPULSIVITY
COMPULSORIES
COMPULSORILY
COMPULSORINESS
COMPULSORY
COMPUNCTION
COMPUNCTIONS
COMPUNCTIOUS
COMPUNCTIOUSLY
COMPURGATION
COMPURGATIONS
COMPURGATOR
COMPURGATORIAL
COMPURGATORS
COMPURGATORY
COMPURSION
COMPURSIONS
COMPUTABILITIES
COMPUTABILITY
COMPUTABLE
COMPUTANTS
COMPUTATION
COMPUTATIONAL
COMPUTATIONALLY
COMPUTATIONS
COMPUTATIVE
COMPUTATOR
COMPUTATORS
COMPUTERATE
COMPUTERDOM

COMPUTERDOMS
COMPUTERESE
COMPUTERESES
COMPUTERISABLE
COMPUTERISATION
COMPUTERISE
COMPUTERISED
COMPUTERISES
COMPUTERISING
COMPUTERIST
COMPUTERISTS
COMPUTERIZABLE
COMPUTERIZATION
COMPUTERIZE
COMPUTERIZED
COMPUTERIZES
COMPUTERIZING
COMPUTERLESS
COMPUTERLIKE
COMPUTERNIK
COMPUTERNIKS
COMPUTERPHOBE
COMPUTERPHOBES
COMPUTERPHOBIA
COMPUTERPHOBIAS
COMPUTERPHOBIC
COMPUTISTS
COMRADELINESS
COMRADELINESSES
COMRADERIES
COMRADESHIP
COMRADESHIPS
COMSTOCKER
COMSTOCKERIES
COMSTOCKERS
COMSTOCKERY
COMSTOCKISM
COMSTOCKISMS
CONACREISM
CONACREISMS
CONATIONAL
CONCANAVALIN
CONCANAVALINS
CONCATENATE
CONCATENATED
CONCATENATES
CONCATENATING
CONCATENATION
CONCATENATIONS
CONCAVENESS
CONCAVENESSES
CONCAVITIES
CONCEALABLE
CONCEALERS
CONCEALING
CONCEALINGLY
CONCEALMENT
CONCEALMENTS

CONCEDEDLY
CONCEITEDLY
CONCEITEDNESS
CONCEITEDNESSES
CONCEITFUL
CONCEITING
CONCEITLESS
CONCEIVABILITY
CONCEIVABLE
CONCEIVABLENESS
CONCEIVABLY
CONCEIVERS
CONCEIVING
CONCELEBRANT
CONCELEBRANTS
CONCELEBRATE
CONCELEBRATED
CONCELEBRATES
CONCELEBRATING
CONCELEBRATION
CONCELEBRATIONS
CONCENTERED
CONCENTERING
CONCENTERS
CONCENTRATE
CONCENTRATED
CONCENTRATEDLY
CONCENTRATES
CONCENTRATING
CONCENTRATION
CONCENTRATIONS
CONCENTRATIVE
CONCENTRATIVELY
CONCENTRATOR
CONCENTRATORS
CONCENTRED
CONCENTRES
CONCENTRIC
CONCENTRICAL
CONCENTRICALLY
CONCENTRICITIES
CONCENTRICITY
CONCENTRING
CONCEPTACLE
CONCEPTACLES
CONCEPTION
CONCEPTIONAL
CONCEPTIONS
CONCEPTIOUS
CONCEPTIVE
CONCEPTUAL
CONCEPTUALISE
CONCEPTUALISED
CONCEPTUALISER
CONCEPTUALISERS
CONCEPTUALISES
CONCEPTUALISING
CONCEPTUALISM

CONCEPTUALISMS
CONCEPTUALIST
CONCEPTUALISTIC
CONCEPTUALISTS
CONCEPTUALITIES
CONCEPTUALITY
CONCEPTUALIZE
CONCEPTUALIZED
CONCEPTUALIZER
CONCEPTUALIZERS
CONCEPTUALIZES
CONCEPTUALIZING
CONCEPTUALLY
CONCEPTUSES
CONCERNANCIES
CONCERNANCY
CONCERNEDLY
CONCERNEDNESS
CONCERNEDNESSES
CONCERNING
CONCERNMENT
CONCERNMENTS
CONCERTANTE
CONCERTANTES
CONCERTANTI
CONCERTEDLY
CONCERTEDNESS
CONCERTEDNESSES
CONCERTGOER
CONCERTGOERS
CONCERTGOING
CONCERTGOINGS
CONCERTINA
CONCERTINAED
CONCERTINAING
CONCERTINAS
CONCERTING
CONCERTINI
CONCERTINIST
CONCERTINISTS
CONCERTINO
CONCERTINOS
CONCERTISE
CONCERTISED
CONCERTISES
CONCERTISING
CONCERTIZE
CONCERTIZED
CONCERTIZES
CONCERTIZING
CONCERTMASTER
CONCERTMASTERS
CONCERTMEISTER
CONCERTMEISTERS
CONCERTSTUCK
CONCERTSTUCKS
CONCESSIBLE
CONCESSION

CONCESSIONAIRE	CONCLUDERS	CONCRETISMS	CONDENSERY
CONCESSIONAIRES	CONCLUDING	CONCRETIST	CONDENSIBILITY
CONCESSIONAL	CONCLUSION	CONCRETISTS	CONDENSIBLE
CONCESSIONARIES	CONCLUSIONARY	CONCRETIVE	CONDENSING
CONCESSIONARY	CONCLUSIONS	CONCRETIVELY	CONDESCEND
CONCESSIONER	CONCLUSIVE	CONCRETIZATION	CONDESCENDED
CONCESSIONERS	CONCLUSIVELY	CONCRETIZATIONS	CONDESCENDENCE
CONCESSIONIST	CONCLUSIVENESS	CONCRETIZE	CONDESCENDENCES
CONCESSIONISTS	CONCLUSORY	CONCRETIZED	CONDESCENDING
CONCESSIONNAIRE	CONCOCTERS	CONCRETIZES	CONDESCENDINGLY
CONCESSIONS	CONCOCTING	CONCRETIZING	CONDESCENDS
CONCESSIVE	CONCOCTION	CONCREWING	CONDESCENSION
CONCESSIVELY	CONCOCTIONS	CONCUBINAGE	CONDESCENSIONS
CONCETTISM	CONCOCTIVE	CONCUBINAGES	CONDIDDLED
CONCETTISMS	CONCOCTORS	CONCUBINARY	CONDIDDLES
CONCETTIST	CONCOLORATE	CONCUBINES	CONDIDDLING
CONCETTISTS	CONCOLOROUS	CONCUBITANCIES	CONDIGNNESS
CONCHIFEROUS	CONCOMITANCE	CONCUBITANCY	CONDIGNNESSES
CONCHIFORM	CONCOMITANCES	CONCUBITANT	CONDIMENTAL
CONCHIGLIE	CONCOMITANCIES	CONCUBITANTS	CONDIMENTED
CONCHIOLIN	CONCOMITANCY	CONCUPISCENCE	CONDIMENTING
CONCHIOLINS	CONCOMITANT	CONCUPISCENCES	CONDIMENTS
CONCHITISES	CONCOMITANTLY	CONCUPISCENT	CONDISCIPLE
CONCHOIDAL	CONCOMITANTS	CONCUPISCIBLE	CONDISCIPLES
CONCHOIDALLY	CONCORDANCE	CONCURRENCE	CONDITIONABLE
CONCHOLOGICAL	CONCORDANCES	CONCURRENCES	CONDITIONAL
CONCHOLOGIES	CONCORDANT	CONCURRENCIES	CONDITIONALITY
CONCHOLOGIST	CONCORDANTLY	CONCURRENCY	CONDITIONALLY
CONCHOLOGISTS	CONCORDATS	CONCURRENT	CONDITIONALS
CONCHOLOGY	CONCORDIAL	CONCURRENTLY	CONDITIONATE
CONCIERGES	CONCORDING	CONCURRENTS	CONDITIONATED
CONCILIABLE	CONCORPORATE	CONCURRING	CONDITIONATES
CONCILIARLY	CONCORPORATED	CONCURRINGLY	CONDITIONATING
CONCILIARY	CONCORPORATES	CONCUSSING	CONDITIONED
CONCILIATE	CONCORPORATING	CONCUSSION	CONDITIONER
CONCILIATED	CONCOURSES	CONCUSSIONS	CONDITIONERS
CONCILIATES	CONCREATED	CONCUSSIVE	CONDITIONING
CONCILIATING	CONCREATES	CONCYCLICALLY	CONDITIONINGS
CONCILIATION	CONCREATING	CONDEMNABLE	CONDITIONS
CONCILIATIONS	CONCREMATION	CONDEMNABLY	CONDOLATORY
CONCILIATIVE	CONCREMATIONS	CONDEMNATION	CONDOLEMENT
CONCILIATOR	CONCRESCENCE	CONDEMNATIONS	CONDOLEMENTS
CONCILIATORILY	CONCRESCENCES	CONDEMNATORY	CONDOLENCE
CONCILIATORS	CONCRESCENT	CONDEMNERS	CONDOLENCES
CONCILIATORY	CONCRETELY	CONDEMNING	CONDOLINGLY
CONCINNITIES	CONCRETENESS	CONDEMNINGLY	CONDOMINIUM
CONCINNITY	CONCRETENESSES	CONDEMNORS	CONDOMINIUMS
CONCINNOUS	CONCRETING	CONDENSABILITY	CONDONABLE
CONCIPIENCIES	CONCRETION	CONDENSABLE	CONDONATION
CONCIPIENCY	CONCRETIONARY	CONDENSATE	CONDONATIONS
CONCIPIENT	CONCRETIONS	CONDENSATED	CONDOTTIERE
CONCISENESS	CONCRETISATION	CONDENSATES	CONDOTTIERI
CONCISENESSES	CONCRETISATIONS	CONDENSATING	CONDUCEMENT
CONCISIONS	CONCRETISE	CONDENSATION	CONDUCEMENTS
CONCLAMATION	CONCRETISED	CONDENSATIONAL	CONDUCIBLE
CONCLAMATIONS	CONCRETISES	CONDENSATIONS	CONDUCINGLY
CONCLAVIST	CONCRETISING	CONDENSERIES	CONDUCIVENESS
CONCLAVISTS	CONCRETISM	CONDENSERS	CONDUCIVENESSES

CONDUCTANCE	CONFEDERATING	CONFIGURATES	CONFLAGRATIONS
CONDUCTANCES	CONFEDERATION	CONFIGURATING	CONFLAGRATIVE
CONDUCTIBILITY	CONFEDERATIONS	CONFIGURATION	CONFLATING
CONDUCTIBLE	CONFEDERATIVE	CONFIGURATIONAL	CONFLATION
CONDUCTIMETRIC	CONFERENCE	CONFIGURATIONS	CONFLATIONS
CONDUCTING	CONFERENCES	CONFIGURATIVE	CONFLICTED
CONDUCTIOMETRIC	CONFERENCIER	CONFIGURED	CONFLICTFUL
CONDUCTION	CONFERENCIERS	CONFIGURES	CONFLICTING
CONDUCTIONAL	CONFERENCING	CONFIGURING	CONFLICTINGLY
CONDUCTIONS	CONFERENCINGS	CONFINABLE	CONFLICTION
CONDUCTIVE	CONFERENTIAL	CONFINEABLE	CONFLICTIONS
CONDUCTIVELY	CONFERMENT	CONFINEDLY	CONFLICTIVE
CONDUCTIVITIES	CONFERMENTS	CONFINEDNESS	CONFLICTORY
CONDUCTIVITY	CONFERRABLE	CONFINEDNESSES	CONFLICTUAL
CONDUCTOMETRIC	CONFERRALS	CONFINELESS	CONFLUENCE
CONDUCTORIAL	CONFERREES	CONFINEMENT	CONFLUENCES
CONDUCTORS	CONFERRENCE	CONFINEMENTS	CONFLUENTLY
CONDUCTORSHIP	CONFERRENCES	CONFIRMABILITY	CONFLUENTS
CONDUCTORSHIPS	CONFERRERS	CONFIRMABLE	CONFOCALLY
CONDUCTRESS	CONFERRING	CONFIRMAND	CONFORMABILITY
CONDUCTRESSES	CONFERVOID	CONFIRMANDS	CONFORMABLE
CONDUPLICATE	CONFERVOIDS	CONFIRMATION	CONFORMABLENESS
CONDUPLICATION	CONFESSABLE	CONFIRMATIONAL	CONFORMABLY
CONDUPLICATIONS	CONFESSANT	CONFIRMATIONS	CONFORMANCE
CONDYLOMAS	CONFESSANTS	CONFIRMATIVE	CONFORMANCES
CONDYLOMATA	CONFESSEDLY	CONFIRMATOR	CONFORMATION
CONDYLOMATOUS	CONFESSING	CONFIRMATORS	CONFORMATIONAL
CONEFLOWER	CONFESSION	CONFIRMATORY	CONFORMATIONS
CONEFLOWERS	CONFESSIONAL	CONFIRMEDLY	CONFORMERS
CONFABBING	CONFESSIONALISM	CONFIRMEDNESS	CONFORMING
CONFABULAR	CONFESSIONALIST	CONFIRMEDNESSES	CONFORMINGLY
CONFABULATE	CONFESSIONALLY	CONFIRMEES	CONFORMISM
CONFABULATED	CONFESSIONALS	CONFIRMERS	CONFORMISMS
CONFABULATES	CONFESSIONARIES	CONFIRMING	CONFORMIST
CONFABULATING	CONFESSIONARY	CONFIRMINGS	CONFORMISTS
CONFABULATION	CONFESSIONS	CONFIRMORS	CONFORMITIES
CONFABULATIONS	CONFESSORESS	CONFISCABLE	CONFORMITY
CONFABULATOR	CONFESSORESSES	CONFISCATABLE	CONFOUNDABLE
CONFABULATORS	CONFESSORS	CONFISCATE	CONFOUNDED
CONFABULATORY	CONFESSORSHIP	CONFISCATED	CONFOUNDEDLY
CONFARREATE	CONFESSORSHIPS	CONFISCATES	CONFOUNDEDNESS
CONFARREATION	CONFIDANTE	CONFISCATING	CONFOUNDER
CONFARREATIONS	CONFIDANTES	CONFISCATION	CONFOUNDERS
CONFECTING	CONFIDANTS	CONFISCATIONS	CONFOUNDING
CONFECTION	CONFIDENCE	CONFISCATOR	CONFOUNDINGLY
CONFECTIONARIES	CONFIDENCES	CONFISCATORS	CONFRATERNAL
CONFECTIONARY	CONFIDENCIES	CONFISCATORY	CONFRATERNITIES
CONFECTIONER	CONFIDENCY	CONFISERIE	CONFRATERNITY
CONFECTIONERIES	CONFIDENTIAL	CONFISERIES	CONFRERIES
CONFECTIONERS	CONFIDENTIALITY	CONFISEURS	CONFRONTAL
CONFECTIONERY	CONFIDENTIALLY	CONFITEORS	CONFRONTALS
CONFECTIONS	CONFIDENTLY	CONFITURES	CONFRONTATION
CONFEDERACIES	CONFIDENTS	CONFLAGRANT	CONFRONTATIONAL
CONFEDERACY	CONFIDINGLY	CONFLAGRATE	CONFRONTATIONS
CONFEDERAL	CONFIDINGNESS	CONFLAGRATED	CONFRONTED
CONFEDERATE	CONFIDINGNESSES	CONFLAGRATES	CONFRONTER
CONFEDERATED	CONFIGURATE	CONFLAGRATING	CONFRONTERS
CONFEDERATES	CONFIGURATED	CONFLAGRATION	CONFRONTING

CONFRONTMENT	CONGLOBULATION	CONGRESSMAN	CONJUNCTION
CONFRONTMENTS	CONGLOBULATIONS	CONGRESSMEN	CONJUNCTIONAL
CONFUSABILITIES	CONGLOMERATE	CONGRESSPEOPLE	CONJUNCTIONALLY
CONFUSABILITY	CONGLOMERATED	CONGRESSPERSON	CONJUNCTIONS
CONFUSABLE	CONGLOMERATES	CONGRESSPERSONS	CONJUNCTIVA
CONFUSABLES	CONGLOMERATEUR	CONGRESSWOMAN	CONJUNCTIVAE
CONFUSEDLY	CONGLOMERATEURS	CONGRESSWOMEN	CONJUNCTIVAL
CONFUSEDNESS	CONGLOMERATIC	CONGRUENCE	CONJUNCTIVAS
CONFUSEDNESSES	CONGLOMERATING	CONGRUENCES	CONJUNCTIVE
CONFUSIBLE	CONGLOMERATION	CONGRUENCIES	CONJUNCTIVELY
CONFUSIBLES	CONGLOMERATIONS	CONGRUENCY	CONJUNCTIVENESS
CONFUSINGLY	CONGLOMERATIVE	CONGRUENTLY	CONJUNCTIVES
CONFUSIONAL	CONGLOMERATOR	CONGRUITIES	CONJUNCTIVITIS
CONFUSIONS	CONGLOMERATORS	CONGRUOUSLY	CONJUNCTLY
CONFUTABLE	CONGLUTINANT	CONGRUOUSNESS	CONJUNCTURAL
CONFUTATION	CONGLUTINATE	CONGRUOUSNESSES	CONJUNCTURE
CONFUTATIONS	CONGLUTINATED	CONICITIES	CONJUNCTURES
CONFUTATIVE	CONGLUTINATES	CONIDIOPHORE	CONJURATION
CONFUTEMENT	CONGLUTINATING	CONIDIOPHORES	CONJURATIONS
CONFUTEMENTS	CONGLUTINATION	CONIDIOPHOROUS	CONJURATOR
CONGEALABLE	CONGLUTINATIONS	CONIDIOSPORE	CONJURATORS
CONGEALABLENESS	CONGLUTINATIVE	CONIDIOSPORES	CONJUREMENT
CONGEALERS	CONGLUTINATOR	CONIFEROUS	CONJUREMENTS
CONGEALING	CONGLUTINATORS	CONIOLOGIES	CONJURINGS
CONGEALMENT	CONGRATTERS	CONIROSTRAL	CONNASCENCE
CONGEALMENTS	CONGRATULABLE	CONJECTING	CONNASCENCES
CONGELATION	CONGRATULANT	CONJECTURABLE	CONNASCENCIES
CONGELATIONS	CONGRATULANTS	CONJECTURABLY	CONNASCENCY
CONGENERIC	CONGRATULATE	CONJECTURAL	CONNASCENT
CONGENERICAL	CONGRATULATED	CONJECTURALLY	CONNATENESS
CONGENERICS	CONGRATULATES	CONJECTURE	CONNATENESSES
CONGENEROUS	CONGRATULATING	CONJECTURED	CONNATIONS
CONGENETIC	CONGRATULATION	CONJECTURER	CONNATURAL
CONGENIALITIES	CONGRATULATIONS	CONJECTURERS	CONNATURALISE
CONGENIALITY	CONGRATULATIVE	CONJECTURES	CONNATURALISED
CONGENIALLY	CONGRATULATOR	CONJECTURING	CONNATURALISES
CONGENIALNESS	CONGRATULATORS	CONJOINERS	CONNATURALISING
CONGENIALNESSES	CONGRATULATORY	CONJOINING	CONNATURALITIES
CONGENITAL	CONGREEING	CONJOINTLY	CONNATURALITY
CONGENITALLY	CONGREETED	CONJUGABLE	CONNATURALIZE
CONGENITALNESS	CONGREETING	CONJUGALITIES	CONNATURALIZED
CONGESTIBLE	CONGREGANT	CONJUGALITY	CONNATURALIZES
CONGESTING	CONGREGANTS	CONJUGALLY	CONNATURALIZING
CONGESTION	CONGREGATE	CONJUGANTS	CONNATURALLY
CONGESTIONS	CONGREGATED	CONJUGATED	CONNATURALNESS
CONGESTIVE	CONGREGATES	CONJUGATELY	CONNATURES
CONGIARIES	CONGREGATING	CONJUGATENESS	CONNECTABLE
CONGLOBATE	CONGREGATION	CONJUGATENESSES	CONNECTEDLY
CONGLOBATED	CONGREGATIONAL	CONJUGATES	CONNECTEDNESS
CONGLOBATES	CONGREGATIONS	CONJUGATING	CONNECTEDNESSES
CONGLOBATING	CONGREGATIVE	CONJUGATINGS	CONNECTERS
CONGLOBATION	CONGREGATOR	CONJUGATION	CONNECTIBLE
CONGLOBATIONS	CONGREGATORS	CONJUGATIONAL	CONNECTING
CONGLOBING	CONGRESSED	CONJUGATIONALLY	CONNECTION
CONGLOBULATE	CONGRESSES	CONJUGATIONS	CONNECTIONAL
CONGLOBULATED	CONGRESSING	CONJUGATIVE	CONNECTIONISM
CONGLOBULATES	CONGRESSIONAL	CONJUGATOR	CONNECTIONISMS
CONGLOBULATING	CONGRESSIONALLY	CONJUGATORS	CONNECTIONS

CONNECTIVE	CONQUISTADORES	CONSENSION	CONSERVATRIXES
CONNECTIVELY	CONQUISTADORS	CONSENSIONS	CONSERVERS
CONNECTIVES	CONSANGUINE	CONSENSUAL	CONSERVING
CONNECTIVITIES	CONSANGUINEOUS	CONSENSUALLY	CONSIDERABLE
CONNECTIVITY	CONSANGUINITIES	CONSENSUSES	CONSIDERABLES
CONNECTORS	CONSANGUINITY	CONSENTANEITIES	CONSIDERABLY
CONNEXIONAL	CONSCIENCE	CONSENTANEITY	CONSIDERANCE
CONNEXIONS	CONSCIENCELESS	CONSENTANEOUS	CONSIDERANCES
CONNIPTION	CONSCIENCES	CONSENTANEOUSLY	CONSIDERATE
CONNIPTIONS	CONSCIENTIOUS	CONSENTERS	CONSIDERATELY
CONNIVANCE	CONSCIENTIOUSLY	CONSENTIENCE	CONSIDERATENESS
CONNIVANCES	CONSCIENTISE	CONSENTIENCES	CONSIDERATION
CONNIVANCIES	CONSCIENTISED	CONSENTIENT	CONSIDERATIONS
CONNIVANCY	CONSCIENTISES	CONSENTING	CONSIDERATIVE
CONNIVENCE	CONSCIENTISING	CONSENTINGLY	CONSIDERATIVELY
CONNIVENCES	CONSCIENTIZE	CONSEQUENCE	CONSIDERED
CONNIVENCIES	CONSCIENTIZED	CONSEQUENCED	CONSIDERER
CONNIVENCY	CONSCIENTIZES	CONSEQUENCES	CONSIDERERS
CONNIVENTLY	CONSCIENTIZING	CONSEQUENCING	CONSIDERING
CONNIVERIES	CONSCIONABLE	CONSEQUENT	CONSIDERINGLY
CONNIVINGLY	CONSCIONABLY	CONSEQUENTIAL	CONSIGLIERE
CONNOISSEUR	CONSCIOUSES	CONSEQUENTIALLY	CONSIGLIERI
CONNOISSEURS	CONSCIOUSLY	CONSEQUENTLY	CONSIGNABLE
CONNOISSEURSHIP	CONSCIOUSNESS	CONSEQUENTS	CONSIGNATION
CONNOTATED	CONSCIOUSNESSES	CONSERVABLE	CONSIGNATIONS
CONNOTATES	CONSCRIBED	CONSERVANCIES	CONSIGNATORIES
CONNOTATING	CONSCRIBES	CONSERVANCY	CONSIGNATORY
CONNOTATION	CONSCRIBING	CONSERVANT	CONSIGNEES
CONNOTATIONAL	CONSCRIPTED	CONSERVATION	CONSIGNERS
CONNOTATIONS	CONSCRIPTING	CONSERVATIONAL	CONSIGNIFIED
CONNOTATIVE	CONSCRIPTION	CONSERVATIONIST	CONSIGNIFIES
CONNOTATIVELY	CONSCRIPTIONAL	CONSERVATIONS	CONSIGNIFY
CONNOTIVELY	CONSCRIPTIONIST	CONSERVATISE	CONSIGNIFYING
CONNUBIALISM	CONSCRIPTIONS	CONSERVATISED	CONSIGNING
CONNUBIALISMS	CONSCRIPTS	CONSERVATISES	CONSIGNMENT
CONNUBIALITIES	CONSECRATE	CONSERVATISING	CONSIGNMENTS
CONNUBIALITY	CONSECRATED	CONSERVATISM	CONSIGNORS
CONNUBIALLY	CONSECRATEDNESS	CONSERVATISMS	CONSILIENCE
CONNUMERATE	CONSECRATES	CONSERVATIVE	CONSILIENCES
CONNUMERATED	CONSECRATING	CONSERVATIVELY	CONSILIENT
CONNUMERATES	CONSECRATION	CONSERVATIVES	CONSIMILAR
CONNUMERATING	CONSECRATIONS	CONSERVATIZE	CONSIMILARITIES
CONNUMERATION	CONSECRATIVE	CONSERVATIZED	CONSIMILARITY
CONNUMERATIONS	CONSECRATOR	CONSERVATIZES	CONSIMILITIES
CONOIDALLY	CONSECRATORS	CONSERVATIZING	CONSIMILITUDE
CONOIDICAL	CONSECRATORY	CONSERVATOIRE	CONSIMILITUDES
CONOMINEES	CONSECTANEOUS	CONSERVATOIRES	CONSIMILITY
CONOSCENTE	CONSECTARIES	CONSERVATOR	CONSISTENCE
CONOSCENTI	CONSECTARY	CONSERVATORIA	CONSISTENCES
CONQUERABLE	CONSECUTION	CONSERVATORIAL	CONSISTENCIES
CONQUERABLENESS	CONSECUTIONS	CONSERVATORIES	CONSISTENCY
CONQUERERS	CONSECUTIVE	CONSERVATORIUM	CONSISTENT
CONQUERESS	CONSECUTIVELY	CONSERVATORIUMS	CONSISTENTLY
CONQUERESSES	CONSECUTIVENESS	CONSERVATORS	CONSISTING
CONQUERING	CONSENESCENCE	CONSERVATORSHIP	CONSISTORIAL
CONQUERINGLY	CONSENESCENCES	CONSERVATORY	CONSISTORIAN
CONQUERORS	CONSENESCENCIES	CONSERVATRICES	CONSISTORIES
CONQUISTADOR	CONSENESCENCY	CONSERVATRIX	CONSISTORY

CONSOCIATE
CONSOCIATED
CONSOCIATES
CONSOCIATING
CONSOCIATION
CONSOCIATIONAL
CONSOCIATIONS
CONSOLABLE
CONSOLATED
CONSOLATES
CONSOLATING
CONSOLATION
CONSOLATIONS
CONSOLATORIES
CONSOLATORY
CONSOLATRICES
CONSOLATRIX
CONSOLATRIXES
CONSOLEMENT
CONSOLEMENTS
CONSOLIDATE
CONSOLIDATED
CONSOLIDATES
CONSOLIDATING
CONSOLIDATION
CONSOLIDATIONS
CONSOLIDATIVE
CONSOLIDATOR
CONSOLIDATORS
CONSOLINGLY
CONSONANCE
CONSONANCES
CONSONANCIES
CONSONANCY
CONSONANTAL
CONSONANTALLY
CONSONANTLY
CONSONANTS
CONSORTABLE
CONSORTERS
CONSORTIAL
CONSORTING
CONSORTISM
CONSORTISMS
CONSORTIUM
CONSORTIUMS
CONSPECIFIC
CONSPECIFICS
CONSPECTUITIES
CONSPECTUITY
CONSPECTUS
CONSPECTUSES
CONSPICUITIES
CONSPICUITY
CONSPICUOUS
CONSPICUOUSLY
CONSPICUOUSNESS
CONSPIRACIES

CONSPIRACY
CONSPIRANT
CONSPIRATION
CONSPIRATIONAL
CONSPIRATIONS
CONSPIRATOR
CONSPIRATORIAL
CONSPIRATORS
CONSPIRATORY
CONSPIRATRESS
CONSPIRATRESSES
CONSPIRERS
CONSPIRING
CONSPIRINGLY
CONSPURCATION
CONSPURCATIONS
CONSTABLES
CONSTABLESHIP
CONSTABLESHIPS
CONSTABLEWICK
CONSTABLEWICKS
CONSTABULARIES
CONSTABULARY
CONSTANCIES
CONSTANTAN
CONSTANTANS
CONSTANTLY
CONSTATATION
CONSTATATIONS
CONSTATING
CONSTATIVE
CONSTATIVES
CONSTELLATE
CONSTELLATED
CONSTELLATES
CONSTELLATING
CONSTELLATION
CONSTELLATIONAL
CONSTELLATIONS
CONSTELLATORY
CONSTERING
CONSTERNATE
CONSTERNATED
CONSTERNATES
CONSTERNATING
CONSTERNATION
CONSTERNATIONS
CONSTIPATE
CONSTIPATED
CONSTIPATES
CONSTIPATING
CONSTIPATION
CONSTIPATIONS
CONSTITUENCIES
CONSTITUENCY
CONSTITUENT
CONSTITUENTLY
CONSTITUENTS

CONSTITUTE
CONSTITUTED
CONSTITUTER
CONSTITUTERS
CONSTITUTES
CONSTITUTING
CONSTITUTION
CONSTITUTIONAL
CONSTITUTIONALS
CONSTITUTIONIST
CONSTITUTIONS
CONSTITUTIVE
CONSTITUTIVELY
CONSTITUTOR
CONSTITUTORS
CONSTRAINABLE
CONSTRAINED
CONSTRAINEDLY
CONSTRAINER
CONSTRAINERS
CONSTRAINING
CONSTRAINS
CONSTRAINT
CONSTRAINTS
CONSTRICTED
CONSTRICTING
CONSTRICTION
CONSTRICTIONS
CONSTRICTIVE
CONSTRICTIVELY
CONSTRICTOR
CONSTRICTORS
CONSTRICTS
CONSTRINGE
CONSTRINGED
CONSTRINGENCE
CONSTRINGENCES
CONSTRINGENCIES
CONSTRINGENCY
CONSTRINGENT
CONSTRINGES
CONSTRINGING
CONSTRUABILITY
CONSTRUABLE
CONSTRUALS
CONSTRUCTABLE
CONSTRUCTED
CONSTRUCTER
CONSTRUCTERS
CONSTRUCTIBLE
CONSTRUCTING
CONSTRUCTION
CONSTRUCTIONAL
CONSTRUCTIONISM
CONSTRUCTIONIST
CONSTRUCTIONS
CONSTRUCTIVE
CONSTRUCTIVELY

CONSTRUCTIVISM
CONSTRUCTIVISMS
CONSTRUCTIVIST
CONSTRUCTIVISTS
CONSTRUCTOR
CONSTRUCTORS
CONSTRUCTS
CONSTRUCTURE
CONSTRUCTURES
CONSTRUERS
CONSTRUING
CONSTUPRATE
CONSTUPRATED
CONSTUPRATES
CONSTUPRATING
CONSTUPRATION
CONSTUPRATIONS
CONSUBSIST
CONSUBSISTED
CONSUBSISTING
CONSUBSISTS
CONSUBSTANTIAL
CONSUBSTANTIATE
CONSUETUDE
CONSUETUDES
CONSUETUDINARY
CONSULAGES
CONSULATES
CONSULSHIP
CONSULSHIPS
CONSULTABLE
CONSULTANCIES
CONSULTANCY
CONSULTANT
CONSULTANTS
CONSULTANTSHIP
CONSULTANTSHIPS
CONSULTATION
CONSULTATIONS
CONSULTATIVE
CONSULTATIVELY
CONSULTATORY
CONSULTEES
CONSULTERS
CONSULTING
CONSULTIVE
CONSULTORS
CONSULTORY
CONSUMABLE
CONSUMABLES
CONSUMEDLY
CONSUMERISM
CONSUMERISMS
CONSUMERIST
CONSUMERISTIC
CONSUMERISTS
CONSUMERSHIP
CONSUMERSHIPS

CONSUMINGLY	CONTAMINANT	CONTEMPTIBLE	CONTEXTURES
CONSUMINGS	CONTAMINANTS	CONTEMPTIBLY	CONTIGNATION
CONSUMMATE	CONTAMINATE	CONTEMPTUOUS	CONTIGNATIONS
CONSUMMATED	CONTAMINATED	CONTEMPTUOUSLY	CONTIGUITIES
CONSUMMATELY	CONTAMINATES	CONTENDENT	CONTIGUITY
CONSUMMATES	CONTAMINATING	CONTENDENTS	CONTIGUOUS
CONSUMMATING	CONTAMINATION	CONTENDERS	CONTIGUOUSLY
CONSUMMATION	CONTAMINATIONS	CONTENDING	CONTIGUOUSNESS
CONSUMMATIONS	CONTAMINATIVE	CONTENDINGLY	CONTINENCE
CONSUMMATIVE	CONTAMINATOR	CONTENDINGS	CONTINENCES
CONSUMMATOR	CONTAMINATORS	CONTENEMENT	CONTINENCIES
CONSUMMATORS	CONTANGOED	CONTENEMENTS	CONTINENCY
CONSUMMATORY	CONTANGOES	CONTENTATION	CONTINENTAL
CONSUMPTION	CONTANGOING	CONTENTATIONS	CONTINENTALISM
CONSUMPTIONS	CONTEMNERS	CONTENTEDLY	CONTINENTALISMS
CONSUMPTIVE	CONTEMNIBLE	CONTENTEDNESS	CONTINENTALIST
CONSUMPTIVELY	CONTEMNIBLY	CONTENTEDNESSES	CONTINENTALISTS
CONSUMPTIVENESS	CONTEMNING	CONTENTING	CONTINENTALLY
CONSUMPTIVES	CONTEMNORS	CONTENTION	CONTINENTALS
CONSUMPTIVITIES	CONTEMPERATION	CONTENTIONS	CONTINENTLY
CONSUMPTIVITY	CONTEMPERATIONS	CONTENTIOUS	CONTINENTS
CONTABESCENCE	CONTEMPERATURE	CONTENTIOUSLY	CONTINGENCE
CONTABESCENCES	CONTEMPERATURES	CONTENTIOUSNESS	CONTINGENCES
CONTABESCENT	CONTEMPERED	CONTENTLESS	CONTINGENCIES
CONTACTABLE	CONTEMPERING	CONTENTMENT	CONTINGENCY
CONTACTEES	CONTEMPERS	CONTENTMENTS	CONTINGENT
CONTACTING	CONTEMPLABLE	CONTERMINAL	CONTINGENTLY
CONTACTORS	CONTEMPLANT	CONTERMINALLY	CONTINGENTS
CONTACTUAL	CONTEMPLANTS	CONTERMINANT	CONTINUABLE
CONTACTUALLY	CONTEMPLATE	CONTERMINATE	CONTINUALITIES
CONTADINAS	CONTEMPLATED	CONTERMINOUS	CONTINUALITY
CONTAGIONIST	CONTEMPLATES	CONTERMINOUSLY	CONTINUALLY
CONTAGIONISTS	CONTEMPLATING	CONTESSERATION	CONTINUALNESS
CONTAGIONS	CONTEMPLATION	CONTESSERATIONS	CONTINUALNESSES
CONTAGIOUS	CONTEMPLATIONS	CONTESTABILITY	CONTINUANCE
CONTAGIOUSLY	CONTEMPLATIST	CONTESTABLE	CONTINUANCES
CONTAGIOUSNESS	CONTEMPLATISTS	CONTESTABLENESS	CONTINUANT
CONTAINABLE	CONTEMPLATIVE	CONTESTABLY	CONTINUANTS
CONTAINERBOARD	CONTEMPLATIVELY	CONTESTANT	CONTINUATE
CONTAINERBOARDS	CONTEMPLATIVES	CONTESTANTS	CONTINUATION
CONTAINERISE	CONTEMPLATOR	CONTESTATION	CONTINUATIONS
CONTAINERISED	CONTEMPLATORS	CONTESTATIONS	CONTINUATIVE
CONTAINERISES	CONTEMPORANEAN	CONTESTERS	CONTINUATIVELY
CONTAINERISING	CONTEMPORANEANS	CONTESTING	CONTINUATIVES
CONTAINERIZE	CONTEMPORANEITY	CONTESTINGLY	CONTINUATOR
CONTAINERIZED	CONTEMPORANEOUS	CONTEXTLESS	CONTINUATORS
CONTAINERIZES	CONTEMPORARIES	CONTEXTUAL	CONTINUEDLY
CONTAINERIZING	CONTEMPORARILY	CONTEXTUALISE	CONTINUEDNESS
CONTAINERLESS	CONTEMPORARY	CONTEXTUALISED	CONTINUEDNESSES
CONTAINERPORT	CONTEMPORISE	CONTEXTUALISES	CONTINUERS
CONTAINERPORTS	CONTEMPORISED	CONTEXTUALISING	CONTINUING
CONTAINERS	CONTEMPORISES	CONTEXTUALIZE	CONTINUINGLY
CONTAINERSHIP	CONTEMPORISING	CONTEXTUALIZED	CONTINUITIES
CONTAINERSHIPS	CONTEMPORIZE	CONTEXTUALIZES	CONTINUITY
CONTAINING	CONTEMPORIZED	CONTEXTUALIZING	CONTINUOUS
CONTAINMENT	CONTEMPORIZES	CONTEXTUALLY	CONTINUOUSLY
CONTAINMENTS	CONTEMPORIZING	CONTEXTURAL	CONTINUOUSNESS
CONTAMINABLE	CONTEMPTIBILITY	CONTEXTURE	CONTINUUMS

CONTORNIATE
CONTORNIATES
CONTORTEDLY
CONTORTEDNESS
CONTORTEDNESSES
CONTORTING
CONTORTION
CONTORTIONAL
CONTORTIONATE
CONTORTIONED
CONTORTIONISM
CONTORTIONISMS
CONTORTIONIST
CONTORTIONISTIC
CONTORTIONISTS
CONTORTIONS
CONTORTIVE
CONTOURING
CONTRABAND
CONTRABANDISM
CONTRABANDISMS
CONTRABANDIST
CONTRABANDISTS
CONTRABANDS
CONTRABASS
CONTRABASSES
CONTRABASSI
CONTRABASSIST
CONTRABASSISTS
CONTRABASSO
CONTRABASSOON
CONTRABASSOONS
CONTRABASSOS
CONTRABBASSI
CONTRABBASSO
CONTRABBASSOS
CONTRACEPTION
CONTRACEPTIONS
CONTRACEPTIVE
CONTRACEPTIVES
CONTRACLOCKWISE
CONTRACTABILITY
CONTRACTABLE
CONTRACTED
CONTRACTEDLY
CONTRACTEDNESS
CONTRACTIBILITY
CONTRACTIBLE
CONTRACTIBLY
CONTRACTILE
CONTRACTILITIES
CONTRACTILITY
CONTRACTING
CONTRACTION
CONTRACTIONAL
CONTRACTIONARY
CONTRACTIONS
CONTRACTIVE

CONTRACTIVELY
CONTRACTIVENESS
CONTRACTOR
CONTRACTORS
CONTRACTUAL
CONTRACTUALLY
CONTRACTURAL
CONTRACTURE
CONTRACTURES
CONTRACYCLICAL
CONTRADANCE
CONTRADANCES
CONTRADICT
CONTRADICTABLE
CONTRADICTED
CONTRADICTER
CONTRADICTERS
CONTRADICTING
CONTRADICTION
CONTRADICTIONS
CONTRADICTIOUS
CONTRADICTIVE
CONTRADICTIVELY
CONTRADICTOR
CONTRADICTORIES
CONTRADICTORILY
CONTRADICTORS
CONTRADICTORY
CONTRADICTS
CONTRAFAGOTTO
CONTRAFAGOTTOS
CONTRAFLOW
CONTRAFLOWS
CONTRAGESTION
CONTRAGESTIONS
CONTRAGESTIVE
CONTRAGESTIVES
CONTRAHENT
CONTRAHENTS
CONTRAINDICANT
CONTRAINDICANTS
CONTRAINDICATE
CONTRAINDICATED
CONTRAINDICATES
CONTRALATERAL
CONTRALTOS
CONTRANATANT
CONTRAOCTAVE
CONTRAOCTAVES
CONTRAPLEX
CONTRAPOSITION
CONTRAPOSITIONS
CONTRAPOSITIVE
CONTRAPOSITIVES
CONTRAPPOSTO
CONTRAPPOSTOS
CONTRAPROP
CONTRAPROPELLER

CONTRAPROPS
CONTRAPTION
CONTRAPTIONS
CONTRAPUNTAL
CONTRAPUNTALIST
CONTRAPUNTALLY
CONTRAPUNTIST
CONTRAPUNTISTS
CONTRARIAN
CONTRARIANS
CONTRARIED
CONTRARIES
CONTRARIETIES
CONTRARIETY
CONTRARILY
CONTRARINESS
CONTRARINESSES
CONTRARIOUS
CONTRARIOUSLY
CONTRARIOUSNESS
CONTRARIWISE
CONTRARYING
CONTRASEXUAL
CONTRASEXUALS
CONTRASTABLE
CONTRASTABLY
CONTRASTED
CONTRASTING
CONTRASTIVE
CONTRASTIVELY
CONTRATERRENE
CONTRAVALLATION
CONTRAVENE
CONTRAVENED
CONTRAVENER
CONTRAVENERS
CONTRAVENES
CONTRAVENING
CONTRAVENTION
CONTRAVENTIONS
CONTRAYERVA
CONTRAYERVAS
CONTRECOUP
CONTRECOUPS
CONTREDANCE
CONTREDANCES
CONTREDANSE
CONTREDANSES
CONTRETEMPS
CONTRIBUTABLE
CONTRIBUTARIES
CONTRIBUTARY
CONTRIBUTE
CONTRIBUTED
CONTRIBUTES
CONTRIBUTING
CONTRIBUTION
CONTRIBUTIONS

CONTRIBUTIVE
CONTRIBUTIVELY
CONTRIBUTOR
CONTRIBUTORIES
CONTRIBUTORS
CONTRIBUTORY
CONTRISTATION
CONTRISTATIONS
CONTRISTED
CONTRISTING
CONTRITELY
CONTRITENESS
CONTRITENESSES
CONTRITION
CONTRITIONS
CONTRITURATE
CONTRITURATED
CONTRITURATES
CONTRITURATING
CONTRIVABLE
CONTRIVANCE
CONTRIVANCES
CONTRIVEMENT
CONTRIVEMENTS
CONTRIVERS
CONTRIVING
CONTROLLABILITY
CONTROLLABLE
CONTROLLABLY
CONTROLLED
CONTROLLER
CONTROLLERS
CONTROLLERSHIP
CONTROLLERSHIPS
CONTROLLING
CONTROLMENT
CONTROLMENTS
CONTROULED
CONTROULING
CONTROVERSE
CONTROVERSES
CONTROVERSIAL
CONTROVERSIALLY
CONTROVERSIES
CONTROVERSY
CONTROVERT
CONTROVERTED
CONTROVERTER
CONTROVERTERS
CONTROVERTIBLE
CONTROVERTIBLY
CONTROVERTING
CONTROVERTIST
CONTROVERTISTS
CONTROVERTS
CONTUBERNAL
CONTUBERNYAL
CONTUMACIES

CONTUMACIOUS
CONTUMACIOUSLY
CONTUMACITIES
CONTUMACITY
CONTUMELIES
CONTUMELIOUS
CONTUMELIOUSLY
CONTUNDING
CONTUSIONED
CONTUSIONS
CONUNDRUMS
CONURBATION
CONURBATIONS
CONVALESCE
CONVALESCED
CONVALESCENCE
CONVALESCENCES
CONVALESCENCIES
CONVALESCENCY
CONVALESCENT
CONVALESCENTLY
CONVALESCENTS
CONVALESCES
CONVALESCING
CONVECTING
CONVECTION
CONVECTIONAL
CONVECTIONS
CONVECTIVE
CONVECTORS
CONVENABLE
CONVENANCE
CONVENANCES
CONVENERSHIP
CONVENERSHIPS
CONVENIENCE
CONVENIENCES
CONVENIENCIES
CONVENIENCY
CONVENIENT
CONVENIENTLY
CONVENORSHIP
CONVENORSHIPS
CONVENTICLE
CONVENTICLED
CONVENTICLER
CONVENTICLERS
CONVENTICLES
CONVENTICLING
CONVENTING
CONVENTION
CONVENTIONAL
CONVENTIONALISE
CONVENTIONALISM
CONVENTIONALIST
CONVENTIONALITY
CONVENTIONALIZE
CONVENTIONALLY

CONVENTIONALS
CONVENTIONARY
CONVENTIONEER
CONVENTIONEERS
CONVENTIONER
CONVENTIONERS
CONVENTIONIST
CONVENTIONISTS
CONVENTIONS
CONVENTUAL
CONVENTUALLY
CONVENTUALS
CONVERGENCE
CONVERGENCES
CONVERGENCIES
CONVERGENCY
CONVERGENT
CONVERGING
CONVERSABLE
CONVERSABLENESS
CONVERSABLY
CONVERSANCE
CONVERSANCES
CONVERSANCIES
CONVERSANCY
CONVERSANT
CONVERSANTLY
CONVERSATION
CONVERSATIONAL
CONVERSATIONISM
CONVERSATIONIST
CONVERSATIONS
CONVERSATIVE
CONVERSAZIONE
CONVERSAZIONES
CONVERSAZIONI
CONVERSELY
CONVERSERS
CONVERSING
CONVERSION
CONVERSIONAL
CONVERSIONARY
CONVERSIONS
CONVERTAPLANE
CONVERTAPLANES
CONVERTEND
CONVERTENDS
CONVERTERS
CONVERTIBILITY
CONVERTIBLE
CONVERTIBLENESS
CONVERTIBLES
CONVERTIBLY
CONVERTING
CONVERTIPLANE
CONVERTIPLANES
CONVERTITE
CONVERTITES

CONVERTIVE
CONVERTOPLANE
CONVERTOPLANES
CONVERTORS
CONVEXEDLY
CONVEXITIES
CONVEXNESS
CONVEXNESSES
CONVEYABLE
CONVEYANCE
CONVEYANCER
CONVEYANCERS
CONVEYANCES
CONVEYANCING
CONVEYANCINGS
CONVEYORISATION
CONVEYORISE
CONVEYORISED
CONVEYORISES
CONVEYORISING
CONVEYORIZATION
CONVEYORIZE
CONVEYORIZED
CONVEYORIZES
CONVEYORIZING
CONVICINITIES
CONVICINITY
CONVICTABLE
CONVICTIBLE
CONVICTING
CONVICTION
CONVICTIONAL
CONVICTIONS
CONVICTISM
CONVICTISMS
CONVICTIVE
CONVICTIVELY
CONVINCEMENT
CONVINCEMENTS
CONVINCERS
CONVINCIBLE
CONVINCING
CONVINCINGLY
CONVINCINGNESS
CONVIVIALIST
CONVIVIALISTS
CONVIVIALITIES
CONVIVIALITY
CONVIVIALLY
CONVOCATED
CONVOCATES
CONVOCATING
CONVOCATION
CONVOCATIONAL
CONVOCATIONIST
CONVOCATIONISTS
CONVOCATIONS
CONVOCATIVE

CONVOCATOR
CONVOCATORS
CONVOLUTED
CONVOLUTEDLY
CONVOLUTEDNESS
CONVOLUTELY
CONVOLUTES
CONVOLUTING
CONVOLUTION
CONVOLUTIONAL
CONVOLUTIONARY
CONVOLUTIONS
CONVOLVING
CONVOLVULACEOUS
CONVOLVULI
CONVOLVULUS
CONVOLVULUSES
CONVULSANT
CONVULSANTS
CONVULSIBLE
CONVULSING
CONVULSION
CONVULSIONAL
CONVULSIONARIES
CONVULSIONARY
CONVULSIONIST
CONVULSIONISTS
CONVULSIONS
CONVULSIVE
CONVULSIVELY
CONVULSIVENESS
COOKHOUSES
COOKSHACKS
COOKSTOVES
COOLHEADED
COOLHOUSES
COOLINGNESS
COOLINGNESSES
COOLNESSES
COOMCEILED
COONHOUNDS
COOPERAGES
COOPERATED
COOPERATES
COOPERATING
COOPERATION
COOPERATIONIST
COOPERATIONISTS
COOPERATIONS
COOPERATIVE
COOPERATIVELY
COOPERATIVENESS
COOPERATIVES
COOPERATIVITIES
COOPERATIVITY
COOPERATOR
COOPERATORS
COOPERINGS

COOPTATION	COPPERPLATES	COPROSPERITY	CORALLIGENOUS
COOPTATIONS	COPPERSKIN	COPROSTEROL	CORALLINES
COOPTATIVE	COPPERSKINS	COPROSTEROLS	CORALLITES
COORDINANCE	COPPERSMITH	COPSEWOODS	CORALLOIDAL
COORDINANCES	COPPERSMITHS	COPUBLISHED	CORALROOTS
COORDINATE	COPPERWORK	COPUBLISHER	CORALWORTS
COORDINATED	COPPERWORKS	COPUBLISHERS	CORBEILLES
COORDINATELY	COPPERWORM	COPUBLISHES	CORBELINGS
COORDINATENESS	COPPERWORMS	COPUBLISHING	CORBELLING
COORDINATES	COPPICINGS	COPULATING	CORBELLINGS
COORDINATING	COPRESENCE	COPULATION	CORBICULAE
COORDINATION	COPRESENCES	COPULATIONS	CORBICULATE
COORDINATIONS	COPRESENTED	COPULATIVE	CORDECTOMIES
COORDINATIVE	COPRESENTING	COPULATIVELY	CORDECTOMY
COORDINATOR	COPRESENTS	COPULATIVES	CORDELLING
COORDINATORS	COPRESIDENT	COPULATORY	CORDGRASSES
COPARCENARIES	COPRESIDENTS	COPURIFIED	CORDIALISE
COPARCENARY	COPRINCIPAL	COPURIFIES	CORDIALISED
COPARCENER	COPRINCIPALS	COPURIFYING	CORDIALISES
COPARCENERIES	COPRISONER	COPYCATTED	CORDIALISING
COPARCENERS	COPRISONERS	COPYCATTING	CORDIALITIES
COPARCENERY	COPROCESSING	COPYEDITED	CORDIALITY
COPARCENIES	COPROCESSOR	COPYEDITING	CORDIALIZE
COPARENTED	COPROCESSORS	COPYGRAPHS	CORDIALIZED
COPARENTING	COPRODUCED	COPYHOLDER	CORDIALIZES
COPARTNERED	COPRODUCER	COPYHOLDERS	CORDIALIZING
COPARTNERIES	COPRODUCERS	COPYREADER	CORDIALNESS
COPARTNERING	COPRODUCES	COPYREADERS	CORDIALNESSES
COPARTNERS	COPRODUCING	COPYREADING	CORDIERITE
COPARTNERSHIP	COPRODUCTION	COPYREADINGS	CORDIERITES
COPARTNERSHIPS	COPRODUCTIONS	COPYRIGHTABLE	CORDILLERA
COPARTNERY	COPRODUCTS	COPYRIGHTED	CORDILLERAN
COPATRIOTS	COPROLALIA	COPYRIGHTER	CORDILLERAS
COPAYMENTS	COPROLALIAC	COPYRIGHTERS	CORDLESSES
COPESETTIC	COPROLALIAS	COPYRIGHTING	CORDOCENTESES
COPESTONES	COPROLITES	COPYRIGHTS	CORDOCENTESIS
COPINGSTONE	COPROLITHS	COPYTAKERS	CORDONNETS
COPINGSTONES	COPROLITIC	COPYWRITER	CORDOTOMIES
COPIOUSNESS	COPROLOGIES	COPYWRITERS	CORDUROYED
COPIOUSNESSES	COPROMOTER	COPYWRITING	CORDUROYING
COPLANARITIES	COPROMOTERS	COPYWRITINGS	CORDWAINER
COPLANARITY	COPROPHAGAN	COQUELICOT	CORDWAINERIES
COPLOTTING	COPROPHAGANS	COQUELICOTS	CORDWAINERS
COPOLYMERIC	COPROPHAGIC	COQUETRIES	CORDWAINERY
COPOLYMERISE	COPROPHAGIES	COQUETTING	CORDYLINES
COPOLYMERISED	COPROPHAGIST	COQUETTISH	CORECIPIENT
COPOLYMERISES	COPROPHAGISTS	COQUETTISHLY	CORECIPIENTS
COPOLYMERISING	COPROPHAGOUS	COQUETTISHNESS	COREDEEMED
COPOLYMERIZE	COPROPHAGY	COQUIMBITE	COREDEEMING
COPOLYMERIZED	COPROPHILIA	COQUIMBITES	COREFERENTIAL
COPOLYMERIZES	COPROPHILIAC	CORACIIFORM	COREGONINE
COPOLYMERIZING	COPROPHILIACS	CORADICATE	CORELATING
COPOLYMERS	COPROPHILIAS	CORALBELLS	CORELATION
COPPERASES	COPROPHILIC	CORALBERRIES	CORELATIONS
COPPERHEAD	COPROPHILOUS	CORALBERRY	CORELATIVE
COPPERHEADS	COPROPRIETOR	CORALLACEOUS	CORELATIVES
COPPERINGS	COPROPRIETORS	CORALLIFEROUS	CORELIGIONIST
COPPERPLATE	COPROSPERITIES	CORALLIFORM	CORELIGIONISTS

COREOPSISES	CORNERWISE	CORPORALITIES	CORPUSCLES
COREPRESSOR	CORNETCIES	CORPORALITY	CORPUSCULAR
COREPRESSORS	CORNETISTS	CORPORALLY	CORPUSCULARIAN
COREQUISITE	CORNETTINO	CORPORALSHIP	CORPUSCULARIANS
COREQUISITES	CORNETTINOS	CORPORALSHIPS	CORPUSCULARITY
CORESEARCHER	CORNETTIST	CORPORASES	CORPUSCULE
CORESEARCHERS	CORNETTISTS	CORPORATELY	CORPUSCULES
CORESIDENT	CORNFIELDS	CORPORATENESS	CORRALLING
CORESIDENTIAL	CORNFLAKES	CORPORATENESSES	CORRASIONS
CORESIDENTS	CORNFLOURS	CORPORATES	CORRECTABLE
CORESPONDENT	CORNFLOWER	CORPORATION	CORRECTEST
CORESPONDENTS	CORNFLOWERS	CORPORATIONS	CORRECTIBLE
CORFHOUSES	CORNHUSKER	CORPORATISE	CORRECTING
CORIACEOUS	CORNHUSKERS	CORPORATISED	CORRECTION
CORIANDERS	CORNHUSKING	CORPORATISES	CORRECTIONAL
CORINTHIANISE	CORNHUSKINGS	CORPORATISING	CORRECTIONER
CORINTHIANISED	CORNICHONS	CORPORATISM	CORRECTIONERS
CORINTHIANISES	CORNICULATE	CORPORATISMS	CORRECTIONS
CORINTHIANISING	CORNICULUM	CORPORATIST	CORRECTITUDE
CORINTHIANIZE	CORNICULUMS	CORPORATISTS	CORRECTITUDES
CORINTHIANIZED	CORNIFEROUS	CORPORATIVE	CORRECTIVE
CORINTHIANIZES	CORNIFICATION	CORPORATIVISM	CORRECTIVELY
CORINTHIANIZING	CORNIFICATIONS	CORPORATIVISMS	CORRECTIVES
CORIVALLED	CORNIFYING	CORPORATIZE	CORRECTNESS
CORIVALLING	CORNIGEROUS	CORPORATIZED	CORRECTNESSES
CORIVALRIES	CORNINESSES	CORPORATIZES	CORRECTORS
CORIVALSHIP	CORNOPEANS	CORPORATIZING	CORRECTORY
CORIVALSHIPS	CORNROWING	CORPORATOR	CORREGIDOR
CORKBOARDS	CORNSTALKS	CORPORATORS	CORREGIDORS
CORKBORERS	CORNSTARCH	CORPOREALISE	CORRELATABLE
CORKINESSES	CORNSTARCHES	CORPOREALISED	CORRELATED
CORKSCREWED	CORNSTONES	CORPOREALISES	CORRELATES
CORKSCREWING	CORNUCOPIA	CORPOREALISING	CORRELATING
CORKSCREWS	CORNUCOPIAN	CORPOREALISM	CORRELATION
CORMOPHYTE	CORNUCOPIAS	CORPOREALISMS	CORRELATIONAL
CORMOPHYTES	COROLLACEOUS	CORPOREALIST	CORRELATIONS
CORMOPHYTIC	COROLLARIES	CORPOREALISTS	CORRELATIVE
CORMORANTS	COROLLIFLORAL	CORPOREALITIES	CORRELATIVELY
CORNACEOUS	COROLLIFLOROUS	CORPOREALITY	CORRELATIVENESS
CORNBORERS	COROLLIFORM	CORPOREALIZE	CORRELATIVES
CORNBRAIDED	COROMANDEL	CORPOREALIZED	CORRELATIVITIES
CORNBRAIDING	COROMANDELS	CORPOREALIZES	CORRELATIVITY
CORNBRAIDS	CORONAGRAPH	CORPOREALIZING	CORRELATOR
CORNBRANDIES	CORONAGRAPHS	CORPOREALLY	CORRELATORS
CORNBRANDY	CORONARIES	CORPOREALNESS	CORRELIGIONIST
CORNBRASHES	CORONATING	CORPOREALNESSES	CORRELIGIONISTS
CORNBREADS	CORONATION	CORPOREITIES	CORREPTION
CORNCOCKLE	CORONATIONS	CORPOREITY	CORREPTIONS
CORNCOCKLES	CORONAVIRUS	CORPORIFICATION	CORRESPOND
CORNCRAKES	CORONAVIRUSES	CORPORIFIED	CORRESPONDED
CORNEITISES	CORONERSHIP	CORPORIFIES	CORRESPONDENCE
CORNELIANS	CORONERSHIPS	CORPORIFYING	CORRESPONDENCES
CORNEMUSES	CORONOGRAPH	CORPOSANTS	CORRESPONDENCY
CORNERBACK	CORONOGRAPHS	CORPULENCE	CORRESPONDENT
CORNERBACKS	COROTATING	CORPULENCES	CORRESPONDENTLY
CORNERSTONE	COROTATION	CORPULENCIES	CORRESPONDENTS
CORNERSTONES	COROTATIONS	CORPULENCY	CORRESPONDING
CORNERWAYS	CORPORALES	CORPULENTLY	CORRESPONDINGLY

CORRESPONDS
CORRESPONSIVE
CORRIGENDA
CORRIGENDUM
CORRIGENTS
CORRIGIBILITIES
CORRIGIBILITY
CORRIGIBLE
CORRIGIBLY
CORRIVALLED
CORRIVALLING
CORRIVALRIES
CORRIVALRY
CORRIVALSHIP
CORRIVALSHIPS
CORROBORABLE
CORROBORANT
CORROBORATE
CORROBORATED
CORROBORATES
CORROBORATING
CORROBORATION
CORROBORATIONS
CORROBORATIVE
CORROBORATIVELY
CORROBORATIVES
CORROBORATOR
CORROBORATORS
CORROBORATORY
CORROBOREE
CORROBOREED
CORROBOREEING
CORROBOREES
CORRODANTS
CORRODENTS
CORRODIBILITIES
CORRODIBILITY
CORRODIBLE
CORROSIBILITIES
CORROSIBILITY
CORROSIBLE
CORROSIONS
CORROSIVELY
CORROSIVENESS
CORROSIVENESSES
CORROSIVES
CORRUGATED
CORRUGATES
CORRUGATING
CORRUGATION
CORRUGATIONS
CORRUGATOR
CORRUGATORS
CORRUPTERS
CORRUPTEST
CORRUPTIBILITY
CORRUPTIBLE
CORRUPTIBLENESS

CORRUPTIBLY
CORRUPTING
CORRUPTION
CORRUPTIONIST
CORRUPTIONISTS
CORRUPTIONS
CORRUPTIVE
CORRUPTIVELY
CORRUPTNESS
CORRUPTNESSES
CORRUPTORS
CORSELETTE
CORSELETTES
CORSETIERE
CORSETIERES
CORSETIERS
CORSETRIES
CORTICALLY
CORTICATED
CORTICATION
CORTICATIONS
CORTICOIDS
CORTICOLOUS
CORTICOSTEROID
CORTICOSTEROIDS
CORTICOSTERONE
CORTICOSTERONES
CORTICOTROPHIC
CORTICOTROPHIN
CORTICOTROPHINS
CORTICOTROPIC
CORTICOTROPIN
CORTICOTROPINS
CORTISONES
CORUSCATED
CORUSCATES
CORUSCATING
CORUSCATION
CORUSCATIONS
CORVETTING
CORYBANTES
CORYBANTIC
CORYBANTISM
CORYBANTISMS
CORYDALINE
CORYDALINES
CORYDALISES
CORYLOPSES
CORYLOPSIS
CORYMBOSELY
CORYNEBACTERIA
CORYNEBACTERIAL
CORYNEBACTERIUM
CORYNEFORM
CORYPHAEUS
CORYPHENES
COSCINOMANCIES
COSCINOMANCY

COSCRIPTED
COSCRIPTING
COSEISMALS
COSEISMICS
COSENTIENT
COSHERINGS
COSIGNATORIES
COSIGNATORY
COSIGNIFICATIVE
COSINESSES
COSMECEUTICAL
COSMECEUTICALS
COSMETICAL
COSMETICALLY
COSMETICIAN
COSMETICIANS
COSMETICISE
COSMETICISED
COSMETICISES
COSMETICISING
COSMETICISM
COSMETICISMS
COSMETICIZE
COSMETICIZED
COSMETICIZES
COSMETICIZING
COSMETICOLOGIES
COSMETICOLOGY
COSMETOLOGIES
COSMETOLOGIST
COSMETOLOGISTS
COSMETOLOGY
COSMICALLY
COSMOCHEMICAL
COSMOCHEMIST
COSMOCHEMISTRY
COSMOCHEMISTS
COSMOCRATIC
COSMOCRATS
COSMODROME
COSMODROMES
COSMOGENIC
COSMOGENIES
COSMOGONAL
COSMOGONIC
COSMOGONICAL
COSMOGONIES
COSMOGONIST
COSMOGONISTS
COSMOGRAPHER
COSMOGRAPHERS
COSMOGRAPHIC
COSMOGRAPHICAL
COSMOGRAPHIES
COSMOGRAPHIST
COSMOGRAPHISTS
COSMOGRAPHY
COSMOLATRIES

COSMOLATRY
COSMOLINED
COSMOLINES
COSMOLINING
COSMOLOGIC
COSMOLOGICAL
COSMOLOGICALLY
COSMOLOGIES
COSMOLOGIST
COSMOLOGISTS
COSMONAUTICS
COSMONAUTS
COSMOPLASTIC
COSMOPOLIS
COSMOPOLISES
COSMOPOLITAN
COSMOPOLITANISM
COSMOPOLITANS
COSMOPOLITE
COSMOPOLITES
COSMOPOLITIC
COSMOPOLITICAL
COSMOPOLITICS
COSMOPOLITISM
COSMOPOLITISMS
COSMORAMAS
COSMORAMIC
COSMOSPHERE
COSMOSPHERES
COSMOTHEISM
COSMOTHEISMS
COSMOTHETIC
COSMOTHETICAL
COSMOTRONS
COSPONSORED
COSPONSORING
COSPONSORS
COSPONSORSHIP
COSPONSORSHIPS
COSTALGIAS
COSTARDMONGER
COSTARDMONGERS
COSTARRING
COSTEANING
COSTEANINGS
COSTERMONGER
COSTERMONGERS
COSTIVENESS
COSTIVENESSES
COSTLESSLY
COSTLINESS
COSTLINESSES
COSTMARIES
COSTOTOMIES
COSTUMERIES
COSTUMIERS
COSURFACTANT
COSURFACTANTS

773

COTANGENTIAL	COULOMBMETERS	COUNTERARGUES	COUNTERCLAIMED
COTANGENTS	COULOMETER	COUNTERARGUING	COUNTERCLAIMING
COTELETTES	COULOMETERS	COUNTERARGUMENT	COUNTERCLAIMS
COTEMPORANEOUS	COULOMETRIC	COUNTERASSAULT	COUNTERCOUP
COTEMPORARY	COULOMETRICALLY	COUNTERASSAULTS	COUNTERCOUPS
COTENANCIES	COULOMETRIES	COUNTERATTACK	COUNTERCRIES
COTERMINOUS	COULOMETRY	COUNTERATTACKED	COUNTERCRY
COTERMINOUSLY	COUMARILIC	COUNTERATTACKER	COUNTERCULTURAL
COTILLIONS	COUMARONES	COUNTERATTACKS	COUNTERCULTURE
COTONEASTER	COUNCILLOR	COUNTERBALANCE	COUNTERCULTURES
COTONEASTERS	COUNCILLORS	COUNTERBALANCED	COUNTERCURRENT
COTRANSDUCE	COUNCILLORSHIP	COUNTERBALANCES	COUNTERCURRENTS
COTRANSDUCED	COUNCILLORSHIPS	COUNTERBASE	COUNTERCYCLICAL
COTRANSDUCES	COUNCILMAN	COUNTERBASES	COUNTERDEMAND
COTRANSDUCING	COUNCILMANIC	COUNTERBID	COUNTERDEMANDS
COTRANSDUCTION	COUNCILMEN	COUNTERBIDDER	COUNTERDRAW
COTRANSDUCTIONS	COUNCILORS	COUNTERBIDDERS	COUNTERDRAWING
COTRANSFER	COUNCILORSHIP	COUNTERBIDS	COUNTERDRAWN
COTRANSFERS	COUNCILORSHIPS	COUNTERBLAST	COUNTERDRAWS
COTRANSPORT	COUNCILWOMAN	COUNTERBLASTS	COUNTERDREW
COTRANSPORTED	COUNCILWOMEN	COUNTERBLOCKADE	COUNTEREFFORT
COTRANSPORTING	COUNSELABLE	COUNTERBLOW	COUNTEREFFORTS
COTRANSPORTS	COUNSELEES	COUNTERBLOWS	COUNTEREVIDENCE
COTRUSTEES	COUNSELING	COUNTERBLUFF	COUNTEREXAMPLE
COTTABUSES	COUNSELINGS	COUNTERBLUFFS	COUNTEREXAMPLES
COTTAGINGS	COUNSELLABLE	COUNTERBOND	COUNTERFACTUAL
COTTERLESS	COUNSELLED	COUNTERBONDS	COUNTERFACTUALS
COTTIERISM	COUNSELLING	COUNTERBORE	COUNTERFECT
COTTIERISMS	COUNSELLINGS	COUNTERBORED	COUNTERFEISANCE
COTTONADES	COUNSELLOR	COUNTERBORES	COUNTERFEIT
COTTONMOUTH	COUNSELLORS	COUNTERBORING	COUNTERFEITED
COTTONMOUTHS	COUNSELLORSHIP	COUNTERBRACE	COUNTERFEITER
COTTONOCRACIES	COUNSELLORSHIPS	COUNTERBRACED	COUNTERFEITERS
COTTONOCRACY	COUNSELORS	COUNTERBRACES	COUNTERFEITING
COTTONSEED	COUNSELORSHIP	COUNTERBRACING	COUNTERFEITLY
COTTONSEEDS	COUNSELORSHIPS	COUNTERBUFF	COUNTERFEITS
COTTONTAIL	COUNTABILITIES	COUNTERBUFFED	COUNTERFESAUNCE
COTTONTAILS	COUNTABILITY	COUNTERBUFFING	COUNTERFIRE
COTTONWEED	COUNTBACKS	COUNTERBUFFS	COUNTERFIRES
COTTONWEEDS	COUNTDOWNS	COUNTERCAMPAIGN	COUNTERFLOW
COTTONWOOD	COUNTENANCE	COUNTERCHANGE	COUNTERFLOWS
COTTONWOODS	COUNTENANCED	COUNTERCHANGED	COUNTERFOIL
COTURNIXES	COUNTENANCER	COUNTERCHANGES	COUNTERFOILS
COTYLEDONAL	COUNTENANCERS	COUNTERCHANGING	COUNTERFORCE
COTYLEDONARY	COUNTENANCES	COUNTERCHARGE	COUNTERFORCES
COTYLEDONOID	COUNTENANCING	COUNTERCHARGED	COUNTERFORT
COTYLEDONOUS	COUNTERACT	COUNTERCHARGES	COUNTERFORTS
COTYLEDONS	COUNTERACTED	COUNTERCHARGING	COUNTERGLOW
COTYLIFORM	COUNTERACTING	COUNTERCHARM	COUNTERGLOWS
COTYLOIDAL	COUNTERACTION	COUNTERCHARMED	COUNTERGUERILLA
COTYLOIDALS	COUNTERACTIONS	COUNTERCHARMING	COUNTERIMAGE
COTYLOSAUR	COUNTERACTIVE	COUNTERCHARMS	COUNTERIMAGES
COTYLOSAURS	COUNTERACTIVELY	COUNTERCHECK	COUNTERING
COUCHETTES	COUNTERACTS	COUNTERCHECKED	COUNTERINSTANCE
COULIBIACA	COUNTERAGENT	COUNTERCHECKING	COUNTERION
COULIBIACAS	COUNTERAGENTS	COUNTERCHECKS	COUNTERIONS
COULIBIACS	COUNTERARGUE	COUNTERCLAIM	COUNTERIRRITANT
COULOMBMETER	COUNTERARGUED	COUNTERCLAIMANT	COUNTERLIGHT

COUNTERLIGHTS	COUNTERPICKETS	COUNTERREFORMS	COUNTERSUIT
COUNTERMAN	COUNTERPLAN	COUNTERRESPONSE	COUNTERSUITS
COUNTERMAND	COUNTERPLANS	COUNTERSANK	COUNTERSUNK
COUNTERMANDABLE	COUNTERPLAY	COUNTERSCARP	COUNTERTACTIC
COUNTERMANDED	COUNTERPLAYER	COUNTERSCARPS	COUNTERTACTICS
COUNTERMANDING	COUNTERPLAYERS	COUNTERSEAL	COUNTERTENDENCY
COUNTERMANDS	COUNTERPLAYS	COUNTERSEALED	COUNTERTENOR
COUNTERMARCH	COUNTERPLEA	COUNTERSEALING	COUNTERTENORS
COUNTERMARCHED	COUNTERPLEAD	COUNTERSEALS	COUNTERTERROR
COUNTERMARCHES	COUNTERPLEADED	COUNTERSHADING	COUNTERTERRORS
COUNTERMARCHING	COUNTERPLEADING	COUNTERSHADINGS	COUNTERTHREAT
COUNTERMARK	COUNTERPLEADS	COUNTERSHAFT	COUNTERTHREATS
COUNTERMARKS	COUNTERPLEAS	COUNTERSHAFTS	COUNTERTHRUST
COUNTERMEASURE	COUNTERPLED	COUNTERSHOT	COUNTERTHRUSTS
COUNTERMEASURES	COUNTERPLOT	COUNTERSHOTS	COUNTERTOP
COUNTERMELODIES	COUNTERPLOTS	COUNTERSIGN	COUNTERTOPS
COUNTERMELODY	COUNTERPLOTTED	COUNTERSIGNED	COUNTERTRADE
COUNTERMEMO	COUNTERPLOTTING	COUNTERSIGNING	COUNTERTRADED
COUNTERMEMOS	COUNTERPLOY	COUNTERSIGNS	COUNTERTRADES
COUNTERMEN	COUNTERPLOYS	COUNTERSINK	COUNTERTRADING
COUNTERMINE	COUNTERPOINT	COUNTERSINKING	COUNTERTREND
COUNTERMINED	COUNTERPOINTED	COUNTERSINKS	COUNTERTRENDS
COUNTERMINES	COUNTERPOINTING	COUNTERSNIPER	COUNTERTYPE
COUNTERMINING	COUNTERPOINTS	COUNTERSNIPERS	COUNTERTYPES
COUNTERMOTION	COUNTERPOISE	COUNTERSPELL	COUNTERVAIL
COUNTERMOTIONS	COUNTERPOISED	COUNTERSPELLS	COUNTERVAILABLE
COUNTERMOVE	COUNTERPOISES	COUNTERSPIES	COUNTERVAILED
COUNTERMOVED	COUNTERPOISING	COUNTERSPY	COUNTERVAILING
COUNTERMOVEMENT	COUNTERPOSE	COUNTERSPYING	COUNTERVAILS
COUNTERMOVES	COUNTERPOSED	COUNTERSPYINGS	COUNTERVIEW
COUNTERMOVING	COUNTERPOSES	COUNTERSTAIN	COUNTERVIEWS
COUNTERMURE	COUNTERPOSING	COUNTERSTAINED	COUNTERVIOLENCE
COUNTERMURED	COUNTERPOWER	COUNTERSTAINING	COUNTERWEIGH
COUNTERMURES	COUNTERPOWERS	COUNTERSTAINS	COUNTERWEIGHED
COUNTERMURING	COUNTERPRESSURE	COUNTERSTATE	COUNTERWEIGHING
COUNTERMYTH	COUNTERPROJECT	COUNTERSTATED	COUNTERWEIGHS
COUNTERMYTHS	COUNTERPROJECTS	COUNTERSTATES	COUNTERWEIGHT
COUNTEROFFER	COUNTERPROOF	COUNTERSTATING	COUNTERWEIGHTED
COUNTEROFFERS	COUNTERPROOFS	COUNTERSTEP	COUNTERWEIGHTS
COUNTERORDER	COUNTERPROPOSAL	COUNTERSTEPS	COUNTERWORD
COUNTERORDERED	COUNTERPROTEST	COUNTERSTRATEGY	COUNTERWORDS
COUNTERORDERING	COUNTERPROTESTS	COUNTERSTREAM	COUNTERWORK
COUNTERORDERS	COUNTERPUNCH	COUNTERSTREAMS	COUNTERWORKED
COUNTERPACE	COUNTERPUNCHED	COUNTERSTRICKEN	COUNTERWORKER
COUNTERPACES	COUNTERPUNCHER	COUNTERSTRIKE	COUNTERWORKERS
COUNTERPANE	COUNTERPUNCHERS	COUNTERSTRIKES	COUNTERWORKING
COUNTERPANES	COUNTERPUNCHES	COUNTERSTRIKING	COUNTERWORKS
COUNTERPART	COUNTERPUNCHING	COUNTERSTROKE	COUNTERWORLD
COUNTERPARTIES	COUNTERQUESTION	COUNTERSTROKES	COUNTERWORLDS
COUNTERPARTS	COUNTERRAID	COUNTERSTRUCK	COUNTESSES
COUNTERPARTY	COUNTERRAIDS	COUNTERSTYLE	COUNTINGHOUSE
COUNTERPEISE	COUNTERRALLIED	COUNTERSTYLES	COUNTINGHOUSES
COUNTERPEISED	COUNTERRALLIES	COUNTERSUBJECT	COUNTLESSLY
COUNTERPEISES	COUNTERRALLY	COUNTERSUBJECTS	COUNTLINES
COUNTERPEISING	COUNTERRALLYING	COUNTERSUE	COUNTRIFIED
COUNTERPETITION	COUNTERREACTION	COUNTERSUED	COUNTROLLED
COUNTERPICKET	COUNTERREFORM	COUNTERSUES	COUNTROLLING
COUNTERPICKETED	COUNTERREFORMER	COUNTERSUING	COUNTRYFIED

COUNTRYISH	COUSINAGES	COWFETERIAS	CRAFTSPERSONS
COUNTRYMAN	COUSINHOOD	COWGRASSES	CRAFTSWOMAN
COUNTRYMEN	COUSINHOODS	COWLSTAFFS	CRAFTSWOMEN
COUNTRYSEAT	COUSINRIES	COWLSTAVES	CRAFTWORKS
COUNTRYSEATS	COUSINSHIP	COWPUNCHER	CRAGGEDNESS
COUNTRYSIDE	COUSINSHIPS	COWPUNCHERS	CRAGGEDNESSES
COUNTRYSIDES	COUTURIERE	COXCOMBICAL	CRAGGINESS
COUNTRYWIDE	COUTURIERES	COXCOMBICALITY	CRAGGINESSES
COUNTRYWOMAN	COUTURIERS	COXCOMBICALLY	CRAIGFLUKE
COUNTRYWOMEN	COVALENCES	COXCOMBRIES	CRAIGFLUKES
COUNTSHIPS	COVALENCIES	COXCOMICAL	CRAKEBERRIES
COUPLEDOMS	COVALENTLY	COXINESSES	CRAKEBERRY
COUPLEMENT	COVARIANCE	COXSWAINED	CRAMBOCLINK
COUPLEMENTS	COVARIANCES	COXSWAINING	CRAMBOCLINKS
COUPONINGS	COVARIANTS	COYISHNESS	CRAMOISIES
COURAGEFUL	COVARIATES	COYISHNESSES	CRAMPBARKS
COURAGEOUS	COVARIATION	COYOTILLOS	CRAMPFISHES
COURAGEOUSLY	COVARIATIONS	COZINESSES	CRAMPONING
COURAGEOUSNESS	COVELLINES	CRABABBLES	CRANBERRIES
COURANTOES	COVELLITES	CRABBEDNESS	CRANEFLIES
COURBARILS	COVENANTAL	CRABBEDNESSES	CRANESBILL
COURBETTES	COVENANTALLY	CRABBINESS	CRANESBILLS
COURGETTES	COVENANTED	CRABBINESSES	CRANIECTOMIES
COURIERING	COVENANTEE	CRABEATERS	CRANIECTOMY
COURSEBOOK	COVENANTEES	CRABGRASSES	CRANIOCEREBRAL
COURSEBOOKS	COVENANTER	CRABSTICKS	CRANIOFACIAL
COURSEWARE	COVENANTERS	CRACKAJACK	CRANIOGNOMIES
COURSEWARES	COVENANTING	CRACKAJACKS	CRANIOGNOMY
COURSEWORK	COVENANTOR	CRACKBACKS	CRANIOLOGICAL
COURSEWORKS	COVENANTORS	CRACKBERRIES	CRANIOLOGICALLY
COURTCRAFT	COVERALLED	CRACKBERRY	CRANIOLOGIES
COURTCRAFTS	COVERMOUNT	CRACKBRAIN	CRANIOLOGIST
COURTEOUSLY	COVERMOUNTED	CRACKBRAINED	CRANIOLOGISTS
COURTEOUSNESS	COVERMOUNTING	CRACKBRAINS	CRANIOLOGY
COURTEOUSNESSES	COVERMOUNTS	CRACKDOWNS	CRANIOMETER
COURTESANS	COVERSINES	CRACKERJACK	CRANIOMETERS
COURTESIED	COVERSLIPS	CRACKERJACKS	CRANIOMETRIC
COURTESIES	COVERTNESS	CRACKHEADS	CRANIOMETRICAL
COURTESYING	COVERTNESSES	CRACKLEWARE	CRANIOMETRIES
COURTEZANS	COVERTURES	CRACKLEWARES	CRANIOMETRIST
COURTHOUSE	COVETINGLY	CRACKLIEST	CRANIOMETRISTS
COURTHOUSES	COVETIVENESS	CRACKLINGS	CRANIOMETRY
COURTIERISM	COVETIVENESSES	CRACOVIENNE	CRANIOPAGI
COURTIERISMS	COVETOUSLY	CRACOVIENNES	CRANIOPAGUS
COURTIERLIKE	COVETOUSNESS	CRADLESONG	CRANIOSACRAL
COURTIERLY	COVETOUSNESSES	CRADLESONGS	CRANIOSCOPIES
COURTLIEST	COWARDICES	CRADLEWALK	CRANIOSCOPIST
COURTLINESS	COWARDLINESS	CRADLEWALKS	CRANIOSCOPISTS
COURTLINESSES	COWARDLINESSES	CRAFTINESS	CRANIOSCOPY
COURTLINGS	COWARDRIES	CRAFTINESSES	CRANIOTOMIES
COURTMARTIALLED	COWARDSHIP	CRAFTMANSHIP	CRANIOTOMY
COURTROOMS	COWARDSHIPS	CRAFTMANSHIPS	CRANKCASES
COURTSHIPS	COWBERRIES	CRAFTSMANLIKE	CRANKHANDLE
COURTSIDES	COWCATCHER	CRAFTSMANLY	CRANKHANDLES
COURTYARDS	COWCATCHERS	CRAFTSMANSHIP	CRANKINESS
COUSCOUSES	COWERINGLY	CRAFTSMANSHIPS	CRANKINESSES
COUSCOUSOU	COWFEEDERS	CRAFTSPEOPLE	CRANKNESSES
COUSCOUSOUS	COWFETERIA	CRAFTSPERSON	CRANKSHAFT

CRANKSHAFTS	CREAMERIES	CREEPMOUSE	CREPUSCULES
CRANREUCHS	CREAMINESS	CREESHIEST	CREPUSCULOUS
CRAPEHANGER	CREAMINESSES	CREMAILLERE	CRESCENDOED
CRAPEHANGERS	CREAMPUFFS	CREMAILLERES	CRESCENDOES
CRAPEHANGING	CREAMWARES	CREMASTERS	CRESCENDOING
CRAPEHANGINGS	CREASELESS	CREMATIONISM	CRESCENDOS
CRAPSHOOTER	CREASOTING	CREMATIONISMS	CRESCENTADE
CRAPSHOOTERS	CREATIANISM	CREMATIONIST	CRESCENTADES
CRAPSHOOTS	CREATIANISMS	CREMATIONISTS	CRESCENTED
CRAPULENCE	CREATININE	CREMATIONS	CRESCENTIC
CRAPULENCES	CREATININES	CREMATORIA	CRESCIVELY
CRAPULENTLY	CREATIONAL	CREMATORIAL	CRESCOGRAPH
CRAPULOSITIES	CREATIONISM	CREMATORIES	CRESCOGRAPHS
CRAPULOSITY	CREATIONISMS	CREMATORIUM	CRESTFALLEN
CRAPULOUSLY	CREATIONIST	CREMATORIUMS	CRESTFALLENLY
CRAPULOUSNESS	CREATIONISTIC	CREMOCARPS	CRESTFALLENNESS
CRAPULOUSNESSES	CREATIONISTS	CRENATIONS	CRETACEOUS
CRAQUELURE	CREATIVELY	CRENATURES	CRETACEOUSES
CRAQUELURES	CREATIVENESS	CRENELATED	CRETACEOUSLY
CRASHINGLY	CREATIVENESSES	CRENELATES	CRETINISED
CRASHLANDED	CREATIVITIES	CRENELATING	CRETINISES
CRASHLANDING	CREATIVITY	CRENELATION	CRETINISING
CRASHLANDS	CREATORSHIP	CRENELATIONS	CRETINISMS
CRASHWORTHINESS	CREATORSHIPS	CRENELLATE	CRETINIZED
CRASHWORTHY	CREATRESSES	CRENELLATED	CRETINIZES
CRASSAMENTA	CREATRIXES	CRENELLATES	CRETINIZING
CRASSAMENTUM	CREATUREHOOD	CRENELLATING	CRETINOIDS
CRASSITUDE	CREATUREHOODS	CRENELLATION	CREVASSING
CRASSITUDES	CREATURELINESS	CRENELLATIONS	CREWELISTS
CRASSNESSES	CREATURELY	CRENELLING	CREWELLERIES
CRASSULACEAN	CREATURESHIP	CRENULATED	CREWELLERY
CRASSULACEOUS	CREATURESHIPS	CRENULATION	CREWELLING
CRATERIFORM	CREDENTIAL	CRENULATIONS	CREWELWORK
CRATERINGS	CREDENTIALED	CREOLISATION	CREWELWORKS
CRATERLESS	CREDENTIALING	CREOLISATIONS	CRIBRATION
CRATERLETS	CREDENTIALISM	CREOLISING	CRIBRATIONS
CRATERLIKE	CREDENTIALISMS	CREOLIZATION	CRIBRIFORM
CRAUNCHABLE	CREDENTIALLED	CREOLIZATIONS	CRICKETERS
CRAUNCHIER	CREDENTIALLING	CREOLIZING	CRICKETING
CRAUNCHIEST	CREDENTIALS	CREOPHAGIES	CRICKETINGS
CRAUNCHINESS	CREDIBILITIES	CREOPHAGOUS	CRIMEWAVES
CRAUNCHINESSES	CREDIBILITY	CREOSOTING	CRIMINALESE
CRAUNCHING	CREDIBLENESS	CREPEHANGER	CRIMINALESES
CRAVATTING	CREDIBLENESSES	CREPEHANGERS	CRIMINALISATION
CRAVENNESS	CREDITABILITIES	CREPEHANGING	CRIMINALISE
CRAVENNESSES	CREDITABILITY	CREPEHANGINGS	CRIMINALISED
CRAWDADDIES	CREDITABLE	CREPINESSES	CRIMINALISES
CRAWFISHED	CREDITABLENESS	CREPITATED	CRIMINALISING
CRAWFISHES	CREDITABLY	CREPITATES	CRIMINALIST
CRAWFISHING	CREDITLESS	CREPITATING	CRIMINALISTICS
CRAWLINGLY	CREDITWORTHY	CREPITATION	CRIMINALISTS
CRAYFISHES	CREDULITIES	CREPITATIONS	CRIMINALITIES
CRAYONISTS	CREDULOUSLY	CREPITATIVE	CRIMINALITY
CRAZINESSES	CREDULOUSNESS	CREPITUSES	CRIMINALIZATION
CRAZYWEEDS	CREDULOUSNESSES	CREPOLINES	CRIMINALIZE
CREAKINESS	CREEPINESS	CREPUSCLES	CRIMINALIZED
CREAKINESSES	CREEPINESSES	CREPUSCULAR	CRIMINALIZES
CREAKINGLY	CREEPINGLY	CREPUSCULE	CRIMINALIZING

CRIMINALLY	CRISTIFORM	CROQUETTES	CROSSHEADS
CRIMINATED	CRISTOBALITE	CROQUIGNOLE	CROSSJACKS
CRIMINATES	CRISTOBALITES	CROQUIGNOLES	CROSSLIGHT
CRIMINATING	CRITERIONS	CROSSABILITIES	CROSSLIGHTS
CRIMINATION	CRITERIUMS	CROSSABILITY	CROSSLINGUISTIC
CRIMINATIONS	CRITHIDIAL	CROSSANDRA	CROSSNESSES
CRIMINATIVE	CRITHOMANCIES	CROSSANDRAS	CROSSOPTERYGIAN
CRIMINATOR	CRITHOMANCY	CROSSBANDED	CROSSOVERS
CRIMINATORS	CRITICALITIES	CROSSBANDING	CROSSPATCH
CRIMINATORY	CRITICALITY	CROSSBANDINGS	CROSSPATCHES
CRIMINOGENIC	CRITICALLY	CROSSBANDS	CROSSPIECE
CRIMINOLOGIC	CRITICALNESS	CROSSBARRED	CROSSPIECES
CRIMINOLOGICAL	CRITICALNESSES	CROSSBARRING	CROSSROADS
CRIMINOLOGIES	CRITICASTER	CROSSBEAMS	CROSSRUFFED
CRIMINOLOGIST	CRITICASTERS	CROSSBEARER	CROSSRUFFING
CRIMINOLOGISTS	CRITICISABLE	CROSSBEARERS	CROSSRUFFS
CRIMINOLOGY	CRITICISED	CROSSBENCH	CROSSTALKS
CRIMINOUSNESS	CRITICISER	CROSSBENCHER	CROSSTREES
CRIMINOUSNESSES	CRITICISERS	CROSSBENCHERS	CROSSWALKS
CRIMSONING	CRITICISES	CROSSBENCHES	CROSSWINDS
CRIMSONNESS	CRITICISING	CROSSBILLS	CROSSWORDS
CRIMSONNESSES	CRITICISINGLY	CROSSBIRTH	CROSSWORTS
CRINGELING	CRITICISMS	CROSSBIRTHS	CROTALARIA
CRINGELINGS	CRITICIZABLE	CROSSBITES	CROTALARIAS
CRINGEWORTHY	CRITICIZED	CROSSBITING	CROTALISMS
CRINGINGLY	CRITICIZER	CROSSBITTEN	CROTCHETED
CRINICULTURAL	CRITICIZERS	CROSSBONES	CROTCHETEER
CRINIGEROUS	CRITICIZES	CROSSBOWER	CROTCHETEERS
CRINKLEROOT	CRITICIZING	CROSSBOWERS	CROTCHETIER
CRINKLEROOTS	CRITICIZINGLY	CROSSBOWMAN	CROTCHETIEST
CRINKLIEST	CRITIQUING	CROSSBOWMEN	CROTCHETINESS
CRINOIDEAN	CROAKINESS	CROSSBREDS	CROTCHETINESSES
CRINOIDEANS	CROAKINESSES	CROSSBREED	CROTONBUGS
CRINOLETTE	CROCHETERS	CROSSBREEDING	CROUPINESS
CRINOLETTES	CROCHETING	CROSSBREEDINGS	CROUPINESSES
CRINOLINED	CROCHETINGS	CROSSBREEDS	CROUSTADES
CRINOLINES	CROCIDOLITE	CROSSBUCKS	CROWBARRED
CRIPPLEDOM	CROCIDOLITES	CROSSCHECK	CROWBARRING
CRIPPLEDOMS	CROCKERIES	CROSSCHECKED	CROWBERRIES
CRIPPLEWARE	CROCODILES	CROSSCHECKING	CROWDEDNESS
CRIPPLEWARES	CROCODILIAN	CROSSCHECKS	CROWDEDNESSES
CRIPPLINGLY	CROCODILIANS	CROSSCLAIM	CROWKEEPER
CRIPPLINGS	CROCOISITE	CROSSCLAIMS	CROWKEEPERS
CRISPATION	CROCOISITES	CROSSCOURT	CROWNLANDS
CRISPATIONS	CROCOSMIAS	CROSSCURRENT	CROWNPIECE
CRISPATURE	CROISSANTS	CROSSCURRENTS	CROWNPIECES
CRISPATURES	CROKINOLES	CROSSCUTTING	CROWNWORKS
CRISPBREAD	CROOKBACKED	CROSSCUTTINGS	CROWSTEPPED
CRISPBREADS	CROOKBACKS	CROSSETTES	CRUCIATELY
CRISPENING	CROOKEDEST	CROSSFALLS	CRUCIFEROUS
CRISPHEADS	CROOKEDNESS	CROSSFIELD	CRUCIFIERS
CRISPINESS	CROOKEDNESSES	CROSSFIRES	CRUCIFIXES
CRISPINESSES	CROOKERIES	CROSSFISHES	CRUCIFIXION
CRISPNESSES	CROOKNECKS	CROSSHAIRS	CRUCIFIXIONS
CRISSCROSS	CROPDUSTER	CROSSHATCH	CRUCIFORMLY
CRISSCROSSED	CROPDUSTERS	CROSSHATCHED	CRUCIFORMS
CRISSCROSSES	CROQUANTES	CROSSHATCHES	CRUCIFYING
CRISSCROSSING	CROQUETING	CROSSHATCHING	CRUCIVERBAL

CRUCIVERBALISM
CRUCIVERBALISMS
CRUCIVERBALIST
CRUCIVERBALISTS
CRUDENESSES
CRUELNESSES
CRUISERWEIGHT
CRUISERWEIGHTS
CRUISEWAYS
CRUISEWEAR
CRUISEWEARS
CRUMBCLOTH
CRUMBCLOTHS
CRUMBLIEST
CRUMBLINESS
CRUMBLINESSES
CRUMBLINGS
CRUMMINESS
CRUMMINESSES
CRUMPLIEST
CRUMPLINGS
CRUNCHABLE
CRUNCHIEST
CRUNCHINESS
CRUNCHINESSES
CRUNCHINGS
CRUSHABILITIES
CRUSHABILITY
CRUSHINGLY
CRUSHPROOF
CRUSTACEAN
CRUSTACEANS
CRUSTACEOUS
CRUSTATION
CRUSTATIONS
CRUSTINESS
CRUSTINESSES
CRUTCHINGS
CRYMOTHERAPIES
CRYMOTHERAPY
CRYOBIOLOGICAL
CRYOBIOLOGIES
CRYOBIOLOGIST
CRYOBIOLOGISTS
CRYOBIOLOGY
CRYOCABLES
CRYOCONITE
CRYOCONITES
CRYOGENICALLY
CRYOGENICS
CRYOGENIES
CRYOGLOBULIN
CRYOGLOBULINS
CRYOHYDRATE
CRYOHYDRATES
CRYOMETERS
CRYOMETRIC
CRYOMETRIES

CRYOPHILIC
CRYOPHORUS
CRYOPHORUSES
CRYOPHYSICS
CRYOPHYTES
CRYOPLANKTON
CRYOPLANKTONS
CRYOPRECIPITATE
CRYOPRESERVE
CRYOPRESERVED
CRYOPRESERVES
CRYOPRESERVING
CRYOPROBES
CRYOPROTECTANT
CRYOPROTECTANTS
CRYOPROTECTIVE
CRYOSCOPES
CRYOSCOPIC
CRYOSCOPIES
CRYOSTATIC
CRYOSURGEON
CRYOSURGEONS
CRYOSURGERIES
CRYOSURGERY
CRYOSURGICAL
CRYOTHERAPIES
CRYOTHERAPY
CRYPTAESTHESIA
CRYPTAESTHESIAS
CRYPTAESTHETIC
CRYPTANALYSES
CRYPTANALYSIS
CRYPTANALYST
CRYPTANALYSTS
CRYPTANALYTIC
CRYPTANALYTICAL
CRYPTARITHM
CRYPTARITHMS
CRYPTESTHESIA
CRYPTESTHESIAS
CRYPTICALLY
CRYPTOBIONT
CRYPTOBIONTS
CRYPTOBIOSES
CRYPTOBIOSIS
CRYPTOCLASTIC
CRYPTOCOCCAL
CRYPTOCOCCI
CRYPTOCOCCOSES
CRYPTOCOCCOSIS
CRYPTOCOCCUS
CRYPTOGAMIAN
CRYPTOGAMIC
CRYPTOGAMIES
CRYPTOGAMIST
CRYPTOGAMISTS
CRYPTOGAMOUS
CRYPTOGAMS

CRYPTOGAMY
CRYPTOGENIC
CRYPTOGRAM
CRYPTOGRAMS
CRYPTOGRAPH
CRYPTOGRAPHER
CRYPTOGRAPHERS
CRYPTOGRAPHIC
CRYPTOGRAPHICAL
CRYPTOGRAPHIES
CRYPTOGRAPHIST
CRYPTOGRAPHISTS
CRYPTOGRAPHS
CRYPTOGRAPHY
CRYPTOLOGIC
CRYPTOLOGICAL
CRYPTOLOGIES
CRYPTOLOGIST
CRYPTOLOGISTS
CRYPTOLOGY
CRYPTOMERIA
CRYPTOMERIAS
CRYPTOMETER
CRYPTOMETERS
CRYPTOMNESIA
CRYPTOMNESIAS
CRYPTOMNESIC
CRYPTONYMOUS
CRYPTONYMS
CRYPTOPHYTE
CRYPTOPHYTES
CRYPTOPHYTIC
CRYPTORCHID
CRYPTORCHIDISM
CRYPTORCHIDISMS
CRYPTORCHIDS
CRYPTORCHISM
CRYPTORCHISMS
CRYPTOSPORIDIA
CRYPTOSPORIDIUM
CRYPTOZOIC
CRYPTOZOITE
CRYPTOZOITES
CRYPTOZOOLOGIES
CRYPTOZOOLOGIST
CRYPTOZOOLOGY
CRYSTALISABLE
CRYSTALISATION
CRYSTALISATIONS
CRYSTALISE
CRYSTALISED
CRYSTALISER
CRYSTALISERS
CRYSTALISES
CRYSTALISING
CRYSTALIZABLE
CRYSTALIZATION
CRYSTALIZATIONS

CRYSTALIZE
CRYSTALIZED
CRYSTALIZER
CRYSTALIZERS
CRYSTALIZES
CRYSTALIZING
CRYSTALLINE
CRYSTALLINES
CRYSTALLINITIES
CRYSTALLINITY
CRYSTALLISABLE
CRYSTALLISATION
CRYSTALLISE
CRYSTALLISED
CRYSTALLISER
CRYSTALLISERS
CRYSTALLISES
CRYSTALLISING
CRYSTALLITE
CRYSTALLITES
CRYSTALLITIC
CRYSTALLITIS
CRYSTALLITISES
CRYSTALLIZABLE
CRYSTALLIZATION
CRYSTALLIZE
CRYSTALLIZED
CRYSTALLIZER
CRYSTALLIZERS
CRYSTALLIZES
CRYSTALLIZING
CRYSTALLOGRAPHY
CRYSTALLOID
CRYSTALLOIDAL
CRYSTALLOIDS
CRYSTALLOMANCY
CTENOPHORAN
CTENOPHORANS
CTENOPHORE
CTENOPHORES
CUADRILLAS
CUBANELLES
CUBBYHOLES
CUBICALNESS
CUBICALNESSES
CUBICITIES
CUBISTICALLY
CUCKOLDING
CUCKOLDISE
CUCKOLDISED
CUCKOLDISES
CUCKOLDISING
CUCKOLDIZE
CUCKOLDIZED
CUCKOLDIZES
CUCKOLDIZING
CUCKOLDOMS
CUCKOLDRIES

CUCKOOFLOWER	CUMBERBUND	CUPRONICKELS	CURRENTNESS
CUCKOOFLOWERS	CUMBERBUNDS	CUPULIFEROUS	CURRENTNESSES
CUCKOOPINT	CUMBERLESS	CURABILITIES	CURRICULAR
CUCKOOPINTS	CUMBERMENT	CURABILITY	CURRICULUM
CUCULIFORM	CUMBERMENTS	CURABLENESS	CURRICULUMS
CUCULLATED	CUMBERSOME	CURABLENESSES	CURRIERIES
CUCULLATELY	CUMBERSOMELY	CURANDERAS	CURRIJONGS
CUCUMIFORM	CUMBERSOMENESS	CURANDEROS	CURRISHNESS
CUCURBITACEOUS	CUMBRANCES	CURARISATION	CURRISHNESSES
CUCURBITAL	CUMBROUSLY	CURARISATIONS	CURRYCOMBED
CUDDLESOME	CUMBROUSNESS	CURARISING	CURRYCOMBING
CUDGELLERS	CUMBROUSNESSES	CURARIZATION	CURRYCOMBS
CUDGELLING	CUMMERBUND	CURARIZATIONS	CURSEDNESS
CUDGELLINGS	CUMMERBUNDS	CURARIZING	CURSEDNESSES
CUFFUFFLES	CUMMINGTONITE	CURATESHIP	CURSELARIE
CUIRASSIER	CUMMINGTONITES	CURATESHIPS	CURSIVENESS
CUIRASSIERS	CUMULATELY	CURATIVELY	CURSIVENESSES
CUIRASSING	CUMULATING	CURATIVENESS	CURSORINESS
CUISINARTS	CUMULATION	CURATIVENESSES	CURSORINESSES
CUISINIERS	CUMULATIONS	CURATORIAL	CURSTNESSES
CULICIFORM	CUMULATIVE	CURATORSHIP	CURTAILERS
CULINARIAN	CUMULATIVELY	CURATORSHIPS	CURTAILING
CULINARIANS	CUMULATIVENESS	CURATRIXES	CURTAILMENT
CULINARILY	CUMULIFORM	CURBSTONES	CURTAILMENTS
CULLENDERS	CUMULOCIRRI	CURCUMINES	CURTAINING
CULMIFEROUS	CUMULOCIRRUS	CURDINESSES	CURTAINLESS
CULMINATED	CUMULONIMBI	CURETTAGES	CURTALAXES
CULMINATES	CUMULONIMBUS	CURETTEMENT	CURTATIONS
CULMINATING	CUMULONIMBUSES	CURETTEMENTS	CURTILAGES
CULMINATION	CUMULOSTRATI	CURFUFFLED	CURTNESSES
CULMINATIONS	CUMULOSTRATUS	CURFUFFLES	CURTSEYING
CULPABILITIES	CUNCTATION	CURFUFFLING	CURVACEOUS
CULPABILITY	CUNCTATIONS	CURIALISMS	CURVACEOUSLY
CULPABLENESS	CUNCTATIOUS	CURIALISTIC	CURVACIOUS
CULPABLENESSES	CUNCTATIVE	CURIALISTS	CURVATIONS
CULTISHNESS	CUNCTATORS	CURIETHERAPIES	CURVATURES
CULTISHNESSES	CUNCTATORY	CURIETHERAPY	CURVEBALLED
CULTIVABILITIES	CUNEIFORMS	CURIOSITIES	CURVEBALLING
CULTIVABILITY	CUNNILINCTUS	CURIOUSEST	CURVEBALLS
CULTIVABLE	CUNNILINCTUSES	CURIOUSNESS	CURVEDNESS
CULTIVATABLE	CUNNILINGUS	CURIOUSNESSES	CURVEDNESSES
CULTIVATED	CUNNILINGUSES	CURLICUING	CURVETTING
CULTIVATES	CUNNINGEST	CURLIEWURLIE	CURVICAUDATE
CULTIVATING	CUNNINGNESS	CURLIEWURLIES	CURVICOSTATE
CULTIVATION	CUNNINGNESSES	CURLINESSES	CURVIFOLIATE
CULTIVATIONS	CUPBEARERS	CURLPAPERS	CURVILINEAL
CULTIVATOR	CUPBOARDED	CURMUDGEON	CURVILINEAR
CULTIVATORS	CUPBOARDING	CURMUDGEONLY	CURVILINEARITY
CULTRIFORM	CUPELLATION	CURMUDGEONS	CURVILINEARLY
CULTURABLE	CUPELLATIONS	CURMURRING	CURVIROSTRAL
CULTURALLY	CUPFERRONS	CURMURRINGS	CUSHINESSES
CULTURELESS	CUPIDINOUS	CURNAPTIOUS	CUSHIONETS
CULTURISTS	CUPIDITIES	CURRAJONGS	CUSHIONING
CULVERINEER	CUPRAMMONIUM	CURRANTIER	CUSHIONLESS
CULVERINEERS	CUPRAMMONIUMS	CURRANTIEST	CUSPIDATED
CULVERTAGE	CUPRESSUSES	CURRAWONGS	CUSPIDATION
CULVERTAGES	CUPRIFEROUS	CURREJONGS	CUSPIDATIONS
CULVERTAILED	CUPRONICKEL	CURRENCIES	CUSPIDORES

CUSSEDNESS	CYANOCOBALAMIN	CYBERSQUATTING	CYCLOMETERS
CUSSEDNESSES	CYANOCOBALAMINE	CYBERSQUATTINGS	CYCLOMETRIES
CUSTODIANS	CYANOCOBALAMINS	CYBERTERRORISM	CYCLOMETRY
CUSTODIANSHIP	CYANOETHYLATE	CYBERTERRORISMS	CYCLONICAL
CUSTODIANSHIPS	CYANOETHYLATED	CYBERTERRORIST	CYCLONICALLY
CUSTODIERS	CYANOETHYLATES	CYBERTERRORISTS	CYCLONITES
CUSTOMABLE	CYANOETHYLATING	CYBRARIANS	CYCLOOLEFIN
CUSTOMARIES	CYANOETHYLATION	CYCADACEOUS	CYCLOOLEFINIC
CUSTOMARILY	CYANOGENAMIDE	CYCADEOIDS	CYCLOOLEFINS
CUSTOMARINESS	CYANOGENAMIDES	CYCADOPHYTE	CYCLOPAEDIA
CUSTOMARINESSES	CYANOGENESES	CYCADOPHYTES	CYCLOPAEDIAS
CUSTOMHOUSE	CYANOGENESIS	CYCLAMATES	CYCLOPAEDIC
CUSTOMHOUSES	CYANOGENETIC	CYCLANDELATE	CYCLOPAEDIST
CUSTOMISATION	CYANOGENIC	CYCLANDELATES	CYCLOPAEDISTS
CUSTOMISATIONS	CYANOHYDRIN	CYCLANTHACEOUS	CYCLOPARAFFIN
CUSTOMISED	CYANOHYDRINS	CYCLAZOCINE	CYCLOPARAFFINS
CUSTOMISER	CYANOMETER	CYCLAZOCINES	CYCLOPEDIA
CUSTOMISERS	CYANOMETERS	CYCLICALITIES	CYCLOPEDIAS
CUSTOMISES	CYANOPHYTE	CYCLICALITY	CYCLOPEDIC
CUSTOMISING	CYANOPHYTES	CYCLICALLY	CYCLOPEDIST
CUSTOMIZATION	CYANOTYPES	CYCLICISMS	CYCLOPEDISTS
CUSTOMIZATIONS	CYANURATES	CYCLICITIES	CYCLOPENTADIENE
CUSTOMIZED	CYATHIFORM	CYCLISATION	CYCLOPENTANE
CUSTOMIZER	CYBERATHLETE	CYCLISATIONS	CYCLOPENTANES
CUSTOMIZERS	CYBERATHLETES	CYCLIZATION	CYCLOPENTOLATE
CUSTOMIZES	CYBERATHLETICS	CYCLIZATIONS	CYCLOPENTOLATES
CUSTOMIZING	CYBERCAFES	CYCLIZINES	CYCLOPLEGIA
CUSTOMSHOUSE	CYBERCASTS	CYCLOADDITION	CYCLOPLEGIAS
CUSTOMSHOUSES	CYBERCRIME	CYCLOADDITIONS	CYCLOPLEGIC
CUSTUMARIES	CYBERCRIMES	CYCLOALIPHATIC	CYCLOPROPANE
CUTABILITIES	CYBERCRIMINAL	CYCLOALKANE	CYCLOPROPANES
CUTABILITY	CYBERCRIMINALS	CYCLOALKANES	CYCLORAMAS
CUTANEOUSLY	CYBERNATED	CYCLOBARBITONE	CYCLORAMIC
CUTCHERIES	CYBERNATES	CYCLOBARBITONES	CYCLOSERINE
CUTCHERRIES	CYBERNATING	CYCLODEXTRIN	CYCLOSERINES
CUTENESSES	CYBERNATION	CYCLODEXTRINS	CYCLOSPERMOUS
CUTGRASSES	CYBERNATIONS	CYCLODIALYSES	CYCLOSPORIN
CUTINISATION	CYBERNAUTS	CYCLODIALYSIS	CYCLOSPORINE
CUTINISATIONS	CYBERNETIC	CYCLODIENE	CYCLOSPORINES
CUTINISING	CYBERNETICAL	CYCLODIENES	CYCLOSPORINS
CUTINIZATION	CYBERNETICALLY	CYCLOGENESES	CYCLOSTOMATE
CUTINIZATIONS	CYBERNETICIAN	CYCLOGENESIS	CYCLOSTOMATOUS
CUTINIZING	CYBERNETICIANS	CYCLOGIROS	CYCLOSTOME
CUTTHROATS	CYBERNETICIST	CYCLOGRAPH	CYCLOSTOMES
CUTTLEBONE	CYBERNETICISTS	CYCLOGRAPHIC	CYCLOSTOMOUS
CUTTLEBONES	CYBERNETICS	CYCLOGRAPHS	CYCLOSTYLE
CUTTLEFISH	CYBERPHOBIA	CYCLOHEXANE	CYCLOSTYLED
CUTTLEFISHES	CYBERPHOBIAS	CYCLOHEXANES	CYCLOSTYLES
CYANAMIDES	CYBERPHOBIC	CYCLOHEXANONE	CYCLOSTYLING
CYANIDATION	CYBERPORNS	CYCLOHEXANONES	CYCLOTHYME
CYANIDATIONS	CYBERPUNKS	CYCLOHEXIMIDE	CYCLOTHYMES
CYANIDINGS	CYBERSECURITIES	CYCLOHEXIMIDES	CYCLOTHYMIA
CYANOACETYLENE	CYBERSECURITY	CYCLOHEXYLAMINE	CYCLOTHYMIAC
CYANOACETYLENES	CYBERSEXES	CYCLOIDALLY	CYCLOTHYMIACS
CYANOACRYLATE	CYBERSPACE	CYCLOIDIAN	CYCLOTHYMIAS
CYANOACRYLATES	CYBERSPACES	CYCLOIDIANS	CYCLOTHYMIC
CYANOBACTERIA	CYBERSQUATTER	CYCLOLITHS	CYCLOTHYMICS
CYANOBACTERIUM	CYBERSQUATTERS	CYCLOMETER	CYCLOTOMIC

CYCLOTRONS
CYLINDERED
CYLINDERING
CYLINDRACEOUS
CYLINDRICAL
CYLINDRICALITY
CYLINDRICALLY
CYLINDRICALNESS
CYLINDRICITIES
CYLINDRICITY
CYLINDRIFORM
CYLINDRITE
CYLINDRITES
CYLINDROID
CYLINDROIDS
CYMAGRAPHS
CYMBALEERS
CYMBALISTS
CYMBIDIUMS
CYMIFEROUS
CYMOGRAPHIC
CYMOGRAPHS
CYMOPHANES
CYMOPHANOUS
CYMOTRICHIES
CYMOTRICHOUS
CYMOTRICHY
CYNGHANEDD
CYNGHANEDDS
CYNICALNESS
CYNICALNESSES
CYNOMOLGUS
CYNOPHILIA
CYNOPHILIAS
CYNOPHILIST
CYNOPHILISTS
CYNOPHOBIA
CYNOPHOBIAS
CYNOPODOUS
CYPERACEOUS
CYPRINODONT
CYPRINODONTS
CYPRINOIDS
CYPRIPEDIA
CYPRIPEDIUM
CYPRIPEDIUMS
CYPROHEPTADINE
CYPROHEPTADINES
CYPROTERONE
CYPROTERONES
CYSTEAMINE
CYSTEAMINES
CYSTECTOMIES
CYSTECTOMY
CYSTICERCI
CYSTICERCOID
CYSTICERCOIDS
CYSTICERCOSES

CYSTICERCOSIS
CYSTICERCUS
CYSTIDEANS
CYSTINOSES
CYSTINOSIS
CYSTINURIA
CYSTINURIAS
CYSTITIDES
CYSTITISES
CYSTOCARPIC
CYSTOCARPS
CYSTOCELES
CYSTOGENOUS
CYSTOGRAPHIES
CYSTOGRAPHY
CYSTOLITHIASES
CYSTOLITHIASIS
CYSTOLITHS
CYSTOSCOPE
CYSTOSCOPES
CYSTOSCOPIC
CYSTOSCOPIES
CYSTOSCOPY
CYSTOSTOMIES
CYSTOSTOMY
CYSTOTOMIES
CYTOCHALASIN
CYTOCHALASINS
CYTOCHEMICAL
CYTOCHEMISTRIES
CYTOCHEMISTRY
CYTOCHROME
CYTOCHROMES
CYTODIAGNOSES
CYTODIAGNOSIS
CYTOGENESES
CYTOGENESIS
CYTOGENETIC
CYTOGENETICAL
CYTOGENETICALLY
CYTOGENETICIST
CYTOGENETICISTS
CYTOGENETICS
CYTOGENIES
CYTOKINESES
CYTOKINESIS
CYTOKINETIC
CYTOKININS
CYTOLOGICAL
CYTOLOGICALLY
CYTOLOGIES
CYTOLOGIST
CYTOLOGISTS
CYTOLYSINS
CYTOMEGALIC
CYTOMEGALOVIRUS
CYTOMEMBRANE
CYTOMEMBRANES

CYTOMETERS
CYTOMETRIC
CYTOMETRIES
CYTOPATHIC
CYTOPATHOGENIC
CYTOPATHOLOGIES
CYTOPATHOLOGY
CYTOPENIAS
CYTOPHILIC
CYTOPHOTOMETRIC
CYTOPHOTOMETRY
CYTOPLASMIC
CYTOPLASMICALLY
CYTOPLASMS
CYTOPLASTIC
CYTOPLASTS
CYTOSKELETAL
CYTOSKELETON
CYTOSKELETONS
CYTOSTATIC
CYTOSTATICALLY
CYTOSTATICS
CYTOTAXONOMIC
CYTOTAXONOMIES
CYTOTAXONOMIST
CYTOTAXONOMISTS
CYTOTAXONOMY
CYTOTECHNOLOGY
CYTOTOXICITIES
CYTOTOXICITY
CYTOTOXINS
CZAREVICHES
CZAREVITCH
CZAREVITCHES

D

DABBLINGLY
DACHSHUNDS
DACOITAGES
DACQUOISES
DACTYLICALLY
DACTYLIOGRAPHY
DACTYLIOLOGIES
DACTYLIOLOGY
DACTYLIOMANCIES
DACTYLIOMANCY
DACTYLISTS
DACTYLOGRAM
DACTYLOGRAMS
DACTYLOGRAPHER
DACTYLOGRAPHERS
DACTYLOGRAPHIC
DACTYLOGRAPHIES
DACTYLOGRAPHY
DACTYLOLOGIES
DACTYLOLOGY
DACTYLOSCOPIES
DACTYLOSCOPY
DAFFADOWNDILLY
DAFFINESSES
DAFFODILLIES
DAFFODILLY
DAFTNESSES
DAGGERBOARD
DAGGERBOARDS
DAGGERLIKE
DAGUERREAN
DAGUERREOTYPE
DAGUERREOTYPED
DAGUERREOTYPER
DAGUERREOTYPERS
DAGUERREOTYPES
DAGUERREOTYPIES
DAGUERREOTYPING
DAGUERREOTYPIST
DAGUERREOTYPY
DAHABEEAHS
DAHABEEYAH
DAHABEEYAHS
DAHABIYAHS
DAHABIYEHS
DAILINESSES
DAILYNESSES
DAINTINESS
DAINTINESSES
DAIRYMAIDS
DAISYWHEEL
DAISYWHEELS
DALLIANCES

DALMATIANS
DALTONISMS
DAMAGEABILITIES
DAMAGEABILITY
DAMAGEABLE
DAMAGINGLY
DAMASCEENE
DAMASCEENED
DAMASCEENES
DAMASCEENING
DAMASCENED
DAMASCENES
DAMASCENING
DAMASCENINGS
DAMASKEENED
DAMASKEENING
DAMASKEENS
DAMASKINED
DAMASKINING
DAMASQUINED
DAMASQUINING
DAMASQUINS
DAMINOZIDE
DAMINOZIDES
DAMNABILITIES
DAMNABILITY
DAMNABLENESS
DAMNABLENESSES
DAMNATIONS
DAMNEDESTS
DAMNIFICATION
DAMNIFICATIONS
DAMNIFYING
DAMOISELLE
DAMOISELLES
DAMPCOURSE
DAMPCOURSES
DAMPISHNESS
DAMPISHNESSES
DAMPNESSES
DAMSELFISH
DAMSELFISHES
DAMSELFLIES
DANCEHALLS
DANDELIONS
DANDIFICATION
DANDIFICATIONS
DANDIFYING
DANDIPRATS
DANDYFUNKS
DANDYISHLY
DANDYPRATS
DANGERLESS

DANGEROUSLY
DANGEROUSNESS
DANGEROUSNESSES
DANGLINGLY
DANKNESSES
DANNEBROGS
DANTHONIAS
DAPPERLING
DAPPERLINGS
DAPPERNESS
DAPPERNESSES
DAREDEVILRIES
DAREDEVILRY
DAREDEVILS
DAREDEVILTRIES
DAREDEVILTRY
DARINGNESS
DARINGNESSES
DARKNESSES
DARLINGNESS
DARLINGNESSES
DARNATIONS
DARNEDESTS
DARRAIGNED
DARRAIGNES
DARRAIGNING
DARRAIGNMENT
DARRAIGNMENTS
DARRAINING
DARRAYNING
DARTBOARDS
DASHBOARDS
DASTARDIES
DASTARDLINESS
DASTARDLINESSES
DASTARDNESS
DASTARDNESSES
DASYMETERS
DASYPAEDAL
DASYPHYLLOUS
DATABASING
DATABUSSES
DATAGLOVES
DATAMATION
DATAMATIONS
DATEDNESSES
DATELINING
DAUGHTERHOOD
DAUGHTERHOODS
DAUGHTERLESS
DAUGHTERLINESS
DAUGHTERLING
DAUGHTERLINGS

DAUGHTERLY
DAUNDERING
DAUNOMYCIN
DAUNOMYCINS
DAUNORUBICIN
DAUNORUBICINS
DAUNTINGLY
DAUNTLESSLY
DAUNTLESSNESS
DAUNTLESSNESSES
DAUNTONING
DAUPHINESS
DAUPHINESSES
DAVENPORTS
DAWDLINGLY
DAWSONITES
DAYCENTRES
DAYDREAMED
DAYDREAMER
DAYDREAMERS
DAYDREAMING
DAYDREAMLIKE
DAYFLOWERS
DAYLIGHTED
DAYLIGHTING
DAYLIGHTINGS
DAYSPRINGS
DAYWORKERS
DAZEDNESSES
DAZZLEMENT
DAZZLEMENTS
DAZZLINGLY
DEACIDIFICATION
DEACIDIFIED
DEACIDIFIES
DEACIDIFYING
DEACONESSES
DEACONHOOD
DEACONHOODS
DEACONRIES
DEACONSHIP
DEACONSHIPS
DEACTIVATE
DEACTIVATED
DEACTIVATES
DEACTIVATING
DEACTIVATION
DEACTIVATIONS
DEACTIVATOR
DEACTIVATORS
DEADENINGLY
DEADENINGS
DEADHEADED

DEADHEADING	DEASPIRATES	DEBONAIRLY	DECANDROUS
DEADHOUSES	DEASPIRATING	DEBONAIRNESS	DECANEDIOIC
DEADLIFTED	DEASPIRATION	DEBONAIRNESSES	DECANICALLY
DEADLIFTING	DEASPIRATIONS	DEBONNAIRE	DECANTATED
DEADLIGHTS	DEATHBLOWS	DEBOUCHING	DECANTATES
DEADLINESS	DEATHLESSLY	DEBOUCHMENT	DECANTATING
DEADLINESSES	DEATHLESSNESS	DEBOUCHMENTS	DECANTATION
DEADLINING	DEATHLESSNESSES	DEBOUCHURE	DECANTATIONS
DEADLOCKED	DEATHLIEST	DEBOUCHURES	DECAPITALISE
DEADLOCKING	DEATHLINESS	DEBRIDEMENT	DECAPITALISED
DEADNESSES	DEATHLINESSES	DEBRIDEMENTS	DECAPITALISES
DEADPANNED	DEATHTRAPS	DEBRIEFERS	DECAPITALISING
DEADPANNER	DEATHWARDS	DEBRIEFING	DECAPITALIZE
DEADPANNERS	DEATHWATCH	DEBRIEFINGS	DECAPITALIZED
DEADPANNING	DEATHWATCHES	DEBRUISING	DECAPITALIZES
DEADSTOCKS	DEATTRIBUTE	DEBUTANTES	DECAPITALIZING
DEADSTROKE	DEATTRIBUTED	DECACHORDS	DECAPITATE
DEADWEIGHT	DEATTRIBUTES	DECADENCES	DECAPITATED
DEADWEIGHTS	DEATTRIBUTING	DECADENCIES	DECAPITATES
DEAERATING	DEBAGGINGS	DECADENTLY	DECAPITATING
DEAERATION	DEBARCATION	DECAFFEINATE	DECAPITATION
DEAERATIONS	DEBARCATIONS	DECAFFEINATED	DECAPITATIONS
DEAERATORS	DEBARKATION	DECAFFEINATES	DECAPITATOR
DEAFENINGLY	DEBARKATIONS	DECAFFEINATING	DECAPITATORS
DEAFENINGS	DEBARMENTS	DECAGONALLY	DECAPODANS
DEAFNESSES	DEBARRASSED	DECAGRAMME	DECAPODOUS
DEALATIONS	DEBARRASSES	DECAGRAMMES	DECAPSULATE
DEALBATION	DEBARRASSING	DECAGYNIAN	DECAPSULATED
DEALBATIONS	DEBASEDNESS	DECAGYNOUS	DECAPSULATES
DEALERSHIP	DEBASEDNESSES	DECAHEDRAL	DECAPSULATING
DEALERSHIPS	DEBASEMENT	DECAHEDRON	DECAPSULATION
DEALFISHES	DEBASEMENTS	DECAHEDRONS	DECAPSULATIONS
DEAMBULATORIES	DEBASINGLY	DECALCIFICATION	DECARBONATE
DEAMBULATORY	DEBATEABLE	DECALCIFIED	DECARBONATED
DEAMINASES	DEBATEMENT	DECALCIFIER	DECARBONATES
DEAMINATED	DEBATEMENTS	DECALCIFIERS	DECARBONATING
DEAMINATES	DEBATINGLY	DECALCIFIES	DECARBONATION
DEAMINATING	DEBAUCHEDLY	DECALCIFYING	DECARBONATIONS
DEAMINATION	DEBAUCHEDNESS	DECALCOMANIA	DECARBONATOR
DEAMINATIONS	DEBAUCHEDNESSES	DECALCOMANIAS	DECARBONATORS
DEAMINISATION	DEBAUCHEES	DECALESCENCE	DECARBONISATION
DEAMINISATIONS	DEBAUCHERIES	DECALESCENCES	DECARBONISE
DEAMINISED	DEBAUCHERS	DECALESCENT	DECARBONISED
DEAMINISES	DEBAUCHERY	DECALITERS	DECARBONISER
DEAMINISING	DEBAUCHING	DECALITRES	DECARBONISERS
DEAMINIZATION	DEBAUCHMENT	DECALOGIST	DECARBONISES
DEAMINIZATIONS	DEBAUCHMENTS	DECALOGISTS	DECARBONISING
DEAMINIZED	DEBEARDING	DECALOGUES	DECARBONIZATION
DEAMINIZES	DEBENTURED	DECAMERONIC	DECARBONIZE
DEAMINIZING	DEBENTURES	DECAMEROUS	DECARBONIZED
DEARBOUGHT	DEBILITATE	DECAMETERS	DECARBONIZER
DEARNESSES	DEBILITATED	DECAMETHONIUM	DECARBONIZERS
DEARTICULATE	DEBILITATES	DECAMETHONIUMS	DECARBONIZES
DEARTICULATED	DEBILITATING	DECAMETRES	DECARBONIZING
DEARTICULATES	DEBILITATION	DECAMETRIC	DECARBOXYLASE
DEARTICULATING	DEBILITATIONS	DECAMPMENT	DECARBOXYLASES
DEASPIRATE	DEBILITATIVE	DECAMPMENTS	DECARBOXYLATE
DEASPIRATED	DEBILITIES	DECANDRIAN	DECARBOXYLATED

DECARBOXYLATES
DECARBOXYLATING
DECARBOXYLATION
DECARBURATION
DECARBURATIONS
DECARBURISATION
DECARBURISE
DECARBURISED
DECARBURISES
DECARBURISING
DECARBURIZATION
DECARBURIZE
DECARBURIZED
DECARBURIZES
DECARBURIZING
DECASTERES
DECASTICHS
DECASTYLES
DECASUALISATION
DECASUALIZATION
DECASYLLABIC
DECASYLLABICS
DECASYLLABLE
DECASYLLABLES
DECATHLETE
DECATHLETES
DECATHLONS
DECAUDATED
DECAUDATES
DECAUDATING
DECEITFULLY
DECEITFULNESS
DECEITFULNESSES
DECEIVABILITIES
DECEIVABILITY
DECEIVABLE
DECEIVABLENESS
DECEIVABLY
DECEIVINGLY
DECELERATE
DECELERATED
DECELERATES
DECELERATING
DECELERATION
DECELERATIONS
DECELERATOR
DECELERATORS
DECELEROMETER
DECELEROMETERS
DECELERONS
DECEMVIRAL
DECEMVIRATE
DECEMVIRATES
DECENARIES
DECENNARIES
DECENNIALLY
DECENNIALS
DECENNIUMS

DECENNOVAL
DECENTERED
DECENTERING
DECENTNESS
DECENTNESSES
DECENTRALISE
DECENTRALISED
DECENTRALISES
DECENTRALISING
DECENTRALIST
DECENTRALISTS
DECENTRALIZE
DECENTRALIZED
DECENTRALIZES
DECENTRALIZING
DECENTRING
DECEPTIBILITIES
DECEPTIBILITY
DECEPTIBLE
DECEPTIONAL
DECEPTIONS
DECEPTIOUS
DECEPTIVELY
DECEPTIVENESS
DECEPTIVENESSES
DECEREBRATE
DECEREBRATED
DECEREBRATES
DECEREBRATING
DECEREBRATION
DECEREBRATIONS
DECEREBRISE
DECEREBRISED
DECEREBRISES
DECEREBRISING
DECEREBRIZE
DECEREBRIZED
DECEREBRIZES
DECEREBRIZING
DECERTIFICATION
DECERTIFIED
DECERTIFIES
DECERTIFYING
DECESSIONS
DECHEANCES
DECHLORINATE
DECHLORINATED
DECHLORINATES
DECHLORINATING
DECHLORINATION
DECHLORINATIONS
DECHRISTIANISE
DECHRISTIANISED
DECHRISTIANISES
DECHRISTIANIZE
DECHRISTIANIZED
DECHRISTIANIZES
DECIDABILITIES

DECIDABILITY
DECIDEDNESS
DECIDEDNESSES
DECIDUOUSLY
DECIDUOUSNESS
DECIDUOUSNESSES
DECIGRAMME
DECIGRAMMES
DECILITERS
DECILITRES
DECILLIONS
DECILLIONTH
DECILLIONTHS
DECIMALISATION
DECIMALISATIONS
DECIMALISE
DECIMALISED
DECIMALISES
DECIMALISING
DECIMALISM
DECIMALISMS
DECIMALIST
DECIMALISTS
DECIMALIZATION
DECIMALIZATIONS
DECIMALIZE
DECIMALIZED
DECIMALIZES
DECIMALIZING
DECIMATING
DECIMATION
DECIMATIONS
DECIMATORS
DECIMETERS
DECIMETRES
DECIMETRIC
DECINORMAL
DECIPHERABILITY
DECIPHERABLE
DECIPHERED
DECIPHERER
DECIPHERERS
DECIPHERING
DECIPHERMENT
DECIPHERMENTS
DECISIONAL
DECISIONED
DECISIONING
DECISIVELY
DECISIVENESS
DECISIVENESSES
DECISTERES
DECITIZENISE
DECITIZENISED
DECITIZENISES
DECITIZENISING
DECITIZENIZE
DECITIZENIZED

DECITIZENIZES
DECITIZENIZING
DECIVILISE
DECIVILISED
DECIVILISES
DECIVILISING
DECIVILIZE
DECIVILIZED
DECIVILIZES
DECIVILIZING
DECKCHAIRS
DECKHOUSES
DECLAIMANT
DECLAIMANTS
DECLAIMERS
DECLAIMING
DECLAIMINGS
DECLAMATION
DECLAMATIONS
DECLAMATORILY
DECLAMATORY
DECLARABLE
DECLARANTS
DECLARATION
DECLARATIONS
DECLARATIVE
DECLARATIVELY
DECLARATOR
DECLARATORILY
DECLARATORS
DECLARATORY
DECLAREDLY
DECLASSIFIABLE
DECLASSIFIED
DECLASSIFIES
DECLASSIFY
DECLASSIFYING
DECLASSING
DECLENSION
DECLENSIONAL
DECLENSIONALLY
DECLENSIONS
DECLINABLE
DECLINATION
DECLINATIONAL
DECLINATIONS
DECLINATOR
DECLINATORS
DECLINATORY
DECLINATURE
DECLINATURES
DECLINISTS
DECLINOMETER
DECLINOMETERS
DECLIVITIES
DECLIVITOUS
DECLUTCHED
DECLUTCHES

DECLUTCHING
DECLUTTERED
DECLUTTERING
DECLUTTERS
DECOCTIBLE
DECOCTIONS
DECOCTURES
DECOHERENCE
DECOHERENCES
DECOHERERS
DECOLLATED
DECOLLATES
DECOLLATING
DECOLLATION
DECOLLATIONS
DECOLLATOR
DECOLLATORS
DECOLLETAGE
DECOLLETAGES
DECOLLETES
DECOLONISATION
DECOLONISATIONS
DECOLONISE
DECOLONISED
DECOLONISES
DECOLONISING
DECOLONIZATION
DECOLONIZATIONS
DECOLONIZE
DECOLONIZED
DECOLONIZES
DECOLONIZING
DECOLORANT
DECOLORANTS
DECOLORATE
DECOLORATED
DECOLORATES
DECOLORATING
DECOLORATION
DECOLORATIONS
DECOLORING
DECOLORISATION
DECOLORISATIONS
DECOLORISE
DECOLORISED
DECOLORISER
DECOLORISERS
DECOLORISES
DECOLORISING
DECOLORIZATION
DECOLORIZATIONS
DECOLORIZE
DECOLORIZED
DECOLORIZER
DECOLORIZERS
DECOLORIZES
DECOLORIZING
DECOLOURED

DECOLOURING
DECOLOURISATION
DECOLOURISE
DECOLOURISED
DECOLOURISES
DECOLOURISING
DECOLOURIZATION
DECOLOURIZE
DECOLOURIZED
DECOLOURIZES
DECOLOURIZING
DECOMMISSION
DECOMMISSIONED
DECOMMISSIONER
DECOMMISSIONERS
DECOMMISSIONING
DECOMMISSIONS
DECOMMITTED
DECOMMITTING
DECOMPENSATE
DECOMPENSATED
DECOMPENSATES
DECOMPENSATING
DECOMPENSATION
DECOMPENSATIONS
DECOMPOSABILITY
DECOMPOSABLE
DECOMPOSED
DECOMPOSER
DECOMPOSERS
DECOMPOSES
DECOMPOSING
DECOMPOSITE
DECOMPOSITION
DECOMPOSITIONS
DECOMPOUND
DECOMPOUNDABLE
DECOMPOUNDED
DECOMPOUNDING
DECOMPOUNDS
DECOMPRESS
DECOMPRESSED
DECOMPRESSES
DECOMPRESSING
DECOMPRESSION
DECOMPRESSIONS
DECOMPRESSIVE
DECOMPRESSOR
DECOMPRESSORS
DECONCENTRATE
DECONCENTRATED
DECONCENTRATES
DECONCENTRATING
DECONCENTRATION
DECONDITION
DECONDITIONED
DECONDITIONING
DECONDITIONS

DECONGESTANT
DECONGESTANTS
DECONGESTED
DECONGESTING
DECONGESTION
DECONGESTIONS
DECONGESTIVE
DECONGESTS
DECONSECRATE
DECONSECRATED
DECONSECRATES
DECONSECRATING
DECONSECRATION
DECONSECRATIONS
DECONSTRUCT
DECONSTRUCTED
DECONSTRUCTING
DECONSTRUCTION
DECONSTRUCTIONS
DECONSTRUCTIVE
DECONSTRUCTOR
DECONSTRUCTORS
DECONSTRUCTS
DECONTAMINANT
DECONTAMINANTS
DECONTAMINATE
DECONTAMINATED
DECONTAMINATES
DECONTAMINATING
DECONTAMINATION
DECONTAMINATIVE
DECONTAMINATOR
DECONTAMINATORS
DECONTROLLED
DECONTROLLING
DECONTROLS
DECORATING
DECORATION
DECORATIONS
DECORATIVE
DECORATIVELY
DECORATIVENESS
DECORATORS
DECOROUSLY
DECOROUSNESS
DECOROUSNESSES
DECORTICATE
DECORTICATED
DECORTICATES
DECORTICATING
DECORTICATION
DECORTICATIONS
DECORTICATOR
DECORTICATORS
DECOUPAGED
DECOUPAGES
DECOUPAGING
DECOUPLERS

DECOUPLING
DECOUPLINGS
DECRASSIFIED
DECRASSIFIES
DECRASSIFY
DECRASSIFYING
DECREASING
DECREASINGLY
DECREEABLE
DECREMENTAL
DECREMENTED
DECREMENTING
DECREMENTS
DECREPITATE
DECREPITATED
DECREPITATES
DECREPITATING
DECREPITATION
DECREPITATIONS
DECREPITLY
DECREPITNESS
DECREPITNESSES
DECREPITUDE
DECREPITUDES
DECRESCENCE
DECRESCENCES
DECRESCENDO
DECRESCENDOS
DECRESCENT
DECRETALIST
DECRETALISTS
DECRETISTS
DECRIMINALISE
DECRIMINALISED
DECRIMINALISES
DECRIMINALISING
DECRIMINALIZE
DECRIMINALIZED
DECRIMINALIZES
DECRIMINALIZING
DECROWNING
DECRUSTATION
DECRUSTATIONS
DECRYPTING
DECRYPTION
DECRYPTIONS
DECUMBENCE
DECUMBENCES
DECUMBENCIES
DECUMBENCY
DECUMBENTLY
DECUMBITURE
DECUMBITURES
DECURIONATE
DECURIONATES
DECURRENCIES
DECURRENCY
DECURRENTLY

DECURSIONS
DECURSIVELY
DECURVATION
DECURVATIONS
DECUSSATED
DECUSSATELY
DECUSSATES
DECUSSATING
DECUSSATION
DECUSSATIONS
DEDICATEDLY
DEDICATEES
DEDICATING
DEDICATION
DEDICATIONAL
DEDICATIONS
DEDICATIVE
DEDICATORIAL
DEDICATORS
DEDICATORY
DEDIFFERENTIATE
DEDRAMATISE
DEDRAMATISED
DEDRAMATISES
DEDRAMATISING
DEDRAMATIZE
DEDRAMATIZED
DEDRAMATIZES
DEDRAMATIZING
DEDUCEMENT
DEDUCEMENTS
DEDUCIBILITIES
DEDUCIBILITY
DEDUCIBLENESS
DEDUCIBLENESSES
DEDUCTIBILITIES
DEDUCTIBILITY
DEDUCTIBLE
DEDUCTIBLES
DEDUCTIONS
DEDUCTIVELY
DEEMSTERSHIP
DEEMSTERSHIPS
DEEPFREEZE
DEEPFREEZES
DEEPFREEZING
DEEPFROZEN
DEEPNESSES
DEEPWATERMAN
DEEPWATERMEN
DEERBERRIES
DEERGRASSES
DEERHOUNDS
DEERSTALKER
DEERSTALKERS
DEERSTALKING
DEERSTALKINGS
DEFACEABLE

DEFACEMENT
DEFACEMENTS
DEFACINGLY
DEFAECATED
DEFAECATES
DEFAECATING
DEFAECATION
DEFAECATIONS
DEFAECATOR
DEFAECATORS
DEFALCATED
DEFALCATES
DEFALCATING
DEFALCATION
DEFALCATIONS
DEFALCATOR
DEFALCATORS
DEFAMATION
DEFAMATIONS
DEFAMATORILY
DEFAMATORY
DEFAULTERS
DEFAULTING
DEFEASANCE
DEFEASANCED
DEFEASANCES
DEFEASIBILITIES
DEFEASIBILITY
DEFEASIBLE
DEFEASIBLENESS
DEFEATISMS
DEFEATISTS
DEFEATURED
DEFEATURES
DEFEATURING
DEFECATING
DEFECATION
DEFECATIONS
DEFECATORS
DEFECTIBILITIES
DEFECTIBILITY
DEFECTIBLE
DEFECTIONIST
DEFECTIONISTS
DEFECTIONS
DEFECTIVELY
DEFECTIVENESS
DEFECTIVENESSES
DEFECTIVES
DEFEMINISATION
DEFEMINISATIONS
DEFEMINISE
DEFEMINISED
DEFEMINISES
DEFEMINISING
DEFEMINIZATION
DEFEMINIZATIONS
DEFEMINIZE

DEFEMINIZED
DEFEMINIZES
DEFEMINIZING
DEFENCELESS
DEFENCELESSLY
DEFENCELESSNESS
DEFENCEMAN
DEFENCEMEN
DEFENDABLE
DEFENDANTS
DEFENESTRATE
DEFENESTRATED
DEFENESTRATES
DEFENESTRATING
DEFENESTRATION
DEFENESTRATIONS
DEFENSATIVE
DEFENSATIVES
DEFENSELESS
DEFENSELESSLY
DEFENSELESSNESS
DEFENSEMAN
DEFENSEMEN
DEFENSIBILITIES
DEFENSIBILITY
DEFENSIBLE
DEFENSIBLENESS
DEFENSIBLY
DEFENSIVELY
DEFENSIVENESS
DEFENSIVENESSES
DEFENSIVES
DEFERENCES
DEFERENTIAL
DEFERENTIALLY
DEFERMENTS
DEFERRABLE
DEFERRABLES
DEFERVESCENCE
DEFERVESCENCES
DEFERVESCENCIES
DEFERVESCENCY
DEFEUDALISE
DEFEUDALISED
DEFEUDALISES
DEFEUDALISING
DEFEUDALIZE
DEFEUDALIZED
DEFEUDALIZES
DEFEUDALIZING
DEFIANTNESS
DEFIANTNESSES
DEFIBRILLATE
DEFIBRILLATED
DEFIBRILLATES
DEFIBRILLATING
DEFIBRILLATION
DEFIBRILLATIONS

DEFIBRILLATOR
DEFIBRILLATORS
DEFIBRINATE
DEFIBRINATED
DEFIBRINATES
DEFIBRINATING
DEFIBRINATION
DEFIBRINATIONS
DEFIBRINISE
DEFIBRINISED
DEFIBRINISES
DEFIBRINISING
DEFIBRINIZE
DEFIBRINIZED
DEFIBRINIZES
DEFIBRINIZING
DEFICIENCE
DEFICIENCES
DEFICIENCIES
DEFICIENCY
DEFICIENTLY
DEFICIENTNESS
DEFICIENTNESSES
DEFICIENTS
DEFILADING
DEFILEMENT
DEFILEMENTS
DEFILIATION
DEFILIATIONS
DEFINABILITIES
DEFINABILITY
DEFINEMENT
DEFINEMENTS
DEFINIENDA
DEFINIENDUM
DEFINIENTIA
DEFINITELY
DEFINITENESS
DEFINITENESSES
DEFINITION
DEFINITIONAL
DEFINITIONS
DEFINITISE
DEFINITISED
DEFINITISES
DEFINITISING
DEFINITIVE
DEFINITIVELY
DEFINITIVENESS
DEFINITIVES
DEFINITIZE
DEFINITIZED
DEFINITIZES
DEFINITIZING
DEFINITUDE
DEFINITUDES
DEFLAGRABILITY
DEFLAGRABLE

DEFLAGRATE

DEFLAGRATE	DEFORESTATION	DEGENDERING	DEGRINGOLADE
DEFLAGRATED	DEFORESTATIONS	DEGENERACIES	DEGRINGOLADED
DEFLAGRATES	DEFORESTED	DEGENERACY	DEGRINGOLADES
DEFLAGRATING	DEFORESTER	DEGENERATE	DEGRINGOLADING
DEFLAGRATION	DEFORESTERS	DEGENERATED	DEGRINGOLER
DEFLAGRATIONS	DEFORESTING	DEGENERATELY	DEGRINGOLERED
DEFLAGRATOR	DEFORMABILITIES	DEGENERATENESS	DEGRINGOLERING
DEFLAGRATORS	DEFORMABILITY	DEGENERATES	DEGRINGOLERS
DEFLATIONARY	DEFORMABLE	DEGENERATING	DEGUSTATED
DEFLATIONIST	DEFORMALISE	DEGENERATION	DEGUSTATES
DEFLATIONISTS	DEFORMALISED	DEGENERATIONIST	DEGUSTATING
DEFLATIONS	DEFORMALISES	DEGENERATIONS	DEGUSTATION
DEFLECTABLE	DEFORMALISING	DEGENERATIVE	DEGUSTATIONS
DEFLECTING	DEFORMALIZE	DEGENEROUS	DEGUSTATORY
DEFLECTION	DEFORMALIZED	DEGLACIATED	DEHISCENCE
DEFLECTIONAL	DEFORMALIZES	DEGLACIATION	DEHISCENCES
DEFLECTIONS	DEFORMALIZING	DEGLACIATIONS	DEHORTATION
DEFLECTIVE	DEFORMATION	DEGLAMORISATION	DEHORTATIONS
DEFLECTORS	DEFORMATIONAL	DEGLAMORISE	DEHORTATIVE
DEFLEXIONAL	DEFORMATIONS	DEGLAMORISED	DEHORTATORY
DEFLEXIONS	DEFORMATIVE	DEGLAMORISES	DEHUMANISATION
DEFLEXURES	DEFORMEDLY	DEGLAMORISING	DEHUMANISATIONS
DEFLOCCULANT	DEFORMEDNESS	DEGLAMORIZATION	DEHUMANISE
DEFLOCCULANTS	DEFORMEDNESSES	DEGLAMORIZE	DEHUMANISED
DEFLOCCULATE	DEFORMITIES	DEGLAMORIZED	DEHUMANISES
DEFLOCCULATED	DEFRAGGERS	DEGLAMORIZES	DEHUMANISING
DEFLOCCULATES	DEFRAGGING	DEGLAMORIZING	DEHUMANIZATION
DEFLOCCULATING	DEFRAGMENT	DEGLUTINATE	DEHUMANIZATIONS
DEFLOCCULATION	DEFRAGMENTED	DEGLUTINATED	DEHUMANIZE
DEFLOCCULATIONS	DEFRAGMENTING	DEGLUTINATES	DEHUMANIZED
DEFLORATED	DEFRAGMENTS	DEGLUTINATING	DEHUMANIZES
DEFLORATES	DEFRAUDATION	DEGLUTINATION	DEHUMANIZING
DEFLORATING	DEFRAUDATIONS	DEGLUTINATIONS	DEHUMIDIFIED
DEFLORATION	DEFRAUDERS	DEGLUTITION	DEHUMIDIFIER
DEFLORATIONS	DEFRAUDING	DEGLUTITIONS	DEHUMIDIFIERS
DEFLOWERED	DEFRAUDMENT	DEGLUTITIVE	DEHUMIDIFIES
DEFLOWERER	DEFRAUDMENTS	DEGLUTITORY	DEHUMIDIFY
DEFLOWERERS	DEFRAYABLE	DEGRADABILITIES	DEHUMIDIFYING
DEFLOWERING	DEFRAYMENT	DEGRADABILITY	DEHYDRATED
DEFLUXIONS	DEFRAYMENTS	DEGRADABLE	DEHYDRATER
DEFOCUSING	DEFREEZING	DEGRADATION	DEHYDRATERS
DEFOCUSSED	DEFROCKING	DEGRADATIONS	DEHYDRATES
DEFOCUSSES	DEFROSTERS	DEGRADATIVE	DEHYDRATING
DEFOCUSSING	DEFROSTING	DEGRADEDLY	DEHYDRATION
DEFOLIANTS	DEFTNESSES	DEGRADINGLY	DEHYDRATIONS
DEFOLIATED	DEFUELLING	DEGRADINGNESS	DEHYDRATOR
DEFOLIATES	DEFUNCTION	DEGRADINGNESSES	DEHYDRATORS
DEFOLIATING	DEFUNCTIONS	DEGRANULATION	DEHYDROGENASE
DEFOLIATION	DEFUNCTIVE	DEGRANULATIONS	DEHYDROGENASES
DEFOLIATIONS	DEFUNCTNESS	DEGREASANT	DEHYDROGENATE
DEFOLIATOR	DEFUNCTNESSES	DEGREASANTS	DEHYDROGENATED
DEFOLIATORS	DEGARNISHED	DEGREASERS	DEHYDROGENATES
DEFORCEMENT	DEGARNISHES	DEGREASING	DEHYDROGENATING
DEFORCEMENTS	DEGARNISHING	DEGREELESS	DEHYDROGENATION
DEFORCIANT	DEGAUSSERS	DEGRESSION	DEHYDROGENISE
DEFORCIANTS	DEGAUSSING	DEGRESSIONS	DEHYDROGENISED
DEFORCIATION	DEGEARINGS	DEGRESSIVE	DEHYDROGENISES
DEFORCIATIONS	DEGENDERED	DEGRESSIVELY	DEHYDROGENISING

DEHYDROGENIZE
DEHYDROGENIZED
DEHYDROGENIZES
DEHYDROGENIZING
DEHYDRORETINOL
DEHYDRORETINOLS
DEHYPNOTISATION
DEHYPNOTISE
DEHYPNOTISED
DEHYPNOTISES
DEHYPNOTISING
DEHYPNOTIZATION
DEHYPNOTIZE
DEHYPNOTIZED
DEHYPNOTIZES
DEHYPNOTIZING
DEICTICALLY
DEIFICATION
DEIFICATIONS
DEINDEXING
DEINDIVIDUATION
DEINDUSTRIALISE
DEINDUSTRIALIZE
DEINONYCHUS
DEINONYCHUSES
DEINOSAURS
DEINOTHERE
DEINOTHERES
DEINOTHERIUM
DEINOTHERIUMS
DEIONISATION
DEIONISATIONS
DEIONISERS
DEIONISING
DEIONIZATION
DEIONIZATIONS
DEIONIZERS
DEIONIZING
DEIPNOSOPHIST
DEIPNOSOPHISTS
DEISTICALLY
DEJECTEDLY
DEJECTEDNESS
DEJECTEDNESSES
DEJECTIONS
DEKALITERS
DEKALITRES
DEKALOGIES
DEKAMETERS
DEKAMETRES
DEKAMETRIC
DELAMINATE
DELAMINATED
DELAMINATES
DELAMINATING
DELAMINATION
DELAMINATIONS
DELAPSIONS

DELASSEMENT
DELASSEMENTS
DELAYERING
DELAYERINGS
DELAYINGLY
DELECTABILITIES
DELECTABILITY
DELECTABLE
DELECTABLENESS
DELECTABLES
DELECTABLY
DELECTATED
DELECTATES
DELECTATING
DELECTATION
DELECTATIONS
DELEGACIES
DELEGATEES
DELEGATING
DELEGATION
DELEGATIONS
DELEGATORS
DELEGITIMATION
DELEGITIMATIONS
DELEGITIMISE
DELEGITIMISED
DELEGITIMISES
DELEGITIMISING
DELEGITIMIZE
DELEGITIMIZED
DELEGITIMIZES
DELEGITIMIZING
DELETERIOUS
DELETERIOUSLY
DELETERIOUSNESS
DELFTWARES
DELIBATING
DELIBATION
DELIBATIONS
DELIBERATE
DELIBERATED
DELIBERATELY
DELIBERATENESS
DELIBERATES
DELIBERATING
DELIBERATION
DELIBERATIONS
DELIBERATIVE
DELIBERATIVELY
DELIBERATOR
DELIBERATORS
DELICACIES
DELICATELY
DELICATENESS
DELICATENESSES
DELICATESSEN
DELICATESSENS
DELICIOUSLY

DELICIOUSNESS
DELICIOUSNESSES
DELIGATION
DELIGATIONS
DELIGHTEDLY
DELIGHTEDNESS
DELIGHTEDNESSES
DELIGHTERS
DELIGHTFUL
DELIGHTFULLY
DELIGHTFULNESS
DELIGHTING
DELIGHTLESS
DELIGHTSOME
DELIMITATE
DELIMITATED
DELIMITATES
DELIMITATING
DELIMITATION
DELIMITATIONS
DELIMITATIVE
DELIMITERS
DELIMITING
DELINEABLE
DELINEATED
DELINEATES
DELINEATING
DELINEATION
DELINEATIONS
DELINEATIVE
DELINEATOR
DELINEATORS
DELINEAVIT
DELINQUENCIES
DELINQUENCY
DELINQUENT
DELINQUENTLY
DELINQUENTS
DELIQUESCE
DELIQUESCED
DELIQUESCENCE
DELIQUESCENCES
DELIQUESCENT
DELIQUESCES
DELIQUESCING
DELIQUIUMS
DELIRATION
DELIRATIONS
DELIRIFACIENT
DELIRIFACIENTS
DELIRIOUSLY
DELIRIOUSNESS
DELIRIOUSNESSES
DELITESCENCE
DELITESCENCES
DELITESCENT
DELIVERABILITY
DELIVERABLE

DELIVERANCE
DELIVERANCES
DELIVERERS
DELIVERIES
DELIVERING
DELIVERYMAN
DELIVERYMEN
DELOCALISATION
DELOCALISATIONS
DELOCALISE
DELOCALISED
DELOCALISES
DELOCALISING
DELOCALIZATION
DELOCALIZATIONS
DELOCALIZE
DELOCALIZED
DELOCALIZES
DELOCALIZING
DELPHICALLY
DELPHINIUM
DELPHINIUMS
DELPHINOID
DELTIOLOGIES
DELTIOLOGIST
DELTIOLOGISTS
DELTIOLOGY
DELTOIDEUS
DELUDINGLY
DELUNDUNGS
DELUSIONAL
DELUSIONARY
DELUSIONIST
DELUSIONISTS
DELUSIVELY
DELUSIVENESS
DELUSIVENESSES
DELUSTERED
DELUSTERING
DELUSTRANT
DELUSTRANTS
DEMAGNETISATION
DEMAGNETISE
DEMAGNETISED
DEMAGNETISER
DEMAGNETISERS
DEMAGNETISES
DEMAGNETISING
DEMAGNETIZATION
DEMAGNETIZE
DEMAGNETIZED
DEMAGNETIZER
DEMAGNETIZERS
DEMAGNETIZES
DEMAGNETIZING
DEMAGOGICAL
DEMAGOGICALLY
DEMAGOGIES

DEMAGOGING
DEMAGOGISM
DEMAGOGISMS
DEMAGOGUED
DEMAGOGUERIES
DEMAGOGUERY
DEMAGOGUES
DEMAGOGUING
DEMAGOGUISM
DEMAGOGUISMS
DEMANDABLE
DEMANDANTS
DEMANDINGLY
DEMANDINGNESS
DEMANDINGNESSES
DEMANNINGS
DEMANTOIDS
DEMARCATED
DEMARCATES
DEMARCATING
DEMARCATION
DEMARCATIONS
DEMARCATOR
DEMARCATORS
DEMARKATION
DEMARKATIONS
DEMARKETED
DEMARKETING
DEMATERIALISE
DEMATERIALISED
DEMATERIALISES
DEMATERIALISING
DEMATERIALIZE
DEMATERIALIZED
DEMATERIALIZES
DEMATERIALIZING
DEMEANOURS
DEMEASNURE
DEMEASNURES
DEMENTATED
DEMENTATES
DEMENTATING
DEMENTEDLY
DEMENTEDNESS
DEMENTEDNESSES
DEMERGERED
DEMERGERING
DEMERITING
DEMERITORIOUS
DEMERITORIOUSLY
DEMERSIONS
DEMIBASTION
DEMIBASTIONS
DEMICANTON
DEMICANTONS
DEMIGODDESS
DEMIGODDESSES
DEMIGRATION

DEMIGRATIONS
DEMILITARISE
DEMILITARISED
DEMILITARISES
DEMILITARISING
DEMILITARIZE
DEMILITARIZED
DEMILITARIZES
DEMILITARIZING
DEMIMONDAINE
DEMIMONDAINES
DEMIMONDES
DEMINERALISE
DEMINERALISED
DEMINERALISER
DEMINERALISERS
DEMINERALISES
DEMINERALISING
DEMINERALIZE
DEMINERALIZED
DEMINERALIZER
DEMINERALIZERS
DEMINERALIZES
DEMINERALIZING
DEMIPIQUES
DEMIRELIEF
DEMIRELIEFS
DEMIREPDOM
DEMIREPDOMS
DEMISEMIQUAVER
DEMISEMIQUAVERS
DEMISSIONS
DEMITASSES
DEMIURGEOUS
DEMIURGICAL
DEMIURGICALLY
DEMIURGUSES
DEMIVEGGES
DEMIVIERGE
DEMIVIERGES
DEMIVOLTES
DEMIWORLDS
DEMOBILISATION
DEMOBILISATIONS
DEMOBILISE
DEMOBILISED
DEMOBILISES
DEMOBILISING
DEMOBILIZATION
DEMOBILIZATIONS
DEMOBILIZE
DEMOBILIZED
DEMOBILIZES
DEMOBILIZING
DEMOCRACIES
DEMOCRATIC
DEMOCRATICAL
DEMOCRATICALLY

DEMOCRATIES
DEMOCRATIFIABLE
DEMOCRATISATION
DEMOCRATISE
DEMOCRATISED
DEMOCRATISER
DEMOCRATISERS
DEMOCRATISES
DEMOCRATISING
DEMOCRATIST
DEMOCRATISTS
DEMOCRATIZATION
DEMOCRATIZE
DEMOCRATIZED
DEMOCRATIZER
DEMOCRATIZERS
DEMOCRATIZES
DEMOCRATIZING
DEMODULATE
DEMODULATED
DEMODULATES
DEMODULATING
DEMODULATION
DEMODULATIONS
DEMODULATOR
DEMODULATORS
DEMOGRAPHER
DEMOGRAPHERS
DEMOGRAPHIC
DEMOGRAPHICAL
DEMOGRAPHICALLY
DEMOGRAPHICS
DEMOGRAPHIES
DEMOGRAPHIST
DEMOGRAPHISTS
DEMOGRAPHY
DEMOISELLE
DEMOISELLES
DEMOLISHED
DEMOLISHER
DEMOLISHERS
DEMOLISHES
DEMOLISHING
DEMOLISHMENT
DEMOLISHMENTS
DEMOLITION
DEMOLITIONIST
DEMOLITIONISTS
DEMOLITIONS
DEMOLOGIES
DEMONESSES
DEMONETARISE
DEMONETARISED
DEMONETARISES
DEMONETARISING
DEMONETARIZE
DEMONETARIZED
DEMONETARIZES

DEMONETARIZING
DEMONETISATION
DEMONETISATIONS
DEMONETISE
DEMONETISED
DEMONETISES
DEMONETISING
DEMONETIZATION
DEMONETIZATIONS
DEMONETIZE
DEMONETIZED
DEMONETIZES
DEMONETIZING
DEMONIACAL
DEMONIACALLY
DEMONIACISM
DEMONIACISMS
DEMONIANISM
DEMONIANISMS
DEMONICALLY
DEMONISATION
DEMONISATIONS
DEMONISING
DEMONIZATION
DEMONIZATIONS
DEMONIZING
DEMONOCRACIES
DEMONOCRACY
DEMONOLATER
DEMONOLATERS
DEMONOLATRIES
DEMONOLATRY
DEMONOLOGIC
DEMONOLOGICAL
DEMONOLOGIES
DEMONOLOGIST
DEMONOLOGISTS
DEMONOLOGY
DEMONOMANIA
DEMONOMANIAS
DEMONSTRABILITY
DEMONSTRABLE
DEMONSTRABLY
DEMONSTRATE
DEMONSTRATED
DEMONSTRATES
DEMONSTRATING
DEMONSTRATION
DEMONSTRATIONAL
DEMONSTRATIONS
DEMONSTRATIVE
DEMONSTRATIVELY
DEMONSTRATIVES
DEMONSTRATOR
DEMONSTRATORS
DEMONSTRATORY
DEMORALISATION
DEMORALISATIONS

DEMORALISE	DEMYTHOLOGISED	DENDROLATRIES	DENOMINATIONS
DEMORALISED	DEMYTHOLOGISER	DENDROLATRY	DENOMINATIVE
DEMORALISER	DEMYTHOLOGISERS	DENDROLOGIC	DENOMINATIVELY
DEMORALISERS	DEMYTHOLOGISES	DENDROLOGICAL	DENOMINATIVES
DEMORALISES	DEMYTHOLOGISING	DENDROLOGIES	DENOMINATOR
DEMORALISING	DEMYTHOLOGIZE	DENDROLOGIST	DENOMINATORS
DEMORALISINGLY	DEMYTHOLOGIZED	DENDROLOGISTS	DENOTATING
DEMORALIZATION	DEMYTHOLOGIZER	DENDROLOGOUS	DENOTATION
DEMORALIZATIONS	DEMYTHOLOGIZERS	DENDROLOGY	DENOTATIONS
DEMORALIZE	DEMYTHOLOGIZES	DENDROMETER	DENOTATIVE
DEMORALIZED	DEMYTHOLOGIZING	DENDROMETERS	DENOTATIVELY
DEMORALIZER	DENATIONALISE	DENDROPHIS	DENOTEMENT
DEMORALIZERS	DENATIONALISED	DENDROPHISES	DENOTEMENTS
DEMORALIZES	DENATIONALISES	DENEGATION	DENOUEMENT
DEMORALIZING	DENATIONALISING	DENEGATIONS	DENOUEMENTS
DEMORALIZINGLY	DENATIONALIZE	DENERVATED	DENOUNCEMENT
DEMOTICIST	DENATIONALIZED	DENERVATES	DENOUNCEMENTS
DEMOTICISTS	DENATIONALIZES	DENERVATING	DENOUNCERS
DEMOTIVATE	DENATIONALIZING	DENERVATION	DENOUNCING
DEMOTIVATED	DENATURALISE	DENERVATIONS	DENSENESSES
DEMOTIVATES	DENATURALISED	DENIABILITIES	DENSIFICATION
DEMOTIVATING	DENATURALISES	DENIABILITY	DENSIFICATIONS
DEMOUNTABLE	DENATURALISING	DENIGRATED	DENSIFIERS
DEMOUNTING	DENATURALIZE	DENIGRATES	DENSIFYING
DEMULCENTS	DENATURALIZED	DENIGRATING	DENSIMETER
DEMULSIFICATION	DENATURALIZES	DENIGRATION	DENSIMETERS
DEMULSIFIED	DENATURALIZING	DENIGRATIONS	DENSIMETRIC
DEMULSIFIER	DENATURANT	DENIGRATIVE	DENSIMETRIES
DEMULSIFIERS	DENATURANTS	DENIGRATOR	DENSIMETRY
DEMULSIFIES	DENATURATION	DENIGRATORS	DENSITOMETER
DEMULSIFYING	DENATURATIONS	DENIGRATORY	DENSITOMETERS
DEMULTIPLEXER	DENATURING	DENISATION	DENSITOMETRIC
DEMULTIPLEXERS	DENATURISE	DENISATIONS	DENSITOMETRIES
DEMURENESS	DENATURISED	DENITRATED	DENSITOMETRY
DEMURENESSES	DENATURISES	DENITRATES	DENTALITIES
DEMURRABLE	DENATURISING	DENITRATING	DENTALIUMS
DEMURRAGES	DENATURIZE	DENITRATION	DENTATIONS
DEMUTUALISATION	DENATURIZED	DENITRATIONS	DENTICULATE
DEMUTUALISE	DENATURIZES	DENITRIFICATION	DENTICULATED
DEMUTUALISED	DENATURIZING	DENITRIFICATOR	DENTICULATELY
DEMUTUALISES	DENAZIFICATION	DENITRIFICATORS	DENTICULATION
DEMUTUALISING	DENAZIFICATIONS	DENITRIFIED	DENTICULATIONS
DEMUTUALIZATION	DENAZIFIED	DENITRIFIER	DENTIFRICE
DEMUTUALIZE	DENAZIFIES	DENITRIFIERS	DENTIFRICES
DEMUTUALIZED	DENAZIFYING	DENITRIFIES	DENTIGEROUS
DEMUTUALIZES	DENDRACHATE	DENITRIFYING	DENTILABIAL
DEMUTUALIZING	DENDRACHATES	DENIZATION	DENTILINGUAL
DEMYELINATE	DENDRIFORM	DENIZATIONS	DENTILINGUALS
DEMYELINATED	DENDRIMERS	DENIZENING	DENTIROSTRAL
DEMYELINATES	DENDRITICAL	DENIZENSHIP	DENTISTRIES
DEMYELINATING	DENDRITICALLY	DENIZENSHIPS	DENTITIONS
DEMYELINATION	DENDROBIUM	DENOMINABLE	DENTURISTS
DEMYELINATIONS	DENDROBIUMS	DENOMINATE	DENUCLEARISE
DEMYSTIFICATION	DENDROGLYPH	DENOMINATED	DENUCLEARISED
DEMYSTIFIED	DENDROGLYPHS	DENOMINATES	DENUCLEARISES
DEMYSTIFIES	DENDROGRAM	DENOMINATING	DENUCLEARISING
DEMYSTIFYING	DENDROGRAMS	DENOMINATION	DENUCLEARIZE
DEMYTHOLOGISE	DENDROIDAL	DENOMINATIONAL	DENUCLEARIZED

DENUCLEARIZES

DENUCLEARIZES
DENUCLEARIZING
DENUDATING
DENUDATION
DENUDATIONS
DENUDEMENT
DENUDEMENTS
DENUMERABILITY
DENUMERABLE
DENUMERABLY
DENUNCIATE
DENUNCIATED
DENUNCIATES
DENUNCIATING
DENUNCIATION
DENUNCIATIONS
DENUNCIATIVE
DENUNCIATOR
DENUNCIATORS
DENUNCIATORY
DEOBSTRUENT
DEOBSTRUENTS
DEODORANTS
DEODORISATION
DEODORISATIONS
DEODORISED
DEODORISER
DEODORISERS
DEODORISES
DEODORISING
DEODORIZATION
DEODORIZATIONS
DEODORIZED
DEODORIZER
DEODORIZERS
DEODORIZES
DEODORIZING
DEONTOLOGICAL
DEONTOLOGIES
DEONTOLOGIST
DEONTOLOGISTS
DEONTOLOGY
DEOPPILATE
DEOPPILATED
DEOPPILATES
DEOPPILATING
DEOPPILATION
DEOPPILATIONS
DEOPPILATIVE
DEORBITING
DEOXIDATED
DEOXIDATES
DEOXIDATING
DEOXIDATION
DEOXIDATIONS
DEOXIDISATION
DEOXIDISATIONS
DEOXIDISED

DEOXIDISER
DEOXIDISERS
DEOXIDISES
DEOXIDISING
DEOXIDIZATION
DEOXIDIZATIONS
DEOXIDIZED
DEOXIDIZER
DEOXIDIZERS
DEOXIDIZES
DEOXIDIZING
DEOXYCORTONE
DEOXYCORTONES
DEOXYGENATE
DEOXYGENATED
DEOXYGENATES
DEOXYGENATING
DEOXYGENATION
DEOXYGENATIONS
DEOXYGENISE
DEOXYGENISED
DEOXYGENISES
DEOXYGENISING
DEOXYGENIZE
DEOXYGENIZED
DEOXYGENIZES
DEOXYGENIZING
DEOXYRIBOSE
DEOXYRIBOSES
DEPAINTING
DEPANNEURS
DEPARTEMENT
DEPARTEMENTS
DEPARTINGS
DEPARTMENT
DEPARTMENTAL
DEPARTMENTALISE
DEPARTMENTALISM
DEPARTMENTALIZE
DEPARTMENTALLY
DEPARTMENTS
DEPARTURES
DEPASTURED
DEPASTURES
DEPASTURING
DEPAUPERATE
DEPAUPERATED
DEPAUPERATES
DEPAUPERATING
DEPAUPERISE
DEPAUPERISED
DEPAUPERISES
DEPAUPERISING
DEPAUPERIZE
DEPAUPERIZED
DEPAUPERIZES
DEPAUPERIZING
DEPEINCTED

DEPEINCTING
DEPENDABILITIES
DEPENDABILITY
DEPENDABLE
DEPENDABLENESS
DEPENDABLY
DEPENDACIE
DEPENDACIES
DEPENDANCE
DEPENDANCES
DEPENDANCIES
DEPENDANCY
DEPENDANTS
DEPENDENCE
DEPENDENCES
DEPENDENCIES
DEPENDENCY
DEPENDENTLY
DEPENDENTS
DEPENDINGLY
DEPEOPLING
DEPERSONALISE
DEPERSONALISED
DEPERSONALISES
DEPERSONALISING
DEPERSONALIZE
DEPERSONALIZED
DEPERSONALIZES
DEPERSONALIZING
DEPHLEGMATE
DEPHLEGMATED
DEPHLEGMATES
DEPHLEGMATING
DEPHLEGMATION
DEPHLEGMATIONS
DEPHLEGMATOR
DEPHLEGMATORS
DEPHLOGISTICATE
DEPHOSPHORYLATE
DEPICTIONS
DEPICTURED
DEPICTURES
DEPICTURING
DEPIGMENTATION
DEPIGMENTATIONS
DEPILATING
DEPILATION
DEPILATIONS
DEPILATORIES
DEPILATORS
DEPILATORY
DEPLETABLE
DEPLETIONS
DEPLORABILITIES
DEPLORABILITY
DEPLORABLE
DEPLORABLENESS
DEPLORABLY

DEPLORATION
DEPLORATIONS
DEPLORINGLY
DEPLOYABLE
DEPLOYMENT
DEPLOYMENTS
DEPLUMATION
DEPLUMATIONS
DEPOLARISATION
DEPOLARISATIONS
DEPOLARISE
DEPOLARISED
DEPOLARISER
DEPOLARISERS
DEPOLARISES
DEPOLARISING
DEPOLARIZATION
DEPOLARIZATIONS
DEPOLARIZE
DEPOLARIZED
DEPOLARIZER
DEPOLARIZERS
DEPOLARIZES
DEPOLARIZING
DEPOLISHED
DEPOLISHES
DEPOLISHING
DEPOLITICISE
DEPOLITICISED
DEPOLITICISES
DEPOLITICISING
DEPOLITICIZE
DEPOLITICIZED
DEPOLITICIZES
DEPOLITICIZING
DEPOLYMERISE
DEPOLYMERISED
DEPOLYMERISES
DEPOLYMERISING
DEPOLYMERIZE
DEPOLYMERIZED
DEPOLYMERIZES
DEPOLYMERIZING
DEPOPULATE
DEPOPULATED
DEPOPULATES
DEPOPULATING
DEPOPULATION
DEPOPULATIONS
DEPOPULATOR
DEPOPULATORS
DEPORTABLE
DEPORTATION
DEPORTATIONS
DEPORTMENT
DEPORTMENTS
DEPOSITARIES
DEPOSITARY

DEPOSITATION
DEPOSITATIONS
DEPOSITING
DEPOSITION
DEPOSITIONAL
DEPOSITIONS
DEPOSITIVE
DEPOSITORIES
DEPOSITORS
DEPOSITORY
DEPRAVATION
DEPRAVATIONS
DEPRAVEDLY
DEPRAVEDNESS
DEPRAVEDNESSES
DEPRAVEMENT
DEPRAVEMENTS
DEPRAVINGLY
DEPRAVITIES
DEPRECABLE
DEPRECATED
DEPRECATES
DEPRECATING
DEPRECATINGLY
DEPRECATION
DEPRECATIONS
DEPRECATIVE
DEPRECATIVELY
DEPRECATOR
DEPRECATORILY
DEPRECATORS
DEPRECATORY
DEPRECIABLE
DEPRECIATE
DEPRECIATED
DEPRECIATES
DEPRECIATING
DEPRECIATINGLY
DEPRECIATION
DEPRECIATIONS
DEPRECIATIVE
DEPRECIATOR
DEPRECIATORS
DEPRECIATORY
DEPREDATED
DEPREDATES
DEPREDATING
DEPREDATION
DEPREDATIONS
DEPREDATOR
DEPREDATORS
DEPREDATORY
DEPREHENDED
DEPREHENDING
DEPREHENDS
DEPRESSANT
DEPRESSANTS
DEPRESSIBLE

DEPRESSING
DEPRESSINGLY
DEPRESSION
DEPRESSIONS
DEPRESSIVE
DEPRESSIVELY
DEPRESSIVENESS
DEPRESSIVES
DEPRESSOMOTOR
DEPRESSOMOTORS
DEPRESSORS
DEPRESSURISE
DEPRESSURISED
DEPRESSURISES
DEPRESSURISING
DEPRESSURIZE
DEPRESSURIZED
DEPRESSURIZES
DEPRESSURIZING
DEPRIVABLE
DEPRIVATION
DEPRIVATIONS
DEPRIVATIVE
DEPRIVEMENT
DEPRIVEMENTS
DEPROGRAMED
DEPROGRAMING
DEPROGRAMME
DEPROGRAMMED
DEPROGRAMMER
DEPROGRAMMERS
DEPROGRAMMES
DEPROGRAMMING
DEPROGRAMS
DEPURATING
DEPURATION
DEPURATIONS
DEPURATIVE
DEPURATIVES
DEPURATORS
DEPURATORY
DEPUTATION
DEPUTATIONS
DEPUTISATION
DEPUTISATIONS
DEPUTISING
DEPUTIZATION
DEPUTIZATIONS
DEPUTIZING
DERACIALISE
DERACIALISED
DERACIALISES
DERACIALISING
DERACIALIZE
DERACIALIZED
DERACIALIZES
DERACIALIZING
DERACINATE

DERACINATED
DERACINATES
DERACINATING
DERACINATION
DERACINATIONS
DERAIGNING
DERAIGNMENT
DERAIGNMENTS
DERAILLEUR
DERAILLEURS
DERAILMENT
DERAILMENTS
DERANGEMENT
DERANGEMENTS
DERATIONED
DERATIONING
DEREALISATION
DEREALISATIONS
DEREALIZATION
DEREALIZATIONS
DERECOGNISE
DERECOGNISED
DERECOGNISES
DERECOGNISING
DERECOGNITION
DERECOGNITIONS
DERECOGNIZE
DERECOGNIZED
DERECOGNIZES
DERECOGNIZING
DEREGISTER
DEREGISTERED
DEREGISTERING
DEREGISTERS
DEREGISTRATION
DEREGISTRATIONS
DEREGULATE
DEREGULATED
DEREGULATES
DEREGULATING
DEREGULATION
DEREGULATIONS
DEREGULATOR
DEREGULATORS
DEREGULATORY
DERELICTION
DERELICTIONS
DERELIGIONISE
DERELIGIONISED
DERELIGIONISES
DERELIGIONISING
DERELIGIONIZE
DERELIGIONIZED
DERELIGIONIZES
DERELIGIONIZING
DEREPRESSED
DEREPRESSES
DEREPRESSING

DEREPRESSION
DEREPRESSIONS
DEREQUISITION
DEREQUISITIONED
DEREQUISITIONS
DERESTRICT
DERESTRICTED
DERESTRICTING
DERESTRICTION
DERESTRICTIONS
DERESTRICTS
DERIDINGLY
DERISIVELY
DERISIVENESS
DERISIVENESSES
DERIVATION
DERIVATIONAL
DERIVATIONIST
DERIVATIONISTS
DERIVATIONS
DERIVATISATION
DERIVATISATIONS
DERIVATISE
DERIVATISED
DERIVATISES
DERIVATISING
DERIVATIVE
DERIVATIVELY
DERIVATIVENESS
DERIVATIVES
DERIVATIZATION
DERIVATIZATIONS
DERIVATIZE
DERIVATIZED
DERIVATIZES
DERIVATIZING
DERMABRASION
DERMABRASIONS
DERMAPTERAN
DERMAPTERANS
DERMATITIS
DERMATITISES
DERMATOGEN
DERMATOGENS
DERMATOGLYPHIC
DERMATOGLYPHICS
DERMATOGRAPHIA
DERMATOGRAPHIAS
DERMATOGRAPHIC
DERMATOGRAPHIES
DERMATOGRAPHY
DERMATOLOGIC
DERMATOLOGICAL
DERMATOLOGIES
DERMATOLOGIST
DERMATOLOGISTS
DERMATOLOGY
DERMATOMAL

DERMATOMES	DESALINIZES	DESEGREGATING	DESICCATIVE
DERMATOMIC	DESALINIZING	DESEGREGATION	DESICCATIVES
DERMATOMICALLY	DESALTINGS	DESEGREGATIONS	DESICCATOR
DERMATOMYOSITIS	DESATURATION	DESELECTED	DESICCATORS
DERMATOPHYTE	DESATURATIONS	DESELECTING	DESIDERATA
DERMATOPHYTES	DESCANTERS	DESELECTION	DESIDERATE
DERMATOPHYTIC	DESCANTING	DESELECTIONS	DESIDERATED
DERMATOPHYTOSES	DESCENDABLE	DESENSITISATION	DESIDERATES
DERMATOPHYTOSIS	DESCENDANT	DESENSITISE	DESIDERATING
DERMATOPLASTIC	DESCENDANTS	DESENSITISED	DESIDERATION
DERMATOPLASTIES	DESCENDENT	DESENSITISER	DESIDERATIONS
DERMATOPLASTY	DESCENDENTS	DESENSITISERS	DESIDERATIVE
DERMATOSES	DESCENDERS	DESENSITISES	DESIDERATIVES
DERMATOSIS	DESCENDEUR	DESENSITISING	DESIDERATUM
DERMESTIDS	DESCENDEURS	DESENSITIZATION	DESIDERIUM
DERMOGRAPHIES	DESCENDIBLE	DESENSITIZE	DESIDERIUMS
DERMOGRAPHY	DESCENDING	DESENSITIZED	DESIGNABLE
DEROGATELY	DESCENDINGS	DESENSITIZER	DESIGNATED
DEROGATING	DESCENSION	DESENSITIZERS	DESIGNATES
DEROGATION	DESCENSIONAL	DESENSITIZES	DESIGNATING
DEROGATIONS	DESCENSIONS	DESENSITIZING	DESIGNATION
DEROGATIVE	DESCHOOLED	DESERPIDINE	DESIGNATIONS
DEROGATIVELY	DESCHOOLER	DESERPIDINES	DESIGNATIVE
DEROGATORILY	DESCHOOLERS	DESERTIFICATION	DESIGNATOR
DEROGATORINESS	DESCHOOLING	DESERTIFIED	DESIGNATORS
DEROGATORY	DESCHOOLINGS	DESERTIFIES	DESIGNATORY
DERRICKING	DESCRAMBLE	DESERTIFYING	DESIGNEDLY
DERRINGERS	DESCRAMBLED	DESERTIONS	DESIGNINGLY
DESACRALISATION	DESCRAMBLER	DESERTISATION	DESIGNINGS
DESACRALISE	DESCRAMBLERS	DESERTISATIONS	DESIGNLESS
DESACRALISED	DESCRAMBLES	DESERTIZATION	DESIGNMENT
DESACRALISES	DESCRAMBLING	DESERTIZATIONS	DESIGNMENTS
DESACRALISING	DESCRIBABLE	DESERTLESS	DESILVERED
DESACRALIZATION	DESCRIBERS	DESERVEDLY	DESILVERING
DESACRALIZE	DESCRIBING	DESERVEDNESS	DESILVERISATION
DESACRALIZED	DESCRIPTION	DESERVEDNESSES	DESILVERISE
DESACRALIZES	DESCRIPTIONS	DESERVINGLY	DESILVERISED
DESACRALIZING	DESCRIPTIVE	DESERVINGNESS	DESILVERISES
DESAGREMENT	DESCRIPTIVELY	DESERVINGNESSES	DESILVERISING
DESAGREMENTS	DESCRIPTIVENESS	DESERVINGS	DESILVERIZATION
DESALINATE	DESCRIPTIVISM	DESEXUALISATION	DESILVERIZE
DESALINATED	DESCRIPTIVISMS	DESEXUALISE	DESILVERIZED
DESALINATES	DESCRIPTIVIST	DESEXUALISED	DESILVERIZES
DESALINATING	DESCRIPTOR	DESEXUALISES	DESILVERIZING
DESALINATION	DESCRIPTORS	DESEXUALISING	DESINENCES
DESALINATIONS	DESCRIVING	DESEXUALIZATION	DESINENTIAL
DESALINATOR	DESECRATED	DESEXUALIZE	DESIPIENCE
DESALINATORS	DESECRATER	DESEXUALIZED	DESIPIENCES
DESALINISATION	DESECRATERS	DESEXUALIZES	DESIPRAMINE
DESALINISATIONS	DESECRATES	DESEXUALIZING	DESIPRAMINES
DESALINISE	DESECRATING	DESHABILLE	DESIRABILITIES
DESALINISED	DESECRATION	DESHABILLES	DESIRABILITY
DESALINISES	DESECRATIONS	DESICCANTS	DESIRABLENESS
DESALINISING	DESECRATOR	DESICCATED	DESIRABLENESSES
DESALINIZATION	DESECRATORS	DESICCATES	DESIRABLES
DESALINIZATIONS	DESEGREGATE	DESICCATING	DESIRELESS
DESALINIZE	DESEGREGATED	DESICCATION	DESIROUSLY
DESALINIZED	DESEGREGATES	DESICCATIONS	DESIROUSNESS

DESIROUSNESSES
DESISTANCE
DESISTANCES
DESISTENCE
DESISTENCES
DESKILLING
DESMODIUMS
DESMODROMIC
DESMOSOMAL
DESMOSOMES
DESNOODING
DESOBLIGEANTE
DESOBLIGEANTES
DESOLATELY
DESOLATENESS
DESOLATENESSES
DESOLATERS
DESOLATING
DESOLATINGLY
DESOLATION
DESOLATIONS
DESOLATORS
DESOLATORY
DESORIENTE
DESORPTION
DESORPTIONS
DESOXYRIBOSE
DESOXYRIBOSES
DESPAIRERS
DESPAIRFUL
DESPAIRING
DESPAIRINGLY
DESPATCHED
DESPATCHER
DESPATCHERS
DESPATCHES
DESPATCHING
DESPERADOES
DESPERADOS
DESPERATELY
DESPERATENESS
DESPERATENESSES
DESPERATION
DESPERATIONS
DESPICABILITIES
DESPICABILITY
DESPICABLE
DESPICABLENESS
DESPICABLY
DESPIRITUALISE
DESPIRITUALISED
DESPIRITUALISES
DESPIRITUALIZE
DESPIRITUALIZED
DESPIRITUALIZES
DESPISABLE
DESPISEDNESS
DESPISEDNESSES

DESPISEMENT
DESPISEMENTS
DESPITEFUL
DESPITEFULLY
DESPITEFULNESS
DESPITEOUS
DESPITEOUSLY
DESPOILERS
DESPOILING
DESPOILMENT
DESPOILMENTS
DESPOLIATION
DESPOLIATIONS
DESPONDENCE
DESPONDENCES
DESPONDENCIES
DESPONDENCY
DESPONDENT
DESPONDENTLY
DESPONDING
DESPONDINGLY
DESPONDINGS
DESPOTATES
DESPOTICAL
DESPOTICALLY
DESPOTICALNESS
DESPOTISMS
DESPOTOCRACIES
DESPOTOCRACY
DESPUMATED
DESPUMATES
DESPUMATING
DESPUMATION
DESPUMATIONS
DESQUAMATE
DESQUAMATED
DESQUAMATES
DESQUAMATING
DESQUAMATION
DESQUAMATIONS
DESQUAMATIVE
DESQUAMATORY
DESSERTSPOON
DESSERTSPOONFUL
DESSERTSPOONS
DESSIATINE
DESSIATINES
DESSIGNMENT
DESSIGNMENTS
DESSYATINE
DESSYATINES
DESTABILISATION
DESTABILISE
DESTABILISED
DESTABILISER
DESTABILISERS
DESTABILISES
DESTABILISING

DESTABILIZATION
DESTABILIZE
DESTABILIZED
DESTABILIZER
DESTABILIZERS
DESTABILIZES
DESTABILIZING
DESTAINING
DESTEMPERED
DESTEMPERING
DESTEMPERS
DESTINATED
DESTINATES
DESTINATING
DESTINATION
DESTINATIONS
DESTITUTED
DESTITUTENESS
DESTITUTENESSES
DESTITUTES
DESTITUTING
DESTITUTION
DESTITUTIONS
DESTOCKING
DESTROYABLE
DESTROYERS
DESTROYING
DESTRUCTED
DESTRUCTIBILITY
DESTRUCTIBLE
DESTRUCTING
DESTRUCTION
DESTRUCTIONAL
DESTRUCTIONIST
DESTRUCTIONISTS
DESTRUCTIONS
DESTRUCTIVE
DESTRUCTIVELY
DESTRUCTIVENESS
DESTRUCTIVES
DESTRUCTIVIST
DESTRUCTIVISTS
DESTRUCTIVITIES
DESTRUCTIVITY
DESTRUCTOR
DESTRUCTORS
DESTRUCTOS
DESUETUDES
DESUGARING
DESULFURED
DESULFURING
DESULFURISATION
DESULFURISE
DESULFURISED
DESULFURISES
DESULFURISING
DESULFURIZATION
DESULFURIZE

DESULFURIZED
DESULFURIZES
DESULFURIZING
DESULPHURATE
DESULPHURATED
DESULPHURATES
DESULPHURATING
DESULPHURATION
DESULPHURATIONS
DESULPHURED
DESULPHURING
DESULPHURISE
DESULPHURISED
DESULPHURISER
DESULPHURISERS
DESULPHURISES
DESULPHURISING
DESULPHURIZE
DESULPHURIZED
DESULPHURIZER
DESULPHURIZERS
DESULPHURIZES
DESULPHURIZING
DESULPHURS
DESULTORILY
DESULTORINESS
DESULTORINESSES
DETACHABILITIES
DETACHABILITY
DETACHABLE
DETACHABLY
DETACHEDLY
DETACHEDNESS
DETACHEDNESSES
DETACHMENT
DETACHMENTS
DETAILEDLY
DETAILEDNESS
DETAILEDNESSES
DETAILINGS
DETAINABLE
DETAINMENT
DETAINMENTS
DETASSELED
DETASSELING
DETASSELLED
DETASSELLING
DETECTABILITIES
DETECTABILITY
DETECTABLE
DETECTIBLE
DETECTIONS
DETECTIVELIKE
DETECTIVES
DETECTIVIST
DETECTIVISTS
DETECTOPHONE
DETECTOPHONES

DETECTORIST	DETERRENCES	DETRIBALISATION	DEUTOPLASMIC
DETECTORISTS	DETERRENTLY	DETRIBALISE	DEUTOPLASMS
DETENTIONS	DETERRENTS	DETRIBALISED	DEUTOPLASTIC
DETENTISTS	DETERSIONS	DETRIBALISES	DEVALORISATION
DETERGENCE	DETERSIVES	DETRIBALISING	DEVALORISATIONS
DETERGENCES	DETESTABILITIES	DETRIBALIZATION	DEVALORISE
DETERGENCIES	DETESTABILITY	DETRIBALIZE	DEVALORISED
DETERGENCY	DETESTABLE	DETRIBALIZED	DEVALORISES
DETERGENTS	DETESTABLENESS	DETRIBALIZES	DEVALORISING
DETERIORATE	DETESTABLY	DETRIBALIZING	DEVALORIZATION
DETERIORATED	DETESTATION	DETRIMENTAL	DEVALORIZATIONS
DETERIORATES	DETESTATIONS	DETRIMENTALLY	DEVALORIZE
DETERIORATING	DETHATCHED	DETRIMENTALS	DEVALORIZED
DETERIORATION	DETHATCHES	DETRIMENTS	DEVALORIZES
DETERIORATIONS	DETHATCHING	DETRITIONS	DEVALORIZING
DETERIORATIVE	DETHRONEMENT	DETRITOVORE	DEVALUATED
DETERIORISM	DETHRONEMENTS	DETRITOVORES	DEVALUATES
DETERIORISMS	DETHRONERS	DETRUNCATE	DEVALUATING
DETERIORITIES	DETHRONING	DETRUNCATED	DEVALUATION
DETERIORITY	DETHRONINGS	DETRUNCATES	DEVALUATIONS
DETERMENTS	DETONABILITIES	DETRUNCATING	DEVANAGARI
DETERMINABILITY	DETONABILITY	DETRUNCATION	DEVANAGARIS
DETERMINABLE	DETONATABLE	DETRUNCATIONS	DEVASTATED
DETERMINABLY	DETONATING	DETRUSIONS	DEVASTATES
DETERMINACIES	DETONATION	DETUMESCENCE	DEVASTATING
DETERMINACY	DETONATIONS	DETUMESCENCES	DEVASTATINGLY
DETERMINANT	DETONATIVE	DETUMESCENT	DEVASTATION
DETERMINANTAL	DETONATORS	DEUTERAGONIST	DEVASTATIONS
DETERMINANTS	DETORSIONS	DEUTERAGONISTS	DEVASTATIVE
DETERMINATE	DETORTIONS	DEUTERANOMALIES	DEVASTATOR
DETERMINATED	DETOXICANT	DEUTERANOMALOUS	DEVASTATORS
DETERMINATELY	DETOXICANTS	DEUTERANOMALY	DEVASTAVIT
DETERMINATENESS	DETOXICATE	DEUTERANOPE	DEVASTAVITS
DETERMINATES	DETOXICATED	DEUTERANOPES	DEVELOPABLE
DETERMINATING	DETOXICATES	DEUTERANOPIA	DEVELOPERS
DETERMINATION	DETOXICATING	DEUTERANOPIAS	DEVELOPING
DETERMINATIONS	DETOXICATION	DEUTERANOPIC	DEVELOPMENT
DETERMINATIVE	DETOXICATIONS	DEUTERATED	DEVELOPMENTAL
DETERMINATIVELY	DETOXIFICATION	DEUTERATES	DEVELOPMENTALLY
DETERMINATIVES	DETOXIFICATIONS	DEUTERATING	DEVELOPMENTS
DETERMINATOR	DETOXIFIED	DEUTERATION	DEVERBATIVE
DETERMINATORS	DETOXIFIES	DEUTERATIONS	DEVERBATIVES
DETERMINED	DETOXIFYING	DEUTERIDES	DEVIANCIES
DETERMINEDLY	DETRACTING	DEUTERIUMS	DEVIATIONISM
DETERMINEDNESS	DETRACTINGLY	DEUTEROGAMIES	DEVIATIONISMS
DETERMINER	DETRACTINGS	DEUTEROGAMIST	DEVIATIONIST
DETERMINERS	DETRACTION	DEUTEROGAMISTS	DEVIATIONISTS
DETERMINES	DETRACTIONS	DEUTEROGAMY	DEVIATIONS
DETERMINING	DETRACTIVE	DEUTEROPLASM	DEVILESSES
DETERMINISM	DETRACTIVELY	DEUTEROPLASMS	DEVILFISHES
DETERMINISMS	DETRACTORS	DEUTEROSCOPIC	DEVILISHLY
DETERMINIST	DETRACTORY	DEUTEROSCOPIES	DEVILISHNESS
DETERMINISTIC	DETRACTRESS	DEUTEROSCOPY	DEVILISHNESSES
DETERMINISTS	DETRACTRESSES	DEUTEROSTOME	DEVILMENTS
DETERRABILITIES	DETRAINING	DEUTEROSTOMES	DEVILSHIPS
DETERRABILITY	DETRAINMENT	DEUTEROTOKIES	DEVILTRIES
DETERRABLE	DETRAINMENTS	DEUTEROTOKY	DEVILWOODS
DETERRENCE	DETRAQUEES	DEUTOPLASM	DEVIOUSNESS

DEVIOUSNESSES	DEXAMETHASONE	DIACAUSTICS	DIAGRAMMABLE
DEVITALISATION	DEXAMETHASONES	DIACHRONIC	DIAGRAMMATIC
DEVITALISATIONS	DEXAMPHETAMINE	DIACHRONICALLY	DIAGRAMMATICAL
DEVITALISE	DEXAMPHETAMINES	DIACHRONIES	DIAGRAMMED
DEVITALISED	DEXIOTROPIC	DIACHRONISM	DIAGRAMMING
DEVITALISES	DEXTERITIES	DIACHRONISMS	DIAGRAPHIC
DEVITALISING	DEXTEROUSLY	DIACHRONISTIC	DIAHELIOTROPIC
DEVITALIZATION	DEXTEROUSNESS	DIACHRONOUS	DIAHELIOTROPISM
DEVITALIZATIONS	DEXTEROUSNESSES	DIACHYLONS	DIAKINESES
DEVITALIZE	DEXTERWISE	DIACHYLUMS	DIAKINESIS
DEVITALIZED	DEXTRALITIES	DIACODIONS	DIALECTALLY
DEVITALIZES	DEXTRALITY	DIACODIUMS	DIALECTICAL
DEVITALIZING	DEXTRANASE	DIACONATES	DIALECTICALLY
DEVITRIFICATION	DEXTRANASES	DIACONICON	DIALECTICIAN
DEVITRIFIED	DEXTROCARDIA	DIACONICONS	DIALECTICIANS
DEVITRIFIES	DEXTROCARDIAC	DIACOUSTIC	DIALECTICISM
DEVITRIFYING	DEXTROCARDIACS	DIACOUSTICS	DIALECTICISMS
DEVOCALISE	DEXTROCARDIAS	DIACRITICAL	DIALECTICS
DEVOCALISED	DEXTROGLUCOSE	DIACRITICALLY	DIALECTOLOGICAL
DEVOCALISES	DEXTROGLUCOSES	DIACRITICS	DIALECTOLOGIES
DEVOCALISING	DEXTROGYRATE	DIACTINISM	DIALECTOLOGIST
DEVOCALIZE	DEXTROGYRE	DIACTINISMS	DIALECTOLOGISTS
DEVOCALIZED	DEXTROPHOSPHATE	DIADELPHOUS	DIALECTOLOGY
DEVOCALIZES	DEXTROROTARY	DIADOCHIES	DIALLAGOID
DEVOCALIZING	DEXTROROTATION	DIADROMOUS	DIALOGICAL
DEVOLUTION	DEXTROROTATIONS	DIAGENESES	DIALOGICALLY
DEVOLUTIONARY	DEXTROROTATORY	DIAGENESIS	DIALOGISED
DEVOLUTIONIST	DEXTRORSAL	DIAGENETIC	DIALOGISES
DEVOLUTIONISTS	DEXTRORSELY	DIAGENETICALLY	DIALOGISING
DEVOLUTIONS	DEXTROUSLY	DIAGEOTROPIC	DIALOGISMS
DEVOLVEMENT	DEXTROUSNESS	DIAGEOTROPISM	DIALOGISTIC
DEVOLVEMENTS	DEXTROUSNESSES	DIAGEOTROPISMS	DIALOGISTICAL
DEVONPORTS	DEZINCKING	DIAGNOSABILITY	DIALOGISTS
DEVOTEDNESS	DHARMSALAS	DIAGNOSABLE	DIALOGITES
DEVOTEDNESSES	DHARMSHALA	DIAGNOSEABLE	DIALOGIZED
DEVOTEMENT	DHARMSHALAS	DIAGNOSING	DIALOGIZES
DEVOTEMENTS	DIABETICAL	DIAGNOSTIC	DIALOGIZING
DEVOTIONAL	DIABETOGENIC	DIAGNOSTICAL	DIALOGUERS
DEVOTIONALIST	DIABETOLOGIST	DIAGNOSTICALLY	DIALOGUING
DEVOTIONALISTS	DIABETOLOGISTS	DIAGNOSTICIAN	DIALYPETALOUS
DEVOTIONALITIES	DIABLERIES	DIAGNOSTICIANS	DIALYSABILITIES
DEVOTIONALITY	DIABOLICAL	DIAGNOSTICS	DIALYSABILITY
DEVOTIONALLY	DIABOLICALLY	DIAGOMETER	DIALYSABLE
DEVOTIONALNESS	DIABOLICALNESS	DIAGOMETERS	DIALYSATES
DEVOTIONALS	DIABOLISED	DIAGONALISABLE	DIALYSATION
DEVOTIONIST	DIABOLISES	DIAGONALISATION	DIALYSATIONS
DEVOTIONISTS	DIABOLISING	DIAGONALISE	DIALYTICALLY
DEVOURINGLY	DIABOLISMS	DIAGONALISED	DIALYZABILITIES
DEVOURMENT	DIABOLISTS	DIAGONALISES	DIALYZABILITY
DEVOURMENTS	DIABOLIZED	DIAGONALISING	DIALYZABLE
DEVOUTNESS	DIABOLIZES	DIAGONALIZABLE	DIALYZATES
DEVOUTNESSES	DIABOLIZING	DIAGONALIZATION	DIALYZATION
DEVVELLING	DIABOLOGIES	DIAGONALIZE	DIALYZATIONS
DEWATERERS	DIABOLOLOGIES	DIAGONALIZED	DIAMAGNETIC
DEWATERING	DIABOLOLOGY	DIAGONALIZES	DIAMAGNETICALLY
DEWATERINGS	DIACATHOLICON	DIAGONALIZING	DIAMAGNETISM
DEWBERRIES	DIACATHOLICONS	DIAGONALLY	DIAMAGNETISMS
DEWINESSES	DIACAUSTIC	DIAGRAMING	DIAMAGNETS

DIAMANTIFEROUS	DIARTHROSES	DIAZOTIZES	DICHROMATIC
DIAMANTINE	DIARTHROSIS	DIAZOTIZING	DICHROMATICISM
DIAMETRALLY	DIASCORDIUM	DIBASICITIES	DICHROMATICISMS
DIAMETRICAL	DIASCORDIUMS	DIBASICITY	DICHROMATICS
DIAMETRICALLY	DIASKEUAST	DIBENZOFURAN	DICHROMATISM
DIAMONDBACK	DIASKEUASTS	DIBENZOFURANS	DICHROMATISMS
DIAMONDBACKS	DIASTALSES	DIBRANCHIATE	DICHROMATS
DIAMONDIFEROUS	DIASTALSIS	DIBRANCHIATES	DICHROMISM
DIAMONDING	DIASTALTIC	DIBROMIDES	DICHROMISMS
DIAMORPHINE	DIASTEMATA	DICACITIES	DICHROOSCOPE
DIAMORPHINES	DIASTEMATIC	DICACODYLS	DICHROOSCOPES
DIANTHUSES	DIASTEREOISOMER	DICARBOXYLIC	DICHROOSCOPIC
DIAPASONAL	DIASTEREOMER	DICARPELLARY	DICHROSCOPE
DIAPASONIC	DIASTEREOMERIC	DICASTERIES	DICHROSCOPES
DIAPAUSING	DIASTEREOMERS	DICENTRICS	DICHROSCOPIC
DIAPEDESES	DIASTROPHIC	DICEPHALISM	DICKCISSEL
DIAPEDESIS	DIASTROPHICALLY	DICEPHALISMS	DICKCISSELS
DIAPEDETIC	DIASTROPHISM	DICEPHALOUS	DICKEYBIRD
DIAPERINGS	DIASTROPHISMS	DICHASIALLY	DICKEYBIRDS
DIAPHANEITIES	DIATESSARON	DICHLAMYDEOUS	DICKYBIRDS
DIAPHANEITY	DIATESSARONS	DICHLORIDE	DICLINISMS
DIAPHANOMETER	DIATHERMACIES	DICHLORIDES	DICOTYLEDON
DIAPHANOMETERS	DIATHERMACY	DICHLOROBENZENE	DICOTYLEDONOUS
DIAPHANOUS	DIATHERMAL	DICHLOROETHANE	DICOTYLEDONS
DIAPHANOUSLY	DIATHERMANCIES	DICHLOROETHANES	DICOUMARIN
DIAPHANOUSNESS	DIATHERMANCY	DICHLOROMETHANE	DICOUMARINS
DIAPHONIES	DIATHERMANEITY	DICHLORVOS	DICOUMAROL
DIAPHORASE	DIATHERMANOUS	DICHLORVOSES	DICOUMAROLS
DIAPHORASES	DIATHERMIA	DICHOGAMIC	DICROTISMS
DIAPHORESES	DIATHERMIAS	DICHOGAMIES	DICTATIONAL
DIAPHORESIS	DIATHERMIC	DICHOGAMOUS	DICTATIONS
DIAPHORETIC	DIATHERMIES	DICHONDRAS	DICTATORIAL
DIAPHORETICS	DIATHERMOUS	DICHOTICALLY	DICTATORIALLY
DIAPHOTOTROPIC	DIATOMACEOUS	DICHOTOMIC	DICTATORIALNESS
DIAPHOTOTROPIES	DIATOMICITIES	DICHOTOMIES	DICTATORSHIP
DIAPHOTOTROPISM	DIATOMICITY	DICHOTOMISATION	DICTATORSHIPS
DIAPHOTOTROPY	DIATOMISTS	DICHOTOMISE	DICTATRESS
DIAPHRAGMAL	DIATOMITES	DICHOTOMISED	DICTATRESSES
DIAPHRAGMATIC	DIATONICALLY	DICHOTOMISES	DICTATRICES
DIAPHRAGMATITIS	DIATONICISM	DICHOTOMISING	DICTATRIXES
DIAPHRAGMED	DIATONICISMS	DICHOTOMIST	DICTATURES
DIAPHRAGMING	DIATRETUMS	DICHOTOMISTS	DICTIONALLY
DIAPHRAGMS	DIATRIBIST	DICHOTOMIZATION	DICTIONARIES
DIAPHYSEAL	DIATRIBISTS	DICHOTOMIZE	DICTIONARY
DIAPHYSIAL	DIATROPISM	DICHOTOMIZED	DICTYOGENS
DIAPIRISMS	DIATROPISMS	DICHOTOMIZES	DICTYOPTERAN
DIAPOPHYSES	DIAZEUCTIC	DICHOTOMIZING	DICTYOPTERANS
DIAPOPHYSIAL	DIAZOMETHANE	DICHOTOMOUS	DICTYOSOME
DIAPOPHYSIS	DIAZOMETHANES	DICHOTOMOUSLY	DICTYOSOMES
DIAPOSITIVE	DIAZONIUMS	DICHOTOMOUSNESS	DICTYOSTELE
DIAPOSITIVES	DIAZOTISATION	DICHROISCOPE	DICTYOSTELES
DIAPYETICS	DIAZOTISATIONS	DICHROISCOPES	DICUMAROLS
DIARCHICAL	DIAZOTISED	DICHROISCOPIC	DICYNODONT
DIARRHETIC	DIAZOTISES	DICHROISMS	DICYNODONTS
DIARRHOEAL	DIAZOTISING	DICHROITES	DIDACTICAL
DIARRHOEAS	DIAZOTIZATION	DICHROITIC	DIDACTICALLY
DIARRHOEIC	DIAZOTIZATIONS	DICHROMATE	DIDACTICISM
DIARTHRODIAL	DIAZOTIZED	DICHROMATES	DIDACTICISMS

DIDACTYLISM
DIDACTYLISMS
DIDACTYLOUS
DIDASCALIC
DIDELPHIAN
DIDELPHIDS
DIDELPHINE
DIDELPHOUS
DIDGERIDOO
DIDGERIDOOS
DIDJERIDOO
DIDJERIDOOS
DIDJERIDUS
DIDRACHMAS
DIDYNAMIAN
DIDYNAMIES
DIDYNAMOUS
DIECIOUSLY
DIECIOUSNESS
DIECIOUSNESSES
DIEFFENBACHIA
DIEFFENBACHIAS
DIELECTRIC
DIELECTRICALLY
DIELECTRICS
DIENCEPHALA
DIENCEPHALIC
DIENCEPHALON
DIENCEPHALONS
DIESELINGS
DIESELISATION
DIESELISATIONS
DIESELISED
DIESELISES
DIESELISING
DIESELIZATION
DIESELIZATIONS
DIESELIZED
DIESELIZES
DIESELIZING
DIESINKERS
DIESTRUSES
DIETARIANS
DIETETICAL
DIETETICALLY
DIETHYLAMIDE
DIETHYLAMIDES
DIETHYLAMINE
DIETHYLAMINES
DIETHYLENE
DIETHYLENES
DIETICIANS
DIETITIANS
DIFFARREATION
DIFFARREATIONS
DIFFERENCE
DIFFERENCED
DIFFERENCES

DIFFERENCIED
DIFFERENCIES
DIFFERENCING
DIFFERENCY
DIFFERENCYING
DIFFERENTIA
DIFFERENTIABLE
DIFFERENTIAE
DIFFERENTIAL
DIFFERENTIALLY
DIFFERENTIALS
DIFFERENTIATE
DIFFERENTIATED
DIFFERENTIATES
DIFFERENTIATING
DIFFERENTIATION
DIFFERENTIATOR
DIFFERENTIATORS
DIFFERENTLY
DIFFERENTNESS
DIFFERENTNESSES
DIFFICULTIES
DIFFICULTLY
DIFFICULTY
DIFFIDENCE
DIFFIDENCES
DIFFIDENTLY
DIFFORMITIES
DIFFORMITY
DIFFRACTED
DIFFRACTING
DIFFRACTION
DIFFRACTIONS
DIFFRACTIVE
DIFFRACTIVELY
DIFFRACTIVENESS
DIFFRACTOMETER
DIFFRACTOMETERS
DIFFRACTOMETRIC
DIFFRACTOMETRY
DIFFRANGIBILITY
DIFFRANGIBLE
DIFFUSEDLY
DIFFUSEDNESS
DIFFUSEDNESSES
DIFFUSENESS
DIFFUSENESSES
DIFFUSIBILITIES
DIFFUSIBILITY
DIFFUSIBLE
DIFFUSIBLENESS
DIFFUSIONAL
DIFFUSIONISM
DIFFUSIONISMS
DIFFUSIONIST
DIFFUSIONISTS
DIFFUSIONS
DIFFUSIVELY

DIFFUSIVENESS
DIFFUSIVENESSES
DIFFUSIVITIES
DIFFUSIVITY
DIFUNCTIONAL
DIFUNCTIONALS
DIGASTRICS
DIGESTANTS
DIGESTEDLY
DIGESTIBILITIES
DIGESTIBILITY
DIGESTIBLE
DIGESTIBLENESS
DIGESTIBLY
DIGESTIONAL
DIGESTIONS
DIGESTIVELY
DIGESTIVES
DIGITALINS
DIGITALISATION
DIGITALISATIONS
DIGITALISE
DIGITALISED
DIGITALISES
DIGITALISING
DIGITALISM
DIGITALISMS
DIGITALIZATION
DIGITALIZATIONS
DIGITALIZE
DIGITALIZED
DIGITALIZES
DIGITALIZING
DIGITATELY
DIGITATION
DIGITATIONS
DIGITIFORM
DIGITIGRADE
DIGITIGRADES
DIGITISATION
DIGITISATIONS
DIGITISERS
DIGITISING
DIGITIZATION
DIGITIZATIONS
DIGITIZERS
DIGITIZING
DIGITONINS
DIGITORIUM
DIGITORIUMS
DIGITOXIGENIN
DIGITOXIGENINS
DIGITOXINS
DIGLADIATE
DIGLADIATED
DIGLADIATES
DIGLADIATING
DIGLADIATION

DIGLADIATIONS
DIGLADIATOR
DIGLADIATORS
DIGLOSSIAS
DIGLYCERIDE
DIGLYCERIDES
DIGNIFICATION
DIGNIFICATIONS
DIGNIFIEDLY
DIGNIFIEDNESS
DIGNIFIEDNESSES
DIGNIFYING
DIGNITARIES
DIGONEUTIC
DIGONEUTISM
DIGONEUTISMS
DIGRAPHICALLY
DIGRESSERS
DIGRESSING
DIGRESSION
DIGRESSIONAL
DIGRESSIONARY
DIGRESSIONS
DIGRESSIVE
DIGRESSIVELY
DIGRESSIVENESS
DIHYBRIDISM
DIHYBRIDISMS
DIJUDICATE
DIJUDICATED
DIJUDICATES
DIJUDICATING
DIJUDICATION
DIJUDICATIONS
DILACERATE
DILACERATED
DILACERATES
DILACERATING
DILACERATION
DILACERATIONS
DILAPIDATE
DILAPIDATED
DILAPIDATES
DILAPIDATING
DILAPIDATION
DILAPIDATIONS
DILAPIDATOR
DILAPIDATORS
DILATABILITIES
DILATABILITY
DILATABLENESS
DILATABLENESSES
DILATANCIES
DILATATION
DILATATIONAL
DILATATIONS
DILATATORS
DILATOMETER

DILATOMETERS	DIMETHYLAMINES	DINOTURBATIONS	DIPHTHONGALLY
DILATOMETRIC	DIMETHYLANILINE	DINUCLEOTIDE	DIPHTHONGED
DILATOMETRIES	DIMIDIATED	DINUCLEOTIDES	DIPHTHONGIC
DILATOMETRY	DIMIDIATES	DIOECIOUSLY	DIPHTHONGING
DILATORILY	DIMIDIATING	DIOECIOUSNESS	DIPHTHONGISE
DILATORINESS	DIMIDIATION	DIOECIOUSNESSES	DIPHTHONGISED
DILATORINESSES	DIMIDIATIONS	DIOESTRUSES	DIPHTHONGISES
DILEMMATIC	DIMINISHABLE	DIOICOUSLY	DIPHTHONGISING
DILETTANTE	DIMINISHED	DIOICOUSNESS	DIPHTHONGIZE
DILETTANTEISH	DIMINISHES	DIOICOUSNESSES	DIPHTHONGIZED
DILETTANTEISM	DIMINISHING	DIOPHYSITE	DIPHTHONGIZES
DILETTANTEISMS	DIMINISHINGLY	DIOPHYSITES	DIPHTHONGIZING
DILETTANTES	DIMINISHINGS	DIOPTOMETER	DIPHTHONGS
DILETTANTI	DIMINISHMENT	DIOPTOMETERS	DIPHYCERCAL
DILETTANTISH	DIMINISHMENTS	DIOPTOMETRIES	DIPHYLETIC
DILETTANTISM	DIMINUENDO	DIOPTOMETRY	DIPHYLLOUS
DILETTANTISMS	DIMINUENDOES	DIOPTRICAL	DIPHYODONT
DILIGENCES	DIMINUENDOS	DIOPTRICALLY	DIPHYODONTS
DILIGENTLY	DIMINUTION	DIORISTICAL	DIPHYSITES
DILLYDALLIED	DIMINUTIONS	DIORISTICALLY	DIPHYSITISM
DILLYDALLIES	DIMINUTIVAL	DIORTHOSES	DIPHYSITISMS
DILLYDALLY	DIMINUTIVE	DIORTHOSIS	DIPLEIDOSCOPE
DILLYDALLYING	DIMINUTIVELY	DIORTHOTIC	DIPLEIDOSCOPES
DILTIAZEMS	DIMINUTIVENESS	DIOSCOREACEOUS	DIPLOBIONT
DILUCIDATE	DIMINUTIVES	DIOSGENINS	DIPLOBIONTIC
DILUCIDATED	DIMORPHISM	DIOTHELETE	DIPLOBIONTS
DILUCIDATES	DIMORPHISMS	DIOTHELETES	DIPLOBLASTIC
DILUCIDATING	DIMORPHOUS	DIOTHELETIC	DIPLOCARDIAC
DILUCIDATION	DIMPLEMENT	DIOTHELETICAL	DIPLOCOCCAL
DILUCIDATIONS	DIMPLEMENTS	DIOTHELISM	DIPLOCOCCI
DILUTABLES	DINANDERIE	DIOTHELISMS	DIPLOCOCCIC
DILUTENESS	DINANDERIES	DIOTHELITE	DIPLOCOCCUS
DILUTENESSES	DINARCHIES	DIOTHELITES	DIPLODOCUS
DILUTIONARY	DINGDONGED	DIOXONITRIC	DIPLODOCUSES
DILUVIALISM	DINGDONGING	DIPEPTIDASE	DIPLOGENESES
DILUVIALISMS	DINGINESSES	DIPEPTIDASES	DIPLOGENESIS
DILUVIALIST	DINGLEBERRIES	DIPEPTIDES	DIPLOIDIES
DILUVIALISTS	DINGLEBERRY	DIPETALOUS	DIPLOMACIES
DIMENHYDRINATE	DINITROBENZENE	DIPHENHYDRAMINE	DIPLOMAING
DIMENHYDRINATES	DINITROBENZENES	DIPHENYLAMINE	DIPLOMATED
DIMENSIONAL	DINITROGEN	DIPHENYLAMINES	DIPLOMATES
DIMENSIONALITY	DINITROPHENOL	DIPHENYLENIMINE	DIPLOMATESE
DIMENSIONALLY	DINITROPHENOLS	DIPHENYLKETONE	DIPLOMATESES
DIMENSIONED	DINNERLESS	DIPHENYLKETONES	DIPLOMATIC
DIMENSIONING	DINNERTIME	DIPHOSGENE	DIPLOMATICAL
DIMENSIONLESS	DINNERTIMES	DIPHOSGENES	DIPLOMATICALLY
DIMENSIONS	DINNERWARE	DIPHOSPHATE	DIPLOMATICS
DIMERCAPROL	DINNERWARES	DIPHOSPHATES	DIPLOMATING
DIMERCAPROLS	DINOCERASES	DIPHTHERIA	DIPLOMATISE
DIMERISATION	DINOFLAGELLATE	DIPHTHERIAL	DIPLOMATISED
DIMERISATIONS	DINOFLAGELLATES	DIPHTHERIAS	DIPLOMATISES
DIMERISING	DINOMANIAS	DIPHTHERIC	DIPLOMATISING
DIMERIZATION	DINOSAURIAN	DIPHTHERITIC	DIPLOMATIST
DIMERIZATIONS	DINOSAURIC	DIPHTHERITIS	DIPLOMATISTS
DIMERIZING	DINOTHERES	DIPHTHERITISES	DIPLOMATIZE
DIMETHOATE	DINOTHERIUM	DIPHTHEROID	DIPLOMATIZED
DIMETHOATES	DINOTHERIUMS	DIPHTHEROIDS	DIPLOMATIZES
DIMETHYLAMINE	DINOTURBATION	DIPHTHONGAL	DIPLOMATIZING

DIPLOMATOLOGIES	DIRIGIBILITIES	DISAFFILIATED	DISANNULLED
DIPLOMATOLOGY	DIRIGIBILITY	DISAFFILIATES	DISANNULLER
DIPLONEMAS	DIRIGIBLES	DISAFFILIATING	DISANNULLERS
DIPLOPHASE	DIRIGISMES	DISAFFILIATION	DISANNULLING
DIPLOPHASES	DIRTINESSES	DISAFFILIATIONS	DISANNULLINGS
DIPLOSTEMONOUS	DISABILITIES	DISAFFIRMANCE	DISANNULMENT
DIPLOTENES	DISABILITY	DISAFFIRMANCES	DISANNULMENTS
DIPNETTING	DISABLEMENT	DISAFFIRMATION	DISANOINTED
DIPPERFULS	DISABLEMENTS	DISAFFIRMATIONS	DISANOINTING
DIPPINESSES	DISABUSALS	DISAFFIRMED	DISANOINTS
DIPRIONIDIAN	DISABUSING	DISAFFIRMING	DISAPPAREL
DIPROPELLANT	DISACCHARID	DISAFFIRMS	DISAPPARELLED
DIPROPELLANTS	DISACCHARIDASE	DISAFFOREST	DISAPPARELLING
DIPROTODON	DISACCHARIDASES	DISAFFORESTED	DISAPPARELS
DIPROTODONS	DISACCHARIDE	DISAFFORESTING	DISAPPEARANCE
DIPROTODONT	DISACCHARIDES	DISAFFORESTMENT	DISAPPEARANCES
DIPROTODONTID	DISACCHARIDS	DISAFFORESTS	DISAPPEARED
DIPROTODONTIDS	DISACCOMMODATE	DISAGGREGATE	DISAPPEARING
DIPROTODONTS	DISACCOMMODATED	DISAGGREGATED	DISAPPEARS
DIPSOMANIA	DISACCOMMODATES	DISAGGREGATES	DISAPPLICATION
DIPSOMANIAC	DISACCORDANT	DISAGGREGATING	DISAPPLICATIONS
DIPSOMANIACAL	DISACCORDED	DISAGGREGATION	DISAPPLIED
DIPSOMANIACS	DISACCORDING	DISAGGREGATIONS	DISAPPLIES
DIPSOMANIAS	DISACCORDS	DISAGGREGATIVE	DISAPPLYING
DIPTERISTS	DISACCREDIT	DISAGREEABILITY	DISAPPOINT
DIPTEROCARP	DISACCREDITED	DISAGREEABLE	DISAPPOINTED
DIPTEROCARPOUS	DISACCREDITING	DISAGREEABLES	DISAPPOINTEDLY
DIPTEROCARPS	DISACCREDITS	DISAGREEABLY	DISAPPOINTING
DIPTEROSES	DISACCUSTOM	DISAGREEING	DISAPPOINTINGLY
DIRECTEDNESS	DISACCUSTOMED	DISAGREEMENT	DISAPPOINTMENT
DIRECTEDNESSES	DISACCUSTOMING	DISAGREEMENTS	DISAPPOINTMENTS
DIRECTIONAL	DISACCUSTOMS	DISALLOWABLE	DISAPPOINTS
DIRECTIONALITY	DISACKNOWLEDGE	DISALLOWANCE	DISAPPROBATION
DIRECTIONLESS	DISACKNOWLEDGED	DISALLOWANCES	DISAPPROBATIONS
DIRECTIONS	DISACKNOWLEDGES	DISALLOWED	DISAPPROBATIVE
DIRECTIVES	DISADORNED	DISALLOWING	DISAPPROBATORY
DIRECTIVITIES	DISADORNING	DISALLYING	DISAPPROPRIATE
DIRECTIVITY	DISADVANCE	DISAMBIGUATE	DISAPPROPRIATED
DIRECTNESS	DISADVANCED	DISAMBIGUATED	DISAPPROPRIATES
DIRECTNESSES	DISADVANCES	DISAMBIGUATES	DISAPPROVAL
DIRECTORATE	DISADVANCING	DISAMBIGUATING	DISAPPROVALS
DIRECTORATES	DISADVANTAGE	DISAMBIGUATION	DISAPPROVE
DIRECTORIAL	DISADVANTAGED	DISAMBIGUATIONS	DISAPPROVED
DIRECTORIALLY	DISADVANTAGEOUS	DISAMENITIES	DISAPPROVER
DIRECTORIES	DISADVANTAGES	DISAMENITY	DISAPPROVERS
DIRECTORSHIP	DISADVANTAGING	DISANALOGIES	DISAPPROVES
DIRECTORSHIPS	DISADVENTURE	DISANALOGOUS	DISAPPROVING
DIRECTRESS	DISADVENTURES	DISANALOGY	DISAPPROVINGLY
DIRECTRESSES	DISADVENTUROUS	DISANCHORED	DISARMAMENT
DIRECTRICE	DISAFFECTED	DISANCHORING	DISARMAMENTS
DIRECTRICES	DISAFFECTEDLY	DISANCHORS	DISARMINGLY
DIRECTRIXES	DISAFFECTEDNESS	DISANIMATE	DISARRANGE
DIREFULNESS	DISAFFECTING	DISANIMATED	DISARRANGED
DIREFULNESSES	DISAFFECTION	DISANIMATES	DISARRANGEMENT
DIREMPTING	DISAFFECTIONATE	DISANIMATING	DISARRANGEMENTS
DIREMPTION	DISAFFECTIONS	DISANNEXED	DISARRANGES
DIREMPTIONS	DISAFFECTS	DISANNEXES	DISARRANGING
DIRENESSES	DISAFFILIATE	DISANNEXING	DISARRAYED

DISARRAYING
DISARTICULATE
DISARTICULATED
DISARTICULATES
DISARTICULATING
DISARTICULATION
DISARTICULATOR
DISARTICULATORS
DISASSEMBLE
DISASSEMBLED
DISASSEMBLER
DISASSEMBLERS
DISASSEMBLES
DISASSEMBLIES
DISASSEMBLING
DISASSEMBLY
DISASSIMILATE
DISASSIMILATED
DISASSIMILATES
DISASSIMILATING
DISASSIMILATION
DISASSIMILATIVE
DISASSOCIATE
DISASSOCIATED
DISASSOCIATES
DISASSOCIATING
DISASSOCIATION
DISASSOCIATIONS
DISASTROUS
DISASTROUSLY
DISATTIRED
DISATTIRES
DISATTIRING
DISATTRIBUTION
DISATTRIBUTIONS
DISATTUNED
DISATTUNES
DISATTUNING
DISAUTHORISE
DISAUTHORISED
DISAUTHORISES
DISAUTHORISING
DISAUTHORIZE
DISAUTHORIZED
DISAUTHORIZES
DISAUTHORIZING
DISAVAUNCE
DISAVAUNCED
DISAVAUNCES
DISAVAUNCING
DISAVENTROUS
DISAVENTURE
DISAVENTURES
DISAVOUCHED
DISAVOUCHES
DISAVOUCHING
DISAVOWABLE
DISAVOWALS

DISAVOWEDLY
DISAVOWERS
DISAVOWING
DISBANDING
DISBANDMENT
DISBANDMENTS
DISBARKING
DISBARMENT
DISBARMENTS
DISBARRING
DISBELIEFS
DISBELIEVE
DISBELIEVED
DISBELIEVER
DISBELIEVERS
DISBELIEVES
DISBELIEVING
DISBELIEVINGLY
DISBENCHED
DISBENCHES
DISBENCHING
DISBENEFIT
DISBENEFITS
DISBOSOMED
DISBOSOMING
DISBOWELED
DISBOWELING
DISBOWELLED
DISBOWELLING
DISBRANCHED
DISBRANCHES
DISBRANCHING
DISBUDDING
DISBURDENED
DISBURDENING
DISBURDENMENT
DISBURDENMENTS
DISBURDENS
DISBURSABLE
DISBURSALS
DISBURSEMENT
DISBURSEMENTS
DISBURSERS
DISBURSING
DISBURTHEN
DISBURTHENED
DISBURTHENING
DISBURTHENS
DISCALCEATE
DISCALCEATES
DISCANDERING
DISCANDERINGS
DISCANDIED
DISCANDIES
DISCANDYING
DISCANDYINGS
DISCANTERS
DISCANTING

DISCAPACITATE
DISCAPACITATED
DISCAPACITATES
DISCAPACITATING
DISCARDABLE
DISCARDERS
DISCARDING
DISCARDMENT
DISCARDMENTS
DISCARNATE
DISCEPTATION
DISCEPTATIONS
DISCEPTATIOUS
DISCEPTATOR
DISCEPTATORIAL
DISCEPTATORS
DISCEPTING
DISCERNABLE
DISCERNABLY
DISCERNERS
DISCERNIBLE
DISCERNIBLY
DISCERNING
DISCERNINGLY
DISCERNMENT
DISCERNMENTS
DISCERPIBILITY
DISCERPIBLE
DISCERPING
DISCERPTIBLE
DISCERPTION
DISCERPTIONS
DISCERPTIVE
DISCHARGEABLE
DISCHARGED
DISCHARGEE
DISCHARGEES
DISCHARGER
DISCHARGERS
DISCHARGES
DISCHARGING
DISCHUFFED
DISCHURCHED
DISCHURCHES
DISCHURCHING
DISCIPLESHIP
DISCIPLESHIPS
DISCIPLINABLE
DISCIPLINAL
DISCIPLINANT
DISCIPLINANTS
DISCIPLINARIAN
DISCIPLINARIANS
DISCIPLINARILY
DISCIPLINARITY
DISCIPLINARIUM
DISCIPLINARIUMS
DISCIPLINARY

DISCIPLINE
DISCIPLINED
DISCIPLINER
DISCIPLINERS
DISCIPLINES
DISCIPLING
DISCIPLINING
DISCIPULAR
DISCISSION
DISCISSIONS
DISCLAIMED
DISCLAIMER
DISCLAIMERS
DISCLAIMING
DISCLAMATION
DISCLAMATIONS
DISCLIMAXES
DISCLOSERS
DISCLOSING
DISCLOSURE
DISCLOSURES
DISCOBOLOS
DISCOBOLUS
DISCOBOLUSES
DISCOGRAPHER
DISCOGRAPHERS
DISCOGRAPHIC
DISCOGRAPHICAL
DISCOGRAPHIES
DISCOGRAPHY
DISCOLOGIES
DISCOLOGIST
DISCOLOGISTS
DISCOLORATION
DISCOLORATIONS
DISCOLORED
DISCOLORING
DISCOLORMENT
DISCOLORMENTS
DISCOLOURATION
DISCOLOURATIONS
DISCOLOURED
DISCOLOURING
DISCOLOURMENT
DISCOLOURMENTS
DISCOLOURS
DISCOMBOBERATE
DISCOMBOBERATED
DISCOMBOBERATES
DISCOMBOBULATE
DISCOMBOBULATED
DISCOMBOBULATES
DISCOMEDUSAN
DISCOMEDUSANS
DISCOMFITED
DISCOMFITER
DISCOMFITERS
DISCOMFITING

DISCOMFITS	DISCONFORMITY	DISCORPORATE	DISCREPANCES
DISCOMFITURE	DISCONNECT	DISCOTHEQUE	DISCREPANCIES
DISCOMFITURES	DISCONNECTED	DISCOTHEQUES	DISCREPANCY
DISCOMFORT	DISCONNECTEDLY	DISCOUNSEL	DISCREPANT
DISCOMFORTABLE	DISCONNECTER	DISCOUNSELLED	DISCREPANTLY
DISCOMFORTED	DISCONNECTERS	DISCOUNSELLING	DISCRETELY
DISCOMFORTING	DISCONNECTING	DISCOUNSELS	DISCRETENESS
DISCOMFORTS	DISCONNECTION	DISCOUNTABLE	DISCRETENESSES
DISCOMMEND	DISCONNECTIONS	DISCOUNTED	DISCRETEST
DISCOMMENDABLE	DISCONNECTIVE	DISCOUNTENANCE	DISCRETION
DISCOMMENDATION	DISCONNECTS	DISCOUNTENANCED	DISCRETIONAL
DISCOMMENDED	DISCONNEXION	DISCOUNTENANCES	DISCRETIONALLY
DISCOMMENDING	DISCONNEXIONS	DISCOUNTER	DISCRETIONARILY
DISCOMMENDS	DISCONSENT	DISCOUNTERS	DISCRETIONARY
DISCOMMISSION	DISCONSENTED	DISCOUNTING	DISCRETIONS
DISCOMMISSIONED	DISCONSENTING	DISCOURAGE	DISCRETIVE
DISCOMMISSIONS	DISCONSENTS	DISCOURAGEABLE	DISCRETIVELY
DISCOMMODE	DISCONSOLATE	DISCOURAGED	DISCRIMINABLE
DISCOMMODED	DISCONSOLATELY	DISCOURAGEMENT	DISCRIMINABLY
DISCOMMODES	DISCONSOLATION	DISCOURAGEMENTS	DISCRIMINANT
DISCOMMODING	DISCONSOLATIONS	DISCOURAGER	DISCRIMINANTS
DISCOMMODIOUS	DISCONTENT	DISCOURAGERS	DISCRIMINATE
DISCOMMODIOUSLY	DISCONTENTED	DISCOURAGES	DISCRIMINATED
DISCOMMODITIES	DISCONTENTEDLY	DISCOURAGING	DISCRIMINATELY
DISCOMMODITY	DISCONTENTFUL	DISCOURAGINGLY	DISCRIMINATES
DISCOMMONED	DISCONTENTING	DISCOURAGINGS	DISCRIMINATING
DISCOMMONING	DISCONTENTMENT	DISCOURING	DISCRIMINATION
DISCOMMONS	DISCONTENTMENTS	DISCOURSAL	DISCRIMINATIONS
DISCOMMUNITIES	DISCONTENTS	DISCOURSED	DISCRIMINATIVE
DISCOMMUNITY	DISCONTIGUITIES	DISCOURSER	DISCRIMINATOR
DISCOMPOSE	DISCONTIGUITY	DISCOURSERS	DISCRIMINATORS
DISCOMPOSED	DISCONTIGUOUS	DISCOURSES	DISCRIMINATORY
DISCOMPOSEDLY	DISCONTINUANCE	DISCOURSING	DISCROWNED
DISCOMPOSES	DISCONTINUANCES	DISCOURSIVE	DISCROWNING
DISCOMPOSING	DISCONTINUATION	DISCOURTEISE	DISCULPATE
DISCOMPOSINGLY	DISCONTINUE	DISCOURTEOUS	DISCULPATED
DISCOMPOSURE	DISCONTINUED	DISCOURTEOUSLY	DISCULPATES
DISCOMPOSURES	DISCONTINUER	DISCOURTESIES	DISCULPATING
DISCOMYCETE	DISCONTINUERS	DISCOURTESY	DISCUMBERED
DISCOMYCETES	DISCONTINUES	DISCOVERABLE	DISCUMBERING
DISCOMYCETOUS	DISCONTINUING	DISCOVERED	DISCUMBERS
DISCONCERT	DISCONTINUITIES	DISCOVERER	DISCURSION
DISCONCERTED	DISCONTINUITY	DISCOVERERS	DISCURSIONS
DISCONCERTEDLY	DISCONTINUOUS	DISCOVERIES	DISCURSIST
DISCONCERTING	DISCONTINUOUSLY	DISCOVERING	DISCURSISTS
DISCONCERTINGLY	DISCOPHILE	DISCOVERTURE	DISCURSIVE
DISCONCERTION	DISCOPHILES	DISCOVERTURES	DISCURSIVELY
DISCONCERTIONS	DISCOPHORAN	DISCREDITABLE	DISCURSIVENESS
DISCONCERTMENT	DISCOPHORANS	DISCREDITABLY	DISCURSORY
DISCONCERTMENTS	DISCOPHOROUS	DISCREDITED	DISCURSUSES
DISCONCERTS	DISCORDANCE	DISCREDITING	DISCUSSABLE
DISCONFIRM	DISCORDANCES	DISCREDITS	DISCUSSANT
DISCONFIRMATION	DISCORDANCIES	DISCREETER	DISCUSSANTS
DISCONFIRMED	DISCORDANCY	DISCREETEST	DISCUSSERS
DISCONFIRMING	DISCORDANT	DISCREETLY	DISCUSSIBLE
DISCONFIRMS	DISCORDANTLY	DISCREETNESS	DISCUSSING
DISCONFORMABLE	DISCORDFUL	DISCREETNESSES	DISCUSSION
DISCONFORMITIES	DISCORDING	DISCREPANCE	DISCUSSIONAL

DISCUSSIONS	DISEMBRANGLING	DISENFRANCHISES	DISENTRAINMENT
DISCUSSIVE	DISEMBROIL	DISENGAGED	DISENTRAINMENTS
DISCUTIENT	DISEMBROILED	DISENGAGEDNESS	DISENTRAINS
DISCUTIENTS	DISEMBROILING	DISENGAGEMENT	DISENTRANCE
DISDAINFUL	DISEMBROILS	DISENGAGEMENTS	DISENTRANCED
DISDAINFULLY	DISEMBURDEN	DISENGAGES	DISENTRANCEMENT
DISDAINFULNESS	DISEMBURDENED	DISENGAGING	DISENTRANCES
DISDAINING	DISEMBURDENING	DISENNOBLE	DISENTRANCING
DISEASEDNESS	DISEMBURDENS	DISENNOBLED	DISENTRAYLE
DISEASEDNESSES	DISEMPLOYED	DISENNOBLES	DISENTRAYLED
DISEASEFUL	DISEMPLOYING	DISENNOBLING	DISENTRAYLES
DISECONOMIES	DISEMPLOYMENT	DISENROLLED	DISENTRAYLING
DISECONOMY	DISEMPLOYMENTS	DISENROLLING	DISENTWINE
DISEMBARKATION	DISEMPLOYS	DISENSHROUD	DISENTWINED
DISEMBARKATIONS	DISEMPOWER	DISENSHROUDED	DISENTWINES
DISEMBARKED	DISEMPOWERED	DISENSHROUDING	DISENTWINING
DISEMBARKING	DISEMPOWERING	DISENSHROUDS	DISENVELOP
DISEMBARKMENT	DISEMPOWERMENT	DISENSLAVE	DISENVELOPED
DISEMBARKMENTS	DISEMPOWERMENTS	DISENSLAVED	DISENVELOPING
DISEMBARKS	DISEMPOWERS	DISENSLAVES	DISENVELOPS
DISEMBARRASS	DISENABLED	DISENSLAVING	DISENVIRON
DISEMBARRASSED	DISENABLEMENT	DISENTAILED	DISENVIRONED
DISEMBARRASSES	DISENABLEMENTS	DISENTAILING	DISENVIRONING
DISEMBARRASSING	DISENABLES	DISENTAILMENT	DISENVIRONS
DISEMBELLISH	DISENABLING	DISENTAILMENTS	DISEPALOUS
DISEMBELLISHED	DISENCHAIN	DISENTAILS	DISEQUILIBRATE
DISEMBELLISHES	DISENCHAINED	DISENTANGLE	DISEQUILIBRATED
DISEMBELLISHING	DISENCHAINING	DISENTANGLED	DISEQUILIBRATES
DISEMBITTER	DISENCHAINS	DISENTANGLEMENT	DISEQUILIBRIA
DISEMBITTERED	DISENCHANT	DISENTANGLES	DISEQUILIBRIUM
DISEMBITTERING	DISENCHANTED	DISENTANGLING	DISEQUILIBRIUMS
DISEMBITTERS	DISENCHANTER	DISENTHRAL	DISESPOUSE
DISEMBODIED	DISENCHANTERS	DISENTHRALL	DISESPOUSED
DISEMBODIES	DISENCHANTING	DISENTHRALLED	DISESPOUSES
DISEMBODIMENT	DISENCHANTINGLY	DISENTHRALLING	DISESPOUSING
DISEMBODIMENTS	DISENCHANTMENT	DISENTHRALLMENT	DISESTABLISH
DISEMBODYING	DISENCHANTMENTS	DISENTHRALLS	DISESTABLISHED
DISEMBOGUE	DISENCHANTRESS	DISENTHRALMENT	DISESTABLISHES
DISEMBOGUED	DISENCHANTS	DISENTHRALMENTS	DISESTABLISHING
DISEMBOGUEMENT	DISENCLOSE	DISENTHRALS	DISESTEEMED
DISEMBOGUEMENTS	DISENCLOSED	DISENTHRONE	DISESTEEMING
DISEMBOGUES	DISENCLOSES	DISENTHRONED	DISESTEEMS
DISEMBOGUING	DISENCLOSING	DISENTHRONES	DISESTIMATION
DISEMBOSOM	DISENCUMBER	DISENTHRONING	DISESTIMATIONS
DISEMBOSOMED	DISENCUMBERED	DISENTITLE	DISFAVORED
DISEMBOSOMING	DISENCUMBERING	DISENTITLED	DISFAVORING
DISEMBOSOMS	DISENCUMBERMENT	DISENTITLES	DISFAVOURED
DISEMBOWEL	DISENCUMBERS	DISENTITLING	DISFAVOURER
DISEMBOWELED	DISENCUMBRANCE	DISENTOMBED	DISFAVOURERS
DISEMBOWELING	DISENCUMBRANCES	DISENTOMBING	DISFAVOURING
DISEMBOWELLED	DISENDOWED	DISENTOMBS	DISFAVOURS
DISEMBOWELLING	DISENDOWER	DISENTRAIL	DISFEATURE
DISEMBOWELMENT	DISENDOWERS	DISENTRAILED	DISFEATURED
DISEMBOWELMENTS	DISENDOWING	DISENTRAILING	DISFEATUREMENT
DISEMBOWELS	DISENDOWMENT	DISENTRAILS	DISFEATUREMENTS
DISEMBRANGLE	DISENDOWMENTS	DISENTRAIN	DISFEATURES
DISEMBRANGLED	DISENFRANCHISE	DISENTRAINED	DISFEATURING
DISEMBRANGLES	DISENFRANCHISED	DISENTRAINING	DISFELLOWSHIP

DISFELLOWSHIPS
DISFIGURATION
DISFIGURATIONS
DISFIGURED
DISFIGUREMENT
DISFIGUREMENTS
DISFIGURER
DISFIGURERS
DISFIGURES
DISFIGURING
DISFLESHED
DISFLESHES
DISFLESHING
DISFLUENCIES
DISFLUENCY
DISFORESTATION
DISFORESTATIONS
DISFORESTED
DISFORESTING
DISFORESTS
DISFORMING
DISFRANCHISE
DISFRANCHISED
DISFRANCHISES
DISFRANCHISING
DISFROCKED
DISFROCKING
DISFUNCTION
DISFUNCTIONS
DISFURNISH
DISFURNISHED
DISFURNISHES
DISFURNISHING
DISFURNISHMENT
DISFURNISHMENTS
DISGARNISH
DISGARNISHED
DISGARNISHES
DISGARNISHING
DISGARRISON
DISGARRISONED
DISGARRISONING
DISGARRISONS
DISGAVELLED
DISGAVELLING
DISGESTING
DISGESTION
DISGESTIONS
DISGLORIFIED
DISGLORIFIES
DISGLORIFY
DISGLORIFYING
DISGORGEMENT
DISGORGEMENTS
DISGORGERS
DISGORGING
DISGOSPELLING
DISGOWNING

DISGRACEFUL
DISGRACEFULLY
DISGRACEFULNESS
DISGRACERS
DISGRACING
DISGRACIOUS
DISGRADATION
DISGRADATIONS
DISGRADING
DISGREGATION
DISGREGATIONS
DISGRUNTLE
DISGRUNTLED
DISGRUNTLEMENT
DISGRUNTLEMENTS
DISGRUNTLES
DISGRUNTLING
DISGUISABLE
DISGUISEDLY
DISGUISEDNESS
DISGUISEDNESSES
DISGUISELESS
DISGUISEMENT
DISGUISEMENTS
DISGUISERS
DISGUISING
DISGUISINGS
DISGUSTEDLY
DISGUSTEDNESS
DISGUSTEDNESSES
DISGUSTFUL
DISGUSTFULLY
DISGUSTFULNESS
DISGUSTING
DISGUSTINGLY
DISGUSTINGNESS
DISHABILITATE
DISHABILITATED
DISHABILITATES
DISHABILITATING
DISHABILITATION
DISHABILLE
DISHABILLES
DISHABITED
DISHABITING
DISHABLING
DISHALLOWED
DISHALLOWING
DISHALLOWS
DISHARMONIC
DISHARMONIES
DISHARMONIOUS
DISHARMONIOUSLY
DISHARMONISE
DISHARMONISED
DISHARMONISES
DISHARMONISING
DISHARMONIZE

DISHARMONIZED
DISHARMONIZES
DISHARMONIZING
DISHARMONY
DISHCLOTHS
DISHCLOUTS
DISHDASHAS
DISHEARTEN
DISHEARTENED
DISHEARTENING
DISHEARTENINGLY
DISHEARTENMENT
DISHEARTENMENTS
DISHEARTENS
DISHELMING
DISHERISON
DISHERISONS
DISHERITED
DISHERITING
DISHERITOR
DISHERITORS
DISHEVELED
DISHEVELING
DISHEVELLED
DISHEVELLING
DISHEVELMENT
DISHEVELMENTS
DISHONESTIES
DISHONESTLY
DISHONESTY
DISHONORABLE
DISHONORABLY
DISHONORARY
DISHONORED
DISHONORER
DISHONORERS
DISHONORING
DISHONOURABLE
DISHONOURABLY
DISHONOURED
DISHONOURER
DISHONOURERS
DISHONOURING
DISHONOURS
DISHORNING
DISHORSING
DISHOUSING
DISHTOWELS
DISHUMOURED
DISHUMOURING
DISHUMOURS
DISHWASHER
DISHWASHERS
DISHWATERS
DISILLUDED
DISILLUDES
DISILLUDING
DISILLUMINATE

DISILLUMINATED
DISILLUMINATES
DISILLUMINATING
DISILLUSION
DISILLUSIONARY
DISILLUSIONED
DISILLUSIONING
DISILLUSIONISE
DISILLUSIONISED
DISILLUSIONISES
DISILLUSIONIZE
DISILLUSIONIZED
DISILLUSIONIZES
DISILLUSIONMENT
DISILLUSIONS
DISILLUSIVE
DISIMAGINE
DISIMAGINED
DISIMAGINES
DISIMAGINING
DISIMMURED
DISIMMURES
DISIMMURING
DISIMPASSIONED
DISIMPRISON
DISIMPRISONED
DISIMPRISONING
DISIMPRISONMENT
DISIMPRISONS
DISIMPROVE
DISIMPROVED
DISIMPROVES
DISIMPROVING
DISINCARCERATE
DISINCARCERATED
DISINCARCERATES
DISINCENTIVE
DISINCENTIVES
DISINCLINATION
DISINCLINATIONS
DISINCLINE
DISINCLINED
DISINCLINES
DISINCLINING
DISINCLOSE
DISINCLOSED
DISINCLOSES
DISINCLOSING
DISINCORPORATE
DISINCORPORATED
DISINCORPORATES
DISINFECTANT
DISINFECTANTS
DISINFECTED
DISINFECTING
DISINFECTION
DISINFECTIONS
DISINFECTOR

DISINFECTORS	DISINTHRAL	DISLIKENING	DISMISSIVELY
DISINFECTS	DISINTHRALLED	DISLIMBING	DISMISSORY
DISINFESTANT	DISINTHRALLING	DISLIMNING	DISMOUNTABLE
DISINFESTANTS	DISINTHRALS	DISLINKING	DISMOUNTED
DISINFESTATION	DISINTOXICATE	DISLOADING	DISMOUNTING
DISINFESTATIONS	DISINTOXICATED	DISLOCATED	DISMUTATION
DISINFESTED	DISINTOXICATES	DISLOCATEDLY	DISMUTATIONS
DISINFESTING	DISINTOXICATING	DISLOCATES	DISNATURALISE
DISINFESTS	DISINTOXICATION	DISLOCATING	DISNATURALISED
DISINFLATION	DISINTRICATE	DISLOCATION	DISNATURALISES
DISINFLATIONARY	DISINTRICATED	DISLOCATIONS	DISNATURALISING
DISINFLATIONS	DISINTRICATES	DISLODGEMENT	DISNATURALIZE
DISINFORMATION	DISINTRICATING	DISLODGEMENTS	DISNATURALIZED
DISINFORMATIONS	DISINURING	DISLODGING	DISNATURALIZES
DISINFORMED	DISINVESTED	DISLODGMENT	DISNATURALIZING
DISINFORMING	DISINVESTING	DISLODGMENTS	DISNATURED
DISINFORMS	DISINVESTITURE	DISLOIGNED	DISNESTING
DISINGENUITIES	DISINVESTITURES	DISLOIGNING	DISOBEDIENCE
DISINGENUITY	DISINVESTMENT	DISLOYALLY	DISOBEDIENCES
DISINGENUOUS	DISINVESTMENTS	DISLOYALTIES	DISOBEDIENT
DISINGENUOUSLY	DISINVESTS	DISLOYALTY	DISOBEDIENTLY
DISINHERISON	DISINVIGORATE	DISLUSTRED	DISOBEYERS
DISINHERISONS	DISINVIGORATED	DISLUSTRES	DISOBEYING
DISINHERIT	DISINVIGORATES	DISLUSTRING	DISOBLIGATION
DISINHERITANCE	DISINVIGORATING	DISMALITIES	DISOBLIGATIONS
DISINHERITANCES	DISINVITED	DISMALLEST	DISOBLIGATORY
DISINHERITED	DISINVITES	DISMALNESS	DISOBLIGED
DISINHERITING	DISINVITING	DISMALNESSES	DISOBLIGEMENT
DISINHERITS	DISINVOLVE	DISMANNING	DISOBLIGEMENTS
DISINHIBIT	DISINVOLVED	DISMANTLED	DISOBLIGES
DISINHIBITED	DISINVOLVES	DISMANTLEMENT	DISOBLIGING
DISINHIBITING	DISINVOLVING	DISMANTLEMENTS	DISOBLIGINGLY
DISINHIBITION	DISJECTING	DISMANTLER	DISOBLIGINGNESS
DISINHIBITIONS	DISJECTION	DISMANTLERS	DISOPERATION
DISINHIBITORY	DISJECTIONS	DISMANTLES	DISOPERATIONS
DISINHIBITS	DISJOINABLE	DISMANTLING	DISORDERED
DISINHUMED	DISJOINING	DISMASKING	DISORDEREDLY
DISINHUMES	DISJOINTED	DISMASTING	DISORDEREDNESS
DISINHUMING	DISJOINTEDLY	DISMASTMENT	DISORDERING
DISINTEGRABLE	DISJOINTEDNESS	DISMASTMENTS	DISORDERLIES
DISINTEGRATE	DISJOINTING	DISMAYEDNESS	DISORDERLINESS
DISINTEGRATED	DISJUNCTION	DISMAYEDNESSES	DISORDERLY
DISINTEGRATES	DISJUNCTIONS	DISMAYFULLY	DISORDINATE
DISINTEGRATING	DISJUNCTIVE	DISMAYINGLY	DISORDINATELY
DISINTEGRATION	DISJUNCTIVELY	DISMAYLING	DISORGANIC
DISINTEGRATIONS	DISJUNCTIVES	DISMEMBERED	DISORGANISATION
DISINTEGRATIVE	DISJUNCTOR	DISMEMBERER	DISORGANISE
DISINTEGRATOR	DISJUNCTORS	DISMEMBERERS	DISORGANISED
DISINTEGRATORS	DISJUNCTURE	DISMEMBERING	DISORGANISER
DISINTEREST	DISJUNCTURES	DISMEMBERMENT	DISORGANISERS
DISINTERESTED	DISLEAFING	DISMEMBERMENTS	DISORGANISES
DISINTERESTEDLY	DISLEAVING	DISMEMBERS	DISORGANISING
DISINTERESTING	DISLIKABLE	DISMISSALS	DISORGANIZATION
DISINTERESTS	DISLIKEABLE	DISMISSIBLE	DISORGANIZE
DISINTERMENT	DISLIKEFUL	DISMISSING	DISORGANIZED
DISINTERMENTS	DISLIKENED	DISMISSION	DISORGANIZER
DISINTERRED	DISLIKENESS	DISMISSIONS	DISORGANIZERS
DISINTERRING	DISLIKENESSES	DISMISSIVE	DISORGANIZES

DISORGANIZING	DISPENSARY	DISPLEASED	DISPRAISING
DISORIENTATE	DISPENSATION	DISPLEASEDLY	DISPRAISINGLY
DISORIENTATED	DISPENSATIONAL	DISPLEASEDNESS	DISPREADING
DISORIENTATES	DISPENSATIONS	DISPLEASES	DISPREDDEN
DISORIENTATING	DISPENSATIVE	DISPLEASING	DISPREDDING
DISORIENTATION	DISPENSATIVELY	DISPLEASINGLY	DISPRINCED
DISORIENTATIONS	DISPENSATOR	DISPLEASINGNESS	DISPRISONED
DISORIENTED	DISPENSATORIES	DISPLEASURE	DISPRISONING
DISORIENTING	DISPENSATORILY	DISPLEASURED	DISPRISONS
DISORIENTS	DISPENSATORS	DISPLEASURES	DISPRIVACIED
DISOWNMENT	DISPENSATORY	DISPLEASURING	DISPRIVILEGE
DISOWNMENTS	DISPENSERS	DISPLENISH	DISPRIVILEGED
DISPARAGED	DISPENSING	DISPLENISHED	DISPRIVILEGES
DISPARAGEMENT	DISPEOPLED	DISPLENISHES	DISPRIVILEGING
DISPARAGEMENTS	DISPEOPLES	DISPLENISHING	DISPRIZING
DISPARAGER	DISPEOPLING	DISPLENISHMENT	DISPROFESS
DISPARAGERS	DISPERMOUS	DISPLENISHMENTS	DISPROFESSED
DTSPARAGES	DISPERSALS	DISPLODING	DISPROFESSES
DISPARAGING	DISPERSANT	DISPLOSION	DISPROFESSING
DISPARAGINGLY	DISPERSANTS	DISPLOSIONS	DISPROFITS
DISPARATELY	DISPERSEDLY	DISPLUMING	DISPROOVED
DISPARATENESS	DISPERSEDNESS	DISPONDAIC	DISPROOVES
DISPARATENESSES	DISPERSEDNESSES	DISPONDEES	DISPROOVING
DISPARATES	DISPERSERS	DISPONGING	DISPROPERTIED
DISPARITIES	DISPERSIBLE	DISPORTING	DISPROPERTIES
DISPARKING	DISPERSING	DISPORTMENT	DISPROPERTY
DISPARTING	DISPERSION	DISPORTMENTS	DISPROPERTYING
DISPASSION	DISPERSIONS	DISPOSABILITIES	DISPROPORTION
DISPASSIONATE	DISPERSIVE	DISPOSABILITY	DISPROPORTIONAL
DISPASSIONATELY	DISPERSIVELY	DISPOSABLE	DISPROPORTIONED
DISPASSIONS	DISPERSIVENESS	DISPOSABLENESS	DISPROPORTIONS
DISPATCHED	DISPERSOID	DISPOSABLES	DISPROPRIATE
DISPATCHER	DISPERSOIDS	DISPOSEDLY	DISPROPRIATED
DISPATCHERS	DISPIRITED	DISPOSINGLY	DISPROPRIATES
DISPATCHES	DISPIRITEDLY	DISPOSINGS	DISPROPRIATING
DISPATCHFUL	DISPIRITEDNESS	DISPOSITION	DISPROVABLE
DISPATCHING	DISPIRITING	DISPOSITIONAL	DISPROVALS
DISPATHIES	DISPIRITINGLY	DISPOSITIONED	DISPROVERS
DISPAUPERED	DISPIRITMENT	DISPOSITIONS	DISPROVIDE
DISPAUPERING	DISPIRITMENTS	DISPOSITIVE	DISPROVIDED
DISPAUPERISE	DISPITEOUS	DISPOSITIVELY	DISPROVIDES
DISPAUPERISED	DISPITEOUSLY	DISPOSITOR	DISPROVIDING
DISPAUPERISES	DISPITEOUSNESS	DISPOSITORS	DISPROVING
DISPAUPERISING	DISPLACEABLE	DISPOSSESS	DISPUNGING
DISPAUPERIZE	DISPLACEMENT	DISPOSSESSED	DISPURSING
DISPAUPERIZED	DISPLACEMENTS	DISPOSSESSES	DISPURVEYANCE
DISPAUPERIZES	DISPLACERS	DISPOSSESSING	DISPURVEYANCES
DISPAUPERIZING	DISPLACING	DISPOSSESSION	DISPURVEYED
DISPAUPERS	DISPLANTATION	DISPOSSESSIONS	DISPURVEYING
DISPELLERS	DISPLANTATIONS	DISPOSSESSOR	DISPURVEYS
DISPELLING	DISPLANTED	DISPOSSESSORS	DISPUTABILITIES
DISPENCING	DISPLANTING	DISPOSSESSORY	DISPUTABILITY
DISPENDING	DISPLAYABLE	DISPOSTING	DISPUTABLE
DISPENSABILITY	DISPLAYERS	DISPOSURES	DISPUTABLENESS
DISPENSABLE	DISPLAYING	DISPRAISED	DISPUTABLY
DISPENSABLENESS	DISPLEASANCE	DISPRAISER	DISPUTANTS
DISPENSABLY	DISPLEASANCES	DISPRAISERS	DISPUTATION
DISPENSARIES	DISPLEASANT	DISPRAISES	DISPUTATIONS

DISPUTATIOUS	DISREPUTABILITY	DISSEMBLINGLY	DISSEVERMENTS
DISPUTATIOUSLY	DISREPUTABLE	DISSEMBLINGS	DISSHEATHE
DISPUTATIVE	DISREPUTABLY	DISSEMINATE	DISSHEATHED
DISPUTATIVELY	DISREPUTATION	DISSEMINATED	DISSHEATHES
DISPUTATIVENESS	DISREPUTATIONS	DISSEMINATES	DISSHEATHING
DISQUALIFIABLE	DISREPUTES	DISSEMINATING	DISSHIVERED
DISQUALIFIED	DISRESPECT	DISSEMINATION	DISSHIVERING
DISQUALIFIER	DISRESPECTABLE	DISSEMINATIONS	DISSHIVERS
DISQUALIFIERS	DISRESPECTED	DISSEMINATIVE	DISSIDENCE
DISQUALIFIES	DISRESPECTFUL	DISSEMINATOR	DISSIDENCES
DISQUALIFY	DISRESPECTFULLY	DISSEMINATORS	DISSIDENTLY
DISQUALIFYING	DISRESPECTING	DISSEMINULE	DISSIDENTS
DISQUANTITIED	DISRESPECTS	DISSEMINULES	DISSILIENCE
DISQUANTITIES	DISROBEMENT	DISSENSION	DISSILIENCES
DISQUANTITY	DISROBEMENTS	DISSENSIONS	DISSILIENT
DISQUANTITYING	DISROOTING	DISSENSUSES	DISSIMILAR
DISQUIETED	DISRUPTERS	DISSENTERISH	DISSIMILARITIES
DISQUIETEDLY	DISRUPTING	DISSENTERISM	DISSIMILARITY
DISQUIETEDNESS	DISRUPTION	DISSENTERISMS	DISSIMILARLY
DISQUIETEN	DISRUPTIONS	DISSENTERS	DISSIMILARS
DISQUIETENED	DISRUPTIVE	DISSENTIENCE	DISSIMILATE
DISQUIETENING	DISRUPTIVELY	DISSENTIENCES	DISSIMILATED
DISQUIETENS	DISRUPTIVENESS	DISSENTIENCIES	DISSIMILATES
DISQUIETFUL	DISRUPTORS	DISSENTIENCY	DISSIMILATING
DISQUIETING	DISSATISFACTION	DISSENTIENT	DISSIMILATION
DISQUIETINGLY	DISSATISFACTORY	DISSENTIENTLY	DISSIMILATIONS
DISQUIETIVE	DISSATISFIED	DISSENTIENTS	DISSIMILATIVE
DISQUIETLY	DISSATISFIEDLY	DISSENTING	DISSIMILATORY
DISQUIETNESS	DISSATISFIES	DISSENTINGLY	DISSIMILES
DISQUIETNESSES	DISSATISFY	DISSENTION	DISSIMILITUDE
DISQUIETOUS	DISSATISFYING	DISSENTIONS	DISSIMILITUDES
DISQUIETUDE	DISSAVINGS	DISSENTIOUS	DISSIMULATE
DISQUIETUDES	DISSEATING	DISSEPIMENT	DISSIMULATED
DISQUISITION	DISSECTIBLE	DISSEPIMENTAL	DISSIMULATES
DISQUISITIONAL	DISSECTING	DISSEPIMENTS	DISSIMULATING
DISQUISITIONARY	DISSECTINGS	DISSERTATE	DISSIMULATION
DISQUISITIONS	DISSECTION	DISSERTATED	DISSIMULATIONS
DISQUISITIVE	DISSECTIONS	DISSERTATES	DISSIMULATIVE
DISQUISITORY	DISSECTIVE	DISSERTATING	DISSIMULATOR
DISRANKING	DISSECTORS	DISSERTATION	DISSIMULATORS
DISREGARDED	DISSEISEES	DISSERTATIONAL	DISSIPABLE
DISREGARDER	DISSEISING	DISSERTATIONIST	DISSIPATED
DISREGARDERS	DISSEISINS	DISSERTATIONS	DISSIPATEDLY
DISREGARDFUL	DISSEISORS	DISSERTATIVE	DISSIPATEDNESS
DISREGARDFULLY	DISSEIZEES	DISSERTATOR	DISSIPATER
DISREGARDING	DISSEIZING	DISSERTATORS	DISSIPATERS
DISREGARDS	DISSEIZINS	DISSERTING	DISSIPATES
DISRELATED	DISSEIZORS	DISSERVICE	DISSIPATING
DISRELATION	DISSELBOOM	DISSERVICEABLE	DISSIPATION
DISRELATIONS	DISSELBOOMS	DISSERVICES	DISSIPATIONS
DISRELISHED	DISSEMBLANCE	DISSERVING	DISSIPATIVE
DISRELISHES	DISSEMBLANCES	DISSEVERANCE	DISSIPATOR
DISRELISHING	DISSEMBLED	DISSEVERANCES	DISSIPATORS
DISREMEMBER	DISSEMBLER	DISSEVERATION	DISSOCIABILITY
DISREMEMBERED	DISSEMBLERS	DISSEVERATIONS	DISSOCIABLE
DISREMEMBERING	DISSEMBLES	DISSEVERED	DISSOCIABLENESS
DISREMEMBERS	DISSEMBLIES	DISSEVERING	DISSOCIABLY
DISREPAIRS	DISSEMBLING	DISSEVERMENT	DISSOCIALISE

DISSOCIALISED	DISSYLLABIC	DISTILLING	DISTRAINMENTS
DISSOCIALISES	DISSYLLABLE	DISTILLINGS	DISTRAINOR
DISSOCIALISING	DISSYLLABLES	DISTILMENT	DISTRAINORS
DISSOCIALITIES	DISSYMMETRIC	DISTILMENTS	DISTRAINTS
DISSOCIALITY	DISSYMMETRICAL	DISTINCTER	DISTRAUGHT
DISSOCIALIZE	DISSYMMETRIES	DISTINCTEST	DISTRAUGHTLY
DISSOCIALIZED	DISSYMMETRY	DISTINCTION	DISTRESSED
DISSOCIALIZES	DISTAINING	DISTINCTIONS	DISTRESSER
DISSOCIALIZING	DISTANCELESS	DISTINCTIVE	DISTRESSERS
DISSOCIATE	DISTANCING	DISTINCTIVELY	DISTRESSES
DISSOCIATED	DISTANTNESS	DISTINCTIVENESS	DISTRESSFUL
DISSOCIATES	DISTANTNESSES	DISTINCTIVES	DISTRESSFULLY
DISSOCIATING	DISTASTEFUL	DISTINCTLY	DISTRESSFULNESS
DISSOCIATION	DISTASTEFULLY	DISTINCTNESS	DISTRESSING
DISSOCIATIONS	DISTASTEFULNESS	DISTINCTNESSES	DISTRESSINGLY
DISSOCIATIVE	DISTASTING	DISTINCTURE	DISTRIBUEND
DISSOLUBILITIES	DISTELFINK	DISTINCTURES	DISTRIBUENDS
DISSOLUBILITY	DISTELFINKS	DISTINGUEE	DISTRIBUTABLE
DISSOLUBLE	DISTEMPERATE	DISTINGUISH	DISTRIBUTARIES
DISSOLUBLENESS	DISTEMPERATURE	DISTINGUISHABLE	DISTRIBUTARY
DISSOLUTELY	DISTEMPERATURES	DISTINGUISHABLY	DISTRIBUTE
DISSOLUTENESS	DISTEMPERED	DISTINGUISHED	DISTRIBUTED
DISSOLUTENESSES	DISTEMPERING	DISTINGUISHER	DISTRIBUTEE
DISSOLUTES	DISTEMPERS	DISTINGUISHERS	DISTRIBUTEES
DISSOLUTION	DISTENDERS	DISTINGUISHES	DISTRIBUTER
DISSOLUTIONISM	DISTENDING	DISTINGUISHING	DISTRIBUTERS
DISSOLUTIONISMS	DISTENSIBILITY	DISTINGUISHMENT	DISTRIBUTES
DISSOLUTIONIST	DISTENSIBLE	DISTORTEDLY	DISTRIBUTING
DISSOLUTIONISTS	DISTENSILE	DISTORTEDNESS	DISTRIBUTION
DISSOLUTIONS	DISTENSION	DISTORTEDNESSES	DISTRIBUTIONAL
DISSOLUTIVE	DISTENSIONS	DISTORTERS	DISTRIBUTIONS
DISSOLVABILITY	DISTENSIVE	DISTORTING	DISTRIBUTIVE
DISSOLVABLE	DISTENTION	DISTORTION	DISTRIBUTIVELY
DISSOLVABLENESS	DISTENTIONS	DISTORTIONAL	DISTRIBUTIVES
DISSOLVENT	DISTHRONED	DISTORTIONS	DISTRIBUTIVITY
DISSOLVENTS	DISTHRONES	DISTORTIVE	DISTRIBUTOR
DISSOLVERS	DISTHRONING	DISTRACTABLE	DISTRIBUTORS
DISSOLVING	DISTHRONISE	DISTRACTED	DISTRICTED
DISSOLVINGS	DISTHRONISED	DISTRACTEDLY	DISTRICTING
DISSONANCE	DISTHRONISES	DISTRACTEDNESS	DISTRINGAS
DISSONANCES	DISTHRONISING	DISTRACTER	DISTRINGASES
DISSONANCIES	DISTHRONIZE	DISTRACTERS	DISTROUBLE
DISSONANCY	DISTHRONIZED	DISTRACTIBILITY	DISTROUBLED
DISSONANTLY	DISTHRONIZES	DISTRACTIBLE	DISTROUBLES
DISSUADABLE	DISTHRONIZING	DISTRACTING	DISTROUBLING
DISSUADERS	DISTICHOUS	DISTRACTINGLY	DISTRUSTED
DISSUADING	DISTICHOUSLY	DISTRACTION	DISTRUSTER
DISSUASION	DISTILLABLE	DISTRACTIONS	DISTRUSTERS
DISSUASIONS	DISTILLAND	DISTRACTIVE	DISTRUSTFUL
DISSUASIVE	DISTILLANDS	DISTRACTIVELY	DISTRUSTFULLY
DISSUASIVELY	DISTILLATE	DISTRAINABLE	DISTRUSTFULNESS
DISSUASIVENESS	DISTILLATES	DISTRAINED	DISTRUSTING
DISSUASIVES	DISTILLATION	DISTRAINEE	DISTRUSTLESS
DISSUASORIES	DISTILLATIONS	DISTRAINEES	DISTURBANCE
DISSUASORY	DISTILLATORY	DISTRAINER	DISTURBANCES
DISSUNDERED	DISTILLERIES	DISTRAINERS	DISTURBANT
DISSUNDERING	DISTILLERS	DISTRAINING	DISTURBANTS
DISSUNDERS	DISTILLERY	DISTRAINMENT	DISTURBATIVE

DISTURBERS	DITHIONITES	DIVERSIFIABLE	DIVINIZATION
DISTURBING	DITHIONOUS	DIVERSIFICATION	DIVINIZATIONS
DISTURBINGLY	DITHYRAMBIC	DIVERSIFIED	DIVINIZING
DISUBSTITUTED	DITHYRAMBICALLY	DIVERSIFIER	DIVISIBILITIES
DISULFATES	DITHYRAMBIST	DIVERSIFIERS	DIVISIBILITY
DISULFIDES	DITHYRAMBISTS	DIVERSIFIES	DIVISIBLENESS
DISULFIRAM	DITHYRAMBS	DIVERSIFORM	DIVISIBLENESSES
DISULFIRAMS	DITRANSITIVE	DIVERSIFYING	DIVISIONAL
DISULFOTON	DITRANSITIVES	DIVERSIONAL	DIVISIONALLY
DISULFOTONS	DITRIGLYPH	DIVERSIONARY	DIVISIONARY
DISULPHATE	DITRIGLYPHIC	DIVERSIONIST	DIVISIONISM
DISULPHATES	DITRIGLYPHS	DIVERSIONISTS	DIVISIONISMS
DISULPHIDE	DITROCHEAN	DIVERSIONS	DIVISIONIST
DISULPHIDES	DITROCHEES	DIVERSITIES	DIVISIONISTS
DISULPHURET	DITSINESSES	DIVERTIBILITIES	DIVISIVELY
DISULPHURETS	DITTANDERS	DIVERTIBILITY	DIVISIVENESS
DISULPHURIC	DITTOGRAPHIC	DIVERTIBLE	DIVISIVENESSES
DISUNIONIST	DITTOGRAPHIES	DIVERTICULA	DIVORCEABLE
DISUNIONISTS	DITTOGRAPHY	DIVERTICULAR	DIVORCEMENT
DISUNITERS	DITTOLOGIES	DIVERTICULATE	DIVORCEMENTS
DISUNITIES	DITZINESSES	DIVERTICULATED	DIVULGATED
DISUNITING	DIURETICALLY	DIVERTICULITIS	DIVULGATER
DISUTILITIES	DIURETICALNESS	DIVERTICULOSES	DIVULGATERS
DISUTILITY	DIURNALIST	DIVERTICULOSIS	DIVULGATES
DISVALUING	DIURNALISTS	DIVERTICULUM	DIVULGATING
DISVOUCHED	DIUTURNITIES	DIVERTIMENTI	DIVULGATION
DISVOUCHES	DIUTURNITY	DIVERTIMENTO	DIVULGATIONS
DISVOUCHING	DIVAGATING	DIVERTIMENTOS	DIVULGATOR
DISWORSHIP	DIVAGATION	DIVERTINGLY	DIVULGATORS
DISWORSHIPS	DIVAGATIONS	DIVERTISEMENT	DIVULGEMENT
DISYLLABIC	DIVALENCES	DIVERTISEMENTS	DIVULGEMENTS
DISYLLABIFIED	DIVALENCIES	DIVERTISSEMENT	DIVULGENCE
DISYLLABIFIES	DIVARICATE	DIVERTISSEMENTS	DIVULGENCES
DISYLLABIFY	DIVARICATED	DIVESTIBLE	DIVULSIONS
DISYLLABIFYING	DIVARICATELY	DIVESTITURE	DIZENMENTS
DISYLLABISM	DIVARICATES	DIVESTITURES	DIZZINESSES
DISYLLABISMS	DIVARICATING	DIVESTMENT	DIZZYINGLY
DISYLLABLE	DIVARICATINGLY	DIVESTMENTS	DJELLABAHS
DISYLLABLES	DIVARICATION	DIVESTURES	DOBSONFLIES
DITCHDIGGER	DIVARICATIONS	DIVIDEDNESS	DOCENTSHIP
DITCHDIGGERS	DIVARICATOR	DIVIDEDNESSES	DOCENTSHIPS
DITCHWATER	DIVARICATORS	DIVIDENDLESS	DOCHMIACAL
DITCHWATERS	DIVEBOMBED	DIVINATION	DOCHMIUSES
DITHEISTIC	DIVEBOMBING	DIVINATIONS	DOCIBILITIES
DITHEISTICAL	DIVELLICATE	DIVINATORIAL	DOCIBILITY
DITHELETES	DIVELLICATED	DIVINATORS	DOCIBLENESS
DITHELETIC	DIVELLICATES	DIVINATORY	DOCIBLENESSES
DITHELETICAL	DIVELLICATING	DIVINENESS	DOCILITIES
DITHELETISM	DIVERGEMENT	DIVINENESSES	DOCIMASIES
DITHELETISMS	DIVERGEMENTS	DIVINERESS	DOCIMASTIC
DITHELISMS	DIVERGENCE	DIVINERESSES	DOCIMOLOGIES
DITHELITISM	DIVERGENCES	DIVINIFIED	DOCIMOLOGY
DITHELITISMS	DIVERGENCIES	DIVINIFIES	DOCKISATION
DITHERIEST	DIVERGENCY	DIVINIFYING	DOCKISATIONS
DITHIOCARBAMATE	DIVERGENTLY	DIVINISATION	DOCKIZATION
DITHIONATE	DIVERGINGLY	DIVINISATIONS	DOCKIZATIONS
DITHIONATES	DIVERSENESS	DIVINISING	DOCKMASTER
DITHIONITE	DIVERSENESSES	DIVINITIES	DOCKMASTERS

DOCKWORKER	DODECAGONAL	DOGMATOLOGIES	DOLOMITISATIONS
DOCKWORKERS	DODECAGONS	DOGMATOLOGY	DOLOMITISE
DOCQUETING	DODECAGYNIAN	DOGNAPPERS	DOLOMITISED
DOCTORANDS	DODECAGYNOUS	DOGNAPPING	DOLOMITISES
DOCTORATED	DODECAHEDRA	DOGROBBERS	DOLOMITISING
DOCTORATES	DODECAHEDRAL	DOGSBODIED	DOLOMITIZATION
DOCTORATING	DODECAHEDRON	DOGSBODIES	DOLOMITIZATIONS
DOCTORESSES	DODECAHEDRONS	DOGSBODYING	DOLOMITIZE
DOCTORLESS	DODECANDROUS	DOGSLEDDED	DOLOMITIZED
DOCTORSHIP	DODECANOIC	DOGSLEDDER	DOLOMITIZES
DOCTORSHIPS	DODECAPHONIC	DOGSLEDDERS	DOLOMITIZING
DOCTRESSES	DODECAPHONIES	DOGSLEDDING	DOLORIFEROUS
DOCTRINAIRE	DODECAPHONISM	DOGTROTTED	DOLORIMETRIES
DOCTRINAIRES	DODECAPHONISMS	DOGTROTTING	DOLORIMETRY
DOCTRINAIRISM	DODECAPHONIST	DOGWATCHES	DOLOROUSLY
DOCTRINAIRISMS	DODECAPHONISTS	DOLABRIFORM	DOLOROUSNESS
DOCTRINALITIES	DODECAPHONY	DOLCELATTE	DOLOROUSNESSES
DOCTRINALITY	DODECASTYLE	DOLCELATTES	DOLOSTONES
DOCTRINALLY	DODECASTYLES	DOLCEMENTE	DOLPHINARIA
DOCTRINARIAN	DODECASYLLABIC	DOLEFULLER	DOLPHINARIUM
DOCTRINARIANISM	DODECASYLLABLE	DOLEFULLEST	DOLPHINARIUMS
DOCTRINARIANS	DODECASYLLABLES	DOLEFULNESS	DOLPHINETS
DOCTRINARISM	DODGEBALLS	DOLEFULNESSES	DOLPHINFISH
DOCTRINARISMS	DODGINESSES	DOLESOMELY	DOLPHINFISHES
DOCTRINISM	DOGARESSAS	DOLICHOCEPHAL	DOLTISHNESS
DOCTRINISMS	DOGBERRIES	DOLICHOCEPHALIC	DOLTISHNESSES
DOCTRINIST	DOGBERRYISM	DOLICHOCEPHALS	DOMESTICABLE
DOCTRINISTS	DOGBERRYISMS	DOLICHOCEPHALY	DOMESTICAL
DOCUDRAMAS	DOGCATCHER	DOLICHOSAURUS	DOMESTICALLY
DOCUMENTABLE	DOGCATCHERS	DOLICHOSAURUSES	DOMESTICATE
DOCUMENTAL	DOGFIGHTING	DOLICHOSES	DOMESTICATED
DOCUMENTALIST	DOGGEDNESS	DOLICHURUS	DOMESTICATES
DOCUMENTALISTS	DOGGEDNESSES	DOLICHURUSES	DOMESTICATING
DOCUMENTARIAN	DOGGINESSES	DOLLARBIRD	DOMESTICATION
DOCUMENTARIANS	DOGGISHNESS	DOLLARBIRDS	DOMESTICATIONS
DOCUMENTARIES	DOGGISHNESSES	DOLLARFISH	DOMESTICATIVE
DOCUMENTARILY	DOGGONEDER	DOLLARFISHES	DOMESTICATOR
DOCUMENTARISE	DOGGONEDEST	DOLLARISATION	DOMESTICATORS
DOCUMENTARISED	DOGLEGGING	DOLLARISATIONS	DOMESTICISE
DOCUMENTARISES	DOGMATICAL	DOLLARISED	DOMESTICISED
DOCUMENTARISING	DOGMATICALLY	DOLLARISES	DOMESTICISES
DOCUMENTARIST	DOGMATICALNESS	DOLLARISING	DOMESTICISING
DOCUMENTARISTS	DOGMATISATION	DOLLARIZATION	DOMESTICITIES
DOCUMENTARIZE	DOGMATISATIONS	DOLLARIZATIONS	DOMESTICITY
DOCUMENTARIZED	DOGMATISED	DOLLARIZED	DOMESTICIZE
DOCUMENTARIZES	DOGMATISER	DOLLARIZES	DOMESTICIZED
DOCUMENTARIZING	DOGMATISERS	DOLLARIZING	DOMESTICIZES
DOCUMENTARY	DOGMATISES	DOLLARLESS	DOMESTICIZING
DOCUMENTATION	DOGMATISING	DOLLAROCRACIES	DOMICILIARY
DOCUMENTATIONAL	DOGMATISMS	DOLLAROCRACY	DOMICILIATE
DOCUMENTATIONS	DOGMATISTS	DOLLARSHIP	DOMICILIATED
DOCUMENTED	DOGMATIZATION	DOLLARSHIPS	DOMICILIATES
DOCUMENTER	DOGMATIZATIONS	DOLLHOUSES	DOMICILIATING
DOCUMENTERS	DOGMATIZED	DOLLINESSES	DOMICILIATION
DOCUMENTING	DOGMATIZER	DOLLISHNESS	DOMICILIATIONS
DODDERIEST	DOGMATIZERS	DOLLISHNESSES	DOMICILING
DODDIPOLLS	DOGMATIZES	DOLLYBIRDS	DOMINANCES
DODDYPOLLS	DOGMATIZING	DOLOMITISATION	DOMINANCIES

DOMINANTLY	DOORSTONES	DOUBTFULNESS	DOWNLINKING
DOMINATING	DOPAMINERGIC	DOUBTFULNESSES	DOWNLOADABLE
DOMINATINGLY	DOPESHEETS	DOUBTINGLY	DOWNLOADED
DOMINATION	DOPEYNESSES	DOUBTLESSLY	DOWNLOADING
DOMINATIONS	DOPINESSES	DOUBTLESSNESS	DOWNLOOKED
DOMINATIVE	DOPPELGANGER	DOUBTLESSNESSES	DOWNPLAYED
DOMINATORS	DOPPELGANGERS	DOUCENESSES	DOWNPLAYING
DOMINATRICES	DOPPLERITE	DOUCEPERES	DOWNREGULATION
DOMINATRIX	DOPPLERITES	DOUCHEBAGS	DOWNREGULATIONS
DOMINATRIXES	DORBEETLES	DOUGHFACED	DOWNRIGHTLY
DOMINEERED	DORKINESSES	DOUGHFACES	DOWNRIGHTNESS
DOMINEERING	DORMANCIES	DOUGHINESS	DOWNRIGHTNESSES
DOMINEERINGLY	DORMITIONS	DOUGHINESSES	DOWNRUSHES
DOMINEERINGNESS	DORMITIVES	DOUGHNUTLIKE	DOWNSCALED
DOMINICKER	DORMITORIES	DOUGHNUTTED	DOWNSCALES
DOMINICKERS	DORONICUMS	DOUGHNUTTING	DOWNSCALING
DOMINIQUES	DORSIBRANCHIATE	DOUGHNUTTINGS	DOWNSHIFTED
DONATARIES	DORSIFEROUS	DOUGHTIEST	DOWNSHIFTER
DONATISTIC	DORSIFIXED	DOUGHTINESS	DOWNSHIFTERS
DONATISTICAL	DORSIFLEXION	DOUGHTINESSES	DOWNSHIFTING
DONATORIES	DORSIFLEXIONS	DOULOCRACIES	DOWNSHIFTINGS
DONENESSES	DORSIGRADE	DOULOCRACY	DOWNSHIFTS
DONKEYWORK	DORSIVENTRAL	DOUPPIONIS	DOWNSIZING
DONKEYWORKS	DORSIVENTRALITY	DOURNESSES	DOWNSLIDES
DONNICKERS	DORSIVENTRALLY	DOUROUCOULI	DOWNSPOUTS
DONNISHNESS	DORSOLATERAL	DOUROUCOULIS	DOWNSTAGES
DONNISHNESSES	DORSOLUMBAR	DOVEISHNESS	DOWNSTAIRS
DONNYBROOK	DORSOVENTRAL	DOVEISHNESSES	DOWNSTAIRSES
DONNYBROOKS	DORSOVENTRALITY	DOVETAILED	DOWNSTATER
DONORSHIPS	DORSOVENTRALLY	DOVETAILING	DOWNSTATERS
DOODLEBUGS	DORTINESSES	DOVETAILINGS	DOWNSTATES
DOOHICKEYS	DOSEMETERS	DOVISHNESS	DOWNSTREAM
DOOHICKIES	DOSIMETERS	DOVISHNESSES	DOWNSTROKE
DOOMSAYERS	DOSIMETRIC	DOWDINESSES	DOWNSTROKES
DOOMSAYING	DOSIMETRICIAN	DOWELLINGS	DOWNSWINGS
DOOMSAYINGS	DOSIMETRICIANS	DOWFNESSES	DOWNTHROWS
DOOMSDAYER	DOSIMETRIES	DOWITCHERS	DOWNTOWNER
DOOMSDAYERS	DOSIMETRIST	DOWNBURSTS	DOWNTOWNERS
DOOMWATCHED	DOSIMETRISTS	DOWNCOMERS	DOWNTRENDED
DOOMWATCHER	DOSIOLOGIES	DOWNDRAFTS	DOWNTRENDING
DOOMWATCHERS	DOSOLOGIES	DOWNDRAUGHT	DOWNTRENDS
DOOMWATCHES	DOSSHOUSES	DOWNDRAUGHTS	DOWNTRODDEN
DOOMWATCHING	DOTCOMMERS	DOWNFALLEN	DOWNTURNED
DOOMWATCHINGS	DOTTINESSES	DOWNFORCES	DOWNWARDLY
DOORFRAMES	DOUBLEHEADER	DOWNGRADED	DOWNWARDNESS
DOORKEEPER	DOUBLEHEADERS	DOWNGRADES	DOWNWARDNESSES
DOORKEEPERS	DOUBLENESS	DOWNGRADING	DOWNWASHES
DOORKNOCKED	DOUBLENESSES	DOWNHEARTED	DOWNZONING
DOORKNOCKER	DOUBLESPEAK	DOWNHEARTEDLY	DOXOGRAPHER
DOORKNOCKERS	DOUBLESPEAKER	DOWNHEARTEDNESS	DOXOGRAPHERS
DOORKNOCKING	DOUBLESPEAKERS	DOWNHILLER	DOXOGRAPHIC
DOORKNOCKS	DOUBLESPEAKS	DOWNHILLERS	DOXOGRAPHIES
DOORPLATES	DOUBLETHINK	DOWNINESSES	DOXOGRAPHY
DOORSTEPPED	DOUBLETHINKS	DOWNLIFTING	DOXOLOGICAL
DOORSTEPPER	DOUBLETONS	DOWNLIGHTER	DOXOLOGICALLY
DOORSTEPPERS	DOUBLETREE	DOWNLIGHTERS	DOXOLOGIES
DOORSTEPPING	DOUBLETREES	DOWNLIGHTS	DOXORUBICIN
DOORSTEPPINGS	DOUBTFULLY	DOWNLINKED	DOXORUBICINS

DOXYCYCLINE
DOXYCYCLINES
DOZINESSES
DRABBINESS
DRABBINESSES
DRABBLINGS
DRABNESSES
DRACONIANISM
DRACONIANISMS
DRACONICALLY
DRACONISMS
DRACONITES
DRACONTIASES
DRACONTIASIS
DRACUNCULUS
DRACUNCULUSES
DRAFTINESS
DRAFTINESSES
DRAFTSMANSHIP
DRAFTSMANSHIPS
DRAFTSPERSON
DRAFTSPERSONS
DRAFTSWOMAN
DRAFTSWOMEN
DRAGGINGLY
DRAGGLETAILED
DRAGHOUNDS
DRAGONESSES
DRAGONFLIES
DRAGONHEAD
DRAGONHEADS
DRAGONISED
DRAGONISES
DRAGONISING
DRAGONISMS
DRAGONIZED
DRAGONIZES
DRAGONIZING
DRAGONLIKE
DRAGONNADE
DRAGONNADED
DRAGONNADES
DRAGONNADING
DRAGONROOT
DRAGONROOTS
DRAGOONAGE
DRAGOONAGES
DRAGOONING
DRAGSTRIPS
DRAINLAYER
DRAINLAYERS
DRAINPIPES
DRAKESTONE
DRAKESTONES
DRAMATICAL
DRAMATICALLY
DRAMATICISM
DRAMATICISMS

DRAMATISABLE
DRAMATISATION
DRAMATISATIONS
DRAMATISED
DRAMATISER
DRAMATISERS
DRAMATISES
DRAMATISING
DRAMATISTS
DRAMATIZABLE
DRAMATIZATION
DRAMATIZATIONS
DRAMATIZED
DRAMATIZER
DRAMATIZERS
DRAMATIZES
DRAMATIZING
DRAMATURGE
DRAMATURGES
DRAMATURGIC
DRAMATURGICAL
DRAMATURGICALLY
DRAMATURGIES
DRAMATURGIST
DRAMATURGISTS
DRAMATURGS
DRAMATURGY
DRAPABILITIES
DRAPABILITY
DRAPEABILITIES
DRAPEABILITY
DRAPERYING
DRASTICALLY
DRATCHELLS
DRAUGHTBOARD
DRAUGHTBOARDS
DRAUGHTERS
DRAUGHTIER
DRAUGHTIEST
DRAUGHTILY
DRAUGHTINESS
DRAUGHTINESSES
DRAUGHTING
DRAUGHTMAN
DRAUGHTMEN
DRAUGHTSMAN
DRAUGHTSMANSHIP
DRAUGHTSMEN
DRAUGHTSWOMAN
DRAUGHTSWOMEN
DRAWBRIDGE
DRAWBRIDGES
DRAWERFULS
DRAWKNIVES
DRAWLINGLY
DRAWLINGNESS
DRAWLINGNESSES
DRAWNWORKS

DRAWPLATES
DRAWSHAVES
DRAWSTRING
DRAWSTRINGS
DRAYHORSES
DREADFULLY
DREADFULNESS
DREADFULNESSES
DREADLESSLY
DREADLESSNESS
DREADLESSNESSES
DREADLOCKS
DREADNAUGHT
DREADNAUGHTS
DREADNOUGHT
DREADNOUGHTS
DREAMBOATS
DREAMERIES
DREAMFULLY
DREAMFULNESS
DREAMFULNESSES
DREAMHOLES
DREAMINESS
DREAMINESSES
DREAMINGLY
DREAMLANDS
DREAMLESSLY
DREAMLESSNESS
DREAMLESSNESSES
DREAMTIMES
DREAMWHILE
DREAMWHILES
DREAMWORLD
DREAMWORLDS
DREARIHEAD
DREARIHEADS
DREARIHOOD
DREARIHOODS
DREARIMENT
DREARIMENTS
DREARINESS
DREARINESSES
DREARISOME
DRECKSILLS
DREGGINESS
DREGGINESSES
DREIKANTER
DREIKANTERS
DRENCHINGS
DREPANIUMS
DRERIHEADS
DRESSGUARD
DRESSGUARDS
DRESSINESS
DRESSINESSES
DRESSMAKER
DRESSMAKERS
DRESSMAKES

DRESSMAKING
DRESSMAKINGS
DRIBBLIEST
DRICKSIEST
DRIFTINGLY
DRIFTWOODS
DRILLABILITIES
DRILLABILITY
DRILLMASTER
DRILLMASTERS
DRILLSHIPS
DRILLSTOCK
DRILLSTOCKS
DRINKABILITIES
DRINKABILITY
DRINKABLENESS
DRINKABLENESSES
DRINKABLES
DRIPSTONES
DRIVABILITIES
DRIVABILITY
DRIVEABILITIES
DRIVEABILITY
DRIVELINES
DRIVELLERS
DRIVELLING
DRIVENNESS
DRIVENNESSES
DRIVERLESS
DRIVESHAFT
DRIVESHAFTS
DRIVETHROUGH
DRIVETHROUGHS
DRIVETRAIN
DRIVETRAINS
DRIZZLIEST
DRIZZLINGLY
DROICHIEST
DROLLERIES
DROLLNESSES
DROMEDARES
DROMEDARIES
DROMOPHOBIA
DROMOPHOBIAS
DRONISHNESS
DRONISHNESSES
DRONKVERDRIET
DROOPINESS
DROOPINESSES
DROOPINGLY
DROPCLOTHS
DROPFORGED
DROPFORGES
DROPFORGING
DROPKICKER
DROPKICKERS
DROPLIGHTS
DROPPERFUL

DROPPERFULS	DUBIOUSNESSES	DUMFOUNDERING	DUPLICATOR
DROPPERSFUL	DUBITANCIES	DUMFOUNDERS	DUPLICATORS
DROPSICALLY	DUBITATING	DUMFOUNDING	DUPLICATURE
DROPSONDES	DUBITATION	DUMMELHEAD	DUPLICATURES
DROPSTONES	DUBITATIONS	DUMMELHEADS	DUPLICIDENT
DROSERACEOUS	DUBITATIVE	DUMMINESSES	DUPLICITIES
DROSOMETER	DUBITATIVELY	DUMORTIERITE	DUPLICITOUS
DROSOMETERS	DUCHESSING	DUMORTIERITES	DUPLICITOUSLY
DROSOPHILA	DUCKBOARDS	DUMOSITIES	DURABILITIES
DROSOPHILAE	DUCKSHOVED	DUMPINESSES	DURABILITY
DROSOPHILAS	DUCKSHOVER	DUMPISHNESS	DURABLENESS
DROSSINESS	DUCKSHOVERS	DUMPISHNESSES	DURABLENESSES
DROSSINESSES	DUCKSHOVES	DUMPTRUCKS	DURALUMINIUM
DROUGHTIER	DUCKSHOVING	DUNDERFUNK	DURALUMINIUMS
DROUGHTIEST	DUCKWALKED	DUNDERFUNKS	DURALUMINS
DROUGHTINESS	DUCKWALKING	DUNDERHEAD	DURATIONAL
DROUGHTINESSES	DUCTILENESS	DUNDERHEADED	DURCHKOMPONIERT
DROUTHIEST	DUCTILENESSES	DUNDERHEADISM	DURCHKOMPONIRT
DROUTHINESS	DUCTILITIES	DUNDERHEADISMS	DURICRUSTS
DROUTHINESSES	DUENNASHIP	DUNDERHEADS	DUROMETERS
DROWSIHEAD	DUENNASHIPS	DUNDERPATE	DUSKINESSES
DROWSIHEADS	DUFFERDOMS	DUNDERPATES	DUSKISHNESS
DROWSIHEDS	DUFFERISMS	DUNDREARIES	DUSKISHNESSES
DROWSINESS	DUIKERBOKS	DUNGEONERS	DUSKNESSES
DROWSINESSES	DUKKERIPEN	DUNGEONING	DUSTCOVERS
DRUCKENNESS	DUKKERIPENS	DUNIEWASSAL	DUSTINESSES
DRUCKENNESSES	DULCAMARAS	DUNIEWASSALS	DUSTSHEETS
DRUDGERIES	DULCETNESS	DUNIWASSAL	DUSTSTORMS
DRUDGINGLY	DULCETNESSES	DUNIWASSALS	DUTEOUSNESS
DRUGMAKERS	DULCIFICATION	DUNNIEWASSAL	DUTEOUSNESSES
DRUGSTORES	DULCIFICATIONS	DUNNIEWASSALS	DUTIABILITIES
DRUIDESSES	DULCIFLUOUS	DUODECENNIAL	DUTIABILITY
DRUMBEATER	DULCIFYING	DUODECILLION	DUTIFULNESS
DRUMBEATERS	DULCILOQUIES	DUODECILLIONS	DUTIFULNESSES
DRUMBEATING	DULCILOQUY	DUODECIMAL	DUUMVIRATE
DRUMBEATINGS	DULCIMORES	DUODECIMALLY	DUUMVIRATES
DRUMBLEDOR	DULCITUDES	DUODECIMALS	DWARFISHLY
DRUMBLEDORS	DULLNESSES	DUODECIMOS	DWARFISHNESS
DRUMBLEDRANE	DULLSVILLE	DUODENECTOMIES	DWARFISHNESSES
DRUMBLEDRANES	DULLSVILLES	DUODENECTOMY	DWARFNESSES
DRUMFISHES	DULOCRACIES	DUODENITIS	DWINDLEMENT
DRUMSTICKS	DUMBFOUNDED	DUODENITISES	DWINDLEMENTS
DRUNKATHON	DUMBFOUNDER	DUOPOLISTIC	DYADICALLY
DRUNKATHONS	DUMBFOUNDERED	DUOPSONIES	DYARCHICAL
DRUNKENNESS	DUMBFOUNDERING	DUPABILITIES	DYEABILITIES
DRUNKENNESSES	DUMBFOUNDERS	DUPABILITY	DYEABILITY
DRUPACEOUS	DUMBFOUNDING	DUPLEXITIES	DYINGNESSES
DRYASDUSTS	DUMBFOUNDS	DUPLICABILITIES	DYNAMETERS
DRYBEATING	DUMBLEDORE	DUPLICABILITY	DYNAMICALLY
DRYOPITHECINE	DUMBLEDORES	DUPLICABLE	DYNAMICIST
DRYOPITHECINES	DUMBNESSES	DUPLICANDS	DYNAMICISTS
DRYSALTERIES	DUMBSTRICKEN	DUPLICATED	DYNAMISING
DRYSALTERS	DUMBSTRUCK	DUPLICATELY	DYNAMISTIC
DRYSALTERY	DUMBWAITER	DUPLICATES	DYNAMITARD
DRYWALLING	DUMBWAITERS	DUPLICATING	DYNAMITARDS
DUALISTICALLY	DUMFOUNDED	DUPLICATION	DYNAMITERS
DUBIOSITIES	DUMFOUNDER	DUPLICATIONS	DYNAMITING
DUBIOUSNESS	DUMFOUNDERED	DUPLICATIVE	DYNAMIZING

DYNAMOELECTRIC
DYNAMOGENESES
DYNAMOGENESIS
DYNAMOGENIES
DYNAMOGENY
DYNAMOGRAPH
DYNAMOGRAPHS
DYNAMOMETER
DYNAMOMETERS
DYNAMOMETRIC
DYNAMOMETRICAL
DYNAMOMETRIES
DYNAMOMETRY
DYNAMOTORS
DYNASTICAL
DYNASTICALLY
DYNORPHINS
DYOPHYSITE
DYOPHYSITES
DYOTHELETE
DYOTHELETES
DYOTHELETIC
DYOTHELETICAL
DYOTHELETISM
DYOTHELETISMS
DYOTHELISM
DYOTHELISMS
DYOTHELITE
DYOTHELITES
DYOTHELITIC
DYOTHELITICAL
DYSAESTHESIA
DYSAESTHESIAS
DYSAESTHETIC
DYSARTHRIA
DYSARTHRIAS
DYSBINDINS
DYSCALCULIA
DYSCALCULIAS
DYSCHROIAS
DYSCRASIAS
DYSCRASITE
DYSCRASITES
DYSENTERIC
DYSENTERIES
DYSFUNCTION
DYSFUNCTIONAL
DYSFUNCTIONS
DYSGENESES
DYSGENESIS
DYSGRAPHIA
DYSGRAPHIAS
DYSGRAPHIC
DYSHARMONIC
DYSKINESIA
DYSKINESIAS
DYSKINETIC
DYSLECTICS

DYSLOGISTIC
DYSLOGISTICALLY
DYSMENORRHEA
DYSMENORRHEAL
DYSMENORRHEAS
DYSMENORRHEIC
DYSMENORRHOEA
DYSMENORRHOEAL
DYSMENORRHOEAS
DYSMENORRHOEIC
DYSMORPHIC
DYSMORPHOPHOBIA
DYSPAREUNIA
DYSPAREUNIAS
DYSPATHETIC
DYSPATHIES
DYSPEPSIAS
DYSPEPSIES
DYSPEPTICAL
DYSPEPTICALLY
DYSPEPTICS
DYSPHAGIAS
DYSPHAGIES
DYSPHASIAS
DYSPHASICS
DYSPHEMISM
DYSPHEMISMS
DYSPHEMISTIC
DYSPHONIAS
DYSPHORIAS
DYSPLASIAS
DYSPLASTIC
DYSPRAXIAS
DYSPROSIUM
DYSPROSIUMS
DYSRHYTHMIA
DYSRHYTHMIAS
DYSRHYTHMIC
DYSSYNERGIA
DYSSYNERGIAS
DYSTELEOLOGICAL
DYSTELEOLOGIES
DYSTELEOLOGIST
DYSTELEOLOGISTS
DYSTELEOLOGY
DYSTHESIAS
DYSTHYMIAC
DYSTHYMIACS
DYSTHYMIAS
DYSTHYMICS
DYSTOPIANS
DYSTROPHIA
DYSTROPHIAS
DYSTROPHIC
DYSTROPHIES
DYSTROPHIN
DYSTROPHINS
DZIGGETAIS

E

EAGERNESSES
EAGLESTONE
EAGLESTONES
EAGLEWOODS
EARBASHERS
EARBASHING
EARBASHINGS
EARLIERISE
EARLIERISED
EARLIERISES
EARLIERISING
EARLIERIZE
EARLIERIZED
EARLIERIZES
EARLIERIZING
EARLINESSES
EARLYWOODS
EARMARKING
EARNESTNESS
EARNESTNESSES
EARSPLITTING
EARTHBOUND
EARTHENWARE
EARTHENWARES
EARTHFALLS
EARTHFLAXES
EARTHINESS
EARTHINESSES
EARTHLIEST
EARTHLIGHT
EARTHLIGHTS
EARTHLINESS
EARTHLINESSES
EARTHLINGS
EARTHMOVER
EARTHMOVERS
EARTHMOVING
EARTHMOVINGS
EARTHQUAKE
EARTHQUAKED
EARTHQUAKES
EARTHQUAKING
EARTHRISES
EARTHSHAKER
EARTHSHAKERS
EARTHSHAKING
EARTHSHAKINGLY
EARTHSHATTERING
EARTHSHINE
EARTHSHINES
EARTHSTARS
EARTHWARDS
EARTHWAXES

EARTHWOLVES
EARTHWOMAN
EARTHWOMEN
EARTHWORKS
EARTHWORMS
EARWIGGING
EARWIGGINGS
EARWITNESS
EARWITNESSES
EASEFULNESS
EASEFULNESSES
EASINESSES
EASSELGATE
EASSELWARD
EASTERLIES
EASTERLING
EASTERLINGS
EASTERMOST
EASTERNERS
EASTERNMOST
EASTWARDLY
EASYGOINGNESS
EASYGOINGNESSES
EAVESDRIPS
EAVESDROPPED
EAVESDROPPER
EAVESDROPPERS
EAVESDROPPING
EAVESDROPPINGS
EAVESDROPS
EAVESTROUGH
EAVESTROUGHS
EBIONISING
EBIONITISM
EBIONITISMS
EBIONIZING
EBOULEMENT
EBOULEMENTS
EBRACTEATE
EBRACTEOLATE
EBRILLADES
EBRIOSITIES
EBULLIENCE
EBULLIENCES
EBULLIENCIES
EBULLIENCY
EBULLIENTLY
EBULLIOMETER
EBULLIOMETERS
EBULLIOMETRIES
EBULLIOMETRY
EBULLIOSCOPE
EBULLIOSCOPES

EBULLIOSCOPIC
EBULLIOSCOPICAL
EBULLIOSCOPIES
EBULLIOSCOPY
EBULLITION
EBULLITIONS
EBURNATION
EBURNATIONS
EBURNIFICATION
EBURNIFICATIONS
ECARDINATE
ECBLASTESES
ECBLASTESIS
ECCALEOBION
ECCALEOBIONS
ECCENTRICAL
ECCENTRICALLY
ECCENTRICITIES
ECCENTRICITY
ECCENTRICS
ECCHYMOSED
ECCHYMOSES
ECCHYMOSIS
ECCHYMOTIC
ECCLESIARCH
ECCLESIARCHS
ECCLESIAST
ECCLESIASTIC
ECCLESIASTICAL
ECCLESIASTICISM
ECCLESIASTICS
ECCLESIASTS
ECCLESIOLATER
ECCLESIOLATERS
ECCLESIOLATRIES
ECCLESIOLATRY
ECCLESIOLOGICAL
ECCLESIOLOGIES
ECCLESIOLOGIST
ECCLESIOLOGISTS
ECCLESIOLOGY
ECCOPROTIC
ECCOPROTICS
ECCREMOCARPUS
ECCREMOCARPUSES
ECCRINOLOGIES
ECCRINOLOGY
ECDYSIASTS
ECHELONING
ECHEVERIAS
ECHIDNINES
ECHINACEAS
ECHINOCOCCI

ECHINOCOCCOSES
ECHINOCOCCOSIS
ECHINOCOCCUS
ECHINODERM
ECHINODERMAL
ECHINODERMATOUS
ECHINODERMS
ECHIUROIDS
ECHOCARDIOGRAM
ECHOCARDIOGRAMS
ECHOGRAPHIES
ECHOGRAPHY
ECHOLALIAS
ECHOLOCATION
ECHOLOCATIONS
ECHOPRAXES
ECHOPRAXIA
ECHOPRAXIAS
ECHOPRAXIS
ECHOVIRUSES
ECLAIRCISSEMENT
ECLAMPSIAS
ECLAMPSIES
ECLECTICALLY
ECLECTICISM
ECLECTICISMS
ECLIPSISES
ECLIPTICALLY
ECOCATASTROPHE
ECOCATASTROPHES
ECOCENTRIC
ECOCLIMATE
ECOCLIMATES
ECOFEMINISM
ECOFEMINISMS
ECOFEMINIST
ECOFEMINISTS
ECOFRIENDLY
ECOLOGICAL
ECOLOGICALLY
ECOLOGISTS
ECOMMERCES
ECONOBOXES
ECONOMETRIC
ECONOMETRICAL
ECONOMETRICALLY
ECONOMETRICIAN
ECONOMETRICIANS
ECONOMETRICS
ECONOMETRIST
ECONOMETRISTS
ECONOMICAL
ECONOMICALLY

ECONOMISATION	ECTOENZYME	EDIBLENESSES	EELGRASSES
ECONOMISATIONS	ECTOENZYMES	EDIFICATION	EERINESSES
ECONOMISED	ECTOGENESES	EDIFICATIONS	EFFACEABLE
ECONOMISER	ECTOGENESIS	EDIFICATORY	EFFACEMENT
ECONOMISERS	ECTOGENETIC	EDIFYINGLY	EFFACEMENTS
ECONOMISES	ECTOGENICALLY	EDITIONING	EFFECTIBLE
ECONOMISING	ECTOGENIES	EDITORIALISE	EFFECTIVELY
ECONOMISMS	ECTOGENOUS	EDITORIALISED	EFFECTIVENESS
ECONOMISTIC	ECTOMORPHIC	EDITORIALISER	EFFECTIVENESSES
ECONOMISTS	ECTOMORPHIES	EDITORIALISERS	EFFECTIVES
ECONOMIZATION	ECTOMORPHS	EDITORIALISES	EFFECTIVITIES
ECONOMIZATIONS	ECTOMORPHY	EDITORIALISING	EFFECTIVITY
ECONOMIZED	ECTOMYCORRHIZA	EDITORIALIST	EFFECTLESS
ECONOMIZER	ECTOMYCORRHIZAE	EDITORIALISTS	EFFECTUALITIES
ECONOMIZERS	ECTOMYCORRHIZAS	EDITORIALIZE	EFFECTUALITY
ECONOMIZES	ECTOPARASITE	EDITORIALIZED	EFFECTUALLY
ECONOMIZING	ECTOPARASITES	EDITORIALIZER	EFFECTUALNESS
ECOPHOBIAS	ECTOPARASITIC	EDITORIALIZERS	EFFECTUALNESSES
ECOPHYSIOLOGIES	ECTOPHYTES	EDITORIALIZES	EFFECTUATE
ECOPHYSIOLOGY	ECTOPHYTIC	EDITORIALIZING	EFFECTUATED
ECOREGIONS	ECTOPICALLY	EDITORIALLY	EFFECTUATES
ECOSPECIES	ECTOPLASMIC	EDITORIALS	EFFECTUATING
ECOSPECIFIC	ECTOPLASMS	EDITORSHIP	EFFECTUATION
ECOSPHERES	ECTOPLASTIC	EDITORSHIPS	EFFECTUATIONS
ECOSSAISES	ECTOPROCTS	EDITRESSES	EFFEMINACIES
ECOSYSTEMS	ECTOSARCOUS	EDRIOPHTHALMIAN	EFFEMINACY
ECOTERRORISM	ECTOTHERMIC	EDRIOPHTHALMIC	EFFEMINATE
ECOTERRORISMS	ECTOTHERMS	EDRIOPHTHALMOUS	EFFEMINATED
ECOTERRORIST	ECTOTROPHIC	EDUCABILITIES	EFFEMINATELY
ECOTERRORISTS	ECTROPIONS	EDUCABILITY	EFFEMINATENESS
ECOTOURISM	ECTROPIUMS	EDUCATABILITIES	EFFEMINATES
ECOTOURISMS	ECTYPOGRAPHIES	EDUCATABILITY	EFFEMINATING
ECOTOURIST	ECTYPOGRAPHY	EDUCATABLE	EFFEMINISE
ECOTOURISTS	ECUMENICAL	EDUCATEDNESS	EFFEMINISED
ECOTOXICOLOGIES	ECUMENICALISM	EDUCATEDNESSES	EFFEMINISES
ECOTOXICOLOGIST	ECUMENICALISMS	EDUCATIONAL	EFFEMINISING
ECOTOXICOLOGY	ECUMENICALLY	EDUCATIONALIST	EFFEMINIZE
ECOTYPICALLY	ECUMENICISM	EDUCATIONALISTS	EFFEMINIZED
ECPHONESES	ECUMENICISMS	EDUCATIONALLY	EFFEMINIZES
ECPHONESIS	ECUMENICIST	EDUCATIONESE	EFFEMINIZING
ECPHRACTIC	ECUMENICISTS	EDUCATIONESES	EFFERENCES
ECPHRACTICS	ECUMENICITIES	EDUCATIONIST	EFFERENTLY
ECRITOIRES	ECUMENICITY	EDUCATIONISTS	EFFERVESCE
ECSTASISED	ECUMENISMS	EDUCATIONS	EFFERVESCED
ECSTASISES	ECUMENISTS	EDUCEMENTS	EFFERVESCENCE
ECSTASISING	ECZEMATOUS	EDULCORANT	EFFERVESCENCES
ECSTASIZED	EDACIOUSLY	EDULCORATE	EFFERVESCENCIES
ECSTASIZES	EDACIOUSNESS	EDULCORATED	EFFERVESCENCY
ECSTASIZING	EDACIOUSNESSES	EDULCORATES	EFFERVESCENT
ECSTASYING	EDAPHICALLY	EDULCORATING	EFFERVESCENTLY
ECSTATICALLY	EDAPHOLOGIES	EDULCORATION	EFFERVESCES
ECTHLIPSES	EDAPHOLOGY	EDULCORATIONS	EFFERVESCIBLE
ECTHLIPSIS	EDELWEISSES	EDULCORATIVE	EFFERVESCING
ECTOBLASTIC	EDENTULATE	EDULCORATOR	EFFERVESCINGLY
ECTOBLASTS	EDENTULOUS	EDULCORATORS	EFFETENESS
ECTOCRINES	EDGINESSES	EDUSKUNTAS	EFFETENESSES
ECTODERMAL	EDIBILITIES	EDUTAINMENT	EFFICACIES
ECTODERMIC	EDIBLENESS	EDUTAINMENTS	EFFICACIOUS

EFFICACIOUSLY
EFFICACIOUSNESS
EFFICACITIES
EFFICACITY
EFFICIENCE
EFFICIENCES
EFFICIENCIES
EFFICIENCY
EFFICIENTLY
EFFICIENTS
EFFIERCING
EFFIGURATE
EFFIGURATION
EFFIGURATIONS
EFFLEURAGE
EFFLEURAGED
EFFLEURAGES
EFFLEURAGING
EFFLORESCE
EFFLORESCED
EFFLORESCENCE
EFFLORESCENCES
EFFLORESCENT
EFFLORESCES
EFFLORESCING
EFFLUENCES
EFFLUVIUMS
EFFLUXIONS
EFFORTFULLY
EFFORTFULNESS
EFFORTFULNESSES
EFFORTLESS
EFFORTLESSLY
EFFORTLESSNESS
EFFRONTERIES
EFFRONTERY
EFFULGENCE
EFFULGENCES
EFFULGENTLY
EFFUSIOMETER
EFFUSIOMETERS
EFFUSIVELY
EFFUSIVENESS
EFFUSIVENESSES
EGALITARIAN
EGALITARIANISM
EGALITARIANISMS
EGALITARIANS
EGAREMENTS
EGGBEATERS
EGGHEADEDNESS
EGGHEADEDNESSES
EGLANDULAR
EGLANDULOSE
EGLANTINES
EGOCENTRIC
EGOCENTRICALLY
EGOCENTRICITIES

EGOCENTRICITY
EGOCENTRICS
EGOCENTRISM
EGOCENTRISMS
EGOISTICAL
EGOISTICALLY
EGOMANIACAL
EGOMANIACALLY
EGOMANIACS
EGOTHEISMS
EGOTISTICAL
EGOTISTICALLY
EGREGIOUSLY
EGREGIOUSNESS
EGREGIOUSNESSES
EGRESSIONS
EGURGITATE
EGURGITATED
EGURGITATES
EGURGITATING
EICOSANOID
EICOSANOIDS
EIDERDOWNS
EIDETICALLY
EIDOGRAPHS
EIGENFREQUENCY
EIGENFUNCTION
EIGENFUNCTIONS
EIGENMODES
EIGENTONES
EIGENVALUE
EIGENVALUES
EIGENVECTOR
EIGENVECTORS
EIGHTBALLS
EIGHTEENMO
EIGHTEENMOS
EIGHTEENTH
EIGHTEENTHLY
EIGHTEENTHS
EIGHTFOILS
EIGHTIETHS
EIGHTPENCE
EIGHTPENCES
EIGHTPENNY
EIGHTSCORE
EIGHTSCORES
EIGHTSOMES
EINSTEINIUM
EINSTEINIUMS
EIRENICALLY
EIRENICONS
EISTEDDFOD
EISTEDDFODAU
EISTEDDFODIC
EISTEDDFODS
EJACULATED
EJACULATES

EJACULATING
EJACULATION
EJACULATIONS
EJACULATIVE
EJACULATOR
EJACULATORS
EJACULATORY
EJECTAMENTA
EJECTIVELY
EJECTMENTS
EKISTICIAN
EKISTICIANS
ELABORATED
ELABORATELY
ELABORATENESS
ELABORATENESSES
ELABORATES
ELABORATING
ELABORATION
ELABORATIONS
ELABORATIVE
ELABORATOR
ELABORATORIES
ELABORATORS
ELABORATORY
ELAEOLITES
ELAEOPTENE
ELAEOPTENES
ELAIOSOMES
ELASMOBRANCH
ELASMOBRANCHS
ELASMOSAUR
ELASMOSAURS
ELASTANCES
ELASTICALLY
ELASTICATE
ELASTICATED
ELASTICATES
ELASTICATING
ELASTICATION
ELASTICATIONS
ELASTICISE
ELASTICISED
ELASTICISES
ELASTICISING
ELASTICITIES
ELASTICITY
ELASTICIZE
ELASTICIZED
ELASTICIZES
ELASTICIZING
ELASTICNESS
ELASTICNESSES
ELASTOMERIC
ELASTOMERS
ELATEDNESS
ELATEDNESSES
ELATERITES

ELATERIUMS
ELBOWROOMS
ELDERBERRIES
ELDERBERRY
ELDERCARES
ELDERLINESS
ELDERLINESSES
ELDERSHIPS
ELECAMPANE
ELECAMPANES
ELECTABILITIES
ELECTABILITY
ELECTIONEER
ELECTIONEERED
ELECTIONEERER
ELECTIONEERERS
ELECTIONEERING
ELECTIONEERINGS
ELECTIONEERS
ELECTIVELY
ELECTIVENESS
ELECTIVENESSES
ELECTIVITIES
ELECTIVITY
ELECTORALLY
ELECTORATE
ELECTORATES
ELECTORESS
ELECTORESSES
ELECTORIAL
ELECTORSHIP
ELECTORSHIPS
ELECTRESSES
ELECTRICAL
ELECTRICALLY
ELECTRICIAN
ELECTRICIANS
ELECTRICITIES
ELECTRICITY
ELECTRIFIABLE
ELECTRIFICATION
ELECTRIFIED
ELECTRIFIER
ELECTRIFIERS
ELECTRIFIES
ELECTRIFYING
ELECTRISATION
ELECTRISATIONS
ELECTRISED
ELECTRISES
ELECTRISING
ELECTRIZATION
ELECTRIZATIONS
ELECTRIZED
ELECTRIZES
ELECTRIZING
ELECTROACOUSTIC
ELECTROACTIVE

ELECTROACTIVITY	ELECTROJETS	ELECTRONVOLTS	ELECTROTYPIES
ELECTROANALYSES	ELECTROKINETIC	ELECTROOSMOSES	ELECTROTYPING
ELECTROANALYSIS	ELECTROKINETICS	ELECTROOSMOSIS	ELECTROTYPIST
ELECTROANALYTIC	ELECTROLESS	ELECTROOSMOTIC	ELECTROTYPISTS
ELECTROBIOLOGY	ELECTROLIER	ELECTROPHILE	ELECTROTYPY
ELECTROCAUTERY	ELECTROLIERS	ELECTROPHILES	ELECTROVALENCE
ELECTROCEMENT	ELECTROLOGIES	ELECTROPHILIC	ELECTROVALENCES
ELECTROCEMENTS	ELECTROLOGIST	ELECTROPHONE	ELECTROVALENCY
ELECTROCHEMIC	ELECTROLOGISTS	ELECTROPHONES	ELECTROVALENT
ELECTROCHEMICAL	ELECTROLOGY	ELECTROPHONIC	ELECTROVALENTLY
ELECTROCHEMIST	ELECTROLYSATION	ELECTROPHORESE	ELECTROWEAK
ELECTROCHEMISTS	ELECTROLYSE	ELECTROPHORESED	ELECTROWINNING
ELECTROCLASH	ELECTROLYSED	ELECTROPHORESES	ELECTROWINNINGS
ELECTROCLASHES	ELECTROLYSER	ELECTROPHORESIS	ELECTUARIES
ELECTROCULTURE	ELECTROLYSERS	ELECTROPHORETIC	ELEDOISINS
ELECTROCULTURES	ELECTROLYSES	ELECTROPHORI	ELEEMOSYNARY
ELECTROCUTE	ELECTROLYSING	ELECTROPHORUS	ELEGANCIES
ELECTROCUTED	ELECTROLYSIS	ELECTROPHORUSES	ELEGIACALLY
ELECTROCUTES	ELECTROLYTE	ELECTROPLATE	ELEMENTALISM
ELECTROCUTING	ELECTROLYTES	ELECTROPLATED	ELEMENTALISMS
ELECTROCUTION	ELECTROLYTIC	ELECTROPLATER	ELEMENTALLY
ELECTROCUTIONS	ELECTROLYTICS	ELECTROPLATERS	ELEMENTALS
ELECTROCYTE	ELECTROLYZATION	ELECTROPLATES	ELEMENTARILY
ELECTROCYTES	ELECTROLYZE	ELECTROPLATING	ELEMENTARINESS
ELECTRODEPOSIT	ELECTROLYZED	ELECTROPLATINGS	ELEMENTARY
ELECTRODEPOSITS	ELECTROLYZER	ELECTROPOLAR	ELEOPTENES
ELECTRODERMAL	ELECTROLYZERS	ELECTROPOSITIVE	ELEPHANTIASES
ELECTRODES	ELECTROLYZES	ELECTRORECEPTOR	ELEPHANTIASIC
ELECTRODIALYSES	ELECTROLYZING	ELECTRORHEOLOGY	ELEPHANTIASIS
ELECTRODIALYSIS	ELECTROMAGNET	ELECTROSCOPE	ELEPHANTINE
ELECTRODIALYTIC	ELECTROMAGNETIC	ELECTROSCOPES	ELEPHANTOID
ELECTRODYNAMIC	ELECTROMAGNETS	ELECTROSCOPIC	ELEUTHERARCH
ELECTRODYNAMICS	ELECTROMER	ELECTROSHOCK	ELEUTHERARCHS
ELECTROFISHING	ELECTROMERIC	ELECTROSHOCKS	ELEUTHERIAN
ELECTROFISHINGS	ELECTROMERISM	ELECTROSONDE	ELEUTHEROCOCCI
ELECTROFLUOR	ELECTROMERISMS	ELECTROSONDES	ELEUTHEROCOCCUS
ELECTROFLUORS	ELECTROMERS	ELECTROSTATIC	ELEUTHERODACTYL
ELECTROFORM	ELECTROMETER	ELECTROSTATICS	ELEUTHEROMANIA
ELECTROFORMED	ELECTROMETERS	ELECTROSURGERY	ELEUTHEROMANIAS
ELECTROFORMING	ELECTROMETRIC	ELECTROSURGICAL	ELEUTHEROPHOBIA
ELECTROFORMINGS	ELECTROMETRICAL	ELECTROTECHNICS	ELEUTHEROPHOBIC
ELECTROFORMS	ELECTROMETRIES	ELECTROTHERAPY	ELEVATIONAL
ELECTROGEN	ELECTROMETRY	ELECTROTHERMAL	ELEVATIONS
ELECTROGENESES	ELECTROMOTANCE	ELECTROTHERMIC	ELEVENTHLY
ELECTROGENESIS	ELECTROMOTANCES	ELECTROTHERMICS	ELFISHNESS
ELECTROGENIC	ELECTROMOTIVE	ELECTROTHERMIES	ELFISHNESSES
ELECTROGENS	ELECTROMOTOR	ELECTROTHERMY	ELICITABLE
ELECTROGILDING	ELECTROMOTORS	ELECTROTINT	ELICITATION
ELECTROGILDINGS	ELECTROMYOGRAM	ELECTROTINTS	ELICITATIONS
ELECTROGRAM	ELECTROMYOGRAMS	ELECTROTONIC	ELIGIBILITIES
ELECTROGRAMS	ELECTROMYOGRAPH	ELECTROTONUS	ELIGIBILITY
ELECTROGRAPH	ELECTRONEGATIVE	ELECTROTONUSES	ELIMINABILITIES
ELECTROGRAPHIC	ELECTRONIC	ELECTROTYPE	ELIMINABILITY
ELECTROGRAPHIES	ELECTRONICA	ELECTROTYPED	ELIMINABLE
ELECTROGRAPHS	ELECTRONICALLY	ELECTROTYPER	ELIMINANTS
ELECTROGRAPHY	ELECTRONICAS	ELECTROTYPERS	ELIMINATED
ELECTROING	ELECTRONICS	ELECTROTYPES	ELIMINATES
ELECTROJET	ELECTRONVOLT	ELECTROTYPIC	ELIMINATING

ELIMINATION	ELUVIATIONS	EMBARQUEMENTS	EMBLEMATIZE
ELIMINATIONS	ELVISHNESS	EMBARRASSABLE	EMBLEMATIZED
ELIMINATIVE	ELVISHNESSES	EMBARRASSED	EMBLEMATIZES
ELIMINATOR	ELYTRIFORM	EMBARRASSEDLY	EMBLEMATIZING
ELIMINATORS	ELYTRIGEROUS	EMBARRASSES	EMBLEMENTS
ELIMINATORY	EMACIATING	EMBARRASSING	EMBLEMISED
ELLIPSOGRAPH	EMACIATION	EMBARRASSINGLY	EMBLEMISES
ELLIPSOGRAPHS	EMACIATIONS	EMBARRASSMENT	EMBLEMISING
ELLIPSOIDAL	EMALANGENI	EMBARRASSMENTS	EMBLEMIZED
ELLIPSOIDS	EMANATIONAL	EMBARRINGS	EMBLEMIZES
ELLIPTICAL	EMANATIONS	EMBASEMENT	EMBLEMIZING
ELLIPTICALLY	EMANATISTS	EMBASEMENTS	EMBLOOMING
ELLIPTICALNESS	EMANCIPATE	EMBASSADES	EMBLOSSOMED
ELLIPTICALS	EMANCIPATED	EMBASSADOR	EMBLOSSOMING
ELLIPTICITIES	EMANCIPATES	EMBASSADORS	EMBLOSSOMS
ELLIPTICITY	EMANCIPATING	EMBASSAGES	EMBODIMENT
ELOCUTIONARY	EMANCIPATION	EMBATTLEMENT	EMBODIMENTS
ELOCUTIONIST	EMANCIPATIONIST	EMBATTLEMENTS	EMBOITEMENT
ELOCUTIONISTS	EMANCIPATIONS	EMBATTLING	EMBOITEMENTS
ELOCUTIONS	EMANCIPATIVE	EMBAYMENTS	EMBOLDENED
ELOIGNMENT	EMANCIPATOR	EMBEDDINGS	EMBOLDENER
ELOIGNMENTS	EMANCIPATORS	EMBEDMENTS	EMBOLDENERS
ELOINMENTS	EMANCIPATORY	EMBELLISHED	EMBOLDENING
ELONGATING	EMANCIPIST	EMBELLISHER	EMBOLECTOMIES
ELONGATION	EMANCIPISTS	EMBELLISHERS	EMBOLECTOMY
ELONGATIONS	EMARGINATE	EMBELLISHES	EMBOLISATION
ELOPEMENTS	EMARGINATED	EMBELLISHING	EMBOLISATIONS
ELOQUENCES	EMARGINATELY	EMBELLISHINGLY	EMBOLISING
ELOQUENTLY	EMARGINATES	EMBELLISHMENT	EMBOLISMAL
ELSEWHITHER	EMARGINATING	EMBELLISHMENTS	EMBOLISMIC
ELUCIDATED	EMARGINATION	EMBEZZLEMENT	EMBOLIZATION
ELUCIDATES	EMARGINATIONS	EMBEZZLEMENTS	EMBOLIZATIONS
ELUCIDATING	EMASCULATE	EMBEZZLERS	EMBOLIZING
ELUCIDATION	EMASCULATED	EMBEZZLING	EMBONPOINT
ELUCIDATIONS	EMASCULATES	EMBITTERED	EMBONPOINTS
ELUCIDATIVE	EMASCULATING	EMBITTERER	EMBORDERED
ELUCIDATOR	EMASCULATION	EMBITTERERS	EMBORDERING
ELUCIDATORS	EMASCULATIONS	EMBITTERING	EMBOSCATAS
ELUCIDATORY	EMASCULATIVE	EMBITTERINGS	EMBOSOMING
ELUCUBRATE	EMASCULATOR	EMBITTERMENT	EMBOSSABLE
ELUCUBRATED	EMASCULATORS	EMBITTERMENTS	EMBOSSMENT
ELUCUBRATES	EMASCULATORY	EMBLAZONED	EMBOSSMENTS
ELUCUBRATING	EMBALLINGS	EMBLAZONER	EMBOTHRIUM
ELUCUBRATION	EMBALMINGS	EMBLAZONERS	EMBOTHRIUMS
ELUCUBRATIONS	EMBALMMENT	EMBLAZONING	EMBOUCHURE
ELUSIVENESS	EMBALMMENTS	EMBLAZONMENT	EMBOUCHURES
ELUSIVENESSES	EMBANKMENT	EMBLAZONMENTS	EMBOUNDING
ELUSORINESS	EMBANKMENTS	EMBLAZONRIES	EMBOURGEOISE
ELUSORINESSES	EMBARCADERO	EMBLAZONRY	EMBOURGEOISED
ELUTRIATED	EMBARCADEROS	EMBLEMATIC	EMBOURGEOISES
ELUTRIATES	EMBARCATION	EMBLEMATICAL	EMBOURGEOISING
ELUTRIATING	EMBARCATIONS	EMBLEMATICALLY	EMBOWELING
ELUTRIATION	EMBARGOING	EMBLEMATISE	EMBOWELLED
ELUTRIATIONS	EMBARKATION	EMBLEMATISED	EMBOWELLING
ELUTRIATOR	EMBARKATIONS	EMBLEMATISES	EMBOWELMENT
ELUTRIATORS	EMBARKMENT	EMBLEMATISING	EMBOWELMENTS
ELUVIATING	EMBARKMENTS	EMBLEMATIST	EMBOWERING
ELUVIATION	EMBARQUEMENT	EMBLEMATISTS	EMBOWERMENT

EMBOWERMENTS
EMBOWMENTS
EMBRACEABLE
EMBRACEMENT
EMBRACEMENTS
EMBRACEORS
EMBRACERIES
EMBRACINGLY
EMBRACINGNESS
EMBRACINGNESSES
EMBRAIDING
EMBRANCHMENT
EMBRANCHMENTS
EMBRANGLED
EMBRANGLEMENT
EMBRANGLEMENTS
EMBRANGLES
EMBRANGLING
EMBRASURED
EMBRASURES
EMBRAZURES
EMBREADING
EMBREATHED
EMBREATHES
EMBREATHING
EMBRITTLED
EMBRITTLEMENT
EMBRITTLEMENTS
EMBRITTLES
EMBRITTLING
EMBROCATED
EMBROCATES
EMBROCATING
EMBROCATION
EMBROCATIONS
EMBROGLIOS
EMBROIDERED
EMBROIDERER
EMBROIDERERS
EMBROIDERIES
EMBROIDERING
EMBROIDERS
EMBROIDERY
EMBROILERS
EMBROILING
EMBROILMENT
EMBROILMENTS
EMBROWNING
EMBRUEMENT
EMBRUEMENTS
EMBRYECTOMIES
EMBRYECTOMY
EMBRYOGENESES
EMBRYOGENESIS
EMBRYOGENETIC
EMBRYOGENIC
EMBRYOGENIES
EMBRYOGENY

EMBRYOLOGIC
EMBRYOLOGICAL
EMBRYOLOGICALLY
EMBRYOLOGIES
EMBRYOLOGIST
EMBRYOLOGISTS
EMBRYOLOGY
EMBRYONATE
EMBRYONATED
EMBRYONICALLY
EMBRYOPHYTE
EMBRYOPHYTES
EMBRYOTOMIES
EMBRYOTOMY
EMBRYULCIA
EMBRYULCIAS
EMENDATING
EMENDATION
EMENDATIONS
EMENDATORS
EMENDATORY
EMERGENCES
EMERGENCIES
EMERGENTLY
EMETICALLY
EMETOPHOBIA
EMETOPHOBIAS
EMICATIONS
EMIGRATING
EMIGRATION
EMIGRATIONAL
EMIGRATIONIST
EMIGRATIONISTS
EMIGRATIONS
EMIGRATORY
EMINENCIES
EMINENTIAL
EMISSARIES
EMISSIVITIES
EMISSIVITY
EMITTANCES
EMMARBLING
EMMENAGOGIC
EMMENAGOGUE
EMMENAGOGUES
EMMENOLOGIES
EMMENOLOGY
EMMETROPES
EMMETROPIA
EMMETROPIAS
EMMETROPIC
EMOLLESCENCE
EMOLLESCENCES
EMOLLIATED
EMOLLIATES
EMOLLIATING
EMOLLIENCE
EMOLLIENCES

EMOLLIENTS
EMOLLITION
EMOLLITIONS
EMOLUMENTAL
EMOLUMENTARY
EMOLUMENTS
EMOTIONABLE
EMOTIONALISE
EMOTIONALISED
EMOTIONALISES
EMOTIONALISING
EMOTIONALISM
EMOTIONALISMS
EMOTIONALIST
EMOTIONALISTIC
EMOTIONALISTS
EMOTIONALITIES
EMOTIONALITY
EMOTIONALIZE
EMOTIONALIZED
EMOTIONALIZES
EMOTIONALIZING
EMOTIONALLY
EMOTIONLESS
EMOTIONLESSLY
EMOTIONLESSNESS
EMOTIVENESS
EMOTIVENESSES
EMOTIVISMS
EMOTIVITIES
EMPACKETED
EMPACKETING
EMPALEMENT
EMPALEMENTS
EMPANELING
EMPANELLED
EMPANELLING
EMPANELMENT
EMPANELMENTS
EMPANOPLIED
EMPANOPLIES
EMPANOPLYING
EMPARADISE
EMPARADISED
EMPARADISES
EMPARADISING
EMPARLAUNCE
EMPARLAUNCES
EMPASSIONATE
EMPASSIONED
EMPATHETIC
EMPATHETICALLY
EMPATHICALLY
EMPATHISED
EMPATHISES
EMPATHISING
EMPATHISTS
EMPATHIZED

EMPATHIZES
EMPATHIZING
EMPATRONED
EMPATRONING
EMPEACHING
EMPENNAGES
EMPEOPLING
EMPERISHED
EMPERISHES
EMPERISHING
EMPERISING
EMPERIZING
EMPERORSHIP
EMPERORSHIPS
EMPHASISED
EMPHASISES
EMPHASISING
EMPHASIZED
EMPHASIZES
EMPHASIZING
EMPHATICAL
EMPHATICALLY
EMPHATICALNESS
EMPHRACTIC
EMPHRACTICS
EMPHYSEMAS
EMPHYSEMATOUS
EMPHYSEMIC
EMPHYSEMICS
EMPHYTEUSES
EMPHYTEUSIS
EMPHYTEUTIC
EMPIECEMENT
EMPIECEMENTS
EMPIERCING
EMPIRICALLY
EMPIRICALNESS
EMPIRICALNESSES
EMPIRICISM
EMPIRICISMS
EMPIRICIST
EMPIRICISTS
EMPIRICUTIC
EMPLACEMENT
EMPLACEMENTS
EMPLASTERED
EMPLASTERING
EMPLASTERS
EMPLASTICS
EMPLASTRON
EMPLASTRONS
EMPLASTRUM
EMPLASTRUMS
EMPLEACHED
EMPLEACHES
EMPLEACHING
EMPLECTONS
EMPLECTUMS

EMPLONGING	EMULSIONIZE	ENCAPSULATION	ENCHANTMENT
EMPLOYABILITIES	EMULSIONIZED	ENCAPSULATIONS	ENCHANTMENTS
EMPLOYABILITY	EMULSIONIZES	ENCAPSULED	ENCHANTRESS
EMPLOYABLE	EMULSIONIZING	ENCAPSULES	ENCHANTRESSES
EMPLOYABLES	EMULSOIDAL	ENCAPSULING	ENCHARGING
EMPLOYMENT	EMUNCTIONS	ENCARNALISE	ENCHARMING
EMPLOYMENTS	EMUNCTORIES	ENCARNALISED	ENCHEASONS
EMPOISONED	ENABLEMENT	ENCARNALISES	ENCHEERING
EMPOISONING	ENABLEMENTS	ENCARNALISING	ENCHEIRIDION
EMPOISONMENT	ENACTMENTS	ENCARNALIZE	ENCHEIRIDIONS
EMPOISONMENTS	ENALAPRILS	ENCARNALIZED	ENCHILADAS
EMPOLDERED	ENAMELISTS	ENCARNALIZES	ENCHIRIDIA
EMPOLDERING	ENAMELLERS	ENCARNALIZING	ENCHIRIDION
EMPOVERISH	ENAMELLING	ENCARPUSES	ENCHIRIDIONS
EMPOVERISHED	ENAMELLINGS	ENCASEMENT	ENCHONDROMA
EMPOVERISHER	ENAMELLIST	ENCASEMENTS	ENCHONDROMAS
EMPOVERISHERS	ENAMELLISTS	ENCASHABLE	ENCHONDROMATA
EMPOVERISHES	ENAMELWARE	ENCASHMENT	ENCHONDROMATOUS
EMPOVERISHING	ENAMELWARES	ENCASHMENTS	ENCINCTURE
EMPOVERISHMENT	ENAMELWORK	ENCAUSTICALLY	ENCINCTURED
EMPOVERISHMENTS	ENAMELWORKS	ENCAUSTICS	ENCINCTURES
EMPOWERING	ENAMORADOS	ENCEPHALALGIA	ENCINCTURING
EMPOWERMENT	ENAMOURING	ENCEPHALALGIAS	ENCIPHERED
EMPOWERMENTS	ENANTIODROMIA	ENCEPHALIC	ENCIPHERER
EMPRESSEMENT	ENANTIODROMIAS	ENCEPHALIN	ENCIPHERERS
EMPRESSEMENTS	ENANTIODROMIC	ENCEPHALINE	ENCIPHERING
EMPTINESSES	ENANTIOMER	ENCEPHALINES	ENCIPHERMENT
EMPURPLING	ENANTIOMERIC	ENCEPHALINS	ENCIPHERMENTS
EMPYREUMATA	ENANTIOMERS	ENCEPHALITIC	ENCIRCLEMENT
EMPYREUMATIC	ENANTIOMORPH	ENCEPHALITIDES	ENCIRCLEMENTS
EMPYREUMATICAL	ENANTIOMORPHIC	ENCEPHALITIS	ENCIRCLING
EMPYREUMATISE	ENANTIOMORPHIES	ENCEPHALITISES	ENCIRCLINGS
EMPYREUMATISED	ENANTIOMORPHISM	ENCEPHALITOGEN	ENCLASPING
EMPYREUMATISES	ENANTIOMORPHOUS	ENCEPHALITOGENS	ENCLITICALLY
EMPYREUMATISING	ENANTIOMORPHS	ENCEPHALOCELE	ENCLOISTER
EMPYREUMATIZE	ENANTIOMORPHY	ENCEPHALOCELES	ENCLOISTERED
EMPYREUMATIZED	ENANTIOPATHIES	ENCEPHALOGRAM	ENCLOISTERING
EMPYREUMATIZES	ENANTIOPATHY	ENCEPHALOGRAMS	ENCLOISTERS
EMPYREUMATIZING	ENANTIOSES	ENCEPHALOGRAPH	ENCLOSABLE
EMULATIONS	ENANTIOSIS	ENCEPHALOGRAPHS	ENCLOSURES
EMULATIVELY	ENANTIOSTYLIES	ENCEPHALOGRAPHY	ENCLOTHING
EMULATRESS	ENANTIOSTYLOUS	ENCEPHALOID	ENCLOUDING
EMULATRESSES	ENANTIOSTYLY	ENCEPHALOMA	ENCODEMENT
EMULGENCES	ENANTIOTROPIC	ENCEPHALOMAS	ENCODEMENTS
EMULOUSNESS	ENANTIOTROPIES	ENCEPHALOMATA	ENCOIGNURE
EMULOUSNESSES	ENANTIOTROPY	ENCEPHALON	ENCOIGNURES
EMULSIFIABLE	ENARRATION	ENCEPHALONS	ENCOLOURED
EMULSIFICATION	ENARRATIONS	ENCEPHALOPATHIC	ENCOLOURING
EMULSIFICATIONS	ENARTHRODIAL	ENCEPHALOPATHY	ENCOLPIONS
EMULSIFIED	ENARTHROSES	ENCEPHALOTOMIES	ENCOLPIUMS
EMULSIFIER	ENARTHROSIS	ENCEPHALOTOMY	ENCOMENDERO
EMULSIFIERS	ENCAMPMENT	ENCEPHALOUS	ENCOMENDEROS
EMULSIFIES	ENCAMPMENTS	ENCHAINING	ENCOMIASTIC
EMULSIFYING	ENCANTHISES	ENCHAINMENT	ENCOMIASTICAL
EMULSIONISE	ENCAPSULATE	ENCHAINMENTS	ENCOMIASTICALLY
EMULSIONISED	ENCAPSULATED	ENCHANTERS	ENCOMIASTS
EMULSIONISES	ENCAPSULATES	ENCHANTING	ENCOMIENDA
EMULSIONISING	ENCAPSULATING	ENCHANTINGLY	ENCOMIENDAS

ENCOMPASSED	ENCUMBRANCE	ENDECAGONS	ENDODONTISTS
ENCOMPASSES	ENCUMBRANCER	ENDEIXISES	ENDOENZYME
ENCOMPASSING	ENCUMBRANCERS	ENDEMICALLY	ENDOENZYMES
ENCOMPASSMENT	ENCUMBRANCES	ENDEMICITIES	ENDOGAMIES
ENCOMPASSMENTS	ENCURTAINED	ENDEMICITY	ENDOGAMOUS
ENCOPRESES	ENCURTAINING	ENDEMIOLOGIES	ENDOGENIES
ENCOPRESIS	ENCURTAINS	ENDEMIOLOGY	ENDOGENOUS
ENCOPRETIC	ENCYCLICAL	ENDENIZENED	ENDOGENOUSLY
ENCOUNTERED	ENCYCLICALS	ENDENIZENING	ENDOLITHIC
ENCOUNTERER	ENCYCLOPAEDIA	ENDENIZENS	ENDOLYMPHATIC
ENCOUNTERERS	ENCYCLOPAEDIAS	ENDERGONIC	ENDOLYMPHS
ENCOUNTERING	ENCYCLOPAEDIC	ENDERMATIC	ENDOMETRIA
ENCOUNTERS	ENCYCLOPAEDISM	ENDERMICAL	ENDOMETRIAL
ENCOURAGED	ENCYCLOPAEDISMS	ENDLESSNESS	ENDOMETRIOSES
ENCOURAGEMENT	ENCYCLOPAEDIST	ENDLESSNESSES	ENDOMETRIOSIS
ENCOURAGEMENTS	ENCYCLOPAEDISTS	ENDOBIOTIC	ENDOMETRITIS
ENCOURAGER	ENCYCLOPEDIA	ENDOBLASTIC	ENDOMETRITISES
ENCOURAGERS	ENCYCLOPEDIAN	ENDOBLASTS	ENDOMETRIUM
ENCOURAGES	ENCYCLOPEDIAS	ENDOCARDIA	ENDOMITOSES
ENCOURAGING	ENCYCLOPEDIC	ENDOCARDIAC	ENDOMITOSIS
ENCOURAGINGLY	ENCYCLOPEDICAL	ENDOCARDIAL	ENDOMITOTIC
ENCOURAGINGS	ENCYCLOPEDISM	ENDOCARDITIC	ENDOMIXISES
ENCRADLING	ENCYCLOPEDISMS	ENDOCARDITIS	ENDOMORPHIC
ENCREASING	ENCYCLOPEDIST	ENDOCARDITISES	ENDOMORPHIES
ENCRIMSONED	ENCYCLOPEDISTS	ENDOCARDIUM	ENDOMORPHISM
ENCRIMSONING	ENCYSTATION	ENDOCARPAL	ENDOMORPHISMS
ENCRIMSONS	ENCYSTATIONS	ENDOCARPIC	ENDOMORPHS
ENCRINITAL	ENCYSTMENT	ENDOCENTRIC	ENDOMORPHY
ENCRINITES	ENCYSTMENTS	ENDOCHONDRAL	ENDOMYCORRHIZA
ENCRINITIC	ENDAMAGEMENT	ENDOCHYLOUS	ENDONEURIA
ENCROACHED	ENDAMAGEMENTS	ENDOCRANIA	ENDONEURIUM
ENCROACHER	ENDAMAGING	ENDOCRANIAL	ENDONUCLEASE
ENCROACHERS	ENDAMOEBAE	ENDOCRANIUM	ENDONUCLEASES
ENCROACHES	ENDAMOEBAS	ENDOCRINAL	ENDONUCLEOLYTIC
ENCROACHING	ENDANGERED	ENDOCRINES	ENDOPARASITE
ENCROACHINGLY	ENDANGERER	ENDOCRINIC	ENDOPARASITES
ENCROACHMENT	ENDANGERERS	ENDOCRINOLOGIC	ENDOPARASITIC
ENCROACHMENTS	ENDANGERING	ENDOCRINOLOGIES	ENDOPARASITISM
ENCRUSTATION	ENDANGERMENT	ENDOCRINOLOGIST	ENDOPARASITISMS
ENCRUSTATIONS	ENDANGERMENTS	ENDOCRINOLOGY	ENDOPEPTIDASE
ENCRUSTING	ENDARCHIES	ENDOCRINOPATHIC	ENDOPEPTIDASES
ENCRUSTMENT	ENDARTERECTOMY	ENDOCRINOPATHY	ENDOPEROXIDE
ENCRUSTMENTS	ENDEARINGLY	ENDOCRINOUS	ENDOPEROXIDES
ENCRYPTING	ENDEARINGNESS	ENDOCRITIC	ENDOPHAGIES
ENCRYPTION	ENDEARINGNESSES	ENDOCUTICLE	ENDOPHAGOUS
ENCRYPTIONS	ENDEARMENT	ENDOCUTICLES	ENDOPHYLLOUS
ENCULTURATE	ENDEARMENTS	ENDOCYTOSES	ENDOPHYTES
ENCULTURATED	ENDEAVORED	ENDOCYTOSIS	ENDOPHYTIC
ENCULTURATES	ENDEAVORER	ENDOCYTOTIC	ENDOPHYTICALLY
ENCULTURATING	ENDEAVORERS	ENDODERMAL	ENDOPLASMIC
ENCULTURATION	ENDEAVORING	ENDODERMIC	ENDOPLASMS
ENCULTURATIONS	ENDEAVOURED	ENDODERMIS	ENDOPLASTIC
ENCULTURATIVE	ENDEAVOURER	ENDODERMISES	ENDOPLEURA
ENCUMBERED	ENDEAVOURERS	ENDODONTAL	ENDOPLEURAS
ENCUMBERING	ENDEAVOURING	ENDODONTIC	ENDOPODITE
ENCUMBERINGLY	ENDEAVOURMENT	ENDODONTICALLY	ENDOPODITES
ENCUMBERMENT	ENDEAVOURMENTS	ENDODONTICS	ENDOPOLYPLOID
ENCUMBERMENTS	ENDEAVOURS	ENDODONTIST	ENDOPOLYPLOIDY

ENDOPROCTS	ENDOTRACHEAL	ENFORCEMENT	ENGRAFTMENT
ENDORADIOSONDE	ENDOTROPHIC	ENFORCEMENTS	ENGRAFTMENTS
ENDORADIOSONDES	ENDOWMENTS	ENFORESTED	ENGRAILING
ENDORHIZAL	ENDPLAYING	ENFORESTING	ENGRAILMENT
ENDORPHINS	ENDUNGEONED	ENFOULDERED	ENGRAILMENTS
ENDORSABLE	ENDUNGEONING	ENFRAMEMENT	ENGRAINEDLY
ENDORSEMENT	ENDUNGEONS	ENFRAMEMENTS	ENGRAINEDNESS
ENDORSEMENTS	ENDURABILITIES	ENFRANCHISE	ENGRAINEDNESSES
ENDOSCOPES	ENDURABILITY	ENFRANCHISED	ENGRAINERS
ENDOSCOPIC	ENDURABLENESS	ENFRANCHISEMENT	ENGRAINING
ENDOSCOPICALLY	ENDURABLENESSES	ENFRANCHISER	ENGRAMMATIC
ENDOSCOPIES	ENDURANCES	ENFRANCHISERS	ENGRASPING
ENDOSCOPIST	ENDURINGLY	ENFRANCHISES	ENGRAVERIES
ENDOSCOPISTS	ENDURINGNESS	ENFRANCHISING	ENGRAVINGS
ENDOSKELETAL	ENDURINGNESSES	ENFREEDOMED	ENGRENAGES
ENDOSKELETON	ENERGETICAL	ENFREEDOMING	ENGRIEVING
ENDOSKELETONS	ENERGETICALLY	ENFREEDOMS	ENGROOVING
ENDOSMOMETER	ENERGETICS	ENFREEZING	ENGROSSEDLY
ENDOSMOMETERS	ENERGISATION	ENGAGEMENT	ENGROSSERS
ENDOSMOMETRIC	ENERGISATIONS	ENGAGEMENTS	ENGROSSING
ENDOSMOSES	ENERGISERS	ENGAGINGLY	ENGROSSINGLY
ENDOSMOSIS	ENERGISING	ENGAGINGNESS	ENGROSSMENT
ENDOSMOTIC	ENERGIZATION	ENGAGINGNESSES	ENGROSSMENTS
ENDOSMOTICALLY	ENERGIZATIONS	ENGARLANDED	ENGUARDING
ENDOSPERMIC	ENERGIZERS	ENGARLANDING	ENGULFMENT
ENDOSPERMS	ENERGIZING	ENGARLANDS	ENGULFMENTS
ENDOSPORES	ENERGUMENS	ENGARRISON	ENGULPHING
ENDOSPOROUS	ENERVATING	ENGARRISONED	ENGYSCOPES
ENDOSTEALLY	ENERVATION	ENGARRISONING	ENHANCEMENT
ENDOSTOSES	ENERVATIONS	ENGARRISONS	ENHANCEMENTS
ENDOSTOSIS	ENERVATIVE	ENGENDERED	ENHARMONIC
ENDOSTYLES	ENERVATORS	ENGENDERER	ENHARMONICAL
ENDOSULFAN	ENFACEMENT	ENGENDERERS	ENHARMONICALLY
ENDOSULFANS	ENFACEMENTS	ENGENDERING	ENHEARSING
ENDOSYMBIONT	ENFEEBLEMENT	ENGENDERMENT	ENHEARTENED
ENDOSYMBIONTS	ENFEEBLEMENTS	ENGENDERMENTS	ENHEARTENING
ENDOSYMBIOSES	ENFEEBLERS	ENGENDRURE	ENHEARTENS
ENDOSYMBIOSIS	ENFEEBLING	ENGENDRURES	ENHUNGERED
ENDOSYMBIOTIC	ENFELONING	ENGENDURES	ENHUNGERING
ENDOTHECIA	ENFEOFFING	ENGINEERED	ENHYDRITES
ENDOTHECIAL	ENFEOFFMENT	ENGINEERING	ENHYDRITIC
ENDOTHECIUM	ENFEOFFMENTS	ENGINEERINGS	ENHYDROSES
ENDOTHELIA	ENFESTERED	ENGINERIES	ENHYPOSTASIA
ENDOTHELIAL	ENFETTERED	ENGIRDLING	ENHYPOSTASIAS
ENDOTHELIOID	ENFETTERING	ENGISCOPES	ENHYPOSTATIC
ENDOTHELIOMA	ENFEVERING	ENGLACIALLY	ENHYPOSTATISE
ENDOTHELIOMAS	ENFIERCING	ENGLISHING	ENHYPOSTATISED
ENDOTHELIOMATA	ENFILADING	ENGLOOMING	ENHYPOSTATISES
ENDOTHELIUM	ENFLESHING	ENGLUTTING	ENHYPOSTATISING
ENDOTHERMAL	ENFLEURAGE	ENGORGEMENT	ENHYPOSTATIZE
ENDOTHERMIC	ENFLEURAGES	ENGORGEMENTS	ENHYPOSTATIZED
ENDOTHERMICALLY	ENFLOWERED	ENGOUEMENT	ENHYPOSTATIZES
ENDOTHERMIES	ENFLOWERING	ENGOUEMENTS	ENHYPOSTATIZING
ENDOTHERMISM	ENFOLDMENT	ENGOUMENTS	ENIGMATICAL
ENDOTHERMISMS	ENFOLDMENTS	ENGRAFFING	ENIGMATICALLY
ENDOTHERMS	ENFORCEABILITY	ENGRAFTATION	ENIGMATISE
ENDOTHERMY	ENFORCEABLE	ENGRAFTATIONS	ENIGMATISED
ENDOTOXINS	ENFORCEDLY	ENGRAFTING	ENIGMATISES

ENIGMATISING	ENNEAHEDRON	ENSCONCING	ENTAILMENT
ENIGMATIST	ENNEAHEDRONS	ENSCROLLED	ENTAILMENTS
ENIGMATISTS	ENNEANDRIAN	ENSCROLLING	ENTAMOEBAE
ENIGMATIZE	ENNEANDROUS	ENSEPULCHRE	ENTAMOEBAS
ENIGMATIZED	ENNEASTYLE	ENSEPULCHRED	ENTANGLEMENT
ENIGMATIZES	ENNOBLEMENT	ENSEPULCHRES	ENTANGLEMENTS
ENIGMATIZING	ENNOBLEMENTS	ENSEPULCHRING	ENTANGLERS
ENIGMATOGRAPHY	ENOKIDAKES	ENSERFMENT	ENTANGLING
ENJAMBEMENT	ENOKITAKES	ENSERFMENTS	ENTELECHIES
ENJAMBEMENTS	ENOLOGICAL	ENSHEATHED	ENTELLUSES
ENJAMBMENT	ENOLOGISTS	ENSHEATHES	ENTENDERED
ENJAMBMENTS	ENORMITIES	ENSHEATHING	ENTENDERING
ENJOINDERS	ENORMOUSLY	ENSHELLING	ENTERCHAUNGE
ENJOINMENT	ENORMOUSNESS	ENSHELTERED	ENTERCHAUNGED
ENJOINMENTS	ENORMOUSNESSES	ENSHELTERING	ENTERCHAUNGES
ENJOYABLENESS	ENOUNCEMENT	ENSHELTERS	ENTERCHAUNGING
ENJOYABLENESSES	ENOUNCEMENTS	ENSHIELDED	ENTERDEALE
ENJOYMENTS	ENPHYTOTIC	ENSHIELDING	ENTERDEALED
ENKEPHALIN	ENQUIRATION	ENSHRINEES	ENTERDEALES
ENKEPHALINE	ENQUIRATIONS	ENSHRINEMENT	ENTERDEALING
ENKEPHALINES	ENRAGEMENT	ENSHRINEMENTS	ENTERECTOMIES
ENKEPHALINS	ENRAGEMENTS	ENSHRINING	ENTERECTOMY
ENKERNELLED	ENRANCKLED	ENSHROUDED	ENTERITIDES
ENKERNELLING	ENRANCKLES	ENSHROUDING	ENTERITISES
ENKINDLERS	ENRANCKLING	ENSIGNCIES	ENTEROBACTERIA
ENKINDLING	ENRAPTURED	ENSIGNSHIP	ENTEROBACTERIAL
ENLACEMENT	ENRAPTURES	ENSIGNSHIPS	ENTEROBACTERIUM
ENLACEMENTS	ENRAPTURING	ENSILABILITIES	ENTEROBIASES
ENLARGEABLE	ENRAUNGING	ENSILABILITY	ENTEROBIASIS
ENLARGEDLY	ENRAVISHED	ENSILAGEING	ENTEROCELE
ENLARGEDNESS	ENRAVISHES	ENSILAGING	ENTEROCELES
ENLARGEDNESSES	ENRAVISHING	ENSLAVEMENT	ENTEROCENTESES
ENLARGEMENT	ENREGIMENT	ENSLAVEMENTS	ENTEROCENTESIS
ENLARGEMENTS	ENREGIMENTED	ENSNAREMENT	ENTEROCOCCAL
ENLARGENED	ENREGIMENTING	ENSNAREMENTS	ENTEROCOCCI
ENLARGENING	ENREGIMENTS	ENSNARLING	ENTEROCOCCUS
ENLEVEMENT	ENREGISTER	ENSORCELED	ENTEROCOEL
ENLEVEMENTS	ENREGISTERED	ENSORCELING	ENTEROCOELE
ENLIGHTENED	ENREGISTERING	ENSORCELLED	ENTEROCOELES
ENLIGHTENER	ENREGISTERS	ENSORCELLING	ENTEROCOELIC
ENLIGHTENERS	ENRHEUMING	ENSORCELLMENT	ENTEROCOELOUS
ENLIGHTENING	ENRICHMENT	ENSORCELLMENTS	ENTEROCOELS
ENLIGHTENMENT	ENRICHMENTS	ENSORCELLS	ENTEROCOLITIS
ENLIGHTENMENTS	ENROLLMENT	ENSOULMENT	ENTEROCOLITISES
ENLIGHTENS	ENROLLMENTS	ENSOULMENTS	ENTEROGASTRONE
ENLIGHTING	ENROLMENTS	ENSPHERING	ENTEROGASTRONES
ENLISTMENT	ENROUGHING	ENSTAMPING	ENTEROHEPATITIS
ENLISTMENTS	ENROUNDING	ENSTATITES	ENTEROKINASE
ENLIVENERS	ENSAMPLING	ENSTEEPING	ENTEROKINASES
ENLIVENING	ENSANGUINATED	ENSTRUCTURED	ENTEROLITH
ENLIVENMENT	ENSANGUINE	ENSWATHEMENT	ENTEROLITHS
ENLIVENMENTS	ENSANGUINED	ENSWATHEMENTS	ENTEROPATHIES
ENLUMINING	ENSANGUINES	ENSWATHING	ENTEROPATHY
ENMESHMENT	ENSANGUINING	ENSWEEPING	ENTEROPNEUST
ENMESHMENTS	ENSCHEDULE	ENTABLATURE	ENTEROPNEUSTAL
ENNEAGONAL	ENSCHEDULED	ENTABLATURES	ENTEROPNEUSTS
ENNEAHEDRA	ENSCHEDULES	ENTABLEMENT	ENTEROPTOSES
ENNEAHEDRAL	ENSCHEDULING	ENTABLEMENTS	ENTEROPTOSIS

ENTEROSTOMAL	ENTHUSIAST	ENTOPLASTRA	ENTWINEMENTS
ENTEROSTOMIES	ENTHUSIASTIC	ENTOPLASTRAL	ENTWISTING
ENTEROSTOMY	ENTHUSIASTICAL	ENTOPLASTRON	ENUCLEATED
ENTEROTOMIES	ENTHUSIASTS	ENTOPROCTS	ENUCLEATES
ENTEROTOMY	ENTHYMEMATIC	ENTOURAGES	ENUCLEATING
ENTEROTOXIN	ENTHYMEMATICAL	ENTRAILING	ENUCLEATION
ENTEROTOXINS	ENTHYMEMES	ENTRAINEMENT	ENUCLEATIONS
ENTEROVIRAL	ENTICEABLE	ENTRAINEMENTS	ENUMERABILITIES
ENTEROVIRUS	ENTICEMENT	ENTRAINERS	ENUMERABILITY
ENTEROVIRUSES	ENTICEMENTS	ENTRAINING	ENUMERABLE
ENTERPRISE	ENTICINGLY	ENTRAINMENT	ENUMERATED
ENTERPRISED	ENTICINGNESS	ENTRAINMENTS	ENUMERATES
ENTERPRISER	ENTICINGNESSES	ENTRAMMELLED	ENUMERATING
ENTERPRISERS	ENTIRENESS	ENTRAMMELLING	ENUMERATION
ENTERPRISES	ENTIRENESSES	ENTRAMMELS	ENUMERATIONS
ENTERPRISING	ENTIRETIES	ENTRANCEMENT	ENUMERATIVE
ENTERPRISINGLY	ENTITATIVE	ENTRANCEMENTS	ENUMERATOR
ENTERTAINED	ENTITLEMENT	ENTRANCEWAY	ENUMERATORS
ENTERTAINER	ENTITLEMENTS	ENTRANCEWAYS	ENUNCIABLE
ENTERTAINERS	ENTOBLASTIC	ENTRANCING	ENUNCIATED
ENTERTAINING	ENTOBLASTS	ENTRAPMENT	ENUNCIATES
ENTERTAININGLY	ENTODERMAL	ENTRAPMENTS	ENUNCIATING
ENTERTAININGS	ENTODERMIC	ENTRAPPERS	ENUNCIATION
ENTERTAINMENT	ENTOILMENT	ENTRAPPING	ENUNCIATIONS
ENTERTAINMENTS	ENTOILMENTS	ENTREASURE	ENUNCIATIVE
ENTERTAINS	ENTOMBMENT	ENTREASURED	ENUNCIATIVELY
ENTERTAKEN	ENTOMBMENTS	ENTREASURES	ENUNCIATOR
ENTERTAKES	ENTOMOFAUNA	ENTREASURING	ENUNCIATORS
ENTERTAKING	ENTOMOFAUNAE	ENTREATABLE	ENUNCIATORY
ENTERTISSUED	ENTOMOFAUNAS	ENTREATIES	ENUREDNESS
ENTHALPIES	ENTOMOLOGIC	ENTREATING	ENUREDNESSES
ENTHRALDOM	ENTOMOLOGICAL	ENTREATINGLY	ENUREMENTS
ENTHRALDOMS	ENTOMOLOGICALLY	ENTREATIVE	ENURESISES
ENTHRALLED	ENTOMOLOGIES	ENTREATMENT	ENVASSALLED
ENTHRALLER	ENTOMOLOGISE	ENTREATMENTS	ENVASSALLING
ENTHRALLERS	ENTOMOLOGISED	ENTRECHATS	ENVAULTING
ENTHRALLING	ENTOMOLOGISES	ENTRECOTES	ENVEIGLING
ENTHRALLMENT	ENTOMOLOGISING	ENTREMESSE	ENVELOPERS
ENTHRALLMENTS	ENTOMOLOGIST	ENTREMESSES	ENVELOPING
ENTHRALMENT	ENTOMOLOGISTS	ENTRENCHED	ENVELOPMENT
ENTHRALMENTS	ENTOMOLOGIZE	ENTRENCHER	ENVELOPMENTS
ENTHRONEMENT	ENTOMOLOGIZED	ENTRENCHERS	ENVENOMING
ENTHRONEMENTS	ENTOMOLOGIZES	ENTRENCHES	ENVENOMISATION
ENTHRONING	ENTOMOLOGIZING	ENTRENCHING	ENVENOMISATIONS
ENTHRONISATION	ENTOMOLOGY	ENTRENCHMENT	ENVENOMIZATION
ENTHRONISATIONS	ENTOMOPHAGIES	ENTRENCHMENTS	ENVENOMIZATIONS
ENTHRONISE	ENTOMOPHAGOUS	ENTREPRENEUR	ENVERMEILED
ENTHRONISED	ENTOMOPHAGY	ENTREPRENEURIAL	ENVERMEILING
ENTHRONISES	ENTOMOPHILIES	ENTREPRENEURS	ENVERMEILS
ENTHRONISING	ENTOMOPHILOUS	ENTREPRENEUSE	ENVIABLENESS
ENTHRONIZATION	ENTOMOPHILY	ENTREPRENEUSES	ENVIABLENESSES
ENTHRONIZATIONS	ENTOMOSTRACAN	ENTROPICALLY	ENVIOUSNESS
ENTHRONIZE	ENTOMOSTRACANS	ENTROPIONS	ENVIOUSNESSES
ENTHRONIZED	ENTOMOSTRACOUS	ENTROPIUMS	ENVIRONICS
ENTHRONIZES	ENTOPHYTAL	ENTRUSTING	ENVIRONING
ENTHRONIZING	ENTOPHYTES	ENTRUSTMENT	ENVIRONMENT
ENTHUSIASM	ENTOPHYTIC	ENTRUSTMENTS	ENVIRONMENTAL
ENTHUSIASMS	ENTOPHYTOUS	ENTWINEMENT	ENVIRONMENTALLY

ENVIRONMENTS	EPEIROGENIC	EPICUREANISM	EPIGENESIS
ENVISAGEMENT	EPEIROGENICALLY	EPICUREANISMS	EPIGENESIST
ENVISAGEMENTS	EPEIROGENIES	EPICUREANS	EPIGENESISTS
ENVISAGING	EPEIROGENY	EPICURISED	EPIGENETIC
ENVISIONED	EPENCEPHALA	EPICURISES	EPIGENETICALLY
ENVISIONING	EPENCEPHALIC	EPICURISING	EPIGENETICIST
ENVOYSHIPS	EPENCEPHALON	EPICURISMS	EPIGENETICISTS
ENWALLOWED	EPENCEPHALONS	EPICURIZED	EPIGENETICS
ENWALLOWING	EPENTHESES	EPICURIZES	EPIGENISTS
ENWHEELING	EPENTHESIS	EPICURIZING	EPIGLOTTAL
ENWRAPMENT	EPENTHETIC	EPICUTICLE	EPIGLOTTIC
ENWRAPMENTS	EPEOLATRIES	EPICUTICLES	EPIGLOTTIDES
ENWRAPPING	EPEXEGESES	EPICUTICULAR	EPIGLOTTIS
ENWRAPPINGS	EPEXEGESIS	EPICYCLICAL	EPIGLOTTISES
ENWREATHED	EPEXEGETIC	EPICYCLOID	EPIGNATHOUS
ENWREATHES	EPEXEGETICAL	EPICYCLOIDAL	EPIGONISMS
ENWREATHING	EPEXEGETICALLY	EPICYCLOIDS	EPIGRAMMATIC
ENZOOTICALLY	EPHEBOPHILIA	EPIDEICTIC	EPIGRAMMATICAL
ENZYMATICALLY	EPHEBOPHILIAS	EPIDEICTICAL	EPIGRAMMATISE
ENZYMICALLY	EPHEDRINES	EPIDEMICAL	EPIGRAMMATISED
ENZYMOLOGICAL	EPHEMERALITIES	EPIDEMICALLY	EPIGRAMMATISER
ENZYMOLOGIES	EPHEMERALITY	EPIDEMICITIES	EPIGRAMMATISERS
ENZYMOLOGIST	EPHEMERALLY	EPIDEMICITY	EPIGRAMMATISES
ENZYMOLOGISTS	EPHEMERALNESS	EPIDEMIOLOGIC	EPIGRAMMATISING
ENZYMOLOGY	EPHEMERALNESSES	EPIDEMIOLOGICAL	EPIGRAMMATISM
ENZYMOLYSES	EPHEMERALS	EPIDEMIOLOGIES	EPIGRAMMATISMS
ENZYMOLYSIS	EPHEMERIDES	EPIDEMIOLOGIST	EPIGRAMMATIST
ENZYMOLYTIC	EPHEMERIDIAN	EPIDEMIOLOGISTS	EPIGRAMMATISTS
EOHIPPUSES	EPHEMERIDS	EPIDEMIOLOGY	EPIGRAMMATIZE
EOSINOPHIL	EPHEMERIST	EPIDENDRONE	EPIGRAMMATIZED
EOSINOPHILE	EPHEMERISTS	EPIDENDRONES	EPIGRAMMATIZER
EOSINOPHILES	EPHEMERONS	EPIDENDRUM	EPIGRAMMATIZERS
EOSINOPHILIA	EPHEMEROPTERAN	EPIDENDRUMS	EPIGRAMMATIZES
EOSINOPHILIAS	EPHEMEROPTERANS	EPIDERMISES	EPIGRAMMATIZING
EOSINOPHILIC	EPHEMEROUS	EPIDERMOID	EPIGRAPHED
EOSINOPHILOUS	EPHORALTIES	EPIDERMOLYSES	EPIGRAPHER
EOSINOPHILS	EPIBLASTIC	EPIDERMOLYSIS	EPIGRAPHERS
EPAGOMENAL	EPICALYCES	EPIDIASCOPE	EPIGRAPHIC
EPANADIPLOSES	EPICALYXES	EPIDIASCOPES	EPIGRAPHICAL
EPANADIPLOSIS	EPICANTHIC	EPIDIDYMAL	EPIGRAPHICALLY
EPANALEPSES	EPICANTHUS	EPIDIDYMIDES	EPIGRAPHIES
EPANALEPSIS	EPICARDIAC	EPIDIDYMIS	EPIGRAPHING
EPANALEPTIC	EPICARDIAL	EPIDIDYMITIS	EPIGRAPHIST
EPANAPHORA	EPICARDIUM	EPIDIDYMITISES	EPIGRAPHISTS
EPANAPHORAL	EPICENISMS	EPIDIORITE	EPILATIONS
EPANAPHORAS	EPICENTERS	EPIDIORITES	EPILEPSIES
EPANODOSES	EPICENTRAL	EPIDOSITES	EPILEPTICAL
EPANORTHOSES	EPICENTRES	EPIDOTISATION	EPILEPTICALLY
EPANORTHOSIS	EPICENTRUM	EPIDOTISATIONS	EPILEPTICS
EPANORTHOTIC	EPICHEIREMA	EPIDOTISED	EPILEPTIFORM
EPARCHATES	EPICHEIREMAS	EPIDOTIZATION	EPILEPTOGENIC
EPAULEMENT	EPICHLOROHYDRIN	EPIDOTIZATIONS	EPILEPTOID
EPAULEMENTS	EPICONDYLE	EPIDOTIZED	EPILIMNION
EPAULETTED	EPICONDYLES	EPIGASTRIA	EPILIMNIONS
EPAULETTES	EPICONDYLITIS	EPIGASTRIAL	EPILOBIUMS
EPEIROGENESES	EPICONDYLITISES	EPIGASTRIC	EPILOGISED
EPEIROGENESIS	EPICONTINENTAL	EPIGASTRIUM	EPILOGISES
EPEIROGENETIC	EPICRANIUM	EPIGENESES	EPILOGISING

EPILOGISTIC
EPILOGISTS
EPILOGIZED
EPILOGIZES
EPILOGIZING
EPILOGUING
EPILOGUISE
EPILOGUISED
EPILOGUISES
EPILOGUISING
EPILOGUIZE
EPILOGUIZED
EPILOGUIZES
EPILOGUIZING
EPIMELETIC
EPIMERASES
EPIMERISMS
EPIMORPHIC
EPIMORPHOSES
EPIMORPHOSIS
EPINASTICALLY
EPINASTIES
EPINEPHRIN
EPINEPHRINE
EPINEPHRINES
EPINEPHRINS
EPINEURIAL
EPINEURIUM
EPINEURIUMS
EPINICIONS
EPINIKIONS
EPIPELAGIC
EPIPETALOUS
EPIPHANIES
EPIPHANOUS
EPIPHENOMENA
EPIPHENOMENAL
EPIPHENOMENALLY
EPIPHENOMENON
EPIPHONEMA
EPIPHONEMAS
EPIPHRAGMS
EPIPHYLLOUS
EPIPHYSEAL
EPIPHYSIAL
EPIPHYTICAL
EPIPHYTICALLY
EPIPHYTISM
EPIPHYTISMS
EPIPHYTOLOGIES
EPIPHYTOLOGY
EPIPHYTOTIC
EPIPHYTOTICS
EPIPLASTRA
EPIPLASTRAL
EPIPLASTRON
EPIPOLISMS
EPIROGENETIC

EPIROGENIC
EPIROGENIES
EPIRRHEMAS
EPIRRHEMATIC
EPISCOPACIES
EPISCOPACY
EPISCOPALIAN
EPISCOPALIANISM
EPISCOPALIANS
EPISCOPALISM
EPISCOPALISMS
EPISCOPALLY
EPISCOPANT
EPISCOPANTS
EPISCOPATE
EPISCOPATED
EPISCOPATES
EPISCOPATING
EPISCOPIES
EPISCOPISE
EPISCOPISED
EPISCOPISES
EPISCOPISING
EPISCOPIZE
EPISCOPIZED
EPISCOPIZES
EPISCOPIZING
EPISEMATIC
EPISEPALOUS
EPISIOTOMIES
EPISIOTOMY
EPISODICAL
EPISODICALLY
EPISOMALLY
EPISPASTIC
EPISPASTICS
EPISTASIES
EPISTAXISES
EPISTEMICALLY
EPISTEMICS
EPISTEMOLOGICAL
EPISTEMOLOGIES
EPISTEMOLOGIST
EPISTEMOLOGISTS
EPISTEMOLOGY
EPISTERNAL
EPISTERNUM
EPISTERNUMS
EPISTILBITE
EPISTILBITES
EPISTOLARIAN
EPISTOLARIANS
EPISTOLARIES
EPISTOLARY
EPISTOLATORY
EPISTOLERS
EPISTOLETS
EPISTOLICAL

EPISTOLISE
EPISTOLISED
EPISTOLISES
EPISTOLISING
EPISTOLIST
EPISTOLISTS
EPISTOLIZE
EPISTOLIZED
EPISTOLIZES
EPISTOLIZING
EPISTOLOGRAPHY
EPISTROPHE
EPISTROPHES
EPITAPHERS
EPITAPHIAL
EPITAPHIAN
EPITAPHING
EPITAPHIST
EPITAPHISTS
EPITAXIALLY
EPITHALAMIA
EPITHALAMIC
EPITHALAMION
EPITHALAMIUM
EPITHALAMIUMS
EPITHELIAL
EPITHELIALISE
EPITHELIALISED
EPITHELIALISES
EPITHELIALISING
EPITHELIALIZE
EPITHELIALIZED
EPITHELIALIZES
EPITHELIALIZING
EPITHELIOID
EPITHELIOMA
EPITHELIOMAS
EPITHELIOMATA
EPITHELIOMATOUS
EPITHELISATION
EPITHELISATIONS
EPITHELISE
EPITHELISED
EPITHELISES
EPITHELISING
EPITHELIUM
EPITHELIUMS
EPITHELIZATION
EPITHELIZATIONS
EPITHELIZE
EPITHELIZED
EPITHELIZES
EPITHELIZING
EPITHEMATA
EPITHERMAL
EPITHETICAL
EPITHETING
EPITHETONS

EPITHYMETIC
EPITOMICAL
EPITOMISATION
EPITOMISATIONS
EPITOMISED
EPITOMISER
EPITOMISERS
EPITOMISES
EPITOMISING
EPITOMISTS
EPITOMIZATION
EPITOMIZATIONS
EPITOMIZED
EPITOMIZER
EPITOMIZERS
EPITOMIZES
EPITOMIZING
EPITRACHELION
EPITRACHELIONS
EPITROCHOID
EPITROCHOIDS
EPIZEUXISES
EPIZOOTICALLY
EPIZOOTICS
EPIZOOTIES
EPIZOOTIOLOGIC
EPIZOOTIOLOGIES
EPIZOOTIOLOGY
EPONYCHIUM
EPONYCHIUMS
EPONYMOUSLY
EPOXIDATION
EPOXIDATIONS
EPOXIDISED
EPOXIDISES
EPOXIDISING
EPOXIDIZED
EPOXIDIZES
EPOXIDIZING
EPROUVETTE
EPROUVETTES
EPULATIONS
EPURATIONS
EQUABILITIES
EQUABILITY
EQUABLENESS
EQUABLENESSES
EQUALISATION
EQUALISATIONS
EQUALISERS
EQUALISING
EQUALITARIAN
EQUALITARIANISM
EQUALITARIANS
EQUALITIES
EQUALIZATION
EQUALIZATIONS
EQUALIZERS

EQUALIZING
EQUALNESSES
EQUANIMITIES
EQUANIMITY
EQUANIMOUS
EQUANIMOUSLY
EQUATABILITIES
EQUATABILITY
EQUATIONAL
EQUATIONALLY
EQUATORIAL
EQUATORIALLY
EQUATORIALS
EQUATORWARD
EQUESTRIAN
EQUESTRIANISM
EQUESTRIANISMS
EQUESTRIANS
EQUESTRIENNE
EQUESTRIENNES
EQUIANGULAR
EQUIANGULARITY
EQUIBALANCE
EQUIBALANCED
EQUIBALANCES
EQUIBALANCING
EQUICALORIC
EQUIDIFFERENT
EQUIDISTANCE
EQUIDISTANCES
EQUIDISTANT
EQUIDISTANTLY
EQUILATERAL
EQUILATERALLY
EQUILATERALS
EQUILIBRANT
EQUILIBRANTS
EQUILIBRATE
EQUILIBRATED
EQUILIBRATES
EQUILIBRATING
EQUILIBRATION
EQUILIBRATIONS
EQUILIBRATOR
EQUILIBRATORS
EQUILIBRATORY
EQUILIBRIA
EQUILIBRIST
EQUILIBRISTIC
EQUILIBRISTS
EQUILIBRITIES
EQUILIBRITY
EQUILIBRIUM
EQUILIBRIUMS
EQUIMOLECULAR
EQUIMULTIPLE
EQUIMULTIPLES
EQUINITIES

EQUINOCTIAL
EQUINOCTIALLY
EQUINOCTIALS
EQUINUMEROUS
EQUIPAGING
EQUIPARATE
EQUIPARATED
EQUIPARATES
EQUIPARATING
EQUIPARATION
EQUIPARATIONS
EQUIPARTITION
EQUIPARTITIONS
EQUIPMENTS
EQUIPOISED
EQUIPOISES
EQUIPOISING
EQUIPOLLENCE
EQUIPOLLENCES
EQUIPOLLENCIES
EQUIPOLLENCY
EQUIPOLLENT
EQUIPOLLENTLY
EQUIPOLLENTS
EQUIPONDERANCE
EQUIPONDERANCES
EQUIPONDERANCY
EQUIPONDERANT
EQUIPONDERATE
EQUIPONDERATED
EQUIPONDERATES
EQUIPONDERATING
EQUIPOTENT
EQUIPOTENTIAL
EQUIPROBABILITY
EQUIPROBABLE
EQUISETACEOUS
EQUISETIFORM
EQUISETUMS
EQUITABILITIES
EQUITABILITY
EQUITABLENESS
EQUITABLENESSES
EQUITATION
EQUITATIONS
EQUIVALENCE
EQUIVALENCES
EQUIVALENCIES
EQUIVALENCY
EQUIVALENT
EQUIVALENTLY
EQUIVALENTS
EQUIVOCALITIES
EQUIVOCALITY
EQUIVOCALLY
EQUIVOCALNESS
EQUIVOCALNESSES
EQUIVOCATE

EQUIVOCATED
EQUIVOCATES
EQUIVOCATING
EQUIVOCATINGLY
EQUIVOCATION
EQUIVOCATIONS
EQUIVOCATOR
EQUIVOCATORS
EQUIVOCATORY
EQUIVOQUES
ERADIATING
ERADIATION
ERADIATIONS
ERADICABLE
ERADICABLY
ERADICANTS
ERADICATED
ERADICATES
ERADICATING
ERADICATION
ERADICATIONS
ERADICATIVE
ERADICATOR
ERADICATORS
ERASABILITIES
ERASABILITY
ERASEMENTS
ERECTILITIES
ERECTILITY
ERECTNESSES
EREMACAUSES
EREMACAUSIS
EREMITICAL
EREMITISMS
EREMURUSES
ERETHISMIC
ERETHISTIC
ERGASTOPLASM
ERGASTOPLASMIC
ERGASTOPLASMS
ERGATANDROMORPH
ERGATANERS
ERGATIVITIES
ERGATIVITY
ERGATOCRACIES
ERGATOCRACY
ERGATOGYNE
ERGATOGYNES
ERGATOMORPH
ERGATOMORPHIC
ERGATOMORPHS
ERGODICITIES
ERGODICITY
ERGOGRAPHS
ERGOMANIAC
ERGOMANIACS
ERGOMANIAS
ERGOMETERS

ERGOMETRIC
ERGOMETRIES
ERGONOMICALLY
ERGONOMICS
ERGONOMIST
ERGONOMISTS
ERGONOVINE
ERGONOVINES
ERGOPHOBIA
ERGOPHOBIAS
ERGOSTEROL
ERGOSTEROLS
ERGOTAMINE
ERGOTAMINES
ERGOTISING
ERGOTIZING
ERICACEOUS
ERINACEOUS
ERIOMETERS
ERIOPHOROUS
ERIOPHORUM
ERIOPHORUMS
ERIOPHYIDS
ERIOSTEMON
ERIOSTEMONS
ERISTICALLY
ERODIBILITIES
ERODIBILITY
EROGENEITIES
EROGENEITY
EROSIONALLY
EROSIVENESS
EROSIVENESSES
EROSIVITIES
EROTICALLY
EROTICISATION
EROTICISATIONS
EROTICISED
EROTICISES
EROTICISING
EROTICISMS
EROTICISTS
EROTICIZATION
EROTICIZATIONS
EROTICIZED
EROTICIZES
EROTICIZING
EROTISATION
EROTISATIONS
EROTIZATION
EROTIZATIONS
EROTOGENIC
EROTOGENOUS
EROTOLOGICAL
EROTOLOGIES
EROTOLOGIST
EROTOLOGISTS
EROTOMANIA

EROTOMANIAC	ERYTHROCYTES	ESCHATOLOGY	ESSENTIALIST
EROTOMANIACS	ERYTHROCYTIC	ESCHEATABLE	ESSENTIALISTS
EROTOMANIAS	ERYTHROMELALGIA	ESCHEATAGE	ESSENTIALITIES
EROTOPHOBIA	ERYTHROMYCIN	ESCHEATAGES	ESSENTIALITY
EROTOPHOBIAS	ERYTHROMYCINS	ESCHEATING	ESSENTIALIZE
ERRANTRIES	ERYTHRONIUM	ESCHEATMENT	ESSENTIALIZED
ERRATICALLY	ERYTHRONIUMS	ESCHEATMENTS	ESSENTIALIZES
ERRATICISM	ERYTHROPENIA	ESCHEATORS	ESSENTIALIZING
ERRATICISMS	ERYTHROPENIAS	ESCHSCHOLTZIA	ESSENTIALLY
ERRONEOUSLY	ERYTHROPHOBIA	ESCHSCHOLTZIAS	ESSENTIALNESS
ERRONEOUSNESS	ERYTHROPHOBIAS	ESCHSCHOLZIA	ESSENTIALNESSES
ERRONEOUSNESSES	ERYTHROPOIESES	ESCHSCHOLZIAS	ESSENTIALS
ERUBESCENCE	ERYTHROPOIESIS	ESCLANDRES	ESTABLISHABLE
ERUBESCENCES	ERYTHROPOIETIC	ESCOPETTES	ESTABLISHED
ERUBESCENCIES	ERYTHROPOIETIN	ESCORTAGES	ESTABLISHER
ERUBESCENCY	ERYTHROPOIETINS	ESCRIBANOS	ESTABLISHERS
ERUBESCENT	ERYTHROPSIA	ESCRITOIRE	ESTABLISHES
ERUBESCITE	ERYTHROPSIAS	ESCRITOIRES	ESTABLISHING
ERUBESCITES	ERYTHROSIN	ESCRITORIAL	ESTABLISHMENT
ERUCTATING	ERYTHROSINE	ESCUTCHEON	ESTABLISHMENTS
ERUCTATION	ERYTHROSINES	ESCUTCHEONED	ESTAFETTES
ERUCTATIONS	ERYTHROSINS	ESCUTCHEONS	ESTAMINETS
ERUCTATIVE	ESCADRILLE	ESEMPLASIES	ESTANCIERO
ERUDITENESS	ESCADRILLES	ESEMPLASTIC	ESTANCIEROS
ERUDITENESSES	ESCALADERS	ESOPHAGEAL	ESTATESMAN
ERUDITIONS	ESCALADING	ESOPHAGOSCOPE	ESTATESMEN
ERUPTIONAL	ESCALADOES	ESOPHAGOSCOPES	ESTERIFICATION
ERUPTIVELY	ESCALATING	ESOPHAGUSES	ESTERIFICATIONS
ERUPTIVENESS	ESCALATION	ESOTERICALLY	ESTERIFIED
ERUPTIVENESSES	ESCALATIONS	ESOTERICISM	ESTERIFIES
ERUPTIVITIES	ESCALATORS	ESOTERICISMS	ESTERIFYING
ERUPTIVITY	ESCALATORY	ESOTERICIST	ESTHESIOGEN
ERVALENTAS	ESCALLONIA	ESOTERICISTS	ESTHESIOGENS
ERYSIPELAS	ESCALLONIAS	ESOTERISMS	ESTHESISES
ERYSIPELASES	ESCALLOPED	ESOTROPIAS	ESTHETICAL
ERYSIPELATOUS	ESCALLOPING	ESPADRILLE	ESTHETICALLY
ERYSIPELOID	ESCALOPING	ESPADRILLES	ESTHETICIAN
ERYSIPELOIDS	ESCAMOTAGE	ESPAGNOLES	ESTHETICIANS
ERYTHEMATIC	ESCAMOTAGES	ESPAGNOLETTE	ESTHETICISM
ERYTHEMATOUS	ESCAPADOES	ESPAGNOLETTES	ESTHETICISMS
ERYTHORBATE	ESCAPELESS	ESPALIERED	ESTIMABLENESS
ERYTHORBATES	ESCAPEMENT	ESPALIERING	ESTIMABLENESSES
ERYTHRAEMIA	ESCAPEMENTS	ESPECIALLY	ESTIMATING
ERYTHRAEMIAS	ESCAPOLOGIES	ESPERANCES	ESTIMATION
ERYTHREMIA	ESCAPOLOGIST	ESPIEGLERIE	ESTIMATIONS
ERYTHREMIAS	ESCAPOLOGISTS	ESPIEGLERIES	ESTIMATIVE
ERYTHRINAS	ESCAPOLOGY	ESPIONAGES	ESTIMATORS
ERYTHRISMAL	ESCARMOUCHE	ESPLANADES	ESTIPULATE
ERYTHRISMS	ESCARMOUCHES	ESPRESSIVO	ESTIVATING
ERYTHRISTIC	ESCARPMENT	ESQUIRESSES	ESTIVATION
ERYTHRITES	ESCARPMENTS	ESSAYETTES	ESTIVATIONS
ERYTHRITIC	ESCHAROTIC	ESSAYISTIC	ESTIVATORS
ERYTHRITOL	ESCHAROTICS	ESSENTIALISE	ESTOPPAGES
ERYTHRITOLS	ESCHATOLOGIC	ESSENTIALISED	ESTRADIOLS
ERYTHROBLAST	ESCHATOLOGICAL	ESSENTIALISES	ESTRAMAZONE
ERYTHROBLASTIC	ESCHATOLOGIES	ESSENTIALISING	ESTRAMAZONES
ERYTHROBLASTS	ESCHATOLOGIST	ESSENTIALISM	ESTRANGEDNESS
ERYTHROCYTE	ESCHATOLOGISTS	ESSENTIALISMS	ESTRANGEDNESSES

ESTRANGELO	ETHEREALITIES	ETHNOGRAPHIC	ETYMOLOGISED
ESTRANGELOS	ETHEREALITY	ETHNOGRAPHICA	ETYMOLOGISES
ESTRANGEMENT	ETHEREALIZATION	ETHNOGRAPHICAL	ETYMOLOGISING
ESTRANGEMENTS	ETHEREALIZE	ETHNOGRAPHIES	ETYMOLOGIST
ESTRANGERS	ETHEREALIZED	ETHNOGRAPHY	ETYMOLOGISTS
ESTRANGHELO	ETHEREALIZES	ETHNOHISTORIAN	ETYMOLOGIZE
ESTRANGHELOS	ETHEREALIZING	ETHNOHISTORIANS	ETYMOLOGIZED
ESTRANGING	ETHEREALLY	ETHNOHISTORIC	ETYMOLOGIZES
ESTRAPADES	ETHEREALNESS	ETHNOHISTORICAL	ETYMOLOGIZING
ESTREATING	ETHEREALNESSES	ETHNOHISTORIES	EUBACTERIA
ESTREPEMENT	ETHERIFICATION	ETHNOHISTORY	EUBACTERIUM
ESTREPEMENTS	ETHERIFICATIONS	ETHNOLINGUIST	EUCALYPTOL
ESTRILDIDS	ETHERIFIED	ETHNOLINGUISTIC	EUCALYPTOLE
ESTROGENIC	ETHERIFIES	ETHNOLINGUISTS	EUCALYPTOLES
ESTROGENICALLY	ETHERIFYING	ETHNOLOGIC	EUCALYPTOLS
ESURIENCES	ETHERISATION	ETHNOLOGICAL	EUCALYPTUS
ESURIENCIES	ETHERISATIONS	ETHNOLOGICALLY	EUCALYPTUSES
ESURIENTLY	ETHERISERS	ETHNOLOGIES	EUCARYOTES
ETEPIMELETIC	ETHERISING	ETHNOLOGIST	EUCARYOTIC
ETERNALISATION	ETHERIZATION	ETHNOLOGISTS	EUCHARISES
ETERNALISATIONS	ETHERIZATIONS	ETHNOMUSICOLOGY	EUCHARISTIC
ETERNALISE	ETHERIZERS	ETHNOSCIENCE	EUCHARISTICAL
ETERNALISED	ETHERIZING	ETHNOSCIENCES	EUCHLORINE
ETERNALISES	ETHEROMANIA	ETHOLOGICAL	EUCHLORINES
ETERNALISING	ETHEROMANIAC	ETHOLOGICALLY	EUCHLORINS
ETERNALIST	ETHEROMANIACS	ETHOLOGIES	EUCHOLOGIA
ETERNALISTS	ETHEROMANIAS	ETHOLOGIST	EUCHOLOGIES
ETERNALITIES	ETHICALITIES	ETHOLOGISTS	EUCHOLOGION
ETERNALITY	ETHICALITY	ETHOXYETHANE	EUCHROMATIC
ETERNALIZATION	ETHICALNESS	ETHOXYETHANES	EUCHROMATIN
ETERNALIZATIONS	ETHICALNESSES	ETHYLAMINE	EUCHROMATINS
ETERNALIZE	ETHICISING	ETHYLAMINES	EUCRYPHIAS
ETERNALIZED	ETHICIZING	ETHYLATING	EUDAEMONIA
ETERNALIZES	ETHIONAMIDE	ETHYLATION	EUDAEMONIAS
ETERNALIZING	ETHIONAMIDES	ETHYLATIONS	EUDAEMONIC
ETERNALNESS	ETHIONINES	ETHYLBENZENE	EUDAEMONICS
ETERNALNESSES	ETHNARCHIES	ETHYLBENZENES	EUDAEMONIES
ETERNISATION	ETHNICALLY	ETIOLATING	EUDAEMONISM
ETERNISATIONS	ETHNICISMS	ETIOLATION	EUDAEMONISMS
ETERNISING	ETHNICITIES	ETIOLATIONS	EUDAEMONIST
ETERNITIES	ETHNOBIOLOGIES	ETIOLOGICAL	EUDAEMONISTIC
ETERNIZATION	ETHNOBIOLOGY	ETIOLOGICALLY	EUDAEMONISTICAL
ETERNIZATIONS	ETHNOBOTANICAL	ETIOLOGIES	EUDAEMONISTS
ETERNIZING	ETHNOBOTANIES	ETIOLOGIST	EUDAIMONISM
ETHAMBUTOL	ETHNOBOTANIST	ETIOLOGISTS	EUDAIMONISMS
ETHAMBUTOLS	ETHNOBOTANISTS	ETIQUETTES	EUDEMONIAS
ETHANEDIOIC	ETHNOBOTANY	ETONOGESTREL	EUDEMONICS
ETHANEDIOL	ETHNOCENTRIC	ETONOGESTRELS	EUDEMONISM
ETHANEDIOLS	ETHNOCENTRICITY	ETOURDERIE	EUDEMONISMS
ETHANOATES	ETHNOCENTRISM	ETOURDERIES	EUDEMONIST
ETHANOLAMINE	ETHNOCENTRISMS	ETRANGERES	EUDEMONISTIC
ETHANOLAMINES	ETHNOCIDES	ETYMOLOGICA	EUDEMONISTICAL
ETHEOSTOMINE	ETHNOGENIC	ETYMOLOGICAL	EUDEMONISTS
ETHEREALISATION	ETHNOGENIES	ETYMOLOGICALLY	EUDIALYTES
ETHEREALISE	ETHNOGENIST	ETYMOLOGICON	EUDICOTYLEDON
ETHEREALISED	ETHNOGENISTS	ETYMOLOGICUM	EUDICOTYLEDONS
ETHEREALISES	ETHNOGRAPHER	ETYMOLOGIES	EUDIOMETER
ETHEREALISING	ETHNOGRAPHERS	ETYMOLOGISE	EUDIOMETERS

EUDIOMETRIC	EUPHAUSIDS	EURODOLLAR	EUTHYROIDS
EUDIOMETRICAL	EUPHAUSIID	EURODOLLARS	EUTRAPELIA
EUDIOMETRICALLY	EUPHAUSIIDS	EUROMARKET	EUTRAPELIAS
EUDIOMETRIES	EUPHEMISED	EUROMARKETS	EUTRAPELIES
EUDIOMETRY	EUPHEMISER	EUROPEANISE	EUTROPHICATION
EUGENECIST	EUPHEMISERS	EUROPEANISED	EUTROPHICATIONS
EUGENECISTS	EUPHEMISES	EUROPEANISES	EUTROPHIES
EUGENICALLY	EUPHEMISING	EUROPEANISING	EVACUATING
EUGENICIST	EUPHEMISMS	EUROPEANIZE	EVACUATION
EUGENICISTS	EUPHEMISTIC	EUROPEANIZED	EVACUATIONS
EUGEOSYNCLINAL	EUPHEMISTICALLY	EUROPEANIZES	EVACUATIVE
EUGEOSYNCLINE	EUPHEMISTS	EUROPEANIZING	EVACUATORS
EUGEOSYNCLINES	EUPHEMIZED	EUROPHILES	EVAGATIONS
EUGLENOIDS	EUPHEMIZER	EUROPHILIA	EVAGINATED
EUGLOBULIN	EUPHEMIZERS	EUROPHILIAS	EVAGINATES
EUGLOBULINS	EUPHEMIZES	EUROPHOBIA	EVAGINATING
EUHARMONIC	EUPHEMIZING	EUROPHOBIAS	EVAGINATION
EUHEMERISE	EUPHONICAL	EUROPHOBIC	EVAGINATIONS
EUHEMERISED	EUPHONICALLY	EUROTERMINAL	EVALUATING
EUHEMERISES	EUPHONIOUS	EUROTERMINALS	EVALUATION
EUHEMERISING	EUPHONIOUSLY	EURYBATHIC	EVALUATIONS
EUHEMERISM	EUPHONIOUSNESS	EURYHALINE	EVALUATIVE
EUHEMERISMS	EUPHONISED	EURYPTERID	EVALUATORS
EUHEMERIST	EUPHONISES	EURYPTERIDS	EVANESCENCE
EUHEMERISTIC	EUPHONISING	EURYPTEROID	EVANESCENCES
EUHEMERISTS	EUPHONISMS	EURYPTEROIDS	EVANESCENT
EUHEMERIZE	EUPHONIUMS	EURYTHERMAL	EVANESCENTLY
EUHEMERIZED	EUPHONIZED	EURYTHERMIC	EVANESCING
EUHEMERIZES	EUPHONIZES	EURYTHERMOUS	EVANGELIAR
EUHEMERIZING	EUPHONIZING	EURYTHERMS	EVANGELIARIES
EUKARYOTES	EUPHORBIACEOUS	EURYTHMICAL	EVANGELIARION
EUKARYOTIC	EUPHORBIAS	EURYTHMICS	EVANGELIARIONS
EULOGISERS	EUPHORBIUM	EURYTHMIES	EVANGELIARIUM
EULOGISING	EUPHORBIUMS	EUSPORANGIATE	EVANGELIARIUMS
EULOGISTIC	EUPHORIANT	EUSTATICALLY	EVANGELIARS
EULOGISTICAL	EUPHORIANTS	EUTECTOIDS	EVANGELIARY
EULOGISTICALLY	EUPHORICALLY	EUTHANASIA	EVANGELICAL
EULOGIZERS	EUPHRASIES	EUTHANASIAS	EVANGELICALISM
EULOGIZING	EUPHUISING	EUTHANASIAST	EVANGELICALISMS
EUMELANINS	EUPHUISTIC	EUTHANASIASTS	EVANGELICALLY
EUNUCHISED	EUPHUISTICAL	EUTHANASIC	EVANGELICALNESS
EUNUCHISES	EUPHUISTICALLY	EUTHANASIES	EVANGELICALS
EUNUCHISING	EUPHUIZING	EUTHANATISE	EVANGELICISM
EUNUCHISMS	EUPLASTICS	EUTHANATISED	EVANGELICISMS
EUNUCHIZED	EUPLOIDIES	EUTHANATISES	EVANGELIES
EUNUCHIZES	EURHYTHMIC	EUTHANATISING	EVANGELISATION
EUNUCHIZING	EURHYTHMICAL	EUTHANATIZE	EVANGELISATIONS
EUNUCHOIDISM	EURHYTHMICS	EUTHANATIZED	EVANGELISE
EUNUCHOIDISMS	EURHYTHMIES	EUTHANATIZES	EVANGELISED
EUNUCHOIDS	EURHYTHMIST	EUTHANATIZING	EVANGELISER
EUONYMUSES	EURHYTHMISTS	EUTHANISED	EVANGELISERS
EUPATORIUM	EUROCHEQUE	EUTHANISES	EVANGELISES
EUPATORIUMS	EUROCHEQUES	EUTHANISING	EVANGELISING
EUPATRIDAE	EUROCREEPS	EUTHANIZED	EVANGELISM
EUPEPTICITIES	EUROCURRENCIES	EUTHANIZES	EVANGELISMS
EUPEPTICITY	EUROCURRENCY	EUTHANIZING	EVANGELIST
EUPHAUSIACEAN	EURODEPOSIT	EUTHENISTS	EVANGELISTARIES
EUPHAUSIACEANS	EURODEPOSITS	EUTHERIANS	EVANGELISTARION

EVANGELISTARY	EVENTUALIZE	EVOLUTIONISTS	EXANTHEMATOUS
EVANGELISTIC	EVENTUALIZED	EVOLUTIONS	EXARATIONS
EVANGELISTS	EVENTUALIZES	EVOLVEMENT	EXARCHATES
EVANGELIZATION	EVENTUALIZING	EVOLVEMENTS	EXARCHISTS
EVANGELIZATIONS	EVENTUALLY	EVONYMUSES	EXASPERATE
EVANGELIZE	EVENTUATED	EVULGATING	EXASPERATED
EVANGELIZED	EVENTUATES	EXACERBATE	EXASPERATEDLY
EVANGELIZER	EVENTUATING	EXACERBATED	EXASPERATER
EVANGELIZERS	EVENTUATION	EXACERBATES	EXASPERATERS
EVANGELIZES	EVENTUATIONS	EXACERBATING	EXASPERATES
EVANGELIZING	EVERBLOOMING	EXACERBATION	EXASPERATING
EVANISHING	EVERDURING	EXACERBATIONS	EXASPERATINGLY
EVANISHMENT	EVERGLADES	EXACERBESCENCE	EXASPERATION
EVANISHMENTS	EVERGREENS	EXACERBESCENCES	EXASPERATIONS
EVANITIONS	EVERLASTING	EXACTINGLY	EXASPERATIVE
EVAPORABILITIES	EVERLASTINGLY	EXACTINGNESS	EXASPERATOR
EVAPORABILITY	EVERLASTINGNESS	EXACTINGNESSES	EXASPERATORS
EVAPORABLE	EVERLASTINGS	EXACTITUDE	EXCAMBIONS
EVAPORATED	EVERYDAYNESS	EXACTITUDES	EXCAMBIUMS
EVAPORATES	EVERYDAYNESSES	EXACTMENTS	EXCARNATED
EVAPORATING	EVERYPLACE	EXACTNESSES	EXCARNATES
EVAPORATION	EVERYTHING	EXACTRESSES	EXCARNATING
EVAPORATIONS	EVERYWHENCE	EXAGGERATE	EXCARNATION
EVAPORATIVE	EVERYWHERE	EXAGGERATED	EXCARNATIONS
EVAPORATOR	EVERYWHITHER	EXAGGERATEDLY	EXCAVATING
EVAPORATORS	EVERYWOMAN	EXAGGERATEDNESS	EXCAVATION
EVAPORIMETER	EVERYWOMEN	EXAGGERATES	EXCAVATIONAL
EVAPORIMETERS	EVIDENCING	EXAGGERATING	EXCAVATIONS
EVAPORITES	EVIDENTIAL	EXAGGERATINGLY	EXCAVATORS
EVAPORITIC	EVIDENTIALLY	EXAGGERATION	EXCEEDABLE
EVAPOROGRAPH	EVIDENTIARY	EXAGGERATIONS	EXCEEDINGLY
EVAPOROGRAPHS	EVILDOINGS	EXAGGERATIVE	EXCELLENCE
EVAPOROMETER	EVILNESSES	EXAGGERATOR	EXCELLENCES
EVAPOROMETERS	EVINCEMENT	EXAGGERATORS	EXCELLENCIES
EVASIVENESS	EVINCEMENTS	EXAGGERATORY	EXCELLENCY
EVASIVENESSES	EVISCERATE	EXAHERTZES	EXCELLENTLY
EVECTIONAL	EVISCERATED	EXALBUMINOUS	EXCELSIORS
EVENEMENTS	EVISCERATES	EXALTATION	EXCENTRICS
EVENHANDED	EVISCERATING	EXALTATIONS	EXCEPTANTS
EVENHANDEDLY	EVISCERATION	EXALTEDNESS	EXCEPTIONABLE
EVENHANDEDNESS	EVISCERATIONS	EXALTEDNESSES	EXCEPTIONABLY
EVENNESSES	EVISCERATOR	EXAMINABILITIES	EXCEPTIONAL
EVENTFULLY	EVISCERATORS	EXAMINABILITY	EXCEPTIONALISM
EVENTFULNESS	EVITATIONS	EXAMINABLE	EXCEPTIONALISMS
EVENTFULNESSES	EVITERNALLY	EXAMINANTS	EXCEPTIONALITY
EVENTISING	EVITERNITIES	EXAMINATES	EXCEPTIONALLY
EVENTIZING	EVITERNITY	EXAMINATION	EXCEPTIONALNESS
EVENTRATED	EVOCATIONS	EXAMINATIONAL	EXCEPTIONALS
EVENTRATES	EVOCATIVELY	EXAMINATIONS	EXCEPTIONS
EVENTRATING	EVOCATIVENESS	EXAMINATOR	EXCEPTIOUS
EVENTRATION	EVOCATIVENESSES	EXAMINATORS	EXCEPTLESS
EVENTRATIONS	EVOLUTIONAL	EXAMINERSHIP	EXCERPTERS
EVENTUALISE	EVOLUTIONARILY	EXAMINERSHIPS	EXCERPTIBLE
EVENTUALISED	EVOLUTIONARY	EXANIMATION	EXCERPTING
EVENTUALISES	EVOLUTIONISM	EXANIMATIONS	EXCERPTINGS
EVENTUALISING	EVOLUTIONISMS	EXANTHEMAS	EXCERPTION
EVENTUALITIES	EVOLUTIONIST	EXANTHEMATA	EXCERPTIONS
EVENTUALITY	EVOLUTIONISTIC	EXANTHEMATIC	EXCERPTORS

833

EXCESSIVELY	EXCOGITABLE	EXCULPATING	EXEMPLARITIES
EXCESSIVENESS	EXCOGITATE	EXCULPATION	EXEMPLARITY
EXCESSIVENESSES	EXCOGITATED	EXCULPATIONS	EXEMPLIFIABLE
EXCHANGEABILITY	EXCOGITATES	EXCULPATORY	EXEMPLIFICATION
EXCHANGEABLE	EXCOGITATING	EXCURSIONED	EXEMPLIFICATIVE
EXCHANGEABLY	EXCOGITATION	EXCURSIONING	EXEMPLIFIED
EXCHANGERS	EXCOGITATIONS	EXCURSIONISE	EXEMPLIFIER
EXCHANGING	EXCOGITATIVE	EXCURSIONISED	EXEMPLIFIERS
EXCHEQUERED	EXCOGITATOR	EXCURSIONISES	EXEMPLIFIES
EXCHEQUERING	EXCOGITATORS	EXCURSIONISING	EXEMPLIFYING
EXCHEQUERS	EXCOMMUNICABLE	EXCURSIONIST	EXEMPTIONS
EXCIPIENTS	EXCOMMUNICATE	EXCURSIONISTS	EXENTERATE
EXCISIONAL	EXCOMMUNICATED	EXCURSIONIZE	EXENTERATED
EXCITABILITIES	EXCOMMUNICATES	EXCURSIONIZED	EXENTERATES
EXCITABILITY	EXCOMMUNICATING	EXCURSIONIZES	EXENTERATING
EXCITABLENESS	EXCOMMUNICATION	EXCURSIONIZING	EXENTERATION
EXCITABLENESSES	EXCOMMUNICATIVE	EXCURSIONS	EXENTERATIONS
EXCITANCIES	EXCOMMUNICATOR	EXCURSIVELY	EXEQUATURS
EXCITATION	EXCOMMUNICATORS	EXCURSIVENESS	EXERCISABLE
EXCITATIONS	EXCOMMUNICATORY	EXCURSIVENESSES	EXERCISERS
EXCITATIVE	EXCOMMUNION	EXCURSUSES	EXERCISING
EXCITATORY	EXCOMMUNIONS	EXCUSABLENESS	EXERCITATION
EXCITEDNESS	EXCORIATED	EXCUSABLENESSES	EXERCITATIONS
EXCITEDNESSES	EXCORIATES	EXCUSATORY	EXERCYCLES
EXCITEMENT	EXCORIATING	EXECRABLENESS	EXFOLIANTS
EXCITEMENTS	EXCORIATION	EXECRABLENESSES	EXFOLIATED
EXCITINGLY	EXCORIATIONS	EXECRATING	EXFOLIATES
EXCLAIMERS	EXCORTICATE	EXECRATION	EXFOLIATING
EXCLAIMING	EXCORTICATED	EXECRATIONS	EXFOLIATION
EXCLAMATION	EXCORTICATES	EXECRATIVE	EXFOLIATIONS
EXCLAMATIONAL	EXCORTICATING	EXECRATIVELY	EXFOLIATIVE
EXCLAMATIONS	EXCORTICATION	EXECRATORS	EXFOLIATOR
EXCLAMATIVE	EXCORTICATIONS	EXECRATORY	EXFOLIATORS
EXCLAMATORILY	EXCREMENTA	EXECUTABLE	EXHALATION
EXCLAMATORY	EXCREMENTAL	EXECUTABLES	EXHALATIONS
EXCLAUSTRATION	EXCREMENTITIAL	EXECUTANCIES	EXHAUSTERS
EXCLAUSTRATIONS	EXCREMENTITIOUS	EXECUTANCY	EXHAUSTIBILITY
EXCLOSURES	EXCREMENTS	EXECUTANTS	EXHAUSTIBLE
EXCLUDABILITIES	EXCREMENTUM	EXECUTARIES	EXHAUSTING
EXCLUDABILITY	EXCRESCENCE	EXECUTIONER	EXHAUSTION
EXCLUDABLE	EXCRESCENCES	EXECUTIONERS	EXHAUSTIONS
EXCLUDIBLE	EXCRESCENCIES	EXECUTIONS	EXHAUSTIVE
EXCLUSIONARY	EXCRESCENCY	EXECUTIVELY	EXHAUSTIVELY
EXCLUSIONISM	EXCRESCENT	EXECUTIVES	EXHAUSTIVENESS
EXCLUSIONISMS	EXCRESCENTIAL	EXECUTORIAL	EXHAUSTIVITIES
EXCLUSIONIST	EXCRESCENTLY	EXECUTORSHIP	EXHAUSTIVITY
EXCLUSIONISTS	EXCRETIONS	EXECUTORSHIPS	EXHAUSTLESS
EXCLUSIONS	EXCRETORIES	EXECUTRESS	EXHAUSTLESSLY
EXCLUSIVELY	EXCRUCIATE	EXECUTRESSES	EXHAUSTLESSNESS
EXCLUSIVENESS	EXCRUCIATED	EXECUTRICES	EXHEREDATE
EXCLUSIVENESSES	EXCRUCIATES	EXECUTRIES	EXHEREDATED
EXCLUSIVES	EXCRUCIATING	EXECUTRIXES	EXHEREDATES
EXCLUSIVISM	EXCRUCIATINGLY	EXEGETICAL	EXHEREDATING
EXCLUSIVISMS	EXCRUCIATION	EXEGETICALLY	EXHEREDATION
EXCLUSIVIST	EXCRUCIATIONS	EXEGETISTS	EXHEREDATIONS
EXCLUSIVISTS	EXCULPABLE	EXEMPLARILY	EXHIBITERS
EXCLUSIVITIES	EXCULPATED	EXEMPLARINESS	EXHIBITING
EXCLUSIVITY	EXCULPATES	EXEMPLARINESSES	EXHIBITION

EXHIBITIONER
EXHIBITIONERS
EXHIBITIONISM
EXHIBITIONISMS
EXHIBITIONIST
EXHIBITIONISTIC
EXHIBITIONISTS
EXHIBITIONS
EXHIBITIVE
EXHIBITIVELY
EXHIBITORS
EXHIBITORY
EXHILARANT
EXHILARANTS
EXHILARATE
EXHILARATED
EXHILARATES
EXHILARATING
EXHILARATINGLY
EXHILARATION
EXHILARATIONS
EXHILARATIVE
EXHILARATOR
EXHILARATORS
EXHILARATORY
EXHORTATION
EXHORTATIONS
EXHORTATIVE
EXHORTATORY
EXHUMATING
EXHUMATION
EXHUMATIONS
EXIGENCIES
EXIGUITIES
EXIGUOUSLY
EXIGUOUSNESS
EXIGUOUSNESSES
EXILEMENTS
EXIMIOUSLY
EXISTENCES
EXISTENTIAL
EXISTENTIALISM
EXISTENTIALISMS
EXISTENTIALIST
EXISTENTIALISTS
EXISTENTIALLY
EXOBIOLOGICAL
EXOBIOLOGIES
EXOBIOLOGIST
EXOBIOLOGISTS
EXOBIOLOGY
EXOCENTRIC
EXOCUTICLE
EXOCUTICLES
EXOCYTOSED
EXOCYTOSES
EXOCYTOSING
EXOCYTOSIS

EXOCYTOTIC
EXODERMISES
EXODONTIAS
EXODONTICS
EXODONTIST
EXODONTISTS
EXOENZYMES
EXOERYTHROCYTIC
EXOGENETIC
EXOGENISMS
EXOGENOUSLY
EXONERATED
EXONERATES
EXONERATING
EXONERATION
EXONERATIONS
EXONERATIVE
EXONERATOR
EXONERATORS
EXONUCLEASE
EXONUCLEASES
EXONUMISTS
EXOPARASITE
EXOPARASITES
EXOPARASITIC
EXOPEPTIDASE
EXOPEPTIDASES
EXOPHAGIES
EXOPHAGOUS
EXOPHTHALMIA
EXOPHTHALMIAS
EXOPHTHALMIC
EXOPHTHALMOS
EXOPHTHALMOSES
EXOPHTHALMUS
EXOPHTHALMUSES
EXOPLANETS
EXOPODITES
EXOPODITIC
EXORABILITIES
EXORABILITY
EXORATIONS
EXORBITANCE
EXORBITANCES
EXORBITANCIES
EXORBITANCY
EXORBITANT
EXORBITANTLY
EXORBITATE
EXORBITATED
EXORBITATES
EXORBITATING
EXORCISERS
EXORCISING
EXORCISTIC
EXORCISTICAL
EXORCIZERS
EXORCIZING

EXOSKELETAL
EXOSKELETON
EXOSKELETONS
EXOSPHERES
EXOSPHERIC
EXOSPHERICAL
EXOSPORIUM
EXOSPOROUS
EXOTERICAL
EXOTERICALLY
EXOTERICISM
EXOTERICISMS
EXOTHERMAL
EXOTHERMALLY
EXOTHERMIC
EXOTHERMICALLY
EXOTHERMICITIES
EXOTHERMICITY
EXOTICALLY
EXOTICISMS
EXOTICISTS
EXOTICNESS
EXOTICNESSES
EXOTROPIAS
EXPANDABILITIES
EXPANDABILITY
EXPANDABLE
EXPANSIBILITIES
EXPANSIBILITY
EXPANSIBLE
EXPANSIBLY
EXPANSIONAL
EXPANSIONARY
EXPANSIONISM
EXPANSIONISMS
EXPANSIONIST
EXPANSIONISTIC
EXPANSIONISTS
EXPANSIONS
EXPANSIVELY
EXPANSIVENESS
EXPANSIVENESSES
EXPANSIVITIES
EXPANSIVITY
EXPATIATED
EXPATIATES
EXPATIATING
EXPATIATION
EXPATIATIONS
EXPATIATIVE
EXPATIATOR
EXPATIATORS
EXPATIATORY
EXPATRIATE
EXPATRIATED
EXPATRIATES
EXPATRIATING
EXPATRIATION

EXPATRIATIONS
EXPATRIATISM
EXPATRIATISMS
EXPECTABLE
EXPECTABLY
EXPECTANCE
EXPECTANCES
EXPECTANCIES
EXPECTANCY
EXPECTANTLY
EXPECTANTS
EXPECTATION
EXPECTATIONAL
EXPECTATIONS
EXPECTATIVE
EXPECTATIVES
EXPECTEDLY
EXPECTEDNESS
EXPECTEDNESSES
EXPECTINGLY
EXPECTINGS
EXPECTORANT
EXPECTORANTS
EXPECTORATE
EXPECTORATED
EXPECTORATES
EXPECTORATING
EXPECTORATION
EXPECTORATIONS
EXPECTORATIVE
EXPECTORATOR
EXPECTORATORS
EXPEDIENCE
EXPEDIENCES
EXPEDIENCIES
EXPEDIENCY
EXPEDIENTIAL
EXPEDIENTIALLY
EXPEDIENTLY
EXPEDIENTS
EXPEDITATE
EXPEDITATED
EXPEDITATES
EXPEDITATING
EXPEDITATION
EXPEDITATIONS
EXPEDITELY
EXPEDITERS
EXPEDITING
EXPEDITION
EXPEDITIONARY
EXPEDITIONS
EXPEDITIOUS
EXPEDITIOUSLY
EXPEDITIOUSNESS
EXPEDITIVE
EXPEDITORS
EXPELLABLE

EXPELLANTS	EXPLAINABLE	EXPORTABILITIES	EXPRESSWAYS
EXPELLENTS	EXPLAINERS	EXPORTABILITY	EXPROBRATE
EXPENDABILITIES	EXPLAINING	EXPORTABLE	EXPROBRATED
EXPENDABILITY	EXPLANATION	EXPORTATION	EXPROBRATES
EXPENDABLE	EXPLANATIONS	EXPORTATIONS	EXPROBRATING
EXPENDABLES	EXPLANATIVE	EXPOSEDNESS	EXPROBRATION
EXPENDITURE	EXPLANATIVELY	EXPOSEDNESSES	EXPROBRATIONS
EXPENDITURES	EXPLANATORILY	EXPOSITING	EXPROBRATIVE
EXPENSIVELY	EXPLANATORY	EXPOSITION	EXPROBRATORY
EXPENSIVENESS	EXPLANTATION	EXPOSITIONAL	EXPROMISSION
EXPENSIVENESSES	EXPLANTATIONS	EXPOSITIONS	EXPROMISSIONS
EXPERIENCE	EXPLANTING	EXPOSITIVE	EXPROMISSOR
EXPERIENCEABLE	EXPLETIVELY	EXPOSITIVELY	EXPROMISSORS
EXPERIENCED	EXPLETIVES	EXPOSITORILY	EXPROPRIABLE
EXPERIENCELESS	EXPLICABLE	EXPOSITORS	EXPROPRIATE
EXPERIENCER	EXPLICABLY	EXPOSITORY	EXPROPRIATED
EXPERIENCERS	EXPLICATED	EXPOSITRESS	EXPROPRIATES
EXPERIENCES	EXPLICATES	EXPOSITRESSES	EXPROPRIATING
EXPERIENCING	EXPLICATING	EXPOSTULATE	EXPROPRIATION
EXPERIENTIAL	EXPLICATION	EXPOSTULATED	EXPROPRIATIONS
EXPERIENTIALISM	EXPLICATIONS	EXPOSTULATES	EXPROPRIATOR
EXPERIENTIALIST	EXPLICATIVE	EXPOSTULATING	EXPROPRIATORS
EXPERIENTIALLY	EXPLICATIVELY	EXPOSTULATINGLY	EXPUGNABLE
EXPERIMENT	EXPLICATOR	EXPOSTULATION	EXPUGNATION
EXPERIMENTAL	EXPLICATORS	EXPOSTULATIONS	EXPUGNATIONS
EXPERIMENTALISE	EXPLICATORY	EXPOSTULATIVE	EXPULSIONS
EXPERIMENTALISM	EXPLICITLY	EXPOSTULATOR	EXPUNCTING
EXPERIMENTALIST	EXPLICITNESS	EXPOSTULATORS	EXPUNCTION
EXPERIMENTALIZE	EXPLICITNESSES	EXPOSTULATORY	EXPUNCTIONS
EXPERIMENTALLY	EXPLOITABLE	EXPOSTURES	EXPURGATED
EXPERIMENTATION	EXPLOITAGE	EXPOUNDERS	EXPURGATES
EXPERIMENTATIVE	EXPLOITAGES	EXPOUNDING	EXPURGATING
EXPERIMENTED	EXPLOITATION	EXPRESSAGE	EXPURGATION
EXPERIMENTER	EXPLOITATIONS	EXPRESSAGES	EXPURGATIONS
EXPERIMENTERS	EXPLOITATIVE	EXPRESSERS	EXPURGATOR
EXPERIMENTING	EXPLOITATIVELY	EXPRESSIBLE	EXPURGATORIAL
EXPERIMENTIST	EXPLOITERS	EXPRESSING	EXPURGATORS
EXPERIMENTISTS	EXPLOITING	EXPRESSION	EXPURGATORY
EXPERIMENTS	EXPLOITIVE	EXPRESSIONAL	EXQUISITELY
EXPERTISED	EXPLORATION	EXPRESSIONISM	EXQUISITENESS
EXPERTISES	EXPLORATIONAL	EXPRESSIONISMS	EXQUISITENESSES
EXPERTISING	EXPLORATIONIST	EXPRESSIONIST	EXQUISITES
EXPERTISMS	EXPLORATIONISTS	EXPRESSIONISTIC	EXSANGUINATE
EXPERTIZED	EXPLORATIONS	EXPRESSIONISTS	EXSANGUINATED
EXPERTIZES	EXPLORATIVE	EXPRESSIONLESS	EXSANGUINATES
EXPERTIZING	EXPLORATIVELY	EXPRESSIONS	EXSANGUINATING
EXPERTNESS	EXPLORATORY	EXPRESSIVE	EXSANGUINATION
EXPERTNESSES	EXPLOSIBLE	EXPRESSIVELY	EXSANGUINATIONS
EXPIATIONS	EXPLOSIONS	EXPRESSIVENESS	EXSANGUINE
EXPIRATION	EXPLOSIVELY	EXPRESSIVITIES	EXSANGUINED
EXPIRATIONS	EXPLOSIVENESS	EXPRESSIVITY	EXSANGUINEOUS
EXPIRATORY	EXPLOSIVENESSES	EXPRESSMAN	EXSANGUINITIES
EXPISCATED	EXPLOSIVES	EXPRESSMEN	EXSANGUINITY
EXPISCATES	EXPONENTIAL	EXPRESSNESS	EXSANGUINOUS
EXPISCATING	EXPONENTIALLY	EXPRESSNESSES	EXSCINDING
EXPISCATION	EXPONENTIALS	EXPRESSURE	EXSECTIONS
EXPISCATIONS	EXPONENTIATION	EXPRESSURES	EXSERTIONS
EXPISCATORY	EXPONENTIATIONS	EXPRESSWAY	EXSICCATED

EXSICCATES
EXSICCATING
EXSICCATION
EXSICCATIONS
EXSICCATIVE
EXSICCATOR
EXSICCATORS
EXSOLUTION
EXSOLUTIONS
EXSTIPULATE
EXSTROPHIES
EXSUFFLATE
EXSUFFLATED
EXSUFFLATES
EXSUFFLATING
EXSUFFLATION
EXSUFFLATIONS
EXSUFFLICATE
EXTEMPORAL
EXTEMPORALLY
EXTEMPORANEITY
EXTEMPORANEOUS
EXTEMPORARILY
EXTEMPORARINESS
EXTEMPORARY
EXTEMPORES
EXTEMPORISATION
EXTEMPORISE
EXTEMPORISED
EXTEMPORISER
EXTEMPORISERS
EXTEMPORISES
EXTEMPORISING
EXTEMPORIZATION
EXTEMPORIZE
EXTEMPORIZED
EXTEMPORIZER
EXTEMPORIZERS
EXTEMPORIZES
EXTEMPORIZING
EXTENDABILITIES
EXTENDABILITY
EXTENDABLE
EXTENDEDLY
EXTENDEDNESS
EXTENDEDNESSES
EXTENDIBILITIES
EXTENDIBILITY
EXTENDIBLE
EXTENSIBILITIES
EXTENSIBILITY
EXTENSIBLE
EXTENSIBLENESS
EXTENSIFICATION
EXTENSIMETER
EXTENSIMETERS
EXTENSIONAL
EXTENSIONALISM

EXTENSIONALISMS
EXTENSIONALITY
EXTENSIONALLY
EXTENSIONIST
EXTENSIONISTS
EXTENSIONS
EXTENSITIES
EXTENSIVELY
EXTENSIVENESS
EXTENSIVENESSES
EXTENSIVISATION
EXTENSIVIZATION
EXTENSOMETER
EXTENSOMETERS
EXTENUATED
EXTENUATES
EXTENUATING
EXTENUATINGLY
EXTENUATINGS
EXTENUATION
EXTENUATIONS
EXTENUATIVE
EXTENUATOR
EXTENUATORS
EXTENUATORY
EXTERIORISATION
EXTERIORISE
EXTERIORISED
EXTERIORISES
EXTERIORISING
EXTERIORITIES
EXTERIORITY
EXTERIORIZATION
EXTERIORIZE
EXTERIORIZED
EXTERIORIZES
EXTERIORIZING
EXTERIORLY
EXTERMINABLE
EXTERMINATE
EXTERMINATED
EXTERMINATES
EXTERMINATING
EXTERMINATION
EXTERMINATIONS
EXTERMINATIVE
EXTERMINATOR
EXTERMINATORS
EXTERMINATORY
EXTERMINED
EXTERMINES
EXTERMINING
EXTERNALISATION
EXTERNALISE
EXTERNALISED
EXTERNALISES
EXTERNALISING
EXTERNALISM

EXTERNALISMS
EXTERNALIST
EXTERNALISTS
EXTERNALITIES
EXTERNALITY
EXTERNALIZATION
EXTERNALIZE
EXTERNALIZED
EXTERNALIZES
EXTERNALIZING
EXTERNALLY
EXTERNSHIP
EXTERNSHIPS
EXTEROCEPTIVE
EXTEROCEPTOR
EXTEROCEPTORS
EXTERRITORIAL
EXTERRITORIALLY
EXTINCTING
EXTINCTION
EXTINCTIONS
EXTINCTIVE
EXTINCTURE
EXTINCTURES
EXTINGUISH
EXTINGUISHABLE
EXTINGUISHANT
EXTINGUISHANTS
EXTINGUISHED
EXTINGUISHER
EXTINGUISHERS
EXTINGUISHES
EXTINGUISHING
EXTINGUISHMENT
EXTINGUISHMENTS
EXTIRPABLE
EXTIRPATED
EXTIRPATES
EXTIRPATING
EXTIRPATION
EXTIRPATIONS
EXTIRPATIVE
EXTIRPATOR
EXTIRPATORS
EXTIRPATORY
EXTOLLINGLY
EXTOLMENTS
EXTORSIVELY
EXTORTIONARY
EXTORTIONATE
EXTORTIONATELY
EXTORTIONER
EXTORTIONERS
EXTORTIONIST
EXTORTIONISTS
EXTORTIONS
EXTRABOLDS
EXTRACANONICAL

EXTRACELLULAR
EXTRACELLULARLY
EXTRACORPOREAL
EXTRACRANIAL
EXTRACTABILITY
EXTRACTABLE
EXTRACTANT
EXTRACTANTS
EXTRACTIBLE
EXTRACTING
EXTRACTION
EXTRACTIONS
EXTRACTIVE
EXTRACTIVELY
EXTRACTIVES
EXTRACTORS
EXTRACURRICULAR
EXTRADITABLE
EXTRADITED
EXTRADITES
EXTRADITING
EXTRADITION
EXTRADITIONS
EXTRADOSES
EXTRADOTAL
EXTRADURAL
EXTRAEMBRYONIC
EXTRAFLORAL
EXTRAFORANEOUS
EXTRAGALACTIC
EXTRAHEPATIC
EXTRAJUDICIAL
EXTRAJUDICIALLY
EXTRALEGAL
EXTRALEGALLY
EXTRALIMITAL
EXTRALIMITARY
EXTRALINGUISTIC
EXTRALITERARY
EXTRALITIES
EXTRALOGICAL
EXTRAMARITAL
EXTRAMETRICAL
EXTRAMUNDANE
EXTRAMURAL
EXTRAMURALLY
EXTRAMUSICAL
EXTRANEITIES
EXTRANEITY
EXTRANEOUS
EXTRANEOUSLY
EXTRANEOUSNESS
EXTRANUCLEAR
EXTRAORDINAIRE
EXTRAORDINARIES
EXTRAORDINARILY
EXTRAORDINARY
EXTRAPOLATE

EXTRAPOLATED	EXTRICATED	EYEPOPPERS
EXTRAPOLATES	EXTRICATES	EYESHADOWS
EXTRAPOLATING	EXTRICATING	EYESTRAINS
EXTRAPOLATION	EXTRICATION	EYESTRINGS
EXTRAPOLATIONS	EXTRICATIONS	EYEWITNESS
EXTRAPOLATIVE	EXTRINSICAL	EYEWITNESSES
EXTRAPOLATOR	EXTRINSICALITY	
EXTRAPOLATORS	EXTRINSICALLY	
EXTRAPOLATORY	EXTROVERSION	
EXTRAPOSED	EXTROVERSIONS	
EXTRAPOSES	EXTROVERSIVE	
EXTRAPOSING	EXTROVERSIVELY	
EXTRAPOSITION	EXTROVERTED	
EXTRAPOSITIONS	EXTROVERTING	
EXTRAPYRAMIDAL	EXTROVERTS	
EXTRASENSORY	EXTRUDABILITIES	
EXTRASOLAR	EXTRUDABILITY	
EXTRASYSTOLE	EXTRUDABLE	
EXTRASYSTOLES	EXTRUSIBLE	
EXTRATEXTUAL	EXTRUSIONS	
EXTRATROPICAL	EXTUBATING	
EXTRAUTERINE	EXUBERANCE	
EXTRAVAGANCE	EXUBERANCES	
EXTRAVAGANCES	EXUBERANCIES	
EXTRAVAGANCIES	EXUBERANCY	
EXTRAVAGANCY	EXUBERANTLY	
EXTRAVAGANT	EXUBERATED	
EXTRAVAGANTLY	EXUBERATES	
EXTRAVAGANZA	EXUBERATING	
EXTRAVAGANZAS	EXUDATIONS	
EXTRAVAGATE	EXULCERATE	
EXTRAVAGATED	EXULCERATED	
EXTRAVAGATES	EXULCERATES	
EXTRAVAGATING	EXULCERATING	
EXTRAVAGATION	EXULCERATION	
EXTRAVAGATIONS	EXULCERATIONS	
EXTRAVASATE	EXULTANCES	
EXTRAVASATED	EXULTANCIES	
EXTRAVASATES	EXULTANTLY	
EXTRAVASATING	EXULTATION	
EXTRAVASATION	EXULTATIONS	
EXTRAVASATIONS	EXULTINGLY	
EXTRAVASCULAR	EXURBANITE	
EXTRAVEHICULAR	EXURBANITES	
EXTRAVERSION	EXUVIATING	
EXTRAVERSIONS	EXUVIATION	
EXTRAVERSIVE	EXUVIATIONS	
EXTRAVERTED	EYEBALLING	
EXTRAVERTING	EYEBRIGHTS	
EXTRAVERTS	EYEBROWING	
EXTREMENESS	EYEBROWLESS	
EXTREMENESSES	EYEDNESSES	
EXTREMISMS	EYEDROPPER	
EXTREMISTS	EYEDROPPERS	
EXTREMITIES	EYEGLASSES	
EXTREMOPHILE	EYELETEERS	
EXTREMOPHILES	EYELETTING	
EXTRICABLE	EYEOPENERS	

F

FABRICANTS	FACTICITIES	FADEDNESSES	FALLACIOUSLY
FABRICATED	FACTIONALISM	FADELESSLY	FALLACIOUSNESS
FABRICATES	FACTIONALISMS	FADOMETERS	FALLALERIES
FABRICATING	FACTIONALIST	FAGGOTINGS	FALLALISHLY
FABRICATION	FACTIONALISTS	FAGGOTRIES	FALLBOARDS
FABRICATIONS	FACTIONALLY	FAGOTTISTS	FALLFISHES
FABRICATIVE	FACTIONARIES	FAINEANCES	FALLIBILISM
FABRICATOR	FACTIONARY	FAINEANCIES	FALLIBILISMS
FABRICATORS	FACTIONIST	FAINEANTISE	FALLIBILIST
FABRICKING	FACTIONISTS	FAINEANTISES	FALLIBILISTS
FABULATING	FACTIOUSLY	FAINNESSES	FALLIBILITIES
FABULATORS	FACTIOUSNESS	FAINTHEARTED	FALLIBILITY
FABULISING	FACTIOUSNESSES	FAINTHEARTEDLY	FALLIBLENESS
FABULISTIC	FACTITIOUS	FAINTINGLY	FALLIBLENESSES
FABULIZING	FACTITIOUSLY	FAINTISHNESS	FALLOWNESS
FABULOSITIES	FACTITIOUSNESS	FAINTISHNESSES	FALLOWNESSES
FABULOSITY	FACTITIVELY	FAINTNESSES	FALSEFACES
FABULOUSLY	FACTORABILITIES	FAIRGROUND	FALSEHOODS
FABULOUSNESS	FACTORABILITY	FAIRGROUNDS	FALSENESSES
FABULOUSNESSES	FACTORABLE	FAIRLEADER	FALSEWORKS
FACECLOTHS	FACTORAGES	FAIRLEADERS	FALSIDICAL
FACELESSNESS	FACTORIALLY	FAIRNESSES	FALSIFIABILITY
FACELESSNESSES	FACTORIALS	FAIRNITICKLE	FALSIFIABLE
FACELIFTED	FACTORINGS	FAIRNITICKLES	FALSIFICATION
FACELIFTING	FACTORISATION	FAIRNITICLE	FALSIFICATIONS
FACEPLATES	FACTORISATIONS	FAIRNITICLES	FALSIFIERS
FACEPRINTS	FACTORISED	FAIRNYTICKLE	FALSIFYING
FACETIOUSLY	FACTORISES	FAIRNYTICKLES	FALTERINGLY
FACETIOUSNESS	FACTORISING	FAIRNYTICLE	FALTERINGS
FACETIOUSNESSES	FACTORIZATION	FAIRNYTICLES	FAMILIARISATION
FACEWORKER	FACTORIZATIONS	FAIRYFLOSS	FAMILIARISE
FACEWORKERS	FACTORIZED	FAIRYFLOSSES	FAMILIARISED
FACILENESS	FACTORIZES	FAIRYHOODS	FAMILIARISER
FACILENESSES	FACTORIZING	FAIRYLANDS	FAMILIARISERS
FACILITATE	FACTORSHIP	FAIRYTALES	FAMILIARISES
FACILITATED	FACTORSHIPS	FAITHCURES	FAMILIARISING
FACILITATES	FACTORYLIKE	FAITHFULLY	FAMILIARITIES
FACILITATING	FACTSHEETS	FAITHFULNESS	FAMILIARITY
FACILITATION	FACTUALISM	FAITHFULNESSES	FAMILIARIZATION
FACILITATIONS	FACTUALISMS	FAITHLESSLY	FAMILIARIZE
FACILITATIVE	FACTUALIST	FAITHLESSNESS	FAMILIARIZED
FACILITATOR	FACTUALISTIC	FAITHLESSNESSES	FAMILIARIZER
FACILITATORS	FACTUALISTS	FAITHWORTHINESS	FAMILIARIZERS
FACILITATORY	FACTUALITIES	FAITHWORTHY	FAMILIARIZES
FACILITIES	FACTUALITY	FALANGISMS	FAMILIARIZING
FACINERIOUS	FACTUALNESS	FALANGISTS	FAMILIARLY
FACINOROUS	FACTUALNESSES	FALCATIONS	FAMILIARNESS
FACINOROUSNESS	FACULTATIVE	FALCONIFORM	FAMILIARNESSES
FACSIMILED	FACULTATIVELY	FALCONRIES	FAMILISTIC
FACSIMILEING	FACUNDITIES	FALDISTORIES	FAMISHMENT
FACSIMILES	FADDINESSES	FALDISTORY	FAMISHMENTS
FACSIMILIST	FADDISHNESS	FALDSTOOLS	FAMOUSNESS
FACSIMILISTS	FADDISHNESSES	FALLACIOUS	FAMOUSNESSES

FANATICALLY	FANTASTRIES	FARTHINGSWORTH	FATALNESSES
FANATICALNESS	FANTASYING	FARTHINGSWORTHS	FATBRAINED
FANATICALNESSES	FANTASYLAND	FASCIATELY	FATEFULNESS
FANATICISE	FANTASYLANDS	FASCIATION	FATEFULNESSES
FANATICISED	FANTOCCINI	FASCIATIONS	FATHEADEDLY
FANATICISES	FARADISATION	FASCICULAR	FATHEADEDNESS
FANATICISING	FARADISATIONS	FASCICULARLY	FATHEADEDNESSES
FANATICISM	FARADISERS	FASCICULATE	FATHERHOOD
FANATICISMS	FARADISING	FASCICULATED	FATHERHOODS
FANATICIZE	FARADIZATION	FASCICULATELY	FATHERLAND
FANATICIZED	FARADIZATIONS	FASCICULATION	FATHERLANDS
FANATICIZES	FARADIZERS	FASCICULATIONS	FATHERLESS
FANATICIZING	FARADIZING	FASCICULES	FATHERLESSNESS
FANCIFULLY	FARANDINES	FASCICULUS	FATHERLIKE
FANCIFULNESS	FARANDOLES	FASCIITISES	FATHERLINESS
FANCIFULNESSES	FARAWAYNESS	FASCINATED	FATHERLINESSES
FANCIFYING	FARAWAYNESSES	FASCINATEDLY	FATHERSHIP
FANCINESSES	FARBOROUGH	FASCINATES	FATHERSHIPS
FANCYWORKS	FARBOROUGHS	FASCINATING	FATHOMABLE
FANDANGLES	FARCEMEATS	FASCINATINGLY	FATHOMETER
FANDANGOES	FARCICALITIES	FASCINATION	FATHOMETERS
FANFARADES	FARCICALITY	FASCINATIONS	FATHOMLESS
FANFARONADE	FARCICALLY	FASCINATIVE	FATHOMLESSLY
FANFARONADED	FARCICALNESS	FASCINATOR	FATHOMLESSNESS
FANFARONADES	FARCICALNESSES	FASCINATORS	FATIDICALLY
FANFARONADING	FARCIFYING	FASCIOLIASES	FATIGABILITIES
FANFARONAS	FAREWELLED	FASCIOLIASIS	FATIGABILITY
FANFOLDING	FAREWELLING	FASCISTICALLY	FATIGABLENESS
FANTABULOUS	FARFETCHEDNESS	FASCITISES	FATIGABLENESSES
FANTASISED	FARINACEOUS	FASHIONABILITY	FATIGATING
FANTASISER	FARINOSELY	FASHIONABLE	FATIGUABLE
FANTASISERS	FARKLEBERRIES	FASHIONABLENESS	FATIGUABLENESS
FANTASISES	FARKLEBERRY	FASHIONABLES	FATIGUELESS
FANTASISING	FARMERESSES	FASHIONABLY	FATIGUINGLY
FANTASISTS	FARMERETTE	FASHIONERS	FATISCENCE
FANTASIZED	FARMERETTES	FASHIONING	FATISCENCES
FANTASIZER	FARMHOUSES	FASHIONIST	FATSHEDERA
FANTASIZERS	FARMSTEADS	FASHIONISTA	FATSHEDERAS
FANTASIZES	FARMWORKER	FASHIONISTAS	FATTENABLE
FANTASIZING	FARMWORKERS	FASHIONISTS	FATTENINGS
FANTASMALLY	FARNARKELED	FASHIONMONGER	FATTINESSES
FANTASMICALLY	FARNARKELING	FASHIONMONGERS	FATUOUSNESS
FANTASQUES	FARNARKELINGS	FASHIONMONGING	FATUOUSNESSES
FANTASTICAL	FARNARKELS	FASHIOUSNESS	FAULCHIONS
FANTASTICALITY	FARRAGINOUS	FASHIOUSNESSES	FAULTFINDER
FANTASTICALLY	FARRANDINE	FASTBALLER	FAULTFINDERS
FANTASTICALNESS	FARRANDINES	FASTBALLERS	FAULTFINDING
FANTASTICATE	FARRIERIES	FASTENINGS	FAULTFINDINGS
FANTASTICATED	FARSIGHTED	FASTIDIOUS	FAULTINESS
FANTASTICATES	FARSIGHTEDLY	FASTIDIOUSLY	FAULTINESSES
FANTASTICATING	FARSIGHTEDNESS	FASTIDIOUSNESS	FAULTLESSLY
FANTASTICATION	FARTHERMORE	FASTIGIATE	FAULTLESSNESS
FANTASTICATIONS	FARTHERMOST	FASTIGIATED	FAULTLESSNESSES
FANTASTICISM	FARTHINGALE	FASTIGIUMS	FAUNISTICALLY
FANTASTICISMS	FARTHINGALES	FASTNESSES	FAUXBOURDON
FANTASTICO	FARTHINGLAND	FATALISTIC	FAUXBOURDONS
FANTASTICOES	FARTHINGLANDS	FATALISTICALLY	FAVORABLENESS
FANTASTICS	FARTHINGLESS	FATALITIES	FAVORABLENESSES

FAVOREDNESS
FAVOREDNESSES
FAVORINGLY
FAVORITISM
FAVORITISMS
FAVOURABLE
FAVOURABLENESS
FAVOURABLY
FAVOUREDNESS
FAVOUREDNESSES
FAVOURINGLY
FAVOURITES
FAVOURITISM
FAVOURITISMS
FAVOURLESS
FAWNINGNESS
FAWNINGNESSES
FAZENDEIRO
FAZENDEIROS
FEARFULLER
FEARFULLEST
FEARFULNESS
FEARFULNESSES
FEARLESSLY
FEARLESSNESS
FEARLESSNESSES
FEARNAUGHT
FEARNAUGHTS
FEARNOUGHT
FEARNOUGHTS
FEARSOMELY
FEARSOMENESS
FEARSOMENESSES
FEASIBILITIES
FEASIBILITY
FEASIBLENESS
FEASIBLENESSES
FEATEOUSLY
FEATHERBED
FEATHERBEDDED
FEATHERBEDDING
FEATHERBEDDINGS
FEATHERBEDS
FEATHERBRAIN
FEATHERBRAINED
FEATHERBRAINS
FEATHEREDGE
FEATHEREDGED
FEATHEREDGES
FEATHEREDGING
FEATHERHEAD
FEATHERHEADED
FEATHERHEADS
FEATHERIER
FEATHERIEST
FEATHERINESS
FEATHERINESSES
FEATHERING

FEATHERINGS
FEATHERLESS
FEATHERLIGHT
FEATHERSTITCH
FEATHERSTITCHED
FEATHERSTITCHES
FEATHERWEIGHT
FEATHERWEIGHTS
FEATLINESS
FEATLINESSES
FEATURELESS
FEATURELESSNESS
FEATURETTE
FEATURETTES
FEBRICITIES
FEBRICULAS
FEBRICULES
FEBRIFACIENT
FEBRIFACIENTS
FEBRIFEROUS
FEBRIFUGAL
FEBRIFUGES
FEBRILITIES
FECKLESSLY
FECKLESSNESS
FECKLESSNESSES
FECULENCES
FECULENCIES
FECUNDATED
FECUNDATES
FECUNDATING
FECUNDATION
FECUNDATIONS
FECUNDATOR
FECUNDATORS
FECUNDATORY
FECUNDITIES
FEDERACIES
FEDERALESE
FEDERALESES
FEDERALISATION
FEDERALISATIONS
FEDERALISE
FEDERALISED
FEDERALISES
FEDERALISING
FEDERALISM
FEDERALISMS
FEDERALIST
FEDERALISTIC
FEDERALISTS
FEDERALIZATION
FEDERALIZATIONS
FEDERALIZE
FEDERALIZED
FEDERALIZES
FEDERALIZING
FEDERARIES

FEDERATING
FEDERATION
FEDERATIONS
FEDERATIVE
FEDERATIVELY
FEDERATORS
FEEBLEMINDED
FEEBLEMINDEDLY
FEEBLENESS
FEEBLENESSES
FEEDGRAINS
FEEDINGSTUFF
FEEDINGSTUFFS
FEEDSTOCKS
FEEDSTUFFS
FEEDTHROUGH
FEEDTHROUGHS
FEEDWATERS
FEELINGLESS
FEELINGNESS
FEELINGNESSES
FEIGNEDNESS
FEIGNEDNESSES
FEIGNINGLY
FEISTINESS
FEISTINESSES
FELDSCHARS
FELDSCHERS
FELDSPATHIC
FELDSPATHOID
FELDSPATHOIDS
FELDSPATHOSE
FELDSPATHS
FELICITATE
FELICITATED
FELICITATES
FELICITATING
FELICITATION
FELICITATIONS
FELICITATOR
FELICITATORS
FELICITIES
FELICITOUS
FELICITOUSLY
FELICITOUSNESS
FELINENESS
FELINENESSES
FELINITIES
FELLATIONS
FELLATRICES
FELLATRIXES
FELLMONGER
FELLMONGERED
FELLMONGERIES
FELLMONGERING
FELLMONGERINGS
FELLMONGERS
FELLMONGERY

FELLNESSES
FELLOWSHIP
FELLOWSHIPED
FELLOWSHIPTNG
FELLOWSHIPPED
FELLOWSHIPPING
FELLOWSHIPS
FELLWALKER
FELLWALKERS
FELONIOUSLY
FELONIOUSNESS
FELONIOUSNESSES
FELSPATHIC
FELSPATHOID
FELSPATHOIDS
FELSPATHOSE
FEMALENESS
FEMALENESSES
FEMALITIES
FEMETARIES
FEMINACIES
FEMINALITIES
FEMINALITY
FEMINEITIES
FEMINILITIES
FEMINILITY
FEMININELY
FEMININENESS
FEMININENESSES
FEMININISM
FEMININISMS
FEMININITIES
FEMININITY
FEMINISATION
FEMINISATIONS
FEMINISING
FEMINISTIC
FEMINITIES
FEMINIZATION
FEMINIZATIONS
FEMINIZING
FEMTOSECOND
FEMTOSECONDS
FENCELESSNESS
FENCELESSNESSES
FENDERLESS
FENESTELLA
FENESTELLAE
FENESTELLAS
FENESTRALS
FENESTRATE
FENESTRATED
FENESTRATION
FENESTRATIONS
FENNELFLOWER
FENNELFLOWERS
FENUGREEKS
FEOFFMENTS

FERACITIES
FERETORIES
FERMENTABILITY
FERMENTABLE
FERMENTATION
FERMENTATIONS
FERMENTATIVE
FERMENTATIVELY
FERMENTERS
FERMENTESCIBLE
FERMENTING
FERMENTITIOUS
FERMENTIVE
FERMENTORS
FERNITICKLE
FERNITICKLES
FERNITICLE
FERNITICLES
FERNTICKLE
FERNTICKLED
FERNTICKLES
FERNTICLED
FERNTICLES
FERNYTICKLE
FERNYTICKLES
FERNYTICLE
FERNYTICLES
FEROCIOUSLY
FEROCIOUSNESS
FEROCIOUSNESSES
FEROCITIES
FERRANDINE
FERRANDINES
FERREDOXIN
FERREDOXINS
FERRELLING
FERRETINGS
FERRICYANIC
FERRICYANIDE
FERRICYANIDES
FERRICYANOGEN
FERRICYANOGENS
FERRIFEROUS
FERRIMAGNET
FERRIMAGNETIC
FERRIMAGNETISM
FERRIMAGNETISMS
FERRIMAGNETS
FERROCENES
FERROCHROME
FERROCHROMES
FERROCHROMIUM
FERROCHROMIUMS
FERROCONCRETE
FERROCONCRETES
FERROCYANIC
FERROCYANIDE
FERROCYANIDES

FERROCYANOGEN
FERROCYANOGENS
FERROELECTRIC
FERROELECTRICS
FERROGRAMS
FERROGRAPHIES
FERROGRAPHY
FERROMAGNESIAN
FERROMAGNET
FERROMAGNETIC
FERROMAGNETISM
FERROMAGNETISMS
FERROMAGNETS
FERROMANGANESE
FERROMANGANESES
FERROMOLYBDENUM
FERRONICKEL
FERRONICKELS
FERRONIERE
FERRONIERES
FERRONNIERE
FERRONNIERES
FERROPRUSSIATE
FERROPRUSSIATES
FERROSILICON
FERROSILICONS
FERROSOFERRIC
FERROTYPED
FERROTYPES
FERROTYPING
FERRUGINEOUS
FERRUGINOUS
FERRYBOATS
FERTIGATED
FERTIGATES
FERTIGATING
FERTIGATION
FERTIGATIONS
FERTILENESS
FERTILENESSES
FERTILISABLE
FERTILISATION
FERTILISATIONS
FERTILISED
FERTILISER
FERTILISERS
FERTILISES
FERTILISING
FERTILITIES
FERTILIZABLE
FERTILIZATION
FERTILIZATIONS
FERTILIZED
FERTILIZER
FERTILIZERS
FERTILIZES
FERTILIZING
FERULACEOUS

FERVENCIES
FERVENTEST
FERVENTNESS
FERVENTNESSES
FERVESCENT
FERVIDITIES
FERVIDNESS
FERVIDNESSES
FESCENNINE
FESTILOGIES
FESTINATED
FESTINATELY
FESTINATES
FESTINATING
FESTINATION
FESTINATIONS
FESTIVALGOER
FESTIVALGOERS
FESTIVENESS
FESTIVENESSES
FESTIVITIES
FESTOLOGIES
FESTOONERIES
FESTOONERY
FESTOONING
FESTSCHRIFT
FESTSCHRIFTEN
FESTSCHRIFTS
FETCHINGLY
FETICHISED
FETICHISES
FETICHISING
FETICHISMS
FETICHISTIC
FETICHISTS
FETICHIZED
FETICHIZES
FETICHIZING
FETIDITIES
FETIDNESSES
FETIPAROUS
FETISHISATION
FETISHISATIONS
FETISHISED
FETISHISES
FETISHISING
FETISHISMS
FETISHISTIC
FETISHISTICALLY
FETISHISTS
FETISHIZATION
FETISHIZATIONS
FETISHIZED
FETISHIZES
FETISHIZING
FETOLOGIES
FETOLOGIST
FETOLOGISTS

FETOPROTEIN
FETOPROTEINS
FETOSCOPES
FETOSCOPIES
FETTERLESS
FETTERLOCK
FETTERLOCKS
FETTUCCINE
FETTUCCINES
FETTUCCINI
FETTUCINES
FETTUCINIS
FEUDALISATION
FEUDALISATIONS
FEUDALISED
FEUDALISES
FEUDALISING
FEUDALISMS
FEUDALISTIC
FEUDALISTS
FEUDALITIES
FEUDALIZATION
FEUDALIZATIONS
FEUDALIZED
FEUDALIZES
FEUDALIZING
FEUDATORIES
FEUILLETES
FEUILLETON
FEUILLETONISM
FEUILLETONISMS
FEUILLETONIST
FEUILLETONISTIC
FEUILLETONISTS
FEUILLETONS
FEVERISHLY
FEVERISHNESS
FEVERISHNESSES
FEVEROUSLY
FEVERROOTS
FEVERWEEDS
FEVERWORTS
FIANCAILLES
FIANCHETTI
FIANCHETTO
FIANCHETTOED
FIANCHETTOES
FIANCHETTOING
FIANCHETTOS
FIBERBOARD
FIBERBOARDS
FIBERFILLS
FIBERGLASS
FIBERGLASSED
FIBERGLASSES
FIBERGLASSING
FIBERISATION
FIBERISATIONS

FIBERISING
FIBERIZATION
FIBERIZATIONS
FIBERIZING
FIBERSCOPE
FIBERSCOPES
FIBREBOARD
FIBREBOARDS
FIBREFILLS
FIBREGLASS
FIBREGLASSES
FIBREOPTIC
FIBRESCOPE
FIBRESCOPES
FIBRILLARY
FIBRILLATE
FIBRILLATED
FIBRILLATES
FIBRILLATING
FIBRILLATION
FIBRILLATIONS
FIBRILLIFORM
FIBRILLINS
FIBRILLOSE
FIBRILLOUS
FIBRINOGEN
FIBRINOGENIC
FIBRINOGENOUS
FIBRINOGENS
FIBRINOIDS
FIBRINOLYSES
FIBRINOLYSIN
FIBRINOLYSINS
FIBRINOLYSIS
FIBRINOLYTIC
FIBRINOPEPTIDE
FIBRINOPEPTIDES
FIBROBLAST
FIBROBLASTIC
FIBROBLASTS
FIBROCARTILAGE
FIBROCARTILAGES
FIBROCEMENT
FIBROCEMENTS
FIBROCYSTIC
FIBROCYTES
FIBROLINES
FIBROLITES
FIBROMATOUS
FIBROMYALGIA
FIBROMYALGIAS
FIBRONECTIN
FIBRONECTINS
FIBROSARCOMA
FIBROSARCOMAS
FIBROSARCOMATA
FIBROSITIS
FIBROSITISES

FIBROUSNESS
FIBROUSNESSES
FIBROVASCULAR
FICKLENESS
FICKLENESSES
FICTIONALISE
FICTIONALISED
FICTIONALISES
FICTIONALISING
FICTIONALITIES
FICTIONALITY
FICTIONALIZE
FICTIONALIZED
FICTIONALIZES
FICTIONALIZING
FICTIONALLY
FICTIONEER
FICTIONEERING
FICTIONEERINGS
FICTIONEERS
FICTIONISATION
FICTIONISATIONS
FICTIONISE
FICTIONISED
FICTIONISES
FICTIONISING
FICTIONIST
FICTIONISTS
FICTIONIZATION
FICTIONIZATIONS
FICTIONIZE
FICTIONIZED
FICTIONIZES
FICTIONIZING
FICTITIOUS
FICTITIOUSLY
FICTITIOUSNESS
FICTIVENESS
FICTIVENESSES
FIDDIOUSED
FIDDIOUSES
FIDDIOUSING
FIDDLEBACK
FIDDLEBACKS
FIDDLEDEDEE
FIDDLEDEEDEE
FIDDLEHEAD
FIDDLEHEADS
FIDDLENECK
FIDDLENECKS
FIDDLESTICK
FIDDLESTICKS
FIDDLEWOOD
FIDDLEWOODS
FIDEICOMMISSA
FIDEICOMMISSARY
FIDEICOMMISSUM
FIDELISMOS

FIDELISTAS
FIDELITIES
FIDGETIEST
FIDGETINESS
FIDGETINESSES
FIDGETINGLY
FIDUCIALLY
FIDUCIARIES
FIDUCIARILY
FIELDBOOTS
FIELDCRAFT
FIELDCRAFTS
FIELDFARES
FIELDMOUSE
FIELDPIECE
FIELDPIECES
FIELDSTONE
FIELDSTONES
FIELDSTRIP
FIELDSTRIPPED
FIELDSTRIPPING
FIELDSTRIPS
FIELDVOLES
FIELDWARDS
FIELDWORKER
FIELDWORKERS
FIELDWORKS
FIENDISHLY
FIENDISHNESS
FIENDISHNESSES
FIERCENESS
FIERCENESSES
FIERINESSES
FIFTEENERS
FIFTEENTHLY
FIFTEENTHS
FIGHTBACKS
FIGURABILITIES
FIGURABILITY
FIGURANTES
FIGURATELY
FIGURATION
FIGURATIONS
FIGURATIVE
FIGURATIVELY
FIGURATIVENESS
FIGUREHEAD
FIGUREHEADS
FIGURELESS
FIGUREWORK
FIGUREWORKS
FILAGREEING
FILAMENTARY
FILAMENTOUS
FILARIASES
FILARIASIS
FILATORIES
FILCHINGLY

FILEFISHES
FILIALNESS
FILIALNESSES
FILIATIONS
FILIBUSTER
FILIBUSTERED
FILIBUSTERER
FILIBUSTERERS
FILIBUSTERING
FILIBUSTERINGS
FILIBUSTERISM
FILIBUSTERISMS
FILIBUSTEROUS
FILIBUSTERS
FILICINEAN
FILIGRAINS
FILIGRANES
FILIGREEING
FILIOPIETISTIC
FILIPENDULOUS
FILLAGREED
FILLAGREEING
FILLAGREES
FILLESTERS
FILLIPEENS
FILLISTERS
FILMICALLY
FILMINESSES
FILMMAKERS
FILMMAKING
FILMMAKINGS
FILMOGRAPHIES
FILMOGRAPHY
FILMSETTER
FILMSETTERS
FILMSETTING
FILMSETTINGS
FILMSTRIPS
FILOPLUMES
FILOPODIUM
FILOSELLES
FILOVIRUSES
FILTERABILITIES
FILTERABILITY
FILTERABLE
FILTERABLENESS
FILTHINESS
FILTHINESSES
FILTRABILITIES
FILTRABILITY
FILTRATABLE
FILTRATING
FILTRATION
FILTRATIONS
FIMBRIATED
FIMBRIATES
FIMBRIATING
FIMBRIATION

FIMBRIATIONS	FINGERPRINT	FIREPOWERS	FISTFIGHTS
FIMBRILLATE	FINGERPRINTED	FIREPROOFED	FISTICUFFS
FIMICOLOUS	FINGERPRINTING	FIREPROOFING	FITFULNESS
FINABLENESS	FINGERPRINTINGS	FIREPROOFINGS	FITFULNESSES
FINABLENESSES	FINGERPRINTS	FIREPROOFS	FITTINGNESS
FINALISATION	FINGERSTALL	FIRESCREEN	FITTINGNESSES
FINALISATIONS	FINGERSTALLS	FIRESCREENS	FIVEFINGER
FINALISERS	FINGERTIPS	FIRESTONES	FIVEFINGERS
FINALISING	FINICALITIES	FIRESTORMS	FIVEPENCES
FINALISTIC	FINICALITY	FIRETHORNS	FIXEDNESSES
FINALITIES	FINICALNESS	FIRETRUCKS	FIXTURELESS
FINALIZATION	FINICALNESSES	FIREWARDEN	FIZZENLESS
FINALIZATIONS	FINICKETIER	FIREWARDENS	FIZZINESSES
FINALIZERS	FINICKETIEST	FIREWATERS	FLABBERGAST
FINALIZING	FINICKIEST	FIRMAMENTAL	FLABBERGASTED
FINANCIALIST	FINICKINESS	FIRMAMENTS	FLABBERGASTING
FINANCIALISTS	FINICKINESSES	FIRMNESSES	FLABBERGASTS
FINANCIALLY	FINICKINGS	FIRSTBORNS	FLABBINESS
FINANCIERED	FINISHINGS	FIRSTFRUITS	FLABBINESSES
FINANCIERING	FINITENESS	FIRSTLINGS	FLABELLATE
FINANCIERS	FINITENESSES	FIRSTNESSES	FLABELLATION
FINANCINGS	FINNICKIER	FISCALISTS	FLABELLATIONS
FINEABLENESS	FINNICKIEST	FISHABILITIES	FLABELLIFORM
FINEABLENESSES	FINNOCHIOS	FISHABILITY	FLABELLUMS
FINENESSES	FINOCCHIOS	FISHBURGER	FLACCIDEST
FINESSINGS	FIORATURAE	FISHBURGERS	FLACCIDITIES
FINGERBOARD	FIREBALLER	FISHERFOLK	FLACCIDITY
FINGERBOARDS	FIREBALLERS	FISHERWOMAN	FLACCIDNESS
FINGERBOWL	FIREBALLING	FISHERWOMEN	FLACCIDNESSES
FINGERBOWLS	FIREBOARDS	FISHFINGER	FLACKERIES
FINGERBREADTH	FIREBOMBED	FISHFINGERS	FLACKERING
FINGERBREADTHS	FIREBOMBING	FISHIFYING	FLAFFERING
FINGERGLASS	FIREBRANDS	FISHINESSES	FLAGELLANT
FINGERGLASSES	FIREBREAKS	FISHMONGER	FLAGELLANTISM
FINGERGUARD	FIREBRICKS	FISHMONGERS	FLAGELLANTISMS
FINGERGUARDS	FIREBUSHES	FISHPLATES	FLAGELLANTS
FINGERHOLD	FIRECRACKER	FISHTAILED	FLAGELLATE
FINGERHOLDS	FIRECRACKERS	FISHTAILING	FLAGELLATED
FINGERHOLE	FIRECRESTS	FISHWIFELY	FLAGELLATES
FINGERHOLES	FIREDRAGON	FISHYBACKS	FLAGELLATING
FINGERINGS	FIREDRAGONS	FISSICOSTATE	FLAGELLATION
FINGERLESS	FIREDRAKES	FISSILINGUAL	FLAGELLATIONS
FINGERLIKE	FIREFANGED	FISSILITIES	FLAGELLATOR
FINGERLING	FIREFANGING	FISSIONABILITY	FLAGELLATORS
FINGERLINGS	FIREFIGHTER	FISSIONABLE	FLAGELLATORY
FINGERMARK	FIREFIGHTERS	FISSIONABLES	FLAGELLIFEROUS
FINGERMARKS	FIREFIGHTING	FISSIONING	FLAGELLIFORM
FINGERNAIL	FIREFIGHTINGS	FISSIPALMATE	FLAGELLINS
FINGERNAILS	FIREFIGHTS	FISSIPARISM	FLAGELLOMANIA
FINGERPICK	FIREFLOATS	FISSIPARISMS	FLAGELLOMANIAC
FINGERPICKED	FIREFLOODS	FISSIPARITIES	FLAGELLOMANIACS
FINGERPICKING	FIREGUARDS	FISSIPARITY	FLAGELLOMANIAS
FINGERPICKINGS	FIREHOUSES	FISSIPAROUS	FLAGELLUMS
FINGERPICKS	FIRELIGHTER	FISSIPAROUSLY	FLAGEOLETS
FINGERPLATE	FIRELIGHTERS	FISSIPAROUSNESS	FLAGGINESS
FINGERPLATES	FIRELIGHTS	FISSIPEDAL	FLAGGINESSES
FINGERPOST	FIREPLACED	FISSIPEDES	FLAGGINGLY
FINGERPOSTS	FIREPLACES	FISSIROSTRAL	FLAGITATED

FLAGITATES
FLAGITATING
FLAGITATION
FLAGITATIONS
FLAGITIOUS
FLAGITIOUSLY
FLAGITIOUSNESS
FLAGRANCES
FLAGRANCIES
FLAGRANTLY
FLAGRANTNESS
FLAGRANTNESSES
FLAGSTAFFS
FLAGSTAVES
FLAGSTICKS
FLAGSTONES
FLAKINESSES
FLAMBEEING
FLAMBOYANCE
FLAMBOYANCES
FLAMBOYANCIES
FLAMBOYANCY
FLAMBOYANT
FLAMBOYANTE
FLAMBOYANTES
FLAMBOYANTLY
FLAMBOYANTS
FLAMEPROOF
FLAMEPROOFED
FLAMEPROOFER
FLAMEPROOFERS
FLAMEPROOFING
FLAMEPROOFS
FLAMETHROWER
FLAMETHROWERS
FLAMINGOES
FLAMINICAL
FLAMMABILITIES
FLAMMABILITY
FLAMMABLES
FLAMMIFEROUS
FLAMMULATED
FLAMMULATION
FLAMMULATIONS
FLANCHINGS
FLANCONADE
FLANCONADES
FLANGELESS
FLANKERING
FLANNELBOARD
FLANNELBOARDS
FLANNELETS
FLANNELETTE
FLANNELETTES
FLANNELGRAPH
FLANNELGRAPHS
FLANNELING
FLANNELINGS

FLANNELLED
FLANNELLING
FLANNELLINGS
FLANNELMOUTHED
FLAPDOODLE
FLAPDOODLES
FLAPPERHOOD
FLAPPERHOODS
FLAPPERISH
FLAPTRACKS
FLAREBACKS
FLASHBACKED
FLASHBACKING
FLASHBACKS
FLASHBOARD
FLASHBOARDS
FLASHBULBS
FLASHCARDS
FLASHCUBES
FLASHFORWARD
FLASHFORWARDED
FLASHFORWARDING
FLASHFORWARDS
FLASHINESS
FLASHINESSES
FLASHLAMPS
FLASHLIGHT
FLASHLIGHTS
FLASHMOBBING
FLASHMOBBINGS
FLASHOVERS
FLASHTUBES
FLATBREADS
FLATFISHES
FLATFOOTED
FLATFOOTING
FLATLANDER
FLATLANDERS
FLATLINERS
FLATLINING
FLATNESSES
FLATSCREEN
FLATSCREENS
FLATSHARES
FLATTENERS
FLATTENING
FLATTERABLE
FLATTERERS
FLATTERIES
FLATTERING
FLATTERINGLY
FLATTEROUS
FLATTEROUSLY
FLATULENCE
FLATULENCES
FLATULENCIES
FLATULENCY
FLATULENTLY

FLATWASHES
FLAUGHTERED
FLAUGHTERING
FLAUGHTERS
FLAUGHTING
FLAUNCHING
FLAUNCHINGS
FLAUNTIEST
FLAUNTINESS
FLAUNTINESSES
FLAUNTINGLY
FLAVANONES
FLAVESCENT
FLAVIVIRUS
FLAVIVIRUSES
FLAVONOIDS
FLAVOPROTEIN
FLAVOPROTEINS
FLAVOPURPURIN
FLAVOPURPURINS
FLAVORFULLY
FLAVORINGS
FLAVORISTS
FLAVORLESS
FLAVORSOME
FLAVOURDYNAMICS
FLAVOURERS
FLAVOURFUL
FLAVOURFULLY
FLAVOURING
FLAVOURINGS
FLAVOURLESS
FLAVOURSOME
FLAWLESSLY
FLAWLESSNESS
FLAWLESSNESSES
FLEAHOPPER
FLEAHOPPERS
FLEAMARKET
FLEAMARKETS
FLECHETTES
FLECKERING
FLECTIONAL
FLECTIONLESS
FLEDGELING
FLEDGELINGS
FLEDGLINGS
FLEECELESS
FLEECHINGS
FLEECHMENT
FLEECHMENTS
FLEECINESS
FLEECINESSES
FLEERINGLY
FLEETINGLY
FLEETINGNESS
FLEETINGNESSES
FLEETNESSES

FLEHMENING
FLEMISHING
FLESHHOODS
FLESHINESS
FLESHINESSES
FLESHLIEST
FLESHLINESS
FLESHLINESSES
FLESHLINGS
FLESHMENTS
FLESHMONGER
FLESHMONGERS
FLESHWORMS
FLETCHINGS
FLEURETTES
FLEXECUTIVE
FLEXECUTIVES
FLEXIBILITIES
FLEXIBILITY
FLEXIBLENESS
FLEXIBLENESSES
FLEXIHOURS
FLEXIONLESS
FLEXITARIAN
FLEXITARIANISM
FLEXITARIANISMS
FLEXITARIANS
FLEXITIMES
FLEXOGRAPHIC
FLEXOGRAPHIES
FLEXOGRAPHY
FLEXTIMERS
FLEXUOUSLY
FLIBBERTIGIBBET
FLICHTERED
FLICHTERING
FLICKERING
FLICKERINGLY
FLICKERTAIL
FLICKERTAILS
FLIGHTIEST
FLIGHTINESS
FLIGHTINESSES
FLIGHTLESS
FLIMFLAMMED
FLIMFLAMMER
FLIMFLAMMERIES
FLIMFLAMMERS
FLIMFLAMMERY
FLIMFLAMMING
FLIMSINESS
FLIMSINESSES
FLINCHINGLY
FLINCHINGS
FLINDERSIA
FLINDERSIAS
FLINTHEADS
FLINTIFIED

FLINTIFIES	FLOORBOARD	FLOWERBEDS	FLUORESCED
FLINTIFYING	FLOORBOARDS	FLOWERETTE	FLUORESCEIN
FLINTINESS	FLOORCLOTH	FLOWERETTES	FLUORESCEINE
FLINTINESSES	FLOORCLOTHS	FLOWERIEST	FLUORESCEINES
FLINTLOCKS	FLOORHEADS	FLOWERINESS	FLUORESCEINS
FLIPFLOPPED	FLOORSHOWS	FLOWERINESSES	FLUORESCENCE
FLIPFLOPPING	FLOORWALKER	FLOWERINGS	FLUORESCENCES
FLIPPANCIES	FLOORWALKERS	FLOWERLESS	FLUORESCENT
FLIPPANTLY	FLOPHOUSES	FLOWERLIKE	FLUORESCENTS
FLIPPANTNESS	FLOPPINESS	FLOWERPOTS	FLUORESCER
FLIPPANTNESSES	FLOPPINESSES	FLOWINGNESS	FLUORESCERS
FLIRTATION	FLORENTINE	FLOWINGNESSES	FLUORESCES
FLIRTATIONS	FLORENTINES	FLOWMETERS	FLUORESCING
FLIRTATIOUS	FLORESCENCE	FLOWSTONES	FLUORIDATE
FLIRTATIOUSLY	FLORESCENCES	FLUCTUATED	FLUORIDATED
FLIRTATIOUSNESS	FLORESCENT	FLUCTUATES	FLUORIDATES
FLIRTINGLY	FLORIATION	FLUCTUATING	FLUORIDATING
FLITTERING	FLORIATIONS	FLUCTUATION	FLUORIDATION
FLITTERMICE	FLORIBUNDA	FLUCTUATIONAL	FLUORIDATIONS
FLITTERMOUSE	FLORIBUNDAS	FLUCTUATIONS	FLUORIDISE
FLOATABILITIES	FLORICANES	FLUEGELHORN	FLUORIDISED
FLOATABILITY	FLORICULTURAL	FLUEGELHORNS	FLUORIDISES
FLOATATION	FLORICULTURE	FLUENTNESS	FLUORIDISING
FLOATATIONS	FLORICULTURES	FLUENTNESSES	FLUORIDIZE
FLOATINGLY	FLORICULTURIST	FLUFFINESS	FLUORIDIZED
FLOATPLANE	FLORICULTURISTS	FLUFFINESSES	FLUORIDIZES
FLOATPLANES	FLORIDEANS	FLUGELHORN	FLUORIDIZING
FLOCCILLATION	FLORIDEOUS	FLUGELHORNIST	FLUORIMETER
FLOCCILLATIONS	FLORIDITIES	FLUGELHORNISTS	FLUORIMETERS
FLOCCULANT	FLORIDNESS	FLUGELHORNS	FLUORIMETRIC
FLOCCULANTS	FLORIDNESSES	FLUIDEXTRACT	FLUORIMETRIES
FLOCCULATE	FLORIFEROUS	FLUIDEXTRACTS	FLUORIMETRY
FLOCCULATED	FLORIFEROUSNESS	FLUIDIFIED	FLUORINATE
FLOCCULATES	FLORIGENIC	FLUIDIFIES	FLUORINATED
FLOCCULATING	FLORILEGIA	FLUIDIFYING	FLUORINATES
FLOCCULATION	FLORILEGIUM	FLUIDISATION	FLUORINATING
FLOCCULATIONS	FLORISTICALLY	FLUIDISATIONS	FLUORINATION
FLOCCULATOR	FLORISTICS	FLUIDISERS	FLUORINATIONS
FLOCCULATORS	FLORISTRIES	FLUIDISING	FLUOROACETATE
FLOCCULENCE	FLOSCULOUS	FLUIDITIES	FLUOROACETATES
FLOCCULENCES	FLOTATIONS	FLUIDIZATION	FLUOROCARBON
FLOCCULENCIES	FLOUNCIEST	FLUIDIZATIONS	FLUOROCARBONS
FLOCCULENCY	FLOUNCINGS	FLUIDIZERS	FLUOROCHROME
FLOCCULENT	FLOUNDERED	FLUIDIZING	FLUOROCHROMES
FLOCCULENTLY	FLOUNDERING	FLUIDNESSES	FLUOROGRAPHIC
FLOODGATES	FLOURISHED	FLUKINESSES	FLUOROGRAPHIES
FLOODLIGHT	FLOURISHER	FLUMMERIES	FLUOROGRAPHY
FLOODLIGHTED	FLOURISHERS	FLUMMOXING	FLUOROMETER
FLOODLIGHTING	FLOURISHES	FLUNITRAZEPAM	FLUOROMETERS
FLOODLIGHTINGS	FLOURISHING	FLUNITRAZEPAMS	FLUOROMETRIC
FLOODLIGHTS	FLOURISHINGLY	FLUNKEYDOM	FLUOROMETRIES
FLOODMARKS	FLOUTINGLY	FLUNKEYDOMS	FLUOROMETRY
FLOODPLAIN	FLOUTINGSTOCK	FLUNKEYISH	FLUOROPHORE
FLOODPLAINS	FLOUTINGSTOCKS	FLUNKEYISM	FLUOROPHORES
FLOODTIDES	FLOWCHARTING	FLUNKEYISMS	FLUOROSCOPE
FLOODWALLS	FLOWCHARTINGS	FLUNKYISMS	FLUOROSCOPED
FLOODWATER	FLOWCHARTS	FLUORAPATITE	FLUOROSCOPES
FLOODWATERS	FLOWERAGES	FLUORAPATITES	FLUOROSCOPIC

FLUOROSCOPIES
FLUOROSCOPING
FLUOROSCOPIST
FLUOROSCOPISTS
FLUOROSCOPY
FLUOROTYPE
FLUOROTYPES
FLUOROURACIL
FLUOROURACILS
FLUORSPARS
FLUOXETINE
FLUOXETINES
FLUPHENAZINE
FLUPHENAZINES
FLUSHNESSES
FLUSHWORKS
FLUSTEREDLY
FLUSTERING
FLUSTERMENT
FLUSTERMENTS
FLUSTRATED
FLUSTRATES
FLUSTRATING
FLUSTRATION
FLUSTRATIONS
FLUTEMOUTH
FLUTEMOUTHS
FLUTTERBOARD
FLUTTERBOARDS
FLUTTERERS
FLUTTERING
FLUTTERINGLY
FLUVIALIST
FLUVIALISTS
FLUVIATILE
FLUVIOMARINE
FLUVOXAMINE
FLUVOXAMINES
FLUXIONALLY
FLUXIONARY
FLUXIONIST
FLUXIONISTS
FLUXMETERS
FLYBLOWING
FLYBRIDGES
FLYCATCHER
FLYCATCHERS
FLYPITCHER
FLYPITCHERS
FLYPITCHES
FLYPOSTING
FLYPOSTINGS
FLYRODDERS
FLYSCREENS
FLYSPECKED
FLYSPECKING
FLYSTRIKES
FLYSWATTER

FLYSWATTERS
FLYWEIGHTS
FOAMFLOWER
FOAMFLOWERS
FOAMINESSES
FOCALISATION
FOCALISATIONS
FOCALISING
FOCALIZATION
FOCALIZATIONS
FOCALIZING
FOCIMETERS
FOCOMETERS
FODDERINGS
FOEDERATUS
FOETATIONS
FOETICIDAL
FOETICIDES
FOETIDNESS
FOETIDNESSES
FOETIPAROUS
FOETOSCOPIES
FOETOSCOPY
FOGGINESSES
FOGRAMITES
FOGRAMITIES
FOISONLESS
FOLIACEOUS
FOLIATIONS
FOLIATURES
FOLKISHNESS
FOLKISHNESSES
FOLKLORISH
FOLKLORIST
FOLKLORISTIC
FOLKLORISTS
FOLKSINESS
FOLKSINESSES
FOLKSINGER
FOLKSINGERS
FOLKSINGING
FOLKSINGINGS
FOLLICULAR
FOLLICULATE
FOLLICULATED
FOLLICULIN
FOLLICULINS
FOLLICULITIS
FOLLICULITISES
FOLLICULOSE
FOLLICULOUS
FOLLOWABLE
FOLLOWERSHIP
FOLLOWERSHIPS
FOLLOWINGS
FOLLOWSHIP
FOLLOWSHIPS
FOMENTATION

FOMENTATIONS
FONCTIONNAIRE
FONCTIONNAIRES
FONDLINGLY
FONDNESSES
FONTANELLE
FONTANELLES
FONTICULUS
FONTICULUSES
FONTINALIS
FONTINALISES
FOODLESSNESS
FOODLESSNESSES
FOODSTUFFS
FOOLBEGGED
FOOLFISHES
FOOLHARDIER
FOOLHARDIEST
FOOLHARDILY
FOOLHARDINESS
FOOLHARDINESSES
FOOLHARDISE
FOOLHARDISES
FOOLHARDIZE
FOOLHARDIZES
FOOLISHEST
FOOLISHNESS
FOOLISHNESSES
FOOTBALLENE
FOOTBALLENES
FOOTBALLER
FOOTBALLERS
FOOTBALLING
FOOTBALLIST
FOOTBALLISTS
FOOTBOARDS
FOOTBREADTH
FOOTBREADTHS
FOOTBRIDGE
FOOTBRIDGES
FOOTCLOTHS
FOOTDRAGGER
FOOTDRAGGERS
FOOTFAULTED
FOOTFAULTING
FOOTFAULTS
FOOTGUARDS
FOOTLAMBERT
FOOTLAMBERTS
FOOTLESSLY
FOOTLESSNESS
FOOTLESSNESSES
FOOTLIGHTS
FOOTLOCKER
FOOTLOCKERS
FOOTNOTING
FOOTPLATEMAN
FOOTPLATEMEN

FOOTPLATES
FOOTPLATEWOMAN
FOOTPLATEWOMEN
FOOTPRINTS
FOOTSLOGGED
FOOTSLOGGER
FOOTSLOGGERS
FOOTSLOGGING
FOOTSLOGGINGS
FOOTSORENESS
FOOTSORENESSES
FOOTSTALKS
FOOTSTALLS
FOOTSTOCKS
FOOTSTONES
FOOTSTOOLED
FOOTSTOOLS
FOPPISHNESS
FOPPISHNESSES
FORAMINATED
FORAMINIFER
FORAMINIFERA
FORAMINIFERAL
FORAMINIFERAN
FORAMINIFERANS
FORAMINIFEROUS
FORAMINIFERS
FORAMINOUS
FORBEARANCE
FORBEARANCES
FORBEARANT
FORBEARERS
FORBEARING
FORBEARINGLY
FORBIDDALS
FORBIDDANCE
FORBIDDANCES
FORBIDDENLY
FORBIDDERS
FORBIDDING
FORBIDDINGLY
FORBIDDINGNESS
FORBIDDINGS
FORCEDNESS
FORCEDNESSES
FORCEFULLY
FORCEFULNESS
FORCEFULNESSES
FORCEMEATS
FORCEPSLIKE
FORCIBILITIES
FORCIBILITY
FORCIBLENESS
FORCIBLENESSES
FORCIPATED
FORCIPATION
FORCIPATIONS
FOREARMING

FOREBITTER	FOREGOINGS	FOREPAYMENT	FORESPEAKING
FOREBITTERS	FOREGONENESS	FOREPAYMENTS	FORESPEAKS
FOREBODEMENT	FOREGONENESSES	FOREPLANNED	FORESPENDING
FOREBODEMENTS	FOREGROUND	FOREPLANNING	FORESPENDS
FOREBODERS	FOREGROUNDED	FOREPOINTED	FORESPOKEN
FOREBODIES	FOREGROUNDING	FOREPOINTING	FORESTAGES
FOREBODING	FOREGROUNDS	FOREPOINTS	FORESTAIRS
FOREBODINGLY	FOREHANDED	FOREQUARTER	FORESTALLED
FOREBODINGNESS	FOREHANDEDLY	FOREQUARTERS	FORESTALLER
FOREBODINGS	FOREHANDEDNESS	FOREREACHED	FORESTALLERS
FOREBRAINS	FOREHANDING	FOREREACHES	FORESTALLING
FORECABINS	FOREHENTING	FOREREACHING	FORESTALLINGS
FORECADDIE	FOREHOOVES	FOREREADING	FORESTALLMENT
FORECADDIES	FOREIGNERS	FOREREADINGS	FORESTALLMENTS
FORECARRIAGE	FOREIGNISM	FORERUNNER	FORESTALLS
FORECARRIAGES	FOREIGNISMS	FORERUNNERS	FORESTALMENT
FORECASTABLE	FOREIGNNESS	FORERUNNING	FORESTALMENTS
FORECASTED	FOREIGNNESSES	FORESAYING	FORESTATION
FORECASTER	FOREJUDGED	FORESEEABILITY	FORESTATIONS
FORECASTERS	FOREJUDGEMENT	FORESEEABLE	FORESTAYSAIL
FORECASTING	FOREJUDGEMENTS	FORESEEING	FORESTAYSAILS
FORECASTLE	FOREJUDGES	FORESEEINGLY	FORESTLAND
FORECASTLES	FOREJUDGING	FORESHADOW	FORESTLANDS
FORECHECKED	FOREJUDGMENT	FORESHADOWED	FORESTLESS
FORECHECKER	FOREJUDGMENTS	FORESHADOWER	FORESTRIES
FORECHECKERS	FOREKNOWABLE	FORESHADOWERS	FORESWEARING
FORECHECKING	FOREKNOWING	FORESHADOWING	FORESWEARS
FORECHECKS	FOREKNOWINGLY	FORESHADOWINGS	FORETASTED
FORECHOSEN	FOREKNOWLEDGE	FORESHADOWS	FORETASTES
FORECLOSABLE	FOREKNOWLEDGES	FORESHANKS	FORETASTING
FORECLOSED	FORELADIES	FORESHEETS	FORETAUGHT
FORECLOSES	FORELAYING	FORESHEWED	FORETEACHES
FORECLOSING	FORELENDING	FORESHEWING	FORETEACHING
FORECLOSURE	FORELIFTED	FORESHOCKS	FORETELLER
FORECLOSURES	FORELIFTING	FORESHORES	FORETELLERS
FORECLOTHS	FORELOCKED	FORESHORTEN	FORETELLING
FORECOURSE	FORELOCKING	FORESHORTENED	FORETHINKER
FORECOURSES	FOREMANSHIP	FORESHORTENING	FORETHINKERS
FORECOURTS	FOREMANSHIPS	FORESHORTENINGS	FORETHINKING
FOREDAMNED	FOREMASTMAN	FORESHORTENS	FORETHINKS
FOREDATING	FOREMASTMEN	FORESHOWED	FORETHOUGHT
FOREDOOMED	FOREMEANING	FORESHOWING	FORETHOUGHTFUL
FOREDOOMING	FOREMENTIONED	FORESIGHTED	FORETHOUGHTS
FOREFATHER	FOREMOTHER	FORESIGHTEDLY	FORETOKENED
FOREFATHERLY	FOREMOTHERS	FORESIGHTEDNESS	FORETOKENING
FOREFATHERS	FORENIGHTS	FORESIGHTFUL	FORETOKENINGS
FOREFEELING	FORENSICALITIES	FORESIGHTLESS	FORETOKENS
FOREFEELINGLY	FORENSICALITY	FORESIGHTS	FORETOPMAN
FOREFENDED	FORENSICALLY	FORESIGNIFIED	FORETOPMAST
FOREFENDING	FOREORDAIN	FORESIGNIFIES	FORETOPMASTS
FOREFINGER	FOREORDAINED	FORESIGNIFY	FORETOPMEN
FOREFINGERS	FOREORDAINING	FORESIGNIFYING	FORETRIANGLE
FOREFRONTS	FOREORDAINMENT	FORESKIRTS	FORETRIANGLES
FOREGATHER	FOREORDAINMENTS	FORESLACKED	FOREVERMORE
FOREGATHERED	FOREORDAINS	FORESLACKING	FOREVERNESS
FOREGATHERING	FOREORDINATION	FORESLACKS	FOREVERNESSES
FOREGATHERS	FOREORDINATIONS	FORESLOWED	FOREVOUCHED
FOREGLEAMS	FOREPASSED	FORESLOWING	FOREWARNED

FOREWARNER	FORKINESSES	FORMLESSLY	FORSWEARERS
FOREWARNERS	FORKLIFTED	FORMLESSNESS	FORSWEARING
FOREWARNING	FORKLIFTING	FORMLESSNESSES	FORSWINKED
FOREWARNINGLY	FORLENDING	FORMULAICALLY	FORSWINKING
FOREWARNINGS	FORLORNEST	FORMULARIES	FORSWORNNESS
FOREWEIGHED	FORLORNNESS	FORMULARISATION	FORSWORNNESSES
FOREWEIGHING	FORLORNNESSES	FORMULARISE	FORSYTHIAS
FOREWEIGHS	FORMABILITIES	FORMULARISED	FORTALICES
FORFAIRING	FORMABILITY	FORMULARISER	FORTEPIANIST
FORFAITERS	FORMALDEHYDE	FORMULARISERS	FORTEPIANISTS
FORFAITING	FORMALDEHYDES	FORMULARISES	FORTEPIANO
FORFAITINGS	FORMALISABLE	FORMULARISING	FORTEPIANOS
FORFEITABLE	FORMALISATION	FORMULARISTIC	FORTHCOMES
FORFEITERS	FORMALISATIONS	FORMULARIZATION	FORTHCOMING
FORFEITING	FORMALISED	FORMULARIZE	FORTHCOMINGNESS
FORFEITURE	FORMALISER	FORMULARIZED	FORTHGOING
FORFEITURES	FORMALISERS	FORMULARIZER	FORTHGOINGS
FORFENDING	FORMALISES	FORMULARIZERS	FORTHINKING
FORFEUCHEN	FORMALISING	FORMULARIZES	FORTHOUGHT
FORFICULATE	FORMALISMS	FORMULARIZING	FORTHRIGHT
FORFOUGHEN	FORMALISTIC	FORMULATED	FORTHRIGHTLY
FORFOUGHTEN	FORMALISTICALLY	FORMULATES	FORTHRIGHTNESS
FORGATHERED	FORMALISTS	FORMULATING	FORTHRIGHTS
FORGATHERING	FORMALITER	FORMULATION	FORTIFIABLE
FORGATHERS	FORMALITIES	FORMULATIONS	FORTIFICATION
FORGEABILITIES	FORMALIZABLE	FORMULATOR	FORTIFICATIONS
FORGEABILITY	FORMALIZATION	FORMULATORS	FORTIFIERS
FORGETFULLY	FORMALIZATIONS	FORMULISED	FORTIFYING
FORGETFULNESS	FORMALIZED	FORMULISES	FORTIFYINGLY
FORGETFULNESSES	FORMALIZER	FORMULISING	FORTILAGES
FORGETTABLE	FORMALIZERS	FORMULISMS	FORTISSIMI
FORGETTERIES	FORMALIZES	FORMULISTIC	FORTISSIMO
FORGETTERS	FORMALIZING	FORMULISTS	FORTISSIMOS
FORGETTERY	FORMALNESS	FORMULIZED	FORTISSISSIMO
FORGETTING	FORMALNESSES	FORMULIZES	FORTITUDES
FORGETTINGLY	FORMAMIDES	FORMULIZING	FORTITUDINOUS
FORGETTINGS	FORMATIONAL	FORNICATED	FORTNIGHTLIES
FORGIVABLE	FORMATIONS	FORNICATES	FORTNIGHTLY
FORGIVABLY	FORMATIVELY	FORNICATING	FORTNIGHTS
FORGIVENESS	FORMATIVENESS	FORNICATION	FORTRESSED
FORGIVENESSES	FORMATIVENESSES	FORNICATIONS	FORTRESSES
FORGIVINGLY	FORMATIVES	FORNICATOR	FORTRESSING
FORGIVINGNESS	FORMATTERS	FORNICATORS	FORTRESSLIKE
FORGIVINGNESSES	FORMATTING	FORNICATRESS	FORTUITIES
FORGOTTENNESS	FORMFITTING	FORNICATRESSES	FORTUITISM
FORGOTTENNESSES	FORMICARIA	FORSAKENLY	FORTUITISMS
FORHAILING	FORMICARIES	FORSAKENNESS	FORTUITIST
FORHENTING	FORMICARIUM	FORSAKENNESSES	FORTUITISTS
FORHOOIEING	FORMICATED	FORSAKINGS	FORTUITOUS
FORINSECAL	FORMICATES	FORSLACKED	FORTUITOUSLY
FORISFAMILIATE	FORMICATING	FORSLACKING	FORTUITOUSNESS
FORISFAMILIATED	FORMICATION	FORSLOEING	FORTUNATELY
FORISFAMILIATES	FORMICATIONS	FORSLOWING	FORTUNATENESS
FORJUDGING	FORMIDABILITIES	FORSPEAKING	FORTUNATENESSES
FORJUDGMENT	FORMIDABILITY	FORSPENDING	FORTUNATES
FORJUDGMENTS	FORMIDABLE	FORSTERITE	FORTUNELESS
FORKEDNESS	FORMIDABLENESS	FORSTERITES	FORTUNISED
FORKEDNESSES	FORMIDABLY	FORSWEARER	FORTUNISES

FORTUNISING	FOUNDEROUS	FRACTIONATING	FRAGRANCING
FORTUNIZED	FOUNDLINGS	FRACTIONATION	FRAGRANTLY
FORTUNIZES	FOUNDRESSES	FRACTIONATIONS	FRAGRANTNESS
FORTUNIZING	FOUNTAINED	FRACTIONATOR	FRAGRANTNESSES
FORWANDERED	FOUNTAINHEAD	FRACTIONATORS	FRAICHEURS
FORWANDERING	FOUNTAINHEADS	FRACTIONED	FRAILNESSES
FORWANDERS	FOUNTAINING	FRACTIONING	FRAMBESIAS
FORWARDERS	FOUNTAINLESS	FRACTIONISATION	FRAMBOESIA
FORWARDEST	FOURCHETTE	FRACTIONISE	FRAMBOESIAS
FORWARDING	FOURCHETTES	FRACTIONISED	FRAMBOISES
FORWARDINGS	FOURDRINIER	FRACTIONISES	FRAMESHIFT
FORWARDNESS	FOURDRINIERS	FRACTIONISING	FRAMESHIFTS
FORWARDNESSES	FOURFOLDNESS	FRACTIONIZATION	FRAMEWORKS
FORWARNING	FOURFOLDNESSES	FRACTIONIZE	FRANCHISED
FORWASTING	FOURPENCES	FRACTIONIZED	FRANCHISEE
FORWEARIED	FOURPENNIES	FRACTIONIZES	FRANCHISEES
FORWEARIES	FOURPLEXES	FRACTIONIZING	FRANCHISEMENT
FORWEARYING	FOURRAGERE	FRACTIONLET	FRANCHISEMENTS
FOSCARNETS	FOURRAGERES	FRACTIONLETS	FRANCHISER
FOSSICKERS	FOURSCORTH	FRACTIOUSLY	FRANCHISERS
FOSSICKING	FOURSQUARE	FRACTIOUSNESS	FRANCHISES
FOSSICKINGS	FOURSQUARELY	FRACTIOUSNESSES	FRANCHISING
FOSSILIFEROUS	FOURSQUARENESS	FRACTOCUMULI	FRANCHISOR
FOSSILISABLE	FOURTEENER	FRACTOCUMULUS	FRANCHISORS
FOSSILISATION	FOURTEENERS	FRACTOGRAPHIES	FRANCISING
FOSSILISATIONS	FOURTEENTH	FRACTOGRAPHY	FRANCIZING
FOSSILISED	FOURTEENTHLY	FRACTOSTRATI	FRANCOLINS
FOSSILISES	FOURTEENTHS	FRACTOSTRATUS	FRANCOMANIA
FOSSILISING	FOVEOLATED	FRACTURABLE	FRANCOMANIAS
FOSSILIZABLE	FOXBERRIES	FRACTURERS	FRANCOPHIL
FOSSILIZATION	FOXHUNTERS	FRACTURING	FRANCOPHILE
FOSSILIZATIONS	FOXHUNTING	FRAGILENESS	FRANCOPHILES
FOSSILIZED	FOXHUNTINGS	FRAGILENESSES	FRANCOPHILS
FOSSILIZES	FOXINESSES	FRAGILITIES	FRANCOPHOBE
FOSSILIZING	FOXTROTTED	FRAGMENTAL	FRANCOPHOBES
FOSTERAGES	FOXTROTTING	FRAGMENTALLY	FRANCOPHOBIA
FOSTERINGLY	FOZINESSES	FRAGMENTARILY	FRANCOPHOBIAS
FOSTERINGS	FRABJOUSLY	FRAGMENTARINESS	FRANCOPHONE
FOSTERLING	FRACTALITIES	FRAGMENTARY	FRANCOPHONES
FOSTERLINGS	FRACTALITY	FRAGMENTATE	FRANGIBILITIES
FOSTRESSES	FRACTIONAL	FRAGMENTATED	FRANGIBILITY
FOTHERGILLA	FRACTIONALISE	FRAGMENTATES	FRANGIBLENESS
FOTHERGILLAS	FRACTIONALISED	FRAGMENTATING	FRANGIBLENESSES
FOUDROYANT	FRACTIONALISES	FRAGMENTATION	FRANGIPANE
FOUGHTIEST	FRACTIONALISING	FRAGMENTATIONS	FRANGIPANES
FOULBROODS	FRACTIONALISM	FRAGMENTED	FRANGIPANI
FOULDERING	FRACTIONALISMS	FRAGMENTING	FRANGIPANIS
FOULMOUTHED	FRACTIONALIST	FRAGMENTISE	FRANGIPANNI
FOULNESSES	FRACTIONALISTS	FRAGMENTISED	FRANKALMOIGN
FOUNDATION	FRACTIONALIZE	FRAGMENTISES	FRANKALMOIGNS
FOUNDATIONAL	FRACTIONALIZED	FRAGMENTISING	FRANKFORTS
FOUNDATIONALLY	FRACTIONALIZES	FRAGMENTIZE	FRANKFURTER
FOUNDATIONARY	FRACTIONALIZING	FRAGMENTIZED	FRANKFURTERS
FOUNDATIONER	FRACTIONALLY	FRAGMENTIZES	FRANKFURTS
FOUNDATIONERS	FRACTIONARY	FRAGMENTIZING	FRANKINCENSE
FOUNDATIONLESS	FRACTIONATE	FRAGRANCED	FRANKINCENSES
FOUNDATIONS	FRACTIONATED	FRAGRANCES	FRANKLINITE
FOUNDERING	FRACTIONATES	FRAGRANCIES	FRANKLINITES

FRANKNESSES	FREEBOOTED	FREEWRITINGS	FRICANDEAUS
FRANKPLEDGE	FREEBOOTER	FREEWRITTEN	FRICANDEAUX
FRANKPLEDGES	FREEBOOTERIES	FREEZINGLY	FRICANDOES
FRANSERIAS	FREEBOOTERS	FREIGHTAGE	FRICASSEED
FRANTICALLY	FREEBOOTERY	FREIGHTAGES	FRICASSEEING
FRANTICNESS	FREEBOOTIES	FREIGHTERS	FRICASSEES
FRANTICNESSES	FREEBOOTING	FREIGHTING	FRICATIVES
FRATCHIEST	FREEBOOTINGS	FREIGHTLESS	FRICTIONAL
FRATERNALISM	FREEDIVING	FREMESCENCE	FRICTIONALLY
FRATERNALISMS	FREEDIVINGS	FREMESCENCES	FRICTIONLESS
FRATERNALLY	FREEDWOMAN	FREMESCENT	FRICTIONLESSLY
FRATERNISATION	FREEDWOMEN	FREMITUSES	FRIEDCAKES
FRATERNISATIONS	FREEHANDED	FRENCHIFICATION	FRIENDINGS
FRATERNISE	FREEHANDEDLY	FRENCHIFIED	FRIENDLESS
FRATERNISED	FREEHANDEDNESS	FRENCHIFIES	FRIENDLESSNESS
FRATERNISER	FREEHEARTED	FRENCHIFYING	FRIENDLIER
FRATERNISERS	FREEHEARTEDLY	FRENETICAL	FRIENDLIES
FRATERNISES	FREEHOLDER	FRENETICALLY	FRIENDLIEST
FRATERNISING	FREEHOLDERS	FRENETICISM	FRIENDLILY
FRATERNITIES	FREELANCED	FRENETICISMS	FRIENDLINESS
FRATERNITY	FREELANCER	FRENETICNESS	FRIENDLINESSES
FRATERNIZATION	FREELANCERS	FRENETICNESSES	FRIENDSHIP
FRATERNIZATIONS	FREELANCES	FRENZIEDLY	FRIENDSHIPS
FRATERNIZE	FREELANCING	FREQUENCES	FRIEZELIKE
FRATERNIZED	FREELOADED	FREQUENCIES	FRIGATOONS
FRATERNIZER	FREELOADER	FREQUENTABLE	FRIGHTENABLE
FRATERNIZERS	FREELOADERS	FREQUENTATION	FRIGHTENED
FRATERNIZES	FREELOADING	FREQUENTATIONS	FRIGHTENER
FRATERNIZING	FREELOADINGS	FREQUENTATIVE	FRIGHTENERS
FRATRICIDAL	FREEMARTIN	FREQUENTATIVES	FRIGHTENING
FRATRICIDE	FREEMARTINS	FREQUENTED	FRIGHTENINGLY
FRATRICIDES	FREEMASONIC	FREQUENTER	FRIGHTFULLY
FRAUDFULLY	FREEMASONRIES	FREQUENTERS	FRIGHTFULNESS
FRAUDSTERS	FREEMASONRY	FREQUENTEST	FRIGHTFULNESSES
FRAUDULENCE	FREEMASONS	FREQUENTING	FRIGHTSOME
FRAUDULENCES	FREENESSES	FREQUENTLY	FRIGIDARIA
FRAUDULENCIES	FREEPHONES	FREQUENTNESS	FRIGIDARIUM
FRAUDULENCY	FREESHEETS	FREQUENTNESSES	FRIGIDITIES
FRAUDULENT	FREESTANDING	FRESCOINGS	FRIGIDNESS
FRAUDULENTLY	FREESTONES	FRESCOISTS	FRIGIDNESSES
FRAUDULENTNESS	FREESTYLER	FRESHENERS	FRIGORIFIC
FRAUGHTAGE	FREESTYLERS	FRESHENING	FRIGORIFICO
FRAUGHTAGES	FREESTYLES	FRESHERDOM	FRIGORIFICOS
FRAUGHTEST	FREESTYLING	FRESHERDOMS	FRIKKADELS
FRAUGHTING	FREESTYLINGS	FRESHMANSHIP	FRILLINESS
FRAXINELLA	FREETHINKER	FRESHMANSHIPS	FRILLINESSES
FRAXINELLAS	FREETHINKERS	FRESHNESSES	FRINGELESS
FREAKERIES	FREETHINKING	FRESHWATER	FRINGILLACEOUS
FREAKINESS	FREETHINKINGS	FRESHWATERS	FRINGILLID
FREAKINESSES	FREEWHEELED	FRETBOARDS	FRINGILLIFORM
FREAKISHLY	FREEWHEELER	FRETFULNESS	FRINGILLINE
FREAKISHNESS	FREEWHEELERS	FRETFULNESSES	FRIPONNERIE
FREAKISHNESSES	FREEWHEELING	FRIABILITIES	FRIPONNERIES
FRECKLIEST	FREEWHEELINGLY	FRIABILITY	FRIPPERERS
FRECKLINGS	FREEWHEELINGS	FRIABLENESS	FRIPPERIES
FREEBASERS	FREEWHEELS	FRIABLENESSES	FRISKINESS
FREEBASING	FREEWRITES	FRIARBIRDS	FRISKINESSES
FREEBOARDS	FREEWRITING	FRICANDEAU	FRISKINGLY

FRITHBORHS	FRONTLINES	FRUCTUATIONS	FUGACIOUSLY
FRITHSOKEN	FRONTLISTS	FRUCTUOUSLY	FUGACIOUSNESS
FRITHSOKENS	FRONTOGENESES	FRUCTUOUSNESS	FUGACIOUSNESSES
FRITHSTOOL	FRONTOGENESIS	FRUCTUOUSNESSES	FUGACITIES
FRITHSTOOLS	FRONTOGENETIC	FRUGALISTS	FUGITATION
FRITILLARIA	FRONTOLYSES	FRUGALITIES	FUGITATIONS
FRITILLARIAS	FRONTOLYSIS	FRUGALNESS	FUGITIVELY
FRITILLARIES	FRONTPAGED	FRUGALNESSES	FUGITIVENESS
FRITILLARY	FRONTPAGES	FRUGIFEROUS	FUGITIVENESSES
FRITTERERS	FRONTPAGING	FRUGIVORES	FUGITOMETER
FRITTERING	FRONTRUNNER	FRUGIVOROUS	FUGITOMETERS
FRIVOLITIES	FRONTRUNNERS	FRUITARIAN	FULFILLERS
FRIVOLLERS	FRONTRUNNING	FRUITARIANISM	FULFILLING
FRIVOLLING	FRONTRUNNINGS	FRUITARIANISMS	FULFILLINGS
FRIVOLOUSLY	FRONTWARDS	FRUITARIANS	FULFILLMENT
FRIVOLOUSNESS	FROSTBITES	FRUITCAKED	FULFILLMENTS
FRIVOLOUSNESSES	FROSTBITING	FRUITCAKES	FULFILMENT
FRIZZINESS	FROSTBITINGS	FRUITERERS	FULFILMENTS
FRIZZINESSES	FROSTBITTEN	FRUITERESS	FULGENCIES
FRIZZLIEST	FROSTBOUND	FRUITERESSES	FULGURATED
FRIZZLINESS	FROSTFISHES	FRUITERIES	FULGURATES
FRIZZLINESSES	FROSTINESS	FRUITFULLER	FULGURATING
FROGFISHES	FROSTINESSES	FRUITFULLEST	FULGURATION
FROGGERIES	FROSTLINES	FRUITFULLY	FULGURATIONS
FROGHOPPER	FROSTWORKS	FRUITFULNESS	FULGURITES
FROGHOPPERS	FROTHERIES	FRUITFULNESSES	FULIGINOSITIES
FROGMARCHED	FROTHINESS	FRUITINESS	FULIGINOSITY
FROGMARCHES	FROTHINESSES	FRUITINESSES	FULIGINOUS
FROGMARCHING	FROUGHIEST	FRUITLESSLY	FULIGINOUSLY
FROGMOUTHS	FROUZINESS	FRUITLESSNESS	FULIGINOUSNESS
FROGSPAWNS	FROUZINESSES	FRUITLESSNESSES	FULLBLOODS
FROLICKERS	FROWARDNESS	FRUITWOODS	FULLERENES
FROLICKING	FROWARDNESSES	FRUMENTACEOUS	FULLERIDES
FROLICSOME	FROWNINGLY	FRUMENTARIOUS	FULLERITES
FROLICSOMELY	FROWSINESS	FRUMENTATION	FULLMOUTHED
FROLICSOMENESS	FROWSINESSES	FRUMENTATIONS	FULLNESSES
FROMENTIES	FROWSTIEST	FRUMENTIES	FULMINANTS
FRONDESCENCE	FROWSTINESS	FRUMPINESS	FULMINATED
FRONDESCENCES	FROWSTINESSES	FRUMPINESSES	FULMINATES
FRONDESCENT	FROWZINESS	FRUMPISHLY	FULMINATING
FRONDIFEROUS	FROWZINESSES	FRUMPISHNESS	FULMINATION
FRONTAGERS	FROZENNESS	FRUMPISHNESSES	FULMINATIONS
FRONTALITIES	FROZENNESSES	FRUSEMIDES	FULMINATOR
FRONTALITY	FRUCTIFEROUS	FRUSTRATED	FULMINATORS
FRONTCOURT	FRUCTIFEROUSLY	FRUSTRATER	FULMINATORY
FRONTCOURTS	FRUCTIFICATION	FRUSTRATERS	FULMINEOUS
FRONTENISES	FRUCTIFICATIONS	FRUSTRATES	FULSOMENESS
FRONTIERED	FRUCTIFIED	FRUSTRATING	FULSOMENESSES
FRONTIERING	FRUCTIFIER	FRUSTRATINGLY	FUMATORIES
FRONTIERSMAN	FRUCTIFIERS	FRUSTRATION	FUMATORIUM
FRONTIERSMEN	FRUCTIFIES	FRUSTRATIONS	FUMATORIUMS
FRONTIERSWOMAN	FRUCTIFYING	FRUTESCENCE	FUMBLINGLY
FRONTIERSWOMEN	FRUCTIVOROUS	FRUTESCENCES	FUMBLINGNESS
FRONTISPIECE	FRUCTUARIES	FRUTESCENT	FUMBLINGNESSES
FRONTISPIECED	FRUCTUATED	FRUTIFYING	FUMIGATING
FRONTISPIECES	FRUCTUATES	FUCIVOROUS	FUMIGATION
FRONTISPIECING	FRUCTUATING	FUCOXANTHIN	FUMIGATIONS
FRONTLESSLY	FRUCTUATION	FUCOXANTHINS	FUMIGATORS

FUMIGATORY
FUMITORIES
FUMOSITIES
FUNAMBULATE
FUNAMBULATED
FUNAMBULATES
FUNAMBULATING
FUNAMBULATION
FUNAMBULATIONS
FUNAMBULATOR
FUNAMBULATORS
FUNAMBULATORY
FUNAMBULISM
FUNAMBULISMS
FUNAMBULIST
FUNAMBULISTS
FUNCTIONAL
FUNCTIONALISM
FUNCTIONALISMS
FUNCTIONALIST
FUNCTIONALISTIC
FUNCTIONALISTS
FUNCTIONALITIES
FUNCTIONALITY
FUNCTIONALLY
FUNCTIONALS
FUNCTIONARIES
FUNCTIONARY
FUNCTIONATE
FUNCTIONATED
FUNCTIONATES
FUNCTIONATING
FUNCTIONED
FUNCTIONING
FUNCTIONLESS
FUNDAMENTAL
FUNDAMENTALISM
FUNDAMENTALISMS
FUNDAMENTALIST
FUNDAMENTALISTS
FUNDAMENTALITY
FUNDAMENTALLY
FUNDAMENTALNESS
FUNDAMENTALS
FUNDAMENTS
FUNDHOLDER
FUNDHOLDERS
FUNDHOLDING
FUNDRAISED
FUNDRAISER
FUNDRAISERS
FUNDRAISES
FUNDRAISING
FUNEREALLY
FUNGIBILITIES
FUNGIBILITY
FUNGICIDAL
FUNGICIDALLY

FUNGICIDES
FUNGISTATIC
FUNGISTATICALLY
FUNGISTATS
FUNGOSITIES
FUNICULARS
FUNICULATE
FUNKINESSES
FUNNELFORM
FUNNELLING
FUNNINESSES
FURACIOUSNESS
FURACIOUSNESSES
FURACITIES
FURALDEHYDE
FURALDEHYDES
FURANOSIDE
FURANOSIDES
FURAZOLIDONE
FURAZOLIDONES
FURBEARERS
FURBELOWED
FURBELOWING
FURBISHERS
FURBISHING
FURCATIONS
FURCIFEROUS
FURFURACEOUS
FURFURACEOUSLY
FURFURALDEHYDE
FURFURALDEHYDES
FURFUROLES
FURIOSITIES
FURIOUSNESS
FURIOUSNESSES
FURLOUGHED
FURLOUGHING
FURMENTIES
FURNIMENTS
FURNISHERS
FURNISHING
FURNISHINGS
FURNISHMENT
FURNISHMENTS
FURNITURES
FUROSEMIDE
FUROSEMIDES
FURRIERIES
FURRINESSES
FURROWLESS
FURSHLUGGINER
FURTHCOMING
FURTHCOMINGS
FURTHERANCE
FURTHERANCES
FURTHERERS
FURTHERING
FURTHERMORE

FURTHERMOST
FURTHERSOME
FURTIVENESS
FURTIVENESSES
FURUNCULAR
FURUNCULOSES
FURUNCULOSIS
FURUNCULOUS
FUSHIONLESS
FUSIBILITIES
FUSIBILITY
FUSIBLENESS
FUSIBLENESSES
FUSILLADED
FUSILLADES
FUSILLADING
FUSILLATION
FUSILLATIONS
FUSIONISMS
FUSIONISTS
FUSIONLESS
FUSSBUDGET
FUSSBUDGETS
FUSSBUDGETY
FUSSINESSES
FUSTANELLA
FUSTANELLAS
FUSTANELLE
FUSTANELLES
FUSTIANISE
FUSTIANISED
FUSTIANISES
FUSTIANISING
FUSTIANIST
FUSTIANISTS
FUSTIANIZE
FUSTIANIZED
FUSTIANIZES
FUSTIANIZING
FUSTIGATED
FUSTIGATES
FUSTIGATING
FUSTIGATION
FUSTIGATIONS
FUSTIGATOR
FUSTIGATORS
FUSTIGATORY
FUSTILARIAN
FUSTILARIANS
FUSTILIRIAN
FUSTILIRIANS
FUSTILLIRIAN
FUSTILLIRIANS
FUSTINESSES
FUSULINIDS
FUTILENESS
FUTILENESSES
FUTILITARIAN

FUTILITARIANISM
FUTILITARIANS
FUTILITIES
FUTURELESS
FUTURELESSNESS
FUTURISTIC
FUTURISTICALLY
FUTURISTICS
FUTURITIES
FUTURITION
FUTURITIONS
FUTUROLOGICAL
FUTUROLOGIES
FUTUROLOGIST
FUTUROLOGISTS
FUTUROLOGY
FUZZINESSES

G

GABAPENTIN
GABAPENTINS
GABARDINES
GABBINESSES
GABBLEMENT
GABBLEMENTS
GABBROITIC
GABERDINES
GABERLUNZIE
GABERLUNZIES
GABIONADES
GABIONAGES
GABIONNADE
GABIONNADES
GADGETEERS
GADGETRIES
GADOLINITE
GADOLINITES
GADOLINIUM
GADOLINIUMS
GADROONING
GADROONINGS
GADZOOKERIES
GADZOOKERY
GAELICISED
GAELICISES
GAELICISING
GAELICISMS
GAELICIZED
GAELICIZES
GAELICIZING
GAILLARDIA
GAILLARDIAS
GAINFULNESS
GAINFULNESSES
GAINGIVING
GAINGIVINGS
GAINLESSNESS
GAINLESSNESSES
GAINLINESS
GAINLINESSES
GAINSAYERS
GAINSAYING
GAINSAYINGS
GAINSTRIVE
GAINSTRIVED
GAINSTRIVEN
GAINSTRIVES
GAINSTRIVING
GAINSTROVE
GAITERLESS
GALABIYAHS
GALACTAGOGUE

GALACTAGOGUES
GALACTOMETER
GALACTOMETERS
GALACTOMETRIES
GALACTOMETRY
GALACTOPHOROUS
GALACTOPOIESES
GALACTOPOIESIS
GALACTOPOIETIC
GALACTOPOIETICS
GALACTORRHEA
GALACTORRHEAS
GALACTORRHOEA
GALACTORRHOEAS
GALACTOSAEMIA
GALACTOSAEMIAS
GALACTOSAMINE
GALACTOSAMINES
GALACTOSEMIA
GALACTOSEMIAS
GALACTOSEMIC
GALACTOSES
GALACTOSIDASE
GALACTOSIDASES
GALACTOSIDE
GALACTOSIDES
GALACTOSYL
GALACTOSYLS
GALANTAMINE
GALANTAMINES
GALANTINES
GALAVANTED
GALAVANTING
GALDRAGONS
GALENGALES
GALENICALS
GALEOPITHECINE
GALEOPITHECOID
GALIMATIAS
GALIMATIASES
GALINGALES
GALIONGEES
GALIVANTED
GALIVANTING
GALLABEAHS
GALLABIAHS
GALLABIEHS
GALLABIYAH
GALLABIYAHS
GALLABIYAS
GALLABIYEH
GALLABIYEHS
GALLAMINES

GALLANTEST
GALLANTING
GALLANTNESS
GALLANTNESSES
GALLANTRIES
GALLBLADDER
GALLBLADDERS
GALLEASSES
GALLERISTS
GALLERYGOER
GALLERYGOERS
GALLERYING
GALLERYITE
GALLERYITES
GALLIAMBIC
GALLIAMBICS
GALLIARDISE
GALLIARDISES
GALLIASSES
GALLICISATION
GALLICISATIONS
GALLICISED
GALLICISES
GALLICISING
GALLICISMS
GALLICIZATION
GALLICIZATIONS
GALLICIZED
GALLICIZES
GALLICIZING
GALLIGASKINS
GALLIMAUFRIES
GALLIMAUFRY
GALLINACEAN
GALLINACEANS
GALLINACEOUS
GALLINAZOS
GALLINIPPER
GALLINIPPERS
GALLINULES
GALLISISED
GALLISISES
GALLISISING
GALLISIZED
GALLISIZES
GALLISIZING
GALLIVANTED
GALLIVANTING
GALLIVANTS
GALLIWASPS
GALLOGLASS
GALLOGLASSES
GALLONAGES

GALLOPADED
GALLOPADES
GALLOPADING
GALLOWGLASS
GALLOWGLASSES
GALLOWSNESS
GALLOWSNESSES
GALLSICKNESS
GALLSICKNESSES
GALLSTONES
GALLUMPHED
GALLUMPHING
GALLYGASKINS
GALRAVAGED
GALRAVAGES
GALRAVAGING
GALRAVITCH
GALRAVITCHED
GALRAVITCHES
GALRAVITCHING
GALUMPHERS
GALUMPHING
GALVANICAL
GALVANICALLY
GALVANISATION
GALVANISATIONS
GALVANISED
GALVANISER
GALVANISERS
GALVANISES
GALVANISING
GALVANISMS
GALVANISTS
GALVANIZATION
GALVANIZATIONS
GALVANIZED
GALVANIZER
GALVANIZERS
GALVANIZES
GALVANIZING
GALVANOMETER
GALVANOMETERS
GALVANOMETRIC
GALVANOMETRICAL
GALVANOMETRIES
GALVANOMETRY
GALVANOPLASTIC
GALVANOPLASTIES
GALVANOPLASTY
GALVANOSCOPE
GALVANOSCOPES
GALVANOSCOPIC
GALVANOSCOPIES

GALVANOSCOPY	GAMOTROPISM	GARIBALDIS	GASOMETRIC
GALVANOTROPIC	GAMOTROPISMS	GARISHNESS	GASOMETRICAL
GALVANOTROPISM	GAMYNESSES	GARISHNESSES	GASOMETRIES
GALVANOTROPISMS	GANDERISMS	GARLANDAGE	GASPEREAUS
GAMAHUCHED	GANGBANGED	GARLANDAGES	GASPEREAUX
GAMAHUCHES	GANGBANGER	GARLANDING	GASPINESSES
GAMAHUCHING	GANGBANGERS	GARLANDLESS	GASSINESSES
GAMARUCHED	GANGBANGING	GARLANDRIES	GASTEROPOD
GAMARUCHES	GANGBOARDS	GARLICKIER	GASTEROPODOUS
GAMARUCHING	GANGBUSTER	GARLICKIEST	GASTEROPODS
GAMBADOING	GANGBUSTERS	GARLICKING	GASTIGHTNESS
GAMBOLLING	GANGBUSTING	GARMENTING	GASTIGHTNESSES
GAMEBREAKER	GANGBUSTINGS	GARMENTLESS	GASTNESSES
GAMEBREAKERS	GANGLIATED	GARMENTURE	GASTRAEUMS
GAMEKEEPER	GANGLIFORM	GARMENTURES	GASTRALGIA
GAMEKEEPERS	GANGLIONATED	GARNETIFEROUS	GASTRALGIAS
GAMEKEEPING	GANGLIONIC	GARNIERITE	GASTRALGIC
GAMEKEEPINGS	GANGLIOSIDE	GARNIERITES	GASTRECTOMIES
GAMENESSES	GANGLIOSIDES	GARNISHEED	GASTRECTOMY
GAMESMANSHIP	GANGPLANKS	GARNISHEEING	GASTRITIDES
GAMESMANSHIPS	GANGRENING	GARNISHEEMENT	GASTRITISES
GAMESOMELY	GANGRENOUS	GARNISHEEMENTS	GASTROCNEMII
GAMESOMENESS	GANGSHAGGED	GARNISHEES	GASTROCNEMIUS
GAMESOMENESSES	GANGSHAGGING	GARNISHERS	GASTROCOLIC
GAMETANGIA	GANGSTERDOM	GARNISHING	GASTRODUODENAL
GAMETANGIAL	GANGSTERDOMS	GARNISHINGS	GASTROENTERIC
GAMETANGIUM	GANGSTERISH	GARNISHMENT	GASTROENTERITIC
GAMETICALLY	GANGSTERISM	GARNISHMENTS	GASTROENTERITIS
GAMETOCYTE	GANGSTERISMS	GARNISHRIES	GASTROLITH
GAMETOCYTES	GANGSTERLAND	GARNITURES	GASTROLITHS
GAMETOGENESES	GANGSTERLANDS	GAROTTINGS	GASTROLOGER
GAMETOGENESIS	GANNETRIES	GARRETEERS	GASTROLOGERS
GAMETOGENIC	GANNISTERS	GARRISONED	GASTROLOGICAL
GAMETOGENIES	GANTELOPES	GARRISONING	GASTROLOGIES
GAMETOGENOUS	GANTLETING	GARROTTERS	GASTROLOGIST
GAMETOGENY	GAOLBREAKS	GARROTTING	GASTROLOGISTS
GAMETOPHORE	GAOLERESSES	GARROTTINGS	GASTROLOGY
GAMETOPHORES	GARAGISTES	GARRULITIES	GASTROMANCIES
GAMETOPHORIC	GARBAGEMAN	GARRULOUSLY	GASTROMANCY
GAMETOPHYTE	GARBAGEMEN	GARRULOUSNESS	GASTRONOME
GAMETOPHYTES	GARBOLOGIES	GARRULOUSNESSES	GASTRONOMER
GAMETOPHYTIC	GARBOLOGIST	GARRYOWENS	GASTRONOMERS
GAMINERIES	GARBOLOGISTS	GASBAGGING	GASTRONOMES
GAMINESQUE	GARDENFULS	GASCONADED	GASTRONOMIC
GAMINESSES	GARDENINGS	GASCONADER	GASTRONOMICAL
GAMMERSTANG	GARDENLESS	GASCONADERS	GASTRONOMICALLY
GAMMERSTANGS	GARDEROBES	GASCONADES	GASTRONOMIES
GAMMOCKING	GARGANTUAN	GASCONADING	GASTRONOMIST
GAMMONINGS	GARGANTUAS	GASCONISMS	GASTRONOMISTS
GAMOGENESES	GARGARISED	GASEOUSNESS	GASTRONOMY
GAMOGENESIS	GARGARISES	GASEOUSNESSES	GASTROPODAN
GAMOGENETIC	GARGARISING	GASHLINESS	GASTROPODANS
GAMOGENETICAL	GARGARISMS	GASHLINESSES	GASTROPODOUS
GAMOGENETICALLY	GARGARIZED	GASHOLDERS	GASTROPODS
GAMOPETALOUS	GARGARIZES	GASIFIABLE	GASTROSCOPE
GAMOPHYLLOUS	GARGARIZING	GASIFICATION	GASTROSCOPES
GAMOSEPALOUS	GARGOYLISM	GASIFICATIONS	GASTROSCOPIC
GAMOTROPIC	GARGOYLISMS	GASOMETERS	GASTROSCOPIES

GASTROSCOPIST	GAZETTEERISH	GELLIFLOWRE	GENECOLOGY
GASTROSCOPISTS	GAZETTEERS	GELLIFLOWRES	GENERALATE
GASTROSCOPY	GAZILLIONAIRE	GELSEMINES	GENERALATES
GASTROSOPH	GAZILLIONAIRES	GELSEMININE	GENERALCIES
GASTROSOPHER	GAZILLIONS	GELSEMININES	GENERALISABLE
GASTROSOPHERS	GAZUNDERED	GELSEMIUMS	GENERALISATION
GASTROSOPHIES	GAZUNDERER	GEMEINSCHAFT	GENERALISATIONS
GASTROSOPHS	GAZUNDERERS	GEMEINSCHAFTEN	GENERALISE
GASTROSOPHY	GAZUNDERING	GEMEINSCHAFTS	GENERALISED
GASTROSTOMIES	GEALOUSIES	GEMFIBROZIL	GENERALISER
GASTROSTOMY	GEANTICLINAL	GEMFIBROZILS	GENERALISERS
GASTROTOMIES	GEANTICLINE	GEMINATELY	GENERALISES
GASTROTOMY	GEANTICLINES	GEMINATING	GENERALISING
GASTROTRICH	GEARCHANGE	GEMINATION	GENERALISSIMO
GASTROTRICHES	GEARCHANGES	GEMINATIONS	GENERALISSIMOS
GASTROTRICHS	GEARSHIFTS	GEMMACEOUS	GENERALIST
GASTROVASCULAR	GEARWHEELS	GEMMATIONS	GENERALISTS
GASTRULATE	GEEKINESSES	GEMMIFEROUS	GENERALITIES
GASTRULATED	GEEKSPEAKS	GEMMINESSES	GENERALITY
GASTRULATES	GEFUFFLING	GEMMIPAROUS	GENERALIZABLE
GASTRULATING	GEGENSCHEIN	GEMMIPAROUSLY	GENERALIZATION
GASTRULATION	GEGENSCHEINS	GEMMOLOGICAL	GENERALIZATIONS
GASTRULATIONS	GEHLENITES	GEMMOLOGIES	GENERALIZE
GATECRASHED	GEITONOGAMIES	GEMMOLOGIST	GENERALIZED
GATECRASHER	GEITONOGAMOUS	GEMMOLOGISTS	GENERALIZER
GATECRASHERS	GEITONOGAMY	GEMMULATION	GENERALIZERS
GATECRASHES	GELANDESPRUNG	GEMMULATIONS	GENERALIZES
GATECRASHING	GELANDESPRUNGS	GEMOLOGICAL	GENERALIZING
GATEHOUSES	GELATINATE	GEMOLOGIES	GENERALLED
GATEKEEPER	GELATINATED	GEMOLOGIST	GENERALLING
GATEKEEPERS	GELATINATES	GEMOLOGISTS	GENERALNESS
GATEKEEPING	GELATINATING	GEMUTLICHKEIT	GENERALNESSES
GATHERABLE	GELATINATION	GEMUTLICHKEITS	GENERALSHIP
GATHERINGS	GELATINATIONS	GENDARMERIE	GENERALSHIPS
GAUCHENESS	GELATINISATION	GENDARMERIES	GENERATING
GAUCHENESSES	GELATINISATIONS	GENDARMERY	GENERATION
GAUCHERIES	GELATINISE	GENDERISED	GENERATIONAL
GAUDEAMUSES	GELATINISED	GENDERISES	GENERATIONALLY
GAUDINESSES	GELATINISER	GENDERISING	GENERATIONISM
GAUFFERING	GELATINISERS	GENDERIZED	GENERATIONISMS
GAUFFERINGS	GELATINISES	GENDERIZES	GENERATIONS
GAULEITERS	GELATINISING	GENDERIZING	GENERATIVE
GAULTHERIA	GELATINIZATION	GENDERLESS	GENERATORS
GAULTHERIAS	GELATINIZATIONS	GENEALOGIC	GENERATRICES
GAUNTLETED	GELATINIZE	GENEALOGICAL	GENERATRIX
GAUNTLETING	GELATINIZED	GENEALOGICALLY	GENERICALLY
GAUNTNESSES	GELATINIZER	GENEALOGIES	GENERICNESS
GAUSSMETER	GELATINIZERS	GENEALOGISE	GENERICNESSES
GAUSSMETERS	GELATINIZES	GENEALOGISED	GENEROSITIES
GAUZINESSES	GELATINIZING	GENEALOGISES	GENEROSITY
GAVELKINDS	GELATINOID	GENEALOGISING	GENEROUSLY
GAWKIHOODS	GELATINOIDS	GENEALOGIST	GENEROUSNESS
GAWKINESSES	GELATINOUS	GENEALOGISTS	GENEROUSNESSES
GAWKISHNESS	GELATINOUSLY	GENEALOGIZE	GENETHLIAC
GAWKISHNESSES	GELATINOUSNESS	GENEALOGIZED	GENETHLIACAL
GAZEHOUNDS	GELIDITIES	GENEALOGIZES	GENETHLIACALLY
GAZETTEERED	GELIDNESSES	GENEALOGIZING	GENETHLIACON
GAZETTEERING	GELIGNITES	GENECOLOGIES	GENETHLIACONS

GENETHLIACS
GENETHLIALOGIC
GENETHLIALOGIES
GENETHLIALOGY
GENETICALLY
GENETICIST
GENETICISTS
GENETOTROPHIC
GENETRICES
GENETRIXES
GENEVRETTE
GENEVRETTES
GENIALISED
GENIALISES
GENIALISING
GENIALITIES
GENIALIZED
GENIALIZES
GENIALIZING
GENIALNESS
GENIALNESSES
GENICULATE
GENICULATED
GENICULATELY
GENICULATES
GENICULATING
GENICULATION
GENICULATIONS
GENISTEINS
GENITALIAL
GENITIVALLY
GENITIVELY
GENITOURINARY
GENITRICES
GENITRIXES
GENOPHOBIA
GENOPHOBIAS
GENOTYPICAL
GENOTYPICALLY
GENOTYPICITIES
GENOTYPICITY
GENOUILLERE
GENOUILLERES
GENSDARMES
GENTAMICIN
GENTAMICINS
GENTEELEST
GENTEELISE
GENTEELISED
GENTEELISES
GENTEELISH
GENTEELISING
GENTEELISM
GENTEELISMS
GENTEELIZE
GENTEELIZED
GENTEELIZES
GENTEELIZING

GENTEELNESS
GENTEELNESSES
GENTIANACEOUS
GENTIANELLA
GENTIANELLAS
GENTILESSE
GENTILESSES
GENTILHOMME
GENTILISED
GENTILISES
GENTILISING
GENTILISMS
GENTILITIAL
GENTILITIAN
GENTILITIES
GENTILITIOUS
GENTILIZED
GENTILIZES
GENTILIZING
GENTILSHOMMES
GENTLEFOLK
GENTLEFOLKS
GENTLEHOOD
GENTLEHOODS
GENTLEMANHOOD
GENTLEMANHOODS
GENTLEMANLIKE
GENTLEMANLINESS
GENTLEMANLY
GENTLEMANSHIP
GENTLEMANSHIPS
GENTLENESS
GENTLENESSE
GENTLENESSES
GENTLEPERSON
GENTLEPERSONS
GENTLEWOMAN
GENTLEWOMANLY
GENTLEWOMEN
GENTRIFICATION
GENTRIFICATIONS
GENTRIFIED
GENTRIFIER
GENTRIFIERS
GENTRIFIES
GENTRIFYING
GENUFLECTED
GENUFLECTING
GENUFLECTION
GENUFLECTIONS
GENUFLECTOR
GENUFLECTORS
GENUFLECTS
GENUFLEXION
GENUFLEXIONS
GENUINENESS
GENUINENESSES
GEOBOTANIC

GEOBOTANICAL
GEOBOTANIES
GEOBOTANIST
GEOBOTANISTS
GEOCACHING
GEOCACHINGS
GEOCARPIES
GEOCENTRIC
GEOCENTRICAL
GEOCENTRICALLY
GEOCENTRICISM
GEOCENTRICISMS
GEOCHEMICAL
GEOCHEMICALLY
GEOCHEMIST
GEOCHEMISTRIES
GEOCHEMISTRY
GEOCHEMISTS
GEOCHRONOLOGIC
GEOCHRONOLOGIES
GEOCHRONOLOGIST
GEOCHRONOLOGY
GEOCORONAE
GEOCORONAS
GEODEMOGRAPHICS
GEODESICAL
GEODESISTS
GEODETICAL
GEODETICALLY
GEODYNAMIC
GEODYNAMICAL
GEODYNAMICIST
GEODYNAMICISTS
GEODYNAMICS
GEOGNOSIES
GEOGNOSTIC
GEOGNOSTICAL
GEOGNOSTICALLY
GEOGRAPHER
GEOGRAPHERS
GEOGRAPHIC
GEOGRAPHICAL
GEOGRAPHICALLY
GEOGRAPHIES
GEOHYDROLOGIC
GEOHYDROLOGIES
GEOHYDROLOGIST
GEOHYDROLOGISTS
GEOHYDROLOGY
GEOLATRIES
GEOLINGUISTICS
GEOLOGIANS
GEOLOGICAL
GEOLOGICALLY
GEOLOGISED
GEOLOGISES
GEOLOGISING
GEOLOGISTS

GEOLOGIZED
GEOLOGIZES
GEOLOGIZING
GEOMAGNETIC
GEOMAGNETICALLY
GEOMAGNETISM
GEOMAGNETISMS
GEOMAGNETIST
GEOMAGNETISTS
GEOMANCERS
GEOMANCIES
GEOMECHANICS
GEOMEDICAL
GEOMEDICINE
GEOMEDICINES
GEOMETRICAL
GEOMETRICALLY
GEOMETRICIAN
GEOMETRICIANS
GEOMETRICS
GEOMETRIDS
GEOMETRIES
GEOMETRISATION
GEOMETRISATIONS
GEOMETRISE
GEOMETRISED
GEOMETRISES
GEOMETRISING
GEOMETRIST
GEOMETRISTS
GEOMETRIZATION
GEOMETRIZATIONS
GEOMETRIZE
GEOMETRIZED
GEOMETRIZES
GEOMETRIZING
GEOMORPHIC
GEOMORPHOGENIC
GEOMORPHOGENIES
GEOMORPHOGENIST
GEOMORPHOGENY
GEOMORPHOLOGIC
GEOMORPHOLOGIES
GEOMORPHOLOGIST
GEOMORPHOLOGY
GEOPHAGIAS
GEOPHAGIES
GEOPHAGISM
GEOPHAGISMS
GEOPHAGIST
GEOPHAGISTS
GEOPHAGOUS
GEOPHILOUS
GEOPHYSICAL
GEOPHYSICALLY
GEOPHYSICIST
GEOPHYSICISTS
GEOPHYSICS

GEOPOLITICAL	GERIATRIST	GERRYMANDERERS	GHOSTWRITING
GEOPOLITICALLY	GERIATRISTS	GERRYMANDERING	GHOSTWRITTEN
GEOPOLITICIAN	GERMANDERS	GERRYMANDERINGS	GHOSTWROTE
GEOPOLITICIANS	GERMANENESS	GERRYMANDERS	GHOULISHLY
GEOPOLITICS	GERMANENESSES	GERUNDIVAL	GHOULISHNESS
GEOPONICAL	GERMANISATION	GERUNDIVELY	GHOULISHNESSES
GEOPRESSURED	GERMANISATIONS	GERUNDIVES	GIANTESSES
GEORGETTES	GERMANISED	GESELLSCHAFT	GIANTHOODS
GEOSCIENCE	GERMANISES	GESELLSCHAFTEN	GIANTLIEST
GEOSCIENCES	GERMANISING	GESELLSCHAFTS	GIANTSHIPS
GEOSCIENTIFIC	GERMANITES	GESNERIADS	GIARDIASES
GEOSCIENTIST	GERMANIUMS	GESSAMINES	GIARDIASIS
GEOSCIENTISTS	GERMANIZATION	GESTALTISM	GIBBERELLIC
GEOSPHERES	GERMANIZATIONS	GESTALTISMS	GIBBERELLIN
GEOSTATICS	GERMANIZED	GESTALTIST	GIBBERELLINS
GEOSTATIONARY	GERMANIZES	GESTALTISTS	GIBBERISHES
GEOSTRATEGIC	GERMANIZING	GESTATIONAL	GIBBETTING
GEOSTRATEGICAL	GERMICIDAL	GESTATIONS	GIBBOSITIES
GEOSTRATEGIES	GERMICIDES	GESTATORIAL	GIBBOUSNESS
GEOSTRATEGIST	GERMINABILITIES	GESTICULANT	GIBBOUSNESSES
GEOSTRATEGISTS	GERMINABILITY	GESTICULATE	GIDDINESSES
GEOSTRATEGY	GERMINABLE	GESTICULATED	GIFTEDNESS
GEOSTROPHIC	GERMINALLY	GESTICULATES	GIFTEDNESSES
GEOSTROPHICALLY	GERMINATED	GESTICULATING	GIFTWRAPPED
GEOSYNCHRONOUS	GERMINATES	GESTICULATION	GIFTWRAPPING
GEOSYNCLINAL	GERMINATING	GESTICULATIONS	GIGACYCLES
GEOSYNCLINE	GERMINATION	GESTICULATIVE	GIGAHERTZES
GEOSYNCLINES	GERMINATIONS	GESTICULATOR	GIGANTESQUE
GEOTACTICAL	GERMINATIVE	GESTICULATORS	GIGANTICALLY
GEOTACTICALLY	GERMINATOR	GESTICULATORY	GIGANTICIDE
GEOTECHNIC	GERMINATORS	GESTURALLY	GIGANTICIDES
GEOTECHNICAL	GERMINESSES	GESUNDHEIT	GIGANTICNESS
GEOTECHNICS	GERMPLASMS	GETTERINGS	GIGANTICNESSES
GEOTECHNOLOGIES	GERONTOCRACIES	GEWURZTRAMINER	GIGANTISMS
GEOTECHNOLOGY	GERONTOCRACY	GEWURZTRAMINERS	GIGANTOLOGIES
GEOTECTONIC	GERONTOCRAT	GEYSERITES	GIGANTOLOGY
GEOTECTONICALLY	GERONTOCRATIC	GHASTFULLY	GIGANTOMACHIA
GEOTECTONICS	GERONTOCRATS	GHASTLIEST	GIGANTOMACHIAS
GEOTEXTILE	GERONTOLOGIC	GHASTLINESS	GIGANTOMACHIES
GEOTEXTILES	GERONTOLOGICAL	GHASTLINESSES	GIGANTOMACHY
GEOTHERMAL	GERONTOLOGIES	GHASTNESSES	GIGGLESOME
GEOTHERMALLY	GERONTOLOGIST	GHETTOISATION	GIGGLINGLY
GEOTHERMIC	GERONTOLOGISTS	GHETTOISATIONS	GIGMANITIES
GEOTHERMOMETER	GERONTOLOGY	GHETTOISED	GILDSWOMAN
GEOTHERMOMETERS	GERONTOMORPHIC	GHETTOISES	GILDSWOMEN
GEOTROPICALLY	GERONTOPHIL	GHETTOISING	GILLFLIRTS
GEOTROPISM	GERONTOPHILE	GHETTOIZATION	GILLIFLOWER
GEOTROPISMS	GERONTOPHILES	GHETTOIZATIONS	GILLIFLOWERS
GERANIACEOUS	GERONTOPHILIA	GHETTOIZED	GILLNETTED
GERATOLOGICAL	GERONTOPHILIAS	GHETTOIZES	GILLNETTER
GERATOLOGIES	GERONTOPHILS	GHETTOIZING	GILLNETTERS
GERATOLOGIST	GERONTOPHOBE	GHOSTLIEST	GILLNETTING
GERATOLOGISTS	GERONTOPHOBES	GHOSTLINESS	GILLRAVAGE
GERATOLOGY	GERONTOPHOBIA	GHOSTLINESSES	GILLRAVAGED
GERFALCONS	GERONTOPHOBIAS	GHOSTWRITE	GILLRAVAGES
GERIATRICIAN	GERRYMANDER	GHOSTWRITER	GILLRAVAGING
GERIATRICIANS	GERRYMANDERED	GHOSTWRITERS	GILLRAVITCH
GERIATRICS	GERRYMANDERER	GHOSTWRITES	GILLRAVITCHED

GILLRAVITCHES	GLABRESCENT	GLAMOURISED	GLAUCONITE
GILLRAVITCHING	GLABROUSNESS	GLAMOURISES	GLAUCONITES
GILLYFLOWER	GLABROUSNESSES	GLAMOURISING	GLAUCONITIC
GILLYFLOWERS	GLACIALIST	GLAMOURIZE	GLAUCOUSLY
GILRAVAGED	GLACIALISTS	GLAMOURIZED	GLAUCOUSNESS
GILRAVAGER	GLACIATING	GLAMOURIZES	GLAUCOUSNESSES
GILRAVAGERS	GLACIATION	GLAMOURIZING	GLAZIERIES
GILRAVAGES	GLACIATIONS	GLAMOURLESS	GLAZINESSES
GILRAVAGING	GLACIOLOGIC	GLAMOUROUS	GLEEFULNESS
GILRAVITCH	GLACIOLOGICAL	GLAMOUROUSLY	GLEEFULNESSES
GILRAVITCHED	GLACIOLOGIES	GLAMOUROUSNESS	GLEEMAIDEN
GILRAVITCHES	GLACIOLOGIST	GLAMOURPUSS	GLEEMAIDENS
GILRAVITCHING	GLACIOLOGISTS	GLAMOURPUSSES	GLEGNESSES
GILSONITES	GLACIOLOGY	GLANCINGLY	GLEISATION
GIMBALLING	GLADDENERS	GLANDEROUS	GLEISATIONS
GIMCRACKERIES	GLADDENING	GLANDIFEROUS	GLEIZATION
GIMCRACKERY	GLADFULNESS	GLANDIFORM	GLEIZATIONS
GIMMICKIER	GLADFULNESSES	GLANDULARLY	GLENDOVEER
GIMMICKIEST	GLADIATORIAL	GLANDULIFEROUS	GLENDOVEERS
GIMMICKING	GLADIATORIAN	GLANDULOUS	GLENGARRIES
GIMMICKRIES	GLADIATORS	GLANDULOUSLY	GLIBNESSES
GINGELLIES	GLADIATORSHIP	GLARINESSES	GLIDEPATHS
GINGERADES	GLADIATORSHIPS	GLARINGNESS	GLIMMERING
GINGERBREAD	GLADIATORY	GLARINGNESSES	GLIMMERINGLY
GINGERBREADED	GLADIOLUSES	GLASNOSTIAN	GLIMMERINGS
GINGERBREADS	GLADNESSES	GLASNOSTIC	GLIOBLASTOMA
GINGERBREADY	GLADSOMELY	GLASSBLOWER	GLIOBLASTOMAS
GINGERLINESS	GLADSOMENESS	GLASSBLOWERS	GLIOBLASTOMATA
GINGERLINESSES	GLADSOMENESSES	GLASSBLOWING	GLIOMATOSES
GINGERROOT	GLADSOMEST	GLASSBLOWINGS	GLIOMATOSIS
GINGERROOTS	GLADSTONES	GLASSHOUSE	GLIOMATOUS
GINGERSNAP	GLADWRAPPED	GLASSHOUSES	GLISSADERS
GINGERSNAPS	GLADWRAPPING	GLASSIFIED	GLISSADING
GINGIVECTOMIES	GLAIKETNESS	GLASSIFIES	GLISSANDOS
GINGIVECTOMY	GLAIKETNESSES	GLASSIFYING	GLISTENING
GINGIVITIS	GLAIKITNESS	GLASSINESS	GLISTENINGLY
GINGIVITISES	GLAIKITNESSES	GLASSINESSES	GLISTERING
GINGLIMOID	GLAIRINESS	GLASSMAKER	GLISTERINGLY
GIPSYHOODS	GLAIRINESSES	GLASSMAKERS	GLITCHIEST
GIPSYWORTS	GLAMORISATION	GLASSMAKING	GLITTERAND
GIRANDOLAS	GLAMORISATIONS	GLASSMAKINGS	GLITTERATI
GIRANDOLES	GLAMORISED	GLASSPAPER	GLITTERIER
GIRDLECAKE	GLAMORISER	GLASSPAPERED	GLITTERIEST
GIRDLECAKES	GLAMORISERS	GLASSPAPERING	GLITTERING
GIRDLESCONE	GLAMORISES	GLASSPAPERS	GLITTERINGLY
GIRDLESCONES	GLAMORISING	GLASSWARES	GLITTERINGS
GIRDLESTEAD	GLAMORIZATION	GLASSWORKER	GLITZINESS
GIRDLESTEADS	GLAMORIZATIONS	GLASSWORKERS	GLITZINESSES
GIRLFRIEND	GLAMORIZED	GLASSWORKS	GLOATINGLY
GIRLFRIENDS	GLAMORIZER	GLASSWORMS	GLOBALISATION
GIRLISHNESS	GLAMORIZERS	GLASSWORTS	GLOBALISATIONS
GIRLISHNESSES	GLAMORIZES	GLASSYHEADED	GLOBALISED
GIRTHLINES	GLAMORIZING	GLAUBERITE	GLOBALISES
GISMOLOGIES	GLAMOROUSLY	GLAUBERITES	GLOBALISING
GITTARONES	GLAMOROUSNESS	GLAUCESCENCE	GLOBALISMS
GITTERNING	GLAMOROUSNESSES	GLAUCESCENCES	GLOBALISTS
GIVENNESSES	GLAMOURING	GLAUCESCENT	GLOBALIZATION
GIZMOLOGIES	GLAMOURISE	GLAUCOMATOUS	GLOBALIZATIONS

GLOBALIZED	GLOSSINESS	GLUTAMATES	GLYCOPHYTES
GLOBALIZES	GLOSSINESSES	GLUTAMINASE	GLYCOPHYTIC
GLOBALIZING	GLOSSINGLY	GLUTAMINASES	GLYCOPROTEIN
GLOBEFISHES	GLOSSITISES	GLUTAMINES	GLYCOPROTEINS
GLOBEFLOWER	GLOSSODYNIA	GLUTAMINIC	GLYCOSIDASE
GLOBEFLOWERS	GLOSSODYNIAS	GLUTARALDEHYDE	GLYCOSIDASES
GLOBESITIES	GLOSSOGRAPHER	GLUTARALDEHYDES	GLYCOSIDES
GLOBETROTS	GLOSSOGRAPHERS	GLUTATHIONE	GLYCOSIDIC
GLOBETROTTED	GLOSSOGRAPHICAL	GLUTATHIONES	GLYCOSIDICALLY
GLOBETROTTER	GLOSSOGRAPHIES	GLUTETHIMIDE	GLYCOSURIA
GLOBETROTTERS	GLOSSOGRAPHY	GLUTETHIMIDES	GLYCOSURIAS
GLOBETROTTING	GLOSSOLALIA	GLUTINOSITIES	GLYCOSURIC
GLOBETROTTINGS	GLOSSOLALIAS	GLUTINOSITY	GLYCOSYLATE
GLOBIGERINA	GLOSSOLALIST	GLUTINOUSLY	GLYCOSYLATED
GLOBIGERINAE	GLOSSOLALISTS	GLUTINOUSNESS	GLYCOSYLATES
GLOBIGERINAS	GLOSSOLOGICAL	GLUTINOUSNESSES	GLYCOSYLATING
GLOBOSENESS	GLOSSOLOGIES	GLUTTINGLY	GLYCOSYLATION
GLOBOSENESSES	GLOSSOLOGIST	GLUTTONIES	GLYCOSYLATIONS
GLOBOSITIES	GLOSSOLOGISTS	GLUTTONISE	GLYOXALINE
GLOBULARITIES	GLOSSOLOGY	GLUTTONISED	GLYOXALINES
GLOBULARITY	GLOTTIDEAN	GLUTTONISES	GLYPHOGRAPH
GLOBULARLY	GLOTTOGONIC	GLUTTONISH	GLYPHOGRAPHER
GLOBULARNESS	GLOTTOLOGIES	GLUTTONISING	GLYPHOGRAPHERS
GLOBULARNESSES	GLOTTOLOGY	GLUTTONIZE	GLYPHOGRAPHIC
GLOBULIFEROUS	GLOWERINGLY	GLUTTONIZED	GLYPHOGRAPHICAL
GLOBULITES	GLOWSTICKS	GLUTTONIZES	GLYPHOGRAPHIES
GLOCHIDIATE	GLUCINIUMS	GLUTTONIZING	GLYPHOGRAPHS
GLOCHIDIUM	GLUCOCORTICOID	GLUTTONOUS	GLYPHOGRAPHY
GLOCKENSPIEL	GLUCOCORTICOIDS	GLUTTONOUSLY	GLYPTODONT
GLOCKENSPIELS	GLUCOKINASE	GLUTTONOUSNESS	GLYPTODONTS
GLOMERATED	GLUCOKINASES	GLYCAEMIAS	GLYPTOGRAPHER
GLOMERATES	GLUCONATES	GLYCERALDEHYDE	GLYPTOGRAPHERS
GLOMERATING	GLUCONEOGENESES	GLYCERALDEHYDES	GLYPTOGRAPHIC
GLOMERATION	GLUCONEOGENESIS	GLYCERIDES	GLYPTOGRAPHICAL
GLOMERATIONS	GLUCONEOGENIC	GLYCERIDIC	GLYPTOGRAPHIES
GLOMERULAR	GLUCOPHORE	GLYCERINATE	GLYPTOGRAPHY
GLOMERULATE	GLUCOPHORES	GLYCERINATED	GLYPTOTHECA
GLOMERULES	GLUCOPROTEIN	GLYCERINATES	GLYPTOTHECAE
GLOMERULUS	GLUCOPROTEINS	GLYCERINATING	GMELINITES
GLOOMFULLY	GLUCOSAMINE	GLYCERINES	GNAPHALIUM
GLOOMINESS	GLUCOSAMINES	GLYCOCOLLS	GNAPHALIUMS
GLOOMINESSES	GLUCOSIDAL	GLYCOGENESES	GNASHINGLY
GLORIFIABLE	GLUCOSIDASE	GLYCOGENESIS	GNATCATCHER
GLORIFICATION	GLUCOSIDASES	GLYCOGENETIC	GNATCATCHERS
GLORIFICATIONS	GLUCOSIDES	GLYCOGENIC	GNATHONICAL
GLORIFIERS	GLUCOSIDIC	GLYCOGENOLYSES	GNATHONICALLY
GLORIFYING	GLUCOSURIA	GLYCOGENOLYSIS	GNATHOSTOMATOUS
GLORIOUSLY	GLUCOSURIAS	GLYCOGENOLYTIC	GNATHOSTOME
GLORIOUSNESS	GLUCOSURIC	GLYCOLIPID	GNATHOSTOMES
GLORIOUSNESSES	GLUCURONIDASE	GLYCOLIPIDS	GNEISSITIC
GLOSSARIAL	GLUCURONIDASES	GLYCOLYSES	GNETOPHYTE
GLOSSARIALLY	GLUCURONIDE	GLYCOLYSIS	GNETOPHYTES
GLOSSARIES	GLUCURONIDES	GLYCOLYTIC	GNOMICALLY
GLOSSARIST	GLUEYNESSES	GLYCONEOGENESES	GNOMONICAL
GLOSSARISTS	GLUINESSES	GLYCONEOGENESIS	GNOMONICALLY
GLOSSATORS	GLUMACEOUS	GLYCOPEPTIDE	GNOMONOLOGIES
GLOSSECTOMIES	GLUMIFEROUS	GLYCOPEPTIDES	GNOMONOLOGY
GLOSSECTOMY	GLUMNESSES	GLYCOPHYTE	GNOSEOLOGIES

GNOSEOLOGY
GNOSIOLOGIES
GNOSIOLOGY
GNOSTICALLY
GNOSTICISM
GNOSTICISMS
GNOTOBIOLOGICAL
GNOTOBIOLOGIES
GNOTOBIOLOGY
GNOTOBIOSES
GNOTOBIOSIS
GNOTOBIOTE
GNOTOBIOTES
GNOTOBIOTIC
GNOTOBIOTICALLY
GNOTOBIOTICS
GOALKEEPER
GOALKEEPERS
GOALKEEPING
GOALKEEPINGS
GOALKICKER
GOALKICKERS
GOALKICKING
GOALKICKINGS
GOALMOUTHS
GOALTENDER
GOALTENDERS
GOALTENDING
GOALTENDINGS
GOATFISHES
GOATISHNESS
GOATISHNESSES
GOATSBEARD
GOATSBEARDS
GOATSUCKER
GOATSUCKERS
GOBBELINES
GOBBLEDEGOOK
GOBBLEDEGOOKS
GOBBLEDYGOOK
GOBBLEDYGOOKS
GOBSMACKED
GOBSTOPPER
GOBSTOPPERS
GODCHILDREN
GODDAMMING
GODDAMNDEST
GODDAMNEDEST
GODDAMNING
GODDAUGHTER
GODDAUGHTERS
GODDESSHOOD
GODDESSHOODS
GODFATHERED
GODFATHERING
GODFATHERS
GODFORSAKEN
GODLESSNESS

GODLESSNESSES
GODLIKENESS
GODLIKENESSES
GODLINESSES
GODMOTHERED
GODMOTHERING
GODMOTHERS
GODPARENTS
GODROONING
GODROONINGS
GOFFERINGS
GOGGLEBOXES
GOITROGENIC
GOITROGENICITY
GOITROGENS
GOLDBEATER
GOLDBEATERS
GOLDBRICKED
GOLDBRICKING
GOLDBRICKS
GOLDCRESTS
GOLDENBERRIES
GOLDENBERRY
GOLDENEYES
GOLDENNESS
GOLDENNESSES
GOLDENRODS
GOLDENSEAL
GOLDENSEALS
GOLDFIELDS
GOLDFINCHES
GOLDFINNIES
GOLDFISHES
GOLDILOCKS
GOLDILOCKSES
GOLDMINERS
GOLDSINNIES
GOLDSMITHERIES
GOLDSMITHERY
GOLDSMITHRIES
GOLDSMITHRY
GOLDSMITHS
GOLDSPINKS
GOLDSTICKS
GOLDSTONES
GOLDTHREAD
GOLDTHREADS
GOLIARDERIES
GOLIARDERY
GOLIARDIES
GOLIATHISE
GOLIATHISED
GOLIATHISES
GOLIATHISING
GOLIATHIZE
GOLIATHIZED
GOLIATHIZES
GOLIATHIZING

GOLLIWOGGS
GOLOMYNKAS
GOLOPTIOUS
GOLUPTIOUS
GOMBEENISM
GOMBEENISMS
GONADECTOMIES
GONADECTOMISED
GONADECTOMIZED
GONADECTOMY
GONADOTROPHIC
GONADOTROPHIN
GONADOTROPHINS
GONADOTROPIC
GONADOTROPIN
GONADOTROPINS
GONDOLIERS
GONENESSES
GONFALONIER
GONFALONIERS
GONGORISTIC
GONIATITES
GONIATITOID
GONIATITOIDS
GONIMOBLAST
GONIMOBLASTS
GONIOMETER
GONIOMETERS
GONIOMETRIC
GONIOMETRICAL
GONIOMETRICALLY
GONIOMETRIES
GONIOMETRY
GONIOSCOPE
GONIOSCOPES
GONOCOCCAL
GONOCOCCIC
GONOCOCCOID
GONOCOCCUS
GONOPHORES
GONOPHORIC
GONOPHOROUS
GONORRHEAL
GONORRHEAS
GONORRHEIC
GONORRHOEA
GONORRHOEAL
GONORRHOEAS
GONORRHOEIC
GOODFELLOW
GOODFELLOWS
GOODFELLOWSHIP
GOODFELLOWSHIPS
GOODINESSES
GOODLIHEAD
GOODLIHEADS
GOODLINESS
GOODLINESSES

GOODLYHEAD
GOODLYHEADS
GOODNESSES
GOODNIGHTS
GOODWILLED
GOOEYNESSES
GOOFINESSES
GOOGLEWHACK
GOOGLEWHACKS
GOOGOLPLEX
GOOGOLPLEXES
GOONEYBIRD
GOONEYBIRDS
GOOSANDERS
GOOSEBERRIES
GOOSEBERRY
GOOSEFISHES
GOOSEFLESH
GOOSEFLESHES
GOOSEFOOTS
GOOSEGRASS
GOOSEGRASSES
GOOSEHERDS
GOOSENECKED
GOOSENECKS
GOOSINESSES
GOPHERWOOD
GOPHERWOODS
GORBELLIES
GOREHOUNDS
GORGEOUSLY
GORGEOUSNESS
GORGEOUSNESSES
GORGONEION
GORGONIANS
GORGONISED
GORGONISES
GORGONISING
GORGONIZED
GORGONIZES
GORGONIZING
GORILLAGRAM
GORILLAGRAMS
GORINESSES
GORMANDISE
GORMANDISED
GORMANDISER
GORMANDISERS
GORMANDISES
GORMANDISING
GORMANDISINGS
GORMANDISM
GORMANDISMS
GORMANDIZE
GORMANDIZED
GORMANDIZER
GORMANDIZERS
GORMANDIZES

GORMANDIZING	GOVERNESSED	GRADUALNESS	GRAMOPHONE
GORMANDIZINGS	GOVERNESSES	GRADUALNESSES	GRAMOPHONES
GOSLARITES	GOVERNESSING	GRADUATESHIP	GRAMOPHONIC
GOSPELISED	GOVERNESSY	GRADUATESHIPS	GRAMOPHONICALLY
GOSPELISES	GOVERNMENT	GRADUATING	GRAMOPHONIES
GOSPELISING	GOVERNMENTAL	GRADUATION	GRAMOPHONIST
GOSPELIZED	GOVERNMENTALISE	GRADUATIONS	GRAMOPHONISTS
GOSPELIZES	GOVERNMENTALISM	GRADUATORS	GRAMOPHONY
GOSPELIZING	GOVERNMENTALIST	GRAECISING	GRANADILLA
GOSPELLERS	GOVERNMENTALIZE	GRAECIZING	GRANADILLAS
GOSPELLING	GOVERNMENTALLY	GRAFFITIED	GRANDADDIES
GOSPELLISE	GOVERNMENTESE	GRAFFITIING	GRANDAUNTS
GOSPELLISED	GOVERNMENTESES	GRAFFITING	GRANDBABIES
GOSPELLISES	GOVERNMENTS	GRAFFITIST	GRANDCHILD
GOSPELLISING	GOVERNORATE	GRAFFITISTS	GRANDCHILDREN
GOSPELLIZE	GOVERNORATES	GRAINFIELD	GRANDDADDIES
GOSPELLIZED	GOVERNORSHIP	GRAINFIELDS	GRANDDADDY
GOSPELLIZES	GOVERNORSHIPS	GRAININESS	GRANDDAUGHTER
GOSPELLIZING	GOWDSPINKS	GRAININESSES	GRANDDAUGHTERS
GOSSIPINGLY	GOWPENFULS	GRALLATORIAL	GRANDEESHIP
GOSSIPINGS	GRACEFULLER	GRALLOCHED	GRANDEESHIPS
GOSSIPMONGER	GRACEFULLEST	GRALLOCHING	GRANDFATHER
GOSSIPMONGERS	GRACEFULLY	GRAMERCIES	GRANDFATHERED
GOSSIPPERS	GRACEFULNESS	GRAMICIDIN	GRANDFATHERING
GOSSIPPING	GRACEFULNESSES	GRAMICIDINS	GRANDFATHERLY
GOSSIPRIES	GRACELESSLY	GRAMINACEOUS	GRANDFATHERS
GOTHICALLY	GRACELESSNESS	GRAMINEOUS	GRANDIFLORA
GOTHICISED	GRACELESSNESSES	GRAMINICOLOUS	GRANDIFLORAS
GOTHICISES	GRACILENESS	GRAMINIVOROUS	GRANDILOQUENCE
GOTHICISING	GRACILENESSES	GRAMINOLOGIES	GRANDILOQUENCES
GOTHICISMS	GRACILITIES	GRAMINOLOGY	GRANDILOQUENT
GOTHICIZED	GRACIOSITIES	GRAMMALOGUE	GRANDILOQUENTLY
GOTHICIZES	GRACIOSITY	GRAMMALOGUES	GRANDILOQUOUS
GOTHICIZING	GRACIOUSES	GRAMMARIAN	GRANDIOSELY
GOURDINESS	GRACIOUSLY	GRAMMARIANS	GRANDIOSENESS
GOURDINESSES	GRACIOUSNESS	GRAMMARLESS	GRANDIOSENESSES
GOURMANDISE	GRACIOUSNESSES	GRAMMATICAL	GRANDIOSITIES
GOURMANDISED	GRADABILITIES	GRAMMATICALITY	GRANDIOSITY
GOURMANDISES	GRADABILITY	GRAMMATICALLY	GRANDMAMAS
GOURMANDISING	GRADABLENESS	GRAMMATICALNESS	GRANDMAMMA
GOURMANDISM	GRADABLENESSES	GRAMMATICASTER	GRANDMAMMAS
GOURMANDISMS	GRADATIONAL	GRAMMATICASTERS	GRANDMASTER
GOURMANDIZE	GRADATIONALLY	GRAMMATICISE	GRANDMASTERS
GOURMANDIZED	GRADATIONED	GRAMMATICISED	GRANDMOTHER
GOURMANDIZES	GRADATIONS	GRAMMATICISES	GRANDMOTHERLY
GOURMANDIZING	GRADDANING	GRAMMATICISING	GRANDMOTHERS
GOUTINESSES	GRADELIEST	GRAMMATICISM	GRANDNEPHEW
GOUVERNANTE	GRADIENTER	GRAMMATICISMS	GRANDNEPHEWS
GOUVERNANTES	GRADIENTERS	GRAMMATICIZE	GRANDNESSES
GOVERNABILITIES	GRADIOMETER	GRAMMATICIZED	GRANDNIECE
GOVERNABILITY	GRADIOMETERS	GRAMMATICIZES	GRANDNIECES
GOVERNABLE	GRADUALISM	GRAMMATICIZING	GRANDPAPAS
GOVERNABLENESS	GRADUALISMS	GRAMMATIST	GRANDPARENT
GOVERNALLS	GRADUALIST	GRAMMATISTS	GRANDPARENTAL
GOVERNANCE	GRADUALISTIC	GRAMMATOLOGIES	GRANDPARENTHOOD
GOVERNANCES	GRADUALISTS	GRAMMATOLOGIST	GRANDPARENTS
GOVERNANTE	GRADUALITIES	GRAMMATOLOGISTS	GRANDSIRES
GOVERNANTES	GRADUALITY	GRAMMATOLOGY	GRANDSTAND

GRANDSTANDED
GRANDSTANDER
GRANDSTANDERS
GRANDSTANDING
GRANDSTANDS
GRANDSTOOD
GRANDUNCLE
GRANDUNCLES
GRANGERISATION
GRANGERISATIONS
GRANGERISE
GRANGERISED
GRANGERISER
GRANGERISERS
GRANGERISES
GRANGERISING
GRANGERISM
GRANGERISMS
GRANGERIZATION
GRANGERIZATIONS
GRANGERIZE
GRANGERIZED
GRANGERIZER
GRANGERIZERS
GRANGERIZES
GRANGERIZING
GRANITELIKE
GRANITEWARE
GRANITEWARES
GRANITIFICATION
GRANITIFORM
GRANITISATION
GRANITISATIONS
GRANITISED
GRANITISES
GRANITISING
GRANITITES
GRANITIZATION
GRANITIZATIONS
GRANITIZED
GRANITIZES
GRANITIZING
GRANIVORES
GRANIVOROUS
GRANNIEING
GRANODIORITE
GRANODIORITES
GRANODIORITIC
GRANOLITHIC
GRANOLITHICS
GRANOLITHS
GRANOPHYRE
GRANOPHYRES
GRANOPHYRIC
GRANTSMANSHIP
GRANTSMANSHIPS
GRANULARITIES
GRANULARITY

GRANULARLY
GRANULATED
GRANULATER
GRANULATERS
GRANULATES
GRANULATING
GRANULATION
GRANULATIONS
GRANULATIVE
GRANULATOR
GRANULATORS
GRANULIFEROUS
GRANULIFORM
GRANULITES
GRANULITIC
GRANULITISATION
GRANULITIZATION
GRANULOCYTE
GRANULOCYTES
GRANULOCYTIC
GRANULOMAS
GRANULOMATA
GRANULOMATOUS
GRANULOSES
GRANULOSIS
GRAPEFRUIT
GRAPEFRUITS
GRAPESEEDS
GRAPESHOTS
GRAPESTONE
GRAPESTONES
GRAPETREES
GRAPEVINES
GRAPHEMICALLY
GRAPHEMICS
GRAPHICACIES
GRAPHICACY
GRAPHICALLY
GRAPHICALNESS
GRAPHICALNESSES
GRAPHICNESS
GRAPHICNESSES
GRAPHITISABLE
GRAPHITISATION
GRAPHITISATIONS
GRAPHITISE
GRAPHITISED
GRAPHITISES
GRAPHITISING
GRAPHITIZABLE
GRAPHITIZATION
GRAPHITIZATIONS
GRAPHITIZE
GRAPHITIZED
GRAPHITIZES
GRAPHITIZING
GRAPHITOID
GRAPHOLECT

GRAPHOLECTS
GRAPHOLOGIC
GRAPHOLOGICAL
GRAPHOLOGIES
GRAPHOLOGIST
GRAPHOLOGISTS
GRAPHOLOGY
GRAPHOMANIA
GRAPHOMANIAS
GRAPHOMOTOR
GRAPHOPHOBIA
GRAPHOPHOBIAS
GRAPINESSES
GRAPLEMENT
GRAPLEMENTS
GRAPPLINGS
GRAPTOLITE
GRAPTOLITES
GRAPTOLITIC
GRASPINGLY
GRASPINGNESS
GRASPINGNESSES
GRASSFINCH
GRASSFINCHES
GRASSHOOKS
GRASSHOPPER
GRASSHOPPERS
GRASSINESS
GRASSINESSES
GRASSLANDS
GRASSPLOTS
GRASSQUITS
GRASSROOTS
GRASSWRACK
GRASSWRACKS
GRATEFULLER
GRATEFULLEST
GRATEFULLY
GRATEFULNESS
GRATEFULNESSES
GRATICULATION
GRATICULATIONS
GRATICULES
GRATIFICATION
GRATIFICATIONS
GRATIFIERS
GRATIFYING
GRATIFYINGLY
GRATILLITIES
GRATILLITY
GRATINATED
GRATINATES
GRATINATING
GRATINEEING
GRATITUDES
GRATUITIES
GRATUITOUS
GRATUITOUSLY

GRATUITOUSNESS
GRATULATED
GRATULATES
GRATULATING
GRATULATION
GRATULATIONS
GRATULATORY
GRAUNCHERS
GRAUNCHING
GRAVADLAXES
GRAVELLING
GRAVENESSES
GRAVEOLENT
GRAVESIDES
GRAVESITES
GRAVESTONE
GRAVESTONES
GRAVEYARDS
GRAVIDITIES
GRAVIDNESS
GRAVIDNESSES
GRAVIMETER
GRAVIMETERS
GRAVIMETRIC
GRAVIMETRICAL
GRAVIMETRICALLY
GRAVIMETRIES
GRAVIMETRY
GRAVIPERCEPTION
GRAVITASES
GRAVITATED
GRAVITATER
GRAVITATERS
GRAVITATES
GRAVITATING
GRAVITATION
GRAVITATIONAL
GRAVITATIONALLY
GRAVITATIONS
GRAVITATIVE
GRAVITINOS
GRAVITOMETER
GRAVITOMETERS
GRAYBEARDED
GRAYBEARDS
GRAYFISHES
GRAYHOUNDS
GRAYNESSES
GRAYWACKES
GRAYWATERS
GREASEBALL
GREASEBALLS
GREASEBAND
GREASEBANDS
GREASEBUSH
GREASEBUSHES
GREASELESS
GREASEPAINT

GREASEPAINTS	GREENLIGHT	GRENADIERS	GRISLINESSES
GREASEPROOF	GREENLIGHTED	GRENADILLA	GRISTLIEST
GREASEPROOFS	GREENLIGHTING	GRENADILLAS	GRISTLINESS
GREASEWOOD	GREENLIGHTS	GRENADINES	GRISTLINESSES
GREASEWOODS	GREENLINGS	GRESSORIAL	GRISTMILLS
GREASINESS	GREENMAILED	GRESSORIOUS	GRITSTONES
GREASINESSES	GREENMAILER	GREVILLEAS	GRITTINESS
GREATCOATED	GREENMAILERS	GREWHOUNDS	GRITTINESSES
GREATCOATS	GREENMAILING	GREWSOMEST	GRIVATIONS
GREATENING	GREENMAILS	GREYBEARDED	GRIZZLIEST
GREATHEARTED	GREENNESSES	GREYBEARDS	GROANINGLY
GREATHEARTEDLY	GREENOCKITE	GREYHOUNDS	GROATSWORTH
GREATNESSES	GREENOCKITES	GREYLISTED	GROATSWORTHS
GRECIANISE	GREENROOMS	GREYLISTING	GROCETERIA
GRECIANISED	GREENSANDS	GREYNESSES	GROCETERIAS
GRECIANISES	GREENSHANK	GREYSTONES	GROGGERIES
GRECIANISING	GREENSHANKS	GREYWACKES	GROGGINESS
GRECIANIZE	GREENSICKNESS	GREYWETHER	GROGGINESSES
GRECIANIZED	GREENSICKNESSES	GREYWETHERS	GROMMETING
GRECIANIZES	GREENSKEEPER	GRIDDLEBREAD	GROOVELESS
GRECIANIZING	GREENSKEEPERS	GRIDDLEBREADS	GROOVELIKE
GREEDINESS	GREENSOMES	GRIDDLECAKE	GROSGRAINS
GREEDINESSES	GREENSPEAK	GRIDDLECAKES	GROSSIERETE
GREENBACKER	GREENSPEAKS	GRIDIRONED	GROSSIERETES
GREENBACKERS	GREENSTICK	GRIDIRONING	GROSSNESSES
GREENBACKISM	GREENSTICKS	GRIDLOCKED	GROSSULARITE
GREENBACKISMS	GREENSTONE	GRIDLOCKING	GROSSULARITES
GREENBACKS	GREENSTONES	GRIEVANCES	GROSSULARS
GREENBELTS	GREENSTUFF	GRIEVINGLY	GROTESQUELY
GREENBONES	GREENSTUFFS	GRIEVOUSLY	GROTESQUENESS
GREENBOTTLE	GREENSWARD	GRIEVOUSNESS	GROTESQUENESSES
GREENBOTTLES	GREENSWARDS	GRIEVOUSNESSES	GROTESQUER
GREENBRIER	GREENWASHED	GRIFFINISH	GROTESQUERIE
GREENBRIERS	GREENWASHES	GRIFFINISM	GROTESQUERIES
GREENCLOTH	GREENWASHING	GRIFFINISMS	GROTESQUERY
GREENCLOTHS	GREENWEEDS	GRILLERIES	GROTESQUES
GREENERIES	GREENWINGS	GRILLROOMS	GROTESQUEST
GREENFIELD	GREENWOODS	GRILLSTEAK	GROUCHIEST
GREENFIELDS	GREGARIANISM	GRILLSTEAKS	GROUCHINESS
GREENFINCH	GREGARIANISMS	GRILLWORKS	GROUCHINESSES
GREENFINCHES	GREGARINES	GRIMACINGLY	GROUNDAGES
GREENFLIES	GREGARINIAN	GRIMALKINS	GROUNDBAIT
GREENGAGES	GREGARIOUS	GRIMINESSES	GROUNDBAITED
GREENGROCER	GREGARIOUSLY	GRIMLOOKED	GROUNDBAITING
GREENGROCERIES	GREGARIOUSNESS	GRIMNESSES	GROUNDBAITS
GREENGROCERS	GREISENISATION	GRINDELIAS	GROUNDBREAKER
GREENGROCERY	GREISENISATIONS	GRINDERIES	GROUNDBREAKERS
GREENHANDS	GREISENISE	GRINDHOUSE	GROUNDBREAKING
GREENHEADS	GREISENISED	GRINDHOUSES	GROUNDBREAKINGS
GREENHEART	GREISENISES	GRINDINGLY	GROUNDBURST
GREENHEARTS	GREISENISING	GRINDSTONE	GROUNDBURSTS
GREENHORNS	GREISENIZATION	GRINDSTONES	GROUNDEDLY
GREENHOUSE	GREISENIZATIONS	GRINNINGLY	GROUNDFISH
GREENHOUSES	GREISENIZE	GRIPPINGLY	GROUNDFISHES
GREENISHNESS	GREISENIZED	GRISAILLES	GROUNDHOGS
GREENISHNESSES	GREISENIZES	GRISEOFULVIN	GROUNDINGS
GREENKEEPER	GREISENIZING	GRISEOFULVINS	GROUNDLESS
GREENKEEPERS	GREMOLATAS	GRISLINESS	GROUNDLESSLY

GROUNDLESSNESS	GRUBSTAKERS	GUBERNATORIAL	GUITARFISH
GROUNDLING	GRUBSTAKES	GUBERNATORS	GUITARFISHES
GROUNDLINGS	GRUBSTAKING	GUBERNIYAS	GUITARISTS
GROUNDMASS	GRUDGELESS	GUDGEONING	GULLIBILITIES
GROUNDMASSES	GRUDGINGLY	GUERDONERS	GULLIBILITY
GROUNDNUTS	GRUELINGLY	GUERDONING	GULOSITIES
GROUNDOUTS	GRUELLINGS	GUERILLAISM	GUMMIFEROUS
GROUNDPLOT	GRUESOMELY	GUERILLAISMS	GUMMINESSES
GROUNDPLOTS	GRUESOMENESS	GUERRILLAISM	GUMMOSITIES
GROUNDPROX	GRUESOMENESSES	GUERRILLAISMS	GUMSHIELDS
GROUNDPROXES	GRUESOMEST	GUERRILLAS	GUMSHOEING
GROUNDSELL	GRUFFNESSES	GUERRILLERO	GUMSUCKERS
GROUNDSELLS	GRUMBLIEST	GUERRILLEROS	GUNCOTTONS
GROUNDSELS	GRUMBLINGLY	GUESSINGLY	GUNFIGHTER
GROUNDSHARE	GRUMBLINGS	GUESSTIMATE	GUNFIGHTERS
GROUNDSHARED	GRUMMETING	GUESSTIMATED	GUNFIGHTING
GROUNDSHARES	GRUMNESSES	GUESSTIMATES	GUNKHOLING
GROUNDSHARING	GRUMPINESS	GUESSTIMATING	GUNMANSHIP
GROUNDSHEET	GRUMPINESSES	GUESSWORKS	GUNMANSHIPS
GROUNDSHEETS	GRUMPISHLY	GUESTENING	GUNNERSHIP
GROUNDSILL	GRUMPISHNESS	GUESTHOUSE	GUNNERSHIPS
GROUNDSILLS	GRUMPISHNESSES	GUESTHOUSES	GUNNYSACKS
GROUNDSKEEPER	GRUNTINGLY	GUESTIMATE	GUNPOWDERS
GROUNDSKEEPERS	GUACAMOLES	GUESTIMATED	GUNPOWDERY
GROUNDSMAN	GUACHAMOLE	GUESTIMATES	GUNRUNNERS
GROUNDSMEN	GUACHAMOLES	GUESTIMATING	GUNRUNNING
GROUNDSPEED	GUACHAROES	GUIDEBOOKS	GUNRUNNINGS
GROUNDSPEEDS	GUANABANAS	GUIDELINES	GUNSLINGER
GROUNDSWELL	GUANAZOLOS	GUIDEPOSTS	GUNSLINGERS
GROUNDSWELLS	GUANETHIDINE	GUIDESHIPS	GUNSLINGING
GROUNDWATER	GUANETHIDINES	GUIDEWORDS	GUNSLINGINGS
GROUNDWATERS	GUANIDINES	GUIDWILLIE	GUNSMITHING
GROUNDWOOD	GUANIFEROUS	GUILDHALLS	GUNSMITHINGS
GROUNDWOODS	GUANOSINES	GUILDSHIPS	GURGITATION
GROUNDWORK	GUARANTEED	GUILDSWOMAN	GURGITATIONS
GROUNDWORKS	GUARANTEEING	GUILDSWOMEN	GUSHINESSES
GROUPTHINK	GUARANTEES	GUILEFULLY	GUSTATIONS
GROUPTHINKS	GUARANTIED	GUILEFULNESS	GUSTATORILY
GROUPUSCULE	GUARANTIES	GUILEFULNESSES	GUSTINESSES
GROUPUSCULES	GUARANTORS	GUILELESSLY	GUTBUCKETS
GROUPWARES	GUARANTYING	GUILELESSNESS	GUTLESSNESS
GROUSELIKE	GUARDEDNESS	GUILELESSNESSES	GUTLESSNESSES
GROVELINGLY	GUARDEDNESSES	GUILLEMETS	GUTSINESSES
GROVELLERS	GUARDHOUSE	GUILLEMOTS	GUTTATIONS
GROVELLING	GUARDHOUSES	GUILLOCHED	GUTTERBLOOD
GROVELLINGLY	GUARDIANSHIP	GUILLOCHES	GUTTERBLOODS
GROWLERIES	GUARDIANSHIPS	GUILLOCHING	GUTTERINGS
GROWLINESS	GUARDRAILS	GUILLOTINE	GUTTERSNIPE
GROWLINESSES	GUARDROOMS	GUILLOTINED	GUTTERSNIPES
GROWLINGLY	GUARDSHIPS	GUILLOTINER	GUTTERSNIPISH
GROWTHIEST	GUARISHING	GUILLOTINERS	GUTTIFEROUS
GROWTHINESS	GUAYABERAS	GUILLOTINES	GUTTURALISATION
GROWTHINESSES	GUBERNACULA	GUILLOTINING	GUTTURALISE
GROWTHISTS	GUBERNACULAR	GUILTINESS	GUTTURALISED
GRUBBINESS	GUBERNACULUM	GUILTINESSES	GUTTURALISES
GRUBBINESSES	GUBERNATION	GUILTLESSLY	GUTTURALISING
GRUBSTAKED	GUBERNATIONS	GUILTLESSNESS	GUTTURALISM
GRUBSTAKER	GUBERNATOR	GUILTLESSNESSES	GUTTURALISMS

GUTTURALITIES
GUTTURALITY
GUTTURALIZATION
GUTTURALIZE
GUTTURALIZED
GUTTURALIZES
GUTTURALIZING
GUTTURALLY
GUTTURALNESS
GUTTURALNESSES
GYMNASIARCH
GYMNASIARCHS
GYMNASIAST
GYMNASIASTS
GYMNASIUMS
GYMNASTICAL
GYMNASTICALLY
GYMNASTICS
GYMNORHINAL
GYMNOSOPHIES
GYMNOSOPHIST
GYMNOSOPHISTS
GYMNOSOPHS
GYMNOSOPHY
GYMNOSPERM
GYMNOSPERMIES
GYMNOSPERMOUS
GYMNOSPERMS
GYMNOSPERMY
GYNAECEUMS
GYNAECOCRACIES
GYNAECOCRACY
GYNAECOCRATIC
GYNAECOLOGIC
GYNAECOLOGICAL
GYNAECOLOGIES
GYNAECOLOGIST
GYNAECOLOGISTS
GYNAECOLOGY
GYNAECOMAST
GYNAECOMASTIA
GYNAECOMASTIAS
GYNAECOMASTIES
GYNAECOMASTS
GYNAECOMASTY
GYNANDRIES
GYNANDRISM
GYNANDRISMS
GYNANDROMORPH
GYNANDROMORPHIC
GYNANDROMORPHS
GYNANDROMORPHY
GYNANDROUS
GYNARCHIES
GYNECOCRACIES
GYNECOCRACY
GYNECOCRATIC
GYNECOLOGIC

GYNECOLOGICAL
GYNECOLOGIES
GYNECOLOGIST
GYNECOLOGISTS
GYNECOLOGY
GYNECOMASTIA
GYNECOMASTIAS
GYNIATRICS
GYNIATRIES
GYNIOLATRIES
GYNIOLATRY
GYNOCRACIES
GYNOCRATIC
GYNODIOECIOUS
GYNODIOECISM
GYNODIOECISMS
GYNOGENESES
GYNOGENESIS
GYNOGENETIC
GYNOMONOECIOUS
GYNOMONOECISM
GYNOMONOECISMS
GYNOPHOBES
GYNOPHOBIA
GYNOPHOBIAS
GYNOPHOBIC
GYNOPHOBICS
GYNOPHORES
GYNOPHORIC
GYNOSTEMIA
GYNOSTEMIUM
GYPSIFEROUS
GYPSOPHILA
GYPSOPHILAS
GYPSYHOODS
GYPSYWORTS
GYRATIONAL
GYRFALCONS
GYROCOMPASS
GYROCOMPASSES
GYROCOPTER
GYROCOPTERS
GYROFREQUENCIES
GYROFREQUENCY
GYROMAGNETIC
GYROMAGNETISM
GYROMAGNETISMS
GYROMANCIES
GYROPILOTS
GYROPLANES
GYROSCOPES
GYROSCOPIC
GYROSCOPICALLY
GYROSCOPICS
GYROSTABILISER
GYROSTABILISERS
GYROSTABILIZER
GYROSTABILIZERS

GYROSTATIC
GYROSTATICALLY
GYROSTATICS
GYROVAGUES

HAANEPOOTS	HACQUETONS	HAEMATOTHERMAL	HAEMORRHAGING
HABERDASHER	HADROSAURS	HAEMATOXYLIC	HAEMORRHOID
HABERDASHERIES	HADROSAURUS	HAEMATOXYLIN	HAEMORRHOIDAL
HABERDASHERS	HADROSAURUSES	HAEMATOXYLINS	HAEMORRHOIDS
HABERDASHERY	HAECCEITIES	HAEMATOXYLON	HAEMOSTASES
HABERDINES	HAEMACHROME	HAEMATOXYLONS	HAEMOSTASIA
HABERGEONS	HAEMACHROMES	HAEMATOZOA	HAEMOSTASIAS
HABILATORY	HAEMACYTOMETER	HAEMATOZOON	HAEMOSTASIS
HABILIMENT	HAEMACYTOMETERS	HAEMATURIA	HAEMOSTATIC
HABILIMENTS	HAEMAGGLUTINATE	HAEMATURIAS	HAEMOSTATICS
HABILITATE	HAEMAGGLUTININ	HAEMATURIC	HAEMOSTATS
HABILITATED	HAEMAGGLUTININS	HAEMOCHROME	HAGBERRIES
HABILITATES	HAEMAGOGUE	HAEMOCHROMES	HAGBUTEERS
HABILITATING	HAEMAGOGUES	HAEMOCOELS	HAGBUTTERS
HABILITATION	HAEMANGIOMA	HAEMOCONIA	HAGGADICAL
HABILITATIONS	HAEMANGIOMAS	HAEMOCONIAS	HAGGADISTIC
HABILITATOR	HAEMANGIOMATA	HAEMOCYANIN	HAGGADISTS
HABILITATORS	HAEMATEINS	HAEMOCYANINS	HAGGARDNESS
HABITABILITIES	HAEMATEMESES	HAEMOCYTES	HAGGARDNESSES
HABITABILITY	HAEMATEMESIS	HAEMOCYTOMETER	HAGGISHNESS
HABITABLENESS	HAEMATINIC	HAEMOCYTOMETERS	HAGGISHNESSES
HABITABLENESSES	HAEMATINICS	HAEMODIALYSER	HAGIARCHIES
HABITATION	HAEMATITES	HAEMODIALYSERS	HAGIOCRACIES
HABITATIONAL	HAEMATITIC	HAEMODIALYSES	HAGIOCRACY
HABITATIONS	HAEMATOBLAST	HAEMODIALYSIS	HAGIOGRAPHER
HABITAUNCE	HAEMATOBLASTIC	HAEMODIALYZER	HAGIOGRAPHERS
HABITAUNCES	HAEMATOBLASTS	HAEMODIALYZERS	HAGIOGRAPHIC
HABITUALLY	HAEMATOCELE	HAEMOFLAGELLATE	HAGIOGRAPHICAL
HABITUALNESS	HAEMATOCELES	HAEMOGLOBIN	HAGIOGRAPHIES
HABITUALNESSES	HAEMATOCRIT	HAEMOGLOBINS	HAGIOGRAPHIST
HABITUATED	HAEMATOCRITS	HAEMOGLOBINURIA	HAGIOGRAPHISTS
HABITUATES	HAEMATOCRYAL	HAEMOLYSES	HAGIOGRAPHY
HABITUATING	HAEMATOGENESES	HAEMOLYSIN	HAGIOLATER
HABITUATION	HAEMATOGENESIS	HAEMOLYSINS	HAGIOLATERS
HABITUATIONS	HAEMATOGENETIC	HAEMOLYSIS	HAGIOLATRIES
HABITUDINAL	HAEMATOGENIC	HAEMOLYTIC	HAGIOLATROUS
HACENDADOS	HAEMATOGENOUS	HAEMOPHILE	HAGIOLATRY
HACIENDADO	HAEMATOLOGIC	HAEMOPHILES	HAGIOLOGIC
HACIENDADOS	HAEMATOLOGICAL	HAEMOPHILIA	HAGIOLOGICAL
HACKAMORES	HAEMATOLOGIES	HAEMOPHILIAC	HAGIOLOGIES
HACKBERRIES	HAEMATOLOGIST	HAEMOPHILIACS	HAGIOLOGIST
HACKBUTEER	HAEMATOLOGISTS	HAEMOPHILIAS	HAGIOLOGISTS
HACKBUTEERS	HAEMATOLOGY	HAEMOPHILIC	HAGIOSCOPE
HACKBUTTER	HAEMATOLYSES	HAEMOPHILIOID	HAGIOSCOPES
HACKBUTTERS	HAEMATOLYSIS	HAEMOPOIESES	HAGIOSCOPIC
HACKMATACK	HAEMATOMAS	HAEMOPOIESIS	HAILSTONES
HACKMATACKS	HAEMATOMATA	HAEMOPOIETIC	HAILSTORMS
HACKNEYING	HAEMATOPHAGOUS	HAEMOPTYSES	HAIRBRAINED
HACKNEYISM	HAEMATOPOIESES	HAEMOPTYSIS	HAIRBREADTH
HACKNEYISMS	HAEMATOPOIESIS	HAEMORRHAGE	HAIRBREADTHS
HACKNEYMAN	HAEMATOPOIETIC	HAEMORRHAGED	HAIRBRUSHES
HACKNEYMEN	HAEMATOSES	HAEMORRHAGES	HAIRCLOTHS
HACKSAWING	HAEMATOSIS	HAEMORRHAGIC	HAIRCUTTER

HAIRCUTTERS	HALLELUJAH	HALTERBROKEN	HANDBRAKES
HAIRCUTTING	HALLELUJAHS	HALTERNECK	HANDBREADTH
HAIRCUTTINGS	HALLMARKED	HALTERNECKS	HANDBREADTHS
HAIRDRESSER	HALLMARKING	HALTINGNESS	HANDCLASPS
HAIRDRESSERS	HALLOWEDNESS	HALTINGNESSES	HANDCRAFTED
HAIRDRESSING	HALLOWEDNESSES	HAMADRYADES	HANDCRAFTING
HAIRDRESSINGS	HALLOYSITE	HAMADRYADS	HANDCRAFTS
HAIRDRIERS	HALLOYSITES	HAMADRYASES	HANDCRAFTSMAN
HAIRDRYERS	HALLSTANDS	HAMAMELIDACEOUS	HANDCRAFTSMEN
HAIRINESSES	HALLUCINATE	HAMAMELISES	HANDCUFFED
HAIRLESSNESS	HALLUCINATED	HAMANTASCH	HANDCUFFING
HAIRLESSNESSES	HALLUCINATES	HAMANTASCHEN	HANDEDNESS
HAIRPIECES	HALLUCINATING	HAMARTHRITIS	HANDEDNESSES
HAIRSBREADTH	HALLUCINATION	HAMARTHRITISES	HANDFASTED
HAIRSBREADTHS	HALLUCINATIONAL	HAMARTIOLOGIES	HANDFASTING
HAIRSPLITTER	HALLUCINATIONS	HAMARTIOLOGY	HANDFASTINGS
HAIRSPLITTERS	HALLUCINATIVE	HAMBURGERS	HANDFEEDING
HAIRSPLITTING	HALLUCINATOR	HAMBURGHER	HANDICAPPED
HAIRSPLITTINGS	HALLUCINATORS	HAMBURGHERS	HANDICAPPER
HAIRSPRAYS	HALLUCINATORY	HAMESUCKEN	HANDICAPPERS
HAIRSPRING	HALLUCINOGEN	HAMESUCKENS	HANDICAPPING
HAIRSPRINGS	HALLUCINOGENIC	HAMFATTERED	HANDICRAFT
HAIRSTREAK	HALLUCINOGENICS	HAMFATTERING	HANDICRAFTER
HAIRSTREAKS	HALLUCINOGENS	HAMFATTERS	HANDICRAFTERS
HAIRSTYLES	HALLUCINOSES	HAMMERCLOTH	HANDICRAFTS
HAIRSTYLING	HALLUCINOSIS	HAMMERCLOTHS	HANDICRAFTSMAN
HAIRSTYLINGS	HALOBIONTIC	HAMMERHEAD	HANDICRAFTSMEN
HAIRSTYLIST	HALOBIONTS	HAMMERHEADED	HANDICUFFS
HAIRSTYLISTS	HALOBIOTIC	HAMMERHEADS	HANDINESSES
HAIRWEAVING	HALOCARBON	HAMMERINGS	HANDIWORKS
HAIRWEAVINGS	HALOCARBONS	HAMMERKOPS	HANDKERCHER
HAIRYBACKS	HALOCLINES	HAMMERLESS	HANDKERCHERS
HALACHISTS	HALOGENATE	HAMMERLOCK	HANDKERCHIEF
HALAKHISTS	HALOGENATED	HAMMERLOCKS	HANDKERCHIEFS
HALBERDIER	HALOGENATES	HAMMERSTONE	HANDKERCHIEVES
HALBERDIERS	HALOGENATING	HAMMERSTONES	HANDLANGER
HALCYONIAN	HALOGENATION	HAMMERTOES	HANDLANGERS
HALENESSES	HALOGENATIONS	HAMMINESSES	HANDLEABLE
HALFENDEALE	HALOGENOID	HAMPEREDNESS	HANDLEBARS
HALFHEARTED	HALOGENOUS	HAMPEREDNESSES	HANDLELESS
HALFHEARTEDLY	HALOGETONS	HAMSHACKLE	HANDMAIDEN
HALFHEARTEDNESS	HALOMORPHIC	HAMSHACKLED	HANDMAIDENS
HALFNESSES	HALOPERIDOL	HAMSHACKLES	HANDPHONES
HALFPENNIES	HALOPERIDOLS	HAMSHACKLING	HANDPICKED
HALFPENNYWORTH	HALOPHILES	HAMSTRINGED	HANDPICKING
HALFPENNYWORTHS	HALOPHILIC	HAMSTRINGING	HANDPRESSES
HALFTRACKS	HALOPHILIES	HAMSTRINGS	HANDPRINTS
HALFWITTED	HALOPHILOUS	HANDBAGGED	HANDSBREADTH
HALFWITTEDLY	HALOPHOBES	HANDBAGGING	HANDSBREADTHS
HALFWITTEDNESS	HALOPHYTES	HANDBAGGINGS	HANDSELING
HALIEUTICS	HALOPHYTIC	HANDBALLED	HANDSELLED
HALIPLANKTON	HALOPHYTISM	HANDBALLER	HANDSELLING
HALIPLANKTONS	HALOPHYTISMS	HANDBALLERS	HANDSHAKES
HALLALLING	HALOTHANES	HANDBALLING	HANDSHAKING
HALLEFLINTA	HALTERBREAK	HANDBARROW	HANDSHAKINGS
HALLEFLINTAS	HALTERBREAKING	HANDBARROWS	HANDSOMELY
HALLELUIAH	HALTERBREAKS	HANDBASKET	HANDSOMENESS
HALLELUIAHS	HALTERBROKE	HANDBASKETS	HANDSOMENESSES

HANDSOMEST	HAPLOGRAPHY	HARDINESSES	HARMONISER
HANDSPIKES	HAPLOIDIES	HARDINGGRASS	HARMONISERS
HANDSPRING	HAPLOLOGIC	HARDINGGRASSES	HARMONISES
HANDSPRINGS	HAPLOLOGIES	HARDLINERS	HARMONISING
HANDSTAFFS	HAPLOSTEMONOUS	HARDMOUTHED	HARMONISTIC
HANDSTAMPED	HAPLOTYPES	HARDNESSES	HARMONISTICALLY
HANDSTAMPING	HAPPENCHANCE	HARDSCRABBLE	HARMONISTS
HANDSTAMPS	HAPPENCHANCES	HARDSTANDING	HARMONIUMIST
HANDSTANDS	HAPPENINGS	HARDSTANDINGS	HARMONIUMISTS
HANDSTAVES	HAPPENSTANCE	HARDSTANDS	HARMONIUMS
HANDSTROKE	HAPPENSTANCES	HARDWAREMAN	HARMONIZABLE
HANDSTROKES	HAPPINESSES	HARDWAREMEN	HARMONIZATION
HANDSTURNS	HAPTOGLOBIN	HARDWIRING	HARMONIZATIONS
HANDTOWELS	HAPTOGLOBINS	HARDWORKING	HARMONIZED
HANDWHEELS	HAPTOTROPIC	HAREBRAINED	HARMONIZER
HANDWORKED	HAPTOTROPISM	HARELIPPED	HARMONIZERS
HANDWORKER	HAPTOTROPISMS	HARESTAILS	HARMONIZES
HANDWORKERS	HARAMZADAS	HARIOLATED	HARMONIZING
HANDWRINGER	HARAMZADIS	HARIOLATES	HARMONOGRAM
HANDWRINGERS	HARANGUERS	HARIOLATING	HARMONOGRAMS
HANDWRITES	HARANGUING	HARIOLATION	HARMONOGRAPH
HANDWRITING	HARASSEDLY	HARIOLATIONS	HARMONOGRAPHS
HANDWRITINGS	HARASSINGLY	HARLEQUINADE	HARMONOMETER
HANDWRITTEN	HARASSINGS	HARLEQUINADES	HARMONOMETERS
HANDWROUGHT	HARASSMENT	HARLEQUINED	HARMOSTIES
HANDYPERSON	HARASSMENTS	HARLEQUINING	HARMOTOMES
HANDYPERSONS	HARBINGERED	HARLEQUINS	HARNESSERS
HANDYWORKS	HARBINGERING	HARLOTRIES	HARNESSING
HANGABILITIES	HARBINGERS	HARMALINES	HARNESSLESS
HANGABILITY	HARBORAGES	HARMATTANS	HARPOONEER
HANKERINGS	HARBORFULS	HARMDOINGS	HARPOONEERS
HANSARDISE	HARBORLESS	HARMFULNESS	HARPOONERS
HANSARDISED	HARBORMASTER	HARMFULNESSES	HARPOONING
HANSARDISES	HARBORMASTERS	HARMLESSLY	HARPSICHORD
HANSARDISING	HARBORSIDE	HARMLESSNESS	HARPSICHORDIST
HANSARDIZE	HARBOURAGE	HARMLESSNESSES	HARPSICHORDISTS
HANSARDIZED	HARBOURAGES	HARMOLODIC	HARPSICHORDS
HANSARDIZES	HARBOURERS	HARMOLODICS	HARQUEBUSE
HANSARDIZING	HARBOURING	HARMONICAL	HARQUEBUSES
HANSELLING	HARBOURLESS	HARMONICALLY	HARQUEBUSIER
HANTAVIRUS	HARDBACKED	HARMONICAS	HARQUEBUSIERS
HANTAVIRUSES	HARDBOARDS	HARMONICHORD	HARQUEBUSS
HAPAXANTHIC	HARDBOUNDS	HARMONICHORDS	HARQUEBUSSES
HAPAXANTHOUS	HARDCOVERS	HARMONICIST	HARROWINGLY
HAPHAZARDLY	HARDENINGS	HARMONICISTS	HARROWMENT
HAPHAZARDNESS	HARDFISTED	HARMONICON	HARROWMENTS
HAPHAZARDNESSES	HARDGRASSES	HARMONICONS	HARRUMPHED
HAPHAZARDRIES	HARDHANDED	HARMONIOUS	HARRUMPHING
HAPHAZARDRY	HARDHANDEDNESS	HARMONIOUSLY	HARSHENING
HAPHAZARDS	HARDHEADED	HARMONIOUSNESS	HARSHNESSES
HAPHTARAHS	HARDHEADEDLY	HARMONIPHON	HARTBEESES
HAPHTAROTH	HARDHEADEDNESS	HARMONIPHONE	HARTBEESTS
HAPLESSNESS	HARDHEARTED	HARMONIPHONES	HARTEBEEST
HAPLESSNESSES	HARDHEARTEDLY	HARMONIPHONS	HARTEBEESTS
HAPLOBIONT	HARDHEARTEDNESS	HARMONISABLE	HARTSHORNS
HAPLOBIONTIC	HARDIHEADS	HARMONISATION	HARUMPHING
HAPLOBIONTS	HARDIHOODS	HARMONISATIONS	HARUSPICAL
HAPLOGRAPHIES	HARDIMENTS	HARMONISED	HARUSPICATE

HARUSPICATED	HAUSTELLUM	HEADPEACES	HEARTBROKE
HARUSPICATES	HAUSTORIAL	HEADPHONES	HEARTBROKEN
HARUSPICATING	HAUSTORIUM	HEADPIECES	HEARTBROKENLY
HARUSPICATION	HAVERSACKS	HEADQUARTER	HEARTBROKENNESS
HARUSPICATIONS	HAVERSINES	HEADQUARTERED	HEARTBURNING
HARUSPICES	HAWFINCHES	HEADQUARTERING	HEARTBURNINGS
HARUSPICIES	HAWKISHNESS	HEADQUARTERS	HEARTBURNS
HARVESTABLE	HAWKISHNESSES	HEADREACHED	HEARTENERS
HARVESTERS	HAWKSBEARD	HEADREACHES	HEARTENING
HARVESTING	HAWKSBEARDS	HEADREACHING	HEARTENINGLY
HARVESTINGS	HAWKSBILLS	HEADSCARVES	HEARTHRUGS
HARVESTLESS	HAWSEHOLES	HEADSHAKES	HEARTHSTONE
HARVESTMAN	HAWSEPIPES	HEADSHEETS	HEARTHSTONES
HARVESTMEN	HAYMAKINGS	HEADSHRINKER	HEARTIKINS
HARVESTTIME	HAZARDABLE	HEADSHRINKERS	HEARTINESS
HARVESTTIMES	HAZARDIZES	HEADSPACES	HEARTINESSES
HASENPFEFFER	HAZARDOUSLY	HEADSPRING	HEARTLANDS
HASENPFEFFERS	HAZARDOUSNESS	HEADSPRINGS	HEARTLESSLY
HASHEESHES	HAZARDOUSNESSES	HEADSQUARE	HEARTLESSNESS
HASTEFULLY	HAZARDRIES	HEADSQUARES	HEARTLESSNESSES
HASTINESSES	HAZINESSES	HEADSTALLS	HEARTLINGS
HATBRUSHES	HEADACHIER	HEADSTANDS	HEARTRENDING
HATCHABILITIES	HEADACHIEST	HEADSTICKS	HEARTRENDINGLY
HATCHABILITY	HEADBANGED	HEADSTOCKS	HEARTSEASE
HATCHBACKS	HEADBANGING	HEADSTONES	HEARTSEASES
HATCHELING	HEADBOARDS	HEADSTREAM	HEARTSEEDS
HATCHELLED	HEADBOROUGH	HEADSTREAMS	HEARTSICKNESS
HATCHELLER	HEADBOROUGHS	HEADSTRONG	HEARTSICKNESSES
HATCHELLERS	HEADCHAIRS	HEADSTRONGLY	HEARTSOMELY
HATCHELLING	HEADCHEESE	HEADSTRONGNESS	HEARTSOMENESS
HATCHERIES	HEADCHEESES	HEADWAITER	HEARTSOMENESSES
HATCHETTITE	HEADCLOTHS	HEADWAITERS	HEARTSTRING
HATCHETTITES	HEADCOUNTS	HEADWATERS	HEARTSTRINGS
HATCHLINGS	HEADDRESSES	HEADWORKER	HEARTTHROB
HATCHMENTS	HEADFISHES	HEADWORKERS	HEARTTHROBS
HATEFULNESS	HEADFOREMOST	HEALTHCARE	HEARTWARMING
HATEFULNESSES	HEADFRAMES	HEALTHCARES	HEARTWATER
HATELESSNESS	HEADGUARDS	HEALTHFULLY	HEARTWATERS
HATELESSNESSES	HEADHUNTED	HEALTHFULNESS	HEARTWOODS
HATEWORTHY	HEADHUNTER	HEALTHFULNESSES	HEARTWORMS
HATLESSNESS	HEADHUNTERS	HEALTHIEST	HEATEDNESS
HATLESSNESSES	HEADHUNTING	HEALTHINESS	HEATEDNESSES
HAUBERGEON	HEADHUNTINGS	HEALTHINESSES	HEATHBERRIES
HAUBERGEONS	HEADINESSES	HEALTHISMS	HEATHBERRY
HAUGHTIEST	HEADLEASES	HEALTHLESS	HEATHBIRDS
HAUGHTINESS	HEADLESSNESS	HEALTHLESSNESS	HEATHCOCKS
HAUGHTINESSES	HEADLESSNESSES	HEALTHSOME	HEATHENDOM
HAUNTINGLY	HEADLIGHTS	HEAPSTEADS	HEATHENDOMS
HAUSFRAUEN	HEADLINERS	HEARKENERS	HEATHENESSE
HAUSSMANNISE	HEADLINING	HEARKENING	HEATHENESSES
HAUSSMANNISED	HEADMASTER	HEARTACHES	HEATHENISE
HAUSSMANNISES	HEADMASTERLY	HEARTBEATS	HEATHENISED
HAUSSMANNISING	HEADMASTERS	HEARTBREAK	HEATHENISES
HAUSSMANNIZE	HEADMASTERSHIP	HEARTBREAKER	HEATHENISH
HAUSSMANNIZED	HEADMASTERSHIPS	HEARTBREAKERS	HEATHENISHLY
HAUSSMANNIZES	HEADMISTRESS	HEARTBREAKING	HEATHENISHNESS
HAUSSMANNIZING	HEADMISTRESSES	HEARTBREAKINGLY	HEATHENISING
HAUSTELLATE	HEADMISTRESSY	HEARTBREAKS	HEATHENISM

HEATHENISMS	HECTOGRAMMES	HEINOUSNESSES	HELIOMETERS
HEATHENIZE	HECTOGRAMS	HEKTOGRAMS	HELIOMETRIC
HEATHENIZED	HECTOGRAPH	HELDENTENOR	HELIOMETRICAL
HEATHENIZES	HECTOGRAPHED	HELDENTENORS	HELIOMETRICALLY
HEATHENIZING	HECTOGRAPHIC	HELIACALLY	HELIOMETRIES
HEATHENNESS	HECTOGRAPHIES	HELIANTHEMUM	HELIOMETRY
HEATHENNESSES	HECTOGRAPHING	HELIANTHEMUMS	HELIOPAUSE
HEATHENRIES	HECTOGRAPHS	HELIANTHUS	HELIOPAUSES
HEATHERIER	HECTOGRAPHY	HELIANTHUSES	HELIOPHILOUS
HEATHERIEST	HECTOLITER	HELIBUSSES	HELIOPHOBIC
HEATHFOWLS	HECTOLITERS	HELICHRYSUM	HELIOPHYTE
HEATHLANDS	HECTOLITRE	HELICHRYSUMS	HELIOPHYTES
HEATSTROKE	HECTOLITRES	HELICITIES	HELIOSCIOPHYTE
HEATSTROKES	HECTOMETER	HELICLINES	HELIOSCIOPHYTES
HEAVENLIER	HECTOMETERS	HELICOGRAPH	HELIOSCOPE
HEAVENLIEST	HECTOMETRE	HELICOGRAPHS	HELIOSCOPES
HEAVENLINESS	HECTOMETRES	HELICOIDAL	HELIOSCOPIC
HEAVENLINESSES	HECTORINGLY	HELICOIDALLY	HELIOSPHERE
HEAVENWARD	HECTORINGS	HELICONIAS	HELIOSPHERES
HEAVENWARDS	HECTORISMS	HELICOPTED	HELIOSTATIC
HEAVINESSES	HECTORSHIP	HELICOPTER	HELIOSTATS
HEAVYHEARTED	HECTORSHIPS	HELICOPTERED	HELIOTACTIC
HEAVYHEARTEDLY	HECTOSTERE	HELICOPTERING	HELIOTAXES
HEAVYWEIGHT	HECTOSTERES	HELICOPTERS	HELIOTAXIS
HEAVYWEIGHTS	HEDGEBILLS	HELICOPTING	HELIOTHERAPIES
HEBDOMADAL	HEDGEHOPPED	HELICTITES	HELIOTHERAPY
HEBDOMADALLY	HEDGEHOPPER	HELIDROMES	HELIOTROPE
HEBDOMADAR	HEDGEHOPPERS	HELILIFTED	HELIOTROPES
HEBDOMADARIES	HEDGEHOPPING	HELILIFTING	HELIOTROPIC
HEBDOMADARS	HEDGEHOPPINGS	HELIOCENTRIC	HELIOTROPICAL
HEBDOMADARY	HEDONICALLY	HELIOCENTRICISM	HELIOTROPICALLY
HEBDOMADER	HEDONISTIC	HELIOCENTRICITY	HELIOTROPIES
HEBDOMADERS	HEDONISTICALLY	HELIOCHROME	HELIOTROPIN
HEBEPHRENIA	HEDYPHANES	HELIOCHROMES	HELIOTROPINS
HEBEPHRENIAC	HEEDFULNESS	HELIOCHROMIC	HELIOTROPISM
HEBEPHRENIACS	HEEDFULNESSES	HELIOCHROMIES	HELIOTROPISMS
HEBEPHRENIAS	HEEDINESSES	HELIOCHROMY	HELIOTROPY
HEBEPHRENIC	HEEDLESSLY	HELIOGRAMS	HELIOTYPED
HEBEPHRENICS	HEEDLESSNESS	HELIOGRAPH	HELIOTYPES
HEBETATING	HEEDLESSNESSES	HELIOGRAPHED	HELIOTYPIC
HEBETATION	HEELPIECES	HELIOGRAPHER	HELIOTYPIES
HEBETATIONS	HEELPLATES	HELIOGRAPHERS	HELIOTYPING
HEBETATIVE	HEFTINESSES	HELIOGRAPHIC	HELIOZOANS
HEBETUDINOSITY	HEGEMONIAL	HELIOGRAPHICAL	HELIPILOTS
HEBETUDINOUS	HEGEMONICAL	HELIOGRAPHIES	HELISPHERIC
HEBRAISATION	HEGEMONIES	HELIOGRAPHING	HELISPHERICAL
HEBRAISATIONS	HEGEMONISM	HELIOGRAPHS	HELLACIOUS
HEBRAISING	HEGEMONISMS	HELIOGRAPHY	HELLACIOUSLY
HEBRAIZATION	HEGEMONIST	HELIOGRAVURE	HELLBENDER
HEBRAIZATIONS	HEGEMONISTS	HELIOGRAVURES	HELLBENDERS
HEBRAIZING	HEGUMENIES	HELIOLATER	HELLBROTHS
HECKELPHONE	HEGUMENOSES	HELIOLATERS	HELLDIVERS
HECKELPHONES	HEIGHTENED	HELIOLATRIES	HELLEBORES
HECOGENINS	HEIGHTENER	HELIOLATROUS	HELLEBORINE
HECTICALLY	HEIGHTENERS	HELIOLATRY	HELLEBORINES
HECTOCOTYLI	HEIGHTENING	HELIOLITHIC	HELLENISATION
HECTOCOTYLUS	HEIGHTISMS	HELIOLOGIES	HELLENISATIONS
HECTOGRAMME	HEINOUSNESS	HELIOMETER	HELLENISED

HELLENISES	HEMATOGENESES	HEMIHEDRISMS	HEMODIALYSIS
HELLENISING	HEMATOGENESIS	HEMIHEDRON	HEMODILUTION
HELLENIZATION	HEMATOGENETIC	HEMIHEDRONS	HEMODILUTIONS
HELLENIZATIONS	HEMATOGENIC	HEMIHYDRATE	HEMODYNAMIC
HELLENIZED	HEMATOGENOUS	HEMIHYDRATED	HEMODYNAMICALLY
HELLENIZES	HEMATOLOGIC	HEMIHYDRATES	HEMODYNAMICS
HELLENIZING	HEMATOLOGICAL	HEMIMETABOLOUS	HEMOFLAGELLATE
HELLGRAMITE	HEMATOLOGIES	HEMIMORPHIC	HEMOFLAGELLATES
HELLGRAMITES	HEMATOLOGIST	HEMIMORPHIES	HEMOGLOBIN
HELLGRAMMITE	HEMATOLOGISTS	HEMIMORPHISM	HEMOGLOBINS
HELLGRAMMITES	HEMATOLOGY	HEMIMORPHISMS	HEMOGLOBINURIA
HELLHOUNDS	HEMATOLYSES	HEMIMORPHITE	HEMOGLOBINURIAS
HELLISHNESS	HEMATOLYSIS	HEMIMORPHITES	HEMOGLOBINURIC
HELLISHNESSES	HEMATOMATA	HEMIMORPHY	HEMOLYMPHS
HELMETLIKE	HEMATOPHAGOUS	HEMIONUSES	HEMOLYSING
HELMINTHIASES	HEMATOPOIESES	HEMIOPSIAS	HEMOLYSINS
HELMINTHIASIS	HEMATOPOIESIS	HEMIPARASITE	HEMOLYZING
HELMINTHIC	HEMATOPOIETIC	HEMIPARASITES	HEMOPHILES
HELMINTHICS	HEMATOPORPHYRIN	HEMIPARASITIC	HEMOPHILIA
HELMINTHOID	HEMATOTHERMAL	HEMIPLEGIA	HEMOPHILIAC
HELMINTHOLOGIC	HEMATOXYLIN	HEMIPLEGIAS	HEMOPHILIACS
HELMINTHOLOGIES	HEMATOXYLINS	HEMIPLEGIC	HEMOPHILIAS
HELMINTHOLOGIST	HEMATOZOON	HEMIPLEGICS	HEMOPHILIC
HELMINTHOLOGY	HEMATURIAS	HEMIPTERAL	HEMOPHILICS
HELMINTHOUS	HEMELYTRAL	HEMIPTERAN	HEMOPHILIOID
HELMSMANSHIP	HEMELYTRON	HEMIPTERANS	HEMOPOIESES
HELMSMANSHIPS	HEMELYTRUM	HEMIPTERON	HEMOPOIESIS
HELOPHYTES	HEMERALOPIA	HEMIPTERONS	HEMOPOIETIC
HELPFULNESS	HEMERALOPIAS	HEMIPTEROUS	HEMOPROTEIN
HELPFULNESSES	HEMERALOPIC	HEMISPACES	HEMOPROTEINS
HELPLESSLY	HEMEROCALLIS	HEMISPHERE	HEMOPTYSES
HELPLESSNESS	HEMEROCALLISES	HEMISPHERES	HEMOPTYSIS
HELPLESSNESSES	HEMERYTHRIN	HEMISPHERIC	HEMORRHAGE
HELVETIUMS	HEMERYTHRINS	HEMISPHERICAL	HEMORRHAGED
HEMACHROME	HEMIACETAL	HEMISPHEROID	HEMORRHAGES
HEMACHROMES	HEMIACETALS	HEMISPHEROIDAL	HEMORRHAGIC
HEMACYTOMETER	HEMIALGIAS	HEMISPHEROIDS	HEMORRHAGING
HEMACYTOMETERS	HEMIANOPIA	HEMISTICHAL	HEMORRHOID
HEMAGGLUTINATE	HEMIANOPIAS	HEMISTICHS	HEMORRHOIDAL
HEMAGGLUTINATED	HEMIANOPSIA	HEMITERPENE	HEMORRHOIDALS
HEMAGGLUTINATES	HEMIANOPSIAS	HEMITERPENES	HEMORRHOIDS
HEMAGGLUTININ	HEMIANOPTIC	HEMITROPAL	HEMOSIDERIN
HEMAGGLUTININS	HEMICELLULOSE	HEMITROPES	HEMOSIDERINS
HEMAGOGUES	HEMICELLULOSES	HEMITROPIC	HEMOSTASES
HEMANGIOMA	HEMICHORDATE	HEMITROPIES	HEMOSTASIA
HEMANGIOMAS	HEMICHORDATES	HEMITROPISM	HEMOSTASIAS
HEMANGIOMATA	HEMICRANIA	HEMITROPISMS	HEMOSTASIS
HEMATEMESES	HEMICRANIAS	HEMITROPOUS	HEMOSTATIC
HEMATEMESIS	HEMICRYPTOPHYTE	HEMIZYGOUS	HEMOSTATICS
HEMATINICS	HEMICRYSTALLINE	HEMOCHROMATOSES	HEMOTOXINS
HEMATOBLAST	HEMICYCLES	HEMOCHROMATOSIS	HEMSTITCHED
HEMATOBLASTIC	HEMICYCLIC	HEMOCHROME	HEMSTITCHER
HEMATOBLASTS	HEMIELYTRA	HEMOCHROMES	HEMSTITCHERS
HEMATOCELE	HEMIELYTRAL	HEMOCYANIN	HEMSTITCHES
HEMATOCELES	HEMIELYTRON	HEMOCYANINS	HEMSTITCHING
HEMATOCRIT	HEMIHEDRAL	HEMOCYTOMETER	HENCEFORTH
HEMATOCRITS	HEMIHEDRIES	HEMOCYTOMETERS	HENCEFORWARD
HEMATOCRYAL	HEMIHEDRISM	HEMODIALYSES	HENCEFORWARDS

HENCHPERSON	HEPATOSCOPIES	HERBIVOROUSLY	HERETICATES
HENCHPERSONS	HEPATOSCOPY	HERBIVOROUSNESS	HERETICATING
HENCHWOMAN	HEPATOTOXIC	HERBOLOGIES	HERETOFORE
HENCHWOMEN	HEPATOTOXICITY	HERBORISATION	HERETRICES
HENDECAGON	HEPHTHEMIMER	HERBORISATIONS	HERETRIXES
HENDECAGONAL	HEPHTHEMIMERAL	HERBORISED	HERIOTABLE
HENDECAGONS	HEPHTHEMIMERS	HERBORISES	HERITABILITIES
HENDECAHEDRA	HEPTACHLOR	HERBORISING	HERITABILITY
HENDECAHEDRON	HEPTACHLORS	HERBORISTS	HERITRESSES
HENDECAHEDRONS	HEPTACHORD	HERBORIZATION	HERITRICES
HENDECASYLLABIC	HEPTACHORDS	HERBORIZATIONS	HERITRIXES
HENDECASYLLABLE	HEPTADECANOIC	HERBORIZED	HERKOGAMIES
HENDIADYSES	HEPTAGLOTS	HERBORIZES	HERMANDADS
HENOTHEISM	HEPTAGONAL	HERBORIZING	HERMAPHRODITE
HENOTHEISMS	HEPTAGYNOUS	HERCOGAMIES	HERMAPHRODITES
HENOTHEIST	HEPTAHEDRA	HERCOGAMOUS	HERMAPHRODITIC
HENOTHEISTIC	HEPTAHEDRAL	HERCULESES	HERMAPHRODITISM
HENOTHEISTS	HEPTAHEDRON	HERCYNITES	HERMATYPIC
HENPECKERIES	HEPTAHEDRONS	HEREABOUTS	HERMENEUTIC
HENPECKERY	HEPTAMEROUS	HEREAFTERS	HERMENEUTICAL
HENPECKING	HEPTAMETER	HEREDITABILITY	HERMENEUTICALLY
HEORTOLOGICAL	HEPTAMETERS	HEREDITABLE	HERMENEUTICS
HEORTOLOGIES	HEPTAMETRICAL	HEREDITABLY	HERMENEUTIST
HEORTOLOGIST	HEPTANDROUS	HEREDITAMENT	HERMENEUTISTS
HEORTOLOGISTS	HEPTANGULAR	HEREDITAMENTS	HERMETICAL
HEORTOLOGY	HEPTAPODIC	HEREDITARIAN	HERMETICALLY
HEPARINISED	HEPTAPODIES	HEREDITARIANISM	HERMETICISM
HEPARINIZED	HEPTARCHAL	HEREDITARIANIST	HERMETICISMS
HEPARINOID	HEPTARCHIC	HEREDITARIANS	HERMETICITIES
HEPATECTOMIES	HEPTARCHIES	HEREDITARILY	HERMETICITY
HEPATECTOMISED	HEPTARCHIST	HEREDITARINESS	HERMETISMS
HEPATECTOMIZED	HEPTARCHISTS	HEREDITARY	HERMETISTS
HEPATECTOMY	HEPTASTICH	HEREDITIES	HERMITAGES
HEPATICOLOGICAL	HEPTASTICHS	HEREDITIST	HERMITESSES
HEPATICOLOGIES	HEPTASYLLABIC	HEREDITISTS	HERMITICAL
HEPATICOLOGIST	HEPTATHLETE	HEREINABOVE	HERMITICALLY
HEPATICOLOGISTS	HEPTATHLETES	HEREINAFTER	HERMITISMS
HEPATICOLOGY	HEPTATHLON	HEREINBEFORE	HERMITRIES
HEPATISATION	HEPTATHLONS	HEREINBELOW	HERNIATING
HEPATISATIONS	HEPTATONIC	HERENESSES	HERNIATION
HEPATISING	HEPTAVALENT	HERESIARCH	HERNIATIONS
HEPATITIDES	HERALDICALLY	HERESIARCHS	HERNIORRHAPHIES
HEPATITISES	HERALDISTS	HERESIOGRAPHER	HERNIORRHAPHY
HEPATIZATION	HERALDRIES	HERESIOGRAPHERS	HERNIOTOMIES
HEPATIZATIONS	HERALDSHIP	HERESIOGRAPHIES	HERNIOTOMY
HEPATIZING	HERALDSHIPS	HERESIOGRAPHY	HEROICALLY
HEPATOCELLULAR	HERBACEOUS	HERESIOLOGIES	HEROICALNESS
HEPATOCYTE	HERBACEOUSLY	HERESIOLOGIST	HEROICALNESSES
HEPATOCYTES	HERBALISMS	HERESIOLOGISTS	HEROICISED
HEPATOGENOUS	HERBALISTS	HERESIOLOGY	HEROICISES
HEPATOLOGIES	HERBARIANS	HERESTHETIC	HEROICISING
HEPATOLOGIST	HERBARIUMS	HERESTHETICAL	HEROICIZED
HEPATOLOGISTS	HERBICIDAL	HERESTHETICIAN	HEROICIZES
HEPATOLOGY	HERBICIDALLY	HERESTHETICIANS	HEROICIZING
HEPATOMATA	HERBICIDES	HERESTHETICS	HEROICNESS
HEPATOMEGALIES	HERBIVORES	HERETICALLY	HEROICNESSES
HEPATOMEGALY	HERBIVORIES	HERETICATE	HEROICOMIC
HEPATOPANCREAS	HERBIVOROUS	HERETICATED	HEROICOMICAL

HEROINISMS	HETEROBLASTY	HETEROGENESIS	HETEROPLASIAS
HERONSHAWS	HETEROCARPOUS	HETEROGENETIC	HETEROPLASTIC
HERPESVIRUS	HETEROCERCAL	HETEROGENIC	HETEROPLASTIES
HERPESVIRUSES	HETEROCERCALITY	HETEROGENIES	HETEROPLASTY
HERPETOFAUNA	HETEROCERCIES	HETEROGENOUS	HETEROPLOID
HERPETOFAUNAE	HETEROCERCY	HETEROGENY	HETEROPLOIDIES
HERPETOFAUNAS	HETEROCHROMATIC	HETEROGONIC	HETEROPLOIDS
HERPETOLOGIC	HETEROCHROMATIN	HETEROGONIES	HETEROPLOIDY
HERPETOLOGICAL	HETEROCHROMOUS	HETEROGONOUS	HETEROPODS
HERPETOLOGIES	HETEROCHRONIC	HETEROGONOUSLY	HETEROPOLAR
HERPETOLOGIST	HETEROCHRONIES	HETEROGONY	HETEROPOLARITY
HERPETOLOGISTS	HETEROCHRONISM	HETEROGRAFT	HETEROPTERAN
HERPETOLOGY	HETEROCHRONISMS	HETEROGRAFTS	HETEROPTEROUS
HERRENVOLK	HETEROCHRONOUS	HETEROGRAPHIC	HETEROSCEDASTIC
HERRENVOLKS	HETEROCHRONY	HETEROGRAPHICAL	HETEROSCIAN
HERRIMENTS	HETEROCLITE	HETEROGRAPHIES	HETEROSCIANS
HERRINGBONE	HETEROCLITES	HETEROGRAPHY	HETEROSEXISM
HERRINGBONED	HETEROCLITIC	HETEROGYNOUS	HETEROSEXISMS
HERRINGBONES	HETEROCLITOUS	HETEROKARYON	HETEROSEXIST
HERRINGBONING	HETEROCONT	HETEROKARYONS	HETEROSEXISTS
HERRINGERS	HETEROCONTS	HETEROKARYOSES	HETEROSEXUAL
HERRYMENTS	HETEROCYCLE	HETEROKARYOSIS	HETEROSEXUALITY
HERSTORIES	HETEROCYCLES	HETEROKARYOTIC	HETEROSEXUALLY
HESITANCES	HETEROCYCLIC	HETEROKONT	HETEROSEXUALS
HESITANCIES	HETEROCYCLICS	HETEROKONTAN	HETEROSOCIAL
HESITANTLY	HETEROCYST	HETEROKONTS	HETEROSOCIALITY
HESITATERS	HETEROCYSTOUS	HETEROLECITHAL	HETEROSOMATOUS
HESITATING	HETEROCYSTS	HETEROLOGIES	HETEROSPECIFIC
HESITATINGLY	HETERODACTYL	HETEROLOGOUS	HETEROSPORIES
HESITATION	HETERODACTYLOUS	HETEROLOGOUSLY	HETEROSPOROUS
HESITATIONS	HETERODACTYLS	HETEROLOGY	HETEROSPORY
HESITATIVE	HETERODONT	HETEROLYSES	HETEROSTROPHIC
HESITATORS	HETERODOXIES	HETEROLYSIS	HETEROSTROPHIES
HESITATORY	HETERODOXY	HETEROLYTIC	HETEROSTROPHY
HESPERIDIA	HETERODUPLEX	HETEROMEROUS	HETEROSTYLED
HESPERIDIN	HETERODUPLEXES	HETEROMORPHIC	HETEROSTYLIES
HESPERIDINS	HETERODYNE	HETEROMORPHIES	HETEROSTYLISM
HESPERIDIUM	HETERODYNED	HETEROMORPHISM	HETEROSTYLISMS
HESPERIDIUMS	HETERODYNES	HETEROMORPHISMS	HETEROSTYLOUS
HESSONITES	HETERODYNING	HETEROMORPHOUS	HETEROSTYLY
HETAERISMIC	HETEROECIOUS	HETEROMORPHY	HETEROTACTIC
HETAERISMS	HETEROECISM	HETERONOMIES	HETEROTACTOUS
HETAERISTIC	HETEROECISMS	HETERONOMOUS	HETEROTAXES
HETAERISTS	HETEROFLEXIBLE	HETERONOMOUSLY	HETEROTAXIA
HETAIRISMIC	HETEROFLEXIBLES	HETERONOMY	HETEROTAXIAS
HETAIRISMS	HETEROGAMETE	HETERONYMOUS	HETEROTAXIC
HETAIRISTIC	HETEROGAMETES	HETERONYMOUSLY	HETEROTAXIES
HETAIRISTS	HETEROGAMETIC	HETERONYMS	HETEROTAXIS
HETERARCHIES	HETEROGAMETIES	HETEROOUSIAN	HETEROTAXY
HETERARCHY	HETEROGAMETY	HETEROOUSIANS	HETEROTHALLIC
HETERAUXESES	HETEROGAMIES	HETEROPHIL	HETEROTHALLIES
HETERAUXESIS	HETEROGAMOUS	HETEROPHILE	HETEROTHALLISM
HETEROATOM	HETEROGAMY	HETEROPHONIES	HETEROTHALLISMS
HETEROATOMS	HETEROGENEITIES	HETEROPHONY	HETEROTHALLY
HETEROAUXIN	HETEROGENEITY	HETEROPHYLLIES	HETEROTHERMAL
HETEROAUXINS	HETEROGENEOUS	HETEROPHYLLOUS	HETEROTOPIA
HETEROBLASTIC	HETEROGENEOUSLY	HETEROPHYLLY	HETEROTOPIAS
HETEROBLASTIES	HETEROGENESES	HETEROPLASIA	HETEROTOPIC

HETEROTOPIES	HEXAHEMERONS	HIBERNATIONS	HIEROCRACY
HETEROTOPOUS	HEXAHYDRATE	HIBERNATOR	HIEROCRATIC
HETEROTOPY	HEXAHYDRATED	HIBERNATORS	HIEROCRATICAL
HETEROTROPH	HEXAHYDRATES	HIBERNICISE	HIEROCRATS
HETEROTROPHIC	HEXAMERISM	HIBERNICISED	HIERODULES
HETEROTROPHIES	HEXAMERISMS	HIBERNICISES	HIERODULIC
HETEROTROPHS	HEXAMEROUS	HIBERNICISING	HIEROGLYPH
HETEROTROPHY	HEXAMETERS	HIBERNICIZE	HIEROGLYPHED
HETEROTYPIC	HEXAMETHONIUM	HIBERNICIZED	HIEROGLYPHIC
HETEROTYPICAL	HEXAMETHONIUMS	HIBERNICIZES	HIEROGLYPHICAL
HETEROUSIAN	HEXAMETRAL	HIBERNICIZING	HIEROGLYPHICS
HETEROUSIANS	HEXAMETRIC	HIBERNISATION	HIEROGLYPHING
HETEROZYGOSES	HEXAMETRICAL	HIBERNISATIONS	HIEROGLYPHIST
HETEROZYGOSIS	HEXAMETRICALLY	HIBERNISED	HIEROGLYPHISTS
HETEROZYGOSITY	HEXAMETRISE	HIBERNISES	HIEROGLYPHS
HETEROZYGOTE	HEXAMETRISED	HIBERNISING	HIEROGRAMMAT
HETEROZYGOTES	HEXAMETRISES	HIBERNIZATION	HIEROGRAMMATE
HETEROZYGOUS	HEXAMETRISING	HIBERNIZATIONS	HIEROGRAMMATES
HETHERWARD	HEXAMETRIST	HIBERNIZED	HIEROGRAMMATIC
HETMANATES	HEXAMETRISTS	HIBERNIZES	HIEROGRAMMATIST
HETMANSHIP	HEXAMETRIZE	HIBERNIZING	HIEROGRAMMATS
HETMANSHIPS	HEXAMETRIZED	HIBISCUSES	HIEROGRAMS
HEULANDITE	HEXAMETRIZES	HICCOUGHED	HIEROGRAPH
HEULANDITES	HEXAMETRIZING	HICCOUGHING	HIEROGRAPHER
HEURISTICALLY	HEXANDRIAN	HICCUPPING	HIEROGRAPHERS
HEURISTICS	HEXANDROUS	HIDALGOISH	HIEROGRAPHIC
HEXACHLORETHANE	HEXANGULAR	HIDALGOISM	HIEROGRAPHICAL
HEXACHLORIDE	HEXAPLARIAN	HIDALGOISMS	HIEROGRAPHIES
HEXACHLORIDES	HEXAPLARIC	HIDDENITES	HIEROGRAPHS
HEXACHLOROPHANE	HEXAPLOIDIES	HIDDENMOST	HIEROGRAPHY
HEXACHLOROPHENE	HEXAPLOIDS	HIDDENNESS	HIEROLATRIES
HEXACHORDS	HEXAPLOIDY	HIDDENNESSES	HIEROLATRY
HEXACOSANOIC	HEXAPODIES	HIDEOSITIES	HIEROLOGIC
HEXACTINAL	HEXARCHIES	HIDEOUSNESS	HIEROLOGICAL
HEXACTINELLID	HEXASTICHAL	HIDEOUSNESSES	HIEROLOGIES
HEXACTINELLIDS	HEXASTICHIC	HIERACIUMS	HIEROLOGIST
HEXADACTYLIC	HEXASTICHON	HIERACOSPHINGES	HIEROLOGISTS
HEXADACTYLOUS	HEXASTICHONS	HIERACOSPHINX	HIEROMANCIES
HEXADECANE	HEXASTICHS	HIERACOSPHINXES	HIEROMANCY
HEXADECANES	HEXASTYLES	HIERARCHAL	HIEROPHANT
HEXADECANOIC	HEXATEUCHAL	HIERARCHIC	HIEROPHANTIC
HEXADECIMAL	HEXAVALENT	HIERARCHICAL	HIEROPHANTS
HEXADECIMALS	HEXOBARBITAL	HIERARCHICALLY	HIEROPHOBIA
HEXAEMERIC	HEXOBARBITALS	HIERARCHIES	HIEROPHOBIAS
HEXAEMERON	HEXOKINASE	HIERARCHISE	HIEROPHOBIC
HEXAEMERONS	HEXOKINASES	HIERARCHISED	HIEROSCOPIES
HEXAFLUORIDE	HEXOSAMINIDASE	HIERARCHISES	HIEROSCOPY
HEXAFLUORIDES	HEXOSAMINIDASES	HIERARCHISING	HIERURGICAL
HEXAGONALLY	HEXYLRESORCINOL	HIERARCHISM	HIERURGIES
HEXAGRAMMOID	HIBAKUSHAS	HIERARCHISMS	HIGHBALLED
HEXAGRAMMOIDS	HIBERNACLE	HIERARCHIZE	HIGHBALLING
HEXAGYNIAN	HIBERNACLES	HIERARCHIZED	HIGHBINDER
HEXAGYNOUS	HIBERNACULA	HIERARCHIZES	HIGHBINDERS
HEXAHEDRAL	HIBERNACULUM	HIERARCHIZING	HIGHBLOODED
HEXAHEDRON	HIBERNATED	HIERATICAL	HIGHBROWED
HEXAHEDRONS	HIBERNATES	HIERATICALLY	HIGHBROWISM
HEXAHEMERIC	HIBERNATING	HIERATICAS	HIGHBROWISMS
HEXAHEMERON	HIBERNATION	HIEROCRACIES	HIGHCHAIRS

HIGHERMOST	HIPPIATRICS	HIRUDINOUS	HISTOLYTIC
HIGHFALUTIN	HIPPIATRIES	HISPANICISE	HISTOLYTICALLY
HIGHFALUTING	HIPPIATRIST	HISPANICISED	HISTOPATHOLOGIC
HIGHFALUTINGS	HIPPIATRISTS	HISPANICISES	HISTOPATHOLOGY
HIGHFALUTINS	HIPPIEDOMS	HISPANICISING	HISTOPHYSIOLOGY
HIGHFLIERS	HIPPIENESS	HISPANICISM	HISTOPLASMOSES
HIGHFLYERS	HIPPIENESSES	HISPANICISMS	HISTOPLASMOSIS
HIGHJACKED	HIPPINESSES	HISPANICIZE	HISTORIANS
HIGHJACKER	HIPPOCAMPAL	HISPANICIZED	HISTORIATED
HIGHJACKERS	HIPPOCAMPI	HISPANICIZES	HISTORICAL
HIGHJACKING	HIPPOCAMPUS	HISPANICIZING	HISTORICALLY
HIGHLANDER	HIPPOCENTAUR	HISPANIDAD	HISTORICALNESS
HIGHLANDERS	HIPPOCENTAURS	HISPANIDADS	HISTORICISE
HIGHLIGHTED	HIPPOCRASES	HISPANIOLISE	HISTORICISED
HIGHLIGHTER	HIPPOCREPIAN	HISPANIOLISED	HISTORICISES
HIGHLIGHTERS	HIPPODAMES	HISPANIOLISES	HISTORICISING
HIGHLIGHTING	HIPPODAMIST	HISPANIOLISING	HISTORICISM
HIGHLIGHTS	HIPPODAMISTS	HISPANIOLIZE	HISTORICISMS
HIGHNESSES	HIPPODAMOUS	HISPANIOLIZED	HISTORICIST
HIGHTAILED	HIPPODROME	HISPANIOLIZES	HISTORICISTS
HIGHTAILING	HIPPODROMES	HISPANIOLIZING	HISTORICITIES
HIGHWAYMAN	HIPPODROMIC	HISPANISMS	HISTORICITY
HIGHWAYMEN	HIPPOGRIFF	HISPIDITIES	HISTORICIZE
HIGHWROUGHT	HIPPOGRIFFS	HISTAMINASE	HISTORICIZED
HILARIOUSLY	HIPPOGRYPH	HISTAMINASES	HISTORICIZES
HILARIOUSNESS	HIPPOGRYPHS	HISTAMINERGIC	HISTORICIZING
HILARIOUSNESSES	HIPPOLOGIES	HISTAMINES	HISTORIETTE
HILARITIES	HIPPOLOGIST	HISTAMINIC	HISTORIETTES
HILLBILLIES	HIPPOLOGISTS	HISTIDINES	HISTORIFIED
HILLCRESTS	HIPPOMANES	HISTIOCYTE	HISTORIFIES
HILLINESSES	HIPPOPHAGIES	HISTIOCYTES	HISTORIFYING
HILLSLOPES	HIPPOPHAGIST	HISTIOCYTIC	HISTORIOGRAPHER
HILLWALKER	HIPPOPHAGISTS	HISTIOLOGIES	HISTORIOGRAPHIC
HILLWALKERS	HIPPOPHAGOUS	HISTIOLOGY	HISTORIOGRAPHY
HILLWALKING	HIPPOPHAGY	HISTIOPHOROID	HISTORIOLOGIES
HILLWALKINGS	HIPPOPHILE	HISTOBLAST	HISTORIOLOGY
HINDBERRIES	HIPPOPHILES	HISTOBLASTS	HISTORISMS
HINDBRAINS	HIPPOPHOBE	HISTOCHEMICAL	HISTORYING
HINDERANCE	HIPPOPHOBES	HISTOCHEMICALLY	HISTRIONIC
HINDERANCES	HIPPOPOTAMI	HISTOCHEMIST	HISTRIONICAL
HINDERINGLY	HIPPOPOTAMIAN	HISTOCHEMISTRY	HISTRIONICALLY
HINDERLAND	HIPPOPOTAMIC	HISTOCHEMISTS	HISTRIONICISM
HINDERLANDS	HIPPOPOTAMUS	HISTOCOMPATIBLE	HISTRIONICISMS
HINDERLANS	HIPPOPOTAMUSES	HISTOGENESES	HISTRIONICS
HINDERLINGS	HIPPURITES	HISTOGENESIS	HISTRIONISM
HINDERLINS	HIPPURITIC	HISTOGENETIC	HISTRIONISMS
HINDERMOST	HIPSTERISM	HISTOGENIC	HITCHHIKED
HINDFOREMOST	HIPSTERISMS	HISTOGENICALLY	HITCHHIKER
HINDQUARTER	HIRCOCERVUS	HISTOGENIES	HITCHHIKERS
HINDQUARTERS	HIRCOCERVUSES	HISTOGRAMS	HITCHHIKES
HINDRANCES	HIRCOSITIES	HISTOLOGIC	HITCHHIKING
HINDSHANKS	HIRSELLING	HISTOLOGICAL	HITHERMOST
HINDSIGHTS	HIRSUTENESS	HISTOLOGICALLY	HITHERSIDE
HINTERLAND	HIRSUTENESSES	HISTOLOGIES	HITHERSIDES
HINTERLANDS	HIRSUTISMS	HISTOLOGIST	HITHERWARD
HIPPEASTRUM	HIRUDINEAN	HISTOLOGISTS	HITHERWARDS
HIPPEASTRUMS	HIRUDINEANS	HISTOLYSES	HOACTZINES
HIPPIATRIC	HIRUDINOID	HISTOLYSIS	HOARFROSTS

HOARHOUNDS
HOARINESSES
HOARSENESS
HOARSENESSES
HOARSENING
HOBBITRIES
HOBBLEBUSH
HOBBLEBUSHES
HOBBLEDEHOY
HOBBLEDEHOYDOM
HOBBLEDEHOYDOMS
HOBBLEDEHOYHOOD
HOBBLEDEHOYISH
HOBBLEDEHOYISM
HOBBLEDEHOYISMS
HOBBLEDEHOYS
HOBBLINGLY
HOBBYHORSE
HOBBYHORSED
HOBBYHORSES
HOBBYHORSING
HOBGOBLINISM
HOBGOBLINISMS
HOBGOBLINRIES
HOBGOBLINRY
HOBGOBLINS
HOBJOBBERS
HOBJOBBING
HOBJOBBINGS
HOBNAILING
HOBNOBBERS
HOBNOBBING
HOCHMAGANDIES
HOCHMAGANDY
HODGEPODGE
HODGEPODGES
HODMANDODS
HODOGRAPHIC
HODOGRAPHS
HODOMETERS
HODOMETRIES
HODOSCOPES
HOGGISHNESS
HOGGISHNESSES
HOIDENISHNESS
HOIDENISHNESSES
HOJATOLESLAM
HOJATOLESLAMS
HOJATOLISLAM
HOJATOLISLAMS
HOKEYNESSES
HOKEYPOKEY
HOKEYPOKEYS
HOKINESSES
HOKYPOKIES
HOLARCHIES
HOLDERBATS
HOLDERSHIP

HOLDERSHIPS
HOLIDAYERS
HOLIDAYING
HOLIDAYMAKER
HOLIDAYMAKERS
HOLINESSES
HOLISTICALLY
HOLLANDAISE
HOLLANDAISES
HOLLOWARES
HOLLOWNESS
HOLLOWNESSES
HOLLOWWARE
HOLLOWWARES
HOLLYHOCKS
HOLOBENTHIC
HOLOBLASTIC
HOLOBLASTICALLY
HOLOCAUSTAL
HOLOCAUSTIC
HOLOCAUSTS
HOLOCRYSTALLINE
HOLODISCUS
HOLODISCUSES
HOLOENZYME
HOLOENZYMES
HOLOGAMIES
HOLOGRAPHED
HOLOGRAPHER
HOLOGRAPHERS
HOLOGRAPHIC
HOLOGRAPHICALLY
HOLOGRAPHIES
HOLOGRAPHING
HOLOGRAPHS
HOLOGRAPHY
HOLOGYNIES
HOLOHEDRAL
HOLOHEDRISM
HOLOHEDRISMS
HOLOHEDRON
HOLOHEDRONS
HOLOMETABOLIC
HOLOMETABOLISM
HOLOMETABOLISMS
HOLOMETABOLOUS
HOLOMORPHIC
HOLOPHOTAL
HOLOPHOTES
HOLOPHRASE
HOLOPHRASES
HOLOPHRASTIC
HOLOPHYTES
HOLOPHYTIC
HOLOPHYTISM
HOLOPHYTISMS
HOLOPLANKTON
HOLOPLANKTONS

HOLOSTERIC
HOLOTHURIAN
HOLOTHURIANS
HOLSTERING
HOLYSTONED
HOLYSTONES
HOLYSTONING
HOMALOGRAPHIC
HOMALOIDAL
HOMEBIRTHS
HOMEBODIES
HOMEBUYERS
HOMECOMERS
HOMECOMING
HOMECOMINGS
HOMECRAFTS
HOMELESSNESS
HOMELESSNESSES
HOMELINESS
HOMELINESSES
HOMEMAKERS
HOMEMAKING
HOMEMAKINGS
HOMEOBOXES
HOMEOMERIC
HOMEOMERIES
HOMEOMEROUS
HOMEOMORPH
HOMEOMORPHIC
HOMEOMORPHIES
HOMEOMORPHISM
HOMEOMORPHISMS
HOMEOMORPHOUS
HOMEOMORPHS
HOMEOMORPHY
HOMEOPATHIC
HOMEOPATHICALLY
HOMEOPATHIES
HOMEOPATHIST
HOMEOPATHISTS
HOMEOPATHS
HOMEOPATHY
HOMEOSTASES
HOMEOSTASIS
HOMEOSTATIC
HOMEOTELEUTON
HOMEOTELEUTONS
HOMEOTHERM
HOMEOTHERMAL
HOMEOTHERMIC
HOMEOTHERMIES
HOMEOTHERMOUS
HOMEOTHERMS
HOMEOTHERMY
HOMEOTYPIC
HOMEOTYPICAL
HOMEOWNERS
HOMEOWNERSHIP

HOMEOWNERSHIPS
HOMEPLACES
HOMEPORTED
HOMEPORTING
HOMESCHOOL
HOMESCHOOLED
HOMESCHOOLER
HOMESCHOOLERS
HOMESCHOOLING
HOMESCHOOLS
HOMESCREETCH
HOMESCREETCHES
HOMESICKNESS
HOMESICKNESSES
HOMESTALLS
HOMESTANDS
HOMESTEADED
HOMESTEADER
HOMESTEADERS
HOMESTEADING
HOMESTEADINGS
HOMESTEADS
HOMESTRETCH
HOMESTRETCHES
HOMEWORKER
HOMEWORKERS
HOMEWORKING
HOMEWORKINGS
HOMEYNESSES
HOMICIDALLY
HOMILETICAL
HOMILETICALLY
HOMILETICS
HOMINESSES
HOMINISATION
HOMINISATIONS
HOMINISING
HOMINIZATION
HOMINIZATIONS
HOMINIZING
HOMOBLASTIC
HOMOBLASTIES
HOMOBLASTY
HOMOCENTRIC
HOMOCENTRICALLY
HOMOCERCAL
HOMOCERCIES
HOMOCHLAMYDEOUS
HOMOCHROMATIC
HOMOCHROMATISM
HOMOCHROMATISMS
HOMOCHROMIES
HOMOCHROMOUS
HOMOCHROMY
HOMOCYCLIC
HOMOCYSTEINE
HOMOCYSTEINES
HOMOEOMERIC

HOMOEOMERIES

HOMOEOMERIES	HOMOGENIZE	HOMONUCLEAR	HOMOTHALLY
HOMOEOMEROUS	HOMOGENIZED	HOMONYMIES	HOMOTHERMAL
HOMOEOMERY	HOMOGENIZER	HOMONYMITIES	HOMOTHERMIC
HOMOEOMORPH	HOMOGENIZERS	HOMONYMITY	HOMOTHERMIES
HOMOEOMORPHIC	HOMOGENIZES	HOMONYMOUS	HOMOTHERMOUS
HOMOEOMORPHIES	HOMOGENIZING	HOMONYMOUSLY	HOMOTHERMY
HOMOEOMORPHISM	HOMOGENOUS	HOMOOUSIAN	HOMOTONIES
HOMOEOMORPHISMS	HOMOGONIES	HOMOOUSIANS	HOMOTONOUS
HOMOEOMORPHOUS	HOMOGONOUS	HOMOPHILES	HOMOTRANSPLANT
HOMOEOMORPHS	HOMOGONOUSLY	HOMOPHOBES	HOMOTRANSPLANTS
HOMOEOMORPHY	HOMOGRAFTS	HOMOPHOBIA	HOMOTYPIES
HOMOEOPATH	HOMOGRAPHIC	HOMOPHOBIAS	HOMOUSIANS
HOMOEOPATHIC	HOMOGRAPHS	HOMOPHOBIC	HOMOZYGOSES
HOMOEOPATHIES	HOMOIOMEROUS	HOMOPHONES	HOMOZYGOSIS
HOMOEOPATHIST	HOMOIOTHERM	HOMOPHONIC	HOMOZYGOSITIES
HOMOEOPATHISTS	HOMOIOTHERMAL	HOMOPHONICALLY	HOMOZYGOSITY
HOMOEOPATHS	HOMOIOTHERMIC	HOMOPHONIES	HOMOZYGOTE
HOMOEOPATHY	HOMOIOTHERMIES	HOMOPHONOUS	HOMOZYGOTES
HOMOEOSTASES	HOMOIOTHERMS	HOMOPHYLIES	HOMOZYGOTIC
HOMOEOSTASIS	HOMOIOTHERMY	HOMOPHYLLIC	HOMOZYGOUS
HOMOEOSTATIC	HOMOIOUSIAN	HOMOPLASIES	HOMOZYGOUSLY
HOMOEOTELEUTON	HOMOIOUSIANS	HOMOPLASMIES	HOMUNCULAR
HOMOEOTELEUTONS	HOMOLOGATE	HOMOPLASMY	HOMUNCULES
HOMOEOTHERMAL	HOMOLOGATED	HOMOPLASTIC	HOMUNCULUS
HOMOEOTHERMIC	HOMOLOGATES	HOMOPLASTICALLY	HONESTNESS
HOMOEOTHERMOUS	HOMOLOGATING	HOMOPLASTIES	HONESTNESSES
HOMOEOTYPIC	HOMOLOGATION	HOMOPLASTY	HONEYBUNCH
HOMOEOTYPICAL	HOMOLOGATIONS	HOMOPOLARITIES	HONEYBUNCHES
HOMOEROTIC	HOMOLOGICAL	HOMOPOLARITY	HONEYCOMBED
HOMOEROTICISM	HOMOLOGICALLY	HOMOPOLYMER	HONEYCOMBING
HOMOEROTICISMS	HOMOLOGIES	HOMOPOLYMERIC	HONEYCOMBINGS
HOMOEROTISM	HOMOLOGISE	HOMOPOLYMERS	HONEYCOMBS
HOMOEROTISMS	HOMOLOGISED	HOMOPTERAN	HONEYCREEPER
HOMOGAMETIC	HOMOLOGISER	HOMOPTERANS	HONEYCREEPERS
HOMOGAMIES	HOMOLOGISERS	HOMOPTEROUS	HONEYDEWED
HOMOGAMOUS	HOMOLOGISES	HOMORGANIC	HONEYEATER
HOMOGENATE	HOMOLOGISING	HOMOSCEDASTIC	HONEYEATERS
HOMOGENATES	HOMOLOGIZE	HOMOSEXUAL	HONEYGUIDE
HOMOGENEITIES	HOMOLOGIZED	HOMOSEXUALISM	HONEYGUIDES
HOMOGENEITY	HOMOLOGIZER	HOMOSEXUALISMS	HONEYMONTH
HOMOGENEOUS	HOMOLOGIZERS	HOMOSEXUALIST	HONEYMONTHED
HOMOGENEOUSLY	HOMOLOGIZES	HOMOSEXUALISTS	HONEYMONTHING
HOMOGENEOUSNESS	HOMOLOGIZING	HOMOSEXUALITIES	HONEYMONTHS
HOMOGENESES	HOMOLOGOUMENA	HOMOSEXUALITY	HONEYMOONED
HOMOGENESIS	HOMOLOGOUS	HOMOSEXUALLY	HONEYMOONER
HOMOGENETIC	HOMOLOGRAPHIC	HOMOSEXUALS	HONEYMOONERS
HOMOGENETICAL	HOMOLOGUES	HOMOSOCIAL	HONEYMOONING
HOMOGENIES	HOMOLOGUMENA	HOMOSOCIALITIES	HONEYMOONS
HOMOGENISATION	HOMOLOSINE	HOMOSOCIALITY	HONEYSUCKER
HOMOGENISATIONS	HOMOMORPHIC	HOMOSPORIES	HONEYSUCKERS
HOMOGENISE	HOMOMORPHIES	HOMOSPOROUS	HONEYSUCKLE
HOMOGENISED	HOMOMORPHISM	HOMOSTYLIES	HONEYSUCKLED
HOMOGENISER	HOMOMORPHISMS	HOMOTAXIAL	HONEYSUCKLES
HOMOGENISERS	HOMOMORPHOSES	HOMOTAXIALLY	HONEYTRAPS
HOMOGENISES	HOMOMORPHOSIS	HOMOTHALLIC	HONORABILITIES
HOMOGENISING	HOMOMORPHOUS	HOMOTHALLIES	HONORABILITY
HOMOGENIZATION	HOMOMORPHS	HOMOTHALLISM	HONORABLENESS
HOMOGENIZATIONS	HOMOMORPHY	HOMOTHALLISMS	HONORABLENESSES

HONORARIES	HORIZONTALNESS	HORRIPILATING	HOSANNAING
HONORARILY	HORIZONTALS	HORRIPILATION	HOSPITABLE
HONORARIUM	HORMOGONIA	HORRIPILATIONS	HOSPITABLENESS
HONORARIUMS	HORMOGONIUM	HORRISONANT	HOSPITABLY
HONORIFICAL	HORMONALLY	HORRISONOUS	HOSPTTAGES
HONORIFICALLY	HORMONELIKE	HORSEBACKS	HOSPITALER
HONORIFICS	HORNBLENDE	HORSEBEANS	HOSPITALERS
HONOURABLE	HORNBLENDES	HORSEBOXES	HOSPITALES
HONOURABLENESS	HORNBLENDIC	HORSEFEATHERS	HOSPITALISATION
HONOURABLY	HORNEDNESS	HORSEFLESH	HOSPITALISE
HONOURLESS	HORNEDNESSES	HORSEFLESHES	HOSPITALISED
HOODEDNESS	HORNINESSES	HORSEFLIES	HOSPITALISES
HOODEDNESSES	HORNLESSNESS	HORSEHAIRS	HOSPITALISING
HOODLUMISH	HORNLESSNESSES	HORSEHIDES	HOSPITALITIES
HOODLUMISM	HORNSTONES	HORSELAUGH	HOSPITALITY
HOODLUMISMS	HORNSWOGGLE	HORSELAUGHS	HOSPITALIZATION
HOODOOISMS	HORNSWOGGLED	HORSELEECH	HOSPTTALIZE
HOODWINKED	HORNSWOGGLES	HORSELEECHES	HOSPITALIZED
HOODWINKER	HORNSWOGGLING	HORSEMANSHIP	HOSPITALIZES
HOODWINKERS	HORNWRACKS	HORSEMANSHIPS	HOSPITALIZING
HOODWINKING	HORNYHEADS	HORSEMEATS	HOSPITALLER
HOOFPRINTS	HORNYWINKS	HORSEMINTS	HOSPITALLERS
HOOKCHECKS	HOROGRAPHER	HORSEPLAYER	HOSTELLERS
HOOKEDNESS	HOROGRAPHERS	HORSEPLAYERS	HOSTELLING
HOOKEDNESSES	HOROGRAPHIES	HORSEPLAYS	HOSTELLINGS
HOOLACHANS	HOROGRAPHY	HORSEPONDS	HOSTELRIES
HOOLIGANISM	HOROLOGERS	HORSEPOWER	HOSTESSING
HOOLIGANISMS	HOROLOGICAL	HORSEPOWERS	HOSTILITIES
HOOPSKIRTS	HOROLOGIES	HORSEPOXES	HOTCHPOTCH
HOOTANANNIE	HOROLOGION	HORSERACES	HOTCHPOTCHES
HOOTANANNIES	HOROLOGIONS	HORSERADISH	HOTDOGGERS
HOOTANANNY	HOROLOGIST	HORSERADISHES	HOTDOGGING
HOOTENANNIE	HOROLOGISTS	HORSESHITS	HOTFOOTING
HOOTENANNIES	HOROLOGIUM	HORSESHOED	HOTHEADEDLY
HOOTENANNY	HOROLOGIUMS	HORSESHOEING	HOTHEADEDNESS
HOOTNANNIE	HOROMETRICAL	HORSESHOEINGS	HOTHEADEDNESSES
HOOTNANNIES	HOROMETRIES	HORSESHOER	HOTHOUSING
HOPEFULNESS	HOROSCOPES	HORSESHOERS	HOTPRESSED
HOPEFULNESSES	HOROSCOPIC	HORSESHOES	HOTPRESSES
HOPELESSLY	HOROSCOPIES	HORSETAILS	HOTPRESSING
HOPELESSNESS	HOROSCOPIST	HORSEWEEDS	HOTTENTOTS
HOPELESSNESSES	HOROSCOPISTS	HORSEWHIPPED	HOUGHMAGANDIE
HOPLOLOGIES	HORRENDOUS	HORSEWHIPPER	HOUGHMAGANDIES
HOPLOLOGIST	HORRENDOUSLY	HORSEWHIPPERS	HOUNDFISHES
HOPLOLOGISTS	HORRENDOUSNESS	HORSEWHIPPING	HOURGLASSES
HOPPERCARS	HORRIBLENESS	HORSEWHIPS	HOURPLATES
HOPSACKING	HORRIBLENESSES	HORSEWOMAN	HOUSEBOATER
HOPSACKINGS	HORRIDNESS	HORSEWOMEN	HOUSEBOATERS
HOPSCOTCHED	HORRIDNESSES	HORSINESSES	HOUSEBOATS
HOPSCOTCHES	HORRIFICALLY	HORTATIONS	HOUSEBOUND
HOPSCOTCHING	HORRIFICATION	HORTATIVELY	HOUSEBREAK
HOREHOUNDS	HORRIFICATIONS	HORTATORILY	HOUSEBREAKER
HORIATIKIS	HORRIFYING	HORTICULTURAL	HOUSEBREAKERS
HORIZONLESS	HORRIFYINGLY	HORTICULTURALLY	HOUSEBREAKING
HORIZONTAL	HORRIPILANT	HORTICULTURE	HOUSEBREAKINGS
HORIZONTALITIES	HORRIPILATE	HORTICULTURES	HOUSEBREAKS
HORIZONTALITY	HORRIPILATED	HORTICULTURIST	HOUSEBROKE
HORIZONTALLY	HORRIPILATES	HORTICULTURISTS	HOUSEBROKEN

HOUSECARLS
HOUSECLEAN
HOUSECLEANED
HOUSECLEANING
HOUSECLEANINGS
HOUSECLEANS
HOUSECOATS
HOUSECRAFT
HOUSECRAFTS
HOUSEDRESS
HOUSEDRESSES
HOUSEFATHER
HOUSEFATHERS
HOUSEFLIES
HOUSEFRONT
HOUSEFRONTS
HOUSEGUEST
HOUSEGUESTS
HOUSEHOLDER
HOUSEHOLDERS
HOUSEHOLDERSHIP
HOUSEHOLDS
HOUSEHUSBAND
HOUSEHUSBANDS
HOUSEKEEPER
HOUSEKEEPERS
HOUSEKEEPING
HOUSEKEEPINGS
HOUSEKEEPS
HOUSELEEKS
HOUSELESSNESS
HOUSELESSNESSES
HOUSELIGHTS
HOUSELINES
HOUSELLING
HOUSELLINGS
HOUSEMAIDS
HOUSEMASTER
HOUSEMASTERS
HOUSEMATES
HOUSEMISTRESS
HOUSEMISTRESSES
HOUSEMOTHER
HOUSEMOTHERS
HOUSEPAINTER
HOUSEPAINTERS
HOUSEPARENT
HOUSEPARENTS
HOUSEPERSON
HOUSEPERSONS
HOUSEPLANT
HOUSEPLANTS
HOUSEROOMS
HOUSESITTING
HOUSEWARES
HOUSEWARMING
HOUSEWARMINGS
HOUSEWIFELINESS

HOUSEWIFELY
HOUSEWIFERIES
HOUSEWIFERY
HOUSEWIFESHIP
HOUSEWIFESHIPS
HOUSEWIFESKEP
HOUSEWIFESKEPS
HOUSEWIFEY
HOUSEWIVES
HOUSEWORKER
HOUSEWORKERS
HOUSEWORKS
HOUSTONIAS
HOVERCRAFT
HOVERCRAFTS
HOVERFLIES
HOVERINGLY
HOVERPORTS
HOVERTRAIN
HOVERTRAINS
HOWLROUNDS
HOWSOMDEVER
HOWSOMEVER
HOWTOWDIES
HOYDENHOOD
HOYDENHOODS
HOYDENISHNESS
HOYDENISHNESSES
HOYDENISMS
HUBRISTICALLY
HUCKABACKS
HUCKLEBERRIES
HUCKLEBERRY
HUCKLEBERRYING
HUCKLEBERRYINGS
HUCKLEBONE
HUCKLEBONES
HUCKSTERAGE
HUCKSTERAGES
HUCKSTERED
HUCKSTERESS
HUCKSTERESSES
HUCKSTERIES
HUCKSTERING
HUCKSTERISM
HUCKSTERISMS
HUCKSTRESS
HUCKSTRESSES
HUDIBRASTIC
HUFFINESSES
HUFFISHNESS
HUFFISHNESSES
HUGENESSES
HUGEOUSNESS
HUGEOUSNESSES
HULLABALLOO
HULLABALLOOS
HULLABALOO

HULLABALOOS
HUMANENESS
HUMANENESSES
HUMANHOODS
HUMANISATION
HUMANISATIONS
HUMANISERS
HUMANISING
HUMANISTIC
HUMANISTICALLY
HUMANITARIAN
HUMANITARIANISM
HUMANITARIANIST
HUMANITARIANS
HUMANITIES
HUMANIZATION
HUMANIZATIONS
HUMANIZERS
HUMANIZING
HUMANKINDS
HUMANNESSES
HUMBLEBEES
HUMBLENESS
HUMBLENESSES
HUMBLESSES
HUMBLINGLY
HUMBUCKERS
HUMBUGGABLE
HUMBUGGERIES
HUMBUGGERS
HUMBUGGERY
HUMBUGGING
HUMDINGERS
HUMDRUMNESS
HUMDRUMNESSES
HUMDUDGEON
HUMDUDGEONS
HUMECTANTS
HUMECTATED
HUMECTATES
HUMECTATING
HUMECTATION
HUMECTATIONS
HUMECTIVES
HUMGRUFFIAN
HUMGRUFFIANS
HUMGRUFFIN
HUMGRUFFINS
HUMICOLOUS
HUMIDIFICATION
HUMIDIFICATIONS
HUMIDIFIED
HUMIDIFIER
HUMIDIFIERS
HUMIDIFIES
HUMIDIFYING
HUMIDISTAT
HUMIDISTATS

HUMIDITIES
HUMIDNESSES
HUMIFICATION
HUMIFICATIONS
HUMILIATED
HUMILIATES
HUMILIATING
HUMILIATINGLY
HUMILIATION
HUMILIATIONS
HUMILIATIVE
HUMILIATOR
HUMILIATORS
HUMILIATORY
HUMILITIES
HUMMELLERS
HUMMELLING
HUMMINGBIRD
HUMMINGBIRDS
HUMMOCKING
HUMORALISM
HUMORALISMS
HUMORALIST
HUMORALISTS
HUMORESQUE
HUMORESQUES
HUMORISTIC
HUMORLESSLY
HUMORLESSNESS
HUMORLESSNESSES
HUMOROUSLY
HUMOROUSNESS
HUMOROUSNESSES
HUMOURLESS
HUMOURLESSNESS
HUMOURSOME
HUMOURSOMENESS
HUMPBACKED
HUMPINESSES
HUNCHBACKED
HUNCHBACKS
HUNDREDERS
HUNDREDFOLD
HUNDREDFOLDS
HUNDREDORS
HUNDREDTHS
HUNDREDWEIGHT
HUNDREDWEIGHTS
HUNGERINGLY
HUNGRINESS
HUNGRINESSES
HUNTIEGOWK
HUNTIEGOWKS
HUNTRESSES
HUNTSMANSHIP
HUNTSMANSHIPS
HUPAITHRIC
HURLBARROW

HURLBARROWS
HURRICANES
HURRICANOES
HURRIEDNESS
HURRIEDNESSES
HURRYINGLY
HURTFULNESS
HURTFULNESSES
HURTLEBERRIES
HURTLEBERRY
HURTLESSLY
HURTLESSNESS
HURTLESSNESSES
HUSBANDAGE
HUSBANDAGES
HUSBANDERS
HUSBANDING
HUSBANDLAND
HUSBANDLANDS
HUSBANDLESS
HUSBANDLIKE
HUSBANDMAN
HUSBANDMEN
HUSBANDRIES
HUSHABYING
HUSHPUPPIES
HUSKINESSES
HYACINTHINE
HYALINISATION
HYALINISATIONS
HYALINISED
HYALINISES
HYALINISING
HYALINIZATION
HYALINIZATIONS
HYALINIZED
HYALINIZES
HYALINIZING
HYALOMELAN
HYALOMELANE
HYALOMELANES
HYALOMELANS
HYALONEMAS
HYALOPHANE
HYALOPHANES
HYALOPLASM
HYALOPLASMIC
HYALOPLASMS
HYALURONIC
HYALURONIDASE
HYALURONIDASES
HYBRIDISABLE
HYBRIDISATION
HYBRIDISATIONS
HYBRIDISED
HYBRIDISER
HYBRIDISERS
HYBRIDISES

HYBRIDISING
HYBRIDISMS
HYBRIDISTS
HYBRIDITIES
HYBRIDIZABLE
HYBRIDIZATION
HYBRIDIZATIONS
HYBRIDIZED
HYBRIDIZER
HYBRIDIZERS
HYBRIDIZES
HYBRIDIZING
HYBRIDOMAS
HYDANTOINS
HYDATHODES
HYDATIDIFORM
HYDNOCARPATE
HYDNOCARPATES
HYDNOCARPIC
HYDRAEMIAS
HYDRAGOGUE
HYDRAGOGUES
HYDRALAZINE
HYDRALAZINES
HYDRANGEAS
HYDRARGYRAL
HYDRARGYRIA
HYDRARGYRIAS
HYDRARGYRIC
HYDRARGYRISM
HYDRARGYRISMS
HYDRARGYRUM
HYDRARGYRUMS
HYDRARTHROSES
HYDRARTHROSIS
HYDRASTINE
HYDRASTINES
HYDRASTININE
HYDRASTININES
HYDRASTISES
HYDRATIONS
HYDRAULICALLY
HYDRAULICKED
HYDRAULICKING
HYDRAULICS
HYDRAZIDES
HYDRAZINES
HYDRICALLY
HYDROACOUSTICS
HYDROBIOLOGICAL
HYDROBIOLOGIES
HYDROBIOLOGIST
HYDROBIOLOGISTS
HYDROBIOLOGY
HYDROBROMIC
HYDROCARBON
HYDROCARBONS
HYDROCASTS

HYDROCELES
HYDROCELLULOSE
HYDROCELLULOSES
HYDROCEPHALIC
HYDROCEPHALICS
HYDROCEPHALIES
HYDROCEPHALOID
HYDROCEPHALOUS
HYDROCEPHALUS
HYDROCEPHALUSES
HYDROCEPHALY
HYDROCHLORIC
HYDROCHLORIDE
HYDROCHLORIDES
HYDROCHORE
HYDROCHORES
HYDROCHORIC
HYDROCOLLOID
HYDROCOLLOIDAL
HYDROCOLLOIDS
HYDROCORAL
HYDROCORALLINE
HYDROCORALLINES
HYDROCORALS
HYDROCORTISONE
HYDROCORTISONES
HYDROCRACK
HYDROCRACKED
HYDROCRACKER
HYDROCRACKERS
HYDROCRACKING
HYDROCRACKINGS
HYDROCRACKS
HYDROCYANIC
HYDRODYNAMIC
HYDRODYNAMICAL
HYDRODYNAMICIST
HYDRODYNAMICS
HYDROELASTIC
HYDROELECTRIC
HYDROEXTRACTOR
HYDROEXTRACTORS
HYDROFLUORIC
HYDROFOILS
HYDROFORMING
HYDROFORMINGS
HYDROGENASE
HYDROGENASES
HYDROGENATE
HYDROGENATED
HYDROGENATES
HYDROGENATING
HYDROGENATION
HYDROGENATIONS
HYDROGENATOR
HYDROGENATORS
HYDROGENISATION
HYDROGENISE

HYDROGENISED
HYDROGENISES
HYDROGENISING
HYDROGENIZATION
HYDROGENIZE
HYDROGENIZED
HYDROGENIZES
HYDROGENIZING
HYDROGENOLYSES
HYDROGENOLYSIS
HYDROGENOUS
HYDROGEOLOGICAL
HYDROGEOLOGIES
HYDROGEOLOGIST
HYDROGEOLOGISTS
HYDROGEOLOGY
HYDROGRAPH
HYDROGRAPHER
HYDROGRAPHERS
HYDROGRAPHIC
HYDROGRAPHICAL
HYDROGRAPHIES
HYDROGRAPHS
HYDROGRAPHY
HYDROKINETIC
HYDROKINETICAL
HYDROKINETICS
HYDROLASES
HYDROLOGIC
HYDROLOGICAL
HYDROLOGICALLY
HYDROLOGIES
HYDROLOGIST
HYDROLOGISTS
HYDROLYSABLE
HYDROLYSATE
HYDROLYSATES
HYDROLYSATION
HYDROLYSATIONS
HYDROLYSED
HYDROLYSER
HYDROLYSERS
HYDROLYSES
HYDROLYSING
HYDROLYSIS
HYDROLYTES
HYDROLYTIC
HYDROLYTICALLY
HYDROLYZABLE
HYDROLYZATE
HYDROLYZATES
HYDROLYZATION
HYDROLYZATIONS
HYDROLYZED
HYDROLYZER
HYDROLYZERS
HYDROLYZES
HYDROLYZING

HYDROMAGNETIC
HYDROMAGNETICS
HYDROMANCER
HYDROMANCERS
HYDROMANCIES
HYDROMANCY
HYDROMANIA
HYDROMANIAS
HYDROMANTIC
HYDROMECHANICAL
HYDROMECHANICS
HYDROMEDUSA
HYDROMEDUSAE
HYDROMEDUSAN
HYDROMEDUSANS
HYDROMEDUSAS
HYDROMEDUSOID
HYDROMEDUSOIDS
HYDROMETALLURGY
HYDROMETEOR
HYDROMETEORS
HYDROMETER
HYDROMETERS
HYDROMETRIC
HYDROMETRICAL
HYDROMETRICALLY
HYDROMETRIES
HYDROMETRY
HYDROMORPHIC
HYDRONAUTS
HYDRONEPHROSES
HYDRONEPHROSIS
HYDRONEPHROTIC
HYDRONICALLY
HYDRONIUMS
HYDROPATHIC
HYDROPATHICAL
HYDROPATHICALLY
HYDROPATHICS
HYDROPATHIES
HYDROPATHIST
HYDROPATHISTS
HYDROPATHS
HYDROPATHY
HYDROPEROXIDE
HYDROPEROXIDES
HYDROPHANE
HYDROPHANES
HYDROPHANOUS
HYDROPHILE
HYDROPHILES
HYDROPHILIC
HYDROPHILICITY
HYDROPHILIES
HYDROPHILITE
HYDROPHILITES
HYDROPHILOUS
HYDROPHILY

HYDROPHOBIA
HYDROPHOBIAS
HYDROPHOBIC
HYDROPHOBICITY
HYDROPHOBOUS
HYDROPHONE
HYDROPHONES
HYDROPHYTE
HYDROPHYTES
HYDROPHYTIC
HYDROPHYTON
HYDROPHYTONS
HYDROPHYTOUS
HYDROPLANE
HYDROPLANED
HYDROPLANES
HYDROPLANING
HYDROPNEUMATIC
HYDROPOLYP
HYDROPOLYPS
HYDROPONIC
HYDROPONICALLY
HYDROPONICS
HYDROPOWER
HYDROPOWERS
HYDROPSIES
HYDROPULTS
HYDROQUINOL
HYDROQUINOLS
HYDROQUINONE
HYDROQUINONES
HYDROSCOPE
HYDROSCOPES
HYDROSCOPIC
HYDROSCOPICAL
HYDROSERES
HYDROSOLIC
HYDROSOMAL
HYDROSOMATA
HYDROSOMATOUS
HYDROSOMES
HYDROSPACE
HYDROSPACES
HYDROSPHERE
HYDROSPHERES
HYDROSPHERIC
HYDROSTATIC
HYDROSTATICAL
HYDROSTATICALLY
HYDROSTATICS
HYDROSTATS
HYDROSULPHATE
HYDROSULPHATES
HYDROSULPHIDE
HYDROSULPHIDES
HYDROSULPHITE
HYDROSULPHITES
HYDROSULPHURIC

HYDROSULPHUROUS
HYDROTACTIC
HYDROTAXES
HYDROTAXIS
HYDROTHECA
HYDROTHECAE
HYDROTHERAPIC
HYDROTHERAPIES
HYDROTHERAPIST
HYDROTHERAPISTS
HYDROTHERAPY
HYDROTHERMAL
HYDROTHERMALLY
HYDROTHORACES
HYDROTHORACIC
HYDROTHORAX
HYDROTHORAXES
HYDROTROPIC
HYDROTROPICALLY
HYDROTROPISM
HYDROTROPISMS
HYDROVANES
HYDROXIDES
HYDROXONIUM
HYDROXONIUMS
HYDROXYAPATITE
HYDROXYAPATITES
HYDROXYBUTYRATE
HYDROXYLAMINE
HYDROXYLAMINES
HYDROXYLAPATITE
HYDROXYLASE
HYDROXYLASES
HYDROXYLATE
HYDROXYLATED
HYDROXYLATES
HYDROXYLATING
HYDROXYLATION
HYDROXYLATIONS
HYDROXYLIC
HYDROXYPROLINE
HYDROXYPROLINES
HYDROXYUREA
HYDROXYUREAS
HYDROXYZINE
HYDROXYZINES
HYDROZINCITE
HYDROZINCITES
HYDROZOANS
HYETOGRAPH
HYETOGRAPHIC
HYETOGRAPHICAL
HYETOGRAPHIES
HYETOGRAPHS
HYETOGRAPHY
HYETOLOGIES
HYETOMETER
HYETOMETERS

HYETOMETROGRAPH
HYGIENICALLY
HYGIENISTS
HYGRISTORS
HYGROCHASIES
HYGROCHASTIC
HYGROCHASY
HYGRODEIKS
HYGROGRAPH
HYGROGRAPHIC
HYGROGRAPHICAL
HYGROGRAPHS
HYGROLOGIES
HYGROMETER
HYGROMETERS
HYGROMETRIC
HYGROMETRICAL
HYGROMETRICALLY
HYGROMETRIES
HYGROMETRY
HYGROPHILE
HYGROPHILES
HYGROPHILOUS
HYGROPHOBE
HYGROPHYTE
HYGROPHYTES
HYGROPHYTIC
HYGROSCOPE
HYGROSCOPES
HYGROSCOPIC
HYGROSCOPICAL
HYGROSCOPICALLY
HYGROSCOPICITY
HYGROSTATS
HYLOGENESES
HYLOGENESIS
HYLOMORPHIC
HYLOMORPHISM
HYLOMORPHISMS
HYLOPATHISM
HYLOPATHISMS
HYLOPATHIST
HYLOPATHISTS
HYLOPHAGOUS
HYLOPHYTES
HYLOTHEISM
HYLOTHEISMS
HYLOTHEIST
HYLOTHEISTS
HYLOTOMOUS
HYLOZOICAL
HYLOZOISMS
HYLOZOISTIC
HYLOZOISTICALLY
HYLOZOISTS
HYMENEALLY
HYMENOPHORE
HYMENOPHORES

HYMENOPTERA	HYPERAESTHESIAS	HYPERCHARGES	HYPERFOCAL
HYMENOPTERAN	HYPERAESTHESIC	HYPERCHARGING	HYPERFUNCTION
HYMENOPTERANS	HYPERAESTHETIC	HYPERCIVILISED	HYPERFUNCTIONAL
HYMENOPTERON	HYPERAGGRESSIVE	HYPERCIVILIZED	HYPERFUNCTIONS
HYMENOPTERONS	HYPERALERT	HYPERCOAGULABLE	HYPERGAMIES
HYMENOPTEROUS	HYPERALGESIA	HYPERCOLOUR	HYPERGAMOUS
HYMNODICAL	HYPERALGESIAS	HYPERCOLOURS	HYPERGEOMETRIC
HYMNODISTS	HYPERALGESIC	HYPERCOMPLEX	HYPERGLYCAEMIA
HYMNOGRAPHER	HYPERAROUSAL	HYPERCONSCIOUS	HYPERGLYCAEMIAS
HYMNOGRAPHERS	HYPERAROUSALS	HYPERCORRECT	HYPERGLYCAEMIC
HYMNOGRAPHIES	HYPERAWARE	HYPERCORRECTION	HYPERGLYCEMIA
HYMNOGRAPHY	HYPERAWARENESS	HYPERCORRECTLY	HYPERGLYCEMIAS
HYMNOLOGIC	HYPERBARIC	HYPERCRITIC	HYPERGLYCEMIC
HYMNOLOGICAL	HYPERBARICALLY	HYPERCRITICAL	HYPERGOLIC
HYMNOLOGIES	HYPERBATIC	HYPERCRITICALLY	HYPERGOLICALLY
HYMNOLOGIST	HYPERBATICALLY	HYPERCRITICISE	HYPERHIDROSES
HYMNOLOGISTS	HYPERBATON	HYPERCRITICISED	HYPERHIDROSIS
HYOPLASTRA	HYPERBATONS	HYPERCRITICISES	HYPERICUMS
HYOPLASTRAL	HYPERBOLAE	HYPERCRITICISM	HYPERIDROSES
HYOPLASTRON	HYPERBOLAS	HYPERCRITICISMS	HYPERIDROSIS
HYOSCYAMINE	HYPERBOLES	HYPERCRITICIZE	HYPERIMMUNE
HYOSCYAMINES	HYPERBOLIC	HYPERCRITICIZED	HYPERIMMUNISE
HYOSCYAMUS	HYPERBOLICAL	HYPERCRITICIZES	HYPERIMMUNISED
HYOSCYAMUSES	HYPERBOLICALLY	HYPERCRITICS	HYPERIMMUNISES
HYPABYSSAL	HYPERBOLISE	HYPERCUBES	HYPERIMMUNISING
HYPABYSSALLY	HYPERBOLISED	HYPERDACTYL	HYPERIMMUNIZE
HYPAESTHESIA	HYPERBOLISES	HYPERDACTYLIES	HYPERIMMUNIZED
HYPAESTHESIAS	HYPERBOLISING	HYPERDACTYLY	HYPERIMMUNIZES
HYPAESTHESIC	HYPERBOLISM	HYPERDORIAN	HYPERIMMUNIZING
HYPAETHRAL	HYPERBOLISMS	HYPERDULIA	HYPERINFLATED
HYPAETHRON	HYPERBOLIST	HYPERDULIAS	HYPERINFLATION
HYPAETHRONS	HYPERBOLISTS	HYPERDULIC	HYPERINFLATIONS
HYPALGESIA	HYPERBOLIZE	HYPERDULICAL	HYPERINOSES
HYPALGESIAS	HYPERBOLIZED	HYPEREFFICIENT	HYPERINOSIS
HYPALGESIC	HYPERBOLIZES	HYPEREMESES	HYPERINOTIC
HYPALLACTIC	HYPERBOLIZING	HYPEREMESIS	HYPERINSULINISM
HYPALLAGES	HYPERBOLOID	HYPEREMETIC	HYPERINTENSE
HYPANTHIAL	HYPERBOLOIDAL	HYPEREMIAS	HYPERINVOLUTION
HYPANTHIUM	HYPERBOLOIDS	HYPEREMOTIONAL	HYPERIRRITABLE
HYPERACIDITIES	HYPERBOREAN	HYPERENDEMIC	HYPERKERATOSES
HYPERACIDITY	HYPERBOREANS	HYPERENERGETIC	HYPERKERATOSIS
HYPERACTION	HYPERCALCAEMIA	HYPERESTHESIA	HYPERKERATOTIC
HYPERACTIONS	HYPERCALCAEMIAS	HYPERESTHESIAS	HYPERKINESES
HYPERACTIVE	HYPERCALCEMIA	HYPERESTHETIC	HYPERKINESIA
HYPERACTIVES	HYPERCALCEMIAS	HYPEREUTECTIC	HYPERKINESIAS
HYPERACTIVITIES	HYPERCALCEMIC	HYPEREUTECTOID	HYPERKINESIS
HYPERACTIVITY	HYPERCAPNIA	HYPEREXCITABLE	HYPERKINETIC
HYPERACUITIES	HYPERCAPNIAS	HYPEREXCITED	HYPERLINKED
HYPERACUITY	HYPERCAPNIC	HYPEREXCITEMENT	HYPERLINKING
HYPERACUSES	HYPERCARBIA	HYPEREXCRETION	HYPERLINKS
HYPERACUSIS	HYPERCARBIAS	HYPEREXCRETIONS	HYPERLIPEMIA
HYPERACUTE	HYPERCATABOLISM	HYPEREXTEND	HYPERLIPEMIAS
HYPERACUTENESS	HYPERCATALECTIC	HYPEREXTENDED	HYPERLIPEMIC
HYPERADRENALISM	HYPERCATALEXES	HYPEREXTENDING	HYPERLIPIDAEMIA
HYPERAEMIA	HYPERCATALEXIS	HYPEREXTENDS	HYPERLIPIDEMIA
HYPERAEMIAS	HYPERCAUTIOUS	HYPEREXTENSION	HYPERLIPIDEMIAS
HYPERAEMIC	HYPERCHARGE	HYPEREXTENSIONS	HYPERLYDIAN
HYPERAESTHESIA	HYPERCHARGED	HYPERFASTIDIOUS	HYPERMANIA

HYPERMANIAS	HYPERPLASIAS	HYPERSENSITISES	HYPERTROPHOUS
HYPERMANIC	HYPERPLASTIC	HYPERSENSITIVE	HYPERTROPHY
HYPERMARKET	HYPERPLOID	HYPERSENSITIZE	HYPERTROPHYING
HYPERMARKETS	HYPERPLOIDIES	HYPERSENSITIZED	HYPERTYPICAL
HYPERMARTS	HYPERPLOIDS	HYPERSENSITIZES	HYPERURBANISM
HYPERMASCULINE	HYPERPLOIDY	HYPERSENSUAL	HYPERURBANISMS
HYPERMEDIA	HYPERPNEAS	HYPERSEXUAL	HYPERURICEMIA
HYPERMEDIAS	HYPERPNEIC	HYPERSEXUALITY	HYPERURICEMIAS
HYPERMETABOLIC	HYPERPNOEA	HYPERSOMNIA	HYPERVELOCITIES
HYPERMETABOLISM	HYPERPNOEAS	HYPERSOMNIAS	HYPERVELOCITY
HYPERMETER	HYPERPOLARISE	HYPERSOMNOLENCE	HYPERVENTILATE
HYPERMETERS	HYPERPOLARISED	HYPERSONIC	HYPERVENTILATED
HYPERMETRIC	HYPERPOLARISES	HYPERSONICALLY	HYPERVENTILATES
HYPERMETRICAL	HYPERPOLARISING	HYPERSONICS	HYPERVIGILANCE
HYPERMETROPIA	HYPERPOLARIZE	HYPERSPACE	HYPERVIGILANCES
HYPERMETROPIAS	HYPERPOLARIZED	HYPERSPACES	HYPERVIGILANT
HYPERMETROPIC	HYPERPOLARIZES	HYPERSPATIAL	HYPERVIRULENT
HYPERMETROPICAL	HYPERPOLARIZING	HYPERSTATIC	HYPERVISCOSITY
HYPERMETROPIES	HYPERPOWER	HYPERSTHENE	HYPESTHESIA
HYPERMETROPY	HYPERPOWERS	HYPERSTHENES	HYPESTHESIAS
HYPERMNESIA	HYPERPRODUCER	HYPERSTHENIA	HYPESTHESIC
HYPERMNESIAS	HYPERPRODUCERS	HYPERSTHENIAS	HYPHENATED
HYPERMNESIC	HYPERPRODUCTION	HYPERSTHENIC	HYPHENATES
HYPERMOBILITIES	HYPERPROSEXIA	HYPERSTHENITE	HYPHENATING
HYPERMOBILITY	HYPERPROSEXIAS	HYPERSTHENITES	HYPHENATION
HYPERMODERN	HYPERPYRETIC	HYPERSTIMULATE	HYPHENATIONS
HYPERMODERNIST	HYPERPYREXIA	HYPERSTIMULATED	HYPHENISATION
HYPERMODERNISTS	HYPERPYREXIAL	HYPERSTIMULATES	HYPHENISATIONS
HYPERMUTABILITY	HYPERPYREXIAS	HYPERSTRESS	HYPHENISED
HYPERMUTABLE	HYPERRATIONAL	HYPERSTRESSES	HYPHENISES
HYPERNATRAEMIA	HYPERREACTIVE	HYPERSURFACE	HYPHENISING
HYPERNATRAEMIAS	HYPERREACTIVITY	HYPERSURFACES	HYPHENISMS
HYPERNOVAE	HYPERREACTOR	HYPERTENSE	HYPHENIZATION
HYPERNOVAS	HYPERREACTORS	HYPERTENSION	HYPHENIZATIONS
HYPERNYMIES	HYPERREALISM	HYPERTENSIONS	HYPHENIZED
HYPEROPIAS	HYPERREALISMS	HYPERTENSIVE	HYPHENIZES
HYPEROREXIA	HYPERREALIST	HYPERTENSIVES	HYPHENIZING
HYPEROREXIAS	HYPERREALISTIC	HYPERTEXTS	HYPHENLESS
HYPEROSMIA	HYPERREALISTS	HYPERTHERMAL	HYPNAGOGIC
HYPEROSMIAS	HYPERREALITIES	HYPERTHERMIA	HYPNOANALYSES
HYPEROSTOSES	HYPERREALITY	HYPERTHERMIAS	HYPNOANALYSIS
HYPEROSTOSIS	HYPERREALS	HYPERTHERMIC	HYPNOANALYTIC
HYPEROSTOTIC	HYPERRESPONSIVE	HYPERTHERMIES	HYPNOGENESES
HYPERPARASITE	HYPERROMANTIC	HYPERTHERMY	HYPNOGENESIS
HYPERPARASITES	HYPERROMANTICS	HYPERTHYMIA	HYPNOGENETIC
HYPERPARASITIC	HYPERSALINE	HYPERTHYMIAS	HYPNOGENIC
HYPERPARASITISM	HYPERSALINITIES	HYPERTHYROID	HYPNOGENIES
HYPERPHAGIA	HYPERSALINITY	HYPERTHYROIDISM	HYPNOGENOUS
HYPERPHAGIAS	HYPERSALIVATION	HYPERTHYROIDS	HYPNOGOGIC
HYPERPHAGIC	HYPERSARCOMA	HYPERTONIA	HYPNOIDISE
HYPERPHRYGIAN	HYPERSARCOMAS	HYPERTONIAS	HYPNOIDISED
HYPERPHYSICAL	HYPERSARCOMATA	HYPERTONIC	HYPNOIDISES
HYPERPHYSICALLY	HYPERSARCOSES	HYPERTONICITIES	HYPNOIDISING
HYPERPIGMENTED	HYPERSARCOSIS	HYPERTONICITY	HYPNOIDIZE
HYPERPITUITARY	HYPERSECRETION	HYPERTROPHIC	HYPNOIDIZED
HYPERPLANE	HYPERSECRETIONS	HYPERTROPHICAL	HYPNOIDIZES
HYPERPLANES	HYPERSENSITISE	HYPERTROPHIED	HYPNOIDIZING
HYPERPLASIA	HYPERSENSITISED	HYPERTROPHIES	HYPNOLOGIC

HYPNOLOGICAL	HYPOCHONDRIASM	HYPOLIMNION	HYPOSENSITIZED
HYPNOLOGIES	HYPOCHONDRIASMS	HYPOLIMNIONS	HYPOSENSITIZES
HYPNOLOGIST	HYPOCHONDRIAST	HYPOLYDIAN	HYPOSENSITIZING
HYPNOLOGISTS	HYPOCHONDRIASTS	HYPOMAGNESAEMIA	HYPOSPADIAS
HYPNOPAEDIA	HYPOCHONDRIUM	HYPOMAGNESEMIA	HYPOSPADIASES
HYPNOPAEDIAS	HYPOCORISM	HYPOMAGNESEMIAS	HYPOSTASES
HYPNOPOMPIC	HYPOCORISMA	HYPOMANIAS	HYPOSTASIS
HYPNOTHERAPIES	HYPOCORISMAS	HYPOMANICS	HYPOSTASISATION
HYPNOTHERAPIST	HYPOCORISMS	HYPOMENORRHEA	HYPOSTASISE
HYPNOTHERAPISTS	HYPOCORISTIC	HYPOMENORRHEAS	HYPOSTASISED
HYPNOTHERAPY	HYPOCORISTICAL	HYPOMENORRHOEA	HYPOSTASISES
HYPNOTICALLY	HYPOCOTYLOUS	HYPOMENORRHOEAS	HYPOSTASISING
HYPNOTISABILITY	HYPOCOTYLS	HYPOMIXOLYDIAN	HYPOSTASIZATION
HYPNOTISABLE	HYPOCRISIES	HYPOMORPHIC	HYPOSTASIZE
HYPNOTISATION	HYPOCRITES	HYPOMORPHS	HYPOSTASIZED
HYPNOTISATIONS	HYPOCRITIC	HYPONASTIC	HYPOSTASIZES
HYPNOTISED	HYPOCRITICAL	HYPONASTICALLY	HYPOSTASIZING
HYPNOTISER	HYPOCRITICALLY	HYPONASTIES	HYPOSTATIC
HYPNOTISERS	HYPOCRYSTALLINE	HYPONATRAEMIA	HYPOSTATICAL
HYPNOTISES	HYPOCYCLOID	HYPONATRAEMIAS	HYPOSTATICALLY
HYPNOTISING	HYPOCYCLOIDAL	HYPONITRITE	HYPOSTATISATION
HYPNOTISMS	HYPOCYCLOIDS	HYPONITRITES	HYPOSTATISE
HYPNOTISTIC	HYPODERMAL	HYPONITROUS	HYPOSTATISED
HYPNOTISTS	HYPODERMAS	HYPONYMIES	HYPOSTATISES
HYPNOTIZABILITY	HYPODERMIC	HYPOPHARYNGES	HYPOSTATISING
HYPNOTIZABLE	HYPODERMICALLY	HYPOPHARYNX	HYPOSTATIZATION
HYPNOTIZATION	HYPODERMICS	HYPOPHARYNXES	HYPOSTATIZE
HYPNOTIZATIONS	HYPODERMIS	HYPOPHOSPHATE	HYPOSTATIZED
HYPNOTIZED	HYPODERMISES	HYPOPHOSPHATES	HYPOSTATIZES
HYPNOTIZER	HYPODIPLOID	HYPOPHOSPHITE	HYPOSTATIZING
HYPNOTIZERS	HYPODIPLOIDIES	HYPOPHOSPHITES	HYPOSTHENIA
HYPNOTIZES	HYPODIPLOIDY	HYPOPHOSPHORIC	HYPOSTHENIAS
HYPNOTIZING	HYPODORIAN	HYPOPHOSPHOROUS	HYPOSTHENIC
HYPOACIDITIES	HYPOEUTECTIC	HYPOPHRYGIAN	HYPOSTOMES
HYPOACIDITY	HYPOEUTECTOID	HYPOPHYSES	HYPOSTRESS
HYPOAEOLIAN	HYPOGAEOUS	HYPOPHYSEAL	HYPOSTRESSES
HYPOALLERGENIC	HYPOGASTRIA	HYPOPHYSECTOMY	HYPOSTROPHE
HYPOBLASTIC	HYPOGASTRIC	HYPOPHYSES	HYPOSTROPHES
HYPOBLASTS	HYPOGASTRIUM	HYPOPHYSIAL	HYPOSTYLES
HYPOCALCEMIA	HYPOGENOUS	HYPOPHYSIS	HYPOSULPHATE
HYPOCALCEMIAS	HYPOGLOSSAL	HYPOPITUITARISM	HYPOSULPHATES
HYPOCALCEMIC	HYPOGLOSSALS	HYPOPITUITARY	HYPOSULPHITE
HYPOCAUSTS	HYPOGLYCAEMIA	HYPOPLASIA	HYPOSULPHITES
HYPOCENTER	HYPOGLYCAEMIAS	HYPOPLASIAS	HYPOSULPHURIC
HYPOCENTERS	HYPOGLYCAEMIC	HYPOPLASTIC	HYPOSULPHUROUS
HYPOCENTRAL	HYPOGLYCEMIA	HYPOPLASTIES	HYPOTACTIC
HYPOCENTRE	HYPOGLYCEMIAS	HYPOPLASTRA	HYPOTENSION
HYPOCENTRES	HYPOGLYCEMIC	HYPOPLASTRON	HYPOTENSIONS
HYPOCHLORITE	HYPOGLYCEMICS	HYPOPLASTY	HYPOTENSIVE
HYPOCHLORITES	HYPOGNATHISM	HYPOPLOIDIES	HYPOTENSIVES
HYPOCHLOROUS	HYPOGNATHISMS	HYPOPLOIDS	HYPOTENUSE
HYPOCHONDRIA	HYPOGNATHOUS	HYPOPLOIDY	HYPOTENUSES
HYPOCHONDRIAC	HYPOGYNIES	HYPOPNOEAS	HYPOTHALAMI
HYPOCHONDRIACAL	HYPOGYNOUS	HYPOSENSITISE	HYPOTHALAMIC
HYPOCHONDRIACS	HYPOKALEMIA	HYPOSENSITISED	HYPOTHALAMUS
HYPOCHONDRIAS	HYPOKALEMIAS	HYPOSENSITISES	HYPOTHECAE
HYPOCHONDRIASES	HYPOKALEMIC	HYPOSENSITISING	HYPOTHECARY
HYPOCHONDRIASIS	HYPOLIMNIA	HYPOSENSITIZE	HYPOTHECATE

HYPOTHECATED
HYPOTHECATES
HYPOTHECATING
HYPOTHECATION
HYPOTHECATIONS
HYPOTHECATOR
HYPOTHECATORS
HYPOTHENUSE
HYPOTHENUSES
HYPOTHERMAL
HYPOTHERMIA
HYPOTHERMIAS
HYPOTHERMIC
HYPOTHESES
HYPOTHESIS
HYPOTHESISE
HYPOTHESISED
HYPOTHESISER
HYPOTHESISERS
HYPOTHESISES
HYPOTHESISING
HYPOTHESIST
HYPOTHESISTS
HYPOTHESIZE
HYPOTHESIZED
HYPOTHESIZER
HYPOTHESIZERS
HYPOTHESIZES
HYPOTHESIZING
HYPOTHETIC
HYPOTHETICAL
HYPOTHETICALLY
HYPOTHETISE
HYPOTHETISED
HYPOTHETISES
HYPOTHETISING
HYPOTHETIZE
HYPOTHETIZED
HYPOTHETIZES
HYPOTHETIZING
HYPOTHYMIA
HYPOTHYMIAS
HYPOTHYROID
HYPOTHYROIDISM
HYPOTHYROIDISMS
HYPOTHYROIDS
HYPOTONIAS
HYPOTONICITIES
HYPOTONICITY
HYPOTROCHOID
HYPOTROCHOIDS
HYPOTYPOSES
HYPOTYPOSIS
HYPOVENTILATION
HYPOXAEMIA
HYPOXAEMIAS
HYPOXAEMIC
HYPOXANTHINE

HYPOXANTHINES
HYPOXEMIAS
HYPSOCHROME
HYPSOCHROMES
HYPSOCHROMIC
HYPSOGRAPHIC
HYPSOGRAPHICAL
HYPSOGRAPHIES
HYPSOGRAPHY
HYPSOMETER
HYPSOMETERS
HYPSOMETRIC
HYPSOMETRICAL
HYPSOMETRICALLY
HYPSOMETRIES
HYPSOMETRIST
HYPSOMETRISTS
HYPSOMETRY
HYPSOPHOBE
HYPSOPHOBES
HYPSOPHOBIA
HYPSOPHOBIAS
HYPSOPHYLL
HYPSOPHYLLARY
HYPSOPHYLLS
HYRACOIDEAN
HYRACOIDEANS
HYSTERANTHOUS
HYSTERECTOMIES
HYSTERECTOMISE
HYSTERECTOMISED
HYSTERECTOMISES
HYSTERECTOMIZE
HYSTERECTOMIZED
HYSTERECTOMIZES
HYSTERECTOMY
HYSTERESES
HYSTERESIAL
HYSTERESIS
HYSTERETIC
HYSTERETICALLY
HYSTERICAL
HYSTERICALLY
HYSTERICKY
HYSTERITIS
HYSTERITISES
HYSTEROGENIC
HYSTEROGENIES
HYSTEROGENY
HYSTEROIDAL
HYSTEROMANIA
HYSTEROMANIAS
HYSTEROTOMIES
HYSTEROTOMY
HYSTRICOMORPH
HYSTRICOMORPHIC
HYSTRICOMORPHS

I

IAMBICALLY
IAMBOGRAPHER
IAMBOGRAPHERS
IATROCHEMICAL
IATROCHEMIST
IATROCHEMISTRY
IATROCHEMISTS
IATROGENIC
IATROGENICALLY
IATROGENICITIES
IATROGENICITY
IATROGENIES
IBUPROFENS
ICEBOATERS
ICEBOATING
ICEBOATINGS
ICEBREAKER
ICEBREAKERS
ICEBREAKING
ICHNEUMONS
ICHNOFOSSIL
ICHNOFOSSILS
ICHNOGRAPHIC
ICHNOGRAPHICAL
ICHNOGRAPHIES
ICHNOGRAPHY
ICHNOLITES
ICHNOLOGICAL
ICHNOLOGIES
ICHTHYOCOLLA
ICHTHYOCOLLAS
ICHTHYODORULITE
ICHTHYODORYLITE
ICHTHYOFAUNA
ICHTHYOFAUNAE
ICHTHYOFAUNAL
ICHTHYOFAUNAS
ICHTHYOIDAL
ICHTHYOIDS
ICHTHYOLATRIES
ICHTHYOLATROUS
ICHTHYOLATRY
ICHTHYOLITE
ICHTHYOLITES
ICHTHYOLITIC
ICHTHYOLOGIC
ICHTHYOLOGICAL
ICHTHYOLOGIES
ICHTHYOLOGIST
ICHTHYOLOGISTS
ICHTHYOLOGY
ICHTHYOPHAGIES
ICHTHYOPHAGIST

ICHTHYOPHAGISTS
ICHTHYOPHAGOUS
ICHTHYOPHAGY
ICHTHYOPSID
ICHTHYOPSIDAN
ICHTHYOPSIDANS
ICHTHYOPSIDS
ICHTHYORNIS
ICHTHYORNISES
ICHTHYOSAUR
ICHTHYOSAURI
ICHTHYOSAURIAN
ICHTHYOSAURIANS
ICHTHYOSAURS
ICHTHYOSAURUS
ICHTHYOSAURUSES
ICHTHYOSES
ICHTHYOSIS
ICHTHYOTIC
ICKINESSES
ICONICALLY
ICONICITIES
ICONIFYING
ICONOCLASM
ICONOCLASMS
ICONOCLAST
ICONOCLASTIC
ICONOCLASTS
ICONOGRAPHER
ICONOGRAPHERS
ICONOGRAPHIC
ICONOGRAPHICAL
ICONOGRAPHIES
ICONOGRAPHY
ICONOLATER
ICONOLATERS
ICONOLATRIES
ICONOLATROUS
ICONOLATRY
ICONOLOGICAL
ICONOLOGIES
ICONOLOGIST
ICONOLOGISTS
ICONOMACHIES
ICONOMACHIST
ICONOMACHISTS
ICONOMACHY
ICONOMATIC
ICONOMATICISM
ICONOMATICISMS
ICONOMETER
ICONOMETERS
ICONOMETRIES

ICONOMETRY
ICONOPHILISM
ICONOPHILISMS
ICONOPHILIST
ICONOPHILISTS
ICONOSCOPE
ICONOSCOPES
ICONOSTASES
ICONOSTASIS
ICOSAHEDRA
ICOSAHEDRAL
ICOSAHEDRON
ICOSAHEDRONS
ICOSANDRIAN
ICOSANDROUS
ICOSITETRAHEDRA
ICTERICALS
ICTERITIOUS
IDEALISATION
IDEALISATIONS
IDEALISERS
IDEALISING
IDEALISTIC
IDEALISTICALLY
IDEALITIES
IDEALIZATION
IDEALIZATIONS
IDEALIZERS
IDEALIZING
IDEALNESSES
IDEALOGIES
IDEALOGUES
IDEATIONAL
IDEATIONALLY
IDEMPOTENCIES
IDEMPOTENCY
IDEMPOTENT
IDEMPOTENTS
IDENTICALLY
IDENTICALNESS
IDENTICALNESSES
IDENTIFIABLE
IDENTIFIABLY
IDENTIFICATION
IDENTIFICATIONS
IDENTIFIED
IDENTIFIER
IDENTIFIERS
IDENTIFIES
IDENTIFYING
IDENTIKITS
IDENTITIES
IDEOGRAMIC

IDEOGRAMMATIC
IDEOGRAMMIC
IDEOGRAPHIC
IDEOGRAPHICAL
IDEOGRAPHICALLY
IDEOGRAPHIES
IDEOGRAPHS
IDEOGRAPHY
IDEOLOGICAL
IDEOLOGICALLY
IDEOLOGIES
IDEOLOGISE
IDEOLOGISED
IDEOLOGISES
IDEOLOGISING
IDEOLOGIST
IDEOLOGISTS
IDEOLOGIZE
IDEOLOGIZED
IDEOLOGIZES
IDEOLOGIZING
IDEOLOGUES
IDEOPHONES
IDEOPRAXIST
IDEOPRAXISTS
IDIOBLASTIC
IDIOBLASTS
IDIOGLOSSIA
IDIOGLOSSIAS
IDIOGRAPHIC
IDIOGRAPHS
IDIOLECTAL
IDIOLECTIC
IDIOMATICAL
IDIOMATICALLY
IDIOMATICALNESS
IDIOMATICNESS
IDIOMATICNESSES
IDIOMORPHIC
IDIOMORPHICALLY
IDIOMORPHISM
IDIOMORPHISMS
IDIOPATHIC
IDIOPATHICALLY
IDIOPATHIES
IDIOPHONES
IDIOPHONIC
IDIOPLASMATIC
IDIOPLASMIC
IDIOPLASMS
IDIORHYTHMIC
IDIORRHYTHMIC
IDIOSYNCRASIES

IDIOSYNCRASY	IGNORANTNESSES	ILLICITNESSES	ILLUSIVENESS
IDIOSYNCRATIC	IGNORATION	ILLIMITABILITY	ILLUSIVENESSES
IDIOSYNCRATICAL	IGNORATIONS	ILLIMITABLE	ILLUSORILY
IDIOTHERMOUS	IGUANODONS	ILLIMITABLENESS	ILLUSORINESS
IDIOTICALLY	ILEOSTOMIES	ILLIMITABLY	ILLUSORINESSES
IDIOTICALNESS	ILLAQUEABLE	ILLIMITATION	ILLUSTRATABLE
IDIOTICALNESSES	ILLAQUEATE	ILLIMITATIONS	ILLUSTRATE
IDIOTICONS	ILLAQUEATED	ILLIQUATION	ILLUSTRATED
IDLENESSES	ILLAQUEATES	ILLIQUATIONS	ILLUSTRATEDS
IDOLATRESS	ILLAQUEATING	ILLIQUIDITIES	ILLUSTRATES
IDOLATRESSES	ILLAQUEATION	ILLIQUIDITY	ILLUSTRATING
IDOLATRIES	ILLAQUEATIONS	ILLITERACIES	ILLUSTRATION
IDOLATRISE	ILLATIVELY	ILLITERACY	ILLUSTRATIONAL
IDOLATRISED	ILLAUDABLE	ILLITERATE	ILLUSTRATIONS
IDOLATRISER	ILLAUDABLY	ILLITERATELY	ILLUSTRATIVE
IDOLATRISERS	ILLEGALISATION	ILLITERATENESS	ILLUSTRATIVELY
IDOLATRISES	ILLEGALISATIONS	ILLITERATES	ILLUSTRATOR
IDOLATRISING	ILLEGALISE	ILLOCUTION	ILLUSTRATORS
IDOLATRIZE	ILLEGALISED	ILLOCUTIONARY	ILLUSTRATORY
IDOLATRIZED	ILLEGALISES	ILLOCUTIONS	ILLUSTRIOUS
IDOLATRIZER	ILLEGALISING	ILLOGICALITIES	ILLUSTRIOUSLY
IDOLATRIZERS	ILLEGALITIES	ILLOGICALITY	ILLUSTRIOUSNESS
IDOLATRIZES	ILLEGALITY	ILLOGICALLY	ILLUSTRISSIMO
IDOLATRIZING	ILLEGALIZATION	ILLOGICALNESS	ILLUVIATED
IDOLATROUS	ILLEGALIZATIONS	ILLOGICALNESSES	ILLUVIATES
IDOLATROUSLY	ILLEGALIZE	ILLUMINABLE	ILLUVIATING
IDOLATROUSNESS	ILLEGALIZED	ILLUMINANCE	ILLUVIATION
IDOLISATION	ILLEGALIZES	ILLUMINANCES	ILLUVIATIONS
IDOLISATIONS	ILLEGALIZING	ILLUMINANT	IMAGINABLE
IDOLIZATION	ILLEGIBILITIES	ILLUMINANTS	IMAGINABLENESS
IDOLIZATIONS	ILLEGIBILITY	ILLUMINATE	IMAGINABLY
IDOLOCLAST	ILLEGIBLENESS	ILLUMINATED	IMAGINARIES
IDOLOCLASTS	ILLEGIBLENESSES	ILLUMINATES	IMAGINARILY
IDONEITIES	ILLEGITIMACIES	ILLUMINATI	IMAGINARINESS
IDOXURIDINE	ILLEGITIMACY	ILLUMINATING	IMAGINARINESSES
IDOXURIDINES	ILLEGITIMATE	ILLUMINATINGLY	IMAGINATION
IDYLLICALLY	ILLEGITIMATED	ILLUMINATION	IMAGINATIONAL
IFFINESSES	ILLEGITIMATELY	ILLUMINATIONAL	IMAGINATIONS
IGNESCENTS	ILLEGITIMATES	ILLUMINATIONS	IMAGINATIVE
IGNIMBRITE	ILLEGITIMATING	ILLUMINATIVE	IMAGINATIVELY
IGNIMBRITES	ILLEGITIMATION	ILLUMINATO	IMAGINATIVENESS
IGNIPOTENT	ILLEGITIMATIONS	ILLUMINATOR	IMAGININGS
IGNITABILITIES	ILLIBERALISE	ILLUMINATORS	IMAGINISTS
IGNITABILITY	ILLIBERALISED	ILLUMINERS	IMAGISTICALLY
IGNITIBILITIES	ILLIBERALISES	ILLUMINING	IMBALANCED
IGNITIBILITY	ILLIBERALISING	ILLUMINISM	IMBALANCES
IGNOBILITIES	ILLIBERALISM	ILLUMINISMS	IMBECILELY
IGNOBILITY	ILLIBERALISMS	ILLUMINIST	IMBECILICALLY
IGNOBLENESS	ILLIBERALITIES	ILLUMINISTS	IMBECILITIES
IGNOBLENESSES	ILLIBERALITY	ILLUSIONAL	IMBECILITY
IGNOMINIES	ILLIBERALIZE	ILLUSIONARY	IMBIBITION
IGNOMINIOUS	ILLIBERALIZED	ILLUSIONED	IMBIBITIONAL
IGNOMINIOUSLY	ILLIBERALIZES	ILLUSIONISM	IMBIBITIONS
IGNOMINIOUSNESS	ILLIBERALIZING	ILLUSIONISMS	IMBITTERED
IGNORAMUSES	ILLIBERALLY	ILLUSIONIST	IMBITTERING
IGNORANCES	ILLIBERALNESS	ILLUSIONISTIC	IMBOLDENED
IGNORANTLY	ILLIBERALNESSES	ILLUSIONISTS	IMBOLDENING
IGNORANTNESS	ILLICITNESS	ILLUSIVELY	IMBORDERED

IMBORDERING	IMMATERIALISE	IMMIGRATIONS	IMMODERACY
IMBOSOMING	IMMATERIALISED	IMMIGRATOR	IMMODERATE
IMBOWERING	IMMATERIALISES	IMMIGRATORS	IMMODERATELY
IMBRANGLED	IMMATERIALISING	IMMIGRATORY	IMMODERATENESS
IMBRANGLES	IMMATERIALISM	IMMINENCES	IMMODERATION
IMBRANGLING	IMMATERIALISMS	IMMINENCIES	IMMODERATIONS
IMBRICATED	IMMATERIALIST	IMMINENTLY	IMMODESTIES
IMBRICATELY	IMMATERIALISTS	IMMINENTNESS	IMMODESTLY
IMBRICATES	IMMATERIALITIES	IMMINENTNESSES	IMMOLATING
IMBRICATING	IMMATERIALITY	IMMINGLING	IMMOLATION
IMBRICATION	IMMATERIALIZE	IMMINUTION	IMMOLATIONS
IMBRICATIONS	IMMATERIALIZED	IMMINUTIONS	IMMOLATORS
IMBROCCATA	IMMATERIALIZES	IMMISCIBILITIES	IMMOMENTOUS
IMBROCCATAS	IMMATERIALIZING	IMMISCIBILITY	IMMORALISM
IMBROGLIOS	IMMATERIALLY	IMMISCIBLE	IMMORALISMS
IMBROWNING	IMMATERIALNESS	IMMISCIBLY	IMMORALIST
IMBRUEMENT	IMMATURELY	IMMISERATION	IMMORALISTS
IMBRUEMENTS	IMMATURENESS	IMMISERATIONS	IMMORALITIES
IMBUEMENTS	IMMATURENESSES	IMMISERISATION	IMMORALITY
IMIDAZOLES	IMMATURITIES	IMMISERISATIONS	IMMORTALISATION
IMINAZOLES	IMMATURITY	IMMISERISE	IMMORTALISE
IMINOUREAS	IMMEASURABILITY	IMMISERISED	IMMORTALISED
IMIPRAMINE	IMMEASURABLE	IMMISERISES	IMMORTALISER
IMIPRAMINES	IMMEASURABLY	IMMISERISING	IMMORTALISERS
IMITABILITIES	IMMEASURED	IMMISERIZATION	IMMORTALISES
IMITABILITY	IMMEDIACIES	IMMISERIZATIONS	IMMORTALISING
IMITABLENESS	IMMEDIATELY	IMMISERIZE	IMMORTALITIES
IMITABLENESSES	IMMEDIATENESS	IMMISERIZED	IMMORTALITY
IMITANCIES	IMMEDIATENESSES	IMMISERIZES	IMMORTALIZATION
IMITATIONAL	IMMEDIATISM	IMMISERIZING	IMMORTALIZE
IMITATIONS	IMMEDIATISMS	IMMISSIONS	IMMORTALIZED
IMITATIVELY	IMMEDICABLE	IMMITIGABILITY	IMMORTALIZER
IMITATIVENESS	IMMEDICABLENESS	IMMITIGABLE	IMMORTALIZERS
IMITATIVENESSES	IMMEDICABLY	IMMITIGABLY	IMMORTALIZES
IMMACULACIES	IMMEMORIAL	IMMITTANCE	IMMORTALIZING
IMMACULACY	IMMEMORIALLY	IMMITTANCES	IMMORTALLY
IMMACULATE	IMMENSENESS	IMMIXTURES	IMMORTELLE
IMMACULATELY	IMMENSENESSES	IMMOBILISATION	IMMORTELLES
IMMACULATENESS	IMMENSITIES	IMMOBILISATIONS	IMMOTILITIES
IMMANACLED	IMMENSURABILITY	IMMOBILISE	IMMOTILITY
IMMANACLES	IMMENSURABLE	IMMOBILISED	IMMOVABILITIES
IMMANACLING	IMMERGENCE	IMMOBILISER	IMMOVABILITY
IMMANATION	IMMERGENCES	IMMOBILISERS	IMMOVABLENESS
IMMANATIONS	IMMERITOUS	IMMOBILISES	IMMOVABLENESSES
IMMANENCES	IMMERSIBLE	IMMOBILISING	IMMOVABLES
IMMANENCIES	IMMERSIONISM	IMMOBILISM	IMMOVEABILITIES
IMMANENTAL	IMMERSIONISMS	IMMOBILISMS	IMMOVEABILITY
IMMANENTISM	IMMERSIONIST	IMMOBILITIES	IMMOVEABLE
IMMANENTISMS	IMMERSIONISTS	IMMOBILITY	IMMOVEABLENESS
IMMANENTIST	IMMERSIONS	IMMOBILIZATION	IMMOVEABLES
IMMANENTISTIC	IMMETHODICAL	IMMOBILIZATIONS	IMMOVEABLY
IMMANENTISTS	IMMETHODICALLY	IMMOBILIZE	IMMUNIFACIENT
IMMANENTLY	IMMIGRANTS	IMMOBILIZED	IMMUNISATION
IMMANITIES	IMMIGRATED	IMMOBILIZER	IMMUNISATIONS
IMMANTLING	IMMIGRATES	IMMOBILIZERS	IMMUNISERS
IMMARCESCIBLE	IMMIGRATING	IMMOBILIZES	IMMUNISING
IMMARGINATE	IMMIGRATION	IMMOBILIZING	IMMUNITIES
IMMATERIAL	IMMIGRATIONAL	IMMODERACIES	IMMUNIZATION

IMMUNIZATIONS	IMMUTABILITIES	IMPASSABLY	IMPENETRATES
IMMUNIZERS	IMMUTABILITY	IMPASSIBILITIES	IMPENETRATING
IMMUNIZING	IMMUTABLENESS	IMPASSIBILITY	IMPENETRATION
IMMUNOASSAY	IMMUTABLENESSES	IMPASSIBLE	IMPENETRATIONS
IMMUNOASSAYABLE	IMPACTIONS	IMPASSIBLENESS	IMPENITENCE
IMMUNOASSAYIST	IMPACTITES	IMPASSIBLY	IMPENITENCES
IMMUNOASSAYISTS	IMPAINTING	IMPASSIONATE	IMPENITENCIES
IMMUNOASSAYS	IMPAIRABLE	IMPASSIONED	IMPENITENCY
IMMUNOBLOT	IMPAIRINGS	IMPASSIONEDLY	IMPENITENT
IMMUNOBLOTS	IMPAIRMENT	IMPASSIONEDNESS	IMPENITENTLY
IMMUNOBLOTTING	IMPAIRMENTS	IMPASSIONING	IMPENITENTNESS
IMMUNOBLOTTINGS	IMPALEMENT	IMPASSIONS	IMPENITENTS
IMMUNOCHEMICAL	IMPALEMENTS	IMPASSIVELY	IMPERATIVAL
IMMUNOCHEMIST	IMPALPABILITIES	IMPASSIVENESS	IMPERATIVE
IMMUNOCHEMISTRY	IMPALPABILITY	IMPASSIVENESSES	IMPERATIVELY
IMMUNOCHEMISTS	IMPALPABLE	IMPASSIVITIES	IMPERATIVENESS
IMMUNOCOMPETENT	IMPALPABLY	IMPASSIVITY	IMPERATIVES
IMMUNOCOMPLEX	IMPALUDISM	IMPASTATION	IMPERATORIAL
IMMUNOCOMPLEXES	IMPALUDISMS	IMPASTATIONS	IMPERATORIALLY
IMMUNODEFICIENT	IMPANATION	IMPATIENCE	IMPERATORS
IMMUNODIAGNOSES	IMPANATIONS	IMPATIENCES	IMPERATORSHIP
IMMUNODIAGNOSIS	IMPANELING	IMPATIENTLY	IMPERATORSHIPS
IMMUNODIFFUSION	IMPANELLED	IMPEACHABILITY	IMPERCEABLE
IMMUNOGENESES	IMPANELLING	IMPEACHABLE	IMPERCEIVABLE
IMMUNOGENESIS	IMPANELMENT	IMPEACHERS	IMPERCEPTIBLE
IMMUNOGENETIC	IMPANELMENTS	IMPEACHING	IMPERCEPTIBLY
IMMUNOGENETICAL	IMPANNELLED	IMPEACHMENT	IMPERCEPTION
IMMUNOGENETICS	IMPANNELLING	IMPEACHMENTS	IMPERCEPTIONS
IMMUNOGENIC	IMPARADISE	IMPEARLING	IMPERCEPTIVE
IMMUNOGENICALLY	IMPARADISED	IMPECCABILITIES	IMPERCEPTIVELY
IMMUNOGENICITY	IMPARADISES	IMPECCABILITY	IMPERCEPTIVITY
IMMUNOGENS	IMPARADISING	IMPECCABLE	IMPERCIPIENCE
IMMUNOGLOBULIN	IMPARIDIGITATE	IMPECCABLY	IMPERCIPIENCES
IMMUNOGLOBULINS	IMPARIPINNATE	IMPECCANCIES	IMPERCIPIENT
IMMUNOLOGIC	IMPARISYLLABIC	IMPECCANCY	IMPERFECTIBLE
IMMUNOLOGICAL	IMPARITIES	IMPECUNIOSITIES	IMPERFECTION
IMMUNOLOGICALLY	IMPARKATION	IMPECUNIOSITY	IMPERFECTIONS
IMMUNOLOGIES	IMPARKATIONS	IMPECUNIOUS	IMPERFECTIVE
IMMUNOLOGIST	IMPARLANCE	IMPECUNIOUSLY	IMPERFECTIVELY
IMMUNOLOGISTS	IMPARLANCES	IMPECUNIOUSNESS	IMPERFECTIVES
IMMUNOLOGY	IMPARTABLE	IMPEDANCES	IMPERFECTLY
IMMUNOMODULATOR	IMPARTATION	IMPEDIMENT	IMPERFECTNESS
IMMUNOPATHOLOGY	IMPARTATIONS	IMPEDIMENTA	IMPERFECTNESSES
IMMUNOPHORESES	IMPARTIALITIES	IMPEDIMENTAL	IMPERFECTS
IMMUNOPHORESIS	IMPARTIALITY	IMPEDIMENTARY	IMPERFORABLE
IMMUNOREACTION	IMPARTIALLY	IMPEDIMENTS	IMPERFORATE
IMMUNOREACTIONS	IMPARTIALNESS	IMPEDINGLY	IMPERFORATED
IMMUNOREACTIVE	IMPARTIALNESSES	IMPEDITIVE	IMPERFORATION
IMMUNOSORBENT	IMPARTIBILITIES	IMPELLENTS	IMPERFORATIONS
IMMUNOSORBENTS	IMPARTIBILITY	IMPENDENCE	IMPERIALISE
IMMUNOSUPPRESS	IMPARTIBLE	IMPENDENCES	IMPERIALISED
IMMUNOTHERAPIES	IMPARTIBLY	IMPENDENCIES	IMPERIALISES
IMMUNOTHERAPY	IMPARTMENT	IMPENDENCY	IMPERIALISING
IMMUNOTOXIC	IMPARTMENTS	IMPENETRABILITY	IMPERIALISM
IMMUNOTOXIN	IMPASSABILITIES	IMPENETRABLE	IMPERIALISMS
IMMUNOTOXINS	IMPASSABILITY	IMPENETRABLY	IMPERIALIST
IMMUREMENT	IMPASSABLE	IMPENETRATE	IMPERIALISTIC
IMMUREMENTS	IMPASSABLENESS	IMPENETRATED	IMPERIALISTS

IMPERIALITIES	IMPERTINENCIES	IMPLAUSIBILITY	IMPOLITEST
IMPERIALITY	IMPERTINENCY	IMPLAUSIBLE	IMPOLITICAL
IMPERIALIZE	IMPERTINENT	IMPLAUSIBLENESS	IMPOLITICALLY
IMPERIALIZED	IMPERTINENTLY	IMPLAUSIBLY	IMPOLITICLY
IMPERIALIZES	IMPERTURBABLE	IMPLEACHED	IMPOLITICNESS
IMPERIALIZING	IMPERTURBABLY	IMPLEACHES	IMPOLITICNESSES
IMPERIALLY	IMPERTURBATION	IMPLEACHING	IMPONDERABILIA
IMPERIALNESS	IMPERTURBATIONS	IMPLEADABLE	IMPONDERABILITY
IMPERIALNESSES	IMPERVIABILITY	IMPLEADERS	IMPONDERABLE
IMPERILING	IMPERVIABLE	IMPLEADING	IMPONDERABLES
IMPERILLED	IMPERVIABLENESS	IMPLEDGING	IMPONDERABLY
IMPERILLING	IMPERVIOUS	IMPLEMENTAL	IMPONDEROUS
IMPERILMENT	IMPERVIOUSLY	IMPLEMENTATION	IMPORTABILITIES
IMPERILMENTS	IMPERVIOUSNESS	IMPLEMENTATIONS	IMPORTABILITY
IMPERIOUSLY	IMPETICOSSED	IMPLEMENTED	IMPORTABLE
IMPERIOUSNESS	IMPETICOSSES	IMPLEMENTER	IMPORTANCE
IMPERIOUSNESSES	IMPETICOSSING	IMPLEMENTERS	IMPORTANCES
IMPERISHABILITY	IMPETIGINES	IMPLEMENTING	IMPORTANCIES
IMPERISHABLE	IMPETIGINOUS	IMPLEMENTOR	IMPORTANCY
IMPERISHABLES	IMPETRATED	IMPLEMENTORS	IMPORTANTLY
IMPERISHABLY	IMPETRATES	IMPLEMENTS	IMPORTATION
IMPERMANENCE	IMPETRATING	IMPLETIONS	IMPORTATIONS
IMPERMANENCES	IMPETRATION	IMPLEXIONS	IMPORTINGS
IMPERMANENCIES	IMPETRATIONS	IMPLEXUOUS	IMPORTUNACIES
IMPERMANENCY	IMPETRATIVE	IMPLICATED	IMPORTUNACY
IMPERMANENT	IMPETRATOR	IMPLICATES	IMPORTUNATE
IMPERMANENTLY	IMPETRATORS	IMPLICATING	IMPORTUNATELY
IMPERMEABILITY	IMPETRATORY	IMPLICATION	IMPORTUNATENESS
IMPERMEABLE	IMPETUOSITIES	IMPLICATIONAL	IMPORTUNED
IMPERMEABLENESS	IMPETUOSITY	IMPLICATIONS	IMPORTUNELY
IMPERMEABLY	IMPETUOUSLY	IMPLICATIVE	IMPORTUNER
IMPERMISSIBLE	IMPETUOUSNESS	IMPLICATIVELY	IMPORTUNERS
IMPERMISSIBLY	IMPETUOUSNESSES	IMPLICATIVENESS	IMPORTUNES
IMPERSCRIPTIBLE	IMPICTURED	IMPLICATURE	IMPORTUNING
IMPERSEVERANT	IMPIERCEABLE	IMPLICATURES	IMPORTUNINGS
IMPERSISTENT	IMPIGNORATE	IMPLICITIES	IMPORTUNITIES
IMPERSONAL	IMPIGNORATED	IMPLICITLY	IMPORTUNITY
IMPERSONALISE	IMPIGNORATES	IMPLICITNESS	IMPOSINGLY
IMPERSONALISED	IMPIGNORATING	IMPLICITNESSES	IMPOSINGNESS
IMPERSONALISES	IMPIGNORATION	IMPLODENTS	IMPOSINGNESSES
IMPERSONALISING	IMPIGNORATIONS	IMPLORATION	IMPOSITION
IMPERSONALITIES	IMPINGEMENT	IMPLORATIONS	IMPOSITIONS
IMPERSONALITY	IMPINGEMENTS	IMPLORATOR	IMPOSSIBILISM
IMPERSONALIZE	IMPIOUSNESS	IMPLORATORS	IMPOSSIBILISMS
IMPERSONALIZED	IMPIOUSNESSES	IMPLORATORY	IMPOSSIBILIST
IMPERSONALIZES	IMPISHNESS	IMPLORINGLY	IMPOSSIBILISTS
IMPERSONALIZING	IMPISHNESSES	IMPLOSIONS	IMPOSSIBILITIES
IMPERSONALLY	IMPLACABILITIES	IMPLOSIVELY	IMPOSSIBILITY
IMPERSONATE	IMPLACABILITY	IMPLOSIVES	IMPOSSIBLE
IMPERSONATED	IMPLACABLE	IMPLUNGING	IMPOSSIBLENESS
IMPERSONATES	IMPLACABLENESS	IMPOCKETED	IMPOSSIBLES
IMPERSONATING	IMPLACABLY	IMPOCKETING	IMPOSSIBLY
IMPERSONATION	IMPLACENTAL	IMPOLDERED	IMPOSTHUMATE
IMPERSONATIONS	IMPLANTABLE	IMPOLDERING	IMPOSTHUMATED
IMPERSONATOR	IMPLANTATION	IMPOLICIES	IMPOSTHUMATES
IMPERSONATORS	IMPLANTATIONS	IMPOLITELY	IMPOSTHUMATING
IMPERTINENCE	IMPLANTERS	IMPOLITENESS	IMPOSTHUMATION
IMPERTINENCES	IMPLANTING	IMPOLITENESSES	IMPOSTHUMATIONS

IMPOSTHUME	IMPREGNANT	IMPROPERLY	IMPUDENTLY
IMPOSTHUMED	IMPREGNANTS	IMPROPERNESS	IMPUDENTNESS
IMPOSTHUMES	IMPREGNATABLE	IMPROPERNESSES	IMPUDENTNESSES
IMPOSTOROUS	IMPREGNATE	IMPROPRIATE	IMPUDICITIES
IMPOSTROUS	IMPREGNATED	IMPROPRIATED	IMPUDICITY
IMPOSTUMATE	IMPREGNATES	IMPROPRIATES	IMPUGNABLE
IMPOSTUMATED	IMPREGNATING	IMPROPRIATING	IMPUGNATION
IMPOSTUMATES	IMPREGNATION	IMPROPRIATION	IMPUGNATIONS
IMPOSTUMATING	IMPREGNATIONS	IMPROPRIATIONS	IMPUGNMENT
IMPOSTUMATION	IMPREGNATOR	IMPROPRIATOR	IMPUGNMENTS
IMPOSTUMATIONS	IMPREGNATORS	IMPROPRIATORS	IMPUISSANCE
IMPOSTUMED	IMPREGNING	IMPROPRIETIES	IMPUISSANCES
IMPOSTUMES	IMPRESARIO	IMPROPRIETY	IMPUISSANT
IMPOSTURES	IMPRESARIOS	IMPROVABILITIES	IMPULSIONS
IMPOSTUROUS	IMPRESCRIPTIBLE	IMPROVABILITY	IMPULSIVELY
IMPOTENCES	IMPRESCRIPTIBLY	IMPROVABLE	IMPULSIVENESS
IMPOTENCIES	IMPRESSERS	IMPROVABLENESS	IMPULSIVENESSES
IMPOTENTLY	IMPRESSIBILITY	IMPROVABLY	IMPULSIVITIES
IMPOTENTNESS	IMPRESSIBLE	IMPROVEMENT	IMPULSIVITY
IMPOTENTNESSES	IMPRESSING	IMPROVEMENTS	IMPUNDULUS
IMPOUNDABLE	IMPRESSION	IMPROVIDENCE	IMPUNITIES
IMPOUNDAGE	IMPRESSIONABLE	IMPROVIDENCES	IMPURENESS
IMPOUNDAGES	IMPRESSIONAL	IMPROVIDENT	IMPURENESSES
IMPOUNDERS	IMPRESSIONALLY	IMPROVIDENTLY	IMPURITIES
IMPOUNDING	IMPRESSIONISM	IMPROVINGLY	IMPURPLING
IMPOUNDMENT	IMPRESSIONISMS	IMPROVISATE	IMPUTABILITIES
IMPOUNDMENTS	IMPRESSIONIST	IMPROVISATED	IMPUTABILITY
IMPOVERISH	IMPRESSIONISTIC	IMPROVISATES	IMPUTABLENESS
IMPOVERISHED	IMPRESSIONISTS	IMPROVISATING	IMPUTABLENESSES
IMPOVERISHER	IMPRESSIONS	IMPROVISATION	IMPUTATION
IMPOVERISHERS	IMPRESSIVE	IMPROVISATIONAL	IMPUTATIONS
IMPOVERISHES	IMPRESSIVELY	IMPROVISATIONS	IMPUTATIVE
IMPOVERISHING	IMPRESSIVENESS	IMPROVISATOR	IMPUTATIVELY
IMPOVERISHMENT	IMPRESSMENT	IMPROVISATORE	INABILITIES
IMPOVERISHMENTS	IMPRESSMENTS	IMPROVISATORES	INABSTINENCE
IMPOWERING	IMPRESSURE	IMPROVISATORI	INABSTINENCES
IMPRACTICABLE	IMPRESSURES	IMPROVISATORIAL	INACCESSIBILITY
IMPRACTICABLY	IMPRIMATUR	IMPROVISATORS	INACCESSIBLE
IMPRACTICAL	IMPRIMATURS	IMPROVISATORY	INACCESSIBLY
IMPRACTICALITY	IMPRINTERS	IMPROVISATRICES	INACCURACIES
IMPRACTICALLY	IMPRINTING	IMPROVISATRIX	INACCURACY
IMPRACTICALNESS	IMPRINTINGS	IMPROVISATRIXES	INACCURATE
IMPRECATED	IMPRISONABLE	IMPROVISED	INACCURATELY
IMPRECATES	IMPRISONED	IMPROVISER	INACCURATENESS
IMPRECATING	IMPRISONER	IMPROVISERS	INACTIVATE
IMPRECATION	IMPRISONERS	IMPROVISES	INACTIVATED
IMPRECATIONS	IMPRISONING	IMPROVISING	INACTIVATES
IMPRECATORY	IMPRISONMENT	IMPROVISOR	INACTIVATING
IMPRECISELY	IMPRISONMENTS	IMPROVISORS	INACTIVATION
IMPRECISENESS	IMPROBABILITIES	IMPROVVISATORE	INACTIVATIONS
IMPRECISENESSES	IMPROBABILITY	IMPROVVISATORES	INACTIVELY
IMPRECISION	IMPROBABLE	IMPROVVISATRICE	INACTIVENESS
IMPRECISIONS	IMPROBABLENESS	IMPRUDENCE	INACTIVENESSES
IMPREDICATIVE	IMPROBABLY	IMPRUDENCES	INACTIVITIES
IMPREGNABILITY	IMPROBATION	IMPRUDENTLY	INACTIVITY
IMPREGNABLE	IMPROBATIONS	IMPSONITES	INADAPTABLE
IMPREGNABLENESS	IMPROBITIES	IMPUDENCES	INADAPTATION
IMPREGNABLY	IMPROMPTUS	IMPUDENCIES	INADAPTATIONS

INADAPTIVE	INAPPREHENSION	INCALESCENCE	INCARNADINED
INADEQUACIES	INAPPREHENSIONS	INCALESCENCES	INCARNADINES
INADEQUACY	INAPPREHENSIVE	INCALESCENT	INCARNADINING
INADEQUATE	INAPPROACHABLE	INCANDESCE	INCARNATED
INADEQUATELY	INAPPROACHABLY	INCANDESCED	INCARNATES
INADEQUATENESS	INAPPROPRIATE	INCANDESCENCE	INCARNATING
INADEQUATES	INAPPROPRIATELY	INCANDESCENCES	INCARNATION
INADMISSIBILITY	INAPTITUDE	INCANDESCENCIES	INCARNATIONS
INADMISSIBLE	INAPTITUDES	INCANDESCENCY	INCARVILLEA
INADMISSIBLY	INAPTNESSES	INCANDESCENT	INCARVILLEAS
INADVERTENCE	INARGUABLE	INCANDESCENTLY	INCASEMENT
INADVERTENCES	INARGUABLY	INCANDESCENTS	INCASEMENTS
INADVERTENCIES	INARTICULACIES	INCANDESCES	INCATENATION
INADVERTENCY	INARTICULACY	INCANDESCING	INCATENATIONS
INADVERTENT	INARTICULATE	INCANTATION	INCAUTIONS
INADVERTENTLY	INARTICULATELY	INCANTATIONAL	INCAUTIOUS
INADVISABILITY	INARTICULATES	INCANTATIONS	INCAUTIOUSLY
INADVISABLE	INARTICULATION	INCANTATOR	INCAUTIOUSNESS
INADVISABLENESS	INARTICULATIONS	INCANTATORS	INCEDINGLY
INADVISABLY	INARTIFICIAL	INCANTATORY	INCENDIARIES
INALIENABILITY	INARTIFICIALLY	INCAPABILITIES	INCENDIARISM
INALIENABLE	INARTISTIC	INCAPABILITY	INCENDIARISMS
INALIENABLENESS	INARTISTICALLY	INCAPABLENESS	INCENDIARY
INALIENABLY	INATTENTION	INCAPABLENESSES	INCENDIVITIES
INALTERABILITY	INATTENTIONS	INCAPABLES	INCENDIVITY
INALTERABLE	INATTENTIVE	INCAPACIOUS	INCENSATION
INALTERABLENESS	INATTENTIVELY	INCAPACIOUSNESS	INCENSATIONS
INALTERABLY	INATTENTIVENESS	INCAPACITANT	INCENSEMENT
INAMORATAS	INAUDIBILITIES	INCAPACITANTS	INCENSEMENTS
INAMORATOS	INAUDIBILITY	INCAPACITATE	INCENSORIES
INANENESSES	INAUDIBLENESS	INCAPACITATED	INCENTIVELY
INANIMATELY	INAUDIBLENESSES	INCAPACITATES	INCENTIVES
INANIMATENESS	INAUGURALS	INCAPACITATING	INCENTIVISATION
INANIMATENESSES	INAUGURATE	INCAPACITATION	INCENTIVISE
INANIMATION	INAUGURATED	INCAPACITATIONS	INCENTIVISED
INANIMATIONS	INAUGURATES	INCAPACITIES	INCENTIVISES
INANITIONS	INAUGURATING	INCAPACITY	INCENTIVISING
INAPPARENT	INAUGURATION	INCAPSULATE	INCENTIVIZATION
INAPPARENTLY	INAUGURATIONS	INCAPSULATED	INCENTIVIZE
INAPPEASABLE	INAUGURATOR	INCAPSULATES	INCENTIVIZED
INAPPELLABLE	INAUGURATORS	INCAPSULATING	INCENTIVIZES
INAPPETENCE	INAUGURATORY	INCAPSULATION	INCENTIVIZING
INAPPETENCES	INAUSPICIOUS	INCAPSULATIONS	INCEPTIONS
INAPPETENCIES	INAUSPICIOUSLY	INCARCERATE	INCEPTIVELY
INAPPETENCY	INAUTHENTIC	INCARCERATED	INCEPTIVES
INAPPETENT	INAUTHENTICITY	INCARCERATES	INCERTAINTIES
INAPPLICABILITY	INBOUNDING	INCARCERATING	INCERTAINTY
INAPPLICABLE	INBREATHED	INCARCERATION	INCERTITUDE
INAPPLICABLY	INBREATHES	INCARCERATIONS	INCERTITUDES
INAPPOSITE	INBREATHING	INCARCERATOR	INCESSANCIES
INAPPOSITELY	INBREEDERS	INCARCERATORS	INCESSANCY
INAPPOSITENESS	INBREEDING	INCARDINATE	INCESSANTLY
INAPPRECIABLE	INBREEDINGS	INCARDINATED	INCESSANTNESS
INAPPRECIABLY	INBRINGING	INCARDINATES	INCESSANTNESSES
INAPPRECIATION	INBRINGINGS	INCARDINATING	INCESTUOUS
INAPPRECIATIONS	INCALCULABILITY	INCARDINATION	INCESTUOUSLY
INAPPRECIATIVE	INCALCULABLE	INCARDINATIONS	INCESTUOUSNESS
INAPPREHENSIBLE	INCALCULABLY	INCARNADINE	INCHARITABLE

893

INCHOATELY	INCLIPPING	INCOMMUTABLY	INCONGRUITY
INCHOATENESS	INCLOSABLE	INCOMPARABILITY	INCONGRUOUS
INCHOATENESSES	INCLOSURES	INCOMPARABLE	INCONGRUOUSLY
INCHOATING	INCLUDABLE	INCOMPARABLY	INCONGRUOUSNESS
INCHOATION	INCLUDEDNESS	INCOMPARED	INCONSCIENT
INCHOATIONS	INCLUDEDNESSES	INCOMPATIBILITY	INCONSCIENTLY
INCHOATIVE	INCLUDIBLE	INCOMPATIBLE	INCONSCIONABLE
INCHOATIVELY	INCLUSIONS	INCOMPATIBLES	INCONSCIOUS
INCHOATIVES	INCLUSIVELY	INCOMPATIBLY	INCONSECUTIVE
INCIDENCES	INCLUSIVENESS	INCOMPETENCE	INCONSECUTIVELY
INCIDENTAL	INCLUSIVENESSES	INCOMPETENCES	INCONSEQUENCE
INCIDENTALLY	INCLUSIVITIES	INCOMPETENCIES	INCONSEQUENCES
INCIDENTALNESS	INCLUSIVITY	INCOMPETENCY	INCONSEQUENT
INCIDENTALS	INCOAGULABLE	INCOMPETENT	INCONSEQUENTIAL
INCINERATE	INCOERCIBLE	INCOMPETENTLY	INCONSEQUENTLY
INCINERATED	INCOGITABILITY	INCOMPETENTS	INCONSIDERABLE
INCINERATES	INCOGITABLE	INCOMPLETE	INCONSIDERABLY
INCINERATING	INCOGITANCIES	INCOMPLETELY	INCONSIDERATE
INCINERATION	INCOGITANCY	INCOMPLETENESS	INCONSIDERATELY
INCINERATIONS	INCOGITANT	INCOMPLETION	INCONSIDERATION
INCINERATOR	INCOGITATIVE	INCOMPLETIONS	INCONSISTENCE
INCINERATORS	INCOGNISABLE	INCOMPLIANCE	INCONSISTENCES
INCIPIENCE	INCOGNISANCE	INCOMPLIANCES	INCONSISTENCIES
INCIPIENCES	INCOGNISANCES	INCOMPLIANCIES	INCONSISTENCY
INCIPIENCIES	INCOGNISANT	INCOMPLIANCY	INCONSISTENT
INCIPIENCY	INCOGNITAS	INCOMPLIANT	INCONSISTENTLY
INCIPIENTLY	INCOGNITOS	INCOMPLIANTLY	INCONSOLABILITY
INCISIFORM	INCOGNIZABLE	INCOMPOSED	INCONSOLABLE
INCISIVELY	INCOGNIZANCE	INCOMPOSITE	INCONSOLABLY
INCISIVENESS	INCOGNIZANCES	INCOMPOSSIBLE	INCONSONANCE
INCISIVENESSES	INCOGNIZANT	INCOMPREHENSION	INCONSONANCES
INCISORIAL	INCOHERENCE	INCOMPREHENSIVE	INCONSONANT
INCITATION	INCOHERENCES	INCOMPRESSIBLE	INCONSONANTLY
INCITATIONS	INCOHERENCIES	INCOMPRESSIBLY	INCONSPICUOUS
INCITATIVE	INCOHERENCY	INCOMPUTABILITY	INCONSPICUOUSLY
INCITATIVES	INCOHERENT	INCOMPUTABLE	INCONSTANCIES
INCITEMENT	INCOHERENTLY	INCOMPUTABLY	INCONSTANCY
INCITEMENTS	INCOHERENTNESS	INCOMUNICADO	INCONSTANT
INCITINGLY	INCOMBUSTIBLE	INCONCEIVABLE	INCONSTANTLY
INCIVILITIES	INCOMBUSTIBLES	INCONCEIVABLES	INCONSTRUABLE
INCIVILITY	INCOMBUSTIBLY	INCONCEIVABLY	INCONSUMABLE
INCLASPING	INCOMMENSURABLE	INCONCINNITIES	INCONSUMABLY
INCLEMENCIES	INCOMMENSURABLY	INCONCINNITY	INCONTESTABLE
INCLEMENCY	INCOMMENSURATE	INCONCINNOUS	INCONTESTABLY
INCLEMENTLY	INCOMMISCIBLE	INCONCLUSION	INCONTIGUOUS
INCLEMENTNESS	INCOMMODED	INCONCLUSIONS	INCONTIGUOUSLY
INCLEMENTNESSES	INCOMMODES	INCONCLUSIVE	INCONTINENCE
INCLINABLE	INCOMMODING	INCONCLUSIVELY	INCONTINENCES
INCLINABLENESS	INCOMMODIOUS	INCONDENSABLE	INCONTINENCIES
INCLINATION	INCOMMODIOUSLY	INCONDENSIBLE	INCONTINENCY
INCLINATIONAL	INCOMMODITIES	INCONDITELY	INCONTINENT
INCLINATIONS	INCOMMODITY	INCONFORMITIES	INCONTINENTLY
INCLINATORIA	INCOMMUNICABLE	INCONFORMITY	INCONTROLLABLE
INCLINATORIUM	INCOMMUNICABLY	INCONGRUENCE	INCONTROLLABLY
INCLINATORY	INCOMMUNICADO	INCONGRUENCES	INCONVENIENCE
INCLININGS	INCOMMUNICATIVE	INCONGRUENT	INCONVENIENCED
INCLINOMETER	INCOMMUTABILITY	INCONGRUENTLY	INCONVENIENCES
INCLINOMETERS	INCOMMUTABLE	INCONGRUITIES	INCONVENIENCIES

INCONVENIENCING
INCONVENIENCY
INCONVENIENT
INCONVENIENTLY
INCONVERSABLE
INCONVERSANT
INCONVERTIBLE
INCONVERTIBLY
INCONVINCIBLE
INCONVINCIBLY
INCOORDINATE
INCOORDINATION
INCOORDINATIONS
INCORONATE
INCORONATED
INCORONATION
INCORONATIONS
INCORPORABLE
INCORPORAL
INCORPORALL
INCORPORATE
INCORPORATED
INCORPORATES
INCORPORATING
INCORPORATION
INCORPORATIONS
INCORPORATIVE
INCORPORATOR
INCORPORATORS
INCORPOREAL
INCORPOREALITY
INCORPOREALLY
INCORPOREITIES
INCORPOREITY
INCORPSING
INCORRECTLY
INCORRECTNESS
INCORRECTNESSES
INCORRIGIBILITY
INCORRIGIBLE
INCORRIGIBLES
INCORRIGIBLY
INCORRODIBLE
INCORROSIBLE
INCORRUPTED
INCORRUPTIBLE
INCORRUPTIBLES
INCORRUPTIBLY
INCORRUPTION
INCORRUPTIONS
INCORRUPTIVE
INCORRUPTLY
INCORRUPTNESS
INCORRUPTNESSES
INCRASSATE
INCRASSATED
INCRASSATES
INCRASSATING

INCRASSATION
INCRASSATIONS
INCRASSATIVE
INCREASABLE
INCREASEDLY
INCREASEFUL
INCREASERS
INCREASING
INCREASINGLY
INCREASINGS
INCREATELY
INCREDIBILITIES
INCREDIBILITY
INCREDIBLE
INCREDIBLENESS
INCREDIBLY
INCREDULITIES
INCREDULITY
INCREDULOUS
INCREDULOUSLY
INCREDULOUSNESS
INCREMATED
INCREMATES
INCREMATING
INCREMATION
INCREMATIONS
INCREMENTAL
INCREMENTALISM
INCREMENTALISMS
INCREMENTALIST
INCREMENTALISTS
INCREMENTALLY
INCREMENTALS
INCREMENTED
INCREMENTING
INCREMENTS
INCRESCENT
INCRETIONARY
INCRETIONS
INCRIMINATE
INCRIMINATED
INCRIMINATES
INCRIMINATING
INCRIMINATION
INCRIMINATIONS
INCRIMINATOR
INCRIMINATORS
INCRIMINATORY
INCROSSBRED
INCROSSBREDS
INCROSSBREED
INCROSSBREEDING
INCROSSBREEDS
INCROSSING
INCRUSTANT
INCRUSTANTS
INCRUSTATION
INCRUSTATIONS

INCRUSTING
INCUBATING
INCUBATION
INCUBATIONAL
INCUBATIONS
INCUBATIVE
INCUBATORS
INCUBATORY
INCULCATED
INCULCATES
INCULCATING
INCULCATION
INCULCATIONS
INCULCATIVE
INCULCATOR
INCULCATORS
INCULCATORY
INCULPABILITIES
INCULPABILITY
INCULPABLE
INCULPABLENESS
INCULPABLY
INCULPATED
INCULPATES
INCULPATING
INCULPATION
INCULPATIONS
INCULPATIVE
INCULPATORY
INCUMBENCIES
INCUMBENCY
INCUMBENTLY
INCUMBENTS
INCUMBERED
INCUMBERING
INCUMBERINGLY
INCUMBRANCE
INCUMBRANCES
INCUNABLES
INCUNABULA
INCUNABULAR
INCUNABULIST
INCUNABULISTS
INCUNABULUM
INCURABILITIES
INCURABILITY
INCURABLENESS
INCURABLENESSES
INCURABLES
INCURIOSITIES
INCURIOSITY
INCURIOUSLY
INCURIOUSNESS
INCURIOUSNESSES
INCURRABLE
INCURRENCE
INCURRENCES
INCURSIONS

INCURVATED
INCURVATES
INCURVATING
INCURVATION
INCURVATIONS
INCURVATURE
INCURVATURES
INCURVITIES
INDAGATING
INDAGATION
INDAGATIONS
INDAGATIVE
INDAGATORS
INDAGATORY
INDAPAMIDE
INDAPAMIDES
INDEBTEDNESS
INDEBTEDNESSES
INDECENCIES
INDECENTER
INDECENTEST
INDECENTLY
INDECIDUATE
INDECIDUOUS
INDECIPHERABLE
INDECIPHERABLY
INDECISION
INDECISIONS
INDECISIVE
INDECISIVELY
INDECISIVENESS
INDECLINABLE
INDECLINABLY
INDECOMPOSABLE
INDECOROUS
INDECOROUSLY
INDECOROUSNESS
INDECORUMS
INDEFATIGABLE
INDEFATIGABLY
INDEFEASIBILITY
INDEFEASIBLE
INDEFEASIBLY
INDEFECTIBILITY
INDEFECTIBLE
INDEFECTIBLY
INDEFENSIBILITY
INDEFENSIBLE
INDEFENSIBLY
INDEFINABILITY
INDEFINABLE
INDEFINABLENESS
INDEFINABLES
INDEFINABLY
INDEFINITE
INDEFINITELY
INDEFINITENESS
INDEFINITES

INDEHISCENCE	INDEXATIONS	INDIGESTION	INDISSUADABLE
INDEHISCENCES	INDEXICALS	INDIGESTIONS	INDISSUADABLY
INDEHISCENT	INDEXTERITIES	INDIGESTIVE	INDISTINCT
INDELIBILITIES	INDEXTERITY	INDIGNANCE	INDISTINCTION
INDELIBILITY	INDICATABLE	INDIGNANCES	INDISTINCTIONS
INDELIBLENESS	INDICATING	INDIGNANTLY	INDISTINCTIVE
INDELIBLENESSES	INDICATION	INDIGNATION	INDISTINCTIVELY
INDELICACIES	INDICATIONAL	INDIGNATIONS	INDISTINCTLY
INDELICACY	INDICATIONS	INDIGNIFIED	INDISTINCTNESS
INDELICATE	INDICATIVE	INDIGNIFIES	INDISTRIBUTABLE
INDELICATELY	INDICATIVELY	INDIGNIFYING	INDITEMENT
INDELICATENESS	INDICATIVES	INDIGNITIES	INDITEMENTS
INDEMNIFICATION	INDICATORS	INDIGOLITE	INDIVERTIBLE
INDEMNIFIED	INDICATORY	INDIGOLITES	INDIVERTIBLY
INDEMNIFIER	INDICOLITE	INDIGOTINS	INDIVIDABLE
INDEMNIFIERS	INDICOLITES	INDINAVIRS	INDIVIDUAL
INDEMNIFIES	INDICTABLE	INDIRECTION	INDIVIDUALISE
INDEMNIFYING	INDICTABLY	INDIRECTIONS	INDIVIDUALISED
INDEMNITIES	INDICTIONAL	INDIRECTLY	INDIVIDUALISER
INDEMONSTRABLE	INDICTIONS	INDIRECTNESS	INDIVIDUALISERS
INDEMONSTRABLY	INDICTMENT	INDIRECTNESSES	INDIVIDUALISES
INDENTATION	INDICTMENTS	INDIRUBINS	INDIVIDUALISING
INDENTATIONS	INDIFFERENCE	INDISCERNIBLE	INDIVIDUALISM
INDENTIONS	INDIFFERENCES	INDISCERNIBLY	INDIVIDUALISMS
INDENTURED	INDIFFERENCIES	INDISCERPTIBLE	INDIVIDUALIST
INDENTURES	INDIFFERENCY	INDISCIPLINABLE	INDIVIDUALISTIC
INDENTURESHIP	INDIFFERENT	INDISCIPLINE	INDIVIDUALISTS
INDENTURESHIPS	INDIFFERENTISM	INDISCIPLINED	INDIVIDUALITIES
INDENTURING	INDIFFERENTISMS	INDISCIPLINES	INDIVIDUALITY
INDEPENDENCE	INDIFFERENTIST	INDISCOVERABLE	INDIVIDUALIZE
INDEPENDENCES	INDIFFERENTISTS	INDISCREET	INDIVIDUALIZED
INDEPENDENCIES	INDIFFERENTLY	INDISCREETLY	INDIVIDUALIZER
INDEPENDENCY	INDIFFERENTS	INDISCREETNESS	INDIVIDUALIZERS
INDEPENDENT	INDIGENCES	INDISCRETE	INDIVIDUALIZES
INDEPENDENTLY	INDIGENCIES	INDISCRETELY	INDIVIDUALIZING
INDEPENDENTS	INDIGENISATION	INDISCRETENESS	INDIVIDUALLY
INDESCRIBABLE	INDIGENISATIONS	INDISCRETION	INDIVIDUALS
INDESCRIBABLES	INDIGENISE	INDISCRETIONARY	INDIVIDUATE
INDESCRIBABLY	INDIGENISED	INDISCRETIONS	INDIVIDUATED
INDESIGNATE	INDIGENISES	INDISCRIMINATE	INDIVIDUATES
INDESTRUCTIBLE	INDIGENISING	INDISPENSABLE	INDIVIDUATING
INDESTRUCTIBLY	INDIGENITIES	INDISPENSABLES	INDIVIDUATION
INDETECTABLE	INDIGENITY	INDISPENSABLY	INDIVIDUATIONS
INDETECTIBLE	INDIGENIZATION	INDISPOSED	INDIVIDUATOR
INDETERMINABLE	INDIGENIZATIONS	INDISPOSEDNESS	INDIVIDUATORS
INDETERMINABLY	INDIGENIZE	INDISPOSES	INDIVIDUUM
INDETERMINACIES	INDIGENIZED	INDISPOSING	INDIVISIBILITY
INDETERMINACY	INDIGENIZES	INDISPOSITION	INDIVISIBLE
INDETERMINATE	INDIGENIZING	INDISPOSITIONS	INDIVISIBLENESS
INDETERMINATELY	INDIGENOUS	INDISPUTABILITY	INDIVISIBLES
INDETERMINATION	INDIGENOUSLY	INDISPUTABLE	INDIVISIBLY
INDETERMINED	INDIGENOUSNESS	INDISPUTABLY	INDOCILITIES
INDETERMINISM	INDIGENTLY	INDISSOCIABLE	INDOCILITY
INDETERMINISMS	INDIGESTED	INDISSOCIABLY	INDOCTRINATE
INDETERMINIST	INDIGESTIBILITY	INDISSOLUBILITY	INDOCTRINATED
INDETERMINISTIC	INDIGESTIBLE	INDISSOLUBLE	INDOCTRINATES
INDETERMINISTS	INDIGESTIBLES	INDISSOLUBLY	INDOCTRINATING
INDEXATION	INDIGESTIBLY	INDISSOLVABLE	INDOCTRINATION

INDOCTRINATIONS	INDURATIONS	INEFFICIENCIES	INERRABLENESSES
INDOCTRINATOR	INDURATIVE	INEFFICIENCY	INERRANCIES
INDOCTRINATORS	INDUSTRIAL	INEFFICIENT	INERTIALLY
INDOLEACETIC	INDUSTRIALISE	INEFFICIENTLY	INERTNESSES
INDOLEBUTYRIC	INDUSTRIALISED	INEFFICIENTS	INESCAPABLE
INDOLENCES	INDUSTRIALISES	INEGALITARIAN	INESCAPABLY
INDOLENCIES	INDUSTRIALISING	INELABORATE	INESCULENT
INDOLENTLY	INDUSTRIALISM	INELABORATELY	INESCUTCHEON
INDOMETHACIN	INDUSTRIALISMS	INELASTICALLY	INESCUTCHEONS
INDOMETHACINS	INDUSTRIALIST	INELASTICITIES	INESSENTIAL
INDOMITABILITY	INDUSTRIALISTS	INELASTICITY	INESSENTIALITY
INDOMITABLE	INDUSTRIALIZE	INELEGANCE	INESSENTIALS
INDOMITABLENESS	INDUSTRIALIZED	INELEGANCES	INESTIMABILITY
INDOMITABLY	INDUSTRIALIZES	INELEGANCIES	INESTIMABLE
INDOPHENOL	INDUSTRIALIZING	INELEGANCY	INESTIMABLENESS
INDOPHENOLS	INDUSTRIALLY	INELEGANTLY	INESTIMABLY
INDORSABLE	INDUSTRIALS	INELIGIBILITIES	INEVITABILITIES
INDORSEMENT	INDUSTRIES	INELIGIBILITY	INEVITABILITY
INDORSEMENTS	INDUSTRIOUS	INELIGIBLE	INEVITABLE
INDRAUGHTS	INDUSTRIOUSLY	INELIGIBLENESS	INEVITABLENESS
INDRENCHED	INDUSTRIOUSNESS	INELIGIBLES	INEVITABLY
INDRENCHES	INDUSTRYWIDE	INELIGIBLY	INEXACTITUDE
INDRENCHING	INDWELLERS	INELOQUENCE	INEXACTITUDES
INDUBITABILITY	INDWELLING	INELOQUENCES	INEXACTNESS
INDUBITABLE	INDWELLINGS	INELOQUENT	INEXACTNESSES
INDUBITABLENESS	INEARTHING	INELOQUENTLY	INEXCITABLE
INDUBITABLY	INEBRIANTS	INELUCTABILITY	INEXCUSABILITY
INDUCEMENT	INEBRIATED	INELUCTABLE	INEXCUSABLE
INDUCEMENTS	INEBRIATES	INELUCTABLY	INEXCUSABLENESS
INDUCIBILITIES	INEBRIATING	INELUDIBILITIES	INEXCUSABLY
INDUCIBILITY	INEBRIATION	INELUDIBILITY	INEXECRABLE
INDUCTANCE	INEBRIATIONS	INELUDIBLE	INEXECUTABLE
INDUCTANCES	INEBRIETIES	INELUDIBLY	INEXECUTION
INDUCTILITIES	INEDIBILITIES	INENARRABLE	INEXECUTIONS
INDUCTILITY	INEDIBILITY	INEPTITUDE	INEXHAUSTED
INDUCTIONAL	INEDUCABILITIES	INEPTITUDES	INEXHAUSTIBLE
INDUCTIONS	INEDUCABILITY	INEPTNESSES	INEXHAUSTIBLY
INDUCTIVELY	INEDUCABLE	INEQUALITIES	INEXHAUSTIVE
INDUCTIVENESS	INEFFABILITIES	INEQUALITY	INEXISTANT
INDUCTIVENESSES	INEFFABILITY	INEQUATION	INEXISTENCE
INDUCTIVITIES	INEFFABLENESS	INEQUATIONS	INEXISTENCES
INDUCTIVITY	INEFFABLENESSES	INEQUIPOTENT	INEXISTENCIES
INDULGENCE	INEFFACEABILITY	INEQUITABLE	INEXISTENCY
INDULGENCED	INEFFACEABLE	INEQUITABLENESS	INEXISTENT
INDULGENCES	INEFFACEABLY	INEQUITABLY	INEXORABILITIES
INDULGENCIES	INEFFECTIVE	INEQUITIES	INEXORABILITY
INDULGENCING	INEFFECTIVELY	INEQUIVALVE	INEXORABLE
INDULGENCY	INEFFECTIVENESS	INEQUIVALVED	INEXORABLENESS
INDULGENTLY	INEFFECTUAL	INERADICABILITY	INEXORABLY
INDULGINGLY	INEFFECTUALITY	INERADICABLE	INEXPANSIBLE
INDUMENTUM	INEFFECTUALLY	INERADICABLY	INEXPECTANCIES
INDUMENTUMS	INEFFECTUALNESS	INERASABLE	INEXPECTANCY
INDUPLICATE	INEFFICACIES	INERASABLY	INEXPECTANT
INDUPLICATED	INEFFICACIOUS	INERASIBLE	INEXPECTATION
INDUPLICATION	INEFFICACIOUSLY	INERASIBLY	INEXPECTATIONS
INDUPLICATIONS	INEFFICACITIES	INERRABILITIES	INEXPEDIENCE
INDURATING	INEFFICACITY	INERRABILITY	INEXPEDIENCES
INDURATION	INEFFICACY	INERRABLENESS	INEXPEDIENCIES

INEXPEDIENCY	INFAMONIZED	INFELICITOUS	INFINITESIMAL
INEXPEDIENT	INFAMONIZES	INFELICITOUSLY	INFINITESIMALLY
INEXPEDIENTLY	INFAMONIZING	INFELICITY	INFINITESIMALS
INEXPENSIVE	INFAMOUSLY	INFEOFFING	INFINITIES
INEXPENSIVELY	INFAMOUSNESS	INFERENCES	INFINITIVAL
INEXPENSIVENESS	INFAMOUSNESSES	INFERENCING	INFINITIVALLY
INEXPERIENCE	INFANGTHIEF	INFERENCINGS	INFINITIVE
INEXPERIENCED	INFANGTHIEFS	INFERENTIAL	INFINITIVELY
INEXPERIENCES	INFANTHOOD	INFERENTIALLY	INFINITIVES
INEXPERTLY	INFANTHOODS	INFERIORITIES	INFINITUDE
INEXPERTNESS	INFANTICIDAL	INFERIORITY	INFINITUDES
INEXPERTNESSES	INFANTICIDE	INFERIORLY	INFIRMARER
INEXPIABLE	INFANTICIDES	INFERNALITIES	INFIRMARERS
INEXPIABLENESS	INFANTILISATION	INFERNALITY	INFIRMARIAN
INEXPIABLY	INFANTILISE	INFERNALLY	INFIRMARIANS
INEXPLAINABLE	INFANTILISED	INFERRABLE	INFIRMARIES
INEXPLAINABLY	INFANTILISES	INFERRIBLE	INFIRMITIES
INEXPLICABILITY	INFANTILISING	INFERTILELY	INFIRMNESS
INEXPLICABLE	INFANTILISM	INFERTILITIES	INFIRMNESSES
INEXPLICABLY	INFANTILISMS	INFERTILITY	INFIXATION
INEXPLICIT	INFANTILITIES	INFESTANTS	INFIXATIONS
INEXPLICITLY	INFANTILITY	INFESTATION	INFLAMABLE
INEXPLICITNESS	INFANTILIZATION	INFESTATIONS	INFLAMINGLY
INEXPRESSIBLE	INFANTILIZE	INFEUDATION	INFLAMMABILITY
INEXPRESSIBLES	INFANTILIZED	INFEUDATIONS	INFLAMMABLE
INEXPRESSIBLY	INFANTILIZES	INFIBULATE	INFLAMMABLENESS
INEXPRESSIVE	INFANTILIZING	INFIBULATED	INFLAMMABLES
INEXPRESSIVELY	INFANTIVORE	INFIBULATES	INFLAMMABLY
INEXPUGNABILITY	INFANTIVORES	INFIBULATING	INFLAMMATION
INEXPUGNABLE	INFANTRIES	INFIBULATION	INFLAMMATIONS
INEXPUGNABLY	INFANTRYMAN	INFIBULATIONS	INFLAMMATORILY
INEXPUNGIBLE	INFANTRYMEN	INFIDELITIES	INFLAMMATORY
INEXTENDED	INFARCTION	INFIDELITY	INFLATABLE
INEXTENSIBILITY	INFARCTIONS	INFIELDERS	INFLATABLES
INEXTENSIBLE	INFATUATED	INFIELDSMAN	INFLATEDLY
INEXTENSION	INFATUATEDLY	INFIELDSMEN	INFLATEDNESS
INEXTENSIONS	INFATUATES	INFIGHTERS	INFLATEDNESSES
INEXTIRPABLE	INFATUATING	INFIGHTING	INFLATINGLY
INEXTRICABILITY	INFATUATION	INFIGHTINGS	INFLATIONARY
INEXTRICABLE	INFATUATIONS	INFILLINGS	INFLATIONISM
INEXTRICABLY	INFEASIBILITIES	INFILTRATE	INFLATIONISMS
INFALLIBILISM	INFEASIBILITY	INFILTRATED	INFLATIONIST
INFALLIBILISMS	INFEASIBLE	INFILTRATES	INFLATIONISTS
INFALLIBILIST	INFEASIBLENESS	INFILTRATING	INFLATIONS
INFALLIBILISTS	INFECTIONS	INFILTRATION	INFLATUSES
INFALLIBILITIES	INFECTIOUS	INFILTRATIONS	INFLECTABLE
INFALLIBILITY	INFECTIOUSLY	INFILTRATIVE	INFLECTEDNESS
INFALLIBLE	INFECTIOUSNESS	INFILTRATOR	INFLECTEDNESSES
INFALLIBLENESS	INFECTIVELY	INFILTRATORS	INFLECTING
INFALLIBLES	INFECTIVENESS	INFINITANT	INFLECTION
INFALLIBLY	INFECTIVENESSES	INFINITARY	INFLECTIONAL
INFAMISING	INFECTIVITIES	INFINITATE	INFLECTIONALLY
INFAMIZING	INFECTIVITY	INFINITATED	INFLECTIONLESS
INFAMONISE	INFECUNDITIES	INFINITATES	INFLECTIONS
INFAMONISED	INFECUNDITY	INFINITATING	INFLECTIVE
INFAMONISES	INFEFTMENT	INFINITELY	INFLECTORS
INFAMONISING	INFEFTMENTS	INFINITENESS	INFLEXIBILITIES
INFAMONIZE	INFELICITIES	INFINITENESSES	INFLEXIBILITY

INFLEXIBLE
INFLEXIBLENESS
INFLEXIBLY
INFLEXIONAL
INFLEXIONALLY
INFLEXIONLESS
INFLEXIONS
INFLEXURES
INFLICTABLE
INFLICTERS
INFLICTING
INFLICTION
INFLICTIONS
INFLICTIVE
INFLICTORS
INFLORESCENCE
INFLORESCENCES
INFLORESCENT
INFLOWINGS
INFLUENCEABLE
INFLUENCED
INFLUENCER
INFLUENCERS
INFLUENCES
INFLUENCING
INFLUENTIAL
INFLUENTIALLY
INFLUENTIALS
INFLUENZAL
INFLUENZAS
INFLUXIONS
INFOLDMENT
INFOLDMENTS
INFOMANIAS
INFOMERCIAL
INFOMERCIALS
INFOPRENEURIAL
INFORMABLE
INFORMALITIES
INFORMALITY
INFORMALLY
INFORMANTS
INFORMATICIAN
INFORMATICIANS
INFORMATICS
INFORMATION
INFORMATIONAL
INFORMATIONALLY
INFORMATIONS
INFORMATIVE
INFORMATIVELY
INFORMATIVENESS
INFORMATORILY
INFORMATORY
INFORMEDLY
INFORMIDABLE
INFORMINGLY
INFORTUNES

INFOSPHERE
INFOSPHERES
INFOTAINMENT
INFOTAINMENTS
INFRACOSTAL
INFRACTING
INFRACTION
INFRACTIONS
INFRACTORS
INFRAGRANT
INFRAHUMAN
INFRAHUMANS
INFRALAPSARIAN
INFRALAPSARIANS
INFRAMAXILLARY
INFRANGIBILITY
INFRANGIBLE
INFRANGIBLENESS
INFRANGIBLY
INFRAORBITAL
INFRAPOSED
INFRAPOSITION
INFRAPOSITIONS
INFRASONIC
INFRASOUND
INFRASOUNDS
INFRASPECIFIC
INFRASTRUCTURAL
INFRASTRUCTURE
INFRASTRUCTURES
INFREQUENCE
INFREQUENCES
INFREQUENCIES
INFREQUENCY
INFREQUENT
INFREQUENTLY
INFRINGEMENT
INFRINGEMENTS
INFRINGERS
INFRINGING
INFRUCTUOUS
INFRUCTUOUSLY
INFUNDIBULA
INFUNDIBULAR
INFUNDIBULATE
INFUNDIBULIFORM
INFUNDIBULUM
INFURIATED
INFURIATELY
INFURIATES
INFURIATING
INFURIATINGLY
INFURIATION
INFURIATIONS
INFUSCATED
INFUSIBILITIES
INFUSIBILITY
INFUSIBLENESS

INFUSIBLENESSES
INFUSIONISM
INFUSIONISMS
INFUSIONIST
INFUSIONISTS
INFUSORIAL
INFUSORIAN
INFUSORIANS
INGATHERED
INGATHERER
INGATHERERS
INGATHERING
INGATHERINGS
INGEMINATE
INGEMINATED
INGEMINATES
INGEMINATING
INGEMINATION
INGEMINATIONS
INGENERATE
INGENERATED
INGENERATES
INGENERATING
INGENERATION
INGENERATIONS
INGENIOUSLY
INGENIOUSNESS
INGENIOUSNESSES
INGENUITIES
INGENUOUSLY
INGENUOUSNESS
INGENUOUSNESSES
INGESTIBLE
INGESTIONS
INGLENEUKS
INGLENOOKS
INGLORIOUS
INGLORIOUSLY
INGLORIOUSNESS
INGRAFTATION
INGRAFTATIONS
INGRAFTING
INGRAFTMENT
INGRAFTMENTS
INGRAINEDLY
INGRAINEDNESS
INGRAINEDNESSES
INGRAINING
INGRATEFUL
INGRATIATE
INGRATIATED
INGRATIATES
INGRATIATING
INGRATIATINGLY
INGRATIATION
INGRATIATIONS
INGRATIATORY
INGRATITUDE

INGRATITUDES
INGRAVESCENCE
INGRAVESCENCES
INGRAVESCENT
INGREDIENT
INGREDIENTS
INGRESSION
INGRESSIONS
INGRESSIVE
INGRESSIVENESS
INGRESSIVES
INGROOVING
INGROSSING
INGROWNNESS
INGROWNNESSES
INGULFMENT
INGULFMENTS
INGULPHING
INGURGITATE
INGURGITATED
INGURGITATES
INGURGITATING
INGURGITATION
INGURGITATIONS
INHABITABILITY
INHABITABLE
INHABITANCE
INHABITANCES
INHABITANCIES
INHABITANCY
INHABITANT
INHABITANTS
INHABITATION
INHABITATIONS
INHABITERS
INHABITING
INHABITIVENESS
INHABITORS
INHABITRESS
INHABITRESSES
INHALATION
INHALATIONAL
INHALATIONS
INHALATORIUM
INHALATORIUMS
INHALATORS
INHARMONIC
INHARMONICAL
INHARMONICITIES
INHARMONICITY
INHARMONIES
INHARMONIOUS
INHARMONIOUSLY
INHAUSTING
INHEARSING
INHERENCES
INHERENCIES
INHERENTLY

INHERITABILITY	INITIALISES	INNAVIGABLE	INOBEDIENTLY
INHERITABLE	INITIALISING	INNAVIGABLY	INOBSERVABLE
INHERITABLENESS	INITIALISM	INNERMOSTS	INOBSERVANCE
INHERITABLY	INITIALISMS	INNERNESSES	INOBSERVANCES
INHERITANCE	INITIALIZATION	INNERSOLES	INOBSERVANT
INHERITANCES	INITIALIZATIONS	INNERSPRING	INOBSERVANTLY
INHERITING	INITIALIZE	INNERVATED	INOBSERVATION
INHERITORS	INITIALIZED	INNERVATES	INOBSERVATIONS
INHERITRESS	INITIALIZES	INNERVATING	INOBTRUSIVE
INHERITRESSES	INITIALIZING	INNERVATION	INOBTRUSIVELY
INHERITRICES	INITIALLED	INNERVATIONS	INOBTRUSIVENESS
INHERITRIX	INITIALLER	INNERWEARS	INOCCUPATION
INHERITRIXES	INITIALLERS	INNKEEPERS	INOCCUPATIONS
INHIBITABLE	INITIALLING	INNOCENCES	INOCULABILITIES
INHIBITERS	INITIALNESS	INNOCENCIES	INOCULABILITY
INHIBITING	INITIALNESSES	INNOCENTER	INOCULABLE
INHIBITION	INITIATING	INNOCENTEST	INOCULANTS
INHIBITIONS	INITIATION	INNOCENTLY	INOCULATED
INHIBITIVE	INITIATIONS	INNOCUITIES	INOCULATES
INHIBITORS	INITIATIVE	INNOCUOUSLY	INOCULATING
INHIBITORY	INITIATIVELY	INNOCUOUSNESS	INOCULATION
INHOLDINGS	INITIATIVES	INNOCUOUSNESSES	INOCULATIONS
INHOMOGENEITIES	INITIATORIES	INNOMINABLE	INOCULATIVE
INHOMOGENEITY	INITIATORS	INNOMINABLES	INOCULATOR
INHOMOGENEOUS	INITIATORY	INNOMINATE	INOCULATORS
INHOSPITABLE	INITIATRESS	INNOVATING	INOCULATORY
INHOSPITABLY	INITIATRESSES	INNOVATION	INODOROUSLY
INHOSPITALITIES	INITIATRICES	INNOVATIONAL	INODOROUSNESS
INHOSPITALITY	INITIATRIX	INNOVATIONIST	INODOROUSNESSES
INHUMANELY	INITIATRIXES	INNOVATIONISTS	INOFFENSIVE
INHUMANITIES	INJECTABLE	INNOVATIONS	INOFFENSIVELY
INHUMANITY	INJECTABLES	INNOVATIVE	INOFFENSIVENESS
INHUMANNESS	INJECTANTS	INNOVATIVELY	INOFFICIOUS
INHUMANNESSES	INJECTIONS	INNOVATIVENESS	INOFFICIOUSLY
INHUMATING	INJELLYING	INNOVATORS	INOFFICIOUSNESS
INHUMATION	INJOINTING	INNOVATORY	INOPERABILITIES
INHUMATIONS	INJUDICIAL	INNOXIOUSLY	INOPERABILITY
INIMICALITIES	INJUDICIALLY	INNOXIOUSNESS	INOPERABLE
INIMICALITY	INJUDICIOUS	INNOXIOUSNESSES	INOPERABLENESS
INIMICALLY	INJUDICIOUSLY	INNUENDOED	INOPERABLY
INIMICALNESS	INJUDICIOUSNESS	INNUENDOES	INOPERATIVE
INIMICALNESSES	INJUNCTING	INNUENDOING	INOPERATIVENESS
INIMICITIOUS	INJUNCTION	INNUMERABILITY	INOPERCULATE
INIMITABILITIES	INJUNCTIONS	INNUMERABLE	INOPERCULATES
INIMITABILITY	INJUNCTIVE	INNUMERABLENESS	INOPPORTUNE
INIMITABLE	INJUNCTIVELY	INNUMERABLY	INOPPORTUNELY
INIMITABLENESS	INJURIOUSLY	INNUMERACIES	INOPPORTUNENESS
INIMITABLY	INJURIOUSNESS	INNUMERACY	INOPPORTUNITIES
INIQUITIES	INJURIOUSNESSES	INNUMERATE	INOPPORTUNITY
INIQUITOUS	INJUSTICES	INNUMERATES	INORDINACIES
INIQUITOUSLY	INKBERRIES	INNUMEROUS	INORDINACY
INIQUITOUSNESS	INKHOLDERS	INNUTRIENT	INORDINATE
INITIALERS	INKINESSES	INNUTRITION	INORDINATELY
INITIALING	INMARRIAGE	INNUTRITIONS	INORDINATENESS
INITIALISATION	INMARRIAGES	INNUTRITIOUS	INORDINATION
INITIALISATIONS	INMIGRANTS	INOBEDIENCE	INORDINATIONS
INITIALISE	INNATENESS	INOBEDIENCES	INORGANICALLY
INITIALISED	INNATENESSES	INOBEDIENT	INORGANISATION

INORGANISATIONS	INSALUBRIOUSLY	INSECTOLOGIST	INSIDIOUSNESS
INORGANISED	INSALUBRITIES	INSECTOLOGISTS	INSIDIOUSNESSES
INORGANIZATION	INSALUBRITY	INSECTOLOGY	INSIGHTFUL
INORGANIZATIONS	INSALUTARY	INSECURELY	INSIGHTFULLY
INORGANIZED	INSANENESS	INSECURENESS	INSIGNIFICANCE
INOSCULATE	INSANENESSES	INSECURENESSES	INSIGNIFICANCES
INOSCULATED	INSANITARINESS	INSECURITIES	INSIGNIFICANCY
INOSCULATES	INSANITARY	INSECURITY	INSIGNIFICANT
INOSCULATING	INSANITATION	INSELBERGE	INSIGNIFICANTLY
INOSCULATION	INSANITATIONS	INSELBERGS	INSIGNIFICATIVE
INOSCULATIONS	INSANITIES	INSEMINATE	INSINCERELY
INPATIENTS	INSATIABILITIES	INSEMINATED	INSINCERITIES
INPAYMENTS	INSATIABILITY	INSEMINATES	INSINCERITY
INPOURINGS	INSATIABLE	INSEMINATING	INSINEWING
INQUIETING	INSATIABLENESS	INSEMINATION	INSINUATED
INQUIETUDE	INSATIABLY	INSEMINATIONS	INSINUATES
INQUIETUDES	INSATIATELY	INSEMINATOR	INSINUATING
INQUILINES	INSATIATENESS	INSEMINATORS	INSINUATINGLY
INQUILINIC	INSATIATENESSES	INSENSATELY	INSINUATION
INQUILINICS	INSATIETIES	INSENSATENESS	INSINUATIONS
INQUILINISM	INSCIENCES	INSENSATENESSES	INSINUATIVE
INQUILINISMS	INSCONCING	INSENSIBILITIES	INSINUATOR
INQUILINITIES	INSCRIBABLE	INSENSIBILITY	INSINUATORS
INQUILINITY	INSCRIBABLENESS	INSENSIBLE	INSINUATORY
INQUILINOUS	INSCRIBERS	INSENSIBLENESS	INSIPIDITIES
INQUINATED	INSCRIBING	INSENSIBLY	INSIPIDITY
INQUINATES	INSCRIPTION	INSENSITIVE	INSIPIDNESS
INQUINATING	INSCRIPTIONAL	INSENSITIVELY	INSIPIDNESSES
INQUINATION	INSCRIPTIONS	INSENSITIVENESS	INSIPIENCE
INQUINATIONS	INSCRIPTIVE	INSENSITIVITIES	INSIPIENCES
INQUIRATION	INSCRIPTIVELY	INSENSITIVITY	INSIPIENTLY
INQUIRATIONS	INSCROLLED	INSENSUOUS	INSISTENCE
INQUIRENDO	INSCROLLING	INSENTIENCE	INSISTENCES
INQUIRENDOS	INSCRUTABILITY	INSENTIENCES	INSISTENCIES
INQUIRINGLY	INSCRUTABLE	INSENTIENCIES	INSISTENCY
INQUISITION	INSCRUTABLENESS	INSENTIENCY	INSISTENTLY
INQUISITIONAL	INSCRUTABLY	INSENTIENT	INSISTINGLY
INQUISITIONIST	INSCULPING	INSEPARABILITY	INSNAREMENT
INQUISITIONISTS	INSCULPTURE	INSEPARABLE	INSNAREMENTS
INQUISITIONS	INSCULPTURED	INSEPARABLENESS	INSOBRIETIES
INQUISITIVE	INSCULPTURES	INSEPARABLES	INSOBRIETY
INQUISITIVELY	INSCULPTURING	INSEPARABLY	INSOCIABILITIES
INQUISITIVENESS	INSECTARIA	INSEPARATE	INSOCIABILITY
INQUISITOR	INSECTARIES	INSERTABLE	INSOCIABLE
INQUISITORIAL	INSECTARIUM	INSERTIONAL	INSOCIABLY
INQUISITORIALLY	INSECTARIUMS	INSERTIONS	INSOLATING
INQUISITORS	INSECTICIDAL	INSESSORIAL	INSOLATION
INQUISITRESS	INSECTICIDALLY	INSEVERABLE	INSOLATIONS
INQUISITRESSES	INSECTICIDE	INSHEATHED	INSOLENCES
INQUISITURIENT	INSECTICIDES	INSHEATHES	INSOLENTLY
INRUSHINGS	INSECTIFORM	INSHEATHING	INSOLIDITIES
INSALIVATE	INSECTIFUGE	INSHELLING	INSOLIDITY
INSALIVATED	INSECTIFUGES	INSHELTERED	INSOLUBILISE
INSALIVATES	INSECTIONS	INSHELTERING	INSOLUBILISED
INSALIVATING	INSECTIVORE	INSHELTERS	INSOLUBILISES
INSALIVATION	INSECTIVORES	INSHIPPING	INSOLUBILISING
INSALIVATIONS	INSECTIVOROUS	INSHRINING	INSOLUBILITIES
INSALUBRIOUS	INSECTOLOGIES	INSIDIOUSLY	INSOLUBILITY

INSOLUBILIZE	INSPIRITINGLY	INSTILLMENT	INSUBJECTION
INSOLUBILIZED	INSPIRITMENT	INSTILLMENTS	INSUBJECTIONS
INSOLUBILIZES	INSPIRITMENTS	INSTILMENT	INSUBORDINATE
INSOLUBILIZING	INSPISSATE	INSTILMENTS	INSUBORDINATELY
INSOLUBLENESS	INSPISSATED	INSTINCTIVE	INSUBORDINATES
INSOLUBLENESSES	INSPISSATES	INSTINCTIVELY	INSUBORDINATION
INSOLUBLES	INSPISSATING	INSTINCTIVITIES	INSUBSTANTIAL
INSOLVABILITIES	INSPISSATION	INSTINCTIVITY	INSUBSTANTIALLY
INSOLVABILITY	INSPISSATIONS	INSTINCTUAL	INSUFFERABLE
INSOLVABLE	INSPISSATOR	INSTINCTUALLY	INSUFFERABLY
INSOLVABLY	INSPISSATORS	INSTITORIAL	INSUFFICIENCE
INSOLVENCIES	INSTABILITIES	INSTITUTED	INSUFFICIENCES
INSOLVENCY	INSTABILITY	INSTITUTER	INSUFFICIENCIES
INSOLVENTS	INSTALLANT	INSTITUTERS	INSUFFICIENCY
INSOMNIACS	INSTALLANTS	INSTITUTES	INSUFFICIENT
INSOMNIOUS	INSTALLATION	INSTITUTING	INSUFFICIENTLY
INSOMNOLENCE	INSTALLATIONS	INSTITUTION	INSUFFLATE
INSOMNOLENCES	INSTALLERS	INSTITUTIONAL	INSUFFLATED
INSOUCIANCE	INSTALLING	INSTITUTIONALLY	INSUFFLATES
INSOUCIANCES	INSTALLMENT	INSTITUTIONARY	INSUFFLATING
INSOUCIANT	INSTALLMENTS	INSTITUTIONS	INSUFFLATION
INSOUCIANTLY	INSTALMENT	INSTITUTIST	INSUFFLATIONS
INSOULMENT	INSTALMENTS	INSTITUTISTS	INSUFFLATOR
INSOULMENTS	INSTANCIES	INSTITUTIVE	INSUFFLATORS
INSPANNING	INSTANCING	INSTITUTIVELY	INSULARISM
INSPECTABLE	INSTANTANEITIES	INSTITUTOR	INSULARISMS
INSPECTING	INSTANTANEITY	INSTITUTORS	INSULARITIES
INSPECTINGLY	INSTANTANEOUS	INSTREAMING	INSULARITY
INSPECTION	INSTANTANEOUSLY	INSTREAMINGS	INSULATING
INSPECTIONAL	INSTANTIAL	INSTRESSED	INSULATION
INSPECTIONS	INSTANTIATE	INSTRESSES	INSULATIONS
INSPECTIVE	INSTANTIATED	INSTRESSING	INSULATORS
INSPECTORAL	INSTANTIATES	INSTRUCTED	INSULINASE
INSPECTORATE	INSTANTIATING	INSTRUCTIBLE	INSULINASES
INSPECTORATES	INSTANTIATION	INSTRUCTING	INSULSITIES
INSPECTORIAL	INSTANTIATIONS	INSTRUCTION	INSULTABLE
INSPECTORS	INSTANTNESS	INSTRUCTIONAL	INSULTINGLY
INSPECTORSHIP	INSTANTNESSES	INSTRUCTIONS	INSULTMENT
INSPECTORSHIPS	INSTARRING	INSTRUCTIVE	INSULTMENTS
INSPHERING	INSTATEMENT	INSTRUCTIVELY	INSUPERABILITY
INSPIRABLE	INSTATEMENTS	INSTRUCTIVENESS	INSUPERABLE
INSPIRATION	INSTAURATION	INSTRUCTOR	INSUPERABLENESS
INSPIRATIONAL	INSTAURATIONS	INSTRUCTORS	INSUPERABLY
INSPIRATIONALLY	INSTAURATOR	INSTRUCTORSHIP	INSUPPORTABLE
INSPIRATIONISM	INSTAURATORS	INSTRUCTORSHIPS	INSUPPORTABLY
INSPIRATIONISMS	INSTIGATED	INSTRUCTRESS	INSUPPRESSIBLE
INSPIRATIONIST	INSTIGATES	INSTRUCTRESSES	INSUPPRESSIBLY
INSPIRATIONISTS	INSTIGATING	INSTRUMENT	INSURABILITIES
INSPIRATIONS	INSTIGATINGLY	INSTRUMENTAL	INSURABILITY
INSPIRATIVE	INSTIGATION	INSTRUMENTALISM	INSURANCER
INSPIRATOR	INSTIGATIONS	INSTRUMENTALIST	INSURANCERS
INSPIRATORS	INSTIGATIVE	INSTRUMENTALITY	INSURANCES
INSPIRATORY	INSTIGATOR	INSTRUMENTALLY	INSURGENCE
INSPIRINGLY	INSTIGATORS	INSTRUMENTALS	INSURGENCES
INSPIRITED	INSTILLATION	INSTRUMENTATION	INSURGENCIES
INSPIRITER	INSTILLATIONS	INSTRUMENTED	INSURGENCY
INSPIRITERS	INSTILLERS	INSTRUMENTING	INSURGENTLY
INSPIRITING	INSTILLING	INSTRUMENTS	INSURGENTS

INSURMOUNTABLE	INTELLECTUALITY	INTENSIFIES	INTERBRAIN
INSURMOUNTABLY	INTELLECTUALIZE	INTENSIFYING	INTERBRAINS
INSURRECTION	INTELLECTUALLY	INTENSIONAL	INTERBRANCH
INSURRECTIONAL	INTELLECTUALS	INTENSIONALITY	INTERBREED
INSURRECTIONARY	INTELLIGENCE	INTENSIONALLY	INTERBREEDING
INSURRECTIONISM	INTELLIGENCER	INTENSIONS	INTERBREEDINGS
INSURRECTIONIST	INTELLIGENCERS	INTENSITIES	INTERBREEDS
INSURRECTIONS	INTELLIGENCES	INTENSITIVE	INTERBROKER
INSUSCEPTIBLE	INTELLIGENT	INTENSITIVES	INTERCALAR
INSUSCEPTIBLY	INTELLIGENTIAL	INTENSIVELY	INTERCALARILY
INSUSCEPTIVE	INTELLIGENTLY	INTENSIVENESS	INTERCALARY
INSUSCEPTIVELY	INTELLIGENTSIA	INTENSIVENESSES	INTERCALATE
INSWATHING	INTELLIGENTSIAS	INTENSIVES	INTERCALATED
INSWINGERS	INTELLIGENTZIA	INTENTIONAL	INTERCALATES
INTACTNESS	INTELLIGENTZIAS	INTENTIONALITY	INTERCALATING
INTACTNESSES	INTELLIGIBILITY	INTENTIONALLY	INTERCALATION
INTAGLIATED	INTELLIGIBLE	INTENTIONED	INTERCALATIONS
INTAGLIOED	INTELLIGIBLY	INTENTIONS	INTERCALATIVE
INTAGLIOING	INTEMERATE	INTENTNESS	INTERCAMPUS
INTANGIBILITIES	INTEMERATELY	INTENTNESSES	INTERCASTE
INTANGIBILITY	INTEMERATENESS	INTERABANG	INTERCEDED
INTANGIBLE	INTEMPERANCE	INTERABANGS	INTERCEDENT
INTANGIBLENESS	INTEMPERANCES	INTERACTANT	INTERCEDER
INTANGIBLES	INTEMPERANT	INTERACTANTS	INTERCEDERS
INTANGIBLY	INTEMPERANTS	INTERACTED	INTERCEDES
INTEGRABILITIES	INTEMPERATE	INTERACTING	INTERCEDING
INTEGRABILITY	INTEMPERATELY	INTERACTION	INTERCELLULAR
INTEGRABLE	INTEMPERATENESS	INTERACTIONAL	INTERCENSAL
INTEGRALITIES	INTEMPESTIVE	INTERACTIONISM	INTERCEPTED
INTEGRALITY	INTEMPESTIVELY	INTERACTIONISMS	INTERCEPTER
INTEGRALLY	INTEMPESTIVITY	INTERACTIONIST	INTERCEPTERS
INTEGRANDS	INTENDANCE	INTERACTIONISTS	INTERCEPTING
INTEGRANTS	INTENDANCES	INTERACTIONS	INTERCEPTION
INTEGRATED	INTENDANCIES	INTERACTIVE	INTERCEPTIONS
INTEGRATES	INTENDANCY	INTERACTIVELY	INTERCEPTIVE
INTEGRATING	INTENDANTS	INTERACTIVITIES	INTERCEPTOR
INTEGRATION	INTENDEDLY	INTERACTIVITY	INTERCEPTORS
INTEGRATIONIST	INTENDERED	INTERAGENCY	INTERCEPTS
INTEGRATIONISTS	INTENDERING	INTERALLELIC	INTERCESSION
INTEGRATIONS	INTENDMENT	INTERALLIED	INTERCESSIONAL
INTEGRATIVE	INTENDMENTS	INTERAMBULACRA	INTERCESSIONS
INTEGRATOR	INTENERATE	INTERAMBULACRAL	INTERCESSOR
INTEGRATORS	INTENERATED	INTERAMBULACRUM	INTERCESSORIAL
INTEGRITIES	INTENERATES	INTERANIMATION	INTERCESSORS
INTEGUMENT	INTENERATING	INTERANIMATIONS	INTERCESSORY
INTEGUMENTAL	INTENERATION	INTERANNUAL	INTERCHAIN
INTEGUMENTARY	INTENERATIONS	INTERARCHED	INTERCHAINED
INTEGUMENTS	INTENSATED	INTERARCHES	INTERCHAINING
INTELLECTED	INTENSATES	INTERARCHING	INTERCHAINS
INTELLECTION	INTENSATING	INTERATOMIC	INTERCHANGE
INTELLECTIONS	INTENSATIVE	INTERBASIN	INTERCHANGEABLE
INTELLECTIVE	INTENSATIVES	INTERBEDDED	INTERCHANGEABLY
INTELLECTIVELY	INTENSENESS	INTERBEDDING	INTERCHANGED
INTELLECTS	INTENSENESSES	INTERBEDDINGS	INTERCHANGEMENT
INTELLECTUAL	INTENSIFICATION	INTERBEHAVIOR	INTERCHANGER
INTELLECTUALISE	INTENSIFIED	INTERBEHAVIORAL	INTERCHANGERS
INTELLECTUALISM	INTENSIFIER	INTERBEHAVIORS	INTERCHANGES
INTELLECTUALIST	INTENSIFIERS	INTERBOROUGH	INTERCHANGING

INTERCHANNEL	INTERCORTICAL	INTERDIFFUSIONS	INTERFIBER
INTERCHAPTER	INTERCOSTAL	INTERDIGITAL	INTERFILED
INTERCHAPTERS	INTERCOSTALS	INTERDIGITATE	INTERFILES
INTERCHURCH	INTERCOUNTRY	INTERDIGITATED	INTERFILING
INTERCIPIENT	INTERCOUNTY	INTERDIGITATES	INTERFLOWED
INTERCIPIENTS	INTERCOUPLE	INTERDIGITATING	INTERFLOWING
INTERCLASS	INTERCOURSE	INTERDIGITATION	INTERFLOWS
INTERCLAVICLE	INTERCOURSES	INTERDINED	INTERFLUENCE
INTERCLAVICLES	INTERCRATER	INTERDINES	INTERFLUENCES
INTERCLAVICULAR	INTERCROPPED	INTERDINING	INTERFLUENT
INTERCLUDE	INTERCROPPING	INTERDISTRICT	INTERFLUOUS
INTERCLUDED	INTERCROPS	INTERDIVISIONAL	INTERFLUVE
INTERCLUDES	INTERCROSS	INTERDOMINION	INTERFLUVES
INTERCLUDING	INTERCROSSED	INTERELECTRODE	INTERFLUVIAL
INTERCLUSION	INTERCROSSES	INTERELECTRON	INTERFOLDED
INTERCLUSIONS	INTERCROSSING	INTERELECTRONIC	INTERFOLDING
INTERCLUSTER	INTERCRURAL	INTEREPIDEMIC	INTERFOLDS
INTERCOASTAL	INTERCULTURAL	INTERESSED	INTERFOLIATE
INTERCOLLEGIATE	INTERCULTURALLY	INTERESSES	INTERFOLIATED
INTERCOLLINE	INTERCULTURE	INTERESSING	INTERFOLIATES
INTERCOLONIAL	INTERCURRENCE	INTERESTED	INTERFOLIATING
INTERCOLONIALLY	INTERCURRENCES	INTERESTEDLY	INTERFRATERNITY
INTERCOLUMNAR	INTERCURRENT	INTERESTEDNESS	INTERFRETTED
INTERCOMMUNAL	INTERCURRENTLY	INTERESTING	INTERFRONTAL
INTERCOMMUNE	INTERCUTTING	INTERESTINGLY	INTERFUSED
INTERCOMMUNED	INTERDASHED	INTERESTINGNESS	INTERFUSES
INTERCOMMUNES	INTERDASHES	INTERETHNIC	INTERFUSING
INTERCOMMUNING	INTERDASHING	INTERFACED	INTERFUSION
INTERCOMMUNION	INTERDEALER	INTERFACES	INTERFUSIONS
INTERCOMMUNIONS	INTERDEALERS	INTERFACIAL	INTERGALACTIC
INTERCOMMUNITY	INTERDEALING	INTERFACIALLY	INTERGENERATION
INTERCOMPANY	INTERDEALS	INTERFACING	INTERGENERIC
INTERCOMPARE	INTERDEALT	INTERFACINGS	INTERGLACIAL
INTERCOMPARED	INTERDENTAL	INTERFACULTY	INTERGLACIALS
INTERCOMPARES	INTERDENTALLY	INTERFAITH	INTERGRADATION
INTERCOMPARING	INTERDEPEND	INTERFAMILIAL	INTERGRADATIONS
INTERCOMPARISON	INTERDEPENDED	INTERFAMILY	INTERGRADE
INTERCONNECT	INTERDEPENDENCE	INTERFASCICULAR	INTERGRADED
INTERCONNECTED	INTERDEPENDENCY	INTERFEMORAL	INTERGRADES
INTERCONNECTING	INTERDEPENDENT	INTERFERED	INTERGRADIENT
INTERCONNECTION	INTERDEPENDING	INTERFERENCE	INTERGRADING
INTERCONNECTOR	INTERDEPENDS	INTERFERENCES	INTERGRAFT
INTERCONNECTORS	INTERDIALECTAL	INTERFERENTIAL	INTERGRAFTED
INTERCONNECTS	INTERDICTED	INTERFERER	INTERGRAFTING
INTERCONNEXION	INTERDICTING	INTERFERERS	INTERGRAFTS
INTERCONNEXIONS	INTERDICTION	INTERFERES	INTERGRANULAR
INTERCONVERSION	INTERDICTIONS	INTERFERING	INTERGROUP
INTERCONVERT	INTERDICTIVE	INTERFERINGLY	INTERGROWING
INTERCONVERTED	INTERDICTIVELY	INTERFEROGRAM	INTERGROWN
INTERCONVERTING	INTERDICTOR	INTERFEROGRAMS	INTERGROWS
INTERCONVERTS	INTERDICTORS	INTERFEROMETER	INTERGROWTH
INTERCOOLED	INTERDICTORY	INTERFEROMETERS	INTERGROWTHS
INTERCOOLER	INTERDICTS	INTERFEROMETRIC	INTERINDIVIDUAL
INTERCOOLERS	INTERDIFFUSE	INTERFEROMETRY	INTERINDUSTRY
INTERCORPORATE	INTERDIFFUSED	INTERFERON	INTERINFLUENCE
INTERCORRELATE	INTERDIFFUSES	INTERFERONS	INTERINFLUENCES
INTERCORRELATED	INTERDIFFUSING	INTERFERTILE	INTERINVOLVE
INTERCORRELATES	INTERDIFFUSION	INTERFERTILITY	INTERINVOLVED

INTERINVOLVES	INTERLAMINATING	INTERLOCUTORILY	INTERMEDIN
INTERINVOLVING	INTERLAMINATION	INTERLOCUTORS	INTERMEDINS
INTERIONIC	INTERLAPPED	INTERLOCUTORY	INTERMEDIUM
INTERIORISATION	INTERLAPPING	INTERLOCUTRESS	INTERMEDIUMS
INTERIORISE	INTERLARDED	INTERLOCUTRICE	INTERMEMBRANE
INTERIORISED	INTERLARDING	INTERLOCUTRICES	INTERMENSTRUAL
INTERIORISES	INTERLARDS	INTERLOCUTRIX	INTERMENTS
INTERIORISING	INTERLAYER	INTERLOCUTRIXES	INTERMESHED
INTERIORITIES	INTERLAYERED	INTERLOOPED	INTERMESHES
INTERIORITY	INTERLAYERING	INTERLOOPING	INTERMESHING
INTERIORIZATION	INTERLAYERS	INTERLOOPS	INTERMETALLIC
INTERIORIZE	INTERLAYING	INTERLOPED	INTERMETALLICS
INTERIORIZED	INTERLEAVE	INTERLOPER	INTERMEZZI
INTERIORIZES	INTERLEAVED	INTERLOPERS	INTERMEZZO
INTERIORIZING	INTERLEAVES	INTERLOPES	INTERMEZZOS
INTERIORLY	INTERLEAVING	INTERLOPING	INTERMIGRATION
INTERISLAND	INTERLENDING	INTERLUDED	INTERMIGRATIONS
INTERJACENCIES	INTERLENDS	INTERLUDES	INTERMINABILITY
INTERJACENCY	INTERLEUKIN	INTERLUDIAL	INTERMINABLE
INTERJACENT	INTERLEUKINS	INTERLUDING	INTERMINABLY
INTERJACULATE	INTERLIBRARY	INTERLUNAR	INTERMINGLE
INTERJACULATED	INTERLINEAL	INTERLUNARY	INTERMINGLED
INTERJACULATES	INTERLINEALLY	INTERLUNATION	INTERMINGLES
INTERJACULATING	INTERLINEAR	INTERLUNATIONS	INTERMINGLING
INTERJACULATORY	INTERLINEARLY	INTERMARGINAL	INTERMISSION
INTERJECTED	INTERLINEARS	INTERMARRIAGE	INTERMISSIONS
INTERJECTING	INTERLINEATE	INTERMARRIAGES	INTERMISSIVE
INTERJECTION	INTERLINEATED	INTERMARRIED	INTERMITOTIC
INTERJECTIONAL	INTERLINEATES	INTERMARRIES	INTERMITTED
INTERJECTIONARY	INTERLINEATING	INTERMARRY	INTERMITTENCE
INTERJECTIONS	INTERLINEATION	INTERMARRYING	INTERMITTENCES
INTERJECTOR	INTERLINEATIONS	INTERMATTED	INTERMITTENCIES
INTERJECTORS	INTERLINED	INTERMATTING	INTERMITTENCY
INTERJECTORY	INTERLINER	INTERMAXILLA	INTERMITTENT
INTERJECTS	INTERLINERS	INTERMAXILLAE	INTERMITTENTLY
INTERJECTURAL	INTERLINES	INTERMAXILLARY	INTERMITTER
INTERJOINED	INTERLINGUA	INTERMEDDLE	INTERMITTERS
INTERJOINING	INTERLINGUAL	INTERMEDDLED	INTERMITTING
INTERJOINS	INTERLINGUALLY	INTERMEDDLER	INTERMITTINGLY
INTERKINESES	INTERLINGUAS	INTERMEDDLERS	INTERMITTOR
INTERKINESIS	INTERLINING	INTERMEDDLES	INTERMITTORS
INTERKNITS	INTERLININGS	INTERMEDDLING	INTERMIXED
INTERKNITTED	INTERLINKED	INTERMEDIA	INTERMIXES
INTERKNITTING	INTERLINKING	INTERMEDIACIES	INTERMIXING
INTERKNOTS	INTERLINKS	INTERMEDIACY	INTERMIXTURE
INTERKNOTTED	INTERLOANS	INTERMEDIAL	INTERMIXTURES
INTERKNOTTING	INTERLOBULAR	INTERMEDIARIES	INTERMODAL
INTERLACED	INTERLOCAL	INTERMEDIARY	INTERMODULATION
INTERLACEDLY	INTERLOCATION	INTERMEDIATE	INTERMOLECULAR
INTERLACEMENT	INTERLOCATIONS	INTERMEDIATED	INTERMONTANE
INTERLACEMENTS	INTERLOCKED	INTERMEDIATELY	INTERMUNDANE
INTERLACES	INTERLOCKER	INTERMEDIATES	INTERMURED
INTERLACING	INTERLOCKERS	INTERMEDIATING	INTERMURES
INTERLACUSTRINE	INTERLOCKING	INTERMEDIATION	INTERMURING
INTERLAMINAR	INTERLOCKS	INTERMEDIATIONS	INTERNALISATION
INTERLAMINATE	INTERLOCUTION	INTERMEDIATOR	INTERNALISE
INTERLAMINATED	INTERLOCUTIONS	INTERMEDIATORS	INTERNALISED
INTERLAMINATES	INTERLOCUTOR	INTERMEDIATORY	

INTERNALISES	INTERPAGING	INTERPOLATED	INTERRADIALLY
INTERNALISING	INTERPANDEMIC	INTERPOLATER	INTERRADII
INTERNALITIES	INTERPARIETAL	INTERPOLATERS	INTERRADIUS
INTERNALITY	INTERPARISH	INTERPOLATES	INTERRADIUSES
INTERNALIZATION	INTERPAROCHIAL	INTERPOLATING	INTERRAILED
INTERNALIZE	INTERPAROXYSMAL	INTERPOLATION	INTERRAILER
INTERNALIZED	INTERPARTICLE	INTERPOLATIONS	INTERRAILERS
INTERNALIZES	INTERPARTY	INTERPOLATIVE	INTERRAILING
INTERNALIZING	INTERPELLANT	INTERPOLATOR	INTERRAILS
INTERNALLY	INTERPELLANTS	INTERPOLATORS	INTERRAMAL
INTERNALNESS	INTERPELLATE	INTERPONED	INTERREGAL
INTERNALNESSES	INTERPELLATED	INTERPONES	INTERREGES
INTERNATIONAL	INTERPELLATES	INTERPONING	INTERREGIONAL
INTERNATIONALLY	INTERPELLATING	INTERPOPULATION	INTERREGNA
INTERNATIONALS	INTERPELLATION	INTERPOSABLE	INTERREGNAL
INTERNECINE	INTERPELLATIONS	INTERPOSAL	INTERREGNUM
INTERNECIVE	INTERPELLATOR	INTERPOSALS	INTERREGNUMS
INTERNEURAL	INTERPELLATORS	INTERPOSED	INTERRELATE
INTERNEURON	INTERPENETRABLE	INTERPOSER	INTERRELATED
INTERNEURONAL	INTERPENETRANT	INTERPOSERS	INTERRELATEDLY
INTERNEURONS	INTERPENETRATE	INTERPOSES	INTERRELATES
INTERNISTS	INTERPENETRATED	INTERPOSING	INTERRELATING
INTERNMENT	INTERPENETRATES	INTERPOSITION	INTERRELATION
INTERNMENTS	INTERPERCEPTUAL	INTERPOSITIONS	INTERRELATIONS
INTERNODAL	INTERPERMEATE	INTERPRETABLE	INTERRELIGIOUS
INTERNODES	INTERPERMEATED	INTERPRETABLY	INTERRENAL
INTERNODIAL	INTERPERMEATES	INTERPRETATE	INTERROBANG
INTERNSHIP	INTERPERMEATING	INTERPRETATED	INTERROBANGS
INTERNSHIPS	INTERPERSONAL	INTERPRETATES	INTERROGABLE
INTERNUCLEAR	INTERPERSONALLY	INTERPRETATING	INTERROGANT
INTERNUCLEON	INTERPETIOLAR	INTERPRETATION	INTERROGANTS
INTERNUCLEONIC	INTERPHALANGEAL	INTERPRETATIONS	INTERROGATE
INTERNUCLEOTIDE	INTERPHASE	INTERPRETATIVE	INTERROGATED
INTERNUNCIAL	INTERPHASES	INTERPRETED	INTERROGATEE
INTERNUNCIO	INTERPHONE	INTERPRETER	INTERROGATEES
INTERNUNCIOS	INTERPHONES	INTERPRETERS	INTERROGATES
INTEROBSERVER	INTERPILASTER	INTERPRETERSHIP	INTERROGATING
INTEROCEAN	INTERPILASTERS	INTERPRETESS	INTERROGATINGLY
INTEROCEANIC	INTERPLANETARY	INTERPRETESSES	INTERROGATION
INTEROCEPTIVE	INTERPLANT	INTERPRETING	INTERROGATIONAL
INTEROCEPTOR	INTERPLANTED	INTERPRETIVE	INTERROGATIONS
INTEROCEPTORS	INTERPLANTING	INTERPRETIVELY	INTERROGATIVE
INTEROCULAR	INTERPLANTS	INTERPRETRESS	INTERROGATIVELY
INTEROFFICE	INTERPLAYED	INTERPRETRESSES	INTERROGATIVES
INTEROPERABLE	INTERPLAYING	INTERPRETS	INTERROGATOR
INTEROPERATIVE	INTERPLAYS	INTERPROVINCIAL	INTERROGATORIES
INTERORBITAL	INTERPLEAD	INTERPROXIMAL	INTERROGATORILY
INTERORGAN	INTERPLEADED	INTERPSYCHIC	INTERROGATORS
INTEROSCULANT	INTERPLEADER	INTERPUNCTION	INTERROGATORY
INTEROSCULATE	INTERPLEADERS	INTERPUNCTIONS	INTERROGEE
INTEROSCULATED	INTERPLEADING	INTERPUNCTUATE	INTERROGEES
INTEROSCULATES	INTERPLEADS	INTERPUNCTUATED	INTERRUPTED
INTEROSCULATING	INTERPLEURAL	INTERPUNCTUATES	INTERRUPTEDLY
INTEROSCULATION	INTERPLUVIAL	INTERPUPILLARY	INTERRUPTER
INTEROSSEAL	INTERPOINT	INTERQUARTILE	INTERRUPTERS
INTEROSSEOUS	INTERPOLABLE	INTERRACIAL	INTERRUPTIBLE
INTERPAGED	INTERPOLAR	INTERRACIALLY	INTERRUPTING
INTERPAGES	INTERPOLATE	INTERRADIAL	INTERRUPTION

INTERRUPTIONS	INTERSTADIAL	INTERTWINING	INTERWEAVEMENT
INTERRUPTIVE	INTERSTADIALS	INTERTWININGLY	INTERWEAVEMENTS
INTERRUPTIVELY	INTERSTAGE	INTERTWININGS	INTERWEAVER
INTERRUPTOR	INTERSTATE	INTERTWIST	INTERWEAVERS
INTERRUPTORS	INTERSTATES	INTERTWISTED	INTERWEAVES
INTERRUPTS	INTERSTATION	INTERTWISTING	INTERWEAVING
INTERSCAPULAR	INTERSTELLAR	INTERTWISTINGLY	INTERWINDING
INTERSCHOLASTIC	INTERSTELLARY	INTERTWISTS	INTERWINDS
INTERSCHOOL	INTERSTERILE	INTERUNION	INTERWORKED
INTERSCRIBE	INTERSTERILITY	INTERUNIONS	INTERWORKING
INTERSCRIBED	INTERSTICE	INTERUNIVERSITY	INTERWORKINGS
INTERSCRIBES	INTERSTICES	INTERURBAN	INTERWORKS
INTERSCRIBING	INTERSTIMULUS	INTERVALES	INTERWOUND
INTERSECTED	INTERSTITIAL	INTERVALLEY	INTERWOVEN
INTERSECTING	INTERSTITIALLY	INTERVALLIC	INTERWREATHE
INTERSECTION	INTERSTITIALS	INTERVALLUM	INTERWREATHED
INTERSECTIONAL	INTERSTRAIN	INTERVALLUMS	INTERWREATHES
INTERSECTIONS	INTERSTRAND	INTERVALOMETER	INTERWREATHING
INTERSECTS	INTERSTRATIFIED	INTERVALOMETERS	INTERWROUGHT
INTERSEGMENT	INTERSTRATIFIES	INTERVARSITY	INTERZONAL
INTERSEGMENTAL	INTERSTRATIFY	INTERVEINED	INTERZONES
INTERSENSORY	INTERSUBJECTIVE	INTERVEINING	INTESTACIES
INTERSEPTAL	INTERSYSTEM	INTERVEINS	INTESTATES
INTERSERTAL	INTERTANGLE	INTERVENED	INTESTINAL
INTERSERTED	INTERTANGLED	INTERVENER	INTESTINALLY
INTERSERTING	INTERTANGLEMENT	INTERVENERS	INTESTINES
INTERSERTS	INTERTANGLES	INTERVENES	INTHRALLED
INTERSERVICE	INTERTANGLING	INTERVENIENT	INTHRALLING
INTERSESSION	INTERTARSAL	INTERVENING	INTHRONING
INTERSESSIONS	INTERTENTACULAR	INTERVENOR	INTIFADAHS
INTERSEXES	INTERTERMINAL	INTERVENORS	INTIFADEHS
INTERSEXUAL	INTERTEXTS	INTERVENTION	INTIMACIES
INTERSEXUALISM	INTERTEXTUAL	INTERVENTIONAL	INTIMATELY
INTERSEXUALISMS	INTERTEXTUALITY	INTERVENTIONISM	INTIMATENESS
INTERSEXUALITY	INTERTEXTUALLY	INTERVENTIONIST	INTIMATENESSES
INTERSEXUALLY	INTERTEXTURE	INTERVENTIONS	INTIMATERS
INTERSIDEREAL	INTERTEXTURES	INTERVENTOR	INTIMATING
INTERSOCIETAL	INTERTIDAL	INTERVENTORS	INTIMATION
INTERSOCIETY	INTERTIDALLY	INTERVERTEBRAL	INTIMATIONS
INTERSPACE	INTERTILLAGE	INTERVIEWED	INTIMIDATE
INTERSPACED	INTERTILLAGES	INTERVIEWEE	INTIMIDATED
INTERSPACES	INTERTILLED	INTERVIEWEES	INTIMIDATES
INTERSPACING	INTERTILLING	INTERVIEWER	INTIMIDATING
INTERSPATIAL	INTERTILLS	INTERVIEWERS	INTIMIDATINGLY
INTERSPATIALLY	INTERTISSUED	INTERVIEWING	INTIMIDATION
INTERSPECIES	INTERTRAFFIC	INTERVIEWS	INTIMIDATIONS
INTERSPECIFIC	INTERTRAFFICS	INTERVILLAGE	INTIMIDATOR
INTERSPERSAL	INTERTRIAL	INTERVISIBILITY	INTIMIDATORS
INTERSPERSALS	INTERTRIBAL	INTERVISIBLE	INTIMIDATORY
INTERSPERSE	INTERTRIGO	INTERVISITATION	INTIMISTES
INTERSPERSED	INTERTRIGOS	INTERVITAL	INTIMITIES
INTERSPERSEDLY	INTERTROOP	INTERVOCALIC	INTINCTION
INTERSPERSES	INTERTROPICAL	INTERVOLVE	INTINCTIONS
INTERSPERSING	INTERTWINE	INTERVOLVED	INTITULING
INTERSPERSION	INTERTWINED	INTERVOLVES	INTOLERABILITY
INTERSPERSIONS	INTERTWINEMENT	INTERVOLVING	INTOLERABLE
INTERSPINAL	INTERTWINEMENTS	INTERWEAVE	INTOLERABLENESS
INTERSPINOUS	INTERTWINES	INTERWEAVED	INTOLERABLY

INTOLERANCE	INTRAMEDULLARY	INTRAVENOUSLY	INTROGRESSIVE
INTOLERANCES	INTRAMERCURIAL	INTRAVITAL	INTROITUSES
INTOLERANT	INTRAMOLECULAR	INTRAVITALLY	INTROJECTED
INTOLERANTLY	INTRAMUNDANE	INTRAVITAM	INTROJECTING
INTOLERANTNESS	INTRAMURAL	INTRAZONAL	INTROJECTION
INTOLERANTS	INTRAMURALLY	INTREATFULL	INTROJECTIONS
INTOLERATION	INTRAMUSCULAR	INTREATING	INTROJECTIVE
INTOLERATIONS	INTRAMUSCULARLY	INTREATINGLY	INTROJECTS
INTONATING	INTRANASAL	INTREATMENT	INTROMISSIBLE
INTONATION	INTRANASALLY	INTREATMENTS	INTROMISSION
INTONATIONAL	INTRANATIONAL	INTRENCHANT	INTROMISSIONS
INTONATIONS	INTRANSIGEANCE	INTRENCHED	INTROMISSIVE
INTONATORS	INTRANSIGEANCES	INTRENCHER	INTROMITTED
INTONINGLY	INTRANSIGEANT	INTRENCHERS	INTROMITTENT
INTORSIONS	INTRANSIGEANTLY	INTRENCHES	INTROMITTER
INTORTIONS	INTRANSIGEANTS	INTRENCHING	INTROMITTERS
INTOXICABLE	INTRANSIGENCE	INTRENCHMENT	INTROMITTING
INTOXICANT	INTRANSIGENCES	INTRENCHMENTS	INTRORSELY
INTOXICANTS	INTRANSIGENCIES	INTREPIDITIES	INTROSPECT
INTOXICATE	INTRANSIGENCY	INTREPIDITY	INTROSPECTED
INTOXICATED	INTRANSIGENT	INTREPIDLY	INTROSPECTING
INTOXICATEDLY	INTRANSIGENTISM	INTREPIDNESS	INTROSPECTION
INTOXICATES	INTRANSIGENTIST	INTREPIDNESSES	INTROSPECTIONAL
INTOXICATING	INTRANSIGENTLY	INTRICACIES	INTROSPECTIONS
INTOXICATINGLY	INTRANSIGENTS	INTRICATELY	INTROSPECTIVE
INTOXICATION	INTRANSITIVE	INTRICATENESS	INTROSPECTIVELY
INTOXICATIONS	INTRANSITIVELY	INTRICATENESSES	INTROSPECTS
INTOXICATIVE	INTRANSITIVITY	INTRIGANTE	INTROSUSCEPTION
INTOXICATOR	INTRANSMISSIBLE	INTRIGANTES	INTROVERSIBLE
INTOXICATORS	INTRANSMUTABLE	INTRIGANTS	INTROVERSION
INTOXIMETER	INTRANUCLEAR	INTRIGUANT	INTROVERSIONS
INTOXIMETERS	INTRAOCULAR	INTRIGUANTE	INTROVERSIVE
INTRACAPSULAR	INTRAOCULARLY	INTRIGUANTES	INTROVERSIVELY
INTRACARDIAC	INTRAPARIETAL	INTRIGUANTS	INTROVERTED
INTRACARDIAL	INTRAPARTUM	INTRIGUERS	INTROVERTING
INTRACARDIALLY	INTRAPERITONEAL	INTRIGUING	INTROVERTIVE
INTRACAVITARY	INTRAPERSONAL	INTRIGUINGLY	INTROVERTS
INTRACELLULAR	INTRAPETIOLAR	INTRINSICAL	INTRUDINGLY
INTRACELLULARLY	INTRAPLATE	INTRINSICALITY	INTRUSIONAL
INTRACEREBRAL	INTRAPOPULATION	INTRINSICALLY	INTRUSIONIST
INTRACEREBRALLY	INTRAPRENEUR	INTRINSICALNESS	INTRUSIONISTS
INTRACOMPANY	INTRAPRENEURIAL	INTRINSICATE	INTRUSIONS
INTRACRANIAL	INTRAPRENEURS	INTRODUCED	INTRUSIVELY
INTRACRANIALLY	INTRAPSYCHIC	INTRODUCER	INTRUSIVENESS
INTRACTABILITY	INTRASEXUAL	INTRODUCERS	INTRUSIVENESSES
INTRACTABLE	INTRASPECIES	INTRODUCES	INTRUSIVES
INTRACTABLENESS	INTRASPECIFIC	INTRODUCIBLE	INTRUSTING
INTRACTABLY	INTRASTATE	INTRODUCING	INTRUSTMENT
INTRACUTANEOUS	INTRATELLURIC	INTRODUCTION	INTRUSTMENTS
INTRADERMAL	INTRATHECAL	INTRODUCTIONS	INTUBATING
INTRADERMALLY	INTRATHECALLY	INTRODUCTIVE	INTUBATION
INTRADERMIC	INTRATHORACIC	INTRODUCTORILY	INTUBATIONS
INTRADERMICALLY	INTRAUTERINE	INTRODUCTORY	INTUITABLE
INTRADOSES	INTRAVASATION	INTROFYING	INTUITIONAL
INTRAFALLOPIAN	INTRAVASATIONS	INTROGRESSANT	INTUITIONALISM
INTRAFASCICULAR	INTRAVASCULAR	INTROGRESSANTS	INTUITIONALISMS
INTRAGALACTIC	INTRAVASCULARLY	INTROGRESSION	INTUITIONALIST
INTRAGENIC	INTRAVENOUS	INTROGRESSIONS	INTUITIONALISTS

INTUITIONALLY	INVAGINATIONS	INVENTORIAL	INVIGILATORS
INTUITIONISM	INVALIDATE	INVENTORIALLY	INVIGORANT
INTUITIONISMS	INVALIDATED	INVENTORIED	INVIGORANTS
INTUITIONIST	INVALIDATES	INVENTORIES	INVIGORATE
INTUITIONISTS	INVALIDATING	INVENTORYING	INVTGORATED
INTUITIONS	INVALIDATION	INVENTRESS	INVIGORATES
INTUITIVELY	INVALIDATIONS	INVENTRESSES	INVIGORATING
INTUITIVENESS	INVALIDATOR	INVERACITIES	INVIGORATINGLY
INTUITIVENESSES	INVALIDATORS	INVERACITY	INVIGORATION
INTUITIVISM	INVALIDHOOD	INVERITIES	INVIGORATIONS
INTUITIVISMS	INVALIDHOODS	INVERNESSES	INVIGORATIVE
INTUMESCED	INVALIDING	INVERSIONS	INVIGORATIVELY
INTUMESCENCE	INVALIDINGS	INVERTASES	INVIGORATOR
INTUMESCENCES	INVALIDISM	INVERTEBRAL	INVIGORATORS
INTUMESCENCIES	INVALIDISMS	INVERTEBRATE	INVINCIBILITIES
INTUMESCENCY	INVALIDITIES	INVERTEBRATES	INVINCIBILITY
INTUMESCENT	INVALIDITY	INVERTEDLY	INVINCIBLE
INTUMESCES	INVALIDNESS	INVERTIBILITIES	INVINCIBLENESS
INTUMESCING	INVALIDNESSES	INVERTIBILITY	INVINCIBLY
INTURBIDATE	INVALUABLE	INVERTIBLE	INVIOLABILITIES
INTURBIDATED	INVALUABLENESS	INVESTABLE	INVIOLABILITY
INTURBIDATES	INVALUABLY	INVESTIBLE	INVIOLABLE
INTURBIDATING	INVARIABILITIES	INVESTIGABLE	INVIOLABLENESS
INTUSSUSCEPT	INVARIABILITY	INVESTIGATE	INVIOLABLY
INTUSSUSCEPTED	INVARIABLE	INVESTIGATED	INVIOLACIES
INTUSSUSCEPTING	INVARIABLENESS	INVESTIGATES	INVIOLATED
INTUSSUSCEPTION	INVARIABLES	INVESTIGATING	INVIOLATELY
INTUSSUSCEPTIVE	INVARIABLY	INVESTIGATION	INVIOLATENESS
INTUSSUSCEPTS	INVARIANCE	INVESTIGATIONAL	INVIOLATENESSES
INTWINEMENT	INVARIANCES	INVESTIGATIONS	INVISIBILITIES
INTWINEMENTS	INVARIANCIES	INVESTIGATIVE	INVISIBILITY
INTWISTING	INVARIANCY	INVESTIGATOR	INVISIBLENESS
INUMBRATED	INVARIANTS	INVESTIGATORS	INVISIBLENESSES
INUMBRATES	INVASIVENESS	INVESTIGATORY	INVISIBLES
INUMBRATING	INVASIVENESSES	INVESTITIVE	INVITATION
INUNCTIONS	INVEAGLING	INVESTITURE	INVITATIONAL
INUNDATING	INVECTIVELY	INVESTITURES	INVITATIONALS
INUNDATION	INVECTIVENESS	INVESTMENT	INVITATIONS
INUNDATIONS	INVECTIVENESSES	INVESTMENTS	INVITATORIES
INUNDATORS	INVECTIVES	INVETERACIES	INVITATORY
INUNDATORY	INVEIGHERS	INVETERACY	INVITEMENT
INURBANELY	INVEIGHING	INVETERATE	INVITEMENTS
INURBANITIES	INVEIGLEMENT	INVETERATELY	INVITINGLY
INURBANITY	INVEIGLEMENTS	INVETERATENESS	INVITINGNESS
INUREDNESS	INVEIGLERS	INVIABILITIES	INVITINGNESSES
INUREDNESSES	INVEIGLING	INVIABILITY	INVOCATING
INUREMENTS	INVENDIBILITIES	INVIABLENESS	INVOCATION
INURNMENTS	INVENDIBILITY	INVIABLENESSES	INVOCATIONAL
INUSITATION	INVENDIBLE	INVIDIOUSLY	INVOCATIONS
INUSITATIONS	INVENTABLE	INVIDIOUSNESS	INVOCATIVE
INUTILITIES	INVENTIBLE	INVIDIOUSNESSES	INVOCATORS
INUTTERABLE	INVENTIONAL	INVIGILATE	INVOCATORY
INVAGINABLE	INVENTIONLESS	INVIGILATED	INVOLUCELLA
INVAGINATE	INVENTIONS	INVIGILATES	INVOLUCELLATE
INVAGINATED	INVENTIVELY	INVIGILATING	INVOLUCELLATED
INVAGINATES	INVENTIVENESS	INVIGILATION	INVOLUCELLUM
INVAGINATING	INVENTIVENESSES	INVIGILATIONS	INVOLUCELS
INVAGINATION	INVENTORIABLE	INVIGILATOR	INVOLUCRAL

INVOLUCRATE	IPECACUANHAS	IRONSMITHS	IRRECONCILED
INVOLUCRES	IPRATROPIUM	IRONSTONES	IRRECONCILEMENT
INVOLUCRUM	IPRATROPIUMS	IRONWORKER	IRRECOVERABLE
INVOLUNTARILY	IPRINDOLES	IRONWORKERS	IRRECOVERABLY
INVOLUNTARINESS	IPRONIAZID	IRRADIANCE	IRRECUSABLE
INVOLUNTARY	IPRONIAZIDS	IRRADIANCES	IRRECUSABLY
INVOLUTEDLY	IPSELATERAL	IRRADIANCIES	IRREDEEMABILITY
INVOLUTELY	IPSILATERAL	IRRADIANCY	IRREDEEMABLE
INVOLUTING	IPSILATERALLY	IRRADIATED	IRREDEEMABLES
INVOLUTION	IRACUNDITIES	IRRADIATES	IRREDEEMABLY
INVOLUTIONAL	IRACUNDITY	IRRADIATING	IRREDENTAS
INVOLUTIONS	IRACUNDULOUS	IRRADIATION	IRREDENTISM
INVOLVEDLY	IRASCIBILITIES	IRRADIATIONS	IRREDENTISMS
INVOLVEMENT	IRASCIBILITY	IRRADIATIVE	IRREDENTIST
INVOLVEMENTS	IRASCIBLENESS	IRRADIATOR	IRREDENTISTS
INVULNERABILITY	IRASCIBLENESSES	IRRADIATORS	IRREDUCIBILITY
INVULNERABLE	IRATENESSES	IRRADICABLE	IRREDUCIBLE
INVULNERABLY	IREFULNESS	IRRADICABLY	IRREDUCIBLENESS
INVULTUATION	IREFULNESSES	IRRADICATE	IRREDUCIBLY
INVULTUATIONS	IRENICALLY	IRRADICATED	IRREDUCTIBILITY
INWARDNESS	IRENICISMS	IRRADICATES	IRREDUCTION
INWARDNESSES	IRENOLOGIES	IRRADICATING	IRREDUCTIONS
INWORKINGS	IRIDACEOUS	IRRATIONAL	IRREFLECTION
INWRAPPING	IRIDECTOMIES	IRRATIONALISE	IRREFLECTIONS
INWREATHED	IRIDECTOMY	IRRATIONALISED	IRREFLECTIVE
INWREATHES	IRIDESCENCE	IRRATIONALISES	IRREFLEXION
INWREATHING	IRIDESCENCES	IRRATIONALISING	IRREFLEXIONS
IODINATING	IRIDESCENT	IRRATIONALISM	IRREFLEXIVE
IODINATION	IRIDESCENTLY	IRRATIONALISMS	IRREFORMABILITY
IODINATIONS	IRIDISATION	IRRATIONALIST	IRREFORMABLE
IODISATION	IRIDISATIONS	IRRATIONALISTIC	IRREFORMABLY
IODISATIONS	IRIDIZATION	IRRATIONALISTS	IRREFRAGABILITY
IODIZATION	IRIDIZATIONS	IRRATIONALITIES	IRREFRAGABLE
IODIZATIONS	IRIDOCYTES	IRRATIONALITY	IRREFRAGABLY
IODOMETRIC	IRIDOLOGIES	IRRATIONALIZE	IRREFRANGIBLE
IODOMETRICAL	IRIDOLOGIST	IRRATIONALIZED	IRREFRANGIBLY
IODOMETRICALLY	IRIDOLOGISTS	IRRATIONALIZES	IRREFUTABILITY
IODOMETRIES	IRIDOSMINE	IRRATIONALIZING	IRREFUTABLE
IONICITIES	IRIDOSMINES	IRRATIONALLY	IRREFUTABLENESS
IONISATION	IRIDOSMIUM	IRRATIONALNESS	IRREFUTABLY
IONISATIONS	IRIDOSMIUMS	IRRATIONALS	IRREGARDLESS
IONIZATION	IRIDOTOMIES	IRREALISABLE	IRREGULARITIES
IONIZATIONS	IRISATIONS	IRREALITIES	IRREGULARITY
IONOPAUSES	IRKSOMENESS	IRREALIZABLE	IRREGULARLY
IONOPHORES	IRKSOMENESSES	IRREBUTTABLE	IRREGULARS
IONOPHORESES	IRONFISTED	IRRECEPTIVE	IRRELATION
IONOPHORESIS	IRONHANDED	IRRECIPROCAL	IRRELATIONS
IONOSONDES	IRONHEARTED	IRRECIPROCITIES	IRRELATIVE
IONOSPHERE	IRONICALLY	IRRECIPROCITY	IRRELATIVELY
IONOSPHERES	IRONICALNESS	IRRECLAIMABLE	IRRELATIVENESS
IONOSPHERIC	IRONICALNESSES	IRRECLAIMABLY	IRRELEVANCE
IONOSPHERICALLY	IRONMASTER	IRRECOGNISABLE	IRRELEVANCES
IONOTROPIC	IRONMASTERS	IRRECOGNITION	IRRELEVANCIES
IONOTROPIES	IRONMONGER	IRRECOGNITIONS	IRRELEVANCY
IONTOPHORESES	IRONMONGERIES	IRRECOGNIZABLE	IRRELEVANT
IONTOPHORESIS	IRONMONGERS	IRRECONCILABLE	IRRELEVANTLY
IONTOPHORETIC	IRONMONGERY	IRRECONCILABLES	IRRELIEVABLE
IPECACUANHA	IRONNESSES	IRRECONCILABLY	IRRELIGION

IRRELIGIONIST	IRRESPECTIVE	ISEIKONIAS	ISOCYANATE
IRRELIGIONISTS	IRRESPECTIVELY	ISENTROPIC	ISOCYANATES
IRRELIGIONS	IRRESPIRABLE	ISENTROPICALLY	ISOCYANIDE
TRRELIGIOUS	IRRESPONSIBLE	ISINGLASSES	ISOCYANIDES
IRRELIGIOUSLY	IRRESPONSIBLES	ISLOMANIAS	ISODIAMETRIC
IRRELIGIOUSNESS	IRRESPONSIBLY	ISMATICALNESS	ISODIAMETRICAL
IRREMEABLE	IRRESPONSIVE	ISMATICALNESSES	ISODIAPHERE
IRREMEABLY	IRRESPONSIVELY	ISOAGGLUTININ	ISODIAPHERES
IRREMEDIABLE	IRRESTRAINABLE	ISOAGGLUTININS	ISODIMORPHIC
IRREMEDIABLY	IRRESUSCITABLE	ISOALLOXAZINE	ISODIMORPHISM
IRREMISSIBILITY	IRRESUSCITABLY	ISOALLOXAZINES	ISODIMORPHISMS
IRREMISSIBLE	IRRETENTION	ISOAMINILE	ISODIMORPHOUS
IRREMISSIBLY	IRRETENTIONS	ISOAMINILES	ISODONTALS
IRREMISSION	IRRETENTIVE	ISOANTIBODIES	ISODYNAMIC
IRREMISSIONS	IRRETENTIVENESS	ISOANTIBODY	ISODYNAMICS
IRREMISSIVE	IRRETRIEVABLE	ISOANTIGEN	ISOELECTRIC
IRREMOVABILITY	IRRETRIEVABLY	ISOANTIGENIC	ISOELECTRONIC
IRREMOVABLE	IRREVERENCE	ISOANTIGENS	ISOENZYMATIC
IRREMOVABLENESS	IRREVERENCES	ISOBARISMS	ISOENZYMES
IRREMOVABLY	IRREVERENT	ISOBAROMETRIC	ISOENZYMIC
IRRENOWNED	IRREVERENTIAL	ISOBILATERAL	ISOFLAVONE
IRREPAIRABLE	IRREVERENTLY	ISOBUTANES	ISOFLAVONES
IRREPARABILITY	IRREVERSIBILITY	ISOBUTENES	ISOGAMETES
IRREPARABLE	IRREVERSIBLE	ISOBUTYLENE	ISOGAMETIC
IRREPARABLENESS	IRREVERSIBLY	ISOBUTYLENES	ISOGENETIC
IRREPARABLY	IRREVOCABILITY	ISOCALORIC	ISOGEOTHERM
IRREPEALABILITY	IRREVOCABLE	ISOCARBOXAZID	ISOGEOTHERMAL
IRREPEALABLE	IRREVOCABLENESS	ISOCARBOXAZIDS	ISOGEOTHERMALS
IRREPEALABLY	IRREVOCABLY	ISOCHASMIC	ISOGEOTHERMIC
IRREPLACEABLE	IRRIDENTAS	ISOCHEIMAL	ISOGEOTHERMICS
IRREPLACEABLY	IRRIGATING	ISOCHEIMALS	ISOGEOTHERMS
IRREPLEVIABLE	IRRIGATION	ISOCHEIMENAL	ISOGLOSSAL
IRREPLEVISABLE	IRRIGATIONAL	ISOCHEIMENALS	ISOGLOSSES
IRREPREHENSIBLE	IRRIGATIONS	ISOCHEIMIC	ISOGLOSSIC
IRREPREHENSIBLY	IRRIGATIVE	ISOCHIMALS	ISOGLOTTAL
IRREPRESSIBLE	IRRIGATORS	ISOCHROMATIC	ISOGLOTTIC
IRREPRESSIBLY	IRRITABILITIES	ISOCHROMOSOME	ISOGRAFTED
IRREPROACHABLE	IRRITABILITY	ISOCHROMOSOMES	ISOGRAFTING
IRREPROACHABLY	IRRITABLENESS	ISOCHRONAL	ISOHYETALS
IRREPRODUCIBLE	IRRITABLENESSES	ISOCHRONALLY	ISOIMMUNISATION
IRREPROVABLE	IRRITANCIES	ISOCHRONES	ISOIMMUNIZATION
IRREPROVABLY	IRRITATING	ISOCHRONISE	ISOKINETIC
IRRESISTANCE	IRRITATINGLY	ISOCHRONISED	ISOKONTANS
IRRESISTANCES	IRRITATION	ISOCHRONISES	ISOLABILITIES
IRRESISTIBILITY	IRRITATIONS	ISOCHRONISING	ISOLABILITY
IRRESISTIBLE	IRRITATIVE	ISOCHRONISM	ISOLATABLE
IRRESISTIBLY	IRRITATORS	ISOCHRONISMS	ISOLATIONISM
IRRESOLUBILITY	IRROTATIONAL	ISOCHRONIZE	ISOLATIONISMS
IRRESOLUBLE	IRRUPTIONS	ISOCHRONIZED	ISOLATIONIST
IRRESOLUBLY	IRRUPTIVELY	ISOCHRONIZES	ISOLATIONISTS
IRRESOLUTE	ISABELLINE	ISOCHRONIZING	ISOLATIONS
IRRESOLUTELY	ISABELLINES	ISOCHRONOUS	ISOLECITHAL
IRRESOLUTENESS	ISALLOBARIC	ISOCHRONOUSLY	ISOLEUCINE
IRRESOLUTION	ISALLOBARS	ISOCHROOUS	ISOLEUCINES
IRRESOLUTIONS	ISAPOSTOLIC	ISOCLINALS	ISOMAGNETIC
IRRESOLVABILITY	ISCHAEMIAS	ISOCLINICS	ISOMAGNETICS
IRRESOLVABLE	ISCHURETIC	ISOCRACIES	ISOMERASES
IRRESOLVABLY	ISCHURETICS	ISOCRYMALS	ISOMERISATION

ISOMERISATIONS	ISOSTATICALLY	ITEROPARITY
ISOMERISED	ISOSTEMONOUS	ITEROPAROUS
ISOMERISES	ISOSTHENURIA	ITHYPHALLI
ISOMERISING	ISOSTHENURIAS	ITHYPHALLIC
ISOMERISMS	ISOTENISCOPE	ITHYPHALLICS
ISOMERIZATION	ISOTENISCOPES	ITHYPHALLUS
ISOMERIZATIONS	ISOTHERALS	ITHYPHALLUSES
ISOMERIZED	ISOTHERMAL	ITINERACIES
ISOMERIZES	ISOTHERMALLY	ITINERANCIES
ISOMERIZING	ISOTHERMALS	ITINERANCY
ISOMETRICAL	ISOTONICALLY	ITINERANTLY
ISOMETRICALLY	ISOTONICITIES	ITINERANTS
ISOMETRICS	ISOTONICITY	ITINERARIES
ISOMETRIES	ISOTOPICALLY	ITINERATED
ISOMETROPIA	ISOTRETINOIN	ITINERATES
ISOMETROPIAS	ISOTRETINOINS	ITINERATING
ISOMORPHIC	ISOTROPICALLY	ITINERATION
ISOMORPHICALLY	ISOTROPIES	ITINERATIONS
ISOMORPHISM	ISOTROPISM	IVERMECTIN
ISOMORPHISMS	ISOTROPISMS	IVERMECTINS
ISOMORPHOUS	ISOTROPOUS	IVORYBILLS
ISONIAZIDE	ISOXSUPRINE	IVORYWOODS
ISONIAZIDES	ISOXSUPRINES	IZVESTIYAS
ISONIAZIDS	ISPAGHULAS	
ISONITRILE	ITACOLUMITE	
ISONITRILES	ITACOLUMITES	
ISOOCTANES	ITALIANATE	
ISOPACHYTE	ITALIANATED	
ISOPACHYTES	ITALIANATES	
ISOPERIMETER	ITALIANATING	
ISOPERIMETERS	ITALIANISE	
ISOPERIMETRICAL	ITALIANISED	
ISOPERIMETRIES	ITALIANISES	
ISOPERIMETRY	ITALIANISING	
ISOPIESTIC	ITALIANIZE	
ISOPIESTICALLY	ITALIANIZED	
ISOPLETHIC	ITALIANIZES	
ISOPOLITIES	ITALIANIZING	
ISOPRENALINE	ITALICISATION	
ISOPRENALINES	ITALICISATIONS	
ISOPRENOID	ITALICISED	
ISOPROPYLS	ITALICISES	
ISOPROTERENOL	ITALICISING	
ISOPROTERENOLS	ITALICIZATION	
ISOPTEROUS	ITALICIZATIONS	
ISOPYCNALS	ITALICIZED	
ISOPYCNICS	ITALICIZES	
ISORHYTHMIC	ITALICIZING	
ISOSEISMAL	ITCHINESSES	
ISOSEISMALS	ITEMISATION	
ISOSEISMIC	ITEMISATIONS	
ISOSEISMICS	ITEMIZATION	
ISOSMOTICALLY	ITEMIZATIONS	
ISOSPONDYLOUS	ITERATIONS	
ISOSPORIES	ITERATIVELY	
ISOSPOROUS	ITERATIVENESS	
ISOSTACIES	ITERATIVENESSES	
ISOSTASIES	ITEROPARITIES	

J

JABBERINGLY
JABBERINGS
JABBERWOCK
JABBERWOCKIES
JABBERWOCKS
JABBERWOCKY
JABORANDIS
JABOTICABA
JABOTICABAS
JACARANDAS
JACKALLING
JACKANAPES
JACKANAPESES
JACKAROOED
JACKAROOING
JACKASSERIES
JACKASSERY
JACKBOOTED
JACKBOOTING
JACKEROOED
JACKEROOING
JACKETLESS
JACKFISHES
JACKFRUITS
JACKHAMMER
JACKHAMMERED
JACKHAMMERING
JACKHAMMERS
JACKKNIFED
JACKKNIFES
JACKKNIFING
JACKKNIVES
JACKLIGHTED
JACKLIGHTING
JACKLIGHTS
JACKPLANES
JACKRABBIT
JACKRABBITS
JACKROLLED
JACKROLLING
JACKSCREWS
JACKSHAFTS
JACKSMELTS
JACKSMITHS
JACKSNIPES
JACKSTONES
JACKSTRAWS
JACQUERIES
JACTATIONS
JACTITATION
JACTITATIONS
JACULATING
JACULATION
JACULATIONS

JACULATORS
JACULATORY
JADEDNESSES
JADISHNESS
JADISHNESSES
JAGGEDNESS
JAGGEDNESSES
JAGGHERIES
JAGHIRDARS
JAGUARONDI
JAGUARONDIS
JAGUARUNDI
JAGUARUNDIS
JAILBREAKS
JAILERESSES
JAILHOUSES
JAILORESSES
JAMAHIRIYA
JAMAHIRIYAS
JAMBALAYAS
JAMBOKKING
JAMBOLANAS
JANISARIES
JANISSARIES
JANITORIAL
JANITORSHIP
JANITORSHIPS
JANITRESSES
JANITRIXES
JANIZARIAN
JANIZARIES
JAPANISING
JAPANIZING
JAPONAISERIE
JAPONAISERIES
JARDINIERE
JARDINIERES
JARGONEERS
JARGONELLE
JARGONELLES
JARGONISATION
JARGONISATIONS
JARGONISED
JARGONISES
JARGONISING
JARGONISTIC
JARGONISTS
JARGONIZATION
JARGONIZATIONS
JARGONIZED
JARGONIZES
JARGONIZING
JARLSBERGS
JAROVISING

JAROVIZING
JASPERISED
JASPERISES
JASPERISING
JASPERIZED
JASPERIZES
JASPERIZING
JASPERWARE
JASPERWARES
JASPIDEOUS
JASPILITES
JAUNDICING
JAUNTINESS
JAUNTINESSES
JAUNTINGLY
JAVELINING
JAWBATIONS
JAWBONINGS
JAWBREAKER
JAWBREAKERS
JAWBREAKING
JAWBREAKINGLY
JAWBREAKINGS
JAWCRUSHER
JAWCRUSHERS
JAWDROPPINGLY
JAYHAWKERS
JAYWALKERS
JAYWALKING
JAYWALKINGS
JAZZINESSES
JEALOUSHOOD
JEALOUSHOODS
JEALOUSIES
JEALOUSING
JEALOUSNESS
JEALOUSNESSES
JEISTIECOR
JEISTIECORS
JEJUNENESS
JEJUNENESSES
JEJUNITIES
JEJUNOSTOMIES
JEJUNOSTOMY
JELLIFICATION
JELLIFICATIONS
JELLIFYING
JELLYBEANS
JELLYFISHES
JELLYGRAPH
JELLYGRAPHED
JELLYGRAPHING
JELLYGRAPHS
JELLYROLLS

JEMMINESSES
JENNETINGS
JEOPARDERS
JEOPARDIED
JEOPARDIES
JEOPARDING
JEOPARDISE
JEOPARDISED
JEOPARDISES
JEOPARDISING
JEOPARDIZE
JEOPARDIZED
JEOPARDIZES
JEOPARDIZING
JEOPARDOUS
JEOPARDOUSLY
JEOPARDYING
JEQUERITIES
JEQUIRITIES
JERFALCONS
JERKINESSES
JERKINHEAD
JERKINHEADS
JERKWATERS
JERRYMANDER
JERRYMANDERED
JERRYMANDERING
JERRYMANDERS
JESSAMINES
JESSERANTS
JESUITICAL
JESUITICALLY
JESUITISMS
JESUITRIES
JETSTREAMS
JETTATURAS
JETTINESSES
JETTISONABLE
JETTISONED
JETTISONING
JEWELFISHES
JEWELLERIES
JEWELWEEDS
JICKAJOGGED
JICKAJOGGING
JIGAJIGGED
JIGAJIGGING
JIGAJOGGED
JIGAJOGGING
JIGAMAREES
JIGGERMAST
JIGGERMASTS
JIGGUMBOBS
JIGJIGGING

JILLFLIRTS	JOLLIFICATIONS	JOYLESSNESSES	JUNKETEERED
JIMPNESSES	JOLLIFYING	JOYOUSNESS	JUNKETEERING
JIMSONWEED	JOLLIMENTS	JOYOUSNESSES	JUNKETEERS
JIMSONWEEDS	JOLLINESSES	JOYPOPPERS	JUNKETINGS
JINGOISTIC	JOLLYBOATS	JOYPOPPING	JUNKETTERS
JINGOISTICALLY	JOLLYHEADS	JOYRIDINGS	JUNKETTING
JINRICKSHA	JOLTERHEAD	JUBILANCES	JUNKINESSES
JINRICKSHAS	JOLTERHEADS	JUBILANCIES	JURIDICALLY
JINRICKSHAW	JONNYCAKES	JUBILANTLY	JURISCONSULT
JINRICKSHAWS	JOSEPHINITE	JUBILARIAN	JURISCONSULTS
JINRIKISHA	JOSEPHINITES	JUBILARIANS	JURISDICTION
JINRIKISHAS	JOSTLEMENT	JUBILATING	JURISDICTIONAL
JINRIKSHAS	JOSTLEMENTS	JUBILATION	JURISDICTIONS
JITTERBUGGED	JOUISANCES	JUBILATIONS	JURISDICTIVE
JITTERBUGGING	JOURNALESE	JUDGEMENTAL	JURISPRUDENCE
JITTERBUGS	JOURNALESES	JUDGEMENTS	JURISPRUDENCES
JITTERIEST	JOURNALING	JUDGESHIPS	JURISPRUDENT
JITTERINESS	JOURNALISATION	JUDGMATICAL	JURISPRUDENTIAL
JITTERINESSES	JOURNALISATIONS	JUDGMATICALLY	JURISPRUDENTS
JOBCENTRES	JOURNALISE	JUDGMENTAL	JURISTICAL
JOBERNOWLS	JOURNALISED	JUDGMENTALLY	JURISTICALLY
JOBHOLDERS	JOURNALISER	JUDICATION	JUSTICESHIP
JOBLESSNESS	JOURNALISERS	JUDICATIONS	JUSTICESHIPS
JOBLESSNESSES	JOURNALISES	JUDICATIVE	JUSTICIABILITY
JOBSEEKERS	JOURNALISING	JUDICATORIAL	JUSTICIABLE
JOBSWORTHS	JOURNALISM	JUDICATORIES	JUSTICIALISM
JOCKEYISMS	JOURNALISMS	JUDICATORS	JUSTICIALISMS
JOCKEYSHIP	JOURNALIST	JUDICATORY	JUSTICIARIES
JOCKEYSHIPS	JOURNALISTIC	JUDICATURE	JUSTICIARS
JOCKSTRAPS	JOURNALISTS	JUDICATURES	JUSTICIARSHIP
JOCKTELEGS	JOURNALIZATION	JUDICIALLY	JUSTICIARSHIPS
JOCOSENESS	JOURNALIZATIONS	JUDICIARIES	JUSTICIARY
JOCOSENESSES	JOURNALIZE	JUDICIOUSLY	JUSTIFIABILITY
JOCOSERIOUS	JOURNALIZED	JUDICIOUSNESS	JUSTIFIABLE
JOCOSITIES	JOURNALIZER	JUDICIOUSNESSES	JUSTIFIABLENESS
JOCULARITIES	JOURNALIZERS	JUGGERNAUT	JUSTIFIABLY
JOCULARITY	JOURNALIZES	JUGGERNAUTS	JUSTIFICATION
JOCULATORS	JOURNALIZING	JUGGLERIES	JUSTIFICATIONS
JOCUNDITIES	JOURNALLED	JUGGLINGLY	JUSTIFICATIVE
JOCUNDNESS	JOURNALLING	JUGLANDACEOUS	JUSTIFICATOR
JOCUNDNESSES	JOURNEYERS	JUGULATING	JUSTIFICATORS
JOHANNESES	JOURNEYING	JUGULATION	JUSTIFICATORY
JOHNNYCAKE	JOURNEYMAN	JUGULATIONS	JUSTIFIERS
JOHNNYCAKES	JOURNEYMEN	JUICEHEADS	JUSTIFYING
JOHNSONGRASS	JOURNEYWORK	JUICINESSES	JUSTNESSES
JOHNSONGRASSES	JOURNEYWORKS	JULIENNING	JUVENESCENCE
JOINTEDNESS	JOUYSAUNCE	JUMBLINGLY	JUVENESCENCES
JOINTEDNESSES	JOUYSAUNCES	JUMBOISING	JUVENESCENT
JOINTNESSES	JOVIALITIES	JUMBOIZING	JUVENILELY
JOINTRESSES	JOVIALNESS	JUMHOURIYA	JUVENILENESS
JOINTURESS	JOVIALNESSES	JUMHOURIYAS	JUVENILENESSES
JOINTURESSES	JOVIALTIES	JUMPINESSES	JUVENILITIES
JOINTURING	JOVYSAUNCE	JUNCACEOUS	JUVENILITY
JOINTWEEDS	JOVYSAUNCES	JUNCTIONAL	JUXTAPOSED
JOINTWORMS	JOWLINESSES	JUNEATINGS	JUXTAPOSES
JOKESMITHS	JOYFULLEST	JUNGLEGYMS	JUXTAPOSING
JOKINESSES	JOYFULNESS	JUNGLELIKE	JUXTAPOSITION
JOLLEYINGS	JOYFULNESSES	JUNIORATES	JUXTAPOSITIONAL
JOLLIFICATION	JOYLESSNESS	JUNIORITIES	JUXTAPOSITIONS

K

KABALISTIC	KAOLINITES	KATHAKALIS	KERATOMATA
KABARAGOYA	KAOLINITIC	KATHAREVOUSA	KERATOMETER
KABARAGOYAS	KAOLINIZED	KATHAREVOUSAS	KERATOMETERS
KABBALISMS	KAOLINIZES	KATHAROMETER	KERATOPHYRE
KABBALISTIC	KAOLINIZING	KATHAROMETERS	KERATOPHYRES
KABBALISTS	KAOLINOSES	KATZENJAMMER	KERATOPLASTIC
KABELJOUWS	KAOLINOSIS	KATZENJAMMERS	KERATOPLASTIES
KADAITCHAS	KAPELLMEISTER	KAWANATANGA	KERATOPLASTY
KAFFEEKLATSCH	KAPELLMEISTERS	KAWANATANGAS	KERATOTOMIES
KAFFEEKLATSCHES	KARABINERS	KAZATSKIES	KERATOTOMY
KAFFIRBOOM	KARANGAING	KAZILLIONS	KERAUNOGRAPH
KAFFIRBOOMS	KARATEISTS	KEELHALING	KERAUNOGRAPHS
KAHIKATEAS	KARSTIFICATION	KEELHAULED	KERBSTONES
KAILYAIRDS	KARSTIFICATIONS	KEELHAULING	KERCHIEFED
KAINOGENESES	KARSTIFIED	KEELHAULINGS	KERCHIEFING
KAINOGENESIS	KARSTIFIES	KEELIVINES	KERCHIEVES
KAINOGENETIC	KARSTIFYING	KEELYVINES	KERFUFFLED
KAIROMONES	KARUHIRUHI	KEENNESSES	KERFUFFLES
KAISERDOMS	KARYOGAMIC	KEEPERLESS	KERFUFFLING
KAISERISMS	KARYOGAMIES	KEEPERSHIP	KERMESITES
KAISERSHIP	KARYOGRAMS	KEEPERSHIPS	KERNELLING
KAISERSHIPS	KARYOKINESES	KEESHONDEN	KERNICTERUS
KAKISTOCRACIES	KARYOKINESIS	KEFUFFLING	KERNICTERUSES
KAKISTOCRACY	KARYOKINETIC	KELYPHITIC	KERNMANTEL
KALAMKARIS	KARYOLOGIC	KENNELLING	KERPLUNKED
KALANCHOES	KARYOLOGICAL	KENNETTING	KERPLUNKING
KALASHNIKOV	KARYOLOGIES	KENOGENESES	KERSANTITE
KALASHNIKOVS	KARYOLOGIST	KENOGENESIS	KERSANTITES
KALEIDOPHONE	KARYOLOGISTS	KENOGENETIC	KERSEYMERE
KALEIDOPHONES	KARYOLYMPH	KENOGENETICALLY	KERSEYMERES
KALEIDOSCOPE	KARYOLYMPHS	KENOPHOBIA	KERYGMATIC
KALEIDOSCOPES	KARYOLYSES	KENOPHOBIAS	KETOGENESES
KALEIDOSCOPIC	KARYOLYSIS	KENOTICIST	KETOGENESIS
KALENDARED	KARYOLYTIC	KENOTICISTS	KETONAEMIA
KALENDARING	KARYOPLASM	KENSPECKLE	KETONAEMIAS
KALIPHATES	KARYOPLASMIC	KENTLEDGES	KETONEMIAS
KALLIKREIN	KARYOPLASMS	KERATINISATION	KETONURIAS
KALLIKREINS	KARYOSOMES	KERATINISATIONS	KETOSTEROID
KALLITYPES	KARYOTYPED	KERATINISE	KETOSTEROIDS
KALSOMINED	KARYOTYPES	KERATINISED	KETTLEDRUM
KALSOMINES	KARYOTYPIC	KERATINISES	KETTLEDRUMMER
KALSOMINING	KARYOTYPICAL	KERATINISING	KETTLEDRUMMERS
KAMELAUKION	KARYOTYPICALLY	KERATINIZATION	KETTLEDRUMS
KAMELAUKIONS	KARYOTYPING	KERATINIZATIONS	KETTLEFULS
KAMERADING	KATABOLICALLY	KERATINIZE	KETTLESTITCH
KANAMYCINS	KATABOLISM	KERATINIZED	KETTLESTITCHES
KANGAROOED	KATABOLISMS	KERATINIZES	KEYBOARDED
KANGAROOING	KATABOTHRON	KERATINIZING	KEYBOARDER
KANTIKOYED	KATABOTHRONS	KERATINOPHILIC	KEYBOARDERS
KANTIKOYING	KATADROMOUS	KERATINOUS	KEYBOARDING
KAOLINISED	KATATHERMOMETER	KERATITIDES	KEYBOARDINGS
KAOLINISES	KATAVOTHRON	KERATITISES	KEYBOARDIST
KAOLINISING	KATAVOTHRONS	KERATOGENOUS	KEYBOARDISTS

KEYBUTTONS	KIESELGURS	KINEMATOGRAPHY	KINNIKINICS
KEYLOGGERS	KIESERITES	KINESCOPED	KINNIKINNICK
KEYPUNCHED	KILDERKINS	KINESCOPES	KINNIKINNICKS
KEYPUNCHER	KILLIFISHES	KINESCOPING	KIRBIGRIPS
KEYPUNCHERS	KILLIKINICK	KINESIATRIC	KIRKYAIRDS
KEYPUNCHES	KILLIKINICKS	KINESIATRICS	KIRSCHWASSER
KEYPUNCHING	KILOCALORIE	KINESIOLOGIES	KIRSCHWASSERS
KEYSTONING	KILOCALORIES	KINESIOLOGIST	KISSAGRAMS
KEYSTROKED	KILOCURIES	KINESIOLOGISTS	KISSOGRAMS
KEYSTROKES	KILOCYCLES	KINESIOLOGY	KITCHENALIA
KEYSTROKING	KILOGAUSSES	KINESIPATH	KITCHENALIAS
KEYSTROKINGS	KILOGRAMME	KINESIPATHIC	KITCHENDOM
KHALIFATES	KILOGRAMMES	KINESIPATHIES	KITCHENDOMS
KHANSAMAHS	KILOHERTZES	KINESIPATHIST	KITCHENERS
KHEDIVATES	KILOJOULES	KINESIPATHISTS	KITCHENETS
KHEDIVIATE	KILOLITERS	KINESIPATHS	KITCHENETTE
KHEDIVIATES	KILOLITRES	KINESIPATHY	KITCHENETTES
KHIDMUTGAR	KILOMETERS	KINESITHERAPIES	KITCHENING
KHIDMUTGARS	KILOMETRES	KINESITHERAPY	KITCHENWARE
KHITMUTGAR	KILOMETRIC	KINESTHESES	KITCHENWARES
KHITMUTGARS	KILOMETRICAL	KINESTHESIA	KITESURFING
KHUSKHUSES	KILOPARSEC	KINESTHESIAS	KITESURFINGS
KIBBITZERS	KILOPARSECS	KINESTHESIS	KITSCHIEST
KIBBITZING	KILOPASCAL	KINESTHETIC	KITSCHIFIED
KIBBUTZNIK	KILOPASCALS	KINESTHETICALLY	KITSCHIFIES
KIBBUTZNIKS	KIMBERLITE	KINETHEODOLITE	KITSCHIFYING
KICKABOUTS	KIMBERLITES	KINETHEODOLITES	KITSCHNESS
KICKAROUND	KINAESTHESES	KINETICALLY	KITSCHNESSES
KICKAROUNDS	KINAESTHESIA	KINETICIST	KITTENISHLY
KICKBOARDS	KINAESTHESIAS	KINETICISTS	KITTENISHNESS
KICKBOXERS	KINAESTHESIS	KINETOCHORE	KITTENISHNESSES
KICKBOXING	KINAESTHETIC	KINETOCHORES	KITTIWAKES
KICKBOXINGS	KINDERGARTEN	KINETOGRAPH	KIWIFRUITS
KICKSHAWSES	KINDERGARTENER	KINETOGRAPHS	KIWISPORTS
KICKSORTER	KINDERGARTENERS	KINETONUCLEI	KLANGFARBE
KICKSORTERS	KINDERGARTENS	KINETONUCLEUS	KLANGFARBES
KICKSTANDS	KINDERGARTNER	KINETONUCLEUSES	KLEBSIELLA
KICKSTARTED	KINDERGARTNERS	KINETOPLAST	KLEBSIELLAS
KICKSTARTING	KINDERSPIEL	KINETOPLASTS	KLEINHUISIE
KICKSTARTS	KINDERSPIELS	KINETOSCOPE	KLEINHUISIES
KIDDIEWINK	KINDHEARTED	KINETOSCOPES	KLENDUSITIES
KIDDIEWINKIE	KINDHEARTEDLY	KINETOSOME	KLENDUSITY
KIDDIEWINKIES	KINDHEARTEDNESS	KINETOSOMES	KLEPHTISMS
KIDDIEWINKS	KINDLESSLY	KINGCRAFTS	KLEPTOCRACIES
KIDDISHNESS	KINDLINESS	KINGDOMLESS	KLEPTOCRACY
KIDDISHNESSES	KINDLINESSES	KINGFISHER	KLEPTOCRATIC
KIDDYWINKS	KINDNESSES	KINGFISHERS	KLEPTOMANIA
KIDNAPINGS	KINDREDNESS	KINGFISHES	KLEPTOMANIAC
KIDNAPPEES	KINDREDNESSES	KINGLIHOOD	KLEPTOMANIACS
KIDNAPPERS	KINDREDSHIP	KINGLIHOODS	KLEPTOMANIAS
KIDNAPPING	KINDREDSHIPS	KINGLINESS	KLETTERSCHUH
KIDNAPPINGS	KINEMATICAL	KINGLINESSES	KLETTERSCHUHE
KIDNEYLIKE	KINEMATICALLY	KINGMAKERS	KLINOSTATS
KIDOLOGIES	KINEMATICS	KINGSNAKES	KLIPSPRINGER
KIDOLOGIST	KINEMATOGRAPH	KINKINESSES	KLIPSPRINGERS
KIDOLOGISTS	KINEMATOGRAPHER	KINNIKINIC	KLONDIKERS
KIESELGUHR	KINEMATOGRAPHIC	KINNIKINICK	KLONDIKING
KIESELGUHRS	KINEMATOGRAPHS	KINNIKINICKS	KLONDYKERS

KLONDYKING
KLOOCHMANS
KLOOTCHMAN
KLOOTCHMANS
KLOOTCHMEN
KLUTZINESS
KLUTZINESSES
KNACKERIES
KNACKERING
KNACKINESS
KNACKINESSES
KNACKWURST
KNACKWURSTS
KNAGGINESS
KNAGGINESSES
KNAPSACKED
KNAVESHIPS
KNAVISHNESS
KNAVISHNESSES
KNEECAPPED
KNEECAPPING
KNEECAPPINGS
KNEEPIECES
KNEVELLING
KNICKERBOCKER
KNICKERBOCKERS
KNICKKNACK
KNICKKNACKS
KNICKPOINT
KNICKPOINTS
KNIFEPOINT
KNIFEPOINTS
KNIFERESTS
KNIGHTAGES
KNIGHTHEAD
KNIGHTHEADS
KNIGHTHOOD
KNIGHTHOODS
KNIGHTLESS
KNIGHTLIER
KNIGHTLIEST
KNIGHTLINESS
KNIGHTLINESSES
KNIPHOFIAS
KNOBBINESS
KNOBBINESSES
KNOBBLIEST
KNOBKERRIE
KNOBKERRIES
KNOBSTICKS
KNOCKABOUT
KNOCKABOUTS
KNOCKDOWNS
KNOCKWURST
KNOCKWURSTS
KNOTGRASSES
KNOTTINESS
KNOTTINESSES

KNOWABLENESS
KNOWABLENESSES
KNOWINGEST
KNOWINGNESS
KNOWINGNESSES
KNOWLEDGABILITY
KNOWLEDGABLE
KNOWLEDGABLY
KNOWLEDGEABLE
KNOWLEDGEABLY
KNOWLEDGED
KNOWLEDGES
KNOWLEDGING
KNUBBLIEST
KNUCKLEBALL
KNUCKLEBALLER
KNUCKLEBALLERS
KNUCKLEBALLS
KNUCKLEBONE
KNUCKLEBONES
KNUCKLEDUSTER
KNUCKLEDUSTERS
KNUCKLEHEAD
KNUCKLEHEADED
KNUCKLEHEADS
KNUCKLIEST
KOEKSISTER
KOEKSISTERS
KOHLRABIES
KOHUTUHUTU
KOLINSKIES
KOLKHOZNIK
KOLKHOZNIKI
KOLKHOZNIKS
KOMONDOROCK
KOMONDOROK
KONIMETERS
KONIOLOGIES
KONISCOPES
KOOKABURRA
KOOKABURRAS
KOOKINESSES
KOTAHITANGA
KOTAHITANGAS
KOTTABOSES
KOTUKUTUKU
KOULIBIACA
KOULIBIACAS
KOURBASHED
KOURBASHES
KOURBASHING
KOUSKOUSES
KOWHAIWHAI
KOWHAIWHAIS
KRAKOWIAKS
KREASOTING
KREMLINOLOGIES
KREMLINOLOGIST

KREMLINOLOGISTS
KREMLINOLOGY
KREOSOTING
KRIEGSPIEL
KRIEGSPIELS
KRIEGSSPIEL
KRIEGSSPIELS
KROMESKIES
KRUGERRAND
KRUGERRANDS
KRUMMHORNS
KRYOMETERS
KUMARAHOUS
KUMMERBUND
KUMMERBUNDS
KUNDALINIS
KURBASHING
KURCHATOVIUM
KURCHATOVIUMS
KURDAITCHA
KURFUFFLED
KURFUFFLES
KURFUFFLING
KURRAJONGS
KURTOSISES
KVETCHIEST
KVETCHINESS
KVETCHINESSES
KWASHIORKOR
KWASHIORKORS
KYANISATION
KYANISATIONS
KYANIZATION
KYANIZATIONS
KYMOGRAPHIC
KYMOGRAPHIES
KYMOGRAPHS
KYMOGRAPHY

L

LABANOTATION
LABANOTATIONS
LABDACISMS
LABEFACTATION
LABEFACTATIONS
LABEFACTION
LABEFACTIONS
LABELLISTS
LABIALISATION
LABIALISATIONS
LABIALISED
LABIALISES
LABIALISING
LABIALISMS
LABIALITIES
LABIALIZATION
LABIALIZATIONS
LABIALIZED
LABIALIZES
LABIALIZING
LABILITIES
LABIODENTAL
LABIODENTALS
LABIONASAL
LABIONASALS
LABIOVELAR
LABIOVELARS
LABORATORIES
LABORATORY
LABOREDNESS
LABOREDNESSES
LABORINGLY
LABORIOUSLY
LABORIOUSNESS
LABORIOUSNESSES
LABORSAVING
LABOUREDLY
LABOUREDNESS
LABOUREDNESSES
LABOURINGLY
LABOURISMS
LABOURISTS
LABOURSOME
LABRADOODLE
LABRADOODLES
LABRADORESCENT
LABRADORITE
LABRADORITES
LABYRINTHAL
LABYRINTHIAN
LABYRINTHIC
LABYRINTHICAL
LABYRINTHICALLY

LABYRINTHINE
LABYRINTHITIS
LABYRINTHITISES
LABYRINTHODONT
LABYRINTHODONTS
LABYRINTHS
LACCOLITES
LACCOLITHIC
LACCOLITHS
LACCOLITIC
LACERABILITIES
LACERABILITY
LACERATING
LACERATION
LACERATIONS
LACERATIVE
LACERTIANS
LACERTILIAN
LACERTILIANS
LACHRYMALS
LACHRYMARIES
LACHRYMARY
LACHRYMATION
LACHRYMATIONS
LACHRYMATOR
LACHRYMATORIES
LACHRYMATORS
LACHRYMATORY
LACHRYMOSE
LACHRYMOSELY
LACHRYMOSITIES
LACHRYMOSITY
LACINESSES
LACINIATED
LACINIATION
LACINIATIONS
LACKADAISICAL
LACKADAISICALLY
LACKADAISY
LACKLUSTER
LACKLUSTERS
LACKLUSTRE
LACKLUSTRES
LACONICALLY
LACONICISM
LACONICISMS
LACQUERERS
LACQUERING
LACQUERINGS
LACQUERWARE
LACQUERWARES
LACQUERWORK
LACQUERWORKS

LACQUEYING
LACRIMATION
LACRIMATIONS
LACRIMATOR
LACRIMATORS
LACRIMATORY
LACRYMATOR
LACRYMATORS
LACRYMATORY
LACTALBUMIN
LACTALBUMINS
LACTARIANS
LACTATIONAL
LACTATIONALLY
LACTATIONS
LACTESCENCE
LACTESCENCES
LACTESCENT
LACTIFEROUS
LACTIFEROUSNESS
LACTIFLUOUS
LACTOBACILLI
LACTOBACILLUS
LACTOFLAVIN
LACTOFLAVINS
LACTOGENIC
LACTOGLOBULIN
LACTOGLOBULINS
LACTOMETER
LACTOMETERS
LACTOPROTEIN
LACTOPROTEINS
LACTOSCOPE
LACTOSCOPES
LACTOSURIA
LACTOSURIAS
LACTOVEGETARIAN
LACUNOSITIES
LACUNOSITY
LACUSTRINE
LADDERLIKE
LADDISHNESS
LADDISHNESSES
LADIESWEAR
LADIESWEARS
LADYFINGER
LADYFINGERS
LADYFISHES
LADYLIKENESS
LADYLIKENESSES
LAEOTROPIC
LAEVIGATED
LAEVIGATES

LAEVIGATING
LAEVOGYRATE
LAEVOROTARY
LAEVOROTATION
LAEVOROTATIONS
LAEVOROTATORY
LAEVULOSES
LAGENIFORM
LAGERPHONE
LAGERPHONES
LAGGARDNESS
LAGGARDNESSES
LAGNIAPPES
LAGOMORPHIC
LAGOMORPHOUS
LAGOMORPHS
LAICISATION
LAICISATIONS
LAICIZATION
LAICIZATIONS
LAIRDSHIPS
LAKEFRONTS
LAKESHORES
LALAPALOOZA
LALAPALOOZAS
LALLAPALOOZA
LALLAPALOOZAS
LALLATIONS
LALLYGAGGED
LALLYGAGGING
LAMASERAIS
LAMASERIES
LAMBASTING
LAMBDACISM
LAMBDACISMS
LAMBDOIDAL
LAMBENCIES
LAMBITIVES
LAMBREQUIN
LAMBREQUINS
LAMBRUSCOS
LAMEBRAINED
LAMEBRAINS
LAMELLARLY
LAMELLATED
LAMELLATELY
LAMELLATION
LAMELLATIONS
LAMELLIBRANCH
LAMELLIBRANCHS
LAMELLICORN
LAMELLICORNS
LAMELLIFORM

LAMELLIROSTRAL	LAMPROPHYRES	LANDOWNERSHIP	LANTERNING
LAMELLIROSTRATE	LAMPROPHYRIC	LANDOWNERSHIPS	LANTERNIST
LAMELLOSITIES	LAMPSHADES	LANDOWNING	LANTERNISTS
LAMELLOSITY	LAMPSHELLS	LANDOWNINGS	LANTHANIDE
LAMENESSES	LANCEJACKS	LANDSCAPED	LANTHANIDES
LAMENTABLE	LANCEOLATE	LANDSCAPER	LANTHANONS
LAMENTABLENESS	LANCEOLATED	LANDSCAPERS	LANTHANUMS
LAMENTABLY	LANCEOLATELY	LANDSCAPES	LANUGINOSE
LAMENTATION	LANCEWOODS	LANDSCAPING	LANUGINOUS
LAMENTATIONS	LANCINATED	LANDSCAPIST	LANUGINOUSNESS
LAMENTEDLY	LANCINATES	LANDSCAPISTS	LANZKNECHT
LAMENTINGLY	LANCINATING	LANDSHARKS	LANZKNECHTS
LAMENTINGS	LANCINATION	LANDSKIPPED	LAODICEANS
LAMINARIAN	LANCINATIONS	LANDSKIPPING	LAPAROSCOPE
LAMINARIANS	LANDAMMANN	LANDSKNECHT	LAPAROSCOPES
LAMINARIAS	LANDAMMANNS	LANDSKNECHTS	LAPAROSCOPIC
LAMINARINS	LANDAMMANS	LANDSLIDDEN	LAPAROSCOPIES
LAMINARISE	LANDAULETS	LANDSLIDES	LAPAROSCOPIST
LAMINARISED	LANDAULETTE	LANDSLIDING	LAPAROSCOPISTS
LAMINARISES	LANDAULETTES	LANDWAITER	LAPAROSCOPY
LAMINARISING	LANDBOARDING	LANDWAITERS	LAPAROTOMIES
LAMINARIZE	LANDBOARDINGS	LANGBEINITE	LAPAROTOMY
LAMINARIZED	LANDBOARDS	LANGBEINITES	LAPIDARIAN
LAMINARIZES	LANDDAMNED	LANGLAUFER	LAPIDARIES
LAMINARIZING	LANDDAMNES	LANGLAUFERS	LAPIDARIST
LAMINATING	LANDDAMNING	LANGOSTINO	LAPIDARISTS
LAMINATION	LANDDROSES	LANGOSTINOS	LAPIDATING
LAMINATIONS	LANDDROSTS	LANGOUSTES	LAPIDATION
LAMINATORS	LANDFILLED	LANGOUSTINE	LAPIDATIONS
LAMINECTOMIES	LANDFILLING	LANGOUSTINES	LAPIDESCENCE
LAMINECTOMY	LANDFILLINGS	LANGRIDGES	LAPIDESCENCES
LAMINGTONS	LANDFORCES	LANGSPIELS	LAPIDESCENT
LAMINITISES	LANDGRAVATE	LANGUAGELESS	LAPIDICOLOUS
LAMMERGEIER	LANDGRAVATES	LANGUAGING	LAPIDIFICATION
LAMMERGEIERS	LANDGRAVES	LANGUESCENT	LAPIDIFICATIONS
LAMMERGEYER	LANDGRAVIATE	LANGUETTES	LAPIDIFIED
LAMMERGEYERS	LANDGRAVIATES	LANGUIDNESS	LAPIDIFIES
LAMPADARIES	LANDGRAVINE	LANGUIDNESSES	LAPIDIFYING
LAMPADEDROMIES	LANDGRAVINES	LANGUISHED	LAPILLIFORM
LAMPADEDROMY	LANDHOLDER	LANGUISHER	LAPSTRAKES
LAMPADEPHORIA	LANDHOLDERS	LANGUISHERS	LAPSTREAKS
LAMPADEPHORIAS	LANDHOLDING	LANGUISHES	LARCENISTS
LAMPADISTS	LANDHOLDINGS	LANGUISHING	LARCENOUSLY
LAMPADOMANCIES	LANDLADIES	LANGUISHINGLY	LARDACEOUS
LAMPADOMANCY	LANDLESSNESS	LANGUISHINGS	LARDALITES
LAMPBLACKS	LANDLESSNESSES	LANGUISHMENT	LARGEHEARTED
LAMPHOLDER	LANDLOCKED	LANGUISHMENTS	LARGEMOUTH
LAMPHOLDERS	LANDLOPERS	LANGUOROUS	LARGEMOUTHS
LAMPLIGHTER	LANDLORDISM	LANGUOROUSLY	LARGENESSES
LAMPLIGHTERS	LANDLORDISMS	LANGUOROUSNESS	LARGHETTOS
LAMPLIGHTS	LANDLUBBER	LANIFEROUS	LARGITIONS
LAMPOONERIES	LANDLUBBERLY	LANIGEROUS	LARKINESSES
LAMPOONERS	LANDLUBBERS	LANKINESSES	LARKISHNESS
LAMPOONERY	LANDLUBBING	LANKNESSES	LARKISHNESSES
LAMPOONING	LANDMARKED	LANOSITIES	LARRIKINISM
LAMPOONIST	LANDMARKING	LANSQUENET	LARRIKINISMS
LAMPOONISTS	LANDMASSES	LANSQUENETS	LARRUPPING
LAMPROPHYRE	LANDOWNERS	LANTERLOOS	LARVICIDAL

LARVICIDES	LATERALITY	LATTERMOST	LAVEROCKED
LARVIKITES	LATERALIZATION	LATTICEWORK	LAVEROCKING
LARVIPAROUS	LATERALIZATIONS	LATTICEWORKS	LAVISHMENT
LARYNGEALLY	LATERALIZE	LATTICINGS	LAVISHMENTS
LARYNGEALS	LATERALIZED	LATTICINIO	LAVISHNESS
LARYNGECTOMEE	LATERALIZES	LAUDABILITIES	LAVISHNESSES
LARYNGECTOMEES	LATERALIZING	LAUDABILITY	LAVOLTAING
LARYNGECTOMIES	LATERALLED	LAUDABLENESS	LAWBREAKER
LARYNGECTOMISED	LATERALLING	LAUDABLENESSES	LAWBREAKERS
LARYNGECTOMIZED	LATERBORNS	LAUDATIONS	LAWBREAKING
LARYNGECTOMY	LATERIGRADE	LAUDATIVES	LAWBREAKINGS
LARYNGISMUS	LATERISATION	LAUDATORIES	LAWFULNESS
LARYNGISMUSES	LATERISATIONS	LAUGHABLENESS	LAWFULNESSES
LARYNGITIC	LATERISING	LAUGHABLENESSES	LAWGIVINGS
LARYNGITIS	LATERITIOUS	LAUGHINGLY	LAWLESSNESS
LARYNGITISES	LATERIZATION	LAUGHINGSTOCK	LAWLESSNESSES
LARYNGOLOGIC	LATERIZATIONS	LAUGHINGSTOCKS	LAWMAKINGS
LARYNGOLOGICAL	LATERIZING	LAUGHLINES	LAWMONGERS
LARYNGOLOGIES	LATEROVERSION	LAUGHWORTHY	LAWNMOWERS
LARYNGOLOGIST	LATEROVERSIONS	LAUNCEGAYE	LAWRENCIUM
LARYNGOLOGISTS	LATESCENCE	LAUNCEGAYES	LAWRENCIUMS
LARYNGOLOGY	LATESCENCES	LAUNCHPADS	LAWYERINGS
LARYNGOPHONIES	LATHERIEST	LAUNDERERS	LAWYERLIKE
LARYNGOPHONY	LATHYRISMS	LAUNDERETTE	LAXATIVENESS
LARYNGOSCOPE	LATHYRITIC	LAUNDERETTES	LAXATIVENESSES
LARYNGOSCOPES	LATHYRUSES	LAUNDERING	LAYBACKING
LARYNGOSCOPIC	LATICIFEROUS	LAUNDRESSES	LAYPERSONS
LARYNGOSCOPIES	LATICIFERS	LAUNDRETTE	LAZARETTES
LARYNGOSCOPIST	LATICLAVES	LAUNDRETTES	LAZARETTOS
LARYNGOSCOPISTS	LATIFUNDIA	LAUNDRYMAN	LAZINESSES
LARYNGOSCOPY	LATIFUNDIO	LAUNDRYMEN	LEACHABILITIES
LARYNGOSPASM	LATIFUNDIOS	LAUNDRYWOMAN	LEACHABILITY
LARYNGOSPASMS	LATIFUNDIUM	LAUNDRYWOMEN	LEADENNESS
LARYNGOTOMIES	LATIMERIAS	LAURACEOUS	LEADENNESSES
LARYNGOTOMY	LATINISATION	LAURDALITE	LEADERBOARD
LASCIVIOUS	LATINISATIONS	LAURDALITES	LEADERBOARDS
LASCIVIOUSLY	LATINISING	LAUREATESHIP	LEADERENES
LASCIVIOUSNESS	LATINITIES	LAUREATESHIPS	LEADERETTE
LASERDISCS	LATINIZATION	LAUREATING	LEADERETTES
LASERDISKS	LATINIZATIONS	LAUREATION	LEADERLESS
LASERWORTS	LATINIZING	LAUREATIONS	LEADERSHIP
LASSITUDES	LATIROSTRAL	LAURELLING	LEADERSHIPS
LASTINGNESS	LATIROSTRATE	LAURUSTINE	LEADPLANTS
LASTINGNESSES	LATISEPTATE	LAURUSTINES	LEADSCREWS
LATCHSTRING	LATITANCIES	LAURUSTINUS	LEAFCUTTER
LATCHSTRINGS	LATITATION	LAURUSTINUSES	LEAFHOPPER
LATECOMERS	LATITATIONS	LAURVIKITE	LEAFHOPPERS
LATEENRIGGED	LATITUDINAL	LAURVIKITES	LEAFINESSES
LATENESSES	LATITUDINALLY	LAVALIERES	LEAFLESSNESS
LATENSIFICATION	LATITUDINARIAN	LAVALLIERE	LEAFLESSNESSES
LATERALING	LATITUDINARIANS	LAVALLIERES	LEAFLETEER
LATERALISATION	LATITUDINOUS	LAVATIONAL	LEAFLETEERS
LATERALISATIONS	LATRATIONS	LAVATORIAL	LEAFLETERS
LATERALISE	LATROCINIA	LAVATORIES	LEAFLETING
LATERALISED	LATROCINIES	LAVENDERED	LEAFLETTED
LATERALISES	LATROCINIUM	LAVENDERING	LEAFLETTING
LATERALISING	LATTERMATH	LAVERBREAD	LEAFSTALKS
LATERALITIES	LATTERMATHS	LAVERBREADS	LEAGUERING

LEAKINESSES
LEANNESSES
LEAPFROGGED
LEAPFROGGING
LEARINESSES
LEARNABILITIES
LEARNABILITY
LEARNEDNESS
LEARNEDNESSES
LEASEBACKS
LEASEHOLDER
LEASEHOLDERS
LEASEHOLDS
LEASTAWAYS
LEATHERBACK
LEATHERBACKS
LEATHERETTE
LEATHERETTES
LEATHERGOODS
LEATHERHEAD
LEATHERHEADS
LEATHERIER
LEATHERIEST
LEATHERINESS
LEATHERINESSES
LEATHERING
LEATHERINGS
LEATHERJACKET
LEATHERJACKETS
LEATHERLEAF
LEATHERLEAVES
LEATHERLIKE
LEATHERNECK
LEATHERNECKS
LEATHERWOOD
LEATHERWOODS
LEAVENINGS
LEBENSRAUM
LEBENSRAUMS
LECHEROUSLY
LECHEROUSNESS
LECHEROUSNESSES
LECITHINASE
LECITHINASES
LECTIONARIES
LECTIONARY
LECTISTERNIA
LECTISTERNIUM
LECTORATES
LECTORSHIP
LECTORSHIPS
LECTOTYPES
LECTRESSES
LECTURESHIP
LECTURESHIPS
LECYTHIDACEOUS
LEDERHOSEN
LEECHCRAFT

LEECHCRAFTS
LEERINESSES
LEFTWARDLY
LEGALISATION
LEGALISATIONS
LEGALISERS
LEGALISING
LEGALISTIC
LEGALISTICALLY
LEGALITIES
LEGALIZATION
LEGALIZATIONS
LEGALIZERS
LEGALIZING
LEGATARIES
LEGATESHIP
LEGATESHIPS
LEGATIONARY
LEGATISSIMO
LEGATORIAL
LEGENDARIES
LEGENDARILY
LEGENDISED
LEGENDISES
LEGENDISING
LEGENDISTS
LEGENDIZED
LEGENDIZES
LEGENDIZING
LEGENDRIES
LEGERDEMAIN
LEGERDEMAINIST
LEGERDEMAINISTS
LEGERDEMAINS
LEGERITIES
LEGGINESSES
LEGIBILITIES
LEGIBILITY
LEGIBLENESS
LEGIBLENESSES
LEGIONARIES
LEGIONELLA
LEGIONELLAE
LEGIONNAIRE
LEGIONNAIRES
LEGISLATED
LEGISLATES
LEGISLATING
LEGISLATION
LEGISLATIONS
LEGISLATIVE
LEGISLATIVELY
LEGISLATIVES
LEGISLATOR
LEGISLATORIAL
LEGISLATORS
LEGISLATORSHIP
LEGISLATORSHIPS

LEGISLATRESS
LEGISLATRESSES
LEGISLATURE
LEGISLATURES
LEGITIMACIES
LEGITIMACY
LEGITIMATE
LEGITIMATED
LEGITIMATELY
LEGITIMATENESS
LEGITIMATES
LEGITIMATING
LEGITIMATION
LEGITIMATIONS
LEGITIMATISE
LEGITIMATISED
LEGITIMATISES
LEGITIMATISING
LEGITIMATIZE
LEGITIMATIZED
LEGITIMATIZES
LEGITIMATIZING
LEGITIMATOR
LEGITIMATORS
LEGITIMISATION
LEGITIMISATIONS
LEGITIMISE
LEGITIMISED
LEGITIMISER
LEGITIMISERS
LEGITIMISES
LEGITIMISING
LEGITIMISM
LEGITIMISMS
LEGITIMIST
LEGITIMISTIC
LEGITIMISTS
LEGITIMIZATION
LEGITIMIZATIONS
LEGITIMIZE
LEGITIMIZED
LEGITIMIZER
LEGITIMIZERS
LEGITIMIZES
LEGITIMIZING
LEGLESSNESS
LEGLESSNESSES
LEGUMINOUS
LEGWARMERS
LEIOMYOMAS
LEIOMYOMATA
LEIOTRICHIES
LEIOTRICHOUS
LEIOTRICHY
LEISHMANIA
LEISHMANIAE
LEISHMANIAL
LEISHMANIAS

LEISHMANIASES
LEISHMANIASIS
LEISHMANIOSES
LEISHMANIOSIS
LEISTERING
LEISURABLE
LEISURABLY
LEISURELINESS
LEISURELINESSES
LEITMOTIFS
LEITMOTIVS
LEMMATISATION
LEMMATISATIONS
LEMMATISED
LEMMATISES
LEMMATISING
LEMMATIZATION
LEMMATIZATIONS
LEMMATIZED
LEMMATIZES
LEMMATIZING
LEMMINGLIKE
LEMNISCATE
LEMNISCATES
LEMONFISHES
LEMONGRASS
LEMONGRASSES
LEMONWOODS
LENGTHENED
LENGTHENER
LENGTHENERS
LENGTHENING
LENGTHIEST
LENGTHINESS
LENGTHINESSES
LENGTHSMAN
LENGTHSMEN
LENGTHWAYS
LENGTHWISE
LENIENCIES
LENITIVELY
LENOCINIUM
LENOCINIUMS
LENTAMENTE
LENTICELLATE
LENTICULAR
LENTICULARLY
LENTICULARS
LENTICULES
LENTIGINES
LENTIGINOSE
LENTIGINOUS
LENTISSIMO
LENTIVIRUS
LENTIVIRUSES
LEONTIASES
LEONTIASIS
LEONTOPODIUM

LEONTOPODIUMS	LESSEESHIP	LEUCODERMA	LEVANTINES
LEOPARDESS	LESSEESHIPS	LEUCODERMAL	LEVELHEADED
LEOPARDESSES	LESSONINGS	LEUCODERMAS	LEVELHEADEDNESS
LEPIDODENDROID	LETHALITIES	LEUCODERMIA	LEVELLINGS
LEPIDODENDROIDS	LETHARGICAL	LEUCODERMIAS	LEVELNESSES
LEPIDOLITE	LETHARGICALLY	LEUCODERMIC	LEVERAGING
LEPIDOLITES	LETHARGIED	LEUCOMAINE	LEVIATHANS
LEPIDOMELANE	LETHARGIES	LEUCOMAINES	LEVIGATING
LEPIDOMELANES	LETHARGISE	LEUCOPENIA	LEVIGATION
LEPIDOPTERA	LETHARGISED	LEUCOPENIAS	LEVIGATIONS
LEPIDOPTERAN	LETHARGISES	LEUCOPENIC	LEVIGATORS
LEPIDOPTERANS	LETHARGISING	LEUCOPLAKIA	LEVIRATICAL
LEPIDOPTERIST	LETHARGIZE	LEUCOPLAKIAS	LEVIRATION
LEPIDOPTERISTS	LETHARGIZED	LEUCOPLAST	LEVIRATIONS
LEPIDOPTEROLOGY	LETHARGIZES	LEUCOPLASTID	LEVITATING
LEPIDOPTERON	LETHARGIZING	LEUCOPLASTIDS	LEVITATION
LEPIDOPTERONS	LETHIFEROUS	LEUCOPLASTS	LEVITATIONAL
LEPIDOPTEROUS	LETTERBOXED	LEUCOPOIESES	LEVITATIONS
LEPIDOSIREN	LETTERBOXES	LEUCOPOIESIS	LEVITATORS
LEPIDOSIRENS	LETTERBOXING	LEUCOPOIETIC	LEVITICALLY
LEPRECHAUN	LETTERBOXINGS	LEUCORRHOEA	LEVOROTARY
LEPRECHAUNISH	LETTERFORM	LEUCORRHOEAL	LEVOROTATORY
LEPRECHAUNS	LETTERFORMS	LEUCORRHOEAS	LEWDNESSES
LEPRECHAWN	LETTERHEAD	LEUCOTOMES	LEXICALISATION
LEPRECHAWNS	LETTERHEADS	LEUCOTOMIES	LEXICALISATIONS
LEPROMATOUS	LETTERINGS	LEUKAEMIAS	LEXICALISE
LEPROSARIA	LETTERLESS	LEUKAEMOGENESES	LEXICALISED
LEPROSARIUM	LETTERPRESS	LEUKAEMOGENESIS	LEXICALISES
LEPROSARIUMS	LETTERPRESSES	LEUKEMOGENESES	LEXICALISING
LEPROSERIE	LETTERSETS	LEUKEMOGENESIS	LEXICALITIES
LEPROSERIES	LETTERSPACING	LEUKEMOGENIC	LEXICALITY
LEPROSITIES	LETTERSPACINGS	LEUKOBLAST	LEXICALIZATION
LEPROUSNESS	LEUCAEMIAS	LEUKOBLASTS	LEXICALIZATIONS
LEPROUSNESSES	LEUCAEMOGEN	LEUKOCYTES	LEXICALIZE
LEPTOCEPHALI	LEUCAEMOGENIC	LEUKOCYTIC	LEXICALIZED
LEPTOCEPHALIC	LEUCAEMOGENS	LEUKOCYTOSES	LEXICALIZES
LEPTOCEPHALOUS	LEUCHAEMIA	LEUKOCYTOSIS	LEXICALIZING
LEPTOCEPHALUS	LEUCHAEMIAS	LEUKOCYTOTIC	LEXICOGRAPHER
LEPTOCERCAL	LEUCITOHEDRA	LEUKODERMA	LEXICOGRAPHERS
LEPTODACTYL	LEUCITOHEDRON	LEUKODERMAL	LEXICOGRAPHIC
LEPTODACTYLOUS	LEUCITOHEDRONS	LEUKODERMAS	LEXICOGRAPHICAL
LEPTODACTYLS	LEUCOBLAST	LEUKODERMIC	LEXICOGRAPHIES
LEPTOKURTIC	LEUCOBLASTS	LEUKODYSTROPHY	LEXICOGRAPHIST
LEPTOPHOSES	LEUCOCIDIN	LEUKOPENIA	LEXICOGRAPHISTS
LEPTOPHYLLOUS	LEUCOCIDINS	LEUKOPENIAS	LEXICOGRAPHY
LEPTORRHINE	LEUCOCRATIC	LEUKOPENIC	LEXICOLOGICAL
LEPTOSOMATIC	LEUCOCYTES	LEUKOPLAKIA	LEXICOLOGICALLY
LEPTOSOMES	LEUCOCYTHAEMIA	LEUKOPLAKIAS	LEXICOLOGIES
LEPTOSOMIC	LEUCOCYTHAEMIAS	LEUKOPLAKIC	LEXICOLOGIST
LEPTOSPIRAL	LEUCOCYTIC	LEUKOPOIESES	LEXICOLOGISTS
LEPTOSPIRE	LEUCOCYTOLYSES	LEUKOPOIESIS	LEXICOLOGY
LEPTOSPIRES	LEUCOCYTOLYSIS	LEUKOPOIETIC	LEXIGRAPHIC
LEPTOSPIROSES	LEUCOCYTOPENIA	LEUKORRHEA	LEXIGRAPHICAL
LEPTOSPIROSIS	LEUCOCYTOPENIAS	LEUKORRHEAL	LEXIGRAPHIES
LEPTOTENES	LEUCOCYTOSES	LEUKORRHEAS	LEXIGRAPHY
LESBIANISM	LEUCOCYTOSIS	LEUKOTOMIES	LHERZOLITE
LESBIANISMS	LEUCOCYTOTIC	LEUKOTRIENE	LHERZOLITES
LESPEDEZAS	LEUCODEPLETED	LEUKOTRIENES	LIABILITIES

LIABLENESS	LIBIDINOSITY	LIFELIKENESS	LIGNOCELLULOSES
LIABLENESSES	LIBIDINOUS	LIFELIKENESSES	LIGNOCELLULOSIC
LIBATIONAL	LIBIDINOUSLY	LIFEMANSHIP	LIGNOSULFONATE
LIBATIONARY	LIBIDINOUSNESS	LIFEMANSHIPS	LIGNOSULFONATES
LIBECCHIOS	LIBRAIRIES	LIFESAVERS	LIGULIFLORAL
LIBELLANTS	LIBRARIANS	LIFESAVING	LIKABILITIES
LIBELLINGS	LIBRARIANSHIP	LIFESAVINGS	LIKABILITY
LIBELLOUSLY	LIBRARIANSHIPS	LIFESTYLER	LIKABLENESS
LIBERALISATION	LIBRATIONAL	LIFESTYLERS	LIKABLENESSES
LIBERALISATIONS	LIBRATIONS	LIFESTYLES	LIKEABLENESS
LIBERALISE	LIBRETTIST	LIFEWORLDS	LIKEABLENESSES
LIBERALISED	LIBRETTISTS	LIGAMENTAL	LIKELIHOOD
LIBERALISER	LICENSABLE	LIGAMENTARY	LIKELIHOODS
LIBERALISERS	LICENSURES	LIGAMENTOUS	LIKELINESS
LIBERALISES	LICENTIATE	LIGATURING	LIKELINESSES
LIBERALISING	LICENTIATES	LIGHTBULBS	LIKENESSES
LIBERALISM	LICENTIATESHIP	LIGHTENERS	LILIACEOUS
LIBERALISMS	LICENTIATESHIPS	LIGHTENING	LILLIPUTIAN
LIBERALIST	LICENTIATION	LIGHTENINGS	LILLIPUTIANS
LIBERALISTIC	LICENTIATIONS	LIGHTERAGE	LILTINGNESS
LIBERALISTS	LICENTIOUS	LIGHTERAGES	LILTINGNESSES
LIBERALITIES	LICENTIOUSLY	LIGHTERING	LIMACIFORM
LIBERALITY	LICENTIOUSNESS	LIGHTERMAN	LIMACOLOGIES
LIBERALIZATION	LICHANOSES	LIGHTERMEN	LIMACOLOGIST
LIBERALIZATIONS	LICHENISMS	LIGHTFACED	LIMACOLOGISTS
LIBERALIZE	LICHENISTS	LIGHTFACES	LIMACOLOGY
LIBERALIZED	LICHENOLOGICAL	LIGHTFASTNESS	LIMBERNESS
LIBERALIZER	LICHENOLOGIES	LIGHTFASTNESSES	LIMBERNESSES
LIBERALIZERS	LICHENOLOGIST	LIGHTHEARTED	LIMBURGITE
LIBERALIZES	LICHENOLOGISTS	LIGHTHEARTEDLY	LIMBURGITES
LIBERALIZING	LICHENOLOGY	LIGHTHOUSE	LIMELIGHTED
LIBERALNESS	LICHTLYING	LIGHTHOUSEMAN	LIMELIGHTER
LIBERALNESSES	LICITNESSES	LIGHTHOUSEMEN	LIMELIGHTERS
LIBERATING	LICKERISHLY	LIGHTHOUSES	LIMELIGHTING
LIBERATION	LICKERISHNESS	LIGHTLYING	LIMELIGHTS
LIBERATIONISM	LICKERISHNESSES	LIGHTNESSES	LIMESCALES
LIBERATIONISMS	LICKPENNIES	LIGHTNINGED	LIMESTONES
LIBERATIONIST	LICKSPITTLE	LIGHTNINGS	LIMEWASHES
LIBERATIONISTS	LICKSPITTLES	LIGHTPLANE	LIMEWATERS
LIBERATIONS	LIDOCAINES	LIGHTPLANES	LIMICOLINE
LIBERATORS	LIEBFRAUMILCH	LIGHTPROOF	LIMICOLOUS
LIBERATORY	LIEBFRAUMILCHS	LIGHTSHIPS	LIMINESSES
LIBERTARIAN	LIENTERIES	LIGHTSOMELY	LIMITABLENESS
LIBERTARIANISM	LIEUTENANCIES	LIGHTSOMENESS	LIMITABLENESSES
LIBERTARIANISMS	LIEUTENANCY	LIGHTSOMENESSES	LIMITARIAN
LIBERTARIANS	LIEUTENANT	LIGHTTIGHT	LIMITARIANS
LIBERTICIDAL	LIEUTENANTRIES	LIGHTWEIGHT	LIMITATION
LIBERTICIDE	LIEUTENANTRY	LIGHTWEIGHTS	LIMITATIONAL
LIBERTICIDES	LIEUTENANTS	LIGHTWOODS	LIMITATIONS
LIBERTINAGE	LIEUTENANTSHIP	LIGNICOLOUS	LIMITATIVE
LIBERTINAGES	LIEUTENANTSHIPS	LIGNIFICATION	LIMITEDNESS
LIBERTINES	LIFEBLOODS	LIGNIFICATIONS	LIMITEDNESSES
LIBERTINISM	LIFEGUARDED	LIGNIFYING	LIMITINGLY
LIBERTINISMS	LIFEGUARDING	LIGNIPERDOUS	LIMITLESSLY
LIBIDINALLY	LIFEGUARDS	LIGNIVOROUS	LIMITLESSNESS
LIBIDINIST	LIFELESSLY	LIGNOCAINE	LIMITLESSNESSES
LIBIDINISTS	LIFELESSNESS	LIGNOCAINES	LIMITROPHE
LIBIDINOSITIES	LIFELESSNESSES	LIGNOCELLULOSE	LIMIVOROUS

LIMNOLOGIC	LINGUISTRY	LIQUEFACIENT	LISTERIOSIS
LIMNOLOGICAL	LINGULATED	LIQUEFACIENTS	LISTLESSLY
LIMNOLOGICALLY	LINISHINGS	LIQUEFACTION	LISTLESSNESS
LIMNOLOGIES	LINKSLANDS	LIQUEFACTIONS	LISTLESSNESSES
LIMNOLOGIST	LINOLEATES	LIQUEFACTIVE	LITENESSES
LIMNOLOGISTS	LINOTYPERS	LIQUEFIABLE	LITERACIES
LIMNOPHILOUS	LINOTYPING	LIQUEFIERS	LITERALISATION
LIMOUSINES	LINTSTOCKS	LIQUEFYING	LITERALISATIONS
LIMPIDITIES	LINTWHITES	LIQUESCENCE	LITERALISE
LIMPIDNESS	LIONCELLES	LIQUESCENCES	LITERALISED
LIMPIDNESSES	LIONFISHES	LIQUESCENCIES	LITERALISER
LIMPNESSES	LIONHEARTED	LIQUESCENCY	LITERALISERS
LINCOMYCIN	LIONHEARTEDNESS	LIQUESCENT	LITERALISES
LINCOMYCINS	LIONISATION	LIQUESCING	LITERALISING
LINCRUSTAS	LIONISATIONS	LIQUEURING	LITERALISM
LINEALITIES	LIONIZATION	LIQUIDAMBAR	LITERALISMS
LINEAMENTAL	LIONIZATIONS	LIQUIDAMBARS	LITERALIST
LINEAMENTS	LIPECTOMIES	LIQUIDATED	LITERALISTIC
LINEARISATION	LIPIDOPLAST	LIQUIDATES	LITERALISTS
LINEARISATIONS	LIPIDOPLASTS	LIQUIDATING	LITERALITIES
LINEARISED	LIPOCHROME	LIQUIDATION	LITERALITY
LINEARISES	LIPOCHROMES	LIQUIDATIONS	LITERALIZATION
LINEARISING	LIPODYSTROPHIES	LIQUIDATOR	LITERALIZATIONS
LINEARITIES	LIPODYSTROPHY	LIQUIDATORS	LITERALIZE
LINEARIZATION	LIPOGENESES	LIQUIDISED	LITERALIZED
LINEARIZATIONS	LIPOGENESIS	LIQUIDISER	LITERALIZER
LINEARIZED	LIPOGRAMMATIC	LIQUIDISERS	LITERALIZERS
LINEARIZES	LIPOGRAMMATISM	LIQUIDISES	LITERALIZES
LINEARIZING	LIPOGRAMMATISMS	LIQUIDISING	LITERALIZING
LINEATIONS	LIPOGRAMMATIST	LIQUIDITIES	LITERALNESS
LINEBACKER	LIPOGRAMMATISTS	LIQUIDIZED	LITERALNESSES
LINEBACKERS	LIPOGRAPHIES	LIQUIDIZER	LITERARILY
LINEBACKING	LIPOGRAPHY	LIQUIDIZERS	LITERARINESS
LINEBACKINGS	LIPOMATOSES	LIQUIDIZES	LITERARINESSES
LINEBREEDING	LIPOMATOSIS	LIQUIDIZING	LITERARYISM
LINEBREEDINGS	LIPOMATOUS	LIQUIDNESS	LITERARYISMS
LINECASTER	LIPOPHILIC	LIQUIDNESSES	LITERATELY
LINECASTERS	LIPOPLASTS	LIQUIDUSES	LITERATENESS
LINECASTING	LIPOPROTEIN	LIQUIFYING	LITERATENESSES
LINECASTINGS	LIPOPROTEINS	LIQUORICES	LITERATION
LINEOLATED	LIPOSCULPTURE	LIQUORISHLY	LITERATIONS
LINERBOARD	LIPOSCULPTURES	LIQUORISHNESS	LITERATORS
LINERBOARDS	LIPOSUCKED	LIQUORISHNESSES	LITERATURE
LINGBERRIES	LIPOSUCKING	LIRIODENDRA	LITERATURED
LINGERINGLY	LIPOSUCTION	LIRIODENDRON	LITERATURES
LINGERINGS	LIPOSUCTIONS	LIRIODENDRONS	LITEROSITIES
LINGONBERRIES	LIPOTROPIC	LISSENCEPHALOUS	LITEROSITY
LINGONBERRY	LIPOTROPIES	LISSOMENESS	LITHENESSES
LINGUIFORM	LIPOTROPIN	LISSOMENESSES	LITHESOMENESS
LINGUISTER	LIPOTROPINS	LISSOMNESS	LITHESOMENESSES
LINGUISTERS	LIPPINESSES	LISSOMNESSES	LITHIFICATION
LINGUISTIC	LIPPITUDES	LISSOTRICHOUS	LITHIFICATIONS
LINGUISTICAL	LIPREADERS	LISTENABILITIES	LITHIFYING
LINGUISTICALLY	LIPREADING	LISTENABILITY	LITHISTIDS
LINGUISTICIAN	LIPREADINGS	LISTENABLE	LITHOCHROMATIC
LINGUISTICIANS	LIPSTICKED	LISTENERSHIP	LITHOCHROMATICS
LINGUISTICS	LIPSTICKING	LISTENERSHIPS	LITHOCHROMIES
LINGUISTRIES	LIQUATIONS	LISTERIOSES	LITHOCHROMY

LITHOCLAST
LITHOCLASTS
LITHOCYSTS
LITHODOMOUS
LITHOGENOUS
LITHOGLYPH
LITHOGLYPHS
LITHOGRAPH
LITHOGRAPHED
LITHOGRAPHER
LITHOGRAPHERS
LITHOGRAPHIC
LITHOGRAPHICAL
LITHOGRAPHIES
LITHOGRAPHING
LITHOGRAPHS
LITHOGRAPHY
LITHOLAPAXIES
LITHOLAPAXY
LITHOLATRIES
LITHOLATROUS
LITHOLATRY
LITHOLOGIC
LITHOLOGICAL
LITHOLOGICALLY
LITHOLOGIES
LITHOLOGIST
LITHOLOGISTS
LITHOMANCIES
LITHOMANCY
LITHOMARGE
LITHOMARGES
LITHOMETEOR
LITHOMETEORS
LITHONTHRYPTIC
LITHONTHRYPTICS
LITHONTRIPTIC
LITHONTRIPTICS
LITHONTRIPTIST
LITHONTRIPTISTS
LITHONTRIPTOR
LITHONTRIPTORS
LITHOPHAGOUS
LITHOPHANE
LITHOPHANES
LITHOPHILOUS
LITHOPHYSA
LITHOPHYSAE
LITHOPHYSE
LITHOPHYSES
LITHOPHYTE
LITHOPHYTES
LITHOPHYTIC
LITHOPONES
LITHOPRINT
LITHOPRINTS
LITHOSPERMUM
LITHOSPERMUMS

LITHOSPHERE
LITHOSPHERES
LITHOSPHERIC
LITHOSTATIC
LITHOTOMES
LITHOTOMIC
LITHOTOMICAL
LITHOTOMIES
LITHOTOMIST
LITHOTOMISTS
LITHOTOMOUS
LITHOTRIPSIES
LITHOTRIPSY
LITHOTRIPTER
LITHOTRIPTERS
LITHOTRIPTIC
LITHOTRIPTICS
LITHOTRIPTIST
LITHOTRIPTISTS
LITHOTRIPTOR
LITHOTRIPTORS
LITHOTRITE
LITHOTRITES
LITHOTRITIC
LITHOTRITICS
LITHOTRITIES
LITHOTRITISE
LITHOTRITISED
LITHOTRITISES
LITHOTRITISING
LITHOTRITIST
LITHOTRITISTS
LITHOTRITIZE
LITHOTRITIZED
LITHOTRITIZES
LITHOTRITIZING
LITHOTRITOR
LITHOTRITORS
LITHOTRITY
LITIGATING
LITIGATION
LITIGATIONS
LITIGATORS
LITIGIOUSLY
LITIGIOUSNESS
LITIGIOUSNESSES
LITTERATEUR
LITTERATEURS
LITTERBAGS
LITTERBUGS
LITTERMATE
LITTERMATES
LITTLENECK
LITTLENECKS
LITTLENESS
LITTLENESSES
LITTLEWORTH
LITURGICAL

LITURGICALLY
LITURGIOLOGIES
LITURGIOLOGIST
LITURGIOLOGISTS
LITURGIOLOGY
LITURGISMS
LITURGISTIC
LITURGISTS
LIVABILITIES
LIVABILITY
LIVABLENESS
LIVABLENESSES
LIVEABILITIES
LIVEABILITY
LIVEABLENESS
LIVEABLENESSES
LIVELIHEAD
LIVELIHEADS
LIVELIHOOD
LIVELIHOODS
LIVELINESS
LIVELINESSES
LIVENESSES
LIVERISHNESS
LIVERISHNESSES
LIVERLEAVES
LIVERWORTS
LIVERWURST
LIVERWURSTS
LIVESTOCKS
LIVETRAPPED
LIVETRAPPING
LIVIDITIES
LIVIDNESSES
LIVINGNESS
LIVINGNESSES
LIVRAISONS
LIXIVIATED
LIXIVIATES
LIXIVIATING
LIXIVIATION
LIXIVIATIONS
LOADMASTER
LOADMASTERS
LOADSAMONEY
LOADSAMONEYS
LOADSAMONIES
LOADSPACES
LOADSTONES
LOAMINESSES
LOANSHIFTS
LOATHEDNESS
LOATHEDNESSES
LOATHFULNESS
LOATHFULNESSES
LOATHINGLY
LOATHLINESS
LOATHLINESSES

LOATHNESSES
LOATHSOMELY
LOATHSOMENESS
LOATHSOMENESSES
LOBECTOMIES
LOBLOLLIES
LOBOTOMIES
LOBOTOMISE
LOBOTOMISED
LOBOTOMISES
LOBOTOMISING
LOBOTOMIZE
LOBOTOMIZED
LOBOTOMIZES
LOBOTOMIZING
LOBSCOUSES
LOBSTERERS
LOBSTERING
LOBSTERINGS
LOBSTERLIKE
LOBSTERMAN
LOBSTERMEN
LOBULATION
LOBULATIONS
LOCALISABILITY
LOCALISABLE
LOCALISATION
LOCALISATIONS
LOCALISERS
LOCALISING
LOCALISTIC
LOCALITIES
LOCALIZABILITY
LOCALIZABLE
LOCALIZATION
LOCALIZATIONS
LOCALIZERS
LOCALIZING
LOCALNESSES
LOCATEABLE
LOCATIONAL
LOCATIONALLY
LOCKHOUSES
LOCKKEEPER
LOCKKEEPERS
LOCKMAKERS
LOCKSMITHERIES
LOCKSMITHERY
LOCKSMITHING
LOCKSMITHINGS
LOCKSMITHS
LOCKSTITCH
LOCKSTITCHED
LOCKSTITCHES
LOCKSTITCHING
LOCOMOBILE
LOCOMOBILES
LOCOMOBILITIES

LOCOMOBILITY	LOGOGRAMMATIC	LONGIPENNATE	LOSABLENESSES
LOCOMOTING	LOGOGRAPHER	LONGIROSTRAL	LOSSMAKERS
LOCOMOTION	LOGOGRAPHERS	LONGITUDES	LOSSMAKING
LOCOMOTIONS	LOGOGRAPHIC	LONGITUDINAL	LOSTNESSES
LOCOMOTIVE	LOGOGRAPHICAL	LONGITUDINALLY	LOTHNESSES
LOCOMOTIVELY	LOGOGRAPHICALLY	LONGJUMPED	LOTUSLANDS
LOCOMOTIVENESS	LOGOGRAPHIES	LONGJUMPING	LOUDHAILER
LOCOMOTIVES	LOGOGRAPHS	LONGLEAVES	LOUDHAILERS
LOCOMOTIVITIES	LOGOGRAPHY	LONGNESSES	LOUDMOUTHED
LOCOMOTIVITY	LOGOGRIPHIC	LONGPRIMER	LOUDMOUTHS
LOCOMOTORS	LOGOGRIPHS	LONGPRIMERS	LOUDNESSES
LOCOMOTORY	LOGOMACHIES	LONGSHOREMAN	LOUDSPEAKER
LOCOPLANTS	LOGOMACHIST	LONGSHOREMEN	LOUDSPEAKERS
LOCORESTIVE	LOGOMACHISTS	LONGSHORING	LOUNDERING
LOCULAMENT	LOGOPAEDIC	LONGSHORINGS	LOUNDERINGS
LOCULAMENTS	LOGOPAEDICS	LONGSIGHTED	LOUNGEWEAR
LOCULATION	LOGOPEDICS	LONGSIGHTEDNESS	LOUNGEWEARS
LOCULATIONS	LOGOPHILES	LONGSOMELY	LOUNGINGLY
LOCULICIDAL	LOGORRHEAS	LONGSOMENESS	LOUSEWORTS
LOCUTIONARY	LOGORRHEIC	LONGSOMENESSES	LOUSINESSES
LOCUTORIES	LOGORRHOEA	LONGSUFFERING	LOUTISHNESS
LODESTONES	LOGORRHOEAS	LONGSUFFERINGS	LOUTISHNESSES
LODGEMENTS	LOGOTHETES	LONGWEARING	LOVABILITIES
LODGEPOLES	LOGOTYPIES	LOOKALIKES	LOVABILITY
LOFTINESSES	LOGROLLERS	LOONINESSES	LOVABLENESS
LOGAGRAPHIA	LOGROLLING	LOOPHOLING	LOVABLENESSES
LOGAGRAPHIAS	LOGROLLINGS	LOOPINESSES	LOVASTATIN
LOGANBERRIES	LOINCLOTHS	LOOSEBOXES	LOVASTATINS
LOGANBERRY	LOITERINGLY	LOOSENESSES	LOVEABILITIES
LOGANIACEOUS	LOITERINGS	LOOSESTRIFE	LOVEABILITY
LOGAOEDICS	LOLLAPALOOZA	LOOSESTRIFES	LOVEABLENESS
LOGARITHMIC	LOLLAPALOOZAS	LOOYENWORK	LOVEABLENESSES
LOGARITHMICAL	LOLLYGAGGED	LOOYENWORKS	LOVELESSLY
LOGARITHMICALLY	LOLLYGAGGING	LOPGRASSES	LOVELESSNESS
LOGARITHMS	LOMENTACEOUS	LOPHOBRANCH	LOVELESSNESSES
LOGGERHEAD	LONELINESS	LOPHOBRANCHIATE	LOVELIGHTS
LOGGERHEADED	LONELINESSES	LOPHOBRANCHS	LOVELIHEAD
LOGGERHEADS	LONENESSES	LOPHOPHORATE	LOVELIHEADS
LOGICALITIES	LONESOMELY	LOPHOPHORE	LOVELINESS
LOGICALITY	LONESOMENESS	LOPHOPHORES	LOVELINESSES
LOGICALNESS	LONESOMENESSES	LOPSIDEDLY	LOVELORNNESS
LOGICALNESSES	LONGAEVOUS	LOPSIDEDNESS	LOVELORNNESSES
LOGICISING	LONGANIMITIES	LOPSIDEDNESSES	LOVEMAKERS
LOGICIZING	LONGANIMITY	LOQUACIOUS	LOVEMAKING
LOGINESSES	LONGANIMOUS	LOQUACIOUSLY	LOVEMAKINGS
LOGISTICAL	LONGBOARDS	LOQUACIOUSNESS	LOVESICKNESS
LOGISTICALLY	LONGBOWMAN	LOQUACITIES	LOVESICKNESSES
LOGISTICIAN	LONGBOWMEN	LORAZEPAMS	LOVESTRUCK
LOGISTICIANS	LONGCLOTHS	LORDLINESS	LOVEWORTHY
LOGJAMMING	LONGEVITIES	LORDLINESSES	LOVINGNESS
LOGNORMALITIES	LONGHAIRED	LORDOLATRIES	LOVINGNESSES
LOGNORMALITY	LONGHEADED	LORDOLATRY	LOWBALLING
LOGNORMALLY	LONGHEADEDNESS	LORGNETTES	LOWBALLINGS
LOGODAEDALIC	LONGHOUSES	LORICATING	LOWBROWISM
LOGODAEDALIES	LONGICAUDATE	LORICATION	LOWBROWISMS
LOGODAEDALUS	LONGICORNS	LORICATIONS	LOWERCASED
LOGODAEDALUSES	LONGINQUITIES	LORNNESSES	LOWERCASES
LOGODAEDALY	LONGINQUITY	LOSABLENESS	LOWERCASING

LOWERCLASSMAN	LUCUBRATION	LUMINIFEROUS	LUTEINISING
LOWERCLASSMEN	LUCUBRATIONS	LUMINOSITIES	LUTEINIZATION
LOWERINGLY	LUCUBRATOR	LUMINOSITY	LUTEINIZATIONS
LOWLANDERS	LUCUBRATORS	LUMINOUSLY	LUTEINIZED
LOWLIGHTED	LUCULENTLY	LUMINOUSNESS	LUTEINIZES
LOWLIGHTING	LUDICROUSLY	LUMINOUSNESSES	LUTEINIZING
LOWLIHEADS	LUDICROUSNESS	LUMISTEROL	LUTEOTROPHIC
LOWLINESSES	LUDICROUSNESSES	LUMISTEROLS	LUTEOTROPHIN
LOWSENINGS	LUETICALLY	LUMPECTOMIES	LUTEOTROPHINS
LOXODROMES	LUFTMENSCH	LUMPECTOMY	LUTEOTROPIC
LOXODROMIC	LUFTMENSCHEN	LUMPFISHES	LUTEOTROPIN
LOXODROMICAL	LUGUBRIOUS	LUMPINESSES	LUTEOTROPINS
LOXODROMICALLY	LUGUBRIOUSLY	LUMPISHNESS	LUTESTRING
LOXODROMICS	LUGUBRIOUSNESS	LUMPISHNESSES	LUTESTRINGS
LOXODROMIES	LUKEWARMISH	LUMPSUCKER	LUXULIANITE
LOYALNESSES	LUKEWARMLY	LUMPSUCKERS	LUXULIANITES
LUBBERLINESS	LUKEWARMNESS	LUNARNAUTS	LUXULLIANITE
LUBBERLINESSES	LUKEWARMNESSES	LUNATICALLY	LUXULLIANITES
LUBRICANTS	LUKEWARMTH	LUNCHBOXES	LUXULYANITE
LUBRICATED	LUKEWARMTHS	LUNCHEONED	LUXULYANITES
LUBRICATES	LULLABYING	LUNCHEONETTE	LUXURIANCE
LUBRICATING	LUMBAGINOUS	LUNCHEONETTES	LUXURIANCES
LUBRICATION	LUMBERINGLY	LUNCHEONING	LUXURIANCIES
LUBRICATIONAL	LUMBERINGNESS	LUNCHMEATS	LUXURIANCY
LUBRICATIONS	LUMBERINGNESSES	LUNCHROOMS	LUXURIANTLY
LUBRICATIVE	LUMBERINGS	LUNCHTIMES	LUXURIATED
LUBRICATOR	LUMBERJACK	LUNGFISHES	LUXURIATES
LUBRICATORS	LUMBERJACKET	LUNINESSES	LUXURIATING
LUBRICIOUS	LUMBERJACKETS	LUNKHEADED	LUXURIATION
LUBRICIOUSLY	LUMBERJACKS	LURIDNESSES	LUXURIATIONS
LUBRICITIES	LUMBERSOME	LUSCIOUSLY	LUXURIOUSLY
LUBRICOUSLY	LUMBERSOMENESS	LUSCIOUSNESS	LUXURIOUSNESS
LUBRITORIA	LUMBERYARD	LUSCIOUSNESSES	LUXURIOUSNESSES
LUBRITORIUM	LUMBERYARDS	LUSHNESSES	LYCANTHROPE
LUBRITORIUMS	LUMBOSACRAL	LUSKISHNESS	LYCANTHROPES
LUCIDITIES	LUMBRICALES	LUSKISHNESSES	LYCANTHROPIC
LUCIDNESSES	LUMBRICALIS	LUSTERLESS	LYCANTHROPIES
LUCIFERASE	LUMBRICALISES	LUSTERWARE	LYCANTHROPIST
LUCIFERASES	LUMBRICALS	LUSTERWARES	LYCANTHROPISTS
LUCIFERINS	LUMBRICIFORM	LUSTFULNESS	LYCANTHROPY
LUCIFEROUS	LUMBRICOID	LUSTFULNESSES	LYCHNOSCOPE
LUCIFUGOUS	LUMBRICUSES	LUSTIHEADS	LYCHNOSCOPES
LUCKENBOOTH	LUMINAIRES	LUSTIHOODS	LYCOPODIUM
LUCKENBOOTHS	LUMINANCES	LUSTINESSES	LYCOPODIUMS
LUCKENGOWAN	LUMINARIAS	LUSTRATING	LYMPHADENITIS
LUCKENGOWANS	LUMINARIES	LUSTRATION	LYMPHADENITISES
LUCKINESSES	LUMINARISM	LUSTRATIONS	LYMPHADENOPATHY
LUCKLESSLY	LUMINARISMS	LUSTRATIVE	LYMPHANGIAL
LUCKLESSNESS	LUMINARIST	LUSTRELESS	LYMPHANGIOGRAM
LUCKLESSNESSES	LUMINARISTS	LUSTREWARE	LYMPHANGIOGRAMS
LUCKPENNIES	LUMINATION	LUSTREWARES	LYMPHANGITIC
LUCRATIVELY	LUMINATIONS	LUSTROUSLY	LYMPHANGITIDES
LUCRATIVENESS	LUMINESCED	LUSTROUSNESS	LYMPHANGITIS
LUCRATIVENESSES	LUMINESCENCE	LUSTROUSNESSES	LYMPHANGITISES
LUCTATIONS	LUMINESCENCES	LUTEINISATION	LYMPHATICALLY
LUCUBRATED	LUMINESCENT	LUTEINISATIONS	LYMPHATICS
LUCUBRATES	LUMINESCES	LUTEINISED	LYMPHOADENOMA
LUCUBRATING	LUMINESCING	LUTEINISES	LYMPHOADENOMAS

LYMPHOADENOMATA
LYMPHOBLAST
LYMPHOBLASTIC
LYMPHOBLASTS
LYMPHOCYTE
LYMPHOCYTES
LYMPHOCYTIC
LYMPHOCYTOPENIA
LYMPHOCYTOSES
LYMPHOCYTOSIS
LYMPHOCYTOTIC
LYMPHOGRAM
LYMPHOGRAMS
LYMPHOGRANULOMA
LYMPHOGRAPHIC
LYMPHOGRAPHIES
LYMPHOGRAPHY
LYMPHOKINE
LYMPHOKINES
LYMPHOMATA
LYMPHOMATOID
LYMPHOMATOSES
LYMPHOMATOSIS
LYMPHOMATOUS
LYMPHOPENIA
LYMPHOPENIAS
LYMPHOPOIESES
LYMPHOPOIESIS
LYMPHOPOIETIC
LYMPHOSARCOMA
LYMPHOSARCOMAS
LYMPHOSARCOMATA
LYMPHOTROPHIC
LYOPHILISATION
LYOPHILISATIONS
LYOPHILISE
LYOPHILISED
LYOPHILISER
LYOPHILISERS
LYOPHILISES
LYOPHILISING
LYOPHILIZATION
LYOPHILIZATIONS
LYOPHILIZE
LYOPHILIZED
LYOPHILIZER
LYOPHILIZERS
LYOPHILIZES
LYOPHILIZING
LYOSORPTION
LYOSORPTIONS
LYRICALNESS
LYRICALNESSES
LYRICISING
LYRICIZING
LYSERGIDES
LYSIGENETIC
LYSIGENOUS

LYSIMETERS
LYSIMETRIC
LYSOGENICITIES
LYSOGENICITY
LYSOGENIES
LYSOGENISATION
LYSOGENISATIONS
LYSOGENISE
LYSOGENISED
LYSOGENISES
LYSOGENISING
LYSOGENIZATION
LYSOGENIZATIONS
LYSOGENIZE
LYSOGENIZED
LYSOGENIZES
LYSOGENIZING
LYSOLECITHIN
LYSOLECITHINS
LYTHRACEOUS

M

MACABRESQUE	MACHINABLE	MACROCOPIES	MACROPHYLUM
MACADAMIAS	MACHINATED	MACROCOSMIC	MACROPHYSICS
MACADAMISATION	MACHINATES	MACROCOSMICALLY	MACROPHYTE
MACADAMISATIONS	MACHINATING	MACROCOSMS	MACROPHYTES
MACADAMISE	MACHINATION	MACROCYCLE	MACROPHYTIC
MACADAMISED	MACHINATIONS	MACROCYCLES	MACROPINAKOID
MACADAMISER	MACHINATOR	MACROCYCLIC	MACROPINAKOIDS
MACADAMISERS	MACHINATORS	MACROCYSTS	MACROPRISM
MACADAMISES	MACHINEABILITY	MACROCYTES	MACROPRISMS
MACADAMISING	MACHINEABLE	MACROCYTIC	MACROPSIAS
MACADAMIZATION	MACHINEGUN	MACROCYTOSES	MACROPTEROUS
MACADAMIZATIONS	MACHINEGUNNED	MACROCYTOSIS	MACROSCALE
MACADAMIZE	MACHINEGUNNING	MACRODACTYL	MACROSCALES
MACADAMIZED	MACHINEGUNS	MACRODACTYLIC	MACROSCOPIC
MACADAMIZER	MACHINELESS	MACRODACTYLIES	MACROSCOPICALLY
MACADAMIZERS	MACHINELIKE	MACRODACTYLOUS	MACROSOCIOLOGY
MACADAMIZES	MACHINEMAN	MACRODACTYLY	MACROSPORANGIA
MACADAMIZING	MACHINEMEN	MACRODIAGONAL	MACROSPORANGIUM
MACARISING	MACHINERIES	MACRODIAGONALS	MACROSPORE
MACARIZING	MACHININGS	MACRODOMES	MACROSPORES
MACARONICALLY	MACHINISTS	MACROECONOMIC	MACROSTRUCTURAL
MACARONICS	MACHMETERS	MACROECONOMICS	MACROSTRUCTURE
MACARONIES	MACHTPOLITIK	MACROEVOLUTION	MACROSTRUCTURES
MACCARONIES	MACHTPOLITIKS	MACROEVOLUTIONS	MACROZAMIA
MACCARONIS	MACINTOSHES	MACROFAUNA	MACROZAMIAS
MACCHERONCINI	MACKINTOSH	MACROFLORA	MACTATIONS
MACCHERONCINIS	MACKINTOSHES	MACROFOSSIL	MACULATING
MACCHIATOS	MACONOCHIE	MACROFOSSILS	MACULATION
MACEBEARER	MACONOCHIES	MACROGAMETE	MACULATIONS
MACEBEARERS	MACRENCEPHALIA	MACROGAMETES	MACULATURE
MACEDOINES	MACRENCEPHALIAS	MACROGLIAS	MACULATURES
MACERANDUBA	MACRENCEPHALIES	MACROGLOBULIN	MADBRAINED
MACERANDUBAS	MACRENCEPHALY	MACROGLOBULINS	MADDENINGLY
MACERATERS	MACROAGGREGATE	MACROGRAPH	MADDENINGNESS
MACERATING	MACROAGGREGATED	MACROGRAPHIC	MADDENINGNESSES
MACERATION	MACROAGGREGATES	MACROGRAPHS	MADEFACTION
MACERATIONS	MACROBIOTA	MACROLOGIES	MADEFACTIONS
MACERATIVE	MACROBIOTE	MACROMERES	MADELEINES
MACERATORS	MACROBIOTES	MACROMOLECULAR	MADEMOISELLE
MACHAIRODONT	MACROBIOTIC	MACROMOLECULE	MADEMOISELLES
MACHAIRODONTS	MACROBIOTICS	MACROMOLECULES	MADERISATION
MACHIAVELIAN	MACROCARPA	MACROMOLES	MADERISATIONS
MACHIAVELIANS	MACROCARPAS	MACRONUCLEAR	MADERISING
MACHIAVELLIAN	MACROCEPHALIA	MACRONUCLEI	MADERIZATION
MACHIAVELLIANS	MACROCEPHALIAS	MACRONUCLEUS	MADERIZATIONS
MACHICOLATE	MACROCEPHALIC	MACRONUTRIENT	MADERIZING
MACHICOLATED	MACROCEPHALIES	MACRONUTRIENTS	MADONNAISH
MACHICOLATES	MACROCEPHALOUS	MACROPHAGE	MADONNAWISE
MACHICOLATING	MACROCEPHALY	MACROPHAGES	MADRASSAHS
MACHICOLATION	MACROCLIMATE	MACROPHAGIC	MADREPORAL
MACHICOLATIONS	MACROCLIMATES	MACROPHAGOUS	MADREPORES
MACHINABILITIES	MACROCLIMATIC	MACROPHOTOGRAPH	MADREPORIAN
MACHINABILITY	MACROCODES	MACROPHYLA	MADREPORIANS

MADREPORIC	MAGNESSTONES	MAGNIFYING	MAINSTREAM
MADREPORITE	MAGNETICAL	MAGNILOQUENCE	MAINSTREAMED
MADREPORITES	MAGNETICALLY	MAGNILOQUENCES	MAINSTREAMING
MADREPORITIC	MAGNETICIAN	MAGNILOQUENT	MAINSTREAMS
MADRIGALESQUE	MAGNETICIANS	MAGNILOQUENTLY	MAINSTREETING
MADRIGALIAN	MAGNETISABLE	MAGNITUDES	MAINSTREETINGS
MADRIGALIST	MAGNETISATION	MAGNITUDINOUS	MAINTAINABILITY
MADRIGALISTS	MAGNETISATIONS	MAGNOLIACEOUS	MAINTAINABLE
MADRILENES	MAGNETISED	MAHARAJAHS	MAINTAINED
MAELSTROMS	MAGNETISER	MAHARANEES	MAINTAINER
MAENADICALLY	MAGNETISERS	MAHARISHIS	MAINTAINERS
MAENADISMS	MAGNETISES	MAHATMAISM	MAINTAINING
MAFFICKERS	MAGNETISING	MAHATMAISMS	MAINTENANCE
MAFFICKING	MAGNETISMS	MAHLSTICKS	MAINTENANCED
MAFFICKINGS	MAGNETISTS	MAHOGANIES	MAINTENANCES
MAGALOGUES	MAGNETITES	MAIASAURAS	MAINTENANCING
MAGAZINIST	MAGNETITIC	MAIDENHAIR	MAINTOPMAST
MAGAZINISTS	MAGNETIZABLE	MAIDENHAIRS	MAINTOPMASTS
MAGDALENES	MAGNETIZATION	MAIDENHEAD	MAINTOPSAIL
MAGGOTIEST	MAGNETIZATIONS	MAIDENHEADS	MAINTOPSAILS
MAGGOTORIA	MAGNETIZED	MAIDENHOOD	MAISONETTE
MAGGOTORIUM	MAGNETIZER	MAIDENHOODS	MAISONETTES
MAGIANISMS	MAGNETIZERS	MAIDENLIKE	MAISONNETTE
MAGISTERIAL	MAGNETIZES	MAIDENLINESS	MAISONNETTES
MAGISTERIALLY	MAGNETIZING	MAIDENLINESSES	MAISTERDOME
MAGISTERIALNESS	MAGNETOCHEMICAL	MAIDENWEED	MAISTERDOMES
MAGISTERIES	MAGNETOELECTRIC	MAIDENWEEDS	MAISTERING
MAGISTERIUM	MAGNETOGRAPH	MAIDISHNESS	MAISTRINGS
MAGISTERIUMS	MAGNETOGRAPHS	MAIDISHNESSES	MAJESTICAL
MAGISTRACIES	MAGNETOMETER	MAIDSERVANT	MAJESTICALLY
MAGISTRACY	MAGNETOMETERS	MAIDSERVANTS	MAJESTICALNESS
MAGISTRALITIES	MAGNETOMETRIC	MAIEUTICAL	MAJESTICNESS
MAGISTRALITY	MAGNETOMETRIES	MAILABILITIES	MAJESTICNESSES
MAGISTRALLY	MAGNETOMETRY	MAILABILITY	MAJOLICAWARE
MAGISTRALS	MAGNETOMOTIVE	MAILCOACHES	MAJOLICAWARES
MAGISTRAND	MAGNETOPAUSE	MAILGRAMMED	MAJORDOMOS
MAGISTRANDS	MAGNETOPAUSES	MAILGRAMMING	MAJORETTES
MAGISTRATE	MAGNETOSPHERE	MAILMERGED	MAJORETTING
MAGISTRATES	MAGNETOSPHERES	MAILMERGES	MAJORETTINGS
MAGISTRATESHIP	MAGNETOSPHERIC	MAILMERGING	MAJORITAIRE
MAGISTRATESHIPS	MAGNETOSTATIC	MAILPOUCHES	MAJORITAIRES
MAGISTRATIC	MAGNETOSTATICS	MAILSHOTTED	MAJORITARIAN
MAGISTRATICAL	MAGNETRONS	MAILSHOTTING	MAJORITARIANISM
MAGISTRATICALLY	MAGNIFIABLE	MAIMEDNESS	MAJORITARIANS
MAGISTRATURE	MAGNIFICAL	MAIMEDNESSES	MAJORITIES
MAGISTRATURES	MAGNIFICALLY	MAINBRACES	MAJORSHIPS
MAGMATISMS	MAGNIFICAT	MAINFRAMES	MAJUSCULAR
MAGNALIUMS	MAGNIFICATION	MAINLANDER	MAJUSCULES
MAGNANIMITIES	MAGNIFICATIONS	MAINLANDERS	MAKEREADIES
MAGNANIMITY	MAGNIFICATS	MAINLINERS	MAKESHIFTS
MAGNANIMOUS	MAGNIFICENCE	MAINLINING	MAKEWEIGHT
MAGNANIMOUSLY	MAGNIFICENCES	MAINLININGS	MAKEWEIGHTS
MAGNANIMOUSNESS	MAGNIFICENT	MAINPERNOR	MAKUNOUCHI
MAGNATESHIP	MAGNIFICENTLY	MAINPERNORS	MAKUNOUCHIS
MAGNATESHIPS	MAGNIFICENTNESS	MAINPRISES	MALABSORPTION
MAGNESITES	MAGNIFICOES	MAINSHEETS	MALABSORPTIONS
MAGNESIUMS	MAGNIFICOS	MAINSPRING	MALACHITES
MAGNESSTONE	MAGNIFIERS	MAINSPRINGS	MALACOLOGICAL

MALACOLOGIES	MALCONFORMATION	MALIGNMENTS	MAMAGUYING
MALACOLOGIST	MALCONTENT	MALIMPRINTED	MAMILLATED
MALACOLOGISTS	MALCONTENTED	MALIMPRINTING	MAMILLATION
MALACOLOGY	MALCONTENTEDLY	MALIMPRINTINGS	MAMILLATIONS
MALACOPHILIES	MALCONTENTS	MALINGERED	MAMILLIFORM
MALACOPHILOUS	MALDEPLOYMENT	MALINGERER	MAMMALIANS
MALACOPHILY	MALDEPLOYMENTS	MALINGERERS	MAMMALIFEROUS
MALACOPHYLLOUS	MALDISTRIBUTION	MALINGERIES	MAMMALITIES
MALACOPTERYGIAN	MALEDICENT	MALINGERING	MAMMALOGICAL
MALACOSTRACAN	MALEDICTED	MALLANDERS	MAMMALOGIES
MALACOSTRACANS	MALEDICTING	MALLEABILITIES	MAMMALOGIST
MALACOSTRACOUS	MALEDICTION	MALLEABILITY	MAMMALOGISTS
MALADAPTATION	MALEDICTIONS	MALLEABLENESS	MAMMECTOMIES
MALADAPTATIONS	MALEDICTIVE	MALLEABLENESSES	MAMMECTOMY
MALADAPTED	MALEDICTORY	MALLEATING	MAMMETRIES
MALADAPTIVE	MALEFACTION	MALLEATION	MAMMIFEROUS
MALADAPTIVELY	MALEFACTIONS	MALLEATIONS	MAMMILLARIA
MALADDRESS	MALEFACTOR	MALLEIFORM	MAMMILLARIAS
MALADDRESSES	MALEFACTORS	MALLEMAROKING	MAMMILLARY
MALADJUSTED	MALEFACTORY	MALLEMAROKINGS	MAMMILLATE
MALADJUSTIVE	MALEFACTRESS	MALLEMUCKS	MAMMILLATED
MALADJUSTMENT	MALEFACTRESSES	MALLENDERS	MAMMITIDES
MALADJUSTMENTS	MALEFFECTS	MALLEOLUSES	MAMMOCKING
MALADMINISTER	MALEFICALLY	MALLOPHAGOUS	MAMMOGENIC
MALADMINISTERED	MALEFICENCE	MALLOWPUFF	MAMMOGRAMS
MALADMINISTERS	MALEFICENCES	MALLOWPUFFS	MAMMOGRAPH
MALADROITLY	MALEFICENT	MALMSTONES	MAMMOGRAPHIC
MALADROITNESS	MALEFICIAL	MALNOURISHED	MAMMOGRAPHIES
MALADROITNESSES	MALENESSES	MALNUTRITION	MAMMOGRAPHS
MALADROITS	MALENGINES	MALNUTRITIONS	MAMMOGRAPHY
MALAGUENAS	MALENTENDU	MALOCCLUDED	MAMMONISMS
MALAGUETTA	MALENTENDUS	MALOCCLUSION	MAMMONISTIC
MALAGUETTAS	MALEVOLENCE	MALOCCLUSIONS	MAMMONISTS
MALAKATOONE	MALEVOLENCES	MALODOROUS	MAMMONITES
MALAKATOONES	MALEVOLENT	MALODOROUSLY	MAMMOPLASTIES
MALAPERTLY	MALEVOLENTLY	MALODOROUSNESS	MAMMOPLASTY
MALAPERTNESS	MALFEASANCE	MALOLACTIC	MANAGEABILITIES
MALAPERTNESSES	MALFEASANCES	MALONYLUREA	MANAGEABILITY
MALAPPORTIONED	MALFEASANT	MALONYLUREAS	MANAGEABLE
MALAPPROPRIATE	MALFEASANTS	MALPIGHIACEOUS	MANAGEABLENESS
MALAPPROPRIATED	MALFORMATION	MALPOSITION	MANAGEABLY
MALAPPROPRIATES	MALFORMATIONS	MALPOSITIONS	MANAGEMENT
MALAPROPIAN	MALFUNCTION	MALPRACTICE	MANAGEMENTAL
MALAPROPISM	MALFUNCTIONED	MALPRACTICES	MANAGEMENTS
MALAPROPISMS	MALFUNCTIONING	MALPRACTITIONER	MANAGERESS
MALAPROPIST	MALFUNCTIONINGS	MALPRESENTATION	MANAGERESSES
MALAPROPISTS	MALFUNCTIONS	MALTALENTS	MANAGERIAL
MALAPROPOS	MALICIOUSLY	MALTINESSES	MANAGERIALISM
MALARIOLOGIES	MALICIOUSNESS	MALTREATED	MANAGERIALISMS
MALARIOLOGIST	MALICIOUSNESSES	MALTREATER	MANAGERIALIST
MALARIOLOGISTS	MALIGNANCE	MALTREATERS	MANAGERIALISTS
MALARIOLOGY	MALIGNANCES	MALTREATING	MANAGERIALLY
MALASSIMILATION	MALIGNANCIES	MALTREATMENT	MANAGERSHIP
MALATHIONS	MALIGNANCY	MALTREATMENTS	MANAGERSHIPS
MALAXATING	MALIGNANTLY	MALVACEOUS	MANCHESTER
MALAXATION	MALIGNANTS	MALVERSATION	MANCHESTERS
MALAXATIONS	MALIGNITIES	MALVERSATIONS	MANCHINEEL
MALAXATORS	MALIGNMENT	MALVOISIES	MANCHINEELS

MANCIPATED	MANGINESSES	MANIPULATOR	MANUFACTORIES
MANCIPATES	MANGOLDWURZEL	MANIPULATORS	MANUFACTORY
MANCIPATING	MANGOLDWURZELS	MANIPULATORY	MANUFACTURABLE
MANCIPATION	MANGOSTANS	MANLINESSES	MANUFACTURAL
MANCIPATIONS	MANGOSTEEN	MANNEQUINS	MANUFACTURE
MANCIPATORY	MANGOSTEENS	MANNERISMS	MANUFACTURED
MANDAMUSED	MANGOUSTES	MANNERISTIC	MANUFACTURER
MANDAMUSES	MANGULATED	MANNERISTICAL	MANUFACTURERS
MANDAMUSING	MANGULATES	MANNERISTICALLY	MANUFACTURES
MANDARINATE	MANGULATING	MANNERISTS	MANUFACTURING
MANDARINATES	MANHANDLED	MANNERLESS	MANUFACTURINGS
MANDARINES	MANHANDLES	MANNERLESSNESS	MANUMISSION
MANDARINIC	MANHANDLING	MANNERLINESS	MANUMISSIONS
MANDARINISM	MANHATTANS	MANNERLINESSES	MANUMITTED
MANDARINISMS	MANHUNTERS	MANNIFEROUS	MANUMITTER
MANDATARIES	MANIACALLY	MANNISHNESS	MANUMITTERS
MANDATORIES	MANICOTTIS	MANNISHNESSES	MANUMITTING
MANDATORILY	MANICURING	MANOEUVRABILITY	MANURANCES
MANDIBULAR	MANICURIST	MANOEUVRABLE	MANUSCRIPT
MANDIBULATE	MANICURISTS	MANOEUVRED	MANUSCRIPTS
MANDIBULATED	MANIFESTABLE	MANOEUVRER	MANZANILLA
MANDILIONS	MANIFESTANT	MANOEUVRERS	MANZANILLAS
MANDIOCCAS	MANIFESTANTS	MANOEUVRES	MANZANITAS
MANDOLINES	MANIFESTATION	MANOEUVRING	MAPMAKINGS
MANDOLINIST	MANIFESTATIONAL	MANOEUVRINGS	MAPPEMONDS
MANDOLINISTS	MANIFESTATIONS	MANOMETERS	MAQUILADORA
MANDRAGORA	MANIFESTATIVE	MANOMETRIC	MAQUILADORAS
MANDRAGORAS	MANIFESTED	MANOMETRICAL	MAQUILLAGE
MANDUCABLE	MANIFESTER	MANOMETRICALLY	MAQUILLAGES
MANDUCATED	MANIFESTERS	MANOMETRIES	MAQUISARDS
MANDUCATES	MANIFESTIBLE	MANORIALISM	MARABUNTAS
MANDUCATING	MANIFESTING	MANORIALISMS	MARANATHAS
MANDUCATION	MANIFESTLY	MANOSCOPIES	MARASCHINO
MANDUCATIONS	MANIFESTNESS	MANRIKIGUSARI	MARASCHINOS
MANDUCATORY	MANIFESTNESSES	MANRIKIGUSARIS	MARASMUSES
MANDYLIONS	MANIFESTOED	MANSERVANT	MARATHONER
MANEUVERABILITY	MANIFESTOES	MANSIONARIES	MARATHONERS
MANEUVERABLE	MANIFESTOING	MANSIONARY	MARATHONING
MANEUVERED	MANIFESTOS	MANSLAUGHTER	MARATHONINGS
MANEUVERER	MANIFOLDED	MANSLAUGHTERS	MARBELISED
MANEUVERERS	MANIFOLDER	MANSLAYERS	MARBELISES
MANEUVERING	MANIFOLDERS	MANSONRIES	MARBELISING
MANEUVERINGS	MANIFOLDING	MANSUETUDE	MARBELIZED
MANFULNESS	MANIFOLDLY	MANSUETUDES	MARBELIZES
MANFULNESSES	MANIFOLDNESS	MANTELLETTA	MARBELIZING
MANGABEIRA	MANIFOLDNESSES	MANTELLETTAS	MARBLEISED
MANGABEIRAS	MANIPULABILITY	MANTELPIECE	MARBLEISES
MANGALSUTRA	MANIPULABLE	MANTELPIECES	MARBLEISING
MANGALSUTRAS	MANIPULARS	MANTELSHELF	MARBLEIZED
MANGANATES	MANIPULATABLE	MANTELSHELVES	MARBLEIZES
MANGANESES	MANIPULATE	MANTELTREE	MARBLEIZING
MANGANESIAN	MANIPULATED	MANTELTREES	MARBLEWOOD
MANGANIFEROUS	MANIPULATES	MANTICALLY	MARBLEWOODS
MANGANITES	MANIPULATING	MANTICORAS	MARCANTANT
MANGELWURZEL	MANIPULATION	MANTICORES	MARCANTANTS
MANGELWURZELS	MANIPULATIONS	MANTLETREE	MARCASITES
MANGEMANGE	MANIPULATIVE	MANTLETREES	MARCASITICAL
MANGETOUTS	MANIPULATIVELY	MANUBRIUMS	MARCATISSIMO

MARCELLERS
MARCELLING
MARCESCENCE
MARCESCENCES
MARCESCENT
MARCESCIBLE
MARCHANTIA
MARCHANTIAS
MARCHIONESS
MARCHIONESSES
MARCHLANDS
MARCHPANES
MARCONIGRAM
MARCONIGRAMS
MARCONIGRAPH
MARCONIGRAPHED
MARCONIGRAPHING
MARCONIGRAPHS
MARCONIING
MARESCHALS
MARGARINES
MARGARITAS
MARGARITES
MARGARITIC
MARGARITIFEROUS
MARGENTING
MARGINALIA
MARGINALISATION
MARGINALISE
MARGINALISED
MARGINALISES
MARGINALISING
MARGINALISM
MARGINALISMS
MARGINALIST
MARGINALISTS
MARGINALITIES
MARGINALITY
MARGINALIZATION
MARGINALIZE
MARGINALIZED
MARGINALIZES
MARGINALIZING
MARGINALLY
MARGINATED
MARGINATES
MARGINATING
MARGINATION
MARGINATIONS
MARGRAVATE
MARGRAVATES
MARGRAVIAL
MARGRAVIATE
MARGRAVIATES
MARGRAVINE
MARGRAVINES
MARGUERITE
MARGUERITES

MARIALITES
MARICULTURE
MARICULTURES
MARICULTURIST
MARICULTURISTS
MARIGRAPHS
MARIHUANAS
MARIJUANAS
MARIMBAPHONE
MARIMBAPHONES
MARIMBISTS
MARINADING
MARINATING
MARINATION
MARINATIONS
MARIONBERRIES
MARIONBERRY
MARIONETTE
MARIONETTES
MARISCHALLED
MARISCHALLING
MARISCHALS
MARIVAUDAGE
MARIVAUDAGES
MARKEDNESS
MARKEDNESSES
MARKETABILITIES
MARKETABILITY
MARKETABLE
MARKETABLENESS
MARKETABLY
MARKETEERS
MARKETINGS
MARKETISATION
MARKETISATIONS
MARKETIZATION
MARKETIZATIONS
MARKETPLACE
MARKETPLACES
MARKSMANSHIP
MARKSMANSHIPS
MARKSWOMAN
MARKSWOMEN
MARLACIOUS
MARLINESPIKE
MARLINESPIKES
MARLINGSPIKE
MARLINGSPIKES
MARLINSPIKE
MARLINSPIKES
MARLSTONES
MARMALADES
MARMALISED
MARMALISES
MARMALISING
MARMALIZED
MARMALIZES
MARMALIZING

MARMARISED
MARMARISES
MARMARISING
MARMARIZED
MARMARIZES
MARMARIZING
MARMAROSES
MARMAROSIS
MARMELISED
MARMELISES
MARMELISING
MARMELIZED
MARMELIZES
MARMELIZING
MARMOREALLY
MAROONINGS
MARPRELATE
MARPRELATED
MARPRELATES
MARPRELATING
MARQUESSATE
MARQUESSATES
MARQUESSES
MARQUETERIE
MARQUETERIES
MARQUETRIES
MARQUISATE
MARQUISATES
MARQUISETTE
MARQUISETTES
MARRIAGEABILITY
MARRIAGEABLE
MARROWBONE
MARROWBONES
MARROWFATS
MARROWLESS
MARROWSKIED
MARROWSKIES
MARROWSKYING
MARSEILLES
MARSHALCIES
MARSHALERS
MARSHALING
MARSHALLED
MARSHALLER
MARSHALLERS
MARSHALLING
MARSHALLINGS
MARSHALSHIP
MARSHALSHIPS
MARSHBUCKS
MARSHINESS
MARSHINESSES
MARSHLANDER
MARSHLANDERS
MARSHLANDS
MARSHLOCKS
MARSHLOCKSES

MARSHMALLOW
MARSHMALLOWS
MARSHMALLOWY
MARSHWORTS
MARSIPOBRANCH
MARSIPOBRANCHS
MARSQUAKES
MARSUPIALIAN
MARSUPIALIANS
MARSUPIALS
MARSUPIANS
MARSUPIUMS
MARTELLANDO
MARTELLANDOS
MARTELLATO
MARTELLING
MARTENSITE
MARTENSITES
MARTENSITIC
MARTENSITICALLY
MARTIALISM
MARTIALISMS
MARTIALIST
MARTIALISTS
MARTIALNESS
MARTIALNESSES
MARTINETISH
MARTINETISM
MARTINETISMS
MARTINGALE
MARTINGALES
MARTINGALS
MARTYRDOMS
MARTYRISATION
MARTYRISATIONS
MARTYRISED
MARTYRISES
MARTYRISING
MARTYRIZATION
MARTYRIZATIONS
MARTYRIZED
MARTYRIZES
MARTYRIZING
MARTYROLOGIC
MARTYROLOGICAL
MARTYROLOGIES
MARTYROLOGIST
MARTYROLOGISTS
MARTYROLOGY
MARVELLING
MARVELLOUS
MARVELLOUSLY
MARVELLOUSNESS
MARVELOUSLY
MARVELOUSNESS
MARVELOUSNESSES
MASCARAING
MASCARPONE

MASCARPONES	MASSOTHERAPY	MASTODONTS	MATERIALISTS
MASCULINELY	MASSPRIEST	MASTODYNIA	MATERIALITIES
MASCULINENESS	MASSPRIESTS	MASTODYNIAS	MATERIALITY
MASCULINENESSES	MASSYMORES	MASTOIDECTOMIES	MATERIALIZATION
MASCULINES	MASTECTOMIES	MASTOIDECTOMY	MATERIALIZE
MASCULINISATION	MASTECTOMY	MASTOIDITIS	MATERIALIZED
MASCULINISE	MASTERATES	MASTOIDITISES	MATERIALIZER
MASCULINISED	MASTERCLASS	MASTOPEXIES	MATERIALIZERS
MASCULINISES	MASTERCLASSES	MASTURBATE	MATERIALIZES
MASCULINISING	MASTERDOMS	MASTURBATED	MATERIALIZING
MASCULINIST	MASTERFULLY	MASTURBATES	MATERIALLY
MASCULINISTS	MASTERFULNESS	MASTURBATING	MATERIALNESS
MASCULINITIES	MASTERFULNESSES	MASTURBATION	MATERIALNESSES
MASCULINITY	MASTERHOOD	MASTURBATIONS	MATERNALISM
MASCULINIZATION	MASTERHOODS	MASTURBATOR	MATERNALISMS
MASCULINIZE	MASTERINGS	MASTURBATORS	MATERNALISTIC
MASCULINIZED	MASTERLESS	MASTURBATORY	MATERNALLY
MASCULINIZES	MASTERLINESS	MATACHINAS	MATERNITIES
MASCULINIZING	MASTERLINESSES	MATAGOURIS	MATEYNESSES
MASCULISTS	MASTERMIND	MATCHBOARD	MATGRASSES
MASHGICHIM	MASTERMINDED	MATCHBOARDING	MATHEMATIC
MASKALLONGE	MASTERMINDING	MATCHBOARDINGS	MATHEMATICAL
MASKALLONGES	MASTERMINDS	MATCHBOARDS	MATHEMATICALLY
MASKALONGE	MASTERPIECE	MATCHBOOKS	MATHEMATICIAN
MASKALONGES	MASTERPIECES	MATCHBOXES	MATHEMATICIANS
MASKANONGE	MASTERSHIP	MATCHLESSLY	MATHEMATICISE
MASKANONGES	MASTERSHIPS	MATCHLESSNESS	MATHEMATICISED
MASKINONGE	MASTERSINGER	MATCHLESSNESSES	MATHEMATICISES
MASKINONGES	MASTERSINGERS	MATCHLOCKS	MATHEMATICISING
MASKIROVKA	MASTERSTROKE	MATCHMAKER	MATHEMATICISM
MASKIROVKAS	MASTERSTROKES	MATCHMAKERS	MATHEMATICISMS
MASOCHISMS	MASTERWORK	MATCHMAKES	MATHEMATICIZE
MASOCHISTIC	MASTERWORKS	MATCHMAKING	MATHEMATICIZED
MASOCHISTICALLY	MASTERWORT	MATCHMAKINGS	MATHEMATICIZES
MASOCHISTS	MASTERWORTS	MATCHMARKED	MATHEMATICIZING
MASONICALLY	MASTHEADED	MATCHMARKING	MATHEMATICS
MASQUERADE	MASTHEADING	MATCHMARKS	MATHEMATISATION
MASQUERADED	MASTHOUSES	MATCHSTICK	MATHEMATISE
MASQUERADER	MASTICABLE	MATCHSTICKS	MATHEMATISED
MASQUERADERS	MASTICATED	MATCHWOODS	MATHEMATISES
MASQUERADES	MASTICATES	MATELASSES	MATHEMATISING
MASQUERADING	MASTICATING	MATELLASSE	MATHEMATIZATION
MASSACRERS	MASTICATION	MATELLASSES	MATHEMATIZE
MASSACRING	MASTICATIONS	MATELOTTES	MATHEMATIZED
MASSAGISTS	MASTICATOR	MATERFAMILIAS	MATHEMATIZES
MASSARANDUBA	MASTICATORIES	MATERFAMILIASES	MATHEMATIZING
MASSARANDUBAS	MASTICATORS	MATERIALISATION	MATINESSES
MASSASAUGA	MASTICATORY	MATERIALISE	MATRESFAMILIAS
MASSASAUGAS	MASTIGOPHORAN	MATERIALISED	MATRIARCHAL
MASSERANDUBA	MASTIGOPHORANS	MATERIALISER	MATRIARCHALISM
MASSERANDUBAS	MASTIGOPHORE	MATERIALISERS	MATRIARCHALISMS
MASSETERIC	MASTIGOPHORES	MATERIALISES	MATRIARCHATE
MASSINESSES	MASTIGOPHORIC	MATERIALISING	MATRIARCHATES
MASSIVENESS	MASTIGOPHOROUS	MATERIALISM	MATRIARCHIC
MASSIVENESSES	MASTITIDES	MATERIALISMS	MATRIARCHICAL
MASSOTHERAPIES	MASTITISES	MATERIALIST	MATRIARCHIES
MASSOTHERAPIST	MASTODONIC	MATERIALISTIC	MATRIARCHS
MASSOTHERAPISTS	MASTODONTIC	MATERIALISTICAL	MATRIARCHY

MATRICIDAL	MATSUTAKES	MAYORALTIES	MECHANICALISM
MATRICIDES	MATTAMORES	MAYORESSES	MECHANICALISMS
MATRICLINIC	MATTERLESS	MAYORSHIPS	MECHANICALLY
MATRICLINOUS	MATTIFYING	MAYSTERDOME	MECHANICALNESS
MATRICULANT	MATTRASSES	MAYSTERDOMES	MECHANICALS
MATRICULANTS	MATTRESSES	MAZARINADE	MECHANICIAN
MATRICULAR	MATURATING	MAZARINADES	MECHANICIANS
MATRICULAS	MATURATION	MAZEDNESSES	MECHANISABLE
MATRICULATE	MATURATIONAL	MAZINESSES	MECHANISATION
MATRICULATED	MATURATIONS	MEADOWLAND	MECHANISATIONS
MATRICULATES	MATURATIVE	MEADOWLANDS	MECHANISED
MATRICULATING	MATURENESS	MEADOWLARK	MECHANISER
MATRICULATION	MATURENESSES	MEADOWLARKS	MECHANISERS
MATRICULATIONS	MATURITIES	MEADOWSWEET	MECHANISES
MATRICULATOR	MATUTINALLY	MEADOWSWEETS	MECHANISING
MATRICULATORS	MAUDLINISM	MEAGERNESS	MECHANISMS
MATRICULATORY	MAUDLINISMS	MEAGERNESSES	MECHANISTIC
MATRIFOCAL	MAUDLINNESS	MEAGRENESS	MECHANISTICALLY
MATRIFOCALITIES	MAUDLINNESSES	MEAGRENESSES	MECHANISTS
MATRIFOCALITY	MAULSTICKS	MEALINESSES	MECHANIZABLE
MATRILINEAL	MAUMETRIES	MEALYMOUTHED	MECHANIZATION
MATRILINEALLY	MAUNDERERS	MEANDERERS	MECHANIZATIONS
MATRILINEAR	MAUNDERING	MEANDERING	MECHANIZED
MATRILINIES	MAUNDERINGS	MEANDERINGLY	MECHANIZER
MATRILOCAL	MAUSOLEUMS	MEANINGFUL	MECHANIZERS
MATRILOCALITIES	MAVERICKED	MEANINGFULLY	MECHANIZES
MATRILOCALITY	MAVERICKING	MEANINGFULNESS	MECHANIZING
MATRILOCALLY	MAVOURNEEN	MEANINGLESS	MECHANOCHEMICAL
MATRIMONIAL	MAVOURNEENS	MEANINGLESSLY	MECHANOMORPHISM
MATRIMONIALLY	MAVOURNINS	MEANINGLESSNESS	MECHANORECEPTOR
MATRIMONIES	MAWKISHNESS	MEANNESSES	MECHANOTHERAPY
MATRIOSHKA	MAWKISHNESSES	MEANWHILES	MECHATRONIC
MATRIOSHKI	MAWMETRIES	MEASLINESS	MECHATRONICS
MATROCLINAL	MAXILLARIES	MEASLINESSES	MECLIZINES
MATROCLINIC	MAXILLIPED	MEASURABILITIES	MECONOPSES
MATROCLINIES	MAXILLIPEDARY	MEASURABILITY	MECONOPSIS
MATROCLINOUS	MAXILLIPEDE	MEASURABLE	MEDAILLONS
MATROCLINY	MAXILLIPEDES	MEASURABLENESS	MEDALLIONED
MATRONAGES	MAXILLIPEDS	MEASURABLY	MEDALLIONING
MATRONHOOD	MAXILLOFACIAL	MEASUREDLY	MEDALLIONS
MATRONHOODS	MAXILLULAE	MEASUREDNESS	MEDALLISTS
MATRONISED	MAXIMALIST	MEASUREDNESSES	MEDDLESOME
MATRONISES	MAXIMALISTS	MEASURELESS	MEDDLESOMELY
MATRONISING	MAXIMAPHILIES	MEASURELESSLY	MEDDLESOMENESS
MATRONIZED	MAXIMAPHILY	MEASURELESSNESS	MEDDLINGLY
MATRONIZES	MAXIMATION	MEASUREMENT	MEDEVACING
MATRONIZING	MAXIMATIONS	MEASUREMENTS	MEDEVACKED
MATRONLINESS	MAXIMISATION	MEASURINGS	MEDEVACKING
MATRONLINESSES	MAXIMISATIONS	MEATINESSES	MEDIAEVALISM
MATRONSHIP	MAXIMISERS	MEATLOAVES	MEDIAEVALISMS
MATRONSHIPS	MAXIMISING	MEATPACKING	MEDIAEVALIST
MATRONYMIC	MAXIMIZATION	MEATPACKINGS	MEDIAEVALISTIC
MATRONYMICS	MAXIMIZATIONS	MEATSCREEN	MEDIAEVALISTS
MATROYSHKA	MAXIMIZERS	MEATSCREENS	MEDIAEVALLY
MATROYSHKAS	MAXIMIZING	MEATSPACES	MEDIAEVALS
MATRYOSHKA	MAYFLOWERS	MECAMYLAMINE	MEDIAGENIC
MATRYOSHKAS	MAYONNAISE	MECAMYLAMINES	MEDIASTINA
MATRYOSHKI	MAYONNAISES	MECHANICAL	MEDIASTINAL

MEDIASTINUM	MEDIEVALISTIC	MEGAKARYOCYTIC	MEGATONNAGE
MEDIATENESS	MEDIEVALISTS	MEGALITHIC	MEGATONNAGES
MEDIATENESSES	MEDIEVALLY	MEGALITRES	MEGAVERTEBRATE
MEDIATIONAL	MEDIOCRACIES	MEGALOBLAST	MEGAVERTEBRATES
MEDIATIONS	MEDIOCRACY	MEGALOBLASTIC	MEGAVITAMIN
MEDIATISATION	MEDIOCRITIES	MEGALOBLASTS	MEGAVITAMINS
MEDIATISATIONS	MEDIOCRITY	MEGALOCARDIA	MEIOFAUNAL
MEDIATISED	MEDITATING	MEGALOCARDIAS	MEIOSPORES
MEDIATISES	MEDITATION	MEGALOCEPHALIC	MEIOTICALLY
MEDIATISING	MEDITATIONS	MEGALOCEPHALIES	MEITNERIUM
MEDIATIZATION	MEDITATIVE	MEGALOCEPHALOUS	MEITNERIUMS
MEDIATIZATIONS	MEDITATIVELY	MEGALOCEPHALY	MEKOMETERS
MEDIATIZED	MEDITATIVENESS	MEGALOMANIA	MELACONITE
MEDIATIZES	MEDITATORS	MEGALOMANIAC	MELACONITES
MEDIATIZING	MEDITERRANEAN	MEGALOMANIACAL	MELALEUCAS
MEDIATORIAL	MEDIUMISTIC	MEGALOMANIACS	MELAMPODES
MEDIATORIALLY	MEDIUMSHIP	MEGALOMANIAS	MELANAEMIA
MEDIATORSHIP	MEDIUMSHIPS	MEGALOMANIC	MELANAEMIAS
MEDIATORSHIPS	MEDIVACING	MEGALOPOLIS	MELANCHOLIA
MEDIATRESS	MEDIVACKED	MEGALOPOLISES	MELANCHOLIAC
MEDIATRESSES	MEDIVACKING	MEGALOPOLITAN	MELANCHOLIACS
MEDIATRICES	MEDRESSEHS	MEGALOPOLITANS	MELANCHOLIAS
MEDIATRIXES	MEDULLATED	MEGALOPSES	MELANCHOLIC
MEDICALISATION	MEDULLOBLASTOMA	MEGALOSAUR	MELANCHOLICALLY
MEDICALISATIONS	MEDUSIFORM	MEGALOSAURIAN	MELANCHOLICS
MEDICALISE	MEEKNESSES	MEGALOSAURIANS	MELANCHOLIES
MEDICALISED	MEERSCHAUM	MEGALOSAURS	MELANCHOLILY
MEDICALISES	MEERSCHAUMS	MEGALOSAURUS	MELANCHOLINESS
MEDICALISING	MEETINGHOUSE	MEGALOSAURUSES	MELANCHOLIOUS
MEDICALIZATION	MEETINGHOUSES	MEGANEWTON	MELANCHOLY
MEDICALIZATIONS	MEETNESSES	MEGANEWTONS	MELANISATION
MEDICALIZE	MEFLOQUINE	MEGAPARSEC	MELANISATIONS
MEDICALIZED	MEFLOQUINES	MEGAPARSECS	MELANISING
MEDICALIZES	MEGACEPHALIC	MEGAPHONED	MELANISTIC
MEDICALIZING	MEGACEPHALIES	MEGAPHONES	MELANIZATION
MEDICAMENT	MEGACEPHALOUS	MEGAPHONIC	MELANIZATIONS
MEDICAMENTAL	MEGACEPHALY	MEGAPHONICALLY	MELANIZING
MEDICAMENTALLY	MEGACITIES	MEGAPHONING	MELANOBLAST
MEDICAMENTARY	MEGACORPORATION	MEGAPHYLLS	MELANOBLASTS
MEDICAMENTED	MEGACURIES	MEGAPIXELS	MELANOCHROI
MEDICAMENTING	MEGACYCLES	MEGAPLEXES	MELANOCHROIC
MEDICAMENTOUS	MEGADEATHS	MEGAPROJECT	MELANOCHROOUS
MEDICAMENTS	MEGAFARADS	MEGAPROJECTS	MELANOCYTE
MEDICASTER	MEGAFAUNAE	MEGASCOPES	MELANOCYTES
MEDICASTERS	MEGAFAUNAL	MEGASCOPIC	MELANOGENESES
MEDICATING	MEGAFAUNAS	MEGASCOPICALLY	MELANOGENESIS
MEDICATION	MEGAFLORAE	MEGASPORANGIA	MELANOMATA
MEDICATIONS	MEGAFLORAS	MEGASPORANGIUM	MELANOPHORE
MEDICATIVE	MEGAGAMETE	MEGASPORES	MELANOPHORES
MEDICINABLE	MEGAGAMETES	MEGASPORIC	MELANOSITIES
MEDICINALLY	MEGAGAMETOPHYTE	MEGASPOROPHYLL	MELANOSITY
MEDICINALS	MEGAGAUSSES	MEGASPOROPHYLLS	MELANOSOME
MEDICINERS	MEGAHERBIVORE	MEGASTORES	MELANOSOMES
MEDICINING	MEGAHERBIVORES	MEGASTRUCTURE	MELANOTROPIN
MEDICOLEGAL	MEGAHERTZES	MEGASTRUCTURES	MELANOTROPINS
MEDIEVALISM	MEGAJOULES	MEGATECHNOLOGY	MELANTERITE
MEDIEVALISMS	MEGAKARYOCYTE	MEGATHERES	MELANTERITES
MEDIEVALIST	MEGAKARYOCYTES	MEGATHERIAN	MELANURIAS

MELAPHYRES	MELODRAMATIST	MEMORIZABLE	MENSTRUATING
MELASTOMACEOUS	MELODRAMATISTS	MEMORIZATION	MENSTRUATION
MELATONINS	MELODRAMATIZE	MEMORIZATIONS	MENSTRUATIONS
MELIACEOUS	MELODRAMATIZED	MEMORIZERS	MENSTRUOUS
MELICOTTON	MELODRAMATIZES	MEMORIZING	MENSTRUUMS
MELICOTTONS	MELODRAMATIZING	MENACINGLY	MENSURABILITIES
MELIORABLE	MELODRAMES	MENADIONES	MENSURABILITY
MELIORATED	MELOMANIAC	MENAGERIES	MENSURABLE
MELIORATES	MELOMANIACS	MENAQUINONE	MENSURATION
MELIORATING	MELOMANIAS	MENAQUINONES	MENSURATIONAL
MELIORATION	MELONGENES	MENARCHEAL	MENSURATIONS
MELIORATIONS	MELPHALANS	MENARCHIAL	MENSURATIVE
MELIORATIVE	MELTABILITIES	MENDACIOUS	MENTALESES
MELIORATOR	MELTABILITY	MENDACIOUSLY	MENTALISMS
MELIORATORS	MELTINGNESS	MENDACIOUSNESS	MENTALISTIC
MELIORISMS	MELTINGNESSES	MENDACITIES	MENTALISTICALLY
MELIORISTIC	MELTWATERS	MENDELEVIUM	MENTALISTS
MELIORISTS	MELUNGEONS	MENDELEVIUMS	MENTALITIES
MELIORITIES	MEMBERLESS	MENDICANCIES	MENTATIONS
MELIPHAGOUS	MEMBERSHIP	MENDICANCY	MENTHACEOUS
MELISMATIC	MEMBERSHIPS	MENDICANTS	MENTHOLATED
MELLIFEROUS	MEMBRANACEOUS	MENDICITIES	MENTICIDES
MELLIFICATION	MEMBRANEOUS	MENINGIOMA	MENTIONABLE
MELLIFICATIONS	MEMBRANOUS	MENINGIOMAS	MENTIONERS
MELLIFLUENCE	MEMBRANOUSLY	MENINGIOMATA	MENTIONING
MELLIFLUENCES	MEMOIRISMS	MENINGITIC	MENTONNIERE
MELLIFLUENT	MEMOIRISTS	MENINGITIDES	MENTONNIERES
MELLIFLUENTLY	MEMORABILE	MENINGITIS	MENTORINGS
MELLIFLUOUS	MEMORABILIA	MENINGITISES	MENTORSHIP
MELLIFLUOUSLY	MEMORABILITIES	MENINGOCELE	MENTORSHIPS
MELLIFLUOUSNESS	MEMORABILITY	MENINGOCELES	MENUISIERS
MELLIPHAGOUS	MEMORABLENESS	MENINGOCOCCAL	MEPACRINES
MELLIVOROUS	MEMORABLENESSES	MENINGOCOCCI	MEPERIDINE
MELLOPHONE	MEMORANDUM	MENINGOCOCCIC	MEPERIDINES
MELLOPHONES	MEMORANDUMS	MENINGOCOCCUS	MEPHITICAL
MELLOTRONS	MEMORATIVE	MENISCECTOMIES	MEPHITICALLY
MELLOWNESS	MEMORIALISATION	MENISCECTOMY	MEPHITISES
MELLOWNESSES	MEMORIALISE	MENISCUSES	MEPHITISMS
MELLOWSPEAK	MEMORIALISED	MENISPERMACEOUS	MEPROBAMATE
MELLOWSPEAKS	MEMORIALISER	MENISPERMUM	MEPROBAMATES
MELOCOTONS	MEMORIALISERS	MENISPERMUMS	MERBROMINS
MELOCOTOON	MEMORIALISES	MENOLOGIES	MERCANTILE
MELOCOTOONS	MEMORIALISING	MENOMINEES	MERCANTILISM
MELODICALLY	MEMORIALIST	MENOPAUSAL	MERCANTILISMS
MELODIOUSLY	MEMORIALISTS	MENOPAUSES	MERCANTILIST
MELODIOUSNESS	MEMORIALIZATION	MENOPAUSIC	MERCANTILISTIC
MELODIOUSNESSES	MEMORIALIZE	MENOPOLISES	MERCANTILISTS
MELODISERS	MEMORIALIZED	MENORRHAGIA	MERCAPTANS
MELODISING	MEMORIALIZER	MENORRHAGIAS	MERCAPTIDE
MELODIZERS	MEMORIALIZERS	MENORRHAGIC	MERCAPTIDES
MELODIZING	MEMORIALIZES	MENORRHEAS	MERCAPTOPURINE
MELODRAMAS	MEMORIALIZING	MENORRHOEA	MERCAPTOPURINES
MELODRAMATIC	MEMORIALLY	MENORRHOEAS	MERCENARIES
MELODRAMATICS	MEMORISABLE	MENSERVANTS	MERCENARILY
MELODRAMATISE	MEMORISATION	MENSTRUALLY	MERCENARINESS
MELODRAMATISED	MEMORISATIONS	MENSTRUATE	MERCENARINESSES
MELODRAMATISES	MEMORISERS	MENSTRUATED	MERCENARISM
MELODRAMATISING	MEMORISING	MENSTRUATES	MERCENARISMS

MERCERISATION	MERCURIALISTS	MERRYMAKERS	MESMERIZERS
MERCERISATIONS	MERCURIALITIES	MERRYMAKING	MESMERIZES
MERCERISED	MERCURIALITY	MERRYMAKINGS	MESMERIZING
MERCERISER	MERCURIALIZE	MERRYTHOUGHT	MESNALTIES
MERCERISERS	MERCURIALIZED	MERRYTHOUGHTS	MESOAMERICAN
MERCERISES	MERCURIALIZES	MERVEILLEUSE	MESOBENTHOS
MERCERISING	MERCURIALIZING	MERVEILLEUSES	MESOBENTHOSES
MERCERIZATION	MERCURIALLY	MERVEILLEUX	MESOBLASTIC
MERCERIZATIONS	MERCURIALNESS	MERVEILLEUXES	MESOBLASTS
MERCERIZED	MERCURIALNESSES	MESALLIANCE	MESOCEPHALIC
MERCERIZER	MERCURIALS	MESALLIANCES	MESOCEPHALICS
MERCERIZERS	MERCURISED	MESATICEPHALIC	MESOCEPHALIES
MERCERIZES	MERCURISES	MESATICEPHALIES	MESOCEPHALISM
MERCERIZING	MERCURISING	MESATICEPHALOUS	MESOCEPHALISMS
MERCHANDISE	MERCURIZED	MESATICEPHALY	MESOCEPHALOUS
MERCHANDISED	MERCURIZES	MESCALINES	MESOCEPHALY
MERCHANDISER	MERCURIZING	MESCALISMS	MESOCRANIES
MERCHANDISERS	MERDIVOROUS	MESDEMOISELLES	MESOCRATIC
MERCHANDISES	MEREOLOGICAL	MESENCEPHALA	MESOCYCLONE
MERCHANDISING	MEREOLOGIES	MESENCEPHALIC	MESOCYCLONES
MERCHANDISINGS	MERESTONES	MESENCEPHALON	MESODERMAL
MERCHANDIZE	MERETRICIOUS	MESENCEPHALONS	MESODERMIC
MERCHANDIZED	MERETRICIOUSLY	MESENCHYMAL	MESOGASTRIA
MERCHANDIZER	MERGANSERS	MESENCHYMATOUS	MESOGASTRIC
MERCHANDIZERS	MERIDIONAL	MESENCHYME	MESOGASTRIUM
MERCHANDIZES	MERIDIONALITIES	MESENCHYMES	MESOGLOEAS
MERCHANDIZING	MERIDIONALITY	MESENTERIAL	MESOGNATHIES
MERCHANDIZINGS	MERIDIONALLY	MESENTERIC	MESOGNATHISM
MERCHANTABILITY	MERIDIONALS	MESENTERIES	MESOGNATHISMS
MERCHANTABLE	MERISTEMATIC	MESENTERITIS	MESOGNATHOUS
MERCHANTED	MERISTICALLY	MESENTERITISES	MESOGNATHY
MERCHANTING	MERITOCRACIES	MESENTERON	MESOHIPPUS
MERCHANTINGS	MERITOCRACY	MESENTERONIC	MESOHIPPUSES
MERCHANTLIKE	MERITOCRAT	MESHUGAASEN	MESOKURTIC
MERCHANTMAN	MERITOCRATIC	MESHUGASEN	MESOMERISM
MERCHANTMEN	MERITOCRATS	MESHUGGENAH	MESOMERISMS
MERCHANTRIES	MERITORIOUS	MESHUGGENAHS	MESOMORPHIC
MERCHANTRY	MERITORIOUSLY	MESHUGGENEH	MESOMORPHIES
MERCHILDREN	MERITORIOUSNESS	MESHUGGENEHS	MESOMORPHISM
MERCIFULLY	MERMAIDENS	MESHUGGENER	MESOMORPHISMS
MERCIFULNESS	MEROBLASTIC	MESHUGGENERS	MESOMORPHOUS
MERCIFULNESSES	MEROBLASTICALLY	MESITYLENE	MESOMORPHS
MERCIFYING	MEROGENESES	MESITYLENES	MESOMORPHY
MERCILESSLY	MEROGENESIS	MESMERICAL	MESONEPHRIC
MERCILESSNESS	MEROGENETIC	MESMERICALLY	MESONEPHROI
MERCILESSNESSES	MEROGONIES	MESMERISATION	MESONEPHROS
MERCURATED	MEROMORPHIC	MESMERISATIONS	MESONEPHROSES
MERCURATES	MEROMYOSIN	MESMERISED	MESOPAUSES
MERCURATING	MEROMYOSINS	MESMERISER	MESOPELAGIC
MERCURATION	MERONYMIES	MESMERISERS	MESOPHILES
MERCURATIONS	MEROPIDANS	MESMERISES	MESOPHILIC
MERCURIALISE	MEROPLANKTON	MESMERISING	MESOPHYLLIC
MERCURIALISED	MEROPLANKTONS	MESMERISMS	MESOPHYLLOUS
MERCURIALISES	MEROZOITES	MESMERISTS	MESOPHYLLS
MERCURIALISING	MERPEOPLES	MESMERIZATION	MESOPHYTES
MERCURIALISM	MERRIMENTS	MESMERIZATIONS	MESOPHYTIC
MERCURIALISMS	MERRINESSES	MESMERIZED	MESOSCAPHE
MERCURIALIST	MERRYMAKER	MESMERIZER	MESOSCAPHES

MESOSPHERE	METACENTRES	METALDEHYDES	METALWORKINGS
MESOSPHERES	METACENTRIC	METALEPSES	METALWORKS
MESOSPHERIC	METACENTRICS	METALEPSIS	METAMATHEMATICS
MESOTHELIA	METACERCARIA	METALEPTIC	METAMERICALLY
MESOTHELIAL	METACERCARIAE	METALEPTICAL	METAMERISM
MESOTHELIOMA	METACERCARIAL	METALHEADS	METAMERISMS
MESOTHELIOMAS	METACHROMATIC	METALINGUISTIC	METAMICTISATION
MESOTHELIOMATA	METACHROMATISM	METALINGUISTICS	METAMICTIZATION
MESOTHELIUM	METACHROMATISMS	METALISING	METAMORPHIC
MESOTHELIUMS	METACHRONISM	METALIZATION	METAMORPHICALLY
MESOTHORACES	METACHRONISMS	METALIZATIONS	METAMORPHISM
MESOTHORACIC	METACHROSES	METALIZING	METAMORPHISMS
MESOTHORAX	METACHROSIS	METALLICALLY	METAMORPHIST
MESOTHORAXES	METACINNABARITE	METALLIDING	METAMORPHISTS
MESOTHORIUM	METACOGNITION	METALLIDINGS	METAMORPHOSE
MESOTHORIUMS	METACOGNITIONS	METALLIFEROUS	METAMORPHOSED
MESOTROPHIC	METACOMPUTER	METALLINGS	METAMORPHOSES
MESQUINERIE	METACOMPUTERS	METALLISATION	METAMORPHOSING
MESQUINERIES	METACOMPUTING	METALLISATIONS	METAMORPHOSIS
MESSAGINGS	METACOMPUTINGS	METALLISED	METAMORPHOUS
MESSALINES	METAETHICAL	METALLISES	METANALYSES
MESSEIGNEURS	METAETHICS	METALLISING	METANALYSIS
MESSENGERED	METAFEMALE	METALLISTS	METANEPHRIC
MESSENGERING	METAFEMALES	METALLIZATION	METANEPHROI
MESSENGERS	METAFICTION	METALLIZATIONS	METANEPHROS
MESSIAHSHIP	METAFICTIONAL	METALLIZED	METAPHASES
MESSIAHSHIPS	METAFICTIONIST	METALLIZES	METAPHORIC
MESSIANICALLY	METAFICTIONISTS	METALLIZING	METAPHORICAL
MESSIANISM	METAFICTIONS	METALLOCENE	METAPHORICALLY
MESSIANISMS	METAGALACTIC	METALLOCENES	METAPHORIST
MESSINESSES	METAGALAXIES	METALLOGENETIC	METAPHORISTS
MESTRANOLS	METAGALAXY	METALLOGENIC	METAPHOSPHATE
METABOLICALLY	METAGENESES	METALLOGENIES	METAPHOSPHATES
METABOLIES	METAGENESIS	METALLOGENY	METAPHOSPHORIC
METABOLISABLE	METAGENETIC	METALLOGRAPHER	METAPHRASE
METABOLISE	METAGENETICALLY	METALLOGRAPHERS	METAPHRASED
METABOLISED	METAGNATHISM	METALLOGRAPHIC	METAPHRASES
METABOLISES	METAGNATHISMS	METALLOGRAPHIES	METAPHRASING
METABOLISING	METAGNATHOUS	METALLOGRAPHIST	METAPHRASIS
METABOLISM	METAGRABOLISE	METALLOGRAPHY	METAPHRAST
METABOLISMS	METAGRABOLISED	METALLOIDAL	METAPHRASTIC
METABOLITE	METAGRABOLISES	METALLOIDS	METAPHRASTICAL
METABOLITES	METAGRABOLISING	METALLOPHONE	METAPHRASTS
METABOLIZABLE	METAGRABOLIZE	METALLOPHONES	METAPHYSIC
METABOLIZE	METAGRABOLIZED	METALLURGIC	METAPHYSICAL
METABOLIZED	METAGRABOLIZES	METALLURGICAL	METAPHYSICALLY
METABOLIZES	METAGRABOLIZING	METALLURGICALLY	METAPHYSICIAN
METABOLIZING	METAGROBOLISE	METALLURGIES	METAPHYSICIANS
METABOLOME	METAGROBOLISED	METALLURGIST	METAPHYSICISE
METABOLOMES	METAGROBOLISES	METALLURGISTS	METAPHYSICISED
METABOLOMICS	METAGROBOLISING	METALLURGY	METAPHYSICISES
METABOTROPIC	METAGROBOLIZE	METALMARKS	METAPHYSICISING
METACARPAL	METAGROBOLIZED	METALSMITH	METAPHYSICIST
METACARPALS	METAGROBOLIZES	METALSMITHS	METAPHYSICISTS
METACARPUS	METAGROBOLIZING	METALWARES	METAPHYSICIZE
METACENTER	METALANGUAGE	METALWORKER	METAPHYSICIZED
METACENTERS	METALANGUAGES	METALWORKERS	METAPHYSICIZES
METACENTRE	METALDEHYDE	METALWORKING	METAPHYSICIZING

METAPHYSICS	METATHESIZED	METHACRYLATE	METHOXYCHLORS
METAPLASES	METATHESIZES	METHACRYLATES	METHOXYFLURANE
METAPLASIA	METATHESIZING	METHACRYLIC	METHOXYFLURANES
METAPLASIAS	METATHETIC	METHADONES	METHYLAMINE
METAPLASIS	METATHETICAL	METHAEMOGLOBIN	METHYLAMINES
METAPLASMIC	METATHETICALLY	METHAEMOGLOBINS	METHYLASES
METAPLASMS	METATHORACES	METHAMPHETAMINE	METHYLATED
METAPLASTIC	METATHORACIC	METHANATION	METHYLATES
METAPOLITICAL	METATHORAX	METHANATIONS	METHYLATING
METAPOLITICS	METATHORAXES	METHANOMETER	METHYLATION
METAPSYCHIC	METAVANADIC	METHANOMETERS	METHYLATIONS
METAPSYCHICAL	METAXYLEMS	METHAQUALONE	METHYLATOR
METAPSYCHICS	METECDYSES	METHAQUALONES	METHYLATORS
METAPSYCHOLOGY	METECDYSIS	METHEDRINE	METHYLCELLULOSE
METARCHONS	METEMPIRIC	METHEDRINES	METHYLDOPA
METASEQUOIA	METEMPIRICAL	METHEGLINS	METHYLDOPAS
METASEQUOIAS	METEMPIRICALLY	METHEMOGLOBIN	METHYLENES
METASILICATE	METEMPIRICISM	METHEMOGLOBINS	METHYLMERCURIES
METASILICATES	METEMPIRICISMS	METHENAMINE	METHYLMERCURY
METASILICIC	METEMPIRICIST	METHENAMINES	METHYLPHENIDATE
METASOMATA	METEMPIRICISTS	METHICILLIN	METHYLPHENOL
METASOMATIC	METEMPIRICS	METHICILLINS	METHYLPHENOLS
METASOMATISM	METEMPSYCHOSES	METHINKETH	METHYLTHIONINE
METASOMATISMS	METEMPSYCHOSIS	METHIONINE	METHYLTHIONINES
METASOMATOSES	METEMPSYCHOSIST	METHIONINES	METHYLXANTHINE
METASOMATOSIS	METENCEPHALA	METHODICAL	METHYLXANTHINES
METASTABILITIES	METENCEPHALIC	METHODICALLY	METHYSERGIDE
METASTABILITY	METENCEPHALON	METHODICALNESS	METHYSERGIDES
METASTABLE	METENCEPHALONS	METHODISATION	METICULOSITIES
METASTABLES	METEORICALLY	METHODISATIONS	METICULOSITY
METASTABLY	METEORISMS	METHODISED	METICULOUS
METASTASES	METEORISTS	METHODISER	METICULOUSLY
METASTASIS	METEORITAL	METHODISERS	METICULOUSNESS
METASTASISE	METEORITES	METHODISES	METOESTROUS
METASTASISED	METEORITIC	METHODISING	METOESTRUS
METASTASISES	METEORITICAL	METHODISMS	METOESTRUSES
METASTASISING	METEORITICIST	METHODISTIC	METONYMICAL
METASTASIZE	METEORITICISTS	METHODISTS	METONYMICALLY
METASTASIZED	METEORITICS	METHODIZATION	METONYMIES
METASTASIZES	METEOROGRAM	METHODIZATIONS	METOPOSCOPIC
METASTASIZING	METEOROGRAMS	METHODIZED	METOPOSCOPICAL
METASTATIC	METEOROGRAPH	METHODIZER	METOPOSCOPIES
METASTATICALLY	METEOROGRAPHIC	METHODIZERS	METOPOSCOPIST
METATARSAL	METEOROGRAPHS	METHODIZES	METOPOSCOPISTS
METATARSALS	METEOROIDAL	METHODIZING	METOPOSCOPY
METATARSUS	METEOROIDS	METHODOLOGICAL	METRALGIAS
METATHEORETICAL	METEOROLITE	METHODOLOGIES	METRICALLY
METATHEORIES	METEOROLITES	METHODOLOGIST	METRICATED
METATHEORY	METEOROLOGIC	METHODOLOGISTS	METRICATES
METATHERIAN	METEOROLOGICAL	METHODOLOGY	METRICATING
METATHERIANS	METEOROLOGIES	METHOMANIA	METRICATION
METATHESES	METEOROLOGIST	METHOMANIAS	METRICATIONS
METATHESIS	METEOROLOGISTS	METHOTREXATE	METRICIANS
METATHESISE	METEOROLOGY	METHOTREXATES	METRICISED
METATHESISED	METESTICKS	METHOXIDES	METRICISES
METATHESISES	METESTROUS	METHOXYBENZENE	METRICISING
METATHESISING	METESTRUSES	METHOXYBENZENES	METRICISMS
METATHESIZE	METFORMINS	METHOXYCHLOR	METRICISTS

METRICIZED	MICROAEROPHILIC	MICROCLIMATES	MICROFAUNA
METRICIZES	MICROAMPERE	MICROCLIMATIC	MICROFAUNAE
METRICIZING	MICROAMPERES	MICROCLINE	MICROFAUNAL
METRIFICATION	MICROANALYSES	MICROCLINES	MICROFAUNAS
METRIFICATIONS	MICROANALYSIS	MICROCOCCAL	MICROFELSITIC
METRIFIERS	MICROANALYST	MICROCOCCI	MICROFIBER
METRIFYING	MICROANALYSTS	MICROCOCCUS	MICROFIBERS
METRITISES	MICROANALYTIC	MICROCODES	MICROFIBRE
METROLOGIC	MICROANALYTICAL	MICROCOMPONENT	MICROFIBRES
METROLOGICAL	MICROANATOMICAL	MICROCOMPONENTS	MICROFIBRIL
METROLOGICALLY	MICROANATOMIES	MICROCOMPUTER	MICROFIBRILLAR
METROLOGIES	MICROANATOMY	MICROCOMPUTERS	MICROFIBRILS
METROLOGIST	MICROARRAY	MICROCOMPUTING	MICROFICHE
METROLOGISTS	MICROARRAYS	MICROCOMPUTINGS	MICROFICHES
METROMANIA	MICROBALANCE	MICROCOPIED	MICROFILAMENT
METROMANIAS	MICROBALANCES	MICROCOPIES	MICROFILAMENTS
METRONIDAZOLE	MICROBAROGRAPH	MICROCOPYING	MICROFILARIA
METRONIDAZOLES	MICROBAROGRAPHS	MICROCOPYINGS	MICROFILARIAE
METRONOMES	MICROBEAMS	MICROCOSMIC	MICROFILARIAL
METRONOMIC	MICROBIOLOGIC	MICROCOSMICAL	MICROFILARIAS
METRONOMICAL	MICROBIOLOGICAL	MICROCOSMICALLY	MICROFILING
METRONOMICALLY	MICROBIOLOGIES	MICROCOSMOS	MICROFILINGS
METRONYMIC	MICROBIOLOGIST	MICROCOSMOSES	MICROFILMABLE
METRONYMICS	MICROBIOLOGISTS	MICROCOSMS	MICROFILMED
METROPLEXES	MICROBIOLOGY	MICROCRACK	MICROFILMER
METROPOLIS	MICROBIOTA	MICROCRACKED	MICROFILMERS
METROPOLISES	MICROBREWER	MICROCRACKING	MICROFILMING
METROPOLITAN	MICROBREWERIES	MICROCRACKINGS	MICROFILMS
METROPOLITANATE	MICROBREWERS	MICROCRACKS	MICROFILTER
METROPOLITANISE	MICROBREWERY	MICROCRYSTAL	MICROFILTERS
METROPOLITANISM	MICROBREWING	MICROCRYSTALS	MICROFLOPPIES
METROPOLITANIZE	MICROBREWINGS	MICROCULTURAL	MICROFLOPPY
METROPOLITANS	MICROBREWS	MICROCULTURE	MICROFLORA
METROPOLITICAL	MICROBUBBLES	MICROCULTURES	MICROFLORAE
METRORRHAGIA	MICROBURST	MICROCURIE	MICROFLORAL
METRORRHAGIAS	MICROBURSTS	MICROCURIES	MICROFLORAS
METROSEXUAL	MICROBUSES	MICROCYTES	MICROFORMS
METROSTYLE	MICROBUSSES	MICROCYTIC	MICROFOSSIL
METROSTYLES	MICROCAPSULE	MICRODETECTION	MICROFOSSILS
METTLESOME	MICROCAPSULES	MICRODETECTIONS	MICROFUNGI
METTLESOMENESS	MICROCARDS	MICRODETECTOR	MICROFUNGUS
MEZCALINES	MICROCASSETTE	MICRODETECTORS	MICROGAMETE
MEZZALUNAS	MICROCASSETTES	MICRODISSECTION	MICROGAMETES
MEZZANINES	MICROCELEBRITY	MICRODONTOUS	MICROGAMETOCYTE
MEZZOTINTED	MICROCEPHAL	MICRODRIVE	MICROGLIAS
MEZZOTINTER	MICROCEPHALIC	MICRODRIVES	MICROGRAMS
MEZZOTINTERS	MICROCEPHALICS	MICROEARTHQUAKE	MICROGRANITE
MEZZOTINTING	MICROCEPHALIES	MICROECONOMIC	MICROGRANITES
MEZZOTINTO	MICROCEPHALOUS	MICROECONOMICS	MICROGRANITIC
MEZZOTINTOS	MICROCEPHALS	MICROELECTRODE	MICROGRAPH
MEZZOTINTS	MICROCEPHALY	MICROELECTRODES	MICROGRAPHED
MIAROLITIC	MICROCHEMICAL	MICROELECTRONIC	MICROGRAPHER
MIASMATICAL	MICROCHEMISTRY	MICROELEMENT	MICROGRAPHERS
MIASMATOUS	MICROCHIPS	MICROELEMENTS	MICROGRAPHIC
MIASMICALLY	MICROCIRCUIT	MICROEVOLUTION	MICROGRAPHICS
MICRIFYING	MICROCIRCUITRY	MICROEVOLUTIONS	MICROGRAPHIES
MICROAEROPHILE	MICROCIRCUITS	MICROFARAD	MICROGRAPHING
MICROAEROPHILES	MICROCLIMATE	MICROFARADS	MICROGRAPHS

MICROGRAPHY
MICROGRAVITIES
MICROGRAVITY
MICROGROOVE
MICROGROOVES
MICROHABITAT
MICROHABITATS
MICROIMAGE
MICROIMAGES
MICROINCHES
MICROINJECT
MICROINJECTED
MICROINJECTING
MICROINJECTION
MICROINJECTIONS
MICROINJECTS
MICROLIGHT
MICROLIGHTING
MICROLIGHTINGS
MICROLIGHTS
MICROLITER
MICROLITERS
MICROLITES
MICROLITHIC
MICROLITHS
MICROLITIC
MICROLOANS
MICROLOGIC
MICROLOGICAL
MICROLOGICALLY
MICROLOGIES
MICROLOGIST
MICROLOGISTS
MICROLUCES
MICROLUXES
MICROMANAGE
MICROMANAGED
MICROMANAGEMENT
MICROMANAGER
MICROMANAGERS
MICROMANAGES
MICROMANAGING
MICROMARKETING
MICROMARKETINGS
MICROMERES
MICROMESHES
MICROMETEORITE
MICROMETEORITES
MICROMETEORITIC
MICROMETEOROID
MICROMETEOROIDS
MICROMETER
MICROMETERS
MICROMETHOD
MICROMETHODS
MICROMETRE
MICROMETRES
MICROMETRIC

MICROMETRICAL
MICROMETRIES
MICROMETRY
MICROMICROCURIE
MICROMICROFARAD
MICROMILLIMETRE
MICROMINIATURE
MICROMINIS
MICROMOLAR
MICROMOLES
MICROMORPHOLOGY
MICRONEEDLE
MICRONEEDLES
MICRONISATION
MICRONISATIONS
MICRONISED
MICRONISES
MICRONISING
MICRONIZATION
MICRONIZATIONS
MICRONIZED
MICRONIZES
MICRONIZING
MICRONUCLEI
MICRONUCLEUS
MICRONUCLEUSES
MICRONUTRIENT
MICRONUTRIENTS
MICROORGANISM
MICROORGANISMS
MICROPARASITE
MICROPARASITES
MICROPARASITIC
MICROPARTICLE
MICROPARTICLES
MICROPAYMENT
MICROPAYMENTS
MICROPEGMATITE
MICROPEGMATITES
MICROPEGMATITIC
MICROPHAGE
MICROPHAGES
MICROPHAGOUS
MICROPHONE
MICROPHONES
MICROPHONIC
MICROPHONICS
MICROPHOTOGRAPH
MICROPHOTOMETER
MICROPHOTOMETRY
MICROPHYLL
MICROPHYLLOUS
MICROPHYLLS
MICROPHYSICAL
MICROPHYSICALLY
MICROPHYSICS
MICROPHYTE
MICROPHYTES

MICROPHYTIC
MICROPIPET
MICROPIPETS
MICROPIPETTE
MICROPIPETTES
MICROPLANKTON
MICROPLANKTONS
MICROPOLIS
MICROPOLISES
MICROPORES
MICROPOROSITIES
MICROPOROSITY
MICROPOROUS
MICROPOWER
MICROPOWERS
MICROPRINT
MICROPRINTED
MICROPRINTING
MICROPRINTINGS
MICROPRINTS
MICROPRISM
MICROPRISMS
MICROPROBE
MICROPROBES
MICROPROCESSING
MICROPROCESSOR
MICROPROCESSORS
MICROPROGRAM
MICROPROGRAMS
MICROPROJECTION
MICROPROJECTOR
MICROPROJECTORS
MICROPSIAS
MICROPTEROUS
MICROPUBLISHER
MICROPUBLISHERS
MICROPUBLISHING
MICROPULSATION
MICROPULSATIONS
MICROPUMPS
MICROPUNCTURE
MICROPUNCTURES
MICROPYLAR
MICROPYLES
MICROPYROMETER
MICROPYROMETERS
MICROQUAKE
MICROQUAKES
MICRORADIOGRAPH
MICROREADER
MICROREADERS
MICROSATELLITE
MICROSATELLITES
MICROSCALE
MICROSCALES
MICROSCOPE
MICROSCOPES
MICROSCOPIC

MICROSCOPICAL
MICROSCOPICALLY
MICROSCOPIES
MICROSCOPIST
MICROSCOPISTS
MICROSCOPY
MICROSECOND
MICROSECONDS
MICROSEISM
MICROSEISMIC
MICROSEISMICAL
MICROSEISMICITY
MICROSEISMS
MICROSITES
MICROSKIRT
MICROSKIRTS
MICROSLEEP
MICROSLEEPS
MICROSMATIC
MICROSOMAL
MICROSOMES
MICROSPECIES
MICROSPHERE
MICROSPHERES
MICROSPHERICAL
MICROSPORANGIA
MICROSPORANGIUM
MICROSPORE
MICROSPORES
MICROSPORIC
MICROSPOROCYTE
MICROSPOROCYTES
MICROSPOROPHYLL
MICROSPOROUS
MICROSTATE
MICROSTATES
MICROSTOMATOUS
MICROSTOMOUS
MICROSTRUCTURAL
MICROSTRUCTURE
MICROSTRUCTURES
MICROSURGEON
MICROSURGEONS
MICROSURGERIES
MICROSURGERY
MICROSURGICAL
MICROSWITCH
MICROSWITCHES
MICROTECHNIC
MICROTECHNICS
MICROTECHNIQUE
MICROTECHNIQUES
MICROTECHNOLOGY
MICROTOMES
MICROTOMIC
MICROTOMICAL
MICROTOMIES
MICROTOMIST

MICROTOMISTS	MIDRASHOTH	MILITARIZING	MILLIHENRYS
MICROTONAL	MIDSAGITTAL	MILITATING	MILLILAMBERT
MICROTONALITIES	MIDSECTION	MILITATION	MILLILAMBERTS
MICROTONALITY	MIDSECTIONS	MILITATIONS	MILLILITER
MICROTONALLY	MIDSHIPMAN	MILITIAMAN	MILLILITERS
MICROTONES	MIDSHIPMATE	MILITIAMEN	MILLILITRE
MICROTUBULAR	MIDSHIPMATES	MILKFISHES	MILLILITRES
MICROTUBULE	MIDSHIPMEN	MILKINESSES	MILLILUCES
MICROTUBULES	MIDSTORIES	MILKSHAKES	MILLILUXES
MICROTUNNELLING	MIDSTREAMS	MILKSOPISM	MILLIMETER
MICROVASCULAR	MIDSUMMERS	MILKSOPISMS	MILLIMETERS
MICROVILLAR	MIDWATCHES	MILKSOPPING	MILLIMETRE
MICROVILLI	MIDWIFERIES	MILKTOASTS	MILLIMETRES
MICROVILLOUS	MIDWINTERS	MILLBOARDS	MILLIMICRON
MICROVILLUS	MIFEPRISTONE	MILLEFEUILLE	MILLIMICRONS
MICROVOLTS	MIFEPRISTONES	MILLEFEUILLES	MILLIMOLAR
MICROWATTS	MIFFINESSES	MILLEFIORI	MILLIMOLES
MICROWAVABLE	MIGHTINESS	MILLEFIORIS	MILLINERIES
MICROWAVEABLE	MIGHTINESSES	MILLEFLEUR	MILLIONAIRE
MICROWAVED	MIGMATITES	MILLEFLEURS	MILLIONAIRES
MICROWAVES	MIGNONETTE	MILLENARIAN	MILLIONAIRESS
MICROWAVING	MIGNONETTES	MILLENARIANISM	MILLIONAIRESSES
MICROWIRES	MIGRAINEUR	MILLENARIANISMS	MILLIONARY
MICROWORLD	MIGRAINEURS	MILLENARIANS	MILLIONFOLD
MICROWORLDS	MIGRAINOUS	MILLENARIES	MILLIONNAIRE
MICROWRITER	MIGRATIONAL	MILLENARISM	MILLIONNAIRES
MICROWRITERS	MIGRATIONIST	MILLENARISMS	MILLIONNAIRESS
MICRURGIES	MIGRATIONISTS	MILLENNIAL	MILLIONTHS
MICTURATED	MIGRATIONS	MILLENNIALISM	MILLIOSMOL
MICTURATES	MILATAINMENT	MILLENNIALISMS	MILLIOSMOLS
MICTURATING	MILATAINMENTS	MILLENNIALIST	MILLIPEDES
MICTURITION	MILDNESSES	MILLENNIALISTS	MILLIPROBE
MICTURITIONS	MILEOMETER	MILLENNIALLY	MILLIPROBES
MIDDELMANNETJIE	MILEOMETERS	MILLENNIANISM	MILLIRADIAN
MIDDENSTEAD	MILESTONES	MILLENNIANISMS	MILLIRADIANS
MIDDENSTEADS	MILITANCES	MILLENNIARISM	MILLIROENTGEN
MIDDLEBREAKER	MILITANCIES	MILLENNIARISMS	MILLIROENTGENS
MIDDLEBREAKERS	MILITANTLY	MILLENNIUM	MILLISECOND
MIDDLEBROW	MILITANTNESS	MILLENNIUMS	MILLISECONDS
MIDDLEBROWED	MILITANTNESSES	MILLEPEDES	MILLISIEVERT
MIDDLEBROWISM	MILITARIES	MILLEPORES	MILLISIEVERTS
MIDDLEBROWISMS	MILITARILY	MILLERITES	MILLIVOLTS
MIDDLEBROWS	MILITARISATION	MILLESIMAL	MILLIWATTS
MIDDLEBUSTER	MILITARISATIONS	MILLESIMALLY	MILLOCRACIES
MIDDLEBUSTERS	MILITARISE	MILLESIMALS	MILLOCRACY
MIDDLEMOST	MILITARISED	MILLHOUSES	MILLOCRATS
MIDDLEWEIGHT	MILITARISES	MILLIAMPERE	MILLSCALES
MIDDLEWEIGHTS	MILITARISING	MILLIAMPERES	MILLSTONES
MIDDLINGLY	MILITARISM	MILLIARIES	MILLSTREAM
MIDFIELDER	MILITARISMS	MILLICURIE	MILLSTREAMS
MIDFIELDERS	MILITARIST	MILLICURIES	MILLWHEELS
MIDINETTES	MILITARISTIC	MILLIDEGREE	MILLWRIGHT
MIDISKIRTS	MILITARISTS	MILLIDEGREES	MILLWRIGHTS
MIDLATITUDE	MILITARIZATION	MILLIGRAMME	MILOMETERS
MIDLATITUDES	MILITARIZATIONS	MILLIGRAMMES	MILQUETOAST
MIDLITTORAL	MILITARIZE	MILLIGRAMS	MILQUETOASTS
MIDLITTORALS	MILITARIZED	MILLIHENRIES	MIMEOGRAPH
MIDNIGHTLY	MILITARIZES	MILLIHENRY	MIMEOGRAPHED

943

MIMEOGRAPHING	MINERALOGISED	MINIMALISM	MINUTENESS
MIMEOGRAPHS	MINERALOGISES	MINIMALISMS	MINUTENESSES
MIMETICALLY	MINERALOGISING	MINIMALIST	MIRABELLES
MIMMICKING	MINERALOGIST	MINIMALISTS	MIRABILISES
MIMOGRAPHER	MINERALOGISTS	MINIMAXING	MIRACIDIAL
MIMOGRAPHERS	MINERALOGIZE	MINIMISATION	MIRACIDIUM
MIMOGRAPHIES	MINERALOGIZED	MINIMISATIONS	MIRACULOUS
MIMOGRAPHY	MINERALOGIZES	MINIMISERS	MIRACULOUSLY
MIMOSACEOUS	MINERALOGIZING	MINIMISING	MIRACULOUSNESS
MINACIOUSLY	MINERALOGY	MINIMIZATION	MIRANDISED
MINACITIES	MINESHAFTS	MINIMIZATIONS	MIRANDISES
MINATORIAL	MINESTONES	MINIMIZERS	MIRANDISING
MINATORIALLY	MINESTRONE	MINIMIZING	MIRANDIZED
MINATORILY	MINESTRONES	MINIRUGBIES	MIRANDIZES
MINAUDERIE	MINESWEEPER	MINISCHOOL	MIRANDIZING
MINAUDERIES	MINESWEEPERS	MINISCHOOLS	MIRIFICALLY
MINAUDIERE	MINESWEEPING	MINISCULES	MIRINESSES
MINAUDIERES	MINESWEEPINGS	MINISERIES	MIRKINESSES
MINCEMEATS	MINGIMINGI	MINISKIRTED	MIRRORLIKE
MINDBLOWER	MINGIMINGIS	MINISKIRTS	MIRRORWISE
MINDBLOWERS	MINGINESSES	MINISTATES	MIRTHFULLY
MINDEDNESS	MINGLEMENT	MINISTERED	MIRTHFULNESS
MINDEDNESSES	MINGLEMENTS	MINISTERIA	MIRTHFULNESSES
MINDFULNESS	MINGLINGLY	MINISTERIAL	MIRTHLESSLY
MINDFULNESSES	MINIATIONS	MINISTERIALIST	MIRTHLESSNESS
MINDLESSLY	MINIATURED	MINISTERIALISTS	MIRTHLESSNESSES
MINDLESSNESS	MINIATURES	MINISTERIALLY	MISACCEPTATION
MINDLESSNESSES	MINIATURING	MINISTERING	MISACCEPTATIONS
MINDSHARES	MINIATURISATION	MINISTERIUM	MISADAPTED
MINEFIELDS	MINIATURISE	MINISTERSHIP	MISADAPTING
MINEHUNTER	MINIATURISED	MINISTERSHIPS	MISADDRESS
MINEHUNTERS	MINIATURISES	MINISTRANT	MISADDRESSED
MINELAYERS	MINIATURISING	MINISTRANTS	MISADDRESSES
MINERALISABLE	MINIATURIST	MINISTRATION	MISADDRESSING
MINERALISATION	MINIATURISTIC	MINISTRATIONS	MISADJUSTED
MINERALISATIONS	MINIATURISTS	MINISTRATIVE	MISADJUSTING
MINERALISE	MINIATURIZATION	MINISTRESS	MISADJUSTS
MINERALISED	MINIATURIZE	MINISTRESSES	MISADVENTURE
MINERALISER	MINIATURIZED	MINISTRIES	MISADVENTURED
MINERALISERS	MINIATURIZES	MINISTROKE	MISADVENTURER
MINERALISES	MINIATURIZING	MINISTROKES	MISADVENTURERS
MINERALISING	MINIBIKERS	MINITOWERS	MISADVENTURES
MINERALIST	MINIBREAKS	MINITRACKS	MISADVENTUROUS
MINERALISTS	MINIBUDGET	MINIVOLLEY	MISADVERTENCE
MINERALIZABLE	MINIBUDGETS	MINIVOLLEYS	MISADVERTENCES
MINERALIZATION	MINIBUSSES	MINNESINGER	MISADVICES
MINERALIZATIONS	MINICABBING	MINNESINGERS	MISADVISED
MINERALIZE	MINICABBINGS	MINNICKING	MISADVISEDLY
MINERALIZED	MINICOMPUTER	MINNOCKING	MISADVISEDNESS
MINERALIZER	MINICOMPUTERS	MINORITAIRE	MISADVISES
MINERALIZERS	MINICOURSE	MINORITAIRES	MISADVISING
MINERALIZES	MINICOURSES	MINORITIES	MISALIGNED
MINERALIZING	MINIDISHES	MINORSHIPS	MISALIGNING
MINERALOGIC	MINIDRESSES	MINOXIDILS	MISALIGNMENT
MINERALOGICAL	MINIFICATION	MINSTRELSIES	MISALIGNMENTS
MINERALOGICALLY	MINIFICATIONS	MINSTRELSY	MISALLEGED
MINERALOGIES	MINIFLOPPIES	MINUSCULAR	MISALLEGES
MINERALOGISE	MINIFLOPPY	MINUSCULES	MISALLEGING

MISALLIANCE	MISARRANGING	MISBESTOWED	MISCELLANEOUS
MISALLIANCES	MISARTICULATE	MISBESTOWING	MISCELLANEOUSLY
MISALLOCATE	MISARTICULATED	MISBESTOWS	MISCELLANIES
MISALLOCATED	MTSARTICULATES	MISBIASING	MISCELLANIST
MISALLOCATES	MISARTICULATING	MISBIASSED	MISCELLANISTS
MISALLOCATING	MISASSAYED	MISBIASSES	MISCELLANY
MISALLOCATION	MISASSAYING	MISBIASSING	MISCHALLENGE
MISALLOCATIONS	MISASSEMBLE	MISBILLING	MISCHALLENGES
MISALLOTMENT	MISASSEMBLED	MISBINDING	MISCHANCED
MISALLOTMENTS	MISASSEMBLES	MISBRANDED	MISCHANCEFUL
MISALLOTTED	MISASSEMBLING	MISBRANDING	MISCHANCES
MISALLOTTING	MISASSIGNED	MISBUILDING	MISCHANCING
MISALLYING	MISASSIGNING	MISBUTTONED	MISCHANNEL
MISALTERED	MISASSIGNS	MISBUTTONING	MISCHANNELED
MISALTERING	MISASSUMPTION	MISBUTTONS	MISCHANNELING
MISANALYSES	MISASSUMPTIONS	MISCALCULATE	MISCHANNELLED
MISANALYSIS	MISATONING	MISCALCULATED	MISCHANNELLING
MISANDRIES	MISATTRIBUTE	MISCALCULATES	MISCHANNELS
MISANDRIST	MISATTRIBUTED	MISCALCULATING	MISCHANTER
MISANDRISTS	MISATTRIBUTES	MISCALCULATION	MISCHANTERS
MISANDROUS	MISATTRIBUTING	MISCALCULATIONS	MISCHARACTERISE
MISANTHROPE	MISATTRIBUTION	MISCALCULATOR	MISCHARACTERIZE
MISANTHROPES	MISATTRIBUTIONS	MISCALCULATORS	MISCHARGED
MISANTHROPIC	MISAUNTERS	MISCALLERS	MISCHARGES
MISANTHROPICAL	MISAVERRED	MISCALLING	MISCHARGING
MISANTHROPIES	MISAVERRING	MISCANTHUS	MISCHIEFED
MISANTHROPIST	MISAWARDED	MISCANTHUSES	MISCHIEFING
MISANTHROPISTS	MISAWARDING	MISCAPTION	MISCHIEVOUS
MISANTHROPOS	MISBALANCE	MISCAPTIONED	MISCHIEVOUSLY
MISANTHROPOSES	MISBALANCED	MISCAPTIONING	MISCHIEVOUSNESS
MISANTHROPY	MISBALANCES	MISCAPTIONS	MISCHMETAL
MISAPPLICATION	MISBALANCING	MISCARRIAGE	MISCHMETALS
MISAPPLICATIONS	MISBECOMES	MISCARRIAGES	MISCHOICES
MISAPPLIED	MISBECOMING	MISCARRIED	MISCHOOSES
MISAPPLIES	MISBECOMINGNESS	MISCARRIES	MISCHOOSING
MISAPPLYING	MISBEGINNING	MISCARRYING	MISCIBILITIES
MISAPPRAISAL	MISBEGOTTEN	MISCASTING	MISCIBILITY
MISAPPRAISALS	MISBEHAVED	MISCATALOG	MISCITATION
MISAPPRECIATE	MISBEHAVER	MISCATALOGED	MISCITATIONS
MISAPPRECIATED	MISBEHAVERS	MISCATALOGING	MISCLAIMED
MISAPPRECIATES	MISBEHAVES	MISCATALOGS	MISCLAIMING
MISAPPRECIATING	MISBEHAVING	MISCEGENATE	MISCLASSED
MISAPPRECIATION	MISBEHAVIOR	MISCEGENATED	MISCLASSES
MISAPPRECIATIVE	MISBEHAVIORS	MISCEGENATES	MISCLASSIFIED
MISAPPREHEND	MISBEHAVIOUR	MISCEGENATING	MISCLASSIFIES
MISAPPREHENDED	MISBEHAVIOURS	MISCEGENATION	MISCLASSIFY
MISAPPREHENDING	MISBELIEFS	MISCEGENATIONAL	MISCLASSIFYING
MISAPPREHENDS	MISBELIEVE	MISCEGENATIONS	MISCLASSING
MISAPPREHENSION	MISBELIEVED	MISCEGENATOR	MISCOINING
MISAPPREHENSIVE	MISBELIEVER	MISCEGENATORS	MISCOLORED
MISAPPROPRIATE	MISBELIEVERS	MISCEGENES	MISCOLORING
MISAPPROPRIATED	MISBELIEVES	MISCEGENETIC	MISCOLOURED
MISAPPROPRIATES	MISBELIEVING	MISCEGENIST	MISCOLOURING
MISARRANGE	MISBESEEMED	MISCEGENISTS	MISCOLOURS
MISARRANGED	MISBESEEMING	MISCEGINES	MISCOMPREHEND
MISARRANGEMENT	MISBESEEMS	MISCELLANARIAN	MISCOMPREHENDED
MISARRANGEMENTS	MISBESTOWAL	MISCELLANARIANS	MISCOMPREHENDS
MISARRANGES	MISBESTOWALS	MISCELLANEA	MISCOMPUTATION

MISCOMPUTATIONS	MISCORRELATION	MISDIAGNOSED	MISERABILIST
MISCOMPUTE	MISCORRELATIONS	MISDIAGNOSES	MISERABILISTS
MISCOMPUTED	MISCOUNSEL	MISDIAGNOSING	MISERABLENESS
MISCOMPUTES	MISCOUNSELLED	MISDIAGNOSIS	MISERABLENESSES
MISCOMPUTING	MISCOUNSELLING	MISDIALING	MISERABLES
MISCONCEIT	MISCOUNSELS	MISDIALLED	MISERABLISM
MISCONCEITED	MISCOUNTED	MISDIALLING	MISERABLISMS
MISCONCEITING	MISCOUNTING	MISDIRECTED	MISERABLIST
MISCONCEITS	MISCREANCE	MISDIRECTING	MISERABLISTS
MISCONCEIVE	MISCREANCES	MISDIRECTION	MISERICORD
MISCONCEIVED	MISCREANCIES	MISDIRECTIONS	MISERICORDE
MISCONCEIVER	MISCREANCY	MISDIRECTS	MISERICORDES
MISCONCEIVERS	MISCREANTS	MISDISTRIBUTION	MISERICORDS
MISCONCEIVES	MISCREATED	MISDIVIDED	MISERLIEST
MISCONCEIVING	MISCREATES	MISDIVIDES	MISERLINESS
MISCONCEPTION	MISCREATING	MISDIVIDING	MISERLINESSES
MISCONCEPTIONS	MISCREATION	MISDIVISION	MISESTEEMED
MISCONDUCT	MISCREATIONS	MISDIVISIONS	MISESTEEMING
MISCONDUCTED	MISCREATIVE	MISDOUBTED	MISESTEEMS
MISCONDUCTING	MISCREATOR	MISDOUBTFUL	MISESTIMATE
MISCONDUCTS	MISCREATORS	MISDOUBTING	MISESTIMATED
MISCONJECTURE	MISCREAUNCE	MISDRAWING	MISESTIMATES
MISCONJECTURED	MISCREAUNCES	MISDRAWINGS	MISESTIMATING
MISCONJECTURES	MISCREDITED	MISDRIVING	MISESTIMATION
MISCONJECTURING	MISCREDITING	MISEDITING	MISESTIMATIONS
MISCONNECT	MISCREDITS	MISEDUCATE	MISEVALUATE
MISCONNECTED	MISCUTTING	MISEDUCATED	MISEVALUATED
MISCONNECTING	MISDEALERS	MISEDUCATES	MISEVALUATES
MISCONNECTION	MISDEALING	MISEDUCATING	MISEVALUATING
MISCONNECTIONS	MISDEEMFUL	MISEDUCATION	MISEVALUATION
MISCONNECTS	MISDEEMING	MISEDUCATIONS	MISEVALUATIONS
MISCONSTER	MISDEEMINGS	MISEMPHASES	MISFALLING
MISCONSTERED	MISDEFINED	MISEMPHASIS	MISFARINGS
MISCONSTERING	MISDEFINES	MISEMPHASISE	MISFEASANCE
MISCONSTERS	MISDEFINING	MISEMPHASISED	MISFEASANCES
MISCONSTRUCT	MISDEMEANANT	MISEMPHASISES	MISFEASORS
MISCONSTRUCTED	MISDEMEANANTS	MISEMPHASISING	MISFEATURE
MISCONSTRUCTING	MISDEMEANED	MISEMPHASIZE	MISFEATURED
MISCONSTRUCTION	MISDEMEANING	MISEMPHASIZED	MISFEATURES
MISCONSTRUCTS	MISDEMEANOR	MISEMPHASIZES	MISFEATURING
MISCONSTRUE	MISDEMEANORS	MISEMPHASIZING	MISFEEDING
MISCONSTRUED	MISDEMEANOUR	MISEMPLOYED	MISFEIGNED
MISCONSTRUES	MISDEMEANOURS	MISEMPLOYING	MISFEIGNING
MISCONSTRUING	MISDEMEANS	MISEMPLOYMENT	MISFIELDED
MISCONTENT	MISDESCRIBE	MISEMPLOYMENTS	MISFIELDING
MISCONTENTED	MISDESCRIBED	MISEMPLOYS	MISFITTING
MISCONTENTING	MISDESCRIBES	MISENROLLED	MISFOCUSED
MISCONTENTMENT	MISDESCRIBING	MISENROLLING	MISFOCUSES
MISCONTENTMENTS	MISDESCRIPTION	MISENROLLS	MISFOCUSING
MISCONTENTS	MISDESCRIPTIONS	MISENTERED	MISFOCUSSED
MISCOOKING	MISDESERTS	MISENTERING	MISFOCUSSES
MISCOPYING	MISDEVELOP	MISENTREAT	MISFOCUSSING
MISCORRECT	MISDEVELOPED	MISENTREATED	MISFORMATION
MISCORRECTED	MISDEVELOPING	MISENTREATING	MISFORMATIONS
MISCORRECTING	MISDEVELOPS	MISENTREATS	MISFORMING
MISCORRECTION	MISDEVOTION	MISENTRIES	MISFORTUNE
MISCORRECTIONS	MISDEVOTIONS	MISERABILISM	MISFORTUNED
MISCORRECTS	MISDIAGNOSE	MISERABILISMS	MISFORTUNES

MISFRAMING	MISIMPROVE	MISLEADINGLY	MISOGAMISTS
MISFUNCTION	MISIMPROVED	MISLEARNED	MISOGYNIES
MISFUNCTIONED	MISIMPROVEMENT	MISLEARNING	MISOGYNIST
MISFUNCTIONING	MISIMPROVEMENTS	MISLEEKING	MISOGYNISTIC
MISFUNCTIONS	MISIMPROVES	MISLIGHTED	MISOGYNISTICAL
MISGAUGING	MISIMPROVING	MISLIGHTING	MISOGYNISTS
MISGIVINGS	MISINFERRED	MISLIKINGS	MISOGYNOUS
MISGOVERNAUNCE	MISINFERRING	MISLIPPENED	MISOLOGIES
MISGOVERNAUNCES	MISINFORMANT	MISLIPPENING	MISOLOGIST
MISGOVERNED	MISINFORMANTS	MISLIPPENS	MISOLOGISTS
MISGOVERNING	MISINFORMATION	MISLOCATED	MISONEISMS
MISGOVERNMENT	MISINFORMATIONS	MISLOCATES	MISONEISTIC
MISGOVERNMENTS	MISINFORMED	MISLOCATING	MISONEISTS
MISGOVERNOR	MISINFORMER	MISLOCATION	MISORDERED
MISGOVERNORS	MISINFORMERS	MISLOCATIONS	MISORDERING
MISGOVERNS	MISINFORMING	MISLODGING	MISORIENTATION
MISGRADING	MISINFORMS	MISLUCKING	MISORIENTATIONS
MISGRAFTED	MISINSTRUCT	MISMANAGED	MISORIENTED
MISGRAFTING	MISINSTRUCTED	MISMANAGEMENT	MISORIENTING
MISGROWING	MISINSTRUCTING	MISMANAGEMENTS	MISORIENTS
MISGROWTHS	MISINSTRUCTION	MISMANAGER	MISPACKAGE
MISGUESSED	MISINSTRUCTIONS	MISMANAGERS	MISPACKAGED
MISGUESSES	MISINSTRUCTS	MISMANAGES	MISPACKAGES
MISGUESSING	MISINTELLIGENCE	MISMANAGING	MISPACKAGING
MISGUGGLED	MISINTENDED	MISMANNERS	MISPAINTED
MISGUGGLES	MISINTENDING	MISMARKING	MISPAINTING
MISGUGGLING	MISINTENDS	MISMARRIAGE	MISPARSING
MISGUIDANCE	MISINTERPRET	MISMARRIAGES	MISPARTING
MISGUIDANCES	MISINTERPRETED	MISMARRIED	MISPATCHED
MISGUIDEDLY	MISINTERPRETER	MISMARRIES	MISPATCHES
MISGUIDEDNESS	MISINTERPRETERS	MISMARRYING	MISPATCHING
MISGUIDEDNESSES	MISINTERPRETING	MISMATCHED	MISPENNING
MISGUIDERS	MISINTERPRETS	MISMATCHES	MISPERCEIVE
MISGUIDING	MISINTERRED	MISMATCHING	MISPERCEIVED
MISHALLOWED	MISINTERRING	MISMATCHMENT	MISPERCEIVES
MISHANDLED	MISJOINDER	MISMATCHMENTS	MISPERCEIVING
MISHANDLES	MISJOINDERS	MISMEASURE	MISPERCEPTION
MISHANDLING	MISJOINING	MISMEASURED	MISPERCEPTIONS
MISHANTERS	MISJUDGEMENT	MISMEASUREMENT	MISPERSUADE
MISHAPPENED	MISJUDGEMENTS	MISMEASUREMENTS	MISPERSUADED
MISHAPPENING	MISJUDGERS	MTSMEASURES	MISPERSUADES
MISHAPPENS	MISJUDGING	MISMEASURING	MISPERSUADING
MISHAPPING	MISJUDGMENT	MISMEETING	MISPERSUASION
MISHEARING	MISJUDGMENTS	MISMETRING	MISPERSUASIONS
MISHEGAASEN	MISKEEPING	MISNOMERED	MISPHRASED
MISHGUGGLE	MISKENNING	MISNOMERING	MISPHRASES
MISHGUGGLED	MISKICKING	MISNUMBERED	MISPHRASING
MISHGUGGLES	MISKNOWING	MISNUMBERING	MISPICKELS
MISHGUGGLING	MISKNOWLEDGE	MISNUMBERS	MISPLACEMENT
MISHITTING	MISKNOWLEDGES	MISOBSERVANCE	MISPLACEMENTS
MISHMASHES	MISLABELED	MISOBSERVANCES	MISPLACING
MISHMOSHES	MISLABELING	MISOBSERVE	MISPLANNED
MISIDENTIFIED	MISLABELLED	MISOBSERVED	MISPLANNING
MISIDENTIFIES	MISLABELLING	MISOBSERVES	MISPLANTED
MISIDENTIFY	MISLABORED	MISOBSERVING	MISPLANTING
MISIDENTIFYING	MISLABORING	MISOCAPNIC	MISPLAYING
MISIMPRESSION	MISLEADERS	MISOGAMIES	MISPLEADED
MISIMPRESSIONS	MISLEADING	MISOGAMIST	MISPLEADING

MISPLEADINGS	MISREFERENCES	MISSIONARISING	MISTAKABLY
MISPLEASED	MISREFERRED	MISSIONARIZE	MISTAKEABLE
MISPLEASES	MISREFERRING	MISSIONARIZED	MISTAKEABLY
MISPLEASING	MISREGARDS	MISSIONARIZES	MISTAKENLY
MISPOINTED	MISREGISTER	MISSIONARIZING	MISTAKENNESS
MISPOINTING	MISREGISTERED	MISSIONARY	MISTAKENNESSES
MISPOISING	MISREGISTERING	MISSIONERS	MISTAKINGS
MISPOSITION	MISREGISTERS	MISSIONING	MISTEACHES
MISPOSITIONED	MISREGISTRATION	MISSIONISATION	MISTEACHING
MISPOSITIONING	MISRELATED	MISSIONISATIONS	MISTELLING
MISPOSITIONS	MISRELATES	MISSIONISE	MISTEMPERED
MISPRAISED	MISRELATING	MISSIONISED	MISTEMPERING
MISPRAISES	MISRELATION	MISSIONISER	MISTEMPERS
MISPRAISING	MISRELATIONS	MISSIONISERS	MISTENDING
MISPRICING	MISRELYING	MISSIONISES	MISTERMING
MISPRINTED	MISREMEMBER	MISSIONISING	MISTHINKING
MISPRINTING	MISREMEMBERED	MISSIONIZATION	MISTHOUGHT
MISPRISERS	MISREMEMBERING	MISSIONIZATIONS	MISTHOUGHTS
MISPRISING	MISREMEMBERS	MISSIONIZE	MISTHROWING
MISPRISION	MISRENDERED	MISSIONIZED	MISTIGRISES
MISPRISIONS	MISRENDERING	MISSIONIZER	MISTINESSES
MISPRIZERS	MISRENDERS	MISSIONIZERS	MISTITLING
MISPRIZING	MISREPORTED	MISSIONIZES	MISTLETOES
MISPROGRAM	MISREPORTER	MISSIONIZING	MISTOUCHED
MISPROGRAMED	MISREPORTERS	MISSISHNESS	MISTOUCHES
MISPROGRAMING	MISREPORTING	MISSISHNESSES	MISTOUCHING
MISPROGRAMMED	MISREPORTS	MISSORTING	MISTRACING
MISPROGRAMMING	MISREPRESENT	MISSOUNDED	MISTRAINED
MISPROGRAMS	MISREPRESENTED	MISSOUNDING	MISTRAINING
MISPRONOUNCE	MISREPRESENTER	MISSPACING	MISTRANSCRIBE
MISPRONOUNCED	MISREPRESENTERS	MISSPEAKING	MISTRANSCRIBED
MISPRONOUNCES	MISREPRESENTING	MISSPELLED	MISTRANSCRIBES
MISPRONOUNCING	MISREPRESENTS	MISSPELLING	MISTRANSCRIBING
MISPROPORTION	MISROUTEING	MISSPELLINGS	MISTRANSLATE
MISPROPORTIONED	MISROUTING	MISSPENDER	MISTRANSLATED
MISPROPORTIONS	MISSAYINGS	MISSPENDERS	MISTRANSLATES
MISPUNCTUATE	MISSEATING	MISSPENDING	MISTRANSLATING
MISPUNCTUATED	MISSEEMING	MISSTAMPED	MISTRANSLATION
MISPUNCTUATES	MISSEEMINGS	MISSTAMPING	MISTRANSLATIONS
MISPUNCTUATING	MISSENDING	MISSTARTED	MISTRAYNED
MISPUNCTUATION	MISSETTING	MISSTARTING	MISTREADING
MISPUNCTUATIONS	MISSHAPENLY	MISSTATEMENT	MISTREADINGS
MISQUOTATION	MISSHAPENNESS	MISSTATEMENTS	MISTREATED
MISQUOTATIONS	MISSHAPENNESSES	MISSTATING	MISTREATING
MISQUOTERS	MISSHAPERS	MISSTEERED	MISTREATMENT
MISQUOTING	MISSHAPING	MISSTEERING	MISTREATMENTS
MISRAISING	MISSHEATHED	MISSTEPPED	MISTRESSED
MISREADING	MISSILEERS	MISSTEPPING	MISTRESSES
MISREADINGS	MISSILEMAN	MISSTOPPED	MISTRESSING
MISRECKONED	MISSILEMEN	MISSTOPPING	MISTRESSLESS
MISRECKONING	MISSILERIES	MISSTRICKEN	MISTRESSLY
MISRECKONINGS	MISSILRIES	MISSTRIKES	MISTRUSTED
MISRECKONS	MISSIOLOGIES	MISSTRIKING	MISTRUSTER
MISRECOLLECTION	MISSIOLOGY	MISSTYLING	MISTRUSTERS
MISRECORDED	MISSIONARIES	MISSUITING	MISTRUSTFUL
MISRECORDING	MISSIONARISE	MISSUMMATION	MISTRUSTFULLY
MISRECORDS	MISSIONARISED	MISSUMMATIONS	MISTRUSTFULNESS
MISREFERENCE	MISSIONARISES	MISTAKABLE	MISTRUSTING

MISTRUSTINGLY	MITOMYCINS	MODERATION	MOISTIFIES
MISTRUSTLESS	MITOTICALLY	MODERATIONS	MOISTIFYING
MISTRYSTED	MITRAILLES	MODERATISM	MOISTNESSES
MISTRYSTING	MITRAILLEUR	MODERATISMS	MOISTURELESS
MISTUTORED	MITRAILLEURS	MODERATORS	MOISTURISE
MISTUTORING	MITRAILLEUSE	MODERATORSHIP	MOISTURISED
MISUNDERSTAND	MITRAILLEUSES	MODERATORSHIPS	MOISTURISER
MISUNDERSTANDS	MITREWORTS	MODERATRICES	MOISTURISERS
MISUNDERSTOOD	MITTIMUSES	MODERATRIX	MOISTURISES
MISUTILISATION	MIXABILITIES	MODERATRIXES	MOISTURISING
MISUTILISATIONS	MIXABILITY	MODERNISATION	MOISTURIZE
MISUTILIZATION	MIXEDNESSES	MODERNISATIONS	MOISTURIZED
MISUTILIZATIONS	MIXMASTERS	MODERNISED	MOISTURIZER
MISVALUING	MIXOBARBARIC	MODERNISER	MOISTURIZERS
MISVENTURE	MIXOLOGIES	MODERNISERS	MOISTURIZES
MISVENTURES	MIXOLOGIST	MODERNISES	MOISTURIZING
MISVENTUROUS	MIXOLOGISTS	MODERNISING	MOITHERING
MISVOCALISATION	MIXOLYDIAN	MODERNISMS	MOLALITIES
MISVOCALIZATION	MIXOTROPHIC	MODERNISTIC	MOLARITIES
MISWANDRED	MIZENMASTS	MODERNISTICALLY	MOLASSESES
MISWEENING	MIZZENMAST	MODERNISTS	MOLDABILITIES
MISWENDING	MIZZENMASTS	MODERNITIES	MOLDABILITY
MISWORDING	MIZZONITES	MODERNIZATION	MOLDAVITES
MISWORDINGS	MNEMONICAL	MODERNIZATIONS	MOLDBOARDS
MISWORSHIP	MNEMONICALLY	MODERNIZED	MOLDINESSES
MISWORSHIPPED	MNEMONISTS	MODERNIZER	MOLECATCHER
MISWORSHIPPING	MNEMOTECHNIC	MODERNIZERS	MOLECATCHERS
MISWORSHIPS	MNEMOTECHNICS	MODERNIZES	MOLECULARITIES
MISWRITING	MNEMOTECHNIST	MODERNIZING	MOLECULARITY
MISWRITTEN	MNEMOTECHNISTS	MODERNNESS	MOLECULARLY
MITERWORTS	MOBILISABLE	MODERNNESSES	MOLEHUNTER
MITHRADATIC	MOBILISATION	MODIFIABILITIES	MOLEHUNTERS
MITHRIDATE	MOBILISATIONS	MODIFIABILITY	MOLENDINAR
MITHRIDATES	MOBILISERS	MODIFIABLE	MOLENDINARIES
MITHRIDATIC	MOBILISING	MODIFIABLENESS	MOLENDINARS
MITHRIDATISE	MOBILITIES	MODIFICATION	MOLENDINARY
MITHRIDATISED	MOBILIZABLE	MODIFICATIONS	MOLESTATION
MITHRIDATISES	MOBILIZATION	MODIFICATIVE	MOLESTATIONS
MITHRIDATISING	MOBILIZATIONS	MODIFICATORY	MOLIMINOUS
MITHRIDATISM	MOBILIZERS	MODILLIONS	MOLLIFIABLE
MITHRIDATISMS	MOBILIZING	MODIOLUSES	MOLLIFICATION
MITHRIDATIZE	MOBLOGGERS	MODISHNESS	MOLLIFICATIONS
MITHRIDATIZED	MOBOCRACIES	MODISHNESSES	MOLLIFIERS
MITHRIDATIZES	MOBOCRATIC	MODULABILITIES	MOLLIFYING
MITHRIDATIZING	MOBOCRATICAL	MODULABILITY	MOLLITIOUS
MITIGATING	MOCHINESSES	MODULARISED	MOLLUSCANS
MITIGATION	MOCKERNUTS	MODULARITIES	MOLLUSCICIDAL
MITIGATIONS	MOCKINGBIRD	MODULARITY	MOLLUSCICIDE
MITIGATIVE	MOCKINGBIRDS	MODULARIZED	MOLLUSCICIDES
MITIGATIVES	MOCKUMENTARIES	MODULATING	MOLLUSCOID
MITIGATORS	MOCKUMENTARY	MODULATION	MOLLUSCOIDAL
MITIGATORY	MODALISTIC	MODULATIONS	MOLLUSCOIDS
MITOCHONDRIA	MODALITIES	MODULATIVE	MOLLUSCOUS
MITOCHONDRIAL	MODELLINGS	MODULATORS	MOLLUSKANS
MITOCHONDRION	MODERATELY	MODULATORY	MOLLYCODDLE
MITOGENETIC	MODERATENESS	MOISTENERS	MOLLYCODDLED
MITOGENICITIES	MODERATENESSES	MOISTENING	MOLLYCODDLER
MITOGENICITY	MODERATING	MOISTIFIED	MOLLYCODDLERS

MOLLYCODDLES	MONASTERIAL	MONGRELIZES	MONOCHROME
MOLLYCODDLING	MONASTERIES	MONGRELIZING	MONOCHROMES
MOLLYHAWKS	MONASTICAL	MONILIASES	MONOCHROMIC
MOLLYMAWKS	MONASTICALLY	MONILIASIS	MONOCHROMICAL
MOLOCHISED	MONASTICISM	MONILIFORM	MONOCHROMIES
MOLOCHISES	MONASTICISMS	MONISTICAL	MONOCHROMIST
MOLOCHISING	MONAURALLY	MONISTICALLY	MONOCHROMISTS
MOLOCHIZED	MONCHIQUITE	MONITORIAL	MONOCHROMY
MOLOCHIZES	MONCHIQUITES	MONITORIALLY	MONOCLINAL
MOLOCHIZING	MONDEGREEN	MONITORIES	MONOCLINALLY
MOLYBDATES	MONDEGREENS	MONITORING	MONOCLINES
MOLYBDENITE	MONECIOUSLY	MONITORSHIP	MONOCLINIC
MOLYBDENITES	MONERGISMS	MONITORSHIPS	MONOCLINISM
MOLYBDENOSES	MONESTROUS	MONITRESSES	MONOCLINISMS
MOLYBDENOSIS	MONETARILY	MONKEYGLAND	MONOCLINOUS
MOLYBDENOUS	MONETARISM	MONKEYISMS	MONOCLONAL
MOLYBDENUM	MONETARISMS	MONKEYPODS	MONOCLONALS
MOLYBDENUMS	MONETARIST	MONKEYPOTS	MONOCOQUES
MOLYBDOSES	MONETARISTS	MONKEYSHINE	MONOCOTYLEDON
MOLYBDOSIS	MONETISATION	MONKEYSHINES	MONOCOTYLEDONS
MOMENTANEOUS	MONETISATIONS	MONKFISHES	MONOCOTYLS
MOMENTARILY	MONETISING	MONKISHNESS	MONOCRACIES
MOMENTARINESS	MONETIZATION	MONKISHNESSES	MONOCRATIC
MOMENTARINESSES	MONETIZATIONS	MONKSHOODS	MONOCRYSTAL
MOMENTOUSLY	MONETIZING	MONOACIDIC	MONOCRYSTALLINE
MOMENTOUSNESS	MONEYCHANGER	MONOAMINERGIC	MONOCRYSTALS
MOMENTOUSNESSES	MONEYCHANGERS	MONOAMINES	MONOCULARLY
MONACHISMS	MONEYGRUBBING	MONOATOMIC	MONOCULARS
MONACHISTS	MONEYGRUBBINGS	MONOBLEPSES	MONOCULOUS
MONACTINAL	MONEYLENDER	MONOBLEPSIS	MONOCULTURAL
MONADELPHOUS	MONEYLENDERS	MONOCARBOXYLIC	MONOCULTURE
MONADICALLY	MONEYLENDING	MONOCARDIAN	MONOCULTURES
MONADIFORM	MONEYLENDINGS	MONOCARPELLARY	MONOCYCLES
MONADISTIC	MONEYMAKER	MONOCARPIC	MONOCYCLIC
MONADNOCKS	MONEYMAKERS	MONOCARPOUS	MONOCYTOID
MONADOLOGIES	MONEYMAKING	MONOCEROSES	MONODACTYLOUS
MONADOLOGY	MONEYMAKINGS	MONOCEROUS	MONODELPHIAN
MONANDRIES	MONEYSPINNING	MONOCHASIA	MONODELPHIC
MONANDROUS	MONEYWORTS	MONOCHASIAL	MONODELPHOUS
MONANTHOUS	MONGERINGS	MONOCHASIUM	MONODICALLY
MONARCHALLY	MONGOLISMS	MONOCHLAMYDEOUS	MONODISPERSE
MONARCHIAL	MONGOLOIDS	MONOCHLORIDE	MONODRAMAS
MONARCHICAL	MONGRELISATION	MONOCHLORIDES	MONODRAMATIC
MONARCHICALLY	MONGRELISATIONS	MONOCHORDS	MONOECIOUS
MONARCHIES	MONGRELISE	MONOCHROIC	MONOECIOUSLY
MONARCHISE	MONGRELISED	MONOCHROICS	MONOECISMS
MONARCHISED	MONGRELISER	MONOCHROMASIES	MONOESTERS
MONARCHISES	MONGRELISERS	MONOCHROMASY	MONOFILAMENT
MONARCHISING	MONGRELISES	MONOCHROMAT	MONOFILAMENTS
MONARCHISM	MONGRELISING	MONOCHROMATE	MONOGAMIES
MONARCHISMS	MONGRELISM	MONOCHROMATES	MONOGAMIST
MONARCHIST	MONGRELISMS	MONOCHROMATIC	MONOGAMISTIC
MONARCHISTIC	MONGRELIZATION	MONOCHROMATICS	MONOGAMISTS
MONARCHISTS	MONGRELIZATIONS	MONOCHROMATISM	MONOGAMOUS
MONARCHIZE	MONGRELIZE	MONOCHROMATISMS	MONOGAMOUSLY
MONARCHIZED	MONGRELIZED	MONOCHROMATOR	MONOGAMOUSNESS
MONARCHIZES	MONGRELIZER	MONOCHROMATORS	MONOGASTRIC
MONARCHIZING	MONGRELIZERS	MONOCHROMATS	MONOGENEAN

MONOGENEANS	MONOLINGUISTS	MONONUCLEATED	MONOPOLISTIC
MONOGENESES	MONOLITHIC	MONONUCLEOSES	MONOPOLISTS
MONOGENESIS	MONOLITHICALLY	MONONUCLEOSIS	MONOPOLIZATION
MONOGENETIC	MONOLOGGED	MONONUCLEOTIDE	MONOPOLIZATIONS
MONOGENICALLY	MONOLOGGING	MONONUCLEOTIDES	MONOPOLIZE
MONOGENIES	MONOLOGICAL	MONOPETALOUS	MONOPOLIZED
MONOGENISM	MONOLOGIES	MONOPHAGIES	MONOPOLIZER
MONOGENISMS	MONOLOGISE	MONOPHAGOUS	MONOPOLIZERS
MONOGENIST	MONOLOGISED	MONOPHASIC	MONOPOLIZES
MONOGENISTIC	MONOLOGISES	MONOPHOBIA	MONOPOLIZING
MONOGENISTS	MONOLOGISING	MONOPHOBIAS	MONOPRIONIDIAN
MONOGENOUS	MONOLOGIST	MONOPHOBIC	MONOPROPELLANT
MONOGLYCERIDE	MONOLOGISTS	MONOPHOBICS	MONOPROPELLANTS
MONOGLYCERIDES	MONOLOGIZE	MONOPHONIC	MONOPSONIES
MONOGONIES	MONOLOGIZED	MONOPHONICALLY	MONOPSONIST
MONOGRAMED	MONOLOGIZES	MONOPHONIES	MONOPSONISTIC
MONOGRAMING	MONOLOGIZING	MONOPHOSPHATE	MONOPSONISTS
MONOGRAMMATIC	MONOLOGUED	MONOPHOSPHATES	MONOPTERAL
MONOGRAMMED	MONOLOGUES	MONOPHTHONG	MONOPTEROI
MONOGRAMMER	MONOLOGUING	MONOPHTHONGAL	MONOPTERON
MONOGRAMMERS	MONOLOGUISE	MONOPHTHONGISE	MONOPTEROS
MONOGRAMMING	MONOLOGUISED	MONOPHTHONGISED	MONOPTEROSES
MONOGRAPHED	MONOLOGUISES	MONOPHTHONGISES	MONOPTOTES
MONOGRAPHER	MONOLOGUISING	MONOPHTHONGIZE	MONOPULSES
MONOGRAPHERS	MONOLOGUIST	MONOPHTHONGIZED	MONORCHIDISM
MONOGRAPHIC	MONOLOGUISTS	MONOPHTHONGIZES	MONORCHIDISMS
MONOGRAPHICAL	MONOLOGUIZE	MONOPHTHONGS	MONORCHIDS
MONOGRAPHICALLY	MONOLOGUIZED	MONOPHYLETIC	MONORCHISM
MONOGRAPHIES	MONOLOGUIZES	MONOPHYLIES	MONORCHISMS
MONOGRAPHING	MONOLOGUIZING	MONOPHYLLOUS	MONORHINAL
MONOGRAPHIST	MONOMACHIA	MONOPHYODONT	MONORHYMED
MONOGRAPHISTS	MONOMACHIAS	MONOPHYODONTS	MONORHYMES
MONOGRAPHS	MONOMACHIES	MONOPHYSITE	MONOSACCHARIDE
MONOGRAPHY	MONOMANIAC	MONOPHYSITES	MONOSACCHARIDES
MONOGYNIAN	MONOMANIACAL	MONOPHYSITIC	MONOSATURATED
MONOGYNIES	MONOMANIACALLY	MONOPHYSITISM	MONOSEMIES
MONOGYNIST	MONOMANIACS	MONOPHYSITISMS	MONOSEPALOUS
MONOGYNISTS	MONOMANIAS	MONOPLANES	MONOSKIERS
MONOGYNOUS	MONOMEROUS	MONOPLEGIA	MONOSKIING
MONOHYBRID	MONOMETALLIC	MONOPLEGIAS	MONOSKIINGS
MONOHYBRIDS	MONOMETALLISM	MONOPLEGIC	MONOSODIUM
MONOHYDRATE	MONOMETALLISMS	MONOPLOIDS	MONOSOMICS
MONOHYDRATED	MONOMETALLIST	MONOPODIAL	MONOSOMIES
MONOHYDRATES	MONOMETALLISTS	MONOPODIALLY	MONOSPACED
MONOHYDRIC	MONOMETERS	MONOPODIES	MONOSPECIFIC
MONOHYDROXY	MONOMETRIC	MONOPODIUM	MONOSPECIFICITY
MONOICOUSLY	MONOMETRICAL	MONOPOLIES	MONOSPERMAL
MONOLATERS	MONOMOLECULAR	MONOPOLISATION	MONOSPERMOUS
MONOLATRIES	MONOMOLECULARLY	MONOPOLISATIONS	MONOSTABLE
MONOLATRIST	MONOMORPHEMIC	MONOPOLISE	MONOSTELES
MONOLATRISTS	MONOMORPHIC	MONOPOLISED	MONOSTELIC
MONOLATROUS	MONOMORPHISM	MONOPOLISER	MONOSTELIES
MONOLAYERS	MONOMORPHISMS	MONOPOLISERS	MONOSTICHIC
MONOLINGUAL	MONOMORPHOUS	MONOPOLISES	MONOSTICHOUS
MONOLINGUALISM	MONOMYARIAN	MONOPOLISING	MONOSTICHS
MONOLINGUALISMS	MONONUCLEAR	MONOPOLISM	MONOSTOMOUS
MONOLINGUALS	MONONUCLEARS	MONOPOLISMS	MONOSTROPHE
MONOLINGUIST	MONONUCLEATE	MONOPOLIST	MONOSTROPHES

MONOSTROPHIC	MONOTREMATOUS	MONUMENTALITY	MORALITIES
MONOSTROPHICS	MONOTREMES	MONUMENTALIZE	MORALIZATION
MONOSTYLAR	MONOTRICHIC	MONUMENTALIZED	MORALIZATIONS
MONOSTYLOUS	MONOTRICHOUS	MONUMENTALIZES	MORALIZERS
MONOSYLLABIC	MONOTROCHS	MONUMENTALIZING	MORALIZING
MONOSYLLABICITY	MONOUNSATURATE	MONUMENTALLY	MORATORIUM
MONOSYLLABISM	MONOUNSATURATED	MONUMENTED	MORATORIUMS
MONOSYLLABISMS	MONOUNSATURATES	MONUMENTING	MORBIDEZZA
MONOSYLLABLE	MONOVALENCE	MONZONITES	MORBIDEZZAS
MONOSYLLABLES	MONOVALENCES	MONZONITIC	MORBIDITIES
MONOSYMMETRIC	MONOVALENCIES	MOODINESSES	MORBIDNESS
MONOSYMMETRICAL	MONOVALENCY	MOONCALVES	MORBIDNESSES
MONOSYMMETRIES	MONOVALENT	MOONCHILDREN	MORBIFEROUS
MONOSYMMETRY	MONOXYLONS	MOONFISHES	MORBIFICALLY
MONOSYNAPTIC	MONOXYLOUS	MOONFLOWER	MORBILLIFORM
MONOTELEPHONE	MONOZYGOTIC	MOONFLOWERS	MORBILLIVIRUS
MONOTELEPHONES	MONOZYGOUS	MOONINESSES	MORBILLIVIRUSES
MONOTERPENE	MONSEIGNEUR	MOONLIGHTED	MORBILLOUS
MONOTERPENES	MONSIGNORI	MOONLIGHTER	MORDACIOUS
MONOTHALAMIC	MONSIGNORIAL	MOONLIGHTERS	MORDACIOUSLY
MONOTHALAMOUS	MONSIGNORS	MOONLIGHTING	MORDACIOUSNESS
MONOTHECAL	MONSTERING	MOONLIGHTINGS	MORDACITIES
MONOTHECOUS	MONSTERINGS	MOONLIGHTS	MORDANCIES
MONOTHEISM	MONSTRANCE	MOONPHASES	MORDANTING
MONOTHEISMS	MONSTRANCES	MOONQUAKES	MORENESSES
MONOTHEIST	MONSTROSITIES	MOONRAKERS	MORGANATIC
MONOTHEISTIC	MONSTROSITY	MOONRAKING	MORGANATICALLY
MONOTHEISTICAL	MONSTROUSLY	MOONRAKINGS	MORGANITES
MONOTHEISTS	MONSTROUSNESS	MOONSCAPES	MORGENSTERN
MONOTHELETE	MONSTROUSNESSES	MOONSHINED	MORGENSTERNS
MONOTHELETES	MONSTRUOSITIES	MOONSHINER	MORIBUNDITIES
MONOTHELETIC	MONSTRUOSITY	MOONSHINERS	MORIBUNDITY
MONOTHELETICAL	MONSTRUOUS	MOONSHINES	MORIBUNDLY
MONOTHELETISM	MONTADALES	MOONSHINING	MORIGERATE
MONOTHELETISMS	MONTAGNARD	MOONSTONES	MORIGERATION
MONOTHELISM	MONTAGNARDS	MOONSTRICKEN	MORIGERATIONS
MONOTHELISMS	MONTBRETIA	MOONSTRIKE	MORIGEROUS
MONOTHELITE	MONTBRETIAS	MOONSTRIKES	MORONICALLY
MONOTHELITES	MONTELIMAR	MOONSTRUCK	MORONITIES
MONOTHELITISM	MONTELIMARS	MOONWALKED	MOROSENESS
MONOTHELITISMS	MONTGOLFIER	MOONWALKER	MOROSENESSES
MONOTOCOUS	MONTGOLFIERS	MOONWALKERS	MOROSITIES
MONOTONICALLY	MONTHLINGS	MOONWALKING	MORPHACTIN
MONOTONICITIES	MONTICELLITE	MOORBUZZARD	MORPHACTINS
MONOTONICITY	MONTICELLITES	MOORBUZZARDS	MORPHALLAXES
MONOTONIES	MONTICOLOUS	MOOSEBIRDS	MORPHALLAXIS
MONOTONING	MONTICULATE	MOOSEWOODS	MORPHEMICALLY
MONOTONISE	MONTICULES	MOOSEYARDS	MORPHEMICS
MONOTONISED	MONTICULOUS	MOOTNESSES	MORPHINISM
MONOTONISES	MONTICULUS	MOPINESSES	MORPHINISMS
MONOTONISING	MONTICULUSES	MOPISHNESS	MORPHINOMANIA
MONOTONIZE	MONTMORILLONITE	MOPISHNESSES	MORPHINOMANIAC
MONOTONIZED	MONUMENTAL	MORALISATION	MORPHINOMANIACS
MONOTONIZES	MONUMENTALISE	MORALISATIONS	MORPHINOMANIAS
MONOTONIZING	MONUMENTALISED	MORALISERS	MORPHOGENESES
MONOTONOUS	MONUMENTALISES	MORALISING	MORPHOGENESIS
MONOTONOUSLY	MONUMENTALISING	MORALISTIC	MORPHOGENETIC
MONOTONOUSNESS	MONUMENTALITIES	MORALISTICALLY	MORPHOGENIC

MORPHOGENIES
MORPHOGENS
MORPHOGENY
MORPHOGRAPHER
MORPHOGRAPHERS
MORPHOGRAPHIES
MORPHOGRAPHY
MORPHOLOGIC
MORPHOLOGICAL
MORPHOLOGICALLY
MORPHOLOGIES
MORPHOLOGIST
MORPHOLOGISTS
MORPHOLOGY
MORPHOMETRIC
MORPHOMETRICS
MORPHOMETRIES
MORPHOMETRY
MORPHOPHONEME
MORPHOPHONEMES
MORPHOPHONEMIC
MORPHOPHONEMICS
MORPHOTROPIC
MORPHOTROPIES
MORPHOTROPY
MORSELLING
MORTADELLA
MORTADELLAS
MORTALISED
MORTALISES
MORTALISING
MORTALITIES
MORTALIZED
MORTALIZES
MORTALIZING
MORTARBOARD
MORTARBOARDS
MORTARLESS
MORTCLOTHS
MORTGAGEABLE
MORTGAGEES
MORTGAGERS
MORTGAGING
MORTGAGORS
MORTICIANS
MORTIFEROUS
MORTIFEROUSNESS
MORTIFICATION
MORTIFICATIONS
MORTIFIERS
MORTIFYING
MORTIFYINGLY
MORTIFYINGS
MORTUARIES
MORULATION
MORULATIONS
MOSAICALLY
MOSAICISMS

MOSAICISTS
MOSAICKING
MOSAICLIKE
MOSASAURUS
MOSBOLLETJIE
MOSBOLLETJIES
MOSCHATELS
MOSCHIFEROUS
MOSKONFYTS
MOSQUITOES
MOSQUITOEY
MOSSBACKED
MOSSBLUITER
MOSSBLUITERS
MOSSBUNKER
MOSSBUNKERS
MOSSINESSES
MOSSPLANTS
MOSSTROOPER
MOSSTROOPERS
MOTETTISTS
MOTHBALLED
MOTHBALLING
MOTHERBOARD
MOTHERBOARDS
MOTHERCRAFT
MOTHERCRAFTS
MOTHERESES
MOTHERFUCKER
MOTHERFUCKERS
MOTHERFUCKING
MOTHERHOOD
MOTHERHOODS
MOTHERHOUSE
MOTHERHOUSES
MOTHERINGS
MOTHERLAND
MOTHERLANDS
MOTHERLESS
MOTHERLESSNESS
MOTHERLINESS
MOTHERLINESSES
MOTHERWORT
MOTHERWORTS
MOTHPROOFED
MOTHPROOFER
MOTHPROOFERS
MOTHPROOFING
MOTHPROOFS
MOTILITIES
MOTIONISTS
MOTIONLESS
MOTIONLESSLY
MOTIONLESSNESS
MOTIVATING
MOTIVATION
MOTIVATIONAL
MOTIVATIONALLY

MOTIVATIONS
MOTIVATIVE
MOTIVATORS
MOTIVELESS
MOTIVELESSLY
MOTIVELESSNESS
MOTIVITIES
MOTOCROSSES
MOTONEURON
MOTONEURONAL
MOTONEURONS
MOTORBICYCLE
MOTORBICYCLES
MOTORBIKED
MOTORBIKES
MOTORBIKING
MOTORBOATED
MOTORBOATER
MOTORBOATERS
MOTORBOATING
MOTORBOATINGS
MOTORBOATS
MOTORBUSES
MOTORBUSSES
MOTORCADED
MOTORCADES
MOTORCADING
MOTORCOACH
MOTORCOACHES
MOTORCYCLE
MOTORCYCLED
MOTORCYCLES
MOTORCYCLING
MOTORCYCLIST
MOTORCYCLISTS
MOTORHOMES
MOTORICALLY
MOTORISATION
MOTORISATIONS
MOTORISING
MOTORIZATION
MOTORIZATIONS
MOTORIZING
MOTORMOUTH
MOTORMOUTHS
MOTORSHIPS
MOTORTRUCK
MOTORTRUCKS
MOUCHARABIES
MOUCHARABY
MOUDIEWART
MOUDIEWARTS
MOUDIEWORT
MOUDIEWORTS
MOUDIWARTS
MOUDIWORTS
MOULDABILITIES
MOULDABILITY

MOULDBOARD
MOULDBOARDS
MOULDERING
MOULDINESS
MOULDINESSES
MOULDWARPS
MOULDYWARP
MOULDYWARPS
MOUNDBIRDS
MOUNTAINBOARD
MOUNTAINBOARDER
MOUNTAINBOARDS
MOUNTAINED
MOUNTAINEER
MOUNTAINEERED
MOUNTAINEERING
MOUNTAINEERINGS
MOUNTAINEERS
MOUNTAINOUS
MOUNTAINOUSLY
MOUNTAINOUSNESS
MOUNTAINSIDE
MOUNTAINSIDES
MOUNTAINTOP
MOUNTAINTOPS
MOUNTEBANK
MOUNTEBANKED
MOUNTEBANKERIES
MOUNTEBANKERY
MOUNTEBANKING
MOUNTEBANKINGS
MOUNTEBANKISM
MOUNTEBANKISMS
MOUNTEBANKS
MOUNTENANCE
MOUNTENANCES
MOUNTENAUNCE
MOUNTENAUNCES
MOURNFULLER
MOURNFULLEST
MOURNFULLY
MOURNFULNESS
MOURNFULNESSES
MOURNINGLY
MOURNIVALS
MOUSEBIRDS
MOUSEOVERS
MOUSEPIECE
MOUSEPIECES
MOUSETAILS
MOUSETRAPPED
MOUSETRAPPING
MOUSETRAPS
MOUSINESSES
MOUSQUETAIRE
MOUSQUETAIRES
MOUSSELINE
MOUSSELINES

MOUSTACHED	MUCKAMUCKED	MUJAHEDDIN	MULTICOLOURED
MOUSTACHES	MUCKAMUCKING	MUJAHEDEEN	MULTICOLOURS
MOUSTACHIAL	MUCKAMUCKS	MUJAHIDEEN	MULTICOLUMN
MOUSTACHIO	MUCKENDERS	MULATTRESS	MULTICOMPONENT
MOUSTACHIOS	MUCKINESSES	MULATTRESSES	MULTICONDUCTOR
MOUTHBREATHER	MUCKRAKERS	MULBERRIES	MULTICOSTATE
MOUTHBREATHERS	MUCKRAKING	MULIEBRITIES	MULTICOUNTY
MOUTHBREEDER	MUCKRAKINGS	MULIEBRITY	MULTICOURSE
MOUTHBREEDERS	MUCKSPREAD	MULISHNESS	MULTICULTURAL
MOUTHBROODER	MUCKSPREADER	MULISHNESSES	MULTICURIE
MOUTHBROODERS	MUCKSPREADERS	MULLAHISMS	MULTICURRENCIES
MOUTHFEELS	MUCKSPREADING	MULLARKIES	MULTICURRENCY
MOUTHPARTS	MUCKSPREADS	MULLIGATAWNIES	MULTICUSPID
MOUTHPIECE	MUCKSWEATS	MULLIGATAWNY	MULTICUSPIDATE
MOUTHPIECES	MUCOCUTANEOUS	MULLIGRUBS	MULTICUSPIDS
MOUTHWASHES	MUCOMEMBRANOUS	MULLIONING	MULTICYCLE
MOUTHWATERING	MUCOPEPTIDE	MULTANGULAR	MULTICYCLES
MOUTHWATERINGLY	MUCOPEPTIDES	MULTANIMOUS	MULTIDENTATE
MOUVEMENTE	MUCOPROTEIN	MULTARTICULATE	MULTIDIALECTAL
MOVABILITIES	MUCOPROTEINS	MULTEITIES	MULTIDIGITATE
MOVABILITY	MUCOPURULENT	MULTIACCESS	MULTIDISCIPLINE
MOVABLENESS	MUCOSANGUINEOUS	MULTIACCESSES	MULTIDIVISIONAL
MOVABLENESSES	MUCOSITIES	MULTIAGENCY	MULTIDOMAIN
MOVEABILITIES	MUCOVISCIDOSES	MULTIANGULAR	MULTIELECTRODE
MOVEABILITY	MUCOVISCIDOSIS	MULTIARMED	MULTIELEMENT
MOVEABLENESS	MUCRONATED	MULTIARTICULATE	MULTIEMPLOYER
MOVEABLENESSES	MUCRONATION	MULTIAUTHOR	MULTIEMPLOYERS
MOVELESSLY	MUCRONATIONS	MULTIAXIAL	MULTIENGINE
MOVELESSNESS	MUDCAPPING	MULTIBARREL	MULTIENZYME
MOVELESSNESSES	MUDDINESSES	MULTIBARRELED	MULTIETHNIC
MOVIEGOERS	MUDDLEDNESS	MULTIBILLION	MULTIETHNICS
MOVIEGOING	MUDDLEDNESSES	MULTIBLADED	MULTIFACED
MOVIEGOINGS	MUDDLEHEAD	MULTIBRANCHED	MULTIFACETED
MOVIELANDS	MUDDLEHEADED	MULTIBUILDING	MULTIFACTOR
MOVIEMAKER	MUDDLEHEADEDLY	MULTICAMERATE	MULTIFACTORIAL
MOVIEMAKERS	MUDDLEHEADS	MULTICAMPUS	MULTIFAMILY
MOVIEMAKING	MUDDLEMENT	MULTICAPITATE	MULTIFARIOUS
MOVIEMAKINGS	MUDDLEMENTS	MULTICARBON	MULTIFARIOUSLY
MOWBURNING	MUDDLINGLY	MULTICASTS	MULTIFIDLY
MOWDIEWART	MUDLARKING	MULTICAULINE	MULTIFIDOUS
MOWDIEWARTS	MUDLOGGERS	MULTICAUSAL	MULTIFILAMENT
MOWDIEWORT	MUDLOGGING	MULTICELLED	MULTIFILAMENTS
MOWDIEWORTS	MUDLOGGINGS	MULTICELLULAR	MULTIFLASH
MOXIBUSTION	MUDPUPPIES	MULTICENTER	MULTIFLORA
MOXIBUSTIONS	MUDSKIPPER	MULTICENTRAL	MULTIFLOROUS
MOYGASHELS	MUDSKIPPERS	MULTICENTRIC	MULTIFOCAL
MOZZARELLA	MUDSLINGER	MULTICHAIN	MULTIFOILS
MOZZARELLAS	MUDSLINGERS	MULTICHAMBERED	MULTIFOLIATE
MRIDAMGAMS	MUDSLINGING	MULTICHANNEL	MULTIFOLIOLATE
MRIDANGAMS	MUDSLINGINGS	MULTICHARACTER	MULTIFORMITIES
MUCEDINOUS	MUFFINEERS	MULTICIDES	MULTIFORMITY
MUCHNESSES	MUGEARITES	MULTICIPITAL	MULTIFORMS
MUCIDITIES	MUGGINESSES	MULTICLIENT	MULTIFREQUENCY
MUCIDNESSES	MUGWUMPERIES	MULTICOATED	MULTIFUNCTION
MUCIFEROUS	MUGWUMPERY	MULTICOLOR	MULTIFUNCTIONAL
MUCILAGINOUS	MUGWUMPISH	MULTICOLORED	MULTIGENIC
MUCILAGINOUSLY	MUGWUMPISM	MULTICOLORS	MULTIGRADE
MUCINOGENS	MUGWUMPISMS	MULTICOLOUR	MULTIGRAIN

MULTIGRAVIDA MULTINOMINAL MULTIPOLARITIES MULTITALENTED
MULTIGRAVIDAE MULTINUCLEAR MULTIPOLARITY MULTITASKED
MULTIGRAVIDAS MULTINUCLEATE MULTIPOLES MULTITASKING
MULTIGROUP MULTINUCLEATED MULTIPOTENT MULTITASKINGS
MULTIHEADED MULTINUCLEOLATE MULTIPOTENTIAL MULTITASKS
MULTIHOSPITAL MULTIORGASMIC MULTIPOWER MULTITERMINAL
MULTIHULLS MULTIPACKS MULTIPRESENCE MULTITHREADING
MULTIJUGATE MULTIPANED MULTIPRESENCES MULTITHREADINGS
MULTIJUGOUS MULTIPARAE MULTIPRESENT MULTITIERED
MULTILANES MULTIPARAMETER MULTIPROBLEM MULTITONES
MULTILATERAL MULTIPARAS MULTIPROCESSING MULTITOWERED
MULTILATERALISM MULTIPARITIES MULTIPROCESSOR MULTITRACK
MULTILATERALIST MULTIPARITY MULTIPROCESSORS MULTITRILLION
MULTILATERALLY MULTIPAROUS MULTIPRODUCT MULTITUDES
MULTILAYER MULTIPARTICLE MULTIPRONGED MULTITUDINARY
MULTILAYERED MULTIPARTITE MULTIPURPOSE MULTITUDINOUS
MULTILEVEL MULTIPARTY MULTIRACIAL MULTITUDINOUSLY
MULTILEVELED MULTIPARTYISM MULTIRACIALISM MULTIUNION
MULTILINEAL MULTIPARTYISMS MULTIRACIALISMS MULTIVALENCE
MULTILINEAR MULTIPEDES MULTIRAMIFIED MULTIVALENCES
MULTILINGUAL MULTIPHASE MULTIRANGE MULTIVALENCIES
MULTILINGUALISM MULTIPHASIC MULTIREGIONAL MULTIVALENCY
MULTILINGUALLY MULTIPHOTON MULTIRELIGIOUS MULTIVALENT
MULTILINGUIST MULTIPICTURE MULTISCIENCE MULTIVALENTS
MULTILINGUISTS MULTIPIECE MULTISCIENCES MULTIVARIABLE
MULTILOBATE MULTIPISTON MULTISCREEN MULTIVARIATE
MULTILOBED MULTIPLANE MULTISENSE MULTIVARIOUS
MULTILOBES MULTIPLANES MULTISENSORY MULTIVERSE
MULTILOBULAR MULTIPLANT MULTISEPTATE MULTIVERSES
MULTILOBULATE MULTIPLAYER MULTISERIAL MULTIVERSITIES
MULTILOCATIONAL MULTIPLAYERS MULTISERIATE MULTIVERSITY
MULTILOCULAR MULTIPLETS MULTISERVICE MULTIVIBRATOR
MULTILOCULATE MULTIPLEXED MULTISIDED MULTIVIBRATORS
MULTILOQUENCE MULTIPLEXER MULTISKILL MULTIVIOUS
MULTILOQUENCES MULTIPLEXERS MULTISKILLED MULTIVITAMIN
MULTILOQUENT MULTIPLEXES MULTISKILLING MULTIVITAMINS
MULTILOQUIES MULTIPLEXING MULTISKILLINGS MULTIVOCAL
MULTILOQUOUS MULTIPLEXOR MULTISKILLS MULTIVOCALS
MULTILOQUY MULTIPLEXORS MULTISONANT MULTIVOLTINE
MULTIMANNED MULTIPLIABLE MULTISOURCE MULTIVOLUME
MULTIMEDIA MULTIPLICABLE MULTISPECIES MULTIWARHEAD
MULTIMEDIAS MULTIPLICAND MULTISPECTRAL MULTIWAVELENGTH
MULTIMEGATON MULTIPLICANDS MULTISPEED MULTIWINDOW
MULTIMEGAWATT MULTIPLICATE MULTISPIRAL MULTIWINDOWS
MULTIMEGAWATTS MULTIPLICATES MULTISPORT MULTOCULAR
MULTIMEMBER MULTIPLICATION MULTISTAGE MULTUNGULATE
MULTIMETALLIC MULTIPLICATIONS MULTISTATE MULTUNGULATES
MULTIMETER MULTIPLICATIVE MULTISTEMMED MUMBLEMENT
MULTIMETERS MULTIPLICATOR MULTISTOREY MUMBLEMENTS
MULTIMILLENNIAL MULTIPLICATORS MULTISTOREYS MUMBLETYPEG
MULTIMILLION MULTIPLICITIES MULTISTORIED MUMBLETYPEGS
MULTIMODAL MULTIPLICITY MULTISTORY MUMBLINGLY
MULTIMOLECULAR MULTIPLIED MULTISTRANDED MUMCHANCES
MULTINATION MULTIPLIER MULTISTRIKE MUMMICHOGS
MULTINATIONAL MULTIPLIERS MULTISTRIKES MUMMIFICATION
MULTINATIONALS MULTIPLIES MULTISULCATE MUMMIFICATIONS
MULTINOMIAL MULTIPLYING MULTISYLLABIC MUMMIFYING
MULTINOMIALS MULTIPOLAR MULTISYSTEM MUMPISHNESS

MUMPISHNESSES

MUMPISHNESSES	MUSCARDINE	MUSKELLUNGES	MUTTERATION
MUMPSIMUSES	MUSCARDINES	MUSKETEERS	MUTTERATIONS
MUNCHABLES	MUSCARINES	MUSKETOONS	MUTTERINGLY
MUNDANENESS	MUSCARINIC	MUSKETRIES	MUTTERINGS
MUNDANENESSES	MUSCATORIA	MUSKINESSES	MUTTONBIRD
MUNDANITIES	MUSCATORIUM	MUSKMELONS	MUTTONBIRDS
MUNDIFICATION	MUSCAVADOS	MUSQUASHES	MUTTONCHOPS
MUNDIFICATIONS	MUSCOLOGIES	MUSQUETOON	MUTTONFISH
MUNDIFICATIVE	MUSCOVADOS	MUSQUETOONS	MUTTONFISHES
MUNDIFYING	MUSCOVITES	MUSSELCRACKER	MUTTONHEAD
MUNDUNGUSES	MUSCULARITIES	MUSSELCRACKERS	MUTTONHEADED
MUNICIPALISE	MUSCULARITY	MUSSINESSES	MUTTONHEADS
MUNICIPALISED	MUSCULARLY	MUSSITATED	MUTUALISATION
MUNICIPALISES	MUSCULATION	MUSSITATES	MUTUALISATIONS
MUNICIPALISING	MUSCULATIONS	MUSSITATING	MUTUALISED
MUNICIPALISM	MUSCULATURE	MUSSITATION	MUTUALISES
MUNICIPALISMS	MUSCULATURES	MUSSITATIONS	MUTUALISING
MUNICIPALIST	MUSCULOSKELETAL	MUSTACHIOED	MUTUALISMS
MUNICIPALISTS	MUSEOLOGICAL	MUSTACHIOS	MUTUALISTIC
MUNICIPALITIES	MUSEOLOGIES	MUSTELINES	MUTUALISTS
MUNICIPALITY	MUSEOLOGIST	MUSTINESSES	MUTUALITIES
MUNICIPALIZE	MUSEOLOGISTS	MUTABILITIES	MUTUALIZATION
MUNICIPALIZED	MUSHINESSES	MUTABILITY	MUTUALIZATIONS
MUNICIPALIZES	MUSHMOUTHS	MUTABLENESS	MUTUALIZED
MUNICIPALIZING	MUSHROOMED	MUTABLENESSES	MUTUALIZES
MUNICIPALLY	MUSHROOMER	MUTAGENESES	MUTUALIZING
MUNICIPALS	MUSHROOMERS	MUTAGENESIS	MUTUALNESS
MUNIFICENCE	MUSHROOMING	MUTAGENICALLY	MUTUALNESSES
MUNIFICENCES	MUSICALISATION	MUTAGENICITIES	MUZZINESSES
MUNIFICENT	MUSICALISATIONS	MUTAGENICITY	MYASTHENIA
MUNIFICENTLY	MUSICALISE	MUTAGENISE	MYASTHENIAS
MUNIFICENTNESS	MUSICALISED	MUTAGENISED	MYASTHENIC
MUNIFIENCE	MUSICALISES	MUTAGENISES	MYASTHENICS
MUNIFIENCES	MUSICALISING	MUTAGENISING	MYCETOLOGIES
MUNITIONED	MUSICALITIES	MUTAGENIZE	MYCETOLOGY
MUNITIONEER	MUSICALITY	MUTAGENIZED	MYCETOMATA
MUNITIONEERS	MUSICALIZATION	MUTAGENIZES	MYCETOMATOUS
MUNITIONER	MUSICALIZATIONS	MUTAGENIZING	MYCETOPHAGOUS
MUNITIONERS	MUSICALIZE	MUTATIONAL	MYCETOZOAN
MUNITIONETTE	MUSICALIZED	MUTATIONALLY	MYCETOZOANS
MUNITIONETTES	MUSICALIZES	MUTATIONIST	MYCOBACTERIA
MUNITIONING	MUSICALIZING	MUTATIONISTS	MYCOBACTERIAL
MURDERESSES	MUSICALNESS	MUTENESSES	MYCOBACTERIUM
MURDEROUSLY	MUSICALNESSES	MUTESSARIF	MYCOBIONTS
MURDEROUSNESS	MUSICIANER	MUTESSARIFAT	MYCODOMATIA
MURDEROUSNESSES	MUSICIANERS	MUTESSARIFATS	MYCODOMATIUM
MURGEONING	MUSICIANLY	MUTESSARIFS	MYCOFLORAE
MURKINESSES	MUSICIANSHIP	MUTILATING	MYCOFLORAS
MURMURATION	MUSICIANSHIPS	MUTILATION	MYCOLOGICAL
MURMURATIONS	MUSICOLOGICAL	MUTILATIONS	MYCOLOGICALLY
MURMURINGLY	MUSICOLOGICALLY	MUTILATIVE	MYCOLOGIES
MURMURINGS	MUSICOLOGIES	MUTILATORS	MYCOLOGIST
MURMUROUSLY	MUSICOLOGIST	MUTINEERED	MYCOLOGISTS
MURTHERERS	MUSICOLOGISTS	MUTINEERING	MYCOPHAGIES
MURTHERING	MUSICOLOGY	MUTINOUSLY	MYCOPHAGIST
MUSCADELLE	MUSICOTHERAPIES	MUTINOUSNESS	MYCOPHAGISTS
MUSCADELLES	MUSICOTHERAPY	MUTINOUSNESSES	MYCOPHAGOUS
MUSCADINES	MUSKELLUNGE	MUTOSCOPES	MYCOPHILES

MYCOPLASMA	MYLONITIZES	MYRMECOLOGISTS	MYTHOGRAPHERS
MYCOPLASMAL	MYLONITIZING	MYRMECOLOGY	MYTHOGRAPHIES
MYCOPLASMAS	MYOBLASTIC	MYRMECOPHAGOUS	MYTHOGRAPHY
MYCOPLASMATA	MYOCARDIAL	MYRMECOPHILE	MYTHOLOGER
MYCOPLASMOSES	MYOCARDIOGRAPH	MYRMECOPHILES	MYTHOLOGERS
MYCOPLASMOSIS	MYOCARDIOGRAPHS	MYRMECOPHILIES	MYTHOLOGIAN
MYCORHIZAE	MYOCARDIOPATHY	MYRMECOPHILOUS	MYTHOLOGIANS
MYCORHIZAL	MYOCARDITIS	MYRMECOPHILY	MYTHOLOGIC
MYCORHIZAS	MYOCARDITISES	MYRMIDONES	MYTHOLOGICAL
MYCORRHIZA	MYOCARDIUM	MYRMIDONIAN	MYTHOLOGICALLY
MYCORRHIZAE	MYOCARDIUMS	MYROBALANS	MYTHOLOGIES
MYCORRHIZAL	MYOCLONUSES	MYRTACEOUS	MYTHOLOGISATION
MYCORRHIZAS	MYOELECTRIC	MYSOPHOBIA	MYTHOLOGISE
MYCOTOXICOSES	MYOELECTRICAL	MYSOPHOBIAS	MYTHOLOGISED
MYCOTOXICOSIS	MYOFIBRILLAR	MYSTAGOGIC	MYTHOLOGISER
MYCOTOXINS	MYOFIBRILS	MYSTAGOGICAL	MYTHOLOGISERS
MYCOTOXOLOGIES	MYOFILAMENT	MYSTAGOGICALLY	MYTHOLOGISES
MYCOTOXOLOGY	MYOFILAMENTS	MYSTAGOGIES	MYTHOLOGISING
MYCOTROPHIC	MYOGLOBINS	MYSTAGOGUE	MYTHOLOGIST
MYCOVIRUSES	MYOGRAPHIC	MYSTAGOGUES	MYTHOLOGISTS
MYDRIATICS	MYOGRAPHICAL	MYSTAGOGUS	MYTHOLOGIZATION
MYELENCEPHALA	MYOGRAPHICALLY	MYSTAGOGUSES	MYTHOLOGIZE
MYELENCEPHALIC	MYOGRAPHIES	MYSTERIOUS	MYTHOLOGIZED
MYELENCEPHALON	MYOGRAPHIST	MYSTERIOUSLY	MYTHOLOGIZER
MYELENCEPHALONS	MYOGRAPHISTS	MYSTERIOUSNESS	MYTHOLOGIZERS
MYELINATED	MYOINOSITOL	MYSTICALLY	MYTHOLOGIZES
MYELITIDES	MYOINOSITOLS	MYSTICALNESS	MYTHOLOGIZING
MYELITISES	MYOLOGICAL	MYSTICALNESSES	MYTHOMANES
MYELOBLAST	MYOLOGISTS	MYSTICETES	MYTHOMANIA
MYELOBLASTIC	MYOMANCIES	MYSTICISMS	MYTHOMANIAC
MYELOBLASTS	MYOMECTOMIES	MYSTIFICATION	MYTHOMANIACS
MYELOCYTES	MYOMECTOMY	MYSTIFICATIONS	MYTHOMANIAS
MYELOCYTIC	MYOPATHIES	MYSTIFIERS	MYTHOPOEIA
MYELOFIBROSES	MYOPHILIES	MYSTIFYING	MYTHOPOEIAS
MYELOFIBROSIS	MYOPHILOUS	MYSTIFYINGLY	MYTHOPOEIC
MYELOFIBROTIC	MYOPICALLY	MYTHICALLY	MYTHOPOEISM
MYELOGENOUS	MYOSITISES	MYTHICISATION	MYTHOPOEISMS
MYELOGRAMS	MYOSOTISES	MYTHICISATIONS	MYTHOPOEIST
MYELOGRAPHIES	MYRIADFOLD	MYTHICISED	MYTHOPOEISTS
MYELOGRAPHY	MYRIADFOLDS	MYTHICISER	MYTHOPOESES
MYELOMATOID	MYRIAPODAN	MYTHICISERS	MYTHOPOESIS
MYELOMATOUS	MYRIAPODOUS	MYTHICISES	MYTHOPOETIC
MYELOPATHIC	MYRINGITIS	MYTHICISING	MYTHOPOETICAL
MYELOPATHIES	MYRINGITISES	MYTHICISMS	MYTHOPOETS
MYELOPATHY	MYRINGOSCOPE	MYTHICISTS	MYTILIFORM
MYIOPHILIES	MYRINGOSCOPES	MYTHICIZATION	MYXAMOEBAE
MYIOPHILOUS	MYRINGOTOMIES	MYTHICIZATIONS	MYXAMOEBAS
MYLOHYOIDS	MYRINGOTOMY	MYTHICIZED	MYXEDEMATOUS
MYLONITISATION	MYRIORAMAS	MYTHICIZER	MYXOEDEMAS
MYLONITISATIONS	MYRIOSCOPE	MYTHICIZERS	MYXOEDEMATOUS
MYLONITISE	MYRIOSCOPES	MYTHICIZES	MYXOEDEMIC
MYLONITISED	MYRISTICIVOROUS	MYTHICIZING	MYXOMATOSES
MYLONITISES	MYRMECOCHORIES	MYTHMAKERS	MYXOMATOSIS
MYLONITISING	MYRMECOCHORY	MYTHMAKING	MYXOMATOUS
MYLONITIZATION	MYRMECOLOGIC	MYTHMAKINGS	MYXOMYCETE
MYLONITIZATIONS	MYRMECOLOGICAL	MYTHOGENESES	MYXOMYCETES
MYLONITIZE	MYRMECOLOGIES	MYTHOGENESIS	MYXOMYCETOUS
MYLONITIZED	MYRMECOLOGIST	MYTHOGRAPHER	MYXOVIRUSES

NABOBERIES
NABOBESSES
NACHTMAALS
NAFFNESSES
NAIFNESSES
NAILBITERS
NAILBRUSHES
NAISSANCES
NAIVENESSES
NAKEDNESSES
NALBUPHINE
NALBUPHINES
NALORPHINE
NALORPHINES
NALTREXONE
NALTREXONES
NAMAYCUSHES
NAMECHECKED
NAMECHECKING
NAMECHECKS
NAMELESSLY
NAMELESSNESS
NAMELESSNESSES
NAMEPLATES
NAMEWORTHY
NANDROLONE
NANDROLONES
NANISATION
NANISATIONS
NANIZATION
NANIZATIONS
NANNOPLANKTON
NANNOPLANKTONS
NANOGRAMME
NANOGRAMMES
NANOMATERIAL
NANOMATERIALS
NANOMETERS
NANOMETRES
NANOPARTICLE
NANOPARTICLES
NANOPHYSICS
NANOPLANKTON
NANOPLANKTONS
NANOSECOND
NANOSECONDS
NANOTECHNOLOGY
NANOTESLAS
NANOWORLDS
NAPHTHALENE
NAPHTHALENES
NAPHTHALIC
NAPHTHALIN

NAPHTHALINE
NAPHTHALINES
NAPHTHALINS
NAPHTHALISE
NAPHTHALISED
NAPHTHALISES
NAPHTHALISING
NAPHTHALIZE
NAPHTHALIZED
NAPHTHALIZES
NAPHTHALIZING
NAPHTHENES
NAPHTHENIC
NAPHTHYLAMINE
NAPHTHYLAMINES
NAPOLEONITE
NAPOLEONITES
NAPPINESSES
NAPRAPATHIES
NAPRAPATHY
NARCISSISM
NARCISSISMS
NARCISSIST
NARCISSISTIC
NARCISSISTS
NARCISSUSES
NARCOANALYSES
NARCOANALYSIS
NARCOCATHARSES
NARCOCATHARSIS
NARCOHYPNOSES
NARCOHYPNOSIS
NARCOLEPSIES
NARCOLEPSY
NARCOLEPTIC
NARCOLEPTICS
NARCOSYNTHESES
NARCOSYNTHESIS
NARCOTERRORISM
NARCOTERRORISMS
NARCOTERRORIST
NARCOTERRORISTS
NARCOTICALLY
NARCOTINES
NARCOTISATION
NARCOTISATIONS
NARCOTISED
NARCOTISES
NARCOTISING
NARCOTISMS
NARCOTISTS
NARCOTIZATION
NARCOTIZATIONS

NARCOTIZED
NARCOTIZES
NARCOTIZING
NARGHILIES
NARGHILLIES
NARRATABLE
NARRATIONAL
NARRATIONS
NARRATIVELY
NARRATIVES
NARRATOLOGICAL
NARRATOLOGIES
NARRATOLOGIST
NARRATOLOGISTS
NARRATOLOGY
NARROWBAND
NARROWBANDS
NARROWCAST
NARROWCASTED
NARROWCASTING
NARROWCASTINGS
NARROWCASTS
NARROWINGS
NARROWNESS
NARROWNESSES
NASALISATION
NASALISATIONS
NASALISING
NASALITIES
NASALIZATION
NASALIZATIONS
NASALIZING
NASCENCIES
NASEBERRIES
NASOFRONTAL
NASOGASTRIC
NASOLACRYMAL
NASOPHARYNGEAL
NASOPHARYNGES
NASOPHARYNX
NASOPHARYNXES
NASTINESSES
NASTURTIUM
NASTURTIUMS
NATALITIAL
NATALITIES
NATATIONAL
NATATORIAL
NATATORIUM
NATATORIUMS
NATHELESSE
NATIONALISATION
NATIONALISE

NATIONALISED
NATIONALISER
NATIONALISERS
NATIONALISES
NATIONALISING
NATIONALISM
NATIONALISMS
NATIONALIST
NATIONALISTIC
NATIONALISTS
NATIONALITIES
NATIONALITY
NATIONALIZATION
NATIONALIZE
NATIONALIZED
NATIONALIZER
NATIONALIZERS
NATIONALIZES
NATIONALIZING
NATIONALLY
NATIONHOOD
NATIONHOODS
NATIONLESS
NATIONWIDE
NATIVENESS
NATIVENESSES
NATIVISTIC
NATIVITIES
NATRIURESES
NATRIURESIS
NATRIURETIC
NATRIURETICS
NATROLITES
NATTERJACK
NATTERJACKS
NATTINESSES
NATURALISATION
NATURALISATIONS
NATURALISE
NATURALISED
NATURALISES
NATURALISING
NATURALISM
NATURALISMS
NATURALIST
NATURALISTIC
NATURALISTS
NATURALIZATION
NATURALIZATIONS
NATURALIZE
NATURALIZED
NATURALIZES
NATURALIZING

NATURALNESS	NEARSIGHTEDLY	NECROGRAPHERS	NECROTOMIES
NATURALNESSES	NEARSIGHTEDNESS	NECROLATER	NECROTROPH
NATURISTIC	NEARTHROSES	NECROLATERS	NECROTROPHIC
NATUROPATH	NEARTHROSIS	NECROLATRIES	NECROTROPHS
NATUROPATHIC	NEATNESSES	NECROLATRY	NECTAREOUS
NATUROPATHIES	NEBBISHERS	NECROLOGIC	NECTAREOUSNESS
NATUROPATHS	NEBENKERNS	NECROLOGICAL	NECTARIFEROUS
NATUROPATHY	NEBUCHADNEZZAR	NECROLOGIES	NECTARINES
NAUGAHYDES	NEBUCHADNEZZARS	NECROLOGIST	NECTARIVOROUS
NAUGHTIEST	NEBULISATION	NECROLOGISTS	NECTOCALYCES
NAUGHTINESS	NEBULISATIONS	NECROMANCER	NECTOCALYX
NAUGHTINESSES	NEBULISERS	NECROMANCERS	NEEDCESSITIES
NAUMACHIAE	NEBULISING	NECROMANCIES	NEEDCESSITY
NAUMACHIAS	NEBULIZATION	NECROMANCY	NEEDFULNESS
NAUMACHIES	NEBULIZATIONS	NECROMANIA	NEEDFULNESSES
NAUPLIIFORM	NEBULIZERS	NECROMANIAC	NEEDINESSES
NAUSEATING	NEBULIZING	NECROMANIACS	NEEDLECORD
NAUSEATINGLY	NEBULOSITIES	NECROMANIAS	NEEDLECORDS
NAUSEATION	NEBULOSITY	NECROMANTIC	NEEDLECRAFT
NAUSEATIONS	NEBULOUSLY	NECROMANTICAL	NEEDLECRAFTS
NAUSEATIVE	NEBULOUSNESS	NECROMANTICALLY	NEEDLEFISH
NAUSEOUSLY	NEBULOUSNESSES	NECROPHAGOUS	NEEDLEFISHES
NAUSEOUSNESS	NECESSAIRE	NECROPHILE	NEEDLEFULS
NAUSEOUSNESSES	NECESSAIRES	NECROPHILES	NEEDLELIKE
NAUTICALLY	NECESSARIAN	NECROPHILIA	NEEDLEPOINT
NAUTILOIDS	NECESSARIANISM	NECROPHILIAC	NEEDLEPOINTS
NAUTILUSES	NECESSARIANISMS	NECROPHILIACS	NEEDLESSLY
NAVARCHIES	NECESSARIANS	NECROPHILIAS	NEEDLESSNESS
NAVELWORTS	NECESSARIES	NECROPHILIC	NEEDLESSNESSES
NAVICULARE	NECESSARILY	NECROPHILIES	NEEDLESTICK
NAVICULARES	NECESSARINESS	NECROPHILISM	NEEDLEWOMAN
NAVICULARS	NECESSARINESSES	NECROPHILISMS	NEEDLEWOMEN
NAVIGABILITIES	NECESSITARIAN	NECROPHILOUS	NEEDLEWORK
NAVIGABILITY	NECESSITARIANS	NECROPHILS	NEEDLEWORKER
NAVIGABLENESS	NECESSITATE	NECROPHILY	NEEDLEWORKERS
NAVIGABLENESSES	NECESSITATED	NECROPHOBE	NEEDLEWORKS
NAVIGATING	NECESSITATES	NECROPHOBES	NEESBERRIES
NAVIGATION	NECESSITATING	NECROPHOBIA	NEFARIOUSLY
NAVIGATIONAL	NECESSITATION	NECROPHOBIAS	NEFARIOUSNESS
NAVIGATIONALLY	NECESSITATIONS	NECROPHOBIC	NEFARIOUSNESSES
NAVIGATIONS	NECESSITATIVE	NECROPHOROUS	NEGATIONAL
NAVIGATORS	NECESSITIED	NECROPOLEIS	NEGATIONIST
NAYSAYINGS	NECESSITIES	NECROPOLES	NEGATIONISTS
NAZIFICATION	NECESSITOUS	NECROPOLIS	NEGATIVELY
NAZIFICATIONS	NECESSITOUSLY	NECROPOLISES	NEGATIVENESS
NEANDERTAL	NECESSITOUSNESS	NECROPSIED	NEGATIVENESSES
NEANDERTALER	NECKCLOTHS	NECROPSIES	NEGATIVING
NEANDERTALERS	NECKERCHIEF	NECROPSYING	NEGATIVISM
NEANDERTALS	NECKERCHIEFS	NECROSCOPIC	NEGATIVISMS
NEANDERTHAL	NECKERCHIEVES	NECROSCOPICAL	NEGATIVIST
NEANDERTHALER	NECKLACING	NECROSCOPIES	NEGATIVISTIC
NEANDERTHALERS	NECKLACINGS	NECROSCOPY	NEGATIVISTS
NEANDERTHALOID	NECKPIECES	NECROTISED	NEGATIVITIES
NEANDERTHALS	NECKVERSES	NECROTISES	NEGATIVITY
NEAPOLITAN	NECROBIOSES	NECROTISING	NEGLECTABLE
NEAPOLITANS	NECROBIOSIS	NECROTIZED	NEGLECTEDNESS
NEARNESSES	NECROBIOTIC	NECROTIZES	NEGLECTEDNESSES
NEARSIGHTED	NECROGRAPHER	NECROTIZING	NEGLECTERS

NEGLECTFUL NEIGHBOURHOODS NEOGOTHICS NEOREALIST
NEGLECTFULLY NEIGHBOURING NEOGRAMMARIAN NEOREALISTIC
NEGLECTFULNESS NEIGHBOURLESS NEOGRAMMARIANS NEOREALISTS
NEGLECTING NEIGHBOURLINESS NEOLIBERAL NEOSTIGMINE
NEGLECTINGLY NEIGHBOURLY NEOLIBERALISM NEOSTIGMINES
NEGLECTION NEIGHBOURS NEOLIBERALISMS NEOTEINIAS
NEGLECTIONS NELUMBIUMS NEOLIBERALS NEOTERICAL
NEGLECTIVE NEMATHELMINTH NEOLOGIANS NEOTERICALLY
NEGLECTORS NEMATHELMINTHIC NEOLOGICAL NEOTERICALS
NEGLIGEABLE NEMATHELMINTHS NEOLOGICALLY NEOTERISED
NEGLIGENCE NEMATICIDAL NEOLOGISED NEOTERISES
NEGLIGENCES NEMATICIDE NEOLOGISES NEOTERISING
NEGLIGENTLY NEMATICIDES NEOLOGISING NEOTERISMS
NEGLIGIBILITIES NEMATOBLAST NEOLOGISMS NEOTERISTS
NEGLIGIBILITY NEMATOBLASTS NEOLOGISTIC NEOTERIZED
NEGLIGIBLE NEMATOCIDAL NEOLOGISTICAL NEOTERIZES
NEGLIGIBLENESS NEMATOCIDE NEOLOGISTICALLY NEOTERIZING
NEGLIGIBLY NEMATOCIDES NEOLOGISTS NEOTROPICS
NEGOCIANTS NEMATOCYST NEOLOGIZED NEOVITALISM
NEGOTIABILITIES NEMATOCYSTIC NEOLOGIZES NEOVITALISMS
NEGOTIABILITY NEMATOCYSTS NEOLOGIZING NEOVITALIST
NEGOTIABLE NEMATODIRIASES NEONATALLY NEOVITALISTS
NEGOTIANTS NEMATODIRIASIS NEONATICIDE NEPENTHEAN
NEGOTIATED NEMATODIRUS NEONATICIDES NEPHALISMS
NEGOTIATES NEMATODIRUSES NEONATOLOGIES NEPHALISTS
NEGOTIATING NEMATOLOGICAL NEONATOLOGIST NEPHELINES
NEGOTIATION NEMATOLOGIES NEONATOLOGISTS NEPHELINIC
NEGOTIATIONS NEMATOLOGIST NEONATOLOGY NEPHELINITE
NEGOTIATOR NEMATOLOGISTS NEONOMIANISM NEPHELINITES
NEGOTIATORS NEMATOLOGY NEONOMIANISMS NEPHELINITIC
NEGOTIATORY NEMATOPHORE NEONOMIANS NEPHELITES
NEGOTIATRESS NEMATOPHORES NEOORTHODOX NEPHELOMETER
NEGOTIATRESSES NEMERTEANS NEOORTHODOXIES NEPHELOMETERS
NEGOTIATRICES NEMERTIANS NEOORTHODOXY NEPHELOMETRIC
NEGOTIATRIX NEMERTINES NEOPAGANISE NEPHELOMETRIES
NEGOTIATRIXES NEMOPHILAS NEOPAGANISED NEPHELOMETRY
NEGRITUDES NEOANTHROPIC NEOPAGANISES NEPHOGRAMS
NEGROHEADS NEOARSPHENAMINE NEOPAGANISING NEPHOGRAPH
NEGROPHILE NEOCLASSIC NEOPAGANISM NEPHOGRAPHS
NEGROPHILES NEOCLASSICAL NEOPAGANISMS NEPHOLOGIC
NEGROPHILISM NEOCLASSICISM NEOPAGANIZE NEPHOLOGICAL
NEGROPHILISMS NEOCLASSICISMS NEOPAGANIZED NEPHOLOGIES
NEGROPHILIST NEOCLASSICIST NEOPAGANIZES NEPHOLOGIST
NEGROPHILISTS NEOCLASSICISTS NEOPAGANIZING NEPHOLOGISTS
NEGROPHILS NEOCOLONIAL NEOPHILIAC NEPHOSCOPE
NEGROPHOBE NEOCOLONIALISM NEOPHILIACS NEPHOSCOPES
NEGROPHOBES NEOCOLONIALISMS NEOPHILIAS NEPHRALGIA
NEGROPHOBIA NEOCOLONIALIST NEOPHOBIAS NEPHRALGIAS
NEGROPHOBIAS NEOCOLONIALISTS NEOPILINAS NEPHRALGIC
NEIGHBORED NEOCONSERVATISM NEOPLASIAS NEPHRALGIES
NEIGHBORHOOD NEOCONSERVATIVE NEOPLASTIC NEPHRECTOMIES
NEIGHBORHOODS NEOCORTEXES NEOPLASTICISM NEPHRECTOMISE
NEIGHBORING NEOCORTICAL NEOPLASTICISMS NEPHRECTOMISED
NEIGHBORLESS NEOCORTICES NEOPLASTICIST NEPHRECTOMISES
NEIGHBORLINESS NEODYMIUMS NEOPLASTICISTS NEPHRECTOMISING
NEIGHBORLY NEOGENESES NEOPLASTIES NEPHRECTOMIZE
NEIGHBOURED NEOGENESIS NEOREALISM NEPHRECTOMIZED
NEIGHBOURHOOD NEOGENETIC NEOREALISMS NEPHRECTOMIZES

NEPHRECTOMIZING	NETHERSTOCKS	NEUROCOMPUTER	NEUROPATHISTS
NEPHRECTOMY	NETHERWARD	NEUROCOMPUTERS	NEUROPATHOLOGIC
NEPHRIDIAL	NETHERWARDS	NEUROCOMPUTING	NEUROPATHOLOGY
NEPHRIDIUM	NETHERWORLD	NEUROCOMPUTINGS	NEUROPATHS
NEPHRITICAL	NETHERWORLDS	NEUROENDOCRINE	NEUROPATHY
NEPHRITICS	NETIQUETTE	NEUROETHOLOGIES	NEUROPEPTIDE
NEPHRITIDES	NETIQUETTES	NEUROETHOLOGY	NEUROPEPTIDES
NEPHRITISES	NETMINDERS	NEUROFEEDBACK	NEUROPHYSIOLOGY
NEPHROBLASTOMA	NETTLELIKE	NEUROFEEDBACKS	NEUROPLASM
NEPHROBLASTOMAS	NETTLESOME	NEUROFIBRIL	NEUROPLASMS
NEPHROLEPIS	NETWORKERS	NEUROFIBRILAR	NEUROPSYCHIATRY
NEPHROLEPISES	NETWORKING	NEUROFIBRILLAR	NEUROPSYCHOLOGY
NEPHROLOGICAL	NETWORKINGS	NEUROFIBRILLARY	NEUROPTERA
NEPHROLOGIES	NEURALGIAS	NEUROFIBRILS	NEUROPTERAN
NEPHROLOGIST	NEURAMINIDASE	NEUROFIBROMA	NEUROPTERANS
NEPHROLOGISTS	NEURAMINIDASES	NEUROFIBROMAS	NEUROPTERIST
NEPHROLOGY	NEURASTHENIA	NEUROFIBROMATA	NEUROPTERISTS
NEPHROPATHIC	NEURASTHENIAC	NEUROGENESES	NEUROPTERON
NEPHROPATHIES	NEURASTHENIACS	NEUROGENESIS	NEUROPTERONS
NEPHROPATHY	NEURASTHENIAS	NEUROGENIC	NEUROPTEROUS
NEPHROPEXIES	NEURASTHENIC	NEUROGENICALLY	NEURORADIOLOGY
NEPHROPEXY	NEURASTHENICS	NEUROGLIAL	NEUROSCIENCE
NEPHROPTOSES	NEURATIONS	NEUROGLIAS	NEUROSCIENCES
NEPHROPTOSIS	NEURECTOMIES	NEUROGRAMS	NEUROSCIENTIFIC
NEPHROSCOPE	NEURECTOMY	NEUROHORMONAL	NEUROSCIENTIST
NEPHROSCOPES	NEURILEMMA	NEUROHORMONE	NEUROSCIENTISTS
NEPHROSCOPIES	NEURILEMMAL	NEUROHORMONES	NEUROSECRETION
NEPHROSCOPY	NEURILEMMAS	NEUROHUMOR	NEUROSECRETIONS
NEPHROSTOME	NEURILITIES	NEUROHUMORAL	NEUROSECRETORY
NEPHROSTOMES	NEURITIDES	NEUROHUMORS	NEUROSENSORY
NEPHROTICS	NEURITISES	NEUROHYPNOLOGY	NEUROSPORA
NEPHROTOMIES	NEUROACTIVE	NEUROHYPOPHYSES	NEUROSPORAS
NEPHROTOMY	NEUROANATOMIC	NEUROHYPOPHYSIS	NEUROSURGEON
NEPHROTOXIC	NEUROANATOMICAL	NEUROLEMMA	NEUROSURGEONS
NEPHROTOXICITY	NEUROANATOMIES	NEUROLEMMAS	NEUROSURGERIES
NEPOTISTIC	NEUROANATOMIST	NEUROLEPTIC	NEUROSURGERY
NEPTUNIUMS	NEUROANATOMISTS	NEUROLEPTICS	NEUROSURGICAL
NERDINESSES	NEUROANATOMY	NEUROLINGUIST	NEUROSURGICALLY
NERVATIONS	NEUROBIOLOGICAL	NEUROLINGUISTIC	NEUROTICALLY
NERVATURES	NEUROBIOLOGIES	NEUROLINGUISTS	NEUROTICISM
NERVELESSLY	NEUROBIOLOGIST	NEUROLOGIC	NEUROTICISMS
NERVELESSNESS	NEUROBIOLOGISTS	NEUROLOGICAL	NEUROTOMIES
NERVELESSNESSES	NEUROBIOLOGY	NEUROLOGICALLY	NEUROTOMIST
NERVINESSES	NEUROBLAST	NEUROLOGIES	NEUROTOMISTS
NERVOSITIES	NEUROBLASTOMA	NEUROLOGIST	NEUROTOXIC
NERVOUSNESS	NEUROBLASTOMAS	NEUROLOGISTS	NEUROTOXICITIES
NERVOUSNESSES	NEUROBLASTOMATA	NEUROLYSES	NEUROTOXICITY
NERVURATION	NEUROBLASTS	NEUROLYSIS	NEUROTOXIN
NERVURATIONS	NEUROCHEMICAL	NEUROMARKETING	NEUROTOXINS
NESCIENCES	NEUROCHEMICALS	NEUROMARKETINGS	NEUROTROPHIC
NESHNESSES	NEUROCHEMIST	NEUROMASTS	NEUROTROPHIES
NESSELRODE	NEUROCHEMISTRY	NEUROMATOUS	NEUROTROPHY
NESSELRODES	NEUROCHEMISTS	NEUROMUSCULAR	NEUROTROPIC
NETBALLERS	NEUROCHIPS	NEUROPATHIC	NEUROVASCULAR
NETHERLINGS	NEUROCOELE	NEUROPATHICAL	NEURULATION
NETHERMORE	NEUROCOELES	NEUROPATHICALLY	NEURULATIONS
NETHERMOST	NEUROCOELS	NEUROPATHIES	NEURYPNOLOGIES
NETHERSTOCK	NEUROCOGNITIVE	NEUROPATHIST	NEURYPNOLOGY

NEUTRALISATION	NEWSINESSES	NICOMPOOPS	NIGHTCLUBBERS
NEUTRALISATIONS	NEWSLETTER	NICOTIANAS	NIGHTCLUBBING
NEUTRALISE	NEWSLETTERS	NICOTINAMIDE	NIGHTCLUBBINGS
NEUTRALISED	NEWSMAGAZINE	NICOTINAMIDES	NIGHTCLUBS
NEUTRALISER	NEWSMAGAZINES	NICOTINISM	NIGHTDRESS
NEUTRALISERS	NEWSMAKERS	NICOTINISMS	NIGHTDRESSES
NEUTRALISES	NEWSMONGER	NICROSILAL	NIGHTFALLS
NEUTRALISING	NEWSMONGERS	NICROSILALS	NIGHTFARING
NEUTRALISM	NEWSPAPERDOM	NICTATIONS	NIGHTFIRES
NEUTRALISMS	NEWSPAPERDOMS	NICTITATED	NIGHTGEARS
NEUTRALIST	NEWSPAPERED	NICTITATES	NIGHTGLOWS
NEUTRALISTIC	NEWSPAPERING	NICTITATING	NIGHTGOWNS
NEUTRALISTS	NEWSPAPERISM	NICTITATION	NIGHTHAWKS
NEUTRALITIES	NEWSPAPERISMS	NICTITATIONS	NIGHTINGALE
NEUTRALITY	NEWSPAPERMAN	NIDAMENTAL	NIGHTINGALES
NEUTRALIZATION	NEWSPAPERMEN	NIDAMENTUM	NIGHTLIFES
NEUTRALIZATIONS	NEWSPAPERS	NIDDERINGS	NIGHTLIVES
NEUTRALIZE	NEWSPAPERWOMAN	NIDDERLING	NIGHTMARES
NEUTRALIZED	NEWSPAPERWOMEN	NIDDERLINGS	NIGHTMARISH
NEUTRALIZER	NEWSPEOPLE	NIDERLINGS	NIGHTMARISHLY
NEUTRALIZERS	NEWSPERSON	NIDICOLOUS	NIGHTMARISHNESS
NEUTRALIZES	NEWSPERSONS	NIDIFICATE	NIGHTPIECE
NEUTRALIZING	NEWSPRINTS	NIDIFICATED	NIGHTPIECES
NEUTRALNESS	NEWSREADER	NIDIFICATES	NIGHTRIDER
NEUTRALNESSES	NEWSREADERS	NIDIFICATING	NIGHTRIDERS
NEUTRETTOS	NEWSSTANDS	NIDIFICATION	NIGHTRIDING
NEUTRINOLESS	NEWSTRADES	NIDIFICATIONS	NIGHTRIDINGS
NEUTROPENIA	NEWSWEEKLIES	NIDIFUGOUS	NIGHTSCOPE
NEUTROPENIAS	NEWSWEEKLY	NIDULATION	NIGHTSCOPES
NEUTROPHIL	NEWSWORTHINESS	NIDULATIONS	NIGHTSHADE
NEUTROPHILE	NEWSWORTHY	NIFEDIPINE	NIGHTSHADES
NEUTROPHILES	NEWSWRITING	NIFEDIPINES	NIGHTSHIRT
NEUTROPHILIC	NEWSWRITINGS	NIFFNAFFED	NIGHTSHIRTS
NEUTROPHILS	NEXTNESSES	NIFFNAFFING	NIGHTSIDES
NEVERMINDS	NIACINAMIDE	NIFTINESSES	NIGHTSPOTS
NEVERTHELESS	NIACINAMIDES	NIGGARDING	NIGHTSTAND
NEVERTHEMORE	NIAISERIES	NIGGARDISE	NIGHTSTANDS
NEWFANGLED	NIALAMIDES	NIGGARDISES	NIGHTSTICK
NEWFANGLEDLY	NIBBLINGLY	NIGGARDIZE	NIGHTSTICKS
NEWFANGLEDNESS	NICCOLITES	NIGGARDIZES	NIGHTTIDES
NEWFANGLENESS	NICENESSES	NIGGARDLINESS	NIGHTTIMES
NEWFANGLENESSES	NICKELIFEROUS	NIGGARDLINESSES	NIGHTWALKER
NEWISHNESS	NICKELINES	NIGGERDOMS	NIGHTWALKERS
NEWISHNESSES	NICKELISED	NIGGERHEAD	NIGHTWEARS
NEWMARKETS	NICKELISES	NIGGERHEADS	NIGRESCENCE
NEWSAGENCIES	NICKELISING	NIGGERISMS	NIGRESCENCES
NEWSAGENCY	NICKELIZED	NIGGERLING	NIGRESCENT
NEWSAGENTS	NICKELIZES	NIGGERLINGS	NIGRIFYING
NEWSBREAKS	NICKELIZING	NIGGLINGLY	NIGRITUDES
NEWSCASTER	NICKELLING	NIGHNESSES	NIGROMANCIES
NEWSCASTERS	NICKELODEON	NIGHTBIRDS	NIGROMANCY
NEWSCASTING	NICKELODEONS	NIGHTBLIND	NIGROSINES
NEWSCASTINGS	NICKNAMERS	NIGHTBLINDNESS	NIHILISTIC
NEWSDEALER	NICKNAMING	NIGHTCLASS	NIHILITIES
NEWSDEALERS	NICKPOINTS	NIGHTCLASSES	NIKETHAMIDE
NEWSFLASHES	NICKSTICKS	NIGHTCLOTHES	NIKETHAMIDES
NEWSGROUPS	NICKUMPOOP	NIGHTCLUBBED	NILPOTENTS
NEWSHOUNDS	NICKUMPOOPS	NIGHTCLUBBER	NIMBLENESS

NIMBLENESSES	NITROGENISE	NOCTILUCENCE	NOMINALIST
NIMBLESSES	NITROGENISED	NOCTILUCENCES	NOMINALISTIC
NIMBLEWITS	NITROGENISES	NOCTILUCENT	NOMINALISTS
NIMBLEWITTED	NITROGENISING	NOCTILUCOUS	NOMINALIZATION
NIMBOSTRATI	NITROGENIZATION	NOCTIVAGANT	NOMINALIZATIONS
NIMBOSTRATUS	NITROGENIZE	NOCTIVAGATION	NOMINALIZE
NIMBYNESSES	NITROGENIZED	NOCTIVAGATIONS	NOMINALIZED
NINCOMPOOP	NITROGENIZES	NOCTIVAGOUS	NOMINALIZES
NINCOMPOOPERIES	NITROGENIZING	NOCTUARIES	NOMINALIZING
NINCOMPOOPERY	NITROGENOUS	NOCTURNALITIES	NOMINATELY
NINCOMPOOPS	NITROGLYCERIN	NOCTURNALITY	NOMINATING
NINEPENCES	NITROGLYCERINE	NOCTURNALLY	NOMINATION
NINEPENNIES	NITROGLYCERINES	NOCTURNALS	NOMINATIONS
NINESCORES	NITROGLYCERINS	NOCUOUSNESS	NOMINATIVAL
NINETEENTH	NITROMETER	NOCUOUSNESSES	NOMINATIVALLY
NINETEENTHLY	NITROMETERS	NODALISING	NOMINATIVE
NINETEENTHS	NITROMETHANE	NODALITIES	NOMINATIVELY
NINETIETHS	NITROMETHANES	NODALIZING	NOMINATIVES
NINHYDRINS	NITROMETRIC	NODOSITIES	NOMINATORS
NINNYHAMMER	NITROPARAFFIN	NODULATION	NOMOCRACIES
NINNYHAMMERS	NITROPARAFFINS	NODULATIONS	NOMOGENIES
NIPCHEESES	NITROPHILOUS	NOEMATICAL	NOMOGRAPHER
NIPPERKINS	NITROSAMINE	NOEMATICALLY	NOMOGRAPHERS
NIPPINESSES	NITROSAMINES	NOISELESSLY	NOMOGRAPHIC
NIPPLEWORT	NITROSATION	NOISELESSNESS	NOMOGRAPHICAL
NIPPLEWORTS	NITROSATIONS	NOISELESSNESSES	NOMOGRAPHICALLY
NISBERRIES	NITROTOLUENE	NOISEMAKER	NOMOGRAPHIES
NITPICKERS	NITROTOLUENES	NOISEMAKERS	NOMOGRAPHS
NITPICKIER	NITWITTEDNESS	NOISEMAKING	NOMOGRAPHY
NITPICKIEST	NITWITTEDNESSES	NOISEMAKINGS	NOMOLOGICAL
NITPICKING	NITWITTERIES	NOISINESSES	NOMOLOGICALLY
NITRAMINES	NITWITTERY	NOISOMENESS	NOMOLOGIES
NITRANILINE	NOBBINESSES	NOISOMENESSES	NOMOLOGIST
NITRANILINES	NOBILESSES	NOMADICALLY	NOMOLOGISTS
NITRATINES	NOBILITATE	NOMADISATION	NOMOTHETES
NITRATIONS	NOBILITATED	NOMADISATIONS	NOMOTHETIC
NITRAZEPAM	NOBILITATES	NOMADISING	NOMOTHETICAL
NITRAZEPAMS	NOBILITATING	NOMADIZATION	NONABRASIVE
NITRIDINGS	NOBILITATION	NOMADIZATIONS	NONABSORBABLE
NITRIFIABLE	NOBILITATIONS	NOMADIZING	NONABSORBENT
NITRIFICATION	NOBILITIES	NOMARCHIES	NONABSORPTIVE
NITRIFICATIONS	NOBLENESSES	NOMENCLATIVE	NONABSTRACT
NITRIFIERS	NOBLEWOMAN	NOMENCLATOR	NONACADEMIC
NITRIFYING	NOBLEWOMEN	NOMENCLATORIAL	NONACADEMICS
NITROBACTERIA	NOCHELLING	NOMENCLATORS	NONACCEPTANCE
NITROBACTERIUM	NOCICEPTIVE	NOMENCLATURAL	NONACCEPTANCES
NITROBENZENE	NOCICEPTOR	NOMENCLATURE	NONACCIDENTAL
NITROBENZENES	NOCICEPTORS	NOMENCLATURES	NONACCOUNTABLE
NITROCELLULOSE	NOCIRECEPTOR	NOMENKLATURA	NONACCREDITED
NITROCELLULOSES	NOCIRECEPTORS	NOMENKLATURAS	NONACCRUAL
NITROCHLOROFORM	NOCTAMBULATION	NOMINALISATION	NONACHIEVEMENT
NITROCOTTON	NOCTAMBULATIONS	NOMINALISATIONS	NONACHIEVEMENTS
NITROCOTTONS	NOCTAMBULISM	NOMINALISE	NONACQUISITIVE
NITROFURAN	NOCTAMBULISMS	NOMINALISED	NONACTIONS
NITROFURANS	NOCTAMBULIST	NOMINALISES	NONACTIVATED
NITROGENASE	NOCTAMBULISTS	NOMINALISING	NONADAPTIVE
NITROGENASES	NOCTILUCAE	NOMINALISM	NONADDICTIVE
NITROGENISATION	NOCTILUCAS	NOMINALISMS	NONADDICTS

NONADDITIVE
NONADDITIVITIES
NONADDITIVITY
NONADHESIVE
NONADIABATIC
NONADJACENT
NONADMIRER
NONADMIRERS
NONADMISSION
NONADMISSIONS
NONAESTHETIC
NONAFFILIATED
NONAFFLUENT
NONAGENARIAN
NONAGENARIANS
NONAGESIMAL
NONAGESIMALS
NONAGGRESSION
NONAGGRESSIONS
NONAGGRESSIVE
NONAGRICULTURAL
NONALCOHOLIC
NONALIGNED
NONALIGNMENT
NONALIGNMENTS
NONALLELIC
NONALLERGENIC
NONALLERGIC
NONALPHABETIC
NONALUMINUM
NONAMBIGUOUS
NONANALYTIC
NONANATOMIC
NONANSWERS
NONANTAGONISTIC
NONANTIBIOTIC
NONANTIBIOTICS
NONANTIGENIC
NONAPPEARANCE
NONAPPEARANCES
NONAQUATIC
NONAQUEOUS
NONARBITRARY
NONARCHITECT
NONARCHITECTS
NONARCHITECTURE
NONARGUMENT
NONARGUMENTS
NONARISTOCRATIC
NONAROMATIC
NONAROMATICS
NONARTISTIC
NONARTISTS
NONASCETIC
NONASPIRIN
NONASSERTIVE
NONASSOCIATED
NONASTRONOMICAL

NONATHLETE
NONATHLETES
NONATHLETIC
NONATTACHED
NONATTACHMENT
NONATTACHMENTS
NONATTENDANCE
NONATTENDANCES
NONATTENDER
NONATTENDERS
NONAUDITORY
NONAUTHORS
NONAUTOMATED
NONAUTOMATIC
NONAUTOMOTIVE
NONAUTONOMOUS
NONAVAILABILITY
NONBACTERIAL
NONBANKING
NONBARBITURATE
NONBARBITURATES
NONBEARING
NONBEHAVIORAL
NONBELIEFS
NONBELIEVER
NONBELIEVERS
NONBELLIGERENCY
NONBELLIGERENT
NONBELLIGERENTS
NONBETTING
NONBINDING
NONBIOGRAPHICAL
NONBIOLOGICAL
NONBIOLOGICALLY
NONBIOLOGIST
NONBIOLOGISTS
NONBONDING
NONBOTANIST
NONBOTANISTS
NONBREAKABLE
NONBREATHING
NONBREEDER
NONBREEDERS
NONBREEDING
NONBROADCAST
NONBUILDING
NONBURNABLE
NONBUSINESS
NONCABINET
NONCALLABLE
NONCALORIC
NONCANCELABLE
NONCANCEROUS
NONCANDIDACIES
NONCANDIDACY
NONCANDIDATE
NONCANDIDATES
NONCAPITAL

NONCAPITALIST
NONCAPITALISTS
NONCARCINOGEN
NONCARCINOGENIC
NONCARCINOGENS
NONCARDIAC
NONCARRIER
NONCARRIERS
NONCELEBRATION
NONCELEBRATIONS
NONCELEBRITIES
NONCELEBRITY
NONCELLULAR
NONCELLULOSIC
NONCENTRAL
NONCERTIFICATED
NONCERTIFIED
NONCHALANCE
NONCHALANCES
NONCHALANT
NONCHALANTLY
NONCHARACTER
NONCHARACTERS
NONCHARISMATIC
NONCHARISMATICS
NONCHAUVINIST
NONCHEMICAL
NONCHEMICALS
NONCHROMOSOMAL
NONCHURCHGOER
NONCHURCHGOERS
NONCIRCULAR
NONCIRCULATING
NONCITIZEN
NONCITIZENS
NONCLANDESTINE
NONCLASSES
NONCLASSICAL
NONCLASSIFIED
NONCLASSROOM
NONCLERICAL
NONCLINICAL
NONCLOGGING
NONCOERCIVE
NONCOGNITIVE
NONCOGNITIVISM
NONCOGNITIVISMS
NONCOHERENT
NONCOINCIDENCE
NONCOINCIDENCES
NONCOLLECTOR
NONCOLLECTORS
NONCOLLEGE
NONCOLLEGIATE
NONCOLLINEAR
NONCOLORED
NONCOLORFAST
NONCOMBATANT

NONCOMBATANTS
NONCOMBATIVE
NONCOMBUSTIBLE
NONCOMMERCIAL
NONCOMMISSIONED
NONCOMMITMENT
NONCOMMITMENTS
NONCOMMITTAL
NONCOMMITTALLY
NONCOMMITTED
NONCOMMUNIST
NONCOMMUNISTS
NONCOMMUNITY
NONCOMMUTATIVE
NONCOMPARABLE
NONCOMPATIBLE
NONCOMPETITION
NONCOMPETITIVE
NONCOMPETITOR
NONCOMPETITORS
NONCOMPLEX
NONCOMPLIANCE
NONCOMPLIANCES
NONCOMPLICATED
NONCOMPLYING
NONCOMPOSER
NONCOMPOSERS
NONCOMPOUND
NONCOMPRESSIBLE
NONCOMPUTER
NONCOMPUTERISED
NONCOMPUTERIZED
NONCONCEPTUAL
NONCONCERN
NONCONCERNS
NONCONCLUSION
NONCONCLUSIONS
NONCONCURRED
NONCONCURRENCE
NONCONCURRENCES
NONCONCURRENT
NONCONCURRING
NONCONCURS
NONCONDENSABLE
NONCONDITIONED
NONCONDUCTING
NONCONDUCTION
NONCONDUCTIVE
NONCONDUCTOR
NONCONDUCTORS
NONCONFERENCE
NONCONFIDENCE
NONCONFIDENCES
NONCONFIDENTIAL
NONCONFLICTING
NONCONFORM
NONCONFORMANCE
NONCONFORMANCES

NONCONFORMED	NONCOVERAGES	NONDESTRUCTIVE	NONELECTRIC
NONCONFORMER	NONCREATIVE	NONDETACHABLE	NONELECTRICAL
NONCONFORMERS	NONCREATIVITIES	NONDEVELOPMENT	NONELECTROLYTE
NONCONFORMING	NONCREATIVITY	NONDEVELOPMENTS	NONELECTROLYTES
NONCONFORMISM	NONCREDENTIALED	NONDEVIANT	NONELECTRONIC
NONCONFORMISMS	NONCRIMINAL	NONDIABETIC	NONELEMENTARY
NONCONFORMIST	NONCRIMINALS	NONDIABETICS	NONEMERGENCIES
NONCONFORMISTS	NONCRITICAL	NONDIALYSABLE	NONEMERGENCY
NONCONFORMITIES	NONCROSSOVER	NONDIALYZABLE	NONEMOTIONAL
NONCONFORMITY	NONCRUSHABLE	NONDIAPAUSING	NONEMPHATIC
NONCONFORMS	NONCRYSTALLINE	NONDIDACTIC	NONEMPIRICAL
NONCONGRUENT	NONCULINARY	NONDIFFUSIBLE	NONEMPLOYEE
NONCONJUGATED	NONCULTIVATED	NONDIMENSIONAL	NONEMPLOYEES
NONCONNECTION	NONCULTIVATION	NONDIPLOMATIC	NONEMPLOYMENT
NONCONNECTIONS	NONCULTIVATIONS	NONDIRECTED	NONEMPLOYMENTS
NONCONSCIOUS	NONCULTURAL	NONDIRECTIONAL	NONENCAPSULATED
NONCONSECUTIVE	NONCUMULATIVE	NONDIRECTIVE	NONENFORCEMENT
NONCONSENSUAL	NONCURRENT	NONDISABLED	NONENFORCEMENTS
NONCONSERVATION	NONCUSTODIAL	NONDISCLOSURE	NONENGAGEMENT
NONCONSERVATIVE	NONCUSTOMER	NONDISCLOSURES	NONENGAGEMENTS
NONCONSOLIDATED	NONCUSTOMERS	NONDISCOUNT	NONENGINEERING
NONCONSTANT	NONCYCLICAL	NONDISCURSIVE	NONENTITIES
NONCONSTRUCTION	NONDANCERS	NONDISJUNCTION	NONENTRIES
NONCONSTRUCTIVE	NONDECEPTIVE	NONDISJUNCTIONS	NONENZYMATIC
NONCONSUMER	NONDECISION	NONDISPERSIVE	NONENZYMIC
NONCONSUMERS	NONDECISIONS	NONDISRUPTIVE	NONEQUILIBRIA
NONCONSUMING	NONDECREASING	NONDISTINCTIVE	NONEQUILIBRIUM
NONCONSUMPTION	NONDEDUCTIBLE	NONDIVERSIFIED	NONEQUILIBRIUMS
NONCONSUMPTIONS	NONDEDUCTIVE	NONDIVIDING	NONEQUIVALENCE
NONCONSUMPTIVE	NONDEFENSE	NONDOCTORS	NONEQUIVALENCES
NONCONTACT	NONDEFERRABLE	NONDOCTRINAIRE	NONEQUIVALENT
NONCONTAGIOUS	NONDEFORMING	NONDOCUMENTARY	NONESSENTIAL
NONCONTEMPORARY	NONDEGENERATE	NONDOGMATIC	NONESSENTIALS
NONCONTIGUOUS	NONDEGRADABLE	NONDOMESTIC	NONESTABLISHED
NONCONTINGENT	NONDELEGATE	NONDOMICILED	NONESTERIFIED
NONCONTINUOUS	NONDELEGATES	NONDOMINANT	NONESUCHES
NONCONTRACT	NONDELIBERATE	NONDORMANT	NONETHELESS
NONCONTRACTUAL	NONDELINQUENT	NONDRAMATIC	NONETHICAL
NONCONTRIBUTORY	NONDELINQUENTS	NONDRINKER	NONETHNICS
NONCONTROLLABLE	NONDELIVERIES	NONDRINKERS	NONEVALUATIVE
NONCONTROLLED	NONDELIVERY	NONDRINKING	NONEVIDENCE
NONCONTROLLING	NONDEMANDING	NONDRIVERS	NONEVIDENCES
NONCONVENTIONAL	NONDEMANDS	NONDURABLE	NONEXCLUSIVE
NONCONVERTIBLE	NONDEMOCRATIC	NONEARNING	NONEXECUTIVE
NONCOOPERATION	NONDEPARTMENTAL	NONECONOMIC	NONEXECUTIVES
NONCOOPERATIONS	NONDEPENDENT	NONECONOMIST	NONEXEMPTS
NONCOOPERATIVE	NONDEPENDENTS	NONECONOMISTS	NONEXISTENCE
NONCOOPERATOR	NONDEPLETABLE	NONEDIBLES	NONEXISTENCES
NONCOOPERATORS	NONDEPLETING	NONEDITORIAL	NONEXISTENT
NONCOPLANAR	NONDEPOSITION	NONEDUCATION	NONEXISTENTIAL
NONCORPORATE	NONDEPOSITIONS	NONEDUCATIONAL	NONEXPENDABLE
NONCORRELATION	NONDEPRESSED	NONEFFECTIVE	NONEXPERIMENTAL
NONCORRELATIONS	NONDERIVATIVE	NONEFFECTIVES	NONEXPERTS
NONCORRODIBLE	NONDESCRIPT	NONELASTIC	NONEXPLANATORY
NONCORRODING	NONDESCRIPTIVE	NONELECTED	NONEXPLOITATION
NONCORROSIVE	NONDESCRIPTLY	NONELECTION	NONEXPLOITATIVE
NONCOUNTRY	NONDESCRIPTNESS	NONELECTIONS	NONEXPLOITIVE
NONCOVERAGE	NONDESCRIPTS	NONELECTIVE	NONEXPLOSIVE

NONEXPOSED	NONHARMONIC	NONINFRINGEMENT	NONLINEARITY
NONFACTORS	NONHAZARDOUS	NONINITIAL	NONLINGUISTIC
NONFACTUAL	NONHEMOLYTIC	NONINITIATE	NONLIQUIDS
NONFACULTY	NONHEREDITARY	NONINITIATES	NONLITERAL
NONFAMILIAL	NONHIERARCHICAL	NONINSECTICIDAL	NONLITERARY
NONFAMILIES	NONHISTONE	NONINSECTS	NONLITERATE
NONFARMERS	NONHISTORICAL	NONINSTALLMENT	NONLITERATES
NONFATTENING	NONHOMOGENEOUS	NONINSTALLMENTS	NONLIVINGS
NONFEASANCE	NONHOMOLOGOUS	NONINSTRUMENTAL	NONLOGICAL
NONFEASANCES	NONHOMOSEXUAL	NONINSURANCE	NONLUMINOUS
NONFEDERAL	NONHOMOSEXUALS	NONINSURED	NONMAGNETIC
NONFEDERATED	NONHORMONAL	NONINTEGRAL	NONMAINSTREAM
NONFEMINIST	NONHOSPITAL	NONINTEGRATED	NONMALIGNANT
NONFEMINISTS	NONHOSPITALISED	NONINTELLECTUAL	NONMALLEABLE
NONFERROUS	NONHOSPITALIZED	NONINTERACTING	NONMANAGEMENT
NONFICTION	NONHOSTILE	NONINTERACTIVE	NONMANAGERIAL
NONFICTIONAL	NONHOUSING	NONINTERCOURSE	NONMARITAL
NONFICTIONALLY	NONHUNTERS	NONINTERCOURSES	NONMARKETS
NONFICTIONS	NONHUNTING	NONINTEREST	NONMATERIAL
NONFIGURATIVE	NONHYGROSCOPIC	NONINTERFERENCE	NONMATHEMATICAL
NONFILAMENTOUS	NONHYSTERICAL	NONINTERSECTING	NONMATRICULATED
NONFILTERABLE	NONIDENTICAL	NONINTERVENTION	NONMEANINGFUL
NONFINANCIAL	NONIDENTITIES	NONINTIMIDATING	NONMEASURABLE
NONFISSIONABLE	NONIDENTITY	NONINTOXICANT	NONMECHANICAL
NONFLAMMABILITY	NONIDEOLOGICAL	NONINTOXICANTS	NONMECHANISTIC
NONFLAMMABLE	NONILLIONS	NONINTOXICATING	NONMEDICAL
NONFLOWERING	NONILLIONTH	NONINTRUSIVE	NONMEETING
NONFLUENCIES	NONILLIONTHS	NONINTUITIVE	NONMEETINGS
NONFLUENCY	NONIMITATIVE	NONINVASIVE	NONMEMBERS
NONFLUORESCENT	NONIMMIGRANT	NONINVOLVED	NONMEMBERSHIP
NONFORFEITABLE	NONIMMIGRANTS	NONINVOLVEMENT	NONMEMBERSHIPS
NONFORFEITURE	NONIMPLICATION	NONINVOLVEMENTS	NONMERCURIAL
NONFORFEITURES	NONIMPLICATIONS	NONIONIZING	NONMETALLIC
NONFREEZING	NONIMPORTATION	NONIRRADIATED	NONMETAMERIC
NONFRIVOLOUS	NONIMPORTATIONS	NONIRRIGATED	NONMETAPHORICAL
NONFULFILLMENT	NONINCLUSION	NONIRRITANT	NONMETRICAL
NONFULFILLMENTS	NONINCLUSIONS	NONIRRITANTS	NONMETROPOLITAN
NONFUNCTIONAL	NONINCREASING	NONIRRITATING	NONMICROBIAL
NONFUNCTIONING	NONINCUMBENT	NONJOINDER	NONMIGRANT
NONGASEOUS	NONINCUMBENTS	NONJOINDERS	NONMIGRATORY
NONGENETIC	NONINDEPENDENCE	NONJOINERS	NONMILITANT
NONGENITAL	NONINDIGENOUS	NONJUDGEMENTAL	NONMILITANTS
NONGEOMETRICAL	NONINDIVIDUAL	NONJUDGMENTAL	NONMILITARY
NONGLAMOROUS	NONINDUCTIVE	NONJUDICIAL	NONMIMETIC
NONGOLFERS	NONINDUSTRIAL	NONJUSTICIABLE	NONMINORITIES
NONGONOCOCCAL	NONINDUSTRY	NONKOSHERS	NONMINORITY
NONGOVERNMENT	NONINFECTED	NONLANDOWNER	NONMODERNS
NONGOVERNMENTAL	NONINFECTIOUS	NONLANDOWNERS	NONMOLECULAR
NONGRADUATE	NONINFECTIVE	NONLANGUAGE	NONMONETARIST
NONGRADUATES	NONINFESTED	NONLANGUAGES	NONMONETARISTS
NONGRAMMATICAL	NONINFLAMMABLE	NONLAWYERS	NONMONETARY
NONGRANULAR	NONINFLAMMATORY	NONLEGUMES	NONMONOGAMOUS
NONGREGARIOUS	NONINFLATIONARY	NONLEGUMINOUS	NONMORTALS
NONGROWING	NONINFLECTIONAL	NONLEXICAL	NONMOTILITIES
NONHALOGENATED	NONINFLUENCE	NONLIBRARIAN	NONMOTILITY
NONHANDICAPPED	NONINFLUENCES	NONLIBRARIANS	NONMOTORISED
NONHAPPENING	NONINFORMATION	NONLIBRARY	NONMOTORIZED
NONHAPPENINGS	NONINFORMATIONS	NONLINEARITIES	NONMUNICIPAL

NONMUSICAL	NONPARENTS	NONPRESCRIPTION	NONRELATIVES
NONMUSICALS	NONPARITIES	NONPROBLEM	NONRELATIVISTIC
NONMUSICIAN	NONPARTICIPANT	NONPROBLEMS	NONRELEVANT
NONMUSICIANS	NONPARTICIPANTS	NONPRODUCING	NONRELIGIOUS
NONMUTANTS	NONPARTIES	NONPRODUCTIVE	NONRENEWABLE
NONMYELINATED	NONPARTISAN	NONPRODUCTIVITY	NONRENEWAL
NONMYSTICAL	NONPARTISANSHIP	NONPROFESSIONAL	NONREPAYABLE
NONNARRATIVE	NONPARTIZAN	NONPROFESSORIAL	NONREPRODUCTIVE
NONNATIONAL	NONPARTIZANSHIP	NONPROFITS	NONRESIDENCE
NONNATIONALS	NONPASSERINE	NONPROGRAM	NONRESIDENCES
NONNATIVES	NONPASSIVE	NONPROGRAMMER	NONRESIDENCIES
NONNATURAL	NONPATHOGENIC	NONPROGRAMMERS	NONRESIDENCY
NONNECESSITIES	NONPAYMENT	NONPROGRESSIVE	NONRESIDENT
NONNECESSITY	NONPAYMENTS	NONPROPRIETARY	NONRESIDENTIAL
NONNEGATIVE	NONPERFORMANCE	NONPROSSED	NONRESIDENTS
NONNEGLIGENT	NONPERFORMANCES	NONPROSSES	NONRESISTANCE
NONNEGOTIABLE	NONPERFORMER	NONPROSSING	NONRESISTANCES
NONNEGOTIABLES	NONPERFORMERS	NONPROTEIN	NONRESISTANT
NONNETWORK	NONPERFORMING	NONPSYCHIATRIC	NONRESISTANTS
NONNITROGENOUS	NONPERISHABLE	NONPSYCHIATRIST	NONRESONANT
NONNORMATIVE	NONPERISHABLES	NONPSYCHOTIC	NONRESPONDENT
NONNUCLEAR	NONPERMANENT	NONPUNITIVE	NONRESPONDENTS
NONNUCLEATED	NONPERMISSIVE	NONPURPOSIVE	NONRESPONDER
NONNUMERICAL	NONPERSISTENT	NONQUANTIFIABLE	NONRESPONDERS
NONNUTRITIOUS	NONPERSONAL	NONQUANTITATIVE	NONRESPONSE
NONNUTRITIVE	NONPERSONS	NONRACIALLY	NONRESPONSES
NONOBJECTIVE	NONPETROLEUM	NONRADIOACTIVE	NONRESPONSIVE
NONOBJECTIVISM	NONPHILOSOPHER	NONRAILROAD	NONRESTRICTED
NONOBJECTIVISMS	NONPHILOSOPHERS	NONRANDOMNESS	NONRESTRICTIVE
NONOBJECTIVIST	NONPHONEMIC	NONRANDOMNESSES	NONRETRACTILE
NONOBJECTIVISTS	NONPHONETIC	NONRATIONAL	NONRETROACTIVE
NONOBJECTIVITY	NONPHOSPHATE	NONREACTIVE	NONRETURNABLE
NONOBSCENE	NONPHOTOGRAPHIC	NONREACTOR	NONRETURNABLES
NONOBSERVANCE	NONPHYSICAL	NONREACTORS	NONREUSABLE
NONOBSERVANCES	NONPHYSICIAN	NONREADERS	NONREVERSIBLE
NONOBSERVANT	NONPHYSICIANS	NONREADING	NONRHOTICITIES
NONOBVIOUS	NONPLASTIC	NONREALISTIC	NONRHOTICITY
NONOCCUPATIONAL	NONPLASTICS	NONRECEIPT	NONRIOTERS
NONOCCURRENCE	NONPLAYERS	NONRECEIPTS	NONRIOTING
NONOCCURRENCES	NONPLAYING	NONRECIPROCAL	NONROTATING
NONOFFICIAL	NONPLUSING	NONRECOGNITION	NONROUTINE
NONOFFICIALS	NONPLUSSED	NONRECOGNITIONS	NONRUMINANT
NONOPERATIC	NONPLUSSES	NONRECOMBINANT	NONRUMINANTS
NONOPERATING	NONPLUSSING	NONRECOMBINANTS	NONSALABLE
NONOPERATIONAL	NONPOISONOUS	NONRECOURSE	NONSAPONIFIABLE
NONOPERATIVE	NONPOLARISABLE	NONRECURRENT	NONSCHEDULED
NONOPTIMAL	NONPOLARIZABLE	NONRECURRING	NONSCIENCE
NONORGANIC	NONPOLITICAL	NONRECYCLABLE	NONSCIENCES
NONORGASMIC	NONPOLITICALLY	NONRECYCLABLES	NONSCIENTIFIC
NONORTHODOX	NONPOLITICIAN	NONREDUCING	NONSCIENTIST
NONOVERLAPPING	NONPOLITICIANS	NONREDUNDANT	NONSCIENTISTS
NONOXIDISING	NONPOLLUTING	NONREFILLABLE	NONSEASONAL
NONOXIDIZING	NONPOSSESSION	NONREFLECTING	NONSECRETOR
NONPAPISTS	NONPOSSESSIONS	NONREFLEXIVE	NONSECRETORS
NONPARALLEL	NONPRACTICAL	NONREFUNDABLE	NONSECRETORY
NONPARAMETRIC	NONPRACTICING	NONREGULATED	NONSECRETS
NONPARASITIC	NONPRACTISING	NONREGULATION	NONSECTARIAN
NONPAREILS	NONPREGNANT	NONRELATIVE	NONSEDIMENTABLE

NONSEGREGATED	NONSTRUCTURAL	NONUNIFORMITY	NORETHISTERONE
NONSEGREGATION	NONSTRUCTURED	NONUNIONISED	NORETHISTERONES
NONSEGREGATIONS	NONSTUDENT	NONUNIONISM	NORMALCIES
NONSELECTED	NONSTUDENTS	NONUNIONISMS	NORMALISABLE
NONSELECTIVE	NONSUBJECT	NONUNIONIST	NORMALISATION
NONSENSATIONAL	NONSUBJECTIVE	NONUNIONISTS	NORMALISATIONS
NONSENSICAL	NONSUBJECTS	NONUNIONIZED	NORMALISED
NONSENSICALITY	NONSUBSIDISED	NONUNIQUENESS	NORMALISER
NONSENSICALLY	NONSUBSIDIZED	NONUNIQUENESSES	NORMALISERS
NONSENSICALNESS	NONSUCCESS	NONUNIVERSAL	NORMALISES
NONSENSITIVE	NONSUCCESSES	NONUNIVERSITY	NORMALISING
NONSENSUOUS	NONSUITING	NONUTILITARIAN	NORMALITIES
NONSENTENCE	NONSUPERVISORY	NONUTILITIES	NORMALIZABLE
NONSENTENCES	NONSUPPORT	NONUTILITY	NORMALIZATION
NONSEPTATE	NONSUPPORTS	NONUTOPIAN	NORMALIZATIONS
NONSEQUENTIAL	NONSURGICAL	NONVALIDITIES	NORMALIZED
NONSERIALS	NONSWIMMER	NONVALIDITY	NORMALIZER
NONSERIOUS	NONSWIMMERS	NONVANISHING	NORMALIZERS
NONSHRINKABLE	NONSYLLABIC	NONVASCULAR	NORMALIZES
NONSIGNERS	NONSYMBOLIC	NONVECTORS	NORMALIZING
NONSIGNIFICANT	NONSYMMETRIC	NONVEGETARIAN	NORMATIVELY
NONSIMULTANEOUS	NONSYMMETRICAL	NONVEGETARIANS	NORMATIVENESS
NONSINKABLE	NONSYNCHRONOUS	NONVENOMOUS	NORMATIVENESSES
NONSKATERS	NONSYSTEMATIC	NONVERBALLY	NORMOTENSIVE
NONSKELETAL	NONSYSTEMIC	NONVETERAN	NORMOTENSIVES
NONSMOKERS	NONSYSTEMS	NONVETERANS	NORMOTHERMIA
NONSMOKING	NONTALKERS	NONVIEWERS	NORMOTHERMIAS
NONSOCIALIST	NONTAXABLE	NONVINTAGE	NORMOTHERMIC
NONSOCIALISTS	NONTEACHING	NONVIOLENCE	NORSELLERS
NONSOLUTION	NONTECHNICAL	NONVIOLENCES	NORSELLING
NONSOLUTIONS	NONTEMPORAL	NONVIOLENT	NORTHBOUND
NONSPATIAL	NONTENURED	NONVIOLENTLY	NORTHCOUNTRYMAN
NONSPEAKER	NONTERMINAL	NONVIRGINS	NORTHCOUNTRYMEN
NONSPEAKERS	NONTERMINALS	NONVISCOUS	NORTHEASTER
NONSPEAKING	NONTERMINATING	NONVOCATIONAL	NORTHEASTERLIES
NONSPECIALIST	NONTHEATRICAL	NONVOLATILE	NORTHEASTERLY
NONSPECIALISTS	NONTHEISTIC	NONVOLCANIC	NORTHEASTERN
NONSPECIFIC	NONTHEISTS	NONVOLUNTARY	NORTHEASTERS
NONSPECIFICALLY	NONTHEOLOGICAL	NONWINNING	NORTHEASTS
NONSPECTACULAR	NONTHEORETICAL	NONWORKERS	NORTHEASTWARD
NONSPECULAR	NONTHERAPEUTIC	NONWORKING	NORTHEASTWARDLY
NONSPECULATIVE	NONTHERMAL	NONWRITERS	NORTHEASTWARDS
NONSPHERICAL	NONTHINKING	NONYELLOWING	NORTHERING
NONSPORTING	NONTHREATENING	NOODLEDOMS	NORTHERLIES
NONSTANDARD	NONTOBACCO	NOOGENESES	NORTHERLINESS
NONSTAPLES	NONTOTALITARIAN	NOOGENESIS	NORTHERLINESSES
NONSTARTER	NONTRADITIONAL	NOOMETRIES	NORTHERMOST
NONSTARTERS	NONTRANSFERABLE	NOOSPHERES	NORTHERNER
NONSTATIONARY	NONTRANSITIVE	NOOTROPICS	NORTHERNERS
NONSTATISTICAL	NONTREATMENT	NORADRENALIN	NORTHERNISE
NONSTATIVE	NONTREATMENTS	NORADRENALINE	NORTHERNISED
NONSTATIVES	NONTRIVIAL	NORADRENALINES	NORTHERNISES
NONSTEROID	NONTROPICAL	NORADRENALINS	NORTHERNISING
NONSTEROIDAL	NONTURBULENT	NORADRENERGIC	NORTHERNISM
NONSTEROIDS	NONTYPICAL	NOREPINEPHRINE	NORTHERNISMS
NONSTORIES	NONUNANIMOUS	NOREPINEPHRINES	NORTHERNIZE
NONSTRATEGIC	NONUNIFORM	NORETHINDRONE	NORTHERNIZED
NONSTRIATED	NONUNIFORMITIES	NORETHINDRONES	NORTHERNIZES

NORTHERNIZING	NOTAPHILISMS	NOUMENALISM	NUCLEARISATION
NORTHERNMOST	NOTAPHILIST	NOUMENALISMS	NUCLEARISATIONS
NORTHLANDS	NOTAPHILISTS	NOUMENALIST	NUCLEARISE
NORTHWARDLY	NOTARIALLY	NOUMENALISTS	NUCLEARISED
NORTHWARDS	NOTARISATION	NOUMENALITIES	NUCLEARISES
NORTHWESTER	NOTARISATIONS	NOUMENALITY	NUCLEARISING
NORTHWESTERLIES	NOTARISING	NOUMENALLY	NUCLEARIZATION
NORTHWESTERLY	NOTARIZATION	NOURISHABLE	NUCLEARIZATIONS
NORTHWESTERN	NOTARIZATIONS	NOURISHERS	NUCLEARIZE
NORTHWESTERS	NOTARIZING	NOURISHING	NUCLEARIZED
NORTHWESTS	NOTARYSHIP	NOURISHINGLY	NUCLEARIZES
NORTHWESTWARD	NOTARYSHIPS	NOURISHMENT	NUCLEARIZING
NORTHWESTWARDLY	NOTATIONAL	NOURISHMENTS	NUCLEATING
NORTHWESTWARDS	NOTCHBACKS	NOURITURES	NUCLEATION
NORTRIPTYLINE	NOTCHELLED	NOURRITURE	NUCLEATIONS
NORTRIPTYLINES	NOTCHELLING	NOURRITURES	NUCLEATORS
NOSEBANDED	NOTEDNESSES	NOUSELLING	NUCLEOCAPSID
NOSEBLEEDING	NOTEPAPERS	NOVACULITE	NUCLEOCAPSIDS
NOSEBLEEDINGS	NOTEWORTHILY	NOVACULITES	NUCLEOLATE
NOSEBLEEDS	NOTEWORTHINESS	NOVELETTES	NUCLEOLATED
NOSEDIVING	NOTEWORTHY	NOVELETTISH	NUCLEONICALLY
NOSEGUARDS	NOTHINGARIAN	NOVELETTIST	NUCLEONICS
NOSEPIECES	NOTHINGARIANISM	NOVELETTISTS	NUCLEOPHILE
NOSEWHEELS	NOTHINGARIANS	NOVELISATION	NUCLEOPHILES
NOSINESSES	NOTHINGISM	NOVELISATIONS	NUCLEOPHILIC
NOSOCOMIAL	NOTHINGISMS	NOVELISERS	NUCLEOPHILICITY
NOSOGRAPHER	NOTHINGNESS	NOVELISING	NUCLEOPLASM
NOSOGRAPHERS	NOTHINGNESSES	NOVELISTIC	NUCLEOPLASMATIC
NOSOGRAPHIC	NOTICEABILITIES	NOVELISTICALLY	NUCLEOPLASMIC
NOSOGRAPHIES	NOTICEABILITY	NOVELIZATION	NUCLEOPLASMS
NOSOGRAPHY	NOTICEABLE	NOVELIZATIONS	NUCLEOPROTEIN
NOSOLOGICAL	NOTICEABLY	NOVELIZERS	NUCLEOPROTEINS
NOSOLOGICALLY	NOTIFIABLE	NOVELIZING	NUCLEOSIDE
NOSOLOGIES	NOTIFICATION	NOVEMDECILLION	NUCLEOSIDES
NOSOLOGIST	NOTIFICATIONS	NOVEMDECILLIONS	NUCLEOSOMAL
NOSOLOGISTS	NOTIONALIST	NOVENARIES	NUCLEOSOME
NOSOPHOBIA	NOTIONALISTS	NOVICEHOOD	NUCLEOSOMES
NOSOPHOBIAS	NOTIONALITIES	NOVICEHOODS	NUCLEOSYNTHESES
NOSTALGIAS	NOTIONALITY	NOVICESHIP	NUCLEOSYNTHESIS
NOSTALGICALLY	NOTIONALLY	NOVICESHIPS	NUCLEOSYNTHETIC
NOSTALGICS	NOTIONISTS	NOVICIATES	NUCLEOTIDASE
NOSTALGIST	NOTOCHORDAL	NOVITIATES	NUCLEOTIDASES
NOSTALGISTS	NOTOCHORDS	NOVOBIOCIN	NUCLEOTIDE
NOSTOLOGIC	NOTODONTID	NOVOBIOCINS	NUCLEOTIDES
NOSTOLOGICAL	NOTODONTIDS	NOVOCAINES	NUDENESSES
NOSTOLOGIES	NOTONECTAL	NOVOCENTENARIES	NUDIBRANCH
NOSTOMANIA	NOTORIETIES	NOVOCENTENARY	NUDIBRANCHIATE
NOSTOMANIAS	NOTORIOUSLY	NOVODAMUSES	NUDIBRANCHIATES
NOSTOPATHIES	NOTORIOUSNESS	NOWCASTING	NUDIBRANCHS
NOSTOPATHY	NOTORIOUSNESSES	NOWCASTINGS	NUDICAUDATE
NOSTRADAMIC	NOTORNISES	NOXIOUSNESS	NUDICAULOUS
NOTABILITIES	NOTOTHERIUM	NOXIOUSNESSES	NUGATORINESS
NOTABILITY	NOTOTHERIUMS	NUBBINESSES	NUGATORINESSES
NOTABLENESS	NOTOUNGULATE	NUBIFEROUS	NUGGETTING
NOTABLENESSES	NOTOUNGULATES	NUBIGENOUS	NUISANCERS
NOTAPHILIC	NOTUNGULATE	NUBILITIES	NULLIFICATION
NOTAPHILIES	NOTUNGULATES	NUCIFEROUS	NULLIFICATIONS
NOTAPHILISM	NOTWITHSTANDING	NUCIVOROUS	NULLIFIDIAN

NULLIFIDIANS

NULLIFIDIANS
NULLIFIERS
NULLIFYING
NULLIPARAE
NULLIPARAS
NULLIPARITIES
NULLIPARITY
NULLIPAROUS
NULLIPORES
NULLNESSES
NUMBERABLE
NUMBERINGS
NUMBERLESS
NUMBERLESSLY
NUMBERLESSNESS
NUMBERPLATE
NUMBERPLATES
NUMBFISHES
NUMBNESSES
NUMBSKULLS
NUMERABILITIES
NUMERABILITY
NUMERACIES
NUMERAIRES
NUMERATING
NUMERATION
NUMERATIONS
NUMERATIVE
NUMERATORS
NUMERICALLY
NUMEROLOGICAL
NUMEROLOGIES
NUMEROLOGIST
NUMEROLOGISTS
NUMEROLOGY
NUMEROSITIES
NUMEROSITY
NUMEROUSLY
NUMEROUSNESS
NUMEROUSNESSES
NUMINOUSES
NUMINOUSNESS
NUMINOUSNESSES
NUMISMATIC
NUMISMATICALLY
NUMISMATICS
NUMISMATIST
NUMISMATISTS
NUMISMATOLOGIES
NUMISMATOLOGIST
NUMISMATOLOGY
NUMMULATED
NUMMULATION
NUMMULATIONS
NUMMULITES
NUMMULITIC
NUMSKULLED
NUNCIATURE

NUNCIATURES
NUNCUPATED
NUNCUPATES
NUNCUPATING
NUNCUPATION
NUNCUPATIONS
NUNCUPATIVE
NUNCUPATORY
NUNNATIONS
NUNNISHNESS
NUNNISHNESSES
NUPTIALITIES
NUPTIALITY
NURSEHOUND
NURSEHOUNDS
NURSELINGS
NURSEMAIDED
NURSEMAIDING
NURSEMAIDS
NURSERYMAID
NURSERYMAIDS
NURSERYMAN
NURSERYMEN
NURTURABLE
NURTURANCE
NURTURANCES
NUTATIONAL
NUTBUTTERS
NUTCRACKER
NUTCRACKERS
NUTGRASSES
NUTHATCHES
NUTJOBBERS
NUTMEGGING
NUTPECKERS
NUTRACEUTICAL
NUTRACEUTICALS
NUTRIMENTAL
NUTRIMENTS
NUTRITIONAL
NUTRITIONALLY
NUTRITIONARY
NUTRITIONIST
NUTRITIONISTS
NUTRITIONS
NUTRITIOUS
NUTRITIOUSLY
NUTRITIOUSNESS
NUTRITIVELY
NUTRITIVES
NUTTINESSES
NYCHTHEMERAL
NYCHTHEMERON
NYCHTHEMERONS
NYCTAGINACEOUS
NYCTALOPES
NYCTALOPIA
NYCTALOPIAS

NYCTALOPIC
NYCTANTHOUS
NYCTINASTIC
NYCTINASTIES
NYCTINASTY
NYCTITROPIC
NYCTITROPISM
NYCTITROPISMS
NYCTOPHOBIA
NYCTOPHOBIAS
NYCTOPHOBIC
NYMPHAEACEOUS
NYMPHAEUMS
NYMPHALIDS
NYMPHETTES
NYMPHOLEPSIES
NYMPHOLEPSY
NYMPHOLEPT
NYMPHOLEPTIC
NYMPHOLEPTS
NYMPHOMANIA
NYMPHOMANIAC
NYMPHOMANIACAL
NYMPHOMANIACS
NYMPHOMANIAS
NYSTAGMOID
NYSTAGMUSES

OAFISHNESS
OAFISHNESSES
OAKENSHAWS
OARSMANSHIP
OARSMANSHIPS
OASTHOUSES
OBBLIGATOS
OBCOMPRESSED
OBDURACIES
OBDURATELY
OBDURATENESS
OBDURATENESSES
OBDURATING
OBDURATION
OBDURATIONS
OBEDIENCES
OBEDIENTIAL
OBEDIENTIARIES
OBEDIENTIARY
OBEDIENTLY
OBEISANCES
OBEISANTLY
OBELISCOID
OBELISKOID
OBESENESSES
OBFUSCATED
OBFUSCATES
OBFUSCATING
OBFUSCATION
OBFUSCATIONS
OBFUSCATORY
OBITUARIES
OBITUARIST
OBITUARISTS
OBJECTIFICATION
OBJECTIFIED
OBJECTIFIES
OBJECTIFYING
OBJECTIONABLE
OBJECTIONABLY
OBJECTIONS
OBJECTIVAL
OBJECTIVATE
OBJECTIVATED
OBJECTIVATES
OBJECTIVATING
OBJECTIVATION
OBJECTIVATIONS
OBJECTIVELY
OBJECTIVENESS
OBJECTIVENESSES
OBJECTIVES
OBJECTIVISE

OBJECTIVISED
OBJECTIVISES
OBJECTIVISING
OBJECTIVISM
OBJECTIVISMS
OBJECTIVIST
OBJECTIVISTIC
OBJECTIVISTS
OBJECTIVITIES
OBJECTIVITY
OBJECTIVIZE
OBJECTIVIZED
OBJECTIVIZES
OBJECTIVIZING
OBJECTLESS
OBJECTLESSNESS
OBJURATION
OBJURATIONS
OBJURGATED
OBJURGATES
OBJURGATING
OBJURGATION
OBJURGATIONS
OBJURGATIVE
OBJURGATOR
OBJURGATORS
OBJURGATORY
OBLANCEOLATE
OBLATENESS
OBLATENESSES
OBLATIONAL
OBLIGATELY
OBLIGATING
OBLIGATION
OBLIGATIONAL
OBLIGATIONS
OBLIGATIVE
OBLIGATORILY
OBLIGATORINESS
OBLIGATORS
OBLIGATORY
OBLIGEMENT
OBLIGEMENTS
OBLIGINGLY
OBLIGINGNESS
OBLIGINGNESSES
OBLIQUATION
OBLIQUATIONS
OBLIQUENESS
OBLIQUENESSES
OBLIQUITIES
OBLIQUITOUS
OBLITERATE

OBLITERATED
OBLITERATES
OBLITERATING
OBLITERATION
OBLITERATIONS
OBLITERATIVE
OBLITERATOR
OBLITERATORS
OBLIVIOUSLY
OBLIVIOUSNESS
OBLIVIOUSNESSES
OBLIVISCENCE
OBLIVISCENCES
OBMUTESCENCE
OBMUTESCENCES
OBMUTESCENT
OBNOXIOUSLY
OBNOXIOUSNESS
OBNOXIOUSNESSES
OBNUBILATE
OBNUBILATED
OBNUBILATES
OBNUBILATING
OBNUBILATION
OBNUBILATIONS
OBREPTIONS
OBREPTITIOUS
OBSCENENESS
OBSCENENESSES
OBSCENITIES
OBSCURANTIC
OBSCURANTISM
OBSCURANTISMS
OBSCURANTIST
OBSCURANTISTS
OBSCURANTS
OBSCURATION
OBSCURATIONS
OBSCUREMENT
OBSCUREMENTS
OBSCURENESS
OBSCURENESSES
OBSCURITIES
OBSECRATED
OBSECRATES
OBSECRATING
OBSECRATION
OBSECRATIONS
OBSEQUIOUS
OBSEQUIOUSLY
OBSEQUIOUSNESS
OBSERVABILITIES
OBSERVABILITY

OBSERVABLE
OBSERVABLENESS
OBSERVABLES
OBSERVABLY
OBSERVANCE
OBSERVANCES
OBSERVANCIES
OBSERVANCY
OBSERVANTLY
OBSERVANTS
OBSERVATION
OBSERVATIONAL
OBSERVATIONALLY
OBSERVATIONS
OBSERVATIVE
OBSERVATOR
OBSERVATORIES
OBSERVATORS
OBSERVATORY
OBSERVINGLY
OBSESSIONAL
OBSESSIONALLY
OBSESSIONIST
OBSESSIONISTS
OBSESSIONS
OBSESSIVELY
OBSESSIVENESS
OBSESSIVENESSES
OBSESSIVES
OBSIDIONAL
OBSIDIONARY
OBSIGNATED
OBSIGNATES
OBSIGNATING
OBSIGNATION
OBSIGNATIONS
OBSIGNATORY
OBSOLESCED
OBSOLESCENCE
OBSOLESCENCES
OBSOLESCENT
OBSOLESCENTLY
OBSOLESCES
OBSOLESCING
OBSOLETELY
OBSOLETENESS
OBSOLETENESSES
OBSOLETING
OBSOLETION
OBSOLETIONS
OBSOLETISM
OBSOLETISMS
OBSTETRICAL

OBSTETRICALLY	OBTRUSIONS	OCCLUSIVENESSES	OCTAHEDRONS
OBSTETRICIAN	OBTRUSIVELY	OCCLUSIVES	OCTAMEROUS
OBSTETRICIANS	OBTRUSIVENESS	OCCULTATION	OCTAMETERS
OBSTETRICS	OBTRUSIVENESSES	OCCULTATIONS	OCTANDRIAN
OBSTINACIES	OBTUNDENTS	OCCULTISMS	OCTANDROUS
OBSTINATELY	OBTUNDITIES	OCCULTISTS	OCTANEDIOIC
OBSTINATENESS	OBTURATING	OCCULTNESS	OCTANGULAR
OBSTINATENESSES	OBTURATION	OCCULTNESSES	OCTAPEPTIDE
OBSTIPATION	OBTURATIONS	OCCUPANCES	OCTAPEPTIDES
OBSTIPATIONS	OBTURATORS	OCCUPANCIES	OCTAPLOIDIES
OBSTREPERATE	OBTUSENESS	OCCUPATING	OCTAPLOIDS
OBSTREPERATED	OBTUSENESSES	OCCUPATION	OCTAPLOIDY
OBSTREPERATES	OBTUSITIES	OCCUPATIONAL	OCTAPODIES
OBSTREPERATING	OBUMBRATED	OCCUPATIONALLY	OCTARCHIES
OBSTREPEROUS	OBUMBRATES	OCCUPATIONS	OCTASTICHON
OBSTREPEROUSLY	OBUMBRATING	OCCUPATIVE	OCTASTICHONS
OBSTRICTION	OBUMBRATION	OCCURRENCE	OCTASTICHOUS
OBSTRICTIONS	OBUMBRATIONS	OCCURRENCES	OCTASTICHS
OBSTROPALOUS	OBVENTIONS	OCCURRENTS	OCTASTROPHIC
OBSTROPULOUS	OBVERSIONS	OCEANARIUM	OCTASTYLES
OBSTRUCTED	OBVIATIONS	OCEANARIUMS	OCTAVALENT
OBSTRUCTER	OBVIOUSNESS	OCEANFRONT	OCTENNIALLY
OBSTRUCTERS	OBVIOUSNESSES	OCEANFRONTS	OCTILLIONS
OBSTRUCTING	OBVOLUTION	OCEANGOING	OCTILLIONTH
OBSTRUCTION	OBVOLUTIONS	OCEANOGRAPHER	OCTILLIONTHS
OBSTRUCTIONAL	OBVOLUTIVE	OCEANOGRAPHERS	OCTINGENARIES
OBSTRUCTIONALLY	OCCASIONAL	OCEANOGRAPHIC	OCTINGENARY
OBSTRUCTIONISM	OCCASIONALISM	OCEANOGRAPHICAL	OCTINGENTENARY
OBSTRUCTIONISMS	OCCASIONALISMS	OCEANOGRAPHIES	OCTOCENTENARIES
OBSTRUCTIONIST	OCCASIONALIST	OCEANOGRAPHY	OCTOCENTENARY
OBSTRUCTIONISTS	OCCASIONALISTS	OCEANOLOGICAL	OCTODECILLION
OBSTRUCTIONS	OCCASIONALITIES	OCEANOLOGIES	OCTODECILLIONS
OBSTRUCTIVE	OCCASIONALITY	OCEANOLOGIST	OCTODECIMO
OBSTRUCTIVELY	OCCASIONALLY	OCEANOLOGISTS	OCTODECIMOS
OBSTRUCTIVENESS	OCCASIONED	OCEANOLOGY	OCTOGENARIAN
OBSTRUCTIVES	OCCASIONER	OCELLATION	OCTOGENARIANS
OBSTRUCTOR	OCCASIONERS	OCELLATIONS	OCTOGENARIES
OBSTRUCTORS	OCCASIONING	OCHLOCRACIES	OCTOGENARY
OBSTRUENTS	OCCIDENTAL	OCHLOCRACY	OCTOGYNOUS
OBTAINABILITIES	OCCIDENTALISE	OCHLOCRATIC	OCTOHEDRON
OBTAINABILITY	OCCIDENTALISED	OCHLOCRATICAL	OCTOHEDRONS
OBTAINABLE	OCCIDENTALISES	OCHLOCRATICALLY	OCTONARIAN
OBTAINMENT	OCCIDENTALISING	OCHLOCRATS	OCTONARIANS
OBTAINMENTS	OCCIDENTALISM	OCHLOPHOBIA	OCTONARIES
OBTEMPERATE	OCCIDENTALISMS	OCHLOPHOBIAC	OCTONARIUS
OBTEMPERATED	OCCIDENTALIST	OCHLOPHOBIACS	OCTONOCULAR
OBTEMPERATES	OCCIDENTALISTS	OCHLOPHOBIAS	OCTOPETALOUS
OBTEMPERATING	OCCIDENTALIZE	OCHLOPHOBIC	OCTOPLOIDS
OBTEMPERED	OCCIDENTALIZED	OCHRACEOUS	OCTOPODANS
OBTEMPERING	OCCIDENTALIZES	OCHROLEUCOUS	OCTOPODOUS
OBTENTIONS	OCCIDENTALIZING	OCTACHORDAL	OCTOPUSHER
OBTESTATION	OCCIDENTALLY	OCTACHORDS	OCTOPUSHERS
OBTESTATIONS	OCCIDENTALS	OCTAGONALLY	OCTOPUSHES
OBTRUDINGS	OCCIPITALLY	OCTAHEDRAL	OCTOSEPALOUS
OBTRUNCATE	OCCIPITALS	OCTAHEDRALLY	OCTOSTICHOUS
OBTRUNCATED	OCCLUDENTS	OCTAHEDRITE	OCTOSTYLES
OBTRUNCATES	OCCLUSIONS	OCTAHEDRITES	OCTOSYLLABIC
OBTRUNCATING	OCCLUSIVENESS	OCTAHEDRON	OCTOSYLLABICS

OCTOSYLLABLE	ODORIMETRIES	OFFICIALDOMS	OLEOMARGARINES
OCTOSYLLABLES	ODORIMETRY	OFFICIALESE	OLEOMARGARINS
OCTOTHORPS	ODORIPHORE	OFFICIALESES	OLEOPHILIC
OCTUPLICATE	ODORIPHORES	OFFICIALISM	OLEORESINOUS
OCTUPLICATES	ODOROUSNESS	OFFICIALISMS	OLEORESINS
OCULARISTS	ODOROUSNESSES	OFFICIALITIES	OLERACEOUS
OCULOMOTOR	OECOLOGICAL	OFFICIALITY	OLFACTIBLE
ODALISQUES	OECOLOGICALLY	OFFICIALLY	OLFACTIONS
ODDSMAKERS	OECOLOGIES	OFFICIALTIES	OLFACTOLOGIES
ODIOUSNESS	OECOLOGIST	OFFICIALTY	OLFACTOLOGIST
ODIOUSNESSES	OECOLOGISTS	OFFICIANTS	OLFACTOLOGISTS
ODOMETRIES	OECUMENICAL	OFFICIARIES	OLFACTOLOGY
ODONATISTS	OECUMENICALLY	OFFICIATED	OLFACTOMETER
ODONATOLOGIES	OEDEMATOSE	OFFICIATES	OLFACTOMETERS
ODONATOLOGIST	OEDEMATOUS	OFFICIATING	OLFACTOMETRIES
ODONATOLOGISTS	OEDOMETERS	OFFICIATION	OLFACTOMETRY
ODONATOLOGY	OENOLOGICAL	OFFICIATIONS	OLFACTORIES
ODONTALGIA	OENOLOGIES	OFFICIATOR	OLFACTRONICS
ODONTALGIAS	OENOLOGIST	OFFICIATORS	OLIGAEMIAS
ODONTALGIC	OENOLOGISTS	OFFICINALLY	OLIGARCHAL
ODONTALGIES	OENOMANCIES	OFFICINALS	OLIGARCHIC
ODONTOBLAST	OENOMANIAS	OFFICIOUSLY	OLIGARCHICAL
ODONTOBLASTIC	OENOMETERS	OFFICIOUSNESS	OLIGARCHICALLY
ODONTOBLASTS	OENOPHILES	OFFICIOUSNESSES	OLIGARCHIES
ODONTOCETE	OENOPHILIES	OFFISHNESS	OLIGOCHAETE
ODONTOCETES	OENOPHILIST	OFFISHNESSES	OLIGOCHAETES
ODONTOGENIC	OENOPHILISTS	OFFLOADING	OLIGOCHROME
ODONTOGENIES	OENOTHERAS	OFFPRINTED	OLIGOCHROMES
ODONTOGENY	OESOPHAGEAL	OFFPRINTING	OLIGOCLASE
ODONTOGLOSSUM	OESOPHAGITIS	OFFSADDLED	OLIGOCLASES
ODONTOGLOSSUMS	OESOPHAGITISES	OFFSADDLES	OLIGOCYTHAEMIA
ODONTOGRAPH	OESOPHAGOSCOPE	OFFSADDLING	OLIGOCYTHAEMIAS
ODONTOGRAPHIES	OESOPHAGOSCOPES	OFFSCOURING	OLIGODENDROCYTE
ODONTOGRAPHS	OESOPHAGOSCOPY	OFFSCOURINGS	OLIGODENDROGLIA
ODONTOGRAPHY	OESOPHAGUS	OFFSEASONS	OLIGOGENES
ODONTOLITE	OESTRADIOL	OFFSETABLE	OLIGOMERIC
ODONTOLITES	OESTRADIOLS	OFFSETTING	OLIGOMERISATION
ODONTOLOGIC	OESTROGENIC	OFFSHORING	OLIGOMERIZATION
ODONTOLOGICAL	OESTROGENICALLY	OFFSHORINGS	OLIGOMEROUS
ODONTOLOGIES	OESTROGENS	OFFSPRINGS	OLIGONUCLEOTIDE
ODONTOLOGIST	OFFENCEFUL	OFTENNESSES	OLIGOPEPTIDE
ODONTOLOGISTS	OFFENCELESS	OFTENTIMES	OLIGOPEPTIDES
ODONTOLOGY	OFFENDEDLY	OILINESSES	OLIGOPHAGIES
ODONTOMATA	OFFENDRESS	OINOLOGIES	OLIGOPHAGOUS
ODONTOMATOUS	OFFENDRESSES	OLDFANGLED	OLIGOPHAGY
ODONTOPHOBIA	OFFENSELESS	OLEAGINOUS	OLIGOPOLIES
ODONTOPHOBIAS	OFFENSIVELY	OLEAGINOUSLY	OLIGOPOLISTIC
ODONTOPHORAL	OFFENSIVENESS	OLEAGINOUSNESS	OLIGOPSONIES
ODONTOPHORAN	OFFENSIVENESSES	OLEANDOMYCIN	OLIGOPSONISTIC
ODONTOPHORE	OFFENSIVES	OLEANDOMYCINS	OLIGOPSONY
ODONTOPHORES	OFFERTORIES	OLECRANONS	OLIGOSACCHARIDE
ODONTOPHOROUS	OFFHANDEDLY	OLEIFEROUS	OLIGOSPERMIA
ODONTORHYNCHOUS	OFFHANDEDNESS	OLEOGRAPHIC	OLIGOSPERMIAS
ODONTORNITHES	OFFHANDEDNESSES	OLEOGRAPHIES	OLIGOTROPHIC
ODONTOSTOMATOUS	OFFICEHOLDER	OLEOGRAPHS	OLIGOTROPHIES
ODORIFEROUS	OFFICEHOLDERS	OLEOGRAPHY	OLIGOTROPHY
ODORIFEROUSLY	OFFICERING	OLEOMARGARIN	OLIGURESES
ODORIFEROUSNESS	OFFICIALDOM	OLEOMARGARINE	OLIGURESIS

OLIGURETIC	OMNIPRESENT	ONEIROSCOPY	OOPHORECTOMIZED
OLIVACEOUS	OMNIRANGES	ONEROUSNESS	OOPHORECTOMIZES
OLIVENITES	OMNISCIENCE	ONEROUSNESSES	OOPHORECTOMY
OLIVINITIC	OMNISCIENCES	ONGOINGNESS	OOPHORITIC
OLOGOANING	OMNISCIENT	ONGOINGNESSES	OOPHORITIS
OLOLIUQUIS	OMNISCIENTLY	ONIONSKINS	OOPHORITISES
OMBROGENOUS	OMNIVORIES	ONOCENTAUR	OOZINESSES
OMBROMETER	OMNIVOROUS	ONOCENTAURS	OPACIFIERS
OMBROMETERS	OMNIVOROUSLY	ONOMASIOLOGIES	OPACIFYING
OMBROPHILE	OMNIVOROUSNESS	ONOMASIOLOGY	OPALESCENCE
OMBROPHILES	OMOPHAGIAS	ONOMASTICALLY	OPALESCENCES
OMBROPHILOUS	OMOPHAGIES	ONOMASTICIAN	OPALESCENT
OMBROPHILS	OMOPHAGOUS	ONOMASTICIANS	OPALESCENTLY
OMBROPHOBE	OMOPHORION	ONOMASTICON	OPALESCING
OMBROPHOBES	OMOPLATOSCOPIES	ONOMASTICONS	OPAQUENESS
OMBROPHOBOUS	OMOPLATOSCOPY	ONOMASTICS	OPAQUENESSES
OMBUDSMANSHIP	OMPHACITES	ONOMATOLOGIES	OPEIDOSCOPE
OMBUDSMANSHIPS	OMPHALOMANCIES	ONOMATOLOGIST	OPEIDOSCOPES
OMINOUSNESS	OMPHALOMANCY	ONOMATOLOGISTS	OPENABILITIES
OMINOUSNESSES	OMPHALOSKEPSES	ONOMATOLOGY	OPENABILITY
OMISSIVENESS	OMPHALOSKEPSIS	ONOMATOPOEIA	OPENHANDED
OMISSIVENESSES	ONAGRACEOUS	ONOMATOPOEIAS	OPENHANDEDLY
OMITTANCES	ONCHOCERCIASES	ONOMATOPOEIC	OPENHANDEDNESS
OMMATIDIAL	ONCHOCERCIASIS	ONOMATOPOESES	OPENHEARTED
OMMATIDIUM	ONCOGENESES	ONOMATOPOESIS	OPENHEARTEDLY
OMMATOPHORE	ONCOGENESIS	ONOMATOPOETIC	OPENHEARTEDNESS
OMMATOPHORES	ONCOGENETICIST	ONOMATOPOIESES	OPENMOUTHED
OMMATOPHOROUS	ONCOGENETICISTS	ONOMATOPOIESIS	OPENMOUTHEDLY
OMNIBENEVOLENCE	ONCOGENICITIES	ONSETTINGS	OPENMOUTHEDNESS
OMNIBENEVOLENT	ONCOGENICITY	ONSHORINGS	OPENNESSES
OMNIBUSSES	ONCOGENOUS	ONSLAUGHTS	OPERABILITIES
OMNICOMPETENCE	ONCOLOGICAL	ONTOGENESES	OPERABILITY
OMNICOMPETENCES	ONCOLOGIES	ONTOGENESIS	OPERAGOERS
OMNICOMPETENT	ONCOLOGIST	ONTOGENETIC	OPERAGOING
OMNIDIRECTIONAL	ONCOLOGISTS	ONTOGENETICALLY	OPERAGOINGS
OMNIFARIOUS	ONCOLYTICS	ONTOGENICALLY	OPERATICALLY
OMNIFARIOUSLY	ONCOMETERS	ONTOGENIES	OPERATIONAL
OMNIFARIOUSNESS	ONCORNAVIRUS	ONTOLOGICAL	OPERATIONALISM
OMNIFEROUS	ONCORNAVIRUSES	ONTOLOGICALLY	OPERATIONALISMS
OMNIFICENCE	ONCOTOMIES	ONTOLOGIES	OPERATIONALIST
OMNIFICENCES	ONCOVIRUSES	ONTOLOGIST	OPERATIONALISTS
OMNIFICENT	ONDOGRAPHS	ONTOLOGISTS	OPERATIONALLY
OMNIFORMITIES	ONEIRICALLY	ONYCHITISES	OPERATIONISM
OMNIFORMITY	ONEIROCRITIC	ONYCHOCRYPTOSES	OPERATIONISMS
OMNIGENOUS	ONEIROCRITICAL	ONYCHOCRYPTOSIS	OPERATIONIST
OMNIPARITIES	ONEIROCRITICISM	ONYCHOMANCIES	OPERATIONISTS
OMNIPARITY	ONEIROCRITICS	ONYCHOMANCY	OPERATIONS
OMNIPAROUS	ONEIRODYNIA	ONYCHOPHAGIES	OPERATISED
OMNIPATIENT	ONEIRODYNIAS	ONYCHOPHAGIST	OPERATISES
OMNIPOTENCE	ONEIROLOGIES	ONYCHOPHAGISTS	OPERATISING
OMNIPOTENCES	ONEIROLOGY	ONYCHOPHAGY	OPERATIVELY
OMNIPOTENCIES	ONEIROMANCER	ONYCHOPHORAN	OPERATIVENESS
OMNIPOTENCY	ONEIROMANCERS	ONYCHOPHORANS	OPERATIVENESSES
OMNIPOTENT	ONEIROMANCIES	OOPHORECTOMIES	OPERATIVES
OMNIPOTENTLY	ONEIROMANCY	OOPHORECTOMISE	OPERATIVITIES
OMNIPOTENTS	ONEIROSCOPIES	OOPHORECTOMISED	OPERATIVITY
OMNIPRESENCE	ONEIROSCOPIST	OOPHORECTOMISES	OPERATIZED
OMNIPRESENCES	ONEIROSCOPISTS	OOPHORECTOMIZE	OPERATIZES

OPERATIZING	OPINICUSES	OPPORTUNISTIC	OPTIMALISING
OPERATORLESS	OPINIONATED	OPPORTUNISTS	OPTIMALITIES
OPERCULARS	OPINIONATEDLY	OPPORTUNITIES	OPTIMALITY
OPERCULATE	OPINIONATEDNESS	OPPORTUNITY	OPTIMALIZATION
OPERCULATED	OPINIONATELY	OPPOSABILITIES	OPTIMALIZATIONS
OPERCULUMS	OPINIONATIVE	OPPOSABILITY	OPTIMALIZE
OPERETTIST	OPINIONATIVELY	OPPOSELESS	OPTIMALIZED
OPERETTISTS	OPINIONATOR	OPPOSINGLY	OPTIMALIZES
OPEROSENESS	OPINIONATORS	OPPOSITELY	OPTIMALIZING
OPEROSENESSES	OPINIONIST	OPPOSITENESS	OPTIMISATION
OPEROSITIES	OPINIONISTS	OPPOSITENESSES	OPTIMISATIONS
OPHICALCITE	OPISOMETER	OPPOSITION	OPTIMISERS
OPHICALCITES	OPISOMETERS	OPPOSITIONAL	OPTIMISING
OPHICLEIDE	OPISTHOBRANCH	OPPOSITIONIST	OPTIMISTIC
OPHICLEIDES	OPISTHOBRANCHS	OPPOSITIONISTS	OPTIMISTICAL
OPHIDIARIA	OPISTHOCOELIAN	OPPOSITIONLESS	OPTIMISTICALLY
OPHIDIARIUM	OPISTHOCOELOUS	OPPOSITIONS	OPTIMIZATION
OPHIDIARIUMS	OPISTHODOMOI	OPPOSITIVE	OPTIMIZATIONS
OPHIOLATER	OPISTHODOMOS	OPPRESSING	OPTIMIZERS
OPHIOLATERS	OPISTHOGLOSSAL	OPPRESSINGLY	OPTIMIZING
OPHIOLATRIES	OPISTHOGNATHISM	OPPRESSION	OPTIONALITIES
OPHIOLATROUS	OPISTHOGNATHOUS	OPPRESSIONS	OPTIONALITY
OPHIOLATRY	OPISTHOGRAPH	OPPRESSIVE	OPTIONALLY
OPHIOLITES	OPISTHOGRAPHIC	OPPRESSIVELY	OPTOACOUSTIC
OPHIOLITIC	OPISTHOGRAPHIES	OPPRESSIVENESS	OPTOELECTRONIC
OPHIOLOGIC	OPISTHOGRAPHS	OPPRESSORS	OPTOELECTRONICS
OPHIOLOGICAL	OPISTHOGRAPHY	OPPROBRIOUS	OPTOKINETIC
OPHIOLOGIES	OPISTHOSOMA	OPPROBRIOUSLY	OPTOLOGIES
OPHIOLOGIST	OPISTHOSOMATA	OPPROBRIOUSNESS	OPTOLOGIST
OPHIOLOGISTS	OPISTHOTONIC	OPPROBRIUM	OPTOLOGISTS
OPHIOMORPH	OPISTHOTONOS	OPPROBRIUMS	OPTOMETERS
OPHIOMORPHIC	OPISTHOTONOSES	OPPUGNANCIES	OPTOMETRIC
OPHIOMORPHOUS	OPOBALSAMS	OPPUGNANCY	OPTOMETRICAL
OPHIOMORPHS	OPODELDOCS	OPPUGNANTLY	OPTOMETRIES
OPHIOPHAGOUS	OPOPANAXES	OPPUGNANTS	OPTOMETRIST
OPHIOPHILIST	OPOTHERAPIES	OPSIMATHIES	OPTOMETRISTS
OPHIOPHILISTS	OPOTHERAPY	OPSIOMETER	OPTOPHONES
OPHIUROIDS	OPPIGNERATE	OPSIOMETERS	OPULENCIES
OPHTHALMIA	OPPIGNERATED	OPSOMANIAC	ORACULARITIES
OPHTHALMIAS	OPPIGNERATES	OPSOMANIACS	ORACULARITY
OPHTHALMIC	OPPIGNERATING	OPSOMANIAS	ORACULARLY
OPHTHALMIST	OPPIGNORATE	OPSONIFICATION	ORACULARNESS
OPHTHALMISTS	OPPIGNORATED	OPSONIFICATIONS	ORACULARNESSES
OPHTHALMITIS	OPPIGNORATES	OPSONIFIED	ORACULOUSLY
OPHTHALMITISES	OPPIGNORATING	OPSONIFIES	ORACULOUSNESS
OPHTHALMOLOGIC	OPPIGNORATION	OPSONIFYING	ORACULOUSNESSES
OPHTHALMOLOGIES	OPPIGNORATIONS	OPSONISATION	ORANGEADES
OPHTHALMOLOGIST	OPPILATING	OPSONISATIONS	ORANGERIES
OPHTHALMOLOGY	OPPILATION	OPSONISING	ORANGEWOOD
OPHTHALMOMETER	OPPILATIONS	OPSONIZATION	ORANGEWOODS
OPHTHALMOMETERS	OPPILATIVE	OPSONIZATIONS	ORANGUTANS
OPHTHALMOMETRY	OPPONENCIES	OPSONIZING	ORATORIANS
OPHTHALMOPHOBIA	OPPORTUNELY	OPTATIVELY	ORATORICAL
OPHTHALMOPLEGIA	OPPORTUNENESS	OPTIMALISATION	ORATORICALLY
OPHTHALMOSCOPE	OPPORTUNENESSES	OPTIMALISATIONS	ORATRESSES
OPHTHALMOSCOPES	OPPORTUNISM	OPTIMALISE	ORBICULARES
OPHTHALMOSCOPIC	OPPORTUNISMS	OPTIMALISED	ORBICULARIS
OPHTHALMOSCOPY	OPPORTUNIST	OPTIMALISES	ORBICULARITIES

ORBICULARITY	ORDINARIER	ORGANOGENESIS	ORIGINALITIES
ORBICULARLY	ORDINARIES	ORGANOGENETIC	ORIGINALITY
ORBICULATE	ORDINARIEST	ORGANOGENIES	ORIGINALLY
ORBICULATED	ORDINARILY	ORGANOGENY	ORIGINATED
ORCHARDING	ORDINARINESS	ORGANOGRAM	ORIGINATES
ORCHARDINGS	ORDINARINESSES	ORGANOGRAMS	ORIGINATING
ORCHARDIST	ORDINATELY	ORGANOGRAPHIC	ORIGINATION
ORCHARDISTS	ORDINATING	ORGANOGRAPHICAL	ORIGINATIONS
ORCHARDMAN	ORDINATION	ORGANOGRAPHIES	ORIGINATIVE
ORCHARDMEN	ORDINATIONS	ORGANOGRAPHIST	ORIGINATIVELY
ORCHESOGRAPHIES	ORDONNANCE	ORGANOGRAPHISTS	ORIGINATOR
ORCHESOGRAPHY	ORDONNANCES	ORGANOGRAPHY	ORIGINATORS
ORCHESTICS	ORECCHIETTE	ORGANOLEPTIC	ORINASALLY
ORCHESTRAL	ORECCHIETTI	ORGANOLOGICAL	ORISMOLOGICAL
ORCHESTRALIST	OREOGRAPHIC	ORGANOLOGIES	ORISMOLOGIES
ORCHESTRALISTS	OREOGRAPHICAL	ORGANOLOGIST	ORISMOLOGY
ORCHESTRALLY	OREOGRAPHIES	ORGANOLOGISTS	ORNAMENTAL
ORCHESTRAS	OREOGRAPHY	ORGANOLOGY	ORNAMENTALLY
ORCHESTRATE	OREOLOGICAL	ORGANOMERCURIAL	ORNAMENTALS
ORCHESTRATED	OREOLOGIES	ORGANOMETALLIC	ORNAMENTATION
ORCHESTRATER	OREOLOGIST	ORGANOMETALLICS	ORNAMENTATIONS
ORCHESTRATERS	OREOLOGISTS	ORGANOPHOSPHATE	ORNAMENTED
ORCHESTRATES	OREPEARCHED	ORGANOSOLS	ORNAMENTER
ORCHESTRATING	OREPEARCHES	ORGANOTHERAPIES	ORNAMENTERS
ORCHESTRATION	OREPEARCHING	ORGANOTHERAPY	ORNAMENTING
ORCHESTRATIONAL	ORGANELLES	ORGANZINES	ORNAMENTIST
ORCHESTRATIONS	ORGANICALLY	ORGIASTICALLY	ORNAMENTISTS
ORCHESTRATOR	ORGANICISM	ORICALCHES	ORNATENESS
ORCHESTRATORS	ORGANICISMS	ORICHALCEOUS	ORNATENESSES
ORCHESTRIC	ORGANICIST	·ORIENTALISE	ORNERINESS
ORCHESTRINA	ORGANICISTIC	ORIENTALISED	ORNERINESSES
ORCHESTRINAS	ORGANICISTS	ORIENTALISES	ORNITHICHNITE
ORCHESTRION	ORGANICITIES	ORIENTALISING	ORNITHICHNITES
ORCHESTRIONS	ORGANICITY	ORIENTALISM	ORNITHINES
ORCHIDACEOUS	ORGANISABILITY	ORIENTALISMS	ORNITHISCHIAN
ORCHIDECTOMIES	ORGANISABLE	ORIENTALIST	ORNITHISCHIANS
ORCHIDECTOMY	ORGANISATION	ORIENTALISTS	ORNITHODELPHIAN
ORCHIDEOUS	ORGANISATIONAL	ORIENTALITIES	ORNITHODELPHIC
ORCHIDISTS	ORGANISATIONS	ORIENTALITY	ORNITHODELPHOUS
ORCHIDLIKE	ORGANISERS	ORIENTALIZE	ORNITHOGALUM
ORCHIDOLOGIES	ORGANISING	ORIENTALIZED	ORNITHOGALUMS
ORCHIDOLOGIST	ORGANISMAL	ORIENTALIZES	ORNITHOLOGIC
ORCHIDOLOGISTS	ORGANISMALLY	ORIENTALIZING	ORNITHOLOGICAL
ORCHIDOLOGY	ORGANISMIC	ORIENTALLY	ORNITHOLOGIES
ORCHIDOMANIA	ORGANISMICALLY	ORIENTATED	ORNITHOLOGIST
ORCHIDOMANIAC	ORGANISTRUM	ORIENTATES	ORNITHOLOGISTS
ORCHIDOMANIACS	ORGANISTRUMS	ORIENTATING	ORNITHOLOGY
ORCHIDOMANIAS	ORGANITIES	ORIENTATION	ORNITHOMANCIES
ORCHIECTOMIES	ORGANIZABILITY	ORIENTATIONAL	ORNITHOMANCY
ORCHIECTOMY	ORGANIZABLE	ORIENTATIONALLY	ORNITHOMANTIC
ORCHITISES	ORGANIZATION	ORIENTATIONS	ORNITHOMORPH
ORDAINABLE	ORGANIZATIONAL	ORIENTATOR	ORNITHOMORPHIC
ORDAINMENT	ORGANIZATIONS	ORIENTATORS	ORNITHOMORPHS
ORDAINMENTS	ORGANIZERS	ORIENTEERED	ORNITHOPHILIES
ORDERLINESS	ORGANIZING	ORIENTEERING	ORNITHOPHILOUS
ORDERLINESSES	ORGANOCHLORINE	ORIENTEERINGS	ORNITHOPHILY
ORDINAIRES	ORGANOCHLORINES	ORIENTEERS	ORNITHOPHOBIA
ORDINANCES	ORGANOGENESES	ORIFLAMMES	ORNITHOPHOBIAS

ORNITHOPOD	ORTHOCHROMATISM	ORTHOGRAPHS	ORTHOSCOPES
ORNITHOPODS	ORTHOCLASE	ORTHOGRAPHY	ORTHOSCOPIC
ORNITHOPTER	ORTHOCLASES	ORTHOHYDROGEN	ORTHOSILTCATE
ORNITHOPTERS	ORTHOCOUSINS	ORTHOHYDROGENS	ORTHOSILICATES
ORNITHORHYNCHUS	ORTHODIAGONAL	ORTHOMOLECULAR	ORTHOSTATIC
ORNITHOSAUR	ORTHODIAGONALS	ORTHOMORPHIC	ORTHOSTICHIES
ORNITHOSAURS	ORTHODONTIA	ORTHONORMAL	ORTHOSTICHOUS
ORNITHOSCOPIES	ORTHODONTIAS	ORTHOPAEDIC	ORTHOSTICHY
ORNITHOSCOPY	ORTHODONTIC	ORTHOPAEDICAL	ORTHOTISTS
ORNITHOSES	ORTHODONTICALLY	ORTHOPAEDICS	ORTHOTONES
ORNITHOSIS	ORTHODONTICS	ORTHOPAEDIES	ORTHOTONESES
OROBANCHACEOUS	ORTHODONTIST	ORTHOPAEDIST	ORTHOTONESIS
OROGENESES	ORTHODONTISTS	ORTHOPAEDISTS	ORTHOTONIC
OROGENESIS	ORTHODOXES	ORTHOPAEDY	ORTHOTOPIC
OROGENETIC	ORTHODOXIES	ORTHOPEDIA	ORTHOTROPIC
OROGENETICALLY	ORTHODOXLY	ORTHOPEDIAS	ORTHOTROPIES
OROGENICALLY	ORTHODROMIC	ORTHOPEDIC	ORTHOTROPISM
OROGRAPHER	ORTHODROMICS	ORTHOPEDICAL	ORTHOTROPISMS
OROGRAPHERS	ORTHODROMIES	ORTHOPEDICALLY	ORTHOTROPOUS
OROGRAPHIC	ORTHODROMY	ORTHOPEDICS	ORTHOTROPY
OROGRAPHICAL	ORTHOEPICAL	ORTHOPEDIES	ORTHOVANADIC
OROGRAPHICALLY	ORTHOEPICALLY	ORTHOPEDIST	ORYCTOLOGIES
OROGRAPHIES	ORTHOEPIES	ORTHOPEDISTS	ORYCTOLOGY
OROLOGICAL	ORTHOEPIST	ORTHOPHOSPHATE	OSCILLATED
OROLOGICALLY	ORTHOEPISTS	ORTHOPHOSPHATES	OSCILLATES
OROLOGISTS	ORTHOGENESES	ORTHOPHOSPHORIC	OSCILLATING
OROPHARYNGEAL	ORTHOGENESIS	ORTHOPHYRE	OSCILLATION
OROPHARYNGES	ORTHOGENETIC	ORTHOPHYRES	OSCILLATIONAL
OROPHARYNX	ORTHOGENIC	ORTHOPHYRIC	OSCILLATIONS
OROPHARYNXES	ORTHOGENICALLY	ORTHOPINAKOID	OSCILLATIVE
OROROTUNDITIES	ORTHOGENICS	ORTHOPINAKOIDS	OSCILLATOR
OROROTUNDITY	ORTHOGNATHIC	ORTHOPNOEA	OSCILLATORS
OROTUNDITIES	ORTHOGNATHIES	ORTHOPNOEAS	OSCILLATORY
OROTUNDITY	ORTHOGNATHISM	ORTHOPRAXES	OSCILLOGRAM
ORPHANAGES	ORTHOGNATHISMS	ORTHOPRAXIES	OSCILLOGRAMS
ORPHANHOOD	ORTHOGNATHOUS	ORTHOPRAXIS	OSCILLOGRAPH
ORPHANHOODS	ORTHOGNATHY	ORTHOPRAXY	OSCILLOGRAPHIC
ORPHANISMS	ORTHOGONAL	ORTHOPRISM	OSCILLOGRAPHIES
ORPHARIONS	ORTHOGONALISE	ORTHOPRISMS	OSCILLOGRAPHS
ORPHEOREON	ORTHOGONALISED	ORTHOPSYCHIATRY	OSCILLOGRAPHY
ORPHEOREONS	ORTHOGONALISES	ORTHOPTERA	OSCILLOSCOPE
ORPHICALLY	ORTHOGONALISING	ORTHOPTERAN	OSCILLOSCOPES
ORRISROOTS	ORTHOGONALITIES	ORTHOPTERANS	OSCILLOSCOPIC
ORTANIQUES	ORTHOGONALITY	ORTHOPTERIST	OSCITANCES
ORTHOBORATE	ORTHOGONALIZE	ORTHOPTERISTS	OSCITANCIES
ORTHOBORATES	ORTHOGONALIZED	ORTHOPTEROID	OSCITANTLY
ORTHOBORIC	ORTHOGONALIZES	ORTHOPTEROIDS	OSCITATING
ORTHOCAINE	ORTHOGONALIZING	ORTHOPTEROLOGY	OSCITATION
ORTHOCAINES	ORTHOGONALLY	ORTHOPTERON	OSCITATIONS
ORTHOCENTER	ORTHOGRADE	ORTHOPTEROUS	OSCULATING
ORTHOCENTERS	ORTHOGRAPH	ORTHOPTERS	OSCULATION
ORTHOCENTRE	ORTHOGRAPHER	ORTHOPTICS	OSCULATIONS
ORTHOCENTRES	ORTHOGRAPHERS	ORTHOPTIST	OSCULATORIES
ORTHOCEPHALIC	ORTHOGRAPHIC	ORTHOPTISTS	OSCULATORY
ORTHOCEPHALIES	ORTHOGRAPHICAL	ORTHOPYROXENE	OSMETERIUM
ORTHOCEPHALOUS	ORTHOGRAPHIES	ORTHOPYROXENES	OSMIDROSES
ORTHOCEPHALY	ORTHOGRAPHIST	ORTHORHOMBIC	OSMIDROSIS
ORTHOCHROMATIC	ORTHOGRAPHISTS	ORTHOSCOPE	OSMIRIDIUM

OSMIRIDIUMS	OSTEOFIBROSIS	OSTRACIZING	OUTBALANCES
OSMOLALITIES	OSTEOGENESES	OSTRACODAN	OUTBALANCING
OSMOLALITY	OSTEOGENESIS	OSTRACODERM	OUTBARGAIN
OSMOLARITIES	OSTEOGENETIC	OSTRACODERMS	OUTBARGAINED
OSMOLARITY	OSTEOGENIC	OSTRACODES	OUTBARGAINING
OSMOMETERS	OSTEOGENIES	OSTRACODOUS	OUTBARGAINS
OSMOMETRIC	OSTEOGENOUS	OSTREACEOUS	OUTBARKING
OSMOMETRICALLY	OSTEOGRAPHIES	OSTREICULTURE	OUTBARRING
OSMOMETRIES	OSTEOGRAPHY	OSTREICULTURES	OUTBAWLING
OSMOREGULATION	OSTEOLOGICAL	OSTREICULTURIST	OUTBEAMING
OSMOREGULATIONS	OSTEOLOGICALLY	OSTREOPHAGE	OUTBEGGING
OSMOREGULATORY	OSTEOLOGIES	OSTREOPHAGES	OUTBIDDERS
OSMOTICALLY	OSTEOLOGIST	OSTREOPHAGIES	OUTBIDDING
OSMUNDINES	OSTEOLOGISTS	OSTREOPHAGOUS	OUTBITCHED
OSSIFEROUS	OSTEOMALACIA	OSTREOPHAGY	OUTBITCHES
OSSIFICATION	OSTEOMALACIAL	OSTRICHISM	OUTBITCHING
OSSIFICATIONS	OSTEOMALACIAS	OSTRICHISMS	OUTBLAZING
OSSIFRAGAS	OSTEOMALACIC	OSTRICHLIKE	OUTBLEATED
OSSIFRAGES	OSTEOMYELITIS	OTHERGATES	OUTBLEATING
OSSIVOROUS	OSTEOMYELITISES	OTHERGUESS	OUTBLESSED
OSTEICHTHYAN	OSTEOPATHIC	OTHERNESSES	OUTBLESSES
OSTEICHTHYANS	OSTEOPATHICALLY	OTHERWHERE	OUTBLESSING
OSTEITIDES	OSTEOPATHIES	OTHERWHILE	OUTBLOOMED
OSTEITISES	OSTEOPATHIST	OTHERWHILES	OUTBLOOMING
OSTENSIBILITIES	OSTEOPATHISTS	OTHERWORLD	OUTBLUFFED
OSTENSIBILITY	OSTEOPATHS	OTHERWORLDISH	OUTBLUFFING
OSTENSIBLE	OSTEOPATHY	OTHERWORLDLY	OUTBLUSHED
OSTENSIBLY	OSTEOPETROSES	OTHERWORLDS	OUTBLUSHES
OSTENSIVELY	OSTEOPETROSIS	OTIOSENESS	OUTBLUSHING
OSTENSORIA	OSTEOPHYTE	OTIOSENESSES	OUTBLUSTER
OSTENSORIES	OSTEOPHYTES	OTIOSITIES	OUTBLUSTERED
OSTENSORIUM	OSTEOPHYTIC	OTOLARYNGOLOGY	OUTBLUSTERING
OSTENTATION	OSTEOPLASTIC	OTOLOGICAL	OUTBLUSTERS
OSTENTATIONS	OSTEOPLASTIES	OTOLOGISTS	OUTBOASTED
OSTENTATIOUS	OSTEOPLASTY	OTOPLASTIES	OUTBOASTING
OSTENTATIOUSLY	OSTEOPOROSES	OTORRHOEAS	OUTBRAGGED
OSTEOARTHRITIC	OSTEOPOROSIS	OTOSCLEROSES	OUTBRAGGING
OSTEOARTHRITICS	OSTEOPOROTIC	OTOSCLEROSIS	OUTBRAVING
OSTEOARTHRITIS	OSTEOSARCOMA	OTOSCOPIES	OUTBRAWLED
OSTEOARTHROSES	OSTEOSARCOMAS	OTOTOXICITIES	OUTBRAWLING
OSTEOARTHROSIS	OSTEOSARCOMATA	OTOTOXICITY	OUTBRAZENED
OSTEOBLAST	OSTEOSISES	OTTRELITES	OUTBRAZENING
OSTEOBLASTIC	OSTEOTOMES	OUANANICHE	OUTBRAZENS
OSTEOBLASTS	OSTEOTOMIES	OUANANICHES	OUTBREAKING
OSTEOCLASES	OSTLERESSES	OUBLIETTES	OUTBREATHE
OSTEOCLASIS	OSTRACEOUS	OUGHTLINGS	OUTBREATHED
OSTEOCLAST	OSTRACISABLE	OUGHTNESSES	OUTBREATHES
OSTEOCLASTIC	OSTRACISED	OUROBOROSES	OUTBREATHING
OSTEOCLASTS	OSTRACISER	OUROLOGIES	OUTBREEDING
OSTEOCOLLA	OSTRACISERS	OUROSCOPIES	OUTBREEDINGS
OSTEOCOLLAS	OSTRACISES	OUTACHIEVE	OUTBRIBING
OSTEOCYTES	OSTRACISING	OUTACHIEVED	OUTBUILDING
OSTEODERMAL	OSTRACISMS	OUTACHIEVES	OUTBUILDINGS
OSTEODERMATOUS	OSTRACIZABLE	OUTACHIEVING	OUTBULGING
OSTEODERMIC	OSTRACIZED	OUTARGUING	OUTBULKING
OSTEODERMOUS	OSTRACIZER	OUTBACKERS	OUTBULLIED
OSTEODERMS	OSTRACIZERS	OUTBALANCE	OUTBULLIES
OSTEOFIBROSES	OSTRACIZES	OUTBALANCED	OUTBULLYING

OUTBURNING	OUTDAZZLING	OUTFISHING	OUTGUESSES
OUTBURSTING	OUTDEBATED	OUTFITTERS	OUTGUESSING
OUTCAPERED	OUTDEBATES	OUTFITTING	OUTGUIDING
OUTCAPERING	OUTDEBATING	OUTFITTINGS	OUTGUNNING
OUTCASTING	OUTDELIVER	OUTFLANKED	OUTGUSHING
OUTCATCHES	OUTDELIVERED	OUTFLANKING	OUTHANDLED
OUTCATCHING	OUTDELIVERING	OUTFLASHED	OUTHANDLES
OUTCAVILED	OUTDELIVERS	OUTFLASHES	OUTHANDLING
OUTCAVILING	OUTDESIGNED	OUTFLASHING	OUTHAULERS
OUTCAVILLED	OUTDESIGNING	OUTFLOATED	OUTHEARING
OUTCAVILLING	OUTDESIGNS	OUTFLOATING	OUTHITTING
OUTCHARGED	OUTDISTANCE	OUTFLOWING	OUTHOMERED
OUTCHARGES	OUTDISTANCED	OUTFLOWINGS	OUTHOMERING
OUTCHARGING	OUTDISTANCES	OUTFLUSHED	OUTHOWLING
OUTCHARMED	OUTDISTANCING	OUTFLUSHES	OUTHUMORED
OUTCHARMING	OUTDODGING	OUTFLUSHING	OUTHUMORING
OUTCHEATED	OUTDOORSMAN	OUTFOOLING	OUTHUNTING
OUTCHEATING	OUTDOORSMANSHIP	OUTFOOTING	OUTHUSTLED
OUTCHIDDEN	OUTDOORSMEN	OUTFROWNED	OUTHUSTLES
OUTCHIDING	OUTDRAGGED	OUTFROWNING	OUTHUSTLING
OUTCLASSED	OUTDRAGGING	OUTFUMBLED	OUTINTRIGUE
OUTCLASSES	OUTDRAWING	OUTFUMBLES	OUTINTRIGUED
OUTCLASSING	OUTDREAMED	OUTFUMBLING	OUTINTRIGUES
OUTCLIMBED	OUTDREAMING	OUTGAINING	OUTINTRIGUING
OUTCLIMBING	OUTDRESSED	OUTGALLOPED	OUTJESTING
OUTCOACHED	OUTDRESSES	OUTGALLOPING	OUTJETTING
OUTCOACHES	OUTDRESSING	OUTGALLOPS	OUTJETTINGS
OUTCOACHING	OUTDRINKING	OUTGAMBLED	OUTJINXING
OUTCOMPETE	OUTDRIVING	OUTGAMBLES	OUTJOCKEYED
OUTCOMPETED	OUTDROPPED	OUTGAMBLING	OUTJOCKEYING
OUTCOMPETES	OUTDROPPING	OUTGASSING	OUTJOCKEYS
OUTCOMPETING	OUTDUELING	OUTGASSINGS	OUTJUGGLED
OUTCOOKING	OUTDUELLED	OUTGENERAL	OUTJUGGLES
OUTCOUNTED	OUTDUELLING	OUTGENERALED	OUTJUGGLING
OUTCOUNTING	OUTDWELLED	OUTGENERALING	OUTJUMPING
OUTCRAFTIED	OUTDWELLING	OUTGENERALLED	OUTJUTTING
OUTCRAFTIES	OUTEARNING	OUTGENERALLING	OUTJUTTINGS
OUTCRAFTYING	OUTECHOING	OUTGENERALS	OUTKEEPING
OUTCRAWLED	OUTERCOATS	OUTGIVINGS	OUTKICKING
OUTCRAWLING	OUTERCOURSE	OUTGLARING	OUTKILLING
OUTCROPPED	OUTERCOURSES	OUTGLEAMED	OUTKISSING
OUTCROPPING	OUTERWEARS	OUTGLEAMING	OUTLANDERS
OUTCROPPINGS	OUTFABLING	OUTGLITTER	OUTLANDISH
OUTCROSSED	OUTFANGTHIEF	OUTGLITTERED	OUTLANDISHLY
OUTCROSSES	OUTFANGTHIEVES	OUTGLITTERING	OUTLANDISHNESS
OUTCROSSING	OUTFASTING	OUTGLITTERS	OUTLASTING
OUTCROSSINGS	OUTFAWNING	OUTGLOWING	OUTLAUGHED
OUTCROWDED	OUTFEASTED	OUTGNAWING	OUTLAUGHING
OUTCROWDING	OUTFEASTING	OUTGOINGNESS	OUTLAUNCED
OUTCROWING	OUTFEELING	OUTGOINGNESSES	OUTLAUNCES
OUTCURSING	OUTFENCING	OUTGRINNED	OUTLAUNCHED
OUTDACIOUS	OUTFIELDER	OUTGRINNING	OUTLAUNCHES
OUTDANCING	OUTFIELDERS	OUTGROSSED	OUTLAUNCHING
OUTDATEDLY	OUTFIGHTING	OUTGROSSES	OUTLAUNCING
OUTDATEDNESS	OUTFIGURED	OUTGROSSING	OUTLAWRIES
OUTDATEDNESSES	OUTFIGURES	OUTGROWING	OUTLEADING
OUTDAZZLED	OUTFIGURING	OUTGROWTHS	OUTLEAPING
OUTDAZZLES	OUTFINDING	OUTGUESSED	OUTLEARNED

OUTLEARNING	OUTPAINTED	OUTPRESSING	OUTRINGING
OUTLODGING	OUTPAINTING	OUTPRICING	OUTRIVALED
OUTLODGINGS	OUTPASSING	OUTPRIZING	OUTRIVALING
OUTLOOKING	OUTPASSION	OUTPRODUCE	OUTRIVALLED
OUTLUSTRED	OUTPASSIONED	OUTPRODUCED	OUTRIVALLING
OUTLUSTRES	OUTPASSIONING	OUTPRODUCES	OUTROARING
OUTLUSTRING	OUTPASSIONS	OUTPRODUCING	OUTROCKING
OUTMANEUVER	OUTPATIENT	OUTPROMISE	OUTROLLING
OUTMANEUVERED	OUTPATIENTS	OUTPROMISED	OUTROOPERS
OUTMANEUVERING	OUTPEEPING	OUTPROMISES	OUTROOTING
OUTMANEUVERS	OUTPEERING	OUTPROMISING	OUTRUNNERS
OUTMANIPULATE	OUTPEOPLED	OUTPULLING	OUTRUNNING
OUTMANIPULATED	OUTPEOPLES	OUTPUNCHED	OUTRUSHING
OUTMANIPULATES	OUTPEOPLING	OUTPUNCHES	OUTSAILING
OUTMANIPULATING	OUTPERFORM	OUTPUNCHING	OUTSAVORED
OUTMANNING	OUTPERFORMED	OUTPURSUED	OUTSAVORING
OUTMANOEUVRE	OUTPERFORMING	OUTPURSUES	OUTSCHEMED
OUTMANOEUVRED	OUTPERFORMS	OUTPURSUING	OUTSCHEMES
OUTMANOEUVRES	OUTPITCHED	OUTPUSHING	OUTSCHEMING
OUTMANOEUVRING	OUTPITCHES	OUTPUTTING	OUTSCOLDED
OUTMANTLED	OUTPITCHING	OUTQUARTERS	OUTSCOLDING
OUTMANTLES	OUTPITYING	OUTQUOTING	OUTSCOOPED
OUTMANTLING	OUTPLACEMENT	OUTRAGEOUS	OUTSCOOPING
OUTMARCHED	OUTPLACEMENTS	OUTRAGEOUSLY	OUTSCORING
OUTMARCHES	OUTPLACERS	OUTRAGEOUSNESS	OUTSCORNED
OUTMARCHING	OUTPLACING	OUTRAISING	OUTSCORNING
OUTMARRIAGE	OUTPLANNED	OUTRANGING	OUTSCREAMED
OUTMARRIAGES	OUTPLANNING	OUTRANKING	OUTSCREAMING
OUTMASTERED	OUTPLAYING	OUTREACHED	OUTSCREAMS
OUTMASTERING	OUTPLODDED	OUTREACHES	OUTSELLING
OUTMASTERS	OUTPLODDING	OUTREACHING	OUTSERVING
OUTMATCHED	OUTPLOTTED	OUTREADING	OUTSETTING
OUTMATCHES	OUTPLOTTING	OUTREASONED	OUTSETTINGS
OUTMATCHING	OUTPOINTED	OUTREASONING	OUTSETTLEMENT
OUTMEASURE	OUTPOINTING	OUTREASONS	OUTSETTLEMENTS
OUTMEASURED	OUTPOLITICK	OUTREBOUND	OUTSHAMING
OUTMEASURES	OUTPOLITICKED	OUTREBOUNDED	OUTSHINING
OUTMEASURING	OUTPOLITICKING	OUTREBOUNDING	OUTSHOOTING
OUTMODEDLY	OUTPOLITICKS	OUTREBOUNDS	OUTSHOUTED
OUTMODEDNESS	OUTPOLLING	OUTRECKONED	OUTSHOUTING
OUTMODEDNESSES	OUTPOPULATE	OUTRECKONING	OUTSIDERNESS
OUTMUSCLED	OUTPOPULATED	OUTRECKONS	OUTSIDERNESSES
OUTMUSCLES	OUTPOPULATES	OUTRECUIDANCE	OUTSINGING
OUTMUSCLING	OUTPOPULATING	OUTRECUIDANCES	OUTSINNING
OUTNIGHTED	OUTPORTERS	OUTREDDENED	OUTSITTING
OUTNIGHTING	OUTPOURERS	OUTREDDENING	OUTSKATING
OUTNUMBERED	OUTPOURING	OUTREDDENS	OUTSLEEPING
OUTNUMBERING	OUTPOURINGS	OUTREDDING	OUTSLICKED
OUTNUMBERS	OUTPOWERED	OUTREIGNED	OUTSLICKING
OUTOFFICES	OUTPOWERING	OUTREIGNING	OUTSMARTED
OUTORGANISE	OUTPRAYING	OUTRELIEFS	OUTSMARTING
OUTORGANISED	OUTPREACHED	OUTREPRODUCE	OUTSMELLED
OUTORGANISES	OUTPREACHES	OUTREPRODUCED	OUTSMELLING
OUTORGANISING	OUTPREACHING	OUTREPRODUCES	OUTSMILING
OUTORGANIZE	OUTPREENED	OUTREPRODUCING	OUTSMOKING
OUTORGANIZED	OUTPREENING	OUTRIGGERS	OUTSNORING
OUTORGANIZES	OUTPRESSED	OUTRIGGING	OUTSOARING
OUTORGANIZING	OUTPRESSES	OUTRIGHTLY	OUTSOURCED

OUTSOURCES	OUTSTRIVING	OUTVAUNTING	OVARIECTOMIZED
OUTSOURCING	OUTSTROKES	OUTVENOMED	OVARIECTOMY
OUTSOURCINGS	OUTSTUDIED	OUTVENOMING	OVARIOTOMIES
OUTSPANNED	OUTSTUDIES	OUTVILLAIN	OVARIOTOMIST
OUTSPANNING	OUTSTUDYING	OUTVILLAINED	OVARIOTOMISTS
OUTSPARKLE	OUTSTUNTED	OUTVILLAINING	OVARIOTOMY
OUTSPARKLED	OUTSTUNTING	OUTVILLAINS	OVARITIDES
OUTSPARKLES	OUTSULKING	OUTVOICING	OVARITISES
OUTSPARKLING	OUTSUMMING	OUTWAITING	OVERABOUND
OUTSPEAKING	OUTSWEARING	OUTWALKING	OVERABOUNDED
OUTSPECKLE	OUTSWEEPING	OUTWARDNESS	OVERABOUNDING
OUTSPECKLES	OUTSWEETEN	OUTWARDNESSES	OVERABOUNDS
OUTSPEEDED	OUTSWEETENED	OUTWARRING	OVERABSTRACT
OUTSPEEDING	OUTSWEETENING	OUTWASTING	OVERABUNDANCE
OUTSPELLED	OUTSWEETENS	OUTWATCHED	OVERABUNDANCES
OUTSPELLING	OUTSWELLED	OUTWATCHES	OVERABUNDANT
OUTSPENDING	OUTSWELLING	OUTWATCHING	OVERACCENTUATE
OUTSPOKENLY	OUTSWIMMING	OUTWEARIED	OVERACCENTUATED
OUTSPOKENNESS	OUTSWINGER	OUTWEARIES	OVERACCENTUATES
OUTSPOKENNESSES	OUTSWINGERS	OUTWEARING	OVERACHIEVE
OUTSPORTED	OUTSWINGING	OUTWEARYING	OVERACHIEVED
OUTSPORTING	OUTSWOLLEN	OUTWEEDING	OVERACHIEVEMENT
OUTSPREADING	OUTTALKING	OUTWEEPING	OVERACHIEVER
OUTSPREADS	OUTTASKING	OUTWEIGHED	OVERACHIEVERS
OUTSPRINGING	OUTTELLING	OUTWEIGHING	OVERACHIEVES
OUTSPRINGS	OUTTHANKED	OUTWELLING	OVERACHIEVING
OUTSPRINTED	OUTTHANKING	OUTWHIRLED	OVERACTING
OUTSPRINTING	OUTTHIEVED	OUTWHIRLING	OVERACTION
OUTSPRINTS	OUTTHIEVES	OUTWICKING	OVERACTIONS
OUTSTANDING	OUTTHIEVING	OUTWILLING	OVERACTIVE
OUTSTANDINGLY	OUTTHINKING	OUTWINDING	OVERACTIVITIES
OUTSTARING	OUTTHOUGHT	OUTWINGING	OVERACTIVITY
OUTSTARTED	OUTTHROBBED	OUTWINNING	OVERADJUSTMENT
OUTSTARTING	OUTTHROBBING	OUTWISHING	OVERADJUSTMENTS
OUTSTATING	OUTTHROWING	OUTWITTING	OVERADVERTISE
OUTSTATION	OUTTHRUSTED	OUTWORKERS	OVERADVERTISED
OUTSTATIONS	OUTTHRUSTING	OUTWORKING	OVERADVERTISES
OUTSTAYING	OUTTHRUSTS	OUTWORTHED	OVERADVERTISING
OUTSTEERED	OUTTONGUED	OUTWORTHING	OVERAGGRESSIVE
OUTSTEERING	OUTTONGUES	OUTWRESTED	OVERAMBITIOUS
OUTSTEPPED	OUTTONGUING	OUTWRESTING	OVERAMPLIFIED
OUTSTEPPING	OUTTOPPING	OUTWRESTLE	OVERANALYSED
OUTSTRAINED	OUTTOWERED	OUTWRESTLED	OVERANALYSES
OUTSTRAINING	OUTTOWERING	OUTWRESTLES	OVERANALYSING
OUTSTRAINS	OUTTRADING	OUTWRESTLING	OVERANALYSIS
OUTSTRETCH	OUTTRAVELED	OUTWRITING	OVERANALYTICAL
OUTSTRETCHED	OUTTRAVELING	OUTWRITTEN	OVERANALYZE
OUTSTRETCHES	OUTTRAVELLED	OUTWROUGHT	OVERANALYZED
OUTSTRETCHING	OUTTRAVELLING	OUTYELLING	OVERANALYZES
OUTSTRIDDEN	OUTTRAVELS	OUTYELPING	OVERANALYZING
OUTSTRIDES	OUTTRICKED	OUTYIELDED	OVERANXIETIES
OUTSTRIDING	OUTTRICKING	OUTYIELDING	OVERANXIETY
OUTSTRIKES	OUTTROTTED	OUVIRANDRA	OVERANXIOUS
OUTSTRIKING	OUTTROTTING	OUVIRANDRAS	OVERAPPLICATION
OUTSTRIPPED	OUTTRUMPED	OVALBUMINS	OVERARCHED
OUTSTRIPPING	OUTTRUMPING	OVALNESSES	OVERARCHES
OUTSTRIVEN	OUTVALUING	OVARIECTOMIES	OVERARCHING
OUTSTRIVES	OUTVAUNTED	OVARIECTOMISED	OVERARMING

OVERAROUSAL	OVERBORROWS	OVERCAPITALISES	OVERCOLORING
OVERAROUSALS	OVERBOUGHT	OVERCAPITALIZE	OVERCOLORS
OVERARRANGE	OVERBOUNDED	OVERCAPITALIZED	OVERCOLOUR
OVERARRANGED	OVERBOUNDING	OVERCAPITALIZES	OVERCOLOURED
OVERARRANGES	OVERBOUNDS	OVERCAREFUL	OVERCOLOURING
OVERARRANGING	OVERBRAKED	OVERCARRIED	OVERCOLOURS
OVERARTICULATE	OVERBRAKES	OVERCARRIES	OVERCOMERS
OVERARTICULATED	OVERBRAKING	OVERCARRYING	OVERCOMING
OVERARTICULATES	OVERBREATHING	OVERCASTED	OVERCOMMIT
OVERASSERT	OVERBREATHINGS	OVERCASTING	OVERCOMMITMENT
OVERASSERTED	OVERBREEDING	OVERCASTINGS	OVERCOMMITMENTS
OVERASSERTING	OVERBREEDS	OVERCATCHES	OVERCOMMITS
OVERASSERTION	OVERBRIDGE	OVERCATCHING	OVERCOMMITTED
OVERASSERTIONS	OVERBRIDGED	OVERCAUGHT	OVERCOMMITTING
OVERASSERTIVE	OVERBRIDGES	OVERCAUTION	OVERCOMMUNICATE
OVERASSERTS	OVERBRIDGING	OVERCAUTIONS	OVERCOMPENSATE
OVERASSESSMENT	OVERBRIEFED	OVERCAUTIOUS	OVERCOMPENSATED
OVERASSESSMENTS	OVERBRIEFING	OVERCENTRALISE	OVERCOMPENSATES
OVERATTENTION	OVERBRIEFS	OVERCENTRALISED	OVERCOMPLEX
OVERATTENTIONS	OVERBRIGHT	OVERCENTRALISES	OVERCOMPLIANCE
OVERATTENTIVE	OVERBRIMMED	OVERCENTRALIZE	OVERCOMPLIANCES
OVERBAKING	OVERBRIMMING	OVERCENTRALIZED	OVERCOMPLICATE
OVERBALANCE	OVERBROWED	OVERCENTRALIZES	OVERCOMPLICATED
OVERBALANCED	OVERBROWING	OVERCHARGE	OVERCOMPLICATES
OVERBALANCES	OVERBROWSE	OVERCHARGED	OVERCOMPRESS
OVERBALANCING	OVERBROWSED	OVERCHARGES	OVERCOMPRESSED
OVERBEARING	OVERBROWSES	OVERCHARGING	OVERCOMPRESSES
OVERBEARINGLY	OVERBROWSING	OVERCHECKS	OVERCOMPRESSING
OVERBEARINGNESS	OVERBRUTAL	OVERCHILLED	OVERCONCERN
OVERBEATEN	OVERBUILDING	OVERCHILLING	OVERCONCERNED
OVERBEATING	OVERBUILDS	OVERCHILLS	OVERCONCERNING
OVERBEJEWELED	OVERBULKED	OVERCIVILISED	OVERCONCERNS
OVERBETTED	OVERBULKING	OVERCIVILIZED	OVERCONFIDENCE
OVERBETTING	OVERBURDEN	OVERCLAIMED	OVERCONFIDENCES
OVERBIDDEN	OVERBURDENED	OVERCLAIMING	OVERCONFIDENT
OVERBIDDER	OVERBURDENING	OVERCLAIMS	OVERCONFIDENTLY
OVERBIDDERS	OVERBURDENS	OVERCLASSES	OVERCONSCIOUS
OVERBIDDING	OVERBURDENSOME	OVERCLASSIFIED	OVERCONSTRUCT
OVERBIDDINGS	OVERBURNED	OVERCLASSIFIES	OVERCONSTRUCTED
OVERBILLED	OVERBURNING	OVERCLASSIFY	OVERCONSTRUCTS
OVERBILLING	OVERBURTHEN	OVERCLASSIFYING	OVERCONSUME
OVERBLANKET	OVERBURTHENED	OVERCLEANED	OVERCONSUMED
OVERBLANKETS	OVERBURTHENING	OVERCLEANING	OVERCONSUMES
OVERBLEACH	OVERBURTHENS	OVERCLEANS	OVERCONSUMING
OVERBLEACHED	OVERBUSIED	OVERCLEARED	OVERCONSUMPTION
OVERBLEACHES	OVERBUSIES	OVERCLEARING	OVERCONTROL
OVERBLEACHING	OVERBUSYING	OVERCLEARS	OVERCONTROLLED
OVERBLOUSE	OVERBUYING	OVERCLOUDED	OVERCONTROLLING
OVERBLOUSES	OVERCALLED	OVERCLOUDING	OVERCONTROLS
OVERBLOWING	OVERCALLING	OVERCLOUDS	OVERCOOKED
OVERBOILED	OVERCANOPIED	OVERCLOYED	OVERCOOKING
OVERBOILING	OVERCANOPIES	OVERCLOYING	OVERCOOLED
OVERBOLDLY	OVERCANOPY	OVERCOACHED	OVERCOOLING
OVERBOOKED	OVERCANOPYING	OVERCOACHES	OVERCORRECT
OVERBOOKING	OVERCAPACITIES	OVERCOACHING	OVERCORRECTED
OVERBORROW	OVERCAPACITY	OVERCOATING	OVERCORRECTING
OVERBORROWED	OVERCAPITALISE	OVERCOATINGS	OVERCORRECTION
OVERBORROWING	OVERCAPITALISED	OVERCOLORED	OVERCORRECTIONS

OVERCORRECTS
OVERCOUNTED
OVERCOUNTING
OVERCOUNTS
OVERCOVERED
OVERCOVERING
OVERCOVERS
OVERCRAMMED
OVERCRAMMING
OVERCRAWED
OVERCRAWING
OVERCREDULITIES
OVERCREDULITY
OVERCREDULOUS
OVERCRITICAL
OVERCROPPED
OVERCROPPING
OVERCROWDED
OVERCROWDING
OVERCROWDINGS
OVERCROWDS
OVERCROWED
OVERCROWING
OVERCULTIVATION
OVERCURING
OVERCUTTING
OVERDARING
OVERDECKED
OVERDECKING
OVERDECORATE
OVERDECORATED
OVERDECORATES
OVERDECORATING
OVERDECORATION
OVERDECORATIONS
OVERDEMANDING
OVERDEPENDENCE
OVERDEPENDENCES
OVERDEPENDENT
OVERDESIGN
OVERDESIGNED
OVERDESIGNING
OVERDESIGNS
OVERDETERMINED
OVERDEVELOP
OVERDEVELOPED
OVERDEVELOPING
OVERDEVELOPMENT
OVERDEVELOPS
OVERDEVIATE
OVERDEVIATED
OVERDEVIATES
OVERDEVIATING
OVERDIRECT
OVERDIRECTED
OVERDIRECTING
OVERDIRECTS
OVERDISCOUNT

OVERDISCOUNTED
OVERDISCOUNTING
OVERDISCOUNTS
OVERDIVERSITIES
OVERDIVERSITY
OVERDOCUMENT
OVERDOCUMENTED
OVERDOCUMENTING
OVERDOCUMENTS
OVERDOMINANCE
OVERDOMINANCES
OVERDOMINANT
OVERDOSAGE
OVERDOSAGES
OVERDOSING
OVERDRAFTS
OVERDRAMATIC
OVERDRAMATISE
OVERDRAMATISED
OVERDRAMATISES
OVERDRAMATISING
OVERDRAMATIZE
OVERDRAMATIZED
OVERDRAMATIZES
OVERDRAMATIZING
OVERDRAUGHT
OVERDRAUGHTS
OVERDRAWING
OVERDRESSED
OVERDRESSES
OVERDRESSING
OVERDRINKING
OVERDRINKS
OVERDRIVEN
OVERDRIVES
OVERDRIVING
OVERDRYING
OVERDUBBED
OVERDUBBING
OVERDUSTED
OVERDUSTING
OVERDYEING
OVEREAGERNESS
OVEREAGERNESSES
OVEREARNEST
OVEREATERS
OVEREATING
OVEREDITED
OVEREDITING
OVEREDUCATE
OVEREDUCATED
OVEREDUCATES
OVEREDUCATING
OVEREDUCATION
OVEREDUCATIONS
OVEREGGING
OVERELABORATE
OVERELABORATED

OVERELABORATES
OVERELABORATING
OVERELABORATION
OVEREMBELLISH
OVEREMBELLISHED
OVEREMBELLISHES
OVEREMOTED
OVEREMOTES
OVEREMOTING
OVEREMOTIONAL
OVEREMPHASES
OVEREMPHASIS
OVEREMPHASISE
OVEREMPHASISED
OVEREMPHASISES
OVEREMPHASISING
OVEREMPHASIZE
OVEREMPHASIZED
OVEREMPHASIZES
OVEREMPHASIZING
OVEREMPHATIC
OVERENAMORED
OVERENCOURAGE
OVERENCOURAGED
OVERENCOURAGES
OVERENCOURAGING
OVERENERGETIC
OVERENGINEER
OVERENGINEERED
OVERENGINEERING
OVERENGINEERS
OVERENROLLED
OVERENTERTAINED
OVERENTHUSIASM
OVERENTHUSIASMS
OVEREQUIPPED
OVERESTIMATE
OVERESTIMATED
OVERESTIMATES
OVERESTIMATING
OVERESTIMATION
OVERESTIMATIONS
OVEREVALUATION
OVEREVALUATIONS
OVEREXAGGERATE
OVEREXAGGERATED
OVEREXAGGERATES
OVEREXCITABLE
OVEREXCITE
OVEREXCITED
OVEREXCITES
OVEREXCITING
OVEREXERCISE
OVEREXERCISED
OVEREXERCISES
OVEREXERCISING
OVEREXERTED
OVEREXERTING

OVEREXERTION
OVEREXERTIONS
OVEREXERTS
OVEREXPAND
OVEREXPANDED
OVEREXPANDING
OVEREXPANDS
OVEREXPANSION
OVEREXPANSIONS
OVEREXPECTATION
OVEREXPLAIN
OVEREXPLAINED
OVEREXPLAINING
OVEREXPLAINS
OVEREXPLICIT
OVEREXPLOIT
OVEREXPLOITED
OVEREXPLOITING
OVEREXPLOITS
OVEREXPOSE
OVEREXPOSED
OVEREXPOSES
OVEREXPOSING
OVEREXPOSURE
OVEREXPOSURES
OVEREXTEND
OVEREXTENDED
OVEREXTENDING
OVEREXTENDS
OVEREXTENSION
OVEREXTENSIONS
OVEREXTRACTION
OVEREXTRACTIONS
OVEREXTRAVAGANT
OVEREXUBERANT
OVEREYEING
OVERFACILE
OVERFALLEN
OVERFALLING
OVERFAMILIAR
OVERFAMILIARITY
OVERFASTIDIOUS
OVERFATIGUE
OVERFATIGUED
OVERFATIGUES
OVERFAVORED
OVERFAVORING
OVERFAVORS
OVERFEARED
OVERFEARING
OVERFEEDING
OVERFERTILISE
OVERFERTILISED
OVERFERTILISES
OVERFERTILISING
OVERFERTILIZE
OVERFERTILIZED
OVERFERTILIZES

OVERFERTILIZING	OVERGARMENT	OVERGRAZED	OVERIDEALISED
OVERFILLED	OVERGARMENTS	OVERGRAZES	OVERIDEALISES
OVERFILLING	OVERGEARED	OVERGRAZING	OVERIDEALISING
OVERFINENESS	OVERGEARING	OVERGRAZINGS	OVERIDEALIZE
OVERFINENESSES	OVERGENERALISE	OVERGREEDY	OVERIDEALIZED
OVERFINISHED	OVERGENERALISED	OVERGREENED	OVERIDEALIZES
OVERFISHED	OVERGENERALISES	OVERGREENING	OVERIDEALIZING
OVERFISHES	OVERGENERALIZE	OVERGREENS	OVERIDENTIFIED
OVERFISHING	OVERGENERALIZED	OVERGROUND	OVERIDENTIFIES
OVERFLIGHT	OVERGENERALIZES	OVERGROWING	OVERIDENTIFY
OVERFLIGHTS	OVERGENEROSITY	OVERGROWTH	OVERIDENTIFYING
OVERFLOODED	OVERGENEROUS	OVERGROWTHS	OVERIMAGINATIVE
OVERFLOODING	OVERGENEROUSLY	OVERHAILED	OVERIMPRESS
OVERFLOODS	OVERGETTING	OVERHAILES	OVERIMPRESSED
OVERFLOURISH	OVERGILDED	OVERHAILING	OVERIMPRESSES
OVERFLOURISHED	OVERGILDING	OVERHALING	OVERIMPRESSING
OVERFLOURISHES	OVERGIRDED	OVERHANDED	OVERINCLINE
OVERFLOURISHING	OVERGIRDING	OVERHANDING	OVERINCLINED
OVERFLOWED	OVERGIVING	OVERHANDLE	OVERINCLINES
OVERFLOWING	OVERGLAMORISE	OVERHANDLED	OVERINCLINING
OVERFLOWINGLY	OVERGLAMORISED	OVERHANDLES	OVERINDULGE
OVERFLOWINGS	OVERGLAMORISES	OVERHANDLING	OVERINDULGED
OVERFLUSHES	OVERGLAMORISING	OVERHANGING	OVERINDULGENCE
OVERFLYING	OVERGLAMORIZE	OVERHARVEST	OVERINDULGENCES
OVERFOCUSED	OVERGLAMORIZED	OVERHARVESTED	OVERINDULGENT
OVERFOCUSES	OVERGLAMORIZES	OVERHARVESTING	OVERINDULGES
OVERFOCUSING	OVERGLAMORIZING	OVERHARVESTS	OVERINDULGING
OVERFOCUSSED	OVERGLANCE	OVERHASTES	OVERINFLATE
OVERFOCUSSES	OVERGLANCED	OVERHASTILY	OVERINFLATED
OVERFOCUSSING	OVERGLANCES	OVERHASTINESS	OVERINFLATES
OVERFOLDED	OVERGLANCING	OVERHASTINESSES	OVERINFLATING
OVERFOLDING	OVERGLAZED	OVERHATING	OVERINFLATION
OVERFONDLY	OVERGLAZES	OVERHAULED	OVERINFLATIONS
OVERFONDNESS	OVERGLAZING	OVERHAULING	OVERINFORM
OVERFONDNESSES	OVERGLOOMED	OVERHEAPED	OVERINFORMED
OVERFORWARD	OVERGLOOMING	OVERHEAPING	OVERINFORMING
OVERFORWARDNESS	OVERGLOOMS	OVERHEARING	OVERINFORMS
OVERFRAUGHT	OVERGOADED	OVERHEATED	OVERINGENIOUS
OVERFREEDOM	OVERGOADING	OVERHEATING	OVERINGENUITIES
OVERFREEDOMS	OVERGOINGS	OVERHEATINGS	OVERINGENUITY
OVERFREELY	OVERGORGED	OVERHENTING	OVERINSISTENT
OVERFREIGHT	OVERGORGES	OVERHITTING	OVERINSURANCE
OVERFREIGHTING	OVERGORGING	OVERHOLDING	OVERINSURANCES
OVERFREIGHTS	OVERGOVERN	OVERHOMOGENISE	OVERINSURE
OVERFULFILL	OVERGOVERNED	OVERHOMOGENISED	OVERINSURED
OVERFULFILLED	OVERGOVERNING	OVERHOMOGENISES	OVERINSURES
OVERFULFILLING	OVERGOVERNS	OVERHOMOGENIZE	OVERINSURING
OVERFULFILLS	OVERGRADED	OVERHOMOGENIZED	OVERINTENSE
OVERFULLNESS	OVERGRADES	OVERHOMOGENIZES	OVERINTENSITIES
OVERFULLNESSES	OVERGRADING	OVERHONORED	OVERINTENSITY
OVERFULNESS	OVERGRAINED	OVERHONORING	OVERINVESTMENT
OVERFULNESSES	OVERGRAINER	OVERHONORS	OVERINVESTMENTS
OVERFUNDED	OVERGRAINERS	OVERHOPING	OVERISSUANCE
OVERFUNDING	OVERGRAINING	OVERHUNTED	OVERISSUANCES
OVERFUNDINGS	OVERGRAINS	OVERHUNTING	OVERISSUED
OVERGALLED	OVERGRASSED	OVERHUNTINGS	OVERISSUES
OVERGALLING	OVERGRASSES	OVERHYPING	OVERISSUING
OVERGANGING	OVERGRASSING	OVERIDEALISE	OVERJOYING

OVERJUMPED
OVERJUMPING
OVERKEEPING
OVERKILLED
OVERKILLING
OVERKINDNESS
OVERKINDNESSES
OVERLABORED
OVERLABORING
OVERLABORS
OVERLABOUR
OVERLABOURED
OVERLABOURING
OVERLABOURS
OVERLADING
OVERLANDED
OVERLANDER
OVERLANDERS
OVERLANDING
OVERLAPPED
OVERLAPPING
OVERLARDED
OVERLARDING
OVERLAUNCH
OVERLAUNCHED
OVERLAUNCHES
OVERLAUNCHING
OVERLAVISH
OVERLAYING
OVERLAYINGS
OVERLEAPED
OVERLEAPING
OVERLEARNED
OVERLEARNING
OVERLEARNS
OVERLEARNT
OVERLEATHER
OVERLEATHERS
OVERLEAVEN
OVERLEAVENED
OVERLEAVENING
OVERLEAVENS
OVERLENDING
OVERLENGTH
OVERLENGTHEN
OVERLENGTHENED
OVERLENGTHENING
OVERLENGTHENS
OVERLENGTHS
OVERLETTING
OVERLIGHTED
OVERLIGHTING
OVERLIGHTS
OVERLITERAL
OVERLITERARY
OVERLIVING
OVERLOADED
OVERLOADING

OVERLOCKED
OVERLOCKER
OVERLOCKERS
OVERLOCKING
OVERLOCKINGS
OVERLOOKED
OVERLOOKER
OVERLOOKERS
OVERLOOKING
OVERLORDED
OVERLORDING
OVERLORDSHIP
OVERLORDSHIPS
OVERLOVING
OVERMANAGE
OVERMANAGED
OVERMANAGES
OVERMANAGING
OVERMANNED
OVERMANNERED
OVERMANNING
OVERMANTEL
OVERMANTELS
OVERMASTED
OVERMASTER
OVERMASTERED
OVERMASTERING
OVERMASTERS
OVERMASTING
OVERMATCHED
OVERMATCHES
OVERMATCHING
OVERMATTER
OVERMATTERS
OVERMATURE
OVERMATURITIES
OVERMATURITY
OVERMEASURE
OVERMEASURED
OVERMEASURES
OVERMEASURING
OVERMEDICATE
OVERMEDICATED
OVERMEDICATES
OVERMEDICATING
OVERMEDICATION
OVERMEDICATIONS
OVERMELTED
OVERMELTING
OVERMIGHTY
OVERMILKED
OVERMILKING
OVERMINING
OVERMIXING
OVERMODEST
OVERMODESTLY
OVERMOUNTED
OVERMOUNTING

OVERMOUNTS
OVERMUCHES
OVERMULTIPLIED
OVERMULTIPLIES
OVERMULTIPLY
OVERMULTIPLYING
OVERMULTITUDE
OVERMULTITUDED
OVERMULTITUDES
OVERMULTITUDING
OVERMUSCLED
OVERNAMING
OVERNETTED
OVERNETTING
OVERNICELY
OVERNICENESS
OVERNICENESSES
OVERNIGHTED
OVERNIGHTER
OVERNIGHTERS
OVERNIGHTING
OVERNIGHTS
OVERNOURISH
OVERNOURISHED
OVERNOURISHES
OVERNOURISHING
OVERNUTRITION
OVERNUTRITIONS
OVEROBVIOUS
OVEROFFICE
OVEROFFICED
OVEROFFICES
OVEROFFICING
OVEROPERATE
OVEROPERATED
OVEROPERATES
OVEROPERATING
OVEROPINIONATED
OVEROPTIMISM
OVEROPTIMISMS
OVEROPTIMIST
OVEROPTIMISTIC
OVEROPTIMISTS
OVERORCHESTRATE
OVERORGANISE
OVERORGANISED
OVERORGANISES
OVERORGANISING
OVERORGANIZE
OVERORGANIZED
OVERORGANIZES
OVERORGANIZING
OVERORNAMENT
OVERORNAMENTED
OVERORNAMENTING
OVERORNAMENTS
OVERPACKAGE
OVERPACKAGED

OVERPACKAGES
OVERPACKAGING
OVERPACKED
OVERPACKING
OVERPAINTED
OVERPAINTING
OVERPAINTS
OVERPARTED
OVERPARTICULAR
OVERPARTING
OVERPASSED
OVERPASSES
OVERPASSING
OVERPAYING
OVERPAYMENT
OVERPAYMENTS
OVERPEDALED
OVERPEDALING
OVERPEDALLED
OVERPEDALLING
OVERPEDALS
OVERPEERED
OVERPEERING
OVERPEOPLE
OVERPEOPLED
OVERPEOPLES
OVERPEOPLING
OVERPERCHED
OVERPERCHES
OVERPERCHING
OVERPERSUADE
OVERPERSUADED
OVERPERSUADES
OVERPERSUADING
OVERPERSUASION
OVERPERSUASIONS
OVERPICTURE
OVERPICTURED
OVERPICTURES
OVERPICTURING
OVERPITCHED
OVERPITCHES
OVERPITCHING
OVERPLACED
OVERPLAIDED
OVERPLAIDS
OVERPLANNED
OVERPLANNING
OVERPLANTED
OVERPLANTING
OVERPLANTS
OVERPLAYED
OVERPLAYING
OVERPLOTTED
OVERPLOTTING
OVERPLUSES
OVERPLUSSES
OVERPLYING

OVERPOISED	OVERPROGRAMMED	OVERREGULATION	OVERSEEDING
OVERPOISES	OVERPROGRAMMING	OVERREGULATIONS	OVERSEEING
OVERPOISING	OVERPROGRAMS	OVERRELIANCE	OVERSELLING
OVERPOPULATE	OVERPROMISE	OVERRELIANCES	OVERSENSITIVE
OVERPOPULATED	OVERPROMISED	OVERRENNING	OVERSENSITIVITY
OVERPOPULATES	OVERPROMISES	OVERREPORT	OVERSERIOUS
OVERPOPULATING	OVERPROMISING	OVERREPORTED	OVERSERIOUSLY
OVERPOPULATION	OVERPROMOTE	OVERREPORTING	OVERSERVICE
OVERPOPULATIONS	OVERPROMOTED	OVERREPORTS	OVERSERVICED
OVERPOSTED	OVERPROMOTES	OVERREPRESENTED	OVERSERVICES
OVERPOSTING	OVERPROMOTING	OVERRESPOND	OVERSERVICING
OVERPOTENT	OVERPROPORTION	OVERRESPONDED	OVERSETTING
OVERPOWERED	OVERPROPORTIONS	OVERRESPONDING	OVERSEWING
OVERPOWERING	OVERPROTECT	OVERRESPONDS	OVERSHADED
OVERPOWERINGLY	OVERPROTECTED	OVERRIDDEN	OVERSHADES
OVERPOWERS	OVERPROTECTING	OVERRIDERS	OVERSHADING
OVERPRAISE	OVERPROTECTION	OVERRIDING	OVERSHADOW
OVERPRAISED	OVERPROTECTIONS	OVERRIPENED	OVERSHADOWED
OVERPRAISES	OVERPROTECTIVE	OVERRIPENESS	OVERSHADOWING
OVERPRAISING	OVERPROTECTS	OVERRIPENESSES	OVERSHADOWS
OVERPRECISE	OVERPUMPED	OVERRIPENING	OVERSHINES
OVERPREPARATION	OVERPUMPING	OVERRIPENS	OVERSHINING
OVERPREPARE	OVERQUALIFIED	OVERROASTED	OVERSHIRTS
OVERPREPARED	OVERRACKED	OVERROASTING	OVERSHOOTING
OVERPREPARES	OVERRACKING	OVERROASTS	OVERSHOOTS
OVERPREPARING	OVERRAKING	OVERRUFFED	OVERSHOWER
OVERPRESCRIBE	OVERRASHLY	OVERRUFFING	OVERSHOWERED
OVERPRESCRIBED	OVERRASHNESS	OVERRULERS	OVERSHOWERING
OVERPRESCRIBES	OVERRASHNESSES	OVERRULING	OVERSHOWERS
OVERPRESCRIBING	OVERRATING	OVERRULINGS	OVERSIGHTS
OVERPRESSED	OVERRAUGHT	OVERRUNNER	OVERSIMPLE
OVERPRESSES	OVERREACHED	OVERRUNNERS	OVERSIMPLIFIED
OVERPRESSING	OVERREACHER	OVERRUNNING	OVERSIMPLIFIES
OVERPRESSURE	OVERREACHERS	OVERSAILED	OVERSIMPLIFY
OVERPRESSURES	OVERREACHES	OVERSAILING	OVERSIMPLIFYING
OVERPRICED	OVERREACHING	OVERSALTED	OVERSIMPLISTIC
OVERPRICES	OVERREACTED	OVERSALTING	OVERSIMPLY
OVERPRICING	OVERREACTING	OVERSANGUINE	OVERSIZING
OVERPRINTED	OVERREACTION	OVERSATURATE	OVERSKIPPED
OVERPRINTING	OVERREACTIONS	OVERSATURATED	OVERSKIPPING
OVERPRINTS	OVERREACTS	OVERSATURATES	OVERSKIRTS
OVERPRIVILEGED	OVERREADING	OVERSATURATING	OVERSLAUGH
OVERPRIZED	OVERRECKON	OVERSATURATION	OVERSLAUGHED
OVERPRIZES	OVERRECKONED	OVERSATURATIONS	OVERSLAUGHING
OVERPRIZING	OVERRECKONING	OVERSAUCED	OVERSLAUGHS
OVERPROCESS	OVERRECKONS	OVERSAUCES	OVERSLEEPING
OVERPROCESSED	OVERREDDED	OVERSAUCING	OVERSLEEPS
OVERPROCESSES	OVERREDDING	OVERSAVING	OVERSLEEVE
OVERPROCESSING	OVERREFINE	OVERSCALED	OVERSLEEVES
OVERPRODUCE	OVERREFINED	OVERSCHUTCHT	OVERSLIPPED
OVERPRODUCED	OVERREFINEMENT	OVERSCORED	OVERSLIPPING
OVERPRODUCES	OVERREFINEMENTS	OVERSCORES	OVERSMOKED
OVERPRODUCING	OVERREFINES	OVERSCORING	OVERSMOKES
OVERPRODUCTION	OVERREFINING	OVERSCRUPULOUS	OVERSMOKING
OVERPRODUCTIONS	OVERREGULATE	OVERSCUTCHED	OVERSOAKED
OVERPROGRAM	OVERREGULATED	OVERSECRETION	OVERSOAKING
OVERPROGRAMED	OVERREGULATES	OVERSECRETIONS	OVERSOLICITOUS
OVERPROGRAMING	OVERREGULATING	OVERSEEDED	OVERSOWING

OVERSPECIALISE	OVERSTIRRED	OVERSWAYED	OVERTOILING
OVERSPECIALISED	OVERSTIRRING	OVERSWAYING	OVERTOPPED
OVERSPECIALISES	OVERSTOCKED	OVERSWEARING	OVERTOPPING
OVERSPECIALIZE	OVERSTOCKING	OVERSWEARS	OVERTOWERED
OVERSPECIALIZED	OVERSTOCKS	OVERSWEETEN	OVERTOWERING
OVERSPECIALIZES	OVERSTORIES	OVERSWEETENED	OVERTOWERS
OVERSPECULATE	OVERSTRAIN	OVERSWEETENING	OVERTRADED
OVERSPECULATED	OVERSTRAINED	OVERSWEETENS	OVERTRADES
OVERSPECULATES	OVERSTRAINING	OVERSWEETNESS	OVERTRADING
OVERSPECULATING	OVERSTRAINS	OVERSWEETNESSES	OVERTRAINED
OVERSPECULATION	OVERSTRESS	OVERSWELLED	OVERTRAINING
OVERSPENDER	OVERSTRESSED	OVERSWELLING	OVERTRAINS
OVERSPENDERS	OVERSTRESSES	OVERSWELLS	OVERTREATED
OVERSPENDING	OVERSTRESSING	OVERSWIMMING	OVERTREATING
OVERSPENDS	OVERSTRETCH	OVERSWINGING	OVERTREATMENT
OVERSPICED	OVERSTRETCHED	OVERSWINGS	OVERTREATMENTS
OVERSPICES	OVERSTRETCHES	OVERSWOLLEN	OVERTREATS
OVERSPICING	OVERSTRETCHING	OVERTAKING	OVERTRICKS
OVERSPILLED	OVERSTREWED	OVERTALKATIVE	OVERTRIMMED
OVERSPILLING	OVERSTREWING	OVERTALKED	OVERTRIMMING
OVERSPILLS	OVERSTREWN	OVERTALKING	OVERTRIPPED
OVERSPREAD	OVERSTREWS	OVERTASKED	OVERTRIPPING
OVERSPREADING	OVERSTRIDDEN	OVERTASKING	OVERTRUMPED
OVERSPREADS	OVERSTRIDE	OVERTAUGHT	OVERTRUMPING
OVERSTABILITIES	OVERSTRIDES	OVERTAXATION	OVERTRUMPS
OVERSTABILITY	OVERSTRIDING	OVERTAXATIONS	OVERTRUSTED
OVERSTAFFED	OVERSTRIKE	OVERTAXING	OVERTRUSTING
OVERSTAFFING	OVERSTRIKES	OVERTEACHES	OVERTRUSTS
OVERSTAFFS	OVERSTRIKING	OVERTEACHING	OVERTURING
OVERSTAINED	OVERSTRODE	OVERTEDIOUS	OVERTURNED
OVERSTAINING	OVERSTRONG	OVERTEEMED	OVERTURNER
OVERSTAINS	OVERSTROOKE	OVERTEEMING	OVERTURNERS
OVERSTANDING	OVERSTRUCK	OVERTHINKING	OVERTURNING
OVERSTANDS	OVERSTRUCTURED	OVERTHINKS	OVERTYPING
OVERSTARED	OVERSTRUNG	OVERTHOUGHT	OVERURGING
OVERSTARES	OVERSTUDIED	OVERTHROWER	OVERUTILISATION
OVERSTARING	OVERSTUDIES	OVERTHROWERS	OVERUTILISE
OVERSTATED	OVERSTUDYING	OVERTHROWING	OVERUTILISED
OVERSTATEMENT	OVERSTUFFED	OVERTHROWN	OVERUTILISES
OVERSTATEMENTS	OVERSTUFFING	OVERTHROWS	OVERUTILISING
OVERSTATES	OVERSTUFFS	OVERTHRUST	OVERUTILIZATION
OVERSTATING	OVERSUBSCRIBE	OVERTHRUSTS	OVERUTILIZE
OVERSTAYED	OVERSUBSCRIBED	OVERTHWART	OVERUTILIZED
OVERSTAYER	OVERSUBSCRIBES	OVERTHWARTED	OVERUTILIZES
OVERSTAYERS	OVERSUBSCRIBING	OVERTHWARTING	OVERUTILIZING
OVERSTAYING	OVERSUBTLE	OVERTHWARTS	OVERVALUATION
OVERSTEERED	OVERSUBTLETIES	OVERTIGHTEN	OVERVALUATIONS
OVERSTEERING	OVERSUBTLETY	OVERTIGHTENED	OVERVALUED
OVERSTEERS	OVERSUDSED	OVERTIGHTENING	OVERVALUES
OVERSTEPPED	OVERSUDSES	OVERTIGHTENS	OVERVALUING
OVERSTEPPING	OVERSUDSING	OVERTIMELY	OVERVEILED
OVERSTIMULATE	OVERSUPPED	OVERTIMERS	OVERVEILING
OVERSTIMULATED	OVERSUPPING	OVERTIMING	OVERVIOLENT
OVERSTIMULATES	OVERSUPPLIED	OVERTIPPED	OVERVOLTAGE
OVERSTIMULATING	OVERSUPPLIES	OVERTIPPING	OVERVOLTAGES
OVERSTIMULATION	OVERSUPPLY	OVERTIRING	OVERVOTING
OVERSTINKING	OVERSUPPLYING	OVERTNESSES	OVERWARMED
OVERSTINKS	OVERSUSPICIOUS	OVERTOILED	OVERWARMING

OVERWASHES	OVERWROUGHT	OXYGENATION
OVERWATCHED	OVERYEARED	OXYGENATIONS
OVERWATCHES	OVERYEARING	OXYGENATOR
OVERWATCHING	OVERZEALOUS	OXYGENATORS
OVERWATERED	OVERZEALOUSNESS	OXYGENISED
OVERWATERING	OVIPARITIES	OXYGENISER
OVERWATERS	OVIPAROUSLY	OXYGENISERS
OVERWEARIED	OVIPOSITED	OXYGENISES
OVERWEARIES	OVIPOSITING	OXYGENISING
OVERWEARING	OVIPOSITION	OXYGENIZED
OVERWEARYING	OVIPOSITIONAL	OXYGENIZER
OVERWEATHER	OVIPOSITIONS	OXYGENIZERS
OVERWEATHERED	OVIPOSITOR	OXYGENIZES
OVERWEATHERING	OVIPOSITORS	OXYGENIZING
OVERWEATHERS	OVIRAPTORS	OXYGENLESS
OVERWEENED	OVOVIVIPARITIES	OXYHAEMOGLOBIN
OVERWEENING	OVOVIVIPARITY	OXYHAEMOGLOBINS
OVERWEENINGLY	OVOVIVIPAROUS	OXYHEMOGLOBIN
OVERWEENINGNESS	OVOVIVIPAROUSLY	OXYHEMOGLOBINS
OVERWEENINGS	OVULATIONS	OXYHYDROGEN
OVERWEIGHED	OVULIFEROUS	OXYMORONIC
OVERWEIGHING	OWERLOUPEN	OXYMORONICALLY
OVERWEIGHS	OWERLOUPING	OXYPHENBUTAZONE
OVERWEIGHT	OWERLOUPIT	OXYRHYNCHUS
OVERWEIGHTED	OWLISHNESS	OXYRHYNCHUSES
OVERWEIGHTING	OWLISHNESSES	OXYSULPHIDE
OVERWEIGHTS	OWNERSHIPS	OXYSULPHIDES
OVERWETTED	OXACILLINS	OXYTETRACYCLINE
OVERWETTING	OXALACETATE	OXYURIASES
OVERWHELMED	OXALACETATES	OXYURIASIS
OVERWHELMING	OXALOACETATE	OYSTERCATCHER
OVERWHELMINGLY	OXALOACETATES	OYSTERCATCHERS
OVERWHELMINGS	OXIDATIONAL	OYSTERINGS
OVERWHELMS	OXIDATIONS	OZOCERITES
OVERWINDING	OXIDATIVELY	OZOKERITES
OVERWINGED	OXIDIMETRIC	OZONATIONS
OVERWINGING	OXIDIMETRIES	OZONIFEROUS
OVERWINTER	OXIDIMETRY	OZONISATION
OVERWINTERED	OXIDISABLE	OZONISATIONS
OVERWINTERING	OXIDISATION	OZONIZATION
OVERWINTERS	OXIDISATIONS	OZONIZATIONS
OVERWISELY	OXIDIZABLE	OZONOLYSES
OVERWITHHELD	OXIDIZATION	OZONOLYSIS
OVERWITHHOLD	OXIDIZATIONS	OZONOSPHERE
OVERWITHHOLDING	OXIDOREDUCTASE	OZONOSPHERES
OVERWITHHOLDS	OXIDOREDUCTASES	
OVERWORKED	OXIMETRIES	
OVERWORKING	OXYACETYLENE	
OVERWRESTED	OXYACETYLENES	
OVERWRESTING	OXYCEPHALIC	
OVERWRESTLE	OXYCEPHALIES	
OVERWRESTLED	OXYCEPHALOUS	
OVERWRESTLES	OXYCEPHALY	
OVERWRESTLING	OXYCODONES	
OVERWRESTS	OXYGENASES	
OVERWRITES	OXYGENATED	
OVERWRITING	OXYGENATES	
OVERWRITTEN	OXYGENATING	

P

PACEMAKERS
PACEMAKING
PACEMAKINGS
PACESETTER
PACESETTERS
PACESETTING
PACESETTINGS
PACHYCARPOUS
PACHYDACTYL
PACHYDACTYLOUS
PACHYDACTYLS
PACHYDERMAL
PACHYDERMATOUS
PACHYDERMIA
PACHYDERMIAS
PACHYDERMIC
PACHYDERMOUS
PACHYDERMS
PACHYMENINGITIS
PACHYMETER
PACHYMETERS
PACHYSANDRA
PACHYSANDRAS
PACHYTENES
PACIFIABLE
PACIFICALLY
PACIFICATE
PACIFICATED
PACIFICATES
PACIFICATING
PACIFICATION
PACIFICATIONS
PACIFICATOR
PACIFICATORS
PACIFICATORY
PACIFICISM
PACIFICISMS
PACIFICIST
PACIFICISTS
PACIFISTIC
PACIFISTICALLY
PACKABILITIES
PACKABILITY
PACKAGINGS
PACKBOARDS
PACKFRAMES
PACKHORSES
PACKINGHOUSE
PACKINGHOUSES
PACKNESSES
PACKSADDLE
PACKSADDLES
PACKSHEETS

PACKSTAFFS
PACKTHREAD
PACKTHREADS
PACLITAXEL
PACLITAXELS
PACTIONING
PADDLEBALL
PADDLEBALLS
PADDLEBOARD
PADDLEBOARDS
PADDLEBOAT
PADDLEBOATS
PADDLEFISH
PADDLEFISHES
PADDOCKING
PADDYMELON
PADDYMELONS
PADDYWACKED
PADDYWACKING
PADDYWACKS
PADDYWHACK
PADDYWHACKS
PADEMELONS
PADEREROES
PADLOCKING
PADRONISMS
PADYMELONS
PAEDAGOGIC
PAEDAGOGUE
PAEDAGOGUES
PAEDERASTIC
PAEDERASTIES
PAEDERASTS
PAEDERASTY
PAEDEUTICS
PAEDIATRIC
PAEDIATRICIAN
PAEDIATRICIANS
PAEDIATRICS
PAEDIATRIES
PAEDIATRIST
PAEDIATRISTS
PAEDOBAPTISM
PAEDOBAPTISMS
PAEDOBAPTIST
PAEDOBAPTISTS
PAEDODONTIC
PAEDODONTICS
PAEDODONTIST
PAEDODONTISTS
PAEDOGENESES
PAEDOGENESIS
PAEDOGENETIC

PAEDOGENIC
PAEDOLOGICAL
PAEDOLOGIES
PAEDOLOGIST
PAEDOLOGISTS
PAEDOMORPHIC
PAEDOMORPHISM
PAEDOMORPHISMS
PAEDOMORPHOSES
PAEDOMORPHOSIS
PAEDOPHILE
PAEDOPHILES
PAEDOPHILIA
PAEDOPHILIAC
PAEDOPHILIACS
PAEDOPHILIAS
PAEDOPHILIC
PAEDOPHILICS
PAEDOTRIBE
PAEDOTRIBES
PAEDOTROPHIES
PAEDOTROPHY
PAGANISATION
PAGANISATIONS
PAGANISERS
PAGANISING
PAGANISTIC
PAGANISTICALLY
PAGANIZATION
PAGANIZATIONS
PAGANIZERS
PAGANIZING
PAGEANTRIES
PAGINATING
PAGINATION
PAGINATIONS
PAIDEUTICS
PAILLASSES
PAILLETTES
PAINFULLER
PAINFULLEST
PAINFULNESS
PAINFULNESSES
PAINKILLER
PAINKILLERS
PAINKILLING
PAINLESSLY
PAINLESSNESS
PAINLESSNESSES
PAINSTAKER
PAINSTAKERS
PAINSTAKING
PAINSTAKINGLY

PAINSTAKINGNESS
PAINSTAKINGS
PAINTBALLS
PAINTBOXES
PAINTBRUSH
PAINTBRUSHES
PAINTERLINESS
PAINTERLINESSES
PAINTINESS
PAINTINESSES
PAINTRESSES
PAINTWORKS
PAKIRIKIRI
PAKIRIKIRIS
PALAEANTHROPIC
PALAEBIOLOGIC
PALAEBIOLOGIES
PALAEBIOLOGIST
PALAEBIOLOGISTS
PALAEBIOLOGY
PALAEETHNOLOGY
PALAEOANTHROPIC
PALAEOBIOLOGIC
PALAEOBIOLOGIES
PALAEOBIOLOGIST
PALAEOBIOLOGY
PALAEOBOTANIC
PALAEOBOTANICAL
PALAEOBOTANIES
PALAEOBOTANIST
PALAEOBOTANISTS
PALAEOBOTANY
PALAEOCLIMATE
PALAEOCLIMATES
PALAEOCLIMATIC
PALAEOCRYSTIC
PALAEOCURRENT
PALAEOCURRENTS
PALAEOECOLOGIC
PALAEOECOLOGIES
PALAEOECOLOGIST
PALAEOECOLOGY
PALAEOETHNOLOGY
PALAEOGAEA
PALAEOGAEAS
PALAEOGEOGRAPHY
PALAEOGRAPHER
PALAEOGRAPHERS
PALAEOGRAPHIC
PALAEOGRAPHICAL
PALAEOGRAPHIES
PALAEOGRAPHIST
PALAEOGRAPHISTS

PALAEOGRAPHY	PALEOBIOLOGICAL	PALINDROMIST	PALMATIFID
PALAEOLIMNOLOGY	PALEOBIOLOGIES	PALINDROMISTS	PALMATIONS
PALAEOLITH	PALEOBIOLOGIST	PALINGENESES	PALMATIPARTITE
PALAEOLITHIC	PALEOBIOLOGISTS	PALINGENESIA	PALMATISECT
PALAEOLITHS	PALEOBIOLOGY	PALINGENESIAS	PALMCORDER
PALAEOMAGNETIC	PALEOBOTANIC	PALINGENESIES	PALMCORDERS
PALAEOMAGNETISM	PALEOBOTANICAL	PALINGENESIS	PALMERWORM
PALAEONTOGRAPHY	PALEOBOTANIES	PALINGENESIST	PALMERWORMS
PALAEONTOLOGIES	PALEOBOTANIST	PALINGENESISTS	PALMETTOES
PALAEONTOLOGIST	PALEOBOTANISTS	PALINGENESY	PALMHOUSES
PALAEONTOLOGY	PALEOBOTANY	PALINGENETIC	PALMIFICATION
PALAEOPATHOLOGY	PALEOECOLOGIC	PALINGENETICAL	PALMIFICATIONS
PALAEOPEDOLOGY	PALEOECOLOGICAL	PALINODIES	PALMIPEDES
PALAEOPHYTOLOGY	PALEOECOLOGIES	PALINOPIAS	PALMISTERS
PALAEOTYPE	PALEOECOLOGIST	PALINOPSIA	PALMISTRIES
PALAEOTYPES	PALEOECOLOGISTS	PALINOPSIAS	PALMITATES
PALAEOTYPIC	PALEOECOLOGY	PALISADING	PALOVERDES
PALAEOZOOLOGIES	PALEOGEOGRAPHIC	PALISADOED	PALPABILITIES
PALAEOZOOLOGIST	PALEOGEOGRAPHY	PALISADOES	PALPABILITY
PALAEOZOOLOGY	PALEOGRAPHER	PALISADOING	PALPABLENESS
PALAESTRAE	PALEOGRAPHERS	PALISANDER	PALPABLENESSES
PALAESTRAL	PALEOGRAPHIC	PALISANDERS	PALPATIONS
PALAESTRAS	PALEOGRAPHICAL	PALLADIOUS	PALPEBRATE
PALAESTRIC	PALEOGRAPHIES	PALLADIUMS	PALPEBRATED
PALAESTRICAL	PALEOGRAPHY	PALLBEARER	PALPEBRATES
PALAFITTES	PALEOLITHS	PALLBEARERS	PALPEBRATING
PALAGONITE	PALEOLOGIES	PALLESCENCE	PALPITATED
PALAGONITES	PALEOMAGNETIC	PALLESCENCES	PALPITATES
PALAMPORES	PALEOMAGNETISM	PALLESCENT	PALPITATING
PALANKEENS	PALEOMAGNETISMS	PALLETISATION	PALPITATION
PALANQUINS	PALEOMAGNETIST	PALLETISATIONS	PALPITATIONS
PALATABILITIES	PALEOMAGNETISTS	PALLETISED	PALSGRAVES
PALATABILITY	PALEONTOLOGIC	PALLETISER	PALSGRAVINE
PALATABLENESS	PALEONTOLOGICAL	PALLETISERS	PALSGRAVINES
PALATABLENESSES	PALEONTOLOGIES	PALLETISES	PALTRINESS
PALATALISATION	PALEONTOLOGIST	PALLETISING	PALTRINESSES
PALATALISATIONS	PALEONTOLOGISTS	PALLETIZATION	PALUDAMENT
PALATALISE	PALEONTOLOGY	PALLETIZATIONS	PALUDAMENTA
PALATALISED	PALEOPATHOLOGY	PALLETIZED	PALUDAMENTS
PALATALISES	PALEOZOOLOGICAL	PALLETIZER	PALUDAMENTUM
PALATALISING	PALEOZOOLOGIES	PALLETIZERS	PALUDAMENTUMS
PALATALIZATION	PALEOZOOLOGIST	PALLETIZES	PALUDICOLOUS
PALATALIZATIONS	PALEOZOOLOGISTS	PALLETIZING	PALUDINOUS
PALATALIZE	PALEOZOOLOGY	PALLIAMENT	PALUSTRIAN
PALATALIZED	PALFRENIER	PALLIAMENTS	PALUSTRINE
PALATALIZES	PALFRENIERS	PALLIASSES	PALYNOLOGIC
PALATALIZING	PALFREYING	PALLIATING	PALYNOLOGICAL
PALATIALLY	PALIFICATION	PALLIATION	PALYNOLOGICALLY
PALATIALNESS	PALIFICATIONS	PALLIATIONS	PALYNOLOGIES
PALATIALNESSES	PALILALIAS	PALLIATIVE	PALYNOLOGIST
PALATINATE	PALILLOGIES	PALLIATIVELY	PALYNOLOGISTS
PALATINATES	PALIMONIES	PALLIATIVES	PALYNOLOGY
PALAVERERS	PALIMPSEST	PALLIATORS	PAMPELMOOSE
PALAVERING	PALIMPSESTS	PALLIATORY	PAMPELMOOSES
PALEACEOUS	PALINDROME	PALLIDITIES	PAMPELMOUSE
PALEMPORES	PALINDROMES	PALLIDNESS	PAMPELMOUSES
PALENESSES	PALINDROMIC	PALLIDNESSES	PAMPEREDNESS
PALEOBIOLOGIC	PALINDROMICAL	PALMACEOUS	PAMPEREDNESSES

PAMPHLETEER
PAMPHLETEERED
PAMPHLETEERING
PAMPHLETEERINGS
PAMPHLETEERS
PAMPOOTIES
PANACHAEAS
PANAESTHESIA
PANAESTHESIAS
PANAESTHETISM
PANAESTHETISMS
PANARITIUM
PANARITIUMS
PANARTHRITIS
PANARTHRITISES
PANATELLAS
PANBROILED
PANBROILING
PANCHAYATS
PANCHROMATIC
PANCHROMATISM
PANCHROMATISMS
PANCOSMISM
PANCOSMISMS
PANCRATIAN
PANCRATIAST
PANCRATIASTS
PANCRATIST
PANCRATISTS
PANCRATIUM
PANCRATIUMS
PANCREASES
PANCREATECTOMY
PANCREATIC
PANCREATIN
PANCREATINS
PANCREATITIDES
PANCREATITIS
PANCREATITISES
PANCREOZYMIN
PANCREOZYMINS
PANCYTOPENIA
PANCYTOPENIAS
PANDAEMONIUM
PANDAEMONIUMS
PANDANACEOUS
PANDANUSES
PANDATIONS
PANDECTIST
PANDECTISTS
PANDEMONIAC
PANDEMONIACAL
PANDEMONIAN
PANDEMONIC
PANDEMONIUM
PANDEMONIUMS
PANDERESSES
PANDERISMS

PANDERMITE
PANDERMITES
PANDICULATION
PANDICULATIONS
PANDOWDIES
PANDURATED
PANDURIFORM
PANEGOISMS
PANEGYRICA
PANEGYRICAL
PANEGYRICALLY
PANEGYRICON
PANEGYRICS
PANEGYRIES
PANEGYRISE
PANEGYRISED
PANEGYRISES
PANEGYRISING
PANEGYRIST
PANEGYRISTS
PANEGYRIZE
PANEGYRIZED
PANEGYRIZES
PANEGYRIZING
PANELLINGS
PANELLISTS
PANENTHEISM
PANENTHEISMS
PANENTHEIST
PANENTHEISTS
PANESTHESIA
PANESTHESIAS
PANETELLAS
PANETTONES
PANGENESES
PANGENESIS
PANGENETIC
PANGENETICALLY
PANGRAMMATIST
PANGRAMMATISTS
PANHANDLED
PANHANDLER
PANHANDLERS
PANHANDLES
PANHANDLING
PANHARMONICON
PANHARMONICONS
PANHELLENIC
PANHELLENION
PANHELLENIONS
PANHELLENIUM
PANHELLENIUMS
PANICKIEST
PANICMONGER
PANICMONGERS
PANICULATE
PANICULATED
PANICULATELY

PANIDIOMORPHIC
PANIFICATION
PANIFICATIONS
PANISLAMIC
PANISLAMISM
PANISLAMISMS
PANISLAMIST
PANISLAMISTS
PANJANDARUM
PANJANDARUMS
PANJANDRUM
PANJANDRUMS
PANLEUCOPENIA
PANLEUCOPENIAS
PANLEUKOPENIA
PANLEUKOPENIAS
PANLOGISMS
PANMIXISES
PANNICULUS
PANNICULUSES
PANNIKELLS
PANOMPHAEAN
PANOPHOBIA
PANOPHOBIAS
PANOPHTHALMIA
PANOPHTHALMIAS
PANOPHTHALMITIS
PANOPTICAL
PANOPTICALLY
PANOPTICON
PANOPTICONS
PANORAMICALLY
PANPHARMACON
PANPHARMACONS
PANPSYCHISM
PANPSYCHISMS
PANPSYCHIST
PANPSYCHISTIC
PANPSYCHISTS
PANRADIOMETER
PANRADIOMETERS
PANSEXUALISM
PANSEXUALISMS
PANSEXUALIST
PANSEXUALISTS
PANSEXUALITIES
PANSEXUALITY
PANSEXUALS
PANSOPHICAL
PANSOPHICALLY
PANSOPHIES
PANSOPHISM
PANSOPHISMS
PANSOPHIST
PANSOPHISTS
PANSPERMATIC
PANSPERMATISM
PANSPERMATISMS

PANSPERMATIST
PANSPERMATISTS
PANSPERMIA
PANSPERMIAS
PANSPERMIC
PANSPERMIES
PANSPERMISM
PANSPERMISMS
PANSPERMIST
PANSPERMISTS
PANTAGAMIES
PANTAGRAPH
PANTAGRAPHS
PANTALEONS
PANTALETTED
PANTALETTES
PANTALONES
PANTALOONED
PANTALOONERIES
PANTALOONERY
PANTALOONS
PANTDRESSES
PANTECHNICON
PANTECHNICONS
PANTHEISMS
PANTHEISTIC
PANTHEISTICAL
PANTHEISTICALLY
PANTHEISTS
PANTHENOLS
PANTHEOLOGIES
PANTHEOLOGIST
PANTHEOLOGISTS
PANTHEOLOGY
PANTHERESS
PANTHERESSES
PANTHERINE
PANTHERISH
PANTILINGS
PANTISOCRACIES
PANTISOCRACY
PANTISOCRAT
PANTISOCRATIC
PANTISOCRATICAL
PANTISOCRATIST
PANTISOCRATISTS
PANTISOCRATS
PANTOFFLES
PANTOGRAPH
PANTOGRAPHER
PANTOGRAPHERS
PANTOGRAPHIC
PANTOGRAPHICAL
PANTOGRAPHIES
PANTOGRAPHS
PANTOGRAPHY
PANTOMIMED
PANTOMIMES

PANTOMIMIC	PAPERMAKERS	PARABOLISE	PARADOXIST
PANTOMIMICAL	PAPERMAKING	PARABOLISED	PARADOXISTS
PANTOMIMICALLY	PAPERMAKINGS	PARABOLISES	PARADOXOLOGIES
PANTOMIMING	PAPERWARES	PARABOLISING	PARADOXOLOGY
PANTOMIMIST	PAPERWEIGHT	PARABOLIST	PARADOXURE
PANTOMIMISTS	PAPERWEIGHTS	PARABOLISTS	PARADOXURES
PANTOPHAGIES	PAPERWORKS	PARABOLIZATION	PARADOXURINE
PANTOPHAGIST	PAPETERIES	PARABOLIZATIONS	PARADROPPED
PANTOPHAGISTS	PAPILIONACEOUS	PARABOLIZE	PARADROPPING
PANTOPHAGOUS	PAPILLATED	PARABOLIZED	PARAENESES
PANTOPHAGY	PAPILLIFEROUS	PARABOLIZES	PARAENESIS
PANTOPHOBIA	PAPILLIFORM	PARABOLIZING	PARAENETIC
PANTOPHOBIAS	PAPILLITIS	PARABOLOID	PARAENETICAL
PANTOPRAGMATIC	PAPILLITISES	PARABOLOIDAL	PARAESTHESIA
PANTOPRAGMATICS	PAPILLOMAS	PARABOLOIDS	PARAESTHESIAS
PANTOSCOPE	PAPILLOMATA	PARABRAKES	PARAESTHETIC
PANTOSCOPES	PAPILLOMATOSES	PARACASEIN	PARAFFINED
PANTOSCOPIC	PAPILLOMATOSIS	PARACASEINS	PARAFFINES
PANTOTHENATE	PAPILLOMATOUS	PARACENTESES	PARAFFINIC
PANTOTHENATES	PAPILLOMAVIRUS	PARACENTESIS	PARAFFINING
PANTOTHENIC	PAPILLOTES	PARACETAMOL	PARAFFINOID
PANTOUFLES	PAPILLULATE	PARACETAMOLS	PARAGENESES
PANTROPICAL	PAPILLULES	PARACHRONISM	PARAGENESIA
PANTRYMAID	PAPISTICAL	PARACHRONISMS	PARAGENESIAS
PANTRYMAIDS	PAPISTICALLY	PARACHUTED	PARAGENESIS
PANTSUITED	PAPISTRIES	PARACHUTES	PARAGENETIC
PANTYWAIST	PAPOVAVIRUS	PARACHUTIC	PARAGENETICALLY
PANTYWAISTS	PAPOVAVIRUSES	PARACHUTING	PARAGLIDED
PANZOOTICS	PAPULATION	PARACHUTIST	PARAGLIDER
PAPALISING	PAPULATIONS	PARACHUTISTS	PARAGLIDERS
PAPALIZING	PAPULIFEROUS	PARACLETES	PARAGLIDES
PAPAPRELATIST	PAPYRACEOUS	PARACROSTIC	PARAGLIDING
PAPAPRELATISTS	PAPYROLOGICAL	PARACROSTICS	PARAGLIDINGS
PAPAVERACEOUS	PAPYROLOGIES	PARACYANOGEN	PARAGLOSSA
PAPAVERINE	PAPYROLOGIST	PARACYANOGENS	PARAGLOSSAE
PAPAVERINES	PAPYROLOGISTS	PARADIDDLE	PARAGLOSSAL
PAPAVEROUS	PAPYROLOGY	PARADIDDLES	PARAGLOSSATE
PAPERBACKED	PARABAPTISM	PARADIGMATIC	PARAGNATHISM
PAPERBACKER	PARABAPTISMS	PARADIGMATICAL	PARAGNATHISMS
PAPERBACKERS	PARABEMATA	PARADISAIC	PARAGNATHOUS
PAPERBACKING	PARABEMATIC	PARADISAICAL	PARAGNOSES
PAPERBACKS	PARABIOSES	PARADISAICALLY	PARAGNOSIS
PAPERBARKS	PARABIOSIS	PARADISEAN	PARAGOGICAL
PAPERBOARD	PARABIOTIC	PARADISIAC	PARAGOGICALLY
PAPERBOARDS	PARABIOTICALLY	PARADISIACAL	PARAGOGUES
PAPERBOUND	PARABLASTIC	PARADISIACALLY	PARAGONING
PAPERBOUNDS	PARABLASTS	PARADISIAL	PARAGONITE
PAPERCLIPS	PARABLEPSES	PARADISIAN	PARAGONITES
PAPERGIRLS	PARABLEPSIES	PARADISICAL	PARAGRAMMATIST
PAPERHANGER	PARABLEPSIS	PARADOCTOR	PARAGRAMMATISTS
PAPERHANGERS	PARABLEPSY	PARADOCTORS	PARAGRAPHED
PAPERHANGING	PARABLEPTIC	PARADOXERS	PARAGRAPHER
PAPERHANGINGS	PARABOLANUS	PARADOXICAL	PARAGRAPHERS
PAPERINESS	PARABOLANUSES	PARADOXICALITY	PARAGRAPHIA
PAPERINESSES	PARABOLICAL	PARADOXICALLY	PARAGRAPHIAS
PAPERKNIFE	PARABOLICALLY	PARADOXICALNESS	PARAGRAPHIC
PAPERKNIVES	PARABOLISATION	PARADOXIDIAN	PARAGRAPHICAL
PAPERMAKER	PARABOLISATIONS	PARADOXIES	PARAGRAPHICALLY

PARAGRAPHING	PARALLELLED	PARAMETERISE	PARANTHELION
PARAGRAPHIST	PARALLELLING	PARAMETERISED	PARANTHROPUS
PARAGRAPHISTS	PARALLELLY	PARAMETERISES	PARANTHROPUSES
PARAGRAPHS	PARALLELOGRAM	PARAMETERISING	PARANYMPHS
PARAHELIOTROPIC	PARALLELOGRAMS	PARAMETERIZE	PARAPARESES
PARAHYDROGEN	PARALLELOPIPED	PARAMETERIZED	PARAPARESIS
PARAHYDROGENS	PARALLELOPIPEDA	PARAMETERIZES	PARAPARETIC
PARAINFLUENZA	PARALLELOPIPEDS	PARAMETERIZING	PARAPENTES
PARAINFLUENZAS	PARALLELWISE	PARAMETERS	PARAPENTING
PARAJOURNALISM	PARALOGIAS	PARAMETRAL	PARAPENTINGS
PARAJOURNALISMS	PARALOGIES	PARAMETRIC	PARAPHASIA
PARAKEELYA	PARALOGISE	PARAMETRICAL	PARAPHASIAS
PARAKEELYAS	PARALOGISED	PARAMETRICALLY	PARAPHASIC
PARAKELIAS	PARALOGISES	PARAMETRISATION	PARAPHERNALIA
PARAKITING	PARALOGISING	PARAMETRISE	PARAPHILIA
PARAKITINGS	PARALOGISM	PARAMETRISED	PARAPHILIAC
PARALALIAS	PARALOGISMS	PARAMETRISES	PARAPHILIACS
PARALANGUAGE	PARALOGIST	PARAMETRISING	PARAPHILIAS
PARALANGUAGES	PARALOGISTIC	PARAMETRIZATION	PARAPHIMOSES
PARALDEHYDE	PARALOGISTS	PARAMETRIZE	PARAPHIMOSIS
PARALDEHYDES	PARALOGIZE	PARAMETRIZED	PARAPHONIA
PARALEGALS	PARALOGIZED	PARAMETRIZES	PARAPHONIAS
PARALEIPOMENA	PARALOGIZES	PARAMETRIZING	PARAPHONIC
PARALEIPOMENON	PARALOGIZING	PARAMILITARIES	PARAPHRASABLE
PARALEIPSES	PARALYMPIC	PARAMILITARY	PARAPHRASE
PARALEIPSIS	PARALYMPICS	PARAMNESIA	PARAPHRASED
PARALEXIAS	PARALYSATION	PARAMNESIAS	PARAPHRASER
PARALIMNION	PARALYSATIONS	PARAMOECIA	PARAPHRASERS
PARALIMNIONS	PARALYSERS	PARAMOECIUM	PARAPHRASES
PARALINGUISTIC	PARALYSING	PARAMORPHIC	PARAPHRASING
PARALINGUISTICS	PARALYSINGLY	PARAMORPHINE	PARAPHRAST
PARALIPOMENA	PARALYTICALLY	PARAMORPHINES	PARAPHRASTIC
PARALIPOMENON	PARALYTICS	PARAMORPHISM	PARAPHRASTICAL
PARALIPSES	PARALYZATION	PARAMORPHISMS	PARAPHRASTS
PARALIPSIS	PARALYZATIONS	PARAMORPHOUS	PARAPHRAXES
PARALLACTIC	PARALYZERS	PARAMORPHS	PARAPHRAXIA
PARALLACTICAL	PARALYZING	PARAMOUNCIES	PARAPHRAXIAS
PARALLACTICALLY	PARALYZINGLY	PARAMOUNCY	PARAPHRAXIS
PARALLAXES	PARAMAECIA	PARAMOUNTCIES	PARAPHRENIA
PARALLELED	PARAMAECIUM	PARAMOUNTCY	PARAPHRENIAS
PARALLELEPIPED	PARAMAGNET	PARAMOUNTLY	PARAPHYSATE
PARALLELEPIPEDA	PARAMAGNETIC	PARAMOUNTS	PARAPHYSES
PARALLELEPIPEDS	PARAMAGNETISM	PARAMYLUMS	PARAPHYSIS
PARALLELING	PARAMAGNETISMS	PARAMYXOVIRUS	PARAPINEAL
PARALLELINGS	PARAMAGNETS	PARAMYXOVIRUSES	PARAPLEGIA
PARALLELISE	PARAMASTOID	PARANEPHRIC	PARAPLEGIAS
PARALLELISED	PARAMASTOIDS	PARANEPHROS	PARAPLEGIC
PARALLELISES	PARAMATTAS	PARANEPHROSES	PARAPLEGICS
PARALLELISING	PARAMECIUM	PARANOEICS	PARAPODIAL
PARALLELISM	PARAMECIUMS	PARANOIACS	PARAPODIUM
PARALLELISMS	PARAMEDICAL	PARANOICALLY	PARAPOPHYSES
PARALLELIST	PARAMEDICALS	PARANOIDAL	PARAPOPHYSIAL
PARALLELISTIC	PARAMEDICO	PARANORMAL	PARAPOPHYSIS
PARALLELISTS	PARAMEDICOS	PARANORMALITIES	PARAPRAXES
PARALLELIZE	PARAMEDICS	PARANORMALITY	PARAPRAXIS
PARALLELIZED	PARAMENSTRUA	PARANORMALLY	PARAPSYCHIC
PARALLELIZES	PARAMENSTRUUM	PARANORMALS	PARAPSYCHICAL
PARALLELIZING	PARAMENSTRUUMS	PARANTHELIA	PARAPSYCHISM

PARAPSYCHISMS	PARASITOLOGIST	PARCHEESIS	PARFOCALITY
PARAPSYCHOLOGY	PARASITOLOGISTS	PARCHMENTISE	PARFOCALIZE
PARAPSYCHOSES	PARASITOLOGY	PARCHMENTISED	PARFOCALIZED
PARAPSYCHOSIS	PARASITOSES	PARCHMENTISES	PARFOCALIZES
PARAQUADRATE	PARASITOSIS	PARCHMENTISING	PARFOCALIZING
PARAQUADRATES	PARASKIING	PARCHMENTIZE	PARGASITES
PARAQUITOS	PARASPHENOID	PARCHMENTIZED	PARGETINGS
PARARHYMES	PARASPHENOIDS	PARCHMENTIZES	PARGETTING
PARAROSANILINE	PARASTATAL	PARCHMENTIZING	PARGETTINGS
PARAROSANILINES	PARASTATALS	PARCHMENTS	PARGYLINES
PARARTHRIA	PARASTICHIES	PARCHMENTY	PARHELIACAL
PARARTHRIAS	PARASTICHOUS	PARCIMONIES	PARHYPATES
PARASAILED	PARASTICHY	PARDALISES	PARIPINNATE
PARASAILING	PARASUICIDE	PARDALOTES	PARISCHANE
PARASAILINGS	PARASUICIDES	PARDONABLE	PARISCHANES
PARASCENDER	PARASYMBIONT	PARDONABLENESS	PARISCHANS
PARASCENDERS	PARASYMBIONTS	PARDONABLY	PARISHIONER
PARASCENDING	PARASYMBIOSES	PARDONINGS	PARISHIONERS
PARASCENDINGS	PARASYMBIOSIS	PARDONLESS	PARISYLLABIC
PARASCENIA	PARASYMBIOTIC	PAREGORICS	PARKINSONIAN
PARASCENIUM	PARASYMPATHETIC	PARENCEPHALA	PARKINSONISM
PARASCEVES	PARASYNAPSES	PARENCEPHALON	PARKINSONISMS
PARASCIENCE	PARASYNAPSIS	PARENCHYMA	PARKLEAVES
PARASCIENCES	PARASYNAPTIC	PARENCHYMAL	PARLEMENTS
PARASELENAE	PARASYNTHESES	PARENCHYMAS	PARLEYVOOED
PARASELENE	PARASYNTHESIS	PARENCHYMATA	PARLEYVOOING
PARASELENIC	PARASYNTHETA	PARENCHYMATOUS	PARLEYVOOS
PARASEXUAL	PARASYNTHETIC	PARENTAGES	PARLIAMENT
PARASEXUALITIES	PARASYNTHETON	PARENTALLY	PARLIAMENTARIAN
PARASEXUALITY	PARATACTIC	PARENTERAL	PARLIAMENTARILY
PARASHIOTH	PARATACTICAL	PARENTERALLY	PARLIAMENTARISM
PARASITAEMIA	PARATACTICALLY	PARENTHESES	PARLIAMENTARY
PARASITAEMIAS	PARATANIWHA	PARENTHESIS	PARLIAMENTING
PARASITICAL	PARATHESES	PARENTHESISE	PARLIAMENTINGS
PARASITICALLY	PARATHESIS	PARENTHESISED	PARLIAMENTS
PARASITICALNESS	PARATHIONS	PARENTHESISES	PARLOUSNESS
PARASITICIDAL	PARATHORMONE	PARENTHESISING	PARLOUSNESSES
PARASITICIDE	PARATHORMONES	PARENTHESIZE	PARMACITIE
PARASITICIDES	PARATHYROID	PARENTHESIZED	PARMACITIES
PARASITISATION	PARATHYROIDS	PARENTHESIZES	PARMIGIANA
PARASITISATIONS	PARATROOPER	PARENTHESIZING	PARMIGIANO
PARASITISE	PARATROOPERS	PARENTHETIC	PAROCCIPITAL
PARASITISED	PARATROOPS	PARENTHETICAL	PAROCHIALISE
PARASITISES	PARATYPHOID	PARENTHETICALLY	PAROCHIALISED
PARASITISING	PARATYPHOIDS	PARENTHOOD	PAROCHIALISES
PARASITISM	PARAWALKER	PARENTHOODS	PAROCHIALISING
PARASITISMS	PARAWALKERS	PARENTINGS	PAROCHIALISM
PARASITIZATION	PARBOILING	PARENTLESS	PAROCHIALISMS
PARASITIZATIONS	PARBREAKED	PARESTHESIA	PAROCHIALITIES
PARASITIZE	PARBREAKING	PARESTHESIAS	PAROCHIALITY
PARASITIZED	PARBUCKLED	PARESTHETIC	PAROCHIALIZE
PARASITIZES	PARBUCKLES	PARFLECHES	PAROCHIALIZED
PARASITIZING	PARBUCKLING	PARFLESHES	PAROCHIALIZES
PARASITOID	PARCELLING	PARFOCALISE	PAROCHIALIZING
PARASITOIDS	PARCELWISE	PARFOCALISED	PAROCHIALLY
PARASITOLOGIC	PARCENARIES	PARFOCALISES	PAROCHINES
PARASITOLOGICAL	PARCHEDNESS	PARFOCALISING	PARODISTIC
PARASITOLOGIES	PARCHEDNESSES	PARFOCALITIES	PAROECIOUS

PAROEMIACS	PARTHENOSPORE	PARTICULARIZERS	PASQUINADED
PAROEMIOGRAPHER	PARTHENOSPORES	PARTICULARIZES	PASQUINADER
PAROEMIOGRAPHY	PARTIALISE	PARTICULARIZING	PASQUINADERS
PAROEMIOLOGIES	PARTIALISED	PARTICULARLY	PASQUINADES
PAROEMIOLOGY	PARTIALISES	PARTICULARNESS	PASQUINADING
PARONOMASIA	PARTIALISING	PARTICULARS	PASSABLENESS
PARONOMASIAS	PARTIALISM	PARTICULATE	PASSABLENESSES
PARONOMASIES	PARTIALISMS	PARTICULATES	PASSACAGLIA
PARONOMASTIC	PARTIALIST	PARTISANLY	PASSACAGLIAS
PARONOMASTICAL	PARTIALISTS	PARTISANSHIP	PASSAGEWAY
PARONOMASY	PARTIALITIES	PARTISANSHIPS	PASSAGEWAYS
PARONYCHIA	PARTIALITY	PARTITIONED	PASSAGEWORK
PARONYCHIAL	PARTIALIZE	PARTITIONER	PASSAGEWORKS
PARONYCHIAS	PARTIALIZED	PARTITIONERS	PASSALONGS
PARONYMIES	PARTIALIZES	PARTITIONING	PASSAMENTED
PARONYMOUS	PARTIALIZING	PARTITIONIST	PASSAMENTING
PARONYMOUSLY	PARTIALNESS	PARTITIONISTS	PASSAMENTS
PAROTIDITIC	PARTIALNESSES	PARTITIONMENT	PASSAMEZZO
PAROTIDITIS	PARTIBILITIES	PARTITIONMENTS	PASSAMEZZOS
PAROTIDITISES	PARTIBILITY	PARTITIONS	PASSEMEASURE
PAROTITISES	PARTICIPABLE	PARTITIVELY	PASSEMEASURES
PAROXETINE	PARTICIPANT	PARTITIVES	PASSEMENTED
PAROXETINES	PARTICIPANTLY	PARTITURAS	PASSEMENTERIE
PAROXYSMAL	PARTICIPANTS	PARTIZANSHIP	PASSEMENTERIES
PAROXYSMALLY	PARTICIPATE	PARTIZANSHIPS	PASSEMENTING
PAROXYSMIC	PARTICIPATED	PARTNERING	PASSEMENTS
PAROXYTONE	PARTICIPATES	PARTNERLESS	PASSENGERS
PAROXYTONES	PARTICIPATING	PARTNERSHIP	PASSEPIEDS
PAROXYTONIC	PARTICIPATION	PARTNERSHIPS	PASSERINES
PARQUETING	PARTICIPATIONAL	PARTRIDGEBERRY	PASSIBILITIES
PARQUETRIES	PARTICIPATIONS	PARTRIDGES	PASSIBILITY
PARQUETTED	PARTICIPATIVE	PARTURIENCIES	PASSIBLENESS
PARQUETTING	PARTICIPATOR	PARTURIENCY	PASSIBLENESSES
PARRAKEETS	PARTICIPATORS	PARTURIENT	PASSIFLORA
PARRAMATTA	PARTICIPATORY	PARTURIENTS	PASSIFLORACEOUS
PARRAMATTAS	PARTICIPIAL	PARTURIFACIENT	PASSIFLORAS
PARRHESIAS	PARTICIPIALLY	PARTURITION	PASSIMETER
PARRICIDAL	PARTICIPLE	PARTURITIONS	PASSIMETERS
PARRICIDES	PARTICIPLES	PARTYGOERS	PASSIONALS
PARRITCHES	PARTICLEBOARD	PARVANIMITIES	PASSIONARIES
PARROCKING	PARTICLEBOARDS	PARVANIMITY	PASSIONARY
PARROQUETS	PARTICULAR	PARVIFOLIATE	PASSIONATE
PARROTFISH	PARTICULARISE	PARVOLINES	PASSIONATED
PARROTFISHES	PARTICULARISED	PARVOVIRUS	PASSIONATELY
PARROTRIES	PARTICULARISER	PARVOVIRUSES	PASSIONATENESS
PARSIMONIES	PARTICULARISERS	PASIGRAPHIC	PASSIONATES
PARSIMONIOUS	PARTICULARISES	PASIGRAPHICAL	PASSIONATING
PARSIMONIOUSLY	PARTICULARISING	PASIGRAPHIES	PASSIONFLOWER
PARSONAGES	PARTICULARISM	PASIGRAPHY	PASSIONFLOWERS
PARSONICAL	PARTICULARISMS	PASODOBLES	PASSIONING
PARTAKINGS	PARTICULARIST	PASQUEFLOWER	PASSIONLESS
PARTHENOCARPIC	PARTICULARISTIC	PASQUEFLOWERS	PASSIONLESSLY
PARTHENOCARPIES	PARTICULARISTS	PASQUILANT	PASSIONLESSNESS
PARTHENOCARPOUS	PARTICULARITIES	PASQUILANTS	PASSIVATED
PARTHENOCARPY	PARTICULARITY	PASQUILERS	PASSIVATES
PARTHENOGENESES	PARTICULARIZE	PASQUILLED	PASSIVATING
PARTHENOGENESIS	PARTICULARIZED	PASQUILLING	PASSIVATION
PARTHENOGENETIC	PARTICULARIZER	PASQUINADE	PASSIVATIONS

PASSIVENESS	PASTURABLE	PATHOGNOMIES	PATRIATING
PASSIVENESSES	PASTURAGES	PATHOGNOMONIC	PATRIATION
PASSIVISMS	PASTURELAND	PATHOGNOMY	PATRIATIONS
PASSIVISTS	PASTURELANDS	PATHOGRAPHIES	PATRICIANLY
PASSIVITIES	PASTURELESS	PATHOGRAPHY	PATRICIANS
PASSMENTED	PATAPHYSICS	PATHOLOGIC	PATRICIATE
PASSMENTING	PATCHBOARD	PATHOLOGICAL	PATRICIATES
PASTEBOARD	PATCHBOARDS	PATHOLOGICALLY	PATRICIDAL
PASTEBOARDS	PATCHCOCKE	PATHOLOGIES	PATRICIDES
PASTEDOWNS	PATCHCOCKES	PATHOLOGISE	PATRICLINIC
PASTELISTS	PATCHERIES	PATHOLOGIST	PATRICLINOUS
PASTELLIST	PATCHINESS	PATHOLOGISTS	PATRIFOCAL
PASTELLISTS	PATCHINESSES	PATHOLOGIZE	PATRIFOCALITIES
PASTEURELLA	PATCHOCKES	PATHOLOGIZED	PATRIFOCALITY
PASTEURELLAE	PATCHOULIES	PATHOLOGIZES	PATRILINEAGE
PASTEURELLAS	PATCHOULIS	PATHOLOGIZING	PATRILINEAGES
PASTEURISATION	PATCHWORKED	PATHOPHOBIA	PATRILINEAL
PASTEURISATIONS	PATCHWORKING	PATHOPHOBIAS	PATRILINEALLY
PASTEURISE	PATCHWORKS	PATHOPHYSIOLOGY	PATRILINEAR
PASTEURISED	PATELLECTOMIES	PATIBULARY	PATRILINEARLY
PASTEURISER	PATELLECTOMY	PATIENTEST	PATRILINIES
PASTEURISERS	PATELLIFORM	PATIENTING	PATRILOCAL
PASTEURISES	PATENTABILITIES	PATINATING	PATRILOCALLY
PASTEURISING	PATENTABILITY	PATINATION	PATRIMONIAL
PASTEURISM	PATENTABLE	PATINATIONS	PATRIMONIALLY
PASTEURISMS	PATERCOVES	PATINISING	PATRIMONIES
PASTEURIZATION	PATEREROES	PATINIZING	PATRIOTICALLY
PASTEURIZATIONS	PATERFAMILIAS	PATISSERIE	PATRIOTISM
PASTEURIZE	PATERFAMILIASES	PATISSERIES	PATRIOTISMS
PASTEURIZED	PATERNALISM	PATISSIERS	PATRISTICAL
PASTEURIZER	PATERNALISMS	PATRESFAMILIAS	PATRISTICALLY
PASTEURIZERS	PATERNALIST	PATRIALISATION	PATRISTICISM
PASTEURIZES	PATERNALISTIC	PATRIALISATIONS	PATRISTICISMS
PASTEURIZING	PATERNALISTS	PATRIALISE	PATRISTICS
PASTICCIOS	PATERNALLY	PATRIALISED	PATROCLINAL
PASTICHEUR	PATERNITIES	PATRIALISES	PATROCLINIC
PASTICHEURS	PATERNOSTER	PATRIALISING	PATROCLINIES
PASTINESSES	PATERNOSTERS	PATRIALISM	PATROCLINOUS
PASTITSIOS	PATHBREAKING	PATRIALISMS	PATROCLINY
PASTMASTER	PATHETICAL	PATRIALITIES	PATROLLERS
PASTMASTERS	PATHETICALLY	PATRIALITY	PATROLLING
PASTNESSES	PATHFINDER	PATRIALIZATION	PATROLOGICAL
PASTORALES	PATHFINDERS	PATRIALIZATIONS	PATROLOGIES
PASTORALISM	PATHFINDING	PATRIALIZE	PATROLOGIST
PASTORALISMS	PATHFINDINGS	PATRIALIZED	PATROLOGISTS
PASTORALIST	PATHLESSNESS	PATRIALIZES	PATROLWOMAN
PASTORALISTS	PATHLESSNESSES	PATRIALIZING	PATROLWOMEN
PASTORALLY	PATHOBIOLOGIES	PATRIARCHAL	PATRONAGED
PASTORALNESS	PATHOBIOLOGY	PATRIARCHALISM	PATRONAGES
PASTORALNESSES	PATHOGENES	PATRIARCHALISMS	PATRONAGING
PASTORATES	PATHOGENESES	PATRIARCHALLY	PATRONESSES
PASTORIUMS	PATHOGENESIS	PATRIARCHATE	PATRONISATION
PASTORSHIP	PATHOGENETIC	PATRIARCHATES	PATRONISATIONS
PASTORSHIPS	PATHOGENIC	PATRIARCHIES	PATRONISED
PASTOURELLE	PATHOGENICITIES	PATRIARCHISM	PATRONISER
PASTOURELLES	PATHOGENICITY	PATRIARCHISMS	PATRONISERS
PASTRYCOOK	PATHOGENIES	PATRIARCHS	PATRONISES
PASTRYCOOKS	PATHOGENOUS	PATRIARCHY	PATRONISING

PATRONISINGLY	PEACEABLENESS	PECKISHNESSES	PEDANTICIZE
PATRONIZATION	PEACEABLENESSES	PECTINACEOUS	PEDANTICIZED
PATRONIZATIONS	PEACEFULLER	PECTINATED	PEDANTICIZES
PATRONIZED	PEACEFULLEST	PECTINATELY	PEDANTICIZING
PATRONIZER	PEACEFULLY	PECTINATION	PEDANTISED
PATRONIZERS	PEACEFULNESS	PECTINATIONS	PEDANTISES
PATRONIZES	PEACEFULNESSES	PECTINESTERASE	PEDANTISING
PATRONIZING	PEACEKEEPER	PECTINESTERASES	PEDANTISMS
PATRONIZINGLY	PEACEKEEPERS	PECTISABLE	PEDANTIZED
PATRONLESS	PEACEKEEPING	PECTISATION	PEDANTIZES
PATRONYMIC	PEACEKEEPINGS	PECTISATIONS	PEDANTIZING
PATRONYMICS	PEACELESSNESS	PECTIZABLE	PEDANTOCRACIES
PATROONSHIP	PEACELESSNESSES	PECTIZATION	PEDANTOCRACY
PATROONSHIPS	PEACEMAKER	PECTIZATIONS	PEDANTOCRAT
PATTERNING	PEACEMAKERS	PECTOLITES	PEDANTOCRATIC
PATTERNINGS	PEACEMAKING	PECTORALLY	PEDANTOCRATS
PATTERNLESS	PEACEMAKINGS	PECTORILOQUIES	PEDANTRIES
PATULOUSLY	PEACETIMES	PECTORILOQUY	PEDDLERIES
PATULOUSNESS	PEACHBLOWS	PECULATING	PEDERASTIC
PATULOUSNESSES	PEACHERINO	PECULATION	PEDERASTIES
PAUCILOQUENT	PEACHERINOS	PECULATIONS	PEDEREROES
PAUGHTIEST	PEACHINESS	PECULATORS	PEDESTALED
PAULOWNIAS	PEACHINESSES	PECULIARISE	PEDESTALING
PAUNCHIEST	PEACOCKERIES	PECULIARISED	PEDESTALLED
PAUNCHINESS	PEACOCKERY	PECULIARISES	PEDESTALLING
PAUNCHINESSES	PEACOCKIER	PECULIARISING	PEDESTRIAN
PAUPERESSES	PEACOCKIEST	PECULIARITIES	PEDESTRIANISE
PAUPERISATION	PEACOCKING	PECULIARITY	PEDESTRIANISED
PAUPERISATIONS	PEACOCKISH	PECULIARIZE	PEDESTRIANISES
PAUPERISED	PEAKEDNESS	PECULIARIZED	PEDESTRIANISING
PAUPERISES	PEAKEDNESSES	PECULIARIZES	PEDESTRIANISM
PAUPERISING	PEARLASHES	PECULIARIZING	PEDESTRIANISMS
PAUPERISMS	PEARLESCENCE	PECULIARLY	PEDESTRIANIZE
PAUPERIZATION	PEARLESCENCES	PECUNIARILY	PEDESTRIANIZED
PAUPERIZATIONS	PEARLESCENT	PEDAGOGICAL	PEDESTRIANIZES
PAUPERIZED	PEARLINESS	PEDAGOGICALLY	PEDESTRIANIZING
PAUPERIZES	PEARLINESSES	PEDAGOGICS	PEDESTRIANS
PAUPERIZING	PEARLWORTS	PEDAGOGIES	PEDETENTOUS
PAUPIETTES	PEARMONGER	PEDAGOGISM	PEDIATRICIAN
PAUSEFULLY	PEARMONGERS	PEDAGOGISMS	PEDIATRICIANS
PAUSELESSLY	PEARTNESSES	PEDAGOGUED	PEDIATRICS
PAVEMENTED	PEASANTRIES	PEDAGOGUERIES	PEDIATRIST
PAVEMENTING	PEASHOOTER	PEDAGOGUERY	PEDIATRISTS
PAVILIONED	PEASHOOTERS	PEDAGOGUES	PEDICELLARIA
PAVILIONING	PEASOUPERS	PEDAGOGUING	PEDICELLARIAE
PAVONAZZOS	PEBBLEDASH	PEDAGOGUISH	PEDICELLATE
PAWKINESSES	PEBBLEDASHED	PEDAGOGUISHNESS	PEDICULATE
PAWNBROKER	PEBBLEDASHES	PEDAGOGUISM	PEDICULATED
PAWNBROKERS	PEBBLEDASHING	PEDAGOGUISMS	PEDICULATES
PAWNBROKING	PECCABILITIES	PEDALLINGS	PEDICULATION
PAWNBROKINGS	PECCABILITY	PEDANTICAL	PEDICULATIONS
PAWNTICKET	PECCADILLO	PEDANTICALLY	PEDICULOSES
PAWNTICKETS	PECCADILLOES	PEDANTICISE	PEDICULOSIS
PAYMASTERS	PECCADILLOS	PEDANTICISED	PEDICULOUS
PAYNIMRIES	PECCANCIES	PEDANTICISES	PEDICURING
PAYROLLING	PECKERWOOD	PEDANTICISING	PEDICURIST
PAYSAGISTS	PECKERWOODS	PEDANTICISM	PEDICURISTS
PEABERRIES	PECKISHNESS	PEDANTICISMS	PEDIMENTAL

PEDIMENTED
PEDIPALPUS
PEDOGENESES
PEDOGENESIS
PEDOGENETIC
PEDOLOGICAL
PEDOLOGIES
PEDOLOGIST
PEDOLOGISTS
PEDOMETERS
PEDOPHILES
PEDOPHILIA
PEDOPHILIAC
PEDOPHILIACS
PEDOPHILIAS
PEDOPHILIC
PEDUNCULAR
PEDUNCULATE
PEDUNCULATED
PEDUNCULATION
PEDUNCULATIONS
PEELGARLIC
PEELGARLICS
PEERLESSLY
PEERLESSNESS
PEERLESSNESSES
PEEVISHNESS
PEEVISHNESSES
PEGMATITES
PEGMATITIC
PEIRASTICALLY
PEJORATING
PEJORATION
PEJORATIONS
PEJORATIVE
PEJORATIVELY
PEJORATIVES
PELARGONIC
PELARGONIUM
PELARGONIUMS
PELECYPODS
PELLAGRINS
PELLAGROUS
PELLETIFIED
PELLETIFIES
PELLETIFYING
PELLETISATION
PELLETISATIONS
PELLETISED
PELLETISER
PELLETISERS
PELLETISES
PELLETISING
PELLETIZATION
PELLETIZATIONS
PELLETIZED
PELLETIZER
PELLETIZERS

PELLETIZES
PELLETIZING
PELLICULAR
PELLITORIES
PELLUCIDITIES
PELLUCIDITY
PELLUCIDLY
PELLUCIDNESS
PELLUCIDNESSES
PELMANISMS
PELOLOGIES
PELOTHERAPIES
PELOTHERAPY
PELTATIONS
PELTMONGER
PELTMONGERS
PELVIMETER
PELVIMETERS
PELVIMETRIES
PELVIMETRY
PELYCOSAUR
PELYCOSAURS
PEMPHIGOID
PEMPHIGOUS
PEMPHIGUSES
PENALISATION
PENALISATIONS
PENALISING
PENALITIES
PENALIZATION
PENALIZATIONS
PENALIZING
PENANNULAR
PENCILINGS
PENCILLERS
PENCILLING
PENCILLINGS
PENDENCIES
PENDENTIVE
PENDENTIVES
PENDICLERS
PENDRAGONS
PENDRAGONSHIP
PENDRAGONSHIPS
PENDULATED
PENDULATES
PENDULATING
PENDULINES
PENDULOSITIES
PENDULOSITY
PENDULOUSLY
PENDULOUSNESS
PENDULOUSNESSES
PENELOPISE
PENELOPISED
PENELOPISES
PENELOPISING
PENELOPIZE

PENELOPIZED
PENELOPIZES
PENELOPIZING
PENEPLAINS
PENEPLANATION
PENEPLANATIONS
PENEPLANES
PENETRABILITIES
PENETRABILITY
PENETRABLE
PENETRABLENESS
PENETRABLY
PENETRALIA
PENETRALIAN
PENETRANCE
PENETRANCES
PENETRANCIES
PENETRANCY
PENETRANTS
PENETRATED
PENETRATES
PENETRATING
PENETRATINGLY
PENETRATION
PENETRATIONS
PENETRATIVE
PENETRATIVELY
PENETRATIVENESS
PENETRATOR
PENETRATORS
PENETROMETER
PENETROMETERS
PENGUINERIES
PENGUINERY
PENGUINRIES
PENHOLDERS
PENICILLAMINE
PENICILLAMINES
PENICILLATE
PENICILLATELY
PENICILLATION
PENICILLATIONS
PENICILLIA
PENICILLIFORM
PENICILLIN
PENICILLINASE
PENICILLINASES
PENICILLINS
PENICILLIUM
PENICILLIUMS
PENINSULAR
PENINSULARITIES
PENINSULARITY
PENINSULAS
PENINSULATE
PENINSULATED
PENINSULATES
PENINSULATING

PENISTONES
PENITENCES
PENITENCIES
PENITENTIAL
PENITENTIALLY
PENITENTIALS
PENITENTIARIES
PENITENTIARY
PENITENTLY
PENMANSHIP
PENMANSHIPS
PENNACEOUS
PENNALISMS
PENNATULACEOUS
PENNATULAE
PENNATULAS
PENNILESSLY
PENNILESSNESS
PENNILESSNESSES
PENNILLION
PENNINITES
PENNONCELLE
PENNONCELLES
PENNONCELS
PENNYCRESS
PENNYCRESSES
PENNYLANDS
PENNYROYAL
PENNYROYALS
PENNYWEIGHT
PENNYWEIGHTS
PENNYWHISTLE
PENNYWHISTLES
PENNYWINKLE
PENNYWINKLES
PENNYWORTH
PENNYWORTHS
PENNYWORTS
PENOLOGICAL
PENOLOGICALLY
PENOLOGIES
PENOLOGIST
PENOLOGISTS
PENONCELLE
PENONCELLES
PENPUSHERS
PENPUSHING
PENSIEROSO
PENSILENESS
PENSILENESSES
PENSILITIES
PENSIONABLE
PENSIONARIES
PENSIONARY
PENSIONEER
PENSIONEERS
PENSIONERS
PENSIONING

PENSIONLESS	PENTAPODIES	PENURIOUSNESS	PEPTONIZING
PENSIONNAT	PENTAPOLIS	PENURIOUSNESSES	PERACIDITIES
PENSIONNATS	PENTAPOLISES	PEOPLEHOOD	PERACIDITY
PENSIVENESS	PENTAPOLITAN	PEOPLEHOODS	PERADVENTURE
PENSIVENESSES	PENTAPRISM	PEOPLELESS	PERADVENTURES
PENSTEMONS	PENTAPRISMS	PEPEROMIAS	PERAEOPODS
PENTABARBITAL	PENTAQUARK	PEPPERBOXES	PERAMBULATE
PENTABARBITALS	PENTAQUARKS	PEPPERCORN	PERAMBULATED
PENTACHORD	PENTARCHICAL	PEPPERCORNS	PERAMBULATES
PENTACHORDS	PENTARCHIES	PEPPERCORNY	PERAMBULATING
PENTACRINOID	PENTASTICH	PEPPERGRASS	PERAMBULATION
PENTACRINOIDS	PENTASTICHES	PEPPERGRASSES	PERAMBULATIONS
PENTACTINAL	PENTASTICHOUS	PEPPERIDGE	PERAMBULATOR
PENTACYCLIC	PENTASTICHS	PEPPERIDGES	PERAMBULATORS
PENTADACTYL	PENTASTYLE	PEPPERIEST	PERAMBULATORY
PENTADACTYLE	PENTASTYLES	PEPPERINESS	PERBORATES
PENTADACTYLES	PENTASYLLABIC	PEPPERINESSES	PERCALINES
PENTADACTYLIC	PENTATEUCHAL	PEPPERINGS	PERCEIVABILITY
PENTADACTYLIES	PENTATHLETE	PEPPERMILL	PERCEIVABLE
PENTADACTYLISM	PENTATHLETES	PEPPERMILLS	PERCEIVABLY
PENTADACTYLISMS	PENTATHLON	PEPPERMINT	PERCEIVERS
PENTADACTYLOUS	PENTATHLONS	PEPPERMINTS	PERCEIVING
PENTADACTYLS	PENTATHLUM	PEPPERMINTY	PERCEIVINGS
PENTADACTYLY	PENTATHLUMS	PEPPERONIS	PERCENTAGE
PENTADELPHOUS	PENTATOMIC	PEPPERTREE	PERCENTAGES
PENTAGONAL	PENTATONIC	PEPPERTREES	PERCENTILE
PENTAGONALLY	PENTAVALENT	PEPPERWORT	PERCENTILES
PENTAGONALS	PENTAZOCINE	PEPPERWORTS	PERCEPTIBILITY
PENTAGRAMS	PENTAZOCINES	PEPPINESSES	PERCEPTIBLE
PENTAGRAPH	PENTECONTER	PEPSINATED	PERCEPTIBLY
PENTAGRAPHS	PENTECONTERS	PEPSINATES	PERCEPTION
PENTAGYNIAN	PENTETERIC	PEPSINATING	PERCEPTIONAL
PENTAGYNOUS	PENTHEMIMER	PEPSINOGEN	PERCEPTIONS
PENTAHEDRA	PENTHEMIMERAL	PEPSINOGENS	PERCEPTIVE
PENTAHEDRAL	PENTHEMIMERS	PEPTALKING	PERCEPTIVELY
PENTAHEDRON	PENTHOUSED	PEPTICITIES	PERCEPTIVENESS
PENTAHEDRONS	PENTHOUSES	PEPTIDASES	PERCEPTIVITIES
PENTALOGIES	PENTHOUSING	PEPTIDOGLYCAN	PERCEPTIVITY
PENTALPHAS	PENTIMENTI	PEPTIDOGLYCANS	PERCEPTUAL
PENTAMERIES	PENTIMENTO	PEPTISABLE	PERCEPTUALLY
PENTAMERISM	PENTLANDITE	PEPTISATION	PERCHERIES
PENTAMERISMS	PENTLANDITES	PEPTISATIONS	PERCHERONS
PENTAMEROUS	PENTOBARBITAL	PEPTIZABLE	PERCHLORATE
PENTAMETER	PENTOBARBITALS	PEPTIZATION	PERCHLORATES
PENTAMETERS	PENTOBARBITONE	PEPTIZATIONS	PERCHLORIC
PENTAMIDINE	PENTOBARBITONES	PEPTONISATION	PERCHLORIDE
PENTAMIDINES	PENTOSANES	PEPTONISATIONS	PERCHLORIDES
PENTANDRIAN	PENTOSIDES	PEPTONISED	PERCHLOROETHENE
PENTANDROUS	PENTOXIDES	PEPTONISER	PERCIPIENCE
PENTANGLES	PENTSTEMON	PEPTONISERS	PERCIPIENCES
PENTANGULAR	PENTSTEMONS	PEPTONISES	PERCIPIENCIES
PENTAPEPTIDE	PENTYLENES	PEPTONISING	PERCIPIENCY
PENTAPEPTIDES	PENULTIMAS	PEPTONIZATION	PERCIPIENT
PENTAPLOID	PENULTIMATE	PEPTONIZATIONS	PERCIPIENTLY
PENTAPLOIDIES	PENULTIMATELY	PEPTONIZED	PERCIPIENTS
PENTAPLOIDS	PENULTIMATES	PEPTONIZER	PERCOIDEAN
PENTAPLOIDY	PENUMBROUS	PEPTONIZERS	PERCOIDEANS
PENTAPODIC	PENURIOUSLY	PEPTONIZES	PERCOLABLE

PERCOLATED	PERENNATIONS	PERFOLIATIONS	PERICHAETIA
PERCOLATES	PERENNIALITIES	PERFORABLE	PERICHAETIAL
PERCOLATING	PERENNIALITY	PERFORANSES	PERICHAETIUM
PERCOLATION	PERENNIALLY	PERFORATED	PERICHONDRAL
PERCOLATIONS	PERENNIALS	PERFORATES	PERICHONDRIA
PERCOLATIVE	PERENNIBRANCH	PERFORATING	PERICHONDRIAL
PERCOLATOR	PERENNIBRANCHS	PERFORATION	PERICHONDRIUM
PERCOLATORS	PERENNITIES	PERFORATIONS	PERICHORESES
PERCURRENT	PERESTROIKA	PERFORATIVE	PERICHORESIS
PERCURSORY	PERESTROIKAS	PERFORATOR	PERICHYLOUS
PERCUSSANT	PERFECTATION	PERFORATORS	PERICLASES
PERCUSSING	PERFECTATIONS	PERFORATORY	PERICLASTIC
PERCUSSION	PERFECTERS	PERFORATUS	PERICLINAL
PERCUSSIONAL	PERFECTEST	PERFORATUSES	PERICLINES
PERCUSSIONIST	PERFECTIBILIAN	PERFORMABILITY	PERICLITATE
PERCUSSIONISTS	PERFECTIBILIANS	PERFORMABLE	PERICLITATED
PERCUSSIONS	PERFECTIBILISM	PERFORMANCE	PERICLITATES
PERCUSSIVE	PERFECTIBILISMS	PERFORMANCES	PERICLITATING
PERCUSSIVELY	PERFECTIBILIST	PERFORMATIVE	PERICRANIA
PERCUSSIVENESS	PERFECTIBILISTS	PERFORMATIVELY	PERICRANIAL
PERCUSSORS	PERFECTIBILITY	PERFORMATIVES	PERICRANIUM
PERCUTANEOUS	PERFECTIBLE	PERFORMATORY	PERICRANIUMS
PERCUTANEOUSLY	PERFECTING	PERFORMERS	PERICULOUS
PERCUTIENT	PERFECTION	PERFORMING	PERICYCLES
PERCUTIENTS	PERFECTIONATE	PERFORMINGS	PERICYCLIC
PERDENDOSI	PERFECTIONATED	PERFUMELESS	PERICYNTHIA
PERDITIONABLE	PERFECTIONATES	PERFUMERIES	PERICYNTHION
PERDITIONS	PERFECTIONATING	PERFUMIERS	PERICYNTHIONS
PERDUELLION	PERFECTIONISM	PERFUNCTORILY	PERIDERMAL
PERDUELLIONS	PERFECTIONISMS	PERFUNCTORINESS	PERIDERMIC
PERDURABILITIES	PERFECTIONIST	PERFUNCTORY	PERIDESMIA
PERDURABILITY	PERFECTIONISTIC	PERFUSATES	PERIDESMIUM
PERDURABLE	PERFECTIONISTS	PERFUSIONIST	PERIDINIAN
PERDURABLY	PERFECTIONS	PERFUSIONISTS	PERIDINIANS
PERDURANCE	PERFECTIVE	PERFUSIONS	PERIDINIUM
PERDURANCES	PERFECTIVELY	PERGAMENEOUS	PERIDINIUMS
PERDURATION	PERFECTIVENESS	PERGAMENTACEOUS	PERIDOTITE
PERDURATIONS	PERFECTIVES	PERGUNNAHS	PERIDOTITES
PEREGRINATE	PERFECTIVITIES	PERIASTRON	PERIDOTITIC
PEREGRINATED	PERFECTIVITY	PERIASTRONS	PERIDROMES
PEREGRINATES	PERFECTNESS	PERIBLASTS	PERIEGESES
PEREGRINATING	PERFECTNESSES	PERICARDIA	PERIEGESIS
PEREGRINATION	PERFECTORS	PERICARDIAC	PERIGASTRIC
PEREGRINATIONS	PERFERVIDITIES	PERICARDIAL	PERIGASTRITIS
PEREGRINATOR	PERFERVIDITY	PERICARDIAN	PERIGASTRITISES
PEREGRINATORS	PERFERVIDLY	PERICARDITIC	PERIGENESES
PEREGRINATORY	PERFERVIDNESS	PERICARDITIS	PERIGENESIS
PEREGRINES	PERFERVIDNESSES	PERICARDITISES	PERIGLACIAL
PEREGRINITIES	PERFERVORS	PERICARDIUM	PERIGONIAL
PEREGRINITY	PERFERVOUR	PERICARDIUMS	PERIGONIUM
PEREIOPODS	PERFERVOURS	PERICARPIAL	PERIGYNIES
PEREMPTORILY	PERFICIENT	PERICARPIC	PERIGYNOUS
PEREMPTORINESS	PERFIDIOUS	PERICENTER	PERIHELIAL
PEREMPTORY	PERFIDIOUSLY	PERICENTERS	PERIHELION
PERENNATED	PERFIDIOUSNESS	PERICENTRAL	PERIHEPATIC
PERENNATES	PERFLUOROCARBON	PERICENTRE	PERIHEPATITIS
PERENNATING	PERFOLIATE	PERICENTRES	PERIHEPATITISES
PERENNATION	PERFOLIATION	PERICENTRIC	PERIKARYAL

PERIKARYON	PERIODONTITISES	PERISHABILITY	PERIVITELLINE
PERILOUSLY	PERIODONTOLOGY	PERISHABLE	PERIWIGGED
PERILOUSNESS	PERIONYCHIA	PERISHABLENESS	PERIWIGGING
PERILOUSNESSES	PERIONYCHIUM	PERISHABLES	PERIWINKLE
PERILYMPHS	PERIOSTEAL	PERISHABLY	PERIWINKLES
PERIMENOPAUSAL	PERIOSTEUM	PERISHINGLY	PERJINKETY
PERIMENOPAUSE	PERIOSTITIC	PERISPERMAL	PERJINKITIES
PERIMENOPAUSES	PERIOSTITIS	PERISPERMIC	PERJINKITY
PERIMETERS	PERIOSTITISES	PERISPERMS	PERJURIOUS
PERIMETRAL	PERIOSTRACUM	PERISPOMENON	PERJURIOUSLY
PERIMETRIC	PERIOSTRACUMS	PERISPOMENONS	PERKINESSES
PERIMETRICAL	PERIPATETIC	PERISSODACTYL	PERLEMOENS
PERIMETRICALLY	PERIPATETICAL	PERISSODACTYLE	PERLOCUTION
PERIMETRIES	PERIPATETICALLY	PERISSODACTYLES	PERLOCUTIONARY
PERIMORPHIC	PERIPATETICISM	PERISSODACTYLIC	PERLOCUTIONS
PERIMORPHISM	PERIPATETICISMS	PERISSODACTYLS	PERLUSTRATE
PERIMORPHISMS	PERIPATETICS	PERISSOLOGIES	PERLUSTRATED
PERIMORPHOUS	PERIPATUSES	PERISSOLOGY	PERLUSTRATES
PERIMORPHS	PERIPETEIA	PERISSOSYLLABIC	PERLUSTRATING
PERIMYSIUM	PERIPETEIAN	PERISTALITH	PERLUSTRATION
PERIMYSIUMS	PERIPETEIAS	PERISTALITHS	PERLUSTRATIONS
PERINAEUMS	PERIPETIAN	PERISTALSES	PERMACULTURE
PERINATALLY	PERIPETIAS	PERISTALSIS	PERMACULTURES
PERINEPHRIA	PERIPETIES	PERISTALTIC	PERMAFROST
PERINEPHRIC	PERIPHERAL	PERISTALTICALLY	PERMAFROSTS
PERINEPHRITIS	PERIPHERALITIES	PERISTERITE	PERMALLOYS
PERINEPHRITISES	PERIPHERALITY	PERISTERITES	PERMANENCE
PERINEPHRIUM	PERIPHERALLY	PERISTERONIC	PERMANENCES
PERINEURAL	PERIPHERALS	PERISTOMAL	PERMANENCIES
PERINEURIA	PERIPHERIC	PERISTOMATIC	PERMANENCY
PERINEURIAL	PERIPHERICAL	PERISTOMES	PERMANENTLY
PERINEURITIC	PERIPHERIES	PERISTOMIAL	PERMANENTNESS
PERINEURITIS	PERIPHONIC	PERISTREPHIC	PERMANENTNESSES
PERINEURITISES	PERIPHRASE	PERISTYLAR	PERMANENTS
PERINEURIUM	PERIPHRASED	PERISTYLES	PERMANGANATE
PERIODATES	PERIPHRASES	PERITECTIC	PERMANGANATES
PERIODICAL	PERIPHRASING	PERITHECIA	PERMANGANIC
PERIODICALIST	PERIPHRASIS	PERITHECIAL	PERMEABILITIES
PERIODICALISTS	PERIPHRASTIC	PERITHECIUM	PERMEABILITY
PERIODICALLY	PERIPHRASTICAL	PERITONAEA	PERMEABLENESS
PERIODICALS	PERIPHYTIC	PERITONAEAL	PERMEABLENESSES
PERIODICITIES	PERIPHYTON	PERITONAEUM	PERMEAMETER
PERIODICITY	PERIPHYTONS	PERITONAEUMS	PERMEAMETERS
PERIODIDES	PERIPLASMS	PERITONEAL	PERMEANCES
PERIODISATION	PERIPLASTS	PERITONEALLY	PERMEATING
PERIODISATIONS	PERIPLUSES	PERITONEOSCOPY	PERMEATION
PERIODIZATION	PERIPROCTS	PERITONEUM	PERMEATIONS
PERIODIZATIONS	PERIPTERAL	PERITONEUMS	PERMEATIVE
PERIODONTAL	PERIPTERIES	PERITONITIC	PERMEATORS
PERIODONTALLY	PERISARCAL	PERITONITIS	PERMETHRIN
PERIODONTIA	PERISARCOUS	PERITONITISES	PERMETHRINS
PERIODONTIAS	PERISCIANS	PERITRACKS	PERMILLAGE
PERIODONTIC	PERISCOPES	PERITRICHA	PERMILLAGES
PERIODONTICALLY	PERISCOPIC	PERITRICHOUS	PERMISSIBILITY
PERIODONTICS	PERISCOPICALLY	PERITRICHOUSLY	PERMISSIBLE
PERIODONTIST	PERISELENIA	PERITRICHS	PERMISSIBLENESS
PERIODONTISTS	PERISELENIUM	PERITYPHLITIS	PERMISSIBLY
PERIODONTITIS	PERISHABILITIES	PERITYPHLITISES	PERMISSION

PERMISSIONS	PEROXISOMES	PERSECUTEES	PERSONALISM
PERMISSIVE	PEROXYSULPHURIC	PERSECUTES	PERSONALISMS
PERMISSIVELY	PERPENDICULAR	PERSECUTING	PERSONALIST
PERMISSIVENESS	PERPENDICULARLY	PERSECUTION	PERSONALISTIC
PERMITTANCE	PERPENDICULARS	PERSECUTIONS	PERSONALISTS
PERMITTANCES	PERPENDING	PERSECUTIVE	PERSONALITIES
PERMITTEES	PERPETRABLE	PERSECUTOR	PERSONALITY
PERMITTERS	PERPETRATE	PERSECUTORS	PERSONALIZATION
PERMITTING	PERPETRATED	PERSECUTORY	PERSONALIZE
PERMITTIVITIES	PERPETRATES	PERSEITIES	PERSONALIZED
PERMITTIVITY	PERPETRATING	PERSELINES	PERSONALIZES
PERMUTABILITIES	PERPETRATION	PERSEVERANCE	PERSONALIZING
PERMUTABILITY	PERPETRATIONS	PERSEVERANCES	PERSONALLY
PERMUTABLE	PERPETRATOR	PERSEVERANT	PERSONALTIES
PERMUTABLENESS	PERPETRATORS	PERSEVERATE	PERSONALTY
PERMUTABLY	PERPETUABLE	PERSEVERATED	PERSONATED
PERMUTATED	PERPETUALISM	PERSEVERATES	PERSONATES
PERMUTATES	PERPETUALISMS	PERSEVERATING	PERSONATING
PERMUTATING	PERPETUALIST	PERSEVERATION	PERSONATINGS
PERMUTATION	PERPETUALISTS	PERSEVERATIONS	PERSONATION
PERMUTATIONAL	PERPETUALITIES	PERSEVERATIVE	PERSONATIONS
PERMUTATIONS	PERPETUALITY	PERSEVERATOR	PERSONATIVE
PERNANCIES	PERPETUALLY	PERSEVERATORS	PERSONATOR
PERNICIOUS	PERPETUALS	PERSEVERED	PERSONATORS
PERNICIOUSLY	PERPETUANCE	PERSEVERES	PERSONHOOD
PERNICIOUSNESS	PERPETUANCES	PERSEVERING	PERSONHOODS
PERNICKETINESS	PERPETUATE	PERSEVERINGLY	PERSONIFIABLE
PERNICKETY	PERPETUATED	PERSICARIA	PERSONIFICATION
PERNOCTATE	PERPETUATES	PERSICARIAS	PERSONIFIED
PERNOCTATED	PERPETUATING	PERSIENNES	PERSONIFIER
PERNOCTATES	PERPETUATION	PERSIFLAGE	PERSONIFIERS
PERNOCTATING	PERPETUATIONS	PERSIFLAGES	PERSONIFIES
PERNOCTATION	PERPETUATOR	PERSIFLEUR	PERSONIFYING
PERNOCTATIONS	PERPETUATORS	PERSIFLEURS	PERSONISED
PERONEUSES	PERPETUITIES	PERSIMMONS	PERSONISES
PERORATING	PERPETUITY	PERSISTENCE	PERSONISING
PERORATION	PERPHENAZINE	PERSISTENCES	PERSONIZED
PERORATIONAL	PERPHENAZINES	PERSISTENCIES	PERSONIZES
PERORATIONS	PERPLEXEDLY	PERSISTENCY	PERSONIZING
PERORATORS	PERPLEXEDNESS	PERSISTENT	PERSONNELS
PEROVSKIAS	PERPLEXEDNESSES	PERSISTENTLY	PERSONPOWER
PEROVSKITE	PERPLEXERS	PERSISTENTS	PERSONPOWERS
PEROVSKITES	PERPLEXING	PERSISTERS	PERSPECTIVAL
PEROXIDASE	PERPLEXINGLY	PERSISTING	PERSPECTIVE
PEROXIDASES	PERPLEXITIES	PERSISTINGLY	PERSPECTIVELY
PEROXIDATION	PERPLEXITY	PERSISTIVE	PERSPECTIVES
PEROXIDATIONS	PERQUISITE	PERSNICKETINESS	PERSPECTIVISM
PEROXIDING	PERQUISITES	PERSNICKETY	PERSPECTIVISMS
PEROXIDISE	PERQUISITION	PERSONABLE	PERSPECTIVIST
PEROXIDISED	PERQUISITIONS	PERSONABLENESS	PERSPECTIVISTS
PEROXIDISES	PERQUISITOR	PERSONABLY	PERSPICACIOUS
PEROXIDISING	PERQUISITORS	PERSONAGES	PERSPICACIOUSLY
PEROXIDIZE	PERRUQUIER	PERSONALIA	PERSPICACITIES
PEROXIDIZED	PERRUQUIERS	PERSONALISATION	PERSPICACITY
PEROXIDIZES	PERSCRUTATION	PERSONALISE	PERSPICUITIES
PEROXIDIZING	PERSCRUTATIONS	PERSONALISED	PERSPICUITY
PEROXISOMAL	PERSECUTED	PERSONALISES	PERSPICUOUS
PEROXISOME	PERSECUTEE	PERSONALISING	PERSPICUOUSLY

PERSPICUOUSNESS
PERSPIRABLE
PERSPIRATE
PERSPIRATED
PERSPIRATES
PERSPIRATING
PERSPIRATION
PERSPIRATIONS
PERSPIRATORY
PERSPIRING
PERSPIRINGLY
PERSTRINGE
PERSTRINGED
PERSTRINGES
PERSTRINGING
PERSUADABILITY
PERSUADABLE
PERSUADERS
PERSUADING
PERSUASIBILITY
PERSUASIBLE
PERSUASION
PERSUASIONS
PERSUASIVE
PERSUASIVELY
PERSUASIVENESS
PERSUASIVES
PERSUASORY
PERSULFURIC
PERSULPHATE
PERSULPHATES
PERSULPHURIC
PERSWADING
PERTAINING
PERTINACIOUS
PERTINACIOUSLY
PERTINACITIES
PERTINACITY
PERTINENCE
PERTINENCES
PERTINENCIES
PERTINENCY
PERTINENTLY
PERTINENTS
PERTNESSES
PERTURBABLE
PERTURBABLY
PERTURBANCE
PERTURBANCES
PERTURBANT
PERTURBANTS
PERTURBATE
PERTURBATED
PERTURBATES
PERTURBATING
PERTURBATION
PERTURBATIONAL
PERTURBATIONS

PERTURBATIVE
PERTURBATOR
PERTURBATORIES
PERTURBATORS
PERTURBATORY
PERTURBEDLY
PERTURBERS
PERTURBING
PERTURBINGLY
PERTUSIONS
PERTUSSISES
PERVASIONS
PERVASIVELY
PERVASIVENESS
PERVASIVENESSES
PERVERSELY
PERVERSENESS
PERVERSENESSES
PERVERSEST
PERVERSION
PERVERSIONS
PERVERSITIES
PERVERSITY
PERVERSIVE
PERVERTEDLY
PERVERTEDNESS
PERVERTEDNESSES
PERVERTERS
PERVERTIBLE
PERVERTING
PERVIATING
PERVICACIES
PERVICACIOUS
PERVICACITIES
PERVICACITY
PERVIOUSLY
PERVIOUSNESS
PERVIOUSNESSES
PESKINESSES
PESSIMISMS
PESSIMISTIC
PESSIMISTICAL
PESSIMISTICALLY
PESSIMISTS
PESTERINGLY
PESTERMENT
PESTERMENTS
PESTHOUSES
PESTICIDAL
PESTICIDES
PESTIFEROUS
PESTIFEROUSLY
PESTIFEROUSNESS
PESTILENCE
PESTILENCES
PESTILENTIAL
PESTILENTIALLY
PESTILENTLY

PESTOLOGICAL
PESTOLOGIES
PESTOLOGIST
PESTOLOGISTS
PETAHERTZES
PETALIFEROUS
PETALODIES
PETALOMANIA
PETALOMANIAS
PETAURINES
PETAURISTS
PETCHARIES
PETERSHAMS
PETHIDINES
PETIOLATED
PETIOLULES
PETITENESS
PETITENESSES
PETITIONARY
PETITIONED
PETITIONER
PETITIONERS
PETITIONING
PETITIONINGS
PETITIONIST
PETITIONISTS
PETNAPINGS
PETNAPPERS
PETNAPPING
PETRIFACTION
PETRIFACTIONS
PETRIFACTIVE
PETRIFICATION
PETRIFICATIONS
PETRIFIERS
PETRIFYING
PETRISSAGE
PETRISSAGES
PETROCHEMICAL
PETROCHEMICALLY
PETROCHEMICALS
PETROCHEMISTRY
PETROCURRENCIES
PETROCURRENCY
PETRODOLLAR
PETRODOLLARS
PETRODROME
PETRODROMES
PETROGENESES
PETROGENESIS
PETROGENETIC
PETROGENIES
PETROGLYPH
PETROGLYPHIC
PETROGLYPHIES
PETROGLYPHS
PETROGLYPHY
PETROGRAMS

PETROGRAPHER
PETROGRAPHERS
PETROGRAPHIC
PETROGRAPHICAL
PETROGRAPHIES
PETROGRAPHY
PETROLAGES
PETROLATUM
PETROLATUMS
PETROLEOUS
PETROLEUMS
PETROLEURS
PETROLEUSE
PETROLEUSES
PETROLHEAD
PETROLHEADS
PETROLIFEROUS
PETROLLING
PETROLOGIC
PETROLOGICAL
PETROLOGICALLY
PETROLOGIES
PETROLOGIST
PETROLOGISTS
PETROMONEY
PETROMONEYS
PETROMONIES
PETRONELLA
PETRONELLAS
PETROPHYSICAL
PETROPHYSICIST
PETROPHYSICISTS
PETROPHYSICS
PETROPOUNDS
PETTEDNESS
PETTEDNESSES
PETTICHAPS
PETTICHAPSES
PETTICOATED
PETTICOATS
PETTIFOGGED
PETTIFOGGER
PETTIFOGGERIES
PETTIFOGGERS
PETTIFOGGERY
PETTIFOGGING
PETTIFOGGINGS
PETTINESSES
PETTISHNESS
PETTISHNESSES
PETULANCES
PETULANCIES
PETULANTLY
PEWHOLDERS
PHACOLITES
PHACOLITHS
PHAELONION
PHAELONIONS

PHAENOGAMIC	PHALLICISM	PHARISEEISM	PHASEOLINS
PHAENOGAMOUS	PHALLICISMS	PHARISEEISMS	PHATICALLY
PHAENOGAMS	PHALLICIST	PHARMACEUTIC	PHEASANTRIES
PHAENOLOGIES	PHALLICISTS	PHARMACEUTICAL	PHEASANTRY
PHAENOLOGY	PHALLOCENTRIC	PHARMACEUTICALS	PHELLODERM
PHAENOMENA	PHALLOCENTRISM	PHARMACEUTICS	PHELLODERMAL
PHAENOMENON	PHALLOCENTRISMS	PHARMACEUTIST	PHELLODERMS
PHAENOTYPE	PHALLOCENTRIST	PHARMACEUTISTS	PHELLOGENETIC
PHAENOTYPED	PHALLOCENTRISTS	PHARMACIES	PHELLOGENIC
PHAENOTYPES	PHALLOCRAT	PHARMACIST	PHELLOGENS
PHAENOTYPING	PHALLOCRATIC	PHARMACISTS	PHELLOPLASTIC
PHAEOMELANIN	PHALLOCRATS	PHARMACODYNAMIC	PHELLOPLASTICS
PHAEOMELANINS	PHALLOIDIN	PHARMACOGENOMIC	PHELONIONS
PHAGEDAENA	PHALLOIDINS	PHARMACOGNOSIES	PHENACAINE
PHAGEDAENAS	PHANEROGAM	PHARMACOGNOSIST	PHENACAINES
PHAGEDAENIC	PHANEROGAMIC	PHARMACOGNOSTIC	PHENACETIN
PHAGEDENAS	PHANEROGAMOUS	PHARMACOGNOSY	PHENACETINS
PHAGEDENIC	PHANEROGAMS	PHARMACOKINETIC	PHENACITES
PHAGOCYTES	PHANEROPHYTE	PHARMACOLOGIC	PHENAKISMS
PHAGOCYTIC	PHANEROPHYTES	PHARMACOLOGICAL	PHENAKISTOSCOPE
PHAGOCYTICAL	PHANSIGARS	PHARMACOLOGIES	PHENAKITES
PHAGOCYTISE	PHANTASIAST	PHARMACOLOGIST	PHENANTHRENE
PHAGOCYTISED	PHANTASIASTS	PHARMACOLOGISTS	PHENANTHRENES
PHAGOCYTISES	PHANTASIED	PHARMACOLOGY	PHENARSAZINE
PHAGOCYTISING	PHANTASIES	PHARMACOPEIA	PHENARSAZINES
PHAGOCYTISM	PHANTASIME	PHARMACOPEIAL	PHENAZINES
PHAGOCYTISMS	PHANTASIMES	PHARMACOPEIAS	PHENCYCLIDINE
PHAGOCYTIZE	PHANTASIMS	PHARMACOPOEIA	PHENCYCLIDINES
PHAGOCYTIZED	PHANTASMAGORIA	PHARMACOPOEIAL	PHENETICIST
PHAGOCYTIZES	PHANTASMAGORIAL	PHARMACOPOEIAN	PHENETICISTS
PHAGOCYTIZING	PHANTASMAGORIAS	PHARMACOPOEIAS	PHENETIDINE
PHAGOCYTOSE	PHANTASMAGORIC	PHARMACOPOEIC	PHENETIDINES
PHAGOCYTOSED	PHANTASMAGORIES	PHARMACOPOEIST	PHENETOLES
PHAGOCYTOSES	PHANTASMAGORY	PHARMACOPOEISTS	PHENFORMIN
PHAGOCYTOSING	PHANTASMAL	PHARMACOPOLIST	PHENFORMINS
PHAGOCYTOSIS	PHANTASMALIAN	PHARMACOPOLISTS	PHENGOPHOBIA
PHAGOCYTOTIC	PHANTASMALITIES	PHARMACOTHERAPY	PHENGOPHOBIAS
PHAGOMANIA	PHANTASMALITY	PHARYNGALS	PHENMETRAZINE
PHAGOMANIAC	PHANTASMALLY	PHARYNGEAL	PHENMETRAZINES
PHAGOMANIACS	PHANTASMAS	PHARYNGITIC	PHENOBARBITAL
PHAGOMANIAS	PHANTASMATA	PHARYNGITIDES	PHENOBARBITALS
PHAGOPHOBIA	PHANTASMIC	PHARYNGITIS	PHENOBARBITONE
PHAGOPHOBIAS	PHANTASMICAL	PHARYNGITISES	PHENOBARBITONES
PHAGOSOMES	PHANTASMICALLY	PHARYNGOLOGICAL	PHENOCOPIES
PHALANGEAL	PHANTASTIC	PHARYNGOLOGIES	PHENOCRYST
PHALANGERS	PHANTASTICS	PHARYNGOLOGIST	PHENOCRYSTIC
PHALANGIDS	PHANTASTRIES	PHARYNGOLOGISTS	PHENOCRYSTS
PHALANGIST	PHANTASTRY	PHARYNGOLOGY	PHENOLATED
PHALANGISTS	PHANTASYING	PHARYNGOSCOPE	PHENOLATES
PHALANSTERIAN	PHANTOMATIC	PHARYNGOSCOPES	PHENOLATING
PHALANSTERIES	PHANTOMISH	PHARYNGOSCOPIC	PHENOLOGICAL
PHALANSTERISM	PHANTOMLIKE	PHARYNGOSCOPIES	PHENOLOGICALLY
PHALANSTERISMS	PHANTOSMES	PHARYNGOSCOPY	PHENOLOGIES
PHALANSTERIST	PHARISAICAL	PHARYNGOTOMIES	PHENOLOGIST
PHALANSTERISTS	PHARISAICALLY	PHARYNGOTOMY	PHENOLOGISTS
PHALANSTERY	PHARISAICALNESS	PHASCOGALE	PHENOLPHTHALEIN
PHALAROPES	PHARISAISM	PHASCOGALES	PHENOMENAL
PHALLICALLY	PHARISAISMS	PHASEDOWNS	PHENOMENALISE

PHENOMENALISED
PHENOMENALISES
PHENOMENALISING
PHENOMENALISM
PHENOMENALISMS
PHENOMENALIST
PHENOMENALISTIC
PHENOMENALISTS
PHENOMENALITIES
PHENOMENALITY
PHENOMENALIZE
PHENOMENALIZED
PHENOMENALIZES
PHENOMENALIZING
PHENOMENALLY
PHENOMENAS
PHENOMENISE
PHENOMENISED
PHENOMENISES
PHENOMENISING
PHENOMENISM
PHENOMENISMS
PHENOMENIST
PHENOMENISTS
PHENOMENIZE
PHENOMENIZED
PHENOMENIZES
PHENOMENIZING
PHENOMENOLOGIES
PHENOMENOLOGIST
PHENOMENOLOGY
PHENOMENON
PHENOMENONS
PHENOTHIAZINE
PHENOTHIAZINES
PHENOTYPED
PHENOTYPES
PHENOTYPIC
PHENOTYPICAL
PHENOTYPICALLY
PHENOTYPING
PHENOXIDES
PHENTOLAMINE
PHENTOLAMINES
PHENYLALANIN
PHENYLALANINE
PHENYLALANINES
PHENYLALANINS
PHENYLAMINE
PHENYLAMINES
PHENYLBUTAZONE
PHENYLBUTAZONES
PHENYLENES
PHENYLEPHRINE
PHENYLEPHRINES
PHENYLKETONURIA
PHENYLKETONURIC
PHENYLMETHYL

PHENYLMETHYLS
PHENYLTHIOUREA
PHENYLTHIOUREAS
PHENYTOINS
PHEROMONAL
PHEROMONES
PHIALIFORM
PHILADELPHUS
PHILADELPHUSES
PHILANDERED
PHILANDERER
PHILANDERERS
PHILANDERING
PHILANDERS
PHILANTHROPE
PHILANTHROPES
PHILANTHROPIC
PHILANTHROPICAL
PHILANTHROPIES
PHILANTHROPIST
PHILANTHROPISTS
PHILANTHROPOID
PHILANTHROPOIDS
PHILANTHROPY
PHILATELIC
PHILATELICALLY
PHILATELIES
PHILATELIST
PHILATELISTS
PHILHARMONIC
PHILHARMONICS
PHILHELLENE
PHILHELLENES
PHILHELLENIC
PHILHELLENISM
PHILHELLENISMS
PHILHELLENIST
PHILHELLENISTS
PHILHORSES
PHILIPPICS
PHILIPPINA
PHILIPPINAS
PHILIPPINE
PHILIPPINES
PHILISTIAS
PHILISTINE
PHILISTINES
PHILISTINISM
PHILISTINISMS
PHILLABEGS
PHILLIBEGS
PHILLIPSITE
PHILLIPSITES
PHILLUMENIES
PHILLUMENIST
PHILLUMENISTS
PHILLUMENY
PHILODENDRA

PHILODENDRON
PHILODENDRONS
PHILOGYNIES
PHILOGYNIST
PHILOGYNISTS
PHILOGYNOUS
PHILOLOGER
PHILOLOGERS
PHILOLOGIAN
PHILOLOGIANS
PHILOLOGIC
PHILOLOGICAL
PHILOLOGICALLY
PHILOLOGIES
PHILOLOGIST
PHILOLOGISTS
PHILOLOGUE
PHILOLOGUES
PHILOMATHIC
PHILOMATHICAL
PHILOMATHIES
PHILOMATHS
PHILOMATHY
PHILOMELAS
PHILOPENAS
PHILOPOENA
PHILOPOENAS
PHILOSOPHASTER
PHILOSOPHASTERS
PHILOSOPHE
PHILOSOPHER
PHILOSOPHERESS
PHILOSOPHERS
PHILOSOPHES
PHILOSOPHESS
PHILOSOPHESSES
PHILOSOPHIC
PHILOSOPHICAL
PHILOSOPHICALLY
PHILOSOPHIES
PHILOSOPHISE
PHILOSOPHISED
PHILOSOPHISER
PHILOSOPHISERS
PHILOSOPHISES
PHILOSOPHISING
PHILOSOPHISM
PHILOSOPHISMS
PHILOSOPHIST
PHILOSOPHISTIC
PHILOSOPHISTS
PHILOSOPHIZE
PHILOSOPHIZED
PHILOSOPHIZER
PHILOSOPHIZERS
PHILOSOPHIZES
PHILOSOPHIZING
PHILOSOPHY

PHILOXENIA
PHILOXENIAS
PHILTERING
PHISNOMIES
PHLEBECTOMIES
PHLEBECTOMY
PHLEBITIDES
PHLEBITISES
PHLEBOGRAM
PHLEBOGRAMS
PHLEBOGRAPHIC
PHLEBOGRAPHIES
PHLEBOGRAPHY
PHLEBOLITE
PHLEBOLITES
PHLEBOLOGIES
PHLEBOLOGY
PHLEBOSCLEROSES
PHLEBOSCLEROSIS
PHLEBOTOMIC
PHLEBOTOMICAL
PHLEBOTOMIES
PHLEBOTOMISE
PHLEBOTOMISED
PHLEBOTOMISES
PHLEBOTOMISING
PHLEBOTOMIST
PHLEBOTOMISTS
PHLEBOTOMIZE
PHLEBOTOMIZED
PHLEBOTOMIZES
PHLEBOTOMIZING
PHLEBOTOMY
PHLEGMAGOGIC
PHLEGMAGOGUE
PHLEGMAGOGUES
PHLEGMASIA
PHLEGMASIAS
PHLEGMATIC
PHLEGMATICAL
PHLEGMATICALLY
PHLEGMATICNESS
PHLEGMIEST
PHLEGMONIC
PHLEGMONOID
PHLEGMONOUS
PHLOGISTIC
PHLOGISTICATE
PHLOGISTICATED
PHLOGISTICATES
PHLOGISTICATING
PHLOGISTON
PHLOGISTONS
PHLOGOPITE
PHLOGOPITES
PHLORIZINS
PHLYCTAENA
PHLYCTAENAE

PHLYCTENAE	PHONETISTS	PHONOTYPING	PHOSPHORESCING
PHOCOMELIA	PHONETIZATION	PHONOTYPIST	PHOSPHORET
PHOCOMELIAS	PHONETIZATIONS	PHONOTYPISTS	PHOSPHORETS
PHOCOMELIC	PHONETIZED	PHORMINGES	PHOSPHORETTED
PHOENIXISM	PHONETIZES	PHOSGENITE	PHOSPHORIC
PHOENIXISMS	PHONETIZING	PHOSGENITES	PHOSPHORISE
PHOENIXLIKE	PHONEYNESS	PHOSPHATASE	PHOSPHORISED
PHOLIDOSES	PHONEYNESSES	PHOSPHATASES	PHOSPHORISES
PHOLIDOSIS	PHONICALLY	PHOSPHATED	PHOSPHORISING
PHONASTHENIA	PHONINESSES	PHOSPHATES	PHOSPHORISM
PHONASTHENIAS	PHONMETERS	PHOSPHATIC	PHOSPHORISMS
PHONATHONS	PHONOCAMPTIC	PHOSPHATIDE	PHOSPHORITE
PHONATIONS	PHONOCAMPTICS	PHOSPHATIDES	PHOSPHORITES
PHONAUTOGRAPH	PHONOCARDIOGRAM	PHOSPHATIDIC	PHOSPHORITIC
PHONAUTOGRAPHIC	PHONOCHEMISTRY	PHOSPHATIDYL	PHOSPHORIZE
PHONAUTOGRAPHS	PHONOFIDDLE	PHOSPHATIDYLS	PHOSPHORIZED
PHONECARDS	PHONOFIDDLES	PHOSPHATING	PHOSPHORIZES
PHONEMATIC	PHONOGRAMIC	PHOSPHATISATION	PHOSPHORIZING
PHONEMATICALLY	PHONOGRAMICALLY	PHOSPHATISE	PHOSPHOROLYSES
PHONEMICALLY	PHONOGRAMMIC	PHOSPHATISED	PHOSPHOROLYSIS
PHONEMICISATION	PHONOGRAMS	PHOSPHATISES	PHOSPHOROLYTIC
PHONEMICISE	PHONOGRAPH	PHOSPHATISING	PHOSPHOROSCOPE
PHONEMICISED	PHONOGRAPHER	PHOSPHATIZATION	PHOSPHOROSCOPES
PHONEMICISES	PHONOGRAPHERS	PHOSPHATIZE	PHOSPHOROUS
PHONEMICISING	PHONOGRAPHIC	PHOSPHATIZED	PHOSPHORUS
PHONEMICIST	PHONOGRAPHIES	PHOSPHATIZES	PHOSPHORUSES
PHONEMICISTS	PHONOGRAPHIST	PHOSPHATIZING	PHOSPHORYL
PHONEMICIZATION	PHONOGRAPHISTS	PHOSPHATURIA	PHOSPHORYLASE
PHONEMICIZE	PHONOGRAPHS	PHOSPHATURIAS	PHOSPHORYLASES
PHONEMICIZED	PHONOGRAPHY	PHOSPHATURIC	PHOSPHORYLATE
PHONEMICIZES	PHONOLITES	PHOSPHENES	PHOSPHORYLATED
PHONEMICIZING	PHONOLITIC	PHOSPHIDES	PHOSPHORYLATES
PHONENDOSCOPE	PHONOLOGIC	PHOSPHINES	PHOSPHORYLATING
PHONENDOSCOPES	PHONOLOGICAL	PHOSPHITES	PHOSPHORYLATION
PHONETICAL	PHONOLOGICALLY	PHOSPHOCREATIN	PHOSPHORYLATIVE
PHONETICALLY	PHONOLOGIES	PHOSPHOCREATINE	PHOSPHORYLS
PHONETICIAN	PHONOLOGIST	PHOSPHOCREATINS	PHOSPHURET
PHONETICIANS	PHONOLOGISTS	PHOSPHOKINASE	PHOSPHURETS
PHONETICISATION	PHONOMETER	PHOSPHOKINASES	PHOSPHURETTED
PHONETICISE	PHONOMETERS	PHOSPHOLIPASE	PHOTICALLY
PHONETICISED	PHONOMETRIC	PHOSPHOLIPASES	PHOTOACTINIC
PHONETICISES	PHONOMETRICAL	PHOSPHOLIPID	PHOTOACTIVE
PHONETICISING	PHONOPHOBIA	PHOSPHOLIPIDS	PHOTOAUTOTROPH
PHONETICISM	PHONOPHOBIAS	PHOSPHONIC	PHOTOAUTOTROPHS
PHONETICISMS	PHONOPHORE	PHOSPHONIUM	PHOTOBATHIC
PHONETICIST	PHONOPHORES	PHOSPHONIUMS	PHOTOBIOLOGIC
PHONETICISTS	PHONOPORES	PHOSPHOPROTEIN	PHOTOBIOLOGICAL
PHONETICIZATION	PHONOSCOPE	PHOSPHOPROTEINS	PHOTOBIOLOGIES
PHONETICIZE	PHONOSCOPES	PHOSPHORATE	PHOTOBIOLOGIST
PHONETICIZED	PHONOTACTIC	PHOSPHORATED	PHOTOBIOLOGISTS
PHONETICIZES	PHONOTACTICS	PHOSPHORATES	PHOTOBIOLOGY
PHONETICIZING	PHONOTYPED	PHOSPHORATING	PHOTOCATALYSES
PHONETISATION	PHONOTYPER	PHOSPHORES	PHOTOCATALYSIS
PHONETISATIONS	PHONOTYPERS	PHOSPHORESCE	PHOTOCATALYTIC
PHONETISED	PHONOTYPES	PHOSPHORESCED	PHOTOCATHODE
PHONETISES	PHONOTYPIC	PHOSPHORESCENCE	PHOTOCATHODES
PHONETISING	PHONOTYPICAL	PHOSPHORESCENT	PHOTOCELLS
PHONETISMS	PHONOTYPIES	PHOSPHORESCES	PHOTOCHEMICAL

PHOTOCHEMICALLY	PHOTOENGRAVING	PHOTOIONIZE	PHOTOOXIDATIVE
PHOTOCHEMIST	PHOTOENGRAVINGS	PHOTOIONIZED	PHOTOOXIDISE
PHOTOCHEMISTRY	PHOTOEXCITATION	PHOTOIONIZES	PHOTOOXIDISED
PHOTOCHEMISTS	PHOTOEXCITED	PHOTOIONIZING	PHOTOOXIDISES
PHOTOCHROMIC	PHOTOFINISHER	PHOTOJOURNALISM	PHOTOOXIDISING
PHOTOCHROMICS	PHOTOFINISHERS	PHOTOJOURNALIST	PHOTOOXIDIZE
PHOTOCHROMIES	PHOTOFINISHING	PHOTOKINESES	PHOTOOXIDIZED
PHOTOCHROMISM	PHOTOFINISHINGS	PHOTOKINESIS	PHOTOOXIDIZES
PHOTOCHROMISMS	PHOTOFISSION	PHOTOKINETIC	PHOTOOXIDIZING
PHOTOCHROMY	PHOTOFISSIONS	PHOTOLITHO	PHOTOPERIOD
PHOTOCOMPOSE	PHOTOFLASH	PHOTOLITHOGRAPH	PHOTOPERIODIC
PHOTOCOMPOSED	PHOTOFLASHES	PHOTOLITHOS	PHOTOPERIODISM
PHOTOCOMPOSER	PHOTOFLOOD	PHOTOLUMINESCE	PHOTOPERIODISMS
PHOTOCOMPOSERS	PHOTOFLOODS	PHOTOLUMINESCED	PHOTOPERIODS
PHOTOCOMPOSES	PHOTOFLUOROGRAM	PHOTOLUMINESCES	PHOTOPHASE
PHOTOCOMPOSING	PHOTOGELATINE	PHOTOLYSABLE	PHOTOPHASES
PHOTOCONDUCTING	PHOTOGENES	PHOTOLYSED	PHOTOPHILIC
PHOTOCONDUCTION	PHOTOGENIC	PHOTOLYSES	PHOTOPHILIES
PHOTOCONDUCTIVE	PHOTOGENICALLY	PHOTOLYSING	PHOTOPHILOUS
PHOTOCONDUCTOR	PHOTOGENIES	PHOTOLYSIS	PHOTOPHILS
PHOTOCONDUCTORS	PHOTOGEOLOGIC	PHOTOLYTIC	PHOTOPHILY
PHOTOCOPIABLE	PHOTOGEOLOGICAL	PHOTOLYTICALLY	PHOTOPHOBE
PHOTOCOPIED	PHOTOGEOLOGIES	PHOTOLYZABLE	PHOTOPHOBES
PHOTOCOPIER	PHOTOGEOLOGIST	PHOTOLYZED	PHOTOPHOBIA
PHOTOCOPIERS	PHOTOGEOLOGISTS	PHOTOLYZES	PHOTOPHOBIAS
PHOTOCOPIES	PHOTOGEOLOGY	PHOTOLYZING	PHOTOPHOBIC
PHOTOCOPYING	PHOTOGLYPH	PHOTOMACROGRAPH	PHOTOPHONE
PHOTOCOPYINGS	PHOTOGLYPHIC	PHOTOMAPPED	PHOTOPHONES
PHOTOCURRENT	PHOTOGLYPHIES	PHOTOMAPPING	PHOTOPHONIC
PHOTOCURRENTS	PHOTOGLYPHS	PHOTOMASKS	PHOTOPHONIES
PHOTODEGRADABLE	PHOTOGLYPHY	PHOTOMECHANICAL	PHOTOPHONY
PHOTODETECTOR	PHOTOGRAMMETRIC	PHOTOMETER	PHOTOPHORE
PHOTODETECTORS	PHOTOGRAMMETRY	PHOTOMETERS	PHOTOPHORES
PHOTODIODE	PHOTOGRAMS	PHOTOMETRIC	PHOTOPHORESES
PHOTODIODES	PHOTOGRAPH	PHOTOMETRICALLY	PHOTOPHORESIS
PHOTODISSOCIATE	PHOTOGRAPHED	PHOTOMETRIES	PHOTOPLAYS
PHOTODUPLICATE	PHOTOGRAPHER	PHOTOMETRIST	PHOTOPOLYMER
PHOTODUPLICATED	PHOTOGRAPHERS	PHOTOMETRISTS	PHOTOPOLYMERS
PHOTODUPLICATES	PHOTOGRAPHIC	PHOTOMETRY	PHOTOPOSITIVE
PHOTODYNAMIC	PHOTOGRAPHICAL	PHOTOMICROGRAPH	PHOTOPRODUCT
PHOTODYNAMICS	PHOTOGRAPHIES	PHOTOMONTAGE	PHOTOPRODUCTION
PHOTOELASTIC	PHOTOGRAPHING	PHOTOMONTAGES	PHOTOPRODUCTS
PHOTOELASTICITY	PHOTOGRAPHIST	PHOTOMOSAIC	PHOTOPSIAS
PHOTOELECTRIC	PHOTOGRAPHISTS	PHOTOMOSAICS	PHOTOPSIES
PHOTOELECTRICAL	PHOTOGRAPHS	PHOTOMULTIPLIER	PHOTOREACTION
PHOTOELECTRODE	PHOTOGRAPHY	PHOTOMURAL	PHOTOREACTIONS
PHOTOELECTRODES	PHOTOGRAVURE	PHOTOMURALS	PHOTOREALISM
PHOTOELECTRON	PHOTOGRAVURES	PHOTONASTIC	PHOTOREALISMS
PHOTOELECTRONIC	PHOTOINDUCED	PHOTONASTIES	PHOTOREALIST
PHOTOELECTRONS	PHOTOINDUCTION	PHOTONASTY	PHOTOREALISTIC
PHOTOEMISSION	PHOTOINDUCTIONS	PHOTONEGATIVE	PHOTOREALISTS
PHOTOEMISSIONS	PHOTOINDUCTIVE	PHOTONEUTRON	PHOTORECEPTION
PHOTOEMISSIVE	PHOTOIONISATION	PHOTONEUTRONS	PHOTORECEPTIONS
PHOTOENGRAVE	PHOTOIONISE	PHOTONOVEL	PHOTORECEPTIVE
PHOTOENGRAVED	PHOTOIONISED	PHOTONOVELS	PHOTORECEPTOR
PHOTOENGRAVER	PHOTOIONISES	PHOTONUCLEAR	PHOTORECEPTORS
PHOTOENGRAVERS	PHOTOIONISING	PHOTOOXIDATION	PHOTOREDUCE
PHOTOENGRAVES	PHOTOIONIZATION	PHOTOOXIDATIONS	PHOTOREDUCED

PHOTOREDUCES

PHOTOREDUCES	PHOTOTONUSES	PHREATOPHYTIC	PHYLACTERIC
PHOTOREDUCING	PHOTOTOPOGRAPHY	PHRENESIAC	PHYLACTERICAL
PHOTOREDUCTION	PHOTOTOXIC	PHRENETICAL	PHYLACTERIES
PHOTOREDUCTIONS	PHOTOTOXICITIES	PHRENETICALLY	PHYLACTERY
PHOTOREFRACTIVE	PHOTOTOXICITY	PHRENETICNESS	PHYLARCHIES
PHOTORESIST	PHOTOTRANSISTOR	PHRENETICNESSES	PHYLAXISES
PHOTORESISTS	PHOTOTROPE	PHRENETICS	PHYLESISES
PHOTOSCANNED	PHOTOTROPES	PHRENITIDES	PHYLETICALLY
PHOTOSCANNING	PHOTOTROPH	PHRENITISES	PHYLLARIES
PHOTOSCANS	PHOTOTROPHIC	PHRENOLOGIC	PHYLLOCLAD
PHOTOSENSITISE	PHOTOTROPHS	PHRENOLOGICAL	PHYLLOCLADE
PHOTOSENSITISED	PHOTOTROPIC	PHRENOLOGICALLY	PHYLLOCLADES
PHOTOSENSITISER	PHOTOTROPICALLY	PHRENOLOGIES	PHYLLOCLADS
PHOTOSENSITISES	PHOTOTROPIES	PHRENOLOGISE	PHYLLODIAL
PHOTOSENSITIVE	PHOTOTROPISM	PHRENOLOGISED	PHYLLODIES
PHOTOSENSITIZE	PHOTOTROPISMS	PHRENOLOGISES	PHYLLODIUM
PHOTOSENSITIZED	PHOTOTROPY	PHRENOLOGISING	PHYLLOMANIA
PHOTOSENSITIZER	PHOTOTUBES	PHRENOLOGIST	PHYLLOMANIAS
PHOTOSENSITIZES	PHOTOTYPED	PHRENOLOGISTS	PHYLLOPHAGOUS
PHOTOSETTER	PHOTOTYPES	PHRENOLOGIZE	PHYLLOPLANE
PHOTOSETTERS	PHOTOTYPESET	PHRENOLOGIZED	PHYLLOPLANES
PHOTOSETTING	PHOTOTYPESETS	PHRENOLOGIZES	PHYLLOPODS
PHOTOSETTINGS	PHOTOTYPESETTER	PHRENOLOGIZING	PHYLLOQUINONE
PHOTOSHOOT	PHOTOTYPIC	PHRENOLOGY	PHYLLOQUINONES
PHOTOSHOOTS	PHOTOTYPICALLY	PHRENSICAL	PHYLLOSILICATE
PHOTOSPHERE	PHOTOTYPIES	PHRENSYING	PHYLLOSILICATES
PHOTOSPHERES	PHOTOTYPING	PHRONTISTERIES	PHYLLOSPHERE
PHOTOSPHERIC	PHOTOTYPOGRAPHY	PHRONTISTERY	PHYLLOSPHERES
PHOTOSTATED	PHOTOVOLTAIC	PHTHALATES	PHYLLOTACTIC
PHOTOSTATIC	PHOTOVOLTAICS	PHTHALEINS	PHYLLOTACTICAL
PHOTOSTATING	PHOTOXYLOGRAPHY	PHTHALOCYANIN	PHYLLOTAXES
PHOTOSTATS	PHOTOZINCOGRAPH	PHTHALOCYANINE	PHYLLOTAXIES
PHOTOSTATTED	PHRAGMOPLAST	PHTHALOCYANINES	PHYLLOTAXIS
PHOTOSTATTING	PHRAGMOPLASTS	PHTHALOCYANINS	PHYLLOTAXY
PHOTOSYNTHATE	PHRASELESS	PHTHIRIASES	PHYLLOXERA
PHOTOSYNTHATES	PHRASEMAKER	PHTHIRIASIS	PHYLLOXERAE
PHOTOSYNTHESES	PHRASEMAKERS	PHTHISICAL	PHYLLOXERAS
PHOTOSYNTHESIS	PHRASEMAKING	PHTHISICKY	PHYLOGENESES
PHOTOSYNTHESISE	PHRASEMAKINGS	PHYCOBILIN	PHYLOGENESIS
PHOTOSYNTHESIZE	PHRASEMONGER	PHYCOBILINS	PHYLOGENETIC
PHOTOSYNTHETIC	PHRASEMONGERING	PHYCOBIONT	PHYLOGENIC
PHOTOSYSTEM	PHRASEMONGERS	PHYCOBIONTS	PHYLOGENIES
PHOTOSYSTEMS	PHRASEOGRAM	PHYCOCYANIN	PHYSALISES
PHOTOTACTIC	PHRASEOGRAMS	PHYCOCYANINS	PHYSHARMONICA
PHOTOTACTICALLY	PHRASEOGRAPH	PHYCOCYANS	PHYSHARMONICAS
PHOTOTAXES	PHRASEOGRAPHIC	PHYCOERYTHRIN	PHYSIATRIC
PHOTOTAXIES	PHRASEOGRAPHIES	PHYCOERYTHRINS	PHYSIATRICAL
PHOTOTAXIS	PHRASEOGRAPHS	PHYCOLOGICAL	PHYSIATRICS
PHOTOTELEGRAPH	PHRASEOGRAPHY	PHYCOLOGIES	PHYSIATRIES
PHOTOTELEGRAPHS	PHRASEOLOGIC	PHYCOLOGIST	PHYSIATRIST
PHOTOTELEGRAPHY	PHRASEOLOGICAL	PHYCOLOGISTS	PHYSIATRISTS
PHOTOTHERAPIES	PHRASEOLOGIES	PHYCOMYCETE	PHYSICALISM
PHOTOTHERAPY	PHRASEOLOGIST	PHYCOMYCETES	PHYSICALISMS
PHOTOTHERMAL	PHRASEOLOGISTS	PHYCOMYCETOUS	PHYSICALIST
PHOTOTHERMALLY	PHRASEOLOGY	PHYCOPHAEIN	PHYSICALISTIC
PHOTOTHERMIC	PHREAKINGS	PHYCOPHAEINS	PHYSICALISTS
PHOTOTONIC	PHREATOPHYTE	PHYCOXANTHIN	PHYSICALITIES
PHOTOTONUS	PHREATOPHYTES	PHYCOXANTHINS	PHYSICALITY

PHYSICALLY	PHYTOALEXINS	PHYTOTOMISTS	PICKELHAUBE
PHYSICALNESS	PHYTOBENTHOS	PHYTOTOXIC	PICKELHAUBES
PHYSICALNESSES	PHYTOBENTHOSES	PHYTOTOXICITIES	PICKERELWEED
PHYSICIANCIES	PHYTOCHEMICAL	PHYTOTOXICITY	PICKERELWEEDS
PHYSICIANCY	PHYTOCHEMICALLY	PHYTOTOXIN	PICKETBOAT
PHYSICIANER	PHYTOCHEMICALS	PHYTOTOXINS	PICKETBOATS
PHYSICIANERS	PHYTOCHEMIST	PHYTOTRONS	PICKETINGS
PHYSICIANS	PHYTOCHEMISTRY	PIACULARITIES	PICKINESSES
PHYSICIANSHIP	PHYTOCHEMISTS	PIACULARITY	PICKPOCKET
PHYSICIANSHIPS	PHYTOCHROME	PIANISSIMI	PICKPOCKETS
PHYSICISMS	PHYTOCHROMES	PIANISSIMO	PICKTHANKS
PHYSICISTS	PHYTOESTROGEN	PIANISSIMOS	PICNICKERS
PHYSICKING	PHYTOESTROGENS	PIANISSISSIMO	PICNICKING
PHYSICOCHEMICAL	PHYTOFLAGELLATE	PIANISTICALLY	PICOCURIES
PHYSIOCRACIES	PHYTOGENESES	PIANOFORTE	PICOFARADS
PHYSIOCRACY	PHYTOGENESIS	PIANOFORTES	PICOMETERS
PHYSIOCRAT	PHYTOGENETIC	PIANOLISTS	PICOMETRES
PHYSIOCRATIC	PHYTOGENETICAL	PICADILLOS	PICORNAVIRUS
PHYSIOCRATS	PHYTOGENIC	PICANINNIES	PICORNAVIRUSES
PHYSIOGNOMIC	PHYTOGENIES	PICARESQUE	PICOSECOND
PHYSIOGNOMICAL	PHYTOGEOGRAPHER	PICARESQUES	PICOSECONDS
PHYSIOGNOMIES	PHYTOGEOGRAPHIC	PICAROONED	PICOWAVING
PHYSIOGNOMIST	PHYTOGEOGRAPHY	PICAROONING	PICQUETING
PHYSIOGNOMISTS	PHYTOGRAPHER	PICAYUNISH	PICROCARMINE
PHYSIOGNOMY	PHYTOGRAPHERS	PICAYUNISHLY	PICROCARMINES
PHYSIOGRAPHER	PHYTOGRAPHIC	PICAYUNISHNESS	PICROTOXIN
PHYSIOGRAPHERS	PHYTOGRAPHIES	PICCADILLIES	PICROTOXINS
PHYSIOGRAPHIC	PHYTOGRAPHY	PICCADILLO	PICTARNIES
PHYSIOGRAPHICAL	PHYTOHORMONE	PICCADILLOES	PICTOGRAMS
PHYSIOGRAPHIES	PHYTOHORMONES	PICCADILLS	PICTOGRAPH
PHYSIOGRAPHY	PHYTOLITHS	PICCADILLY	PICTOGRAPHIC
PHYSIOLATER	PHYTOLOGICAL	PICCALILLI	PICTOGRAPHIES
PHYSIOLATERS	PHYTOLOGICALLY	PICCALILLIS	PICTOGRAPHS
PHYSIOLATRIES	PHYTOLOGIES	PICCANINNIES	PICTOGRAPHY
PHYSIOLATRY	PHYTOLOGIST	PICCANINNY	PICTORIALISE
PHYSIOLOGIC	PHYTOLOGISTS	PICCOLOIST	PICTORIALISED
PHYSIOLOGICAL	PHYTONADIONE	PICCOLOISTS	PICTORIALISES
PHYSIOLOGICALLY	PHYTONADIONES	PICHICIAGO	PICTORIALISING
PHYSIOLOGIES	PHYTOPATHOGEN	PICHICIAGOS	PICTORIALISM
PHYSIOLOGIST	PHYTOPATHOGENIC	PICHICIEGO	PICTORIALISMS
PHYSIOLOGISTS	PHYTOPATHOGENS	PICHICIEGOS	PICTORIALIST
PHYSIOLOGUS	PHYTOPATHOLOGY	PICHOLINES	PICTORIALISTS
PHYSIOLOGUSES	PHYTOPHAGIC	PICKABACKED	PICTORIALIZE
PHYSIOLOGY	PHYTOPHAGIES	PICKABACKING	PICTORIALIZED
PHYSIOPATHOLOGY	PHYTOPHAGOUS	PICKABACKS	PICTORIALIZES
PHYSIOTHERAPIES	PHYTOPHAGY	PICKADILLIES	PICTORIALIZING
PHYSIOTHERAPIST	PHYTOPLANKTER	PICKADILLO	PICTORIALLY
PHYSIOTHERAPY	PHYTOPLANKTERS	PICKADILLOES	PICTORIALNESS
PHYSITHEISM	PHYTOPLANKTON	PICKADILLS	PICTORIALNESSES
PHYSITHEISMS	PHYTOPLANKTONIC	PICKADILLY	PICTORIALS
PHYSITHEISTIC	PHYTOPLANKTONS	PICKANINNIES	PICTORICAL
PHYSOCLISTOUS	PHYTOSOCIOLOGY	PICKANINNY	PICTORICALLY
PHYSOSTIGMIN	PHYTOSTEROL	PICKAPACKS	PICTUREGOER
PHYSOSTIGMINE	PHYTOSTEROLS	PICKAROONS	PICTUREGOERS
PHYSOSTIGMINES	PHYTOTHERAPIES	PICKEDNESS	PICTUREPHONE
PHYSOSTIGMINS	PHYTOTHERAPY	PICKEDNESSES	PICTUREPHONES
PHYSOSTOMOUS	PHYTOTOMIES	PICKEERERS	PICTURESQUE
PHYTOALEXIN	PHYTOTOMIST	PICKEERING	PICTURESQUELY

PICTURESQUENESS

PICTURESQUENESS
PICTURISATION
PICTURISATIONS
PICTURISED
PICTURISES
PICTURISING
PICTURIZATION
PICTURIZATIONS
PICTURIZED
PICTURIZES
PICTURIZING
PIDDLINGLY
PIDGINISATION
PIDGINISATIONS
PIDGINISED
PIDGINISES
PIDGINISING
PIDGINIZATION
PIDGINIZATIONS
PIDGINIZED
PIDGINIZES
PIDGINIZING
PIECEMEALED
PIECEMEALING
PIECEMEALS
PIECEWORKER
PIECEWORKERS
PIECEWORKS
PIEDMONTITE
PIEDMONTITES
PIEDNESSES
PIEMONTITE
PIEMONTITES
PIEPOWDERS
PIERCEABLE
PIERCINGLY
PIERCINGNESS
PIERCINGNESSES
PIERRETTES
PIETISTICAL
PIETISTICALLY
PIEZOCHEMISTRY
PIEZOELECTRIC
PIEZOMAGNETIC
PIEZOMAGNETISM
PIEZOMAGNETISMS
PIEZOMETER
PIEZOMETERS
PIEZOMETRIC
PIEZOMETRICALLY
PIEZOMETRIES
PIEZOMETRY
PIGEONHOLE
PIGEONHOLED
PIGEONHOLER
PIGEONHOLERS
PIGEONHOLES
PIGEONHOLING

PIGEONITES
PIGEONRIES
PIGEONWING
PIGEONWINGS
PIGGINESSES
PIGGISHNESS
PIGGISHNESSES
PIGGYBACKED
PIGGYBACKING
PIGGYBACKS
PIGHEADEDLY
PIGHEADEDNESS
PIGHEADEDNESSES
PIGMENTARY
PIGMENTATION
PIGMENTATIONS
PIGMENTING
PIGNERATED
PIGNERATES
PIGNERATING
PIGNORATED
PIGNORATES
PIGNORATING
PIGNORATION
PIGNORATIONS
PIGSCONCES
PIGSTICKED
PIGSTICKER
PIGSTICKERS
PIGSTICKING
PIGTAILING
PIKEPERCHES
PIKESTAFFS
PIKESTAVES
PILASTERED
PILEORHIZA
PILEORHIZAS
PILFERABLE
PILFERAGES
PILFERINGLY
PILFERINGS
PILFERPROOF
PILGARLICK
PILGARLICKS
PILGARLICKY
PILGARLICS
PILGRIMAGE
PILGRIMAGED
PILGRIMAGER
PILGRIMAGERS
PILGRIMAGES
PILGRIMAGING
PILGRIMERS
PILGRIMISE
PILGRIMISED
PILGRIMISES
PILGRIMISING
PILGRIMIZE

PILGRIMIZED
PILGRIMIZES
PILGRIMIZING
PILIFEROUS
PILLARISTS
PILLARLESS
PILLICOCKS
PILLIONING
PILLIONIST
PILLIONISTS
PILLIWINKS
PILLORISED
PILLORISES
PILLORISING
PILLORIZED
PILLORIZES
PILLORIZING
PILLORYING
PILLOWCASE
PILLOWCASES
PILLOWSLIP
PILLOWSLIPS
PILNIEWINKS
PILOCARPIN
PILOCARPINE
PILOCARPINES
PILOCARPINS
PILOSITIES
PILOTFISHES
PILOTHOUSE
PILOTHOUSES
PIMPERNELS
PIMPLINESS
PIMPLINESSES
PIMPMOBILE
PIMPMOBILES
PINACOIDAL
PINACOTHECA
PINACOTHECAE
PINAFORING
PINAKOIDAL
PINAKOTHEK
PINAKOTHEKS
PINBALLING
PINCERLIKE
PINCHBECKS
PINCHCOCKS
PINCHCOMMONS
PINCHCOMMONSES
PINCHFISTS
PINCHINGLY
PINCHPENNIES
PINCHPENNY
PINCHPOINT
PINCHPOINTS
PINCUSHION
PINCUSHIONS
PINEALECTOMIES

PINEALECTOMISE
PINEALECTOMISED
PINEALECTOMISES
PINEALECTOMIZE
PINEALECTOMIZED
PINEALECTOMIZES
PINEALECTOMY
PINEAPPLES
PINFEATHER
PINFEATHERS
PINFOLDING
PINGRASSES
PINGUEFIED
PINGUEFIES
PINGUEFYING
PINGUIDITIES
PINGUIDITY
PINGUITUDE
PINGUITUDES
PINHEADEDNESS
PINHEADEDNESSES
PINHOOKERS
PINKERTONS
PINKINESSES
PINKISHNESS
PINKISHNESSES
PINKNESSES
PINNACLING
PINNATIFID
PINNATIFIDLY
PINNATIONS
PINNATIPARTITE
PINNATIPED
PINNATISECT
PINNIEWINKLE
PINNIEWINKLES
PINNIPEDES
PINNIPEDIAN
PINNIPEDIANS
PINNULATED
PINNYWINKLE
PINNYWINKLES
PINOCYTOSES
PINOCYTOSIS
PINOCYTOTIC
PINOCYTOTICALLY
PINPOINTED
PINPOINTING
PINPRICKED
PINPRICKING
PINSETTERS
PINSPOTTER
PINSPOTTERS
PINSTRIPES
PINTADERAS
PINWHEELED
PINWHEELING
PINWRENCHES

PIONEERING	PISTACHIOS	PIWAKAWAKA	PLAGIOCEPHALY
PIOUSNESSES	PISTAREENS	PIXELATION	PLAGIOCLASE
PIPECLAYED	PISTILLARY	PIXELATIONS	PLAGIOCLASES
PIPECLAYING	PISTILLATE	PIXELLATED	PLAGIOCLASTIC
PIPEFISHES	PISTILLODE	PIXILATION	PLAGIOCLIMAX
PIPEFITTER	PISTILLODES	PIXILATIONS	PLAGIOCLIMAXES
PIPEFITTERS	PISTOLEERS	PIXILLATED	PLAGIOSTOMATOUS
PIPEFITTING	PISTOLEROS	PIXILLATION	PLAGIOSTOME
PIPEFITTINGS	PISTOLIERS	PIXILLATIONS	PLAGIOSTOMES
PIPELINING	PISTOLLING	PIXINESSES	PLAGIOSTOMOUS
PIPELININGS	PITAPATTED	PIZZAIOLAS	PLAGIOTROPIC
PIPERACEOUS	PITAPATTING	PIZZICATOS	PLAGIOTROPISM
PIPERAZINE	PITCHBENDS	PLACABILITIES	PLAGIOTROPISMS
PIPERAZINES	PITCHBLENDE	PLACABILITY	PLAGIOTROPOUS
PIPERIDINE	PITCHBLENDES	PLACABLENESS	PLAGUESOME
PIPERIDINES	PITCHERFUL	PLACABLENESSES	PLAINCHANT
PIPERONALS	PITCHERFULS	PLACARDING	PLAINCHANTS
PIPESTONES	PITCHERSFUL	PLACATINGLY	PLAINCLOTHES
PIPINESSES	PITCHFORKED	PLACATIONS	PLAINCLOTHESMAN
PIPISTRELLE	PITCHFORKING	PLACEHOLDER	PLAINCLOTHESMEN
PIPISTRELLES	PITCHFORKS	PLACEHOLDERS	PLAINNESSES
PIPISTRELS	PITCHINESS	PLACEKICKED	PLAINSONGS
PIPIWHARAUROA	PITCHINESSES	PLACEKICKER	PLAINSPOKEN
PIPIWHARAUROAS	PITCHOMETER	PLACEKICKERS	PLAINSPOKENNESS
PIPSISSEWA	PITCHOMETERS	PLACEKICKING	PLAINSTANES
PIPSISSEWAS	PITCHPERSON	PLACEKICKS	PLAINSTONES
PIPSQUEAKS	PITCHPERSONS	PLACELESSLY	PLAINTEXTS
PIQUANCIES	PITCHPINES	PLACEMENTS	PLAINTIFFS
PIQUANTNESS	PITCHPIPES	PLACENTALS	PLAINTIVELY
PIQUANTNESSES	PITCHPOLED	PLACENTATE	PLAINTIVENESS
PIRACETAMS	PITCHPOLES	PLACENTATION	PLAINTIVENESSES
PIRATICALLY	PITCHPOLING	PLACENTATIONS	PLAINTLESS
PIRLICUING	PITCHSTONE	PLACENTIFORM	PLAINWORKS
PIROPLASMA	PITCHSTONES	PLACENTOLOGIES	PLAISTERED
PIROPLASMATA	PITCHWOMAN	PLACENTOLOGY	PLAISTERING
PIROPLASMS	PITCHWOMEN	PLACIDITIES	PLANARIANS
PIROUETTED	PITEOUSNESS	PLACIDNESS	PLANARITIES
PIROUETTER	PITEOUSNESSES	PLACIDNESSES	PLANATIONS
PIROUETTERS	PITHECANTHROPI	PLACODERMS	PLANCHETTE
PIROUETTES	PITHECANTHROPUS	PLAGIARIES	PLANCHETTES
PIROUETTING	PITHINESSES	PLAGIARISE	PLANELOADS
PISCATORIAL	PITIABLENESS	PLAGIARISED	PLANENESSES
PISCATORIALLY	PITIABLENESSES	PLAGIARISER	PLANESIDES
PISCATRIXES	PITIFULLER	PLAGIARISERS	PLANETARIA
PISCICOLOUS	PITIFULLEST	PLAGIARISES	PLANETARIES
PISCICULTURAL	PITIFULNESS	PLAGIARISING	PLANETARIUM
PISCICULTURALLY	PITIFULNESSES	PLAGIARISM	PLANETARIUMS
PISCICULTURE	PITILESSLY	PLAGIARISMS	PLANETESIMAL
PISCICULTURES	PITILESSNESS	PLAGIARIST	PLANETESIMALS
PISCICULTURIST	PITILESSNESSES	PLAGIARISTIC	PLANETICAL
PISCICULTURISTS	PITTOSPORUM	PLAGIARISTS	PLANETLIKE
PISCIFAUNA	PITTOSPORUMS	PLAGIARIZE	PLANETOIDAL
PISCIFAUNAE	PITUITARIES	PLAGIARIZED	PLANETOIDS
PISCIFAUNAS	PITUITRINS	PLAGIARIZER	PLANETOLOGICAL
PISCIVORES	PITYRIASES	PLAGIARIZERS	PLANETOLOGIES
PISCIVOROUS	PITYRIASIS	PLAGIARIZES	PLANETOLOGIST
PISSASPHALT	PITYROSPORUM	PLAGIARIZING	PLANETOLOGISTS
PISSASPHALTS	PITYROSPORUMS	PLAGIOCEPHALIES	PLANETOLOGY

PLANETWIDE	PLASMODESM	PLASTIDIAL	PLATITUDINISER
PLANGENCIES	PLASMODESMA	PLASTIDULE	PLATITUDINISERS
PLANGENTLY	PLASMODESMAS	PLASTIDULES	PLATITUDINISES
PLANIGRAPH	PLASMODESMATA	PLASTILINA	PLATITUDINISING
PLANIGRAPHS	PLASMODESMS	PLASTILINAS	PLATITUDINIZE
PLANIMETER	PLASMODIAL	PLASTIQUES	PLATITUDINIZED
PLANIMETERS	PLASMODIUM	PLASTISOLS	PLATITUDINIZER
PLANIMETRIC	PLASMOGAMIES	PLASTOCYANIN	PLATITUDINIZERS
PLANIMETRICAL	PLASMOGAMY	PLASTOCYANINS	PLATITUDINIZES
PLANIMETRICALLY	PLASMOLYSE	PLASTOGAMIES	PLATITUDINIZING
PLANIMETRIES	PLASMOLYSED	PLASTOGAMY	PLATITUDINOUS
PLANIMETRY	PLASMOLYSES	PLASTOMETER	PLATITUDINOUSLY
PLANISHERS	PLASMOLYSING	PLASTOMETERS	PLATONICALLY
PLANISHING	PLASMOLYSIS	PLASTOMETRIC	PLATONISMS
PLANISPHERE	PLASMOLYTIC	PLASTOMETRIES	PLATOONING
PLANISPHERES	PLASMOLYTICALLY	PLASTOMETRY	PLATTELAND
PLANISPHERIC	PLASMOLYZE	PLASTOQUINONE	PLATTELANDS
PLANKTONIC	PLASMOLYZED	PLASTOQUINONES	PLATTERFUL
PLANLESSLY	PLASMOLYZES	PLATANACEOUS	PLATTERFULS
PLANLESSNESS	PLASMOLYZING	PLATEAUING	PLATTERSFUL
PLANLESSNESSES	PLASMOSOMA	PLATEGLASS	PLATYCEPHALIC
PLANOBLAST	PLASMOSOMATA	PLATELAYER	PLATYCEPHALOUS
PLANOBLASTS	PLASMOSOME	PLATELAYERS	PLATYFISHES
PLANOGAMETE	PLASMOSOMES	PLATEMAKER	PLATYHELMINTH
PLANOGAMETES	PLASTERBOARD	PLATEMAKERS	PLATYHELMINTHIC
PLANOGRAPHIC	PLASTERBOARDS	PLATEMAKING	PLATYHELMINTHS
PLANOGRAPHIES	PLASTERERS	PLATEMAKINGS	PLATYKURTIC
PLANOGRAPHY	PLASTERINESS	PLATEMARKED	PLATYPUSES
PLANOMETER	PLASTERINESSES	PLATEMARKING	PLATYRRHINE
PLANOMETERS	PLASTERING	PLATEMARKS	PLATYRRHINES
PLANOMETRIC	PLASTERINGS	PLATERESQUE	PLATYRRHINIAN
PLANOMETRICALLY	PLASTERSTONE	PLATFORMED	PLATYRRHINIANS
PLANOMETRIES	PLASTERSTONES	PLATFORMING	PLAUDITORY
PLANOMETRY	PLASTERWORK	PLATFORMINGS	PLAUSIBILITIES
PLANTAGINACEOUS	PLASTERWORKS	PLATINIFEROUS	PLAUSIBILITY
PLANTATION	PLASTICALLY	PLATINIRIDIUM	PLAUSIBLENESS
PLANTATIONS	PLASTICENE	PLATINIRIDIUMS	PLAUSIBLENESSES
PLANTIGRADE	PLASTICENES	PLATINISATION	PLAYABILITIES
PLANTIGRADES	PLASTICINE	PLATINISATIONS	PLAYABILITY
PLANTLINGS	PLASTICINES	PLATINISED	PLAYACTING
PLANTOCRACIES	PLASTICISATION	PLATINISES	PLAYACTINGS
PLANTOCRACY	PLASTICISATIONS	PLATINISING	PLAYACTORS
PLANTSWOMAN	PLASTICISE	PLATINIZATION	PLAYBUSSES
PLANTSWOMEN	PLASTICISED	PLATINIZATIONS	PLAYFELLOW
PLANULIFORM	PLASTICISER	PLATINIZED	PLAYFELLOWS
PLAQUETTES	PLASTICISERS	PLATINIZES	PLAYFIELDS
PLASMAGELS	PLASTICISES	PLATINIZING	PLAYFULNESS
PLASMAGENE	PLASTICISING	PLATINOCYANIC	PLAYFULNESSES
PLASMAGENES	PLASTICITIES	PLATINOCYANIDE	PLAYGOINGS
PLASMAGENIC	PLASTICITY	PLATINOCYANIDES	PLAYGROUND
PLASMALEMMA	PLASTICIZATION	PLATINOIDS	PLAYGROUNDS
PLASMALEMMAS	PLASTICIZATIONS	PLATINOTYPE	PLAYGROUPS
PLASMAPHERESES	PLASTICIZE	PLATINOTYPES	PLAYHOUSES
PLASMAPHERESIS	PLASTICIZED	PLATITUDES	PLAYLEADER
PLASMASOLS	PLASTICIZER	PLATITUDINAL	PLAYLEADERS
PLASMATICAL	PLASTICIZERS	PLATITUDINARIAN	PLAYLISTED
PLASMINOGEN	PLASTICIZES	PLATITUDINISE	PLAYLISTING
PLASMINOGENS	PLASTICIZING	PLATITUDINISED	PLAYMAKERS

PLAYMAKING	PLEINAIRISMS	PLEROPHORIES	PLOUGHABLE
PLAYMAKINGS	PLEINAIRIST	PLEROPHORY	PLOUGHBOYS
PLAYSCHOOL	PLEINAIRISTS	PLESIOSAUR	PLOUGHGATE
PLAYSCHOOLS	PLEIOCHASIA	PLESIOSAURIAN	PLOUGHGATES
PLAYTHINGS	PLEIOCHASIUM	PLESIOSAURS	PLOUGHHEAD
PLAYWRIGHT	PLEIOMERIES	PLESSIMETER	PLOUGHHEADS
PLAYWRIGHTING	PLEIOMEROUS	PLESSIMETERS	PLOUGHINGS
PLAYWRIGHTINGS	PLEIOTAXIES	PLESSIMETRIC	PLOUGHLAND
PLAYWRIGHTS	PLEIOTROPIC	PLESSIMETRIES	PLOUGHLANDS
PLAYWRITING	PLEIOTROPIES	PLESSIMETRY	PLOUGHMANSHIP
PLAYWRITINGS	PLEIOTROPISM	PLETHORICAL	PLOUGHMANSHIPS
PLEADINGLY	PLEIOTROPISMS	PLETHORICALLY	PLOUGHSHARE
PLEASANCES	PLEIOTROPY	PLETHYSMOGRAM	PLOUGHSHARES
PLEASANTER	PLENARTIES	PLETHYSMOGRAMS	PLOUGHSTAFF
PLEASANTEST	PLENILUNAR	PLETHYSMOGRAPH	PLOUGHSTAFFS
PLEASANTLY	PLENILUNES	PLETHYSMOGRAPHS	PLOUGHTAIL
PLEASANTNESS	PLENIPOTENCE	PLETHYSMOGRAPHY	PLOUGHTAILS
PLEASANTNESSES	PLENIPOTENCES	PLEURAPOPHYSES	PLOUGHWISE
PLEASANTRIES	PLENIPOTENCIES	PLEURAPOPHYSIS	PLOUGHWRIGHT
PLEASANTRY	PLENIPOTENCY	PLEURISIES	PLOUGHWRIGHTS
PLEASINGLY	PLENIPOTENT	PLEURITICAL	PLOUTERING
PLEASINGNESS	PLENIPOTENTIAL	PLEURITICS	PLOWMANSHIP
PLEASINGNESSES	PLENIPOTENTIARY	PLEURITISES	PLOWMANSHIPS
PLEASURABILITY	PLENISHERS	PLEUROCARPOUS	PLOWSHARES
PLEASURABLE	PLENISHING	PLEUROCENTESES	PLOWSTAFFS
PLEASURABLENESS	PLENISHINGS	PLEUROCENTESIS	PLOWTERING
PLEASURABLY	PLENISHMENT	PLEURODONT	PLUCKINESS
PLEASUREFUL	PLENISHMENTS	PLEURODONTS	PLUCKINESSES
PLEASURELESS	PLENITUDES	PLEURODYNIA	PLUGBOARDS
PLEASURERS	PLENITUDINOUS	PLEURODYNIAS	PLUGUGLIES
PLEASURING	PLENTEOUSLY	PLEUROPNEUMONIA	PLUMASSIER
PLEBEIANISE	PLENTEOUSNESS	PLEUROTOMIES	PLUMASSIERS
PLEBEIANISED	PLENTEOUSNESSES	PLEUROTOMY	PLUMBAGINACEOUS
PLEBEIANISES	PLENTIFULLY	PLEUSTONIC	PLUMBAGINOUS
PLEBEIANISING	PLENTIFULNESS	PLEXIGLASS	PLUMBERIES
PLEBEIANISM	PLENTIFULNESSES	PLEXIGLASSES	PLUMBIFEROUS
PLEBEIANISMS	PLENTITUDE	PLEXIMETER	PLUMBISOLVENCY
PLEBEIANIZE	PLENTITUDES	PLEXIMETERS	PLUMBISOLVENT
PLEBEIANIZED	PLEOCHROIC	PLEXIMETRIC	PLUMBNESSES
PLEBEIANIZES	PLEOCHROISM	PLEXIMETRIES	PLUMBOSOLVENCY
PLEBEIANIZING	PLEOCHROISMS	PLEXIMETRY	PLUMBOSOLVENT
PLEBEIANLY	PLEOMORPHIC	PLIABILITIES	PLUMDAMASES
PLEBIFICATION	PLEOMORPHIES	PLIABILITY	PLUMIGEROUS
PLEBIFICATIONS	PLEOMORPHISM	PLIABLENESS	PLUMMETING
PLEBIFYING	PLEOMORPHISMS	PLIABLENESSES	PLUMOSITIES
PLEBISCITARY	PLEOMORPHOUS	PLIANTNESS	PLUMPENING
PLEBISCITE	PLEOMORPHY	PLIANTNESSES	PLUMPNESSES
PLEBISCITES	PLEONASTES	PLICATENESS	PLUMULACEOUS
PLECOPTERAN	PLEONASTIC	PLICATENESSES	PLUMULARIAN
PLECOPTERANS	PLEONASTICAL	PLICATIONS	PLUMULARIANS
PLECOPTEROUS	PLEONASTICALLY	PLICATURES	PLUNDERABLE
PLECTOGNATH	PLEONECTIC	PLODDINGLY	PLUNDERAGE
PLECTOGNATHIC	PLEONEXIAS	PLODDINGNESS	PLUNDERAGES
PLECTOGNATHOUS	PLEROCERCOID	PLODDINGNESSES	PLUNDERERS
PLECTOGNATHS	PLEROCERCOIDS	PLOTLESSNESS	PLUNDERING
PLECTOPTEROUS	PLEROMATIC	PLOTLESSNESSES	PLUNDEROUS
PLEDGEABLE	PLEROPHORIA	PLOTTERING	PLUPERFECT
PLEINAIRISM	PLEROPHORIAS	PLOTTINGLY	PLUPERFECTS

PLURALISATION	PNEUMATICALLY	POCKETKNIVES	PODZOLIZATION
PLURALISATIONS	PNEUMATICITIES	POCKETLESS	PODZOLIZATIONS
PLURALISED	PNEUMATICITY	POCKETPHONE	PODZOLIZED
PLURALISER	PNEUMATICS	POCKETPHONES	PODZOLIZES
PLURALISERS	PNEUMATOLOGICAL	POCKETSFUL	PODZOLIZING
PLURALISES	PNEUMATOLOGIES	POCKMANKIES	POENOLOGIES
PLURALISING	PNEUMATOLOGIST	POCKMANTIE	POETASTERIES
PLURALISMS	PNEUMATOLOGISTS	POCKMANTIES	POETASTERING
PLURALISTIC	PNEUMATOLOGY	POCKMARKED	POETASTERINGS
PLURALISTICALLY	PNEUMATOLYSES	POCKMARKING	POETASTERS
PLURALISTS	PNEUMATOLYSIS	POCKPITTED	POETASTERY
PLURALITIES	PNEUMATOLYTIC	POCKPITTING	POETASTRIES
PLURALIZATION	PNEUMATOMETER	POCOCURANTE	POETICALLY
PLURALIZATIONS	PNEUMATOMETERS	POCOCURANTEISM	POETICALNESS
PLURALIZED	PNEUMATOMETRIES	POCOCURANTEISMS	POETICALNESSES
PLURALIZER	PNEUMATOMETRY	POCOCURANTES	POETICISED
PLURALIZERS	PNEUMATOPHORE	POCOCURANTISM	POETICISES
PLURALIZES	PNEUMATOPHORES	POCOCURANTISMS	POETICISING
PLURALIZING	PNEUMECTOMIES	POCOCURANTIST	POETICISMS
PLURILITERAL	PNEUMECTOMY	POCOCURANTISTS	POETICIZED
PLURILOCULAR	PNEUMOBACILLI	POCULIFORM	POETICIZES
PLURIPARAE	PNEUMOBACILLUS	PODAGRICAL	POETICIZING
PLURIPARAS	PNEUMOCOCCAL	PODARGUSES	POETICULES
PLURIPOTENT	PNEUMOCOCCI	PODCASTERS	POETRESSES
PLURIPRESENCE	PNEUMOCOCCUS	PODCASTING	POGONOPHORAN
PLURIPRESENCES	PNEUMOCONIOSES	PODCASTINGS	POGONOPHORANS
PLURISERIAL	PNEUMOCONIOSIS	PODGINESSES	POGONOTOMIES
PLURISERIATE	PNEUMOCONIOTIC	PODIATRIES	POGONOTOMY
PLUSHINESS	PNEUMOCONIOTICS	PODIATRIST	POGROMISTS
PLUSHINESSES	PNEUMOCYSTIS	PODIATRISTS	POHUTUKAWA
PLUSHNESSES	PNEUMOCYSTISES	PODOCONIOSES	POHUTUKAWAS
PLUTOCRACIES	PNEUMODYNAMICS	PODOCONIOSIS	POIGNADOES
PLUTOCRACY	PNEUMOGASTRIC	PODOLOGIES	POIGNANCES
PLUTOCRATIC	PNEUMOGASTRICS	PODOLOGIST	POIGNANCIES
PLUTOCRATICAL	PNEUMOGRAM	PODOLOGISTS	POIGNANTLY
PLUTOCRATICALLY	PNEUMOGRAMS	PODOPHTHALMOUS	POIKILITIC
PLUTOCRATS	PNEUMOGRAPH	PODOPHYLIN	POIKILOCYTE
PLUTOLATRIES	PNEUMOGRAPHS	PODOPHYLINS	POIKILOCYTES
PLUTOLATRY	PNEUMOKONIOSES	PODOPHYLLI	POIKILOTHERM
PLUTOLOGIES	PNEUMOKONIOSIS	PODOPHYLLIN	POIKILOTHERMAL
PLUTOLOGIST	PNEUMONECTOMIES	PODOPHYLLINS	POIKILOTHERMIC
PLUTOLOGISTS	PNEUMONECTOMY	PODOPHYLLUM	POIKILOTHERMIES
PLUTONISMS	PNEUMONIAS	PODOPHYLLUMS	POIKILOTHERMISM
PLUTONIUMS	PNEUMONICS	PODSOLISATION	POIKILOTHERMS
PLUTONOMIES	PNEUMONITIS	PODSOLISATIONS	POIKILOTHERMY
PLUTONOMIST	PNEUMONITISES	PODSOLISED	POINCIANAS
PLUTONOMISTS	PNEUMOTHORACES	PODSOLISES	POINSETTIA
PLUVIOMETER	PNEUMOTHORAX	PODSOLISING	POINSETTIAS
PLUVIOMETERS	PNEUMOTHORAXES	PODSOLIZATION	POINTEDNESS
PLUVIOMETRIC	POACHINESS	PODSOLIZATIONS	POINTEDNESSES
PLUVIOMETRICAL	POACHINESSES	PODSOLIZED	POINTELLES
PLUVIOMETRIES	POCKETABLE	PODSOLIZES	POINTILLISM
PLUVIOMETRY	POCKETBIKE	PODSOLIZING	POINTILLISME
PLYOMETRIC	POCKETBIKES	PODZOLISATION	POINTILLISMES
PLYOMETRICS	POCKETBOOK	PODZOLISATIONS	POINTILLISMS
PNEUMATHODE	POCKETBOOKS	PODZOLISED	POINTILLIST
PNEUMATHODES	POCKETFULS	PODZOLISES	POINTILLISTE
PNEUMATICAL	POCKETKNIFE	PODZOLISING	POINTILLISTES

POINTILLISTIC	POLEMONIACEOUS	POLLENATING	POLYALCOHOLS
POINTILLISTS	POLEMONIUM	POLLENIFEROUS	POLYAMIDES
POINTLESSLY	POLEMONIUMS	POLLENISER	POLYAMINES
POINTLESSNESS	POLIANITES	POLLENISERS	POLYANDRIES
POINTLESSNESSES	POLICEWOMAN	POLLENIZER	POLYANDROUS
POISONABLE	POLICEWOMEN	POLLENIZERS	POLYANTHAS
POISONOUSLY	POLICYHOLDER	POLLENOSES	POLYANTHUS
POISONOUSNESS	POLICYHOLDERS	POLLENOSIS	POLYANTHUSES
POISONOUSNESSES	POLIOMYELITIDES	POLLICITATION	POLYARCHIES
POISONWOOD	POLIOMYELITIS	POLLICITATIONS	POLYATOMIC
POISONWOODS	POLIOMYELITISES	POLLINATED	POLYAXIALS
POKEBERRIES	POLIORCETIC	POLLINATES	POLYAXONIC
POKELOGANS	POLIORCETICS	POLLINATING	POLYBASITE
POKERISHLY	POLIOVIRUS	POLLINATION	POLYBASITES
POKERWORKS	POLIOVIRUSES	POLLINATIONS	POLYBUTADIENE
POKINESSES	POLISHABLE	POLLINATOR	POLYBUTADIENES
POLARTMETER	POLISHINGS	POLLINATORS	POLYCARBONATE
POLARIMETERS	POLISHMENT	POLLINIFEROUS	POLYCARBONATES
POLARIMETRIC	POLISHMENTS	POLLINISED	POLYCARBOXYLATE
POLARIMETRIES	POLITBUROS	POLLINISER	POLYCARBOXYLIC
POLARIMETRY	POLITENESS	POLLINISERS	POLYCARPELLARY
POLARISABLE	POLITENESSES	POLLINISES	POLYCARPIC
POLARISATION	POLITESSES	POLLINISING	POLYCARPIES
POLARISATIONS	POLITICALISE	POLLINIZED	POLYCARPOUS
POLARISCOPE	POLITICALISED	POLLINIZER	POLYCENTRIC
POLARISCOPES	POLITICALISES	POLLINIZERS	POLYCENTRISM
POLARISCOPIC	POLITICALISING	POLLINIZES	POLYCENTRISMS
POLARISERS	POLITICALIZE	POLLINIZING	POLYCHAETE
POLARISING	POLITICALIZED	POLLINOSES	POLYCHAETES
POLARITIES	POLITICALIZES	POLLINOSIS	POLYCHAETOUS
POLARIZABILITY	POLITICALIZING	POLLTAKERS	POLYCHASIA
POLARIZABLE	POLITICALLY	POLLUCITES	POLYCHASIUM
POLARIZATION	POLITICASTER	POLLUSIONS	POLYCHETES
POLARIZATIONS	POLITICASTERS	POLLUTANTS	POLYCHLORINATED
POLARIZERS	POLITICIAN	POLLUTEDLY	POLYCHLOROPRENE
POLARIZING	POLITICIANS	POLLUTEDNESS	POLYCHOTOMIES
POLAROGRAM	POLITICISATION	POLLUTEDNESSES	POLYCHOTOMOUS
POLAROGRAMS	POLITICISATIONS	POLLUTIONS	POLYCHOTOMY
POLAROGRAPH	POLITICISE	POLLYANNAISH	POLYCHREST
POLAROGRAPHIC	POLITICISED	POLLYANNAISM	POLYCHRESTS
POLAROGRAPHIES	POLITICISES	POLLYANNAISMS	POLYCHROIC
POLAROGRAPHS	POLITICISING	POLLYANNAS	POLYCHROISM
POLAROGRAPHY	POLITICIZATION	POLLYANNISH	POLYCHROISMS
POLEMARCHES	POLITICIZATIONS	POLONAISES	POLYCHROMATIC
POLEMARCHS	POLITICIZE	POLONISING	POLYCHROMATISM
POLEMICALLY	POLITICIZED	POLONIZING	POLYCHROMATISMS
POLEMICISE	POLITICIZES	POLTERGEIST	POLYCHROME
POLEMICISED	POLITICIZING	POLTERGEISTS	POLYCHROMED
POLEMICISES	POLITICKED	POLTFOOTED	POLYCHROMES
POLEMICISING	POLITICKER	POLTROONERIES	POLYCHROMIC
POLEMICIST	POLITICKERS	POLTROONERY	POLYCHROMIES
POLEMICISTS	POLITICKING	POLVERINES	POLYCHROMING
POLEMICIZE	POLITICKINGS	POLYACRYLAMIDE	POLYCHROMOUS
POLEMICIZED	POLITICOES	POLYACRYLAMIDES	POLYCHROMY
POLEMICIZES	POLITIQUES	POLYACTINAL	POLYCISTRONIC
POLEMICIZING	POLLARDING	POLYACTINE	POLYCLINIC
POLEMISING	POLLENATED	POLYADELPHOUS	POLYCLINICS
POLEMIZING	POLLENATES	POLYALCOHOL	POLYCLONAL

POLYCOTTON	POLYGAMIZING	POLYHYBRID	POLYOLEFIN
POLYCOTTONS	POLYGAMOUS	POLYHYBRIDS	POLYOLEFINS
POLYCOTYLEDON	POLYGAMOUSLY	POLYHYDRIC	POLYOMINOS
POLYCOTYLEDONS	POLYGENESES	POLYHYDROXY	POLYONYMIC
POLYCROTIC	POLYGENESIS	POLYIMIDES	POLYONYMIES
POLYCROTISM	POLYGENETIC	POLYISOPRENE	POLYONYMOUS
POLYCROTISMS	POLYGENETICALLY	POLYISOPRENES	POLYPARIES
POLYCRYSTAL	POLYGENIES	POLYLEMMAS	POLYPARIUM
POLYCRYSTALLINE	POLYGENISM	POLYLYSINE	POLYPEPTIDE
POLYCRYSTALS	POLYGENISMS	POLYLYSINES	POLYPEPTIDES
POLYCULTURE	POLYGENIST	POLYMASTIA	POLYPEPTIDIC
POLYCULTURES	POLYGENISTS	POLYMASTIAS	POLYPETALOUS
POLYCYCLIC	POLYGENOUS	POLYMASTIC	POLYPHAGIA
POLYCYCLICS	POLYGLOTISM	POLYMASTIES	POLYPHAGIAS
POLYCYSTIC	POLYGLOTISMS	POLYMASTISM	POLYPHAGIES
POLYCYTHAEMIA	POLYGLOTTAL	POLYMASTISMS	POLYPHAGOUS
POLYCYTHAEMIAS	POLYGLOTTIC	POLYMATHIC	POLYPHARMACIES
POLYCYTHEMIA	POLYGLOTTISM	POLYMATHIES	POLYPHARMACY
POLYCYTHEMIAS	POLYGLOTTISMS	POLYMERASE	POLYPHASIC
POLYCYTHEMIC	POLYGLOTTOUS	POLYMERASES	POLYPHENOL
POLYDACTYL	POLYGLOTTS	POLYMERIDE	POLYPHENOLIC
POLYDACTYLIES	POLYGONACEOUS	POLYMERIDES	POLYPHENOLS
POLYDACTYLISM	POLYGONALLY	POLYMERIES	POLYPHLOESBOEAN
POLYDACTYLISMS	POLYGONATUM	POLYMERISATION	POLYPHLOISBIC
POLYDACTYLOUS	POLYGONATUMS	POLYMERISATIONS	POLYPHONES
POLYDACTYLS	POLYGONIES	POLYMERISE	POLYPHONIC
POLYDACTYLY	POLYGONUMS	POLYMERISED	POLYPHONICALLY
POLYDAEMONISM	POLYGRAPHED	POLYMERISES	POLYPHONIES
POLYDAEMONISMS	POLYGRAPHER	POLYMERISING	POLYPHONIST
POLYDEMONISM	POLYGRAPHERS	POLYMERISM	POLYPHONISTS
POLYDEMONISMS	POLYGRAPHIC	POLYMERISMS	POLYPHONOUS
POLYDIPSIA	POLYGRAPHICALLY	POLYMERIZATION	POLYPHONOUSLY
POLYDIPSIAS	POLYGRAPHIES	POLYMERIZATIONS	POLYPHOSPHORIC
POLYDIPSIC	POLYGRAPHING	POLYMERIZE	POLYPHYLETIC
POLYDISPERSE	POLYGRAPHIST	POLYMERIZED	POLYPHYLLOUS
POLYDISPERSITY	POLYGRAPHISTS	POLYMERIZES	POLYPHYODONT
POLYELECTROLYTE	POLYGRAPHS	POLYMERIZING	POLYPIDOMS
POLYEMBRYONATE	POLYGRAPHY	POLYMEROUS	POLYPLOIDAL
POLYEMBRYONIC	POLYGYNIAN	POLYMORPHIC	POLYPLOIDIC
POLYEMBRYONIES	POLYGYNIES	POLYMORPHICALLY	POLYPLOIDIES
POLYEMBRYONY	POLYGYNIST	POLYMORPHISM	POLYPLOIDS
POLYESTERS	POLYGYNISTS	POLYMORPHISMS	POLYPLOIDY
POLYESTROUS	POLYGYNOUS	POLYMORPHOUS	POLYPODIES
POLYETHENE	POLYHALITE	POLYMORPHOUSLY	POLYPODOUS
POLYETHENES	POLYHALITES	POLYMORPHS	POLYPROPENE
POLYETHYLENE	POLYHEDRAL	POLYMYOSITIS	POLYPROPENES
POLYETHYLENES	POLYHEDRIC	POLYMYOSITISES	POLYPROPYLENE
POLYGALACEOUS	POLYHEDRON	POLYMYXINS	POLYPROPYLENES
POLYGAMIES	POLYHEDRONS	POLYNEURITIS	POLYPROTODONT
POLYGAMISE	POLYHEDROSES	POLYNEURITISES	POLYPROTODONTS
POLYGAMISED	POLYHEDROSIS	POLYNOMIAL	POLYPTYCHS
POLYGAMISES	POLYHISTOR	POLYNOMIALISM	POLYRHYTHM
POLYGAMISING	POLYHISTORIAN	POLYNOMIALISMS	POLYRHYTHMIC
POLYGAMIST	POLYHISTORIANS	POLYNOMIALS	POLYRHYTHMS
POLYGAMISTS	POLYHISTORIC	POLYNUCLEAR	POLYRIBOSOMAL
POLYGAMIZE	POLYHISTORIES	POLYNUCLEATE	POLYRIBOSOME
POLYGAMIZED	POLYHISTORS	POLYNUCLEOTIDE	POLYRIBOSOMES
POLYGAMIZES	POLYHISTORY	POLYNUCLEOTIDES	POLYSACCHARIDE

POLYSACCHARIDES	POLYTONALIST	PONDERANCE	POPPERINGS
POLYSACCHAROSE	POLYTONALISTS	PONDERANCES	POPPYCOCKS
POLYSACCHAROSES	POLYTONALITIES	PONDERANCIES	POPPYHEADS
POLYSEMANT	POLYTONALITY	PONDERANCY	POPULARISATION
POLYSEMANTS	POLYTONALLY	PONDERATED	POPULARISATIONS
POLYSEMIES	POLYTROPHIC	PONDERATES	POPULARISE
POLYSEMOUS	POLYTUNNEL	PONDERATING	POPULARISED
POLYSEPALOUS	POLYTUNNELS	PONDERATION	POPULARISER
POLYSILOXANE	POLYTYPICAL	PONDERATIONS	POPULARISERS
POLYSILOXANES	POLYUNSATURATED	PONDERINGLY	POPULARISES
POLYSOMICS	POLYURETHAN	PONDERMENT	POPULARISING
POLYSOMIES	POLYURETHANE	PONDERMENTS	POPULARITIES
POLYSORBATE	POLYURETHANES	PONDEROSAS	POPULARITY
POLYSORBATES	POLYURETHANS	PONDEROSITIES	POPULARIZATION
POLYSTICHOUS	POLYVALENCE	PONDEROSITY	POPULARIZATIONS
POLYSTYLAR	POLYVALENCES	PONDEROUSLY	POPULARIZE
POLYSTYLES	POLYVALENCIES	PONDEROUSNESS	POPULARIZED
POLYSTYRENE	POLYVALENCY	PONDEROUSNESSES	POPULARIZER
POLYSTYRENES	POLYVALENT	PONDOKKIES	POPULARIZERS
POLYSULFIDE	POLYVINYLIDENE	PONEROLOGIES	POPULARIZES
POLYSULFIDES	POLYVINYLIDENES	PONEROLOGY	POPULARIZING
POLYSULPHIDE	POLYVINYLS	PONIARDING	POPULATING
POLYSULPHIDES	POLYWATERS	PONTIANACS	POPULATION
POLYSYLLABIC	POLYZOARIA	PONTIANAKS	POPULATIONAL
POLYSYLLABICAL	POLYZOARIAL	PONTICELLO	POPULATIONS
POLYSYLLABICISM	POLYZOARIES	PONTICELLOS	POPULISTIC
POLYSYLLABISM	POLYZOARIUM	PONTIFICAL	POPULOUSLY
POLYSYLLABISMS	POMEGRANATE	PONTIFICALITIES	POPULOUSNESS
POLYSYLLABLE	POMEGRANATES	PONTIFICALITY	POPULOUSNESSES
POLYSYLLABLES	POMICULTURE	PONTIFICALLY	PORBEAGLES
POLYSYLLOGISM	POMICULTURES	PONTIFICALS	PORCELAINEOUS
POLYSYLLOGISMS	POMIFEROUS	PONTIFICATE	PORCELAINISE
POLYSYNAPTIC	POMMELLING	PONTIFICATED	PORCELAINISED
POLYSYNDETON	POMOERIUMS	PONTIFICATES	PORCELAINISES
POLYSYNDETONS	POMOLOGICAL	PONTIFICATING	PORCELAINISING
POLYSYNTHESES	POMOLOGICALLY	PONTIFICATION	PORCELAINIZE
POLYSYNTHESIS	POMOLOGIES	PONTIFICATIONS	PORCELAINIZED
POLYSYNTHESISM	POMOLOGIST	PONTIFICATOR	PORCELAINIZES
POLYSYNTHESISMS	POMOLOGISTS	PONTIFICATORS	PORCELAINIZING
POLYSYNTHETIC	POMOSEXUAL	PONTIFICES	PORCELAINLIKE
POLYSYNTHETICAL	POMOSEXUALS	PONTIFYING	PORCELAINOUS
POLYSYNTHETISM	POMPADOURED	PONTLEVISES	PORCELAINS
POLYSYNTHETISMS	POMPADOURS	PONTONEERS	PORCELANEOUS
POLYTECHNIC	POMPELMOOSE	PONTONIERS	PORCELLANEOUS
POLYTECHNICAL	POMPELMOOSES	PONTONNIER	PORCELLANISE
POLYTECHNICS	POMPELMOUS	PONTONNIERS	PORCELLANISED
POLYTENIES	POMPELMOUSE	PONTOONERS	PORCELLANISES
POLYTHALAMOUS	POMPELMOUSES	PONTOONING	PORCELLANISING
POLYTHEISM	POMPHOLYGOUS	PONYTAILED	PORCELLANITE
POLYTHEISMS	POMPHOLYXES	POORHOUSES	PORCELLANITES
POLYTHEIST	POMPOSITIES	POORMOUTHED	PORCELLANIZE
POLYTHEISTIC	POMPOUSNESS	POORMOUTHING	PORCELLANIZED
POLYTHEISTICAL	POMPOUSNESSES	POORMOUTHS	PORCELLANIZES
POLYTHEISTS	PONDERABILITIES	POORNESSES	PORCELLANIZING
POLYTHENES	PONDERABILITY	POPLINETTE	PORCELLANOUS
POLYTOCOUS	PONDERABLE	POPLINETTES	PORCUPINES
POLYTONALISM	PONDERABLES	POPMOBILITIES	PORCUPINISH
POLYTONALISMS	PONDERABLY	POPMOBILITY	PORIFERANS

PORIFEROUS	PORTAMENTO	POSITIVENESS	POSTCLASSIC
PORINESSES	PORTAPACKS	POSITIVENESSES	POSTCLASSICAL
PORISMATIC	PORTATIVES	POSITIVEST	POSTCODING
PORISMATICAL	PORTCULLIS	POSITIVISM	POSTCOITAL
PORISTICAL	PORTCULLISED	POSITIVISMS	POSTCOLLEGE
PORKINESSES	PORTCULLISES	POSITIVIST	POSTCOLLEGIATE
PORLOCKING	PORTCULLISING	POSITIVISTIC	POSTCOLONIAL
PORLOCKINGS	PORTENDING	POSITIVISTS	POSTCONCEPTION
PORNOCRACIES	PORTENTOUS	POSITIVITIES	POSTCONCERT
PORNOCRACY	PORTENTOUSLY	POSITIVITY	POSTCONQUEST
PORNOGRAPHER	PORTENTOUSNESS	POSITRONIUM	POSTCONSONANTAL
PORNOGRAPHERS	PORTEOUSES	POSITRONIUMS	POSTCONVENTION
PORNOGRAPHIC	PORTERAGES	POSOLOGICAL	POSTCOPULATORY
PORNOGRAPHIES	PORTERESSES	POSOLOGIES	POSTCORONARY
PORNOGRAPHY	PORTERHOUSE	POSSESSABLE	POSTCRANIAL
PORNOTOPIA	PORTERHOUSES	POSSESSEDLY	POSTCRANIALLY
PORNOTOPIAN	PORTFOLIOS	POSSESSEDNESS	POSTCRISIS
PORNOTOPIAS	PORTHORSES	POSSESSEDNESSES	POSTDATING
POROGAMIES	PORTHOUSES	POSSESSING	POSTDEADLINE
POROMERICS	PORTIONERS	POSSESSION	POSTDEBATE
POROSCOPES	PORTIONING	POSSESSIONAL	POSTDEBUTANTE
POROSCOPIC	PORTIONIST	POSSESSIONARY	POSTDELIVERY
POROSCOPIES	PORTIONISTS	POSSESSIONATE	POSTDEPRESSION
POROSITIES	PORTIONLESS	POSSESSIONATES	POSTDEVALUATION
POROUSNESS	PORTLINESS	POSSESSIONED	POSTDILUVIAL
POROUSNESSES	PORTLINESSES	POSSESSIONLESS	POSTDILUVIAN
PORPENTINE	PORTMANTEAU	POSSESSIONS	POSTDILUVIANS
PORPENTINES	PORTMANTEAUS	POSSESSIVE	POSTDIVESTITURE
PORPHYRIAS	PORTMANTEAUX	POSSESSIVELY	POSTDIVORCE
PORPHYRIES	PORTMANTLE	POSSESSIVENESS	POSTDOCTORAL
PORPHYRINS	PORTMANTLES	POSSESSIVES	POSTDOCTORATE
PORPHYRIOS	PORTMANTUA	POSSESSORS	POSTEDITING
PORPHYRITE	PORTMANTUAS	POSSESSORSHIP	POSTELECTION
PORPHYRITES	PORTOBELLO	POSSESSORSHIPS	POSTEMBRYONAL
PORPHYRITIC	PORTOBELLOS	POSSESSORY	POSTEMBRYONIC
PORPHYROGENITE	PORTOLANOS	POSSIBILISM	POSTEMERGENCE
PORPHYROGENITES	PORTRAITED	POSSIBILISMS	POSTEMERGENCY
PORPHYROID	PORTRAITING	POSSIBILIST	POSTEPILEPTIC
PORPHYROIDS	PORTRAITIST	POSSIBILISTS	POSTERIORITIES
PORPHYROPSIN	PORTRAITISTS	POSSIBILITIES	POSTERIORITY
PORPHYROPSINS	PORTRAITURE	POSSIBILITY	POSTERIORLY
PORPHYROUS	PORTRAITURES	POSSIBLEST	POSTERIORS
PORPOISING	PORTRAYABLE	POSTABORTION	POSTERISATION
PORRACEOUS	PORTRAYALS	POSTACCIDENT	POSTERISATIONS
PORRECTING	PORTRAYERS	POSTADOLESCENT	POSTERITIES
PORRECTION	PORTRAYING	POSTAMPUTATION	POSTERIZATION
PORRECTIONS	PORTREEVES	POSTAPOCALYPTIC	POSTERIZATIONS
PORRENGERS	PORTRESSES	POSTARREST	POSTEROLATERAL
PORRIGINOUS	PORTULACACEOUS	POSTATOMIC	POSTERUPTIVE
PORRINGERS	PORTULACAS	POSTATTACK	POSTEXERCISE
PORTABELLA	PORWIGGLES	POSTBELLUM	POSTEXILIAN
PORTABELLAS	POSHNESSES	POSTBIBLICAL	POSTEXILIC
PORTABELLO	POSIGRADES	POSTBOURGEOIS	POSTEXPERIENCE
PORTABELLOS	POSITIONAL	POSTBUSSES	POSTEXPOSURE
PORTABILITIES	POSITIONALLY	POSTCAPITALIST	POSTFEMINISM
PORTABILITY	POSITIONED	POSTCARDED	POSTFEMINISMS
PORTALLING	POSITIONING	POSTCARDING	POSTFEMINIST
PORTAMENTI	POSITIVELY	POSTCARDLIKE	POSTFEMINISTS

POSTFIXING	POSTLIMINIUM	POSTPRODUCTION	POSTWEANING
POSTFLIGHT	POSTLIMINOUS	POSTPRODUCTIONS	POSTWORKSHOP
POSTFORMED	POSTLIMINY	POSTPUBERTY	POTABILITIES
POSTFORMING	POSTLITERATE	POSTPUBESCENT	POTABILITY
POSTFRACTURE	POSTMARITAL	POSTRECESSION	POTABLENESS
POSTFREEZE	POSTMARKED	POSTRETIREMENT	POTABLENESSES
POSTGANGLIONIC	POSTMARKING	POSTRIDERS	POTAMOGETON
POSTGLACIAL	POSTMASTECTOMY	POSTROMANTIC	POTAMOGETONS
POSTGRADUATE	POSTMASTER	POSTSCENIUM	POTAMOLOGICAL
POSTGRADUATES	POSTMASTERS	POSTSCENIUMS	POTAMOLOGIES
POSTGRADUATION	POSTMASTERSHIP	POSTSCRIPT	POTAMOLOGIST
POSTHARVEST	POSTMASTERSHIPS	POSTSCRIPTS	POTAMOLOGISTS
POSTHASTES	POSTMATING	POSTSEASON	POTAMOLOGY
POSTHEMORRHAGIC	POSTMEDIEVAL	POSTSEASONS	POTASSIUMS
POSTHOLDER	POSTMENOPAUSAL	POSTSECONDARY	POTATOBUGS
POSTHOLDERS	POSTMENSTRUAL	POSTSTIMULATION	POTBELLIED
POSTHOLIDAY	POSTMERIDIAN	POSTSTIMULATORY	POTBELLIES
POSTHOLOCAUST	POSTMIDNIGHT	POSTSTIMULUS	POTBOILERS
POSTHORSES	POSTMILLENARIAN	POSTSTRIKE	POTBOILING
POSTHOSPITAL	POSTMILLENNIAL	POSTSURGICAL	POTENTATES
POSTHOUSES	POSTMISTRESS	POSTSYNAPTIC	POTENTIALITIES
POSTHUMOUS	POSTMISTRESSES	POSTSYNCED	POTENTIALITY
POSTHUMOUSLY	POSTMODERN	POSTSYNCING	POTENTIALLY
POSTHUMOUSNESS	POSTMODERNISM	POSTTENSION	POTENTIALS
POSTHYPNOTIC	POSTMODERNISMS	POSTTENSIONED	POTENTIARIES
POSTICALLY	POSTMODERNIST	POSTTENSIONING	POTENTIARY
POSTILIONS	POSTMODERNISTS	POSTTENSIONS	POTENTIATE
POSTILLATE	POSTMORTEM	POSTTRANSFUSION	POTENTIATED
POSTILLATED	POSTMORTEMS	POSTTRAUMATIC	POTENTIATES
POSTILLATES	POSTNATALLY	POSTTREATMENT	POTENTIATING
POSTILLATING	POSTNEONATAL	POSTULANCIES	POTENTIATION
POSTILLATION	POSTNUPTIAL	POSTULANCY	POTENTIATIONS
POSTILLATIONS	POSTOCULAR	POSTULANTS	POTENTIATOR
POSTILLATOR	POSTOPERATIVE	POSTULANTSHIP	POTENTIATORS
POSTILLATORS	POSTOPERATIVELY	POSTULANTSHIPS	POTENTILLA
POSTILLERS	POSTORBITAL	POSTULATED	POTENTILLAS
POSTILLING	POSTORGASMIC	POSTULATES	POTENTIOMETER
POSTILLION	POSTPARTUM	POSTULATING	POTENTIOMETERS
POSTILLIONS	POSTPERSON	POSTULATION	POTENTIOMETRIC
POSTIMPACT	POSTPERSONS	POSTULATIONAL	POTENTIOMETRIES
POSTIMPERIAL	POSTPOLLINATION	POSTULATIONALLY	POTENTIOMETRY
POSTINAUGURAL	POSTPONABLE	POSTULATIONS	POTENTISED
POSTINDUSTRIAL	POSTPONEMENT	POSTULATOR	POTENTISES
POSTINFECTION	POSTPONEMENTS	POSTULATORS	POTENTISING
POSTINJECTION	POSTPONENCE	POSTULATORY	POTENTIZED
POSTINOCULATION	POSTPONENCES	POSTULATUM	POTENTIZES
POSTIRRADIATION	POSTPONERS	POSTURISED	POTENTIZING
POSTISCHEMIC	POSTPONING	POSTURISES	POTENTNESS
POSTISOLATION	POSTPOSING	POSTURISING	POTENTNESSES
POSTLANDING	POSTPOSITION	POSTURISTS	POTHECARIES
POSTLAPSARIAN	POSTPOSITIONAL	POSTURIZED	POTHOLDERS
POSTLAUNCH	POSTPOSITIONS	POSTURIZES	POTHOLINGS
POSTLIBERATION	POSTPOSITIVE	POSTURIZING	POTHUNTERS
POSTLIMINARY	POSTPOSITIVELY	POSTVACCINAL	POTHUNTING
POSTLIMINIA	POSTPOSITIVES	POSTVACCINATION	POTHUNTINGS
POSTLIMINIARY	POSTPRANDIAL	POSTVAGOTOMY	POTICARIES
POSTLIMINIES	POSTPRIMARY	POSTVASECTOMY	POTICHOMANIA
POSTLIMINIOUS	POSTPRISON	POSTVOCALIC	POTICHOMANIAS

POTLATCHED	POWERLIFTER	PRAEPOSTORS	PRATFALLING
POTLATCHES	POWERLIFTERS	PRAESIDIUM	PRATINCOLE
POTLATCHING	POWERLIFTING	PRAESIDIUMS	PRATINCOLES
POTOMETERS	POWERLIFTINGS	PRAETORIAL	PRATTLEBOX
POTPOURRIS	POWERPLAYS	PRAETORIAN	PRATTLEBOXES
POTSHOTTING	POWERTRAIN	PRAETORIANS	PRATTLEMENT
POTTERINGLY	POWERTRAINS	PRAETORIUM	PRATTLEMENTS
POTTERINGS	POWSOWDIES	PRAETORIUMS	PRATTLINGLY
POTTINESSES	POXVIRUSES	PRAETORSHIP	PRAXEOLOGICAL
POTTINGARS	POZZOLANAS	PRAETORSHIPS	PRAXEOLOGIES
POTTINGERS	POZZOLANIC	PRAGMATICAL	PRAXEOLOGY
POTTYMOUTH	POZZUOLANA	PRAGMATICALITY	PRAXINOSCOPE
POTTYMOUTHS	POZZUOLANAS	PRAGMATICALLY	PRAXINOSCOPES
POTWALLERS	PRACHARAKS	PRAGMATICALNESS	PRAYERFULLY
POULDERING	PRACTICABILITY	PRAGMATICISM	PRAYERFULNESS
POULTERERS	PRACTICABLE	PRAGMATICISMS	PRAYERFULNESSES
POULTICING	PRACTICABLENESS	PRAGMATICIST	PRAYERLESS
POULTROONE	PRACTICABLY	PRAGMATICISTS	PRAYERLESSLY
POULTROONES	PRACTICALISM	PRAGMATICS	PRAYERLESSNESS
POULTRYMAN	PRACTICALISMS	PRAGMATISATION	PREABSORBED
POULTRYMEN	PRACTICALIST	PRAGMATISATIONS	PREABSORBING
POUNDCAKES	PRACTICALISTS	PRAGMATISE	PREABSORBS
POURBOIRES	PRACTICALITIES	PRAGMATISED	PREACCUSED
POURPARLER	PRACTICALITY	PRAGMATISER	PREACCUSES
POURPARLERS	PRACTICALLY	PRAGMATISERS	PREACCUSING
POURPOINTS	PRACTICALNESS	PRAGMATISES	PREACHABLE
POURSEWING	PRACTICALNESSES	PRAGMATISING	PREACHERSHIP
POURTRAHED	PRACTICALS	PRAGMATISM	PREACHERSHIPS
POURTRAICT	PRACTICERS	PRAGMATISMS	PREACHIEST
POURTRAICTS	PRACTICIAN	PRAGMATIST	PREACHIFIED
POURTRAYED	PRACTICIANS	PRAGMATISTIC	PREACHIFIES
POURTRAYING	PRACTICING	PRAGMATISTS	PREACHIFYING
POUSOWDIES	PRACTICUMS	PRAGMATIZATION	PREACHIFYINGS
POUSSETTED	PRACTIQUES	PRAGMATIZATIONS	PREACHINESS
POUSSETTES	PRACTISANT	PRAGMATIZE	PREACHINESSES
POUSSETTING	PRACTISANTS	PRAGMATIZED	PREACHINGLY
POUTHERING	PRACTISERS	PRAGMATIZER	PREACHINGS
POWDERIEST	PRACTISING	PRAGMATIZERS	PREACHMENT
POWDERLESS	PRACTITIONER	PRAGMATIZES	PREACHMENTS
POWDERLIKE	PRACTITIONERS	PRAGMATIZING	PREACQUAINT
POWELLISED	PRACTIVELY	PRAISEACHS	PREACQUAINTANCE
POWELLISES	PRACTOLOLS	PRAISELESS	PREACQUAINTED
POWELLISING	PRAEAMBLES	PRAISEWORTHILY	PREACQUAINTING
POWELLITES	PRAECOCIAL	PRAISEWORTHY	PREACQUAINTS
POWELLIZED	PRAECORDIAL	PRAISINGLY	PREACQUISITION
POWELLIZES	PRAEDIALITIES	PRALLTRILLER	PREADAMITE
POWELLIZING	PRAEDIALITY	PRALLTRILLERS	PREADAMITES
POWERBOATING	PRAEFECTORIAL	PRANAYAMAS	PREADAPTATION
POWERBOATINGS	PRAELECTED	PRANCINGLY	PREADAPTATIONS
POWERBOATS	PRAELECTING	PRANDIALLY	PREADAPTED
POWERFULLY	PRAELUDIUM	PRANKINGLY	PREADAPTING
POWERFULNESS	PRAEMUNIRE	PRANKISHLY	PREADAPTIVE
POWERFULNESSES	PRAEMUNIRES	PRANKISHNESS	PREADJUSTED
POWERHOUSE	PRAENOMENS	PRANKISHNESSES	PREADJUSTING
POWERHOUSES	PRAENOMINA	PRANKSTERS	PREADJUSTS
POWERLESSLY	PRAENOMINAL	PRASEODYMIUM	PREADMISSION
POWERLESSNESS	PRAENOMINALLY	PRASEODYMIUMS	PREADMISSIONS
POWERLESSNESSES	PRAEPOSTOR	PRATFALLEN	PREADMITTED

PREADMITTING	PREATTUNED	PRECEDENTIALLY	PRECIPITANCES
PREADMONISH	PREATTUNES	PRECEDENTLY	PRECIPITANCIES
PREADMONISHED	PREATTUNING	PRECEDENTS	PRECIPITANCY
PREADMONISHES	PREAUDIENCE	PRECENSORED	PRECIPITANT
PREADMONISHING	PREAUDIENCES	PRECENSORING	PRECIPITANTLY
PREADMONITION	PREAUDITED	PRECENSORS	PRECIPITANTNESS
PREADMONITIONS	PREAUDITING	PRECENTING	PRECIPITANTS
PREADOLESCENCE	PREAVERRED	PRECENTORIAL	PRECIPITATE
PREADOLESCENCES	PREAVERRING	PRECENTORS	PRECIPITATED
PREADOLESCENT	PREAXIALLY	PRECENTORSHIP	PRECIPITATELY
PREADOLESCENTS	PREBENDARIES	PRECENTORSHIPS	PRECIPITATENESS
PREADOPTED	PREBENDARY	PRECENTRESS	PRECIPITATES
PREADOPTING	PREBIBLICAL	PRECENTRESSES	PRECIPITATING
PREAGRICULTURAL	PREBIDDING	PRECENTRICES	PRECIPITATION
PREALLOTTED	PREBILLING	PRECENTRIX	PRECIPITATIONS
PREALLOTTING	PREBINDING	PRECENTRIXES	PRECIPITATIVE
PREALTERED	PREBIOLOGIC	PRECEPTIAL	PRECIPITATOR
PREALTERING	PREBIOLOGICAL	PRECEPTIVE	PRECIPITATORS
PREAMBLING	PREBLESSED	PRECEPTIVELY	PRECIPITIN
PREAMBULARY	PREBLESSES	PRECEPTORAL	PRECIPITINOGEN
PREAMBULATE	PREBLESSING	PRECEPTORATE	PRECIPITINOGENS
PREAMBULATED	PREBOARDED	PRECEPTORATES	PRECIPITINS
PREAMBULATES	PREBOARDING	PRECEPTORIAL	PRECIPITOUS
PREAMBULATING	PREBOILING	PRECEPTORIALS	PRECIPITOUSLY
PREAMBULATORY	PREBOOKING	PRECEPTORIES	PRECIPITOUSNESS
PREAMPLIFIER	PREBREAKFAST	PRECEPTORS	PRECISENESS
PREAMPLIFIERS	PREBUDGETS	PRECEPTORSHIP	PRECISENESSES
PREANESTHETIC	PREBUILDING	PRECEPTORSHIPS	PRECISIANISM
PREANNOUNCE	PREBUTTALS	PRECEPTORY	PRECISIANISMS
PREANNOUNCED	PRECALCULI	PRECEPTRESS	PRECISIANIST
PREANNOUNCES	PRECALCULUS	PRECEPTRESSES	PRECISIANISTS
PREANNOUNCING	PRECALCULUSES	PRECESSING	PRECISIANS
PREAPPLIED	PRECANCELED	PRECESSION	PRECISIONISM
PREAPPLIES	PRECANCELING	PRECESSIONAL	PRECISIONISMS
PREAPPLYING	PRECANCELLATION	PRECESSIONALLY	PRECISIONIST
PREAPPOINT	PRECANCELLED	PRECESSIONS	PRECISIONISTS
PREAPPOINTED	PRECANCELLING	PRECHARGED	PRECISIONS
PREAPPOINTING	PRECANCELS	PRECHARGES	PRECLASSICAL
PREAPPOINTS	PRECANCEROUS	PRECHARGING	PRECLEANED
PREAPPROVE	PRECANCERS	PRECHECKED	PRECLEANING
PREAPPROVED	PRECAPITALIST	PRECHECKING	PRECLEARANCE
PREAPPROVES	PRECARIOUS	PRECHILLED	PRECLEARANCES
PREAPPROVING	PRECARIOUSLY	PRECHILLING	PRECLEARED
PREARRANGE	PRECARIOUSNESS	PRECHOOSES	PRECLEARING
PREARRANGED	PRECASTING	PRECHOOSING	PRECLINICAL
PREARRANGEMENT	PRECAUTION	PRECHRISTIAN	PRECLINICALLY
PREARRANGEMENTS	PRECAUTIONAL	PRECIEUSES	PRECLUDABLE
PREARRANGES	PRECAUTIONARY	PRECIOSITIES	PRECLUDING
PREARRANGING	PRECAUTIONED	PRECIOSITY	PRECLUSION
PREASSEMBLED	PRECAUTIONING	PRECIOUSES	PRECLUSIONS
PREASSIGNED	PRECAUTIONS	PRECIOUSLY	PRECLUSIVE
PREASSIGNING	PRECAUTIOUS	PRECIOUSNESS	PRECLUSIVELY
PREASSIGNS	PRECEDENCE	PRECIOUSNESSES	PRECOCIALS
PREASSURANCE	PRECEDENCES	PRECIPICED	PRECOCIOUS
PREASSURANCES	PRECEDENCIES	PRECIPICES	PRECOCIOUSLY
PREASSURED	PRECEDENCY	PRECIPITABILITY	PRECOCIOUSNESS
PREASSURES	PRECEDENTED	PRECIPITABLE	PRECOCITIES
PREASSURING	PRECEDENTIAL	PRECIPITANCE	PRECOGNISANT

PRECOGNISE	PRECONISES	PREDECESSORS	PREDEVELOPMENT
PRECOGNISED	PRECONISING	PREDEDUCTED	PREDEVELOPMENTS
PRECOGNISES	PRECONIZATION	PREDEDUCTING	PREDEVELOPS
PRECOGNISING	PRECONIZATIONS	PREDEDUCTS	PREDIABETES
PRECOGNITION	PRECONIZED	PREDEFINED	PREDIABETESES
PRECOGNITIONS	PRECONIZES	PREDEFINES	PREDIABETIC
PRECOGNITIVE	PRECONIZING	PREDEFINING	PREDIABETICS
PRECOGNIZANT	PRECONQUEST	PREDEFINITION	PREDIALITIES
PRECOGNIZE	PRECONSCIOUS	PREDEFINITIONS	PREDIALITY
PRECOGNIZED	PRECONSCIOUSES	PREDELIVERY	PREDICABILITIES
PRECOGNIZES	PRECONSCIOUSLY	PREDENTATE	PREDICABILITY
PRECOGNIZING	PRECONSONANTAL	PREDEPARTURE	PREDICABLE
PRECOGNOSCE	PRECONSTRUCT	PREDEPOSIT	PREDICABLENESS
PRECOGNOSCED	PRECONSTRUCTED	PREDEPOSITED	PREDICABLES
PRECOGNOSCES	PRECONSTRUCTING	PREDEPOSITING	PREDICAMENT
PRECOGNOSCING	PRECONSTRUCTION	PREDEPOSITS	PREDICAMENTAL
PRECOLLEGE	PRECONSTRUCTS	PREDESIGNATE	PREDICAMENTS
PRECOLLEGIATE	PRECONSUME	PREDESIGNATED	PREDICANTS
PRECOLONIAL	PRECONSUMED	PREDESIGNATES	PREDICATED
PRECOMBUSTION	PRECONSUMES	PREDESIGNATING	PREDICATES
PRECOMBUSTIONS	PRECONSUMING	PREDESIGNATION	PREDICATING
PRECOMMITMENT	PRECONTACT	PREDESIGNATIONS	PREDICATION
PRECOMMITMENTS	PRECONTRACT	PREDESIGNATORY	PREDICATIONS
PRECOMPETITIVE	PRECONTRACTED	PREDESIGNED	PREDICATIVE
PRECOMPOSE	PRECONTRACTING	PREDESIGNING	PREDICATIVELY
PRECOMPOSED	PRECONTRACTS	PREDESIGNS	PREDICATOR
PRECOMPOSES	PRECONVENTION	PREDESTINABLE	PREDICATORS
PRECOMPOSING	PRECONVICTION	PREDESTINARIAN	PREDICATORY
PRECOMPUTE	PRECONVICTIONS	PREDESTINARIANS	PREDICTABILITY
PRECOMPUTED	PRECOOKERS	PREDESTINATE	PREDICTABLE
PRECOMPUTER	PRECOOKING	PREDESTINATED	PREDICTABLENESS
PRECOMPUTES	PRECOOLING	PREDESTINATES	PREDICTABLY
PRECOMPUTING	PRECOPULATORY	PREDESTINATING	PREDICTERS
PRECONCEIT	PRECORDIAL	PREDESTINATION	PREDICTING
PRECONCEITS	PRECREASED	PREDESTINATIONS	PREDICTION
PRECONCEIVE	PRECREASES	PREDESTINATIVE	PREDICTIONS
PRECONCEIVED	PRECREASING	PREDESTINATOR	PREDICTIVE
PRECONCEIVES	PRECRITICAL	PREDESTINATORS	PREDICTIVELY
PRECONCEIVING	PRECURRERS	PREDESTINE	PREDICTORS
PRECONCEPTION	PRECURSIVE	PREDESTINED	PREDIGESTED
PRECONCEPTIONS	PRECURSORS	PREDESTINES	PREDIGESTING
PRECONCERT	PRECURSORY	PREDESTINIES	PREDIGESTION
PRECONCERTED	PRECUTTING	PREDESTINING	PREDIGESTIONS
PRECONCERTEDLY	PREDACEOUS	PREDESTINY	PREDIGESTS
PRECONCERTING	PREDACEOUSNESS	PREDETERMINABLE	PREDIKANTS
PRECONCERTS	PREDACIOUS	PREDETERMINATE	PREDILECTED
PRECONCILIAR	PREDACIOUSNESS	PREDETERMINE	PREDILECTING
PRECONDEMN	PREDACITIES	PREDETERMINED	PREDILECTION
PRECONDEMNED	PREDATIONS	PREDETERMINER	PREDILECTIONS
PRECONDEMNING	PREDATISMS	PREDETERMINERS	PREDILECTS
PRECONDEMNS	PREDATORILY	PREDETERMINES	PREDINNERS
PRECONDITION	PREDATORINESS	PREDETERMINING	PREDISCHARGE
PRECONDITIONED	PREDATORINESSES	PREDETERMINISM	PREDISCOVERIES
PRECONDITIONING	PREDECEASE	PREDETERMINISMS	PREDISCOVERY
PRECONDITIONS	PREDECEASED	PREDEVALUATION	PREDISPOSAL
PRECONISATION	PREDECEASES	PREDEVELOP	PREDISPOSALS
PRECONISATIONS	PREDECEASING	PREDEVELOPED	PREDISPOSE
PRECONISED	PREDECESSOR	PREDEVELOPING	PREDISPOSED

PREDISPOSES	PREESTABLISHING	PREFIGURATIONS	PREGNANCIES
PREDISPOSING	PREETHICAL	PREFIGURATIVE	PREGNANTLY
PREDISPOSITION	PREEXCITED	PREFIGURATIVELY	PREGNENOLONE
PREDISPOSITIONS	PREEXCITES	PREFIGURED	PREGNENOLONES
PREDNISOLONE	PREEXCITING	PREFIGUREMENT	PREGROWTHS
PREDNISOLONES	PREEXEMPTED	PREFIGUREMENTS	PREGUIDING
PREDNISONE	PREEXEMPTING	PREFIGURES	PREGUSTATION
PREDNISONES	PREEXEMPTS	PREFIGURING	PREGUSTATIONS
PREDOCTORAL	PREEXISTED	PREFILLING	PREHALLUCES
PREDOMINANCE	PREEXISTENCE	PREFINANCE	PREHALLUXES
PREDOMINANCES	PREEXISTENCES	PREFINANCED	PREHANDLED
PREDOMINANCIES	PREEXISTENT	PREFINANCES	PREHANDLES
PREDOMINANCY	PREEXISTING	PREFINANCING	PREHANDLING
PREDOMINANT	PREEXPERIMENT	PREFIXALLY	PREHARDENED
PREDOMINANTLY	PREEXPOSED	PREFIXIONS	PREHARDENING
PREDOMINATE	PREEXPOSES	PREFIXTURE	PREHARDENS
PREDOMINATED	PREEXPOSING	PREFIXTURES	PREHARVEST
PREDOMINATELY	PREFABBING	PREFLIGHTED	PREHEADACHE
PREDOMINATES	PREFABRICATE	PREFLIGHTING	PREHEATERS
PREDOMINATING	PREFABRICATED	PREFLIGHTS	PREHEATING
PREDOMINATION	PREFABRICATES	PREFLORATION	PREHEMINENCE
PREDOMINATIONS	PREFABRICATING	PREFLORATIONS	PREHEMINENCES
PREDOMINATOR	PREFABRICATION	PREFOCUSED	PREHENDING
PREDOMINATORS	PREFABRICATIONS	PREFOCUSES	PREHENSIBLE
PREDOOMING	PREFABRICATOR	PREFOCUSING	PREHENSILE
PREDRILLED	PREFABRICATORS	PREFOCUSSED	PREHENSILITIES
PREDRILLING	PREFASCIST	PREFOCUSSES	PREHENSILITY
PREDYNASTIC	PREFATORIAL	PREFOCUSSING	PREHENSION
PREECLAMPSIA	PREFATORIALLY	PREFOLIATION	PREHENSIONS
PREECLAMPSIAS	PREFATORILY	PREFOLIATIONS	PREHENSIVE
PREECLAMPTIC	PREFECTORIAL	PREFORMATION	PREHENSORIAL
PREEDITING	PREFECTSHIP	PREFORMATIONISM	PREHENSORS
PREELECTED	PREFECTSHIPS	PREFORMATIONIST	PREHENSORY
PREELECTING	PREFECTURAL	PREFORMATIONS	PREHISTORIAN
PREELECTION	PREFECTURE	PREFORMATIVE	PREHISTORIANS
PREELECTRIC	PREFECTURES	PREFORMATS	PREHISTORIC
PREEMBARGO	PREFERABILITIES	PREFORMATTED	PREHISTORICAL
PREEMERGENCE	PREFERABILITY	PREFORMATTING	PREHISTORICALLY
PREEMERGENT	PREFERABLE	PREFORMING	PREHISTORIES
PREEMINENCE	PREFERABLENESS	PREFORMULATE	PREHISTORY
PREEMINENCES	PREFERABLY	PREFORMULATED	PREHOLIDAY
PREEMINENT	PREFERENCE	PREFORMULATES	PREHOMINID
PREEMINENTLY	PREFERENCES	PREFORMULATING	PREHOMINIDS
PREEMPLOYMENT	PREFERENTIAL	PREFRANKED	PREIGNITION
PREEMPTING	PREFERENTIALISM	PREFRANKING	PREIGNITIONS
PREEMPTION	PREFERENTIALIST	PREFREEZES	PREIMPLANTATION
PREEMPTIONS	PREFERENTIALITY	PREFREEZING	PREIMPOSED
PREEMPTIVE	PREFERENTIALLY	PREFRESHMAN	PREIMPOSES
PREEMPTIVELY	PREFERMENT	PREFRONTAL	PREIMPOSING
PREEMPTORS	PREFERMENTS	PREFRONTALS	PREINAUGURAL
PREENACTED	PREFERRABLE	PREFULGENT	PREINDUCTION
PREENACTING	PREFERRERS	PREFUNDING	PREINDUSTRIAL
PREENROLLMENT	PREFERRING	PREGANGLIONIC	PREINFORMED
PREERECTED	PREFIGURATE	PREGENITAL	PREINFORMING
PREERECTING	PREFIGURATED	PREGLACIAL	PREINFORMS
PREESTABLISH	PREFIGURES	PREGNABILITIES	PREINSERTED
PREESTABLISHED	PREFIGURATING	PREGNABILITY	PREINSERTING
PREESTABLISHES	PREFIGURATION	PREGNANCES	PREINSERTS

PREINTERVIEW	PRELIMINARY	PREMEDITATEDLY	PRENOMINATING
PREINTERVIEWED	PRELIMITED	PREMEDITATES	PRENOMINATION
PREINTERVIEWING	PRELIMITING	PREMEDITATING	PRENOMINATIONS
PREINTERVIEWS	PRELINGUAL	PREMEDITATION	PRENOTIFICATION
PREINVASION	PRELINGUALLY	PREMEDITATIONS	PRENOTIFIED
PREINVITED	PRELITERACIES	PREMEDITATIVE	PRENOTIFIES
PREINVITES	PRELITERACY	PREMEDITATOR	PRENOTIFYING
PREINVITING	PRELITERARY	PREMEDITATORS	PRENOTIONS
PREJUDGEMENT	PRELITERATE	PREMEIOTIC	PRENTICESHIP
PREJUDGEMENTS	PRELITERATES	PREMENOPAUSAL	PRENTICESHIPS
PREJUDGERS	PRELOADING	PREMENSTRUAL	PRENTICING
PREJUDGING	PRELOCATED	PREMENSTRUALLY	PRENUMBERED
PREJUDGMENT	PRELOCATES	PREMIERING	PRENUMBERING
PREJUDGMENTS	PRELOCATING	PREMIERSHIP	PRENUMBERS
PREJUDICANT	PRELOGICAL	PREMIERSHIPS	PRENUPTIAL
PREJUDICATE	PRELUDIOUS	PREMIGRATION	PREOBTAINED
PREJUDICATED	PRELUNCHEON	PREMILLENARIAN	PREOBTAINING
PREJUDICATES	PRELUSIONS	PREMILLENARIANS	PREOBTAINS
PREJUDICATING	PRELUSIVELY	PREMILLENNIAL	PREOCCUPANCIES
PREJUDICATION	PRELUSORILY	PREMILLENNIALLY	PREOCCUPANCY
PREJUDICATIONS	PREMALIGNANT	PREMODIFICATION	PREOCCUPANT
PREJUDICATIVE	PREMANDIBULAR	PREMODIFIED	PREOCCUPANTS
PREJUDICED	PREMANDIBULARS	PREMODIFIES	PREOCCUPATE
PREJUDICES	PREMANUFACTURE	PREMODIFYING	PREOCCUPATED
PREJUDICIAL	PREMANUFACTURED	PREMOISTEN	PREOCCUPATES
PREJUDICIALLY	PREMANUFACTURES	PREMOISTENED	PREOCCUPATING
PREJUDICIALNESS	PREMARITAL	PREMOISTENING	PREOCCUPATION
PREJUDICING	PREMARITALLY	PREMOISTENS	PREOCCUPATIONS
PREJUDIZES	PREMARKETED	PREMOLDING	PREOCCUPIED
PREKINDERGARTEN	PREMARKETING	PREMONISHED	PREOCCUPIES
PRELAPSARIAN	PREMARKETS	PREMONISHES	PREOCCUPYING
PRELATESHIP	PREMARRIAGE	PREMONISHING	PREOCULARS
PRELATESHIPS	PREMATURELY	PREMONISHMENT	PREOPENING
PRELATESSES	PREMATURENESS	PREMONISHMENTS	PREOPERATIONAL
PRELATICAL	PREMATURENESSES	PREMONITION	PREOPERATIVE
PRELATICALLY	PREMATURES	PREMONITIONS	PREOPERATIVELY
PRELATIONS	PREMATURITIES	PREMONITIVE	PREOPTIONS
PRELATISED	PREMATURITY	PREMONITOR	PREORDAINED
PRELATISES	PREMAXILLA	PREMONITORILY	PREORDAINING
PRELATISING	PREMAXILLAE	PREMONITORS	PREORDAINMENT
PRELATISMS	PREMAXILLARIES	PREMONITORY	PREORDAINMENTS
PRELATISTS	PREMAXILLARY	PREMOTIONS	PREORDAINS
PRELATIZED	PREMAXILLAS	PREMOVEMENT	PREORDERED
PRELATIZES	PREMEASURE	PREMOVEMENTS	PREORDERING
PRELATIZING	PREMEASURED	PREMUNITION	PREORDINANCE
PRELATURES	PREMEASURES	PREMUNITIONS	PREORDINANCES
PRELAUNCHED	PREMEASURING	PREMYCOTIC	PREORDINATION
PRELAUNCHES	PREMEDICAL	PRENATALLY	PREORDINATIONS
PRELAUNCHING	PREMEDICALLY	PRENEGOTIATE	PREOVULATORY
PRELECTING	PREMEDICATE	PRENEGOTIATED	PREPACKAGE
PRELECTION	PREMEDICATED	PRENEGOTIATES	PREPACKAGED
PRELECTIONS	PREMEDICATES	PRENEGOTIATING	PREPACKAGES
PRELECTORS	PREMEDICATING	PRENEGOTIATION	PREPACKAGING
PRELEXICAL	PREMEDICATION	PRENEGOTIATIONS	PREPACKING
PRELIBATION	PREMEDICATIONS	PRENOMINAL	PREPARATION
PRELIBATIONS	PREMEDIEVAL	PRENOMINATE	PREPARATIONS
PRELIMINARIES	PREMEDITATE	PRENOMINATED	PREPARATIVE
PRELIMINARILY	PREMEDITATED	PRENOMINATES	PREPARATIVELY

PREPARATIVES	PREPOSSESSINGLY	PREQUALIFYING	PRESBYTERIALS
PREPARATOR	PREPOSSESSION	PREREADING	PRESBYTERIAN
PREPARATORILY	PREPOSSESSIONS	PRERECESSION	PRESBYTERIANISE
PREPARATORS	PREPOSTEROUS	PRERECORDED	PRESBYTERIANISM
PREPARATORY	PREPOSTEROUSLY	PRERECORDING	PRESBYTERIANIZE
PREPAREDLY	PREPOSTORS	PRERECORDS	PRESBYTERIANS
PREPAREDNESS	PREPOTENCE	PREREGISTER	PRESBYTERIES
PREPAREDNESSES	PREPOTENCES	PREREGISTERED	PRESBYTERS
PREPASTING	PREPOTENCIES	PREREGISTERING	PRESBYTERSHIP
PREPATELLAR	PREPOTENCY	PREREGISTERS	PRESBYTERSHIPS
PREPAYABLE	PREPOTENTLY	PREREGISTRATION	PRESBYTERY
PREPAYMENT	PREPPINESS	PREREHEARSAL	PRESBYTISM
PREPAYMENTS	PREPPINESSES	PRERELEASE	PRESBYTISMS
PREPENSELY	PREPRANDIAL	PRERELEASED	PRESCHEDULE
PREPENSING	PREPREPARED	PRERELEASES	PRESCHEDULED
PREPENSIVE	PREPRESIDENTIAL	PRERELEASING	PRESCHEDULES
PREPERFORMANCE	PREPRICING	PREREQUIRE	PRESCHEDULING
PREPLACING	PREPRIMARIES	PREREQUIRED	PRESCHOOLER
PREPLANNED	PREPRIMARY	PREREQUIRES	PRESCHOOLERS
PREPLANNING	PREPRINTED	PREREQUIRING	PRESCHOOLS
PREPLANTED	PREPRINTING	PREREQUISITE	PRESCIENCE
PREPLANTING	PREPROCESS	PREREQUISITES	PRESCIENCES
PREPOLLENCE	PREPROCESSED	PRERETIREMENT	PRESCIENTIFIC
PREPOLLENCES	PREPROCESSES	PREREVISIONIST	PRESCIENTLY
PREPOLLENCIES	PREPROCESSING	PREREVOLUTION	PRESCINDED
PREPOLLENCY	PREPROCESSOR	PRERINSING	PRESCINDENT
PREPOLLENT	PREPROCESSORS	PREROGATIVE	PRESCINDING
PREPOLLICES	PREPRODUCTION	PREROGATIVED	PRESCISSION
PREPONDERANCE	PREPRODUCTIONS	PREROGATIVELY	PRESCISSIONS
PREPONDERANCES	PREPROFESSIONAL	PREROGATIVES	PRESCORING
PREPONDERANCIES	PREPROGRAM	PREROMANTIC	PRESCREENED
PREPONDERANCY	PREPROGRAMED	PRESAGEFUL	PRESCREENING
PREPONDERANT	PREPROGRAMING	PRESAGEFULLY	PRESCREENS
PREPONDERANTLY	PREPROGRAMMED	PRESAGEMENT	PRESCRIBED
PREPONDERATE	PREPROGRAMMING	PRESAGEMENTS	PRESCRIBER
PREPONDERATED	PREPROGRAMS	PRESANCTIFIED	PRESCRIBERS
PREPONDERATELY	PREPSYCHEDELIC	PRESANCTIFIES	PRESCRIBES
PREPONDERATES	PREPUBERAL	PRESANCTIFY	PRESCRIBING
PREPONDERATING	PREPUBERTAL	PRESANCTIFYING	PRESCRIBINGS
PREPONDERATION	PREPUBERTIES	PRESBYACOUSES	PRESCRIPTIBLE
PREPONDERATIONS	PREPUBERTY	PRESBYACOUSIS	PRESCRIPTION
PREPORTION	PREPUBESCENCE	PRESBYACUSES	PRESCRIPTIONS
PREPORTIONED	PREPUBESCENCES	PRESBYACUSIS	PRESCRIPTIVE
PREPORTIONING	PREPUBESCENT	PRESBYCOUSES	PRESCRIPTIVELY
PREPORTIONS	PREPUBESCENTS	PRESBYCOUSIS	PRESCRIPTIVISM
PREPOSITION	PREPUBLICATION	PRESBYCUSES	PRESCRIPTIVISMS
PREPOSITIONAL	PREPUBLICATIONS	PRESBYCUSIS	PRESCRIPTIVIST
PREPOSITIONALLY	PREPUNCHED	PRESBYOPES	PRESCRIPTIVISTS
PREPOSITIONS	PREPUNCHES	PRESBYOPIA	PRESCRIPTS
PREPOSITIVE	PREPUNCHING	PRESBYOPIAS	PRESEASONS
PREPOSITIVELY	PREPUNCTUAL	PRESBYOPIC	PRESELECTED
PREPOSITIVES	PREPURCHASE	PRESBYOPICS	PRESELECTING
PREPOSITOR	PREPURCHASED	PRESBYOPIES	PRESELECTION
PREPOSITORS	PREPURCHASES	PRESBYTERAL	PRESELECTIONS
PREPOSSESS	PREPURCHASING	PRESBYTERATE	PRESELECTOR
PREPOSSESSED	PREQUALIFIED	PRESBYTERATES	PRESELECTORS
PREPOSSESSES	PREQUALIFIES	PRESBYTERIAL	PRESELECTS
PREPOSSESSING	PREQUALIFY	PRESBYTERIALLY	PRESELLING

PRESENSION
PRESENSIONS
PRESENTABILITY
PRESENTABLE
PRESENTABLENESS
PRESENTABLY
PRESENTATION
PRESENTATIONAL
PRESENTATIONISM
PRESENTATIONIST
PRESENTATIONS
PRESENTATIVE
PRESENTEEISM
PRESENTEEISMS
PRESENTEES
PRESENTENCE
PRESENTENCED
PRESENTENCES
PRESENTENCING
PRESENTERS
PRESENTIAL
PRESENTIALITIES
PRESENTIALITY
PRESENTIALLY
PRESENTIENT
PRESENTIMENT
PRESENTIMENTAL
PRESENTIMENTS
PRESENTING
PRESENTISM
PRESENTISMS
PRESENTIST
PRESENTIVE
PRESENTIVENESS
PRESENTMENT
PRESENTMENTS
PRESENTNESS
PRESENTNESSES
PRESERVABILITY
PRESERVABLE
PRESERVABLY
PRESERVATION
PRESERVATIONIST
PRESERVATIONS
PRESERVATIVE
PRESERVATIVES
PRESERVATORIES
PRESERVATORY
PRESERVERS
PRESERVICE
PRESERVING
PRESETTING
PRESETTLED
PRESETTLEMENT
PRESETTLES
PRESETTLING
PRESHAPING
PRESHIPPED

PRESHIPPING
PRESHOWING
PRESHRINKING
PRESHRINKS
PRESHRUNKEN
PRESIDENCIES
PRESIDENCY
PRESIDENTESS
PRESIDENTESSES
PRESIDENTIAL
PRESIDENTIALLY
PRESIDENTS
PRESIDENTSHIP
PRESIDENTSHIPS
PRESIDIARY
PRESIDIUMS
PRESIFTING
PRESIGNALED
PRESIGNALING
PRESIGNALLED
PRESIGNALLING
PRESIGNALS
PRESIGNIFIED
PRESIGNIFIES
PRESIGNIFY
PRESIGNIFYING
PRESLAUGHTER
PRESLICING
PRESOAKING
PRESOLVING
PRESORTING
PRESPECIFIED
PRESPECIFIES
PRESPECIFY
PRESPECIFYING
PRESSBOARD
PRESSBOARDS
PRESSGANGS
PRESSINGLY
PRESSINGNESS
PRESSINGNESSES
PRESSMARKS
PRESSROOMS
PRESSURELESS
PRESSURING
PRESSURISATION
PRESSURISATIONS
PRESSURISE
PRESSURISED
PRESSURISER
PRESSURISERS
PRESSURISES
PRESSURISING
PRESSURIZATION
PRESSURIZATIONS
PRESSURIZE
PRESSURIZED
PRESSURIZER

PRESSURIZERS
PRESSURIZES
PRESSURIZING
PRESSWOMAN
PRESSWOMEN
PRESSWORKS
PRESTAMPED
PRESTAMPING
PRESTATION
PRESTATIONS
PRESTERILISE
PRESTERILISED
PRESTERILISES
PRESTERILISING
PRESTERILIZE
PRESTERILIZED
PRESTERILIZES
PRESTERILIZING
PRESTERNUM
PRESTERNUMS
PRESTIDIGITATOR
PRESTIGEFUL
PRESTIGIATOR
PRESTIGIATORS
PRESTIGIOUS
PRESTIGIOUSLY
PRESTIGIOUSNESS
PRESTISSIMO
PRESTISSIMOS
PRESTORAGE
PRESTORING
PRESTRESSED
PRESTRESSES
PRESTRESSING
PRESTRICTION
PRESTRICTIONS
PRESTRUCTURE
PRESTRUCTURED
PRESTRUCTURES
PRESTRUCTURING
PRESUMABLE
PRESUMABLY
PRESUMEDLY
PRESUMINGLY
PRESUMMITS
PRESUMPTION
PRESUMPTIONS
PRESUMPTIVE
PRESUMPTIVELY
PRESUMPTIVENESS
PRESUMPTUOUS
PRESUMPTUOUSLY
PRESUPPOSE
PRESUPPOSED
PRESUPPOSES
PRESUPPOSING
PRESUPPOSITION
PRESUPPOSITIONS

PRESURGERY
PRESURMISE
PRESURMISES
PRESURVEYED
PRESURVEYING
PRESURVEYS
PRESWEETEN
PRESWEETENED
PRESWEETENING
PRESWEETENS
PRESYMPTOMATIC
PRESYNAPTIC
PRESYNAPTICALLY
PRETASTING
PRETELEVISION
PRETELLING
PRETENCELESS
PRETENDANT
PRETENDANTS
PRETENDEDLY
PRETENDENT
PRETENDENTS
PRETENDERS
PRETENDERSHIP
PRETENDERSHIPS
PRETENDING
PRETENDINGLY
PRETENSION
PRETENSIONED
PRETENSIONING
PRETENSIONLESS
PRETENSIONS
PRETENSIVE
PRETENTIOUS
PRETENTIOUSLY
PRETENTIOUSNESS
PRETERHUMAN
PRETERISTS
PRETERITENESS
PRETERITENESSES
PRETERITES
PRETERITION
PRETERITIONS
PRETERITIVE
PRETERMINAL
PRETERMINATION
PRETERMINATIONS
PRETERMISSION
PRETERMISSIONS
PRETERMITS
PRETERMITTED
PRETERMITTER
PRETERMITTERS
PRETERMITTING
PRETERNATURAL
PRETERNATURALLY
PRETERPERFECT
PRETERPERFECTS

PRETESTING
PRETEXTING
PRETHEATER
PRETORIANS
PRETORSHIP
PRETORSHIPS
PRETOURNAMENT
PRETRAINED
PRETRAINING
PRETREATED
PRETREATING
PRETREATMENT
PRETREATMENTS
PRETRIMMED
PRETRIMMING
PRETTIFICATION
PRETTIFICATIONS
PRETTIFIED
PRETTIFIER
PRETTIFIERS
PRETTIFIES
PRETTIFYING
PRETTINESS
PRETTINESSES
PRETTYISMS
PREUNIFICATION
PREUNITING
PREUNIVERSITY
PREVAILERS
PREVAILING
PREVAILINGLY
PREVAILMENT
PREVAILMENTS
PREVALENCE
PREVALENCES
PREVALENCIES
PREVALENCY
PREVALENTLY
PREVALENTNESS
PREVALENTNESSES
PREVALENTS
PREVALUING
PREVARICATE
PREVARICATED
PREVARICATES
PREVARICATING
PREVARICATION
PREVARICATIONS
PREVARICATOR
PREVARICATORS
PREVENANCIES
PREVENANCY
PREVENIENCE
PREVENIENCES
PREVENIENT
PREVENIENTLY
PREVENTABILITY
PREVENTABLE

PREVENTABLY
PREVENTATIVE
PREVENTATIVES
PREVENTERS
PREVENTIBILITY
PREVENTIBLE
PREVENTIBLY
PREVENTING
PREVENTION
PREVENTIONS
PREVENTIVE
PREVENTIVELY
PREVENTIVENESS
PREVENTIVES
PREVIEWERS
PREVIEWING
PREVIOUSLY
PREVIOUSNESS
PREVIOUSNESSES
PREVISIONAL
PREVISIONARY
PREVISIONED
PREVISIONING
PREVISIONS
PREVISITED
PREVISITING
PREVOCALIC
PREVOCALICALLY
PREVOCATIONAL
PREWARMING
PREWARNING
PREWASHING
PREWEANING
PREWEIGHED
PREWEIGHING
PREWORKING
PREWRAPPED
PREWRAPPING
PREWRITING
PREWRITINGS
PRTCELESSLY
PRICELESSNESS
PRICELESSNESSES
PRICINESSES
PRICKLIEST
PRICKLINESS
PRICKLINESSES
PRICKLINGS
PRICKWOODS
PRIDEFULLY
PRIDEFULNESS
PRIDEFULNESSES
PRIESTCRAFT
PRIESTCRAFTS
PRIESTESSES
PRIESTHOOD
PRIESTHOODS
PRIESTLIER

PRIESTLIEST
PRIESTLIKE
PRIESTLINESS
PRIESTLINESSES
PRIESTLING
PRIESTLINGS
PRIESTSHIP
PRIESTSHIPS
PRIGGERIES
PRIGGISHLY
PRIGGISHNESS
PRIGGISHNESSES
PRIMAEVALLY
PRIMALITIES
PRIMAQUINE
PRIMAQUINES
PRIMARINESS
PRIMARINESSES
PRIMATESHIP
PRIMATESHIPS
PRIMATIALS
PRIMATICAL
PRIMATOLOGICAL
PRIMATOLOGIES
PRIMATOLOGIST
PRIMATOLOGISTS
PRIMATOLOGY
PRIMAVERAS
PRIMENESSES
PRIMEVALLY
PRIMIGENIAL
PRIMIGRAVIDA
PRIMIGRAVIDAE
PRIMIGRAVIDAS
PRIMIPARAE
PRIMIPARAS
PRIMIPARITIES
PRIMIPARITY
PRIMIPAROUS
PRIMITIVELY
PRIMITIVENESS
PRIMITIVENESSES
PRIMITIVES
PRIMITIVISM
PRIMITIVISMS
PRIMITIVIST
PRIMITIVISTIC
PRIMITIVISTS
PRIMITIVITIES
PRIMITIVITY
PRIMNESSES
PRIMOGENIAL
PRIMOGENIT
PRIMOGENITAL
PRIMOGENITARY
PRIMOGENITIVE
PRIMOGENITIVES
PRIMOGENITOR

PRIMOGENITORS
PRIMOGENITRICES
PRIMOGENITRIX
PRIMOGENITRIXES
PRIMOGENITS
PRIMOGENITURE
PRIMOGENITURES
PRIMORDIAL
PRIMORDIALISM
PRIMORDIALISMS
PRIMORDIALITIES
PRIMORDIALITY
PRIMORDIALLY
PRIMORDIALS
PRIMORDIUM
PRIMROSING
PRIMULACEOUS
PRIMULINES
PRINCEDOMS
PRINCEHOOD
PRINCEHOODS
PRINCEKINS
PRINCELETS
PRINCELIER
PRINCELIEST
PRINCELIKE
PRINCELINESS
PRINCELINESSES
PRINCELING
PRINCELINGS
PRINCESHIP
PRINCESHIPS
PRINCESSES
PRINCESSLY
PRINCIFIED
PRINCIPALITIES
PRINCIPALITY
PRINCIPALLY
PRINCIPALNESS
PRINCIPALNESSES
PRINCIPALS
PRINCIPALSHIP
PRINCIPALSHIPS
PRINCIPATE
PRINCIPATES
PRINCIPIAL
PRINCIPIUM
PRINCIPLED
PRINCIPLES
PRINCIPLING
PRINTABILITIES
PRINTABILITY
PRINTABLENESS
PRINTABLENESSES
PRINTERIES
PRINTHEADS
PRINTMAKER
PRINTMAKERS

PRINTMAKING	PRIVATIZER	PROBUSINESS	PROCIDENCES
PRINTMAKINGS	PRIVATIZERS	PROCACIOUS	PROCLAIMANT
PRINTWHEEL	PRIVATIZES	PROCACITIES	PROCLAIMANTS
PRINTWHEELS	PRIVATIZING	PROCAMBIAL	PROCLAIMED
PRINTWORKS	PRIVILEGED	PROCAMBIUM	PROCLAIMER
PRIORESSES	PRIVILEGES	PROCAMBIUMS	PROCLAIMERS
PRIORITIES	PRIVILEGING	PROCAPITALIST	PROCLAIMING
PRIORITISATION	PRIZEFIGHT	PROCAPITALISTS	PROCLAMATION
PRIORITISATIONS	PRIZEFIGHTER	PROCARBAZINE	PROCLAMATIONS
PRIORITISE	PRIZEFIGHTERS	PROCARBAZINES	PROCLAMATORY
PRIORITISED	PRIZEFIGHTING	PROCARYONS	PROCLITICS
PRIORITISES	PRIZEFIGHTINGS	PROCARYOTE	PROCLIVITIES
PRIORITISING	PRIZEFIGHTS	PROCARYOTES	PROCLIVITY
PRIORITIZATION	PRIZEWINNER	PROCARYOTIC	PROCOELOUS
PRIORITIZATIONS	PRIZEWINNERS	PROCATHEDRAL	PROCONSULAR
PRIORITIZE	PRIZEWINNING	PROCATHEDRALS	PROCONSULATE
PRIORITIZED	PRIZEWOMAN	PROCEDURAL	PROCONSULATES
PRIORITIZES	PRIZEWOMEN	PROCEDURALLY	PROCONSULS
PRIORITIZING	PROABORTION	PROCEDURALS	PROCONSULSHIP
PRIORSHIPS	PROACTIONS	PROCEDURES	PROCONSULSHIPS
PRISMATICAL	PROAIRESES	PROCEEDERS	PROCRASTINATE
PRISMATICALLY	PROAIRESIS	PROCEEDING	PROCRASTINATED
PRISMATOID	PROBABILIORISM	PROCEEDINGS	PROCRASTINATES
PRISMATOIDAL	PROBABILIORISMS	PROCELEUSMATIC	PROCRASTINATING
PRISMATOIDS	PROBABILIORIST	PROCELEUSMATICS	PROCRASTINATION
PRISMOIDAL	PROBABILIORISTS	PROCELLARIAN	PROCRASTINATIVE
PRISONMENT	PROBABILISM	PROCEPHALIC	PROCRASTINATOR
PRISONMENTS	PROBABILISMS	PROCERCOID	PROCRASTINATORS
PRISSINESS	PROBABILIST	PROCERCOIDS	PROCRASTINATORY
PRISSINESSES	PROBABILISTIC	PROCEREBRA	PROCREANTS
PRISTINELY	PROBABILISTS	PROCEREBRAL	PROCREATED
PRIVATDOCENT	PROBABILITIES	PROCEREBRUM	PROCREATES
PRIVATDOCENTS	PROBABILITY	PROCEREBRUMS	PROCREATING
PRIVATDOZENT	PROBATIONAL	PROCERITIES	PROCREATION
PRIVATDOZENTS	PROBATIONALLY	PROCESSABILITY	PROCREATIONAL
PRIVATEERED	PROBATIONARIES	PROCESSABLE	PROCREATIONS
PRIVATEERING	PROBATIONARY	PROCESSERS	PROCREATIVE
PRIVATEERINGS	PROBATIONER	PROCESSIBILITY	PROCREATIVENESS
PRIVATEERS	PROBATIONERS	PROCESSIBLE	PROCREATOR
PRIVATEERSMAN	PROBATIONERSHIP	PROCESSING	PROCREATORS
PRIVATEERSMEN	PROBATIONS	PROCESSINGS	PROCRUSTEAN
PRIVATENESS	PROBATIVELY	PROCESSION	PROCRYPSES
PRIVATENESSES	PROBENECID	PROCESSIONAL	PROCRYPSIS
PRIVATIONS	PROBENECIDS	PROCESSIONALIST	PROCRYPTIC
PRIVATISATION	PROBIOTICS	PROCESSIONALLY	PROCRYPTICALLY
PRIVATISATIONS	PROBLEMATIC	PROCESSIONALS	PROCTALGIA
PRIVATISED	PROBLEMATICAL	PROCESSIONARY	PROCTALGIAS
PRIVATISER	PROBLEMATICALLY	PROCESSIONED	PROCTITIDES
PRIVATISERS	PROBLEMATICS	PROCESSIONER	PROCTITISES
PRIVATISES	PROBLEMIST	PROCESSIONERS	PROCTODAEA
PRIVATISING	PROBLEMISTS	PROCESSIONING	PROCTODAEAL
PRIVATISMS	PROBOSCIDEAN	PROCESSIONINGS	PROCTODAEUM
PRIVATISTS	PROBOSCIDEANS	PROCESSIONS	PROCTODAEUMS
PRIVATIVELY	PROBOSCIDES	PROCESSORS	PROCTODEUM
PRIVATIVES	PROBOSCIDIAN	PROCESSUAL	PROCTODEUMS
PRIVATIZATION	PROBOSCIDIANS	PROCHRONISM	PROCTOLOGIC
PRIVATIZATIONS	PROBOSCISES	PROCHRONISMS	PROCTOLOGICAL
PRIVATIZED	PROBOULEUTIC	PROCIDENCE	PROCTOLOGIES

PROCTOLOGIST	PRODNOSING	PROFICIENCY	PROGESTOGENIC
PROCTOLOGISTS	PRODROMATA	PROFICIENT	PROGESTOGENS
PROCTOLOGY	PRODUCEMENT	PROFICIENTLY	PROGGINSES
PROCTORAGE	PRODUCEMENTS	PROFICIENTS	PROGLOTTIC
PROCTORAGES	PRODUCIBILITIES	PROFILINGS	PROGLOTTID
PROCTORIAL	PRODUCIBILITY	PROFILISTS	PROGLOTTIDEAN
PROCTORIALLY	PRODUCIBLE	PROFITABILITIES	PROGLOTTIDES
PROCTORING	PRODUCTIBILITY	PROFITABILITY	PROGLOTTIDS
PROCTORISE	PRODUCTILE	PROFITABLE	PROGLOTTIS
PROCTORISED	PRODUCTION	PROFITABLENESS	PROGNATHIC
PROCTORISES	PRODUCTIONAL	PROFITABLY	PROGNATHISM
PROCTORISING	PRODUCTIONS	PROFITEERED	PROGNATHISMS
PROCTORIZE	PRODUCTIVE	PROFITEERING	PROGNATHOUS
PROCTORIZED	PRODUCTIVELY	PROFITEERINGS	PROGNOSING
PROCTORIZES	PRODUCTIVENESS	PROFITEERS	PROGNOSTIC
PROCTORIZING	PRODUCTIVITIES	PROFITEROLE	PROGNOSTICATE
PROCTORSHIP	PRODUCTIVITY	PROFITEROLES	PROGNOSTICATED
PROCTORSHIPS	PROEMBRYOS	PROFITINGS	PROGNOSTICATES
PROCTOSCOPE	PROENZYMES	PROFITLESS	PROGNOSTICATING
PROCTOSCOPES	PROESTRUSES	PROFITLESSLY	PROGNOSTICATION
PROCTOSCOPIC	PROFANATION	PROFITWISE	PROGNOSTICATIVE
PROCTOSCOPIES	PROFANATIONS	PROFLIGACIES	PROGNOSTICATOR
PROCTOSCOPY	PROFANATORY	PROFLIGACY	PROGNOSTICATORS
PROCUMBENT	PROFANENESS	PROFLIGATE	PROGNOSTICS
PROCURABLE	PROFANENESSES	PROFLIGATELY	PROGRADATION
PROCURACIES	PROFANITIES	PROFLIGATES	PROGRADATIONS
PROCURANCE	PROFASCIST	PROFLUENCE	PROGRADING
PROCURANCES	PROFECTITIOUS	PROFLUENCES	PROGRAMABLE
PROCURATION	PROFEMINIST	PROFOUNDER	PROGRAMERS
PROCURATIONS	PROFESSEDLY	PROFOUNDEST	PROGRAMING
PROCURATOR	PROFESSING	PROFOUNDLY	PROGRAMINGS
PROCURATORIAL	PROFESSION	PROFOUNDNESS	PROGRAMMABILITY
PROCURATORIES	PROFESSIONAL	PROFOUNDNESSES	PROGRAMMABLE
PROCURATORS	PROFESSIONALISE	PROFULGENT	PROGRAMMABLES
PROCURATORSHIP	PROFESSIONALISM	PROFUNDITIES	PROGRAMMATIC
PROCURATORSHIPS	PROFESSIONALIST	PROFUNDITY	PROGRAMMED
PROCURATORY	PROFESSIONALIZE	PROFUSENESS	PROGRAMMER
PROCUREMENT	PROFESSIONALLY	PROFUSENESSES	PROGRAMMERS
PROCUREMENTS	PROFESSIONALS	PROFUSIONS	PROGRAMMES
PROCURESSES	PROFESSIONS	PROGENITIVE	PROGRAMMING
PROCUREURS	PROFESSORATE	PROGENITIVENESS	PROGRAMMINGS
PRODIGALISE	PROFESSORATES	PROGENITOR	PROGRESSED
PRODIGALISED	PROFESSORESS	PROGENITORIAL	PROGRESSES
PRODIGALISES	PROFESSORESSES	PROGENITORS	PROGRESSING
PRODIGALISING	PROFESSORIAL	PROGENITORSHIP	PROGRESSION
PRODIGALITIES	PROFESSORIALLY	PROGENITORSHIPS	PROGRESSIONAL
PRODIGALITY	PROFESSORIAT	PROGENITRESS	PROGRESSIONALLY
PRODIGALIZE	PROFESSORIATE	PROGENITRESSES	PROGRESSIONARY
PRODIGALIZED	PROFESSORIATES	PROGENITRICES	PROGRESSIONISM
PRODIGALIZES	PROFESSORIATS	PROGENITRIX	PROGRESSIONISMS
PRODIGALIZING	PROFESSORS	PROGENITRIXES	PROGRESSIONIST
PRODIGALLY	PROFESSORSHIP	PROGENITURE	PROGRESSIONISTS
PRODIGIOSITIES	PROFESSORSHIPS	PROGENITURES	PROGRESSIONS
PRODIGIOSITY	PROFFERERS	PROGESTATIONAL	PROGRESSISM
PRODIGIOUS	PROFFERING	PROGESTERONE	PROGRESSISMS
PRODIGIOUSLY	PROFICIENCE	PROGESTERONES	PROGRESSIST
PRODIGIOUSNESS	PROFICIENCES	PROGESTINS	PROGRESSISTS
PRODITORIOUS	PROFICIENCIES	PROGESTOGEN	PROGRESSIVE

PROGRESSIVELY	PROKARYOTIC	PROLOCUTIONS	PROMISCUITY
PROGRESSIVENESS	PROKARYOTS	PROLOCUTOR	PROMISCUOUS
PROGRESSIVES	PROLACTINS	PROLOCUTORS	PROMISCUOUSLY
PROGRESSIVISM	PROLAMINES	PROLOCUTORSHIP	PROMISCUOUSNESS
PROGRESSIVISMS	PROLAPSING	PROLOCUTORSHIPS	PROMISEFUL
PROGRESSIVIST	PROLAPSUSES	PROLOCUTRICES	PROMISELESS
PROGRESSIVISTIC	PROLATENESS	PROLOCUTRIX	PROMISINGLY
PROGRESSIVISTS	PROLATENESSES	PROLOCUTRIXES	PROMISSIVE
PROGRESSIVITIES	PROLATIONS	PROLOGISED	PROMISSORILY
PROGRESSIVITY	PROLEGOMENA	PROLOGISES	PROMISSORS
PROGYMNASIA	PROLEGOMENAL	PROLOGISING	PROMISSORY
PROGYMNASIUM	PROLEGOMENARY	PROLOGISTS	PROMONARCHIST
PROGYMNASIUMS	PROLEGOMENON	PROLOGIZED	PROMONTORIES
PROHIBITED	PROLEGOMENOUS	PROLOGIZES	PROMONTORY
PROHIBITER	PROLEPTICAL	PROLOGIZING	PROMOTABILITIES
PROHIBITERS	PROLEPTICALLY	PROLOGUING	PROMOTABILITY
PROHIBITING	PROLETARIAN	PROLOGUISE	PROMOTABLE
PROHIBITION	PROLETARIANISE	PROLOGUISED	PROMOTIONAL
PROHIBITIONARY	PROLETARIANISED	PROLOGUISES	PROMOTIONS
PROHIBITIONISM	PROLETARIANISES	PROLOGUISING	PROMOTIVENESS
PROHIBITIONISMS	PROLETARIANISM	PROLOGUIZE	PROMOTIVENESSES
PROHIBITIONIST	PROLETARIANISMS	PROLOGUIZED	PROMPTBOOK
PROHIBITIONISTS	PROLETARIANIZE	PROLOGUIZES	PROMPTBOOKS
PROHIBITIONS	PROLETARIANIZED	PROLOGUIZING	PROMPTINGS
PROHIBITIVE	PROLETARIANIZES	PROLONGABLE	PROMPTITUDE
PROHIBITIVELY	PROLETARIANNESS	PROLONGATE	PROMPTITUDES
PROHIBITIVENESS	PROLETARIANS	PROLONGATED	PROMPTNESS
PROHIBITOR	PROLETARIAT	PROLONGATES	PROMPTNESSES
PROHIBITORS	PROLETARIATE	PROLONGATING	PROMPTUARIES
PROHIBITORY	PROLETARIATES	PROLONGATION	PROMPTUARY
PROINSULIN	PROLETARIATS	PROLONGATIONS	PROMPTURES
PROINSULINS	PROLETARIES	PROLONGERS	PROMULGATE
PROJECTABLE	PROLICIDAL	PROLONGING	PROMULGATED
PROJECTILE	PROLICIDES	PROLONGMENT	PROMULGATES
PROJECTILES	PROLIFERATE	PROLONGMENTS	PROMULGATING
PROJECTING	PROLIFERATED	PROLUSIONS	PROMULGATION
PROJECTINGS	PROLIFERATES	PROMACHOSES	PROMULGATIONS
PROJECTION	PROLIFERATING	PROMENADED	PROMULGATOR
PROJECTIONAL	PROLIFERATION	PROMENADER	PROMULGATORS
PROJECTIONIST	PROLIFERATIONS	PROMENADERS	PROMULGING
PROJECTIONISTS	PROLIFERATIVE	PROMENADES	PROMUSCIDATE
PROJECTIONS	PROLIFEROUS	PROMENADING	PROMUSCIDES
PROJECTISATION	PROLIFEROUSLY	PROMETHAZINE	PROMYCELIA
PROJECTISATIONS	PROLIFICACIES	PROMETHAZINES	PROMYCELIAL
PROJECTIVE	PROLIFICACY	PROMETHEUM	PROMYCELIUM
PROJECTIVELY	PROLIFICAL	PROMETHEUMS	PRONATIONS
PROJECTIVITIES	PROLIFICALLY	PROMETHIUM	PRONATORES
PROJECTIVITY	PROLIFICATION	PROMETHIUMS	PRONENESSES
PROJECTIZATION	PROLIFICATIONS	PROMILITARY	PRONEPHRIC
PROJECTIZATIONS	PROLIFICITIES	PROMIMENTLY	PRONEPHROI
PROJECTMENT	PROLIFICITY	PROMINENCE	PRONEPHROS
PROJECTMENTS	PROLIFICNESS	PROMINENCES	PRONEPHROSES
PROJECTORS	PROLIFICNESSES	PROMINENCIES	PRONGBUCKS
PROJECTURE	PROLIXIOUS	PROMINENCY	PRONGHORNS
PROJECTURES	PROLIXITIES	PROMINENTLY	PRONOMINAL
PROKARYONS	PROLIXNESS	PROMINENTNESS	PRONOMINALISE
PROKARYOTE	PROLIXNESSES	PROMINENTNESSES	PRONOMINALISED
PROKARYOTES	PROLOCUTION	PROMISCUITIES	PRONOMINALISES

PRONOMINALISING	PROPAGANDIZERS	PROPHETICALLY	PROPOSITAE
PRONOMINALIZE	PROPAGANDIZES	PROPHETICISM	PROPOSITION
PRONOMINALIZED	PROPAGANDIZING	PROPHETICISMS	PROPOSTTIONAL
PRONOMINALIZES	PROPAGATED	PROPHETISM	PROPOSITIONALLY
PRONOMINALIZING	PROPAGATES	PROPHETISMS	PROPOSITIONED
PRONOMINALLY	PROPAGATING	PROPHETSHIP	PROPOSITIONING
PRONOUNCEABLE	PROPAGATION	PROPHETSHIPS	PROPOSITIONS
PRONOUNCED	PROPAGATIONAL	PROPHYLACTIC	PROPOSITUS
PRONOUNCEDLY	PROPAGATIONS	PROPHYLACTICS	PROPOUNDED
PRONOUNCEMENT	PROPAGATIVE	PROPHYLAXES	PROPOUNDER
PRONOUNCEMENTS	PROPAGATOR	PROPHYLAXIS	PROPOUNDERS
PRONOUNCER	PROPAGATORS	PROPINQUITIES	PROPOUNDING
PRONOUNCERS	PROPAGULES	PROPINQUITY	PROPOXYPHENE
PRONOUNCES	PROPAGULUM	PROPIONATE	PROPOXYPHENES
PRONOUNCING	PROPANEDIOIC	PROPIONATES	PROPRAETOR
PRONOUNCINGS	PROPANONES	PROPITIABLE	PROPRAETORIAL
PRONUCLEAR	PROPAROXYTONE	PROPITIATE	PROPRAETORIAN
PRONUCLEARIST	PROPAROXYTONES	PROPITIATED	PROPRAETORS
PRONUCLEARISTS	PROPELLANT	PROPITIATES	PROPRANOLOL
PRONUCLEUS	PROPELLANTS	PROPITIATING	PROPRANOLOLS
PRONUCLEUSES	PROPELLENT	PROPITIATION	PROPRETORS
PRONUNCIAMENTO	PROPELLENTS	PROPITIATIONS	PROPRIETARIES
PRONUNCIAMENTOS	PROPELLERS	PROPITIATIOUS	PROPRIETARILY
PRONUNCIATION	PROPELLING	PROPITIATIVE	PROPRIETARY
PRONUNCIATIONAL	PROPELLORS	PROPITIATOR	PROPRIETIES
PRONUNCIATIONS	PROPELMENT	PROPITIATORIES	PROPRIETOR
PRONUNCIOS	PROPELMENTS	PROPITIATORILY	PROPRIETORIAL
PROOEMIONS	PROPENDENT	PROPITIATORS	PROPRIETORIALLY
PROOEMIUMS	PROPENDING	PROPITIATORY	PROPRIETORS
PROOFREADER	PROPENSELY	PROPITIOUS	PROPRIETORSHIP
PROOFREADERS	PROPENSENESS	PROPITIOUSLY	PROPRIETORSHIPS
PROOFREADING	PROPENSENESSES	PROPITIOUSNESS	PROPRIETRESS
PROOFREADINGS	PROPENSION	PROPLASTID	PROPRIETRESSES
PROOFREADS	PROPENSIONS	PROPLASTIDS	PROPRIETRICES
PROOFROOMS	PROPENSITIES	PROPODEONS	PROPRIETRIX
PROPAEDEUTIC	PROPENSITY	PROPODEUMS	PROPRIETRIXES
PROPAEDEUTICAL	PROPENSIVE	PROPOLISES	PROPRIOCEPTION
PROPAEDEUTICS	PROPERDINS	PROPONENTS	PROPRIOCEPTIONS
PROPAGABILITIES	PROPERISPOMENON	PROPORTION	PROPRIOCEPTIVE
PROPAGABILITY	PROPERNESS	PROPORTIONABLE	PROPRIOCEPTOR
PROPAGABLE	PROPERNESSES	PROPORTIONABLY	PROPRIOCEPTORS
PROPAGABLENESS	PROPERTIED	PROPORTIONAL	PROPROCTOR
PROPAGANDA	PROPERTIES	PROPORTIONALITY	PROPROCTORS
PROPAGANDAS	PROPERTYING	PROPORTIONALLY	PROPUGNATION
PROPAGANDISE	PROPERTYLESS	PROPORTIONALS	PROPUGNATIONS
PROPAGANDISED	PROPHECIES	PROPORTIONATE	PROPULSION
PROPAGANDISER	PROPHESIABLE	PROPORTIONATED	PROPULSIONS
PROPAGANDISERS	PROPHESIED	PROPORTIONATELY	PROPULSIVE
PROPAGANDISES	PROPHESIER	PROPORTIONATES	PROPULSORS
PROPAGANDISING	PROPHESIERS	PROPORTIONATING	PROPULSORY
PROPAGANDISM	PROPHESIES	PROPORTIONED	PROPYLAEUM
PROPAGANDISMS	PROPHESYING	PROPORTIONING	PROPYLAMINE
PROPAGANDIST	PROPHESYINGS	PROPORTIONINGS	PROPYLAMINES
PROPAGANDISTIC	PROPHETESS	PROPORTIONLESS	PROPYLENES
PROPAGANDISTS	PROPHETESSES	PROPORTIONMENT	PROPYLITES
PROPAGANDIZE	PROPHETHOOD	PROPORTIONMENTS	PROPYLITISATION
PROPAGANDIZED	PROPHETHOODS	PROPORTIONS	PROPYLITISE
PROPAGANDIZER	PROPHETICAL	PROPOSABLE	PROPYLITISED

PROPYLITISES	PROSELYTED	PROSPECTINGS	PROSTRATION
PROPYLITISING	PROSELYTES	PROSPECTION	PROSTRATIONS
PROPYLITIZATION	PROSELYTIC	PROSPECTIONS	PROSYLLOGISM
PROPYLITIZE	PROSELYTING	PROSPECTIVE	PROSYLLOGISMS
PROPYLITIZED	PROSELYTISATION	PROSPECTIVELY	PROTACTINIUM
PROPYLITIZES	PROSELYTISE	PROSPECTIVENESS	PROTACTINIUMS
PROPYLITIZING	PROSELYTISED	PROSPECTIVES	PROTAGONISM
PRORATABLE	PROSELYTISER	PROSPECTLESS	PROTAGONISMS
PRORATIONS	PROSELYTISERS	PROSPECTOR	PROTAGONIST
PRORECTORS	PROSELYTISES	PROSPECTORS	PROTAGONISTS
PROROGATED	PROSELYTISING	PROSPECTUS	PROTAMINES
PROROGATES	PROSELYTISM	PROSPECTUSES	PROTANDRIES
PROROGATING	PROSELYTISMS	PROSPERING	PROTANDROUS
PROROGATION	PROSELYTIZATION	PROSPERITIES	PROTANOMALIES
PROROGATIONS	PROSELYTIZE	PROSPERITY	PROTANOMALOUS
PROROGUING	PROSELYTIZED	PROSPEROUS	PROTANOMALY
PROSAICALLY	PROSELYTIZER	PROSPEROUSLY	PROTANOPES
PROSAICALNESS	PROSELYTIZERS	PROSPEROUSNESS	PROTANOPIA
PROSAICALNESSES	PROSELYTIZES	PROSTACYCLIN	PROTANOPIAS
PROSAICISM	PROSELYTIZING	PROSTACYCLINS	PROTANOPIC
PROSAICISMS	PROSEMINAR	PROSTAGLANDIN	PROTEACEOUS
PROSAICNESS	PROSEMINARS	PROSTAGLANDINS	PROTECTANT
PROSAICNESSES	PROSENCEPHALA	PROSTANTHERA	PROTECTANTS
PROSATEURS	PROSENCEPHALIC	PROSTANTHERAS	PROTECTERS
PROSAUROPOD	PROSENCEPHALON	PROSTATECTOMIES	PROTECTING
PROSAUROPODS	PROSENCHYMA	PROSTATECTOMY	PROTECTINGLY
PROSCENIUM	PROSENCHYMAS	PROSTATISM	PROTECTION
PROSCENIUMS	PROSENCHYMATA	PROSTATISMS	PROTECTIONISM
PROSCIUTTI	PROSENCHYMATOUS	PROSTATITIS	PROTECTIONISMS
PROSCIUTTO	PROSEUCHAE	PROSTATITISES	PROTECTIONIST
PROSCIUTTOS	PROSIFYING	PROSTERNUM	PROTECTIONISTS
PROSCRIBED	PROSILIENCIES	PROSTERNUMS	PROTECTIONS
PROSCRIBER	PROSILIENCY	PROSTHESES	PROTECTIVE
PROSCRIBERS	PROSILIENT	PROSTHESIS	PROTECTIVELY
PROSCRIBES	PROSIMIANS	PROSTHETIC	PROTECTIVENESS
PROSCRIBING	PROSINESSES	PROSTHETICALLY	PROTECTIVES
PROSCRIPTION	PROSLAMBANOMENE	PROSTHETICS	PROTECTORAL
PROSCRIPTIONS	PROSLAVERY	PROSTHETIST	PROTECTORATE
PROSCRIPTIVE	PROSOBRANCH	PROSTHETISTS	PROTECTORATES
PROSCRIPTIVELY	PROSOBRANCHS	PROSTHODONTIA	PROTECTORIAL
PROSCRIPTS	PROSODIANS	PROSTHODONTIAS	PROTECTORIES
PROSECTING	PROSODICAL	PROSTHODONTICS	PROTECTORLESS
PROSECTORIAL	PROSODICALLY	PROSTHODONTIST	PROTECTORS
PROSECTORS	PROSODISTS	PROSTHODONTISTS	PROTECTORSHIP
PROSECTORSHIP	PROSOPAGNOSIA	PROSTITUTE	PROTECTORSHIPS
PROSECTORSHIPS	PROSOPAGNOSIAS	PROSTITUTED	PROTECTORY
PROSECUTABLE	PROSOPOGRAPHER	PROSTITUTES	PROTECTRESS
PROSECUTED	PROSOPOGRAPHERS	PROSTITUTING	PROTECTRESSES
PROSECUTES	PROSOPOGRAPHIES	PROSTITUTION	PROTECTRICES
PROSECUTING	PROSOPOGRAPHY	PROSTITUTIONS	PROTECTRIX
PROSECUTION	PROSOPOPEIA	PROSTITUTOR	PROTECTRIXES
PROSECUTIONS	PROSOPOPEIAL	PROSTITUTORS	PROTEIFORM
PROSECUTOR	PROSOPOPEIAS	PROSTOMIAL	PROTEINACEOUS
PROSECUTORIAL	PROSOPOPOEIA	PROSTOMIUM	PROTEINASE
PROSECUTORS	PROSOPOPOEIAL	PROSTOMIUMS	PROTEINASES
PROSECUTRICES	PROSOPOPOEIAS	PROSTRATED	PROTEINOUS
PROSECUTRIX	PROSPECTED	PROSTRATES	PROTEINURIA
PROSECUTRIXES	PROSPECTING	PROSTRATING	PROTEINURIAS

PROTENDING
PROTENSION
PROTENSIONS
PROTENSITIES
PROTENSITY
PROTENSIVE
PROTENSIVELY
PROTEOCLASTIC
PROTEOGLYCAN
PROTEOGLYCANS
PROTEOLYSE
PROTEOLYSED
PROTEOLYSES
PROTEOLYSING
PROTEOLYSIS
PROTEOLYTIC
PROTEOLYTICALLY
PROTEOMICS
PROTERANDRIES
PROTERANDROUS
PROTERANDRY
PROTEROGYNIES
PROTEROGYNOUS
PROTEROGYNY
PROTERVITIES
PROTERVITY
PROTESTANT
PROTESTANTS
PROTESTATION
PROTESTATIONS
PROTESTERS
PROTESTING
PROTESTINGLY
PROTESTORS
PROTHALAMIA
PROTHALAMION
PROTHALAMIUM
PROTHALLIA
PROTHALLIAL
PROTHALLIC
PROTHALLIUM
PROTHALLOID
PROTHALLUS
PROTHALLUSES
PROTHETICALLY
PROTHONOTARIAL
PROTHONOTARIAT
PROTHONOTARIATS
PROTHONOTARIES
PROTHONOTARY
PROTHORACES
PROTHORACIC
PROTHORAXES
PROTHROMBIN
PROTHROMBINS
PROTISTANS
PROTISTOLOGIES
PROTISTOLOGIST

PROTISTOLOGISTS
PROTISTOLOGY
PROTOACTINIUM
PROTOACTINIUMS
PROTOAVISES
PROTOCHORDATE
PROTOCHORDATES
PROTOCOCCAL
PROTOCOLED
PROTOCOLIC
PROTOCOLING
PROTOCOLISE
PROTOCOLISED
PROTOCOLISES
PROTOCOLISING
PROTOCOLIST
PROTOCOLISTS
PROTOCOLIZE
PROTOCOLIZED
PROTOCOLIZES
PROTOCOLIZING
PROTOCOLLED
PROTOCOLLING
PROTOCTIST
PROTOCTISTS
PROTODERMS
PROTOGALAXIES
PROTOGALAXY
PROTOGENIC
PROTOGINES
PROTOGYNIES
PROTOGYNOUS
PROTOHISTORIAN
PROTOHISTORIANS
PROTOHISTORIC
PROTOHISTORIES
PROTOHISTORY
PROTOHUMAN
PROTOHUMANS
PROTOLANGUAGE
PROTOLANGUAGES
PROTOLITHIC
PROTOMARTYR
PROTOMARTYRS
PROTOMORPHIC
PROTONATED
PROTONATES
PROTONATING
PROTONATION
PROTONATIONS
PROTONEMAL
PROTONEMATA
PROTONEMATAL
PROTONOTARIAL
PROTONOTARIAT
PROTONOTARIATS
PROTONOTARIES
PROTONOTARY

PROTOPATHIC
PROTOPATHIES
PROTOPATHY
PROTOPHILIC
PROTOPHLOEM
PROTOPHLOEMS
PROTOPHYTE
PROTOPHYTES
PROTOPHYTIC
PROTOPLANET
PROTOPLANETARY
PROTOPLANETS
PROTOPLASM
PROTOPLASMAL
PROTOPLASMATIC
PROTOPLASMIC
PROTOPLASMS
PROTOPLAST
PROTOPLASTIC
PROTOPLASTS
PROTOPORPHYRIN
PROTOPORPHYRINS
PROTOSPATAIRE
PROTOSPATAIRES
PROTOSPATHAIRE
PROTOSPATHAIRES
PROTOSPATHARIUS
PROTOSTARS
PROTOSTELE
PROTOSTELES
PROTOSTELIC
PROTOSTOME
PROTOSTOMES
PROTOTHERIAN
PROTOTHERIANS
PROTOTROPH
PROTOTROPHIC
PROTOTROPHIES
PROTOTROPHS
PROTOTROPHY
PROTOTYPAL
PROTOTYPED
PROTOTYPES
PROTOTYPIC
PROTOTYPICAL
PROTOTYPICALLY
PROTOTYPING
PROTOXIDES
PROTOXYLEM
PROTOXYLEMS
PROTOZOANS
PROTOZOOLOGICAL
PROTOZOOLOGIES
PROTOZOOLOGIST
PROTOZOOLOGISTS
PROTOZOOLOGY
PROTOZOONS
PROTRACTED

PROTRACTEDLY
PROTRACTEDNESS
PROTRACTIBLE
PROTRACTILE
PROTRACTING
PROTRACTION
PROTRACTIONS
PROTRACTIVE
PROTRACTOR
PROTRACTORS
PROTREPTIC
PROTREPTICAL
PROTREPTICS
PROTRUDABLE
PROTRUDENT
PROTRUDING
PROTRUSIBLE
PROTRUSILE
PROTRUSION
PROTRUSIONS
PROTRUSIVE
PROTRUSIVELY
PROTRUSIVENESS
PROTUBERANCE
PROTUBERANCES
PROTUBERANCIES
PROTUBERANCY
PROTUBERANT
PROTUBERANTLY
PROTUBERATE
PROTUBERATED
PROTUBERATES
PROTUBERATING
PROTUBERATION
PROTUBERATIONS
PROUDHEARTED
PROUDNESSES
PROUSTITES
PROVABILITIES
PROVABILITY
PROVABLENESS
PROVABLENESSES
PROVANTING
PROVASCULAR
PROVECTION
PROVECTIONS
PROVEDITORE
PROVEDITORES
PROVEDITORS
PROVEDORES
PROVENANCE
PROVENANCES
PROVENDERED
PROVENDERING
PROVENDERS
PROVENIENCE
PROVENIENCES

PROVENTRICULAR	PROVOCATEUR	PSALMODICAL	PSEUDOCLASSICS
PROVENTRICULI	PROVOCATEURS	PSALMODIES	PSEUDOCODE
PROVENTRICULUS	PROVOCATION	PSALMODISE	PSEUDOCODES
PROVERBIAL	PROVOCATIONS	PSALMODISED	PSEUDOCOEL
PROVERBIALISE	PROVOCATIVE	PSALMODISES	PSEUDOCOELOMATE
PROVERBIALISED	PROVOCATIVELY	PSALMODISING	PSEUDOCOELS
PROVERBIALISES	PROVOCATIVENESS	PSALMODIST	PSEUDOCYESES
PROVERBIALISING	PROVOCATIVES	PSALMODISTS	PSEUDOCYESIS
PROVERBIALISM	PROVOCATOR	PSALMODIZE	PSEUDOEPHEDRINE
PROVERBIALISMS	PROVOCATORS	PSALMODIZED	PSEUDOGRAPH
PROVERBIALIST	PROVOCATORY	PSALMODIZES	PSEUDOGRAPHIES
PROVERBIALISTS	PROVOKABLE	PSALMODIZING	PSEUDOGRAPHS
PROVERBIALIZE	PROVOKEMENT	PSALTERIAN	PSEUDOGRAPHY
PROVERBIALIZED	PROVOKEMENTS	PSALTERIES	PSEUDOLOGIA
PROVERBIALIZES	PROVOKINGLY	PSALTERIUM	PSEUDOLOGIAS
PROVERBIALIZING	PROVOLONES	PSALTRESSES	PSEUDOLOGIES
PROVERBIALLY	PROVOSTRIES	PSAMMOPHIL	PSEUDOLOGUE
PROVERBING	PROVOSTSHIP	PSAMMOPHILE	PSEUDOLOGUES
PROVIDABLE	PROVOSTSHIPS	PSAMMOPHILES	PSEUDOLOGY
PROVIDENCE	PROWLINGLY	PSAMMOPHILOUS	PSEUDOMARTYR
PROVIDENCES	PROXIMALLY	PSAMMOPHILS	PSEUDOMARTYRS
PROVIDENTIAL	PROXIMATELY	PSAMMOPHYTE	PSEUDOMEMBRANE
PROVIDENTIALLY	PROXIMATENESS	PSAMMOPHYTES	PSEUDOMEMBRANES
PROVIDENTLY	PROXIMATENESSES	PSAMMOPHYTIC	PSEUDOMONAD
PROVINCEWIDE	PROXIMATION	PSELLISMUS	PSEUDOMONADES
PROVINCIAL	PROXIMATIONS	PSELLISMUSES	PSEUDOMONADS
PROVINCIALISE	PROXIMITIES	PSEPHOANALYSES	PSEUDOMONAS
PROVINCIALISED	PROZYMITES	PSEPHOANALYSIS	PSEUDOMORPH
PROVINCIALISES	PRUDENTIAL	PSEPHOLOGICAL	PSEUDOMORPHIC
PROVINCIALISING	PRUDENTIALISM	PSEPHOLOGICALLY	PSEUDOMORPHISM
PROVINCIALISM	PRUDENTIALISMS	PSEPHOLOGIES	PSEUDOMORPHISMS
PROVINCIALISMS	PRUDENTIALIST	PSEPHOLOGIST	PSEUDOMORPHOUS
PROVINCIALIST	PRUDENTIALISTS	PSEPHOLOGISTS	PSEUDOMORPHS
PROVINCIALISTS	PRUDENTIALITIES	PSEPHOLOGY	PSEUDOMUTUALITY
PROVINCIALITIES	PRUDENTIALITY	PSEUDAESTHESIA	PSEUDONYMITIES
PROVINCIALITY	PRUDENTIALLY	PSEUDAESTHESIAS	PSEUDONYMITY
PROVINCIALIZE	PRUDENTIALS	PSEUDARTHROSES	PSEUDONYMOUS
PROVINCIALIZED	PRUDISHNESS	PSEUDARTHROSIS	PSEUDONYMOUSLY
PROVINCIALIZES	PRUDISHNESSES	PSEUDEPIGRAPH	PSEUDONYMS
PROVINCIALIZING	PRURIENCES	PSEUDEPIGRAPHA	PSEUDOPODAL
PROVINCIALLY	PRURIENCIES	PSEUDEPIGRAPHIC	PSEUDOPODIA
PROVINCIALS	PRURIENTLY	PSEUDEPIGRAPHON	PSEUDOPODIAL
PROVIRUSES	PRURIGINOUS	PSEUDEPIGRAPHS	PSEUDOPODIUM
PROVISIONAL	PRURITUSES	PSEUDEPIGRAPHY	PSEUDOPODS
PROVISIONALLY	PRUSSIANISATION	PSEUDERIES	PSEUDOPREGNANCY
PROVISIONALS	PRUSSIANISE	PSEUDIMAGINES	PSEUDOPREGNANT
PROVISIONARIES	PRUSSIANISED	PSEUDIMAGO	PSEUDORANDOM
PROVISIONARY	PRUSSIANISES	PSEUDIMAGOS	PSEUDOSCALAR
PROVISIONED	PRUSSIANISING	PSEUDOACID	PSEUDOSCALARS
PROVISIONER	PRUSSIANIZATION	PSEUDOACIDS	PSEUDOSCHOLARLY
PROVISIONERS	PRUSSIANIZE	PSEUDOALLELE	PSEUDOSCIENCE
PROVISIONING	PRUSSIANIZED	PSEUDOALLELES	PSEUDOSCIENCES
PROVISIONS	PRUSSIANIZES	PSEUDOBULB	PSEUDOSCIENTIST
PROVISORILY	PRUSSIANIZING	PSEUDOBULBS	PSEUDOSCOPE
PROVITAMIN	PRUSSIATES	PSEUDOCARP	PSEUDOSCOPES
PROVITAMINS	PSALIGRAPHIES	PSEUDOCARPOUS	PSEUDOSCORPION
PROVOCABLE	PSALIGRAPHY	PSEUDOCARPS	PSEUDOSCORPIONS
PROVOCANTS	PSALMBOOKS	PSEUDOCLASSIC	PSEUDOSOLUTION

PSEUDOSOLUTIONS	PSYCHOANALYSIS	PSYCHOHISTORIES	PSYCHOPHYSICIST
PSEUDOSYMMETRY	PSYCHOANALYST	PSYCHOHISTORY	PSYCHOPHYSICS
PSEUDOVECTOR	PSYCHOANALYSTS	PSYCHOKINESES	PSYCHOPOMP
PSEUDOVECTORS	PSYCHOANALYTIC	PSYCHOKINESIS	PSYCHOPOMPS
PSILANTHROPIC	PSYCHOANALYZE	PSYCHOKINETIC	PSYCHOSEXUAL
PSILANTHROPIES	PSYCHOANALYZED	PSYCHOLINGUIST	PSYCHOSEXUALITY
PSILANTHROPISM	PSYCHOANALYZER	PSYCHOLINGUISTS	PSYCHOSEXUALLY
PSILANTHROPISMS	PSYCHOANALYZERS	PSYCHOLOGIC	PSYCHOSOCIAL
PSILANTHROPIST	PSYCHOANALYZES	PSYCHOLOGICAL	PSYCHOSOCIALLY
PSILANTHROPISTS	PSYCHOANALYZING	PSYCHOLOGICALLY	PSYCHOSOMATIC
PSILANTHROPY	PSYCHOBABBLE	PSYCHOLOGIES	PSYCHOSOMATICS
PSILOCYBIN	PSYCHOBABBLER	PSYCHOLOGISE	PSYCHOSOMIMETIC
PSILOCYBINS	PSYCHOBABBLERS	PSYCHOLOGISED	PSYCHOSURGEON
PSILOMELANE	PSYCHOBABBLES	PSYCHOLOGISES	PSYCHOSURGEONS
PSILOMELANES	PSYCHOBILLIES	PSYCHOLOGISING	PSYCHOSURGERIES
PSILOPHYTE	PSYCHOBILLY	PSYCHOLOGISM	PSYCHOSURGERY
PSILOPHYTES	PSYCHOBIOGRAPHY	PSYCHOLOGISMS	PSYCHOSURGICAL
PSILOPHYTIC	PSYCHOBIOLOGIC	PSYCHOLOGIST	PSYCHOSYNTHESES
PSITTACINE	PSYCHOBIOLOGIES	PSYCHOLOGISTIC	PSYCHOSYNTHESIS
PSITTACINES	PSYCHOBIOLOGIST	PSYCHOLOGISTS	PSYCHOTECHNICS
PSITTACOSES	PSYCHOBIOLOGY	PSYCHOLOGIZE	PSYCHOTHERAPIES
PSITTACOSIS	PSYCHOCHEMICAL	PSYCHOLOGIZED	PSYCHOTHERAPIST
PSITTACOTIC	PSYCHOCHEMICALS	PSYCHOLOGIZES	PSYCHOTHERAPY
PSORIATICS	PSYCHOCHEMISTRY	PSYCHOLOGIZING	PSYCHOTICALLY
PSYCHAGOGUE	PSYCHODELIA	PSYCHOLOGY	PSYCHOTICISM
PSYCHAGOGUES	PSYCHODELIAS	PSYCHOMACHIA	PSYCHOTICISMS
PSYCHASTHENIA	PSYCHODELIC	PSYCHOMACHIAS	PSYCHOTICS
PSYCHASTHENIAS	PSYCHODELICALLY	PSYCHOMACHIES	PSYCHOTOMIMETIC
PSYCHASTHENIC	PSYCHODRAMA	PSYCHOMACHY	PSYCHOTOXIC
PSYCHASTHENICS	PSYCHODRAMAS	PSYCHOMETER	PSYCHOTROPIC
PSYCHEDELIA	PSYCHODRAMATIC	PSYCHOMETERS	PSYCHOTROPICS
PSYCHEDELIAS	PSYCHODYNAMIC	PSYCHOMETRIC	PSYCHROMETER
PSYCHEDELIC	PSYCHODYNAMICS	PSYCHOMETRICAL	PSYCHROMETERS
PSYCHEDELICALLY	PSYCHOGALVANIC	PSYCHOMETRICIAN	PSYCHROMETRIC
PSYCHEDELICS	PSYCHOGASES	PSYCHOMETRICS	PSYCHROMETRICAL
PSYCHIATER	PSYCHOGENESES	PSYCHOMETRIES	PSYCHROMETRIES
PSYCHIATERS	PSYCHOGENESIS	PSYCHOMETRIST	PSYCHROMETRY
PSYCHIATRIC	PSYCHOGENETIC	PSYCHOMETRISTS	PSYCHROPHILIC
PSYCHIATRICAL	PSYCHOGENETICAL	PSYCHOMETRY	PTARMIGANS
PSYCHIATRICALLY	PSYCHOGENETICS	PSYCHOMOTOR	PTERANODON
PSYCHIATRIES	PSYCHOGENIC	PSYCHONEUROSES	PTERANODONS
PSYCHIATRIST	PSYCHOGENICALLY	PSYCHONEUROSIS	PTERIDINES
PSYCHIATRISTS	PSYCHOGERIATRIC	PSYCHONEUROTIC	PTERIDOLOGICAL
PSYCHIATRY	PSYCHOGNOSES	PSYCHONEUROTICS	PTERIDOLOGIES
PSYCHICALLY	PSYCHOGNOSIS	PSYCHONOMIC	PTERIDOLOGIST
PSYCHICISM	PSYCHOGNOSTIC	PSYCHONOMICS	PTERIDOLOGISTS
PSYCHICISMS	PSYCHOGONIES	PSYCHOPATH	PTERIDOLOGY
PSYCHICIST	PSYCHOGONY	PSYCHOPATHIC	PTERIDOMANIA
PSYCHICISTS	PSYCHOGRAM	PSYCHOPATHICS	PTERIDOMANIAS
PSYCHOACOUSTIC	PSYCHOGRAMS	PSYCHOPATHIES	PTERIDOPHILIST
PSYCHOACOUSTICS	PSYCHOGRAPH	PSYCHOPATHIST	PTERIDOPHILISTS
PSYCHOACTIVE	PSYCHOGRAPHIC	PSYCHOPATHISTS	PTERIDOPHYTE
PSYCHOANALYSE	PSYCHOGRAPHICAL	PSYCHOPATHOLOGY	PTERIDOPHYTES
PSYCHOANALYSED	PSYCHOGRAPHICS	PSYCHOPATHS	PTERIDOPHYTIC
PSYCHOANALYSER	PSYCHOGRAPHIES	PSYCHOPATHY	PTERIDOPHYTOUS
PSYCHOANALYSERS	PSYCHOGRAPHS	PSYCHOPHILIES	PTERIDOSPERM
PSYCHOANALYSES	PSYCHOGRAPHY	PSYCHOPHILY	PTERIDOSPERMS
PSYCHOANALYSING	PSYCHOHISTORIAN	PSYCHOPHYSICAL	PTERODACTYL

PTERODACTYLE	PUERPERIUM	PULVERISATION	PUNCTUATIONS
PTERODACTYLES	PUERPERIUMS	PULVERISATIONS	PUNCTUATIVE
PTERODACTYLS	PUFFINESSES	PULVERISED	PUNCTUATOR
PTEROSAURIAN	PUFFTALOONAS	PULVERISER	PUNCTUATORS
PTEROSAURIANS	PUFTALOONIES	PULVERISERS	PUNCTULATE
PTEROSAURS	PUFTALOONS	PULVERISES	PUNCTULATED
PTERYGIALS	PUGGINESSES	PULVERISING	PUNCTULATION
PTERYGIUMS	PUGILISTIC	PULVERIZABLE	PUNCTULATIONS
PTERYGOIDS	PUGILISTICAL	PULVERIZATION	PUNCTURABLE
PTERYLOGRAPHIC	PUGILISTICALLY	PULVERIZATIONS	PUNCTURATION
PTERYLOGRAPHIES	PUGNACIOUS	PULVERIZED	PUNCTURATIONS
PTERYLOGRAPHY	PUGNACIOUSLY	PULVERIZER	PUNCTURERS
PTERYLOSES	PUGNACIOUSNESS	PULVERIZERS	PUNCTURING
PTERYLOSIS	PUGNACITIES	PULVERIZES	PUNDIGRION
PTOCHOCRACIES	PUISSANCES	PULVERIZING	PUNDIGRIONS
PTOCHOCRACY	PUISSANTLY	PULVERULENCE	PUNDITRIES
PTYALAGOGIC	PUISSAUNCE	PULVERULENCES	PUNDONORES
PTYALAGOGUE	PUISSAUNCES	PULVERULENT	PUNGENCIES
PTYALAGOGUES	PULCHRITUDE	PULVILISED	PUNICACEOUS
PTYALISING	PULCHRITUDES	PULVILIZED	PUNINESSES
PTYALIZING	PULCHRITUDINOUS	PULVILLIFORM	PUNISHABILITIES
PUBCRAWLER	PULLULATED	PULVILLING	PUNISHABILITY
PUBCRAWLERS	PULLULATES	PULVILLIOS	PUNISHABLE
PUBERULENT	PULLULATING	PULVINATED	PUNISHINGLY
PUBERULOUS	PULLULATION	PULVINULES	PUNISHMENT
PUBESCENCE	PULLULATIONS	PUMICATING	PUNISHMENTS
PUBESCENCES	PULMOBRANCH	PUMMELLING	PUNITIVELY
PUBLICALLY	PULMOBRANCHIATE	PUMPERNICKEL	PUNITIVENESS
PUBLICATION	PULMOBRANCHS	PUMPERNICKELS	PUNITIVENESSES
PUBLICATIONS	PULMONATES	PUMPKINSEED	PUNKINESSES
PUBLICISED	PULPBOARDS	PUMPKINSEEDS	PUPIGEROUS
PUBLICISES	PULPIFYING	PUNCHBALLS	PUPILABILITIES
PUBLICISING	PULPINESSES	PUNCHBOARD	PUPILABILITY
PUBLICISTS	PULPITEERS	PUNCHBOARDS	PUPILARITIES
PUBLICITIES	PULPITRIES	PUNCHBOWLS	PUPILARITY
PUBLICIZED	PULPSTONES	PUNCHINELLO	PUPILLAGES
PUBLICIZES	PULSATANCE	PUNCHINELLOES	PUPILLARITIES
PUBLICIZING	PULSATANCES	PUNCHINELLOS	PUPILLARITY
PUBLICNESS	PULSATILITIES	PUNCHINESS	PUPILLATED
PUBLICNESSES	PULSATILITY	PUNCHINESSES	PUPILLATES
PUBLISHABLE	PULSATILLA	PUNCTATION	PUPILLATING
PUBLISHERS	PULSATILLAS	PUNCTATIONS	PUPILSHIPS
PUBLISHING	PULSATIONS	PUNCTATORS	PUPIPAROUS
PUBLISHINGS	PULSATIVELY	PUNCTILIOS	PUPPETEERED
PUBLISHMENT	PULSELESSNESS	PUNCTILIOUS	PUPPETEERING
PUBLISHMENTS	PULSELESSNESSES	PUNCTILIOUSLY	PUPPETEERS
PUCCINIACEOUS	PULSIMETER	PUNCTILIOUSNESS	PUPPETLIKE
PUCKERIEST	PULSIMETERS	PUNCTUALIST	PUPPETRIES
PUCKISHNESS	PULSOMETER	PUNCTUALISTS	PUPPYHOODS
PUCKISHNESSES	PULSOMETERS	PUNCTUALITIES	PURBLINDLY
PUDDENINGS	PULTACEOUS	PUNCTUALITY	PURBLINDNESS
PUDGINESSES	PULTRUSION	PUNCTUALLY	PURBLINDNESSES
PUDIBUNDITIES	PULTRUSIONS	PUNCTUATED	PURCHASABILITY
PUDIBUNDITY	PULVERABLE	PUNCTUATES	PURCHASABLE
PUDICITIES	PULVERATION	PUNCTUATING	PURCHASERS
PUERILISMS	PULVERATIONS	PUNCTUATION	PURCHASING
PUERILITIES	PULVERINES	PUNCTUATIONIST	PURDONIUMS
PUERPERALLY	PULVERISABLE	PUNCTUATIONISTS	PUREBLOODS

PURENESSES	PURSUINGLY	PUZZLEHEADED	PYRANOMETER
PURGATIONS	PURSUIVANT	PUZZLEMENT	PYRANOMETERS
PURGATIVELY	PURSUIVANTS	PUZZLEMENTS	PYRANOSIDE
PURGATIVES	PURTENANCE	PUZZLINGLY	PYRANOSIDES
PURGATORIAL	PURTENANCES	PUZZOLANAS	PYRARGYRITE
PURGATORIALLY	PURTRAYING	PYCNIDIOSPORE	PYRARGYRITES
PURGATORIAN	PURULENCES	PYCNIDIOSPORES	PYRENEITES
PURGATORIES	PURULENCIES	PYCNOCONIDIA	PYRENOCARP
PURIFICATION	PURULENTLY	PYCNOCONIDIUM	PYRENOCARPS
PURIFICATIONS	PURVEYANCE	PYCNODYSOSTOSES	PYRENOMYCETOUS
PURIFICATIVE	PURVEYANCES	PYCNODYSOSTOSIS	PYRETHRINS
PURIFICATOR	PUSCHKINIA	PYCNOGONID	PYRETHROID
PURIFICATORS	PUSCHKINIAS	PYCNOGONIDS	PYRETHROIDS
PURIFICATORY	PUSHCHAIRS	PYCNOGONOID	PYRETHRUMS
PURISTICAL	PUSHFULNESS	PYCNOMETER	PYRETOLOGIES
PURISTICALLY	PUSHFULNESSES	PYCNOMETERS	PYRETOLOGY
PURITANICAL	PUSHINESSES	PYCNOMETRIC	PYRETOTHERAPIES
PURITANICALLY	PUSHINGNESS	PYCNOSPORE	PYRETOTHERAPY
PURITANICALNESS	PUSHINGNESSES	PYCNOSPORES	PYRGEOMETER
PURITANISE	PUSILLANIMITIES	PYCNOSTYLE	PYRGEOMETERS
PURITANISED	PUSILLANIMITY	PYCNOSTYLES	PYRHELIOMETER
PURITANISES	PUSILLANIMOUS	PYELITISES	PYRHELIOMETERS
PURITANISING	PUSILLANIMOUSLY	PYELOGRAMS	PYRHELIOMETRIC
PURITANISM	PUSSYFOOTED	PYELOGRAPHIC	PYRIDOXALS
PURITANISMS	PUSSYFOOTER	PYELOGRAPHIES	PYRIDOXAMINE
PURITANIZE	PUSSYFOOTERS	PYELOGRAPHY	PYRIDOXAMINES
PURITANIZED	PUSSYFOOTING	PYELONEPHRITIC	PYRIDOXINE
PURITANIZES	PUSSYFOOTS	PYELONEPHRITIS	PYRIDOXINES
PURITANIZING	PUSTULANTS	PYGOSTYLES	PYRIDOXINS
PURLICUING	PUSTULATED	PYKNODYSOSTOSES	PYRIMETHAMINE
PURLOINERS	PUSTULATES	PYKNODYSOSTOSIS	PYRIMETHAMINES
PURLOINING	PUSTULATING	PYKNOMETER	PYRIMIDINE
PUROMYCINS	PUSTULATION	PYKNOMETERS	PYRIMIDINES
PURPLEHEART	PUSTULATIONS	PYKNOSOMES	PYRITHIAMINE
PURPLEHEARTS	PUTANGITANGI	PYLORECTOMIES	PYRITHIAMINES
PURPLENESS	PUTATIVELY	PYLORECTOMY	PYRITIFEROUS
PURPLENESSES	PUTONGHUAS	PYOGENESES	PYRITISING
PURPLISHNESS	PUTREFACIENT	PYOGENESIS	PYRITIZING
PURPLISHNESSES	PUTREFACTION	PYORRHOEAL	PYRITOHEDRA
PURPORTEDLY	PUTREFACTIONS	PYORRHOEAS	PYRITOHEDRAL
PURPORTING	PUTREFACTIVE	PYORRHOEIC	PYRITOHEDRON
PURPORTLESS	PUTREFIABLE	PYRACANTHA	PYROBALLOGIES
PURPOSEFUL	PUTREFIERS	PYRACANTHAS	PYROBALLOGY
PURPOSEFULLY	PUTREFYING	PYRACANTHS	PYROCATECHIN
PURPOSEFULNESS	PUTRESCENCE	PYRALIDIDS	PYROCATECHINS
PURPOSELESS	PUTRESCENCES	PYRAMIDALLY	PYROCATECHOL
PURPOSELESSLY	PUTRESCENT	PYRAMIDICAL	PYROCATECHOLS
PURPOSELESSNESS	PUTRESCIBILITY	PYRAMIDICALLY	PYROCERAMS
PURPOSIVELY	PUTRESCIBLE	PYRAMIDING	PYROCHEMICAL
PURPOSIVENESS	PUTRESCIBLES	PYRAMIDION	PYROCHEMICALLY
PURPOSIVENESSES	PUTRESCINE	PYRAMIDIONS	PYROCLASTIC
PURPRESTURE	PUTRESCINES	PYRAMIDIST	PYROCLASTICS
PURPRESTURES	PUTRIDITIES	PYRAMIDISTS	PYROCLASTS
PURSERSHIP	PUTRIDNESS	PYRAMIDOLOGIES	PYROELECTRIC
PURSERSHIPS	PUTRIDNESSES	PYRAMIDOLOGIST	PYROELECTRICITY
PURSINESSES	PUTSCHISTS	PYRAMIDOLOGISTS	PYROELECTRICS
PURSUANCES	PUTTYROOTS	PYRAMIDOLOGY	PYROGALLATE
PURSUANTLY	PUZZLEDOMS	PYRAMIDONS	PYROGALLATES

PYROGALLIC
PYROGALLOL
PYROGALLOLS
PYROGENETIC
PYROGENICITIES
PYROGENICITY
PYROGENOUS
PYROGNOSTIC
PYROGNOSTICS
PYROGRAPHER
PYROGRAPHERS
PYROGRAPHIC
PYROGRAPHIES
PYROGRAPHY
PYROGRAVURE
PYROGRAVURES
PYROKINESES
PYROKINESIS
PYROLATERS
PYROLATRIES
PYROLIGNEOUS
PYROLIGNIC
PYROLISING
PYROLIZING
PYROLOGIES
PYROLUSITE
PYROLUSITES
PYROLYSABLE
PYROLYSATE
PYROLYSATES
PYROLYSERS
PYROLYSING
PYROLYTICALLY
PYROLYZABLE
PYROLYZATE
PYROLYZATES
PYROLYZERS
PYROLYZING
PYROMAGNETIC
PYROMANCER
PYROMANCERS
PYROMANCIES
PYROMANIAC
PYROMANIACAL
PYROMANIACS
PYROMANIAS
PYROMANTIC
PYROMERIDE
PYROMERIDES
PYROMETALLURGY
PYROMETERS
PYROMETRIC
PYROMETRICAL
PYROMETRICALLY
PYROMETRIES
PYROMORPHITE
PYROMORPHITES
PYRONINOPHILIC

PYROPHOBIA
PYROPHOBIAS
PYROPHOBIC
PYROPHOBICS
PYROPHONES
PYROPHORIC
PYROPHOROUS
PYROPHORUS
PYROPHORUSES
PYROPHOSPHATE
PYROPHOSPHATES
PYROPHOSPHORIC
PYROPHOTOGRAPH
PYROPHOTOGRAPHS
PYROPHOTOGRAPHY
PYROPHOTOMETER
PYROPHOTOMETERS
PYROPHOTOMETRY
PYROPHYLLITE
PYROPHYLLITES
PYROSCOPES
PYROSTATIC
PYROSULPHATE
PYROSULPHATES
PYROSULPHURIC
PYROTARTRATE
PYROTARTRATES
PYROTECHNIC
PYROTECHNICAL
PYROTECHNICALLY
PYROTECHNICIAN
PYROTECHNICIANS
PYROTECHNICS
PYROTECHNIES
PYROTECHNIST
PYROTECHNISTS
PYROTECHNY
PYROVANADIC
PYROXENITE
PYROXENITES
PYROXENITIC
PYROXENOID
PYROXENOIDS
PYROXYLINE
PYROXYLINES
PYROXYLINS
PYRRHICIST
PYRRHICISTS
PYRRHOTINE
PYRRHOTINES
PYRRHOTITE
PYRRHOTITES
PYRRHULOXIA
PYRRHULOXIAS
PYRROLIDINE
PYRROLIDINES
PYTHOGENIC
PYTHONESSES

PYTHONOMORPH
PYTHONOMORPHS

Q

QABALISTIC
QINGHAOSUS
QUACKERIES
QUACKSALVER
QUACKSALVERS
QUACKSALVING
QUADPLEXES
QUADRAGENARIAN
QUADRAGENARIANS
QUADRAGESIMAL
QUADRANGLE
QUADRANGLES
QUADRANGULAR
QUADRANGULARLY
QUADRANTAL
QUADRANTES
QUADRAPHONIC
QUADRAPHONICS
QUADRAPHONIES
QUADRAPHONY
QUADRAPLEGIA
QUADRAPLEGIAS
QUADRAPLEGIC
QUADRAPLEGICS
QUADRATICAL
QUADRATICALLY
QUADRATICS
QUADRATING
QUADRATRIX
QUADRATRIXES
QUADRATURA
QUADRATURE
QUADRATURES
QUADRATUSES
QUADRELLAS
QUADRENNIA
QUADRENNIAL
QUADRENNIALLY
QUADRENNIALS
QUADRENNIUM
QUADRENNIUMS
QUADRICEPS
QUADRICEPSES
QUADRICIPITAL
QUADRICONE
QUADRICONES
QUADRIENNIA
QUADRIENNIAL
QUADRIENNIUM
QUADRIFARIOUS
QUADRIFOLIATE
QUADRIFORM
QUADRIGEMINAL

QUADRIGEMINATE
QUADRIGEMINOUS
QUADRILATERAL
QUADRILATERALS
QUADRILINGUAL
QUADRILITERAL
QUADRILITERALS
QUADRILLED
QUADRILLER
QUADRILLERS
QUADRILLES
QUADRILLING
QUADRILLION
QUADRILLIONS
QUADRILLIONTH
QUADRILLIONTHS
QUADRILOCULAR
QUADRINGENARIES
QUADRINGENARY
QUADRINOMIAL
QUADRINOMIALS
QUADRIPARTITE
QUADRIPARTITION
QUADRIPHONIC
QUADRIPHONICS
QUADRIPLEGIA
QUADRIPLEGIAS
QUADRIPLEGIC
QUADRIPLEGICS
QUADRIPOLE
QUADRIPOLES
QUADRIREME
QUADRIREMES
QUADRISECT
QUADRISECTED
QUADRISECTING
QUADRISECTION
QUADRISECTIONS
QUADRISECTS
QUADRISYLLABIC
QUADRISYLLABLE
QUADRISYLLABLES
QUADRIVALENCE
QUADRIVALENCES
QUADRIVALENCIES
QUADRIVALENCY
QUADRIVALENT
QUADRIVALENTS
QUADRIVIAL
QUADRIVIUM
QUADRIVIUMS
QUADROPHONIC
QUADROPHONICS

QUADROPHONIES
QUADROPHONY
QUADRUMANE
QUADRUMANES
QUADRUMANOUS
QUADRUMANS
QUADRUMVIR
QUADRUMVIRATE
QUADRUMVIRATES
QUADRUMVIRS
QUADRUPEDAL
QUADRUPEDS
QUADRUPLED
QUADRUPLES
QUADRUPLET
QUADRUPLETS
QUADRUPLEX
QUADRUPLEXED
QUADRUPLEXES
QUADRUPLEXING
QUADRUPLICATE
QUADRUPLICATED
QUADRUPLICATES
QUADRUPLICATING
QUADRUPLICATION
QUADRUPLICITIES
QUADRUPLICITY
QUADRUPLIES
QUADRUPLING
QUADRUPOLE
QUADRUPOLES
QUAESITUMS
QUAESTIONARIES
QUAESTIONARY
QUAESTORIAL
QUAESTORSHIP
QUAESTORSHIPS
QUAESTUARIES
QUAESTUARY
QUAGGINESS
QUAGGINESSES
QUAGMIRIER
QUAGMIRIEST
QUAGMIRING
QUAINTNESS
QUAINTNESSES
QUAKINESSES
QUALIFIABLE
QUALIFICATION
QUALIFICATIONS
QUALIFICATIVE
QUALIFICATIVES
QUALIFICATOR

QUALIFICATORS
QUALIFICATORY
QUALIFIEDLY
QUALIFIERS
QUALIFYING
QUALIFYINGS
QUALITATIVE
QUALITATIVELY
QUALMISHLY
QUALMISHNESS
QUALMISHNESSES
QUANDARIES
QUANGOCRACIES
QUANGOCRACY
QUANTIFIABLE
QUANTIFICATION
QUANTIFICATIONS
QUANTIFIED
QUANTIFIER
QUANTIFIERS
QUANTIFIES
QUANTIFYING
QUANTISATION
QUANTISATIONS
QUANTISERS
QUANTISING
QUANTITATE
QUANTITATED
QUANTITATES
QUANTITATING
QUANTITATION
QUANTITATIONS
QUANTITATIVE
QUANTITATIVELY
QUANTITIES
QUANTITIVE
QUANTITIVELY
QUANTIVALENCE
QUANTIVALENCES
QUANTIVALENT
QUANTIZATION
QUANTIZATIONS
QUANTIZERS
QUANTIZING
QUANTOMETER
QUANTOMETERS
QUAQUAVERSAL
QUAQUAVERSALLY
QUARANTINE
QUARANTINED
QUARANTINES
QUARANTINING
QUARENDENS

QUARENDERS	QUARTZIEST	QUERCETUMS	QUICKSTEPPING
QUARRELERS	QUARTZIFEROUS	QUERCITINS	QUICKSTEPS
QUARRELING	QUARTZITES	QUERCITRON	QUICKTHORN
QUARRELLED	QUARTZITIC	QUERCITRONS	QUICKTHORNS
QUARRELLER	QUASICRYSTAL	QUERIMONIES	QUIDDANIES
QUARRELLERS	QUASICRYSTALS	QUERIMONIOUS	QUIDDITATIVE
QUARRELLING	QUASIPARTICLE	QUERIMONIOUSLY	QUIDDITCHES
QUARRELLINGS	QUASIPARTICLES	QUERNSTONE	QUIDDITIES
QUARRELLOUS	QUASIPERIODIC	QUERNSTONES	QUIESCENCE
QUARRELSOME	QUATERCENTENARY	QUERSPRUNG	QUIESCENCES
QUARRELSOMELY	QUATERNARIES	QUERSPRUNGS	QUIESCENCIES
QUARRELSOMENESS	QUATERNARY	QUERULOUSLY	QUIESCENCY
QUARRENDER	QUATERNATE	QUERULOUSNESS	QUIESCENTLY
QUARRENDERS	QUATERNION	QUERULOUSNESSES	QUIETENERS
QUARRIABLE	QUATERNIONIST	QUERYINGLY	QUIETENING
QUARRINGTON	QUATERNIONISTS	QUESADILLA	QUIETENINGS
QUARRINGTONS	QUATERNIONS	QUESADILLAS	QUIETISTIC
QUARRYINGS	QUATERNITIES	QUESTINGLY	QUIETNESSES
QUARRYMASTER	QUATERNITY	QUESTIONABILITY	QUILLBACKS
QUARRYMASTERS	QUATORZAIN	QUESTIONABLE	QUILLWORKS
QUARTATION	QUATORZAINS	QUESTIONABLY	QUILLWORTS
QUARTATIONS	QUATREFEUILLE	QUESTIONARIES	QUINACRINE
QUARTERAGE	QUATREFEUILLES	QUESTIONARY	QUINACRINES
QUARTERAGES	QUATREFOIL	QUESTIONED	QUINAQUINA
QUARTERBACK	QUATREFOILS	QUESTIONEE	QUINAQUINAS
QUARTERBACKED	QUATTROCENTISM	QUESTIONEES	QUINCENTENARIES
QUARTERBACKING	QUATTROCENTISMS	QUESTIONER	QUINCENTENARY
QUARTERBACKS	QUATTROCENTIST	QUESTIONERS	QUINCENTENNIAL
QUARTERDECK	QUATTROCENTISTS	QUESTIONING	QUINCENTENNIALS
QUARTERDECKER	QUATTROCENTO	QUESTIONINGLY	QUINCUNCIAL
QUARTERDECKERS	QUATTROCENTOS	QUESTIONINGS	QUINCUNCIALLY
QUARTERDECKS	QUAVERIEST	QUESTIONIST	QUINCUNXES
QUARTERERS	QUAVERINGLY	QUESTIONISTS	QUINCUNXIAL
QUARTERFINAL	QUAVERINGS	QUESTIONLESS	QUINDECAGON
QUARTERFINALIST	QUEACHIEST	QUESTIONLESSLY	QUINDECAGONS
QUARTERFINALS	QUEASINESS	QUESTIONNAIRE	QUINDECAPLET
QUARTERING	QUEASINESSES	QUESTIONNAIRES	QUINDECAPLETS
QUARTERINGS	QUEBRACHOS	QUESTORIAL	QUINDECENNIAL
QUARTERLIES	QUEECHIEST	QUESTORSHIP	QUINDECENNIALS
QUARTERLIFE	QUEENCAKES	QUESTORSHIPS	QUINDECILLION
QUARTERLIGHT	QUEENCRAFT	QUESTRISTS	QUINDECILLIONS
QUARTERLIGHTS	QUEENCRAFTS	QUIBBLINGLY	QUINGENTENARIES
QUARTERMASTER	QUEENHOODS	QUIBBLINGS	QUINGENTENARY
QUARTERMASTERS	QUEENLIEST	QUICKBEAMS	QUINIDINES
QUARTERMISTRESS	QUEENLINESS	QUICKENERS	QUINOLINES
QUARTEROON	QUEENLINESSES	QUICKENING	QUINOLONES
QUARTEROONS	QUEENSHIPS	QUICKENINGS	QUINQUAGENARIAN
QUARTERSAW	QUEENSIDES	QUICKLIMES	QUINQUAGESIMAL
QUARTERSAWED	QUEERCORES	QUICKNESSES	QUINQUECOSTATE
QUARTERSAWING	QUEERITIES	QUICKSANDS	QUINQUEFARIOUS
QUARTERSAWN	QUEERNESSES	QUICKSILVER	QUINQUEFOLIATE
QUARTERSAWS	QUELQUECHOSE	QUICKSILVERED	QUINQUENNIA
QUARTERSTAFF	QUELQUECHOSES	QUICKSILVERING	QUINQUENNIAD
QUARTERSTAFFS	QUENCHABLE	QUICKSILVERINGS	QUINQUENNIADS
QUARTERSTAVES	QUENCHINGS	QUICKSILVERISH	QUINQUENNIAL
QUARTETTES	QUENCHLESS	QUICKSILVERS	QUINQUENNIALLY
QUARTODECIMAN	QUENCHLESSLY	QUICKSILVERY	QUINQUENNIALS
QUARTODECIMANS	QUERCETINS	QUICKSTEPPED	QUINQUENNIUM

QUINQUENNIUMS QUIZZIFYING
QUINQUEPARTITE QUIZZINESS
QUINQUEREME QUIZZINESSES
QUINQUEREMES QUODLIBETARIAN
QUINQUEVALENCE QUODLIBETARIANS
QUINQUEVALENCES QUODLIBETIC
QUINQUEVALENCY QUODLIBETICAL
QUINQUEVALENT QUODLIBETICALLY
QUINQUINAS QUODLIBETS
QUINQUIVALENT QUOTABILITIES
QUINTESSENCE QUOTABILITY
QUINTESSENCES QUOTABLENESS
QUINTESSENTIAL QUOTABLENESSES
QUINTETTES QUOTATIONS
QUINTILLION QUOTATIOUS
QUINTILLIONS QUOTATIVES
QUINTILLIONTH QUOTEWORTHY
QUINTILLIONTHS QUOTIDIANS
QUINTROONS QUOTITIONS
QUINTUPLED
QUINTUPLES
QUINTUPLET
QUINTUPLETS
QUINTUPLICATE
QUINTUPLICATED
QUINTUPLICATES
QUINTUPLICATING
QUINTUPLICATION
QUINTUPLING
QUIRISTERS
QUIRKINESS
QUIRKINESSES
QUISLINGISM
QUISLINGISMS
QUITCLAIMED
QUITCLAIMING
QUITCLAIMS
QUITTANCED
QUITTANCES
QUITTANCING
QUIVERFULS
QUIVERIEST
QUIVERINGLY
QUIVERINGS
QUIXOTICAL
QUIXOTICALLY
QUIXOTISMS
QUIXOTRIES
QUIZMASTER
QUIZMASTERS
QUIZZERIES
QUIZZICALITIES
QUIZZICALITY
QUIZZICALLY
QUIZZIFICATION
QUIZZIFICATIONS
QUIZZIFIED
QUIZZIFIES

R

RABATMENTS
RABATTEMENT
RABATTEMENTS
RABATTINGS
RABBINATES
RABBINICAL
RABBINICALLY
RABBINISMS
RABBINISTIC
RABBINISTS
RABBINITES
RABBITBRUSH
RABBITBRUSHES
RABBITFISH
RABBITFISHES
RABBITRIES
RABBLEMENT
RABBLEMENTS
RABIDITIES
RABIDNESSES
RACCAHOUTS
RACECOURSE
RACECOURSES
RACEGOINGS
RACEHORSES
RACEMATION
RACEMATIONS
RACEMISATION
RACEMISATIONS
RACEMISING
RACEMIZATION
RACEMIZATIONS
RACEMIZING
RACEMOSELY
RACEMOUSLY
RACETRACKER
RACETRACKERS
RACETRACKS
RACEWALKED
RACEWALKER
RACEWALKERS
RACEWALKING
RACEWALKINGS
RACHIOTOMIES
RACHIOTOMY
RACHISCHISES
RACHISCHISIS
RACHITIDES
RACHITISES
RACIALISED
RACIALISES
RACIALISING
RACIALISMS

RACIALISTIC
RACIALISTS
RACIALIZED
RACIALIZES
RACIALIZING
RACIATIONS
RACINESSES
RACKABONES
RACKETEERED
RACKETEERING
RACKETEERINGS
RACKETEERS
RACKETIEST
RACKETRIES
RACONTEURING
RACONTEURINGS
RACONTEURS
RACONTEUSE
RACONTEUSES
RACQUETBALL
RACQUETBALLS
RACQUETING
RADARSCOPE
RADARSCOPES
RADIALISATION
RADIALISATIONS
RADIALISED
RADIALISES
RADIALISING
RADIALITIES
RADIALIZATION
RADIALIZATIONS
RADIALIZED
RADIALIZES
RADIALIZING
RADIANCIES
RADIATIONAL
RADIATIONLESS
RADIATIONS
RADICALISATION
RADICALISATIONS
RADICALISE
RADICALISED
RADICALISES
RADICALISING
RADICALISM
RADICALISMS
RADICALISTIC
RADICALITIES
RADICALITY
RADICALIZATION
RADICALIZATIONS
RADICALIZE

RADICALIZED
RADICALIZES
RADICALIZING
RADICALNESS
RADICALNESSES
RADICATING
RADICATION
RADICATIONS
RADICCHIOS
RADICELLOSE
RADICICOLOUS
RADICIFORM
RADICIVOROUS
RADICULOSE
RADIESTHESIA
RADIESTHESIAS
RADIESTHESIST
RADIESTHESISTS
RADIESTHETIC
RADIOACTIVATE
RADIOACTIVATED
RADIOACTIVATES
RADIOACTIVATING
RADIOACTIVATION
RADIOACTIVE
RADIOACTIVELY
RADIOACTIVITIES
RADIOACTIVITY
RADIOAUTOGRAPH
RADIOAUTOGRAPHS
RADIOAUTOGRAPHY
RADIOBIOLOGIC
RADIOBIOLOGICAL
RADIOBIOLOGIES
RADIOBIOLOGIST
RADIOBIOLOGISTS
RADIOBIOLOGY
RADIOCARBON
RADIOCARBONS
RADIOCHEMICAL
RADIOCHEMICALLY
RADIOCHEMIST
RADIOCHEMISTRY
RADIOCHEMISTS
RADIOECOLOGIES
RADIOECOLOGY
RADIOELEMENT
RADIOELEMENTS
RADIOGENIC
RADIOGONIOMETER
RADIOGRAMS
RADIOGRAPH
RADIOGRAPHED

RADIOGRAPHER
RADIOGRAPHERS
RADIOGRAPHIC
RADIOGRAPHIES
RADIOGRAPHING
RADIOGRAPHS
RADIOGRAPHY
RADIOISOTOPE
RADIOISOTOPES
RADIOISOTOPIC
RADIOLABEL
RADIOLABELED
RADIOLABELING
RADIOLABELLED
RADIOLABELLING
RADIOLABELS
RADIOLARIAN
RADIOLARIANS
RADIOLOCATION
RADIOLOCATIONAL
RADIOLOCATIONS
RADIOLOGIC
RADIOLOGICAL
RADIOLOGICALLY
RADIOLOGIES
RADIOLOGIST
RADIOLOGISTS
RADIOLUCENCIES
RADIOLUCENCY
RADIOLUCENT
RADIOLYSES
RADIOLYSIS
RADIOLYTIC
RADIOMETER
RADIOMETERS
RADIOMETRIC
RADIOMETRICALLY
RADIOMETRIES
RADIOMETRY
RADIOMICROMETER
RADIOMIMETIC
RADIONUCLIDE
RADIONUCLIDES
RADIOPACITIES
RADIOPACITY
RADIOPAGER
RADIOPAGERS
RADIOPAGING
RADIOPAGINGS
RADIOPAQUE
RADIOPHONE
RADIOPHONES
RADIOPHONIC

RADIOPHONICALLY
RADIOPHONICS
RADIOPHONIES
RADIOPHONIST
RADIOPHONISTS
RADIOPHONY
RADIOPHOTO
RADIOPHOTOS
RADIOPROTECTION
RADIOPROTECTIVE
RADIORESISTANT
RADIOSCOPE
RADIOSCOPES
RADIOSCOPIC
RADIOSCOPICALLY
RADIOSCOPIES
RADIOSCOPY
RADIOSENSITISE
RADIOSENSITISED
RADIOSENSITISES
RADIOSENSITIVE
RADIOSENSITIZE
RADIOSENSITIZED
RADIOSENSITIZES
RADIOSONDE
RADIOSONDES
RADIOSTRONTIUM
RADIOSTRONTIUMS
RADIOTELEGRAM
RADIOTELEGRAMS
RADIOTELEGRAPH
RADIOTELEGRAPHS
RADIOTELEGRAPHY
RADIOTELEMETER
RADIOTELEMETERS
RADIOTELEMETRIC
RADIOTELEMETRY
RADIOTELEPHONE
RADIOTELEPHONES
RADIOTELEPHONIC
RADIOTELEPHONY
RADIOTELETYPE
RADIOTELETYPES
RADIOTHERAPIES
RADIOTHERAPIST
RADIOTHERAPISTS
RADIOTHERAPY
RADIOTHERMIES
RADIOTHERMY
RADIOTHONS
RADIOTHORIUM
RADIOTHORIUMS
RADIOTOXIC
RADIOTRACER
RADIOTRACERS
RADULIFORM
RAFFINATES
RAFFINOSES

RAFFISHNESS
RAFFISHNESSES
RAFFLESIAS
RAFTERINGS
RAGAMUFFIN
RAGAMUFFINS
RAGGAMUFFIN
RAGGAMUFFINS
RAGGEDIEST
RAGGEDNESS
RAGGEDNESSES
RAGMATICAL
RAGPICKERS
RAILBUSSES
RAILLERIES
RAILROADED
RAILROADER
RAILROADERS
RAILROADING
RAILROADINGS
RAILWAYMAN
RAILWAYMEN
RAINBOWLIKE
RAINCHECKS
RAINFOREST
RAINFORESTS
RAININESSES
RAINMAKERS
RAINMAKING
RAINMAKINGS
RAINPROOFED
RAINPROOFING
RAINPROOFS
RAINSPOUTS
RAINSQUALL
RAINSQUALLS
RAINSTORMS
RAINWASHED
RAINWASHES
RAINWASHING
RAINWATERS
RAISONNEUR
RAISONNEURS
RAIYATWARI
RAIYATWARIS
RAJAHSHIPS
RAJPRAMUKH
RAJPRAMUKHS
RAKESHAMES
RAKISHNESS
RAKISHNESSES
RALLENTANDO
RALLENTANDOS
RALLYCROSS
RALLYCROSSES
RALLYINGLY
RAMAPITHECINE
RAMAPITHECINES

RAMBLINGLY
RAMBOUILLET
RAMBOUILLETS
RAMBUNCTIOUS
RAMBUNCTIOUSLY
RAMENTACEOUS
RAMGUNSHOCH
RAMIFICATION
RAMIFICATIONS
RAMMISHNESS
RAMMISHNESSES
RAMOSITIES
RAMPACIOUS
RAMPAGEOUS
RAMPAGEOUSLY
RAMPAGEOUSNESS
RAMPAGINGS
RAMPALLIAN
RAMPALLIANS
RAMPANCIES
RAMPARTING
RAMPAUGING
RAMRODDING
RAMSHACKLE
RANCHERIAS
RANCHERIES
RANCIDITIES
RANCIDNESS
RANCIDNESSES
RANCOROUSLY
RANCOROUSNESS
RANCOROUSNESSES
RANDINESSES
RANDOMISATION
RANDOMISATIONS
RANDOMISED
RANDOMISER
RANDOMISERS
RANDOMISES
RANDOMISING
RANDOMIZATION
RANDOMIZATIONS
RANDOMIZED
RANDOMIZER
RANDOMIZERS
RANDOMIZES
RANDOMIZING
RANDOMNESS
RANDOMNESSES
RANDOMWISE
RANGATIRAS
RANGATIRATANGA
RANGATIRATANGAS
RANGEFINDER
RANGEFINDERS
RANGEFINDING
RANGEFINDINGS
RANGELANDS

RANGERSHIP
RANGERSHIPS
RANGINESSES
RANIVOROUS
RANKNESSES
RANKSHIFTED
RANKSHIFTING
RANKSHIFTS
RANSACKERS
RANSACKING
RANSHACKLE
RANSHACKLED
RANSHACKLES
RANSHACKLING
RANSHAKLED
RANSHAKLES
RANSHAKLING
RANSOMABLE
RANSOMLESS
RANTERISMS
RANTIPOLED
RANTIPOLES
RANTIPOLING
RANUNCULACEOUS
RANUNCULUS
RANUNCULUSES
RAPACIOUSLY
RAPACIOUSNESS
RAPACIOUSNESSES
RAPACITIES
RAPIDITIES
RAPIDNESSES
RAPPELLING
RAPPELLINGS
RAPPORTAGE
RAPPORTAGES
RAPPORTEUR
RAPPORTEURS
RAPPROCHEMENT
RAPPROCHEMENTS
RAPSCALLION
RAPSCALLIONS
RAPTATORIAL
RAPTNESSES
RAPTURELESS
RAPTURISED
RAPTURISES
RAPTURISING
RAPTURISTS
RAPTURIZED
RAPTURIZES
RAPTURIZING
RAPTUROUSLY
RAPTUROUSNESS
RAPTUROUSNESSES
RAREFACTION
RAREFACTIONAL
RAREFACTIONS

RAREFACTIVE	RATIONALES	RAWINSONDE	REACQUIRING
RAREFIABLE	RATIONALISABLE	RAWINSONDES	REACQUISITION
RAREFICATION	RATIONALISATION	RAWMAISHES	REACQUISITIONS
RAREFICATIONAL	RATIONALISE	RAYGRASSES	REACTANCES
RAREFICATIONS	RATIONALISED	RAYLESSNESS	REACTIONAL
RARENESSES	RATIONALISER	RAYLESSNESSES	REACTIONARIES
RASCAILLES	RATIONALISERS	RAZMATAZES	REACTIONARISM
RASCALDOMS	RATIONALISES	RAZORBACKS	REACTIONARISMS
RASCALISMS	RATIONALISING	RAZORBILLS	REACTIONARIST
RASCALLIEST	RATIONALISM	RAZZAMATAZZ	REACTIONARISTS
RASCALLION	RATIONALISMS	RAZZAMATAZZES	REACTIONARY
RASCALLIONS	RATIONALIST	RAZZBERRIES	REACTIONARYISM
RASHNESSES	RATIONALISTIC	RAZZMATAZZ	REACTIONARYISMS
RASPATORIES	RATIONALISTS	RAZZMATAZZES	REACTIONISM
RASPBERRIES	RATIONALITIES	REABSORBED	REACTIONISMS
RASPINESSES	RATIONALITY	REABSORBING	REACTIONIST
RASTAFARIAN	RATIONALIZABLE	REABSORPTION	REACTIONISTS
RASTAFARIANS	RATIONALIZATION	REABSORPTIONS	REACTIVATE
RASTERISED	RATIONALIZE	REACCEDING	REACTIVATED
RASTERISES	RATIONALIZED	REACCELERATE	REACTIVATES
RASTERISING	RATIONALIZER	REACCELERATED	REACTIVATING
RASTERIZED	RATIONALIZERS	REACCELERATES	REACTIVATION
RASTERIZES	RATIONALIZES	REACCELERATING	REACTIVATIONS
RASTERIZING	RATIONALIZING	REACCENTED	REACTIVELY
RATABILITIES	RATIONALLY	REACCENTING	REACTIVENESS
RATABILITY	RATIONALNESS	REACCEPTED	REACTIVENESSES
RATABLENESS	RATIONALNESSES	REACCEPTING	REACTIVITIES
RATABLENESSES	RATTENINGS	REACCESSION	REACTIVITY
RATAPLANNED	RATTINESSES	REACCESSIONS	REACTUATED
RATAPLANNING	RATTLEBAGS	REACCLAIMED	REACTUATES
RATATOUILLE	RATTLEBOXES	REACCLAIMING	REACTUATING
RATATOUILLES	RATTLEBRAIN	REACCLAIMS	READABILITIES
RATBAGGERIES	RATTLEBRAINED	REACCLIMATISE	READABILITY
RATBAGGERY	RATTLEBRAINS	REACCLIMATISED	READABLENESS
RATCHETING	RATTLESNAKE	REACCLIMATISES	READABLENESSES
RATEABILITIES	RATTLESNAKES	REACCLIMATISING	READAPTATION
RATEABILITY	RATTLETRAP	REACCLIMATIZE	READAPTATIONS
RATEABLENESS	RATTLETRAPS	REACCLIMATIZED	READAPTING
RATEABLENESSES	RATTLINGLY	REACCLIMATIZES	READDICTED
RATEMETERS	RATTOONING	REACCLIMATIZING	READDICTING
RATEPAYERS	RAUCOUSNESS	REACCREDIT	READDRESSED
RATHERIPES	RAUCOUSNESSES	REACCREDITATION	READDRESSES
RATHSKELLER	RAUNCHIEST	REACCREDITED	READDRESSING
RATHSKELLERS	RAUNCHINESS	REACCREDITING	READERSHIP
RATIFIABLE	RAUNCHINESSES	REACCREDITS	READERSHIPS
RATIFICATION	RAUWOLFIAS	REACCUSING	READINESSES
RATIFICATIONS	RAVAGEMENT	REACCUSTOM	READJUSTABLE
RATIOCINATE	RAVAGEMENTS	REACCUSTOMED	READJUSTED
RATIOCINATED	RAVELLINGS	REACCUSTOMING	READJUSTER
RATIOCINATES	RAVELMENTS	REACCUSTOMS	READJUSTERS
RATIOCINATING	RAVENINGLY	REACQUAINT	READJUSTING
RATIOCINATION	RAVENOUSLY	REACQUAINTANCE	READJUSTMENT
RATIOCINATIONS	RAVENOUSNESS	REACQUAINTANCES	READJUSTMENTS
RATIOCINATIVE	RAVENOUSNESSES	REACQUAINTED	READMISSION
RATIOCINATOR	RAVIGOTTES	REACQUAINTING	READMISSIONS
RATIOCINATORS	RAVISHINGLY	REACQUAINTS	READMITTANCE
RATIOCINATORY	RAVISHMENT	REACQUIRED	READMITTANCES
	RAVISHMENTS	REACQUIRES	READMITTED

READMITTING	REALLOCATIONS	REAPPRAISEMENTS	REASSERTION
READOPTING	REALLOTMENT	REAPPRAISER	REASSERTIONS
READOPTION	REALLOTMENTS	REAPPRAISERS	REASSESSED
READOPTIONS	REALLOTTED	REAPPRAISES	REASSESSES
READORNING	REALLOTTING	REAPPRAISING	REASSESSING
READVANCED	REALNESSES	REAPPROPRIATE	REASSESSMENT
READVANCES	REALPOLITIK	REAPPROPRIATED	REASSESSMENTS
READVANCING	REALPOLITIKER	REAPPROPRIATES	REASSIGNED
READVERTISE	REALPOLITIKERS	REAPPROPRIATING	REASSIGNING
READVERTISED	REALPOLITIKS	REAPPROVED	REASSIGNMENT
READVERTISEMENT	REALTERING	REAPPROVES	REASSIGNMENTS
READVERTISES	REAMENDING	REAPPROVING	REASSORTED
READVERTISING	REAMENDMENT	REARGUARDS	REASSORTING
READVISING	REAMENDMENTS	REARGUMENT	REASSORTMENT
READYMADES	REANALYSED	REARGUMENTS	REASSORTMENTS
REAEDIFIED	REANALYSES	REARHORSES	REASSUMING
REAEDIFIES	REANALYSING	REARMAMENT	REASSUMPTION
REAEDIFYED	REANALYSIS	REARMAMENTS	REASSUMPTIONS
REAEDIFYES	REANALYZED	REAROUSALS	REASSURANCE
REAEDIFYING	REANALYZES	REAROUSING	REASSURANCES
REAFFIRMATION	REANALYZING	REARRANGED	REASSURERS
REAFFIRMATIONS	REANIMATED	REARRANGEMENT	REASSURING
REAFFIRMED	REANIMATES	REARRANGEMENTS	REASSURINGLY
REAFFIRMING	REANIMATING	REARRANGER	REASTINESS
REAFFIXING	REANIMATION	REARRANGERS	REASTINESSES
REAFFOREST	REANIMATIONS	REARRANGES	REATTACHED
REAFFORESTATION	REANNEXATION	REARRANGING	REATTACHES
REAFFORESTED	REANNEXATIONS	REARRESTED	REATTACHING
REAFFORESTING	REANNEXING	REARRESTING	REATTACHMENT
REAFFORESTS	REANOINTED	REARTICULATE	REATTACHMENTS
REAGENCIES	REANOINTING	REARTICULATED	REATTACKED
REAGGREGATE	REANSWERED	REARTICULATES	REATTACKING
REAGGREGATED	REANSWERING	REARTICULATING	REATTAINED
REAGGREGATES	REAPPARELLED	REASCENDED	REATTAINING
REAGGREGATING	REAPPARELLING	REASCENDING	REATTEMPTED
REAGGREGATION	REAPPARELS	REASCENSION	REATTEMPTING
REAGGREGATIONS	REAPPEARANCE	REASCENSIONS	REATTEMPTS
REALIGNING	REAPPEARANCES	REASONABILITIES	REATTRIBUTE
REALIGNMENT	REAPPEARED	REASONABILITY	REATTRIBUTED
REALIGNMENTS	REAPPEARING	REASONABLE	REATTRIBUTES
REALISABILITIES	REAPPLICATION	REASONABLENESS	REATTRIBUTING
REALISABILITY	REAPPLICATIONS	REASONABLY	REATTRIBUTION
REALISABLE	REAPPLYING	REASONEDLY	REATTRIBUTIONS
REALISABLY	REAPPOINTED	REASONINGS	REAUTHORISATION
REALISATION	REAPPOINTING	REASONLESS	REAUTHORISE
REALISATIONS	REAPPOINTMENT	REASONLESSLY	REAUTHORISED
REALISTICALLY	REAPPOINTMENTS	REASSAILED	REAUTHORISES
REALIZABILITIES	REAPPOINTS	REASSAILING	REAUTHORISING
REALIZABILITY	REAPPORTION	REASSEMBLAGE	REAUTHORIZATION
REALIZABLE	REAPPORTIONED	REASSEMBLAGES	REAUTHORIZE
REALIZABLY	REAPPORTIONING	REASSEMBLE	REAUTHORIZED
REALIZATION	REAPPORTIONMENT	REASSEMBLED	REAUTHORIZES
REALIZATIONS	REAPPORTIONS	REASSEMBLES	REAUTHORIZING
REALLOCATE	REAPPRAISAL	REASSEMBLIES	REAVAILING
REALLOCATED	REAPPRAISALS	REASSEMBLING	REAWAKENED
REALLOCATES	REAPPRAISE	REASSEMBLY	REAWAKENING
REALLOCATING	REAPPRAISED	REASSERTED	REAWAKENINGS
REALLOCATION	REAPPRAISEMENT	REASSERTING	REBALANCED

REBALANCES

REBALANCES
REBALANCING
REBAPTISED
REBAPTISES
REBAPTISING
REBAPTISMS
REBAPTIZED
REBAPTIZES
REBAPTIZING
REBARBATIVE
REBARBATIVELY
REBATEABLE
REBATEMENT
REBATEMENTS
REBBETZINS
REBEGINNING
REBELLIONS
REBELLIOUS
REBELLIOUSLY
REBELLIOUSNESS
REBELLOWED
REBELLOWING
REBIRTHING
REBIRTHINGS
REBLENDING
REBLOOMING
REBLOSSOMED
REBLOSSOMING
REBLOSSOMS
REBOARDING
REBOATIONS
REBORROWED
REBORROWING
REBOTTLING
REBOUNDERS
REBOUNDING
REBRANCHED
REBRANCHES
REBRANCHING
REBRANDING
REBREEDING
REBROADCAST
REBROADCASTED
REBROADCASTING
REBROADCASTS
REBUILDING
REBUKEFULLY
REBUKINGLY
REBUTMENTS
REBUTTABLE
REBUTTONED
REBUTTONING
RECALCITRANCE
RECALCITRANCES
RECALCITRANCIES
RECALCITRANCY
RECALCITRANT
RECALCITRANTS

RECALCITRATE
RECALCITRATED
RECALCITRATES
RECALCITRATING
RECALCITRATION
RECALCITRATIONS
RECALCULATE
RECALCULATED
RECALCULATES
RECALCULATING
RECALCULATION
RECALCULATIONS
RECALESCED
RECALESCENCE
RECALESCENCES
RECALESCENT
RECALESCES
RECALESCING
RECALIBRATE
RECALIBRATED
RECALIBRATES
RECALIBRATING
RECALIBRATION
RECALIBRATIONS
RECALLABILITIES
RECALLABILITY
RECALLABLE
RECALLMENT
RECALLMENTS
RECALMENTS
RECANALISATION
RECANALISATIONS
RECANALISE
RECANALISED
RECANALISES
RECANALISING
RECANALIZATION
RECANALIZATIONS
RECANALIZE
RECANALIZED
RECANALIZES
RECANALIZING
RECANTATION
RECANTATIONS
RECAPITALISE
RECAPITALISED
RECAPITALISES
RECAPITALISING
RECAPITALIZE
RECAPITALIZED
RECAPITALIZES
RECAPITALIZING
RECAPITULATE
RECAPITULATED
RECAPITULATES
RECAPITULATING
RECAPITULATION
RECAPITULATIONS

RECAPITULATIVE
RECAPITULATORY
RECAPPABLE
RECAPTIONS
RECAPTURED
RECAPTURER
RECAPTURERS
RECAPTURES
RECAPTURING
RECARPETED
RECARPETING
RECARRYING
RECATALOGED
RECATALOGING
RECATALOGS
RECATCHING
RECAUTIONED
RECAUTIONING
RECAUTIONS
RECEIPTING
RECEIPTORS
RECEIVABILITIES
RECEIVABILITY
RECEIVABLE
RECEIVABLENESS
RECEIVABLES
RECEIVERSHIP
RECEIVERSHIPS
RECEIVINGS
RECEMENTED
RECEMENTING
RECENSIONS
RECENSORED
RECENSORING
RECENTNESS
RECENTNESSES
RECENTRIFUGE
RECENTRIFUGED
RECENTRIFUGES
RECENTRIFUGING
RECENTRING
RECEPTACLE
RECEPTACLES
RECEPTACULA
RECEPTACULAR
RECEPTACULUM
RECEPTIBILITIES
RECEPTIBILITY
RECEPTIBLE
RECEPTIONIST
RECEPTIONISTS
RECEPTIONS
RECEPTIVELY
RECEPTIVENESS
RECEPTIVENESSES
RECEPTIVITIES
RECEPTIVITY
RECERTIFICATION

RECERTIFIED
RECERTIFIES
RECERTIFYING
RECESSIONAL
RECESSIONALS
RECESSIONARY
RECESSIONS
RECESSIVELY
RECESSIVENESS
RECESSIVENESSES
RECESSIVES
RECHALLENGE
RECHALLENGED
RECHALLENGES
RECHALLENGING
RECHANGING
RECHANNELED
RECHANNELING
RECHANNELLED
RECHANNELLING
RECHANNELS
RECHARGEABLE
RECHARGERS
RECHARGING
RECHARTERED
RECHARTERING
RECHARTERS
RECHARTING
RECHAUFFES
RECHEATING
RECHECKING
RECHOOSING
RECHOREOGRAPH
RECHOREOGRAPHED
RECHOREOGRAPHS
RECHRISTEN
RECHRISTENED
RECHRISTENING
RECHRISTENS
RECHROMATOGRAPH
RECIDIVISM
RECIDIVISMS
RECIDIVIST
RECIDIVISTIC
RECIDIVISTS
RECIDIVOUS
RECIPIENCE
RECIPIENCES
RECIPIENCIES
RECIPIENCY
RECIPIENTS
RECIPROCAL
RECIPROCALITIES
RECIPROCALITY
RECIPROCALLY
RECIPROCALS
RECIPROCANT
RECIPROCANTS

RECIPROCATE
RECIPROCATED
RECIPROCATES
RECIPROCATING
RECIPROCATION
RECIPROCATIONS
RECIPROCATIVE
RECIPROCATOR
RECIPROCATORS
RECIPROCATORY
RECIPROCITIES
RECIPROCITY
RECIRCLING
RECIRCULATE
RECIRCULATED
RECIRCULATES
RECIRCULATING
RECIRCULATION
RECIRCULATIONS
RECITALIST
RECITALISTS
RECITATION
RECITATIONIST
RECITATIONISTS
RECITATIONS
RECITATIVE
RECITATIVES
RECITATIVI
RECITATIVO
RECITATIVOS
RECKLESSLY
RECKLESSNESS
RECKLESSNESSES
RECKONINGS
RECLADDING
RECLAIMABLE
RECLAIMABLY
RECLAIMANT
RECLAIMANTS
RECLAIMERS
RECLAIMING
RECLAMATION
RECLAMATIONS
RECLASPING
RECLASSIFIED
RECLASSIFIES
RECLASSIFY
RECLASSIFYING
RECLEANING
RECLIMBING
RECLINABLE
RECLINATION
RECLINATIONS
RECLOSABLE
RECLOTHING
RECLUSENESS
RECLUSENESSES
RECLUSIONS

RECLUSIVELY
RECLUSIVENESS
RECLUSIVENESSES
RECLUSORIES
RECODIFICATION
RECODIFICATIONS
RECODIFIED
RECODIFIES
RECODIFYING
RECOGNISABILITY
RECOGNISABLE
RECOGNISABLY
RECOGNISANCE
RECOGNISANCES
RECOGNISANT
RECOGNISED
RECOGNISEE
RECOGNISEES
RECOGNISER
RECOGNISERS
RECOGNISES
RECOGNISING
RECOGNISOR
RECOGNISORS
RECOGNITION
RECOGNITIONS
RECOGNITIVE
RECOGNITORY
RECOGNIZABILITY
RECOGNIZABLE
RECOGNIZABLY
RECOGNIZANCE
RECOGNIZANCES
RECOGNIZANT
RECOGNIZED
RECOGNIZEE
RECOGNIZEES
RECOGNIZER
RECOGNIZERS
RECOGNIZES
RECOGNIZING
RECOGNIZOR
RECOGNIZORS
RECOILLESS
RECOINAGES
RECOLLECTED
RECOLLECTEDLY
RECOLLECTEDNESS
RECOLLECTING
RECOLLECTION
RECOLLECTIONS
RECOLLECTIVE
RECOLLECTIVELY
RECOLLECTS
RECOLONISATION
RECOLONISATIONS
RECOLONISE
RECOLONISED

RECOLONISES
RECOLONISING
RECOLONIZATION
RECOLONIZATIONS
RECOLONIZE
RECOLONIZED
RECOLONIZES
RECOLONIZING
RECOLORING
RECOLOURED
RECOLOURING
RECOMBINANT
RECOMBINANTS
RECOMBINATION
RECOMBINATIONAL
RECOMBINATIONS
RECOMBINED
RECOMBINES
RECOMBINING
RECOMFORTED
RECOMFORTING
RECOMFORTLESS
RECOMFORTS
RECOMFORTURE
RECOMFORTURES
RECOMMENCE
RECOMMENCED
RECOMMENCEMENT
RECOMMENCEMENTS
RECOMMENCES
RECOMMENCING
RECOMMENDABLE
RECOMMENDABLY
RECOMMENDATION
RECOMMENDATIONS
RECOMMENDATORY
RECOMMENDED
RECOMMENDER
RECOMMENDERS
RECOMMENDING
RECOMMENDS
RECOMMISSION
RECOMMISSIONED
RECOMMISSIONING
RECOMMISSIONS
RECOMMITMENT
RECOMMITMENTS
RECOMMITTAL
RECOMMITTALS
RECOMMITTED
RECOMMITTING
RECOMPACTED
RECOMPACTING
RECOMPACTS
RECOMPENCE
RECOMPENCES
RECOMPENSABLE
RECOMPENSE

RECOMPENSED
RECOMPENSER
RECOMPENSERS
RECOMPENSES
RECOMPENSING
RECOMPILATION
RECOMPILATIONS
RECOMPILED
RECOMPILES
RECOMPILING
RECOMPOSED
RECOMPOSES
RECOMPOSING
RECOMPOSITION
RECOMPOSITIONS
RECOMPRESS
RECOMPRESSED
RECOMPRESSES
RECOMPRESSING
RECOMPRESSION
RECOMPRESSIONS
RECOMPUTATION
RECOMPUTATIONS
RECOMPUTED
RECOMPUTES
RECOMPUTING
RECONCEIVE
RECONCEIVED
RECONCEIVES
RECONCEIVING
RECONCENTRATE
RECONCENTRATED
RECONCENTRATES
RECONCENTRATING
RECONCENTRATION
RECONCEPTION
RECONCEPTIONS
RECONCEPTUALISE
RECONCEPTUALIZE
RECONCILABILITY
RECONCILABLE
RECONCILABLY
RECONCILED
RECONCILEMENT
RECONCILEMENTS
RECONCILER
RECONCILERS
RECONCILES
RECONCILIATION
RECONCILIATIONS
RECONCILIATORY
RECONCILING
RECONDENSATION
RECONDENSATIONS
RECONDENSE
RECONDENSED
RECONDENSES
RECONDENSING

RECONDITELY	RECONSIDERATION	RECONVERSION	RECREMENTITIOUS
RECONDITENESS	RECONSIDERED	RECONVERSIONS	RECREMENTS
RECONDITENESSES	RECONSIDERING	RECONVERTED	RECRIMINATE
RECONDITION	RECONSIDERS	RECONVERTING	RECRIMINATED
RECONDITIONED	RECONSIGNED	RECONVERTS	RECRIMINATES
RECONDITIONING	RECONSIGNING	RECONVEYANCE	RECRIMINATING
RECONDITIONS	RECONSIGNS	RECONVEYANCES	RECRIMINATION
RECONDUCTED	RECONSOLED	RECONVEYED	RECRIMINATIONS
RECONDUCTING	RECONSOLES	RECONVEYING	RECRIMINATIVE
RECONDUCTS	RECONSOLIDATE	RECONVICTED	RECRIMINATOR
RECONFERRED	RECONSOLIDATED	RECONVICTING	RECRIMINATORS
RECONFERRING	RECONSOLIDATES	RECONVICTION	RECRIMINATORY
RECONFIGURATION	RECONSOLIDATING	RECONVICTIONS	RECROSSING
RECONFIGURE	RECONSOLIDATION	RECONVICTS	RECROWNING
RECONFIGURED	RECONSOLING	RECONVINCE	RECRUDESCE
RECONFIGURES	RECONSTITUENT	RECONVINCED	RECRUDESCED
RECONFIGURING	RECONSTITUENTS	RECONVINCES	RECRUDESCENCE
RECONFINED	RECONSTITUTABLE	RECONVINCING	RECRUDESCENCES
RECONFINES	RECONSTITUTE	RECORDABLE	RECRUDESCENCIES
RECONFINING	RECONSTITUTED	RECORDATION	RECRUDESCENCY
RECONFIRMATION	RECONSTITUTES	RECORDATIONS	RECRUDESCENT
RECONFIRMATIONS	RECONSTITUTING	RECORDERSHIP	RECRUDESCES
RECONFIRMED	RECONSTITUTION	RECORDERSHIPS	RECRUDESCING
RECONFIRMING	RECONSTITUTIONS	RECORDINGS	RECRUITABLE
RECONFIRMS	RECONSTRUCT	RECORDISTS	RECRUITALS
RECONNAISSANCE	RECONSTRUCTED	RECOUNTALS	RECRUITERS
RECONNAISSANCES	RECONSTRUCTIBLE	RECOUNTERS	RECRUITING
RECONNECTED	RECONSTRUCTING	RECOUNTING	RECRUITMENT
RECONNECTING	RECONSTRUCTION	RECOUNTMENT	RECRUITMENTS
RECONNECTION	RECONSTRUCTIONS	RECOUNTMENTS	RECRYSTALLISE
RECONNECTIONS	RECONSTRUCTIVE	RECOUPABLE	RECRYSTALLISED
RECONNECTS	RECONSTRUCTOR	RECOUPLING	RECRYSTALLISES
RECONNOISSANCE	RECONSTRUCTORS	RECOUPMENT	RECRYSTALLISING
RECONNOISSANCES	RECONSTRUCTS	RECOUPMENTS	RECRYSTALLIZE
RECONNOITER	RECONSULTED	RECOURSING	RECRYSTALLIZED
RECONNOITERED	RECONSULTING	RECOVERABILITY	RECRYSTALLIZES
RECONNOITERER	RECONSULTS	RECOVERABLE	RECRYSTALLIZING
RECONNOITERERS	RECONTACTED	RECOVERABLENESS	RECTANGLED
RECONNOITERING	RECONTACTING	RECOVEREES	RECTANGLES
RECONNOITERS	RECONTACTS	RECOVERERS	RECTANGULAR
RECONNOITRE	RECONTAMINATE	RECOVERIES	RECTANGULARITY
RECONNOITRED	RECONTAMINATED	RECOVERING	RECTANGULARLY
RECONNOITRER	RECONTAMINATES	RECOVERORS	RECTIFIABILITY
RECONNOITRERS	RECONTAMINATING	RECOWERING	RECTIFIABLE
RECONNOITRES	RECONTAMINATION	RECREANCES	RECTIFICATION
RECONNOITRING	RECONTEXTUALISE	RECREANCIES	RECTIFICATIONS
RECONQUERED	RECONTEXTUALIZE	RECREANTLY	RECTIFIERS
RECONQUERING	RECONTINUE	RECREATING	RECTIFYING
RECONQUERS	RECONTINUED	RECREATION	RECTILINEAL
RECONQUEST	RECONTINUES	RECREATIONAL	RECTILINEALLY
RECONQUESTS	RECONTINUING	RECREATIONIST	RECTILINEAR
RECONSECRATE	RECONTOURED	RECREATIONISTS	RECTILINEARITY
RECONSECRATED	RECONTOURING	RECREATIONS	RECTILINEARLY
RECONSECRATES	RECONTOURS	RECREATIVE	RECTIPETALIES
RECONSECRATING	RECONVALESCENCE	RECREATIVELY	RECTIPETALITIES
RECONSECRATION	RECONVENED	RECREATORS	RECTIPETALITY
RECONSECRATIONS	RECONVENES	RECREMENTAL	RECTIPETALY
RECONSIDER	RECONVENING	RECREMENTITIAL	RECTIROSTRAL

RECTISERIAL	REDBAITERS	REDEPLOYING	REDISCOUNTED
RECTITISES	REDBAITING	REDEPLOYMENT	REDISCOUNTING
RECTITUDES	REDBELLIES	REDEPLOYMENTS	REDISCOUNTS
RECTITUDINOUS	REDBREASTS	REDEPOSITED	REDISCOVER
RECTOCELES	REDCURRANT	REDEPOSITING	REDISCOVERED
RECTORATES	REDCURRANTS	REDEPOSITS	REDISCOVERER
RECTORESSES	REDDISHNESS	REDESCENDED	REDISCOVERERS
RECTORIALS	REDDISHNESSES	REDESCENDING	REDISCOVERIES
RECTORSHIP	REDECIDING	REDESCENDS	REDISCOVERING
RECTORSHIPS	REDECORATE	REDESCRIBE	REDISCOVERS
RECTRESSES	REDECORATED	REDESCRIBED	REDISCOVERY
RECTRICIAL	REDECORATES	REDESCRIBES	REDISCUSSED
RECULTIVATE	REDECORATING	REDESCRIBING	REDISCUSSES
RECULTIVATED	REDECORATION	REDESCRIPTION	REDISCUSSING
RECULTIVATES	REDECORATIONS	REDESCRIPTIONS	REDISPLAYED
RECULTIVATING	REDECORATOR	REDESIGNED	REDISPLAYING
RECUMBENCE	REDECORATORS	REDESIGNING	REDISPLAYS
RECUMBENCES	REDECRAFTS	REDETERMINATION	REDISPOSED
RECUMBENCIES	REDEDICATE	REDETERMINE	REDISPOSES
RECUMBENCY	REDEDICATED	REDETERMINED	REDISPOSING
RECUMBENTLY	REDEDICATES	REDETERMINES	REDISPOSITION
RECUPERABLE	REDEDICATING	REDETERMINING	REDISPOSITIONS
RECUPERATE	REDEDICATION	REDEVELOPED	REDISSOLUTION
RECUPERATED	REDEDICATIONS	REDEVELOPER	REDISSOLUTIONS
RECUPERATES	REDEEMABILITIES	REDEVELOPERS	REDISSOLVE
RECUPERATING	REDEEMABILITY	REDEVELOPING	REDISSOLVED
RECUPERATION	REDEEMABLE	REDEVELOPMENT	REDISSOLVES
RECUPERATIONS	REDEEMABLENESS	REDEVELOPMENTS	REDISSOLVING
RECUPERATIVE	REDEEMABLY	REDEVELOPS	REDISTILLATION
RECUPERATOR	REDEEMLESS	REDIALLING	REDISTILLATIONS
RECUPERATORS	REDEFEATED	REDICTATED	REDISTILLED
RECUPERATORY	REDEFEATING	REDICTATES	REDISTILLING
RECURELESS	REDEFECTED	REDICTATING	REDISTILLS
RECURRENCE	REDEFECTING	REDIGESTED	REDISTRIBUTE
RECURRENCES	REDEFINING	REDIGESTING	REDISTRIBUTED
RECURRENCIES	REDEFINITION	REDIGESTION	REDISTRIBUTES
RECURRENCY	REDEFINITIONS	REDIGESTIONS	REDISTRIBUTING
RECURRENTLY	REDELIVERANCE	REDIGRESSED	REDISTRIBUTION
RECURRINGLY	REDELIVERANCES	REDIGRESSES	REDISTRIBUTIONS
RECURSIONS	REDELIVERED	REDIGRESSING	REDISTRIBUTIVE
RECURSIVELY	REDELIVERER	REDINGOTES	REDISTRICT
RECURSIVENESS	REDELIVERERS	REDINTEGRATE	REDISTRICTED
RECURSIVENESSES	REDELIVERIES	REDINTEGRATED	REDISTRICTING
RECURVIROSTRAL	REDELIVERING	REDINTEGRATES	REDISTRICTS
RECUSANCES	REDELIVERS	REDINTEGRATING	REDIVIDING
RECUSANCIES	REDELIVERY	REDINTEGRATION	REDIVISION
RECUSATION	REDEMANDED	REDINTEGRATIONS	REDIVISIONS
RECUSATIONS	REDEMANDING	REDINTEGRATIVE	REDIVORCED
RECYCLABLE	REDEMPTIBLE	REDIRECTED	REDIVORCES
RECYCLABLES	REDEMPTION	REDIRECTING	REDIVORCING
RECYCLATES	REDEMPTIONAL	REDIRECTION	REDLININGS
RECYCLEABLE	REDEMPTIONER	REDIRECTIONS	REDOLENCES
RECYCLISTS	REDEMPTIONERS	REDISBURSE	REDOLENCIES
REDACTIONAL	REDEMPTIONS	REDISBURSED	REDOLENTLY
REDACTIONS	REDEMPTIVE	REDISBURSES	REDOUBLEMENT
REDACTORIAL	REDEMPTIVELY	REDISBURSING	REDOUBLEMENTS
REDAMAGING	REDEMPTORY	REDISCOUNT	REDOUBLERS
REDARGUING	REDEPLOYED	REDISCOUNTABLE	REDOUBLING

REDOUBTABLE	REEDUCATIONS	REENERGIZED	REEVALUATED
REDOUBTABLENESS	REEDUCATIVE	REENERGIZES	REEVALUATES
REDOUBTABLY	REEJECTING	REENERGIZING	REEVALUATING
REDOUBTING	REELECTING	REENFORCED	REEVALUATION
REDOUNDING	REELECTION	REENFORCES	REEVALUATIONS
REDOUNDINGS	REELECTIONS	REENFORCING	REEXAMINATION
REDRAFTING	REELEVATED	REENGAGEMENT	REEXAMINATIONS
REDREAMING	REELEVATES	REENGAGEMENTS	REEXAMINED
REDRESSABILITY	REELEVATING	REENGAGING	REEXAMINES
REDRESSABLE	REELIGIBILITIES	REENGINEER	REEXAMINING
REDRESSERS	REELIGIBILITY	REENGINEERED	REEXECUTED
REDRESSIBLE	REELIGIBLE	REENGINEERING	REEXECUTES
REDRESSING	REEMBARKED	REENGINEERS	REEXECUTING
REDRESSIVE	REEMBARKING	REENGRAVED	REEXHIBITED
REDRESSORS	REEMBODIED	REENGRAVES	REEXHIBITING
REDRILLING	REEMBODIES	REENGRAVING	REEXHIBITS
REDRUTHITE	REEMBODYING	REENJOYING	REEXPELLED
REDRUTHITES	REEMBRACED	REENLARGED	REEXPELLING
REDSHIFTED	REEMBRACES	REENLARGES	REEXPERIENCE
REDSHIRTED	REEMBRACING	REENLARGING	REEXPERIENCED
REDSHIRTING	REEMBROIDER	REENLISTED	REEXPERIENCES
REDSTREAKS	REEMBROIDERED	REENLISTING	REEXPERIENCING
REDUCIBILITIES	REEMBROIDERING	REENLISTMENT	REEXPLAINED
REDUCIBILITY	REEMBROIDERS	REENLISTMENTS	REEXPLAINING
REDUCIBLENESS	REEMERGENCE	REENROLLED	REEXPLAINS
REDUCIBLENESSES	REEMERGENCES	REENROLLING	REEXPLORED
REDUCTANTS	REEMERGING	REENSLAVED	REEXPLORES
REDUCTASES	REEMISSION	REENSLAVES	REEXPLORING
REDUCTIONAL	REEMISSIONS	REENSLAVING	REEXPORTATION
REDUCTIONISM	REEMITTING	REENTERING	REEXPORTATIONS
REDUCTIONISMS	REEMPHASES	REENTHRONE	REEXPORTED
REDUCTIONIST	REEMPHASIS	REENTHRONED	REEXPORTING
REDUCTIONISTIC	REEMPHASISE	REENTHRONES	REEXPOSING
REDUCTIONISTS	REEMPHASISED	REENTHRONING	REEXPOSURE
REDUCTIONS	REEMPHASISES	REENTRANCE	REEXPOSURES
REDUCTIVELY	REEMPHASISING	REENTRANCES	REEXPRESSED
REDUCTIVENESS	REEMPHASIZE	REENTRANTS	REEXPRESSES
REDUCTIVENESSES	REEMPHASIZED	REEQUIPMENT	REEXPRESSING
REDUNDANCE	REEMPHASIZES	REEQUIPMENTS	REFASHIONED
REDUNDANCES	REEMPHASIZING	REEQUIPPED	REFASHIONING
REDUNDANCIES	REEMPLOYED	REEQUIPPING	REFASHIONMENT
REDUNDANCY	REEMPLOYING	REERECTING	REFASHIONMENTS
REDUNDANTLY	REEMPLOYMENT	REESCALATE	REFASHIONS
REDUPLICATE	REEMPLOYMENTS	REESCALATED	REFASTENED
REDUPLICATED	REENACTING	REESCALATES	REFASTENING
REDUPLICATES	REENACTMENT	REESCALATING	REFECTIONER
REDUPLICATING	REENACTMENTS	REESCALATION	REFECTIONERS
REDUPLICATION	REENACTORS	REESCALATIONS	REFECTIONS
REDUPLICATIONS	REENCOUNTER	REESTABLISH	REFECTORIAN
REDUPLICATIVE	REENCOUNTERED	REESTABLISHED	REFECTORIANS
REDUPLICATIVELY	REENCOUNTERING	REESTABLISHES	REFECTORIES
REEDIFYING	REENCOUNTERS	REESTABLISHING	REFEREEING
REEDINESSES	REENDOWING	REESTABLISHMENT	REFERENCED
REEDITIONS	REENERGISE	REESTIMATE	REFERENCER
REEDUCATED	REENERGISED	REESTIMATED	REFERENCERS
REEDUCATES	REENERGISES	REESTIMATES	REFERENCES
REEDUCATING	REENERGISING	REESTIMATING	REFERENCING
REEDUCATION	REENERGIZE	REEVALUATE	REFERENDARIES

REFERENDARY	REFLECTORISING	REFORMATTED	REFRESHFULLY
REFERENDUM	REFLECTORIZE	REFORMATTING	REFRESHING
REFERENDUMS	REFLECTORIZED	REFORMINGS	REFRESHINGLY
REFERENTIAL	REFLECTORIZES	REFORMISMS	REFRESHMENT
REFERENTIALITY	REFLECTORIZING	REFORMISTS	REFRESHMENTS
REFERENTIALLY	REFLECTORS	REFORMULATE	REFRIGERANT
REFERRABLE	REFLEXIBILITIES	REFORMULATED	REFRIGERANTS
REFERRIBLE	REFLEXIBILITY	REFORMULATES	REFRIGERATE
REFIGHTING	REFLEXIBLE	REFORMULATING	REFRIGERATED
REFIGURING	REFLEXIONAL	REFORMULATION	REFRIGERATES
REFILLABLE	REFLEXIONS	REFORMULATIONS	REFRIGERATING
REFILTERED	REFLEXIVELY	REFORTIFICATION	REFRIGERATION
REFILTERING	REFLEXIVENESS	REFORTIFIED	REFRIGERATIONS
REFINANCED	REFLEXIVENESSES	REFORTIFIES	REFRIGERATIVE
REFINANCES	REFLEXIVES	REFORTIFYING	REFRIGERATOR
REFINANCING	REFLEXIVITIES	REFOUNDATION	REFRIGERATORIES
REFINANCINGS	REFLEXIVITY	REFOUNDATIONS	REFRIGERATORS
REFINEDNESS	REFLEXOLOGICAL	REFOUNDERS	REFRIGERATORY
REFINEDNESSES	REFLEXOLOGIES	REFOUNDING	REFRINGENCE
REFINEMENT	REFLEXOLOGIST	REFRACTABLE	REFRINGENCES
REFINEMENTS	REFLEXOLOGISTS	REFRACTARIES	REFRINGENCIES
REFINERIES	REFLEXOLOGY	REFRACTARY	REFRINGENCY
REFINISHED	REFLOATING	REFRACTILE	REFRINGENT
REFINISHER	REFLOODING	REFRACTING	REFRINGING
REFINISHERS	REFLOWERED	REFRACTION	REFRONTING
REFINISHES	REFLOWERING	REFRACTIONS	REFUELABLE
REFINISHING	REFLOWERINGS	REFRACTIVE	REFUELLABLE
REFITMENTS	REFLOWINGS	REFRACTIVELY	REFUELLING
REFITTINGS	REFLUENCES	REFRACTIVENESS	REFUGEEISM
REFLAGGING	REFOCILLATE	REFRACTIVITIES	REFUGEEISMS
REFLATIONARY	REFOCILLATED	REFRACTIVITY	REFULGENCE
REFLATIONS	REFOCILLATES	REFRACTOMETER	REFULGENCES
REFLECTANCE	REFOCILLATING	REFRACTOMETERS	REFULGENCIES
REFLECTANCES	REFOCILLATION	REFRACTOMETRIC	REFULGENCY
REFLECTERS	REFOCILLATIONS	REFRACTOMETRIES	REFULGENTLY
REFLECTING	REFOCUSING	REFRACTOMETRY	REFUNDABILITIES
REFLECTINGLY	REFOCUSSED	REFRACTORIES	REFUNDABILITY
REFLECTION	REFOCUSSES	REFRACTORILY	REFUNDABLE
REFLECTIONAL	REFOCUSSING	REFRACTORINESS	REFUNDMENT
REFLECTIONLESS	REFORESTATION	REFRACTORS	REFUNDMENTS
REFLECTIONS	REFORESTATIONS	REFRACTORY	REFURBISHED
REFLECTIVE	REFORESTED	REFRACTURE	REFURBISHER
REFLECTIVELY	REFORESTING	REFRACTURES	REFURBISHERS
REFLECTIVENESS	REFORMABILITIES	REFRAINERS	REFURBISHES
REFLECTIVITIES	REFORMABILITY	REFRAINING	REFURBISHING
REFLECTIVITY	REFORMABLE	REFRAINMENT	REFURBISHINGS
REFLECTOGRAM	REFORMADES	REFRAINMENTS	REFURBISHMENT
REFLECTOGRAMS	REFORMADOES	REFRANGIBILITY	REFURBISHMENTS
REFLECTOGRAPH	REFORMADOS	REFRANGIBLE	REFURNISHED
REFLECTOGRAPHS	REFORMATES	REFRANGIBLENESS	REFURNISHES
REFLECTOGRAPHY	REFORMATION	REFREEZING	REFURNISHING
REFLECTOMETER	REFORMATIONAL	REFRESHENED	REFUSENIKS
REFLECTOMETERS	REFORMATIONIST	REFRESHENER	REFUTABILITIES
REFLECTOMETRIES	REFORMATIONISTS	REFRESHENERS	REFUTABILITY
REFLECTOMETRY	REFORMATIONS	REFRESHENING	REFUTATION
REFLECTORISE	REFORMATIVE	REFRESHENS	REFUTATIONS
REFLECTORISED	REFORMATORIES	REFRESHERS	REGAINABLE
REFLECTORISES	REFORMATORY	REFRESHFUL	REGAINMENT

REGAINMENTS	REGISSEURS	REGULARISING	REHUMANISE
REGALEMENT	REGISTERABLE	REGULARITIES	REHUMANISED
REGALEMENTS	REGISTERED	REGULARITY	REHUMANISES
REGALITIES	REGISTERER	REGULARIZATION	REHUMANISING
REGALNESSES	REGISTERERS	REGULARIZATIONS	REHUMANIZE
REGARDABLE	REGISTERING	REGULARIZE	REHUMANIZED
REGARDFULLY	REGISTRABLE	REGULARIZED	REHUMANIZES
REGARDFULNESS	REGISTRANT	REGULARIZES	REHUMANIZING
REGARDFULNESSES	REGISTRANTS	REGULARIZING	REHYDRATABLE
REGARDLESS	REGISTRARIES	REGULATING	REHYDRATED
REGARDLESSLY	REGISTRARS	REGULATION	REHYDRATES
REGARDLESSNESS	REGISTRARSHIP	REGULATIONS	REHYDRATING
REGATHERED	REGISTRARSHIPS	REGULATIVE	REHYDRATION
REGATHERING	REGISTRARY	REGULATIVELY	REHYDRATIONS
REGELATING	REGISTRATION	REGULATORS	REHYPNOTISE
REGELATION	REGISTRATIONAL	REGULATORY	REHYPNOTISED
REGELATIONS	REGISTRATIONS	REGULISING	REHYPNOTISES
REGENERABLE	REGISTRIES	REGULIZING	REHYPNOTISING
REGENERACIES	REGLORIFIED	REGURGITANT	REHYPNOTIZE
REGENERACY	REGLORIFIES	REGURGITANTS	REHYPNOTIZED
REGENERATE	REGLORIFYING	REGURGITATE	REHYPNOTIZES
REGENERATED	REGLOSSING	REGURGITATED	REHYPNOTIZING
REGENERATELY	REGNANCIES	REGURGITATES	REICHSMARK
REGENERATENESS	REGRAFTING	REGURGITATING	REICHSMARKS
REGENERATES	REGRANTING	REGURGITATION	REIDENTIFIED
REGENERATING	REGRATINGS	REGURGITATIONS	REIDENTIFIES
REGENERATION	REGREDIENCE	REHABILITANT	REIDENTIFY
REGENERATIONS	REGREDIENCES	REHABILITANTS	REIDENTIFYING
REGENERATIVE	REGREENING	REHABILITATE	REIFICATION
REGENERATIVELY	REGREETING	REHABILITATED	REIFICATIONS
REGENERATOR	REGRESSING	REHABILITATES	REIFICATORY
REGENERATORS	REGRESSION	REHABILITATING	REIGNITING
REGENERATORY	REGRESSIONS	REHABILITATION	REIGNITION
REGENTSHIP	REGRESSIVE	REHABILITATIONS	REIGNITIONS
REGENTSHIPS	REGRESSIVELY	REHABILITATIVE	REILLUMINE
REGIMENTAL	REGRESSIVENESS	REHABILITATOR	REILLUMINED
REGIMENTALLY	REGRESSIVITIES	REHABILITATORS	REILLUMINES
REGIMENTALS	REGRESSIVITY	REHAMMERED	REILLUMING
REGIMENTATION	REGRESSORS	REHAMMERING	REILLUMINING
REGIMENTATIONS	REGRETFULLY	REHANDLING	REIMAGINED
REGIMENTED	REGRETFULNESS	REHANDLINGS	REIMAGINES
REGIMENTING	REGRETFULNESSES	REHARDENED	REIMAGINING
REGIONALISATION	REGRETTABLE	REHARDENING	REIMBURSABLE
REGIONALISE	REGRETTABLY	REHEARINGS	REIMBURSED
REGIONALISED	REGRETTERS	REHEARSALS	REIMBURSEMENT
REGIONALISES	REGRETTING	REHEARSERS	REIMBURSEMENTS
REGIONALISING	REGRINDING	REHEARSING	REIMBURSER
REGIONALISM	REGROOMING	REHEARSINGS	REIMBURSERS
REGIONALISMS	REGROOVING	REHEATINGS	REIMBURSES
REGIONALIST	REGROUPING	REHOSPITALISE	REIMBURSING
REGIONALISTIC	REGUERDONED	REHOSPITALISED	REIMMERSED
REGIONALISTS	REGUERDONING	REHOSPITALISES	REIMMERSES
REGIONALIZATION	REGUERDONS	REHOSPITALISING	REIMMERSING
REGIONALIZE	REGULARISATION	REHOSPITALIZE	REIMPLANTATION
REGIONALIZED	REGULARISATIONS	REHOSPITALIZED	REIMPLANTATIONS
REGIONALIZES	REGULARISE	REHOSPITALIZES	REIMPLANTED
REGIONALIZING	REGULARISED	REHOSPITALIZING	REIMPLANTING
REGIONALLY	REGULARISES	REHOUSINGS	REIMPLANTS

REIMPORTATION	REINFORCERS	REINSTATEMENTS	REINVESTING
REIMPORTATIONS	REINFORCES	REINSTATES	REINVESTMENT
REIMPORTED	REINFORCING	REINSTATING	RFTNVESTMENTS
REIMPORTER	REINFORMED	REINSTATION	REINVIGORATE
REIMPORTERS	REINFORMING	REINSTATIONS	REINVIGORATED
REIMPORTING	REINFUNDED	REINSTATOR	REINVIGORATES
REIMPOSING	REINFUNDING	REINSTATORS	REINVIGORATING
REIMPOSITION	REINFUSING	REINSTITUTE	REINVIGORATION
REIMPOSITIONS	REINHABITED	REINSTITUTED	REINVIGORATIONS
REIMPRESSION	REINHABITING	REINSTITUTES	REINVIGORATOR
REIMPRESSIONS	REINHABITS	REINSTITUTING	REINVIGORATORS
REINCARNATE	REINITIATE	REINSURANCE	REINVITING
REINCARNATED	REINITIATED	REINSURANCES	REINVOKING
REINCARNATES	REINITIATES	REINSURERS	REINVOLVED
REINCARNATING	REINITIATING	REINSURING	REINVOLVES
REINCARNATION	REINJECTED	REINTEGRATE	REINVOLVING
REINCARNATIONS	REINJECTING	REINTEGRATED	REIOYNDURE
REINCITING	REINJECTION	REINTEGRATES	REIOYNDURES
REINCORPORATE	REINJECTIONS	REINTEGRATING	REISSUABLE
REINCORPORATED	REINJURIES	REINTEGRATION	REISTAFELS
REINCORPORATES	REINJURING	REINTEGRATIONS	REITERANCE
REINCORPORATING	REINNERVATE	REINTEGRATIVE	REITERANCES
REINCORPORATION	REINNERVATED	REINTERMENT	REITERATED
REINCREASE	REINNERVATES	REINTERMENTS	REITERATEDLY
REINCREASED	REINNERVATING	REINTERPRET	REITERATES
REINCREASES	REINNERVATION	REINTERPRETED	REITERATING
REINCREASING	REINNERVATIONS	REINTERPRETING	REITERATION
REINCURRED	REINOCULATE	REINTERPRETS	REITERATIONS
REINCURRING	REINOCULATED	REINTERRED	REITERATIVE
REINDEXING	REINOCULATES	REINTERRING	REITERATIVELY
REINDICTED	REINOCULATING	REINTERROGATE	REITERATIVES
REINDICTING	REINOCULATION	REINTERROGATED	REJACKETED
REINDICTMENT	REINOCULATIONS	REINTERROGATES	REJACKETING
REINDICTMENTS	REINSERTED	REINTERROGATING	REJECTABLE
REINDUCING	REINSERTING	REINTERROGATION	REJECTAMENTA
REINDUCTED	REINSERTION	REINTERVIEW	REJECTIBLE
REINDUCTING	REINSERTIONS	REINTERVIEWED	REJECTINGLY
REINDUSTRIALISE	REINSPECTED	REINTERVIEWING	REJECTIONIST
REINDUSTRIALIZE	REINSPECTING	REINTERVIEWS	REJECTIONISTS
REINFECTED	REINSPECTION	REINTRODUCE	REJECTIONS
REINFECTING	REINSPECTIONS	REINTRODUCED	REJIGGERED
REINFECTION	REINSPECTS	REINTRODUCES	REJIGGERING
REINFECTIONS	REINSPIRED	REINTRODUCING	REJOICEFUL
REINFESTATION	REINSPIRES	REINTRODUCTION	REJOICEMENT
REINFESTATIONS	REINSPIRING	REINTRODUCTIONS	REJOICEMENTS
REINFLAMED	REINSPIRIT	REINVADING	REJOICINGLY
REINFLAMES	REINSPIRITED	REINVASION	REJOICINGS
REINFLAMING	REINSPIRITING	REINVASIONS	REJOINDERS
REINFLATED	REINSPIRITS	REINVENTED	REJOINDURE
REINFLATES	REINSTALLATION	REINVENTING	REJOINDURES
REINFLATING	REINSTALLATIONS	REINVENTION	REJONEADOR
REINFLATION	REINSTALLED	REINVENTIONS	REJONEADORA
REINFLATIONS	REINSTALLING	REINVESTED	REJONEADORAS
REINFORCEABLE	REINSTALLS	REINVESTIGATE	REJONEADORES
REINFORCED	REINSTALMENT	REINVESTIGATED	REJOURNING
REINFORCEMENT	REINSTALMENTS	REINVESTIGATES	REJUGGLING
REINFORCEMENTS	REINSTATED	REINVESTIGATING	REJUSTIFIED
REINFORCER	REINSTATEMENT	REINVESTIGATION	REJUSTIFIES

REJUSTIFYING	RELATIVISED	RELIEFLESS	RELUBRICATIONS
REJUVENATE	RELATIVISES	RELIEVABLE	RELUCTANCE
REJUVENATED	RELATIVISING	RELIEVEDLY	RELUCTANCES
REJUVENATES	RELATIVISM	RELIGHTING	RELUCTANCIES
REJUVENATING	RELATIVISMS	RELIGIEUSE	RELUCTANCY
REJUVENATION	RELATIVIST	RELIGIEUSES	RELUCTANTLY
REJUVENATIONS	RELATIVISTIC	RELIGIONARIES	RELUCTATED
REJUVENATOR	RELATIVISTS	RELIGIONARY	RELUCTATES
REJUVENATORS	RELATIVITIES	RELIGIONER	RELUCTATING
REJUVENESCE	RELATIVITIST	RELIGIONERS	RELUCTATION
REJUVENESCED	RELATIVITISTS	RELIGIONISE	RELUCTATIONS
REJUVENESCENCE	RELATIVITY	RELIGIONISED	RELUCTIVITIES
REJUVENESCENCES	RELATIVIZATION	RELIGIONISES	RELUCTIVITY
REJUVENESCENT	RELATIVIZATIONS	RELIGIONISING	RELUMINING
REJUVENESCES	RELATIVIZE	RELIGIONISM	REMAINDERED
REJUVENESCING	RELATIVIZED	RELIGIONISMS	REMAINDERING
REJUVENISE	RELATIVIZES	RELIGIONIST	REMAINDERMAN
REJUVENISED	RELATIVIZING	RELIGIONISTS	REMAINDERMEN
REJUVENISES	RELAUNCHED	RELIGIONIZE	REMAINDERS
REJUVENISING	RELAUNCHES	RELIGIONIZED	REMANDMENT
REJUVENIZE	RELAUNCHING	RELIGIONIZES	REMANDMENTS
REJUVENIZED	RELAUNDERED	RELIGIONIZING	REMANENCES
REJUVENIZES	RELAUNDERING	RELIGIONLESS	REMANENCIES
REJUVENIZING	RELAUNDERS	RELIGIOSELY	REMANUFACTURE
REKEYBOARD	RELAXATION	RELIGIOSITIES	REMANUFACTURED
REKEYBOARDED	RELAXATIONS	RELIGIOSITY	REMANUFACTURER
REKEYBOARDING	RELAXATIVE	RELIGIOUSES	REMANUFACTURERS
REKEYBOARDS	RELAXEDNESS	RELIGIOUSLY	REMANUFACTURES
REKINDLING	RELAXEDNESSES	RELIGIOUSNESS	REMANUFACTURING
REKNITTING	RELEARNING	RELIGIOUSNESSES	REMARKABILITIES
REKNOTTING	RELEASABLE	RELINQUISH	REMARKABILITY
RELABELING	RELEASEMENT	RELINQUISHED	REMARKABLE
RELABELLED	RELEASEMENTS	RELINQUISHER	REMARKABLENESS
RELABELLING	RELEGATABLE	RELINQUISHERS	REMARKABLES
RELACQUERED	RELEGATING	RELINQUISHES	REMARKABLY
RELACQUERING	RELEGATION	RELINQUISHING	REMARKETED
RELACQUERS	RELEGATIONS	RELINQUISHMENT	REMARKETING
RELANDSCAPE	RELENTINGS	RELINQUISHMENTS	REMARRIAGE
RELANDSCAPED	RELENTLESS	RELIQUAIRE	REMARRIAGES
RELANDSCAPES	RELENTLESSLY	RELIQUAIRES	REMARRYING
RELANDSCAPING	RELENTLESSNESS	RELIQUARIES	REMASTERED
RELATEDNESS	RELENTMENT	RELIQUEFIED	REMASTERING
RELATEDNESSES	RELENTMENTS	RELIQUEFIES	REMATCHING
RELATIONAL	RELETTERED	RELIQUEFYING	REMATERIALISE
RELATIONALLY	RELETTERING	RELISHABLE	REMATERIALISED
RELATIONISM	RELEVANCES	RELIVERING	REMATERIALISES
RELATIONISMS	RELEVANCIES	RELLISHING	REMATERIALISING
RELATIONIST	RELEVANTLY	RELOCATABLE	REMATERIALIZE
RELATIONISTS	RELIABILITIES	RELOCATEES	REMATERIALIZED
RELATIONLESS	RELIABILITY	RELOCATING	REMATERIALIZES
RELATIONSHIP	RELIABLENESS	RELOCATION	REMATERIALIZING
RELATIONSHIPS	RELIABLENESSES	RELOCATIONS	REMEASURED
RELATIVELY	RELICENSED	RELOCATORS	REMEASUREMENT
RELATIVENESS	RELICENSES	RELUBRICATE	REMEASUREMENTS
RELATIVENESSES	RELICENSING	RELUBRICATED	REMEASURES
RELATIVISATION	RELICENSURE	RELUBRICATES	REMEASURING
RELATIVISATIONS	RELICENSURES	RELUBRICATING	REMEDIABILITIES
RELATIVISE	RELICTIONS	RELUBRICATION	REMEDIABILITY

REMEDIABLE	REMISSIBILITIES	REMONSTRATE	REMUNERABILITY
REMEDIABLY	REMISSIBILITY	REMONSTRATED	REMUNERABLE
REMEDIALLY	REMISSIBLE	REMONSTRATES	REMUNERATE
REMEDIATED	REMISSIBLENESS	REMONSTRATING	REMUNERATED
REMEDIATES	REMISSIBLY	REMONSTRATINGLY	REMUNERATES
REMEDIATING	REMISSIONS	REMONSTRATION	REMUNERATING
REMEDIATION	REMISSIVELY	REMONSTRATIONS	REMUNERATION
REMEDIATIONS	REMISSNESS	REMONSTRATIVE	REMUNERATIONS
REMEDILESS	REMISSNESSES	REMONSTRATIVELY	REMUNERATIVE
REMEDILESSLY	REMITMENTS	REMONSTRATOR	REMUNERATIVELY
REMEDILESSNESS	REMITTABLE	REMONSTRATORS	REMUNERATOR
REMEMBERABILITY	REMITTANCE	REMONSTRATORY	REMUNERATORS
REMEMBERABLE	REMITTANCES	REMONTANTS	REMUNERATORY
REMEMBERABLY	REMITTENCE	REMONTOIRE	REMURMURED
REMEMBERED	REMITTENCES	REMONTOIRES	REMURMURING
REMEMBERER	REMITTENCIES	REMONTOIRS	REMYTHOLOGISE
REMEMBERERS	REMITTENCY	REMORALISATION	REMYTHOLOGISED
REMEMBERING	REMITTENTLY	REMORALISATIONS	REMYTHOLOGISES
REMEMBRANCE	REMIXTURES	REMORALISE	REMYTHOLOGISING
REMEMBRANCER	REMOBILISATION	REMORALISED	REMYTHOLOGIZE
REMEMBRANCERS	REMOBILISATIONS	REMORALISES	REMYTHOLOGIZED
REMEMBRANCES	REMOBILISE	REMORALISING	REMYTHOLOGIZES
REMERCYING	REMOBILISED	REMORALIZATION	REMYTHOLOGIZING
REMIGATING	REMOBILISES	REMORALIZATIONS	RENAISSANCE
REMIGATION	REMOBILISING	REMORALIZE	RENAISSANCES
REMIGATIONS	REMOBILIZATION	REMORALIZED	RENASCENCE
REMIGRATED	REMOBILIZATIONS	REMORALIZES	RENASCENCES
REMIGRATES	REMOBILIZE	REMORALIZING	RENATIONALISE
REMIGRATING	REMOBILIZED	REMORSEFUL	RENATIONALISED
REMIGRATION	REMOBILIZES	REMORSEFULLY	RENATIONALISES
REMIGRATIONS	REMOBILIZING	REMORSEFULNESS	RENATIONALISING
REMILITARISE	REMODELERS	REMORSELESS	RENATIONALIZE
REMILITARISED	REMODELING	REMORSELESSLY	RENATIONALIZED
REMILITARISES	REMODELLED	REMORSELESSNESS	RENATIONALIZES
REMILITARISING	REMODELLING	REMORTGAGE	RENATIONALIZING
REMILITARIZE	REMODIFIED	REMORTGAGED	RENATURATION
REMILITARIZED	REMODIFIES	REMORTGAGES	RENATURATIONS
REMILITARIZES	REMODIFYING	REMORTGAGING	RENATURING
REMILITARIZING	REMOISTENED	REMOTENESS	RENCONTRES
REMINERALISE	REMOISTENING	REMOTENESSES	RENCOUNTER
REMINERALISED	REMOISTENS	REMOTIVATE	RENCOUNTERED
REMINERALISES	REMONETISATION	REMOTIVATED	RENCOUNTERING
REMINERALISING	REMONETISATIONS	REMOTIVATES	RENCOUNTERS
REMINERALIZE	REMONETISE	REMOTIVATING	RENDERABLE
REMINERALIZED	REMONETISED	REMOTIVATION	RENDERINGS
REMINERALIZES	REMONETISES	REMOTIVATIONS	RENDEZVOUS
REMINERALIZING	REMONETISING	REMOULADES	RENDEZVOUSED
REMINISCED	REMONETIZATION	REMOULDING	RENDEZVOUSES
REMINISCENCE	REMONETIZATIONS	REMOUNTING	RENDEZVOUSING
REMINISCENCES	REMONETIZE	REMOVABILITIES	RENDITIONS
REMINISCENT	REMONETIZED	REMOVABILITY	RENEGADING
REMINISCENTIAL	REMONETIZES	REMOVABLENESS	RENEGADOES
REMINISCENTLY	REMONETIZING	REMOVABLENESSES	RENEGATION
REMINISCENTS	REMONSTRANCE	REMOVALIST	RENEGATIONS
REMINISCER	REMONSTRANCES	REMOVALISTS	RENEGOTIABLE
REMINISCERS	REMONSTRANT	REMOVEABLE	RENEGOTIATE
REMINISCES	REMONSTRANTLY	REMOVEDNESS	RENEGOTIATED
REMINISCING	REMONSTRANTS	REMOVEDNESSES	RENEGOTIATES

RENEGOTIATING	RENUNICATES	REORIENTATED	REPATRIATING
RENEGOTIATION	RENVERSEMENT	REORIENTATES	REPATRIATION
RENEGOTIATIONS	RENVERSEMENTS	REORIENTATING	REPATRIATIONS
RENEWABILITIES	RENVERSING	REORIENTATION	REPATRIATOR
RENEWABILITY	REOBJECTED	REORIENTATIONS	REPATRIATORS
RENEWABLES	REOBJECTING	REORIENTED	REPATTERNED
RENEWEDNESS	REOBSERVED	REORIENTING	REPATTERNING
RENEWEDNESSES	REOBSERVES	REOUTFITTED	REPATTERNS
RENFORCING	REOBSERVING	REOUTFITTING	REPAYMENTS
RENITENCES	REOBTAINED	REOVIRUSES	REPEALABLE
RENITENCIES	REOBTAINING	REOXIDATION	REPEATABILITIES
RENOGRAPHIC	REOCCUPATION	REOXIDATIONS	REPEATABILITY
RENOGRAPHIES	REOCCUPATIONS	REOXIDISED	REPEATABLE
RENOGRAPHY	REOCCUPIED	REOXIDISES	REPEATEDLY
RENOMINATE	REOCCUPIES	REOXIDISING	REPEATINGS
RENOMINATED	REOCCUPYING	REOXIDIZED	REPECHAGES
RENOMINATES	REOCCURRED	REOXIDIZES	REPELLANCE
RENOMINATING	REOCCURRENCE	REOXIDIZING	REPELLANCES
RENOMINATION	REOCCURRENCES	REPACIFIED	REPELLANCIES
RENOMINATIONS	REOCCURRING	REPACIFIES	REPELLANCY
RENORMALISATION	REOFFENDED	REPACIFYING	REPELLANTLY
RENORMALISE	REOFFENDER	REPACKAGED	REPELLANTS
RENORMALISED	REOFFENDERS	REPACKAGER	REPELLENCE
RENORMALISES	REOFFENDING	REPACKAGERS	REPELLENCES
RENORMALISING	REOFFERING	REPACKAGES	REPELLENCIES
RENORMALIZATION	REOPERATED	REPACKAGING	REPELLENCY
RENORMALIZE	REOPERATES	REPAGINATE	REPELLENTLY
RENORMALIZED	REOPERATING	REPAGINATED	REPELLENTS
RENORMALIZES	REOPERATION	REPAGINATES	REPELLINGLY
RENORMALIZING	REOPERATIONS	REPAGINATING	REPENTANCE
RENOSTERVELD	REOPPOSING	REPAGINATION	REPENTANCES
RENOSTERVELDS	REORCHESTRATE	REPAGINATIONS	REPENTANTLY
RENOTIFIED	REORCHESTRATED	REPAINTING	REPENTANTS
RENOTIFIES	REORCHESTRATES	REPAINTINGS	REPENTINGLY
RENOTIFYING	REORCHESTRATING	REPAIRABILITIES	REPEOPLING
RENOUNCEABLE	REORCHESTRATION	REPAIRABILITY	REPERCUSSED
RENOUNCEMENT	REORDAINED	REPAIRABLE	REPERCUSSES
RENOUNCEMENTS	REORDAINING	REPANELING	REPERCUSSING
RENOUNCERS	REORDERING	REPANELLED	REPERCUSSION
RENOUNCING	REORDINATION	REPANELLING	REPERCUSSIONS
RENOVASCULAR	REORDINATIONS	REPAPERING	REPERCUSSIVE
RENOVATING	REORGANISATION	REPARABILITIES	REPERTOIRE
RENOVATION	REORGANISATIONS	REPARABILITY	REPERTOIRES
RENOVATIONS	REORGANISE	REPARATION	REPERTORIAL
RENOVATIVE	REORGANISED	REPARATIONS	REPERTORIES
RENOVATORS	REORGANISER	REPARATIVE	REPERUSALS
RENSSELAERITE	REORGANISERS	REPARATORY	REPERUSING
RENSSELAERITES	REORGANISES	REPARTEEING	REPETITEUR
RENTABILITIES	REORGANISING	REPARTITION	REPETITEURS
RENTABILITY	REORGANIZATION	REPARTITIONED	REPETITEUSE
RENTALLERS	REORGANIZATIONS	REPARTITIONING	REPETITEUSES
RENUMBERED	REORGANIZE	REPARTITIONS	REPETITION
RENUMBERING	REORGANIZED	REPASSAGES	REPETITIONAL
RENUNCIATE	REORGANIZER	REPASTURES	REPETITIONARY
RENUNCIATION	REORGANIZERS	REPATCHING	REPETITIONS
RENUNCIATIONS	REORGANIZES	REPATRIATE	REPETITIOUS
RENUNCIATIVE	REORGANIZING	REPATRIATED	REPETITIOUSLY
RENUNCIATORY	REORIENTATE	REPATRIATES	REPETITIOUSNESS

REPETITIVE	REPLUNGING	REPOTTINGS	REPRESSURIZES
REPETITIVELY	REPOINTING	REPOUSSAGE	REPRESSURIZING
REPETITIVENESS	REPOLARISATION	REPOUSSAGES	REPRIEVABLE
REPHOTOGRAPH	REPOLARISATIONS	REPOUSSOIR	REPRIEVALS
REPHOTOGRAPHED	REPOLARISE	REPOUSSOIRS	REPRIEVERS
REPHOTOGRAPHING	REPOLARISED	REPOWERING	REPRIEVING
REPHOTOGRAPHS	REPOLARISES	REPREEVING	REPRIMANDED
REPHRASING	REPOLARISING	REPREHENDABLE	REPRIMANDING
REPIGMENTED	REPOLARIZATION	REPREHENDED	REPRIMANDS
REPIGMENTING	REPOLARIZATIONS	REPREHENDER	REPRINTERS
REPIGMENTS	REPOLARIZE	REPREHENDERS	REPRINTING
REPINEMENT	REPOLARIZED	REPREHENDING	REPRISTINATE
REPINEMENTS	REPOLARIZES	REPREHENDS	REPRISTINATED
REPININGLY	REPOLARIZING	REPREHENSIBLE	REPRISTINATES
REPLACEABILITY	REPOLISHED	REPREHENSIBLY	REPRISTINATING
REPLACEABLE	REPOLISHES	REPREHENSION	REPRISTINATION
REPLACEMENT	REPOLISHING	REPREHENSIONS	REPRISTINATIONS
REPLACEMENTS	REPOPULARISE	REPREHENSIVE	REPRIVATISATION
REPLANNING	REPOPULARISED	REPREHENSIVELY	REPRIVATISE
REPLANTATION	REPOPULARISES	REPREHENSORY	REPRIVATISED
REPLANTATIONS	REPOPULARISING	REPRESENTABLE	REPRIVATISES
REPLANTING	REPOPULARIZE	REPRESENTAMEN	REPRIVATISING
REPLASTERED	REPOPULARIZED	REPRESENTAMENS	REPRIVATIZATION
REPLASTERING	REPOPULARIZES	REPRESENTANT	REPRIVATIZE
REPLASTERS	REPOPULARIZING	REPRESENTANTS	REPRIVATIZED
REPLEADERS	REPOPULATE	REPRESENTATION	REPRIVATIZES
REPLEADING	REPOPULATED	REPRESENTATIONS	REPRIVATIZING
REPLEDGING	REPOPULATES	REPRESENTATIVE	REPROACHABLE
REPLENISHABLE	REPOPULATING	REPRESENTATIVES	REPROACHABLY
REPLENISHED	REPOPULATION	REPRESENTED	REPROACHED
REPLENISHER	REPOPULATIONS	REPRESENTEE	REPROACHER
REPLENISHERS	REPORTABLE	REPRESENTEES	REPROACHERS
REPLENISHES	REPORTAGES	REPRESENTER	REPROACHES
REPLENISHING	REPORTEDLY	REPRESENTERS	REPROACHFUL
REPLENISHMENT	REPORTINGLY	REPRESENTING	REPROACHFULLY
REPLENISHMENTS	REPORTINGS	REPRESENTMENT	REPROACHFULNESS
REPLETENESS	REPORTORIAL	REPRESENTMENTS	REPROACHING
REPLETENESSES	REPORTORIALLY	REPRESENTOR	REPROACHINGLY
REPLETIONS	REPOSEDNESS	REPRESENTORS	REPROACHLESS
REPLEVIABLE	REPOSEDNESSES	REPRESENTS	REPROBACIES
REPLEVINED	REPOSEFULLY	REPRESSERS	REPROBANCE
REPLEVINING	REPOSEFULNESS	REPRESSIBILITY	REPROBANCES
REPLEVISABLE	REPOSEFULNESSES	REPRESSIBLE	REPROBATED
REPLEVYING	REPOSITING	REPRESSIBLY	REPROBATER
REPLICABILITIES	REPOSITION	REPRESSING	REPROBATERS
REPLICABILITY	REPOSITIONED	REPRESSION	REPROBATES
REPLICABLE	REPOSITIONING	REPRESSIONIST	REPROBATING
REPLICASES	REPOSITIONS	REPRESSIONS	REPROBATION
REPLICATED	REPOSITORIES	REPRESSIVE	REPROBATIONARY
REPLICATES	REPOSITORS	REPRESSIVELY	REPROBATIONS
REPLICATING	REPOSITORY	REPRESSIVENESS	REPROBATIVE
REPLICATION	REPOSSESSED	REPRESSORS	REPROBATIVELY
REPLICATIONS	REPOSSESSES	REPRESSURISE	REPROBATOR
REPLICATIVE	REPOSSESSING	REPRESSURISED	REPROBATORS
REPLICATOR	REPOSSESSION	REPRESSURISES	REPROBATORY
REPLICATORS	REPOSSESSIONS	REPRESSURISING	REPROCESSED
REPLOTTING	REPOSSESSOR	REPRESSURIZE	REPROCESSES
REPLUMBING	REPOSSESSORS	REPRESSURIZED	REPROCESSING

REPRODUCED	REPUBLISHERS	REQUIRABLE	REREVISING
REPRODUCER	REPUBLISHES	REQUIREMENT	REROUTEING
REPRODUCERS	REPUBLISHING	REQUIREMENTS	RESADDLING
REPRODUCES	REPUDIABLE	REQUIRINGS	RESALEABLE
REPRODUCIBILITY	REPUDIATED	REQUISITELY	RESALUTING
REPRODUCIBLE	REPUDIATES	REQUISITENESS	RESAMPLING
REPRODUCIBLES	REPUDIATING	REQUISITENESSES	RESCHEDULE
REPRODUCIBLY	REPUDIATION	REQUISITES	RESCHEDULED
REPRODUCING	REPUDIATIONIST	REQUISITION	RESCHEDULES
REPRODUCTION	REPUDIATIONISTS	REQUISITIONARY	RESCHEDULING
REPRODUCTIONS	REPUDIATIONS	REQUISITIONED	RESCHEDULINGS
REPRODUCTIVE	REPUDIATIVE	REQUISITIONING	RESCHOOLED
REPRODUCTIVELY	REPUDIATOR	REQUISITIONIST	RESCHOOLING
REPRODUCTIVES	REPUDIATORS	REQUISITIONISTS	RESCINDABLE
REPRODUCTIVITY	REPUGNANCE	REQUISITIONS	RESCINDERS
REPROGRAMED	REPUGNANCES	REQUISITOR	RESCINDING
REPROGRAMING	REPUGNANCIES	REQUISITORS	RESCINDMENT
REPROGRAMMABLE	REPUGNANCY	REQUISITORY	RESCINDMENTS
REPROGRAMME	REPUGNANTLY	REQUITABLE	RESCISSIBLE
REPROGRAMMED	REPULSIONS	REQUITEFUL	RESCISSION
REPROGRAMMES	REPULSIVELY	REQUITELESS	RESCISSIONS
REPROGRAMMING	REPULSIVENESS	REQUITEMENT	RESCISSORY
REPROGRAMS	REPULSIVENESSES	REQUITEMENTS	RESCREENED
REPROGRAPHER	REPUNCTUATION	REQUITTING	RESCREENING
REPROGRAPHERS	REPUNCTUATIONS	REQUOYLING	RESCRIPTED
REPROGRAPHIC	REPURCHASE	RERADIATED	RESCRIPTING
REPROGRAPHICS	REPURCHASED	RERADIATES	RESCULPTED
REPROGRAPHIES	REPURCHASES	RERADIATING	RESCULPTING
REPROGRAPHY	REPURCHASING	RERADIATION	RESEALABLE
REPROOFING	REPURIFIED	RERADIATIONS	RESEARCHABLE
REPROVABLE	REPURIFIES	REREADINGS	RESEARCHED
REPROVINGLY	REPURIFYING	REREBRACES	RESEARCHER
REPROVINGS	REPURPOSED	RERECORDED	RESEARCHERS
REPROVISION	REPURPOSES	RERECORDING	RESEARCHES
REPROVISIONED	REPURPOSING	REREDORTER	RESEARCHFUL
REPROVISIONING	REPURSUING	REREDORTERS	RESEARCHING
REPROVISIONS	REPUTABILITIES	REREDOSSES	RESEARCHIST
REPTATIONS	REPUTABILITY	REREGISTER	RESEARCHISTS
REPTILIANLY	REPUTATION	REREGISTERED	RESEASONED
REPTILIANS	REPUTATIONAL	REREGISTERING	RESEASONING
REPTILIFEROUS	REPUTATIONLESS	REREGISTERS	RESECTABILITIES
REPTILIOUS	REPUTATIONS	REREGISTRATION	RESECTABILITY
REPUBLICAN	REPUTATIVE	REREGISTRATIONS	RESECTABLE
REPUBLICANISE	REPUTATIVELY	REREGULATE	RESECTIONAL
REPUBLICANISED	REPUTELESS	REREGULATED	RESECTIONS
REPUBLICANISES	REQUALIFIED	REREGULATES	RESECURING
REPUBLICANISING	REQUALIFIES	REREGULATING	RESEGREGATE
REPUBLICANISM	REQUALIFYING	REREGULATION	RESEGREGATED
REPUBLICANISMS	REQUESTERS	REREGULATIONS	RESEGREGATES
REPUBLICANIZE	REQUESTING	RERELEASED	RESEGREGATING
REPUBLICANIZED	REQUESTORS	RERELEASES	RESEGREGATION
REPUBLICANIZES	REQUICKENED	RERELEASING	RESEGREGATIONS
REPUBLICANIZING	REQUICKENING	REREMINDED	RESEIZURES
REPUBLICANS	REQUICKENS	REREMINDING	RESELECTED
REPUBLICATION	REQUIESCAT	REREPEATED	RESELECTING
REPUBLICATIONS	REQUIESCATS	REREPEATING	RESELECTION
REPUBLISHED	REQUIGHTED	REREVIEWED	RESELECTIONS
REPUBLISHER	REQUIGHTING	REREVIEWING	RESEMBLANCE

RESEMBLANCES	RESHUFFLES	RESISTIVENESSES	RESOLVEDNESSES
RESEMBLANT	RESHUFFLING	RESISTIVITIES	RESOLVENTS
RESEMBLERS	RESIDENCES	RESISTIVITY	RESONANCES
RESEMBLING	RESIDENCIES	RESISTLESS	RESONANTLY
RESENSITISE	RESIDENTER	RESISTLESSLY	RESONATING
RESENSITISED	RESIDENTERS	RESISTLESSNESS	RESONATION
RESENSITISES	RESIDENTIAL	RESITTINGS	RESONATIONS
RESENSITISING	RESIDENTIALLY	RESITUATED	RESONATORS
RESENSITIZE	RESIDENTIARIES	RESITUATES	RESORBENCE
RESENSITIZED	RESIDENTIARY	RESITUATING	RESORBENCES
RESENSITIZES	RESIDENTSHIP	RESKETCHED	RESORCINAL
RESENSITIZING	RESIDENTSHIPS	RESKETCHES	RESORCINOL
RESENTENCE	RESIDUALLY	RESKETCHING	RESORCINOLS
RESENTENCED	RESIGHTING	RESKILLING	RESORPTION
RESENTENCES	RESIGNATION	RESKILLINGS	RESORPTIONS
RESENTENCING	RESIGNATIONS	RESMELTING	RESORPTIVE
RESENTFULLY	RESIGNEDLY	RESMOOTHED	RESOUNDING
RESENTFULNESS	RESIGNEDNESS	RESMOOTHING	RESOUNDINGLY
RESENTFULNESSES	RESIGNEDNESSES	RESNATRONS	RESOURCEFUL
RESENTINGLY	RESIGNMENT	RESOCIALISATION	RESOURCEFULLY
RESENTMENT	RESIGNMENTS	RESOCIALISE	RESOURCEFULNESS
RESENTMENTS	RESILEMENT	RESOCIALISED	RESOURCELESS
RESERPINES	RESILEMENTS	RESOCIALISES	RESOURCING
RESERVABLE	RESILIENCE	RESOCIALISING	RESPEAKING
RESERVATION	RESILIENCES	RESOCIALIZATION	RESPECIFIED
RESERVATIONIST	RESILIENCIES	RESOCIALIZE	RESPECIFIES
RESERVATIONISTS	RESILIENCY	RESOCIALIZED	RESPECIFYING
RESERVATIONS	RESILIENTLY	RESOCIALIZES	RESPECTABILISE
RESERVATORIES	RESILVERED	RESOCIALIZING	RESPECTABILISED
RESERVATORY	RESILVERING	RESOFTENED	RESPECTABILISES
RESERVEDLY	RESINATING	RESOFTENING	RESPECTABILITY
RESERVEDNESS	RESINIFEROUS	RESOLDERED	RESPECTABILIZE
RESERVEDNESSES	RESINIFICATION	RESOLDERING	RESPECTABILIZED
RESERVICED	RESINIFICATIONS	RESOLIDIFIED	RESPECTABILIZES
RESERVICES	RESINIFIED	RESOLIDIFIES	RESPECTABLE
RESERVICING	RESINIFIES	RESOLIDIFY	RESPECTABLENESS
RESERVISTS	RESINIFYING	RESOLIDIFYING	RESPECTABLES
RESERVOIRED	RESINISING	RESOLUBILITIES	RESPECTABLY
RESERVOIRING	RESINIZING	RESOLUBILITY	RESPECTANT
RESERVOIRS	RESINOUSLY	RESOLUBLENESS	RESPECTERS
RESETTABLE	RESINOUSNESS	RESOLUBLENESSES	RESPECTFUL
RESETTLEMENT	RESINOUSNESSES	RESOLUTELY	RESPECTFULLY
RESETTLEMENTS	RESIPISCENCE	RESOLUTENESS	RESPECTFULNESS
RESETTLING	RESIPISCENCES	RESOLUTENESSES	RESPECTING
RESHARPENED	RESIPISCENCIES	RESOLUTEST	RESPECTIVE
RESHARPENING	RESIPISCENCY	RESOLUTION	RESPECTIVELY
RESHARPENS	RESIPISCENT	RESOLUTIONER	RESPECTIVENESS
RESHINGLED	RESISTANCE	RESOLUTIONERS	RESPECTLESS
RESHINGLES	RESISTANCES	RESOLUTIONIST	RESPELLING
RESHINGLING	RESISTANTS	RESOLUTIONISTS	RESPELLINGS
RESHIPMENT	RESISTENTS	RESOLUTIONS	RESPIRABILITIES
RESHIPMENTS	RESISTIBILITIES	RESOLUTIVE	RESPIRABILITY
RESHIPPERS	RESISTIBILITY	RESOLVABILITIES	RESPIRABLE
RESHIPPING	RESISTIBLE	RESOLVABILITY	RESPIRATION
RESHOOTING	RESISTIBLY	RESOLVABLE	RESPIRATIONAL
RESHOWERED	RESISTINGLY	RESOLVABLENESS	RESPIRATIONS
RESHOWERING	RESISTIVELY	RESOLVEDLY	RESPIRATOR
RESHUFFLED	RESISTIVENESS	RESOLVEDNESS	RESPIRATORS

RESPIRATORY	RESSENTIMENTS	RESTIVENESS	RESTRIVING
RESPIRITUALISE	RESTABILISE	RESTIVENESSES	RESTRUCTURE
RESPIRITUALISED	RESTABILISED	RESTLESSLY	RESTRUCTURED
RESPIRITUALISES	RESTABILISES	RESTLESSNESS	RESTRUCTURES
RESPIRITUALIZE	RESTABILISING	RESTLESSNESSES	RESTRUCTURING
RESPIRITUALIZED	RESTABILIZE	RESTOCKING	RESTRUCTURINGS
RESPIRITUALIZES	RESTABILIZED	RESTORABLE	RESTUDYING
RESPIROMETER	RESTABILIZES	RESTORABLENESS	RESTUFFING
RESPIROMETERS	RESTABILIZING	RESTORATION	RESTUMPING
RESPIROMETRIC	RESTABLING	RESTORATIONISM	RESUBJECTED
RESPIROMETRIES	RESTACKING	RESTORATIONISMS	RESUBJECTING
RESPIROMETRY	RESTAFFING	RESTORATIONIST	RESUBJECTS
RESPITELESS	RESTAMPING	RESTORATIONISTS	RESUBMISSION
RESPLENDED	RESTARTABLE	RESTORATIONS	RESUBMISSIONS
RESPLENDENCE	RESTARTERS	RESTORATIVE	RESUBMITTED
RESPLENDENCES	RESTARTING	RESTORATIVELY	RESUBMITTING
RESPLENDENCIES	RESTATEMENT	RESTORATIVES	RESULTANTLY
RESPLENDENCY	RESTATEMENTS	RESTRAINABLE	RESULTANTS
RESPLENDENT	RESTATIONED	RESTRAINED	RESULTATIVE
RESPLENDENTLY	RESTATIONING	RESTRAINEDLY	RESULTLESS
RESPLENDING	RESTATIONS	RESTRAINEDNESS	RESULTLESSNESS
RESPLICING	RESTAURANT	RESTRAINER	RESUMMONED
RESPLITTING	RESTAURANTEUR	RESTRAINERS	RESUMMONING
RESPONDENCE	RESTAURANTEURS	RESTRAINING	RESUMPTION
RESPONDENCES	RESTAURANTS	RESTRAININGS	RESUMPTIONS
RESPONDENCIES	RESTAURATEUR	RESTRAINTS	RESUMPTIVE
RESPONDENCY	RESTAURATEURS	RESTRENGTHEN	RESUMPTIVELY
RESPONDENT	RESTAURATION	RESTRENGTHENED	RESUPINATE
RESPONDENTIA	RESTAURATIONS	RESTRENGTHENING	RESUPINATION
RESPONDENTIAS	RESTEMMING	RESTRENGTHENS	RESUPINATIONS
RESPONDENTS	RESTFULLER	RESTRESSED	RESUPPLIED
RESPONDERS	RESTFULLEST	RESTRESSES	RESUPPLIES
RESPONDING	RESTFULNESS	RESTRESSING	RESUPPLYING
RESPONSELESS	RESTFULNESSES	RESTRETCHED	RESURFACED
RESPONSERS	RESTHARROW	RESTRETCHES	RESURFACER
RESPONSIBILITY	RESTHARROWS	RESTRETCHING	RESURFACERS
RESPONSIBLE	RESTIMULATE	RESTRICKEN	RESURFACES
RESPONSIBLENESS	RESTIMULATED	RESTRICTED	RESURFACING
RESPONSIBLY	RESTIMULATES	RESTRICTEDLY	RESURGENCE
RESPONSIONS	RESTIMULATING	RESTRICTEDNESS	RESURGENCES
RESPONSIVE	RESTIMULATION	RESTRICTING	RESURRECTED
RESPONSIVELY	RESTIMULATIONS	RESTRICTION	RESURRECTING
RESPONSIVENESS	RESTITCHED	RESTRICTIONISM	RESURRECTION
RESPONSORIAL	RESTITCHES	RESTRICTIONISMS	RESURRECTIONAL
RESPONSORIALS	RESTITCHING	RESTRICTIONIST	RESURRECTIONARY
RESPONSORIES	RESTITUTED	RESTRICTIONISTS	RESURRECTIONISE
RESPONSORS	RESTITUTES	RESTRICTIONS	RESURRECTIONISM
RESPONSORY	RESTITUTING	RESTRICTIVE	RESURRECTIONIST
RESPONSUMS	RESTITUTION	RESTRICTIVELY	RESURRECTIONIZE
RESPOOLING	RESTITUTIONISM	RESTRICTIVENESS	RESURRECTIONS
RESPOTTING	RESTITUTIONISMS	RESTRICTIVES	RESURRECTIVE
RESPRAYING	RESTITUTIONIST	RESTRIKING	RESURRECTOR
RESPREADING	RESTITUTIONISTS	RESTRINGED	RESURRECTORS
RESPRINGING	RESTITUTIONS	RESTRINGEING	RESURRECTS
RESPROUTED	RESTITUTIVE	RESTRINGENT	RESURVEYED
RESPROUTING	RESTITUTOR	RESTRINGENTS	RESURVEYING
RESSALDARS	RESTITUTORS	RESTRINGES	RESUSCITABLE
RESSENTIMENT	RESTITUTORY	RESTRINGING	RESUSCITANT

RESUSCITANTS
RESUSCITATE
RESUSCITATED
RESUSCITATES
RESUSCITATING
RESUSCITATION
RESUSCITATIONS
RESUSCITATIVE
RESUSCITATOR
RESUSCITATORS
RESUSPENDED
RESUSPENDING
RESUSPENDS
RESVERATROL
RESVERATROLS
RESWALLOWED
RESWALLOWING
RESWALLOWS
RESYNCHRONISE
RESYNCHRONISED
RESYNCHRONISES
RESYNCHRONISING
RESYNCHRONIZE
RESYNCHRONIZED
RESYNCHRONIZES
RESYNCHRONIZING
RESYNTHESES
RESYNTHESIS
RESYNTHESISE
RESYNTHESISED
RESYNTHESISES
RESYNTHESISING
RESYNTHESIZE
RESYNTHESIZED
RESYNTHESIZES
RESYNTHESIZING
RESYSTEMATISE
RESYSTEMATISED
RESYSTEMATISES
RESYSTEMATISING
RESYSTEMATIZE
RESYSTEMATIZED
RESYSTEMATIZES
RESYSTEMATIZING
RETACKLING
RETAILINGS
RETAILMENT
RETAILMENTS
RETAILORED
RETAILORING
RETAINABLE
RETAINERSHIP
RETAINERSHIPS
RETAINMENT
RETAINMENTS
RETALIATED
RETALIATES
RETALIATING

RETALIATION
RETALIATIONIST
RETALIATIONISTS
RETALIATIONS
RETALIATIVE
RETALIATOR
RETALIATORS
RETALIATORY
RETALLYING
RETARDANTS
RETARDATES
RETARDATION
RETARDATIONS
RETARDATIVE
RETARDATORY
RETARDMENT
RETARDMENTS
RETARGETED
RETARGETING
RETEACHING
RETELLINGS
RETEMPERED
RETEMPERING
RETENTIONIST
RETENTIONISTS
RETENTIONS
RETENTIVELY
RETENTIVENESS
RETENTIVENESSES
RETENTIVITIES
RETENTIVITY
RETESTIFIED
RETESTIFIES
RETESTIFYING
RETEXTURED
RETEXTURES
RETEXTURING
RETHINKERS
RETHINKING
RETHREADED
RETHREADING
RETIARIUSES
RETICELLAS
RETICENCES
RETICENCIES
RETICENTLY
RETICULARLY
RETICULARY
RETICULATE
RETICULATED
RETICULATELY
RETICULATES
RETICULATING
RETICULATION
RETICULATIONS
RETICULOCYTE
RETICULOCYTES
RETICULUMS

RETIGHTENED
RETIGHTENING
RETIGHTENS
RETINACULA
RETINACULAR
RETINACULUM
RETINALITE
RETINALITES
RETINISPORA
RETINISPORAS
RETINITIDES
RETINITISES
RETINOBLASTOMA
RETINOBLASTOMAS
RETINOPATHIES
RETINOPATHY
RETINOSCOPE
RETINOSCOPES
RETINOSCOPIC
RETINOSCOPIES
RETINOSCOPIST
RETINOSCOPISTS
RETINOSCOPY
RETINOSPORA
RETINOSPORAS
RETINOTECTAL
RETIRACIES
RETIREDNESS
RETIREDNESSES
RETIREMENT
RETIREMENTS
RETIRINGLY
RETIRINGNESS
RETIRINGNESSES
RETORSIONS
RETORTIONS
RETOTALING
RETOTALLED
RETOTALLING
RETOUCHABLE
RETOUCHERS
RETOUCHING
RETRACEABLE
RETRACEMENT
RETRACEMENTS
RETRACKING
RETRACTABILITY
RETRACTABLE
RETRACTATION
RETRACTATIONS
RETRACTIBILITY
RETRACTIBLE
RETRACTILE
RETRACTILITIES
RETRACTILITY
RETRACTING
RETRACTION
RETRACTIONS

RETRACTIVE
RETRACTIVELY
RETRACTORS
RETRAINABLE
RETRAINEES
RETRAINING
RETRANSFER
RETRANSFERRED
RETRANSFERRING
RETRANSFERS
RETRANSFORM
RETRANSFORMED
RETRANSFORMING
RETRANSFORMS
RETRANSLATE
RETRANSLATED
RETRANSLATES
RETRANSLATING
RETRANSLATION
RETRANSLATIONS
RETRANSMISSION
RETRANSMISSIONS
RETRANSMIT
RETRANSMITS
RETRANSMITTED
RETRANSMITTING
RETREADING
RETREATANT
RETREATANTS
RETREATERS
RETREATING
RETRENCHABLE
RETRENCHED
RETRENCHES
RETRENCHING
RETRENCHMENT
RETRENCHMENTS
RETRIBUTED
RETRIBUTES
RETRIBUTING
RETRIBUTION
RETRIBUTIONS
RETRIBUTIVE
RETRIBUTIVELY
RETRIBUTOR
RETRIBUTORS
RETRIBUTORY
RETRIEVABILITY
RETRIEVABLE
RETRIEVABLENESS
RETRIEVABLY
RETRIEVALS
RETRIEVEMENT
RETRIEVEMENTS
RETRIEVERS
RETRIEVING
RETRIEVINGS
RETRIMMING

RETROACTED	RETROJECTED	REUNIONISMS	REVARNISHES
RETROACTING	RETROJECTING	REUNIONIST	REVARNISHING
RETROACTION	RETROJECTION	REUNIONISTIC	REVEALABILITIES
RETROACTIONS	RETROJECTIONS	REUNIONISTS	REVEALABILITY
RETROACTIVE	RETROJECTS	REUNITABLE	REVEALABLE
RETROACTIVELY	RETROLENTAL	REUPHOLSTER	REVEALINGLY
RETROACTIVENESS	RETROMINGENCIES	REUPHOLSTERED	REVEALINGNESS
RETROACTIVITIES	RETROMINGENCY	REUPHOLSTERING	REVEALINGNESSES
RETROACTIVITY	RETROMINGENT	REUPHOLSTERS	REVEALINGS
RETROBULBAR	RETROMINGENTS	REUSABILITIES	REVEALMENT
RETROCEDED	RETROPACKS	REUSABILITY	REVEALMENTS
RETROCEDENCE	RETROPERITONEAL	REUTILISATION	REVEGETATE
RETROCEDENCES	RETROPHILIA	REUTILISATIONS	REVEGETATED
RETROCEDENT	RETROPHILIAC	REUTILISED	REVEGETATES
RETROCEDES	RETROPHILIACS	REUTILISES	REVEGETATING
RETROCEDING	RETROPHILIAS	REUTILISING	REVEGETATION
RETROCESSION	RETROPULSION	REUTILIZATION	REVEGETATIONS
RETROCESSIONS	RETROPULSIONS	REUTILIZATIONS	REVELATION
RETROCESSIVE	RETROPULSIVE	REUTILIZED	REVELATIONAL
RETROCHOIR	RETROREFLECTION	REUTILIZES	REVELATIONIST
RETROCHOIRS	RETROREFLECTIVE	REUTILIZING	REVELATIONISTS
RETROCOGNITION	RETROREFLECTOR	REUTTERING	REVELATIONS
RETROCOGNITIONS	RETROREFLECTORS	REVACCINATE	REVELATIVE
RETRODICTED	RETROROCKET	REVACCINATED	REVELATORS
RETRODICTING	RETROROCKETS	REVACCINATES	REVELATORY
RETRODICTION	RETRORSELY	REVACCINATING	REVELLINGS
RETRODICTIONS	RETROSEXUAL	REVACCINATION	REVELMENTS
RETRODICTIVE	RETROSEXUALS	REVACCINATIONS	REVENDICATE
RETRODICTS	RETROSPECT	REVALENTAS	REVENDICATED
RETROFIRED	RETROSPECTED	REVALIDATE	REVENDICATES
RETROFIRES	RETROSPECTING	REVALIDATED	REVENDICATING
RETROFIRING	RETROSPECTION	REVALIDATES	REVENDICATION
RETROFITTED	RETROSPECTIONS	REVALIDATING	REVENDICATIONS
RETROFITTING	RETROSPECTIVE	REVALIDATION	REVENGEFUL
RETROFITTINGS	RETROSPECTIVELY	REVALIDATIONS	REVENGEFULLY
RETROFLECTED	RETROSPECTIVES	REVALORISATION	REVENGEFULNESS
RETROFLECTION	RETROSPECTS	REVALORISATIONS	REVENGELESS
RETROFLECTIONS	RETROUSSAGE	REVALORISE	REVENGEMENT
RETROFLEXED	RETROUSSAGES	REVALORISED	REVENGEMENTS
RETROFLEXES	RETROVERSE	REVALORISES	REVENGINGLY
RETROFLEXION	RETROVERSION	REVALORISING	REVENGINGS
RETROFLEXIONS	RETROVERSIONS	REVALORIZATION	REVERBERANT
RETROGRADATION	RETROVERTED	REVALORIZATIONS	REVERBERANTLY
RETROGRADATIONS	RETROVERTING	REVALORIZE	REVERBERATE
RETROGRADE	RETROVERTS	REVALORIZED	REVERBERATED
RETROGRADED	RETROVIRAL	REVALORIZES	REVERBERATES
RETROGRADELY	RETROVIRUS	REVALORIZING	REVERBERATING
RETROGRADES	RETROVIRUSES	REVALUATED	REVERBERATION
RETROGRADING	RETURNABILITIES	REVALUATES	REVERBERATIONS
RETROGRESS	RETURNABILITY	REVALUATING	REVERBERATIVE
RETROGRESSED	RETURNABLE	REVALUATION	REVERBERATOR
RETROGRESSES	RETURNABLES	REVALUATIONS	REVERBERATORIES
RETROGRESSING	RETURNLESS	REVAMPINGS	REVERBERATORS
RETROGRESSION	RETWISTING	REVANCHISM	REVERBERATORY
RETROGRESSIONAL	REUNIFICATION	REVANCHISMS	REVERENCED
RETROGRESSIONS	REUNIFICATIONS	REVANCHIST	REVERENCER
RETROGRESSIVE	REUNIFYING	REVANCHISTS	REVERENCERS
RETROGRESSIVELY	REUNIONISM	REVARNISHED	REVERENCES

REVERENCING	REVISITANT	REVOLUTIONARIES	RHABDOVIRUSES
REVERENTIAL	REVISITANTS	REVOLUTIONARILY	RHACHIDIAL
REVERENTIALLY	REVISITATION	REVOLUTIONARY	RHACHILLAS
REVERENTLY	REVISITATIONS	REVOLUTIONER	RHACHITISES
REVERENTNESS	REVISITING	REVOLUTIONERS	RHADAMANTHINE
REVERENTNESSES	REVISUALISATION	REVOLUTIONISE	RHAGADIFORM
REVERIFIED	REVISUALIZATION	REVOLUTIONISED	RHAMNACEOUS
REVERIFIES	REVITALISATION	REVOLUTIONISER	RHAMPHOTHECA
REVERIFYING	REVITALISATIONS	REVOLUTIONISERS	RHAMPHOTHECAE
REVERSEDLY	REVITALISE	REVOLUTIONISES	RHAPONTICS
REVERSELESS	REVITALISED	REVOLUTIONISING	RHAPSODICAL
REVERSIBILITIES	REVITALISES	REVOLUTIONISM	RHAPSODICALLY
REVERSIBILITY	REVITALISING	REVOLUTIONISMS	RHAPSODIES
REVERSIBLE	REVITALIZATION	REVOLUTIONIST	RHAPSODISE
REVERSIBLES	REVITALIZATIONS	REVOLUTIONISTS	RHAPSODISED
REVERSIBLY	REVITALIZE	REVOLUTIONIZE	RHAPSODISES
REVERSINGS	REVITALIZED	REVOLUTIONIZED	RHAPSODISING
REVERSIONAL	REVITALIZES	REVOLUTIONIZER	RHAPSODIST
REVERSIONALLY	REVITALIZING	REVOLUTIONIZERS	RHAPSODISTIC
REVERSIONARIES	REVIVABILITIES	REVOLUTIONIZES	RHAPSODISTS
REVERSIONARY	REVIVABILITY	REVOLUTIONIZING	RHAPSODIZE
REVERSIONER	REVIVALISM	REVOLUTIONS	RHAPSODIZED
REVERSIONERS	REVIVALISMS	REVOLVABLE	RHAPSODIZES
REVERSIONS	REVIVALIST	REVOLVABLY	RHAPSODIZING
REVERSISES	REVIVALISTIC	REVOLVENCIES	RHEOCHORDS
REVERTANTS	REVIVALISTS	REVOLVENCY	RHEOLOGICAL
REVERTIBLE	REVIVEMENT	REVOLVINGLY	RHEOLOGICALLY
REVESTIARIES	REVIVEMENTS	REVOLVINGS	RHEOLOGIES
REVESTIARY	REVIVESCENCE	REVULSIONARY	RHEOLOGIST
REVESTRIES	REVIVESCENCES	REVULSIONS	RHEOLOGISTS
REVETMENTS	REVIVESCENCIES	REVULSIVELY	RHEOMETERS
REVIBRATED	REVIVESCENCY	REVULSIVES	RHEOMETRIC
REVIBRATES	REVIVESCENT	REWAKENING	RHEOMETRICAL
REVIBRATING	REVIVIFICATION	REWARDABLE	RHEOMETRIES
REVICTUALED	REVIVIFICATIONS	REWARDABLENESS	RHEOMORPHIC
REVICTUALING	REVIVIFIED	REWARDINGLY	RHEOMORPHISM
REVICTUALLED	REVIVIFIES	REWARDLESS	RHEOMORPHISMS
REVICTUALLING	REVIVIFYING	REWEIGHING	RHEOPHILES
REVICTUALS	REVIVINGLY	REWIDENING	RHEORECEPTOR
REVIEWABLE	REVIVISCENCE	REWRAPPING	RHEORECEPTORS
REVILEMENT	REVIVISCENCES	RHABDOCOELE	RHEOSTATIC
REVILEMENTS	REVIVISCENCIES	RHABDOCOELES	RHEOTACTIC
REVILINGLY	REVIVISCENCY	RHABDOLITH	RHEOTROPES
REVINDICATE	REVIVISCENT	RHABDOLITHS	RHEOTROPIC
REVINDICATED	REVOCABILITIES	RHABDOMANCER	RHEOTROPISM
REVINDICATES	REVOCABILITY	RHABDOMANCERS	RHEOTROPISMS
REVINDICATING	REVOCABLENESS	RHABDOMANCIES	RHETORICAL
REVINDICATION	REVOCABLENESSES	RHABDOMANCY	RHETORICALLY
REVINDICATIONS	REVOCATION	RHABDOMANTIST	RHETORICIAN
REVIOLATED	REVOCATIONS	RHABDOMANTISTS	RHETORICIANS
REVIOLATES	REVOCATORY	RHABDOMERE	RHETORISED
REVIOLATING	REVOKABILITIES	RHABDOMERES	RHETORISES
REVISIONAL	REVOKABILITY	RHABDOMYOMA	RHETORISING
REVISIONARY	REVOKEMENT	RHABDOMYOMAS	RHETORIZED
REVISIONISM	REVOKEMENTS	RHABDOMYOMATA	RHETORIZES
REVISIONISMS	REVOLTINGLY	RHABDOSPHERE	RHETORIZING
REVISIONIST	REVOLUTION	RHABDOSPHERES	RHEUMATEESE
REVISIONISTS	REVOLUTIONAL	RHABDOVIRUS	RHEUMATEESES

RHEUMATICAL	RHINOSCOPIES	RHODOPHANE	RHYTHMISING
RHEUMATICALLY	RHINOSCOPY	RHODOPHANES	RHYTHMISTS
RHEUMATICKY	RHINOTHECA	RHODOPSINS	RHYTHMIZATION
RHEUMATICS	RHINOTHECAE	RHOEADINES	RHYTHMIZATIONS
RHEUMATISE	RHINOVIRUS	RHOICISSUS	RHYTHMIZED
RHEUMATISES	RHINOVIRUSES	RHOICISSUSES	RHYTHMIZES
RHEUMATISM	RHIPIDIONS	RHOMBENCEPHALA	RHYTHMIZING
RHEUMATISMAL	RHIPIDIUMS	RHOMBENCEPHALON	RHYTHMLESS
RHEUMATISMS	RHIZANTHOUS	RHOMBENPORPHYR	RHYTHMOMETER
RHEUMATIZE	RHIZOCARPIC	RHOMBENPORPHYRS	RHYTHMOMETERS
RHEUMATIZES	RHIZOCARPOUS	RHOMBENPORPHYRY	RHYTHMOPOEIA
RHEUMATOID	RHIZOCARPS	RHOMBOHEDRA	RHYTHMOPOEIAS
RHEUMATOIDALLY	RHIZOCAULS	RHOMBOHEDRAL	RHYTHMUSES
RHEUMATOLOGICAL	RHIZOCEPHALAN	RHOMBOHEDRON	RHYTIDECTOMIES
RHEUMATOLOGIES	RHIZOCEPHALANS	RHOMBOHEDRONS	RHYTIDECTOMY
RHEUMATOLOGIST	RHIZOCEPHALOUS	RHOMBOIDAL	RHYTIDOMES
RHEUMATOLOGISTS	RHIZOCTONIA	RHOMBOIDEI	RIBALDRIES
RHEUMATOLOGY	RHIZOCTONIAS	RHOMBOIDES	RIBATTUTAS
RHIGOLENES	RHIZOGENETIC	RHOMBOIDEUS	RIBAUDRIES
RHINENCEPHALA	RHIZOGENIC	RHOMBPORPHYRIES	RIBAVIRINS
RHINENCEPHALIC	RHIZOGENOUS	RHOMBPORPHYRY	RIBBONFISH
RHINENCEPHALON	RHIZOMATOUS	RHOPALISMS	RIBBONFISHES
RHINENCEPHALONS	RHIZOMORPH	RHOPALOCERAL	RIBBONLIKE
RHINESTONE	RHIZOMORPHOUS	RHOPALOCEROUS	RIBBONRIES
RHINESTONED	RHIZOMORPHS	RHOTACISED	RIBBONWOOD
RHINESTONES	RHIZOPHAGOUS	RHOTACISES	RIBBONWOODS
RHINITIDES	RHIZOPHILOUS	RHOTACISING	RIBGRASSES
RHINITISES	RHIZOPHORE	RHOTACISMS	RIBOFLAVIN
RHINOCERICAL	RHIZOPHORES	RHOTACISTIC	RIBOFLAVINE
RHINOCEROS	RHIZOPLANE	RHOTACISTS	RIBOFLAVINES
RHINOCEROSES	RHIZOPLANES	RHOTACIZED	RIBOFLAVINS
RHINOCEROT	RHIZOPODAN	RHOTACIZES	RIBONUCLEASE
RHINOCEROTE	RHIZOPODANS	RHOTACIZING	RIBONUCLEASES
RHINOCEROTES	RHIZOPODOUS	RHOTICITIES	RIBONUCLEIC
RHINOCEROTIC	RHIZOPUSES	RHUBARBING	RIBONUCLEOSIDE
RHINOLALIA	RHIZOSPHERE	RHUBARBINGS	RIBONUCLEOSIDES
RHINOLALIAS	RHIZOSPHERES	RHUMBATRON	RIBONUCLEOTIDE
RHINOLITHS	RHIZOTOMIES	RHUMBATRONS	RIBONUCLEOTIDES
RHINOLOGICAL	RHODAMINES	RHYMESTERS	RICERCARES
RHINOLOGIES	RHODANATES	RHYNCHOCOEL	RICERCATAS
RHINOLOGIST	RHODANISED	RHYNCHOCOELS	RICHNESSES
RHINOLOGISTS	RHODANISES	RHYNCHODONT	RICINOLEIC
RHINOPHYMA	RHODANISING	RHYNCHOPHORE	RICKBURNER
RHINOPHYMAS	RHODANIZED	RHYNCHOPHORES	RICKBURNERS
RHINOPLASTIC	RHODANIZES	RHYNCHOPHOROUS	RICKETIEST
RHINOPLASTIES	RHODANIZING	RHYPAROGRAPHER	RICKETINESS
RHINOPLASTY	RHODOCHROSITE	RHYPAROGRAPHERS	RICKETINESSES
RHINORRHAGIA	RHODOCHROSITES	RHYPAROGRAPHIC	RICKETTIER
RHINORRHAGIAS	RHODODAPHNE	RHYPAROGRAPHIES	RICKETTIEST
RHINORRHOEA	RHODODAPHNES	RHYPAROGRAPHY	RICKETTSIA
RHINORRHOEAL	RHODODENDRON	RHYTHMICAL	RICKETTSIAE
RHINORRHOEAS	RHODODENDRONS	RHYTHMICALLY	RICKETTSIAL
RHINOSCLEROMA	RHODOLITES	RHYTHMICITIES	RICKETTSIAS
RHINOSCLEROMAS	RHODOMONTADE	RHYTHMICITY	RICKSTANDS
RHINOSCLEROMATA	RHODOMONTADED	RHYTHMISATION	RICKSTICKS
RHINOSCOPE	RHODOMONTADES	RHYTHMISATIONS	RICOCHETED
RHINOSCOPES	RHODOMONTADING	RHYTHMISED	RICOCHETING
RHINOSCOPIC	RHODONITES	RHYTHMISES	RICOCHETTED

RICOCHETTING	RIJKSDAALERS	RITUALISING	ROBOTIZATION
RIDABILITIES	RIJSTAFELS	RITUALISMS	ROBOTIZATIONS
RIDABILITY	RIJSTTAFEL	RITUALISTIC	ROBOTIZING
RIDDLINGLY	RIJSTTAFELS	RITUALISTICALLY	ROBUSTIOUS
RIDERSHIPS	RIMINESSES	RITUALISTS	ROBUSTIOUSLY
RIDGEBACKS	RIMOSITIES	RITUALIZATION	ROBUSTIOUSNESS
RIDGELINES	RINDERPEST	RITUALIZATIONS	ROBUSTNESS
RIDGELINGS	RINDERPESTS	RITUALIZED	ROBUSTNESSES
RIDGEPOLES	RINFORZANDO	RITUALIZES	ROCAMBOLES
RIDGETREES	RINGBARKED	RITUALIZING	ROCKABILLIES
RIDICULERS	RINGBARKING	RITZINESSES	ROCKABILLY
RIDICULING	RINGHALSES	RIVALESSES	ROCKCRESSES
RIDICULOUS	RINGLEADER	RIVALISING	ROCKETEERS
RIDICULOUSLY	RINGLEADERS	RIVALITIES	ROCKETRIES
RIDICULOUSNESS	RINGMASTER	RIVALIZING	ROCKFISHES
RIEBECKITE	RINGMASTERS	RIVALSHIPS	ROCKHOPPER
RIEBECKITES	RINGSIDERS	RIVERBANKS	ROCKHOPPERS
RIFACIMENTI	RINGSTANDS	RIVERBOATS	ROCKHOUNDING
RIFACIMENTO	RINGSTRAKED	RIVERCRAFT	ROCKHOUNDINGS
RIFAMPICIN	RINGTOSSES	RIVERCRAFTS	ROCKHOUNDS
RIFAMPICINS	RINKHALSES	RIVERFRONT	ROCKINESSES
RIFAMYCINS	RINSABILITIES	RIVERFRONTS	ROCKSHAFTS
RIFENESSES	RINSABILITY	RIVERHEADS	ROCKSLIDES
RIFLEBIRDS	RINSIBILITIES	RIVERSCAPE	ROCKSTEADIES
RIGAMAROLE	RINSIBILITY	RIVERSCAPES	ROCKSTEADY
RIGAMAROLES	RINTHEREOUT	RIVERSIDES	ROCKWATERS
RIGHTABLENESS	RINTHEREOUTS	RIVERWARDS	RODENTICIDE
RIGHTABLENESSES	RIOTOUSNESS	RIVERWEEDS	RODENTICIDES
RIGHTENING	RIOTOUSNESSES	RIVERWORTHINESS	RODFISHERS
RIGHTEOUSLY	RIPENESSES	RIVERWORTHY	RODFISHING
RIGHTEOUSNESS	RIPIDOLITE	RIVETINGLY	RODFISHINGS
RIGHTEOUSNESSES	RIPIDOLITES	ROADABILITIES	RODGERSIAS
RIGHTFULLY	RIPIENISTS	ROADABILITY	RODOMONTADE
RIGHTFULNESS	RIPPLINGLY	ROADBLOCKED	RODOMONTADED
RIGHTFULNESSES	RIPRAPPING	ROADBLOCKING	RODOMONTADER
RIGHTNESSES	RIPSNORTER	ROADBLOCKS	RODOMONTADERS
RIGHTSIZED	RIPSNORTERS	ROADCRAFTS	RODOMONTADES
RIGHTSIZES	RIPSNORTING	ROADHEADER	RODOMONTADING
RIGHTSIZING	RISIBILITIES	ROADHEADERS	ROENTGENISATION
RIGHTWARDS	RISIBILITY	ROADHOLDING	ROENTGENISE
RIGIDIFICATION	RISKINESSES	ROADHOLDINGS	ROENTGENISED
RIGIDIFICATIONS	RISORGIMENTO	ROADHOUSES	ROENTGENISES
RIGIDIFIED	RISORGIMENTOS	ROADROLLER	ROENTGENISING
RIGIDIFIES	RITARDANDO	ROADROLLERS	ROENTGENIZATION
RIGIDIFYING	RITARDANDOS	ROADRUNNER	ROENTGENIZE
RIGIDISING	RITONAVIRS	ROADRUNNERS	ROENTGENIZED
RIGIDITIES	RITORNELLE	ROADSTEADS	ROENTGENIZES
RIGIDIZING	RITORNELLES	ROADWORTHINESS	ROENTGENIZING
RIGIDNESSES	RITORNELLI	ROADWORTHY	ROENTGENOGRAM
RIGMAROLES	RITORNELLO	ROBERDSMAN	ROENTGENOGRAMS
RIGORISTIC	RITORNELLOS	ROBERDSMEN	ROENTGENOGRAPH
RIGOROUSLY	RITORNELLS	ROBERTSMAN	ROENTGENOGRAPHS
RIGOROUSNESS	RITOURNELLE	ROBERTSMEN	ROENTGENOGRAPHY
RIGOROUSNESSES	RITOURNELLES	ROBORATING	ROENTGENOLOGIC
RIGSDALERS	RITUALISATION	ROBOTICALLY	ROENTGENOLOGIES
RIGWIDDIES	RITUALISATIONS	ROBOTISATION	ROENTGENOLOGIST
RIGWOODIES	RITUALISED	ROBOTISATIONS	ROENTGENOLOGY
RIJKSDAALER	RITUALISES	ROBOTISING	ROENTGENOPAQUE

ROENTGENOSCOPE	ROMELDALES	ROSANILINE	ROUGHCASTERS
ROENTGENOSCOPES	ROMPISHNESS	ROSANILINES	ROUGHCASTING
ROENTGENOSCOPIC	ROMPISHNESSES	ROSANILINS	ROUGHCASTS
ROENTGENOSCOPY	RONDOLETTO	ROSEBUSHES	ROUGHDRIED
ROGUESHIPS	RONDOLETTOS	ROSEFINCHES	ROUGHDRIES
ROGUISHNESS	RONTGENISATION	ROSEFISHES	ROUGHDRYING
ROGUISHNESSES	RONTGENISATIONS	ROSEMALING	ROUGHENING
ROISTERERS	RONTGENISE	ROSEMALINGS	ROUGHHEWED
ROISTERING	RONTGENISED	ROSEMARIES	ROUGHHEWING
ROISTERINGS	RONTGENISES	ROSEWATERS	ROUGHHOUSE
ROISTEROUS	RONTGENISING	ROSINESSES	ROUGHHOUSED
ROISTEROUSLY	RONTGENIZATION	ROSINWEEDS	ROUGHHOUSES
ROLLCOLLAR	RONTGENIZATIONS	ROSMARINES	ROUGHHOUSING
ROLLCOLLARS	RONTGENIZE	ROSTELLATE	ROUGHNECKED
ROLLERBALL	RONTGENIZED	ROSTELLUMS	ROUGHNECKING
ROLLERBALLS	RONTGENIZES	ROSTERINGS	ROUGHNECKS
ROLLERBLADE	RONTGENIZING	ROSTROCARINATE	ROUGHNESSES
ROLLERBLADED	RONTGENOGRAM	ROSTROCARINATES	ROUGHRIDER
ROLLERBLADER	RONTGENOGRAMS	ROTACHUTES	ROUGHRIDERS
ROLLERBLADERS	RONTGENOGRAPH	ROTAMETERS	ROULETTING
ROLLERBLADES	RONTGENOGRAPHS	ROTAPLANES	ROUNCEVALS
ROLLERBLADING	RONTGENOGRAPHY	ROTATIONAL	ROUNDABOUT
ROLLERBLADINGS	RONTGENOLOGICAL	ROTATIVELY	ROUNDABOUTATION
ROLLERCOASTER	RONTGENOLOGIES	ROTAVATING	ROUNDABOUTED
ROLLERCOASTERED	RONTGENOLOGIST	ROTAVATORS	ROUNDABOUTEDLY
ROLLERCOASTERS	RONTGENOLOGISTS	ROTAVIRUSES	ROUNDABOUTILITY
ROLLICKING	RONTGENOLOGY	ROTGRASSES	ROUNDABOUTING
ROLLICKINGS	RONTGENOPAQUE	ROTIFERANS	ROUNDABOUTLY
ROLLOCKING	RONTGENOSCOPE	ROTIFEROUS	ROUNDABOUTNESS
ROLLOCKINGS	RONTGENOSCOPES	ROTISSERIE	ROUNDABOUTS
ROMANCICAL	RONTGENOSCOPIC	ROTISSERIES	ROUNDARCHED
ROMANCINGS	RONTGENOSCOPIES	ROTOGRAPHED	ROUNDBALLS
ROMANICITE	RONTGENOSCOPY	ROTOGRAPHING	ROUNDEDNESS
ROMANICITES	RONTGENOTHERAPY	ROTOGRAPHS	ROUNDEDNESSES
ROMANISATION	ROOFLESSNESS	ROTOGRAVURE	ROUNDELAYS
ROMANISATIONS	ROOFLESSNESSES	ROTOGRAVURES	ROUNDHANDS
ROMANISING	ROOFSCAPES	ROTORCRAFT	ROUNDHEADED
ROMANIZATION	ROOMINESSES	ROTORCRAFTS	ROUNDHEADEDNESS
ROMANIZATIONS	ROOTEDNESS	ROTOTILLED	ROUNDHEELS
ROMANIZING	ROOTEDNESSES	ROTOTILLER	ROUNDHOUSE
ROMANTICAL	ROOTINESSES	ROTOTILLERS	ROUNDHOUSES
ROMANTICALITIES	ROOTLESSNESS	ROTOTILLING	ROUNDNESSES
ROMANTICALITY	ROOTLESSNESSES	ROTOVATING	ROUNDTABLE
ROMANTICALLY	ROOTSERVER	ROTOVATORS	ROUNDTABLES
ROMANTICISATION	ROOTSERVERS	ROTTENNESS	ROUNDTRIPPING
ROMANTICISE	ROOTSINESS	ROTTENNESSES	ROUNDTRIPPINGS
ROMANTICISED	ROOTSINESSES	ROTTENSTONE	ROUNDTRIPS
ROMANTICISES	ROOTSTALKS	ROTTENSTONED	ROUNDWOODS
ROMANTICISING	ROOTSTOCKS	ROTTENSTONES	ROUNDWORMS
ROMANTICISM	ROPEDANCER	ROTTENSTONING	ROUSEABOUT
ROMANTICISMS	ROPEDANCERS	ROTTWEILER	ROUSEABOUTS
ROMANTICIST	ROPEDANCING	ROTTWEILERS	ROUSEDNESS
ROMANTICISTS	ROPEDANCINGS	ROTUNDITIES	ROUSEDNESSES
ROMANTICIZATION	ROPEWALKER	ROTUNDNESS	ROUSEMENTS
ROMANTICIZE	ROPEWALKERS	ROTUNDNESSES	ROUSSETTES
ROMANTICIZED	ROPINESSES	ROUGHBACKS	ROUSTABOUT
ROMANTICIZES	ROQUELAURE	ROUGHCASTED	ROUSTABOUTS
ROMANTICIZING	ROQUELAURES	ROUGHCASTER	ROUTEMARCH

ROUTEMARCHED
ROUTEMARCHES
ROUTEMARCHING
ROUTINEERS
ROUTINISATION
ROUTINISATIONS
ROUTINISED
ROUTINISES
ROUTINISING
ROUTINISMS
ROUTINISTS
ROUTINIZATION
ROUTINIZATIONS
ROUTINIZED
ROUTINIZES
ROUTINIZING
ROWANBERRIES
ROWANBERRY
ROWDINESSES
ROYALISING
ROYALISTIC
ROYALIZING
ROYALMASTS
ROYSTERERS
ROYSTERING
ROYSTEROUS
RUBBERIEST
RUBBERISED
RUBBERISES
RUBBERISING
RUBBERIZED
RUBBERIZES
RUBBERIZING
RUBBERLIKE
RUBBERNECK
RUBBERNECKED
RUBBERNECKER
RUBBERNECKERS
RUBBERNECKING
RUBBERNECKS
RUBBERWEAR
RUBBERWEARS
RUBBISHING
RUBBLEWORK
RUBBLEWORKS
RUBEFACIENT
RUBEFACIENTS
RUBEFACTION
RUBEFACTIONS
RUBELLITES
RUBESCENCE
RUBESCENCES
RUBIACEOUS
RUBICELLES
RUBICONING
RUBICUNDITIES
RUBICUNDITY
RUBIGINOSE

RUBIGINOUS
RUBRICALLY
RUBRICATED
RUBRICATES
RUBRICATING
RUBRICATION
RUBRICATIONS
RUBRICATOR
RUBRICATORS
RUBRICIANS
RUBYTHROAT
RUBYTHROATS
RUCTATIONS
RUDBECKIAS
RUDDERHEAD
RUDDERHEADS
RUDDERLESS
RUDDERPOST
RUDDERPOSTS
RUDDERSTOCK
RUDDERSTOCKS
RUDDINESSES
RUDENESSES
RUDIMENTAL
RUDIMENTALLY
RUDIMENTARILY
RUDIMENTARINESS
RUDIMENTARY
RUEFULNESS
RUEFULNESSES
RUFESCENCE
RUFESCENCES
RUFFIANING
RUFFIANISH
RUFFIANISM
RUFFIANISMS
RUGGEDISATION
RUGGEDISATIONS
RUGGEDISED
RUGGEDISES
RUGGEDISING
RUGGEDIZATION
RUGGEDIZATIONS
RUGGEDIZED
RUGGEDIZES
RUGGEDIZING
RUGGEDNESS
RUGGEDNESSES
RUGOSITIES
RUINATIONS
RUINOUSNESS
RUINOUSNESSES
RULERSHIPS
RUMBLEDETHUMP
RUMBLEDETHUMPS
RUMBLEGUMPTION
RUMBLEGUMPTIONS
RUMBLINGLY

RUMBULLION
RUMBULLIONS
RUMBUSTICAL
RUMBUSTIOUS
RUMBUSTIOUSLY
RUMBUSTIOUSNESS
RUMELGUMPTION
RUMELGUMPTIONS
RUMFUSTIAN
RUMFUSTIANS
RUMGUMPTION
RUMGUMPTIONS
RUMINANTLY
RUMINATING
RUMINATINGLY
RUMINATION
RUMINATIONS
RUMINATIVE
RUMINATIVELY
RUMINATORS
RUMLEGUMPTION
RUMLEGUMPTIONS
RUMMELGUMPTION
RUMMELGUMPTIONS
RUMMINESSES
RUMMLEGUMPTION
RUMMLEGUMPTIONS
RUMORMONGER
RUMORMONGERING
RUMORMONGERINGS
RUMORMONGERS
RUMRUNNERS
RUNAROUNDS
RUNECRAFTS
RUNNINESSES
RUNTINESSES
RUPESTRIAN
RUPICOLINE
RUPICOLOUS
RUPTURABLE
RUPTUREWORT
RUPTUREWORTS
RURALISATION
RURALISATIONS
RURALISING
RURALITIES
RURALIZATION
RURALIZATIONS
RURALIZING
RURALNESSES
RURIDECANAL
RUSHINESSES
RUSHLIGHTS
RUSSETINGS
RUSSETTING
RUSSETTINGS
RUSSIFYING
RUSTBUCKET

RUSTICALLY
RUSTICATED
RUSTICATES
RUSTICATING
RUSTICATINGS
RUSTICATION
RUSTICATIONS
RUSTICATOR
RUSTICATORS
RUSTICISED
RUSTICISES
RUSTICISING
RUSTICISMS
RUSTICITIES
RUSTICIZED
RUSTICIZES
RUSTICIZING
RUSTICWORK
RUSTICWORKS
RUSTINESSES
RUSTLINGLY
RUSTPROOFED
RUSTPROOFING
RUSTPROOFS
RUTHENIOUS
RUTHENIUMS
RUTHERFORD
RUTHERFORDIUM
RUTHERFORDIUMS
RUTHERFORDS
RUTHFULNESS
RUTHFULNESSES
RUTHLESSLY
RUTHLESSNESS
RUTHLESSNESSES
RUTTINESSES
RUTTISHNESS
RUTTISHNESSES
RYBAUDRYES
RYEGRASSES

S

SABADILLAS
SABBATARIAN
SABBATICAL
SABBATICALS
SABBATISED
SABBATISES
SABBATISING
SABBATISMS
SABBATIZED
SABBATIZES
SABBATIZING
SABERMETRICIAN
SABERMETRICIANS
SABERMETRICS
SABLEFISHES
SABOTAGING
SABRETACHE
SABRETACHES
SABULOSITIES
SABULOSITY
SABURRATION
SABURRATIONS
SACAHUISTA
SACAHUISTAS
SACAHUISTE
SACAHUISTES
SACCADICALLY
SACCHARASE
SACCHARASES
SACCHARATE
SACCHARATED
SACCHARATES
SACCHARIDE
SACCHARIDES
SACCHARIFEROUS
SACCHARIFIED
SACCHARIFIES
SACCHARIFY
SACCHARIFYING
SACCHARIMETER
SACCHARIMETERS
SACCHARIMETRIES
SACCHARIMETRY
SACCHARINE
SACCHARINELY
SACCHARINES
SACCHARINITIES
SACCHARINITY
SACCHARINS
SACCHARISATION
SACCHARISATIONS
SACCHARISE
SACCHARISED
SACCHARISES

SACCHARISING
SACCHARIZATION
SACCHARIZATIONS
SACCHARIZE
SACCHARIZED
SACCHARIZES
SACCHARIZING
SACCHAROID
SACCHAROIDAL
SACCHAROIDS
SACCHAROMETER
SACCHAROMETERS
SACCHAROMYCES
SACCHAROMYCETES
SACCHAROSE
SACCHAROSES
SACCHARUMS
SACCULATED
SACCULATION
SACCULATIONS
SACCULIFORM
SACERDOTAL
SACERDOTALISE
SACERDOTALISED
SACERDOTALISES
SACERDOTALISING
SACERDOTALISM
SACERDOTALISMS
SACERDOTALIST
SACERDOTALISTS
SACERDOTALIZE
SACERDOTALIZED
SACERDOTALIZES
SACERDOTALIZING
SACERDOTALLY
SACHEMDOMS
SACHEMSHIP
SACHEMSHIPS
SACKCLOTHS
SACRALGIAS
SACRALISATION
SACRALISATIONS
SACRALISED
SACRALISES
SACRALISING
SACRALIZATION
SACRALIZATIONS
SACRALIZED
SACRALIZES
SACRALIZING
SACRAMENTAL
SACRAMENTALISM
SACRAMENTALISMS
SACRAMENTALIST

SACRAMENTALISTS
SACRAMENTALITY
SACRAMENTALLY
SACRAMENTALNESS
SACRAMENTALS
SACRAMENTARIAN
SACRAMENTARIES
SACRAMENTARY
SACRAMENTED
SACRAMENTING
SACRAMENTS
SACREDNESS
SACREDNESSES
SACRIFICEABLE
SACRIFICED
SACRIFICER
SACRIFICERS
SACRIFICES
SACRIFICIAL
SACRIFICIALLY
SACRIFICING
SACRIFYING
SACRILEGES
SACRILEGIOUS
SACRILEGIOUSLY
SACRILEGIST
SACRILEGISTS
SACRISTANS
SACRISTIES
SACROCOCCYGEAL
SACROCOSTAL
SACROCOSTALS
SACROILIAC
SACROILIACS
SACROILIITIS
SACROILIITISES
SACROSANCT
SACROSANCTITIES
SACROSANCTITY
SACROSANCTNESS
SADDLEBACK
SADDLEBACKED
SADDLEBACKS
SADDLEBAGS
SADDLEBILL
SADDLEBILLS
SADDLEBOWS
SADDLEBRED
SADDLEBREDS
SADDLECLOTH
SADDLECLOTHS
SADDLELESS
SADDLERIES
SADDLEROOM

SADDLEROOMS
SADDLETREE
SADDLETREES
SADISTICALLY
SADOMASOCHISM
SADOMASOCHISMS
SADOMASOCHIST
SADOMASOCHISTIC
SADOMASOCHISTS
SAFECRACKER
SAFECRACKERS
SAFECRACKING
SAFECRACKINGS
SAFEGUARDED
SAFEGUARDING
SAFEGUARDS
SAFEKEEPING
SAFEKEEPINGS
SAFELIGHTS
SAFENESSES
SAFFLOWERS
SAFRANINES
SAGACIOUSLY
SAGACIOUSNESS
SAGACIOUSNESSES
SAGACITIES
SAGANASHES
SAGAPENUMS
SAGEBRUSHES
SAGENESSES
SAGINATING
SAGINATION
SAGINATIONS
SAGITTALLY
SAGITTARIAN
SAGITTARIANS
SAGITTARIES
SAGITTIFORM
SAILBOARDED
SAILBOARDER
SAILBOARDERS
SAILBOARDING
SAILBOARDINGS
SAILBOARDS
SAILBOATER
SAILBOATERS
SAILBOATING
SAILBOATINGS
SAILCLOTHS
SAILFISHES
SAILMAKERS
SAILORINGS
SAILORLESS
SAILORLIKE

SAILPLANED	SALICYLATED	SALPINGITIC	SALVABLENESSES
SAILPLANER	SALICYLATES	SALPINGITIS	SALVAGEABILITY
SAILPLANERS	SALICYLATING	SALPINGITISES	SALVAGEABLE
SAILPLANES	SALICYLISM	SALSOLACEOUS	SALVARSANS
SAILPLANING	SALICYLISMS	SALSUGINOUS	SALVATIONAL
SAINTESSES	SALIENCIES	SALTARELLI	SALVATIONISM
SAINTFOINS	SALIENTIAN	SALTARELLO	SALVATIONISMS
SAINTHOODS	SALIENTIANS	SALTARELLOS	SALVATIONIST
SAINTLIEST	SALIFEROUS	SALTATIONISM	SALVATIONISTS
SAINTLINESS	SALIFIABLE	SALTATIONISMS	SALVATIONS
SAINTLINESSES	SALIFICATION	SALTATIONIST	SALVATORIES
SAINTLINGS	SALIFICATIONS	SALTATIONISTS	SALVERFORM
SAINTPAULIA	SALIMETERS	SALTATIONS	SALVIFICAL
SAINTPAULIAS	SALIMETRIC	SALTATORIAL	SALVIFICALLY
SAINTSHIPS	SALIMETRIES	SALTATORIOUS	SALVINIACEOUS
SALABILITIES	SALINISATION	SALTBUSHES	SAMARIFORM
SALABILITY	SALINISATIONS	SALTCELLAR	SAMARITANS
SALABLENESS	SALINISING	SALTCELLARS	SAMARSKITE
SALABLENESSES	SALINITIES	SALTCHUCKER	SAMARSKITES
SALACIOUSLY	SALINIZATION	SALTCHUCKERS	SAMENESSES
SALACIOUSNESS	SALINIZATIONS	SALTCHUCKS	SAMNITISES
SALACIOUSNESSES	SALINIZING	SALTFISHES	SAMPLERIES
SALACITIES	SALINOMETER	SALTIGRADE	SANATORIUM
SALAMANDER	SALINOMETERS	SALTIGRADES	SANATORIUMS
SALAMANDERS	SALINOMETRIC	SALTIMBANCO	SANBENITOS
SALAMANDRIAN	SALINOMETRIES	SALTIMBANCOS	SANCTIFIABLE
SALAMANDRINE	SALINOMETRY	SALTIMBOCCA	SANCTIFICATION
SALAMANDROID	SALIVATING	SALTIMBOCCAS	SANCTIFICATIONS
SALAMANDROIDS	SALIVATION	SALTINESSES	SANCTIFIED
SALANGANES	SALIVATIONS	SALTIREWISE	SANCTIFIEDLY
SALBUTAMOL	SALIVATORS	SALTISHNESS	SANCTIFIER
SALBUTAMOLS	SALLENDERS	SALTISHNESSES	SANCTIFIERS
SALEABILITIES	SALLOWNESS	SALTNESSES	SANCTIFIES
SALEABILITY	SALLOWNESSES	SALTPETERS	SANCTIFYING
SALEABLENESS	SALLYPORTS	SALTPETREMAN	SANCTIFYINGLY
SALEABLENESSES	SALMAGUNDI	SALTPETREMEN	SANCTIFYINGS
SALERATUSES	SALMAGUNDIES	SALTPETRES	SANCTIMONIES
SALESCLERK	SALMAGUNDIS	SALTSHAKER	SANCTIMONIOUS
SALESCLERKS	SALMAGUNDY	SALTSHAKERS	SANCTIMONIOUSLY
SALESGIRLS	SALMANASER	SALUBRIOUS	SANCTIMONY
SALESLADIES	SALMANASERS	SALUBRIOUSLY	SANCTIONABLE
SALESMANSHIP	SALMANAZAR	SALUBRIOUSNESS	SANCTIONED
SALESMANSHIPS	SALMANAZARS	SALUBRITIES	SANCTIONEER
SALESPEOPLE	SALMONBERRIES	SALURETICS	SANCTIONEERS
SALESPERSON	SALMONBERRY	SALUTARILY	SANCTIONER
SALESPERSONS	SALMONELLA	SALUTARINESS	SANCTIONERS
SALESROOMS	SALMONELLAE	SALUTARINESSES	SANCTIONING
SALESWOMAN	SALMONELLAS	SALUTATION	SANCTIONLESS
SALESWOMEN	SALMONELLOSES	SALUTATIONAL	SANCTITIES
SALIAUNCES	SALMONELLOSIS	SALUTATIONS	SANCTITUDE
SALICACEOUS	SALMONOIDS	SALUTATORIAN	SANCTITUDES
SALICETUMS	SALOMETERS	SALUTATORIANS	SANCTUARIES
SALICIONAL	SALOPETTES	SALUTATORIES	SANCTUARISE
SALICIONALS	SALPIGLOSSES	SALUTATORILY	SANCTUARISED
SALICORNIA	SALPIGLOSSIS	SALUTATORY	SANCTUARISES
SALICORNIAS	SALPIGLOSSISES	SALUTIFEROUS	SANCTUARISING
SALICYLAMIDE	SALPINGECTOMIES	SALVABILITIES	SANCTUARIZE
SALICYLAMIDES	SALPINGECTOMY	SALVABILITY	SANCTUARIZED
SALICYLATE	SALPINGIAN	SALVABLENESS	SANCTUARIZES

SANCTUARIZING	SANGUINELY	SAPIDNESSES	SARCOCARPS
SANDALLING	SANGUINENESS	SAPIENCIES	SARCOCOLLA
SANDALWOOD	SANGUINENESSES	SAPIENTIAL	SARCOCOLLAS
SANDALWOODS	SANGUINEOUS	SAPIENTIALLY	SARCOCYSTIS
SANDARACHS	SANGUINEOUSNESS	SAPINDACEOUS	SARCOCYSTISES
SANDBAGGED	SANGUINING	SAPLESSNESS	SARCOIDOSES
SANDBAGGER	SANGUINITIES	SAPLESSNESSES	SARCOIDOSIS
SANDBAGGERS	SANGUINITY	SAPODILLAS	SARCOLEMMA
SANDBAGGING	SANGUINIVOROUS	SAPOGENINS	SARCOLEMMAL
SANDBLASTED	SANGUINOLENCIES	SAPONACEOUS	SARCOLEMMAS
SANDBLASTER	SANGUINOLENCY	SAPONACEOUSNESS	SARCOLEMMATA
SANDBLASTERS	SANGUINOLENT	SAPONARIAS	SARCOLOGIES
SANDBLASTING	SANGUIVOROUS	SAPONIFIABLE	SARCOMATOID
SANDBLASTINGS	SANITARIAN	SAPONIFICATION	SARCOMATOSES
SANDBLASTS	SANITARIANISM	SAPONIFICATIONS	SARCOMATOSIS
SANDCASTLE	SANITARIANISMS	SAPONIFIED	SARCOMATOUS
SANDCASTLES	SANITARIANS	SAPONIFIER	SARCOMERES
SANDCRACKS	SANITARIES	SAPONIFIERS	SARCOPHAGAL
SANDERLING	SANITARILY	SAPONIFIES	SARCOPHAGI
SANDERLINGS	SANITARINESS	SAPONIFYING	SARCOPHAGOUS
SANDERSWOOD	SANITARINESSES	SAPOTACEOUS	SARCOPHAGUS
SANDERSWOODS	SANITARIST	SAPPANWOOD	SARCOPHAGUSES
SANDFISHES	SANITARISTS	SAPPANWOODS	SARCOPLASM
SANDGLASSES	SANITARIUM	SAPPERMENT	SARCOPLASMIC
SANDGROPER	SANITARIUMS	SAPPHIRINE	SARCOPLASMS
SANDGROPERS	SANITATING	SAPPHIRINES	SARCOSOMAL
SANDGROUSE	SANITATION	SAPPINESSES	SARCOSOMES
SANDGROUSES	SANITATIONIST	SAPRAEMIAS	SARDONICAL
SANDINESSES	SANITATIONISTS	SAPROBIONT	SARDONICALLY
SANDLOTTER	SANITATIONS	SAPROBIONTS	SARDONICISM
SANDLOTTERS	SANITISATION	SAPROBIOTIC	SARDONICISMS
SANDPAINTING	SANITISATIONS	SAPROGENIC	SARDONYXES
SANDPAINTINGS	SANITISERS	SAPROGENICITIES	SARGASSUMS
SANDPAPERED	SANITISING	SAPROGENICITY	SARMENTACEOUS
SANDPAPERING	SANITIZATION	SAPROGENOUS	SARMENTOSE
SANDPAPERS	SANITIZATIONS	SAPROLEGNIA	SARMENTOUS
SANDPAPERY	SANITIZERS	SAPROLEGNIAS	SARPANCHES
SANDPIPERS	SANITIZING	SAPROLITES	SARRACENIA
SANDSPOUTS	SANITORIUM	SAPROLITIC	SARRACENIACEOUS
SANDSTONES	SANITORIUMS	SAPROPELIC	SARRACENIAS
SANDSTORMS	SANNYASINS	SAPROPELITE	SARRUSOPHONE
SANDSUCKER	SANSCULOTTE	SAPROPELITES	SARRUSOPHONES
SANDSUCKERS	SANSCULOTTERIE	SAPROPHAGOUS	SARSAPARILLA
SANDWICHED	SANSCULOTTERIES	SAPROPHYTE	SARSAPARILLAS
SANDWICHES	SANSCULOTTES	SAPROPHYTES	SARTORIALLY
SANDWICHING	SANSCULOTTIC	SAPROPHYTIC	SARTORIUSES
SANENESSES	SANSCULOTTIDES	SAPROPHYTICALLY	SASKATOONS
SANGFROIDS	SANSCULOTTISH	SAPROPHYTISM	SASQUATCHES
SANGUIFEROUS	SANSCULOTTISM	SAPROPHYTISMS	SASSAFRASES
SANGUIFICATION	SANSCULOTTISMS	SAPROTROPH	SASSARARAS
SANGUIFICATIONS	SANSCULOTTIST	SAPROTROPHIC	SASSINESSES
SANGUIFIED	SANSCULOTTISTS	SAPROTROPHS	SASSOLITES
SANGUIFIES	SANSEVIERIA	SAPSUCKERS	SASSYWOODS
SANGUIFYING	SANSEVIERIAS	SARABANDES	SATANICALLY
SANGUINARIA	SANTALACEOUS	SARBACANES	SATANICALNESS
SANGUINARIAS	SANTOLINAS	SARCASTICALLY	SATANICALNESSES
SANGUINARILY	SANTONICAS	SARCENCHYMATOUS	SATANITIES
SANGUINARINESS	SAPANWOODS	SARCENCHYME	SATANOLOGIES
SANGUINARY	SAPIDITIES	SARCENCHYMES	SATANOLOGY

SATANOPHANIES	SATURABILITY	SAVINGNESS	SCALEBOARD
SATANOPHANY	SATURATERS	SAVINGNESSES	SCALEBOARDS
SATANOPHOBIA	SATURATING	SAVORINESS	SCALENOHEDRA
SATANOPHOBIAS	SATURATION	SAVORINESSES	SCALENOHEDRON
SATCHELFUL	SATURATIONS	SAVOURIEST	SCALENOHEDRONS
SATCHELFULS	SATURATORS	SAVOURINESS	SCALETAILS
SATCHELLED	SATURNALIA	SAVOURINESSES	SCALEWORKS
SATCHELSFUL	SATURNALIAN	SAVOURLESS	SCALINESSES
SATEDNESSES	SATURNALIANLY	SAVVINESSES	SCALLAWAGS
SATELLITED	SATURNALIAS	SAWBONESES	SCALLOPERS
SATELLITES	SATURNIIDS	SAWDUSTING	SCALLOPING
SATELLITIC	SATURNINELY	SAWTIMBERS	SCALLOPINI
SATELLITING	SATURNINITIES	SAXICAVOUS	SCALLOPINIS
SATELLITISE	SATURNINITY	SAXICOLINE	SCALLYWAGS
SATELLITISED	SATURNISMS	SAXICOLOUS	SCALOGRAMS
SATELLITISES	SATURNISTS	SAXIFRAGACEOUS	SCALOPPINE
SATELLITISING	SATYAGRAHA	SAXIFRAGES	SCALOPPINES
SATELLITIUM	SATYAGRAHAS	SAXITOXINS	SCALOPPINI
SATELLITIUMS	SATYAGRAHI	SAXOPHONES	SCALPELLIC
SATELLITIZE	SATYAGRAHIS	SAXOPHONIC	SCALPELLIFORM
SATELLITIZED	SATYRESQUE	SAXOPHONIST	SCALPRIFORM
SATELLITIZES	SATYRESSES	SAXOPHONISTS	SCAMBAITING
SATELLITIZING	SATYRIASES	SCABBARDED	SCAMBAITINGS
SATIABILITIES	SATYRIASIS	SCABBARDING	SCAMBLINGLY
SATIABILITY	SAUCEBOATS	SCABBARDLESS	SCAMBLINGS
SATIATIONS	SAUCEBOXES	SCABBEDNESS	SCAMMONIATE
SATINETTAS	SAUCERFULS	SCABBEDNESSES	SCAMMONIES
SATINETTES	SAUCERLESS	SCABBINESS	SCAMPERERS
SATINFLOWER	SAUCERLIKE	SCABBINESSES	SCAMPERING
SATINFLOWERS	SAUCINESSES	SCABERULOUS	SCAMPISHLY
SATINWOODS	SAUCISSONS	SCABIOUSES	SCAMPISHNESS
SATIRICALLY	SAUERBRATEN	SCABRIDITIES	SCAMPISHNESSES
SATIRICALNESS	SAUERBRATENS	SCABRIDITY	SCANDALING
SATIRICALNESSES	SAUERKRAUT	SCABROUSLY	SCANDALISATION
SATIRISABLE	SAUERKRAUTS	SCABROUSNESS	SCANDALISATIONS
SATIRISATION	SAUNTERERS	SCABROUSNESSES	SCANDALISE
SATIRISATIONS	SAUNTERING	SCAFFOLAGE	SCANDALISED
SATIRISERS	SAUNTERINGLY	SCAFFOLAGES	SCANDALISER
SATIRISING	SAUNTERINGS	SCAFFOLDAGE	SCANDALISERS
SATIRIZABLE	SAURISCHIAN	SCAFFOLDAGES	SCANDALISES
SATIRIZATION	SAURISCHIANS	SCAFFOLDED	SCANDALISING
SATIRIZATIONS	SAUROGNATHOUS	SCAFFOLDER	SCANDALIZATION
SATIRIZERS	SAUROPODOUS	SCAFFOLDERS	SCANDALIZATIONS
SATIRIZING	SAUROPSIDAN	SCAFFOLDING	SCANDALIZE
SATISFACTION	SAUROPSIDANS	SCAFFOLDINGS	SCANDALIZED
SATISFACTIONS	SAUROPTERYGIAN	SCAGLIOLAS	SCANDALIZER
SATISFACTORILY	SAUSSURITE	SCAITHLESS	SCANDALIZERS
SATISFACTORY	SAUSSURITES	SCALABILITIES	SCANDALIZES
SATISFIABLE	SAUSSURITIC	SCALABILITY	SCANDALIZING
SATISFICED	SAVABLENESS	SCALABLENESS	SCANDALLED
SATISFICER	SAVABLENESSES	SCALABLENESSES	SCANDALLING
SATISFICERS	SAVAGEDOMS	SCALARIFORM	SCANDALMONGER
SATISFICES	SAVAGENESS	SCALARIFORMLY	SCANDALMONGERS
SATISFICING	SAVAGENESSES	SCALATIONS	SCANDALOUS
SATISFICINGS	SAVAGERIES	SCALDBERRIES	SCANDALOUSLY
SATISFIERS	SAVEABLENESS	SCALDBERRY	SCANDALOUSNESS
SATISFYING	SAVEABLENESSES	SCALDFISHES	SCANSORIAL
SATISFYINGLY	SAVEGARDED	SCALDHEADS	SCANTINESS
SATURABILITIES	SAVEGARDING	SCALDSHIPS	SCANTINESSES

SCANTITIES	SCARFISHES	SCAVENGINGS	SCHEMATISING
SCANTLINGS	SCARFSKINS	SCAZONTICS	SCHEMATISM
SCANTNESSES	SCARIFICATION	SCELERATES	SCHEMATISMS
SCAPEGALLOWS	SCARIFICATIONS	SCENARISATION	SCHEMATIST
SCAPEGALLOWSES	SCARIFICATOR	SCENARISATIONS	SCHEMATISTS
SCAPEGOATED	SCARIFICATORS	SCENARISED	SCHEMATIZATION
SCAPEGOATING	SCARIFIERS	SCENARISES	SCHEMATIZATIONS
SCAPEGOATINGS	SCARIFYING	SCENARISING	SCHEMATIZE
SCAPEGOATISM	SCARIFYINGLY	SCENARISTS	SCHEMATIZED
SCAPEGOATISMS	SCARINESSES	SCENARIZATION	SCHEMATIZES
SCAPEGOATS	SCARLATINA	SCENARIZATIONS	SCHEMATIZING
SCAPEGRACE	SCARLATINAL	SCENARIZED	SCHEMINGLY
SCAPEGRACES	SCARLATINAS	SCENARIZES	SCHEMOZZLE
SCAPEMENTS	SCARLETING	SCENARIZING	SCHEMOZZLED
SCAPEWHEEL	SCARPERING	SCENESHIFTER	SCHEMOZZLES
SCAPEWHEELS	SCATHEFULNESS	SCENESHIFTERS	SCHEMOZZLING
SCAPHOCEPHALI	SCATHEFULNESSES	SCENICALLY	SCHERZANDI
SCAPHOCEPHALIC	SCATHELESS	SCENOGRAPHER	SCHERZANDO
SCAPHOCEPHALIES	SCATHINGLY	SCENOGRAPHERS	SCHERZANDOS
SCAPHOCEPHALISM	SCATOLOGIC	SCENOGRAPHIC	SCHIAVONES
SCAPHOCEPHALOUS	SCATOLOGICAL	SCENOGRAPHICAL	SCHILLERISATION
SCAPHOCEPHALUS	SCATOLOGIES	SCENOGRAPHIES	SCHILLERISE
SCAPHOCEPHALY	SCATOLOGIST	SCENOGRAPHY	SCHILLERISED
SCAPHOPODS	SCATOLOGISTS	SCENTLESSNESS	SCHILLERISES
SCAPIGEROUS	SCATOPHAGIES	SCENTLESSNESSES	SCHILLERISING
SCAPOLITES	SCATOPHAGOUS	SCEPTERING	SCHILLERIZATION
SCAPULARIES	SCATOPHAGY	SCEPTERLESS	SCHILLERIZE
SCAPULATED	SCATTERABLE	SCEPTICALLY	SCHILLERIZED
SCAPULIMANCIES	SCATTERATION	SCEPTICISM	SCHILLERIZES
SCAPULIMANCY	SCATTERATIONS	SCEPTICISMS	SCHILLERIZING
SCAPULIMANTIC	SCATTERBRAIN	SCEPTRELESS	SCHILLINGS
SCAPULOMANCIES	SCATTERBRAINED	SCEUOPHYLACIA	SCHINDYLESES
SCAPULOMANCY	SCATTERBRAINS	SCEUOPHYLACIUM	SCHINDYLESIS
SCAPULOMANTIC	SCATTEREDLY	SCEUOPHYLAX	SCHINDYLETIC
SCARABAEAN	SCATTERERS	SCEUOPHYLAXES	SCHIPPERKE
SCARABAEANS	SCATTERGOOD	SCHADENFREUDE	SCHIPPERKES
SCARABAEID	SCATTERGOODS	SCHADENFREUDES	SCHISMATIC
SCARABAEIDS	SCATTERGRAM	SCHALSTEIN	SCHISMATICAL
SCARABAEIST	SCATTERGRAMS	SCHALSTEINS	SCHISMATICALLY
SCARABAEISTS	SCATTERGUN	SCHAPPEING	SCHISMATICALS
SCARABAEOID	SCATTERGUNS	SCHATCHENS	SCHISMATICS
SCARABAEOIDS	SCATTERING	SCHECHITAH	SCHISMATISE
SCARABAEUS	SCATTERINGLY	SCHECHITAHS	SCHISMATISED
SCARABAEUSES	SCATTERINGS	SCHECHITAS	SCHISMATISES
SCARABOIDS	SCATTERLING	SCHECKLATON	SCHISMATISING
SCARAMOUCH	SCATTERLINGS	SCHECKLATONS	SCHISMATIZE
SCARAMOUCHE	SCATTERMOUCH	SCHEDULERS	SCHISMATIZED
SCARAMOUCHES	SCATTERMOUCHES	SCHEDULING	SCHISMATIZES
SCARCEMENT	SCATTERSHOT	SCHEELITES	SCHISMATIZING
SCARCEMENTS	SCATTINESS	SCHEFFLERA	SCHISTOSITIES
SCARCENESS	SCATTINESSES	SCHEFFLERAS	SCHISTOSITY
SCARCENESSES	SCATURIENT	SCHEMATICAL	SCHISTOSOMAL
SCARCITIES	SCAVENGERED	SCHEMATICALLY	SCHISTOSOME
SCARECROWS	SCAVENGERIES	SCHEMATICS	SCHISTOSOMES
SCAREHEADS	SCAVENGERING	SCHEMATISATION	SCHISTOSOMIASES
SCAREMONGER	SCAVENGERINGS	SCHEMATISATIONS	SCHISTOSOMIASIS
SCAREMONGERING	SCAVENGERS	SCHEMATISE	SCHIZAEACEOUS
SCAREMONGERINGS	SCAVENGERY	SCHEMATISED	SCHIZANTHUS
SCAREMONGERS	SCAVENGING	SCHEMATISES	SCHIZANTHUSES

SCHIZOCARP	SCHMOOSING	SCHOOLMAID	SCIENTIZING
SCHIZOCARPIC	SCHMOOZERS	SCHOOLMAIDS	SCINCOIDIAN
SCHIZOCARPOUS	SCHMOOZIER	SCHOOLMARM	SCINCOIDIANS
SCHIZOCARPS	SCHMOOZIEST	SCHOOLMARMISH	SCINDAPSUS
SCHIZOGENESES	SCHMOOZING	SCHOOLMARMS	SCINDAPSUSES
SCHIZOGENESIS	SCHMUTTERS	SCHOOLMASTER	SCINTIGRAM
SCHIZOGENETIC	SCHNAPPERS	SCHOOLMASTERED	SCINTIGRAMS
SCHIZOGENIC	SCHNAPPSES	SCHOOLMASTERING	SCINTIGRAPHIC
SCHIZOGNATHOUS	SCHNAUZERS	SCHOOLMASTERISH	SCINTIGRAPHIES
SCHIZOGONIC	SCHNITZELS	SCHOOLMASTERLY	SCINTIGRAPHY
SCHIZOGONIES	SCHNORKELED	SCHOOLMASTERS	SCINTILLAE
SCHIZOGONOUS	SCHNORKELING	SCHOOLMATE	SCINTILLANT
SCHIZOGONY	SCHNORKELLED	SCHOOLMATES	SCINTILLANTLY
SCHIZOIDAL	SCHNORKELLER	SCHOOLMISTRESS	SCINTILLAS
SCHIZOMYCETE	SCHNORKELLERS	SCHOOLMISTRESSY	SCINTILLASCOPE
SCHIZOMYCETES	SCHNORKELLING	SCHOOLROOM	SCINTILLASCOPES
SCHIZOMYCETIC	SCHNORKELS	SCHOOLROOMS	SCINTILLATE
SCHIZOMYCETOUS	SCHNORRERS	SCHOOLTEACHER	SCINTILLATED
SCHIZOPHRENE	SCHNORRING	SCHOOLTEACHERS	SCINTILLATES
SCHIZOPHRENES	SCHNOZZLES	SCHOOLTEACHING	SCINTILLATING
SCHIZOPHRENETIC	SCHOLARCHS	SCHOOLTEACHINGS	SCINTILLATINGLY
SCHIZOPHRENIA	SCHOLARLIER	SCHOOLTIDE	SCINTILLATION
SCHIZOPHRENIAS	SCHOLARLIEST	SCHOOLTIDES	SCINTILLATIONS
SCHIZOPHRENIC	SCHOLARLINESS	SCHOOLTIME	SCINTILLATOR
SCHIZOPHRENICS	SCHOLARLINESSES	SCHOOLTIMES	SCINTILLATORS
SCHIZOPHYCEOUS	SCHOLARSHIP	SCHOOLWARD	SCINTILLISCAN
SCHIZOPHYTE	SCHOLARSHIPS	SCHOOLWARDS	SCINTILLISCANS
SCHIZOPHYTES	SCHOLASTIC	SCHOOLWORK	SCINTILLOMETER
SCHIZOPHYTIC	SCHOLASTICAL	SCHOOLWORKS	SCINTILLOMETERS
SCHIZOPODAL	SCHOLASTICALLY	SCHORLACEOUS	SCINTILLON
SCHIZOPODOUS	SCHOLASTICATE	SCHORLOMITE	SCINTILLONS
SCHIZOPODS	SCHOLASTICATES	SCHORLOMITES	SCINTILLOSCOPE
SCHIZOTHYMIA	SCHOLASTICISM	SCHOTTISCHE	SCINTILLOSCOPES
SCHIZOTHYMIAS	SCHOLASTICISMS	SCHOTTISCHES	SCINTISCAN
SCHIZOTHYMIC	SCHOLASTICS	SCHRECKLICH	SCINTISCANNER
SCHIZZIEST	SCHOLIASTIC	SCHUSSBOOMER	SCINTISCANNERS
SCHLEMIELS	SCHOLIASTS	SCHUSSBOOMERS	SCINTISCANS
SCHLEMIHLS	SCHOOLBAGS	SCHUTZSTAFFEL	SCIOLISTIC
SCHLEPPERS	SCHOOLBOOK	SCHUTZSTAFFELS	SCIOMACHIES
SCHLEPPIER	SCHOOLBOOKS	SCHVARTZES	SCIOMANCER
SCHLEPPIEST	SCHOOLBOYISH	SCHWARMEREI	SCTOMANCERS
SCHLEPPING	SCHOOLBOYS	SCHWARMEREIS	SCIOMANCIES
SCHLIMAZEL	SCHOOLCHILD	SCHWARMERISCH	SCIOMANTIC
SCHLIMAZELS	SCHOOLCHILDREN	SCHWARTZES	SCIOPHYTES
SCHLOCKERS	SCHOOLCRAFT	SCHWARZLOT	SCIOPHYTIC
SCHLOCKIER	SCHOOLCRAFTS	SCHWARZLOTS	SCIOSOPHIES
SCHLOCKIEST	SCHOOLDAYS	SCIAENOIDS	SCIRRHOSITIES
SCHLUMBERGERA	SCHOOLERIES	SCIAMACHIES	SCIRRHOSITY
SCHLUMBERGERAS	SCHOOLFELLOW	SCIENTIFIC	SCIRRHUSES
SCHLUMPIER	SCHOOLFELLOWS	SCIENTIFICAL	SCISSIPARITIES
SCHLUMPIEST	SCHOOLGIRL	SCIENTIFICALLY	SCISSIPARITY
SCHLUMPING	SCHOOLGIRLISH	SCIENTISED	SCISSORERS
SCHMALTZES	SCHOOLGIRLS	SCIENTISES	SCISSORING
SCHMALTZIER	SCHOOLGOING	SCIENTISING	SCISSORTAIL
SCHMALTZIEST	SCHOOLGOINGS	SCIENTISMS	SCISSORTAILS
SCHMALZIER	SCHOOLHOUSE	SCIENTISTIC	SCISSORWISE
SCHMALZIEST	SCHOOLHOUSES	SCIENTISTS	SCITAMINEOUS
SCHMEARING	SCHOOLINGS	SCIENTIZED	SCLAUNDERS
SCHMEERING	SCHOOLKIDS	SCIENTIZES	SCLEREIDES

SCLERENCHYMA	SCOLECIFORM	SCORODITES	SCRAPPINESS
SCLERENCHYMAS	SCOLECITES	SCORPAENID	SCRAPPINESSES
SCLERENCHYMATA	SCOLLOPING	SCORPAENIDS	SCRAPYARDS
SCLERIASES	SCOLOPACEOUS	SCORPAENOID	SCRATCHBACK
SCLERIASIS	SCOLOPENDRA	SCORPAENOIDS	SCRATCHBACKS
SCLERITISES	SCOLOPENDRAS	SCORPIOIDS	SCRATCHBOARD
SCLEROCAULIES	SCOLOPENDRID	SCORPIONIC	SCRATCHBOARDS
SCLEROCAULOUS	SCOLOPENDRIDS	SCORZONERA	SCRATCHBUILD
SCLEROCAULY	SCOLOPENDRIFORM	SCORZONERAS	SCRATCHBUILDER
SCLERODERM	SCOLOPENDRINE	SCOTODINIA	SCRATCHBUILDERS
SCLERODERMA	SCOLOPENDRIUM	SCOTODINIAS	SCRATCHBUILDING
SCLERODERMAS	SCOLOPENDRIUMS	SCOTOMATOUS	SCRATCHBUILDS
SCLERODERMATA	SCOLYTOIDS	SCOTOMETER	SCRATCHBUILT
SCLERODERMATOUS	SCOMBROIDS	SCOTOMETERS	SCRATCHCARD
SCLERODERMIA	SCOMFISHED	SCOUNDRELLY	SCRATCHCARDS
SCLERODERMIAS	SCOMFISHES	SCOUNDRELS	SCRATCHERS
SCLERODERMIC	SCOMFISHING	SCOUTCRAFT	SCRATCHIER
SCLERODERMITE	SCONCHEONS	SCOUTCRAFTS	SCRATCHIES
SCLERODERMITES	SCOOTCHING	SCOUTHERED	SCRATCHIEST
SCLERODERMOUS	SCOOTERIST	SCOUTHERING	SCRATCHILY
SCLERODERMS	SCOOTERISTS	SCOUTHERINGS	SCRATCHINESS
SCLEROMALACIA	SCOPELOIDS	SCOUTMASTER	SCRATCHINESSES
SCLEROMALACIAS	SCOPOLAMINE	SCOUTMASTERS	SCRATCHING
SCLEROMATA	SCOPOLAMINES	SCOWDERING	SCRATCHINGLY
SCLEROMETER	SCOPOLINES	SCOWDERINGS	SCRATCHINGS
SCLEROMETERS	SCOPOPHILIA	SCOWLINGLY	SCRATCHLESS
SCLEROMETRIC	SCOPOPHILIAC	SCOWTHERED	SCRATCHPLATE
SCLEROPHYLL	SCOPOPHILIACS	SCOWTHERING	SCRATCHPLATES
SCLEROPHYLLIES	SCOPOPHILIAS	SCRABBLERS	SCRATTLING
SCLEROPHYLLOUS	SCOPOPHILIC	SCRABBLIER	SCRAUCHING
SCLEROPHYLLS	SCOPOPHOBIA	SCRABBLIEST	SCRAUGHING
SCLEROPHYLLY	SCOPOPHOBIAS	SCRABBLING	SCRAWLIEST
SCLEROPROTEIN	SCOPTOPHILIA	SCRAGGEDNESS	SCRAWLINGLY
SCLEROPROTEINS	SCOPTOPHILIAS	SCRAGGEDNESSES	SCRAWLINGS
SCLEROSING	SCOPTOPHOBIA	SCRAGGIEST	SCRAWNIEST
SCLEROTALS	SCOPTOPHOBIAS	SCRAGGINESS	SCRAWNINESS
SCLEROTIAL	SCORBUTICALLY	SCRAGGINESSES	SCRAWNINESSES
SCLEROTICS	SCORCHINGLY	SCRAGGLIER	SCREAKIEST
SCLEROTINS	SCORCHINGNESS	SCRAGGLIEST	SCREAMINGLY
SCLEROTIOID	SCORCHINGNESSES	SCRAGGLING	SCREECHERS
SCLEROTISATION	SCORCHINGS	SCRAICHING	SCREECHIER
SCLEROTISATIONS	SCORDATURA	SCRAIGHING	SCREECHIEST
SCLEROTISE	SCORDATURAS	SCRAMBLERS	SCREECHING
SCLEROTISED	SCOREBOARD	SCRAMBLING	SCREEDINGS
SCLEROTISES	SCOREBOARDS	SCRAMBLINGLY	SCREENABLE
SCLEROTISING	SCORECARDS	SCRAMBLINGS	SCREENAGER
SCLEROTITIS	SCOREKEEPER	SCRANCHING	SCREENAGERS
SCLEROTITISES	SCOREKEEPERS	SCRANNIEST	SCREENCRAFT
SCLEROTIUM	SCORELINES	SCRAPBOOKS	SCREENCRAFTS
SCLEROTIZATION	SCORESHEET	SCRAPEGOOD	SCREENFULS
SCLEROTIZATIONS	SCORESHEETS	SCRAPEGOODS	SCREENINGS
SCLEROTIZE	SCORIACEOUS	SCRAPEGUTS	SCREENLAND
SCLEROTIZED	SCORIFICATION	SCRAPEPENNIES	SCREENLANDS
SCLEROTIZES	SCORIFICATIONS	SCRAPEPENNY	SCREENLIKE
SCLEROTIZING	SCORIFIERS	SCRAPERBOARD	SCREENPLAY
SCLEROTOMIES	SCORIFYING	SCRAPERBOARDS	SCREENPLAYS
SCLEROTOMY	SCORNFULLY	SCRAPHEAPS	SCREENSAVER
SCOFFINGLY	SCORNFULNESS	SCRAPPAGES	SCREENSAVERS
SCOLDINGLY	SCORNFULNESSES	SCRAPPIEST	SCREENSHOT

SCREENSHOTS	SCRIPOPHILIST	SCRUBBINESSES	SCULDUDDERIES
SCREENWRITER	SCRIPOPHILISTS	SCRUBBINGS	SCULDUDDERY
SCREENWRITERS	SCRIPOPHILY	SCRUBLANDS	SCULDUDDRIES
SCREEVINGS	SCRIPPAGES	SCRUBWOMAN	SCULDUDDRY
SCREICHING	SCRIPTORIA	SCRUBWOMEN	SCULDUGGERIES
SCREIGHING	SCRIPTORIAL	SCRUFFIEST	SCULDUGGERY
SCREWBALLS	SCRIPTORIUM	SCRUFFINESS	SCULLERIES
SCREWBEANS	SCRIPTORIUMS	SCRUFFINESSES	SCULPTRESS
SCREWDRIVER	SCRIPTURAL	SCRUMDOWNS	SCULPTRESSES
SCREWDRIVERS	SCRIPTURALISM	SCRUMMAGED	SCULPTURAL
SCREWINESS	SCRIPTURALISMS	SCRUMMAGER	SCULPTURALLY
SCREWINESSES	SCRIPTURALIST	SCRUMMAGERS	SCULPTURED
SCREWWORMS	SCRIPTURALISTS	SCRUMMAGES	SCULPTURES
SCRIBACIOUS	SCRIPTURALLY	SCRUMMAGING	SCULPTURESQUE
SCRIBACIOUSNESS	SCRIPTURES	SCRUMMIEST	SCULPTURESQUELY
SCRIBBLEMENT	SCRIPTURISM	SCRUMPLING	SCULPTURING
SCRIBBLEMENTS	SCRIPTURISMS	SCRUMPOXES	SCULPTURINGS
SCRIBBLERS	SCRIPTURIST	SCRUMPTIOUS	SCUMBERING
SCRIBBLIER	SCRIPTURISTS	SCRUMPTIOUSLY	SCUMBLINGS
SCRIBBLIEST	SCRIPTWRITER	SCRUMPTIOUSNESS	SCUMFISHED
SCRIBBLING	SCRIPTWRITERS	SCRUNCHEON	SCUMFISHES
SCRIBBLINGLY	SCRIPTWRITING	SCRUNCHEONS	SCUMFISHING
SCRIBBLINGS	SCRIPTWRITINGS	SCRUNCHIER	SCUNCHEONS
SCRIECHING	SCRITCHING	SCRUNCHIES	SCUNGILLIS
SCRIEVEBOARD	SCRIVEBOARD	SCRUNCHIEST	SCUNNERING
SCRIEVEBOARDS	SCRIVEBOARDS	SCRUNCHING	SCUPPERING
SCRIGGLIER	SCRIVENERS	SCRUNCHION	SCUPPERNONG
SCRIGGLIEST	SCRIVENERSHIP	SCRUNCHIONS	SCUPPERNONGS
SCRIGGLING	SCRIVENERSHIPS	SCRUNTIEST	SCURFINESS
SCRIMMAGED	SCRIVENING	SCRUPLELESS	SCURFINESSES
SCRIMMAGER	SCRIVENINGS	SCRUPULOSITIES	SCURRILITIES
SCRIMMAGERS	SCROBICULAR	SCRUPULOSITY	SCURRILITY
SCRIMMAGES	SCROBICULATE	SCRUPULOUS	SCURRILOUS
SCRIMMAGING	SCROBICULATED	SCRUPULOUSLY	SCURRILOUSLY
SCRIMPIEST	SCROBICULE	SCRUPULOUSNESS	SCURRILOUSNESS
SCRIMPINESS	SCROBICULES	SCRUTABILITIES	SCURRIOURS
SCRIMPINESSES	SCROFULOUS	SCRUTABILITY	SCURVINESS
SCRIMPNESS	SCROFULOUSLY	SCRUTATORS	SCURVINESSES
SCRIMPNESSES	SCROFULOUSNESS	SCRUTINEER	SCUTATIONS
SCRIMSHANDER	SCROGGIEST	SCRUTINEERS	SCUTCHEONLESS
SCRIMSHANDERED	SCROLLABLE	SCRUTINIES	SCUTCHEONS
SCRIMSHANDERING	SCROLLWISE	SCRUTINISE	SCUTCHINGS
SCRIMSHANDERS	SCROLLWORK	SCRUTINISED	SCUTELLATE
SCRIMSHANDIED	SCROLLWORKS	SCRUTINISER	SCUTELLATED
SCRIMSHANDIES	SCROOCHING	SCRUTINISERS	SCUTELLATION
SCRIMSHANDY	SCROOTCHED	SCRUTINISES	SCUTELLATIONS
SCRIMSHANDYING	SCROOTCHES	SCRUTINISING	SCUTTERING
SCRIMSHANK	SCROOTCHING	SCRUTINISINGLY	SCUTTLEBUTT
SCRIMSHANKED	SCROPHULARIA	SCRUTINIZE	SCUTTLEBUTTS
SCRIMSHANKING	SCROPHULARIAS	SCRUTINIZED	SCUTTLEFUL
SCRIMSHANKS	SCROUNGERS	SCRUTINIZER	SCUTTLEFULS
SCRIMSHAWED	SCROUNGIER	SCRUTINIZERS	SCUZZBALLS
SCRIMSHAWING	SCROUNGIEST	SCRUTINIZES	SCYPHIFORM
SCRIMSHAWS	SCROUNGING	SCRUTINIZING	SCYPHISTOMA
SCRIMSHONER	SCROUNGINGS	SCRUTINIZINGLY	SCYPHISTOMAE
SCRIMSHONERS	SCROWDGING	SCRUTINOUS	SCYPHISTOMAS
SCRIPOPHILE	SCRUBBABLE	SCRUTINOUSLY	SCYPHOZOAN
SCRIPOPHILES	SCRUBBIEST	SCRUTOIRES	SCYPHOZOANS
SCRIPOPHILIES	SCRUBBINESS	SCUDDALERS	SCYTHELIKE

SDEIGNFULL	SEBORRHOEAL	SECTARIANIZE	SECULARIZATION
SDEIGNFULLY	SEBORRHOEAS	SECTARIANIZED	SECULARIZATIONS
SDRUCCIOLA	SEBORRHOEIC	SECTARIANIZES	SECULARIZE
SEABEACHES	SECERNENTS	SECTARIANIZING	SECULARIZED
SEABORGIUM	SECERNMENT	SECTARIANS	SECULARIZER
SEABORGIUMS	SECERNMENTS	SECTILITIES	SECULARIZERS
SEABOTTLES	SECESSIONAL	SECTIONALISE	SECULARIZES
SEACUNNIES	SECESSIONISM	SECTIONALISED	SECULARIZING
SEAFARINGS	SECESSIONISMS	SECTIONALISES	SECUNDINES
SEALIFTING	SECESSIONIST	SECTIONALISING	SECUNDOGENITURE
SEALPOINTS	SECESSIONISTS	SECTIONALISM	SECURANCES
SEAMANLIKE	SECESSIONS	SECTIONALISMS	SECUREMENT
SEAMANSHIP	SECLUDEDLY	SECTIONALIST	SECUREMENTS
SEAMANSHIPS	SECLUDEDNESS	SECTIONALISTS	SECURENESS
SEAMINESSES	SECLUDEDNESSES	SECTIONALIZE	SECURENESSES
SEAMLESSLY	SECLUSIONIST	SECTIONALIZED	SECURIFORM
SEAMLESSNESS	SECLUSIONISTS	SECTIONALIZES	SECURITANS
SEAMLESSNESSES	SECLUSIONS	SECTIONALIZING	SECURITIES
SEAMSTRESS	SECLUSIVELY	SECTIONALLY	SECURITISATION
SEAMSTRESSES	SECLUSIVENESS	SECTIONALS	SECURITISATIONS
SEAMSTRESSIES	SECLUSIVENESSES	SECTIONING	SECURITISE
SEAMSTRESSY	SECOBARBITAL	SECTIONISATION	SECURITISED
SEANNACHIE	SECOBARBITALS	SECTIONISATIONS	SECURITISES
SEANNACHIES	SECONDARIES	SECTIONISE	SECURITISING
SEAQUARIUM	SECONDARILY	SECTIONISED	SECURITIZATION
SEAQUARIUMS	SECONDARINESS	SECTIONISES	SECURITIZATIONS
SEARCHABLE	SECONDARINESSES	SECTIONISING	SECURITIZE
SEARCHINGLY	SECONDHAND	SECTIONIZATION	SECURITIZED
SEARCHINGNESS	SECONDMENT	SECTIONIZATIONS	SECURITIZES
SEARCHINGNESSES	SECONDMENTS	SECTIONIZE	SECURITIZING
SEARCHLESS	SECRETAGES	SECTIONIZED	SECUROCRAT
SEARCHLIGHT	SECRETAGOGIC	SECTIONIZES	SECUROCRATS
SEARCHLIGHTS	SECRETAGOGUE	SECTIONIZING	SEDATENESS
SEAREDNESS	SECRETAGOGUES	SECTORIALS	SEDATENESSES
SEAREDNESSES	SECRETAIRE	SECTORISATION	SEDENTARILY
SEARNESSES	SECRETAIRES	SECTORISATIONS	SEDENTARINESS
SEASICKEST	SECRETARIAL	SECTORISED	SEDENTARINESSES
SEASICKNESS	SECRETARIAT	SECTORISES	SEDGELANDS
SEASICKNESSES	SECRETARIATE	SECTORISING	SEDIGITATED
SEASONABLE	SECRETARIATES	SECTORIZATION	SEDIMENTABLE
SEASONABLENESS	SECRETARIATS	SECTORIZATIONS	SEDIMENTARILY
SEASONABLY	SECRETARIES	SECTORIZED	SEDIMENTARY
SEASONALITIES	SECRETARYSHIP	SECTORIZES	SEDIMENTATION
SEASONALITY	SECRETARYSHIPS	SECTORIZING	SEDIMENTATIONS
SEASONALLY	SECRETIONAL	SECULARISATION	SEDIMENTED
SEASONALNESS	SECRETIONARY	SECULARISATIONS	SEDIMENTING
SEASONALNESSES	SECRETIONS	SECULARISE	SEDIMENTOLOGIC
SEASONINGS	SECRETIVELY	SECULARISED	SEDIMENTOLOGIES
SEASONLESS	SECRETIVENESS	SECULARISER	SEDIMENTOLOGIST
SEASTRANDS	SECRETIVENESSES	SECULARISERS	SEDIMENTOLOGY
SEAWORTHIER	SECRETNESS	SECULARISES	SEDIMENTOUS
SEAWORTHIEST	SECRETNESSES	SECULARISING	SEDITIONARIES
SEAWORTHINESS	SECRETORIES	SECULARISM	SEDITIONARY
SEAWORTHINESSES	SECTARIANISE	SECULARISMS	SEDITIOUSLY
SEBIFEROUS	SECTARIANISED	SECULARIST	SEDITIOUSNESS
SEBORRHEAL	SECTARIANISES	SECULARISTIC	SEDITIOUSNESSES
SEBORRHEAS	SECTARIANISING	SECULARISTS	SEDUCEABLE
SEBORRHEIC	SECTARIANISM	SECULARITIES	SEDUCEMENT
SEBORRHOEA	SECTARIANISMS	SECULARITY	SEDUCEMENTS

SEDUCINGLY	SEIGNIORSHIP	SELENIFEROUS	SEMEIOLOGIST
SEDUCTIONS	SEIGNIORSHIPS	SELENOCENTRIC	SEMEIOLOGISTS
SEDUCTIVELY	SEIGNORAGE	SELENODONT	SEMEIOLOGY
SEDUCTIVENESS	SEIGNORAGES	SELENODONTS	SEMEIOTICIAN
SEDUCTIVENESSES	SEIGNORIAL	SELENOGRAPH	SEMEIOTICIANS
SEDUCTRESS	SEIGNORIES	SELENOGRAPHER	SEMEIOTICS
SEDUCTRESSES	SEISMICALLY	SELENOGRAPHERS	SEMELPARITIES
SEDULITIES	SEISMICITIES	SELENOGRAPHIC	SEMELPARITY
SEDULOUSLY	SEISMICITY	SELENOGRAPHICAL	SEMELPAROUS
SEDULOUSNESS	SEISMOGRAM	SELENOGRAPHIES	SEMESTRIAL
SEDULOUSNESSES	SEISMOGRAMS	SELENOGRAPHIST	SEMIABSTRACT
SEECATCHIE	SEISMOGRAPH	SELENOGRAPHISTS	SEMIABSTRACTION
SEEDEATERS	SEISMOGRAPHER	SELENOGRAPHS	SEMIANGLES
SEEDINESSES	SEISMOGRAPHERS	SELENOGRAPHY	SEMIANNUAL
SEEDNESSES	SEISMOGRAPHIC	SELENOLOGICAL	SEMIANNUALLY
SEEDSTOCKS	SEISMOGRAPHICAL	SELENOLOGIES	SEMIAQUATIC
SEEMELESSE	SEISMOGRAPHIES	SELENOLOGIST	SEMIARBOREAL
SEEMINGNESS	SEISMOGRAPHS	SELENOLOGISTS	SEMIARIDITIES
SEEMINGNESSES	SEISMOGRAPHY	SELENOLOGY	SEMIARIDITY
SEEMLIHEAD	SEISMOLOGIC	SELFISHNESS	SEMIAUTOMATIC
SEEMLIHEADS	SEISMOLOGICAL	SELFISHNESSES	SEMIAUTOMATICS
SEEMLIHEDS	SEISMOLOGICALLY	SELFLESSLY	SEMIAUTONOMOUS
SEEMLINESS	SEISMOLOGIES	SELFLESSNESS	SEMIBREVES
SEEMLINESSES	SEISMOLOGIST	SELFLESSNESSES	SEMICARBAZIDE
SEEMLYHEDS	SEISMOLOGISTS	SELFNESSES	SEMICARBAZIDES
SEERSUCKER	SEISMOLOGY	SELFSAMENESS	SEMICARBAZONE
SEERSUCKERS	SEISMOMETER	SELFSAMENESSES	SEMICARBAZONES
SEETHINGLY	SEISMOMETERS	SELLOTAPED	SEMICENTENNIAL
SEGHOLATES	SEISMOMETRIC	SELLOTAPES	SEMICENTENNIALS
SEGMENTALLY	SEISMOMETRICAL	SELLOTAPING	SEMICHORUS
SEGMENTARY	SEISMOMETRIES	SELTZOGENE	SEMICHORUSES
SEGMENTATE	SEISMOMETRY	SELTZOGENES	SEMICIRCLE
SEGMENTATION	SEISMONASTIC	SELVEDGING	SEMICIRCLED
SEGMENTATIONS	SEISMONASTIES	SEMAINIERS	SEMICIRCLES
SEGMENTING	SEISMONASTY	SEMANTEMES	SEMICIRCULAR
SEGREGABLE	SEISMOSCOPE	SEMANTICAL	SEMICIRCULARLY
SEGREGANTS	SEISMOSCOPES	SEMANTICALLY	SEMICIRQUE
SEGREGATED	SEISMOSCOPIC	SEMANTICIST	SEMICIRQUES
SEGREGATES	SELACHIANS	SEMANTICISTS	SEMICIVILISED
SEGREGATING	SELAGINELLA	SEMANTIDES	SEMICIVILIZED
SEGREGATION	SELAGINELLAS	SEMAPHORED	SEMICLASSIC
SEGREGATIONAL	SELDOMNESS	SEMAPHORES	SEMICLASSICAL
SEGREGATIONIST	SELDOMNESSES	SEMAPHORIC	SEMICLASSICS
SEGREGATIONISTS	SELECTABLE	SEMAPHORICAL	SEMICOLONIAL
SEGREGATIONS	SELECTIONIST	SEMAPHORICALLY	SEMICOLONIALISM
SEGREGATIVE	SELECTIONISTS	SEMAPHORING	SEMICOLONIES
SEGREGATOR	SELECTIONS	SEMASIOLOGICAL	SEMICOLONS
SEGREGATORS	SELECTIVELY	SEMASIOLOGIES	SEMICOLONY
SEGUIDILLA	SELECTIVENESS	SEMASIOLOGIST	SEMICOMATOSE
SEGUIDILLAS	SELECTIVENESSES	SEMASIOLOGISTS	SEMICOMMERCIAL
SEIGNEURIAL	SELECTIVITIES	SEMASIOLOGY	SEMICONDUCTING
SEIGNEURIE	SELECTIVITY	SEMATOLOGIES	SEMICONDUCTION
SEIGNEURIES	SELECTNESS	SEMATOLOGY	SEMICONDUCTIONS
SEIGNIORAGE	SELECTNESSES	SEMBLABLES	SEMICONDUCTOR
SEIGNIORAGES	SELECTORATE	SEMBLANCES	SEMICONDUCTORS
SEIGNIORALTIES	SELECTORATES	SEMBLATIVE	SEMICONSCIOUS
SEIGNIORALTY	SELECTORIAL	SEMEIOLOGIC	SEMICONSCIOUSLY
SEIGNIORIAL	SELEGILINE	SEMEIOLOGICAL	SEMICRYSTALLIC
SEIGNIORIES	SELEGILINES	SEMEIOLOGIES	SEMICRYSTALLINE

SEMICYLINDER	SEMIMONTHLIES	SEMIPRECIOUS	SENECTITUDES
SEMICYLINDERS	SEMIMONTHLY	SEMIPRIVATE	SENESCENCE
SEMICYLINDRICAL	SEMIMYSTICAL	SEMIPUBLIC	SENESCENCES
SEMIDARKNESS	SEMINALITIES	SEMIQUAVER	SENESCHALS
SEMIDARKNESSES	SEMINALITY	SEMIQUAVERS	SENESCHALSHIP
SEMIDEIFIED	SEMINARIAL	SEMIRELIGIOUS	SENESCHALSHIPS
SEMIDEIFIES	SEMINARIAN	SEMIRETIRED	SENHORITAS
SEMIDEIFYING	SEMINARIANS	SEMIRETIREMENT	SENILITIES
SEMIDEPONENT	SEMINARIES	SEMIRETIREMENTS	SENIORITIES
SEMIDEPONENTS	SEMINARIST	SEMIROUNDS	SENNACHIES
SEMIDESERT	SEMINARISTS	SEMISACRED	SENSATIONAL
SEMIDESERTS	SEMINATING	SEMISECRET	SENSATIONALISE
SEMIDETACHED	SEMINATION	SEMISEDENTARY	SENSATIONALISED
SEMIDIAMETER	SEMINATIONS	SEMISHRUBBY	SENSATIONALISES
SEMIDIAMETERS	SEMINATURAL	SEMISKILLED	SENSATIONALISM
SEMIDIURNAL	SEMINIFEROUS	SEMISOLIDS	SENSATIONALISMS
SEMIDIVINE	SEMINOMADIC	SEMISOLUSES	SENSATIONALIST
SEMIDOCUMENTARY	SEMINOMADS	SEMISUBMERSIBLE	SENSATIONALISTS
SEMIDOMINANT	SEMINOMATA	SEMISYNTHETIC	SENSATIONALIZE
SEMIDRYING	SEMINUDITIES	SEMITERETE	SENSATIONALIZED
SEMIDWARFS	SEMINUDITY	SEMITERRESTRIAL	SENSATIONALIZES
SEMIDWARVES	SEMIOCHEMICAL	SEMITONALLY	SENSATIONALLY
SEMIELLIPTICAL	SEMIOCHEMICALS	SEMITONICALLY	SENSATIONISM
SEMIEMPIRICAL	SEMIOFFICIAL	SEMITRAILER	SENSATIONISMS
SEMIEVERGREEN	SEMIOFFICIALLY	SEMITRAILERS	SENSATIONIST
SEMIFEUDAL	SEMIOLOGIC	SEMITRANSLUCENT	SENSATIONISTS
SEMIFINALIST	SEMIOLOGICAL	SEMITRANSPARENT	SENSATIONLESS
SEMIFINALISTS	SEMIOLOGICALLY	SEMITROPIC	SENSATIONS
SEMIFINALS	SEMIOLOGIES	SEMITROPICAL	SENSELESSLY
SEMIFINISHED	SEMIOLOGIST	SEMITROPICS	SENSELESSNESS
SEMIFITTED	SEMIOLOGISTS	SEMITRUCKS	SENSELESSNESSES
SEMIFLEXIBLE	SEMIOPAQUE	SEMIVITREOUS	SENSIBILIA
SEMIFLUIDIC	SEMIOTICIAN	SEMIVOCALIC	SENSIBILITIES
SEMIFLUIDITIES	SEMIOTICIANS	SEMIVOWELS	SENSIBILITY
SEMIFLUIDITY	SEMIOTICIST	SEMIWEEKLIES	SENSIBLENESS
SEMIFLUIDS	SEMIOTICISTS	SEMIWEEKLY	SENSIBLENESSES
SEMIFORMAL	SEMIOVIPAROUS	SEMIYEARLY	SENSIBLEST
SEMIFREDDO	SEMIPALMATE	SEMPERVIVUM	SENSITISATION
SEMIFREDDOS	SEMIPALMATED	SEMPERVIVUMS	SENSITISATIONS
SEMIGLOBULAR	SEMIPALMATION	SEMPITERNAL	SENSITISED
SEMIGLOSSES	SEMIPALMATIONS	SEMPITERNALLY	SENSITISER
SEMIGROUPS	SEMIPARASITE	SEMPITERNITIES	SENSITISERS
SEMIHOBOES	SEMIPARASITES	SEMPITERNITY	SENSITISES
SEMILEGENDARY	SEMIPARASITIC	SEMPITERNUM	SENSITISING
SEMILETHAL	SEMIPARASITISM	SEMPITERNUMS	SENSITIVELY
SEMILETHALS	SEMIPARASITISMS	SEMPSTERING	SENSITIVENESS
SEMILIQUID	SEMIPELLUCID	SEMPSTERINGS	SENSITIVENESSES
SEMILIQUIDS	SEMIPERIMETER	SEMPSTRESS	SENSITIVES
SEMILITERATE	SEMIPERIMETERS	SEMPSTRESSES	SENSITIVITIES
SEMILITERATES	SEMIPERMANENT	SEMPSTRESSING	SENSITIVITY
SEMILOGARITHMIC	SEMIPERMEABLE	SEMPSTRESSINGS	SENSITIZATION
SEMILUCENT	SEMIPLUMES	SENARMONTITE	SENSITIZATIONS
SEMILUNATE	SEMIPOLITICAL	SENARMONTITES	SENSITIZED
SEMILUSTROUS	SEMIPOPULAR	SENATORIAL	SENSITIZER
SEMIMANUFACTURE	SEMIPORCELAIN	SENATORIALLY	SENSITIZERS
SEMIMENSTRUAL	SEMIPORCELAINS	SENATORIAN	SENSITIZES
SEMIMETALLIC	SEMIPORNOGRAPHY	SENATORSHIP	SENSITIZING
SEMIMETALS	SEMIPOSTAL	SENATORSHIPS	SENSITOMETER
SEMIMONASTIC	SEMIPOSTALS	SENECTITUDE	SENSITOMETERS

SENSITOMETRIC	SENTINELED	SEPTICAEMIAS	SEQUESTERS
SENSITOMETRIES	SENTINELING	SEPTICAEMIC	SEQUESTRABLE
SENSITOMETRY	SENTINELLED	SEPTICALLY	SEQUESTRAL
SENSOMOTOR	SENTINELLING	SEPTICEMIA	SEQUESTRANT
SENSORIALLY	SEPALODIES	SEPTICEMIAS	SEQUESTRANTS
SENSORIMOTOR	SEPARABILITIES	SEPTICEMIC	SEQUESTRATE
SENSORINEURAL	SEPARABILITY	SEPTICIDAL	SEQUESTRATED
SENSORIUMS	SEPARABLENESS	SEPTICIDALLY	SEQUESTRATES
SENSUALISATION	SEPARABLENESSES	SEPTICITIES	SEQUESTRATING
SENSUALISATIONS	SEPARATELY	SEPTIFEROUS	SEQUESTRATION
SENSUALISE	SEPARATENESS	SEPTIFRAGAL	SEQUESTRATIONS
SENSUALISED	SEPARATENESSES	SEPTILATERAL	SEQUESTRATOR
SENSUALISES	SEPARATING	SEPTILLION	SEQUESTRATORS
SENSUALISING	SEPARATION	SEPTILLIONS	SEQUESTRUM
SENSUALISM	SEPARATIONISM	SEPTILLIONTH	SEQUESTRUMS
SENSUALISMS	SEPARATIONISMS	SEPTILLIONTHS	SERAPHICAL
SENSUALIST	SEPARATIONIST	SEPTIMOLES	SERAPHICALLY
SENSUALISTIC	SEPARATIONISTS	SEPTIVALENT	SERAPHINES
SENSUALISTS	SEPARATIONS	SEPTUAGENARIAN	SERASKIERATE
SENSUALITIES	SEPARATISM	SEPTUAGENARIANS	SERASKIERATES
SENSUALITY	SEPARATISMS	SEPTUAGENARIES	SERASKIERS
SENSUALIZATION	SEPARATIST	SEPTUAGENARY	SERENADERS
SENSUALIZATIONS	SEPARATISTIC	SEPTUPLETS	SERENADING
SENSUALIZE	SEPARATISTS	SEPTUPLICATE	SERENDIPITIES
SENSUALIZED	SEPARATIVE	SEPTUPLICATES	SERENDIPITIST
SENSUALIZES	SEPARATIVELY	SEPTUPLING	SERENDIPITISTS
SENSUALIZING	SEPARATIVENESS	SEPULCHERED	SERENDIPITOUS
SENSUALNESS	SEPARATORIES	SEPULCHERING	SERENDIPITOUSLY
SENSUALNESSES	SEPARATORS	SEPULCHERS	SERENDIPITY
SENSUOSITIES	SEPARATORY	SEPULCHRAL	SERENENESS
SENSUOSITY	SEPARATRICES	SEPULCHRALLY	SERENENESSES
SENSUOUSLY	SEPARATRIX	SEPULCHRED	SERENITIES
SENSUOUSNESS	SEPARATUMS	SEPULCHRES	SERGEANCIES
SENSUOUSNESSES	SEPIOLITES	SEPULCHRING	SERGEANTIES
SENTENCERS	SEPIOSTAIRE	SEPULCHROUS	SERGEANTSHIP
SENTENCING	SEPIOSTAIRES	SEPULTURAL	SERGEANTSHIPS
SENTENTIAE	SEPTATIONS	SEPULTURED	SERIALISATION
SENTENTIAL	SEPTAVALENT	SEPULTURES	SERIALISATIONS
SENTENTIALLY	SEPTEMVIRATE	SEPULTURING	SERIALISED
SENTENTIOUS	SEPTEMVIRATES	SEQUACIOUS	SERIALISES
SENTENTIOUSLY	SEPTEMVIRI	SEQUACIOUSLY	SERIALISING
SENTENTIOUSNESS	SEPTEMVIRS	SEQUACIOUSNESS	SERIALISMS
SENTIENCES	SEPTENARIES	SEQUACITIES	SERIALISTS
SENTIENCIES	SEPTENARII	SEQUELISED	SERIALITIES
SENTIENTLY	SEPTENARIUS	SEQUELISES	SERIALIZATION
SENTIMENTAL	SEPTENDECILLION	SEQUELISING	SERIALIZATIONS
SENTIMENTALISE	SEPTENNATE	SEQUELIZED	SERIALIZED
SENTIMENTALISED	SEPTENNATES	SEQUELIZES	SERIALIZES
SENTIMENTALISES	SEPTENNIAL	SEQUELIZING	SERIALIZING
SENTIMENTALISM	SEPTENNIALLY	SEQUENCERS	SERIATIONS
SENTIMENTALISMS	SEPTENNIUM	SEQUENCIES	SERICICULTURE
SENTIMENTALIST	SEPTENNIUMS	SEQUENCING	SERICICULTURES
SENTIMENTALISTS	SEPTENTRIAL	SEQUENCINGS	SERICICULTURIST
SENTIMENTALITY	SEPTENTRION	SEQUENTIAL	SERICITISATION
SENTIMENTALIZE	SEPTENTRIONAL	SEQUENTIALITIES	SERICITISATIONS
SENTIMENTALIZED	SEPTENTRIONALLY	SEQUENTIALITY	SERICITIZATION
SENTIMENTALIZES	SEPTENTRIONES	SEQUENTIALLY	SERICITIZATIONS
SENTIMENTALLY	SEPTENTRIONS	SEQUESTERED	SERICTERIA
SENTIMENTS	SEPTICAEMIA	SEQUESTERING	SERICTERIUM

SERICULTURAL	SEROTAXONOMY	SERRIEDNESS	SESQUITERTIAS
SERICULTURE	SEROTHERAPIES	SERRIEDNESSES	SESSILITIES
SERICULTURES	SEROTHERAPY	SERRULATED	SESSIONALLY
SERICULTURIST	SEROTINIES	SERRULATION	SESTERTIUM
SERICULTURISTS	SEROTINOUS	SERRULATIONS	SESTERTIUS
SERIGRAPHER	SEROTONERGIC	SERTULARIAN	SETACEOUSLY
SERIGRAPHERS	SEROTONINERGIC	SERTULARIANS	SETIFEROUS
SERIGRAPHIC	SEROTONINS	SERVANTHOOD	SETIGEROUS
SERIGRAPHIES	SEROTYPING	SERVANTHOODS	SETTERWORT
SERIGRAPHS	SEROTYPINGS	SERVANTING	SETTERWORTS
SERIGRAPHY	SEROUSNESS	SERVANTLESS	SETTLEABLE
SERINETTES	SEROUSNESSES	SERVANTRIES	SETTLEDNESS
SERIOCOMIC	SERPENTIFORM	SERVANTSHIP	SETTLEDNESSES
SERIOCOMICAL	SERPENTINE	SERVANTSHIPS	SETTLEMENT
SERIOCOMICALLY	SERPENTINED	SERVICEABILITY	SETTLEMENTS
SERIOUSNESS	SERPENTINELY	SERVICEABLE	SEVENPENCE
SERIOUSNESSES	SERPENTINES	SERVICEABLENESS	SEVENPENCES
SERJEANCIES	SERPENTINIC	SERVICEABLY	SEVENPENNIES
SERJEANTIES	SERPENTINING	SERVICEBERRIES	SEVENPENNY
SERJEANTRIES	SERPENTININGLY	SERVICEBERRY	SEVENTEENS
SERJEANTRY	SERPENTININGS	SERVICELESS	SEVENTEENTH
SERJEANTSHIP	SERPENTINISE	SERVICEMAN	SEVENTEENTHLY
SERJEANTSHIPS	SERPENTINISED	SERVICEMEN	SEVENTEENTHS
SERMONEERS	SERPENTINISES	SERVICEWOMAN	SEVENTIETH
SERMONETTE	SERPENTINISING	SERVICEWOMEN	SEVENTIETHS
SERMONETTES	SERPENTINITE	SERVIETTES	SEVERABILITIES
SERMONICAL	SERPENTINITES	SERVILENESS	SEVERABILITY
SERMONINGS	SERPENTINIZE	SERVILENESSES	SEVERALFOLD
SERMONISED	SERPENTINIZED	SERVILISMS	SEVERALTIES
SERMONISER	SERPENTINIZES	SERVILITIES	SEVERANCES
SERMONISERS	SERPENTINIZING	SERVITORIAL	SEVERENESS
SERMONISES	SERPENTINOUS	SERVITORSHIP	SEVERENESSES
SERMONISING	SERPENTISE	SERVITORSHIPS	SEVERITIES
SERMONIZED	SERPENTISED	SERVITRESS	SEWABILITIES
SERMONIZER	SERPENTISES	SERVITRESSES	SEWABILITY
SERMONIZERS	SERPENTISING	SERVITUDES	SEXAGENARIAN
SERMONIZES	SERPENTIZE	SERVOCONTROL	SEXAGENARIANS
SERMONIZING	SERPENTIZED	SERVOCONTROLS	SEXAGENARIES
SEROCONVERSION	SERPENTIZES	SERVOMECHANICAL	SEXAGENARY
SEROCONVERSIONS	SERPENTIZING	SERVOMECHANISM	SEXAGESIMAL
SEROCONVERT	SERPENTLIKE	SERVOMECHANISMS	SEXAGESIMALLY
SEROCONVERTED	SERPENTRIES	SERVOMOTOR	SEXAGESIMALS
SEROCONVERTING	SERPIGINES	SERVOMOTORS	SEXAHOLICS
SEROCONVERTS	SERPIGINOUS	SESQUIALTER	SEXANGULAR
SERODIAGNOSES	SERPIGINOUSLY	SESQUIALTERA	SEXANGULARLY
SERODIAGNOSIS	SERPULITES	SESQUIALTERAS	SEXAVALENT
SERODIAGNOSTIC	SERRADELLA	SESQUICARBONATE	SEXCENTENARIES
SEROLOGICAL	SERRADELLAS	SESQUICENTENARY	SEXCENTENARY
SEROLOGICALLY	SERRADILLA	SESQUIOXIDE	SEXDECILLION
SEROLOGIES	SERRADILLAS	SESQUIOXIDES	SEXDECILLIONS
SEROLOGIST	SERRANOIDS	SESQUIPEDAL	SEXENNIALLY
SEROLOGISTS	SERRASALMO	SESQUIPEDALIAN	SEXENNIALS
SERONEGATIVE	SERRASALMOS	SESQUIPEDALITY	SEXERCISES
SERONEGATIVITY	SERRATIONS	SESQUIPLICATE	SEXINESSES
SEROPOSITIVE	SERRATIROSTRAL	SESQUISULPHIDE	SEXIVALENT
SEROPOSITIVITY	SERRATULATE	SESQUISULPHIDES	SEXLESSNESS
SEROPURULENT	SERRATURES	SESQUITERPENE	SEXLESSNESSES
SEROSITIES	SERRATUSES	SESQUITERPENES	SEXLOCULAR
SEROTAXONOMIES	SERREFILES	SESQUITERTIA	SEXOLOGICAL

SEXOLOGIES	SHADOWINESSES	SHANKPIECES	SHEATHIEST
SEXOLOGIST	SHADOWINGS	SHANTYTOWN	SHEATHINGS
SEXOLOGISTS	SHADOWLESS	SHANTYTOWNS	SHEATHLESS
SEXPARTITE	SHADOWLIKE	SHAPELESSLY	SHEBEENERS
SEXPLOITATION	SHAGGEDNESS	SHAPELESSNESS	SHEBEENING
SEXPLOITATIONS	SHAGGEDNESSES	SHAPELESSNESSES	SHEBEENINGS
SEXTILLION	SHAGGINESS	SHAPELIEST	SHECHITAHS
SEXTILLIONS	SHAGGINESSES	SHAPELINESS	SHECKLATON
SEXTILLIONTH	SHAGGYMANE	SHAPELINESSES	SHECKLATONS
SEXTILLIONTHS	SHAGGYMANES	SHARAWADGI	SHEEPBERRIES
SEXTODECIMO	SHAGREENED	SHARAWADGIS	SHEEPBERRY
SEXTODECIMOS	SHAGTASTIC	SHARAWAGGI	SHEEPCOTES
SEXTONESSES	SHAHTOOSHES	SHARAWAGGIS	SHEEPFOLDS
SEXTONSHIP	SHAKEDOWNS	SHAREABILITIES	SHEEPHEADS
SEXTONSHIPS	SHAKINESSES	SHAREABILITY	SHEEPHERDER
SEXTUPLETS	SHAKUHACHI	SHARECROPPED	SHEEPHERDERS
SEXTUPLICATE	SHAKUHACHIS	SHARECROPPER	SHEEPHERDING
SEXTUPLICATED	SHALLOWEST	SHARECROPPERS	SHEEPHERDINGS
SEXTUPLICATES	SHALLOWING	SHARECROPPING	SHEEPISHLY
SEXTUPLICATING	SHALLOWINGS	SHARECROPS	SHEEPISHNESS
SEXTUPLING	SHALLOWNESS	SHAREFARMER	SHEEPISHNESSES
SEXUALISATION	SHALLOWNESSES	SHAREFARMERS	SHEEPSHANK
SEXUALISATIONS	SHAMANISMS	SHAREHOLDER	SHEEPSHANKS
SEXUALISED	SHAMANISTIC	SHAREHOLDERS	SHEEPSHEAD
SEXUALISES	SHAMANISTS	SHAREHOLDING	SHEEPSHEADS
SEXUALISING	SHAMATEURISM	SHAREHOLDINGS	SHEEPSHEARER
SEXUALISMS	SHAMATEURISMS	SHAREMILKER	SHEEPSHEARERS
SEXUALISTS	SHAMATEURS	SHAREMILKERS	SHEEPSHEARING
SEXUALITIES	SHAMBLIEST	SHAREWARES	SHEEPSHEARINGS
SEXUALIZATION	SHAMBLINGS	SHARKSKINS	SHEEPSKINS
SEXUALIZATIONS	SHAMEFACED	SHARKSUCKER	SHEEPTRACK
SEXUALIZED	SHAMEFACEDLY	SHARKSUCKERS	SHEEPTRACKS
SEXUALIZES	SHAMEFACEDNESS	SHARPBENDER	SHEEPWALKS
SEXUALIZING	SHAMEFASTNESS	SHARPBENDERS	SHEERNESSES
SFORZANDOS	SHAMEFASTNESSES	SHARPENERS	SHEETROCKED
SHABBINESS	SHAMEFULLY	SHARPENING	SHEETROCKING
SHABBINESSES	SHAMEFULNESS	SHARPNESSES	SHEETROCKS
SHABRACQUE	SHAMEFULNESSES	SHARPSHOOTER	SHEIKHDOMS
SHABRACQUES	SHAMELESSLY	SHARPSHOOTERS	SHELDDUCKS
SHACKLEBONE	SHAMELESSNESS	SHARPSHOOTING	SHELDRAKES
SHACKLEBONES	SHAMELESSNESSES	SHARPSHOOTINGS	SHELFROOMS
SHADBERRIES	SHAMEWORTHY	SHASHLICKS	SHELFTALKER
SHADBUSHES	SHAMIANAHS	SHATTERERS	SHELFTALKERS
SHADCHANIM	SHAMIYANAH	SHATTERING	SHELLACKED
SHADINESSES	SHAMIYANAHS	SHATTERINGLY	SHELLACKER
SHADKHANIM	SHAMMASHIM	SHATTERPROOF	SHELLACKERS
SHADOWBOXED	SHAMPOOERS	SHAUCHLIER	SHELLACKING
SHADOWBOXES	SHAMPOOING	SHAUCHLIEST	SHELLACKINGS
SHADOWBOXING	SHANACHIES	SHAUCHLING	SHELLBACKS
SHADOWCAST	SHANDRYDAN	SHAVELINGS	SHELLBARKS
SHADOWCASTING	SHANDRYDANS	SHAVETAILS	SHELLBOUND
SHADOWCASTINGS	SHANDYGAFF	SHEARLINGS	SHELLCRACKER
SHADOWCASTS	SHANDYGAFFS	SHEARWATER	SHELLCRACKERS
SHADOWGRAPH	SHANGHAIED	SHEARWATERS	SHELLDRAKE
SHADOWGRAPHIES	SHANGHAIER	SHEATFISHES	SHELLDRAKES
SHADOWGRAPHS	SHANGHAIERS	SHEATHBILL	SHELLDUCKS
SHADOWGRAPHY	SHANGHAIING	SHEATHBILLS	SHELLFIRES
SHADOWIEST	SHANKBONES	SHEATHFISH	SHELLFISHERIES
SHADOWINESS	SHANKPIECE	SHEATHFISHES	SHELLFISHERY

SHELLFISHES	SHIELDRAKE	SHIPWRECKING	SHOEBLACKS
SHELLINESS	SHIELDRAKES	SHIPWRECKS	SHOEHORNED
SHELLINESSES	SHIELDWALL	SHIPWRIGHT	SHOEHORNING
SHELLPROOF	SHIELDWALLS	SHIPWRIGHTS	SHOEMAKERS
SHELLSHOCK	SHIFTINESS	SHIRRALEES	SHOEMAKING
SHELLSHOCKED	SHIFTINESSES	SHIRTBANDS	SHOEMAKINGS
SHELLSHOCKS	SHIFTLESSLY	SHIRTDRESS	SHOESHINES
SHELLWORKS	SHIFTLESSNESS	SHIRTDRESSES	SHOESTRING
SHELLYCOAT	SHIFTLESSNESSES	SHIRTFRONT	SHOESTRINGS
SHELLYCOATS	SHIFTWORKS	SHIRTFRONTS	SHOGGLIEST
SHELTERBELT	SHIGELLOSES	SHIRTINESS	SHOGUNATES
SHELTERBELTS	SHIGELLOSIS	SHIRTINESSES	SHONGOLOLO
SHELTERERS	SHIKARRING	SHIRTLIFTER	SHONGOLOLOS
SHELTERING	SHILLABERS	SHIRTLIFTERS	SHOOGIEING
SHELTERINGS	SHILLALAHS	SHIRTMAKER	SHOOGLIEST
SHELTERLESS	SHILLELAGH	SHIRTMAKERS	SHOOTAROUND
SHEMOZZLED	SHILLELAGHS	SHIRTSLEEVE	SHOOTAROUNDS
SHEMOZZLES	SHILLELAHS	SHIRTSLEEVED	SHOOTDOWNS
SHEMOZZLING	SHILLINGLESS	SHIRTSLEEVES	SHOPAHOLIC
SHENANIGAN	SHILLINGSWORTH	SHIRTTAILED	SHOPAHOLICS
SHENANIGANS	SHILLINGSWORTHS	SHIRTTAILING	SHOPAHOLISM
SHEPHERDED	SHILLYSHALLIED	SHIRTTAILS	SHOPAHOLISMS
SHEPHERDESS	SHILLYSHALLIER	SHIRTWAIST	SHOPBOARDS
SHEPHERDESSES	SHILLYSHALLIERS	SHIRTWAISTER	SHOPBREAKER
SHEPHERDING	SHILLYSHALLIES	SHIRTWAISTERS	SHOPBREAKERS
SHEPHERDLESS	SHILLYSHALLY	SHIRTWAISTS	SHOPBREAKING
SHEPHERDLING	SHILLYSHALLYING	SHITTIMWOOD	SHOPBREAKINGS
SHEPHERDLINGS	SHIMMERING	SHITTIMWOODS	SHOPFRONTS
SHERARDISATION	SHIMMERINGLY	SHITTINESS	SHOPKEEPER
SHERARDISATIONS	SHIMMERINGS	SHITTINESSES	SHOPKEEPERS
SHERARDISE	SHIMOZZLES	SHIVAREEING	SHOPKEEPING
SHERARDISED	SHINGLIEST	SHIVERIEST	SHOPKEEPINGS
SHERARDISES	SHINGLINGS	SHIVERINGLY	SHOPLIFTED
SHERARDISING	SHINGUARDS	SHIVERINGS	SHOPLIFTER
SHERARDIZATION	SHININESSES	SHLEMIEHLS	SHOPLIFTERS
SHERARDIZATIONS	SHININGNESS	SHLEMOZZLE	SHOPLIFTING
SHERARDIZE	SHININGNESSES	SHLEMOZZLED	SHOPSOILED
SHERARDIZED	SHINLEAVES	SHLEMOZZLES	SHOPWALKER
SHERARDIZES	SHINNERIES	SHLEMOZZLING	SHOPWALKERS
SHERARDIZING	SHINNEYING	SHLIMAZELS	SHOPWINDOW
SHEREEFIAN	SHINPLASTER	SHLOCKIEST	SHOPWINDOWS
SHERGOTTITE	SHINPLASTERS	SHMALTZIER	SHOREBIRDS
SHERGOTTITES	SHINSPLINTS	SHMALTZIEST	SHOREFRONT
SHERIFFALTIES	SHIPBOARDS	SHOALINESS	SHOREFRONTS
SHERIFFALTY	SHIPBROKER	SHOALINESSES	SHORELINES
SHERIFFDOM	SHIPBROKERS	SHOALNESSES	SHOREWARDS
SHERIFFDOMS	SHIPBUILDER	SHOCKABILITIES	SHOREWEEDS
SHERIFFSHIP	SHIPBUILDERS	SHOCKABILITY	SHORTBOARD
SHERIFFSHIPS	SHIPBUILDING	SHOCKHEADED	SHORTBOARDS
SHEWBREADS	SHIPBUILDINGS	SHOCKINGLY	SHORTBREAD
SHIBBOLETH	SHIPFITTER	SHOCKINGNESS	SHORTBREADS
SHIBBOLETHS	SHIPFITTERS	SHOCKINGNESSES	SHORTCAKES
SHIBUICHIS	SHIPLAPPED	SHOCKPROOF	SHORTCHANGE
SHIDDUCHIM	SHIPLAPPING	SHOCKSTALL	SHORTCHANGED
SHIELDINGS	SHIPMASTER	SHOCKSTALLS	SHORTCHANGER
SHIELDLESS	SHIPMASTERS	SHOCKUMENTARIES	SHORTCHANGERS
SHIELDLIKE	SHIPOWNERS	SHOCKUMENTARY	SHORTCHANGES
SHIELDLING	SHIPPOUNDS	SHODDINESS	SHORTCHANGING
SHIELDLINGS	SHIPWRECKED	SHODDINESSES	SHORTCOMING

SHORTCOMINGS	SHOWERHEADS	SHROUDLESS	SICKENINGLY
SHORTCRUST	SHOWERIEST	SHRUBBERIED	SICKENINGS
SHORTCUTTING	SHOWERINESS	SHRUBBERIES	SICKERNESS
SHORTENERS	SHOWERINESSES	SHRUBBIEST	SICKERNESSES
SHORTENING	SHOWERINGS	SHRUBBINESS	SICKISHNESS
SHORTENINGS	SHOWERLESS	SHRUBBINESSES	SICKISHNESSES
SHORTFALLS	SHOWERPROOF	SHRUBLANDS	SICKLEBILL
SHORTGOWNS	SHOWERPROOFED	SHTETELACH	SICKLEBILLS
SHORTHAIRED	SHOWERPROOFING	SHTICKIEST	SICKLEMIAS
SHORTHAIRS	SHOWERPROOFINGS	SHUBUNKINS	SICKLINESS
SHORTHANDED	SHOWERPROOFS	SHUDDERING	SICKLINESSES
SHORTHANDS	SHOWGROUND	SHUDDERINGLY	SICKNESSES
SHORTHEADS	SHOWGROUNDS	SHUDDERINGS	SICKNURSES
SHORTHORNS	SHOWINESSES	SHUDDERSOME	SICKNURSING
SHORTLISTED	SHOWJUMPER	SHUFFLEBOARD	SICKNURSINGS
SHORTLISTING	SHOWJUMPERS	SHUFFLEBOARDS	SIDDHUISMS
SHORTLISTS	SHOWJUMPING	SHUFFLINGLY	SIDEBOARDS
SHORTNESSES	SHOWJUMPINGS	SHUFFLINGS	SIDEBURNED
SHORTSIGHTED	SHOWMANSHIP	SHUNAMITISM	SIDECHECKS
SHORTSIGHTEDLY	SHOWMANSHIPS	SHUNAMITISMS	SIDEDNESSES
SHORTSTOPS	SHOWPIECES	SHUNPIKERS	SIDEDRESSES
SHORTSWORD	SHOWPLACES	SHUNPIKING	SIDELEVERS
SHORTSWORDS	SHOWSTOPPER	SHUNPIKINGS	SIDELIGHTS
SHORTWAVED	SHOWSTOPPERS	SHUTTERBUG	SIDELINERS
SHORTWAVES	SHOWSTOPPING	SHUTTERBUGS	SIDELINING
SHORTWAVING	SHREDDIEST	SHUTTERING	SIDEPIECES
SHOTFIRERS	SHREDDINGS	SHUTTERINGS	SIDERATING
SHOTGUNNED	SHREWDNESS	SHUTTERLESS	SIDERATION
SHOTGUNNER	SHREWDNESSES	SHUTTLECOCK	SIDERATIONS
SHOTGUNNERS	SHREWISHLY	SHUTTLECOCKED	SIDEREALLY
SHOTGUNNING	SHREWISHNESS	SHUTTLECOCKING	SIDEROLITE
SHOTMAKERS	SHREWISHNESSES	SHUTTLECOCKS	SIDEROLITES
SHOTMAKING	SHREWMOUSE	SHUTTLELESS	SIDEROPENIA
SHOTMAKINGS	SHRIECHING	SHUTTLEWISE	SIDEROPENIAS
SHOULDERED	SHRIEKIEST	SHYLOCKING	SIDEROPHILE
SHOULDERING	SHRIEKINGLY	SIALAGOGIC	SIDEROPHILES
SHOULDERINGS	SHRIEKINGS	SIALAGOGUE	SIDEROPHILIC
SHOUTHERED	SHRIEVALTIES	SIALAGOGUES	SIDEROPHILIN
SHOUTHERING	SHRIEVALTY	SIALOGOGIC	SIDEROPHILINS
SHOUTINGLY	SHRILLIEST	SIALOGOGUE	SIDEROSTAT
SHOUTLINES	SHRILLINGS	SIALOGOGUES	SIDEROSTATIC
SHOVELBOARD	SHRILLNESS	SIALOGRAMS	SIDEROSTATS
SHOVELBOARDS	SHRILLNESSES	SIALOGRAPHIES	SIDESADDLE
SHOVELFULS	SHRIMPIEST	SIALOGRAPHY	SIDESADDLES
SHOVELHEAD	SHRIMPINGS	SIALOLITHS	SIDESHOOTS
SHOVELHEADS	SHRIMPLIKE	SIALORRHOEA	SIDESLIPPED
SHOVELLERS	SHRINELIKE	SIALORRHOEAS	SIDESLIPPING
SHOVELLING	SHRINKABLE	SIBILANCES	SIDESPLITTING
SHOVELNOSE	SHRINKAGES	SIBILANCIES	SIDESPLITTINGLY
SHOVELNOSES	SHRINKINGLY	SIBILANTLY	SIDESTEPPED
SHOVELSFUL	SHRINKPACK	SIBILATING	SIDESTEPPER
SHOWBIZZES	SHRINKPACKS	SIBILATION	SIDESTEPPERS
SHOWBOATED	SHRITCHING	SIBILATIONS	SIDESTEPPING
SHOWBOATER	SHRIVELING	SIBILATORS	SIDESTREAM
SHOWBOATERS	SHRIVELLED	SIBILATORY	SIDESTREET
SHOWBOATING	SHRIVELLING	SICCATIVES	SIDESTREETS
SHOWBREADS	SHROFFAGES	SICILIANOS	SIDESTROKE
SHOWCASING	SHROUDIEST	SICILIENNE	SIDESTROKES
SHOWERHEAD	SHROUDINGS	SICILIENNES	SIDESWIPED

SIDESWIPER	SIGNALLINGS	SILKGROWERS	SIMARUBACEOUS
SIDESWIPERS	SIGNALMENT	SILKINESSES	SIMILARITIES
SIDESWIPES	SIGNALMENTS	SILKOLINES	SIMILARITY
SIDESWIPING	SIGNATORIES	SILKSCREEN	SIMILATIVE
SIDETRACKED	SIGNATURES	SILKSCREENS	SIMILISING
SIDETRACKING	SIGNBOARDS	SILLIMANITE	SIMILITUDE
SIDETRACKS	SIGNEURIES	SILLIMANITES	SIMILITUDES
SIDEWHEELER	SIGNIFIABLE	SILLINESSES	SIMILIZING
SIDEWHEELERS	SIGNIFICANCE	SILTATIONS	SIMILLIMUM
SIDEWHEELS	SIGNIFICANCES	SILTSTONES	SIMILLIMUMS
SIDEWINDER	SIGNIFICANCIES	SILVERBACK	SIMONIACAL
SIDEWINDERS	SIGNIFICANCY	SILVERBACKS	SIMONIACALLY
SIEGECRAFT	SIGNIFICANT	SILVERBERRIES	SIMONISING
SIEGECRAFTS	SIGNIFICANTLY	SILVERBERRY	SIMONIZING
SIEGEWORKS	SIGNIFICANTS	SILVERBILL	SIMPERINGLY
SIFFLEUSES	SIGNIFICATE	SILVERBILLS	SIMPLEMINDED
SIGHTLESSLY	SIGNIFICATES	SILVEREYES	SIMPLEMINDEDLY
SIGHTLESSNESS	SIGNIFICATION	SILVERFISH	SIMPLENESS
SIGHTLESSNESSES	SIGNIFICATIONS	SILVERFISHES	SIMPLENESSES
SIGHTLIEST	SIGNIFICATIVE	SILVERHORN	SIMPLESSES
SIGHTLINES	SIGNIFICATIVELY	SILVERHORNS	SIMPLETONS
SIGHTLINESS	SIGNIFICATOR	SILVERIEST	SIMPLICIAL
SIGHTLINESSES	SIGNIFICATORS	SILVERINESS	SIMPLICIALLY
SIGHTSCREEN	SIGNIFICATORY	SILVERINESSES	SIMPLICIDENTATE
SIGHTSCREENS	SIGNIFIEDS	SILVERINGS	SIMPLICITER
SIGHTSEEING	SIGNIFIERS	SILVERISED	SIMPLICITIES
SIGHTSEEINGS	SIGNIFYING	SILVERISES	SIMPLICITY
SIGHTSEERS	SIGNIFYINGS	SILVERISING	SIMPLIFICATION
SIGHTWORTHY	SIGNIORIES	SILVERIZED	SIMPLIFICATIONS
SIGILLARIAN	SIGNORINAS	SILVERIZES	SIMPLIFICATIVE
SIGILLARIANS	SIGNPOSTED	SILVERIZING	SIMPLIFICATOR
SIGILLARID	SIGNPOSTING	SILVERLING	SIMPLIFICATORS
SIGILLARIDS	SIKORSKIES	SILVERLINGS	SIMPLIFIED
SIGILLATION	SILENTIARIES	SILVERPOINT	SIMPLIFIER
SIGILLATIONS	SILENTIARY	SILVERPOINTS	SIMPLIFIERS
SIGMATIONS	SILENTNESS	SILVERSIDE	SIMPLIFIES
SIGMATISMS	SILENTNESSES	SILVERSIDES	SIMPLIFYING
SIGMATRONS	SILHOUETTE	SILVERSIDESES	SIMPLISTIC
SIGMOIDALLY	SILHOUETTED	SILVERSKIN	SIMPLISTICALLY
SIGMOIDECTOMIES	SILHOUETTES	SILVERSKINS	SIMULACRES
SIGMOIDECTOMY	SILHOUETTING	SILVERSMITH	SIMULACRUM
SIGMOIDOSCOPE	SILHOUETTIST	SILVERSMITHING	SIMULACRUMS
SIGMOIDOSCOPES	SILHOUETTISTS	SILVERSMITHINGS	SIMULATING
SIGMOIDOSCOPIC	SILICATING	SILVERSMITHS	SIMULATION
SIGMOIDOSCOPIES	SILICICOLOUS	SILVERTAIL	SIMULATIONS
SIGMOIDOSCOPY	SILICIFEROUS	SILVERTAILS	SIMULATIVE
SIGNALINGS	SILICIFICATION	SILVERWARE	SIMULATIVELY
SIGNALISATION	SILICIFICATIONS	SILVERWARES	SIMULATORS
SIGNALISATIONS	SILICIFIED	SILVERWEED	SIMULATORY
SIGNALISED	SILICIFIES	SILVERWEEDS	SIMULCASTED
SIGNALISES	SILICIFYING	SILVESTRIAN	SIMULCASTING
SIGNALISING	SILICONISED	SILVICULTURAL	SIMULCASTS
SIGNALIZATION	SILICONIZED	SILVICULTURALLY	SIMULTANEITIES
SIGNALIZATIONS	SILICOTICS	SILVICULTURE	SIMULTANEITY
SIGNALIZED	SILICULOSE	SILVICULTURES	SIMULTANEOUS
SIGNALIZES	SILIQUACEOUS	SILVICULTURIST	SIMULTANEOUSES
SIGNALIZING	SILKALENES	SILVICULTURISTS	SIMULTANEOUSLY
SIGNALLERS	SILKALINES	SIMAROUBACEOUS	SINANTHROPUS
SIGNALLING	SILKGROWER	SIMAROUBAS	SINANTHROPUSES

SINARCHISM	SINGULARIZING	SIPUNCULID	SKATEPARKS
SINARCHISMS	SINGULARLY	SIPUNCULIDS	SKEDADDLED
SINARCHIST	SINGULARNESS	SIPUNCULOID	SKEDADDLER
SINARCHISTS	SINGULARNESSES	SIPUNCULOIDS	SKEDADDLERS
SINARQUISM	SINGULTUSES	SIRENISING	SKEDADDLES
SINARQUISMS	SINICISING	SIRENIZING	SKEDADDLING
SINARQUIST	SINICIZING	SIRONISING	SKELDERING
SINARQUISTS	SINISTERITIES	SIRONIZING	SKELETALLY
SINCERENESS	SINISTERITY	SISERARIES	SKELETOGENOUS
SINCERENESSES	SINISTERLY	SISSINESSES	SKELETONIC
SINCERITIES	SINISTERNESS	SISSYNESSES	SKELETONISE
SINCIPITAL	SINISTERNESSES	SISTERHOOD	SKELETONISED
SINDONOLOGIES	SINISTERWISE	SISTERHOODS	SKELETONISER
SINDONOLOGIST	SINISTRALITIES	SISTERLESS	SKELETONISERS
SINDONOLOGISTS	SINISTRALITY	SISTERLIKE	SKELETONISES
SINDONOLOGY	SINISTRALLY	SISTERLINESS	SKELETONISING
SINDONOPHANIES	SINISTRALS	SISTERLINESSES	SKELETONIZE
SINDONOPHANY	SINISTRODEXTRAL	SITATUNGAS	SKELETONIZED
SINECURISM	SINISTRORSAL	SITIOLOGIES	SKELETONIZER
SINECURISMS	SINISTRORSALLY	SITIOPHOBIA	SKELETONIZERS
SINECURIST	SINISTRORSE	SITIOPHOBIAS	SKELETONIZES
SINECURISTS	SINISTRORSELY	SITOLOGIES	SKELETONIZING
SINEWINESS	SINISTROUS	SITOPHOBIA	SKELLOCHED
SINEWINESSES	SINISTROUSLY	SITOPHOBIAS	SKELLOCHING
SINFONIETTA	SINLESSNESS	SITOSTEROL	SKELTERING
SINFONIETTAS	SINLESSNESSES	SITOSTEROLS	SKEPTICALLY
SINFULNESS	SINNINGIAS	SITUATIONAL	SKEPTICALNESS
SINFULNESSES	SINOATRIAL	SITUATIONALLY	SKEPTICALNESSES
SINGABLENESS	SINOLOGICAL	SITUATIONISM	SKEPTICISM
SINGABLENESSES	SINOLOGIES	SITUATIONISMS	SKEPTICISMS
SINGALONGS	SINOLOGIST	SITUATIONS	SKETCHABILITIES
SINGLEDOMS	SINOLOGISTS	SITUTUNGAS	SKETCHABILITY
SINGLEHOOD	SINOLOGUES	SITZKRIEGS	SKETCHABLE
SINGLEHOODS	SINSEMILLA	SIXPENNIES	SKETCHBOOK
SINGLENESS	SINSEMILLAS	SIXTEENERS	SKETCHBOOKS
SINGLENESSES	SINTERABILITIES	SIXTEENMOS	SKETCHIEST
SINGLESTICK	SINTERABILITY	SIXTEENTHLY	SKETCHINESS
SINGLESTICKS	SINUATIONS	SIXTEENTHS	SKETCHINESSES
SINGLETONS	SINUITISES	SIZABLENESS	SKETCHPADS
SINGLETREE	SINUOSITIES	SIZABLENESSES	SKEUOMORPH
SINGLETREES	SINUOUSNESS	SIZARSHIPS	SKEUOMORPHIC
SINGSONGED	SINUOUSNESSES	SIZEABLENESS	SKEUOMORPHISM
SINGSONGING	SINUPALLIAL	SIZEABLENESSES	SKEUOMORPHISMS
SINGSPIELS	SINUPALLIATE	SIZINESSES	SKEUOMORPHS
SINGULARISATION	SINUSITISES	SIZZLINGLY	SKEWBACKED
SINGULARISE	SINUSOIDAL	SJAMBOKING	SKEWNESSES
SINGULARISED	SINUSOIDALLY	SJAMBOKKED	SKIAGRAPHS
SINGULARISES	SIPHONAGES	SJAMBOKKING	SKIAMACHIES
SINGULARISING	SIPHONOGAM	SKAITHLESS	SKIASCOPES
SINGULARISM	SIPHONOGAMIES	SKALDSHIPS	SKIASCOPIES
SINGULARISMS	SIPHONOGAMS	SKANKINESS	SKIBOBBERS
SINGULARIST	SIPHONOGAMY	SKANKINESSES	SKIBOBBING
SINGULARISTS	SIPHONOPHORE	SKATEBOARD	SKIBOBBINGS
SINGULARITIES	SIPHONOPHORES	SKATEBOARDED	SKIDDOOING
SINGULARITY	SIPHONOPHOROUS	SKATEBOARDER	SKIJORINGS
SINGULARIZATION	SIPHONOSTELE	SKATEBOARDERS	SKIKJORING
SINGULARIZE	SIPHONOSTELES	SKATEBOARDING	SKIKJORINGS
SINGULARIZED	SIPHONOSTELIC	SKATEBOARDINGS	SKILFULNESS
SINGULARIZES	SIPHUNCLES	SKATEBOARDS	SKILFULNESSES

SKILLCENTRE	SKULDUDDERIES	SLANGINGLY	SLEEPINESSES
SKILLCENTRES	SKULDUDDERY	SLANGUAGES	SLEEPLESSLY
SKILLESSNESS	SKULDUGGERIES	SLANTENDICULAR	SLEEPLESSNESS
SKILLESSNESSES	SKULDUGGERY	SLANTINDICULAR	SLEEPLESSNESSES
SKILLFULLY	SKULKINGLY	SLANTINGLY	SLEEPOVERS
SKILLFULNESS	SKULLDUGGERIES	SLANTINGWAYS	SLEEPSUITS
SKILLFULNESSES	SKULLDUGGERY	SLAPDASHES	SLEEPWALKED
SKILLIGALEE	SKUMMERING	SLAPHAPPIER	SLEEPWALKER
SKILLIGALEES	SKUNKBIRDS	SLAPHAPPIEST	SLEEPWALKERS
SKILLIGOLEE	SKUNKWEEDS	SLAPSTICKS	SLEEPWALKING
SKILLIGOLEES	SKUTTERUDITE	SLASHFESTS	SLEEPWALKINGS
SKIMBOARDED	SKUTTERUDITES	SLASHINGLY	SLEEPWALKS
SKIMBOARDER	SKYBRIDGES	SLATHERING	SLEEPYHEAD
SKIMBOARDERS	SKYDIVINGS	SLATINESSES	SLEEPYHEADED
SKIMBOARDING	SKYJACKERS	SLATTERING	SLEEPYHEADS
SKIMBOARDINGS	SKYJACKING	SLATTERNLINESS	SLEETINESS
SKIMBOARDS	SKYJACKINGS	SLATTERNLY	SLEETINESSES
SKIMMINGLY	SKYLARKERS	SLAUGHTERABLE	SLEEVEHAND
SKIMMINGTON	SKYLARKING	SLAUGHTERED	SLEEVEHANDS
SKIMMINGTONS	SKYLARKINGS	SLAUGHTERER	SLEEVELESS
SKIMOBILED	SKYLIGHTED	SLAUGHTERERS	SLEEVELETS
SKIMOBILES	SKYROCKETED	SLAUGHTERHOUSE	SLEEVELIKE
SKIMOBILING	SKYROCKETING	SLAUGHTERHOUSES	SLEIGHINGS
SKIMPINESS	SKYROCKETS	SLAUGHTERIES	SLENDEREST
SKIMPINESSES	SKYSCRAPER	SLAUGHTERING	SLENDERISE
SKIMPINGLY	SKYSCRAPERS	SLAUGHTERMAN	SLENDERISED
SKINFLICKS	SKYSURFERS	SLAUGHTERMEN	SLENDERISES
SKINFLINTS	SKYSURFING	SLAUGHTEROUS	SLENDERISING
SKINFLINTY	SKYSURFINGS	SLAUGHTEROUSLY	SLENDERIZE
SKINNINESS	SKYWRITERS	SLAUGHTERS	SLENDERIZED
SKINNINESSES	SKYWRITING	SLAUGHTERY	SLENDERIZES
SKIPPERING	SKYWRITINGS	SLAVEHOLDER	SLENDERIZING
SKIPPERINGS	SKYWRITTEN	SLAVEHOLDERS	SLENDERNESS
SKIPPINGLY	SLABBERERS	SLAVEHOLDING	SLENDERNESSES
SKIRMISHED	SLABBERING	SLAVEHOLDINGS	SLEUTHHOUND
SKIRMISHER	SLABBINESS	SLAVERINGLY	SLEUTHHOUNDS
SKIRMISHERS	SLABBINESSES	SLAVISHNESS	SLICKENERS
SKIRMISHES	SLABSTONES	SLAVISHNESSES	SLICKENING
SKIRMISHING	SLACKENERS	SLAVOCRACIES	SLICKENSIDE
SKIRMISHINGS	SLACKENING	SLAVOCRACY	SLICKENSIDED
SKITTERIER	SLACKENINGS	SLAVOCRATS	SLICKENSIDES
SKITTERIEST	SLACKNESSES	SLAVOPHILE	SLICKNESSES
SKITTERING	SLAISTERED	SLAVOPHILES	SLICKROCKS
SKITTISHLY	SLAISTERIES	SLAVOPHILS	SLICKSTERS
SKITTISHNESS	SLAISTERING	SLEAZEBAGS	SLICKSTONE
SKITTISHNESSES	SLALOMISTS	SLEAZEBALL	SLICKSTONES
SKREEGHING	SLAMDANCED	SLEAZEBALLS	SLIDDERING
SKREIGHING	SLAMDANCES	SLEAZINESS	SLIGHTINGLY
SKRIECHING	SLAMDANCING	SLEAZINESSES	SLIGHTNESS
SKRIEGHING	SLAMMAKINS	SLEDGEHAMMER	SLIGHTNESSES
SKRIMMAGED	SLAMMERKIN	SLEDGEHAMMERED	SLIMEBALLS
SKRIMMAGES	SLAMMERKINS	SLEDGEHAMMERING	SLIMINESSES
SKRIMMAGING	SLANDERERS	SLEDGEHAMMERS	SLIMNASTICS
SKRIMSHANK	SLANDERING	SLEECHIEST	SLIMNESSES
SKRIMSHANKED	SLANDEROUS	SLEEKENING	SLIMPSIEST
SKRIMSHANKER	SLANDEROUSLY	SLEEKNESSES	SLINGBACKS
SKRIMSHANKERS	SLANDEROUSNESS	SLEEKSTONE	SLINGSHOTS
SKRIMSHANKING	SLANGINESS	SLEEKSTONES	SLINGSTONE
SKRIMSHANKS	SLANGINESSES	SLEEPINESS	SLINGSTONES

SLINKINESS	SLOGANISES	SLUMBERINGS	SMATTERINGS
SLINKINESSES	SLOGANISING	SLUMBERLAND	SMEARCASES
SLINKSKINS	SLOGANISINGS	SLUMBERLANDS	SMEARINESS
SLINKWEEDS	SLOGANIZED	SLUMBERLESS	SMEARINESSES
SLIPCOVERED	SLOGANIZES	SLUMBEROUS	SMELLINESS
SLIPCOVERING	SLOGANIZING	SLUMBEROUSLY	SMELLINESSES
SLIPCOVERS	SLOGANIZINGS	SLUMBEROUSNESS	SMELTERIES
SLIPDRESSES	SLOMMOCKED	SLUMBERSOME	SMICKERING
SLIPFORMED	SLOMMOCKING	SLUMBROUSLY	SMICKERINGS
SLIPFORMING	SLOPINGNESS	SLUMGULLION	SMIERCASES
SLIPNOOSES	SLOPINGNESSES	SLUMGULLIONS	SMIFLIGATE
SLIPPERIER	SLOPPINESS	SLUMMOCKED	SMIFLIGATED
SLIPPERIEST	SLOPPINESSES	SLUMMOCKING	SMIFLIGATES
SLIPPERILY	SLOPWORKER	SLUMPFLATION	SMIFLIGATING
SLIPPERINESS	SLOPWORKERS	SLUMPFLATIONARY	SMILACACEOUS
SLIPPERINESSES	SLOTHFULLY	SLUMPFLATIONS	SMILINGNESS
SLIPPERING	SLOTHFULNESS	SLUNGSHOTS	SMILINGNESSES
SLIPPERWORT	SLOTHFULNESSES	SLUSHINESS	SMIRKINGLY
SLIPPERWORTS	SLOUCHIEST	SLUSHINESSES	SMITHCRAFT
SLIPPINESS	SLOUCHINESS	SLUTCHIEST	SMITHCRAFTS
SLIPPINESSES	SLOUCHINESSES	SLUTTERIES	SMITHEREEN
SLIPSHEETED	SLOUCHINGLY	SLUTTISHLY	SMITHEREENED
SLIPSHEETING	SLOUGHIEST	SLUTTISHNESS	SMITHEREENING
SLIPSHEETS	SLOVENLIER	SLUTTISHNESSES	SMITHEREENS
SLIPSHODDINESS	SLOVENLIEST	SMACKHEADS	SMITHERIES
SLIPSHODNESS	SLOVENLIKE	SMALLCLOTHES	SMITHSONITE
SLIPSHODNESSES	SLOVENLINESS	SMALLHOLDER	SMITHSONITES
SLIPSLOPPY	SLOVENLINESSES	SMALLHOLDERS	SMOKEBOARD
SLIPSTREAM	SLOVENRIES	SMALLHOLDING	SMOKEBOARDS
SLIPSTREAMED	SLOWCOACHES	SMALLHOLDINGS	SMOKEBUSHES
SLIPSTREAMING	SLOWNESSES	SMALLMOUTH	SMOKEHOODS
SLIPSTREAMS	SLUBBERING	SMALLMOUTHS	SMOKEHOUSE
SLITHERIER	SLUBBERINGLY	SMALLNESSES	SMOKEHOUSES
SLITHERIEST	SLUBBERINGS	SMALLPOXES	SMOKEJACKS
SLITHERING	SLUGGABEDS	SMALLSWORD	SMOKELESSLY
SLIVOVICAS	SLUGGARDISE	SMALLSWORDS	SMOKELESSNESS
SLIVOVICES	SLUGGARDISED	SMALMINESS	SMOKELESSNESSES
SLIVOVITZES	SLUGGARDISES	SMALMINESSES	SMOKEPROOF
SLIVOWITZES	SLUGGARDISING	SMARAGDINE	SMOKESCREEN
SLOBBERERS	SLUGGARDIZE	SMARAGDITE	SMOKESCREENS
SLOBBERIER	SLUGGARDIZED	SMARAGDITES	SMOKESTACK
SLOBBERIEST	SLUGGARDIZES	SMARMINESS	SMOKESTACKS
SLOBBERING	SLUGGARDIZING	SMARMINESSES	SMOKETIGHT
SLOBBISHNESS	SLUGGARDLINESS	SMARTARSED	SMOKETREES
SLOBBISHNESSES	SLUGGARDLY	SMARTARSES	SMOKINESSES
SLOCKDOLAGER	SLUGGARDNESS	SMARTASSES	SMOLDERING
SLOCKDOLAGERS	SLUGGARDNESSES	SMARTENING	SMOOTHABLE
SLOCKDOLIGER	SLUGGISHLY	SMARTMOUTH	SMOOTHBORE
SLOCKDOLIGERS	SLUGGISHNESS	SMARTMOUTHS	SMOOTHBORED
SLOCKDOLOGER	SLUGGISHNESSES	SMARTNESSES	SMOOTHBORES
SLOCKDOLOGERS	SLUGHORNES	SMARTPHONE	SMOOTHENED
SLOCKENING	SLUICEGATE	SMARTPHONES	SMOOTHENING
SLOEBUSHES	SLUICEGATES	SMARTWEEDS	SMOOTHINGS
SLOETHORNS	SLUICELIKE	SMARTYPANTS	SMOOTHNESS
SLOGANEERED	SLUICEWAYS	SMASHEROOS	SMOOTHNESSES
SLOGANEERING	SLUMBERERS	SMASHINGLY	SMOOTHPATE
SLOGANEERINGS	SLUMBERFUL	SMATTERERS	SMOOTHPATES
SLOGANEERS	SLUMBERING	SMATTERING	SMORGASBORD
SLOGANISED	SLUMBERINGLY	SMATTERINGLY	SMORGASBORDS

SMORREBROD	SNAPSHOOTINGS	SNIVELLERS	SNOWMOBILE
SMORREBRODS	SNAPSHOTTED	SNIVELLING	SNOWMOBILER
SMOTHERERS	SNAPSHOTTING	SNOBBERIES	SNOWMOBILERS
SMOTHERINESS	SNARLINGLY	SNOBBISHLY	SNOWMOBILES
SMOTHERINESSES	SNATCHIEST	SNOBBISHNESS	SNOWMOBILING
SMOTHERING	SNATCHINGLY	SNOBBISHNESSES	SNOWMOBILINGS
SMOTHERINGLY	SNATCHINGS	SNOBBOCRACIES	SNOWMOBILIST
SMOTHERINGS	SNAZZINESS	SNOBBOCRACY	SNOWMOBILISTS
SMOULDERED	SNAZZINESSES	SNOBOCRACIES	SNOWPLOUGH
SMOULDERING	SNEAKINESS	SNOBOCRACY	SNOWPLOUGHED
SMOULDERINGS	SNEAKINESSES	SNOBOGRAPHER	SNOWPLOUGHING
SMUDGELESS	SNEAKINGLY	SNOBOGRAPHERS	SNOWPLOUGHS
SMUDGINESS	SNEAKINGNESS	SNOBOGRAPHIES	SNOWPLOWED
SMUDGINESSES	SNEAKINGNESSES	SNOBOGRAPHY	SNOWPLOWING
SMUGGERIES	SNEAKISHLY	SNOLLYGOSTER	SNOWSCAPES
SMUGGLINGS	SNEAKISHNESS	SNOLLYGOSTERS	SNOWSHOEING
SMUGNESSES	SNEAKISHNESSES	SNOOKERING	SNOWSHOERS
SMUTCHIEST	SNEAKSBIES	SNOOPERSCOPE	SNOWSLIDES
SMUTTINESS	SNEERINGLY	SNOOPERSCOPES	SNOWSTORMS
SMUTTINESSES	SNEESHINGS	SNOOTINESS	SNOWSURFING
SNACKETTES	SNEEZELESS	SNOOTINESSES	SNOWSURFINGS
SNAGGLETEETH	SNEEZEWEED	SNORKELERS	SNOWTUBING
SNAGGLETOOTH	SNEEZEWEEDS	SNORKELING	SNOWTUBINGS
SNAGGLETOOTHED	SNEEZEWOOD	SNORKELLED	SNUBBINESS
SNAILERIES	SNEEZEWOODS	SNORKELLING	SNUBBINESSES
SNAILFISHES	SNEEZEWORT	SNORKELLINGS	SNUBBINGLY
SNAKEBIRDS	SNEEZEWORTS	SNORTINGLY	SNUBNESSES
SNAKEBITES	SNICKERERS	SNOTTERIES	SNUFFBOXES
SNAKEBITTEN	SNICKERING	SNOTTERING	SNUFFINESS
SNAKEFISHES	SNICKERSNEE	SNOTTINESS	SNUFFINESSES
SNAKEHEADS	SNICKERSNEED	SNOTTINESSES	SNUFFLIEST
SNAKEMOUTH	SNICKERSNEEING	SNOWBALLED	SNUFFLINGS
SNAKEMOUTHS	SNICKERSNEES	SNOWBALLING	SNUGGERIES
SNAKEROOTS	SNIDENESSES	SNOWBERRIES	SNUGNESSES
SNAKESKINS	SNIFFINESS	SNOWBLADER	SOAPBERRIES
SNAKESTONE	SNIFFINESSES	SNOWBLADERS	SOAPBOXING
SNAKESTONES	SNIFFINGLY	SNOWBLADES	SOAPINESSES
SNAKEWEEDS	SNIFFISHLY	SNOWBLADING	SOAPOLALLIE
SNAKEWOODS	SNIFFISHNESS	SNOWBLADINGS	SOAPOLALLIES
SNAKINESSES	SNIFFISHNESSES	SNOWBLINKS	SOAPSTONES
SNAKISHNESS	SNIFFLIEST	SNOWBLOWER	SOBERINGLY
SNAKISHNESSES	SNIFTERING	SNOWBLOWERS	SOBERISING
SNAPDRAGON	SNIGGERERS	SNOWBOARDED	SOBERIZING
SNAPDRAGONS	SNIGGERING	SNOWBOARDER	SOBERNESSES
SNAPHANCES	SNIGGERINGLY	SNOWBOARDERS	SOBERSIDED
SNAPHAUNCE	SNIGGERINGS	SNOWBOARDING	SOBERSIDEDNESS
SNAPHAUNCES	SNIGGLINGS	SNOWBOARDINGS	SOBERSIDES
SNAPHAUNCH	SNIPEFISHES	SNOWBOARDS	SOBOLIFEROUS
SNAPHAUNCHES	SNIPERSCOPE	SNOWBRUSHES	SOBRIETIES
SNAPPERING	SNIPERSCOPES	SNOWBUSHES	SOBRIQUETS
SNAPPINESS	SNIPPERSNAPPER	SNOWCAPPED	SOCDOLAGER
SNAPPINESSES	SNIPPERSNAPPERS	SNOWDRIFTS	SOCDOLAGERS
SNAPPINGLY	SNIPPETIER	SNOWFIELDS	SOCDOLIGER
SNAPPISHLY	SNIPPETIEST	SNOWFLAKES	SOCDOLIGERS
SNAPPISHNESS	SNIPPETINESS	SNOWFLECKS	SOCDOLOGER
SNAPPISHNESSES	SNIPPETINESSES	SNOWFLICKS	SOCDOLOGERS
SNAPSHOOTER	SNIPPINESS	SNOWINESSES	SOCIABILITIES
SNAPSHOOTERS	SNIPPINESSES	SNOWMAKERS	SOCIABILITY
SNAPSHOOTING	SNITCHIEST	SNOWMAKING	SOCIABLENESS

SOCIABLENESSES	SOCIOPATHS	SOLDERABILITIES	SOLICITORSHIPS
SOCIALISABLE	SOCIOPATHY	SOLDERABILITY	SOLICITOUS
SOCIALISATION	SOCIOPOLITICAL	SOLDERABLE	SOLICITOUSLY
SOCIALISATIONS	SOCIORELIGIOUS	SOLDERINGS	SOLICITOUSNESS
SOCIALISED	SOCIOSEXUAL	SOLDIERIES	SOLICITUDE
SOCIALISER	SOCKDOLAGER	SOLDIERING	SOLICITUDES
SOCIALISERS	SOCKDOLAGERS	SOLDIERINGS	SOLIDARISM
SOCIALISES	SOCKDOLIGER	SOLDIERLIKE	SOLIDARISMS
SOCIALISING	SOCKDOLIGERS	SOLDIERLINESS	SOLIDARIST
SOCIALISMS	SOCKDOLOGER	SOLDIERLINESSES	SOLIDARISTIC
SOCIALISTIC	SOCKDOLOGERS	SOLDIERSHIP	SOLIDARISTS
SOCIALISTICALLY	SODALITIES	SOLDIERSHIPS	SOLIDARITIES
SOCIALISTS	SODBUSTERS	SOLECISING	SOLIDARITY
SOCIALITES	SODDENNESS	SOLECISTIC	SOLIDATING
SOCIALITIES	SODDENNESSES	SOLECISTICAL	SOLIDIFIABLE
SOCIALIZABLE	SODICITIES	SOLECISTICALLY	SOLIDIFICATION
SOCIALIZATION	SODOMISING	SOLECIZING	SOLIDIFICATIONS
SOCIALIZATIONS	SODOMITICAL	SOLEMNESSES	SOLIDIFIED
SOCIALIZED	SODOMITICALLY	SOLEMNIFICATION	SOLIDIFIER
SOCIALIZER	SODOMIZING	SOLEMNIFIED	SOLIDIFIERS
SOCIALIZERS	SOFTBALLER	SOLEMNIFIES	SOLIDIFIES
SOCIALIZES	SOFTBALLERS	SOLEMNIFYING	SOLIDIFYING
SOCIALIZING	SOFTBOUNDS	SOLEMNISATION	SOLIDITIES
SOCIALNESS	SOFTCOVERS	SOLEMNISATIONS	SOLIDNESSES
SOCIALNESSES	SOFTENINGS	SOLEMNISED	SOLIDUNGULATE
SOCIATIONS	SOFTHEADED	SOLEMNISER	SOLIDUNGULOUS
SOCIETALLY	SOFTHEADEDLY	SOLEMNISERS	SOLIFIDIAN
SOCIOBIOLOGICAL	SOFTHEADEDNESS	SOLEMNISES	SOLIFIDIANISM
SOCIOBIOLOGIES	SOFTHEARTED	SOLEMNISING	SOLIFIDIANISMS
SOCIOBIOLOGIST	SOFTHEARTEDLY	SOLEMNITIES	SOLIFIDIANS
SOCIOBIOLOGISTS	SOFTHEARTEDNESS	SOLEMNIZATION	SOLIFLUCTION
SOCIOBIOLOGY	SOFTNESSES	SOLEMNIZATIONS	SOLIFLUCTIONS
SOCIOCULTURAL	SOFTSHELLS	SOLEMNIZED	SOLIFLUXION
SOCIOCULTURALLY	SOGDOLAGER	SOLEMNIZER	SOLIFLUXIONS
SOCIOECONOMIC	SOGDOLAGERS	SOLEMNIZERS	SOLILOQUIES
SOCIOGRAMS	SOGDOLIGER	SOLEMNIZES	SOLILOQUISE
SOCIOHISTORICAL	SOGDOLIGERS	SOLEMNIZING	SOLILOQUISED
SOCIOLECTS	SOGDOLOGER	SOLEMNNESS	SOLILOQUISER
SOCIOLINGUIST	SOGDOLOGERS	SOLEMNNESSES	SOLILOQUISERS
SOCIOLINGUISTIC	SOGGINESSES	SOLENESSES	SOLILOQUISES
SOCIOLINGUISTS	SOILINESSES	SOLENETTES	SOLILOQUISING
SOCIOLOGESE	SOJOURNERS	SOLENODONS	SOLILOQUIST
SOCIOLOGESES	SOJOURNING	SOLENOIDAL	SOLILOQUISTS
SOCIOLOGIC	SOJOURNINGS	SOLENOIDALLY	SOLILOQUIZE
SOCIOLOGICAL	SOJOURNMENT	SOLEPLATES	SOLILOQUIZED
SOCIOLOGICALLY	SOJOURNMENTS	SOLEPRINTS	SOLILOQUIZER
SOCIOLOGIES	SOKEMANRIES	SOLFATARAS	SOLILOQUIZERS
SOCIOLOGISM	SOLACEMENT	SOLFATARIC	SOLILOQUIZES
SOCIOLOGISMS	SOLACEMENTS	SOLFEGGIOS	SOLILOQUIZING
SOCIOLOGIST	SOLANACEOUS	SOLFERINOS	SOLIPEDOUS
SOCIOLOGISTIC	SOLARIMETER	SOLICITANT	SOLIPSISMS
SOCIOLOGISTS	SOLARIMETERS	SOLICITANTS	SOLIPSISTIC
SOCIOMETRIC	SOLARISATION	SOLICITATION	SOLIPSISTICALLY
SOCIOMETRIES	SOLARISATIONS	SOLICITATIONS	SOLIPSISTS
SOCIOMETRIST	SOLARISING	SOLICITIES	SOLITAIRES
SOCIOMETRISTS	SOLARIZATION	SOLICITING	SOLITARIAN
SOCIOMETRY	SOLARIZATIONS	SOLICITINGS	SOLITARIANS
SOCIOPATHIC	SOLARIZING	SOLICITORS	SOLITARIES
SOCIOPATHIES	SOLDATESQUE	SOLICITORSHIP	SOLITARILY

SOLITARINESS	SOMATICALLY	SOMEWHILES	SONGOLOLOS
SOLITARINESSES	SOMATOGENIC	SOMEWHITHER	SONGSMITHS
SOLITUDINARIAN	SOMATOLOGIC	SOMMELIERS	SONGSTRESS
SOLITUDINARIANS	SOMATOLOGICAL	SOMNAMBULANCE	SONGSTRESSES
SOLITUDINOUS	SOMATOLOGICALLY	SOMNAMBULANCES	SONGWRITER
SOLIVAGANT	SOMATOLOGIES	SOMNAMBULANT	SONGWRITERS
SOLIVAGANTS	SOMATOLOGIST	SOMNAMBULANTS	SONGWRITING
SOLLICKERS	SOMATOLOGISTS	SOMNAMBULAR	SONGWRITINGS
SOLMISATION	SOMATOLOGY	SOMNAMBULARY	SONICATING
SOLMISATIONS	SOMATOMEDIN	SOMNAMBULATE	SONICATION
SOLMIZATION	SOMATOMEDINS	SOMNAMBULATED	SONICATIONS
SOLMIZATIONS	SOMATOPLASM	SOMNAMBULATES	SONICATORS
SOLONCHAKS	SOMATOPLASMS	SOMNAMBULATING	SONIFEROUS
SOLONETSES	SOMATOPLASTIC	SOMNAMBULATION	SONNETEERING
SOLONETZES	SOMATOPLEURAL	SOMNAMBULATIONS	SONNETEERINGS
SOLONETZIC	SOMATOPLEURE	SOMNAMBULATOR	SONNETEERS
SOLONISATION	SOMATOPLEURES	SOMNAMBULATORS	SONNETISED
SOLONISATIONS	SOMATOPLEURIC	SOMNAMBULE	SONNETISES
SOLONIZATION	SOMATOSENSORY	SOMNAMBULES	SONNETISING
SOLONIZATIONS	SOMATOSTATIN	SOMNAMBULIC	SONNETIZED
SOLSTITIAL	SOMATOSTATINS	SOMNAMBULISM	SONNETIZES
SOLSTITIALLY	SOMATOTENSIC	SOMNAMBULISMS	SONNETIZING
SOLUBILISATION	SOMATOTONIA	SOMNAMBULIST	SONNETTING
SOLUBILISATIONS	SOMATOTONIAS	SOMNAMBULISTIC	SONOFABITCH
SOLUBILISE	SOMATOTONIC	SOMNAMBULISTS	SONOGRAPHER
SOLUBILISED	SOMATOTROPHIC	SOMNIATING	SONOGRAPHERS
SOLUBILISES	SOMATOTROPHIN	SOMNIATIVE	SONOGRAPHIES
SOLUBILISING	SOMATOTROPHINS	SOMNIATORY	SONOGRAPHS
SOLUBILITIES	SOMATOTROPIC	SOMNIFACIENT	SONOGRAPHY
SOLUBILITY	SOMATOTROPIN	SOMNIFACIENTS	SONOMETERS
SOLUBILIZATION	SOMATOTROPINS	SOMNIFEROUS	SONORITIES
SOLUBILIZATIONS	SOMATOTYPE	SOMNIFEROUSLY	SONOROUSLY
SOLUBILIZE	SOMATOTYPED	SOMNILOQUENCE	SONOROUSNESS
SOLUBILIZED	SOMATOTYPES	SOMNILOQUENCES	SONOROUSNESSES
SOLUBILIZES	SOMATOTYPING	SOMNILOQUIES	SOOTERKINS
SOLUBILIZING	SOMBERNESS	SOMNILOQUISE	SOOTFLAKES
SOLUBLENESS	SOMBERNESSES	SOMNILOQUISED	SOOTHERING
SOLUBLENESSES	SOMBRENESS	SOMNILOQUISES	SOOTHFASTLY
SOLUTIONAL	SOMBRENESSES	SOMNILOQUISING	SOOTHFASTNESS
SOLUTIONED	SOMBRERITE	SOMNILOQUISM	SOOTHFASTNESSES
SOLUTIONING	SOMBRERITES	SOMNILOQUISMS	SOOTHINGLY
SOLUTIONIST	SOMEBODIES	SOMNILOQUIST	SOOTHINGNESS
SOLUTIONISTS	SOMEPLACES	SOMNILOQUISTS	SOOTHINGNESSES
SOLVABILITIES	SOMERSAULT	SOMNILOQUIZE	SOOTHSAYER
SOLVABILITY	SOMERSAULTED	SOMNILOQUIZED	SOOTHSAYERS
SOLVABLENESS	SOMERSAULTING	SOMNILOQUIZES	SOOTHSAYING
SOLVABLENESSES	SOMERSAULTS	SOMNILOQUIZING	SOOTHSAYINGS
SOLVATIONS	SOMERSETED	SOMNILOQUOUS	SOOTINESSES
SOLVENCIES	SOMERSETING	SOMNILOQUY	SOPAIPILLA
SOLVENTLESS	SOMERSETTED	SOMNOLENCE	SOPAIPILLAS
SOLVOLYSES	SOMERSETTING	SOMNOLENCES	SOPAPILLAS
SOLVOLYSIS	SOMESTHESIA	SOMNOLENCIES	SOPHISTERS
SOLVOLYTIC	SOMESTHESIAS	SOMNOLENCY	SOPHISTICAL
SOMAESTHESIA	SOMESTHESIS	SOMNOLENTLY	SOPHISTICALLY
SOMAESTHESIAS	SOMESTHESISES	SOMNOLESCENT	SOPHISTICATE
SOMAESTHESIS	SOMESTHETIC	SONGCRAFTS	SOPHISTICATED
SOMAESTHESISES	SOMETHINGS	SONGFULNESS	SOPHISTICATEDLY
SOMAESTHETIC	SOMEWHENCE	SONGFULNESSES	SOPHISTICATES
SOMASCOPES	SOMEWHERES	SONGLESSLY	SOPHISTICATING

SOPHISTICATION	SOTERIOLOGICAL	SOUTHEASTERLIES	SOVIETISING
SOPHISTICATIONS	SOTERIOLOGIES	SOUTHEASTERLY	SOVIETISMS
SOPHISTICATOR	SOTERIOLOGY	SOUTHEASTERN	SOVIETISTIC
SOPHISTICATORS	SOTTISHNESS	SOUTHEASTERS	SOVIETISTS
SOPHISTRIES	SOTTISHNESSES	SOUTHEASTS	SOVIETIZATION
SOPHOMORES	SOTTISIERS	SOUTHEASTWARD	SOVIETIZATIONS
SOPHOMORIC	SOUBRETTES	SOUTHEASTWARDS	SOVIETIZED
SOPHOMORICAL	SOUBRETTISH	SOUTHERING	SOVIETIZES
SOPORIFEROUS	SOUBRIQUET	SOUTHERLIES	SOVIETIZING
SOPORIFEROUSLY	SOUBRIQUETS	SOUTHERLINESS	SOVIETOLOGICAL
SOPORIFICALLY	SOULDIERED	SOUTHERLINESSES	SOVIETOLOGIST
SOPORIFICS	SOULDIERING	SOUTHERMOST	SOVIETOLOGISTS
SOPPINESSES	SOULFULNESS	SOUTHERNER	SOVRANTIES
SOPRANINOS	SOULFULNESSES	SOUTHERNERS	SOWBELLIES
SOPRANISTS	SOULLESSLY	SOUTHERNISE	SPACEBANDS
SORBABILITIES	SOULLESSNESS	SOUTHERNISED	SPACEBORNE
SORBABILITY	SOULLESSNESSES	SOUTHERNISES	SPACECRAFT
SORBEFACIENT	SOUNDALIKE	SOUTHERNISING	SPACECRAFTS
SORBEFACIENTS	SOUNDALIKES	SOUTHERNISM	SPACEFARING
SORBITISATION	SOUNDBITES	SOUTHERNISMS	SPACEFARINGS
SORBITISATIONS	SOUNDBOARD	SOUTHERNIZE	SPACEFLIGHT
SORBITISED	SOUNDBOARDS	SOUTHERNIZED	SPACEFLIGHTS
SORBITISES	SOUNDBOXES	SOUTHERNIZES	SPACEPLANE
SORBITISING	SOUNDCARDS	SOUTHERNIZING	SPACEPLANES
SORBITIZATION	SOUNDINGLY	SOUTHERNLY	SPACEPORTS
SORBITIZATIONS	SOUNDLESSLY	SOUTHERNMOST	SPACESHIPS
SORBITIZED	SOUNDLESSNESS	SOUTHERNNESS	SPACESUITS
SORBITIZES	SOUNDLESSNESSES	SOUTHERNNESSES	SPACEWALKED
SORBITIZING	SOUNDNESSES	SOUTHERNWOOD	SPACEWALKER
SORCERESSES	SOUNDPOSTS	SOUTHERNWOODS	SPACEWALKERS
SORDAMENTE	SOUNDPROOF	SOUTHLANDER	SPACEWALKING
SORDIDNESS	SOUNDPROOFED	SOUTHLANDERS	SPACEWALKS
SORDIDNESSES	SOUNDPROOFING	SOUTHLANDS	SPACEWOMAN
SOREHEADED	SOUNDPROOFINGS	SOUTHSAYING	SPACEWOMEN
SOREHEADEDLY	SOUNDPROOFS	SOUTHWARDLY	SPACINESSES
SOREHEADEDNESS	SOUNDSCAPE	SOUTHWARDS	SPACIOUSLY
SORENESSES	SOUNDSCAPES	SOUTHWESTER	SPACIOUSNESS
SORICIDENT	SOUNDSTAGE	SOUTHWESTERLIES	SPACIOUSNESSES
SORORIALLY	SOUNDSTAGES	SOUTHWESTERLY	SPADASSINS
SORORICIDAL	SOUNDTRACK	SOUTHWESTERN	SPADEFISHES
SORORICIDE	SOUNDTRACKS	SOUTHWESTERS	SPADEWORKS
SORORICIDES	SOUPSPOONS	SOUTHWESTS	SPADICEOUS
SORORISING	SOURCEBOOK	SOUTHWESTWARD	SPADICIFLORAL
SORORITIES	SOURCEBOOKS	SOUTHWESTWARDLY	SPADILLIOS
SORORIZING	SOURCELESS	SOUTHWESTWARDS	SPAGERISTS
SORRINESSES	SOURDELINE	SOUVENIRED	SPAGHETTILIKE
SORROWFULLY	SOURDELINES	SOUVENIRING	SPAGHETTINI
SORROWFULNESS	SOURDOUGHS	SOUVLAKIAS	SPAGHETTINIS
SORROWFULNESSES	SOURNESSES	SOVENANCES	SPAGHETTIS
SORROWINGS	SOURPUSSES	SOVEREIGNLY	SPAGIRISTS
SORROWLESS	SOUSAPHONE	SOVEREIGNS	SPAGYRICAL
SORTATIONS	SOUSAPHONES	SOVEREIGNTIES	SPAGYRICALLY
SORTILEGER	SOUSAPHONIST	SOVEREIGNTIST	SPAGYRISTS
SORTILEGERS	SOUSAPHONISTS	SOVEREIGNTISTS	SPALLATION
SORTILEGES	SOUTENEURS	SOVEREIGNTY	SPALLATIONS
SORTILEGIES	SOUTERRAIN	SOVIETISATION	SPANAEMIAS
SORTITIONS	SOUTERRAINS	SOVIETISATIONS	SPANAKOPITA
SOSTENUTOS	SOUTHBOUND	SOVIETISED	SPANAKOPITAS
SOTERIOLOGIC	SOUTHEASTER	SOVIETISES	SPANCELING

SPANCELLED	SPASTICALLY	SPECIALIZER	SPECTATRICES
SPANCELLING	SPASTICITIES	SPECIALIZERS	SPECTATRIX
SPANGHEWED	SPASTICITY	SPECIALIZES	SPECTATRIXES
SPANGHEWING	SPATANGOID	SPECIALIZING	SPECTINOMYCIN
SPANGLIEST	SPATANGOIDS	SPECIALLED	SPECTINOMYCINS
SPANGLINGS	SPATCHCOCK	SPECIALLING	SPECTRALITIES
SPANIELLED	SPATCHCOCKED	SPECIALNESS	SPECTRALITY
SPANIELLING	SPATCHCOCKING	SPECIALNESSES	SPECTRALLY
SPANIOLATE	SPATCHCOCKS	SPECIALOGUE	SPECTRALNESS
SPANIOLATED	SPATHACEOUS	SPECIALOGUES	SPECTRALNESSES
SPANIOLATES	SPATHIPHYLLUM	SPECIALTIES	SPECTROGRAM
SPANIOLATING	SPATHIPHYLLUMS	SPECIATING	SPECTROGRAMS
SPANIOLISE	SPATHULATE	SPECIATION	SPECTROGRAPH
SPANIOLISED	SPATIALITIES	SPECIATIONAL	SPECTROGRAPHIC
SPANIOLISES	SPATIALITY	SPECIATIONS	SPECTROGRAPHIES
SPANIOLISING	SPATIOTEMPORAL	SPECIESISM	SPECTROGRAPHS
SPANIOLIZE	SPATTERDASH	SPECIESISMS	SPECTROGRAPHY
SPANIOLIZED	SPATTERDASHES	SPECIESIST	SPECTROLOGICAL
SPANIOLIZES	SPATTERDOCK	SPECIESISTS	SPECTROLOGIES
SPANIOLIZING	SPATTERDOCKS	SPECIFIABLE	SPECTROLOGY
SPANKINGLY	SPATTERING	SPECIFICAL	SPECTROMETER
SPANOKOPITA	SPATTERWORK	SPECIFICALLY	SPECTROMETERS
SPANOKOPITAS	SPATTERWORKS	SPECIFICATE	SPECTROMETRIC
SPARAGMATIC	SPEAKEASIES	SPECIFICATED	SPECTROMETRIES
SPARAGRASS	SPEAKERINE	SPECIFICATES	SPECTROMETRY
SPARAGRASSES	SPEAKERINES	SPECIFICATING	SPECTROSCOPE
SPARAXISES	SPEAKERPHONE	SPECIFICATION	SPECTROSCOPES
SPARENESSES	SPEAKERPHONES	SPECIFICATIONS	SPECTROSCOPIC
SPARGANIUM	SPEAKERSHIP	SPECIFICATIVE	SPECTROSCOPICAL
SPARGANIUMS	SPEAKERSHIPS	SPECIFICITIES	SPECTROSCOPIES
SPARINGNESS	SPEAKINGLY	SPECIFICITY	SPECTROSCOPIST
SPARINGNESSES	SPEAKINGLY	SPECIFIERS	SPECTROSCOPISTS
SPARKISHLY	SPEARFISHED	SPECIFYING	SPECTROSCOPY
SPARKLESSLY	SPEARFISHES	SPECIOCIDE	SPECULARITIES
SPARKLIEST	SPEARFISHING	SPECIOCIDES	SPECULARITY
SPARKLINGLY	SPEARHEADED	SPECIOSITIES	SPECULARLY
SPARKLINGS	SPEARHEADING	SPECIOSITY	SPECULATED
SPARKPLUGGED	SPEARHEADS	SPECIOUSLY	SPECULATES
SPARKPLUGGING	SPEARMINTS	SPECIOUSNESS	SPECULATING
SPARKPLUGS	SPEARWORTS	SPECIOUSNESSES	SPECULATION
SPARROWFART	SPECIALEST	SPECKLEDNESS	SPECULATIONS
SPARROWFARTS	SPECIALISATION	SPECKLEDNESSES	SPECULATIST
SPARROWGRASS	SPECIALISATIONS	SPECKSIONEER	SPECULATISTS
SPARROWGRASSES	SPECIALISE	SPECKSIONEERS	SPECULATIVE
SPARROWHAWK	SPECIALISED	SPECKTIONEER	SPECULATIVELY
SPARROWHAWKS	SPECIALISER	SPECKTIONEERS	SPECULATIVENESS
SPARROWLIKE	SPECIALISERS	SPECTACLED	SPECULATOR
SPARSENESS	SPECIALISES	SPECTACLES	SPECULATORS
SPARSENESSES	SPECIALISING	SPECTACULAR	SPECULATORY
SPARSITIES	SPECIALISM	SPECTACULARITY	SPECULATRICES
SPARTEINES	SPECIALISMS	SPECTACULARLY	SPECULATRIX
SPARTERIES	SPECIALIST	SPECTACULARS	SPECULATRIXES
SPASMATICAL	SPECIALISTIC	SPECTATING	SPEECHCRAFT
SPASMODICAL	SPECIALISTS	SPECTATORIAL	SPEECHCRAFTS
SPASMODICALLY	SPECIALITIES	SPECTATORS	SPEECHFULNESS
SPASMODIST	SPECIALITY	SPECTATORSHIP	SPEECHFULNESSES
SPASMODISTS	SPECIALIZATION	SPECTATORSHIPS	SPEECHIFICATION
SPASMOLYTIC	SPECIALIZATIONS	SPECTATRESS	SPEECHIFIED
SPASMOLYTICS	SPECIALIZE	SPECTATRESSES	SPEECHIFIER

SPEECHIFIERS	SPELLCHECKS	SPERMATORRHOEAS	SPHENDONES
SPEECHIFIES	SPELLDOWNS	SPERMATOTHECA	SPHENODONS
SPEECHIFYING	SPELLICANS	SPERMATOTHECAE	SPHENODONT
SPEECHLESS	SPELLINGLY	SPERMATOZOA	SPHENOGRAM
SPEECHLESSLY	SPELLSTOPT	SPERMATOZOAL	SPHENOGRAMS
SPEECHLESSNESS	SPELUNKERS	SPERMATOZOAN	SPHENOIDAL
SPEECHMAKER	SPELUNKING	SPERMATOZOANS	SPHENOPSID
SPEECHMAKERS	SPELUNKINGS	SPERMATOZOIC	SPHENOPSIDS
SPEECHMAKING	SPENDTHRIFT	SPERMATOZOID	SPHERELESS
SPEECHMAKINGS	SPENDTHRIFTS	SPERMATOZOIDS	SPHERELIKE
SPEECHWRITER	SPERMACETI	SPERMATOZOON	SPHERICALITIES
SPEECHWRITERS	SPERMACETIS	SPERMICIDAL	SPHERICALITY
SPEEDBALLED	SPERMADUCT	SPERMICIDE	SPHERICALLY
SPEEDBALLING	SPERMADUCTS	SPERMICIDES	SPHERICALNESS
SPEEDBALLINGS	SPERMAGONIA	SPERMIDUCT	SPHERICALNESSES
SPEEDBALLS	SPERMAGONIUM	SPERMIDUCTS	SPHERICITIES
SPEEDBOATING	SPERMAPHYTE	SPERMIOGENESES	SPHERICITY
SPEEDBOATINGS	SPERMAPHYTES	SPERMIOGENESIS	SPHERISTERION
SPEEDBOATS	SPERMAPHYTIC	SPERMIOGENETIC	SPHERISTERIONS
SPEEDFREAK	SPERMARIES	SPERMOGONE	SPHEROCYTE
SPEEDFREAKS	SPERMARIUM	SPERMOGONES	SPHEROCYTES
SPEEDFULLY	SPERMATHECA	SPERMOGONIA	SPHEROCYTOSES
SPEEDINESS	SPERMATHECAE	SPERMOGONIUM	SPHEROCYTOSIS
SPEEDINESSES	SPERMATHECAL	SPERMOPHILE	SPHEROIDAL
SPEEDOMETER	SPERMATIAL	SPERMOPHILES	SPHEROIDALLY
SPEEDOMETERS	SPERMATICAL	SPERMOPHYTE	SPHEROIDICALLY
SPEEDREADING	SPERMATICALLY	SPERMOPHYTES	SPHEROIDICITIES
SPEEDREADS	SPERMATICS	SPERMOPHYTIC	SPHEROIDICITY
SPEEDSKATING	SPERMATIDS	SPERRYLITE	SPHEROIDISATION
SPEEDSKATINGS	SPERMATIUM	SPERRYLITES	SPHEROIDISE
SPEEDSTERS	SPERMATOBLAST	SPESSARTINE	SPHEROIDISED
SPEEDWELLS	SPERMATOBLASTIC	SPESSARTINES	SPHEROIDISES
SPELAEOLOGICAL	SPERMATOBLASTS	SPESSARTITE	SPHEROIDISING
SPELAEOLOGIES	SPERMATOCELE	SPESSARTITES	SPHEROIDIZATION
SPELAEOLOGIST	SPERMATOCELES	SPETSNAZES	SPHEROIDIZE
SPELAEOLOGISTS	SPERMATOCIDAL	SPETZNAZES	SPHEROIDIZED
SPELAEOLOGY	SPERMATOCIDE	SPEWINESSES	SPHEROIDIZES
SPELAEOTHEM	SPERMATOCIDES	SPHACELATE	SPHEROIDIZING
SPELAEOTHEMS	SPERMATOCYTE	SPHACELATED	SPHEROMETER
SPELDERING	SPERMATOCYTES	SPHACELATES	SPHEROMETERS
SPELDRINGS	SPERMATOGENESES	SPHACELATING	SPHEROPLAST
SPELEOLOGICAL	SPERMATOGENESIS	SPHACELATION	SPHEROPLASTS
SPELEOLOGIES	SPERMATOGENETIC	SPHACELATIONS	SPHERULITE
SPELEOLOGIST	SPERMATOGENIC	SPHACELUSES	SPHERULITES
SPELEOLOGISTS	SPERMATOGENIES	SPHAERIDIA	SPHERULITIC
SPELEOLOGY	SPERMATOGENOUS	SPHAERIDIUM	SPHINCTERAL
SPELEOTHEM	SPERMATOGENY	SPHAERITES	SPHINCTERIAL
SPELEOTHEMS	SPERMATOGONIA	SPHAEROCRYSTAL	SPHINCTERIC
SPELEOTHERAPIES	SPERMATOGONIAL	SPHAEROCRYSTALS	SPHINCTERS
SPELEOTHERAPY	SPERMATOGONIUM	SPHAEROSIDERITE	SPHINGOMYELIN
SPELLBINDER	SPERMATOPHORAL	SPHAGNICOLOUS	SPHINGOMYELINS
SPELLBINDERS	SPERMATOPHORE	SPHAGNOLOGIES	SPHINGOSINE
SPELLBINDING	SPERMATOPHORES	SPHAGNOLOGIST	SPHINGOSINES
SPELLBINDINGLY	SPERMATOPHYTE	SPHAGNOLOGISTS	SPHINXLIKE
SPELLBINDS	SPERMATOPHYTES	SPHAGNOLOGY	SPHRAGISTIC
SPELLBOUND	SPERMATOPHYTIC	SPHAIRISTIKE	SPHRAGISTICS
SPELLCHECK	SPERMATORRHEA	SPHAIRISTIKES	SPHYGMOGRAM
SPELLCHECKER	SPERMATORRHEAS	SPHALERITE	SPHYGMOGRAMS
SPELLCHECKERS	SPERMATORRHOEA	SPHALERITES	SPHYGMOGRAPH

SPHYGMOGRAPHIC	SPINELESSLY	SPIRITLESSNESS	SPIRONOLACTONES
SPHYGMOGRAPHIES	SPINELESSNESS	SPIRITOUSNESS	SPIROPHORE
SPHYGMOGRAPHS	SPINELESSNESSES	SPIRITOUSNESSES	SPIROPHORES
SPHYGMOGRAPHY	SPINESCENCE	SPIRITUALISE	SPIRULINAS
SPHYGMOLOGIES	SPINESCENCES	SPIRITUALISED	SPISSITUDE
SPHYGMOLOGY	SPINESCENT	SPIRITUALISER	SPISSITUDES
SPHYGMOMETER	SPINIFEROUS	SPIRITUALISERS	SPITCHCOCK
SPHYGMOMETERS	SPINIFEXES	SPIRITUALISES	SPITCHCOCKED
SPHYGMOPHONE	SPINIGEROUS	SPIRITUALISING	SPITCHCOCKING
SPHYGMOPHONES	SPINIGRADE	SPIRITUALISM	SPITCHCOCKS
SPHYGMOSCOPE	SPININESSES	SPIRITUALISMS	SPITEFULLER
SPHYGMOSCOPES	SPINMEISTER	SPIRITUALIST	SPITEFULLEST
SPHYGMUSES	SPINMEISTERS	SPIRITUALISTIC	SPITEFULLY
SPICEBERRIES	SPINNAKERS	SPIRITUALISTS	SPITEFULNESS
SPICEBERRY	SPINNERETS	SPIRITUALITIES	SPITEFULNESSES
SPICEBUSHES	SPINNERETTE	SPIRITUALITY	SPITSTICKER
SPICILEGES	SPINNERETTES	SPIRITUALIZE	SPITSTICKERS
SPICINESSES	SPINNERIES	SPIRITUALIZED	SPITTLEBUG
SPICULATION	SPINNERULE	SPIRITUALIZER	SPITTLEBUGS
SPICULATIONS	SPINNERULES	SPIRITUALIZERS	SPIVVERIES
SPIDERIEST	SPINOSITIES	SPIRITUALIZES	SPLANCHNIC
SPIDERLIKE	SPINSTERDOM	SPIRITUALIZING	SPLANCHNOCELE
SPIDERWEBS	SPINSTERDOMS	SPIRITUALLY	SPLANCHNOCELES
SPIDERWOOD	SPINSTERHOOD	SPIRITUALNESS	SPLANCHNOLOGIES
SPIDERWOODS	SPINSTERHOODS	SPIRITUALNESSES	SPLANCHNOLOGY
SPIDERWORK	SPINSTERIAL	SPIRITUALS	SPLASHBACK
SPIDERWORKS	SPINSTERIAN	SPIRITUALTIES	SPLASHBACKS
SPIDERWORT	SPINSTERISH	SPIRITUALTY	SPLASHBOARD
SPIDERWORTS	SPINSTERLY	SPIRITUELLE	SPLASHBOARDS
SPIEGELEISEN	SPINSTERSHIP	SPIRITUOSITIES	SPLASHDOWN
SPIEGELEISENS	SPINSTERSHIPS	SPIRITUOSITY	SPLASHDOWNS
SPIFFINESS	SPINSTRESS	SPIRITUOUS	SPLASHIEST
SPIFFINESSES	SPINSTRESSES	SPIRITUOUSNESS	SPLASHINESS
SPIFFLICATE	SPINTHARISCOPE	SPIRITUSES	SPLASHINESSES
SPIFFLICATED	SPINTHARISCOPES	SPIRKETTING	SPLASHINGS
SPIFFLICATES	SPINULESCENT	SPIRKETTINGS	SPLASHPROOF
SPIFFLICATING	SPINULIFEROUS	SPIROCHAETAEMIA	SPLATCHING
SPIFFLICATION	SPIRACULAR	SPIROCHAETE	SPLATTERED
SPIFFLICATIONS	SPIRACULATE	SPIROCHAETES	SPLATTERING
SPIFLICATE	SPIRACULUM	SPIROCHAETOSES	SPLATTERPUNK
SPIFLICATED	SPIRALIFORM	SPIROCHAETOSIS	SPLATTERPUNKS
SPIFLICATES	SPIRALISMS	SPIROCHETAL	SPLATTINGS
SPIFLICATING	SPIRALISTS	SPIROCHETE	SPLAYFOOTED
SPIFLICATION	SPIRALITIES	SPIROCHETES	SPLAYFOOTEDLY
SPIFLICATIONS	SPIRALLING	SPIROCHETOSES	SPLEENFULLY
SPIKEFISHES	SPIRASTERS	SPIROCHETOSIS	SPLEENIEST
SPIKENARDS	SPIRATIONS	SPIROGRAMS	SPLEENLESS
SPIKINESSES	SPIRIFEROUS	SPIROGRAPH	SPLEENSTONE
SPILLIKINS	SPIRILLOSES	SPIROGRAPHIC	SPLEENSTONES
SPILLOVERS	SPIRILLOSIS	SPIROGRAPHIES	SPLEENWORT
SPILOSITES	SPIRITEDLY	SPIROGRAPHS	SPLEENWORTS
SPINACENES	SPIRITEDNESS	SPIROGRAPHY	SPLENATIVE
SPINACEOUS	SPIRITEDNESSES	SPIROGYRAS	SPLENDIDER
SPINACHLIKE	SPIRITINGS	SPIROMETER	SPLENDIDEST
SPINDLELEGS	SPIRITISMS	SPIROMETERS	SPLENDIDIOUS
SPINDLESHANKS	SPIRITISTIC	SPIROMETRIC	SPLENDIDLY
SPINDLIEST	SPIRITISTS	SPIROMETRIES	SPLENDIDNESS
SPINDLINGS	SPIRITLESS	SPIROMETRY	SPLENDIDNESSES
SPINDRIFTS	SPIRITLESSLY	SPIRONOLACTONE	SPLENDIDOUS

SPLENDIFEROUS	SPOKESHAVE	SPOONBAITS	SPORTFISHERMEN
SPLENDIFEROUSLY	SPOKESHAVES	SPOONBILLS	SPORTFISHING
SPLENDOROUS	SPOKESMANSHIP	SPOONDRIFT	SPORTFISHINGS
SPLENDOURS	SPOKESMANSHIPS	SPOONDRIFTS	SPORTFULLY
SPLENDROUS	SPOKESPEOPLE	SPOONERISM	SPORTFULNESS
SPLENECTOMIES	SPOKESPERSON	SPOONERISMS	SPORTFULNESSES
SPLENECTOMISE	SPOKESPERSONS	SPORADICAL	SPORTINESS
SPLENECTOMISED	SPOKESWOMAN	SPORADICALLY	SPORTINESSES
SPLENECTOMISES	SPOKESWOMEN	SPORADICALNESS	SPORTINGLY
SPLENECTOMISING	SPOLIATING	SPORANGIAL	SPORTIVELY
SPLENECTOMIZE	SPOLIATION	SPORANGIOLA	SPORTIVENESS
SPLENECTOMIZED	SPOLIATIONS	SPORANGIOLE	SPORTIVENESSES
SPLENECTOMIZES	SPOLIATIVE	SPORANGIOLES	SPORTSCAST
SPLENECTOMIZING	SPOLIATORS	SPORANGIOLUM	SPORTSCASTER
SPLENECTOMY	SPOLIATORY	SPORANGIOPHORE	SPORTSCASTERS
SPLENETICAL	SPONDAICAL	SPORANGIOPHORES	SPORTSCASTS
SPLENETICALLY	SPONDOOLICKS	SPORANGIOSPORE	SPORTSMANLIKE
SPLENETICS	SPONDULICKS	SPORANGIOSPORES	SPORTSMANLY
SPLENISATION	SPONDYLITIC	SPORANGIUM	SPORTSMANSHIP
SPLENISATIONS	SPONDYLITICS	SPORICIDAL	SPORTSMANSHIPS
SPLENITISES	SPONDYLITIS	SPORICIDES	SPORTSPEOPLE
SPLENIUSES	SPONDYLITISES	SPORIDESMS	SPORTSPERSON
SPLENIZATION	SPONDYLOLYSES	SPOROCARPS	SPORTSPERSONS
SPLENIZATIONS	SPONDYLOLYSIS	SPOROCYSTIC	SPORTSWEAR
SPLENOMEGALIES	SPONDYLOSES	SPOROCYSTS	SPORTSWEARS
SPLENOMEGALY	SPONDYLOSIS	SPOROCYTES	SPORTSWOMAN
SPLEUCHANS	SPONDYLOUS	SPOROGENESES	SPORTSWOMEN
SPLINTERED	SPONGEABLE	SPOROGENESIS	SPORTSWRITER
SPLINTERIER	SPONGEBAGS	SPOROGENIC	SPORTSWRITERS
SPLINTERIEST	SPONGELIKE	SPOROGENIES	SPORTSWRITING
SPLINTERING	SPONGEWARE	SPOROGENOUS	SPORTSWRITINGS
SPLINTLIKE	SPONGEWARES	SPOROGONIA	SPORULATED
SPLINTWOOD	SPONGEWOOD	SPOROGONIAL	SPORULATES
SPLINTWOODS	SPONGEWOODS	SPOROGONIC	SPORULATING
SPLODGIEST	SPONGICOLOUS	SPOROGONIES	SPORULATION
SPLODGINESS	SPONGIFORM	SPOROGONIUM	SPORULATIONS
SPLODGINESSES	SPONGINESS	SPOROPHORE	SPORULATIVE
SPLOOSHING	SPONGINESSES	SPOROPHORES	SPOTLESSLY
SPLOTCHIER	SPONGIOBLAST	SPOROPHORIC	SPOTLESSNESS
SPLOTCHIEST	SPONGIOBLASTIC	SPOROPHOROUS	SPOTLESSNESSES
SPLOTCHILY	SPONGIOBLASTS	SPOROPHYLL	SPOTLIGHTED
SPLOTCHINESS	SPONGOLOGIES	SPOROPHYLLS	SPOTLIGHTING
SPLOTCHINESSES	SPONGOLOGIST	SPOROPHYLS	SPOTLIGHTS
SPLOTCHING	SPONGOLOGISTS	SPOROPHYTE	SPOTTEDNESS
SPLURGIEST	SPONGOLOGY	SPOROPHYTES	SPOTTEDNESSES
SPLUTTERED	SPONSIONAL	SPOROPHYTIC	SPOTTINESS
SPLUTTERER	SPONSORIAL	SPOROPOLLENIN	SPOTTINESSES
SPLUTTERERS	SPONSORING	SPOROPOLLENINS	SPOUSELESS
SPLUTTERING	SPONSORSHIP	SPOROTRICHOSES	SPOYLEFULL
SPLUTTERINGLY	SPONSORSHIPS	SPOROTRICHOSIS	SPRACHGEFUHL
SPLUTTERINGS	SPONTANEITIES	SPOROZOANS	SPRACHGEFUHLS
SPODOGRAMS	SPONTANEITY	SPOROZOITE	SPRACKLING
SPODOMANCIES	SPONTANEOUS	SPOROZOITES	SPRADDLING
SPODOMANCY	SPONTANEOUSLY	SPORTABILITIES	SPRANGLING
SPODOMANTIC	SPONTANEOUSNESS	SPORTABILITY	SPRATTLING
SPODUMENES	SPOOFERIES	SPORTANCES	SPRAUCHLED
SPOILFIVES	SPOOKERIES	SPORTCASTER	SPRAUCHLES
SPOILSPORT	SPOOKINESS	SPORTCASTERS	SPRAUCHLING
SPOILSPORTS	SPOOKINESSES	SPORTFISHERMAN	SPRAUNCIER

SPRAUNCIEST	SPRINGTIMES	SQUALIDITY	SQUEAKINGLY
SPRAWLIEST	SPRINGWATER	SQUALIDNESS	SQUEAKINGS
SPREADABILITIES	SPRINGWATERS	SQUALIDNESSES	SQUEALINGS
SPREADABILITY	SPRINGWOOD	SQUALLIEST	SQUEAMISHLY
SPREADABLE	SPRINGWOODS	SQUALLINGS	SQUEAMISHNESS
SPREADINGLY	SPRINGWORT	SQUAMATION	SQUEAMISHNESSES
SPREADINGS	SPRINGWORTS	SQUAMATIONS	SQUEEGEEING
SPREADSHEET	SPRINKLERED	SQUAMELLAS	SQUEEZABILITIES
SPREADSHEETS	SPRINKLERING	SQUAMIFORM	SQUEEZABILITY
SPREAGHERIES	SPRINKLERS	SQUAMOSALS	SQUEEZABLE
SPREAGHERY	SPRINKLING	SQUAMOSELY	SQUEEZIEST
SPREATHING	SPRINKLINGS	SQUAMOSENESS	SQUEEZINGS
SPRECHERIES	SPRINTINGS	SQUAMOSENESSES	SQUEGGINGS
SPRECHGESANG	SPRITELIER	SQUAMOSITIES	SQUELCHERS
SPRECHGESANGS	SPRITELIEST	SQUAMOSITY	SQUELCHIER
SPRECHSTIMME	SPRITSAILS	SQUAMOUSLY	SQUELCHIEST
SPRECHSTIMMES	SPROUTINGS	SQUAMOUSNESS	SQUELCHING
SPREETHING	SPRUCENESS	SQUAMOUSNESSES	SQUELCHINGS
SPREKELIAS	SPRUCENESSES	SQUAMULOSE	SQUETEAGUE
SPRIGGIEST	SPRYNESSES	SQUANDERED	SQUETEAGUES
SPRIGHTFUL	SPUILZIEING	SQUANDERER	SQUIBBINGS
SPRIGHTFULLY	SPULEBLADE	SQUANDERERS	SQUIDGIEST
SPRIGHTFULNESS	SPULEBLADES	SQUANDERING	SQUIFFIEST
SPRIGHTING	SPULYIEING	SQUANDERINGLY	SQUIGGLERS
SPRIGHTLESS	SPULZIEING	SQUANDERINGS	SQUIGGLIER
SPRIGHTLIER	SPUMESCENCE	SQUANDERMANIA	SQUIGGLIEST
SPRIGHTLIEST	SPUMESCENCES	SQUANDERMANIAS	SQUIGGLING
SPRIGHTLINESS	SPUMESCENT	SQUAREHEAD	SQUILGEEING
SPRIGHTLINESSES	SPUNBONDED	SQUAREHEADS	SQUILLIONS
SPRIGTAILS	SPUNKINESS	SQUARENESS	SQUINANCIES
SPRINGALDS	SPUNKINESSES	SQUARENESSES	SQUINCHING
SPRINGBOARD	SPURGALLED	SQUAREWISE	SQUINNIEST
SPRINGBOARDS	SPURGALLING	SQUARISHLY	SQUINNYING
SPRINGBOKS	SPURIOSITIES	SQUARISHNESS	SQUINTIEST
SPRINGBUCK	SPURIOSITY	SQUARISHNESSES	SQUINTINGLY
SPRINGBUCKS	SPURIOUSLY	SQUARSONAGE	SQUINTINGS
SPRINGEING	SPURIOUSNESS	SQUARSONAGES	SQUIRALITIES
SPRINGHAAS	SPURIOUSNESSES	SQUASHABLE	SQUIRALITY
SPRINGHALT	SPUTTERERS	SQUASHIEST	SQUIRALTIES
SPRINGHALTS	SPUTTERING	SQUASHINESS	SQUIRARCHAL
SPRINGHASE	SPUTTERINGLY	SQUASHINESSES	SQUIRARCHICAL
SPRINGHEAD	SPUTTERINGS	SQUATNESSES	SQUIRARCHIES
SPRINGHEADS	SPYGLASSES	SQUATTERED	SQUIRARCHS
SPRINGHOUSE	SPYMASTERS	SQUATTERING	SQUIRARCHY
SPRINGHOUSES	SQUABASHED	SQUATTIEST	SQUIREAGES
SPRINGIEST	SQUABASHER	SQUATTINESS	SQUIREARCH
SPRINGINESS	SQUABASHERS	SQUATTINESSES	SQUIREARCHAL
SPRINGINESSES	SQUABASHES	SQUATTLING	SQUIREARCHICAL
SPRINGINGS	SQUABASHING	SQUATTOCRACIES	SQUIREARCHIES
SPRINGKEEPER	SQUABBIEST	SQUATTOCRACY	SQUIREARCHS
SPRINGKEEPERS	SQUABBLERS	SQUAWBUSHES	SQUIREARCHY
SPRINGLESS	SQUABBLING	SQUAWFISHES	SQUIREDOMS
SPRINGLETS	SQUADRONAL	SQUAWKIEST	SQUIREHOOD
SPRINGLIKE	SQUADRONED	SQUAWKINGS	SQUIREHOODS
SPRINGTAIL	SQUADRONES	SQUAWROOTS	SQUIRELIKE
SPRINGTAILS	SQUADRONING	SQUEAKERIES	SQUIRELING
SPRINGTIDE	SQUAILINGS	SQUEAKIEST	SQUIRELINGS
SPRINGTIDES	SQUALIDEST	SQUEAKINESS	SQUIRESHIP
SPRINGTIME	SQUALIDITIES	SQUEAKINESSES	SQUIRESHIPS

SQUIRESSES	STADHOLDERSHIP	STAKHANOVISM	STANCHELLED
SQUIRMIEST	STADHOLDERSHIPS	STAKHANOVISMS	STANCHELLING
SQUIRMINGLY	STADIOMETER	STAKHANOVITE	STANCHERED
SQUIRRELED	STADIOMETERS	STAKHANOVITES	STANCHERING
SQUIRRELFISH	STADTHOLDER	STAKTOMETER	STANCHINGS
SQUIRRELFISHES	STADTHOLDERATE	STAKTOMETERS	STANCHIONED
SQUIRRELING	STADTHOLDERATES	STALACTICAL	STANCHIONING
SQUIRRELLED	STADTHOLDERS	STALACTIFORM	STANCHIONS
SQUIRRELLING	STADTHOLDERSHIP	STALACTITAL	STANCHLESS
SQUIRRELLY	STAFFROOMS	STALACTITE	STANCHNESS
SQUIRTINGS	STAGECOACH	STALACTITED	STANCHNESSES
SQUISHIEST	STAGECOACHES	STALACTITES	STANDARDBRED
SQUISHINESS	STAGECOACHING	STALACTITIC	STANDARDBREDS
SQUISHINESSES	STAGECOACHINGS	STALACTITICAL	STANDARDISATION
SQUOOSHIER	STAGECOACHMAN	STALACTITICALLY	STANDARDISE
SQUOOSHIEST	STAGECOACHMEN	STALACTITIFORM	STANDARDISED
SQUOOSHING	STAGECRAFT	STALACTITIOUS	STANDARDISER
STABBINGLY	STAGECRAFTS	STALAGMITE	STANDARDISERS
STABILATES	STAGEHANDS	STALAGMITES	STANDARDISES
STABILISATION	STAGESTRUCK	STALAGMITIC	STANDARDISING
STABILISATIONS	STAGFLATION	STALAGMITICAL	STANDARDIZATION
STABILISATOR	STAGFLATIONARY	STALAGMITICALLY	STANDARDIZE
STABILISATORS	STAGFLATIONS	STALAGMOMETER	STANDARDIZED
STABILISED	STAGGERBUSH	STALAGMOMETERS	STANDARDIZER
STABILISER	STAGGERBUSHES	STALAGMOMETRIES	STANDARDIZERS
STABILISERS	STAGGERERS	STALAGMOMETRY	STANDARDIZES
STABILISES	STAGGERING	STALEMATED	STANDARDIZING
STABILISING	STAGGERINGLY	STALEMATES	STANDARDLESS
STABILITIES	STAGGERINGS	STALEMATING	STANDARDLY
STABILIZATION	STAGHOUNDS	STALENESSES	STANDDOWNS
STABILIZATIONS	STAGINESSES	STALKINESS	STANDFASTS
STABILIZATOR	STAGNANCES	STALKINESSES	STANDFIRST
STABILIZATORS	STAGNANCIES	STALLENGER	STANDFIRSTS
STABILIZED	STAGNANTLY	STALLENGERS	STANDGALES
STABILIZER	STAGNATING	STALLHOLDER	STANDISHES
STABILIZERS	STAGNATION	STALLHOLDERS	STANDOFFISH
STABILIZES	STAGNATIONS	STALLINGER	STANDOFFISHLY
STABILIZING	STAIDNESSES	STALLINGERS	STANDOFFISHNESS
STABLEBOYS	STAINABILITIES	STALLMASTER	STANDOVERS
STABLEMATE	STAINABILITY	STALLMASTERS	STANDPATTER
STABLEMATES	STAINLESSES	STALWARTLY	STANDPATTERS
STABLENESS	STAINLESSLY	STALWARTNESS	STANDPATTISM
STABLENESSES	STAINLESSNESS	STALWARTNESSES	STANDPATTISMS
STABLISHED	STAINLESSNESSES	STALWORTHS	STANDPIPES
STABLISHES	STAINPROOF	STAMINEOUS	STANDPOINT
STABLISHING	STAIRCASED	STAMINIFEROUS	STANDPOINTS
STABLISHMENT	STAIRCASES	STAMINODES	STANDSTILL
STABLISHMENTS	STAIRCASING	STAMINODIA	STANDSTILLS
STACCATISSIMO	STAIRCASINGS	STAMINODIES	STANNARIES
STACKROOMS	STAIRFOOTS	STAMINODIUM	STANNATORS
STACKYARDS	STAIRHEADS	STAMMERERS	STANNIFEROUS
STACTOMETER	STAIRLIFTS	STAMMERING	STANNOTYPE
STACTOMETERS	STAIRSTEPPED	STAMMERINGLY	STANNOTYPES
STADDLESTONE	STAIRSTEPPING	STAMMERINGS	STAPEDECTOMIES
STADDLESTONES	STAIRSTEPS	STAMPEDERS	STAPEDECTOMY
STADHOLDER	STAIRWELLS	STAMPEDING	STAPEDIUSES
STADHOLDERATE	STAIRWORKS	STAMPEDOED	STAPHYLINE
STADHOLDERATES	STAKEHOLDER	STAMPEDOING	STAPHYLINID
STADHOLDERS	STAKEHOLDERS	STANCHABLE	STAPHYLINIDS

STAPHYLITIS	STASIMORPHIES	STAUNCHABLE	STEATOMATOUS
STAPHYLITISES	STASIMORPHY	STAUNCHERS	STEATOPYGA
STAPHYLOCOCCAL	STATECRAFT	STAUNCHEST	STEATOPYGAS
STAPHYLOCOCCI	STATECRAFTS	STAUNCHING	STEATOPYGIA
STAPHYLOCOCCIC	STATEHOODS	STAUNCHINGS	STEATOPYGIAS
STAPHYLOCOCCUS	STATEHOUSE	STAUNCHLESS	STEATOPYGIC
STAPHYLOMA	STATEHOUSES	STAUNCHNESS	STEATOPYGOUS
STAPHYLOMAS	STATELESSNESS	STAUNCHNESSES	STEATORRHEA
STAPHYLOMATA	STATELESSNESSES	STAUROLITE	STEATORRHEAS
STAPHYLOPLASTIC	STATELIEST	STAUROLITES	STEATORRHOEA
STAPHYLOPLASTY	STATELINESS	STAUROLITIC	STEATORRHOEAS
STAPHYLOPLASY	STATELINESSES	STAUROSCOPE	STEDFASTLY
STAPHYLORRHAPHY	STATEMENTED	STAUROSCOPES	STEDFASTNESS
STARBOARDED	STATEMENTING	STAUROSCOPIC	STEDFASTNESSES
STARBOARDING	STATEMENTINGS	STAVESACRE	STEELHEADS
STARBOARDS	STATEMENTS	STAVESACRES	STEELINESS
STARBURSTS	STATEROOMS	STAVUDINES	STEELINESSES
STARCHEDLY	STATESMANLIKE	STAYMAKERS	STEELMAKER
STARCHEDNESS	STATESMANLY	STEADFASTLY	STEELMAKERS
STARCHEDNESSES	STATESMANSHIP	STEADFASTNESS	STEELMAKING
STARCHIEST	STATESMANSHIPS	STEADFASTNESSES	STEELMAKINGS
STARCHINESS	STATESPEOPLE	STEADICAMS	STEELWARES
STARCHINESSES	STATESPERSON	STEADINESS	STEELWORKER
STARCHLIKE	STATESPERSONS	STEADINESSES	STEELWORKERS
STARDRIFTS	STATESWOMAN	STEAKHOUSE	STEELWORKING
STARFISHED	STATESWOMEN	STEAKHOUSES	STEELWORKINGS
STARFISHES	STATICALLY	STEALINGLY	STEELWORKS
STARFLOWER	STATIONARIES	STEALTHFUL	STEELYARDS
STARFLOWERS	STATIONARILY	STEALTHIER	STEENBRASES
STARFRUITS	STATIONARINESS	STEALTHIEST	STEENBUCKS
STARFUCKER	STATIONARY	STEALTHILY	STEENKIRKS
STARFUCKERS	STATIONERIES	STEALTHINESS	STEEPDOWNE
STARFUCKING	STATIONERS	STEALTHINESSES	STEEPEDOWNE
STARFUCKINGS	STATIONERY	STEALTHING	STEEPENING
STARGAZERS	STATIONING	STEALTHINGS	STEEPINESS
STARGAZING	STATIONMASTER	STEAMBOATS	STEEPINESSES
STARGAZINGS	STATIONMASTERS	STEAMERING	STEEPLEBUSH
STARKENING	STATISTICAL	STEAMFITTER	STEEPLEBUSHES
STARKNESSES	STATISTICALLY	STEAMFITTERS	STEEPLECHASE
STARLIGHTED	STATISTICIAN	STEAMINESS	STEEPLECHASED
STARLIGHTS	STATISTICIANS	STEAMINESSES	STEEPLECHASER
STARMONGER	STATISTICS	STEAMROLLED	STEEPLECHASERS
STARMONGERS	STATOBLAST	STEAMROLLER	STEEPLECHASES
STAROSTIES	STATOBLASTS	STEAMROLLERED	STEEPLECHASING
STARRINESS	STATOCYSTS	STEAMROLLERING	STEEPLECHASINGS
STARRINESSES	STATOLATRIES	STEAMROLLERS	STEEPLEJACK
STARSHINES	STATOLATRY	STEAMROLLING	STEEPLEJACKS
STARSTONES	STATOLITHIC	STEAMROLLS	STEEPNESSES
STARSTRUCK	STATOLITHS	STEAMSHIPS	STEERAGEWAY
STARTINGLY	STATOSCOPE	STEAMTIGHT	STEERAGEWAYS
STARTLEMENT	STATOSCOPES	STEAMTIGHTNESS	STEERLINGS
STARTLEMENTS	STATUARIES	STEAROPTENE	STEERSMATE
STARTLINGLY	STATUESQUE	STEAROPTENES	STEERSMATES
STARTLINGS	STATUESQUELY	STEARSMATE	STEGANOGRAM
STARVATION	STATUESQUENESS	STEARSMATES	STEGANOGRAMS
STARVATIONS	STATUETTES	STEATOCELE	STEGANOGRAPH
STARVELING	STATUTABLE	STEATOCELES	STEGANOGRAPHER
STARVELINGS	STATUTABLY	STEATOLYSES	STEGANOGRAPHERS
STASIDIONS	STATUTORILY	STEATOLYSIS	STEGANOGRAPHIC

STEGANOGRAPHIES	STENOGRAPHER	STEPSISTER	STEREOMETRIES
STEGANOGRAPHIST	STENOGRAPHERS	STEPSISTERS	STEREOMETRY
STEGANOGRAPHS	STENOGRAPHIC	STEPSTOOLS	STEREOPHONIC
STEGANOGRAPHY	STENOGRAPHICAL	STERADIANS	STEREOPHONIES
STEGANOPOD	STENOGRAPHIES	STERCORACEOUS	STEREOPHONY
STEGANOPODOUS	STENOGRAPHING	STERCORANISM	STEREOPSES
STEGANOPODS	STENOGRAPHIST	STERCORANISMS	STEREOPSIS
STEGOCARPOUS	STENOGRAPHISTS	STERCORANIST	STEREOPTICON
STEGOCEPHALIAN	STENOGRAPHS	STERCORANISTS	STEREOPTICONS
STEGOCEPHALIANS	STENOGRAPHY	STERCORARIOUS	STEREOPTICS
STEGOCEPHALOUS	STENOHALINE	STERCORARY	STEREOREGULAR
STEGODONTS	STENOPAEIC	STERCORATE	STEREOSCOPE
STEGOMYIAS	STENOPETALOUS	STERCORATED	STEREOSCOPES
STEGOPHILIST	STENOPHAGOUS	STERCORATES	STEREOSCOPIC
STEGOPHILISTS	STENOPHYLLOUS	STERCORATING	STEREOSCOPICAL
STEGOSAURIAN	STENOTHERM	STERCORICOLOUS	STEREOSCOPIES
STEGOSAURS	STENOTHERMAL	STERCULIACEOUS	STEREOSCOPIST
STEGOSAURUS	STENOTHERMS	STERCULIAS	STEREOSCOPISTS
STEGOSAURUSES	STENOTOPIC	STEREOACUITIES	STEREOSCOPY
STEINBOCKS	STENOTROPIC	STEREOACUITY	STEREOSONIC
STEINKIRKS	STENOTYPED	STEREOBATE	STEREOSPECIFIC
STELLARATOR	STENOTYPER	STEREOBATES	STEREOTACTIC
STELLARATORS	STENOTYPERS	STEREOBATIC	STEREOTACTICAL
STELLATELY	STENOTYPES	STEREOBLIND	STEREOTAXES
STELLERIDAN	STENOTYPIC	STEREOCARD	STEREOTAXIA
STELLERIDANS	STENOTYPIES	STEREOCARDS	STEREOTAXIAS
STELLERIDS	STENOTYPING	STEREOCHEMICAL	STEREOTAXIC
STELLIFEROUS	STENOTYPIST	STEREOCHEMISTRY	STEREOTAXICALLY
STELLIFIED	STENOTYPISTS	STEREOCHROME	STEREOTAXIS
STELLIFIES	STENTMASTER	STEREOCHROMED	STEREOTOMIES
STELLIFORM	STENTMASTERS	STEREOCHROMES	STEREOTOMY
STELLIFYING	STENTORIAN	STEREOCHROMIES	STEREOTROPIC
STELLIFYINGS	STEPBAIRNS	STEREOCHROMING	STEREOTROPISM
STELLIONATE	STEPBROTHER	STEREOCHROMY	STEREOTROPISMS
STELLIONATES	STEPBROTHERS	STEREOGNOSES	STEREOTYPE
STELLULARLY	STEPCHILDREN	STEREOGNOSIS	STEREOTYPED
STELLULATE	STEPDANCER	STEREOGRAM	STEREOTYPER
STEMMATOUS	STEPDANCERS	STEREOGRAMS	STEREOTYPERS
STEMMERIES	STEPDANCING	STEREOGRAPH	STEREOTYPES
STEMWINDER	STEPDANCINGS	STEREOGRAPHED	STEREOTYPIC
STEMWINDERS	STEPDAUGHTER	STEREOGRAPHIC	STEREOTYPICAL
STENCHIEST	STEPDAUGHTERS	STEREOGRAPHICAL	STEREOTYPICALLY
STENCILERS	STEPFAMILIES	STEREOGRAPHIES	STEREOTYPIES
STENCILING	STEPFAMILY	STEREOGRAPHING	STEREOTYPING
STENCILLED	STEPFATHER	STEREOGRAPHS	STEREOTYPINGS
STENCILLER	STEPFATHERS	STEREOGRAPHY	STEREOTYPIST
STENCILLERS	STEPHANITE	STEREOISOMER	STEREOTYPISTS
STENCILLING	STEPHANITES	STEREOISOMERIC	STEREOTYPY
STENCILLINGS	STEPHANOTIS	STEREOISOMERISM	STEREOVISION
STENOBATHIC	STEPHANOTISES	STEREOISOMERS	STEREOVISIONS
STENOBATHS	STEPLADDER	STEREOISOMETRIC	STERICALLY
STENOCARDIA	STEPLADDERS	STEREOLOGICAL	STERIGMATA
STENOCARDIAS	STEPMOTHER	STEREOLOGICALLY	STERILANTS
STENOCHROME	STEPMOTHERLY	STEREOLOGIES	STERILISABLE
STENOCHROMES	STEPMOTHERS	STEREOLOGY	STERILISATION
STENOCHROMIES	STEPPARENT	STEREOMETER	STERILISATIONS
STENOCHROMY	STEPPARENTING	STEREOMETERS	STERILISED
STENOGRAPH	STEPPARENTINGS	STEREOMETRIC	STERILISER
STENOGRAPHED	STEPPARENTS	STEREOMETRICAL	STERILISERS

STERILISES	STEWARDING	STIGMARIANS	STIMULANCIES
STERILISING	STEWARDRIES	STIGMASTEROL	STIMULANCY
STERILITIES	STEWARDSHIP	STIGMASTEROLS	STIMULANTS
STERILIZABLE	STEWARDSHIPS	STIGMATICAL	STIMULATED
STERILIZATION	STEWARTRIES	STIGMATICALLY	STIMULATER
STERILIZATIONS	STIACCIATO	STIGMATICS	STIMULATERS
STERILIZED	STIACCIATOS	STIGMATIFEROUS	STIMULATES
STERILIZER	STIBIALISM	STIGMATISATION	STIMULATING
STERILIZERS	STIBIALISMS	STIGMATISATIONS	STIMULATINGLY
STERILIZES	STICCADOES	STIGMATISE	STIMULATION
STERILIZING	STICCATOES	STIGMATISED	STIMULATIONS
STERLINGLY	STICHARION	STIGMATISER	STIMULATIVE
STERLINGNESS	STICHARIONS	STIGMATISERS	STIMULATIVES
STERLINGNESSES	STICHICALLY	STIGMATISES	STIMULATOR
STERNALGIA	STICHIDIUM	STIGMATISING	STIMULATORS
STERNALGIAS	STICHOLOGIES	STIGMATISM	STIMULATORY
STERNALGIC	STICHOLOGY	STIGMATISMS	STINGAREES
STERNBOARD	STICHOMETRIC	STIGMATIST	STINGBULLS
STERNBOARDS	STICHOMETRICAL	STIGMATISTS	STINGFISHES
STERNEBRAE	STICHOMETRIES	STIGMATIZATION	STINGINESS
STERNFASTS	STICHOMETRY	STIGMATIZATIONS	STINGINESSES
STERNFOREMOST	STICHOMYTHIA	STIGMATIZE	STINGINGLY
STERNNESSES	STICHOMYTHIAS	STIGMATIZED	STINGINGNESS
STERNOCOSTAL	STICHOMYTHIC	STIGMATIZER	STINGINGNESSES
STERNOTRIBE	STICHOMYTHIES	STIGMATIZERS	STINKEROOS
STERNPORTS	STICHOMYTHY	STIGMATIZES	STINKHORNS
STERNPOSTS	STICKABILITIES	STIGMATIZING	STINKINGLY
STERNSHEET	STICKABILITY	STIGMATOPHILIA	STINKINGNESS
STERNSHEETS	STICKBALLS	STIGMATOPHILIAS	STINKINGNESSES
STERNUTATION	STICKERING	STIGMATOPHILIST	STINKSTONE
STERNUTATIONS	STICKHANDLE	STIGMATOSE	STINKSTONES
STERNUTATIVE	STICKHANDLED	STILBESTROL	STINKWEEDS
STERNUTATIVES	STICKHANDLER	STILBESTROLS	STINKWOODS
STERNUTATOR	STICKHANDLERS	STILBOESTROL	STINTEDNESS
STERNUTATORIES	STICKHANDLES	STILBOESTROLS	STINTEDNESSES
STERNUTATORS	STICKHANDLING	STILETTOED	STINTINGLY
STERNUTATORY	STICKINESS	STILETTOES	STIPELLATE
STERNWARDS	STICKINESSES	STILETTOING	STIPENDIARIES
STERNWORKS	STICKLEADER	STILLATORIES	STIPENDIARY
STEROIDOGENESES	STICKLEADERS	STILLATORY	STIPENDIATE
STEROIDOGENESIS	STICKLEBACK	STILLBIRTH	STIPENDIATED
STEROIDOGENIC	STICKLEBACKS	STILLBIRTHS	STIPENDIATES
STERTOROUS	STICKSEEDS	STILLBORNS	STIPENDIATING
STERTOROUSLY	STICKTIGHT	STILLHOUSE	STIPITIFORM
STERTOROUSNESS	STICKTIGHTS	STILLHOUSES	STIPPLINGS
STETHOSCOPE	STICKWEEDS	STILLICIDE	STIPULABLE
STETHOSCOPES	STICKWORKS	STILLICIDES	STIPULACEOUS
STETHOSCOPIC	STICKYBEAK	STILLIFORM	STIPULATED
STETHOSCOPIES	STICKYBEAKED	STILLNESSES	STIPULATES
STETHOSCOPIST	STICKYBEAKING	STILLROOMS	STIPULATING
STETHOSCOPISTS	STICKYBEAKS	STILPNOSIDERITE	STIPULATION
STETHOSCOPY	STIDDIEING	STILTBIRDS	STIPULATIONS
STEVEDORED	STIFFENERS	STILTEDNESS	STIPULATOR
STEVEDORES	STIFFENING	STILTEDNESSES	STIPULATORS
STEVEDORING	STIFFENINGS	STILTINESS	STIPULATORY
STEVENGRAPH	STIFFNESSES	STILTINESSES	STIRABOUTS
STEVENGRAPHS	STIFFWARES	STIMPMETER	STIRPICULTURE
STEWARDESS	STIFLINGLY	STIMPMETERS	STIRPICULTURES
STEWARDESSES	STIGMARIAN	STIMULABLE	STIRRINGLY

STITCHCRAFT	STOCKROUTE	STOMATOPOD	STOREHOUSE
STITCHCRAFTS	STOCKROUTES	STOMATOPODS	STOREHOUSES
STITCHERIES	STOCKTAKEN	STOMODAEAL	STORFKEEPER
STITCHINGS	STOCKTAKES	STOMODAEUM	STOREKEEPERS
STITCHWORK	STOCKTAKING	STOMODAEUMS	STOREKEEPING
STITCHWORKS	STOCKTAKINGS	STOMODEUMS	STOREKEEPINGS
STITCHWORT	STOCKWORKS	STONEBOATS	STOREROOMS
STITCHWORTS	STOCKYARDS	STONEBORER	STORESHIPS
STOCHASTIC	STODGINESS	STONEBORERS	STORIETTES
STOCHASTICALLY	STODGINESSES	STONEBRASH	STORIOLOGIES
STOCKADING	STOECHIOLOGICAL	STONEBRASHES	STORIOLOGIST
STOCKBREEDER	STOECHIOLOGIES	STONEBREAK	STORIOLOGISTS
STOCKBREEDERS	STOECHIOLOGY	STONEBREAKS	STORIOLOGY
STOCKBREEDING	STOECHIOMETRIC	STONECASTS	STORKSBILL
STOCKBREEDINGS	STOECHIOMETRIES	STONECHATS	STORKSBILLS
STOCKBROKER	STOECHIOMETRY	STONECROPS	STORMBIRDS
STOCKBROKERAGE	STOICALNESS	STONECUTTER	STORMBOUND
STOCKBROKERAGES	STOICALNESSES	STONECUTTERS	STORMFULLY
STOCKBROKERS	STOICHEIOLOGIES	STONECUTTING	STORMFULNESS
STOCKBROKING	STOICHEIOLOGY	STONECUTTINGS	STORMFULNESSES
STOCKBROKINGS	STOICHEIOMETRIC	STONEFISHES	STORMINESS
STOCKFISHES	STOICHEIOMETRY	STONEFLIES	STORMINESSES
STOCKHOLDER	STOICHIOLOGICAL	STONEGROUND	STORMPROOF
STOCKHOLDERS	STOICHIOLOGIES	STONEHANDS	STORYBOARD
STOCKHOLDING	STOICHIOLOGY	STONEHORSE	STORYBOARDED
STOCKHOLDINGS	STOICHIOMETRIC	STONEHORSES	STORYBOARDING
STOCKHORNS	STOICHIOMETRIES	STONELESSNESS	STORYBOARDS
STOCKHORSE	STOICHIOMETRY	STONELESSNESSES	STORYBOOKS
STOCKHORSES	STOITERING	STONEMASON	STORYETTES
STOCKINESS	STOKEHOLDS	STONEMASONRIES	STORYLINES
STOCKINESSES	STOKEHOLES	STONEMASONRY	STORYTELLER
STOCKINETS	STOLENWISE	STONEMASONS	STORYTELLERS
STOCKINETTE	STOLIDITIES	STONESHOTS	STORYTELLING
STOCKINETTES	STOLIDNESS	STONEWALLED	STORYTELLINGS
STOCKINGED	STOLIDNESSES	STONEWALLER	STOTTERING
STOCKINGER	STOLONIFEROUS	STONEWALLERS	STOUTENING
STOCKINGERS	STOMACHACHE	STONEWALLING	STOUTHEARTED
STOCKINGLESS	STOMACHACHES	STONEWALLINGS	STOUTHEARTEDLY
STOCKISHLY	STOMACHERS	STONEWALLS	STOUTHERIE
STOCKISHNESS	STOMACHFUL	STONEWARES	STOUTHERIES
STOCKISHNESSES	STOMACHFULNESS	STONEWASHED	STOUTHRIEF
STOCKJOBBER	STOMACHFULS	STONEWASHES	STOUTHRIEFS
STOCKJOBBERIES	STOMACHICAL	STONEWASHING	STOUTNESSES
STOCKJOBBERS	STOMACHICS	STONEWORKER	STOVEPIPES
STOCKJOBBERY	STOMACHING	STONEWORKERS	STRABISMAL
STOCKJOBBING	STOMACHLESS	STONEWORKS	STRABISMIC
STOCKJOBBINGS	STOMACHOUS	STONEWORTS	STRABISMICAL
STOCKKEEPER	STOMATITIC	STONINESSES	STRABISMOMETER
STOCKKEEPERS	STOMATITIDES	STONISHING	STRABISMOMETERS
STOCKLISTS	STOMATITIS	STONKERING	STRABISMUS
STOCKLOCKS	STOMATITISES	STONYHEARTED	STRABISMUSES
STOCKPILED	STOMATODAEA	STOOLBALLS	STRABOMETER
STOCKPILER	STOMATODAEUM	STOOPBALLS	STRABOMETERS
STOCKPILERS	STOMATOGASTRIC	STOOPINGLY	STRABOTOMIES
STOCKPILES	STOMATOLOGICAL	STOPLIGHTS	STRABOTOMY
STOCKPILING	STOMATOLOGIES	STOPPERING	STRACCHINI
STOCKPILINGS	STOMATOLOGY	STOPWATCHES	STRACCHINO
STOCKPUNISHT	STOMATOPLASTIES	STOREFRONT	STRADDLEBACK
STOCKROOMS	STOMATOPLASTY	STOREFRONTS	STRADDLERS

STRADDLING	STRAMONIUMS	STRATHSPEY	STRAYLINGS
STRAGGLERS	STRANDEDNESS	STRATHSPEYS	STREAKIEST
STRAGGLIER	STRANDEDNESSES	STRATICULATE	STREAKINESS
STRAGGLIEST	STRANDFLAT	STRATICULATION	STREAKINESSES
STRAGGLING	STRANDFLATS	STRATICULATIONS	STREAKINGS
STRAGGLINGLY	STRANDLINE	STRATIFICATION	STREAKLIKE
STRAGGLINGS	STRANDLINES	STRATIFICATIONS	STREAMBEDS
STRAICHTER	STRANDWOLF	STRATIFIED	STREAMERED
STRAICHTEST	STRANDWOLVES	STRATIFIES	STREAMIEST
STRAIGHTAWAY	STRANGENESS	STRATIFORM	STREAMINESS
STRAIGHTAWAYS	STRANGENESSES	STRATIFYING	STREAMINESSES
STRAIGHTBRED	STRANGERED	STRATIGRAPHER	STREAMINGLY
STRAIGHTBREDS	STRANGERING	STRATIGRAPHERS	STREAMINGS
STRAIGHTED	STRANGLEHOLD	STRATIGRAPHIC	STREAMLESS
STRAIGHTEDGE	STRANGLEHOLDS	STRATIGRAPHICAL	STREAMLETS
STRAIGHTEDGED	STRANGLEMENT	STRATIGRAPHIES	STREAMLIKE
STRAIGHTEDGES	STRANGLEMENTS	STRATIGRAPHIST	STREAMLINE
STRAIGHTEN	STRANGLERS	STRATIGRAPHISTS	STREAMLINED
STRAIGHTENED	STRANGLING	STRATIGRAPHY	STREAMLINER
STRAIGHTENER	STRANGULATE	STRATOCRACIES	STREAMLINERS
STRAIGHTENERS	STRANGULATED	STRATOCRACY	STREAMLINES
STRAIGHTENING	STRANGULATES	STRATOCRAT	STREAMLING
STRAIGHTENS	STRANGULATING	STRATOCRATIC	STREAMLINGS
STRAIGHTER	STRANGULATION	STRATOCRATS	STREAMLINING
STRAIGHTEST	STRANGULATIONS	STRATOCUMULI	STREAMSIDE
STRAIGHTFORTH	STRANGURIES	STRATOCUMULUS	STREAMSIDES
STRAIGHTFORWARD	STRAPHANGED	STRATOPAUSE	STREETAGES
STRAIGHTING	STRAPHANGER	STRATOPAUSES	STREETBOYS
STRAIGHTISH	STRAPHANGERS	STRATOSPHERE	STREETCARS
STRAIGHTJACKET	STRAPHANGING	STRATOSPHERES	STREETFULS
STRAIGHTJACKETS	STRAPHANGS	STRATOSPHERIC	STREETIEST
STRAIGHTLACED	STRAPLESSES	STRATOSPHERICAL	STREETKEEPER
STRAIGHTLY	STRAPLINES	STRATOTANKER	STREETKEEPERS
STRAIGHTNESS	STRAPONTIN	STRATOTANKERS	STREETLAMP
STRAIGHTNESSES	STRAPONTINS	STRATOVOLCANO	STREETLAMPS
STRAIGHTWAY	STRAPPADOED	STRATOVOLCANOES	STREETLIGHT
STRAIGHTWAYS	STRAPPADOES	STRATOVOLCANOS	STREETLIGHTS
STRAINEDLY	STRAPPADOING	STRAUCHTED	STREETROOM
STRAININGS	STRAPPADOS	STRAUCHTER	STREETROOMS
STRAITENED	STRAPPIEST	STRAUCHTEST	STREETSCAPE
STRAITENING	STRAPPINGS	STRAUCHTING	STREETSCAPES
STRAITJACKET	STRAPWORTS	STRAUGHTED	STREETSMART
STRAITJACKETED	STRATAGEMS	STRAUGHTER	STREETWALKER
STRAITJACKETING	STRATEGETIC	STRAUGHTEST	STREETWALKERS
STRAITJACKETS	STRATEGETICAL	STRAUGHTING	STREETWALKING
STRAITLACED	STRATEGICAL	STRAVAGING	STREETWALKINGS
STRAITLACEDLY	STRATEGICALLY	STRAVAIGED	STREETWARD
STRAITLACEDNESS	STRATEGICS	STRAVAIGER	STREETWARDS
STRAITNESS	STRATEGIES	STRAVAIGERS	STREETWEAR
STRAITNESSES	STRATEGISE	STRAVAIGING	STREETWEARS
STRAITWAISTCOAT	STRATEGISED	STRAWBERRIES	STREETWISE
STRAMACONS	STRATEGISES	STRAWBERRY	STREIGNING
STRAMASHED	STRATEGISING	STRAWBOARD	STRELITZES
STRAMASHES	STRATEGIST	STRAWBOARDS	STRELITZIA
STRAMASHING	STRATEGISTS	STRAWFLOWER	STRELITZIAS
STRAMAZONS	STRATEGIZE	STRAWFLOWERS	STRENGTHEN
STRAMINEOUS	STRATEGIZED	STRAWWEIGHT	STRENGTHENED
STRAMONIES	STRATEGIZES	STRAWWEIGHTS	STRENGTHENER
STRAMONIUM	STRATEGIZING	STRAWWORMS	STRENGTHENERS

STRENGTHENING	STRETCHLESS	STRINGHALT	STROMBULIFEROUS
STRENGTHENINGS	STRETCHMARKS	STRINGHALTED	STROMBULIFORM
STRENGTHENS	STREWMENTS	STRINGHALTS	STROMBUSES
STRENGTHFUL	STRIATIONS	STRINGIEST	STRONGARMED
STRENGTHLESS	STRIATURES	STRINGINESS	STRONGARMING
STRENUITIES	STRICKENLY	STRINGINESSES	STRONGARMS
STRENUOSITIES	STRICKLING	STRINGINGS	STRONGBOXES
STRENUOSITY	STRICTIONS	STRINGLESS	STRONGHOLD
STRENUOUSLY	STRICTNESS	STRINGLIKE	STRONGHOLDS
STRENUOUSNESS	STRICTNESSES	STRINGPIECE	STRONGNESS
STRENUOUSNESSES	STRICTURED	STRINGPIECES	STRONGNESSES
STREPEROUS	STRICTURES	STRINGYBARK	STRONGPOINT
STREPHOSYMBOLIA	STRIDDLING	STRINGYBARKS	STRONGPOINTS
STREPITANT	STRIDELEGGED	STRINKLING	STRONGROOM
STREPITATION	STRIDELEGS	STRINKLINGS	STRONGROOMS
STREPITATIONS	STRIDENCES	STRIPAGRAM	STRONGYLES
STREPITOSO	STRIDENCIES	STRTPAGRAMS	STRONGYLOID
STREPITOUS	STRIDENTLY	STRIPELESS	STRONGYLOIDOSES
STREPSIPTEROUS	STRIDEWAYS	STRIPINESS	STRONGYLOIDOSIS
STREPTOBACILLI	STRIDULANCE	STRIPINESSES	STRONGYLOIDS
STREPTOBACILLUS	STRIDULANCES	STRIPLINGS	STRONGYLOSES
STREPTOCARPUS	STRIDULANT	STRIPPABLE	STRONGYLOSIS
STREPTOCARPUSES	STRIDULANTLY	STRIPPERGRAM	STRONTIANITE
STREPTOCOCCAL	STRIDULATE	STRIPPERGRAMS	STRONTIANITES
STREPTOCOCCI	STRIDULATED	STRIPPINGS	STRONTIANS
STREPTOCOCCIC	STRIDULATES	STRIPTEASE	STRONTIUMS
STREPTOCOCCUS	STRIDULATING	STRIPTEASER	STROPHANTHIN
STREPTOKINASE	STRIDULATION	STRIPTEASERS	STROPHANTHINS
STREPTOKINASES	STRIDULATIONS	STRIPTEASES	STROPHANTHUS
STREPTOLYSIN	STRIDULATOR	STRIVINGLY	STROPHANTHUSES
STREPTOLYSINS	STRIDULATORS	STROBILACEOUS	STROPHICAL
STREPTOMYCES	STRIDULATORY	STROBILATE	STROPHIOLATE
STREPTOMYCETE	STRIDULOUS	STROBILATED	STROPHIOLATED
STREPTOMYCETES	STRIDULOUSLY	STROBILATES	STROPHIOLE
STREPTOMYCIN	STRIDULOUSNESS	STROBILATING	STROPHIOLES
STREPTOMYCINS	STRIFELESS	STROBILATION	STROPHOIDS
STREPTOSOLEN	STRIGIFORM	STROBILATIONS	STROPHULUS
STREPTOSOLENS	STRIKEBOUND	STROBILIFORM	STROPPIEST
STREPTOTHRICIN	STRIKEBREAKER	STROBILINE	STROPPINESS
STREPTOTHRICINS	STRIKEBREAKERS	STROBILISATION	STROPPINESSES
STRESSBUSTER	STRIKEBREAKING	STROBILISATIONS	STROUDINGS
STRESSBUSTERS	STRIKEBREAKINGS	STROBILIZATION	STROUPACHS
STRESSBUSTING	STRIKELESS	STROBILIZATIONS	STRUCTURAL
STRESSFULLY	STRIKEOUTS	STROBILOID	STRUCTURALISE
STRESSFULNESS	STRIKEOVER	STROBILUSES	STRUCTURALISED
STRESSFULNESSES	STRIKEOVERS	STROBOSCOPE	STRUCTURALISES
STRESSLESS	STRIKINGLY	STROBOSCOPES	STRUCTURALISING
STRESSLESSNESS	STRIKINGNESS	STROBOSCOPIC	STRUCTURALISM
STRETCHABILITY	STRIKINGNESSES	STROBOSCOPICAL	STRUCTURALISMS
STRETCHABLE	STRINGBOARD	STROBOTRON	STRUCTURALIST
STRETCHERED	STRINGBOARDS	STROBOTRONS	STRUCTURALISTS
STRETCHERING	STRINGCOURSE	STRODDLING	STRUCTURALIZE
STRETCHERS	STRINGCOURSES	STROGANOFF	STRUCTURALIZED
STRETCHIER	STRINGENCIES	STROGANOFFS	STRUCTURALIZES
STRETCHIEST	STRINGENCY	STROLLINGS	STRUCTURALIZING
STRETCHINESS	STRINGENDO	STROMATOLITE	STRUCTURALLY
STRETCHINESSES	STRINGENTLY	STROMATOLITES	STRUCTURATION
STRETCHING	STRINGENTNESS	STROMATOLITIC	STRUCTURATIONS
STRETCHINGS	STRINGENTNESSES	STROMATOUS	STRUCTURED

STRUCTURELESS	STUMBLIEST	STYLOPHONES	SUBAQUEOUS
STRUCTURES	STUMBLINGLY	STYLOPISED	SUBARACHNOID
STRUCTURING	STUMPINESS	STYLOPISES	SUBARACHNOIDAL
STRUGGLERS	STUMPINESSES	STYLOPISING	SUBARBOREAL
STRUGGLING	STUMPWORKS	STYLOPIZED	SUBARBORESCENT
STRUGGLINGLY	STUNNINGLY	STYLOPIZES	SUBARCTICS
STRUGGLINGS	STUNTEDNESS	STYLOPIZING	SUBARCUATE
STRUMITISES	STUNTEDNESSES	STYLOPODIA	SUBARCUATION
STRUMPETED	STUNTWOMAN	STYLOPODIUM	SUBARCUATIONS
STRUMPETING	STUNTWOMEN	STYLOSTIXES	SUBARRATION
STRUTHIOID	STUPEFACIENT	STYLOSTIXIS	SUBARRATIONS
STRUTHIOIDS	STUPEFACIENTS	STYPTICITIES	SUBARRHATION
STRUTHIOUS	STUPEFACTION	STYPTICITY	SUBARRHATIONS
STRUTTINGLY	STUPEFACTIONS	STYRACACEOUS	SUBARTICLE
STRUTTINGS	STUPEFACTIVE	STYROFOAMS	SUBARTICLES
STRYCHNIAS	STUPEFIERS	SUABILITIES	SUBASSEMBLE
STRYCHNINE	STUPEFYING	SUASIVENESS	SUBASSEMBLED
STRYCHNINED	STUPEFYINGLY	SUASIVENESSES	SUBASSEMBLES
STRYCHNINES	STUPENDIOUS	SUAVENESSES	SUBASSEMBLIES
STRYCHNINING	STUPENDOUS	SUAVEOLENT	SUBASSEMBLING
STRYCHNINISM	STUPENDOUSLY	SUBABDOMINAL	SUBASSEMBLY
STRYCHNINISMS	STUPENDOUSNESS	SUBACETATE	SUBASSOCIATION
STRYCHNISM	STUPIDITIES	SUBACETATES	SUBASSOCIATIONS
STRYCHNISMS	STUPIDNESS	SUBACIDITIES	SUBATMOSPHERIC
STUBBINESS	STUPIDNESSES	SUBACIDITY	SUBATOMICS
STUBBINESSES	STUPRATING	SUBACIDNESS	SUBAUDIBLE
STUBBLIEST	STUPRATION	SUBACIDNESSES	SUBAUDITION
STUBBORNED	STUPRATIONS	SUBACTIONS	SUBAUDITIONS
STUBBORNER	STURDINESS	SUBACUTELY	SUBAURICULAR
STUBBORNEST	STURDINESSES	SUBADOLESCENT	SUBAVERAGE
STUBBORNING	STUTTERERS	SUBADOLESCENTS	SUBAXILLARY
STUBBORNLY	STUTTERING	SUBAERIALLY	SUBBASEMENT
STUBBORNNESS	STUTTERINGLY	SUBAFFLUENT	SUBBASEMENTS
STUBBORNNESSES	STUTTERINGS	SUBAGENCIES	SUBBITUMINOUS
STUCCOWORK	STYLEBOOKS	SUBAGGREGATE	SUBBRANCHES
STUCCOWORKS	STYLELESSNESS	SUBAGGREGATES	SUBBUREAUS
STUDDINGSAIL	STYLELESSNESSES	SUBAGGREGATION	SUBBUREAUX
STUDDINGSAILS	STYLIFEROUS	SUBAGGREGATIONS	SUBCABINET
STUDENTRIES	STYLISATION	SUBAHDARIES	SUBCABINETS
STUDENTSHIP	STYLISATIONS	SUBAHSHIPS	SUBCALIBER
STUDENTSHIPS	STYLISHNESS	SUBALLIANCE	SUBCALIBRE
STUDFISHES	STYLISHNESSES	SUBALLIANCES	SUBCANTORS
STUDHORSES	STYLISTICALLY	SUBALLOCATION	SUBCAPSULAR
STUDIEDNESS	STYLISTICS	SUBALLOCATIONS	SUBCARDINAL
STUDIEDNESSES	STYLITISMS	SUBALTERNANT	SUBCARDINALS
STUDIOUSLY	STYLIZATION	SUBALTERNANTS	SUBCARRIER
STUDIOUSNESS	STYLIZATIONS	SUBALTERNATE	SUBCARRIERS
STUDIOUSNESSES	STYLOBATES	SUBALTERNATES	SUBCATEGORIES
STUFFINESS	STYLOGRAPH	SUBALTERNATION	SUBCATEGORISE
STUFFINESSES	STYLOGRAPHIC	SUBALTERNATIONS	SUBCATEGORISED
STULTIFICATION	STYLOGRAPHICAL	SUBALTERNITIES	SUBCATEGORISES
STULTIFICATIONS	STYLOGRAPHIES	SUBALTERNITY	SUBCATEGORISING
STULTIFIED	STYLOGRAPHS	SUBALTERNS	SUBCATEGORIZE
STULTIFIER	STYLOGRAPHY	SUBANGULAR	SUBCATEGORIZED
STULTIFIERS	STYLOLITES	SUBANTARCTIC	SUBCATEGORIZES
STULTIFIES	STYLOLITIC	SUBAPOSTOLIC	SUBCATEGORIZING
STULTIFYING	STYLOMETRIES	SUBAPPEARANCE	SUBCATEGORY
STUMBLEBUM	STYLOMETRY	SUBAPPEARANCES	SUBCAVITIES
STUMBLEBUMS	STYLOPHONE	SUBAQUATIC	SUBCEILING

SUBCEILINGS	SUBCOMPACTS	SUBDELIRIA	SUBERIZATION
SUBCELESTIAL	SUBCOMPONENT	SUBDELIRIOUS	SUBERIZATIONS
SUBCELESTIALS	SUBCOMPONENTS	SUBDELIRTUM	SUBERIZING
SUBCELLARS	SUBCONSCIOUS	SUBDELIRIUMS	SUBFACTORIAL
SUBCELLULAR	SUBCONSCIOUSES	SUBDEPARTMENT	SUBFACTORIALS
SUBCENTERS	SUBCONSCIOUSLY	SUBDEPARTMENTS	SUBFAMILIES
SUBCENTRAL	SUBCONSULS	SUBDEPUTIES	SUBFERTILE
SUBCENTRALLY	SUBCONTIGUOUS	SUBDERMALLY	SUBFERTILITIES
SUBCEPTION	SUBCONTINENT	SUBDEVELOPMENT	SUBFERTILITY
SUBCEPTIONS	SUBCONTINENTAL	SUBDEVELOPMENTS	SUBFEUDATION
SUBCHANTER	SUBCONTINENTS	SUBDIACONAL	SUBFEUDATIONS
SUBCHANTERS	SUBCONTINUOUS	SUBDIACONATE	SUBFEUDATORY
SUBCHAPTER	SUBCONTRACT	SUBDIACONATES	SUBFOSSILS
SUBCHAPTERS	SUBCONTRACTED	SUBDIALECT	SUBFREEZING
SUBCHARTER	SUBCONTRACTING	SUBDIALECTS	SUBFUSCOUS
SUBCHARTERS	SUBCONTRACTINGS	SUBDIRECTOR	SUBGENERATION
SUBCHASERS	SUBCONTRACTOR	SUBDIRECTORS	SUBGENERATIONS
SUBCHELATE	SUBCONTRACTORS	SUBDISCIPLINE	SUBGENERIC
SUBCHLORIDE	SUBCONTRACTS	SUBDISCIPLINES	SUBGENERICALLY
SUBCHLORIDES	SUBCONTRAOCTAVE	SUBDISTRICT	SUBGENUSES
SUBCIRCUIT	SUBCONTRARIES	SUBDISTRICTS	SUBGLACIAL
SUBCIRCUITS	SUBCONTRARIETY	SUBDIVIDABLE	SUBGLACIALLY
SUBCIVILISATION	SUBCONTRARY	SUBDIVIDED	SUBGLOBOSE
SUBCIVILISED	SUBCOOLING	SUBDIVIDER	SUBGLOBULAR
SUBCIVILIZATION	SUBCORDATE	SUBDIVIDERS	SUBGOVERNMENT
SUBCIVILIZED	SUBCORIACEOUS	SUBDIVIDES	SUBGOVERNMENTS
SUBCLASSED	SUBCORTEXES	SUBDIVIDING	SUBGROUPED
SUBCLASSES	SUBCORTICAL	SUBDIVISIBLE	SUBGROUPING
SUBCLASSIFIED	SUBCORTICES	SUBDIVISION	SUBHARMONIC
SUBCLASSIFIES	SUBCOSTALS	SUBDIVISIONAL	SUBHARMONICS
SUBCLASSIFY	SUBCOUNTIES	SUBDIVISIONS	SUBHASTATION
SUBCLASSIFYING	SUBCRANIAL	SUBDIVISIVE	SUBHASTATIONS
SUBCLASSING	SUBCRITICAL	SUBDOMINANT	SUBHEADING
SUBCLAUSES	SUBCRUSTAL	SUBDOMINANTS	SUBHEADINGS
SUBCLAVIAN	SUBCULTURAL	SUBDUCTING	SUBIMAGINAL
SUBCLAVIANS	SUBCULTURALLY	SUBDUCTION	SUBIMAGINES
SUBCLAVICULAR	SUBCULTURE	SUBDUCTIONS	SUBIMAGOES
SUBCLIMACTIC	SUBCULTURED	SUBDUEDNESS	SUBINCISED
SUBCLIMAXES	SUBCULTURES	SUBDUEDNESSES	SUBINCISES
SUBCLINICAL	SUBCULTURING	SUBDUEMENT	SUBINCISING
SUBCLINICALLY	SUBCURATIVE	SUBDUEMENTS	SUBINCISION
SUBCLUSTER	SUBCUTANEOUS	SUBDUPLICATE	SUBINCISIONS
SUBCLUSTERED	SUBCUTANEOUSLY	SUBECONOMIC	SUBINDEXES
SUBCLUSTERING	SUBCUTISES	SUBECONOMIES	SUBINDICATE
SUBCLUSTERS	SUBDEACONATE	SUBECONOMY	SUBINDICATED
SUBCOLLECTION	SUBDEACONATES	SUBEDITING	SUBINDICATES
SUBCOLLECTIONS	SUBDEACONRIES	SUBEDITORIAL	SUBINDICATING
SUBCOLLEGE	SUBDEACONRY	SUBEDITORS	SUBINDICATION
SUBCOLLEGIATE	SUBDEACONS	SUBEDITORSHIP	SUBINDICATIONS
SUBCOLONIES	SUBDEACONSHIP	SUBEDITORSHIPS	SUBINDICATIVE
SUBCOMMISSION	SUBDEACONSHIPS	SUBEMPLOYED	SUBINDICES
SUBCOMMISSIONED	SUBDEALERS	SUBEMPLOYMENT	SUBINDUSTRIES
SUBCOMMISSIONER	SUBDEANERIES	SUBEMPLOYMENTS	SUBINDUSTRY
SUBCOMMISSIONS	SUBDEANERY	SUBENTRIES	SUBINFEUDATE
SUBCOMMITTEE	SUBDEBUTANTE	SUBEPIDERMAL	SUBINFEUDATED
SUBCOMMITTEES	SUBDEBUTANTES	SUBEQUATORIAL	SUBINFEUDATES
SUBCOMMUNITIES	SUBDECANAL	SUBERISATION	SUBINFEUDATING
SUBCOMMUNITY	SUBDECISION	SUBERISATIONS	SUBINFEUDATION
SUBCOMPACT	SUBDECISIONS	SUBERISING	SUBINFEUDATIONS

SUBINFEUDATORY	SUBJECTIVIZES	SUBLIMISES	SUBMICRONS
SUBINFEUDED	SUBJECTIVIZING	SUBLIMISING	SUBMICROSCOPIC
SUBINFEUDING	SUBJECTLESS	SUBLIMITIES	SUBMILLIMETER
SUBINFEUDS	SUBJECTSHIP	SUBLIMIZED	SUBMINIATURE
SUBINHIBITORY	SUBJECTSHIPS	SUBLIMIZES	SUBMINIATURES
SUBINSINUATION	SUBJOINDER	SUBLIMIZING	SUBMINIATURISE
SUBINSINUATIONS	SUBJOINDERS	SUBLINEATION	SUBMINIATURISED
SUBINSPECTOR	SUBJOINING	SUBLINEATIONS	SUBMINIATURISES
SUBINSPECTORS	SUBJUGABLE	SUBLINGUAL	SUBMINIATURIZE
SUBINTELLECTION	SUBJUGATED	SUBLITERACIES	SUBMINIATURIZED
SUBINTELLIGENCE	SUBJUGATES	SUBLITERACY	SUBMINIATURIZES
SUBINTELLIGITUR	SUBJUGATING	SUBLITERARY	SUBMINIMAL
SUBINTERVAL	SUBJUGATION	SUBLITERATE	SUBMINISTER
SUBINTERVALS	SUBJUGATIONS	SUBLITERATES	SUBMINISTERS
SUBINTRANT	SUBJUGATOR	SUBLITERATURE	SUBMISSIBLE
SUBINTRODUCE	SUBJUGATORS	SUBLITERATURES	SUBMISSION
SUBINTRODUCED	SUBJUNCTION	SUBLITTORAL	SUBMISSIONS
SUBINTRODUCES	SUBJUNCTIONS	SUBLITTORALS	SUBMISSIVE
SUBINTRODUCING	SUBJUNCTIVE	SUBLUXATED	SUBMISSIVELY
SUBINVOLUTION	SUBJUNCTIVELY	SUBLUXATES	SUBMISSIVENESS
SUBINVOLUTIONS	SUBJUNCTIVES	SUBLUXATING	SUBMISSNESS
SUBIRRIGATE	SUBKINGDOM	SUBLUXATION	SUBMISSNESSES
SUBIRRIGATED	SUBKINGDOMS	SUBLUXATIONS	SUBMITTABLE
SUBIRRIGATES	SUBLANCEOLATE	SUBMANAGER	SUBMITTALS
SUBIRRIGATING	SUBLANGUAGE	SUBMANAGERS	SUBMITTERS
SUBIRRIGATION	SUBLANGUAGES	SUBMANDIBULAR	SUBMITTING
SUBIRRIGATIONS	SUBLAPSARIAN	SUBMANDIBULARS	SUBMITTINGS
SUBITANEOUS	SUBLAPSARIANISM	SUBMARGINAL	SUBMOLECULE
SUBITISING	SUBLAPSARIANS	SUBMARGINALLY	SUBMOLECULES
SUBITIZING	SUBLATIONS	SUBMARINED	SUBMONTANE
SUBJACENCIES	SUBLEASING	SUBMARINER	SUBMONTANELY
SUBJACENCY	SUBLESSEES	SUBMARINERS	SUBMUCOSAE
SUBJACENTLY	SUBLESSORS	SUBMARINES	SUBMUCOSAL
SUBJECTABILITY	SUBLETHALLY	SUBMARINING	SUBMUCOSAS
SUBJECTABLE	SUBLETTERS	SUBMARKETS	SUBMULTIPLE
SUBJECTIFIED	SUBLETTING	SUBMATRICES	SUBMULTIPLES
SUBJECTIFIES	SUBLETTINGS	SUBMATRIXES	SUBMUNITION
SUBJECTIFY	SUBLIBRARIAN	SUBMAXILLARIES	SUBMUNITIONS
SUBJECTIFYING	SUBLIBRARIANS	SUBMAXILLARY	SUBNASCENT
SUBJECTING	SUBLICENSE	SUBMAXIMAL	SUBNATIONAL
SUBJECTION	SUBLICENSED	SUBMEDIANT	SUBNATURAL
SUBJECTIONS	SUBLICENSES	SUBMEDIANTS	SUBNETWORK
SUBJECTIVE	SUBLICENSING	SUBMERGEMENT	SUBNETWORKED
SUBJECTIVELY	SUBLIEUTENANCY	SUBMERGEMENTS	SUBNETWORKING
SUBJECTIVENESS	SUBLIEUTENANT	SUBMERGENCE	SUBNETWORKS
SUBJECTIVES	SUBLIEUTENANTS	SUBMERGENCES	SUBNORMALITIES
SUBJECTIVISE	SUBLIMABLE	SUBMERGIBILITY	SUBNORMALITY
SUBJECTIVISED	SUBLIMATED	SUBMERGIBLE	SUBNORMALLY
SUBJECTIVISES	SUBLIMATES	SUBMERGIBLES	SUBNORMALS
SUBJECTIVISING	SUBLIMATING	SUBMERGING	SUBNUCLEAR
SUBJECTIVISM	SUBLIMATION	SUBMERSIBILITY	SUBNUCLEUS
SUBJECTIVISMS	SUBLIMATIONS	SUBMERSIBLE	SUBNUCLEUSES
SUBJECTIVIST	SUBLIMENESS	SUBMERSIBLES	SUBOCCIPITAL
SUBJECTIVISTIC	SUBLIMENESSES	SUBMERSING	SUBOCEANIC
SUBJECTIVISTS	SUBLIMINAL	SUBMERSION	SUBOCTAVES
SUBJECTIVITIES	SUBLIMINALLY	SUBMERSIONS	SUBOCTUPLE
SUBJECTIVITY	SUBLIMINALS	SUBMETACENTRIC	SUBOFFICER
SUBJECTIVIZE	SUBLIMINGS	SUBMETACENTRICS	SUBOFFICERS
SUBJECTIVIZED	SUBLIMISED	SUBMICROGRAM	SUBOFFICES

SUBOPERCULA	SUBPRINCIPAL	SUBSECRETARY	SUBSISTERS
SUBOPERCULAR	SUBPRINCIPALS	SUBSECTION	SUBSISTING
SUBOPERCULUM	SUBPRIORESS	SUBSECTIONS	SUBSOCIALLY
SUBOPTIMAL	SUBPRIORESSES	SUBSECTORS	SUBSOCIETIES
SUBOPTIMISATION	SUBPROBLEM	SUBSEGMENT	SUBSOCIETY
SUBOPTIMISE	SUBPROBLEMS	SUBSEGMENTS	SUBSOILERS
SUBOPTIMISED	SUBPROCESS	SUBSEIZURE	SUBSOILING
SUBOPTIMISES	SUBPROCESSES	SUBSEIZURES	SUBSOILINGS
SUBOPTIMISING	SUBPRODUCT	SUBSELLIUM	SUBSONICALLY
SUBOPTIMIZATION	SUBPRODUCTS	SUBSENSIBLE	SUBSPECIALISE
SUBOPTIMIZE	SUBPROFESSIONAL	SUBSENTENCE	SUBSPECIALISED
SUBOPTIMIZED	SUBPROGRAM	SUBSENTENCES	SUBSPECIALISES
SUBOPTIMIZES	SUBPROGRAMS	SUBSEQUENCE	SUBSPECIALISING
SUBOPTIMIZING	SUBPROJECT	SUBSEQUENCES	SUBSPECIALIST
SUBOPTIMUM	SUBPROJECTS	SUBSEQUENT	SUBSPECIALISTS
SUBORBICULAR	SUBPROLETARIAT	SUBSEQUENTIAL	SUBSPECIALITIES
SUBORBITAL	SUBPROLETARIATS	SUBSEQUENTLY	SUBSPECIALITY
SUBORDINAL	SUBRATIONAL	SUBSEQUENTNESS	SUBSPECIALIZE
SUBORDINANCIES	SUBREFERENCE	SUBSEQUENTS	SUBSPECIALIZED
SUBORDINANCY	SUBREFERENCES	SUBSERVIENCE	SUBSPECIALIZES
SUBORDINARIES	SUBREGIONAL	SUBSERVIENCES	SUBSPECIALIZING
SUBORDINARY	SUBREGIONS	SUBSERVIENCIES	SUBSPECIALTIES
SUBORDINATE	SUBREPTION	SUBSERVIENCY	SUBSPECIALTY
SUBORDINATED	SUBREPTIONS	SUBSERVIENT	SUBSPECIES
SUBORDINATELY	SUBREPTITIOUS	SUBSERVIENTLY	SUBSPECIFIC
SUBORDINATENESS	SUBREPTITIOUSLY	SUBSERVIENTS	SUBSPECIFICALLY
SUBORDINATES	SUBREPTIVE	SUBSERVING	SUBSPINOUS
SUBORDINATING	SUBROGATED	SUBSESSILE	SUBSPONTANEOUS
SUBORDINATION	SUBROGATES	SUBSHRUBBY	SUBSTANCELESS
SUBORDINATIONS	SUBROGATING	SUBSIDENCE	SUBSTANCES
SUBORDINATIVE	SUBROGATION	SUBSIDENCES	SUBSTANDARD
SUBORDINATOR	SUBROGATIONS	SUBSIDENCIES	SUBSTANTIAL
SUBORDINATORS	SUBROUTINE	SUBSIDENCY	SUBSTANTIALISE
SUBORGANISATION	SUBROUTINES	SUBSIDIARIES	SUBSTANTIALISED
SUBORGANIZATION	SUBSAMPLED	SUBSIDIARILY	SUBSTANTIALISES
SUBORNATION	SUBSAMPLES	SUBSIDIARINESS	SUBSTANTIALISM
SUBORNATIONS	SUBSAMPLING	SUBSIDIARITIES	SUBSTANTIALISMS
SUBORNATIVE	SUBSATELLITE	SUBSIDIARITY	SUBSTANTIALIST
SUBOSCINES	SUBSATELLITES	SUBSIDIARY	SUBSTANTIALISTS
SUBPANATION	SUBSATURATED	SUBSIDISABLE	SUBSTANTIALITY
SUBPANATIONS	SUBSATURATION	SUBSIDISATION	SUBSTANTIALIZE
SUBPARAGRAPH	SUBSATURATIONS	SUBSIDISATIONS	SUBSTANTIALIZED
SUBPARAGRAPHS	SUBSCAPULAR	SUBSIDISED	SUBSTANTIALIZES
SUBPARALLEL	SUBSCAPULARS	SUBSIDISER	SUBSTANTIALLY
SUBPENAING	SUBSCHEMATA	SUBSIDISERS	SUBSTANTIALNESS
SUBPERIODS	SUBSCIENCE	SUBSIDISES	SUBSTANTIALS
SUBPHRENIC	SUBSCIENCES	SUBSIDISING	SUBSTANTIATE
SUBPOENAED	SUBSCRIBABLE	SUBSIDIZABLE	SUBSTANTIATED
SUBPOENAING	SUBSCRIBED	SUBSIDIZATION	SUBSTANTIATES
SUBPOPULATION	SUBSCRIBER	SUBSIDIZATIONS	SUBSTANTIATING
SUBPOPULATIONS	SUBSCRIBERS	SUBSIDIZED	SUBSTANTIATION
SUBPOTENCIES	SUBSCRIBES	SUBSIDIZER	SUBSTANTIATIONS
SUBPOTENCY	SUBSCRIBING	SUBSIDIZERS	SUBSTANTIATIVE
SUBPREFECT	SUBSCRIBINGS	SUBSIDIZES	SUBSTANTIATOR
SUBPREFECTS	SUBSCRIPTION	SUBSIDIZING	SUBSTANTIATORS
SUBPREFECTURE	SUBSCRIPTIONS	SUBSISTENCE	SUBSTANTIVAL
SUBPREFECTURES	SUBSCRIPTIVE	SUBSISTENCES	SUBSTANTIVALLY
SUBPRIMATE	SUBSCRIPTS	SUBSISTENT	SUBSTANTIVE
SUBPRIMATES	SUBSECRETARIES	SUBSISTENTIAL	SUBSTANTIVELY

SUBSTANTIVENESS
SUBSTANTIVES
SUBSTANTIVISE
SUBSTANTIVISED
SUBSTANTIVISES
SUBSTANTIVISING
SUBSTANTIVITIES
SUBSTANTIVITY
SUBSTANTIVIZE
SUBSTANTIVIZED
SUBSTANTIVIZES
SUBSTANTIVIZING
SUBSTATION
SUBSTATIONS
SUBSTELLAR
SUBSTERNAL
SUBSTITUENT
SUBSTITUENTS
SUBSTITUTABLE
SUBSTITUTE
SUBSTITUTED
SUBSTITUTES
SUBSTITUTING
SUBSTITUTION
SUBSTITUTIONAL
SUBSTITUTIONARY
SUBSTITUTIONS
SUBSTITUTIVE
SUBSTITUTIVELY
SUBSTITUTIVITY
SUBSTRACTED
SUBSTRACTING
SUBSTRACTION
SUBSTRACTIONS
SUBSTRACTOR
SUBSTRACTORS
SUBSTRACTS
SUBSTRATAL
SUBSTRATES
SUBSTRATIVE
SUBSTRATOSPHERE
SUBSTRATUM
SUBSTRATUMS
SUBSTRUCTED
SUBSTRUCTING
SUBSTRUCTION
SUBSTRUCTIONS
SUBSTRUCTS
SUBSTRUCTURAL
SUBSTRUCTURE
SUBSTRUCTURES
SUBSULTIVE
SUBSULTORILY
SUBSULTORY
SUBSULTUSES
SUBSUMABLE
SUBSUMPTION
SUBSUMPTIONS
SUBSUMPTIVE

SUBSURFACE
SUBSURFACES
SUBSYSTEMS
SUBTACKSMAN
SUBTACKSMEN
SUBTANGENT
SUBTANGENTS
SUBTEMPERATE
SUBTENANCIES
SUBTENANCY
SUBTENANTS
SUBTENDING
SUBTENURES
SUBTERFUGE
SUBTERFUGES
SUBTERMINAL
SUBTERNATURAL
SUBTERRAIN
SUBTERRAINS
SUBTERRANE
SUBTERRANEAN
SUBTERRANEANLY
SUBTERRANEANS
SUBTERRANEOUS
SUBTERRANEOUSLY
SUBTERRANES
SUBTERRENE
SUBTERRENES
SUBTERRESTRIAL
SUBTERRESTRIALS
SUBTEXTUAL
SUBTHERAPEUTIC
SUBTHRESHOLD
SUBTILENESS
SUBTILENESSES
SUBTILISATION
SUBTILISATIONS
SUBTILISED
SUBTILISER
SUBTILISERS
SUBTILISES
SUBTILISIN
SUBTILISING
SUBTILISINS
SUBTILITIES
SUBTILIZATION
SUBTILIZATIONS
SUBTILIZED
SUBTILIZER
SUBTILIZERS
SUBTILIZES
SUBTILIZING
SUBTILTIES
SUBTITLING
SUBTITULAR
SUBTLENESS
SUBTLENESSES
SUBTLETIES
SUBTOTALED

SUBTOTALING
SUBTOTALLED
SUBTOTALLING
SUBTOTALLY
SUBTRACTED
SUBTRACTER
SUBTRACTERS
SUBTRACTING
SUBTRACTION
SUBTRACTIONS
SUBTRACTIVE
SUBTRACTOR
SUBTRACTORS
SUBTRAHEND
SUBTRAHENDS
SUBTREASURER
SUBTREASURERS
SUBTREASURIES
SUBTREASURY
SUBTRIANGULAR
SUBTRIPLICATE
SUBTROPICAL
SUBTROPICALLY
SUBTROPICS
SUBTRUDING
SUBTYPICAL
SUBUMBRELLA
SUBUMBRELLAR
SUBUMBRELLAS
SUBUNGULATE
SUBUNGULATES
SUBURBANISATION
SUBURBANISE
SUBURBANISED
SUBURBANISES
SUBURBANISING
SUBURBANISM
SUBURBANISMS
SUBURBANITE
SUBURBANITES
SUBURBANITIES
SUBURBANITY
SUBURBANIZATION
SUBURBANIZE
SUBURBANIZED
SUBURBANIZES
SUBURBANIZING
SUBURBICARIAN
SUBVARIETIES
SUBVARIETY
SUBVASSALS
SUBVENTION
SUBVENTIONARY
SUBVENTIONS
SUBVERSALS
SUBVERSING
SUBVERSION
SUBVERSIONARIES
SUBVERSIONARY

SUBVERSIONS
SUBVERSIVE
SUBVERSIVELY
SUBVERSIVENESS
SUBVERSIVES
SUBVERTEBRAL
SUBVERTERS
SUBVERTICAL
SUBVERTING
SUBVIRUSES
SUBVISIBLE
SUBVITREOUS
SUBVOCALISATION
SUBVOCALISE
SUBVOCALISED
SUBVOCALISES
SUBVOCALISING
SUBVOCALIZATION
SUBVOCALIZE
SUBVOCALIZED
SUBVOCALIZES
SUBVOCALIZING
SUBVOCALLY
SUBWARDENS
SUBWOOFERS
SUBWRITERS
SUCCEDANEA
SUCCEDANEOUS
SUCCEDANEUM
SUCCEDANEUMS
SUCCEEDABLE
SUCCEEDERS
SUCCEEDING
SUCCEEDINGLY
SUCCENTORS
SUCCENTORSHIP
SUCCENTORSHIPS
SUCCESSANTLY
SUCCESSFUL
SUCCESSFULLY
SUCCESSFULNESS
SUCCESSION
SUCCESSIONAL
SUCCESSIONALLY
SUCCESSIONIST
SUCCESSIONISTS
SUCCESSIONLESS
SUCCESSIONS
SUCCESSIVE
SUCCESSIVELY
SUCCESSIVENESS
SUCCESSLESS
SUCCESSLESSLY
SUCCESSLESSNESS
SUCCESSORAL
SUCCESSORS
SUCCESSORSHIP
SUCCESSORSHIPS
SUCCINATES

SUCCINCTER	SUFFERANCE	SUGARCOATS	SULFATASES
SUCCINCTEST	SUFFERANCES	SUGARHOUSE	SULFATHIAZOLE
SUCCINCTLY	SUFFERINGLY	SUGARHOUSES	SULFATHIAZOLES
SUCCINCTNESS	SUFFERINGS	SUGARINESS	SULFATIONS
SUCCINCTNESSES	SUFFICIENCE	SUGARINESSES	SULFHYDRYL
SUCCINCTORIA	SUFFICIENCES	SUGARLOAVES	SULFHYDRYLS
SUCCINCTORIES	SUFFICIENCIES	SUGARPLUMS	SULFINPYRAZONE
SUCCINCTORIUM	SUFFICIENCY	SUGGESTERS	SULFINPYRAZONES
SUCCINCTORY	SUFFICIENT	SUGGESTIBILITY	SULFONAMIDE
SUCCINITES	SUFFICIENTLY	SUGGESTIBLE	SULFONAMIDES
SUCCINYLCHOLINE	SUFFICIENTS	SUGGESTIBLENESS	SULFONATED
SUCCORABLE	SUFFICINGNESS	SUGGESTIBLY	SULFONATES
SUCCORLESS	SUFFICINGNESSES	SUGGESTING	SULFONATING
SUCCOTASHES	SUFFIGANCE	SUGGESTION	SULFONATION
SUCCOURABLE	SUFFIGANCES	SUGGESTIONISE	SULFONATIONS
SUCCOURERS	SUFFISANCE	SUGGESTIONISED	SULFONIUMS
SUCCOURING	SUFFISANCES	SUGGESTIONISES	SULFONYLUREA
SUCCOURLESS	SUFFIXATION	SUGGESTIONISING	SULFONYLUREAS
SUCCUBUSES	SUFFIXATIONS	SUGGESTIONISM	SULFOXIDES
SUCCULENCE	SUFFIXIONS	SUGGESTIONISMS	SULFURATED
SUCCULENCES	SUFFLATING	SUGGESTIONIST	SULFURATES
SUCCULENCIES	SUFFLATION	SUGGESTIONISTS	SULFURATING
SUCCULENCY	SUFFLATIONS	SUGGESTIONIZE	SULFURETED
SUCCULENTLY	SUFFOCATED	SUGGESTIONIZED	SULFURETING
SUCCULENTS	SUFFOCATES	SUGGESTIONIZES	SULFURETTED
SUCCUMBERS	SUFFOCATING	SUGGESTIONIZING	SULFURETTING
SUCCUMBING	SUFFOCATINGLY	SUGGESTIONS	SULFURISATION
SUCCURSALE	SUFFOCATINGS	SUGGESTIVE	SULFURISATIONS
SUCCURSALES	SUFFOCATION	SUGGESTIVELY	SULFURISED
SUCCURSALS	SUFFOCATIONS	SUGGESTIVENESS	SULFURISES
SUCCUSSATION	SUFFOCATIVE	SUICIDALLY	SULFURISING
SUCCUSSATIONS	SUFFRAGANS	SUICIDOLOGIES	SULFURIZED
SUCCUSSING	SUFFRAGANSHIP	SUICIDOLOGIST	SULFURIZES
SUCCUSSION	SUFFRAGANSHIPS	SUICIDOLOGISTS	SULFURIZING
SUCCUSSIONS	SUFFRAGETTE	SUICIDOLOGY	SULFUROUSLY
SUCCUSSIVE	SUFFRAGETTES	SUITABILITIES	SULFUROUSNESS
SUCHNESSES	SUFFRAGETTISM	SUITABILITY	SULFUROUSNESSES
SUCKERFISH	SUFFRAGETTISMS	SUITABLENESS	SULKINESSES
SUCKERFISHES	SUFFRAGISM	SUITABLENESSES	SULLENNESS
SUCKFISHES	SUFFRAGISMS	SUITRESSES	SULLENNESSES
SUCRALFATE	SUFFRAGIST	SULCALISED	SULPHACETAMIDE
SUCRALFATES	SUFFRAGISTS	SULCALISES	SULPHACETAMIDES
SUCRALOSES	SUFFRUTESCENT	SULCALISING	SULPHADIAZINE
SUCTIONING	SUFFRUTICOSE	SULCALIZED	SULPHADIAZINES
SUCTORIANS	SUFFUMIGATE	SULCALIZES	SULPHANILAMIDE
SUDATORIES	SUFFUMIGATED	SULCALIZING	SULPHANILAMIDES
SUDATORIUM	SUFFUMIGATES	SULCATIONS	SULPHATASE
SUDATORIUMS	SUFFUMIGATING	SULFACETAMIDE	SULPHATASES
SUDDENNESS	SUFFUMIGATION	SULFACETAMIDES	SULPHATHIAZOLE
SUDDENNESSES	SUFFUMIGATIONS	SULFADIAZINE	SULPHATHIAZOLES
SUDDENTIES	SUFFUSIONS	SULFADIAZINES	SULPHATING
SUDORIFEROUS	SUGARALLIE	SULFADIMIDINE	SULPHATION
SUDORIFICS	SUGARALLIES	SULFADIMIDINES	SULPHATIONS
SUDORIPAROUS	SUGARBERRIES	SULFADOXINE	SULPHHYDRYL
SUEABILITIES	SUGARBERRY	SULFADOXINES	SULPHHYDRYLS
SUEABILITY	SUGARBUSHES	SULFAMETHAZINE	SULPHINPYRAZONE
SUFFERABLE	SUGARCANES	SULFAMETHAZINES	SULPHINYLS
SUFFERABLENESS	SUGARCOATED	SULFANILAMIDE	SULPHONAMIDE
SUFFERABLY	SUGARCOATING	SULFANILAMIDES	SULPHONAMIDES

SULPHONATE	SUMMARISATION	SUNBONNETS	SUPERAGENT
SULPHONATED	SUMMARISATIONS	SUNBURNING	SUPERAGENTS
SULPHONATES	SUMMARISED	SUNDERABLE	SUPERALLOY
SULPHONATING	SUMMARISER	SUNDERANCE	SUPERALLOYS
SULPHONATION	SUMMARISERS	SUNDERANCES	SUPERALTAR
SULPHONATIONS	SUMMARISES	SUNDERINGS	SUPERALTARS
SULPHONIUM	SUMMARISING	SUNDERMENT	SUPERALTERN
SULPHONIUMS	SUMMARISTS	SUNDERMENTS	SUPERALTERNS
SULPHONMETHANE	SUMMARIZABLE	SUNDOWNERS	SUPERAMBITIOUS
SULPHONMETHANES	SUMMARIZATION	SUNDOWNING	SUPERANNUABLE
SULPHONYLS	SUMMARIZATIONS	SUNDRENCHED	SUPERANNUATE
SULPHONYLUREA	SUMMARIZED	SUNDRESSES	SUPERANNUATED
SULPHONYLUREAS	SUMMARIZER	SUNFLOWERS	SUPERANNUATES
SULPHURATE	SUMMARIZERS	SUNGLASSES	SUPERANNUATING
SULPHURATED	SUMMARIZES	SUNLESSNESS	SUPERANNUATION
SULPHURATES	SUMMARIZING	SUNLESSNESSES	SUPERANNUATIONS
SULPHURATING	SUMMATIONAL	SUNLOUNGER	SUPERATHLETE
SULPHURATION	SUMMATIONS	SUNLOUNGERS	SUPERATHLETES
SULPHURATIONS	SUMMERHOUSE	SUNNINESSES	SUPERATING
SULPHURATOR	SUMMERHOUSES	SUNPORCHES	SUPERATION
SULPHURATORS	SUMMERIEST	SUNRISINGS	SUPERATIONS
SULPHUREOUS	SUMMERINESS	SUNSCREENING	SUPERATOMS
SULPHUREOUSLY	SUMMERINESSES	SUNSCREENS	SUPERBANKS
SULPHUREOUSNESS	SUMMERINGS	SUNSEEKERS	SUPERBAZAAR
SULPHURETED	SUMMERLESS	SUNSETTING	SUPERBAZAARS
SULPHURETING	SUMMERLIKE	SUNSETTINGS	SUPERBAZAR
SULPHURETS	SUMMERLONG	SUNSPOTTED	SUPERBAZARS
SULPHURETTED	SUMMERSAULT	SUNSTROKES	SUPERBIKES
SULPHURETTING	SUMMERSAULTED	SUNTANNING	SUPERBITCH
SULPHURING	SUMMERSAULTING	SUNWORSHIPPER	SUPERBITCHES
SULPHURISATION	SUMMERSAULTS	SUNWORSHIPPERS	SUPERBITIES
SULPHURISATIONS	SUMMERSETS	SUOVETAURILIA	SUPERBLOCK
SULPHURISE	SUMMERSETTED	SUPERABILITIES	SUPERBLOCKS
SULPHURISED	SUMMERSETTING	SUPERABILITY	SUPERBNESS
SULPHURISES	SUMMERTIDE	SUPERABLENESS	SUPERBNESSES
SULPHURISING	SUMMERTIDES	SUPERABLENESSES	SUPERBOARD
SULPHURIZATION	SUMMERTIME	SUPERABOUND	SUPERBOARDS
SULPHURIZATIONS	SUMMERTIMES	SUPERABOUNDED	SUPERBOMBER
SULPHURIZE	SUMMERWEIGHT	SUPERABOUNDING	SUPERBOMBERS
SULPHURIZED	SUMMERWOOD	SUPERABOUNDS	SUPERBOMBS
SULPHURIZES	SUMMERWOODS	SUPERABSORBENT	SUPERBRAIN
SULPHURIZING	SUMMITEERS	SUPERABSORBENTS	SUPERBRAINS
SULPHUROUS	SUMMITLESS	SUPERABUNDANCE	SUPERBRATS
SULPHUROUSLY	SUMMITRIES	SUPERABUNDANCES	SUPERBRIGHT
SULPHUROUSNESS	SUMMONABLE	SUPERABUNDANT	SUPERBUREAUCRAT
SULPHURWORT	SUMMONSING	SUPERABUNDANTLY	SUPERCABINET
SULPHURWORTS	SUMPHISHNESS	SUPERACHIEVER	SUPERCABINETS
SULPHURYLS	SUMPHISHNESSES	SUPERACHIEVERS	SUPERCALENDER
SULTANATES	SUMPSIMUSES	SUPERACTIVE	SUPERCALENDERED
SULTANESSES	SUMPTUOSITIES	SUPERACTIVITIES	SUPERCALENDERS
SULTANSHIP	SUMPTUOSITY	SUPERACTIVITY	SUPERCARGO
SULTANSHIPS	SUMPTUOUSLY	SUPERACUTE	SUPERCARGOES
SULTRINESS	SUMPTUOUSNESS	SUPERADDED	SUPERCARGOS
SULTRINESSES	SUMPTUOUSNESSES	SUPERADDING	SUPERCARGOSHIP
SUMMABILITIES	SUNBATHERS	SUPERADDITION	SUPERCARGOSHIPS
SUMMABILITY	SUNBATHING	SUPERADDITIONAL	SUPERCARRIER
SUMMARINESS	SUNBATHINGS	SUPERADDITIONS	SUPERCARRIERS
SUMMARINESSES	SUNBERRIES	SUPERAGENCIES	SUPERCAUTIOUS
SUMMARISABLE	SUNBONNETED	SUPERAGENCY	SUPERCEDED

SUPERCEDES
SUPERCEDING
SUPERCELESTIAL
SUPERCENTER
SUPERCENTERS
SUPERCHARGE
SUPERCHARGED
SUPERCHARGER
SUPERCHARGERS
SUPERCHARGES
SUPERCHARGING
SUPERCHERIE
SUPERCHERIES
SUPERCHURCH
SUPERCHURCHES
SUPERCILIARIES
SUPERCILIARY
SUPERCILIOUS
SUPERCILIOUSLY
SUPERCITIES
SUPERCIVILISED
SUPERCIVILIZED
SUPERCLASS
SUPERCLASSES
SUPERCLEAN
SUPERCLUBS
SUPERCLUSTER
SUPERCLUSTERS
SUPERCOILED
SUPERCOILING
SUPERCOILS
SUPERCOLLIDER
SUPERCOLLIDERS
SUPERCOLOSSAL
SUPERCOLUMNAR
SUPERCOMPUTER
SUPERCOMPUTERS
SUPERCOMPUTING
SUPERCOMPUTINGS
SUPERCONDUCT
SUPERCONDUCTED
SUPERCONDUCTING
SUPERCONDUCTION
SUPERCONDUCTIVE
SUPERCONDUCTOR
SUPERCONDUCTORS
SUPERCONDUCTS
SUPERCONFIDENCE
SUPERCONFIDENT
SUPERCONTINENT
SUPERCONTINENTS
SUPERCONVENIENT
SUPERCOOLED
SUPERCOOLING
SUPERCOOLS
SUPERCRIMINAL
SUPERCRIMINALS
SUPERCRITICAL
SUPERCURRENT

SUPERCURRENTS
SUPERDAINTY
SUPERDELUXE
SUPERDENSE
SUPERDIPLOMAT
SUPERDIPLOMATS
SUPERDOMINANT
SUPERDOMINANTS
SUPEREFFECTIVE
SUPEREFFICIENCY
SUPEREFFICIENT
SUPEREGOIST
SUPEREGOISTS
SUPERELASTIC
SUPERELEVATE
SUPERELEVATED
SUPERELEVATES
SUPERELEVATING
SUPERELEVATION
SUPERELEVATIONS
SUPERELITE
SUPEREMINENCE
SUPEREMINENCES
SUPEREMINENT
SUPEREMINENTLY
SUPEREROGANT
SUPEREROGATE
SUPEREROGATED
SUPEREROGATES
SUPEREROGATING
SUPEREROGATION
SUPEREROGATIONS
SUPEREROGATIVE
SUPEREROGATOR
SUPEREROGATORS
SUPEREROGATORY
SUPERESSENTIAL
SUPERETTES
SUPEREVIDENT
SUPEREXALT
SUPEREXALTATION
SUPEREXALTED
SUPEREXALTING
SUPEREXALTS
SUPEREXCELLENCE
SUPEREXCELLENT
SUPEREXPENSIVE
SUPEREXPRESS
SUPEREXPRESSES
SUPERFAMILIES
SUPERFAMILY
SUPERFARMS
SUPERFATTED
SUPERFECTA
SUPERFECTAS
SUPERFEMALE
SUPERFEMALES
SUPERFETATE
SUPERFETATED

SUPERFETATES
SUPERFETATING
SUPERFETATION
SUPERFETATIONS
SUPERFICIAL
SUPERFICIALISE
SUPERFICIALISED
SUPERFICIALISES
SUPERFICIALITY
SUPERFICIALIZE
SUPERFICIALIZED
SUPERFICIALIZES
SUPERFICIALLY
SUPERFICIALNESS
SUPERFICIALS
SUPERFICIES
SUPERFINENESS
SUPERFINENESSES
SUPERFIRMS
SUPERFIXES
SUPERFLACK
SUPERFLACKS
SUPERFLUID
SUPERFLUIDITIES
SUPERFLUIDITY
SUPERFLUIDS
SUPERFLUITIES
SUPERFLUITY
SUPERFLUOUS
SUPERFLUOUSLY
SUPERFLUOUSNESS
SUPERFLUXES
SUPERFOETATION
SUPERFOETATIONS
SUPERFRONTAL
SUPERFRONTALS
SUPERFUNDS
SUPERFUSED
SUPERFUSES
SUPERFUSING
SUPERFUSION
SUPERFUSIONS
SUPERGENES
SUPERGIANT
SUPERGIANTS
SUPERGLACIAL
SUPERGLUED
SUPERGLUES
SUPERGLUING
SUPERGOVERNMENT
SUPERGRAPHICS
SUPERGRASS
SUPERGRASSES
SUPERGRAVITIES
SUPERGRAVITY
SUPERGROUP
SUPERGROUPS
SUPERGROWTH
SUPERGROWTHS

SUPERHARDEN
SUPERHARDENED
SUPERHARDENING
SUPERHARDENS
SUPERHEATED
SUPERHEATER
SUPERHEATERS
SUPERHEATING
SUPERHEATS
SUPERHEAVIES
SUPERHEAVY
SUPERHELICAL
SUPERHELICES
SUPERHELIX
SUPERHELIXES
SUPERHEROES
SUPERHEROINE
SUPERHEROINES
SUPERHETERODYNE
SUPERHIGHWAY
SUPERHIGHWAYS
SUPERHIVES
SUPERHUMAN
SUPERHUMANISE
SUPERHUMANISED
SUPERHUMANISES
SUPERHUMANISING
SUPERHUMANITIES
SUPERHUMANITY
SUPERHUMANIZE
SUPERHUMANIZED
SUPERHUMANIZES
SUPERHUMANIZING
SUPERHUMANLY
SUPERHUMANNESS
SUPERHUMERAL
SUPERHUMERALS
SUPERHYPED
SUPERHYPES
SUPERHYPING
SUPERIMPORTANT
SUPERIMPOSABLE
SUPERIMPOSE
SUPERIMPOSED
SUPERIMPOSES
SUPERIMPOSING
SUPERIMPOSITION
SUPERINCUMBENCE
SUPERINCUMBENCY
SUPERINCUMBENT
SUPERINDIVIDUAL
SUPERINDUCE
SUPERINDUCED
SUPERINDUCEMENT
SUPERINDUCES
SUPERINDUCING
SUPERINDUCTION
SUPERINDUCTIONS
SUPERINFECT

SUPERINFECTED	SUPERMEMBRANE	SUPERORDINATING	SUPERPRAISES
SUPERINFECTING	SUPERMEMBRANES	SUPERORDINATION	SUPERPRAISING
SUPERINFECTION	SUPERMICRO	SUPERORGANIC	SUPERPREMIUM
SUPERINFECTIONS	SUPERMICROS	SUPERORGANICISM	SUPERPREMIUMS
SUPERINFECTS	SUPERMILITANT	SUPERORGANICIST	SUPERPROFIT
SUPERINSULATED	SUPERMILITANTS	SUPERORGANISM	SUPERPROFITS
SUPERINTEND	SUPERMINDS	SUPERORGANISMS	SUPERQUALITY
SUPERINTENDED	SUPERMINIS	SUPERORGASM	SUPERRACES
SUPERINTENDENCE	SUPERMINISTER	SUPERORGASMS	SUPERREALISM
SUPERINTENDENCY	SUPERMINISTERS	SUPEROVULATE	SUPERREALISMS
SUPERINTENDENT	SUPERMODEL	SUPEROVULATED	SUPERREALIST
SUPERINTENDENTS	SUPERMODELS	SUPEROVULATES	SUPERREALISTS
SUPERINTENDING	SUPERMODERN	SUPEROVULATING	SUPERREFINE
SUPERINTENDS	SUPERMOTOS	SUPEROVULATION	SUPERREFINED
SUPERINTENSITY	SUPERMUNDANE	SUPEROVULATIONS	SUPERREFINES
SUPERIORESS	SUPERNACULA	SUPEROXIDE	SUPERREFINING
SUPERIORESSES	SUPERNACULAR	SUPEROXIDES	SUPERREGIONAL
SUPERIORITIES	SUPERNACULUM	SUPERPARASITISM	SUPERREGIONALS
SUPERIORITY	SUPERNALLY	SUPERPARTICLE	SUPERROADS
SUPERIORLY	SUPERNATANT	SUPERPARTICLES	SUPERROMANTIC
SUPERIORSHIP	SUPERNATANTS	SUPERPATRIOT	SUPERSAFETIES
SUPERIORSHIPS	SUPERNATATION	SUPERPATRIOTIC	SUPERSAFETY
SUPERJACENT	SUPERNATATIONS	SUPERPATRIOTISM	SUPERSALES
SUPERJOCKS	SUPERNATES	SUPERPATRIOTS	SUPERSALESMAN
SUPERJUMBO	SUPERNATION	SUPERPERSON	SUPERSALESMEN
SUPERJUMBOS	SUPERNATIONAL	SUPERPERSONAL	SUPERSALTS
SUPERKINGDOM	SUPERNATIONALLY	SUPERPERSONS	SUPERSATURATE
SUPERKINGDOMS	SUPERNATIONS	SUPERPHENOMENA	SUPERSATURATED
SUPERLARGE	SUPERNATURAL	SUPERPHENOMENON	SUPERSATURATES
SUPERLATIVE	SUPERNATURALISE	SUPERPHOSPHATE	SUPERSATURATING
SUPERLATIVELY	SUPERNATURALISM	SUPERPHOSPHATES	SUPERSATURATION
SUPERLATIVENESS	SUPERNATURALIST	SUPERPHYLA	SUPERSAURS
SUPERLATIVES	SUPERNATURALIZE	SUPERPHYLUM	SUPERSAVER
SUPERLAWYER	SUPERNATURALLY	SUPERPHYSICAL	SUPERSAVERS
SUPERLAWYERS	SUPERNATURALS	SUPERPIMPS	SUPERSCALAR
SUPERLIGHT	SUPERNATURE	SUPERPLANE	SUPERSCALE
SUPERLINER	SUPERNATURES	SUPERPLANES	SUPERSCHOOL
SUPERLINERS	SUPERNORMAL	SUPERPLASTIC	SUPERSCHOOLS
SUPERLOADS	SUPERNORMALITY	SUPERPLASTICITY	SUPERSCOUT
SUPERLOBBYIST	SUPERNORMALLY	SUPERPLASTICS	SUPERSCOUTS
SUPERLOBBYISTS	SUPERNOVAE	SUPERPLAYER	SUPERSCREEN
SUPERLOYALIST	SUPERNOVAS	SUPERPLAYERS	SUPERSCREENS
SUPERLOYALISTS	SUPERNUMERARIES	SUPERPLUSES	SUPERSCRIBE
SUPERLUMINAL	SUPERNUMERARY	SUPERPOLITE	SUPERSCRIBED
SUPERLUNAR	SUPERNURSE	SUPERPOLYMER	SUPERSCRIBES
SUPERLUNARY	SUPERNURSES	SUPERPOLYMERS	SUPERSCRIBING
SUPERLUXURIOUS	SUPERNUTRIENT	SUPERPORTS	SUPERSCRIPT
SUPERLUXURY	SUPERNUTRIENTS	SUPERPOSABLE	SUPERSCRIPTION
SUPERLYING	SUPERNUTRITION	SUPERPOSED	SUPERSCRIPTIONS
SUPERMACHO	SUPERNUTRITIONS	SUPERPOSES	SUPERSCRIPTS
SUPERMAJORITIES	SUPEROCTAVE	SUPERPOSING	SUPERSECRECIES
SUPERMAJORITY	SUPEROCTAVES	SUPERPOSITION	SUPERSECRECY
SUPERMALES	SUPERORDER	SUPERPOSITIONS	SUPERSECRET
SUPERMARKET	SUPERORDERS	SUPERPOWER	SUPERSEDABLE
SUPERMARKETS	SUPERORDINAL	SUPERPOWERED	SUPERSEDEAS
SUPERMARTS	SUPERORDINARY	SUPERPOWERFUL	SUPERSEDEASES
SUPERMASCULINE	SUPERORDINATE	SUPERPOWERS	SUPERSEDED
SUPERMASSIVE	SUPERORDINATED	SUPERPRAISE	SUPERSEDENCE
SUPERMAXES	SUPERORDINATES	SUPERPRAISED	SUPERSEDENCES

SUPERSEDER
SUPERSEDERE
SUPERSEDERES
SUPERSEDERS
SUPERSEDES
SUPERSEDING
SUPERSEDURE
SUPERSEDURES
SUPERSELLER
SUPERSELLERS
SUPERSELLING
SUPERSELLS
SUPERSENSIBLE
SUPERSENSIBLY
SUPERSENSITIVE
SUPERSENSORY
SUPERSENSUAL
SUPERSESSION
SUPERSESSIONS
SUPERSEXES
SUPERSEXUALITY
SUPERSHARP
SUPERSHOWS
SUPERSINGER
SUPERSINGERS
SUPERSIZED
SUPERSIZES
SUPERSIZING
SUPERSLEUTH
SUPERSLEUTHS
SUPERSLICK
SUPERSMART
SUPERSMOOTH
SUPERSONIC
SUPERSONICALLY
SUPERSONICS
SUPERSOUND
SUPERSOUNDS
SUPERSPECIAL
SUPERSPECIALIST
SUPERSPECIALS
SUPERSPECIES
SUPERSPECTACLE
SUPERSPECTACLES
SUPERSPEED
SUPERSPEEDS
SUPERSPIES
SUPERSTARDOM
SUPERSTARDOMS
SUPERSTARS
SUPERSTATE
SUPERSTATES
SUPERSTATION
SUPERSTATIONS
SUPERSTIMULATE
SUPERSTIMULATED
SUPERSTIMULATES
SUPERSTITION
SUPERSTITIONS

SUPERSTITIOUS
SUPERSTITIOUSLY
SUPERSTOCK
SUPERSTOCKS
SUPERSTORE
SUPERSTORES
SUPERSTRATA
SUPERSTRATUM
SUPERSTRATUMS
SUPERSTRENGTH
SUPERSTRENGTHS
SUPERSTRIKE
SUPERSTRIKES
SUPERSTRING
SUPERSTRINGS
SUPERSTRONG
SUPERSTRUCT
SUPERSTRUCTED
SUPERSTRUCTING
SUPERSTRUCTION
SUPERSTRUCTIONS
SUPERSTRUCTIVE
SUPERSTRUCTS
SUPERSTRUCTURAL
SUPERSTRUCTURE
SUPERSTRUCTURES
SUPERSTUDS
SUPERSUBTILE
SUPERSUBTLE
SUPERSUBTLETIES
SUPERSUBTLETY
SUPERSURGEON
SUPERSURGEONS
SUPERSWEET
SUPERSYMMETRIC
SUPERSYMMETRIES
SUPERSYMMETRY
SUPERSYSTEM
SUPERSYSTEMS
SUPERTANKER
SUPERTANKERS
SUPERTAXES
SUPERTEACHER
SUPERTEACHERS
SUPERTERRANEAN
SUPERTERRIFIC
SUPERTHICK
SUPERTHRILLER
SUPERTHRILLERS
SUPERTIGHT
SUPERTITLE
SUPERTITLES
SUPERTONIC
SUPERTONICS
SUPERTRUCK
SUPERTRUCKS
SUPERTWIST
SUPERTWISTS
SUPERVENED

SUPERVENES
SUPERVENIENCE
SUPERVENIENCES
SUPERVENIENT
SUPERVENING
SUPERVENTION
SUPERVENTIONS
SUPERVIRILE
SUPERVIRTUOSI
SUPERVIRTUOSO
SUPERVIRTUOSOS
SUPERVIRULENT
SUPERVISAL
SUPERVISALS
SUPERVISED
SUPERVISEE
SUPERVISEES
SUPERVISES
SUPERVISING
SUPERVISION
SUPERVISIONS
SUPERVISOR
SUPERVISORS
SUPERVISORSHIP
SUPERVISORSHIPS
SUPERVISORY
SUPERVOLUTE
SUPERWAIFS
SUPERWAVES
SUPERWEAPON
SUPERWEAPONS
SUPERWEEDS
SUPERWIDES
SUPERWIVES
SUPERWOMAN
SUPERWOMEN
SUPINATING
SUPINATION
SUPINATIONS
SUPINATORS
SUPINENESS
SUPINENESSES
SUPPEAGOES
SUPPEDANEA
SUPPEDANEUM
SUPPERLESS
SUPPERTIME
SUPPERTIMES
SUPPLANTATION
SUPPLANTATIONS
SUPPLANTED
SUPPLANTER
SUPPLANTERS
SUPPLANTING
SUPPLEJACK
SUPPLEJACKS
SUPPLEMENT
SUPPLEMENTAL
SUPPLEMENTALLY

SUPPLEMENTALS
SUPPLEMENTARIES
SUPPLEMENTARILY
SUPPLEMENTARY
SUPPLEMENTATION
SUPPLEMENTED
SUPPLEMENTER
SUPPLEMENTERS
SUPPLEMENTING
SUPPLEMENTS
SUPPLENESS
SUPPLENESSES
SUPPLETION
SUPPLETIONS
SUPPLETIVE
SUPPLETIVES
SUPPLETORILY
SUPPLETORY
SUPPLIABLE
SUPPLIANCE
SUPPLIANCES
SUPPLIANTLY
SUPPLIANTS
SUPPLICANT
SUPPLICANTS
SUPPLICATE
SUPPLICATED
SUPPLICATES
SUPPLICATING
SUPPLICATINGLY
SUPPLICATION
SUPPLICATIONS
SUPPLICATORY
SUPPLICATS
SUPPLICAVIT
SUPPLICAVITS
SUPPLYMENT
SUPPLYMENTS
SUPPORTABILITY
SUPPORTABLE
SUPPORTABLENESS
SUPPORTABLY
SUPPORTANCE
SUPPORTANCES
SUPPORTERS
SUPPORTING
SUPPORTINGS
SUPPORTIVE
SUPPORTIVELY
SUPPORTIVENESS
SUPPORTLESS
SUPPORTMENT
SUPPORTMENTS
SUPPORTRESS
SUPPORTRESSES
SUPPORTURE
SUPPORTURES
SUPPOSABLE
SUPPOSABLY

SUPPOSEDLY	SUPRARATIONAL	SURFEITERS	SURREBUTTED
SUPPOSINGS	SUPRARENAL	SURFEITING	SURREBUTTER
SUPPOSITION	SUPRARENALS	SURFEITINGS	SURREBUTTERS
SUPPOSITIONAL	SUPRASEGMENTAL	SURFFISHES	SURREBUTTING
SUPPOSITIONALLY	SUPRASENSIBLE	SURFPERCHES	SURREJOINDER
SUPPOSITIONARY	SUPRATEMPORAL	SURFRIDERS	SURREJOINDERS
SUPPOSITIONLESS	SUPRAVITAL	SURGEONCIES	SURREJOINED
SUPPOSITIONS	SUPRAVITALLY	SURGEONFISH	SURREJOINING
SUPPOSITIOUS	SUPREMACIES	SURGEONFISHES	SURREJOINS
SUPPOSITIOUSLY	SUPREMACISM	SURGEONSHIP	SURRENDERED
SUPPOSITITIOUS	SUPREMACISMS	SURGEONSHIPS	SURRENDEREE
SUPPOSITIVE	SUPREMACIST	SURGICALLY	SURRENDEREES
SUPPOSITIVELY	SUPREMACISTS	SURJECTION	SURRENDERER
SUPPOSITIVES	SUPREMATISM	SURJECTIONS	SURRENDERERS
SUPPOSITORIES	SUPREMATISMS	SURJECTIVE	SURRENDERING
SUPPOSITORY	SUPREMATIST	SURLINESSES	SURRENDEROR
SUPPRESSANT	SUPREMATISTS	SURMASTERS	SURRENDERORS
SUPPRESSANTS	SUPREMENESS	SURMISABLE	SURRENDERS
SUPPRESSED	SUPREMENESSES	SURMISINGS	SURRENDRIES
SUPPRESSEDLY	SUPREMITIES	SURMISTRESS	SURREPTITIOUS
SUPPRESSER	SURADDITION	SURMISTRESSES	SURREPTITIOUSLY
SUPPRESSERS	SURADDITIONS	SURMOUNTABLE	SURROGACIES
SUPPRESSES	SURBASEMENT	SURMOUNTED	SURROGATED
SUPPRESSIBILITY	SURBASEMENTS	SURMOUNTER	SURROGATES
SUPPRESSIBLE	SURBEDDING	SURMOUNTERS	SURROGATESHIP
SUPPRESSING	SURCEASING	SURMOUNTING	SURROGATESHIPS
SUPPRESSION	SURCHARGED	SURMOUNTINGS	SURROGATING
SUPPRESSIONS	SURCHARGEMENT	SURMULLETS	SURROGATION
SUPPRESSIVE	SURCHARGEMENTS	SURNOMINAL	SURROGATIONS
SUPPRESSIVENESS	SURCHARGER	SURPASSABLE	SURROGATUM
SUPPRESSOR	SURCHARGERS	SURPASSERS	SURROGATUMS
SUPPRESSORS	SURCHARGES	SURPASSING	SURROUNDED
SUPPURATED	SURCHARGING	SURPASSINGLY	SURROUNDING
SUPPURATES	SURCINGLED	SURPASSINGNESS	SURROUNDINGS
SUPPURATING	SURCINGLES	SURPLUSAGE	SURTARBRAND
SUPPURATION	SURCINGLING	SURPLUSAGES	SURTARBRANDS
SUPPURATIONS	SURCULUSES	SURPLUSING	SURTURBRAND
SUPPURATIVE	SUREFOOTED	SURPLUSSED	SURTURBRANDS
SUPPURATIVES	SUREFOOTEDLY	SURPLUSSES	SURVEILING
SUPRACHIASMIC	SUREFOOTEDNESS	SURPLUSSING	SURVEILLANCE
SUPRACILIARY	SURENESSES	SURPRINTED	SURVEILLANCES
SUPRACOSTAL	SURETYSHIP	SURPRINTING	SURVEILLANT
SUPRACRUSTAL	SURETYSHIPS	SURPRISALS	SURVEILLANTS
SUPRAGLOTTAL	SURFACELESS	SURPRISEDLY	SURVEILLED
SUPRALAPSARIAN	SURFACEMAN	SURPRISERS	SURVEILLES
SUPRALAPSARIANS	SURFACEMEN	SURPRISING	SURVEILLING
SUPRALIMINAL	SURFACINGS	SURPRISINGLY	SURVEYABLE
SUPRALIMINALLY	SURFACTANT	SURPRISINGNESS	SURVEYANCE
SUPRALUNAR	SURFACTANTS	SURPRISINGS	SURVEYANCES
SUPRAMAXILLARY	SURFBOARDED	SURPRIZING	SURVEYINGS
SUPRAMOLECULAR	SURFBOARDER	SURQUEDIES	SURVEYORSHIP
SUPRAMOLECULE	SURFBOARDERS	SURQUEDRIES	SURVEYORSHIPS
SUPRAMOLECULES	SURFBOARDING	SURREALISM	SURVEYING
SUPRAMUNDANE	SURFBOARDINGS	SURREALISMS	SURVIVABILITIES
SUPRANATIONAL	SURFBOARDS	SURREALIST	SURVIVABILITY
SUPRANATIONALLY	SURFCASTER	SURREALISTIC	SURVIVABLE
SUPRAOPTIC	SURFCASTERS	SURREALISTS	SURVIVALISM
SUPRAORBITAL	SURFCASTING	SURREBUTTAL	SURVIVALISMS
SUPRAPUBIC	SURFCASTINGS	SURREBUTTALS	SURVIVALIST

SURVIVALISTS	SUSPERCOLLATING	SWAGGERINGS	SWEETBRIER
SURVIVANCE	SUSPICIONAL	SWAINISHNESS	SWEETBRIERS
SURVIVANCES	SUSPICIONED	SWAINISHNESSES	SWEETCORNS
SURVIVORSHIP	SUSPICIONING	SWALLOWABLE	SWEETENERS
SURVIVORSHIPS	SUSPICIONLESS	SWALLOWERS	SWEETENING
SUSCEPTANCE	SUSPICIONS	SWALLOWING	SWEETENINGS
SUSCEPTANCES	SUSPICIOUS	SWALLOWTAIL	SWEETFISHES
SUSCEPTIBILITY	SUSPICIOUSLY	SWALLOWTAILS	SWEETHEART
SUSCEPTIBLE	SUSPICIOUSNESS	SWALLOWWORT	SWEETHEARTED
SUSCEPTIBLENESS	SUSPIRATION	SWALLOWWORTS	SWEETHEARTING
SUSCEPTIBLY	SUSPIRATIONS	SWAMPINESS	SWEETHEARTS
SUSCEPTIVE	SUSPIRIOUS	SWAMPINESSES	SWEETIEWIFE
SUSCEPTIVENESS	SUSTAINABILITY	SWAMPLANDS	SWEETIEWIVES
SUSCEPTIVITIES	SUSTAINABLE	SWANKINESS	SWEETISHLY
SUSCEPTIVITY	SUSTAINEDLY	SWANKINESSES	SWEETISHNESS
SUSCEPTORS	SUSTAINERS	SWANNERIES	SWEETISHNESSES
SUSCIPIENT	SUSTAINING	SWANSDOWNS	SWEETMEATS
SUSCIPIENTS	SUSTAININGLY	SWARAJISMS	SWEETNESSES
SUSCITATED	SUSTAININGS	SWARAJISTS	SWEETSHOPS
SUSCITATES	SUSTAINMENT	SWARTHIEST	SWEETWATER
SUSCITATING	SUSTAINMENTS	SWARTHINESS	SWEETWATERS
SUSCITATION	SUSTENANCE	SWARTHINESSES	SWEETWOODS
SUSCITATIONS	SUSTENANCES	SWARTHNESS	SWEIRNESSES
SUSPECTABLE	SUSTENTACULA	SWARTHNESSES	SWELLFISHES
SUSPECTEDLY	SUSTENTACULAR	SWARTNESSES	SWELLHEADED
SUSPECTEDNESS	SUSTENTACULUM	SWASHBUCKLE	SWELLHEADEDNESS
SUSPECTEDNESSES	SUSTENTATE	SWASHBUCKLED	SWELLHEADS
SUSPECTERS	SUSTENTATED	SWASHBUCKLER	SWELLINGLY
SUSPECTFUL	SUSTENTATES	SWASHBUCKLERS	SWELTERING
SUSPECTING	SUSTENTATING	SWASHBUCKLES	SWELTERINGLY
SUSPECTLESS	SUSTENTATION	SWASHBUCKLING	SWELTERINGS
SUSPENDERED	SUSTENTATIONS	SWASHWORKS	SWELTRIEST
SUSPENDERS	SUSTENTATIVE	SWATCHBOOK	SWEPTWINGS
SUSPENDIBILITY	SUSTENTATOR	SWATCHBOOKS	SWERVELESS
SUSPENDIBLE	SUSTENTATORS	SWATHEABLE	SWIFTNESSES
SUSPENDING	SUSTENTION	SWATTERING	SWIMFEEDER
SUSPENSEFUL	SUSTENTIONS	SWAYBACKED	SWIMFEEDERS
SUSPENSEFULLY	SUSTENTIVE	SWEARWORDS	SWIMMERETS
SUSPENSEFULNESS	SUSURRATED	SWEATBANDS	SWIMMINGLY
SUSPENSELESS	SUSURRATES	SWEATBOXES	SWIMMINGNESS
SUSPENSERS	SUSURRATING	SWEATERDRESS	SWIMMINGNESSES
SUSPENSIBILITY	SUSURRATION	SWEATERDRESSES	SWINDLINGS
SUSPENSIBLE	SUSURRATIONS	SWEATINESS	SWINEHERDS
SUSPENSION	SUSURRUSES	SWEATINESSES	SWINEHOODS
SUSPENSIONS	SUTLERSHIP	SWEATPANTS	SWINEPOXES
SUSPENSIVE	SUTLERSHIPS	SWEATSHIRT	SWINESTONE
SUSPENSIVELY	SUTTEEISMS	SWEATSHIRTS	SWINESTONES
SUSPENSIVENESS	SUTTLETIES	SWEATSHOPS	SWINGBEATS
SUSPENSOID	SUTURATION	SWEATSUITS	SWINGBOATS
SUSPENSOIDS	SUTURATIONS	SWEEPBACKS	SWINGEINGLY
SUSPENSORIA	SUZERAINTIES	SWEEPINGLY	SWINGINGEST
SUSPENSORIAL	SUZERAINTY	SWEEPINGNESS	SWINGINGLY
SUSPENSORIES	SVARABHAKTI	SWEEPINGNESSES	SWINGLETREE
SUSPENSORIUM	SVARABHAKTIS	SWEEPSTAKE	SWINGLETREES
SUSPENSORS	SVELTENESS	SWEEPSTAKES	SWINGLINGS
SUSPENSORY	SVELTENESSES	SWEETBREAD	SWINGOMETER
SUSPERCOLLATE	SWAGGERERS	SWEETBREADS	SWINGOMETERS
SUSPERCOLLATED	SWAGGERING	SWEETBRIAR	SWINGTREES
SUSPERCOLLATES	SWAGGERINGLY	SWEETBRIARS	SWINISHNESS

SWINISHNESSES	SYCOPHANTICALLY	SYLLOGISTICALLY	SYMMETALLISMS
SWIRLINGLY	SYCOPHANTISE	SYLLOGISTICS	SYMMETRIAN
SWISHINGLY	SYCOPHANTISED	SYLLOGISTS	SYMMETRIANS
SWITCHABLE	SYCOPHANTISES	SYLLOGIZATION	SYMMETRICAL
SWITCHBACK	SYCOPHANTISH	SYLLOGIZATIONS	SYMMETRICALLY
SWITCHBACKED	SYCOPHANTISHLY	SYLLOGIZED	SYMMETRICALNESS
SWITCHBACKING	SYCOPHANTISING	SYLLOGIZER	SYMMETRIES
SWITCHBACKS	SYCOPHANTISM	SYLLOGIZERS	SYMMETRISATION
SWITCHBLADE	SYCOPHANTISMS	SYLLOGIZES	SYMMETRISATIONS
SWITCHBLADES	SYCOPHANTIZE	SYLLOGIZING	SYMMETRISE
SWITCHBOARD	SYCOPHANTIZED	SYLPHIDINE	SYMMETRISED
SWITCHBOARDS	SYCOPHANTIZES	SYLVANITES	SYMMETRISES
SWITCHEROO	SYCOPHANTIZING	SYLVESTRAL	SYMMETRISING
SWITCHEROOS	SYCOPHANTLY	SYLVESTRIAN	SYMMETRIZATION
SWITCHGEAR	SYCOPHANTRIES	SYLVICULTURAL	SYMMETRIZATIONS
SWITCHGEARS	SYCOPHANTRY	SYLVICULTURE	SYMMETRIZE
SWITCHGIRL	SYCOPHANTS	SYLVICULTURES	SYMMETRIZED
SWITCHGIRLS	SYLLABARIA	SYLVINITES	SYMMETRIZES
SWITCHGRASS	SYLLABARIES	SYMBIONTIC	SYMMETRIZING
SWITCHGRASSES	SYLLABARIUM	SYMBIONTICALLY	SYMMETROPHOBIA
SWITCHIEST	SYLLABICAL	SYMBIOTICAL	SYMMETROPHOBIAS
SWITCHINGS	SYLLABICALLY	SYMBIOTICALLY	SYMPATHECTOMIES
SWITCHLIKE	SYLLABICATE	SYMBOLICAL	SYMPATHECTOMY
SWITCHOVER	SYLLABICATED	SYMBOLICALLY	SYMPATHETIC
SWITCHOVERS	SYLLABICATES	SYMBOLICALNESS	SYMPATHETICAL
SWITCHYARD	SYLLABICATING	SYMBOLISATION	SYMPATHETICALLY
SWITCHYARDS	SYLLABICATION	SYMBOLISATIONS	SYMPATHETICS
SWITHERING	SYLLABICATIONS	SYMBOLISED	SYMPATHIES
SWIVELBLOCK	SYLLABICITIES	SYMBOLISER	SYMPATHINS
SWIVELBLOCKS	SYLLABICITY	SYMBOLISERS	SYMPATHIQUE
SWIVELLING	SYLLABIFICATION	SYMBOLISES	SYMPATHISE
SWOLLENNESS	SYLLABIFIED	SYMBOLISING	SYMPATHISED
SWOLLENNESSES	SYLLABIFIES	SYMBOLISMS	SYMPATHISER
SWOONINGLY	SYLLABIFYING	SYMBOLISTIC	SYMPATHISERS
SWOOPSTAKE	SYLLABISED	SYMBOLISTICAL	SYMPATHISES
SWORDBEARER	SYLLABISES	SYMBOLISTICALLY	SYMPATHISING
SWORDBEARERS	SYLLABISING	SYMBOLISTS	SYMPATHIZE
SWORDBILLS	SYLLABISMS	SYMBOLIZATION	SYMPATHIZED
SWORDCRAFT	SYLLABIZED	SYMBOLIZATIONS	SYMPATHIZER
SWORDCRAFTS	SYLLABIZES	SYMBOLIZED	SYMPATHIZERS
SWORDFISHES	SYLLABIZING	SYMBOLIZER	SYMPATHIZES
SWORDPLAYER	SYLLABLING	SYMBOLIZERS	SYMPATHIZING
SWORDPLAYERS	SYLLABOGRAM	SYMBOLIZES	SYMPATHOLYTIC
SWORDPLAYS	SYLLABOGRAMS	SYMBOLIZING	SYMPATHOLYTICS
SWORDPROOF	SYLLABOGRAPHIES	SYMBOLLING	SYMPATHOMIMETIC
SWORDSMANSHIP	SYLLABOGRAPHY	SYMBOLOGICAL	SYMPATRICALLY
SWORDSMANSHIPS	SYLLABUSES	SYMBOLOGIES	SYMPATRIES
SWORDSTICK	SYLLEPTICAL	SYMBOLOGIST	SYMPETALIES
SWORDSTICKS	SYLLEPTICALLY	SYMBOLOGISTS	SYMPETALOUS
SWORDTAILS	SYLLOGISATION	SYMBOLOGRAPHIES	SYMPHILIES
SYBARITICAL	SYLLOGISATIONS	SYMBOLOGRAPHY	SYMPHILISM
SYBARITICALLY	SYLLOGISED	SYMBOLOLATRIES	SYMPHILISMS
SYBARITISH	SYLLOGISER	SYMBOLOLATRY	SYMPHILOUS
SYBARITISM	SYLLOGISERS	SYMBOLOLOGIES	SYMPHONICALLY
SYBARITISMS	SYLLOGISES	SYMBOLOLOGY	SYMPHONIES
SYCOPHANCIES	SYLLOGISING	SYMMETALISM	SYMPHONION
SYCOPHANCY	SYLLOGISMS	SYMMETALISMS	SYMPHONIONS
SYCOPHANTIC	SYLLOGISTIC	SYMMETALLIC	SYMPHONIOUS
SYCOPHANTICAL	SYLLOGISTICAL	SYMMETALLISM	SYMPHONIOUSLY

SYMPHONIST	SYNANTHOUS	SYNCHRONOUS	SYNDICATIONS
SYMPHONISTS	SYNAPHEIAS	SYNCHRONOUSLY	SYNDICATOR
SYMPHYLOUS	SYNAPOSEMATIC	SYNCHRONOUSNESS	SYNDICATORS
SYMPHYSEAL	SYNAPOSEMATISM	SYNCHROSCOPE	SYNDICSHIP
SYMPHYSEOTOMIES	SYNAPOSEMATISMS	SYNCHROSCOPES	SYNDICSHIPS
SYMPHYSEOTOMY	SYNAPTASES	SYNCHROTRON	SYNDIOTACTIC
SYMPHYSIAL	SYNAPTICAL	SYNCHROTRONS	SYNDYASMIAN
SYMPHYSIOTOMIES	SYNAPTICALLY	SYNCLASTIC	SYNECDOCHE
SYMPHYSIOTOMY	SYNAPTOSOMAL	SYNCLINALS	SYNECDOCHES
SYMPHYSTIC	SYNAPTOSOME	SYNCLINORIA	SYNECDOCHIC
SYMPIESOMETER	SYNAPTOSOMES	SYNCLINORIUM	SYNECDOCHICAL
SYMPIESOMETERS	SYNARCHIES	SYNCOPATED	SYNECDOCHICALLY
SYMPLASTIC	SYNARTHRODIAL	SYNCOPATES	SYNECDOCHISM
SYMPODIALLY	SYNARTHRODIALLY	SYNCOPATING	SYNECDOCHISMS
SYMPOSIACS	SYNARTHROSES	SYNCOPATION	SYNECOLOGIC
SYMPOSIARCH	SYNARTHROSIS	SYNCOPATIONS	SYNECOLOGICAL
SYMPOSIARCHS	SYNASTRIES	SYNCOPATIVE	SYNECOLOGICALLY
SYMPOSIAST	SYNAXARION	SYNCOPATOR	SYNECOLOGIES
SYMPOSIASTS	SYNCARPIES	SYNCOPATORS	SYNECOLOGIST
SYMPOSIUMS	SYNCARPOUS	SYNCRETISATION	SYNECOLOGISTS
SYMPTOMATIC	SYNCHONDROSES	SYNCRETISATIONS	SYNECOLOGY
SYMPTOMATICAL	SYNCHONDROSIS	SYNCRETISE	SYNECPHONESES
SYMPTOMATICALLY	SYNCHORESES	SYNCRETISED	SYNECPHONESIS
SYMPTOMATISE	SYNCHORESIS	SYNCRETISES	SYNECTICALLY
SYMPTOMATISED	SYNCHROFLASH	SYNCRETISING	SYNEIDESES
SYMPTOMATISES	SYNCHROFLASHES	SYNCRETISM	SYNEIDESIS
SYMPTOMATISING	SYNCHROMESH	SYNCRETISMS	SYNERGETIC
SYMPTOMATIZE	SYNCHROMESHES	SYNCRETIST	SYNERGETICALLY
SYMPTOMATIZED	SYNCHRONAL	SYNCRETISTIC	SYNERGICALLY
SYMPTOMATIZES	SYNCHRONEITIES	SYNCRETISTS	SYNERGISED
SYMPTOMATIZING	SYNCHRONEITY	SYNCRETIZATION	SYNERGISES
SYMPTOMATOLOGIC	SYNCHRONIC	SYNCRETIZATIONS	SYNERGISING
SYMPTOMATOLOGY	SYNCHRONICAL	SYNCRETIZE	SYNERGISMS
SYMPTOMLESS	SYNCHRONICALLY	SYNCRETIZED	SYNERGISTIC
SYMPTOMOLOGICAL	SYNCHRONICITIES	SYNCRETIZES	SYNERGISTICALLY
SYMPTOMOLOGIES	SYNCHRONICITY	SYNCRETIZING	SYNERGISTS
SYMPTOMOLOGY	SYNCHRONIES	SYNDACTYLIES	SYNERGIZED
SYNADELPHITE	SYNCHRONISATION	SYNDACTYLISM	SYNERGIZES
SYNADELPHITES	SYNCHRONISE	SYNDACTYLISMS	SYNERGIZING
SYNAERESES	SYNCHRONISED	SYNDACTYLOUS	SYNESTHESIA
SYNAERESIS	SYNCHRONISER	SYNDACTYLS	SYNESTHESIAS
SYNAESTHESES	SYNCHRONISERS	SYNDACTYLY	SYNESTHETIC
SYNAESTHESIA	SYNCHRONISES	SYNDERESES	SYNGENESES
SYNAESTHESIAS	SYNCHRONISING	SYNDERESIS	SYNGENESIOUS
SYNAESTHESIS	SYNCHRONISM	SYNDESISES	SYNGENESIS
SYNAESTHETIC	SYNCHRONISMS	SYNDESMOSES	SYNGENETIC
SYNAGOGICAL	SYNCHRONISTIC	SYNDESMOSIS	SYNGNATHOUS
SYNAGOGUES	SYNCHRONISTICAL	SYNDESMOTIC	SYNKARYONIC
SYNALEPHAS	SYNCHRONIZATION	SYNDETICAL	SYNKARYONS
SYNALLAGMATIC	SYNCHRONIZE	SYNDETICALLY	SYNODICALLY
SYNALOEPHA	SYNCHRONIZED	SYNDICALISM	SYNOECETES
SYNALOEPHAS	SYNCHRONIZER	SYNDICALISMS	SYNOECIOSES
SYNANDRIUM	SYNCHRONIZERS	SYNDICALIST	SYNOECIOSIS
SYNANDROUS	SYNCHRONIZES	SYNDICALISTIC	SYNOECIOUS
SYNANTHEROUS	SYNCHRONIZING	SYNDICALISTS	SYNOECISED
SYNANTHESES	SYNCHRONOLOGIES	SYNDICATED	SYNOECISES
SYNANTHESIS	SYNCHRONOLOGY	SYNDICATES	SYNOECISING
SYNANTHETIC	SYNCHRONOSCOPE	SYNDICATING	SYNOECISMS
SYNANTHIES	SYNCHRONOSCOPES	SYNDICATION	SYNOECIZED

SYNOECIZES
SYNOECIZING
SYNOECOLOGIES
SYNOECOLOGY
SYNOEKETES
SYNONYMATIC
SYNONYMICAL
SYNONYMICON
SYNONYMICONS
SYNONYMIES
SYNONYMISE
SYNONYMISED
SYNONYMISES
SYNONYMISING
SYNONYMIST
SYNONYMISTS
SYNONYMITIES
SYNONYMITY
SYNONYMIZE
SYNONYMIZED
SYNONYMIZES
SYNONYMIZING
SYNONYMOUS
SYNONYMOUSLY
SYNONYMOUSNESS
SYNOPSISED
SYNOPSISES
SYNOPSISING
SYNOPSIZED
SYNOPSIZES
SYNOPSIZING
SYNOPTICAL
SYNOPTICALLY
SYNOPTISTIC
SYNOPTISTS
SYNOSTOSES
SYNOSTOSIS
SYNOVIALLY
SYNOVITISES
SYNSEPALOUS
SYNTACTICAL
SYNTACTICALLY
SYNTACTICS
SYNTAGMATA
SYNTAGMATIC
SYNTAGMATITE
SYNTAGMATITES
SYNTECTICAL
SYNTENOSES
SYNTENOSIS
SYNTERESES
SYNTERESIS
SYNTEXISES
SYNTHESISATION
SYNTHESISATIONS
SYNTHESISE
SYNTHESISED
SYNTHESISER
SYNTHESISERS

SYNTHESISES
SYNTHESISING
SYNTHESIST
SYNTHESISTS
SYNTHESIZATION
SYNTHESIZATIONS
SYNTHESIZE
SYNTHESIZED
SYNTHESIZER
SYNTHESIZERS
SYNTHESIZES
SYNTHESIZING
SYNTHESPIAN
SYNTHESPIANS
SYNTHETASE
SYNTHETASES
SYNTHETICAL
SYNTHETICALLY
SYNTHETICISM
SYNTHETICISMS
SYNTHETICS
SYNTHETISATION
SYNTHETISATIONS
SYNTHETISE
SYNTHETISED
SYNTHETISER
SYNTHETISERS
SYNTHETISES
SYNTHETISING
SYNTHETISM
SYNTHETISMS
SYNTHETIST
SYNTHETISTS
SYNTHETIZATION
SYNTHETIZATIONS
SYNTHETIZE
SYNTHETIZED
SYNTHETIZER
SYNTHETIZERS
SYNTHETIZES
SYNTHETIZING
SYNTHRONUS
SYNTONICALLY
SYNTONISED
SYNTONISES
SYNTONISING
SYNTONIZED
SYNTONIZES
SYNTONIZING
SYPHILISATION
SYPHILISATIONS
SYPHILISED
SYPHILISES
SYPHILISING
SYPHILITIC
SYPHILITICALLY
SYPHILITICS
SYPHILIZATION
SYPHILIZATIONS

SYPHILIZED
SYPHILIZES
SYPHILIZING
SYPHILOLOGIES
SYPHILOLOGIST
SYPHILOLOGISTS
SYPHILOLOGY
SYPHILOMAS
SYPHILOMATA
SYPHILOPHOBIA
SYPHILOPHOBIAS
SYRINGITIS
SYRINGITISES
SYRINGOMYELIA
SYRINGOMYELIAS
SYRINGOMYELIC
SYRINGOTOMIES
SYRINGOTOMY
SYSSARCOSES
SYSSARCOSIS
SYSSARCOTIC
SYSTEMATIC
SYSTEMATICAL
SYSTEMATICALLY
SYSTEMATICIAN
SYSTEMATICIANS
SYSTEMATICNESS
SYSTEMATICS
SYSTEMATISATION
SYSTEMATISE
SYSTEMATISED
SYSTEMATISER
SYSTEMATISERS
SYSTEMATISES
SYSTEMATISING
SYSTEMATISM
SYSTEMATISMS
SYSTEMATIST
SYSTEMATISTS
SYSTEMATIZATION
SYSTEMATIZE
SYSTEMATIZED
SYSTEMATIZER
SYSTEMATIZERS
SYSTEMATIZES
SYSTEMATIZING
SYSTEMATOLOGIES
SYSTEMATOLOGY
SYSTEMICALLY
SYSTEMISATION
SYSTEMISATIONS
SYSTEMISED
SYSTEMISER
SYSTEMISERS
SYSTEMISES
SYSTEMISING
SYSTEMIZATION
SYSTEMIZATIONS
SYSTEMIZED

SYSTEMIZER
SYSTEMIZERS
SYSTEMIZES
SYSTEMIZING
SYSTEMLESS
SYZYGETICALLY

TABASHEERS	TACHEOMETRICAL	TACITURNLY	TAILSPINNING
TABBOULEHS	TACHEOMETRIES	TACKBOARDS	TAILSTOCKS
TABBYHOODS	TACHEOMETRY	TACKIFIERS	TAILWATERS
TABEFACTION	TACHISTOSCOPE	TACKIFYING	TAILWHEELS
TABEFACTIONS	TACHISTOSCOPES	TACKINESSES	TAINTLESSLY
TABELLIONS	TACHISTOSCOPIC	TACMAHACKS	TAKINGNESS
TABERNACLE	TACHOGRAMS	TACTFULNESS	TAKINGNESSES
TABERNACLED	TACHOGRAPH	TACTFULNESSES	TALBOTYPES
TABERNACLES	TACHOGRAPHS	TACTICALLY	TALEBEARER
TABERNACLING	TACHOMETER	TACTICIANS	TALEBEARERS
TABERNACULAR	TACHOMETERS	TACTICITIES	TALEBEARING
TABESCENCE	TACHOMETRIC	TACTILISTS	TALEBEARINGS
TABESCENCES	TACHOMETRICAL	TACTILITIES	TALEGALLAS
TABLANETTE	TACHOMETRICALLY	TACTLESSLY	TALENTLESS
TABLANETTES	TACHOMETRIES	TACTLESSNESS	TALISMANIC
TABLATURES	TACHOMETRY	TACTLESSNESSES	TALISMANICAL
TABLECLOTH	TACHYARRHYTHMIA	TACTUALITIES	TALISMANICALLY
TABLECLOTHS	TACHYCARDIA	TACTUALITY	TALKABILITIES
TABLELANDS	TACHYCARDIAC	TAEKWONDOS	TALKABILITY
TABLEMATES	TACHYCARDIAS	TAENIACIDE	TALKATHONS
TABLESPOON	TACHYGRAPH	TAENIACIDES	TALKATIVELY
TABLESPOONFUL	TACHYGRAPHER	TAENIAFUGE	TALKATIVENESS
TABLESPOONFULS	TACHYGRAPHERS	TAENIAFUGES	TALKATIVENESSES
TABLESPOONS	TACHYGRAPHIC	TAFFETASES	TALKINESSES
TABLESPOONSFUL	TACHYGRAPHICAL	TAFFETIZED	TALLGRASSES
TABLETOPPED	TACHYGRAPHIES	TAGLIARINI	TALLIATING
TABLETTING	TACHYGRAPHIST	TAGLIARINIS	TALLNESSES
TABLEWARES	TACHYGRAPHISTS	TAGLIATELLE	TALLYHOING
TABOGGANED	TACHYGRAPHS	TAGLIATELLES	TALLYSHOPS
TABOGGANING	TACHYGRAPHY	TAHSILDARS	TALLYWOMAN
TABOPARESES	TACHYLITES	TAIKONAUTS	TALLYWOMEN
TABOPARESIS	TACHYLITIC	TAILBOARDS	TALMUDISMS
TABULARISATION	TACHYLYTES	TAILCOATED	TAMABILITIES
TABULARISATIONS	TACHYLYTIC	TAILENDERS	TAMABILITY
TABULARISE	TACHYMETER	TAILGATERS	TAMABLENESS
TABULARISED	TACHYMETERS	TAILGATING	TAMABLENESSES
TABULARISES	TACHYMETRIC	TAILLESSLY	TAMARILLOS
TABULARISING	TACHYMETRICAL	TAILLESSNESS	TAMBOURERS
TABULARIZATION	TACHYMETRICALLY	TAILLESSNESSES	TAMBOURINE
TABULARIZATIONS	TACHYMETRIES	TAILLIGHTS	TAMBOURINES
TABULARIZE	TACHYMETRY	TAILORBIRD	TAMBOURING
TABULARIZED	TACHYPHASIA	TAILORBIRDS	TAMBOURINIST
TABULARIZES	TACHYPHASIAS	TAILORESSES	TAMBOURINISTS
TABULARIZING	TACHYPHRASIA	TAILORINGS	TAMBOURINS
TABULATING	TACHYPHRASIAS	TAILORMADE	TAMEABILITIES
TABULATION	TACHYPHYLAXES	TAILORMAKE	TAMEABILITY
TABULATIONS	TACHYPHYLAXIS	TAILORMAKES	TAMEABLENESS
TABULATORS	TACHYPNEAS	TAILORMAKING	TAMEABLENESSES
TABULATORY	TACHYPNOEA	TAILPIECES	TAMELESSNESS
TACAMAHACS	TACHYPNOEAS	TAILPIPING	TAMELESSNESSES
TACHEOMETER	TACITNESSES	TAILPLANES	TAMENESSES
TACHEOMETERS	TACITURNITIES	TAILSLIDES	TAMOXIFENS
TACHEOMETRIC	TACITURNITY	TAILSPINNED	TAMPERINGS

TAMPERPROOF	TAPERSTICK	TARGETITISES	TASTEMAKER
TAMPONADES	TAPERSTICKS	TARGETLESS	TASTEMAKERS
TAMPONAGES	TAPESCRIPT	TARIFFICATION	TASTINESSES
TANDEMWISE	TAPESCRIPTS	TARIFFICATIONS	TATAHASHES
TANGENCIES	TAPESTRIED	TARIFFLESS	TATPURUSHA
TANGENTALLY	TAPESTRIES	TARMACADAM	TATPURUSHAS
TANGENTIAL	TAPESTRYING	TARMACADAMS	TATTERDEMALION
TANGENTIALITIES	TAPHEPHOBIA	TARMACKING	TATTERDEMALIONS
TANGENTIALITY	TAPHEPHOBIAS	TARNATIONS	TATTERDEMALLION
TANGENTIALLY	TAPHEPHOBIC	TARNISHABLE	TATTERSALL
TANGERINES	TAPHONOMIC	TARNISHERS	TATTERSALLS
TANGHININS	TAPHONOMICAL	TARNISHING	TATTINESSES
TANGIBILITIES	TAPHONOMIES	TARPAULING	TATTLETALE
TANGIBILITY	TAPHONOMIST	TARPAULINGS	TATTLETALES
TANGIBLENESS	TAPHONOMISTS	TARPAULINS	TATTLINGLY
TANGIBLENESSES	TAPHOPHOBIA	TARRADIDDLE	TATTOOISTS
TANGINESSES	TAPHOPHOBIAS	TARRADIDDLES	TAUNTINGLY
TANGLEFOOT	TAPHROGENESES	TARRIANCES	TAUROBOLIA
TANGLEFOOTS	TAPHROGENESIS	TARRINESSES	TAUROBOLIUM
TANGLEMENT	TAPOTEMENT	TARSALGIAS	TAUROMACHIAN
TANGLEMENTS	TAPOTEMENTS	TARSOMETATARSAL	TAUROMACHIES
TANGLESOME	TAPSALTEERIE	TARSOMETATARSI	TAUROMACHY
TANGLEWEED	TAPSALTEERIES	TARSOMETATARSUS	TAUROMORPHOUS
TANGLEWEEDS	TAPSIETEERIE	TARTANALIA	TAUTNESSES
TANGLINGLY	TAPSIETEERIES	TARTANALIAS	TAUTOCHRONE
TANISTRIES	TAPSTRESSES	TARTANRIES	TAUTOCHRONES
TANKBUSTER	TARADIDDLE	TARTAREOUS	TAUTOCHRONISM
TANKBUSTERS	TARADIDDLES	TARTARISATION	TAUTOCHRONISMS
TANKBUSTING	TARAMASALATA	TARTARISATIONS	TAUTOCHRONOUS
TANKBUSTINGS	TARAMASALATAS	TARTARISED	TAUTOLOGIC
TANTALATES	TARANTARAED	TARTARISES	TAUTOLOGICAL
TANTALISATION	TARANTARAING	TARTARISING	TAUTOLOGICALLY
TANTALISATIONS	TARANTARAS	TARTARIZATION	TAUTOLOGIES
TANTALISED	TARANTASES	TARTARIZATIONS	TAUTOLOGISE
TANTALISER	TARANTASSES	TARTARIZED	TAUTOLOGISED
TANTALISERS	TARANTELLA	TARTARIZES	TAUTOLOGISES
TANTALISES	TARANTELLAS	TARTARIZING	TAUTOLOGISING
TANTALISING	TARANTISMS	TARTINESSES	TAUTOLOGISM
TANTALISINGLY	TARANTISTS	TARTNESSES	TAUTOLOGISMS
TANTALISINGS	TARANTULAE	TARTRAZINE	TAUTOLOGIST
TANTALISMS	TARANTULAS	TARTRAZINES	TAUTOLOGISTS
TANTALITES	TARATANTARA	TASEOMETER	TAUTOLOGIZE
TANTALIZATION	TARATANTARAED	TASEOMETERS	TAUTOLOGIZED
TANTALIZATIONS	TARATANTARAING	TASIMETERS	TAUTOLOGIZES
TANTALIZED	TARATANTARAS	TASIMETRIC	TAUTOLOGIZING
TANTALIZER	TARAXACUMS	TASIMETRIES	TAUTOLOGOUS
TANTALIZERS	TARBOGGINED	TASKMASTER	TAUTOLOGOUSLY
TANTALIZES	TARBOGGINING	TASKMASTERS	TAUTOMERIC
TANTALIZING	TARBOGGINS	TASKMISTRESS	TAUTOMERISM
TANTALIZINGLY	TARBOOSHES	TASKMISTRESSES	TAUTOMERISMS
TANTALIZINGS	TARBOUCHES	TASSELLING	TAUTOMETRIC
TANTALUSES	TARBOUSHES	TASSELLINGS	TAUTOMETRICAL
TANTAMOUNT	TARDIGRADE	TASTEFULLY	TAUTONYMIC
TANTARARAS	TARDIGRADES	TASTEFULNESS	TAUTONYMIES
TANZANITES	TARDINESSES	TASTEFULNESSES	TAUTONYMOUS
TAOISEACHS	TARGETABLE	TASTELESSLY	TAUTOPHONIC
TAPERINGLY	TARGETEERS	TASTELESSNESS	TAUTOPHONICAL
TAPERNESSES	TARGETITIS	TASTELESSNESSES	TAUTOPHONIES

TAUTOPHONY	TEARSHEETS	TECHNOGRAPHIES	TEENYBOPPER
TAWDRINESS	TEARSTAINED	TECHNOGRAPHY	TEENYBOPPERS
TAWDRINESSES	TEARSTAINS	TECHNOJUNKIE	TEFTERBOARD
TAWHEOWHEO	TEARSTRIPS	TECHNOJUNKIES	TEETERBOARDS
TAWHEOWHEOS	TEASELINGS	TECHNOLOGIC	TEETHRIDGE
TAWNINESSES	TEASELLERS	TECHNOLOGICAL	TEETHRIDGES
TAXABILITIES	TEASELLING	TECHNOLOGICALLY	TEETOTALED
TAXABILITY	TEASELLINGS	TECHNOLOGIES	TEETOTALER
TAXABLENESS	TEASPOONFUL	TECHNOLOGISE	TEETOTALERS
TAXABLENESSES	TEASPOONFULS	TECHNOLOGISED	TEETOTALING
TAXAMETERS	TEASPOONSFUL	TECHNOLOGISES	TEETOTALISM
TAXATIONAL	TEATASTERS	TECHNOLOGISING	TEETOTALISMS
TAXIDERMAL	TEAZELLING	TECHNOLOGIST	TEETOTALIST
TAXIDERMIC	TECHINESSES	TECHNOLOGISTS	TEETOTALISTS
TAXIDERMIES	TECHNETIUM	TECHNOLOGIZE	TEETOTALLED
TAXIDERMISE	TECHNETIUMS	TECHNOLOGIZED	TEETOTALLER
TAXIDERMISED	TECHNETRONIC	TECHNOLOGTZES	TEETOTALLERS
TAXIDERMISES	TECHNICALISE	TECHNOLOGIZING	TEETOTALLING
TAXIDERMISING	TECHNICALISED	TECHNOLOGY	TEETOTALLY
TAXIDERMIST	TECHNICALISES	TECHNOMANIA	TEGUMENTAL
TAXIDERMISTS	TECHNICALISING	TECHNOMANIAC	TEGUMENTARY
TAXIDERMIZE	TECHNICALITIES	TECHNOMANIACS	TEICHOPSIA
TAXIDERMIZED	TECHNICALITY	TECHNOMANIAS	TEICHOPSIAS
TAXIDERMIZES	TECHNICALIZE	TECHNOMUSIC	TEINOSCOPE
TAXIDERMIZING	TECHNICALIZED	TECHNOMUSICS	TEINOSCOPES
TAXIMETERS	TECHNICALIZES	TECHNOPHILE	TEKNONYMIES
TAXIPLANES	TECHNICALIZING	TECHNOPHILES	TEKNONYMOUS
TAXONOMERS	TECHNICALLY	TECHNOPHOBE	TELAESTHESIA
TAXONOMICAL	TECHNICALNESS	TECHNOPHOBES	TELAESTHESIAS
TAXONOMICALLY	TECHNICALNESSES	TECHNOPHOBIA	TELAESTHETIC
TAXONOMIES	TECHNICALS	TECHNOPHOBIAS	TELANGIECTASES
TAXONOMIST	TECHNICIAN	TECHNOPHOBIC	TELANGIECTASIA
TAXONOMISTS	TECHNICIANS	TECHNOPHOBICS	TELANGIECTASIAS
TAXPAYINGS	TECHNICISE	TECHNOPOLE	TELANGIECTASIS
TAYASSUIDS	TECHNICISED	TECHNOPOLES	TELANGIECTATIC
TAYBERRIES	TECHNICISES	TECHNOPOLIS	TELAUTOGRAPH
TCHOTCHKES	TECHNICISING	TECHNOPOLISES	TELAUTOGRAPHIC
TCHOUKBALL	TECHNICISM	TECHNOPOLITAN	TELAUTOGRAPHIES
TCHOUKBALLS	TECHNICISMS	TECHNOPOLITANS	TELAUTOGRAPHY
TEABERRIES	TECHNICIST	TECHNOPOPS	TELEARCHICS
TEACHABILITIES	TECHNICISTS	TECHNOSPEAK	TELEBANKING
TEACHABILITY	TECHNICIZE	TECHNOSPEAKS	TELEBANKINGS
TEACHABLENESS	TECHNICIZED	TECHNOSTRESS	TELEBRIDGE
TEACHABLENESSES	TECHNICIZES	TECHNOSTRESSES	TELEBRIDGES
TEACHERLESS	TECHNICIZING	TECHNOSTRUCTURE	TELECAMERA
TEACHERSHIP	TECHNICOLOUR	TECTIBRANCH	TELECAMERAS
TEACHERSHIPS	TECHNICOLOURED	TECTIBRANCHIATE	TELECASTED
TEACUPFULS	TECHNIKONS	TECTIBRANCHS	TELECASTER
TEACUPSFUL	TECHNIQUES	TECTONICALLY	TELECASTERS
TEAKETTLES	TECHNOBABBLE	TECTONISMS	TELECASTING
TEARFULNESS	TECHNOBABBLES	TECTRICIAL	TELECHIRIC
TEARFULNESSES	TECHNOCRACIES	TEDIOSITIES	TELECOMMAND
TEARGASSED	TECHNOCRACY	TEDIOUSNESS	TELECOMMANDS
TEARGASSES	TECHNOCRAT	TEDIOUSNESSES	TELECOMMUTE
TEARGASSING	TECHNOCRATIC	TEDIOUSOME	TELECOMMUTED
TEARINESSES	TECHNOCRATS	TEEMINGNESS	TELECOMMUTER
TEARJERKER	TECHNOFEAR	TEEMINGNESSES	TELECOMMUTERS
TEARJERKERS	TECHNOFEARS	TEENTSIEST	TELECOMMUTES

TELECOMMUTING	TELEMARKETING	TELEPHONICALLY	TELESURGERIES
TELECOMMUTINGS	TELEMARKETINGS	TELEPHONIES	TELESURGERY
TELECONFERENCE	TELEMARKING	TELEPHONING	TELETYPESETTING
TELECONFERENCES	TELEMATICS	TELEPHONIST	TELETYPEWRITER
TELECONNECTION	TELEMEDICINE	TELEPHONISTS	TELETYPEWRITERS
TELECONNECTIONS	TELEMEDICINES	TELEPHOTOGRAPH	TELETYPING
TELECONTROL	TELEMETERED	TELEPHOTOGRAPHS	TELEUTOSPORE
TELECONTROLS	TELEMETERING	TELEPHOTOGRAPHY	TELEUTOSPORES
TELECONVERTER	TELEMETERS	TELEPHOTOS	TELEUTOSPORIC
TELECONVERTERS	TELEMETRIC	TELEPOINTS	TELEVANGELICAL
TELECOTTAGE	TELEMETRICAL	TELEPORTATION	TELEVANGELISM
TELECOTTAGES	TELEMETRICALLY	TELEPORTATIONS	TELEVANGELISMS
TELECOTTAGING	TELEMETRIES	TELEPORTED	TELEVANGELIST
TELECOTTAGINGS	TELENCEPHALA	TELEPORTING	TELEVANGELISTS
TELECOURSE	TELENCEPHALIC	TELEPRESENCE	TELEVERITE
TELECOURSES	TELENCEPHALON	TELEPRESENCES	TELEVERITES
TELEDILDONICS	TELENCEPHALONS	TELEPRINTER	TELEVIEWED
TELEFACSIMILE	TELEOLOGIC	TELEPRINTERS	TELEVIEWER
TELEFACSIMILES	TELEOLOGICAL	TELEPROCESSING	TELEVIEWERS
TELEFAXING	TELEOLOGICALLY	TELEPROCESSINGS	TELEVIEWING
TELEFERIQUE	TELEOLOGIES	TELEPROMPTER	TELEVISERS
TELEFERIQUES	TELEOLOGISM	TELEPROMPTERS	TELEVISING
TELEGENICALLY	TELEOLOGISMS	TELERECORD	TELEVISION
TELEGNOSES	TELEOLOGIST	TELERECORDED	TELEVISIONAL
TELEGNOSIS	TELEOLOGISTS	TELERECORDING	TELEVISIONALLY
TELEGNOSTIC	TELEONOMIC	TELERECORDINGS	TELEVISIONARY
TELEGONIES	TELEONOMIES	TELERECORDS	TELEVISIONS
TELEGONOUS	TELEOSAURIAN	TELERGICALLY	TELEVISORS
TELEGRAMMATIC	TELEOSAURIANS	TELESCIENCE	TELEVISUAL
TELEGRAMMED	TELEOSAURS	TELESCIENCES	TELEVISUALLY
TELEGRAMMIC	TELEOSTEAN	TELESCOPED	TELEWORKER
TELEGRAMMING	TELEOSTEANS	TELESCOPES	TELEWORKERS
TELEGRAPHED	TELEOSTOME	TELESCOPIC	TELEWORKING
TELEGRAPHER	TELEOSTOMES	TELESCOPICAL	TELEWORKINGS
TELEGRAPHERS	TELEOSTOMOUS	TELESCOPICALLY	TELEWRITER
TELEGRAPHESE	TELEPATHED	TELESCOPIES	TELEWRITERS
TELEGRAPHESES	TELEPATHIC	TELESCOPIFORM	TELFERAGES
TELEGRAPHIC	TELEPATHICALLY	TELESCOPING	TELIOSPORE
TELEGRAPHICALLY	TELEPATHIES	TELESCOPIST	TELIOSPORES
TELEGRAPHIES	TELEPATHING	TELESCOPISTS	TELLERSHIP
TELEGRAPHING	TELEPATHISE	TELESCREEN	TELLERSHIPS
TELEGRAPHIST	TELEPATHISED	TELESCREENS	TELLURATES
TELEGRAPHISTS	TELEPATHISES	TELESELLING	TELLURETTED
TELEGRAPHS	TELEPATHISING	TELESELLINGS	TELLURIANS
TELEGRAPHY	TELEPATHIST	TELESERVICES	TELLURIDES
TELEHEALTH	TELEPATHISTS	TELESHOPPED	TELLURIONS
TELEHEALTHS	TELEPATHIZE	TELESHOPPING	TELLURISED
TELEJOURNALISM	TELEPATHIZED	TELESHOPPINGS	TELLURISES
TELEJOURNALISMS	TELEPATHIZES	TELESMATIC	TELLURISING
TELEJOURNALIST	TELEPATHIZING	TELESMATICAL	TELLURITES
TELEJOURNALISTS	TELEPHEMES	TELESMATICALLY	TELLURIUMS
TELEKINESES	TELEPHERIQUE	TELESOFTWARE	TELLURIZED
TELEKINESIS	TELEPHERIQUES	TELESOFTWARES	TELLURIZES
TELEKINETIC	TELEPHONED	TELESTEREOSCOPE	TELLURIZING
TELEKINETICALLY	TELEPHONER	TELESTHESIA	TELLUROMETER
TELEMARKED	TELEPHONERS	TELESTHESIAS	TELLUROMETERS
TELEMARKETER	TELEPHONES	TELESTHETIC	TELNETTING
TELEMARKETERS	TELEPHONIC	TELESTICHS	TELOCENTRIC

TELOCENTRICS	TEMPORALIZE	TENANTRIES	TENEBRISTS
TELOMERASE	TEMPORALIZED	TENANTSHIP	TENEBRITIES
TELOMERASES	TEMPORALIZES	TENANTSHIPS	TENEBROSITIES
TELOMERISATION	TEMPORALTZING	TENDENCIALLY	TENEBROSITY
TELOMERISATIONS	TEMPORALLY	TENDENCIES	TENEBROUSNESS
TELOMERIZATION	TEMPORALNESS	TENDENCIOUS	TENEBROUSNESSES
TELOMERIZATIONS	TEMPORALNESSES	TENDENCIOUSLY	TENEMENTAL
TELOPHASES	TEMPORALTIES	TENDENCIOUSNESS	TENEMENTARY
TELOPHASIC	TEMPORALTY	TENDENTIAL	TENEMENTED
TELPHERAGE	TEMPORANEOUS	TENDENTIALLY	TENESMUSES
TELPHERAGES	TEMPORARIES	TENDENTIOUS	TENIACIDES
TELPHERING	TEMPORARILY	TENDENTIOUSLY	TENIAFUGES
TELPHERLINE	TEMPORARINESS	TENDENTIOUSNESS	TENNANTITE
TELPHERLINES	TEMPORARINESSES	TENDERABLE	TENNANTITES
TELPHERMAN	TEMPORISATION	TENDERFEET	TENORRHAPHIES
TELPHERMEN	TEMPORISATIONS	TENDERFOOT	TENORRHAPHY
TELPHERWAY	TEMPORISED	TENDERFOOTS	TENOSYNOVITIS
TELPHERWAYS	TEMPORISER	TENDERHEARTED	TENOSYNOVITISES
TEMAZEPAMS	TEMPORISERS	TENDERHEARTEDLY	TENOTOMIES
TEMERARIOUS	TEMPORISES	TENDERINGS	TENOTOMIST
TEMERARIOUSLY	TEMPORISING	TENDERISATION	TENOTOMISTS
TEMERARIOUSNESS	TEMPORISINGLY	TENDERISATIONS	TENOVAGINITIS
TEMERITIES	TEMPORISINGS	TENDERISED	TENOVAGINITISES
TEMEROUSLY	TEMPORIZATION	TENDERISER	TENPOUNDER
TEMPERABILITIES	TEMPORIZATIONS	TENDERISERS	TENPOUNDERS
TEMPERABILITY	TEMPORIZED	TENDERISES	TENSENESSES
TEMPERABLE	TEMPORIZER	TENDERISING	TENSIBILITIES
TEMPERALITIE	TEMPORIZERS	TENDERIZATION	TENSIBILITY
TEMPERALITIES	TEMPORIZES	TENDERIZATIONS	TENSIBLENESS
TEMPERAMENT	TEMPORIZING	TENDERIZED	TENSIBLENESSES
TEMPERAMENTAL	TEMPORIZINGLY	TENDERIZER	TENSILENESS
TEMPERAMENTALLY	TEMPORIZINGS	TENDERIZERS	TENSILENESSES
TEMPERAMENTFUL	TEMPTABILITIES	TENDERIZES	TENSILITIES
TEMPERAMENTS	TEMPTABILITY	TENDERIZING	TENSIMETER
TEMPERANCE	TEMPTABLENESS	TENDERLING	TENSIMETERS
TEMPERANCES	TEMPTABLENESSES	TENDERLINGS	TENSIOMETER
TEMPERATED	TEMPTATION	TENDERLOIN	TENSIOMETERS
TEMPERATELY	TEMPTATIONS	TENDERLOINS	TENSIOMETRIC
TEMPERATENESS	TEMPTATIOUS	TENDERNESS	TENSIOMETRIES
TEMPERATENESSES	TEMPTINGLY	TENDERNESSES	TENSIOMETRY
TEMPERATES	TEMPTINGNESS	TENDEROMETER	TENSIONALLY
TEMPERATING	TEMPTINGNESSES	TENDEROMETERS	TENSIONERS
TEMPERATIVE	TEMPTRESSES	TENDINITIS	TENSIONING
TEMPERATURE	TEMULENCES	TENDINITISES	TENSIONLESS
TEMPERATURES	TEMULENCIES	TENDONITIS	TENTACULAR
TEMPERINGS	TEMULENTLY	TENDONITISES	TENTACULATE
TEMPESTING	TENABILITIES	TENDOVAGINITIS	TENTACULIFEROUS
TEMPESTIVE	TENABILITY	TENDRESSES	TENTACULITE
TEMPESTUOUS	TENABLENESS	TENDRILLAR	TENTACULITES
TEMPESTUOUSLY	TENABLENESSES	TENDRILLED	TENTACULOID
TEMPESTUOUSNESS	TENACIOUSLY	TENDRILLOUS	TENTACULUM
TEMPOLABILE	TENACIOUSNESS	TENDRILOUS	TENTATIONS
TEMPORALISE	TENACIOUSNESSES	TENEBRIFIC	TENTATIVELY
TEMPORALISED	TENACITIES	TENEBRIONID	TENTATIVENESS
TEMPORALISES	TENACULUMS	TENEBRIONIDS	TENTATIVENESSES
TEMPORALISING	TENAILLONS	TENEBRIOUS	TENTATIVES
TEMPORALITIES	TENANTABLE	TENEBRIOUSNESS	TENTERHOOK
TEMPORALITY	TENANTLESS	TENEBRISMS	TENTERHOOKS

TENTIGINOUS	TERGIVERSATED	TERRAFORMING	TERSANCTUS
TENTMAKERS	TERGIVERSATES	TERRAFORMINGS	TERSANCTUSES
TENTORIUMS	TERGIVERSATING	TERRAFORMS	TERSENESSES
TENUIROSTRAL	TERGIVERSATION	TERRAMARES	TERTIARIES
TENUOUSNESS	TERGIVERSATIONS	TERRAQUEOUS	TERVALENCIES
TENUOUSNESSES	TERGIVERSATOR	TERRARIUMS	TERVALENCY
TENURIALLY	TERGIVERSATORS	TERREMOTIVE	TESCHENITE
TEPEFACTION	TERGIVERSATORY	TERREPLEIN	TESCHENITES
TEPEFACTIONS	TERMAGANCIES	TERREPLEINS	TESSARAGLOT
TEPHIGRAMS	TERMAGANCY	TERRESTRIAL	TESSELATED
TEPHROITES	TERMAGANTLY	TERRESTRIALLY	TESSELATES
TEPHROMANCIES	TERMAGANTS	TERRESTRIALNESS	TESSELATING
TEPHROMANCY	TERMINABILITIES	TERRESTRIALS	TESSELLATE
TEPIDARIUM	TERMINABILITY	TERRIBILITIES	TESSELLATED
TEPIDITIES	TERMINABLE	TERRIBILITY	TESSELLATES
TEPIDNESSES	TERMINABLENESS	TERRIBLENESS	TESSELLATING
TERAHERTZES	TERMINABLY	TERRIBLENESSES	TESSELLATION
TERATOCARCINOMA	TERMINALLY	TERRICOLES	TESSELLATIONS
TERATOGENESES	TERMINATED	TERRICOLOUS	TESSERACTS
TERATOGENESIS	TERMINATES	TERRIFICALLY	TESSITURAS
TERATOGENIC	TERMINATING	TERRIFIERS	TESTABILITIES
TERATOGENICIST	TERMINATION	TERRIFYING	TESTABILITY
TERATOGENICISTS	TERMINATIONAL	TERRIFYINGLY	TESTACEANS
TERATOGENICITY	TERMINATIONS	TERRIGENOUS	TESTACEOUS
TERATOGENIES	TERMINATIVE	TERRITORIAL	TESTAMENTAL
TERATOGENS	TERMINATIVELY	TERRITORIALISE	TESTAMENTAR
TERATOGENY	TERMINATOR	TERRITORIALISED	TESTAMENTARILY
TERATOLOGIC	TERMINATORS	TERRITORIALISES	TESTAMENTARY
TERATOLOGICAL	TERMINATORY	TERRITORIALISM	TESTAMENTS
TERATOLOGIES	TERMINISMS	TERRITORIALISMS	TESTATIONS
TERATOLOGIST	TERMINISTS	TERRITORIALIST	TESTATRICES
TERATOLOGISTS	TERMINOLOGICAL	TERRITORIALISTS	TESTATRIXES
TERATOLOGY	TERMINOLOGIES	TERRITORIALITY	TESTCROSSED
TERATOMATA	TERMINOLOGIST	TERRITORIALIZE	TESTCROSSES
TERATOMATOUS	TERMINOLOGISTS	TERRITORIALIZED	TESTCROSSING
TERATOPHOBIA	TERMINOLOGY	TERRITORIALIZES	TESTERNING
TERATOPHOBIAS	TERMINUSES	TERRITORIALLY	TESTICULAR
TERCENTENARIES	TERMITARIA	TERRITORIALS	TESTICULATE
TERCENTENARY	TERMITARIES	TERRITORIED	TESTICULATED
TERCENTENNIAL	TERMITARIUM	TERRITORIES	TESTIFICATE
TERCENTENNIALS	TERMITARIUMS	TERRORISATION	TESTIFICATES
TEREBINTHINE	TERNEPLATE	TERRORISATIONS	TESTIFICATION
TEREBINTHS	TERNEPLATES	TERRORISED	TESTIFICATIONS
TEREBRANTS	TEROTECHNOLOGY	TERRORISER	TESTIFICATOR
TEREBRATED	TERPENELESS	TERRORISERS	TESTIFICATORS
TEREBRATES	TERPENOIDS	TERRORISES	TESTIFICATORY
TEREBRATING	TERPINEOLS	TERRORISING	TESTIFIERS
TEREBRATION	TERPOLYMER	TERRORISMS	TESTIFYING
TEREBRATIONS	TERPOLYMERS	TERRORISTIC	TESTIMONIAL
TEREBRATULA	TERPSICHOREAL	TERRORISTS	TESTIMONIALISE
TEREBRATULAE	TERPSICHOREAN	TERRORIZATION	TESTIMONIALISED
TEREBRATULAS	TERRACELESS	TERRORIZATIONS	TESTIMONIALISES
TEREPHTHALATE	TERRACETTE	TERRORIZED	TESTIMONIALIZE
TEREPHTHALATES	TERRACETTES	TERRORIZER	TESTIMONIALIZED
TEREPHTHALIC	TERRACINGS	TERRORIZERS	TESTIMONIALIZES
TERGIVERSANT	TERRACOTTA	TERRORIZES	TESTIMONIALS
TERGIVERSANTS	TERRACOTTAS	TERRORIZING	TESTIMONIED
TERGIVERSATE	TERRAFORMED	TERRORLESS	TESTIMONIES

TESTIMONYING	TETRAFLUORIDES	TETRASPORANGIUM	THALASSAEMIAS
TESTINESSES	TETRAGONAL	TETRASPORE	THALASSAEMIC
TESTOSTERONE	TETRAGONALLY	TETRASPORES	THALASSEMIA
TESTOSTERONES	TETRAGONALNESS	TETRASPORIC	THALASSEMIAS
TESTUDINAL	TETRAGONOUS	TETRASPOROUS	THALASSEMIC
TESTUDINARY	TETRAGRAMMATON	TETRASTICH	THALASSEMICS
TESTUDINEOUS	TETRAGRAMMATONS	TETRASTICHAL	THALASSIAN
TESTUDINES	TETRAGRAMS	TETRASTICHIC	THALASSIANS
TETANICALLY	TETRAGYNIAN	TETRASTICHOUS	THALASSOCRACIES
TETANISATION	TETRAGYNOUS	TETRASTICHS	THALASSOCRACY
TETANISATIONS	TETRAHEDRA	TETRASTYLE	THALASSOCRAT
TETANISING	TETRAHEDRAL	TETRASTYLES	THALASSOCRATS
TETANIZATION	TETRAHEDRALLY	TETRASYLLABIC	THALASSOGRAPHER
TETANIZATIONS	TETRAHEDRITE	TETRASYLLABICAL	THALASSOGRAPHIC
TETANIZING	TETRAHEDRITES	TETRASYLLABLE	THALASSOGRAPHY
TETARTOHEDRAL	TETRAHEDRON	TETRASYLLABLES	THALASSOTHERAPY
TETARTOHEDRALLY	TETRAHEDRONS	TETRATHEISM	THALATTOCRACIES
TETARTOHEDRISM	TETRAHYDROFURAN	TETRATHEISMS	THALATTOCRACY
TETARTOHEDRISMS	TETRAHYMENA	TETRATHLON	THALICTRUM
TETCHINESS	TETRAHYMENAS	TETRATHLONS	THALICTRUMS
TETCHINESSES	TETRALOGIES	TETRATOMIC	THALIDOMIDE
TETHERBALL	TETRAMERAL	TETRAVALENCIES	THALIDOMIDES
TETHERBALLS	TETRAMERIC	TETRAVALENCY	THALLIFORM
TETRABASIC	TETRAMERISM	TETRAVALENT	THALLOPHYTE
TETRABASICITIES	TETRAMERISMS	TETRAVALENTS	THALLOPHYTES
TETRABASICITY	TETRAMEROUS	TETRAZOLIUM	THALLOPHYTIC
TETRABRACH	TETRAMETER	TETRAZOLIUMS	THANATISMS
TETRABRACHS	TETRAMETERS	TETRAZZINI	THANATISTS
TETRABRANCHIATE	TETRAMETHYLLEAD	TETRODOTOXIN	THANATOGNOMONIC
TETRACAINE	TETRAMORPHIC	TETRODOTOXINS	THANATOGRAPHIES
TETRACAINES	TETRANDRIAN	TETROTOXIN	THANATOGRAPHY
TETRACHLORIDE	TETRANDROUS	TETROTOXINS	THANATOLOGICAL
TETRACHLORIDES	TETRAPLEGIA	TETROXIDES	THANATOLOGIES
TETRACHORD	TETRAPLEGIAS	TEUTONISED	THANATOLOGIST
TETRACHORDAL	TETRAPLEGIC	TEUTONISES	THANATOLOGISTS
TETRACHORDS	TETRAPLOID	TEUTONISING	THANATOLOGY
TETRACHOTOMIES	TETRAPLOIDIES	TEUTONIZED	THANATOPHOBIA
TETRACHOTOMOUS	TETRAPLOIDS	TEUTONIZES	THANATOPHOBIAS
TETRACHOTOMY	TETRAPLOIDY	TEUTONIZING	THANATOPSES
TETRACTINAL	TETRAPODIC	TEXTBOOKISH	THANATOPSIS
TETRACTINE	TETRAPODIES	TEXTPHONES	THANATOSES
TETRACYCLIC	TETRAPODOUS	TEXTUALISM	THANATOSIS
TETRACYCLINE	TETRAPOLIS	TEXTUALISMS	THANEHOODS
TETRACYCLINES	TETRAPOLISES	TEXTUALIST	THANESHIPS
TETRADACTYL	TETRAPOLITAN	TEXTUALISTS	THANKFULLER
TETRADACTYLIES	TETRAPTERAN	TEXTUARIES	THANKFULLEST
TETRADACTYLOUS	TETRAPTEROUS	TEXTURALLY	THANKFULLY
TETRADACTYLS	TETRAPTOTE	TEXTURELESS	THANKFULNESS
TETRADACTYLY	TETRAPTOTES	TEXTURISED	THANKFULNESSES
TETRADITES	TETRAPYRROLE	TEXTURISES	THANKLESSLY
TETRADRACHM	TETRAPYRROLES	TEXTURISING	THANKLESSNESS
TETRADRACHMS	TETRARCHATE	TEXTURIZED	THANKLESSNESSES
TETRADYMITE	TETRARCHATES	TEXTURIZES	THANKSGIVER
TETRADYMITES	TETRARCHIC	TEXTURIZING	THANKSGIVERS
TETRADYNAMOUS	TETRARCHICAL	THALAMENCEPHALA	THANKSGIVING
TETRAETHYL	TETRARCHIES	THALAMICALLY	THANKSGIVINGS
TETRAETHYLS	TETRASEMIC	THALAMIFLORAL	THANKWORTHILY
TETRAFLUORIDE	TETRASPORANGIA	THALASSAEMIA	THANKWORTHINESS

THANKWORTHY	THEATRICALIZE	THEODOLITE	THEOPHANOUS
THARBOROUGH	THEATRICALIZED	THEODOLITES	THEOPHOBIA
THARBOROUGHS	THEATRICALIZES	THEODOLITIC	THEOPHOBIAC
THATCHIEST	THEATRICALIZING	THEOGONICAL	THEOPHOBIACS
THATCHINGS	THEATRICALLY	THEOGONIES	THEOPHOBIAS
THATCHLESS	THEATRICALNESS	THEOGONIST	THEOPHOBIST
THATNESSES	THEATRICALS	THEOGONISTS	THEOPHOBISTS
THAUMASITE	THEATRICISE	THEOLOGASTER	THEOPHORIC
THAUMASITES	THEATRICISED	THEOLOGASTERS	THEOPHYLLINE
THAUMATINS	THEATRICISES	THEOLOGATE	THEOPHYLLINES
THAUMATOGENIES	THEATRICISING	THEOLOGATES	THEOPNEUST
THAUMATOGENY	THEATRICISM	THEOLOGERS	THEOPNEUSTIC
THAUMATOGRAPHY	THEATRICISMS	THEOLOGIAN	THEOPNEUSTIES
THAUMATOLATRIES	THEATRICIZE	THEOLOGIANS	THEOPNEUSTY
THAUMATOLATRY	THEATRICIZED	THEOLOGICAL	THEORBISTS
THAUMATOLOGIES	THEATRICIZES	THEOLOGICALLY	THEOREMATIC
THAUMATOLOGY	THEATRICIZING	THEOLOGIES	THEOREMATICAL
THAUMATROPE	THEATROMANIA	THEOLOGISATION	THEOREMATICALLY
THAUMATROPES	THEATROMANIAS	THEOLOGISATIONS	THEOREMATIST
THAUMATROPICAL	THEATROPHONE	THEOLOGISE	THEOREMATISTS
THAUMATURGE	THEATROPHONES	THEOLOGISED	THEORETICAL
THAUMATURGES	THECODONTS	THEOLOGISER	THEORETICALLY
THAUMATURGIC	THEFTUOUSLY	THEOLOGISERS	THEORETICIAN
THAUMATURGICAL	THEIRSELVES	THEOLOGISES	THEORETICIANS
THAUMATURGICS	THEISTICAL	THEOLOGISING	THEORETICS
THAUMATURGIES	THEISTICALLY	THEOLOGIST	THEORIQUES
THAUMATURGISM	THELEMENTS	THEOLOGISTS	THEORISATION
THAUMATURGISMS	THELITISES	THEOLOGIZATION	THEORISATIONS
THAUMATURGIST	THELYTOKIES	THEOLOGIZATIONS	THEORISERS
THAUMATURGISTS	THELYTOKOUS	THEOLOGIZE	THEORISING
THAUMATURGUS	THEMATICALLY	THEOLOGIZED	THEORIZATION
THAUMATURGUSES	THEMATISATION	THEOLOGIZER	THEORIZATIONS
THAUMATURGY	THEMATISATIONS	THEOLOGIZERS	THEORIZERS
THEANTHROPIC	THEMATIZATION	THEOLOGIZES	THEORIZING
THEANTHROPIES	THEMATIZATIONS	THEOLOGIZING	THEOSOPHER
THEANTHROPISM	THEMSELVES	THEOLOGOUMENA	THEOSOPHERS
THEANTHROPISMS	THENABOUTS	THEOLOGOUMENON	THEOSOPHIC
THEANTHROPIST	THENARDITE	THEOLOGUES	THEOSOPHICAL
THEANTHROPISTS	THENARDITES	THEOMACHIES	THEOSOPHICALLY
THEANTHROPY	THENCEFORTH	THEOMACHIST	THEOSOPHIES
THEARCHIES	THENCEFORWARD	THEOMACHISTS	THEOSOPHISE
THEATERGOER	THENCEFORWARDS	THEOMANCIES	THEOSOPHISED
THEATERGOERS	THEOBROMINE	THEOMANIAC	THEOSOPHISES
THEATERGOING	THEOBROMINES	THEOMANIACS	THEOSOPHISING
THEATERGOINGS	THEOCENTRIC	THEOMANIAS	THEOSOPHISM
THEATREGOER	THEOCENTRICISM	THEOMANTIC	THEOSOPHISMS
THEATREGOERS	THEOCENTRICISMS	THEOMORPHIC	THEOSOPHIST
THEATREGOING	THEOCENTRICITY	THEOMORPHISM	THEOSOPHISTICAL
THEATREGOINGS	THEOCENTRISM	THEOMORPHISMS	THEOSOPHISTS
THEATRICAL	THEOCENTRISMS	THEONOMIES	THEOSOPHIZE
THEATRICALISE	THEOCRACIES	THEONOMOUS	THEOSOPHIZED
THEATRICALISED	THEOCRASIES	THEOPATHETIC	THEOSOPHIZES
THEATRICALISES	THEOCRATIC	THEOPATHIC	THEOSOPHIZING
THEATRICALISING	THEOCRATICAL	THEOPATHIES	THEOTECHNIC
THEATRICALISM	THEOCRATICALLY	THEOPHAGIES	THEOTECHNIES
THEATRICALISMS	THEODICEAN	THEOPHAGOUS	THEOTECHNY
THEATRICALITIES	THEODICEANS	THEOPHANIC	THERALITES
THEATRICALITY	THEODICIES	THEOPHANIES	THERAPEUSES

THERAPEUSIS	THERMOBALANCE	THERMOMETERS	THERMOTHERAPY
THERAPEUTIC	THERMOBALANCES	THERMOMETRIC	THERMOTICAL
THERAPEUTICALLY	THERMOBARIC	THERMOMETRICAL	THERMOTICS
THERAPEUTICS	THERMOBAROGRAPH	THERMOMETRIES	THERMOTOLERANT
THERAPEUTIST	THERMOBAROMETER	THERMOMETRY	THERMOTROPIC
THERAPEUTISTS	THERMOCHEMICAL	THERMOMOTOR	THERMOTROPICS
THERAPISTS	THERMOCHEMIST	THERMOMOTORS	THERMOTROPISM
THERAPSIDS	THERMOCHEMISTRY	THERMONASTIES	THERMOTROPISMS
THEREABOUT	THERMOCHEMISTS	THERMONASTY	THEROLOGIES
THEREABOUTS	THERMOCHROMIC	THERMONUCLEAR	THEROPHYTE
THEREAFTER	THERMOCHROMIES	THERMOPERIODIC	THEROPHYTES
THEREAGAINST	THERMOCHROMISM	THERMOPERIODISM	THEROPODAN
THEREAMONG	THERMOCHROMISMS	THERMOPHIL	THEROPODANS
THEREANENT	THERMOCHROMY	THERMOPHILE	THERSITICAL
THEREBESIDE	THERMOCLINE	THERMOPHILES	THESAURUSES
THEREINAFTER	THERMOCLINES	THERMOPHILIC	THESMOTHETE
THEREINBEFORE	THERMOCOUPLE	THERMOPHILOUS	THESMOTHETES
THERENESSES	THERMOCOUPLES	THERMOPHILS	THETICALLY
THERETHROUGH	THERMODURIC	THERMOPHYLLOUS	THEURGICAL
THERETOFORE	THERMODYNAMIC	THERMOPILE	THEURGICALLY
THEREUNDER	THERMODYNAMICAL	THERMOPILES	THEURGISTS
THEREWITHAL	THERMODYNAMICS	THERMOPLASTIC	THIABENDAZOLE
THEREWITHIN	THERMOELECTRIC	THERMOPLASTICS	THIABENDAZOLES
THERIANTHROPIC	THERMOELECTRON	THERMORECEPTOR	THIAMINASE
THERIANTHROPISM	THERMOELECTRONS	THERMORECEPTORS	THIAMINASES
THERIOLATRIES	THERMOELEMENT	THERMOREGULATE	THICKENERS
THERIOLATRY	THERMOELEMENTS	THERMOREGULATED	THICKENING
THERIOMORPH	THERMOFORM	THERMOREGULATES	THICKENINGS
THERIOMORPHIC	THERMOFORMABLE	THERMOREGULATOR	THICKHEADED
THERIOMORPHISM	THERMOFORMED	THERMOREMANENCE	THICKHEADEDNESS
THERIOMORPHISMS	THERMOFORMING	THERMOREMANENT	THICKHEADS
THERIOMORPHOSES	THERMOFORMS	THERMOSCOPE	THICKLEAVES
THERIOMORPHOSIS	THERMOGENESES	THERMOSCOPES	THICKNESSES
THERIOMORPHOUS	THERMOGENESIS	THERMOSCOPIC	THICKSKINS
THERIOMORPHS	THERMOGENETIC	THERMOSCOPICAL	THIEVERIES
THERMAESTHESIA	THERMOGENIC	THERMOSETS	THIEVISHLY
THERMAESTHESIAS	THERMOGENOUS	THERMOSETTING	THIEVISHNESS
THERMALISATION	THERMOGRAM	THERMOSIPHON	THIEVISHNESSES
THERMALISATIONS	THERMOGRAMS	THERMOSIPHONS	THIGHBONES
THERMALISE	THERMOGRAPH	THERMOSPHERE	THIGMOTACTIC
THERMALISED	THERMOGRAPHER	THERMOSPHERES	THIGMOTAXES
THERMALISES	THERMOGRAPHERS	THERMOSPHERIC	THIGMOTAXIS
THERMALISING	THERMOGRAPHIC	THERMOSTABILITY	THIGMOTROPIC
THERMALIZATION	THERMOGRAPHIES	THERMOSTABLE	THIGMOTROPISM
THERMALIZATIONS	THERMOGRAPHS	THERMOSTAT	THIGMOTROPISMS
THERMALIZE	THERMOGRAPHY	THERMOSTATED	THIMBLEBERRIES
THERMALIZED	THERMOHALINE	THERMOSTATIC	THIMBLEBERRY
THERMALIZES	THERMOJUNCTION	THERMOSTATICS	THIMBLEFUL
THERMALIZING	THERMOJUNCTIONS	THERMOSTATING	THIMBLEFULS
THERMESTHESIA	THERMOLABILE	THERMOSTATS	THIMBLERIG
THERMESTHESIAS	THERMOLABILITY	THERMOSTATTED	THIMBLERIGGED
THERMETTES	THERMOLOGIES	THERMOSTATTING	THIMBLERIGGER
THERMICALLY	THERMOLOGY	THERMOTACTIC	THIMBLERIGGERS
THERMIDORS	THERMOLYSES	THERMOTAXES	THIMBLERIGGING
THERMIONIC	THERMOLYSIS	THERMOTAXIC	THIMBLERIGGINGS
THERMIONICS	THERMOLYTIC	THERMOTAXIS	THIMBLERIGS
THERMISTOR	THERMOMAGNETIC	THERMOTENSILE	THIMBLESFUL
THERMISTORS	THERMOMETER	THERMOTHERAPIES	THIMBLEWEED

THIMBLEWEEDS	THIORIDAZINE	THORNHEDGES	THREADWORM
THIMBLEWIT	THIORIDAZINES	THORNINESS	THREADWORMS
THIMBLEWITS	THIOSINAMINE	THORNINESSES	THREATENED
THIMBLEWITTED	THIOSINAMINES	THORNPROOFS	THREATENER
THIMEROSAL	THIOSULFATE	THORNTREES	THREATENERS
THIMEROSALS	THIOSULFATES	THOROUGHBASS	THREATENING
THINGAMABOB	THIOSULPHATE	THOROUGHBASSES	THREATENINGLY
THINGAMABOBS	THIOSULPHATES	THOROUGHBRACE	THREATENINGS
THINGAMAJIG	THIOSULPHURIC	THOROUGHBRACED	THREEFOLDNESS
THINGAMAJIGS	THIOURACIL	THOROUGHBRACES	THREEFOLDNESSES
THINGAMIES	THIOURACILS	THOROUGHBRED	THREENESSES
THINGAMYBOB	THIRDBOROUGH	THOROUGHBREDS	THREEPENCE
THINGAMYBOBS	THIRDBOROUGHS	THOROUGHER	THREEPENCES
THINGAMYJIG	THIRDSTREAM	THOROUGHEST	THREEPENCEWORTH
THINGAMYJIGS	THIRDSTREAMS	THOROUGHFARE	THREEPENNIES
THINGHOODS	THIRSTIEST	THOROUGHFARES	THREEPENNY
THINGINESS	THIRSTINESS	THOROUGHGOING	THREEPENNYWORTH
THINGINESSES	THIRSTINESSES	THOROUGHGOINGLY	THREESCORE
THINGLINESS	THIRSTLESS	THOROUGHLY	THREESCORES
THINGLINESSES	THIRTEENTH	THOROUGHNESS	THREESOMES
THINGNESSES	THIRTEENTHLY	THOROUGHNESSES	THREMMATOLOGIES
THINGUMABOB	THIRTEENTHS	THOROUGHPACED	THREMMATOLOGY
THINGUMABOBS	THIRTIETHS	THOROUGHPIN	THRENETICAL
THINGUMAJIG	THIRTYFOLD	THOROUGHPINS	THRENODIAL
THINGUMAJIGS	THIRTYSOMETHING	THOROUGHWAX	THRENODIES
THINGUMBOB	THISNESSES	THOROUGHWAXES	THRENODIST
THINGUMBOBS	THISTLEDOWN	THOROUGHWORT	THRENODISTS
THINGUMMIES	THISTLEDOWNS	THOROUGHWORTS	THREONINES
THINGUMMYBOB	THISTLIEST	THOUGHTCAST	THRESHINGS
THINGUMMYBOBS	THITHERWARD	THOUGHTCASTS	THRESHOLDS
THINGUMMYJIG	THITHERWARDS	THOUGHTFUL	THRIFTIEST
THINGUMMYJIGS	THIXOTROPE	THOUGHTFULLY	THRIFTINESS
THINKABLENESS	THIXOTROPES	THOUGHTFULNESS	THRIFTINESSES
THINKABLENESSES	THIXOTROPIC	THOUGHTLESS	THRIFTLESS
THINKINGLY	THIXOTROPIES	THOUGHTLESSLY	THRIFTLESSLY
THINKINGNESS	THIXOTROPY	THOUGHTLESSNESS	THRIFTLESSNESS
THINKINGNESSES	THOLEIITES	THOUGHTWAY	THRILLIEST
THINKPIECE	THOLEIITIC	THOUGHTWAYS	THRILLINGLY
THINKPIECES	THOLOBATES	THOUSANDFOLD	THRILLINGNESS
THINNESSES	THORACENTESES	THOUSANDFOLDS	THRILLINGNESSES
THIOALCOHOL	THORACENTESIS	THOUSANDTH	THRIVELESS
THIOALCOHOLS	THORACICALLY	THOUSANDTHS	THRIVINGLY◦
THIOBACILLI	THORACOCENTESES	THRAIPINGS	THRIVINGNESS
THIOBACILLUS	THORACOCENTESIS	THRALLDOMS	THRIVINGNESSES
THIOBARBITURATE	THORACOPLASTIES	THRAPPLING	THROATIEST
THIOCARBAMIDE	THORACOPLASTY	THRASHINGS	THROATINESS
THIOCARBAMIDES	THORACOSCOPE	THRASONICAL	THROATINESSES
THIOCYANATE	THORACOSCOPES	THRASONICALLY	THROATLASH
THIOCYANATES	THORACOSTOMIES	THREADBARE	THROATLASHES
THIOCYANIC	THORACOSTOMY	THREADBARENESS	THROATLATCH
THIODIGLYCOL	THORACOTOMIES	THREADFINS	THROATLATCHES
THIODIGLYCOLS	THORACOTOMY	THREADIEST	THROATWORT
THIOFURANS	THORIANITE	THREADINESS	THROATWORTS
THIOPENTAL	THORIANITES	THREADINESSES	THROBBINGLY
THIOPENTALS	THORNBACKS	THREADLESS	THROBBINGS
THIOPENTONE	THORNBILLS	THREADLIKE	THROMBOCYTE
THIOPENTONES	THORNBUSHES	THREADMAKER	THROMBOCYTES
THIOPHENES	THORNHEDGE	THREADMAKERS	THROMBOCYTIC

THROMBOEMBOLIC	THUMBLINGS	THURIFYING	TICKETTYBOO
THROMBOEMBOLISM	THUMBNAILS	THUSNESSES	TICKLISHLY
THROMBOGEN	THUMBPIECE	THWACKINGS	TICKLISHNESS
THROMBOGENS	THUMBPIECES	THWARTEDLY	TICKLISHNESSES
THROMBOKINASE	THUMBPRINT	THWARTINGLY	TICKTACKED
THROMBOKINASES	THUMBPRINTS	THWARTINGS	TICKTACKING
THROMBOLYSES	THUMBSCREW	THWARTSHIP	TICKTACKTOE
THROMBOLYSIS	THUMBSCREWS	THWARTSHIPS	TICKTACKTOES
THROMBOLYTIC	THUMBSTALL	THWARTWAYS	TICKTOCKED
THROMBOLYTICS	THUMBSTALLS	THWARTWISE	TICKTOCKING
THROMBOPHILIA	THUMBTACKED	THYLACINES	TICTACKING
THROMBOPHILIAS	THUMBTACKING	THYLAKOIDS	TICTOCKING
THROMBOPLASTIC	THUMBTACKS	THYMECTOMIES	TIDDLEDYWINK
THROMBOPLASTIN	THUMBWHEEL	THYMECTOMISE	TIDDLEDYWINKS
THROMBOPLASTINS	THUMBWHEELS	THYMECTOMISED	TIDDLEYWINK
THROMBOSED	THUMPINGLY	THYMECTOMISES	TIDDLEYWINKS
THROMBOSES	THUNBERGIA	THYMECTOMISING	TIDDLYWINK
THROMBOSING	THUNBERGIAS	THYMECTOMIZE	TIDDLYWINKS
THROMBOSIS	THUNDERBIRD	THYMECTOMIZED	TIDEWAITER
THROMBOTIC	THUNDERBIRDS	THYMECTOMIZES	TIDEWAITERS
THROMBOXANE	THUNDERBOLT	THYMECTOMIZING	TIDEWATERS
THROMBOXANES	THUNDERBOLTS	THYMECTOMY	TIDINESSES
THRONELESS	THUNDERBOX	THYMELAEACEOUS	TIDIVATING
THRONGINGS	THUNDERBOXES	THYMIDINES	TIDIVATION
THROPPLING	THUNDERCLAP	THYMIDYLIC	TIDIVATIONS
THROTTLEABLE	THUNDERCLAPS	THYMOCYTES	TIEBREAKER
THROTTLEHOLD	THUNDERCLOUD	THYRATRONS	TIEBREAKERS
THROTTLEHOLDS	THUNDERCLOUDS	THYRISTORS	TIEMANNITE
THROTTLERS	THUNDERERS	THYROCALCITONIN	TIEMANNITES
THROTTLING	THUNDERFLASH	THYROGLOBULIN	TIERCELETS
THROTTLINGS	THUNDERFLASHES	THYROGLOBULINS	TIERCERONS
THROUGHFARE	THUNDERHEAD	THYROIDECTOMIES	TIGERISHLY
THROUGHFARES	THUNDERHEADS	THYROIDECTOMY	TIGERISHNESS
THROUGHGAUN	THUNDERIER	THYROIDITIS	TIGERISHNESSES
THROUGHGAUNS	THUNDERIEST	THYROIDITISES	TIGGYWINKLE
THROUGHITHER	THUNDERING	THYROTOXICOSES	TIGGYWINKLES
THROUGHOTHER	THUNDERINGLY	THYROTOXICOSIS	TIGHTASSED
THROUGHOUT	THUNDERINGS	THYROTROPHIC	TIGHTASSES
THROUGHPUT	THUNDERLESS	THYROTROPHIN	TIGHTENERS
THROUGHPUTS	THUNDEROUS	THYROTROPHINS	TIGHTENING
THROUGHWAY	THUNDEROUSLY	THYROTROPIC	TIGHTFISTED
THROUGHWAYS	THUNDEROUSNESS	THYROTROPIN	TIGHTFISTEDNESS
THROWAWAYS	THUNDERSHOWER	THYROTROPINS	TIGHTISHLY
THROWBACKS	THUNDERSHOWERS	THYROXINES	TIGHTNESSES
THROWSTERS	THUNDERSTONE	THYRSOIDAL	TIGHTROPES
THRUMMIEST	THUNDERSTONES	THYSANOPTEROUS	TIGHTWIRES
THRUMMINGLY	THUNDERSTORM	THYSANURAN	TIGRISHNESS
THRUMMINGS	THUNDERSTORMS	THYSANURANS	TIGRISHNESSES
THRUPPENCE	THUNDERSTRICKEN	THYSANUROUS	TIKOLOSHES
THRUPPENCES	THUNDERSTRIKE	TIBIOFIBULA	TILEFISHES
THRUPPENNIES	THUNDERSTRIKES	TIBIOFIBULAE	TILIACEOUS
THRUPPENNY	THUNDERSTRIKING	TIBIOFIBULAS	TILLANDSIA
THRUSTINGS	THUNDERSTROKE	TIBIOTARSI	TILLANDSIAS
THRUTCHING	THUNDERSTROKES	TIBIOTARSUS	TILLERLESS
THUDDINGLY	THUNDERSTRUCK	TIBOUCHINA	TILTMETERS
THUGGERIES	THURIFEROUS	TIBOUCHINAS	TILTROTORS
THUMBHOLES	THURIFICATION	TICHORRHINE	TIMBERDOODLE
THUMBIKINS	THURIFICATIONS	TICKETLESS	TIMBERDOODLES

TIMBERHEAD	TIMOROUSLY	TITHINGMAN	TOBOGGANERS
TIMBERHEADS	TIMOROUSNESS	TITHINGMEN	TOBOGGANING
TIMBERINGS	TIMOROUSNESSES	TITILLATED	TOBOGGANINGS
TIMBERLAND	TIMPANISTS	TITILLATES	TOBOGGANIST
TIMBERLANDS	TINCTORIAL	TITILLATING	TOBOGGANISTS
TIMBERLINE	TINCTORIALLY	TITILLATINGLY	TOBOGGINED
TIMBERLINES	TINCTURING	TITILLATION	TOBOGGINING
TIMBERWORK	TINDERBOXES	TITILLATIONS	TOCCATELLA
TIMBERWORKS	TINGLINGLY	TITILLATIVE	TOCCATELLAS
TIMBERYARD	TINGUAITES	TITILLATOR	TOCCATINAS
TIMBERYARDS	TININESSES	TITILLATORS	TOCHERLESS
TIMBRELLED	TINKERINGS	TITIPOUNAMU	TOCOLOGIES
TIMBROLOGIES	TINKERTOYS	TITIVATING	TOCOPHEROL
TIMBROLOGIST	TINKLINGLY	TITIVATION	TOCOPHEROLS
TIMBROLOGISTS	TINNINESSES	TITIVATIONS	TODDLERHOOD
TIMBROLOGY	TINNITUSES	TITIVATORS	TODDLERHOODS
TIMBROMANIA	TINPLATING	TITLEHOLDER	TOENAILING
TIMBROMANIAC	TINSELLING	TITLEHOLDERS	TOERAGGERS
TIMBROMANIACS	TINSELRIES	TITLEHOLDING	TOFFISHNESS
TIMBROMANIAS	TINSMITHING	TITRATABLE	TOFFISHNESSES
TIMBROPHILIES	TINSMITHINGS	TITRATIONS	TOGAVIRUSES
TIMBROPHILIST	TINTINESSES	TITRIMETRIC	TOGETHERNESS
TIMBROPHILISTS	TINTINNABULA	TITTERINGLY	TOGETHERNESSES
TIMBROPHILY	TINTINNABULANT	TITTERINGS	TOILETRIES
TIMEFRAMES	TINTINNABULAR	TITTIVATED	TOILFULNESS
TIMEKEEPER	TINTINNABULARY	TITTIVATES	TOILFULNESSES
TIMEKEEPERS	TINTINNABULATE	TITTIVATING	TOILINETTE
TIMEKEEPING	TINTINNABULATED	TITTIVATION	TOILINETTES
TIMEKEEPINGS	TINTINNABULATES	TITTIVATIONS	TOILSOMELY
TIMELESSLY	TINTINNABULOUS	TITTIVATOR	TOILSOMENESS
TIMELESSNESS	TINTINNABULUM	TITTIVATORS	TOILSOMENESSES
TIMELESSNESSES	TINTOMETER	TITTLEBATS	TOKENISTIC
TIMELINESS	TINTOMETERS	TITTUPPING	TOKOLOGIES
TIMELINESSES	TINTOOKIES	TITUBANCIES	TOKOLOSHES
TIMENOGUYS	TIPPYTOEING	TITUBATING	TOKOLOSHIS
TIMEPASSED	TIPSIFYING	TITUBATION	TOKTOKKIES
TIMEPASSES	TIPSINESSES	TITUBATIONS	TOLBUTAMIDE
TIMEPASSING	TIPTRONICS	TITULARIES	TOLBUTAMIDES
TIMEPIECES	TIRAILLEUR	TITULARITIES	TOLERABILITIES
TIMEPLEASER	TIRAILLEURS	TITULARITY	TOLERABILITY
TIMEPLEASERS	TIREDNESSES	TOADEATERS	TOLERABLENESS
TIMESAVERS	TIRELESSLY	TOADFISHES	TOLERABLENESSES
TIMESAVING	TIRELESSNESS	TOADFLAXES	TOLERANCES
TIMESCALES	TIRELESSNESSES	TOADGRASSES	TOLERANTLY
TIMESERVER	TIRESOMELY	TOADRUSHES	TOLERATING
TIMESERVERS	TIRESOMENESS	TOADSTONES	TOLERATION
TIMESERVING	TIRESOMENESSES	TOADSTOOLS	TOLERATIONISM
TIMESERVINGS	TIROCINIUM	TOASTMASTER	TOLERATIONISMS
TIMETABLED	TIROCINIUMS	TOASTMASTERS	TOLERATIONIST
TIMETABLES	TITANESSES	TOASTMISTRESS	TOLERATIONISTS
TIMETABLING	TITANICALLY	TOASTMISTRESSES	TOLERATIONS
TIMEWORKER	TITANIFEROUS	TOBACCANALIAN	TOLERATIVE
TIMEWORKERS	TITANOSAUR	TOBACCANALIANS	TOLERATORS
TIMIDITIES	TITANOSAURS	TOBACCOLESS	TOLLBOOTHS
TIMIDNESSES	TITANOTHERE	TOBACCONIST	TOLLBRIDGE
TIMOCRACIES	TITANOTHERES	TOBACCONISTS	TOLLBRIDGES
TIMOCRATIC	TITARAKURA	TOBOGGANED	TOLLDISHES
TIMOCRATICAL	TITARAKURAS	TOBOGGANER	TOLLHOUSES

TOLUIDIDES	TOOTHACHES	TOPOGRAPHICALLY	TORRENTIAL
TOLUIDINES	TOOTHBRUSH	TOPOGRAPHIES	TORRENTIALITIES
TOMAHAWKED	TOOTHBRUSHES	TOPOGRAPHS	TORRENTIALITY
TOMAHAWKING	TOOTHBRUSHING	TOPOGRAPHY	TORRENTIALLY
TOMATILLOES	TOOTHBRUSHINGS	TOPOLOGICAL	TORRENTUOUS
TOMATILLOS	TOOTHCOMBS	TOPOLOGICALLY	TORRIDITIES
TOMBOYISHLY	TOOTHFISHES	TOPOLOGIES	TORRIDNESS
TOMBOYISHNESS	TOOTHINESS	TOPOLOGIST	TORRIDNESSES
TOMBOYISHNESSES	TOOTHINESSES	TOPOLOGISTS	TORRIFYING
TOMBSTONES	TOOTHPASTE	TOPONYMICAL	TORSIBILITIES
TOMCATTING	TOOTHPASTES	TOPONYMICS	TORSIBILITY
TOMFOOLERIES	TOOTHPICKS	TOPONYMIES	TORSIOGRAPH
TOMFOOLERY	TOOTHSHELL	TOPONYMIST	TORSIOGRAPHS
TOMFOOLING	TOOTHSHELLS	TOPONYMISTS	TORSIONALLY
TOMFOOLISH	TOOTHSOMELY	TOPOPHILIA	TORTELLINI
TOMFOOLISHNESS	TOOTHSOMENESS	TOPOPHILIAS	TORTELLINIS
TOMOGRAPHIC	TOOTHSOMENESSES	TOPSOILING	TORTFEASOR
TOMOGRAPHIES	TOOTHWASHES	TOPSOILINGS	TORTFEASORS
TOMOGRAPHS	TOOTHWORTS	TOPSTITCHED	TORTICOLLAR
TOMOGRAPHY	TOPAGNOSES	TOPSTITCHES	TORTICOLLIS
TONALITIES	TOPAGNOSIA	TOPSTITCHING	TORTICOLLISES
TONALITIVE	TOPAGNOSIAS	TOPWORKING	TORTILITIES
TONELESSLY	TOPAGNOSIS	TORBANITES	TORTILLONS
TONELESSNESS	TOPARCHIES	TORBERNITE	TORTIOUSLY
TONELESSNESSES	TOPAZOLITE	TORBERNITES	TORTOISESHELL
TONETICALLY	TOPAZOLITES	TORCHBEARER	TORTOISESHELLS
TONGUELESS	TOPCROSSES	TORCHBEARERS	TORTRICIDS
TONGUELETS	TOPDRESSING	TORCHIERES	TORTUOSITIES
TONGUELIKE	TOPDRESSINGS	TORCHLIGHT	TORTUOSITY
TONGUESTER	TOPECTOMIES	TORCHLIGHTS	TORTUOUSLY
TONGUESTERS	TOPGALLANT	TORCHWOODS	TORTUOUSNESS
TONICITIES	TOPGALLANTS	TORMENTEDLY	TORTUOUSNESSES
TONISHNESS	TOPHACEOUS	TORMENTERS	TORTUREDLY
TONISHNESSES	TOPHEAVINESS	TORMENTILS	TORTURESOME
TONNISHNESS	TOPHEAVINESSES	TORMENTING	TORTURINGLY
TONNISHNESSES	TOPIARISTS	TORMENTINGLY	TORTURINGS
TONOMETERS	TOPICALITIES	TORMENTINGS	TORTUROUSLY
TONOMETRIC	TOPICALITY	TORMENTORS	TOSSICATED
TONOMETRIES	TOPKNOTTED	TORMENTUMS	TOSTICATED
TONOPLASTS	TOPLESSNESS	TOROIDALLY	TOSTICATION
TONSILITIS	TOPLESSNESSES	TOROSITIES	TOSTICATIONS
TONSILITISES	TOPLOFTICAL	TORPEDINOUS	TOTALISATION
TONSILLARY	TOPLOFTIER	TORPEDOERS	TOTALISATIONS
TONSILLECTOMIES	TOPLOFTIEST	TORPEDOING	TOTALISATOR
TONSILLECTOMY	TOPLOFTILY	TORPEDOIST	TOTALISATORS
TONSILLITIC	TOPLOFTINESS	TORPEDOISTS	TOTALISERS
TONSILLITIS	TOPLOFTINESSES	TORPEFYING	TOTALISING
TONSILLITISES	TOPMAKINGS	TORPESCENCE	TOTALISTIC
TONSILLOTOMIES	TOPMINNOWS	TORPESCENCES	TOTALITARIAN
TONSILLOTOMY	TOPNOTCHER	TORPESCENT	TOTALITARIANISE
TOOLHOLDER	TOPNOTCHERS	TORPIDITIES	TOTALITARIANISM
TOOLHOLDERS	TOPOCENTRIC	TORPIDNESS	TOTALITARIANIZE
TOOLHOUSES	TOPOCHEMISTRIES	TORPIDNESSES	TOTALITARIANS
TOOLMAKERS	TOPOCHEMISTRY	TORPITUDES	TOTALITIES
TOOLMAKING	TOPOGRAPHER	TORPORIFIC	TOTALIZATION
TOOLMAKINGS	TOPOGRAPHERS	TORREFACTION	TOTALIZATIONS
TOOLPUSHER	TOPOGRAPHIC	TORREFACTIONS	TOTALIZATOR
TOOLPUSHERS	TOPOGRAPHICAL	TORREFYING	TOTALIZATORS

TOTALIZERS	TOWELHEADS	TRABECULATED	TRACTILITIES
TOTALIZING	TOWELLINGS	TRACASSERIE	TRACTILITY
TOTAQUINES	TOWERINGLY	TRACASSERIES	TRACTIONAL
TOTEMICALLY	TOWNHOUSES	TRACEABILITIES	TRACTORATION
TOTEMISTIC	TOWNSCAPED	TRACEABILITY	TRACTORATIONS
TOTIPALMATE	TOWNSCAPES	TRACEABLENESS	TRACTORFEED
TOTIPALMATION	TOWNSCAPING	TRACEABLENESSES	TRACTORFEEDS
TOTIPALMATIONS	TOWNSCAPINGS	TRACELESSLY	TRACTRICES
TOTIPOTENCIES	TOWNSFOLKS	TRACHEARIAN	TRADECRAFT
TOTIPOTENCY	TOWNSPEOPLE	TRACHEARIANS	TRADECRAFTS
TOTIPOTENT	TOWNSPEOPLES	TRACHEARIES	TRADEMARKED
TOTTERINGLY	TOWNSWOMAN	TRACHEATED	TRADEMARKING
TOTTERINGS	TOWNSWOMEN	TRACHEATES	TRADEMARKS
TOUCHABLENESS	TOXALBUMIN	TRACHEIDAL	TRADENAMES
TOUCHABLENESSES	TOXALBUMINS	TRACHEIDES	TRADERSHIP
TOUCHBACKS	TOXAPHENES	TRACHEITIS	TRADERSHIPS
TOUCHDOWNS	TOXICATION	TRACHEITISES	TRADESCANTIA
TOUCHHOLES	TOXICATIONS	TRACHELATE	TRADESCANTIAS
TOUCHINESS	TOXICITIES	TRACHEOLAR	TRADESFOLK
TOUCHINESSES	TOXICOGENIC	TRACHEOLES	TRADESFOLKS
TOUCHINGLY	TOXICOLOGIC	TRACHEOPHYTE	TRADESMANLIKE
TOUCHINGNESS	TOXICOLOGICAL	TRACHEOPHYTES	TRADESPEOPLE
TOUCHINGNESSES	TOXICOLOGICALLY	TRACHEOSCOPIES	TRADESPEOPLES
TOUCHLINES	TOXICOLOGIES	TRACHEOSCOPY	TRADESWOMAN
TOUCHMARKS	TOXICOLOGIST	TRACHEOSTOMIES	TRADESWOMEN
TOUCHPAPER	TOXICOLOGISTS	TRACHEOSTOMY	TRADITIONAL
TOUCHPAPERS	TOXICOLOGY	TRACHEOTOMIES	TRADITIONALISE
TOUCHSTONE	TOXICOMANIA	TRACHEOTOMY	TRADITIONALISED
TOUCHSTONES	TOXICOMANIAS	TRACHINUSES	TRADITIONALISES
TOUCHTONES	TOXICOPHAGOUS	TRACHITISES	TRADITIONALISM
TOUCHWOODS	TOXICOPHOBIA	TRACHOMATOUS	TRADITIONALISMS
TOUGHENERS	TOXICOPHOBIAS	TRACHYPTERUS	TRADITIONALIST
TOUGHENING	TOXIGENICITIES	TRACHYPTERUSES	TRADITIONALISTS
TOUGHENINGS	TOXIGENICITY	TRACHYTOID	TRADITIONALITY
TOUGHNESSES	TOXIPHAGOUS	TRACKBALLS	TRADITIONALIZE
TOURBILLION	TOXIPHOBIA	TRACKERBALL	TRADITIONALIZED
TOURBILLIONS	TOXIPHOBIAC	TRACKERBALLS	TRADITIONALIZES
TOURBILLON	TOXIPHOBIACS	TRACKLAYER	TRADITIONALLY
TOURBILLONS	TOXIPHOBIAS	TRACKLAYERS	TRADITIONARILY
TOURISTICALLY	TOXOCARIASES	TRACKLAYING	TRADITIONARY
TOURMALINE	TOXOCARIASIS	TRACKLAYINGS	TRADITIONER
TOURMALINES	TOXOPHILIES	TRACKLEMENT	TRADITIONERS
TOURMALINIC	TOXOPHILITE	TRACKLEMENTS	TRADITIONIST
TOURNAMENT	TOXOPHILITES	TRACKLESSLY	TRADITIONISTS
TOURNAMENTS	TOXOPHILITIC	TRACKLESSNESS	TRADITIONLESS
TOURNEYERS	TOXOPLASMA	TRACKLESSNESSES	TRADITIONS
TOURNEYING	TOXOPLASMAS	TRACKROADS	TRADITORES
TOURNIQUET	TOXOPLASMIC	TRACKSIDES	TRADUCEMENT
TOURNIQUETS	TOXOPLASMOSES	TRACKSUITS	TRADUCEMENTS
TOURTIERES	TOXOPLASMOSIS	TRACKWALKER	TRADUCIANISM
TOVARICHES	TOYISHNESS	TRACKWALKERS	TRADUCIANISMS
TOVARISCHES	TOYISHNESSES	TRACTABILITIES	TRADUCIANIST
TOVARISHES	TRABEATION	TRACTABILITY	TRADUCIANISTIC
TOWARDLINESS	TRABEATIONS	TRACTABLENESS	TRADUCIANISTS
TOWARDLINESSES	TRABECULAE	TRACTABLENESSES	TRADUCIANS
TOWARDNESS	TRABECULAR	TRACTARIAN	TRADUCIBLE
TOWARDNESSES	TRABECULAS	TRACTARIANS	TRADUCINGLY
TOWELETTES	TRABECULATE	TRACTATORS	TRADUCINGS

TRADUCTION	TRAITORISM	TRANQUILIZING	TRANSCENDINGLY
TRADUCTIONS	TRAITORISMS	TRANQUILIZINGLY	TRANSCENDS
TRADUCTIVE	TRAITOROUS	TRANQUILLER	TRANSCRANIAL
TRAFFICABILITY	TRAITOROUSLY	TRANQUILLEST	TRANSCRIBABLE
TRAFFICABLE	TRAITOROUSNESS	TRANQUILLISE	TRANSCRIBE
TRAFFICATOR	TRAITORSHIP	TRANQUILLISED	TRANSCRIBED
TRAFFICATORS	TRAITORSHIPS	TRANQUILLISER	TRANSCRIBER
TRAFFICKED	TRAITRESSES	TRANQUILLISERS	TRANSCRIBERS
TRAFFICKER	TRAJECTILE	TRANQUILLISES	TRANSCRIBES
TRAFFICKERS	TRAJECTING	TRANQUILLISING	TRANSCRIBING
TRAFFICKING	TRAJECTION	TRANQUILLITIES	TRANSCRIPT
TRAFFICKINGS	TRAJECTIONS	TRANQUILLITY	TRANSCRIPTASE
TRAFFICLESS	TRAJECTORIES	TRANQUILLIZE	TRANSCRIPTASES
TRAGACANTH	TRAJECTORY	TRANQUILLIZED	TRANSCRIPTION
TRAGACANTHS	TRALATICIOUS	TRANQUILLIZER	TRANSCRIPTIONAL
TRAGEDIANS	TRALATITIOUS	TRANQUILLIZERS	TRANSCRIPTIONS
TRAGEDIENNE	TRAMELLING	TRANQUILLIZES	TRANSCRIPTIVE
TRAGEDIENNES	TRAMMELERS	TRANQUILLIZING	TRANSCRIPTIVELY
TRAGELAPHINE	TRAMMELING	TRANQUILLY	TRANSCRIPTS
TRAGELAPHS	TRAMMELLED	TRANQUILNESS	TRANSCULTURAL
TRAGICALLY	TRAMMELLER	TRANQUILNESSES	TRANSCURRENT
TRAGICALNESS	TRAMMELLERS	TRANSACTED	TRANSCUTANEOUS
TRAGICALNESSES	TRAMMELLING	TRANSACTING	TRANSDERMAL
TRAGICOMEDIES	TRAMONTANA	TRANSACTINIDE	TRANSDUCED
TRAGICOMEDY	TRAMONTANAS	TRANSACTINIDES	TRANSDUCER
TRAGICOMIC	TRAMONTANE	TRANSACTION	TRANSDUCERS
TRAGICOMICAL	TRAMONTANES	TRANSACTIONAL	TRANSDUCES
TRAGICOMICALLY	TRAMPETTES	TRANSACTIONALLY	TRANSDUCING
TRAILBASTON	TRAMPLINGS	TRANSACTIONS	TRANSDUCTANT
TRAILBASTONS	TRAMPOLINE	TRANSACTOR	TRANSDUCTANTS
TRAILBLAZER	TRAMPOLINED	TRANSACTORS	TRANSDUCTION
TRAILBLAZERS	TRAMPOLINER	TRANSALPINE	TRANSDUCTIONAL
TRAILBLAZING	TRAMPOLINERS	TRANSALPINES	TRANSDUCTIONS
TRAILBREAKER	TRAMPOLINES	TRANSAMINASE	TRANSDUCTOR
TRAILBREAKERS	TRAMPOLINING	TRANSAMINASES	TRANSDUCTORS
TRAILERABLE	TRAMPOLININGS	TRANSAMINATION	TRANSECTED
TRAILERING	TRAMPOLINIST	TRANSAMINATIONS	TRANSECTING
TRAILERINGS	TRAMPOLINISTS	TRANSANDEAN	TRANSECTION
TRAILERIST	TRAMPOLINS	TRANSANDINE	TRANSECTIONS
TRAILERISTS	TRANCELIKE	TRANSATLANTIC	TRANSENNAS
TRAILERITE	TRANQUILER	TRANSAXLES	TRANSEPTAL
TRAILERITES	TRANQUILEST	TRANSCALENCIES	TRANSEPTATE
TRAILHEADS	TRANQUILISATION	TRANSCALENCY	TRANSEXUAL
TRAILINGLY	TRANQUILISE	TRANSCALENT	TRANSEXUALISM
TRAINABILITIES	TRANQUILISED	TRANSCAUCASIAN	TRANSEXUALISMS
TRAINABILITY	TRANQUILISER	TRANSCEIVER	TRANSEXUALS
TRAINBANDS	TRANQUILISERS	TRANSCEIVERS	TRANSFECTED
TRAINBEARER	TRANQUILISES	TRANSCENDED	TRANSFECTING
TRAINBEARERS	TRANQUILISING	TRANSCENDENCE	TRANSFECTION
TRAINEESHIP	TRANQUILISINGLY	TRANSCENDENCES	TRANSFECTIONS
TRAINEESHIPS	TRANQUILITIES	TRANSCENDENCIES	TRANSFECTS
TRAINLOADS	TRANQUILITY	TRANSCENDENCY	TRANSFERABILITY
TRAINSPOTTERISH	TRANQUILIZATION	TRANSCENDENT	TRANSFERABLE
TRAIPSINGS	TRANQUILIZE	TRANSCENDENTAL	TRANSFERAL
TRAITORESS	TRANQUILIZED	TRANSCENDENTALS	TRANSFERALS
TRAITORESSES	TRANQUILIZER	TRANSCENDENTLY	TRANSFERASE
TRAITORHOOD	TRANQUILIZERS	TRANSCENDENTS	TRANSFERASES
TRAITORHOODS	TRANQUILIZES	TRANSCENDING	TRANSFEREE

TRANSFEREES	TRANSGENDERED	TRANSITABLE	TRANSMARINE
TRANSFERENCE	TRANSGENDERS	TRANSITING	TRANSMEMBRANE
TRANSFERENCES	TRANSGENES	TRANSITION	TRANSMEWED
TRANSFERENTIAL	TRANSGENESES	TRANSITIONAL	TRANSMEWING
TRANSFEROR	TRANSGENESIS	TRANSITIONALLY	TRANSMIGRANT
TRANSFERORS	TRANSGENIC	TRANSITIONALS	TRANSMIGRANTS
TRANSFERRABLE	TRANSGENICS	TRANSITIONARY	TRANSMIGRATE
TRANSFERRAL	TRANSGRESS	TRANSITIONS	TRANSMIGRATED
TRANSFERRALS	TRANSGRESSED	TRANSITIVE	TRANSMIGRATES
TRANSFERRED	TRANSGRESSES	TRANSITIVELY	TRANSMIGRATING
TRANSFERRER	TRANSGRESSING	TRANSITIVENESS	TRANSMIGRATION
TRANSFERRERS	TRANSGRESSION	TRANSITIVES	TRANSMIGRATIONS
TRANSFERRIBLE	TRANSGRESSIONAL	TRANSITIVITIES	TRANSMIGRATIVE
TRANSFERRIN	TRANSGRESSIONS	TRANSITIVITY	TRANSMIGRATOR
TRANSFERRING	TRANSGRESSIVE	TRANSITORILY	TRANSMIGRATORS
TRANSFERRINS	TRANSGRESSIVELY	TRANSITORINESS	TRANSMIGRATORY
TRANSFIGURATION	TRANSGRESSOR	TRANSITORY	TRANSMISSIBLE
TRANSFIGURE	TRANSGRESSORS	TRANSLATABILITY	TRANSMISSION
TRANSFIGURED	TRANSHIPMENT	TRANSLATABLE	TRANSMISSIONAL
TRANSFIGUREMENT	TRANSHIPMENTS	TRANSLATED	TRANSMISSIONS
TRANSFIGURES	TRANSHIPPED	TRANSLATES	TRANSMISSIVE
TRANSFIGURING	TRANSHIPPER	TRANSLATING	TRANSMISSIVELY
TRANSFINITE	TRANSHIPPERS	TRANSLATION	TRANSMISSIVITY
TRANSFIXED	TRANSHIPPING	TRANSLATIONAL	TRANSMISSOMETER
TRANSFIXES	TRANSHIPPINGS	TRANSLATIONALLY	TRANSMITTABLE
TRANSFIXING	TRANSHISTORICAL	TRANSLATIONS	TRANSMITTAL
TRANSFIXION	TRANSHUMANCE	TRANSLATIVE	TRANSMITTALS
TRANSFIXIONS	TRANSHUMANCES	TRANSLATIVES	TRANSMITTANCE
TRANSFORMABLE	TRANSHUMANT	TRANSLATOR	TRANSMITTANCES
TRANSFORMATION	TRANSHUMANTS	TRANSLATORIAL	TRANSMITTANCIES
TRANSFORMATIONS	TRANSHUMED	TRANSLATORS	TRANSMITTANCY
TRANSFORMATIVE	TRANSHUMES	TRANSLATORY	TRANSMITTED
TRANSFORMED	TRANSHUMING	TRANSLEITHAN	TRANSMITTER
TRANSFORMER	TRANSIENCE	TRANSLITERATE	TRANSMITTERS
TRANSFORMERS	TRANSIENCES	TRANSLITERATED	TRANSMITTIBLE
TRANSFORMING	TRANSIENCIES	TRANSLITERATES	TRANSMITTING
TRANSFORMINGS	TRANSIENCY	TRANSLITERATING	TRANSMITTIVITY
TRANSFORMISM	TRANSIENTLY	TRANSLITERATION	TRANSMOGRIFIED
TRANSFORMISMS	TRANSIENTNESS	TRANSLITERATOR	TRANSMOGRIFIES
TRANSFORMIST	TRANSIENTNESSES	TRANSLITERATORS	TRANSMOGRIFY
TRANSFORMISTIC	TRANSIENTS	TRANSLOCATE	TRANSMOGRIFYING
TRANSFORMISTS	TRANSILIENCE	TRANSLOCATED	TRANSMONTANE
TRANSFORMS	TRANSILIENCES	TRANSLOCATES	TRANSMONTANES
TRANSFUSABLE	TRANSILIENCIES	TRANSLOCATING	TRANSMOUNTAIN
TRANSFUSED	TRANSILIENCY	TRANSLOCATION	TRANSMOVED
TRANSFUSER	TRANSILIENT	TRANSLOCATIONS	TRANSMOVES
TRANSFUSERS	TRANSILLUMINATE	TRANSLUCENCE	TRANSMOVING
TRANSFUSES	TRANSISTHMIAN	TRANSLUCENCES	TRANSMUNDANE
TRANSFUSIBLE	TRANSISTOR	TRANSLUCENCIES	TRANSMUTABILITY
TRANSFUSING	TRANSISTORISE	TRANSLUCENCY	TRANSMUTABLE
TRANSFUSION	TRANSISTORISED	TRANSLUCENT	TRANSMUTABLY
TRANSFUSIONAL	TRANSISTORISES	TRANSLUCENTLY	TRANSMUTATION
TRANSFUSIONIST	TRANSISTORISING	TRANSLUCID	TRANSMUTATIONAL
TRANSFUSIONISTS	TRANSISTORIZE	TRANSLUCIDITIES	TRANSMUTATIONS
TRANSFUSIONS	TRANSISTORIZED	TRANSLUCIDITY	TRANSMUTATIVE
TRANSFUSIVE	TRANSISTORIZES	TRANSLUNAR	TRANSMUTED
TRANSFUSIVELY	TRANSISTORIZING	TRANSLUNARY	TRANSMUTER
TRANSGENDER	TRANSISTORS	TRANSMANCHE	TRANSMUTERS

TRANSMUTES	TRANSPORTATIONS	TRANSUMPTIVE	TRAPNESTED
TRANSMUTING	TRANSPORTED	TRANSUMPTS	TRAPNESTING
TRANSNATIONAL	TRANSPORTEDLY	TRANSURANIAN	TRAPPINESS
TRANSNATURAL	TRANSPORTEDNESS	TRANSURANIC	TRAPPINESSES
TRANSOCEANIC	TRANSPORTER	TRANSURANICS	TRAPSHOOTER
TRANSONICS	TRANSPORTERS	TRANSURANIUM	TRAPSHOOTERS
TRANSPACIFIC	TRANSPORTING	TRANSVAGINAL	TRAPSHOOTING
TRANSPADANE	TRANSPORTINGLY	TRANSVALUATE	TRAPSHOOTINGS
TRANSPARENCE	TRANSPORTINGS	TRANSVALUATED	TRASHERIES
TRANSPARENCES	TRANSPORTIVE	TRANSVALUATES	TRASHINESS
TRANSPARENCIES	TRANSPORTS	TRANSVALUATING	TRASHINESSES
TRANSPARENCY	TRANSPOSABILITY	TRANSVALUATION	TRASHTRIES
TRANSPARENT	TRANSPOSABLE	TRANSVALUATIONS	TRATTORIAS
TRANSPARENTISE	TRANSPOSAL	TRANSVALUE	TRAUCHLING
TRANSPARENTISED	TRANSPOSALS	TRANSVALUED	TRAUMATICALLY
TRANSPARENTISES	TRANSPOSED	TRANSVALUER	TRAUMATISATION
TRANSPARENTIZE	TRANSPOSER	TRANSVALUERS	TRAUMATISATIONS
TRANSPARENTIZED	TRANSPOSERS	TRANSVALUES	TRAUMATISE
TRANSPARENTIZES	TRANSPOSES	TRANSVALUING	TRAUMATISED
TRANSPARENTLY	TRANSPOSING	TRANSVERSAL	TRAUMATISES
TRANSPARENTNESS	TRANSPOSINGS	TRANSVERSALITY	TRAUMATISING
TRANSPERSONAL	TRANSPOSITION	TRANSVERSALLY	TRAUMATISM
TRANSPICUOUS	TRANSPOSITIONAL	TRANSVERSALS	TRAUMATISMS
TRANSPICUOUSLY	TRANSPOSITIONS	TRANSVERSE	TRAUMATIZATION
TRANSPIERCE	TRANSPOSITIVE	TRANSVERSED	TRAUMATIZATIONS
TRANSPIERCED	TRANSPOSON	TRANSVERSELY	TRAUMATIZE
TRANSPIERCES	TRANSPOSONS	TRANSVERSENESS	TRAUMATIZED
TRANSPIERCING	TRANSPUTER	TRANSVERSES	TRAUMATIZES
TRANSPIRABLE	TRANSPUTERS	TRANSVERSING	TRAUMATIZING
TRANSPIRATION	TRANSSEXUAL	TRANSVERSION	TRAUMATOLOGICAL
TRANSPIRATIONAL	TRANSSEXUALISM	TRANSVERSIONS	TRAUMATOLOGIES
TRANSPIRATIONS	TRANSSEXUALISMS	TRANSVERTER	TRAUMATOLOGY
TRANSPIRATORY	TRANSSEXUALITY	TRANSVERTERS	TRAUMATONASTIES
TRANSPIRED	TRANSSEXUALS	TRANSVESTED	TRAUMATONASTY
TRANSPIRES	TRANSSHAPE	TRANSVESTIC	TRAVAILING
TRANSPIRING	TRANSSHAPED	TRANSVESTING	TRAVELATOR
TRANSPLACENTAL	TRANSSHAPES	TRANSVESTISM	TRAVELATORS
TRANSPLANT	TRANSSHAPING	TRANSVESTISMS	TRAVELINGS
TRANSPLANTABLE	TRANSSHIPMENT	TRANSVESTIST	TRAVELLERS
TRANSPLANTATION	TRANSSHIPMENTS	TRANSVESTISTS	TRAVELLING
TRANSPLANTED	TRANSSHIPPED	TRANSVESTITE	TRAVELLINGS
TRANSPLANTER	TRANSSHIPPER	TRANSVESTITES	TRAVELOGUE
TRANSPLANTERS	TRANSSHIPPERS	TRANSVESTITISM	TRAVELOGUES
TRANSPLANTING	TRANSSHIPPING	TRANSVESTITISMS	TRAVERSABLE
TRANSPLANTINGS	TRANSSHIPPINGS	TRANSVESTS	TRAVERSALS
TRANSPLANTS	TRANSSHIPS	TRAPANNERS	TRAVERSERS
TRANSPOLAR	TRANSSONIC	TRAPANNING	TRAVERSING
TRANSPONDER	TRANSTHORACIC	TRAPESINGS	TRAVERSINGS
TRANSPONDERS	TRANSUBSTANTIAL	TRAPEZIFORM	TRAVERTINE
TRANSPONDOR	TRANSUDATE	TRAPEZISTS	TRAVERTINES
TRANSPONDORS	TRANSUDATES	TRAPEZIUMS	TRAVERTINS
TRANSPONTINE	TRANSUDATION	TRAPEZIUSES	TRAVESTIED
TRANSPORTABLE	TRANSUDATIONS	TRAPEZOHEDRA	TRAVESTIES
TRANSPORTAL	TRANSUDATORY	TRAPEZOHEDRAL	TRAVESTYING
TRANSPORTALS	TRANSUDING	TRAPEZOHEDRON	TRAVOLATOR
TRANSPORTANCE	TRANSUMING	TRAPEZOHEDRONS	TRAVOLATORS
TRANSPORTANCES	TRANSUMPTION	TRAPEZOIDAL	TRAWLERMAN
TRANSPORTATION	TRANSUMPTIONS	TRAPEZOIDS	TRAWLERMEN

TRAYMOBILE	TRELLISWORKS	TREPONEMATOSIS	TRIBOLOGICAL
TRAYMOBILES	TREMATODES	TREPONEMATOUS	TRIBOLOGIES
TRAZODONES	TREMATOIDS	TREPONEMES	TRIBOLOGIST
TREACHERER	TREMBLEMENT	TRESPASSED	TRIBOLOGISTS
TREACHERERS	TREMBLEMENTS	TRESPASSER	TRIBOMETER
TREACHERIES	TREMBLIEST	TRESPASSERS	TRIBOMETERS
TREACHEROUS	TREMBLINGLY	TRESPASSES	TRIBRACHIAL
TREACHEROUSLY	TREMBLINGS	TRESPASSING	TRIBRACHIC
TREACHEROUSNESS	TREMENDOUS	TRESTLETREE	TRIBROMOETHANOL
TREACHETOUR	TREMENDOUSLY	TRESTLETREES	TRIBROMOMETHANE
TREACHETOURS	TREMENDOUSNESS	TRESTLEWORK	TRIBULATED
TREACHOURS	TREMOLANDI	TRESTLEWORKS	TRIBULATES
TREACLIEST	TREMOLANDO	TRETINOINS	TRIBULATING
TREACLINESS	TREMOLANDOS	TREVALLIES	TRIBULATION
TREACLINESSES	TREMOLANTS	TRIABLENESS	TRIBULATIONS
TREADLINGS	TREMOLITES	TRIABLENESSES	TRIBUNATES
TREADMILLS	TREMOLITIC	TRIACETATE	TRIBUNESHIP
TREADWHEEL	TREMORLESS	TRIACETATES	TRIBUNESHIPS
TREADWHEELS	TREMULANTS	TRIACONTER	TRIBUNICIAL
TREASONABLE	TREMULATED	TRIACONTERS	TRIBUNICIAN
TREASONABLENESS	TREMULATES	TRIACTINAL	TRIBUNITIAL
TREASONABLY	TREMULATING	TRIADELPHOUS	TRIBUNITIAN
TREASONOUS	TREMULOUSLY	TRIADICALLY	TRIBUTARIES
TREASURABLE	TREMULOUSNESS	TRIALITIES	TRIBUTARILY
TREASURELESS	TREMULOUSNESSES	TRIALLISTS	TRIBUTARINESS
TREASURERS	TRENCHANCIES	TRIALOGUES	TRIBUTARINESSES
TREASURERSHIP	TRENCHANCY	TRIALWARES	TRICAMERAL
TREASURERSHIPS	TRENCHANTLY	TRIAMCINOLONE	TRICARBOXYLIC
TREASURIES	TRENCHARDS	TRIAMCINOLONES	TRICARPELLARY
TREASURING	TRENCHERMAN	TRIANDRIAN	TRICENTENARIES
TREATABILITIES	TRENCHERMEN	TRIANDROUS	TRICENTENARY
TREATABILITY	TRENDIFIED	TRIANGULAR	TRICENTENNIAL
TREATMENTS	TRENDIFIES	TRIANGULARITIES	TRICENTENNIALS
TREATYLESS	TRENDIFYING	TRIANGULARITY	TRICEPHALOUS
TREBBIANOS	TRENDINESS	TRIANGULARLY	TRICERATOPS
TREBLENESS	TRENDINESSES	TRIANGULATE	TRICERATOPSES
TREBLENESSES	TRENDSETTER	TRIANGULATED	TRICERIONS
TREBUCHETS	TRENDSETTERS	TRIANGULATELY	TRICHIASES
TREBUCKETS	TRENDSETTING	TRIANGULATES	TRICHIASIS
TRECENTIST	TRENDSETTINGS	TRIANGULATING	TRICHINELLA
TRECENTISTS	TRENDYISMS	TRIANGULATION	TRICHINELLAE
TREDECILLION	TREPANATION	TRIANGULATIONS	TRICHINELLAS
TREDECILLIONS	TREPANATIONS	TRIAPSIDAL	TRICHINIASES
TREDRILLES	TREPANNERS	TRIARCHIES	TRICHINIASIS
TREEHOPPER	TREPANNING	TRIATHLETE	TRICHINISATION
TREEHOPPERS	TREPANNINGS	TRIATHLETES	TRICHINISATIONS
TREEHOUSES	TREPHINATION	TRIATHLONS	TRICHINISE
TREELESSNESS	TREPHINATIONS	TRIATOMICALLY	TRICHINISED
TREELESSNESSES	TREPHINERS	TRIAXIALITIES	TRICHINISES
TREENWARES	TREPHINING	TRIAXIALITY	TRICHINISING
TREGETOURS	TREPHININGS	TRIBADISMS	TRICHINIZATION
TREHALOSES	TREPIDATION	TRIBALISMS	TRICHINIZATIONS
TREILLAGED	TREPIDATIONS	TRIBALISTIC	TRICHINIZE
TREILLAGES	TREPIDATORY	TRIBALISTS	TRICHINIZED
TREKSCHUIT	TREPONEMAL	TRIBESPEOPLE	TRICHINIZES
TREKSCHUITS	TREPONEMAS	TRIBESWOMAN	TRICHINIZING
TRELLISING	TREPONEMATA	TRIBESWOMEN	TRICHINOSE
TRELLISWORK	TREPONEMATOSES	TRIBOELECTRIC	TRICHINOSED

TRICHINOSES	TRICHOTOMY	TRIDACTYLOUS	TRIHALOMETHANE
TRICHINOSING	TRICHROISM	TRIDENTATE	TRIHALOMETHANES
TRICHINOSIS	TRICHROISMS	TRIDIMENSIONAL	TRIHEDRALS
TRICHINOTIC	TRICHROMAT	TRIDOMINIA	TRIHEDRONS
TRICHINOUS	TRICHROMATIC	TRIDOMINIUM	TRIHYBRIDS
TRICHLORFON	TRICHROMATISM	TRIDYMITES	TRIHYDRATE
TRICHLORFONS	TRICHROMATISMS	TRIENNIALLY	TRIHYDRATED
TRICHLORIDE	TRICHROMATS	TRIENNIALS	TRIHYDRATES
TRICHLORIDES	TRICHROMIC	TRIENNIUMS	TRIHYDROXY
TRICHLOROACETIC	TRICHROMICS	TRIERARCHAL	TRIIODOMETHANE
TRICHLOROETHANE	TRICHRONOUS	TRIERARCHIES	TRIIODOMETHANES
TRICHLORPHON	TRICHURIASES	TRIERARCHS	TRILATERAL
TRICHLORPHONS	TRICHURIASIS	TRIERARCHY	TRILATERALISM
TRICHOBACTERIA	TRICKERIES	TRIETHYLAMINE	TRILATERALISMS
TRICHOCYST	TRICKINESS	TRIETHYLAMINES	TRILATERALIST
TRICHOCYSTIC	TRICKINESSES	TRIFACIALS	TRILATERALISTS
TRICHOCYSTS	TRICKISHLY	TRIFARIOUS	TRILATERALLY
TRICHOGYNE	TRICKISHNESS	TRIFFIDIAN	TRILATERALS
TRICHOGYNES	TRICKISHNESSES	TRIFLINGLY	TRILATERATION
TRICHOGYNIAL	TRICKLIEST	TRIFLINGNESS	TRILATERATIONS
TRICHOGYNIC	TRICKLINGLY	TRIFLINGNESSES	TRILINEATE
TRICHOLOGICAL	TRICKLINGS	TRIFLUOPERAZINE	TRILINGUAL
TRICHOLOGIES	TRICKSIEST	TRIFLURALIN	TRILINGUALISM
TRICHOLOGIST	TRICKSINESS	TRIFLURALINS	TRILINGUALISMS
TRICHOLOGISTS	TRICKSINESSES	TRIFOLIATE	TRILINGUALLY
TRICHOLOGY	TRICKSTERING	TRIFOLIATED	TRILITERAL
TRICHOMONACIDAL	TRICKSTERINGS	TRIFOLIOLATE	TRILITERALISM
TRICHOMONACIDE	TRICKSTERS	TRIFOLIUMS	TRILITERALISMS
TRICHOMONACIDES	TRICKTRACK	TRIFURCATE	TRILITERALS
TRICHOMONAD	TRICKTRACKS	TRIFURCATED	TRILITHONS
TRICHOMONADAL	TRICLINIUM	TRIFURCATES	TRILLIONAIRE
TRICHOMONADS	TRICLOSANS	TRIFURCATING	TRILLIONAIRES
TRICHOMONAL	TRICOLETTE	TRIFURCATION	TRILLIONTH
TRICHOMONIASES	TRICOLETTES	TRIFURCATIONS	TRILLIONTHS
TRICHOMONIASIS	TRICOLORED	TRIGAMISTS	TRILOBATED
TRICHOPHYTON	TRICOLOURED	TRIGEMINAL	TRILOBITES
TRICHOPHYTONS	TRICOLOURS	TRIGEMINALS	TRILOBITIC
TRICHOPHYTOSES	TRICONSONANTAL	TRIGGERFISH	TRILOCULAR
TRICHOPHYTOSIS	TRICONSONANTIC	TRIGGERFISHES	TRIMERISMS
TRICHOPTERAN	TRICORNERED	TRIGGERING	TRIMESTERS
TRICHOPTERANS	TRICORPORATE	TRIGGERLESS	TRIMESTRAL
TRICHOPTERIST	TRICORPORATED	TRIGGERMAN	TRIMESTRIAL
TRICHOPTERISTS	TRICOSTATE	TRIGGERMEN	TRIMETHADIONE
TRICHOPTEROUS	TRICOTEUSE	TRIGLYCERIDE	TRIMETHADIONES
TRICHOTHECENE	TRICOTEUSES	TRIGLYCERIDES	TRIMETHOPRIM
TRICHOTHECENES	TRICOTINES	TRIGLYPHIC	TRIMETHOPRIMS
TRICHOTOMIC	TRICROTISM	TRIGLYPHICAL	TRIMETHYLAMINE
TRICHOTOMIES	TRICROTISMS	TRIGNESSES	TRIMETHYLAMINES
TRICHOTOMISE	TRICROTOUS	TRIGONALLY	TRIMETHYLENE
TRICHOTOMISED	TRICUSPIDAL	TRIGONOMETER	TRIMETHYLENES
TRICHOTOMISES	TRICUSPIDATE	TRIGONOMETERS	TRIMETRICAL
TRICHOTOMISING	TRICUSPIDS	TRIGONOMETRIC	TRIMETROGON
TRICHOTOMIZE	TRICYCLERS	TRIGONOMETRICAL	TRIMETROGONS
TRICHOTOMIZED	TRICYCLICS	TRIGONOMETRIES	TRIMMINGLY
TRICHOTOMIZES	TRICYCLING	TRIGONOMETRY	TRIMNESSES
TRICHOTOMIZING	TRICYCLINGS	TRIGRAMMATIC	TRIMOLECULAR
TRICHOTOMOUS	TRICYCLIST	TRIGRAMMIC	TRIMONTHLY
TRICHOTOMOUSLY	TRICYCLISTS	TRIGRAPHIC	TRIMORPHIC

TRIMORPHISM	TRIPHOSPHATES	TRISTEARIN	TRIUMPHALISMS
TRIMORPHISMS	TRIPHTHONG	TRISTEARINS	TRIUMPHALIST
TRIMORPHOUS	TRIPHTHONGAL	TRISTESSES	TRIUMPHALISTS
TRINACRIAN	TRIPHTHONGS	TRISTFULLY	TRIUMPHALS
TRINACRIFORM	TRIPHYLITE	TRISTFULNESS	TRIUMPHANT
TRINISCOPE	TRIPHYLITES	TRISTFULNESSES	TRIUMPHANTLY
TRINISCOPES	TRIPHYLLOUS	TRISTICHIC	TRIUMPHERIES
TRINITARIAN	TRIPINNATE	TRISTICHOUS	TRIUMPHERS
TRINITRATE	TRIPINNATELY	TRISTIMULUS	TRIUMPHERY
TRINITRATES	TRIPITAKAS	TRISUBSTITUTED	TRIUMPHING
TRINITRINS	TRIPLENESS	TRISULCATE	TRIUMPHINGS
TRINITROBENZENE	TRIPLENESSES	TRISULFIDE	TRIUMVIRAL
TRINITROCRESOL	TRIPLETAIL	TRISULFIDES	TRIUMVIRATE
TRINITROCRESOLS	TRIPLETAILS	TRISULPHIDE	TRIUMVIRATES
TRINITROPHENOL	TRIPLICATE	TRISULPHIDES	TRIUMVIRIES
TRINITROPHENOLS	TRIPLICATED	TRISYLLABIC	TRIUNITIES
TRINITROTOLUENE	TRIPLICATES	TRISYLLABICAL	TRIVALENCE
TRINITROTOLUOL	TRIPLICATING	TRISYLLABICALLY	TRIVALENCES
TRINITROTOLUOLS	TRIPLICATION	TRISYLLABLE	TRIVALENCIES
TRINKETERS	TRIPLICATIONS	TRISYLLABLES	TRIVALENCY
TRINKETING	TRIPLICITIES	TRITAGONIST	TRIVALVULAR
TRINKETINGS	TRIPLICITY	TRITAGONISTS	TRIVIALISATION
TRINKETRIES	TRIPLOBLASTIC	TRITANOPIA	TRIVIALISATIONS
TRINOCULAR	TRIPLOIDIES	TRITANOPIAS	TRIVIALISE
TRINOMIALISM	TRIPPERISH	TRITANOPIC	TRIVIALISED
TRINOMIALISMS	TRIPPINGLY	TRITENESSES	TRIVIALISES
TRINOMIALIST	TRIPTEROUS	TRITERNATE	TRIVIALISING
TRINOMIALISTS	TRIPTYQUES	TRITHEISMS	TRIVIALISM
TRINOMIALLY	TRIPUDIARY	TRITHEISTIC	TRIVIALISMS
TRINOMIALS	TRIPUDIATE	TRITHEISTICAL	TRIVIALIST
TRINUCLEOTIDE	TRIPUDIATED	TRITHEISTS	TRIVIALISTS
TRINUCLEOTIDES	TRIPUDIATES	TRITHIONATE	TRIVIALITIES
TRIOECIOUS	TRIPUDIATING	TRITHIONATES	TRIVIALITY
TRIOXOBORIC	TRIPUDIATION	TRITHIONIC	TRIVIALIZATION
TRIOXYGENS	TRIPUDIATIONS	TRITIATING	TRIVIALIZATIONS
TRIPALMITIN	TRIPUDIUMS	TRITIATION	TRIVIALIZE
TRIPALMITINS	TRIQUETRAL	TRITIATIONS	TRIVIALIZED
TRIPARTISM	TRIQUETRAS	TRITICALES	TRIVIALIZES
TRIPARTISMS	TRIQUETROUS	TRITICALLY	TRIVIALIZING
TRIPARTITE	TRIQUETROUSLY	TRITICALNESS	TRIVIALNESS
TRIPARTITELY	TRIQUETRUM	TRITICALNESSES	TRIVIALNESSES
TRIPARTITION	TRIRADIATE	TRITICEOUS	TRIWEEKLIES
TRIPARTITIONS	TRIRADIATELY	TRITICISMS	TROCHAICALLY
TRIPEHOUND	TRISACCHARIDE	TRITUBERCULAR	TROCHANTER
TRIPEHOUNDS	TRISACCHARIDES	TRITUBERCULATE	TROCHANTERAL
TRIPERSONAL	TRISAGIONS	TRITUBERCULIES	TROCHANTERIC
TRIPERSONALISM	TRISECTING	TRITUBERCULISM	TROCHANTERS
TRIPERSONALISMS	TRISECTION	TRITUBERCULISMS	TROCHEAMETER
TRIPERSONALIST	TRISECTIONS	TRITUBERCULY	TROCHEAMETERS
TRIPERSONALISTS	TRISECTORS	TRITURABLE	TROCHELMINTH
TRIPERSONALITY	TRISECTRICES	TRITURATED	TROCHELMINTHS
TRIPETALOUS	TRISECTRIX	TRITURATES	TROCHILUSES
TRIPHAMMER	TRISKELION	TRITURATING	TROCHISCUS
TRIPHAMMERS	TRISKELIONS	TRITURATION	TROCHISCUSES
TRIPHENYLAMINE	TRISOCTAHEDRA	TRITURATIONS	TROCHLEARS
TRIPHENYLAMINES	TRISOCTAHEDRAL	TRITURATOR	TROCHOIDAL
TRIPHIBIOUS	TRISOCTAHEDRON	TRITURATORS	TROCHOIDALLY
TRIPHOSPHATE	TRISOCTAHEDRONS	TRIUMPHALISM	TROCHOMETER

TROCHOMETERS	TROPHOTAXES	TROUBLESHOOTERS	TRUNCHEONING
TROCHOPHORE	TROPHOTAXIS	TROUBLESHOOTING	TRUNCHEONS
TROCHOPHORES	TROPHOTROPIC	TROUBLESHOOTS	TRUNKFISHES
TROCHOSPHERE	TROPHOTROPISM	TROUBLESHOT	TRUNKSLEEVE
TROCHOSPHERES	TROPHOTROPISMS	TROUBLESOME	TRUNKSLEEVES
TROCHOTRON	TROPHOZOITE	TROUBLESOMELY	TRUNNIONED
TROCHOTRONS	TROPHOZOITES	TROUBLESOMENESS	TRUSTABILITIES
TROCTOLITE	TROPICALISATION	TROUBLINGS	TRUSTABILITY
TROCTOLITES	TROPICALISE	TROUBLOUSLY	TRUSTAFARIAN
TROGLODYTE	TROPICALISED	TROUBLOUSNESS	TRUSTAFARIANS
TROGLODYTES	TROPICALISES	TROUBLOUSNESSES	TRUSTBUSTER
TROGLODYTIC	TROPICALISING	TROUGHLIKE	TRUSTBUSTERS
TROGLODYTICAL	TROPICALITIES	TROUNCINGS	TRUSTBUSTING
TROGLODYTISM	TROPICALITY	TROUSERING	TRUSTBUSTINGS
TROGLODYTISMS	TROPICALIZATION	TROUSERINGS	TRUSTEEING
TROLLEYBUS	TROPICALIZE	TROUSERLESS	TRUSTEESHIP
TROLLEYBUSES	TROPICALIZED	TROUSSEAUS	TRUSTEESHIPS
TROLLEYBUSSES	TROPICALIZES	TROUSSEAUX	TRUSTFULLY
TROLLEYING	TROPICALIZING	TROUTLINGS	TRUSTFULNESS
TROLLIUSES	TROPICALLY	TROUTSTONE	TRUSTFULNESSES
TROLLOPEES	TROPICBIRD	TROUTSTONES	TRUSTINESS
TROLLOPING	TROPICBIRDS	TROUVAILLE	TRUSTINESSES
TROLLOPISH	TROPISMATIC	TROUVAILLES	TRUSTINGLY
TROMBICULID	TROPOCOLLAGEN	TROWELLERS	TRUSTINGNESS
TROMBICULIDS	TROPOCOLLAGENS	TROWELLING	TRUSTINGNESSES
TROMBIDIASES	TROPOLOGIC	TRUANTRIES	TRUSTLESSLY
TROMBIDIASIS	TROPOLOGICAL	TRUANTSHIP	TRUSTLESSNESS
TROMBONIST	TROPOLOGICALLY	TRUANTSHIPS	TRUSTLESSNESSES
TROMBONISTS	TROPOLOGIES	TRUCKLINES	TRUSTWORTHILY
TROMOMETER	TROPOMYOSIN	TRUCKLINGS	TRUSTWORTHINESS
TROMOMETERS	TROPOMYOSINS	TRUCKLOADS	TRUSTWORTHY
TROMOMETRIC	TROPOPAUSE	TRUCKMASTER	TRUTHFULLY
TROOPSHIPS	TROPOPAUSES	TRUCKMASTERS	TRUTHFULNESS
TROOSTITES	TROPOPHILOUS	TRUCKSTOPS	TRUTHFULNESSES
TROPAEOLIN	TROPOPHYTE	TRUCULENCE	TRUTHLESSNESS
TROPAEOLINS	TROPOPHYTES	TRUCULENCES	TRUTHLESSNESSES
TROPAEOLUM	TROPOPHYTIC	TRUCULENCIES	TRYINGNESS
TROPAEOLUMS	TROPOSCATTER	TRUCULENCY	TRYINGNESSES
TROPEOLINS	TROPOSCATTERS	TRUCULENTLY	TRYPAFLAVINE
TROPHALLACTIC	TROPOSPHERE	TRUEHEARTED	TRYPAFLAVINES
TROPHALLAXES	TROPOSPHERES	TRUEHEARTEDNESS	TRYPANOCIDAL
TROPHALLAXIS	TROPOSPHERIC	TRUENESSES	TRYPANOCIDE
TROPHESIAL	TROPOTAXES	TRUEPENNIES	TRYPANOCIDES
TROPHESIES	TROPOTAXIS	TRUFFLINGS	TRYPANOSOMAL
TROPHICALLY	TROTHPLIGHT	TRUMPERIES	TRYPANOSOME
TROPHOBIOSES	TROTHPLIGHTED	TRUMPETERS	TRYPANOSOMES
TROPHOBIOSIS	TROTHPLIGHTING	TRUMPETING	TRYPANOSOMIASES
TROPHOBIOTIC	TROTHPLIGHTS	TRUMPETINGS	TRYPANOSOMIASIS
TROPHOBLAST	TROUBADOUR	TRUMPETLIKE	TRYPANOSOMIC
TROPHOBLASTIC	TROUBADOURS	TRUMPETWEED	TRYPARSAMIDE
TROPHOBLASTS	TROUBLEDLY	TRUMPETWEEDS	TRYPARSAMIDES
TROPHOLOGIES	TROUBLEFREE	TRUNCATELY	TRYPSINOGEN
TROPHOLOGY	TROUBLEMAKER	TRUNCATING	TRYPSINOGENS
TROPHONEUROSES	TROUBLEMAKERS	TRUNCATION	TRYPTAMINE
TROPHONEUROSIS	TROUBLEMAKING	TRUNCATIONS	TRYPTAMINES
TROPHOPLASM	TROUBLEMAKINGS	TRUNCHEONED	TRYPTOPHAN
TROPHOPLASMS	TROUBLESHOOT	TRUNCHEONER	TRYPTOPHANE
TROPHOTACTIC	TROUBLESHOOTER	TRUNCHEONERS	TRYPTOPHANES

TRYPTOPHANS

TRYPTOPHANS	TUBEROSITY	TUMESCENCES	TURBINATED
TSAREVICHES	TUBICOLOUS	TUMIDITIES	TURBINATES
TSAREVITCH	TUBIFICIDS	TUMIDNESSES	TURBINATION
TSAREVITCHES	TUBIFLOROUS	TUMORGENIC	TURBINATIONS
TSCHERNOSEM	TUBOCURARINE	TUMORGENICITIES	TURBOCHARGED
TSCHERNOSEMS	TUBOCURARINES	TUMORGENICITY	TURBOCHARGER
TSESAREVICH	TUBOPLASTIES	TUMORIGENESES	TURBOCHARGERS
TSESAREVICHES	TUBOPLASTY	TUMORIGENESIS	TURBOCHARGING
TSESAREVITCH	TUBULARIAN	TUMORIGENIC	TURBOCHARGINGS
TSESAREVITCHES	TUBULARIANS	TUMORIGENICITY	TURBOELECTRIC
TSESAREVNA	TUBULARITIES	TUMULOSITIES	TURBOGENERATOR
TSESAREVNAS	TUBULARITY	TUMULOSITY	TURBOGENERATORS
TSESAREWICH	TUBULATING	TUMULTUARY	TURBOMACHINERY
TSESAREWICHES	TUBULATION	TUMULTUATE	TURBOPROPS
TSESAREWITCH	TUBULATIONS	TUMULTUATED	TURBOSHAFT
TSESAREWITCHES	TUBULATORS	TUMULTUATES	TURBOSHAFTS
TSOTSITAAL	TUBULATURE	TUMULTUATING	TURBULATOR
TSOTSITAALS	TUBULATURES	TUMULTUATION	TURBULATORS
TSUTSUGAMUSHI	TUBULIFLORAL	TUMULTUATIONS	TURBULENCE
TSUTSUGAMUSHIS	TUBULIFLOROUS	TUMULTUOUS	TURBULENCES
TUBBINESSES	TUBULOUSLY	TUMULTUOUSLY	TURBULENCIES
TUBECTOMIES	TUCKERBAGS	TUMULTUOUSNESS	TURBULENCY
TUBERACEOUS	TUCKERBOXES	TUNABILITIES	TURBULENTLY
TUBERCULAR	TUFFACEOUS	TUNABILITY	TURCOPOLES
TUBERCULARLY	TUFFTAFFETA	TUNABLENESS	TURCOPOLIER
TUBERCULARS	TUFFTAFFETAS	TUNABLENESSES	TURCOPOLIERS
TUBERCULATE	TUFFTAFFETIES	TUNBELLIED	TURFGRASSES
TUBERCULATED	TUFFTAFFETY	TUNBELLIES	TURFINESSES
TUBERCULATELY	TUFTAFFETA	TUNEFULNESS	TURFSKIING
TUBERCULATION	TUFTAFFETAS	TUNEFULNESSES	TURFSKIINGS
TUBERCULATIONS	TUFTAFFETIES	TUNELESSLY	TURGENCIES
TUBERCULES	TUFTAFFETY	TUNELESSNESS	TURGESCENCE
TUBERCULIN	TUILLETTES	TUNELESSNESSES	TURGESCENCES
TUBERCULINS	TUILYIEING	TUNESMITHS	TURGESCENCIES
TUBERCULISATION	TUILZIEING	TUNGSTATES	TURGESCENCY
TUBERCULISE	TUITIONARY	TUNGSTITES	TURGESCENT
TUBERCULISED	TULARAEMIA	TUNNELINGS	TURGIDITIES
TUBERCULISES	TULARAEMIAS	TUNNELLERS	TURGIDNESS
TUBERCULISING	TULARAEMIC	TUNNELLIKE	TURGIDNESSES
TUBERCULIZATION	TULAREMIAS	TUNNELLING	TURMOILING
TUBERCULIZE	TULIPOMANIA	TUNNELLINGS	TURNABOUTS
TUBERCULIZED	TULIPOMANIAS	TUPPENNIES	TURNAGAINS
TUBERCULIZES	TULIPWOODS	TURACOVERDIN	TURNAROUND
TUBERCULIZING	TUMATAKURU	TURACOVERDINS	TURNAROUNDS
TUBERCULOID	TUMBLEBUGS	TURANGAWAEWAE	TURNBROACH
TUBERCULOMA	TUMBLEDOWN	TURANGAWAEWAES	TURNBROACHES
TUBERCULOMAS	TUMBLEHOME	TURBELLARIAN	TURNBUCKLE
TUBERCULOMATA	TUMBLEHOMES	TURBELLARIANS	TURNBUCKLES
TUBERCULOSE	TUMBLERFUL	TURBIDIMETER	TURNROUNDS
TUBERCULOSED	TUMBLERFULS	TURBIDIMETERS	TURNSTILES
TUBERCULOSES	TUMBLERSFUL	TURBIDIMETRIC	TURNSTONES
TUBERCULOSIS	TUMBLESETS	TURBIDIMETRIES	TURNTABLES
TUBERCULOUS	TUMBLEWEED	TURBIDIMETRY	TURNVEREIN
TUBERCULOUSLY	TUMBLEWEEDS	TURBIDITES	TURNVEREINS
TUBERCULUM	TUMEFACIENT	TURBIDITIES	TUROPHILES
TUBERIFEROUS	TUMEFACTION	TURBIDNESS	TURPENTINE
TUBERIFORM	TUMEFACTIONS	TURBIDNESSES	TURPENTINED
TUBEROSITIES	TUMESCENCE	TURBINACIOUS	TURPENTINES

TURPENTINING	TWINKLINGS	TYPICALNESS
TURPENTINY	TWISTABILITIES	TYPICALNESSES
TURPITUDES	TWISTABILITY	TYPIFICATION
TURQUOISES	TWITCHIEST	TYPIFICATIONS
TURRIBANTS	TWITCHINGS	TYPOGRAPHED
TURRICULATE	TWITTERERS	TYPOGRAPHER
TURRICULATED	TWITTERING	TYPOGRAPHERS
TURTLEBACK	TWITTERINGLY	TYPOGRAPHIA
TURTLEBACKS	TWITTERINGS	TYPOGRAPHIC
TURTLEDOVE	TWITTINGLY	TYPOGRAPHICAL
TURTLEDOVES	TWOFOLDNESS	TYPOGRAPHICALLY
TURTLEHEAD	TWOFOLDNESSES	TYPOGRAPHIES
TURTLEHEADS	TWOPENCEWORTH	TYPOGRAPHING
TURTLENECK	TWOPENCEWORTHS	TYPOGRAPHIST
TURTLENECKED	TWOPENNIES	TYPOGRAPHISTS
TURTLENECKS	TWOSEATERS	TYPOGRAPHS
TUTELARIES	TYCOONATES	TYPOGRAPHY
TUTIORISMS	TYCOONERIES	TYPOLOGICAL
TUTIORISTS	TYLECTOMIES	TYPOLOGICALLY
TUTORESSES	TYMPANIFORM	TYPOLOGIES
TUTORIALLY	TYMPANISTS	TYPOLOGIST
TUTORISING	TYMPANITES	TYPOLOGISTS
TUTORIZING	TYMPANITESES	TYPOMANIAS
TUTORSHIPS	TYMPANITIC	TYPOTHETAE
TUTOYERING	TYMPANITIS	TYRANNESSES
TUTWORKERS	TYMPANITISES	TYRANNICAL
TUTWORKMAN	TYNDALLIMETRIES	TYRANNICALLY
TUTWORKMEN	TYNDALLIMETRY	TYRANNICALNESS
TWADDLIEST	TYPECASTER	TYRANNICIDAL
TWADDLINGS	TYPECASTERS	TYRANNICIDE
TWALPENNIES	TYPECASTING	TYRANNICIDES
TWANGINGLY	TYPEFOUNDER	TYRANNISED
TWANGLINGLY	TYPEFOUNDERS	TYRANNISER
TWANGLINGS	TYPEFOUNDING	TYRANNISERS
TWATTLINGS	TYPEFOUNDINGS	TYRANNISES
TWAYBLADES	TYPESCRIPT	TYRANNISING
TWEEDINESS	TYPESCRIPTS	TYRANNIZED
TWEEDINESSES	TYPESETTER	TYRANNIZER
TWEEDLEDEE	TYPESETTERS	TYRANNIZERS
TWEEDLEDEED	TYPESETTING	TYRANNIZES
TWEEDLEDEEING	TYPESETTINGS	TYRANNIZING
TWEEDLEDEES	TYPESTYLES	TYRANNOSAUR
TWEENAGERS	TYPEWRITER	TYRANNOSAURS
TWEENESSES	TYPEWRITERS	TYRANNOSAURUS
TWELVEFOLD	TYPEWRITES	TYRANNOSAURUSES
TWELVEMONTH	TYPEWRITING	TYRANNOUSLY
TWELVEMONTHS	TYPEWRITINGS	TYRANNOUSNESS
TWENTIETHS	TYPEWRITTEN	TYRANNOUSNESSES
TWENTYFOLD	TYPHACEOUS	TYROCIDINE
TWENTYFOLDS	TYPHLITISES	TYROCIDINES
TWICHILDREN	TYPHLOLOGIES	TYROCIDINS
TWIDDLIEST	TYPHLOLOGY	TYROGLYPHID
TWIDDLINGS	TYPHLOSOLE	TYROGLYPHIDS
TWILIGHTED	TYPHLOSOLES	TYROPITTAS
TWILIGHTING	TYPHOGENIC	TYROSINASE
TWINBERRIES	TYPHOIDINS	TYROSINASES
TWINFLOWER	TYPICALITIES	TYROTHRICIN
TWINFLOWERS	TYPICALITY	TYROTHRICINS

U

UBIQUARIAN	ULTRACIVILISED	ULTRAMARINES	ULTRASENSUAL
UBIQUINONE	ULTRACIVILIZED	ULTRAMASCULINE	ULTRASERIOUS
UBIQUINONES	ULTRACLEAN	ULTRAMICRO	ULTRASHARP
UBIQUITARIAN	ULTRACOMMERCIAL	ULTRAMICROMETER	ULTRASHORT
UBIQUITARIANISM	ULTRACOMPACT	ULTRAMICROSCOPE	ULTRASIMPLE
UBIQUITARIANS	ULTRACOMPETENT	ULTRAMICROSCOPY	ULTRASLICK
UBIQUITARY	ULTRACONVENIENT	ULTRAMICROTOME	ULTRASMALL
UBIQUITIES	ULTRACREPIDATE	ULTRAMICROTOMES	ULTRASMART
UBIQUITINATION	ULTRACREPIDATED	ULTRAMICROTOMY	ULTRASMOOTH
UBIQUITINATIONS	ULTRACREPIDATES	ULTRAMILITANT	ULTRASONIC
UBIQUITINS	ULTRACRITICAL	ULTRAMILITANTS	ULTRASONICALLY
UBIQUITOUS	ULTRADEMOCRATIC	ULTRAMINIATURE	ULTRASONICS
UBIQUITOUSLY	ULTRADENSE	ULTRAMODERN	ULTRASONOGRAPHY
UBIQUITOUSNESS	ULTRADISTANCE	ULTRAMODERNISM	ULTRASOUND
UDOMETRIES	ULTRADISTANT	ULTRAMODERNISMS	ULTRASOUNDS
UFOLOGICAL	ULTRAEFFICIENT	ULTRAMODERNIST	ULTRASTRUCTURAL
UFOLOGISTS	ULTRAENERGETIC	ULTRAMODERNISTS	ULTRASTRUCTURE
UGLIFICATION	ULTRAEXCLUSIVE	ULTRAMONTANE	ULTRASTRUCTURES
UGLIFICATIONS	ULTRAFAMILIAR	ULTRAMONTANES	ULTRAVACUA
UGLINESSES	ULTRAFASTIDIOUS	ULTRAMONTANISM	ULTRAVACUUM
UGSOMENESS	ULTRAFEMININE	ULTRAMONTANISMS	ULTRAVACUUMS
UGSOMENESSES	ULTRAFICHE	ULTRAMONTANIST	ULTRAVIOLENCE
UINTAHITES	ULTRAFICHES	ULTRAMONTANISTS	ULTRAVIOLENCES
UINTATHERE	ULTRAFILTER	ULTRAMUNDANE	ULTRAVIOLENT
UINTATHERES	ULTRAFILTERED	ULTRANATIONAL	ULTRAVIOLET
UITLANDERS	ULTRAFILTERING	ULTRAORTHODOX	ULTRAVIOLETS
ULCERATING	ULTRAFILTERS	ULTRAPATRIOTIC	ULTRAVIRILE
ULCERATION	ULTRAFILTRATE	ULTRAPHYSICAL	ULTRAVIRILITIES
ULCERATIONS	ULTRAFILTRATES	ULTRAPOWERFUL	ULTRAVIRILITY
ULCERATIVE	ULTRAFILTRATION	ULTRAPRACTICAL	ULTRAVIRUS
ULCEROGENIC	ULTRAGLAMOROUS	ULTRAPRECISE	ULTRAVIRUSES
ULCEROUSLY	ULTRAHAZARDOUS	ULTRAPRECISION	ULTRAWIDEBAND
ULCEROUSNESS	ULTRAHEATED	ULTRAQUIET	ULTRAWIDEBANDS
ULCEROUSNESSES	ULTRAHEATING	ULTRARADICAL	ULTRONEOUS
ULOTRICHIES	ULTRAHEATS	ULTRARADICALS	ULTRONEOUSLY
ULOTRICHOUS	ULTRAHEAVY	ULTRARAPID	ULTRONEOUSNESS
ULSTERETTE	ULTRAHUMAN	ULTRARAREFIED	ULULATIONS
ULSTERETTES	ULTRAISTIC	ULTRARATIONAL	UMBELLATED
ULTERIORLY	ULTRALARGE	ULTRAREALISM	UMBELLATELY
ULTIMACIES	ULTRALEFTISM	ULTRAREALISMS	UMBELLIFER
ULTIMATELY	ULTRALEFTISMS	ULTRAREALIST	UMBELLIFEROUS
ULTIMATENESS	ULTRALEFTIST	ULTRAREALISTIC	UMBELLIFERS
ULTIMATENESSES	ULTRALEFTISTS	ULTRAREALISTS	UMBELLULATE
ULTIMATING	ULTRALIBERAL	ULTRAREFINED	UMBELLULES
ULTIMATUMS	ULTRALIBERALISM	ULTRARELIABLE	UMBILICALLY
ULTIMOGENITURE	ULTRALIBERALS	ULTRARIGHT	UMBILICALS
ULTIMOGENITURES	ULTRALIGHT	ULTRARIGHTIST	UMBILICATE
ULTRABASIC	ULTRALIGHTS	ULTRARIGHTISTS	UMBILICATED
ULTRABASICS	ULTRAMAFIC	ULTRAROMANTIC	UMBILICATION
ULTRACAREFUL	ULTRAMARATHON	ULTRAROYALIST	UMBILICATIONS
ULTRACASUAL	ULTRAMARATHONER	ULTRAROYALISTS	UMBILICUSES
ULTRACAUTIOUS	ULTRAMARATHONS	ULTRASECRET	UMBILIFORM
ULTRACENTRIFUGE	ULTRAMARINE	ULTRASENSITIVE	UMBONATION

UMBONATIONS	UNACTUATED	UNAMORTIZED	UNAPPREHENSIBLE
UMBRACULATE	UNADAPTABLE	UNAMPLIFIED	UNAPPREHENSIVE
UMBRACULIFORM	UNADDRESSED	UNAMUSABLE	UNAPPRISED
UMBRACULUM	UNADJUDICATED	UNAMUSINGLY	UNAPPROACHABLE
UMBRAGEOUS	UNADJUSTED	UNANALYSABLE	UNAPPROACHABLY
UMBRAGEOUSLY	UNADMIRING	UNANALYSED	UNAPPROACHED
UMBRAGEOUSNESS	UNADMITTED	UNANALYTIC	UNAPPROPRIATE
UMBRATICAL	UNADMONISHED	UNANALYTICAL	UNAPPROPRIATED
UMBRATILOUS	UNADOPTABLE	UNANALYZABLE	UNAPPROVED
UMBRELLAED	UNADULTERATE	UNANALYZED	UNAPPROVING
UMBRELLAING	UNADULTERATED	UNANCHORED	UNAPPROVINGLY
UMBRELLOES	UNADULTERATEDLY	UNANCHORING	UNAPTNESSES
UMBRIFEROUS	UNADVENTROUS	UNANESTHETISED	UNARGUABLE
UMPIRESHIP	UNADVENTUROUS	UNANESTHETIZED	UNARGUABLY
UMPIRESHIPS	UNADVERTISED	UNANIMATED	UNARMOURED
UNABASHEDLY	UNADVISABLE	UNANIMITIES	UNARRANGED
UNABATEDLY	UNADVISABLENESS	UNANIMOUSLY	UNARROGANT
UNABBREVIATED	UNADVISABLY	UNANIMOUSNESS	UNARTFULLY
UNABOLISHED	UNADVISEDLY	UNANIMOUSNESSES	UNARTICULATE
UNABRIDGED	UNADVISEDNESS	UNANNEALED	UNARTICULATED
UNABROGATED	UNADVISEDNESSES	UNANNOTATED	UNARTIFICIAL
UNABSOLVED	UNAESTHETIC	UNANNOUNCED	UNARTIFICIALLY
UNABSORBED	UNAFFECTED	UNANSWERABILITY	UNARTISTIC
UNABSORBENT	UNAFFECTEDLY	UNANSWERABLE	UNARTISTLIKE
UNACADEMIC	UNAFFECTEDNESS	UNANSWERABLY	UNASCENDABLE
UNACADEMICALLY	UNAFFECTING	UNANSWERED	UNASCENDED
UNACCENTED	UNAFFECTIONATE	UNANTICIPATED	UNASCENDIBLE
UNACCENTUATED	UNAFFILIATED	UNANTICIPATEDLY	UNASCERTAINABLE
UNACCEPTABILITY	UNAFFLUENT	UNAPOLOGETIC	UNASCERTAINED
UNACCEPTABLE	UNAFFORDABLE	UNAPOLOGISING	UNASHAMEDLY
UNACCEPTABLY	UNAGGRESSIVE	UNAPOLOGIZING	UNASHAMEDNESS
UNACCEPTANCE	UNAGREEABLE	UNAPOSTOLIC	UNASHAMEDNESSES
UNACCEPTANCES	UNALIENABLE	UNAPOSTOLICAL	UNASPIRATED
UNACCEPTED	UNALIENABLY	UNAPOSTOLICALLY	UNASPIRING
UNACCLIMATED	UNALIENATED	UNAPPALLED	UNASPIRINGLY
UNACCLIMATISED	UNALLEVIATED	UNAPPARELLED	UNASPIRINGNESS
UNACCLIMATIZED	UNALLOCATED	UNAPPARELLING	UNASSAILABILITY
UNACCOMMODATED	UNALLOTTED	UNAPPARELS	UNASSAILABLE
UNACCOMMODATING	UNALLOWABLE	UNAPPARENT	UNASSAILABLY
UNACCOMPANIED	UNALLURING	UNAPPEALABLE	UNASSAILED
UNACCOMPLISHED	UNALTERABILITY	UNAPPEALABLY	UNASSEMBLED
UNACCOUNTABLE	UNALTERABLE	UNAPPEALING	UNASSERTIVE
UNACCOUNTABLY	UNALTERABLENESS	UNAPPEALINGLY	UNASSERTIVELY
UNACCOUNTED	UNALTERABLY	UNAPPEASABLE	UNASSIGNABLE
UNACCREDITED	UNALTERING	UNAPPEASABLY	UNASSIGNED
UNACCULTURATED	UNAMBIGUOUS	UNAPPEASED	UNASSIMILABLE
UNACCUSABLE	UNAMBIGUOUSLY	UNAPPETISING	UNASSIMILATED
UNACCUSABLY	UNAMBITIOUS	UNAPPETISINGLY	UNASSISTED
UNACCUSTOMED	UNAMBITIOUSLY	UNAPPETIZING	UNASSISTEDLY
UNACCUSTOMEDLY	UNAMBIVALENT	UNAPPETIZINGLY	UNASSISTING
UNACHIEVABLE	UNAMBIVALENTLY	UNAPPLAUSIVE	UNASSOCIATED
UNACHIEVED	UNAMENABLE	UNAPPLICABLE	UNASSUAGEABLE
UNACKNOWLEDGED	UNAMENDABLE	UNAPPOINTED	UNASSUAGED
UNACQUAINT	UNAMIABILITIES	UNAPPRECIATED	UNASSUMING
UNACQUAINTANCE	UNAMIABILITY	UNAPPRECIATION	UNASSUMINGLY
UNACQUAINTANCES	UNAMIABLENESS	UNAPPRECIATIONS	UNASSUMINGNESS
UNACQUAINTED	UNAMIABLENESSES	UNAPPRECIATIVE	UNATHLETIC
UNACTORISH	UNAMORTISED	UNAPPREHENDED	UNATONABLE

UNATTACHED	UNBARRICADES	UNBETTERABLE	UNBREAKABLE
UNATTAINABLE	UNBARRICADING	UNBETTERED	UNBREATHABLE
UNATTAINABLY	UNBATTERED	UNBEWAILED	UNBREATHED
UNATTAINTED	UNBEARABLE	UNBIASEDLY	UNBREATHING
UNATTEMPTED	UNBEARABLENESS	UNBIASEDNESS	UNBREECHED
UNATTENDED	UNBEARABLY	UNBIASEDNESSES	UNBREECHES
UNATTENDING	UNBEATABLE	UNBIASSEDLY	UNBREECHING
UNATTENTIVE	UNBEATABLY	UNBIASSEDNESS	UNBRIBABLE
UNATTENUATED	UNBEAUTIFUL	UNBIASSEDNESSES	UNBRIDGEABLE
UNATTESTED	UNBEAUTIFULLY	UNBIASSING	UNBRIDLEDLY
UNATTRACTIVE	UNBEAVERED	UNBIBLICAL	UNBRIDLEDNESS
UNATTRACTIVELY	UNBECOMING	UNBINDINGS	UNBRIDLEDNESSES
UNATTRIBUTABLE	UNBECOMINGLY	UNBIRTHDAY	UNBRIDLING
UNATTRIBUTED	UNBECOMINGNESS	UNBIRTHDAYS	UNBRILLIANT
UNAUGMENTED	UNBECOMINGS	UNBISHOPED	UNBROKENLY
UNAUSPICIOUS	UNBEDIMMED	UNBISHOPING	UNBROKENNESS
UNAUTHENTIC	UNBEDINNED	UNBLAMABLE	UNBROKENNESSES
UNAUTHENTICATED	UNBEFITTING	UNBLAMABLY	UNBROTHERLIKE
UNAUTHENTICITY	UNBEFRIENDED	UNBLAMEABLE	UNBROTHERLY
UNAUTHORISED	UNBEGETTING	UNBLAMEABLY	UNBUCKLING
UNAUTHORITATIVE	UNBEGINNING	UNBLEACHED	UNBUDGEABLE
UNAUTHORIZED	UNBEGOTTEN	UNBLEMISHED	UNBUDGEABLY
UNAUTOMATED	UNBEGUILED	UNBLENCHED	UNBUDGETED
UNAVAILABILITY	UNBEGUILES	UNBLENCHING	UNBUDGINGLY
UNAVAILABLE	UNBEGUILING	UNBLESSEDNESS	UNBUFFERED
UNAVAILABLENESS	UNBEHOLDEN	UNBLESSEDNESSES	UNBUILDABLE
UNAVAILABLY	UNBEKNOWNST	UNBLESSING	UNBUILDING
UNAVAILING	UNBELIEVABILITY	UNBLINDFOLD	UNBUNDLERS
UNAVAILINGLY	UNBELIEVABLE	UNBLINDFOLDED	UNBUNDLING
UNAVAILINGNESS	UNBELIEVABLY	UNBLINDFOLDING	UNBUNDLINGS
UNAVERTABLE	UNBELIEVED	UNBLINDFOLDS	UNBURDENED
UNAVERTIBLE	UNBELIEVER	UNBLINDING	UNBURDENING
UNAVOIDABILITY	UNBELIEVERS	UNBLINKING	UNBUREAUCRATIC
UNAVOIDABLE	UNBELIEVES	UNBLINKINGLY	UNBURNABLE
UNAVOIDABLENESS	UNBELIEVING	UNBLISSFUL	UNBURNISHED
UNAVOIDABLY	UNBELIEVINGLY	UNBLOCKING	UNBURROWED
UNAVOWEDLY	UNBELIEVINGNESS	UNBLOODIED	UNBURROWING
UNAWAKENED	UNBELLIGERENT	UNBLUSHING	UNBURTHENED
UNAWAKENING	UNBENDABLE	UNBLUSHINGLY	UNBURTHENING
UNAWARENESS	UNBENDINGLY	UNBLUSHINGNESS	UNBURTHENS
UNAWARENESSES	UNBENDINGNESS	UNBOASTFUL	UNBUSINESSLIKE
UNBAILABLE	UNBENDINGNESSES	UNBONNETED	UNBUTTERED
UNBALANCED	UNBENDINGS	UNBONNETING	UNBUTTONED
UNBALANCES	UNBENEFICED	UNBORROWED	UNBUTTONING
UNBALANCING	UNBENEFICIAL	UNBOSOMERS	UNCALCIFIED
UNBALLASTED	UNBENEFITED	UNBOSOMING	UNCALCINED
UNBANDAGED	UNBENIGHTED	UNBOTTLING	UNCALCULATED
UNBANDAGES	UNBENIGNANT	UNBOTTOMED	UNCALCULATING
UNBANDAGING	UNBENIGNLY	UNBOUNDEDLY	UNCALIBRATED
UNBAPTISED	UNBESEEMED	UNBOUNDEDNESS	UNCALLOUSED
UNBAPTISES	UNBESEEMING	UNBOUNDEDNESSES	UNCANCELED
UNBAPTISING	UNBESEEMINGLY	UNBOWDLERISED	UNCANDIDLY
UNBAPTIZED	UNBESOUGHT	UNBOWDLERIZED	UNCANDIDNESS
UNBAPTIZES	UNBESPEAKING	UNBRACKETED	UNCANDIDNESSES
UNBAPTIZING	UNBESPEAKS	UNBRAIDING	UNCANDOURS
UNBARBERED	UNBESPOKEN	UNBRANCHED	UNCANNIEST
UNBARRICADE	UNBESTOWED	UNBREACHABLE	UNCANNINESS
UNBARRICADED	UNBETRAYED	UNBREACHED	UNCANNINESSES

UNCANONICAL	UNCHARITABLY	UNCIPHERED	UNCLUBBABLE
UNCANONICALNESS	UNCHARITIES	UNCIPHERING	UNCLUTCHED
UNCANONISE	UNCHARMING	UNCIRCULATED	UNCLUTCHES
UNCANONISED	UNCHARNELLED	UNCIRCUMCISED	UNCLUTCHING
UNCANONISES	UNCHARNELLING	UNCIRCUMCISION	UNCLUTTERED
UNCANONISING	UNCHARNELS	UNCIRCUMCISIONS	UNCLUTTERING
UNCANONIZE	UNCHARTERED	UNCIRCUMSCRIBED	UNCLUTTERS
UNCANONIZED	UNCHASTELY	UNCIVILISED	UNCOALESCE
UNCANONIZES	UNCHASTENED	UNCIVILISEDLY	UNCOALESCED
UNCANONIZING	UNCHASTENESS	UNCIVILISEDNESS	UNCOALESCES
UNCAPITALISED	UNCHASTENESSES	UNCIVILITIES	UNCOALESCING
UNCAPITALIZED	UNCHASTEST	UNCIVILITY	UNCOATINGS
UNCAPSIZABLE	UNCHASTISABLE	UNCIVILIZED	UNCODIFIED
UNCAPTIONED	UNCHASTISED	UNCIVILIZEDLY	UNCOERCIVE
UNCAPTURABLE	UNCHASTITIES	UNCIVILIZEDNESS	UNCOERCIVELY
UNCARPETED	UNCHASTITY	UNCIVILNESS	UNCOFFINED
UNCASTRATED	UNCHASTIZABLE	UNCIVILNESSES	UNCOFFINING
UNCATALOGED	UNCHASTIZED	UNCLAMPING	UNCOLLECTED
UNCATALOGUED	UNCHAUVINISTIC	UNCLARIFIED	UNCOLLECTIBLE
UNCATCHABLE	UNCHECKABLE	UNCLARITIES	UNCOLLECTIBLES
UNCATEGORISABLE	UNCHECKING	UNCLASPING	UNCOLOURED
UNCATEGORIZABLE	UNCHEERFUL	UNCLASSICAL	UNCOMATABLE
UNCEASINGLY	UNCHEERFULLY	UNCLASSIFIABLE	UNCOMBATIVE
UNCEASINGNESS	UNCHEERFULNESS	UNCLASSIFIED	UNCOMBINED
UNCEASINGNESSES	UNCHEWABLE	UNCLEANEST	UNCOMBINES
UNCELEBRATED	UNCHILDING	UNCLEANLIER	UNCOMBINING
UNCENSORED	UNCHILDLIKE	UNCLEANLIEST	UNCOMEATABLE
UNCENSORIOUS	UNCHIVALROUS	UNCLEANLINESS	UNCOMELINESS
UNCENSURED	UNCHIVALROUSLY	UNCLEANLINESSES	UNCOMELINESSES
UNCEREBRAL	UNCHLORINATED	UNCLEANNESS	UNCOMFORTABLE
UNCEREMONIOUS	UNCHOREOGRAPHED	UNCLEANNESSES	UNCOMFORTABLY
UNCEREMONIOUSLY	UNCHRISTEN	UNCLEANSED	UNCOMFORTED
UNCERTAINLY	UNCHRISTENED	UNCLEAREST	UNCOMMENDABLE
UNCERTAINNESS	UNCHRISTENING	UNCLEARNESS	UNCOMMENDABLY
UNCERTAINNESSES	UNCHRISTENS	UNCLEARNESSES	UNCOMMENDED
UNCERTAINTIES	UNCHRISTIAN	UNCLENCHED	UNCOMMERCIAL
UNCERTAINTY	UNCHRISTIANED	UNCLENCHES	UNCOMMITTED
UNCERTIFICATED	UNCHRISTIANING	UNCLENCHING	UNCOMMONER
UNCERTIFIED	UNCHRISTIANISE	UNCLERICAL	UNCOMMONEST
UNCHAINING	UNCHRISTIANISED	UNCLESHIPS	UNCOMMONLY
UNCHAIRING	UNCHRISTIANISES	UNCLIMBABLE	UNCOMMONNESS
UNCHALLENGEABLE	UNCHRISTIANIZE	UNCLIMBABLENESS	UNCOMMONNESSES
UNCHALLENGEABLY	UNCHRISTIANIZED	UNCLINCHED	UNCOMMUNICABLE
UNCHALLENGED	UNCHRISTIANIZES	UNCLINCHES	UNCOMMUNICATED
UNCHALLENGING	UNCHRISTIANLIKE	UNCLINCHING	UNCOMMUNICATIVE
UNCHANCIER	UNCHRISTIANLY	UNCLIPPING	UNCOMMUTED
UNCHANCIEST	UNCHRISTIANS	UNCLOAKING	UNCOMPACTED
UNCHANGEABILITY	UNCHRONICLED	UNCLOGGING	UNCOMPANIED
UNCHANGEABLE	UNCHRONOLOGICAL	UNCLOISTER	UNCOMPANIONABLE
UNCHANGEABLY	UNCHURCHED	UNCLOISTERED	UNCOMPANIONED
UNCHANGING	UNCHURCHES	UNCLOISTERING	UNCOMPASSIONATE
UNCHANGINGLY	UNCHURCHING	UNCLOISTERS	UNCOMPELLED
UNCHANGINGNESS	UNCHURCHLY	UNCLOTHING	UNCOMPELLING
UNCHANNELED	UNCILIATED	UNCLOUDEDLY	UNCOMPENSATED
UNCHAPERONED	UNCINARIAS	UNCLOUDEDNESS	UNCOMPETITIVE
UNCHARGING	UNCINARIASES	UNCLOUDEDNESSES	UNCOMPLACENT
UNCHARISMATIC	UNCINARIASIS	UNCLOUDING	UNCOMPLAINING
UNCHARITABLE	UNCINEMATIC	UNCLUBABLE	UNCOMPLAININGLY

UNCOMPLAISANT	UNCONGENIALITY	UNCONVERSABLE	UNCTUOUSNESSES
UNCOMPLAISANTLY	UNCONJECTURED	UNCONVERSANT	UNCUCKOLDED
UNCOMPLETED	UNCONJUGAL	UNCONVERTED	UNCULTIVABLE
UNCOMPLIANT	UNCONJUGATED	UNCONVERTIBLE	UNCULTIVATABLE
UNCOMPLICATED	UNCONJUNCTIVE	UNCONVICTED	UNCULTIVATED
UNCOMPLIMENTARY	UNCONNECTED	UNCONVINCED	UNCULTURED
UNCOMPLYING	UNCONNECTEDLY	UNCONVINCING	UNCUMBERED
UNCOMPOSABLE	UNCONNECTEDNESS	UNCONVINCINGLY	UNCURBABLE
UNCOMPOUNDED	UNCONNIVING	UNCONVOYED	UNCURTAILED
UNCOMPREHENDED	UNCONQUERABLE	UNCOOPERATIVE	UNCURTAINED
UNCOMPREHENDING	UNCONQUERABLY	UNCOOPERATIVELY	UNCURTAINING
UNCOMPREHENSIVE	UNCONQUERED	UNCOORDINATED	UNCURTAINS
UNCOMPROMISABLE	UNCONSCIENTIOUS	UNCOPYRIGHTABLE	UNCUSTOMARILY
UNCOMPROMISING	UNCONSCIONABLE	UNCOQUETTISH	UNCUSTOMARY
UNCOMPUTERISED	UNCONSCIONABLY	UNCORRECTABLE	UNCUSTOMED
UNCOMPUTERIZED	UNCONSCIOUS	UNCORRECTED	UNCYNICALLY
UNCONCEALABLE	UNCONSCIOUSES	UNCORRELATED	UNDANCEABLE
UNCONCEALED	UNCONSCIOUSLY	UNCORROBORATED	UNDAUNTABLE
UNCONCEALING	UNCONSCIOUSNESS	UNCORRUPTED	UNDAUNTEDLY
UNCONCEIVABLE	UNCONSECRATE	UNCORSETED	UNDAUNTEDNESS
UNCONCEIVABLY	UNCONSECRATED	UNCOUNSELLED	UNDAUNTEDNESSES
UNCONCEIVED	UNCONSECRATES	UNCOUNTABLE	UNDAZZLING
UNCONCERNED	UNCONSECRATING	UNCOUPLERS	UNDEBARRED
UNCONCERNEDLY	UNCONSENTANEOUS	UNCOUPLING	UNDEBATABLE
UNCONCERNEDNESS	UNCONSENTING	UNCOURAGEOUS	UNDEBATABLY
UNCONCERNING	UNCONSIDERED	UNCOURTEOUS	UNDEBAUCHED
UNCONCERNMENT	UNCONSIDERING	UNCOURTLINESS	UNDECADENT
UNCONCERNMENTS	UNCONSOLED	UNCOURTLINESSES	UNDECAGONS
UNCONCERNS	UNCONSOLIDATED	UNCOUTHEST	UNDECEIVABLE
UNCONCERTED	UNCONSTANT	UNCOUTHNESS	UNDECEIVED
UNCONCILIATORY	UNCONSTRAINABLE	UNCOUTHNESSES	UNDECEIVER
UNCONCLUSIVE	UNCONSTRAINED	UNCOVENANTED	UNDECEIVERS
UNCONCOCTED	UNCONSTRAINEDLY	UNCOVERING	UNDECEIVES
UNCONDITIONAL	UNCONSTRAINT	UNCREATEDNESS	UNDECEIVING
UNCONDITIONALLY	UNCONSTRAINTS	UNCREATEDNESSES	UNDECIDABILITY
UNCONDITIONED	UNCONSTRICTED	UNCREATING	UNDECIDABLE
UNCONFEDERATED	UNCONSTRUCTED	UNCREATIVE	UNDECIDEDLY
UNCONFESSED	UNCONSTRUCTIVE	UNCREDENTIALED	UNDECIDEDNESS
UNCONFINABLE	UNCONSUMED	UNCREDIBLE	UNDECIDEDNESSES
UNCONFINED	UNCONSUMMATED	UNCREDITABLE	UNDECIDEDS
UNCONFINEDLY	UNCONTAINABLE	UNCREDITED	UNDECILLION
UNCONFINES	UNCONTAMINATED	UNCRIPPLED	UNDECILLIONS
UNCONFINING	UNCONTEMNED	UNCRITICAL	UNDECIMOLE
UNCONFIRMED	UNCONTEMPLATED	UNCRITICALLY	UNDECIMOLES
UNCONFORMABLE	UNCONTEMPORARY	UNCROSSABLE	UNDECIPHERABLE
UNCONFORMABLY	UNCONTENTIOUS	UNCROSSING	UNDECIPHERED
UNCONFORMING	UNCONTESTABLE	UNCROWNING	UNDECISIVE
UNCONFORMITIES	UNCONTESTED	UNCRUMPLED	UNDECLARED
UNCONFORMITY	UNCONTRACTED	UNCRUMPLES	UNDECLINING
UNCONFOUNDED	UNCONTRADICTED	UNCRUMPLING	UNDECOMPOSABLE
UNCONFUSED	UNCONTRIVED	UNCRUSHABLE	UNDECOMPOSED
UNCONFUSEDLY	UNCONTROLLABLE	UNCRYSTALLISED	UNDECORATED
UNCONFUSES	UNCONTROLLABLY	UNCRYSTALLIZED	UNDEDICATED
UNCONFUSING	UNCONTROLLED	UNCTIONLESS	UNDEFEATED
UNCONGEALED	UNCONTROLLEDLY	UNCTUOSITIES	UNDEFENDED
UNCONGEALING	UNCONTROVERSIAL	UNCTUOSITY	UNDEFINABLE
UNCONGEALS	UNCONTROVERTED	UNCTUOUSLY	UNDEFOLIATED
UNCONGENIAL	UNCONVENTIONAL	UNCTUOUSNESS	UNDEFORMED

UNDEIFYING	UNDERBLANKETS	UNDERCLUBBED	UNDEREARTH
UNDELAYING	UNDERBODIES	UNDERCLUBBING	UNDEREATEN
UNDELECTABLE	UNDERBORNE	UNDERCLUBS	UNDEREATING
UNDELEGATED	UNDERBOSSES	UNDERCOATED	UNDEREDUCATED
UNDELIBERATE	UNDERBOUGH	UNDERCOATING	UNDEREMPHASES
UNDELIGHTED	UNDERBOUGHS	UNDERCOATINGS	UNDEREMPHASIS
UNDELIGHTFUL	UNDERBOUGHT	UNDERCOATS	UNDEREMPHASISE
UNDELIGHTS	UNDERBREATH	UNDERCOOKED	UNDEREMPHASISED
UNDELIVERABLE	UNDERBREATHS	UNDERCOOKING	UNDEREMPHASISES
UNDELIVERED	UNDERBREEDING	UNDERCOOKS	UNDEREMPHASIZE
UNDEMANDING	UNDERBREEDINGS	UNDERCOOLED	UNDEREMPHASIZED
UNDEMOCRATIC	UNDERBRIDGE	UNDERCOOLING	UNDEREMPHASIZES
UNDEMONSTRABLE	UNDERBRIDGES	UNDERCOOLS	UNDEREMPLOYED
UNDEMONSTRATIVE	UNDERBRIMS	UNDERCOUNT	UNDEREMPLOYMENT
UNDENIABLE	UNDERBRUSH	UNDERCOUNTED	UNDERESTIMATE
UNDENIABLENESS	UNDERBRUSHED	UNDERCOUNTING	UNDERESTIMATED
UNDENIABLY	UNDERBRUSHES	UNDERCOUNTS	UNDERESTIMATES
UNDEPENDABLE	UNDERBRUSHING	UNDERCOVER	UNDERESTIMATING
UNDEPENDING	UNDERBUDDED	UNDERCOVERT	UNDERESTIMATION
UNDEPLORED	UNDERBUDDING	UNDERCOVERTS	UNDEREXPOSE
UNDEPRAVED	UNDERBUDGET	UNDERCREST	UNDEREXPOSED
UNDEPRECIATED	UNDERBUDGETED	UNDERCRESTED	UNDEREXPOSES
UNDEPRESSED	UNDERBUDGETING	UNDERCRESTING	UNDEREXPOSING
UNDEPRIVED	UNDERBUDGETS	UNDERCRESTS	UNDEREXPOSURE
UNDERACHIEVE	UNDERBUILD	UNDERCROFT	UNDEREXPOSURES
UNDERACHIEVED	UNDERBUILDER	UNDERCROFTS	UNDERFEEDING
UNDERACHIEVER	UNDERBUILDERS	UNDERCURRENT	UNDERFEEDS
UNDERACHIEVERS	UNDERBUILDING	UNDERCURRENTS	UNDERFELTS
UNDERACHIEVES	UNDERBUILDS	UNDERCUTTING	UNDERFINANCED
UNDERACHIEVING	UNDERBUILT	UNDERDAMPER	UNDERFINISHED
UNDERACTED	UNDERBURNT	UNDERDAMPERS	UNDERFIRED
UNDERACTING	UNDERBUSHED	UNDERDECKS	UNDERFIRES
UNDERACTION	UNDERBUSHES	UNDERDEVELOP	UNDERFIRING
UNDERACTIONS	UNDERBUSHING	UNDERDEVELOPED	UNDERFISHED
UNDERACTIVE	UNDERBUYING	UNDERDEVELOPING	UNDERFISHES
UNDERACTIVITIES	UNDERCAPITALISE	UNDERDEVELOPS	UNDERFISHING
UNDERACTIVITY	UNDERCAPITALIZE	UNDERDOERS	UNDERFLOOR
UNDERACTOR	UNDERCARDS	UNDERDOING	UNDERFLOWS
UNDERACTORS	UNDERCARRIAGE	UNDERDOSED	UNDERFONGED
UNDERAGENT	UNDERCARRIAGES	UNDERDOSES	UNDERFONGING
UNDERAGENTS	UNDERCARTS	UNDERDOSING	UNDERFONGS
UNDERBAKED	UNDERCASTS	UNDERDRAIN	UNDERFOOTED
UNDERBAKES	UNDERCHARGE	UNDERDRAINAGE	UNDERFOOTING
UNDERBAKING	UNDERCHARGED	UNDERDRAINAGES	UNDERFOOTS
UNDERBEARER	UNDERCHARGES	UNDERDRAINED	UNDERFULFIL
UNDERBEARERS	UNDERCHARGING	UNDERDRAINING	UNDERFULFILLED
UNDERBEARING	UNDERCLASS	UNDERDRAINS	UNDERFULFILLING
UNDERBEARINGS	UNDERCLASSES	UNDERDRAWERS	UNDERFULFILS
UNDERBEARS	UNDERCLASSMAN	UNDERDRAWING	UNDERFUNDED
UNDERBELLIES	UNDERCLASSMEN	UNDERDRAWINGS	UNDERFUNDING
UNDERBELLY	UNDERCLAYS	UNDERDRAWN	UNDERFUNDINGS
UNDERBIDDER	UNDERCLIFF	UNDERDRAWS	UNDERFUNDS
UNDERBIDDERS	UNDERCLIFFS	UNDERDRESS	UNDERGARMENT
UNDERBIDDING	UNDERCLOTHE	UNDERDRESSED	UNDERGARMENTS
UNDERBITES	UNDERCLOTHED	UNDERDRESSES	UNDERGIRDED
UNDERBITING	UNDERCLOTHES	UNDERDRESSING	UNDERGIRDING
UNDERBITTEN	UNDERCLOTHING	UNDERDRIVE	UNDERGIRDS
UNDERBLANKET	UNDERCLOTHINGS	UNDERDRIVES	UNDERGLAZE

UNDERGLAZES	UNDERLINED	UNDERPEOPLED	UNDERREPORTED
UNDERGOERS	UNDERLINEN	UNDERPERFORM	UNDERREPORTING
UNDERGOING	UNDERLINENS	UNDERPERFORMED	UNDERREPORTS
UNDERGOWNS	UNDERLINES	UNDERPERFORMING	UNDERRUNNING
UNDERGRADS	UNDERLINGS	UNDERPERFORMS	UNDERRUNNINGS
UNDERGRADUATE	UNDERLINING	UNDERPINNED	UNDERSATURATED
UNDERGRADUATES	UNDERLOADED	UNDERPINNING	UNDERSAYING
UNDERGRADUETTE	UNDERLOADING	UNDERPINNINGS	UNDERSCORE
UNDERGRADUETTES	UNDERLOADS	UNDERPITCH	UNDERSCORED
UNDERGROUND	UNDERLOOKER	UNDERPLANT	UNDERSCORES
UNDERGROUNDER	UNDERLOOKERS	UNDERPLANTED	UNDERSCORING
UNDERGROUNDERS	UNDERLYING	UNDERPLANTING	UNDERSCRUB
UNDERGROUNDS	UNDERLYINGLY	UNDERPLANTS	UNDERSCRUBS
UNDERGROVE	UNDERMANNED	UNDERPLAYED	UNDERSEALED
UNDERGROVES	UNDERMANNING	UNDERPLAYING	UNDERSEALING
UNDERGROWN	UNDERMASTED	UNDERPLAYS	UNDERSEALINGS
UNDERGROWTH	UNDERMEANING	UNDERPLOTS	UNDERSEALS
UNDERGROWTHS	UNDERMEANINGS	UNDERPOPULATED	UNDERSECRETARY
UNDERHAIRS	UNDERMENTIONED	UNDERPOWERED	UNDERSELLER
UNDERHANDED	UNDERMINDE	UNDERPRAISE	UNDERSELLERS
UNDERHANDEDLY	UNDERMINDED	UNDERPRAISED	UNDERSELLING
UNDERHANDEDNESS	UNDERMINDES	UNDERPRAISES	UNDERSELLS
UNDERHANDS	UNDERMINDING	UNDERPRAISING	UNDERSELVES
UNDERHEATED	UNDERMINED	UNDERPREPARED	UNDERSENSE
UNDERHEATING	UNDERMINER	UNDERPRICE	UNDERSENSES
UNDERHEATS	UNDERMINERS	UNDERPRICED	UNDERSERVED
UNDERHONEST	UNDERMINES	UNDERPRICES	UNDERSETTING
UNDERINFLATED	UNDERMINING	UNDERPRICING	UNDERSEXED
UNDERINFLATION	UNDERMININGS	UNDERPRISE	UNDERSHAPEN
UNDERINFLATIONS	UNDERNAMED	UNDERPRISED	UNDERSHERIFF
UNDERINSURED	UNDERNEATH	UNDERPRISES	UNDERSHERIFFS
UNDERINVESTMENT	UNDERNEATHS	UNDERPRISING	UNDERSHIRT
UNDERJAWED	UNDERNICENESS	UNDERPRIVILEGED	UNDERSHIRTED
UNDERKEEPER	UNDERNICENESSES	UNDERPRIZE	UNDERSHIRTS
UNDERKEEPERS	UNDERNOTED	UNDERPRIZED	UNDERSHOOT
UNDERKEEPING	UNDERNOTES	UNDERPRIZES	UNDERSHOOTING
UNDERKEEPS	UNDERNOTING	UNDERPRIZING	UNDERSHOOTS
UNDERKILLS	UNDERNOURISH	UNDERPRODUCTION	UNDERSHORTS
UNDERKINGDOM	UNDERNOURISHED	UNDERPROOF	UNDERSHRUB
UNDERKINGDOMS	UNDERNOURISHES	UNDERPROPPED	UNDERSHRUBS
UNDERKINGS	UNDERNOURISHING	UNDERPROPPER	UNDERSIDES
UNDERLAPPED	UNDERNTIME	UNDERPROPPERS	UNDERSIGNED
UNDERLAPPING	UNDERNTIMES	UNDERPROPPING	UNDERSIGNING
UNDERLAYER	UNDERNUTRITION	UNDERPROPS	UNDERSIGNS
UNDERLAYERS	UNDERNUTRITIONS	UNDERPUBLICISED	UNDERSIZED
UNDERLAYING	UNDERPAINTING	UNDERPUBLICIZED	UNDERSKIES
UNDERLAYMENT	UNDERPAINTINGS	UNDERQUOTE	UNDERSKINKER
UNDERLAYMENTS	UNDERPANTS	UNDERQUOTED	UNDERSKINKERS
UNDERLEASE	UNDERPARTS	UNDERQUOTES	UNDERSKIRT
UNDERLEASED	UNDERPASSES	UNDERQUOTING	UNDERSKIRTS
UNDERLEASES	UNDERPASSION	UNDERRATED	UNDERSLEEVE
UNDERLEASING	UNDERPASSIONS	UNDERRATES	UNDERSLEEVES
UNDERLEAVES	UNDERPAYING	UNDERRATING	UNDERSLUNG
UNDERLETTER	UNDERPAYMENT	UNDERREACT	UNDERSOILS
UNDERLETTERS	UNDERPAYMENTS	UNDERREACTED	UNDERSONGS
UNDERLETTING	UNDERPEEPED	UNDERREACTING	UNDERSPEND
UNDERLETTINGS	UNDERPEEPING	UNDERREACTS	UNDERSPENDING
UNDERLIERS	UNDERPEEPS	UNDERREPORT	UNDERSPENDS

UNDERSPENT	UNDERTAXED	UNDERWIRES	UNDEVELOPED
UNDERSPINS	UNDERTAXES	UNDERWIRING	UNDEVIATING
UNDERSTAFFED	UNDERTAXING	UNDERWIRINGS	UNDEVIATINGLY
UNDERSTAFFING	UNDERTENANCIES	UNDERWOODS	UNDIAGNOSABLE
UNDERSTAFFINGS	UNDERTENANCY	UNDERWOOLS	UNDIAGNOSED
UNDERSTAND	UNDERTENANT	UNDERWORKED	UNDIALECTICAL
UNDERSTANDABLE	UNDERTENANTS	UNDERWORKER	UNDIDACTIC
UNDERSTANDABLY	UNDERTHINGS	UNDERWORKERS	UNDIFFERENCED
UNDERSTANDED	UNDERTHIRST	UNDERWORKING	UNDIGESTED
UNDERSTANDER	UNDERTHIRSTS	UNDERWORKS	UNDIGESTIBLE
UNDERSTANDERS	UNDERTHRUST	UNDERWORLD	UNDIGHTING
UNDERSTANDING	UNDERTHRUSTING	UNDERWORLDS	UNDIGNIFIED
UNDERSTANDINGLY	UNDERTHRUSTS	UNDERWRITE	UNDIGNIFIES
UNDERSTANDINGS	UNDERTIMED	UNDERWRITER	UNDIGNIFYING
UNDERSTANDS	UNDERTIMES	UNDERWRITERS	UNDIMINISHABLE
UNDERSTATE	UNDERTINTS	UNDERWRITES	UNDIMINISHED
UNDERSTATED	UNDERTONED	UNDERWRITING	UNDIPLOMATIC
UNDERSTATEDLY	UNDERTONES	UNDERWRITINGS	UNDIRECTED
UNDERSTATEMENT	UNDERTRICK	UNDERWRITTEN	UNDISAPPOINTING
UNDERSTATEMENTS	UNDERTRICKS	UNDERWROTE	UNDISCERNED
UNDERSTATES	UNDERTRUMP	UNDERWROUGHT	UNDISCERNEDLY
UNDERSTATING	UNDERTRUMPED	UNDESCENDABLE	UNDISCERNIBLE
UNDERSTEER	UNDERTRUMPING	UNDESCENDED	UNDISCERNIBLY
UNDERSTEERED	UNDERTRUMPS	UNDESCENDIBLE	UNDISCERNING
UNDERSTEERING	UNDERUSING	UNDESCRIBABLE	UNDISCERNINGS
UNDERSTEERS	UNDERUTILISE	UNDESCRIBED	UNDISCHARGED
UNDERSTOCK	UNDERUTILISED	UNDESCRIED	UNDISCIPLINABLE
UNDERSTOCKED	UNDERUTILISES	UNDESERVED	UNDISCIPLINE
UNDERSTOCKING	UNDERUTILISING	UNDESERVEDLY	UNDISCIPLINED
UNDERSTOCKS	UNDERUTILIZE	UNDESERVEDNESS	UNDISCIPLINES
UNDERSTOOD	UNDERUTILIZED	UNDESERVER	UNDISCLOSED
UNDERSTOREY	UNDERUTILIZES	UNDESERVERS	UNDISCOMFITED
UNDERSTOREYS	UNDERUTILIZING	UNDESERVES	UNDISCORDANT
UNDERSTORIES	UNDERVALUATION	UNDESERVING	UNDISCORDING
UNDERSTORY	UNDERVALUATIONS	UNDESERVINGLY	UNDISCOURAGED
UNDERSTRAPPER	UNDERVALUE	UNDESIGNATED	UNDISCOVERABLE
UNDERSTRAPPERS	UNDERVALUED	UNDESIGNED	UNDISCOVERABLY
UNDERSTRAPPING	UNDERVALUER	UNDESIGNEDLY	UNDISCOVERED
UNDERSTRATA	UNDERVALUERS	UNDESIGNEDNESS	UNDISCUSSABLE
UNDERSTRATUM	UNDERVALUES	UNDESIGNING	UNDISCUSSED
UNDERSTRENGTH	UNDERVALUING	UNDESIRABILITY	UNDISCUSSIBLE
UNDERSTUDIED	UNDERVESTS	UNDESIRABLE	UNDISGUISABLE
UNDERSTUDIES	UNDERVIEWER	UNDESIRABLENESS	UNDISGUISED
UNDERSTUDY	UNDERVIEWERS	UNDESIRABLES	UNDISGUISEDLY
UNDERSTUDYING	UNDERVOICE	UNDESIRABLY	UNDISHONOURED
UNDERSUPPLIED	UNDERVOICES	UNDESIRING	UNDISMANTLED
UNDERSUPPLIES	UNDERVOTES	UNDESIROUS	UNDISMAYED
UNDERSUPPLY	UNDERWATER	UNDESPAIRING	UNDISORDERED
UNDERSUPPLYING	UNDERWATERS	UNDESPAIRINGLY	UNDISPATCHED
UNDERSURFACE	UNDERWEARS	UNDESPOILED	UNDISPENSED
UNDERSURFACES	UNDERWEIGHT	UNDESTROYED	UNDISPOSED
UNDERTAKABLE	UNDERWEIGHTS	UNDETECTABLE	UNDISPUTABLE
UNDERTAKEN	UNDERWHELM	UNDETECTED	UNDISPUTED
UNDERTAKER	UNDERWHELMED	UNDETERMINABLE	UNDISPUTEDLY
UNDERTAKERS	UNDERWHELMING	UNDETERMINATE	UNDISSEMBLED
UNDERTAKES	UNDERWHELMS	UNDETERMINATION	UNDISSOCIATED
UNDERTAKING	UNDERWINGS	UNDETERMINED	UNDISSOLVED
UNDERTAKINGS	UNDERWIRED	UNDETERRED	UNDISSOLVING

UNDISTEMPERED	UNDULATIONISTS	UNENDINGNESS	UNEXCEPTIONABLY
UNDISTILLED	UNDULATIONS	UNENDINGNESSES	UNEXCEPTIONAL
UNDISTINCTIVE	UNDULATORS	UNENDURABLE	UNEXCEPTIONALLY
UNDISTINGUISHED	UNDULATORY	UNENDURABLENESS	UNEXCITABLE
UNDISTORTED	UNDUPLICATED	UNENDURABLY	UNEXCITING
UNDISTRACTED	UNDUTIFULLY	UNENFORCEABLE	UNEXCLUDED
UNDISTRACTEDLY	UNDUTIFULNESS	UNENFORCED	UNEXCLUSIVE
UNDISTRACTING	UNDUTIFULNESSES	UNENJOYABLE	UNEXCLUSIVELY
UNDISTRIBUTED	UNDYINGNESS	UNENLARGED	UNEXECUTED
UNDISTURBED	UNDYINGNESSES	UNENLIGHTENED	UNEXEMPLIFIED
UNDISTURBEDLY	UNEARMARKED	UNENLIGHTENING	UNEXERCISED
UNDISTURBING	UNEARTHING	UNENQUIRING	UNEXHAUSTED
UNDIVERSIFIED	UNEARTHLIER	UNENRICHED	UNEXPANDED
UNDIVERTED	UNEARTHLIEST	UNENSLAVED	UNEXPECTANT
UNDIVERTING	UNEARTHLINESS	UNENTAILED	UNEXPECTED
UNDIVESTED	UNEARTHLINESSES	UNENTERPRISING	UNEXPECTEDLY
UNDIVESTEDLY	UNEASINESS	UNENTERTAINED	UNEXPECTEDNESS
UNDIVIDABLE	UNEASINESSES	UNENTERTAINING	UNEXPENDED
UNDIVIDEDLY	UNEATABLENESS	UNENTHRALLED	UNEXPENSIVE
UNDIVIDEDNESS	UNEATABLENESSES	UNENTHUSIASTIC	UNEXPENSIVELY
UNDIVIDEDNESSES	UNECCENTRIC	UNENTITLED	UNEXPERIENCED
UNDIVORCED	UNECLIPSED	UNENVIABLE	UNEXPERIENT
UNDIVULGED	UNECOLOGICAL	UNENVIABLY	UNEXPIATED
UNDOCTORED	UNECONOMIC	UNEQUALLED	UNEXPLAINABLE
UNDOCTRINAIRE	UNECONOMICAL	UNEQUIPPED	UNEXPLAINED
UNDOCUMENTED	UNEDIFYING	UNEQUITABLE	UNEXPLODED
UNDOGMATIC	UNEDUCABLE	UNEQUIVOCABLY	UNEXPLOITED
UNDOGMATICALLY	UNEDUCATED	UNEQUIVOCAL	UNEXPLORED
UNDOMESTIC	UNEFFECTED	UNEQUIVOCALLY	UNEXPRESSED
UNDOMESTICATE	UNELABORATE	UNEQUIVOCALNESS	UNEXPRESSIBLE
UNDOMESTICATED	UNELABORATED	UNERASABLE	UNEXPRESSIVE
UNDOMESTICATES	UNELECTABLE	UNERRINGLY	UNEXPUGNABLE
UNDOMESTICATING	UNELECTRIFIED	UNERRINGNESS	UNEXPURGATED
UNDOUBLING	UNEMBARRASSED	UNERRINGNESSES	UNEXTENDED
UNDOUBTABLE	UNEMBELLISHED	UNESCAPABLE	UNEXTENUATED
UNDOUBTEDLY	UNEMBITTERED	UNESCORTED	UNEXTINGUISHED
UNDOUBTFUL	UNEMBODIED	UNESSENCED	UNEXTRAORDINARY
UNDOUBTING	UNEMOTIONAL	UNESSENCES	UNFADINGLY
UNDOUBTINGLY	UNEMOTIONALLY	UNESSENCING	UNFADINGNESS
UNDRAINABLE	UNEMOTIONED	UNESSENTIAL	UNFADINGNESSES
UNDRAMATIC	UNEMPHATIC	UNESSENTIALLY	UNFAILINGLY
UNDRAMATICALLY	UNEMPHATICALLY	UNESSENTIALS	UNFAILINGNESS
UNDRAMATISED	UNEMPIRICAL	UNESTABLISHED	UNFAILINGNESSES
UNDRAMATIZED	UNEMPLOYABILITY	UNEVALUATED	UNFAIRNESS
UNDREADING	UNEMPLOYABLE	UNEVANGELICAL	UNFAIRNESSES
UNDREAMING	UNEMPLOYABLES	UNEVENNESS	UNFAITHFUL
UNDRESSING	UNEMPLOYED	UNEVENNESSES	UNFAITHFULLY
UNDRESSINGS	UNEMPLOYEDS	UNEVENTFUL	UNFAITHFULNESS
UNDRINKABLE	UNEMPLOYMENT	UNEVENTFULLY	UNFALLIBLE
UNDRIVEABLE	UNEMPLOYMENTS	UNEVENTFULNESS	UNFALSIFIABLE
UNDROOPING	UNENCHANTED	UNEVIDENCED	UNFALTERING
UNDULANCES	UNENCLOSED	UNEXACTING	UNFALTERINGLY
UNDULANCIES	UNENCOURAGING	UNEXAGGERATED	UNFAMILIAR
UNDULATELY	UNENCUMBERED	UNEXAMINED	UNFAMILIARITIES
UNDULATING	UNENDANGERED	UNEXAMPLED	UNFAMILIARITY
UNDULATINGLY	UNENDEARED	UNEXCAVATED	UNFAMILIARLY
UNDULATION	UNENDEARING	UNEXCELLED	UNFASHIONABLE
UNDULATIONIST	UNENDINGLY	UNEXCEPTIONABLE	UNFASHIONABLY

UNFASHIONED	UNFIXITIES	UNFOSSILIFEROUS	UNGENTEELLY
UNFASTENED	UNFLAGGING	UNFOSSILISED	UNGENTILITIES
UNFASTENING	UNFLAGGINGLY	UNFOSSILIZED	UNGENTILITY
UNFASTIDIOUS	UNFLAMBOYANT	UNFOSTERED	UNGENTLEMANLIKE
UNFATHERED	UNFLAPPABILITY	UNFOUGHTEN	UNGENTLEMANLY
UNFATHERLY	UNFLAPPABLE	UNFOUNDEDLY	UNGENTLENESS
UNFATHOMABLE	UNFLAPPABLENESS	UNFOUNDEDNESS	UNGENTLENESSES
UNFATHOMABLY	UNFLAPPABLY	UNFOUNDEDNESSES	UNGENTRIFIED
UNFATHOMED	UNFLATTERING	UNFRANCHISED	UNGENUINENESS
UNFAVORABLE	UNFLATTERINGLY	UNFRAUGHTED	UNGENUINENESSES
UNFAVORABLENESS	UNFLAVOURED	UNFRAUGHTING	UNGERMINATED
UNFAVORABLY	UNFLESHING	UNFRAUGHTS	UNGETATABLE
UNFAVORITE	UNFLINCHING	UNFREEDOMS	UNGIMMICKY
UNFAVOURABLE	UNFLINCHINGLY	UNFREEZING	UNGIRTHING
UNFAVOURABLY	UNFLUSHING	UNFREQUENT	UNGLAMORISED
UNFAVOURED	UNFLUSTERED	UNFREQUENTED	UNGLAMORIZED
UNFEARFULLY	UNFOCUSSED	UNFREQUENTLY	UNGLAMOROUS
UNFEASIBLE	UNFOLDINGS	UNFRIENDED	UNGODLIEST
UNFEATHERED	UNFOLDMENT	UNFRIENDEDNESS	UNGODLINESS
UNFEATURED	UNFOLDMENTS	UNFRIENDLIER	UNGODLINESSES
UNFEELINGLY	UNFORBIDDEN	UNFRIENDLIEST	UNGOVERNABLE
UNFEELINGNESS	UNFORCEDLY	UNFRIENDLILY	UNGOVERNABLY
UNFEELINGNESSES	UNFORCIBLE	UNFRIENDLINESS	UNGOVERNED
UNFEIGNEDLY	UNFORDABLE	UNFRIENDLY	UNGRACEFUL
UNFEIGNEDNESS	UNFOREBODING	UNFRIENDSHIP	UNGRACEFULLY
UNFEIGNEDNESSES	UNFOREKNOWABLE	UNFRIENDSHIPS	UNGRACEFULNESS
UNFEIGNING	UNFOREKNOWN	UNFRIGHTED	UNGRACIOUS
UNFELLOWED	UNFORESEEABLE	UNFRIGHTENED	UNGRACIOUSLY
UNFEMININE	UNFORESEEING	UNFRIVOLOUS	UNGRACIOUSNESS
UNFERMENTED	UNFORESEEN	UNFROCKING	UNGRAMMATIC
UNFERTILISED	UNFORESKINNED	UNFRUCTUOUS	UNGRAMMATICAL
UNFERTILIZED	UNFORESTED	UNFRUITFUL	UNGRAMMATICALLY
UNFETTERED	UNFORETOLD	UNFRUITFULLY	UNGRASPABLE
UNFETTERING	UNFOREWARNED	UNFRUITFULNESS	UNGRATEFUL
UNFEUDALISE	UNFORFEITED	UNFULFILLABLE	UNGRATEFULLY
UNFEUDALISED	UNFORGETTABLE	UNFULFILLED	UNGRATEFULNESS
UNFEUDALISES	UNFORGETTABLY	UNFURNISHED	UNGRATIFIED
UNFEUDALISING	UNFORGIVABLE	UNFURNISHES	UNGROUNDED
UNFEUDALIZE	UNFORGIVEN	UNFURNISHING	UNGROUNDEDLY
UNFEUDALIZED	UNFORGIVENESS	UNFURROWED	UNGROUNDEDNESS
UNFEUDALIZES	UNFORGIVENESSES	UNFUSSIEST	UNGRUDGING
UNFEUDALIZING	UNFORGIVING	UNGAINLIER	UNGRUDGINGLY
UNFILIALLY	UNFORGIVINGNESS	UNGAINLIEST	UNGUARDEDLY
UNFILLABLE	UNFORGOTTEN	UNGAINLINESS	UNGUARDEDNESS
UNFILLETED	UNFORMALISED	UNGAINLINESSES	UNGUARDEDNESSES
UNFILTERABLE	UNFORMALIZED	UNGAINSAID	UNGUARDING
UNFILTERED	UNFORMATTED	UNGAINSAYABLE	UNGUENTARIA
UNFILTRABLE	UNFORMIDABLE	UNGALLANTLY	UNGUENTARIES
UNFINDABLE	UNFORMULATED	UNGARMENTED	UNGUENTARIUM
UNFINISHED	UNFORSAKEN	UNGARNERED	UNGUENTARY
UNFINISHING	UNFORTHCOMING	UNGARNISHED	UNGUERDONED
UNFINISHINGS	UNFORTIFIED	UNGARTERED	UNGUESSABLE
UNFITNESSES	UNFORTUNATE	UNGATHERED	UNGUICULATE
UNFITTEDNESS	UNFORTUNATELY	UNGENEROSITIES	UNGUICULATED
UNFITTEDNESSES	UNFORTUNATENESS	UNGENEROSITY	UNGUICULATES
UNFITTINGLY	UNFORTUNATES	UNGENEROUS	UNGULIGRADE
UNFIXEDNESS	UNFORTUNED	UNGENEROUSLY	UNHABITABLE
UNFIXEDNESSES	UNFORTUNES	UNGENITURED	UNHABITUATED

UNHACKNEYED	UNHOLINESS	UNIFICATION	UNIMPOSING
UNHALLOWED	UNHOLINESSES	UNIFICATIONS	UNIMPREGNATED
UNHALLOWING	UNHOMELIKE	UNIFLOROUS	UNIMPRESSED
UNHAMPERED	UNHOMOGENISED	UNIFOLIATE	UNIMPRESSIBLE
UNHANDIEST	UNHOMOGENIZED	UNIFOLIOLATE	UNIMPRESSIVE
UNHANDINESS	UNHONOURED	UNIFORMEST	UNIMPRISONED
UNHANDINESSES	UNHOPEFULLY	UNIFORMING	UNIMPROVED
UNHANDSELED	UNHOSPITABLE	UNIFORMITARIAN	UNIMPUGNABLE
UNHANDSOME	UNHOUSELED	UNIFORMITARIANS	UNINAUGURATED
UNHANDSOMELY	UNHOUZZLED	UNIFORMITIES	UNINCHANTED
UNHANDSOMENESS	UNHUMANISE	UNIFORMITY	UNINCLOSED
UNHAPPIEST	UNHUMANISED	UNIFORMNESS	UNINCORPORATED
UNHAPPINESS	UNHUMANISES	UNIFORMNESSES	UNINCUMBERED
UNHAPPINESSES	UNHUMANISING	UNIGENITURE	UNINDEARED
UNHAPPYING	UNHUMANIZE	UNIGENITURES	UNINDICTED
UNHARBOURED	UNHUMANIZED	UNIGNORABLE	UNINFECTED
UNHARBOURING	UNHUMANIZES	UNILABIATE	UNINFLAMED
UNHARBOURS	UNHUMANIZING	UNILATERAL	UNINFLAMMABLE
UNHARDENED	UNHUMOROUS	UNILATERALISM	UNINFLATED
UNHARMFULLY	UNHURRIEDLY	UNILATERALISMS	UNINFLECTED
UNHARMONIOUS	UNHURRYING	UNILATERALIST	UNINFLUENCED
UNHARNESSED	UNHURTFULLY	UNILATERALISTS	UNINFLUENTIAL
UNHARNESSES	UNHURTFULNESS	UNILATERALITIES	UNINFORCEABLE
UNHARNESSING	UNHURTFULNESSES	UNILATERALITY	UNINFORCED
UNHARVESTED	UNHUSBANDED	UNILATERALLY	UNINFORMATIVE
UNHATTINGS	UNHYDROLYSED	UNILINGUAL	UNINFORMATIVELY
UNHAZARDED	UNHYDROLYZED	UNILINGUALISM	UNINFORMED
UNHAZARDOUS	UNHYGIENIC	UNILINGUALISMS	UNINFORMING
UNHEALABLE	UNHYPHENATED	UNILINGUALS	UNINGRATIATING
UNHEALTHFUL	UNHYSTERICAL	UNILITERAL	UNINHABITABLE
UNHEALTHFULLY	UNHYSTERICALLY	UNILLUMINATED	UNINHABITED
UNHEALTHFULNESS	UNIAXIALLY	UNILLUMINATING	UNINHIBITED
UNHEALTHIER	UNICAMERAL	UNILLUMINED	UNINHIBITEDLY
UNHEALTHIEST	UNICAMERALISM	UNILLUSIONED	UNINHIBITEDNESS
UNHEALTHILY	UNICAMERALISMS	UNILLUSTRATED	UNINITIATE
UNHEALTHINESS	UNICAMERALIST	UNILOBULAR	UNINITIATED
UNHEALTHINESSES	UNICAMERALISTS	UNILOCULAR	UNINITIATES
UNHEARSING	UNICAMERALLY	UNIMAGINABLE	UNINOCULATED
UNHEARTING	UNICELLULAR	UNIMAGINABLY	UNINQUIRING
UNHEEDEDLY	UNICELLULARITY	UNIMAGINATIVE	UNINQUISITIVE
UNHEEDFULLY	UNICENTRAL	UNIMAGINATIVELY	UNINSCRIBED
UNHEEDINGLY	UNICOLORATE	UNIMAGINED	UNINSPECTED
UNHELMETED	UNICOLOROUS	UNIMMORTAL	UNINSPIRED
UNHELPABLE	UNICOLOURED	UNIMMUNISED	UNINSPIRING
UNHELPFULLY	UNICOSTATE	UNIMMUNIZED	UNINSTALLED
UNHERALDED	UNICYCLING	UNIMOLECULAR	UNINSTALLING
UNHEROICAL	UNICYCLIST	UNIMPAIRED	UNINSTALLS
UNHEROICALLY	UNICYCLISTS	UNIMPARTED	UNINSTRUCTED
UNHESITATING	UNIDEALISM	UNIMPASSIONED	UNINSTRUCTIVE
UNHESITATINGLY	UNIDEALISMS	UNIMPEACHABLE	UNINSULATED
UNHIDEBOUND	UNIDEALISTIC	UNIMPEACHABLY	UNINSURABLE
UNHINDERED	UNIDENTIFIABLE	UNIMPEACHED	UNINSUREDS
UNHINGEMENT	UNIDENTIFIED	UNIMPEDEDLY	UNINTEGRATED
UNHINGEMENTS	UNIDEOLOGICAL	UNIMPLORED	UNINTELLECTUAL
UNHISTORIC	UNIDIMENSIONAL	UNIMPORTANCE	UNINTELLIGENCE
UNHISTORICAL	UNIDIOMATIC	UNIMPORTANCES	UNINTELLIGENCES
UNHITCHING	UNIDIOMATICALLY	UNIMPORTANT	UNINTELLIGENT
UNHOARDING	UNIDIRECTIONAL	UNIMPORTUNED	UNINTELLIGENTLY

UNINTELLIGIBLE
UNINTELLIGIBLY
UNINTENDED
UNINTENTIONAL
UNINTENTIONALLY
UNINTEREST
UNINTERESTED
UNINTERESTEDLY
UNINTERESTING
UNINTERESTINGLY
UNINTERESTS
UNINTERMITTED
UNINTERMITTEDLY
UNINTERMITTING
UNINTERPRETABLE
UNINTERRUPTED
UNINTERRUPTEDLY
UNINTIMIDATED
UNINTOXICATING
UNINTRODUCED
UNINUCLEAR
UNINUCLEATE
UNINVENTIVE
UNINVESTED
UNINVIDIOUS
UNINVITING
UNINVOLVED
UNIONISATION
UNIONISATIONS
UNIONISERS
UNIONISING
UNIONISTIC
UNIONIZATION
UNIONIZATIONS
UNIONIZERS
UNIONIZING
UNIPARENTAL
UNIPARENTALLY
UNIPARTITE
UNIPERSONAL
UNIPERSONALITY
UNIPOLARITIES
UNIPOLARITY
UNIQUENESS
UNIQUENESSES
UNIRONICALLY
UNIRRADIATED
UNIRRIGATED
UNISEPTATE
UNISERIALLY
UNISERIATE
UNISERIATELY
UNISEXUALITIES
UNISEXUALITY
UNISEXUALLY
UNISONALLY
UNISONANCE
UNISONANCES

UNITARIANISM
UNITARIANISMS
UNITARIANS
UNITEDNESS
UNITEDNESSES
UNITHOLDER
UNITHOLDERS
UNITISATION
UNITISATIONS
UNITIZATION
UNITIZATIONS
UNIVALENCE
UNIVALENCES
UNIVALENCIES
UNIVALENCY
UNTVALENTS
UNIVALVULAR
UNIVARIANT
UNIVARIATE
UNIVERSALISE
UNIVERSALISED
UNIVERSALISES
UNIVERSALISING
UNIVERSALISM
UNIVERSALISMS
UNIVERSALIST
UNIVERSALISTIC
UNIVERSALISTS
UNIVERSALITIES
UNIVERSALITY
UNIVERSALIZE
UNIVERSALIZED
UNIVERSALIZES
UNIVERSALIZING
UNIVERSALLY
UNIVERSALNESS
UNIVERSALNESSES
UNIVERSALS
UNIVERSITARIAN
UNIVERSITIES
UNIVERSITY
UNIVOCALLY
UNIVOLTINE
UNJAUNDICED
UNJOINTING
UNJUSTIFIABLE
UNJUSTIFIABLY
UNJUSTIFIED
UNJUSTNESS
UNJUSTNESSES
UNKEMPTNESS
UNKEMPTNESSES
UNKENNELED
UNKENNELING
UNKENNELLED
UNKENNELLING
UNKINDLIER
UNKINDLIEST

UNKINDLINESS
UNKINDLINESSES
UNKINDNESS
UNKINDNESSES
UNKINGLIER
UNKINGLIEST
UNKINGLIKE
UNKNIGHTED
UNKNIGHTING
UNKNIGHTLINESS
UNKNIGHTLY
UNKNITTING
UNKNOTTING
UNKNOWABILITIES
UNKNOWABILITY
UNKNOWABLE
UNKNOWABLENESS
UNKNOWABLES
UNKNOWABLY
UNKNOWINGLY
UNKNOWINGNESS
UNKNOWINGNESSES
UNKNOWINGS
UNKNOWLEDGEABLE
UNKNOWNNESS
UNKNOWNNESSES
UNLABELLED
UNLABORIOUS
UNLABOURED
UNLABOURING
UNLADYLIKE
UNLAMENTED
UNLATCHING
UNLAUNDERED
UNLAWFULLY
UNLAWFULNESS
UNLAWFULNESSES
UNLEARNABLE
UNLEARNEDLY
UNLEARNEDNESS
UNLEARNEDNESSES
UNLEARNING
UNLEASHING
UNLEAVENED
UNLEISURED
UNLEISURELY
UNLESSONED
UNLETTABLE
UNLETTERED
UNLEVELING
UNLEVELLED
UNLEVELLING
UNLIBERATED
UNLIBIDINOUS
UNLICENSED
UNLIFELIKE
UNLIGHTENED
UNLIGHTSOME

UNLIKEABLE
UNLIKELIER
UNLIKELIEST
UNLIKELIHOOD
UNLIKELIHOODS
UNLIKELINESS
UNLIKELINESSES
UNLIKENESS
UNLIKENESSES
UNLIMBERED
UNLIMBERING
UNLIMITEDLY
UNLIMITEDNESS
UNLIMITEDNESSES
UNLIQUEFIED
UNLIQUIDATED
UNLIQUORED
UNLISTENABLE
UNLISTENED
UNLISTENING
UNLITERARY
UNLIVEABLE
UNLIVELINESS
UNLIVELINESSES
UNLOADINGS
UNLOCALISED
UNLOCALIZED
UNLOCKABLE
UNLOOSENED
UNLOOSENING
UNLOVEABLE
UNLOVELIER
UNLOVELIEST
UNLOVELINESS
UNLOVELINESSES
UNLOVERLIKE
UNLOVINGLY
UNLOVINGNESS
UNLOVINGNESSES
UNLUCKIEST
UNLUCKINESS
UNLUCKINESSES
UNLUXURIANT
UNLUXURIOUS
UNMACADAMISED
UNMACADAMIZED
UNMAGNIFIED
UNMAIDENLY
UNMAILABLE
UNMAINTAINABLE
UNMAINTAINED
UNMALICIOUS
UNMALICIOUSLY
UNMALLEABILITY
UNMALLEABLE
UNMANACLED
UNMANACLES
UNMANACLING

UNMANAGEABLE	UNMENTIONABLY	UNMOTHERLY	UNOBJECTIONABLY
UNMANAGEABLY	UNMENTIONED	UNMOTIVATED	UNOBNOXIOUS
UNMANFULLY	UNMERCENARY	UNMOULDING	UNOBSCURED
UNMANIPULATED	UNMERCHANTABLE	UNMOUNTING	UNOBSERVABLE
UNMANLIEST	UNMERCIFUL	UNMOVEABLE	UNOBSERVANCE
UNMANLINESS	UNMERCIFULLY	UNMOVEABLY	UNOBSERVANCES
UNMANLINESSES	UNMERCIFULNESS	UNMUFFLING	UNOBSERVANT
UNMANNERED	UNMERITABLE	UNMUNITIONED	UNOBSERVED
UNMANNEREDLY	UNMERITEDLY	UNMURMURING	UNOBSERVEDLY
UNMANNERLINESS	UNMERITING	UNMURMURINGLY	UNOBSERVING
UNMANNERLY	UNMETABOLISED	UNMUSICALLY	UNOBSTRUCTED
UNMANTLING	UNMETABOLIZED	UNMUSICALNESS	UNOBSTRUCTIVE
UNMANUFACTURED	UNMETALLED	UNMUSICALNESSES	UNOBTAINABLE
UNMARKETABLE	UNMETAPHORICAL	UNMUTILATED	UNOBTAINED
UNMARRIABLE	UNMETAPHYSICAL	UNMUZZLING	UNOBTRUSIVE
UNMARRIAGEABLE	UNMETHODICAL	UNMUZZLINGS	UNOBTRUSIVELY
UNMARRIEDS	UNMETHODISED	UNMYELINATED	UNOBTRUSIVENESS
UNMARRYING	UNMETHODIZED	UNNAMEABLE	UNOCCUPIED
UNMASCULINE	UNMETRICAL	UNNATURALISE	UNOFFENDED
UNMASKINGS	UNMILITARY	UNNATURALISED	UNOFFENDING
UNMASTERED	UNMINDFULLY	UNNATURALISES	UNOFFENSIVE
UNMATCHABLE	UNMINDFULNESS	UNNATURALISING	UNOFFICERED
UNMATERIAL	UNMINDFULNESSES	UNNATURALIZE	UNOFFICIAL
UNMATERIALISED	UNMINGLING	UNNATURALIZED	UNOFFICIALLY
UNMATERIALIZED	UNMINISTERIAL	UNNATURALIZES	UNOFFICIOUS
UNMATERNAL	UNMIRACULOUS	UNNATURALIZING	UNOPENABLE
UNMATHEMATICAL	UNMISSABLE	UNNATURALLY	UNOPERATIVE
UNMATRICULATED	UNMISTAKABLE	UNNATURALNESS	UNOPPRESSIVE
UNMEANINGLY	UNMISTAKABLY	UNNATURALNESSES	UNORDAINED
UNMEANINGNESS	UNMISTAKEABLE	UNNAVIGABLE	UNORDERING
UNMEANINGNESSES	UNMISTAKEABLY	UNNAVIGATED	UNORDINARY
UNMEASURABLE	UNMISTRUSTFUL	UNNECESSARILY	UNORGANISED
UNMEASURABLY	UNMITERING	UNNECESSARINESS	UNORGANIZED
UNMEASURED	UNMITIGABLE	UNNECESSARY	UNORIGINAL
UNMEASUREDLY	UNMITIGABLY	UNNEEDFULLY	UNORIGINALITIES
UNMECHANIC	UNMITIGATED	UNNEGOTIABLE	UNORIGINALITY
UNMECHANICAL	UNMITIGATEDLY	UNNEIGHBOURED	UNORIGINATE
UNMECHANISE	UNMITIGATEDNESS	UNNEIGHBOURLY	UNORIGINATED
UNMECHANISED	UNMODERATED	UNNERVINGLY	UNORNAMENTAL
UNMECHANISES	UNMODERNISED	UNNEUROTIC	UNORNAMENTED
UNMECHANISING	UNMODERNIZED	UNNEWSWORTHY	UNORTHODOX
UNMECHANIZE	UNMODIFIABLE	UNNILHEXIUM	UNORTHODOXIES
UNMECHANIZED	UNMODIFIED	UNNILHEXIUMS	UNORTHODOXLY
UNMECHANIZES	UNMODULATED	UNNILPENTIUM	UNORTHODOXY
UNMECHANIZING	UNMOISTENED	UNNILPENTIUMS	UNOSSIFIED
UNMEDIATED	UNMOLESTED	UNNILQUADIUM	UNOSTENTATIOUS
UNMEDICATED	UNMONITORED	UNNILQUADIUMS	UNOVERCOME
UNMEDICINABLE	UNMORALISED	UNNILSEPTIUM	UNOVERTHROWN
UNMEDITATED	UNMORALISING	UNNILSEPTIUMS	UNOXIDISED
UNMEETNESS	UNMORALITIES	UNNOTICEABLE	UNOXIDIZED
UNMEETNESSES	UNMORALITY	UNNOTICEABLY	UNOXYGENATED
UNMELLOWED	UNMORALIZED	UNNOTICING	UNPACIFIED
UNMELODIOUS	UNMORALIZING	UNNOURISHED	UNPACKINGS
UNMELODIOUSNESS	UNMORTGAGED	UNNOURISHING	UNPAINTABLE
UNMEMORABLE	UNMORTIFIED	UNNUMBERED	UNPAINTING
UNMEMORABLY	UNMORTISED	UNNURTURED	UNPALATABILITY
UNMENTIONABLE	UNMORTISES	UNOBEDIENT	UNPALATABLE
UNMENTIONABLES	UNMORTISING	UNOBJECTIONABLE	UNPALATABLY

UNPAMPERED	UNPERFECTLY	UNPOETICALNESS	UNPREPAREDLY
UNPANELLED	UNPERFECTNESS	UNPOISONED	UNPREPAREDNESS
UNPANELLING	UNPERFECTNESSES	UNPOISONING	UNPREPARES
UNPANNELLED	UNPERFORATED	UNPOLARISABLE	UNPREPARING
UNPANNELLING	UNPERFORMABLE	UNPOLARISED	UNPREPOSSESSED
UNPAPERING	UNPERFORMED	UNPOLARIZABLE	UNPREPOSSESSING
UNPARADISE	UNPERFORMING	UNPOLARIZED	UNPRESCRIBED
UNPARADISED	UNPERFUMED	UNPOLICIED	UNPRESENTABLE
UNPARADISES	UNPERILOUS	UNPOLISHABLE	UNPRESSURED
UNPARADISING	UNPERISHABLE	UNPOLISHED	UNPRESSURISED
UNPARAGONED	UNPERISHED	UNPOLISHES	UNPRESSURIZED
UNPARALLEL	UNPERISHING	UNPOLISHING	UNPRESUMING
UNPARALLELED	UNPERJURED	UNPOLITELY	UNPRESUMPTUOUS
UNPARASITISED	UNPERPETRATED	UNPOLITENESS	UNPRETENDING
UNPARASITIZED	UNPERPLEXED	UNPOLITENESSES	UNPRETENDINGLY
UNPARDONABLE	UNPERPLEXES	UNPOLITICAL	UNPRETENTIOUS
UNPARDONABLY	UNPERPLEXING	UNPOLLUTED	UNPRETENTIOUSLY
UNPARDONED	UNPERSECUTED	UNPOPULARITIES	UNPRETTINESS
UNPARDONING	UNPERSONED	UNPOPULARITY	UNPRETTINESSES
UNPARENTAL	UNPERSONING	UNPOPULARLY	UNPREVAILING
UNPARENTED	UNPERSUADABLE	UNPOPULATED	UNPREVENTABLE
UNPARLIAMENTARY	UNPERSUADED	UNPOPULOUS	UNPREVENTED
UNPASSABLE	UNPERSUASIVE	UNPORTIONED	UNPRIESTED
UNPASSABLENESS	UNPERTURBED	UNPOSSESSED	UNPRIESTING
UNPASSIONATE	UNPERVERTED	UNPOSSESSING	UNPRIESTLY
UNPASSIONED	UNPERVERTING	UNPOSSIBLE	UNPRINCELY
UNPASTEURISED	UNPERVERTS	UNPOWDERED	UNPRINCIPLED
UNPASTEURIZED	UNPHILOSOPHIC	UNPRACTICABLE	UNPRINTABLE
UNPASTORAL	UNPHILOSOPHICAL	UNPRACTICAL	UNPRINTABLENESS
UNPASTURED	UNPHONETIC	UNPRACTICALITY	UNPRINTABLY
UNPATENTABLE	UNPICKABLE	UNPRACTICALLY	UNPRISABLE
UNPATENTED	UNPICTURESQUE	UNPRACTICALNESS	UNPRISONED
UNPATHETIC	UNPILLARED	UNPRACTICED	UNPRISONING
UNPATHWAYED	UNPILLOWED	UNPRACTISED	UNPRIVILEGED
UNPATRIOTIC	UNPITIFULLY	UNPRACTISEDNESS	UNPRIZABLE
UNPATRIOTICALLY	UNPITIFULNESS	UNPRAISEWORTHY	UNPROBLEMATIC
UNPATRONISED	UNPITIFULNESSES	UNPRAISING	UNPROCEDURAL
UNPATRONIZED	UNPITYINGLY	UNPREACHED	UNPROCESSED
UNPATTERNED	UNPLAITING	UNPREACHES	UNPROCLAIMED
UNPAVILIONED	UNPLASTERED	UNPREACHING	UNPROCURABLE
UNPEACEABLE	UNPLAUSIBLE	UNPRECEDENTED	UNPRODUCED
UNPEACEABLENESS	UNPLAUSIBLY	UNPRECEDENTEDLY	UNPRODUCTIVE
UNPEACEFUL	UNPLAUSIVE	UNPREDICTABLE	UNPRODUCTIVELY
UNPEACEFULLY	UNPLAYABLE	UNPREDICTABLES	UNPRODUCTIVITY
UNPEDANTIC	UNPLEASANT	UNPREDICTABLY	UNPROFANED
UNPEDIGREED	UNPLEASANTLY	UNPREDICTED	UNPROFESSED
UNPEERABLE	UNPLEASANTNESS	UNPREDICTING	UNPROFESSIONAL
UNPENSIONED	UNPLEASANTRIES	UNPREDICTS	UNPROFESSIONALS
UNPEOPLING	UNPLEASANTRY	UNPREFERRED	UNPROFITABILITY
UNPEPPERED	UNPLEASING	UNPREGNANT	UNPROFITABLE
UNPERCEIVABLE	UNPLEASINGLY	UNPREJUDICED	UNPROFITABLY
UNPERCEIVABLY	UNPLEASURABLE	UNPREJUDICEDLY	UNPROFITED
UNPERCEIVED	UNPLEASURABLY	UNPRELATICAL	UNPROFITING
UNPERCEIVEDLY	UNPLOUGHED	UNPREMEDITABLE	UNPROGRAMMABLE
UNPERCEPTIVE	UNPLUGGING	UNPREMEDITATED	UNPROGRAMMED
UNPERCHING	UNPLUMBING	UNPREMEDITATION	UNPROGRESSIVE
UNPERFECTION	UNPOETICAL	UNPREOCCUPIED	UNPROGRESSIVELY
UNPERFECTIONS	UNPOETICALLY	UNPREPARED	UNPROHIBITED

UNPROJECTED	UNPUTDOWNABLE	UNREALISMS	UNREFLECTIVE
UNPROLIFIC	UNPUZZLING	UNREALISTIC	UNREFLECTIVELY
UNPROMISED	UNQUALIFIABLE	UNREALISTICALLY	UNREFORMABLE
UNPROMISING	UNQUALIFIED	UNREALITIES	UNREFORMED
UNPROMISINGLY	UNQUALIFIEDLY	UNREALIZABLE	UNREFRACTED
UNPROMPTED	UNQUALIFIEDNESS	UNREALIZED	UNREFRESHED
UNPRONOUNCEABLE	UNQUALIFIES	UNREALIZES	UNREFRESHING
UNPRONOUNCED	UNQUALIFYING	UNREALIZING	UNREFRIGERATED
UNPROPERLY	UNQUALITED	UNREASONABLE	UNREGARDED
UNPROPERTIED	UNQUALITIED	UNREASONABLY	UNREGARDING
UNPROPHETIC	UNQUANTIFIABLE	UNREASONED	UNREGENERACIES
UNPROPHETICAL	UNQUANTIFIED	UNREASONING	UNREGENERACY
UNPROPITIOUS	UNQUANTISED	UNREASONINGLY	UNREGENERATE
UNPROPITIOUSLY	UNQUANTIZED	UNRECALLABLE	UNREGENERATED
UNPROPORTIONATE	UNQUARRIED	UNRECALLED	UNREGENERATELY
UNPROPORTIONED	UNQUEENING	UNRECALLING	UNREGENERATES
UNPROPOSED	UNQUEENLIER	UNRECAPTURABLE	UNREGIMENTED
UNPROPPING	UNQUEENLIEST	UNRECEIPTED	UNREGISTERED
UNPROSPEROUS	UNQUEENLIKE	UNRECEIVED	UNREGULATED
UNPROSPEROUSLY	UNQUENCHABLE	UNRECEPTIVE	UNREHEARSED
UNPROTECTED	UNQUENCHABLY	UNRECIPROCATED	UNREINFORCED
UNPROTECTEDNESS	UNQUENCHED	UNRECKONABLE	UNREJOICED
UNPROTESTANTISE	UNQUESTIONABLE	UNRECKONED	UNREJOICING
UNPROTESTANTIZE	UNQUESTIONABLY	UNRECLAIMABLE	UNRELATIVE
UNPROTESTED	UNQUESTIONED	UNRECLAIMABLY	UNRELENTING
UNPROTESTING	UNQUESTIONING	UNRECLAIMED	UNRELENTINGLY
UNPROVABLE	UNQUESTIONINGLY	UNRECOGNISABLE	UNRELENTINGNESS
UNPROVIDED	UNQUICKENED	UNRECOGNISABLY	UNRELENTOR
UNPROVIDEDLY	UNQUIETEST	UNRECOGNISED	UNRELENTORS
UNPROVIDENT	UNQUIETING	UNRECOGNISING	UNRELIABILITIES
UNPROVIDES	UNQUIETNESS	UNRECOGNIZABLE	UNRELIABILITY
UNPROVIDING	UNQUIETNESSES	UNRECOGNIZABLY	UNRELIABLE
UNPROVISIONED	UNQUOTABLE	UNRECOGNIZED	UNRELIABLENESS
UNPROVOCATIVE	UNRANSOMED	UNRECOGNIZING	UNRELIEVABLE
UNPROVOKED	UNRATIFIED	UNRECOLLECTED	UNRELIEVED
UNPROVOKEDLY	UNRAVELING	UNRECOMMENDABLE	UNRELIEVEDLY
UNPROVOKES	UNRAVELLED	UNRECOMMENDED	UNRELIGIOUS
UNPROVOKING	UNRAVELLER	UNRECOMPENSED	UNRELIGIOUSLY
UNPUBLICISED	UNRAVELLERS	UNRECONCILABLE	UNRELISHED
UNPUBLICIZED	UNRAVELLING	UNRECONCILABLY	UNRELUCTANT
UNPUBLISHABLE	UNRAVELLINGS	UNRECONCILED	UNREMAINING
UNPUBLISHED	UNRAVELMENT	UNRECONCILIABLE	UNREMARKABLE
UNPUCKERED	UNRAVELMENTS	UNRECONSTRUCTED	UNREMARKABLY
UNPUCKERING	UNRAVISHED	UNRECORDED	UNREMARKED
UNPUNCTUAL	UNREACHABLE	UNRECOUNTED	UNREMEDIED
UNPUNCTUALITIES	UNREACTIVE	UNRECOVERABLE	UNREMEMBERED
UNPUNCTUALITY	UNREADABILITIES	UNRECOVERABLY	UNREMEMBERING
UNPUNCTUATED	UNREADABILITY	UNRECOVERED	UNREMINISCENT
UNPUNISHABLE	UNREADABLE	UNRECTIFIED	UNREMITTED
UNPUNISHABLY	UNREADABLENESS	UNRECURING	UNREMITTEDLY
UNPUNISHED	UNREADABLY	UNRECYCLABLE	UNREMITTENT
UNPURCHASABLE	UNREADIEST	UNREDEEMABLE	UNREMITTENTLY
UNPURCHASEABLE	UNREADINESS	UNREDEEMED	UNREMITTING
UNPURCHASED	UNREADINESSES	UNREDRESSED	UNREMITTINGLY
UNPURIFIED	UNREALISABLE	UNREDUCIBLE	UNREMITTINGNESS
UNPURPOSED	UNREALISED	UNREFLECTED	UNREMORSEFUL
UNPURVAIDE	UNREALISES	UNREFLECTING	UNREMORSEFULLY
UNPURVEYED	UNREALISING	UNREFLECTINGLY	UNREMORSELESS

UNREMOVABLE	UNRESOLVEDNESS	UNRIPENESSES	UNSATURATES
UNREMUNERATIVE	UNRESPECTABLE	UNRIPPINGS	UNSATURATION
UNRENDERED	UNRESPECTED	UNRIVALLED	UNSATURATIONS
UNREPAIRABLE	UNRESPECTIVE	UNRIVETING	UNSAVORILY
UNREPAIRED	UNRESPITED	UNROMANISED	UNSAVORINESS
UNREPEALABLE	UNRESPONSIVE	UNROMANIZED	UNSAVORINESSES
UNREPEALED	UNRESPONSIVELY	UNROMANTIC	UNSAVOURILY
UNREPEATABLE	UNRESTFULNESS	UNROMANTICAL	UNSAVOURINESS
UNREPEATED	UNRESTFULNESSES	UNROMANTICALLY	UNSAVOURINESSES
UNREPELLED	UNRESTINGLY	UNROMANTICISED	UNSAYABLES
UNREPENTANCE	UNRESTINGNESS	UNROMANTICIZED	UNSCABBARD
UNREPENTANCES	UNRESTINGNESSES	UNROOSTING	UNSCABBARDED
UNREPENTANT	UNRESTORED	UNROUNDING	UNSCABBARDING
UNREPENTANTLY	UNRESTRAINABLE	UNRUFFABLE	UNSCABBARDS
UNREPENTED	UNRESTRAINED	UNRUFFLEDNESS	UNSCALABLE
UNREPENTING	UNRESTRAINEDLY	UNRUFFLEDNESSES	UNSCAVENGERED
UNREPENTINGLY	UNRESTRAINT	UNRUFFLING	UNSCEPTRED
UNREPINING	UNRESTRAINTS	UNRULIMENT	UNSCHEDULED
UNREPININGLY	UNRESTRICTED	UNRULIMENTS	UNSCHOLARLIKE
UNREPLACEABLE	UNRESTRICTEDLY	UNRULINESS	UNSCHOLARLY
UNREPLENISHED	UNRETARDED	UNRULINESSES	UNSCHOOLED
UNREPORTABLE	UNRETENTIVE	UNSADDLING	UNSCIENTIFIC
UNREPORTED	UNRETIRING	UNSAFENESS	UNSCISSORED
UNREPOSEFUL	UNRETOUCHED	UNSAFENESSES	UNSCORCHED
UNREPOSING	UNRETURNABLE	UNSAFETIES	UNSCOTTIFIED
UNREPRESENTED	UNRETURNED	UNSAILORLIKE	UNSCRAMBLE
UNREPRESSED	UNRETURNING	UNSAINTING	UNSCRAMBLED
UNREPRIEVABLE	UNRETURNINGLY	UNSAINTLIER	UNSCRAMBLER
UNREPRIEVED	UNREVEALABLE	UNSAINTLIEST	UNSCRAMBLERS
UNREPRIMANDED	UNREVEALED	UNSAINTLINESS	UNSCRAMBLES
UNREPROACHED	UNREVEALING	UNSAINTLINESSES	UNSCRAMBLING
UNREPROACHFUL	UNREVENGED	UNSALABILITIES	UNSCRATCHED
UNREPROACHING	UNREVENGEFUL	UNSALABILITY	UNSCREENED
UNREPRODUCIBLE	UNREVEREND	UNSALARIED	UNSCREWING
UNREPROVABLE	UNREVERENT	UNSALEABILITIES	UNSCRIPTED
UNREPROVED	UNREVERSED	UNSALEABILITY	UNSCRIPTURAL
UNREPROVING	UNREVERTED	UNSALEABLE	UNSCRIPTURALLY
UNREPUGNANT	UNREVIEWABLE	UNSALVAGEABLE	UNSCRUPLED
UNREPULSABLE	UNREVIEWED	UNSANCTIFIED	UNSCRUPULOSITY
UNREQUIRED	UNREVOLUTIONARY	UNSANCTIFIES	UNSCRUPULOUS
UNREQUISITE	UNREWARDED	UNSANCTIFY	UNSCRUPULOUSLY
UNREQUITED	UNREWARDEDLY	UNSANCTIFYING	UNSCRUTINISED
UNREQUITEDLY	UNREWARDING	UNSANCTIONED	UNSCRUTINIZED
UNRESCINDED	UNRHETORICAL	UNSANDALLED	UNSCULPTURED
UNRESENTED	UNRHYTHMIC	UNSANITARY	UNSEALABLE
UNRESENTFUL	UNRHYTHMICAL	UNSATIABLE	UNSEARCHABLE
UNRESENTING	UNRHYTHMICALLY	UNSATIATED	UNSEARCHABLY
UNRESERVED	UNRIDDLEABLE	UNSATIATING	UNSEARCHED
UNRESERVEDLY	UNRIDDLERS	UNSATIRICAL	UNSEASONABLE
UNRESERVEDNESS	UNRIDDLING	UNSATISFACTION	UNSEASONABLY
UNRESERVES	UNRIDEABLE	UNSATISFACTIONS	UNSEASONED
UNRESISTANT	UNRIGHTEOUS	UNSATISFACTORY	UNSEASONEDNESS
UNRESISTED	UNRIGHTEOUSLY	UNSATISFIABLE	UNSEASONING
UNRESISTIBLE	UNRIGHTEOUSNESS	UNSATISFIED	UNSEAWORTHINESS
UNRESISTING	UNRIGHTFUL	UNSATISFIEDNESS	UNSEAWORTHY
UNRESISTINGLY	UNRIGHTFULLY	UNSATISFYING	UNSECONDED
UNRESOLVABLE	UNRIGHTFULNESS	UNSATURATE	UNSECTARIAN
UNRESOLVED	UNRIPENESS	UNSATURATED	UNSECTARIANISM

UNSECTARIANISMS	UNSHAKEABLE	UNSMIRCHED	UNSPIRITUAL
UNSEEMINGS	UNSHAKEABLENESS	UNSMOOTHED	UNSPIRITUALISE
UNSEEMLIER	UNSHAKEABLY	UNSMOOTHING	UNSPIRITUALISED
UNSEEMLIEST	UNSHAKENLY	UNSMOTHERABLE	UNSPIRITUALISES
UNSEEMLINESS	UNSHAPELIER	UNSNAGGING	UNSPIRITUALIZE
UNSEEMLINESSES	UNSHAPELIEST	UNSNAPPING	UNSPIRITUALIZED
UNSEGMENTED	UNSHARPENED	UNSNARLING	UNSPIRITUALIZES
UNSEGREGATED	UNSHEATHED	UNSNECKING	UNSPIRITUALLY
UNSEISABLE	UNSHEATHES	UNSOCIABILITIES	UNSPLINTERABLE
UNSEIZABLE	UNSHEATHING	UNSOCIABILITY	UNSPOOLING
UNSELECTED	UNSHELLING	UNSOCIABLE	UNSPORTING
UNSELECTIVE	UNSHELTERED	UNSOCIABLENESS	UNSPORTSMANLIKE
UNSELECTIVELY	UNSHIELDED	UNSOCIABLY	UNSPOTTEDNESS
UNSELFCONSCIOUS	UNSHIFTING	UNSOCIALISED	UNSPOTTEDNESSES
UNSELFISHLY	UNSHINGLED	UNSOCIALISM	UNSPRINKLED
UNSELFISHNESS	UNSHIPPING	UNSOCIALISMS	UNSTABLENESS
UNSELFISHNESSES	UNSHOCKABLE	UNSOCIALITIES	UNSTABLENESSES
UNSELLABLE	UNSHOOTING	UNSOCIALITY	UNSTABLEST
UNSEMINARIED	UNSHOUTING	UNSOCIALIZED	UNSTACKING
UNSENSATIONAL	UNSHOWERED	UNSOCIALLY	UNSTAIDNESS
UNSENSIBLE	UNSHRINKABLE	UNSOCKETED	UNSTAIDNESSES
UNSENSIBLY	UNSHRINKING	UNSOCKETING	UNSTAINABLE
UNSENSITISED	UNSHRINKINGLY	UNSOFTENED	UNSTANCHABLE
UNSENSITIVE	UNSHROUDED	UNSOFTENING	UNSTANCHED
UNSENSITIZED	UNSHROUDING	UNSOLDERED	UNSTANDARDISED
UNSENSUALISE	UNSHRUBBED	UNSOLDERING	UNSTANDARDIZED
UNSENSUALISED	UNSHUNNABLE	UNSOLDIERLIKE	UNSTARCHED
UNSENSUALISES	UNSHUTTERED	UNSOLDIERLY	UNSTARCHES
UNSENSUALISING	UNSHUTTERING	UNSOLICITED	UNSTARCHING
UNSENSUALIZE	UNSHUTTERS	UNSOLICITOUS	UNSTARTLING
UNSENSUALIZED	UNSHUTTING	UNSOLIDITIES	UNSTATESMANLIKE
UNSENSUALIZES	UNSIGHTEDLY	UNSOLIDITY	UNSTATUTABLE
UNSENSUALIZING	UNSIGHTING	UNSOLVABLE	UNSTATUTABLY
UNSENTENCED	UNSIGHTLIER	UNSOPHISTICATE	UNSTAUNCHABLE
UNSENTIMENTAL	UNSIGHTLIEST	UNSOPHISTICATED	UNSTAUNCHED
UNSEPARABLE	UNSIGHTLINESS	UNSOUNDABLE	UNSTEADFAST
UNSEPARATED	UNSIGHTLINESSES	UNSOUNDEST	UNSTEADFASTLY
UNSEPULCHRED	UNSINEWING	UNSOUNDNESS	UNSTEADFASTNESS
UNSERIOUSNESS	UNSINKABLE	UNSOUNDNESSES	UNSTEADIED
UNSERIOUSNESSES	UNSINNOWED	UNSPARINGLY	UNSTEADIER
UNSERVICEABLE	UNSISTERED	UNSPARINGNESS	UNSTEADIES
UNSETTLEDLY	UNSISTERLINESS	UNSPARINGNESSES	UNSTEADIEST
UNSETTLEDNESS	UNSISTERLY	UNSPARRING	UNSTEADILY
UNSETTLEDNESSES	UNSIZEABLE	UNSPEAKABLE	UNSTEADINESS
UNSETTLEMENT	UNSKILFULLY	UNSPEAKABLENESS	UNSTEADINESSES
UNSETTLEMENTS	UNSKILFULNESS	UNSPEAKABLY	UNSTEADYING
UNSETTLING	UNSKILFULNESSES	UNSPEAKING	UNSTEELING
UNSETTLINGLY	UNSKILLFUL	UNSPECIALISED	UNSTEPPING
UNSETTLINGS	UNSKILLFULLY	UNSPECIALIZED	UNSTERCORATED
UNSHACKLED	UNSKILLFULNESS	UNSPECIFIABLE	UNSTERILISED
UNSHACKLES	UNSLAKABLE	UNSPECIFIC	UNSTERILIZED
UNSHACKLING	UNSLEEPING	UNSPECIFIED	UNSTICKING
UNSHADOWABLE	UNSLINGING	UNSPECTACLED	UNSTIGMATISED
UNSHADOWED	UNSLIPPING	UNSPECTACULAR	UNSTIGMATIZED
UNSHADOWING	UNSLUICING	UNSPECULATIVE	UNSTIMULATED
UNSHAKABLE	UNSLUMBERING	UNSPELLING	UNSTINTING
UNSHAKABLENESS	UNSLUMBROUS	UNSPHERING	UNSTINTINGLY
UNSHAKABLY	UNSMILINGLY	UNSPIRITED	UNSTITCHED

UNSTITCHES	UNSUPPLENESS	UNSYSTEMATICAL	UNTHINKINGLY
UNSTITCHING	UNSUPPLENESSES	UNSYSTEMATISED	UNTHINKINGNESS
UNSTOCKING	UNSUPPLIED	UNSYSTEMATIZED	UNTHOROUGH
UNSTOCKINGED	UNSUPPORTABLE	UNTACKLING	UNTHOUGHTFUL
UNSTOOPING	UNSUPPORTED	UNTAINTEDLY	UNTHOUGHTFULLY
UNSTOPPABLE	UNSUPPORTEDLY	UNTAINTEDNESS	UNTHREADED
UNSTOPPABLY	UNSUPPOSABLE	UNTAINTEDNESSES	UNTHREADING
UNSTOPPERED	UNSUPPRESSED	UNTAINTING	UNTHREATENED
UNSTOPPERING	UNSURFACED	UNTALENTED	UNTHREATENING
UNSTOPPERS	UNSURMISED	UNTAMABLENESS	UNTHRIFTILY
UNSTOPPING	UNSURMOUNTABLE	UNTAMABLENESSES	UNTHRIFTINESS
UNSTRAINED	UNSURPASSABLE	UNTAMEABLE	UNTHRIFTINESSES
UNSTRAPPED	UNSURPASSABLY	UNTAMEABLENESS	UNTHRIFTYHEAD
UNSTRAPPING	UNSURPASSED	UNTAMEABLY	UNTHRIFTYHEADS
UNSTRATIFIED	UNSURPRISED	UNTAMEDNESS	UNTHRIFTYHED
UNSTREAMED	UNSURPRISING	UNTAMEDNESSES	UNTHRIFTYHEDS
UNSTRENGTHENED	UNSURPRISINGLY	UNTANGIBLE	UNTHRONING
UNSTRESSED	UNSURVEYED	UNTANGLING	UNTIDINESS
UNSTRESSES	UNSUSCEPTIBLE	UNTARNISHED	UNTIDINESSES
UNSTRIATED	UNSUSPECTED	UNTASTEFUL	UNTILLABLE
UNSTRINGED	UNSUSPECTEDLY	UNTEACHABLE	UNTIMBERED
UNSTRINGING	UNSUSPECTEDNESS	UNTEACHABLENESS	UNTIMELIER
UNSTRIPPED	UNSUSPECTING	UNTEACHING	UNTIMELIEST
UNSTRIPPING	UNSUSPECTINGLY	UNTEARABLE	UNTIMELINESS
UNSTRUCTURED	UNSUSPENDED	UNTECHNICAL	UNTIMELINESSES
UNSUBDUABLE	UNSUSPICION	UNTELLABLE	UNTIMEOUSLY
UNSUBJECTED	UNSUSPICIONS	UNTEMPERED	UNTINCTURED
UNSUBLIMATED	UNSUSPICIOUS	UNTEMPERING	UNTIRINGLY
UNSUBLIMED	UNSUSPICIOUSLY	UNTENABILITIES	UNTOCHERED
UNSUBMERGED	UNSUSTAINABLE	UNTENABILITY	UNTOGETHER
UNSUBMISSIVE	UNSUSTAINED	UNTENABLENESS	UNTORMENTED
UNSUBMITTING	UNSUSTAINING	UNTENABLENESSES	UNTORTURED
UNSUBSCRIBE	UNSWADDLED	UNTENANTABLE	UNTOUCHABILITY
UNSUBSCRIBED	UNSWADDLES	UNTENANTED	UNTOUCHABLE
UNSUBSCRIBES	UNSWADDLING	UNTENANTING	UNTOUCHABLES
UNSUBSCRIBING	UNSWALLOWED	UNTENDERED	UNTOWARDLINESS
UNSUBSIDISED	UNSWATHING	UNTENDERLY	UNTOWARDLY
UNSUBSIDIZED	UNSWAYABLE	UNTERMINATED	UNTOWARDNESS
UNSUBSTANTIAL	UNSWEARING	UNTERRESTRIAL	UNTOWARDNESSES
UNSUBSTANTIALLY	UNSWEARINGS	UNTERRIFIED	UNTRACEABLE
UNSUBSTANTIATED	UNSWEETENED	UNTERRIFYING	UNTRACKING
UNSUCCEEDED	UNSWERVING	UNTESTABLE	UNTRACTABLE
UNSUCCESSES	UNSWERVINGLY	UNTETHERED	UNTRACTABLENESS
UNSUCCESSFUL	UNSYLLABLED	UNTETHERING	UNTRADITIONAL
UNSUCCESSFULLY	UNSYMMETRICAL	UNTHANKFUL	UNTRADITIONALLY
UNSUCCESSIVE	UNSYMMETRICALLY	UNTHANKFULLY	UNTRAMMELED
UNSUCCOURED	UNSYMMETRIES	UNTHANKFULNESS	UNTRAMMELLED
UNSUFFERABLE	UNSYMMETRISED	UNTHATCHED	UNTRAMPLED
UNSUFFICIENT	UNSYMMETRIZED	UNTHATCHES	UNTRANQUIL
UNSUITABILITIES	UNSYMMETRY	UNTHATCHING	UNTRANSFERABLE
UNSUITABILITY	UNSYMPATHETIC	UNTHEOLOGICAL	UNTRANSFERRABLE
UNSUITABLE	UNSYMPATHIES	UNTHEORETICAL	UNTRANSFORMED
UNSUITABLENESS	UNSYMPATHISING	UNTHICKENED	UNTRANSLATABLE
UNSUITABLY	UNSYMPATHIZING	UNTHINKABILITY	UNTRANSLATABLY
UNSUMMERED	UNSYMPATHY	UNTHINKABLE	UNTRANSLATED
UNSUMMONED	UNSYNCHRONISED	UNTHINKABLENESS	UNTRANSMIGRATED
UNSUPERFLUOUS	UNSYNCHRONIZED	UNTHINKABLY	UNTRANSMISSIBLE
UNSUPERVISED	UNSYSTEMATIC	UNTHINKING	UNTRANSMITTED

UNTRANSMUTABLE

UNTRANSMUTABLE	UNUTTERABLE	UNWATCHFUL	UNWITHERING
UNTRANSMUTED	UNUTTERABLENESS	UNWATCHFULLY	UNWITHHELD
UNTRANSPARENT	UNUTTERABLES	UNWATCHFULNESS	UNWITHHOLDEN
UNTRAVELED	UNUTTERABLY	UNWATERING	UNWITHHOLDING
UNTRAVELLED	UNVACCINATED	UNWAVERING	UNWITHSTOOD
UNTRAVERSABLE	UNVALUABLE	UNWAVERINGLY	UNWITNESSED
UNTRAVERSED	UNVANQUISHABLE	UNWEAKENED	UNWITTINGLY
UNTREADING	UNVANQUISHED	UNWEAPONED	UNWITTINGNESS
UNTREASURE	UNVARIABLE	UNWEAPONING	UNWITTINGNESSES
UNTREASURED	UNVARIEGATED	UNWEARABLE	UNWOMANING
UNTREASURES	UNVARNISHED	UNWEARIABLE	UNWOMANLIER
UNTREASURING	UNVEILINGS	UNWEARIABLY	UNWOMANLIEST
UNTREATABLE	UNVENDIBLE	UNWEARIEDLY	UNWOMANLINESS
UNTREMBLING	UNVENERABLE	UNWEARIEDNESS	UNWOMANLINESSES
UNTREMBLINGLY	UNVENTILATED	UNWEARIEDNESSES	UNWONTEDLY
UNTREMENDOUS	UNVERACIOUS	UNWEARYING	UNWONTEDNESS
UNTREMULOUS	UNVERACITIES	UNWEARYINGLY	UNWONTEDNESSES
UNTRENCHED	UNVERACITY	UNWEATHERED	UNWORKABILITIES
UNTRESPASSING	UNVERBALISED	UNWEDGABLE	UNWORKABILITY
UNTRIMMING	UNVERBALIZED	UNWEDGEABLE	UNWORKABLE
UNTROUBLED	UNVERIFIABILITY	UNWEETINGLY	UNWORKMANLIKE
UNTROUBLEDLY	UNVERIFIABLE	UNWEIGHING	UNWORLDLIER
UNTRUENESS	UNVERIFIED	UNWEIGHTED	UNWORLDLIEST
UNTRUENESSES	UNVIOLATED	UNWEIGHTING	UNWORLDLINESS
UNTRUSSERS	UNVIRTUOUS	UNWELCOMED	UNWORLDLINESSES
UNTRUSSING	UNVIRTUOUSLY	UNWELCOMELY	UNWORSHIPFUL
UNTRUSSINGS	UNVISITABLE	UNWELCOMENESS	UNWORSHIPPED
UNTRUSTFUL	UNVISORING	UNWELCOMENESSES	UNWORTHIER
UNTRUSTINESS	UNVITIATED	UNWELLNESS	UNWORTHIES
UNTRUSTINESSES	UNVITRIFIABLE	UNWELLNESSES	UNWORTHIEST
UNTRUSTING	UNVITRIFIED	UNWHISTLEABLE	UNWORTHILY
UNTRUSTWORTHILY	UNVIZARDED	UNWHOLESOME	UNWORTHINESS
UNTRUSTWORTHY	UNVIZARDING	UNWHOLESOMELY	UNWORTHINESSES
UNTRUTHFUL	UNVOCALISED	UNWHOLESOMENESS	UNWOUNDABLE
UNTRUTHFULLY	UNVOCALIZED	UNWIELDIER	UNWRAPPING
UNTRUTHFULNESS	UNVOICINGS	UNWIELDIEST	UNWREATHED
UNTUCKERED	UNVOYAGEABLE	UNWIELDILY	UNWREATHES
UNTUMULTUOUS	UNVULGARISE	UNWIELDINESS	UNWREATHING
UNTUNABLENESS	UNVULGARISED	UNWIELDINESSES	UNWRINKLED
UNTUNABLENESSES	UNVULGARISES	UNWIELDLILY	UNWRINKLES
UNTUNEABLE	UNVULGARISING	UNWIELDLINESS	UNWRINKLING
UNTUNEFULLY	UNVULGARIZE	UNWIELDLINESSES	UNYIELDING
UNTUNEFULNESS	UNVULGARIZED	UNWIFELIER	UNYIELDINGLY
UNTUNEFULNESSES	UNVULGARIZES	UNWIFELIEST	UNYIELDINGNESS
UNTURNABLE	UNVULGARIZING	UNWIFELIKE	UPBRAIDERS
UNTWISTING	UNVULNERABLE	UNWILLINGLY	UPBRAIDING
UNTWISTINGS	UNWANDERING	UNWILLINGNESS	UPBRAIDINGLY
UNTYPICALLY	UNWARENESS	UNWILLINGNESSES	UPBRAIDINGS
UNTYREABLE	UNWARENESSES	UNWINDABLE	UPBREAKING
UNUNUNIUMS	UNWARINESS	UNWINDINGS	UPBRINGING
UNUPLIFTED	UNWARINESSES	UNWINKINGLY	UPBRINGINGS
UNUSEFULLY	UNWARRANTABLE	UNWINNABLE	UPBUILDERS
UNUSEFULNESS	UNWARRANTABLY	UNWINNOWED	UPBUILDING
UNUSEFULNESSES	UNWARRANTED	UNWISENESS	UPBUILDINGS
UNUSUALNESS	UNWARRANTEDLY	UNWISENESSES	UPBUOYANCE
UNUSUALNESSES	UNWASHEDNESS	UNWITCHING	UPBUOYANCES
UNUTILISED	UNWASHEDNESSES	UNWITHDRAWING	UPBURSTING
UNUTILIZED	UNWATCHABLE	UNWITHERED	UPCATCHING

UPCHEERING	UPPROPPING	URALITISES	URIBILINOGEN
UPCHUCKING	UPREACHING	URALITISING	URIBILINOGENS
UPCLIMBING	UPRIGHTEOUSLY	URALITIZATION	URICOSURIC
UPCOUNTRIES	UPRIGHTING	URALITIZATIONS	URICOTELIC
UPDATEABLE	UPRIGHTNESS	URALITIZED	URICOTELISM
UPDRAGGING	UPRIGHTNESSES	URALITIZES	URICOTELISMS
UPDRAUGHTS	UPROARIOUS	URALITIZING	URINALYSES
UPFILLINGS	UPROARIOUSLY	URANALYSES	URINALYSIS
UPFLASHING	UPROARIOUSNESS	URANALYSIS	URINATIONS
UPFLINGING	UPROOTEDNESS	URANINITES	URINIFEROUS
UPFOLLOWED	UPROOTEDNESSES	URANOGRAPHER	URINIPAROUS
UPFOLLOWING	UPROOTINGS	URANOGRAPHERS	URINOGENITAL
UPGATHERED	UPSETTABLE	URANOGRAPHIC	URINOLOGIES
UPGATHERING	UPSETTINGLY	URANOGRAPHICAL	URINOMETER
UPGRADABILITIES	UPSETTINGS	URANOGRAPHIES	URINOMETERS
UPGRADABILITY	UPSHIFTING	URANOGRAPHIST	URINOSCOPIES
UPGRADABLE	UPSHOOTING	URANOGRAPHISTS	URINOSCOPY
UPGRADATION	UPSIDEOWNE	URANOGRAPHY	UROCHORDAL
UPGRADATIONS	UPSITTINGS	URANOLOGIES	UROCHORDATE
UPGRADEABILITY	UPSKILLING	URANOMETRIES	UROCHORDATES
UPGRADEABLE	UPSPEAKING	URANOMETRY	UROCHROMES
UPGROWINGS	UPSPEARING	URANOPLASTIES	URODYNAMICS
UPHEAPINGS	UPSPRINGING	URANOPLASTY	UROGENITAL
UPHILLWARD	UPSTANDING	URBANENESS	UROGRAPHIC
UPHOARDING	UPSTANDINGNESS	URBANENESSES	UROGRAPHIES
UPHOISTING	UPSTARTING	URBANISATION	UROKINASES
UPHOLDINGS	UPSTEPPING	URBANISATIONS	UROLAGNIAS
UPHOLSTERED	UPSTIRRING	URBANISING	UROLITHIASES
UPHOLSTERER	UPSTREAMED	URBANISTIC	UROLITHIASIS
UPHOLSTERERS	UPSTREAMING	URBANISTICALLY	UROLOGICAL
UPHOLSTERIES	UPSTRETCHED	URBANITIES	UROLOGISTS
UPHOLSTERING	UPSURGENCE	URBANIZATION	UROPOIESES
UPHOLSTERS	UPSURGENCES	URBANIZATIONS	UROPOIESIS
UPHOLSTERY	UPSWARMING	URBANIZING	UROPYGIUMS
UPHOLSTRESS	UPSWEEPING	URBANOLOGIES	UROSCOPIES
UPHOLSTRESSES	UPSWELLING	URBANOLOGIST	UROSCOPIST
UPHOORDING	UPSWINGING	URBANOLOGISTS	UROSCOPISTS
UPKNITTING	UPTHROWING	URBANOLOGY	UROSTEGITE
UPLIFTINGLY	UPTHRUSTED	URCEOLUSES	UROSTEGITES
UPLIFTINGS	UPTHRUSTING	UREDINIOSPORE	UROSTHENIC
UPLIGHTERS	UPTHUNDERED	UREDINIOSPORES	UROSTOMIES
UPLIGHTING	UPTHUNDERING	UREDIOSPORE	URTICACEOUS
UPLINKINGS	UPTHUNDERS	UREDIOSPORES	URTICARIAL
UPMANSHIPS	UPTIGHTEST	UREDOSORUS	URTICARIAS
UPPERCASED	UPTIGHTNESS	UREDOSPORE	URTICARIOUS
UPPERCASES	UPTIGHTNESSES	UREDOSPORES	URTICATING
UPPERCASING	UPTITLINGS	UREOTELISM	URTICATION
UPPERCLASSMAN	UPTRAINING	UREOTELISMS	URTICATIONS
UPPERCLASSMEN	UPTURNINGS	URETERITIS	USABILITIES
UPPERCUTTING	UPVALUATION	URETERITISES	USABLENESS
UPPERPARTS	UPVALUATIONS	URETHRITIC	USABLENESSES
UPPERWORKS	UPWARDNESS	URETHRITIS	USEABILITIES
UPPISHNESS	UPWARDNESSES	URETHRITISES	USEABILITY
UPPISHNESSES	UPWELLINGS	URETHROSCOPE	USEABLENESS
UPPITINESS	UPWHIRLING	URETHROSCOPES	USEABLENESSES
UPPITINESSES	URALITISATION	URETHROSCOPIC	USEFULNESS
UPPITYNESS	URALITISATIONS	URETHROSCOPIES	USEFULNESSES
UPPITYNESSES	URALITISED	URETHROSCOPY	USELESSNESS

USELESSNESSES
USHERESSES
USHERETTES
USHERSHIPS
USQUEBAUGH
USQUEBAUGHS
USTILAGINEOUS
USTILAGINOUS
USTULATION
USTULATIONS
USUALNESSES
USUCAPIENT
USUCAPIENTS
USUCAPIONS
USUCAPTIBLE
USUCAPTING
USUCAPTION
USUCAPTIONS
USUFRUCTED
USUFRUCTING
USUFRUCTUARIES
USUFRUCTUARY
USURIOUSLY
USURIOUSNESS
USURIOUSNESSES
USURPATION
USURPATIONS
USURPATIVE
USURPATORY
USURPATURE
USURPATURES
USURPINGLY
UTERECTOMIES
UTERECTOMY
UTERITISES
UTEROGESTATION
UTEROGESTATIONS
UTEROTOMIES
UTILISABLE
UTILISATION
UTILISATIONS
UTILITARIAN
UTILITARIANISE
UTILITARIANISED
UTILITARIANISES
UTILITARIANISM
UTILITARIANISMS
UTILITARIANIZE
UTILITARIANIZED
UTILITARIANIZES
UTILITARIANS
UTILIZABLE
UTILIZATION
UTILIZATIONS
UTOPIANISE
UTOPIANISED
UTOPIANISER
UTOPIANISERS

UTOPIANISES
UTOPIANISING
UTOPIANISM
UTOPIANISMS
UTOPIANIZE
UTOPIANIZED
UTOPIANIZER
UTOPIANIZERS
UTOPIANIZES
UTOPIANIZING
UTRICULARIA
UTRICULARIAS
UTRICULATE
UTRICULITIS
UTRICULITISES
UTTERABLENESS
UTTERABLENESSES
UTTERANCES
UTTERMOSTS
UTTERNESSES
UVAROVITES
UVULITISES
UXORICIDAL
UXORICIDES
UXORILOCAL
UXORIOUSLY
UXORIOUSNESS
UXORIOUSNESSES

V

VACANTNESS
VACANTNESSES
VACATIONED
VACATIONER
VACATIONERS
VACATIONING
VACATIONIST
VACATIONISTS
VACATIONLAND
VACATIONLANDS
VACATIONLESS
VACCINATED
VACCINATES
VACCINATING
VACCINATION
VACCINATIONS
VACCINATOR
VACCINATORS
VACCINATORY
VACCINIUMS
VACILLATED
VACILLATES
VACILLATING
VACILLATINGLY
VACILLATION
VACILLATIONS
VACILLATOR
VACILLATORS
VACILLATORY
VACUATIONS
VACUOLATED
VACUOLATION
VACUOLATIONS
VACUOLISATION
VACUOLISATIONS
VACUOLIZATION
VACUOLIZATIONS
VACUOUSNESS
VACUOUSNESSES
VAGABONDAGE
VAGABONDAGES
VAGABONDED
VAGABONDING
VAGABONDISE
VAGABONDISED
VAGABONDISES
VAGABONDISH
VAGABONDISING
VAGABONDISM
VAGABONDISMS
VAGABONDIZE
VAGABONDIZED
VAGABONDIZES

VAGABONDIZING
VAGARIOUSLY
VAGILITIES
VAGINECTOMIES
VAGINECTOMY
VAGINICOLINE
VAGINICOLOUS
VAGINISMUS
VAGINISMUSES
VAGINITISES
VAGOTOMIES
VAGOTONIAS
VAGOTROPIC
VAGRANCIES
VAGRANTNESS
VAGRANTNESSES
VAGUENESSES
VAINGLORIED
VAINGLORIES
VAINGLORIOUS
VAINGLORIOUSLY
VAINGLORYING
VAINNESSES
VAIVODESHIP
VAIVODESHIPS
VALEDICTION
VALEDICTIONS
VALEDICTORIAN
VALEDICTORIANS
VALEDICTORIES
VALEDICTORY
VALENTINES
VALERIANACEOUS
VALETUDINARIAN
VALETUDINARIANS
VALETUDINARIES
VALETUDINARY
VALIANCIES
VALIANTNESS
VALIANTNESSES
VALIDATING
VALIDATION
VALIDATIONS
VALIDATORY
VALIDITIES
VALIDNESSES
VALLATIONS
VALLECULAE
VALLECULAR
VALLECULATE
VALORISATION
VALORISATIONS
VALORISING

VALORIZATION
VALORIZATIONS
VALORIZING
VALOROUSLY
VALPOLICELLA
VALPOLICELLAS
VALPROATES
VALUABLENESS
VALUABLENESSES
VALUATIONAL
VALUATIONALLY
VALUATIONS
VALUELESSNESS
VALUELESSNESSES
VALVASSORS
VALVULITIS
VALVULITISES
VAMPIRISED
VAMPIRISES
VAMPIRISING
VAMPIRISMS
VAMPIRIZED
VAMPIRIZES
VAMPIRIZING
VANADIATES
VANADINITE
VANADINITES
VANASPATIS
VANCOMYCIN
VANCOMYCINS
VANDALISATION
VANDALISATIONS
VANDALISED
VANDALISES
VANDALISING
VANDALISMS
VANDALISTIC
VANDALIZATION
VANDALIZATIONS
VANDALIZED
VANDALIZES
VANDALIZING
VANGUARDISM
VANGUARDISMS
VANGUARDIST
VANGUARDISTS
VANISHINGLY
VANISHINGS
VANISHMENT
VANISHMENTS
VANITORIES
VANPOOLING
VANPOOLINGS

VANQUISHABLE
VANQUISHED
VANQUISHER
VANQUISHERS
VANQUISHES
VANQUISHING
VANQUISHMENT
VANQUISHMENTS
VANTAGELESS
VANTBRACES
VAPIDITIES
VAPIDNESSES
VAPORABILITIES
VAPORABILITY
VAPORESCENCE
VAPORESCENCES
VAPORESCENT
VAPORETTOS
VAPORIFORM
VAPORIMETER
VAPORIMETERS
VAPORISABLE
VAPORISATION
VAPORISATIONS
VAPORISERS
VAPORISHNESS
VAPORISHNESSES
VAPORISING
VAPORIZABLE
VAPORIZATION
VAPORIZATIONS
VAPORIZERS
VAPORIZING
VAPOROSITIES
VAPOROSITY
VAPOROUSLY
VAPOROUSNESS
VAPOROUSNESSES
VAPORWARES
VAPOURABILITIES
VAPOURABILITY
VAPOURABLE
VAPOURINGLY
VAPOURINGS
VAPOURISHNESS
VAPOURISHNESSES
VAPOURLESS
VAPOURWARE
VAPOURWARES
VAPULATING
VAPULATION
VAPULATIONS
VARIABILITIES

VARIABILITY	VARNISHING	VASSALISING	VEGETATIOUS
VARIABLENESS	VARNISHINGS	VASSALIZED	VEGETATIVE
VARIABLENESSES	VARSOVIENNE	VASSALIZES	VEGETATIVELY
VARIATIONAL	VARSOVIENNES	VASSALIZING	VEGETATIVENESS
VARIATIONALLY	VASCULARISATION	VASSALLING	VEGGIEBURGER
VARIATIONIST	VASCULARISE	VASSALRIES	VEGGIEBURGERS
VARIATIONISTS	VASCULARISED	VASTIDITIES	VEHEMENCES
VARIATIONS	VASCULARISES	VASTITUDES	VEHEMENCIES
VARICELLAR	VASCULARISING	VASTNESSES	VEHEMENTLY
VARICELLAS	VASCULARITIES	VATICINATE	VEILLEUSES
VARICELLATE	VASCULARITY	VATICINATED	VEINSTONES
VARICELLOID	VASCULARIZATION	VATICINATES	VEINSTUFFS
VARICELLOUS	VASCULARIZE	VATICINATING	VELARISATION
VARICOCELE	VASCULARIZED	VATICINATION	VELARISATIONS
VARICOCELES	VASCULARIZES	VATICINATIONS	VELARISING
VARICOLORED	VASCULARIZING	VATICINATOR	VELARIZATION
VARICOLOURED	VASCULARLY	VATICINATORS	VELARIZATIONS
VARICOSITIES	VASCULATURE	VATICINATORY	VELARIZING
VARICOSITY	VASCULATURES	VAUDEVILLE	VELDSCHOEN
VARICOTOMIES	VASCULIFORM	VAUDEVILLEAN	VELDSCHOENS
VARICOTOMY	VASCULITIDES	VAUDEVILLEANS	VELDSKOENS
VARIEDNESS	VASCULITIS	VAUDEVILLES	VELITATION
VARIEDNESSES	VASECTOMIES	VAUDEVILLIAN	VELITATIONS
VARIEGATED	VASECTOMISE	VAUDEVILLIANS	VELLEITIES
VARIEGATES	VASECTOMISED	VAUDEVILLIST	VELLENAGES
VARIEGATING	VASECTOMISES	VAUDEVILLISTS	VELLICATED
VARIEGATION	VASECTOMISING	VAULTINGLY	VELLICATES
VARIEGATIONS	VASECTOMIZE	VAUNTERIES	VELLICATING
VARIEGATOR	VASECTOMIZED	VAUNTINGLY	VELLICATION
VARIEGATORS	VASECTOMIZES	VAVASORIES	VELLICATIONS
VARIETALLY	VASECTOMIZING	VECTOGRAPH	VELLICATIVE
VARIFOCALS	VASOACTIVE	VECTOGRAPHS	VELOCIMETER
VARIFORMLY	VASOACTIVITIES	VECTORIALLY	VELOCIMETERS
VARIOLATED	VASOACTIVITY	VECTORINGS	VELOCIMETRIES
VARIOLATES	VASOCONSTRICTOR	VECTORISATION	VELOCIMETRY
VARIOLATING	VASODILATATION	VECTORISATIONS	VELOCIPEDE
VARIOLATION	VASODILATATIONS	VECTORISED	VELOCIPEDEAN
VARIOLATIONS	VASODILATATORY	VECTORISES	VELOCIPEDEANS
VARIOLATOR	VASODILATION	VECTORISING	VELOCIPEDED
VARIOLATORS	VASODILATIONS	VECTORIZATION	VELOCIPEDER
VARIOLISATION	VASODILATOR	VECTORIZATIONS	VELOCIPEDERS
VARIOLISATIONS	VASODILATORS	VECTORIZED	VELOCIPEDES
VARIOLITES	VASODILATORY	VECTORIZES	VELOCIPEDIAN
VARIOLITIC	VASOINHIBITOR	VECTORIZING	VELOCIPEDIANS
VARIOLIZATION	VASOINHIBITORS	VECTORSCOPE	VELOCIPEDING
VARIOLIZATIONS	VASOINHIBITORY	VECTORSCOPES	VELOCIPEDIST
VARIOLOIDS	VASOPRESSIN	VEGEBURGER	VELOCIPEDISTS
VARIOMETER	VASOPRESSINS	VEGEBURGERS	VELOCIRAPTOR
VARIOMETERS	VASOPRESSOR	VEGETABLES	VELOCIRAPTORS
VARIOUSNESS	VASOPRESSORS	VEGETARIAN	VELOCITIES
VARIOUSNESSES	VASOSPASMS	VEGETARIANISM	VELODROMES
VARISCITES	VASOSPASTIC	VEGETARIANISMS	VELOUTINES
VARITYPING	VASOTOCINS	VEGETARIANS	VELUTINOUS
VARITYPIST	VASOTOMIES	VEGETATING	VELVETEENED
VARITYPISTS	VASSALAGES	VEGETATINGS	VELVETEENS
VARLETESSES	VASSALESSES	VEGETATION	VELVETIEST
VARLETRIES	VASSALISED	VEGETATIONAL	VELVETINESS
VARNISHERS	VASSALISES	VEGETATIONS	VELVETINESSES

VELVETINGS	VENOLOGIES	VENTURINGS	VERGEBOARD
VELVETLIKE	VENOMOUSLY	VENTUROUSLY	VERGEBOARDS
VENALITIES	VENOMOUSNESS	VENTUROUSNESS	VERGENCIES
VENATICALLY	VENOMOUSNESSES	VENTUROUSNESSES	VERGERSHIP
VENATIONAL	VENOSCLEROSES	VERACIOUSLY	VERGERSHIPS
VENATORIAL	VENOSCLEROSIS	VERACIOUSNESS	VERIDICALITIES
VENDETTIST	VENOSITIES	VERACIOUSNESSES	VERIDICALITY
VENDETTISTS	VENOUSNESS	VERACITIES	VERIDICALLY
VENDIBILITIES	VENOUSNESSES	VERANDAHED	VERIDICOUS
VENDIBILITY	VENTIDUCTS	VERAPAMILS	VERIFIABILITIES
VENDIBLENESS	VENTIFACTS	VERATRIDINE	VERIFIABILITY
VENDIBLENESSES	VENTILABLE	VERATRIDINES	VERIFIABLE
VENDITATION	VENTILATED	VERATRINES	VERIFIABLENESS
VENDITATIONS	VENTILATES	VERBALISATION	VERIFIABLY
VENDITIONS	VENTILATING	VERBALISATIONS	VERIFICATION
VENEERTNGS	VENTILATION	VERBALISED	VERIFICATIONS
VENEFICALLY	VENTILATIONS	VERBALISER	VERIFICATIVE
VENEFICIOUS	VENTILATIVE	VERBALISERS	VERIFICATORY
VENEFICIOUSLY	VENTILATOR	VERBALISES	VERISIMILAR
VENEFICOUS	VENTILATORS	VERBALISING	VERISIMILARLY
VENEFICOUSLY	VENTILATORY	VERBALISMS	VERISIMILITIES
VENENATING	VENTOSITIES	VERBALISTIC	VERISIMILITUDE
VENEPUNCTURE	VENTRICLES	VERBALISTS	VERISIMILITUDES
VENEPUNCTURES	VENTRICOSE	VERBALITIES	VERISIMILITY
VENERABILITIES	VENTRICOSITIES	VERBALIZATION	VERISIMILOUS
VENERABILITY	VENTRICOSITY	VERBALIZATIONS	VERITABLENESS
VENERABLENESS	VENTRICOUS	VERBALIZED	VERITABLENESSES
VENERABLENESSES	VENTRICULAR	VERBALIZER	VERJUICING
VENERABLES	VENTRICULE	VERBALIZERS	VERKRAMPTE
VENERATING	VENTRICULES	VERBALIZES	VERKRAMPTES
VENERATION	VENTRICULI	VERBALIZING	VERMEILING
VENERATIONAL	VENTRICULUS	VERBALLING	VERMEILLED
VENERATIONS	VENTRILOQUAL	VERBARIANS	VERMEILLES
VENERATIVENESS	VENTRILOQUIAL	VERBASCUMS	VERMEILLING
VENERATORS	VENTRILOQUIALLY	VERBENACEOUS	VERMICELLI
VENEREOLOGICAL	VENTRILOQUIES	VERBERATED	VERMICELLIS
VENEREOLOGIES	VENTRILOQUISE	VERBERATES	VERMICIDAL
VENEREOLOGIST	VENTRILOQUISED	VERBERATING	VERMICIDES
VENEREOLOGISTS	VENTRILOQUISES	VERBERATION	VERMICULAR
VENEREOLOGY	VENTRILOQUISING	VERBERATIONS	VERMICULARLY
VENESECTION	VENTRILOQUISM	VERBICIDES	VERMICULATE
VENESECTIONS	VENTRILOQUISMS	VERBIFICATION	VERMICULATED
VENGEANCES	VENTRILOQUIST	VERBIFICATIONS	VERMICULATES
VENGEFULLY	VENTRILOQUISTIC	VERBIFYING	VERMICULATING
VENGEFULNESS	VENTRILOQUISTS	VERBIGERATE	VERMICULATION
VENGEFULNESSES	VENTRILOQUIZE	VERBIGERATED	VERMICULATIONS
VENGEMENTS	VENTRILOQUIZED	VERBIGERATES	VERMICULES
VENIALITIES	VENTRILOQUIZES	VERBIGERATING	VERMICULITE
VENIALNESS	VENTRILOQUIZING	VERBIGERATION	VERMICULITES
VENIALNESSES	VENTRILOQUOUS	VERBIGERATIONS	VERMICULOUS
VENIPUNCTURE	VENTRILOQUY	VERBOSENESS	VERMICULTURE
VENIPUNCTURES	VENTRIPOTENT	VERBOSENESSES	VERMICULTURES
VENISECTION	VENTROLATERAL	VERBOSITIES	VERMIFUGAL
VENISECTIONS	VENTROMEDIAL	VERDANCIES	VERMIFUGES
VENOGRAPHIC	VENTURESOME	VERDIGRISED	VERMILIONED
VENOGRAPHICAL	VENTURESOMELY	VERDIGRISES	VERMILIONING
VENOGRAPHIES	VENTURESOMENESS	VERDIGRISING	VERMILIONS
VENOGRAPHY	VENTURINGLY	VERDURELESS	VERMILLING

VERMILLION	VERSIFICATOR	VESPERTILIONID	VIBRATILITY
VERMILLIONS	VERSIFICATORS	VESPERTILIONIDS	VIBRATINGLY
VERMINATED	VERSIFIERS	VESPERTILIONINE	VIBRATIONAL
VERMINATES	VERSIFYING	VESPERTINAL	VIBRATIONLESS
VERMINATING	VERSIONERS	VESPERTINE	VIBRATIONS
VERMINATION	VERSIONING	VESPIARIES	VIBRATIUNCLE
VERMINATIONS	VERSIONINGS	VESTIARIES	VIBRATIUNCLES
VERMINOUSLY	VERSIONIST	VESTIBULAR	VIBRATOLESS
VERMINOUSNESS	VERSIONISTS	VESTIBULED	VIBROFLOTATION
VERMINOUSNESSES	VERSLIBRIST	VESTIBULES	VIBROFLOTATIONS
VERMIVOROUS	VERSLIBRISTE	VESTIBULING	VIBROGRAPH
VERNACULAR	VERSLIBRISTES	VESTIBULITIS	VIBROGRAPHS
VERNACULARISE	VERSLIBRISTS	VESTIBULITISES	VIBROMETER
VERNACULARISED	VERTEBRALLY	VESTIBULUM	VIBROMETERS
VERNACULARISES	VERTEBRATE	VESTIGIALLY	VICARESSES
VERNACULARISING	VERTEBRATED	VESTIMENTAL	VICARIANCE
VERNACULARISM	VERTEBRATES	VESTIMENTARY	VICARIANCES
VERNACULARISMS	VERTEBRATION	VESTIMENTS	VICARIANTS
VERNACULARIST	VERTEBRATIONS	VESTITURES	VICARIATES
VERNACULARISTS	VERTICALITIES	VESTMENTAL	VICARIOUSLY
VERNACULARITIES	VERTICALITY	VESTMENTED	VICARIOUSNESS
VERNACULARITY	VERTICALLY	VESUVIANITE	VICARIOUSNESSES
VERNACULARIZE	VERTICALNESS	VESUVIANITES	VICARSHIPS
VERNACULARIZED	VERTICALNESSES	VETCHLINGS	VICEGERENCIES
VERNACULARIZES	VERTICILLASTER	VETERINARIAN	VICEGERENCY
VERNACULARIZING	VERTICILLASTERS	VETERINARIANS	VICEGERENT
VERNACULARLY	VERTICILLATE	VETERINARIES	VICEGERENTS
VERNACULARS	VERTICILLATED	VETERINARY	VICEREGALLY
VERNALISATION	VERTICILLATELY	VEXATIOUSLY	VICEREGENT
VERNALISATIONS	VERTICILLATION	VEXATIOUSNESS	VICEREGENTS
VERNALISED	VERTICILLATIONS	VEXATIOUSNESSES	VICEREINES
VERNALISES	VERTICILLIUM	VEXEDNESSES	VICEROYALTIES
VERNALISING	VERTICILLIUMS	VEXILLARIES	VICEROYALTY
VERNALITIES	VERTICITIES	VEXILLATION	VICEROYSHIP
VERNALIZATION	VERTIGINES	VEXILLATIONS	VICEROYSHIPS
VERNALIZATIONS	VERTIGINOUS	VEXILLOLOGIC	VICHYSSOIS
VERNALIZED	VERTIGINOUSLY	VEXILLOLOGICAL	VICHYSSOISE
VERNALIZES	VERTIGINOUSNESS	VEXILLOLOGIES	VICHYSSOISES
VERNALIZING	VERTIPORTS	VEXILLOLOGIST	VICINITIES
VERNATIONS	VERUMONTANA	VEXILLOLOGISTS	VICIOSITIES
VERNISSAGE	VERUMONTANUM	VEXILLOLOGY	VICIOUSNESS
VERNISSAGES	VERUMONTANUMS	VEXINGNESS	VICIOUSNESSES
VERRUCIFORM	VESICATING	VEXINGNESSES	VICISSITUDE
VERRUCOSITIES	VESICATION	VIABILITIES	VICISSITUDES
VERRUCOSITY	VESICATIONS	VIBRACULAR	VICISSITUDINARY
VERSABILITIES	VESICATORIES	VIBRACULARIA	VICISSITUDINOUS
VERSABILITY	VESICATORY	VIBRACULARIUM	VICOMTESSE
VERSATILELY	VESICULARITIES	VIBRACULOID	VICOMTESSES
VERSATILENESS	VESICULARITY	VIBRACULUM	VICTIMHOOD
VERSATILENESSES	VESICULARLY	VIBRAHARPIST	VICTIMHOODS
VERSATILITIES	VESICULATE	VIBRAHARPISTS	VICTIMISATION
VERSATILITY	VESICULATED	VIBRAHARPS	VICTIMISATIONS
VERSICOLOR	VESICULATES	VIBRANCIES	VICTIMISED
VERSICOLOUR	VESICULATING	VIBRAPHONE	VICTIMISER
VERSICOLOURED	VESICULATION	VIBRAPHONES	VICTIMISERS
VERSICULAR	VESICULATIONS	VIBRAPHONIST	VICTIMISES
VERSIFICATION	VESICULOSE	VIBRAPHONISTS	VICTIMISING
VERSIFICATIONS	VESPERTILIAN	VIBRATILITIES	VICTIMIZATION

VICTIMIZATIONS	VIEWINESSES	VILLICATIONS	VINOLOGIST
VICTIMIZED	VIEWLESSLY	VILLOSITIES	VINOLOGISTS
VICTIMIZER	VIEWPHONES	VINAIGRETTE	VINOSITIES
VICTIMIZERS	VIEWPOINTS	VINAIGRETTES	VINTAGINGS
VICTIMIZES	VIGILANCES	VINBLASTINE	VINYLCYANIDE
VICTIMIZING	VIGILANTES	VINBLASTINES	VINYLCYANIDES
VICTIMLESS	VIGILANTISM	VINCIBILITIES	VINYLIDENE
VICTIMOLOGIES	VIGILANTISMS	VINCIBILITY	VINYLIDENES
VICTIMOLOGIST	VIGILANTLY	VINCIBLENESS	VIOLABILITIES
VICTIMOLOGISTS	VIGILANTNESS	VINCIBLENESSES	VIOLABILITY
VICTIMOLOGY	VIGILANTNESSES	VINCRISTINE	VIOLABLENESS
VICTORESSES	VIGINTILLION	VINCRISTINES	VIOLABLENESSES
VICTORIANA	VIGINTILLIONS	VINDEMIATE	VIOLACEOUS
VICTORINES	VIGNETTERS	VINDEMIATED	VIOLATIONS
VICTORIOUS	VIGNETTING	VINDEMIATES	VIOLENTING
VICTORIOUSLY	VIGNETTIST	VINDEMIATING	VIOLINISTIC
VICTORIOUSNESS	VIGNETTISTS	VINDICABILITIES	VIOLINISTICALLY
VICTORYLESS	VIGORISHES	VINDICABILITY	VIOLINISTS
VICTRESSES	VIGOROUSLY	VINDICABLE	VIOLONCELLI
VICTROLLAS	VIGOROUSNESS	VINDICATED	VIOLONCELLIST
VICTUALAGE	VIGOROUSNESSES	VINDICATES	VIOLONCELLISTS
VICTUALAGES	VIKINGISMS	VINDICATING	VIOLONCELLO
VICTUALERS	VILDNESSES	VINDICATION	VIOLONCELLOS
VICTUALING	VILENESSES	VINDICATIONS	VIOSTEROLS
VICTUALLAGE	VILIFICATION	VINDICATIVE	VIPERFISHES
VICTUALLAGES	VILIFICATIONS	VINDICATIVENESS	VIPERIFORM
VICTUALLED	VILIPENDED	VINDICATOR	VIPERISHLY
VICTUALLER	VILIPENDER	VINDICATORILY	VIPEROUSLY
VICTUALLERS	VILIPENDERS	VINDICATORS	VIRAGINIAN
VICTUALLESS	VILIPENDING	VINDICATORY	VIRAGINOUS
VICTUALLING	VILLAGERIES	VINDICATRESS	VIREONINES
VIDEOCASSETTE	VILLAGIOES	VINDICATRESSES	VIRESCENCE
VIDEOCASSETTES	VILLAGISATION	VINDICTIVE	VIRESCENCES
VIDEOCONFERENCE	VILLAGISATIONS	VINDICTIVELY	VIRGINALIST
VIDEODISCS	VILLAGIZATION	VINDICTIVENESS	VIRGINALISTS
VIDEODISKS	VILLAGIZATIONS	VINEDRESSER	VIRGINALLED
VIDEOGRAMS	VILLAGREES	VINEDRESSERS	VIRGINALLING
VIDEOGRAPHER	VILLAINAGE	VINEGARETTE	VIRGINALLY
VIDEOGRAPHERS	VILLAINAGES	VINEGARETTES	VIRGINHOOD
VIDEOGRAPHIES	VILLAINESS	VINEGARING	VIRGINHOODS
VIDEOGRAPHY	VILLAINESSES	VINEGARISH	VIRGINITIES
VIDEOLANDS	VILLAINIES	VINEGARRETTE	VIRGINIUMS
VIDEOPHILE	VILLAINOUS	VINEGARRETTES	VIRIDESCENCE
VIDEOPHILES	VILLAINOUSLY	VINEGARROON	VIRIDESCENCES
VIDEOPHONE	VILLAINOUSNESS	VINEGARROONS	VIRIDESCENT
VIDEOPHONES	VILLANAGES	VINEYARDIST	VIRIDITIES
VIDEOPHONIC	VILLANELLA	VINEYARDISTS	VIRILESCENCE
VIDEOTAPED	VILLANELLAS	VINICULTURAL	VIRILESCENCES
VIDEOTAPES	VILLANELLE	VINICULTURE	VIRILESCENT
VIDEOTAPING	VILLANELLES	VINICULTURES	VIRILISATION
VIDEOTELEPHONE	VILLANOUSLY	VINICULTURIST	VIRILISATIONS
VIDEOTELEPHONES	VILLEGGIATURA	VINICULTURISTS	VIRILISING
VIDEOTEXES	VILLEGGIATURAS	VINIFEROUS	VIRILITIES
VIDEOTEXTS	VILLEINAGE	VINIFICATION	VIRILIZATION
VIEWERSHIP	VILLEINAGES	VINIFICATIONS	VIRILIZATIONS
VIEWERSHIPS	VILLENAGES	VINIFICATOR	VIRILIZING
VIEWFINDER	VILLIAGOES	VINIFICATORS	VIROLOGICAL
VIEWFINDERS	VILLICATION	VINOLOGIES	VIROLOGICALLY

VIROLOGIES	VISCOSIMETRY	VITALIZERS	VITRIFACTIONS
VIROLOGIST	VISCOSITIES	VITALIZING	VITRIFACTURE
VIROLOGISTS	VISCOUNTCIES	VITALNESSES	VITRIFACTURES
VIRTUALISE	VISCOUNTCY	VITAMINISE	VITRIFIABILITY
VIRTUALISED	VISCOUNTESS	VITAMINISED	VITRIFIABLE
VIRTUALISES	VISCOUNTESSES	VITAMINISES	VITRIFICATION
VIRTUALISING	VISCOUNTIES	VITAMINISING	VITRIFICATIONS
VIRTUALISM	VISCOUNTSHIP	VITAMINIZE	VITRIFYING
VIRTUALISMS	VISCOUNTSHIPS	VITAMINIZED	VITRIOLATE
VIRTUALIST	VISCOUSNESS	VITAMINIZES	VITRIOLATED
VIRTUALISTS	VISCOUSNESSES	VITAMINIZING	VITRIOLATES
VIRTUALITIES	VISIBILITIES	VITASCOPES	VITRIOLATING
VIRTUALITY	VISIBILITY	VITATIVENESS	VITRIOLATION
VIRTUALIZE	VISIBLENESS	VITATIVENESSES	VITRIOLATIONS
VIRTUALIZED	VISIBLENESSES	VITELLICLE	VITRIOLING
VIRTUALIZES	VISIOGENIC	VITELLICLES	VITRIOLISATION
VIRTUALIZING	VISIONALLY	VITELLIGENOUS	VITRIOLISATIONS
VIRTUELESS	VISIONARIES	VITELLINES	VITRIOLISE
VIRTUOSITIES	VISIONARINESS	VITELLOGENESES	VITRIOLISED
VIRTUOSITY	VISIONARINESSES	VITELLOGENESIS	VITRIOLISES
VIRTUOSOSHIP	VISIONINGS	VITELLOGENIC	VITRIOLISING
VIRTUOSOSHIPS	VISIONISTS	VITELLUSES	VITRIOLIZATION
VIRTUOUSLY	VISIONLESS	VITIATIONS	VITRIOLIZATIONS
VIRTUOUSNESS	VISIOPHONE	VITICETUMS	VITRIOLIZE
VIRTUOUSNESSES	VISIOPHONES	VITICOLOUS	VITRIOLIZED
VIRULENCES	VISITATION	VITICULTURAL	VITRIOLIZES
VIRULENCIES	VISITATIONAL	VITICULTURALLY	VITRIOLIZING
VIRULENTLY	VISITATIONS	VITICULTURE	VITRIOLLED
VIRULIFEROUS	VISITATIVE	VITICULTURER	VITRIOLLING
VISAGISTES	VISITATORIAL	VITICULTURERS	VITUPERABLE
VISCACHERA	VISITATORS	VITICULTURES	VITUPERATE
VISCACHERAS	VISITORIAL	VITICULTURIST	VITUPERATED
VISCERALLY	VISITRESSES	VITICULTURISTS	VITUPERATES
VISCERATED	VISUALISATION	VITIFEROUS	VITUPERATING
VISCERATES	VISUALISATIONS	VITILITIGATE	VITUPERATION
VISCERATING	VISUALISED	VITILITIGATED	VITUPERATIONS
VISCEROMOTOR	VISUALISER	VITILITIGATES	VITUPERATIVE
VISCEROPTOSES	VISUALISERS	VITILITIGATING	VITUPERATIVELY
VISCEROPTOSIS	VISUALISES	VITILITIGATION	VITUPERATOR
VISCEROTONIA	VISUALISING	VITILITIGATIONS	VITUPERATORS
VISCEROTONIAS	VISUALISTS	VITIOSITIES	VITUPERATORY
VISCEROTONIC	VISUALITIES	VITRAILLED	VIVACIOUSLY
VISCIDITIES	VISUALIZATION	VITRAILLIST	VIVACIOUSNESS
VISCIDNESS	VISUALIZATIONS	VITRAILLISTS	VIVACIOUSNESSES
VISCIDNESSES	VISUALIZED	VITRECTOMIES	VIVACISSIMO
VISCOELASTIC	VISUALIZER	VITRECTOMY	VIVACITIES
VISCOELASTICITY	VISUALIZERS	VITREOSITIES	VIVANDIERE
VISCOMETER	VISUALIZES	VITREOSITY	VIVANDIERES
VISCOMETERS	VISUALIZING	VITREOUSES	VIVANDIERS
VISCOMETRIC	VITALISATION	VITREOUSLY	VIVERRINES
VISCOMETRICAL	VITALISATIONS	VITREOUSNESS	VIVIANITES
VISCOMETRIES	VITALISERS	VITREOUSNESSES	VIVIDITIES
VISCOMETRY	VITALISING	VITRESCENCE	VIVIDNESSES
VISCOSIMETER	VITALISTIC	VITRESCENCES	VIVIFICATION
VISCOSIMETERS	VITALISTICALLY	VITRESCENT	VIVIFICATIONS
VISCOSIMETRIC	VITALITIES	VITRESCIBILITY	VIVIPARIES
VISCOSIMETRICAL	VITALIZATION	VITRESCIBLE	VIVIPARISM
VISCOSIMETRIES	VITALIZATIONS	VITRIFACTION	VIVIPARISMS

VIVIPARITIES	VOCIFERATED	VOLCANISES	VOLUNTARILY
VIVIPARITY	VOCIFERATES	VOLCANISING	VOLUNTARINESS
VIVIPAROUS	VOCIFERATING	VOLCANISMS	VOLUNTARINESSES
VIVIPAROUSLY	VOCIFERATION	VOLCANISTS	VOLUNTARISM
VIVIPAROUSNESS	VOCIFERATIONS	VOLCANIZATION	VOLUNTARISMS
VIVISECTED	VOCIFERATOR	VOLCANIZATIONS	VOLUNTARIST
VIVISECTING	VOCIFERATORS	VOLCANIZED	VOLUNTARISTIC
VIVISECTION	VOCIFEROSITIES	VOLCANIZES	VOLUNTARISTS
VIVISECTIONAL	VOCIFEROSITY	VOLCANIZING	VOLUNTARYISM
VIVISECTIONALLY	VOCIFEROUS	VOLCANOLOGIC	VOLUNTARYISMS
VIVISECTIONIST	VOCIFEROUSLY	VOLCANOLOGICAL	VOLUNTARYIST
VIVISECTIONISTS	VOCIFEROUSNESS	VOLCANOLOGIES	VOLUNTARYISTS
VIVISECTIONS	VOETGANGER	VOLCANOLOGIST	VOLUNTATIVE
VIVISECTIVE	VOETGANGERS	VOLCANOLOGISTS	VOLUNTEERED
VIVISECTOR	VOETSTOETS	VOLCANOLOGY	VOLUNTEERING
VIVISECTORIUM	VOETSTOOTS	VOLITATING	VOLUNTEERISM
VIVISECTORIUMS	VOGUISHNESS	VOLITATION	VOLUNTEERISMS
VIVISECTORS	VOGUISHNESSES	VOLITATIONAL	VOLUNTEERS
VIVISEPULTURE	VOICEFULNESS	VOLITATIONS	VOLUPTUARIES
VIVISEPULTURES	VOICEFULNESSES	VOLITIONAL	VOLUPTUARY
VIXENISHLY	VOICELESSLY	VOLITIONALLY	VOLUPTUOSITIES
VIXENISHNESS	VOICELESSNESS	VOLITIONARY	VOLUPTUOSITY
VIXENISHNESSES	VOICELESSNESSES	VOLITIONLESS	VOLUPTUOUS
VIZIERATES	VOICEMAILS	VOLITORIAL	VOLUPTUOUSLY
VIZIERSHIP	VOICEOVERS	VOLKSLIEDER	VOLUPTUOUSNESS
VIZIERSHIPS	VOICEPRINT	VOLKSRAADS	VOLUTATION
VIZIRSHIPS	VOICEPRINTS	VOLLEYBALL	VOLUTATIONS
VOCABULARIAN	VOIDABLENESS	VOLLEYBALLS	VOLVULUSES
VOCABULARIANS	VOIDABLENESSES	VOLPLANING	VOMERONASAL
VOCABULARIED	VOIDNESSES	VOLTAMETER	VOMITORIES
VOCABULARIES	VOISINAGES	VOLTAMETERS	VOMITORIUM
VOCABULARY	VOITURIERS	VOLTAMETRIC	VOMITURITION
VOCABULIST	VOIVODESHIP	VOLTAMMETER	VOMITURITIONS
VOCABULISTS	VOIVODESHIPS	VOLTAMMETERS	VOODOOISMS
VOCALICALLY	VOLATILENESS	VOLTIGEURS	VOODOOISTIC
VOCALISATION	VOLATILENESSES	VOLTINISMS	VOODOOISTS
VOCALISATIONS	VOLATILISABLE	VOLTMETERS	VOORKAMERS
VOCALISERS	VOLATILISATION	VOLUBILITIES	VOORTREKKER
VOCALISING	VOLATILISATIONS	VOLUBILITY	VOORTREKKERS
VOCALITIES	VOLATILISE	VOLUBLENESS	VORACIOUSLY
VOCALIZATION	VOLATILISED	VOLUBLENESSES	VORACIOUSNESS
VOCALIZATIONS	VOLATILISES	VOLUMENOMETER	VORACIOUSNESSES
VOCALIZERS	VOLATILISING	VOLUMENOMETERS	VORACITIES
VOCALIZING	VOLATILITIES	VOLUMETERS	VORAGINOUS
VOCALNESSES	VOLATILITY	VOLUMETRIC	VORTICALLY
VOCATIONAL	VOLATILIZABLE	VOLUMETRICAL	VORTICELLA
VOCATIONALISM	VOLATILIZATION	VOLUMETRICALLY	VORTICELLAE
VOCATIONALISMS	VOLATILIZATIONS	VOLUMETRIES	VORTICELLAS
VOCATIONALIST	VOLATILIZE	VOLUMINOSITIES	VORTICISMS
VOCATIONALISTS	VOLATILIZED	VOLUMINOSITY	VORTICISTS
VOCATIONALLY	VOLATILIZES	VOLUMINOUS	VORTICITIES
VOCATIVELY	VOLATILIZING	VOLUMINOUSLY	VORTICULAR
VOCICULTURAL	VOLCANICALLY	VOLUMINOUSNESS	VORTIGINOUS
VOCIFERANCE	VOLCANICITIES	VOLUMISING	VOTARESSES
VOCIFERANCES	VOLCANICITY	VOLUMIZING	VOTIVENESS
VOCIFERANT	VOLCANISATION	VOLUMOMETER	VOTIVENESSES
VOCIFERANTS	VOLCANISATIONS	VOLUMOMETERS	VOUCHERING
VOCIFERATE	VOLCANISED	VOLUNTARIES	VOUCHSAFED

VOUCHSAFEMENT
VOUCHSAFEMENTS
VOUCHSAFES
VOUCHSAFING
VOUCHSAFINGS
VOUSSOIRED
VOUSSOIRING
VOUTSAFING
VOWELISATION
VOWELISATIONS
VOWELISING
VOWELIZATION
VOWELIZATIONS
VOWELIZING
VOYAGEABLE
VOYEURISMS
VOYEURISTIC
VOYEURISTICALLY
VRAICKINGS
VRAISEMBLANCE
VRAISEMBLANCES
VULCANICITIES
VULCANICITY
VULCANISABLE
VULCANISATE
VULCANISATES
VULCANISATION
VULCANISATIONS
VULCANISED
VULCANISER
VULCANISERS
VULCANISES
VULCANISING
VULCANISMS
VULCANISTS
VULCANITES
VULCANIZABLE
VULCANIZATE
VULCANIZATES
VULCANIZATION
VULCANIZATIONS
VULCANIZED
VULCANIZER
VULCANIZERS
VULCANIZES
VULCANIZING
VULCANOLOGICAL
VULCANOLOGIES
VULCANOLOGIST
VULCANOLOGISTS
VULCANOLOGY
VULGARIANS
VULGARISATION
VULGARISATIONS
VULGARISED
VULGARISER
VULGARISERS
VULGARISES

VULGARISING
VULGARISMS
VULGARITIES
VULGARIZATION
VULGARIZATIONS
VULGARIZED
VULGARIZER
VULGARIZERS
VULGARIZES
VULGARIZING
VULNERABILITIES
VULNERABILITY
VULNERABLE
VULNERABLENESS
VULNERABLY
VULNERARIES
VULNERATED
VULNERATES
VULNERATING
VULNERATION
VULNERATIONS
VULPECULAR
VULPICIDES
VULPINISMS
VULPINITES
VULTURISMS
VULVITISES
VULVOVAGINAL
VULVOVAGINITIS

W

WACKINESSES
WADSETTERS
WADSETTING
WAFFLESTOMPER
WAFFLESTOMPERS
WAGELESSNESS
WAGELESSNESSES
WAGENBOOMS
WAGEWORKER
WAGEWORKERS
WAGGISHNESS
WAGGISHNESSES
WAGGLINGLY
WAGGONETTE
WAGGONETTES
WAGGONLESS
WAGGONLOAD
WAGGONLOADS
WAGHALTERS
WAGONETTES
WAGONLOADS
WAGONWRIGHT
WAGONWRIGHTS
WAINSCOTED
WAINSCOTING
WAINSCOTINGS
WAINSCOTTED
WAINSCOTTING
WAINSCOTTINGS
WAINWRIGHT
WAINWRIGHTS
WAISTBANDS
WAISTBELTS
WAISTCLOTH
WAISTCLOTHS
WAISTCOATED
WAISTCOATEER
WAISTCOATEERS
WAISTCOATING
WAISTCOATINGS
WAISTCOATS
WAISTLINES
WAITERAGES
WAITERHOOD
WAITERHOODS
WAITERINGS
WAITLISTED
WAITLISTING
WAITPERSON
WAITPERSONS
WAITRESSED
WAITRESSES
WAITRESSING
WAITRESSINGS
WAITSTAFFS

WAKEBOARDER
WAKEBOARDERS
WAKEBOARDING
WAKEBOARDINGS
WAKEBOARDS
WAKEFULNESS
WAKEFULNESSES
WALDFLUTES
WALDGRAVES
WALDGRAVINE
WALDGRAVINES
WALDSTERBEN
WALDSTERBENS
WALKABOUTS
WALKATHONS
WALKINGSTICK
WALKINGSTICKS
WALKSHORTS
WALLBOARDS
WALLCHARTS
WALLCLIMBER
WALLCLIMBERS
WALLCOVERING
WALLCOVERINGS
WALLFISHES
WALLFLOWER
WALLFLOWERS
WALLOPINGS
WALLOWINGS
WALLPAPERED
WALLPAPERING
WALLPAPERS
WALLPOSTER
WALLPOSTERS
WALLYBALLS
WALLYDRAGS
WALLYDRAIGLE
WALLYDRAIGLES
WALNUTWOOD
WALNUTWOODS
WAMBENGERS
WAMBLINESS
WAMBLINESSES
WAMBLINGLY
WAMPISHING
WAMPUMPEAG
WAMPUMPEAGS
WANCHANCIE
WANDERINGLY
WANDERINGS
WANDERLUST
WANDERLUSTS
WANRESTFUL
WANTHRIVEN
WANTONISED

WANTONISES
WANTONISING
WANTONIZED
WANTONIZES
WANTONIZING
WANTONNESS
WANTONNESSES
WAPENSCHAW
WAPENSCHAWS
WAPENSHAWS
WAPENTAKES
WAPINSCHAW
WAPINSCHAWS
WAPINSHAWS
WAPPENSCHAW
WAPPENSCHAWING
WAPPENSCHAWINGS
WAPPENSCHAWS
WAPPENSHAW
WAPPENSHAWING
WAPPENSHAWINGS
WAPPENSHAWS
WARBLINGLY
WARBONNETS
WARCHALKER
WARCHALKERS
WARCHALKING
WARCHALKINGS
WARDENRIES
WARDENSHIP
WARDENSHIPS
WARDERSHIP
WARDERSHIPS
WARDRESSES
WARDROBERS
WARDROBING
WAREHOUSED
WAREHOUSEMAN
WAREHOUSEMEN
WAREHOUSER
WAREHOUSERS
WAREHOUSES
WAREHOUSING
WAREHOUSINGS
WARFARINGS
WARIBASHIS
WARINESSES
WARLIKENESS
WARLIKENESSES
WARLOCKRIES
WARLORDISM
WARLORDISMS
WARMBLOODS
WARMHEARTED
WARMHEARTEDNESS

WARMNESSES
WARMONGERING
WARMONGERINGS
WARMONGERS
WARRANDICE
WARRANDICES
WARRANDING
WARRANTABILITY
WARRANTABLE
WARRANTABLENESS
WARRANTABLY
WARRANTEES
WARRANTERS
WARRANTIED
WARRANTIES
WARRANTING
WARRANTINGS
WARRANTISE
WARRANTISES
WARRANTLESS
WARRANTORS
WARRANTYING
WARRIORESS
WARRIORESSES
WASHABILITIES
WASHABILITY
WASHATERIA
WASHATERIAS
WASHBASINS
WASHBOARDS
WASHCLOTHS
WASHERWOMAN
WASHERWOMEN
WASHETERIA
WASHETERIAS
WASHHOUSES
WASHINESSES
WASHINGTONIA
WASHINGTONIAS
WASHSTANDS
WASPINESSES
WASPISHNESS
WASPISHNESSES
WASSAILERS
WASSAILING
WASSAILINGS
WASSAILRIES
WASTEBASKET
WASTEBASKETS
WASTEFULLY
WASTEFULNESS
WASTEFULNESSES
WASTELANDS
WASTENESSES
WASTEPAPER

WASTEPAPERS	WATERFINDER	WATERTHRUSH	WEAPONLESS
WASTERFULLY	WATERFINDERS	WATERTHRUSHES	WEAPONRIES
WASTERFULNESS	WATERFLOOD	WATERTIGHT	WEARABILITIES
WASTERFULNESSES	WATERFLOODED	WATERTIGHTNESS	WEARABILITY
WASTEWATER	WATERFLOODING	WATERWEEDS	WEARIFULLY
WASTEWATERS	WATERFLOODINGS	WATERWHEEL	WEARIFULNESS
WASTEWEIRS	WATERFLOODS	WATERWHEELS	WEARIFULNESSES
WASTNESSES	WATERFOWLER	WATERWORKS	WEARILESSLY
WATCHABLES	WATERFOWLERS	WATERZOOIS	WEARINESSES
WATCHBANDS	WATERFOWLING	WATTLEBARK	WEARISOMELY
WATCHBOXES	WATERFOWLINGS	WATTLEBARKS	WEARISOMENESS
WATCHCASES	WATERFOWLS	WATTLEBIRD	WEARISOMENESSES
WATCHCRIES	WATERFRONT	WATTLEBIRDS	WEARYINGLY
WATCHDOGGED	WATERFRONTS	WATTLEWORK	WEASELLERS
WATCHDOGGING	WATERGLASS	WATTLEWORKS	WEASELLING
WATCHFULLY	WATERGLASSES	WATTMETERS	WEATHERABILITY
WATCHFULNESS	WATERHEADS	WAULKMILLS	WEATHERABLE
WATCHFULNESSES	WATERINESS	WAVEFRONTS	WEATHERBOARD
WATCHGLASS	WATERINESSES	WAVEGUIDES	WEATHERBOARDED
WATCHGLASSES	WATERISHNESS	WAVELENGTH	WEATHERBOARDING
WATCHGUARD	WATERISHNESSES	WAVELENGTHS	WEATHERBOARDS
WATCHGUARDS	WATERLEAFS	WAVELESSLY	WEATHERCAST
WATCHLISTS	WATERLESSNESS	WAVELLITES	WEATHERCASTER
WATCHMAKER	WATERLESSNESSES	WAVEMETERS	WEATHERCASTERS
WATCHMAKERS	WATERLILIES	WAVERINGLY	WEATHERCASTS
WATCHMAKING	WATERLINES	WAVERINGNESS	WEATHERCLOTH
WATCHMAKINGS	WATERLOGGED	WAVERINGNESSES	WEATHERCLOTHS
WATCHSPRING	WATERLOGGING	WAVESHAPES	WEATHERCOCK
WATCHSPRINGS	WATERMANSHIP	WAVINESSES	WEATHERCOCKED
WATCHSTRAP	WATERMANSHIPS	WAXBERRIES	WEATHERCOCKING
WATCHSTRAPS	WATERMARKED	WAXFLOWERS	WEATHERCOCKS
WATCHTOWER	WATERMARKING	WAXINESSES	WEATHERERS
WATCHTOWERS	WATERMARKS	WAXWORKERS	WEATHERGIRL
WATCHWORDS	WATERMELON	WAYFARINGS	WEATHERGIRLS
WATERBIRDS	WATERMELONS	WAYMARKING	WEATHERGLASS
WATERBORNE	WATERPOWER	WAYMENTING	WEATHERGLASSES
WATERBRAIN	WATERPOWERS	WAYWARDNESS	WEATHERING
WATERBRAINS	WATERPOXES	WAYWARDNESSES	WEATHERINGS
WATERBUCKS	WATERPROOF	WAYZGOOSES	WEATHERISATION
WATERBUSES	WATERPROOFED	WEAKFISHES	WEATHERISATIONS
WATERBUSSES	WATERPROOFER	WEAKHEARTED	WEATHERISE
WATERCOLOR	WATERPROOFERS	WEAKISHNESS	WEATHERISED
WATERCOLORIST	WATERPROOFING	WEAKISHNESSES	WEATHERISES
WATERCOLORISTS	WATERPROOFINGS	WEAKLINESS	WEATHERISING
WATERCOLORS	WATERPROOFNESS	WEAKLINESSES	WEATHERIZATION
WATERCOLOUR	WATERPROOFS	WEAKNESSES	WEATHERIZATIONS
WATERCOLOURIST	WATERQUAKE	WEALTHIEST	WEATHERIZE
WATERCOLOURISTS	WATERQUAKES	WEALTHINESS	WEATHERIZED
WATERCOLOURS	WATERSCAPE	WEALTHINESSES	WEATHERIZES
WATERCOOLER	WATERSCAPES	WEALTHLESS	WEATHERIZING
WATERCOOLERS	WATERSHEDS	WEAPONEERED	WEATHERLINESS
WATERCOURSE	WATERSIDER	WEAPONEERING	WEATHERLINESSES
WATERCOURSES	WATERSIDERS	WEAPONEERINGS	WEATHERMAN
WATERCRAFT	WATERSIDES	WEAPONEERS	WEATHERMEN
WATERCRAFTS	WATERSKIING	WEAPONISED	WEATHERMOST
WATERCRESS	WATERSKIINGS	WEAPONISES	WEATHEROMETER
WATERCRESSES	WATERSMEET	WEAPONISING	WEATHEROMETERS
WATERDRIVE	WATERSMEETS	WEAPONIZED	WEATHERPERSON
WATERDRIVES	WATERSPOUT	WEAPONIZES	WEATHERPERSONS
WATERFALLS	WATERSPOUTS	WEAPONIZING	WEATHERPROOF

WEATHERPROOFED
WEATHERPROOFING
WEATHERPROOFS
WEATHERWORN
WEAVERBIRD
WEAVERBIRDS
WEBCASTERS
WEBCASTING
WEBLOGGERS
WEBMASTERS
WEEDICIDES
WEEDINESSES
WEEDKILLER
WEEDKILLERS
WEEKENDERS
WEEKENDING
WEEKENDINGS
WEEKNIGHTS
WEELDLESSE
WEEPINESSES
WEIGHBOARD
WEIGHBOARDS
WEIGHBRIDGE
WEIGHBRIDGES
WEIGHTIEST
WEIGHTINESS
WEIGHTINESSES
WEIGHTINGS
WEIGHTLESS
WEIGHTLESSLY
WEIGHTLESSNESS
WEIGHTLIFTER
WEIGHTLIFTERS
WEIGHTLIFTING
WEIGHTLIFTINGS
WEIMARANER
WEIMARANERS
WEIRDNESSES
WEISENHEIMER
WEISENHEIMERS
WELCOMENESS
WELCOMENESSES
WELCOMINGLY
WELDABILITIES
WELDABILITY
WELDMESHES
WELFARISMS
WELFARISTIC
WELFARISTS
WELLBEINGS
WELLHOUSES
WELLINGTON
WELLINGTONIA
WELLINGTONIAS
WELLINGTONS
WELLNESSES
WELLSPRING
WELLSPRINGS
WELTANSCHAUUNG
WELTANSCHAUUNGS

WELTERWEIGHT
WELTERWEIGHTS
WELTSCHMERZ
WELTSCHMERZES
WELWITSCHIA
WELWITSCHIAS
WENSLEYDALE
WENSLEYDALES
WENTLETRAP
WENTLETRAPS
WEREWOLFERIES
WEREWOLFERY
WEREWOLFISH
WEREWOLFISM
WEREWOLFISMS
WEREWOLVES
WERNERITES
WERWOLFISH
WESTERINGS
WESTERLIES
WESTERLINESS
WESTERLINESSES
WESTERNERS
WESTERNISATION
WESTERNISATIONS
WESTERNISE
WESTERNISED
WESTERNISES
WESTERNISING
WESTERNISM
WESTERNISMS
WESTERNIZATION
WESTERNIZATIONS
WESTERNIZE
WESTERNIZED
WESTERNIZES
WESTERNIZING
WESTERNMOST
WESTWARDLY
WETTABILITIES
WETTABILITY
WHAIKORERO
WHAIKOREROS
WHAKAPAPAS
WHALEBACKS
WHALEBOATS
WHALEBONES
WHAREPUNIS
WHARFINGER
WHARFINGERS
WHARFMASTER
WHARFMASTERS
WHATABOUTS
WHATCHAMACALLIT
WHATNESSES
WHATSHERNAME
WHATSHERNAMES
WHATSHISNAME
WHATSHISNAMES
WHATSITSNAME

WHATSITSNAMES
WHATSOEVER
WHATSOMEVER
WHEATFIELD
WHEATFIELDS
WHEATGRASS
WHEATGRASSES
WHEATLANDS
WHEATMEALS
WHEATSHEAF
WHEATSHEAVES
WHEATWORMS
WHEEDLESOME
WHEEDLINGLY
WHEEDLINGS
WHEELBARROW
WHEELBARROWED
WHEELBARROWING
WHEELBARROWS
WHEELBASES
WHEELCHAIR
WHEELCHAIRS
WHEELHORSE
WHEELHORSES
WHEELHOUSE
WHEELHOUSES
WHEELWORKS
WHEELWRIGHT
WHEELWRIGHTS
WHEESHTING
WHEEZINESS
WHEEZINESSES
WHENCEFORTH
WHENCESOEVER
WHENSOEVER
WHEREABOUT
WHEREABOUTS
WHEREAFTER
WHEREAGAINST
WHEREFORES
WHEREINSOEVER
WHERENESSES
WHERESOEER
WHERESOEVER
WHERETHROUGH
WHEREUNDER
WHEREUNTIL
WHEREWITHAL
WHEREWITHALS
WHEREWITHS
WHERRETING
WHERRITING
WHETSTONES
WHEWELLITE
WHEWELLITES
WHEYISHNESS
WHEYISHNESSES
WHICHSOEVER
WHICKERING
WHIDDERING

WHIFFLERIES
WHIFFLETREE
WHIFFLETREES
WHIFFLINGS
WHIGGAMORE
WHIGGAMORES
WHIGMALEERIE
WHIGMALEERIES
WHIGMALEERY
WHILLYWHAED
WHILLYWHAING
WHILLYWHAS
WHILLYWHAW
WHILLYWHAWED
WHILLYWHAWING
WHILLYWHAWS
WHIMBERRIES
WHIMPERERS
WHIMPERING
WHIMPERINGLY
WHIMPERINGS
WHIMSICALITIES
WHIMSICALITY
WHIMSICALLY
WHIMSICALNESS
WHIMSICALNESSES
WHIMSINESS
WHIMSINESSES
WHINBERRIES
WHINGDINGS
WHINGEINGS
WHININESSES
WHINSTONES
WHIPLASHED
WHIPLASHES
WHIPLASHING
WHIPPERSNAPPER
WHIPPERSNAPPERS
WHIPPETING
WHIPPETINGS
WHIPPINESS
WHIPPINESSES
WHIPPLETREE
WHIPPLETREES
WHIPPOORWILL
WHIPPOORWILLS
WHIPSAWING
WHIPSNAKES
WHIPSTAFFS
WHIPSTALLED
WHIPSTALLING
WHIPSTALLS
WHIPSTITCH
WHIPSTITCHED
WHIPSTITCHES
WHIPSTITCHING
WHIPSTOCKS
WHIPTAILED
WHIRLABOUT
WHIRLABOUTS

WHIRLBLAST	WHITHERING	WICKEDNESS	WILLOWLIKE
WHIRLBLASTS	WHITHERSOEVER	WICKEDNESSES	WILLOWWARE
WHIRLIGIGS	WHITHERWARD	WICKERWORK	WILLOWWARES
WHIRLINGLY	WHITHERWARDS	WICKERWORKS	WILLPOWERS
WHIRLPOOLS	WHITISHNESS	WICKETKEEPER	WIMPINESSES
WHIRLWINDS	WHITISHNESSES	WICKETKEEPERS	WIMPISHNESS
WHIRLYBIRD	WHITLEATHER	WICKTHINGS	WIMPISHNESSES
WHIRLYBIRDS	WHITLEATHERS	WIDDERSHINS	WINCEYETTE
WHIRRETING	WHITTAWERS	WIDEAWAKES	WINCEYETTES
WHISKERANDO	WHITTERICK	WIDEBODIES	WINCHESTER
WHISKERANDOED	WHITTERICKS	WIDECHAPPED	WINCHESTERS
WHISKERANDOS	WHITTERING	WIDEMOUTHED	WINCOPIPES
WHISKEYFIED	WHITTLINGS	WIDENESSES	WINDBAGGERIES
WHISKIFIED	WHIZZBANGS	WIDERSHINS	WINDBAGGERY
WHISPERERS	WHIZZINGLY	WIDESCREEN	WINDBLASTS
WHISPERING	WHODUNITRIES	WIDESPREAD	WINDBREAKER
WHISPERINGLY	WHODUNITRY	WIDOWBIRDS	WINDBREAKERS
WHISPERINGS	WHODUNNITRIES	WIDOWERHOOD	WINDBREAKS
WHISPEROUSLY	WHODUNNITRY	WIDOWERHOODS	WINDBURNED
WHISTLEABLE	WHODUNNITS	WIDOWHOODS	WINDBURNING
WHISTLINGLY	WHOLEFOODS	WIELDINESS	WINDCHEATER
WHISTLINGS	WHOLEGRAIN	WIELDINESSES	WINDCHEATERS
WHITEBAITS	WHOLEHEARTED	WIENERWURST	WINDCHILLS
WHITEBASSES	WHOLEHEARTEDLY	WIENERWURSTS	WINDFALLEN
WHITEBEAMS	WHOLEMEALS	WIFELINESS	WINDFLOWER
WHITEBEARD	WHOLENESSES	WIFELINESSES	WINDFLOWERS
WHITEBEARDS	WHOLESALED	WIGWAGGERS	WINDGALLED
WHITEBOARD	WHOLESALER	WIGWAGGING	WINDHOVERS
WHITEBOARDS	WHOLESALERS	WILDCATTED	WINDINESSES
WHITEBOYISM	WHOLESALES	WILDCATTER	WINDJAMMER
WHITEBOYISMS	WHOLESALING	WILDCATTERS	WINDJAMMERS
WHITECOATS	WHOLESOMELY	WILDCATTING	WINDJAMMING
WHITECOMBS	WHOLESOMENESS	WILDEBEEST	WINDJAMMINGS
WHITEDAMPS	WHOLESOMENESSES	WILDEBEESTS	WINDLASSED
WHITEFACES	WHOLESOMER	WILDERMENT	WINDLASSES
WHITEFISHES	WHOLESOMEST	WILDERMENTS	WINDLASSING
WHITEFLIES	WHOLESTITCH	WILDERNESS	WINDLESSLY
WHITEHEADS	WHOLESTITCHES	WILDERNESSES	WINDLESSNESS
WHITENESSES	WHOLEWHEAT	WILDFLOWER	WINDLESSNESSES
WHITENINGS	WHOMSOEVER	WILDFLOWERS	WINDLESTRAE
WHITESMITH	WHOREHOUSE	WILDFOWLER	WINDLESTRAES
WHITESMITHS	WHOREHOUSES	WILDFOWLERS	WINDLESTRAW
WHITETAILS	WHOREMASTER	WILDFOWLING	WINDLESTRAWS
WHITETHORN	WHOREMASTERIES	WILDFOWLINGS	WINDMILLED
WHITETHORNS	WHOREMASTERLY	WILDGRAVES	WINDMILLING
WHITETHROAT	WHOREMASTERS	WILDNESSES	WINDOWINGS
WHITETHROATS	WHOREMASTERY	WILFULNESS	WINDOWLESS
WHITEWALLS	WHOREMISTRESS	WILFULNESSES	WINDOWPANE
WHITEWARES	WHOREMISTRESSES	WILINESSES	WINDOWPANES
WHITEWASHED	WHOREMONGER	WILLEMITES	WINDOWSILL
WHITEWASHER	WHOREMONGERIES	WILLFULNESS	WINDOWSILLS
WHITEWASHERS	WHOREMONGERS	WILLFULNESSES	WINDROWERS
WHITEWASHES	WHOREMONGERY	WILLIEWAUGHT	WINDROWING
WHITEWASHING	WHORISHNESS	WILLIEWAUGHTS	WINDSCREEN
WHITEWASHINGS	WHORISHNESSES	WILLINGEST	WINDSCREENS
WHITEWATER	WHORTLEBERRIES	WILLINGNESS	WINDSHAKES
WHITEWINGS	WHORTLEBERRY	WILLINGNESSES	WINDSHIELD
WHITEWOODS	WHOSESOEVER	WILLOWHERB	WINDSHIELDS
WHITEYWOOD	WHUNSTANES	WILLOWHERBS	WINDSTORMS
WHITEYWOODS	WHYDUNNITS	WILLOWIEST	WINDSUCKER

WINDSUCKERS	WINTERLESS	WITCHHOODS	WOLFBERRIES
WINDSURFED	WINTERLINESS	WITCHINGLY	WOLFFISHES
WINDSURFER	WINTERLINESSES	WTTCHKNOTS	WOLFHOUNDS
WINDSURFERS	WINTERTIDE	WITCHWEEDS	WOLFISHNESS
WINDSURFING	WINTERTIDES	WITENAGEMOT	WOLFISHNESSES
WINDSURFINGS	WINTERTIME	WITENAGEMOTE	WOLFRAMITE
WINDTHROWS	WINTERTIMES	WITENAGEMOTES	WOLFRAMITES
WINEBERRIES	WINTERWEIGHT	WITENAGEMOTS	WOLFSBANES
WINEBIBBER	WINTRINESS	WITGATBOOM	WOLLASTONITE
WINEBIBBERS	WINTRINESSES	WITGATBOOMS	WOLLASTONITES
WINEBIBBING	WIREDRAWER	WITHDRAWABLE	WOLVERENES
WINEBIBBINGS	WIREDRAWERS	WITHDRAWAL	WOLVERINES
WINEGLASSES	WIREDRAWING	WITHDRAWALS	WOMANFULLY
WINEGLASSFUL	WIREDRAWINGS	WITHDRAWER	WOMANHOODS
WINEGLASSFULS	WIREGRASSES	WITHDRAWERS	WOMANISERS
WINEGROWER	WIREHAIRED	WITHDRAWING	WOMANISHLY
WINEGROWERS	WIRELESSED	WITHDRAWMENT	WOMANISHNESS
WINEMAKERS	WIRELESSES	WITHDRAWMENTS	WOMANISHNESSES
WINEPRESSES	WIRELESSING	WITHDRAWNNESS	WOMANISING
WINGCHAIRS	WIREPHOTOS	WITHDRAWNNESSES	WOMANISINGS
WINGLESSNESS	WIREPULLER	WITHEREDNESS	WOMANIZERS
WINGLESSNESSES	WIREPULLERS	WITHEREDNESSES	WOMANIZING
WINGSPREAD	WIREPULLING	WITHERINGLY	WOMANIZINGS
WINGSPREADS	WIREPULLINGS	WITHERINGS	WOMANKINDS
WINNABILITIES	WIRETAPPED	WITHERITES	WOMANLIEST
WINNABILITY	WIRETAPPER	WITHERSHINS	WOMANLINESS
WINNINGNESS	WIRETAPPERS	WITHHOLDEN	WOMANLINESSES
WINNINGNESSES	WIRETAPPING	WITHHOLDER	WOMANNESSES
WINNOWINGS	WIRETAPPINGS	WITHHOLDERS	WOMANPOWER
WINSOMENESS	WIREWALKER	WITHHOLDING	WOMANPOWERS
WINSOMENESSES	WIREWALKERS	WITHHOLDMENT	WOMENFOLKS
WINTERBERRIES	WIREWORKER	WITHHOLDMENTS	WOMENKINDS
WINTERBERRY	WIREWORKERS	WITHINDOORS	WOMENSWEAR
WINTERBOURNE	WIREWORKING	WITHOUTDOORS	WOMENSWEARS
WINTERBOURNES	WIREWORKINGS	WITHSTANDER	WONDERFULLY
WINTERCRESS	WIRINESSES	WITHSTANDERS	WONDERFULNESS
WINTERCRESSES	WISECRACKED	WITHSTANDING	WONDERFULNESSES
WINTERFEED	WISECRACKER	WITHSTANDS	WONDERINGLY
WINTERFEEDING	WISECRACKERS	WITHYWINDS	WONDERINGS
WINTERFEEDS	WISECRACKING	WITLESSNESS	WONDERKIDS
WINTERGREEN	WISECRACKS	WITLESSNESSES	WONDERLAND
WINTERGREENS	WISENESSES	WITNESSABLE	WONDERLANDS
WINTERIEST	WISENHEIMER	WITNESSERS	WONDERLESS
WINTERINESS	WISENHEIMERS	WITNESSING	WONDERMENT
WINTERINESSES	WISHFULNESS	WITTICISMS	WONDERMENTS
WINTERISATION	WISHFULNESSES	WITTINESSES	WONDERMONGER
WINTERISATIONS	WISHTONWISH	WITWANTONED	WONDERMONGERING
WINTERISED	WISHTONWISHES	WITWANTONING	WONDERMONGERS
WINTERISES	WISPINESSES	WITWANTONS	WONDERWORK
WINTERISING	WISTFULNESS	WIZARDRIES	WONDERWORKS
WINTERIZATION	WISTFULNESSES	WOADWAXENS	WONDROUSLY
WINTERIZATIONS	WITBLITSES	WOBBEGONGS	WONDROUSNESS
WINTERIZED	WITCHBROOM	WOBBLINESS	WONDROUSNESSES
WINTERIZES	WITCHBROOMS	WOBBLINESSES	WONTEDNESS
WINTERIZING	WITCHCRAFT	WOEBEGONENESS	WONTEDNESSES
WINTERKILL	WITCHCRAFTS	WOEBEGONENESSES	WOODBLOCKS
WINTERKILLED	WITCHERIES	WOEFULLEST	WOODBORERS
WINTERKILLING	WITCHETTIES	WOEFULNESS	WOODBURYTYPE
WINTERKILLINGS	WITCHGRASS	WOEFULNESSES	WOODBURYTYPES
WINTERKILLS	WITCHGRASSES	WOFULNESSES	WOODCARVER

WOODCARVERS

WOODCARVERS
WOODCARVING
WOODCARVINGS
WOODCHOPPER
WOODCHOPPERS
WOODCHUCKS
WOODCRAFTS
WOODCRAFTSMAN
WOODCRAFTSMEN
WOODCUTTER
WOODCUTTERS
WOODCUTTING
WOODCUTTINGS
WOODENHEAD
WOODENHEADED
WOODENHEADS
WOODENNESS
WOODENNESSES
WOODENTOPS
WOODENWARE
WOODENWARES
WOODGRAINS
WOODGROUSE
WOODGROUSES
WOODHORSES
WOODHOUSES
WOODINESSES
WOODLANDER
WOODLANDERS
WOODLESSNESS
WOODLESSNESSES
WOODNESSES
WOODPECKER
WOODPECKERS
WOODPIGEON
WOODPIGEONS
WOODPRINTS
WOODREEVES
WOODRUSHES
WOODSCREWS
WOODSHEDDED
WOODSHEDDING
WOODSHEDDINGS
WOODSHOCKS
WOODSHRIKE
WOODSHRIKES
WOODSPITES
WOODSTONES
WOODSTOVES
WOODSWALLOW
WOODSWALLOWS
WOODTHRUSH
WOODTHRUSHES
WOODWAXENS
WOODWORKER
WOODWORKERS
WOODWORKING
WOODWORKINGS
WOOLGATHERER
WOOLGATHERERS

WOOLGATHERING
WOOLGATHERINGS
WOOLGROWER
WOOLGROWERS
WOOLGROWING
WOOLGROWINGS
WOOLINESSES
WOOLLINESS
WOOLLINESSES
WOOLLYBACK
WOOLLYBACKS
WOOLLYBUTT
WOOLLYBUTTS
WOOLLYFOOT
WOOLLYFOOTS
WOOLSORTER
WOOLSORTERS
WOOMERANGS
WOOZINESSES
WORCESTERBERRY
WORCESTERS
WORDBREAKS
WORDINESSES
WORDISHNESS
WORDISHNESSES
WORDLESSLY
WORDLESSNESS
WORDLESSNESSES
WORDMONGER
WORDMONGERS
WORDSEARCH
WORDSEARCHES
WORDSMITHERIES
WORDSMITHERY
WORDSMITHS
WORKABILITIES
WORKABILITY
WORKABLENESS
WORKABLENESSES
WORKAHOLIC
WORKAHOLICS
WORKAHOLISM
WORKAHOLISMS
WORKAROUND
WORKAROUNDS
WORKBASKET
WORKBASKETS
WORKBENCHES
WORKERISTS
WORKERLESS
WORKFELLOW
WORKFELLOWS
WORKFORCES
WORKGROUPS
WORKHORSES
WORKHOUSES
WORKINGMAN
WORKINGMEN
WORKINGWOMAN
WORKINGWOMEN

WORKLESSNESS
WORKLESSNESSES
WORKMANLIKE
WORKMANSHIP
WORKMANSHIPS
WORKMASTER
WORKMASTERS
WORKMISTRESS
WORKMISTRESSES
WORKPEOPLE
WORKPIECES
WORKPLACES
WORKPRINTS
WORKSHEETS
WORKSHOPPED
WORKSHOPPING
WORKSPACES
WORKSTATION
WORKSTATIONS
WORKTABLES
WORKWATCHER
WORKWATCHERS
WORLDBEATS
WORLDLIEST
WORLDLINESS
WORLDLINESSES
WORLDLINGS
WORLDSCALE
WORLDSCALES
WORLDVIEWS
WORMINESSES
WORNNESSES
WORRIMENTS
WORRISOMELY
WORRISOMENESS
WORRISOMENESSES
WORRYINGLY
WORRYWARTS
WORSENESSES
WORSHIPABLE
WORSHIPERS
WORSHIPFUL
WORSHIPFULLY
WORSHIPFULNESS
WORSHIPING
WORSHIPLESS
WORSHIPPED
WORSHIPPER
WORSHIPPERS
WORSHIPPING
WORTHINESS
WORTHINESSES
WORTHLESSLY
WORTHLESSNESS
WORTHLESSNESSES
WORTHWHILE
WORTHWHILENESS
WOUNDINGLY
WOUNDWORTS
WRAITHLIKE

WRANGLERSHIP
WRANGLERSHIPS
WRANGLESOME
WRANGLINGS
WRAPAROUND
WRAPAROUNDS
WRAPPERING
WRAPROUNDS
WRATHFULLY
WRATHFULNESS
WRATHFULNESSES
WRATHINESS
WRATHINESSES
WREATHIEST
WREATHLESS
WREATHLIKE
WRECKFISHES
WRECKMASTER
WRECKMASTERS
WRENCHINGLY
WRENCHINGS
WRESTLINGS
WRETCHEDER
WRETCHEDEST
WRETCHEDLY
WRETCHEDNESS
WRETCHEDNESSES
WRIGGLIEST
WRIGGLINGS
WRINKLELESS
WRINKLIEST
WRISTBANDS
WRISTLOCKS
WRISTWATCH
WRISTWATCHES
WRITERESSES
WRITERSHIP
WRITERSHIPS
WRITHINGLY
WRONGDOERS
WRONGDOING
WRONGDOINGS
WRONGFULLY
WRONGFULNESS
WRONGFULNESSES
WRONGHEADED
WRONGHEADEDLY
WRONGHEADEDNESS
WRONGNESSES
WRONGOUSLY
WULFENITES
WUNDERKIND
WUNDERKINDER
WUNDERKINDS
WYANDOTTES
WYLIECOATS

X

XANTHATION
XANTHATIONS
XANTHOCHROIA
XANTHOCHROIAS
XANTHOCHROIC
XANTHOCHROID
XANTHOCHROIDS
XANTHOCHROISM
XANTHOCHROISMS
XANTHOCHROMIA
XANTHOCHROMIAS
XANTHOCHROOUS
XANTHOMATA
XANTHOMATOUS
XANTHOMELANOUS
XANTHOPHYL
XANTHOPHYLL
XANTHOPHYLLOUS
XANTHOPHYLLS
XANTHOPHYLS
XANTHOPSIA
XANTHOPSIAS
XANTHOPTERIN
XANTHOPTERINE
XANTHOPTERINES
XANTHOPTERINS
XANTHOXYLS
XENARTHRAL
XENOBIOTIC
XENOBIOTICS
XENOBLASTS
XENOCRYSTS
XENODIAGNOSES
XENODIAGNOSIS
XENODIAGNOSTIC
XENODOCHIUM
XENODOCHIUMS
XENOGAMIES
XENOGAMOUS
XENOGENEIC
XENOGENESES
XENOGENESIS
XENOGENETIC
XENOGENIES
XENOGENOUS
XENOGLOSSIA
XENOGLOSSIAS
XENOGLOSSIES
XENOGLOSSY
XENOGRAFTS
XENOLITHIC
XENOMANIAS
XENOMENIAS

XENOMORPHIC
XENOMORPHICALLY
XENOPHILES
XENOPHOBES
XENOPHOBIA
XENOPHOBIAS
XENOPHOBIC
XENOPHOBICALLY
XENOPHOBIES
XENOPLASTIC
XENOTRANSPLANT
XENOTRANSPLANTS
XENOTROPIC
XERANTHEMUM
XERANTHEMUMS
XERISCAPES
XEROCHASIES
XERODERMAE
XERODERMAS
XERODERMATIC
XERODERMATOUS
XERODERMIA
XERODERMIAS
XERODERMIC
XEROGRAPHER
XEROGRAPHERS
XEROGRAPHIC
XEROGRAPHICALLY
XEROGRAPHIES
XEROGRAPHY
XEROMORPHIC
XEROMORPHOUS
XEROMORPHS
XEROPHAGIES
XEROPHILES
XEROPHILIES
XEROPHILOUS
XEROPHTHALMIA
XEROPHTHALMIAS
XEROPHTHALMIC
XEROPHYTES
XEROPHYTIC
XEROPHYTICALLY
XEROPHYTISM
XEROPHYTISMS
XERORADIOGRAPHY
XEROSTOMAS
XEROSTOMATA
XEROSTOMIA
XEROSTOMIAS
XEROTHERMIC
XEROTRIPSES
XEROTRIPSIS

XIPHIHUMERALIS
XIPHIPLASTRA
XIPHIPLASTRAL
XIPHIPLASTRALS
XIPHIPLASTRON
XIPHISTERNA
XIPHISTERNUM
XIPHISTERNUMS
XIPHOPAGIC
XIPHOPAGOUS
XIPHOPAGUS
XIPHOPAGUSES
XIPHOPHYLLOUS
XIPHOSURAN
XIPHOSURANS
XYLOBALSAMUM
XYLOBALSAMUMS
XYLOCARPOUS
XYLOCHROME
XYLOCHROMES
XYLOGENOUS
XYLOGRAPHED
XYLOGRAPHER
XYLOGRAPHERS
XYLOGRAPHIC
XYLOGRAPHICAL
XYLOGRAPHIES
XYLOGRAPHING
XYLOGRAPHS
XYLOGRAPHY
XYLOIDINES
XYLOLOGIES
XYLOMETERS
XYLOPHAGAN
XYLOPHAGANS
XYLOPHAGES
XYLOPHAGOUS
XYLOPHILOUS
XYLOPHONES
XYLOPHONIC
XYLOPHONIST
XYLOPHONISTS
XYLOPYROGRAPHY
XYLORIMBAS
XYLOTOMIES
XYLOTOMIST
XYLOTOMISTS
XYLOTOMOUS
XYLOTYPOGRAPHIC
XYLOTYPOGRAPHY
XYRIDACEOUS

Y

YACHTSMANSHIP
YACHTSMANSHIPS
YACHTSWOMAN
YACHTSWOMEN
YAFFINGALE
YAFFINGALES
YAMMERINGS
YARBOROUGH
YARBOROUGHS
YARDMASTER
YARDMASTERS
YARDSTICKS
YATTERINGLY
YATTERINGS
YEARNINGLY
YEASTINESS
YEASTINESSES
YELLOCHING
YELLOWBACK
YELLOWBACKS
YELLOWBARK
YELLOWBARKS
YELLOWBIRD
YELLOWBIRDS
YELLOWCAKE
YELLOWCAKES
YELLOWFINS
YELLOWHAMMER
YELLOWHAMMERS
YELLOWHEAD
YELLOWHEADS
YELLOWIEST
YELLOWISHNESS
YELLOWISHNESSES
YELLOWLEGS
YELLOWNESS
YELLOWNESSES
YELLOWTAIL
YELLOWTAILS
YELLOWTHROAT
YELLOWTHROATS
YELLOWWARE
YELLOWWARES
YELLOWWEED
YELLOWWEEDS
YELLOWWOOD
YELLOWWOODS
YELLOWWORT
YELLOWWORTS
YEOMANRIES
YERSINIOSES
YERSINIOSIS
YESTERDAYS

YESTEREVEN
YESTEREVENING
YESTEREVENINGS
YESTEREVENS
YESTEREVES
YESTERMORN
YESTERMORNING
YESTERMORNINGS
YESTERMORNS
YESTERNIGHT
YESTERNIGHTS
YESTERYEAR
YESTERYEARS
YIELDABLENESS
YIELDABLENESSES
YIELDINGLY
YIELDINGNESS
YIELDINGNESSES
YOCTOSECOND
YOCTOSECONDS
YOHIMBINES
YOKEFELLOW
YOKEFELLOWS
YOTTABYTES
YOUNGBERRIES
YOUNGBERRY
YOUNGLINGS
YOUNGNESSES
YOUNGSTERS
YOURSELVES
YOUTHENING
YOUTHFULLY
YOUTHFULNESS
YOUTHFULNESSES
YOUTHHEADS
YOUTHHOODS
YOUTHQUAKE
YOUTHQUAKES
YPSILIFORM
YTHUNDERED
YTTERBITES
YTTERBIUMS
YTTRIFEROUS
YUCKINESSES
YUMMINESSES
YUPPIEDOMS
YUPPIFICATION
YUPPIFICATIONS
YUPPIFYING

Z

ZABAGLIONE
ZABAGLIONES
ZALAMBDODONT
ZALAMBDODONTS
ZAMBOORAKS
ZAMINDARIES
ZAMINDARIS
ZANINESSES
ZANTEDESCHIA
ZANTEDESCHIAS
ZANTHOXYLS
ZANTHOXYLUM
ZANTHOXYLUMS
ZAPATEADOS
ZAPOTILLAS
ZEALOTISMS
ZEALOTRIES
ZEALOUSNESS
ZEALOUSNESSES
ZEBRAFISHES
ZEBRAWOODS
ZEBRINNIES
ZEITGEBERS
ZEITGEISTS
ZELATRICES
ZELATRIXES
ZELOPHOBIA
ZELOPHOBIAS
ZELOPHOBIC
ZELOPHOBICS
ZELOTYPIAS
ZEMINDARIES
ZEMINDARIS
ZEOLITIFORM
ZEPTOSECOND
ZEPTOSECONDS
ZESTFULNESS
ZESTFULNESSES
ZETTABYTES
ZEUGLODONT
ZEUGLODONTS
ZEUGMATICALLY
ZIBELLINES
ZIDOVUDINE
ZIDOVUDINES
ZIGZAGGEDNESS
ZIGZAGGEDNESSES
ZIGZAGGERIES
ZIGZAGGERS
ZIGZAGGERY
ZIGZAGGING
ZILLIONAIRE
ZILLIONAIRES

ZILLIONTHS
ZINCIFEROUS
ZINCIFICATION
ZINCIFICATIONS
ZINCIFYING
ZINCKENITE
ZINCKENITES
ZINCKIFICATION
ZINCKIFICATIONS
ZINCKIFIED
ZINCKIFIES
ZINCKIFYING
ZINCOGRAPH
ZINCOGRAPHER
ZINCOGRAPHERS
ZINCOGRAPHIC
ZINCOGRAPHICAL
ZINCOGRAPHIES
ZINCOGRAPHS
ZINCOGRAPHY
ZINCOLYSES
ZINCOLYSIS
ZINFANDELS
ZINGIBERACEOUS
ZINJANTHROPI
ZINJANTHROPUS
ZINJANTHROPUSES
ZINKENITES
ZINKIFEROUS
ZINKIFICATION
ZINKIFICATIONS
ZINKIFYING
ZINZIBERACEOUS
ZIRCALLOYS
ZIRCONIUMS
ZITHERISTS
ZIZYPHUSES
ZOANTHARIAN
ZOANTHARIANS
ZOANTHROPIC
ZOANTHROPIES
ZOANTHROPY
ZOECHROMES
ZOMBIELIKE
ZOMBIFICATION
ZOMBIFICATIONS
ZOMBIFYING
ZOOCEPHALIC
ZOOCHEMICAL
ZOOCHEMISTRIES
ZOOCHEMISTRY
ZOOCHORIES
ZOOCHOROUS

ZOOCULTURE
ZOOCULTURES
ZOODENDRIA
ZOODENDRIUM
ZOOGAMETES
ZOOGEOGRAPHER
ZOOGEOGRAPHERS
ZOOGEOGRAPHIC
ZOOGEOGRAPHICAL
ZOOGEOGRAPHIES
ZOOGEOGRAPHY
ZOOGLOEOID
ZOOGONIDIA
ZOOGONIDIUM
ZOOGRAFTING
ZOOGRAFTINGS
ZOOGRAPHER
ZOOGRAPHERS
ZOOGRAPHIC
ZOOGRAPHICAL
ZOOGRAPHIES
ZOOGRAPHIST
ZOOGRAPHISTS
ZOOKEEPERS
ZOOLATRIAS
ZOOLATRIES
ZOOLATROUS
ZOOLOGICAL
ZOOLOGICALLY
ZOOLOGISTS
ZOOMAGNETIC
ZOOMAGNETISM
ZOOMAGNETISMS
ZOOMANCIES
ZOOMETRICAL
ZOOMETRIES
ZOOMORPHIC
ZOOMORPHIES
ZOOMORPHISM
ZOOMORPHISMS
ZOONOMISTS
ZOOPATHIES
ZOOPATHOLOGIES
ZOOPATHOLOGY
ZOOPERISTS
ZOOPHAGANS
ZOOPHAGIES
ZOOPHAGOUS
ZOOPHILIAS
ZOOPHILIES
ZOOPHILISM
ZOOPHILISMS
ZOOPHILIST

ZOOPHILISTS
ZOOPHILOUS
ZOOPHOBIAS
ZOOPHOBOUS
ZOOPHYSIOLOGIES
ZOOPHYSIOLOGIST
ZOOPHYSIOLOGY
ZOOPHYTICAL
ZOOPHYTOID
ZOOPHYTOLOGICAL
ZOOPHYTOLOGIES
ZOOPHYTOLOGIST
ZOOPHYTOLOGISTS
ZOOPHYTOLOGY
ZOOPLANKTER
ZOOPLANKTERS
ZOOPLANKTON
ZOOPLANKTONIC
ZOOPLANKTONS
ZOOPLASTIC
ZOOPLASTIES
ZOOPSYCHOLOGIES
ZOOPSYCHOLOGY
ZOOSCOPIES
ZOOSPERMATIC
ZOOSPERMIA
ZOOSPERMIUM
ZOOSPORANGIA
ZOOSPORANGIAL
ZOOSPORANGIUM
ZOOSPOROUS
ZOOSTEROLS
ZOOTECHNICAL
ZOOTECHNICS
ZOOTECHNIES
ZOOTHAPSES
ZOOTHAPSIS
ZOOTHECIAL
ZOOTHECIUM
ZOOTHEISMS
ZOOTHEISTIC
ZOOTHERAPIES
ZOOTHERAPY
ZOOTOMICAL
ZOOTOMICALLY
ZOOTOMISTS
ZOOTROPHIC
ZOOTROPHIES
ZOOTSUITER
ZOOTSUITERS
ZOOXANTHELLA
ZOOXANTHELLAE
ZORBONAUTS

ZUCCHETTOS
ZUGZWANGED
ZUGZWANGING
ZUMBOORUKS
ZWISCHENZUG
ZWISCHENZUGS
ZWITTERION
ZWITTERIONIC
ZWITTERIONS
ZYGANTRUMS
ZYGAPOPHYSEAL
ZYGAPOPHYSES
ZYGAPOPHYSIAL
ZYGAPOPHYSIS
ZYGOBRANCH
ZYGOBRANCHIATE
ZYGOBRANCHIATES
ZYGOBRANCHS
ZYGOCACTUS
ZYGOCACTUSES
ZYGOCARDIAC
ZYGODACTYL
ZYGODACTYLIC
ZYGODACTYLISM
ZYGODACTYLISMS
ZYGODACTYLOUS
ZYGODACTYLS
ZYGOMATICS
ZYGOMORPHIC
ZYGOMORPHIES
ZYGOMORPHISM
ZYGOMORPHISMS
ZYGOMORPHOUS
ZYGOMORPHY
ZYGOMYCETE
ZYGOMYCETES
ZYGOMYCETOUS
ZYGOPHYLLACEOUS
ZYGOPHYTES
ZYGOPLEURAL
ZYGOSITIES
ZYGOSPERMS
ZYGOSPHENE
ZYGOSPHENES
ZYGOSPORES
ZYGOSPORIC
ZYGOTICALLY
ZYMOGENESES
ZYMOGENESIS
ZYMOLOGICAL
ZYMOLOGIES
ZYMOLOGIST
ZYMOLOGISTS
ZYMOMETERS
ZYMOSIMETER
ZYMOSIMETERS
ZYMOTECHNIC
ZYMOTECHNICAL

ZYMOTECHNICS
ZYMOTICALLY